ROCKWOOD AND GREEN'S
FRACTURES
IN ADULTS

VOLUME 1

SEVENTH EDITION

EDITORS

Robert W. Bucholz, MD
Professor
Department of Orthopaedic Surgery
The University of Texas Southwestern Medical Center
Dallas, Texas

James D. Heckman, MD
Editor-in-Chief
The Journal of Bone and Joint Surgery
Needham, Massachusetts
Clinical Professor of Orthopaedic Surgery
Harvard Medical School
Visiting Orthopaedic Surgeon
Department of Orthopaedic Surgery
Massachusetts General Hospital
Boston, Massachusetts

Charles M. Court-Brown, MD, FRCS Ed
(Orth)
Professor of Orthopaedic Trauma
Royal Infirmary of Edinburgh
Edinburgh, United Kingdom

Paul Tornetta, III, MD
Professor and Vice Chairman
Department of Orthopaedic Surgery
Boston University Medical Center
Director of Orthopaedic Trauma
Boston University Medical Center
Boston, Massachusetts

ASSOCIATE EDITORS

Margaret M. McQueen, MD, FRCS Ed
(Orth)
Consultant Orthopaedic Trauma Surgeon
Royal Infirmary of Edinburgh
Edinburgh, United Kingdom

William M. Ricci, MD
Associate Professor
Chief, Orthopaedic Trauma Service
Department of Orthopaedic Surgery
Washington University School of Medicine
St. Louis, Missouri

 Wolters Kluwer | Lippincott Williams & Wilkins
Health
Philadelphia • Baltimore • New York • London
Buenos Aires • Hong Kong • Sydney • Tokyo

Acquisitions Editor: Robert Hurley
Product Manager: Dave Murphy
Senior Manufacturing Manager: Benjamin Rivera
Marketing Manager: Lisa Lawrence
Design Coordinator: Doug Smock
Production Service: Absolute Service/Maryland Composition

Printed in China
Not authorised for Sale in North America or the Caribbean
CIP data available upon request

ISBN-13: 9781609130169
ISBN-10: 1609130162

Care has been taken to confirm the accuracy of the information presented and to describe generally accepted practices. However, the authors, editors, and publisher are not responsible for errors or omissions or for any consequences from application of the information in this book and make no warranty, expressed or implied, with respect to the currency, completeness, or accuracy of the contents of the publication. Application of the information in a particular situation remains the professional responsibility of the practitioner.

The authors, editors, and publisher have exerted every effort to ensure that drug selection and dosage set forth in this text are in accordance with current recommendations and practice at the time of publication. However, in view of ongoing research, changes in government regulations, and the constant flow of information relating to drug therapy and drug reactions, the reader is urged to check the package insert for each drug for any change in indications and dosage and for added warnings and precautions. This is particularly important when the recommended agent is a new or infrequently employed drug.

Some drugs and medical devices presented in the publication have Food and Drug Administration (FDA) clearance for limited use in restricted research settings. It is the responsibility of the health care provider to ascertain the FDA status of each drug or device planned for use in their clinical practice.

To purchase additional copies of this book, call our customer service department at (800) 638-3030 or fax orders to (301) 223-2320. International customers should call (301) 223-2300.

Visit Lippincott Williams & Wilkins on the Internet: at LWW.com. Lippincott Williams & Wilkins customer service representatives are available from 8:30 am to 6 pm, EST.

10 9 8 7 6 5 4 3 2

We dedicate this Seventh Edition of *Rockwood and Green's Fractures in Adults* to Charles A. Rockwood, Jr, MD, and David P. Green, MD, who served as our inspiration and mentors for carrying on the revision and update of this textbook.

To Marybeth for her unwavering support over the years.

RWB

To Susan for her encouragement and understanding.

JDH

To my family for their help and support.

CCB

To my mother, Phyllis, who found the best in people, had compassion for all, and whose insight, guidance, and love have always made me believe that anything is possible.

PT3

CONTENTS

This book is due for return on or before the last date shown below.

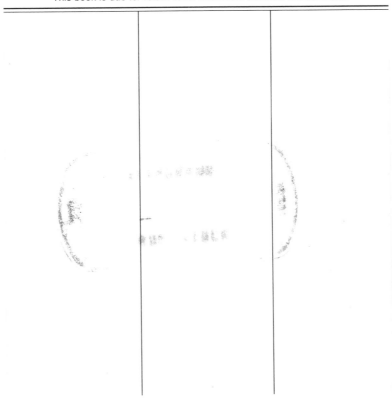

ROCKWOOD AND GREEN'S
FRACTURES
IN ADULTS

SEVENTH EDITION

CONTRIBUTING AUTHORS

Stuart A. Aitken, MRCS, Ed Registrar in Orthopaedic and Traumatology, Royal Infirmary of Edinburgh, Edinburgh, United Kingdom

George S. Athwal, MD FRCSC Assistant Professor of Orthopaedic Surgery, University of Western Ontario, Consultant, Hands and Upper Limbs Centre, St. Joseph's Health Care, London, Ontario, Canada

Roger M. Atkins, MA DM, FRCS Professor of Orthopaedic Surgery, British Royal Infirmary, Bristol, England

T. William Axelrad, MD, PhD Chief Resident of Orthopaedics, Boston University, Boston, Massachusetts

David P. Barei, MD Associate Professor of Orthopaedics and Sports Medicine, University of Washington, Attending Surgeon, Department of Orthopaedics and Sports Medicine, Harborview Medical Center, Seattle, Washington

Asheesh Bedi, MD Assistant Professor of Sports Medicine and Shoulder Surgery, University of Michigan and University of Michigan Hospitals, Ann Arbor, Michigan

Mohit Bhandari, MD, MSc, FRCSC Associate Professor and Canada Research Chair, Division of Orthopaedic Surgery, McMaster University, Consultant Surgeon, Hamilton Health Sciences-General Hospital, Hamilton, Ontario, Canada

Brett R. Bolhofner, MD Assistant Clinical Professor of Orthopaedic Surgery, University of South Florida, Director of Orthopaedic Trauma Service, Bayfront Medical Center, St. Petersburg, Florida

Christopher M. Bono, MD Assistant Professor of Orthopaedic Surgery, Harvard Medical School, Chief of Orthopaedic Spine Service, Department of Orthopaedic Surgery, Brigham and Women's Hospital, Boston, Massachusetts

Michael J. Bosse, MD Department of Orthopaedic Surgery, Carolinas Medical Center, Charlotte, North Carolina

Mark R. Brinker, MD Clinical Professor of Orthopaedic Surgery, Baylor College of Medicine, Director of Acute and Reconstructive Trauma, Center for Problem Fractures and Limb Restoration, Texas Orthopaedic Hospital, Houston, Texas

Joseph A. Buckwalter, MS, MD Arthur Steindler Chair and Head of Orthopaedic Surgery, Department of Orthopaedics and Rehabilitation, University of Iowa, Iowa City, Iowa

Lisa K. Cannada, MD Associate Professor of Orthopaedics, Saint Louis University, Orthopaedic Traumatologist, Saint Louis University Hospital, St. Louis, Missouri

Edward Carreras, MD Boston University School of Medicine, Boston, Massachusetts

Shew-Ping Chow, FRCS, FHKAM Chair Professor, Department of Orthopaedics and Traumatology, The University of Hong Kong, Honorary Consultant, Department of Orthopaedics and Traumatology, Queen Mary Hospital, Hong Kong

Michael P. Clare, MD Director of Fellowship Education, Foot & Ankle Fellowship, Florida Orthopaedic Institute, Tampa, Florida

Cory A. Collinge, MD Director of Orthopaedic Trauma, Harris Methodist Forth Worth Hospital, Fort Worth, Texas

Roy I. Davidovitch, MD Assistant Professor of Orthopaedic Surgery, New York University Hospital for Joint Diseases, Chief of Orthopaedic Trauma Service, Jamaica Hospital Medical Center, Jamaica, New York

Douglas R. Dirschl, MD Professor and Chairman, Department of Orthopaedics, North Carolina School of Medicine, Chief, Department of Orthopaedics, University of North Carolina Hospitals, Chapel Hill, North Carolina

Paul J. Dougherty, MD Residency Program Director, Department of Orthopaedic Surgery, University of Michigan, Residency Program Director, Department of Orthopaedic Surgery, University of Michigan Hospital, Ann Arbor, Michigan

Robert P. Dunbar, Jr., MD Assistant Professor of Orthopaedics and Sports Medicine, Harborview Medical Center, University of Washington, Seattle, Washington

Anil K. Dutta, MD Department of Orthopaedics, University of Texas Health Science Center, San Antonio, Texas

John S. Early, MD Clinical Professor of Orthopaedic Surgery, University of Texas Southwestern Medical Center, Attending, Department of Orthopaedics, Texas Health Dallas, Dallas, Texas

Kenneth A. Egol, MD Professor and Vice Chairman of Orthopaedic Surgery, Chief of Division of Trauma Service, New York University Hospital for Joint Diseases, New York, New York

Thomas A. Einhorn, MD Professor and Chairman of Orthopaedic Surgery, Boston University School of Medicine, Chief of Orthopaedic Surgery, Boston Medical Center, Boston, Massachusetts

William J. J. Ertl, MD Assistant Professor, Department of Orthopaedics and Rehabilitation, University of Oklahoma College of Medicine, Oklahoma City, Oklahoma

Gregory C. Fanelli, MD Geisinger Health System Sports Medicine and Orthopaedic Surgery, Danville, Pennsylvania

Daren Forward, MA, FRCS, DM Trauma Fellow, R Adams Cowley Shock Trauma Center, University of Maryland School of Medicine, Baltimore, Consultant Orthopaedic Trauma Surgeon, Nottingham University Hospital, Nottingham, United Kingdom

Christian Gaebler, MD, PhD Sports Trauma Surgeon, Private Practice, Vienna, Austria

Leesa M. Galatz, MD Associate Professor of Shoulder and Elbow Service, Department of Orthopaedic Surgery, Washington University, Barnes-Jewish Hospital, St. Louis, Missouri

Michael J. Gardner, MD Assistant Professor of Orthopaedic Surgery, Washington University School of Medicine, Attending Surgeon, Department of Orthopaedic Trauma Service, Barnes-Jewish Hospital, St. Louis, Missouri

Peter V. Giannoudis, MD, FRCS, EEC (Orth) Professor of Trauma and Orthopaedic Surgery, University of Leeds, St. James University Hospital, Leeds, United Kingdom

Larry Gulotta, MD Sports Medicine/Shoulder Service Fellow, Department of Orthopaedic Surgery, Hospital for Special Surgery, New York, New York

George J. Haidukewych, MD Professor of Orthopaedic Surgery, University of Central Florida, Co-Director of Orthopaedic Trauma, Chief of Complex Adult Reconstruction, Orlando Health, Orlando, Florida

Mark H. Henry, MD Hand and Wrist Center of Houston, Houston, Texas

Ronald F. Hollis, Jr., MD Department of Orthopaedic Surgery, Washington University School of Medicine, St. Louis, Missouri

Per Olof Josefsson, MD, PhD Associate Professor of Clinical Sciences, Lund University, Senior Consultant and Head of Traumatology, Department of Orthopaedic Surgery, Malmö University Hospital, Malmö, Sweden

Leo Joskowicz, PhD Professor and Director, Computer Aided Surgery and Medical Image Processing Laboratory, School of Engineering and Computer Science, The Hebrew University of Jerusalem, Jerusalem, Israel

Michael S.H. Kain, MD Department of Orthopaedic Surgery, Boston University, Orthopaedic Surgeon, Lahey Clinic, Burlington, Massachusetts

Sanjeev Kakar, MD, MRCS, MBA Hand and Upper Extremity Fellow, Mayo Clinic, Rochester, Minnesota

Kerry M. Kallas, MD Musculoskeletal Radiologist, Center of Diagnostic Imaging, Sartell, Minnesota

Magnus K. Karlsson, MD, PhD Professor, Clinical and Molecular Osteoporosis Research Unit, Department of Clinical Sciences, Lund University, Senior Consultant and Professor, Department of Orthopaedic Surgery, Malmö University Hospital, Malmö, Sweden

Madhav A. Karunakar, MD Orthopaedic Traumatologist, Department of Orthopaedic Surgery, Carolinas Medical Center, Charlotte, North Carolina

John Keating, FRCS, Ed (Orth) Consultant Orthopaedic Surgeon, Royal Infirmary of Edinburgh, Edinburgh, United Kingdom

Kevin J. Kulwicki, MD Shoulder and Elbow Surgery Fellow, Department of Orthopaedic Surgery, New York University Hospital for Joint Diseases, Staff Orthopaedic Surgeon, Columbia-Saint Mary's Hospital, Ozaukee Campus, Mequon, Wisconsin

Young W. Kwon, MD, PhD Assistant Professor of Orthopaedic Surgery, New York University School of Medicine, Shoulder and Elbow Service, Department of Orthopaedic Surgery, Hospital for Joint Disease, New York University, New York, New York

Joseph Lane, MD Attending Orthopaedic Surgeon, Hospital for Special Surgery, Professor of Orthopaedic Surgery, Weill Cornell Medical College, New York, New York

Joshua Langford, MD Instructor of Orthopaedic Surgery, University of Central Florida College of Medicine, Attending Orthopaedic Traumatologist, Orlando Health Orthopaedic Residency Program, Orlando Regional Medical Center, Orlando, Florida

Sune Larsson, MD Professor of Orthopaedics, Uppsala University, Director of Research, Uppsala University Hospital, Uppsala, Sweden

Frankie Leung, FRCS, FHKAM Clinical Associate Professor of Orthopaedics and Traumatology, The University of Hong Kong, Chief of Division of Orthopaedic Trauma, Department of Orthopaedics and Traumatology, Queen Mary Hospital, Hong Kong

Meir Liebergall, MD Professor of Orthopaedic Surgery, Hebrew University, Chairman, Department of Orthopaedic Surgery, The Hadassah-Hebrew University Medical Center, Jerusalem, Israel

Ellen J. MacKenzie, PhD Center for Injury Research and Health Policy, Johns Hopkins University Bloomberg School of Hygiene and Public Health, Baltimore, Maryland

Samir Mardini, MD Associate Professor of Surgery, Department of Plastic Surgery, Mayo Clinic, Rochester, Minnesota

J. L. Marsh, MD Carroll B. Larson Professor of Orthopaedics and Rehabilitation, University of Iowa Hospitals and Clinics, Iowa City, Iowa

Michael D. McKee, MD, FRCS(C) Professor, Upper Extremity Reconstructive Service, Division of Orthopaedics, Department of Surgery, St. Michael's Hospital and the University of Toronto, Toronto, Canada

Sohail K. Mirza, MD, MPH Professor of Orthopaedics, Dartmouth Medical School, Attending Surgeon and Vice Chair of Orthopaedics, Dartmouth-Hitchcock Medical Center, Lebanon, New Hampshire

Berton R. Moed, MD Professor and Chairman, Department of Orthopaedic Surgery, Saint Louis University School of Medicine, Chief of Orthopaedic Surgery, Saint Louis University Hospital, St. Louis, Missouri

Eric S. Moghadamian, MD Assistant Professor, Department of Orthopaedic Surgery, University of Kentucky, Lexington, Kentucky

Steven L. Moran, MD Associate Professor of Orthopaedics and Division of Plastic Surgery, Mayo Clinic, Rochester, Minnesota

Rami Mosheiff, MD Associate Professor of Orthopaedic Surgery, Hebrew University, Head of Orthopaedic Trauma Center, The Hadassah-Hebrew University Medical Center, Jerusalem, Israel

Soheil Najibi, MD, PhD Senior Staff Orthopaedic Surgeon, Henry Ford Hospital, Detroit, Michigan

Sean E. Nork, MD Associate Professor of Orthopaedic Surgery, Harborview Medical Center at the University of Washington, Seattle, Washington

Daniel P. O'Connor, PhD Assistant Professor, Laboratory of Integrated Physiology, University of Houston, Joe W. King Orthopaedic Institute, Texas University Hospital, Houston, Texas

Robert V. O'Toole III, MD Associate Professor, R Adams Cowley Shock Trauma Center, University of Maryland School of Medicine, Baltimore

Christina V. Oleson, MD Assistant Professor of Orthopaedics, Section of Physical Medicine and Rehabilitation, Dartmouth Medical School and Dartmouth-Hitchcock Medical Center, Lebanon, New Hampshire

Hans Christoph Pape, MD W Pauwels Professor and Chairman, Department of Orthopaedics and Trauma, University of Aachen Medical Centre, Aachen, Germany

Brad A. Petrisor, MSc, MD, FRCSC Assistant Professor, McMaster University, Consultant Orthopaedic Surgeon, Hamilton Health-Sciences General Hospital, Hamilton, Ontario, Canada

Anil S. Ranawat, MD Assistant Attending Orthopaedic Surgeon Hospital for Special Surgery, Instructor in Orthopaedic Surgery, Weill Comell Medical College, New York, New York

Nalini Rao, MD Clinical Professor of Medicine and Orthopaedic Surgery, University of Pittsburgh School of Medicine, Chief, Division of Infectious Disease, UPMC Shadyside Hospital Pittsburgh, Pennsylvania

James J. Reid, MD Private practice Los Angeles, California

Mark C. Reilly, MD Associate Professor, Co-Chief of Orthopaedic Trauma Service, Department of Orthopaedics, New Jersey Medical School, Newark, New Jersey

David Ring, MD, PhD Associate Professor of Orthopaedic Surgery, Harvard Medical School, Director of Research, Orthopaedic Hand and Upper Extremity Service, Massachusetts General Hospital, Boston, Massachusetts

C. Michael Robinson, BMed Sci, FRCS, Ed (Orth) Honorary Senior Lecturer, Department of Orthopaedic and Trauma Surgery, University of Edinburgh, Consultant Orthopaedic Trauma Surgeon, Orthopaedic Trauma Unit, Royal Infirmary of Edinburgh, Edinburgh, United Kingdom

Charles A. Rockwood, Jr., MD Professor and Chairman Emeritus of Orthopaedics, University of Texas Health Science Center, San Antonio, Texas

David S. Ruch, MD Professor, Director of Orthopaedic Hand Surgery, Duke University Medical Center, Durham, North Carolina

Thomas P. Rüedi, MD, FACS Professor Dr med, FACS Founding Member of the AO Foundation, Davos, Switzerland

Thomas A. Russell, MD Professor, Campbell Clinic Department of Orthopaedics, University of Tennessee, Staff Surgeon, Department of Orthopaedic Surgery, Elvis Presley Trauma Center, Memphis, Tennessee

Claude Sagi, MD Associate Clinical Professor of Orthopaedic Surgery, University of South Florida, Fellowship Director, Department of Orthopaedic Trauma Service, Tampa General Hospital, Tampa, Florida

Christopher J. Salgado, MD Assistant Professor of Surgery, Division of Plastic Surgery Cooper University Hospital, Camden, New Jersey

David W. Sanders, MD, MSc, FRCSC Associate Professor of Orthopaedic Surgery, University of Western Ontario, Orthopaedic Surgeon, Victoria Hospital, London, Ontario, Canada

Roy W. Sanders, MD Clinical Professor of Orthopaedic Surgery, University of South Florida, Chief of Orthopaedic Surgery, Tampa General Hospital, Tampa, Florida

Emil Schemitsch, MD, FRCS (C) Professor of Surgery, University of Toronto, Head of Division of Orthopaedic Surgery, St. Michael's Hospital, Toronto, Ontario, Canada

Robert C. Schenk, Jr., MD Professor and Chair of Department of Orthopaedics, University of New Mexico School of Medicine, University of New Mexico Lobos Team Physician, Department of Sports Medicine, University of New Mexico Hospitals, Albuquerque, New Mexico

Andrew H. Schmidt, MD Professor of Orthopaedic Surgery, University of Minnesota, Faculty, Department of Orthopaedic Surgery, Hennepin County Medical Center, Minneapolis, Minnesota

Michael A. Schütz, MD, PhD, FRACS, FAOrthA Chair of Trauma, Faculty of Built Environment and Engineering, Queensland University of Technology, Director of Trauma and Orthopaedics, Princess Alexandra Hospital, Brisbane, Queensland, Australia

Alexander Y. Shin, MD Professor of Orthopaedic Surgery, Mayo Clinic, Consultant, Department of Orthopaedic Surgery, Mayo Clinic, Rochester, Minnesota

Nathan E. Simmons, MD Associate Professor of Neurosurgery, Dartmouth Medical School and Dartmouth-Hitchcock Medical Center, Lebanon, New Hampshire

Wade Smith, MD Director of Orthopaedic Trauma, Department of Orthopaedic Surgery, Geisinger Medical Center, Danville, Pennsylvania

James P. Stannard, MD Professor and Chairman, J. Vernon Luck Distinguished Professor, Department of Orthopaedic Surgery, University of Missouri, Columbia, Missouri

David C. Teague, MD Professor and Don H. O'Donoghue Chair, Department of Orthopaedic Surgery and Rehabilitation, University of Oklahoma Health Science Center, Chief of Department of Orthopaedics, OU Medical Center, Oklahoma City, Oklahoma

Allan F. Tencer, PhD Professor of Orthopaedics and Sports Medicine, University of Washington, Professor, Orthopaedic Sciences Laboratory, Harborview Medical Center, Seattle, Washington

Alexander R. Vaccaro, MD, PhD Vice-Chairman of Orthopaedics, The Rothman Institute, Professor and Co-Director, Delaware Valley Regional Spine Cord Injury Center, Co-Chief of Spine Surgery and Spine Fellowship Program, Department of Orthopaedics and Neurosurgery, Thomas Jefferson Hospital, Philadelphia, Pennsylvania

Arthur van Noort, MD, PhD Department of Orthopaedic Surgery, Spaarne Hospital, Hoofddorp, The Netherlands

J. Tracy Watson, MD Professor of Orthopaedic Surgery, St. Louis University School of Medicine, Chief of Division of Orthopaedic Traumatology, Saint Louis University Hospital, St. Louis, Missouri

Adam Watts, BSc, MBBS, FRCS (Tr and Ortho) Royal Infirmary of Edinburgh, Edinburgh, United Kingdom

Kristy L. Weber, MD Professor of Orthopaedic Surgery and Oncology, Johns Hopkins University, Chief of Division of Orthopaedic Surgery, Johns Hopkins University, Baltimore, Maryland

Peter G. Whang, MD Assistant Professor of Orthopaedics and Rehabilitation, Yale University School of Medicine, Attending Physician, Department of Orthopaedics and Rehabilitation, Yale-New Haven Hospital, New Haven, Connecticut

Tim White, MD, FRCS (Tr and Orth) Honorary Senior Lecturer, Department of Orthopaedic and Trauma Surgery, University of Edinburgh, Consultant Orthopaedic Trauma Surgeon, Orthopaedic Trauma Unit, Royal Infirmary of Edinburgh, Edinburgh, United Kingdom

Gerald R. Williams, Jr., MD   Professor of Orthopaedic Surgery, Chief of Shoulder and Elbow Service, The Rothman Institute, Jefferson Medical College, Philadelphia, Pennsylvania

Michael A. Wirth, MD   Professor and Charles A. Rockwood, Jr., MD Chair of Orthopaedics, University of Texas Health Science Center at San Antonio, Staff, Department of Orthopaedics, University Hospital, San Antonio, Texas

Donald A. Wiss, MD   Director of Orthopaedic Trauma at Cedars-Sinai Medical Center, Los Angeles, California

Bruce H. Ziran, MD   Director of Orthopaedic Trauma, Orthopaedic Surgery Residency Program, Atlanta Medical Center, Atlanta, Georgia

Joseph D. Zuckerman, MD   Walter A.L. Thompson Professor of Orthopaedic Surgery, Department of Orthopaedic Surgery, New York University School of Medicine, Chairman; Surgeon-in-Chief, Department of Orthopaedic Surgery, New York University Hospital for Joint Diseases, New York, New York

PREFACE

The 7th edition of *Rockwood and Green's Fractures in Adults* continues with the changes that were instituted in the 6th edition. In this edition there are four more chapters and 53 new authors drawn from three continents and ten different countries. Eleven new chapters focus on topics that have not been covered in separate chapters in previous editions of *Rockwood and Green*. To allow us to cope with the advances and changes in Orthopaedic Trauma, Paul Tornetta has become an Editor, and Margaret McQueen from Edinburgh and Bill Ricci from St Louis have been appointed Associate Editors. All three are accomplished orthopaedic trauma surgeons and their complementary interests and areas of expertise have greatly assisted the production of the 7th edition. In addition, many of the new authors represent the next generation of orthopaedic trauma surgeons who will be determining the direction of trauma management over the next two or three decades.

Orthopaedic trauma continues to be an expanding discipline, with change occurring more quickly than is often realized. When Drs. Rockwood and Green published the 1st edition in 1975, there were virtually no orthopaedic trauma specialists in most countries, fractures were usually treated nonoperatively, and mortality following severe trauma was considerable. In one generation the changes in orthopaedic surgery, as in the rest of medicine, have been formidable. We have worked to incorporate these changes in this edition. The continuing importance of wartime and severe civilian injuries is reflected in new chapters on gunshot and wartime injuries, the principles of mangled extremity management, bone and soft tissue reconstruction, and amputation. There is expanded coverage in this edition of the inevitable complications that all orthopaedic surgeons have to deal with, and we have included new chapters that discuss systemic complications, complex regional pain syndrome, infec-

tion, nonunion, and malunion. We have also separated distal tibial fractures into pilon and ankle fractures.

The other area of orthopaedic trauma that is expanding quickly, particularly in the developed countries, is the treatment of osteoporotic (or fragility) fractures. These fractures are assuming a greater medical and political importance, and orthopaedic implants are now being designed specifically to treat elderly patients. It is likely that this trend will continue over the next few decades; many of the chapters in this edition reflect this change in emphasis.

The changes in the 7th edition are highlighted by the altered presentation of the book. Many of the operative pictures and diagrams are now in color, as are all the tables. This edition is strengthened by the inclusion online of 20 new videos of surgical procedures done by Drs. Tornetta, Ricci, and Schmidt. Twelve additional videos will be created in the next year. The user will be able to download clips from these videos for lectures and presentations. We have also made available videos of many surgical approaches useful for trauma procedures. Two features that we have not changed are the Pearls and Pitfalls and the Authors' Preferred Treatment, these features having been present in the last edition. It is perhaps a paradox that we ask our authors to emphasize Level 1 evidence in the form of randomized double blind studies but we promote the authors' preferred methods, which is Level V evidence! However, we continue to believe that it is the function of *Rockwood and Green* to feature the world's leading orthopaedic trauma surgeons and to listen to what they say.

Robert W. Bucholz
James D. Heckman
Charles M. Court-Brown
Paul Tornetta, III

GENERAL PRINCIPLES: BASICS

1

BIOMECHANICS OF FRACTURES
AND FRACTURE FIXATION

Allan F. Tencer

INTRODUCTION

This chapter provides a basic discussion of the concepts of biomechanics, and demonstrates how these concepts can be used to understand the basic functions of bone fracture fixation devices and to avoid clinical problems associated with the mechanics of fracture fixation. Emphasis has been placed on addressing practical problems. First, fundamental concepts of mechanics as they apply to the practice of orthopaedic fracture fixation are explained. This is followed by a short discussion on the mechanical organization of bone, its ability to carry load, and the relationship of applied forces and specific fracture patterns. A discussion of mechanisms of bone and joint injury, including specific mechanisms observed in car crashes is next presented. Description of the mechanics of healing bone follows, which is relevant to understanding the timing of applying progressive load to healing fractures in patients. Finally, the performance of various types of fixation systems is discussed, with emphasis on fixation of difficult fractures, such as the femoral neck and the tibial plateau, and those involving osteoporotic bone. The focus of the discussion is not on comparing the various specific devices available, but rather on demonstrating the common mechanical principles involved in fracture fixation so that potential problems common to various devices can be recognized and avoided.

In the study of biomechanics as it relates to fracture fixation, the fundamental mechanical question remains: is the fixation system stiff and strong enough to allow the patient early mobility, before bony union is complete, without delaying healing, creating bone deformity, or damaging the implant, and yet flexible enough to allow transmission of force to the healing fracture to stimulate union? The issue of which brand of fixation is strongest or stiffest is not specifically addressed because that is not the standard by which different devices should be judged. Within a range of fixation stiffness it has been shown that bone will heal, with the amount of stabilizing callus compensating for more flexible fixation.

BASIC CONCEPTS

Before describing the performance of fracture fixation systems, some basic concepts used in biomechanics will be introduced. As Figure 1-1 demonstrates, loads in many different directions may act on a fixed fracture, including body weight, and forces induced by muscle contraction and ligament tension. A *force* causes an object to either accelerate or decelerate. It has *magnitude* (strength) and acts in a specific direction, therefore it is termed a *vector*. However complex the system of forces acting on a bone, each force may be separated into its vector components (which form a 90-degree triangle with the force). Any of several components, acting in the same direction, can be summed to yield the net or *resultant force*. As a simple example, consider the resultant force acting at the shoe/floor interface during ambulation. It can be separated into a vertical force because of

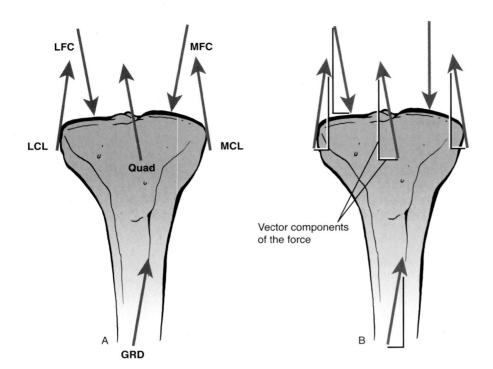

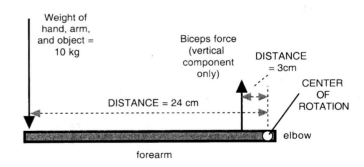

FIGURE 1-1 Force vectors acting on a long bone during functional use as a result of muscle, tendon, and external forces. A vector indicates that the force has both magnitude and direction. The complex system of forces can be divided into components acting perpendicular and parallel to the ground, or the axis of the bone, then added to arrive at an overall resultant force.

body weight and a horizontal frictional force that produces the forward thrust. Similarly, muscle forces can be separated in the same manner—one force along the axis of the long bone and one perpendicular. The components of the different forces that act in the same direction can be added, and the resultant force acting on the bone can then be found. This concept is important when designing fracture fixation systems because it allows the designer to size the implants so that they can withstand the mechanical loads applied without failure.

The two major loads acting on a long bone are those that cause it to displace in a linear direction (translation) and those that cause it to rotate around a joint center. Muscles typically cause a bone to rotate (e.g., the biceps causes the forearm to rotate, the anterior tibialis causes the foot to dorsiflex). When a force causes rotation, it is termed a *moment* and has a *moment arm*. The moment arm is the lever arm against which the force acts to cause rotation. It is the perpendicular distance of the muscle force from the center of rotation of the joint. As shown in Figure 1-2, the moment or rotary force is affected not only by the magnitude of the force applied, but also by its distance from the center of rotation. In the example, two moments act on the outstretched arm. The weight carried in the hand rotates the arm downward, while the balancing muscle force rotates the arm upward. Equilibrium is reached by balancing the moments so that the arm does not rotate and the weight can be carried. Note that to achieve this, the muscle force must be 8 times as large as the weight of the object, arm, and hand because its moment arm or distance from the center of the joint is only one eighth as long.

The basic forces—compression, transverse loading, torsion, and bending—cause bone to behave in predictable ways. A *compressive force* (Fig. 1-3) results in shortening the length of the bone, while *tension* elongates it. *Torsion* causes twisting of a bone about its long axis, while *bending* causes it to bow at the center. The forces and moments that act on a long bone during functional use produce three basic stresses on the healing fracture region: tension, compression, and *shear* (as shown previously, all forces can be reduced to their basic components). *Stress*, as shown in Figure 1-4, is simply the force divided by the area on an object over which it acts. This is a convenient way to express how the force affects a material locally. For example, comparing two bones, one with half the cross-sectional area of the other, if the smaller bone is subjected to half the force of the larger bone, the stress experienced by each bone would be the same. Therefore, a smaller woman with less weight

FIGURE 1-2 In this example the outstretched arm is a lever. The moment or load that rotates the arm downward around the elbow, the center of rotation, is defined as the product of the weight of the object arm and hand X distance from the elbow (for simplicity the center of gravity of the hand, arm, and object are combined). This moment must be counteracted by a moment in the opposite direction, because of the vertical component of the biceps muscle acting through its lever, which is smaller than the lever arm of the weight arm and hand. The biceps force is then calculated from (10 kg × 24 cm)/3 cm = 80 kg. The biceps force is much greater than the weight of the object arm and hand because its lever arm is smaller.

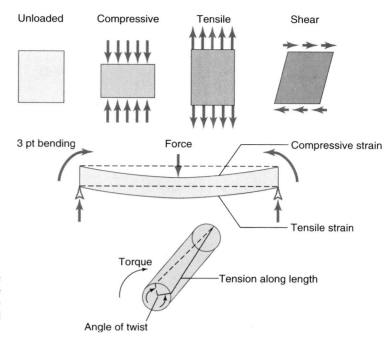

FIGURE 1-3 Top: Basic forces acting on a long bone and the deflection of the bone in response. Compression shortens the length, tension increases the length, and shear deforms the shape of the bone **(middle)**, bending causes the bone to bow, and **(bottom)** torsion results in twisting about the long axis.

has proportionally smaller bones to keep the stresses on the bone tissue similar to that of a larger and heavier man. The stresses acting on fracture callus as a result of the different forces are shown (in an idealized case) in Figure 1-5. Just as stress is normalized force (force per unit area), so can length changes be normalized. *Strain* is simply the change in height or length that a bone undergoes during loading divided by its original height or length, as shown in Figure 1-4. Under the same force and for bones of similar composition, a bone twice as long will experience twice the length change. Nevertheless, the strain will be the same in both cases because the strain (in the longer bone) will be twice the change in length divided by twice the original length.

Mechanical testing of fractured long bones with fixation devices applied demonstrates a specific type of behavior, as shown in Figure 1-6. This diagram represents the data measured in an experimental test of the *structural properties* of the bone-fixation construct; that is, the properties of the fixation device and bone combined. *Material properties* relate to the properties of the substances that make up each component (bone, stainless steel, titanium). As load is applied to the construct in a testing machine, the construct deforms. This deformation is termed *elastic* because when the load is removed, the construct will return to its original shape (an important consideration in preventing malalignment of the bone fracture components). At some load, however, the construct becomes overloaded, entering the *plastic*

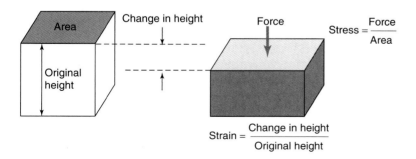

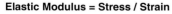

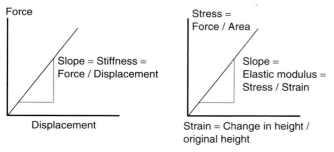

FIGURE 1-4 The stress is defined as the force acting on a surface divided by the area over which it acts. Strain is the change in height or length of the object under load divided by its original height or length. Stiffness is defined as the slope of a force versus displacement graph; that is, the change in force divided by the corresponding change in displacement. Elastic modulus is the corresponding slope but of a stress versus strain graph.

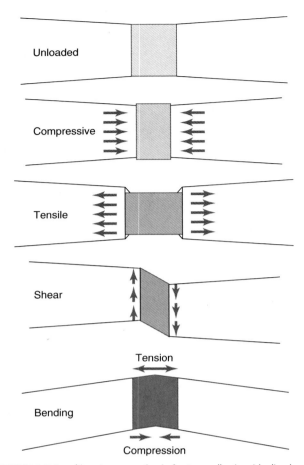

FIGURE 1-5 Resulting stresses acting in fracture callus in a idealized case with each of the basic forces applied (top to bottom): unloaded, compressive stresses along the bone axis and expansive stresses perpendicular to the bone axis as a result of compression, tensile and contraction stresses caused by tension, distortion as a result of shearing; and tension on the convex side, compression on the concave side, and internal shearing caused by bending.

range. If the load is released after loading in the plastic range but before failure, some *permanent deformation* remains in the construct. Practically, this represents a bent plate, fixator, or rod and a malaligned fracture. The point at which elastic behavior changes to plastic is termed the *yield point*. The elastic range represents the working range for the fixation construct. Its two most important properties are its yield point, which defines its safe maximum functional load, and its stiffness, or the amount it deforms under load in the elastic range. (A third very important property, fatigue, will be discussed later.)

Note that a fixation construct may have different yield points and stiffnesses for loads acting in different directions. An example is a half-pin external fixator construct applied to a tibia, with the pins oriented anterior-posteriorly. The stiffness is much greater in anterior-posterior bending than medial-lateral bending for this construct. Another property to consider is the *work done* in deforming a fixation construct. The product of the force applied and the distance the construct bends is defined as the work done, and is represented by the area under the force-displacement graph of Figure 1-6. *Toughness* can be defined as the work done to fracture a construct or material, including both the elastic and plastic regions of deformation. A material

may be flexible and tough (e.g., rubber, or a child's bone that deforms but is difficult to break) or stiff but brittle (e.g., glass, elderly bone), if it cannot absorb much deformation without fracturing.

The factors that govern stiffness and yield point are the material from which the fixation device is made and its shape (considering an ununited fracture in which the fracture callus contributes little to structural properties). A construct made of higher elastic modulus materials will be stiffer (for example, stainless steel as compared to titanium). The stiffness of a construct is found by dividing the force applied by the deformation that the construct exhibited. The *elastic* (or *Young*) modulus is determined by dividing the stress applied by the resulting strain. Unlike whole constructs, in which case it is difficult to determine stress (because it is hard to define the area over which the force is applied and at least two different materials are involved), uniform blocks of materials can be characterized by their elastic modulus. The moduli of some common orthopaedic materials are given in Table 1-1. As shown, the elastic modulus of titanium alloy is about one half that of stainless steel, so given two plates of the same size and shape, the titanium plate has about one half the stiffness of the stainless steel plate. This can be important to consider when using new devices made of different materials.

The shape of the implant is important in determining the loads that it can support. As shown in Figure 1-7, the same wooden 2×4 beam that bends easily when load is applied to its wider surface becomes much stiffer when load is applied to its narrower surface. This is because, in the latter case, the material of the 2×4 resisting the load is distributed further away from the center of the beam (note that in this example, the material of the beam did not change, just its orientation relative to the load applied). This concept of distribution of material is reflected in the shape property, *moment of inertia*. The moment of inertia provides a measure of how the material is distributed in the cross section of the object relative to the load applied to it. The farther away the material is from the center of the beam, the greater its stiffness. Steel I-beams were developed to take advantage of this concept; that is, gaining greater stiffness for the same amount of material. For cylindrical objects like rods, pins, or screws, their stiffness is related to the 4th power of their diameter. This is why, as shown in Figure 1-7, for rods made of the same materials and of similar thickness, a 16-mm diameter intramedullary rod is 1.7 times as stiff as a 14-mm rod $[(16/14)^4]$, and a 7-mm diameter pedicle screw is 1.85 times as stiff as a 6-mm diameter screw.

A third important property of a fracture fixation construct is its ability to resist *fatigue* under cyclic loading. Load can be applied that remains below the yield point of the construct, yet progressively creates a crack that grows until the local stress in the region of the crack exceeds the yield point and the construct fails. Some materials have an *endurance limit* such that they can support a certain level of load indefinitely without failure. An important aspect to fatigue performance of a fixation construct is the effect of a *stress concentrator*. In completely uniform materials, the stresses, in tension for example, will be almost identical throughout the material. Fixation devices have holes, screw threads, and other features in which shape changes occur. A very radical change in shape (as shown in Figure 1-8, the sharp corner between threads of different diameter in a fixation screw) causes a stress concentrator at the corner. This explains why

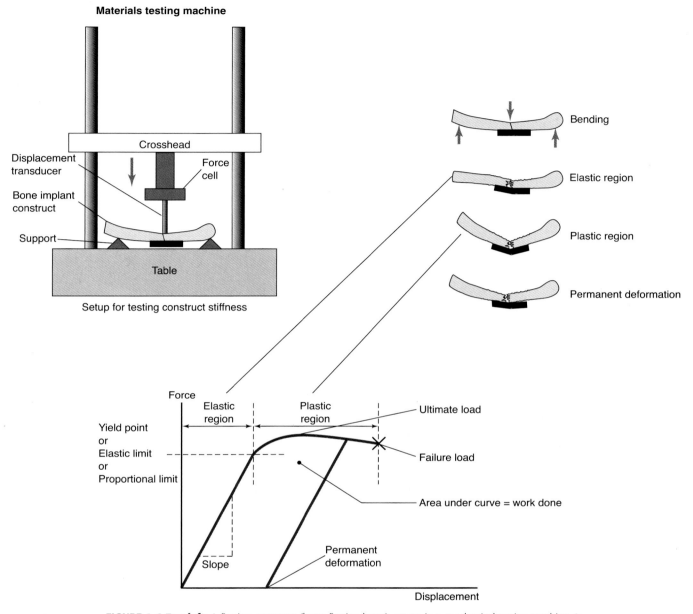

FIGURE 1-6 Top left: A fixation construct (bone-fixation-bone) set up in a mechanical testing machine. In this example a long bone is fixed with a plate and subjected to bending. **Top right:** The construct during loading in the elastic region, plastic region, and with permanent deformation. **Bottom:** The resulting measurements from the testing machine, which measures force applied and displacement at the point of the applied load. The graph demonstrates the elastic region, in which the construct acts like a spring, returning to its original shape after the load is released; the plastic region, in which the plate may have permanently bent; and the failure load, in which the fixation fails.

the base of a screw thread, the place at which it meets the shaft of the screw, has rounded corners. The stresses on a fracture construct are increased when applied in heavier patients, with poor bone-to-bone contact across the fracture site, delayed union, early weight bearing before the fracture has united, and when smaller low-profile fixation devices are used. For these circumstances, consider the use of larger implants, taking care not to create stress concentrators by scuffing or scratching the implant, and delay weight bearing until some fracture consolidation is apparent. These steps can increase the amount of load cycles that the implant can bear without fatigue failure.

A scratch can also cause a local small stress concentrator. When immersed in the saline environment of the body, *stress corrosion* can occur. Stress corrosion combines the effects of the local growth of the crack resulting from cyclic loading with galvanic corrosion. A *galvanic cell* describes a local environment in which electrons flow from the more negative to the more positive material when immersed in a liquid conductor (saline in this case) (Fig. 1-9). Material is actually removed from the more negative electrode, such as the surface of the plate during galvanic corrosion. In a fixed fracture, the dissimilar materials are the surface of the plate (for example, stainless steel), which

TABLE 1-1 | Basic Engineering Properties of Common Biologic and Implant Materials

Material	Ultimate Strength Tensile (MPa)	Ultimate Strength Compressive (MPa)	Yield Strength 0.2% Offset (MPa)	Elastic Modulus (MPa)
Muscle	0.2			
Skin	8			50
Cartilage	4	10		20
Fascia	10			
Tendon	70			400
Cortical bone	100	175	80	15,000
Cancellous bone	2	3		1000
Plaster of Paris	70	75	20	
Polyethylene	40	20	20	1000
PTFE Teflon	25			500
Acrylic bone cement	40	80		2000
Titanium (pure, cold worked)	500		400	100,000
Titanium (Al-4V) (alloy F 136)	900		800	100,000
Stainless steel (316 L) (annealed)	>500		>200	200,000
Stainless steel (cold worked)	>850		>700	200,000
Cobalt chrome (cast)	>450		>50	20,000
Cobalt chrome (wrought, annealed)	>300		>300	230,000
Cobalt chrome (wrought, cold work)	1500		1000	230,000
Super alloys (CoNiMo)	1800		1600	230,000

(Ultimate tensile strength or maximum force in tension, yield strength at 0.2% offset, the strength at which the strain in the material [change in length / original length] is 0.2%, a usual standard for metals, elastic modulus, or stress/strain.)

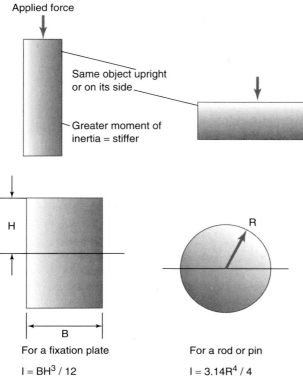

For a fixation plate

$$I = BH^3 / 12$$

For a rod or pin

$$I = 3.14R^4 / 4$$

FIGURE 1-7 Concept of moment of inertia or the effect of the geometry of an object on its stiffness. **Top:** Looking at the edge of a wood 2 × 4 (used in home building); left, the 2 × 4 with the load applied on the narrower side is stiffer than the same 2 × 4 with the load applied on its wider side. The area of the 2 × 4 is farther away from the central axis when the load is applied on the narrower side. **Bottom:** The moment of inertia is a term used to describe how the material is distributed within an object. Left, for a plate, looking at its edge, the moment of inertia and the stiffness increase directly with the width of the plate and the cube of its height. For a tube, such as an intramedullary rod, the moment of inertia increases with the 4th power of its diameter. Therefore a 16-mm diameter IM rod is 1.7 times as stiff as a 14-mm rod, and 2.3 times as stiff as a 13-mm rod, if all the rods have the same thickness and are made of the same material.

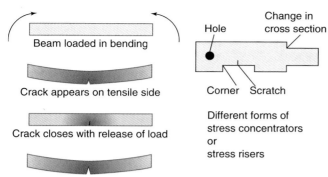

FIGURE 1-8 A stress concentrator is a region of an object in which stresses are higher than in the surrounding material. **Left:** Taking the example of a fracture plate subjected to bending, the bottom surface elongates under load. In the region of highest tensile forces, a scratch starts to grow into a crack that closes when the load is released, then reopens slightly larger with the next load cycle, eventually growing to a point at which the plate fails. Crack growth is accentuated by stress corrosion, poor bone-to-bone contact at the fracture, and by loads applied by heavier patients. **Right:** Stress concentrators (sometimes referred to as stress risers) occur around holes, sharp corners, from scratches, and at corners from changes in cross section.

creates an oxide surface coating, and the same material within the just opening crack, which has not yet developed the oxide film. The conductive fluid is the blood and saline found in the surrounding tissues. Galvanic corrosion can accelerate the failure of an implant, even when the implant is loaded well below its yield point, by increasing the rate at which the crack grows, because along with yielding at the site of the crack, material at the crack is being removed by the corrosion process. Another mechanism of corrosion, termed *fretting*, results when the surfaces of two implants rub together, such as the head of a screw against the surface of the plate through which it passes. *Crevice corrosion*, which is not common in modern orthopaedic materials, results from small galvanic cells formed by impurities in the surface of the implant, causing crevices as the material corrodes.[23]

Another basic property is *viscoelasticity*. Biologic materials do not act as pure springs when load is applied to them. (A spring deforms under load, then returns to its original shape when the load is released.) For example, if a load is applied to a tendon, and the load is maintained for a period of time, the tissue will continue to deform or *creep*. This is the basic principle behind stretching exercises. Under a constant load, a metal fixation plate will deform and remain at that deformation until the load is removed (elastic behavior). In contrast the tendon both deforms elastically and creeps, exhibiting both viscous and elastic behavior. This property has important implications for certain types of fixation, especially those that rely on loading of

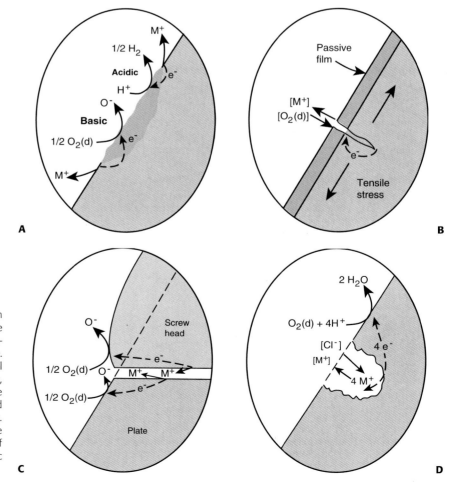

FIGURE 1-9 A. Illustration of crevice corrosion, with a local galvanic cell caused by an impurity in the surface of a plate and ions, M+, being released, resulting in loss of material and formation of a crevice. **B.** Stress corrosion occurs by a local galvanic cell setup between the material at the tip of the crack, which just opened and has not oxidized, and the remaining oxidized surface of the plate. The released ions enhance crack growth occurring from loading. **C.** Fretting corrosion caused by the loss of the oxide layer on the surface of a plate caused by rubbing of the base of the screw against the plate. **D.** Galvanic corrosion around a scratch or pit in the plate.[23]

soft tissues, such as in certain types of spinal fixation (to be discussed later).

A second characteristic of viscoelastic behavior is *loading rate dependence*. In simple terms, stretching a soft tissue can be thought of as stretching two components, an elastic one and a viscous one, which make up that tissue. For example, consider a spring connected in series to the handle of a syringe (Fig. 1-10). When a compressive force is applied, the spring instantly compresses, representing the elastic response of the tissue. The syringe plunger starts to displace and continues as it pushes fluid through the orifice. If the force is held constant, the plunger will continue to move, representing the viscous creep of the tissue. If the compressive force is applied slowly, the syringe handle offers little resistance. As the rate of force application increases, the resistance of the syringe to motion increases. This represents the increase in stiffness of the tissue at higher loading rates. That is, the stiffness of the tissue depends upon the rate at which the load is applied.

A well-known example of loading rate dependence relates to failure of ligament and bone. At low loading rates, ligament is weaker than bone and the ligament fails generally in midsubstance. At higher loading rates, the ligament becomes stiffer, and failure may occur by avulsion of the bony attachment of the ligament. *Stress relaxation* occurs if the applied force, instead of increasing, is held constant. As the fluid flows out of the syringe, without further movement of the plunger, the internal force decreases. These three properties—creep, stress relaxation, and load rate dependence—make up the basic tissue viscoelastic properties. It should be appreciated that the model used in this discussion is a simple linear series model, for explanation purposes only. Nevertheless, more complex models using com-

binations of these basic components have successfully described the observed properties of tissues. Another example of tissue viscoelasticity, besides tendon and other soft tissues, is found in trabecular bone (for example, spinal vertebrae). In this case, the trabecular structure acts as the spring component, while forcing the interstitial fluid through the porous matrix as the trabeculae deform represents the viscous component. Under higher loading rates, there is resistance to flow, increasing the internal pressure and therefore the stiffness of the structure. These effects have been observed at high loading rates, such as during fracture (Fig. 1-11).[32]

In summary, bones and joints can be subjected to various forces, but these forces can be resolved into basic components that create tension, compression, shearing, twisting, and bending. These forces cause internal, compressive, tensile, and shear stresses in the tissue. The stiffness of a fixation construct used to stabilize a fracture describes how much it deforms under a given load acting in a specific direction. Stiffness may vary with direction and is highly dependent on the shape of the fixation construct. The effect of shape is described by the moment of inertia. In combination with the moment of inertia, the elastic modulus of the material describes how stiff the fixation will be under load, and its ability to withstand the forces of, for example the patient's weight during ambulation. Failure of fixation can come not only from loading above its yield point but also as a result of repetitive stress. Repetitive loading can cause growth of a crack at a stress concentrator, and can be significantly accentuated by corrosion when the implant is immersed in bodily fluids. Biologic tissues behave viscoelastically; that is, they creep under constant load, stress relax when the elongation is fixed, and increase in stiffness as the rate of load application increases.

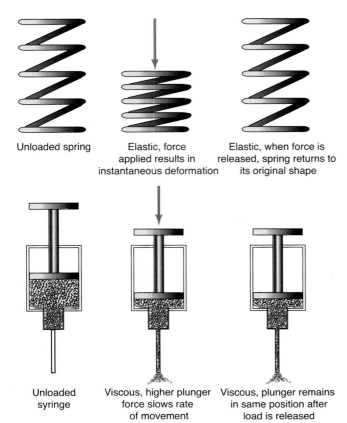

Unloaded spring

Elastic, force applied results in instantaneous deformation

Elastic, when force is released, spring returns to its original shape

Unloaded syringe

Viscous, higher plunger force slows rate of movement

Viscous, plunger remains in same position after load is released

FIGURE 1-10 Viscoelastic response in a biological tissue can be explained by considering and combining the properties of two devices, a simple spring and a fluid-filled syringe. The elastic or spring component instantly compresses when a load is applied to it. When the load is released, the spring returns to its original shape. When a load is applied to the viscous component, represented by the syringe, fluid is forced out the needle. If the load is released, the plunger does not return, but remains in its final position, representing the creep property of the tissue. Further, if the force is applied to the plunger more rapidly, there is greater resistance to motion, explaining the increased stiffness of tissue to increased rates of loading. Combinations of these simple components can be used to describe the mechanical properties of biologic tissues.

Compressive loading
resulting in large deformations

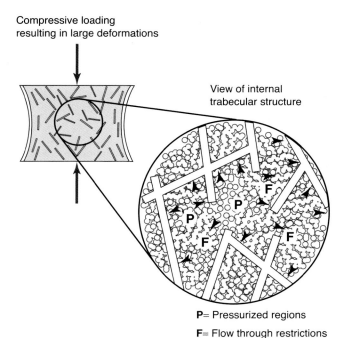

View of internal
trabecular structure

P = Pressurized regions

F = Flow through restrictions

FIGURE 1-11 Trabecular bone possesses some features of the spring and syringe viscoelastic model described in Figure 1-10, although it should be appreciated that this is an idealized model. The trabecular structure acts as the spring element. At higher loading rates, the interstitial fluid resists flowing through the trabecular spaces, causing increased internal pressure and greater bone stiffness. This anatomical feature allows vertebrae and the metaphyseal ends of long bones to resist dynamic loads caused by rapidly applied forces.[32]

TABLE 1-2	**Definitions of the Units Used to Describe the Basic Properties of Fracture Constructs**

Force, newtons (N) 1 N ~ 0.254 lb

Displacement, millimeters (mm)

Stress, pressure, modulus, megapascals (MPa) with 1 MPa = force of 1 N/area of 1 mm^2

Modulus = stress/strain, in which stress units are MPa; strain has no units

Strain (no units), strain = change in length (mm)/original length (mm)

In this chapter, these mechanical properties are described in basic units of measurements, defined in Table 1-2.

BIOMECHANICS OF INTACT AND HEALING BONE

Bone has a hierarchical structure. As shown in Figure 1-12, the lowest level of the structure consists of single collagen fibrils with embedded apatite crystals. At this level of structure, changing the collagen to mineral ratio has a significant effect on the elastic modulus of bone,[30,32,42] because it decreases with loss of mineral (Fig. 1-13). This is important from a fracture healing perspective because mineralizing healing callus goes through phases of increasing mineral density and corresponding increased modulus as healing occurs. At the next level of structural organization, the orientation of the collagen fibrils is important.[9–12,55–57] As demonstrated in Figure 1-14, the orientation of its fibers affects the ability of bone to support loads in specific

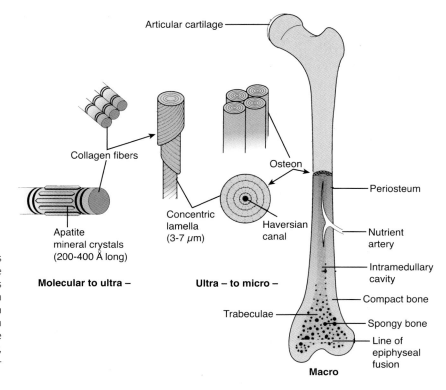

FIGURE 1-12 The hierarchical structure of bone is demonstrated. At the lowest level of organization, the ratio of mineral crystals to collagen fibrils determines elastic modulus of the combined material, as shown in Figure 1-13. At the next level, the fiber orientation is important in determining the difference in strength of bone in different directions. At the final level, the lamella of bone fibers form haversian systems that, particularly in cortical bone, are oriented in the direction of the major loads the bone must support.

Articular cartilage

Collagen fibers

Osteon

Periosteum

Concentric
lamella
(3-7 μm)

Haversian
canal

Nutrient
artery

Apatite
mineral crystals
(200-400 Å long)

Molecular to ultra –

Ultra – to micro –

Intramedullary
cavity

Compact bone

Trabeculae

Spongy bone

Line of
epiphyseal
fusion

Macro

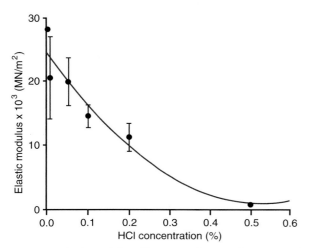

FIGURE 1-13 Elastic modulus of bone samples tested in tension after exposure to different concentrations of HCl. Greater HCl concentration progressively demineralizes bone, ultimately leaving only collagen. This diagram illustrates the contribution of bone mineral to the tensile elastic modulus of whole bone.[30]

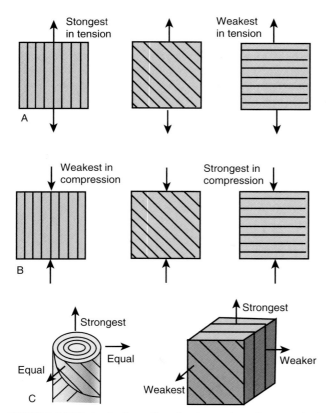

FIGURE 1-14 Effects of collagen fiber direction on the resistance to loads applied in different directions. **A.** Under tensile loading, the strongest arrangement is having the collagen fibers parallel to the load. **B.** Under compressive loading, the strongest arrangement is having the collagen fibers perpendicular to the load. **C.** In bone that must accommodate different loading directions, the arrangement of the haversian system produces one strongest direction along the axis, with proximately equal strengths in other directions.[57]

directions. During fracture healing, the callus initially starts as a disorganized random array of fibers, which progressively reorganize to become stiffest along the directions of the major applied loads (body weight and muscle forces) to which the bone is exposed. At the next level, the density of the haversian systems affects bone strength. It has been repeatedly demonstrated that a power law relationship exists between bone density and strength at this level of structure (Fig. 1-15). This means that as bone density decreases, its strength decreases as the square of its density (as density decreases by half, strength decreases by a factor of 4). This forms the basis for predicting changes in bone strength as a result of conditions such as osteoporosis. Similarly, the modulus changes with bone density by a power of between 2 and 3.[19,21,29,35,62] Noninvasive measures of bone density such as quantitative computed tomography (qCT) have been shown to have a significant predictive relationship to bone strength.[3,43–44,103]

Several additional factors can affect the strength of bone. As discussed previously, bone is a viscoelastic material whose strength and modulus both increase as loading rate increases (for example, in fracture impact loading as compared with normal ambulation).[29,38–40,108,163] The geometry of bone, specifically the size of the cross section and thickness of the cortex, affects its moment of inertia and therefore its strength.[124] Age also affects bone properties. The bending strength and modulus increase as bone mineralizes and matures from childhood to adulthood and slowly decrease thereafter[39,43,157] and the capacity to absorb impact energy decreases with age[41] as bone becomes more brittle. Defects or holes in bone (for example from drilling for screws) also affect its strength.[27,30,47,97,106] The torsional strength of bone decreases as the diameter of the hole or defect increases (Fig. 1-16). As the hole increases in size to 30% of the diameter of the bone, bone strength decreases to about 50% of that of the bone without a defect. An important consideration, applicable in the resection of bone (such as in removal of a tumor) is the shape of the hole or defect left after tumor removal. Leaving a hole with square corners significantly decreases bone strength compared to the same hole with rounded corners, because the square corner is a large stress concentrator. Oval or circular holes, while themselves still stress risers, do not contribute the additional effect of the sharp corner.[34] Table 1-3 summarizes the strength of cortical and cancellous bone material as well as the ultimate strengths of various whole bones.

As a fracture heals, its strength is affected by changes in its mineral content, callus diameter, and fiber organization, as discussed previously. The initial callus forms from the periosteal surface outward, which is beneficial mechanically, because as the outer diameter of the healing area enlarges, its moment of inertia and therefore its initial stiffness both increase, as shown in Figure 1-17.[122] The cross-sectional area increases progressively, as shown in Figure 1-18, as does the mineral content of the callus.[8] The mechanical results of these changes to bone as the fracture heals are shown in Figure 1-19. From torsional tests of healing rabbit long bones, progressive increases were observed in stiffness and peak torque to failure with time.[159] Interestingly, in that experiment, the stiffness appeared to gain normal values before the peak torque to failure, showing that stiffness and strength are related but not directly. Figure 1-19 shows that beyond 4 weeks (in rats, whose bones heal rapidly),

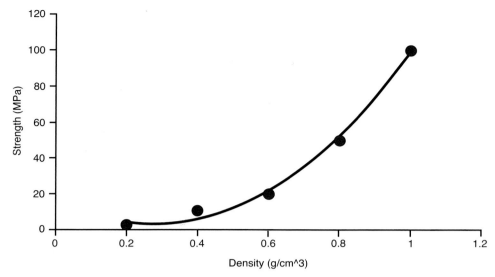

FIGURE 1-15 The relationship of trabecular bone density to compressive strength and modulus demonstrates a power law relationship so that these properties decrease by a factor of about 4 when density decreases by half.[32]

the cross-sectional area starts to decrease as the bone remodels to normal shape, while the bone tissue continues to mineralize.

The mechanical environment created by the fixation system along with the available blood supply affects the type of tissue formed in a healing fracture. The theory of interfragmentary strain attempts to relate the types of tissues formed to the amount of strain experienced by the tissue between the healing bone fragments.[122] This theory is a simple representation and cannot describe the complex stresses that the tissue is exposed to during actual healing. Nonetheless, within the limitations of the theory, when large strains occur in the tissues between healing bone surfaces, granulation tissue is formed. Intermediate level strains produce cartilage and small strains result in primary bone healing, or direct deposition of bone tissue with limited callus formation.

Among the limitations of this theory, one should recognize that it doesn't follow that zero strain will result in maximum bone formation. Load and some resulting strain are necessary within the healing fracture to stimulate bone formation. In a study in which controlled daily displacements in compression were applied to healing long bones using an external fixator, and the bone mineral within the healing fracture was measured with time, there was an optimal displacement above or below which less mineral was created in the fracture callus (Fig. 1-20).[158] Further, compression rather than tension is the preferred direction of loading.[16] Fracture fixation constructs of different stiffnesses within a certain range produce healed fractures with similar mechanical properties, however, they may reach this endpoint by different routes. In a study of femoral fixation using intramedullary rods of either 5% or 50% of the torsional stiffness of the intact femur, the femurs fixed with the lower stiffness rods produced an abundance of stabilizing callus, as opposed to the femurs with more rigid fixation, see Figure 1-21. This is because with more rigid fixation there was less necessity for biological fracture stabilization. In both cases, however, the mechanical properties of the healed fractures were ultimately similar.[162] These studies demonstrate that some strain as a result of loading the fracture stimulates healing, and that bone will adapt and heal within a relatively wide range of mechanical stability environments.

In summary, several factors affect the strength of bone and healing fractures. Increasing mineral content increases fracture stiffness. Callus that forms on the periosteal surface is beneficial in increasing the moment of inertia and therefore the stiffness of the fractured region. Healing fractures exhibit several stages, with stiffness returning to normal followed later by peak load to failure. Bone will heal within a range of mechanical environments. To a certain extent, healing bone will compensate for more flexible fixation by forming a greater quantity of fracture callus; however, there is a range of loading of a healing callus, sufficient to stimulate bone formation, which increases as the callus matures.

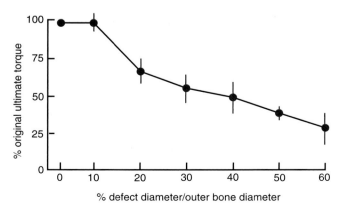

FIGURE 1-16 The relationship of ultimate torque (failure torque) of a long bone to the diameter of the hole divided by the outer diameter of the bone. There is no change in ultimate torque until the defect size increase beyond greater than 10% of the diameter of the bone.[47]

BIOMECHANICS OF BONE FRACTURE

To appreciate why bone fractures in certain patterns, one must understand that, as shown in Table 1-3, bone is weakest in

TABLE 1-3 **Mechanical Properties of Bone Material and Whole Bones in Different Loading Directions**

Bone Type	Load Type	Elastic Modulus ($\times$ 10 E9 N/m²)	Ultimate Stress ($\times$ 10 E6 N/m²)	Reference
Cortical	Tension	11.4–19.1	107–146	Evans Acta Anat 1958;35:285 Evans Am J Anat 1967;120:79 Kotani Spine 1999;24:1406 Wright Med Biol Eng 1976;14:671 Reilly, J Biomech 1974;7:271
	Compression	15.1–19.7	156–212	Curry 1984, Princeton University Press
	Shear		73–82	Yamada 1970, Williams and Wilkins
Cancellous	Tension	~0.2–5.0	~3–20	Curry J Biomech 1976;12:459
	Compression	0.1–3	1.5–50	Carter J Bone Jt Surg 1977;59A:954 Weaver J Bone Jt Surg 1966;48A:289 Galante Calcif Tissue Res 1970;5:236
	Shear		6.6 +/− 1.7	Stone J Biomech 1983;16:743

Bone Type	Loading Direction and Type	Ultimate Strength	Reference
Cervical spine	Axial compressive impact	980–7400N	Kotani Spine 1999;24:1406 McElhaney Soc Auto Eng 1983;83:1615 Nusholtz 25th STAPP car crash conf 1981:1197 Yoganandan J Spinal Disorders 1991;4:73
	Extension	57 N-m	Nahum Accidental Injury 1993 Springer-Verlag
	Flexion	120 N-m	Nahum Accidental Injury 1993 Springer-Verlag
	Lateral Bending	54 N-m	Nahum Accidental Injury 1993 Springer-Verlag
Lumbar Spine	Axial compressive impact	1400–9000 N	Bell Calcif Tissue Res 1967;1:75 Brassow Eur J Radiol 1982;2:99 Cody Spine 1991;16:146 Hansson Spine 1980;5:46 Halton J Anat 1979;129:753 Tran Spine 1994;20:1984
Sacroiliac Joint	Axial compressive impact	3450–3694 N	Fasola 1955; Wright Patterson AFB
Femoral neck	Lateral to medial at trochanter	1000–4000 N	Smith J Bone Jt Surg 1953;35A:367
	Vertical impact at femoral head	725–10,570 N	Alho Clin Orthop 1988;227:292 Leicher Clin Orthop 1982;163:272 Stankewitz J Orthop Res 1996;14:786
Femur	Torsion	183 N-m	Martens J Biomech 1980;13:667
	From impact at knee along axis	6230–17,130 N	Patrick 9th STAPP car crash conf 1966:237 Viano J Biomech 1980;13:701
	Three-point bending, posterior	21.2–31.3 N-m	Mather J Biomech 1968;1:331
Patella	Impact perpendicular to anterior	6900–10,012N	Patrick 9th STAPP car crash conf 1966:237
Tibia	Axial torsion	101 +/− 35 Nm	Martens J Biomech 1980;13:667
Foot and ankle	Impact perpendicular to sole	4107–6468 N	Assal 46th AAAM 2002:273 Yoganandan Soc Auto Eng 1996;96:2426 Schueler In Soc Auto Eng 1996;PT-56:551 Kitagawa Soc Auto Eng 1998;983145 Funk Soc Auto Eng; 2000;2000-01-0155 McMaster; STAPP car crash conf 2000;44:357

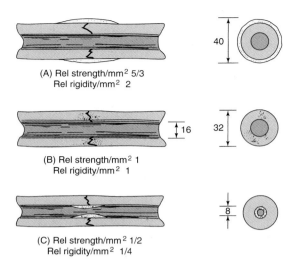

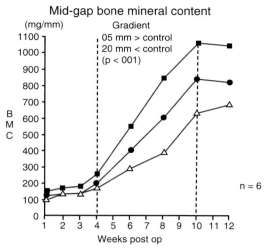

Mid-gap bone mineral content

FIGURE 1-17 A comparison of the moments of inertia and resulting strengths when fracture callus is located **(A)** on the outer surface, **(B)** on the bone surfaces, or **(C)** in the medullary canal. The strength and rigidity are significantly increased when callus is located over the periosteal surface, compared to within the medullary canal.[118]

FIGURE 1-20 The effect on bone mineral of different cyclic displacements applied daily within a healing fracture (upper curve, 0.5 mm; middle curve, 1.0 mm; lower curve, 2.0 mm for 500 cycles/day). This shows that some displacement (in this experiment, 0.5 mm) stimulates bone formation, but that greater displacements (1.0 mm and 2.0 mm) do not enhance bone formation. These results point to an optimal range of displacements for maximum bone formation.[158]

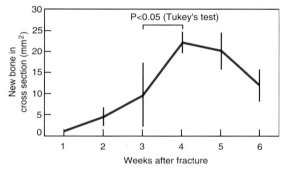

FIGURE 1-18 Changes in the cross-sectional area of a healing femoral fracture, which peaks and slowly decreases. There is a similar increase in the mineral content. (The data come from rats, which heal more rapidly than humans, indicated by the 4-week time to peak mineralization.[8])

tension and strongest in compression. Therefore, when a force creates tensile stresses in a particular region of a loaded bone, failure will generally occur first in that region. The simplest example, shown in Figure 1-22, is the transverse fracture created in a long bone subjected to pure bending. Because in this example the upper, convex surface undergoes the greatest elongation, it is subjected to the largest tensile stresses, and failure, indicated by a crack, initiates here. The crack then progresses transversely through the material, and layers just below the outer layer become subjected to high tensile stress until they crack as well. In this manner, the crack progresses through the bone transversely until it fails. The concave surface is subjected to compression so the crack does not initiate there. A second example is the fracture line or crack that occurs when a bone

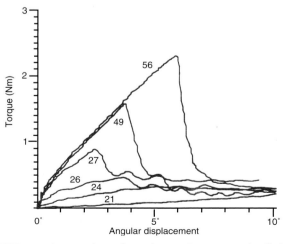

FIGURE 1-19 A comparison of superimposed torque-angular displacement plots taken from experimental long bones at different stages of healing shows the significant increase in both stiffness and peak torque to failure with increased duration of healing. Numerical values are time in days postfracture in rabbits.[159]

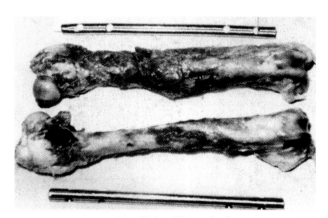

FIGURE 1-21 A comparison of the different healing responses of dog femurs with midshaft fractures fixed with **(top)** IM rods of 5%, or **(bottom)** 50% of the torsional stiffness of the intact femur. The femurs fixed with rods of lower stiffness produced more callus as additional stabilization against functional loads, but there was ultimately no difference in mechanical properties between the femurs fixed with rods of different stiffnesses.[162]

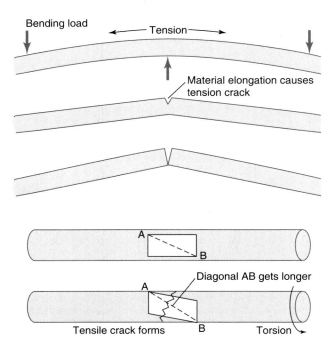

FIGURE 1-22 **Top:** A transverse fracture is created by the progressive tensile failure of bone material starting from the convex surface in which elongation and therefore stress is greatest, with the crack progressing to the concave side. **Bottom:** A spiral fracture is created by the progressive failure in tension of fibers on the bone surface along the diagonal that elongates as the material on the surface distorts when torque is applied. (A rectangle on the surface becomes a parallelogram, with one diagonal elongating. The crack will be transverse to the diagonal.)

is subjected to torsion or axial twisting. In those cases, a spiral fracture results. Consider, as shown in Figure 1-22, a rectangular area on the surface of a long bone that is loaded in torsion. The rectangle distorts as the bone twists, with one diagonal of the rectangle elongating and the other shortening, depending on the direction of twist. A crack will form perpendicular to the diagonal that is elongating, and progresses around the perimeter of the bone resulting in a spiral fracture. The region of bone with the smallest diameter is usually the least stiff region, resulting in the greatest distortion of the surface and is generally the location of the fracture. This explains why torsional fractures of the tibia often occur in the narrow distal third, see Figure 1-23.

A compressive load results in failure of cortical bone by shear, indicated by slippage along the diagonal, because bone is weaker in shear than in compression (Fig. 1-24). In this case, compressive loading causes an interface within the bone at 45 degrees to the applied load to slide along another at an oblique angle. At very high loads, such as during impact fractures, crushing or comminution of bone also occurs, especially at the weaker metaphyseal ends of a long bone. The trabecular bone at the metaphyseal ends is weaker in compression than the diaphyseal cortical bone is in shear. Because of this, it is unlikely that shearing failure will occur in the diaphysis caused by pure compressive forces. The butterfly fracture (Fig. 1-24) results from combined bending and compression. Bending load causes the fracture to start to fail in tension producing a transverse crack, but as the crack progresses and the remaining intact bone weakens, it starts to fail in compression, causing an oblique (shear) fracture line. As the ends of the failing bone are driven together, a third fragment—the butterfly—may result as the

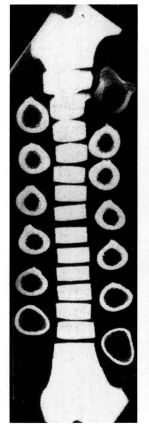

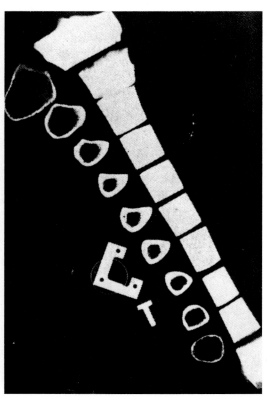

FIGURE 1-23 Cross sections through **(left)** a femur, and **(right)** a tibia. The small cross section of the distal third of the tibia results in more distortion and higher stresses and explains why torsional failure often occurs in this area.

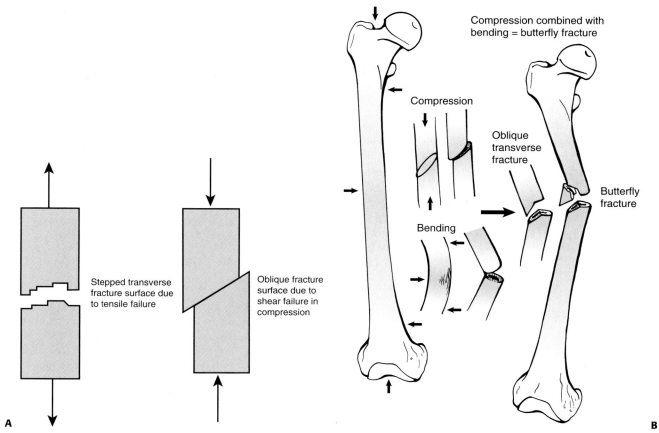

FIGURE 1-24 A. Left: Tensile fracture causes a stepped surface as fibers pull apart. The crack progresses, then steps to an adjacent region in which failure continues. **Right:** Pure compression of cortical bone results in failure by shearing or sliding along oblique surfaces. In reality, pure compression of a long bone (in a fall for example) results in crushing of the much weaker metaphyseal trabecular bone with a pilon fracture of the distal tibia or a tibial plateau fracture as the result. **B.** Some fractures that combine bending and compression demonstrate transverse cracking as a result of bending followed by an oblique crack characteristic of compressive failure. The butterfly fracture with additional splitting of the fragment secondary to the initial fracture is an example.

oblique fragment splits off. The production of a butterfly fragment probably depends on the timing and magnitude of the two basic applied loads: compression and bending.

Aging, especially with osteoporotic changes, alters the force required to fracture bone and the types of fractures that occur. As shown in Figure 1-15, trabecular bone stiffness varies with the cube (3rd power) of its density and strength approximately with the square of its density.[32] Bone mass normally peaks around age 25 to 30 years and decreases up to 1% annually thereafter. If the density of trabecular bone is decreased by 30% in a 60- to 70-year-old as a result of osteoporosis, the bone compressive strength is about half of that of a 30-year-old. Typically, fractures as a result of osteoporosis occur in the vertebrae, the distal radius, and the femoral neck. In addition, osteoporosis changes the cross-sectional shape of long bones, decreasing thickness by increasing the endosteal diameter while causing the periosteal diameter to increase. If cortical outer diameter—for example, in the femur—increased and cortical thickness decreased at the same rate, the moment of inertia of the bone cross section would be larger. That is why large-diameter thin tubing can be substituted for smaller diameter thicker tubing in structures (for example, sailboat masts), saving weight while

not sacrificing strength. However, in the femur, the inner surface of the cortex also becomes more irregular and porous, decreasing its material strength. A common result of loss of femoral bone mass combined with other factors, such as poor balance, is a hip fracture usually resulting from a fall.[1]

Auto crashes account for many fractures. Some particular mechanisms have been observed. Fracture of the calcaneus or the malleoli of the foot and ankle can occur through a combination of the foot being forced against the brake pedal by the weight of the occupant during a high speed frontal collision, or in combination with the floor pan of the auto crushing into the space in which the foot resides.[127] Drivers who were braking during a crash were shown to be much more likely to injure their right foot compared with their left foot.[15] If the Achilles tendon applies load to resist the forced dorsiflexion of the foot on the brake pedal, the combination of these two loads make cause three point bending loading of the calcaneus, with the posterior facet of the talus as the fulcrum. A crack initiates on the plantar or tensile side of the calcaneus and a tongue type calcaneus fracture can occur. Inversion or eversion, in which the foot is not securely planted on the brake pedal and rotates with compression, is likely to result in a malleolar fracture,[61] although the combinations of forces causing these high energy fractures are not entirely predictable.

A major mechanism of midshaft femur fractures is impact with the dashboard of the vehicle in a frontal collision, especially for unrestrained drivers who submarine or slide forward in the seat.[154] Tensing the quadriceps and hamstrings muscles during a crash applies significant additional compression along the femur.[154] The anterior bow of the femur causes the external compressive force from contact of the knee with the dashboard, and internal muscle forces to bend the femur, resulting in bending and transverse or oblique fractures. If the femur of the occupant hits the dashboard in an adducted orientation, the femur can be displaced from the acetabulum, causing a fracture of the acetabular roof and dislocation of the hip joint. Pelvic fractures result from loading in side impact crashes, in which the door punches inward against the hip and pelvis. The actual fracture pattern (symphysis, sacroiliac joint, or both) is probably the result of the specific alignment of the pelvis with the applied loads at impact. Pelvic fracture classifications are based on the presumed mechanism of injury and specific forces applied.[139,141,166,167] Bilateral hip fractures have been found to occur in crashes in which the vehicle has a large center console that tends to trap the pelvis as force is also applied on the hip opposite that which contacts the door. Auto crashes also create, in occupants with lap but not shoulder belts, the classic "Chance fracture," which is combined compression and flexion failure of a lumbar vertebra, usually at the level in which the lap belt forms a fulcrum. Upper extremity injuries in auto crashes have been found to be related to airbag deployment and entrapment of the arm in the steering wheel.[65]

BIOMECHANICS OF FRACTURE IMPLANTS

Avoiding Mechanical Problems with Fracture Fixation Devices

In this section, the functions of commonly used fixation devices for skeletal fracture fixation are discussed. Observed fixation problems with devices such as wire, cable, screws plates, IM rods, and external fixators are explained with the objective of reducing the potential for mechanical damage or failure of these devices during use.

Cerclage Wire Breakage

The tensile strength of surgical wire has been shown to increase directly with its diameter,[150] and when twisted, the optimal number of turns is between four and eight.[132] However, solid wire is very sensitive to notches or scratches. Testing shows that notches as small as 1% of the diameter of the wire can reduce its fatigue life by 63%.[132] For this reason, cable has been introduced for cerclage applications. Cable has significantly better fatigue performance compared to wire, as shown in Figure 1-25.[64] Because cables consist of multiple strands of single thin wires, damage to any particular strand does not result in failure of the whole cable. Single loops of suture such as Ethibond are about 30% as strong as 18-gage stainless steel wire in tension, and Merseline tape is about 50% as strong. Four loops of Ethibond were shown to have tensile strength equivalent to stainless steel wire.[70]

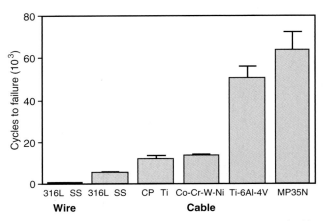

FIGURE 1-25 A comparison of the fatigue resistance of wire and cables made of the indicated materials. Wire, 316 SS (stainless steel), cable 316 SS, Cp Ti, commercially pure titanium, Co-Cr-W-Ni, cobalt chrome, Ti 6Al 4V, titanium alloy, MP35N, nickel alloy.[64]

Screw Breakage by Shearing during Insertion

A screw is a mechanical device that is used to convert rotary load (torque) into compression between a plate and bone, or between bone fragments. As shown in Figure 1-26, the thread of a screw, if unwound from the shaft, is really a ramp or inclined plane that pulls, for example, underlying bone toward

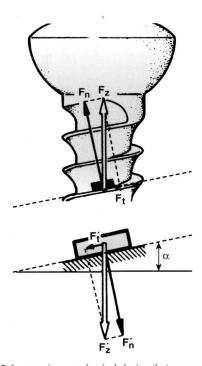

FIGURE 1-26 A screw is a mechanical device that converts torque into compression between objects. The screw thread is actually an inclined plane that slowly pulls the objects it is embedded into together. For this reason, the head and screw shaft in one part must be free to rotate. If this part of the screw is threaded into the hole of the first part (for example, the plate) it will not allow the surfaces to compress (F_n, normal or compressive force acting against the screw head; F_t, tangential or frictional force acting along the screw thread; F_z, resultant of the two forces, α, angle of the screw thread. The smaller the angle α [finer thread] the lower the frictional force).

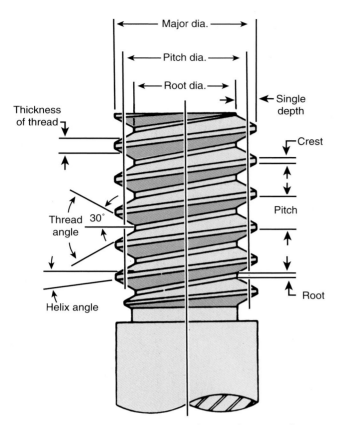

FIGURE 1-27 Nomenclature of screws. The root diameter is the inner diameter of the screw and the pitch defines the distance between threads.

screw to turn freely. Tapping is necessary in cortical bone so that the torque applied by the surgeon is converted into compression instead of cutting threads and overcoming friction between the screw thread and bone (F_t in Figure 1-26) that it is being driven into (Fig. 1-28).[75] At the same time, self-tapping screws are available and, when used, those with multiple cutting flutes at the tip of the screw appeared to be the easiest to insert and had greater holding power.[165] With cancellous bone, as discussed later, tapping is less advantageous, unless the bone is very dense. One common problem during screw placement is shear failure of the screw, typically the head twisting off leaving the shaft embedded in bone and difficult to remove. This can occur especially when using smaller (less than 4 mm diameter) screws in dense bone, especially without tapping. The stiffness and strength of a screw are related to the 4th power of its diameter (the effect of moment of inertia, for screws of the same material). A 6-mm diameter screw is approximately 5 times as stiff as a 3-mm diameter screw and 16 times as resistant to shear failure by over-torquing the screw during insertion.

Screw Pullout

Particularly in cancellous bone, the maximum force that a screw can withstand along its axis, the pullout force, depends upon the size of the screw and the density of the bone it is placed into. As shown in Figure 1-29, when the force acting on the screw exceeds its pullout strength, the screw will pull or shear out of the hole, carrying the sheared bone within its threads, because it is usually the bone that fails and not the screw. The pullout force increases with larger screw diameter, a longer embedded length of screw shaft, and greater density of the bone it is placed into.[33,45,58,134] The diameter and length of the embedded screw can be thought of as defining the outer surface of a cylinder along which the screw shears. Given the maximum stress that bone of a particular density can withstand, increasing the surface area of the screw cylinder increases the pullout force (because force = stress × area over which it acts). To enhance screw purchase, consider embedding the largest diameter screw possible into bone of the greatest density over as long a purchase length as possible.[33,45] Pullout strength also increases significantly if the screw is placed through both bone cortices.

In cancellous bone, screw pullout becomes a more significant

the fixation plate, causing compression between them.[123] The basic components of a screw are shown in Figure 1-27. Because of its function, the screw head and shaft should be free to turn in the plate; otherwise the compressive force generated may be limited. (This doesn't apply to screws that are designed to be threaded into the plate holes in locking plates.) One common problem is that sometimes threads are tapped into both bone components. The bone component in which the screw head will rest should be drilled oversize to allow the shaft of the

FIGURE 1-28 Schematic diagram showing the approximate distribution of torque acting on screw placed into cortical bone. With a pretapped hole, about 65% of the applied torque goes to produce compression and 35% to overcome the friction associated with driving the screw. When the hole is not tapped, only about 5% of the torque is used to produce compression, the rest going to overcome friction and to cut threads in bone. These observations do not apply in cancellous bone.

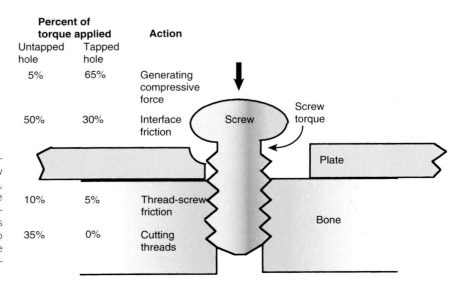

Percent of torque applied		Action
Untapped hole	Tapped hole	
5%	65%	Generating compressive force
50%	30%	Interface friction
10%	5%	Thread-screw friction
35%	0%	Cutting threads

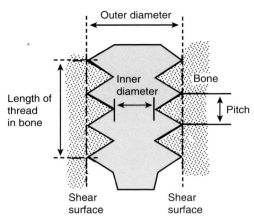

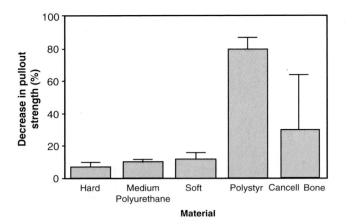

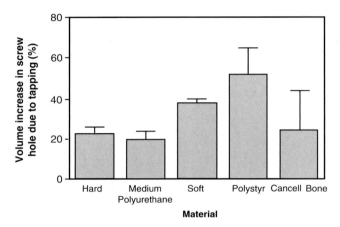

FIGURE 1-29 The factors that determine the pullout strength of a screw are its outer diameter and length of engagement (this defines the dimensions of a cylinder of bone that is carried in the threads and is sheared out as the screw is pulled out of bone) and the shear strength of bone at the screw/bone interface, which is directly related to its density. A finer pitch screw produces a small gain in purchase.[33]

problem because the porosity of cancellous bone reduces its density and therefore its shear strength.[148] Hole preparation, specifically drilling but not tapping, improves the pullout strength of screws placed into cancellous bone (such as pedicle screws in the vertebral body).[33] The reason that tapping reduces strength in cancellous bone, as shown in Figure 1-30, is that running the tap in and out of the hole removes bone, effectively increasing the diameter of the hole and reducing the amount of bone material that interacts with the screw threads. Tapping has more effect as bone density decreases and can reduce the pullout strength from 10% to as much as 30%. It should also be noted that the findings of studies related to pullout strength relate to the time immediately after insertion. As the bone heals, it also remodels around the screw, possibly doubling its initial pullout strength.[134]

FIGURE 1-30 Top: The decrease in pullout strength in various types of foam used to test bone screws demonstrating the percentage decrease in pullout strength between screws placed into holes that were either drilled only or drilled and tapped. **Bottom:** The percentage increase in volume comparing holes that were drilled only and those that were drilled and tapped. Tapping in cancellous bone increases hole volume, which decreases pullout strength.[33]

Screw Breakage by Cyclic Loading

A mechanism exists through which cortical screws can fail because of cyclic bending, shown in Figure 1-31. This mode of loading could occur during functional use; for example, with a dynamic compression plate (DCP) but not a locking plate. The screw should be tightened against the DCP plate to the maximum extent possible and the tightening torque effectively transferred to compressive force between plate and bone (see Fig. 1-28). The screw holds the plate against bone partly by frictional contact, which depends on the frictional force generated between the undersurface of the plate and bone. The frictional force is directly dependent on the compressive force generated by the screws. If any sliding occurs between the plate and bone, bending load will be transferred from the head of the screw into the plate, where screw-plate contact occurs. Bending loads perpendicular to the axis of the screw, along with possible stress corrosion and fretting corrosion, may cause the screws to fail rapidly in fatigue. Zand et al[168] showed that screws tightened against a plate with only 10% to 15% less force than the maximum possible failed in less than 1000 loading cycles, by bending fatigue, compared with fully tightened screws that were able to sustain over 2.5 million loading cycles. Screws that lock into the plate reduce this problem. Small fragment screws, around

4 mm outside diameter, can fatigue because their core diameters are small. The trade-off in use of these devices is choosing a screw with a larger core diameter and shallower thread to reduce the possibility of fatigue, or a smaller core diameter and deeper thread to increase purchase strength in bone.[111]

Cannulated screws are commonly used for fixation, having the significant advantage that they can be precisely guided into position over a guide wire, which itself may aid in reduction of a fracture fragment. Nevertheless, drilling precision for the screw or guide wire is decreased with increasing density of bone, and the use of longer and smaller diameter drill bits.[74] Cannulated screws follow the same mechanical principles as solid screws, however, to create the central hole, material must be removed from the center of the screw. Manufacturers commonly increase the minor diameter (the diameter of the screw at the base of the thread) to accommodate the loss of this material. The same size cannulated screws usually have less thread depth compared with solid screws. The result—depending on the screw size—is less pullout strength. For 4-mm diameter screws, cannulated screws of the same outside diameter had about 16% less pullout strength.[151] Alternatively, to keep the same thread depth, the outer diameter of the screw may be increased.

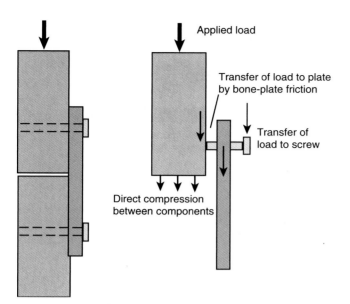

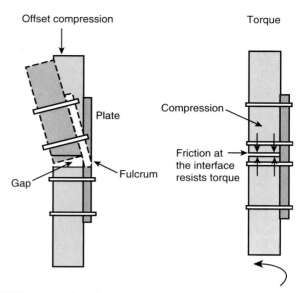

FIGURE 1-31 A mechanism for rapid failure of screws in cyclic bending occurs when the screw has not been tightened sufficiently to keep the plate from sliding along the bone surface (the plate-bone gap shown here is exaggerated for clarity). The result is that bending loads are applied transverse to the long axis of the screw, which in combination with fretting corrosion caused by the screws rubbing against the plate results in early failure of the screw.

FIGURE 1-33 Left: When a gap is left on the cortex opposite that to which the plate is attached, bending of the plate at the fracture site can cause the plate to fail rapidly in bending. **Right:** Compressing the fracture surfaces not only allows the bone cortices to resist bending loads but the frictional contact and interdigitation help resist torsion.

Breakage of Fracture Fixation Plates

The fracture fixation plate is designed to stabilize a fracture by driving the ends of the fracture together, compressing them. This is beneficial to fracture healing because it improves stability, opening the possibility for primary bone healing with minimal callus formation, and by enhancing the resistance of the plate to bending fatigue failure. Observing the cross section of an oval hole in a dynamic compression fracture plate, Figure 1-32, shows that one border of the hole actually has an inclined surface. When the head of the screw displaces downward toward the bone surface, the screw and the fragment of bone it is attached to slide toward the center of the plate. This action, which occurs in both fracture components, causes the fracture surfaces to be driven together [2] and creates significant compressive forces across the ends of the fracture.[37] Compressing the

ends of the fracture significantly improves the stability of the construct and reduces bending and torsional stresses applied to the plate, increasing its life. Stability is improved because the bone ends resist bending forces that close the fracture gap, and torsional loads are resisted by the frictional force and interlock between the ends of the fracture components. Also, the fracture gap that must be healed is smaller.

It is important to appreciate that the plate is vulnerable to bending failure, because plates are thin, relatively easy to bend (compared to bone), and have low moments of inertia. They are designed to apply compressive force to the ends of the fracture, and the stabilized bone can then resist the bending loads applied during functional use. If a gap is left on the side opposite the plate, Figure 1-33, the fracture site becomes a fulcrum around which the plate bends under combined compressive and bending loads such as those which occur during ambulation (if the compressive force is not located directly down the tibial

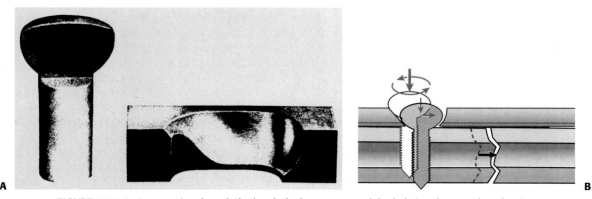

FIGURE 1-32 A. Cross section through the head of a bone screw and the hole in a fracture plate showing the geometry. **B.** As the screw is tightened, the head slides down the inclined border of the plate, which displaces the screw sideways, and therefore the screw and the bone fragment to which the screw is attached are displaced toward the opposite fragment.

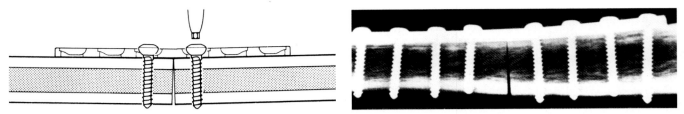

FIGURE 1-34 A demonstration of the gapping that occurs on the opposite cortex when a flat plate is applied to a flat bone surface. Slightly prebending the plate causes the ends of the opposite cortices to be driven together when the plate is applied.[118]

shaft, which occurs during heel strike and toe off, then bending loads will be applied along with the compressive force). Gapping can also occur when a segment of bone is missing at the fracture site, or if the plate is not properly contoured during application. Figure 1-34 demonstrates how a flat, noncontoured plate tightened against a flat bone surface will cause a gap to appear on the opposite cortex.[118] This is why a plate should be prebent sufficiently to create an initial gap between it and the bone surface it will be applied to.[68,119,136] Gapping at the fracture also occurs when the plate is applied to the predominantly compressive side instead of the tensile side of a long bone during functional loading that causes bending. Figure 1-35 demonstrates that placing the plate on the compressive side will cause a gap to open under load.

Plate stresses are significantly increased by gapping at the fracture.[14] In comminuted fractures in which it is difficult to approximate the fracture ends, screws should be placed as close as possible across the fracture gap to reduce strains in the plate.[53] Torsional and bending stiffness of a fracture construct can be significantly increased, and therefore plate strain reduced, by increasing the length of the plate itself[133] as well as with several cortices of fixation (i.e., screw-cortex contact).

However, as shown in Figure 1-36, there is an optimum number of cortices, eight for DCP plates and nine for LC-DCP plates, beyond which there is little additional gain in torsional stiffness[54]. Figure 1-37 shows several interesting aspects related to plate fixation with screws. First, plate strains are highest at the two holes adjacent to the fracture gap and become very small five holes away. Second, this occurs regardless of whether the screws were placed near the fracture (locations 2, 3, 4, and 5), far from the fracture (locations 7, 8, 9, and 10), or were mixed (locations 2, 6, and 9).[53] This data also indicates that not all holes of the plate need to be filled with screws to provide similar fixation stiffness.

A significant recent development in plate design is the locking or LISS (less invasive stabilization system) plate,[60] also called the noncontact plate or internal fixator,[83] in which the screw head has a machine thread, separate from the bone thread, which locks it to the plate. The screws and plate form a rigid connection. In addition, the screws have been designed with a finer thread for unicortical fixation.[53] The LISS plate functions differently biomechanically from the dynamic compression plate (DCP). The DCP plate is compressed against the bone fragments by the screws and requires bone to plate contact to produce a stable fracture construct. Buttressing of the opposite cortex is important in maintaining fracture stability and reducing plate stresses with the DCP plate. Bending loads applied to the screws in the nonlocking DCP plate caused the screws to rotate within the plate resulting in fracture fragment motion, higher plate stresses, and reduced stability at the fracture site.

The LISS plate acts conceptually like an external fixator,[60] in which the pins (screws) are rigidly connected to the side bar (the plate) and bone to fixator contact is reduced in the low contact plate version. This produces less interference with the biological processes of fracture healing, especially helping to preserve the blood supply near the fracture site. Also, the LISS plate provides more stability in comminuted fractures[142] in which cortical buttressing and compression are difficult to achieve and fracture mechanical stability occurs mainly from the hardware.[50] LISS plates do not allow the screws to be directed obliquely, except when specifically designed into the implant, and do not generally develop interfragmentary compression at the fracture site. Bending loads applied to the screws from bone are resisted by the locking interface between the threads in the screw head and the threads in the plate. Therefore, these plates are not as dependent on cortical buttressing for stability as the DCP plate. Dynamic fatigue testing has shown that LISS plates have fatigue strengths similar to other systems and are able to support loads comparable to 1 bodyweight for 2 million cycles, which should be sufficient for normal fracture healing. Because

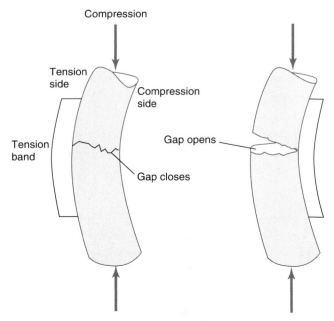

FIGURE 1-35 The application of a plate on the compressive as opposed to the tensile side of a bone subjected to bending causes a gap to open on the opposite side of the plate during functional loading.

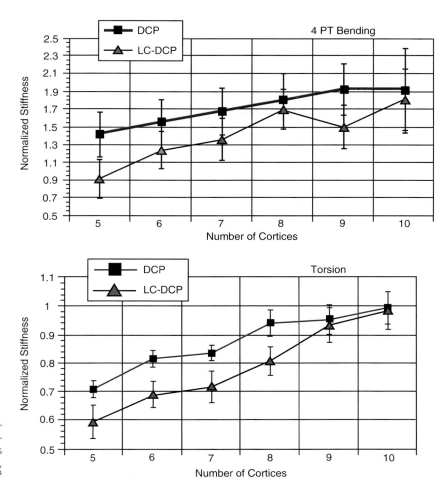

FIGURE 1-36 Relative stiffness of a plate-bone construct in **(top)** torsion and **(bottom)** bending as a function of the number of cortices through which screws have been placed (DCP, dynamic compression plate, LC-DCP, limited contact dynamic compression plate).[54]

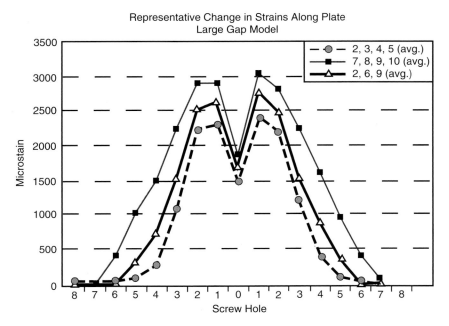

FIGURE 1-37 Distribution of strain (measured in microstrain or strain $\times 10^{-6}$) at various locations along a plate regardless of placement of the screws in different locations (holes 2, 3, 45), (holes 7, 8, 9, 10), or holes (2, 6, 9).[53]

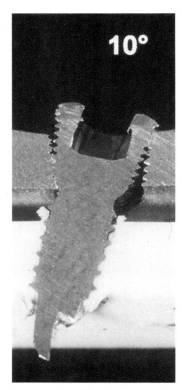

FIGURE 1-38 A demonstration of the importance of accurate placement of locking screws into the plate.[81]

screw pullout strength is related directly to the length of screw purchase in bone cortex, the unicortical screws used in some systems have lower pullout strength than bicortical screws. More screws must be used to compensate for the inherent lower pullout strength of the unicortical screw. As with other systems, the LISS plates have mechanical sensitivities. For example, accurate placement of the locking screws is important. As Figure 1-38 shows, angulation of the screw causes incomplete engagement and, therefore, lower mechanical stability of the construct. In fact, comparatively, the bending stability of a 4.5-mm LISS plate was reduced to 63% and 31%, respectively, caused by a 5- or 10-degree misalignment of the locking screws in the plate.[81]

Plate Failure through a Screw Hole
Many plates are long with multiple screw holes to provide flexibility of fixation of bone fractures with complex geometries. It is not necessary to place screws in every hole in the plate,[46] but the effects of screw placement on fixation stiffness should be understood. The screw hole will be an area of elevated stresses on the plate, unless the plate is made thicker near the holes to compensate, as is the case with some plates. Placing the plate so that an empty screw hole is located over the fracture will significantly increase the potential for fatigue fracture of the plate. The plate material around the holes will have higher material stresses than occurs in the solid regions of the plate. Around the holes, the force acts through a smaller cross-sectional area, so the material stresses must be higher. A second consideration related to multihole plates is that separating the screws so that there is a greater distance between them across the fracture site results in lower stiffness of the plate-fracture

construct. As with any beam (plate), the greater the distance between the supports (screws), the greater the bending displacement and the higher the stresses will be for the same applied load. It is best to avoid placing screw holes over or near the fracture site and it is beneficial, in terms of improving fixation stiffness, to place screws as close together across the fracture site as possible.

Fully Threaded Lag Screws
The lag screw is a very effective device for generating large compressive forces across fracture fragments, and these forces are applied directly across the fracture site. The head and upper part of the shaft of the screw must be allowed to glide in one fracture component so that it pulls the other fracture component towards it to create compression across the two. As shown in Figure 1-39, a fully threaded lag screw blocks the gliding action between the two components. Comparing the compressive forces across the fracture site using fully and partly threaded lag screws demonstrated that the average compressive force at the opposite cortex (i.e., the force in the screw itself) was about 50% greater when a partly threaded screw was used.[86]

Femoral Splitting as a Result of IM Rod Insertion
Insertion of an intramedullary (IM) rod into the femur can lead to difficulties because the femur has a significant anterior curvature,[169] shown in Figure 1-40. Current femoral nails have radii of curvature that range from 186 to 300 cm, compared with the average for a large sample of femora, which was 120 +/− 36 cm. Therefore, current femoral nails are considerably straighter than the femora they are inserted into.[49] The rod, which also has a curved shape to accommodate the femoral bow, must conform to the curvature of the femur as insertion progresses. Placing a rod, which is essentially a steel curved spring, down the femoral canal causes the rod to bend, because the femur is generally much stiffer than the rod, Figure 1-41. In fact, the nail must conform not only to an anterior-posterior

FIGURE 1-39 Using a fully threaded lag screw causes the threads to engage in bone on both sides of the fracture. This inhibits the screw from compressing the bone fragments together.[86]

FIGURE 1-40 Cross sections of various femora demonstrate the curvature that an IM rod must conform to when it is fully inserted.[169]

bow but also canal curvature medially and laterally.[51] Figure 1-42 demonstrates that rod contact with the internal surfaces of the femur generates forces which resist insertion. These rod-femur contact forces, directed perpendicular to the surface of the medullary canal cause the femur to expand and will result in splitting if they become too large.[80]

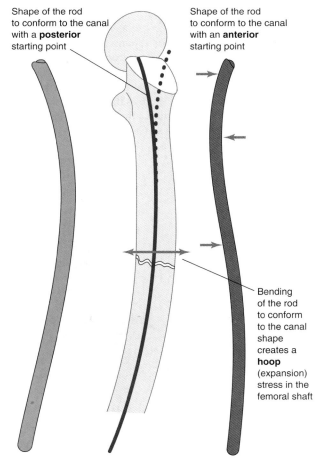

Shape of the rod to conform to the canal with a **posterior** starting point

Shape of the rod to conform to the canal with an **anterior** starting point

Bending of the rod to conform to the canal shape creates a **hoop** (expansion) stress in the femoral shaft

FIGURE 1-41 Mismatch of the curvature between the IM rod and the medullary canal results in bending stresses that could cause splitting of the femur during insertion.[80]

The factors that govern the amount of bending of the rod during insertion and the resulting internal forces acting within the femur are the proximal starting hole position, the length of the proximal fragment, the initial curvature of the IM rod compared with the curvature of the femur, and the rod bending stiffness. Stiffnesses of rods can vary considerably.[131] Figure 1-42 demonstrates examples in which rod proximal starting hole position resulted in femoral splitting during rod insertion.[80] Some newer IM nails employ a valgus bend to be used with a femoral trochanteric entry portal.[120] The optimal entry point for retrograde nailing, used selectively when antegrade nailing is not possible, was found to be about 1.2 cm anterior to the femoral origin of the posterior cruciate ligament and at the midpoint of the intracondylar sulcus.[91]

IM Rod and Locking Screw Breakage

Fractures of IM rods and locking screws occur occasionally during healing. The most demanding mechanical situation for IM rod fixation of the femur or tibia occurs when the fracture is very distal. Figure 1-43 compares the forces acting on idealized femora with more proximal and more distal fractures. For a specific location of the external load (muscle load or body weight), the more distal fracture results in a longer moment arm (the perpendicular distance from the load to the fracture site) creating a greater moment, and therefore higher stresses in the rod. The highest stresses in the rod occur near the fracture site. With a distal fracture, in addition to the greater moment, the locking holes—which are significant stress risers—are usually located just distal to the fracture site. It has been shown that the maximum stresses acting in the rod increase rapidly once the distance between the fracture and the most superior of the distal screw holes is reduced to less than about 4 cm.[28] Cyclic loading of nails used to fixed distal fractures, with peak loading of about 1 times bodyweight, confirm that titanium alloy nails can survive more than 1 million loading cycles when the more proximal of the distal locking screws is more than 3 cm from the fracture site.[7] In addition, placing the distal locking screws can be difficult because they must be inserted freehand under fluoroscopic guidance. Sometimes the corner of the screw hole of the rod can be nicked by the drill or while driving the screw, creating an additional stress riser that can accentuate the fatigue process. Awareness of these potential problems has led to design changes such as closing the proximal section of the rod, increasing material thickness around the screw holes, and cold forming, which increases the strength of the rod material.

Screw bending and breakage can also occur. When distal screws are placed into bone with relatively low bone density, the screw is supported mostly by the cortices. The distal end of the femur widens rapidly (Fig. 1-44), so the unsupported length of the screw between the cortices can be quite variable. For the same diameter and material, the stiffness and strength of a screw subjected to bending decreases with the third power of its unsupported length (the distance between cortices, assuming no support from the trabecular bone). If the unsupported length of one screw is twice as long as that of another, and assuming that the trabecular bone does not contribute to support of the screw, one can expect the stiffness and strength of the screw with the longer unsupported length to be 8 times less than that of the screw with the shorter length between cortical supports, and therefore the deformation will be 8 times greater under the same load. This does create a tradeoff in fixation of

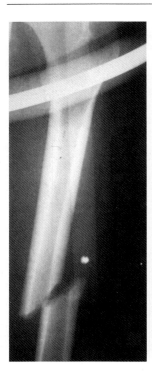
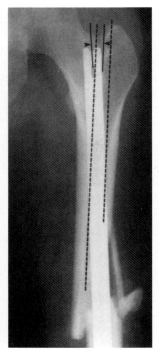
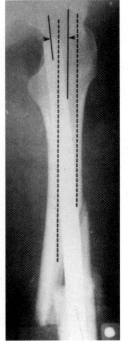

FIGURE 1-42 The starting position selected for rod entry into the medullary canal affects the degree to which it must bend and the internal forces generated in the femur. A starting position offset from the axis of the medullary canal, coupled with a stiff rod and a longer proximal segment that requires the rod to bend more during insertion, generate higher insertion forces and internal femoral forces. In this example of a midshaft femoral fracture **(left)**, the starting hole was selected medial relative to the axis of the medullary canal **(middle)** and posterior **(right)**. The medullary canal is outlined in dashed lines. Therefore the rod must bend both medially and posteriorly as it is inserted into the canal and has created internal stresses which have split the distal end of the femur.[80]

these fractures with respect to screw placement. If the screws are too close to the fracture, the stresses in the rod increase, while if they are located within the flair of the metaphysis, with poor trabecular bone, their unsupported length increases, decreasing stiffness and strength. The fatigue life of the distal locking screws is directly related to the diameter of the root of the thread and the resulting moment of inertia, so it has been proposed to remove the threads to increase fatigue life by 10 to 100 times.[73]

Loosening of External Fixator Pins

Loosening of fixator pins in bone is thought to result from several causes. The shape of the end of the pin itself, because it is self-tapping, can affect the local heat generated in bone during insertion, potentially causing thermal necrosis around the pin hole site,[160] along with bone microcracking. In addition, high

Lateral force

Moment arm of lateral force

Fulcrum

Moment arm of resisting load

FIGURE 1-43 If the same force acts on IM rods placed in femora with more proximal **(left)** or more distal **(right)** fractures, the moment arm of the force will be longer in the case of the more distal fracture and therefore the moment acting at the fracture site on the implant will be larger. For the more distal fracture, the high stress region close to the fracture site is also significantly closer to the distal locking screw holes which are significant stress risers.

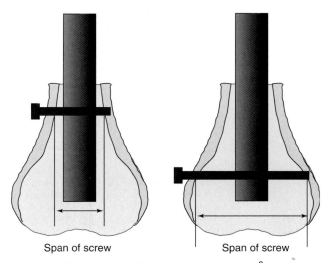

Span of screw   Span of screw

Screw deformation proportional to (span)^3

FIGURE 1-44 Because the distal end of the femur flares rapidly, the length of the locking screw required to crosslock the rod can be quite variable. If the screw is not well supported by trabecular bone but mainly by cortex, then its stiffness and strength decrease with the 3rd power of its length between cortices. If the screw length doubles, the deformation of the screw under the same load increases by a factor of 8.

Pin loosening

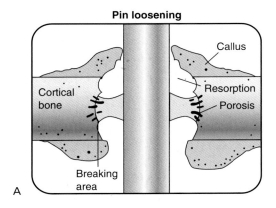

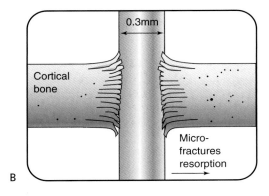

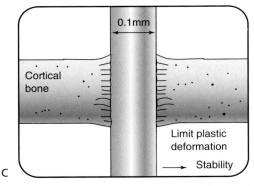

FIGURE 1-45 A proposed mechanism for loosening of external fixation pins involves under- or oversizing the diameter of the pin relative to the bone hole. **A.** If the pin and bone hole are the same diameter, micromotion can occur with bone resorption. **B.** If the pin is more than 0.3 mm smaller in diameter than the hole in bone, microfracture may occur during insertion. **C.** If the bone hole diameter is about 0.1 mm smaller than the pin diameter, the bone is prestressed but does not fracture, micromotion is eliminated, and pin stability is maintained.[118]

local stresses can occur in the pins and bone if the hole through which the pin is inserted is undersized.[78] A third mechanism, Figure 1-45, is micromotion, which induces bone resorption at the pin/bone interface if the pin is a loose fit in the hole. To reduce these problems, slight undersizing of the bone hole by about 0.1 mm in diameter has been advocated. If the bone hole is undersized by 0.3 mm in diameter, the yield strength of bone may be exceeded when the pin is inserted.[118]

Excessively Flexible External Fixation
An external fixator is an assembly of pins attached to bone fragments, along with clamps and sidebars that couple the pins.

This assembly allows considerable variation in construction of a frame to accommodate the fracture. The optimal stiffness of a fixator is not specifically known. The stiffness necessary to stabilize the fracture and induce healing changes as the fracture consolidates. It must be rigid enough to initially support the forces applied by the patient during ambulation without causing malalignment of the fracture. On the other hand, it should not be so stiff that the fracture is shielded from the stresses required to stimulate healing. Some basic mechanical guidelines in the construction of the frame, explained below, will ensure that frames are adequately constructed for the loads they are subjected to. Figure 1-46 demonstrates that when the diameter of a pin or sidebar increases, its stiffness and strength increase to the 4th power of the relative change in diameter (actually the ratio of the larger to the smaller diameter). As its length (distance between bone surface and sidebar) decreases, stiffness and strength increase to the 3rd power of the length change. This principle also holds also for the pins spanning the fracture, which affect the unsupported length of the sidebar across the fracture.

In construction of a frame, it is beneficial to decrease the sidebar to bone distance, which decreases the unsupported lengths of the pins, increases the pin diameter, and decreases the distance between the pins which span the fracture—for example, increasing the number of pins applied also increases frame stiffness. In terms of actual effects, for example in bending, doubling the sidebar distance from bone decreases frame stiffness by about 67%, doubling the separation distance of the pins across the fracture decreases stiffness by 50%, and decreasing pin diameter by 1 mm (from 6 to 5 mm, for example) also decreases frame stiffness by about 50%.[152] Using a partly threaded pin and burying the pin thread completely within the cortex enhances the stiffness of the pin, because the smaller diameter of the root of the pin thread is not exposed. Also, using hydroxyapatite coated external fixation pins to enhance the screw-bone interface[117] can be a good option.

The comments above pertain to uniplane fixators, which are constructed to resist the major loads, axial compression, and anterior-posterior bending, acting on a long bone such as the tibia during walking, with the sidebar usually aligned with the anterior-posterior plane. To resist torsion and out-of-plane (medial-lateral) bending, the fixator can be assembled with additional pins and sidebars in other planes. A comparison of the relative stiffnesses of different fixator assemblies is given in Figure 1-47. The unilateral half pin frame with sidebars mounted at right angles provides the greatest overall resistance to bending, compression, and torsional loads.[20] Hybrid fixation devices have adopted components of both unilateral bar fixators and ring fixators with wire transfixing pins. Both axial compression and torsional stiffnesses have been found to increase significantly with increases in the number and diameter of the transfixing wires, and pretensioning the wires.[31] More anterior placement of wires, or addition of an anteromedial halfpin have been found to increase anterior-posterior bending stiffness.[63] Testing of several different configurations (see Figure 1-48) showed that the box type (two rings above and two below the fracture, along with anterior half pins, two connecting rods and a unilateral bar) was the stiffest configuration, compared with a unilateral frame alone or a unilateral frame with rings only proximal to the fracture site. The addition of an anterior half pin significantly increased fixation stiffness.[128]

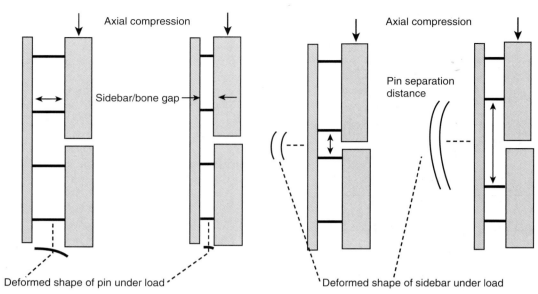

FIGURE 1-46 To produce more rigidity in construction of an external fixator, the basic principles that should be considered are that for pin and rod type sidebars, stiffness increases with the 4th power of the cross-sectional area (the moment of inertia, Fig. 1-7) and decreases with the 3rd power of their span or unsupported length (Fig. 1-44). This explains why it is beneficial to decrease sidebar to bone distance, increase pin diameter, place pins as close together across the fracture site, and use larger diameter or multiple sidebars in frame construction.[77,152]

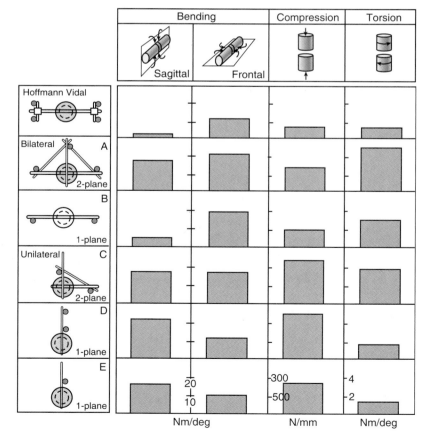

FIGURE 1-47 A comparison of the bending, compression, and torsional stiffnesses of different external fixation constructs for multiplane load resistance.[20]

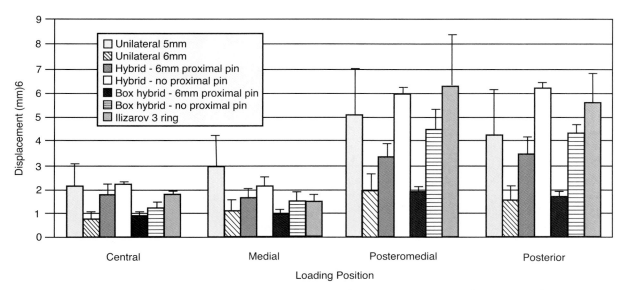

FIGURE 1-48 A comparison of displacement of the proximal fragment in a simulated tibia fracture under 100N load with various unilateral and hybrid external fixators (the box type uses both a large unilateral frame connecting bar and two smaller diameter connecting rods).[128]

Fixation in Osteoporotic Bone

Because the attachment strength of a fixation device to bone, a screw for example, is directly related to the local bone density, and because a dominant mechanical characteristic of osteoporotic bone is low density, several strategies can be used when osteoporotic bone is encountered. These include cortical buttressing by impaction; wide buttressing, which spreads the load over a larger surface area; long splintage; improved anchoring; and increasing the local bone density by injection of, for example, hydroyapatite or methylmethacrylate, see Figure 1-49.[71] Impaction strategies can be applied in fractures of the distal radius, femoral neck, and lumbar vertebrae. The dynamic hip screw is an example of a device which allows controlled impaction of the fracture of the femoral neck. An angled blade plate applied to supracondylar femur fractures, as compared with a condylar screw, provides wider buttressing—that is, a larger surface area of contact with bone. The rafter plate, which permits placement of numerous cancellous screws for tibial plateau fractures, is another example of the application of this principle.[25] Long splinting with a longer, more flexible plate has been applied in humerus fractures, and the interlocked intramedullary rod is a second example of long splinting. Enhanced anchoring of pedicle screws using augmenting laminar hooks is an example of augmentation of anchoring.[17] The locking plate, in which the screws are threaded into the plate and fixed so they cannot rotate, can be useful in stabilizing osteoporotic fractures when cortical buttressing is not practical because of low bone density and the fixation hardware must support most of the load. Hydroxyapatite coated external fixation pins have been shown to enhance the screw-bone interface.[117] Interlocking

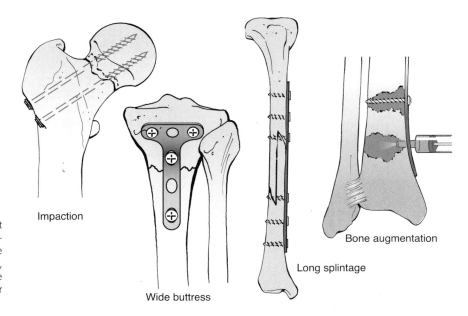

FIGURE 1-49 Some basic strategies to augment fixation strength in osteoporotic bone include impaction of the fracture components using a device that allows sliding, buttressing with a wide plate, increasing the plate length, and augmenting the bone locally by injection of methylmethacrylate or a calcium phosphate cement.[71]

Impaction

Wide buttress

Long splintage

Bone augmentation

screws, in which a standard screw has a 45-degree hole drilled into the shaft to accept an interlocking pin, can be used to reduce screw backout.[107]

Enhancement of local bone density using either PMMA or, more recently, absorbable hydroxyapatite cements has been studied, particularly in relation to fixation of femoral and vertebral osteoporotic fractures. PMMA injection has been widely employed in vertebroplasty through a transpedicular approach[99] and has been shown to restore the stiffness of fractured vertebrae to that of intact vertebrae. Biomechanical studies have shown significantly improved strength of the fixation of femoral neck fractures, up to 170%,[147] and similar findings, including decreased shortening and greater stability were noted when hydroxyapatite cement was applied to unstable three-part intertrochanteric fractures fixed with a dynamic hip screw.[52] Calcium phosphate cements used in vertebroplasty instead of PMMA also restored the stiffness of fractured vertebrae to intact levels.[102] Calcium phosphate cement injection into the pedicle has been shown to improve the bending stiffness of pedicle screws by up to 125%.[18]

Biomechanical Aspects of Fracture Fixation in Specific Locations

In the previous discussion, common problems such as screw pullout and plate breakage common to fracture fixation mainly in the long bones were discussed. In this section, the focus is placed on specific challenging problems in fixation, including the femoral neck, tibial plateau, pelvis, and spine.

Fixation in the Proximal Femur

Fixation of fractures of the proximal femur is particularly challenging because the compressive force acting through the femoral head can range from 4 to 8 times body weight during normal activities.[121] This force acts through a significant moment arm (the length of the femoral neck), which causes large bending loads on the fixation hardware. In addition, many of these fractures occur in the elderly, who are likely to have trabecular bone of low density and poor mechanical quality.[100] Also, it is generally not possible to gain screw purchase in the cortical bone of the femoral head.

The major force acting in, for example, a basicervical fracture of the femoral neck, fixed with a sliding hip screw is the joint reaction force through the femoral head, which derives from body weight and forces generated by muscle action during ambulation. The joint reaction force can be divided into two components. One (Fig. 1-50) is perpendicular to the axis of the sliding screw and causes shearing of the fracture surfaces along the fracture line, which results in inferior displacement and varus angulation of the femoral head, and increases the resistance of the screw to sliding. The other is parallel to the screw, driving the surfaces together and enhancing stability by frictional and mechanical interlocking of the fracture. Therefore, the aim of femoral neck fixation systems is to utilize the component of the joint force parallel to the femoral neck to encourage the fracture surfaces to slide together. This is the basic principle behind selection of a higher angle hip screw when possible.

When using the compression (or sliding) hip screw, or a nail with a sliding lag screw, it is important to ensure that the screw can slide freely in the barrel of the side plate or the hole in the nail. The following comments related to sliding hip screw

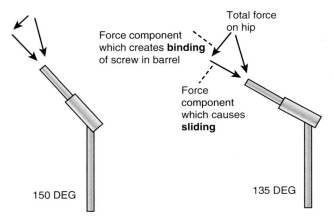

FIGURE 1-50 The joint reaction force in the femoral head can be divided into two major components. The one parallel of the axis of the femoral neck produces sliding and impaction of the fracture components and the other, transverse to the femoral neck, causes the screw component of the femoral hip screw to bind, resisting sliding. The higher-angle hip screw has a screw axis more closely aligned with the joint reaction force so the force component that produces sliding is larger while the transverse force component resisting sliding is smaller.

devices apply as well to nail/lag screw constructs. When screw sliding occurs, the screw is supported by the barrel against inferior bending of the femoral head because the construct is buttressed by fracture interdigitation. Adherence to two basic mechanical principles will enhance the ability of the screw to slide in the bore of the side plate or nail. As mentioned above, the higher angle hip screw is more effective at accommodating sliding. Also, the screw should be engaged as deeply as possible within the barrel. For the same force acting at the femoral end of the screw, the internal force where the screw contacts the barrel is increased if less of the screw shaft remains in the barrel. This occurs because the moment (bending load) caused by the force transverse to the axis of the screw (F_h in Fig. 1-51) (at the femoral head) acts over a longer moment arm or perpendicular distance, L_e (force X perpendicular distance to the edge of the barrel, which is the fulcrum). The balancing moment arm, L_b, is shorter because less of the screw remains in the barrel. Because F_h acts over a longer moment arm while F_e acts over a shorter moment arm, F_b increases. The internal force, F_b, where the screw contacts the barrel causes a greater frictional resistance force, which requires more force to overcome to permit sliding.[93] Sliding hip screws with either two- or four-hole side plates appear to provide equivalent resistance to physiologic compressive loading.[110]

Several factors affect the strength of femoral neck fixation using multiple screws, but the number of screws used (three or four) is not a significant factor.[155] Factors that do increase the strength of this type of fixation include a more horizontal fracture line with respect to the long axes of the screws,[48] placement of the screws in areas of greater femoral head bone density,[145,149] fractures with less comminution[129] and a shorter moment arm for the joint load (shorter distance from the center of the femoral head to the fracture line).[145] However, the most important factor has been found to be the quality of the reduction because of the importance of cortical buttressing in reducing fracture displacement.[143] Under physiological load, several mechanisms of failure of fixation have been observed, see Figure

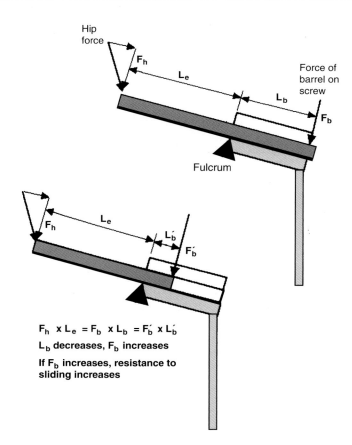

FIGURE 1-51 The greater the length of the sliding screw within the barrel, the lower its resistance to sliding. In this diagram Fh is the component of the joint reaction force perpendicular to the axis of the screw. The inferior edge of the proximal end of the barrel is the location of the fulcrum in bending. An internal force, Fb, from the surface of the barrel acts against the screw to counteract Fh. For equilibrium, the moments produced by Fh (Fh × Le) and Fb (Fb × Lb) must be equal. If Lb, the distance from the point of application of internal force Fb to the fulcrum, decreases, Fb must increase to produce the same moment. If Fb is larger, the frictional force and therefore the resistance to screw sliding will increase. (Le is the length of the screw beyond the barrel).[93]

1-52. In some cases the screws bend inferiorly, especially if buttressing of the fracture surfaces inferior to the screws is not possible because of comminution of the fracture. The fixation screw heads, if no washers are used to distribute the screw load against bone, have been found to pull through cortex near the greater trochanter when the cortex is thin. Finally, if the screws are not well supported inferiorly where they cross the fracture, they may rotate inferiorly carrying the femoral head into a varus orientation.[145] Supporting at least one screw against the inferior cortex may help prevent this from occurring.

With respect to the biomechanical performance of different devices, the actual stiffness provided by the sliding hip screw, the reconstruction nail, and multiple pin constructs are quite similar, except that the reconstruction nail offers significantly greater torsional stiffness than the other forms of fixation because of its tubular shape.[66,130] New techniques applied to proximal fracture fixation include the femoral locking plate and percutaneous compression plating. In fixation of the challenging vertical shear fracture of the proximal femur, the proximal femoral locking plate was found to produce considerably stiffer constructs than cannulated screws, a dynamic hip screw, or a dynamic condylar screw.[6] Percutaneous compression plating has been found to provide adequate bending and torsional stability[92] and was equivalent to the trochanteric antegrade nail in fracture site stability, though it failed at about 2100N (about 3 times body weight) compared to the antegrade nail at 3200N.[67]

Fixation around the Metaphyseal Region of the Knee
Both supracondylar femur and tibial plateau fractures are challenging to stabilize because they may involve fixation of multiple

small fragments of primarily cancellous bone. Supracondylar fixation alternatives that have been compared mechanically include condylar plates, plates with lag screws across the fracture site, and blade plates. All devices tested appeared to provide similar construct stiffnesses. The most important factor identified for plate fixation was maintaining contact at the cortex opposite that to which the fixation device was applied. Fixation constructs without cortical contact were only about 20% as stiff as those with cortical buttressing.[59,140] Using a retrograde intramedullary supracondylar nail was found to produce constructs that were 14% less stiff in axial compression and 17% less stiff in torsion, compared with a fixed angle side plate.[112] However, longer nails (36 cm) enhanced fixation stability compared to shorter nails (20 cm).[144] Several newer fixation systems have been described for femoral supracondylar fracture stabilization. The less invasive stabilization system (LISS) uses a low-profile plate with monocortical screws distally which also lock to the plate. LISS plates produced constructs with more elastic deformation and less subsidence than those with a condylar screw or buttress plate.[105,156]

Tibial plateau fractures are challenging to stabilize. Considering patient outcomes, the loss of reduction was related to patients being more than 60 years old, premature weight bearing, fracture fragmentation, and severe osteoporosis.[4] Different methods of fixation include using wires or screws alone, Figure 1-53, or screws placed through an L- or T-shaped plate, which buttresses the cortex. Various configurations of wires have been tested[24] and show that the stiffness of the construct increases with the number of wires, regardless of their specific orientations. As Figure 1-53 shows, fixation with screws alone requires

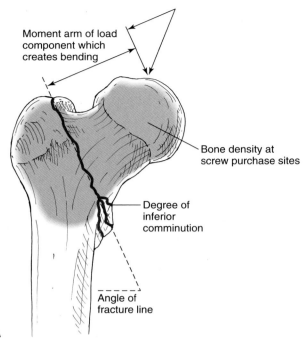

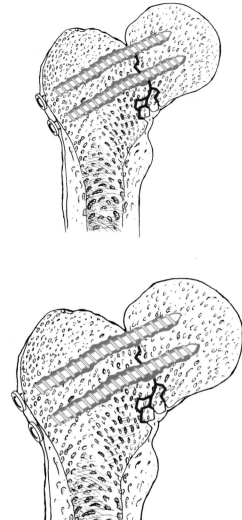

Moment arm of load component which creates bending

Bone density at screw purchase sites

Degree of inferior comminution

Angle of fracture line

A

B

FIGURE 1-52 A. Some factors that decrease the strength of femoral neck fracture fixation include decreased bone density; a more vertical fracture surface, which facilitates sliding of the fracture components; comminution at the inferior cortex, which reduces buttressing against bending; and a longer moment arm or distance of the center of the femoral head to the fracture line. **B.** Observed mechanisms of failure of femoral neck fixation using screws include bending of the pins, displacement of the screw heads through the thin cortex of the greater trochanter, especially if washers are not used, and rotation of the screws inferiorly through the low density cancellous bone of the Ward triangle area until they settle against the inferior cortex.[145]

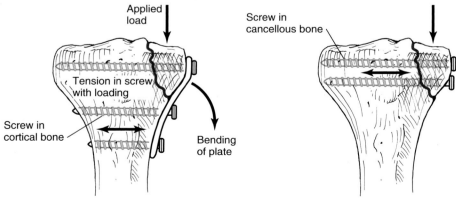

Applied load

Screw in cancellous bone

Tension in screw with loading

Screw in cortical bone

Bending of plate

A,B

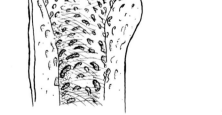

FIGURE 1-53 Two alternative methods of fixation of tibial plateau fractures: **(A)** transverse screws combined with a buttress plate and **(B)** transverse screws alone. The buttress plate provides additional support in bending as the tibial fracture component is loaded in an inferior direction and allows the screws to engage the thicker, more distal cortical bone.

that the screw resist bending forces as the tibial fragment is loaded distally in compression through the joint. With the addition of a plate, not only is the load distributed to the plate, but additional screws can be placed in the stronger cortical bone distal to the metaphyseal region of the tibia. One disadvantage of a buttress plate is the additional invasiveness that it requires for installation with potential compromise of blood supply. Fixation with T plates and screws showed the greatest resistance to an axial compressive load,[46] regardless of the specific configuration of the screws.[84] Investigations of different plate configurations found that for bicondylar tibial plateau fractures, dual (lateral and medial) side plating reduced subsidence under axial loading by about 50% compared with single-sided lateral locking plating.[72] For medial plateau fractures, the medial buttress plate, which supports the load directly, is superior mechanically to a lateral locked plate.[126] A new alternative is the short proximal tibial nail with multiple interlocking screws. In combined axial loading, bending and rotation, the nail provided stability equivalent to that of double plating and was greater than constructs with a locking plate, external fixator, or conventional unreamed tibial nail.[69]

Fixation of the Spine

The halo apparatus is an external fixation device for cervical spine injuries that are stable in compression. It stabilizes the injured cervical spine mainly in bending but not in compression. Factors that affect its mechanical performance include (Fig. 1-54) the fit of the jacket on the torso and the frictional

characteristics of the lining. High friction linings decrease slip at the vest lining/torso interface, more rigid vests reduce deflection under loads, and less flexible superstructures all decrease cervical spine motion at the injury level. While stiffening the vest enhances its ability to stabilize the injury, this property must be balanced with enough flexibility to provide reasonable comfort for the wearer and to accommodate expansion and contraction of the chest. Because the injured cervical segment is relatively distant from the vest, small motions of the vest can result in relatively large displacements at the injury site.[114] A very rigid halo superstructure attaching the vest to the halo ring may not increase injury stability if connected to a poorly fitting vest.

Several methods are available to reconstruct cervical spine injuries. The major differences between them relate to the location of the fixation device itself on the vertebra—anterior, lateral, or posterior—and to the method by which the fixation is attached to bone. Generally the most rigid fixation is the one with the longest moment arm from the center of rotation of the injured segment. For a specific applied moment, say flexion, a posteriorly located fixation, being located further from the center of rotation, results in greater rigidity. Figure 1-55 shows the approximate locations of the centers of rotation at different cervical spine levels when the posterior elements have been

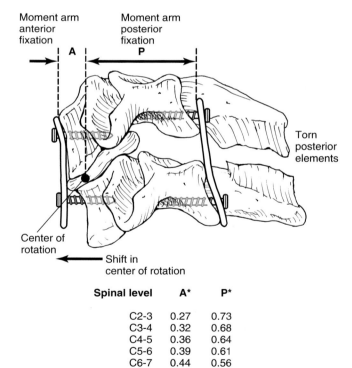

Spinal level	A*	P*
C2-3	0.27	0.73
C3-4	0.32	0.68
C4-5	0.36	0.64
C5-6	0.39	0.61
C6-7	0.44	0.56

*In % of anterior-posterior diameter of vertebra

FIGURE 1-55 The ratios, in terms of anterior-posterior diameter of the vertebra, of the location of the center of rotation at each vertebral level, from the anterior and posterior surfaces. A fixation device must resist bending moments caused by flexion, extension, lateral bending, and torsion. The resisting moment in the fixation is the product of the force acting in the fixation (for example, at the screw-plate junction) and the distance of that point on the fixation to the center of rotation of the motion segment. The longer the moment arm for the same bending load, the smaller the force on the fixation components. Posterior fixation, by its location, will have lower moments in its components.[5]

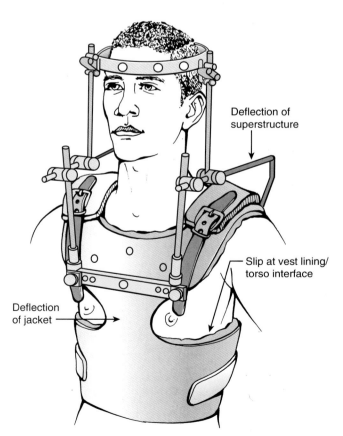

FIGURE 1-54 A schematic diagram showing possible sources of deformation in the halo apparatus. The large distance from the vest to chest contact points to the cervical injury site results in relatively large motions at the injury site for small motions of the vest.[114]

disrupted.[5] After corpectomy, testing has shown that posterior rods provide the greatest stability, which is unchanged after augmentation with an anterior plate, while anterior plating alone offers the least stability.[146] Similarly, another test showed that after corpectomy, sagittal plane motion was most rigid after supplementation with lateral mass plates, less rigid with an anterior plate alone, and least with strut grafting alone.[85] Anterior plates provide relatively similar stability, especially if augmented with a bone graft, however, with multilevel corpectomy, anterior plate constructs were more prone to fatigue loosening than single level corpectomies.[79] Some of the newer semiconstrained anterior plates, most of which offer devices to lock the screws to prevent backout, allow screw rotation which results in more load sharing with the graft.[125] By comparison, the compressive load estimated to be transmitted through the graft increased from about 40% with a fully constrained device to about 80% when a semiconstrained device was used.[125] Wiring or plating with lateral mass screws generally reduces anterior-posterior motion across the fixed segment by 20% to 70%, so none of the techniques can be considered as entirely rigid.[113]

The type of attachment of the fixation system to the vertebra is fundamental to its performance. Wires, hooks, screws, or combinations of them all produce different types of force transfer between the fixation and the vertebra, Figure 1-56.[36] A wire can resist only tension, while a screw can resist forces in all directions (tension, compression, bending transverse to the axis of the screw) except for rotation about its longitudinal axis. A hook only resists forces that drive the surface of the hook against bone, and depends also on the shape of the hook and the bone surface it rests against. For this reason, screws are biomechanically superior to other forms of vertebral attachments.

In general, pedicle screws resist pullout in the same manner as bone screws described elsewhere, therefore pullout strength increases with increased density of the bone it is embedded into,[33,104,161,164] a greater depth of insertion,[95] engagement of the anterior cortex,[115] and a larger screw diameter. Single screws placed into pedicles and loaded in a caudal-cephalad direction, which occurs during flexion and extension of the vertebra, are vulnerable to toggling, and eventual loosening, even under relatively small forces. As demonstrated in Figure 1-57, the screw tends to toggle about the base of the pedicle, which is the stiffest region, being comprised mainly of cortical bone. Toggling tends to open the screw hole in a "windshield wiper" fashion.[13,95] Toggling can be reduced if the screw head is locked to the plate or rod, and the plate or rod contacts the vertebra over a wide area.[95]

Some fundamental principles should be considered when applying lumbar spinal fixation. Longer fixation, attached to more vertebrae, reduces forces acting on the screws because of the effect of the greater lever arm of a longer plate or rod. A longer fusion, although biomechanically advantageous, is not necessarily beneficial from a clinical perspective because remaining spinal motion is significantly reduced. Adding an anterior strut graft or a fusion cage is important because it buttresses a posterior fixation system against flexion moments, reducing forces in the fixation.[89] Coupler bars, which connect the fixation rods to form an H configuration, prevent the rods from rotating medial and lateral when torsion is applied to the motion segment, Figure 1-58. This significantly enhances the torsional and lateral bending stability of the implant.[72]

Extensive testing has been performed on various posterior and anterior thoracolumbar fixation devices as they continue

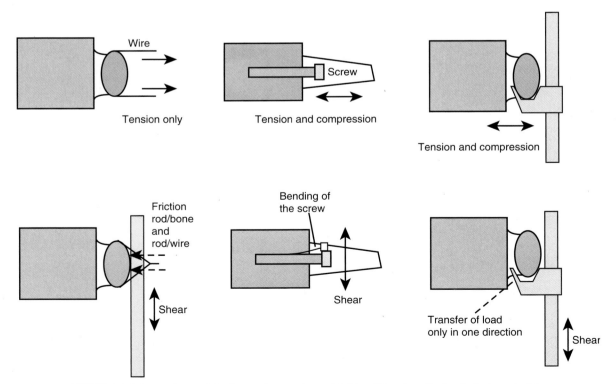

FIGURE 1-56 Comparisons of the forces that can be resisted by different methods of attachment of the fixation to the vertebra. A sublaminar wire resists only tension, while a screw can resist forces in all directions except for rotation about its long axis. A hook resists only forces that drive it against the bone surfaces.

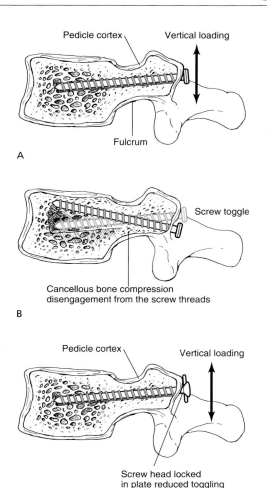

Pedicle cortex | Vertical loading

Fulcrum

A

Screw toggle

Cancellous bone compression
disengagement from the screw threads

B

Pedicle cortex | Vertical loading

Screw head locked
in plate reduced toggling

C

FIGURE 1-57 A. The mechanism of toggling of a single pedicle screw subjected to a caudo-cephalad loading. **B.** The fulcrum is at the base of the pedicle, the narrowest region with little cancellous bone. The screw toggle compresses bone within the vertebral body. **C.** Toggling is reduced if the plate or rod to which the screw connects contacts the vertebra over a wide surface, which prevents it from rotating, while the screw head is locked to the plate or rod.[95]

to be developed. Testing of anterior fixation systems with and without an augmented strut graft showed that load sharing with the graft ranged from 63% to 89% for six systems tested, three being plates and three based on locked rods. These tests demonstrated the significant effect of the graft in sagittal plane stability of the fixation. The most rigid systems, not significantly different in performance, relied on either a thick rigid plate or large rods.[26] In cases of delayed or nonunion the cyclic performance of the implant can be very important, more so than its static stiffness or maximum load to failure. A comparison test of 12 fixation systems showed that only three could withstand 2 million load cycles with 600N of compressive force. The two fixations with greatest bending strength also did not fail after cycling, however, there was no correlation between bending strength and cyclic failure for the other 10 systems, indicating that particular design aspects could cause fatigue failure regardless of static strength.[88] Three devices failed in less than 10,000 cycles. Currently, most posterior devices use essentially the same principles, including pedicle screws with an interface clamp to the rod that allows variable orientation of the screw, a low profile assembly, and crosslinks. They provide similar fixation stiffness. Lumbosacral fixation using sacral screws was most rigid and demonstrated the least screw strain when supplemented with iliac screws, and was more effective than using screws at S1 supplemented with screws at S2.[96]

The biomechanical properties of fusion cages have been investigated. A fusion cage is a hollow threaded insert that can be applied from anterior, lateral, or posterior directions in single or double units. Various fusion cages are available for the cervical spine. The devices fall into one of three categories: screw designs with a horizontal cylinder and external threads, box shapes, and vertical cylinders. In general, all cage designs increased flexion stiffness by 130% to 180%. Only a few box or cylinder designs increased extension stiffness, and box designs were most effective in increasing axial rotation and lateral bending stiffnesses, ranging from 140% to 180% of intact values.[82] Testing of lumbar fusion cages has shown that placement of cages in lateral, posterolateral, or posterior orientations had little effect on stiffness, except for torsional loading with posterior cage placement, because posterior insertion damaged the lamina

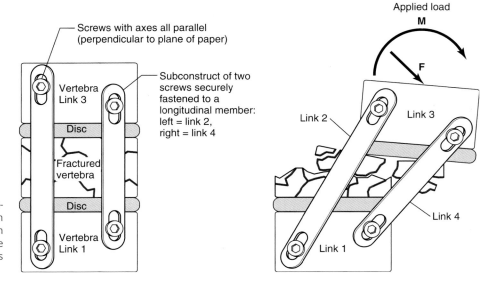

FIGURE 1-58 Without a coupler bar between two longitudinal rods **(left)**, they can rotate when a lateral moment or axial torsion is applied **(right)**. A coupler connecting the rods to form an H configuration reduces this effect.[72]

Screws with axes all parallel
(perpendicular to plane of paper)

Vertebra
Link 3

Subconstruct of two
screws securely
fastened to a
longitudinal member:
left = link 2,
right = link 4

Disc

Fractured
vertebra

Disc

Vertebra
Link 1

Applied load
M

F

Link 2 | Link 3

Link 4

Link 1

or facets, reducing the inherent torsional stability of the motion segment. Fixation with cages alone did not significantly increase lumbar motion segment stability, so augmentation with posterior fixation in cases of motion segment instability is necessary. Because cage fixation relies on the combination of distraction of the soft tissues and the strength of the vertebral cancellous bone, the properties of these tissues will have a significant effect on the performance of cage implant constructs.[153]

Fixation of the Humerus

Proximal humerus fractures fixed with locking plates provided greater stability against torsional loading but were similar to blade plate constructs in bending, because both fixation devices are loaded as tension bands in bending.[116,137,138] In comparing different types of blade plate constructs, the stiffest construct employed an eight-hole, low-contact dynamic compression plate, contoured into a blade configuration, and fixed with a diagonal screw that triangulates with the end of the blade. This arrangement was considerably stiffer than other blade plates or T plate and screw constructs.[101] One potential problem is penetration of the screws through the subchondral bone in osteoporotic patients.

SUMMARY

Effective fracture fixation requires a biomechanical appreciation of the forces applied to a damaged bone or joint and the basic mechanisms by which these loads are transferred through the bridging fixation and the implant-bone interface. In particular, the importance of the contribution of cortex-to-cortex contact across the fracture site in resisting both compressive and bending forces must be emphasized. This contact creates a buttress that contributes significantly to the stability of the construct and the functional life of the implant. Many of the observations used to formulate these basic principles have been made using cadaveric bone in experimental laboratory simulations, and conclusions are based on comparisons of the most rigid mechanical construct. Other aspects such as the compromise of blood flow or the extent of the incision during installation should also be considered. Further, even if one construct is more rigid than another, within a certain range of mechanical stiffness, both may perform equally well in producing fracture healing with anatomic alignment. It is important to correlate the biomechanical findings to clinical observations of the performance of the implant during fracture healing.

REFERENCES

1. Aharonoff GB, Dennis MG, Elshinawy A, et al. Circumstances of falls causing hip fractures in the elderly. Clin Orthop Rel Res 1998;348:10–14.
2. Allgower M. Cinderella of surgery-fractures? Surg Clin North Am 1978;58:1071–1093.
3. Alho A, Husby T, Hoiseth A. Bone mineral content and mechanical strength. An ex-vivo study on human femora at autopsy. Clin Orthop Rel Res 1988;227:292–297.
4. Ali AM, El-Shafie M, Willett KM. Failure of fixation of tibial plateau fractures. J Orthop Trauma 2002;16:323–329.
5. Amevo B, Aprill C, Bogduk N. Abnormal instantaneous axes of rotation in patients with neck pain. Spine 1992;17:748–756.
6. Aminian A, Gao F, Fedoriw WW, et al. Vertically oriented femoral neck fractures: mechanical analysis of four fixation techniques. J Orthop Trauma 2007;21:544–548.
7. Antekeier SB, Burden RL, Voor MJ, et al. Mechanical study of the safe distance between distal femoral fracture site and distal locking screws in antegrade intraeduallary nailing. J Orthop Trauma 2005;19:693–697.
8. Aro HT, Wippenman BW, Hodgson SF, et al. Prediction of properties of fracture callus by measurement of mineral density using microbone densitometry. J Bone Jt Surg 1989;71A:1020–1030.
9. Ascenzi A, Bonucci E. The compressive properties of single osteons. Anat Rec 1968; 161:377–392.
10. Ascenzi A, Bonucci E. The shearing properties of single osteons. Anat Rec 1972;172: 499–510.
11. Ascenzi A, Bonucci E. The tensile properties of single osteons. Anat Rec 1967;158: 375–386.
12. Ascenzi A, Bonucci E, Simkin A. An approach to the mechanical properties of single osteonic lamellae. J Biomech 1973;6:227–235.
13. Ashman RB, Galpin RD, Corin JD, et al. Biomechanical analysis of pedicle screw instrumentation in a corpectomy model. Spine 1989;14:1398–1405.
14. Askew MJ, Mow VC, Wirth CR. Analysis of the intraosseus stress field due to compression plating. J Biomech 1975;8:203–212.
15. Assal M, Huber P, Rohr E, et al. Are drivers more likely to injure their right or left foot in a frontal car crash: a car crash and biomechanical investigation. 46th Annual Proceedings, Association for the Advancement of Automotive Medicine 2002:273–288.
16. Augat P, Merk J, Wolf S, et al. Mechanical stimulation by external application of cyclic tensile strains does not effectively enhance bone healing. J Orthop Trauma 2001;15: 54–60.
17. Ayerby SA, Harrington JR, McLain RF. Offset laminar hooks decrease bending moments of pedicle screws during in situ contouring. Spine 1997;22:376–381.
18. Bai B, Kummer FJ, Spivak J. Augmentation of anterior vertebral body screw fixation by an injectable biodegradable calcium phosphate bone substitute. Spine 2001;24: 2679–2683.
19. Bartley MH Jr., Arnold JS, Haslam RK, et al. The relationship of bone strength and bone quantity in health, disease, and aging. J Gerontol 1996;21:517–521.
20. Behrens F, Johnson WD. Unilateral external fixation methods to increase and reduce frame stiffness. Clin Orthop Rel Res 1989;241:48–56.
21. Bell GH, Dunbar O, Beck JS, et al. Variations in strength of vertebrae with age and their relation to osteoporosis. Calcif Tissue Res 1967;1:75–86.
22. Benjamin J, Bried J, Dohm M, et al. Biomechanical evaluation of various forms of fixation of transverse patellar fractures. J Orthop Trauma 1987;1:219–222.
23. Black J. Orthopedic Biomaterials in Research and Practice. New York: Churchill Livingstone, 1988.
24. Beris AE, Glisson RR, Seaber AV, et al. Load tolerance of tibial plateau depressions reinforced with a cluster of K-wires. 34th Annual Meeting of the Orthopedic Research Society. 1988;13:301.
25. Benirschke SK, Swiontkowski MF. Knee. In: Hansen ST, Swiontkowski, MF, eds. Orthopedic Trauma Protocols. New York: Raven Press, 1993.
26. Brodke DS, Gollogly S, Bachus KN, et al. Anterior thoracolumbar instrumentation: stiffness and load sharing characteristics of plate and rod systems. Spine 2003: 1794–1801.
27. Brooks DB, Burstein AH, Frankel UH. The biomechanics of torsional fractures. J Bone Jt Surg 1970;52A:507–514.
28. Bucholz RW, Ross SE, Lawrence KL. Fatigue fracture of the interlocking nail in the treatment of fractures of the distal part of the femoral shaft. J Bone Jt Surg 1987;69A: 1391–1399.
29. Burstein AH, Reilly DL, Martens M. Aging of bone tissue: mechanical properties. J Bone Jt Surg 1976;58A:82–86.
30. Burstein AH, Zika IM, Heiple KG, et al. Contribution of collagen and mineral to the elastic-plastic properties of bone. J Bone Jt Surg 1975;57A:956–961.
31. Calhoun JH, Li F, Ledbetter BR, et al. Biomechanics of Ilizarov for fracture fixation. 37th Annual Meeting of the Orthopedic Research Society 1991;16:439.
32. Carter DR, Hayes WC. The compressive behavior of bone as a two-phase porous structure. J Bone Jt Surg 1977;59A:954–962.
33. Chapman JR, Harrington RM, Lee KM, et al. Factors affecting the pullout strength of cancellous bone screws. ASME J Biomech Eng 1996;118:391–398.
34. Clark CR, Morgan C, Sonstegard DA, et al. The effect of biopsy-hole shape and size on bone strength. J Bone Jt Surg 1977,59A:213–217.
35. Cody DD, Goldstein SA, Flynn MJ, et al. Correlations between vertebral regional bone mineral density (rBMD) and whole bone fracture load. Spine 1991;16:146–154.
36. Coe JD, Herzig MA, Warden KE, et al. Load to failure of spinal implants in osteoporotic spines; a comparison of pedicle screws, laminar hooks, and spinous process wires. 35th Annual Meeting of the Orthopedic Research Society 1989;14:71.
37. Cordey J, Florin P, Klaue K, et al. Compression achieved with the dynamic compression plate: effects of the inclined sloping cylinder and inclination of the screw. In: Uhthoff HK, ed. Current Concepts of Internal Fixation of Fractures. Berlin: Springer-Verlag, 1980:192–200.
38. Crowninshield RD, Pope MH. The response of compact bone in tension at various strain rates. Ann Biomed Eng 1974;2:217–225.
39. Currey JD. The Mechanical Adaptation of Bones. Princeton, NJ: Princeton University Press, 1984.
40. Currey JD. The effects of strain rate, reconstruction, and mineral content on some mechanical properties of bovine bone. J Biomech 1975;8:81–86.
41. Currey JD. Changes in the impact energy absorption of bone with age. J Biomech 1979; 12:459–469.
42. Currey JD. The mechanical consequences of variation in the mineral content of bone. J Biomech 1969;2:1–11.
43. Currey JD, Butler G. The mechanical properties of the bone tissue in children. J Bone Jt Surg 1975;57A:810–814.
44. Dalen N, Hellstrom LG, Jacobson B. Bone mineral content and mechanical strength of the femoral neck. Acta Orthop Scand 1976;47:503–508.
45. DeCoster TA, Heetderks DB, Downey DJ, et al. Optimizing bone screw pullout force. J Orthop Trauma 1990;4:169–174.
46. Denny LD, Keating EM, Engelhardt JA, et al. A comparison of fixation techniques in tibial plateau fractures. 30th Annual Meeting of the Orthopedic Research Society 1984; 9:314.
47. Edgarton BC, An K-A, Morrey BF. Torsional strength reduction due to cortical defects in bone. J Orthop Res 1990;8:851–855.
48. Edwards WT, Lewallen DG, Hayes WC. The effect of pin number and fracture pattern on immediate mechanical fixation of a subcapital hip fracture model. 31st Annual Meeting of the Orthopedic Research Society 1985;10:219.
49. Egol KA, Chang EY, Cvitkovic J, et al. Mismatch of current intramedullary nails with the anterior bow of the femur. J Orthop Trauma 2004;18:410–415.

50. Egol KA, Kubiak EN, Fulkerson E, et al. Biomechanics of locked plates and screws. J Orthop Trauma 2004;18:488–493.
51. Ehmke LW, Polzin BMI, Madey SM, et al. Femoral nailing through the trochanter: the reamer pathway indicates a helical shaped nail. J Orthop Trauma 2006;20:668–674.
52. Elder S, Frankenberg E, Yetkilner DN, et al. Biomechanical evaluation of calcium phosphate cement augmented fixation of unstable intertrochanteric fractures. 43rd Annual Meeting of the Orthopedic Research Society 1998;23:432.
53. Ellis T, Bourgeault CA, Kyle RF. Screw position affects dynamic compression plate strain in an in vitro fracture model. J Orthop Trauma 2001;15:333–337.
54. El Maraghy AW, Elmaraghy MW, Nousiainen M, et al. Influence of the number of cortices on the stiffness of plate fixation of diaphyseal fractures. J Orthop Trauma 2001; 15:186–191.
55. Evans FG. Relations between the microscopic structure and tensile strength of human bone. Acta Anat 1958;35:285–301.
56. Evans FG, Bang S. Differences and relationships between the physical properties and the structure of human femoral, tibial, and fibular cortical bone. Am J Anat 1967;120: 79–88.
57. Evans FG, Vincentelli R. Relation of collagen fiber orientation to some mechanical properties of human cortical bone. J Biomech 1969;2:63–71.
58. Finlay JB, Jarada I, Boune RB, et al. Analysis of the pull-out strength of screws and pegs used to secure tibial components following total knee arthroplasty. Clin Orthop Rel Res 1989;247:220–231.
59. Frankenburg EP, Robinson AP, Urquhart AG, et al. Supracondylar femur fractures: a biomechanical analysis of four fixation devices. 38th Annual Meeting of the Orthopedic Research Society 1992;17:413.
60. Frigg R, Appenzeller A, Christensen R, et al. The development of the distal femur Less Invasive Stabilization System (LISS). Injury 2001;32:S-C-24–31.
61. Funk JR, Tourret LJ, George SE, et al. The role of axial loading in malleolar fractures. SAE Transactions 2000-01-0155, 2000.
62. Galante J, Rostoker W, Ray RD. Physical properties of trabecular bone. Calcif Tissue Res 1970;5:236–246.
63. Geller J, Tornetta III P, Tiburzi D, et al. Tension wire position for hybrid external fixation of the proximal tibia. J Orthop Trauma 2000;14:502–504.
64. Georgette FS, Sander TW, Oh I. The fatigue resistance of orthopedic wire and cable systems. Second World Congress on Biomaterials, Washington DC, 1984:146.
65. Goldman MW, MacLennan PA, McGwin G, et al. The association between restraint system and upper extremity injury after motor vehicle collisions. J Orthop Trauma 2005;19:529–534.
66. Goodman SB, Davidson JA, Locke L, et al. A biomechanical study of two methods of internal fixation of unstable fractures of the femoral neck. J Orthop Trauma 1992;6: 66–72.
67. Gotfried Y, Cohen B, Rotem A. Biomechanical evaluation of the percutaneous compression plating system for hip fractures. J Orthop Trauma 2002;16:644–650.
68. Gotzen L, Hutter J, Haas N. The prebending of AO plates in compression osteosynthesis. In: Uhthoff HK, ed. Current Concepts of Internal Fixation of Fractures. Berlin: Springer-Verlag, 1980:201–210.
69. Hansen M, Mehler D, Hessmann MH, et al. Intramedullary stabilization of extra-articular proximal tibial fractures: a biomechanical comparison of intramedullary and extramedullary implants including a new proximal tibial nail (PTN). J Orthop Trauma 2007; 21:701–709.
70. Harrell RM, Tong J, Weinhold PS, et al. Comparison of the mechanical properties of different tension band materials and suture techniques. J Orthop Trauma 2003;17: 119–122.
71. Hertel R, Jost B. Basic principles and techniques of internal fixation in osteoporotic bone. In: Yhu An, ed. Internal Fixation in Osteoporotic Bone. New York: Thieme, 2002:108–115.
72. Higgans TF, Klatt J, Bachus KN. Biomechanical analysis of bicondylar tibial plateau fixation: how does lateral locking plate fixation compare to dual plate fixation? J Orthop Trauma 2007;21:301–306.
73. Hou S-H, Wang J-L, Lin J. Mechanical strength, fatigue life, and failure analysis of two prototypes and five conventional tibial locking screws. J Orthop Res 2002;16:701–708.
74. Hufner T, Geerling J, Oldag G, et al. Accuracy study of computer assisted drilling: the effect of bone density, drill bit characteristics, and use of a mechanical guide. J Orthop Trauma 2005;19:317–322.
75. Hughes AN, Jordan BA. The mechanical properties of surgical bone screws and some aspects of insertion practice. Injury 1972;4:25–38.
76. Hungerford DS, Barry M. Biomechanics of the patellofemoral joint. Clin Orthop Rel Res 1979;144:9–15.
77. Huiskes R, Chao EYS. Guidelines for external fixation frame rigidity and stresses. J Orthop Res 1986;4:68–75.
78. Huiskes R, Chao EYS, Crippen TE. Parametric analyses of pin-bone stresses in external fracture fixation. J Orthop Res 1985;3:341–349.
79. Isomi T, Panjabi MM, Wang J-L, et al. Stabilizing potential of anterior cervical plates in multilevel corpectomies. Spine 1999;24:2219–2223.
80. Johnson KD, Tencer AF, Sherman MC. Biomechanical factors affecting fracture stability and femoral bursting in closed intramedullary nailing of femoral shaft fractures, with illustrative case presentations. J Orthop Trauma 1987;1:1–11.
81. Kaab MJ, Frenk A, Schmeling A, et al. Locked internal fixator, sensitivity of screw-plate stability to the correct insertion angle of the screw. J Orthop Trauma 2004;18: 483–487.
82. Kandziora F, Pflugmacher R, Schafer J, et al. Biomechanical comparison of cervical spine interbody fusion cages. Spine 2001;26:1850–1857.
83. Karnezis IA, Miles AW, Cunningham JL, et al. Biological internal fixation of long bone fractures: a biomechanical study of a noncontact plate system. Injury 1998;29: 689–695.
84. Karunaker MA, Egol KA, Peindl R, et al. Split depression tibial plateau fractures: a biomechanical study. J Orthop Trauma 2002;16:172–177.
85. Kirkpatrick JS, Levy JA, Carillo J, et al. Reconstruction after multilevel corpectomy in the cervical spine. Spine 1999;24:1186–1191.
86. Klaue K, Perren SM, Kowalski M. Internal fixation with a self-compressing plate and screw: improvements of the plate hole and screw design. I. Mechanical investigation. J Orthop Trauma 1991;5:280–288.
87. Korner J, Diederichs G, Arzdorf M, et al. A biomechanical evaluation of methods of distal humerus fracture fixation using locking compression plates versus conventional reconstruction plates. J Orthop Trauma 2004;18:286–293.
88. Kotani Y, Cunningham BW, Parker LM, et al. Static and fatigue biomechanical properties of anterior thoracolumbar instrumentation systems. Spine 1999;24:1406–1413.
89. Krag MH. Biomechanics of thoracolumbar spinal fixation. A review. Spine 1991;16: S85–S98.
90. Krag MH, Beynnan BD, Pope MH, et al. An internal fixator for posterior application to short segments of the thoracic, lumbar, or lumbosacral spine. Design and testing. Clin Orthop Rel Res 1986;203:75–98.
91. Krupp RJ, Malkani AL, Goodin RA, et al. Optimal entry point for retrograde femoral nailing. J Orthop Trauma 2003;17:100–105.
92. Kubiak EN, Bong M, Park SS, et al. Intramedullary fixation of unstable intertrochanteric hip fractures. J Orthop Trauma 2004;18:12–17.
93. Kyle RF, Wright TM, Burstein AH. Biomechanical analysis of the sliding characteristics of compression hip screws. J Bone Jt Surg 1980;62A:1308–1314.
94. Laurence M, Freeman MA, Swanson SA. Engineering considerations in the internal fixation of fractures of the tibial shaft. J Bone Jt Surg 1969;51B:754–768.
95. Law M, Tencer AF, Anderson PA. Caudo-cephalad loading of pedicle screws: mechanisms of loosening and methods of augmentation. Spine 1993;18:2438–2443.
96. Lebwohl NH, Cunningham BW, Dmitriev A, et al. Biomechanical comparison of lumbosacral fixation techniques in a calf spine model. Spine 2002;27:2312–2320.
97. Leggon RE, Lindsey RW, Panjabi MM. Strength reduction and the effects of treatment of long bones with diaphyseal defects involving 50% of the cortex. J Orthop Res 1988; 6:540–546.
98. Leighton RK, Waddell JP, Bray TJ, et al. Biomechanical testing of new and old fixation devices for vertical shear fracture of the pelvis. J Orthop Trauma 1991;5:313–317.
99. Liebschner MAK, Rosenberg WS, Keaveny TM. Effects of bone cement volume and distribution on vertebral stiffness after vertebroplasty. Spine 2001;26:1547–1554.
100. Leicher I, Margulies JY, Weinreb A, et al. The relationship between bone density, mineral content, and mechanical strength in the femoral neck. Clin Orthop Rel Res 1982;163:272–281.
101. Lever JP, Aksenov SA, Zdero R, et al. Biomechanical analysis of plate osteosynthesis systems for proximal humerus fractures. J Orthop Trauma 2008;22:23–29.
102. Lim TH, Breback GT, Renner SM, et al. Biomechanical evaluation of an injectable calcium phosphate cement for vertebroplasty. Spine 2002;27:1297–1302.
103. Lotz JC, Gerhart TN, Hayes WC. Mechanical properties of trabecular bone from the proximal femur by single-energy quantitative computed tomography. J Computer Assisted Tomogr 1990;14:107–114.
104. Mann KA, Bartel DL. A structural analysis of the fixation of pedicle screws to vertebrae. 36th Annual Meeting of the Orthopedic Research Society 1990;15:611.
105. Marti A, Fankhauser C, Frenk A, et al. Biomechanical evaluation of the less invasive stabilization system for the internal fixation of distal femur fractures. J Orthop Res 2001;15:482–487.
106. McBroom, RJ, Cheal EJ, Hayes WC. Strength reductions from metastatic cortical defects in long bones. J Orthop Res 1988;6:369–378.
107. McKoy BE, Conner GS, An YH. An interlocking screw for fixation in osteoporotic bone. In: An YH, ed., Internal Fixation in Osteoporotic Bone.New York: Thieme, 2002: 237–241.
108. McElhaney JH. Dynamic response of bone and muscle tissue. J Appl Physiol 1966;21: 1231–1236.
109. McElhaney JH, Alem NM, Roberts VL. A porous block model for cancellous bone. Am Soc Mech Eng 1970;70-WA/BHF-2:1–9.
110. McLoughlin SW, Wheeler DL, Rider J, et al. Biomechanical evaluation of the dynamic hip screw with two- and four-hole side plates. J Orthop Trauma 2000;14:318–323.
111. Merk BR, Stern SH, Cordes S, et al. A fatigue life analysis of small fragment screws. J Orthop Trauma 2001;15:494–499.
112. Meyer RW, Plaxton NA, Postak PD, et al. Mechanical comparison of a distal femoral side plate and a retrograde intramedullary nail. J Orthop Trauma 2000;14:398–404.
113. Mihara H, Cheng BC, David SM, et al. Biomechanical comparison of posterior cervical fixation. Spine 2001;26:1662–1667.
114. Mirza SK, Moquin RR, Anderson PA, et al. Stabilizing properties of the halo apparatus. Spine 1997;22:727–733.
115. Misenhimer GR, Peek RD, Wiltze LL, et al. Anatomic analysis of pedicle canal and cancellous diameter related to screw size. Spine 1989;14:367–372.
116. Molloy S, Jasper LE, Elliott DS, et al. Biomechanical evaluation of intramedullary nail versus tension band fixation for transverse olecranon fractures J Orthop Trauma 2004; 18:170–174.
117. Moroni A, Aspenberg P, Toksvig-Larsen S, et al. Enhanced fixation with hydroxapatite coated pins. Clin Orthop Rel Res 1998;346:171–177.
118. Muller ME, Allgower M, Schneider R, et al. Manual of Internal Fixation. Berlin: Springer-Verlag, 1979:85–96.
119. Nunamaker DM, Perren SM. A radiological and histological analysis of fracture healing using prebending of compression plates. Clin Orthop Rel Res 1979;138:167–174.
120. Ostrum RF, Marcantonio A, Marburger R. A critical analysis of the eccentric starting point for trochanteric intramedullary femoral nailing. J Orthop Trauma 2005;19: 681–686.
121. Paul JP. Approaches to design, force actions transmitted by joints in the human body. Proc Roy Soc London 1976;192:163–172.
122. Perren SM. Physical and biological aspects of fracture healing with special reference to internal fixation. Clin Orthop Rel Res 1975;138:175–194.
123. Perren SM, Cordey J, Baumgart F, et al. Technical and biomechanical aspects of screws used for bone surgery. Int J Orthop Trauma 1992;2:31–48.
124. Pierce MC, Valdevit A, Anderson L, et al. Biomechanical evaluation of dual energy A-ray absorptiometry for predicting fracture loads of the infant femur for injury investigation: an in vitro porcine model. J Orthop Trauma 2000;14:571–576.
125. Rapoff AJ, Conrad BP, Johnson WM, et al. Load sharing in Premier and Zephir anterior cervical plates. Spine 2003;28:2648–2651.
126. Ratcliff JR, Werner FW, Green JK, et al. Medial buttress versus lateral locked plating in a cadaver medial tibial plateau fracture model. J Orthop Trauma 2007;21:444–448.
127. Richter M, Thermann H, Wippermann B, et al. Foot fractures in restrained front seat car occupants: a long-term study over 23 years. J Orthop Trauma 2001;15:287–293.
128. Roberts CS, Dodds JC, Perry K, et al. Hybrid external fixation of the proximal tibia: strategies to improve frame stability. J Orthop Trauma 2003;17:415–420.

129. Rubin R, Trent P, Arnold W, et al. Knowles pinning of experimental femoral neck fractures: a biomechanical study. J Trauma 1981;21:1036–1039.

130. Russell TA, Dingman CA, Wisnewski P. Mechanical and clinical rationale for femoral neck fracture fixation with a cephalomedullary interlocking nail. 37th Annual Meeting of the Orthopedic Research Society 1992;17:177.

131. Russell TA, Taylor JC, LaVelle DG, et al. Mechanical characterization of femoral interlocking intramedullary nailing systems. J Orthop Trauma 1991;5:332–340.

132. Sander TW, Treharne RW, Baswell I, et al. Development of a new orthopedic wire tester. J Biomed Mat Res 1983;17:587–596.

133. Sanders R, Haidukewych GJ, Milne T, et al. Minimal versus maximal plate fixation techniques of the ulna: the biomechanical effect of number of screws and plate length. J Orthop Res. 2002;16:166–171.

134. Schatzker J, Sanderson R, Murnaghan JP. The holding power of orthopedic screws in vivo. Clin Orthop Rel Res 1975;108:115–126.

135. Schildhauer TA, LeDoux WR, Chapman JR, et al. Triangular osteosynthesis and iliosacral screw fixation for unstable sacral fractures: a cadaveric and biomechanical evaluation under cyclic loads. J Orthop Trauma 2003;17:22–31.

136. Schawecker F. The Practise of Osteosynthesis. A Manual of Accident Surgery. Chicago: Yearbook Medical Publishers, 1974.

137. Schuster I, Korner J, Arsdorf M, et al. Mechanical comparison in cadaver specimens of three different 90-degree double-plate osteosyntheses for simulated C2-type distal humerus fractures with varying bone densities. J Orthop Trauma 2008;22:113–120.

138. Siffri PC, Peindl RD, Coley ER, et al. Biomechanical analysis of blade plate versus locking plate fixation for a proximal humerus fracture: comparison using cadaveric and synthetic humeri. J Orthop Trauma 2006;20:547–554.

139. Simonian PT, Routt ML, Harrington RM, et al. The unstable iliac fracture: a biomechanical evaluation of internal fixation. Injury 1997;28:469–475.

140. Simonian PT, Thomson GT, Emley W, et al. Angled screw placement in the lateral condyle buttress plate for supracondylar femur fractures. 43th Annual Meeting of the Orthopedic Research Society, 1998.

141. Simonian PT, Schwappach JR, Routt Jr MLC, et al. Evaluation of new plate designs for symphysis pubis internal fixation. J Trauma 1996;41:498–502.

142. Snow M, Thompson G, Turner PG. A mechanical comparison of the locking compression plate (LCP) and the low contact dynamic compression plate (DCP) in an osteoporotic bone model. J Orthop Trauma 2008;22:121–125.

143. Spangler L, Cummings P, Tencer AF, et al. Biomechanical factors and failure of transcervical hip fracture repair. Injury 2001;32:223–228.

144. Spears BR, Ostrum RF, Litsky AS. A mechanical study of gap motion in cadaver femurs using short and long supracondylar nails. J Orthop Trauma 2004;18:354–360.

145. Stankewitz CJ, Chapman J, Muthusamy R, et al. Relationship of mechanical factors to the strength of proximal femur fractures fixed with cancellous screws. J Ortho Trauma 1996;10:248–257.

146. Singh K, Vaccaro AR, Kim J, et al. Biomechanical comparison of cervical spine reconstructive techniques after a multilevel corpectomy of the cervical spine. Spine 2003; 28:2352–2358.

147. Stankewich CJ, Swiontkowski MF, Tencer AF, et al. Augmentation of femoral neck fracture fixation with an injectable calcium-phosphate bone mineral cement. J Orthop Res 1996;14:786–793.

148. Stone JL, Beaupre GS, Hayes WC. Multiaxial strength characteristics of trabecular bone. J Biomech 1983;16:743–752.

149. Swiontkowski MF, Harrington RM, Keller TS, et al. Torsion and bending analysis of internal fixation techniques for femoral neck fractures: the role of implant design and bone density. J Orthop Res 1987;5:433–444.

150. Taitsman J, Saha S. Tensile properties of reinforced bone cement. J Bone Jt Surg 1976; 59A:419–425.

151. Tencer AF, Asnis SE, Harrington RM, et al. Biomechanics of cannulated and noncannulated screws. In: Asnis SE, Kyle RF, eds. Cannulated Screw Fixation, Principles, and Operative Techniques. New York: Springer-Verlag, 1996.

152. Tencer AF, Claudi B, Pearce S, et al. Development of a variable stiffness fixation system for stabilization of segmental defects of the tibia. J Orthop Res 1984;l:395–404.

153. Tencer AF, Hampton D, Eddy S. Biomechanical properties of threaded inserts for lumbar interbody spinal fusion. Spine 1995;20:2408–2414.

154. Tencer AF, Kaufman R, Ryan K, et al. Estimating the loads in femurs of occupants in actual motor vehicle crashes using frontal crash test data. Accident Analysis and Prevention 2002;34(1):1–11.

155. Van Audekercke R, Martens M, Mulier JC, et al. Experimental study on internal fixation of femoral neck fractures. Clin Orthop Rel Res 1979;141:203–212.

156. Watford KE, Kregor PJ, Hartsock LA. LISS plate fixation of periprosthtic supracondylar femur fractures. In: An YH, ed. Internal Fixation in Osteoporotic Bone. New York: Thieme, 2002:271–278.

157. Weaver JK, Chalmers J. Cancellous bone: its strength and changes with aging and an evaluation of some methods for measuring its mineral content 1. Age changes in cancellous bone. J Bone Jt Surg 1966:48A:289–299.

158. White III AA, Panjabi MM, Southwick WO. Effects of compression and cyclical loading on fracture healing—a quantitative biomechanical study. J Biomech 1977;10:233–239.

159. White III AA, Panjabi MM, Southwick WO. The four biomechanical stages of fracture repair. J Bone Jt Surg 1977;59A:188–192.

160. Wikenheiser MA, Lewallen DG, Markel MD. In vitro mechanical, thermal, and microstructural performance of five external fixation pins. 38th Annual Meeting of the Orthopedic Research Society 1992:17:409.

161. Wittenberg RH, Shea M, Swartz DE, et al. Importance of bone mineral density in instrumented spinal fusions. Spine 1991;16:648–652.

162. Woodard Pl, Self J, Calhoun JH, et al. The effect of implant axial and torsional stiffness on fracture healing. J Orthop Trauma 1987;l:33l–340.

163. Wright TM, Hayes WC. Tensile testing of bone over a wide range of strain rates: effects of strain rate, microstructure, and density. Med Biol Eng 1976;14:671–680.

164. Wu S-S, Edwards WT, Zou D, et al. Transpedicular vertebral screws in human vertebrae: effect on screw-vertebra interface stiffness. 38th Annual Meeting of the Orthopedic Research Society 1992;17:459.

165. Yerby S, Scott CC, Evans NJ, et al. Effect of cutting flute design on cortical bone screw insertion torque and pullout strength. J Orthop Trauma 2001;15:216–221.

166. Yinger K, Scalise J, Olson SA, et al. Biomechanical comparison of posterior pelvic ring fixation. J Orthop Trauma 2003;17:481–487.

167. Young JWR, Burgess AR, Brumback RJ. Lateral compression fractures of the pelvis; the importance of plain radiographs in the diagnosis and surgical management. Skeletal Radiol 1986:15:103–109.

168. Zand MS, Goldstein SA, Matthews LS. Fatigue failure of cortical bone screws. J Biomech 1983;16:305–311.

169. Zuber K, Schneider E, Eulenberger J, et al. Form und Dimension der Markhohle menschlicher Femora in Hinblick auf die Passung von Marknagelimplantaten. Unfallchirurg 1988;91:314–319.

2

CLASSIFICATION OF FRACTURES

Douglas R. Dirschl and Lisa K. Cannada

INTRODUCTION

Fracture classification systems have been in existence for nearly as long as people have identified fractures; they certainly predate the advent of radiography. Even in the earliest written surviving medical text, the Edwin Smith Papyrus, there was a rudimentary classification of fractures. If a fracture could be characterized as "having a wound over it, piercing through"—in other words, an open fracture—it was determined to be an "ailment not to be treated." This early form of one of the earliest systems of fracture classification served both to characterize the fracture and to guide the treatment.

Throughout the ages, all systems of fracture classification have served numerous purposes: to characterize fractures as far as certain general and specific features, to guide treatment, and to predict outcomes. This chapter will review the purposes and goals of fracture classification, the history of the use of such systems, and the general types of fracture classification systems in common use today. This chapter will also provide a critical analysis of the effectiveness of fracture classification systems, as well as some of the limitations of these systems. Finally, it will comment on the possible future of fracture classification systems.

PURPOSES OF FRACTURE CLASSIFICATION SYSTEMS

Taxonomy, or the naming and categorization of things, is not unique to orthopaedics or to fractures. Taxonomy is a universal phenomenon that occurs in all fields of science and art. One clear and simple example is the system of taxonomy that has been used to divide the natural world into three kingdoms: animals, plants, and bacteria (Fig. 2-1). This taxonomy, though simple, is a perfect example of the kinds of classification that permeate the world of arts and sciences and of the first general purpose of classification systems—to name things.

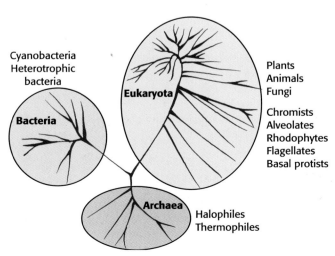

FIGURE 2-1 Balloon diagram of taxonomy of the natural world.

TABLE 2-1	**Purposes of Classification Systems**
To Name	High validity and reliability
To Describe and Compare	not required
To Guide Action	High validity and reliability
To Predict Outcomes	recommended

A second purpose of classification systems has been to describe things according to characteristics and to provide a hierarchy of those characteristics. A group of common descriptors are created so that individual items can be classified into various groups. Groups are then ordered into a hierarchy according to some definition of complexity. A simple example of this is the phylogeny used to describe the animal kingdom; this system describes and groups animals according to common characteristics, and then orders those groups in a hierarchy of complexity of the organism. This is, in principle, analogous to many fracture classification systems, which provide a group of common descriptors for fractures that are ordered according to complexity.

A third purpose of classification systems is to guide action or intervention. This feature of classification systems is not universally seen, and it is generally present only in classification systems that are diagnostic in nature. This introduces one of the key distinctions among classification systems—that between systems used for description and characterization and those used to guide actions and predict outcomes. For example, the classification system for the animal kingdom names and classifies animals, but it is descriptive only—it does not guide the observer in any suggested action. In orthopaedic practice, however, physicians use fracture classification systems to assist in making treatment decisions. In fact, many fracture classification systems were designed specifically for the purpose of guiding treatment. We should have higher expectations of the validity and integrity of systems that are used to guide actions than those used purely as descriptive tools.

The fourth purpose of classification systems is to assist in predicting outcomes of an intervention or treatment. The ability to reliably predict an outcome from a fracture classification alone would be of tremendous benefit, for it would allow physicians to counsel patients, beginning at the time of injury, about the expected outcome. This ability would also assist greatly in clinical research, as it would allow the comparison of the results from one clinical study of a particular fracture to that of another. It should be clear to the reader that, for a classification system to reliably predict outcome, a rigorous analysis of the reliability and validity of the classification system is necessary. Table 2-1 summarizes the purposes of classification systems, along with the level of reliability and validity necessary for high performance of the system.

HISTORY OF FRACTURE CLASSIFICATION

Fracture classifications have existed much longer than have radiographs. The Edmund Smith Papyrus, while it did not make a clear distinction between comminuted and noncomminuted fractures, clearly classified fractures as open or closed, and pro-

vided guidelines for treatment based on that classification. Open fractures, for example, were synonymous with early death in the Ancient Egypt, and these fractures were "ailments not to be treated."

In the 18th and 19th centuries, still prior to the discovery of radiographs, there were in existence fracture classification systems that were based on the clinical appearance of the limb alone. The Colles fracture of the distal radius, in which the distal fragment was displaced dorsally—causing the dinner fork deformity of the distal radius—was a common fracture. Any fracture with this clinical deformity was considered a Colles fracture and was treated with correction of the deformity and immobilization of the limb.[15] The Pott fracture, a fracture of the distal tibia and fibula with varus deformity, was likewise a fracture classification that was based only on the clinical appearance of the limb.[58] These are but two examples of fracture classifications that were accepted and in widespread use prior to the development of radiographic imaging.

After the advent of radiography, fracture classification systems expanded in number and came into common usage. Radiography so altered the understanding of fractures and the methods of fracture care that nearly all fracture classification systems in use today are based solely on a characterization of the fracture fragments on plain radiographs. Most modern fracture classification systems are based on a description of the location, number, and displacement of fracture lines viewed on radiographs, rather than on the clinical appearance of the fractured limb. While countless fracture classification systems based on radiographs have been described in the past century for fractures in all parts of the skeleton, only the most enduring classification systems remain in common usage today. Examples of these enduring classification systems are the Garden[30] and Neer[51] classification systems of proximal femoral and proximal humeral fractures, respectively. These and other commonly used classification systems will be discussed in more detail in a later part of this chapter.

Nearly all fracture classification systems in use today are based upon having observers—usually orthopaedic physicians—make judgments and interpretations based on the analysis of plain radiographs of the fractured bone. Usually, anteroposterior and lateral radiographs are used, although some fracture classification systems allow for or encourage the use of additional x-ray views, such as oblique radiographs, or internal and external rotation radiographs. It is evident that each decision made in the process of classifying a fracture is based on a human's interpretation of the often complex patterns of shadows evident on a plain radiograph of the fractured limb. This, in turn, requires that the observer have a detailed and fundamental understanding of the osteology of the bone being imaged and of the fracture being classified. The observer must have the ability to accurately and completely identify all of the fracture lines, understand the origin and nature of all of the fracture fragments, and delineate the relationship of all of the fracture fragments to one another. Finally, the procedure of fracture classification requires that the observer very accurately quantify the amount of displacement or angulation of each fracture fragment from the location in which it should be in the nonfractured situation.

More recently, computed tomography (CT) scanning has been added by many observers to assist in classifying fractures. In most cases, the CT scan data has been used and applied

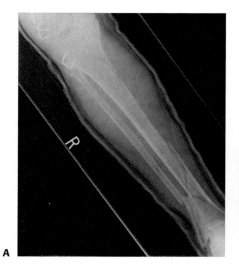
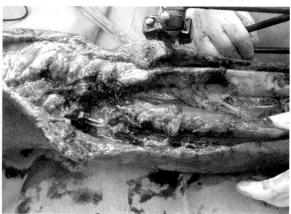

FIGURE 2-2 Tibial fracture as seen on radiograph **(A)** and intraoperatively **(B)**. The x-ray appearance greatly underestimates the overall severity of the injury.

to a classification system that was devised for use with plain radiographs alone. There are a few classification systems, however, that are specifically designed for use with CT imaging data. The most well-known example of such a system is the Sanders classification system for fractures of the calcaneus,[61] which was designed for use with a carefully defined semicoronal CT sequence through the posterior facet of the subtalar joint.

Most fracture classification systems until very recently relied solely on radiographic images to classify the fracture, guide treatment, and predict outcomes. It is becoming increasingly appreciated, however, that nonradiographic factors such as the extent of soft tissue injury when there are other injuries (skeletal or nonskeletal), medical comorbidities, and various other nonradiographic factors have a large effect on treatment decisions and on the outcomes of fracture treatment.[23,42] These factors, however, are not accounted for in radiographic systems for fracture classification.

In reviewing a radiograph of a fracture, it is difficult to fully appreciate the extent of soft tissue damage that has occurred, and the image provides no information about the patient's medical history. For example, if one views a radiograph of the transverse tibial shaft fracture shown in Figure 2-2, one may conclude that this is a simple, low-energy injury. In this example, however, the fracture occurred as a result of very high energy, and the patient sustained extensive soft tissue damage. In addition, the patient was an insulin-dependent diabetic with severe peripheral neuropathy and skin ulcerations on the fractured limb. There is no way, from view of the plain radiographs or application of a fracture classification based on radiographs alone, to account for these additional factors. The patient in this example required amputation, a treatment that would not be predicted by review of the radiographs alone. Some discussion of the role of classifying the soft tissue injury in characterizing fractures will take place later in this chapter.

TYPES OF FRACTURE CLASSIFICATION SYSTEMS

Classification systems used to characterize fractures can be characterized into three broad categories: (i) those that are fracture specific, which evolved around and were generated for the classification of a single fracture in a single location in the skeleton; (ii) those that are generic or universal fracture classification systems, which apply a single, consistent methodology to the classification of fractures in all parts of the human skeleton; and (iii) those that attempt to classify the soft tissue injury. It is beyond the scope of this chapter to discuss individually all the fracture classification systems now in common usage, but it is important for the reader to understand the differences between the general types of classification systems. For that reason, some examples of each of the three types of fracture classification systems will be discussed.

Examples of Fracture-Specific Classification Systems

The Garden classification of femoral neck fractures[30] is a long-standing fracture classification system that describes the displacement and angulation of the femoral head on anteroposterior (AP) and lateral radiographs of the hip (see Fig. 47-2). The classification is essentially a descriptive one, describing the location and displacement of the fractured femoral neck and head. The fracture types are ordered, however, to indicate increasing fracture severity, greater fracture instability, and higher risk of complications with attempts at reduction and stabilization of the fracture. This feature of ordering fracture types by severity takes the classification system from a nominal system to an ordinal system. Garden types 1 and 2 fractures are considered to be stable injuries and are frequently treated with percutaneous internal fixation. Garden 3 and 4 fractures have been grouped as unstable fracture patterns and, while closed reduction and internal fixation are used in some circumstances, most Garden 3 and 4 fractures in elderly patients are treated with arthroplasty.

The Schatzker classification of proximal tibia fractures[62,63] is an example of another descriptive classification system that has been widely utilized and is based on the location of the major fracture line in the proximal tibia and the presence or absence of a depressed segment of the articular surface of the proximal tibia (see Fig. 53-9). This fracture classification is not dependent on the amount of displacement or depression of the articular fractures, but only on the location of the fracture lines. The Schatzker classification seems very simple, but it also demonstrates some of the areas of confusion that can result from fracture classifications. For example, Schatzker V and VI fractures are distinct fracture types in the system, but observers have a great deal of difficulty in distinguishing these two fracture types from one another when viewing fracture radiographs. Also, the Schatzker VI fracture group includes fractures classified as types C1 and C3 by the AO/OTA system (described below), thus demonstrating an area of inconsistency between two commonly used but different systems for classifying the same fracture that can lead to confusion among observers.

The Neer classification system for proximal humeral fractures[51] is a descriptive fracture classification system that has been widely utilized and widely taught (Fig. 2-3). It is based on how many fracture "parts" there are—a part is defined as a fracture fragment that is either displaced more than one centimeter or angulated more than 45 degrees. The Neer classification groups fractures into nondisplaced (one-part), two-part, three-part, or four-part fractures. Nondisplaced fractures in the Neer system involve several fracture lines, none of which meet the displacement or angulation criteria to be considered a "part." Two-part fractures in the Neer system can represent either a fracture across the surgical neck of the humerus or greater tuberosity fracture that is displaced. Three-part fractures classically involve the humeral head, in greater tuberosity fragments being displaced or angulated. Four-part fractures involve displacement or angulation of the humeral head and greater and lesser tuberosities. The reader should note that, in addition to correct identification of the fracture fragments, this classification system requires the observer to make careful and accurate measurements of fragment displacement and angulation to determine if a fragment constitutes a part.

The Lauge-Hansen classification of malleolar fractures of the ankle[42] is an example of a widely used system that is based primarily on the mechanism of injury. The system makes use of the fact that particular mechanisms of injury to the ankle will result in predictable patterns of fracture to the malleoli. The appearance of the fracture on the radiographs, then, is used to infer the mechanism of the injury. The injuries are classified according to the position of the foot at the time of injury and the direction of the deforming force at the time of fracture. The position of the foot is described as pronation or supination, and the deforming force is categorized as external rotation, inversion, or eversion. This creates six general fracture types, which are essentially nominal—they are not ordered into increasing injury severity. Within each fracture type, however, there is an ordinal scale, with varying degrees of severity being assigned to each type (1–4) according to the fracture pattern. With this classification system, correct determination of the fracture type can guide the manipulations necessary to affect fracture reduction—the treating physician must reverse the direction of the injuring forces to achieve a reduction. For example, internal rotation is required to achieve reduction of a supination external rotation fracture pattern.

Generic or Universal Classification Systems

The AO/OTA (Orthopaedic Trauma Association) fracture classification[44,78] is essentially the only generic or universal system in wide usage today. It is universal in the sense that the same

fracture classification system can be applied to any bone within the body. This classification system was devised through a consensus panel of orthopaedic traumatologists who were members of the Orthopaedic Trauma Association and is based upon a classification system initially developed and proposed by the AO/ASIF group in Europe.[49,50] The Orthopaedic Trauma Association believed there was a need for a detailed universal system for classification of fractures to allow for standardization of research and communication among orthopaedic surgeons. The AO/OTA fracture classification system is an alphanumeric system that can be applied to most bones within the body.

In applying the OTA fracture classification system, there are five questions that must be answered for each fracture:

1. *Which bone?* The major bones in the body are numbered, with the humerus being #1, the forearm #2, the femur #3, the tibia #4, and so on (Fig. 2-4).

2. *Where in the bone is the fracture?* The answer to this question identifies a specific segment within the bone. The second number of the coding system is applied to the location in the bone. In most long bones, the diaphyseal segment (2) is located between the proximal (1) and distal (3) segments. The dividing lines between the shaft segment and the proximal and distal segments occur in metaphysis of the bone. The tibia is assigned a fourth segment, which is the malleolar segment. An example of the application of answering the first two questions of the AO/OTA classification is that a fracture of the midshaft of the femur will be given a numeric classification of 32 (3 for femur, 2 for the diaphyseal segment) (Fig. 2-4).

3. *Which fracture type?* The fracture type in this system can be A, B, or C, but these three types are defined differently in diaphyseal fractures and fractures at either end of the bone. For diaphyseal fractures, the type A fracture is a simple fracture with two fragments. The type B diaphyseal fracture has some comminution, but there can still be contact between the proximal and distal fragments. The type C diaphyseal fracture is a highly comminuted or segmental fracture with no contact possible between proximal and distal fragments. For proximal and distal segment fractures, type A fractures are considered extra-articular, type B fractures are partial articular (there is some continuity between the shaft and some portion of the articular surface), and Type C fractures involve complete disruption of the articular surface from the diaphysis. An example of this portion of the classification system is shown in Figure 2-4.

4. *Which group do the fractures belong to?* Grouping further divides the fractures according to more specific descriptive details. Fracture groups are not consistently defined; that is, fracture groups are different for each fracture type. Complete description of the fracture groups is beyond the scope of this chapter.

5. *Which subgroup?* This is the most detailed determination in the AO/OTA classification system. As is the case with groups, subgroups differ from bone to bone and depend upon key features for any given bone in its classification. The intended purpose of the subgroups is to increase the precision of the classification system. An in-depth discussion of this fracture classification is beyond the scope of this chapter, and the reader is referred to the references for a more detailed description of this universal fracture classification system.

Displaced fractures

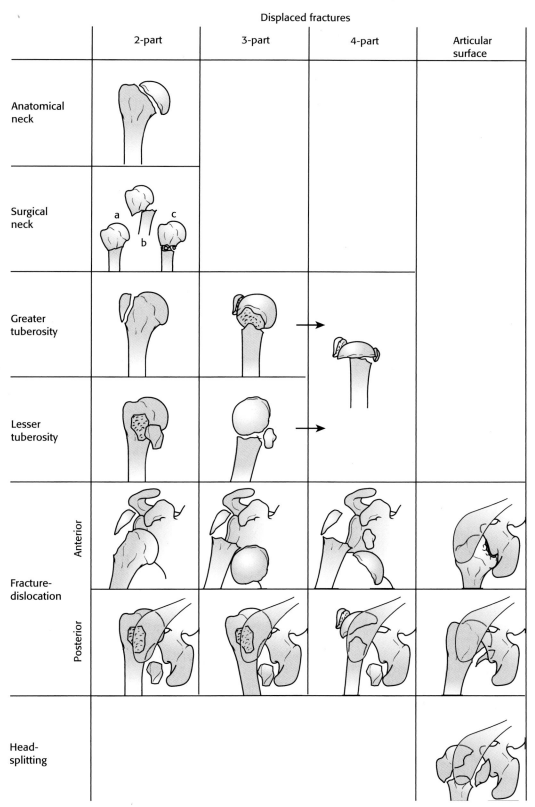

FIGURE 2-3 The Neer four-part classification of proximal humerus fractures. A fracture is displaced if the fracture fragments are separated 1 cm or greater, or if angulation between the fracture fragments is more than 45 degrees. A displaced fracture is either a two-, three-, or four-part fracture. (From Neer CS. Displaced proximal humeral fractures: I. classification and evaluation. J Bone Joint Surg 1970;52A:1077–1089, reprinted with permission from Journal of Bone and Joint Surgery.)

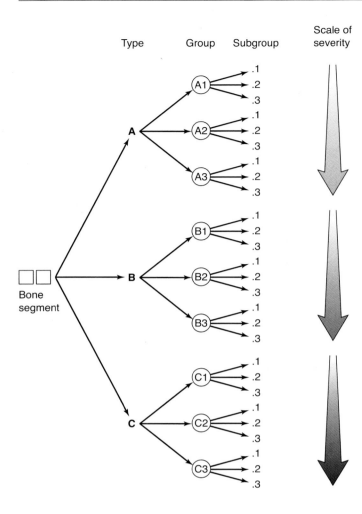

Type   Group   Subgroup   Scale of severity

FIGURE 2-4 The AO/ASIF Comprehensive Long Bone Classification applied to proximal humeral fractures. This system describes three types of proximal humerus fractures (types A, B, and C). Type A fractures are described as unifocal extra-articular (two-segment) fractures, type B as bifocal extra-articular (three-segment) fractures, and type C as anatomic neck or articular segment fractures. Each type includes three fracture patterns, with nine subgroups for each type of fracture. The subgroup classification indicates the degree of displacement. (Adapted from Müller ME, Allgower M, Schneider R, et al. Manual of Internal Fixation. New York: Springer-Verlag, 1991, with permission.)

The AO/OTA classification system is an evolving system. It is continually evaluated by a committee of the OTA, and is open for change where appropriate. The reader should note that the AO/OTA classification system of fractures, and its precursor, the AO/ASIF system, were designed for delineation and recording of the maximum possible amount of detail about the individual fracture pattern and appearance on radiographs. The assumption made during the development of these classification systems is that with specific definitions/diagrams and a high degree of detail come greater accuracy and a superior fracture classification system that could be applied by any orthopaedic surgeon. It was believed such a system could potentially result in better prognostic and research capabilities. As will be discussed later in the chapter, greater specificity and detail in a fracture classification system does not necessarily correlate well with good performance of the classification system.

Classifications of Soft Tissue Injury Associated with Fractures

The skin and soft tissue represent an organ system. The energy of the injury may be reflected in the soft tissue damage to the extremity involved. If one sees a radiograph demonstrating a comminuted fracture, it is often thought that it is a high-energy injury. However, there may be other patient factors that come into consideration and may lead to a comminuted fracture from a lower-energy mechanism. This may be evident in an elderly

patient with ground-level falls who has a significantly comminuted distal humerus fracture. The energy of the injury itself resulted only from a ground-level fall, but led to a complex fracture type as a result of underlying osteoporotic bone. Some of the value in the soft tissue classification system is in planning the treatment as well as in predicting the outcome.

The clearest example of a fracture with an associated soft tissue injury is the open fracture. Early classification systems for open fractures focused only on the size of the opening in the skin. With time, however, it was recognized that the extent of muscle injury, local vascular damage, and periosteal stripping are also of paramount significance. Gustilo et al.[32,33] developed the classification system now used by most North American orthopaedists to describe open fractures. This classification system takes into account the skin wound, the extent of local soft tissue injury and contamination, and the severity of the fracture pattern (see Table 12-2). The Gustilo classification system originally included type I, type II, and type III fractures. However, this system was modified later to expand the type III open fractures into subtypes A, B, and C. It is important to note that the type III-C fracture is defined as any open fracture in which there is an accompanying vascular injury that *requires repair*. The Gustilo classification system has been applied to open fractures in nearly all long bones. It is important to recognize that this classification system only can be applied fully after surgical debridement of the open fracture has been performed. This system

TABLE 2-2	**Oestern and Tscherne Classification of Closed Fractures**	
Grade	Soft Tissue Injury	Bony Injury
Grade 0	Minimal soft tissue damage Indirect injury to limb	Simple fracture pattern
Grade 1	Superficial abrasion/contusion	Mild fracture pattern
Grade 2	Deep abrasion with skin or muscle contusion Direct trauma to limb	Severe fracture pattern
Grade 3	Extensive skin contusion or crush Severe damage to underlying muscle Subcutaneous avulsion Compartmental syndrome may be present	Severe fracture pattern

has proven useful in predicting risk of infection in open tibial fractures.[32]

Interobserver agreement in grading open tibial fractures according to the classification of Gustilo was investigated by Brumback and Jones,[10] who presented radiographs and videotapes of surgical debridements to a group of orthopaedic traumatologists who classified the fractures. They reported an average interobserver agreement of 60%. The range of agreement, however, was wide, ranging from 42% to 94%. Percentage agreement was best for the most severe and the least severe injuries, and was poorer for fractures in the middle range of the classification system. That the classification system did not have similar reliability across the spectrum of injury severity has been a criticism of this classification system as a prognostic indicator for any but the least severe and most severe injuries.

The classification of Oestern and Tscherne can be used to characterize the severity of closed fractures (Table 2-2).[54] This system remains the only published classification system for the soft tissue injury associated with closed fractures. Fractures are assigned one of four grades, from 0 to 3. Figure 2-5 is an example of a patient with a Tscherne Grade 2 closed tibial plateau fracture. Deep abrasions of the skin, muscle contusion, fracture blisters, and massive soft tissue swelling, as in this patient, may lead the surgeon away from immediate articular stabilization and toward temporary spanning external fixation. No studies have been done to determine the interobserver reliability of the Tscherne system for the classification of the soft tissue injury associated with closed fractures.

The value of a classification system is greatly enhanced if it can assist in predicting outcome. A prospective study completed by Gaston et al.[31] assessed various fracture classification schemes against several validated functional outcome measures in patients with tibial shaft fractures. The Tscherne classification system of closed fractures was more predictive of outcome than the other classification systems used. The Tscherne system was most strongly predictive of time to return to prolonged walking or running.

Limitations of Fracture Classification Systems

To be successful and valuable as a predictive tool, a classification system must be both reliable and valid.[11,29,45] Reliability reflects the ability of a classification system to return the same result for the same fracture radiographs over multiple observers or by the same observer when viewing the fracture on multiple occasions. The former is termed interobserver reliability, or the agreement between different observers using the classification system to assess the same cases. The latter is termed intraobserver reproducibility—the agreement of the same observer's assessment, using the classification system, for the same cases on repeated occasions. The validity of a classification system reflects the accuracy with which the system describes the true fracture entity. A valid classification system would correctly categorize the fracture in a large percentage of cases, when compared to a "gold standard." Unfortunately, there is no such gold standard for fracture classification—not even observation at surgery can be considered infallible—so the assessment of the performance of fracture classification systems must be confined to assessing interobserver reliability and intraobserver reproducibility.

There has been discussion over the appropriate use of the terms "agreement" and "accuracy" in reference to the performance of fracture classification systems, as well as which of these terms is the best measure of a system's performance. The term "accuracy" implies that there is a correct answer or a gold standard against which comparisons can be made, validated, and determined to be true or false. However, the term "agreement" indicates that there is no defined gold standard and that unanimous agreement among all observers that might classify a given fracture is the highest measure of performance of a classification system. These two terms are not congruent and they are not interchangeable. Each is tested by a vastly different statistical method and to optimize each would require a radically different method for generating and validating a fracture classifi-

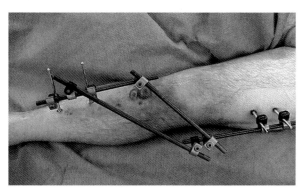

FIGURE 2-5 Example of a Tscherne II fracture of the proximal tibia.

cation system. It has been unclear at times whether those developing and applying classification systems today are expecting the classification to serve as a gold standard or they are attempting to develop the classification to achieve optimal agreement among observers.

In the late 1980s and early 1990s, studies began to appear in the orthopaedic literature assessing the interobserver reliability of various fracture classifications systems.[2,3,28,39,53,59,67,73] In a controversial editorial published in 1993, *Fracture Classification Systems: Do They Work and Are They Useful*, Albert Burstein, Ph.D., arrayed some important issues and considerations for fracture classification systems.[11] He stated that classification systems are tools, and that the measure of whether such a tool works is if it produces the same result, time after time, in the hands of anyone who employs the tool. Dr. Burstein went on to say that "any classification scheme, be it nominal, ordinal, or scalar, should be proved to be a workable tool before it is used in a discriminatory or predictive manner." He emphasized that the key distinction for a classification system was between its use to describe and characterize fractures and its use to guide treatment or predict outcomes. It is the latter use that requires a system to be proven to be a valid tool; the minimum criteria for acceptable performance of any classification system should be a demonstration of a high degree of interobserver reliability and intraobserver reproducibility.

Several studies have been published since Dr. Burstein's editorial appeared, and nearly all concluded that fracture classification systems had substantial interobserver variability. Classification systems for fractures of the proximal femur,[2,28,53,56,64,73] proximal humerus,[7,9,39,67,68] ankle,[16,52,59,64,73] distal tibia,[22,45,71] and tibial plateau[12,46,75–77] among others, were all shown to have poor to slight interobserver reliability. The earliest of these studies looked only at the observed percentage of agreement—the percentage of times that individual pairs of observers categorized fractures into the same category. Subsequent studies, however, have most frequently used a statistical test known as the kappa statistic, a test that analyzes pair-wise comparisons between observers applying the same classification system to a specific set of fracture cases. The kappa statistic was originally introduced by Cohen in 1960,[13] and the kappa statistic and its variants are the most recognized and widely used methods for measuring reliability for fracture classification systems. The kappa statistic adjusts the proportion of agreement between any two observers by correcting for the proportion of agreement that could have occurred by chance alone. Kappa values can range from + 1.0 (perfect agreement) to 0.0 (chance agreement) to − 1.0 (perfect disagreement) (Table 2-3).

The original kappa statistic is appropriate when there are only two choices of fracture categories or when the fracture classification system is nominal—all categorical differences are equally important. In most situations, however, there are more than two categories into which a fracture can be classified, and fracture classification systems are ordinal—the categorical differences are ranked according to injury severity, treatment method, or presumed outcome. In these cases, the most appropriate variant of the kappa statistic to be used is the weighted kappa statistic, described by Fleiss,[26,27] in which some credit is given to partial agreement and not all disagreements are treated equally. For example, in the Neer classification of proximal humeral fractures, disagreement between a nondisplaced and a two-part fracture has far fewer treatment implications than disagreement between a nondisplaced and a four-part fracture. By weighting kappa values, one can account for the different levels of importance between levels of disagreement. However, the most appropriate use of the weighted kappa statistic should include a clear explanation of the weighting scheme selected, since the results of the kappa statistic will vary—even with the same observations—if the weighting scheme varies.[29] Thus, without specific knowledge of the weighting scheme used, it is difficult to compare the results of fracture classification system reliability across different studies.

In most studies, the guidelines proposed by Landis and Koch[40] have been used to categorize kappa values; values less than 0.00 indicate poor reliability, 0.01 to 0.20 indicate slight reliability, 0.21 to 0.40 indicate fair reliability, 0.41 to 0.60 indicate moderate reliability, 0.61 to 0.80 indicate substantial reliability, and 0.81 to 1.00 indicate nearly perfect agreement. Although these criteria have gained widespread acceptance, the values were chosen arbitrarily and were never intended to serve as general benchmarks. A second set of criteria, also arbitrary, have been proposed by Svanholm et al.: less than 0.50 indicate poor reliability; 0.51 to 0.74 indicate good reliability, and greater than 0.75 indicate excellent reliability.[69]

Observer variability, using the kappa statistic, has been found to be a limitation of many fracture classification systems. Many studies have documented only fair to poor intraobserver reliability for a wide range of fracture classification systems. Systems tested have included, among others, the Neer fracture classification system of proximal humeral fractures,[7,8,39,67] the Garden classification systems of proximal femoral fractures,[2,28,53,56,64] the Rüedi and Allgöwer and AO classification systems of distal tibial fractures,[22,45,71] the Lauge-Hansen and Weber classification of malleolar fractures,[16,52,72,73] and the Schatzker and AO fracture classification system of proximal tibial fractures.[12,46,75–77] Even the Gustilo-Anderson classification system for classifying open fractures has been shown to have only fair interobserver reliability.[10] Additionally, studies have shown observer variability in classifying various other orthopaedic injuries, such as fractures of the acetabulum,[6,57,74] the distal radius,[1,3,36] the scaphoid,[20] the spine,[5,55] the calcaneus,[35,41] and gunshot fractures of the femur.[66]

More recent studies have attempted to isolate the sources of this variability, but the root cause for the variability has not been identified. It remains unknown if any system for the classification of fractures can perform with excellent intraobserver reliability when it will be used by many observers. A methodology for validation for fracture classification systems has been proposed, but it is highly detailed and extremely time consuming and it is unknown if it can be practically applied.[4]

The use of the weighted kappa statistic in studies assessing

TABLE 2-3	**Range of the Kappa Statistic**
Value of Kappa Statistic	Level of Agreement
+ 1.00	Perfect agreement
0.00	Agreement equal to chance
− 1.00	Perfect disagreement

the reliability of fracture classification systems should clearly state the weighting scheme used. Methodological issues such as this were evaluated in a systematic review of 44 published studies assessing the reliability of fracture classification systems.[4] Various methodological issues were identified, including a failure to assure that the study sample of fracture radiographs was representative of the spectrum and frequency of injury severity seen for the particular fracture in 61% of the studies, a failure to justify the size of the study group in 100% of the studies, and inadequate statistical analysis of the data in 61% of the studies. While the authors of this study used very rigid and, some would argue, unfairly rigorous criteria to evaluate these studies, the authors' conclusion that reliability studies of fracture classification cannot be easily compared to one another is valid and appropriate. The development and adoption of a systematic methodological approach to the development and validation of new fracture classification systems seems appropriate and is needed.

Only one study to date has attempted to validate whether a fracture classification scheme correlates well with outcomes following fracture care.[70] In a prospective, multicenter study, 200 patients with unilateral isolated lower extremity fractures (acetabulum, femur, tibia, talus, or calcaneus) underwent various functional outcome measurements at 6 and 12 months, including the Sickness Impact Profile and the AMA Impairment rating. The AO/OTA fracture classification for each of these patients was correlated with the functional outcome measures. While the study indicated some significant differences in functional outcome between type C and type B fractures, there was no significant difference between type C and type A fractures. The authors concluded that the AO/OTA code for fracture classification may not be a good predictor of 6- and 12-month functional performance and impairment for patients with isolated lower extremity fractures.

Additional, deeper research has attempted to elucidate some of the reasons for interobserver variation in the classification of fractures. These studies have generally focused on a few specific variables or tasks involved in the fracture classification process. Some of those which have been investigated are discussed in the following paragraphs.

Quality of Fracture Radiographs

The quality of the radiographs varies normally in clinical practice and may affect the observer's ability to accurately or reproducibly identify and classify the fracture. Many have attributed observed intraobserver variability in fracture classifications systems to variations in the quality of radiographs.[1,7,28,37,39,67] Studies looking specifically at this variable, however, have not demonstrated it to be a significant source of intraobserver variability.[16,22] In one such study involving classification of tibial plafond fractures using the Rüedi and Allgöwer system, observers were asked to classify the fractures, but also asked to make a determination of whether the radiographs were of adequate quality to classify the fracture.[22] In that study, observers agreed less on the quality of the radiographs (mean kappa 0.38 + 0.046) than on the classification of the fractures themselves (mean kappa 0.43 + 0.048). In addition, the extent of interobserver agreement on the quality of the radiographs had no correlation with the extent of agreement in classifying the fractures. The authors concluded that, based on the results of their investigation, it appeared that improving the quality of plain radiographic images would be unlikely to improve the reliability of classification of fractures of the tibial plafond.

Further studies using advanced imaging modalities, such as CT or magnetic resonance imaging (MRI) scanning, in which high-quality images should always be obtained, have generally not demonstrated improved intra-observer reliability over studies that have used plain radiographs alone. Bernstein et al. found that CT scans did not improve interobserver agreement for the Neer classification of proximal humerus fractures.[7] Chan et al., in a study of the impact of a CT scan on determining treatment plan and fracture classification for tibial plateau fractures, found that viewing the CT scans did not improve interobserver agreement on classification, but did increase agreement regarding treatment plan.[12] Two studies investigating the effect of adding CT information to plain radiographs on the interobserver agreement in classifying fractures of the tibial plateau and tibial plafond failed to show a significant improvement in agreement after the addition of CT scan information.[12,46,47] Katz et al.,[35] studying fractures of the distal radius, found the addition of a CT scan occasionally resulted in changes in treatment plans and also increased agreement among observers on the surgical plan in treating these injuries. A study investigating the use of three-dimensional CT scanning in distal humeral fractures concluded that three-dimensional CT did not improve interobserver reliability over plain radiographs or two-dimensional CT scans, but that it did improve intra-observer reproducibility.[25] These authors and others have concluded that CT scan information may be a useful adjunct in surgical planning for a severe articular fracture, but is probably not required for the purpose of fracture classification.

Some contradictory data was recently published in Germany.[18] Thirty-five distal radius fractures that had been classified as AO/OTA A2 and A3 (extra-articular types) after radiographic review underwent CT scanning. The scans revealed that 57% of the fractures had an intra-articular component and had been inappropriately classified at AO/OTA type A fractures. The reader should note that this study did not attempt to determine interobserver reliability of the classification, but simply that a single observer reviewing the CT scans disagreed with the original fracture classification in 57% of cases. It remains unproven whether CT scanning is a useful adjunct to improve interobserver agreement in the classification of fractures.

One study reported on the impact of MRI scanning on the interobserver reliability of classification of tibial plateau fractures according to the Schatzker classification system.[77] Three orthopaedic trauma surgeons classified tibial plateau fractures first with plain radiographs, and then with either the addition of a CT and an MRI scan. Kappa values averaged 0.68 with plain radiographs alone, 0.73 with the addition of a CT scan, and 0.85 with addition of an MRI scan. No statistical analysis was reported to indicate whether the addition of CT and MRI information resulted in a statistically significant improvement in reliability.

Difficulty Identifying Fracture Lines on Radiographs

All fracture classification systems require the use of a diagnostic image, usually a radiograph, on which the observer must make observations, measurements, or both. Even with high-quality radiographs, however, overlapping osseous fragments or densities can make the accurate identification of each fracture fragment difficult. Osteopenia can also increase the difficulty in accurate classification of fractures. Osteopenic bone casts a much fainter "shadow" on radiographic films, making the delineation of fine trabecular or articular details a much more difficult task for the observer. Osteopenia represents a physiologic parameter that may affect treatment plans and outcomes, but is not mentioned in any classification system.

Periarticular fractures also may be difficult to accurately classify with plain radiographs. Articular fractures tend to occur in areas of the skeleton with complex three-dimensional osteology, may be highly comminuted, and the classification systems used for these fractures are predicated on the accurate identification of each fracture fragment and determination of its relationship to the other fragments and/or its position in the nonfracture situation. Observer variability in the identification of these small fracture fragments in complex fractures would be expected to lead to poorer interobserver reliability of the fracture classification system. Dirschl et al. investigated the observers' ability to identify small articular fragments in classifying tibial plafond fractures according to the Rüedi and Allgöwer classification.[22] Observers classified 25 tibial plafond fractures on radiographs and then on line drawings that had been made from those radiographs by the senior author; interobserver reliability was no different in the two situations. At a second classification session, observers were asked to first mark, on the fracture radiographs, the articular fragments and then to classify the fractures; in a final session, the observers classified the radiographs after the fracture fragments had been premarked by the senior author. Having observers mark the fracture fragments resulted in no improvement in interobserver reliability of the fracture classification system. When identification of the articular fragments was removed from the fracture classification process, however, by having the fragments premarked by the senior author, the interobserver reliability was significantly improved (mean kappa value increased from 0.43 to 0.54, $P<0.025$). The authors believed the results of this study indicated that observers classifying fractures of the tibial plafond have great difficulty identifying the fragments of the tibial articular surface on radiographs. They went on to postulate that fracture classification system predicated on the identification of the number and displacement of small articular fragments may inherently perform poorly on reliability analyses, because of observer difficulty in reliably identifying the fracture fragments.

Variability Making Measurements on Radiographs

The amount of displacement of fracture fragments, particularly articular fragments, has long been felt to be important in characterizing fractures and has been used by many to make decisions regarding treatment. Additionally, some classification systems for fractures are predicated on the observer accurately identifying the amount of displacement and/or angulation of fracture fragments; the Neer classification system for proximal humeral fractures is an example. Finally, the quality of fracture care has frequently been judged by measuring the amount of displacement of articular fracture fragments on posttreatment radiographs.

Numerous studies have shown, however, that there is variability among observers in making measurements on radiographs and that this may be a source for variability in fracture classification. One such study assessed the error of measurement of articular incongruity of tibial plateau fractures.[47] In this study, five orthopaedic traumatologists measured the maximum articular depression and the maximum condylar widening on

56 sets of tibial plateau fracture radiographs. For 38 of the cases, the observers also had a computed tomography scan of the knee to assist in making measurements. The results of the study indicated that the 95% tolerance limits for measuring maximum articular depression were ± 12 millimeters, and for measuring maximum condylar widening were ± 9 millimeters. This result indicates that there is substantial variability in making these seemingly simple measurements.

Tolerance limits, of course, will decrease as the range of measurements decreases (the range of articular depression in the study above was 35 millimeters). Thus, it would be expected that lower tolerance limits would result from the measurement of reduced tibial plateau than those observed in the reported study, which measured injury films. However, in a study looking at the tolerance limits for measuring articular congruity in healed distal radial fractures, tolerance limits of ± 3 millimeters were identified, when the range of articular congruity measurements was only 4 millimeters.[36]

It has been suggested that CT scanning may improve the reliability of measurement of articular fracture displacements. In one study of intra-articular fractures of the distal radius, there was poor correlation between measurement of gap widths or step deformities on plain radiographs as compared to CT scans.[14] Nearly one third of measurements made from plain radiographs were significantly different than those made from CT scans. Another study extended these findings by examining known intra-articular displacements made in the hip joints of cadaveric specimens.[8] The authors observed that CT-generated data were far more accurate and reproducible than were data obtained from plain films. Moed et al. reported on a series of posterior wall acetabular fractures treated with open reduction and internal fixation in which reduction was assessed on both plain radiographs and on CT scans.[48] Of 59 patients who were graded as having an anatomic reduction based on plain radiographs and for whom postoperative CT scans were obtained, 46 had a gap or step-off greater than 2 millimeters. These results may not be characteristic of all fractures, since the posterior wall of the acetabulum may be more difficult to profile using plain radiographs than most areas of other joints.

From this work, it appears that there is significant observer variability in the routine measurement of articular incongruity on radiographs. It also seems highly unlikely that observers using plain radiographs can reliably measure small amounts of incongruity. This suggests that improvements in our ability to reliably assess the displacement of fracture fragments are necessary to reduce variability in articular fracture assessment.

Complexity of Decision-Making in Applying a Fracture Classification

Some fracture classification systems are quite complex, requiring the observer to choose between many possible categories in characterizing a fracture. The AO/OTA system, for example, has up to 27 possible classifications for a fracture of a single bone segment (there are three choices each for fracture type, group, and subgroup). It seems reasonable that observers would find it easier to classify a fracture if there were fewer choices to be made, and studies of the AO/OTA fracture classification system have confirmed this. In nearly all cases, for various fractures, classification of type can be performed much more reliably than classification into groups or subgroups.[16,36,43,45,56,71,75] These studies concluded that, for optimal reliability, the use of this classification beyond characterization of type was not recommended.

It has also been proposed that limiting observers' choices to no more than two for any step in the classification of fractures would improve the ability of the observer to classify the fracture and would improve interobserver reliability. In 1996, the developers of the AO/ASIF comprehensive classification of fractures (CCF) modified to incorporate binary decision-making.[50] The reasoning was that, if observers could answer a series of "yes or no" questions about the fracture, they could more precisely and reliably classify the fracture. The modification was planned, announced, and implemented without any sort of validation that the modification would achieve the desired outcomes or that binary decision making would improve reliability in fracture classification.

Since 1997, however, two investigations of specific fracture types have evaluated whether binary decision making improves reliability in the classification of fractures. The first of these studies developed a binary modification of the Rüedi and Allgöwer classification of tibial plafond fractures and had observers classify 25 fractures according to the original classification system and the binary modification.[22] The binary modification was applied rigidly in fracture classification sessions that were proctored by the author; observers were forced to make binary decisions about the fracture radiographs, and not permitted to jump to the final fracture classification. The results of this study indicated that the binary modification of this classification system did not perform with greater reliability than the standard classification system (mean kappa 0.43 ± 0.048 standard and 0.35 ± 0.038 binary). Another investigation compared the interobserver reliability of classification of malleolar fractures of the tibia (segment 44) according to the classic and binary modification of the AO/ASIF CCF.[16] Six observers classified 50 malleolar fractures according to both the standard and binary systems, and no difference in interobserver reliability could be demonstrated between the two systems (mean kappa 0.61 standard and 0.62 binary). The authors concluded that strictly enforced binary decision-making did not improve reliability in the classification of malleolar fractures according to the AO/ASIF CCF. The results of these two studies cast doubt on the effectiveness of binary decision making in improving interobserver reliability in the classification of fractures.

A recent study tested the hypothesis that perhaps the amount of information provided an observer could be overwhelming and limit reliability of fracture classification.[35] This group tested the Sanders classification of calcaneal fractures and, rather than providing observers with the full CT scan data for each of the 30 cases, they provided each observer with only one carefully selected CT image from which to make a classification decision. The results indicated that the overall interobserver reliability was no better with only one CT cut than with the full series of CT cuts. The results clearly showed, however, that interobserver agreement was much better for the most and least severe fractures in the series and poorest for fractures in the midrange of severity. This finding is probably applicable to all classification schemes, in which observers are much better at differentiating the best from the worst than they are at cases in the middle of the spectrum of injury severity.

Categorization of a Continuous Variable

All fracture classification systems in common use today are categorical; regardless of the nature or complexity of the classifica-

tion system, each group's fractures are grouped into discreet categories. Injuries to individual patients, however, occur on a continuum of energy and severity of injury; fractures follow this same pattern, occurring on a spectrum of injury severity. The process of fracture classification can therefore be said to be a process by which a continuous variable, such as fracture severity, is made a categorical one. This "categorization" of a continuous variable may be a source of intraobserver variability in fracture classification systems.[29,45] One recent study concluded that "it has become clear that these deficiencies are related to the fact that the infinite variation of injury is a continuous variable and to force this continuous variable into a classification scheme, a dichotomous variable, will result in the discrepancies that have been documented."[29] The authors further suggested that "multiple classifiers, blinded to the treatment selected and clinical outcomes, and consensus methodology should be used to optimize the utility of injury classification schemes for research and publication purposes."

In an effort to address this issue, some authors have proposed that, instead of classifying fractures, perhaps fractures should merely be rank ordered from the least severe to the most severe. This would serve as a means to preserve the continuum of fracture severity and has been proposed as a means of potentially improving interobserver reliability. An initial study using this methodology in tibial plafond fracture showed promise.[19] Twenty-five tibial plafond fractures were ranked by three orthopaedic traumatologists from the least severe to the most severe, and the group demonstrated outstanding interobserver reliability, with a Cronbach alpha statistic[17] of 0.94 (nearly perfect agreement). In a subsequent study, the rank order concept was expanded and a series of 10 tibial plafond fractures were ranked by 69 observers.[21] The intraclass correlation coefficient was 0.62, representing substantial agreement, but also represented some deterioration from the results with only three observers. Based on these results, which are superior to those of most categorical fracture classification systems that have been evaluated, further study of this sort of classification system appears to be warranted.

It has been postulated that one means of implementing a fracture classification system that ranks cases on a continuum of injury severity would be to approach the matter much in the same way as clinicians determine bone age in children.[21] A series of radiographs would be published that represent the spectrum of fracture severity, from the least severe to the most severe, and then an observer would simply review these examples and determine where the fracture under review lay on this spectrum of severity. This concept is markedly different from any scheme used to date to classify fractures, would be unlikely to completely replace other systems of fracture classification, and may have weaknesses that have not yet been determined. Such a system will require extensive testing and validation before it could be widely used.

Poor Attention to Classification of Nonradiographic Factors

Measuring the injury severity and predicting the outcome following a fracture depends on much more than radiographic factors.[23,24,43] Recently, many have come to question whether any system for fracture classification that relies solely on radiographic data will be highly reliable or highly predictive of the outcome of severe fractures. There is strong evidence that the extent of injury to the soft tissues (cartilage, muscle, tendon, skin, etc.), the magnitude and durations of the patient's physiologic response to injury, the presence of comorbid conditions, and the patient's socioeconomic background and lifestyle may all play critical roles in influencing outcomes following severe fractures.

As an example, it is well recognized that injury to articular cartilage is a critical and significant contributor to the overall severity of an articular fracture, as evidenced by studies documenting poor outcomes after osteochondritis dissecans and other chondral injuries. The information present in the orthopaedic clinical literature indicates that the severity of injury to the articular surface during fracture has an important bearing on outcome and the eventual development of posttraumatic osteoarthrosis. A better understanding of the impaction injury to the articular cartilage and the prognosis of such injury will be critical to improving our assessment and understanding of severe intra-articular fractures. Unfortunately, there currently are no imaging modalities that have been validated to indicate to the clinician the extent of injury to the cartilage of the articular surface and/or the potential for repair or the risk of posttraumatic degeneration of the articular cartilage. Plain radiographs and CT scans provide very little information about the current and future health of the articular cartilage in a joint with a fracture.

Inherent Variability in Human Observations

It is to be expected that human observers, no matter how well-trained, will have some level of variability in applying any tool—no matter how reliable—in classifying fractures. The magnitude of the "baseline" level of inherent human variability in fracture classification is entirely unknown. As such, it is extremely difficult for investigators to know with precision what represents excellent interobserver reliability in fracture classification. There is disagreement over the best statistical analysis to use in assessing reliability or what level of agreement is acceptable in studies on fracture classification. Statistics such as the intraclass correlation coefficient are very good as indicators of when a laboratory test, such as the hematocrit or serum calcium level, has acceptable reliability and reproducibility. Whether the same threshold level of reliability should be applied to a process such as fracture classification is unknown. Similarly, the interpretation of the weighted kappa statistic for fracture classification is somewhat difficult, since there are few guidelines to aid in interpreting their results. Landis and Koch admit that their widely accepted reference intervals for the kappa statistic were chosen arbitrarily. Additionally, a recent investigation seemed to indicate that using the kappa statistic with a small number of observers introduces the possibility of "sampling error" causing an increased variance in the kappa statistic itself.[4,57] Having many different observers causes stabilization of the kappa value around a "mean value" for the agreement among the population of observers. Invariably, however, using more observers results in a lower mean kappa value and indicated poorer interobserver reliability of the classification system being tested. Therefore, studies with a small amount of observers that reported excellent reliability in fracture classification systems may be reporting spuriously high results for the kappa statistic—results that would be much lower if more observers were used. Unfortunately, there are currently no better or more reliable methods for reporting and interpreting interobserver reliability than the use of the ICC or the kappa statistic.

CURRENT USEFULNESS OF FRACTURE CLASSIFICATION SYSTEMS

Fracture classification systems are highly useful for describing fractures; this has been one of the best uses for fracture classification systems. Using a well-known fracture classification to describe a fracture to an orthopaedist or colleague who cannot immediately view the fracture radiographs immediately invokes in the orthopaedist a visual image of the fracture. This visual image, even if it is not highly reliable to statistical testing, enhances communication between orthopaedic physicians.

Fracture classification systems are also useful as educational tools. Educating orthopaedic trainees in systems of fracture classification is highly valuable, for many systems are devised from the mechanism of injury or from the anatomical alignment of the fracture fragments. These are important educational tools to assist orthopaedic trainees in better understanding the osteology of different parts of the skeleton and the various mechanisms of injury that can result in fractures. Educational systems using fracture classification methodologies can assist orthopaedic trainees in formulating a context in which to make treatment decisions, and can also provide an important historical context of fracture care and fracture classification in orthopaedics.

Fracture classification systems may be useful in guiding treatment, and it is clearly the intent of many fracture classification systems to do so. It is unclear, however, from much of the literature that has been published, whether fracture classification systems are valid tools to guide treatment. The fact that there is so much observer variability in fracture classification adds an element of doubt to comparative clinical studies that have used fracture classification as a guide to treatment.

Fracture classification systems have also been said to be useful in predicting outcomes following fracture care. The orthopaedic literature to date, however, does not seem to clearly indicate that fracture classification systems can be used to predict patient outcomes in any sort of valid or reproducible way. The interobserver variability of many fracture classification systems is one of the key reasons that the literature cannot clearly show this correlation. One exception to this, however, is that most fracture classification system have good reliability in characterizing the most severe and least severe injuries—those that correlate with the best and worst outcomes. It is in the mid-range of injury severity that classification systems demonstrate the poorest reliability and the poorest ability to predict outcomes.

THE FUTURE OF FRACTURE CLASSIFICATION SYSTEMS

There will be in the future a more comprehensive determination of injury severity than merely classifying a fracture according to plain radiographs. It has become clear in recent years that variables other than radiograph appearance of the fracture play a huge role in determining patient outcome, and these variables will be utilized in new systems of determining injury severity in patients with fractures. Objective measures of energy of injury include CT scans, finite element models or volumetric measures,

measures of the extent of injury to soft tissues, objective measures of the patient's physiologic reserve and response to injury, and serum lactate levels. An assessment of overall health status and the existence of comorbid conditions are other ways that may be used to make more comprehensive the determination of fracture severity. These factors will likely be combined with the radiographic appearance of the fracture to better guide treatment and to better predict outcomes of fracture care.

Better imaging modalities will also assist us in better and more reliably determining and characterizing the injury severity in patients with fractures. Newer uses for CT scanning and MRI imaging and ultrasound will be instrumental in providing the treating surgeon more information about the extent of soft tissue injury, the health of the bone and cartilage, and the biology at the fracture site. In addition, we may gain additional information about the patient's ability to heal well. All of these will advance the orthopaedist's ability to determine injury severity. For example it is possible with very high-energy MRI scans to determine the proteoglycan content of articular cartilage. Since articular cartilage is not imaged on CT or plain radiographic imaging, its health has been generally excluded from the classification of fractures. However, the long-term health of the articular cartilage is crucial to the patient's outcome following a severe articular injury. In the future, the ability to use advanced imaging modalities to better characterize the current health and predict the future health of the articular cartilage will be a great advancement in our ability to accurately classify fractures and to use fracture classification as a predictive measure.

Newer fracture classification schemes will be devised that will better assure that fractures can be measured and characterized on a continuum, which is how they occur. These new classification systems will better represent the continual aspects of injury severity than do systems in use today, many of which were based simply on anatomical consideration rather than on injury severity. Ideas such as rank-ordering fractures, putting fractures on a continuum, sending fractures to a fracture classification clearing house (for classification by one or just a few observers) are but a few possible future approaches to advancing and making more reproducible the classification of fractures.

There will be better agreement about what sort of process of validation a fracture classification system should undergo before becoming available for general use. Most classification systems in general use have had no formal validation. Most of them have come into general use because of the reputation or influence of the person or group that devised them, or perhaps because the system has been in use so long that it has simply become part of the vernacular in fracture classification and fracture care. One study has proposed a formal, detailed, and very time-consuming methodology for the validation of all fracture classification systems, very similar to that which was performed for patient-based outcome measures, such as the short form 36 and the musculoskeletal functional assessment.[4] It is as of yet unclear whether such validation methods would improve the interobserver reliability of fracture classification systems. It is clear, however, that such methods would be exhaustive and very time consuming, and that many orthopaedic surgeons do not believe that such detailed validation is necessary for fracture classification systems.

The use of imaging processing and analysis techniques will advance our understanding and ability to classify fractures. Advances in imaging processes and image analysis, perhaps when coupled with neural nets and other learning technologies, may make it possible for computers to be taught to classify fractures with a high degree of reliability and reproducibility. One could envision a system by which digital images of a fracture are classified according to any of several classification systems and that will be done automatically by a computer system at the time the radiographs are obtained, much as electrocardiograph (EKG) readings are currently generated by a computer at the time the patient's cardiac tracing is obtained.

Finally, there will be more rigorous validation of fracture classification systems. Rigorous statistical methods—or at least consensus statistical methodologies—will be developed and implemented that, while detailed, time consuming, and involved, will result in greatly improved validation of many fracture classification systems.

REFERENCES

1. Andersen DJ, Blair WF, Steyers CM, et al. Classification of distal radius fractures: an analysis of interobserver reliability and intraobserver reproducibility. J Hand Surg 1996; 21A:574–582.
2. Andersen E, Jorgensen LG, Hededam LT. Evans classification of trochanteric fractures: an assessment for the interobserver reliability and intraobserver reproducibility. Injury 1990;21:377–378.
3. Anderson GR, Rasmussen JB, Dahl B, et al. Older's classification of Colle fractures: good intraobserver and interobserver reproducibility in 185 cases. Acta Orthop Scan 1991; 62:463–464.
4. Audige L, Bhandari M, Kellam J. How reliabile are reliability studies of fracture classifications? A systematic review of their methodologies. Acta Orthop Scand 2004;75:184–194.
5. Barker L, Anderson J, Chesnut R, et al. Reliability and reproducibility of dens fracture classification with use of plain radiography and reformatted computer-aided tomography. J Bone Joint Surg Am 2006;88:106–112.
6. Beaule PE, Dorey FJ, Matta JM. Letournel classification for acetabular fractures: assessment of interobserver and intraobserver reliability. J Bone Joint Surg Am 2003;85: 1704–1709.
7. Bernstein J, Adler LM, Blank JE, et al. Evaluation of the Neer system of classification of proximal humeral fractures with computerized tomographic scans and plain radiographs. J Bone Joint Surg Am 1996;78:1371–1375.
8. Borrelli J Jr, Goldfarb C, Catalano L, et al. Assessment of articular fragment displacement in acetabular fractures: a comparison of computed tomography and plain radiographs. J Orthop Trauma 2002;16:449–456.
9. Brorson S, Bagger J, Sylvest A, et al. Low agreement among 24 doctors using the Neer classification; only moderate agreement on displacement, even between specialists. International Orthop 2002;26:271–273.
10. Brumback RJ, Jones AL. Interobserver agreement in the classification of open fractures of the tibia. J Bone Joint Surg Am 1994;76:1162–1166.
11. Burstein AH. Fracture classification systems: do they work and are they useful? J Bone Joint Surg Am 1993;75:1743–1744.
12. Chan PSH, Klimkiewicz JJ, Luchette WT, et al. Impact of CT scan on treatment plan and fracture classification of tibial plateau fractures. J Orthop Trauma 1997;11:484–489.
13. Cohen J. A coefficient of agreement for nominal scales. Educ Psych Meas 1960;20: 37–46.
14. Cole RJ, Bindra RR, Evanoff BA, et al. Radiographic evaluation of osseous displacement following intraarticular fracture of the distal radius: reliability of plain radiographs versus computed tomography. J Hand Surg (Am) 1997;22:792–800.
15. Colles, A. On the fracture of the carpal extremity of the radius. Edinb Med Surg J 1814; 10:182–186.
16. Craig III, WL, Dirschl DR. An assessment of the effectiveness of binary decision-making in improving the reliability of the AO/ASIF classification of fractures of the ankle. J Orthop Trauma 1998;12:280–284.
17. Cronbach LJ. Coefficient alpha and the internal structure of tests. Psychometrika 1951; 16:297–334.
18. Dahlen HC, Franck WM, Sabauri G, et al. Incorrect classification of extra-articular distal radius fractures by conventional x-rays: comparison between biplanar radiologic diagnostics and CT assessment of fracture morphology. Unfallchirurg 2004;107(6):491–498.
19. DeCoster TA, Willis MC, Marsh JL, et al. Rank order analysis of tibial plafond fracture: does injury or reduction predict outcome? Foot and Ankle International 1999;20:44–49.
20. Desai VV, Davis TRC, Barton NJ. The prognostic value and reproducibility of the radiological features of the fractured scaphoid. J Hand Surg Br 1999;5:586–590.
21. Dirschl DR, Ferry ST. Reliability of classification of fractures of the tibial plafond according to a rank order method. J Trauma 2006;61:1463–1466.
22. Dirschl DR, Adams GL. A critical assessment of methods to improve reliability in the classification of fractures, using fractures of the tibial plafond as a model. J Orthop Trauma 1997;11:471–476.
23. Dirschl DR, Dawson PA. Assessment of injury severity in tibial plateau fractures. Clin Orthop Rel Res 2004;423:85–92.
24. Dirschl DR, Marsh JL, Buckwalter J, et al. The clinical and basic science of articular fractures. Accepted by J American Acad Orthop Surg, September 2002, 30 pages.
25. Doornberg J, Lindenhovius A, Kloen P, et al. Two- and three-dimensional computed tomography for the classification and management of distal humeral fractures. J Bone Joint Surg Am 2006;88:1795–1801.

26. Fleiss JL. In: Statistical Methods for Rates and Proportions. 2nd Ed. New York: John Wiley & Sons, 1981:218.

27. Fleiss JL, Stakter MJ, Fischman SL, et al. Interexaminer reliability in caries trials. J Dent Res 1979;58:604–609.

28. Frandsen PA, Andersen E, Madsen F, et al. Garden classification of femoral neck fractures: an assessment of interobserver variation. J Bone Joint Surg Br 1988;70:588–590.

29. Garbuz DS, Masri BA, Esdaile J, et al. Classification systems in orthopaedics. J Am Acad Orthop Surg 2002;10:290–297.

30. Garden RS. Low-angle fixation in fractures of the femoral neck. J Bone Joint Surg Br 1961;43:647–663.

31. Gaston P, Will R, Elton RA, et al. Fractures of the tibia: can their outcome be predicted? J Bone Joint Surg 1999;81B:71–76.

32. Gustilo RB, Anderson JT. Prediction of infection in the treatment of 1025 open fractures in long bones. J Bone Joint Surg 1976;58A:453-458.

33. Gustilo RB, Mendoza RM, Williams DN. Problems in the management of Type III (severe) open fractures: a new classification of type III open fractures. J Trauma 1984;24(8): 742–746.

34. Gustillo RB, Merkow RL, Templeman D. Current concepts review: the management of open fractures. J Bone Joint Surg Am 1990;72:299–303.

35. Humphrey CA, Dirschl DR, Ellis TJ. Interobserver reliability of a CT-based fracture classification system. J Orthop Trauma 2005;19:616–622.

36. Katz MA, Beredjiklian PK, Bozentka DJ, et al. Computed tomography scanning of intraarticular distal radius fractures: does it influence treatment? J Hand Surg Am 2001;26(3): 415–421.

37. Kreder HJ, Hanel DP, McKee M, et al. Consistency of AO fracture classification for the distal radius. J Bone Joint Surg Br 1996;78:726–731.

38. Kreder HJ, Hanel DP, McKee M, et al. X-ray film measurements for healed distal radius fractures. J Hand Surg 1996;21A:31–39.

39. Kristiansen B, Andersen ULS, Olsen CA, et al. The Neer classification of fractures of the proximal humerus: an assessment of interobserver variation. Skeletal Radiol 1988;17: 420–422.

40. Landis JR, Koch GG. The measurement of observer agreement for categorical data. Biometrics 1977;33:159–174.

41. Lauder AJ, Inda DJ, Bott AM, et al. Interobserver and intraobserver reliability of two classification systems for intra-articular calcaneal fractures. Foot and Ankle International 2006;27:251–255.

42. Lauge-Hansen N. Fractures of the ankle. III: Genetic roentgenologic diagnosis of fractures of the ankle. AJR 1954;71:456–471.

43. Marsh J, Buckwalter J, Gelberman RC, et al. Does an anatomic reduction really change the result in the management of articular fractures? J Bone Joint Surg 2002;84-A: 1259–1271.

44. Marsh JL, Slongo TF, Agel J, et al. Fracture and dislocation classification compendium—2007. F Orthop Trauma 2007;21:S1–S160.

45. Martin JS, Marsh JL. Current classification of fractures; rationale and utility. Radiol Clin North Am 1997;35:491–506.

46. Martin JS, Marsh JL, Bonar SK, et al. Assessment of the AO/ASIF fracture classification for the distal tibia. J Orthop Trauma 1997;11:477–483.

47. Martin J, Marsh JL, Nepola JV, et al. Radiographic fracture assessments: which ones can we reliably make? J Orthop Trauma 2000;14(6):379–385.

48. Moed RB, Carr SEW, Watson JT. Open reduction and internal fixation of posterior wall fractures of the acetabulum. Clin Orthop and Rel Res 2000;377:57–67.

49. Muller ME. The comprehensive classification of fractures of long bone. In: Muller ME, Allgower M, Schneider R, et al, eds. Manual of Internal Fixation: Techniques Recommended by the AO-ASIF Group. 3rd Ed. Heidelberg: Springer-Verlag, 1991.

50. Muller ME, Nazarian S, Kack P. CCF: comprehensive classification of fractures. Bern: Maurice E Muller Foundation, 1996.

51. Neer CS. Displaced proximal humeral fractures. Part I: classification and evaluation. J Bone Joint Surg Am 1970;52:1077–1089.

52. Nielsen JO, Dons-Jensen H, Sorensen HT. Lauge-Hansen classification of malleolar fractures: an assessment of the reproducibility of 118 cases. Acta Orthop Scand 1990;61: 385–387.

53. Oakes DA, Jackson KR, Davies MR, et al. The impact of the Garden classification on proposed operative treatment. Clin Orthop and Rel Res 2003;409:232–240.

54. Oestern HJ, Txcherne H. Pathophysiology and classification of soft tissue injuries associated with fractures. In: Tscherne H, ed. Fracture With Soft Tissue Injuries. New York: Springer-Verlag, 1984:1–9.

55. Oner FC, Ramos LMP, Simmermacher RKJ, et al. Classification of thoracic and lumbar spine fractures: problems of reproducibility. Eur Spine J 2002;11:235–245.

56. Pervez H, Parker MJ, Pryor GA, et al. Classification of trochanteric fracture of the proximal femur: a study of the reliability of current systems. Injury 2002;33:713–715.

57. Petrisor BA, Bhandari M, Orr RD, et al. Improving reliability in the classification of fractures of the acetabulum. Arch Orthop Trauma Surg 2003;123:228–233.

58. Pott, P. In: Hanes L, Clarke W, Callius R. eds. Some Few General Remarks on Fractures and Dislocations. London, 1765.

59. Rasmussen S, Madsen PV, Bennicke K. Observer variation in the Lauge-Hansen classification of ankle fractures: precision improved by instruction. Actat Orthop Scand 1993; 64:693–694.

60. Remington RD, Schork MA. Statistics with Applications to the Biological and Health Sciences. Englewood Cliffs, NJ: Prentice-Hall, 1970.

61. Sanders R. Displaced intra-articular fractures of the calcaneus. Journal of Bone and Joint Surgery American 2000;225–250.

62. Schatzker J. Fractures of the tibial plateau. In Schatzker M, Tile M, eds. Rationale of Operative Fractures Care. Berlin: Springer-Verlag, 1988:279–295.

63. Schatzker J, McBroom R. Tibial plateau fractures: the Toronto experience 1968–1975. Clin Orthop and Rel Res 1979;138:94–104.

64. Schipper IB, Steyerberg EW, Castelein RM, et al. Reliability of the AO/ASIF classification for peritrochanteric femoral fractures. Acta Orthop Scand 2001;72:36–41.

65. Seigel G, Podgor MJ, Remaley NA. Acceptable values of kappa for comparison of two groups. Am J Epidemiol 1992;135:571–578.

66. Shepherd LE, Zalavras CG, Jaki K, et al. Gunshot femoral shaft fractures: is the current classification system reliable? Clin Orthop and Rel Res 2003;408:101–109.

67. Sidor JL, Zuckerman JD, Lyon T, et al. The Neer classification system for proximal humeral fractures: an assessment of interobserver reliability and intraobserver reproducibility. J Bone Joint Surg Am 1993;75:1745–1750.

68. Siebenrock KA, Gerber C. The reproducibility of classification of fractures of the proximal end of the humerus. J Bone Joint Surg Am 1993;75:1751–1755.

69. Svanholm H, Starklint H, Gundersen HJ, et al. Reproducibility of histomorphologic diagnoses with special reference to the kappa statistic. APMIS 97 1989;689–698.

70. Swiontkowski JF, Agel J, McAndrew MP, et al. Outcome validation of the AO/OTA fracture classification system. J Orthop Trauma 2000;14:534–541.

71. Swiontkowski JF, Sands AK, Agel J, et al. Interobserver variation in the AO/OTA fracture classification system for pilon fractures: is there a problem? J Orthop Trauma 1997;11: 467–470.

72. Thomsen NOB, Olsen LH, Nielsen ST. Kappa statistics in the assessment of observer variation: the significance of multiple observers classifying ankle fractures. J Orthop Sci 2002;7:163–166.

73. Thomsen NOB, Overgaard S, Olen LH, et al. Observer variation in the radiographic classification of ankle fractures. J Bone and Joint Surg Br 1991;73:676–678.

74. Visutipol B, Chobrangsin P, Ketmalasiri B, et al. Evaluation of Letournel and Judet classification of acetabular fracture with plain radiographs and three-dimensional computerized tomographic scan. J Orthop Surg 2000;8:33–37.

75. Walton NP, Harish S, Roberts C, et al. AO or Schatzker? How reliable is classification of tibial plateau fractures? Arch Orthop Trauma Surg 2003;123:396–398.

76. Wicky S, Blaser PF, Blanc CH, et al. Comparison between standard radiography and spiral CT with 3D reconstruction in the evaluation, classification and management of tibial plateau fractures. Eur Radiol 2000;10:1227–1232 (showed change in surgical plan in 59% of cases, but no diff in classification).

77. Yacoubian SV, Nevins RT, Sallis JG, et al. Impact of MRI on treatment plan and fracture classification of tibial plateau fractures. J Orthop Trauma 2002;16:632–637.

78. Fracture and dislocation compendium (Orthopaedic Trauma Association Committee for Coding and Classification). J Orthop Trauma 1996;10:Suppl. 1.

3

THE EPIDEMIOLOGY OF FRACTURES

Charles M. Court-Brown, Stuart A. Aitken, Daren Forward, and Robert V. O'Toole III

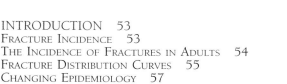

INTRODUCTION

The sixth edition of Rockwood and Green[8] was the first edition to publish a chapter dealing with the epidemiology of fractures. There were two sections: the first section contained information about the overall epidemiology of fractures in a defined population, and the second section examined the overall fracture epidemiology in the United States. In this edition, we have changed the focus of the chapter to try to compare two different types of orthopaedic trauma unit. In the first part of the chapter, the epidemiology of fractures presenting to the Royal Infirmary of Edinburgh in Scotland in a 1-year period in 2007–2008 will be analyzed. This hospital is the only hospital admitting orthopaedic trauma in a well-defined population containing the City of Edinburgh, Midlothian, and East Lothian, and therefore its data can be used to calculate the prevalence and incidence of different fractures in the population. The Royal Infirmary of Edinburgh is the largest orthopaedic trauma hospital in the United Kingdom, and we believe that the epidemiological results should be applicable to many developed countries. We accept that there will be some epidemiological differences in different countries mainly depending on social demographics, but it is likely that the epidemiological results from the Royal Infirmary of Edinburgh will reflect the fracture epidemiology in similar countries.

In the second part of the chapter, the fracture epidemiology from the R. Adams Cowley Shock Trauma Center in Baltimore, Maryland, USA, will be presented. This is a Level I Trauma Center that is the main primary adult resource center for the Maryland Emergency Medical Services System. It is the highest volume Trauma Center in the United States, and its trauma and critical care admissions average 7800 patients per year. Unlike the Royal Infirmary of Edinburgh, the R. Adams Cowley Shock Trauma Center mainly treats severely injured patients; the less severely injured patients being treated in other hospitals in the Baltimore area. There are three Level I Trauma Centers in Baltimore; therefore, the population that is treated in the R. Adams Cowley Shock Trauma Center is a subset of the overall population and the overall prevalences and incidences of different fractures in the community cannot be calculated. However, we believe that a comparison of the results of these two large hospitals will be of interest to many orthopaedic surgeons, many of whom work in institutions that are similar to either the Royal Infirmary of Edinburgh or the R. Adams Cowley Shock Trauma Center.

Fracture Incidence

Despite the frequency with which fractures occur, it has proven to be very difficult to accurately estimate their incidence within

TABLE 3-1	The Fracture Incidence Reported in Various Studies					
				Incidence (n/10^5/yr)		
	Years of Study	Country	Overall	Male	Female
Donaldson et al.[12]	1980–1982	UK	9.05	10.0	8.1
Johansen et al.[23]	1994–1995	UK	21.1	23.5	18.8
Court-Brown and Caesar[8]	2000	UK	12.6	13.6	11.6
Rennie et al.[35]					
Donaldson et al.[13]	2002–2004	UK	36.0	41.0	31.0
Sahlin[36]	1985–1986	Norway	22.8	22.9	21.3
Fife and Barancik[14]	1977	USA	21.0	26.0	16.0

To obtain the overall incidence in Scotland in 2000, the adult fractures reported by Court-Brown and Caesar[8] have been combined with the children's fractures reported by Rennie et al.[35]

the population and there are very few studies where this has been done.[7,12–14,23,35,36] Table 3-1 shows the results of several analyses of fracture epidemiology in the United Kingdom,[7,12,13,23,35] Norway,[36] and the United States.[14] The difference in results is striking. All the studies shown in Table 3-1 have included both children and adults, but the studies use different methodologies and we believe that this is one of the principal reasons for the significant discrepancies in the results.

Donaldson et al.[12] examined a geographically well-defined population in England and looked at both the inpatient and outpatient fractures in the area. They observed that they might be missing a few toe fractures and some spinal fractures in the elderly, but they felt that they had missed very few fractures. A very similar methodology was employed by Court-Brown and Caesar in the sixth edition of Rockwood and Green.[8] They assessed the number of adult fractures in the well-defined population served by the Royal Infirmary of Edinburgh in 2000. The pediatric fractures were also recorded in the same year.[35] When the pediatric and adult databases are combined, the overall database gives figures that, given the 20-year gap between the two studies, must be regarded as being equivalent to those of Donaldson et al.[12]

Table 3-1 shows that other studies have demonstrated a much higher incidence of fractures in the population, although all have agreed that more fractures occur in males than females. The studies by Johansen et al. in Wales,[23] Sahlin in Norway,[36] and Fife and Barancik in the United States[14] all record similar fracture incidences. The notable difference between these studies and the Edinburgh studies is that in the Edinburgh studies all diagnoses were made from radiographs by experienced surgeons or radiologists. In the other studies, the outpatient fractures in particular were often diagnosed by junior doctors who were not orthopaedic surgeons and were inexperienced in diagnosing fractures. These studies analyze hospital or community data but do not check the veracity of fracture diagnosis. We believe that this leads to an overestimate of a number of fractures particularly in locations where soft tissue injuries are relatively common such as the hand, wrist, ankle, and foot. It is of interest that the incidence of fractures of the forearm, wrist, and hand in the Welsh study[23] was 9.2/1000/year compared with 6.1/1000/year in Edinburgh where all the radiographs were re-

viewed by an experienced surgeon or radiologist. This is also true of ankle fractures (1.42/1000/year in Wales and 0.96/1000/year in Edinburgh) and foot fractures (2.41/1000/year in Wales and 1.3/1000/year in Edinburgh), but not of the more obvious fractures of the femur, where the incidence in the two studies were virtually identical (1.6/1000/year in Wales and 1.4/1000/year in Edinburgh).

The third type of methodological analysis that has been employed is where patients are asked to complete a questionnaire regarding whether they have had a fracture in a given period. This type of methodology was adopted by Donaldson et al.[13] in a later study. Table 3-1 shows that when this type of survey is used, even higher estimates of fracture incidence are achieved. We think it unlikely that the overall incidence of fractures is as high as 36/1000/year, and we believe that the difference is attributable to the type of methodology used. Many patients are told that recurrent or continuing pain may be secondary to undiagnosed fractures by family physicians, physiotherapists, nurses, osteopaths, or other paramedical professionals without there being any proof; we believe that this has skewed the results of this study.

The Incidence of Fractures in Adults

For this edition of Rockwood and Green, we have analyzed a further year of fracture treatment at the Royal Infirmary of Edinburgh in Scotland. In the sixth edition,[8] all fractures presenting to the Royal Infirmary in 2000 were analyzed. For this chapter, we have analyzed the fractures presenting to the hospital between July 1, 2007, and June 30, 2008. We have concentrated on adults aged 16 years or older and used the 2001 United Kingdom census[15] to calculate incidence. This is the most recent United Kingdom census. No patients aged less than 16 years have been included, and all soft tissue injuries and dislocations have been excluded. We have not included spinal fractures as these are treated both by the Edinburgh orthopaedic surgeons and neurosurgeons, and patients with spinal injuries are treated at the National Spinal Injuries Centre in Glasgow. Local patients injured outside the catchment area of the Royal Infirmary of Edinburgh but treated in the Royal Infirmary have been included, and all patients injured in Edinburgh but living outside the catchment area have been excluded.

The overall incidence of fractures in patients aged 16 years or more was 13.7/1000/year in 2007–2008. The incidence of fractures in males was 13.7/1000/year and in females it was 13.6/1000/year. There were 6986 fractures of which 3304 (47.3%) occurred in males and 3687 (52.7%) in females. The overall average age was 52.9 years with an average of 41.4 years in males and 63.0 years in females.

All studies since the classic epidemiological study of Buhr and Cooke[2] have highlighted the fact that men have a bimodal distribution of fractures and women have a unimodal distribution with a significant progressive increase in fracture incidence in the postmenopausal years.[7,12,14,23,28] The overall fracture distribution curve shown in Figure 3-1 is no different. It shows the overall age and gender-specific fracture incidence curves. In males, the incidence of fractures between 16–19 years of age is 26.2/1000/year compared with 5.9/1000/year in females. The lowest incidence in males is 8.1/1000/year, which occurs between 50–59 years. In females, the lowest incidence is 4.8/1000/year, which occurs between 30–39 years of age. In older males, the incidence rises to 65.7/1000/year in males aged at least 90 years of age, compared with 80.3/1000/year in females aged at least 90 years of age. The later male peak has become more obvious in recent years because males are now living longer and they are at greater risk of osteopenic or osteoporotic fractures.[24]

Fracture Distribution Curves

The earliest fracture distribution curves, based on age and gender, were proposed by Buhr and Cooke.[2] They analyzed 8539 fractures over a 5-year period in Oxford, England, and proposed five basic curves. Their Type A curve affected young and middle-aged men and they referred to it as a "wage earners" curve. They suggested that this occurred in patients who presented with fractures of the hand, medial malleolus, metatarsus, foot phalanges, and spine. Their J-shaped curve affected older males and females and obviously described fragility, or osteoporotic, fractures. It is equivalent to our Type F curve (Fig. 3-2). They stated that fractures of the proximal humerus, humeral diaphysis, proximal femur, and pelvis together with bimalleolar ankle fracture had a J-shaped curve.

Buhr and Cooke's[2] third curve was an L-shaped curve that affected younger males and females and was equivalent to our Type C curve (see Fig. 3-2). This was said to occur in distal

humeral fractures, tibial diaphyseal fractures, and clavicular fractures. They also described two composite curves with either a bimodal male and unimodal female distribution or a unimodal male and bimodal female distribution. These are equivalent to our Type D and G curves (see Fig. 3-2). They said that these curves described fractures of the proximal and distal radius, femoral diaphysis, proximal tibia and fibular, and the lateral malleolus.

Later studies produced similar distribution curves.[12,23,28] Knowelden et al.[28] analyzed only patients who were at least 35 years of age. They showed that fractures of the proximal humerus, pelvis, and proximal femur all demonstrated an osteoporotic Type F curve (see Fig. 3-2). It is interesting to note that they had a Type A curve (see Fig. 3-2) for femoral diaphyseal fractures, but they recorded that the highest incidence of femoral diaphyseal fractures occurred in the elderly. Donaldson et al.[12] constructed four curves for proximal femoral, proximal humeral, distal radial and tibial, and fibular diaphyseal fractures that were very similar to the curves shown in Figure 3-2, although there were fewer older females with fractures of the tibia and fibular diaphysis than we would see now. Johansen et al.[33] also constructed eight curves covering different body areas these being the hip, spine, upper arm, pelvis, forearm and wrist, ankle, hand, finger and thumb, and foot and toes. These are very similar to the curves shown in Figure 3-2.

Analysis of individual fracture incidence shows that there are eight basic fracture distribution curves, shown in Figure 3-2. Most fractures have a unimodal distribution affecting either younger or older patients. Some fractures, however, have a bimodal distribution whereby younger and older patients are affected but there is a lower incidence in middle age. If one analyzes males and females separately, the distribution curves shown in Figure 3-2 can be constructed. The eight distribution curves define all fractures. It should be remembered that the curves shown in Figure 3-2 are diagrammatic. The relative heights of the peaks of the curves will vary, but the overall curve patterns remain appropriate for all fractures.

A Type A curve is often thought of as the typical fracture curve with a unimodal distribution in younger males and in older females. Generally, the younger male peak is higher than the older female peak, though this is not the case in all fractures. An example is the metatarsal fracture where the younger male peak and the older female peak are at a similar height. Type A curves are seen in fractures of the scapula, distal radius, femoral diaphysis, tibial diaphysis, ankle, and metatarsus. In Type B curves, there is also a young male unimodal distribution, but fractures in females occur in smaller numbers throughout the decades. Type B fractures are generally seen in the hand and affect the carpus, metacarpus, and fingers. However, they are also characteristic of femoral head fractures and those isolated fractures of the fibula which do not involve the ankle joint.

In Type C fractures, both males and females show a unimodal distribution. These fractures are rare after middle age. These fractures tend to occur in the foot and affect the toes, midfoot, and talus. In Type D fractures, there is a young male unimodal distribution but the female distribution is bimodal affecting younger and older females. Generally the second peak starts around the time of the menopause. Type D curves are seen in fractures of the proximal forearm, forearm diaphysis, and tibial plafond.

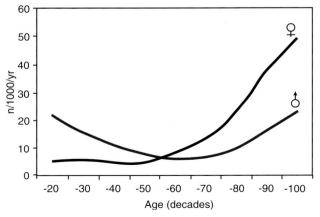

FIGURE 3-1 The overall age and gender fracture distribution curves.

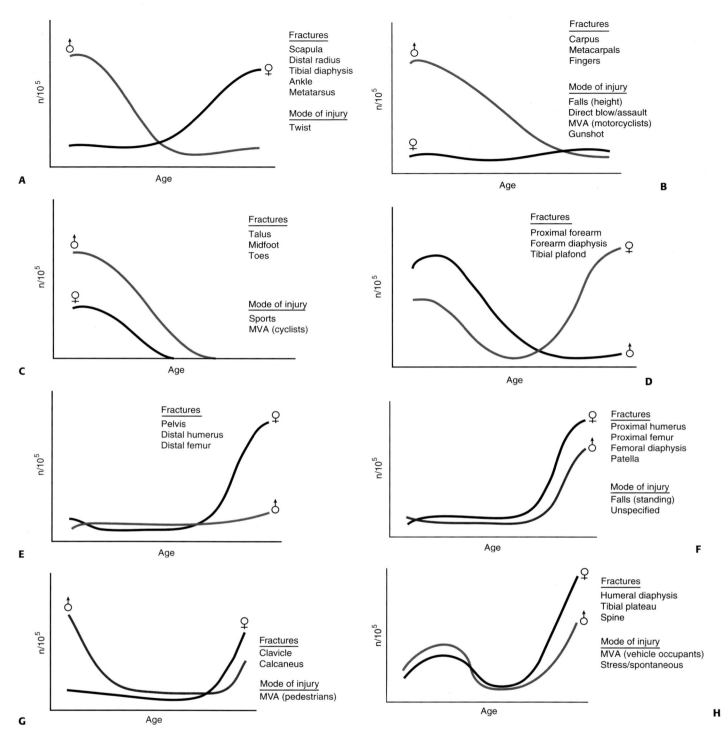

FIGURE 3-2 The eight fracture distribution curves. See Table 3-2 for list of distribution curves for different fractures.

Type E fractures are the opposite of Type B fractures. They show a unimodal female distribution affecting older females with a relatively constant, lower incidence of fractures in males throughout the decades. The Type E pattern is seen in pelvic fractures, distal humeral fractures, and distal femoral fractures. This may be surprising to orthopaedic surgeons who see young male patients with these fractures after high-energy trauma. However, if the complete epidemiology of these fractures is analyzed across the community, it is apparent that the high-energy fractures are relatively rare compared with the lower-energy fractures seen in later life.

Type F fractures are the opposite of Type C fractures. In Type F fractures, both males and females show a unimodal distribution affecting older patients with the incidence being higher in females. This pattern is characteristic of fractures of the proximal humerus, humeral diaphysis, proximal femur, femoral diaphysis, and patella. There is some variation regarding when the rise in fracture incidence occurs. Generally, it is earlier in females than males and usually occurs around the time of the menopause in proximal humeral fracture, humeral diaphyseal fractures, and patella fractures but later in femoral diaphyseal fractures and proximal femoral fractures.

In Type G fractures, females show a unimodal distribution affecting older females, and males show a bimodal distribution affecting both younger and older males with the incidence being higher in younger males. This distribution is seen in calcaneal and clavicular fractures. Type H fractures are unusual in that both males and females show a bimodal distribution. This fracture pattern is seen in fractures of the humeral diaphysis, tibial plateau, and cervical spine.[8]

One can use the system of eight curves shown in Table 3-2 to define other fractures. Although Figure 3-2 shows that

ankle fractures have a Type A distribution, analysis of the different types of ankle fractures shows that only lateral malleolar fractures have a Type A distribution. Medial malleolar fractures have a Type D distribution, and suprasyndesmotic ankle fractures have a Type C distribution. Both bimalleolar and trimalleolar are fragility fractures showing a Type E distribution. Similarly, proximal forearm fractures have a Type D distribution when they are all considered together, but further analysis shows that radial neck fractures have a Type A distribution, whereas radial head fractures have a Type H distribution. Both olecranon fractures and fractures of both the proximal radius and ulnar have a Type F distribution and should be regarded as fragility fractures. The distribution curves for different fractures are listed in Table 3-2.

Changing Epidemiology

A review of the literature and of the patients attending fracture clinics and hospitals around the world indicates that fracture epidemiology is changing very quickly.[1,16,17,19,22,24–27,37,43] It is apparent that the most obvious change is the increased numbers of older women who now present with fractures. This not only represents an increase in the incidence of fragility fractures, but it has also been caused by the fact that older women now present with fractures that 50–60 years ago were usually seen in younger patients. This is best illustrated by using the fracture distribution curves shown in Figure 3-2. Buhr and Cooke,[2] in 1959, showed that fractures of the medial malleolus, metatarsus, spine, distal humerus, tibial diaphysis, and clavicle all had a Type C distribution curve and affected younger people. These fractures are now Types A, D, G, or H, and a significant number of older patients, usually female, present with them. We suspect that this is also the case with fractures of the scapula, tibial plateau, and calcaneus, amongst others.

It is interesting to compare the data from Knowelden et al.[28] with the modern data from the Edinburgh Trauma Unit. Knowelden and his associates[28] examined the epidemiology of patients who were at least 35 years of age in Dundee, Scotland, and Oxford, England, between 1954 and 1958. The results are shown in Table 3-3, which also shows comparative results from Minnesota, United States, and Edinburgh. Comparison of the 1954–1958 overall results for Dundee with the 2007–2008 results from Edinburgh indicate that the overall incidence of fractures is rising. Dundee and Edinburgh are only 60 miles apart and are not dissimilar in their social demography. What is most interesting is that the incidence of fractures in males aged 35 years or more has not changed in 50 years, although it seems likely that the spectrum of fractures has. This should be compared with females where the incidence of fractures in this age group has almost doubled. This suggests that while it is undoubtedly true that males are living longer, the problem of osteoporotic fragility fractures is still mainly seen in female patients. The figures from Minnesota[31] are clearly very different from those of the United Kingdom. A review of the methodology employed in this study indicates that the radiographs for each fracture were reviewed and that the study does not suffer from the deficiencies of other studies. It seems odd that there should be such a considerable discrepancy between two not dissimilar groups of people and we have no good explanation for the difference.

TABLE 3-2 **The Distribution Curves Shown in Figure 3-2 Applied to a Number of Commonly Seen Fractures**

Fracture Location

Clavicle	G	Proximal femur	F
Medial	A	Head	B
Diaphyseal	G	Neck	F
Lateral	A	Intertrochanteric	F
Scapula	A	Subtrochanteric	F
Intra-articular	A	Femoral diaphysis	A
Extra-articular	A	Distal femur	E
Proximal humerus	F	Patella	F
Humeral diaphysis	H	Proximal tibia	H
Distal humerus	E	Tibia and fibular diaphyses	A
Proximal forearm	D	Tibial diaphysis	B
Radial head	H	Fibular diaphysis	B
Radial neck	A	Distal tibia	D
Olecranon	F	Ankle	A
Radius and ulna	F	Medial malleolus	D
Forearm diaphysis	D	Lateral malleolus	A
Radius	A	Bimalleolar	E
Ulna	H	Trimalleolar	E
Radius and ulna	A	Suprasyndesmotic	C
Distal radius/ulna	A	Talus	C
Distal ulna	A	Neck	C
Carpus	A	Body	C
Scaphoid	B	Calcaneus	G
Triquetrum	A	Intra-articular	B
Hamate	B	Extra-articular	G
Trapezium	B	Midfoot	C
Metacarpus	B	Metatarsus	A
Finger phalanges	B	Toe phalanges	C
Pelvis	E	Cervical spine	H
Acetabulum	G	Thoracolumbar spine	A

Fracture Types

Periprosthetic	F
Open	G
Multiple	A
Fatigue	C
Insufficiency	F

In the fracture type section, "Multiple" refers to multiple fractures and not to multiple injuries.

TABLE 3-3	A Review of Studies Employing Similar Methodologies for the Assessment of Fracture Incidence					
			Incidence (n/10^5/yr)			
	Years of Study	Country	Overall	Male	Female	
Melton et al.[31]	1989–1991	USA	22.05	18.11	24.75	
Knowleden et al.[28]	1954–1958	Scotland	10.0	10.8	9.5	
	1954–1958	England	8.9	8.7	9.0	
Court-Brown and Aitken	2007–2008	Scotland	14.2	10.8	17.3	

A comparison of the 2000 Edinburgh fracture database published in the sixth edition of Rockwood and Green[8] and the 2007–2008 database shows that in the 8-year gap, there was an increase in the numbers of fractures presenting to the Edinburgh Orthopaedic Trauma Unit. In the sixth edition, the results of patients aged 12 years or more were published, but if this database is adjusted to be equivalent to the 2007–2008 database and to include only patients of at least 16 years of age, it can be seen that there is an overall increase of incidence from 107.7/10^4/year to 136.7/10^4/year. If the data is broken down by age and gender, it can be seen that there was no change in the incidence of fractures in females aged 16–34 years. However, the incidence of male fractures in this age group rose from 156.4/10^4/year to 172.5/10^4/year. In patients aged 35–49 years, the incidence of fractures in females rose from 45.3/10^4/year to 66.4/10^4/year, and in males it rose from 81.4/10^4/year to 108.7/10^4/year. In the group aged 50 years or older, the incidence of fractures in females rose from 228.7/10^4/year to 289.4/10^4/year and from 80.8/10^4/year to 110.1/10^4/year in males. The methodology used to collect and analyze the data was the same in both years, and it would therefore seem that the incidence of fractures has risen in a relatively short period but with the incidence of fragility fractures in females showing the greatest increase.

This apparent increase in the age of patients who present with fractures is also suggested by an analysis of the age at which patients present with different fractures. The average age of the patients of at least 16 years of age who presented with fractures in 2000 was 51.5 years compared with 52.9 years in 2007–2008. Of the 27 different fracture types shown in Table 3-4, 20 presented with a higher average age in 2007–2008 than in 2000. We appreciate that this might be a fortuitous occurrence, but it does seem likely that the average age of patients who present with fractures is continuing to rise.

Variation in Epidemiology

We have pointed out that the epidemiology of fractures varies widely. We believe that some of the variations are accounted for by the different methods used to collect, and in particular, to diagnose fractures. However, despite this, there are significant differences in the incidence of fractures in different communities. These differences have mainly been studied in osteoporotic or fragility fractures and the literature is consistent in pointing out that the population of Scandinavia has the highest incidences of these fractures.[1,26,27,30] The reason for this is unknown. However, there is evidence that the incidence of frac-

tures varies with racial type,[3,4,39] domicile,[17,19] season of the year,[22] and social deprivation.[32] The literature consistently details a higher incidence of fractures in urban, rather than rural, communities,[17,19,31,38] which points to the important of environmental factors. There is also evidence that the incidence of certain fractures, such as hip fractures, varies in different parts of the same country.[19,37]

How Common Are Different Fractures?

There is a surprising amount of debate about which fractures are most commonly seen. Surgeons often analyze their own hospital patients to see which fractures they most commonly treat and then extrapolate their findings to the whole population. This is clearly inappropriate as many hospitals deal with a specific type or complexity of fracture and the spectrum of fractures presenting to Edinburgh and Baltimore is different in many respects.

Table 3-4 shows the fractures that were seen in 2007–2008 in the Royal Infirmary of Edinburgh. Fractures of the distal radius are by far the most common, followed by fractures of the proximal femur, metacarpus, finger phalanges, and ankle. Altogether, these fractures account for 57.5% of all the fractures treated in the unit. Some fractures are relatively rare, but because of the trouble that surgeons have in treating them, they receive a great deal of attention in the literature. Examples of these are fractures of the distal tibia, talus, and calcaneus which together accounted for 2% of the fractures seen in the study year.

In Table 3-5, the fractures have been arranged in order of decreasing age, with the prevalence of fracture in patients aged over 65 and 80 years also being shown. If the gender ratio in Table 3-4 is compared with the average age of the different fractures shown in Table 3-5, it can be seen that fractures with a high female preponderance tend to occur in patients with an older average age.

Which Fractures Are Fragility Fractures?

The importance of osteoporotic fractures has been highlighted by many authors, but in a recent study, Cauley et al.[3] compared the absolute risk of fractures with the risk of different cardiovascular events and breast cancer in women aged 50–79 years in the United States. They found that the projected number of women who would experience a fracture exceeded the combined number of women who would experience invasive breast cancer or a range of different cardiovascular events in all ethnic groups except black women. They found that the annualized

TABLE 3-4	The Prevalence, Incidence, and Gender Ratios of Fractures Treated in Edinburgh in 2007/2008			
	Number	Prevalence (%)	Incidence (n/10⁵/yr)	Gender Ratio (Male/Female) (%)
Distal radius/ulna	1147	16.4	224.5	29/71
Proximal femur	817	11.7	159.8	27/73
Metacarpal	738	10.6	144.4	78/22
Finger phalanx	679	9.7	132.8	63/37
Ankle	633	9.1	123.8	47/53
Proximal humerus	510	7.3	99.8	31/69
Metatarsal	498	7.1	97.4	38/62
Proximal forearm	354	5.1	69.2	47/53
Clavicle	263	3.8	51.4	70/30
Toe phalanx	250	3.6	48.9	53/47
Carpus	203	2.9	39.7	70/30
Pelvis	127	1.8	24.8	39/61
Femoral diaphysis	91	1.3	17.8	44/56
Proximal tibia	80	1.1	15.6	45/55
Tibial diaphysis	73	1.0	14.3	78/22
Humeral diaphysis	68	1.0	13.3	51/49
Forearm diaphyses	60	0.9	11.7	73/27
Patella	56	0.8	11.1	34/66
Calcaneus	54	0.8	10.6	78/22
Distal tibia	52	0.7	10.2	62/38
Scapula	52	0.7	10.2	44/56
Distal humerus	46	0.7	9.0	30/70
Distal femur	39	0.6	7.6	33/67
Midfoot	37	0.5	7.2	46/54
Talus	32	0.5	6.3	66/34
Fibula	26	0.3	5.1	73/27
Sesamoid	1	0.01	0.2	100/0
	6986	100	1366.7	47/53

incidence of fracture was greatest in white and American Indian women and lowest in black women.

There has been some debate as to which fractures are osteoporotic fragility fractures. Traditionally, four fractures have been regarded as osteoporotic or fragility fractures; these being fractures of the proximal femur, proximal humerus, distal radius, and thoracolumbar spine. However, it is self-evident that there are many fractures that commonly occur in osteopenic or osteoporotic bone and should also be regarded as fragility fractures. Buhr and Cooke[2] indicated that humeral diaphyseal fractures, bimalleolar ankle fractures, and pelvic fractures had a Type F distribution, and they also demonstrated that proximal radial, femoral diaphyseal, proximal tibial, and lateral malleolar fractures had a bimodal distribution with a significant proportion of the fractures occurring in older patients. Other workers have also shown that there are a considerable number of fractures that should be regarded as fragility fractures.[24,25]

Recently, Kanis et al.[25] defined osteoporotic fractures as occurring at a site associated with a low-bone-mineral density (BMD) and that also increased in incidence after the age of 50 years. Based on this definition, Johnell and Kanis[24] proposed that vertebral fractures, hip fractures, all other femoral fractures, wrist and forearm fractures, humeral fractures, rib fractures, pelvic fractures, clavicular fractures, scapular fractures, and sternal fractures should be regarded as osteoporotic fractures. They also suggested that fractures of the tibia and fibula should be regarded as osteoporotic in women.

If Table 3-5 and Figure 3-2 are examined, a list of the fragility fractures that may occur in osteopenic and osteoporotic bone can be drawn up. These are shown in Table 3-6. Table 3-5 shows that there are eight fractures where patients present with an average age of more than that of patients with distal radial fractures, this fracture being widely accepted as a fragility fracture. If these patients are combined with patients who present

TABLE 3-5 The Fractures Treated in Edinburgh in 2007–2008 Arranged in Order of Decreasing Average Age

	Number	Average Age (yrs)	>65 yrs (%)	>80 yrs (%)
Proximal femur	817	80.4	90.2	64.7
Femoral diaphysis	91	69.5	71.4	39.6
Pelvis	127	68.2	66.1	46.4
Proximal humerus	510	66.7	60.6	26.0
Distal femur	39	63.3	60.0	35.9
Distal humerus	46	62.6	54.3	21.1
Patella	56	58.6	46.4	19.6
Humeral diaphysis	68	58.3	38.2	16.2
Distal radius/ulna	1147	57.8	46.0	19.0
Proximal tibia	80	56.0	37.5	20.0
Scapula	52	52.1	36.5	15.4
Ankle	633	49.5	24.3	5.7
Proximal forearm	354	47.3	22.0	7.1
Metatarsal	498	46.6	19.2	3.9
Distal tibia	52	44.6	15.4	5.8
Clavicle	263	44.4	22.1	10.3
Midfoot	37	44.1	18.9	2.7
Finger phalanges	679	40.9	14.5	5.5
Forearm diaphyses	60	40.1	20.0	8.3
Tibial diaphysis	73	39.6	19.2	9.6
Toe phalanges	250	38.9	10.6	1.6
Calcaneus	54	38.5	10.6	1.9
Talus	32	37.0	6.2	0
Carpus	203	35.9	9.4	1.5
Metacarpal	738	32.2	7.5	2.1
Fibula	26	30.7	7.7	3.8
Sesamoid	1	21.0	0	0
	6986	52.9	36.9	18.4

The percentages of fractures in patients aged more than 65 and 80 years is also shown.

TABLE 3-6 A List of the Fractures Which Should Be Considered as Fragility Fractures

Proximal humerus	Femoral diaphysis
Humeral diaphysis	Distal femur
Distal humerus	Patella
Olecranon	Bimalleolar ankle
Proximal radius and ulna	Trimalleolar ankle
Distal radius	Pelvis
Proximal femur	Thoracolumbar spine

of inpatient fractures were potentially fragility fractures. This illustrates the scale of the current problem. It seems likely that the problem will increase and that with increasing aging of the population other fractures will be regarded as fragility fractures and will be added to the list shown in Table 3-6. We believe that this particularly applies to fractures of the proximal tibia and scapula although all Type A, D, G, and H fractures will present more commonly in elderly patients in the future.

Open Fractures

The epidemiology of open fractures is shown in Table 3-7. Altogether, 2.6% of the fractures were open with 19.9% being Gustilo[18] Type III in severity. The overall incidence of open fractures in 2007–2008 was 35.4/10⁵/year with an incidence of 53.1/10⁵/year in males and 19.6/10⁵/year in females. The open fractures had a Type G distribution curve with the expected increase in young males but also an increased incidence in older males and females. Further analysis shows that in patients aged 65 years or older, 48.5% of the open fractures occurred following a fall from standing height with a further 33% being caused by a direct blow or assault. Only 3 (9.1%) open fractures in this age group were caused by motor vehicle accidents and all 3 patients were pedestrians. The fact that most open fractures in the elderly are caused by low-energy trauma suggests that the aging soft tissues have the same inherent problems as aging bone!

Table 3-7 shows that the highest prevalence of open fractures occurs in tibial diaphyseal fractures. In the sixth edition of Rockwood and Green,[8] it was noted that there was a high incidence of open distal tibial fractures in 2000. We do not know if the change in the 8-year period is coincidental. Open fractures of the finger phalanges are relatively common but rarely severe with the most severe open fractures generally being seen in the pelvis and lower limb. A number of fractures, such as those of the proximal femur, proximal humerus, and scapula, did not present with open wounds during the study period. They may present as open fractures, but their prevalence is low. The mode of injury also affects the prevalence of open fractures. In motor vehicle accidents, pedestrians and motorcyclists will present with more open fractures than vehicle occupants and cyclists (see Table 3-12). In addition, it is worth noting the very high prevalence of open fractures which occur in the distal femoral diaphysis (see Table 3-22).

with fracture Types E and F and with those patients over 50 years of age who present with fracture Types A, D, G, and H, an estimate of the true scale of the fragility fractures in a developed country can be obtained. It is interesting to note that all humeral and all femoral fractures, with the exception of the very rare femoral head fracture, should now be regarded as fragility fractures as should many long bone metaphyseal fractures. Based on the fractures shown in Table 3-6 and the patients who presented with Type A, D, G, and H fractures and were over 50 years of age, Court-Brown and Caesar[7] estimated that 30.1% of male fractures and 66.3% of female fractures were potentially fragility fractures. They also pointed out that in a large Orthopaedic Trauma Unit, 34.7% of outpatient fractures and 70.4%

TABLE 3-7	The Epidemiology of Open Fractures in Edinburgh in 2007 to 2008		
	Number	Open (%)	Gustilo[18] III (%)
Tibial diaphysis	73	21.9	56.2
Finger phalanges	679	13.7	9.7
Forearm diaphyses	60	11.7	0
Distal femur	39	7.7	66.6
Toe phalanges	250	6.8	29.4
Talus	32	6.2	100
Femoral diaphysis	91	5.5	60
Midfoot	37	5.4	100
Distal tibia	52	3.8	50
Proximal tibia	80	2.5	0
Proximal forearm	354	2.3	12.5
Patella	56	1.8	0
Calcaneus	54	1.8	100
Humeral diaphysis	68	1.5	0
Metacarpus	738	1.1	12.5
Carpus	203	1.0	50
Ankle	633	0.8	20
Pelvis	127	0.8	100
Metatarsus	498	0.6	100
Distal radius	1147	0.6	0
	5271	2.6	19.9

Multiple Fractures

Orthopaedic surgeons will be aware that although most fractures present as isolated injuries, patients may present with more than one fracture and that there are certain accepted patterns, such as the association between calcaneal and spinal fractures in a fall from a height or the association between fractures of the proximal femur and distal radius in the elderly who present after a fall from a standing height. Table 3-8 lists the common associated fractures for each index fracture. The numbers of index and associated fractures are given as well as their ratio. The higher the ratio, the more fractures the patient presents with. Table 3-8 shows that fractures of the feet are associated with the highest fracture ratios, although fractures of the pelvis and scapula are also associated with a number of other fractures.

The 6986 fractures occurred in 6414 patients. One hundred and eighty-two (2.8%) presented with multiple fractures of the hands or feet, and 328 (5.1%) presented with more than one fracture in different anatomical sites. Of these, 286 patients presented with 2 fractures and the rest presented with up to 7 fractures. The gender ratio was 49/51 but the male and female patients who presented with more than one fracture in different sites were very different. The average age was 33.5 years in males and 50.8 years in females, and the overall distribution was Type A. Only 20.5% of females who presented with more than one fracture were less than 50 years of age.

Mode of Injury

In the sixth edition of Rockwood and Green,[8] nine basic modes of injury were discussed with motor vehicle injuries being divided into four different categories: vehicle occupants, pedestrians, motorcyclists, and cyclists. In this edition, we have divided the basic modes of injury into eight categories and we have combined twisting injuries with falls from a standing height as it is often difficult for patients to separate the two. In the sixth edition,[8] falls down stairs and slopes were combined, but in this edition falls down slopes have been combined with falls from a standing height and therefore falls down stairs are presented separately. The eight basic modes of injury are shown in Table 3-9. Gunshot injuries are very uncommon in Scotland and there were none admitted during the study year. The "Other" mode in Table 3-9 contains the patients who could or would not remember their cause of injury. Many of these were intoxicated at the time of presentation.

The most common cause of injury is a fall from a standing height. About 57% of fractures were caused by a simple fall, with 83% of fractures in patients of at least 50 years of age being caused by a simple fall. The other common causes of injury are sporting activities and direct blows, assaults, or crush injuries. Sporting injuries provide a heterogeneous collection of fractures caused by direct blows, twisting injuries, and falls. They predominantly affect young males. Direct blows, assaults, or crush injuries accounted for 12.5% of the fractures and these also usually occur in young males.

Motor vehicle accidents are often perceived to cause the majority of fractures but this is not the case. In 2000, 7.2% of the fractures admitted to the Royal Infirmary of Edinburgh followed a motor vehicle accident, but in 2007–2008 this was reduced to 5.2%. The United Kingdom has one of the lowest incidences of mortality from motor vehicle accidents in the world, and it is likely that the morbidity is also lower than in other countries. Given the fact that unlike the United States, Germany, and other countries, the United Kingdom does not have a formalized trauma system, this illustrates the importance of accident prevention. In Baltimore in a very large U.S. Level I trauma center, about 60% of fractures are caused by motor vehicle accidents (see Table 3-33). It is possible to construct age and gender curves for modes of injury in the same way as can be done for individual fractures. The eight curves (see Fig. 3-2) used to describe fractures can also be used to describe their mode of injury.

Falls from a Standing Height

This is the most common mode of injury, and there is little doubt that with increasing age and infirmity in the population, fractures resulting from falls from a standing height will become even more common in the next few decades. Table 3-9 shows that overall, 57.2% of fractures were caused by a simple fall and that the patients had an average age of 60.2 years. Further analysis shows that 77.8% of fractures in females followed a simple fall, compared with 33.8% of fractures in males. The average age was 68.5 years for females and 56.4 years for males, showing that this mode of injury is common in elderly males and females. Overall fractures caused by a simple fall have a Type F distribution.

TABLE 3-8	The Number of Index Fractures, Associated Fractures, and the Ratio of the Two*			
	Index Fracture	Other Fractures	Ratio	Associated Fractures
Midfoot	37	36	0.97	Other Midfoot (30.6%) Calcaneus (16.7%) Ankle (13.9%)
Calcaneus	54	34	0.63	Other Calcaneus (22.2%) Midfoot (9.3%) Ankle (7.4%)
Scapula	52	32	0.62	Proximal Humerus (23.5%) Clavicle (17.6%) Ribs (17.6%)
Pelvis	127	78	0.61	Proximal Femur (11.5%) Distal Radius (11.5%) Ribs (11.5%)
Talus	32	14	0.44	Metatarsal (21.4%) Midfoot (21.4%)
Proximal Tibia	80	35	0.44	Other Proximal Tibia (17.1%) Pelvis (14.3%)
Femoral Diaphysis	91	33	0.36	Pelvis (30.3%) Proximal Femur (15.2%) Tibial Diaphysis (6.0%)
Fibula	26	9	0.35	Distal Radius (22.2%)
Distal Femur	39	11	0.28	Proximal Humerus (18.2%) Pelvis (18.2%) Femoral Diaphysis (18.2%)
Tibial Diaphysis	73	19	0.26	Femoral Diaphysis (15.8%)
Distal Tibia	52	13	0.25	Other Distal Tibia (30.8%) Proximal Forearm (30.8%)
Distal Humerus	46	11	0.24	Proximal Forearm (27.3%) Metacarpal (18.2%)
Patella	56	13	0.23	Metacarpal (23.1%) Distal Radius (23.1%)
Proximal Forearm	354	78	0.22	Other Proximal Forearm (46.2%) Distal Radius (11.5%) Carpus (6.4%)
Metacarpals	738	119	0.16	Other Metacarpal (62.2%) Finger Phalanges (14.3%) Carpus (4.2%)
Metatarsals	498	74	0.15	Other Metatarsal (50.0%) Ankle (14.9%) Midfoot (9.5%)
Humeral Diaphysis	68	10	0.15	Proximal Humerus (20.0%) Pelvis (20.0%) Distal Radius (20.0%)
Proximal Humerus	510	68	0.13	Proximal Femur (25.0%) Distal Radius (11.8%) Scapula (10.3%)
Forearm Diaphysis	60	8	0.13	Metacarpal (30.0%) Proximal Forearm (20.0%)
Carpus	203	25	0.12	Distal Radius (32.0%) Proximal Forearm (24.0%) Metacarpal (24.0%)
Distal Radius	1147	123	0.11	Other Distal Radius (29.3%) Proximal Femur (8.9%) Carpus (8.9%)

(continued)

TABLE 3-8 **(Continued) The Number of Index Fractures, Associated Fractures, and the Ratio of the Two***

	Index Fracture	Other Fractures	Ratio	Associated Fractures
Finger Phalanges	679	65	0.10	Other Finger Phalanges (38.5%) Metacarpals (27.7%) Distal Radius (12.3%)
Toe Phalanges	250	24	0.10	Other Toe Phalanges (25.0%) Metatarsals (25.0%)
Clavicle	263	22	0.08	Scapula (22.7%) Ribs (18.2%)
Ankle	633	48	0.08	Metatarsals (27.1%) Other Ankle (16.7%) Midfoot (10.4%)
Proximal Femur	817	53	0.06	Proximal Humerus (32.1%) Distal Radius (22.6%) Pelvis (11.3%)

*The more common associated fractures are also shown.

Table 3-10 shows that the highest prevalence of fractures following a standing fall is in the upper limbs. However, this underplays the importance of falls in the elderly. Analysis of the data concerning the common fragility fractures shows that 94.2% of proximal femoral fractures, 81.8% of proximal humeral fractures, 81.7% of pelvic fractures, and 69.6% of distal radial fractures are caused by simple falls. However, with the changes in the spectrum of osteoporotic fractures that have already been documented, it is also interesting to note that 63.2% of humeral diaphyseal fractures, 84.8% of distal humeral fractures, 65.9% of femoral diaphyseal fractures, and 74.3% of distal femoral fractures were also caused by falls. The common fractures caused by falls from a standing height at different ages are shown in Table 3-11.

Falls down Stairs

In the sixth edition of Rockwood and Green,[8] a ninth distribution curve was used to describe those fractures caused by a fall down stairs or slopes. If the falls down slopes are removed, it becomes apparent that falls down stairs, like falls from a standing height, have a Type F distribution and affect older patients. Tables 3-9 to 3-11 show that the overall distribution of fractures is very similar to those caused by a simple fall, although the average age of the patients is slightly younger. Table 3-9 shows that the average age of the patients is 54.6 years, with an average age of 56.6 years in females and 50.8 years in males. The most common fracture following a fall down stairs is a fracture of the distal radius and ulna (20.3%), followed by ankle fractures

TABLE 3-9 **The Average Age, Prevalence, and Gender Ratio for the Eight Basic Modes of Injury in Edinburgh**

	Average Age (yr)	Prevalence (%)	Gender Ratio (Male/Female) (%)
Fall (standing)	60.2	57.2	28/72
Fall (stairs)	54.6	3.9	38/62
Fall (height)	38.6	3.6	78/22
Direct blow/assault/crush	34.2	12.5	77/23
Sport	29.5	13.3	81/19
Motor vehicle accident	39.8	5.2	79/21
Stress/spontaneous	68.0	0.6	26/74
Other	38.6	3.6	57/43

TABLE 3-10 **The Prevalence of Upper Limb, Lower Limb, and Pelvic Fractures for the Eight Basic Modes of Injury in Edinburgh**

	Upper Limb (%)	Lower Limb (%)	Pelvis (%)
Fall (standing)	52.8	45.1	2.1
Fall (stairs)	52.5	46.0	1.5
Fall (height)	40.2	50.4	9.4
Direct blow/assault/crush	84.3	15.3	0.4
Sport	76.4	23.0	0.7
Motor vehicle accident	61.3	35.5	3.2
Stress/spontaneous	25.6	74.4	0
Other	76.3	23.7	0

TABLE 3-11	The Prevalences of the Most Common Fractures Associated with the Different Modes of Injury		
	16–39 Years (%)	40–59 Years (%)	60–99 Years (%)
Fall (standing)	Metatarsal (18.1) Distal radius (16.8) Ankle (15.9)	Ankle (19.8) Distal radius (19.0) Metatarsal (11.0)	Proximal femur (29.2) Distal radius (22.4) Proximal humerus (12.9)
Fall (stairs)	Distal radius (43.6) Ankle (20.5) Proximal forearm (17.9)	Ankle (25.3) Distal radius (13.9) Metatarsal (10.1)	Distal radius (22.1) Ankle (18.9) Proximal femur (15.0)
Fall (height)	Calcaneus (19.7) Distal radius (11.8) Pelvis (11.0)	Distal radius (14.1) Proximal femur (13.0) Ankle (8.7)	Distal radius (20.0) Scapula (16.0) Ankle (12.0)
Direct blow/ assault/ crush	Metacarpal (55.1) Finger phalanx (19.6) Toe phalanx (7.6)	Finger phalanx (44.3) Metacarpal (26.6) Toe phalanx (9.8)	Finger phalanx (43.2) Toe phalanx (17.9) Distal radius (11.9)
Sport	Finger phalanx (21.9) Distal radius (15.4) Metacarpal (13.7)	Distal radius (20.5) Finger phalanx (19.9) Ankle (9.9)	Distal radius (37.9) Ankle (13.8) Proximal humerus (10.3)
MVA	Proximal forearm (11.6) Clavicle (10.0) Distal radius (10.0)	Clavicle (13.6) Ankle (11.0) Proximal forearm (10.2)	Distal radius (14.2) Tibial plateau (11.9) Pelvis (9.5)
Stress/ spontaneous	Distal radius (50.0) Metatarsal (50.0) Finger phalanx (20.0)	Femur diaphysis (40.0) Metatarsal (40.0) Humeral diaphysis (15.6)	Proximal femur (43.7) Femur diaphysis (21.9)
Other	Finger phalanx (21.9) Distal radius (15.4) Metacarpal (13.7)	Distal radius (20.5) Finger phalanx (19.9) Ankle (9.9)	Distal radius (37.9) Ankle (13.8) Proximal humerus (10.3)

(18.8%) and proximal femoral fractures (7.3%). The common fractures caused by falls down stairs at different ages are shown in Table 3-11.

Falls from a Height

This category contains all falls from more than 6 feet, so the type of injury will vary with the height of the fall. Table 3-9 shows that they are relatively uncommon and usually occur in younger males, giving them a Type B distribution. This mode of injury is unusual in that the average age of males and females is virtually identical. The average for males was 38.7 years and for females 38.1 years. In younger patients, Table 3-11 shows that falls from a height are associated with a high prevalence of calcaneal fractures and pelvic fractures (also see Table 3-10). These tend to be replaced by distal radial and ankle fractures in older patient groups, but there is a surprisingly high prevalence of scapular fractures in the over 60 age group. The other fracture that must be looked for following a fall from a height is that of the thoracolumbar spine,[29] which may also be associated with a calcaneal fracture.

Direct Blows, Assaults, or Crush Injuries

Like falls from a height, these are more common in young males and have a Type B distribution. The average age of males was 31.9 years and 40.4 years in females. In young males, direct blows are usually punch injuries or kicks which accounts for the high prevalence of metacarpal, finger, and toe fractures. In older patients, it tends to be finger fractures that present more commonly than metacarpal fractures. Altogether, 50% of all

metacarpal fractures and 33.8% of all finger phalangeal fractures were caused by a direct blow or assault. They are a particular problem in adolescence and will be discussed further in the section dealing with the epidemiology of adolescent fractures. They are not infrequently associated with social deprivation.[32]

Sporting Injuries

This is a very heterogeneous group of patients who present after twisting injuries, falls, direct blows, motor vehicle accidents, and cycling accidents. In addition, there is an association between stress fractures and sporting activity. Stress fractures are discussed further in Chapter 19. In general, sports fractures show a Type C distribution with young males and females being affected, though Table 3-9 shows that more fractures occur in males. Table 3-10 shows that most sports injuries affect the upper limb, though Table 3-11 indicates that ankle fractures are relatively common in older sportsmen and women.

It is obvious that the epidemiology of sports-related fractures will vary throughout the world depending on the degree of affluence, availability of resources, and the popularity of different sports. Thus, an analysis of sports fractures from Edinburgh will not include injuries from sports such as baseball, American football, ice hockey, or cross country skiing. However, many sports are universally popular. Examples of these are soccer, rugby, skiing, field hockey, basketball, athletics, and horse riding. Court-Brown et al.[11] examined the epidemiology of sports-related fractures in depth. They found that in the United Kingdom, 10 sports accounted for 86.8% of the fractures, with soccer and rugby together being responsible for 59.2% of fractures.

Soccer is the world's most popular sport. It is probably the second most common cause of tibial diaphyseal fractures after motor vehicle accidents,[10] but 47% of soccer-related fractures are in the hand and wrist, with a further 26% occurring in the foot and ankle.[11]

Motor Vehicle Accidents

It is often assumed that motor vehicle accidents are responsible for the majority of fractures, but Table 3-9 shows that this is not the case. Our results will not be equivalent to other parts of the world, as the United Kingdom has fairly strict laws regarding alcohol consumption and speeding. The importance of accident prevention has already been alluded to. Overall motor vehicle accident fractures have a Type B distribution with a unimodal peak in young males and a constant low incidence in females. Upper limb fractures are more commonly seen (see Table 3-10) but the spectrum of fractures varies with the type of injury. See Tables 3-34 and 3-35 for further information about motor vehicle accidents in Baltimore.

Vehicle Occupants. With improved automobile design and stricter seatbelt, speeding, and alcohol legislation, vehicle occupants now have the lowest prevalence of fractures in motor vehicle accidents. Table 3-12 shows only 11.2% of motor vehicle accident fractures occurred in vehicle occupants. There is a Type H distribution of fractures with a bimodal distribution being seen in both males and females. Analysis of the fractures showed that 48.7% occurred in the upper limb, 46.1% in the lower limb, and 5.1% were pelvic fractures. It should be remembered that spinal fractures may also occur in vehicle occupants.

Pedestrians. On average, pedestrians tend to be slightly older than vehicle occupants (see Table 3-12) and further analysis shows that they have Type G distribution of fractures with bimodal peaks in younger and older males but a unimodal peak in older women. In fact, 58.3 % of female pedestrians presenting with fractures were over 70 years of age compared with 19% of males. Not unexpectedly, there was a higher prevalence of lower limb fractures in pedestrians, with 50.6% of fractures being in the lower limb compared with 44% in the upper limb and 5.3% in the pelvis. The most common fractures associated with pedestrian injuries are shown in Table 3-12, which also shows that 12% of the fractures were open.

Motorcyclists. Predictably, motorcycle fractures show a Type B distribution with most motorcycle fractures occurring in young men. Table 3-12 shows that there are relatively few motorcycle fractures in women. Many of the fractures that occur in motorcyclists are severe but overall, Table 3-12 shows that metacarpal, ankle, and clavicular fractures are most commonly seen. However, the severity of the fractures is indicated by the fact that 13.9% were open fractures. Overall, 53% of the fractures were in the upper limb, 43.4% were in the lower limb, and 6.6% were pelvic fractures.

Cyclists. Unlike motorcycle fractures, there is a significant number of female cyclists who present with fractures. Overall, there is a Type C distribution. These fractures show a different distribution from other motor vehicle accident fractures as 84.2% are in the upper limb with only 15% occurring in the lower limb. Pelvic fractures are very rare. The most common fracture types are shown in Table 3-12, which also shows that open fractures are unusual.

Stress/Spontaneous Fractures

These two fracture types have been combined as many spontaneous fractures are in fact insufficiency fractures occurring in older patients. In this study, there were few fatigue fractures in

TABLE 3-12	The Prevalence, Average Age, and Gender Ratio of Patients who Sustained Fractures in Road Traffic Accidents*				
	Prevalence (%)	Average Age (yrs)	Gender Ratio (Male/ Female) (%)	Open Fractures (%)	Associated Injuries (%)
Vehicle occupant	11.2	41.6	64/36	2.6	Finger phalanx (15.4) Tibial plateau (12.8) Clavicle (10.2)
Pedestrian	21.5	45.1	84/16	12.0	Tibial diaphysis (12.0) Distal radius (12.0) Tibial plateau (9.3)
Motorcyclist	32.9	34.2	94/6	13.9	Metacarpal (13.9) Ankle (9.6) Clavicle (8.7)
Cyclist	34.4	39.8	67/33	3.3	Proximal forearm (25.0) Clavicle (14.2) Distal radius (12.5)
		39.4		8.6	

*The rate of open fractures and the most common associated injuries are also shown.

younger patients and it seems likely that with increasing numbers of elderly in the population more insufficiency fractures will be seen. In the sixth edition of Rockwood and Green,[8] spontaneous/stress fractures were noted to have a Type H distribution with fatigue fractures occurring in younger patients and insufficiency fractures in older patients. In this study, the distribution showed a Type F curve, and it seems likely that this will continue to be the case as there will be many more insufficiency fractures in the elderly than fatigue fractures in the young. The distribution of fatigue fractures is a Type C curve affecting younger males and females. Table 3-11 shows that in the over 60 age group, insufficiency fractures tend to occur in the proximal femur, femoral diaphysis, or humeral diaphysis.

Other Modes of Injury

Approximately 4% of patients presented with no definite history as to how their fracture occurred. The two most common causes of this are excessive alcohol intake or dementia. In this study, 93.4% of patients were intoxicated on presentation. Many of the fractures will have been sustained in falls or fights, and a review of the 16–39 year age group (see Table 3-11) shows that the fracture distribution is similar to that seen in direct blows or assaults. In the 40–59 year age group, we suspect that many fractures followed falls, and it is interesting to note that distal radial fractures were not a significant problem, suggesting that alcohol prevented the patients from putting their hand out to stop their fall!

Gunshot Injuries

Information regarding the epidemiology of fractures caused by firearms is sparse. They are relatively uncommon in Europe, but the North American literature strongly suggests that they have a Type B distribution and most commonly occur in young males. Gunshot mortality and morbidity are greater in the United States, where the large urban Level I trauma centers see a disproportionate number of fractures caused by firearms. See Table 3-39 for information about the epidemiology of fractures caused by gunshot injuries in Baltimore.

Specific Fracture Types

Clavicle

Table 3-4 shows that fractures of the clavicle account for about 4% of all fractures. Overall, they have a Type G distribution occurring in young males but in both older males and females. However, if they are subdivided according to their location within the clavicle, fractures of the medial and lateral thirds of the clavicle have a Type A distribution while the more common middle third fracture has a Type G distribution (see Table 3-2). Table 3-13 shows that fractures of the medial third of the clavicle are rare, and it should be remembered that in young patients they may well be physeal fractures. The more common middle and lateral third fractures are different with lateral third fractures tending to occur in slightly older patients although the gender ratio is very similar. Overall, Table 3-13 shows that falls from a standing height, sporting injuries, and motor vehicle accidents account for about 85% of clavicle fractures. However, if one compares the mode of injury of middle and lateral third fractures, sporting injuries cause most middle third fractures (39.7%) and falls from a standing height cause most lateral third fractures (58.4%). This is a reflection of the different averages ages of the patients who present with the two fractures.

TABLE 3-13	The Basic Epidemiological Characteristics of Clavicle Fractures		
Clavicle Fracture	Prevalence (%)	Average Age (yrs)	Gender Ratio (Male/Female) (%)
Medial third	2.3	46.6	60/40
Middle third	59.3	39.3	73/27
Lateral third	38.4	51.8	66/34
Common causes	Fall standing height 40.3% Sport 31.2% Motor vehicle accident 13.3%		

Scapula

Table 3-4 shows that scapular fractures are comparatively rare, accounting for 0.7% of all the fractures seen during the year. We believe that their epidemiology is changing and that there are now many more elderly patients presenting with scapular fractures. They have a Type A distribution, and Table 3-5 shows that 36.5% occur in patients aged at least 65 years. We have subdivided the scapula into fractures of the body, neck, acromion, coracoid, and glenoid, and the epidemiology for the different fractures is shown in Table 3-14. This shows that the most common scapular fractures are those in the glenoid and body. Coracoid fractures are rare with acromion and neck fractures each accounting for 11%–14% of scapular fractures. About 65% of glenoid fractures were associated with shoulder dislocations. It is interesting to note that all fracture types have a similar average age and further analysis showed that acromion, body, neck, and glenoid fractures all had a Type A distribution. Most fractures are caused by a simple fall. The average age for this group was 60.4 years and 50% presented with an associated dislocation. The average age of the patients injured in motor vehicle accidents was 30.1 years and 85.7% were male.

Proximal Humerus

Table 3-4 shows that these are common fractures accounting for 7.3% of all the fractures seen in the year. They have a Type

TABLE 3-14	The Basic Epidemiological Characteristics of Scapular Fractures		
Scapular Fracture	Prevalence (%)	Average Age (yrs)	Gender Ratio (Male/Female) (%)
Acromion	13.5	54.1	71/29
Coracoid	1.9	75.0	0/100
Glenoid	39.6	52.1	31/69
Neck	11.5	53.1	50/50
Body	28.8	50.4	53/47
Common causes	Fall (standing height) 42.3% Motor vehicle accident 13.5% Fall (height) 13.5%		

F distribution and are accepted to be fragility fractures. In this study, 81.8% resulted from a fall from a standing height and the average age of this group was 70.7 years. The second most common cause was motor vehicle accidents, with 4.7% of fractures being caused in this way. The average age of this group was 42.1 years. The third most common cause was sporting injuries, with 3.9% of fractures occurring in patients with an average age of 39.4 years.

Humeral Diaphysis

We believe that humeral diaphyseal fractures should be regarded as fragility fractures. The average age of the patients was older than in those patients who presented with distal radial fractures (see Table 3-5), and although humeral diaphyseal fractures have a Type H distribution, we think it likely that this will change to a Type F distribution in decades to come. Table 3-5 shows that over 38% of patients are aged at least 65 years. This accounts for the fact that 63% of the fractures were caused by a simple fall. A further 11.8% were sport injuries, with 37.5% of these being caused by arm wrestling, a recognized cause of distal diaphyseal fractures of the humerus. All 3 patients were intoxicated! In 5 patients (7.3%), the fractures were spontaneous and surgeons should be aware of the possibility of pathological fractures following humeral metastases.

Distal Humerus

Table 3-4 shows that distal humeral fractures are relatively uncommon, accounting for only 0.7% of the fractures in this study. Surgeons may be surprised that overall they have a Type E distribution as much of the literature has centered on the complex intra-articular distal humeral fractures seen in younger patients after high-energy trauma. However, Table 3-5 shows that about 55% of patients are at least 65 years of age on presentation. In fact, 63% of the patients in this study presented with extra-articular supracondylar fractures, with 28.2% presenting with partial articular fractures and only 8.7% with complete articular fractures. The average ages were 68.8, 51.5, and 52.7 years, respectively, indicating that if supracondylar distal humeral fractures were graded separately in Table 3-5, they would be third in terms of age after proximal femoral and femoral diaphyseal fractures. Given these average ages, it will not be surprising that 84.8% of distal humeral fractures were caused by simple falls with the average age of this group being 69.1 years. A further 6.5% of fractures occurred as the result of sports injuries with 6.5% also occurring in motor vehicle accidents. These occurred in younger patients the average ages being 26 and 30 years respectively.

Proximal Forearm

Proximal forearm fractures comprise about 5% of all fractures (see Table 3-4). Overall, they show a Type D distribution. As has already been pointed out, however, if one analyzes the different proximal forearm fractures, it is evident that there are a number of different fracture types. Table 3-2 shows that radial head fractures have a Type H distribution while radial neck fractures have a Type A distribution. The two remaining fractures of the proximal forearm, those of the olecranon and combined fractures of the proximal radius and ulna, are both Type F fractures and should be regarded as fragility fractures.

TABLE 3-15	**The Basic Epidemiological Characteristics of Proximal Forearm Fractures**		
	Prevalence (%)	Average Age (yrs)	Gender Ratio (Male/Female) (%)
Olecranon	19.2	57.0	46/54
Radial head	53.1	43.2	50/50
Radial neck	22.5	44.9	54/46
Proximal radius and ulna	5.1	65.0	33/67
Common causes	Fall (standing height)	59.6%	
	Sport	13.6%	
	Motor vehicle accident	10.5%	

Table 3-15 shows that falls from a standing height account for about 60% of proximal forearm fractures. The average age of this group was 55 years. A further 24% of fractures were caused in motor vehicle accidents or by sports injuries. The average ages of these two groups were 36.2 and 29.7 years, respectively.

Forearm Diaphyses

Table 3-4 shows that fractures of the diaphyses of the radius and ulna account for 0.9% of all fractures in this study. Overall, they have a Type D pattern that is made up of three different patterns seen in the three different types of forearm fractures. Isolated ulnar fractures have a Type H distribution, whereas isolated radial fractures have a Type A distribution. Fractures of both the ulna and radial diaphyses also have a Type A distribution. This actually differs from the fracture distribution noted in the sixth edition of Rockwood and Green,[8] where radial and ulna fractures had a Type B distribution curve affecting young males. Table 3-16 shows that this is not the case in this study. The change may simply be fortuitous or it may represent increasing age in patients with forearm fractures. The most com-

TABLE 3-16	**The Basic Epidemiological Characteristics of Forearm Fractures**		
	Prevalence (%)	Average Age (yrs)	Gender Ratio (Male/Female) (%)
Ulna diaphysis	65.0	40.6	77/23
Radial diaphysis	13.3	30.5	88/12
Radial and ulnar diaphyses	21.7	44.5	54/46
Common causes	Fall (standing height)	28.3%	
	Direct blow/ assault	21.7%	
	Sport	18.3%	

mon causes of forearm fractures are listed in Table 3-16. The most common cause of isolated radial fractures was sports injury, which accounted for 50% of these fractures. In isolated ulnar fractures, the most common causes were direct blows and simple falls, which both caused 25.6% of fractures. In radial and ulna fractures, the most common cause was a simple fall, which caused 38.5% of fractures. The average of age of this group was 60 years.

Distal Radius and Ulna

Fractures of the distal radius and ulna are the most common fractures that orthopaedic surgeons have to treat, accounting for about 16% of all fractures (see Table 3-4). In this study, isolated distal ulnar fractures were included with fractures of the distal radius and fractures of the distal radius and ulna. There were 32 (2.8%) isolated distal ulna fractures compared with 1115 (97.2%) distal radial fractures. Both have a Type A distribution, but there are slight epidemiological differences that are shown in Table 3-17. This shows that about 70% of distal radial and ulna fractures are caused by a simple fall. The average age of this group was 65.7 years and 84.7% were female. Predictably, the average age of the patients whose distal radial fractures and ulna fractures were caused by sporting injuries was less at 40 years and only 28% were female.

There has been considerable interest in the incidence of distal radial fractures in different parts of the world. Sakuma et al.[37] analyzed the incidence in Japan in 2004 and showed it to be $108.6/10^5$/year with an average age of 60.2 years. Hagino et al.[19] also examined distal radial fractures in a region of Japan and showed that between 1986 and 1995, the incidence of distal radial fracture rose in women but not in men. Brogren et al.[1] examined the incidence of distal radial fracture in Southern Sweden in 2001 in patients aged 18 or older and showed it to be $260/10^5$/year. They stressed that it was lower than earlier series, and they wondered whether the incidence of distal radial fractures was declining. A further Scandinavian study compared the incidence of distal radial fractures in Oslo, Norway, in 1978 and 1998 and found no difference. They observed that Oslo had the highest rates of hip and distal radial fractures in the world but that the risk was lower in immigrant Asians than in ethnic Norwegians.

Carpus

Carpal fractures are relatively common and account for about 3% of all fractures (see Table 3-4). The most common carpal

TABLE 3-17	The Basic Epidemiological Characteristics of Fractures of the Distal Radius and Ulna		
	Prevalence (%)	Average Age (yrs)	Gender Ratio (Male/Female) (%)
Distal radius (+/− distal ulna)	97.2	58.0	28/72
Distal ulna	2.8	51.3	59/41
Common causes	Fall (standing height)	69.6%	
	Sport	13.3%	
	Fall (stairs)	4.6%	

TABLE 3-18	The Basic Epidemiological Characteristics of Carpal Fractures		
	Prevalence (%)	Average Age (yrs)	Gender Ratio (Male/Female) (%)
Scaphoid	69.3	34.8	71/29
Triquetrum	15.3	45.2	58/42
Hamate	6.4	23.4	92/8
Trapezium	2.8	25.4	100/0
Common causes	Fall (standing height)	41.6%	
	Sport	26.2%	
	Direct blow/ assault	14.8%	

bone to be fractured in the scaphoid (carpal navicular), but in this study, there were also fractures in the capitate, hamate, lunate, pisiform, trapezium, trapezoid, and triquetrum. Most of these fractures were very unusual, but there were sufficient fractures of the triquetrum, hamate, and trapezium to warrant further analysis. Table 3-18 shows the epidemiology of the four most commonly fractured carpal bones. Although the carpal bones have a Type A distribution curve overall, fractures of the scaphoid, hamate, and trapezium tend to occur in young males. They all have Type B distribution curves whereas the triquetrum has a Type A distribution (see Table 3-2). The average age is particularly young in hamate and trapezium fractures. Table 3-18 also shows that over 80% of carpal fractures are caused by simple falls, sports injuries, or direct blows or assaults. As might be guessed from the gender ratio and average age, 80% of trapezium fractures and 54% of hamate fractures were caused by direct blows compared with 11% of scaphoid fractures. Most scaphoid fractures (40.7%) were caused by simple falls onto the wrist although 32.8% followed sporting injuries.

Metacarpus

Table 3-4 shows that metacarpal fractures are the third most common fractures seen by orthopaedic surgeons, comprising about 10% of all fractures. They are common in young males and have a Type B distribution. In this study, there were 738 separate metacarpal fractures, with 86.2% presenting as a single metacarpal fracture. The remaining 13.8% presented as fractures of two, three, or four metacarpals with fractures of three and four metacarpals being rare (Table 3-19). If one considers just the single metacarpal fractures, 52.6% were fractures of the fifth metacarpal and 15% involved the fourth metacarpal. Table 3-19 shows that the average age of patients who present with metacarpal fractures is very similar no matter which metacarpal is fractured and all have Type B distributions.

The most common cause of metacarpal fractures is a direct blow or assault, with 54.1% of the patients admitting to this. It is likely that not all patients were honest and the figure may be higher! In fifth metacarpal fractures, 64.2% were caused by a direct blow or assault compared with 17.8% of first metacarpal fractures, 51.4% of second metacarpal fracture, 30.9% of third metacarpal fractures, and 52.3% of fourth metacarpal fractures. Unsurprisingly, the gender ratio for metacarpal fractures caused by an assault was 90:10 (male:female).

TABLE 3-19	**The Basic Epidemiological Characteristics of Metacarpal Fractures**		
	Prevalence (%)	Average Age (yrs)	Gender Ratio (Male/Female) (%)
First	7.6	33.5	87/13
Second	5.0	29.6	78/22
Third	5.7	32.1	76/24
Fourth	15.0	31.9	73/27
Fifth	52.6	31.1	78/22
Two metacarpals	5.4	37.8	85/15
Three metacarpals	0.7	31.6	60/40
Four metacarpals	0.3	60.0	50/50
Common causes	Direct blow/ assault	54.1%	
	Fall (standing height)	18.7%	
	Sport	17.6%	

In the patients who presented with two metacarpal fractures, the most common combination was fractures of the fourth and fifth metacarpals (56.4%), followed by fractures of the third and fourth metacarpals (30.8%). As with single metacarpal fractures, direct blows or assaults were the most common cause of two metacarpal fractures, with 46.1% being so caused compared with 17.9% following a sports injury or a simple fall.

Finger Fractures

The epidemiology of finger phalangeal fractures is not too dissimilar to that of metacarpal fractures. They account for about 10% of all fractures (see Table 3-4) and, like metacarpal fractures, they tend to occur in young males and have a Type B distribution. Table 3-20 shows an analysis of the epidemiology of the individual fingers. As with metacarpal fractures, the index and middle fingers are least affected, and it is the little finger

TABLE 3-20	**The Basic Epidemiological Characteristics of Finger Phalangeal Fractures**		
	Prevalence (%)	Average Age (yrs)	Gender Ratio (Male/Female) (%)
Thumb	20.0	38.6	64/36
Index	12.1	34.5	74/26
Long	14.4	39.3	67/33
Ring	16.3	43.3	59/41
Little	29.6	41.9	60/40
Two fingers	3.1	45.7	48/52
Three fingers	0.6	64.0	33/67
Common causes	Direct blow/ assault	35.2%	
	Sport	28.6%	
	Fall (Standing height)	23.4%	

that is most affected. However, unlike metacarpal fractures, the thumb phalanges are more commonly affected than those of the ring finger. The average age and gender ratio of fractures of the individual fingers is very similar and all have a Type B distribution. Fractures of more than one finger are relatively rare but, as with patients who have fractures of two or more metacarpals (see Table 3-19), it is interesting to note that the higher average age and the different gender ratio suggest that multiple fractures of the fingers tend to occur in older patients.

The causes of finger fractures are also similar to those of metacarpal fractures. Direct blows or assaults accounted for 35.2% of fractures. If this combined with fractures caused by sporting injuries and falls from a standing height, it is apparent that 87.2% of finger fractures are caused by these three modes of injury. Analysis of the modes of injuries of individual finger fractures does show some differences from metacarpal fractures. The two fingers most commonly fractured by direct blows or assaults are the middle (46.9%) and ring (45.0%) fingers, whereas it is the thumb (35.2%) and index finger (35.4%), that are most commonly affected in sporting injuries. Falls from a standing height most commonly cause fractures of the ring (27.0%) and little fingers (27.8%).

Proximal Femur

Proximal femoral fractures have been extensively studied in different parts of the world.[4,5,17,19,22,26] Not only are proximal femoral fractures the most common fracture to be operatively treated, but the high average age of patients who present with these fractures means that the patients are often very frail and have extensive medical comorbidities. Thus, all health systems incur considerable expense in looking after these patients.

Table 3-4 shows that the incidence of proximal femoral fractures was $159.8/10^5$/year in 2007–2008. In males, the incidence was $90.9/10^5$/year, and in females, it was $221.2/10^5$/year. In males aged 50 years or more, the incidence was $234.3/10^5$/year, and in females aged 50 years or more, it was $537.3/10^5$ year. A comparison with data from the Edinburgh Trauma Unit from 1998, 10 years earlier, shows that the overall incidence for hip fractures was the same in 1998 but that the overall incidence of hip fractures in males of all ages was $70.5/10^5$/year and $240.1/10^5$/year for females. This indicates a change in the incidence of hip fractures such that the incidence in males is rising while it appears to be falling in females.

A review of the literature shows that this trend has been documented in other parts of the world. Chevally et al.[5] studied hip fractures in Switzerland between 1991 and 2000. In patients aged at least 50 years, the incidence of hip fractures in males was $153/10^5$/year and $455/10^5$/year in females. Overall, the incidence in females fell over the study period but rose slightly in males. In Australia, Chang et al.[4] observed a decreased incidence of hip fractures in both males and females between 1989 and 2000. Kannus et al.[26] studied the incidence of hip fractures in older adults in Finland between 1970 and 2004. They showed that the number of hip fractures in Finns aged at least 50 years rose between 1970 and 1997 but that the rise then levelled off in both sexes although the decline was greater in women. They postulated that the reasons for the decline might be a cohort effect towards healthier elderly populations in the developed countries, but they also suggested that it might relate to increased bone mass, improved functional ability, and campaigns to treat osteoporosis.

There is no doubt that the incidence of hip fractures varies throughout the world for reasons discussed earlier in this chapter. However, in developed countries it seems that the high rise in the incidence of hip fractures noted after the second World War is gradually levelling off. This has been well documented in Finland,[26] and presumably other countries will show the same epidemiological changes in years to come.

The epidemiology of different fractures of the proximal femur is shown in Table 3-21. Femoral head fractures are extremely rare even in Level I Trauma Centers. The unit actually treated two during the study year, but they were both from outside the study area and were not included in the study. A review of a recent paper dealing with the management of femoral head fractures indicates that they are a Type B fracture occurring mainly in young males.[21] In this study, intracapsular fractures were more commonly seen than extracapsular fractures, but both are very common and both have a Type F distribution. Their descriptive criteria are very similar and virtually all are caused by falls from a standing height.

Femoral Diaphysis

We think it likely that few fractures have undergone such a major change in their epidemiology in the last 20–30 years. The femoral diaphyseal fracture was essentially the fracture that caused many surgeons to change from operative to nonoperative management in the 1970s. It was associated with young patients and high-energy trauma, but it is educational to review the papers of Buhr and Cooke[2] and Knowelden et al.[28] who recognized that, even in the 1950s, femoral diaphyseal fractures had a bimodal distribution and often occurred in older patients. The change in their epidemiology is highlighted by the fact that in 1990, the average age of patients presenting to the Edinburgh Orthopaedic Trauma Unit with femoral diaphyseal fractures was 44 years. Table 3-5 shows that in 2007–2008, the average age was 69.5 years. However, they have a Type A distribution (see Table 3-2). A review of the database in the Edinburgh Orthopaedic Trauma Unit shows that there was a decline in the incidence of femoral diaphyseal fracture throughout the 1990s, but we think it possible that the incidence is rising again mainly because of the increasing numbers of periprosthetic fractures that orthopaedic surgeons are seeing.

TABLE 3-22	The Basic Epidemiological Characteristics of Femoral Diaphyseal Fractures			
	Prevalence (%)	Average Age (yrs)	Open (%)	Gender Ratio (Male/Female) (%)
Subtrochanteric	58.2	76.1	0	38/62
Middle third	22.0	64.7	5.0	37/63
Distal third	19.8	55.4	22.2	67/33
Periprosthetic	38.5	72.6	0	49/51
Nonperiprosthetic	61.5	65.4	5.5	41/59
Common causes	Fall (standing height)	65.9%		
	Motor vehicle accident	8.8%		
	Fall (height)	7.7%		

In Table 3-22, the femoral diaphyseal fractures have been divided in two ways. We have divided them according to their location within the diaphysis but also by whether they were periprosthetic fractures or not. Table 3-22 shows that subtrochanteric fractures have a similar age to those of the proximal femur, and it is interesting to observe that 58.7% of the femoral fractures were subtrochanteric. In previous years, there were higher rates of middle and distal third fractures. Table 3-22 also shows that fractures of the distal femoral diaphysis tend to be more severe, with 22.2% being open. In this group, 44.4% of the fractures were caused by a simple fall, but 27.7% resulted from a motor vehicle accident. In middle third fractures, 55% resulted from a simple fall, 20% were sports injuries, and 5% followed a motor vehicle accident.

Table 3-22 shows that 38.5% of the femoral fractures were periprosthetic. These have a Type F distribution. It is clear that the prevalence of periprosthetic fractures is rising. In 2000, 29.1% of our femoral fractures were periprosthetic and, in years to come, it is likely that their prevalence will continue to rise. More detailed analysis of the periprosthetic fractures shows that 82.5% of these fractures were related to hip and knee implants and 17.2% to implants used to treat previous fractures.

Distal Femur

Distal femoral fractures are relatively uncommon accounting for only 0.6% of the fractures seen in 2007–2008. As with all femoral fractures, with the exception of the rare femoral head fracture, they should now be regarded as fragility fractures as Table 3-5 shows the average age for patients was 63.3 years. They have a Type E distribution (see Table 3-2). As with femoral diaphyseal fractures, there is an increased prevalence of periprosthetic fractures of the distal femur and 15.4% of distal femoral fractures were periprosthetic. Table 3-23 shows the epidemiology of both periprosthetic and nonperiprosthetic distal femoral fractures. It also indicates that most distal femoral fractures, whether or not they are related to a prosthesis, are low-energy injuries in older patients. As with femoral diaphyseal fractures, the majority (83.3%) of periprosthetic distal femoral fractures were related to prostheses rather than to trauma implants.

TABLE 3-21	The Basic Epidemiological Characteristics of Proximal Femoral Fractures		
	Prevalence (%)	Average Age (yrs)	Gender Ratio (Male/Female) (%)
Femoral head	0	—	—
Intracapsular	62.1	80.1	28/72
Extracapsular	37.9	81.0	25/75
Common causes	Fall (standing height)	94.2%	
	Fall (stairs)	2.3%	
	Spontaneous	1.7%	

TABLE 3-23	The Basic Epidemiological Characteristics of Distal Femoral Fractures			
	Prevalence (%)	Average Age (yrs)	Open (%)	Gender Ratio (Male/ Female) (%)
Periprosthetic	15.4	80.8	0	0/100
Nonperiprosthetic	84.6	62.0	9.1	39/61
Common causes	Fall (standing height)		74.4%	
	Motor vehicle accident		7.7%	
	Fall (height)		7.7%	

Patella

Patella fractures accounted for 0.8% of all fractures in this study. They should be regarded as fragility fractures, and they have a Type F distribution. Most are caused by a fall from a standing height (73.2%), although 8.9% were caused by motor vehicle accidents and 7.1% by falls down stairs.

Proximal Tibia

Fractures of the proximal tibia account for about 1% of all fractures. They have a Type H distribution with bimodal peaks in both males and females. However, it is likely that in years to come they will be regarded as fragility fractures as the proportions of older and younger patients change. Analysis of the proximal tibia fractures shows that 22.5% were extra-articular fractures, 57.5% were partial articular fractures, and the remaining 10% were complete articular fractures. The most common cause of a proximal tibia fracture was a fall from a standing height (51.2%), followed by motor vehicle accidents (23.7%) and sports injuries (7.5%). The average ages of these patients were 66.0, 45.2, and 36.2 years, respectively.

Tibial Diaphysis

We believe that the incidence of tibial diaphyseal fractures is declining presumably as the result of improved road safety measures. Analysis of tibial diaphyseal fractures between 1988 and 1990 in our unit showed that 37.5% of fractures followed motor vehicle accidents, 30.9% were caused by sports injuries, and a further 17.8% were caused by falls from a standing height.[10] Almost 20 years later, 27.4% of our tibial diaphyseal fractures followed sports injuries, 20.5% occurred as a result of a motor vehicle accident, and 32.8% followed a fall from a standing height. This emphasizes the significant changes in the epidemiology of this fracture.

A review of the literature shows that there are reports of a decreasing incidence of tibial diaphyseal fractures. Weiss et al.[43] analyzed tibial diaphyseal fractures in Sweden between 1998 and 2000. They had an overall incidence of $17/10^5$/year, but this decreased from $18.7/10^5$/year in 1998 to $16.1/10^5$/year in 2004. They had a lower prevalence of open fractures with an overall rate of 12%, but they also found that the rate decreased through their study period. They found that 48% of their fractures were caused by a fall from a standing height, with only 21% being caused by a motor vehicle accident. Sweden is an affluent country and it is likely that other countries will have the same changes in epidemiology in the future. Our results clearly suggest that it is occurring in the United Kingdom.

Tibial diaphyseal fractures have a Type A distribution curve (see Table 3-2). We had a higher rate of open fractures than seen in the Swedish study, but the epidemiology of both closed and open fractures were very similar. The average ages for the closed and open fracture groups were 38.9 and 43.1 years, respectively, with gender ratios of 79/21 and 75/25 (male/female). In the open fracture group, 62.5% were caused by motor vehicle accidents with 80% of these fractures being Gustilo[18] Type III in severity. In the closed fracture group, 36.8% followed a simple fall, 35.1% occurred in sports accidents, and only 8.8% were caused by motor vehicle accidents.

There is an important subgroup of tibial diaphyseal fractures: those with an intact fibula. These comprised 21.9% of the tibial fracture group. Their epidemiological characteristics are different in that the average age was 29.1 years and the gender ratio was 88/12 (male/female). This group of fractures has a Type B distribution.

Fibula

A fracture that has received little attention in the orthopaedic literature is the isolated fibular fracture which is not related to an ankle fracture or a tibial diaphyseal fracture. These are rare injuries, and Table 3-4 shows that they accounted for only 0.3% of the fractures seen in the study year. The average age of the patients was 40.6 years, and the fracture has a Type B distribution. There are two basic types of fibular fracture with 57.7% occurring in the fibular diaphysis and 42.3% in the proximal fibula. The average ages and gender ratios were 38.4 years for males and 42.2 years for females and 87/13 and 64/36, respectively. Most of the fractures (34.6%) followed sport injuries, with 26.9% occurring as a result of a motor vehicle accident and 19.2% as a result of a fall from a standing height.

Distal Tibia

Distal tibia, or tibial plafond, fractures are comparatively uncommon, accounting for only 0.7% of all fractures. They have a Type D distribution occurring in younger and older males but also in older females. We were surprised by the low rate of open distal tibial fractures (see Table 3-7) compared with 2000,[8] when 16.6% of distal tibial fractures were open. This suggests that there are fewer fractures being caused by high-energy injuries when compared with 8 years ago. The most common cause of distal tibial fractures in 2007–2008 was falls from a standing height (32.6%), followed by falls from a height (26.9%) and sporting injuries (21.1%). The average ages of these groups was 61.1, 34.1, and 35.4 years, respectively, showing the increasing incidence of these fractures in the elderly.

Ankle

Ankle fractures are common, accounting for about 9% of all fractures (see Table 3-4). Overall, they have a Type A distribution. If they are classified according to the location of the fracture, it is apparent that lateral malleolar fractures have a Type A distribution whereas medial malleolar fractures have a Type D distribution. Suprasyndesmotic fractures have a Type C distribution and both bimalleolar and trimalleolar fractures have a Type E distribution and should be regarded as fragility fractures. This should not be a surprise as 50 years ago, Buhr and Cooke[2] drew attention to the numbers of elderly patients who presented with bimalleolar fractures.

Recently, Kannus et al.[27] have drawn attention to the increased incidence of ankle fractures in patients aged at least 60 years since the early 1970s. Like hip fractures, a review of the Finnish hospital register has shown that the incidence of elderly ankle fractures stabilized in Finland in the 1990s. The authors recorded an overall incidence of $57/10^5$/year in 1970, compared with $169/10^5$/year in 1997. Since then, the incidence has declined. In women, it has declined from $199/10^5$/year in 1997 to $173/10^5$/year in 2006, and in men, the equivalent values were $123/10^5$/year and $100/10^5$/year. In 2007–2008, our incidence in women aged 60 years or more was $214.1/10^5$/year with $95.5/10^5$/year being recorded in males. Thus, the incidence in the United Kingdom appears to be somewhat more than in Finland.

Table 3-24 shows the basic epidemiological criteria for ankle fractures divided according to the traditional Weber classification.[42] It shows that ankle fractures tend to occur as a result of low-energy trauma as might be expected from the average ages and gender ratios. Suprasyndesmotic fractures are less commonly caused by simple falls (50.6%). They are more commonly caused by sports injuries (20.7%) and motor vehicle accidents (7.8%).

Talus

Fractures of the talus are relatively uncommon. They account for 0.5% of fractures and have a Type C distribution, being commonly seen in young males and females. For the purposes of describing their basic epidemiology, Table 3-25 shows talar fractures divided into head, neck, and body fractures. Head fractures are very rare and only one was treated in the study year. The other talar fractures were fairly evenly divided between talar body and talar neck fractures. Those fractures caused by a simple fall tend to be minor avulsion fractures of the neck, occurring in the few elderly patients who presented with talar fractures. The average age of this group was 56.1 years compared with 26.0 years for the sports injury group and 23.2 years for the patients injured in motor vehicle accidents.

Calcaneus

Calcaneal fractures are relatively uncommon and account for 0.8% of fractures. They have a different distribution from talar fractures, and they have a Type G distribution curve with an increasing number of elderly females presenting with calcaneal

fractures. Conventionally, calcaneal fractures are separated into intra-articular fractures, involving the posterior facet, extra-articular fractures, and fractures of the processes or tuberosities. In Table 3-26, the latter two fracture types have been combined and the epidemiological characteristics of intra-articular posterior facet fractures and extra-articular fractures are presented. Intra-articular fractures have a Type B distribution and tend to affect younger men. Extra-articular fractures have a Type G distribution curve, and there are a number of older men and women who present with these fractures. The most common mode of injury is a fall from a height, and if the intra-articular group is examined, it can be seen that 70.6% of these fractures were caused by a fall from a height.

Midfoot

Fractures of the cuboid, navicular, and cuneiform bones are unusual and together they comprise 0.5% of fractures. They have a Type C distribution mainly affecting younger males and females. Table 3-27 shows the epidemiological characteristics for fractures of the cuboid, navicular, and cuneiform. It shows that fractures of the cuboid are the most common midfoot fractures. Fractures of the cuneiform most commonly affect the medial cuneiform, with 80% of the cuneiform fractures being located in the medial cuneiform. In 20% of patients with cuneiform fractures, more than one cuneiform was fractured.

Metatarsus

Altogether, there were 498 metatarsal fractures comprising about 7% of all the fractures seen in the study year. In fact,

TABLE 3-25 The Basic Epidemiological Characteristics of Talar Fractures

	Prevalence (%)	Average Age (yrs)	Gender Ratio (Male/Female) (%)
Neck	50.0	40.2	56/44
Body	46.8	36.2	67/33
Head	3.2	21.0	100/0
Common causes	Fall (standing height)	28.1%	
	Sport	21.8%	
	Motor vehicle accident	18.7%	

TABLE 3-24 The Basic Epidemiological Characteristics of Ankle Fractures

	Prevalence (%)	Average Age (yrs)	Gender Ratio (Male/Female) (%)
Infrasyndesmotic	26.3	50.8	40/60
Transsyndesmotic	61.4	49.9	47/53
Suprasyndesmotic	12.2	42.7	58/42
Common causes	Fall (standing height)	65.1%	
	Sport	14.2%	
	Fall (stairs)	7.7%	

TABLE 3-26 The Basic Characteristics of Calcaneal Fractures

	Prevalence (%)	Average Age (yrs)	Gender Ratio (Male/Female) (%)
Extra-articular	68.5	38.6	76/24
Intra-articular	31.5	39.8	88/12
Common causes	Fall (height)	61.8%	
	Fall (standing height)	16.4%	
	Fall (stairs)	9.1%	

TABLE 3-27	The Basic Epidemiological Characteristics of Midfoot Fractures		
	Prevalence (%)	Average Age (yrs)	Gender Ratio (Male/Female) (%)
Cuboid	45.9	41.9	59/41
Navicular	27.0	41.3	30/70
Cuneiform	27.0	50.7	40/60
Common causes	Fall (standing height) 43.2% Fall (stairs) 18.9% Motor vehicle accident 16.2%		

there were only 359 isolated metatarsal fractures with a further 40 patients presenting with multiple fractures having fractured between two and five metatarsals. Overall, patients who present with metatarsal fractures have a Type A distribution. The basic epidemiology of the different isolated metatarsals and the multiple group is shown in Table 3-28. Fractures of the fifth metatarsal are by far the most common, and they have a slightly different epidemiological profile from other isolated metatarsal fractures. They more commonly occur in women, and patients with fractures of the fourth and fifth metatarsals tend to have a higher average age than patients with fractures of the first, second, and third metatarsals. The most common combination of multiple metatarsal fractures are fractures of the second and third metatarsals, which accounted for 32.5% of the multiple fractures. The most common combination of three metatarsal fractures was seen in the second, third, and fourth metatarsals, which made up 40% of the multiple fracture group. Ten percent of patients with multiple metatarsal fractures presented with fractures of the second, third, fourth, and fifth metatarsals. As with metacarpal and finger phalangeal fractures, it is interesting to observe that patients who present with multiple metatarsal fractures tend to be older. In fractures of the fifth metatarsal,

TABLE 3-28	The Basic Epidemiological Characteristics of Metatarsal Fractures		
	Prevalence (%)	Average Age (yrs)	Gender Ratio (Male/Female) (%)
First	3.4	35.4	82/18
Second	3.8	41.8	58/42
Third	3.6	35.9	59/41
Fourth	2.8	45.1	50/50
Fifth	58.4	45.6	31/69
Multiple	28.0	65.2	60/40
Common causes	Fall (standing height) 67.6% Sport 9.2% Direct blow/ crush 6.6%		

78.4% resulted from a simple fall, 8.6% from a sports injury, and 2.1% from a fall from a height.

Toe Phalanges
Toe fractures are fairly common, accounting for 3%–4% of all fractures. They have a Type C distribution affecting young males and females, and unsurprisingly, 53.7% were caused by direct blows.

Pelvis and Acetabulum
Pelvic fractures account for about 2% of all fractures. There has been considerable interest in their management over the last 20–25 years, and the implication is that they occur as the result of high-energy trauma. Some clearly do but the vast majority of pelvic fractures are simple pubic rami fractures occurring in the frail elderly. There is a marked female preponderance and overall they have a Type E distribution. In Table 3-29, pelvic fractures have been divided into pelvic and acetabular fractures to permit a more detailed analysis. If acetabular fractures are considered separately, it is apparent that they have a Type G distribution with younger and older males and older females presenting with these injuries. Pelvic fractures have a Type E distribution. A review of the common causes indicates that the majority of patients are injured in a simple fall and the average age of this group is 82.6 years. This is the highest average age for a particular fracture caused by an individual mode of injury in the study and suggests that the patients who present with pubic rami fractures following a simple fall are very frail indeed. Patients who sustain a pelvic fracture as a result of a fall from a height have an average age of 38.6 years, and those who sustain a pelvic fracture as a result of a motor vehicle accident have an average age of 47.2 years.

Vertebral Fractures
We did not analyze spinal fractures in 2007–2008 because of the difficulty in retrieving them and the impossibility of producing accurate figures. In 2000,[8] we documented the prevalence of spinal fractures to be 0.7% and the incidence to be $7.5/10^5/$ year but of course the correct figures must be much higher. Most thoracolumbar fractures are fragility fractures occurring in older patients and the majority are not admitted to hospital. We assessed thoracolumbar fractures that were admitted to hospital as having a Type B distribution, but we felt that the correct distribution was Type A when the osteoporotic fractures were

TABLE 3-29	The Basic Epidemiological Characteristics of Pelvic Fractures		
	Prevalence (%)	Average Age (yrs)	Gender Ratio (Male/Female) (%)
Pelvis	86.6	70.0	33/67
Acetabulum	13.4	56.7	76/24
Common causes	Fall (standing height) 63.0% Fall (height) 18.1% Motor vehicle accident 8.7%		

included. One could even argue that there are so many osteoporotic thoracolumbar fractures in elderly women that the correct distribution curve is in fact Type E. We documented that cervical fractures had a Type H distribution. See Table 3-40 for the epidemiological characteristics of traumatic spine fractures admitted to Baltimore in 2007.

Cooper et al.[6] estimated the age and gender adjusted incidence of clinically diagnosed vertebral fractures in the United States as $117/10^5$/year, but the figure is likely to vary considerably in different parts of the world. In a recent study, Grados et al.[16] analyzed the prevalence of vertebral fractures in elderly French women. They found that 22.8% of women with an average age of 80.1 years had a vertebral fracture. The prevalence and the number of fractures increased with age such that 41.4% of women aged at least 85 years had vertebral fractures.

Epidemiology of Adolescent Fractures

There is very little information available about adolescent fractures. This is because epidemiological studies tend to concentrate on adult or pediatric fractures with a dividing age of 14, 16, or 18 years. Unfortunately, adolescent fractures are lost in the division. They are an important group because fractures in adolescent males in particular are common and the curves shown in Figure 3-2 do not emphasize this. To study adolescent fracture epidemiology, the epidemiological data from the year 2000,[8] which was presented in the sixth edition of Rockwood and Green, was combined with the pediatric data from the same year.[35] Adolescent fractures were defined as being between 10–19 years.

Figure 3-3 shows the age and gender distribution curves for the adolescent population. It can be see that there is a significant rise in the incidence of adolescent male fractures from 10–13 years. In fact, male adolescents had a fracture incidence of $38.3/10^3$/year, which was second only to the incidence of fractures in females over 80 years of age which, in 2000, was $45.5/10^3$/year. There was a progressive decrease in fracture incidence in boys after 13 years and in girls after 11 years, and at 19 years of age, the fracture incidence in males was 3.6 times that in females. The overall incidence in adolescents was $24.3/10^3$/year and the gender ratio was 72/28 (male/female).

Table 3-30 shows the incidence of the different fractures seen in children, adolescents, and adults in 2000. What is striking is the very high incidence of fractures of the distal radius, finger phalanges, metacarpus, clavicle, metatarsus, and ankle in adolescents. Some fractures have a lower incidence in adolescents and these tend to be the fragility fractures, although calcaneal fractures are rare in the adolescent period. In other fractures, such as distal humerus fractures, the adolescent group is clearly midway between the high incidence in childhood and the lower incidence in adulthood. Menon et al.[32] divided the adolescents into male and female junior and senior adolescents of 10–14 years and 15–19 years. They examined the influence of social deprivation in these groups and showed a correlation between social deprivation and fracture incidence in senior male and female adolescents and junior male adolescents. They also found that social deprivation was an independent predictor of fractures of the hand in senior adolescent males, fractures of the upper limb in junior adolescent males, and in fractures of the upper limb and distal radius in senior adolescent females.

Epidemiology of Patients Aged at Least 90 Years

The other important cohort of patients that has not previously been analyzed are those patients aged 90 years or more, the 90+ group. Nonogenarians and centenarians are becoming an increasingly important part of society, and the National Office of Statistics in the United Kingdom has shown that they are the age group that is increasing most quickly.[34] In the last United States census,[41] it was estimated that 90+ patients comprised 0.65% of the population, the equivalent figure in the United Kingdom being 0.58%. In 2025, it is estimated that the 90+ group will represent 1.2% of the population of the United Kingdom. Thus, the orthopaedic surgeons of the future will have to treat more fractures in this difficult group of patients.

Unfortunately, this increase in the population is not being matched by better health in most countries. In 2008, the National Office of Statistics in the United Kingdom[33] stated that while the population had been living longer in the previous 23 years, the time that both sexes could be in poorer health or have a limiting illness or disability had risen between 1981 and 2004. There was a slight improvement after 2004, which may tally with the decline in osteoporotic fractures in Finland[26,27]

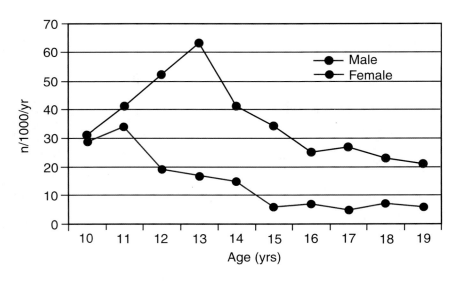

FIGURE 3-3 The age and gender specific fracture distribution curves for adolescents. Data from Menon et al.[32]

TABLE 3-30	Fracture-Specific Incidences in Adolescents, Children, and Adults		
	Adolescents (10–19 yrs)	Children (0–13 yrs)	Adults (≥14 yrs)
Distal radius	659.0	689.7	195.2
Finger phalanges	439.9	294.7	107.3
Metacarpus	405.3	111.8	130.3
Clavicle	139.8	137.9	36.5
Metatarsus	132.7	99.3	75.4
Ankle	118.6	60.6	100.8
Toe phalanges	110.1	63.7	39.6
Carpus	69.2	19.9	29.7
Forearm diaphysis	63.5	111.8	13.8
Proximal forearm	55.1	59.6	55.5
Tibial diaphysis	52.2	44.9	21.5
Distal tibia	35.3	33.4	7.9
Proximal humerus	29.7	38.7	63.0
Distal humerus	32.5	166.2	5.8
Spine	12.7	5.2	7.5
Proximal tibia	11.3	4.2	13.3
Humeral diaphysis	11.3	5.2	12.9
Patella	9.9	4.2	10.7
Femoral diaphysis	8.5	16.7	10.3
Pelvis	9.9	4.2	17.0
Calcaneus	7.1	2.1	13.7
Midfoot	5.7	4.2	5.0
Talus	5.7	1.0	3.2
Proximal femur	5.7	1.0	129.4
Distal femur	2.8	5.2	4.5
Scapula	2.8	0	3.2
	2430.2	1986.5	1113.3

The data used in this table is from Court-Brown and Caesar[8] and Rennie et al.[35]

that has already been discussed, but it seems likely that increasing longevity is going to be paired with increasing morbidity and hospitalization for a range of different conditions including orthopaedic trauma. The data from the Edinburgh Orthopaedic Trauma Unit in 2000 suggests that this is already occurring in orthopaedic trauma. Court-Brown and Clement[9] showed that in 2000, 0.58% of the population aged 90 years or more accounted for 3.02% of the fractures, 8.7% of the inpatient admissions, and 7.6% of the orthopaedic trauma surgery.

Table 3-31 shows the epidemiology of fractures in the 90+ group in 2007–2008. Altogether, they accounted for 4.4% of all fractures, which represents an increase compared with 2000. The prevalence of male fractures was 1.8% compared with 6.8% in females. The overall incidence was 7707.7/10⁵/year with the male incidence being 6568.5/10⁵/year and the female incidence 8032.3/10⁵/year. The high incidence relates to the relatively low numbers of 90+ patients in the population, with 22.2% of the group being male and 77.8% being female. As expected, proximal femoral fractures are by far the most common fractures seen by orthopaedic surgeons, but 12.1% of fractures were other lower limb fractures, 30.9% were upper limb fractures, and 7.2% were pelvic fractures. Fractures of the proximal femur, distal radius and ulna, proximal humerus, pelvis, and femoral diaphysis account for 83.1% of all the fractures. The ankle fractures were all transsyndesmotic fractures and the proximal forearm fractures were either olecranon fractures or fractures of the proximal radius and ulna, both of which have a Type F distribution. Fractures of the foot and hand are extremely rare in this group, there being only 1 (0.1%) foot fracture and 6 (0.4%) hand fractures. As might be predicted, 95.4% of the 90+ group sustained their fractures as a result of a fall from a standing height. A further 2.3% had a fall down stairs and only 2 (0.7%) patients were involved in a motor vehicle accident. Both were pedestrians. Only 5 (1.6%) of the fractures were open.

TABLE 3-31	The Prevalence, Incidence, and Gender Ratios of Fractures in the 90+ Group in 2007–2008			
	Number	Prevalence (%)	Incidence (n/10⁵/yr)	Gender Ratio (Male/Female) (%)
Proximal femur	153	49.8	3841.3	21/79
Distal radius/ulna	35	11.4	878.7	9/91
Proximal humerus	33	10.7	828.5	37/63
Pelvis	22	5.9	552.3	16/84
Femoral diaphysis	12	3.9	301.3	17/83
Ankle	9	2.9	226.0	0/100
Distal femur	6	1.9	150.6	17/83
Proximal forearm	6	1.9	150.6	17/83
Tibial plateau	6	1.9	150.6	0/100
Clavicle	5	1.6	126.5	20/80
Distal humerus	5	1.6	126.5	20/80
Finger phalanges	5	1.6	126.5	40/60
Humeral diaphysis	4	1.3	100.4	25/75
Distal tibia	1	0.3	25.1	0/100
Metacarpal	1	0.3	25.1	0/100
Metatarsal	1	0.3	25.1	100/0
Patella	1	0.3	25.1	0/100
Scapula	1	0.3	25.1	100/0
Tibial diaphysis	1	0.3	25.1	0/100
	307	100	7707.7	19/81

R. Adams Cowley Shock Trauma Center, Baltimore, Maryland

A review of the patients treated in the R. Adams Cowley Shock Trauma Center in Baltimore in 2007 showed that there were 2325 patients who presented with 4744 fractures. The gender ratio was 71/29 (male/female), and 70% of the patients were admitted directly from the accident with a further 30% being transferred from another hospital. The average age of the patients was 41.7 years, with the average age of males and females being 39.3 years and 47.6 years, respectively. The average Injury Severity Score (ISS) was 17, with a range of 1–75 and a mode of 9. There was a diverse racial mix of patients with 65.9% being Caucasian. A further 25.8% were Black, 4.2% were Hispanic, and 1.2% were Asian. The remaining 2.1% of patients were from other races. The relative severity of injury in patients admitted to Baltimore is highlighted by the fact that 16.5% of the fractures were open and the hospital mortality was 4.2%.

Table 3-32 shows the prevalence of the fractures admitted to Baltimore in 2007. There is a considerable difference between Tables 3-4 and 3-32, illustrating the differences between Baltimore and Edinburgh. In Baltimore, 32.5% of all the fractures involved the spine and pelvis, whereas in Edinburgh 28.1% of fractures involved the distal radius and ulna and the proximal femur. This difference encapsulates the different populations treated by Baltimore and Edinburgh. Another significant difference is the high prevalence of diaphyseal fractures in Baltimore. Fractures of the forearm, femoral, and tibial diaphyses consti-

tute 18.3% of the Baltimore fractures compared with 3.2% of the Edinburgh fractures. However, the prevalence of humeral diaphyseal fractures was similar, although many more humeral diaphyseal fractures were open in Baltimore. Predictably, the prevalence of lower energy metaphyseal fractures, such as those of the proximal femur, proximal humerus, proximal forearm, and distal radius, was much less in Baltimore as were fractures of the hand and forefoot.

Open Fractures

A comparison of Tables 3-7 and 3-32 shows a significant difference in the numbers of open fractures in Baltimore compared with Edinburgh. In Baltimore, 16.5% of fractures were open compared with 2.6% in Edinburgh. In Baltimore, 60% of the open fractures were in the lower limb or pelvis with the largest number, as in Edinburgh, being in the tibial diaphysis. However, the highest prevalence of all open fractures was in the distal humerus where 55% were open and 20% were caused by gunshot wounds. In the pelvis, the overall figure of 5.2% open fractures was made up of 23 (8.7%) open pelvic fractures and 5 (1.9%) open acetabular fractures, but it is interesting to note that all 5 open acetabular fractures were caused by gunshot wounds (see Table 3-39).

Multiple Fractures

As with open fractures, the data regarding multiple fractures is very different between Baltimore and Edinburgh. In Baltimore,

TABLE 3-32	The Numbers and Prevalence of Fractures Admitted to Baltimore in 2007*			
	Number	Prevalence (%)	(#)	Open Fractures (%)
Spine	1004	21.2	24	2.4
Pelvis	535	11.3	28	55.2
Tibial diaphysis	313	6.6	155	49.5
Forearm diaphyses	303	6.4	85	28.1
Distal tibia/ankle	255	5.4	73	28.6
Femoral diaphysis	253	5.3	55	21.7
Clavicle	201	4.2	6	3.0
Scapula	192	4.0	21	10.9
Distal radius/ ulna	186	3.9	21	11.3
Proximal tibia	146	3.1	27	18.5
Metacarpal	132	2.8	29	22.0
Proximal femur	120	2.5	13	10.8
Finger phalanx	105	2.2	35	33.3
Proximal humerus	102	2.1	10	9.8
Metatarsal	98	2.1	14	14.3
Calcaneus	96	2.0	14	14.6
Distal femur	93	2.0	35	37.6
Proximal forearm	89	1.9	27	30.3
Talus	80	1.7	8	10.0
Sternum	75	1.6	3	4.0
Humeral diaphysis	70	1.5	14	20.0
Patella	64	1.3	30	46.9
Midfoot	61	1.3	3	4.9
Distal humerus	60	1.3	33	55.0
Carpus	56	1.2	5	8.9
Toe phalanx	55	1.2	16	29.1
	4744	100	784	16.5

*The numbers and prevalence of open fractures are also shown.

only 23.5% of patients presented with an isolated injury with a further 22.4% presenting with two fractures, 16.1% with three fractures, and 12.9% with four fractures. The remaining 25.1% presented with between 5 and 15 fractures, with 3.1% of patients presenting with at least 10 fractures.

Distribution Curves
It is impossible to produce accurate distribution curves from the Baltimore data because there is no knowledge as to the size of the captive population. However, Figure 3-4 shows age and gender specific frequency curves of the fractures presenting to Baltimore in 2007. It can be seen that there is a slight increase in fractures in older females, and, if one takes into account the fact that there is a markedly reduced number of older females in the population, it is likely that in fact the overall distribution of the fractures in Baltimore is a Type A distribution with a unimodal distribution in younger men and in older females. This is also suggested by a review of the frequency curves of

other Level I Trauma Centers.[40] It should be noted that in a number of the fractures in Baltimore, there is a dip in frequency between the ages of 30 and 45, particularly in males. This is shown in Figure 3-4.

Mode of Injury
The different modes of injury are recorded in Table 3-33. This shows that about 60% of the fractures treated in Baltimore occurred as the result of motor vehicle accidents with a further 12.3% occurring as the result of a fall from a height and 7.5% following a fall from a standing height. Sports injuries are relatively rare as they are usually low-energy injuries and are treated elsewhere. In Baltimore, 51.8% of the sports injuries were caused by horse riding accidents and were associated with more severe fractures.

The data is obviously very different to that of Edinburgh (see Table 3-9) and emphasizes the role of Level I Trauma Centers in treating severely injured patients who are usually injured as

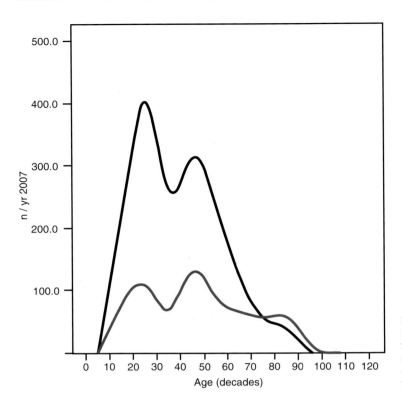

FIGURE 3-4 The age and gender frequency curves from Baltimore. These are not incidence curves and given the increase in frequency in older females and the relatively small number of older females in the population, it is likely that this is a Type A curve (see Figure 3-2) although the younger male peak is greater than the older female peak.

the result of motor vehicle accidents. The other major difference is that 6.5% of fractures are caused by gunshot wounds. In fact, the only similarity between the two hospitals is in the prevalence of fractures caused by falls down stairs, although there was a similar number of fractures for which there was no information about the mode of injury.

Motor Vehicle Accidents

Table 3-33 shows that motor vehicle accidents are responsible for the majority of fractures admitted to Baltimore. Again, there are considerable differences from the Edinburgh data. Table 3-34 shows that in Baltimore, vehicle occupants were most commonly admitted after motor vehicle accidents with 64% of the patients being either vehicle drivers or passengers. A further 19.7% of patients were motorcyclists, with 13.3% being pedes-

trians and only 3.1% being cyclists. Table 3-34 shows the average ISS for each type of patient. This indicates that the pedestrians were the most seriously injured followed by vehicle occupants and motor cyclists. These figures are considerably different from the Edinburgh figures shown in Table 3-12, and they suggest that there may be considerable differences in the type of transport used in Edinburgh and Baltimore. It is interesting to note that the prevalence of fractures in pedestrians is not dissimilar between the two hospitals, but a comparison of the numbers of fractures in other patients suggests that there are relatively more cyclists and motorcyclists in Edinburgh than in Baltimore. The Edinburgh figures for the prevalence of open fracture in pedestrians also indicate the severity of injury in this group of patients.

Table 3-35 shows the importance of protective equipment for vehicle occupants and motorcyclists involved in motor vehicle accidents. Unrestrained drivers with no air bags fitted in their cars had an average ISS of 22.3. This dropped to 17.4 if a seatbelt was used and, interestingly, it dropped to 15.4 if a seatbelt was not used but the air bag deployed in the accident. If both a seatbelt was used and an air bag deployed in the accident the average ISS was lower at 14.5. These figures emphasize the importance of both seatbelts and air bags in preventing injuries. The relative figures were the same for vehicle occupants. Almost 20% of motorcyclists were not wearing protective headgear when they were involved in the motor vehicle accident. These motorcyclists had a higher ISS than those wearing headgear.

The review of Tables 3-32 and 3-34 illustrates the relative severity of the injuries admitted to Baltimore. Table 3-34 shows that the most common fracture seen in vehicle occupants, pedestrians, and motorcyclists was a tibial diaphyseal fracture, while Table 3-32 shows the prevalence of open fractures indicat-

TABLE 3-33	**The Numbers and Prevalences of Fractures for the Eight Basic Modes of Injury in Baltimore**	
	Number	Prevalence (%)
Fall (standing)	173	7.5
Fall (stairs)	96	4.1
Fall (height)	285	12.3
Direct blow/assault/crush	76	3.3
Sport	43	1.8
Motor vehicle accident	1410	60.6
Gunshot	151	6.5
Others	91	3.9

TABLE 3-34	The Epidemiology of Patients Involved in Motor Vehicle Accidents in Baltimore in 2007*				
	Number	Prevalence (%)	ISS (Average)	ISS (Range)	
Vehicle driver	679	48.2	18.1	1–75	Tibial diaphysis Pneumothorax Cervical spine injury
Vehicle passenger	223	15.8	20.2	4–75	Tibial diaphysis Pneumothorax Cervical spine injury
Pedestrian	187	13.3	21.5	1–75	Tibial diaphysis Pneumothorax Brain injury
Motorcyclist	278	19.7	17.5	2–75	Tibial diaphysis Pneumothorax Clavicle
Cyclist	43	3.1	17.2	4–75	Cervical spine injury Clavicle Acetabulum

*The most common fractures are shown.

ing that the fractures admitted to Baltimore were usually very severe. The contrast with the Edinburgh data shown in Tables 3-7 and 3-12 is remarkable, but it is difficult to know whether the contrast is because of a different spectrum of injury in Baltimore or because the less severely injured patients go to other hospitals. However, it is likely that both vehicle occupants and motorcyclists make more use of protective equipment in Edinburgh than in Baltimore, and this may well account for some of the differences in the spectrum of injuries between the two hospitals.

Gunshot Fractures

A review of the fractures caused by gunshot injuries in Baltimore in 2007 shows that they accounted for 6.5% of all fractures. Gunshot fractures had a Type B distribution; the patients having an average age of 28 years and 93% of them being male. There were racial differences with 83% of the patients being Black and 15% being Caucasian. The average ISS was 16 and the mortality was 5%. There were fewer injuries to other body systems than seen with blunt trauma (Tables 3-34, 3-36, 3-37, and 3-38). Overall, 7% of patients had an injury to the central nervous system, 30% had thoracic injuries, 33% had abdominal

injuries, and 22% had associated spinal injuries. Table 3-39 shows the fractures were caused by gunshot injuries. The most common fractures were in the tibia and fibula, pelvis, and hand.

There have been relatively few analyses of civilian gunshot fractures in adults but Hakenson et al.[20] also noted a Type B distribution. They also recorded that, in 1994, 56% of the males were unemployed, 79% were uninsured, 68% were documented substance abusers, and 65% of the injuries were probably related to illicit drug activity. The situation is probably not dissimilar now.

Upper Limb Fractures

Upper limb fractures represented 31.5% of the fractures admitted to Baltimore during 2007. The epidemiological characteristics of the commonest four upper limb fractures are shown in Table 3-36.

Clavicle Fractures

The most common upper limb fracture was that of the clavicle which interestingly had a similar prevalence and average age to those seen in Edinburgh (see Tables 3-4 and 3-5). The gender ratio is also similar, but there was a slightly higher prevalence

TABLE 3-35	The Use of Protective Equipment in Baltimore in 2007					
Protective Equipment	Vehicle Drivers		Vehicle Passengers		Motorcyclists	
	%	Average ISS	%	Average ISS	%	Average ISS
None	21.5	22.3	41.2	22.7	19.0	22.2
Seatbelt	36.7	17.4	35.0	20.1		
Airbag	6.4	15.4	4.0	16.1		
Seatbelt and airbag	28.5	14.5	13.9	15.6		
Helmet					78.0	16.7

TABLE 3-36   **The Epidemiology of the Four Most Common Upper Limb Fractures That Presented to Baltimore in 2007**

	Clavicle	Scapula	Distal Radius	Humeral Diaphysis
Prevalence (%)	4.2	4.0	3.9	1.5
Average age (yr)	41	42	44	38
Gender ratio (male/female, %)	70/30	83/17	65/35	74/26
Open (%)	3.0	10.9	11.3	20.0
Average ISS	21	24	17	21
Mode of injury	MVA driver 24% Motorcyclist 23% Passenger 16%	MVA driver 30% Motorcyclist 22% Fall (Height) 13%	Fall 40% MVA driver 26% Motorcyclist 15%	MVA driver 24% Fall 16% Motorcyclist 13%
Associated fractures	Scapula 20% Thoracic spine 20% Pelvis 17%	Clavicle 20% Thoracic spine 20% Skull 19%	Ulna 54% Skull 16% Face 13%	Proximal humerus 19% Lumbar spine 17% Tibial diaphysis 14%
Associated injuries (%)				
Central nervous system	43	50	32	39
Chest	67	74	34	43
Abdomen	23	40	23	31
Spine	22	43	28	30
Lower limb	53	55	39	37

TABLE 3-37   **The Epidemiology of the Four Most Common Lower Limb Fractures That Presented to Baltimore in 2007**

	Tibial Diaphysis	Femoral Diaphysis	Calcaneus	Distal Femur
Prevalence (%)	6.6	4.5	2.0	2.0
Average age (yr)	39	34	38	47
Gender ratio (male/female, %)	74/26	71/29	70/30	55/45
Open (%)	49.5	23.6	14.6	37.6
Average ISS	18	21	13	19
Mode of injury	Pedestrian 24% MVA driver 23% Motorcyclist 16%	MVA driver 36% Motorcyclist 19% Passenger 17%	Fall (Height) 41% MVA driver 34% Passenger 8%	MVA driver 26% Fall 21% Motorcyclist 19%
Associated fractures	Pelvis 16% Femoral diaphysis 15% Lumbar spine 13%	Tibial diaphysis 22% Pelvis 19% Acetabulum 13%	Fibula 30% Talus 26% Tarsus 26%	Femoral diaphysis 19% Tibial diaphysis 16% Lumbar spine 14%
Associated injuries (%)				
Central nervous system	26	31	27	15
Chest	36	43	33	48
Abdomen	28	36	22	38
Spine	25	20	26	25
Upper limb	42	42	41	53

TABLE 3-38	The Epidemiology of Pelvic and Acetabular Fractures in Baltimore in 2007	
	Acetabulum	Pelvis
Prevalence (%)	5.7	5.6
Average age (yr)	42	39
Gender ratio (male/female, %)	70/30	68/32
Open (%)	1.9	8.7
Average ISS	21	23
Mode of injury	MVA driver 43% Fall 17% Passenger 12%	MVA driver 29% Fall 21% Pedestrian 13%
Associated fractures	Lumbar spine 17% Tibial diaphysis 12% Femoral diaphysis 12%	Lumbar spine 32% Thoracic spine 13% Cervical spine 13%
Associated injuries (%)		
Central nervous system	32	33
Chest	46	54
Abdomen	42	52
Spine	27	41
Upper limb	46	49

of open fractures. Given the high-energy nature of the fractures admitted to Baltimore and the subcutaneous location of the clavicle, a rate of 3% open clavicle fractures is surprisingly low. The mean ISS for patients who had clavicle fractures was 21, and Table 3-36 shows that motor vehicle accidents account for the majority of clavicle fractures. It also shows that there was a high rate of associated chest and lower limb injuries and that 20% of the patients who presented with clavicle fractures actually had a floating shoulder because of an associated scapular fracture. The other commonly associated fractures were pelvic and spinal. It is difficult to assess the overall distribution curve because of the impossibility of calculating incidence in the Baltimore population. However, there was a unimodal distribution affecting younger and middle-aged males and a bimodal distribution affecting younger and older females suggesting that the clavicle fracture in Baltimore had a Type D distribution. It is worth noting, however, that there was a dip in the frequency of clavicle fractures between the ages of 20 and 50 in males.

Scapular Fractures

Unlike the clavicle, there were significant differences in the prevalence and spectrum of scapular fractures in Baltimore and Edinburgh. In Edinburgh, it is apparent that the scapula is becoming much more common in older patients, but in Baltimore it remains a high-energy injury predominantly seen in younger males. The average age of patients who presented with scapular fractures was 42 years and the gender ratio was 83/17 (male/female). The severity of injury associated with scapular fractures is highlighted in Table 3-36 by the comparatively high average ISS of 24 and the very high prevalence of open fractures. Table 3-36 also shows that the majority of scapular fractures occur as a result of motor vehicle accidents, although it is apparent that a number were caused by falls from a height. There was also a high rate of associated injuries to the central nervous

system, chest, and lower limb in particular. The high male prevalence and the relatively low average age suggests that the distribution curve for scapular fractures in Baltimore is Type B.

Distal Radial Fractures

Distal radial fractures have a very different epidemiology to that seen in Edinburgh. They occur in 3.9% of patients in Baltimore, and the average age is 44 years. There was a high prevalence of open fractures, but Table 3-36 shows that the average ISS of the patients who presented with distal radial fractures was lower than in other upper limb fractures. The majority of patients were injured in a fall, but the high-energy nature of these fractures, when compared to Edinburgh, is highlighted by the numbers of patients who were injured in motor vehicle accidents. Table 3-36 shows that the patients had fewer associated injuries than patients with clavicle or scapular fractures. The distribution curve is essentially a Type D curve with a bimodal distribution in younger men and women, accentuating the high-energy nature of this fracture in Baltimore.

Humeral Diaphyseal Fractures

These fractures have a similar prevalence to that seen in Edinburgh but otherwise the epidemiology was very different. The average age was only 38 years, and there was a marked preponderance of males, unlike in Edinburgh where humeral diaphyseal fractures showed all the characteristics of a fragility fracture. In Baltimore, 20% of the humeral diaphyseal fractures were open and a considerable number were caused by motor vehicle accidents. The relative severity of these injuries was highlighted by the number that had associated proximal humeral or spinal fractures. In Baltimore, the distribution curve for humeral diaphyseal fractures was Type B.

TABLE 3-39 The Epidemiology of Fractures Caused by Gunshot Wounds in Baltimore in 2007

	Number	Prevalence (%)
Tibial and fibular diaphyses	24	9.8
Pelvis	23	9.4
Hand	23	9.4
Forearm diaphyses	16	6.6
Lumbar spine	15	6.1
Femoral diaphysis	13	5.3
Scapula	11	4.5
Distal humerus	10	4.1
Distal femur	10	4.1
Cervical spine	9	3.7
Skull	9	3.7
Thoracic spine	9	3.7
Proximal forearm	9	3.7
Humeral diaphysis	8	3.3
Proximal humerus	8	3.3
Foot	8	3.3
Proximal femur	8	3.3
Face	7	2.9
Acetabulum	5	2.0
Clavicle	5	2.0
Proximal tibia	5	2.0
Ankle	4	1.6
Calcaneus	1	0.4
Distal radius	1	0.4

Lower Limb Fractures

Overall, lower limb fractures accounted for 34.5% of the fractures treated in Baltimore in 2007. The epidemiological features of the four most common lower limb fractures are shown in Table 3-37.

Tibial Diaphyseal Fractures

Fractures of the tibial diaphysis were the most common long bone fracture to be treated in Baltimore and accounted for 6.6% of all fractures. The average age and gender ratio were virtually identical to Edinburgh but otherwise the epidemiological characteristics were very different. In both hospitals, tibial diaphyseal fractures were associated with the highest rate of open injuries. In Baltimore, 49.5% of tibial diaphyseal fractures were open compared with 21.9% in Edinburgh (see Table 3-7). The average ISS of the patients who presented with a tibial diaphyseal fracture was 18, and Table 3-37 shows that the patients often had other associated lower limb or pelvic fractures and that 42% of the patients presented with an associated upper limb fracture. Table 3-37 also shows that the majority of fractures were caused by motor vehicle accidents. As one might expect,

the overall distribution for tibial fractures in Baltimore was a Type C curve.

Femoral Diaphyseal Fractures

The epidemiological characteristics of femoral diaphyseal fracture in Baltimore are very different from Edinburgh. As one would expect in a Level I Trauma Center, the patients tend to be young and predominantly male. However, there are a number of younger females who present with femoral diaphyseal fractures in Baltimore. Overall, femoral fractures in Baltimore show a Type C distribution. As with tibial diaphyseal fractures, Table 3-37 shows that there is a high prevalence of open fractures (23.6%), and the average ISS was higher than seen with tibial diaphyseal fractures. Many patients were injured in motor vehicle accidents, and there was a high rate of pelvic fractures and other lower limb injuries.

Calcaneal Fractures

Calcaneal fractures were also more commonly seen in Baltimore than in Edinburgh with 2% of the fractures involving the calcaneus. The average age was lower than in Edinburgh (see Table 3-5), but the gender ratio was very similar. As in Edinburgh, the majority of patients were injured in a fall from a height, although there was a greater association with motor vehicle accidents in Baltimore. Overall, the patients were less significantly injured when compared with patients who presented with other lower limb injuries. However, not unexpectedly, there was a high rate of associated lower limb fractures, and 41% of patients presented with associated upper limb fractures (see Table 3-37). Relatively, more females presented with calcaneal fractures in Baltimore. Overall, the distribution showed a Type C curve, but there was a dip in frequency in both males and females between the ages of 30 and 45 years.

Distal Femoral Fractures

The epidemiology of distal femoral fractures in Baltimore was very different to that seen in Edinburgh, although it was the only fracture dealt with in Baltimore that had a true Type A distribution with a late peak in elderly females suggesting that these very difficult fractures may be transferred to the major Trauma Center from other hospitals in the area. The late female increase in frequency of distal femoral fractures accounts for the higher average age of 47 years, and Table 3-37 shows that 45% of the fractures occurred in females. A large number were caused by simple falls, but in younger patients, the fractures were often associated with motor vehicle accidents. Any associated injury was usually either spinal or another lower limb fracture. However, 53% of the patients presented with other upper limb fractures.

Pelvic and Acetabular Fractures

Although 11.3% of the fractures admitted to Baltimore involved the pelvis, Table 3-38 shows that there was an equal distribution between pelvic and acetabular fractures and, in fact, the epidemiological characteristics for both fractures were very similar with similar average ages, gender ratios, and average ISS. The only significant difference in the basic epidemiological criteria was that open pelvic fractures were much more common than open acetabular fractures. However, further analysis of Table

3-38 shows that there are other differences with more acetabular fractures occurring in vehicle drivers. The overall distribution curves for both pelvic and acetabular fractures in Baltimore are similar with both showing a Type C distribution although, as with other fracture in Baltimore, the pelvic distribution curve shows a drop in incidence between 30 and 45 years. This is not apparent in the acetabular group.

Spinal Fractures

Table 3-40 shows that spinal fractures were the most common fractures seen in Baltimore in 2007, accounting for 21.2% of the fractures. Table 3-40 shows the epidemiological characteristics of the fractures with particular reference to their location in the spine. It shows that the highest prevalence of fractures was in the cervical spine and that 20.1% of cervical spine fractures were associated with a dislocation. The epidemiological characteristics of thoracic and lumbar fractures are very similar, although there is a higher rate of dislocation in the thoracic spine. The mode of injury was very similar for all spinal fractures, but unsurprisingly there were different associated injuries depending on the location of the fracture.

The Baltimore data is somewhat different from data obtained from a large German Level I Trauma Center. Leucht et al.[29] analyzed 562 patients with a traumatic spine fracture. They found that 39% were associated with a high-energy fall, and 25.6% were caused by a motor vehicle accident. They showed that while fall-related spinal fractures were evenly distributed throughout the spine, motor vehicle-related fractures were more commonly seen in the cervical and thoracic spines. Overall, they found that L1 was most commonly affected (28.5%), followed by T12 (14.1%), and L2 (12.1%). The lowest prevalence of fractures were in T1 (0.4%) and T2 (0.2%). They also found that 54.8% of patients sustained a compression fracture, while 16.9% sustained a distraction fracture and 18.5% a rotation fracture.

It seems likely that the incidence of fractures in the population will continue to change fairly quickly, mainly as a result of aging in the population although improved road safety measures, industrial legislation, and osteoporosis treatment will also play a part. In developed countries, there is evidence that the increasing incidence of a number of fractures that has been apparent in the last 50 years or so is now tailing off, but it is likely that other fractures will continue to increase in incidence. Some of the fractures listed in Table 3-5 are likely to be associated with a higher average age in the future and quite a few fractures will convert from a Type A, D, G, or H distribution to a Type E or F distribution and will become fragility fractures. Indeed, a comparison of the Edinburgh 2000 data base detailed in the sixth edition of Rockwood and Green[8] with the 2007–2008 database used in this chapter shows increasing patient age and a tendency for the frequency of high-energy fractures to decrease. There is also evidence of an increasing incidence of a number of the fragility fractures listed in Table 3-6.

We doubt that many surgeons realize the speed at which the epidemiology of fractures is changing. The prime example of change is the femoral diaphyseal fracture which is commonly assumed to affect young patients involved in motor vehicle accidents. This is clearly still the case in fractures admitted to Level I Trauma Centers such as Baltimore, but if the whole population is considered, it is obvious that the epidemiology of this fracture has changed markedly in the last 30–40 years so that the average age of patients with femoral diaphyseal fractures is now about 70 and almost 40% are presenting with periprosthetic femoral diaphyseal fractures, which usually occur after low-energy trauma.

It also seems likely that Level I Trauma Centers will be treating more elderly patients in the future. There is already a Type A distribution in the fractures that are treated and, while there will always be a significant number of young people who will require treatment mainly because of injuries in motor vehicle

TABLE 3-40	**The Epidemiology of the Spinal Fractures That Presented to Baltimore in 2007**		
	Cervical Spine	Thoracic Spine	Lumbar Spine
Prevalence (%)	39	27	34
Average age (yr)	47	42	43
Gender ratio (male/female, %)	69/31	74/26	69/31
Open (%)	1.8	2.3	2.4
Average ISS	22	25	22
Dislocation (%)	20.1	9.7	2.4
Mode of injury	MVA driver 31% Fall 28% Passenger 14%	MVA driver 31% Fall 26% Motorcyclist 14%	MVA driver 33% Fall 23% Passenger 14%
Associated injuries (%)			
Central nervous system	51	46	33
Chest	41	73	56
Abdomen	24	35	47
Upper limb	41	54	47
Lower limb	36	45	60

accidents, it does seem likely that specialist Trauma Units will be called on to treat the increasingly difficult fractures caused by osteopenia and osteoporosis in elderly patients. We believe that the Type A distribution of distal femoral fractures in Baltimore suggests that this is already happening.

REFERENCES

1. Brogren E, Petranek M, Atroshi I. Incidence and characteristics of distal radius fractures in a southern Swedish region. BMC Musculoskelet Disord 2007;8:48.
2. Buhr AJ, Cooke AM. Fracture patterns. Lancet 1959;1(7072):531–536.
3. Cauley JA, Wampler NS, Barnhart JN, et al. Incidence of fractures compared to cardiovascular disease and breast cancer: the Women's Health Initiative observational study. Osteoporos Int 2008;19(12);1717–1723.
4. Chang KP, Center JR, Nguyen TV, et al. Incidence of hip and other osteoporotic fractures in elderly men and women: Dubbo osteoporosis epidemiology study. J Bone Min Res 2004;19(4):532–536.
5. Chevally T, Guilley E, Herrmann FR, et al. Incidence of hip fracture over a 10-year period (1991–2000): reversal of a secular trend. Bone 2007;40(5):1284–1289.
6. Cooper C, Atkinson EJ, O'Fallon WM et al. Incidence of clinically diagnosed vertebral fractures: a population-based study in Rochester, Minnesota, 1985–1989. J Bone Miner Res 1992;7(2): 221–227.
7. Court-Brown CM, Caesar B. Epidemiology of adult fractures: a review. Int J Care Injured 2006;38(11):691–697.
8. Court-Brown CM, Caesar B. The epidemiology of fractures. In Heckman JD, Bucholz RW, Court-Brown C, eds. Rockwood and Green's Fractures in Adults. 6th ed. Philadelphia: Lippincott Williams & Wilkins; 2006:95–113.
9. Court-Brown CM, Clement N. Four score years and ten. An analysis of the epidemiology of fractures in the very elderly. Inj J Care Injured 2009;Jul 9 (Epub).
10. Court-Brown CM, McBirnie J. The epidemiology of tibial fractures. J Bone Joint Surg Br 1995;77B:417–421.
11. Court-Brown CM, Wood AM, Aitken S. The epidemiology of acute sports-related fractures in adults. Injury 2008;39(12):1365–1372.
12. Donaldson LJ, Cook A, Thomson RG. Incidence of fractures in a geographically defined population. J Epidemiol Community Health 1990;44(3):241–245.
13. Donaldson LJ, Reckless IP, Scholes S, et al. The epidemiology of fractures in England. J Epidemiol Community Health 2008;62(2):174–180.
14. Fife D, Barancik J. Northeastern Ohio trauma study. III. Incidence of fractures. Ann Emerg Med 1985;14(3):244–248.
15. General Register Office for Scotland. 2001 Census. Available at: http://www.gro-scotland.gov.uk/census/censushm/index/html. Accessed June 4, 2009.
16. Grados F, Marcelli C, Dargent-Molina P, et al. Prevalence of vertebral fractures in French women older than 75 years from the EPIDOS study. Bone 2004;34(2):362–367.
17. Guilley E, Chevalley F, Herrmann D, et al. Reversal of the hip fracture secular trend is related to a decrease in the incidence in institution-dwelling elderly women. Osteoporos Int 2008;19(12);1741–1748.
18. Gustilo RB, Mendoza RM, Williams DM. Problems in the management of type III (severe) open fractures. A new classification of type III open fractures. J Trauma 1984;24(8); 742–746.
19. Hagino H, Yamamoto K, Ohshiro H, et al. Changing incidence of hip, distal radius, and proximal humerus fractures in Tottori Prefecture, Japan. Bone 1999;24(3):265–270.
20. Hakanson R, Nussman D, Gorman RA, et al. Gunshot fractures: a medical, social, and economic analysis. Orthopaedics 1994;17(6):519–523.
21. Henle P, Kloen P, Siebenrock KA. Femoral head injuries: which treatment strategy can be recommended? Injury 2007;38(4):478–488.
22. Jacobsen SJ, Goldberg J, Miles TP, et al. Seasonal variation in the incidence of hip fracture among white persons aged 65 years or older in the United States, 1984–1987. Am J Epidemiol 1991;133(10):996–1004.
23. Johansen A, Evans RJ, Stone MD, et al. Fracture incidence in England and Wales: a study based on the population of Cardiff. Injury 1997;28(9–10):655–660.
24. Johnell O, Kanis J. Epidemiology of osteoporotic fractures. Osteoporos Int 2005; 16(Suppl 2):S3–S7
25. Kanis J, Oden A, Johnell O, et al The burden of osteoporotic fractures: a method for setting intervention thresholds. Osteoporos Int 2001;12(5):417–427.
26. Kannus P, Niemi S, Palvanen M, et al. Stabilizing influence of low-trauma ankle fractures in elderly people Finnish statistics for 1970 to 2006 and prediction for the future. Bone 2008;43(2):340–342.
27. Kannus P, Niemi S, Parkkari J, et al. Nationwide decline in incidence of hip fracture. J Bone Min Res 2006;21(12):1836–1838.
28. Knowelden J, Buhr AJ, Dunbar O. Incidence of fractures in persons over 35 years of age. Brit J Prev Soc Med 1964;18:130–141.
29. Leucht P, Fischer K, Muhr G, et al. Epidemiology of traumatic spine fracture. Injury 2009;40:166–172.
30. Lofthus CM, Frihagen F, Meyer HE, et al. Epidemiology of distal forearm fractures in Oslo, Norway. Osteoporos Int 2008;19(6):781–786.
31. Melton LJ 3rd, Crowson CS, O'Fallon WM. Fracture incidence in Olmstesd County, Minnesota: comparison of urban with rural rates and changes in urban rates over time. Osteoporos Int 1999;9(1):29–37.
32. Menon MRG, Walker JL, Court-Brown CM. The epidemiology of fractures in adolescents with reference to social deprivation. J Bone Joinr Surg Br 2008;90B:1482–1486.
33. National Statistics. Centenarians: the fastest increasing age group. Available at: http://www.statistics.gov.uk/cci/nugget_print.asp?ID = 1875. Accessed June 4, 2009.
34. National Statistics. Health expectancy: live longer, more years in poor health. Available at: http://www.statistics.gov.uk/cci/nugget_print.asp?ID = 934. Accessed June 4, 2009.
35. Rennie L, Court-Brown CM, Mok JY, et al. The epidemiology of fractures in children. Injury 2007;38(8):913–922.
36. Sahlin Y. Occurrence of fractures in a defined population: a 1-year study. Injury 1990; 21(3):158–160.
37. Sakuma M, Endo N, Oinuma T, et al. Incidence and outcome of osteoporotic fractures in 2004 in Sado City, Niigata Prefecture, Japan. J Bone Miner Metab 2008;26(4):373–378.
38. Sanders KM, Nicholson GC, Ugoni AM, et al. Fracture rates lower in rural than urban communities: the Geelong osteoporosis study. J Epidemiol Community Health 2002: 56(6);466–470.
39. Tracy JK, Meyer WA, Flores RH, et al. Racial differences in rate of decline in bone mass in older men: the Baltimore men's osteoporosis study. J Bone Min Res 2005;20(7): 1228–1234.
40. Urquhart DM, Edwards ER, Graves SE, et al. Characterisation of orthopaedic trauma admitted to adult Level 1 Trauma Centres. Int J Care Injured 2006;37(2);120–127.
41. U.S. Census Bureau. International data base (IDB). Available at: http://www.census.gov/ipc/www/idb. Accessed June 4, 2009.
42. Weber BG. Die verletzungen des oberen sprungglenkes. Bern: Hans Huber;1966.
43. Weiss RJ, Montgomery SM, Ehlin A, et al. Decreasing incidence of tibial shaft fractures between 1998 and 2004: information based on 10,627 Swedish patients. Acta Orthop 2008;79(4):526–533.

4

BONE AND JOINT HEALING

Joseph A. Buckwalter, Thomas A. Einhorn, J. L. Marsh,
Larry Gulotta, Anil Ranawat, and Joseph Lane

INTRODUCTION

Over the last 2 decades, orthopaedic surgeons have dramatically advanced their ability to restore the structure and function of damaged bones and joints. Using new methods of internal fixation, external fixation, and rehabilitation, they now successfully treat even the most severe fractures and many severe joint injuries. New biologic approaches to promoting tissue repair and regeneration will further improve treatment of these injuries.[11] Yet ultimately the result of the treatment of any musculoskeletal injury depends on the skill of the surgeon in taking advantage of the natural healing potential of the tissues that form the skeleton. Surgeons can treat bone and joint injuries without extensive knowledge of these tissues, but they are better able to select the optimal treatment if they have this knowledge. Furthermore, they can treat, and in some instances prevent, complications of musculoskeletal injuries or problems of failed or inadequate healing more effectively when they are as skilled in applying the knowledge of tissue healing as they are in the use of surgical techniques.

BONE TISSUE

The mechanical properties of bone are readily apparent. Its tensile strength nearly equals that of cast iron, but it is three times lighter and ten times more flexible. Yet bone is not a homogenous inert material like iron, or the plastics and metals that form most orthopaedic implants. Its matrix consists of organic and inorganic components, and it is covered on its internal and external surfaces by cells and cell processes.[13] An elaborate system of lacunae, canals or tunnels containing cells and cell processes, blood vessels, lymphatics, and nerves permeates the matrix, and various specialized cell populations responsible for maintaining the tissue lie within the matrix lacunae and on the bone surfaces.[13] In most people bone appears to remain unchanged for decades, but this appearance is deceptive; it is constantly changing in response to mechanical and hormonal signals.[14] Over a lifetime, the skeleton is fully turned over multiple times, adjusting its alignment to altered loads.

Mature bones consist of a central fatty or hematopoietic marrow supported and surrounded by bone tissue and periosteum. Although the three component tissues of bone differ in composition, structure, and function, they are not independent. Marrow can serve as a source of bone cells, marrow blood vessels form a critical part of the bone circulatory system, and disorders or mechanical disruption of the marrow can affect the activities of bone and periosteal cells.

Bone consists of mesenchymal cells embedded within an abundant extracellular matrix.[13,14] The matrix contains mineral that gives the tissue great strength and stiffness in compression and bending. The organic component of the bone matrix, primarily type I collagen, and contributes to bone strength, but also gives bone the plasticity that allows substantial deformation without fracture. Bone matrix also contains various cytokines, including growth factors that stimulate bone formation.[13,14] These growth factors appear to have important roles in normal bone metabolism and in fracture healing. The periosteum, consisting of two layers—an outer fibrous layer and an inner, more cellular and vascular cambium layer—covers the external bone surfaces and participates in the healing of many types of fractures. The thicker, more cellular periosteum of infants and children has a more extensive vascular supply than that of adults. Perhaps because of these differences, the periosteum of children is more active in fracture healing. Two types of bone can be distinguished by their mechanical and biological properties: woven or immature bone, and lamellar or mature bone.[13] Woven bone forms the embryonic skeleton and is replaced by lamellar bone during development and growth.[14] Woven bone also forms the initial fracture repair tissue and is replaced by lamellar bone as the fracture remodels under mechanical load. Compared with lamellar bone, woven bone has a more rapid rate of deposition and resorption, an irregular woven pattern of matrix collagen fibrils consistent with its name, approximately four times the amount of osteocytes per unit volume, and an irregular pattern of matrix mineralization. The frequent patchwork formation of woven bone and the spotty pattern of mineralization create an irregular radiographic appearance that distinguishes the woven bone found in fracture callus from lamellar bone. Because of its lack of collagen fibril orientation, irregular mineralization, and relatively high cell content and water concentration, woven bone is less stiff and more easily deformed than lamellar bone.

JOINT TISSUES

All synovial joints share the same basic structure: congruent articulating cartilaginous surfaces supported by subchondral and metaphyseal bone, joint capsules and ligaments that link the bones supporting the articular surfaces, and synovial membranes that cover the inner surfaces of the joint except for the area of articular cartilage. Some joints also have dense fibrous tissue menisci that lie between the cartilaginous surfaces and attach to the joint capsule.

Articular cartilage consists of sparsely distributed chondrocytes surrounded by an elaborate, highly organized macromolecular framework filled with water.[16] Three classes of molecules (collagens, proteoglycans, and noncollagenous proteins) form the macromolecular framework. Type II collagen fibrils give the cartilage its form and tensile strength, and various quantitatively minor collagens help organize and maintain the meshwork of type II collagen fibrils. The interaction of proteoglycans with water gives the tissue its stiffness to compression and its resiliency, thereby contributing to its durability.[87] The noncollagenous proteins are less well understood than the proteoglycans and collagens, but they appear to help organize and stabilize the matrix, attach chondrocytes to the matrix macromolecules, and possibly help stabilize the chondrocyte phenotype. Unlike the other primary musculoskeletal tissues, cartilage lacks blood, nerve, and lymphatic supplies.

BONE AND JOINT INJURIES

Acute bone and joint injuries result from the application of forces to the skeleton that exceed the strength of the tissues. Disruptions of bone tissue are called *fractures*. Visible disruptions of articular cartilage also generally are referred to as fractures when they involve both the articular cartilage and subchondral bone. These are called *osteochondral* or *intra-articular fractures*, and when they involve only the cartilage they are called *chondral fractures*.

FRACTURE HEALING

Inflammation and Repair

A fracture initiates a sequence of inflammation, repair, and remodeling that can restore the injured bone to its original state.[30] Inflammation begins immediately after injury and is followed rapidly by repair.[12] After repair has replaced the lost and damaged cells and matrix, a prolonged remodeling phase ensues. The energy requirements of fracture healing increase rapidly during inflammation and reach a peak during repair, when the cells in the fracture callus are proliferating and synthesizing large volumes of new matrix. These energy requirements remain high until cell density and cell activity begin to decline as remodeling starts.[48]

An injury that fractures bone not only damages its cells, blood vessels, and bone matrix (Fig. 4-1) but also the surrounding soft tissues, including the periosteum and muscle. A hematoma accumulates within the medullary canal, between the fracture ends and beneath the elevated periosteum. The damage to the bone blood vessels deprives osteocytes of their nutrition, and they die as far back as the junction of collateral vascular channels, leaving the immediate ends of the fracture without living cells (Fig. 4-2). Severely damaged periosteum and marrow, as well as other surrounding soft tissues, may also contribute necrotic material to the fracture site.

Inflammatory mediators released from platelets and from dead and injured cells cause blood vessels to dilate and exude plasma leading to the acute edema seen in the region of a fresh fracture. Inflammatory cells migrate to the region, including polymorphonuclear leukocytes, followed by macrophages and lymphocytes. These cells also release cytokines that stimulate angiogenesis.[53] As the inflammatory response subsides, necrotic tissue and exudates are resorbed, and fibroblasts and chondrocytes appear and start producing a new matrix, the fracture callus (Figs. 4-2 and 4-3).

The factors that stimulate fracture repair probably include the chemotactic and growth factors released during inflammation at the fracture site and bone matrix proteins, including growth factors exposed by disruption of the bone tissue and the fracture hematoma.[92] Although the inflammation caused by a fracture follows the same sequence for almost every fracture, the amount and composition of repair tissue and the rate of repair may differ depending on (i) whether the fracture occurs through primarily cancellous bone or through primarily cortical bone, (ii) the extent of the soft tissue disruption surrounding the fracture, and (iii) other factors that are discussed under the section titled "Variables That Influence Fracture Healing."

The mechanical stability of the fracture site also influences the repair process. The summaries of fracture repair and remodeling that follow first describe healing of closed fractures that

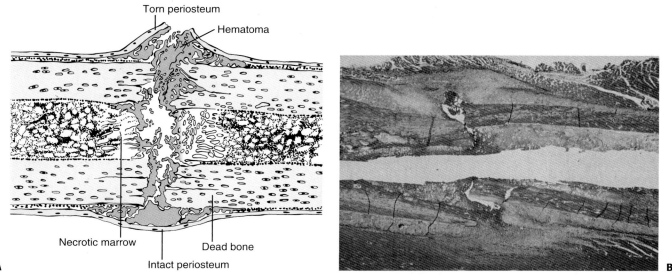

FIGURE 4-1 Initial events following fracture of a long bone diaphysis. **A.** Drawing showing that the periosteum is torn opposite the point of impact, and may remain intact on the other side. A hematoma accumulates beneath the periosteum and between the fracture ends. There is necrotic marrow and cortical bone close to the fracture line. **B.** A photomicrograph of a fractured rat femur 3 days after injury showing the proliferation of the periosteal repair tissue.

are not rigidly stabilized; that is, fractures in which repair proceeds in the presence of motion at the fracture site (Fig. 4-4). A closed clavicle fracture that is not treated by internal fixation provides an example of repair and remodeling of an unstable fracture. The second summary describes the healing of stable fractures; that is, fractures in which repair proceeds at a rigidly stable fracture site with the fracture surfaces held in contact. Transverse diaphyseal fractures of the radius and ulna treated by open anatomic reduction and rigid internal fixation provide examples of the repair and remodeling of stable fractures.

Repair and Remodeling of Unstable Fractures

Disruption of blood vessels in the bone, bone marrow, periosteum, and surrounding tissue at the time of injury results in the extravasation of blood at the fracture site and the formation

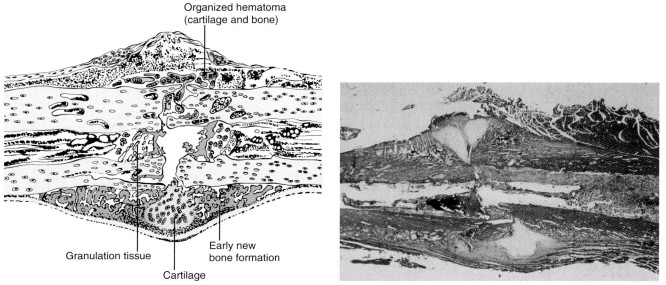

FIGURE 4-2 Early repair of a diaphyseal fracture of a long bone. **A.** Drawing showing organization of the hematoma, early woven bone formation in the subperiosteal regions, and cartilage formation in other areas. Periosteal cells contribute to healing this type of injury. If the fracture is rigidly immobilized or if it occurs primarily through cancellous bone and the cancellous surfaces lie in close apposition, there will be little evidence of fracture callus. **B.** Photomicrograph of a fractured rat femur 9 days after injury showing cartilage and bone formation in the subperiosteal regions. (Reprinted from Einhorn TA. The cell and molecular biology of fracture healing. Clin Ortho 1998;335(Suppl):S7–S21, with permission.)

Persistent cartilage

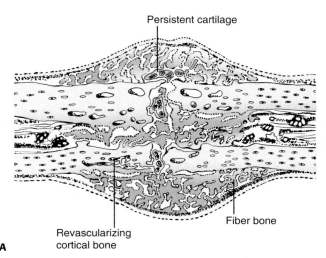

Revascularizing
cortical bone

Fiber bone

A

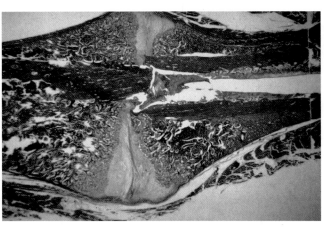

B

FIGURE 4-3 Progressive fracture healing by fracture callus. **A.** Drawing showing woven or fiber bone bridging the fracture gap and uniting the fracture fragments. Cartilage remains in the regions most distant from ingrowing capillary buds. In many instances, the capillaries are surrounded by new bone. Vessels revascularize the cortical bone at the fracture site. **B.** Photomicrograph of a fractured rat femur 21 days after injury showing fracture callus united the fracture fragments. (Reprinted from Einhorn TA. The cell and molecular biology of fracture healing. Clin Ortho 1998;335(Suppl):S7–S21, with permission.)

of a hematoma. Organization of this hematoma is usually recognized as the first step in fracture repair (see Fig. 4-2). Experimental work indicates that loss of the hematoma impairs or slows fracture healing,[36,37] suggesting that the hematoma and an intact surrounding periosteal soft tissue envelope that contains the hematoma may facilitate the initial stages of repair. Open fractures or the treatment of fractures by open reduction disrupts organization of the hematoma and may slow the repair process. The precise reasons why a hematoma may affect fracture healing remain uncertain. Presumably, the intact fracture hematoma provides a fibrin scaffold that facilitates migration of repair cells. In addition, growth factors such as parathyroid growth factors (PGGA) and transforming growth factors (TGF-β) and other proteins released by platelets and cells in the frac-

ture hematoma mediate the critical initial events in fracture repair. These include cell migration and proliferation, and the synthesis of a repair tissue matrix.[53,92] A breakdown product of thrombin provides strong stem cell attraction.[6]

Although the volume of the vascular bed of an extremity increases shortly after fracture, presumably because of vasodilatation, vascular proliferation also occurs in the region of the fracture. It appears that, under ordinary circumstances, the periosteal vessels contribute most of the capillary buds early in normal bone healing, with the nutrient medullary artery becoming more important later in the process. The invading vessels carry along pericytes that provide a large source of mesenchymal stem cells.[7] Fibroblastic growth factors may be important mediators of the angiogenesis in fracture healing, but the exact stimuli responsible for vascular invasion and endothelial cell proliferation have not been defined. When the surgeon interferes with the blood supply to the fracture site, either by stripping the periosteum excessively or by destroying the medullary system through reaming and the insertion of intramedullary nails, repair must depend upon the remaining, intact blood vessels.

The bone ends at the fracture site, deprived of their blood supply, become necrotic and the surrounding bone is resorbed. In some fractures this may create a radiographically apparent gap at the fracture site several weeks or more after the fracture. The cells responsible for this function, the osteoclasts, come from a different cell line than the cells responsible for bone formation.[13,14] They are derived from circulating monocytes in the blood and monocytic precursor cells from the bone marrow, in which the osteoblasts develop from the periosteum or from undifferentiated mesenchymal cells that migrate into the fracture site.

Pluripotential mesenchymal cells, probably of a common origin, form the fibrous tissue, cartilage, and eventually bone at the fracture site. Some of these cells originate in the injured tissues, while others migrate to the injury site with the incoming

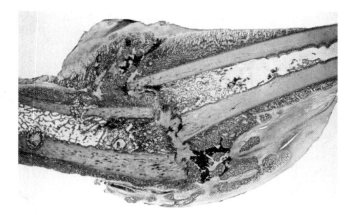

FIGURE 4-4 Light micrograph showing healing of a diaphyseal fracture under conditions of loading and motion. This femur fracture occurred in a pig that continued to use the limb for 3 weeks. Even though the fracture was not stabilized, it is healing. A large fracture callus consisting primarily of woven bone surrounds and unites the two fracture fragments. As the callus matures it progressively stabilizes the fracture. Notice that the fracture callus contains areas of mineralized and unmineralized cartilage.

blood vessels. Accompanying the neoangiogenesis are pericytes that provide a large pool of undifferentiated mesenchymal stem cells capable of differentiating into different tissue cell types. In addition, these undifferentiated cells are productive sources of bone morphogenic protein (BMP)—the growth factor that drives the differentiation process.[2] Cells from the cambium layer of the periosteum form the earliest bone (see Fig. 4-1A). Periosteal cells have an especially prominent role in healing fractures in children because the periosteum is thicker and more cellular in younger individuals. With increasing age, the periosteum becomes thinner and its contribution to fracture healing becomes less apparent. Osteoblasts from the endosteal surface also participate in bone formation, but surviving osteocytes do not appear to form repair tissue. Most of the cells responsible for osteogenesis during fracture healing appear in the fracture site with the granulation tissue that replaces the fracture hematoma.

The mesenchymal cells at the fracture site proliferate, differentiate, and produce the fracture callus consisting of fibrous tissue, cartilage, and woven bone (see Fig. 4-3). Biological growth factors, notably members of the BMP family, drive the early differention process.[6] The fracture callus fills and surrounds the fracture site, and in the early stages of healing can be divided into the hard or bony callus and the softer fibrous and cartilaginous callus. The bone formed initially at the periphery of the callus by intramembranous bone formation is the hard callus. The soft callus forms in the central regions, in which there is relatively low oxygen tension, and it consists primarily of cartilage and fibrous tissue. Bone gradually replaces this cartilage through the process of endochondral ossification, enlarging the hard callus and increasing the stability of the fracture fragments (see Fig. 4-4). This process continues until new bone bridges the fracture site, reestablishing continuity between the cortical bone ends.

The composition of the fracture callus matrix changes as repair progresses (Fig. 4-5). The cells replace the fibrin clot with a loose fibrous matrix containing glycosaminoglycans, proteoglycans, and types I and III collagen. In many regions they convert this tissue to denser fibrocartilage or hyaline-like cartilage. With formation of the hyaline-like cartilage, type II collagen, cartilage-specific proteoglycan, and link protein content increase. Newly formed woven bone remodels to lamellar bone,

and with remodeling the content of collagen and other proteins returns to normal levels.

An analysis of fracture repair demonstrates a close correlation between the activation of genes for blood vessel, cartilage, and bone-specific proteins in the cells and the development of granulation tissue, cartilage, and bone, respectively,[82] demonstrating that fracture repair depends on the regulation of gene expression in the repair cells. The simultaneous occurrence of chondrogenesis, endochondral ossification, and intramembranous bone formation in different regions of the fracture callus suggests that local mediators and small variations in the microenvironment, including mechanical stresses, determine what genes will be expressed and therefore the type of tissue the repair cells form. Local mediators that may influence repair cell function include growth factors released from cells and platelets. BMPs influence this differentiation process.[6] These factors are closely related to the WNT pathway. Acidic fibroblast growth factor (FGF), basic FGF, and transforming growth factor beta (TGF-β) may stimulate chondrocyte proliferation and cartilage formation, osteoblast proliferation, and bone synthesis. TGF-β released from platelets immediately after injury may initiate formation of fracture callus. TGF-β synthesis is also associated with cartilage hypertrophy and calcification at the endochondral ossification front. Local oxygen tension is also an important factor. Hypoxia strongly inhibits in vitro chondrogenesis and osteogenesis in mesenchymal stem cells.[52] Conversely, hypoxia promotes chondrocytic differentiation and cartilage matrix synthesis and suppresses terminal chondrocyte differentiation.[40] These hypoxia-induced phenomena may act on chondrocytes to enhance and preserve their phenotype and function during chondrocyte differentiation and endochondral ossification. Proteoglycan synthesis and aggregation in the various zones and stages of endochondral ossification are differentially affected by the ambient oxygen environment.[23]

As mineralization of fracture callus proceeds, the bone ends gradually become enveloped in a fusiform mass of callus containing increasing amounts of woven bone. Increasing mineral content is closely associated with increasing stiffness of the fracture callus.[3] The stability of the fracture fragments progressively increases because of the internal and external callus formation, and eventually *clinical union* occurs—that is, the fracture site becomes stable and pain-free. *Radiographic union* occurs when plain radiographs show bone trabeculae or cortical bone crossing the fracture site, and this often occurs later than clinical union. However, even at this stage healing is not complete. The immature fracture callus is weaker than normal bone, and it only gains full strength during remodeling.

During the final stages of repair, remodeling of the repair tissue begins with replacement of the woven bone by lamellar bone and resorption of unneeded callus. Radioisotope studies[62] show increased activity in fracture sites long after the patient has full restoration of function and plain radiographs show bone union, demonstrating that fracture remodeling continues for years after clinical and radiographic union. Remodeling of fracture repair tissue after all woven bone has been replaced presumably consists of osteoclastic resorption of superfluous or poorly placed bone and formation of new bony trabeculae along lines of stress.

Although fracture callus remodeling results from an elaborate sequence of cellular and matrix changes, the important functional result for the patient is an increase in mechanical

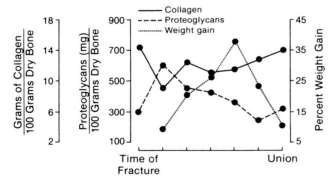

FIGURE 4-5 A schematic representation of the changing composition and mass of fracture callus. Collagen formation precedes significant accumulation of mineral. After an initial rise, proteoglycan concentration falls gradually as fracture healing progresses. The total mass of the fracture callus increases during repair and then decreases during remodeling.

stability. The progressive increase in fracture stability consists of four stages.[90] During stage I, a healing bone subjected to torsional testing fails through the original fracture site with a low-stiffness pattern. In stage II, the bone still fails through the fracture site, but the characteristics of failure indicate a high-stiffness, hard-tissue pattern. In stage III, the bone fails partly through the original fracture site and partly through the previously intact bone with a high-stiffness, hard-tissue pattern. Finally, in stage IV, failure does not occur through the fracture site, indicating that new tissue at the fracture site duplicates the mechanical properties of the uninjured tissue. The sequence of repair depends upon the mechanical environment. Loose connective tissue abundant in collagen can tolerate the marked tensile demands. As the callus progresses, cartilage appears in response to compression. The fracture repair process then moves toward rigid stability by progressing through calcified cartilage, woven bone, and ultimately lamellar bone. If the initial fracture environment is stable, the initial repair matrix will be woven bone and then lamellar bone, which is produced along lines of stress.

Despite successful fracture healing, the bone density of the involved limb may be decreased for years.[45,93] In one study, patients with healed tibial fractures had decreased bone density in the involved limb decades after the injury.[45] The clinical significance of these observations remains unclear, but they suggest that fractures, and possibly the decreased loading of a limb after fracture, may cause long-lasting changes in the tissues.

Repair and Remodeling of Stabilized Fractures (Primary Bone Healing)

As described above, when motion occurs within certain limits at a fracture site, fracture callus progressively stabilizes the bone fragments and remodeling of the fracture callus eventually produces lamellar bone. When the fracture surfaces are rigidly held in contact, fracture healing can occur without any grossly visible callus. This type of fracture healing has been referred to as *primary bone healing*, indicating that it occurs without the formation and replacement of visible fracture callus (Fig. 4-6).

In most fractures that are rigidly stabilized with the bone ends directly apposed, there are regions of the fracture line where the bone ends are in contact and other areas where there are small gaps. Where there is contact between the bone ends, lamellar bone can form directly across the fracture line by extension of osteons. A cluster of osteoclasts cuts across the fracture line; osteoblasts following the osteoclasts deposit new bone; and blood vessels follow the osteoblasts. The new bone matrix, enclosed osteocytes, and blood vessels form new haversian systems (Fig. 4-7). Where gaps exist that prevent direct extension of osteons across the fracture site, osteoblasts first fill the defects with woven bone. After the gap fills with woven bone, haversian remodeling begins, reestablishing the normal cortical bone structure. Cutting cones consisting of osteoclasts followed by osteoblasts and blood vessels traverse the woven bone in the fracture gap, depositing lamellar bone and reestablishing the cortical bone blood supply across the fracture site without the formation of grossly visible fracture callus. If a segment of cortical bone is necrotic, gap healing by direct extension of osteons still can occur but at a slower rate, and the areas of necrotic cortical bone will remain unremodeled for a prolonged period.

Many impacted epiphyseal, metaphyseal, and vertebral body fractures, where cancellous and, in some regions, cortical bone surfaces, interlock have sufficient stability to permit primary bone healing where the bone surfaces are in direct contact. The same type of cancellous bone healing can occur at rigidly stabilized osteotomies through metaphyseal bone, intra-articular fractures, and surgical arthrodesis sites. Most diaphyseal osteotomies, acute diaphyseal fractures of long bones, and unstable metaphyseal fractures require the use of devices that compress and rigidly stabilize the fracture site to allow primary healing.

Failure of Fracture Healing

Despite optimal treatment, some fractures heal slowly or fail to heal.[54] It is difficult to set the time when a given fracture should be united, but when healing progresses more slowly than average, the slow progress is referred to as delayed union. Watson-Jones[89] described a condition he called slow union, in which the fracture line remains clearly visible radiographically but there is no undue separation of the fragments, no cavitation of the surfaces, no calcification, and no sclerosis. This indolent fracture healing may be related to the severity of the injury, poor blood supply, the age and nutritional status of the patient, or other factors. It is not a nonunion but rather a variation of normal healing. In contrast, failure of bone healing, or nonunion, results from an arrest of the healing process. This arrest of healing should be documented clinically and radiographically over time. Most experts agree that there should be no evidence of healing clinically or radiographically for at least 3 months before the term "nonunion" is used to describe the fracture.[72] A nonunion that occurs despite the formation of a large volume of callus around the fracture site is commonly referred to as a hypertrophic nonunion (Fig. 4-8). This is in contrast to an atrophic nonunion (Fig. 4-9), in which little or no callus forms and bone resorption occurs at the fracture site. In some nonunions, cartilagenous tissue forms over the fracture surfaces and the cavity between the surfaces fills with a clear fluid resembling normal joint or bursal fluid creating a pseudarthrosis, or false joint (Fig. 4-10). Pseudarthroses may or may not be painful, but they almost uniformly remain unstable indefinitely. In other nonunions the gap between the bone ends fills with fibrous or fibrocartilaginous tissue. Occasionally, dense fibrous and cartilaginous tissue firmly stabilizes a fracture, creating a fibrous union. Although fibrous unions may be painless and unite the fracture fragments, they fail to restore the normal strength of the bone.

Variables That Influence Fracture Healing

Occasionally delayed unions or nonunions occur without apparent cause, but in many instances injury, patient, and treatment variables that adversely influenced fracture healing can be identified. These variables include severe soft tissue damage associated with open and high-energy closed fractures; infection; segmental fractures; pathologic fractures; fractures with soft tissue interposition; poor local blood supply; systemic diseases; malnutrition; vitamin D deficiency; corticosteroid use; poor mechanical fixation; and iatrogenic interference with healing. Many other variables have been reported to retard bone healing.[12] Some of them exert an adverse influence that can be measured in experimental studies, but may not cause clinically significant impairment of fracture healing. Others, like distraction of a fracture site or interposition of soft tissues in the frac-

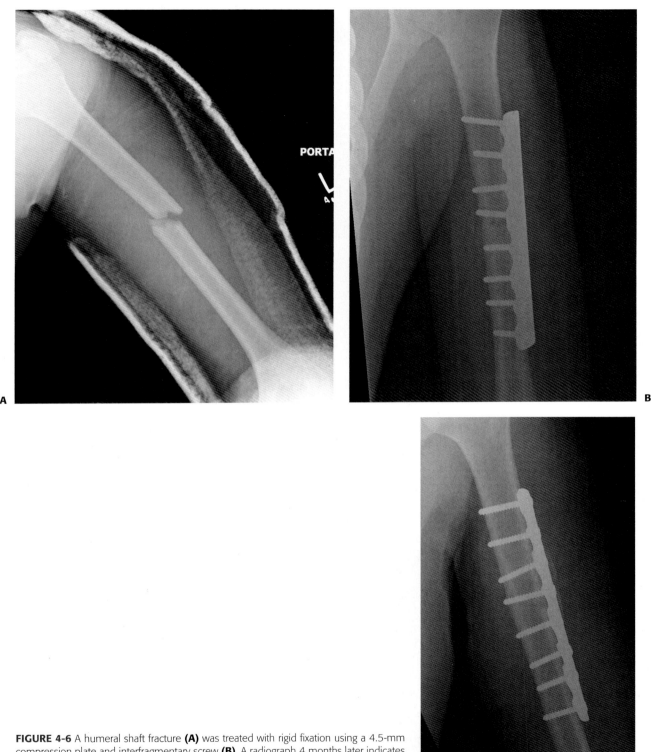

FIGURE 4-6 A humeral shaft fracture **(A)** was treated with rigid fixation using a 4.5-mm compression plate and interfragmentary screw **(B)**. A radiograph 4 months later indicates healing without visible fracture callus. This represents primary bone healing **(C)**.

ture site have not been examined systematically in experimental studies, but clinical experience shows that they can impair fracture healing.

Injury Variables
Open Fractures. Severe open fractures cause soft tissue disruption, fracture displacement, and, in some instances, significant

bone loss. Extensive tearing or crushing of the soft tissue disrupts the blood supply to the fracture site, leaving substantial volumes of necrotic bone and soft tissue, impeding or preventing formation of a fracture hematoma and delaying formation of repair tissue (Fig. 4-11). Exposed bone and soft tissue become desiccated, increasing the volume of necrotic tissue and the risk of infection. Early use of vascularized soft tissue flaps to cover

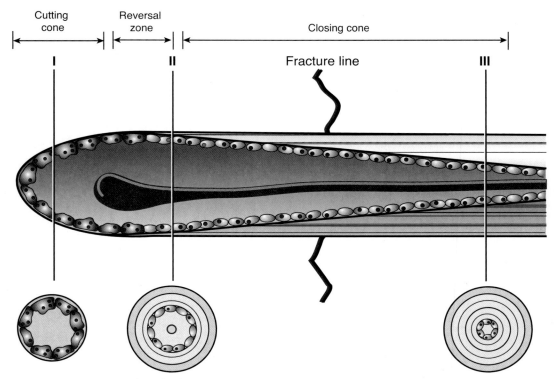

FIGURE 4-7 Primary bone healing utilizes an osteoclastic cutting cone crossing the fracture gap (**I**) followed by bone reconstitution by the trailing osteoblasts (**II, III**).

bone exposed by severe open fractures can prevent desiccation and facilitate healing of these injuries.[72] In addition to the problems created by the soft tissue damage, open fractures may become infected. Management of this complication usually requires debriding infected bone and soft tissue along with providing appropriate antibiotic treatment. Although infection compromises bone healing, infected fractures can unite if they are stabilized and the infection is suppressed. This may leave the patient with chronic osteomyelitis, but in most instances bone union with a chronic infection is a better result than an infected nonunion.

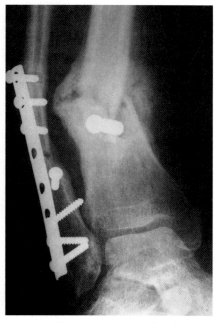

FIGURE 4-8 Hypertrophic delayed union of a distal tibial fracture 5 months after injury. Note the abundant callus but incomplete bridging of the fracture gap.

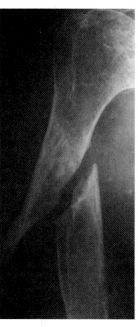

FIGURE 4-9 Atrophic nonunion of a humeral shaft fracture 18 months after fracture. Note the absence of callus.

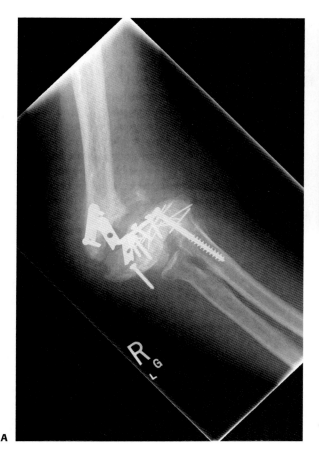

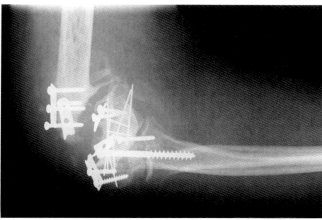

A

B

FIGURE 4-10 A,B. A synovial pseudoarthrosis of the distal humerus is demonstrated in these radiographs taken after failed internal fixation. The nonunion is grossly mobile and the elbow joint is stiff.

Severity of Injury. High-energy injury leads to extensive local tissue necrosis. A severe fracture, open or closed, may be associated with extensive soft tissue loss, displacement and comminution of the bone fragments, loss of bone, and decreased blood supply to the fracture site. Comminution of bone fragments generally indicates that there is also extensive soft tissue injury. However, some patients with osteopenic bone may sustain comminuted fractures from low-energy injuries that have minimal soft tissue injury. Displacement of the fracture fragments and severe trauma to the soft tissues retard fracture healing, probably because the extensive tissue damage increases the volume of

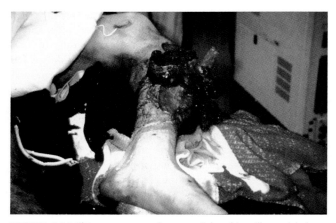

FIGURE 4-11 This severe open fracture of the tibia will certainly have delayed healing because of disrupted blood supply and the extensive amount of necrotic bone and soft tissue.

necrotic tissue, impedes the migration of mesenchymal cells, compromises vascular invasion, decreases the amount of viable mesenchymal cells, and disrupts the local blood supply. Less severe injuries leave an intact soft tissue envelope that contains the fracture hematoma, provides a ready source of mesenchymal cells, acts as a soft tissue tube to direct the repair efforts of these cells, and serves as an internal splint that contributes to immobilization of the fragments.

Intra-articular Fractures. Because they extend into joint surfaces and because joint motion or loading may cause movement of the fracture fragments, intra-articular fractures can present challenging treatment problems. Most intra-articular fractures heal, but if the alignment and congruity of the joint surface is not restored, the joint surface will be incongruous and the joint may be unstable. In some instances, especially if the fracture is not rigidly stabilized, healing may be delayed or nonunion may occur. However, prolonged immobilization of a joint with an intra-articular fracture frequently causes joint stiffness. For these reasons, surgeons usually attempt to reduce and securely fix unstable intra-articular fractures. This approach ideally restores joint alignment and congruity and allows for at least some joint motion while the fracture heals. Unfortunately, restoring joint alignment, congruity, and stability in patients with severe intra-articular fractures may require extensive surgical exposure that further compromises the blood supply to the fracture site. Even after reduction and adequate initial stabilization, intra-articular fractures may displace as a result of high transarticular forces, failure of the stabilization, or collapse of the subchondral cancellous bone. This late loss of reduction occurs most frequently after comminuted fractures of the proximal and distal tibia and distal radius. The creation of either a gap or a step-off exceeding 2 millimeters will lead to secondary osteoarthritis.[60]

Segmental Fractures. A segmental fracture of a long bone implies that a large amount of energy was absorbed by this type of injury and the two-level fracture pattern impairs or disrupts the intramedullary blood supply to the middle fragment. If there is severe soft tissue trauma, the periosteal blood supply to the middle fragment may also be compromised. Possibly because of this, the probability of delayed union or nonunion, proximally or distally, may be increased. These problems occur most frequently in segmental fractures of the tibia, especially at the distal fracture site.[80,94] In contrast, segmental fractures of the femur less commonly develop nonunions, presumably because of the better soft tissue coverage and resulting better blood supply. When internal fixation of a segmental fracture is performed, the soft tissue attachments of the middle fragment should be preserved whenever possible.

Soft Tissue Interposition. Interposition of soft tissue including muscle, fascia, tendon, and occasionally nerves and vessels between fracture fragments will compromise fracture healing. Soft tissue interposition should be suspected when the bone fragments cannot be brought into apposition or alignment during attempted closed reduction. If this occurs, an open reduction may be needed to extricate the interposed tissue and achieve an acceptable position of the fracture fragments.

Damage to the Blood Supply. Lack of an adequate vascular supply can significantly delay or prevent fracture healing in part related to a deficiency of stem cells. An insufficient blood supply for fracture healing may result from a severe soft tissue and bone injury or from the normally limited blood supply to some bones or bone regions. For example, the vulnerable blood supplies of the femoral head, proximal scaphoid, and talar body may predispose these bones to delayed union or nonunion, even in the absence of severe soft tissue damage or fracture displacement. Extensive surgical dissection may also compromise the vascular supply to a fracture site, especially in regions of the skeleton with a vulnerable blood supply, or in fractures with associated severe soft tissue injuries, or in regions with minimal surrounding soft tissue, for example, the distal tibia.

Patient Variables

Diseases/Disorders. Disease state can influence fracture healing both at the site of fracture and for the patient systemically. Patients with Parkinson's disease have a longer hospital stay and a higher rate of referral to a nursing facility. Yet the rates of complications, recovery of ambulation, and 1-year mortality are comparable to those of non-Parkinson patient.[42] Diabetes in animals and man results in impaired fracture healing in part associated with increased rates of cartilage resorption and diminished callus size.[46] Fracture healing is also impaired in HIV-positive populations. Apart from directly impeding cellular function in bone remodeling, HIV infection is reported to cause derangement in the levels of cytokines involved in fracture repair.[79]

Age. Patient age significantly influences the rate of fracture healing. Infants have the most rapid rate of fracture healing.

The rate of healing declines with increasing age, and the ability to achieve secure mechanical fixation of the fracture fragments decreases with the development of osteoporosis. Multiple factors contribute to age-related changes in fracture healing, including decreased number and function of stem cells, decreased chondrogenic potential of the periosteum, changes in the local signaling milieu at the fracture site, and impaired vascularization.[51] Biologic augmentation may partially remedy this phenomenon. The ability to achieve stable fixation, however, declines in osteoporotic patients resulting in bone fragment drift and malalignment.[41,85,86] One possible reason for the greater healing potential of children may be an increased availability of cells that produce repair tissue: younger cells may differentiate more rapidly from the mesenchymal pool and the pool of undifferentiated mesenchymal cells may be larger in children.

Nutrition. The cell migration, proliferation, and matrix synthesis necessary to heal a fracture requires substantial energy. Furthermore, to synthesize large volumes of collagens, proteoglycans, and other matrix macromolecules, the cells need a steady supply of the components of these molecules: proteins and carbohydrates. As a result, the metabolic state of the patient can alter the outcome of injury, and in severely malnourished patients injuries that usually heal rapidly may fail to heal. Although few surgeons in economically developed countries see many severely malnourished patients, they may see relatively large numbers of patients with milder forms of protein-calorie malnutrition and other dietary deficiencies. Jensen and associates[44] found a 42.4% incidence of clinical or subclinical malnutrition in patients undergoing orthopaedic surgical procedures. A study of 490 patients with hip fractures found that 87 of these patients (18%) suffered from malnutrition and that the malnourished patients stayed in the hospital longer, were less likely to recover their prefracture level of activity, and were more likely to die within 1 year of their hip fracture.[47] Low serum albumin levels, low iron-binding capacity, and low lymphocyte counts markedly increase perioperative complications in fragility fracture patients.[54] Both vitamin D insufficiency (<32 ng/mL) and deficiency (<20 ng/mL) occur in more than 60% of patients with low-energy fractures.[37]

Because trauma and major surgery can cause malnutrition and decrease immunocompetence,[44] surgeons must pay careful attention to nutrition and metabolic balance in patients with multiple injuries.[63] Even in well-nourished patients, the nutritional demands of healing multiple injuries can exceed intake.[44] Leung and colleagues[48] reported that the adenosine triphosphate (ATP) content of a 2-week rabbit fracture callus was a thousand times greater than the ATP content of normal bone. Others have suggested that a single long-bone fracture can temporarily increase metabolic requirements 20% to 25%, and that multiple injuries and infection can increase metabolic requirements by more than 50%.[21,44] Failure to meet these increased nutritional demands may be associated with increased mortality; more frequent surgical complications such as infection, wound dehiscence, and impaired healing; and slower rehabilitation. An experimental study of fracture healing demonstrated that fracture callus does not achieve normal strength in states of dietary deficiency, and that a dietary deficiency of protein reduces fracture callus strength and energy storage capacity.[33] For these reasons, the optimal treatment of injured patients requires an assessment of their nutritional status and appropriate treatment, which may include nutritional support.

Systemic Hormones. Many different hormones can influence fracture healing.[12] Corticosteroids may compromise fracture healing,[26] possibly by inhibiting the differentiation of osteoblasts from mesenchymal cells[83] and decreasing the synthesis of bone organic matrix components[26] necessary for repair. Prolonged corticosteroid administration may also decrease bone density and compromise the surgeon's ability to achieve stable internal fixation, leading to nonunion.[1] The role of growth hormone in fracture healing remains uncertain. Some experimental work suggests that growth hormone deficiency adversely affects fracture healing and that growth hormone replacement can improve healing.[4,69] Other investigations indicate that excess amounts of growth hormone may have little or no effect[22,70] and that normal alterations in the level of circulating growth hormone have little effect on fracture healing. Thyroid hormone, calcitonin, insulin, and anabolic steroids have been reported in experimental situations to enhance the rate of fracture healing.[12] Diabetes, hypovitaminosis D, and rickets have been shown to retard fracture healing in experimental situations. However, clinical experience shows that fractures heal in patients with hormonal disturbances, although union may be slower than normal.

Nicotine and Other Agents. In addition to hormones, various other agents may adversely affect fracture healing. Clinical experience suggests that cigarette smoking inhibits fracture healing, and a study of tibial osteotomy healing in rabbits showed that animals exposed to nicotine healed fractures more slowly and had a higher percentage of nonunions.[76] The mechanism of the nicotine effect on bone healing remains unknown, but a study of bone graft incorporation in rabbits showed that nicotine inhibited vascularization of autogenous cancellous bone grafts.[77] Agents used to treat malignancies may also inhibit bone healing.[66]

Tissue Variables
Form of Bone (Cancellous or Cortical).
Healing of fractures in cancellous and cortical bone differs, probably because of the differences in surface area, cellularity, and vascularity. Well-apposed and impacted cancellous bone surfaces usually unite rapidly, probably because the large surface area of cancellous bone creates many points of bone contact rich in cells and blood supply and because osteoblasts can form new bone directly on existing trabeculae. Because woven bone forms across points of cancellous bone contact, stable fractures located primarily in cancellous regions, especially impacted fractures in which the trabeculae of the fracture fragments have been forced together so that they interdigitate, form little or no visible external callus, and rarely fail to heal. Where fractured cancellous bone surfaces are not impacted, new bone spreads from the points of contact to fill gaps. When a gap is excessively large, two bone-forming fronts grow from the fracture fragments and eventually meet, but if excessive motion occurs, external callus (including cartilage) may develop. In contrast, cortical bone has a much smaller surface area per unit volume and generally a less extensive internal blood supply, and regions of necrotic cortical bone must be removed before new bone can form.

Bone Necrosis. Normally, healing proceeds from both sides of a fracture, but if one fracture fragment has lost its blood supply, healing depends entirely on in-growth of capillaries from the living side or the surrounding soft tissues. If one fracture fragment is avascular the fracture can heal, but the rate is slower and the incidence of healing is lower than if both fragments have a normal blood supply.[54] If both fragments are avascular, the chances for union decrease further (Fig. 4-12). Traumatic or surgical disruption of blood vessels, infection, prolonged use of corticosteroids, and radiation treatment can cause bone necrosis. Irradiated bone, even when it is not obviously necrotic, often heals at a slower rate than normal bone.[75,91] Nonunion occurs in radiated bones[44] probably because of radiation-induced cell death, thrombosis of vessels, and fibrosis of the marrow. These changes may reduce the population of cells that can participate in repair, increase the volume of necrotic tissue, and interfere with the in-growth of capillaries and the migration of fibroblasts into the fracture site.

Bone Disease. Pathologic fractures occur through diseased bone and therefore require less force than that necessary to break normal bone. Commonly recognized causes of pathologic fractures include osteoporosis, osteomalacia, primary malignant bone tumors, metastatic bone tumors, benign bone tumors, bone cysts, osteogenesis imperfecta, fibrous dysplasia, Paget disease, hyperparathyroidism, and infections. Fractures through bone involved with primary or secondary malignancies usually will not heal if the neoplasm is not treated. Subperiosteal new bone and fracture callus may form, but the mass of malignant cells impairs or prevents fracture healing, particularly if the malignant cells continue to destroy bone. Fractures through infected bone present a similar problem. Thus, the healing of a fracture through a malignancy or infection usually requires treatment of the underlying local disease or removal of the involved portion of the bone. Depending on the extent of bone involvement and the aggressiveness of the lesion, fractures through bones with nonmalignant conditions like simple bone cysts and Paget disease will heal. The most prevalent bone disease, osteoporosis, may impair fracture healing beyond the simple consequences of aging.[32,67,85,88] When there is diminished surface contact of apposing cortical or cancellous bone surfaces due to decreased bone mass, the time required to restore normal

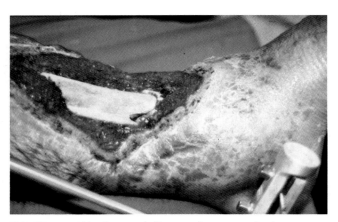

FIGURE 4-12 This photograph illustrates bone necrosis after a severe open tibia fracture with failure of soft tissue coverage. Fracture healing will not occur without aggressive intervention.

bone mechanical strength may be increased. Furthermore, decreased bone mass reduces the strength and stability of the interface between the bone and compromises internal fixation. This may lead to failure of internal fixation and subsequent delayed healing or nonunion or malunion.[85]

Infection. Infection can slow or prevent bone healing. For fracture healing to proceed at the maximum rate, the local cells must be devoted primarily to healing the fracture. If infection occurs following a fracture or if the fracture occurs as a result of the infection, many cells must be diverted to wall off and eliminate the infection and energy consumption increases. Furthermore, infection may cause necrosis of normal tissue and thrombosis of blood vessels, thereby retarding or preventing healing. Surgical debridement of infected fractures may cause further tissue damage.

Treatment Variables

Apposition of Fracture Fragments. Decreasing the fracture gap decreases the volume of repair tissue needed to heal a fracture. Restoring fracture fragment apposition is especially important if the surrounding soft tissues have been disrupted or when soft tissues are interposed between the fracture fragments. When a significant portion of the periosteum and other soft tissue components remains intact or can be rapidly restored, lack of bone fragment apposition may not impair healing.

Loading and Micromotion. The optimal conditions for fracture healing include loading of the repair tissue. Based on the available evidence it appears that loading a fracture site stimulates bone formation while decreased loading slows fracture healing.[15] In addition, experimental work and clinical experience have shown that early or even almost-immediate controlled loading and limb movement, including induced micromotion at long bone fracture sites, may promote fracture healing.[15] However, the optimal timing, intensity, and pattern of loading for specific fractures have not been defined and these factors probably vary not only among fractures, but among patients.

Fracture Stabilization. Fracture stabilization by traction, cast immobilization, external fixation, or internal fixation can facilitate fracture healing by preventing repeated disruption of repair tissue. Some fractures (e.g., displaced femoral neck and scaphoid fractures) rarely heal if they are not rigidly stabilized. Fracture stability appears to be particularly important for healing when there is extensive associated soft tissue injury, when the blood supply to the fracture site is marginal, and when the fracture occurs within a synovial joint. Excessive motion secondary to ineffective stabilization, repeated manipulation, or excessive loading and motion retards fracture healing and may cause nonunion (Fig. 4-13). In these injuries it is probable that the repeated excessive motion disrupts the initial fracture hematoma or granulation tissue, delaying or preventing formation of fracture callus. A hypertrophied callus response suggests impaired fracture fixation. If excessive motion continues, a cleft forms between the fracture ends, and a pseudarthrosis develops.

Despite the importance of stability for healing of some fractures, motion does not impair healing of all fractures. During the early part of repair, motion occurs at most fractures except for those treated by rigid internal fixation. Fractures with intact surrounding soft tissues that provide some stability in a well-vascularized region of bone may heal rapidly even though palpable motion of the fracture site persists for weeks after injury. For example, closed rib, clavicle, metacarpal, and metatarsal fractures heal even though the fracture fragments remain mobile until the fracture callus stabilizes them.

Unlike traction and cast immobilization, some forms of external fixation and internal fixation of the fractures with metallic plates can rigidly stabilize a fracture (<3% strain). Although rigid stabilization of a fracture makes possible primary bone repair without cartilage or connective tissue intermediates, it does not accelerate fracture healing. Rigid fixation of fractures makes it possible to restore and maintain anatomic apposition of the fracture fragments. This approach has proven especially beneficial in the treatment of intra-articular fractures, diaphyseal fractures of the radius and ulna, and other selected diaphyseal and metaphyseal fractures.

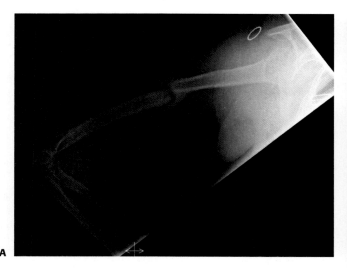

A

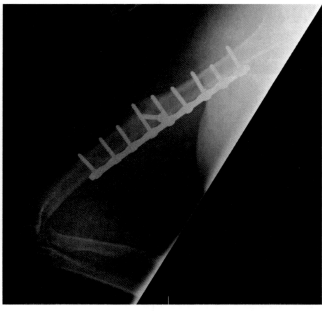

B

FIGURE 4-13 In this humeral shaft fracture, excessive motion led to a hypertrophic nonunion **(A)**. Elimination of motion with a compression plate led to healing **(B)**.

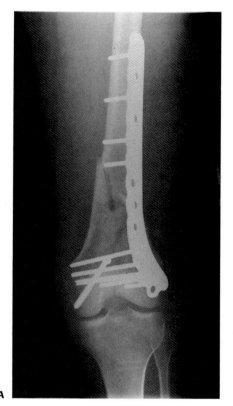 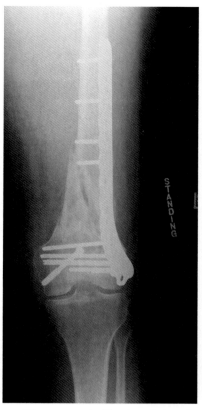 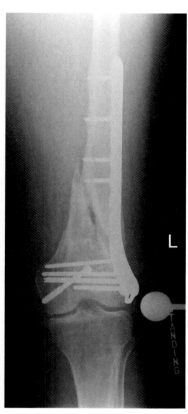

FIGURE 4-14 This distal femur fracture **(A)** was treated with a laterally based stainless steel locking plate. Radiographs 1 year **(B)** and 2 years **(C)** after surgery demonstrate absence of medial callus and a delayed union or nonunion. Using a very stiff implant may have contributed to this complication.

Although rigid internal stabilization of fractures with metallic implants has multiple advantages, it also has potential disadvantages (Fig. 4-14). Rigid fixation can alter fracture remodeling and decrease bone density because the stiffness of most implants differs from that of bone. For example, steel is more than 10 times as stiff as bone. When a fractured bone, rigidly fixed with a stiff implant, is loaded, the bone is shielded from normal stresses by the more rigid implant. Regional loss of bone mass may occur, which increases the probability of refracture following removal of the plate,[39] although refractures following removal of plates may also be due the presence of screw holes that act as stress risers.

Treatment That Interferes with Healing

Most fractures will heal when treated by various methods. Furthermore, the healing potential of many fractures, especially those in children, can overcome less than optimal treatment, but some surgical and nonsurgical interventions interfere with healing and may cause delayed union or nonunion. Surgical exposure of a fracture site can interfere with healing. The fracture hematoma is disrupted, the blood supply to the fracture site and the surrounding soft tissues may be damaged, and opening a closed fracture may lead to infection. Inadequate immobilization of some fractures (for example, scaphoid and femoral neck fractures), distraction of fracture fragments by internal or external fixation devices or traction, and repeated manipulations or excessive early motion of a fracture all may interfere with healing.

Treatment of osteoporosis can prevent subsequent fragility fractures. In the setting of an acute fracture these agents can also affect the repair process. Osteoporotic therapy initially consists of correcting vitamin D and calcium deficiency. Approximately 60% to 70% of fracture patients have either $25-(OH)$ vitamin D insufficiency (<32mg/mL) or deficiency (<20ng/mL).[34] Calcium (800 mg/day) and vitamin D (800 units/day) can decrease fracture risk by 25%. Forty-five percent of women and 66% of men with osteoporosis have secondary causes that require identification and treatment. Osteoporosis therapy is either antiresorptive (estrogen, calcitonin, selective estrogen receptor modulators, or bisphosphonates) or anabolic (parathyroid hormone [PTH]).[29,57] In the setting of an active fracture, PTH has been demonstrated in multiple animal studies to enhance the repair process.[5] Both bisphosphonates and PTH increase the callus size. Bisphosphonates delay cellular maturation while PTH speeds up callus maturation, especially the chondroid stages. Hence, in fresh fractures and osteoporosis, PTH not only treats the osteoporosis but can also enhance the repair. In the steady nonfracture state, both the bisphosphonates and PTH decrease the risk for subsequent fractures. However, after prolonged bisphosphonate use (approximately 2 years), particularly if the patient has not received adequate calcium and vitamin D supplementation, the bone turnover becomes profoundly depressed and subtrochanteric and femoral shaft stress fractures may occur in diaphyseal bone.[33,63,68] These fractures are best treated by correcting the calcium and vitamin D deficiency, halting the bisphosphonate treatment, and initiating anabolic PTH therapy.

SYNOVIAL JOINT HEALING

Because articular cartilage lacks blood vessels, it cannot respond to injury with inflammation. However, injuries that disrupt subchondral bone as well as the overlying cartilage initiate the fracture healing process in the subcondral bone, and the repair tissue from bone will fill an articular cartilage defect. Cartilage healing then follows the sequence of inflammation, repair, and remodeling like that seen in bone or dense fibrous tissue.[9,12,19,20] Even after remodeling, the articular surface usually heals with fibrocartilage that has weaker mechanical properties than the original articular cartilage.

In addition to direct mechanical injury, articular cartilage can sustain damage following disruption of the synovial membrane exposing it to the outside environment. Because of these special features, acute traumatic injuries to synovial joints can be separated into the following two categories: disruption of the soft tissues of the synovial joint without direct mechanical cartilage injury, and mechanical injury of the articular cartilage.

Healing Following Disruption of Synovial Joint Soft Tissues

Exposure of articular cartilage to air by traumatic or surgical disruption of the joint capsule and synovial membrane, or by blood in a hemarthrosis, can alter cartilage matrix composition by stimulating degradation or suppressing synthesis of proteoglycans.[18,91] A decrease in matrix proteoglycan concentration decreases cartilage stiffness and may make the tissue more vulnerable to damage from impact loading. Prompt restoration of the synovial environment by closure of the synovial membrane will allow chondrocytes to repair the damage to the macromolecular framework of the matrix, and the tissue may regain its normal composition and function. However, prolonged exposure of the articular surface to air can desiccate the tissue and kill chondrocytes.[65]

It is not clear what duration of exposure causes irreversible damage. The available evidence, based on animal experiments, suggests that damage to the matrix macromolecular framework may occur with any disruption of the synovial membrane,[19] but clinical experience suggests that permanent or progressive damage in human joints rarely occurs following temporary disruption of the synovial cavity. Furthermore, articular cartilage can be restored to its normal condition if the loss of matrix proteoglycans does not exceed the amount the cells can replenish, if a sufficient number chondrocytes remain viable, and if the collagenous meshwork of the matrix remains intact.[84]

Exposure injury to articular cartilage can be minimized by decreasing the period of time that the cartilage is unprotected by synovium or other soft tissues. If the cartilage must remain unprotected, keeping the surface moist with a physiologic solution may be helpful. Because cartilage that has sustained exposure injury may be temporarily more vulnerable to mechanical injury, it seems advisable to minimize immediate impact loading of cartilage that has experienced this type of injury.

Healing Following Damage to the Articular Surface

Acute traumatic injury to articular cartilage may occur through several mechanisms. Osteochondral fractures mechanically disrupt cartilage and bone tissue at the fracture site, but on the other hand, the injury may be limited to the cartilage with abrasion of the articular surface or the creation of chondral fractures.[18,19,20] Alternatively, blunt trauma to a synovial joint may occur without an associated bone or cartilage fracture. Therefore, acute articular cartilage injuries can be separated into those caused by blunt trauma that does not disrupt or fracture tissue and those caused by blunt trauma or other mechanisms that mechanically disrupt or fracture the tissue. Injuries that fracture or disrupt cartilage can be further divided into those limited to articular cartilage and those affecting both cartilage and subchondral bone.

Blunt Trauma without Tissue Disruption

Although the effects of acute blunt trauma on articular cartilage have not been extensively studied clinically or experimentally, blunt trauma to joints occurs frequently as an isolated injury or in association with a fracture or dislocation. Among the reasons for the limited amount of studies are the lack of clearly defined clinically significant consequences of blunt trauma to cartilage, the ability of cartilage to withstand large acute loads without apparent immediate damage, the frequent lack of a clinically detectable injury and repair response in cartilage following blunt trauma, and difficulty in defining the relationship between the intensity of blunt trauma and the extent of cartilage injury.[18] Despite these limitations, current information suggests that acute blunt trauma to articular cartilage may damage it even when there is no grossly apparent tissue disruption, and these injuries may lead to later degeneration of the articular surface.

Physiologic levels of impact loading have not been demonstrated to produce cartilage injury, and clinical experience suggests that acute impact loading considerably greater than physiologic loading but less than that necessary to produce detectable fractures rarely causes significant articular cartilage injury. However, acute impact loading less than that necessary to produce visible tissue disruption may cause chondrocyte necrosis, apoptosis, release of matrix metalloproteinases, cartilage swelling, and altered relationships between collagen fibrils and proteoglycans.[17,92,93,94] This observation suggests that blunt trauma, under at least some conditions, may disrupt the macromolecular framework of the cartilage matrix and possibly injure cells without producing a detectable fracture of the cartilage or bone. Presumably this tissue damage would make cartilage more vulnerable to subsequent injury and progressive deterioration if the cells could not rapidly restore the matrix. This type of injury may help explain the development of articular cartilage degeneration following joint dislocations or other types of acute joint trauma that do not cause visible damage to the articular surface. Blunt trauma may cause a bone bruise as evidenced by marrow edema on MRI (T2, S71R sequence). This often occurs in conjunction with a cartilage injury.[49]

Trauma That Disrupts Cartilage

Injuries Limited to Articular Cartilage. Lacerations, traumatically induced splits of articular cartilage perpendicular to the surface, or chondral fractures kill chondrocytes at the site of the injury and disrupt the matrix. Viable chondrocytes near the injury may proliferate, form clusters of new cells, and synthesize new matrix.[15] They do not migrate to the site of the injury, and the matrix they synthesize does not fill the defect. A hematoma does not form, and inflammatory cells and fibroblasts do not migrate to the site of injury. This minimal response may be due to the inability of chondrocytes to respond effectively to injury, the inability of undifferentiated mesenchymal cells to invade the tissue defect, and the lack of a clot that attracts cells and gives them a temporary matrix to adhere to and replace with more permanent tissue. Although the very limited response of chondrocytes to injury will not heal a clinically significant cartilage defect, most traumatic defects limited to small areas of articular cartilage do not progress.

Lacerations, fractures, or abrasions of the articular surface tangential or parallel to the surface presumably follow a similar course. Cells directly adjacent to the injury site may die and others may show signs of increased proliferative or synthetic activity. A thin acellular layer of nonfibrillar material may form over an injured surface, but there is no evidence that the cell activity stimulated by the injury restores the articular cartilage to its original state.

Osteochondral Injury. An articular cartilage injury that also damages subchondral bone stimulates a fracture healing response in the subchondral bone that includes inflammation, repair, and remodeling.[10,17,55] Blood from ruptured bone blood vessels fills the injury site with a hematoma that extends from the bony injury into the chondral defect. The clot may fill a small chondral defect, generally one less than several millimeters wide, but it usually does not completely fill larger defects. Inflammatory cells migrate through the clot followed by fibroblasts that begin to synthesize a collagenous matrix. In the combined bone and chondral defect some of the mesenchymal cells assume a rounded shape and begin to synthesize a matrix that closely resembles the matrix of articular cartilage.

Within weeks of injury the repair tissue forming in the chondral portion of the defect and the tissue forming in the bony portion of the defect begin to differ. Tissue in the chondral defect has a higher proportion of repair cells and matrix that resemble hyaline cartilage, while the repair tissue in the bone defect has started to form new bone. Within 6 weeks of injury repair tissue in the two locations is distinguished by the new bone formed in the bone defect, the absence of bone in the chondral defect, and the higher proportion of hyaline cartilage repair tissue in the chondral defect.

While the initial repair of an osteochondral injury usually follows a predictable course, subsequent changes in the cartilage repair tissue vary considerably among similar defects. In some chondral defects the production of a cartilaginous matrix continues and the cells may retain the appearance and some of the functions of chondrocytes, including the production of type II collagen and proteoglycans. They rarely if ever restore the matrix to the original state but they may succeed in producing a form of fibrocartilaginous scar that maintains the integrity of the articular surface and provides clinically satisfactory joint function for years. Unfortunately, in many other injuries, particularly larger ones, the cartilage repair tissue deteriorates rather than remodeling. It becomes progressively more fibrillar, and the cells lose the appearance of chondrocytes and appear to become more fibroblastic. The fibrous matrix may begin to fibrillate and fragment, eventually leaving exposed bone (Fig. 4-15). The reasons why healing of some osteochondral injuries results in the formation of fibrocartilage that may provide at

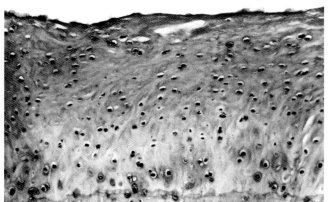

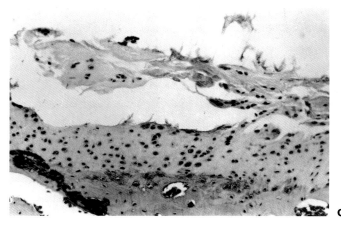

FIGURE 4-15 **A.** Normal rabbit articular cartilage showing the homogenous extracellular matrix. The chondrocytes near the articular surface are relatively small and flattened, in which those in the middle and deeper zones of the articular cartilage have a more spherical shape. **B.** Well-formed fibrocartilaginous repair cartilage. Notice that the extracellular matrix is more fibrillar and the chondrocytes do not show the same organization as normal articular cartilage. Nonetheless, this repair cartilage does fill the defect in the articular surface. In most instances after osteochondral injury, this type of tissue forms within 6 to 8 weeks. **C.** Photomicrograph showing fibrillation and fragmentation of fibrocartilaginous repair tissue. Because fibrocartilaginous repair tissue lacks the mechanical properties of normal articular cartilage, it often degenerates over time. (Reprinted from Buckwalter JA, Mow VC. Cartilage repair and osteoarthritis. In: Moskowitz RW, Howell DS, Goldberg VM, et al eds. Osteoarthritis Diagnosis and Medical/Surgical Management. 2nd Ed. Philadelphia: WB Saunders, 1992:86–87, with permission.)

least temporary joint function, while others fail to repair, have not been well defined.

Variables That Influence Cartilage Healing

Injury Variables

The volume and surface area of cartilage injury and the degrees of disruption of joint congruity and stability can influence joint healing (Fig. 4-16).[9,19] Furthermore, clinical experience suggests that high-intensity joint trauma may cause articular cartilage damage that is not detectable by current imaging methods. Although it is generally accepted that more severe joint injuries are more likely to lead to progressive joint degeneration and osteoarthritis, the relationships between specific injury variables including the intensity of force applied to the joint surface, the degree of articular surface comminution and incongruity, and the degree of joint instability and the risk of osteoarthritis have not been defined.

Patient Variables

As in other tissues, patient age may influence the healing potential of cartilage injuries.[10,21,55,56,57,58] That is, infants or young children have a greater potential to heal and remodel chondral and osteochondral injuries than older individuals, although this has not been thoroughly investigated. Other patient variables such as weight, activity level, and systemic disease may be clinically important, but their influence has not been demonstrated.

Treatment Variables

Apposition. Because experimental work indicates that smaller defects in articular cartilage tend to heal more successfully,[19,24]

it seems reasonable to expect that treatments that decrease the volume and surface area of a chondral defect, such as open reduction and internal fixation of osteochondral fractures, will increase the probability of successful cartilage repair. Experimental work indicates that 1-mm or smaller defects tend to heal more successfully than larger defects[19,24] and eliminating the gap between articular fracture fragments results in better anatomic restoration of an articular surface. Therefore, decreasing the width of an osteochondral fracture gap should increase the probability of a clinically successful result. However, depending on the location of the chondral injury within the joint and the presence or absence of other injuries to the joint, some persistent separation of osteochondral fractures or loss of segments of the articular surface may not produce clinically significant disturbances of synovial joint function or rapid cartilage deterioration.[55]

The clinical results of the treatment of intra-articular fractures show that articular surfaces can sustain limited traumatic loss of cartilage without immediate disturbance of joint function and possibly without long-term consequences. However, the extent of tolerable loss of the articular surface has not been defined and may vary among joints.[55]

Loading and Motion. Prolonged immobilization of a joint following osteochondral fractures can lead to significant adhesion formation as well as deterioration of the uninjured cartilage, resulting in poor synovial joint function. Early motion during the repair and remodeling phases of healing decreases or prevents adhesions and the immobilization-induced deterioration of uninjured cartilage. However, loading and motion must be used carefully following injury, because these measures alone

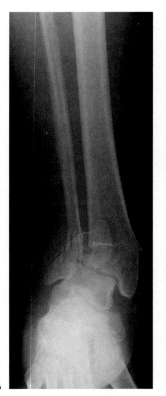
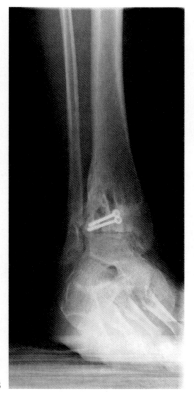
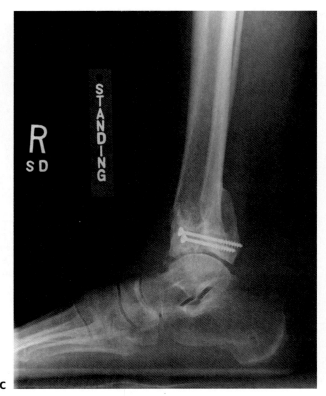

A   **B**   **C**

FIGURE 4-16 A severe tibial plafond fracture **(A)** has extensive cartilage injury and is at high risk to progress to posttraumatic arthritis despite surgical treatment **(B,C)**.

will not predictably restore normal articular cartilage structure and composition in clinically significant defects, and excessive loading and motion may damage chondral repair tissue and displace fracture fragments.

Restoration of Joint Congruity. Significant traumatically induced joint incongruity causes mechanical joint dysfunction including instability, locking, catching, and restricted range of motion, and may be associated with progressive deterioration of the articular cartilage. It is not clear how much of the long-term cartilage deterioration following injuries that cause joint incongruity is secondary to the traumatic cartilage damage at the time of injury and how much is related to the long-term effects of incongruity. However, in most injuries restoration of acceptable joint congruity avoids immediate problems with mechanical joint dysfunction and may delay or decrease the severity and rate of cartilage deterioration.

Unfortunately, the degree of joint incongruity that can be tolerated without causing long-term joint deterioration has not been well defined. A study of contact stress aberrations following imprecise reduction of experimental human cadaver tibial plateau fractures showed that, in general, peak local cartilage pressure increased with increasing joint incongruity (fracture fragment step-off), but the results varied among specimens.[8] In most specimens, cartilage pressure did not increase significantly until the fragment step-off exceeded 1.5 mm. When the step-off was increased to 3 mm, the peak cartilage pressure averaged 75% greater than normal. The authors estimated that the long-term "pressure tolerance level'" of cartilage may be much higher, probably about twice the normal level, indicating that simple incongruities of several millimeters should not cause immediate or long-term problems. However, they also found that in some specimens even minor incongruities, as little as 0.25 mm, caused apparently deleterious peak local pressure elevations, suggesting that results may vary even among individuals with the same degree of articular incongruity. Experimental study of intra-articular fractures stabilized with a step-off shows that the articular surface can remodel, thereby decreasing the original incongruity.[50] The long-term results of traumatically induced articular incongruity may also depend on the age of the patient. Skeletally immature individuals may have a greater capacity to remodel incongruities, and age-related alterations in articular cartilage[21] may decrease its capacity to repair injuries or withstand alterations in loading caused by joint incongruity.

Stabilization. Mechanical stabilization of an osteochondral injury in an acceptable position increases the likelihood of satisfactory healing by preventing disruption of the repair tissue and restoring articular cartilage congruity. An equally important benefit of stabilizing osteochondral fractures is that it allows early controlled loading and motion. Continuous passive motion enhances soft tissue healing, especially healing of the cartilage injury.[71]

SUMMARY

The primary tissues that form bones and joints, bone, and articular cartilage differ in their composition, structure, and capacity for healing. Bone fractures initiate a response that begins with inflammation (the cellular and vascular response to injury), pro-

ceeds through repair (the replacement of damaged or lost cells and matrices with new cells and matrices), and ends with remodeling (removal, replacement, and reorganization of the repair tissue, usually along the lines of mechanical stress). Injury to articular cartilage does not trigger an inflammatory response, but the cells respond to injury with an effort at cell proliferation and the synthesis of new matrix. This effort rarely, if ever, restores a normal articular surface. When injuries extend through articular cartilage into bone, the repair tissue that forms in the bone extends into the region of the chondral injury and produces a fibrocartilaginous tissue that in some instances restores a functional articular surface.

The principles of treating acute bone and joint injuries include preventing further tissue damage, avoiding treatments that compromise the natural healing process, and creating the optimal mechanical and biological conditions for healing. This may include removing necrotic tissue, preventing infection, rapidly restoring blood supply when necessary, and in some circumstances providing apposition, alignment, and stabilization of the injured tissues. One of the most important recent advances in the treatment of bone and joint injuries has been the recognition that early controlled loading and motion of the repair and remodeling tissues improves healing of many injuries. However, as with all treatments, this intervention must be used with care, since uncontrolled or excessive loading and motion can adversely affect or even prevent healing. At the tissue level, the effect of the mechanical environment on repair and the function of the repair tissue cells are not well understood, and at the clinical level the optimal protocols for loading and motion of musculoskeletal tissue injuries have not been well defined. Although future improvements in the treatment of musculoskeletal tissue injuries, including controlled motion and loading of repair and remodeling tissue, use of ultrasound and electrical fields, and surgical restoration of apposition and mechanical stability of injured tissue undoubtedly will advance the practice of orthopedics, it is not likely that they will restore the original state of the tissue for patients with the most severe musculoskeletal tissue injuries. In particular, large segmental losses of bone and many articular cartilage injuries will continue to present especially difficult treatment problems. Future developments that may help improve healing of these injuries include the creation and implantation of synthetic matrices and the use of growth factors and implanted mesenchymal cells to guide and promote regeneration of bone and articular cartilage.

REFERENCES

1. Adinoff AD, Hollister JR. Steroid induced fractures and bone loss in patients with asthma. N Eng J Med 1983;309:265–268.
2. Anderson HC, Hodges PT, Agieilera XM, et al. Bone morphogenetic protein (BMP) localization in developing human and rat growth plate methaphyses, epiphysis, and articular cartilage. J Histochem Cytochem 2000;48:1493–1502.
3. Aro HT, Wippermann BW, Hodgson SF, et al. Prediction of properties of fracture callus by measurement of mineral density using microbone densitometry. J Bone Joint Surg 1989;71A:1020–1030.
4. Bak B, Jorgensen PH, Andreassen TT. The stimulating effect of growth hormone on fracture healing is dependent on onset and duration of administration. Clin Orthop 1991;264:295–301.
5. Barnes GL, Kakar S, Vora S, et al. Stimulation of fracture healing with systemic intermitten parathyroid hormone treatment. JBJS Am 2008;90S:120–127.
6. Bishop GB, Einhorn TA. Current and future clinical applications of bone morphogenetic proteins in orthopaedic trauma surgery. Int Orthop 2007;31:721–727.
7. Brighton CT, Hunt RM. Early histologic and ultrastructural changes in microvessels of periosteal callus. J Orthop Trauma 1997;71:244–253.
8. Brown TD, Anderson DD, Nepola JV, et al. Contact stress aberrations following imprecise reduction of simple tibial plateau fractures. J Orthop Res 1988;6:851–862.

9. Buckwalter JA. Articular cartilage injuries. Clin Orthop 2002;21–37.

10. Buckwalter JA, Brown TD. Joint injury, repair, and remodeling: roles in posttraumatic osteoarthritis. Clin Orthop 2004;7–16.

11. Buckwalter JA. Can tissue engineering help orthopaedic patients? Clinical needs and criteria for success. In: Sandell LJ, Grodzinsky AJ, eds. Tissue Engineering in Musculoskeletal Clinical Practice. Rosemont IL: American Academy of Orthopaedic Surgeons, 2004:3–16.

12. Buckwalter JA, Einhorn TA, Bolander ME, et al. Healing of musculoskeletal tissues. In Rockwood CA, Green D, eds. Fractures. Philadelphia: Lippincott, 1996:261–304.

13. Buckwalter JA, Glimcher MJ, Cooper RR, et al. Bone biology. Part I. Structure, blood supply, cells, matrix, and mineralization. J Bone Joint Surg 1995;77A:1256–1275.

14. Buckwalter JA, Glimcher MM, Cooper RR, et al. Bone biology. Part II. Formation, form, modeling, and remodeling. J Bone Joint Surg 1995;77A:1276–1289.

15. Buckwalter JA, Grodzinsky AJ. Loading of healing bone, fibrous tissue, and muscle: implications for orthopedic practice. J Am Acad Orthop Surg 1999;7:291–299.

16. Buckwalter JA, Mankin HJ. Articular cartilage I. Tissue design and chondrocyte-matrix interactions. J Bone Joint Surg 1997;79A:600–611.

17. Buckwalter JA, Martin JA, Olmstead M, et al. Osteochondral repair of primate knee femoral and patellar articular surfaces: implications for preventing posttraumatic osteoarthritis. Iowa Orthop J 2003;23:66–74.

18. Buckwalter JA. Mechanical injuries of articular cartilage. In: Finerman G, ed. Biology and Biomechanics of the Traumatized Synovial Joint. Park Ridge IL: American Academy of Orthopaedic Surgeons, 1992:83–96.

19. Buckwalter JA, Rosenberg LA, Hunziker EB. Articular cartilage: composition, structure, response to injury, and methods of facilitation repair. In: Ewing JW, ed. Articular Cartilage and Knee Joint Function: Basic Science and Arthroscopy. New York: Raven Press, 1990:19–56.

20. Buckwalter JA, Rosenberg LC, R.Coutts, et al. Articular cartilage: injury and repair. In Woo SL, Buckwalter JA, eds. Injury and Repair of the Musculoskeletal Soft Tissues. Park Ridge, IL: American Academy of Orthopaedic Surgeons, 1988:465–482.

21. Buckwalter JA, Woo SL-Y, Goldberg VM, et al. Soft tissue aging and musculoskeletal function. J Bone Joint Surg 1993;75A:1533–1548.

22. Carpenter JE, Hipp JA, Gerhart TN, et al. Failure of growth hormone to alter the biomechanics of fracture-healing in a rabbit model. J Bone Joint Surg 1992;74A:359–367.

23. Clark CC, Tolin BS, Brighton CT. The effect of oxygen tension on progeoglycan synthesis and aggregation in mammalian growth plate chondrocytes. J Orthop Res 1991;9:477–484.

24. Convery FR, Akeson WH, Keown GH. The repair of large osteochondral defects: an experimental study in horses. Clin Orthop 1972;82:253–262.

25. Covas, DT, Panepucci RA, Fortes AM, et al. Multipatent mesenchymal stromal cells obtained from diverse human tissues share functional properties and gene-expression profile with CD 146⁺ perivascular cells and fibroblasts. Exp. Mematol 2008;36:642–654.

26. Cruess RL, Sakai T. Effect of cortisone upon synthesis rates of some components of rat bone matrix. Clin Orthop 1972;86:253–259.

27. Cuthbertson DP. Further observations of the disturbance of metabolism caused by injury, with particular reference to the dietary requirements of fracture cases. Br J Surg 1936;23:505–520.

28. Efron PA, Martins A, Minnich D, et al. Characterization of the systemic loss of dendritic cells in murine lymph nodes during polymicrobial sepsis. J Orthop Trauma 2003;17(9):635–641.

29. Einhorn TA, Bonnarens F, Burstein AH. The contributions of dietary protein and mineral to the healing of experimental fractures. A biomechanical study. J Bone Joint Surg 1986;68A:1389–1395.

30. Einhorn TA. The cell and molecular biology of fracture healing. Clin Ortho 1998;335 (Suppl):S7–S21.

31. Gardner MJ, Demetrakopoulos D, Shindle MK, et al. Prevention and treatment of osteoporotic fractures. Minerva Med 2005;96:343–352.

32. Giannoudis P, Tzioupis C, Almalki T, et al. Fracture healing in osteoporotic fractures: is it really different? A basic science perspective. Injury 2007;38:590–599.

33. Goodman AH, Sherman MS. Postirradiation fractures of the femoral neck. J Bone Joint Surg 1963;45A:723–730.

34. Glowacki J, LeBoff MS, Kolatkar NS, et al. Importance of vitamin D in hospital-based fracture care pathways. J Nutri Health Aging 2008;12:291–293.

35. Goh SK, Yong K-Y, Koh JS, et al. Subtrochanteric insufficiency fractures in patients on alendronate therapy: a caution. JBJS Br 2007;89:349–353.

36. Gruber R, Koch H, Doll BA, et al. Fracture healing in elderly patients. Exp Gerontol 2006;41:1080–1093.

37. Grundnes O, Reikeras O. The importance of the hematoma for fracture healing in rats. Acat Orthop Scand 1993;64:340–342.

38. Grundnes O, Reikeras O. The role of the hematoma and periosteal sealing for fracture healing in rats. Acat Orthop Scand 1993;64:47–49.

39. Hidaka S, Gustilo RB. Refracture of bones of the forearm after plate removal. J Bone Joint Surg 1984;66A:1241–1243.

40. Hirao M, Tamai N, Tsumaki N, et al. Oxygen tension regulates chondrocyte differentiation and function during endochondral ossification. J Biol Chem 2006;281:31079–31092.

41. Hollinger JO, Anikepe AO, MacKrell J, et al. Accelerated fracture healing in the geriatric, osteoporotic rat with recombinant human platelet-derived growth factor—BB and an injectable beta-tricalcium phosphate/collagen matrix. J Orthop Res 2008;26:83–90.

42. Idjadi JA, Aharonoff GB, Su H, et al. Hip fracture outcomes in patients with Parkinson disease. Am J Orthop 2005;34:341–346.

43. Jansen NW, Roosendaal G, Bijlsma JW, et al. Exposure of human cartilage tissue to low concentrations of blood for a short period of time leads to prolonged cartilage damage: an in vitro study. Arthritis Rheum 2007;56(1):199–207.

44. Jensen JE, Jensen TG, Smith TK, et al. Nutrition in orthopedic surgery. J Bone Joint Surg 1982;64A:1263–1272.

45. Karlsson MK, Nilsson BE, Obrant KJ. Bone mineral loss after lower extremity trauma: 62 cases followed for 15–38 years. Acta Orthop Scand 1993;64:362–364.

46. Kayal RA, Tsatsas D, Bauer MA, et al. Diminished bone formation during diabetic fracture healing is related to premature resorption of cartilage associated with increased osteoclast activity. J Bone Miner Res 2007;22:560–568.

47. Koval KJ, Maurer SG, Su ET, et al. The effects of nutritional status on outcome after hip fracture. J Ortho Trauma 1999;13:164–169.

48. Leung KS, Sher AH, Lam TSW, et al. Energy metabolism in fracture healing. J Bone Joint Surg 1989;71B:567–660.

49. Li X, MA BC, Bolbos RI, et al. Quantitation assessment of bone marrow edema-like lesion and overlying cartilage in knees with osteoarthritis and anterior cruciate ligament tear using MR imaging and spectroscopic imaging at 3 Testa. J Magn Reson Imaging 2008;28:453–461.

50. Llinas A, McKellop HA, Marshall GJ, et al. Healing and remodeling of articular incongruities in a rabbit fracture model. J Bone Joint Surg 1993;75:1508–1523.

51. Lu C, Hansen E, Sapozhnikova A, et al. Effect of age on vascularization during fracture repair. J Orthop Res 2008;26:1384–1389.

52. Malladi P, Xu Y, Chiou M, et al. Effect of reduced oxygen tension on chondrogenesis and osteogenesis in adipose-derived mesenchymal cells. Am J Physiol Cell Physiol 2006;290:1139–1146.

53. Mark H, Penington A, Nannmark U, et al. Microvascular invasion during endochondral ossification in experimental fractures in rats. Bone 2004;35:535–542.

54. Marsh JL, Buckwalter JA, Evarts CM. Nonunion, delayed union, malunion, and avascular necrosis. In: Epps CH, ed. Complications in Orthopaedic Surgery. Philadelphia: Lippincott, 1994:183–211.

55. Marsh JL, Buckwalter J, Gelberman R, et al. Articular fractures: does an anatomic reduction really change the result? J Bone Joint Surg Am 2002;84-A:1259–1271.

56. Martin JA, Buckwalter JA. Telomere erosion and senescence in human articular cartilage chondrocytes. J Gerontol A Biol Sci Med Sci 2001;56-B:172–179.

57. Martin JA, Buckwalter JA. The role of chondrocyte senescence in the pathogenesis of osteoarthritis and in limiting cartilage repair. J Bone Joint Surg Am 2003;85-A(Suppl 2):106–110.

58. Martin JA, Ellerbroek SM, Buckwalter JA. Age-related decline in chondrocyte response to insulin-like growth factor-I: the role of growth factor binding proteins. J Orthop Res 1997;15:491–498.

59. Martin JA, Klingelhutz AJ, Moussavi-Harami F, et al. Effects of oxidative damage and telomerase activity on human articular cartilage chondrocyte senescence. J Gerontol A Biol Sci Med Sci 2004;59:324–337.

60. Matta JM. Fracturing of the acetabulum: accuracy of reduction and clinical results in patients managed operatively within 3 weeks after the injuries. J Bone Jt Surg 1996;78A:1632–1645.

61. Mauck KF, Clarke BL. Diagnosis, screening, prevention, and treatment of osteoporosis. Mayo Clin Proc 2006;81:662–672.

62. McKibbin B. The biology of fracture healing in long bones. J Bone Jt Surg 1978;60B:150–162.

63. Michelsen CG, Askanazi J. Current concepts review: the metabolic response to injury: mechanism and clinical implantations. J Bone Joint Surg 1986;68A:782–787.

64. Milentijevic D, Rubel IF, Liew AS, et al. An in vivo rabbit model for cartilage trauma: a preliminary study of the influence of impact stress magnitude on chondrocyte death and matrix damage. J Orthop Trauma 2005;19(7):466–473.

65. Mitchell N, Shepard N. The deleterious effects of drying on articular cartilage. J Bone Joint Surg 1989;71A:89–95.

66. Morcuende JA, Gomez P, Stack J, et al. Effect of chemotherapy on segmental bone healing enhanced by rhBMP-2. Iowa Orthop J 2004;24:36–42.

67. Namkung-Matthai H, Appleyard R, Jansen J, et al. Osteoporosis influences the early period of fracture healing in a rat osteoporotic model. Bone 2001;28:80–86.

68. Neviaser As, Lane JM, Lenart BA, et al. Low-energy femoral shaft fractures associated with alendronateuse. J Orthop Trauma 2008;22:346–350.

69. Nielson HM, Bak B, Jorgensen PH, et al. Growth hormone promotes healing of tibial fractures in the rat. Acta Orthop Scand 1991;62:244–247.

70. Northmore-Ball MD, Wood MR, Meggitt BF. A biomechanical study of the effects of growth hormone in experimental fracture healing. J Bone Joint Surg 1980;62B:391–396.

71. Nugent-Derfus GE, Takara T, O'Neill JK, et al. Continuous passive motion applied to whole joints stimulated chondrocyte biosynthesis of PRG4. Osteoarthritis Cartilage 2007;15:566–574.

72. Olson SA. Open fractures of the tibial shaft: current treatment. J Bone Jt Surg 1996;78A:1428–1437.

73. Parvumal V, Roberts CS. Factors contributing to nonunion of fractures. Current Orthopaedics 2007;21:258–261.

74. Patterson BM, Cornell CN, Carbone B, et al. Protein depletion and metabolic stress in elderly patients who have a fracture of the hip. JBJS Am 1992;74:251–260.

75. Pelker RR, Friedlaender GE. Fracture healing: radiation-induced alterations. Clin Ortho 1997;341:267–282.

76. Raikin SM, Landsman JC, Alexander VA, et al. Effect of nicotine on the rate and strength of long bone fracture healing. Clin Ortho 1998;353:231–237.

77. Riebel GD, Boden SD, Whitesides TE, et al. The effect of nicotine on incorporation of cancellous bone graft in an animal model. Spine 1995;20:2198–2202.

78. Reilly TM, Seldes R, Lunchetti W, Brighton CT. Similarities in the phenotype expression of pericytes and bone cells. CORR 1998;346:95–103.

79. Richardson J, Mill AM, Johnston CJ, et al. Fracture healing in HIV-positive populations. J Bone Jt Surg 2008;90:988–994.

80. Rommens PM, Coosemans W, Broos PL. The difficult healing of segmental fractures of the tibial shaft. Arch Orthop Traum Surg 1989;108:238–242.

81. Ryaby JT, Sheller MR, Levine BP, et al. Thrombin peptide TP 508 stimulates cellular events leading to angiogenesis, revascularization, and repair of dermal and musculoskeletal tissues. JBJS Am 2006;88S:7:32–39.

82. Sandberg MJ, Aro HT, Vuorio EL. Gene expression during bone repair. Clin Orthop 1993;289:292–312.

83. Simmons DJ, Kunvin AS. Autoradiographic and biochemical investigations of the effect of cortisone on the bones of the rat. Clin Orthop 1967;55:201–215.

84. Speer KP, Callaghan JJ, Seaber AV, et al. The effects of exposure of articular cartilage to air. A histochemical and ultrastructural investigation. J Bone Joint Surg 1990;72A:1442–1450.

85. Stromsoe K. Fracture fixation problems in osteoporosis. Injury 2004;35:107–113.

86. Strube P, Sentuerk U, Riha T, et al. Influence of age and mechanical stability on bone defect healing: age reverses mechanical effects. Bone 2008;42:758–764.

87. Torzilli PA, Grigiene R, Borrelli J Jr, et al. Effect of impact load on articular cartilage:

cell metabolism and viability, and matrix water content. J Biomech Eng 1999;121(5): 433–441.

88. Wang JW, Li W, Xu SW, et al. Osteoporosis influences the middle and late periods of fracture healing in a rat osteoporotic model. Chin J Traumatol 2005;8:111–116.

89. Watson-Jones R. Fractures and Joint Injuries, vol 2. 4th Ed. Edinburgh: Livingstone, 1955.

90. White AA, Panjabi MM, Southwick WO. The four biomechanical stages of fracture repair. J Bone Joint Surg 1977;59A:188–192.

91. Widmann RF, Pelker RR, Friedlander GE, et al. Effects of prefracture irradiation on the biomechanical parameters of fracture healing. J Orthop Res 1993;11:422–428.

92. Wildemann B, Schmidmaier G, Brenner N, et al. Quantification, localization, and expression of IGF-I and TGF-beta1 during growth factor–stimulated fracture healing. Calcif Tissue Int 2004;74:388–397.

93. Wiel HE, Lips P, Nauta J, et al. Loss of bone in the proximal part of the femur following unstable fractures of the leg. J Bone Joint Surg 1994;76A:230–236.

94. Woll TS, Duwelius PJ. The segmental tibia fracture. Clin Orthop 1992;281:204–207.

5

BIOLOGICAL AND BIOPHYSICAL TECHNOLOGIES FOR THE ENHANCEMENT OF FRACTURE REPAIR

T. William Axelrad, Sanjeev Kakar, and Thomas A. Einhorn

INTRODUCTION

Fractures heal and remodel during a well-orchestrated biological process that includes multiple signaling pathways and is regulated by both local and systemic factors. Despite this physiologic control, it is estimated that between 5% and 10% of the fractures occurring annually in the United States exhibit some degree of impaired healing.[67] In many instances, the cause of the impairment is unknown and may be related to inadequate reduction, instability,[48] the systemic state of the patient,[68,151] or the nature and extent of energy associated with the traumatic insult itself.[170,228] In addition, there are certain areas within the appendicular skeleton that have a predilection to impaired healing because of aspects of the local biomechanical environment or anatomy of the blood supply. Examples include open fractures of the tibia that have delayed union rates of between 16% and 100% depending on the grade of injury[92]; the scaphoid and femoral neck, where the repair processes are influenced by the anatomy of arterial blood flow[60,93,177]; and the subtrochanteric region of the femur, where mechanical loads are among the highest in the appendicular skeleton.[114]

While fracture healing typically occurs without incident, complications related to delay in union or nonunion can be severe with regard to patient morbidity and medical treatment costs. Direct costs for treatments of tibia nonunions have been estimated to be approximately $7500, and these can escalate to $17,000 when indirect costs such as loss of work productivity are taken into account.[38] To improve and expedite repair, surgeons may consider the use of bone grafts or orthobiologic agents. This chapter will review the current use and development of these materials in the restoration of skeletal function.

BONE GRAFTS AND BONE GRAFT SUBSTITUTES

The use of bone grafts for the treatment of bone defects is increasing, and the indications are growing with rising numbers of spinal fusions, primary and revision arthroplasties, and periprosthetic fractures.[10,154,198,236] It is estimated that more than 2.2 million bone grafts are performed worldwide each year, with 450,000 performed in the United States.[140] In addition to the treatment of musculoskeletal injuries and conditions, a significant number of grafts are used in the repair and reconstruction of the craniofacial bones.[218]

The gold standard for bone grafting remains autogenous bone graft because it provides the basic components required to stimulate skeletal repair, including osteoinductive factors, an osteoconductive extracellular matrix, and osteogenic stem cells present in the form of bone marrow elements. *Osteoinduction* refers to the process by which pluripotent mesenchymal stem cells are recruited from the surrounding host tissues and differentiate into bone-forming osteoprogenitor cells. This is mediated by graft-derived growth factors such as bone morphogenetic proteins and other peptide signaling molecules.[211,229] *Osteoconduction* is a process in which the macroscopic and microscopic architecture of bone, as well as its surface chemistry and charge, serves as a scaffold to support the ingrowth of blood vessels and the attachment of osteoprogenitor cells. This occurs in an ordered sequence determined by the three-dimensional structure of the graft, the local blood supply, and the biomechanical forces exerted on the graft and surrounding tissues.[211] *Osteogenesis* refers to the process of bone formation and is conducted by fully mature osteoblasts. With regard to bone grafting, an osteogenic material is one that contains live donor osteoblasts capable of producing bone or osteoprogenitor cells that have the ability to differentiate into osteoblasts in the host.

Autogenous bone grafting provides consistent results with regard to healing and integration[21,137,195,209]; however, the morbidity associated with graft harvesting, such as donor site pain, nerve or arterial injury, and infection rates of between 8% and 10%,[15,77,91,219,242] have prompted extensive research into alternatives. One alternative that has gained acceptance for a variety of procedures is allograft bone.[35,65,94,108,200] While the problems related to autogenous graft harvesting are avoided, limitations such as decreased or absent osteoinductive potential[20] and increased cost have restricted its use.[176] In addition, although current methods of donor selection and screening have greatly reduced the risk, the issue of disease transmission remains a concern for many patients and surgeons.[16,110] For these reasons, the development of effective bone graft substitutes and strategies for tissue engineering of bone have led to a new field of study for the future of fracture management.

Autologous Bone

Autologous bone grafting is the standard to which all materials and technologies to enhance bone healing are compared. It provides the ideal graft requirements in terms of osteoinductivity, osteoconductivity, and osteogenicity. The most common and best-described sources of autologous bone include the pelvis, the distal radius,[216] the fibula,[137] the proximal tibia,[171] and the ribs.[145]

Through the harvesting of the patient's own bone, the potential for a graft-versus-host reaction is eliminated, as is

the risk of disease transmission. Based on the type of graft needed, either cancellous or cortical bone can be harvested. There is also the potential to harvest a vascularized graft, particularly from the fibula or the rib. Careful planning is needed to ensure that the proposed harvest site will contain both the correct type and amount of graft. For example, a large segmental defect in the tibia would need a large structural graft,[73,159] whereas a tibia plateau fracture with a depressed fragment may just require a small amount of cancellous graft.

The sequences of events that occur after bone grafting are similar to those involved in the normal repair process and include hematoma formation and recruitment of circulating progenitor cells in response to the release of proinflammatory and proangiogenic factors.[24] The recruited cells then begin the process of graft incorporation, and osteoclasts begin resorption of necrotic graft material. Pluripotential mesenchymal cells respond to local growth factors and differentiate into osteoblasts that produce osteoid. While osteoblasts and endosteal lining cells on the surface of the graft may survive the transplantation and contribute to the healing, it is likely that the main contribution of the graft is to act as an osteoinductive and osteoconductive substrate. These properties provide the necessary physical and chemical requirements to support the attachment, spreading, division, and differentiation of the cells that form bone. The final stages in the process involve mineralization of the osteoid, remodeling of the callus, and incorporation of the remaining graft. The process of remodeling of the callus (composed of woven bone) involves the coordinated activities of osteoblastic bone formation and osteoclastic bone resorption, with woven bone ultimately being replaced by lamellar bone.

Autologous Cancellous Bone Graft

Cancellous bone is an effective graft material for specific types of fractures, particularly those that do not require immediate structural support from the graft. Its main function is to act as a scaffold for the attachment of host cells and to provide the osteoconductive and osteoinductive functions required for the laying down of new bone. The process by which the graft is replaced by new bone is known as "creeping substitution"[210] and is usually complete within 1 year (Fig. 5-1, Table 5-1).

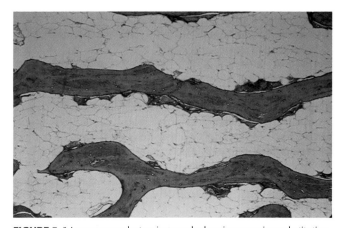

FIGURE 5-1 Low-power photomicrograph showing creeping substitution. Newly formed woven bone, containing osteoblasts with basophilic-staining nuclei, is laid down upon dead lamellar bone identified by the presence of empty osteocytic lacunae (hematoxylin and eosin stain, original magnification ×10).

TABLE 5-1	Properties of Types of Autologous Bone Grafts		
Property	Cancellous	Nonvascularized Cortical	Vascularized Cortical
Osteoconduction	+ + +	+	+
Osteoinduction	+ +*	+/−	+/−
Osteoprogenitor cells	+ + +	−	+ +
Immediate strength	−	+ + +	+ + +
Strength at 6 months	+ +	+ +, + + +	+ + +
Strength at 1 year	+ + +	+ + +	+ + +

*Although cancellous bone is widely believed to be osteoinductive, there is no evidence to critically demonstrate that inductive proteins and cytokines are active in autologous cancellous bone graft.
Reprinted with permission from Finkemeier CG. Bone grafting and bone graft substitutes. J Bone J Surg Am 2002;84:454 – 464.

Commonly used sources of cancellous graft include the iliac crest, distal radius, greater trochanter, and proximal tibial and distal femoral metaphyses.[130,171] While cancellous graft does not provide structural support by itself, it can be impacted into skeletal defects and, in conjunction with internal fixation devices, support areas of bone loss. Examples of this use are in the treatment of depressed fractures of the tibial plateau and in revision hip and knee arthroplasty where there is bone loss.[224,225]

Autologous Cortical Bone Graft

Cortical bone can provide structural support as well as osteoconductive and osteoinductive properties. Cortical bone grafts are usually harvested from the ribs, fibula, or crest of the ilium (as a so-called tricortical graft) and can be transplanted with or without a vascular pedicle. Nonvascularized grafts are mostly osteoconductive and possibly provide some osteoinductive properties but possess little or no osteogenic properties because they contain very few osteoblasts or osteoprogenitor cells (Table 5-1). Diffusion of nutrients is limited by the thickness of the cortical matrix, and, as such, the survival of transplanted osteocytes is limited.[57] The density of the graft also plays a role in the incorporation and remodeling process. Revascularization of the graft is slow as the dense cortical bone must be resorbed. Remodeling proceeds as it does for cancellous bone but can require up to 2 years for completion.[37,72,203]

Vascularized bone graft biology is different from its nonvascularized counterpart, not only in terms of the rate of repair but also in the way in which remodeling occurs.[57] Once implanted with its viable vascular pedicle, there is the provision of an immediate blood supply that is independent of the surrounding bone. Using a canine model, Shaffer et al.[203] demonstrated that at 1 week after transplantation, six of eight vascularized grafts contained patent cortical vessels, while the cortices of contralateral nonvascularized grafts did not show evidence of vascularity until 6 weeks. In addition, osteocyte survival was greater after vascularized transplantation. Dell et al.[57] examined vascularized and nonvascularized grafts histologically and graded the amount of necrosis based on the presence or absence of osteocytes. At 2 weeks, the vascularized graft remained mostly viable, with the only area of necrosis noted at the periphery. In comparison, conventional nonvascularized grafts showed diffuse necrosis of the medullary cavity and it was not until 24 weeks that the histologic appearance of the two became

similar. The increase in osteocyte survival and the early vascularity seen in vascularized grafts are consistent with the observation of more rapid incorporation of vascularized bone graft compared with nonvascularized grafts.[86,203]

The differences in the remodeling of nonvascularized and vascularized grafts are the result of the vascular source. Nonvascularized grafts are incorporated from the outside in through creeping substitution, resulting in substantial callus formation. In contrast, vascularized grafts do not induce the vast angiogenic response seen at the cortex of nonvascularized grafts and most of the early mechanical strength is derived from the graft itself. By 6 weeks, in a canine model, both grafts demonstrate comparable strength but through vastly different processes.[57]

In the treatment of bone defects that will not heal without grafting, also known as critical-sized defects, both vascularized and nonvascularized grafts are indicated. For defects up to 6 cm in length where immediate structural support is desired, nonvascularized grafts can be used.[75] Controversy exists regarding the best alternative for defects between 6 and 12 cm, while defects greater than 12 cm are good candidates for vascularized grafting procedures.[57,73] Vascularized grafts are also indicated for reconstruction of defects where the microenvironment of the host is inadequate to initiate an effective biological response. Examples of this include acute traumatic injuries with extensive soft tissue damage and impairment of blood supply, atrophic nonunions, and irradiated or severely scarred tissue.[57,73]

Mesenchymal Stem Cells

Fracture repair requires that progenitor cells be present or recruited to the site of injury to provide a source of cells to differentiate into chondroblasts and osteoblasts during endochondral and intramembranous bone formation. Progenitor cells have the capability of differentiating into different cell types. At first these cells are totipotent, in which case they have the ability to form any cell type in the body, and then they progress toward more committed, or monopotent cells. In contrast, multipotent cells, such as mesenchymal stem cells (MSCs), can be directed toward cells of a specific germ layer only.[185]

In the elderly, the pool of available progenitor cells may be diminished, leading to delayed or possibly impaired fracture healing.[95,214] The aging process affects the available pool of stems cells, specifically the endothelial progenitor cells (EPCs) and MSCs.[55,222]

Adult MSCs obtained from bone marrow have been shown

to be a source of autologous graft material. When Muschler et al.[163] aspirated MSCs from the iliac crest, they noted that the mean prevalence of colony-forming units expressing alkaline phosphatase (CFU-APs), a marker of osteoblast progenitors, was 55 per 1 million nucleated cells (57 patients; 31 men and 16 women; age range, 15 to 83 years and 13 to 79 years). The investigators also demonstrated an age-related decline in the number of progenitor cells for both men and women. When considered as graft material, these investigators showed that the volume of aspirate used for grafting can affect the number of CFU-APs. As the aspirate volume increases, so does the number of CFU-APs. Contamination of the sample by peripheral blood, however, increases as the aspiration volume increases. Increasing the aspirate volume from 1 to 4 mL caused an approximate 50% decrease in the final concentration of CFU-APs, resulting in the need to aspirate multiple sites to obtain the needed number of progenitor cells.[162] These and other findings have resulted in the search for alternatives to standard autogenous bone marrow grafting, including the use of allogeneic MSCs and expansion of autogenous cells in vitro.

Several animal models have been developed that demonstrate improved bone healing with grafts of autogenous bone marrow containing MSCs.[33,174,180] Early reports in patients with the use of unconcentrated bone marrow showed promising results. Healy et al.[100] treated eight patients with nine nonunions using injections of freshly harvested, unconcentrated autologous bone marrow. The nonunions were the result of failed bone grafting with internal fixation following en bloc resection of lower extremity sarcomas of bone. The results showed that five of nine constructs had achieved union, with new bone formation evident in seven of the patients.

Hernigou et al.[104] studied percutaneous injection of concentrated autologous bone marrow aspirated from the iliac crests in 60 patients with established nonunions of the tibia. Analysis of the patients at 6 months found that bony union had occurred in 53 of the patients as determined by clinical and radiographic criteria. A retrospective analysis of the composition of the graft found that osteogenic progenitor cell concentration was significantly lower (<1000 cells/cm^3) in the seven patients who failed to achieve union in comparison to the 53 who did. In light of these findings, the authors recommend the use of greater than 1000 progenitors/cm^3 in the treatment of tibial nonunions.

The early work on isolation and culturing of autologous MSCs was performed by Bruder et al.[31,32] and Jaiswal et al.[117] The ability to concentrate stems cells and to culture and expand them in vitro were two major accomplishments in the development of this technology. Work in several laboratories demonstrated that MSCs could also be isolated, cryopreserved, and expanded without the loss of osteogenic potential.[32,99,117] An important breakthrough in the use of MSCs as a bone graft substitute occurred through a series of experiments in both humans and animals. It was shown that allogenic MSC xenografts placed in utero would differentiate and persist for up to 13 months. Others found, in humans, autologous culture expanded MSCs could be infused without clinically significant adverse events.[136,145] Le Blanc et al. studied this phenomenon by combining MSCs with allogenic mixed lymphocyte cultures and found that the lymphocytes actually inhibited proliferation of the MCSs and that this suppression was most significant for MSCs that had differentiated into the osteoblastic lineage.[137] Critical-sized defects in dogs treated with allogenic stem cells

loaded onto ceramic carriers have demonstrated healing similar to those treated with autologous cells, and no immunologic responses were observed at any time points.[9]

In addition to adult stem cells, it has been hypothesized that embryonic stem cells are deposited during embryogenesis in various organs, including bone marrow, and may persist in these locations into adulthood as pluripotent stem cells.[85,132] These cells have the capability to both respond to a normal repair process in the body and participate in the repair of soft tissue and bone. Examples of such cells include very small embryonic-like (VSEL) cells, multipotent adult progenitor cells (MAPCs), MSCs, and marrow-isolated adult multilineage inducible (MIAMI) cells.[184] These cells express the embryonic specific gene *Oct-4*$^+$, a gene that is downregulated during development. Although there is little known about the use of these cells for skeletal grafting, there is currently great interest in gaining a better understanding of their potential because the use of embryonic stems cells in other organ systems has yielded impressive results.[186]

Allogeneic Bone

The morbidity associated with harvesting autogenous bone grafts, as well as the limited amount of bone available to fill large defects, has led to the use of alternative methods of treating skeletal defects and promoting bony union. A popular alternative is the use of allograft or allogeneic bone, because it is relatively abundant and has shown good healing potential in several studies.[46,108,274] Allografts are frequently used in spinal surgery[64] and in joint arthroplasty[71,160] and account for approximately one third of the bone grafts performed in the United States.[28] Despite their widespread use in elective procedures, considerably less is known about their use in the repair of fresh fractures or nonunions.

Limitations of the efficacy of allogeneic bone as a bone graft material may be attributed to its storage and sterilization procedures such as freeze-drying or freezing that are used to lower the rate of disease transmission. Freeze-drying, or lyophilization, involves removal of water and vacuum packing of the tissue and has been shown to significantly reduce immunogenicity, including the expression of the major histocompatibility complex (MHC) class I antigen in osteoblasts.[80,243] Conversely, Pelker et al.[178] demonstrated that such treatment of the graft reduces its mechanical integrity, thereby diminishing its load-bearing properties. In addition, freeze-drying reduces the osteoinductive potential of the allograft by inducing the death of its osteogenic cells. Allogeneic bone is available in many preparations including morselized and cancellous chips, cortico-cancellous and cortical grafts, osteochondral segments, and demineralized bone matrix.[75]

The processes involved in allograft incorporation are similar to those seen with nonvascularized autografts, except that they occur much more slowly, particularly when large grafts are used.[87] This is in part related to the lack of viable donor cells that contribute to healing and the immune response that occurs during the inflammatory process of allograft incorporation. This results in limited revascularization, creeping substitution, and remodeling of the graft.[36,212] Studies have suggested that this lack of vascularization may account for the high incidence of fractures seen with these grafts, which has been reported to occur in between 16% and 50% of cases.[74,221] Histologically, mononuclear cells invade the graft and surround newly developing blood vessels. Necrotic graft bone remains in the host tissue much longer compared with autograft bone and may be seen for many years after implantation depending on the size of the graft and its anatomic location.[88,211]

Enneking et al.[74] reported the histologic evaluation of 73 retrieved allografts. Of these specimens, 24 (33%) were obtained at autopsy or after amputation. The investigators were able to study the incorporation of grafts over time and found that, overall, vascular penetration of the graft and healing were poor. During the first 2 years, new vessel penetration rarely exceeded a depth of 5 mm, and new bone apposition occupied no more than 20% of the graft. The depth of penetration after 2 years was typically less than 10 mm, although 80% of the surface area of the graft was found to be attached to the local soft tissues. Overall, necrotic tissue remained in the central aspects of the allograft, and these areas appeared to be isolated from the remodeling process.

The biological nature of the recipient host bed is a critical factor in facilitating allograft incorporation. A well-vascularized bed aids in the incorporation of the allograft through a combination of revascularization, osteoconduction, and remodeling.[123]

Cortical allografts are harvested from a number of sites including the pelvis, ribs, and fibula. They are available as whole bone segments for limb salvage procedures or they may be cut longitudinally to yield struts that can be used to fill bone defects or reconstitute cortical bone after periprosthetic fractures.[97] The relative inertness of cortical allografts limits their potential to achieve graft–host union. To improve this, autogenous graft harvested from the iliac crest can be placed at the allograft–host bone interface. This technique was described by Wang and Weng[235] in the treatment of distal femoral nonunions. Thirteen patients with femoral nonunions were treated with open reduction and internal fixation with deep-frozen cortical allograft struts. Seven unicortical, five bicortical, and one tricortical allograft, with an average length of 10 cm, were used. Autogenous bone grafts were inserted into the defect between the allograft and host femur. All nonunions united at an average of 5 months.

Demineralized Bone Matrix

Demineralized bone matrix (DBM) is produced by acid extraction of allograft bone.[231] It contains type I collagen, noncollagenous proteins, and osteoinductive growth factors but provides little structural support.[150] The bioavailability of the growth factors contained in DBM results in its greater osteoinductive potential than conventional allografts.[76] These properties can be affected by different storage, processing, and sterilization procedures. Donor-to-donor variability in the osteoinductive capacity of DBM exists, resulting in the requirement by the American Association of Tissue Banks and the U.S. Food and Drug Administration (FDA) that each batch of DBM be obtained from a single human donor.[12]

Studies in rats have shown that implantation of DBM is followed by hematoma formation and an inflammatory process characterized by polymorphonuclear cell migration into the implant within 18 hours. MSCs differentiate into cartilage-producing chondrocytes by day 5. The cartilage becomes mineralized and is then invaded by new blood vessels by 10 to 12 days. The accompanying perivascular cells differentiate into osteoblasts, leading to new bone formation. Remodeling then occurs with all implanted DBM being eventually resorbed and replaced by host bone.[211]

Tiedeman et al.[223] reported a case series on the use of DBM in conjunction with bone marrow in the treatment of 39 patients with either fresh fractures associated with bone loss or comminution, nonunions, joint arthrodesis, or cavitary lesions resulting from tumor or joint revisions. All 39 patients were available for follow-up and review, and 30 demonstrated bony union. Patients with fracture nonunion represented the most recalcitrant group clinically, with union being achieved in only 11 of 18 patients. Because no control patients were included in the study, the efficacy of the DBM–bone marrow composite could not be determined. Ziran et al.[244] followed 107 patients treated with DBM and cancellous allograft bone chips for the treatment of acute fractures with bone loss or atrophic nonunions, the majority (18 of 25) of which occurred in smokers. They found that 87 fractures healed at a mean of 32 months.

Numerous DBM formulations exist based on refinements of the manufacturing processes. They are available as a freeze-dried powder, granules, gel, putty, or strips. All have osteoinductive effects in animal studies, while human studies have shown mixed results. A prospective nonrandomized study comparing the use of autograft and human DBM (Grafton, Osteotech, Inc., Eatontown, NJ) in anterior cervical spine fusion found higher rates of pseudarthrosis and graft collapse with DBM, although the differences did not reach statistical significance.[4] Ziran et al.[245] retrospectively reviewed 41 patients with atrophic and oligotrophic nonunions treated with human DBM (AlloMatrix; Wright Medical Technologies, Memphis, TN). Postoperative complications were high, with 51% experiencing wound complications, of which 32% required operative debridement. Of the 41 treated patients, only 22 went on to heal without the need for additional bone grafting. Bibbo et al.[23] studied the use of human DBM and calcium sulfate compound (AlloMatrix Wright Medical, Arlington, TN) combined with vancomycin for the treatment of calcaneal fractures. Their results demonstrated that fractures treated with AlloMatrix and vancomycin healed at a mean of 8.2 weeks, compared with 10.4 weeks needed for those that were not grafted. It is interesting to note that while the study was not randomized, the fractures that received DBM and calcium sulfate represented more significant injuries in that they had substantial bone loss and included six open fractures (Gustilo grade 1). Hierholzer et al.[106] retrospectively reviewed the results of the treatment of 45 aseptic nonunions of the humerus treated with either autograft or DBM allograft (Grafton; Osteotech, Inc., Eatontown, NJ). The union rate in the 45 patients treated with autograft was 100%, which was similar to the 97% union rate in 33 patients treated with DBM. Donor site pain was a significant problem in the patients treated with autograft, with 44% of the patients experiencing prolonged pain or paresthesias and one patient having a superficial infection requiring operative debridement.

AUTHORS' PREFERRED METHOD OF TREATMENT

Autologous Cancellous Bone Graft

We prefer the use of autologous cancellous bone graft for the augmentation of fractures associated with bone loss, nonunions, and small bone defects requiring grafting (e.g., a metaphyseal or middiaphyseal cyst that has undergone curettage). Diaphyseal defects up to 12 cm in length can be treated with nonvascularized cortical autografts. For defects of more than 12 centimeters, vascularized cortical autografts are recommended. We do not believe there is sufficient information, nor have there been sufficient studies providing good evidence, to support the use of freshly harvested, unconcentrated autologous bone marrow in traumatic or reconstructive orthopaedic surgery. Because the number of osteoprogenitor cells in any human bone marrow aspirate is very small, it is unclear if this complement of cells can support a robust osteogenic response. However, freshly harvested autologous bone marrow, obtained by multiple aspirations of no more than 5 mL each, in conjunction with the use of so-called selective retention methods or methods involving centrifugation of the freshly harvested bone marrow may optimize the concentration of osteoprogenitor cells and serve as an effective graft material.[103,105]

There is not much information on the use of allogeneic bone to enhance the healing of fresh fractures or nonunions. We suggest that allogeneic cancellous bone chips be used to augment the healing of fresh fractures associated with bone loss or to treat nonunions when used in conjunction with autologous bone to make up a sufficient volume of graft material. Incorporation of allogeneic strut grafts may also be enhanced by the use of autogenous cancellous bone at the junction with the host bone.

The efficacy of human DBM as a graft material remains unclear. Although widely available and known to contain bone morphogenetic protein (BMP), we do not believe there is sufficient evidence demonstrating its efficacy when used alone in the treatment of fresh fractures or nonunions or the reconstruction of bone defects. However, we and others have used DBM in conjunction with autologous cancellous bone to increase the volume of graft material. We have also used DBM as a delivery vehicle for bone marrow aspirate concentrate. In these settings, we believe that DBM provides an osteogenic advantage and may enhance the ability of a fixed volume of autologous graft or bone marrow to be effective.

Bone Graft Substitutes

The ideal bone graft substitute would provide three elements: scaffolding for osteoconduction, growth factors for osteoinduction, and progenitor cells for osteogenesis.[233] The currently available materials, including calcium phosphate ceramics, calcium sulfate, bioactive glass, biodegradable polymers, recombinant human BMPs (osteogenic protein 1 [OP-1] and BMP-2), and autologous bone marrow cells, each fulfill only some of these criteria.[139]

Calcium Phosphate Ceramics

An ideal osteoconductive scaffold should have the appropriate three-dimensional structure to allow for osteointegration and invasion by cells and blood vessels. It should also be biocompatible and biodegradable with biomechanical properties similar to those of the surrounding bone. Many of the ceramics used as bone grafts enable osteoconduction to occur.[69,234] Despite this, their brittleness and poor tensile strength limit their use as bone graft materials.

The first clinical use of calcium phosphate ceramics for the repair of bony defects was reported by Albee in 1920.[2] Since then, several animal studies have reported favorable results. Despite these early experiments, it was not until the 1970s that calcium phosphates, and in particular, hydroxyapatite (HA), were synthesized, characterized, and used clinically.[118,156,191] Calcium phosphate ceramics are osteoconductive materials produced by a sintering process in which mineral salts are heated to over 1000°C. Sintering reduces the amount of carbonated apatite, an unstable and weakly soluble form of HA.

Hydroxyapatite. Calcium phosphate ceramics can be divided into slow and rapid resorbing ceramics, and this difference is important with regard to whether the compound will need to provide long-term structural support or is acting as a void filler that will be quickly replaced.[76] HA is a slow resorbing compound that is derived from several sources, both animal[153] and synthetic.[102,187] Interpore (Interpore International, Irvine, CA) is a coralline hydroxyapatite and was the first calcium phosphate–based bone graft substitute approved by the FDA. A simple hydrothermal treatment process converts it from its native coral state to the more·stable HA form with pore diameters of between 200 and 500 μm, a structure very similar to human trabecular bone. Bucholz et al.[34] investigated its use to treat tibial plateau fractures. Forty patients with metaphyseal defects needing operative reduction were randomized into a control group treated with autogenous bone graft or a group treated with Interpore HA. Indications for surgery included valgus instability of the knee secondary to a lateral tibial plateau fracture, varus instability because of a medial plateau injury, articular incongruence of 10 mm or greater, and translation of the major condylar fragment of greater than 5 mm. After insertion of the graft, cortical fracture fragments were reduced, and a standard AO interfragmentary screw and plate fixation device was used to stabilize the reduction. With an average of 15.4 months for the autograft and 34.5 months for the Interpore-treated groups, radiographic and functional knee joint assessments revealed no differences between the two groups. No evidence of ceramic resorption was found in the radiographic follow-up 3 years after implantation, highlighting the potential use of HA as a bone filler. Attempts at using HA as a stand-alone implant for fixation in distal radius fractures did not show such promising results.[119] Compared with Kapandji wiring, those fractures treated with HA only showed substantial loss of reduction at 6, 12, and 26 weeks. Clinical parameters were also decreased for the HA-treated patients with regard to decreased grip strength and palmar flexion.

Tricalcium Phosphate. Tricalcium phosphate (TCP) undergoes partial resorption and some of it may be converted to HA once implanted in the body. The composition of TCP is very similar to the calcium and phosphate phase of human bone. This combined with its porous nature appears to facilitate incorporation with host bone in both animals and humans by 24 months.[11,84]

Reports have demonstrated the efficacy of TCP as a bone graft substitute. McAndrew et al.[156] investigated the suitability of TCP to treat bony defects in a case series of 43 patients with 33 acute fractures and 13 nonunions. Patients were followed for an average of 1 year. Healing was demonstrated in 90% of the fracture patients and 85% of those with nonunions. Radiographic analysis showed complete resorption of TCP between 6 and 24 months after implantation.

Anker et al.[8] retrospectively reviewed 24 patients with 24 bone defects treated with TCP. Most of the defects were metaphyseal and located in the lower extremity. The average defect size was 43 cm^3, and the patients were followed for an average of 10 months. Full weight bearing in patients with a lower extremity defect occurred at a mean of 7 weeks, and radiographic follow-up showed that the graft had completely resorbed in all but except patient at 6 months.

Calcium Phosphate–Collagen Composite. Collagen is the most abundant protein in the extracellular matrix of bone and promotes mineral deposition by providing binding sites for matrix proteins. Types I and III collagen have been combined with HA, TCP, and autologous bone marrow to form a graft material devoid of structural support but able to function as an effective bone graft substitute or bone graft expander to augment fracture healing. This was demonstrated by Chapman et al.,[45] who conducted a multicenter prospective randomized controlled study comparing autogenous bone graft and a composite of bovine collagen, calcium phosphate, and autogenous bone marrow (Collagraft; Zimmer, Inc., Warsaw, IN) in the treatment of acute long bone fractures. Two hundred forty-nine fractures were grafted and followed for a minimum of 2 years. The authors observed no significant differences between the two treatment groups in terms of union rates, functional outcomes, or impairment of activities of daily living. The prevalence of complications was similar in the two groups except for higher infection rates in patients receiving autogenous bone grafts. Antibodies to the bovine collagen developed in 12% of the patients in the Collagraft-treated group but no specific allergic problems were identified. Similar results using this material have been reported by others.[52,128,134]

Calcium Sulfate. Calcium sulfate, or plaster of Paris, was first used as a bone filler in the early 1900s.[217] It acts as an osteoconductive material, which completely resorbs as newly formed bone remodels and restores anatomic features and structural properties.

Moed et al.[158] investigated the use of calcium sulfate as a bone graft substitute in a prospective nonrandomized clinical study for the treatment of acetabular fractures with intra-articular comminution, marginal impaction, or both. Thirty-two fractures were treated with calcium sulfate pellets. Radiographic analysis demonstrated that the majority of fractures healed successfully with most of the pellets being replaced by bone. Two groups of investigators reported the use of calcium sulfate as a material that augments or extends the use of autologous bone graft. In a prospective nonrandomized multicenter study, Kelly et al.[121] treated 109 patients with bone defects with calcium sulfate pellets alone or mixed with unconcentrated bone marrow aspirate, demineralized bone, or autograft. After 6 months, the radiographic results showed that 99% of the pellets were resorbed and 88% of the defects were filled with trabeculated bone. Borrelli et al.[26] treated 26 patients with persistent long bone nonunions or osseous defects after an open fracture, with a mixture of autogenous iliac crest bone graft and medical-grade calcium sulfate. Twenty-two patients achieved healing after the primary surgery, while an additional two demonstrated union after a second procedure. Persistent nonunions were seen in two patients.

Combinations of DBM and calcium sulfate have been tested with the thought that they would be both osteoconductive and osteoinductive, as well as provide structural support. Early results in animals indicate that this combination may have benefits.[23] Despite these encouraging reports, there have been no randomized controlled trials to study the efficacy of calcium sulfate in the treatment of skeletal injuries.

Calcium Phosphate Cements
Calcium phosphate cements (CPCs) can be used as bone-void fillers in the treatment of bony defects associated with acute fractures. Inorganic calcium and phosphate are combined to form an injectable paste that can be delivered into the fracture site.

Sanchez-Sotelo et al.[194] conducted a prospective randomized controlled study examining the use of a commercially available CPC, Norian SRS (Norian Corporation, Cupertino, CA), in the treatment of distal radius fractures. Under physiologic conditions, this material begins to harden within minutes, forming a mineral known as dahllite. By 12 hours, dahllite formation is nearly complete, providing the cement with an ultimate compressive strength of 55 megapascals (MPa).[89] In comparison, proximal tibia trabecular bone from human cadavers has an ultimate stress that varies with age.[63] Younger patients (16 to 39 years) had an average ultimate stress of 10.6 MPa, while older individuals (60 to 83 years) had significantly lower values at 7.27 MPa. Studies in animals have shown that it is remodeled in vivo and, in some cases, is completely resorbed and replaced by host bone.[50] One hundred ten patients, who were between 50 and 85 years of age and who had sustained either an AO type A3 or C2 distal radius fracture, were enrolled. Patients were prospectively randomized to receive either closed reduction with a short arm cast for 6 weeks or closed reduction and stabilization with Norian SRS for 2 weeks. They were followed for a 12-month period and assessed by radiography, range of motion, and grip strength. The results showed improved functional and radiographic outcomes in the patients treated with Norian SRS. In a subsequent randomized controlled study, Cassidy et al.[44] compared the use of Norian SRS and closed reduction to closed reduction and the application of a cast or external fixation in 323 patients with fractures of the distal radius. Significant clinical differences were seen at 6 to 8 weeks postoperatively, with better grip strength, wrist and digit range of motion, and hand function and less swelling in the patients treated with Norian SRS. By 1 year, these differences had disappeared.

In light of the promising results seen with distal radius fractures, Norian SRS has been used to treat other fractures. Schildhauer et al.[197] reported its use in the treatment of complex calcaneal fractures. Thirty-six joint depression fractures were treated with Norian SRS after standard open reduction and internal fixation. Patients were allowed to bear weight fully as early as 3 weeks postoperatively. Results demonstrated no statistical difference in clinical outcome scores in patients who bore full weight before or after 6 weeks postoperatively, suggesting that this cement may permit early full weight bearing after treatment of this fracture.

Biomechanical studies in vivo and in vitro have also found improved function of calcium phosphate cements compared with the gold standard of autograft with regard to structural support in tibial plateau fractures. Yetkinler et al.[241] evaluated the compressive strength of TCP compared with autograft in experimentally created centrally depressed tibial plateau fractures treated with two screws. The cadaveric tibia were then subjected to 10,000 cycles of load, after which they were loaded to failure. Results showed no difference in the load to failure; however, the TCP-treated specimens showed significantly less displacement than control subjects. Welch et al.[237] created bilateral subchondral defects that were 8 mm in diameter and 10 mm deep beneath the subchondral bone of the articular cartilage in the lateral tibial plateau of goats. These defects were filled with cancellous autograft or TCP and the tibias were harvested at varying time points during the healing process. At all times, the subsidence at the fracture site was significantly less in those treated with TCP, with a mean subsidence of 0.3 mm at 6 months compared with 3.7 mm in the control group.

Lobenhoffer and coworkers[147] used Norian SRS in the treatment of 26 tibial plateau fractures (OTA types B2, B3, and C3) followed for a mean of 19.7 months. Successive radiographs were obtained and clinical parameters were measured using the Lysholm knee score and Tegner activity scale. Twenty-two fractures healed without any displacement or complications. Two cases required early wound revision secondary to sterile drainage, and two cases developed partial loss of fracture reduction between 4 and 8 weeks postoperatively requiring revision surgery. The high mechanical strength of the cement allowed earlier weight bearing after a mean postoperative period of 4.5 weeks (Fig. 5-2). Similar results supporting the use of Norian SRS for filling metaphyseal defects in the treatment of displaced tibial plateau fractures have been reported by others.[109,237] Simpson et al.[206] followed 13 tibial plateau fractures treated with either limited internal fixation and injectable Norian SRS or buttress plating and cancellous autograft. At 1-year follow-up, the mean subsidence of the autograft-treated group was 4 mm, while the SRS-treated group had only subsided 0.7 mm.

A recent metaanalysis by Bajammal et al.[13] reviewed 14 randomized controlled trials that evaluated calcium phosphate cement. They found that the use of calcium phosphate cement was associated with a lower incidence of pain compared with control subjects. They also found a 68% relative risk reduction in the loss of fracture reduction compared with fractures supplemented with autograft. Despite this, sterile serous drainage was reported in at least three of the papers.[146,155,232] The exact cause for the sterile drainage is not known but may be related to

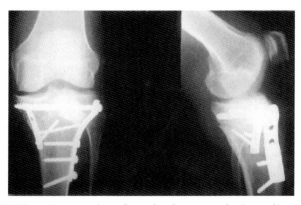

FIGURE 5-2 Postoperative radiographs after open reduction and internal fixation and injection of 19.5 mL of the calcium phosphate cement Norian SRS in the lateral tibail plateau defect. The patient used crutches and walked bearing partial weight for 6 weeks. (Reprinted with permission from Lobenhoffer P, Gerich T, Witte F, et al. Use of an injectable calcium phosphate bone cement in the treatment of tibial plateau fractures: a prospective study of 26 cases with 27 mean follow-up. J Orthop Trauma 2002;16:143–149.)

local reaction to cement particles or loose bodies secondary to hematoma formation before complete curing of the cement.

AUTHORS' PREFERRED METHOD OF TREATMENT

Calcium-Based Bone Graft Substitutes and Calcium Phosphate–Based Cement

The calcium-based bone graft substitutes are best used as bone void fillers when it is possible to implant them such that they are surrounded by host bone on all sides. It is preferable to use them in parts of the skeleton where tensile strains are low or nonexistent. Calcium sulfate, which is much more rapidly resorbed than the other calcium-based materials, must be used in parts of the skeleton where compressive strength is required for only short periods. These materials should not be used to bridge segmental diaphyseal defects or as onlay grafts where the majority of the surface is exposed to soft tissues.

Calcium phosphate–based cement has been tested in several randomized controlled clinical trials. Based on these data, its use to shorten the time in a cast during treatment of distal radius fractures or to shorten the time to weight bearing in the augmentation of tibial plateau and calcaneal fractures is supported by clinical evidence and this is a viable treatment options for these indications. It may be useful in other applications such as acetabular fractures and fractures of the hip, but sufficient evidence is not yet available for its use in these settings.

ENHANCEMENT OF FRACTURE HEALING WITH GROWTH FACTORS AND RELATED MOLECULES

The regulation of cell growth and tissue repair occurs through a host of signaling molecules, including systemic hormones, peptide growth factors, and proinflammatory cytokines. These molecules have autocrine, paracrine, or endocrine effects through actions on appropriate target cells. In addition to promoting cell differentiation, some have direct effects on cell adhesion, proliferation, and migration by modulating the synthesis of proteins, other growth factors, and receptors.[120]

Bone Morphogenetic Proteins

Since the discovery of the osteoinductive properties of BMP,[230] attention has focused on the role of these proteins in embryologic development and bone repair in the postnatal skeleton.[47,120,188] BMPs are a group of noncollagenous glycoproteins that belong to the transforming growth factor beta (TGF-β) superfamily. They are synthesized locally and predominantly exert their effects by autocrine and paracrine mechanisms. Fifteen different human BMPs have been identified and their genes cloned.[54] For clinical applications, the most extensively studied among these are BMP-2 and BMP-7 (also called OP-1).

The importance of BMPs in bone repair has been the subject of much investigation. Cho et al.[47] characterized the temporal expression of BMPs during fracture healing in mice, defining specific periods when individual BMPs may exert important roles in normal skeletal repair. BMP-2 showed maximal expression on day 1 after fracture, suggesting its role as an early response gene in the cascade of healing events. BMP-3, -4, -7, and -8 exhibited a restricted period of expression from day 14 through day 21, when the resorption of calcified cartilage and osteoblastic recruitment were most active. BMP-5 and -6 were constitutively expressed from day 3 to day 21.

Initial human studies were undertaken to determine if BMPs were likely to play a key role during fracture healing in patients. Kloen et al.[126] demonstrated the presence of BMPs and their various receptors in human fracture callus. Tissue was obtained from the fracture site of malunions in five patients undergoing a corrective osteotomy. Immunohistochemical analysis was performed and results demonstrated consistent positive staining for all BMPs and BMP receptors, with immunoreactivity most intense for BMP-3 and -7. More recently, Rosen et al. demonstrated the importance of BMP-2 in the fracture repair cascade. Tibia fractures were produced in transgenic mice in which BMP-2 was deleted in a limb-specific manner, before the onset of skeletal development. Mice heterozygous for this mutation were shown to have impaired healing during the earliest stages of repair with reduced periosteal reaction and decreased formation of other BMPs involved in the repair process (e.g., BMP-4 and BMP-7). However, in mice homozygous for this mutation, fracture healing was completely abolished. This study demonstrated that BMP-2 is essential for fracture healing.[226]

Several investigations have tested the use of recombinant human BMPs (BMPs synthesized by recombinant gene technology using human BMP DNA) in the treatment of fractures and nonunions. In a large prospective randomized controlled, partially blinded, multicenter study, Friedlaender et al.[81] assessed the efficacy of recombinant human (rh)BMP-7 (OP-1) versus iliac crest bone graft in the treatment of 122 patients with 124 tibial nonunions. All of the nonunions were treated with reduction and fixation with an intramedullary nail and were randomized to receive either autologous bone graft or implantation of rhBMP-7 (OP-1) in a type I collagen carrier. Clinical assessment at 9 months indicated equivalent rates of union, with 81% of the 63 patients treated with BMP-7 and 85% of the 61 control patients demonstrating evidence of healing. Radiographic assessments showed bridging callus in 75% and 84% of these patients, respectively. As these results showed equivalent efficacy between OP-1 and autogenous bone graft, the authors concluded that OP-1 was a safe and effective alternative to bone graft in the treatment of tibial nonunions (Fig. 5-3).

Bong et al.[25] prospectively followed 23 patients with humeral nonunions treated with plate and screw or intramedullary nail fixation in conjunction with various combinations of autograft, allograft, or DBM. In addition, patients were treated with recombinant human (rh)OP-1 contained within a type I collagen matrix implant. The investigators found that all patients had healed at an average of 144.3 days. They concluded that OP-1 used in conjunction with allograft and/or DBM was an effective alternative to autograft for the treatment of humeral nonunions. A similar study was performed in 26 fracture nonunions in 25 patients treated with OP-1 and followed to union.[62] Of the 26 fractures, 17 also received autologous bone graft at the time of final fixation. Radiographic union occurred in 24 of the 26 fractures at an average of 5.6 months. The two cases of persistent nonunion occurred in open fractures that were complicated by infection prior to the application of OP-1.

Another TGF-β family member, BMP-2, has shown promise in the treatment of acute fractures in several human studies. The BMP-2 Evaluation in Surgery for Tibial Trauma (BESTT)

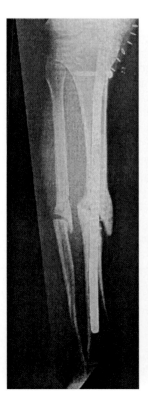
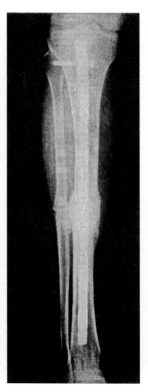
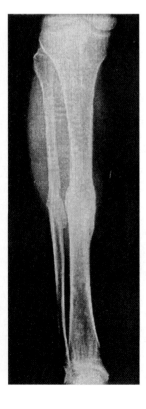

FIGURE 5-3 Sequential radiographs of a tibial nonunion treated with recombinant human OP-1 immediately postoperatively and at 9 months and 24 months after intramedullary nailing. Note the bridging callus and subsequent tibial union. [Reprinted with permission from Friedlaender GE, Perry CR, Cole JD, et al. Osteogenic protein 1 (bone morphogenetic protein 7) in the treatment of tibial nonunions. J Bone Joint Surg Am 2001;83:S151–S158].

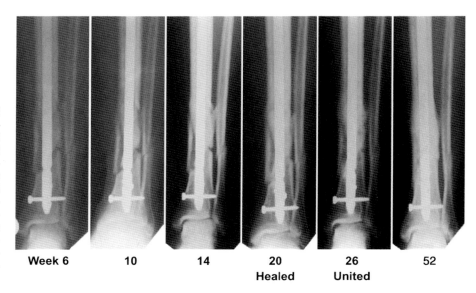

FIGURE 5-4 Radiographs of a patient who had sustained an open fracture of the left tibia (Gustilo and Anderson type IIIB) and was treated with an unreamed intramedullary nail and 1.50 mg/mL recombinant human BMP-2. The fracture was considered to be clinically healed by 20 weeks and healed radiographically by 26 weeks. (Reprinted with permission from Govender S, Csimma C, Genant HK, et al. Recombinant human bone morphogenetic protein 2 for treatment of open tibial fractures. A prospective, controlled, randomized study of 450 patients. J Bone Joint Surg Am 2002;84:2123–2134).

Week 6   10   14   20 Healed   26 United   52

Study Group reported on a large prospective randomized controlled multicenter trial evaluating the effects of rhBMP-2 in the treatment of open tibial fractures.[92] Four hundred fifty patients with these injuries were randomized to receive either initial irrigation and debridement followed by treatment with intramedullary (IM) nail fixation alone or IM fixation plus an implant containing either 0.75 mg/kg or 1.5 mg/ kg rhBMP-2. The implant was placed over the fracture site at the time of wound closure. After 1 year, there were fewer secondary interventions (returns to the operating room for additional treatment) in the group treated with 1.5 mg/kg rhBMP-2. In addition, those patients treated with 1.5 mg/kg rhBMP-2 had accelerated times to union, improved wound healing, and reduced infection rates (Fig. 5-4). A subgroup analysis was performed on this cohort by Swiontkowski et al.,[215] who also included results in 60 additional patients treated in a similar manner. The investigators analyzed 113 patients with either type IIIA or IIIB open fractures and included only patients who received placebo (65 patients) or 1.5 mg/ml of rhBMP-2 (66 patients). The results showed that the treatment group required significantly fewer bone grafts to achieve union and had a lower incidence of infection.

Despite numerous studies of the positive effects of BMPs in animal models of fracture healing and critical-sized defect repair, results of the use of BMPs in patients have been less impressive. Diefenderfer et al.[61] noted that one of the reasons may be a differential response of human bone marrow stromal cells to BMPs. Bone marrow cells isolated from patients undergoing hip replacement were cultured and grown to confluence with or without dexamethasone and treated with BMPs. The results demonstrated no significant osteogenic response to BMP-2, -4, or -7 as determined by alkaline phosphatase induction, unless the cells were pretreated with dexamethasone. Moreover, even when the cells were pretreated, the alkaline phosphatase response to BMPs was only about 50% of that measured in mouse bone marrow cell cultures. The authors concluded that the ability of human bone marrow cells to respond to BMPs may differ substantially from that which exists in lower mammalian species.

Other Peptide Signaling Molecules

In addition to the BMPs, other growth factors act on both the progenitor cells and local inflammatory cells that create the rich

vascular network at the site of fracture repair. Some of the factors directly enhance the effects of local BMPs, whereas others stimulate local inflammation and angiogenesis, both of which are prerequisites for bone healing. While none of these factors are currently available for clinical treatment of fractures, each has shown promise in animal models and in the treatment of other disease processes.

Transforming Growth Factor-β

TGF-β is similar in structure to the BMPs and has many similar functions. It is known to influence a number of cell processes including the stimulation of MSC growth and differentiation, enhancement of collagen, and other extracellular matrix protein synthesis, and it functions as a chemotactic factor for fibroblast and macrophage recruitment.[124]

Several studies have found dose-dependent effects of TGF-β on fracture healing, with high and low doses having different effects. Lind et al.[146] tested two doses of TGF-β in rabbits in which tibial defects had undergone unilateral plate fixation. After 6 weeks of healing, the investigators found that bending stiffness was only improved in the group treated with the low dose, while callus formation was significantly improved for both doses. Critchlow et al.[53] performed a study of tibial defect healing in rabbits to test the hypothesis that the anabolic effects of TGF-β on bone repair are dependent on mechanical stability at the fracture site. The results showed that under stable mechanical conditions, a low dose of TGF-β_2 had an insignificant effect on callus development, whereas the higher dose, which was closer to the low dose used by Lind et al.,[170] led to a larger callus.

From these studies, TGF-β appears to have some efficacy in augmenting fracture healing; however, the effects are highly dose dependent and not especially robust. Although its application to directly influence fracture repair has not been as promising as those of several of the BMPs, a recombinant fusion protein with TGF-β, containing a collagen binding domain, has been shown to induce osteogenic differentiation of bone marrow cells in rats.[5] Becerra et al.[18] presented a case report of a 69-year-old man with a proximal tibial defect from resection of long-standing osteomyelitis. Bone marrow cells were cultured in the presence of the TGF-β fusion protein after they were obtained from the iliac crest. Expanded cells were then placed in the tibial defect in conjunction with an HA carrier. Imaging at 90 days was consistent with new bone formation including bridging callus, and biopsy samples taken at the 8 weeks showed new bone formation.

Vascular Endothelial Growth Factor

Angiogenesis is required for bone healing to occur, as this is the way cells receive nutrients and oxygen. Early in the fracture repair process, vascular endothelial growth factor (VEGF) has been shown to be upregulated.[213] Eckhart et al.[66] tested the ability of recombinant human VEGF (rhVEGF) to heal critical-sized defects in rabbits. They compared the healing at 7 weeks with autograft and vehicle-treated controls. Biomechanical testing of the treated bones found that the amount of torque required to failure and the stiffness were significantly greater in the rhVEGF-treated animals compared with controls and equivalent to autograft treatment. Micro–computed tomography analysis showed abundant callus in both the rhVEGF- and autograft-treated groups, and this callus was absent in the control groups.

As discussed earlier, remodeling of allograft bone is a slow process that occurs through creeping substitution. Surface healing can leave large central areas of necrotic bone that contributes to the 25% to 35% failure rate with this type of grafting.[22,148] Ito et al.[115] found that VEGF and receptor activator of nuclear factor–κB ligand (RANKL) were downregulated during allograft healing. They developed a method by which RANKL and VEGF were combined with a viral vector and attached to the surface of allografts. Theses allografts were then used in a mouse fracture model, where histologic analysis at 4 weeks showed periosteal resorption with new bone formation and medullary neovascularization that was not seen in untreated controls. These preliminary results demonstrate a novel way to increase allograft healing and warrant further study.

Fibroblast Growth Factor

Basic fibroblast growth factor (bFGF), also known as FGF-2, belongs to a class of growth factors that have an affinity for heparin and of which at least 22 members have been described.[116] It is one of the most potent stimulators of angiogenesis, partially through its influence on endothelial cell migration and upregulation of integrin expression.[125] During growth, wound healing, and fracture repair, it acts as a mitogen for fibroblasts, chondrocytes, and osteoblasts.[111,114]

During fracture repair, FGFs differ in their temporal and spatial expression.[192] In the early stages, FGF-1 and -2 are localized to the proliferating periosteum. This expression is then limited to osteoblasts during intramembranous bone formation and to the chondrocytes and osteoblasts during endochondral bone formation. In light of their active involvement during fracture repair, investigators have studied the potential therapeutic roles of FGFs in bone formation. Nakamura and associates[165] studied these effects by injecting bFGF into middiaphyseal transverse tibial fractures in dogs. Controls were injected with carrier molecules. Results showed that bFGF enlarged the callus area at 4 weeks and increased the callus bone mineral content at 8 weeks. Subsequent to the reporting of these findings in animals, at least one biotechnology company initiated preliminary studies in humans to set the stage for a multicenter randomized controlled trial in patients with closed tibia fractures. Those preliminary results have not been reported and the multi-

center clinical trial has not been conducted. At this time, the status of the FGFs in the enhancement of fracture healing in patients is unknown.

Platelet-Derived Growth Factor

Platelet-derived growth factor (PDGF) is a large polypeptide that consists of two chains that share 60% amino acid sequence homology.[208] Its potential role in bone healing is related to its mitogenic and chemotactic properties for osteoblasts.[39,42] A positive effect of PDGF on fracture healing was demonstrated in a rabbit tibial osteotomy model in which the fractures were injected with either 80 μg of PDGF in a collagen carrier or collagen alone.[167] Results showed an increase in callus formation and a more advanced stage of endosteal and periosteal osteogenic differentiation in the PDGF-treated group compared with the controls. However, the treatment had no effect on the mechanical properties of the calluses compared with controls.

While these early results were mixed, a more recent study by Hollinger et al.[107] in a geriatric, osteoporotic rat model found significant gains in mechanical strength in fractures treated with PDGF combined with an injectable beta-tricalcium phosphate–collagen matrix. At 5 weeks after the initial injury, the torsion to failure in the PDGF-treated tibias was comparable to that of the uninjured extremity, while control and untreated fractures remained unhealed. These preclinical data and encouraging results from clinical studies of PDGF treatment of dental implants[169] and diabetic foot ulcers[238] suggest a potential role for PDGF in skeletal trauma.

Prostaglandin Agonists

Prostaglandins (PGs) comprise a group of unsaturated long-chain fatty acids that are known to have profound osteogenic effects when implanted into skeletal sites[142,175] or infused systemically.[227] The release of arachidonate from alkyl-arachidonyl phospholcholine produces the precursor of several potent pro-angiogenic and proinflammatory mediators. Arachidonate is converted to several types of PGs by either of two known prostaglandin synthases (cyclooxygenases): COX1 or the inducible COX2. In a study of rabbit tibial fractures, Dekel et al.[56] demonstrated that PGE_2 caused a dose-dependent stimulation of callus formation and an increase in total bone mineral content. Its effects were also shown to be greatest during the latter stages of fracture healing, suggesting that the primary effect may be to stimulate osteoblasts and osteoprogenitor cells as opposed to undifferentiated MSCs.

A limiting factor for the development of PGs for the treatment of fractures is its undesirable systemic effects. These include nausea, pyrexia, diarrhea, lethargy, and flushing, and they are mitigated by the binding of PGs to all of its four receptors (EP1, EP2, EP3, and EP4). Recently, Li and coworkers[142] reported on enhanced fracture repair by the nonprostanoid PGE_2 agonist CP-533,536. Using this more selective approach, binding of the synthetic PG agonist to its EP2 receptor was shown to lessen the systemic effects while targeting the receptor that primarily regulates bone anabolic activity. In models of both rat and canine fracture healing, they delivered CP-533,536 in a poly(DL-lactide-coglycolide) matrix to fractures sites in a dose-dependent fashion. Each dose increased callus size, density, and strength compared with the controls. Histologic examination showed extensive endochondral and intramembranous ossification. These data suggest that a selective EP2-receptor agonist may have a therapeutic role in the augmentation of the fracture repair process. Clinical trials are currently under way to investigate this application.

AUTHORS' PREFERRED METHOD OF TREATMENT
Bone Morphogenetic Proteins

We recommend the use of OP-1 (BMP-7) for the treatment of recalcitrant nonunions of long bones and BMP-2 for the treatment of open tibia fractures. The other molecules discussed in this section have not been fully tested for their clinical efficacies, and therefore it is not possible to consider their use at this time.

SYSTEMIC ENHANCEMENT OF FRACTURE HEALING

Parathyroid Hormone

Calcium and phosphate homeostasis is a complex process that involves multiple signaling pathways and organ systems. The largest storage site of calcium and phosphate is the skeletal system, and the release of these ions and their accumulation within this system are largely regulated by the coordinated stimulation and suppression of osteoblasts and osteoclasts. Parathyroid hormone (PTH) is a major regulator of mineral homeostasis and exerts its effects by binding to its receptor on osteoblasts.[189,190] PTH is an 84–amino acid peptide that is produced in response to depressed serum calcium levels. Its major effects are in the kidneys, where it regulates phosphate diuresis and 1,25-dihydroxyvitamin D synthesis with its subsequent enhancement of gastrointestinal calcium and phosphate absorption.[181] The actions of PTH on bone metabolism can be both stimulatory and inhibitory. It has been found that continuous release of PTH leads to an increase in osteoclast numbers and activity,[143] while intermittent exposure results in increased bone formation in both rats and humans.[59,168]

Clinical trials using PTH(1–34) have shown an increase in bone mass in osteoporotic men and an increase in bone mineral density and a reduction of vertebral and other osteoporotic related fractures in postmenopausal women.[58,168] Neer et al.[168] assessed the efficacy of PTH(1–34) for improving bone mineral density in a clinical trial involving 1673 postmenopausal women with prior nontraumatic vertebral fractures. Results demonstrated that PTH increased bone mineral density and reduced the risk of fracture.

Based on this anabolic effect of PTH on the skeleton, several animal studies have been conducted examining the effects of PTH on the repair of bone. All have demonstrated an enhancement of fracture healing when doses where given intermittently.[164,166] Manabe et al.[152] studied PTH in a primate model of fracture repair. Seventeen female cynomolgus monkeys underwent a femoral osteotomy with plate fixation. Treatment groups consisted of either low-dose (0.77 μg/kg) or high-dose (7.5 μg/kg) PTH or placebo for control, and injections were given twice weekly for 3 weeks. All groups healed by 26 weeks, at which time the animals were killed. Ultimate stress and elastic modulus of the healing osteotomy were significantly higher in PTH-treated animals, while the callus size was larger but had

lower density in control animals. Alkhiary et al.[3] reported on the use of PTH(1–34) in the treatment experimental femur fractures in Sprague-Dawley rats. Animals were treated with either 5 or 30 μg/kg/day PTH(1–34) for a total of 35 days beginning at the time of fracture creation. Animals were killed at various time points, and the fracture callus was analyzed for bone mineral content and density as well as undergoing mechanical testing to failure. Results compared with control animals demonstrated significant increases in strength and bone mineral content for the 30 μg/kg group as early as 3 weeks, and these differences where sustained at 85 days.

A recent clinical trial on the use of PTH(1–34) in the treatment of fractures of the distal radius in humans showed that time to fracture healing was shorter in the PTH-treated patients.[1] These findings suggest that PTH(1–34), as well as other PTH fragments, may have role in the clinical treatment of fractures.

Growth Hormone and Insulin-Like Growth Factor I

Growth hormone (GH) and insulin-like growth factors (IGFs) play an important role in skeletal development and remodeling. GH is currently used clinically to treat patients with short stature[172] because it stimulates endochondral ossification, periosteal bone formation, and linear growth. It mediates these effects through the IGF system including the ligands, receptors, IGF binding proteins (IGFBPs), IGFBP proteases and activators, and inhibitors of IGFBP proteases.

Two IGFs have been identified: IGF-I (somatomedin C) and IGF-II. Although IGF-II is the most abundant growth factor in bone, IGF-I has the greater potency for promoting growth and has been localized in healing fractures of humans.[7,40,41] IGF-I and IGF-II promote bone matrix formation (type I collagen and noncollagenous matrix proteins) by fully differentiated osteoblasts, inhibit collagen degradation, and promote osteoblast maturation and replication.[43] Expression of the IGF-I increases with expression of GH,[183] and it is likely responsible for the anabolic effects of GH.

Several studies have reported moderate enhancement of skeletal repair using either GH[6,14] or IGF-I.[220] Kolbeck et al.[129] showed that GH significantly improves the mechanical properties of fracture callus in minipigs. A recent randomized clinical trial was presented by Raschke et al.[183] in which 406 patients with tibia fractures were treated daily with varying concentrations of GH or placebo for up to 26 weeks. Dosages were gradually increased to the assigned dose over a 3-week period in an attempt to decrease adverse events such as water retention. With regard to the primary outcome of radiographic union, no significant difference was seen in the open fractures between control and GH-treated patients. On the other hand, the relative risk for healing a closed fracture was greatest in the group treated with the highest dose of GH (60 μg/day; relative risk [RR], 1.44; 95% confidence interval [CI], 1.01–2.05; $P = 0.045$). Patients treated with 60 μg/day GH were able to bear full weight at an average of 87 days versus 108 days in the placebo-treated controls. However, the benefits of GH might have been overshadowed by the high number of adverse events: 58% in the 60 μg/day GH–treated group compared with 35% in placebo-treated controls. These adverse events included arthralgias, edema, and, to a lesser extent, wound infection.

Statins

Statins, HMG-CoA reductase inhibitors, are lipid-lowering drugs that block cholesterol synthesis through the inhibition of mevalonic acid production. The conversion of HMG-CoA to mevalonic acid occurs early in the pathway and also inhibits the production of farnesyl pyrophosphate (FPP) and geranylgeranyl pyrophosphate (GGPP). Small GTP-binding proteins such as Rho and Ras require GGPP and FPP, respectively, for translocation to the plasma membrane.[134] Inhibition of this process by statins may block osteoclast maturation and subsequent bone catabolism.[203] In addition, studies have shown that statins stimulate the BMP-2 promoter in osteoblasts leading to enhanced bone formation.[161]

In mice, Skoglund et al.[207] showed that daily injections of simvastatin had no effect on fracture healing, while a continuous systemic infusion and continuous local delivery improved the force to failure by 160% and 170%, respectively. The large systemic doses were likely required because commercially available statins target the liver, and little is available to the skeletal tissues at standard doses. Garret el al.[84] addressed this by developing poly(lactic-coglycolide acid) nanoparticle beads containing various concentrations of lovastatin. They then created femur fractures in Sprague-Dawley rats that were treated immediately with injection of nanoparticles that eluted either 0, 0.2, 1, 1.5, or 7.5 μg/day lovastatin. Their results showed at 4 weeks that doses of 1 and 1.5 μg/day significantly accelerated fracture healing as measured by size of the fracture gap and biomechanical strength.

PHYSICAL ENHANCEMENT OF SKELETAL REPAIR

The mechanical environment has a direct impact on fracture healing. Direct mechanical perturbation and biophysical modalities such as electrical and ultrasound stimulation have been shown to affect fracture healing. To enhance fracture repair by these mechanical measures, it is necessary to develop a fundamental understanding of the ways by which the mechanical environment impacts cellular and molecular signaling.

Mechanical and Biophysical Stimulation

Mechanical forces play a crucial role in the healing process. Sarmiento and associates[196] found that early weight bearing accelerates the fracture-healing process. Standardized femoral fractures were produced in rats and stabilized by nonrigid intramedullary fixation. The animals were either allowed to bear weight at an early stage or were kept non–weight bearing by cast immobilization. Histologic, radiographic, and mechanical differences were present by the second week after fracture. These differences became progressively greater during the next 3 weeks. The authors attributed these findings to early mobilization facilitating the maturation of callus tissue produced by endochondral ossification.

The degree of stability at the fracture site has a direct impact on the repair process.[139] Using a standardized, bilateral tibial canine osteotomy model, compression plating of the fracture was compared with the less stable external fixation performed on the opposite side. At 120 days after injury, bone formation was biomechanically less mature on the external fixator side. These tibias had significantly less intracortical new-bone formation and more bone porosity compared with those that had been treated with compression plates. Endosteal new bone formation was greater on the plated side. Because the in vitro

stiffness of the external fixator was less in all modes tested (compression, distraction, torsion, and anteroposterior bending) except lateral bending, the authors concluded that the rigidity of the fixation may be an important factor in early remodeling of a healing osteotomy.

Several investigators have attempted to modulate fracture healing by altering the mechanical strain environment. In a prospective randomized clinical trial, Kenwright et al.[122] compared the effects of controlled axial micromotion on tibial diaphyseal fracture healing in patients who were treated with external fixation and stratified according to fracture severity and extent of soft tissue injury. A specially designed pneumatic pump was attached to the unilateral external fixation frame of one group of patients and delivered a cyclic axial displacement of 1.0 mm at 0.5 Hz for 20 to 30 minutes a day. Fracture healing was assessed clinically, radiographically, and by measurement of the mechanical stiffness of the fracture. Both clinical and mechanical healing was enhanced in the group subjected to micromovement, compared with those treated with frames without micromotion. The differences in healing times were statistically significant and independently related to the treatment method. There was no difference in complication rates between treatment groups.

Distraction Osteogenesis

Limb lengthening was first described by Codivilla[49] in 1904 for the treatment of limb length discrepancies. It was not until the work of Ilizarov[112,113] 50 years later that the technique of distraction osteogenesis gained popularity as a method for enhancing bone regeneration.

Distraction osteogenesis generates new tissue through the application of tensile forces to developing callus via a controlled osteotomy.[141,157] The controlled distraction of bone fragments results in the expression of various growth factors, including those involved in angiogenesis. Pacicca et al.[173] demonstrated the expression of several of these molecules localized to the leading edge of the distraction gap, where nascent osteogenesis was occurring. The greatest levels were seen during the active phase, consistent with the apposition of new bone matrix. Others have shown that robust angiogenesis, under VEGF control, occurs during the active and consolidation phase and is supported by the recruitment of endothelial progenitor cells.[138]

Several investigators have used the technique of distraction osteogenesis to stimulate new bone formation in the clinical setting. Kocaoglu et al.[127] treated 16 patients with hypertrophic nonunions with the Ilizarov distraction method. All patients had at least 1 cm of shortening, three patients had a deformity in one plane, and the remainder had a deformity in two planes. Distraction was begun on the first postoperative day at the rate of 0.25 mm/day divided into four equal increments. Once the desired length had been obtained, the fixator was left in place until at least three of four cortices showed bridging callus. All nonunions had healed at an average follow-up of 38.1 months, with correction of all preoperative length inequalities and limb angulation to normal alignment. A similar study of 17 patients with tibial nonunions with bone loss found an average treatment time of 8 months, with functional results being reported as excellent in 15 and good in 2.[201]

Open fractures have also been managed successfully with distraction osteogenesis. Sen et al.[202] managed 24 patients with Gustilo and Anderson[96] grade III open tibia fractures with

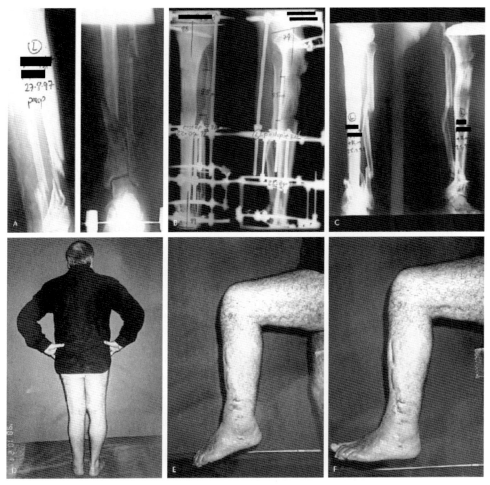

FIGURE 5-5 A 53-year-old man sustained a grade IIIB open fracture of his left distal tibia with 8.5 cm of bone loss. **A.** Preoperative anteroposterior and lateral radiographs. **B.** Late postoperative radiographs taken at the end of the distraction period. **C.** Radiographs after frame removal displaying complete union of the fracture and completed lengthening through the proximal tibia. **D.** Leg length equality at the end of treatment. **E,F.** Ankle range of motion during the last follow-up examination. (Reprinted with permission from Sen C, Kocaoglu M, Levent E, et al. Bifocal compression-distraction in the acute treatment of grade III open tibia fractures with bone and soft-tissue loss-a report of 24 cases. J Orthop Trauma 2004;18:150–157.)

compression-distraction osteogenesis using the Ilizarov-type circular external fixator. After an average of 30-month follow-up, results were excellent in 21 and good in 3 patients. Functional assessment scores were excellent in 19, good in 4, and fair in 1 patient (Fig. 5-5).

Electrical Stimulation

Electrical potentials were first described in mechanically loaded bone by Fukada and Yasuda[82] in 1957. With this discovery, investigators began to study the influence that electrical current might have on the healing of bone. In 1971, Freidenberg et al.[79] found that the healing of nonunions could be affected by the use of direct current. Within 5 years, more than 119 articles had been published highlighting the use of electrical stimulation on bone growth and repair.[29]

There are currently three methods for the electrical stimulation of bone healing: (i) constant direct-current (DC) stimulation with the use of percutaneous or implanted electrodes (invasive), (ii) capacitive coupling (noninvasive), or (iii) time-varying inductive coupling produced by a magnetic field (noninvasive;

also known as pulsed electromagnetic field [PEMF] stimulation). DC stimulation uses stainless steel cathodes placed in the tissues near the fracture site. New bone formation is directly proportional to the level of applied current, with a threshold level above which cellular necrosis may occur.[78] With pulsed electromagnetic stimulation, there is an alternating current that is produced by externally applied coils. This produces a time-varying magnetic and electrical field within the bone. In capacitively coupled electric fields (CCEFs), an electrical field is induced in bone through the use of an external capacitor—that is, two electrically charged metal plates placed on either side of a limb.[30]

Electrical stimulation has primarily been used in orthopaedics for the treatment of nonunions. Brighton and coworkers[30] used DC for the treatment of 178 nonunions in 175 patients at a single center. Union was achieved in 84% of the patients. Interestingly, the investigators found that even in the presence of osteomyelitis the healing rate was nearly 75%. The presence of previously inserted metallic fixation devices did not affect the healing rate. The study began with two treatment groups, one receiving 10 microamperes and the other 20 receiving microamperes of current. The first 11 patients failed to heal by 12 weeks, and thereafter all patients received the higher dose of current. When this study was expanded to include other centers, an additional 58 of 89 nonunions achieved similar results. Treatment failures were attributed to inadequate electricity, the presence of a synovial pseudarthrosis or infection, and dislodgment of the electrodes. Complications were minor and, with the exception of patients with previous osteomyelitis, no deep infections resulting from this treatment were noted. The authors concluded that given proper electrical parameters and cast immobilization, a rate of bone union comparable to that seen with bone-graft surgery could be achieved.

Scott and King[199] reported similar results in a prospective, double-blind trial using capacitive coupling in patients with established nonunions. In a population of 21 patients, 10 were actively managed and 11 were treated with a placebo unit. Healing was achieved in 60% of the patients who received electrical stimulation (Fig. 5-6). Patients managed with the placebo unit showed a complete lack of bone formation.

Bassett et al.[17] reported on the use of PEMF in the treatment of nonunited tibial diaphyseal fractures. One hundred twenty-five patients with 127 nonunions underwent long-leg plaster cast immobilization. Patients were treated with non–weight-bearing ambulation and a total of 10 hours of PEMF stimulation daily. Bony union occurred in 87% of the patients and was independent of patient age or sex, the number of previous operations, and the presence of infection or metal fixation.

Sharrard[205] conducted a double-blind, multicenter trial of the use of PEMFs in patients who had developed delayed union of tibial fractures. Forty-five tibial fractures that had not united for more than 16 weeks but less than 32 weeks were treated with immobilization in a plaster cast that incorporated the coils of an electromagnetic stimulation unit. The unit was activated for 20 of these fractures and was not active for 25. There was radiographic evidence of union in nine of the fractures that had

been subjected to electromagnetic stimulation compared with only three of the fractures in the control group.

Despite the promising results seen in patients with nonunions and delayed unions, the application of this technology to the treatment of fresh fractures has not been clearly defined. Although some studies have shown that PEMFs favorably influence fracture healing in experimental animals[78] and osteotomies in patients,[27,151] other studies have failed to demonstrate clinically significant effects.[17] Beck et al.[19] found no difference in healing time in 44 patients who were randomly assigned to either CCEF or placebo. At present, there continues to be a paucity of published clinical studies showing that electrical stimulation enhances the healing of fresh fractures.

Ultrasound Stimulation

Low-intensity pulsed ultrasound (LIPUS) has been shown to promote fracture repair and increase the mechanical strength of fracture callus in both animal[179,240] and clinical[101,131] studies. In a prospective randomized double-blind trial, Heckman et al.[101] examined the use of LIPUS as an adjunct to conventional treatment with a cast in 67 patients with closed or open grade I tibial shaft fractures. Thirty-three fractures were treated with the active device and 34 with the placebo. Using clinical and radiographic criteria, the authors noted that there was a statistically significant decrease in the time to union (86 ± 5.8 days in the LIPUS treatment group versus 114 ± 10.4 days in the control group) and in the time to overall healing (96 ± 4.9 days in the ultrasound treatment group versus 154 ± 13.7 days in the controls). There were no issues with patient compliance in the treatment group and no serious complications reported with its use.

In a subsequent multicenter prospective randomized double-blind study, Kristiansen and coworkers[131] evaluated the efficacy of LIPUS in the treatment of dorsally angulated distal radius fractures that had been treated with closed reduction and a cast.

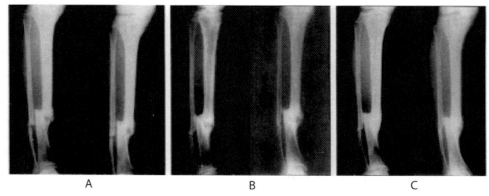

| A | B | C |

FIGURE 5-6 Anteroposterior and oblique radiographs of the tibia of a 23-year-old man who had sustained a closed fracture of the tibial diaphysis while playing soccer. He underwent closed intramedullary nailing of the tibia on the day of the injury, but an infection developed at the site of the fixation within a few months. The fixation device was removed but a low-grade infection with wound drainage persisted despite antibiotic treatment. The fracture was mobile and tender. The patient was entered into a placebo-controlled study of electrical capacitive coupling. **A.** Radiographs made at the beginning of treatment with a placebo unit. **B.** After 9 months of treatment with the placebo unit, the fracture site was still mobile, clinically painful, and discharging pus. No progress toward healing was seen. **C.** Six months after a 14-week period of electrical capacitive coupling, there was no longer any drainage and the fracture had united. (Reprinted with permission from Scott G, King JB. A prospective, double-blind trial of electrical capacitive coupling in the treatment of nonunion of long bones. J Bone Joint Surg Am 1994;76A:820–826.)

The time to union was significantly shorter for the fractures that were treated with LIPUS compared with the controls (61 ± 3 days versus 98 ± 5 days). The authors further noted that treatment with LIPUS was associated with significantly less loss of reduction (20% ± 6% versus 43% ± 8%) as determined by the degree of volar angulation as well as with a significant decrease in the mean time until the loss of reduction ceased (12 ± 4 days versus 25 ± 4 days).

There are several known risks factors for delayed or nonunion, and one of the most common is tobacco use. Cook et al.[56] studied LIPUS for the treatment of acute tibial and distal radius fractures in smokers. Healing time in this patient population is typically delayed, with tibial and distal radius fractures requiring 175 ± 27 days and 98 ± 30 days, respectively, to achieve bony union. Treatment with LIPUS was able to reduce this time to 103 ± 8.3 days in the tibial fracture group and 48 ± 5.1 days in the patients with distal radius fractures. Treatment with LIPUS also substantially reduced the incidence of delayed unions in tibias in smokers and nonsmokers. These results are important because they suggest that LIPUS can override some of the detrimental effects that smoking has on fracture healing. Rutten et al.[193] prospectively analyzed 71 cases of tibial nonunion and found that treatment with LIPUS resulted in a healing rate of 73%, and that this was significantly higher than the rate of spontaneous healing. Within the subgroups analyzed, the rate of healing in smokers and nonsmokers was not found to be statistically significant.

In contrast to these findings, the effects of LIPUS on fracture healing may be affected by the presence of fixation devices. Emami et al.[70] noted that ultrasound did not appear to have a stimulatory role on tibial fracture repair in a prospective randomized controlled double-blinded study to evaluate its effects in patients with fresh tibial fractures who were treated with a reamed and statically locked intramedullary rod. Patients were divided into an ultrasound group and placebo group. They all underwent treatment with an ultrasound device for 20 minutes daily for 75 days without knowing whether it was active. Standardized radiographs were taken every third week until healing and at 6 and 12 months. Results showed that low-intensity ultrasound treatment did not shorten the healing time.

AUTHORS' PREFERRED METHOD OF TREATMENT

Distraction Osteogenesis, Electrical Stimulation, Ultrasound Stimulation

The use of controlled micromotion to enhance fracture healing, as described by Goodship and Kenwright[90] has not been widely used and we have no experience with this method. The use of appropriately applied distraction osteogenesis for the treatment of nonunions is recommended for surgeons who are experienced with the use of small-pin, ring fixation.

There are clearly good data to support the use of electrical stimulation for the treatment of nonunions and delayed unions. DC, capacitive coupling, and PEMFs have all been demonstrated, in randomized controlled trials, to enhance the healing of nonunions. PEMFs can also be used for the treatment of delayed unions. There is no evidence that electrical stimulation of any type enhances the healing of fresh fractures.

Ultrasound stimulation can be used for the treatment of fresh closed fractures of the distal radius and tibia when treated in a cast or external fixation device. We also recommend this treatment as an adjunct to the management of closed fractures of long bones in patients who smoke. We have also had good results in the treatment of tibia fractures that show delayed union (Fig. 5-7). Until there is evidence to support the use of LIPUS in patients treated with fixation devices, we do not recommend the use of ultrasound in the treatment of fractures of patients who have undergone an operation in which fixation devices have been implanted.

CONCLUSIONS AND FUTURE DIRECTIONS

The repair of fractures is a predictable event for most skeletal injuries. There are, however, instances when fracture repair is delayed or fails to occur. With improved understanding of the intracellular and extracellular pathways involved in bone heal-

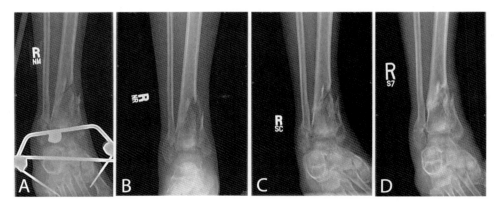

FIGURE 5-7 Sequential radiographs of a patient who sustained a grade II distal tibia fracture that underwent irrigation and debridement with placement of an external fixator. **A.** At 4 months, the external fixator was removed and the patient was believed to have a delayed union. Daily treatments with Exogen (Smith and Nephew, Memphis, TN) ultrasound stimulation was started. **B.** At 1 month of treatment, the patient progressed to partial weight bearing. **C.** At 2 months, radiographs showed continued progression of healing. **D.** At 6 months, the patient was bearing full weight without pain. (Courtesy Paul Tornetta III, MD.)

ing, our ability to successfully augment this repair process continuously evolves.

Currently, the ability to promote fracture healing is limited. Accepted options include returning to the operating room to perform an open procedure supplemented with some type of physiologic or synthetic graft, recombinant human OP-1 or BMP-2, or the use of LIPUS. Systemic treatments, such as the use of statins or hormones, are still in the development stages, but these types of treatments may allow earlier interventions, especially in at-risk patients. Current advances, including improved methods for obtaining autogenous and allogenic MSCs, development of delivery mechanisms for gene therapy, and improvements in synthetic bone graft materials, will greatly enhance the ability to improve fracture repair.

REFERENCES

1. Abstracts of the 35th European Symposium on Calcified Tissues. Calcif Tissue Int 2008;April 11.
2. Albee FH. Studies in bone growth: triple calcium phosphate as a stimulus to osteogenesis. Ann Surg 1920;71:32–39.
3. Alkhiary YM, Gerstenfeld LC, Krall E, et al. Enhancement of experimental fracture-healing by systemic administration of recombinant human parathyroid hormone (PTH 1–34). J Bone Joint Surg Am 2005;87:731–741.
4. An HS, Simpson JM, Glover JM, et al. Comparison between allograft plus demineralized bone matrix versus autograft in anterior cervical fusion. A prospective multicenter study. Spine 1995;20:2211–2216.
5. Andrades JA, Han B, Becerra J, et al. A recombinant human TGF-beta1 fusion protein with collagen-binding domain promotes migration, growth, and differentiation of bone marrow mesenchymal cells. Exp Cell Res 1999;250:485–498.
6. Andreassen TT, Oxlund H. Local anabolic effects of growth hormone on intact bone and healing fractures in rats. Calcif Tissue Int 2003;73:258–264.
7. Andrew JG, Hoyland J, Freemont AJ, et al. Insulin-like growth factor gene expression in human fracture callus. Calcif Tissue Int 1993;53:97–102.
8. Anker CJ, Holdridge SP, Baird B, et al. Ultraporous beta-tricalcium phosphate is well incorporated in small cavitary defects. Clin Orthop Relat Res 2005;May:251–257.
9. Arinzeh TL, Peter SJ, Archambault MP, et al. Allogeneic mesenchymal stem cells regenerate bone in a critical-sized canine segmental defect. J Bone Joint Surg Am 2003;85A:1927–1935.
10. Arts JJ, Verdonschot N, Buma P, et al. Larger bone graft size and washing of bone grafts prior to impaction enhances the initial stability of cemented cups: experiments using a synthetic acetabular model. Acta Orthop 2006;77:227–233.
11. Artzi Z, Weinreb M, Givol N, et al. Biomaterial resorption rate and healing site morphology of inorganic bovine bone and beta-tricalcium phosphate in the canine: a 24-month longitudinal histologic study and morphometric analysis. Int J Oral Maxillofac Implants 2004;19:357–368.
12. Bae HW, Zhao L, Kanim LE, et al. Intervariability and intravariability of bone morphogenetic proteins in commercially available demineralized bone matrix products. Spine 2006;31:1299–1306.
13. Bajammal SS, Zlowodzki M, Schmitz-Lelwica AE, et al. The use of calcium phosphate bone cement in fracture treatment: a meta-analysis of randomized trials. Orthop Trauma Assoc 2007.
14. Bak B, Jorgensen PH, Andreassen TT. The stimulating effect of growth hormone on fracture healing is dependent on onset and duration of administration. Clin Orthop Relat Res 1991;March:295–301.
15. Banwart JC, Asher MA, Hassanein RS. Iliac crest bone graft harvest donor site morbidity. A statistical evaluation. Spine 1995;20:1055–1060.
16. Barriga A, az-de-Rada P, Barroso JL, et al. Frozen cancellous bone allografts: positive cultures of implanted grafts in posterior fusions of the spine. Eur Spine J 2004;13:152–156.
17. Bassett CA, Mitchell SN, Gaston SR. Treatment of ununited tibial diaphyseal fractures with pulsing electromagnetic fields. J Bone Joint Surg Am 1981;63A:511–523.
18. Becerra J, Guerado E, Claros S, et al. Autologous human-derived bone marrow cells exposed to a novel TGF-beta1 fusion protein for the treatment of critically sized tibial defect. Regen Med 2006;1:267–278.
19. Beck BR, Matheson GO, Bergman G, et al. Do capacitively coupled electric fields accelerate tibial stress fracture healing? A randomized controlled trial. Am J Sports Med 2008;36:545–553.
20. Becker W, Becker BE, Caffesse R. A comparison of demineralized freeze-dried bone and autologous bone to induce bone formation in human extraction sockets. J Periodontol 1994;65:1128–1133.
21. Beredjiklian PK, Hotchkiss RN, Athanasian EA, et al. Recalcitrant nonunion of the distal humerus: treatment with free vascularized bone grafting. Clin Orthop Relat Res 2005:134–139.
22. Berrey BH Jr, Lord CF, Gebhardt MC, et al. Fractures of allografts. Frequency, treatment, and end-results. J Bone Joint Surg Am 1990;72:825–833.
23. Bibbo C, Patel DV. The effect of demineralized bone matrix-calcium sulfate with vancomycin on calcaneal fracture healing and infection rates: a prospective study. Foot Ankle Int 2006;27:487–493.
24. Bolander ME. Regulation of fracture repair by growth factors. Proc Soc Exp Biol Med 1992;200:165–170.
25. Bong MR, Capla EL, Egol KA, et al. Osteogenic protein-1 (bone morphogenic protein-

7) combined with various adjuncts in the treatment of humeral diaphyseal nonunions. Bull Hosp Jt Dis 2005;63:20–23.
26. Borrelli J Jr, Prickett WD, Ricci WM. Treatment of nonunions and osseous defects with bone graft and calcium sulfate. Clin Orthop Relat Res 2003;June:245–254.
27. Borsalino G, Bagnacani M, Bettati E, et al. Electrical stimulation of human femoral intertrochanteric osteotomies. Double-blind study. Clin Orthop Relat Res 1988;December:256–63.
28. Boyce T, Edwards J, Scarborough N. Allograft bone. The influence of processing on safety and performance. Orthop Clin North Am 1999;30:571–581.
29. Brighton CT. The treatment of nonunions with electricity. J Bone Joint Surg Am 1981;63A:847–851.
30. Brighton CT, Black J, Friedenberg ZB, et al. A multicenter study of the treatment of nonunion with constant direct current. J Bone Joint Surg Am 1981;63A:2–13.
31. Bruder SP, Fink DJ, Caplan AI. Mesenchymal stem cells in bone development, bone repair, and skeletal regeneration therapy. J Cell Biochem 1994;56:283–294.
32. Bruder SP, Jaiswal N, Haynesworth SE. Growth kinetics, self-renewal, and the osteogenic potential of purified human mesenchymal stem cells during extensive subcultivation and following cryopreservation. J Cell Biochem 1997;64:278–294.
33. Bruder SP, Kraus KH, Goldberg VM, et al. The effect of implants loaded with autologous mesenchymal stem cells on the healing of canine segmental bone defects. J Bone Joint Surg Am 1998;80:985–996.
34. Bucholz RW, Carlton A, Holmes R. Interporous hydroxyapatite as a bone graft substitute in tibial plateau fractures. Clin Orthop Relat Res 1989;March:53–62.
35. Buecker PJ, Gebhardt MC. Are fibula strut allografts a reliable alternative for periarticular reconstruction after curettage for bone tumors? Clin Orthop Relat Res 2007;461:170–174.
36. Burchardt H. Biology of bone transplantation. Orthop Clin North Am 1987;18:187–196.
37. Burchardt H, Busbee GA III, Enneking WF. Repair of experimental autologous grafts of cortical bone. J Bone Joint Surg Am 1975;57A:814–819.
38. Busse JW, Bhandari M, Sprague S, et al. An economic analysis of management strategies for closed and open grade I tibial shaft fractures. Acta Orthop 2005;76:705–712.
39. Canalis E. Effect of platelet-derived growth factor on DNA and protein synthesis in cultured rat calvaria. Metabolism 1981;30:970–975.
40. Canalis E, Centrella M, McCarthy TL. Regulation of insulin-like growth factor-II production in bone cultures. Endocrinology 1991;129:2457–2462.
41. Canalis E, McCarthy T, Centrella M. Isolation and characterization of insulin-like growth factor I (somatomedin-C) from cultures of fetal rat calvariae. Endocrinology 1988;122:22–27.
42. Canalis E, McCarthy TL, Centrella M. Effects of platelet-derived growth factor on bone formation in vitro. J Cell Physiol 1989;140:530–537.
43. Canalis E, Pash J, Gabbitas B, et al. Growth factors regulate the synthesis of insulin-like growth factor-I in bone cell cultures. Endocrinology 1993;133:33–38.
44. Cassidy C, Jupiter JB, Cohen M, et al. Norian SRS cement compared with conventional fixation in distal radial fractures. A randomized study. J Bone Joint Surg Am 2003;85A:2127–2137.
45. Chapman MW, Bucholz R, Cornell C. Treatment of acute fractures with a collagen-calcium phosphate graft material. A randomized clinical trial. J Bone Joint Surg Am 1997;79A:495–502.
46. Chmell MJ, McAndrew MP, Thomas R, et al. Structural allografts for reconstruction of lower extremity open fractures with 10 centimeters or more of acute segmental defects. J Orthop Trauma 1995;9:222–226.
47. Cho TJ, Gerstenfeld LC, Einhorn TA. Differential temporal expression of members of the transforming growth factor beta superfamily during murine fracture healing. J Bone Miner Res 2002;17:513–520.
48. Claes L, Augat P, Suger G, et al. Influence of size and stability of the osteotomy gap on the success of fracture healing. J Orthop Res 1997;15:577–584.
49. Codivilla A. On the means of lengthening, in the lower limbs, the muscles and tissues which are shortened through deformity. 1904. Clin Orthop Relat Res 1994;April:4–9.
50. Constantz BR, Ison IC, Fulmer MT, et al. Skeletal repair by in situ formation of the mineral phase of bone. Science 1995;267:1796–1799.
51. Cook SD, Ryaby JP, McCabe J, et al. Acceleration of tibia and distal radius fracture healing in patients who smoke. Clin Orthop Relat Res 1997;April:198–207.
52. Cornell CN, Lane JM, Chapman M, et al. Multicenter trial of Collagraft as bone graft substitute. J Orthop Trauma 1991;5:1–8.
53. Critchlow MA, Bland YS, Ashhurst DE. The effect of exogenous transforming growth factor-beta 2 on healing fractures in the rabbit. Bone 1995;16:521–527.
54. Croteau S, Rauch F, Silvestri A, et al. Bone morphogenetic proteins in orthopedics: from basic science to clinical practice. Orthopedics 1999;22:686–695.
55. D'Ippolito G, Schiller PC, Ricordi C, et al. Age-related osteogenic potential of mesenchymal stromal cells from human vertebral bone marrow. J Bone Miner Res 1999;14:1115–1122.
56. Dekel S, Lenthall G, Francis MJ. Release of prostaglandins from bone and muscle after tibial fracture. An experimental study in rabbits. J Bone Joint Surg Br 1981;63B:185–189.
57. Dell PC, Burchardt H, Glowczewskie FP Jr. A roentgenographic, biomechanical, and histological evaluation of vascularized and nonvascularized segmental fibular canine autografts. J Bone Joint Surg Am 1985;67A:105–112.
58. Dempster DW, Cosman F, Kurland ES, et al. Effects of daily treatment with parathyroid hormone on bone microarchitecture and turnover in patients with osteoporosis: a paired biopsy study. J Bone Miner Res 2001;16:1846–1853.
59. Dempster DW, Cosman F, Parisien M, et al. Anabolic actions of parathyroid hormone on bone. Endocr Rev 1993;14:690–709.
60. Dias JJ, Wildin CJ, Bhowal B, et al. Should acute scaphoid fractures be fixed? A randomized controlled trial. J Bone Joint Surg Am 2005;87A:2160–2168.
61. Diefenderfer DL, Osyczka AM, Garino JP, et al. Regulation of BMP-induced transcription in cultured human bone marrow stromal cells. J Bone Joint Surg Am 2003;85A(suppl 3):19–28.
62. Dimitriou R, Dahabreh Z, Katsoulis E, et al. Application of recombinant BMP-7 on persistent upper and lower limb nonunions. Injury 2005;36(suppl 4):S51–S59.
63. Ding M, Dalstra M, Danielsen CC, et al. Age variations in the properties of human tibial trabecular bone. J Bone Joint Surg Br 1997;79B:995–1002.

64. Dodd CA, Fergusson CM, Freedman L, et al. Allograft versus autograft bone in scoliosis surgery. J Bone Joint Surg Br 1988;70B:431–434.

65. Dolan CM, Henning JA, Anderson JG, et al. Randomized prospective study comparing tricortical iliac crest autograft to allograft in the lateral column lengthening component for operative correction of adult acquired flatfoot deformity. Foot Ankle Int 2007;28:8–12.

66. Eckardt H, Ding M, Lind M, et al. Recombinant human vascular endothelial growth factor enhances bone healing in an experimental nonunion model. J Bone Joint Surg Br 2005;87:1434–1438.

67. Einhorn TA. Enhancement of fracture-healing. J Bone Joint Surg Am 1995;77:940–956.

68. Einhorn TA, Bonnarens F, Burstein AH. The contributions of dietary protein and mineral to the healing of experimental fractures. A biomechanical study. J Bone Joint Surg Am 1986;68A:1389–1395.

69. Ellies LG, Nelson DG, Featherstone JD. Crystallographic structure and surface morphology of sintered carbonated apatites. J Biomed Mater Res 1988;22:541–553.

70. Emami A, Petren-Mallmin M, Larsson S. No effect of low-intensity ultrasound on healing time of intramedullary fixed tibial fractures. J Orthop Trauma 1999;13:252–257.

71. Engh GA, Ammeen DJ. Use of structural allograft in revision total knee arthroplasty in knees with severe tibial bone loss. J Bone Joint Surg Am 2007;89:2640–2647.

72. Enneking WF, Burchardt H, Puhl JJ, et al. Physical and biological aspects of repair in dog cortical-bone transplants. J Bone Joint Surg Am 1975;57:237–252.

73. Enneking WF, Eady JL, Burchardt H. Autogenous cortical bone grafts in the reconstruction of segmental skeletal defects. J Bone Joint Surg Am 1980;62:1039–1058.

74. Enneking WF, Mindell ER. Observations on massive retrieved human allografts. J Bone Joint Surg Am 1991;73A:1123–1142.

75. Finkemeier CG. Bone-grafting and bone-graft substitutes. J Bone Joint Surg Am 2002;84A:454–464.

76. Fleming JE Jr, Cornell CN, Muschler GF. Bone cells and matrices in orthopedic tissue engineering. Orthop Clin North Am 2000;31:357–374.

77. Fowler BL, Dall BE, Rowe DE. Complications associated with harvesting autogenous iliac bone graft. Am J Orthop 1995 December;24:895–903.

78. Friedenberg ZB, Andrews ET, Smolenski BI, et al. Bone reaction to varying amounts of direct current. Surg Gynecol Obstet 1970;131:894–899.

79. Friedenberg ZB, Harlow MC, Brighton CT. Healing of nonunion of the medial malleolus by means of direct current: a case report. J Trauma 1971;11:883–885.

80. Friedlaender GE. Immune responses to osteochondral allografts. Current knowledge and future directions. Clin Orthop Relat Res 1983;April:58–68.

81. Friedlaender GE, Perry CR, Cole JD, et al. Osteogenic protein-1 (bone morphogenetic protein-7) in the treatment of tibial nonunions. J Bone Joint Surg Am 2001;83A(suppl 1, pt 2):S151–S158.

82. Fukada E, Yasuda I. On the peizoelectric effects of bone. J Phys Soc Japan 1957;12:1158.

83. Gaasbeek RD, Toonen HG, van Heerwaarden RJ, et al. Mechanism of bone incorporation of beta-TCP bone substitute in open wedge tibial osteotomy in patients. Biomaterials 2005;26:6713–6719.

84. Garrett IR, Gutierrez GE, Rossini G, et al. Locally delivered lovastatin nanoparticles enhance fracture healing in rats. J Orthop Res 2007;25:1351–1357.

85. Garvin K, Feschuk C, Sharp JG, et al. Does the number or quality of pluripotent bone marrow stem cells decrease with age? Clin Orthop Relat Res 2007;465:202–207.

86. Goldberg VM, Shaffer JW, Field G, et al. Biology of vascularized bone grafts. Orthop Clin North Am 1987;18:197–205.

87. Goldberg VM, Stevenson S. Natural history of autografts and allografts. Clin Orthop Relat Res 1987;December:7–16.

88. Goldberg VM, Stevenson S. The biology of bone grafts. Semin Arthroplasty 1993;4:58–63.

89. Goodman SB, Bauer TW, Carter D, et al. Norian SRS cement augmentation in hip fracture treatment. Laboratory and initial clinical results. Clin Orthop Relat Res 1998;March:42–50.

90. Goodship AE, Cunningham JL, Kenwright J. Strain rate and timing of stimulation in mechanical modulation of fracture healing. Clin Orthop Relat Res 1998;355(suppl):S105–S115.

91. Goulet JA, Senunas LE, DeSilva GL, et al. Autogenous iliac crest bone graft. Complications and functional assessment. Clin Orthop Relat Res 1997;June:76–81.

92. Govender S, Csimma C, Genant HK, et al. Recombinant human bone morphogenetic protein-2 for treatment of open tibial fractures: a prospective, controlled, randomized study of 450 patients. J Bone Joint Surg Am 2002;84A:2123–2134.

93. Griffith JF, Yeung DK, Tsang PH, et al. Compromised bone marrow perfusion in osteoporosis. J Bone Miner Res 2008;23:1068–1075.

94. Grogan DP, Kalen V, Ross TI, et al. Use of allograft bone for posterior spinal fusion in idiopathic scoliosis. Clin Orthop Relat Res 1999;December:273–278.

95. Gruber R, Koch H, Doll BA, et al. Fracture healing in the elderly patient. Exp Gerontol 2006;41:1080–1093.

96. Gustilo RB, Anderson JT. Prevention of infection in the treatment of 1025 open fractures of long bones: retrospective and prospective analyses. J Bone Joint Surg Am 1976;58:453–458.

97. Haddad FS, Duncan CP. Cortical onlay allograft struts in the treatment of periprosthetic femoral fractures. Instr Course Lect 2003;52:291–300.

98. Haidukewych GJ, Berry DJ. Nonunion of fractures of the subtrochanteric region of the femur. Clin Orthop Relat Res 2004;February:185–188.

99. Haynesworth SE, Goshima J, Goldberg VM, et al. Characterization of cells with osteogenic potential from human marrow. Bone 1992;13:81–88.

100. Healey JH, Zimmerman PA, McDonnell JM, et al. Percutaneous bone marrow grafting of delayed union and nonunion in cancer patients. Clin Orthop Relat Res 1990;July:280–285.

101. Heckman JD, Ryaby JP, McCabe J, et al. Acceleration of tibial fracture-healing by noninvasive, low-intensity pulsed ultrasound. J Bone Joint Surg Am 1994;76A:26–34.

102. Hee SL, Nik Intan NI, Fazan F. Comparison of hydroxyapatite powders derived from different resources. Med J Malaysia 2004;59(suppl B):77–78.

103. Hernigou P, Mathieu G, Poignard A, et al. Percutaneous autologous bone-marrow grafting for nonunions. Surgical technique. J Bone Joint Surg Am 2006;88(suppl 1, pt 2):322–327.

104. Hernigou P, Poignard A, Beaujean F, et al. Percutaneous autologous bone-marrow grafting for nonunions. Influence of the number and concentration of progenitor cells. J Bone Joint Surg Am 2005;87A:1430–1437.

105. Hernigou P, Poignard A, Manicom O, et al. The use of percutaneous autologous bone marrow transplantation in nonunion and avascular necrosis of bone. J Bone Joint Surg Br 2005;87B:896–902.

106. Hierholzer C, Sama D, Toro JB, et al. Plate fixation of ununited humeral shaft fractures: effect of type of bone graft on healing. J Bone Joint Surg Am 2006;88A:1442–1447.

107. Hollinger JO, Onikepe AO, MacKrell J, et al. Accelerated fracture healing in the geriatric, osteoporotic rat with recombinant human platelet-derived growth factor-BB and an injectable beta-tricalcium phosphate/collagen matrix. J Orthop Res 2008;26:83–90.

108. Hornicek FJ, Zych GA, Hutson JJ, et al. Salvage of humeral nonunions with onlay bone plate allograft augmentation. Clin Orthop Relat Res 2001;May:203–209.

109. Horstmann WG, Verheyen CC, Leemans R. An injectable calcium phosphate cement as a bone-graft substitute in the treatment of displaced lateral tibial plateau fractures. Injury 2003;34:141–144.

110. Hou CH, Yang RS, Hou SM. Hospital-based allogenic bone bank—10-year experience. J Hosp Infect 2005;59:41–45.

111. Hurley MM, Abreu C, Harrison JR, et al. Basic fibroblast growth factor inhibits type I collagen gene expression in osteoblastic MC3T3-E1 cells. J Biol Chem 1993;268:5588–5593.

112. Ilizarov GA, Khelimskii AM, Saks RG. [Characteristics of systemic growth regulation of the limbs under the effect of various factors influencing their growth and length]. Ortop Travmatol Protez 1978;August:37–41.

113. Ilizarov GA, Pereslitskikh PF, Barabash AP. [Closed directed longitudino-oblique or spinal osteoclasia of the long tubular bones (experimental study)]. Ortop Travmatol Protez 1978;November:20–23.

114. Ingber DE, Folkman J. Mechanochemical switching between growth and differentiation during fibroblast growth factor-stimulated angiogenesis in vitro: role of extracellular matrix. J Cell Biol 1989;109:317–330.

115. Ito H, Koefoed M, Tiyapatanaputi P, et al. Remodeling of cortical bone allografts mediated by adherent rAAV-RANKL and VEGF gene therapy. Nat Med 2005;11:291–297.

116. Itoh N, Ornitz DM. Evolution of the Fgf and Fgfr gene families. Trends Genet 2004;20:563–569.

117. Jaiswal N, Haynesworth SE, Caplan AI, et al. Osteogenic differentiation of purified, culture-expanded human mesenchymal stem cells in vitro. J Cell Biochem 1997;64:295–312.

118. Jarcho M, Kay JF, Gumaer KI, et al. Tissue, cellular, and subcellular events at a bone-ceramic hydroxylapatite interface. J Bioeng 1977;1:79–92.

119. Jeyam M, Andrew JG, Muir LT, et al. Controlled trial of distal radial fractures treated with a resorbable bone mineral substitute. J Hand Surg [Br] 2002;27:146–149.

120. Johnson EE, Urist MR, Finerman GA. Repair of segmental defects of the tibia with cancellous bone grafts augmented with human bone morphogenetic protein. A preliminary report. Clin Orthop Relat Res 1988;November:249–257.

121. Kelly CM, Wilkins RM, Gitelis S, et al. The use of a surgical grade calcium sulfate as a bone graft substitute: results of a multicenter trial. Clin Orthop Relat Res 2001;January:42–50.

122. Kenwright J, Richardson JB, Goodship AE, et al. Effect of controlled axial micromovement on healing of tibial fractures. Lancet 1986;2:1185–1187.

123. Kerry RM, Masri BA, Garbuz DS, et al. The biology of bone grafting. Instr Course Lect 1999;48:645–652.

124. Khan SN, Bostrom MP, Lane JM. Bone growth factors. Orthop Clin North Am 2000;31:375–388.

125. Klein S, Giancotti FG, Presta M, et al. Basic fibroblast growth factor modulates integrin expression in microvascular endothelial cells. Mol Biol Cell 1993;4:973–982.

126. Kloen P, Di PM, Borens O, et al. BMP signaling components are expressed in human fracture callus. Bone 2003;33:362–371.

127. Kocaoglu M, Eralp L, Sen C, et al. Management of stiff hypertrophic nonunions by distraction osteogenesis: a report of 16 cases. J Orthop Trauma 2003;17:543–548.

128. Kocialkowski A, Wallace WA, Prince HG. Clinical experience with a new artificial bone graft: preliminary results of a prospective study. Injury 1990;21:142–144.

129. Kolbeck S, Bail H, Schmidmaier G, et al. Homologous growth hormone accelerates bone healing: a biomechanical and histological study. Bone 2003;33:628–637.

130. Krause JO, Perry CR. Distal femur as a donor site of autogenous cancellous bone graft. J Orthop Trauma 1995;9:145–151.

131. Kristiansen TK, Ryaby JP, McCabe J, et al. Accelerated healing of distal radial fractures with the use of specific, low-intensity ultrasound. A multicenter, prospective, randomized, double-blind, placebo-controlled study. J Bone Joint Surg Am 1997;79:961–973.

132. Kucia M, Machalinski B, Ratajczak MZ. The developmental deposition of epiblast/germ cell-line derived cells in various organs as a hypothetical explanation of stem cell plasticity? Acta Neurobiol Exp (Wars) 2006;66:331–341.

133. Lassus J, Tulikoura I, Konttinen YT, et al. Treatment of infection and nonunion after bilateral complicated proximal tibial fracture. Ann Chir Gynaecol 2000;89:325–328.

134. Laufs U, Liao JK. Direct vascular effects of HMG-CoA reductase inhibitors. Trends Cardiovasc Med 2000;10:143–148.

135. Lazarus HM, Haynesworth SE, Gerson SL, et al. Ex vivo expansion and subsequent infusion of human bone marrow-derived stromal progenitor cells (mesenchymal progenitor cells): implications for therapeutic use. Bone Marrow Transplant 1995;16:557–564.

136. Le BK, Tammik C, Rosendahl K, et al. HLA expression and immunologic properties of differentiated and undifferentiated mesenchymal stem cells. Exp Hematol 2003;31:890–896.

137. LeCroy CM, Rizzo M, Gunneson EE, et al. Free vascularized fibular bone grafting in the management of femoral neck nonunion in patients younger than 50 years. J Orthop Trauma 2002;16:464–472.

138. Lee DY, Cho TJ, Kim JA, et al. Mobilization of endothelial progenitor cells in fracture healing and distraction osteogenesis. Bone 2008;January 26.

139. Lewallen DG, Chao EY, Kasman RA, et al. Comparison of the effects of compression plates and external fixators on early bone-healing. J Bone Joint Surg Am 1984;66A:1084–1091.

140. Lewandrowski KU, Gresser JD, Wise DL, et al. Bioresorbable bone graft substitutes of different osteoconductivities: a histologic evaluation of osteointegration of poly(propylene glycol-co-fumaric acid)-based cement implants in rats. Biomaterials 2000;21:757–764.

141. Lewinson D, Maor G, Rozen N, et al. Expression of vascular antigens by bone cells during bone regeneration in a membranous bone distraction system. Histochem Cell Biol 2001;116:381–388.

142. Li M, Ke HZ, Qi H, et al. A novel, nonprostanoid EP2 receptor-selective prostaglandin E2 agonist stimulates local bone formation and enhances fracture healing. J Bone Miner Res 2003;18:2033–2042.

143. Li X, Qin L, Bergenstock M, et al. Parathyroid hormone stimulates osteoblastic expression of MCP-1 to recruit and increase the fusion of pre/osteoclasts. J Biol Chem 2007; 282:33098–33106.

144. Liechty KW, MacKenzie TC, Shaaban AF, et al. Human mesenchymal stem cells engraft and demonstrate site-specific differentiation after in utero transplantation in sheep. Nat Med 2000;6:1282–1286.

145. Lin CH, Wei FC, Levin LS, et al. Free composite serratus anterior and rib flaps for tibial composite bone and soft-tissue defect. Plast Reconstr Surg 1997;99:1656–1665.

146. Lind M, Schumacker B, Soballe K, et al. Transforming growth factor-beta enhances fracture healing in rabbit tibiae. Acta Orthop Scand 1993;64:553–556.

147. Lobenhoffer P, Gerich T, Witte F, et al. Use of an injectable calcium phosphate bone cement in the treatment of tibial plateau fractures: a prospective study of 26 cases with 20-month mean follow-up. J Orthop Trauma 2002;16:143–149.

148. Lord CF, Gebhardt MC, Tomford WW, et al. Infection in bone allografts. Incidence, nature, and treatment. J Bone Joint Surg Am 1988;70A:369–376.

149. Ludwig SC, Boden SD. Osteoinductive bone graft substitutes for spinal fusion: a basic science summary. Orthop Clin North Am 1999;30:635–645.

150. Macey LR, Kana SM, Jingushi S, et al. Defects of early fracture-healing in experimental diabetes. J Bone Joint Surg Am 1989;71A:722–733.

151. Mammi GI, Rocchi R, Cadossi R, et al. The electrical stimulation of tibial osteotomies. Double-blind study. Clin Orthop Relat Res 1993;March:246–253.

152. Manabe T, Mori S, Mashiba T, et al. Human parathyroid hormone (1–34) accelerates natural fracture healing process in the femoral osteotomy model of cynomolgus monkeys. Bone 2007;40:1475–1482.

153. Manjubala I, Sivakumar M, Sampath Kumar TS, et al. Synthesis and characterization of functional gradient materials using Indian corals. J Mater Sci Mater Med 2000;11: 705–709.

154. Masri BA, Meek RM, Duncan CP. Periprosthetic fractures evaluation and treatment. Clin Orthop Relat Res 2004;March:80–95.

155. Matsumine A, Kusuzaki K, Matsubara T, et al. Calcium phosphate cement in musculoskeletal tumor surgery. J Surg Oncol 2006;93:212–220.

156. McAndrew MP, Gorman PW, Lange TA. Tricalcium phosphate as a bone graft substitute in trauma: preliminary report. J Orthop Trauma 1988;2:333–339.

157. Meyer U, Meyer T, Wiesmann HP, et al. Mechanical tension in distraction osteogenesis regulates chondrocytic differentiation. Int J Oral Maxillofac Surg 2001;30:522–530.

158. Moed BR, Willson Carr SE, Craig JG, et al. Calcium sulfate used as bone graft substitute in acetabular fracture fixation. Clin Orthop Relat Res 2003;May:303–309.

159. Moore JR, Weiland AJ, Daniel RK. Use of free vascularized bone grafts in the treatment of bone tumors. Clin Orthop Relat Res 1983;May:37–44.

160. Moucha CS, Einhorn TA. Enhancement of skeletal repair. In: Browner BD, Jupiter JB, Levine AM, eds. Skeletal Trauma. Basic Science, Management, and Reconstruction. 3rd Ed. Philadelphia: Saunders; 2003:639.

161. Mundy G, Garrett R, Harris S, et al. Stimulation of bone formation in vitro and in rodents by statins. Science 1999;286:1946–1949.

162. Muschler GF, Boehm C, Easley K. Aspiration to obtain osteoblast progenitor cells from human bone marrow: the influence of aspiration volume. J Bone Joint Surg Am 1997; 79A:1699–1709.

163. Muschler GF, Nitto H, Boehm CA, et al. Age- and gender-related changes in the cellularity of human bone marrow and the prevalence of osteoblastic progenitors. J Orthop Res 200119:117–125.

164. Nakajima A, Shimoji N, Shiomi K, et al. Mechanisms for the enhancement of fracture healing in rats treated with intermittent low-dose human parathyroid hormone (1–34). J Bone Miner Res 2002;17:2038–2047.

165. Nakamura T, Hara Y, Tagawa M, et al. Recombinant human basic fibroblast growth factor accelerates fracture healing by enhancing callus remodeling in experimental dog tibial fracture. J Bone Miner Res 1998;13:942–949.

166. Nakazawa T, Nakajima A, Shiomi K, et al. Effects of low-dose, intermittent treatment with recombinant human parathyroid hormone (1–34) on chondrogenesis in a model of experimental fracture healing. Bone 2005;37:711–719.

167. Nash TJ, Howlett CR, Martin C, et al. Effect of platelet-derived growth factor on tibial osteotomies in rabbits. Bone 1994;15:20320–20328.

168. Neer RM, Arnaud CD, Zanchetta JR, et al. Effect of parathyroid hormone (1–34) on fractures and bone mineral density in postmenopausal women with osteoporosis. N Engl J Med 2001;344:1434–1441.

169. Nevins M, Camelo M, Nevins ML, Schenk RK, Lynch SE. Periodontal regeneration in humans using recombinant human platelet-derived growth factor-BB (rhPDGF-BB) and allogenic bone. J Periodontol 2003;74:1282–1292.

170. Nicoll EA. Fractures of the tibial shaft. A survey of 705 cases. J Bone Joint Surg Br 1964;46B:373–387.

171. O'Keeffe RM Jr, Riemer BL, Butterfield SL. Harvesting of autogenous cancellous bone graft from the proximal tibial metaphysis. A review of 230 cases. J Orthop Trauma 1991;5:469–474.

172. Ohlsson C, Bengtsson BA, Isaksson OG, et al. Growth hormone and bone. Endocr Rev 1998;19:55–79.

173. Pacicca DM, Patel N, Lee C, et al. Expression of angiogenic factors during distraction osteogenesis. Bone 2003;33:889–898.

174. Paley D, Young MC, Wiley AM, et al. Percutaneous bone marrow grafting of fractures and bony defects. An experimental study in rabbits. Clin Orthop Relat Res 1986;July: 300–312.

175. Paralkar VM, Borovecki F, Ke HZ, et al. An EP2 receptor-selective prostaglandin E2 agonist induces bone healing. Proc Natl Acad Sci U S A 2003;100:6736–6740.

176. Parikh SN. Bone graft substitutes: past, present, future. J Postgrad Med 2002;48: 142–148.

177. Parker MJ, Raghavan R, Gurusamy K. Incidence of fracture-healing complications after femoral neck fractures. Clin Orthop Relat Res 2007;458:175–179.

178. Pelker RR, Friedlaender GE, Markham TC, et al. Effects of freezing and freeze-drying on the biomechanical properties of rat bone. J Orthop Res 1984;1:405–411.

179. Pilla AA, Mont MA, Nasser PR, et al. Noninvasive low-intensity pulsed ultrasound accelerates bone healing in the rabbit. J Orthop Trauma 1990;4:246–253.

180. Plenk H Jr, Hollmann K, Wilfert KH. Experimental bridging of osseous defects in rats by the implantation of Kiel bone containing fresh autologous marrow. J Bone Joint Surg Br 1972;54B:735–743.

181. Raisz LG. Physiology and pathophysiology of bone remodeling. Clin Chem 1999;45: 1353–1358.

182. Raschke M, Kolbeck S, Bail H, et al. Homologous growth hormone accelerates healing of segmental bone defects. Bone 2001;29:368–373.

183. Raschke M, Rasmussen MH, Govender S, et al. Effects of growth hormone in patients with tibial fracture: a randomized, double-blind, placebo-controlled clinical trial. Eur J Endocrinol 2007;156:341–351.

184. Ratajczak MZ, Machalinski B, Wojakowski W, et al. A hypothesis for an embryonic origin of pluripotent Oct-4(+) stem cells in adult bone marrow and other tissues. Leukemia 2007;21:860–867.

185. Ratajczak MZ, Zuba-Surma EK, Machalinski B, et al. Bone marrow–derived stem cells: our key to longevity? J Appl Genet 2007;48:307–319.

186. Ratajczak MZ, Zuba-Surma EK, Shin DM, et al. Very small embryonic-like (VSEL) stem cells in adult organs and their potential role in rejuvenation of tissues and longevity. Exp Gerontol 2008;June 14.

187. Rhee SH. Synthesis of hydroxyapatite via mechanochemical treatment. Biomaterials 2002;23:1147–1152.

188. Ripamonti U, Duneas N. Tissue morphogenesis and regeneration by bone morphogenetic proteins. Plast Reconstr Surg 1998;101:227–239.

189. Rouleau MF, Mitchell J, Goltzman D. In vivo distribution of parathyroid hormone receptors in bone: evidence that a predominant osseous target cell is not the mature osteoblast. Endocrinology 1988;123:187–191.

190. Rouleau MF, Mitchell J, Goltzman D. Characterization of the major parathyroid hormone target cell in the endosteal metaphysis of rat long bones. J Bone Miner Res 1990; 5:1043–1053.

191. Roy DM, Linnehan SK. Hydroxyapatite formed from coral skeletal carbonate by hydrothermal exchange. Nature 1974;247:220–222.

192. Rundle CH, Miyakoshi N, Ramirez E, et al. Expression of the fibroblast growth factor receptor genes in fracture repair. Clin Orthop Relat Res 2002;October:253–263.

193. Rutten S, Nolte PA, Guit GL, et al. Use of low-intensity pulsed ultrasound for posttraumatic nonunions of the tibia: a review of patients treated in the Netherlands. J Trauma 2007;62:902–908.

194. Sanchez-Sotelo J, Munuera L, Madero R. Treatment of fractures of the distal radius with a remodellable bone cement: a prospective, randomized study using Norian SRS. J Bone Joint Surg Br 2000;82:856–863.

195. Sanders RA, Sackett JR. Open reduction and internal fixation of delayed union and nonunion of the distal humerus. J Orthop Trauma 1990;4:254–259.

196. Sarmiento A, Schaeffer JF, Beckerman L, et al. Fracture healing in rat femora as affected by functional weight-bearing. J Bone Joint Surg Am 1977;59A:369–375.

197. Schildhauer TA, Bauer TW, Josten C, et al. Open reduction and augmentation of internal fixation with an injectable skeletal cement for the treatment of complex calcaneal fractures. J Orthop Trauma 2000;14:309–317.

198. Schreurs BW, Arts JJ, Verdonschot N, et al. Femoral component revision with use of impaction bone-grafting and a cemented polished stem. Surgical technique. J Bone Joint Surg Am 2006;88(suppl 1, pt 2):259–274.

199. Scott G, King JB. A prospective, double-blind trial of electrical capacitive coupling in the treatment of non-union of long bones. J Bone Joint Surg Am 1994;76A:820–826.

200. Segur JM, Torner P, Garcia S, et al. Use of bone allograft in tibial plateau fractures. Arch Orthop Trauma Surg 1998;117:357–359.

201. Sen C, Eralp L, Gunes T, et al. An alternative method for the treatment of nonunion of the tibia with bone loss. J Bone Joint Surg Br 2006;88B:783–789.

202. Sen C, Kocaoglu M, Eralp L, et al. compression-distraction in the acute treatment of grade III open tibia fractures with bone and soft-tissue loss: a report of 24 cases. J Orthop Trauma 2004;18:150–157.

203. Shaffer JW, Field GA, Goldberg VM, et al. Fate of vascularized and nonvascularized autografts. Clin Orthop Relat Res 1985;July:32–43.

204. Shanbhag AS. Use of bisphosphonates to improve the durability of total joint replacements. J Am Acad Orthop Surg 2006;14:215–225.

205. Sharrard WJ. A double-blind trial of pulsed electromagnetic fields for delayed union of tibial fractures. J Bone Joint Surg Br 1990;72B:347–355.

206. Simpson D, Keating JF. Outcome of tibial plateau fractures managed with calcium phosphate cement. Injury 2004;35:913–918.

207. Skoglund B, Aspenberg P. Locally applied Simvastatin improves fracture healing in mice. BMC Musculoskelet Disord 2007;8:98.

208. Solheim E. Growth factors in bone. Int Orthop 1998;22:410–416.

209. Souter WA. Autogenous cancellous strip grafts in the treatment of delayed union of long bone fractures. J Bone Joint Surg Br 1969;51B:63–75.

210. Springfield DS. Massive autogenous bone grafts. Orthop Clin North Am 1987;18: 249–256.

211. Stevenson S. Biology of bone grafts. Orthop Clin North Am 1999;30:543–552.

212. Stevenson S, Li XQ, Martin B. The fate of cancellous and cortical bone after transplantation of fresh and frozen tissue-antigen-matched and mismatched osteochondral allografts in dogs. J Bone Joint Surg Am 1991;73:1143–1156.

213. Street J, Winter D, Wang JH, et al. Is human fracture hematoma inherently angiogenic? Clin Orthop Relat Res 2000;September:224–237.

214. Street JT, Wang JH, Wu QD, et al. The angiogenic response to skeletal injury is preserved in the elderly. J Orthop Res 2001;19:1057–1066.

215. Swiontkowski MF, Aro HT, Donell S, et al. Recombinant human bone morphogenetic protein-2 in open tibial fractures. A subgroup analysis of data combined from two prospective randomized studies. J Bone Joint Surg Am 2006;88A:1258–1265.

216. Tambe AD, Cutler L, Murali SR, et al. In scaphoid nonunion, does the source of graft affect outcome? Iliac crest versus distal end of radius bone graft. J Hand Surg [Br] 2006;31:47–51.

217. Tay BK, Patel VV, Bradford DS. Calcium sulfate- and calcium phosphate-based bone substitutes. Mimicry of the mineral phase of bone. Orthop Clin North Am 1999;30: 615–623.

218. Tessier P, Kawamoto H, Matthews D, et al. Autogenous bone grafts and bone substi-

tutes—tools and techniques: I. A 20,000-case experience in maxillofacial and craniofacial surgery. Plast Reconstr Surg 2005;116(5 suppl):6S–24S.

219. Tessier P, Kawamoto H, Posnick J, et al. Complications of harvesting autogenous bone grafts: a group experience of 20,000 cases. Plast Reconstr Surg 2005;116(5 suppl): 72S–3S.

220. Thaller SR, Dart A, Tesluk H. The effects of insulin-like growth factor-1 on critical-size calvarial defects in Sprague-Dawley rats. Ann Plast Surg 1993;31:429–433.

221. Thompson RC Jr, Pickvance EA, Garry D. Fractures in large-segment allografts. J Bone Joint Surg Am 1993;75:1663–1673.

222. Thum T, Hoeber S, Froese S, et al. Age-dependent impairment of endothelial progenitor cells is corrected by growth-hormone-mediated increase of insulin-like growth-factor-1. Circ Res 2007;100:434–443.

223. Tiedeman JJ, Garvin KL, Kile TA, et al. The role of a composite, demineralized bone matrix and bone marrow in the treatment of osseous defects. Orthopedics 1995;18: 1153–1158.

224. Toms AD, Barker RL, Jones RS, et al. Impaction bone-grafting in revision joint replacement surgery. J Bone Joint Surg Am 2004;86A:2050–2060.

225. Toms AD, McClelland D, Chua L, et al. Mechanical testing of impaction bone grafting in the tibia: initial stability and design of the stem. J Bone Joint Surg Br 2005;87B: 656–663.

226. Tsuji K, Bandyopadhyay A, Harfe BD, et al. BMP2 activity, although dispensable for bone formation, is required for the initiation of fracture healing. Nat Genet 2006;38: 1424–1429.

227. Ueda K, Saito A, Nakano H, et al. Cortical hyperostosis following long-term administration of prostaglandin E1 in infants with cyanotic congenital heart disease. J Pediatr 1980;97:834–836.

228. Uhthoff HK, Rahn BA. Healing patterns of metaphyseal fractures. Clin Orthop Relat Res 1981;October:295–303.

229. Urist MR. Osteoinduction in undemineralized bone implants modified by chemical inhibitors of endogenous matrix enzymes. A preliminary report. Clin Orthop Relat Res 1972;87:132–137.

230. Urist MR. Bone: formation by autoinduction. 1965. Clin Orthop Relat Res 2002;February:4–10.

231. Urist MR, Silverman BF, Buring K, et al. The bone induction principle. Clin Orthop Relat Res 1967;53:243–283.

232. Uygur F, Ulkur E, Pehlivan O, et al. Soft tissue necrosis following using calcium phosphate cement in calcaneal bone cyst: case report. Arch Orthop Trauma Surg 2007; December 4.

233. Vaccaro AR. The role of the osteoconductive scaffold in synthetic bone graft. Orthopedics 2002;25(5 suppl):s571–s578.

234. Vaes G. Cellular biology and biochemical mechanism of bone resorption. A review of recent developments on the formation, activation, and mode of action of osteoclasts. Clin Orthop Relat Res 1988;June:239–271.

235. Wang JW, Weng LH. Treatment of distal femoral nonunion with internal fixation, cortical allograft struts, and autogenous bone-grafting. J Bone Joint Surg Am 2003; 85A:436–440.

236. Waters PM, Stewart SL. Surgical treatment of nonunion and avascular necrosis of the proximal part of the scaphoid in adolescents. J Bone Joint Surg Am 2002;84A:915–920.

237. Welch RD, Zhang H, Bronson DG. Experimental tibial plateau fractures augmented with calcium phosphate cement or autologous bone graft. J Bone Joint Surg Am 2003; 85A:222–231.

238. Wieman TJ, Smiell JM, Su Y. Efficacy and safety of a topical gel formulation of recombinant human platelet-derived growth factor-BB (becaplermin) in patients with chronic neuropathic diabetic ulcers. A phase III randomized placebo-controlled double-blind study. Diabetes Care 1998;21:822–827.

239. Yacobucci GN, Cocking MR. Union of medial opening-wedge high tibial osteotomy using a corticocancellous proximal tibial wedge allograft. Am J Sports Med 2008;January 28.

240. Yang KH, Parvizi J, Wang SJ, et al. Exposure to low-intensity ultrasound increases aggrecan gene expression in a rat femur fracture model. J Orthop Res 1996;14: 802–809.

241. Yetkinler DN, McClellan RT, Reindel ES, et al. Biomechanical comparison of conventional open reduction and internal fixation versus calcium phosphate cement fixation of a central depressed tibial plateau fracture. J Orthop Trauma 2001;15:197–206.

242. Younger EM, Chapman MW. Morbidity at bone graft donor sites. J Orthop Trauma 1989;3:192–195.

243. Yu HB, Shen GF, Wei FC. Effect of cryopreservation on the immunogenicity of osteoblasts. Transplant Proc 2007;39:3030–3031.

244. Ziran BH, Hendi P, Smith WR, et al. Osseous healing with a composite of allograft and demineralized bone matrix: adverse effects of smoking. Am J Orthop 2007;36: 207–209.

245. Ziran BH, Smith WR, Morgan SJ. Use of calcium-based demineralized bone matrix/allograft for nonunions and posttraumatic reconstruction of the appendicular skeleton: preliminary results and complications. J Trauma 2007;63:1324–1328.

6

PRINCIPLES OF NONOPERATIVE FRACTURE TREATMENT

Charles M. Court-Brown

INTRODUCTION

onoperative fracture management was the only method of fracture management until about 1750. Since then there have been advances in operative fracture treatment, which accelerated considerably after World War II because of improved surgical techniques, better anesthesia and postoperative treatment, and the introduction of antibiotics. Even today, nonoperative management remains a very important tool in the armamentarium of the orthopaedic trauma surgeon. The concentration of severe injuries into specialized trauma centers in many countries has unquestionably improved their treatment but has also caused surgeons to overestimate the role of operative treatment in the full spectrum of fractures. In fact, nonoperative fracture treatment remains the most common method of fracture management, although its role has changed significantly during the last 20 to 30 years. This chapter presents an epidemiological analysis of nonoperative fracture management from a major trauma center, illustrates common nonoperative techniques, and discusses indications for their use.

HISTORY OF NONOPERATIVE FRACTURE TREATMENT

The ancient Egyptians were the first to document how fractures should be managed and to record the basic results of their management.[69] The Edwin Smith Papyrus dates from 2800 to 3000 BC and was translated in 1930 in the United States.[12] It is composed of a series of case reports of specific injuries and their associated prognoses, good and bad. Case 37 describes a coexisting humeral fracture and wound over the upper arm. It suggests that if the two are not connected the arm should be splinted and the wound dressed. If the wound and fracture connect the prognosis is poor and the ailment should not be treated! In those days, splintage relied on bandaging over splints of wood and linen and using glue to stiffen the bandages.

There does not appear to have been any significant advance in fracture management until the Ancient Greek Empire, with Hippocrates being credited with many advances that were probably the results of clinical work of many doctors. Hippocrates describes six different methods of applying roller bandages depending on the fracture location. The bandages were stiffened with cerate, which was an ointment consisting of lard or oil mixed with wax, resin, or pitch to essentially create a cast. It was customary to defer definitive management, usually fracture manipulation, until the swelling had diminished, which often took about 7 days. It is interesting to note that delayed management still remains popular in the treatment of some fractures. The Ancient Greeks also used mechanical aids to facilitate the reduction of fractures and dislocations, and Hippocrates is credited with the first audit of fracture healing time. However, he was either an optimist or the ancient Greeks had a superior genetic makeup because he said that femoral fractures and tibial fractures united in 50 and 40 days, respectively![45]

Further progress occurred in Ancient Rome and in Asia, but it is Albucasis, an Arabic physician, who is credited with advancing nonoperative fracture treatment and for acting as a conduit through which the philosophies of Ancient Rome and Greece could be transferred to Western Europe. Albucasis clearly upset his colleagues by suggesting that in femoral diaphyseal fractures the knee should be placed in full flexion.[69] His cast was a mixture of mill dust and egg whites or mixtures of grain, herbs, clay, and egg whites that were supported by bandages. He also introduced the somewhat radical practice of maintaining his casts for a longer period rather than changing them every few days, as had been done up to that time.

Following the introduction of gun powder in 1338, cannon shot in 1346, and half-pound gunshot in 1364, it was obvious that surgeons were going to be faced with many more open fractures than they had encountered before. As one would expect this stimulated innovation and surgeons began to challenge the views that open wounds should be encouraged to suppurate and that "laudable pus" was essential for wound healing. Paré and others demonstrated that wounds could be cleaned and sometimes closed primarily. Paré made the discovery that primary wound cleaning using a paste of oil of roses, turpentine, and egg yolk gave better results than the use of boiling oil. Paré's views were very influential, and the management of open wounds improved considerably.[2] He and others realized that devitalized bone fragments should be removed from open wounds but it was Desault and Larrey who introduced debridement at the l'Hotel Dieu in Paris at the end of the 18th century.[69]

Despite considerable progress being achieved in the management of open wounds, surgeons were essentially still left with the fracture treatment principles outlined by Albucasis around 1000 AD. Seutin,[87] a Belgian surgeon, had introduced a method of applying rigid dressings which could be left in position for a longer period, but it was the introduction of plaster of Paris bandages that revolutionized fracture treatment. These were introduced by Pirogov from Russia and Mathijsen from Holland in the early 1800s.[69] A better method of fracture management had become essential because of the carnage caused by the Napoleonic wars in Europe and the increased urbanization associated with the Industrial Revolution. While plaster of Paris bandages were not used during the American Civil War, Sayre[85] and Stimson[93] in New York together with Scudder[86] in Boston promoted the use of plaster of Paris bandages in the United States. Volkmann[103] was a particular enthusiast of the use of plaster of Paris in the management of fractures in Europe.

As with all new inventions, it took time for most surgeons to accept plaster of Paris bandaging, and the use of supportive splints such as the Thomas splint remained popular in the United Kingdom. They were strongly supported by Hugh Owen Thomas[94] and Robert Jones.[50] Eventually plaster casts became the routine method of managing most fractures and the arguments between surgeons centered around the amount of padding that should be used, the use of early weight bearing, and whether early joint motion could be allowed. Lorenz Böhler of Vienna[7] was a particular proponent of plaster of Paris cast treatment, believing in accurate reduction, the use of skintight casts, and intensive physical therapy. He was also very influential in developing a system of fracture treatment that was adopted throughout the world.

Sarmiento[80–84] was a particular advocate of nonoperative management, particularly of tibial fractures. He introduced a lower-leg functional brace to permit early joint mobilization. Credit must be given to Sarmiento for continuing to popularize nonoperative management of diaphyseal fractures and for providing a counterargument to those surgeons who felt that operative management was always indicated. Sarmiento's tibial functional brace became popular but its introduction coincided with the explosion of interest in operative lower-limb fracture treatment, which started in the 1960s.

The operative treatment of fractures first started around 1775 in France, and the first operative textbook detailing techniques of fracture fixation was published by Bérenger-Féraud in 1870.[6] He described six methods of fracture management, of which three are still in use today—cerclage wiring, interosseous sutures, and external fixation. In the 20th century operative management rapidly increased in popularity in both the United States and Europe. Pioneers such as Lambotte, Hey-Groves, Lane, Hoffman, Kuntscher, Ilizarov, and Müller and his colleagues in Europe and Parkhill, the Rush brothers, and Sherman in the United States promoted internal and external fixation.[69] However, it was the introduction of antibiotics and the development of modern anesthesia and improved surgical techniques that altered the way orthopaedic surgeons considered fracture management. The prevalence of operative fracture management has now increased significantly but is not used in all fractures. It is instructive to review the current use of nonoperative fracture management and to compare it with 50 or 60 years ago, when many surgeons were beginning to think seriously about operative management for the first time.

EPIDEMIOLOGY OF NONOPERATIVE FRACTURE TREATMENT

There has been no previous study of the use of nonoperative management in a defined population of adults, although there have been studies of the use of nonoperative treatment in more specialized hospitals, which were not responsible for treating all fractures in an entire community.[31,39,59,95] These studies have mainly dealt with pediatric fractures[39,59,95] but in 1958 Emmett and Breck[31] published a paper detailing the treatment of almost 11,000 fresh fractures in El Paso, Texas. To analyze the current role of nonoperative management, a study of the primary treatment of 7863 consecutive fractures in Edinburgh, Scotland, in 2000 was undertaken. To allow the examination of the role of nonoperative management in the complete population, the fractures in adults and children have been combined.

The data includes all inpatients and outpatients treated in

the Royal Infirmary of Edinburgh and The Royal Hospital for Sick Children in Edinburgh. These two hospitals provide the only trauma care for a defined population in the East of Scotland. In 2000 the catchment population of the area was 643,702 patients. In the study all patients treated in the catchment area but residing outside were excluded, and all patients who had primary treatment outside the catchment area but were subsequently treated within the area were included. All inpatient and outpatient fractures were included except spinal fractures. As in other centers these are treated by both orthopaedic surgeons and neurosurgeons in Edinburgh, with spinal cord injury patients being transferred to a specialized national center outside Edinburgh.

In this study manipulation under anesthesia was defined as nonoperative management but the soft tissue surgery inherent in the management of open fractures was defined as operative treatment regardless of whether fixation was used. Secondary procedures were not analyzed and the management of pure dislocations and soft tissue damage was not considered. In the study children were defined as being less than 16 years of age, with all patients 16 years and older being defined as adults. The basic demographic details of all patients were included in the database. Fracture location was defined using regional descriptors familiar to all orthopaedic surgeons. The OTA classification[34] was used to classify all long bone fractures and the Carstairs and Morris index[15] was used to define social deprivation. This index has been used extensively to investigate correlation between disease and social deprivation.[27,32] In this study, it was used to test whether social deprivation determined the choice of treatment method in different fractures. Several measures were used to analyze fracture severity and the subsequent decision to use operative treatment. Fracture severity was assessed using the OTA classification[34] in metaphyseal and intra-articular fractures of the long bones. OTA type A fractures are extra-articular, type B fractures are partial-articular, and type C fractures are complete articular fractures. This system does not apply to proximal humeral, proximal forearm, or proximal femoral fractures, and fracture severity was therefore assessed in fractures of the distal humerus, distal radius, distal femur, proximal tibia, and distal tibia. Nowadays the degree of severity of diaphyseal fractures is often not a major factor in determining management. This is particularly true of lower limb diaphyseal fractures for which intramedullary nailing is now commonly used regardless of the degree of displacement, comminution, or soft tissue damage.

The type of fracture treatment was also assessed with reference to the mode of injury and the presence of multiple fractures. The seven most common modes of injury were examined to see if particular modes of injury were associated with a higher prevalence of operative treatment. These were motor vehicle accidents, twisting injuries, falls, falls down stairs or slopes, falls from a height, assaults or direct blows, and sporting injuries. The association between operative treatment and the presence of multiple fractures was also examined.

Table 6-1 shows that, in adults, 67.6% of fractures were nonoperatively managed in 2000 with 63% of fractures in females and 72.8% of fractures in males being treated nonoperatively. There is a significant difference between upper and lower limb fractures, with 81.7% of upper limb fractures and 46.8% of

TABLE 6-1	**Number and Prevalence of Surgically Treated Adult Fractures Showing Gender and Regional Differences**		
		Operatively Treated	
	Total Number	Number	%
Adult fractures	**5576**	**1804**	**32.4**
Males	2650	720	27.2
Females	2926	1084	37.0
Upper limb	**3232**	**590**	**18.3**
Lower limb	**2255**	**1200**	**53.2**
Pelvis	**89**	**14**	**15.7**

lower limb fractures being treated nonoperatively. In addition, 84.3% of pelvic fractures were treated nonoperatively but most of these were pubic rami fractures occurring in elderly patients.

Age is an important predictor of the role of operative fracture treatment, as illustrated in Figure 6-1. To allow for a complete analysis of the relationship between age and the requirement for operative fracture treatment, the children's data from 2000 has been combined with the adult data. Figure 6-1 shows a gradual increase in operative treatment with age. Only 7.3% of patients younger than 5 years were treated operatively compared with 56.9% of patients aged 95 years or more. At about 80 years the prevalence of operative management overtakes nonoperative management and the highest prevalence of operative management is seen between 90 and 94 years of age when 67.4% of patients were treated operatively. Analysis of the equivalent results for males and females shows that both sexes have a similar distribution to the overall distribution shown in Figure 6-1.

Figures 6-2A and 6-2B show the equivalent age-related curves for upper and lower limb fractures. These are very different from Figure 6-1 and from each other. In the upper limb (Fig. 6-2A) there is a progressive increase in surgery from 9.1% in patients aged less than 5 years to 27.9% in patients aged 70 to 75 years. Older patients show a gradual reduction in surgical treatment. In the lower limb (Fig. 6-2B) there was no surgery undertaken in patients less than 5 years old but in older patients there was a gradual increase in operative treatment up to 95.1% in patients aged 95 years or more. The prevalence of lower limb operative surgery overtakes nonoperative treatment between 65 and 70 years of age. Analysis of the gender-specific curves for upper and lower limb fractures shows no difference to the overall distribution curves shown in Figure 6-2.

When considering fracture treatment nowadays it is important to look carefully at the elderly. There has been an increase in the incidence of osteoporotic fractures[23,48] as well as an appreciation that many fractures that formerly occurred in younger patients now commonly occur in the elderly.[21] Figure 6-3A shows the prevalence of operative treatment in adults aged 80 years or more, and it can be seen that there is a gradual increase in the use of surgery to treat fractures in this group up to about 93 years of age, when the use of surgical management begins to decline. Figures 6-3B and 6-3C show the relationship between old age and surgery in upper and lower limb fractures.

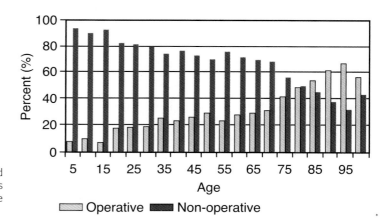

FIGURE 6-1 The prevalence of operatively and nonoperatively treated fractures according to patient age. The children's fracture data has been included and all patients have been divided into 5-year age bands.

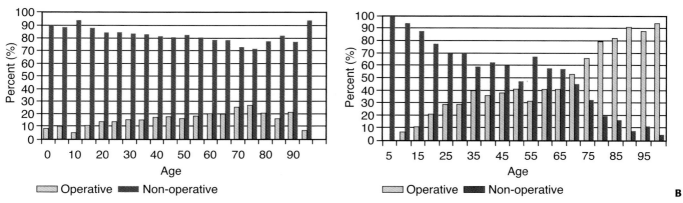

FIGURE 6-2 The prevalence of operatively and nonoperatively treated upper limb **(A)** and lower limb **(B)** fractures according to patient age. Patients are divided into 5-year age bands. The children's data has been added to the adult data.

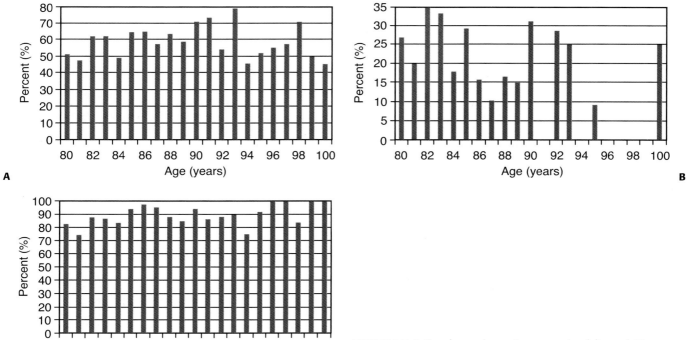

FIGURE 6-3 A. Prevalence of operative surgery in adults aged 80 years or more. **B,C.** Equivalent graphs for upper limb **(B)** and lower limb **(C)** fractures.

In the upper limb, Figure 6-3B shows that 25% to 35% of adults in their early eighties who present with upper limb fractures are treated surgically, but the prevalence declines to the extent that only 7.4% of upper limb fractures in patients aged 95 years or more were treated surgically. The situation is very different in lower limb fractures, and Figure 6-3C shows that the operative treatment of lower limb fractures gradually increases in the ninth and tenth decades of life.

Table 6-2 shows the prevalence of nonoperative management in different fractures. It indicates that virtually all proximal femoral, femoral diaphyseal, and tibial diaphyseal fractures are now treated operatively, with a very high prevalence of surgery in forearm diaphyseal fractures. There is a very low prevalence of surgery in proximal humeral, proximal radial, clavicular, metatarsal, and toe phalangeal fractures, and in this study no scapular surgery was undertaken—although obviously it is sometimes required. In the remaining fractures shown in Table 6-2, the prevalence of operative treatment varies between 11% and 71%, suggesting that both operative and nonoperative treatments are commonly used. In all fractures the surgeon clearly has to decide whether to treat the fracture operatively or nonoperatively based on many objective and subjective criteria, in-

TABLE 6-2	**The Prevalence of Operatively Treated Fractures in Adults in Decreasing Order**					
	Fractures			Average age		
		Treated operatively				
	Total	n	%	Surgery	Nonop	P
Proximal femur	693	676	97.5	80.4	79.7	Ns
Femoral diaphysis	54	51	94.4	67.9	89.0	Ns
Tibial diaphysis	102	96	94.1	42.0	62.7	0.022
Radius/ulna diaphyses	10	9	90.0	33.5	16.0	Ns
Radial diaphysis	11	9	81.2	46.2	54.5	Ns
Distal tibia	35	25	71.4	43.6	44.9	Ns
Proximal tibia	70	48	68.6	48.1	52.1	Ns
Proximal ulna	59	36	61.0	65.4	49.3	<0.001
Distal femur	23	14	60.9	61.7	65.0	Ns
Proximal radius/ulna	12	7	58.3	60.3	64.8	Ns
Talus	15	8	53.3	31.2	34.1	Ns
Distal humerus	28	14	50.0	60.5	61.1	Ns
Ankle	517	206	39.8	48.0	46.9	Ns
Humeral diaphysis	66	24	36.4	45.6	63.0	<0.001
Patella	56	20	35.7	55.1	58.5	Ns
Calcaneus	72	25	34.7	43.5	39.2	Ns
Ulnar diaphysis	38	12	31.6	32.2	43.0	Ns
Midfoot	27	8	29.6	48.0	46.9	Ns
Distal radius	977	285	29.2	61.8	56.9	<0.001
Pelvis	89	14	15.7	56.1	73.2	<0.001
Carpus	151	18	15.7	26.7	34.9	Ns
Finger phalanges	516	59	11.4	37.7	38.9	Ns
Metacarpus	626	69	11.0	28.8	32.1	Ns
Proximal humerus	336	25	7.4	61.5	65.0	Ns
Proximal radius	223	14	6.3	44.4	41.5	Ns
Clavicle	162	9	5.6	42.0	43.2	Ns
Metatarsus	381	15	3.9	42.0	44.4	Ns
Toe phalanges	209	8	3.8	37.6	35.8	Ns
Scapula	17	0	—	—	—	—
Sesamoid	1	0	—	—	—	—

The average age of patients treated operatively and nonoperatively is shown as is the probability of the age differences being significant.

cluding the location and severity of the fracture and any associated soft tissue damage; the age and medical condition of the patient; the ability to cooperate with a postoperative treatment regime; and any social habits such as smoking, drinking, and drug taking. Tables 6-1 and 6-2 both show that more surgical intervention is undertaken in lower limb fractures than in upper limb fractures. Table 6-2 also shows the five fractures for which multivariate analysis showed that age was an independent predictor of fracture management. In three fractures—those of the tibial diaphysis, humeral diaphysis, and the pelvis—increasing age was associated with the use of nonoperative treatment but for fractures of the proximal ulna and the distal radius increasing age predicted surgical management.

Empirically it seems clear that there must be a relationship between the prevalence of operative surgery and the severity of the fracture that has been treated. It is quite difficult to define such a relationship in diaphyseal fractures, as Table 6-2 shows that most diaphyseal fractures tend to be treated operatively now regardless of how serious they are. This does not apply to isolated fractures of the ulnar diaphysis or to humeral diaphyseal fractures but femoral, tibial, and other forearm diaphyseal fractures are now usually treated by internal fixation. On the other hand, an analysis of the severity of the five metaphyseal or intra-articular fractures classified by the OTA[34] shows that fracture severity is an independent predictor of surgery (Table 6-3). The only fracture that does not appear to show such a relationship is the distal femoral fracture and many of the patients that present with this fracture are very elderly and frail. It is also interesting to note that ankle fractures show a relationship between fracture severity and the requirement for operative treatment, although the classification basis is different from the fractures listed in Table 6-3. In the 517 ankle fractures shown in Table 6-2, 12.3% of the OTA type A ankle fractures were operatively treated compared with 49.1% of type B fractures and 70% of type C fractures.

An analysis of the role of surgery in the treatment of patients who present with multiple fractures shows that 42.1% of fractures that occur in adults who present with multiple fractures were treated surgically. Statistical analysis showed that the presence of more than one fracture was an independent predictor of surgery in fractures of the midfoot, distal radius, and metatarsus. Table 6-4 shows the prevalence of surgical treatment for the seven most common modes of injury for those fractures in which multivariate analysis showed that the mode of injury was an independent predictor of surgical treatment. The seven modes of injury shown in Table 6-4 accounted for 93.4% of adult fractures. As one might expect, the highest prevalence of surgical fracture treatment is often, but not exclusively, related to motor vehicle accidents. Ankle fractures following falls were more commonly treated operatively than ankle fractures that occurred as a result of motor vehicle accidents, but further analysis showed a higher prevalence of OTA Type C fractures in the older population who sustained an ankle fracture as a result of a fall. The only fracture in which social deprivation independently determined treatment was the metacarpal. These fractures often occur in socially deprived male adolescents and in the Edinburgh study 46.3% followed a fight or an assault. As in many centers, these fractures were most frequently treated nonoperatively.

Many surgeons will probably be surprised that in 2000 67.6% of fractures were treated nonoperatively in a major trauma unit. One assumes that the prevalence of nonoperative management is declining, and almost certainly this is the case, but this study indicates that in fact nonoperative management is still the most common overall treatment method for fractures in general. However, the overall figure of 67.6% disguises the overall trends. Figures 6-2 and 6-3 show a difference between upper and lower limb fractures, particularly in the elderly. It would be interesting to know if the prevalence of surgery in different fractures is changing in response to a changing population and to improved treatment methods.

There is very little data by which the changing prevalence can be assessed. There has been no previous complete epidemiological study in adults but in a remarkable paper Emmet and Breck[31] working in El Paso, Texas, before, during, and after World War II analyzed about 11,000 fresh fractures. They combined their pediatric and adult fractures and detailed the management of different fractures. The epidemiology of their population was different from the Edinburgh population, but they analyzed a very large number of fractures and it is interesting to compare their results between 1937 and 1955 with the Edinburgh results in 2000. To permit this the data from the pediatric fractures that were treated in Edinburgh in 2000 have been combined with the adult data.

TABLE 6-3	**Prevalence of Surgical Treatment in Different Severities of Metaphyseal and Intra-articular Fractures**			
	OTA Fracture type			
	Type A Extra-articular %	Type B Partial articular %	Type C Complete articular %	P
Distal humerus	15.4	88.9	66.7	0.002
Distal radius	28.0	10.7	51.8	<0.001
Distal femur	58.3	66.7	62.5	ns
Proximal tibia	18.2	78.0	77.8	<0.001
Distal tibia	30.0	76.9	100.0	0.001

The probability of increasing fracture complexity being a predictive factor for surgical treatment is shown.

TABLE 6-4	Prevalence of Surgical Treatment in Different Modes of Injury and the Probability of a Statistical Association							
	Twist	Fall	Fall stairs	Fall height	Assault/ direct blow	Sport	MVA	P
ADULTS								
Proximal humerus	—	5.1	22.2	25.0	25.0	7.1	10.5	0.01
Humeral diaphysis	—	23.1	—	60.0	50.0	100	100	0.003
Distal radius	0	28.2	39.4	32.0	11.1	21.9	56.1	0.001
Metacarpus	—	5.2	0	15.3	11.7	15.8	21.7	0.035
Distal tibia	0	66.6	50.0	88.9	0	100	100	0.005
Ankle	22.4	52.8	33.3	36.4	52.2	48.9	38.1	<0.001
Midfoot	0	—	0	37.5	0	66.0	100	0.003
Metatarsus	1.3	3.1	3.2	4.3	11.1	0	16.6	<0.001
CHILDREN								
Clavicle	—	0	0	0	0	0	10.0	0.011
Proximal radius	0	3.6	—	9.1	100	0	0	0.015
Proximal ulna	—	0	100	—	0	—	—	0.012
Distal radius	0	5.4	0	18.3	0	15.7	4.2	<0.001
Finger phalanges	50.0	0	0	0	0	4.6	0	<0.001

If the fracture is not listed there was no correlation between fracture treatment and mode of injury.

Emmet and Breck categorized their fractures differently from the fractures listed in Table 6-2. They combined all of their tibial fractures, except for ankle fractures, and they also combined talar, calcaneal, and midfoot fractures as tarsal fractures. They separated forearm fractures into radius and ulna fractures as well as isolated radius and ulna fractures but they combined proximal and diaphyseal forearm fractures together. Using Emmet and Breck's fracture criteria the comparative data between 1937 and 1955 and 2000 are shown in Tables 6-5 and 6-6.

Table 6-5 shows those fractures in which there is an increased prevalence of surgery in 2000 and Table 6-6 shows those fractures for which there is no evidence that we now operate more frequently than surgeons in the early 1950s. Table 6-5 indicates that we operate on many more diaphyseal fractures than in the early 1950s. The only exception appears to be the isolated radial fracture (Table 6-6). It must be remembered that proximal radial fractures have been combined with radial diaphyseal fractures and if one looks at Table 6-2 it is obvious that we now operate on many more diaphyseal fractures than were operated on in the 1950s. Table 6-5 also shows that we operate on four or five times the amount of distal radial fractures and this difference is undoubtedly greater if adults alone are examined.

It is probably more instructive to examine Table 6-6 and see which fractures we do not operate on any more frequently than in the 1950s. It would seem that we in fact treat fewer hand fractures nonoperatively, and this is presumably because of the beneficial effects of industrial legislation, which has significantly decreased the incidence of crushed hand injuries in many countries. However, in some parts of the world serious hand injuries are still relatively common and operative treatment will be more common.

One should consider that, with the possible exception of toe and patella fractures, surgeons now have access to superior implants and techniques than surgeons in the 1950s. It is therefore interesting that the treatment of fractures of the clavicle and proximal humerus in particular seem to be much the same as 50 or 60 years ago. There are now studies suggesting that more of these fractures may be treated surgically in the future, but only time will tell if this occurs.[14,62] Many clavicle fractures have a relatively simple morphology and the early results of locked plating of proximal humeral fractures have not been as encouraging as was hoped.[67] Therefore, it seems likely that nonoperative management of the fractures listed in Table 6-6 will continue to be a popular treatment method. The fractures in Table 6-6 comprise 46.2% of all the fractures treated in Edinburgh in 2000 and this explains the relatively low overall operation rate for this year. The demographic characteristics of nonoperative fracture treatment are summarized in Table 6-7.

TECHNIQUES OF NONOPERATIVE MANAGEMENT

Currently, we tend to use nonoperative techniques to treat stable fractures rather than to facilitate the reduction and stabilization of unstable fractures. It tends to be used to treat undisplaced or minimally displaced fractures or in patients who are elderly, frail, or who have significant medical or social comorbidities. However, in parts of the world with less access to operative fixation techniques, it remains an important treatment method for all fractures, and it is therefore important that surgeons understand the rationale behind the use of all nonoperative techniques.

TABLE 6-5	Comparison of Edinburgh Data with Emmet and Breck, Fractures with an Increased Prevalence of Surgery in 2000			
	Emmett and Breck[21]			Edinburgh
	1937–1945 %	1946–1950 %	1951–1955 %	2000 %
Humeral diaphysis	22.2	10.6	20.8	33.3
Distal humerus	8.5	17.8	25.3	32.9
Radius and ulna	6.0	13.6	14.9	26.4
Ulna	20.7	17.7	19.8	38.3
Distal radius	6.0	4.2	4.6	20.3
Carpus	0	4.9	7.3	10.1
Proximal femur	47.1	72.3	73.3	97.4
Femoral diaphysis	27.5	41.8	52.1	76.1
Distal femur	50.0	26.1	36.0	65.5
Tibia and fibula	27.5	22.9	30.4	61.8
Ankle	13.0	20.4	22.5	35.8
Tarsus	4.3	5.9	17.4	35.2

The Edinburgh data have been adjusted to correspond with Emmet and Breck's fracture definitions. See text for details.

There have been several advances in nonoperative fracture management in the last 20 to 30 years, although the basic tenets of management remain unchanged. The use of plaster of Paris casts remains widespread as they are inexpensive and easy to apply. However fiberglass casts are now more frequently used as they are lighter and more radiolucent. In addition, plastic orthoses, braces, and splints are now more frequently used.

Their design has improved but their overall function remains unchanged.

Traction

The initial argument regarding the role of internal fixation of fractures after World War II centered on femoral diaphyseal fractures. Intramedullary nailing gradually grew more popular

TABLE 6-6	Comparison of Edinburgh Data with Emmet and Breck Detailing the Fractures without an Increased Prevalence of Surgery in 2000			
	Emmett and Breck[21]			Edinburgh
	1937–1945 %	1946–1950 %	1951–1955 %	2000 %
Clavicle	1.7	2.8	8.7	3.0
Scapula	0	0	3.0	0
Proximal humerus	2.9	7.9	9.6	6.9
Radius	5.5	8.8	10.6	10.4
Metacarpus	7.9	15.7	16.6	9.2
Finger phalanges	13.5	13.6	20.9	7.5
Patella	35.3	38.3	32.1	32.8
Metatarsus	0	6.2	8.5	3.6
Toe phalanges	0	8.4	7.6	3.2
Pelvis	0	22.2	18.2	15.7
Total (Tables 65 and 66)	12.2	17.1	21.6	25.4

The Edinburgh data have been adjusted to correspond with Emmet and Breck's fracture definitions. See text for details.

TABLE 6-7	**Essential Demographics of Nonoperative Management**

Prevalence of nonoperative management (%)

	All adults (>16 years)	Adults (≥ 80 years)
Overall	67.6	59.5
Males	72.8	68.3
Females	63.0	57.9
Upper limb	81.7	78.4
Lower limb	46.8	12.2

Fractures most commonly treated

Nonoperatively (>90%)	Operatively (>70%)
Scapula	Proximal femur
Toe phalanges	Femoral diaphysis
Metatarsus	Tibial diaphysis
Clavicle	Radius and ulnar diaphyses
Proximal radius	Radial diaphysis
Proximal humerus	Distal tibia

Factors affecting decision to operate

Age

Severity of fracture (metaphyseal and intra-articular fractures)

Multiple fractures

Mode of injury (some fractures)

and essentially superceded traction as the treatment of choice for femoral fractures in the 1970s and 1980s, but traction is still used in parts of the world and surgeons should understand the rationale behind its use and its complications. In addition to the treatment of femoral diaphyseal fractures, traction was used to treat acetabular fractures and fracture dislocations of the hip as well as comminuted fractures of the tibial diaphysis and distal tibia, although its role in the management of these fractures is now extremely limited and essentially confined to situations when internal and external fixation techniques are unavailable. It is still used for the acute management of cervical spine fractures.

There are six basic methods of skeletal traction that are shown in Figure 6-4. Most traction methods rely on a splint on which the leg is placed. The proximal end or ring of the splint is placed in the patient's groin and traction is applied by placing a transosseous pin through the distal femur or proximal tibia. Fixed traction is undertaken when the pin is secured to the distal end of the splint by traction cords. In balanced traction the splint is suspended by a pulley system and a second pulley system is applied to the transosseous pin. Traction, using a variable weight, then alters the fracture position with countertraction being achieved by placing the patient head down and raising the end of the bed. Once traction is established the fracture alignment is checked radiologically and pads inserted appropriately to push the femur into correct alignment. A poste-

rior pad under the distal femur is almost always required because of the posterior sag produced by the effect of gravity.

Many types of traction have been described but the six basic types are shown in Figure 6-4. The first of these is a Thomas splint with a Pearson knee piece attached to the splint (Fig. 6-4A). The Thomas splint supports the leg and balanced traction is applied. After 4 to 6 weeks the knee piece is applied and knee mobilization commenced. This was a commonly used traction apparatus.

A second type of traction is Braun traction and a weight and pulley system (Fig. 6-4B). This is a very simple traction system that permits traction in the longitudinal axis of the femur. Control of the femoral fragments was difficult. The system, using skin rather than skeletal traction, is still used for temporary traction prior to femoral diaphyseal surgery.

Another type of traction is Hamilton-Russell traction, which uses a one-pulley system to provide support for the femur and to apply traction (Fig. 6-4C). The mechanical advantage offered by two pulleys at the foot of the bed theoretically meant that the longitudinal pull was twice as great as the upward pull and the resulting traction was at an axis of 30 degrees to the horizontal, approximately in line with the femur. This method of traction does not adequately control the femoral fragments and it was sometimes used after a period of skeletal traction.

A fourth type of traction is Perkins traction (Fig. 6-4D). This is essentially a straight pull along the axis of the femur through a proximal pin but without a splint. The control of femoral alignment was poor and malunion was common. Perkins believed in early knee mobilization and advocated the use of a split bed later in the treatment of femoral diaphyseal fractures. In this system the patients sat on a bed with the knee flexed over the mattress and knee movement was encouraged while longitudinal traction was maintained.

A fifth variety of traction is Fisk traction (Fig. 6-4E). This consists of a short Thomas splint and a hinged knee piece. Traction in the axis of the femur was maintained using a proximal tibial transosseous pin but the patient could flex the hip and knee by pulling on a separate cord attached to the end of the thigh splint.

Finally, there is 90–90 traction (Fig. 6-4F). In this method, the thigh is pulled upward and both hip and knee are at 90 degrees. The advantage of this method is that gravity does not cause posterior sag of the femoral fragments. It was used for proximal femoral diaphyseal fractures when the proximal femoral fracture was flexed by the unopposed action of iliopsoas. The method is still used for pediatric femoral fractures.

Treatment of femoral diaphyseal fractures by traction should be reserved for cases for which no other method is available. There is considerable morbidity associated with its use. The main complications are failure to maintain normal femoral alignment and significant knee stiffness. Charnley[16] documented 34 cases in patients between 20 and 45 years of age with middle and distal third diaphyseal fractures. On average, knee mobilization was commenced at 10 to 25 weeks and the final range of motion was 120 degrees. He also quoted very similar results from Massachusetts General Hospital stating that 44.4% of patients, with an average age of 37 years, had actually regained full knee function. Keep in mind that these were selected series of patients and Charnley's results were not matched by other surgeons. Connolly et al.[17] reported that the use of traction was associated with malunion and nonunion requiring

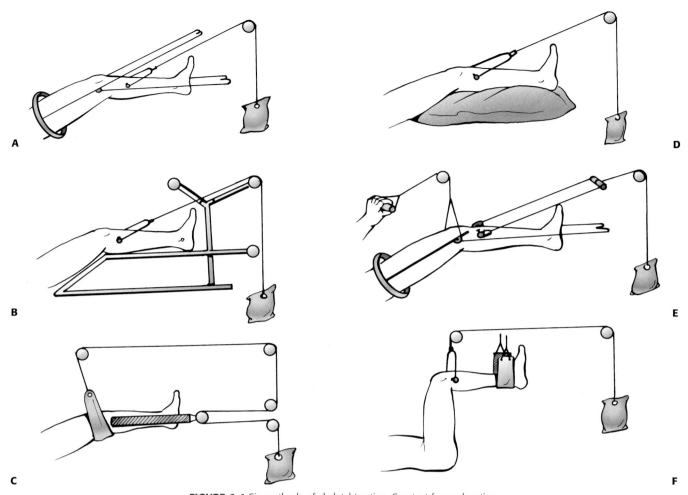

FIGURE 6-4 Six methods of skeletal traction. See text for explanation.

operative treatment in 11% to 29% of cases. Shortening of more than 2 cm occurred in 14% to 30% of cases and refracture in 4% to 17% of cases. They pointed out that the most significant complication was knee stiffness, which occurred in 30% to 50% of cases and affected both elderly and younger patients. In addition to these complications, prolonged traction is associated with significant medical problems and decubitus ulcers. Younger patients also suffered significantly with loss of employment and financial hardship. Psychological problems associated with prolonged bed rest were not uncommon.

To minimize these complications surgeons turned to the use of a cast brace, which is essentially a long leg cast with knee hinges to facilitate knee mobilization. This was applied after a few weeks of bed rest but its use was far from problem free. If the surgeon used prolonged bed rest prior to the application of the cast, patients tended to have the problems associated with traction, and if they shortened the period of bed rest it was difficult to apply the cast and mobilize the patient without losing fracture alignment. Using a regime of early application of a cast brace and mobilization, Connolly et al.[17] documented a 0.7% prevalence of nonunion and malunion with 13% shortening of more than 2 cm and 5.4% symptomatic loss of knee motion, 2% refracture, and 3% pulmonary emboli. They found the method particularly useful for distal fractures, comminuted

middiaphyseal fractures, and open fractures. Hardy[42] used a similar regime and quoted femoral malalignment in 72.2% of patients, significant knee disfunction in 7.4%, and knee instability in 35.2% of patients. As with femoral traction, the cast brace has now essentially disappeared and should only be used if surgical treatment is unavailable.

Tibial traction should not be used. It was used in cases of middiaphyseal comminution or if it was considered that a tibial plafond fracture was too complex to be treated surgically. Traction was applied through a transosseous calcaneal pin. Unfortunately, the use of excessive traction has been shown to increase the risk of compartment syndrome[88] and even if this complication does not occur, traction is associated with the same complications as femoral fractures, these being malalignment, joint stiffness, and nonunion. There is now no indication for tibial traction unless appropriate internal or external fixation techniques are unavailable.

Spinal Traction

Cervical Spine
Unlike skeletal traction spinal traction remains popular and is in widespread use for the management of cervical fractures and dislocations. It has been shown to be effective in various cervical

FIGURE 6-5 The use of cranial tongs to apply traction.

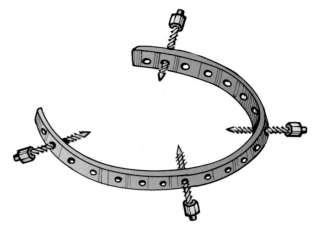

FIGURE 6-6 A halo ring.

fractures. Traction is commonly used to reduce a fracture or dislocation, thereby decompressing the neural elements and providing a degree of spinal stability. Spinal traction is rarely used for definitive management and it is usually changed to a halo-body cast or vest, or the surgeon may opt for later surgical stabilization. There are two principal types of cervical traction. These are cranial tongs, of which the best known are the Gardner-Wells tongs, and halo traction.

Cranial Tongs. Cranial tongs consist of a hemi-circular frame with two spring-loaded angulated pins (Fig. 6-5) that are placed into the outer table of the skull at points about 1 cm posterior to the external auditory meatus and 1 cm superior to the pinna of each ear. Because this is below the widest diameter of the skull the upward pin angulation means that traction can be applied. Each spring loaded pin is applied with an insertion torque of 6 to 8 inch pounds, and once the tongs are in position a simple pulley system can be set up with a weight hanging over the end of the frame or bed. Care must be exercised in applying weights in case overdistraction and neural damage occurs.

The weight required to reduce the spine varies with the position of the fracture, the degree of ligamentous damage, and the size of the patient. As a rule the surgeon should start with an initial weight of 10 pounds. Approximately 5 pounds per spinal segment are required to reduce the fracture in most patients, although this is only a guide. Thus a load of about 40 pounds will be required for a C5–C6 injury although the exact weight varies and serial imaging is required to check the position as the load is increased. It is important to obtain a lateral radiograph or fluoroscopic image to visualize fracture reduction.

Halo Rings. Closed or open halo rings are now a more popular choice for cervical traction (Fig. 6-6) because they can tolerate higher loading than cranial tongs and can be incorporated into a cast or brace to allow definitive treatment. The halo is attached with four pins: two anterior and two posterior. The pins should be inserted below the widest diameter of the skull with two anterior pins being placed through stab incisions under local anesthetic about 1 cm above the lateral third of the orbital rim. In this location they are lateral to the supraorbital and supra-trochlear nerves. The posterior pins are placed about 1 cm above the helix of the ear and to prevent skin necrosis they should not make contact with the ear. Opposing pins should be tightened at the same time to avoid pin displacement, with the pins then being retightened 24 to 48 hours after the initial application. If a pin loosens it can be retightened once to 8 inch pounds.

Halo-Body Fixation. The original halo-body device was a body cast attached to a halo. It was devised by Perry and Nickel.[70] Halo casts may still be useful if the appropriate bracing materials are not available or if the patient is uncooperative, but nowadays the halo is usually attached to a vest or orthosis (Fig. 6-7), which is made of plastic and tightened with buckles or straps. It is attached to the halo by two anterior and two posterior rods and it is worn until union occurs or a cervical brace is used.

Complications. As with skeletal traction, cervical traction is associated with several complications. It has been estimated that up to 31% of normal cervical spinal motion is permitted by halo-body orthoses and about 10% of patients lose fracture re-

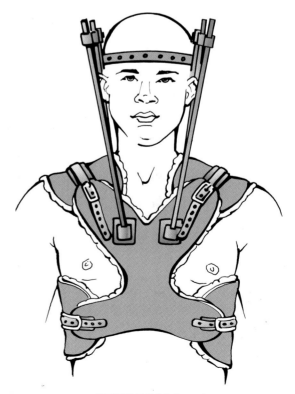

FIGURE 6-7 A halo vest.

duction.[53] Thus serial radiographs are essential during treatment. As with external skeletal fixation, pin track sepsis is a problem with it occurring in up to 20% of patients. As the fixation is unicortical, pin loosening is also a problem and rates of 36% to 60% have been recorded.[35,60] Nerve damage, dural puncture, skull perforation, and brain abscesses have all been reported, and when halo-body fixation is used in quadriplegic patients there is a high incidence of pressure sores, decubitus ulcers, and respiratory complications.[35,60] Dysphagia has also been reported.

Thoracolumbar Spine

Traction is not used for the definitive management of thoracolumbar fractures although prolonged bed rest is still used despite an increasing prevalence of surgical stabilization. Prolonged immobilization necessitates the use of a rotating bed, such as a Stryker bed, which is designed to facilitate skin care, physiotherapy, and personal hygiene. Complications include respiratory problems and decubitus ulcers, and intensive nursing is required. In less severe thoracolumbar fractures the surgeon may opt for a short period of bed rest followed by surgical stabilization or the use of a thoracolumbar brace or orthosis.

The use of a short period of thoracolumbar traction is sometimes used as a method of reducing thoracolumbar and lumbar burst fractures prior to the application of a thoracolumbar cast.[97] This technique involves the use of a Cotrel frame for a few days to facilitate fracture reduction. At this time, this technique is not in widespread use.

Casts

Unlike skeletal traction, casts remain popular for fracture treatment and probably remain the most common method of fracture treatment throughout the world. Figures 6-2 and 6-3 and Table 6-2 show that casts are more commonly used to treat upper limb fractures but Table 6-2 also indicates that many less-severe lower limb fractures continue to be treated with casts. Nowadays casts are less commonly used to control the position of a diaphyseal fracture after closed reduction but in some metaphyseal and intra-articular fractures, such as distal radial fractures and ankle fractures, this method of treatment is still widely used. Casts are often used for pain management and to facilitate mobilization in less severe fractures. The decision between cast management and surgery is frequently subjective and influenced by the patient's age, physical condition, mental status, and degree of prefracture mobility. In decades to come, it is likely that this decision will become more difficult as the age of the patients increases and they get progressively less fit.

There are three principles that apply to the treatment of unstable fractures with a cast. These are

1. Utilization of intact soft tissues
2. Three-point fixation
3. Hydrostatic pressure

These are illustrated in Figure 6-8 with reference to a fracture of the tibia and fibula. In theory there will often be a hinge of intact soft tissue on one side of the fracture, which can be used to assist with fracture reduction. If three-point fixation is applied through the cast the fracture will be maintained in a reduced position. This theory is somewhat naïve, although it may well work in the OTA A3.3 tibial fracture illustrated in Figure 6-8. However, many tibial fractures are not transverse, and obviously

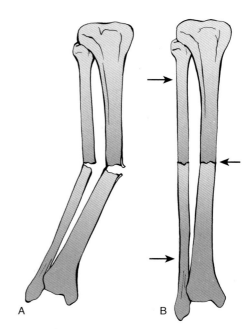

FIGURE 6-8 A. An OTA A3.3 fracture with valgus angulation. **B.** Three-point fixation or pressure, will reduce fracture if a soft tissue hinge is present.

the theoretical concept of a soft tissue hinge will be less applicable in spiral, butterfly, segmental, or comminuted fractures. In addition, there may well be soft tissue stripping from the diaphysis adjacent to the fracture and the fracture ends may overlap, which makes reduction more difficult. The last point to bear in mind is that while the soft tissue hinge may be intact in low velocity fractures in younger patients, it is unlikely to be intact after high energy injury or in older patients. The periosteum becomes thinner with increasing age and is more easily damaged. As many fractures occur in older patients, the fracture reduction concepts promoted by Charnley[16] and others are less applicable. This is illustrated in Figure 6-9. It shows the theoretical use of the soft tissue hinge in a metaphyseal distal radial fracture compared with the more common distal radial fracture in an older person, which is associated with metaphyseal comminution and a poor or absent soft tissue hinge.

The principle of hydrostatic pressure is illustrated in Figure 6-10. Hydrostatic pressure relies on the fact that the soft tissues and the diaphysis of the bone are not compressible. Thus, when they are encased in a complete cast or brace they essentially become rigid and maintain the position of the fracture. As with the soft tissue hinge, the explanation is somewhat simplistic and does not take into account active muscle contraction around the fracture.

Cast Application

All casts are applied in a similar manner no matter whether the traditional plaster of Paris or more modern fiberglass materials are used. Both types of cast material are frequently used as "slabs," which are often applied to a limb soon after injury to give temporary support. A full cast is rarely applied immediately after injury because of the potential of swelling associated with the injury to lead to compartment syndrome if the limb is encased in a rigid cast. Slabs are applied by using a layer of protective stockinette and layers of synthetic wool padding (Fig. 6-11). A slab of the appropriate length is then cut and, after

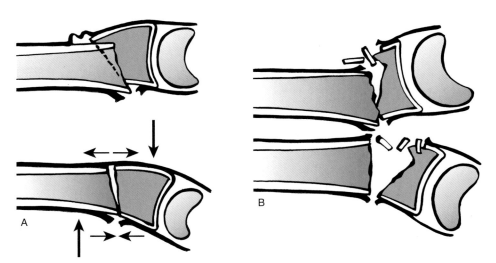

FIGURE 6-9 A. The use of an intact soft tissue hinge and three-point fixation in a distal radial fracture in a young patient. **B.** The same situation in an older patient with poor soft tissues and bone comminution.

soaking, applied to the limb. The location of the slab depends on the fracture. In the lower limb, backslabs or dorsal slabs are usually used, these being applied to the posterior leg and calf to support the fracture until a full cast can be applied or surgery is undertaken. In the upper limb, humeral diaphyseal fractures are often supported with a laterally located slab, fractures around the elbow and forearm being supported with a posteriorly located backslab, and distal radial and carpal fractures with a dorsal slab.

Full casts are applied by wrapping plaster of Paris or fiberglass bandages around the limb after stockinette and synthetic wool have been applied (Fig. 6-12). Up to 30 years ago there was considerable debate regarding how much padding should be used, as surgeons recognized that too much padding permit-

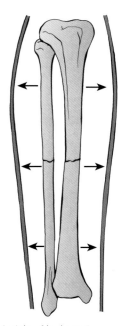

FIGURE 6-10 The principle of hydrostatic pressure in cast use. See text for explanation.

ted secondary fracture displacement but too little padding caused skin problems and increased the risk of compartment syndrome. On the other hand, if the cast is being used to control the position of a reduced fracture, excessive padding should be avoided because redisplacement of the fracture may occur. Cast bandages should be applied carefully, keeping the bandages flat to avoid soft tissue damage. As the cast hardens the surgeon should manipulate the fracture, taking care not to indent the cast material, thereby compressing the underlying soft tissue. Care must be taken not to obstruct joint motion or, if a joint is encased by the cast, it should be placed in the correct position. Once the cast has been applied, radiographs should be obtained to confirm the fracture is in an acceptable position. Cast management of unstable fractures is very labor intensive. Followup must be assiduous until callus starts to stabilize the fracture, as it is easy to miss secondary fracture displacement. If this occurs, the position of the fracture must be corrected without undue delay as soft tissue contracture occurs fairly quickly and secondary reduction becomes progressively more difficult. If this occurs, it is important that the surgeon knows how to deal with it.

In diaphyseal fractures angular malalignment can be corrected by wedging the cast. In this technique (Fig. 6-13) radiographs, or preferably fluoroscopy, are used to identify the fracture site and the cast is cut leaving a hinge of 2 to 3 cm of the cast intact, the location of the hinge depending on the direction of the necessary correction. Thus if the fracture is in valgus a medial hinge is left and a varus force applied to the distal cast to open the window. Once opened, the position is maintained until more cast material can be applied to maintain the reduced position. In years gone by, plaster rooms would keep a jar of wooden dowling to insert into the cast window to maintain the reduced fracture position while the supplementary plaster of Paris dried. Theoretically, rotational deformity is also correctible by cutting the cast. Again a cut is made in the cast at the level of the fracture and the rotation is corrected, but it is easy to lose position and sometimes it is better to remove the cast and reapply it. Surgeons should be aware that it is difficult to maintain the position of an unstable fracture in a cast, and that is why earlier surgeons defined levels of "acceptable" malunion. If

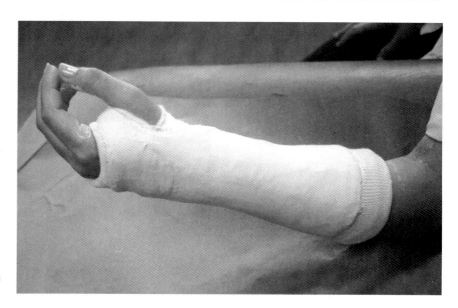

FIGURE 6-11 A forearm back slab used to treat an undisplaced distal radial fracture.

the fracture position is not maintained by the cast, consideration should be given to operative treatment.

Types of Cast
Upper Limb Casts
Long Arm Cast. The classic long arm cast with the elbow at 90 degrees and the wrist included in the cast (Fig. 6-14) is less commonly used now because forearm and elbow fractures are often internally fixed, but it is still used for less severe fractures. The cast is applied from just below the axilla to just proximal to the metacarpophalangeal joints of the digits but leaving the thumb free. The wrist is placed in 30 degrees of dorsiflexion and the elbow in 90 degrees of flexion. In more minor fractures the wrist may not be included and a full arm cylinder is then applied.

Hanging Cast or U-Slab. These casts are routinely used to treat humeral diaphyseal fractures in the acute phase. The arm is placed over the lower chest with the elbow at 90 degrees. A collar and cuff support can be used to maintain the position. A cast is then applied as shown in Figure 6-15, so that the top of the humeral component of the cast is above the humeral

fracture. Gravity is used to regain humeral length and the alignment of the fracture can be theoretically adjusted by altering the length of the cast between the neck and forearm. The shorter the cuff the more varus is applied to the fracture. An alternative to the hanging cast is the U-slab or sugar-tong splint, in which a plaster is placed from just below the axilla on the medial side of the arm down and around the elbow and then upwards to just below the shoulder. The slab is then bandaged into position. In proximal humeral fractures the slab can be extended above the shoulder but surgeons should be aware that this will negate any beneficial reduction effects of gravity. These casts are often replaced at 2 to 4 weeks by a functional brace (see Fig. 6-23).

Colles Cast (Forearm Cast). The Colles, or forearm cast, is the most widely used upper limb cast and is used for most distal radial and ulnar fractures as well as for some carpal injuries. The cast extends from below the elbow to just proximal to the metacarpal necks of the digits with the thumb left free (Fig. 6-16). The application of the Colles cast is frequently preceded by the use of a dorsal plaster slab, which is replaced by the cast once the swelling has reduced.

Scaphoid Cast. The scaphoid cast is commonly used to treat scaphoid fractures and pain in the anatomical snuff box on the radial border of the wrist when radiographs do not confirm the presence of a fracture. The wrist is held in slight dorsiflexion and the thumb is in abduction and slight flexion as if a glass is being held between the index finger and thumb (Fig. 6-17). The cast extends from just below the elbow to just proximal to the metacarpal necks of the digits. On the thumb the cast extends to just proximal to the interphalangeal joint. A modification of the scaphoid cast is the extended scaphoid cast, which may be used for fractures distal to the metacarpophalangeal joint of the thumb. In the extended scaphoid cast the whole thumb is included.

Bruner Cast. The Bruner cast is a variant of the extended scaphoid cast that is cut short to release the wrist joint. It is particularly useful for the treatment of ligamentous injuries of

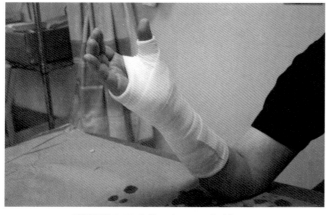

FIGURE 6-12 A fiberglass scaphoid cast.

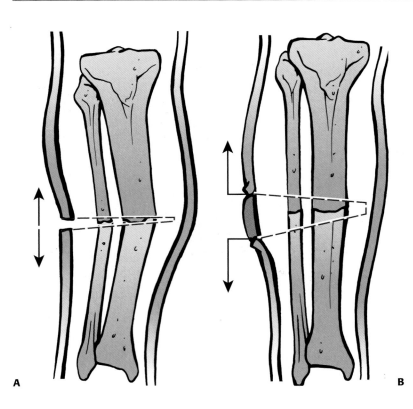

A   **B**

FIGURE 6-13 Wedging a cast to straighten a diaphyseal fracture of the tibia and fibula. **A.** The fracture is in valgus. The cast is cut at the level of the fracture to leave a medial hinge. **B.** The fracture is straightened and the gap in the cast kept open while the cast is completed.

the thumb metacarpophalangeal joint but may be used to treat associated minor avulsion fractures.

Burkhalter Cast. This cast is used to treat metacarpal or phalangeal fractures. The wrist is placed in 40 degrees of extension and the metacarpophalangeal joints are placed in 70 to 90 degrees of flexion (Fig. 6-18). The cast relies on the intact dorsal hood of the fingers acting as a tension band or a soft tissue hinge. It is usually applied by placing a slab over the dorsum of the forearm and the hand, with the wrist and fingers in the correct position and then applying a forearm cast to secure the slab. Finger extension is not permitted by the dorsal slab but some flexion is allowed.

James Cast. In this cast the fingers are kept in the "position of function" of the hand. The wrist is maintained at 40 degrees of extension with the metacarpophalangeal joints at 90 degrees and the interphalangeal joints of the fingers at 70 to 90 degrees. In this position the collateral ligaments of the metacarpophalangeal joints and the interphalangeal joints are stretched maximally and thus contractures will not occur (Fig. 6-19). As with the Burkhalter cast, the James cast is in fact a combination of a slab and a cast. Initially a volar slab is applied to the forearm

FIGURE 6-14 A long-arm cast.

FIGURE 6-15 A hanging cast.

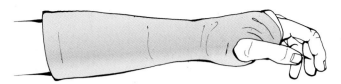

FIGURE 6-16 A Colles, or forearm, cast.

FIGURE 6-17 A scaphoid cast.

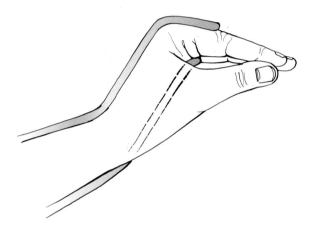

FIGURE 6-18 A Burkhalter cast. This is a combination of a forearm cast and a dorsal slab.

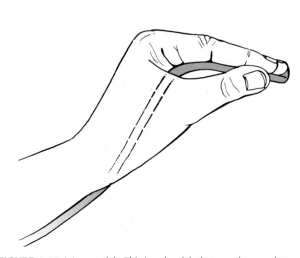

FIGURE 6-19 A James slab. This is volar slab that may be supplemented by a forearm cast.

and hand with the joints in the correct position. A forearm cast is then applied.

Other Upper Limb Casts. Surgeons used to use shoulder spicas to treat factures around the shoulder girdle. These were mainly used for clavicle or proximal humeral fractures. Sometimes a shoulder was placed at 90 degrees of abduction with the elbow at 90 degrees of flexion and the forearm pronated in the "policeman's halt position." These casts are now very rarely used with surgeons favoring operative management for the fractures that they were employed to treat.

Lower Limb Casts

Below Knee Cast. This is the most common cast used for lower limb injury including ankle fractures, foot fractures, and soft tissue injuries. It is occasionally used to treat undisplaced lower tibial diaphyseal fractures or minor pilon fractures. The cast is applied from below the level of the fibular neck proximally to the level of the metatarsal heads distally with the ankle at 90 degrees and the foot in the plantigrade position (Fig. 6-20). The below knee cast may be applied as a first stage in a long leg cast used to treat an unstable tibial diaphyseal fracture.

Long Leg Cast. Surgeons usually use a long leg cast to treat unstable tibial diaphyseal fracture in the acute phase changing to a patellar tendon-bearing cast after a few weeks. They may also be used to treat fractures around the knee. A long leg cast is best constituted by applying a below knee cast and then flexing the knee to about 10 degrees, following which the thigh extension is applied (Fig. 6-21).

Patellar Tendon-Bearing Cast. The other variant of the below knee cast is the patellar tendon-bearing cast, which is usually used to treat tibial diaphyseal fractures after a few weeks in a long leg cast. In this cast the proximal end of a below knee cast

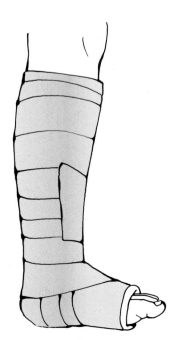

FIGURE 6-20 A below knee cast.

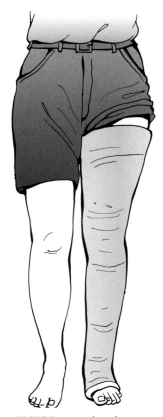

FIGURE 6-21 A long leg cast.

is extended upward as far as the lower pole in the patella and moulded around the patellar tendon to provide a degree of rotational stability (Fig. 6-22). Care must be taken not to apply pressure over the common peroneal nerve running around the neck of the fibula.

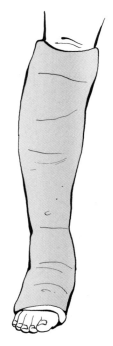

FIGURE 6-22 A patella tendon–bearing cast.

Spinal Casts. Spinal casts are now rarely used. The basic cast is a plaster jacket that extends from the sternal notch to the symphysis pubis and is carefully moulded. If fractures lower than L3 are to be treated, the cast should be extended downwards to include one thigh. If cervical fractures are treated in a cast, the cast is extended upward into a collar but the use of cervical casts is now extremely unusual and they would only be used if no other treatment method was available. Thoracolumbar casts are still used by some surgeons,[97] but the results are no better than those associated with spinal braces.

Braces

Limb Braces

Many different limb braces have been designed but they fall into four main types used to treat fractures of the humeral diaphysis, distal radius, metacarpus, and lower leg. Most braces are made of polyethylene or plastic and secured by Velcro, plastic straps, and buckles. Braces tend to be lighter than casts and are often used after a short period of cast immobilization once the fracture is more stable. Other advantages are that braces can be tightened as the soft tissue swelling decreases and they can be removed for personal hygiene and radiological evaluation of the fracture.

Upper Limb

Humeral Brace. A simple polyethylene or plastic brace is often used to treat humeral diaphyseal fractures after the initial cast management. The brace fits around the arm and is usually wider laterally than medially to support the humerus proximally (Fig. 6-23).

Distal Forearm Brace. These are used to treat distal radial fractures and may be used after a period of cast immobilization or they may be applied primarily to the forearm. There are two basic types. Figure 6-24 shows a conventional distal forearm brace, which extends to the radiocarpal joint. Alternatively, the brace may have a dorsal extension to just proximal to the metacarpophalangeal joints of all digits except the thumb.

Metacarpal Brace. Metacarpal braces are usually either made up of a strap worn around the hand under which padding is

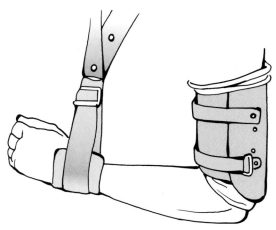

FIGURE 6-23 A humeral brace. The sling length can be altered to change the fracture position.

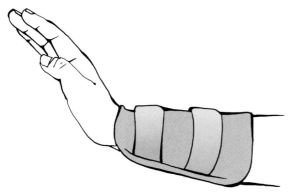

FIGURE 6-24 A distal forearm brace. A modification of this brace includes an extension to just proximal to the MCPJs, except the thumb.

placed to maintain fracture reduction or they take the form of a heat-molded plastic brace which is placed around the hand and then molded into an appropriate shape to maintain fracture reduction (Fig. 6-25). They can be used for the primary treatment of metacarpal fractures[40] or to protect the metacarpus after operative fracture treatment.[55] Skin necrosis has been reported.[36]

Lower Limb

Below Knee Brace. The most popular lower limb brace is the equivalent of the below knee cast. There are many available but all tend to be made of plastic and fasten with Velcro or straps (Fig. 6-26). They are used for the same indications as below knee casts and may be used after an initial period of cast management. They are most commonly used after internal fixation of ankle and foot fractures or to allow mobilization after a soft tissue injury to the ankle, hindfoot, or midfoot.

Patellar Tendon-Bearing Brace. This is the equivalent of the tendon-bearing cast but it permits ankle movement (Fig. 6-27). The plastic brace is fitted with an ankle hinge and a heel cup and can therefore be worn inside a shoe.

Knee Brace. This is the modern equivalent of the old cast brace but it is no longer used to treat femoral diaphyseal fractures. Now it is made from synthetic material and fitted with adjust-

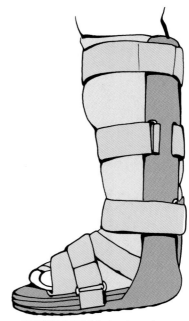

FIGURE 6-26 A below knee brace.

able integral knee hinges (Fig. 6-28). These are often used to treat soft tissue injuries around the knee but may be used to facilitate mobilization after internal fixation of distal femoral or proximal tibial fractures. In some minor fractures around the knee they may be used for definitive treatment.

Spinal Braces

Cervical Braces. There are three types of cervical braces: soft and hard collars, high cervicothoracic orthoses, and low cervicothoracic orthoses (Fig. 6-29A). Within these three types there are many different designs but they all have the same basic function. Standard soft and hard collars are not generally used for the treatment of acute cervical fractures or dislocations but they are useful for the treatment of minor soft tissue sprains and whiplash injuries. They allow up to 80% of normal cervical movement and therefore confer little stability to the cervical spine.[49,60] Their main function is to act as a proprioceptive stimulus to remind patients to take care. Rigid cervical collars

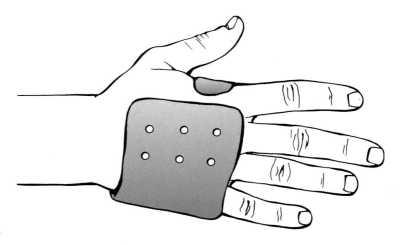

FIGURE 6-25 A metacarpal brace.

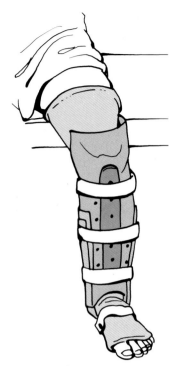

FIGURE 6-27 A patella tendon—bearing brace.

may be used for emergency stabilization of the injured cervical spine but the most effective way of stabilizing the cervical spine is by strapping the chin and forehead to a rigid spinal board.

High cervicothoracic orthoses (Fig. 6-29B) have molded occipito-mandibular supports that extend to the upper part of

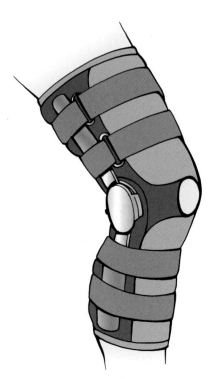

FIGURE 6-28 A knee brace.

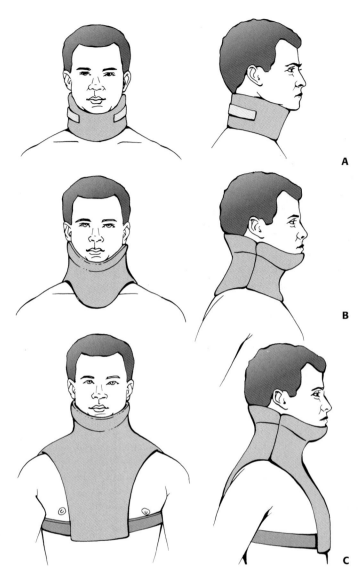

FIGURE 6-29 Different types of cervical braces. **A.** A cervical collar. **B.** A high cervicothoracic orthosis. **C.** A low cervicothoracic orthosis.

the thorax. The best-known example of this orthosis is the Philadelphia collar. Studies indicate that the Philadelphia collar resists 71% or normal cervical flexion and extension, 34% of lateral bending, and 54% of rotation.[60] Other similar orthoses show similar results. These types of braces are useful for the management of cervical sprains or to provide temporary immobilization during transport or after surgical stabilization of the cervical spine.

Low cervicothoracic orthoses have the same molded upper support but extend to the lower part of the thorax (Fig. 6-29C). Examples of these braces are the Minerva and SOMI (sternal-occipital-mandibular immobilizer) braces. Low cervicothoracic orthoses are better than high cervicothoracic orthoses in resisting cervical rotation and sagittal movement in the mid and lower cervical spine but they do not prevent all cervical movement. If any type of neck brace is used to treat an unstable or potentially unstable cervical fracture serial radiographs must be taken to check that fracture reduction is maintained until union.

The complications of cervical braces are essentially the same

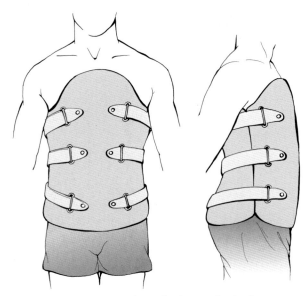

FIGURE 6-30 A thoracolumbarsacral orthosis.

as those associated with limb braces. As cervical movement is not prevented, loss of fracture reduction may occur in unstable fractures. In addition, a poorly fitting brace may be uncomfortable and cause skin and soft tissue irritation and damage.[60]

Thoracic and Lumbar Braces. The role of thoracolumbar braces is to support the spine by limiting overall trunk motion, decreasing muscular activity, increasing the intra-abdominal pressure, resisting spinal loading, and limiting spinal motion. Several braces are available; the simplest is a lumbosacral corset and the most complex is an individually moulded thoracolumbar-sacral orthosis made from plastic and tightened by buckles and straps (Fig. 6-30). A useful intermediate brace is the Jewett brace (Fig. 6-31), which provides three-point fixation and permits spinal extension but not flexion.

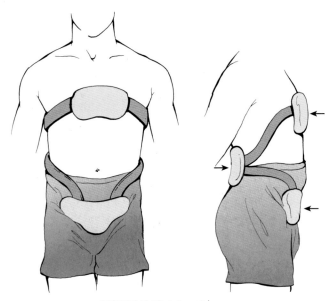

FIGURE 6-31 A Jewett brace.

Lumbar corsets, like cervical collars, are essentially proprioceptive and serve to remind the patient to take care. They are used in the management of low back pain but their only use in spinal injury is in the management of minor stable fractures or soft tissue injury. The Jewett brace is useful in the treatment of injuries between T6 and L3, which are unstable in flexion. Studies have shown that it reduces intersegmental motion and flexion at the thoracolumbar joint while lateral bending and axial rotation remain unaffected.[9] They are more effective in the treatment of one- and two-column spinal fractures than in the treatment of three-column fractures. Thoracolumbar-sacral orthoses provide more stability but maintenance of reduction of unstable thoracolumbar fractures cannot be guaranteed and serial radiographs are required to confirm the maintenance of fracture reduction.

Casts or Braces?

There has been a lot of debate whether casts or braces are more useful and which gives better results. The debate is mainly centered on tibial diaphyseal fractures, distal radial fractures, and ankle fractures. In ankle fractures the debate has mainly concerned the management of internally fixed fractures in the postoperative phase, whereas in the other fractures surgeons have compared the use of casts and braces in nonoperatively managed patients.

Tibial Diaphyseal Fractures

The comparative usefulness of casts and braces in the treatment of tibial diaphyseal fractures was a subject of considerable debate until about 15 years ago, when intramedullary nailing became the treatment of choice for these fractures. The implication in the literature is that functional bracing produced better results, with Sarmiento and colleagues being particular proponents of functional bracing.[80–82] Table 6-8 shows a comparison of the results of tibial fractures treated with long leg casts, patellar tendon-bearing casts, and functional bracing. It shows the results of the major papers published between 1965 and 1992, when patellar tendon-bearing casts and functional braces were popular. It must be remembered that the importance of functional outcome following tibial diaphyseal fracture became more widely recognized during this period, and several earlier papers extolled the virtues of their chosen method without analyzing functional outcome to any significant degree.

The papers shown in Table 6-8 that discuss the use of long leg casts confirm that the method is associated with significant knee stiffness, particularly if used for complex fractures, open fractures, or in fractures that were associated with nonunion. Few modern surgeons would treat open tibial diaphyseal fractures with a long leg cast but it is interesting to note that Nicoll[63] reported 60% delayed or nonunion in open tibial fractures managed in a long leg cast in 1965. He also reported 25% joint stiffness rising to 70% in tibial nonunions associated with an open fracture. The results of the use of long leg casts were reported as late as 1991, when Kyrö et al[56] analyzed the use of long leg casts in 165 consecutive tibial fractures. Traction was used in severe open fractures and a calcaneal pin was incorporated into the cast of 23% of the patients. They found that 26% of patients had impaired knee flexion and 9% had impaired knee extension. In addition, 42% had impaired ankle flexion and 37% had impaired toe movement. Only 21% of the patients

| TABLE 6-8 | Comparison of Use of Long Leg Casts, Patellar Tendon–Bearing Casts and Functional Braces | | | | |

	No	Open (%)	Union (wks)	Malunion (%)	Joint stiffness (%)
Long leg casts					
Nicoll[63]	674	22.5	15.9	8.6	25.0
Slätis and Rokkanen[90]	198	33.3	19.8	?	?
Karahaju et al.[51]	80	23.7	?	11.2	27.5
Steen Jensen et al.[91]	102	?	?	21.0	7.0
Van der Linden and Larsson[100]	50	12.0	17.0	50.0	24.0
Haines et al.[38]	91	36.3	16.3	25.3	33.0
Kay et al.[52]	79	22.8	19.1	9.1	?
Kyrö et al.[56]	165	21.0	13.7	30.0	42.0
Patellar tendon–bearing casts					
Sarmiento[80]	69	0	13.6	?	?
Austin[4]	132	11.4	16.7	39.0	?
Böstmann and Hanninen[10]	114	16.0	15.3	40.0	?
Puno et al.[73]	141	17.0	16.7	4.4	?
Oni et al.[66]	100	0	?	21.0	43.0
Hooper et al.[46]	33	21.0	18.3	27.3	15.0
Bone et al.[8]	25	0	26.0	27.0	Yes
Functional braces					
Sarmiento[80]	135	24.4	15.5	?	?
Sarmiento et al.[81]	780	31.0	18.7	13.7	?
Digby et al.[25]	82	20.7	17.4	9.0	45.0
Den Outer et al.[24]	94	11.7	?	40.0	?
Pun et al.[72]	97	7.2	17.1	23.7	28.9
Alho et al.[1]	35	31.4	17.0	8.6	26.0

thought that they had an excellent result. The other papers listed in Table 6-8 show the significant problems of malunion and joint stiffness associated with the use of long leg casts.

There is no doubt that the use of patellar tendon-bearing casts and functional braces facilitated knee mobilization but it should be remembered that during the period when these methods of management were introduced surgeons had turned to operative treatment for open and more severe closed fractures, and thus the results presented in Table 6-8 for patellar tendon-bearing casts and functional braces may well have been achieved in more straightforward fractures than those treated by long leg casts in earlier years. However, comparison of the results of tendon-bearing casts with long leg casts shows a similar prevalence of malunion and probably joint stiffness. Functional braces were introduced to facilitate hindfoot mobility but again one must remember that the patients analyzed in these studies almost certainly had more benign fractures than those treated previously in long leg casts. Sarmiento et al.[82] analyzed 780 patients treated with a functional brace but selected ambulatory patients and excluded fractures with excessive initial shortening and those that showed an increasing angular deformity in the initial cast. Their results were good but they did not assess

malunion or joint stiffness. Table 6-8 shows that other studies have found significant levels of malunion and joint stiffness. Digby et al.[25] reviewed 103 adult tibial fractures and reported that 11% had restricted ankle motion and 45% had reduced subtalar function. These results match those of the other papers listed in Table 6-8, and it is salutary to observe that a comparison of the three methods of casting and bracing does not show that functional bracing gives superior results, although long leg casts are associated with greater knee stiffness.

Distal Radial Fractures

Stewart et al.[92] undertook a prospective study comparing a conventional Colles cast with an above elbow cast brace and a below elbow cast brace in the treatment of displaced distal radial fractures. In both the above elbow and below elbow cast brace they used a dorsal extension of the brace beyond the wrist joint, which extended as far as the metacarpophalangeal joints of the fingers. The brace only extended to the carpometacarpal joint of the thumb. The authors undertook a radiographic and functional analysis of the patients and found no statistical difference in either the radiographic or functional results between the three different methods of management. They also noted no difference in the prevalence of complications between the three groups of patients. They did comment that there was better patient tolerance of casts than braces with the main problem of bracing being pressure over the distal radial border and the head of the ulna. They felt that in most patients there was no reason to change from the traditional Colles cast.

In a later study, Tumia et al.[99] compared the traditional Colles cast with a forearm functional brace that did not have an extension beyond the wrist joint (see Fig. 6-24). They treated both minimally displaced fractures, which did not require manipulation, and displaced fractures which did require manipulation. The results were assessed using a functional and anatomical scoring system. They found that the brace-treated patients had lower functional scores than the cast-treated group at 12 weeks, but the difference was not statistically significant. By 24 weeks the results were similar. Grip strength was initially higher in both manipulated and nonmanipulated brace-treated groups, but by 12 weeks there was no difference with cast-managed fractures. There was also more pain associated with the brace during the first five weeks, but this settled later. Their conclusion was that a brace could be used effectively in treating Colles fractures. In a similar study O'Connor et al.[65] compared a plastic cast with a lightweight removable splint in 66 patients with minimally displaced radial fractures. They also used both anatomical and functional evaluation systems and found no significant differences between the two groups, but patients tended to prefer the brace.

Ankle Fractures

There have been several studies comparing the use of casts and braces after operative management of ankle fractures. Tropp and Norlon[98] compared the use of a plaster cast for 6 weeks with an ankle brace applied 1 to 2 weeks after surgery. They permitted early weight bearing in both groups and showed that by 10 weeks there was improved function in the brace-managed group. This had disappeared by 12 months but they did report impaired dorsiflexion in the cast group, compared with the functional brace group.

DiStasio et al.[26] examined a group of U.S. military personnel with operatively treated ankle fractures. They compared the use of a non–weight-bearing cast for 6 weeks with the use of a non–weight-bearing removable orthosis, and showed that the orthosis group had better subjective scores for pain, function, cosmesis, and motion 3 and 6 months after injury, but there was no difference in objective assessment of function on return to duty. Simanski et al.[89] compared the use of a functional brace with early weight bearing with a standard cast without weight bearing after ankle fixation. Both groups did well and most of the patients achieved their preinjury level of activity. The authors of both these studies stated that braces were useful but emphasized the requirement of reliable, cooperative patients! In a prospective randomized study Lehtonen et al.[57] compared the use of a below knee cast and a functional brace in Weber type A and B fractures treated operatively. There were no significant differences between the study groups in the final subjective and objective evaluations, but there were more wound complications in the brace-managed group. In all studies dealing with casts or braces in operatively managed ankle fractures, differences in outcome have been shown to be relatively minor.

The comparative results of the use of casts or braces in tibial diaphyseal fractures, distal radial fractures, and ankle fractures indicate that there is no advantage of either method. The studies suggest return of joint movement is slightly faster if a brace is used but there is no evidence that overall function is better with a brace. There is also some evidence that early complications are higher if a brace is used. The choice between a brace and a cast is determined by the surgeon and patient. Braces are obviously useful. Personal hygiene is easier, and physical therapy, if indicated, can be more easily undertaken, but braces are also more expensive and are not freely available in all countries. The decision should be based on these factors but also on the reliability of the patient. Casts have a great advantage in that they are difficult, although not impossible, to remove and are therefore advantageous in the treatment of many young males in particular!

Slings, Bandages, and Support Strapping

Several types of minor injuries, soft tissue sprains, and minor fractures are treated by support and analgesia with mobilization of the affected area encouraged after a relatively short period. Tubular elastic support bandages are frequently used to treat minor soft tissue injuries such as ankle and foot sprains, wrist sprains, or minor ligament damage in other joints. Several upper limb fractures are treated by the use of slings, which may be supplemented by bandaging.

Fractures of the clavicle, proximal humerus, and radial head and neck are often treated by sling support until the discomfort settles enough to allow joint movement. Several different methods of bandaging have been used to treat clavicle fractures in an effort to reduce pain and maintain fracture reduction. The figure-of-eight bandage remains popular in the treatment of clavicle fractures. This is placed anteriorly around both shoulders and crossed over at the level of the upper thoracic spine. Theoretically, tightening the bandage reduces and stabilizes the fracture, but unfortunately it loosens quickly and clinical evidence suggests that it is no better than a sling.[3] Fractures of the clavicle, proximal humerus, and proximal radius that are treated nonoperatively are best treated by the use of a sling for 2 weeks followed by mobilization of the affected joint.

Another area for which strapping is useful is in the management of stable undisplaced fractures of the phalanges of the hand and foot. These fractures can be treated by buddy strapping the affected digit to an adjacent digit (Fig. 6-32). Usually two strips of half-inch tape are placed around the proximal and middle phalanges with protective gauze between the fingers. The joints should be left free to permit mobilization. It should be remembered that this type of strapping loosens quickly and the patient, or companion, should be taught how to replace it.

The use of an elastoplast thumb spica (Fig. 6-33) may be helpful in treating sprains or minor tears of the collateral ligaments of the thumb. It can also be used for treating minor associated avulsion fractures. These are constructed of elastoplast tape, which is placed around the thumb and extends down to the carpometacarpal area. As with buddy strapping, they tend to loosen quickly and need to be replaced. Neither buddy strapping nor elastoplast spicas should be used to treat unstable fractures.

Splints

Many different splints have been designed, usually for the treatment of metacarpal and phalangeal fractures. The two most

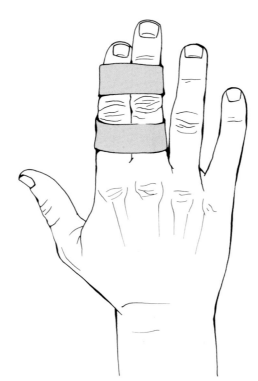

FIGURE 6-32 Buddy strapping.

popular splints are the aluminium-backed foam splint (Fig. 6-34) and the mallet finger splint (Fig. 6-35). Aluminium-backed foam splints are used for phalangeal fractures. They are commonly applied to the volar or dorsal aspects of the digits to immobilize fractures or joints after reduction of a dislocation. They are also useful for immobilizing the finger after soft tissue injuries, and a volar splint may be particularly helpful for main-

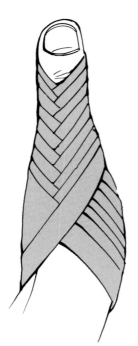

FIGURE 6-33 A thumb spica.

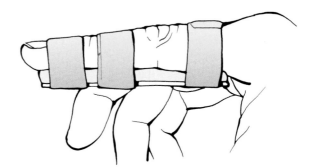

FIGURE 6-34 An aluminium-backed foam splint.

taining extension after a volar plate injury. In more unstable fractures the surgeon may elect to use an aluminium-backed splint in the same way as a Burkhalter (Fig. 6-18) or James (Fig. 6-19) cast might be used. This is appropriate for a single digit fracture and the splint is extended across the wrist joint maintaining the position of the wrist as described for the Burkhalter or James splint.

Mallet fingers caused by either avulsion of the extensor tendons from the distal phalanx or by a fracture of the distal phalanx are well treated by the use of a Mallet finger splint (Fig. 6-35). An appropriately sized splint is applied to the digit with the distal interphalangeal joint in full extension. If this method of management is used the patient is taught that the distal interphalangeal joint must be kept extended for a period of 6 weeks. The main problem with the technique is failure of the patient to follow the treatment protocol, with the splint being removed too early.

SPECIFIC FRACTURES

Upper Limb

Suggested guidelines for the nonoperative management of upper limb fractures are shown in Table 6-9.

Shoulder Girdle

Clavicle. The management of clavicular fractures is described in detail in Chapter 36. Historically most clavicle fractures have been managed nonoperatively (Fig. 6-36) and Table 6-2 shows that this continues to be the case. In recent years there has been considerable interest in primary internal fixation of clavicle fractures, with both plating and intramedullary pinning being

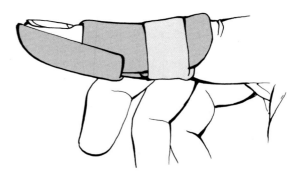

FIGURE 6-35 A mallet finger splint.

TABLE 6-9	Guidelines for Nonoperative Management for Different Upper Limb Fractures if Nonoperative Management Is Chosen as the Treatment Method*
Fracture Type	**Nonoperative Management**
Scapula	Sling and mobilize at 2 weeks
Clavicle	Sling and mobilize at 2 weeks
Proximal humerus	Sling and mobilize at 2 weeks
Humeral diaphysis	Hanging U-slab or sugar-tong cast. Brace at 2 to 3 weeks
Distal humerus	Long arm cast for 4 to 8 weeks
Olecranon	Long arm cast for 6 weeks
Proximal radius	Sling and mobilize at 2 weeks
Forearm diaphysis	
Both bones (undisplaced)	Long arm cast. Forearm cast at 4 weeks
Radius only	Forearm cast 6 weeks
Ulna only	Forearm cast 6 weeks
Distal radius and ulna	Forearm cast or brace for 6 weeks
Scaphoid	Scaphoid cast for 6 to 12 weeks
Other carpal bones	Forearm cast for 3 to 6 weeks
Metacarpal fractures	
Undisplaced	Mobilize
Displaced	Burkhalter or James splint. Mobilize at 3 weeks.
Phalangeal fractures	
Proximal and middle phalanges	
Undisplaced	Buddy strapping and mobilize
Displaced	Burkhalter, James, or aluminium splint. Mobilize at 3 weeks.
Distal phalanx	Mobilize or mallet splint

* See relevant chapters for suggested management for different fractures.

used.[14,37,64] Not surprisingly, opinion continues to be divided regarding the best method of treatment. Nordquist et al.[64] analyzed 225 consecutive clavicle fractures treated nonoperatively and showed that 185 were symptomatic, 39 had moderate pain, and 1 patient had a poor result. There were seven nonunions in displaced fractures. They advocated nonoperative manage-

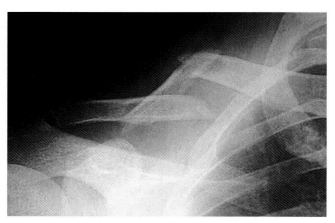

FIGURE 6-36 A clavicular fracture with a large intermediate fragment. There is debate about operative or nonoperative treatment for these fractures, but in this case union and good function was successfully achieved with nonoperative management.

ment as did Grassi et al., who compared nonoperative treatment and intramedullary pinning in 80 clavicle fractures.[37] They found no difference in the outcome scores between the two groups.

Recently the Canadian Orthopaedic Trauma Society[14] pointed out that several studies indicated there was a high prevalence of symptomatic malunion and nonunion after nonoperative management of midshaft clavicle fractures, and they undertook a prospective study comparing plate fixation with nonoperative management in displaced clavicle fractures. They found that the outcome scores were significantly improved in the operatively managed group at all time points and that there was a reduced union time and prevalence of nonunion in the operatively managed fractures. They advocated plate fixation of completely displaced midshaft clavicle fractures in active adult patients.

It seems likely that more midshaft clavicle fractures will be primarily plated in the future but clearly more work is required to establish the precise indications for operative treatment. As many clavicle fractures are undisplaced or minimally displaced nonoperative management will continue to be an important treatment method and it is important to review the alternative methods of nonoperative management.

Most surgeons use a sling when treating clavicle fractures nonoperatively. The sling is usually maintained for 2 weeks and then physical therapy is started. The historical alternative to the sling was the figure-of-eight bandage. The rationale behind the use of a figure-of-eight bandage was that the shoulders were extended and fracture reduction thereby facilitated, but comparative studies have shown no advantage of the figure-of-eight bandage over a simple sling. Andersen et al.[3] actually found that the sling caused less discomfort and fewer complications. If nonoperative management is used to treat a clavicle fracture, it is suggested that a sling should be worn for about 2 weeks and then a physical therapy regime instituted.

Approximately 28% of clavicle fractures occur in the distal third of the bone.[76] As with midshaft clavicle fractures, there has been debate about how lateral clavicular fractures should be treated, with interest centring on the Neer type 2 distal clavicle fractures associated with transection of the coronoid and trapezoid ligaments. The treatment of the condition will be discussed in detail in Chapter 36, but the literature suggests that nonoperative management is a good alternative for lateral third clavicle fractures, particularly in middle-aged and elderly patients.[76,77] As with middiaphyseal clavicle fractures, if nonoperative management is chosen to treat a distal clavicle fracture a sling should be used for 2 weeks and a physical therapy regime then commenced.

Scapula Fractures. Scapula fractures are very rare and are predominantly treated nonoperatively. The implication is that they occur in high energy injuries and they have been documented to occur in 7% of multiple-injured patients.[102] However, Chapter 3 shows that they actually have a type A distribution with a proportion of scapula fractures occurring in the elderly and, in general, nonoperative treatment will be used.

There are four basic types of scapula fractures: intra-articular and extra articular glenoid fractures, acromion fractures, coracoid fractures, and fractures of the scapula body. Most scapular fractures do not require operative management, the obvious exception being the displaced glenoid rim fracture associated with instability of the glenohumeral joint. Most coracoid and acromion fractures are undisplaced and few require surgical treatment. In addition, there is little evidence that scapular body fractures need operative treatment, with a metaanalysis of scapula fractures showing that 99% of body fractures were treated nonoperatively.[106] The same study also showed that the literature indicates that 83% of scapula neck fractures are treated nonoperatively.[106] Van Noort and van Kampen[101] examined 13 patients with scapula neck fractures and found an average Constant score[18] of 90 after nonoperative management with no correlation between functional outcome and malunion. Pace et al.[68] confirmed the good outcome associated with nonoperative management but pointed out that most patients had some activity-related pain and minor cuff tendinopathy which, they thought, related to glenoid neck malunion.

It is likely that most scapula fractures will continue to be treated nonoperatively and if this method of treatment is chosen, it is suggested a sling is used for about 2 weeks to provide pain relief, following which a physical therapy program should be instituted. Scapular fractures are discussed in detail in Chapter 37.

Floating Shoulder. The term "floating shoulder" is given to a combination of clavicle and scapular neck fractures. It was initially felt that clavicle stabilization would minimize scapular neck malunion[44] but later papers suggest that nonoperative

treatment of the floating shoulder gives equivalent or better results. Egol et al.[29] compared operative and nonoperative management and showed no significant difference between the two methods. They did note that internal and external rotation was weaker in the operatively treated group although there was improved forward flexion in this group. Edwards et al.[28] reported similar results but stressed that more severely displaced fractures were associated with poorer results. Thus the literature suggests that most floating shoulders should be treated nonoperatively using a sling for 2 weeks followed by a course of physical therapy.

Proximal Humeral Fractures

Most proximal humeral fractures are treated nonoperatively (Fig. 6-37) and a comparison with the prevalence of surgery in the 1950s (see Table 6-6) suggests that there has been little change for a considerable period. The recent introduction of locking plates may increase the rate of surgical treatment but this must be balanced against the increasing age and infirmity of the elderly population who tend to present with this fracture. It seems logical to assume that most proximal humeral fractures will continue to be treated nonoperatively for the foreseeable future. The overall management of this fracture is discussed in Chapter 35.

The debate about the treatment of proximal humeral fractures is centered around three- and four-part fractures and fracture dislocations, which comprise about 12.5% of proximal humeral fractures.[20] Neer[61] stated that 85% of proximal humeral fractures were minimally displaced fractures, although a more recent study showed that 49% of proximal humeral fractures were minimally displaced.[19] The difference probably relates to

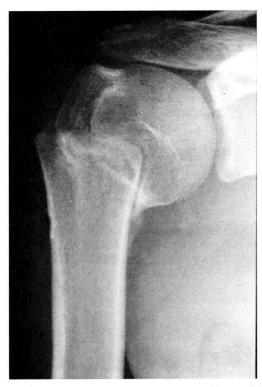

FIGURE 6-37 A varus impacted (OTA A2.2) proximal humeral fracture. This united well with a good clinical result.

the increased incidence of osteopenic and osteoporotic fractures in the population since Neer's study. These fractures should be managed nonoperatively. There is debate about the management of two-part fractures, particularly with the introduction of the locking proximal humeral plate, but these plates have only been partially successful[67] and it seems likely that many two-part fractures will continue to be managed nonoperatively. If further information about the results of nonoperative treatment of two-part proximal humeral fractures and fracture dislocations is required, the 1-year Neer[61] and Constant[18] scores of all two-part fractures classified according to the OTA classification has been published.[22]

Nonoperative management is undertaken by placing the patient in a sling for 2 weeks and then gradually introducing a program of physical therapy. The patient should be warned that progress is slow and that it is often more than 1 year before maximum shoulder motion is regained.

Humeral Diaphyseal Fractures

Table 6-2 shows that together with isolated ulnar diaphyseal fractures, humeral diaphyseal fractures are the only diaphyseal fractures that are now commonly treated nonoperatively. Table 6-2 also shows that there is a significant age difference between the patients treated operatively and those treated nonoperatively, with younger patients tending to be treated operatively. About two thirds of patients with humeral diaphyseal fractures are treated nonoperatively (Fig. 6-38) and this figure is sup-

ported by an analysis of the literature. In 1988, Zagorski et al.[105] reported on the use of a functional brace in humeral diaphyseal fracture. They analyzed 170 patients and showed that 167 had excellent or good functional results. Since then, further studies[30,33,47,74,78,96] have accepted that nonoperative management gives good results but they have tried to analyze which fractures, if any, are better treated surgically. Clearly open fractures, irreducible fractures, pathological fractures, fractures in the multiply injured, and floating elbows may well be treated surgically, but Ekholm et al.[30] also noted that OTA type A fractures seemed to have a high prevalence of nonunion and often required revision surgery. Ring et al.[74] took a similar view stating that spiral or oblique fractures that involved the middle or proximal third had a high rate of nonunion after treatment with a functional brace. Toivanen et al.[96] treated 93 consecutive fractures with a brace but found that 23% required surgery. Again they found a higher rate of nonunion in proximal third diaphyseal fractures.

The other disadvantage of nonoperative management that has been highlighted recently is impairment of shoulder function. Fjalestad et al.[93] reported that 38% of patients treated with a humeral brace lost external rotation of the shoulder, which they attributed to malrotation at the fracture site. Rosenberg and Soudry[78] analyzed 15 patients treated by bracing and showed that the Constant shoulder scores were significantly lower in the injured shoulder. The average age was only 43 years and only 40% of the patients returned to their previous professional activities.

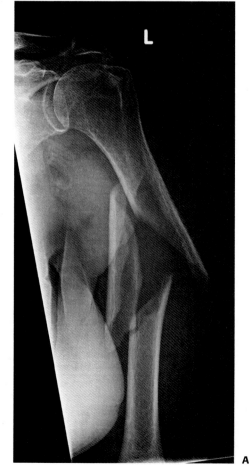
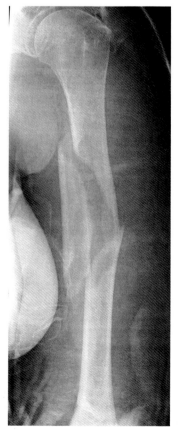

FIGURE 6-38 A. An OTA B1.2 humeral diaphyseal fracture. **B.** After the application of a U-slab the fracture has reduced and union occurred.

There has been a particular interest in bracing fractures of the distal third of the humeral diaphysis. Fracture alignment can be difficult to maintain and there is concern about elbow stiffness.[47] Sarmiento et al.[83] analyzed 85 distal third fractures, of which 15% were open. They recorded 96% union with no infections. In a recent study Jawa et al.[47] compared operative and nonoperative management and found very similar results between them, although they stated that operative treatment gives more predictable alignment and potentially a quicker return of function, although there was as risk of nerve damage and infection.

It seems likely that the prevalence of surgical treatment of humeral diaphyseal fractures will increase. As studies have become more refined it is becoming apparent that there are advantages to surgery in some fractures. Nonoperative management will probably continue to be an important method of management for reducible middle-third closed fractures but other fracture types will probably be treated operatively more frequently than they are now. If nonoperative management is selected, it is suggested that a U-slab or sugar-tong cast is used for about 2 weeks and a functional brace then applied. The brace is usually used for 8 to 12 weeks with serial radiographs used to determine union. Active elbow motion is usually allowed by about 4 weeks. The treatment of humeral diaphyseal fractures is discussed in Chapter 34.

Distal Humeral Fractures

It is perhaps surprising to note that Table 6-2 shows only 50% of distal humeral fractures were treated nonoperatively in a major trauma center in a 1-year period. However, Table 6-3 shows there is a considerable difference in surgery based on the OTA classification. A review of the OTA Type 1 extra-articular distal humeral fractures shows that nonoperative management was mainly reserved for undisplaced or minimally displaced epicondylar fractures or supracondylar fractures in the elderly. Most OTA Type B and C fractures were treated operatively. The average age of the patients with Type C fractures who were treated nonoperatively was 92 years! Thus most displaced distal humeral fractures are treated operatively.

There is little literature dealing with type A extra-articular distal humeral fractures. A1 fractures affecting the epicondyle tend to occur in younger patients and A2 and A3 supracondylar fractures tend to occur in the elderly. There is debate about whether these should be managed nonoperatively as there is a relatively high rate of nonunion. It is likely that some Type A distal humeral fractures will continue to be treated nonoperatively. If nonoperative management is used for A1 fractures, a long arm cast should be used for 4 to 6 weeks. If an A2 or A3 fracture is treated in the elderly the cast may need to be worn for up to 8 weeks. Distal humeral fractures are discussed in Chapter 33.

Proximal Forearm Fractures

Proximal Radial Fractures. Table 6-2 shows that most radial head and neck fractures continue to be treated nonoperatively, and a review of Table 6-6 suggests that the treatment has changed little for many years. The 6.3% primary surgery listed in Table 6-2 related mainly to complex fracture dislocations of the elbow and the relatively uncommon OTA C2 and C3 fractures. Most surgeons accept that most proximal radial fractures should be treated nonoperatively. If nonoperative management is used, all that is required is a sling with joint mobilization being started as soon as pain permits.

Olecranon Fractures. Table 6-2 shows that most olecranon fractures are treated by internal fixation. It also shows that those fractures treated nonoperatively tended to occur in younger patients. Nonoperative treatment is usually used for undisplaced fractures or if there is only a minor avulsion fracture from the tip of the olecranon. If nonoperative management is used for a potentially unstable olecranon fracture, a long arm cast should be applied for 6 weeks following which a physical therapy regime is instituted. If there is a minor avulsion fracture from the tip of the olecranon treatment should be symptomatic and mobilization commenced about 2 weeks after fracture. The treatment of proximal forearm fractures is discussed in Chapter 32.

Forearm Fractures

Most forearm fractures are treated by internal fixation as detailed in Chapter 30. Table 6-2 shows that over 80% of isolated radial diaphyseal and 90% of radial and ulna diaphyseal fractures will be treated operatively. The only exceptions are stable undisplaced fractures, which can be treated in a cast or brace. Isolated ulna diaphyseal fractures are frequently treated nonoperatively, with Table 6-2 indicating that about 30% are treated operatively. Many isolated ulna diaphyseal fractures are undisplaced or minimally displaced and the use of a cast or brace will give good results (Fig. 6-39). Sarmiento et al.[84] reported on 287 ulnar shaft fractures and recorded 99% union. They found that proximal third ulna fractures were associated with an average loss of pronation of 12 degrees but overall there were good or

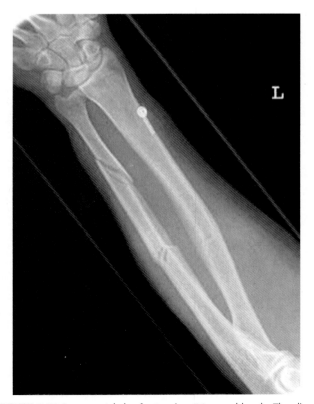

FIGURE 6-39 A segmental ulna fracture in a 54-year-old male. The alignment is well maintained and operative treatment is not required.

excellent results in 96% of patients. If nonoperative management is used for undisplaced fractures of the radius and ulna, a long arm cast should be applied, which can be converted to a forearm cast or brace at about 6 weeks if further immobilization is required. For undisplaced isolated fractures of the radius, a forearm cast or brace can be used, usually for 6 weeks, and if isolated ulna fractures are to be treated nonoperatively a forearm cast or brace can be applied for 6 weeks.

Distal Radial Fractures

Table 6-2 shows that about 70% of distal radial fractures are treated nonoperatively (Fig. 6-40) and Table 6-5 shows that there has been an increase in operative management over the years. There is an increased appreciation of the importance of fracture reduction and carpal alignment and progressively more distal radial fractures are being treated operatively. The introduction of locked plates and different types of external fixation has altered the management of these fractures but a substantial proportion of distal radial fractures are stable and will continue to be managed nonoperatively. As with other osteopenic and osteoporotic fractures the epidemiology of distal radial fractures will be change significantly in a rapidly aging population, who will present with more medical comorbidities. As a result of changing patient demographics it may well be that more distal radial fractures will be treated nonoperatively in the future. Distal radial fracture treatment is discussed in Chapter 30.

If a stable distal radial fracture is to be treated nonoperatively, a forearm cast or brace should be applied for 6 weeks, and following removal a physical education program instituted. If an unstable fracture is to be treated nonoperatively, reduction needs to be undertaken using a haematoma block, regional block, or general anesthetic. The classic reduction technique is to apply traction, flexion, and ulnar deviation and to check the fracture position on radiographs or fluoroscopy. If the fracture does not reduce, the Agee maneuver can be used (Fig. 6-41). Once the fracture has been reduced a dorsal slab or short forearm cast is applied. The fracture must be x-rayed 7 to 10 days after the initial reduction to check that the reduction has been maintained. If it has not been maintained, the surgeon must decide on further fracture management based on the age of the patient, his or her functional state, and the presence of medical comorbidities. Remanipulation is generally unsuccessful in older patients, and in most cases of redisplacement the surgeon will have to consider operative treatment, although in very elderly demented patients the fracture will often be left in the malreduced position. If the fracture position is maintained the cast or slab is completed and worn for 6 weeks. Alternatively, a functional brace can be used. Following removal of the cast or brace, a physical therapy regime should be instituted.

Carpal Fractures

Table 6-2 shows that about 15% of carpal fractures are treated surgically, and Table 6-5 indicates that the prevalence of operative treatment has recently increased. There has been increasing interest in primary scaphoid fixation after fracture and it seems likely that the number of scaphoid fractures treated surgically will increase. Still, many scaphoid fractures are minor stable fractures and it is likely that nonoperative management will continue to be popular. A recent analysis[20] showed that scaphoid fractures comprise about 82% of carpal fractures suggesting that nonoperative management for carpal fractures will continue

to be used. A further 9% of carpal fractures were triquetral fractures, which are also treated nonoperatively. Complex carpal fractures and dislocations do require surgical treatment but are relatively uncommon.

If nonoperative management is used a scaphoid cast is applied (see Fig. 6-17). It usually needs to be worn for 6 to 8 weeks but union can be slow and the cast may need to be worn for up to 12 weeks. If other carpal fractures are treated a cast or brace is usually worn for 3 to 6 weeks, depending on the type of fracture. Flake fractures of the triquetrum usually require only 3 weeks in a forearm cast. The treatment of carpal fractures is discussed in Chapter 29.

Metacarpal Fractures

Metacarpal fractures are very unusual in that it would seem that they are more frequently treated nonoperatively than they were 60 years ago, despite the availability of mini-plates and minifixators. Table 6-2 shows than only about 11% of metacarpal fractures had primary operative treatment in 2000 in a major trauma unit. It is likely that the reduction in operative treatment relates to improved industrial and workplace safety legislation in many countries. Crushed hands are much less common than in the post–World War II period and an analysis of metacarpal fractures in 2000 shows that they are mainly low energy fractures with about 50% being caused by a direct blow. About 60% of fractures affect the little finger metacarpal (Fig. 6-42) and 54% of these affect the metacarpal neck.[20]

Nonoperative treatment of isolated stable undisplaced or minimally displaced metacarpal fractures usually involves the use of buddy strapping and mobilization, although not infrequently no supportive strapping is actually required at all. If closed reduction is required, it can be achieved by flexing the metacarpophalangeal joint to 90 degrees and using the proximal phalanx to push the metacarpal head dorsally and to control rotation. This is known as the Jahss technique. The indications for fracture reduction mainly relate to angulation, rotation, and shortening and are discussed in Chapter 28. Surgeons may elect to treat malreduced or unstable fractures operatively but if nonoperative management is undertaken a Burkhalter or James type of cast or splint should be used. These are usually maintained for about 3 weeks, following which a physical therapy regime is organized. Fractures of the neck, diaphyses, and bases of metacarpals are similarly treated but basal fractures or fracture dislocations of the thumb metacarpal may well be treated by the application of a Brunner cast, which may be maintained for 4 to 6 weeks.

Phalangeal Fractures

The prevalence of operative treatment of phalangeal fractures is similar to metacarpal fractures (Table 6-2) and, as with metacarpal fractures, comparison with Emmett and Breck's data from 60 years ago[31] shows that we seem to operate less now. Presumably, as with metacarpal fractures, this is because the incidence of crushed hands and severe hand injuries has declined mainly as a result of improved workplace legislation. As with metacarpal fractures, many phalangeal fractures are stable and require no more than buddy strapping or the application of an aluminium foam backed splint to minimize pain and the possibility of secondary displacement. If phalangeal fractures are stable after reduction they can be treated by the application of a Burkhalter or James type splint, or by the use of a longer aluminium

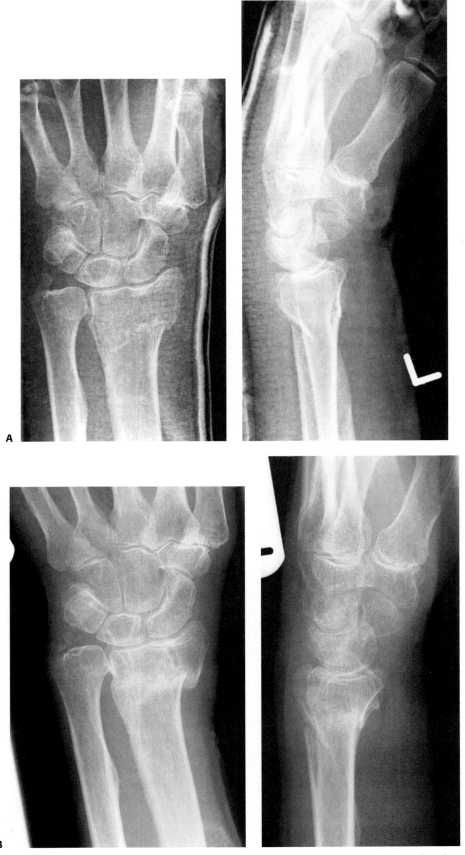

FIGURE 6-40 A. A-P and lateral radiographs of a distal radial fracture in a 68-year-old male. Note the relative lack of dorsal comminution. **B.** Closed manipulation was undertaken and A-P and lateral radiographs at 6 weeks show that good alignment has been maintained.

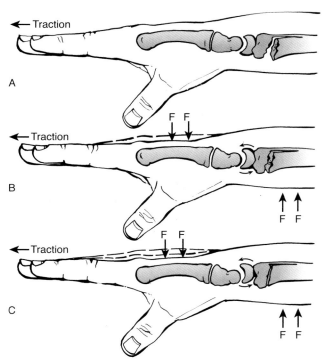

FIGURE 6-41 The Agee maneuver. This places a volar translation force on the distal radial fragment, which allows the lunate to tilt the distal fragment in a volar direction.

backed foam splint bent to maintain the finger in the same position as achieved by the splint. Again the splint will be maintained for 2 to 3 weeks.

Fractures of the distal phalanges are frequently treated nonoperatively. Tuft fractures and closed diaphyseal fractures tend

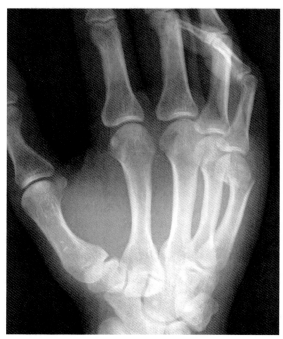

FIGURE 6-42 A fracture of the neck of the little finger metacarpal. Most of these fractures are treated nonoperatively.

to be stable and are often treated by local splintage for pain relief. Basal fractures of the distal phalanx are often unstable but can frequently be treated in full extension on a splint for 4 weeks. Bony mallet injuries are treated similarly in a mallet splint. For further information about the treatment of phalangeal fractures see Chapter 28.

Lower Limb Fractures

Suggested guidelines for the nonoperative treatment of lower limb fractures are shown in Table 6-10.

Femoral Neck Fractures

Table 6-2 indicates that proximal femoral fractures are treated operatively unless the patient's medical condition means that surgery is contraindicated. In undisplaced intracapsular femoral neck fractures, there is a higher prevalence of nonunion, avascular necrosis, and fracture displacement in nonoperatively treated fractures.[20] In addition, nonoperative management means that an elderly patient, often with significant medical comorbidities, is confined to bed for 4 to 6 weeks, which is clearly undesirable. The only proximal femoral fracture for which nonoperative management may be the treatment of choice is the greater trochanter fracture, when there may be little or no displacement. Even in these fractures, surgeons should be aware that there may be an intertrochanteric extension. Lesser trochanter fractures are very rare but may be treated nonoperatively. In older patients these fractures should be assumed to be metastatic fractures until proven otherwise. The treatment of proximal femoral fractures is discussed in Chapters 47 through 49.

Femoral Diaphyseal Fractures

Femoral diaphyseal fractures should no longer be treated nonoperatively unless the patient is not fit for surgery or the facilities to allow operative treatment are unavailable. The results from nonoperative treatment are significantly inferior to operative management. If nonoperative management is used then one of the methods of traction illustrated in Figure 6-4 should be used. There is probably no other fracture in which there is such a strong consensus in favor of one treatment method, and intramedullary nailing is generally used for all femoral diaphyseal fractures (see Chapter 50).

Distal Femoral Fractures

Table 6-2 shows that most distal femoral fractures are treated operatively, which is what one would expect, although in recent years there has been a significant change in the epidemiology of distal femoral fractures. These fractures now commonly occur in the elderly, with the epidemiological review in Chapter 3 giving an average age of 61 years for patients with this fracture. A review of the 39.1% of distal femoral fractures that were treated nonoperatively as detailed in Table 6-2 shows that virtually all were undisplaced fractures in older or clinically unwell patients. Thus, nonoperative management is now mainly used for low-energy undisplaced fractures that commonly occur in elderly patients. Nonoperative management will usually involve the application of a long leg cast for about 4 weeks following which a hinged knee brace can be applied. As fractures treated nonoperatively are usually undisplaced, union may be fairly rapid. This is particularly true for OTA type B partial articular fractures, which are not infrequently undisplaced or minimally

TABLE 6-10	Guidelines for Nonoperative Management for Different Lower Limb Fractures if Nonoperative Management Is Chosen as the Treatment Method*

Fracture Type	Nonoperative Management
Pelvis	
Insufficiency fracture (elderly patient)	Mobilize as pain permits
APC Type 1 and LC Type 1	Mobilize as pain permits
Undisplaced acetabulum (except transtectal type)	Mobilize as pain permits
Proximal femur	Not recommended
Femoral diaphysis	Not recommended
Distal femur (undisplaced)	Hinged knee brace for 6 to 8 weeks
Patella (undisplaced)	Long leg cylinder cast or brace. Mobilize at 4 to 6 weeks.
Proximal tibia (undisplaced)	Hinged knee brace for 6 to 8 weeks
Tibial diaphysis	Long leg cast. Patellar tendon–bearing cast or brace at 4 to 6 weeks
Distal tibia (undisplaced)	Lower leg cast or brace for 6 to 8 weeks
Ankle	Lower leg cast or brace for 6 weeks
Talus	Lower leg cast or brace for 6 weeks
Calcaneus	Lower leg cast or brace for 6 weeks
Midfoot	Lower leg cast or brace for 4 to 6 weeks
Metatarsus	Mobilize or lower leg cast or brace for 4 to 6 weeks
Toes	Buddy strapping and mobilize

*See relevant chapters for suggested management for different fractures.

displaced. Under these circumstances a cast or brace may well only need to be used for 6 to 8 weeks. The treatment of distal femoral fractures is detailed in Chapter 51.

Patella Fractures

Patella fractures are discussed in Chapter 52. Most occur in older patients as a result of a fall.[20] Therefore, undisplaced or minimally displaced patella fractures are relatively common and these are usually treated nonoperatively. Table 6-2 shows that about 35% to 40% of patella fractures are treated operatively, these being the more serious fractures. Nonoperative management usually involves the use of a long leg cylinder cast or brace, which is worn for about 6 weeks. A physical therapy program is then instituted.

Proximal Tibial Fractures

Proximal tibial fractures have a somewhat unusual distribution with a bimodal distribution in both males and females (Chapter 3). About 48% of the fractures detailed in Table 6-2 were high energy injuries that occurred in younger patients, which explains the higher incidence of operative treatment, compared with distal femoral fractures, with almost 70% of patients being treated operatively. As with distal femoral fractures, the patients treated nonoperatively tend to present with undisplaced or minimally displaced fractures (Fig. 6-43). If nonoperative management is used for proximal tibial fractures, a hinged knee brace should be applied for 6 to 8 weeks. If this is unavailable a long

leg cylinder cast can be used. The treatment of proximal tibial fractures is discussed in Chapter 53.

Tibial Diaphyseal Fractures

The treatment of tibial diaphyseal fractures has changed considerably in the last 20 years. The treatment of these fractures was the subject of much debate until relatively recently. Long leg casts, patellar tendon–bearing casts and functional braces have all been used to treat both closed and open tibial diaphyseal fractures (Table 6-8) but the results were relatively poor and intramedullary nailing has become the treatment of choice for these fractures. This is discussed in Chapter 55. Table 6-2 shows that about 94% of tibial diaphyseal fractures were treated operatively in Edinburgh, with nonoperative management being mainly reserved for stable OTA A3.1 transverse tibial fractures with an intact fibula that occur mainly in younger patients. These unite quickly and are treated in a below knee cast.

If nonoperative management is to be used for an unstable tibial diaphyseal fracture it is recommended that a long leg cast is applied initially and that a patellar tendon–bearing cast or brace be applied after 4 to 6 weeks. Serial radiographs will be required to determine when union has occurred and, therefore, when to remove the cast. Traction should not be used to stabilize tibial diaphyseal fractures as it is associated with increased intracompartmental pressure and the effects of prolonged bed rest. There is now no indication for traction. If internal fixation can-

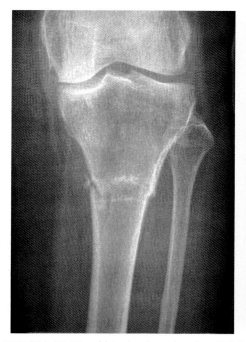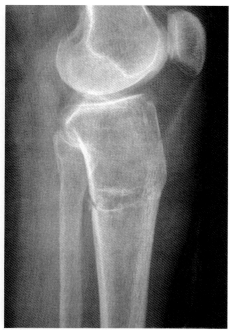

FIGURE 6-43 AP and lateral radiographs of an OTA A2.3 extra-articular proximal tibial fracture in a 78-year-old female with significant medical cormorbidities. A long leg cast was used.

not be used to treat a tibial diaphyseal fracture, external fixation is usually possible.

Distal Tibial Fractures

Much of the literature dealing with distal tibial or pilon fractures concerns displaced high energy fractures occurring in younger patients. These fractures are treated operatively as detailed in Chapter 56. Further analysis of the distal tibial fractures shown in Table 6-2 shows that about 40% of them were OTA type A extra-articular fractures and 31% were OTA type B partial artic- ular fractures. Table 6-3 shows the prevalence of surgery in the different OTA fracture types, and it can be seen that while most type B and all type C fractures are treated operatively only 30% of type A fractures were treated surgically. Of these patients, 47% were 14 to 16 years of age and had physeal fractures, and the remaining 53% had an average age of 59 years and presented mainly with low energy undisplaced or minimally displaced fractures. Thus, as with other lower limb fractures, there is a distinct difference in fracture treatment based on age, mode of injury, and fracture displacement. If nonoperative management is to be used for an undisplaced or a minimally displaced type A or type B pilon fracture, a non–weight-bearing below-knee cast or brace is adequate and it may need to be worn for 8 to 10 weeks depending on the speed of union. In younger patients with physeal fractures the use of a cast or brace for 4 to 6 weeks is adequate.

Ankle Fractures

Table 6-2 shows that overall about 40% of ankle fractures are treated operatively. As has already been pointed out, the preva- lence of operative treatment of metaphyseal and intra-articular fractures varies with the degree of severity of the fracture as defined by the OTA classification (Table 6-3). This principle also applies to ankle fractures, although their OTA classification

is somewhat different from the classifications of the fractures shown in Table 6-3. Further analysis of the ankle fractures shown in Table 6-2 shows that about 12% of type A infrasyndes- motic fractures were treated operatively, these mainly being iso- lated medial malleolar fractures. This compares with 49% of transsyndesmotic type B fractures and 70% of suprasyndesmotic type C fractures. Thus most type A and about half of type B fractures will be treated nonoperatively. A review of the patients who present with type C fractures but were treated nonopera- tively shows that most had external rotation rather than abduc- tion injuries and it was felt that the posterior tibio-fibula liga- ments were intact. They were considered to be stable after the application of a cast. If this method of management is chosen, serial radiographs must be undertaken to make sure there is no evidence of late syndesmotic widening.

Analysis of the type B fractures shows that 84.3% of the bimalleolar fractures and 94.3% of the trimalleolar fractures were treated operatively. A review of the lateral malleolar frac- ture associated with talar shift, the OTA B2.1 fracture, showed that 91.4% of fractures were treated operatively but an analysis of the prevalence of operative management in the common OTA B1.1 spiral lateral malleolar fracture caused by external rotation shows that only 16.8% of these fractures were treated opera- tively. It is important to realize that B1.1 fractures associated with 2 to 3 mm of displacement do not require operative treat- ment and that an excellent result can be obtained with cast or brace management (Figure 6-44).[5,54] Care must be taken to be certain that the patient does not actually have an OTA B2.1 fracture with talar shift, and radiographs should be obtained after the application of the cast and at 2 weeks to check for this. If nonoperative ankle fracture treatment is undertaken a below knee cast or brace is applied for 6 weeks. Many surgeons do not permit weight bearing for 6 weeks after cast application but there is no good evidence to support this regime[41] and

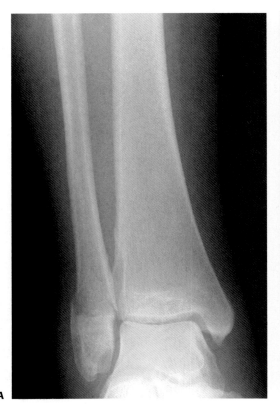

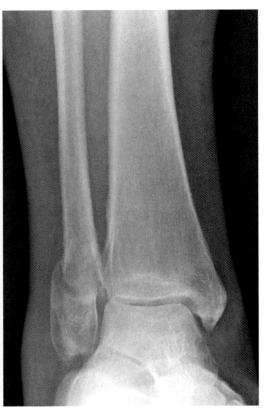

A   B

FIGURE 6-44 A. An OTA B1.1 ankle fracture in a 50-year-old female. Note the slight lateral translation of the distal fibula. **B.** Surgery is not required. Union occurred with good ankle function.

weight bearing can be allowed in most ankle fractures. Ankle fractures are discussed in Chapter 57.

Talar Fractures

Fractures of the talus are relatively uncommon, but Table 6-2 shows that about 50% are treated operatively. A review of the epidemiology of talar fractures has shown that about 70% are body fractures and 30% are neck fractures.[20] Further analysis of the body fractures shows that about 42% are shear or crush injuries but 50% are fractures of the lateral or posterior processes, which are often treated nonoperatively (Fig. 6-45).

A review of the talar neck fractures showed that about 30% were Hawkins type I[43] fractures, which are also commonly treated nonoperatively. Thus while displaced neck and body fractures will usually be treated operatively, there are several talar fractures that will be managed nonoperatively. If non-operative management is to be undertaken, the use of a non–weight-bearing below knee cast or brace for 6 to 8 weeks is recommended. Following its removal a physical therapy regime should be instituted. Talar fractures are discussed in Chapter 58.

Calcaneal Fractures

There has been considerable recent discussion about the management of calcaneal fractures.[13,71] These are often displaced intra-articular fractures and as such should benefit from operative treatment. There is continued debate about the indications for surgery and many calcaneal fractures continue to be managed nonoperatively.[13] Table 6-2 shows that in a trauma unit

where fracture fixation of intra-articular calcaneal fractures remains routine about 35% of fractures are treated by primary operative fixation. As with talar fractures, it is important to understand the epidemiology of calcaneal fractures in order to understand why only 35% of fractures are treated operatively. Analysis of the calcaneal fractures included in Table 6-2 shows that about 60% are intra-articular; the remaining 40% are extra-articular calcaneal body fractures (Fig. 6-46) or fractures of the anterior, medial, or lateral processes or of the posterior tuberos-

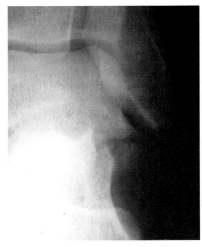

FIGURE 6-45 A talar lateral process fracture. Most of these fractures are treated nonoperatively as are fractures of the posterior process.

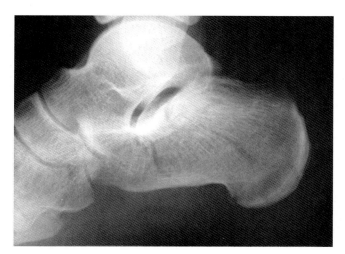

FIGURE 6-46 A calcaneal body fracture with an undisplaced fracture entering the posterior facet. Surgery is not required.

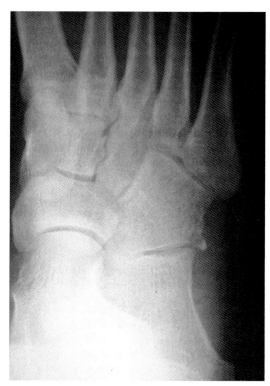

FIGURE 6-47 A minor avulsion fracture of the cuboid. This type of midfoot fracture is very common and does not require surgery.

ity.[20] Many of these fractures will be treated nonoperatively. Also, an analysis of types of intra-articular calcaneal fracture using the Sanders classification[79] shows that about 16% of intra-articular calcaneal fractures are undisplaced Sanders type 1 that do not require surgery. In addition, there are other factors that affect the choice of management in calcaneal fractures. It is assumed that intra-articular calcaneal fractures occur in young patients and many do, but there has been an increasing prevalence of these fractures in older patients, with 12.7% of the calcaneal fractures included in Table 6-2 occurring in patients of at least 65 years of age. Surgeons often treat these patients nonoperatively.

If nonoperative treatment is used for calcaneal fractures it is suggested that a non–weight-bearing below knee cast or brace be used for 6 weeks, and then weight bearing and a physical therapy regime instituted. Calcaneal fractures are discussed in Chapter 59.

Midfoot Fractures

Table 6-2 indicates that about 30% of midfoot fractures are treated operatively. A review of the epidemiology of midfoot fractures shows that there are four basic fracture types, these being avulsion fractures, shear fractures, uni-articular impaction fractures, and biarticular impaction fractures.[20] About 45% of midfoot fractures are avulsion fractures, which are generally treated nonoperatively (Fig. 6-47) as operative treatment tends to be used mainly for shear fractures or for maintaining length in the medial and lateral columns of the midfoot in more severe fractures or fracture dislocations. The other indication for operative treatment is if the fracture is associated with a Lisfranc dislocation of the tarso-metatarsal joint. Thus, more severe midfoot injuries tend to be treated operatively. If nonoperative treatment is used it is usually for less severe injuries and the use of a non–weight-bearing cast or brace for 6 weeks is adequate. Midfoot fractures are discussed in Chapter 60.

Metatarsal Fractures

Metatarsal fractures are relatively common but Table 6-2 shows that very few are treated operatively. About 90% of metatarsal fractures are isolated injuries, with about 75% affecting the fifth

metatarsal.[20] Most are low-energy injuries and are treated nonoperatively (Chapter 60). Some multiple metatarsal fractures or fractures associated with significant displacement or with a Lisfranc dislocation of the tarso-metatarsal joint require operative treatment but these are frequently associated with high energy injuries to the foot. Stress fractures of the metatarsal are not uncommon and are also treated nonoperatively. Treatment of metatarsal fractures is essentially symptomatic. No treatment is required if the patient can manage to mobilize without significant discomfort. If the fracture is painful, it is suggested that a below knee cast or brace be applied for 3 weeks and then reapplied if the pain continues. Mobilization can be allowed when the patient can manage this.

Toe Fractures

Table 6-2 shows that, as with metatarsal fractures, nonoperative treatment of toe fractures is very common. Analysis of the toe phalangeal fractures in Table 6-2 shows that about 20% involved the hallux, and that five of the eight fractures that were treated operatively were in the hallux. Surgical treatment of the other toes is rarely required. If nonoperative management is used, buddy strapping to the adjacent toe is usually all that is needed, although the treatment is usually symptomatic and frequently no treatment is actually required.

Pelvic and Acetabular Fractures

Table 6-2 shows that the prevalence of operative management of pelvic and acetabular fractures is relatively low. This may be surprising to surgeons working in Level I trauma centers but it must be remembered that most fractures involving the pelvis are insufficiency fractures of the pubic rami and occur in the elderly. In the last 30 years there has been an explosion of interest in the surgical treatment of pelvic and acetabular fractures. The pelvic fractures that occur in younger patients that are still frequently treated nonoperatively are the anterior posterior compression type I injuries and the lateral compression[104] type I injuries. Treatment is restricted weight bearing depending on the degree of discomfort. Most acetabular fractures are treated operatively with nonoperative management reserved for undisplaced fractures with the exception of transtectal transverse fractures, which may displace later.[20] Treatment is restricted weight bearing for 10 to 12 weeks and a physical therapy program. Pelvic and acetabular fractures are discussed in Chapters 44 and 45.

Spinal Fractures

Very little is known about the prevalence of nonoperative management of all cervical and thoracolumbar fractures, but it is a very common method of treatment with many of the perceived advantages of spinal fixation not having been proven in clinical trials. The management of spinal fractures is discussed in detail in Chapters 42 and 43.

SPECIFIC FRACTURE TYPES

Periprosthetic Fractures

Increasing longevity, with associated osteopenia and osteoporosis, together with an increased use of arthroplasty and fracture fixation have lead to a rapid increase in the incidence of periprosthetic fractures. These usually occur in older patients and can be very difficult to treat. Many periprosthetic fractures will be treated operatively but there is a role for nonoperative management in certain circumstances. Most periprosthetic fractures associated with arthroplasty will occur in the femur following hip or knee replacement. The classification and management of these is detailed in Chapter 21 but if the Vancouver classification[11] of proximal femoral periprosthetic fractures is employed, most Type B and C fractures will be treated operatively with nonoperative treatment being reserved for stable Type A fractures (Fig. 6-48). The basic principle governing the use of nonoperative management is that the fractures should be undisplaced or minimally displaced and the implant should not be loose. If these conditions apply, type A proximal femoral periprosthetic fractures can be treated by a period of restricted weight bearing.

The same basic principle applies to periprosthetic fractures affecting the acetabulum or distal femur. Minor undisplaced perioperative acetabular fractures are sometimes caused by the insertion of hemiarthroplasty prosthesis in the treatment of proximal femoral fractures. These can be treated nonoperatively with a period of restricted weight bearing. More severe displaced acetabular fractures are usually treated operatively. In the distal femur Lewis and Rorabeck[58] type I fractures can be treated nonoperatively as they are undisplaced and stable, but type II and III fractures are best treated operatively. Again a period of restricted weight bearing is used. The same principles are applied to periprosthetic patellar and proximal tibial fractures.

Humeral periprosthetic fractures can be very difficult to treat. They occur in elderly patients and analysis of implant failure has shown that loosening is relatively rare.[75] Thus the surgeon may be faced with a type B[104] periprosthetic fracture

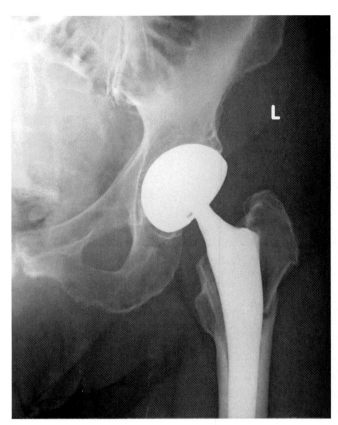

FIGURE 6-48 A Vancouver Type A fracture around the proximal stem of a stable bipolar prosthesis. This type of periprosthetic fracture generally does not need surgical treatment.

in osteopenic bone and a stable implant. An example of this is shown in Figure 6-49 in which there had been an earlier humeral diaphyseal fracture as well. Nonoperative management may be the only realistic option under these circumstances. Periprosthetic fractures associated with elbow or ankle arthroplasties are treated using the basic principles of fracture displacement and implant stability that have already been outlined.

In recent years there has been an increasing prevalence of femoral fractures associated with proximal femoral fracture fixation. These are most commonly associated with proximal femoral nails but may occur after the use of compression and dynamic hip screws. These fractures are usually displaced and there is little role for nonoperative management.

Stress Fractures

There are two types of stress fracture: fatigue fractures and insufficiency fractures. They are discussed in Chapter 19. Fatigue fractures usually occur in younger patients and, with the exception of some fractures of the proximal femur, femoral diaphysis, distal femur, and tibial diaphysis they are usually undisplaced and are managed nonoperatively (Fig. 6-50). The general principles of management are the same as described for other fractures and the same treatment regimes outlined in Tables 6-9 and 6-10 should be followed. Insufficiency fractures occur in abnormal bone and obviously the most common causes for these fractures are osteopenia and osteoporosis. Many of these fractures are undisplaced and nonoperative management will be

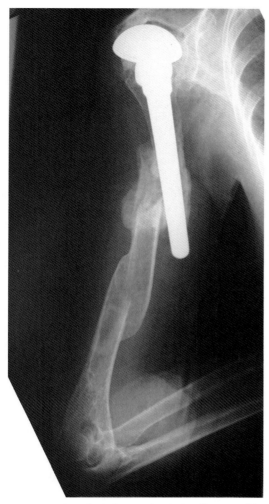

FIGURE 6-49 A periprosthetic fracture that is virtually impossible to treat surgically. A Vancouver Type B fracture in a humerus with a old nonoperatively managed diaphyseal fracture in an 89-year-old female. The shoulder was already very stiff.

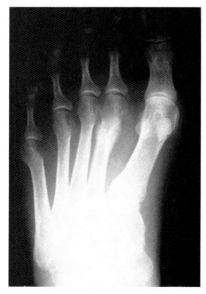

FIGURE 6-50 A stress fracture of the second metatarsal. The treatment is nonoperative.

used. The treatments outlined in Tables 6-9 and 6-10 should be followed.

Metastatic Fractures

Metastatic fractures are discussed in Chapter 20. It is difficult to be prescriptive about the role of nonoperative treatment as it largely depends on the location of the fracture, the type of tumor, and the medical condition of the patient. Generally speaking, most metastatic fractures are treated operatively unless the patient has a very short life expectancy as surgical stabilization will diminish pain and improve the quality of the patient's remaining life.

THE FUTURE OF NONOPERATIVE FRACTURE TREATMENT

There are two principal competing factors that will determine the role of nonoperative management of fractures in the future. It is likely that fracture fixation techniques will become more sophisticated and fractures that we now treat nonoperatively may be shown in the future to have better results if treated operatively. It is certain that in many parts of the world the population that is going to present with fractures is the elderly population and it is highly likely that the patients who present with fractures in the future will be older and less fit than current patients. Future fracture research will need to determine the role of operative management in elderly patients who already have functional impairment and significant medical comorbidities. It seems likely that as we develop into a "super-elderly" population we will re-evaluate the role of nonoperative management in many fractures.

Surgeons have analyzed the properties of osteoporotic bone in the belief that better fixation methods will improve the outcome of fractures in the elderly, but it is also necessary to consider the effect of aging on soft tissues and their recovery after injury and surgery. It may well be that the effect of increasing age on muscles, tendons, ligaments, and other soft tissues will negate any advantages gained by improved operative fixation but only time will tell.

Overall it seems likely that the prevalence of operative treatment will rise, but probably not as quickly as has been the case in the last 30 to 40 years. Improved vehicle design together with enhanced industrial legislation, speed restrictions, and drinking and driving laws will probably reduce the incidence of severe injuries but there is no doubt that orthopaedic surgeons will be faced with an epidemic of less severe fractures in the elderly.

REFERENCES

1. Alho A, Benterud JG, Hogevold HE, et al. Comparison of functional bracing and locked intramedullary nailing in the treatment of displaced tibial shaft fractures. Clin Orthop 1992;277:243–250.
2. Ambroise Paré. The Apologie and Treatise of Ambroise Paré. Geoffrey Keynes, ed. London: Falcon, 1951.
3. Andersen K, Jensen PO, Lauritzen J. Treatment of clavicular fractures. Figure-of-eight bandage versus a simple sling. Acta Orthop Scand 1987;58:71–74.
4. Austin RT. The Sarmiento tibial plaster: a prospective study of 145 tibial fractures. Injury 1981;13:12–22.
5. Bauer M, Jonsson K, Nilsson B. Thirty-year follow-up of ankle fractures. Acta Orthop Scand 1985;56:103–106.
6. Bérenger-Féraud LJB. Traité de l'immobilisation directe. Paris. Adrien Delahaye. 1870.
7. Böhler L. The Treatment of Fractures. New York: Grune and Stratton, 1956.
8. Bone LB, Sucato D, Stegemann PM, et al. Displaced isolated fractures of the tibial shaft

treated with either a cast or intramedullary nailing. J Bone Joint Surg (Am) 1997;79A: 1336–1341.
9. Bono CM, Rinaldi M. Thoracolumbar fractures and dislocations. In: Court-Brown CM, McQueen MM, Tornetta P, eds. Trauma. Philadelphia: Lippincott Williams and Wilkins, 2006:226–237.
10. Böstmann O, Hänninen A. Tibial shaft fractures caused by indirect violence. Acta Orthop Scand 1982;53:981–990.
11. Brady OH, Kerry R, Masri BA, et al. The Vancouver classification of periprosthetic fractures of the hip: a rational approach to treatment. Tech Orthop 1999;14:107–114.
12. Breasted JF. The Edwin Smith Papyrus. Chicago: University of Chicago Press, 1930.
13. Buckley R, Tough S, McCormack R, et al. Operative compared with nonoperative treatment of displaced intra-articular calcaneal fractures: a prospective, randomized, controlled multicenter trial. J Bone Joint Surg (Am) 2002;84A:1733–1744.
14. Canadian Orthopaedic Trauma Society. Nonoperative treatment compared with plate fixation of displaced midshaft clavicular fractures. A multicenter, randomized clinical trial. J Bone Joint Surg (Am) 2007;89:1–10.
15. Carstairs V, Morris R. Deprivation and health in Scotland. Health Bulletin 1990;48: 162–175.
16. Charnley J. The closed treatment of common fractures. 3rd Ed. Edinburgh: E&S Livingstone, 1972.
17. Connolly JF, Dehne E, Lafollette B. Closed reduction and early cast-brace ambulation in the treatment of femoral fractures. Part II: results in one hundred and forty-three fractures. J Bone Joint Surg (Am) 1973;55A:1581–1599.
18. Constant CR. Age related recovery of shoulder function after injury. Thesis. University College, Cork, 1986.
19. Court-Brown CM, Garg A, McQueen MM. The epidemiology of proximal humeral fractures. Acta Orthop Scand 2001;72:365–371.
20. Court-Brown CM, McQueen MM, Tornetta P. Trauma. Philadelphia: Lippincott Williams and Wilkins, 2006.
21. Court-Brown CM, Caesar B. The epidemiology of adult fractures: a review. Injury 2006; 37:691–697.
22. Court-Brown CM, McQueen MM. Two-part fractures and fracture dislocations. Nand Clin 2007;23:397–414.
23. Dennison E, Cooper C. Epidemiology of osteoporotic fractures. Horm Res 2000; 54(Suppl 1):58–63.
24. Den Outer AG, Meeuwis JD, Hermans J, et al. Conservative versus operative treatment of displaced noncomminute tibial shaft fractures. Clin Orthop 1990;252:231–237.
25. Digby JM, Holloway GMN, Webb JK. A study of function after tibial cast bracing. Injury 1993;14:432–439.
26. DiStasio AJ, Jaggears FR, DePasquale LV, et al. Protected early motion versus cast immobilization in postoperative management of ankle fractures. Contemp Orthop 1994;29:273–277.
27. Dunn L, Henry J, Beard D. Socal deprivation and adult head injury: a national study. J Neurol Neurosurg Psychiatry 2003;74:1060–1064.
28. Edwards SG, Whittle AP, Wood GW. Nonoperative treatment of ipsilateral fractures of the scapula and clavicle. J Bone Joint Surg (Am) 2000;82A:774–780.
29. Egol KA, Connor PM, Karunakar MA, et al. The floating shoulder: clinical and functional results. J Bone Joint Surg (Am) 2001;83A:1188–1194.
30. Ekholm R, Tidermark J, Törnkvist H, etc. Outcome after closed functional bracing of humeral shaft fractures. J Orthop Trauma 2006;20:591–596.
31. Emmett JE, Breck LW. A review and analysis of 11,000 fractures seen in a private practice of orthopaedic surgery 1937–1956. J Bone Joint Surg (Am) 1958;40: 1169–1175.
32. Evans JMM, Newton RW, Ruta DA, et al. Socioeconomic status, obesity, and prevalence of Type 1 and Type 2 diabetes mellitus. Diabetic Med 2000;17:478–480.
33. Fjalestad T, Strømsøe K, Salvesen P, et al. Functional results of braced humeral diaphyseal fractures; why do 38% lose external rotation of the shoulder? Arch Orthop Trauma Surg 2000;120:281–285.
34. Fracture and dislocation classification compendium. J Trauma 2007;21:10(Suppl).
35. Garfin SR. Botte MJ, Centeno RS, et al. Osteology of the skull as it affects halo pin placement. Spine 1985;10:696–698.
36. Geiger KR, Karpman RR. Necrosis of the skin over the metacarpal as a result of functional fracture-bracing. J Bone Joint Surg (Am) 1989;71:1199–1202.
37. Grassi FA, Tajana MS, D'Angelo F. Management of midclavicular fractures: comparison between nonoperative reatment and open intramedullary fixation in 80 patients. J Trauma 2001;50:1096–1100.
38. Haines JF, Williams EA, Hargadon ES, et al. Is conservative treatment of displaced tibial shaft fractures justified? J Bone Joint Surg (Br) 1984;66B:84–88.
39. Hanlon CR, Estes WL. Fractures in childhood. A statistical analysis. Am J Surg 1954; 87:312–323.
40. Hansen PB, Hansen TB. The treatment of fractures of the ring and little metacarpal necks. A prospective randomized study of three different types of treatment. J Hand Surg (Br) 1998;23B:245–247.
41. Harager K, Hviid K, Jensen CM, et al. Successful immediate weight-bearing of internally fixated ankle fractures in a general population. J Orthop Sci 2000;5:52–54.
42. Hardy AE. The treatment of femoral fractures by cast-brace application and early ambulation. A prospective review of 106 patients. J Bone Joint Surg (Am) 1983;65A:56–65.
43. Hawkins LG. Fractures of the neck of the talus. J Bone Joint Surg (Am) 1970;52A: 991–1002.
44. Herscovici D, Fiennes AG, Allgöwer M, et al. The floating shoulder: ipsilateral clavicle and scapular neck fractures. J Bone Joint Surg (Br) 1992;74B:362–364.
45. Hippocrates. The Genuine Works of Hippocrates, trans Francis Adams. Baltimore: Williams and Wilkins, 1939.
46. Hooper GJ, Keddell RG, Penny ID. Conservative management or closed nailing for tibial shaft fractures. A randomized prospective trial. J Bone Joint Surg (Br) 1991;73B: 83–85.
47. Jawa A, McCarty P, Doornberg J, et al. Extra-articular distal-third diaphyseal fractures of the humerus. A comparison of functional bracing and plate fixation. J Bone Joint Surg (Am) 2006;88A:2343–2347.
48. Johnell O, Kanis JA. An estimate of the worldwide prevalence and disability associated with osteoporotic fractures. Osteoporos Int 2006;17:1726–1733.
49. Johnson RM, Hart DL, Simmons BF, et al. Cervical orthoses: a study comparing their effectiveness in restricting cervical movement in normal subjects. J Bone Joint Surg (Am) 1977;59A:332–339.
50. Jones R. An orthopaedic view of the treatment of fractures. Am J Orthop 1913;11:314.
51. Karaharju EO, Alho A, Neimenen J. Results of operative and nonoperative management of tibial fractures. Injury 1979;7:49–52.
52. Kay L, Hansen BA, Raaschou HO. Fractures of the tibial shaft conservatively treated. Injury 1986;17:P5–11.
53. Koch RA, Nickel VL. The halo vest: An evaluation of motion and forces across the neck. Spine 1978;3:103–107.
54. Kristensen KD, Hansen T. Closed treatment of ankle fractures. Stage II supination-eversion fractures followed for 20 years. Acta Orthop Scand 1985;56:107–109.
55. Küntscher M, Blazek J, Brüner S, et al. Functional bracing after operative treatment of metacarpal fractures. Unfallchirurg 2002;105:1109–1114.
56. Kyrö A, Tunturi T, Soukka A. Conservative treatment of tibial fractures. Results in a series of 163 patients. Ann Chir Gynaecol 1991;80:294–300.
57. Lehtonen H, Järvinen TLN, Honkonen S, et al. Use of a cast compared with a functional ankle brace after operative treatment of an ankle fracture: a prospective, randomized study. J Bone Joint Surg (Am) 2003;85A:205–211.
58. Lewis PL, Rorabeck CH. Periprosthetic fractures. In: Engh GA, Rorabeck CH, eds. Revision Total Knee Arthroplasty. Baltimore: Wiliams and Wilkins, 1997.
59. Lichtenberg RP. A study of 2532 fractures in children. Am J Surg 1954;87:330–338.
60. Lindsay RW, Pneumaticos SG, Gugala Z. Management techniques for spinal injuries. In: Browner BD, Jupiter JB, Levine AM, et al., eds. Skeletal Trauma. 3rd Ed. Philadelphia: WB Saunders, 2003:746–776.
61. Neer CS. Displaced proximal humeral fractures. I. Classification and evaluation. J Bone Joint Surg (Am) 1970;52A:1077–1089.
62. Nho SJ, Brophy RH, Barker JU, et al. Management of proximal humeral fractures based on current literature. J Bone Joint Surg 2007;89(Suppl 3):44–58.
63. Nicoll EA. Fractures of the tibial shaft. A survey of 705 cases. J Bone Joint Surg (Br) 1965;46B:373–387.
64. Nordqvist A, Pettersson CJ, Redlund-Johnell I. Midclavicle fractures in adults: end result study after conservative treatment. J Orthop Trauma 1998;12:572–576.
65. O'Connor D, Mullett H, Doyle M, et al. Minimally displaced Colles fractures: a prospective randomized trial of treatment with a wrist splint or a plaster cast. J Hand Surg (Br) 2003;28:50–53.
66. Oni OOA, Hui A, Gregg PJ. The healing of closed tibial shaft fractures. J Bone Joint Surg (Br) 1988;70B:787–790.
67. Owsley KC, Gorczyca JT. Fracture displacement and screw cutout after open reduction and locked plate fixation of proximal humeral fractures. J Bone Joint Surg (Am) 2008; 90:233–240.
68. Pace AM, Stuart R, Brownlow H. Outcome of glenoid neck fractures. J Shoulder Elbow Surg 2005;14:585–590.
69. Peltier LF. Fractures. A History and Short Iconography of their Treatment. San Francisco: Norman Publishing, 1990.
70. Perry J, Nickel VL. Total cervical spine fusion for neck paralysis. J Bone Joint Surg (Am) 1959;41A:37–60.
71. Poeze M, Verbruggen JP, Brink PR. The relationship between the outcome of operatively treated calcaneal fractures and institutional fracture load. A systematic review of the literature. J Bone Joint Surg (Am) 2008;90A:1013–1021.
72. Pun WK, Chow SP, Fang D, et al. A study of function and residual joint stiffness after functional bracing of tibial shaft fractures. Clin Orthop 1991;267:157–163.
73. Puno RM, Teynor JT, Nagano J, et al. Critical analysis of results of treatment of 201 tibial shaft fractures. Clin Orthop 1986;212:113–121.
74. Ring D, Chin K, Taghinia AH, et al. Nonunion after functional brace treatment of diaphyseal humerus fractures. J Trauma 2007;62:1157–1158.
75. Robinson CM, Page RS, Hill RM. Primary hemiarthroplasty for treatment of proximal humerus fractures. J Bone Joint Surg (Am) 2003;85A:1215–1223.
76. Robinson CM. Cairns DA. Primary nonoperative treatment of displaced lateral fractures of the clavicle. J Bone Joint Surg 2004;86A:778–782.
77. Rokito AS, Zuckerman JD, Shaari JM, et al. A comparison of nonoperative and operative treatment of type II distal clavicle fractures. Bull Hosp Jt Dis 2002;61:32–39.
78. Rosenberg N, Soudry M. Shoulder impairment following treatment of diaphyseal fractures of humerus by functional brace. Arch Orthop Trauma Surg 2006;126:437–440.
79. Sanders R, Fortin P, DiPasquale T, et al. Operative treatment in 120 displaced intraarticular calcaneal fractures: results using a prognostic computed tomography scan classification. Clin Orthop 1993;290:87–95.
80. Sarmiento A. A functional below-the-knee cast for tibial fractures. J Bone Joint Surg 1967;49A:855–875.
81. Sarmiento A. A functional below-the-knee cast for tibial fractures. J Bone Joint Surg (Am) 1970;52A:295–311.
82. Sarmiento A. Gersten LM, Sobol PA. Tibial shaft fractures treated with functional braces. Experience with 780 fractures. J Bone Joint Surg (Br) 1989;71B:602–609.
83. Sarmiento A, Horowitch A, Aboulafia A, et al. Functional bracing for comminuted extra-articular fractures of the distal third of the humerus. J Bone Joint Surg (Br) 1990; 72B:283–287.
84. Sarmiento A, Latta LL, Zych GA, et al. Isolated ulnar shaft fractures treated with functional braces. J Orthop Trauma 1998;12:420–423.
85. Sayre LA. Report on fractures. Trans Am Med Assoc 1874;25:301.
86. Scudder CL. The ambulatory treatment of fractures. Boston Med Surg J 1898;138:102.
87. Seutin LJG. Du traitement des fractures par l'appareil inamovible. Bruxelles. 1835.
88. Shakespeare DT, Henderson NJ. Compartment pressure changes during calcaneal traction in tibial fractures. J Bone Joint Surg (Br) 1982:64:498–499.
89. Simanski CJ, Maegele MG, Lefering R, et al. Functional treatment and early weightbearing after an ankle fracture: a prospective study. J Orthop Trauma 2006;20:108–114.
90. Slätis P, Rokkanen P. Conservative treatment of tibial shaft fractures. Acta Chir Scand 1967;134:41–47.
91. Steen Jensen J, Wang Hansen S, Johansen J. Tibial shaft fractures: a comparison of conservative treatment and internal fixation with conventional plates or AO compression plates. Acta Orthop Scand 1977;48:204–212.
92. Stewart HD, Innes AR, Burke FD. Functional cast-bracing for Colles fractures. A comparison between cast-bracing and conventional plaster casts. J Bone Joint Surg (Br) 1984;66B:749–753.
93. Stimson LA. A treatise on fractures. Philadelphia: Henry C. Lea, 1883.

94. Thomas HO. The principles of the treatment of fractures and dislocations. London: HK Lewis, 1886.

95. Thompson GH, Wilber JH, Marcus RE. Internal fixation of fractures in children and adolescents. Clin Orthop 1984;188:10–20.

96. Toivanen JAK, Niemenen J, Laine HJ, et al. Functional treatment of closed humeral shaft fractures. Int Orthop 2005;29:10–13.

97. Tropiano P, Huang RC, Louis CA, et al. Functional and radiographic outcome of thoracolumbar and lumbar burst fractures managed by closed orthopaedic reduction and casting. Spine 2003;28:2459–2465.

98. Tropp H, Norlin R. Ankle performance after ankle fracture: a randomized study of early mobilization. Foot Ankle Int 1995;16:79–83.

99. Tumia N, Wardlaw D, Hallett J, et al. Aberdeen Colles brace as a treatment for Colles fracture. A multicenter, prospective, randomized, controlled trial. J Bone Joint Surg (Br) 2003;85:78–82.

100. Van der Linden W, Larsson K. Plate fixation versus conservative treatment of tibial shaft fractures. A randomized trial. J Bone Joint Surg (Am) 1979;61A:873–878.

101. Van Noort A, van Kampen A. Fractures of the scapula surgical neck: outcome after conservative treatment in 13 cases. Arch Orthop Trauma Surg 2005;125:696–700.

102. Veysi VT, Mittal R, Agarwal S, et al. Multiple trauma and scapula fractures: so what? J Trauma 2003;55:1145–1147.

103. Volkmann R. Verletzungen der knochen (knochenbruchen und knochenwunden). In: Pithia and Billroth, eds. Handbuch der Allemeinen und Speziellen Chirurgie. vol 2. Erlangen: Ferdinand Enke, 1865.

104. Young JWR, Burgess AR, Brumback RJ, et al. Pelvic fractures: value of plain radiography in early assessment and management. Radiology 1986;160:445–451.

105. Zagorski JB, Latta LL, Zych GA, et al. Diaphyseal fracture of the humerus. Treatment with prefabricated braces. J Bone Joint Surg (Am) 1988;70A:607–610.

106. Zlowodzki M, Bhandari M, Zelle BA, et al. Treatment of scapula fractures: systematic review of 520 fractures in 22 case series. J Orthop Trauma 2006;20:230–233.

7

PRINCIPLES OF INTERNAL FIXATION

Michael Schütz and Thomas P. Rüedi

HISTORICAL BACKGROUND AND THE GOALS OF INTERNAL FIXATION

By 3000 BC, the ancient Egyptians knew that splinting of a fractured limb not only reduces pain but also supports the healing process. However, the first reports on modern techniques of internal fixation are only about 100 years old. The brothers Elie and Albin Lambotte from Belgium described in detail the essentials of what they called "osteosynthesis" of fractures with plates and screws, wire loops, and external fixators. Albin Lambotte (1866–1955) highlighted the importance of anatomic reduction and stable fixation of articular fractures as the only way to regain good joint function.[44] While he planned and drew every fracture in detail, he also emphasized the importance of careful soft tissue handling to preserve vascularity and prevent infection. His pupil Robert Danis (1880–1962) introduced the term "soudure autogéné", or primary bone healing without visible callus, which he observed when the fracture was anatomically reduced and fixed with his compression plate. In 1950, the 32-year-old Swiss orthopaedic surgeon Maurice Müller spent one day in the clinic of Danis and was deeply impressed by the patients he saw and the results of compression plating. Back in Fribourg, he got permission to treat a patient with the new technique and compression plates, which he soon modified and technically improved. Together with 13 other young Swiss surgeons, he founded in 1958 the Arbeitsgemeinschaft für

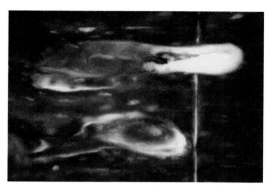

FIGURE 7-1 Direct or primary fracture healing as observed with absolute stability. A new Havers osteon transversing the osteotomy, thereby interdigitating across the osteotomy line.

Osteosynthesefragen (AO). The main representatives were Martin Allgöwer, Walter Bandi, Robert Schneider, and Hans Willenegger.[54] They agreed on and adhered to strict rules and principles of surgery and, thanks to a meticulous follow-up of every single fracture, they were able to document their results and learn from the mistakes and complications. Parallel to the Swiss AO, Gerhard Küntscher (1900–1972) in Germany had developed the technique of intramedullary nailing, which soon revolutionized the treatment of diaphyseal fractures especially of the femur and tibia.[43] In contrast to the rigid fixation by interfragmentary compression, intramedullary nailing was a splinting technique, which allowed for some motion at the fracture site and therefore healing by callus formation. Rigid fixation on one hand and the more elastic internal splinting on the other have often been considered as competing techniques, while they are actually complementary, each having its pros and cons and specific indications.

The ultimate goal of operative fracture fixation must be (i) to obtain full restoration of function of the injured limb and (ii) for the patient to return to his preinjury status of activities, as well as to minimize the risk and incidence of complications. The purpose of the use of implants is to provide a temporary support, to maintain alignment during the fracture healing, and to allow for a functional rehabilitation.

INFLUENCE OF BIOLOGY AND BIOMECHANICS ON FRACTURE HEALING

The biological and biomechanical influences on fracture treatment will be considered in this chapter. Any procedure will alter the biological and biomechanical environment for fracture healing, and every surgeon treating fractures should be familiar with those alterations. From a mechanical and biological point of view, a fractured bone needs a certain degree of immobilization, an optimally preserved blood supply, and biological or hormonal stimuli in order to unite. All three factors are important; the mechanical part is however the easiest to quantify. We may distinguish two types of mechanical stability: absolute and relative. Absolute stability is defined as rigid fixation that does not allow any micromotion between the fractured fragments under physiologic loading. It is best obtained by interfragmentary compression and is based on preload and friction. More elastic fixation as provided by internal or external splinting of the bone is defined as relative stability which allows limited motion at the fracture site under functional loading. The degree of stability determines the type of fracture healing, which is either by primary or direct bone remodelling (Fig. 7-1), or by secondary or indirect healing with callus formation. Indirect fracture healing by callus can take place in a much wider spectrum of mechanical environments than primary or direct bone remodelling (Fig. 7-2). Callus will not form if there is no motion; however, if there is excessive movement, healing will equally be delayed.

The strain theory[11,63] describes, in a simplified manner, what occurs at a cellular level in a fracture gap. Strain is the deformation of a material (e.g., granulation tissue within a gap) when a given force is applied relative to its original form, thus it has no dimension. The amount of deformation a tissue can tolerate before it breaks varies greatly. The strain of normal intact bone until it breaks is "low," about 2%, while granulation tissue has a high strain tolerance of 100%.[63] In a narrow fracture gap, a defined distracting force will disrupt the few cells within it (Fig. 7-3). The same force applied to a wider gap filled with granulation tissue will, however, only deform this tissue and not cause any rupture. In a simple transverse or short oblique fracture, any deforming force is acting very locally on the single fracture gap corresponding to a concentration of stress, while in complex, multifragmentary fractures the same force will be distrib-

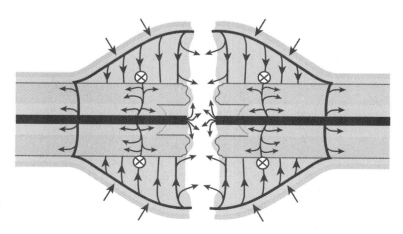

FIGURE 7-2 Secondary healing by callus as observed with relative stability. Schematic drawing of vessel ingrowth from the periphery to the fracture gap.

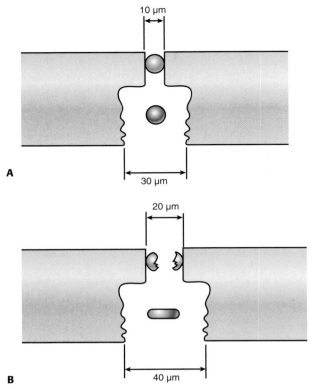

FIGURE 7-3 Strain theory by Perren: Panel **(A)** shows two cells (*red and blue circles*) in two different sized fracture gaps (10 pm and 30 pm). Panel **(B)** is after 10 pm of distraction. The single red cell in a narrow gap will rupture upon minimal distraction (high strain), while the blue cell in a wide gap with the same distraction will just deform or extend (low strain).

uted over a wide range of different fracture fragments or gaps (stress distribution). By applying the strain theory, a simple type A diaphyseal fracture has a situation of "high strain." Therefore, such a fracture is best reduced anatomically and fixed by inter-fragmentary compression (lag screw and plate), a method that produces a high degree or absolute stability (Fig. 7-4).

On the other hand, a more complex, multifragmentary diaphyseal fracture corresponds to a "low strain" situation, which profits from correct axial and rotational alignment and less rigid fixation (locked intramedullary nail, bridge plate, or external fixator) providing relative stability (Fig. 7-5). It appears most important in simple fracture types treated with rigid fixation that persistent gaps at the fracture site are avoided, while in complex fractures treated with less rigid fixation such small gaps may be tolerated (Table 7-1). Larger gaps are less well tolerated. Bhandari[6] and Audigé[1] have independently shown in large clinical series of surgically stabilized tibia shaft fractures that persistent fracture gaps of over 2 mm were closely related or predictive for the development of a healing delay or nonunion.

In articular fractures, the anatomic congruity of the joint surface must be restored and the fragments should be fixed rigidly by interfragmentary compression, while associated metaphyseal comminution or a diaphyseal extension of the fracture can be correctly aligned in all planes and bridged by an appropriate device (see Fig. 7-28).

SOFT TISSUE INJURY AND FRACTURE HEALING

Every fracture is associated to a certain extent with injury to the tissues surrounding the bone. The energy, direction, and

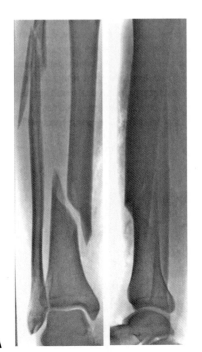
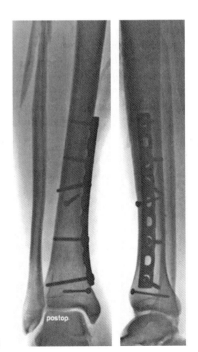
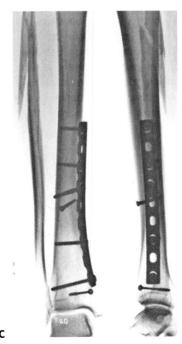

FIGURE 7-4 A simple tibia and fibula spiral fracture by indirect trauma **(A)** is reduced anatomically and fixed with interfragmentary compression (lag screw and protection plate) providing absolute stability **(B)**. **C.** Healing occurs without callus formation at 1-year follow-up.

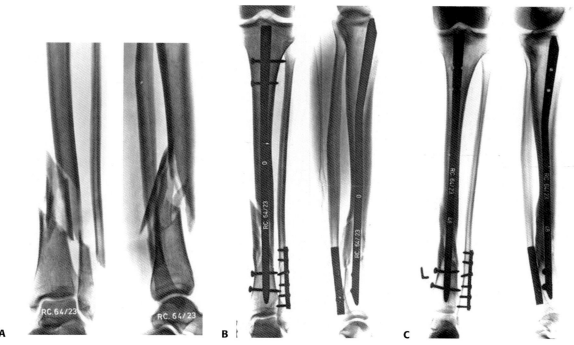

FIGURE 7-5 A. Complex, distal tibia and fibula fractures by direct trauma **B.** Fixed after axial and rotational alignment with a locked intramedullary nail providing relative stability. **C.** Healing occurred after proximal dynamization with callus formation. The fibula fracture was fixed because of the vicinity to the ankle joint.

concentration of forces inducing the fracture will determine the fracture type and the associated soft tissue lesions.[56] As a result of the displacement of the fragments, periosteal and endosteal blood vessels maybe disrupted and the periosteum will be stripped.[71] The statement that "every fracture is a soft tissue injury where the bone happens to be broken," should emphasize the great importance of the soft parts, which unfortunately are still often not considered and respected enough.

The healing process of a fracture starts with the formation of granulation tissue within the fracture hematoma and is dependent on a preserved or restored blood supply to the area. The more extensive the zone of injury and the tissue destruction, the higher is the risk for a delay of the healing process or for other complications. Depending on the mechanism and the magnitude or energy of the insult that caused the bone to break, direct and indirect fracture mechanisms are distinguished which can usually be deducted from the

radiographic appearance of the fracture pattern. An indirect fracture mechanism, like a rotation or bend, will cause a spiral or butterfly fracture, respectively, with relatively little soft tissue injury. These fractures generally heal rather uneventfully when adequately reduced and immobilized by nonoperative or operative means (see Fig. 7-4). In contrast, a direct blow will induce a local contusion of the skin at a minimum, or more often will result in an open transverse or wedge type fracture with an extensive area of soft tissue injury (Fig. 7-6). In open fractures, the severity or extent of the lesion is usually much more evident than in closed fractures.[20] The latter may also involve important neurovascular structures surrounding the bone. In closed fractures, occult injuries are therefore more often missed.[51] A careful assessment, classification, and documentation of the fracture and the soft tissue injury is therefore of great importance in the planning, especially for correct timing, of surgery. As a rule,

TABLE 7-1	**Relation of the Stability of Fixation (Absolute vs. Relative), the Type of Fracture (Simple or Complex), and the Size of the Fracture Gap to Fracture Healing**	
	Fracture Gap	
	Simple Small (<2 mm)	Multifragmentary Large (>2 mm)
Relative stability	Bone resorption, healing delay, or nonunion	Secondary bone healing (callus)
Absolute stability	Primary bone healing, osteonal remodeling	Bone resorption, healing delay, or nonunion

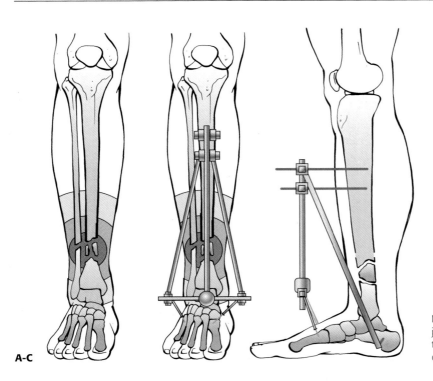

FIGURE 7-6 A. Schematic drawing showing zone of injury around a tibia and fibula fracture caused by direct trauma. **B,C.** Bridging external fixator to protect the zone of injury in a severely contused distal tibia fracture.

it is much safer to temporarily immobilize the zone of injury by traction or more adequately by an external fixator, postponing definitive fixation until the soft tissues have recovered.

In open fractures with a soft tissue defect or an associated vascular injury, it may be advisable to perform emergency fixation of the bone, followed by vessel repair and immediate or early plastic reconstructive procedure to cover the tissue defect. Decision-making under such circumstances requires much experience, and it may be advisable to involve a senior surgeon or the entire team including a plastic-reconstructive surgeon (see also Chapter 10).

As we cannot influence the extent of soft tissue lesions caused by the accident, we must do our best to limit any additional injury to the blood supply of the bone and surrounding structures. Minimally invasive surgical approaches without exposure of the fracture, indirect reduction techniques, and fixation devices that do not additionally harm the blood supply to the bone should be used wherever possible.

PREOPERATIVE PLANNING

Every fracture needs a careful preoperative assessment and planning process, which is essential in order to obtain a predictable outcome and to prevent intraoperative problems, hazards, and unnecessary delays.

The preoperative assessment should take into consideration the patient, the fracture, and the soft tissues. Planning includes the evaluation not only of the fracture and limb per se, but of the whole patient. Factors like the history and mechanism of the accident, the age of the patient, pre-existing vascular and metabolic diseases, and the use of drugs, alcohol, and nicotine all may greatly influence the outcome and therefore must be included in the decision-making. The expectations of the patient, their profession, and recreational activities should be known and discussed. The treatment plan is adapted accordingly.

For the fracture, plain radiographs are studied and additional imaging requested if considered necessary. Computed tomography (CT) scans with two- or three-dimensional reconstruction usually give more information,[10,47,57] while traction views (under anesthesia) may still be helpful in greatly displaced articular fractures. The classification of the fracture will help to communicate and discuss the type of treatment, to evaluate the problems, and to make a prognosis as to the outcome. The soft tissues and neurovascular conditions are then assessed carefully, as closed fractures may also have severe involvement of these structures. The timely diagnosis of a compartment syndrome and its correct treatment may save a critically injured limb. The assessment and classification of the soft tissue injury is often more difficult than that of the fracture and requires much experience.

Preoperative plan:

- Timing of surgery
- Surgical approach
- Reduction maneuvers
- Fixation construct
- Intraoperative imaging
- Wound closure/coverage
- Postoperative care
- Rehabilitation

PRE-, PERI-, AND POSTOPERATIVE CARE

While the anatomic location and pattern of a fracture may dictate a certain method of fixation, for example a complete articular fracture will require open reduction and stable internal fixation, other fracture types may be approached by different fixation techniques or even by nonoperative treatment. The conditions of the soft tissue, such as severe swelling or a skin contusion, may preclude immediate surgery and make a staged procedure recommendable. Once the indication and best time for surgery has been established, the type of anesthesia, positioning of the patient, use of a tourniquet, and the need for prophylactic antibiotics or a bone graft has to be communicated to the anaesthesia and operating room (OR) team as well as the method of fixation, approach, reduction aids, type of implant, and intraoperative imaging. The more complex the fracture and the procedure, the more detailed the planning must be. Drawing the outlines of a fracture on tracing paper will help to recognize the number, shape, position, and relationship of the different fragments. Thereby, the character and challenges of a fracture will be appreciated and the experienced surgeon will be able to decide how to reduce and fix the fracture without additional damage to the most vulnerable blood supply of the area.

Planning Technique on Paper

Two good orthogonal radiographs of the injured and the uninjured side including the adjacent joints, tracing paper, colored pens, templates of the implants, a set of goniometers, and an x-ray screen are needed for preoperative templating. Step one: the outlines of the intact bone(s) are drawn. Step two: the outlines of the fractured bone(s) are drawn, with the different fragments separated from each other. Step three: the main fragments and the intermediate pieces are reassembled on the drawing of the intact bones. To do so, the separate fragments can be copied on different pieces of drawing paper or cut with scissors. The restored fracture on paper helps indicate how to best reduce the fracture and which function of the fixation device (absolute or relative stability) will be utilized (Fig. 7-7). The plan also indicates what size implant is needed and where and how to place or introduce it to minimize additional soft tissue injury. Finally, the reduced fracture with the implant in place is drawn, and the different steps of applying the fixation device are numbered. For an open fracture, the question of wound closure or coverage should be addressed. The OR team will be grateful if a list of the required equipment, instrument sets, reduction tools, intraoperative imaging, and so forth, is provided.

Digital x-ray imaging is becoming standard equipment in most newer radiology departments and online planning tools and templates are under development and will soon be available, which will hopefully make the whole planning process on personal laptops more attractive, easier, and less time consuming. A good preoperative plan will reduce OR time, make a procedure more efficient and thus be beneficial to the patient.

Prophylactic Antibiotics and Thromboembolic Prophylaxis

While the use of prophylactic antibiotics in operative fracture fixation of open as well as closed fractures is an evidence-based standard treatment today,[7,57] much discussion centers around the kind of antibiotic and the duration of application. As there is a large variation in the recommendations depending on national, regional, and local factors, we suggest that the infectious disease specialist of a specific hospital should be consulted. In general, a second generation cephalosporin with a broad spectrum is recommended, applied as single dose 30 minutes before the start of surgery or initiated before surgery and continued for

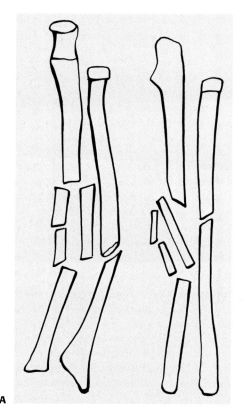
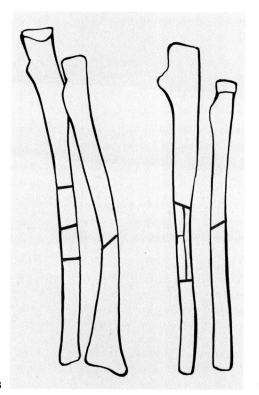
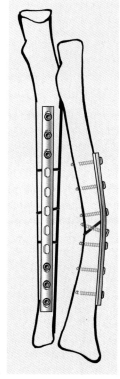

A   **B**   **C**

FIGURE 7-7 Planning on paper: first, the different fracture fragments are drawn separately on tracing paper **(A)**. **B.** They may be cut out with scissors to be assembled again, or they may be copied onto the outlines of the intact bones of the opposite side. **C.** Finally, the implants are added in the correct position, length, and function providing absolute (compression) or relative (bridging) stability.

24 to 48 hours postoperatively. Furthermore, frequent wound irrigation with saline during surgery is recommended ("Keep the soft tissues wet and they will love you") to reduce the risk of infection.[3] The addition of antibiotics or antiseptics to irrigate solutions is however debatable and not proven to be effective. The detailed treatment of open fractures is discussed in Chapter 10.

The risk of venous thromboembolism depends on multiple factors including age, type of surgery, duration of immobilization, and pre-existing disposition. The incidence of deep vein thrombosis (DVT) is high in patients with fractures of the hip, pelvis, spine, and lower extremity, while upper limb injuries are rarely the source of thrombosis. DVT has a considerable morbidity with significant complications and mortality. Similar to the use of antibiotics, the recommendations for a thromboembolic prophylaxis vary greatly from one institution to the other. Early postoperative mobilization of the entire patient is probably the most effective prophylaxis but not always possible. Low molecular heparin, aspirin, and intermittent compression devices applied to the feet, as well as warfarin or coumarin, are all recommended by some but also rejected by others, as there is no evidence of superiority of one single method.

Postoperative Care and Rehabilitation

The postoperative care starts with the wound bandage and/or splinting, positioning of the injured limb, and the initiation of physiotherapy exercises. A general goal is to move the joints, the injured limb, and the whole patient as soon as possible, usually by 24 hours after surgery, provided the fixation of the fracture is stable and the soft tissues permit such an aggressive management. In the case of lower limb injuries and if the patient is considered compliant, a plan for early start of partial weight bearing should be made. In patients that are not compliant, the fixation must be able to tolerate early full weight bearing or the fracture has to be protected externally by a splint or cast.

FRACTURE REDUCTION

The gentle and atraumatic reduction of a fracture is not only one of the most important and most challenging steps in fracture management, operative as well as nonoperative, but probably also the most difficult part to teach and practice. The goal of reduction is to restore the anatomic relationship of the fractured bone and of the limb by reversing the mechanism of fragment displacement during the injury. It seems a fact that due to the muscle insertions to the bone, a fracture tends to redisplace in the direction and degree of the original displacement. It is therefore important not only to assess the radiographs and CT scans carefully, but also to appreciate the vectors and forces of fragment displacement by muscle pull (Fig. 7-8).

In the diaphysis and regardless of whether the fracture is simple, multifragmentary, or has a bone defect, the correct restoration of length, axial alignment, and rotation is considered an adequate reduction. In the epiphyseal segment, however, a meticulous, anatomic reconstruction of the articular surface and joint congruency is advocated in order to obtain a good functional result. As such, ambitious aims are sometimes difficult to achieve without risks, such as long incisions and a wide exposure. A careful balance between a perfect reconstruction and the necessary respect for the soft tissue biology has to be

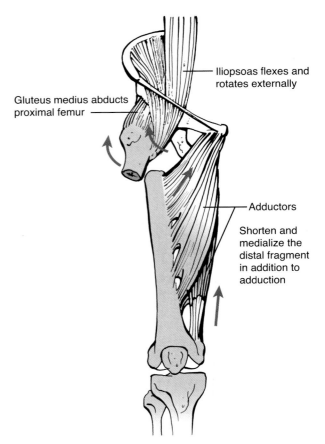

FIGURE 7-8 Typical displacement of a subtrochanteric fracture with external rotation, abduction, and flexion of the proximal and adduction of the distal fragment.

Labels: Iliopsoas flexes and rotates externally; Gluteus medius abducts proximal femur; Adductors; Shorten and medialize the distal fragment in addition to adduction

chosen. Furthermore, irreparable damage to the joint cartilage may be a limiting factor.

Mast et al.[48] created the term of "biological fracture fixation" which refers not only to the method of fixation, but also to the reduction techniques. Accordingly, distinctions between direct and indirect as well as open and closed reduction will be made. Although direct and open reduction and indirect and closed techniques are usually associated, they are not necessarily synonymous. At the end, the essentials are that any reduction or fragment manipulation occurs atraumatic and gently, not causing any additional harm to the vascularity of the already compromised fracture fragments and soft tissues envelope.

Direct Reduction

Direct reduction means that the fracture fragments are manipulated directly by the application of different instruments or hands, which usually requires an open exposure of the fracture site. Some newly developed instruments and devices, such as joy sticks, large pointed reduction forceps, the ingenious colinear clamp, or new cerclage wire tools, may also be applied directly to the bone through very small incisions and without wide exposure of the fracture (Fig. 7-9). The application of these new techniques is called minimally invasive surgery or minimally invasive plate osteosynthesis in spite of the fact that thanks to the new instruments, direct fragment manipulation has occurred.

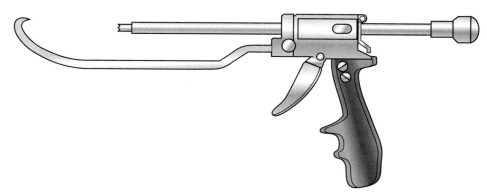

FIGURE 7-9 Colinear reduction clamp for minimally invasive approaches.

The advantages of direct reduction are a precise restoration of anatomy, though at the cost of more interference with bone and soft tissue biology. A higher risk of infection and possibly a delay in bony union that accompany stripping of the soft tissues are further potential disadvantages.

Indirect Reduction

Indirect reduction means that the reduction and alignment of the fracture fragments is being achieved without exposing the fracture site as such by applying reduction forces indirectly—via the soft tissue envelope—to the main fragments by manual or skeletal traction, a distractor or some other means. The classic example of indirect reduction is the "closed" insertion of an intramedullary nail on a fracture table, where reduction has been obtained by traction on the lower leg, while the nail provides the final alignment of the fragments. The advantage of indirect reduction is that there is virtually no exposure of the fracture site, which reduces the risk of additional damage to the vascularity of the tissues, as well as that of an infection. The disadvantages are that it is a demanding technique and that the correct overall alignment of the fracture is more difficult to assess, especially in rotation.

Open Reduction

Open reduction implies that the fracture site is exposed, allowing to watch and inspect the adequacy of reduction with our eyes. It is usually combined with direct manipulation of some fragments, but can also involve indirect techniques such as the use of a joint bridging distractor in an articular fracture.

Indications for open reductions are:

- Displaced articular fractures with impaction of the joint surface
- Fractures that require exact axial alignment (e.g., forearm fractures, simple metaphyseal fractures)
- Failed closed reduction due to soft tissue interposition
- Delayed surgery where granulation tissue or early callus has to be removed
- Where there is a high risk for harming neurovascular structures
- In cases of no or limited access to perioperative imaging to check reduction

Careful preoperative planning including adequate imaging is essential to choose the best approach, the tools for a gentle reduction, and the appropriate implant. In articular fractures, it is usually sufficient to be able to see into the joint in order to carefully clear it from hematoma and debris and to judge the cartilage damage as well as the quality of reduction after the reconstruction. The periosteum and any soft tissue attachments must be preserved wherever possible, while separate stab incisions may help the placement of pointed reduction clamps, temporary Kirschner wires (K-wires), or the insertion of lag screws.

Closed Reduction

Closed reduction relies entirely on indirect fragment alignment by ligamentotaxis or the pull of the soft tissue envelope. Longitudinal traction is the main force that may be modified by add- or abduction, flexion or extension, and rotation as well as supporting bolsters, etc. These maneuvers may be quite demanding and usually require the presence of an image intensifier. Profound knowledge of the anatomy (location of muscle insertion and direction of muscle pull) as well as careful planning are prerequisites. Percutaneously applied joysticks and special instruments may be helpful.[19,41] If correctly applied, the advantages are minimal additional damage to the soft tissues, safer and more rapid fracture repair, as well as lower risk of infection.

Indications for closed reduction:

- Most diaphyseal fractures, where correct axial alignment, length, and rotation is considered sufficient for a good outcome
- Minimally displaced articular fractures suited for percutaneous fixation
- Femoral neck and trochanteric fractures, subcapital humerus fractures, and certain distal radius fractures

The size of an incision will not necessarily be indicative of the amount of damage done to the biology of a fracture. Much harm can be done through a short incision, but also little harm through a larger exposure. All that matters is the gentleness of the surgeon's hands and his or her skills in managing the reduction process.

TECHNIQUES AND INSTRUMENTS FOR FRACTURE REDUCTION

Traction and Distraction

Traction is the most common means to reduce a fracture. This can occur manually with the help of a fracture table or by applying a distractor directly to the main fragments of a long bone or, in an articular fracture, across the joint (Fig. 7-10). While longitudinal traction will usually correct shortening, it may be difficult to align the fragments in both the sagittal and coronal

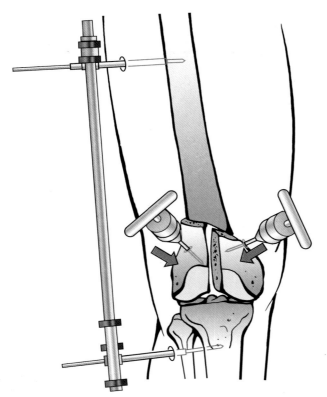

FIGURE 7-10 Joint bridging distractor to support reduction of a distal femur fracture with joysticks.

osteopenic bone, they can, however, penetrate through the thin cortex. Occasionally, a small hole created with a drill or K-wire is helpful to gain purchase for the tip. The forceps may be applied directly or percutaneously through stab incisions.

Two special forceps (Faraboeuf and Jungbluth) have originally been developed for pelvic and acetabular fractures. Both are applied to the heads of two screws that are inserted on either side of a fracture (Fig. 7-13). The newest reduction forceps is the collinear forceps which is no longer based on a hinge between the two branches but on a sliding mechanism that allows a linear movement (see Fig. 7-9). Thanks to this, the new reduction tool can be introduced through very short incisions or through narrow openings in the pelvis, which makes it ideal for minimally invasive techniques.

Other reduction tools include joysticks (preferably Schanz screws), Hohman retractors for intrafocal manipulation, and cerclage wires, while every surgeon has additional tricks and tools in his or her personal armamentarium (Fig. 7-14).

There are situations in which the implant, intramedullary nail, plate, or modular external fixator may be used for the reduction and fixation at the same time. Especially in conventional nonlocked plating, angle blades and precontoured plates can be used to reduce the fracture toward the plate.

Computer assisted surgery with navigation software has promised to open completely new applications especially for hip and knee replacement, but appears to still be in an early stage for acute fracture reduction and management.[29,35]

Intra- and Postoperative Assessment of the Reduction

After the reduction of a fracture, the position of the fragments should be held reduced with temporary K-wires and/or a forceps and then the reconstruction and axial alignment must be carefully assessed in at least two planes preferably with the image intensifier. However, the resolution of the images is not as precise as that of radiographs, and the size of the field or picture is usually too small to allow evaluation of the longitudinal axis of a bone or its rotation. Another shortcoming of the image intensifier is the often prolonged exposure to radiation for the patient, surgeon, and staff. Several tricks have been described to overcome these drawbacks, and some of them will be described in the chapter on intramedullary nailing, where axial and rotational alignment is particularly difficult. In articular fractures, inspection of the joint surface occurs best either with the image intensifier or without any imaging at all. The most

planes. There are a number of tricks described to overcome the problem. The fracture table has the disadvantage that traction is usually applied across a joint and that there are limited possibilities to move the limb. The distractor, on the other hand, offers many possibilities and more freedom of movement, but it is quite demanding to manipulate and requires considerable practice (Fig. 7-11).[2,4]

Reduction Forceps

There is a great variety of reduction forceps available, some for general use, others for rather specific applications (Table 7-2). The reduction forceps with sharp points (Weber forceps) (Fig. 7-12) is the most commonly used as it comes in many different dimensions. The points provide an excellent purchase on the fragments without stripping or squeezing the periosteum; in

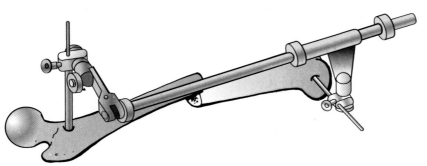

FIGURE 7-11 Femoral distractor applied in two planes to allow axial and rotational alignment such as for intramedullary nailing or minimally invasive plating.

TABLE 7-2 **Useful and Frequently Used Instruments for Reduction**

Instrument	Image of Instrument	Description	Application Technique, Degrees of Freedom
Reduction forceps with points (Weber forceps)		Different sizes and angulations of the branches available, different mechanisms	On-forceps technique, two-forceps technique, three linear, and two rotational degrees of freedom
Reduction forceps, toothed		Different sizes	Mainly used for alignment of a plate on a diaphyseal bone and reduction
Bone holding forceps, self-centering (Verbrugge forceps)		Four different sizes	
Bone spreader		Different sizes and angulations	Only for distraction, one linear degree of freedom
Colinear reduction forceps		Different insertable branches (hooks)	Only for compression, one linear degree of freedom
Pelvic reduction forceps with ballpoints ("King Tong," "Queen Tong")		Symmetric and asymmetric, two spikes and three spikes, spiked mountable washer	
Angled pelvic reduction forceps (Matta forceps)		Large and small	
Pelvic reduction forceps (Faraboeuf forceps)		Different sizes, 3.5- and 4.5-mm screws	
Pelvic reduction forceps (Jungbluth forceps)		Two different sizes, 3.5- and 4.5-mm screws	Can be used in different directions as the screw directly links the forceps to the bone fragment

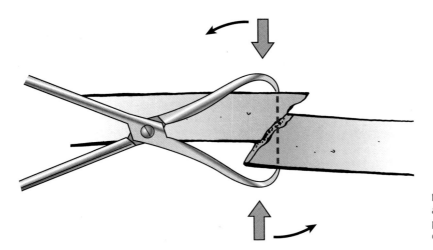

FIGURE 7-12 Pointed reduction forceps (Weber), which allow safe purchase of the bone without stripping of the periosteum. By manipulating the forceps (*arrows*), a simple oblique fracture can be easily reduced.

reliable way to assess an articular reconstruction is with a CT scan, which is becoming more available in the OR integrated into the new two- and three-dimensional fluoroscopes. Arthroscopy has also been advocated for minimally invasive surgical control of articular fractures.[28,49] It offers advantages to evaluate menisci and ligaments as well as the consistency of articular cartilage; however for the judgement of axial alignment, open reduction usually appears to be superior.

TECHNIQUES AND DEVICES FOR INTERNAL FIXATION

Operative fracture fixation can be performed with devices applied either externally (percutaneously) or internally (under-

neath the soft tissue cover). The former includes the many different types of external fixators that will be described in Chapter 8. Internal fixation devices stabilize the bone from within the medullary canal (intramedullary nails) or are fixed to the exterior of the bone (conventional nonlocked screws and plates and locked plates as well as tension band wires).

Screws

Screws are the basic and most efficient tool for internal fixation, especially in combination with plates. A screw is a powerful element that converts rotation into linear motion.

Most screws are characterized by some common design features (Fig. 7-15).

- A central core that provides strength
- A thread that engages the bone and is responsible for the function and purchase
- A tip that may be blunt or sharp, self-cutting or self-drilling and -cutting
- A head that engages in bone or a plate
- A recess in the head to attach the screwdriver

Screws are provided in different forms, sizes, and materials. They are typically named according to their design, function, or way of application.

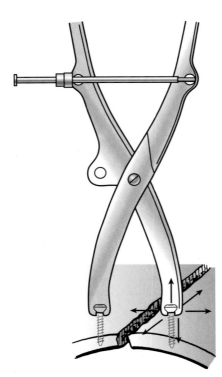

FIGURE 7-13 The Jungbluth forceps is applied with the help of the head of two screws that are inserted close to the fracture. Distraction as well as translation movements may be performed, which is especially helpful in the pelvis.

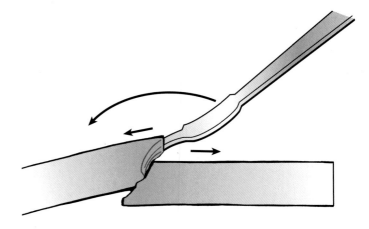

FIGURE 7-14 Hohman retractor for direct reduction of a simple fracture.

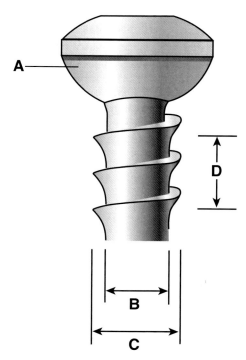

FIGURE 7-15 Schematic illustration of a conventional 4.5-mm cortex screw. **A.** Spherical screw head allowing a congruous fit in the plate hole. The minor diameter **(B)**. The major diameter **(C)**, and the thread pitch **(D)** are commonly referenced screw design parameters.

- Design (partial or fully threaded, cannulated, self tapping, etc.)
- Dimension of major thread diameter (most commonly used: 1.5-mm, 2.0-mm, 2.7-mm, 3.5-mm, 4.5-mm, 6.5-mm, 7.3-mm, etc.)

- Area of typical application (cortex, cancellous bone, bicortical or monocortical)
- Function (lag screw, locking head screw, position screw, etc.)

One and the same screw can have different functions, depending on the screw design and way of application. The two basic principles of a conventional screw are to compress a fracture plane (lag screw) and to fix a plate to the bone (plate screw). The more recent designed locking head screws provide angular stability between the implant and the bone (Fig. 7-16). The locking head screws have a head with a thread that engages with the reciprocal thread of the plate hole.[16] This creates a screw–plate device with angular stability. Screw tightening does not press plate against the bone surface. The load transfer occurs through the locking head screws and the plate, similarly to an external fixator, and not by friction and preload. As the locked plate lies underneath the soft tissues, the principle of this purely locked construct has been termed internal fixator (Fig. 7-17). If a combination of conventional and locked screws are used in one plate ("hybrid fixation"), the principle must be followed that in each fragment, all conventional screws are inserted before inserting locked screws. Lag screws (Fig. 7-18) can be applied independently or through a plate hole. In both situations, compression between two fragments or between the plate and the bone produces preload and friction, which oppose fragment displacement by other forces including shear force. Interfragmentary compression is the basic element responsible for absolute stability of fracture fixation.

To insert a screw, a hole has to be drilled into the bone with a drill bit slightly larger in diameter than the minor diameter of the selected screw. To ensure safe purchase of the screw, it is recommended to cut a thread with a matching tap before the screw is inserted especially in cortical as well as in hard cancellous bone in young patients. In bone of softer quality, such as

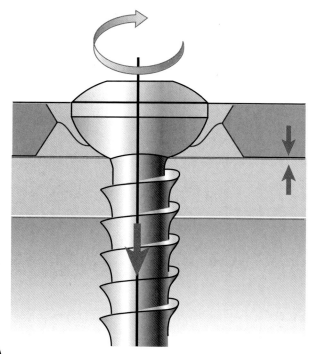

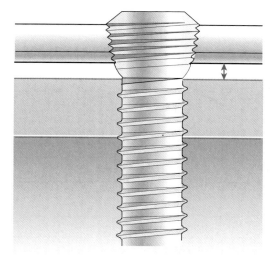

FIGURE 7-16 A. A conventional cortical screw applied as a plate screw. It presses the plate against the bone surface thereby creating friction and preload. **B.** Locking head screw. The screw head is firmly locked in the screw hole without pressing the plate against the bone. It provides angular stability.

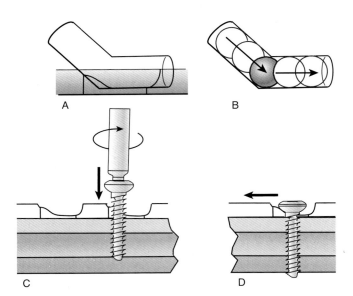

FIGURE 7-17 A. Dynamic compression principle: the holes of the DCP are shaped like an inclined and transverse cylinder. **B.** Like a ball, the screw head slides down the inclined cylinder. **C,D.** Because of the shape of the plate hole, the plate is being moved horizontally relative to bone when the screw is driven home.

cancellous bone, screw insertion may be done without tapping. Alternatively, there are also self-tapping screws, which reduce insertion time but require some practice. The screw design and the technique of screw insertion influence the amount of damage done and ultimately the holding power of a screw. Thermal necrosis may be caused by dull drill bits or by inserting pins and wires with a diameter larger than 2 mm without predrilling, leading to loosening and ring sequester. It is the surgeon's responsibility to adequately prepare the holes.

In general, three different types of screws are differentiated:

1. The cortex screw thread is designed for use in cortical bone (see Fig. 7-15). It is typically fully threaded but maybe partially threaded and is commonly available in diameters from 1.0 to 4.5 mm. Each size has a pair of drill bits corresponding to the screw's major and minor diameter and a tap. The drill corresponding to the major diameter is used for drilling the gliding hole for a lag screw while the drill corresponding to the minor diameter is used for drilling the threaded hole. Today, self-tapping cortex screws are available and also recommended, except for hard cortical bone of the young adult. Some of the screws are also available in a cannulated version.

2. The cancellous bone screw has a deeper thread, a larger pitch, and typically a larger outer diameter (4.0- to 8.0-mm) than the cortex screws. They are indicated for metaepiphyseal cancellous bone. The screw may be partially or fully threaded. Tapping is recommend to open the cortex and in dense bone of the young adult.

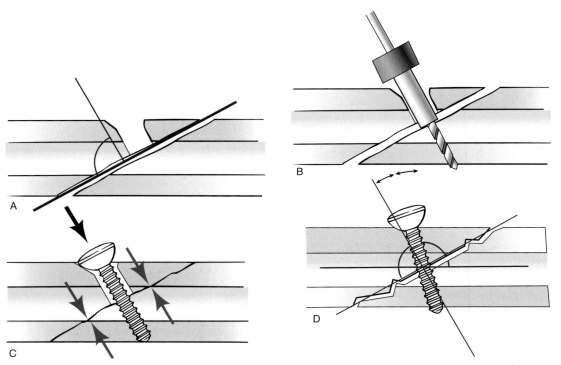

FIGURE 7-18 A. The first step of inserting a lag screw involves drilling the glide hole in the near cortex with a drill bit slightly larger than the major screw diameter. **B.** Into this hole, a drill sleeve is inserted to correctly center the pilot or threaded hole on the opposite or far cortex, which is drilled with a drill bit the same size as the minor diameter of the screw. After measuring the screw length with the depth gauge and tapping the thread in the far cortex, the cortex screw is inserted. **C.** Driving home the screw, the fracture surfaces will be compressed (interfragmentary compression). While the ideal screw direction to generate compression is at right angles to the fracture plane, this is only rarely possible. **D.** Therefore, the screw is directed between the perpendicular to the fracture plane and to that of the bone.

3. The locking head screws of locking plate systems (see Fig. 7-16B) are primarily characterized by the threaded screw head. They may have a larger core diameter and a relatively shallow thread with blunt edges. This increases the strength and interface between screw and cortical bone compared to conventional screws.[73] Locking screws are used in combination with plates that have holes able to accommodate the threaded screw head.

Different Functions of a Screw

Various different screw functions are listed in Table 7-3. Three examples are given in more depth due to their importance in daily operative fracture care.

Lag Screw. One of the basic principles of modern internal fixation is absolute stability thanks to interfragmentary compression provided by a lag screw.[64] A fully threaded conventional cortex screw is acting as a lag screw when the thread engages only in the cortex opposite to the fracture line (far cortex) and not in the cortex close to the screw head (near cortex). This is obtained by first drilling a glide hole with a drill bit slightly larger than the major diameter of the cortex screw. Next, a drill sleeve is inserted into the gliding hole to precisely center the threaded or pilot hole in the opposite cortex colinear with the gliding hole, which is drilled with a smaller drill bit corresponding to the minor diameter of the screw. After measuring the screw length with a depth gauge, the thread in the far cortex is cut with a tap or a self-tapping screw is inserted. As the screw advances in the threaded hole, the head will engage in the near cortex and create preload and compression between the two fragments. It is advisable to apply only about two thirds of the possible torque to a lag screw corresponding to about 2000 to 3000 N.[61,72] The ideal direction of a lag screw, for generation of compressive force, is perpendicular to the fracture plane. As this is often not practical, an inclination halfway between the perpendiculars to the fracture and to the long axis of the bone is typically chosen (see Fig. 7-18). The head of a plate independent lag screw should be countersunk in the underlying cortex, which increases the area of contact between the screw and bone and reduces the risk of stress risers producing cracks. A further advantage of countersinking is reducing the protuberance of the large screw head underneath the skin (e.g., on the tibial crest).

The partially threaded cancellous bone screw will also produce interfragmentary compression, provided that the thread engages only in the fragment opposite to the fracture plane. A

TABLE 7-3	Various Screw Functions and Clinical Examples	
	Function	
Name	**Mechanism**	**Clinical Example**
Nonlocked plate screw	Preload and friction is applied to create force between the plate and the bone	Forearm plating
Lag screw	The glide hole allows compression between bone fragments	Fixation of a butterfly or wedge fragment or medial malleolus fracture
Position screw	Holds anatomic parts in correct relation to each other without compression (i.e., thread hole only, no glide hole)	Syndesmotic screw
Locking head screw	Used exclusively with locked plates; threads in the screw head allow mechanical coupling to a reciprocal thread in the plate and provide angular stability	Complex metaphyseal fracture Osteoporotic
Interlocking screw	Couples an intramedullary nail to the bone to maintain length, alignment, and rotation	Interlocked femoral or tibial intramedullary nail
Anchor screw	A point of fixation used to anchor a wire loop or strong suture	Tension band anchor in a proximal humerus fracture
Push-pull screw	A temporary point of fixation used to reduce a fracture by distraction and/or compression	Use of an articulated compression device
Reduction screw	Conventional screw used through a plate to pull fracture fragments towards the plate; the screw may be removed or exchanged once alignment is obtained	Minimally invasive plate osteosynthesis technique to reduce multifragmentary fracture onto the plate
Poller screw	Screw used as a fulcrum to redirect an intramedullary nail	Proximal tibial fracture during intramedullary nailing

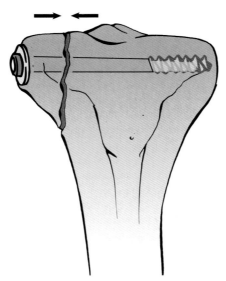

FIGURE 7-19 A partially threaded 6.5-mm cancellous bone screw will act as a lag screw, provided that the thread has its purchase opposite to the fracture line only.

washer may prevent the screw head from sinking into the thin metaphyseal cortex (Fig. 7-19).

Plate Screws. Conventional nonlocked cortex screws used to fix a plate to the bone are called plate screws. They are introduced with a special drill guide that fits into the plate hole either centrally or eccentrically depending on whether axial compression is demanded. The drill bit has the diameter of the minor diameter of the screw, which may be self-tapping or not. By driving home the plate screws, the plate is pressed against the bone which produces preload and friction between the two surfaces.

Positioning Screw. A positioning screw is a fully threaded screw that joins two anatomic parts at a defined distance without compression. The thread is therefore tapped in both cortices. An example is a screw placed between fibula and tibia in a malleolar fracture to secure the syndesmotic ligaments (Fig. 7-20).

Plates

Besides the lag screw as a basic principle of operative fracture fixation, conventional compression plating (Fig. 7-21) is the other principle providing absolute stability and inducing primary or direct bone healing without visible callus. Today, the classical open reduction with considerable exposure of the fracture and internal fixation by plates and screws is being challenged by less invasive and more elastic fixation methods, so called biological techniques. Nevertheless, plating with absolute stability still has its definitive place in operative fracture treatment, especially since we have learned to better protect the delicate soft tissues during open approaches. Fractures of the forearm bones as well as simple metaphyseal fractures of other long bones are good indications for conventional nonlocked plating, so are mal- and nonunions. In articular fractures that require anatomic reduction and rigid fixation by interfragmen-

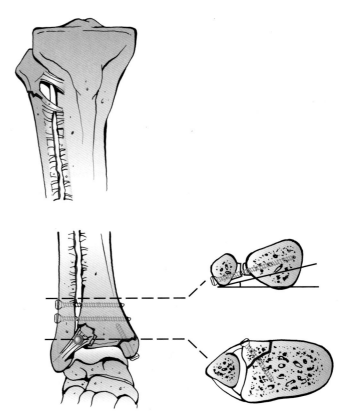

FIGURE 7-20 Example of a cortex screw in the function as a position screw between fibula and tibia to secure the ruptured syndesmosis. A thread is cut in every cortex, thus preventing compression between the two bones. The other screws are lag screws.

tary compression, plates will often support lag screws and/or buttress the metaphysis. However, for most diaphyseal fractures of the femur and tibia, intramedullary nailing is the criterion standard.

Absolute stability results in direct fracture healing, which generally takes longer than healing by callus. Appearance of callus after attempted rigid plate fixation is unexpected and a sign of unplanned instability, which may lead to implant failure, healing delay, or nonunion. The classical technique of compression plating relies on pressing the plate to the bone surface, which may disturb the blood flow to the underlying cortex, leading to local cortical necrosis. This so called footprint of the plate induces a slow cortical remodelling by creeping substitution and revascularization. What was once considered stress protection is now interpreted as disturbed vascularity of the cortex and has been addressed by new plate designs with limited bone contact or more effectively by the internal fixator principle, where there is no direct contact between plate and bone.[60]

Plate Design

Early modern plates had round holes in which the conical screw head had a firm fit. Axial compression was obtained with a removable external device. In 1967, the dynamic compression plate (DCP) designed by Perren introduced a new principle of applying axial compression by leveraging the interaction of a spherical screw head and an inclined oval screw hole (see Fig. 7-17). The oval hole also allowed angulation of the screw in

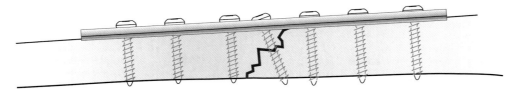

FIGURE 7-21 Protection or neutralization plate to protect a simple fracture. The oblique screw inserted through the plate is a lag screw crossing the fracture plane, which adds to the absolute stability of the fixation.

different directions.[66] The use of special drill guides precisely placed the screws in relation to the plate hole in neutral or compression mode. These features of the DCP greatly extended and facilitated the possibilities of application of plates.

While the original plates were all straight and of two sizes only (4.5-mm narrow and broad), smaller sizes soon followed, as did different designs for special applications such as the angle blade plates for the proximal and distal femur, tubular plates, reconstruction plates, the sliding hip screw, dynamic condylar screws, and other form plates (Fig. 7-22).

A further advancement was the limited contact-DCP which featured a new design of the under surface reducing the area of contact between the plate and the bone to reduce the adverse effects of pressure and friction on bone vascularity (Fig. 7-23). This plate generation, designed with finite element analysis, displayed an even distribution of strength throughout its length, irrespective of the plate holes.[65] All conventional plates usually had to be contoured to match the shape of the bone, as the plate was either pressed against the bone or the bone was pulled towards the plate.

The most recent and most revolutionary design changes to modern plates that also introduced a completely new principles of fixation, the internal fixators or locking plates, will be discussed later in a separate section of this chapter.

Plate Functions

While there are many different designs and dimensions of plates, the function that is assigned to a plate by the surgeon and how it is applied is decisive for the outcome. There are five key functions or modes any plate can have. In order to assign a specific function to a plate, the preoperative plan has to take into account the fracture pattern, its location, the soft tissues, and biomechanical surrounding.

The five functions are:

1. Neutralization or protection
2. Compression
3. Buttressing
4. Tension band
5. Bridging

Neutralization or Protection Plate for Absolute Stability. A simple, torsion, or butterfly fracture of the diaphysis or metaphysis, caused by indirect rotational forces, is best reduced anatomically and fixed by one or two lag screws providing interfragmentary compression. It is normally recommended to protect the lag screw fixation with the addition of a plate in order to protect it or to neutralize any shearing or rotational forces, thereby improving the stability (Fig. 7-24). This type of classical plate application can also be performed with minimal exposure of the fracture site and percutaneous reduction with the help of pointed reduction forceps.

Compression Plate. Axial compression of a transverse fracture of a forearm bone is best obtained by a compression plate. By slightly overbending the plate in relation the shape of the bone and by eccentric placement of the screws, axial compression is obtained. In short oblique fractures, in addition to axial compression, a lag screw inserted through the plate and across the oblique fracture plane will significantly increase the stability of the fixation (see Fig. 7-24). In oblique fractures, the plate is fixed first to the fragment with an obtuse angle, so that when compression is added on the opposite side of the fracture, the fragment locks in the axilla between plate and bone.

Buttress Plate (Antiglide Function). In articular fractures such as malleolar fractures, tibia plateau, or distal radius fractures,

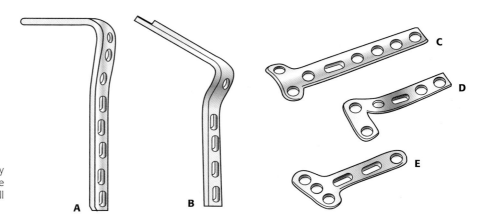

FIGURE 7-22 Different types and forms of early plates: 95 degree **(A)** and 130 degree **(B)** angle blade plates, T **(C)** and L **(D)** plates, and small fragment 3.5 distal radius plates **(E)**.

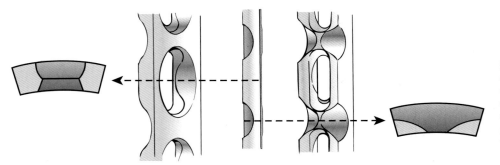

FIGURE 7-23 More recent plate designs (like the limited contact-DCP) feature the dynamic compression unit and have undercuts between the screw holes to reduce the area of contact between the plate and bone. This plate design has uniform strength of the plate throughout the plate.[62]

we can observe how a large fragment has been displaced by shearing forces.[8] To counteract these forces and keep the reduced fragment in place, a plate is best applied in a position that locks the spike of the fragment back in place, thereby preventing any further shearing or gliding of the fragment. Buttress plates are often combined with lag screws either through the plate or independently (Fig. 7-25).

Tension Band Plate. Certain bones such as the femur are loaded eccentrically. The studies of Pauwels[59] revealed that, with weight-bearing, the concave, medial side of the femur is undergoing compressive forces, while the convex, lateral cortex is under tension. An eccentrically applied plate on the convex side of the bone will theoretically convert tensile forces into compression, provided the opposite medial cortex is stable. In a subtrochanteric fracture that is fixed with a plate, this implant will function as a tension band provided the medial cortex, opposite to the plate, has been reduced anatomically without any residual gap (Fig. 7-26).

Bridge Plate. Since the introduction of more biological indirect reduction and minimally invasive techniques with less rigid or elastic fixations providing relative stability, a plate can also be applied as an internal bridging device, similar to an external fixator.[23,76] The best indications for bridge plating are comminuted diaphyseal or metaphyseal fractures that are not suited for intramedullary nailing. While we do not know the ideal working length of a plate precisely, it is recommended to choose a plate about three times as long as the fracture zone and to fix it with only a few firmly anchored screws proximally and distally (Fig. 7-27).

From Biological to Minimally Invasive Plate Fixation

Although the protagonists of modern operative fracture fixation, starting with Albin Lambotte, stressed 100 years ago the importance of gentle soft tissue handling and minimal stripping of the periosteum in order to preserve bone vascularity, the request for anatomic reduction seemed somehow in contradiction with this principle. In inexperienced hands, too wide exposures and extensive denudation of bone occurred all too often, resulting in catastrophes such as delayed or nonunions, infections, or the combination of the two. Mast et al.[48] described in detail the advantages of indirect reduction techniques without exposing the fracture fragments and created the term of "biological plate fixation" with long bridging angle blade or straight plates. In a study comparing a series of subtrochanteric fractures treated by conventional open technique with indirection and bridge plating, it was demonstrated that in the bridge plating group, the time for union was shorter and predictable even without bone graft, the complication rate was lower, and the functional outcome better.[36] An important prerequisite was, however, that the procedure was carefully planned and well performed.

We have learned from closed intramedullary nailing with interlocking that in complex diaphyseal fractures, correct axial and rotational alignment is all that is needed for early callus formation and that anatomic reduction of every fragment is not required.

Krettek et al.[42] further developed these observations and ideas by minimizing the approaches to short incisions far away from the fracture focus and by inserting extra long plates via a bluntly prepared submuscular space close to the bone and across the fracture (Fig. 7-28). The screws were inserted through equally short incisions and straight through the muscles. In

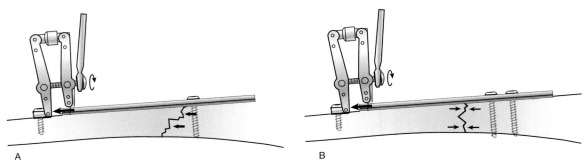

A   B

FIGURE 7-24 Axial compression with a plate can be obtained with the removable, articulated tension device. The plate is first fixed on one side of the fracture and then compressed in the axial direction. In case of an oblique fracture, a lag screw across the fracture plane will increase stability and compress the opposite cortex **(A)**. To obtain an equal compression of both cortices of a transverse fracture, the plate is slightly over contoured before axial compression is applied **(B)**.

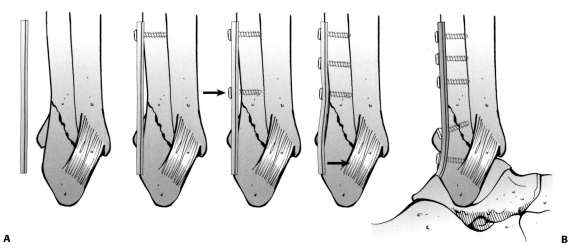

FIGURE 7-25 A buttress plate or antiglide plate has the function of preventing any secondary displacement of an oblique fracture in the metaphysis of a bone. The example shows the application in a malleolar fracture, where the plate is positioned on the posterolateral aspect of the distal fibula. **A.** The different steps and the sequence of introducing the screws are illustrated. **B.** Final construct after addition of lag screw.

cadaver studies, Farouk et al.[15] could show that the perforator vessels were not injured by these tunnelling maneuvers. Similar to the rapid appearance of callus in intramedullary nailing, the healing of these minimally exposed fractures fixed with only relatively stable bridge plates occurred very consistently with early callus formation.

The drawback of minimally invasive techniques is the higher incidence of axial and rotational malalignment just as in intramedullary nailing,[75] especially in the femur. Furthermore, the intraoperative radiation exposure of the patient and staff is higher, but may be reduced when navigation techniques are refined and used more in the future.

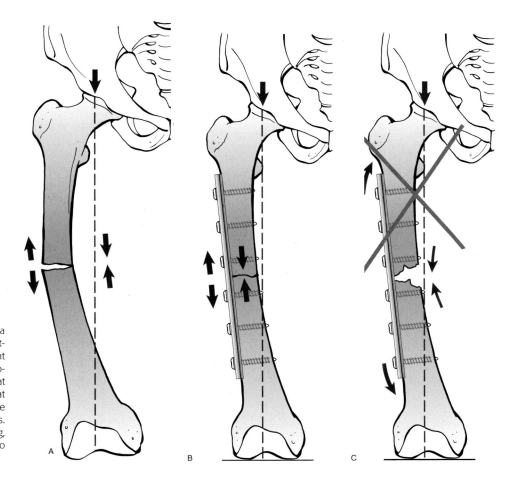

FIGURE 7-26 By placing the plate in a transverse femur fracture **(A)** to the lateral aspect of the femur **(B)**, this implant will undergo tensile forces that are theoretically converted into compression at the fracture site. A precondition is that the bone opposite to the plate has close contact to resist the compressive forces. If the essential medial support is missing, the plate is more likely to break due to fatigue **(C)**.

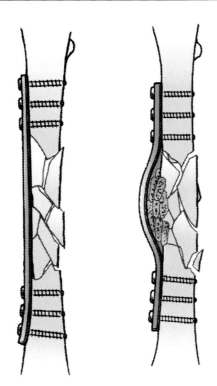

FIGURE 7-27 Bridge plating can be performed with any plate of adequate length. Nevertheless, the new locking plate systems are considered ideally suited for bridge plating and simplify the technique of minimal invasive application. The bridging device should be about three times the length of the fracture zone providing relative stability.

For high-energy articular fractures of the distal femur and proximal and distal tibia that often show extensions into the diaphysis, a combination of open anatomic reduction and stable fixation of the articular block with minimally invasive bridging fixation of the metadiaphysis can be recommended (Fig. 7-29).

LOCKED PLATING—INTERNAL FIXATOR PRINCIPLE

In an endeavour to further reduce or abolish the area of contact and friction between a plate and the bone surface, Tepic and Perren[78] reported about a new principle of fracture fixation based on what they called the internal fixator (Fig. 7-30A,B). The first development was the point-contact fixator (PC-Fix), where every screw head was locked in the plate hole through a tight fit between the conical shape of the head and the plate hole (Fig. 7-30C). The stability of the fixation was therefore not based on compressing the plate onto the bone or on preload and friction, but depended on the stiffness of the plate screw construct. As the locked plate is not based on friction between the plate and the bone, there is no requirement for contact with the bone surface. Leaving a narrow free space between the implant and the bone preserves the periosteal blood flow and the underlying cortex remains vital, which appears to increase resistance against infection.[14] A further feature of the locking head screws is the angular stability of the construct, which prevents any secondary displacement or collapse of fixation.[13] There is no need for a precise contouring of the plate to the shape of the bone with a pure locked plate construct, as plate is not pressed against bone as in conventional nonlocked plating. Last but not least, the locking head screws often have a larger core diameter (4.0- vs. 3.0-mm), which increases their strength, while the thread may be shallow as it adds very little to the resistance to pullout. Thanks to the angular stability of the screws, any bending forces will have to displace and pullout

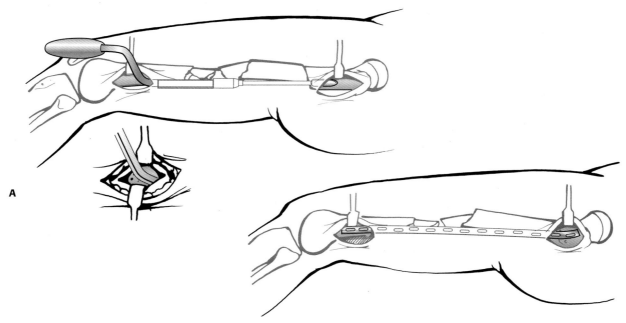

FIGURE 7-28 Minimally invasive plate osteosynthesis with blunt percutaneous tunnelling distally **(A)** and insertion of a plate without exposing the comminuted fracture zone **(B)**.

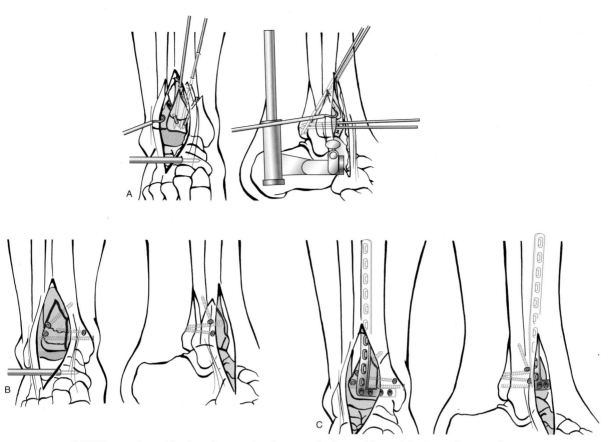

FIGURE 7-29 A combination of conventional open reduction and internal fixation with minimally invasive plate osteosynthesis in a pilon fracture. **A.** After initial provisional treatment with a bridging external fixator, the articular block is reconstructed anatomically and held with K-wires. **B.** The articular fragments are then fixed by lag screws. **C.** To secure the screw fixation and to bridge the metaphysis, an anterolateral L-shaped pilon plate is inserted percutaneously with minimally invasive plate osteosynthesis technique.

the entire screw–plate construct together and not one screw after the other as in conventional plating (Fig. 7-30D,E).[121] This feature has proven most useful in poor quality or osteoporotic bone as well as in periprosthetic fractures, where often only monocortical screws can be inserted beside the shaft of a prosthesis.[31]

Advantages of the internal fixator due to angular stability of the construct:

- No requirement for direct contact to the underlying bone, preservation of periosteal blood flow
- Improved construct stability in osteopenic bone
- Resistance to secondary collapse or screw displacement
- No need for precise plate contouring

About 10 years before Tepic and Perren,[78] a group of Polish surgeons[67] had developed a similar system with conventional plates and screws, which was applied to the medial aspect of the tibia but outside the skin and where the so called "platform screws" were locked with some sort of washers in the screw holes (Fig. 7-31). Also, Reinhold in 1931 and Wolter in 1927 had already described the idea of angular stability or locked plating.

The clinical applicability and validity of the internal fixator principle was shown in a series of over 350 forearm fractures

that were fixed with the PC-Fix.[21] The next development was the locked plate less invasive stabilization system (LISS) for the distal femur.[39] It combines the fixed angle device with the possibility of a minimally invasive plate insertion technique using a special jig and monocortical and self-drilling and self-tapping screws that are introduced through short stab incisions. The advantages of the monocortical screws were seen in the single step insertion through stab incisions and a jig. They, however, lack torsional control seen with bicortical screws. Locked plating systems (Figs. 7-32 and 7-33) have improved the surgical fixation of distal femur fractures by making the clinical results more reliable especially in complex fracture situations, such as osteoporotic and periprosthetic fractures.[39,41,42,75] While the original LISS only accepted locking head screws, there was a rising demand for the ability to also use conventional screws in a plate with locking capability.[16,41] With the further development of locked plates, more and more plates have become precontoured to fit the periarticular anatomic regions (Fig. 7-34).

Available plates now cover the full range of plate functions, including the advantages of both locked and nonlocked plating.[22,78]

- Conventional compression, protection, or buttress plates with conventional nonlocked screws

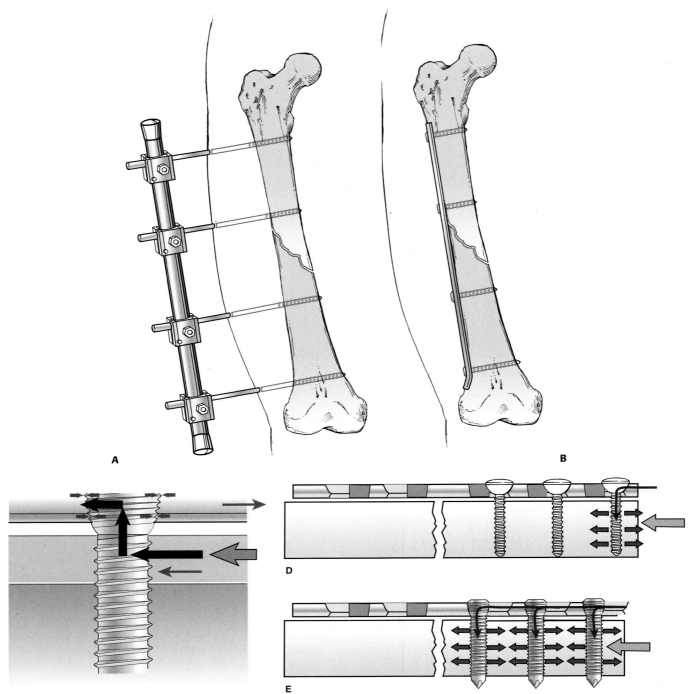

FIGURE 7-30 The principle of the "internal fixator" is based on moving an external fixator **(A)** close to the bone and underneath the soft tissue envelope **(B)**. A plate replaces the longitudinal rod and the locking head screws provide the angular stability of the clamps and Schanz screws. **C.** The force transfer in the internal fixator principle occurs primarily through the locking head screws across the plate and fracture. It is not dependent on preload and friction as in conventional plating, but rather on the stiffness of the fixator device. The locked plate does not have to touch the bone surface and therefore interferes less with the periosteal blood flow.[79] **D.** In conventional plating, the screw head is allowed to toggle under loading. This process of load concentration starts at the end screw and continues from one screw to the next until the plate is completely pulled out. **E.** In locked plates, the angular stable screws prevent a load concentration at a single bone screw interface by distributing the load more evenly. To pull out a locked plate, much greater forces are needed as all screws have to be loosened at the same time.[18,67]

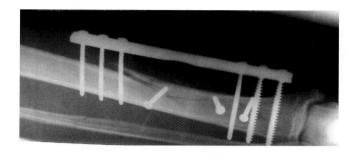

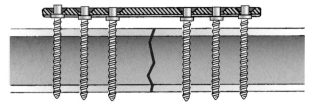

FIGURE 7-31 A locked plate as it was developed by the Polish Zespol Group in the 1980s, where the plate remains outside the skin cover. The screws are locked with some sort of washers in the plate holes.

- Pure locked plating with all locking head screws
- Hybrid plating with a combination of conventional non-locked screws (to use plate as template for reduction) and locked screws (for advantages of fixed angle support of end segment fractures and improved fixation in osteoporotic bone)

When using hybrid plating technique, certain technical aspects

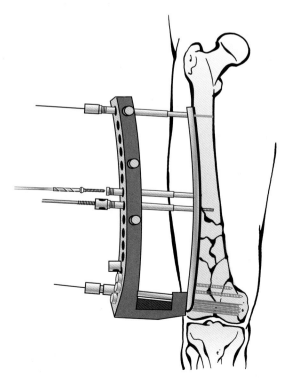

FIGURE 7-32 Locked plate fixation for distal femur fractures. After reconstruction and preliminary fixation of the articular fracture components under direct vision, the plate can be inserted in a submuscular space with a special jig. The locking head screws are introduced percutaneously through the jig.

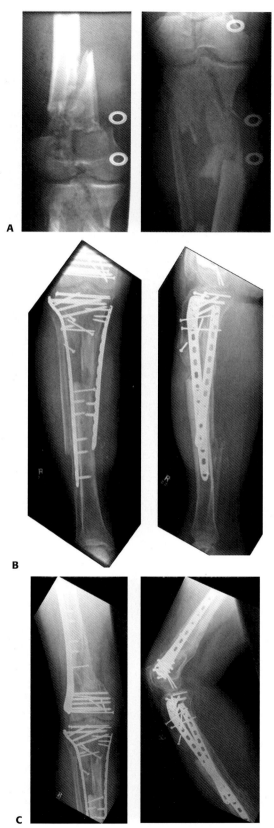

FIGURE 7-33 Clinical example of a "floating knee," proximal tibia combined with a distal femur fractures, extending into both shafts and extensive open soft tissue injury **(A)**, fixed by locking plates **(B)**. After reconstruction of articular congruency with lag screws, the locking plates were placed percutaneously to the lateral aspect of the tibia. **C.** Follow-up after 1 year with good restitution of function.

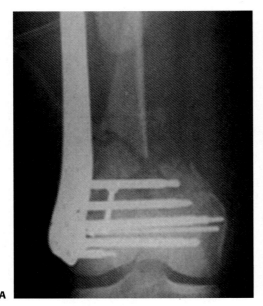
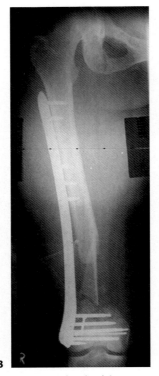
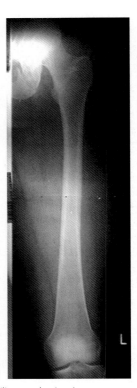

A   B   C

FIGURE 7-34 Precontoured implants, like the locking plate for the distal femur, can facilitate reduction in complex fracture situations. This open fracture had significant metaphyseal bone loss. In accordance to the anatomic fit of the plate, the distal screws were placed parallel to the anteroposterior joint line of the distal femur. **(A)** Following this intraoperative guideline, the postoperative films show a good alignment **(B)** similar to the uninjured contralateral side **(C)** (further secondary bone graft was required to bridge the defect).

have to be followed to avoid failures. Once a locking head screw has been inserted in a bone segment, no conventional screws should be added in the same segment, as this would create unwanted tension forces within the plate and bone. The sequence should be "lag first, lock second." A reduction screw may be used to approximate a fragment to the locked plate as an indirect reduction tool and then locking screws are added to keep the fragment in place to the plate.

INTRAMEDULLARY FIXATION TECHNIQUES

Introduction and History

The medullary canal of a long bone offers itself to accept splinting devices of different designs and sizes. The major advantage is the biomechanical ideal position of the implant in the center of the bone. On the other hand, a major problem is how to control axial displacement or neutralize rotational forces. The interlocking techniques have helped to solve these drawbacks to a great extent. Depending on the anatomy, the insertion can usually occur closed, without exposure of the fracture focus, in an ante- or retrograde direction. A closed procedure would require the availability of an image intensifier in the operating room for reduction and interlocking.

Today, intramedullary nails are the implant of choice for the femoral and tibial diaphysis. Recently, with new nail designs, the spectrum of indications has been extended to even intra-

articular fractures of these bones (Fig. 7-35). For the humeral shaft, intramedullary nails are an option competing with the still very popular and more versatile plating techniques. Flexible nails as used in pediatric fractures[45] have been advocated for the clavicle, while nailing of the forearm bones has not yet proved to be equal or superior for the fixation for ulna and radius fractures due to the difficulty of reliable locking systems that can control the rotational forces.

Historically, the first description of an intramedullary splinting with ivory pegs goes back to the nineteenth century.[76] Hey-Groves[26] used solid metal rods for femur fractures and pointed to the rapid healing, preservation of soft tissues, and periosteum as well as the abolition of prolonged plaster cast immobilization. The Rush brothers[69] presented their technique with multiple flexible intramedullary pins in 1927. The most important contributions to intramedullary fixation, however, came from Gerhard Küntscher[43] (1900–1972) who performed a number of animal experiments and perfected not only the nailing technique but also the implant shape and design. He requested a tight fit between nail and bone to achieve a higher stability and to allow compression of the mostly transverse fractures under load. To extend the area of contact within the medullary cavity, he started to ream the canal in order to insert thicker, longer, and slotted cloverleaf nails. Herzog,[25] in 1950, introduced the tibia nail with a proximal bend and lateral slots at the distal end to accept antirotational wires. Shortly before his death, Küntscher[43] designed the "detensor nail" for comminuted femur

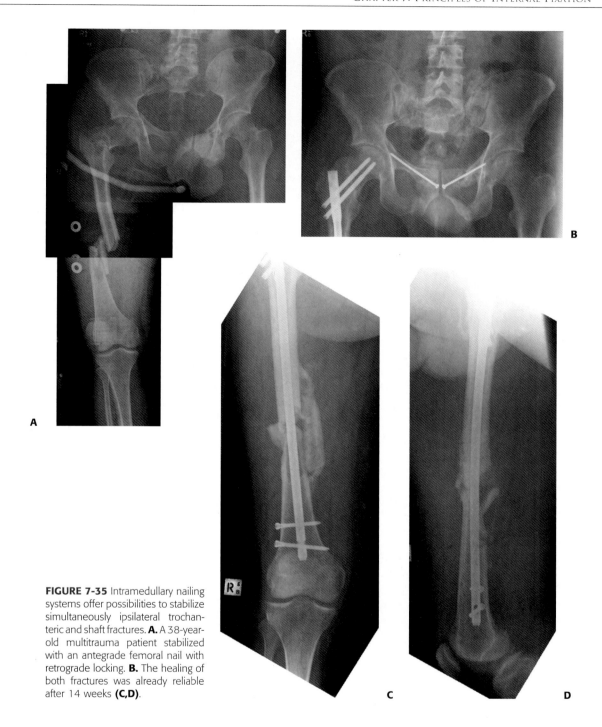

FIGURE 7-35 Intramedullary nailing systems offer possibilities to stabilize simultaneously ipsilateral trochanteric and shaft fractures. **A.** A 38-year-old multitrauma patient stabilized with an antegrade femoral nail with retrograde locking. **B.** The healing of both fractures was already reliable after 14 weeks **(C,D).**

fractures with a sort of interlocking device. This idea was further developed by Klemm and Schnellmann[38] in Germany and Kempf et al.[34] in France and were precursors to today's interlocking nails.

Mechanics of Intramedullary Nailing

Küntscher's[43] original concept was based on the principle of elastic deformation or "elastic locking" of the nail within the medullary canal. To increase the elasticity, the hollow cloverleaf nail was slotted, and reaming of the canal enlarged the area of contact and friction between the nail and the bone (working

length). Nails with larger diameters had an increased bending and torsional stiffness. The weak point of the first nails remained the poor resistance to axial (telescoping) forces and rotation, especially in comminuted fractures. The introduction of interlocking screws and bolts at the proximal and distal end of the nail addressed these issues rather well; there remains, however, the problem of the strength and purchase of the locking screws in the bone. This problem is not yet completely solved as twisted blades and an increase in screw diameter and number (larger and more holes) may weaken the nail ends. Based on the positive experience and data of Lottes,[46] who presented very low infection rates in open tibia fractures with the use of solid nails that were introduced without reaming, thinner, solid tibia nails with holes for interlocking were developed. At the beginning, those thin nails were to be inserted without reaming but with mandatory interlocking as a temporary splint in open tibia fractures.[70] Animal experiments showed that after nail insertion, the endosteal blood supply was not destroyed to the same extent as after reaming and also that the resistance to infection was much higher if solid nails were compared with tubular ones.[50] The clinical experience as to the infection rate in open fractures was most encouraging; however, the time to union took longer, especially in the majority of cases where the original concept of secondary exchange nailing to a thicker nail was not followed. The enthusiasm for the new nails without reaming rapidly extended their indications and use also to closed and highly complex tibia and femur fractures. This resulted in a higher incidence of delayed and malunions due to a poorer mechanical stiffness of the construct, especially in long bone fractures of the lower extremity.[9,12,70]

Pathophysiology of Intramedullary Nailing

Depending on the surgical technique, nail design, and anatomic region, the use of intramedullary nails has both local and systemic effects, some of which may be beneficial while others may be detrimental to the patient and fracture healing.

Local Effects

The insertion of a nail into the medullary canal is inevitably associated with damage to the endosteal blood supply, which was shown to be reversible within 8 to 12 weeks.[74] Experimental data have also shown that the cortical blood perfusion is significantly reduced after reaming of the medullary canal, if compared to a series without reaming.[37] Accordingly, the return of cortical blood flow takes considerably longer after reaming than in the unreamed cases, which may have an influence on the resistance to infection, especially in open fractures. Furthermore, tight fitting nails appear to compromise the cortical blood flow to a higher degree than loose fitting ones.[30] Reaming of a narrow medullary canal may be associated with a risk of heat necrosis of the bone and surrounding tissues especially if blunt reamers and/or a tourniquet are used.[32,56] On the other hand, the bone debris produced during the reaming has been shown to act like an autogenous bone graft, enhancing fracture healing.[17,27] Meta-analysis of current clinical studies found "gentle" reaming superior to the undreamed technique for reliable healing of long bone fractures in closed and low degree open fractures.[9]

Systemic Response

Reaming of the medullary canal has been associated with pulmonary embolization, coagulation disorders, humoral, neural, immunologic, and inflammatory reactions. The development of posttraumatic pulmonary failure after early femoral nailing in the polytrauma patient with chest injury appears to be more frequent following reaming of the medullary canal than without it.[58] In clinical and experimental studies, the passage of large thrombi into pulmonary circulation has been demonstrated with intraoperative echocardiography especially during the reaming process and, to lesser extent, when introducing the reaming guide.[80] Measurements of the intramedullary pressure have shown values between 420 and 1510 mm Hg during ream-

ing procedures compared with 40 to 70 mm Hg when thin solid nails were inserted without reaming.[52,53] Nevertheless, there is an ongoing controversy between the advocators of reamed nailing also in the multiply injured patient and those who are recommending the use of thinner solid or cannulated nails without reaming. The young adult with a simple transverse femoral shaft fracture and a high injury severity score (>25) appears to have an increased risk for pulmonary complications, which is why there is the recommendation for a staged nailing procedure according to the concept of damage control surgery (DCS) under such circumstances. DCS starts as soon as possible with the stabilization of the femoral shaft fracture with an external fixator followed by a conversion to an intramedullary nail after 5 to 10 days (window of opportunity).[33] The described systemic responses of intramedullary nailing of femoral shaft fractures seem to be much more critical than in tibial shaft fractures, where such effects have hardly ever been observed.

Implants for Nailing

There is a great variety of intramedullary nails and entire nailing systems available for the femur, tibia, and humerus. Forearm nails are also on the market, but they have not proven to be superior or as versatile as the fixation with plates. Originally, intramedullary nails were offered in a tubular, usually slotted form, while today solid and especially cannulated nails are most popular. In children, the elastic nails have become the implant of choice for long bone fractures.[45] The implant material is either stainless steel or a titanium alloy. The holes or openings for interlocking devices are usually situated at either end of the implant and oriented in different directions; some nails also have locking possibilities throughout the entire nail length.

Accordingly, the indications have increased from midshaft fractures to fractures involving the proximal and distal femur and tibia as well as the proximal humerus.

The nail design and the dimensions have to be adapted to the shape of the medullary cavity and the bone. The correct diameter and length of the nail should to be selected beforehand; unfortunately, the accuracy of templates is rather poor. The best tool is probably a radiolucent ruler placed on the intact contralateral leg under C-arm control or measurement with the intramedullary guidewire.

A very important issue is the correct entry point and starting trajectory of the nail, which varies from one type of nail to the other (Fig. 7-36). A misplaced starting point may lead to axial and/or rotational malalignment that is usually tricky to correct; even additional stress fractures have been described. It is therefore advisable to study the technical guide of a specific type of nail carefully and to check the correct entry point and direction of the guidewire with the image intensifier preferably in two planes.

Positioning of the Patient for Intramedullary Nailing and Reduction

Every surgeon has a preferred way of how to nail a specific bone, with or without a fracture table, with the help of a distractor, or in a supine or in a lateral decubitus position, etc. As each way has its pros and cons, much depends on the experience of the OR team and the surgeon. It appears most important for any patient positioning that the nail entry point can be clearly seen in two projections with the C-arm and the same holds true for the distal locking procedure.

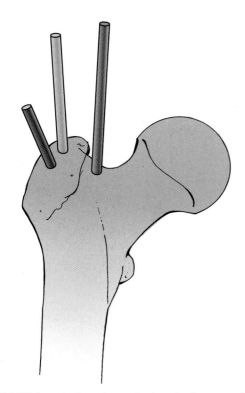

FIGURE 7-36 Various starting points and trajectories for antegrade femoral nailing. The correct entry point is crucial, but may vary from one type of nail to the other. (Always study the recommendations of the manufacturer as to the recommended nail entry point!)

Reduction of fresh diaphyseal fractures is rarely a problem. The guidewire can usually be inserted easily into the opposite fragment or a solid nail or reduction device can be used as a joystick. In metaphyseal fractures, the correct alignment may be much more difficult especially in the proximal or distal tibia. Blocking or Poller screws[40] may be helpful to guide the nail in the right direction (Fig. 7-37). The technique of the Poller screws can be used to decrease the functional width of a wide metaphyseal cavity or to force and redirect the nail into a particular direction for a better alignment or improved stabilization. The use of the screw can be temporary or definitive. This technique is especially helpful to steer the nail into the "right" direction, after being misplaced in the first attempt.

Locking Technique

Most nails are inserted with a special handle which also serves as an aiming device for locking the driving end of the nail with bolts, blades, or locking screws. Placement of the far locking device is usually more difficult as during the insertion, most nails are more or less distorted so that the locking holes are not in the original alignment anymore. Far locking must therefore be done in a "free hand" technique or with the aid of aiming devices usually mounted on the drill. Tight fitting nails tend to distract the fractures resulting in wide gaps, which may lead to increased compartment pressure as well as to delayed or nonunion.[5] It is therefore recommended to lock first at the far end, then to backslap the nail, and then to lock the driving end. Finally, locking can be done in a static or dynamic mode,

while it is advisable to use at least two locking screws at either end of the nail to control rotation in a reliable way. Static locking is recommended for complex fractures to prevent telescoping, while dynamic locking is advisable in short oblique or transverse fracture to allow fracture compression during weight-bearing.

Assessment of Axial Alignment and Rotation in Intramedullary Nailing

In simple fractures, axial alignment is not a problem. However, in more complex, segmental, or comminuted fractures or in floating knee injuries, it may be difficult to judge the correct axial alignment. The most useful intraoperative indicator of an acceptable coronal plane alignment is when the nail entrance point is correct and the nail is centrally placed in the distal fragment (or proximal segment in retrograde nailing). In the lower extremity, the long cable of electrocautery, a C-arm, and the patient in supine position is helpful to judge the right direction. The cable is centered to the femoral head and distally to the middle of the ankle joint under radiographic view. At the level of the knee, the cable should now run exactly through the center of the joint as well. Any deviation indicates an axial malalignment in the coronal plane.

The clinical assessment of the rotation intraoperatively is more difficult and less accurate. There are several radiologic signs like the size of the diameter of two adjacent fragments or the projection of the greater trochanter in relation to the patella in the anteroposterior view, but they are not very reliable. With the patient still on the OR table, internal and external rotation can be performed to reliably check the rotation in comparison with the uninjured side. The most accurate evaluation is with a few CT slices through the knee and the hip joint allowing a comparison with the uninjured side.[24]

The intramedullary nail to fix diaphyseal fractures of the long bones is the criterion standard. It is a minimally invasive procedure allowing early weight-bearing and has a good chance of rapid and undisturbed fracture healing.

TENSION BAND PRINCIPLE

Pauwels[59] was the one who observed that a curved tubular structure when subjected to an axial load always presents a tension side on the convexity and a compression side on the concavity. The same occurs when a straight tube or bone is loaded eccentrically like in the femur, where tensile forces are on the lateral and compression on the medial side. By applying a tension band device laterally, these tensile forces are converted to compression forces, assuming the opposite side is stable and has good contact.

In fractures where muscle pull tends to displace fragments as in the olecranon, patella, or the avulsion fracture of the greater tuberosity of the humerus, a tension band will neutralize the distraction forces and underflexion of the joint the fragments will be compressed (Fig. 7-38). We therefore speak of dynamic tension bands providing absolute stability and encourage the patients with tension band fixation of one of these joints to regularly perform flexion exercises.

In principle, any fixation device, plate, wire loop, and even an external fixator, if applied correctly to the tension of a fractured bone, can act as a tension band. The tension band device

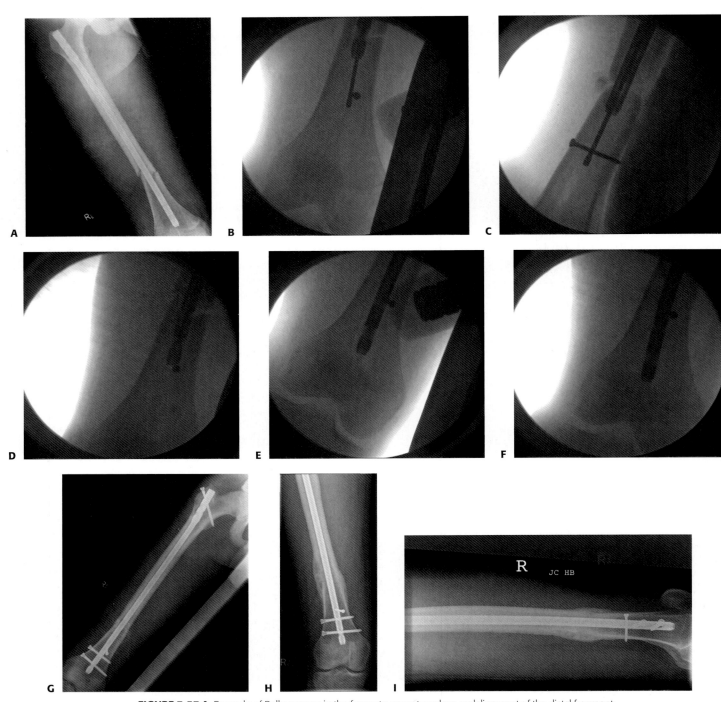

FIGURE 7-37 A. Example of Poller screws in the femur to correct a valgus malalignment of the distal fragment. After the nail was backed out, a 3.5-mm cortical screw was placed **(B,C)** to steer the nail into the appropriate position **(D–F)**. **G–I.** Postoperative control and healing after 1 year. In this case, to correct valgus with a blocking screw, the screw must be placed lateral to the nail and near the fracture or medial to the nail and far from the fracture.

must withstand tensile forces, the bone must resist compressive forces, and the cortex opposite to the tension band must be exactly reduced without a gap.

The most commonly used 1.4- or 1.6-mm metal wire can be inserted through a drill hole in the bone, or it can be placed through the Sharpey fibers of a tendon insertion such as at the patella or it may be looped around a screw head or a K-wire. The wire loop should always be placed eccentrically to the load axis (e.g., in front of the patella and not around it) (see Fig. 7-38). Wire withstands tensile forces quite well; however, if bending forces are added it will easily break. The same is true for any type of plate.

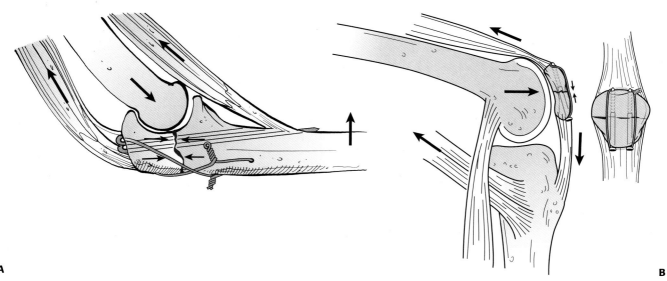

A   B

FIGURE 7-38 A. An atypical example of tension band fixation of the olecranon with two K-wires and a figure of eight tension band wiring. **B.** Tension band fixation of a transverse patella fracture with a tension band wire loop. Note that the tension band device must lie eccentrically on the tensile side of the bone and that this dynamic fixation is enhanced by flexion of the joint.

In mal- and nonunions, we often can observe an angular deformity. Any fixation device should therefore be applied to the convex side of the deformity, in such a way as to act as a tension band, which then automatically induces compression and enhances bony union (Fig. 7-39).

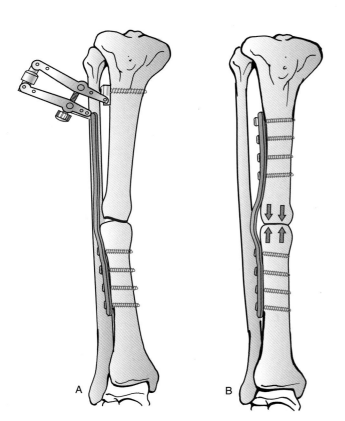

FIGURE 7-39 In mal- and nonunions with deformity **(A)**, the plate applied to the convex or tension side of the bone acts as a tension band and compresses the bone ends **(B)**.

REFERENCES

1. Audigé L, Griffin D, Bhandari M, et al. Path analysis of factors for delayed healing and nonunion in 416 operatively treated tibial shaft fractures. Clin Orthop Relat Res 2005;438:221–232.
2. Babst R, Hehl M, Regazzoni P. LISS Tractor. Kombination des less invasive stabilization systems (LISS) mit dem AO-Distraktor fuer distale Femur- und proximale Tibiafrakturen. Unfallchirurg 2001;104:530–535.
3. Badia JM, Torres JM, Tur C, et al. Saline wound irrigation reduces the postoperative infection rate in guinea pigs. J Surg Res 1996;63:457–459.
4. Baumgaertel F, Dahlen C, Stiletto R, et al. Technique of using the AO-femoral distractor for femoral IM nailing. J Orthop Trauma 1994;8:315–321.
5. Bhandari M, Guyatt GH, Tong D, et al. Reamed versus nonreamed IM nailing of lower extremity long bone fractures: a systematic overview and meta-analysis. J Orthop Trauma 2000;14:2–9.
6. Bhandari M, Tornetta P 3rd, Sprague S, et al. Predictors of reoperation following operative management of fractures of the tibial shaft. J Orthop Trauma 2003;17(5):353–361.
7. Boxma H, Broekhuizen T, Patka P, et al. Randomized controlled trial of single dose antibiotic prophylaxis in surgical treatment of closed fractures: the Dutch Trauma Trial. Lancet 1996;347:1133–1137
8. Brunner CF, Weber BG. Antigleitplatte, In: Brunner CF, Weber BG, eds. Besondere Osteosynthesetechniken. Berlin: Springer, 1981.
9. Canadian Orthopedic Trauma Society. Nonunion following intramedullary nailing of the femur with and without reaming. Results of a multicenter randomized clinical trial. J Bone Joint Surg Am 2003;85-A(11):2093–2096.
10. Chan PS, Klimkiewicz JJ, Luchetti WT, et al. Impact of CT scan on treatment plan and fracture classification of tibial plateau fractures. J Orthop Trauma 1997;11:484–489.
11. Claes LE, Augat P, Suger G, et al. Influence of size and stability of the osteotomy gap on the success of fracture healing. J Orthop Res 1997;15(4):577–584.
12. Court-Brown CM, Christie J, McQueen MM. Closed intramedullary tibial nailing. Its use in closed and type I open fractures. J Bone Joint Surg Br 1990;72(4):605–611.
13. Egol KA, Kubiak EN, Fulkerson E, et al. Biomechanics of locked plates and screws. J Orthop Trauma 2004;18(8):488–493.
14. Eijer H, Hanke C, Arens S, et al. PC Fix and local infection resistance—influence of implant design on postoperative infection development, clinical and experimental results. Injury 2001;32(Suppl 2):38–42.
15. Farouk O, Krettek C, Miclau T, et al. Minimally invasive plate osteosynthesis: does percutaneous plating disrupt femoral blood supply less than the traditional technique? J Orthop Trauma 1999;13(6):401–406.
16. Frigg R. Locking compression plate (LCP). An osteosynthesis plate based on the dynamic compression plate and the point contact fixator (PC-Fix). Injury 2001;32(Suppl 2):63–66.
17. Frolke JP, Bakker FC, Patka P, et al. Reaming debris in osteotomized sheep tibiae. J Trauma 2001;50:65–69.
18. Gautier E, Sommer C. Guidelines for the clinical application of the LCP. Injury 2003;34(Suppl 2):B63–B76.
19. Georgiadis GM, Burgar AM. Percutaneous skeletal joysticks for closed reduction of femoral shaft fractures during IM nailing. J Orthop Trauma 2001;15:570–571.
20. Gustilo RB, Mendoza RM, Williams DN. Problems in the management of type III (severe) open fractures: a new classification of type III open fractures. J Trauma 1984;24:742–746.
21. Haas N, Hauke C, Schutz M, et al. Treatment of diaphyseal fractures of the forearm using the Point Contact Fixator (PC-Fix): results of 387 fractures of a prospective multicentric study (PC-Fix II). Injury 2001;32(Suppl 2):B51–B62.

22. Haidukewych GJ, Ricci W. Locked plating in orthopaedic trauma: a clinical update. J Am Acad Orthop Surg 2008;16(6):347–355.
23. Heitemeyer U, Kemper F, Hierholzer G, et al. Severely comminuted femoral shaft fractures: treatment by bridging-plate osteosynthesis. Arch Orthop Trauma Surg 1987;106:327–330.
24. Hernandez RJ, Tachdjian MO, Poznanski AK, et al. CT determination of femoral torsion. AJR Am.J Roentgenol 1981;137:97–101.
25. Herzog K. Die Technik der geschlossenen Marknagelung frischer Tibiafrakturen mit dem Rohrschlitznagel. Chirurg 1958;29:501–506.
26. Hey-Groves EW. Ununited fractures with special reference to gunshot injuries and the use of bone grafting. J Bone Joint Surg Br 1918;6:203–228.
27. Hoegel F, Mueller CA, Peter R, et al. Bone debris: dead matter or vital osteoblasts. J Trauma 2004;56:363–367.
28. Holzach P, Matter P, Minter J. Arthroscopically assisted treatment of lateral tibial plateau fractures in skiers: use of a cannulated reduction system. J Orthop Trauma 1994;8:273–281.
29. Hüfner T, Gebhard F, Grützner PA, et al. Which navigation when? Injury 2004;35(Suppl 1):30–34.
30. Hupel TM, Aksenov SA, Schemitsch EH. Cortical bone blood flow in loose- and tight-fitting unreamed locked IM nailing: a canine segmental tibia fracture model. J Orthop Trauma 1998;12:127–135.
31. Kaab MJ, Stockle U, Schutz M, et al. Stabilization of periprosthetic fractures with angular stable internal fixation: a report of 13 cases. Arch Orthop Trauma Surg 2006;126(2):105–110.
32. Karunakar MA, Frankenburg EP, Le TT, et al. The thermal effects of intramedullary reaming. J Orthop Trauma 2004;18(10):674–679.
33. Keel M, Trentz O. Pathophysiology of polytrauma. Injury 2005;36(6):691–709.
34. Kempf I, Jaeger JH, North J, et al. L'enclouage centro-medullaire du femur et du tibia selon la technique de Kuntscher. Interet du verrouillage du clou. Etude experimentale. Acta Orthop Belg 1976;42(Suppl 1):29–43.
35. Kendoff D, Citak M, Gardner MJ, et al. Navigated femoral nailing using noninvasive registration of the contralateral intact femur to restore anteversion. Technique and clinical use. J Orthop Trauma 2007;21(10):725–730.
36. Kinast C, Bolhofner BR, Mast JW, et al. Subtrochanteric fractures of the femur. Results of treatment with the 95 degrees condylar blade-plate. Clin Orthop Relat Res 1989;238:122–130.
37. Klein MP, Rahn BA, Frigg R, et al. Reaming versus nonreaming in medullary nailing: interference with cortical circulation of the canine tibia. Arch Orthop Trauma Surg 1990;109:314–316.
38. Klemm K, Schellmann WD. Dynamische und statische Verriegelung des Marknagels. Monatsschr Unfallheilkd Versicher Versorg Verkehrsmed 1972;75:568–575.
39. Kregor PJ, Hughes JL, Cole PA. Fixation of distal femoral fractures above total knee arthroplasty utilizing the less invasive stabilization system (L.I.S.S.). Injury 2001;32(Suppl 3):SC64–SC75.
40. Krettek C, Miclau T, Schandelmaier P, et al. The mechanical effect of blocking screws ("Poller screws") in stabilizing tibia fractures with short proximal or distal fragments after insertion of small-diameter IM nails. J Orthop Trauma 1999;13:550–553.
41. Krettek C, Muller M, Miclau T. Evolution of minimally invasive plate osteosynthesis (MIPO) in the femur. Injury 2001;32(Suppl 3):SC14–SC23.
42. Krettek C, Schandelmaier P, Miclau T, et al. Transarticular joint reconstruction and indirect plate osteosynthesis for complex distal supracondylar femoral fractures. Injury 1997;28(Suppl 1):A31–A41.
43. Kuntscher G. Praxis der Marknagelung. Stuttgart, Germany: Schattauer, 1962.
44. Lambotte A. Chirurgie Operatoire des Fractures. Paris, France: Masson Editors, 1913.
45. Ligier JN, Metaizeau JP, Prevot J, et al. Elastic stable IM nailing of femoral shaft fractures in children. J Bone Joint Surg Br 1988;70:74–77.
46. Lottes JO. Medullary nailing of the tibia with the triflange nail. Clin Orthop Relat Res 1974;105:53–66.
47. Magid D, Michelson JD, Ney DR, et al. Adult ankle fractures: comparison of plain films and interactive two- and three-dimensional CT scans. AJR Am J Roentgenol 1990;154:1017–1023.
48. Mast J, Jakob R, Ganz R. Planning and Reduction Technique in Fracture Surgery. Berlin: Springer-Verlag, 1996.
49. Mehta JA, Bain GI, Heptinstall RJ. Anatomical reduction of intra-articular fractures of the distal radius. An arthroscopically assisted approach. J Bone Joint Surg Br 2000;82:79–86.
50. Melcher GA, Metzdorf A, Schlegel U, et al. Influence of reaming versus nonreaming in intramedullary nailing on local infection rate: experimental investigation in rabbits. J Trauma 1995;39(6):1123–1128.
51. Mubarak SJ, Hargens AR. Acute compartment syndromes. Surg Clin North Am 1983;63(3):539–565.
52. Muller C, Frigg R, Pfister U. Effect of flexible drive diameter and reamer design on the increase of pressure in the medullary cavity during reaming. Injury 1993;24(Suppl 3):S40–S47.
53. Muller C, McIff T, Rahn BA, et al. Influence of the compression force on the IM pressure development in reaming of the femoral medullary cavity. Injury 1993;24(Suppl 3):S36–S39.
54. Muller ME, Allgower M, Schneider R, et al. Manual of Internal Fixation. Heidelberg: Springer; 1991.
55. Ochsner PE, Baumgart F, Kohler G. Heat-induced segmental necrosis after reaming of one humeral and two tibial fractures with a narrow medullary canal. Injury 1998;29(Suppl 2):B1–10.
56. Oestern HJ, Tscherne H. Pathophysiology and classification of soft tissue injuries associated with fractures. In: Tscherne H, Gotzen L, eds. Fractures with Soft Tissue Injury. Berlin: Springer, 1984.
57. Paiement GD, Renaud E, Dagenais G, et al. Double-blind randomized prospective study of the efficacy of antibiotic prophylaxis for open reduction and internal fixation of closed ankle fractures. J Orthop Trauma 1994;8:64–66.
58. Pape HC, Giannoudis PV, Grimme K, et al. Effects of IM femoral fracture fixation: what is the impact of experimental studies in regards to the clinical knowledge? Shock 2002;18:291–300.
59. Pauwels F. Biomechanics of the Locomotor Apparatus. Berlin: Springer, 1980.
60. Perren SM. Evolution of the internal fixation of long bone fractures. The scientific basis of biological internal fixation: choosing a new balance between stability and biology. J Bone Joint Surg Br 2002;84(8):1093–1110.
61. Perren SM. Force measurements in screw fixation. J Biomech 1976;9:669–675.
62. Perren SM. The concept of biological plating using the limited contact-dynamic compression plate (LC-DCP). Scientific background, design, and application. Injury 1991;22(Suppl 1):1–41.
63. Perren SM, Cordey J. The Concept of Interfragmentary Strain. Berlin: Springer-Verlag, 1980.
64. Perren SM, Frigg R, Hehli M, et al. Lag screw. In: Ruedi TP, Murphy WM, eds. AO Principles of Fracture Management. Stuttgart: Thieme, 2000.
65. Perren SM., Klaue K., Pohler O, et al. The limited contact dynamic compression plate (LC-DCP). Arch Orthop Trauma Surg 1990;109(6):304–310.
66. Perren SM, Russenberger M, Steinemann S, et al. A dynamic compression plate. Acta Orthop Scand Suppl 1969;125:31–41.
67. Ramotowski W, Granowski R. Das "Zespol"—osteosynthesesystem: mechanische grundlage und klinische anwendung. Orthop Praxis 1984;9:750–758.
68. Ricci WM, Loftus T, Cox C, et al. Locked plates combined with minimally invasive insertion technique for the treatment of periprosthetic supracondylar femur fractures above a total knee arthroplasty. J Orthop Trauma 2006;20(3):190–196.
69. Rush LV, Rush HC. A reconstruction operation for a comminuted fracture of the upper third of the ulna. Am J Surg 1937;38:332–333.
70. Schandelmaier P, Krettek C, Tscherne H. Biomechanical study of nine different tibia locking nails. J Orthop Trauma 1996;10:37–44.
71. Schaser KD, Zhang L, Haas NP, et al. Temporal profile of microvascular disturbances in rat tibial periosteum following closed soft tissue trauma. Langenbecks Arch Surg 2003;388:323–330.
72. Schatzker J, Sanderson R, Murnaghan JP. The holding power of orthopedic screws in vivo. Clin Orthop Relat Res 1975;108:115–126.
73. Schavan R. Mechanische testung von schanzschen schrauben. Fachhochsule Aachen (Thesis) 1994.
74. Schemitsch EH, Kowalski MJ, Swiontkowski MF, et al. Cortical bone blood flow in reamed and unreamed locked IM nailing: a fractured tibia model in sheep. J Orthop Trauma 1994;8:373–382.
75. Schutz M, Muller M, Krettek C, et al. Minimally invasive fracture stabilization of distal femoral fractures with the LISS: a prospective multicenter study. Results of a clinical study with special emphasis on difficult cases. Injury 2001;32(Suppl 3):SC48–SC54.
76. Stimson LA. A Treatise on Fractures. London; Churchill, 1893.
77. Sturmer KM. Die elastische Plattenosteo-synthese, ihre Biomechanik, Indikation und Technik im Vergleich zur rigiden Osteosynthese. Unfallchirurg 1996;99:816–829.
78. Tepic S, Perren SM. The biomechanics of the PC-Fix internal fixator. Injury 1995;26(Suppl 2):5–10.
79. Wagner M. General principles for the clinical use of the LCP. Injury 2003;34:31–42.
80. Wenda K, Runkel M, Degreif J, et al. Pathogenesis and clinical relevance of bone marrow embolism in medullary nailing: demonstrated by intraoperative echocardiography. Injury 1993;24(Suppl 3):S73–S81.

8

PRINCIPLES OF EXTERNAL FIXATION

J. Tracy Watson

HISTORICAL PERSPECTIVE

External fixation was described by Hippocrates almost 2400 years ago, when he wrote on a method to immobilize a fracture of the tibia, at the same time allowing for the inspection of the soft tissue injury. This was accomplished by wrapping the proximal and distal tibia with leather wraps, "such as are worn by persons confined for a length of time in large shackles, and they should have a thickened coat on each side, and they would be well stuffed and fit well, the one above the ankle, and the other below the knee."[182] "Four flexible rods made of the cornel tree, (European dogwood) of equal length should be placed between the knee and ankle wrap. If these things be properly contrived, they should occasion a proper and equable extension in a straight line. And the rods are commodiously arranged on either side of the ankle so as not to interfere with the position of the limb; and the wound is easily examined and arranged"[107,182] (Fig. 8-1).

The history of modern external fixation dates to the nineteenth century with Malgaigne's description of an ingenious mechanism consisting of a clamp that approximated four transcutaneous metal prongs for use in reducing and maintaining patellar fractures. This was described in 1843, a full 12 years before the introduction of plaster casting techniques.[93,182]

MONOLATERAL EXTERNAL FIXATION

In 1897, Clayton Parkhill, a Denver surgeon, reported on the results of nine patients treated with an external device consisting of four screws, two of which were inserted into each fragment above and below the fracture. The ends of the screws were fixed

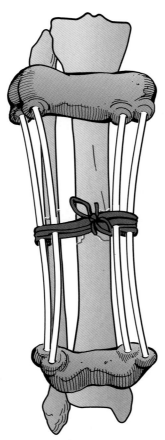

FIGURE 8-1 Hippocrates "shackle" external device for maintaining a tibia fracture at length.

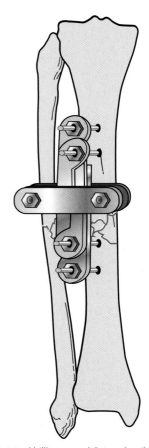

FIGURE 8-2 Parkhill's external fixator for tibia fractures.

together by interlocking small plates and bolts. He did require supplemental plaster immobilization to provide additional support to the construct (Fig. 8-2). He treated eight nonunions and one unstable tibial shaft fracture. Union of the fractures occurred in eight of the nine patients.[179,180] His career was unfortunately cut short when he died from appendicitis. Although he a surgeon, he would not undergo surgery for his condition and died in Denver in 1902.

Belgian surgeon Lambotte recognized Parkhill's work but was unable to obtain a copy of Parkhill's paper. In 1902, he expanded external fixation further and was the first to apply a simple unilateral frame in a systematic fashion. He recognized that the metal pins that penetrated bone and protruded through the skin were remarkably well tolerated and could be connected to an external clamp device, which would allow for stabilization of these pins and thus the bone fragments to which they were attached[134] (Fig. 8-3). Lambott's concepts and design evolved and eventually allowed for frame adjustments to occur, including compression and distraction at the fracture site. In Europe, Lambott's original concepts were expanded significantly, and in 1938, Raul Hoffman, who was a doctor of theology and a carpenter in his free time, devised an external fixator that incorporated a universal ball joint connecting the external ball of the fixator to strong pin griping clamps. This universal joint permitted fracture reduction to occur in three planes, while the fixator was in place. Hoffman could substitute a sliding compression–distraction bar connecting the pin griping clamps,

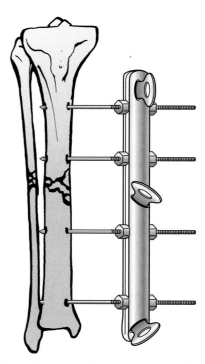

FIGURE 8-3 Lambotte's external fixator, using simple pins and a clamp device.

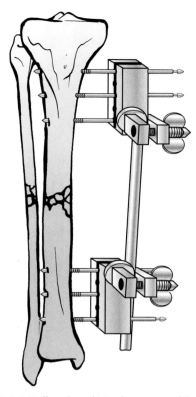

FIGURE 8-4 Hoffman's multipin clamp external fixator.

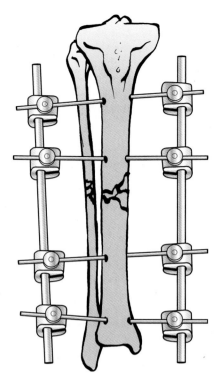

FIGURE 8-5 Anderson device with through-and-through transfixion pins.

and interfragmentary compression or limb length restoration could be performed[108,109] (Fig. 8-4).

In the United States, Roger Anderson devised an apparatus for the mechanical reduction of fractures, using transcutaneous pins connected to metal clamps. Anderson's early concept called for application of through-and-through transfixion pins. This permitted multiplanar adjustment of the fracture fragments and allowed compression at the fracture site. Following reduction, a cast was applied while the limb was still held by the external device.[7] After the cast was applied, the external device was removed and reused on additional patients. Later, Anderson extended this concept and designed an entire external system that connected transcutaneous pins to bars, eliminating the need for a plaster cast[93] (Fig. 8-5).

In 1937, Otto Stader devised a system of fracture management for use in his veterinary practice, which permitted stabilization of fractures and allowed the independent reduction of fracture fragments to occur in three planes.[93,182] Stader's work was observed by surgeons from Bellevue Hospital in New York City. They persuaded him to adapt his fixator for use in humans, and thus the Stader device was refined and enlarged for use in human long bones. In 1942, Lewis and Briedenbach reported their experience with this device for treating 20 patients with fractures of long bones at Bellevue Hospital. They were encouraged by the frame's ability to achieve excellent alignment and early ambulation without the need for adjunctive casting.[144] (Fig. 8-6). They were the first to describe the technique of placing pins as far from the fracture as possible and avoiding pins placed near the site of fracture. This was done to improve the fixator's ability to gradually reduce a malaligned extremity by adjusting the device. They thought that a wide pin spread increased the overall mechanical stability of the construct. They

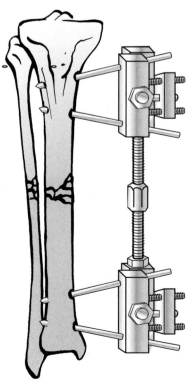

FIGURE 8-6 The Stader device.

also were one of the first investigators, along with Schanz, Riedel, and Anderson, to point out the advantages of inserting the fixation pins at an angle to each other (not parallel) as a means of firmer control over the bone fragments.[144,182]

The use of external fixation techniques by the United States during World War II was documented by Shaar and Kreuz with their use of the Stader splint.[210,211] Although there were some favorable reports on the use of external fixation techniques and their use at base hospitals, experience showed that the techniques were too specialized and time consuming for use in an active combat zone. Because of the high incidence of significant complications associated with external fixation, this technique fell into general disfavor because these complications were by and large attributed to the external fixation device and not necessarily to the problems of treating high-energy open fractures.[99] This resulted in a directive issued to military surgeons of the U.S. Armed Forces to discontinue the use of external fixation.[93]

Following World War II, a study was commissioned by the Committee on Fracture and Trauma Surgery of the American Academy of Orthopaedic Surgeons (AAOS) to investigate the efficacy and indications for external fixation in clinical fracture management. The study was based on 3082 questionnaires sent to practicing clinicians who were members of the American Academy of Orthopaedic Surgeons (AAOS), the American Association of Surgery and Trauma, and the Iowa Medical Association. Only 395 replies were analyzed by the committee. Twenty-eight percent of the respondents thought that external skeletal fixation had a definite place for fracture management, while 29.4% thought that external fixation was not inadvisable except in select rare instances.[118] Over 43% of respondents had used external fixation at one time but had abandoned it completely at the time of the survey. Based on the results of the survey and concerns that practitioners had with the potential mechanical difficulty associated with these frames, as well as the prospect of converting a closed fracture to an open fracture, the committee concluded that any physicians who contemplated the use of external skeletal fixation required special training under the supervision of a surgeon who had treated at least 200 cases by this method.[93] As a consequence, by 1950 the majority of American surgeons were not using this modality. From 1950 to 1970, external fixators were generally unpopular with American orthopedists, although pins and plaster were still widely used for wrist and tibial fractures.

In Europe, Vidal and his coworkers were the first to subject the various assemblies of the external fixator frames to mechanical testing. Vidal used Hoffman's equipment but designed a quadrilateral frame to provide rigid stabilization of complex fracture problems. His biomechanical studies determined that the quadrilateral configuration was quite stable.[93,227]

Similarly, Franz Bernie continued with Dr. Hoffman's original concept of a unilateral frame using a single connecting bar and half-pins. His extensive clinical experience with a half-pin frame documented the success of this device when treating several large series of fracture problems.[35,36]

The European experience in the late 1960s and early 1970s demonstrated that the use of external fixation could not only treat fractures but also be extended to the treatment of pseudoarthrosis, as well as infections and arthrodesis.

During the 1970s, De Bastiani developed the "Dynamic Axial Fixator," and Gotzen, the "Monofixator." These were simple four pin frames with large pin clusters positioned at either ends of the bone. These were then connected to each other by a large-

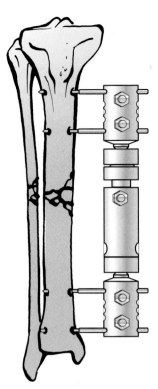

FIGURE 8-7 Large body monotube external fixator.

diameter telescoping tubular rod (Fig. 8-7). This innovation allowed the frames to be more patient friendly compared with the complex fixators of Vidal-Adrey. These frames would promote axial loading with full weight bearing and would accentuate micromotion and dynamization at the fracture site to enhance healing.

The outstanding basic science work on external fixation, which was emanating from Europe in the early 1970s, along with the promising clinical results from European centers, stimulated renewed interest in the use of these techniques in North America. This also coincided with the publication of the second edition of the *A/O Manual* in 1977.[106] It was at this time that external fixation was recommended for the treatment of acute open fractures. Simultaneous with the recommendations, the second *A/O Manual* showed a new tubular monolateral external fixation system. The tubular system of the ASIF gained wide acceptance very rapidly, because of improved pin design and frame biomechanics, as well as precise indications for their use. These factors contributed to many North American surgeons revisiting and adopting this technique, as well as reporting good clinical results (Fig. 8-8).

Circular External Fixation

External fixation as a modality for fracture treatment continued to remain viable in Russia following World War II. Instead of concentrating on half-pin– and monolateral–type configurations, their techniques focused on the use of very thin transfixion wires, which were tensioned to maintain bone segment fixation. In the early 1950s, Gavril Abramovitch Ilizarov developed a circular fixator, which permitted surgeons to stabilize bone fragments but also made three-dimensional reconstructions possible.

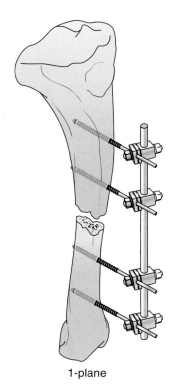

1-plane

FIGURE 8-8 The "simple monolateral" multicomponent external fixation system that helped renew interest in contemporary external fixation techniques.

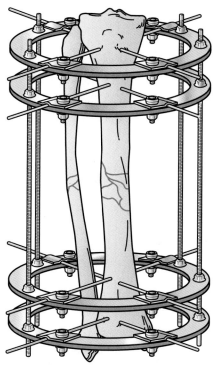

FIGURE 8-9 Ilizarov's circular fixator using small tensioned wires attached to individual rings.

By attaching these wires to separate rings, the rings could be individually manipulated to provide for three planes of correction, similar to the concepts pioneered by Hoffman, Bernie, and Vidal. This ability to achieve precise ring positioning resulted in significant flexibility of the device[1,112] (Fig. 8-9).

In 1975, Volkoff and Oganesian published a series of patients treated with distraction arthroplasty at the knee and elbow using small transfixion wires attached to ring fixators. Their work went largely unnoticed in North America even though it was published in the *American Journal of Bone and Joint Surgery*.[230]

Dr. David Fisher was exposed to Volkoff's circular apparatus and designed a circular-type fixator. Instead of using thin tensioned wires as with the Russian device, he designed a fixator configuration, which allowed for significant pin separation, deviation of pins at various angles, and a semicircular configuration. He determined that fracture site stability could be increased using these circular configuration concepts.[80,93]

As the traditional Soviet Ilizarov-type devices were quite cumbersome and complex compared with the more straightforward A/O- and Hoffman-type fixators, Kroner in 1978 refined and modified the Russian devices by using plastic components and transfixion pins in place of the thin wires used with the Ilizarov technique.[93,112]

For many years, this method was restricted to the region of Kurgan in Siberia. In 1980, the technique was introduced to western Europe thanks to the innovative[l] treatment of world famous Italian explorer Carlo Mauri. Mauri traveled exclusively to Russia for this technique and was successfully treated for an infected pseudarthrosis of the tibia by Ilizarov. Through the friendship established by Mauri with Prof. Ilizarov, the technique was brought back to Italy under the guidance of Prof.

Roberto Cattaneoto and his associates, Drs. Villa, Catagni, and Tentori. They began the first Western clinical trials with transosseous osteosynthesis using Ilizarov's fixator in Lecco, Italy, in 1981.[1,112]

When the political climate in the Soviet Union changed under different leadership in the 1980s, the possibilities of the Ilizarov method and biology that had previously been unrecognized in the West became more apparent. These techniques were presented at various orthopaedic meetings in Italy and other centers in western Europe in the early 1980s.[1,93,112]

A few select North American surgeons, notably Victor Frankel, James Aronson, Dror Paley, and Stewart Green, were exposed to Ilizarov's work and determined that the methodology applied to difficult contemporary orthopaedic problems had vast potential and began clinical applications in the mid 1980s.[1,112] In 1989, Green, who had significant expertise in treating nonunions and osteomyelitis with external fixation techniques, was entrusted by Ilizarov to translate his original basic science work into English. This was published in *Clinical Orthopaedics and Related Research* in 1989.[112–114]

The North American experience was popularized by a small cadre of American surgeons in the late 1980s. This technique today has become widely accepted for complex problems in traumatology, reconstructive surgery, and limb lengthening. In an effort to simplify and apply these techniques to traumatology, the tensioned ring concept was married to the unilateral fixator and the hybrid external fixator was developed to address periarticular injuries with all the advantages of tensioned wires, while limiting the disadvantages of tethering large musculotendinous units with through and through transfixion wire constructs[1,96] (Fig. 8-10).

Recent advancements in deformity correction and precise

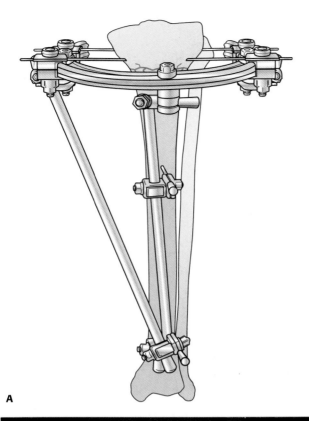

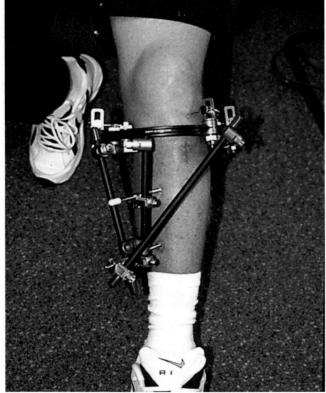

FIGURE 8-10 A. An early version of a hybrid external fixator that combines periarticular tensioned wires and diaphyseal half-pin configurations. **B.** Clinical picture of the same hybrid frame on a patient with a tibial plateau fracture.

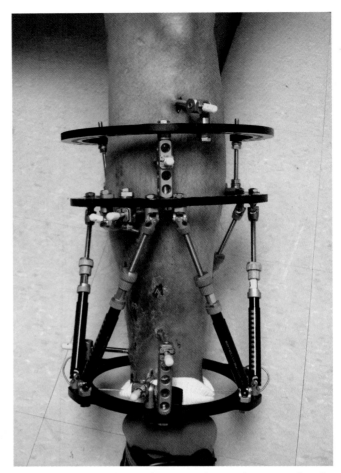

FIGURE 8-11 Hexapod external fixator (Taylor Spatial Frame), with multiple oblique connecting struts through which the limb segments can be manipulated for simultaneous correction of multiple deformities.

fracture reductions have been developed by Charles Taylor and others to correct complex deformities through the use of simple ring constructs using half-pin fixation. These "hexapod" fixators are ring fixators with the rings interconnected and manipulated by a system of adjustable struts, which allow for six axis correction of bone fragments (Fig. 8-11). The development of this concept, as well as the ability to interface deformity correction with web-based software, has continued the progression and advancement of contemporary external fixation techniques.

FRAME TYPES

External fixation systems in current clinical use can be categorized according to the type of bone anchorage used. This is accomplished by using either large threaded pins, which are screwed into the bone, or by drilling small-diameter transfixion wires through the bone and then placing the wires under tension to maintain bone fragment position.

The pins or wires are then connected to one another through the use of longitudinal bars or circular rings. Thus, the distinction is made between monolateral external fixation (longitudinal connecting bars) and circular external fixation (wires and/or pins connecting to rings). Circular fixation may use either threaded pins or small tensioned wires to attach the bone to the frame. Monolateral fixation is accomplished using various-diameter threaded pins; however, these may occasionally involve the use of centrally threaded through-and-through transfixion pins.

FRAME BIOMECHANICS

Large Pin Fixation

Large pin fixator constructs are attached to the bone using various sizes of terminally threaded pins. The half-pins have a

wide range of diameter ranging from 2 mm to 6 mm with all intermediate sizes available. Additionally, there are large-diameter pins with threads in the midportion of the device (i.e., centrally threaded pins) for use in transfixion-type constructs (i.e., Hoffman/Vidal configurations) (Fig. 8-12, A–E).

The basic indications for large pin external skeletal fixation are numerous. The actual biomechanical function that a monolateral frame will perform is dependent on the placement of the pins and orientation of the connecting bars applied. These factors, as well the inherent skeletal pathology treated, combine

FIGURE 8-12 A. Large centrally threaded Schanz pin placed as a transfixion pin in a temporary knee-spanning external fixator. Pins with larger thread diameter are suitable for cancellous bone insertion as in this case. **B.** Multiple pin types (from left) with 5-mm self-tapping predrilled pins with a short thread length. The small pitch angle and narrow thread diameter of this pin are ideal for application in cortical bone. **C.** A 5-mm self-tapping predrilled pin with long threads. **D.** A 6-mm hydroxyapatite self-drilling pin; note self-drilling tip. Hydroxyapatite-coated pins improve the pin–bone interface by encouraging direct bone apposition and ingrowth. **E.** A 6-mm self-tapping predrilled titanium pin.

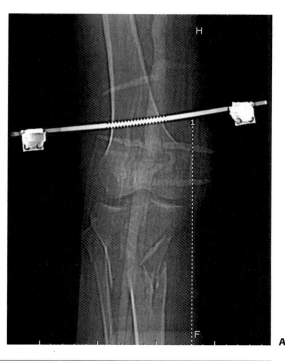

A

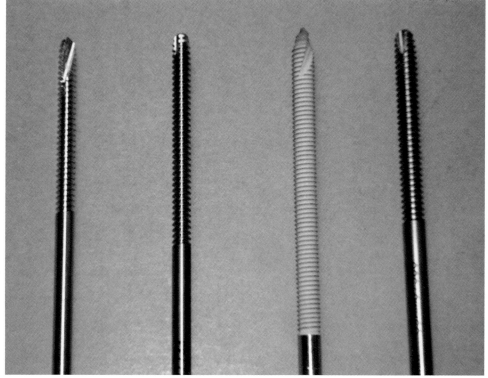

B–E

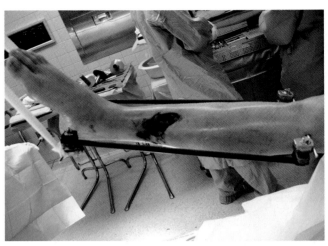

FIGURE 8-13 Simple "spanning" fixator with a transfixion pin above and below the midtibial injury. This maintains the reduction but is not "rigid" and requires additional temporary splinting.

to impart a specific biomechanical function to the fixation construct. The ability to neutralize deforming forces is the most common mechanical principle exploited with external fixation. This is especially true for fresh fractures accompanied by severe soft tissue damage. The use of monolateral fixation for the stabilization of fresh fractures is used emergently as a way of dealing with soft tissue compromise in the immediate posttrauma/postoperative period.[78] Following resolution of the soft tissue injury, secondary procedures such as bone grafting or delayed internal fixation are commonly considered. The primary function of fixators used in this way is to provide relative stability to maintain the temporary fracture reduction at length to avoid collapse of the fracture construct. It should be noted, however, that this type of stabilization is reasonably "flexible" as it is nearly impossible to achieve absolute rigidity to achieve primary bone healing using monolateral or less flexible external fixation (Fig. 8-13).

Monolateral as well as circular frames can also be used to bring areas of metaphyseal or metadiaphyseal bone into close contact through the use of compression techniques. This may be useful in arthrodesis, osteotomy, or nonunion repair[175] (Fig. 8-14). Similarly, distraction forces can also be applied across pin groups to effect deformity correction, intercalary bone transport, or limb lengthening.

Components

Regardless of the biomechanical function of the frame type, the most important factors regarding the longevity and performance of the frame are the strength and competency of the pin–bone interface. Pin loosening with subsequent pin sepsis continues to be problematic. There are many biomechanical factors, which have been evaluated for the prevention of pin tract problems. All pin types and designs are based on these concepts.[14,22,59,90,92,101]

1. Pin geometry and thread design
2. Pin biomaterials and biocompatibility
3. Pin insertion techniques
4. Pin bone stresses

Pin Design

It has been determined that both the screw thread design and the type of cutting head have a significant effect on the holding power of screws. Screw diameter is crucial in determining the stiffness of the frame, as well as in determining the risk of stress fracture at the pin site entry portal. The bending stiffness of the screw increases as a function of the pin's radius raised to the fourth power ($S = r^4$). Calculations have determined that in adult bone, a pin diameter of 6 mm is the maximum that can be used to achieve a stable implant without suffering the consequences of stress fracture through the pinhole itself.[41,185,207] In addition to the variable diameter of the pin, the screw thread may have differing pitch angle and pitch height. The screw design must make allowances for the quality and location of bone to which the screw is applied. Pins, which have a small pitch height and low pitch angle, are usually applied in regions of dense cortical bone, such as femoral and tibial diaphysis.

As the pitch vertex angle increases and the curvature and the diameter of the thread increase, the area captured by each individual thread is broader and more likely to be applied in cancellous bone rather than in hard cortical bone. Conical pins have been designed so that the threads taper and increase in diameter from the tip of the pin to the shaft. This allows the pins to increase their purchase, theoretically by cutting a new larger path in the bone with each advance of the pin. This conical taper also produces a gradual increase in radial preload and thus the screw–bone contact is optimized. Micromotion typical of a straight cylindrical screw is avoided.[136,164,166]

Pin Biomaterials

Traditionally, external fixator pins have been composed of stainless steel offering substantial stiffness.[123] Finite element analyses of the near pin–bone interface cortex revealed stress values that were significantly increased by the use of deep threads and by the use of stainless steel as opposed to titanium pins. Titanium has a much a lower modulus of elasticity. Because of the better biocompatibility afforded with titanium and titanium alloys, there are some investigators who prefer the lower pin–bone interface stresses, as well as the better biocompatibility when using titanium, because they believe there is a lower rate of pin sepsis. This may be due to many factors, including an actual bone ingrowth phenomenon seen at the pin–bone interface.[158,160,164] In a prospective trial, 80 patients (320 pins) with unstable distal radius fractures were treated with external wrist fixators. The external fixator pins were either stainless steel or titanium alloy. The rate of premature fixator removal because of severe pin tract infection (5% versus 0%) and the rate of pin loosening (10% versus 5%) were higher in the stainless steel pin group. The authors concluded that the use of titanium alloy external fixator pins in distal radial fractures yields a trend of reduced pin-related complications and significantly reduced pain levels compared with the stainless steel pin fixators.[184]

Among the many different techniques to enhance the pin–bone interface fixation, coating the pins with hydroxyapatite (HA) has been shown to be one of the most effective.[20,38,147] Moroni demonstrated that HA-coated tapered pins improved the strength of fixation at the pin–bone interface, which corresponded to a lower rate of pin tract infection.[163] The HA coating provides a significant increase in direct bone apposition with a decrease in the fibrous tissue interposition at the pin–one interface. These advantages provided by HA coating appear to be clinically more relevant when these pins are used in cancellous bone rather than in cortical bone[38,161,162] (see Fig. 8-12, B–E). In subsequent studies, HA coating on fixator pins has been

FIGURE 8-14 A. A simple "compression" monolateral system constructed to achieve arthrodesis of the knee. **B.** Complex ring external fixator to effect similar compression forces for an infected knee fusion intramedullary nail. Solid arthrodesis was achieved following frame removal, débridement, and compression treatment.

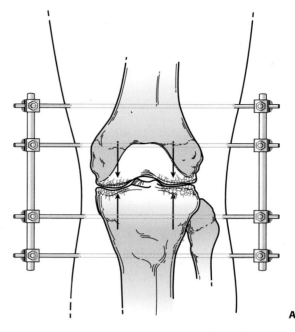

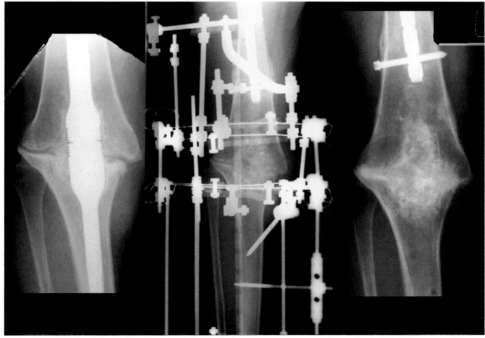

shown to be more important for optimal pin fixation than the particular combination of design parameters used in each pin type (i.e., thread pitch, thread configuration, tapered, etc.).[159]

Insertion Technique and Pin–Bone Stress

Preloading the implant–bone interface has an effect on pin loosening. Radial preload is a concept that prestresses the pin–bone interface in a circumferential fashion rather than in just one direction.[27,67]

Fixator pins are placed with a slight mismatch in the greater thread diameter versus the core diameter of the pilot hole. The small mismatch increases insertion and removal torque, with a decrease in signs of clinical loosening. There is a point at which insertion of pins with a mismatch of greater than 0.4 mm can

result in significant microscopic structural damage to the bone surrounding the pin. High degrees of radial preload or large pilot hole thread diameter mismatch will exceed the elastic limit of cortical bone, with subsequent stress fracture. Thus, the use of oversize pins producing excessive radial preloads must be questioned.[27,86,121]

Screw insertion technique also has an effect on the pin–bone interface. The pins typically come in two types: predrilled pins and self-drilling pins (see Fig. 12B–E). Predrilled pins, by their name, require a drill to be used to produce a pilot hole *prior* to insertion of the pin. The pilot hole has a root diameter equal to or somewhat less than the core diameter of the pin itself.[112,207] As a better pilot hole is drilled with a precise cutting tip, the radial preload is also affected, which will also affect the overall pullout strength. The advantage of predrilling using very sharp drills for pilot holes is that it minimizes the risk of thermal necrosis and subsequent bone damage.[67] The use of self-tapping cortical pins allows each thread to purchase bone as the pin is slowly advanced by hand[50,59] (see Fig. 8-12).

Self-drilling pins have a drill tip point and are driven under power into the bone to engage the threads in cortical or cancellous bone. There is some concern that when using self-drilling pins, the near cortex thread purchase may be stripped as the drill tip of the pin engages the far cortex. As the drill tip on the pin spins to cut the far cortex, the newly purchased bone in the near threads is stripped and the pin stability is compromised. Some studies indicate a 25% reduction in bone purchase of self-drilling, self-tapping pins compared with that of predrilled pins.[8] This is also accompanied by a marked increase in depth of insertion required to achieve a similar pin purchase or pin "feel," when a self-drilling pin has a long, sharp-tipped drilling portion adjacent to the actual threads.[150] To have both cortices engaged with full threads, the pin must be advanced through the far cortex enough to capture the fully threaded portion of the pin and avoid the tapered drill tip. This may leave the tip of the pin "proud" for 2 to 3 mm, which may be problematic in certain anatomic areas where neurovascular structures are directly adjacent to the bone (Fig. 8-15).

Reduction in the length of the drilling portion of the pin means that less of the pin tip needs to project through the far cortex before a firm grip is achieved on the bone. The flutes for tapping the bone run obliquely back down the shaft of the pin. The helical or spiral nature of the flutes steers the bone debris back along the pins and out into the soft tissue. The efficient removal of this bone is mandatory to avoid compacting and jamming the cutting flutes with bone debris and thus compromising their cutting ability, increasing the heat of insertion.[86] The potential disadvantages of self-drilling pins are, therefore, increased heat of insertion; increased microfracture at both cortices, specifically at the near cortex with increased bone resorption; and subsequent decreased pull-out strength with decreased insertion and extraction torque.[50,164] Studies have noted elevations of temperature on heat of insertion with a direct drill technique, where temperatures in excess of 55° C can occur during insertion of self-drilling pins.[153] The complication of thermal necrosis with secondary loosening caused by the resorption of nonviable bone is a real theoretic concern (Fig. 8-16). Clinically, there does not appear to be any increased incidence of pin tract infection or other pin-associated complications reported with the use of self-drilling pins.[206]

Monolateral Frame Types

Monolateral frames are subdivided into those fixators that come with individual separate components (i.e., separate bars, attachable pin bar clamps, bar-to-bar clamps, and separate Schanz pins). These "simple monolateral" frames allow for a wide range of flexibility with "build-up" or "build-down" capabilities. These components are available with various diameter connection bars as well as multiple clamp sizes and pin clamp configurations. These often are also available in "mini" configurations for stabilization of smaller areas of involvement such as for the wrist and hand as well as foot and ankle involvement. This allows the surgeon to apply a frame specific to the clinical and biomechanical needs of the pathology addressed (Fig. 8-17).

This is in distinction to a more constrained type of fixator, which comes preassembled with a multipin clamp at each end of a long rigid tubular body. The telescoping tube will allow for axial compression or distraction of this "monotube"-type fixator. "Simple monolateral fixators" have the distinct advantage of allowing individual pins to be placed at different angles and varying obliquities while still connecting to the bar. This is helpful when altering the pin position relative to areas of soft tissue compromise. The advantage of the monotube-type fixator is its simplicity. Pin placement is predetermined by the multipin clamps. Loosening the universal articulations between the body and the clamps allows these frames to be easily manipulated to reduce a fracture. Similarly, compression (dynamization) or distraction can be accomplished by a simple adjustment of the monotube body (see Fig. 8-7).

"Simple" Monolateral Fixators

The stability of all monolateral fixators is based on the concept of a simple "four-pin frame." Pin number, pin separation, and pin

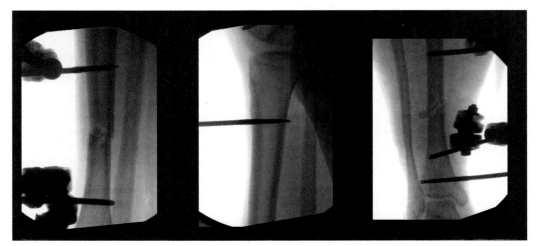

FIGURE 8-15 Pin insertion technique should include the evaluation of the far cortex–pin interface to determine the appropriate depth pin penetration. Excessive penetration can result in potential neurovascular injury if self-drilling pins "pull" the pin too far in order to gain adequate thread purchase. These pins are placed correctly and do not protrude excessively beyond the far cortex.

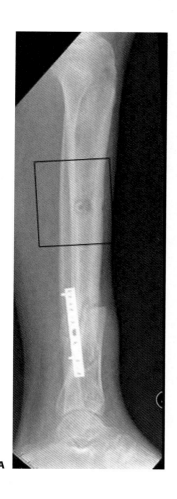

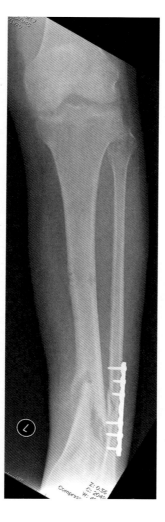

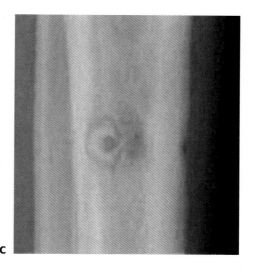

FIGURE 8-16 A,B. Nonunion with varus deformity following failure of hybrid external fixation. Self-drilling pins used in the diaphysis resulted in a ring sequestrum at proximal pin site (*black box*). **C.** Sclerotic bone (dead) at old pin location, with circumferential lucency characteristic of ring sequestrum. This complication required excision of the infected sequestrum.

A

B

C

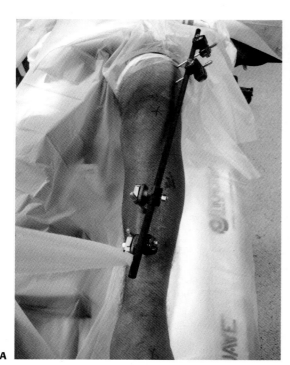

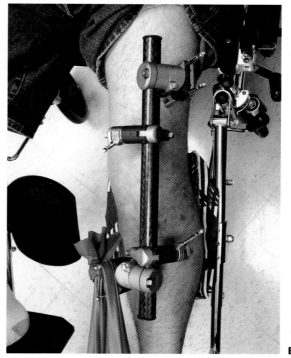

A

B

FIGURE 8-17 A,B. Two similar monolateral external fixators both used to span knee dislocations. Note similar components: separate pin clamps and bars. (**A.** Jet-X monolateral fixator, **B.** Hoffman Monotube fixator.) (*continues*)

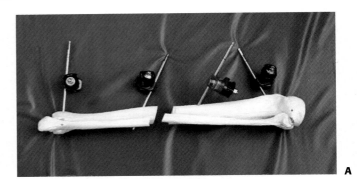

A

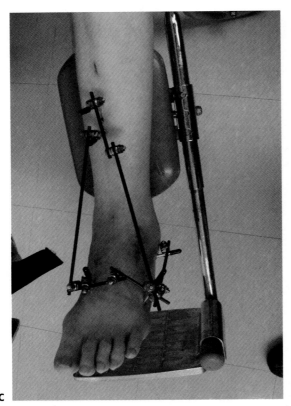

C

FIGURE 8-17 (*continued*) **C.** "Mini" monolateral frame used to span an ankle (Mini-Hoffman ex-fix).

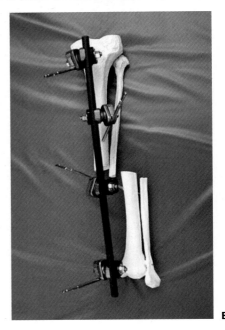

B

proximity to the fracture site, as well as bone bar distance and the diameter of the pins and connecting bars, all influence the final mechanical stability of the external fixator frame (Fig. 8-18).

Most simple monolateral frames allow for individual placement of pins prior to the application of the connecting bars. This permits the surgeon to place pins out of the zone compromised skin or away from the fracture hematoma. The versatility of contemporary pin/bar clamps is based on multiple degrees of freedom built into the clamp that allow a single bar to attach to all four clamps while still retaining the ability to reduce the fracture. The pins do not have to be placed in precise alignment as was required by earlier monolateral frame designs (Fig. 8-19). If aligned pin placement positioning is contraindicated because of

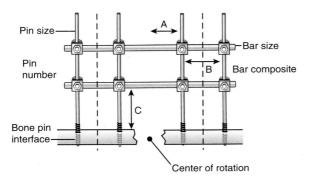

FIGURE 8-18 Factors affecting the stability of monolateral external fixation include pin distance from fracture site, pin separation, bone–bar distance, connecting bar size and composition, pin diameter, pin number, and pin–bone interface. **A.** Pin to center of rotation; **B.** pin separation; **C.** bone–bar distance.

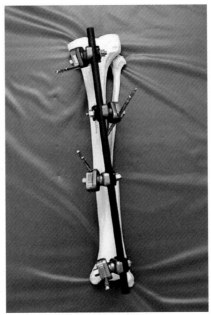

C

FIGURE 8-19 A. Versatility of a monolateral frame is demonstrated. Pins can be positioned out of plane with respect to each other. **B.** A solitary connecting bar is able to connect to all pin bar clamps. **C.** Reduction can be accomplished by manipulating each limb segment and then tightening the clamps to lock the reduction in place.

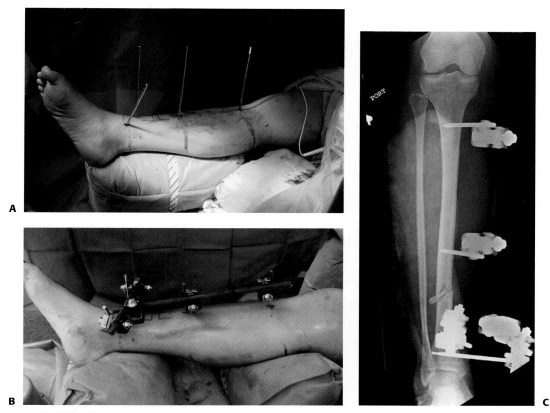

FIGURE 8-20 A. Tibia fracture is grossly reduced and two pins each placed above and below the fracture. **B.** Each two-pin segment is connected with a single bar. The reduction is fine tuned and the two bars are connected to each other to lock in the reduction. **C.** Final postreduction radiograph demonstrating two pins in each limb segment

soft tissue or other concerns, the fractures can still be reduced by simply adding additional connecting bars and using the proximal and distal pin groupings as reduction handles; once reduction is achieved, the bar-to-bar connecting clamp is tightened and reduction is maintained (Fig. 8-20).

Simple four-pin system rigidity can be increased by maximizing pin separation distance on each side of the fracture component as well as the number of pins used. In the case of a four-pin system, the use of two pins on each limb segment with maximal pin spread minimizing the bone-correcting bar distance also increases stability[172] (see Fig. 8-18). Behrens demonstrated unilateral configurations with stiffness characteristics similar to those of the most rigid one- and two-plane bilateral constructs that are easily built using the "four-pin frame" as a basic building block[22–24] (Fig. 8-19). Mechanically, most effective were the "delta" plane configurations, when two simple four-pin fixators are applied at 90-degree angles to each other and connected (Fig. 8-21). However, single and double stacked bar anterior four-pin frames have the best combination of clinical and mechanical features (Fig. 8-22). The complex delta frames allow for gradual frame build-down on a rational basis to slowly transfer more load to the bone. This stepwise frame reduction leads from the most rigid unilateral constructs to frames that allow the most complete force transmission across the fracture site while still providing adequate protection against sagittal bending movements.[22–24] Studies have shown that a unilateral biplanar delta frame without transfixion pins can be

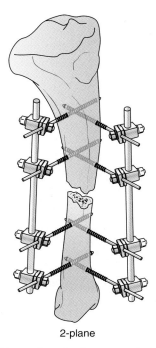

2-plane

FIGURE 8-21 A delta configuration is composed of two "simple" four-pin frames connected at 90 degrees to each other.

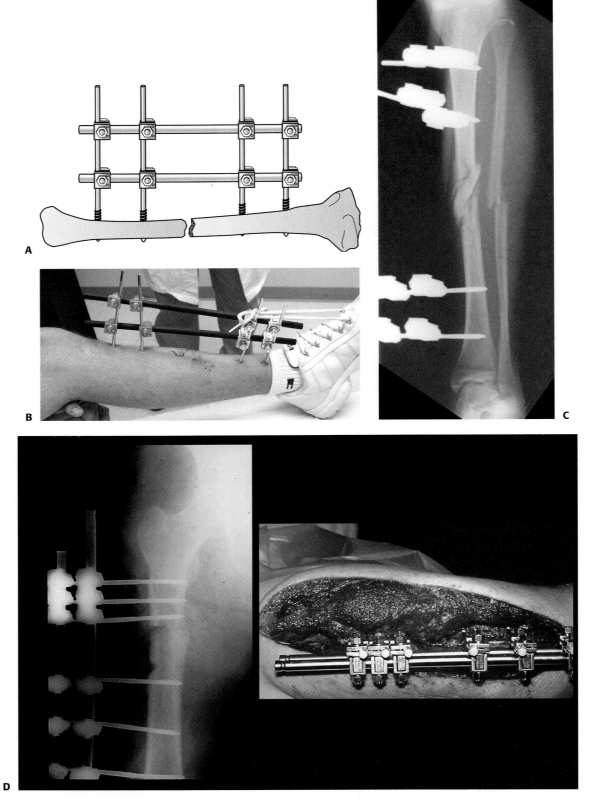

FIGURE 8-22 A. Stability of a "simple" four-pin frame can be increased by adding a second connecting bar. A "double-stacked" frame. **B.** The bone-connecting bar distance was increased to avoid soft tissue impingement on the bars. Because of the increased distance to the bone an additional connecting bar was added to increase the stability of the frame. **C.** Reduction maintained with "simple" four-pin double stack frame. Early consolidation is noted in this comminuted open fracture. **D.** Infected femur fracture with severe soft tissue injury and bone loss required additional pins, and a double stack frame to achieve stability was necessary to treat this injury.

set up with an overall rigidity as good as that of a bilateral transfixion-type device.[221]

When the connecting bars to bone distance increases, implant stability decreases. This is clinically significant when dealing with patients who present with wide areas of soft tissue compromise, which may preclude the ability to place the connecting bar close to the subcutaneous border of the bone. To counteract this, a standard four-pin fixator should be altered to increase the number of pins applied in each fracture segment[31] (Fig. 8-22).

The materials of which the connecting bars are constructed have a significant effect on overall frame stability. Kowalski et al.[131] demonstrated that carbon fiber bars were approximately 15% stiffer than stainless steel tubes and that the external fixator with carbon fiber bars achieved 85% of the fixation stiffness compared with that achieved with stainless steel tubes. They thought that the loss of stiffness of the external fixator construct was likely due to the clamps being less effective in connecting the carbon fiber rods to the pins.

The weakest part of the system is the junction between the fixator body and the clamp or between the fixator clamp and the Schanz pins. Insufficient holding strength on a pin by a clamp may result in a decrease in the overall fixation rigidity, as well as increased motion and cortical bone reaction at the pin–bone interface.[14] Cyclic loading of external fixators has been shown to loosen the tightened screws in the pin clamps. Thus, one needs to be aware of the mechanical yield characteristics of the clamps, bars, and pins throughout the course of treatment.[68]

Because of the gradual fatigue of components and loosening of pin-to-bar and bar-to-bar connections, the clinical practice of regular tightening of the device during the course of treatment should be routine.[68,101,250]

Monotube Fixators

Stability of the large monotube fixators is accomplished in a distinctly different way compared with the simpler monolateral fixators. Most monotube fixators have fixed location for their pins mounted in pin clusters. These are connected to the body, and thus the ability to vary pin location is substantially less compared with simple monolateral fixators. Because the pin clusters are fixed at either end of the monotube body, the ability to maximize pin spread in relation to the fracture site is limited by the monotype body's length. There is little variability to lower the large monotube connection bar closer to the bone in an effort to increase stability. These frames are very stable and accomplish their inherent rigidity by having a large-diameter monotube connecting body, which are 3 to 4 times the diameter of the simpler monolateral connecting bars. Because of the large body configuration, these devices offer higher bending stiffness, as well as equal torsional stiffness and variable axial stiffness compared with standard Hoffman-Vidal quadrilateral frames with transfixion pins[31,44,105,117,119] (Fig. 8-23).

These frames have ball joints at either end connecting the large fixator bodies to their respective pin clamp configurations. There has been concern about the ability to achieve stability due to the ball locking mechanism. Chao and Hein[44] determined that the ball joint locking cam and fixation screw clamp required periodic tightening during clinical application to prevent loss of frame stiffness under repetitive loading. However,

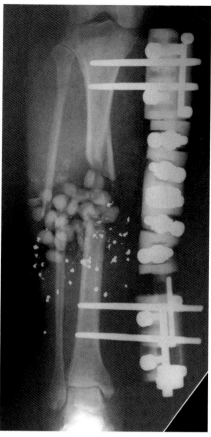

FIGURE 8-23 Large pin "monotube" fixator. Device has fixed proximal and distal pin clamps and a large telescoping body.

frank clinical failure with these types of ball joint devices has not been demonstrated.[12,44,105]

Insufficient holding strength on a pin within a constrained pin clamp may result in the diminution of the overall construct rigidity, as well as pin movement at the pin–bone interface. This is a distinct disadvantage compared with the single component simple monolateral frames where each pin has its own pin–bone clamp.[12] When using monotube fixators, the use of six pins increased torsional rigidity, but this configuration fails at lower bending loads compared with the four-pin configuration, reflecting the uneven holding strength of the pin clamp on three pins.[12]

Pin Orientation and Frame Stability

The rigidity of a half-pin system is maximal in the plane of the pins and is minimal at right angles to this plane. Thus, a simple four-pin frame placed along the anterior border of the tibia will resist the anterior and posterior forces generated with normal stride, while this frame is weakest in mediolateral bending.[221,224,248] The biomechanical advantage of adding an additional two to four pins perpendicular (90 degrees) to the anterior pins is that it increases the mediolateral bending forces as well (delta configuration) (see Fig. 8-21).

If half the pins are oriented out plane in relation to the remaining pins, this decreases the overall strength of the construct in the primary plane of the pins; however, this would be compensated for by increasing the strength of the construct in

FIGURE 8-24 Frames with nonlinear pin placement neutralize forces similar to the normal forces developed in a tibia. This frame demonstrates pins out of plane to each in the transverse and sagittal orientations. The 6-mm hydroxyapatite-coated pins were used, which gives this simple frame very stable mechanics requiring only three pins on each side of the fracture line.

the plane at right angles.[22,23,213] Thus, overall frame rigidity would be improved.

Shear and Eagan demonstrated a system in which the pins were placed at 60 degrees to each other and offered substantial advantages. With only a 10-degree separation between the pin angles, displacement and response to torsional stress are reduced by 97%. This increase in torsional rigidity occurs up until about 30 degrees of pin divergence angle, at which time torsional displacement has all but stopped. The effects on compressive forces are much less. When fixator pins are spread out, the fixator was 91% stronger for resisting angular displacements and torsion compared with the traditional monolateral orientation.[213] A rigid frame configuration is not generally perceived as undesirable, but far preferable to merely reducing rigidity in all planes is the production of a frame, which more closely mimics the biomechanics of normal bone. An external fixator, which allows an offset pin angle of 60 degrees, demonstrates the ability to equalize forces in the sagittal and coronal planes, providing mechanical stimuli much closer to those normally encountered in the sagittal and coronal planes[45,157,172,204,212] (Fig. 8-24).

Many investigators are currently examining alternative pin placement as a way to achieve maximal fracture stability with relative frame simplicity.* A simplified two-ring circular frame

*References 22,23,157,212,221,224,248.

using only three 6-mm half-pins has been shown to increase circular frame stability compared with more complex ring constructs. The pins for these simple frames were applied at divergent angles of at least 60 degrees to the perpendicular. These divergent 6-mm half-pin frames demonstrated similar mechanical performance compared with standardized multiple tensioned wire and 5-mm half-pin frames in terms of axial micromotion and angular deflection.[137] Based on the mechanical performance of these simplified divergent half-pin frames, surgeons can now reliably improve frame stability by simply placing pins out of plane to the long axis of the bone (i.e., not perpendicular to the long axis) (Fig. 8-25).

Frame stability is most problematic when treating highly comminuted fractures or in fractures with significant fracture obliquity and increased shear stresses. Standard half-pin application with pins placed perpendicular to the long axis of the bone fails to oppose the shear force vector directly, because the pins are placed oblique to the shear force vector, and thus it does not neutralize the cantilever forces induced by this standard pin insertion angle.

Alternatively, when half-pins are placed parallel to the fracture line and thus in direct opposition to the shear force vector, the shear force is actively converted into one of compression manifesting a dynamic stabilization of the fracture edges (Fig. 8-26). In this way, compression is *dependent* on axial load, and the shear phenomenon is dramatically reduced, thereby yielding nearly zero shear. For fracture obliquities less than or equal to 30 degrees, there is inherent stability such that standard modes of fixation can be utilized without undue concern.[106,157] However, at fracture obliquities greater than 30 degrees, one must respect the inherent shear present with axial loading at the fracture ends. Added steps should therefore be considered to help minimize this shear component, such as the application of the steerage pin concept. At fracture obliquities greater than 60 degrees, shear is a dominating force and one must be aware that even with steerage pins, the forces may be extreme. Frames should be modified to perform strictly as a neutralization device as interfragmentary compression will be difficult to achieve even with the most complex devices[106] (Fig. 8-26).

Small Wire Fixation

A major advantage of a monolateral system is that it can be applied in a uniplanar fashion, minimizing the transfixion of soft tissues. The ring-type systems have the disadvantage of transfixion-type wires tethering soft tissues, as the wires pass from one side of the limb to the other.[93,112] Because of the smaller wire diameter, the trauma to the soft tissue and bony reaction and intolerance to the wires are minimized. Large pin monolateral fixators rely on stiff pins for frame stability. Upon loading, these pins act as cantilevers and do produce eccentric loading characteristics. Shear forces are regarded to be inhibitory to fracture healing and bone formation, which may be accentuated with certain types of monolateral half-pin stabilization, especially when pins are all in line.[10,11,13,19,43,178,251] Thus, the advantages of having half-pins placed out of plane. Circular or semicircular fixators allow for multiple planes of fixation, which produces frame behavior largely eliminating the harmful effects of cantilever loading and shear forces, yet accentuating axial micromotion and dynamization.[80,145,154,172,186,248]

FIGURE 8-25 A. Oblique (out of plane) pin testing construct that confirms oblique orientation of pins allows for fewer pins to be used with no decline in relative fixator stability. **B,C.** "Simple" construct with only 3- to 6-mm pins above and below the nonunion. All pins were placed out of plane to each other to affect larger pin spread and confer stability.

A

B

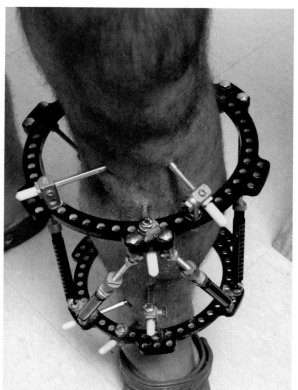

C

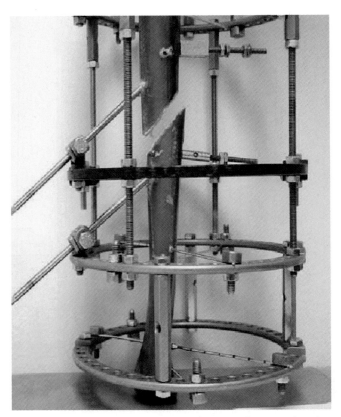

FIGURE 8-26 Steerage pin experimental set up demonstrating pins placed parallel to the major fracture line, dramatically reducing the shear forces and accentuating compressive forces with axial weight bearing. (Courtesy of David Lowenberg, MD.)

Components

Ring fixators are built with longitudinal connecting rods and rings to which the small-diameter tensioned wires are attached. Alternatively, the bone fragments may be attached to the rings by half-pins. The connecting rods may incorporate universal joints, which give these frames their ability to produce gradual multiplanar angular and axial adjustments.

There are several component related factors, which can be manipulated to affect an increase in the stability of the ring fixation construct:

1. Increase wire diameter
2. Increase wire tension
3. Increase pin crossing angle to approach 90 degrees
4. Decrease ring size (distance of ring to bone)
5. Increase number of wires
6. Use of olive wires/drop wires
7. Close ring position to either side of fracture (pathology) site
8. Centering bone in middle of ring

Wires

Thin smooth wires of 1.5, 1.8, and 2 mm are the most basic component used in a circular small wire fixator (Fig. 8-27A). Wire strength and stiffness increase as the square of the diameter of the wire ($S = d^2$). As these wires are tensioned, they provide increased stability. This occurs by increasing wire stiffness, which simultaneously decreases the axial excursion of the wires during loading. The amount of tension in the wires directly affects the stiffness of the frame. Compression and bending resistance increase as a function of wire tension as tension is gradually increased up to 130 kg. Beyond this threshold, further wire tensioning is difficult to accomplish because commercially available wire tensioning devices are unable to stop the slippage of the wire in the device as the wire is tensioned.[1,16,193]

Beaded wires (olive wires) perform many specialized functions. During insertion, the beaded portion of the wire is juxtaposed onto the cortex. As the far side of the wire is tensioned, the bead is compressed into the near cortex. This allows olive wires to be inserted to perform interfragmentary compression, which may be useful in fracture applications (Fig. 8-28). These wires act as a source of additional transverse force to help stabilize and correct malunions/nonunions and provide additional support to a limb segment that a smooth wire cannot achieve.[1,112]

Wire Tension

As you perform limb lengthening, tension in the wire will inherently be generated from the soft tissue forces achieved through distraction. This may generate tension in the wire up to as much as 50 kg. If the patient is weight bearing, and the limb is loaded, then further wire deflection (tension) occurs. This generates additional tension in the wire. Additional rigidity of the entire construct is also demonstrated (the "self stiffening effect of tensioned wires"). If the wire was initially tensioned to 130 kg and additional tension is added through lengthening and weight bearing, then the yield point of the wire may be approached with possible wire breakage occurring (see Fig. 8-27). A fracture frame is essentially a static fixator where additional wire tension will only occur through weight bearing. Thus, the degree of initial wire tension should take into account the pathology being treated and the treatment forces being generated.[1,15,39,40,52]

Ring Diameter

The diameter of the ring also affects the stiffness of frame, as the diameter of the ring increases, so does the distance of the ring to the bone, similar to the bone bar distance when discussing half-pin monolateral fixators (see Fig. 8-27). Because of this increased distance, the frame becomes less stable. Ring diameter and wire tension have a dramatic effect on overall frame stability. As ring diameter increases, the effect of increasing wire tension on gap stiffness and gap displacement is decreased. Decreased ring diameter has a greater affect on all variables compared with simply increasing wire tension. Although the effect of wire tension decreases as ring diameter increases, tensioning wires on frames with larger ring constructs is important because these constructs are inherently less stiff due to longer wires.[1,15,37,39,40,52]

Wire Orientation

Wires placed parallel to each other, and parallel to the applied forces, provide little resistance to deformation. The bone can slide along this axis much like a central axle in a wheel. In bending stresses, the frames can be much less rigid due to bowing of the transverse wires and slippage of the bone along these wires. The most stable configuration occurs when two wires intersect as close to 90 degrees as possible. The bending stiffness in the plane of the wire is decreased by a factor of 2 as the angles between the wires converge from 90 to 45 degrees (Fig.

FIGURE 8-27 A. Smooth and beaded (olive) wires come in the common sizes of 1.5-mm, 1.8-mm, and 2-mm diameters. **B.** A wire tensioning device is used to increase the overall rigidity of the frame construct. **C.** Multiple ring diameters are available to match the diameter of the applied extremity. Too large a ring increases the distance from bone to ring and thus makes the frame less rigid.

A

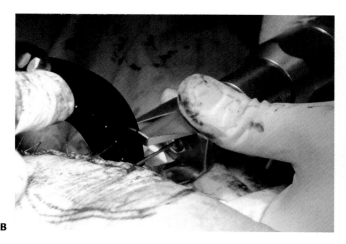

B

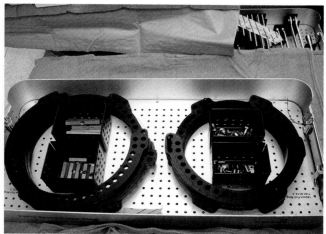

C

8-29). Therefore, changing pin orientation to a less acute angle decreases the stiffness in AP bending but has a lesser effect on lateral bending, torsion, and axial compression.[39,40,83,173]

Clinically, a wire divergence angle of at least 60 degrees should be attempted. Because this is not always possible due to anatomic constraints of passing transfixion wires, the use of olive wires or the addition of a wire at a distance off of the primary ring (drop wires) significantly improves bending stiffness. The use of two counteropposed olive wires also improves the shear stiffness (olive wires placed at the same level but from opposite directions achieve an olive on each side of the bone, thus "locking" in the segment)[39,40,83,95,112,186,238,240] (see Fig. 8-28).

Limb Positioning in the Ring

The location of the tibial bone in the limb is actually eccentric in nature compared with the humerus or the femur. This is important when placing the rings around the particular extremity. One should be aware that the center of the ring applied may not be located over the actual center of the bone. It may be positioned eccentric with respect to the ring, affecting the overall stiffness of the frame. If the bone is located off center, this position provides greater stiffness to loading in axial

compression, compared with a construct where the center of the ring is positioned exactly over the center of the bone. This center/center configuration demonstrates lowered axial stiffness at the fracture site during axial loading.* Clinically, because most of these types of frames are applied to the tibia, this is usually not an issue because the bone is routinely eccentric in the limb as long as you center the ring on the leg itself. The eccentric location of the muscular compartments ensures this offset bone position. To place a frame on a tibia with the center/center orientation, a very large ring would be needed. This would vastly increase the ring–bone distance and further decrease the frame stiffness (Fig. 8-30).

A typical four-ring frame consists of eight crossed wires, two wires at each level and four rings with supporting struts connecting two rings on either side of the fracture (see Fig. 8-9). When this four-ring frame is tested against the standard Hoffman-Vidal quadrilateral transfixion frame, the circular-type frame was noted to be relatively stiff in compression. However, the circular fixators are less rigid than all other monolateral-type fixators in all modes of loading, most particularly in axial

*References 1,15,37,39,40,41,83,173.

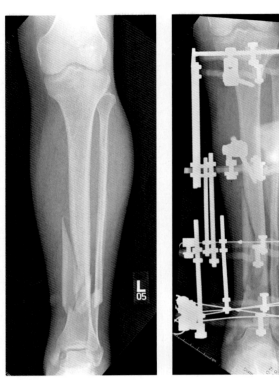

A

B

FIGURE 8-28 A. Fracture extending over distal third of tibia with large medial butterfly fragment is an ideal indication for a small wire fixator. **B.** Olive wires were used as a "lag screw" to achieve additional stability of the butterfly and distally in the metaphyseal region.

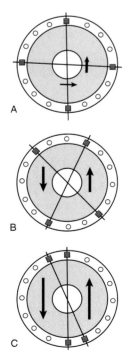

A

B

C

FIGURE 8-29 A. Wire crossing angle of 90 degrees provides the most stable configuration with small mediolateral translations and a rigid frame. **B.** A wire convergence angle of 45 to 60 degrees allows acceptable amounts of translations to occur with satisfactory frame stability. **C.** As the convergence angle decreases, the translation increases dramatically to the point where the bone slides along a single axis. Parallel wires produce a grossly unstable frame configuration.

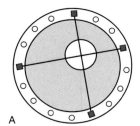

A

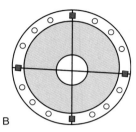

B

FIGURE 8-30 A. Eccentric bone location in the ring, simulating a tibial mounting. **B.** Center/center location of bone in the ring mounting simulating a femoral or humeral mounting.

compression.[1,15,39,52] Nevertheless, this may prove to be clinically beneficial to allow for axial micromotion and facilitate secondary bone healing.[69] The Ilizarov fixator allowed significantly more axial motion at the fracture site during axial compression than the other fixators tested, but the device controlled shear at the fracture site as well as other half-pin frames.[69,119] The overall stiffness and shear rigidity of the Ilizarov external fixator are similar to those of the half-pin fixators in bending and torsion.[83,112,128,154,186,203,249]

Wire Connecting Bolts

Mechanical slippage between wire and fixation bolt is the primary reason for loss of wire tension and thus frame instability. Studies demonstrate that when clamping a wire to the frame, the wire tension is reduced by approximately 7%.[246] This may be due to wire deformation by the bolts and as such can reduce wire tension during fixator assembly.[245] Slippage can be avoided by adequate torque on the fixation bolt (i.e., greater than 20 Newton meters [Nm]). Material yield accompanied by some wire slippage through the clamps is responsible for the decreased tension at the pin–clamp interface. Although, the initial wire tension has an appreciable effect on the wire stiffness, it does not affect the elastic load range of the clamp wire system. To prevent yield of the clamp wire system in clinical practice, the fixator should be assembled with sufficient wires to ensure that the load transmitted to each wire by the patient does not exceed 15 N.[250] Adding additional wires will increase frame stiffness directly proportional to the number of wires in the system. Stiffness of an Ilizarov frame is more dependent on bone preload than on wire number, wire type, or frame design. Preload stiffness can be increased simply by compressing the rings together and achieving bone-on-bone contact.[1,15,16,37,40,41,83]

Hybrid Fixators

Because of the complexity involved in the assembly of a full circular ring fixator, hybrid configurations were developed to take advantage of tensioned wires' ability to stabilize complex periarticular fractures. Early designs married a periarticular ring using few tensioned wires to a monolateral bar connected to the shaft using two or three half-pins. Unfortunately, these simple frames were shown to be mechanically inferior in their abilities to alleviate cantilever loading with resultant malunion/nonunion[128,187,188,194,238] (see Fig. 8-10B). Mechanical instability was especially pronounced when the frames were applied with two prominent errors in technique. (a) Insertion of only two transfixion wires in periarticular locations. Because of anatomic constraints, the wires cannot be placed at 90 degrees to each other in most periarticular locations. As noted previously, if the two wires are not at 90 degrees, then the bone can translate easily along the two wires. (b) Half-pins placed too far from the site of pathology put significant strain on the connecting clamps to maintain frame stability (Fig. 8-31).

The term "hybrid techniques" now denotes the use of half-pins and wires in the same frame mounting as well as using a combination of rings and monolateral connecting bars. Stable hybrid frames should include a ring incorporating multiple levels of fixation in the periarticular fragment. This is accomplished with a minimum of three or more tensioned wires and, if possible, an additional level of periarticular fixation using adjunctive half-pins augments the stability.[5,6,15,34,128]

The use of a single bar connecting the shaft to the periarticular ring places significant stresses on the single connecting clamp and accentuating the harmful off-axis forces generated with weight bearing. Multiple connecting bars or a full circular frame is preferred with a minimum of four half-pins attached to the shaft component.[5,6,37,187,188,194,249]

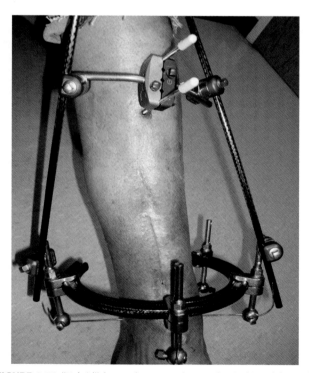

FIGURE 8-31 "Hybrid" frame demonstrating mechanical instability with only two periarticular tensioned wires on the distal ring and two small monolateral bars connecting only two diaphyseal half-pins located at an extreme distance from the fracture. This unstable fracture fixation went onto nonunion.

BIOLOGY OF EXTERNAL FIXATION AND DISTRACTION HISTOGENESIS

The fracture repair process proceeds through constant physiologic stages depending on external forces imparted onto the fracture site. There are four distinct types of fracture healing that have been identified. External fixation facilitates external bridging callus.

External bridging callus is largely under the control of mechanical and other humoral factors and is highly dependent on the integrity of the surrounding soft tissue envelope. The critical cells necessary for healing are derived from the surrounding soft tissues and from the revascularization response that occurs during the inflammatory phase of fracture healing.[1,33,112]

This type of fracture healing has the ability to bridge large gaps and is very tolerant of movement. It results in the development of a large callus with formation of cartilage due to the greater inflammatory response caused by increased micromovement of the fragments.[126,136] Migrating mesenchymal cells from the surrounding area reach the fracture ends where they differentiate into various cell types, primarily cartilage. The cartilage is formed in the well-vascularized granulation tissue due to its ability to repel vessels. These early cartilaginous elements undergo remodeling through endochondral bone formation. It is well known that this type of indirect bone healing occurs under less-rigid interfragmentary stabilization.[125–127] The rate of this type of healing and the extent of callus in this type of repair can be modulated by mechanical conditions at the fracture site.[143] It has been shown that applying cyclic interfragmentary micromotion for short periods of time influences the repair process and leads to a larger area of callus formation compared with those fractures that are rigidly fixed.* Alternatively, efforts to reduce micromotion by increasing frame stiffness can cause a significant reduction in the rate of healing.[21,43,248,251]

Larger interfragmentary movements lead to more fibrocartilage, as well as an increase in the number of blood vessels.[49,232] However, as the amount of fibrocartilage increases, the ability to remodel and form bone is simultaneously decreased. There appears to be some threshold at which the degree of micromotion becomes inhibitory to this overall remodeling process and thus hypertrophic nonunion can result. It should be noted, however, that fractures requiring external fixation in general are usually more complex, which may result in a higher rate of nonunion. Healing problems encountered in these severe injuries may reflect the severity of the local soft tissue and periosteal injury and should not be attributed solely to the inherent features of the external fixation device.

Bony healing is not complete until remodeling of the fracture has been achieved. At this stage, the visible fracture lines in the callus decrease and subsequently disappear. The bone transmits mechanical forces to the encapsulating callus as the tissue differentiates from granulation tissue to collagen and hyaline cartilage, and then to woven intramedullary bone through the process of endochondral bone formation.[1,112,233]

Dynamization

Dynamization converts a static fixator, which seeks to neutralize all forces including axial motion and allows the passage of forces

*References 10,11,49,69,89,90,102,119,125–127,178,183.

across the fracture site to occur. As the elasticity of the callus decreases, bone stiffness and strength increase and larger loads can be supported. Thus, the advantages of axial dynamization are that it helps to restore cortical contact and produces a stable fracture pattern with inherent mechanical support. Aro and colleagues[11,13] described a uniform distribution of callus following dynamization and noted this as "secondary contact healing." By increasing cortical contact, dynamization attempts to decrease the translational shear forces.[10,11,13] These forces are accepted by most to be the leading factor in producing a predominance of fibrous tissue at the fracture site with resultant delayed or nonunion.[19,22,37,45]

Frames are distinguished between static and dynamic fixators. Active dynamization occurs with weight bearing or with loading when there is progressive closure of the fracture gap. This usually occurs by making adjustments in the pin bar clamps with simple monolateral fixators or releasing the body on a monotube-type fixator. Dynamization also decreases the pin–bone stresses and prolongs the lifetime of the frame.[1,119,125,152]

There is a race between the gradually increasing load-carrying capacity of the healing bone and failure of the pin–bone interface. In unstable fractures, very high stresses can occur at the pin–bone interface, which may create localized yielding failure. In half-pin frames, these high stresses are generated primarily at the entry cortex and stress-related pin–bone failures of half-pins occur mainly in this location.[185]

It is well accepted that the relative motion of the bone ends at the fracture site is a very important parameter in the healing of the fracture. However, the threshold at which this motion becomes deleterious is as yet unknown. Micromotion is the fundamental mechanical force seen by the fracture construct, which is imparted to the periosteal callus, and distinctions need to be made in terms of quality, extent, and time of micromotion application.[53,112]

Limited Open Reduction Internal Fixation with External Fixation

Inherent with the use of external fixation is the desire to perform limited internal fixation in combination with an external fixator. While this type of methodology is very useful in metaphyseal bone and has been demonstrated to work well in periarticular fractures, its use in diaphyseal regions must be questioned.

The use of interfragmentary screws seeks to achieve direct bone healing through the use of constant compression. Primary cortical healing occurs only when mechanical immobilization is absolute and bony apposition is perfect. It is very intolerant of movement and is not dependent on external soft tissues. This type of healing is very slow and has no ability to cross gaps, as opposed to external bridging callus.[102,125]

In many ways, it represents bone healing through gradual remodeling. Primary cortical healing is characterized by sequential cutting cones of osteoclast across the fracture line with subsequent reestablishment of new osteons. The vasculature develops from a budding process sprouting from the intramedullary blood vessels, which are very fragile and intolerant of motion. The external fixator, on the other hand, does not entirely eliminate extraneous forces but seeks to limit the degree of micromotion but still allow movement to occur along a number of vectors.[49,102,106,112,119,125,232] Therefore, because the bone is rigidly

fixed with lag screws, very poor bridging callus develops. Because external fixators do not produce absolute rigidity, insufficient cortical healing occurs, demonstrating the worst of both biological entities.[178] This technique has been abandoned for use in diaphyseal regions, because of the increased incidence of pseudoarthrosis. A combination of internal and external fixation for diaphyseal fractures may at first appear to be desirable but is in fact often disastrous and should be avoided.[215]

Distraction Osteogenesis

Distraction osteogenesis is the mechanical induction of new bone that occurs between bony surfaces that are gradually pulled apart. Ilizarov described this as, "the tension stress effect."[1,112–114] Osteogenesis in the distraction gap of a distracted bone takes place by the formation of a physis-like structure. New bone forms in parallel columns extending in both directions from a central growth region known as the *interzone* (Fig. 8-32). Recruitment of the tissue-forming cells for the interzone originates in the periosteum.[1,16,17,112] Under the influence of tension stress, fibroblast-like cells found in the middle of the growth zone have an elongated shape and are orientated along the tension stress vector during distraction. Surrounding the fibroblast-like cells are collagen fibers aligning parallel to the direction of the tension vector. The fibroblastic cells transform into osteoblasts, which deposit osteoid tissue upon these collagen fibers. They further differentiate to become osteocytes within the bone matrix laid down upon the longitudinal collagen bundles. These cells will become incorporated into their own HA matrix as the collagen bundles are consolidated into bone. This tissue gradually blends into the newly formed bone trabeculae in the regions farthest away from the central interzone. Thus, newly formed bone grows both proximally and distally away from the middle of the distraction zone during elongation. These columns of bone will eventually cross the fibrous interzone to bridge the osteogenic surfaces following distraction[1,112–114] (Fig. 8-32B).

With stable fixation, osteogenesis in the distraction zone proceeds via direct intermembranous ossification omitting the cartilaginous phase characteristic of endochondral ossification. Distraction osteogenesis also provides a significant neovascularization effect. The fibroblast precursors are concentrated around sinusoidal capillaries. The growth of these newly formed capillaries under the influence of tension stress proceeds very rapidly and in some instances overgrows development of bony distraction, resulting in enfolding of this tremendous capillary response. This dense network of newly formed blood cells has a longitudinal orientation connecting to the surrounding soft tissue vessels by numerous arteries that perforate the regenerate bone. Thus, the regenerate distraction gap is very vascular, with large vascular channels that surround each longitudinal column of distracted collagen. Neovascularization extends from each bone end surface toward the central fibrous interzone. This intense formation of new blood vessels under the influence of tension stress occurs not only in bone but also in the soft tissues. These vessels contain a thin lining of endothelial cells very similar to the neovascular response that occurs in a centripetal fashion during routine fracture healing (Fig. 8-32B).

The rate and rhythm of distraction are crucial in achieving viable tissue following distraction histogenesis. Histologic and biochemical studies have determined that a distraction rate of

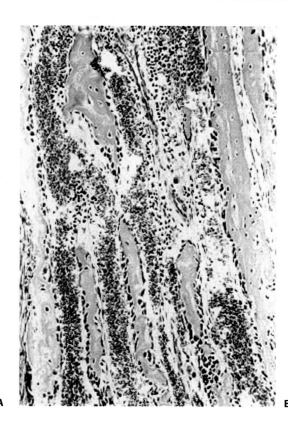

FIGURE 8-32 A. Interzone (box) is the central growth region involved in the genesis of new bone formation during distraction. **B.** Collagen fibrils line up along the vector of distraction. Osteoblasts line the collagen bundles forming new bone. There are large vascular channels surrounding each collagen bundle.

0.5 mm per day or less leads to premature consolidation of the lengthening bone, while a distraction rate of 2 mm or greater often results in undesirable changes within the distracted tissues. Faster rates of distraction will disrupt the small vascular channels and areas of cysts can occur inhibiting mineralization.[1,16,17,112–114]

For osteogenesis to proceed more rapidly, optimum preservation of the periosteal tissues, bone marrow, and surrounding soft tissue blood supply at the time of osteotomy is mandatory.[1,112,253] The new bone or soft tissues are formed parallel to the tension vector even when the vector is perpendicular to the limb's overall mechanical axis.

Ilizarov recommended achieving a goal of 1-mm total distraction (rate of distraction) per day. The actual number of distractions (rhythm of distraction) should be at least four each day, achieving the total daily distraction in four divided doses. His work has also demonstrated that constant distraction over a 24-hour period produces a significant increase in the regenerate quality compared with other variables.[1,112–114]

When motion is present at the fracture site, bone resorption always occurs. The greater the interfragmentary motion at the site of the fracture, the greater is the resorption of the fragment and the slower is the consolidation. The healing process depends on arterial revascularization, and if the fracture fragments are excessively mobile, the local blood supply is traumatized by the moving bone ends.[49,178,232] Instability that introduces translational shear across the distraction gap will result in an atrophic fibrous nonunion with mixed cartilage and incomplete vascular channels, interspersed within the longitudinal collagen columns. In these areas of mechanical instability, intramembranous ossification is irregular with islands of endochondral ossification seen, and if local vascularity is insufficient, mineralization will be inhibited, leaving necrotic fibrous areas or vascular cysts.

Circular frames are able to limit the magnitude of abnormal forces, when they are placed in compression.[1,16,69,128] This stabilizes the small blood vessels and allows for neutralization of the forces that are destructive to the neovascular region.[16,17] This allows endochondral bone remodeling to proceed.

Compression osteosynthesis with constant compression on the bone does not suppress the reparative process and does not cause damage to or resorption of the bone tissues. Under conditions of both compression and distraction in the presence of stable fixation, bone is actively formed by cellular elements of the endosteum, bone marrow, and periosteum. The osteogenic activity of connective tissue is stimulated by tension stress when the tissue is stabilized. Soon after the end of distraction, the connective tissue is replaced by bone. Therefore, compression (i.e., active compression) or dynamization can facilitate healing of delayed or nonunions under this mechanical environment. Increase in axial loading is accompanied by enhanced blood supply that activates osteogenesis.[1,112–114,232] Many authors have demonstrated the positive benefit that axial loading combined with muscular activity has on new bone formation.[125–127,135]

As noted by Ilizarov, all tissues will respond to a slow application of prolonged tension with metaplasia and the differentiation into the corresponding tissue type. Bone responds best followed by muscle, ligament, and tendons in that order. Neurovascular structures will respond with gradual new vessels and some degree of nerve and vessel lengthening. However, they respond very slowly and are intolerant of acute distraction forces.[1,112–114]

As such, this phenomenon of histogenesis can occur indirectly via traction on living tissue, as well as with tension stress simulated by nonviable implants (i.e., the implantation of soft tissue expandable prosthetics).[102]

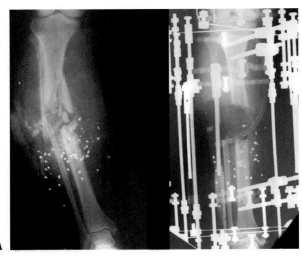

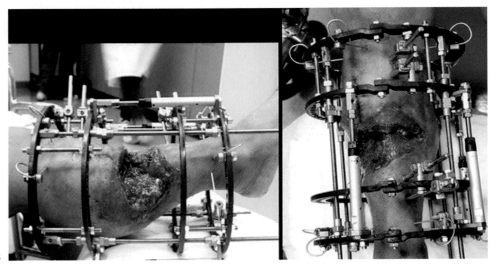

FIGURE 8-33 A. Severe bone and soft tissue loss stabilized with a ring fixator. **B.** Gradual distraction (compression) across defect gradually closes down the defect via soft tissue transport.

(continues)

Muscle growth results from the tension stress effect by increasing the number of myofibrils in preexisting muscle. Muscle also responds by the formation of new muscle tissue through the increased numbers of muscle satellite cells, the appearance of myoblasts, and their fusion into myotubes as well as differentiation of the sarcoplasmic components of the existing muscle fibers into new muscle tissue. Within the newly formed muscle fibers, active formation of myofibrils and sarcomeres also occurs.[1,112–114]

Smooth muscle tissue and blood vessels walls are also stimulated by tension stress. Smooth muscle activity and proliferation are accompanied by an increase in the extent and number of intercellular contacts between myocytes and by the formation of new elastic structures. These morphologic changes in the ultrastructure of arterial smooth wall muscle cells resemble the changes seen in the walls of arteries elongated during active prenatal and early postnatal growth.[1,112–114]

A similar response also occurs in the connective tissue of fascia, tendons, and dermis. The number of fibroblasts is increased during distraction and an increase in the density of intracellular junctions is multiplied, which is characteristic of fibroblasts in the developing connective tissue of embryos, fetuses, and newborn animals. The adventitial blood vessels in

the epineurium and perineurium of major nerve trunks also undergo similar changes.[1,112–114]

Distraction, accomplished through the use of a ring fixator, or a stable monotube device, initiates the histogenesis of bone, muscle, nerves, and skin.[1,16,17,112–114] This facilitates the treatment of complex orthopaedic diseases, including pathologic conditions such as osteomyelitis and fibrous dysplasia. Other conditions that have been historically refractory to standard treatments, such as congenital pseudoarthrosis and severe hemimelias, can also be addressed.*

Bone transport methodologies can replace large skeletal defects with normal healthy bone structure, which is well vascularized and is relatively impervious to stress fractures. The ability to correct significant angular, translational, and axial deformities simultaneously through relative percutaneous techniques, as well as perform these corrections in an ambulatory outpatient setting, adds to the attractiveness of this methodology** (Fig. 8-33).

*References 54,58,112,122,156,169,197,216,222.
**References 48,70,94,95,112,147,174,202,203,226,234,235,237,242.

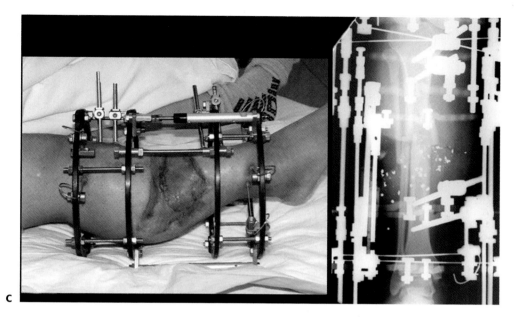

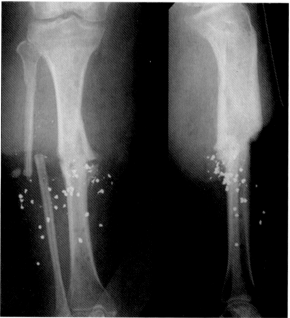

FIGURE 8-33 (*continued*) **C.** Skin grafting was performed over reconstructed soft tissues, once docking of the bone ends had been completed. **D.** Healed tibia later underwent limb lengthening.

CONTEMPORARY EXTERNAL FIXATOR APPLICATIONS*

Traditionally, indications for external fixation were primarily for trauma applications. This included the treatment of open fractures and closed fractures with high-grade soft tissue injury or compartment syndrome. For patients with multiple long bone fractures, external fixation has been used as a method for temporary, if not definitive, stabilization of these long bone injuries.

Following the launch of circular and hybrid techniques, indications have been expanded to include the definitive treatment of complex periarticular injuries, which include high-energy tibial plateau and distal tibial pilon fractures. With the introduc-

tion of minimally invasive techniques, combined with locking plate technologies, the indications for use of circular fixation for the definitive fixation of periarticular fractures has narrowed. Circular fixator use in periarticular injuries is largely restricted to the most severe fractures patterns with extensive comminution, bone loss, or critical soft tissue injury.

Given the mechanical and biological advantages of external fixation, their use in reconstructive orthopaedics has gained wider acceptance and is currently used for limb lengthening, osteotomy, fusion, and deformity correction, as well as bone transport for the reconstruction of bone defects (see Fig. 8-14B).

Damage Control External Fixation

The concept of temporary spanning fixation for complex articular injuries has become widely accepted. The ability to achieve

*References 32,94,133,147,175,195,234,235.

an initial ligamentotaxis reduction substantially decreases the amount of injury-related swelling and edema by reducing large fracture gaps. It is important to achieve an early ligamentotaxis reduction, as a delay for more than a few days will result in an inability to disimpact displaced metaphyseal fragments. When definitive stabilization is attempted, reduction will be more difficult by indirect means and may require larger or more extensile types of incisions.[181,209,239,241,243]

Many types of temporary "traveling traction" have been described. Most commonly used are the knee- or ankle-bridging constructs. This may be a simple quadrilateral frame, constructed by applying medial and lateral radiolucent external bars to proximal and distal threaded transfixion pins placed across the respective joint. Manual distraction is carried out and a ligamentotaxis reduction is achieved. A simple anterior monolateral frame can be used to maintain similar reduction across the knee joint for temporizing the management knee dislocations, complex distal femoral fractures, and tibial plateau fractures[181,209,239,241,243,244] (Fig. 8-34).

A simple monolateral frame can be configured in a triangular-type construct about the distal tibial and ankle region in an effort to achieve relative stability. With temporary fixation in place, the patient is then able to have other procedures or tests performed while effective distraction is maintained and the soft tissues are put to rest (Fig. 8-35).

Application of these techniques in a polytraumatized patient is valuable when rapid stabilization is necessary for a patient in extremis, so-called damage control orthopaedics (DCO). Simple monolateral or monotube fixators can be placed very rapidly across long bone injuries, providing adequate stabilization to facilitate the management and resuscitation of the polytraumatized patient.[98,219] Excessive traction across a joint should be avoided when applying these temporary joint-spanning frames. By overdistracting these extremities, the muscular compartments can become stretched, effectively compressing the compartments, and lead to late compartment syndrome.[72]

For periarticular fractures, the decision to convert to definitive stabilization is usually based on the adequacy of soft tissues. A latency period of at least 10 to 14 days is required to allow the soft tissues to recover to the extent where contemporary internal fixation techniques can be undertaken safely. Many series have demonstrated excellent results achieved with a staged approach consisting of early fracture stabilization using spanning external fixation. This is followed by careful preoperative planning based on traction computed tomography scans and the judicious clinical evaluation of the soft tissue injury prior to definitive internal fixation.[4,141,177,181,209,239]

The timing of conversion of a DCO external fixator to an intramedullary nail is determined by the condition of the soft tissues and the overall stability of the patient. With the temporary stabilization of long bone fractures, definitive conversion to intramedullary nailing has demonstrated variable success especially in the tibia.[61] Most authors would suggest early (within the first 2 to 3 weeks of frame application) conversion to intramedullary nailing to avoid colonization of the medullary canal by the external fixator pins. Increased infection rates have been documented when conversion is done after 2 weeks of external fixation. It has been shown that the longer the external fixator remains in place, the greater is the risk of complications occurring following conversion to intramedullary devices, especially if the pins are removed and the nail exchanged at the same operative setting[115,156] (Fig. 8-36).

In the femur, conversion from external fixation to nailing has demonstrated good rates of success if the exchange is done when the patient's overall physical condition has improved. Acute conversion to an intramedullary device for the femur in a single procedure is preferred in patients without evidence of pin track infection. However, studies have shown that infection rates after DCO for femoral fractures are comparable to those after primary intramedullary nailing. There appears to be no contraindication to the implementation of a damage control approach for severely injured patients with femoral shaft fractures where appropriate. Pin-site contamination was more common where the fixator was in place for longer than 2 weeks.

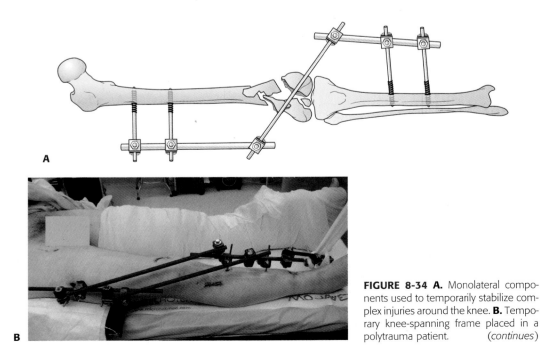

FIGURE 8-34 A. Monolateral components used to temporarily stabilize complex injuries around the knee. **B.** Temporary knee-spanning frame placed in a polytrauma patient. (*continues*)

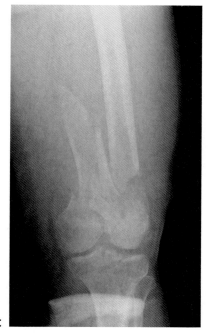

C

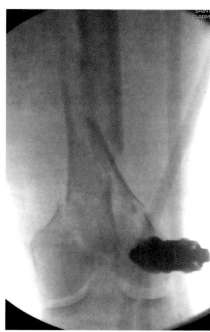

D

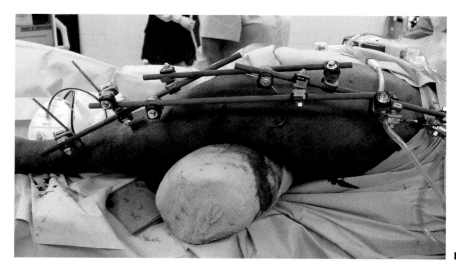

E

F

FIGURE 8-34 (*continued*) **C–E.** Open distal femoral and proximal tibial fracture stabilized with a knee-spanning frame. **F.** Patient with a severe crush injury to lower extremity with multiple fractures and compartment syndrome. Entire limb was spanned to include the patient's knee and ankle.

For patients treated by using a DCO approach, conversion to definitive fixation should be performed in a timely fashion. Delayed conversion requires a period of traction before nailing to avoid significant shortening of the fracture. Certainly, prolonged traction while awaiting pin site contamination to resolve is contraindicated in the multiply injured patient.[26,103]

Stabilization of unstable pelvic fractures has been achieved by the rapid application of simple external fixation for use in the immediate resuscitative period. The application of an external frame affords significant reduction in the volume of the true pelvis, as well as stabilizing the movement of large bony cancellous surfaces along the posterior aspect of the pelvic ring. The ability to provide stabilization and decrease the pelvic volume allows the surgeon to control hemorrhage and has helped to contribute to the low mortality seen with these injuries.[56,124]

Anterior pelvic external fixator constructs provide excellent adequate fixation, and traditional constructs include single and multiple pin placements in several locations in each iliac crest. However, anterior frame application, specifically the anterior superior iliac crest pins that course between the inner and outer iliac tables, may be problematic. These frames may be difficult to apply in a large obese patient.[97] As well, these pins may loosen very rapidly due to the variable pin purchase in cancellous bone (Fig. 8-37).

Biomechanical and anatomic studies have focused on pin placement lower on the pelvis, specifically in the supra-acetabu-

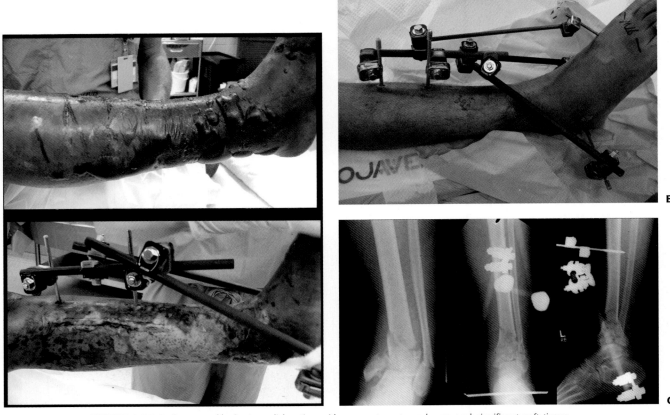

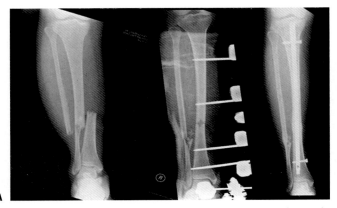

FIGURE 8-35 A. Severe ankle fracture dislocation with compartment syndrome and significant soft tissue compromise was spanned with a triangular ankle-spanning external fixator (*top*). Open pilon fracture stabilized with triangular ankle spanning configuration (*bottom*). The reduction achieved with the simple frame facilitates the definitive reconstructive procedures once soft tissue recovery has occurred and the fasciotomy incisions have healed. **B.** Pilon fracture stabilized with an ankle-spanning frame. The forefoot was maintained in neutral with the addition of a metatarsal pin. **C.** A ligamentotaxis reduction maintained alignment and allowed definitive reconstruction once the soft tissues had recovered.

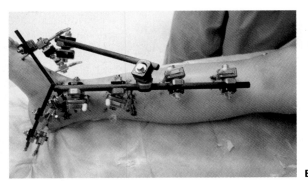

FIGURE 8-36 A. Open tibial shaft fracture with complex foot injury is temporarily stabilized with a spanning monolateral fixator. **B.** An anatomic reduction was achieved and maintained with the frame. Once soft tissues recovered and the patient's condition stabilized, the frame was converted to an intramedullary nail at 10 days postinjury.

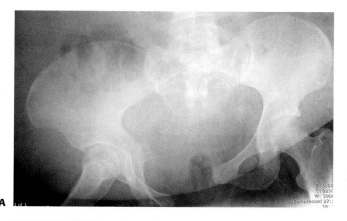

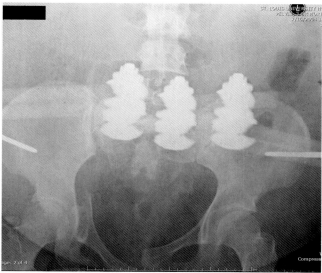

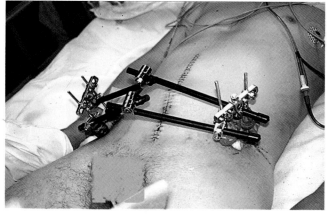

FIGURE 8-37 A. Pelvic injury with anteroposterior disruption and hemodynamic instability. Note large pannus prohibiting supra-acetabular pin placement. **B.** This patient underwent simple anterior frame application to help in the resuscitation of the patient and provide temporary pelvic stabilization. **C.** Another patient with a different anterior iliac wing frame, which was modified with additional iliac crest pins and additional bars to increase stability.

lar region. Pins in this location are more stable biomechanically because of the improved purchase in the hard cortical bone of the posterior column (Fig. 8-38). This pin placement allows for pelvic reduction in the transverse plane of deformity and may allow improved reduction of the posterior elements. In addition the location of the pins and frame can facilitate concurrent or subsequent laparotomy procedures.[85,138]

Pelvic frames are most useful in those fractures that are vertically stable.[155] Rotationally unstable fracture such as AP compression and lateral compression injuries are best suited to application of an anterior pelvic frame.[56] At times, the application of an anterior frame may be complicated, cumbersome, and time consuming and may be contraindicated as an emergency application. For this reason, a modification of pelvic external fixation, the so-called C-clamp, is used to provide posterior stability temporarily in the patient with massive pelvic ring injuries and massive hemorrhage.

DEFINITIVE FRACTURE MANAGEMENT

The choice of external fixator type depends on the location and complexity of the fracture, as well as the type of wound present when dealing with open injuries. The less stable the fracture pattern, the more complex a frame needs to be applied to control motion at the bone ends. If possible, weight bearing should be a consideration. If periarticular extension or involvement is present, the ability to bridge the joint with the frame provides satisfactory stability for both hard and soft tissues. It is important that the frame be constructed and applied to allow for

multiple débridements and subsequent soft tissue reconstruction. This demands that the pins are placed away from the zone of injury to avoid potential pin site contamination with the operative field.

Ring fixators have a definite advantage for extra-articular injuries in that they allow for immediate weight bearing and can gradually correct deformity and malalignment, as well as achieve active compression or distraction at the fracture site.

Monolateral Applications

The largest indication for the use of monolateral frames for fracture management occurs in the distal radius and in the tibial shaft. This is followed closely by temporary application of trauma frames for complex femoral and humeral shaft injuries. Much less likely is the use of monolateral frames for forearm injuries.

Wrist External Fixation
Specific fixators have been designed for use in the distal radiu, and may be either joint bridging or joint sparing. Following the restoration of palmar tilt by closed fracture manipulation, wrist position can be adjusted into neutral or extension to help avoid finger stiffness and carpal tunnel syndrome without compromising fracture reduction.[2] For unstable fractures, it has been shown that augmentation of the fixator construct with multiple dorsal and radial percutaneous pins corrects the dorsal tilt and maintains the reduction in those fractures that are difficult to maintain with distraction ligamentotaxis alone[51,148,166] (Fig. 8-39).

The use of dynamic external fixation devices across the wrist

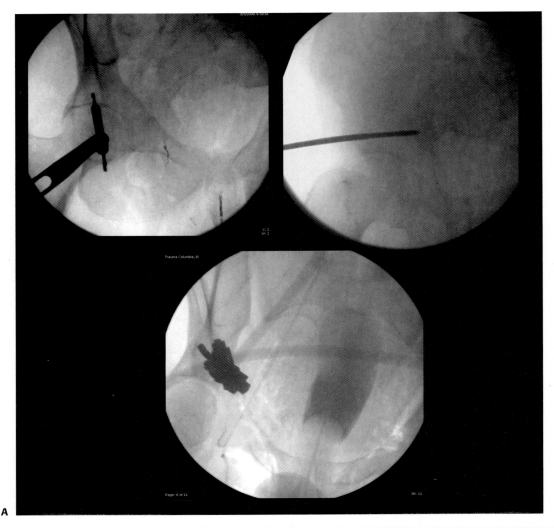

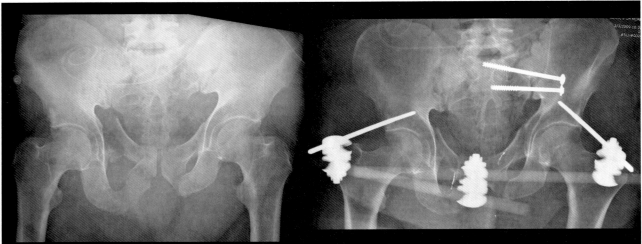

FIGURE 8-38 A. Correct location of supra-acetabular pins localized with intraoperative fluoroscopy. Pins traverse the area just superior to the dome of the hip joint and gain purchase in the dense cortical bone of the posterior column. **B,C.** Use of supra-acetabular pins in conjunction with posterior ring fixation necessary to stabilize this complex pelvic injury with bladder rupture.

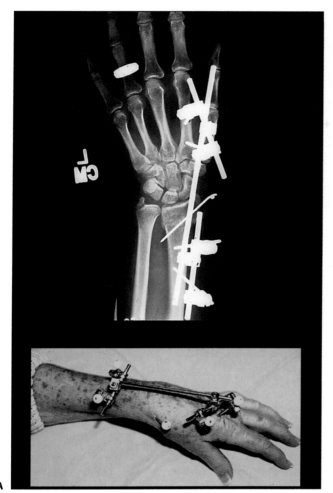

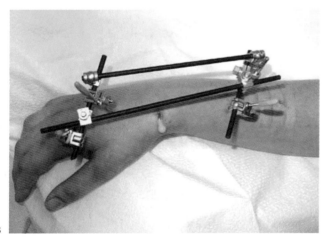

A

B

FIGURE 8-39 A. Mini fixator used in combination with percutaneous pins to maintain reduction of a distal radius fracture. Solitary connecting bar placed between the metacarpal and radial pins. **B.** Alternative configuration using quadrilateral frame construct with percutaneous pins.

has demonstrated mixed results. The concept behind this was to achieve a ligamentotaxis reduction, as well as initiate early range of motion by uncoupling the device.[91] For distal radius fractures with metaphyseal displacement but with a congruous joint, there exists a trend for better functional, clinical, and radiographic outcomes when treated by immediate external

fixation and optional K-wire fixation. Although there is insufficient evidence to confirm a better functional outcome, external fixation reduces re-displacement and provides improved anatomic results, and most of the surgically related complications are minor, probably related to technique of pin insertion.[100,129,142,217] External fixation devices function best when maintaining radial length alone.[84]

Joint-bridging external fixation allows the radial length to be restored with the fixator; however, the anatomic reduction of articular fragments and restoration of the normal volar tilt prove to be more difficult when using a joint-spanning frame. A method of nonbridging external fixation combined with percutaneous pinning facilitates fracture reduction and allows for free wrist movements (Fig. 8-40). This method has demonstrated no clinical differences when used for both intra- and extra-articular distal radius fractures compared with wrist bridging fixation.[18,92,130,170] The ability to maintain the reduction and minimize the total load transmitted from the wrist joint to the fracture site is fixator dependent and will differ from manufacturer to manufacturer.[84,252]

Femoral External Fixation

The use of external fixation for the management of acute femur fractures is primarily limited to pediatric indications or to those fractures with significant soft tissue or neurovascular compromise or to those severely injured patients who cannot tolerate more extensive surgery (DCO). Commonly, femoral applications include the use of a minimum of four pins placed along the anterolateral aspect of the femoral shaft. These simple monolateral frames have been shown to provide adequate stabilization for most complex femoral fracture patterns[28,57] (Fig. 8-41). Fixator constructs with independent pins placed out of plane relative to one another allow for safer pin insertion and demonstrate increased stability over monotube or simple monolateral frames where pins are placed in a straight line orientation.[29,66]

In a large part of the world, external fixation of femoral shaft fractures is often the definitive treatment. Monolateral or monotube fixators are commonly used with four- or six-pin configurations. A pin tract infection with occasional pin loosening is the most commonly reported complication and, although a common occurrence, is not a major problem and can be treated with local wound care and antibiotic therapy. The most common problem is significant decrease in the range of motion of the knee, which can be difficult to treat successfully and is the major drawback to using this routinely when other methods are available.[75,257]

Other complications include the high rate of refracture following frame removal, especially when used in a pediatric population for definitive femoral shaft fracture treatment.[42,189]

Knee Dislocation

Knee dislocation is always a difficult topic mainly with regard to the structures that have been damaged and the best treatment option. Knee dislocation in the polytrauma patient is also problematic in the context of open knee dislocations or dislocation in association with arterial disruption, or compartment syndrome.

In an effort to maintain the reduction and allow for arterial repair, compartmental release, or the treatment of other injuries, spanning external fixation is a valuable option. Simple knee-spanning monolateral or monotube fixators can be easily applied with two pins above the knee located in the distal femur

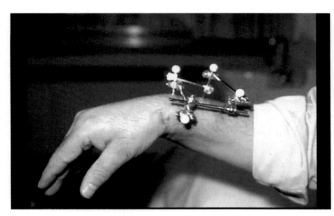
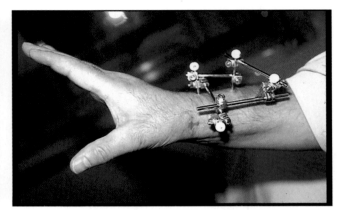

FIGURE 8-40 Fracture-spanning wrist fixator allows for range of motion with no loss in stability. This joint-sparing configuration is indicated in certain select distal radius fractures.

and two pins in the midtibia. The knee is reduced under fluoroscopy and the fixator locked, maintaining the reduction to facilitate other procedures and avoid the phenomenon of redislocation that can occur when stabilizing these severe injuries with temporary splinting or casting (Fig. 8-42).

Following initial surgical repair (usually posterior cruciate ligament or acute posterolateral reconstruction) of the globally unstable knee, some investigators advocate the immediate application of an articulated hinged knee fixator to protect these extensive repairs. Articulated external fixation has been proposed as a method to protect ligament reconstructions while allowing aggressive and early postoperative rehabilitation after knee dislocation.[116,256]

Mechanical studies have evaluated the additional stability afforded to knees by these monolateral or bilateral hinged knee frames.[214] Application of articulated external fixators to specimens with intact ligaments significantly reduced cruciate ligament forces for Lachman, anterior drawer, and posterior drawer tests.

Articulated external fixation of the knee can reduce stresses in the cruciate ligaments after multiligament reconstructions and can decrease anteroposterior translation in the cruciate-deficient knee.[82]

Humerus External Fixation

External fixation is an infrequent treatment option for the management of acute humeral shaft fractures. Unlike the tibia, in which fixator half-pins can be placed perpendicular to the subcutaneous medial tibial surface, external fixation in the humerus often involves transfixion of crucial musculotendinous units.

FIGURE 8-41 A–C. Severe soft tissue injury prevents acute intramedullary nailing of the femoral shaft fracture. Stability required spanning across the knee to maintain reduction. Secondary conversion to intramedullary nailing occurred at 12 days postinjury with no secondary infection noted.

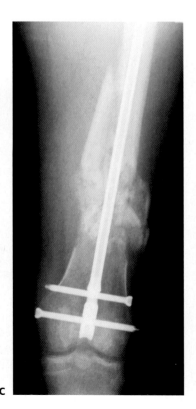
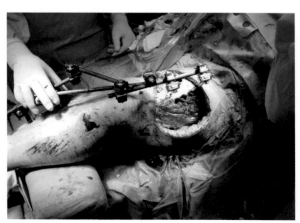
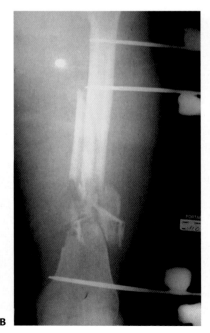

A   **B**   **C**

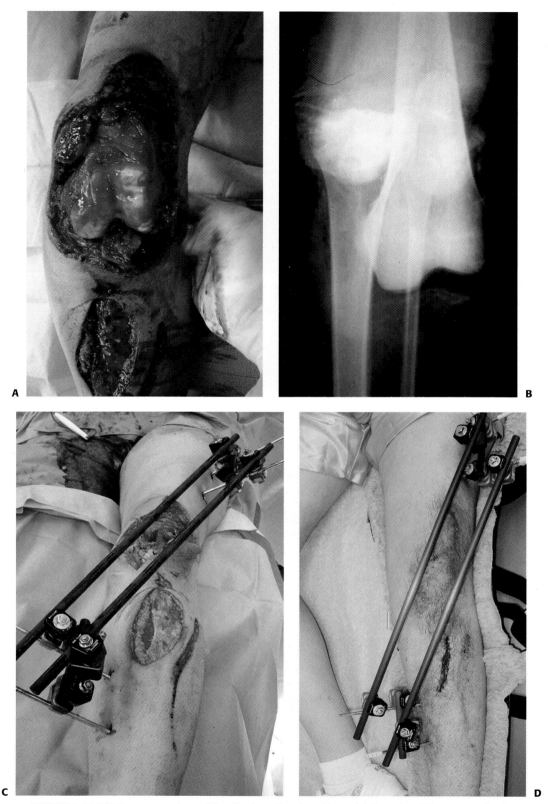

FIGURE 8-42 A,B. Severe open knee dislocation in conjunction with arterial disruption. **C,D.** Emergent knee-spanning fixator was applied at the time of initial surgical management, which included arterial repair and multiple débridements. The wound was eventually closed, and the patient underwent delayed ligamentous reconstruction at 10 weeks postinjury.

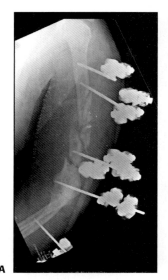
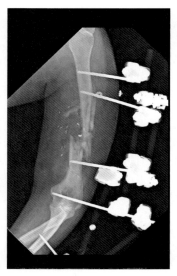
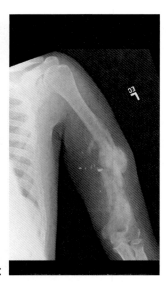

FIGURE 8-43 A. Segmental humerus fracture in association with arterial injury. The fracture was emergently stabilized with spanning external fixator and arterial repair. **B.** At 6 weeks postinjury, demonstrates callus formation. **C.** Frame was removed at 10 weeks postinjury with translation and angulation but complete healing of this segmental injury.

Complications related to these frames may include pin tract sequelae and an inhibition of shoulder and elbow motion. However, with contemporary fixation devices, indications for use in the humerus continue to expand. In addition to their initial use for shaft injuries, many series now report the successful treatment of supracondylar and proximal humerus fractures treated with monolateral, circular, and hinge fixators.[46,104151]

The most frequent indication for use in the humerus is for the stabilization of severely contaminated open fractures or in gunshot wounds that occur in association with vascular disruption (Fig. 8-43). Rapid application of a simple four-pin external fixator provides excellent stability such that the limb may be manipulated during subsequent vascular arterial repair without concern for disruption of the repair. External fixation together with radical debridement has reduced the incidence of chronic infection and improved the prognosis for the vascular repair

(Fig. 8-44). Average fixator time is dependent on associated extremity injures and has been reported to be an average 16 weeks for these severe injuries. Secondary surgical procedures for soft tissue and bony reconstruction are facilitated and reported rates of pin tract infection are relatively low.[78,106,165,172]

When treating polytrauma or multiply injured patients, complex shaft fractures, supracondlyar, intracondylar, and other fracture-dislocations about the elbow can be temporized by the application of a provisional elbow-spanning fixator. This reduces the fracture at length with a generalized repositioning of the fragments and can maintain the reduction of a grossly unstable elbow dislocation. When the patient's status improves, or the soft tissues recover, formal treatment of the injuries can be safely undertaken (Fig. 8-45).

In select severe elbow injuries that undergo internal fixation, the construct may be further augmented by the application of

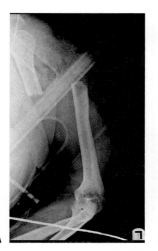
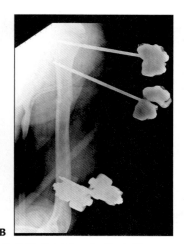

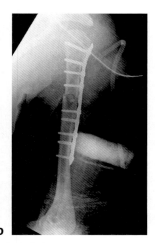

FIGURE 8-44 A. Multiply injured patient with open proximal humerus. **B,C.** Damage control measures included application of fracture-spanning external fixator. **D.** When patient had recovered from initial injuries, definitive fixation was carried out at 9 days postinjury using plate fixation in conjunction with frame removal.

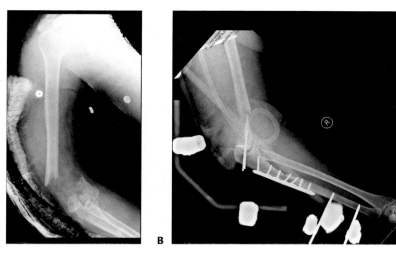

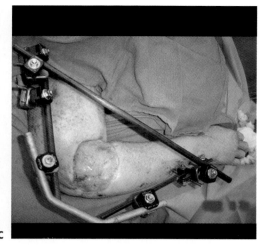

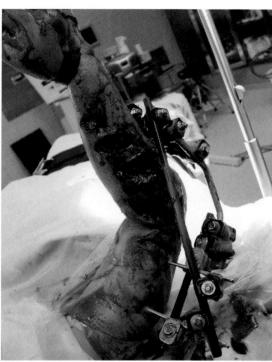

FIGURE 8-45 (A–C) Severe open elbow injury with substantial bone and soft tissue loss. Stability was maintained with an elbow-spanning fixator which allowed free flap procedures as well as reconstruction of the elbow to proceed. **(D)** Multiple soft tissue and skeletal injuries of the entire upper extremity from a boat propeller injury. Stabilization accomplished emergently with a spanning fixator.

a hinge-type elbow fixator, or a static elbow-spanning fixator. The use of a hinged external fixator for supplemental fixation of distal humerus fractures may be effective in cases where internal fixation is severely compromised by comminution or bone loss or in conjunction with an unstable elbow joint.[62] Other indications for the application of an elbow hinge fixator are related to elbow instability as the primary pathology. This includes recurrent dislocation or subluxation of the elbow after repair or tenuous fixation of large coronoid fractures due to fragmentation or osteopenia. The hinge fixator has also been used to augment the reconstruction of bony, capsuloligamentous, and/or musculotendinous stabilizers following the open stabilization of the joint. A relative indication for use of an elbow hinge includes providing stability following fascial arthroplasty or débridement for infection, if the débridement destabilizes the elbow.[168,191,192,255]

Many investigators using hinge fixators document the resto-

ration of stability and excellent motion after relocation of a chronic elbow dislocation. Good results have also demonstrated its usefulness as a tool following the reconstruction of acute and chronic elbow instability or instability after fracture-dislocation (Fig. 8-46).

In some cases of nonunion of the humerus shaft, standard treatment options such as intramedullary nailing or compression plating and bone grafting may not applicable or recommended, due to subclinical infection, severe osteoporosis, poor soft tissues, or other confounding variables. Many authors have advocated a one-stage debridement, with or without autogenous bone grafting, and application of an Ilizarov external fixator. The frame is then acutely compressed in the operating room followed by slow gradual compression (0.25 to 0.50 mm per day) for several weeks postoperatively (Fig. 8-47). Some series report that the Ilizarov treatment of complex distal humeral and midshaft nonunions that have failed internal fixation has been

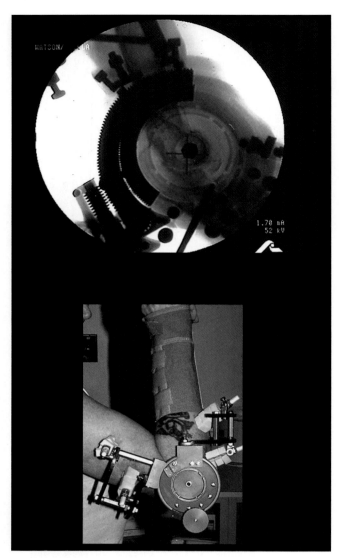

FIGURE 8-46 Elbow hinge placed to augment repair of a chronically dislocated elbow. Hinge assists in providing concentric reduction while the repair heals. Patient is able to continue to perform therapy without fear of re-dislocation. Hinge devices are very technique dependent, and placement of axis pin in the center of rotation of the distal humerus is crucial to maintain a concentric reduction of the elbow with range of motion (note fluoroscopy image documenting accurate center of rotation).

successful and has restored function, decreased pain, and improved quality of life. The Ilizarov method may offer a salvage procedure with a successful clinical outcome.[32,190,225]

Tibial Fractures

Open tibial diaphyseal fractures are primarily candidates for closed intramedullary nailing; however, there are occasions when external fixation is indicated. External fixation is favored when there is significant contamination and severe soft tissue injury or when the fracture configuration extends into the metaphyseal/diaphyseal junction or the joint itself, making intramedullary nailing problematic.

Monolateral external fixation allows for rapid closed reduction, which also helps to limit the amount of operative time and blood loss. It is useful in patients with multiple injuries or

in the patients where prolonged anesthesia is contraindicated. A simple single or double bar unilateral system allows for independent pin placement, while the larger Monotube frames facilitate rapid application with fixed pin couples.[26,47,71,78,80]

Contemporary simple monolateral fixators have clamps that allow independent adjustments at each pin–bar interface, allowing wide variability in pin placement, which helps to avoid areas of soft tissue compromise. Because of this feature, simple four-pin placement may be random on either side of the fracture. In general, the most proximal and most distal pins are first inserted as far away from the fracture line as possible and the connecting rod is attached. The rod is positioned close to the bone to increase the strength of the system. The intermediate pins can then be inserted using the multiaxial pin fixation clamps as templates with drill sleeves as guides. Upon placement of these two additional pins, the reduction can then be achieved with minimal difficulty (see Figs. 8-19 and 8-20).

Alternatively, the proximal two pins can be connected by a solitary bar and the distal two pins are connected to a solitary bar. Both proximal and distal bars are then used as reduction tools to manipulate the fracture into alignment. Once reduction has been achieved, an additional bar to bar construct between the two fixed pin couples is connected.

Use of the large Monotube fixators facilitates rapid placement of these devices with the fixed pin couple acting as pin templates. Two pins are placed through the fixator pin couple proximal to the fracture and two pins are placed through the pin couple distal to the fracture. Care must be taken to allow adequate length of the Monotube frame prior to final reduction and tightening of the body (Fig. 8-48).

Most Monotube bodies have a very large diameter, which limits the amount of shearing, torsional and bending movements of the fixation construct. Axial compression is achieved by releasing the telescoping mechanism. Dynamic weight bearing is initiated at an early stage once the fracture is deemed stable. In fractures that are highly comminuted, weight bearing is delayed until visible callus is achieved and sufficient stability has been maintained. The telescopic body allows dynamic movement in an axial direction, which is a stimulus for early periosteal healing.[12–14]

Because external fixators offer the ability to compress actively across fracture fragments, fracture gaps secondary to comminution and minimal bone loss can be closed directly by this maneuver. Fracture gaps secondary to malalignment can be corrected sequentially as bone union takes place. This can be accomplished with most circular and select monolateral fixators with three-dimensional adjustability.[13,15,174]

Closed tibial fractures treated with external fixation heal on an average in 4 to 5 months. In an effort to accelerate this rate, most proponents of external tibial fixation believe that early dynamization or gradual frame disassembly should be performed in an effort to effect load transfer to the fracture and promote secondary callus formation. Research and clinical studies have been inconclusive on the advantages of passive dynamization. However, dynamization does seem to facilitate fracture healing if it is used within the first 6 to 8 weeks following the fracture. Kenwright and colleagues demonstrated significant improvement in the time to union with active dynamization.[125–127]

If a major bone defect exists at the fracture site, dynamization may result in permanent shortening. If more than 1.5- to

FIGURE 8-47 A. Segmental bone loss with small distal supra condylar remnant precluding traditional plate fixation of this injury. Ring fixator applied with sequential compression across comminution to achieve bone contact. **B.** Continued compression allowed healing of the humeral shaft fracture with approximately 1.5 cm of shortening; however, no bone grafting was necessary.

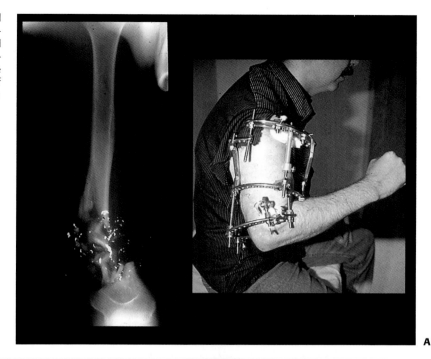

A

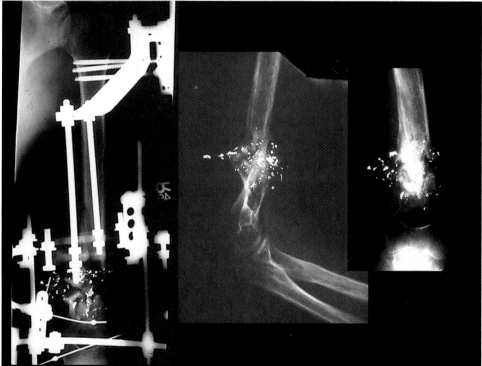

B

2-cm discrepancy will be the result, then dynamization is not indicated. Most external fixators have bone transport capabilities as an option to regain limb length and skeletal continuity.[234,237]

Often tibia fractures with severe soft tissue injury have concomitant foot injuries as well. These patients require multiple reconstructive procedures and are often initially treated with external fixation techniques such as a bridging frame. It is advantageous to extend these frames down onto the hindfoot and forefoot to avoid the common complication of equinous defor-

mity. This can develop over time specifically in those patients with a wide zone of injury, which can cause the posterior compartment and other tissues to contract (see Fig. 8-35B).

Small Wire External Fixation

Diaphyseal long bone injuries are best managed using half-pin techniques. This is easily accomplished when the fracture occurs in the mid portion of the long bone, allowing adequate regions of diaphyseal bone above and below the fracture to be stabilized by half-pins, which achieve solid bicortical pin purchase.

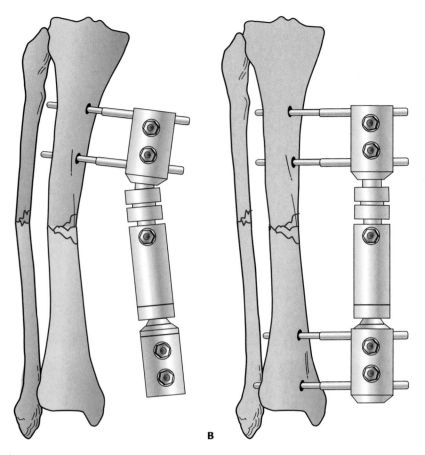

A

B

FIGURE 8-48 A. Monotube fixator allows rapid reduction and stabilization for complex tibia fractures. Fixed pin connectors act as templates to place proximal pins. **B.** Distal pins are then applied again through the distal pin clamp. The Monotube allows for reduction in all three planes. Once reduction has been achieved, the Monotube is locked and reduction is maintained.

However, as many high-energy fractures involve the tibial metaphyseal regions, transfixion techniques using small tensioned wires are ideally suited to this region. They demonstrate better mechanical stability and longevity compared with traditional half-pin techniques.

Because of the tension exerted on the small periarticular wires, this approach may avoid the need to span the ankle or the knee joint to maintain the reduction. The small tensioned wires may be used in concert with limited open reduction if necessary. Olive wires can be used to achieve and maintain "tension compression fixation" across small metaphyseal fragments, similar to the effect achieved with small lag screws. Therefore, the combination of smooth and olive wires are be used to neutralize deforming forces across the fracture lines and help to achieve and maintain compression across the fracture lines[1,112] (Fig. 8-49).

In contrast to other hybrid techniques, a completely circular frame offers more adjustability and will not incur detrimental mechanical forces such as cantilever bending. These detrimental forces are commonly generated with traditional hybrid techniques if performed incorrectly. The "hybrid" has evolved to include a traditional monolateral diaphyseal bar attached to a solitary circular periarticular ring. Full ring stabilization is preferable to monolateral shaft stabilization because of the cantilever loading accentuated with this construct. Specifically in the proximal tibia, this type of frame configuration functions similar to a diving board, producing tremendous loads at the metaphyseal diaphyseal junction with associated development of nonunion or malunion.[4,5,6,240,241,243,244] If monolateral adaptations are to

be used, it is recommended that at least three divergent connecting bars be attached to the periarticular ring.[6] The bars should be oriented to achieve at least 270 degrees of separation to alleviate cantilever loading. An additional disadvantage of this standard "hybrid" construct is the inability to easily dynamize the fixator.[187,188,238,249]

Surgical application of a circular hybrid periarticular fixator can be performed with the patient on either a fracture or radiolucent table with calcaneal pin or distal tibial pin traction. Following a ligamentotaxis reduction of the metaphyseal fragments, olive wires or percutaneous small fragment screws can be used to achieve interfragmentary compression of these metaphyseal components. If necessary, limited incisions are used to elevate

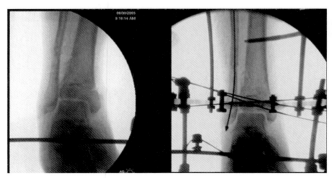

FIGURE 8-49 Ring construct using tensioned smooth and olive wires to stabilize small periarticular fracture fragments.

FIGURE 8-50 Anatomic specimen showing the capsular reflections around the knee joint. Care must be taken to avoid capsular penetration when placing periarticular wires around the knee. (Courtesy of Spence Reid, MD.)

the depressed articular fragments as well as bone graft the subchondral defects. It has been shown that at least three periarticular wires are necessary to stabilize these injuries. Most authors using small wire techniques recommend that as many wires as can be inserted safely should be used for maximal stability.[6,76,229,239,241,244,254] Biomechanical data support the use of tensioned wire fixation stabilizing complex fractures of the proximal tibia. The stability achieved with a four-wire fixation construct is comparable to that of dual plating for bicondylar tibial plateau fractures.[5,240,241]

When using transfixion wires, care should be taken to avoid the proximal tibial capsular reflection, as well as the distal ankle joint to avoid tethering the capsule.[87,229,231] This maintains the wires in an extra-articular location and avoids secondary contamination of the joints, which can result in knee or ankle sepsis (Fig. 8-50).

The treatment of these injuries has also included the use of monotube ankle bridging and simple monolateral external fixator designs.[25,81] These are applied to achieve a distraction reduction across their respective joints, followed by limited open reduction and internal fixation. The advantage of using monotube constructs for either plateau or pilon fractures is that articular fixation is achieved and maintained without the use of small tensioned wires and the potential for articular contamination is avoided[224] (Fig. 8-51).

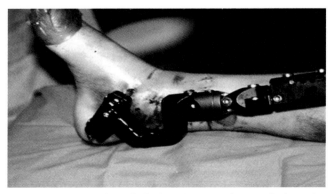

FIGURE 8-51 Monotube ankle-bridging fixator used to provide distraction in combination with limited internal fixation for pilon fractures.

Bone Transport

Treatment of acute bone loss following severe tibial shaft fractures continues to be a complex reconstructive problem. Many procedures have been devised to reconstitute bone stock, obtain fracture union, and provide a stable functional limb. Cancellous grafting, whether placed directly into the defect or through a posterolateral approach, has been the most common methodology; however, often this technique requires numerous grafting procedures.[47,48,223] Fibular bypass, tibial fibular synostosis, ipsilateral direct fibular transfer, and free vascularized fibular transfer have been used to reconstruct these large defects.[48,71,77] Internal bone transport has been developed as a primary method of bony reconstruction in acute tibial fractures with bone loss. This technique is indicated for reconstruction of defects greater than 4 cm.*

Bone transport can be carried out with a modified Monotube monolateral fixator that has an intercalary sliding mechanism to transport the bone segment. Likewise, ring fixators can also be configured to perform successful intercalary bone transport.

The basic transport frame using a ring fixator consists of four or five rings. A stable proximal and distal ring block is placed at the level of the knee and ankle joints. A transport ring is placed in the midportion of the tibia. Orientation of the frame on the limb is crucial to ensure that the proposed docking site is aligned and will provide sufficient cortical contact for union to occur. Likewise, appropriate alignment using a monotube construct is also critical to ensure docking site alignment. The intercalary transport component is attached to bone using either transfixion wires or half-pin techniques. An antibiotic cement spacer is also placed across the defect. This block provides additional stability to the frame–bone construct and acts to maintain the transport space. The block remains in place until the next debridement, free flap procedure, or delayed primary closure of the wound (Fig. 8-52A).

At the time of definitive wound coverage, the antibiotic block spacer is removed and a solitary string of antibiotic cement beads is placed in the defect. The beads provide and maintain a "potential space" or fibrous tunnel through which the transport segment will travel. This space allows relative unencumbered movement of the transport segment underneath the flap. If no flap is needed, the wound is closed primarily and antibiotics beads are still used to maintain the potential space and prevent invagination of the intact soft tissue envelope into the transport pathway** (Fig. 8-52B–D).

If soft tissue loss is not sufficient to expose bone at the site of skeletal defect, then soft tissue transport in conjunction with the bone transport is possible.[48,57,113,114] Tissue loss that exposes bone is not amenable to combined soft tissue–bone transport without first addressing the exposed bone. This is accomplished through rotational or free tissue transfer to cover the bone. Alternatively, the bone should be resected back until healthy soft tissue covers the bony segment.[167,200,234,235] At this time, acute shortening or gradual shortening can be accomplished and the soft tissue defect allowed to heal without additional coverage procedures. Following soft tissue healing, relengthening or deformity correction can then be carried out through the use of the frame.

*References 1,17,48,94,95,112,120,174,203,234,235,237,242.
**References 94,95,112,203,234,235,237,243.

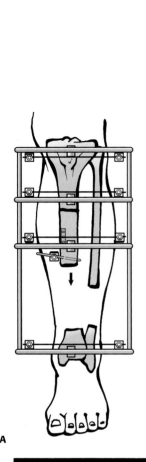

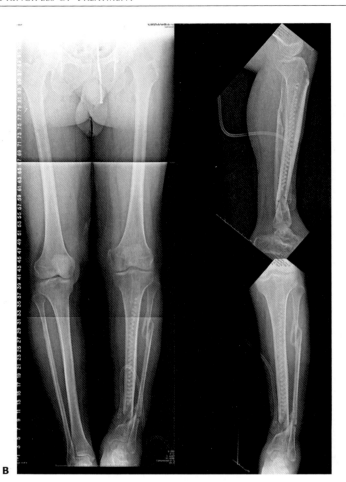

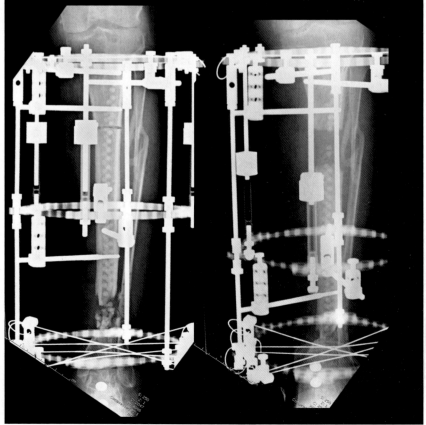

FIGURE 8-52 A. A typical four-ring transport frame attaching the rings to the bone with either transfixion wires or half-pins. **B.** Long alignment and plain films document the infected distal tibial defect. Previous intramedullary débridement was performed along with the application of antibiotic beads down the medullary canal, which had become ingrown and could not be removed. **C.** Transport frame applied with proximal tibial corticotomy. Resorbable calcium sulfate antibiotic beads maintain the potential space in the transport tract. As docking approaches, the beads were compressed and autografting to the docking site was carried out.

(continues)

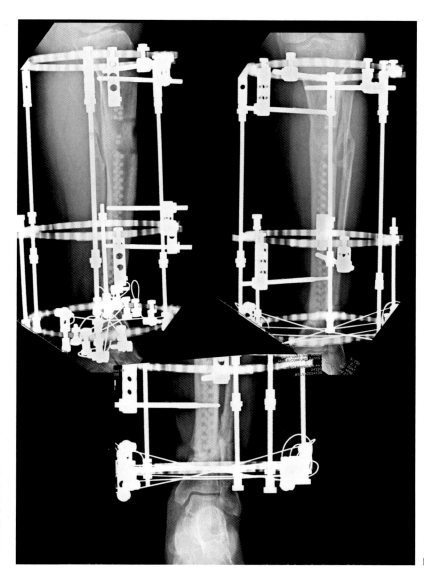

FIGURE 8-52 (*continued*) **D.** The regenerate and docking sites appear healed. The regenerate is mature as is indicated by the reconstitution of the medial and lateral cortices, as well as reconstitution of the posterior cortex and nearly complete restoration of the anterior cortex. The frame was successfully removed without docking site nonunion or late deformity of the regenerate.

D

Transport is delayed for at least 3 weeks following free flap coverage. If no flap is used, corticotomy and transport can be undertaken immediately at the time of wound closure. This 3-week delay allows for healing of the flap over the bony defect, as well as early neovascularization of the zone of injury. The delay also allows the free flap anastomosis site to become fully epithelialized, which is then able to withstand the inevitable tension forces that it is subjected to during the bone transport process.[1,112] The location of the transport Schanz pins should be in the inferior portion of the transport segment, so that it will "pull" the bone into docking position" rather than "push" the transport segment. This is the case if the pins were located more proximal in the transport segment. This construct results in an unstable situation where the transport segment will have a tendency to deviate during transport.[1,94,95,112,242]

Following fixation of the transport segment, a proximal or distal corticotomy is performed. Because of the wide zone of injury that often occurs following open tibial fractures, it is better to perform the corticotomy away from any region of soft tissue compromise. A latency period of 7 to 10 days is allowed prior to the initiation of transport. The initial rate of distraction

begins slowly at 0.25 to 0.5 mm per day. A slower distraction rate is recommended initially because of the wide variability in injury patterns and vascularity of the limb. In more extensive fractures with a wide zone of injury, transport should be undertaken very slowly and the regenerate bone visualized by approximately 2 to 3 weeks postcorticotomy. The distraction rate can then be adjusted depending on the quality of the regenerative bone. Transport in the acute fracture proceeds at a much slower rate, 0.5 to 0.75 mm per day, as opposed to the standard rate of 1 mm a day typical for standard limb lengthening.

To decrease the transport distance, the limb can be shortened acutely at the time of frame application.[48] This shortening aids in soft tissue coverage by decreasing tension and gaps in the soft tissues. Shortening acutely can be accomplished safely for defects up to 3 to 4 cm in the tibia and humerus. More shortening can be tolerated acutely in a femoral defect up to 5 to 7 cm. In some situations, it is advantageous to decrease the transport distance, and thus time, in the frame. Shortening aids in soft tissue coverage by decreasing tension and gaps in the open wound; this approach combined with vacuum-assisted closure (VAC) may allow wounds to be closed by delayed primary closure or healed by secondary intention or simple skin grafting. With this technique, one may avoid extensive free flap coverage.[48,57,113,114,167,200,234,235]

However, acute shortening greater than 4 cm is not recommended due to distortion of the neurovascular elements, which results in the development of edema and inability of the musculotendinous units to function properly[242] (see Fig. 8-33). Bone transport continues until the antibiotic beads have been compressed to the width of one bead. At this time, the patient is returned to surgery and the docking site is exposed. The beads are removed and the bone ends are freshened to achieve punctate bleeding surfaces. A high-speed burr can be used to fashion congruent surfaces on the ends of the proposed docking segments. This ensures maximal cortical contact and increases stability at the docking site. Autogenous iliac crest bone graft is placed directly into the docking site at this time, and distal transport is resumed within 24 hours of the procedure.[1,48,94,95,234-236]

The docking site is impacted and gradually compressed 0.25 mm every 48 hours until the docking site is radiographically healed. Numerous authors have found that grafting the atrophic docking site aids in the speed of union with a subsequent decrease in the overall time the patient must remain in the fixator.[48,94,95,237] Bone transport is a reliable technique; however, it is very time consuming and requires extreme patient compliance. The principles of transport include a stable external fixation system above and below the defect. The primary importance is the ability to develop a biologically sound wound at the transport location.

Hexpod Fixators

As external fixation devices and techniques have become more sophisticated, the ability to simultaneously correct a complex deformity with a simplistic device has become more attractive. The Taylor Spatial Frame was designed to allow simultaneous correction in six axes (i.e., coronal angulation, translation, sagittal angulation and translation, rotation and shortening). To achieve this with conventional frames, a complex customized frame mounting would be required. Additionally, the mounting of these traditional frames would be fairly difficult due to the fact that the rings need to be placed parallel to the respective reference joints, as well perpendicular to the long axis of the limb. In cases of deformity or fracture, this can be very problematic. The hexapod-type frames allow the rings to be positioned in any orientation within their respective limb segment (i.e., above the fracture site). It is not necessary that the rings be parallel with respect to joints or perpendicular to the long axis of the bones. This demanding technique has been vastly simplified using this six-axis "hexapod" concept.[205]

The hexapod is a ring fixator Ilizarov-type design with a configuration consisting of 6 distractors and 12 ball joints, which allows for 6 degrees of freedom of bone fragment displacement. By adjusting the simple distractors, gradual three-dimensional corrections or acute reductions are possible without the need for complicated frame mechanisms.[205]

As a fixation device, it is unique in that its optimal use depends on the use of computer software. Once the rings are mounted, the deformity parameters are calculated with respect to angulation, translation, in both the anteroposterior and lateral planes. Additional information about rotational and axial mal-

alignment is also computed. These deformity parameters are then placed into the software program along with the frame mounting parameters. The frame mounting parameters include data points such as height of the distance of the frame from the deformity or fracture site location. The overall length of the six struts is also a variable, which is entered into the software calculations. The program will then calculate the final strut lengths necessary to achieve a corrected limb alignment. In addition, daily strut adjustments can also be calculated to affect a very gradual correction over a specific time period that the surgeon wishes to achieve. The final alignment can be further adjusted using the same software applying similar deformity and strut parameters to the program.[196]

In the acute application, this frame allows emergent placement of a relatively simple frame. The frame can be attached using either transfixion wires or a minimum of three half-pins on either side of the fracture. At this point, an approximate reduction can be achieved grossly at the time of surgery and the final reduction can be completed over a short period of time using the software program and gradual adjustment of the six struts (Fig. 8-53). The hexapod frames and Internet software offer the advantage of very accurate and precise control of multiple deformities without significant soft tissue dissection. A relatively straightforward and simple external device is applied to effect these corrections.

Studies now have documented the hexapod frames' ability to achieve gradual realignment of complex pediatric fractures and deformities.[3,74,79,213] One can comprehensively approach tibial nonunions with the Taylor spatial frame (TSF). This is particularly useful in the setting of stiff hypertrophic nonunion, infection, bone loss, leg length descrepancy (LLD), and poor soft tissue envelope. Investigators have determined that previously infected nonunions have a higher risk of failure than non-infected cases; however, these results are consistent with most studies treating infected nonunions by any modality.[198,199] What is unique is the hexapod frames' ability to resolve multiple deformities and restore leg length equality with a relatively simplistic frame application[79,198,199,205,228] (Fig. 8-54).

FRAME MANAGEMENT

Often during treatment using external fixators, secondary procedures are required. This may include soft tissue coverage procedures or delayed bone grafting. Most external fixator frames can easily be modified or placed out of the zone of injury. Most surgeons find it problematic to drape the fixator out of the operative field and maintain this unusually small area as sterile throughout an entire procedure. The benefits of safely prepping an external frame into the operative field include the ability to maintain reduction during secondary conversion procedures, decreasing the time, material cost, and frustration in trying to drape a fixator safely out of the operative field. It has been shown that following standardized protocol, preclensing the external fixator frame, followed by alcohol wash, sequential povidone-iodine prep, paint, and spray with air drying followed by draping the extremity and fixator directly into the operative field, additional surgery can be safely performed without the risk of an increased rate of postoperative wound infection.[93,236] It is possible to perform free flaps and other soft tissue procedures directly around the external fixator pins as long as the pins do not communicate directly with the operative site.

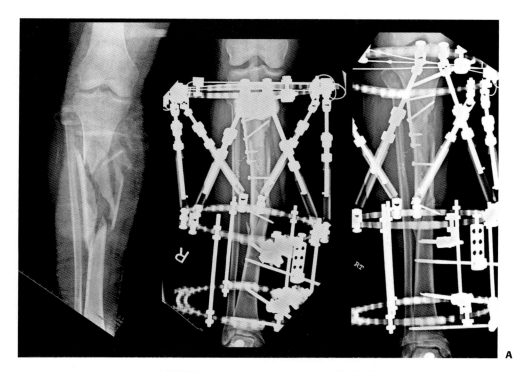

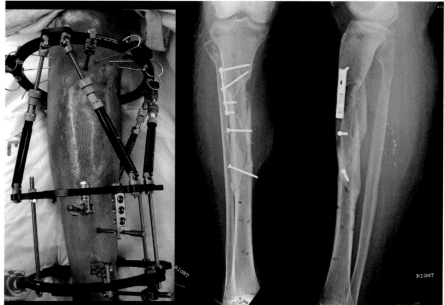

FIGURE 8-53 A. Complex open proximal tibial fracture with bone and soft tissue loss. Acute management includes conversion of a spanning fixator to a Taylor Spatial Frame, with limited internal fixation at the time of free flap coverage. The valgus malalign-ment was gradually corrected over 10 days to restore the correct mechanical axis. **B.** The pin sites did not encroach into the flap region and required minimal pin care. The frame was removed at 14 weeks postinjury with alignment maintained.

Pin Insertion Technique

The integrity of the pin–bone interface is the critical link in the stability of the external fixation system. External fixation pins placed in cancellous metaphyseal bone frequently loosen over time, resulting in fixation failure and increased risk for infection. The fixation pin in cortical/diaphyseal regions can remain intact and infection free for extended periods of time. Thus, each pin in the fixation construct should be continually evaluated for these potential problems to avoid an unstable fixator.

The correct insertion technique involves incising the skin directly at the side of pin insertion. Following generous incision, dissection is carried directly down to bone and the periosteum is incised where anatomically feasible. A small Penfield-type elevator is used to gently reflect the periosteum off of the bone at the site of insertion. Extraneous soft tissue tethering and necrosis are avoided by minimizing soft tissue at the site of insertion. A trocar and drill sleeve are advanced directly to bone, minimizing the amount of soft tissue entrapment that might be encountered during predrilling. The drill sleeve should be centered in the midportion of the medullary canal (Fig. 8-55). One needs to ensure that the pin trajectory traverses the near cortex, then the medullary canal, and finally exits the far cortex. In this fashion, you avoid a transcortical pin, which is a stress riser and can be a site of fracture once the frame has been removed. A sleeve should also be used if a self-drilling pin is selected. Following predrilling, a pin of appropriate depth is

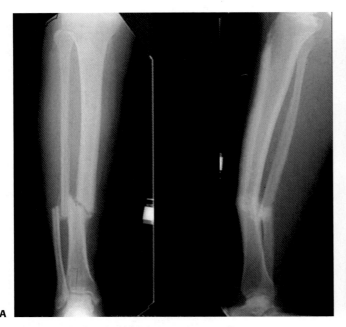

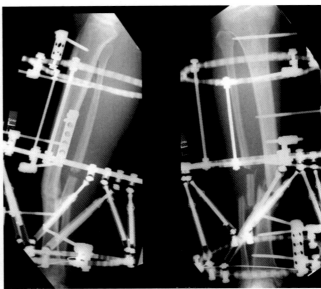

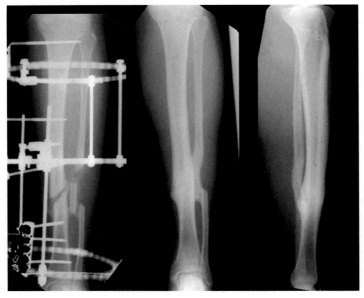

FIGURE 8-54 A. Complex tibial nonunion with malrotation, angulation, translation, and leg length discrepancy. **B.** Taylor Spatial Frame applied to limb using primarily half-pin attachments. Patient's self-adjustment of the six oblique struts will gradually correct all deformity parameters. **C.** Complete realignment and consolidation via gradual distraction osteogenesis; no grafting was required to achieve these results.

advanced to achieve bicortical purchase and any offending soft tissue tethering should be released with a small scalpel.[1,93]

Pin Care

The universal standard for pin care has yet to be identified. Pin site recommendations are based more often on clinical preference rather than on strict research findings. The pin care protocol should be based on the pathophysiologic processes involved in the development of pin site infection.[93] It should be noted that correct pin site insertion technique removes most of the factors that cause pin site infection and subsequent pin loosening.[93,176] If appropriate insertion technique is used, the pin sites will completely heal around each individual pin, much like a pierced earring insertion site heals. Once healed, only showering, without any other pin cleansing procedures, is necessary.[247] The occasional removal of a serous crust around the pins using dilute hydrogen peroxide and saline may be necessary.[1,25,88,93]

In general, recommendations include using normal saline as the cleansing agent in concert with dilute hydrogen peroxide.[88,93] Review of the Cochrane database with regard to the most effective pin care regimen was undertaken. All randomized controlled trials comparing the effect on infection and other complication rates of different methods of cleansing or dressing orthopaedic percutaneous pin sites were evaluated. Three trials compared a cleansing regimen with no cleansing, two trials compared cleansing solutions, one trial compared identical pin site care performed daily or weekly, and four trials compared dressings. One of these trials reported that infection rates were lower (9%) with a regimen that included cleansing with half-strength hydrogen peroxide and application of Xeroform dressing compared with other regimens.[220] However, the authors agree with the conclusions of other investigators that there is insufficient evidence for a particular strategy of pin site care that minimizes infection rates.[73,140]

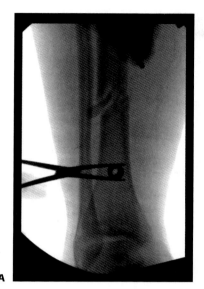
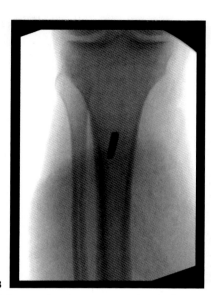
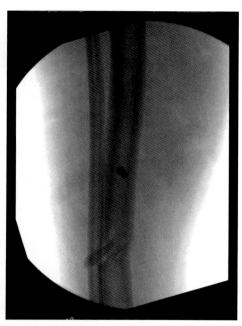

A   B   C

FIGURE 8-55 A. The drill sleeve and trochar are centered on the bone to ensure that the pin is not eccentrically located and traverses both cortices and the medullary canal. The pin must engage the posterior cortex and be central in the bone to avoid postframe stress fracture through an errant transcortical pin tract. **B,C.** Central location of diaphyseal pins.

One should avoid ointments for postcleansing care, as these tend to inhibit the normal skin flora and alter the normal skin bacteria, and thus can lead to superinfection or pin site colonization.[149] It is important to remove the buildup of crusted material, which will tend to stiffen the pin–skin interface and increase shear forces at the pin–bone interface (Fig. 8-56A). This leads to the development of additional necrotic tissues and fluid buildup around the pin.[51] Immediate postoperative compressive dressing should be applied to the pin sites to stabilize the pin–skin interface and thus minimize pin–skin motion, which can lead to additional necrotic debris. By "training" the skin, the pin site remains stable.[1,112] This allows the skin to heal around the pin undisturbed. Compressive dressings can be removed within 10 days to 2 weeks' time once the pin sites are healed (Fig. 8-56B,C). If pin drainage does develop, then providing pin care three times per day should be undertaken. This may also involve rewrapping and compressing the offending pin site in an effort to minimize the abnormal pin–skin motion.[112]

Review of large pin site registries has documented a significant difference in the rates of pin tract infection between large Schanz half-pins and small transfixion wires. For acute fracture fixation fixators, patients with hybrid external fixators demonstrated a similar risk of pin tract infection as patients who had unilateral fixators. The infection rate in the ring fixator (using small transfixion wires) group was significantly lower than the hybrid external and unilateral fixator groups (using primarily Schanz half-pins).[176]

Similar pin registries evaluating the rates of pin tract infection for limb-lengthening procedures demonstrated similar results. The rate of half-pin site infection was significantly ($P < .05$) higher in half-pin fixators (100%) compared with hybrid fixators (78%) where a combination of thin wire and half-pins was used. When half-pins were compared exclusively to thin wires, a

significantly ($P < .05$) higher incidence of half-pin site infection (78%) over fine-wire site infection (33%) was revealed.[9]

These findings highlight the need to insert half-pins with correct technique (as described earlier) to avoid excessive soft tissue impingement, incarceration, or development of necrotic tissue at the site of half-pin insertion.

Frame Removal

Definitive treatment with an external fixator demands closed scrutiny of the radiographs to ensure that the fracture or distraction site has completely healed prior to frame removal. Numerous authors have described various techniques including computed tomography scans, ultrasound, and bone densitometry to determine the adequacy of fracture healing.[1,16,17,112] In general, the patient should be fully weight bearing with a minimal amount of pain noted at the fracture site. The frame should be fully dynamized such that the load is being borne by the patient's limb rather than by the external fixator (Fig. 8-57). For distraction osteogenesis, the patient's radiographs are visualized in the anteroposterior and lateral planes. It is necessary to see three of four neocortices in the regenerate zone reconstituted to ensure that the bone is mechanically stable and able to tolerate frame removal[1,15,17,94,95] (Fig. 8-52D). Late deformity following frame removal is very common and usually is the result of incomplete healing of the distraction regenerate.[1,112] In the tibia, this is because the subcutaneous border anteriorly has the least amount of soft tissue coverage and thus blood supply. However, mechanical stability requires only three of four reconstituted cortices.

With standard external fixation techniques, similar precautions should be adhered to in order to avoid refracture or the development of nonunion. Four oblique views should be obtained to determine the adequacy of fracture healing prior to frame removal.

A

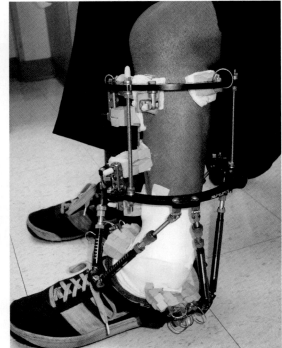

B

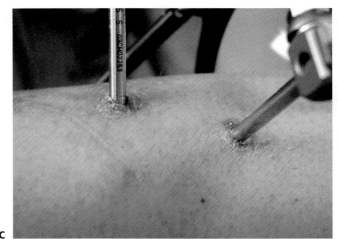

C

D

E

FIGURE 8-56 A. While the pin sites are healing, the serous fluid that develops at the pin site develops crusting that should be removed with mild peroxide or mild soap and water. **B.** The pin–skin interface should be compressed and stabilized to minimize motion and subsequent development of any necrotic material. Gauze wraps around the pins or pin sponges can be used to provide the stabilization. **C.** Healed pin sites require no special care other than mild soap and water. No ointments or antiseptics are required for the maintenance of a healed/sealed pin site. **D.** Long-term pins develop painful hypertrophic keratosis surrounding the pin sites and should be excised at the time of pin removal. **E.** Grade 4 pin tract infection with seropurlulent drainage and redness requires vigorous pin care and antibiotics.   *(continues)*

Ease of frame removal in an outpatient or office setting is variable depending on the type of fixator pins used. A study evaluated the ability to remove stainless steel pin fixators in the office setting without anesthesia. Removal of these particular external fixators without anesthesia was well tolerated by the great majority of patients. Inflammation at pin sites was associated with a higher degree of discomfort during external fixator removal. Despite the higher pain score, most patients with pin site inflammation report that they would repeat the procedure without anesthesia.[201]

This study confirms the concept that stainless steel pins are usually easily removed; however, newer pin designs, including titanium pins, as well as HA-coated pins, are more problematic. With the biological ingrowth nature of these biomaterials, pin removal is often difficult, requiring sufficient force to loosen (break) the intact pin–bone interface. This may inflict a signifi-

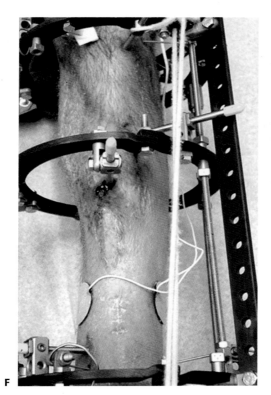

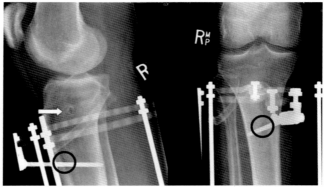

FIGURE 8-56 (*continued*) **F.** Grade 5 pin tract infection with surrounding erythema, inflammation, and purulent drainage. Radiographs of this region must be examined for radiographic signs, suggestive of pin loosening. **G.** Radiographic evidence of pin sepsis and loosening includes pin sequestrum (*white arrow*) and cortical lucencies (*black circle*).

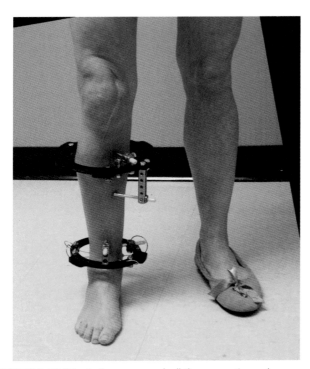

FIGURE 8-57 Prior to frame removal, all the connecting rods were removed and only the rings remain. The frame has been fully dynamized, and the patient was allowed to ambulate full weight bearing. The patient is instructed to be aware of any signs of pain or deformity, which would indicate incomplete healing. If this occurs, the connecting bars can easily be reapplied and the frame not removed at this time.

cant amount of pain, which may preclude this procedure occurring in an office setting.[160,164] In patients whose treatment time has been prolonged, there is often a large overgrowth of heterotopic pin keratosis that has built up around the pin sites. This can leave an unsightly painful scar if not removed and therefore should be excised at the time of pin removal (Fig. 8-56D).

Frame Reuse

In this era of cost containment for health care, the practice of recycling external fixator components makes economic sense. Dirschl and Smith reported on a single center's experience with a reuse program. Components in good repair were returned to the operating room stock for reuse, whereas those showing signs of wear were discarded. No component was used more than three times. The institution charged patients a "loaner fee" equal to the hospital's cost for the inspection, processing, and recycling of fixator components. The mean hospital cost for a fixator decreased 34% as a result of this program. There were no differences in the rates of reoperation or complications before and after institution of the reuse program. No patient had mechanical failure of a new or reused component.[63,64,132]

Many investigators have evaluated the mechanical properties of recycled fixator components.[63,64,110,132] A thorough examination of clinically removed frames, including static mechanical testing, has shown no reduction in performance or catastrophic mechanical failure of recycled parts that showed no visual signs of wear. The potential cost savings, combined with the documented safety of recycled components, makes reuse of these devices attractive.

August 2000 marked a significant change for hospitals or companies that perform in-house reprocessing of single use medical devices (external fixator components). The U.S Food and Drug Administration (FDA) announced new guidelines for hospitals as well as third party reprocessing companies that now holds them to the same rigorous premarket submission requirements as manufacturers. For every device a hospital wants to reprocess, it must submit information to the FDA that demonstrates the safety and effectiveness of that device following reprocessing. This means that hospitals now face tough choices, with a wide range of factors to consider, such as cost liability, quality assurance, and device tracking. Since this ruling went into effect, many hospitals have determined that they lack the resources to meet the arduous premarket submission requirements (510K approval). Hospitals that performed their own reprocessing have been forced to decide whether to continue to recycle at great expense, stop using reprocessed devices, or outsource to a third party preprocessor. Many have decided to outsource the service.

Preprocessing, whether in-house or by a third party company, can result in cost savings over the purchase price of new fixator components. Data currently suggest that this does not compromise a hospital's standard of care or patient outcomes. A recent study at Boston University evaluated reuse of reprocessed external fixation frames at the time of removal, for efficacy of function and potential complications of their use such as pin tract infections, loss of fixation, or loosening of components.[218] The authors found no statistical differences in the incidence of pin tract infections, loss of fixation, or loosening of the components, compared with those patients treated with new fixators. Their study demonstrated that this type of reuse program was safe and effective with a potential savings of 25% compared with the cost of all new frames.

Devices must be tested and recertified prior to redeployment in hospital stock. Horwitz and colleagues, using a conservative pass rate and the assumption of a maximum of three recertifications for each component, calculated the total potential hospital savings on external fixation components when this program was instituted.[110] Components were returned to the original manufacturer for reprocessing. The first-pass rate was 76% for initial reprocessing. The second-pass rate (i.e., the rate for components that had already been recertified once and had been sent for a second recertification) was 83%. On the basis of a conservative pass-rate estimate of 75%, the predicted average number of uses of a recyclable component was 2.7. The recertified components were sold back to their institution at 50% of the original price. Because carbon-fiber bars and half-pins were not recycled, 85% of the charges expended on new external fixation components were spent on portions of the system that were recyclable. The potential total savings on reusable components was found to be 32%, with a total savings of 27% for the whole external fixation system. The investigators noted that no recertified components failed in clinical use over the course of the study.

These studies demonstrate the real cost savings associated with a manufacturer-based testing and recertification program. However, issues of voluntary participation in reuse programs by the patient as well as informed consent of the use of reprocessed components, component ownership, and the impact of savings on patient charges have yet to be worked out by individual institutions.

Pin Complications

Wire and pin site complications include pin site inflammation, chronic infection, loosening, and metal fatigue failure. Most

authors agree that infection rates from external fixation pins have steadily decreased, as pin technology has increased, but are still very far from zero.[60] The rates of frank pin tract infection have been chronicled as antidotal observations mentioned off hand in many studies regarding external fixation given as the basis for a pin tract infection and pin failure. The major problem inherent in all external fixator studies has been the definition of what exactly an infected pin site consists of. Histologic examination of the tissues surrounding the inflamed pin site might lead to the conclusion that almost every pin tract is infected. The most common wire and pin site complications are now graded by the classification as described by Dahl et al[55] (Table 8-1).

The *Grade 0* pin site appears normal other than marginal erythema and requires only weekly pin care (see Fig. 8-56C).
Grade 1 infection does show marginal inflammation; however, no drainage is apparent and treatment requires more frequent pin care consisting of daily cleansing with mild soap or half-strength peroxide and saline solution.
Grade 2 pin tract infection consists of an inflamed pin site with serous type discharge.
Grade 3 pin tract infections consist of an inflamed pin site with purulent discharge; both *grade 2* and *grade 3* pin tract infections require placement of the patient on antibiotics and continued daily pin care.
Grade 4 pin tract infection consists of serous or seropurulent drainage in concert with redness, inflammation, and radiographs demonstrating osteolysis of both the near and far cortices (see Fig. 8-56E). Once osteolysis is visible demonstrating bicortical involvement, removal of the offending pin should be carried out immediately. Local soft tissue debridement of the pin tract with peroxide or other astringent irrigant should be performed. Formal surgical management is unnecessary as long as there is no obvious radiolucencies noted on the plain radiographs at the side of osteolysis (Fig. 8-56G)
Grade 5 pin tract inflammation consists of inflamed purulent drainage and osteolysis, as well as sequestrum noted around these abscesses within the medullary canal. Deep-seated infection is present, and this requires formal irrigation and debridement procedures with delivery of culture-specific antibiotics (Fig. 8-56F). In an effort to avoid collapse of the external fixation construct and the establishment of biomechanical frame instability, pin exchange should be carried out in conjunction with the pin removal process.

Premature Consolidation

In patients undergoing distraction osteogenesis techniques, the problem of premature consolidation is most commonly diagnosed as a failure of the corticotomy site to open and lengthen following initiation of distraction. In most instances, the problem is actually an incomplete osteotomy rather than the premature healing of the osteotomy site.[1,112,242] When this occurs in the tibia, it is a failure to completely osteotomize the posterior lateral cortex. This complication occurs primarily with surgeons who do not have a large amount of experience in performing percutaneous corticotomy techniques. Most experienced surgeons will perform the corticotomy and then manually distract the corticotomy site acutely for 1 to 2 mm under fluoroscopic control to ensure that the corticotomy is complete and can man-

TABLE 8-1	**DAHL Pin Site Classification**			
Grade	Inflammation	Drainage	Radiographic Findings	Treatment
0	None or marginal	None	None	Weekly care
1	Marginal inflammation	None	None	Frequent pin care with mild soap or half-strength peroxide
2	Inflamed	Serous	None	Same as for grade 1 plus oral antibiotics
3	Inflamed	Purulent	None	Same as for grade 2
4	Inflamed with induration	Seropurulent	Osteolysis at near and far cortices	Pin removal local wound care
5	Inflamed with induration, tenderness, surrounding erythema	Gross purulent drainage	Sequestrum and medullary abscess	Formal surgical debridement with culture-specific antibiotics

ually be distracted. Using the fixator pins half above and below the corticotomy as joysticks, the limb segments can be counterrotated one against the other under fluoroscopy to ensure that a complete osteotomy has occurred.[1,94–96,112,242]

Premature consolidation does occur most commonly in a pediatric population where distraction must begin much sooner compared with a mature patient. It is usually due to a prolonged latency period allowing significant callus formation to bridge across the corticotomy site. This is seen clinically, when examining the frame and seeing excessive deflection of the wires or half-pins with a concomitant lack of a distraction gap on radiography; if this is recognized early in the treatment phase, continued slow distraction can be carried out until the premature area of consolidation ruptures.[1,112] The patient should be warned, however, that he may feel or hear an audible ache, snap, or pop in the limb with sudden pain and concomitant swelling. Should this occur, the patient should immediately reverse the distraction and compress the region until the pain has subsided. If the patient continues to distract following the fracture of the premature consolidation zone, significant diastasis in the distraction gap will be created causing rupture of the neovascular channels. This may result in the formation of cysts with incomplete regenerate formation and possible regenerate failure.[1,15,16,112–114,174]

Should the slow distraction fail to achieve disruption of the premature consolidation, the patient should be returned to the operating room where closed manipulation can sometimes be successful in achieving complete corticotomy. Should this fail, a repeat corticotomy should be carried out.

The most common cause of incomplete regenerate healing includes disruption of the periosteum and soft tissues during corticotomy, too rapid a distraction, and frame instability.[15,16,112–114]

The rate and rhythm of distraction should be modulated in accordance with the radiographic visualization of the regenerate bone including the formation of the interzone and longitudinal orientation of trabecular bone. Any evidence of disruption or nonlinear orientation of the trabecular bone should be a clear sign that frame instability has occurred. Each pin, wire, and ring connection should be checked and, if necessary, additional pins or wires added to assure adequate frame stability. This will help to avoid formation of intercalary cartilaginous elements.

Regenerate refracture or late deformity following removal of the apparatus usually presents as a gradual deviation of the limb. This often occurs as a result of the patient and treating surgeon becoming "frame weary," which results in premature frame removal prior to complete healing of the regenerate or fracture.[1,112] Certainly, one should always error on the conservative side and leave the frame on for an extended period of time to ensure that the fracture has healed.

Refracture through a docking site is unusual and is usually the result of incomplete healing. What is more common is fracturing through an osteoporotic stress fracture or through a previous pin or wire hole site.

When late deformity or regenerate collapse occurs, this usually leads to an unsatisfactory outcome unless collapse is detected early and the frame reapplied. Untreated, the resulting malunion requires secondary osteotomy procedures.

Pin and wire site fracture, as well as docking site or fracture site refractures, can usually be treated with a cast if detected early before significant malalignment occurs. However, in complex cases, frame reapplication is required.

Contractures

Muscle contractures usually result from excessive joint distraction. This can occur over an extended period of time such as the use of an ankle bridging monotube fixator or temporary traveling traction spanning the knee or ankle.[208] A common complication when using lower extremity external fixators is the development of equinus contractures of the foot and ankle. To prevent this, prophylaxis should be encouraged by spanning the tibial frame down onto the forefoot in a neutral position.

Contractures result when the resting muscle length becomes relatively short compared with that of the newly lengthened bone. Thus, tibial lengthening or bone transport can cause flexion contractures at the knee and equinus contractures of the ankle. Measures should be taken to provide prophylaxis against severe muscle contractures when dealing with correction of leg length discrepancy.[1,112] This also occurs during the correction of malunions or nonunions where, following the deformity correction, relative length is restored. Preventive measures include avoiding transfixion of tendons and maximizing muscle excursion before placing transfixion wires or half-pins. Physical therapy throughout the course of treatment is helpful as is splinting and maintaining a plantigrade foot in neutral and the knee in full extension when the patient is at rest.

CONCLUSION

Advances in biomechanics and biomaterials continue to result in improvements in pin and frame technology. External fixation frames can now remain in place for prolonged periods of time without degradation in the pin–bone interface. Simplified frame mountings have extended the indications for use of these devices, not only for acute fracture management but also for the reconstruction of complex posttraumatic conditions. Cutting edge technologies such as web-based software interfacing with digital radiographs, combined with uncomplicated frame adjustments, can now produce anatomic restoration of limbs that previously could not be achieved with external devices. External fixation continues to provide a powerful means to treat a variety of challenging conditions as the ultimate noninvasive tool.

REFERENCES

1. ASAMI Group, Maiocchi AB, Aronson J, eds. Operative Principles of Ilizarov: Fracture Treatment, Nonunion, Osteomyelitis, Lengthening, Deformity Correction. Baltimore, MD: Williams & Wilkins, 1991.
2. Agee JM. External fixation. Technical advances based upon multiplanar ligamentotaxis. Orthop Clin North Am 1993;24:265–274.
3. Al-Sayyad MJ. Taylor Spatial Frame in the treatment of pediatric and adolescent tibial shaft fractures. J Pediatr Orthop 2006;26:164–170.
4. Ali AM, Burton M, Hashmi M, et al. Outcome of complex fractures of the tibial plateau treated with a beam-loading ring fixation system. J Bone Joint Surg Br 2003;85B:691–699.
5. Ali AM, Saleh M, Bolongaro S, et al. The strength of different fixation techniques for bicondylar tibial plateau fractures: a biomechanical study. Clin Biomech (Bristol, Avon) 2003;18:864–870.
6. Ali AM, Yang L, Hashmi M, et al. Bicondylar tibial plateau fractures managed with the Sheffield Hybrid Fixator. Biomechanical study and operative technique. Injury 2001;32 suppl 4:SD86–SD91.
7. Anderson R. An automatic method of treatment for fractures of the tibia and the fibula. Surg Gynecol Obstet 1936;62:865–869.
8. Andrianne Y, Wagenknecht M, Donkerwolcke M, et al. External fixation pin: an in vitro general investigation. Orthopedics 1987;10:1507–1516.
9. Antoci V, Ono CM, Antoci V Jr, et al. Pin-tract infection during limb lengthening using external fixation. Am J Orthop 2008;37:E150–E154.
10. Arazi M, Yalcin H, Tarakcioglu N, et al. The effects of dynamization and destabilization of the external fixator on fracture healing: a comparative biomechanical study in dogs. Orthopedics 2002;25:521–524.
11. Aro HT, Chao EY. Bone-healing patterns affected by loading, fracture fragment stability, fracture type, and fracture site compression. Clin Orthop 1993;8–17.
12. Aro HT, Hein TJ, Chao EY. Mechanical performance of pin clamps in external fixators. Clin Orthop 1989;246–253.
13. Aro HT, Kelly PJ, Lewallen DG, et al. The effects of physiologic dynamic compression on bone healing under external fixation. Clin Orthop 1990;260–273.
14. Aro HT, Markel MD, Chao EY. Cortical bone reactions at the interface of external fixation half-pins under different loading conditions. J Trauma 1993;35:776–785.
15. Aronson J, Harp JH Jr. Mechanical considerations in using tensioned wires in a transosseous external fixation system. Clin Orthop 1992;23–29.
16. Aronson J, Harrison B, Boyd CM, et al. Mechanical induction of osteogenesis: the importance of pin rigidity. J Pediatr Orthop 1988;8:396–401.
17. Aronson J, Johnson E, Harp JH. Local bone transportation for treatment of intercalary defects by the Ilizarov technique. Biomechanical and clinical considerations. Clin Orthop 1989;71–79.
18. Atroshi I, Brogren E, Larsson GU, et al. Wrist-bridging versus nonbridging external fixation for displaced distal radius fractures: a randomized assessor-blind clinical trial of 38 patients followed for 1 year. Acta Orthop 2006;77:445–453.
19. Augat P, Burger J, Schorlemmer S, et al. Shear movement at the fracture site delays healing in a diaphyseal fracture model. J Orthop Res 2003;21:1011–1017.
20. Augat P, Claes L, Hanselmann KF, et al. Increase of stability in external fracture fixation by hydroxyapatite-coated bone screws. J Appl Biomater 1995;6:99–104.
21. Augat P, Merk J, Wolf S, et al. Mechanical stimulation by external application of cyclic tensile strains does not effectively enhance bone healing. J Orthop Trauma 2001;15:54–60.
22. Behrens F. General theory and principles of external fixation. Clin Orthop 1989;241:15–23.
23. Behrens F, Johnson W. Unilateral external fixation. Methods to increase and reduce frame stiffness. Clin Orthop 1989;48–56.
24. Behrens F, Johnson WD, Koch TW, et al. Bending Stiffness of Unilateral and Bilateral Fixator Frames. Clin Orthop 1983;178:103–110.
25. Bereton V. Pin-site care and the rate of local infection. J Wound Care 1998;7:42–44.
26. Bhandari M, Zlowodzki M, Tornetta P 3rd, et al. Intramedullary nailing following external fixation in femoral and tibial shaft fractures. J Orthop Trauma 2005;19:140–144.
27. Biliouris TL, Schneider E, Rahn BA, et al. The effect of radial preload on the implant-bone interface: a cadaveric study. J Orthop Trauma 1989;3:323–332.
28. Blasier RD, Aronson J, Tursky EA. External fixation of pediatric femur fractures. J Pediatr Orthop 1997;17:342–346.
29. Bosse MJ, Holmes C, Vossoughi J, et al. Comparison of the Howmedica and Synthes military external fixation frames. J Orthop Trauma 1994;8:119–126.
30. Bottlang M, Marsh JL, Brown TD. Articulated external fixation of the ankle: minimizing motion resistance by accurate axis alignment. J Biomech 1999;32:63–70.
31. Briggs BT, Chao EY. The mechanical performance of the standard Hoffmann-Vidal external fixation apparatus. J Bone Joint Surg Am 1982;64A:566–473.
32. Brinker MR, O'Connor DP, Crouch CC, et al. Ilizarov treatment of infected nonunions of the distal humerus after failure of internal fixation: an outcomes study. J Orthop Trauma 2007;21:178–184.
33. Broos PLO, Sermon A. From unstable internal fixation to biological osteosynthesis: a historical overview of operative fracture treatment. Acta Chir Belg 2004;104:396–400.
34. Bronson DG, Samchukov ML, Birch JG. Stabilization of a short juxta-articular bone segment with a circular external fixator. J Pediatr Orthop B 2002;11:143–149.
35. Burny F, Bourgois R. [Biomechanical study of the Hoffman external fixation device]. Acta Orthop Belg 1972;38:265–279.
36. Burny F. Elastic external fixation of fractures of the long bones. Arch Putti Chir Organi Mov 1986;36:323–329.
37. Caja VL, Larsson S, Kim W, et al. Mechanical performance of the Monticelli-Spinelli external fixation system. Clin Orthop 1994;257–266.
38. Caja VL, Piza G, Navarro A. Hydroxyapatite coating of external fixation pins to decrease axial deformity during tibial lengthening for short stature. J Bone Joint Surg Am 2003;85A:1527–1531.
39. Calhoun JH, Li F, Ledbetter BR, et al. Biomechanics of the Ilizarov fixator for fracture fixation. Clin Orthop 1992;15–22.
40. Calhoun JL, Li F, Bauford WL, et al. Rigidity of half-pins for the Ilizarov external fixator. Bull Hosp Jt Dis 1992;52:21–26.
41. Capper M, Soutis C, Oni OO. Pin-hole shear stresses generated by conical and standard external fixation pins. Biomaterials 1993;14:876–878.
42. Carmichael KD, Bynum J, Goucher N. Rates of refracture associated with external fixation in pediatric femur fractures. Am J Orthop 2005;34:439–444; discussion 444.
43. Chao EY, Aro HT, Lewallen DG, et al. The effect of rigidity on fracture healing in external fixation. Clin Orthop 1989;24–35.
44. Chao EY, Hein TJ. Mechanical performance of the standard Orthofix external fixator. Orthopedics 1988;11:1057–1069.
45. Chao EY, Kasman RA, An KN. Rigidity and stress analyses of external fracture fixation devices—a theoretical approach. J Biomech 1982;15:971–983.
46. Chaudhary S, Patil N, Bagaria V, et al. Open intercondylar fractures of the distal humerus: Management using a miniexternal fixator construct. J Shoulder Elbow Surg 2008;17:465–470.
47. Christian EP, Bosse MJ, Robb G. Reconstruction of large diaphyseal defects, without free fibular transfer, in grade IIIB tibial fractures. J Bone Joint Surg 1989;71A:994–1002.
48. Cierny G, Zorn KE. Segmental tibial defects. Comparing conventional and Ilizarov methodologies. Clin Orthop 1994;301:118–123.
49. Claes L, Eckert-Hubner K, Augat P. The effect of mechanical stability on local vascularization and tissue differentiation in callus healing. J Orthop Res 2002;20:1099–105.
50. Clary EM, Roe SC. In vitro biomechanical and histological assessment of pilot hole diameter for positive-profile external skeletal fixation pins in canine tibiae. Vet Surg 1996;25:453–462.
51. Clasper JC, Cannon LB, Stapley SA, et al. Fluid accumulation and the rapid spread of bacteria in the pathogenesis of external fixator pin track infection. Injury 2001;32:377–381.
52. Cross AR, Lewis DD, Murphy ST, et al. Effects of ring diameter and wire tension on the axial biomechanics of four-ring circular external skeletal fixator constructs. Am J Vet Res 2001;62:1025–1030.
53. Cunningham JL, Evans M, Harris JD, et al. The measurement of stiffness of fractures treated with external fixation. Eng Med 1987;16:229–232.
54. Dahl MT. The gradual correction of forearm deformities in multiple hereditary exostoses. Hand Clin 1993;9:707–718.
55. Dahl MT, Gulli B, Berg T. Complications of limb lengthening a learning curve. Clin Orthop 1994;301:10–18.
56. Dahners LE, Jacobs RR, McKenzie EB, et al. Biomechanical studies of an anterior pelvic external fixation frame intended for control of vertical shear fractures. South Med J 1986;79:815–817.
57. D'Hooghe P, Defoort K, Lammens J, et al. Management of a large posttraumatic skin and bone defect using an Ilizarov frame. Acta Orthop Belg 2006;72:214–218.
58. De la Huerta F. Correction of the neglected clubfoot by the Ilizarov method. Clin Orthop 1994;89–93.
59. Degernes LA, Roe SC, Abrams CF Jr. Holding power of different pin designs and pin insertion methods in avian cortical bone. Vet Surg 1998;27:301–306.
60. DeJong ES, DeBerardino TM, Brooks DE, et al. Antimicrobial efficacy of external fixator pins coated with a lipid stabilized hydroxyapatite/chlorhexidine complex to prevent pin tract infection in a goat model. J Trauma 2001;50:1008–1014.
61. Della Rocca GJ, Crist BD. External fixation versus conversion to intramedullary nailing for definitive management of closed fractures of the femoral and tibial shaft. J Am Acad Orthop Surg 2006;14(10 suppl):S131–S135.
62. Deuel CR, Wolinsky P, Shepherd E, et al. The use of hinged external fixation to provide additional stabilization for fractures of the distal humerus. J Orthop Trauma 2007;21:323–329.
63. Dirschl DR, Smith IJ. Reuse of external fixator components: effects on costs and complications. J Trauma 1998;44:855–858.

64. Dirschl DR, Obremskey WT. Mechanical strength and wear of used EBI external fixators. Orthopaedics 2002;25:1059–1062.
65. Dodds SD, Cornelissen S, Jossan S, et al. A biomechanical comparison of fragment-specific fixation and augmented external fixation for intra-articular distal radius fractures. J Hand Surg [Am] 2002;27:953–964.
66. Dougherty PJ, Vickaryous B, Conley E, et al. A comparison of two military temporary femoral external fixators. Clin Orthop 2003;176–183.
67. Doyle J, Hayes P, Fenlon G. Experimental analysis of effects of pin pretensioning on external fixator rigidity. Arch Orthop Trauma Surg 1988;107:377–380.
68. Drijber FL, Finlay JB. Universal joint slippage as a cause of Hoffmann half-frame external fixator failure [erratum in J Biomed Eng 1993;15:174]. J Biomed Eng 1992;14: 509–515.
69. Duda GN, Sollmann M, Sporrer S, et al. Interfragmentary motion in tibial osteotomies stabilized with ring fixators. Clin Orthop 2002;163–172.
70. Easley ME, Montijo HE, Wilson JB, et al. Revision tibiotalar arthrodesis. J Bone Joint Surg Am 2008;90A:1212–1223.
71. Edwards CC. Staged reconstruction of complex open tibial fractures using Hoffmann external fixation: clinical decisions and dilemmas. Clin Orthop 1983;178:130–161.
72. Egol KA, Bazzi J, McLaurin TM, et al. The effect of knee-spanning external fixation on compartment pressures in the leg. J Orthop Trauma 2008;22:680–685.
73. Egol KA, Paksima N, Puopolo S, et al. Treatment of external fixation pins about the wrist: a prospective, randomized trial. J Bone Joint Surg Am 2006;88A:349–354.
74. Eidelman M, Bialik V, Katzman A. Correction of deformities in children using the Taylor spatial frame. J Pediatr Orthop B 2006;15:387–395.
75. El Hayek T, Daher AA, Meouchy W, et al. External fixators in the treatment of fractures in children. J Pediatr Orthop B 2004;13:103–109.
76. Endres T, Grass R, Biewener A, et al. [Advantages of minimally invasive reposition, retention, and hybrid Ilizarov fixation for tibial pilon fractures with particular emphasis on C2/C3 fractures]. Unfallchirurg 2004;107:273–284.
77. Enneking WF, Eady JL, Burchardt H. Autogenous cortical bone grafts in the reconstruction of segmental skeletal defects. J Bone Joint Surg Am 1980;62A:1039–1058.
78. Etter C, Burri C, Claes L, et al. Treatment by external fixation of open fractures associated with severe sof tissue damage of the leg. Biomechanical principles and clinical experience. Clin Orthop 1983;80–88.
79. Feldman DS, Madan SS, Koval KJ, et al. Correction of tibia vara with six-axis deformity analysis and the Taylor Spatial Frame. J Pediatr Orthop 2003;23:387–391.
80. Fischer DA. Skeletal stabilization with a multiplane external fixation device. Design rationale and preliminary clinical experience. Clin Orthop 1983;:50–62.
81. Fitzpatrick DC, Foels WS, Pedersen DR, et al. An articulated ankle external fixation system that can be aligned with the ankle axis. Iowa Orthop J 1995;15:197–203.
82. Fitzpatrick DC, Sommers MB, Kam BC, et al. Knee stability after articulated external fixation. Am J Sports Med 2005;33:1735–1741.
83. Fleming B, Paley D, Kristiansen T, et al. A biomechanical analysis of the Ilizarov external fixator. Clin Orthop 1989;95–105.
84. Flinkkila T, Ristiniemi J, Hyvonen P, et al. Nonbridging external fixation in the treatment of unstable fractures of the distal forearm. Arch Orthop Trauma Surg 2003;123: 349–352. Epub 2003 Jun 14.
85. Gardner MJ, Nork SE. Stabilization of unstable pelvic fractures with supra-acetabular compression external fixation. J Orthop Trauma 2007;21:269–273.
86. Gantous A, Phillips JH. The effects of varying pilot hole size on the holding power of miniscrews and microscrews. Plast Reconstr Surg 1995;95:1165–1169.
87. Geller J, Tornetta P 3rd, Tiburzi D, et al. Tension wire position for hybrid external fixation of the proximal tibia. J Orthop Trauma 2000;14:502–504.
88. Gordon JE, Kelly-Hahn J, Carpenter CJ, et al. Pin site care during external fixation in children: results of nihilistic approach. J Pediatr Orthop 2000;20:163.
89. Goodship AE, Cunningham JL, Kenwright J. Strain rate and timing of stimulation in mechanical modulation of fracture healing. Clin Orthop 1998;(355 suppl):S105–S115.
90. Goodship AE, Watkins PE, Rigby HS, et al. The role of fixator frame stiffness in the control of fracture healing. An experimental study. J Biomech 1993;26:1027–1035.
91. Goslings JC, DaSilva MF, Viegas SF, et al. Kinematics of the wrist with a new dynamic external fixation device. Clin Orthop 2001;226–234.
92. Gradl G, Jupiter JB, Gierer P, et al. Fractures of the distal radius treated with a nonbridging external fixation technique using multiplanar K-wires. J Hand Surg [Am] 2005;30: 960–968.
93. Green SA. Complications of External Skeletal Fixation: Causes Prevention, and Treatment. Springfield, IL: Charles C Thomas, 1981.
94. Green SA. Skeletal defects: a comparison of bone grafting and bone transport for skeletal defects. Clin Orthop 1994;310:111–117.
95. Green SA, Jackson JM, Wall DM, et al. Management of segmental defects by the Ilizarov intercalary bone transport method. Clin Orthop 1992;280:136–142.
96. Green SA. The Ilizarov method: Rancho technique. Orthop Clin North Am 1991;22: 677–688.
97. Haidukewych GJ, Kumar S, Prpa B. Placement of half-pins for supra-acetabular external fixation: an anatomic study. Clin Orthop 2003;269–273.
98. Haidukewych GJ. Temporary external fixation for the management of complex intra- and periarticular fractures of the lower extremity. J Orthop Trauma 2002;16:678–685.
99. Hampton OP, ed. Orthopaedic Surgery in the Mediterranean Theatre of Operations. Washington, DC: Office of the Surgeon General, Department of the Army; 1957: 203–210. Bradford C, Wilson PD. Mechanical skeletal fixation in war surgery, with a report of 61 cases. SGO 1942;75:486–476.
100. Handoll HH, Huntley JS, Madhok R. Different methods of external fixation for treating distal radial fractures in adults. Cochrane Database Syst Rev 2008:CD006522.
101. Harer T, Hontzsch D, Stohr E, et al. [How much are external fixator nuts tightened in general practice?] Aktuelle Traumatol 1993;23:212–213.
102. Hart MB, Wu JJ, Chao EY, et al. External skeletal fixation of canine tibial osteotomies. Compression compared with no compression. J Bone Joint Surg Am 1985;67:598–605.
103. Harwood PJ, Giannoudis PV, Probst C, et al. The risk of local infective complications after damage control procedures for femoral shaft fracture. J Orthop Trauma 2006;20: 181–189.
104. Haasper C, Jagodzinski M, Krettek C, et al. Hinged external fixation and closed reduction for distal humerus fracture. Arch Orthop Trauma Surg 2006;126:188–191.
105. Hein TJ, Chao EY. Biomechanical analysis of the Orthofix axial external fixator. Biomed Sci Instrum 1987;23:39–42.
106. Hierholzer G, Ruedi Th, Allgower M, et al., eds. Manual on the AO/ASIF Tubular External Fixator. Berlin: Springer-Verlag, 1985.
107. Hippocrates: An abridged report on external skeletal fixation. Clin Orthop 1989;241: 3–4.
108. Hoffmann R. Closed osteosynthesis with special references to war surgery. Acta Chir Scand 1942;86:255–261.
109. Hoffman R. Osteotaxis: Transcutaneous Osteosynthesis by Means of Screws and Ball and Socket Joints. Paris: Gead, 1953.
110. Horwitz DS, Schabel KL, Higgins TF. The economic impact of reprocessing external fixation components. J Bone Joint Surg Am 2007;89A:2132–2136.
111. Hutchinson DT, Bachus KN, Higgenbotham T. External fixation of the distal radius: to predrill or not to predrill. J Hand Surg [Am] 2000;25:1064–1068.
112. Ilizarov GA. Transosseous osteosynthesis. In: Green S, ed. Theoretical and Clinical Aspects of the Regeneration and Growth of Tissue. Berlin: Springer Verlag, 1992.
113. Ilizarov GA. The tension-stress effect on the genesis and growth of tissues: part II. The influence of the rate and frequency of distraction. Clin Orthop 1989;263–285.
114. Ilizarov GA. The tension-stress effect on the genesis and growth of tissues: part I. The influence of stability of fixation and soft-tissue preservation. Clin Orthop 1989; 249–281.
115. Jackson M, Topliss CJ, Atkins RM. Fine wire frame-assisted intramedullary nailing of the tibia. J Orthop Trauma 2003;17:222–224.
116. Jagodzinski M, Haasper C, Knobloch C, Krettek C [Treatment of chronic knee dislocation with an external fixator]. Unfallchirurg 2005;108:597–600.
117. Jaskulka RA, Egkher E, Wielke B. Comparison of the mechanical performance of three types of unilateral, dynamizable external fixators. An experimental study. Arch Orthop Trauma Surg 1994;113:271–275.
118. Johnson HF, Stovall SL. External fixation of fractures. J Bone Joint Surg Am 1950;32A: 466–471.
119. Juan JA, Prat J, Vera P, et al. Biomechanical consequences of callus development in Hoffmann, Wagner, Orthofix, and Ilizarov external fixators. J Biomech 1992;25: 995–1006.
120. Kabata T, Tsuchiya H, Sakurakichi K, et al. Reconstruction with distraction osteogenesis for juxta-articular nonunions with bone loss. J Trauma 2005;58:1213–1222.
121. Karnezis IA, Miles AW, Cunningham JL, et al. Axial preload in external fixator half-pins: a preliminary mechanical study of an experimental bone anchorage system. Clin Biomech (Bristol, Avon) 1999;14:69–73.
122. Kashiwagi N, Suzuki S, Seto Y, et al. Bilateral humeral lengthening in achondroplasia. Clin Orthop 2001;251–257.
123. Kasman RA, Chao EY. Fatigue performance of external fixator pins. J Orthop Res 1984; 2:377–384.
124. Kellam JF. The role of external fixation in pelvic disruptions. Clin Orthop 1989;66–82.
125. Kenwright J, Gardner T. Mechanical influences on tibial fracture healing. Clin Orthop 1998;(355 suppl):S179–S190.
126. Kenwright J, Goodship AE. Controlled mechanical stimulation in the treatment of tibial fractures. Clin Orthop 1989;36–47.
127. Kenwright J, Richardson JB, Cunningham JL, et al. Axial movement and tibial fractures. A controlled randomised trial of treatment. J Bone Joint Surg Br 1991;73B:654–659.
128. Khalily C, Voor MJ, Seligson D. Fracture site motion with Ilizarov and "hybrid" external fixation. J Orthop Trauma 1998;12:21–26.
129. Kreder HJ, Agel J, McKee MD, et al. A randomized, controlled trial of distal radius fractures with metaphyseal displacement but without joint incongruity: closed reduction and casting versus closed reduction, spanning external fixation, and optional percutaneous K-wires. J Orthop Trauma 2006;20:115–121.
130. Krishnan J, Wigg AE, Walker RW, et al. Intra-articular fractures of the distal radius: a prospective randomized controlled trial comparing static bridging and dynamic non-bridging external fixation. J Hand Surg [Br] 2003;28:417–421.
131. Kowalski M, Schemitsch EH, Harrington RM, et al. Comparative biomechanical evaluation of different external fixation sidebars: stainless-steel tubes versus carbon fiber rods. J Orthop Trauma 1996;10:470–475.
132. Kummer FJ, Frankel VH, Catagni MA. Reuse of Ilizarov frame components: A potential cost savings? Contemp Orthop 1992;25:125–128.
133. Lai D, Chen CM, Chiu FY, et al. Reconstruction of juxta-articular huge defects of distal femur with vascularized fibular bone graft and Ilizarov's distraction osteogenesis. J Trauma 2007;62:166–173.
134. Lambotte A. The operative treatment of fractures: report of fractures committee. Br Med J 1912;2:1530.
135. Larsson S, Kim W, Caja VL, et al. Effect of early axial dynamization on tibial bone healing: a study in dogs. Clin Orthop 2001;240–251.
136. Lavini FM, Brivio LR, Leso P. Biomechanical factors in designing screws for the Orthofix system. Clin Orthop 1994;63–67.
137. Lenarz C, Bledsoe G, Watson JT. Circular external fixation frames with divergent half-pins: a pilot biomechanical Study. Clin Orthop Relat Res 2008;466:2933–2939.
138. Lerner A, Fodor L, Keren Y, et al. External fixation for temporary stabilization and wound management of an open pelvic ring injury with extensive soft tissue damage: case report and review of the literature. J Trauma 2008;65:715–718.
139. Lerner A, Ullmann Y, Stein H, et al. Using the Ilizarov external fixation device for skin expansion. Ann Plast Surg 2000;45:535–537.
140. Lethaby A, Temple J, Santy J. Pin site care for preventing infections associated with external bone fixators and pins. Cochrane Database Syst Rev 2008;CD004551.
141. Leung F, Kwok HY, Pun TS, et al. Limited open reduction and Ilizarov external fixation in the treatment of distal tibial fractures. Injury 2004;35:278–283.
142. Leung F, Tu YK, Chew WY, et al. Comparison of external and percutaneous pin fixation with plate fixation for intra-articular distal radial fractures. A randomized study. J Bone Joint Surg Am 2008;90A:16–22.
143. Lewallen DG, Chao EY, Kasman RA, et al. Comparison of the effects of compression plates and external fixators on early bone-healing. J Bone Joint Surg Am 1984;66A: 1084–1091.
144. Lewis KM, Breidenbach L, Stader O. The Stader reduction splint for treating fractures of the shafts of the long bones. Ann Surg 1942;116:623–631.
145. Lowenberg DW, Nork S, Abruzzo FM. Correlation of shear to compression for progressive fracture obliquity. Clin Orthop Relat Res 2008;466:2947–2954.
146. Magyar G, Toksvig-Larsen S, Moroni A. Hydroxyapatite coating of threaded pins enhances fixation. J Bone Joint Surg Br 1997;79B:487–479.

147. Manzotti A, Pullen C, Deromedis B, et al. Knee arthrodesis after infected total knee arthroplasty using the Ilizarov method. Clin Orthop 2001;143–149.

148. Markiewitz AD, Gellman H. Five-pin external fixation and early range of motion for distal radius fractures. Orthop Clin North Am 2001;32:329–335, ix.

149. Marotta JS, Coupe KJ, Milner R, et al. Long-term bactericidal properties of a gentamicin-coated antimicrobial external fixation pin sleeve. J Bone Joint Surg Am 2003;85A(suppl 4):129–131.

150. Marti JM, Roe SC. Biomechanical comparison of the trocar tip point and the hollow ground tip point for smooth external skeletal fixation pins. Vet Surg 1998;27:423–428.

151. Martin C, Guillen M, Lopez G. Treatment of two- and three-part fractures of the proximal humerus using external fixation: a retrospective evaluation of 62 patients. Acta Orthop 2006;77:275–278.

152. Matsushita T, Nakamura K, Ohnishi I, et al. Sliding performance of unilateral external fixators for tibia. Med Eng Phys 1998;20:66–69.

153. Matthews LS, Green CA, Goldstein SA. The thermal effects of skeletal fixation-pin insertion in bone. J Bone Joint Surg Am 1984;66A:1077–1083.

154. McCoy MT, Chao EY, Kasman RA. Comparison of mechanical performance in four types of external fixators. Clin Orthop 1983;23–33.

155. Mears DC, Rubash HE. External and internal fixation of the pelvic ring. Instr Course Lect 1984;33:144–158.

156. Menon DK, Dougall TW, Pool RD, et al. Augmentative Ilizarov external fixation after failure of diaphyseal union with intramedullary nailing. J Orthop Trauma 2002;16:491–497.

157. Metcalfe AJ, Saleh M, Yang L. Techniques for improving stability in oblique fractures treated by circular fixation with particular reference to the sagittal plane. J Bone Joint Surg Br 2005;87B:868–872.

158. Moroni A, Caja VL, Maltarello MC, et al. Biomechanical, scanning electron microscopy, and microhardness analyses of the bone-pin interface in hydroxyapatite coated versus uncoated pins. J Orthop Trauma 1997;11:154–161.

159. Moroni A, Cadossi M, Romagnoli M, et al. A biomechanical and histological analysis of standard versus hydroxyapatite-coated pins for external fixation. J Biomed Mater Res B Appl Biomater 2008;86B:417–421.

160. Moroni A, Faldini C, Marchetti S, et al. Improvement of the bone-pin interface strength in osteoporotic bone with use of hydroxyapatite-coated tapered external-fixation pins. A prospective, randomized clinical study of wrist fractures. J Bone Joint Surg Am 2001;83A:717–721.

161. Moroni A, Faldini C, Pegreffi F, et al. Fixation strength of tapered versus bicylindrical hydroxyapatite-coated external fixation pins: an animal study. J Biomed Mater Res 2002;63:61–64.

162. Moroni A, Faldini C, Pegreffi F, et al. Dynamic hip screw compared with external fixation for treatment of osteoporotic pertrochanteric fractures. A prospective, randomized study. J Bone Joint Surg Am 2005;87A:753–759.

163. Moroni A, Heikkila J, Magyar G, et al. Fixation strength and pin tract infection of hydroxyapatite-coated tapered pins. Clin Orthop 2001;209–217.

164. Moroni A, Vannini F, Mosca M, et al. State of the art review: techniques to avoid pin loosening and infection in external fixation. J Orthop Trauma 2002;16:189–195.

165. Mostafavi HR, Tornetta P 3rd. Open fractures of the humerus treated with external fixation. Clin Orthop Relat Res 1997;187–197.

166. Nakata RY, Chand Y, Matiko JD, et al. External fixators for wrist fractures: a biomechanical and clinical study. J Hand Surg [Am] 1985;10(6 Pt 1):845–851.

167. Nho SJ, Helfet DL, Rozbruch SR. Temporary intentional leg shortening and deformation to facilitate wound closure using the Ilizarov/Taylor spatial frame. J Orthop Trauma 2006;20:419–424.

168. Nolla J, Ring D, Lozano-Calderon S, et al. Interposition arthroplasty of the elbow with hinged external fixation for post-traumatic arthritis. J Shoulder Elbow Surg 2008;17:459–464.

169. Noonan KJ, Price CT. Pearls and pitfalls of deformity correction and limb lengthening via monolateral external fixation. Iowa Orthop J 1996;16:58–69.

170. Ochman S, Frerichmann U, Armsen N, et al. [Is use of the fixateur externe no longer indicated for the treatment of unstable radial fracture in the elderly?] Unfallchirurg 2006;109:1050–1057.

171. Oni OO, Capper M, Soutis C. A finite element analysis of the effect of pin distribution on the rigidity of a unilateral external fixation system. Injury 1993;24:525–527.

172. Oni OO, Capper M, Soutis C. External fixation of upper limb fractures: the effect of pin offset on fixator stability. Biomaterials 1995;16:263–264.

173. Orbay GL, Frankel VH, Kummer FJ. The effect of wire configuration on the stability of the Ilizarov external fixator. Clin Orthop 1992;:299–302.

174. Paley D, Catagni MA, Argnani F, et al. Ilizarov treatment of tibial nonunions with bone loss. Clin Orthop 1989;146–165.

175. Paley D, Lamm BM, Katsenis D, et al. Treatment of malunion and nonunion at the site of an ankle fusion with the Ilizarov apparatus. Surgical technique. J Bone Joint Surg Am 2006;88A(suppl 1, pt 1):119–134.

176. Parameswaran AD, Roberts CS, Seligson D, et al. Pin tract infection with contemporary external fixation: how much of a problem? J Orthop Trauma 2003;17:503–507.

177. Parekh AA, Smith WR, Silva S, et al. Treatment of distal femur and proximal tibia fractures with external fixation followed by planned conversion to internal fixation. J Trauma 2008;64:736–739.

178. Park SH, O'Connor K, McKellop H, et al. The influence of active shear or compressive motion on fracture-healing. J Bone Joint Surg Am 1998;80A:868–878.

179. Parkhill C. A new apparatus for the fixation of bones after resection and in fractures with a tendency to displacement. Trans Am Surg Assoc 1897;15:251–256.

180. Parkhill C. Further observations regarding the use of the bone clamp in ununited fractures with malunion and recent fractures with a tendency to displacement. Ann Surg 1898;27:59–67.

181. Patterson MJ, Cole JD. Two-staged delayed open reduction and internal fixation of severe pilon fractures. J Orthop Trauma 1999;13:85–91.

182. Peltier LM. External skeletal fixation for the treatment of fractures. In: Peltier LM, ed. Fractures: A History and Iconography of Their Treatment. San Francisco: Norman Publishing; 1990:183-196.

183. Pettila MH, Sarna S, Paavolainen P, et al. Short-term external support promotes healing in semirigidly fixed fractures. Clin Orthop 1997;157–163.

184. Pieske O, Geleng P, Zaspel J, et al. Titanium alloy pins versus stainless steel pins in external fixation at the wrist: a randomized prospective study. J Trauma 2008;64:1275–1280.

185. Pettine KA, Chao EY, Kelly PJ. Analysis of the external fixator pin-bone interface. Clin Orthop 1993;18–27.

186. Podolsky A, Chao EY. Mechanical performance of Ilizarov circular external fixators in comparison with other external fixators. Clin Orthop 1993;61–70.

187. Pugh KJ, Wolinsky PR, Dawson JM, et al. The biomechanics of hybrid external fixation. J Orthop Trauma 1999;13:20–26.

188. Pugh KJ, Wolinsky PR, Pienkowski D, et al. Comparative biomechanics of hybrid external fixation. J Orthop Trauma 1999;13:418–425.

189. Ramseier LE, Bhaskar AR, Cole WG, et al. Treatment of open femur fractures in children: comparison between external fixator and intramedullary nailing. J Pediatr Orthop 2007;27:748–750.

190. Raschke M, Khodadadyan C, Maitino PD, et al. Nonunion of the humerus following intramedullary nailing treated by Ilizarov hybrid fixation. J Orthop Trauma 1998;12:138–141.

191. Ring D, Hotchkiss RN, Guss D, et al. Hinged elbow external fixation for severe elbow contracture. J Bone Joint Surg Am 2005;87A:1293–1296.

192. Ring D, Jupiter JB. Compass hinge fixator for acute and chronic instability of the elbow. Oper Orthop Traumatol 2005;17:143–157.

193. Roberts CS, Antoci V, Antoci V Jr, et al. The accuracy of fine wire tensioners: a comparison of five tensioners used in hybrid and ring external fixation. J Orthop Trauma 2004;18:158–162.

194. Roberts CS, Dodds JC, Perry K, et al. Hybrid external fixation of the proximal tibia: strategies to improve frame stability. J Orthop Trauma 2003;17:415–420.

195. Rochman R, Jackson Hutson J, et al. Tibiocalcaneal arthrodesis using the Ilizarov technique in the presence of bone loss and infection of the talus. Foot Ankle Int 2008;29:1001–1008.

196. Rogers MJ, McFadyen I, Livingstone JA, et al. Computer hexapod assisted orthopaedic surgery (CHAOS) in the correction of long bone fracture and deformity. J Orthop Trauma 2007;21:337–342.

197. Rozbruch SR, DiPaola M, Blyakher A. Fibula lengthening using a modified Ilizarov method. Orthopedics 2002;25:1241–1244.

198. Rozbruch SR, Fragomen AT, Ilizarov S. Correction of tibial deformity with use of the Ilizarov-Taylor spatial frame. J Bone Joint Surg Am 2006;88A(suppl 4):156–174.

199. Rozbruch SR, Pugsley JS, Fragomen AT, et al. Repair of tibial nonunions and bone defects with the Taylor Spatial Frame. J Orthop Trauma 2008;22:88–95.

200. Rozbruch S, Weitzman AM, Watson JT, et al. Simultaneous treatment of tibial bone and soft-tissue defects with the Ilizarov method. J Orthop Trauma 2006;20:197–205.

201. Ryder S, Gorczyca JT. Routine removal of external fixators without anesthesia. J Orthop Trauma 2007;21:571–573.

202. Sakurakichi K, Tsuchiya H, Uehara K, et al. Ankle arthrodesis combined with tibial lengthening using the Ilizarov apparatus. J Orthop Sci 2003;8:20–25.

203. Saleh M, Rees A. Bifocal surgery for deformity and bone loss after lower-limb fractures. Comparison of bone-transport and compression-distraction methods. J Bone Joint Surg Br 1995;77:429–434.

204. Schuind FA, Burny F, Chao EY. Biomechanical properties and design considerations in upper extremity external fixation. Hand Clin 1993;9:543–553.

205. Seide K, Wolter D, Kortmann HR. Fracture reduction and deformity correction with the hexapod Ilizarov fixator. Clin Orthop 1999;186–195.

206. Seitz WH Jr, Froimson AI, Brooks DB, et al. External fixator pin insertion techniques: biomechanical analysis and clinical relevance. J Hand Surg [Am] 1991;16:560–563.

207. Seligson D, Donald GD, Stanwyck TS, et al. Consideration of pin diameter and insertion technique for external fixation in diaphyseal bone. Acta Orthop Belg 1984;50:441–450.

208. Simpson AH, Cunningham JL, Kenwright J. The forces which develop in the tissues during leg lengthening. A clinical study. J Bone Joint Surg Br 1996;78B:979–983.

209. Sirkin M, Sanders R, DiPasquale T, et al. A staged protocol for soft tissue management in the treatment of complex pilon fractures. J Orthop Trauma 1999;13:78–84.

210. Shaar CM, Kreuz FP. Manual of Fractures. Treatment by External Skeletal Fixation. Philadelphia: WB Saunders, 1943.

211. Shaar CM, Kreuz FP, Jones DT. End results of treatment of fresh fractures by the use of the Stader apparatus. J Bone Joint Surg 1944;26:471–474.

212. Shearer J, Egan J. Computerized analysis of pin geometry. In: Coombs R, Green SA, Sarmeinto A, eds. External Fixation and Functional Bracing. London: Orthotext, 1989:129–135.

213. Sluga M, Pfeiffer M, Kotz R, et al. Lower limb deformities in children: two-stage correction using the Taylor spatial frame. J Pediatr Orthop B 2003;12:123–128.

214. Sommers MB, Fitzpatrick DC, Kahn KM, et al. Hinged external fixation of the knee: intrinsic factors influencing passive joint motion. J Orthop Trauma 2004;18:163–169.

215. Spiegel PG, VanderSchilden JL. Minimal internal and external fixation in the treatment of open tibia fractures. Clin Orthop 1983;96–102.

216. Stanitski DF, Dahl M, Louie K, et al. Management of late-onset tibia vara in the obese patient by using circular external fixation. J Pediatr Orthop 1997;17:691–694.

217. Strauss EJ, Banerjee D, Kummer FJ, et al. Evaluation of a novel, nonspanning external fixator for treatment of unstable extra-articular fractures of the distal radius: biomechanical comparison with a volar locking plate. J Trauma 2008;64:975–981.

218. Sung JK, Levin R, Siegel J, et al. Reuse of external fixation components: a randomized trial. J Orthop Trauma 2008;22:126–301.

219. Taeger G, Ruchholtz S, Zettl R, et al. Primary external fixation with consecutive procedural modification in Polytrauma. Unfallchirurg 2002;105:315–321.

220. Temple J, Santy J. Pin site care for preventing infections associated with external bone fixators and pins. Cochrane Database Syst Rev 2008;CD004551.

221. Tencer AF, Claudi B, Pearce S, et al. Development of a variable stiffness external fixation system for stabilization of segmental defects of the tibia. J Orthop Res 1984;1:395–404.

222. Tetsworth KD, Paley D. Accuracy of correction of complex lower-extremity deformities by the Ilizarov method. Clin Orthop 1994;102–110.

223. Thakur AJ, Patankar J. Open tibial fractures. Treatment by uniplanar external fixation and early bone grafting. J Bone Joint Surg Br 1991;73B:448–451.

224. Thordarson DB, Markolf KL, Cracchiolo A 3rd. External fixation in arthrodesis of the ankle. A biomechanical study comparing a unilateral frame with a modified transfixion frame. J Bone Joint Surg Am 1994;76A:1541–1544.

225. Tomić S, Bumbasirević M, Lesić A, et al. Ilizarov frame fixation without bone graft for

atrophic humeral shaft nonunion: 28 patients with a minimum 2-year follow-up. J Orthop Trauma 2007;21:549–556.

226. Tsuchiya H, Uehara K, Abdel-Wanis ME, et al. Deformity correction followed by lengthening with the Ilizarov method. Clin Orthop 2002;402:176–183.

227. Vidal J. External fixation. Clin Orthop 1983;180:7–14.

228. Viskontas DG, MacLeod MD, Sanders DW. High tibial osteotomy with use of the Taylor Spatial Frame external fixator for osteoarthritis of the knee. Can J Surg 2006; 49:245–250.

229. Vives MJ, Abidi NA, Ishikawa SN, et al. Soft tissue injuries with the use of safe corridors for transfixion wire placement during external fixation of distal tibia fractures: an anatomic study. J Orthop Trauma 2001;15:555–559.

230. Volkov MV, Oganesian OV. Restoration of function in the knee and elbow with a hinge-distractor apparatus. J Bone Joint Surg Am 1975;57A:591–600.

231. Vora AM, Haddad SL, Kadakia A, et al. Extracapsular placement of distal tibial transfixation wires. J Bone Joint Surg Am 2004;86A:988–993.

232. Wallace AL, Draper ER, Strachan RK, et al. The vascular response to fracture micromovement. Clin Orthop 1994;281–290.

233. Wang ZG, Peng CL, Zheng XL, et al. Force measurement on fracture site with external fixation. Med Biol Eng Comput 1997;35:289–290.

234. Watson JT. Distraction osteogenesis. J AAOS 2006;14:168–174.

235. Watson JT. Nonunion with extensive bone loss: reconstruction with ilizarov techniques and orthobiologics. Opin Tech Orthop 2009;18:95–107.

236. Watson JT, Occhietti M, Parmar V. Rate of postoperative wound infections in patients with pre-existing external fixators treated with secondary open procedures. Presented at the Proceedings of the 15th Annual Meeting Orthopaedic Trauma Association, Charlotte, NC, October 22–24, 1999.

237. Watson JT, Anders M, Moed BR: Bone loss in tibial shaft fractures: management strategies. Clin Orthop 1995;316:1–17.

238. Watson JT, Karges DE, Cramer KE, et al. Analysis of failure of hybrid external fixation techniques for the treatment of distal tibial pilon fractures. Presented at the Proceedings of the 16th Annual Meeting Orthopaedic Trauma Association, San Antonio, TX, October 12–14, 1999.

239. Watson JT, Moed BR, Karges DE, et al. Pilon fractures: treatment protocol based on severity of soft tissue injury. Clin Orthop 2000;375:78–90.

240. Watson JT, Ripple S, Hoshaw SJ, et al. Hybrid external fixation for tibial plateau fractures: clinical and biomechanical correlation. Orthop Clin North Am 2002;33: 199–209.

241. Watson JT. Hybrid external fixation for tibial plateau fractures. Am J Knee Surg 2001; 14:135–140.

242. Watson JT. Bone transport. Tech Orthop 1996;11:132–143.

243. Watson JT. High-energy fractures of the tibial plateau. Ortho Clin N Am 1994;25: 723–752.

244. Watson JT. Tibial pilon fractures. Tech Orthop 1996;11:150–159.

245. Watson MA, Mathias KJ, Maffulli N, et al. The effect of clamping a tensioned wire: implications for the Ilizarov external fixation system. Proc Inst Mech Eng [H] 2003; 217:91–98.

246. Watson MA, Matthias KJ, Maffulli N, et al. Yielding of the clamped-wire system in the Ilizarov external fixator. Proc Inst Mech Eng [H] 2003;217:367–374.

247. W-Dahl A, Toksvig-Larsen S, Lindstrand A. No difference between daily and weekly pin site care: a randomized study of 50 patients with external fixation. Acta Orthop Scand 2003;74:704–708.

248. Williams EA, Rand JA, An KN, et al. The early healing of tibial osteotomies stabilized by one-plane or two-plane external fixation. J Bone Joint Surg Am 1987;69A:355–365.

249. Windhagen H, Glockner R, Bail H, et al. Stiffness characteristics of composite hybrid external fixators. Clin Orthop 2002;267–276.

250. Wosar MA, Marcellin-Little DJ, Roe SC. Influence of bolt tightening torque, wire size, and component reuse on wire fixation in circular external fixation. Vet Surg 2002;31: 571–576.

251. Wu JJ, Shyr HS, Chao EY, et al. Comparison of osteotomy healing under external fixation devices with different stiffness characteristics. J Bone Joint Surg Am 1984;66A: 1258–1264.

252. Yamako G, Ishii Y, Matsuda Y, et al. Biomechanical characteristics of nonbridging external fixators for distal radius fractures. J Hand Surg [Am] 2008;33:322–326.

253. Yasui N, Nakase T, Kawabata H, et al. A technique of percutaneous multidrilling osteotomy for limb lengthening and deformity correction. J Orthop Sci 2000;5:104–107.

254. Yildiz C, Atesalp AS, Demiralp B, et al. High-velocity gunshot wounds of the tibial plafond managed with Ilizarov external fixation: a report of 13 cases. J Orthop Trauma 2003;17:421–429.

255. Yu JR, Throckmorton TW, Bauer RM, et al. Management of acute complex instability of the elbow with hinged external fixation. J Shoulder Elbow Surg 2007;16:60–67.

256. Zaffagnini S, Iacono F, Lo Presti M, et al. A new hinged dynamic distractor, for immediate mobilization after knee dislocations: technical note. Arch Orthop Trauma Surg 2007;Dec 6:78.

257. Zlowodzki M, Prakash JS, Aggarwal NK. External fixation of complex femoral shaft fractures. Int Orthop 2007;31:409–413. Epub 2006 Aug 15.

9

MANAGEMENT OF THE MULTIPLY INJURED PATIENT

Peter V. Giannoudis and Hans Christoph Pape

POLYTRAUMA: INCIDENCE, EPIDEMIOLOGY, AND MORTALITY

Trauma is a major worldwide cause of death and disability that mainly affects young adults and the elderly population.[411] In the United Kingdom, it causes more than 14,500 deaths each year.[371] The definition of *multiple trauma* varies among surgeons from different specialties and between different centers and countries. This has lead to the development of standardized scoring systems to allow comparable stratification of injuries between centers and to aid prediction of morbidity and mortality. Polytrauma patients are the subgroup of injured patients who have sustained injuries to more than one body region and organ with at least one of the injuries being life-threatening. The cumulative severity of this trauma load on the victim's anatomy and physiology is usually expressed as an Injury Severity Score (ISS) of 16 or greater or of 18 or greater.[7,346] Trentz emphasized the pathophysiologic systemic impact of multiple trauma when he defined polytrauma as "a syndrome of multiple injuries exceeding a defined severity (ISS ≥17) with sequential systemic reactions (systemic inflammatory response syndrome [SIRS] for at least 1 day) that may lead to dysfunction or failure of remote organs and vital systems, which have not themselves been directly injured."[185,380]

Polytrauma is reported to occur in 15% to 20% and about 10% of the overall trauma population in the United States[7] and the United Kingdom,[371] respectively. According to the National Trauma Data Bank Annual Report in 2007, which reported on 1,485,098 cases between 2002 and 2006 in the United States, 45.2% of patients sustained minor injuries (ISS 1 to 8) with 32.4% sustaining moderate injuries (ISS 9 to 15), 12.8% severe injuries (ISS 16 to 24), and 9.6% very severe injuries (ISS >24).[368] Motor vehicle–related injuries accounted for 37.9% of all cases, followed by falls at 30.2%. Blunt trauma accounted for 86.2% of all cases with penetrating trauma comprising a further 11.1% and burns 1.7% of the remaining cases. Major peaks occurred in the 16 to 24 years age group because of motor vehicle– and firearm-related injuries and in the 35 to 44 years age group because of motor vehicle–related injuries. Males were more prone to trauma, with only 35% of the trauma victims being female. A review of the mortality rates showed that 3.8% of females died compared with 4.8% of males. A review of the different grades of injury severity shows that the mortality rate for patients with an ISS of 1 to 8 is 0.7%. This compares with 1.9% for an ISS of 9 to 15, 5.3% for an ISS of 16 to 24, and 29.3% for an ISS greater than 24. A review of the mortality rates by organ system shows that patients with abdominal and thoracic injuries have the highest rates at 10.9% and 10.1%, respectively, followed by pelvic injuries at 8.4% and brain and skull injuries at 7.8%. Overall, motor vehicle accidents are associated with the highest mortality, being responsible for about 40% of deaths.[368]

Recent reports of polytrauma in the elderly are somewhat limited and the subject has been given only cursory attention. With an aging, increasingly active elderly population, it is likely that such patients will be seen with increasing frequency. The elderly with diminished physiologic reserve, often in association with significant comorbidities, require special consideration. The distribution of injuries and type of injury mechanism are likely to be different in a population with a high incidence of osteoporosis. Elderly patients can become multiply injured following low-energy trauma and these injuries may have worse outcomes. For example, while falls have been reported to account for only 9% to 11% of injury-related deaths in the general population, they comprise more than 50% of traumatic deaths in persons over 65 years of age.[9] Patients with limited mental or physical capacity are also more likely to be involved in accidents as they are slower to identify and respond to dangerous situations.[181,198] One must also consider the likelihood of a medical emergency such as a myocardial infarction or stroke precipitating an accident, making it necessary to treat this pathology together with the patient's injuries.

Over a 5-year period, of 24,560 patients who were admitted to our institution, 3172 (13%) were severely injured having an ISS equal to or greater than 16. Within this severely injured group, 438 (14%) were over 65 years of age. Therefore, elderly patients with severe injuries accounted for 1.8% of our overall admissions. The median age in the elderly group was 75 years (range, 65 to 100 years) and the median ISS was 25 (range, 16 to 75). Figure 9-1 illustrates the overall distribution of injuries sustained in the elderly and adult age groups. It can be seen that the overall injury distribution is similar, although adults sustained more facial, neck, and abdominal injuries overall and more severe (Abbreviated Injury Score [AIS] 3 or greater) facial, chest, and abdominal injuries compared with the elderly patients. Elderly patients sustained more severe (AIS of 3 or greater) external injuries, all of which were severe burns. High-energy injuries were responsible for the majority of these injuries, although relatively minor trauma became increasingly important in older patients. In patients aged over 65 years who were operated on in the first 24 hours, 47% underwent neurosurgical, 34% extremity or spinal, 15% abdominal, and 7% cardiothoracic interventions. This was not significantly different from the pattern of interventions undertaken in the adult group with rates of 50%, 36%, 19%, and 12%, respectively. The mortality rate was significantly higher in the elderly patients than the adults (42% versus 20%, P <0.0001). Figure 9-2 shows inpatient mortality by age group. This increased significantly with age from 19% in patients younger than 40 years to almost 50% in the over-75 year age group. The difference between consecutive age groups is statistically significant at each point until the final two groups. There was no difference observed between the mortality in the 75- to 85-year-old and the over-85 group (48.2% versus 47.4%, P = NS). Figure 9-3 shows the percentage of those who died in each time period, by age group. It can be seen that in both adult and elderly patients, the majority died within the first 24 hours, falling off progressively with time after this. However, the overall trend was for a greater proportion of the elderly patients to die later compared with the adults. This difference was only statistically significant for the 24- to 72-hour and 2- to 3-week periods (P <0.05 and P <0.001, respectively). Age, ISS, and Glasgow Coma Scale (GCS) score continued to be predictive of mortality in elderly patients but other factors relevant in younger adults were not (Table 9-1).

THE EFFECT OF LEGISLATION AND MOTOR VEHICLE DESIGN ON PREVALENCE AND MORTALITY RATES

In 1997, in the United States, motor vehicle accidents resulted in 41,967 deaths (16 per 100,000 population/year) and 3.4

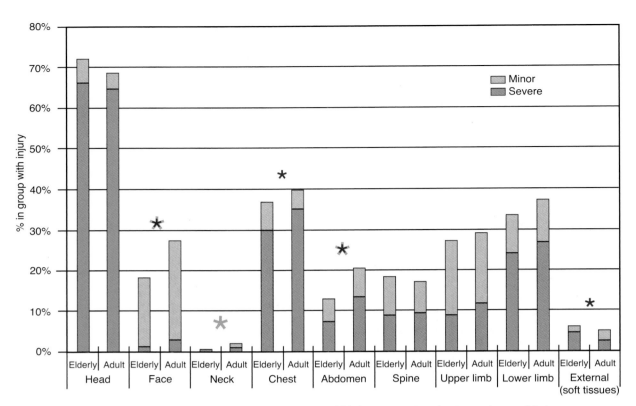

FIGURE 9-1 Distribution of regional injuries by age group (elderly >65 years). Both minor and severe injuries are shown. The asterisks denote statistical significance with the color of the asterisk denoting the severity of the injury.

million nonfatal injuries (1270 per 100,000 population/ year).[256] Motor vehicle–related injuries were the leading cause of death among persons aged 1 to 24 years.[256]

Between 1982 and 2001, in a review of 858,741 traffic deaths in the United States, five risk factors were noted to contribute to mortality: (a) alcohol use by drivers and pedestrians (43%),

(b) failure to wear a seat belt (30%), (c) failure to have an air bag (4%), (d) failure to wear a motorcycle helmet (1%), and (e) failure to wear a bicycle helmet (1%).[73] Over these 20 years, the mortality rates attributed to each risk factor declined because of legislation. There were 153,168 lives saved by decreased drinking and driving, 129,297 by increased use of seat belts,

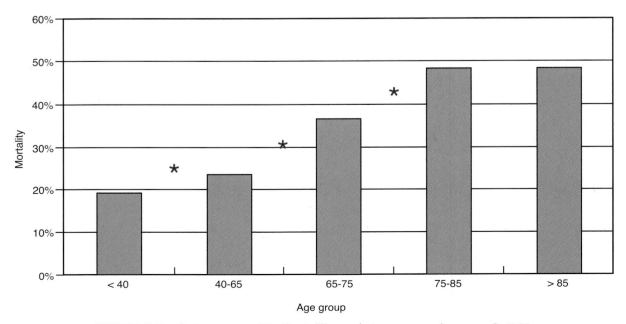

FIGURE 9-2 Mortality by age group. *Significant difference between consecutive groups, $P < 0.05$.

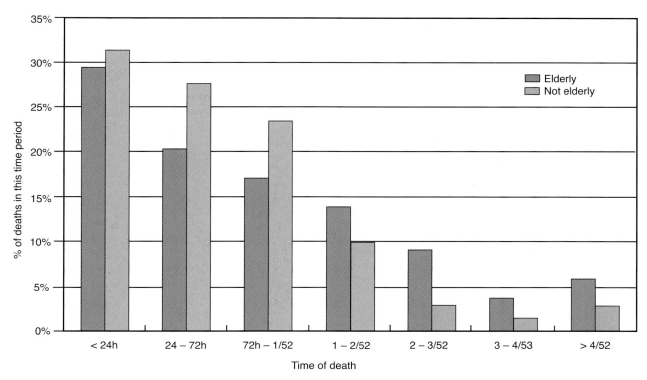

FIGURE 9-3 Percentage of deaths occurring in each time period.

4305 by increased use of air bags, 6475 by increased use of motorcycle helmets, and 239 by increased use of bicycle helmets. Sufficient evidence was found to prove the effectiveness of lower blood alcohol concentration laws for young and inexperienced drivers and of intervention training programs for servers of alcoholic beverages.[404] All 50 states and the District of Columbia have laws defining it as a crime to drive with a blood alcohol concentration (BAC) at or above a proscribed level, this being 0.08%.

Seat belts stop the occupant with the car and therefore prevent the body from being ejected when the car stops. Deceleration energy is spread over more energy-absorbing parts of the body such as the pelvis, chest, and shoulders. Safety belts are the single most effective means of reducing fatal and nonfatal injuries in motor vehicle accidents, and primary enforcement seat belt laws where police officers are allowed to stop a driver and issue a ticket for the sole reason of not wearing a seatbelt are likely to be more effective than secondary laws that permit nonbelted occupants or drivers to be ticketed only after being stopped for another moving violation.[88,306,342,343] According to the National Highway Traffic Safety Administration (NHTSA).[257] seat belt use nationwide was 82% in 2007, ranging from 63.8% in New Hampshire to 97.6% in Hawaii. Twenty-eight states had primary enforcement seat belt laws.

TABLE 9-1	**Comparison of Continuous Variables between Survivors and Those Who Died, by Age Group**					
	Elderly Adults			Adult		
	Survived, Median	Died, Median	P	Survived, Median	Died, Median	P
Age (yr)	74	76*	.013	33	35*	.045
Injury Severity Score	20	26*	.001	25	30*	.001
Glasgow Coma Scale score	14	9*	.001	14	3*	.001
Emergency fluids (mL)	2000	2000	NS	2000	2500	.001
Pulse (/min)	80	88*	NS	86	80*	.001
Blood pressure (mm Hg)	140	130*	.024	130	110*	.001
Respirations (/min)	18	18	NS	18	14	.001

*Statistically significant difference between elderly and adult patients who died (Mann-Whitney U test, P <0.001).

However, almost 70% of the 16- to 34-year-old passenger vehicle occupant fatalities killed during nighttime hours were unrestrained.[257] All states have child passenger protection laws. These vary widely in age and size requirements and penalties for noncompliance. Child-restraint use in 1996 was 85% for children younger than 1 year and 60% for children aged 1 to 4 years. Since 1975, deaths among children younger than 5 years have decreased by 30% to 3.1 per 100,000 population/year, but rates for age groups of 5 to 15 years have declined by only 11% to 13%.[255] In a study reviewing accidents involving 4243 children aged 4 to 7 years, between 1998 and 2002, injuries occurred among 1.81% of all 4- to 7-year-olds, including 1.95% of those in seat belts and 0.77% of those in belt-positioning booster seats. The odds of injury were 59% lower for children in belt-positioning boosters than in seat belts. Children in booster seats sustained no injuries to the abdomen, spine, or lower extremities, while children in seat belts alone had injuries to all body regions.[92,93]

Driver air bags have been shown to reduce mortality by 8%, whether the driver was belted or not. However, seat belts provide much greater protection, with seat belt use reducing the risk of death by 65%, or by 68% if the seat belt is used in combination with an air bag[72] (see Table 3-35). No differences in the risk of frontal crash deaths were observed between adult occupants with sled-certified and first-generation air bags. Consistent with reports of decreases in air bag–related deaths, significant reductions in frontal deaths among child passengers seated in the right-front position in sled-certified vehicles were seen.[36] Airbags have been reported to be associated with reduced in-hospital mortality and decreased injury severity.[402] In a systematic review, helmets have been shown to reduce the risk of death by 42% and the risk of head injury by around 69% in motorcycle riders.[213]

Current evidence supports the view that reduced speed limits, speed-camera networks, and speed-calming measures substantially reduce the absolute numbers of road deaths. This is apparent in the United Kingdom, Australia, France, and other countries.[302] There is also evidence that speed enforcement detection devices are a promising intervention for reducing the number of road traffic injuries and deaths.[404] It is of note, however, that in the United States, there are no speed-camera networks.[302]

With regard to pedestrians, cars and light trucks (vans, pickups, and sport utility vehicles) are responsible for 85.2% pedestrian deaths in the United States. Heavy trucks, buses, and motorcycles are responsible for the remainder.[288] Buses kill eight times as many pedestrians as cars per mile of vehicle travel. Vehicle characteristics such as mass, front end design, visibility,[59] and degree of interaction with pedestrians probably determine their risk per mile.[288] Therefore, one option to reduce pedestrian fatalities might be the modification of motor vehicles. However, every type of motor vehicle has to be evaluated on an individual basis. Thus, lowering the front end of light trucks, and consequently the point of impact with a pedestrian's body, might reduce the likelihood of serious head and chest injuries.[57]

In an effort to assess the effect of modern vehicle design on the mechanism and pattern of injury for vehicular trauma victims, patients (restrained car occupants, bicyclists, pedestrians) injured between 1973 and 1978 and between 1994 and 1999 in a specific region in Germany were compared.[303] A lower injury severity (ISS 5.0 versus 12.1), lower incidence of poly-trauma (4.5% versus 15%), and a lower mortality rate (3.4% versus 14%) were measured for all groups during the later period. Given the same crash severity, these reductions were also related to improvements in vehicle design rather than just seat-belt use.[303]

PREHOSPITAL CARE AND TRAUMA CARE SYSTEMS: THEIR IMPACT ON OUTCOMES

Organized civilian trauma care in the United States has its origins in the late 1960s when it was stated that the quality of civilian trauma care in the United States was below the standard in combat zones in Vietnam: "If seriously wounded, the chances of survival would be better in the zone of combat than on the average city street." A trauma system organizes the full range of coordinated care to all injured patients in a defined geographic area. It includes injury prevention, prehospital and in-hospital care, and rehabilitation. The concepts of organized trauma care[5] have proved to be one of the most important advances in the care of the injured patient over the last 30 years.[157,208] The number of U.S. states with a trauma system increased from 7 in 1981 to 36 in 2002.[340] Nevertheless, in 2000 approximately 40% of the U.S. population still lived in states without a trauma system.[254]

The use of an established trauma system network also might facilitate the care of victims of natural disasters[279] or terrorist attacks.[167] The performance of hospitals and health providers in a trauma system is subjected to review from outside and within the system.[6,226,249] Research and constant reevaluation are necessary for continuous assessment of the system and improvement of its outcomes and efficiency.[209,340] According to a systematic review of published evidence[224] of the effectiveness of trauma systems in the United States until 1999, the implementation of trauma systems decreased hospital mortality of patients who are severely injured to approximately 15%.[49,179, 218,224,248] The relative risk of death caused by motor vehicle accidents was 10% lower in states with organized systems of trauma care than in states without such systems.[254] However, it took about 10 years to establish an organized system of trauma that was effective in reducing mortality. Nathens et al.[253] concluded that this is consistent with the maturation and development of trauma triage protocols, interhospital transfer agreements, organization of trauma centers, and ongoing quality assurance. U.S. counties with 24-hour availability of surgical specialties, CT scanners, and operating rooms have a decreased motor vehicle accident mortality, compared with counties without those resources. Counties with designated trauma centers have lower motor vehicle–related mortality rates.[232] Recently published prospectively collected data comparing mortality in trauma centers to nontrauma centers shows a 25% mortality reduction for patients younger than 55 years when treated in a trauma center.[215]

Outcome results obviously depend on every single part of the chain in trauma system as well as on the interplay of these elements and there is a lack of evidence of the understanding of the contribution of individual components on the efficiency of the system. However, prehospital notification protocols and performance improvement programs appear to be most associated with decreased risk-adjusted odds of death.[208] With regard to prehospital trauma care, there are ongoing national and

TABLE 9-2	**Prehospital Trauma Care Systems**

1. Basic Life Support (BLS) systems
   - Noninvasive supportive care to trauma patients by emergency medical technicians (splinting)
   - Transport trauma patients rapidly to a medical care facility
2. Paramedic-Performed Advanced Life Support (PARAALS) systems
   - Perform invasive procedures such as intubation and intravenous fluid therapy, administer drugs
3. Physician-Performed Advanced Life Support (PHYSALS) systems

international debates and studies as to which system is most favorable[35,87] and how prehospital trauma care can be improved.[43,61,99,128,293]

Worldwide, three different types of prehospital trauma care systems or emergency medical services (EMS) systems can be differentiated (Table 9-2).

The prehospital trauma system in the United States results from the experience in the Vietnam Conflict, where trained paramedical personnel were responsible for the initial treatment in the combat zone, whereas physicians were thought to be most effective in a hospital setting.[252] Extensive medical care at the scene was almost impossible because of combat, so that "load and go" or "scoop and run" was favored. In contrast, Franco-German[87] EMS systems are physician directed and in most cases associated with a longer time at the scene of the accident ("stay and play") to facilitate stabilization of the patient before transport to an appropriate hospital.

An international study comparing these systems[252] by using shock rate in the emergency department and early trauma fatality rate as parameters to assess prehospital outcome, found out that the emergency department shock rate did not vary significantly between physician-performed Advanced Life Support (PHYSALS) systems and paramedic-performed Advanced Life Support (PARAALS) systems. Early trauma fatality rate was significantly lower in PHYSALS EMS systems compared to the PARAALS EMS systems. Therefore, a physician at the scene may be associated with lower early trauma fatality rates. However, there are a lack of data to allow proper comparison of outcomes between the EMS systems of different countries.[87]

Several other studies and reviews focusing on prehospital trauma care systems have concluded that there is no evidence supporting advanced prehospital trauma care. Almost all of these studies used hospital trauma fatality as the main outcome parameter and only compared advanced life support (ALS) systems with basic life support (BLS) systems.[47,206,207,315] One further study also compared PARAALS EMS in Montreal to PHYSALS EMS in Toronto and BLS EMS in Quebec using in-hospital mortality as their outcome parameter.[207] PHYSALS EMS system was not associated with a reduction in risk of in-hospital death, and the conclusion was that in urban centers with highly specialized level I trauma centers, there is no benefit in having on-site ALS for the prehospital management of trauma patients.[207]

TRAUMA SCORING SYSTEMS AND THEIR VALUE

Trauma patients represent a grossly heterogeneous population. The need for comparative analysis of the injury-, management-, and outcome-related parameters among the different patient groups, hospitals, trauma management strategies, and health systems has stimulated the development of many trauma scoring systems and scales over the last 40 years.[10,34,38,52,191,401]

These scoring systems represent a means of quantifying the injuries that have been sustained together with other independent parameters such as comorbidities, age, and mechanism of injury. They serve as a common language between clinicians and researchers. Initially, they were designed for the purpose of field triage and in that regard they needed to be simple and user friendly. Subsequently, they have evolved to more complex and research-focused systems. Their concept is based on converting many independent factors into a one-dimensional numeric value that ideally represents the patient's degree of critical illness. They are often based on complex mathematical models derived from large data sets and registries such as the Major Trauma Outcome Study (MTOS) or the Trauma Audit and Research Network (TARN).[54,371]

Ideally, a complete trauma scoring system should reflect the severity of the anatomic trauma, the level of the physiologic response, the inherent patient reserves in terms of comorbidities, and age and, as proved recently, should incorporate immunologic aspects and genetic predisposition parameters.[14,107,118,119,121,122,349] The variety of the potential applications of such scoring systems ranges from basic prehospital and interhospital triage and mortality prediction to other prognostic parameters such as length of hospital stay and risk of disability. They can be used as a tool for comparison of diagnostic or therapeutic methods and for the auditing of trauma management.

Some of the existing injury-scoring systems can be classified based on anatomic parameters. Examples of these are the AIS,[370] the ISS,[10] the Maximum Abbreviated Injury Severity Scale (MAIS),[370] the New Injury Severity Scale (NISS),[273] the Anatomic Profile (AP),[69] the modified Anatomic Profile (mAP),[320] the Organ Severity Scale (OIS),[367] and the ICD-9 Severity Score ICISS.[319] Other scoring systems are based on physiologic parameters. Examples of these are the Trauma Score (TS),[55] the Revised Trauma Score (RTS),[56] and the Acute Physiology and Chronic Health Evaluation (APACHE).[416] Some scoring systems are based on a combination of these parameters. Examples of these are the Trauma and Injury Severity Score (TRISS),[38] A Severity Characterisation of Trauma (ASCOT),[191] and the Physiologic Trauma Score (PTS).[199] Numerous studies have assessed the accuracy, reliability, and specificity of the different trauma scores.[53,118]

Anatomical-Based Scales and Scoring Systems

The AIS was initially introduced in 1971.[297] It has been revised a number of times and is continuously monitored and evolved by a committee of the Association of Advancement of Automotive Medicine (AAAM).[370] Its latest version was published in 2005,[106] but the most used versions are the AIS90 and AIS98. In general, the AIS is an anatomically based, consensus-derived, global severity scoring system that classifies each injury by body region according to its relative significance. All different anatomic injuries are matched with a different seven-digit number-code. They are classified according to the affected *body region* (first digit, with body region 1 = head, 2 = face, 3 = neck, 4 = thorax, 5 = abdomen, 6 = spine, 7 = upper extremities,

8 = pelvis and lower extremities, and 9 = external and thermal injuries), *type of anatomic structure* (second digit, range 1 to 6), *specific anatomic structure* (third and fourth digits, range from 02 to 90), and *level of the injury* (fifth and sixth digits, range from 00 to 99). The last digit of each seven-digit AIS code follows a dot and represents the injury severity of the specific injury on a scale of 1 to 6 (1 = minor, 2 = moderate, 3 = serious, 4 = severe, 5 = critical, and 6 = maximal-currently untreatable injury). This last severity digit has been developed by a consensus of many experts and is continuously monitored by the committee.

The ISS was introduced by Baker et al. in 1974.[10] Each injury in the patient is allocated an AIS code and the codes are grouped in six ISS body regions: head and neck, face, chest, abdomen, extremities and pelvis and external. Only the highest AIS severity score (post dot digit–seventh digit of the AIS code) in each ISS body region is used. The ISS is the sum of the squared AIS scores for the three most severely injured ISS body regions. It can take values from 1 to 75. A value of 75 can be assigned either by the sum of three AIS severities of 5 in three different ISS body regions, or by the presence of at least one AIS severity of 6. Any AIS severity 6 is an automatic ISS 75 independent of any other injuries. The ISS score is virtually the only anatomic scoring system in widespread use. It has been validated on numerous occasions and it has been shown to have a linear correlation with mortality, morbidity, hospital stay, and other measures of injury severity. Currently, it represents the gold standard of anatomic trauma scoring systems.[32,217,233] However, it has certain weaknesses in that any error in AIS coding or scoring increases the ISS error. In addition, it is not weighted over the different body regions and injury patterns, and it often underestimates the overall anatomic injury, particularly in penetrating trauma or if there are multiple injuries in one body region. The ISS is not a useful triage tool as a full description of patient's injuries is usually not initially available.

The Maximum AIS (MAIS) is another anatomic injury score often used in daily clinical practice and research that originates from the AIS. It is the highest AIS code in a multitrauma patient and is used by researchers to describe the overall injury in a particular body region and to compare frequencies of specific injuries and their relative severity.[171,238]

To address some of the disadvantages of the ISS, in 1997, Osler et al.[273] described the New ISS (NISS). This is the sum of the squares of the three highest AIS severity scores regardless of the ISS body regions. It has been found to be an improvement on the ISS especially for orthopaedic trauma and penetrating injuries.[12,13,146,168] However, it has still not been extensively evaluated and has the disadvantage of requiring an accurate injury diagnosis before an exact calculation can be made.

The Anatomic Profile (AP)[68,107] was also introduced to address the weaknesses of the ISS. It was described as one of the components of the ASCOT and includes all the serious injuries (AIS severity 3 or greater) in all the body regions. It is also weighted more toward the head and the torso. All serious injuries are grouped into four categories (A = head and spine, B = thorax and anterior neck, C = all remaining serious injuries, D = all nonserious injuries). The square root of the sum of squares of the AIS scores of all the injuries in each of the four categories is computed and by logistic-regression analysis a probability of survival is calculated. The AP has been proved to be superior to the ISS in discriminating survivors from non-

survivors. However, up to now, its complex computational model has restricted its application and limited its use.

A modified Anatomic Profile (mAP)[320] was subsequently introduced. This is a four-number characterization of injury. These four numbers are the maximum AIS scores across all body regions together with the modified A, B, C component scores of the original AP (mA = head and spine, mB = thorax and neck, mC = all other serious injuries).[68] The mAP component score values (A, B, C) are equal to the square root of the sum of the squares of the AIS values for all serious injuries (AIS 3 to 6) in the specified body region groups. This leads to an Anatomic Profile Score, a single number defined as the weighted sum of the four mAP components. The coefficients are derived from logistic regression analysis of 14,392 consecutive admissions to four Level I trauma centres of the Major Trauma Outcome Study.[54]

The Organ Injury Scaling (OIS) was originally designed in 1987. It is a scale of anatomic injury within an organ system or body structure. The OIS offers a common language between trauma surgeons, but it is not designed to correlate with patient outcomes. The organ injury scaling committee of the American Association for the Surgery of Trauma (AAST) is responsible for revising and auditing the OIS tables that can be found on the AAST Web site.[367] The severity of each organ injury may be graded from 1 to 6 using the severity subcategories of the AIS. The injuries can also be divided by mechanism such as blunt or penetrating or by anatomic descriptions such as hematoma, laceration, contusion, or vascular.

Recently, another anatomic injury scoring system was introduced. It was based on the well-accepted and popular coding system of the *ICD-9* instead of the AIS. The *International Classification of Diseases, Ninth Edition (ICD)* is a standard taxonomy used by most hospitals and health care providers. The ICD-9 Severity Score (ICISS)[319] uses survival risk ratios (SRRs) calculated for each *ICD-9* discharge diagnosis. The SRRs are calculated by dividing the number of survivors of each different *ICD-9* code by the total number of patients with such an injury. The product of all the different SRRs of a patient's injuries produces the ICISS. Neural networking has been used to further improve ICISS accuracy. ICISS has been shown to be better than ISS and to outperform TRISS in identifying outcomes and resource utilization. However, in several studies, the AP, mAP, and NISS scores appear to outperform ICISS in predicting hospital mortality.[144,243,244,359]

Physiology-Based Scores

Initially, the trauma-scoring systems based on physiologic parameters were introduced as field triage tools. The basic characteristic of these physiology-based scores is that they are comparatively simple but also time dependent. In 1981, Champion et al.[55] hypothesized that early trauma deaths are associated with one of the three basic systems: the central nervous, cardiovascular, and respiratory systems. They designed a scoring system, the TS, based on a large cohort of patients, which focused on five parameters: GCS score, the unassisted respiratory rate (RR), respiratory expansion, the systolic blood pressure (SBP), and capillary refill. All contributed equally in the calculation of this score. It was proved useful in predicting survival outcomes, with good interrater reliability, but it was shown to underestimate head injuries and it also incorporated parameters such as

TABLE 9-3	Unweighted Revised Trauma Score as Used in Field Triage		
GCS Score	RR (/min)	SBP (mm Hg)	Coded value
13 to 15	10 to 29	>89	4
9 to 12	>29	76 to 89	3
6 to 8	6 to 9	50 to 75	2
4 to 5	1 to 5	1 to 49	1
3	0	0	0

GCS, Glasgow Coma Scale; RR, respiratory rate; SBP, systolic blood pressure.

respiratory expansion and capillary refill, which were difficult to assess in the field.[56] Consequently, the same authors developed an RTS 8 years later,[56] which was internationally adopted and is still in clinical use as both a field triage and a clinical research tool. It includes three variables (GCS, RR, SBP), and a coded value from 0 to 4 can be assigned to each (Table 9-3). An RTS score may range from 0 to 12, with lower scores representing a more critical status. In its initial validation, this physiologic scoring system identified 97% of the fatally injured as those having an RTS of 11 or less. It also indicated certain weaknesses, which suggested that it should be used in combination with an anatomic based score.[245,313] Currently, the threshold of 11 is used as a decision-making tool for transferring an injured patient to a dedicated trauma center.

In clinical research, auditing, and accurate outcome prediction, the RTS is used in its weighted form and is called coded RTS (RTSc). It is calculated with the following mathematical formula that allows weighting of the three contributing parameters (GCS, RR, SBP) and their significance:

$$RTSc = 0.9368\ GCS + 0.2908\ RR + 0.7326\ SBP$$

The RTSc emphasizes the significance of head trauma and ranges from 0 to 7.8408, with lower values representing worse physiologic derangement. The threshold for transfer to dedicated trauma centers for the RTSc is 4. Besides the obvious calculation difficulties that this formula may impose, the use of the RTS or the RTSc is compromised by the fact that the GCS score cannot be estimated in intubated and mechanically ventilated patients or in intoxicated patients. Also, the calculated score may vary with the physiologic parameters, which are often rapidly changing. It may well also underestimate the severity of trauma in a well-resuscitated patient.

The Acute Physiology and Chronic Health Evaluation (APACHE) was introduced in 1981,[193] and its latest revision in 2006 (APACHE IV) represents the most modern scoring system utilized in the demanding environment of intensive care units (ICUs) and therefore also in intensive trauma units (ITUs). The evaluated parameters include the age of the injured patient, any chronic health comorbidities, several physiologicl elements required for the calculation of the Acute Physiology Score (APS),[416] previous length of ITU stay, emergency surgery, admission source, and diagnosis on admission to ITU. These parameters are responsible for both the complexity of the APACHE score and its superior prognostic accuracy.

Combined Scores

The individual deficiencies of the anatomic scales and the physiologic based trauma scores led researchers to develop combined approaches to more accurately translate the overall injury load of a trauma victim to a single score or value. The TRISS[34] incorporates both the ISS and the RTS, as well as the patient's age, to predict survival. The probability for survival (Ps) is expressed via a specific formula $Ps = 1/(1 + e^{-b})$, where e is a constant (approximately 2.718282) and $b = b_0 + b_1(RTS) + b_2(ISS) + b_3(age\ factor)$. The b coefficients are derived by regression analysis from the MTOS database.[54] The probability of survival according to this model ranges from 0 to 1.000 for a patient with a 100% expectation of survival. TRISS has been used in numerous studies.* Its value as a predictor of survival or death has been shown to vary from 75% to 90% depending on the patient data set used. However, the deficiencies that govern the ISS and the RTS were also found in their derivative, the TRISS. This is particularly true of its inability to account for multiple injuries in the same anatomic region, the variability of the RTS value, the inability to calculate a value in intubated patients because of the inaccuracy of the GCS and RR, and the difficulty of assessing comorbidities and the physiologic reserve of the injured patient.

In 1990, another, more inclusive trauma scoring system was introduced. ASCOT[52] attempts to incorporate anatomic (AP) and physiology (RTS) parameters, as well as the patient's age, in a more efficient way than TRISS. The ASCOT score is derived from the same formula $(Ps = 1/(1 + e^{-b})$ as the TRISS but has different coefficients for blunt and penetrating injury. The principal claimed advantage of ASCOT was the use of the AP instead of the ISS, which better reflected the cumulative anatomic injury load of the patient. However, while the predictive performance of the ASCOT was marginally better than that of the TRISS, its complexity is considerably higher.[143,225,274]

In 2002 the PTS was described. This incorporated the systemic inflammatory response syndrome (SIRS) score on admission (range, 0 to 4; 1 point for the presence of each of the following: temperature greater than 38° C or less than 36° C; heart rate greater than 90 beats/minute; RR greater than 20/min; neutrophil count greater than 12,000 or less than 4000/mm^3; or the presence of 10% bands), the age, and the GCS score into a simple calculation to predict mortality. This new statistical model appeared to be accurate and has been shown to be comparable with the TRISS, or the ICISS, in subsequent studies.[199]

It must be remembered that despite the considerable effort expended in designing these different assessment methodologies, there are always going to be difficulties in translating the multifactorial problems inherent in the multiply injured patient into a number and all scores have advantages and disadvantages. In the future, it is likely that additional factors such as the immunologic response to trauma, and possibly genetic predisposition, will be assessed. Until the development of an "ideal" scoring model, we should be cautious in our conclusions regarding the existing systems and the prediction of outcome in the injured patient.

*References 30,31,45,84,220,270,352,395.

PATHOPHYSIOLOGY AND IMMUNE RESPONSE TO TRAUMA

In the past century, descriptions of the physiologic response to injury have delineated three phases. First, there is a hypodynamic ebb phase (shock) where the body initially attempts to limit the blood loss and to maintain perfusion to the vital organs. This is followed by a hyperdynamic flow phase lasting for up to 2 weeks, which is characterized by increased blood flow to remove waste products and to allow nutrients to reach the site of injury for repair. The last phase is a recuperation phase that may last for several months in an attempt to allow the human body to return to its preinjury level.[108] However, with more recent knowledge, accumulated mainly during the past 20 years, it has become clear that the physiologic response to injury is not as simplistic as was initially thought but instead represents a complex phenomenon involving the immune system, and even today it is still not fully understood. With the advances made in every field of medicine and particularly in the disciplines of molecular biology and molecular medicine, it is now possible not only to characterize, but also to quantify, the cellular elements and molecular mediators involved in this dynamic physiologic process.

The first physiologic reaction after injury involves the neuroendocrine system and leads to an adrenocortical response characterized by the increased release of adrenocorticosteroids and catecholamines. Subsequently, the work of Hans Selye further illustrated the importance of this neuroendocrine response to trauma, pointing out that this was involved in what he named "the general adaptation syndrome."[337] This is now considered as a forerunner of SIRS.[28] This activation of the neuroendocrine system is responsible for the increase in heart rate, RR, fever, and leukocytosis observed in trauma patients after major injury. Besides trauma, SIRS can be induced by other insults such as burns, infection, or major surgery and is defined as being present when two or more of the criteria shown in Table 9-4 apply.[28]

The activation of the immune system following a traumatic insult is necessary for hemostasis, protection against invading microorganisms, and the initiation of tissue repair and tissue healing. Restoration of homeostasis is dependent on the magnitude of the injury sustained and the vulnerability of the host, who may possess an abnormal or defective local and systemic immune response and therefore may fail to control the destructive process. Multiple alterations in inflammatory and immunologic functions have been demonstrated in clinical and experimental situations following trauma and hemorrhage, suggesting that a cascade of abnormalities that ultimately leads to adult respiratory distress syndrome (ARDS) and multiple organ dysfunction syndrome (MODS) is initiated in the immediate postinjury period.[116,120,122,123,147] Blood loss and tissue damage caused by fractures and soft tissue crush injuries induce generalized hypoxemia in the entire vascular bed of the body. Hypoxemia is the leading cause of damage as it causes all endothelial membranes to alter their shape. Subsequently, the circulating immune system, namely the neutrophil and macrophage defense systems, identify these altered membranes. The damaged endothelial cell walls, by trying to seal the damaged tissue, induce activation of the coagulatory system. This explains why these patients develop a drop in their platelet count. Further cascade mechanisms, such as activation of the complement system, the prostaglandin system, the specific immune system, and others, are set in motion.

The release of mediators of both a proinflammatory and an anti-inflammatory nature (Fig. 9-4) is dependent primarily on the severity of the "first-hit phenomenon" related to the initial trauma and secondarily on the activation of the various molecular cascades during therapeutic or diagnostic interventions, surgical procedures, and posttraumatic or postoperative complications ("second" or "third" hits).[109,117] The mediators that are involved in the sequelae of posttraumatic events are initially released from the local cells at the site of injury and subsequently systemically. The sequestration and the activation mainly of polymorphonuclear (PMN) granulocytes, monocytes, and leukocytes trigger a multifocal molecular and pathophysiologic process. The mechanism of complement activation, leukostasis, and macrophage activation has been associated with the concept of the "low flow syndrome"[298] and more recently with endothelial and PMN leukocyte activation.[156,205] The cells interact and adhere to the endothelium via adhesion molecules like L-selectin, ICAM-1, and integrin β2, these being representatives of the selectin, immunoglobulin, and integrin superfamilies, respectively.

After firm adhesion, PMN leukocytes can extravasate and, by losing their autoregulatory mechanisms, can release toxic enzymes, causing remote organ injury in the form of ARDS or MODS.[117,147]

If the systemic immune response is not able to restore the integrity of the host, dysregulation of the immune system will occur, leading initially to an exaggerated systemic inflammation and, at a later stage, immune paralysis. The availability of techniques to measure molecular mediators has allowed different research groups to search for inflammatory markers that could detect patients in a borderline condition who are at risk of developing posttraumatic complications. Alternate treatments may then prevent the onset of adverse sequelae. Serum markers of immune reactivity can be selectively grouped into markers of acute phase reactants, mediator activity, and cellular activity[112,231,259,283,360] (Table 9-5).

Interleukin-6 (IL-6) has perhaps been the most useful and widely used of these, partly because of its more consistent pattern of expression and plasma half-life.[286] A measurement of greater than 500 pg/dL in combination with early surgery has been associated with adverse outcome.[137] Clinical parameters are also useful in assessing the response to trauma and SIRS was developed for this purpose.[222] Although both systems have previously been correlated with injury severity and early elevation is associated with adverse outcome,[309] there has been little

TABLE 9-4	Defined Parameters of the Systemic Inflammatory Response Syndrome (SIRS)
Body temperature	>38° or <36° C
Heart rate	>90 beats/min
Respiratory rate	>20 /min or Paco$_2$ <32 mm Hg
White blood cell count	>12,000 or <4000 mm^{-3} or >10% band forms

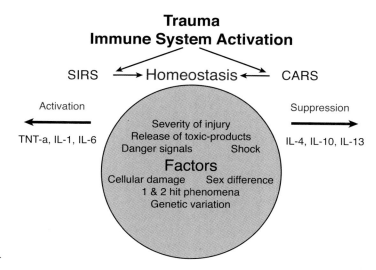

FIGURE 9-4 Diagrammatic representation of the release of mediators.

work examining the relationship between these two assessments in detail. In a recent study, it was found that in the early phase, both IL-6 and SIRS are closely correlated with the NISS and with each other. A cutoff value of 200 pg/dL was shown to be significantly diagnostic of an "SIRS state." Significant correlations between adverse events and both the IL-6 level and SIRS state were demonstrated.[14]

Lately, the quest to discover new biomarkers of immune reactivity has led to the discovery of signaling substances termed alarmins.[20] The alarmins are endogenous molecules capable of activating innate immune responses as a signal of tissue damage and cell injury. To this group of endogenous triggers belong such molecules as the high-mobility group box 1 (HMGB1), heat shock proteins (HSPs), defensins, cathelicidin, eosinophil-derived neurotoxin (EDN), and others. These structurally diverse proteins function as endogenous mediators of innate immunity, chemoattractants, and activators of antigen presenting cells (APCs).[272] HMGB1 is a nuclear protein that influences nuclear transactions and plays a role in signaling after tissue damage. In contrast to alarmins, the PAMPs (pathogen-associated molecular patterns) represent inflammatory molecules of a microbial nature being recognized by the immune system as foreign because of their peculiar molecular patterns.

Both PAMPs and alarmins are currently considered to belong to the larger family of damage-associated molecular patterns (DAMPs).[20] PAMPs and DAMPs are recognized by our immune system by the expression of multiligand receptors such as the Toll-like receptors (TLRs).[413] Overall, these molecules represent a newly documented superfamily capable of activating innate immune responses after trauma. The molecules categorized in this superfamily are expanding but their pathophysiologic contribution is currently not fully understood.

The evolution of molecular biology has allowed scientists to monitor different variables related to the endothelial-cell activation and interaction process. We can now achieve characterization and quantification of the endothelial response to the initial trauma and to the subsequent stress events, thus monitoring the clinical course of the patient.[101,210] It is now becoming clear that the problem of managing patients with multiple injuries has shifted from early and effective resuscitation to the treatment of the host response to injury. The quantification of the resulting activity of the different circulating mediators may predict a potential disaster but does not necessarily contribute to the salvage of the patient at risk. Too much, or too little immune response? Which one of the two opposites is worse or better? Can we intervene, at what stage, in which direction, and to which of the affected individuals? The real question may well be whether all these markers and molecules are just epiphenomena or related to the outcome. Currently, the effort is being made to better understand all the processes and the cascade of events that regulate these responses. Research has been aimed at describing responses to surgery at the molecular level and in developing and evaluating techniques to modify surgical stress responses. The release mechanisms of the surgical stress response as well as the factors that could amplify the response should be considered by surgeons. The severity of the injury, type of anesthesia, administration of adequate pain relief, type of surgical procedure, timing and length of surgery, preexisting comorbid conditions, any genetic influences that might lead to an adverse outcome, expertise of the operating room staff, and expertise of the surgeon are some of the important factors to be taken into account.

TABLE 9-5	Serum Inflammatory Markers
Group	**Serum Inflammatory Markers**
Acute phase reactants	LBP, CRP, procalcitonin
Mediator activity	TNF, IL-1, IL-6, IL-10, IL-18
Cellular activity	TNF-RI, TNF-RII, IL-1RI, IL-1RII, sIL-6R, mIL-6R, ICAM-1 E-selectin, CD11b Elastase, HLA-DR class II antigens, DNA

LBP, lipopolysaccharide-binding protein; CRP, C-reactive protein; TNF, tumor necrosis factor; IL-1, -6, -10, -18, interleukin 1, 6, 10, 18; TNF-RI, RII, tumor necrosis factor receptor I, II; IL-1 RI, RII, interleukin 1 receptor antagonist I, II; sIL6-R, soluble form interleukin 6 receptor; mIL-6R, membrane-bound soluble interleukin 6 receptor.

INITIAL EVALUATION AND MANAGEMENT OF THE MULTIPLY INJURED PATIENT

The management of a polytrauma patient can be basically divided into the prehospital and the in-hospital phases. The chance of survival and the extent of recovery are highly dependent on the medical care that follows the injury. The speed with which lethal processes are identified and halted makes the difference between life and death and between recovery and disability. Time is an independent and cynical challenger of any physician managing multiply injured patients. Thus, the adopted approach to this peculiar clinical setting should be based on getting most things right and very few things wrong. Due to the inherent imperfections of the human nature of the medical personnel, this approach should be based on simple and practical principles and be well organized and standardized.

Starting from the prehospital phases of extrication and transfer to the hospital, the initial evaluation and management, despite its inherent limitations because of lack of time and means, have been shown to be decisive for the severely injured patient.[276] The effect on survival of early extrication,[403] the initial management from trained emergency personnel whether they be physicians or paramedics,[176,338,374] and, equally important, the fast transfer to the designated trauma centers[304,372] have been evaluated and highlighted in numerous studies. The introduction and the universal acceptance of the Advanced Trauma Life Support (ATLS)[369] and, to a lesser degree, the Prehospital Trauma Life Support (PHTLS)[4,408] protocols have contributed immensely toward improved and standardized initial evaluation and management of the trauma patient.

It is important to follow the accepted principles and a structured initial evaluation of the traumatized patient. The initial priorities are airway maintenance, breathing, circulation, and neurologic deficit.

Together with direct triage to an appropriate health center, protection of the spine, early aggressive prehospital resuscitation, the implications of telemedicine and informatics, the advances of the means of transport, and the rationalization of the location of trauma centers have resulted in minimizing prehospital mortality and achieving mortality rates that are lower than those predicted by mathematical models such as TRISS and ASCOT).[43,275,323]

There are, however, are several continuing debates regarding the prehospital component of trauma management, as listed in Table 9-6.

Staged Approach to Hospital Care

The in-hospital period in the evaluation and management of the trauma patient is divided into four different periods (Table 9-7).

This division allows anticipation of potential problems and sensible decision making regarding the timing of interventions using a systematic approach.

Acute "Reanimation" Period

This phase includes the time from admission to the control of the acute life-threatening conditions. Rapid systematic assessment is performed to immediately identify potentially life-threatening conditions. Diagnosis should be followed by prioritized management of the airway and any breathing disorders

---

TABLE 9-6	Subjects of Debate in Prehospital Trauma Management

A. The management of the airway
   Should we use prehospital endotracheal intubation (ETI) or not?[41,78,89]
   The use of neuromuscular blocking agents[77,79]
   The effect of hyperventilation on the outcome of patients in shock[223] or with head trauma[64]

B. The control of hemorrhage and circulatory resuscitation
   The control of hemorrhage with modern dressings[258]
   Appropriate prehospital fluid resuscitation?
      Limited fluid resuscitation or standard aggressive strategy?[21,58]
      Optimal type of resuscitation fluid?[42,67,130,132,310,390]
      Should we use standard crystalloid fluids, hypertonic fluids, or polymerized hemoglobin blood substitutes?

C. The management of potential spinal injuries[18,39,148]

D. How do we improve triage systems?
   How do we assess the most appropriate hospital-based on the sustained injury load and the patient-related reserves?[113,215] The use of models combining physiologic data and patient- and mechanism of injury–related parameters is of current interest.[66,161,162]

---

followed by circulatory support as set down in ATLS. This is followed by the "secondary survey," this being a complete acute diagnostic "check-up." However, this should only be undertaken if there is no acute life-threatening situation, which would make immediate surgery necessary. In these cases, this secondary assessment should be delayed until the patient is properly stabilized.

Primary "Stabilization" Period

This phase begins when any acute life-threatening situation has been treated, and there is complete stability of the respiratory, hemodynamic, and neurologic systems of the patient. This is the usual phase where major extremity injuries are managed, including the acute management of fractures associated with arterial injuries or the presence of acute compartment syndrome. Fractures can be temporarily stabilized with external fixation and the compartments released where required. This primary period may last up to 48 hours.

Secondary "Regeneration" Period

In this phase, the general condition of the patient is stabilized and monitored. It is vital to regularly reevaluate the constantly evolving clinical picture to avoid harmful impact from intensive

---

TABLE 9-7	In-Hospital Periods in the Evaluation and Management of the Trauma Patient

1. Acute "reanimation" period (1 to 3 hours)
2. Primary "stabilization" period (1 to 48 hours)
3. Secondary "regeneration" period (2 to 10 days)
4. Tertiary "reconstruction and rehabilitation" period (weeks)

treatment or the burden of complex operative procedures. Unnecessary surgical interventions should not be performed during the acute response phase following trauma. Physiologic and intensive care scoring systems may be used to monitor clinical progress. In the presence of systemic inflammation and MODS, appropriate supportive measures should be undertaken in an intensive care environment.

Tertiary "Reconstruction and Rehabilitation" Period

This final rehabilitation period is accompanied by any necessary surgical procedures, including final reconstructive measures. Only when adequate recovery is demonstrated should complex surgical procedures be contemplated. Such interventions include the definitive management of complex midface fractures, spinal or pelvic fractures, or joint reconstruction.

The acute period of "reanimation" originally included the initial 1 to 3 hours after admission, but because of the improvement of prehospital trauma care, it is now considered to extend from the arrival of the emergency services at the scene until control of the acutely threatening conditions has been achieved. In many countries, this first period of trauma management is governed by the principles of the ATLS.[372] The concept of a dedicated trauma team coordinated by a person experienced in trauma and emergency management has been adopted in most of the trauma centers.[131,268,296] Rapid primary assessment and simultaneous interventions to control the airway and the cervical spine (a), to facilitate breathing (b), and to maintain the circulation and the vital blood flow (c) is started immediately. After establishing a non–life-threatening situation, the secondary survey follows, where a thorough evaluation aims to identify all injuries and clinically relevant conditions in the injured patients.

During this process, the clinicians should use, in a systematic and timely manner, several diagnostic means to assist the decision making process.[150,200,212,299,388,410] The use of standardized diagnostic and therapeutic protocols has been shown to improve the timing of the acute process, as well as its quality, and the overall clinical outcome.[417] It has been shown that the use of predefined and validated algorithms effectively guides inexperienced personnel and reduces the mortality, especially of the moderately severe polytrauma patients (ISS between 20 and 50).[23] The primary goal of the initial management is to diagnose quickly and immediately treat all the life-threatening conditions, including airway obstruction or injury causing asphyxia, tension pneumothorax or hemothorax, cardiac tamponade, open thoracic trauma or flail chest, and massive internal or external hemorrhage. The acute management of these conditions may necessitate an urgent transfer to the operating theaters, before further investigations can be undertaken, thus delaying the diagnostic algorithms and the secondary survey. A pertinent example would be the neglect of an intra-abdominal or pelvic hemorrhage, while attempting to deal with a severe extremity injury. Of particular importance is the fact that the condition of a polytrauma patient is dynamic and potentially unstable at any moment. The treating team needs to be continuously alert, especially at the initial stages of management, as a previously controlled situation may deteriorate rapidly. The continuous awareness of the team and the flexibility to change the current management process are essential.[40,63,126,312,354]

There has been a continuous evolution of the initial evaluation of multiple injured patients, which has been reflected in continuing debate about the standing ATLS protocols. The continuous monitoring of the blood pressure, electrocardiogram, oxygen saturation (pulse oximetry), ventilatory rate, the insertion of urine and/or gastric catheters, and the acquisition of an initial full blood count, arterial blood gases, and cross-matching of the patient have been generally accepted as gold standards of the acute phase. There is also debate about the extent of the initial radiographic evaluation and imaging that may be useful in the first stages of the patient's evaluation and management. The current ATLS course manual recommends initial anteroposterior (AP) chest, AP pelvic, and lateral cervical spine radiographs, and the use of diagnostic peritoneal lavage (DPL) or an abdominal ultrasonogram.

The introduction of modern imaging modalities such as multislice computed tomography (MSCT)[25] and total body digital radiography[26] has caused a change in the initial radiographic assessment protocols in many trauma centers and sometimes there is a degree of confusion between the trauma and emergency personnel. The necessity for AP pelvic radiography[187,264] and lateral cervical spine radiography[183,386] has been disputed by advocates of these new imaging modalities. Existing studies[97,100,294,344] demonstrate promising results, and it would seem that despite the additional cost that these modalities impose, the expected benefits from their use in time and trauma management effectiveness are significant. The advantages and pitfalls of these new tools have to be further evaluated in comparison to current practice, and their use has to be incorporated in specific protocols. They also need to be investigated regarding their effect on the overall outcome of the injured patient and on the rationalization of acute trauma management.

Respiratory Function Assessment

Treatment should prioritize removal of any airway obstruction (Table 9-8). If the obstruction is subglottic emergency cricothyroidotomy or tracheostomy can be lifesaving. Obstruction of the trachea in the region of the mediastinum can also cause severe respiratory impairment. This can lead to severe mediastinal emphysema and tracheal perforation. The next priority is to maintain respiration, which can be compromised by thoracic or central nervous dysfunction. Disorders of the respiratory system can be diagnosed clinically from symptoms and signs including dyspnea, cyanosis, stridor, depressed conscious level, abnormal chest expansion, and the presence of major thoracic injuries. Thoracic injury can cause acute respiratory derangement, including lung contusion, tension pneumothorax, and hemothorax. Tension pneumothorax is an acute life-threatening condition. The management of pneumothorax and hemothorax

---

TABLE 9-8 Conditions That Cause Airway Obstruction

1. Midfacial fractures with obstruction of the nasopharynx
2. Mandibular fractures with the obstruction of the pharynx by the base of the tongue
3. Direct laryngeal or tracheal injury
4. Blood or vomit aspiration
5. Foreign bodies (e.g., dentures)

should include the insertion of a chest drain to decompress the chest.

Pulmonary edema can be caused by cardiac dysfunction, occurring as a consequence of direct cardiac trauma[383] or secondary myocardial infarction. Alternatively, isolated blunt thoracic trauma may cause high-pressure edema, which has been observed following thoracic compression. Management of these two conditions differs. One requires fluid replacement therapy and the other requires the use of diuretics. However, the initial management of both types of edema involves continues suction and the use of PEEP pressures.

Severe head injury can cause central respiratory impairment, which can be best verified through the use of PCS. Severe shock may result in severe cerebral hypoxia and subsequent respiratory impairment. It is important that the emergency physician does not underestimate the effect of hemorrhagic shock. Continuous observation of the spontaneously breathing patient with minor injuries can be justified in these cases. In the severely or multiply injured patient, immediate intubation and ventilation for adequate oxygenation are indicated. A tidal volume of 8 to 10 mL/kg of body weight, PEEP of 5 mL, and 50% O_2 saturation of the air are prerequisites for adequate ventilation.

Management of Hemorrhagic Shock

Using a parallel approach, it is usual to commence immediate management of posttraumatic shock while full evaluation of respiratory, neurologic, and cardiovascular status is ongoing. Prolonged shock can lead to further posttraumatic complications and therefore impact negatively on the patient's prognosis. Two large-bore intravenous cannulas should be inserted during the preclinical phase and rapid fluid replacement therapy should commence as soon as possible. The cannulas are usually placed in the antecubital fossas and fastened securely to prevent dislodgement.

On arrival to the emergency department, further intravenous lines can be inserted as appropriate. Single internal jugular or subclavian vein lines have the disadvantage of being too long and narrow to allow rapid transfusion of large amounts of fluid. If lines in the peripheral veins are not feasible, venous cutdown can be conducted by using the long saphenous vein around the ankle.

The choice of fluid for trauma resuscitation remains a controversial issue.[242] Historically, crystalloid solutions were considered unsuitable as they were rapidly lost from circulation with plasma or serum being preferred. In the 1960s, it was discovered that resuscitation with crystalloid solutions was associated with lower rates of renal impairment and mortality.

It was considered that losses into the interstitial space occurred because of edema formation and required additional replacement. Therefore, infusion of a combination of crystalloid and blood at a 3:1 ratio was recommended. The application of these principles, particularly in military conflicts, coincided with the emergence of "adult respiratory distress syndrome" or "shock lung" as a clinical entity in survivors of major trauma. Whether this was a consequence of large-volume crystalloid infusion was unclear. Interest in the use of colloid products was therefore renewed. However, early results were conflicting, partly because of shortcomings in trial design. Meta-analyses of these smaller studies revealed no overall difference in the rate of pulmonary insufficiency following resuscitation with either

fluid type. Moreover, when final mortality was considered, particularly in the subgroup of trauma patients, a significant improvement in the overall survival rate was observed in the group administered crystalloid.[60,327] Crystalloid fluid is, therefore, considered to be the first treatment choice in most centers and is particularly favored in U.S. trauma centers. Ringer's lactate has various theoretical advantages over isotonic saline, although clinical trials have not shown differences in outcome. Research into fluid selection for resuscitation is ongoing, particularly as much early evidence is based on the use of albumin as a colloid. Since then, newer products with higher molecular weights have become available that should be more efficient in maintaining fluid in the intravascular space. There is further evidence, however, that in cases of severe hemorrhagic shock, increased capillary permeability allows these molecules to leak into the interstitium, worsening tissue edema and oxygen delivery.[242]

Animal studies demonstrating that small bolus administration of hypertonic saline was as effective as large volume crystalloid have provoked considerable interest in potential clinical applications.[241] This effect was enhanced by combination with dextran.[347] Although improvements in microvascular circulation were observed, this also appeared to increase bleeding. A meta-analysis of early clinical trials revealed that hypertonic saline offered no advantage over standard crystalloid resuscitation, although hypertonic saline dextran might.[390] This effect was particularly striking in those with closed head injury, and further animal studies have revealed that hypertonic saline can increase cerebral perfusion while decreasing cerebral edema.[339]

Frequent Sources of Hemorrhage

External blood loss is usually obvious though the volume lost prior to admission is usually unclear. Furthermore, the identification of external sites of hemorrhage should not distract from a rigorous search for internal bleeding, the identification of which can be more problematic. Internal blood loss should be suspected in all patients, particularly where shock is recalcitrant. This usually occurs in the thorax, abdomen, or pelvis. Differentiation of the site of internal bleeding can usually be made by using a combination of clinical judgment, thoracic and pelvic AP radiographs, and abdominal ultrasonography. Abdominal ultrasound should be conducted in the first few minutes of the patient's arrival to the emergency department where this is possible. Increasingly, emergency department and trauma personnel are being trained in ultrasound examination and appropriate equipment is being made available.

Endpoints of Volume Therapy

An adequate clinical response includes improvement in the pulse, blood pressure, capillary refill, and urine output. In the severely injured or complex patient, invasive techniques including invasive arterial monitoring and central venous or pulmonary artery pressure recording should be considered at an early stage. Although controversy still exists in specific situations, current goals include normalization of vital signs and maintenance of central venous pressure between 8 and 15 mm Hg. Serial recording of acid-base parameters, the base excess and serum lactate in particular, have been shown to be a particularly useful in assessing response to therapy and detecting the presence of occult hypoperfusion in apparently stable patients.[24,62,234] Ongoing requirement for blood transfusion should be monitored by regular measurement of the hemoglobin concentration. This can be rapidly estimated, where necessary, using the majority of bedside arterial blood gas analyzers. Ongoing excessive fluid or blood requirement should always prompt a repeated search for sources of hemorrhage. Shock treatment is a dynamic process, and in cases where there is ongoing bleeding, surgical intervention is often indicated.

More recently, several methods for improved monitoring of cardiovascular status have been introduced including gastric tonometry, near infrared spectroscopy, transthoracic impedance, cardiography, central venous oximetry, and skeletal muscle acid-base estimation. Many of these techniques remain experimental and they are currently not available on a widespread basis. They may be available in certain centers and expert advice is essential.

Replacement of Blood and Coagulation Products

It is essential not only to maintain the intravascular volume but also to preserve the patient's oxygen carrying capacity. In cases of massive hemorrhage, this will inevitably require the replacement of red blood cells. Furthermore, lost, depleted, and diluted components of the coagulation cascade will also require replacement. However, it should be noted that it is becoming increasingly apparent that, particularly in young healthy trauma victims, much lower hemoglobin concentrations than previously thought optimal are tolerated and indeed may be beneficial.[292] Not only is blood a precious resource, but transfusion also carries the risk of various complications including the transmission of infective agents. Traditionally, target hemoglobin concentrations of 10 g/L were advocated, but it has recently been shown that concentrations as low as 5 g/L are acceptable in normovolemic healthy volunteers.[399] Randomized trials in selected normovolemic intensive care patients showed that the maintenance of hemoglobin concentrations between 7 and 9 g/L resulted in equivalent and perhaps superior outcomes to maintenance above 10 g/L[154] and transfusion requirement has been shown to constitute an independent risk factor for mortality in trauma.[221] This may be related to the potential of blood products to cause an inflammatory response in the recipient.[3,153]

In cases with severe blood loss, there is no clear point where continued administration becomes futile.[385] Ideally, fully cross-matched blood should be used but in an emergency universal donor O-negative blood can be utilized immediately. A sample should be drawn for cross-match prior to administration as the transfusion of O-negative blood can interfere with subsequent analysis. The blood bank should be able to deliver type specific blood within 15 to 20 minutes of the patient's arrival in the emergency department. This blood is not fully cross-matched and therefore still carries a relative risk of transfusion reaction. Cross-matched blood should be available within 30 to 40 minutes in most cases. Administration of platelets, fresh-frozen plasma, and other blood products should be guided by laboratory results and clinical judgment. Expert hematologic advice is often required.[83,145] Procoagulant therapy for severe coagulopathy remains experimental, although early results are promising.

The cost and potential adverse effects of autologous blood transfusion are becoming increasingly relevant, but so far no convincing evidence has been found that tetrameric polymerized human hemoglobin can be used on a routine basis.[242]

Instead, the use of factor VII appears to be a promising alternative in patients who present with uncontrollable coagulopathy if there is no surgical source of bleeding. The first randomized prospective trial documented that no severe side effects appear to occur in trauma patients. In addition, numerous case reports where the substance was applied as a bailout demonstrated that it appeared to have an acute, yet difficult to prove, effect.[227,331]

Differential Diagnosis of Hemorrhagic Shock

Hemorrhagic shock should be distinguished from other causes of shock such as cardiogenic and neurogenic shock. The presence of flat jugular veins might indicate the presence of hemorrhagic shock. An elevated jugular venous pressure (JVP) can be diagnostic of cardiogenic shock, caused by coronary heart disease, myocardial infarction, cardiac contusion, tension pneumothorax, or cardiac tamponade. To establish this diagnosis, the insertion of a pulmonary artery catheter may be necessary.

Neurogenic Shock.   Relative hypovolemia is the cause of neurogenic shock, and it is usually because of spinal injury. Loss of autonomic supply leads to a decrease in vascular tone with blood pooling in the peripheries. This can occur without significant blood loss. The resultant increase in skin perfusion leads to warm peripheries and a decrease in central blood delivery. This type of shock may be difficult to distinguish from hypovolemia.

Cardiogenic Shock.   Cardiogenic shock requires immediate attention and often immediate surgical intervention. The heart can be impaired by cardiac tamponade, tension pneumothorax, and hemothorax or, in rare cases, by intra-abdominal bleeding. These pathologies may necessitate immediate surgical intervention including placement of a chest drain, pericardiocentesis, or emergency thoracotomy. If there is indirect impairment of cardiac function, medical treatment should be introduced and normovolemia should be restored. A raised JVP in cardiogenic shock may be the result of right-sided heart failure. This should be confirmed by measurement of the central venous pressure. Impaired right-sided cardiac function may result in blood pooling in the pulmonary system. This can be difficult to distinguish from peripheral blood loss. The two can coexist and may impair cardiac function. Conditions that cause this include cardiac tamponade, tension pneumothorax, myocardial infarction, and cardiac contusion.

The presence of penetrating cardiac trauma associated with an elevated central pressure and a decreased peripheral systemic pressure should alert the treating physician to the possibility of cardiac tamponade. A normal chest radiograph may not rule out this possibility, but ultrasound can provide an immediate diagnosis. The treatment of this condition should include emergency pericardiocentesis. Following aspiration of 10 mL of fluid from the pericardial sac, an immediate improvement of the heart stroke volume is seen with an increase in the peripheral systemic perfusion. Emergency thoracotomy is rarely indicated. If required, it can be performed through an incision between the fourth and fifth ribs on the left side, and then by opening the pericardium in a craniocaudal direction to avoid injury to the phrenic nerve. One or two transmural stitches allow temporary cardiac closure and cardiac massage can then be conducted.

Tension pneumothorax causes rapidly increasing cyanosis

and a rapid deterioration of respiratory function, and it can cause acute right ventricular failure. As the condition progresses, raised intrathoracic pressure causes reduced right-sided venous return to the heart. As mediastinal shift occurs, kinking or obstruction of the vena caval system can lead to complete obstruction resulting in cardiac arrest. Rapid diagnosis followed by immediate decompression is a lifesaving measure.

Cardiac failure may cause myocardial infarction (MI) independent from the trauma. This diagnosis should be considered in elderly people after road traffic accidents. In these patients, MI may have been caused by hypovolemia, hypoxia, or the acute release of catecholamines in the bloodstream at the time of the accident or, alternatively, the MI may have occurred incidentally and actually caused the accident. A diagnosis of MI can be confirmed from acute changes on the ECG and an increase of blood markers (CK-MB). The treatment of MI should include medical therapy to control arrhythmias. Patients with MI should be treated in the ICU with continuous monitoring from the medical team.

Cardiac contusion can be difficult to differentiate from MI. Contusion is usually seen following a blunt anterior thoracic wall trauma associated with a fracture of the sternum. Differentiating this condition from MI in the acute setting is of secondary importance to the initial management as both diagnoses require similar management, including control of cardiac arrhythmias and heart failure with continuous invasive monitoring.

Neurologic Status Assessment

If a patient has to be intubated and sedated, it is important for the emergency physician to evaluate their neurologic status fully prior to this. The size and reaction of the pupils are important indicators of the presence of any central impairment and abnormal pupillary reaction and size may be seen. The light reflex reflects the function of the second and third cranial nerves, the oculocephalic reflex depends on the integrity of the third and fourth cranial nerves and the corneal reflex represents intact fifth and seventh cranial nerves. The GCS also provides important information regarding the neurologic status of patients, particularly where serial measurements are possible. It can provide a useful aid in clinical decision making:

It has been argued that computed tomography (CT) should be performed if the GCS score is less than 10, and if the GCS score is less than 8, continuous intracranial pressure monitoring may be necessary. This indication represents a rough estimate and the severity of impact and the clinical condition of the patient should also be used for evaluation.

Staging of Patient's Physiologic Status

Once the initial assessment and intervention are complete, patients should be placed into one of four categories in order to guide the subsequent approach to their care. This is done on the basis of overall injury severity, the presence of specific injuries, and current hemodynamic status as detailed in Table 9-9. Any deterioration in the patient's clinical state or physiologic parameters should prompt rapid reassessment and adjustment of the management approach as appropriate. Achieving end points of resuscitation is of paramount importance for the stratification of the patient into the appropriate category. End points of resuscitation include stable hemodynamics, stable oxygen saturation, lactate level less than 2 mmol/L, no coagulation disturbances, normal temperature, urinary output greater than 1 mL/kg/hr, and no requirement for inotropic support.

Stable

Stable patients have no immediately life-threatening injuries, respond to initial therapy, and are hemodynamically stable without inotropic support. There is no evidence of physiologic disturbance such as coagulopathy or respiratory distress or ongoing occult hypoperfusion manifesting as abnormalities of acid-base status. They are not hypothermic. These patients have

---

TABLE 9-9 **Use of Preexisting Classification Systems to Assess Whether Patients Are Stable or Can Be Stabilized to Permit Definitive Fracture Fixation***

	Parameter	Stable (Grade I)	Borderline (Grade II)	Unstable (Grade III)	In extremis (Grade IV)
Shock	Blood pressure (mm Hg)	100 or more	80 to 100	60 to 90	<50 to 60
	Blood units (2 hours)	0 to 2	2 to 8	5 to 15	>15
	Lactate levels	Normal range	Around 2.5	>2.5	Severe acidosis
	Base deficit (mmol/L)	Normal range	No data	No data	>6 to 8
	ATLS Classification	I	II to III	III to IV	IV
Coagulation	Platelet count (μg/mL)	>110.000	90.000 to 110.000	<70.000 to 90.000	<70.000
	Factor II and V (%)	90 to 100	70 to 80	50 to 70	<50
	Fibrinogen (g/dL)	>1	Around 1	<1	DIC
	D-dimer	Normal range	Abnormal	Abnormal	DIC
Temperature		<33° C	33° to 35° C	30° to 32° C	30° C or less
Soft tissue injuries	Lung function; Pao_2/Fio_2	350 to 400	300 to 350	200 to 300	<200
	Chest trauma scores; AIS	AIS I or II	AIS 2 or greater	AIS 2 or greater	AIS 3 or greater
	Chest trauma score; TTS	0	I to II	II to III	IV
	Abdominal trauma (Moore)	II or less	III or less	III	III or greater
	Pelvic trauma (AO class)	A type (AO)	B or C	C	C (crush, rollover abdomen)
	Extremities	AIS I to II	AIS II to III	AIS III to IV	Crush, rollover extremities

*Three of the four categories must be met to allow classification into for a particular category. Patients who respond to resuscitation qualify for early definitive care as long as prolonged surgery is avoided.

the physiologic reserve to withstand prolonged operative intervention where this is appropriate and can be managed using an early total care approach, with reconstruction of complex injuries.

Borderline

Borderline patients have stabilized in response to initial resuscitative attempts but have clinical features, or combinations of injury, which have been associated with poor outcome and put them at risk of rapid deterioration. These have been defined as follows:

- ISS greater than 40
- Hypothermia below 35° C
- Initial mean pulmonary arterial pressure greater than 24 mm Hg or a greater than 6 mm Hg rise in pulmonary artery pressure during intramedullary nailing or other operative intervention
- Multiple injuries (ISS greater than 20) in association with thoracic trauma (AIS greater than 2)
- Multiple injuries in association with severe abdominal or pelvic injury and hemorrhagic shock at presentation (systolic BP less than 90 mm Hg)
- Radiographic evidence of pulmonary contusion
- Patients with bilateral femoral fracture
- Patients with moderate or severe head injuries (AIS 3 or greater)

This group of patients can be initially managed using an early total care approach, but this should be undertaken with caution and forethought given to operative strategy should the patient require a rapid change of treatment rationale. Additional invasive monitoring should be instituted and provision made for ICU admission. A low threshold should be used for conversion to a damage control approach to management, as detailed later.

Unstable

Patients who remain hemodynamically unstable despite initial intervention are at greatly increased risk of rapid deterioration, subsequent multiple organ failure, and death. Treatment in these cases has evolved to utilize a "damage control" approach. This entails rapid lifesaving surgery only if absolutely necessary and timely transfer to the intensive care unit for further stabilization and monitoring. Temporary stabilization of fractures using external fixation, hemorrhage control, and exteriorization of gastrointestinal injuries where possible is advocated. Complex reconstructive procedures should be delayed until stability is achieved and the acute immunoinflammatory response to injury has subsided. This rationale is intended to reduce the magnitude of the "second hit" of operative intervention or at least delay it until the patient is physiologically equipped to cope.

In Extremis

These patients are very close to death, having suffered severe injuries, and often have ongoing uncontrolled blood loss. They remain severely unstable despite ongoing resuscitative efforts and are usually suffering from the effects of a "deadly triad" of hypothermia, acidosis, and coagulopathy. A damage control approach is certainly advocated. Only absolutely lifesaving procedures are attempted in order not to exhaust the biological reserve of these patients. The patients should then be transferred directly to intensive care for invasive monitoring and advanced hematologic, pulmonary, and cardiovascular support. Ortho-

paedic injuries can be stabilized rapidly in the emergency department or ICU using external fixation and this should not delay other therapy. Further reconstructive surgery is delayed and can be performed if the patient survives.

THE ROLE OF THE EARLY PHASE RADIOLOGIC INVESTIGATIONS

The technologic advances of MSCT scanning have revolutionized the early radiologic diagnostics in most Level I trauma centers. Nowadays, the availability of such imaging is standard of care in these institutions. Nevertheless, many other diagnostic tools are available to allow a complete picture of all injuries. While clinical examination and judgment still represent the fundamental basis of contemporary trauma management, the role of emergency radiology is continuously expanding and evolving. In the current emergency trauma setting, the 24/7 availability and immediate proximity of emergency radiology units (ERUs) to the emergency departments are considered essential. The architectural design and the infrastructure planning demand close coordination of the four components of acute trauma services, these being the resuscitation room, emergency radiology unit, trauma theaters, and intensive trauma unit.[98,227,406]

Conventional Radiography

Conventional radiography is currently used in the acute setting in most of the institutions that have adopted the ATLS concepts. It consists of the standard three radiographs: AP radiographs of the chest and pelvis and a lateral radiograph of the cervical spine. These are often taken using portable bedside radiograph machines as adjuncts of the primary survey. These are followed by abdominal ultrasound, and in many cases by CT scans and additional plain radiographs of the extremities. This standard protocol represents the international consensus of dedicated trauma centers or trauma-treating general hospitals worldwide.

An initial bedside lateral C-spine radiograph is considered necessary because an urgent intubation may be required and the patient's GCS score may not allow for clinical screening. A bedside lateral C-spine radiograph is considered accurate enough for severe or unstable fractures and fracture dislocations but has significant disadvantages in identifying more subtle fractures or clearing the thoracocervical area.[197,278]

The supine chest radiograph remains the most important of the three initial bedside radiographs. Its sensitivity is very high (greater than 95%) for identifying a large hemothorax, flail chest, pneumothorax, hemomediastinum, pulmonary contusions, and lacerations. However, its specificity is quite low and there are injuries that are likely to be missed, such as diaphragm ruptures or a small hemothorax.[48,253,334]

The routine use of pelvic radiography in the first phases of trauma evaluation and management has received most criticism. In general, pelvic trauma occurs in the multiply injured population who present with potential hemodynamic compromise and, in fact, it can be used as a paradigm of polytrauma.[110] Now that CT scanning is widely used in the secondary survey of moderately or severely injured trauma patients, it is considered by many that the routine bedside pelvic radiography for hemodynamically stable patients may be abandoned. In contrast, in hemodynamically unstable patients, it is still considered a useful screening tool to facilitate early notification of the orthopaedic team and the interventional radiologist. It also encourages the use of simple measures of reduction of the disrupted pelvis such as pelvic binders, plain sheet wrapping, or keeping the lower extremities adducted in internal rotation.[281,301]

The introduction of digital radiography imaging appears to offer certain advantages even in the acute setting of the resuscitation room.[48] Recently, the use of total-body radiographs in the acute evaluation of multiply injured patients was introduced. Despite the escalating role of modern CTs, this new technology appears to offer additional vital and quick information in the resuscitation room setting. This new technology is based on an enhanced linear slot-scanning device that produces high quality radiographic two-plane whole body images of any size in seconds. It has been evaluated in a number of centers,[16,247] and its usefulness is expected to be proven in the near future.

Ultrasonography

The ultrasound scan has gained a significant role in the acute trauma setting and is considered a vital tool in the hands of the trained emergency physician or trauma surgeon.[317] Although it is operator dependent, it can be carried out at the patient's bedside and is quick and noninvasive and can be easily repeated. The focused assessment with sonography for trauma (FAST) scan, introduced in 1990, offers a quick, comprehensive, and sensitive method of detecting free intra-abdominal fluid, or pericardial effusion. It has a number of useful views, which are detailed in Table 9-10. The reported sensitivity for intra-abdominal free fluid is high (70% to 98%) but is highly dependent on the volume of the free fluid and on the completion of scanning of all the areas listed in Table 9-10.[37,190] As far as the diagnosis of solid organ injuries is concerned, its sensitivity is poor (45% to 85%).[262] Its specificity for either free fluid or visceral injuries is high (86% to 100%).[37,190] It has been shown to be more sensitive in detecting pneumothorax than plain radiographs,[350] and it is excellent in detecting cardiac injuries and pericardial collections (97% to 100%).[316] Its limitations are mainly in the identification of solid organ injuries, which are usually underestimated. The technique is highly operator dependent,[51] and it requires free access to the anatomic areas listed in Table 9-10. Its accuracy is also affected by patient movement.[250,326]

Computed Tomography

Since the use of CT scanning in trauma management became widespread in the 1980s, its contribution has been immense.

TABLE 9-10 Views Used in FAST Scans*

- Transverse subxiphoid view (pericardial effusion, left liver lobe)
- Right upper quadrant view (right liver lobe, right kidney, free fluid in Morrison's pouch)
- Longitudinal left upper quadrant view (spleen, left kidney, free fluid)
- Transverse and longitudinal suprapubic views (bladder, free fluid in Pouch of Douglas)
- Bilateral longitudinal thoracic views (pleural effusions)

*The organs and areas of fluid delineated by the scans are also shown.

When used in combination with the ATLS secondary survey, it is the best method of detecting head, spine, chest, and abdominal injury. Its disadvantages are the length of time it takes to transfer and scan the patient and then assess the images, its inaccuracy in noncompliant patients, and its radiation dose.[405] Currently, in certain trauma centers, its use is moving to even earlier phases of acute trauma management. The use of intravenous contrast enhancement, the advances in software, and the image reconstruction ability of modern scanners have shortened the duration and significantly enhanced the quality of a trauma whole body scan. In particular, the contemporary MSCT scanners are able to produce high-quality whole body images in only a few minutes.[400]

Compared with MSCT, the traditional techniques of acute diagnostic evaluation have certain disadvantages. This is particularly true for blunt trauma. The standard clinical examination has a diagnostic accuracy for abdominal trauma of about 60% to 65%.[219,336] Deep peritoneal lavage (DPL), despite its high sensitivity, has a low specificity and was replaced by FAST; although FAST is limited by the fact that it provides an overview of intra-abdominal trauma rather than an accurate diagnosis. Whole body scanning offers additional diagnostic information regarding the head, spine, pelvis, and chest. Thus, MSCT minimizes the time to accurate diagnosis, this being particularly true in hemodynamically stable patients.[155] Another advantage of this new CT scanning modality is that it can also be used after a more traditional approach involving an initial bedside chest radiograph, a FAST scan, and the initial resuscitation of the unstable patient, or even after urgent surgery of the patients in extremis.[282,311] The evidence related to the new MSCT-based protocols is encouraging, especially for intubated, sedated, and hemodynamically stable patients. Nevertheless, further proof from well-designed randomized prospective trials is needed before radically changing the established ATLS protocols.

Angiography

Angiography, including CT angiography, has assumed a central role in the diagnosis and management of injured patients. It constitutes the gold standard in the detection of traumatic aortic and vascular injuries. In addition to the detection of these life-threatening injuries, it offers the possibility of intervening to halt the hemorrhage, although this requires the presence of a trained vascular radiologist.[103,142] Its inherent disadvantages are the infrastructure that is required, the low rate of allergic reactions to the contrast, the requirement for an experienced vascular radiologist given the inconsistent time schedule of trauma, and, most important, its duration, this being the time taken to transfer the injured patient to the angiographic suite and perform the investigation and any intervention that are required.

Initially, angiography and closed intervention were undertaken in patients who were stable hemodynamically.[140,333] The indications then expanded to include those patients who responded transiently to fluid resuscitation,[141] and more recently, it has been used as the ultimate salvage procedure in cases where hemodynamic instability persists even after a laparotomy or thoracotomy has been undertaken.[321,375] It is often used successfully in patients with pelvic trauma,[387] arterial injury,[138,289,379] and abdominal solid organ injuries.[19,211,240,330,348]

The radiologic interventional techniques that may be used in acute trauma management are either embolization of moderate to small vessels and injured solid organs, with gelfoam slurry or coils, or percutaneous endovascular stenting of larger vessels. They are considered to be procedures that are associated with minimal risk, especially in trauma management where they may be potentially lifesaving interventions. Currently, the protocols of angiography with or without radiologic vascular intervention vary significantly between different designated centers and trauma care systems. Controversies center on the main issues that have already been discussed these being the timing of its use, the availability of a vascular radiologist, the financial implications and its long-term consequences. Further prospective randomized studies are required to investigate its use.

SURGICAL PRIORITIES FOR LIFESAVING SURGERIES

In polytrauma patients, correct decision making can be lifesaving. Examples of conditions requiring emergent operative treatment that does not permit the use of prolonged diagnostic procedures are cardiac tamponade, arterial injuries to major vessels, and head trauma with imminent incarceration. Furthermore, injuries to cavities associated with severe hemorrhage and shock must be addressed promptly. Close communication within a cooperative multidisciplinary approach is, therefore, crucial.

Hemothorax

Hemothorax is usually easily diagnosed from the chest radiograph. However, in the presence of extensive lung contusion or atelectasis, the diagnosis can be difficult. Ultrasound examination has shown the potential to identify free thoracic fluid, although CT remains the gold standard and often reveals the source of any bleeding.[1]

Significant bleeding into the pleural space with a resultant hemothorax is treated during the primary survey by the insertion of a chest tube. Usually, the indication for a chest tube comes from examination of the chest radiograph and only occasionally are clinical findings the sole basis for chest tube insertion, as a chest radiograph can usually be performed very rapidly. It is standard practice to insert the chest tube in the mid-axillary line at the fifth intercostal space. Lower insertion risks injury to the diaphragm or intra-abdominal organs. Blunt dissection should be undertaken to prevent further injury to other organs. This is important, even where the operator is confident of correctly positioning the chest drain, as intra-abdominal injuries may lead to increased intra-abdominal pressure and diaphragmatic elevation or even rupture.

A traditional chest tube, measuring at least 28 gauge, should be used to drain a hemothorax. Modern percutaneous drains used in thoracic medicine are not sufficient for this purpose. The large diameter reduces the risk of coagulation and allows for rapid blood evacuation, and the surgeon can be relatively confident that the drained contents are representative of thoracic blood loss. It is usual to direct the tube caudally to drain blood and cranially in the presence of a pneumothorax.

The presence of a haemothorax is not diagnostic of major thoracic hemorrhage. In most cases, bleeding is the result of injury to one intercostal vessel and this will usually arrest spontaneously. Indications for emergency department thoracotomy remain controversial, although recognized indications include traumatic arrest and recalcitrant profound hypotension in penetrating trauma, rapid exsanguination with more than 1500 mL of blood initially or 250 mL/hr after chest tube insertion and unresponsive hypotension in blunt thoracic trauma. As a last resort, catastrophic subdiaphragmatic hemorrhage may be controlled by cross-clamping the aorta. These interventions are regarded as useless in patients who present with blunt thoracic trauma and where there has been no witnessed cardiac output or in patients with severe head injuries. There is recent evidence that increased caution should be used before undertaking emergency thoracotomy in blunt trauma patients for all indications, particularly in the emergency department, because of a relatively high rate of nontherapeutic procedures and poor outcome.[11,165]

Mediastinal Hemorrhage and Thoracic Aortic Injury

Mediastinal hemorrhage because of injury to the thoracic aorta is commonly diagnosed erroneously because of poor-quality chest radiography obtained in emergency situations with a supine position and insufficient inspiratory effort. The mediastinal enlargement observed on chest radiographs is often rather nonspecific. Clinically, one should pay careful attention to the presence of dilated jugular veins, which helps to differentiate cardiac from aortic injuries. However, further imaging should be rapidly obtained in the hemodynamically stable patient, ideally using contrast-enhanced thoracic CT. Angiography has been regarded as the gold standard in diagnosis, but although traditional CT scanning sometimes leads to false-positive results, many centers now prefer contrast-enhanced high-resolution spiral CT as an investigative modality.[50,90,329]

Thoracic aortic rupture is exceedingly rare in patients surviving long enough to reach the emergency department alive. In most cases, the adventitia is preserved and further intrathoracic blood loss is prevented by the parietal pleura. Furthermore, there is increasing evidence that repair can be delayed in the presence of other life-threatening injuries, and occasionally conservative management can be successful.[163,202,363] These patients should, however, always be treated in a center with an acute thoracic surgical service.

Nonoperative treatment of incomplete aortic ruptures in hemodynamically stable patients consists of permissive hypotension or active reduction of blood pressure while controlling for a difference in blood pressure between the upper and lower body parts. Indications for immediate intervention include the development of hemodynamic instability without an alternative explanation, hemorrhage via the chest tubes of more than 500 mL/hr, or a blood pressure gradient between upper and lower extremities leading to impaired perfusion of the lower limbs (difference of mean blood pressure greater than 30 mm Hg). Given the high mortality of emergency repair in cases of traumatic aortic injury, there is increasing interest in the use of endovascular stenting in such situations.[169,201,322]

If the clinical situation suggests cardiac injury in the presence of radiologic mediastinal abnormality, the diagnosis is generally cardiac tamponade. Pericardiocentesis should be performed. If there is acute decompensation, an emergent thoracocentesis is indicated. Further diagnostic tests are too time consuming in this immediately life-threatening situation. If the patient is still hemodynamically stable, a very sensitive and readily available test is the transthoracic echocardiogram.

Severe Pelvic Trauma: Application of Sheets, Binders, External Fixators, and Packing

Pelvic fracture is often seen in conjunction with multisystem trauma and can lead to rapid occult hemorrhage. Treatment should be regarded as part of the resuscitative effort and early intervention can be lifesaving.[215] Bleeding is more common from multiple small vessels rather than from injured major vessels and, because of the large volume of the retroperitoneum, spontaneous arrest of the hemorrhage is unlikely in severe cases.[135] It is also common for the retroperitoneum to be breached during the injury, further decreasing the barriers to ongoing hematoma expansion. Treatment with the pneumatic antishock garment or pelvic belt-straps can give some temporary stabilization,[394] but results are inconclusive and severe complications have been reported in relation to their use.

Although there has been increasing interest in the use of selective angiography in these cases to embolize bleeding vessels, this intervention is often time consuming to organize and perform. Patients must be relatively stable and careful selection is crucial. Embolization can be used as an adjunct to other interventions where continued arterial hemorrhage is suspected. In severe injuries with profound hemodynamic instability the use of external fixation, a pelvic C-clamp and open tamponade by packing is recommended.[358,366] With the patient supine, the area from the subcostal margin to the pubic symphysis is prepared with the abdomen and pelvis completely exposed. If a C-clamp has already been applied for posterior pelvic instability, it should be rendered mobile. In a C-type injury with vertical pelvic instability, the lower extremity of the appropriate side should be accessible to allow reduction where necessary.

If there is prior evidence of free intraperitoneal fluid, an external fixation device should be applied and a midline laparotomy should be performed. The intra-abdominal organs should then be examined for bleeding following standard management protocols for blunt abdominal trauma (Fig. 9-5). If, however, initial diagnostic imaging has shown no evidence of intra-abdominal fluid and a major source of pelvic hemorrhage is suspected, a lower midline laparotomy can be used. Initial attention should be directed to the retroperitoneum. Following the skin incision, ruptured pelvic soft tissues are usually readily visible. Any hematoma is evacuated and the paravesical space is explored for bleeding sources. Large bleeding vessels should be ligated where possible. In diffuse bleeding, well-directed packing with external stabilization is recommended.

If the hemorrhage is obviously originating from a deep dorsal source, particularly in cases of posterior pelvic instability, attempts at further extraperitoneal exploration should be made in the presacral region. Large bleeding sources can be identified and treated appropriately. In cases of catastrophic arterial hemorrhage, temporary control can be achieved by cross-clamping the aorta. Often in venous hemorrhage, no single bleeding source is identifiable. Usually, bleeding originates from disruption of the presacral venous plexus or from the fracture site itself. Again, well-directed packing can often adequately control hemorrhage. Recent studies have reported mortalities rates between 25% and 30% following pelvic packing in unstable patients.[70,377]

Following exploration and packing, temporary abdominal closure is performed and correction of physiologic derangements should be undertaken without delay, with particular regard being paid to coagulopathy and hypothermia. Packing is left in situ and changed routinely at 24 to 48 hours, although in cases of suspected ongoing hemorrhage and recalcitrant shock, earlier reintervention should be considered. At planned revision, the cavity should be debrided as required and any hematoma excised. It should then be thoroughly examined for sites of ongoing hemorrhage. Further bleeding points can be dealt with, but if diffuse hemorrhage persists, further packing should be used and later planned surgical revision undertaken.

Exsanguinating Abdominal Hemorrhage versus Expanding Intracranial Hematoma

There is still controversy regarding these difficult situations, with a number of compelling arguments being presented. There is increasing evidence for conservative management of abdominal injuries except in the most unstable patients and it should be remembered that apparent intra-abdominal hemorrhage is often pelvic in origin. Evacuating an intracranial hematoma, if the patient exsanguinates, is obviously futile. However, there is equally little, and some would say less, benefit in saving a patient's life if the result is profoundly disabling brain injury or death from tentorial herniation. Once compensatory autoregulatory mechanisms are overwhelmed, intracranial pressure rapidly increases. There is evidence that in people with head injury, mortality from extracranial causes alone is unusual. In a study

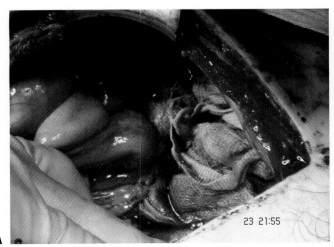 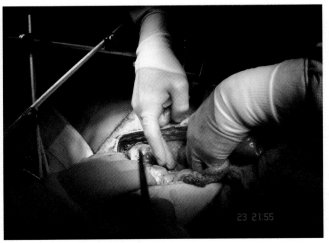

FIGURE 9-5 A. Midline laparotomy following application of an anterior external fixator. **B.** Packing of the lower abdominal cavity is shown to address retroperitoneal bleeding.

of almost 50,000 trauma patients, 70% of deaths were attributed to the head injury alone and only 7% to extracranial trauma, with the rest caused by a combination of both.[105] However, craniotomy should not be undertaken without imaging to confirm an operable lesion except in very rare circumstances. CT scanning is time consuming and can cause a significant delay in treatment. This time might be better spent rapidly attempting hemodynamic stabilization. There is also evidence that in hypotensive patients undergoing head CT, emergency laparotomy is required far more frequently than craniotomy (21% versus 2.5%).[407] Furthermore, inferior outcome has been demonstrated in head-injured patients with shock, suggesting that early correction of hypotension may protect the patient from secondary brain injury.[391]

It is clear that in these patients rapid complex management decisions must be made and clinical experience is essential. Thankfully, it would appear that such dilemmas seldom occur. In a review of 800 patients with significant head and abdominal injuries, 52 required craniotomy, 40 required laparotomy, and only 3 required both.[373]

SURGICAL STRATEGY AND DECISION MAKING FOR MAJOR INJURIES: EARLY DEFINITIVE FIXATION OR DAMAGE-CONTROL SURGERY?

Before fracture fixation in polytrauma patients was routinely performed, patients fared badly and the mortality rate secondary to fat embolism syndrome and organ failure was high. The major fear of surgeons treating these patients was the development of fat embolism syndrome. Pulmonary dysfunction is the hallmark of this syndrome and usually develops several days after trauma. Once the fat embolism syndrome becomes full blown, treatment is often unsuccessful and mortality rates of about 50% have been reported.[15]

Fat embolism syndrome was found to be caused by fat and intramedullary contents liberated from an unstabilized fracture. It was therefore concluded that fixation of major fractures could prevent this complication in addition to being an effective way of minimizing soft tissue damage and ongoing blood loss. Multiple authors reported dramatic improvements in the clinical condition when fracture fixation was performed routinely.[175,305,382] A decrease in the incidence of pneumonia and ARDS, a shorter stay in the ICU, and better survival rates were reported. The first prospective, randomized trial by Bone et al.[27] demonstrated the advantages of early fracture stabilization; this is now referred to as early total care (ETC). Patients with delayed fracture stabilization had a prolonged duration of ventilatory therapy and stayed longer in both intensive care and hospital.[27,305] It was therefore accepted that a major aim of the treatment of the multiple trauma patient with fractures was rapid stabilization of the pelvic and extremity injuries. An essential prerequisite for ETC was optimization of retrieval conditions and a reduction of the retrieval time. Furthermore, the improvements of intensive care medicine with improved cardiovascular monitoring and facilities for prolonged ventilatory support facilitated the development of a more aggressive surgical approach.

The strict application of ETC, even in patients with a high ISS, brain injury, or severe chest trauma limited discussion about the best management for these polytraumatized patients.

As it became evident that these specific subgroups of polytraumatized patients do not benefit from ETC, the borderline patient was identified. These patients were demonstrated to be at particular risk of a poor late outcome. The clinical and laboratory characteristics of the borderline patient have been previously described.[123]

The concept of damage control provided solutions to the management of these borderline patients together with patients who were unstable or in an extremis condition. The term *damage control* was initially described by the U.S. Navy as "the capacity of the ship to absorb damage and maintain mission integrity." In the polytraumatized patient, this concept of surgical treatment seeks to control but not to definitively repair the trauma-induced injuries early after trauma. After restoration of normal physiology (core temperature, coagulation, hemodynamics, respiratory status), the definitive management of injuries is performed.[341] The damage control concept consists of three separate components: resuscitative surgery for rapid hemorrhage control, restoration of normal physiologic parameters, and definitive surgical management.

Within the damage control orthopaedics framework, the first stage involves early temporary stabilization of unstable fractures and the control of hemorrhage. The second stage consists of resuscitation of the patients in the ICU with optimization of their condition, and the third stage involves delayed definitive fracture management when the patient's condition allows. The most popular tool of the trauma surgeon, to achieve temporary stabilization of a fractured pelvis or long bone, is the external fixator. External fixation is a quick and minimally invasive method of providing stabilization, and it can be very effective in accomplishing early fracture stabilization but postponing the additional biological stresses posed by prolonged surgical procedures. The delayed definitive procedure used for the stabilization of long bone fractures, and in particular the femur, is most frequently intramedullary nailing, which is carried out when the condition of the patient allows. Recent studies have reported that the damage control orthopaedics approach was a safe treatment method for fractures of the shaft of the femur in selected multiply injured patients.[261,284,325] The application of DCO in multiply injured patients is illustrated in Figure 9-6.

In patients with additional severe injuries to the head, chest, and pelvis who present with life-threatening hemorrhage, an acute change in the clinical condition may rapidly occur. Unfortunately, no level I study is available for these patient subsets. The EAST evidence-based work group conducted a systematic review of the literature regarding the timing of fracture fixation in different subsets of patients with multiple trauma.[91] They concluded that there is no compelling evidence that early long bone stabilization either enhances or worsens outcome for patients with severe head injury or for patients with associated pulmonary trauma. While the available data suggest that early fracture fixation may reduce associated morbidity for certain patients with polytrauma, the work group stopped short of recommending early fixation for all patients. It is questionable whether a level I study can be obtained in these variable patient groups.

The practice of delaying the definitive surgery in damage control orthopaedics attempts to reduce the biological load of surgical trauma in the already traumatized patient. This hypothesis was assessed in a prospective randomized study by means of measuring proinflammatory cytokines. Clinically stable patients with an ISS greater than 16 and a femoral shaft fracture were

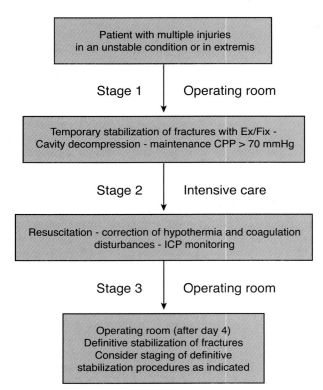

FIGURE 9-6 The staging of damage control orthopaedics (DCO).

randomized to ETC this being primary intramedullary nailing of the femur within 24 hours and damage control orthopaedics where the femoral fracture was initially stabilized with an external fixator and subsequently by intramedullary nailing. A sustained inflammatory response (higher levels of IL-6) was measured after primary intramedullary femoral nailing but not after initial external fixation followed by secondary conversion to an intramedullary implant. The authors concluded that damage control orthopaedic surgery appears to minimize the additional surgical impact induced by the acute stabilization of the femur.[283]

Other issues that have been discussed with regard to the DCO concept include the ideal timing of secondary definitive surgery and whether it is safe to convert an external fixator to an intramedullary nail or whether this associated with an unacceptably high infection rate. It has been shown that days 2 to 4 do not offer optimal conditions for definitive surgery. In general, during this period, marked immune reactions are ongoing and enhanced generalized edema is observed.[398] Nevertheless, these patients represent a highly diverse group and individual clinical judgment is more reliable, especially when combined with information from the newer laboratory tests. In a retrospective analysis of 4314 patients treated in our clinic, it was found that a secondary procedure lasting longer than 3 hours was associated with the development of MODS. Also, the patients who developed complications had their surgery performed between days 2 and 4, whereas patients who did not go on to develop MODS were operated between days 6 and 8 ($P < 0.001$).[285]

With regard to the issue of whether external fixation can be converted safely to an intramedullary nail, the infection rates reported in the literature are low ranging from 1.7% to

3%.[261,325] According to these reports, conversion of the external fixator to a nail should be done within the first 2 weeks as this minimizes the risk of developing deep sepsis.

In general terms, the measurement of inflammatory mediators has been shown to be sensitive in predicting the clinical course, morbidity, and mortality in trauma patients.[65,170,203] Based on the latest available studies, recommendations can be made in terms of patient selection for ETC and DCO. These are shown in Tables 9-11 and 9-12.

STANDARD OF CARE FOR THE TREATMENT OF SKELETAL INJURIES

The sequence of fracture treatment in multiply injured patients with multifocal injuries to an extremity is a crucial part of the management concept. Some areas of the body are prone to progressive soft tissue damage because of their anatomy. Therefore, the recommended sequence of treatment is tibia, femur, pelvis, spine, and upper extremity.

In this context, the simultaneous treatment of different extremity injuries should be considered. Initially, trauma surgeons must undertake the shortest possible interventions in these patients to minimize the second-hit phenomenon.[107,108] The simultaneous employment of different surgical approaches and different specialties, where this is feasible, will minimize the risks and facilitate the transfer of the unstable patient to the controlled environment of the ITU as soon as possible. Even at the later reconstructive phase of treatment, it may well be possible to undertake simultaneous operations at different anatomic sites. This is straightforward if there are contralateral fractures of the upper and lower extremities or a combination of facial/thoracic and lower extremity trauma. These combinations of injuries allow two different surgical teams, such as orthopaedic and plastic surgeons or orthopaedic and maxillofacial surgeons, to work together, minimizing the duration of anesthe-

---

TABLE 9-11 Indications for Early Total Care

- Stable hemodynamics
- No need for vasoactive/inotropic stimulation
- No hypoxemia, no hypercapnia
- Lactate less than 2 mmol/L
- Normal coagulation
- Normothermia
- Urinary output greater than 1 mL/kg/hr

TABLE 9-12 Indications for "Damage Control" Surgery

1. Physiological criteria—hypothermia, coagulopathy, acidosis = "lethal triad"
2. Complex pattern of severe injuries—probable major blood loss and a prolonged reconstructive procedure in a physiologically unstable patient

sia, the surgical stress on the injured, and at the same time optimizing the operation theatre time and the financial implications.[108,113,281]

As the main goal of trauma systems is to provide definitive, specialized care for the injured in the shortest possible time, the preservation of high standards in acute trauma services implies complex clinical capabilities, particular infrastructure logistics, and, even more important, algorithms facilitating simultaneous activity in diagnosis and treatment. Unfortunately, the existing evidence regarding the role of simultaneous surgery for polytraumatized patients is not of adequate quality and quantity to justify generalized conclusions. However, it is anticipated that further study will define its role.

Management of Unilateral Fracture Patterns

In multifocal injuries of the upper extremity, the surgeon should be aware of the overall distribution of the fractures rather than merely consider each fracture as an isolated problem. Even though an early definitive osteosynthesis would be preferred in all fractures, the general status of the multiply injured patient or the local fracture conditions may not permit this. In these cases, it is recommended that careful immobilization of diaphyseal fractures is the first phase of fracture management.

If there are periarticular fractures of the large joints, and urgent open reduction and fixation is impossible, transarticular external fixation (TEF) should be performed. In any case with concomitant vascular injury or any evidence of a developing compartment syndrome, a fasciotomy should be undertaken.

In multifocal injuries of the lower extremity such as ipsilateral distal femoral and proximal tibial fractures, known as a floating knee, a similar flexible but nonetheless structured and priority-oriented management system should be applied. The overall clinical status of the patients is crucial to the implementation of this concept. If the floating knee occurs in a stable patient, the femoral fracture can be treated with a retrograde unreamed nail inserted through a small incision in the knee joint, which is flexed at 30 degrees. An antegrade tibial nail can then be inserted through the same incision. If the same fracture pattern occurs in an unstable patient, the fractures are best treated by the application of a transarticular external fixator, which spans both fractures. This is performed as a temporary stabilizing procedure to minimize additional damage, especially to the soft tissues. A secondary definitive osteosynthesis can be done, when the patient has safely recovered from the initial potentially life-threatening injuries. During the whole procedure, good communication between the anesthesiologist and the surgeon is very important, because the procedure may have to be adapted to any change in the patient's vital parameters.

In periarticular and metaphyseal fractures, the priorities of treatment are often dictated by the state of the soft tissues. A high priority is given to femoral head and talar fractures. Other periarticular fractures have a lower priority unless complicating factors such as vascular dysfunction, compartment syndrome, or an open wound are evident. The apparently "minor" injuries to the hand, fingers, tarsus, and toes are also important. They should also be considered in the overall management concept and treated appropriately.

Management of Bilateral Fracture Patterns

In bilateral fractures, simultaneous treatment is ideal. Particularly in bilateral tibial fractures, both legs are surgically cleaned and draped at the same time. However, the operative procedure is performed sequentially because of the problems of space and handling inherent in the use of fluoroscopy. If the vital signs of the patient deteriorate during the operation, the second leg may be temporarily stabilized using an external fixator. Definitive osteosynthesis can then be delayed until the general status of the patient is stabilized again. The priorities in the treatment of bilateral fracture patterns follow the evaluation of the injury severity with more severe injuries being stabilized first.

Upper Extremity Injuries

The management of upper extremity fractures in multiply injured patients is usually undertaken secondary to the treatment of injuries to the head and trunk or of the lower extremity. If there is a closed fracture of the upper extremity without any associated injury, such as vascular or nerve damage or compartment syndrome, fractures of the shoulder girdle, proximal humerus, and humeral shaft are can be stabilized by a shoulder body bandage known as a Gilchrist bandage. If definitive osteosynthesis is required, it may be performed during the secondary management phase, possibly after further imaging. External fixation is an alternative for the temporary stabilization of humeral diaphyseal fractures, and transarticular external fixation may be used to stabilize fractures about the elbow if definitive stabilization has to be delayed. Primary management of fractures of the forearm wrist and hand is often with a cast, but, again, temporary external fixator may be used.

Lower Extremity Injuries

Our experience suggests that long bone fractures associated with a severe head injury or chest trauma (lung contusions) require a specially modified strategy. We strongly recommend expanded monitoring of respiratory function, ventilation (capnography), and pulmonary hemodynamics. Additionally, intracranial pressure monitoring is mandatory in patients with severe head injury.[44]

Unstable Pelvic Injuries

The management of the rare unstable pelvic injury is much easier if a standardized protocol is followed. A thorough clinical and radiologic examination is essential for the assessment of pelvic injuries. This examination is usually done during the initial examination phase. As a consequence of this, the classification of the pelvic injury may be approximate. However, sophisticated alphanumeric classifications of pelvic injuries in this context are not of much use. Instead, the simple AO classification, the ABC system (Fig. 9-7), can assist in the decision-making process.[246] In this classification, type A injuries include stable fractures such as fractures of the pelvic rim, avulsion fractures, and undisplaced anterior pelvic ring fractures. The posterior rim is not injured at all. Type B injuries comprise fractures with only partially intact posterior structures and rotational dislocations may be possible. Sometimes, this injury may initially be an internal rotational dislocation resulting in excellent bony compression and stabilization of the pelvis. On the other hand, they still carry a high risk of intra-abdominal injuries. If the injury results in the open book type of fracture with both alae being externally rotated, urogenital lesions and hemorrhagic complications are much more common.

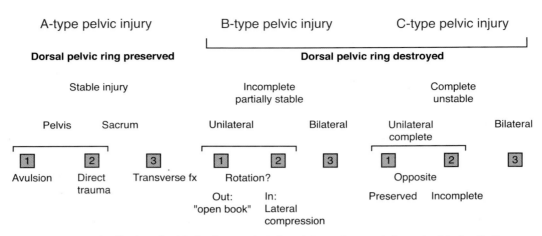

A-type pelvic injury   B-type pelvic injury   C-type pelvic injury

Dorsal pelvic ring preserved

Dorsal pelvic ring destroyed

Stable injury   Incomplete partially stable   Complete unstable

Pelvis   Sacrum   Unilateral   Bilateral   Unilateral complete   Bilateral

| 1 | 2 | 3 | 1 | 2 | 3 | 1 | 2 | 3 |

Avulsion   Direct trauma   Transverse fx   Rotation?   Opposite

Out: "open book"   In: Lateral compression   Preserved   Incomplete

FIGURE 9-7 Classification of pelvic ring fractures in A, B, and C type fracture similar to the AO classification.

Because the differentiation of type B and C injuries may be difficult, a CT scan of the pelvis is strongly recommended. If there is no CT available, diagonal inlet and outlet radiographs may serve as an alternative. In C type injuries, the pelvis shows translational instability of the dorsal pelvic ring, such that the stabilizing structures are all divided (Fig. 9-8). One or both hemipelves are separated from the trunk. This injury is associated with an extremely high rate of hemorrhagic complications and other pelvic injuries.

This simple classification has significant therapeutic implications. In type A injuries, operative treatment is generally not required, whereas in type B injuries, adequate stabilization is obtained by osteosynthesis of the anterior pelvic ring only. Type C injuries require anterior and posterior osteosynthesis for adequate stability.

In addition, the differentiation of several sectors of injury

has proved useful. Here, transsymphyseal, transpubic, transacetabular, and transiliacal fractures are differentiated from the transiliosacral and transsacral fractures. This process is easy to memorize and requires a structured analysis of the radiographs. For each of the injured regions, we have standardized the recommendations for the osteosynthesis. Thus, an adequate management plan is available for the small numbers of unstable pelvic fractures that will be seen. Because more than 80% of unstable pelvic injuries are associated with multiple injuries, stabilization in the supine position is preferred during the primary period. Additionally, the supine position offers the advantage of facilitating repair of both parts of the common combined symphyseal and iliosacral rupture. Generally speaking, we recommend the earliest stabilization possible for fractures of the pelvic ring to avoid ongoing blood loss and to simplify ICU care and early ambulation.[288]

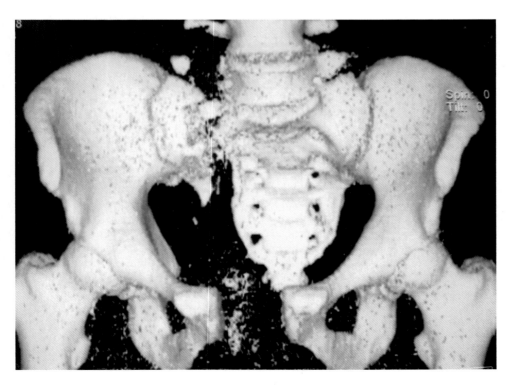

FIGURE 9-8 Type C pelvic fracture. Three-dimensional computed tomography scan.

Complex Pelvic Injuries

Pelvic injuries associated with any other injury to local pelvic organs are called complex pelvic injuries.[29] These injuries comprise about 10% of pelvic injuries and they are associated with a significantly higher mortality of between 30% and 60%, in comparison with simple pelvic injuries. During the early phase, hemorrhage is the most common cause of death. Later on, ARDS and MODS occur as sequelae of blood loss, and initially persistent shock determines the further course and eventual outcome of the patient.

During the acute therapy phase, only immediate priority-guided management concepts save the lives of these severely injured patients and improve their prognosis. A variety of methods for hemorrhage control in pelvic injuries are discussed in the literature. With these techniques, several complex therapeutic protocols have been developed. Our experience has resulted in a rather simple algorithm requiring three decisions to be made within the first 30 minutes after admission. The therapeutic goal is based on a combined strategy of intensive shock treatment, early stabilization of the pelvic ring, and potential operative hemorrhage control and packing rather than a single treatment option. Once hemorrhage control is satisfactory, the associated urogenital and intestinal injuries should be treated expeditiously to avoid septic complications.

In urogenital injuries, reliable drainage of the urine is the primary goal. During the first laparotomy, intraperitoneal ruptures of the bladder are repaired. In injuries of the urethra, it is recommended that the urethra be splinted with a transurethral catheter in the acute phase and the definitive reconstructive procedure be undertaken during the secondary period to reduce the rate of late strictures. If early realignment is not possible, then a suprapubic catheter should be inserted.

In open pelvic fractures with injuries to the rectum or anus, a temporary colostomy of the transverse colon generally guarantees proper excretion and safeguards the healing process in the pelvis. At the end of the procedure, an extensive antegrade washout of the distal part is assumed to reduce the microbial load. Any potential muscular or skin necrosis is radically debrided to reduce the risk of infection.

Unstable Injuries of the Spine

In general, operative treatment of unstable spine injuries in multiply injured patients is mandatory, if only for intensive care nursing purposes. Nonoperative treatment using a plaster jacket or a halo-body fixator is unsuitable for multiply injured patients, because the immobilization of the patients carries a high risk. Not only are the intensive care nursing procedures much easier after internal stabilization, but also the period of immobilization and the period of intensive care stay are significantly reduced. Spinal fractures associated with neurologic dysfunction are usually stabilized at the same time as the spinal cord is decompressed. However, in recent years, there has been a move toward stabilizing more unstable injuries of the spine in patients who present without neurologic symptoms for the same reasons. It is our experience that after diagnosing an unstable injury of the spine in a patient who does not have neurologic symptoms, a closed reduction should be undertaken if there is a fracture of the cervical spine or an AO type C rotational injury of the lower thoracic or lumbar spines.

In any other injury, the reduction is performed in the operating room just before the actual procedure. It is important to realize that even if there is a slight suspicion that a fracture fragment or a protruding intervertebral disc may narrow the spinal canal after closed reduction, further diagnostic imaging with CT or MRI should be carried out preoperatively.

In multiply injured patients in particular, closed reduction may be difficult because of coexisting extremity injuries. In these cases, the proper correction of rotation and axis should be obtained intraoperatively.

If there is interposition of a bone fragment or an intervertebral disc, open reduction is always indicated to avoid spinal cord compression.

We routinely use the ventral approach for operative management of the upper (C1-3) and lower (C4-7) cervical spine. The patient's head is fixed to a special reduction apparatus using the rim of the halo fixator. In thoracic or lumbar spine injuries, associated injuries to the chest and abdomen have to be considered. Nonetheless, in our experience, injuries requiring dorsal and ventral stabilization may usually be fixed with a dorsal internal fixator in the acute management period. Depending on the general status of the patient, the ventral stabilization may be performed during the secondary period. Even intrathoracic or intra-abdominal injuries are not necessarily a contraindication to the use of the prone position, which is required for dorsal instrumentation. The prone position can even be used successfully in patients with severe lung injury.

Assessment of Fracture Severity

Closed Fractures

Fractures in polytrauma patients managed either with the ETC or the DCO approach must be stabilized before being admitted to the ITU. Stabilized fractures not only reduce pain but also minimize the release of intramedullary contents into the circulation and secondary damage to the soft tissues. Furthermore, nursing is easier and early functional treatment can be initiated.

Assessment of the degree of soft tissue damage in closed fractures is often difficult. A skin contusion over an otherwise closed fracture may present more therapeutic and prognostic problems than an inside-out puncture wound in an open fracture. Although the skin wound may not be particularly impressive, this type of blunt injury can lead to a significant weakening of the natural skin barrier. As necrosis is the main complication of a skin contusion infection can occur, particularly in the ICU environment. This issue has been addressed by the development of a classification system that allows the clinician to decide the appropriate therapeutic approach that would be beneficial to the patient's overall condition.[267] The classification of soft tissue injuries is detailed in Table 9-13.

Open Fractures

In polytrauma patients, prompt evaluation and treatment of open fractures are of paramount importance. It involves careful assessment of the damage to the soft tissues, radical débridement, extensive irrigation, and finally stable fracture fixation. Careful assessment of the injury severity is the first step in the development of a treatment strategy. The time and mechanism of injury, the energy of the causative force, and the severity of the fracture should be considered. The extent of any coexisting vascular and nerve damage and the general condition of the patient are also of great importance. In high-energy trauma, the soft tissues may be severely damaged and may require careful evaluation and extensive débridement during the initial assessment.

TABLE 9-13 **Classification of Soft Tissue Injury in Closed Fractures[267]**

- **Closed fracture C0:** No injury or very minor soft tissue injury. The C0 classification covers simple fractures caused by indirect mechanisms of injury.

- **Closed fracture C1:** Superficial abrasions or contusions from internal fragment pressure. Simple to moderate fracture types are included.

- **Closed fracture C2:** Deep, contaminated abrasions or local dermal and muscular contusions because of tangential forces are included. An incipient compartment syndrome is also classified as C2. These injuries usually are caused by direct forces, resulting in moderate to severe fracture types. The closed segmental tibial fracture occurring after a typical bumper impact is a good illustrative example.

- **Closed fracture C3:** Extensive skin contusions or muscular destruction, subcutaneous degloving and obvious compartment syndrome in any closed fracture are graded C3. Severe and comminuted fractures occur in this subgroup.

- **Closed fracture C4:** The same injuries as C3 closed fractures but the C4 group are associated with significant vascular damage requiring operative treatment.

Open fractures resulting from low-energy trauma are usually associated with less soft tissue damage and may almost be treated like closed injuries. After the initial débridement, the fracture may be appropriately stabilized.

Open fractures resulting from high-energy trauma often have the particular problem of extensive soft tissue damage combined with significant bone destruction. This injury requires a graded concept of care. The treatment plan considers an adequate débridement, initial temporary stabilization followed by definitive secondary stabilization, as well as the closure of the wound. Our experience with this type of injury indicates that each fracture has almost unique characteristics, which require individual management. In multiply injured patients, the overall injury severity has to be considered, as do the extent of the shock and the initial blood loss. Once these factors have been taken into account, a clear therapeutic plan should be established for each patient. Open fractures are discussed further in Chapters 10 and 12.

Classification of Soft Tissue Damage

Several classifications have been proposed over the years for the grading of open fractures, but the standard system of classifying the soft tissue component of a fracture remains that of Gustilo and Anderson.[139] Despite the doubts that have been raised over its reliability, it seems likely to remain in common use as it is fairly simple to remember and to apply.

In multiply injured patients, a thorough assessment of soft tissue damage is even more crucial. In this group, the prognosis for the soft tissue damage depends on a multitude of parameters, including tissue hypoxia, acidosis, and hypoperfusion of the extremities caused by secondary to hemorrhagic shock. All these factors should be taken into account in clinical decision making and planning.

Reconstruction versus Amputation?

With advances in free tissue transfer and microsurgical techniques and a better appreciation of the usefulness of the Ilizarov

technique, limb preservation, especially in Grade IIIb and IIIc fractures of the lower extremity, is more commonly attempted nowadays. Reconstructive bone and soft tissue surgery usually requires repeated operations, long-term hospital stays, and prolonged periods of treatment. The surgeon must appreciate that this is very difficult for the patient and his or her family and there are often significant social and economic consequences. Several authors have therefore looked into criteria to help guide surgeons in their decision between reconstruction and amputation of a severely injured extremity. From the surgical point of view, an attempt to preserve the limb often seems to be the best decision for the patient. However, from a socioeconomic point, multiple prolonged hospital stays may have severe effects on the patient. The financial loss for the patient from prolonged hospital stays and time off work may prove to be higher than that associated with a primary amputation, and not infrequently multiple attempts at reconstruction leave patients incapable of earning their living for more than 2 years.[335] Additionally, it should be remembered that patients with reconstructed limbs often find it difficult to return to their occupations at all.

If a severely injured patient survives after a primary amputation, the question that arises is whether the amputation was unavoidable or whether reconstruction was possible. If the patient dies, the question is whether the severity of the injuries was underestimated initially and would an early amputation have saved the patient's life. Last, if the patient survives after primary reconstruction but suffers from complications requiring prolonged treatment, the question is whether the bad outcome justified the resources that were expended.

Several classification systems have been developed to help surgeons in this decision-making process.[133,151,166] Recently, McNamara et al.[229] evaluated the Mangled Extremity Severity Score (MESS) by retrospectively studying 24 patients with Gustilo III-C fractures. The results confirmed high predictability. To improve the predictive value, nerve damage and a detailed assessment of the bone and soft tissue damage were included. The new score that resulted from this is called the Nerve Injury, Ischemia, Soft Tissue Injury, Skeletal Injury, Shock and Age (NISSSA) score. It has been shown to have a sensitivity of 81.8% and a specificity of 92.3%.[229] Amputations are discussed further in Chapter 13.

Débridement

After deciding to salvage the limb, extensive careful debridement is the first step in the operative treatment plan. All soft tissues have to be considered. If the debridement is overcautious, this may lead to a deterioration of the patient's condition and even organ failure. Adequate surgical exposure of the injury is essential to both assess and treat the soft tissue damage. In multiply injured patients, there is a high risk of late soft tissue necrosis secondary to impaired soft tissue perfusion, which may occur with posttraumatic edema, increased capillary permeability, massive volume resuscitation, and an unstable circulation. Therefore, in many patients, regular operative explorations need to be scheduled. These second-look surgeries allow for continuous assessment of the soft tissues. This strategy enables the surgeon to undertake redébridement procedures every 48 hours if required.

Operative Strategy Depending on the Overall Injury Severity

Clearly, the ability of the multiply injured patient to tolerate reconstructive surgery depends mostly on the overall condition of the patient and the extent of the coexisting injuries. Any lengthy reconstruction or reimplantation procedure may potentially harm the patient and induce a life-threatening situation. Attention also has to be paid to the long-term prognosis of an open injury in the multiply injured patient. All these parameters need to be considered when constructing a therapeutic plan.

Patients with an ISS of 1 to 15 Points or 16 to 25 Points and Grade IIIa, b, and c Soft Tissue Injuries. In this subgroup of multiply injured patients, reconstruction is indicated. The surgical process is now largely standardized. After a radical débridement, the second step consists of vascular repair, if this is required. This may necessitate the use of an interposition vein graft. Following this, the fractures should be stabilized, ideally using intramedullary osteosynthesis. Intramedullary implants are much less damaging to the soft tissues than direct osteosynthesis. There is less soft tissue stripping and only minimal impairment of the circulation of the bone.[196]

The closure of any associated soft tissue defect depends on the extent of the injury. In most cases, the wound will be temporarily covered with synthetic skin grafts or vacuum systems, before final closure using plastic reconstructive surgery techniques. This is discussed further in Chapter 14. In general, the expected result of reconstructive limb-saving strategy should be better than that of amputation.

Patients with an ISS of 1 to 15 Points and 16 to 25 Points with Complete or Incomplete Amputations. The surgical management of these injuries is very similar. The option of reimplantation has to be considered and this may require referral to a specialized center. If reimplantation is anticipated, appropriate preparations must be made. Hemorrhage should be stopped by elevation and application of a pressure bandage. The treatment of the amputated limb follows clear emergency medicine guidelines.[362]

Amputation injuries in children always have to be considered for replantation. Children have an improved tissue regenerative ability and have better functional outcome results than similarly injured adults.

Patients with an ISS of 26 to 50 Points and More Than 50 Points. In recent years, Level 1 trauma centers have improved their critical care and fracture management techniques and they now succeed in saving most severely traumatized extremities. Unfortunately, these limbs still sometimes require secondary amputation because of insufficient planning.[174] In this subgroup of most severely injured patients with extremity injuries, the preservation of the extremity should not be attempted at all. The principle "life before limb" should hold true and the indications for amputation are generous. If the decision to amputate a limb is made, the actual procedure should ideally be performed quickly through healthy tissue using a guillotine method. Under these circumstances, primary closure is associated with an extremely high rate of complications because the overall extent of the soft tissue damage and posttraumatic edema cannot be adequately estimated.

Open Intra-articular Fractures

A two-step strategy has been advocated for the management of open intra-articular fractures. First, the injury is débrided and the joint surface is reconstructed using a minimal invasive osteosynthesis technique (MIO). The joint is then immobilized by bridging, or transarticular, external fixation. The definitive osteosynthesis is carried out secondarily following soft tissue healing. In this procedure, the previously reconstructed articular segment is attached to the metaphysis. Sometimes bone shortening has to be accepted, at least temporarily, to close potential bony or soft tissue defects. The Ilizarov frame is often used under these circumstances. This is discussed further in Chapter 14.

Timing of Soft Tissue Defect Reconstruction

In many multiply injured patients, primary wound closure represents bad practice. The relative hypoxia of the tissues may lead to impaired and delayed wound healing associated with a higher risk of wound infection. In small soft tissue injuries, we recommend secondary closure of the wound after covering the wound with artificial skin until the swelling decreases. An absolute prerequisite for wound closure is to completely cover implants with well-perfused soft tissues. In these defects, artificial skin replacements are used primarily and the wound is secondarily closed later over a period of several days. In some selected cases, continuous wound closure may also be an option.

In medium-sized soft tissue defects, secondary closure is often achieved by local soft tissue transpositions following appropriate mobilization of the soft tissues. In extensive soft tissue defects associated with exposure of bone with significant periosteal damage, the soft tissues used to cover the defect require to be very well perfused. Soft tissue reconstruction should be undertaken within 72 hours of the trauma or there is danger of further damage.

Large posttraumatic soft tissue defects are very challenging for the surgeon and require a well-defined therapeutic strategy. The overall concept of soft tissue coverage depends on the extent of uncovered bone, tendons, and nerves. For bone associated with significant periosteal stripping, damaged neurovascular structures, and injuries involving open joints, soft tissue cover with well-perfused tissues is essential. To achieve satisfactory results, timely communication and continuous cooperation between trauma and plastic surgeons are essential.

Soft Tissue Reconstruction

There are numerous local and distant flaps described in the literature to cover soft tissue defects.

Local Flaps

Rotational flaps are used to cover small and medium-sized soft tissue defects. These flaps consist of different combinations of muscle, fascia, and skin, which are usually well perfused. They are very adaptable but are associated with a number of disadvantages. In multiply injured patients, it may be difficult to use local flaps because of coexisting injuries to the adjacent soft tissues. Meticulous preoperative planning is mandatory. Local flaps are discussed in more detail in Chapter 14.

Distant Flaps

For the reasons stated earlier, distant flaps are commonly used in multiply injured patients. However, the choice of flap is often difficult. On the one hand, the patient may need urgent soft tissue closure, but on the other hand, a prolonged procedure may be contraindicated. Carefully planning is essential; see Chapter 14.

INTENSIVE CARE UNIT

Ventilation Strategies

Multiple trauma patients often present with blunt thoracic trauma and suffer from a variable degree of respiratory insufficiency. Management strategies for these patients should begin on arrival at the trauma center. The objective is to initiate treatment early to minimize the risk of development of atelectasis and/or parenchymal damage. Mechanical ventilation should facilitate alveolar recruitment and enhance intrapulmonary gas distribution. Modern ventilation strategies with low tidal volume (4 to 8 mL/kg), best positive end-expiratory pressure (PEEP), low airway pressures (less than 35 cm H$_2$O), and an inspiratory oxygen concentration of 55% to 60% are often ideal. Hypercapnia may be allowed up to a certain degree. This is known as permissive hypercapnia (PHC).[384] It is well tolerated in patients with ARDS and a P$_{CO_2}$ of 60 to 120 mm Hg. Clinical experience shows that the pressure controlled ventilation with inversed ratio ventilation (I:E [1:1 to 4:1]), low tidal volumes (4 to 8 mL/kg), frequencies of 10 to 15/min, PHC (P$_{CO_2}$ about 70 mm Hg), and an individual PEEP (5 to 12 cm H$_2$O), a high oxygen concentration (F$_{IO_2}$ less than 0.5) and a high airway pressure can prevent the lung from further ventilation damage.[409] Early experiences using other ventilation strategies, such as bilevel positive airway pressure (BiPAP), demonstrate that they are also feasible, although there may be problems with BiPAP in cases where long-term sedation is required. One of the most recent concepts developed for the prevention of pulmonary failure is the recruitment of alveoli by a temporary increase in PEEP (open lung concept).[2] It does not cause sustained cardiovascular side effects and also does not lead to the development of bronchopleural fistulas. However, the clinical relevance of this new concept remains to be proved in larger series.[239]

Recently, a new study compared an established low-tidal-volume ventilation strategy with an experimental strategy based on the original "open-lung approach," combining low tidal volume, lung recruitment maneuvers, and high PEEP. The authors concluded that for patients with acute lung injury and ARDS, a multifaceted ventilation strategy designed to recruit and open the lung resulted in no significant difference in all-cause hospital mortality or barotrauma compared with an established low-tidal-volume ventilation strategy. This "open-lung" strategy did appear to improve secondary end points related to hypoxemia and the use of rescue therapies.[230]

Adult Respiratory Distress Syndrome

Acute lung injury can be caused by severe pneumonia or trauma, and ARDS is its most critical form. In ARDS, the lungs become swollen with water and protein, and breathing becomes impossible, leading to death in 3% to 40% of cases. Activated blood cells, cytokines, toxins, cell debris, and local tissue damage facilitate endothelial cell damage leading to decompensation of lymph drainage and pulmonary interstitial edema. Patients with ARDS have higher hospital mortality rates and reduced long-term pulmonary function and quality of life. ARDS is treated with mechanical ventilation, which can provide life support but often at the expense of further lung injury. Ventilation that employs a low tidal volume inhaled in each breath reduces the risk of death in patients who are critically ill with ARDS. The use of steroids has been controversial despite the fact that published trails support the administration of low- to moderate-

dose corticosteroids in the treatment of early- and late-phase ARDS.[80] The impact of clinical risk factors in the conversion from acute lung injury to acute ARDS in severe multiple trauma patients has also been evaluated. It has been shown that the impact of pulmonary contusion, the APACHE II score and disseminated intravascular coagulation may help to predict the conversion of acute lung injury to ARDS in severe multiple trauma.[412] Historically, three phases of ARDS have been differentiated, the third leading to a state of scarring of pulmonary tissue and often irreversible loss of organ function. Currently, we believe that the formation of scar tissue is often the result of high intra-alveolar pressures because of inadequate ventilation techniques. Because of the improved ventilation strategies described earlier, the late form is usually no longer seen.[290]

Multiple Organ Dysfunction Syndrome

MODS is the result of an inappropriate generalized inflammatory response of the host to a variety of insults. Currently, it is believed that in the early phase of MODS, circulating cytokines cause universal endothelium injury in organs. In the later phase of MODS, overexpression of inflammatory mediators in the interstitial space of various organs is considered a main mechanism of parenchymal injury. The difference in constitutive expression and the upregulation of adhesion molecules in vascular beds and the density and potency of intrinsic inflammatory cells in different organs are the key factors determining the sequence and severity of organ dysfunction.[393]

The sequence of organ failures is variable. The most commonly reported sequence is pulmonary failure followed by the liver and intestine.[82,95]

GENETIC PREDISPOSITION TO ADVERSE OUTCOME

We believe that there are still patients that do not conform to the roles set by the predictive parameters following trauma. Some patients do worse while some others fare better than predicted. In the early 1990s, it was recognized that these differences in the clinical course of the patients and their outcomes are subject to biological variation in the context of trauma or surgery.[137] This biological variation is highly dependent on the genetic constitution of the patient, and the importance of genes as the cause of diseases or as predisposing factors has become indisputable. The observed polymorphisms are of different natures. Some of them are mutations located within endonuclease restriction sites, whereas others are single nucleotide polymorphisms or consist of insertions or deletions of larger fragments, as detected by polymerase chain reaction techniques.[121] The polymorphism can be located within the gene or in the promoter region. Polymorphisms are different alleles, none of which is predominant in the population. A specific polymorphism variation can be associated with a genetic disease. The polymorphism can also interact with the environment and then exert detrimental actions.

With the availability of molecular diagnostic techniques, there has been increased interest in conducting disease–gene association studies determining the role of genetic variations in the inflammatory response to injury and infection.

The existence of genotypes susceptible to postoperative sepsis is no longer a myth. A growing body of evidence suggests that genetic susceptibility influences the development of surgical sepsis and its sequelae, ARDS and MODS. The identification of functional polymorphisms in several cytokine genes and other important molecules provides a potential mechanism whereby these variations may exist. Several studies have reported the relationship between different polymorphic variants and the risk of developing posttraumatic complications.[127,129,180,300]

However, when investigating genetic polymorphisms, it is not enough just to determine the presence of a polymorphism. One has to take several criteria into account. Patients have different genetic constitutions. Investigating polymorphisms linked to disease can be blurred by the existing genetic variation. Therefore, it is necessary to determine the overall genetic constellation of the population under investigation. Furthermore, the power of the study has to be sufficient to achieve specific results. One has to consider whether other genes may be involved. These genes might be the actual cause for the differences investigated. The gene investigated is then just an epiphenomenon. It is therefore important to study family genetics at the same time. The family constitution can tell more about the underlying genes that are involved in the disease process. If differences in disease outcome are linked to one or more genetic polymorphisms, one has to perform a subsequent study in another cohort. This cohort has to show similar linkage of genes to outcome. A number of studies[214,300,307,332,397] have indicated the influence of specific polymorphic variants of important genes in the development of posttraumatic sepsis. However, most of the studies have been undertaken on small populations, which are not necessarily geographically or ethnically distinct, and for this reason the results may be difficult to interpret. Because of these problems, multicenter, international studies will be required to investigate the application of genetic information to patients.

Future research should focus on a broad array of genes. Single nucleotide polymorphism genotyping assays using microarray techniques are suitable for this. Early identification of patients at risk would permit direct interventions with biological response modifiers in an attempt to improve morbidity and mortality rates. Early positive results have been achieved in septic patients and goal-directed therapeutic low-dose steroid supplementation, blood glucose control, and activated protein C therapy appears to be associated with an improved outcome after sepsis.[75,307,308] Hopefully, similar achievements can be made for patients with acute trauma in the future.

REHABILITATION

The aftercare of polytrauma patients has to start during the immediate postoperative period. This requires mobilization of the extremities during the course of the intensive care treatment. Passive continuous motion may be used, but mobilization of all major joints must be performed and should be part of a standardized rehabilitation program.

Once the patient has been returned to the normal ward, these measures must be maintained and they may be accompanied by active exercises by the patient. These should be performed under the supervision of a trained physiotherapist. The modes of mobilization and the degree of weight bearing should be carefully discussed between the treating surgeon and the physical therapist. Patients tend to be cautious about mobilization and there is often a particular fear about weight bearing. This

can often be explained by the severe psychological impact induced by the traumatic insult. Reassurance of the patient is an important additional factor if adequate mobilization is going to be achieved. These factors are important not only with regard to the maintenance of joint mobility but also to prevent osteoporosis induced by immobility. It is crucial that patients realize the importance of muscular activity, joint mobility, and weight bearing with reference to neuromuscular function and the maintenance of an optimal osseous microstructure.

Patients with Head Trauma

When treating patients who have had significant head trauma, special care must be taken to avoid the development of secondary brain damage. These patients also benefit from early rehabilitation measures. An appropriate transfer to a rehabilitation center is advisable. Although it may be considered appropriate to commence treatment in the primary center, the patients are often still under the influence of sedative drugs or undergoing withdrawal symptoms from these drugs. In this situation, a thorough workup cannot be performed and cognitive training is useless. In an ideal situation, transfer to a specialized facility may overlap with the normalization of the withdrawal symptoms and thus forms the basis of a timely beginning of the rehabilitation program.

Outcome Studies

Evaluation of the effectiveness of trauma care was traditionally focused on mortality rates, the incidence of preventable deaths, complication rates, in-hospital morbidity, and length of hospital stay.[34,319] However, because of the advances of acute trauma management and the increased survival rates over the last few decades, long-term functional recovery, health-related quality-of-life, return to work, and patient's satisfaction have been added to the classic trauma evaluation endpoints.

The long-term outcome of major trauma reflects the result of multiple phases and factors, including diagnostic procedures, therapeutic interventions, inherent characteristics of the patient, and effectiveness of the trauma services over a long period of time, from the time of the accident until rehabilitation or even later. It is the end result of this multifactorial and complicated system that is of most concern to the patient. In the last two decades, the importance of the patient's point of view and his or her perception of health outcomes have been acknowledged and have led to the development of a large number of functional and patient-related outcome scores.[33]

However, the increasingly high priority of assessing the long-term functional outcome of trauma is not only based on patients' concerns as proper assessment facilitates the development and improvement of management guidelines, discharge and rehabilitation planning, and the optimal allocation of resources. Additionally, the long-term outcome of trauma management has significant social and economic implications.[33]

Recovery following polytrauma is often prolonged, and thus the appropriate time interval for assessment of long-term outcomes is usually longer than the customary time-frame of 2 years. In particular, social rehabilitation, including return-to-work or hobbies, change of occupation or retirement, appears to be a long-term process. This suggests that the evaluation of the functional outcome following polytrauma should be based on a lengthened follow-up period by which time surgical outpatient review is sporadic, if it is still occurring at all. This fact together with the complexity of parameters associated with the outcome of polytrauma explains the difficulty of long-term assessment and the scarcity of comprehensive clinical studies and adequate data.

Currently, the long-term outcome evaluation of trauma care encompasses parameters related to quality-of-life, return to work or sports, persistent physical or psychological complaints, and restrictions and acquired disabilities. The term "quality of life" entered *Index Medicus* in 1977.[134,415] To apply its concept in the specific clinical setting of trauma, four basic areas should be considered: physical function, psychological function, social function, and symptoms.[381] The unique character of this outcome assessment is that it relies largely on subjective variables judged by the patients themselves.

A large number of validated scoring systems are used to quantify outcome after mainly isolated injuries in almost all anatomic areas. In the case of polytrauma, they are often used to objectively quantify the anatomic and physical components of the final outcome. Examples are the Lysholm and Merle d'Aubigne scores. For patients with multiple musculoskeletal disorders, patient-assessed scales have been developed that describe self-reported complaints and subjective parameters. In addition, numerous scoring systems have been developed to determine psychological outcome after trauma.

In most of the large series, it is musculoskeletal injuries of the lower extremity below the knee,[335,378,414] together with injuries of the spine,[114,149,228] the pelvis,[280,376] and brain injury,[204,216] that are identified as those most influencing the long-term functional outcome of polytrauma patients.[356] According to most published series, they seem to determine a major proportion of the patient's quality of life with respect to functional status and pain.

Predictors of disability, such as mechanism of injury, gender, injury severity, sociodemographic status, social support, and psychological sequelae, have also been reported.[46,160,164] Clinically relevant psychological impairments such as anxiety, depression, and posttraumatic stress disorder have been reported, especially within the first year after injury, when they have a prevalence of 30% to 60%. In succeeding years, the prevalence drops and has been reported to be 7% to 22%.[235] The importance of psychological outcomes, particularly posttraumatic stress disorder, has been highlighted in many series.[324,357] It is described as an anxiety disorder that can develop after exposure to a terrifying event or ordeal in which grave physical harm occurred or was threatened.

In general, despite the differences in injury pattern, severity of injury, trauma management practices, and rehabilitation, there is strong evidence that the quality of life and the overall outcome are significantly impaired after major trauma. In the past, the principal aim of treatment was the prevention of late organ failure and death. In contrast, today, the ultimate goal of trauma care is to restore patients to the previous functional status and role in society. A number of studies reporting on the functional outcome after multiple trauma are shown in Table 9-14,* whereas in Table 9-15[124,173,355,396] the commonly used functional outcome scores are presented. The measurement of outcome still lacks accuracy, but we anticipate significant improvement in this important aspect of trauma.

REIMBURSEMENT

Health economics is an important issue in every national health system around the world. In patients with multiple injuries, the issue of reimbursement is still unresolved and has been the subject of much recent debate.

Most health systems continue to be in deficit as a result of their disproportionate funding and inadequacy of reimbursement policies.** Before, however, one decides to evaluate the real cost of a specific procedure to a national health system, one must be familiar with the factors that a thorough economic analysis should include. A thorough economic analysis of any medical condition measures direct, indirect, and intangible costs.[182,365] It incorporates both fixed and variable costs, direct expenses and indirect expenses associated with the duration of therapy, final functional outcome, disability payments, and quality of life.[76,186,295]

Fixed costs are related to the hospital's overheads, and it is these costs that the clinician has least control over. The variable costs are mostly related to clinical practice and they have been more extensively studied. Direct medical and nonmedical costs are easier to record compared with the indirect ones, and most of the literature focuses on them. The indirect and intangible costs are more difficult to estimate and they require longer patient follow-up. However, they can be significantly larger than the direct costs. A major deficiency of the existing health economics studies is their lack of an all-inclusive cost analysis.

The assessment of health economics in orthopaedic trauma is complicated as it has to encompass the entire trauma system, including prehospital, in-hospital, and posthospital care. Because of this, the financial implications are difficult to assess, and they are especially difficult in polytrauma patients, where there are many aspects to evaluate. Examples of these are the prehospital and emergency services; the intensity of the medical and nursing staff workload, which varies with each patient; and the element of "trauma readiness."[96] "Trauma readiness" is related to the expertise of the personnel involved in patient care, the effectiveness of the infrastructure, and the efficiency of coordination of the trauma team. The expense of maintaining a dedicated trauma team on a 24/7 schedule has proved to be the most difficult economic parameter to assess, rate, and reimburse.[364] Over the years, several authors have attempted to address the issue of trauma and polytrauma costs.[†] In all of these studies, it was evident that conventional cost accounting methods were inadequate to assess the costs despite recent advances in "operations management" and health economics. The necessary components of an all-inclusive economic analysis of a trauma system were first outlined in the Model Trauma Care Systems Plan published by the U.S. Bureau of Health Resources Development in 1992.[94] Table 9-16 presents a description of the different aspects of trauma-related health economics.

Allowing for the restrictions already outlined, medical spending on injuries in the United States in 1987 was $64.7 billion. In 2000, it accounted for 10.3% of the total medical expenditure and had reached $117.2 billion. In the United Kingdom, in 1994 the cost of treating trauma was £20 billion, and in 2003 it was reported to be £34 billion.[236,269,389] Major increases in the socioeconomic costs of trauma and polytrauma

---

*References 8,102,158,159,178,195,277,287.

**References 136,198,291,314,328,346,351.
†References 71,152,177,192,237,263,345,392.

TABLE 9-14 **Fifteen Representative Studies Focused on Long-term Outcome of Major Trauma Patients**

Authors, Origin, Year	No. of Patients	ISS — Follow-Up	Outcome Parameters	Conclusions
Bull JV,[367] Birmingham, UK, 1975	1268	NA — On discharge	• Disability: 5-point scale	• Of the 1268 cases, 264 suffered some residual disability. • The ISS rating may be a useful measure of disability when applied to groups of cases, but should be used with great caution in forecasting the outcome of an individual patient.
MacKenzie EJ, et al.,[365] Baltimore, USA, 1986	473	NA — 6 months	• Activities of daily living (ADL) • Instrumental activities of daily living (IADL) • Mobility	• AIS of the most severe extremity and spinal cord injury carries considerably more weight when predicting functional status than do the AIS scores of injuries to any other body region.
Horne G and Schemitsch E,[368] Wellington, NZ, 1989	90	Mean ISS 23.3 — Mean 3.2 years	• Modified Glasgow scale	• Correlation between outcome and the severity of brain injury, the severity of skeletal injuries, and the ISS • ISS <24, no physical impairment ISS of 25 to 30, slight impairment ISS >30, at least one moderate impairment
Gaillard M, et al.,[374] Creteil, France, 1990	250	Mean ISS 25 — Minimum 2 years	• Long-term survey	• No correlation between sequelae and the duration of work, extent of injury, or ISS
Jurkovich G, et al.,[375] Seattle, Baltimore, Nashville, USA 1995	329	NA — 12 months	• Sickness Impact Profile (SIP)	• 48% had some form of disability, even at 12 months. • Disability was present for a wide spectrum of activities of daily life, including ambulation, psychosocial health, sleep, home management, and return to work and leisure activities. • Need for psychological intervention and social support long into the recovery period of patients who might not at first seem to require them.
Ott R, et al.,[376] Nurnberg, Germany, 1996	73	PTS ≥40 — Range 1 to 13 years	• Aachen Longtime Outcome Score (ALOS) • Spitzer Index (SI) • Self-assessment • Return to work	• Handicaps mainly resulted from permanent physical disability, in particular in the lower extremities. • Head injuries, extremity trauma, severity of injury, and increasing age correlated with worse outcome.
Anke AGW, et al.,[377] Oslo, Norway, 1997	69	Mean ISS 25 (range 17 to 50) — 35 ± 4 months	• Checklist on social network • Occurrence of impairments and disabilities	• 74% had physical impairments; 32% of the subjects had cognitive impairments. • Significant correlation between ISS and degree of impairment • High prevalence of impairment after severe multiple trauma
Holbrook TL, et al.,[378] San Diego, USA, 1999	780	Mean ISS 13 ± 8.5 — 18 months	• Quality of Well-being (QWB) scale • Functional Disability Score • Center for Epidemiologic Studies Depression (CES-D) scale • Impact of Events Scale	• Depression, posttraumatic stress disorder, and serious extremity injury play an important role in determining outcome. • A prolonged and profound level of functional limitation after major trauma was identified at 12-month and 18-month follow-up.
Korosec-Jagodic H, et al.,[379] Celje, Slovenia, 2000	98	APACHE II 14.3 ± 6.6 — 2 years	• EuroQol 5D questionnaire • Health-related quality of life (HRQOL)	• Trauma patients had a tendency toward anxiety and depression. • Survival and quality of life after critical illness are independent.

(continues)

TABLE 9-14 **Fifteen Representative Studies Focused on Long-term Outcome of Major Trauma Patients (*Continued*)**

Authors, Origin, Year	No. of Patients	ISS — Follow-Up	Outcome Parameters	Conclusions
Holbrook TL, et al.,[380] San Diego, USA, 2001	1048	Mean ISS 13.5 — 18 months	• QWB scale • CES-D scale • Impact of Events Scale	• Gender may play a strong and independent role in predicting functional outcome and quality of life after major trauma. • Functional outcome and quality of life were markedly lower in women compared with men, as measured by the QWB scale.
Stalp M, et al.,[366] Hannover, Germany, 2002	254	Mean ISS 24 ± 6 — Mean 2.1 years ± 0.1	• Hannover Score for Polytrauma Outcome (HASPOC) • Musculoskeletal Function Assessment (MFA) • 12-Item Health Survey (SF-12) • Functional Independence Measurement (FIM) • Glasgow Outcome Scale • Evaluation of specific body regions	• The most severe impairment in functional outcome occurs after injuries of the lower extremities, spine, and pelvis. • The main problems in patients with multiple injuries, with skeletal injuries, 2 years after trauma, were secondary to injuries of the lower extremity below the knee, the spine, and the pelvis.
Tran T and Thordarson D,[356] Los Angeles, USA 2002	24	Mean ISS 17 — Minimum 12 months	• 36-Item Health Survey (SF-36) • AAOS lower limb • Foot and Ankle Score	• Significant negative impact on outcome in multiply injured patients who have also sustained a foot injury. • Multiply injured patients with foot injuries had significantly more limitations in physical and social activities, increased bodily pain.
Zelle BA, et al.,[354] Hannover, Germany 2005	637	Mean ISS 20.7 ± 9.7 — Mean 17.5 (range 10 to 28)	• HASPOC • SF-12 • Self-reported requirement for medical aids and devices • Self-reported requirement for inpatient rehabilitation • Self-reported length of rehabilitation • Retired because of injury	• Psychosocial factors play a major role in recovery following polytrauma. • Workers' compensation patients were significantly more likely to use medical aids and devices, be retired because of their injury, and have inpatient rehabilitation. • Workers' compensation status has a significant impact on the long-term subjective and objective outcome following polytrauma.
Zelle BA, et al.,[357] Hannover, Germany 2005	389	Mean ISS 20.2 ± 4.3 Mean PTS 29.5 ± 13.3 — Mean 17.3 ± 4.8 years	• Lower-extremity-specific outcome measurements • HASPOC • SF-12 • Tegner activity score • Inability to work	• Injuries below the knee have a major impact on the functional recovery following polytrauma. • The analysis of general outcome and lower-extremity-specific outcome measurements suggests that patients with fractures above the knee joint achieve superior outcomes than patients with fractures below the knee joint.
Pape HC, et al.,[373] Hannover, Germany, 2006	637	Mean ISS 20.7 (range 4 to 54) — Mean 17.5 years (range 0 to 28)	• Lower-extremity-specific outcome measurements • General outcome measurements • SF-12 • Inability to work • Subjective outcome questionnaires	• The injury most often responsible for physical disability was head trauma, followed by injuries to the lower extremities. • A high percentage of patients can be recruited for follow-up even 10 years after polytrauma.

can be seen in studies from Germany, Switzerland, and the rest of Europe.*

When the rising costs of trauma care are appreciated, one can easily understand why providing trauma services is not really sustainable. The issue of reimbursement is still unresolved

and has been the focus of much debate recently. Most health care organizations and trauma systems apply a predetermined charge for their trauma services, which does not relate to each patient's direct or indirect medical and nonmedical costs. It is therefore no surprise that, especially for complex cases and polytrauma patients, such cost estimation has proved to be inaccurate. It has been estimated that a comparison of the actual direct costs of polytrauma and its relative reimbursement has

*References 17,104,125,251,265,266,271,318,361.

TABLE 9-15	Commonly Used Functional Outcome Scores in the Clinical Setting of Polytrauma		
Name—Abbreviation	Characteristics	Range of Values	Studies
Quality of Well Being scale— QWB scale	1 symptom scale and 3 function scales (mobility, physical activity, social activity)	0 to 1.0 Death to asymptomatic full function	378, 380
Glasgow Outcome Score— GOS	5-item score	1 to 5 Dead to good recovery	366, 368, 381
Activities of Daily Living scale— ADL scale	21 items of basic capacities of self-care (BADL) and higher levels of performance (IADL)	0 to 21 Worst to best	365, 377
Sickness Impact Profile—SIP	12 categories physical and psychosocial	0 to 210 Worst to best	375, 382
Functional Independence Measurement—FIM	13 motor items and 5 cognitive items	1 to 7 Total assist to complete independence	366
Hannover Score for Polytrauma Outcome—HASPOC score	Part 1 (113 questions) patient questionnaire (HASPOC-Subjective) and Part 2 (191 questions) physical examination (HASPOC-Objective)	5 to 411 points Best to worst	357, 366, 383
Health Survey Short-Form 36 or 12 items—SF-3 /12	36/12 health-related aspects	0 to 100 points	357, 373, 384
EuroQol 5D questionnaire— EQ-5D	Part I, descriptive system Part II, visual-analog scale Part III, EuroQol 5D Index	Minus 0.11 to 1 Worse imaginable to best imaginable heath state	379

resulted in a negative balance of 80% to 900% in different health systems.[346] In England, the cost of treatment of any multiple injured patient is estimated using the "polytrauma tariff." This tariff is used in all patients with multiple injuries instead of calculating the costs of the different interventions in each individual polytrauma case. The concept of Payment by Results was introduced across the National Health Service (NHS) in England in 2005 and is based on the average cost of providing a particular treatment or health service. The dominant diagnosis or procedural code determines the tariff, as well as the length of hospital stay.[85] In 2000, the NHS fiscal services calculated this tariff to be £1500.00.[346] According to the website of the Department of Health[86] for the financial year 2006 to 2007, the polytrauma tariff is a standard sum of £3004 for those younger than 69 years and £5716 for older than 70 years. Additional costs are calculated depending on the length of hospital stay for these patients if their hospitalization is prolonged for longer than 1 week for the older-than-69-years group or longer than 4 weeks for the older-than-70-years group. However, poor documentation, inefficient coding, and the inherent weaknesses of using

TABLE 9-16	Different Aspects of Health Economics That Needs to Be Evaluated in an All-Inclusive Financial Profile of Trauma and Polytrauma Care		
Direct Costs			
Medical	Nonmedical	Indirect Costs	Intangible Costs
Personnel costs	Transportation	Lost productivity	Quality of life (pain, suffering, grief)
Supply costs	Lodging of patients and relatives	Lost earnings	
Length of hospitalization		Impairment payments	QALY evaluation (quality-adjusted life years lost)
Diagnostic interventions		Residential and nursing care	
Medications		Insurance costs	
Surgical interventions		Legal costs	Psychosocial parameters
Outpatient attendances			
Rehabilitation			
Prehospital costs			
Trauma readiness			
Trauma training			

average costs in complex and multisystem diseases like polytrauma have resulted in incorrect tariffs and therefore significant loss of revenue for the hospitals.[260]

Besides the polytrauma tariff, one has to consider other factors that are contributing to this inadequate system of cost evaluation of medical treatment. The absence of a single formal trauma network in the United Kingdom and the existence of many small informal networks centered on teaching or large general hospitals has almost certainly hindered efforts to achieve a complete financial assessment of the trauma services. Without an accurate assessment of the overall services, it is difficult to quantify full reimbursement and less easy to justify adequate resources.

The workload of the hospitals receiving trauma in these networks varies significantly. It is often unrecognized and underfunded by the authorities. These units often function under significant pressure. The continuous use of their resources for trauma and polytrauma patients prolongs the elective waiting lists and limits the level of service that can provided to local patients for the more financially rewarding routine elective treatments.[74,81,172,287] Thus, these centers often present a worse profile according to strict financial and managerial criteria in comparison to smaller hospitals with a smaller trauma workload. Moreover, NHS revenues from elective orthopaedic cases have been recorded to be more than those of acute trauma cases, emphasizing the problem of the insufficiency of the "trauma tariffs."[22] Unfortunately, as the numbers of trauma patients increases, the administrative focus is directed more toward problems with elective waiting lists, thus reducing the resources of the specialist trauma services even further.[22]

Patients with pelvic trauma represent an almost ideal paradigm of polytrauma cases from a clinical perspective.[184] The health economics implications of these patients were evaluated in 2004.[22] The authors identified one of the main problems as the establishment of the out-of-area transfer system (OATS) for pelvic trauma in 1999. Analysis showed that only 60% of treated cases were reimbursed because of the retrospective manner of the calculation.

The increasing numbers of trauma cases treated in such centers demands a more accurate and up-to-date estimation of the actual volume of the trauma care services and their direct medical burdens.

It is of note that, currently, a comprehensive and complete evaluation of the financial implications of polytrauma does not exist. The assessment of the cost-effectiveness of any trauma system must be correlated with the return of trauma victims to a productive life. The complexity and multiplicity of the different aspects of these patients and their treatment represent the main reason for this deficiency. However, its necessity cannot be overstressed to facilitate the development and monitoring of the required services and to demonstrate the deficiency of the associated financial frameworks. Trauma centers must identify and understand their cost structure not only to improve their efficiency but also to survive. In this context, medical and financial researchers must focus on all the different aspects of polytrauma expenses. More specifically, the following recommendations can be made:

1. The direct medical costs should include all the diagnostic and therapeutic procedures and interventions incurred by these patients and avoid the limitations of the "polytrauma tariff." The target should be to achieve an accurate assessment of all the expenses of the trauma hospital services to claim satisfactory reimbursement.

2. The concept of "trauma readiness" is of particular importance for the hospital personnel and services. The variability and intensity of the trauma workload cannot be compared with those of any other medical service. The 24/7 availability of a trauma team and the financial implications of this must be included at any economic analysis and should be reimbursed.

3. At the same time, the costs of prehospital services related to trauma and polytrauma should also be assessed on a prospective and all-inclusive basis taking into account the aspects of "readiness" and also the secondary transportation of individual polytrauma patients to tertiary specialized centers with established pelvic and spine treatment units.

4. The health authorities should evaluate the tertiary referral centers of expert trauma services using different criteria and financial algorithms than those applied to the referring hospital centers. The criteria defining success in these hospitals should be compared with those of similar trauma centers with similar workloads and multidisciplinary readiness, and not with those of hospitals that provide services of a more elective nature.

5. The difficulties of evaluating the quality of life and psychosocial costs of trauma and polytrauma should not discourage the researchers. A prospective study following these patients until their final outcome should be initiated as soon as possible. It would provide all the necessary information about the real socioeconomic burden of contemporary trauma.

6. The fragmentation of health services and trauma networks dealing with the assessment of the economics of polytrauma must be avoided. The conclusions of a prospective study estimating the socioeconomic burden of trauma should include all the health care providers that are involved with polytrauma care.

REFERENCES

1. Abboud PA, Kendall J. Emergency department ultrasound for hemothorax after blunt traumatic injury. J Emerg Med 2003;25:181–184.
2. Agro F, Barzoi G, Doyle DJ, et al. Reduction in pulmonary shunt using the Open Lung Concept. Anaesthesia 2004;59:625–626.
3. Aiboshi J, Moore EE, Ciesla DJ, et al. Blood transfusion and the two-insult model of post-injury multiple organ failure. Shock 2001;15:302–306.
4. Ali J, Adam RU, Gana TJ, et al. Trauma patient outcome after the Prehospital Trauma Life Support program. J Trauma 1997;42:1018–1021.
5. American College of Emergency Physicians. Guidelines for trauma care systems. Ann Emerg Med 1987;16:459–463.
6. American College of Emergency Physicians. Trauma care systems development, evaluation, and funding. Ann Emerg Med Clin North Am 1999;34:308.
7. American College of Surgeons/Committee of Trauma. National Trauma Data Bank annual report 2005, dataset version 5.0. Chicago: American College of Surgeons Committee on Trauma 2005.
8. Anke AG, Stanghelle JK, Finset A, et al. Long-term prevalence of impairments and disabilities after multiple trauma. J Trauma 1997;42:54–61.
9. Baker SP, Harvey AH. Fall injuries in the elderly. Clin Geriatr Med 1985;1:501–512.
10. Baker SP, O'Neill B, Haddon W Jr, et al. The Injury Severity Score: a method for describing patients with multiple injuries and evaluating emergency care. J Trauma 1974;14:187–196.
11. Balkan ME, Oktar GL, Kayi-Cangir A, et al. Emergency thoracotomy for blunt thoracic trauma. Ann Thorac Cardiovasc Surg 2002;8:78–82.
12. Balogh Z, Offner PJ, Moore EE, et al. NISS predicts post injury multiple organ failure better than the ISS. J Trauma 2000;48:624–627.
13. Balogh ZJ, Varga E, Tomka J, et al. The New Injury Severity Score is a better predictor of extended hospitalization and intensive care unit admission than the Injury Severity Score in patients with multiple orthopaedic injuries. J Orthop Trauma 2003;17:508–512.
14. Barber RC, Chang LY, Purdue GF, et al. Detecting genetic predisposition for complicated clinical outcomes after burn injury. Burns 2006;32:821–827.
15. Beck JP, Colins JA. Theoretical and clinical aspects of post traumatic fat embolism syndrome. AAOS Instr Course Lett 1973;22:38–44.

16. Beningfield S, Potgieter H, Nicol A, et al. Report on a new type of trauma full-body digital x-ray machine. Emerg Radiol 2003;10:23–29.
17. Berg J, Tagliaferri F, Servadei F. Cost of trauma in Europe. Eur J Neurol 2005;12(suppl 1):85–90.
18. Bernhard M, Gries A, Kremer P, et al. Spinal cord injury (SCI): prehospital management. Resuscitation 2005;66:127–139.
19. Bessoud B, Duchosal MA, Siegrist CA, et al. Proximal splenic artery embolization for blunt splenic injury: clinical, immunologic, and ultrasound-Doppler follow-up. J Trauma 2007;62:1481–1486.
20. Bianchi ME. DAMPs, PAMPs, and alarmins: all we need to know about danger. J Leukoc Biol 2007;81:1–5.
21. Bickell WH, Wall MJ Jr, Pepe PE, et al. Immediate versus delayed fluid resuscitation for hypotensive patients with penetrating torso injuries. N Engl J Med 1994;331: 1105–1109.
22. Bircher M, Giannoudis PV. Pelvic trauma management within the UK: a reflection of a failing trauma service. Injury 2004;35:2–6.
23. Bishop M, Shoemaker WC, Avakian S, et al. Evaluation of a comprehensive algorithm for blunt and penetrating thoracic and abdominal trauma. Am Surg 1991;57:737–746.
24. Blow O, Magliore L, Claridge JA, et al. The golden hour and the silver day: detection and correction of occult hypoperfusion within 24 hours improves outcome from major trauma. J Trauma 1999;47-5:964–969.
25. Boehm T, Alkadhi H, Schertler T, et al. [Application of multislice spiral CT (MSCT) in multiple injured patients and its effect on diagnostic and therapeutic algorithms]. Rofo 2004;176:1734–1742.
26. Boffard KD, Goosen J, Plani F, et al. The use of low dosage x-ray (Lodox/Statscan) in major trauma: comparison between low dose x-ray and conventional x-ray techniques. J Trauma 2006;60:1175–1181; discussion 1181–1183.
27. Bone L, Johnson K, Weigelt J, et al. Early versus delayed stabilization of femoral fractures. A prospective randomized study. J Bone Joint Surg Am 1989;71A:336–40.
28. Bone RC, Balk RA, Cerra FB, et al. Definitions for sepsis and organ failure and guidelines for the use of innovative therapies in sepsis. The ACCP/SCCM Consensus Conference Committee. American College of Chest Physicians/Society of Critical Care Medicine, Chest 1992;101:1644–1655.
29. Bosch U, Pohlemann T, Tscherne H. Primary management of pelvic injuries. Orthopäde 1992;21:385–392.
30. Bothig R. [TRISS: a method of assessment of the prognosis in multiple trauma patients]. Zentralbl Chir 1991;116:831–844.
31. Bouamra O, Wrotchford A, Hollis S, et al. A new approach to outcome prediction in trauma: a comparison with the TRISS model. J Trauma 2006;61:701–710.
32. Bouillon B, Lefering R, Vorweg M, et al. Trauma score systems: Cologne Validation Study. J Trauma 1997;42:652–658.
33. Bouillon B, Neugebauer E. Outcome after polytrauma. Langenbecks Arch Surg 1998; 383:228–234.
34. Boyd CR, Tolson MA, Copes WS. Evaluating trauma care: the TRISS method. Trauma Score and the Injury Severity Score. J Trauma 1987;27:370–378.
35. Braver ER, Kyrychenko SY, Ferguson SA. Driver mortality in frontal crashes: comparison of newer and older airbag designs. Traffic Inj Prev 2005;6:24–30.
36. Braver ER, Scerbo M, Kufera JA, et al. Deaths among drivers and right-front passengers in frontal collisions: redesigned air bags relative to first-generation air bags. Traffic Inj Prev 2008;9:48–58.
37. Brenchley J, Walker A, Sloan JP, et al. Evaluation of focused assessment with sonography in trauma (FAST) by UK emergency physicians. Emerg Med J 2006;23:446–448.
38. Brenneman FD, Boulanger BR, McLellan BA, et al. Measuring injury severity: time for a change? J Trauma 1998;44:580–582.
39. Brouhard R. To immobilize or not immobilize: that is the question. Emerg Med Serv 2006;35:81–82.
40. Bruns B, Lindsey M, Rowe K, et al. Hemoglobin drops within minutes of injuries and predicts need for an intervention to stop hemorrhage. J Trauma 2007;63:312–315.
41. Bulger EM, Copass MK, Maier RV, et al. An analysis of advanced prehospital airway management. J Emerg Med 2002;23:183–189.
42. Bulger EM, Jurkovich GJ, Nathens AB, et al. Hypertonic resuscitation of hypovolemic shock after blunt trauma: a randomized controlled trial. Arch Surg 2008;143:139–148; discussion 149.
43. Bulger EM, Maier RV. Prehospital care of the injured: what's new? Surg Clin North Am 2007;87:37–53.
44. Bulger EM, Nathens AB, Rivara FP, et al. Brain Trauma Foundation. Management of severe head injury: institutional variations in care and effect on outcome. Crit Care Med 2002;30:1870–1876.
45. Bull JP, Dickson GR. Injury scoring by TRISS and ISS/age. Injury 1991;22:127–131.
46. Bull JP. The Injury Severity Score of road traffic casualties in relation to mortality, time of death, hospital treatment time, and disability. Accid Anal Prev 1975;7:249–255.
47. Bunn F, Kwan I, Roberts IRW. Effectiveness of prehospital trauma care. London: Cochrane Injuries Group, 2001.
48. Burger C, Zwingmann J, Kabir K, et al. [Faster diagnostics by digital x-ray imaging in the emergency room: a prospective study in multiple trauma patients]. Z Orthop Unfall 2007;145:772–777.
49. Cales RH. Trauma mortality in Orange County: the effect of implementation of a regional trauma system. Ann Emerg Med 1984;13:1–10.
50. Cardarelli MG, McLaughlin JS, Downing SW, et al. Management of traumatic aortic rupture: a 30-year experience. Ann Surg 2002;236:465–469.
51. Catalano O, Siani A. Focused assessment with sonography for trauma (FAST): what it is, how it is carried out, and why we disagree. Radiol Med (Torino) 2004;108:443–453.
52. Champion HR, Copes WS, Sacco WJ, et al. A new characterization of injury severity. J Trauma 1990;30:539–545.
53. Champion HR, Copes WS, Sacco WJ, et al. Improved predictions from a Severity Characterization Of Trauma (ASCOT) over Trauma and Injury Severity Score (TRISS): results of an independent evaluation. J Trauma 1996;40:42–48.
54. Champion HR, Copes WS, Sacco WJ, et al. The Major Trauma Outcome Study: establishing national norms for trauma care. J Trauma 1990;30:1356–1365.
55. Champion HR, Sacco WJ, Carnazzo AJ, et al. Trauma score. Crit Care Med 1981;9: 672–676.
56. Champion HR, Sacco WJ, Copes WS, et al. A revision of the Trauma Score. J Trauma 1989;29:623–629.
57. Chawla A, Mohan D, Sharma V. Safer truck front design for pedestrian impacts. J Crash Prev Inj Cont 2000;2:33–43.
58. Chesnut RM, Marshall SB, Piek J, et al. Early and late systemic hypotension as a frequent and fundamental source of cerebral ischemia following severe brain injury in the Traumatic Coma Data Bank. Acta Neurochir Suppl (Wien) 1993;59:121–125.
59. Choi CB, Park P, Kim YH, et al. Comparison of visibility measurement techniques for forklift truck design factors. Appl Ergon 2009;40:280–285.
60. Choi P-L, Yip G, Quinonez LG. Crystalloids vs. colloids in fluid resuscitation: a systematic review. Crit Care Med 1999;27:200–210.
61. Ciesla DJ, Sava JA, Street JH 3rd, Jordan MH. Secondary overtriage: a consequence of an immature trauma system. J Am Coll Surg 2008;206:131–137.
62. Claridge JA, Crabtree TD, Pelletier SJ, et al. Persistent occult hypoperfusion is associated with a significant increase in infection rate and mortality in major trauma patients. J Trauma 2000;48:8–14; discussion 15.
63. Cocchi MN, Kimlin E, Walsh M, et al. Identification and resuscitation of the trauma patient in shock. Emerg Med Clin North Am 2007;25:623–642.
64. Coles JP, Minhas PS, Fryer TD, et al. Effect of hyperventilation on cerebral blood flow in traumatic head injury: clinical relevance and monitoring correlates. Crit Care Med 2002;30:1950–1959.
65. Collighan N, Giannoudis PV, Kourgeraki O, et al. Interleukin 13 and inflammatory markers in human sepsis. Br J Surg 2004;91:762–768.
66. Cooke WH, Salinas J, Convertino VA, et al. Heart rate variability and its association with mortality in prehospital trauma patients. J Trauma 2006;60:363–370; discussion 370.
67. Cooper DJ, Myles PS, McDermott FT, et al. Prehospital hypertonic saline resuscitation of patients with hypotension and severe traumatic brain injury: a randomized controlled trial. JAMA 2004;291:1350–1357.
68. Copes WS, Champion HR, Sacco WJ, et al. The Injury Severity Score revisited. J Trauma 1988;28:69–77.
69. Copes WS, Champion HR, Sacco WJ, et al. Progress in characterizing anatomic injury. J Trauma 1990;30:1200–1207.
70. Cothren CC, Osborn PM, Moore EE, et al. Preperitoneal pelvic packing for hemodynamically unstable pelvic fractures: a paradigm shift. J Trauma 2007;62:834–839.
71. Cummings G, O'Keefe G. Scene disposition and mode of transport following rural trauma: a prospective cohort study comparing patient costs. J Emerg Med 2000;18: 349–354.
72. Cummings P, McKnight B, Rivara FP, Grossman DC. Association of driver air bags with driver fatality: a matched cohort study. BMJ 2002;324:1119–1122.
73. Cummings P, Rivara FP, Olson CM, Smith KM. Changes in traffic crash mortality rates attributed to use of alcohol, or lack of a seat belt, air bag, motorcycle helmet, or bicycle helmet, United States, 1982–2001. Inj Prev 2006;12:148–154.
74. Curtis K, Zou Y, Morris R, Black D. Trauma case management: improving patient outcomes. Injury 2006;37:626–632.
75. Dahabreh Z, Dimitriou R, Chalidis B, Giannoudis PV. Coagulopathy and the role of recombinant human activated protein C in sepsis and following polytrauma. Expert Opin Drug Saf 2006;5:67–82.
76. Dahabreh Z, Dimitriou R, Giannoudis PV. Health economics: a cost analysis of treatment of persistent fracture nonunions using bone morphogenetic protein-7. Injury 2007;38:371–377.
77. Davis DP, Ochs M, Hoyt DB, et al. Paramedic-administered neuromuscular blockade improves prehospital intubation success in severely head-injured patients. J Trauma 2003;55:713–719.
78. Davis DP, Stern J, Sise MJ, et al. A follow-up analysis of factors associated with head-injury mortality after paramedic rapid sequence intubation. J Trauma 2005;59:486–90.
79. Davis DP, Valentine C, Ochs M, et al. The Combitube as a salvage airway device for paramedic rapid sequence intubation. Ann Emerg Med 2003;42:697–704.
80. Deal EN, Hollands JM, Schramm GE, Micek ST. Role of corticosteroids in the management of acute respiratory distress syndrome. Clin Ther 2008;30:787–799.
81. DeBritz JN, Pollak AN. The impact of trauma centre accreditation on patient outcome. Injury 2006;37:1166–1171.
82. Deitch EA. Multiple organ failure. Adv Surg 1993;26:333–356.
83. DeLoughery. Coagulation defects in trauma patients: etiology, recognition, and therapy. Crit Care Clin 2004;20:13–24.
84. Demetriades D, Sofianos C. Penetrating trauma audit: TRISS analysis. S Afr J Surg 1992;30:142–144.
85. Department of Health. Chief executive's report to the NHS. Retrieved April 15, 2009, from http://www.dh.gov.uk/en/Publicationsandstatistics/Publications/AnnualReports/DH_4134613.
86. Department of Health. NHS costing manual 2006–07. Retrieved April 15, 2009, from http://www.dh.gov.uk/en/index.htm.
87. Dick WF. Anglo-American vs. Franco-German emergency medical services system. Prehosp Disaster Med 2003;18:29–35.
88. Dinh-Zarr TB, Sleet DA, Shults RA, et al. Reviews of evidence regarding interventions to increase the use of safety belts. Am J Prev Med 2001;21(suppl 4):48–65.
89. Doran JV, Tortella BJ, Drivet WJ, et al. Factors influencing successful intubation in the prehospital setting. Prehosp Disaster Med 1995;10:259–264.
90. Downing SW, Sperling JS, Mirvis SE, et al. Experience with spiral computed tomography as the sole diagnostic method for traumatic aortic rupture. Ann Thorac Surg 2001; 72:495–501.
91. Dunham CM, Bosse MJ, Clancy TV, et al. EAST Practice Management Guidelines Work Group. Practice management guidelines for the optimal timing of long-bone fracture stabilization in polytrauma patients: the EAST Practice Management Guidelines Work Group. J Trauma 2001;50:958–967.
92. Durbin DR, Elliott MR, Winston FK. Belt-positioning booster seats and reduction in risk of injury among children in vehicle crashes. JAMA 2003;289:2835–40.
93. Durbin DR, Runge J, Mackay M, et al. Booster seats for children: closing the gap between science and public policy in the United States. Traffic Inj Prev 2003;4:5–8.
94. Durham R, Pracht E, Orban B, et al. Evaluation of a mature trauma system. Ann Surg 2006;243:775–783.
95. Durham RM, Moran JJ, Mazuski JE, et al. Multiple organ failure in trauma patients. J Trauma 2003;55:608–616.
96. Eastman AB, Bishop GS, Walsh JC, et al. The economic status of trauma centers on the eve of health care reform. J Trauma 1994;36:835–844.

97. Exadaktylos AK, Benneker LM, Jeger V, et al. Total-body digital x-ray in trauma. An experience report on the first operational full body scanner in Europe and its possible role in ATLS. Injury 2008;39:525–529.

98. Finefrock SC. Designing and building a new emergency department: the experience of one chest pain, stroke, and trauma center in Columbus, Ohio. J Emerg Nurs 2006; 32:144–148.

99. Frink M, Probst C, Hildebrand F, et al. [The influence of transportation mode on mortality in polytraumatized patients. An analysis based on the German Trauma Registry]. Unfallchirurg 2007;110:334–340.

100. Fung Kon Jin PH, Goslings JC, Ponsen KJ, et al. Assessment of a new trauma workflow concept implementing a sliding CT scanner in the trauma room: the effect on workup times. J Trauma 2008;64:1320–1326.

101. Furst DE, Breedveld FC, Kalden JR, et al. Updated consensus statement on biological agents, specifically tumour necrosis factor α (TNFα) blocking agents and interleukin-1 receptor antagonist (IL-1ra), for the treatment of rheumatic diseases. Ann Rheum Dis 2005;64(suppl 4):iv2–iv14.

102. Gaillard M, Pasquier C, Guerrini P, et al. [Short- and long-term outcome of 250 patients admitted in surgical intensive care units after multiple injuries]. Agressologie 1990;31: 633–636.

103. Gansslen A, Giannoudis P, Pape HC. Hemorrhage in pelvic fracture: who needs angiography? Curr Opin Crit Care 2003;9:515–523.

104. Ganzoni D, Zellweger R, Trentz O. [Cost analysis of acute therapy of polytrauma patients]. Swiss Surg 2003;9:268–274.

105. Gennarelli TA, Champion HR, Sacco WJ, et al. Mortality of patients with head injury and extracranial injury treated in trauma centers. J Trauma 1989;29-9:1193–1201.

106. Gennarelli TA, Wodzin E. AIS 2005: a contemporary injury scale. Injury 2006;37: 1083–1091.

107. Giannoudis PV, Abbott C, Stone M, et al. Fatal systemic inflammatory response syndrome following early bilateral femoral nailing. Intensive Care Med 1998;24:641–642.

108. Giannoudis PV, Dinopoulos H, Chalidis B, Hall GM. Surgical stress response. Injury 2006;37(suppl):S3–S9.

109. Giannoudis PV, Fogerty S. Initial care of the severely injured patient: predicting morbidity from subclinical findings and clinical proteomics. Injury 2007;38:261–262.

110. Giannoudis PV, Grotz MR, Tzioupis C, et al. Prevalence of pelvic fractures, associated injuries, and mortality: the United Kingdom perspective. J Trauma 2007;63:875–883.

111. Giannoudis PV, Harwood PJ, van Griensven M, et al. Correlation between IL-6 levels and the SIRS score: can an IL-6 cut off predict a SIRS state? J Trauma 2008;65:646–652.

112. Giannoudis PV, Hildebrand F, Pape HC. Inflammatory serum markers in patients with multiple trauma. Can they predict outcome? J Bone Joint Surg Br 2004;86B:313–323.

113. Giannoudis PV, Kanakaris NK. The unresolved issue of health economics and polytrauma: the UK perspective. Injury 2008;39:705–709.

114. Giannoudis PV, Mehta SS, Tsiridis E. Incidence and outcome of whiplash injury after multiple trauma. Spine 2007;32:776–781.

115. Giannoudis PV, Pape HC. Damage control orthopaedics in unstable pelvic ring injuries. Injury 2004;35-7:671–677.

116. Giannoudis PV, Pape HC. Trauma and immune reactivity: too much, or too little immune response? Injury 2007;38:1333–1335.

117. Giannoudis PV, Smith RM, Banks RE, et al. Stimulation of inflammatory markers after blunt trauma. Br J Surg 1998;85:986–990.

118. Giannoudis PV, Smith RM, Perry SL, et al. Immediate IL-10 expression following major orthopaedic trauma: relationship to anti-inflammatory response and subsequent development of sepsis. Intens Care Med 2000;26:1076–1081.

119. Giannoudis PV, Smith RM, Windsor AC, et al. Monocyte human leukocyte antigen-DR expression correlates with intrapulmonary shunting after major trauma. Am J Surg 1999;177:454–459.

120. Giannoudis PV, Tosounidis TI, Kanakaris NK, Kontakis G. Quantification and characterisation of endothelial injury after trauma. Injury 2007;38:1373–1381.

121. Giannoudis PV, van Griensven M, Tsiridis E, et al. The genetic predisposition to adverse outcome after trauma. J Bone Joint Surg Br 2007;89B:1273–1279.

122. Giannoudis PV. Current concepts of the inflammatory response after major trauma: an update. Injury 2003;34:397–404.

123. Giannoudis PV. Surgical priorities in damage control in polytrauma. J Bone Joint Surg 2003;85B:478–844.

124. Gilson BS, Gilson JS, Bergner M, et al. The Sickness Impact Profile. Development of an outcome measure of health care. Am J Public Health 1975;65:1304–1310.

125. Goldfarb MG, Bazzoli GJ, Coffey RM. Trauma systems and the costs of trauma care. Health Serv Res 1996;31:71–95.

126. Goldschlager T, Rosenfeld JV, Winter CD. "Talk and die" patients presenting to a major trauma centre over a 10-year period: a critical review. J Clin Neurosci 2007;14: 618–623.

127. Gong MN, Zhou W, Williams PL, et al. −308GA and TNFB polymorphisms in acute respiratory distress syndrome. Eur Respir J 2005;26:382–389.

128. Gonzalez RP, Cummings GR, Phelan HA, et al. Does increased emergency medical services prehospital time affect patient mortality in rural motor vehicle crashes? A statewide analysis. Am J Surg 2009;197:30–34.

129. Gordon AC, Lagan AL, Aganna E, et al. TNF and TNFR polymorphisms in severe sepsis and septic shock: a prospective multicentre study. Genes Immun 2004;5:631–640.

130. Gould SA, Moore EE, Hoyt DB, et al. The life-sustaining capacity of human polymerized hemoglobin when red cells might be unavailable. J Am Coll Surg 2002;195:445–452.

131. Green SM, Steele R. Mandatory surgeon presence on trauma patient arrival. Ann Emerg Med 2008;51:334–335.

132. Greenburg AG, Kim HW. Hemoglobin-based oxygen carriers. Crit Care 2004;8(suppl 2):S61–S64.

133. Gregory RT, Gould RJ, Peclet M, et al. The mangled extremity syndrome (MES): a severity grading system for multisystem injury of the extremity. J Trauma 1985;25: 1147–1150.

134. Grieco A, Long CJ. Investigation of the Karnofsky Performance Status as a measure of quality of life. Health Psychol 1984;3:129–142.

135. Grimm MR, Vrahas MS, Thomas KA. Pressure-volume characteristics of the intact and disrupted pelvic retroperitoneum. J Trauma 1998;44-3:454–459.

136. Grotz M, Schwermann T, Lefering R, et al. [DRG reimbursement for multiple trauma patients: a comparison with the comprehensive hospital costs using the German trauma registry]. Unfallchirurg 2004;107:68–75.

137. Guillou PJ. Biological variation in the development of sepsis after surgery or trauma. Lancet 1993;342:217–220.

138. Gunn M, Campbell M, Hoffer EK. Traumatic abdominal aortic injury treated by endovascular stent placement. Emerg Radiol 2007;13:329–331.

139. Gustilo RB, Mendoza RM, Williams DN. Problems in the management of type III (severe) open fractures: a new classification of type III open fractures. J Trauma 1984; 24:742–746.

140. Haan J, Scott J, Boyd-Kranis RL, et al. Admission angiography for blunt splenic injury: advantages and pitfalls. J Trauma 2001;51:1161–1165.

141. Hagiwara A, Murata A, Matsuda T, et al. The efficacy and limitations of transarterial embolization for severe hepatic injury. J Trauma 2002;52:1091–1096.

142. Hagiwara A, Murata A, Matsuda T, et al. The usefulness of transcatheter arterial embolization for patients with blunt polytrauma showing transient response to fluid resuscitation. J Trauma 2004;57:271–276.

143. Hannan EL, Mendeloff J, Farrell LS, et al. Validation of TRISS and ASCOT using a non-MTOS trauma registry. J Trauma 1995;38:83–88.

144. Hannan EL, Waller CH, Farrell LS, et al. A comparison among the abilities of various injury severity measures to predict mortality with and without accompanying physiologic information. J Trauma 2005;58:244–251.

145. Hardy JD, de Moerloose P, Samma M. Perioperatoire GdieH. Massive transfusion and coagulopathy: pathophysiology and implications for clinical management. Can J Anaesth 2004;51-4:293–310.

146. Harwood PJ, Giannoudis PV, Probst C, et al. Which AIS based scoring system is the best predictor of outcome in orthopaedic blunt trauma patients? J Trauma 2006;60: 334–340.

147. Harwood PJ, Giannoudis PV, van Griensven M, et al. Alterations in the systemic inflammatory response after early total care and damage control procedures for femoral shaft fracture in severely injured patients. J Trauma 2005;58:446–452.

148. Hauswald M, Ong G, Tandberg D, et al. Out-of-hospital spinal immobilization: its effect on neurologic injury. Acad Emerg Med 1998;5:214–219.

149. Hebert JS, Burnham RS. The effect of polytrauma in persons with traumatic spine injury. A prospective database of spine fractures. Spine 2000;25:55–60.

150. Heinzelmann M, Imhof HG, Trentz O. [Shock trauma room management of the multiple-traumatized patient with skull-brain injuries. A systematic review of the literature]. Unfallchirurg 2004;107:871–880.

151. Helfet DL, Howey T, Sanders R, Johansen K. Limb salvage versus amputation. Preliminary results of the Mangled Extremity Severity Score. Clin Orthop 1990;256:80–86.

152. Helling TS, Watkins M, Robb CV. Improvement in cost recovery at an urban level I trauma center. J Trauma 1995;39:980–983.

153. Hensler T, Heinemann B, Sauerland S, et al. Immunologic alterations associated with high blood transfusion volume after multiple injury: effects on plasmatic cytokine and cytokine receptor concentrations. Shock 2003;20:497–502.

154. Herbert PC, Wells G, Blajchmann MA. A multicentre randomized controlled clinical trial of transfusion requirements in critical care. N Engl J Med 1999;54:898–905.

155. Herzog C, Ahle H, Mack MG, et al. Traumatic injuries of the pelvis and thoracic and lumbar spine: does thin-slice multidetector-row CT increase diagnostic accuracy? Eur Radiol 2004;14:1751–1760.

156. Hildebrand F, Pape HC, Krettek C. [The importance of cytokines in the posttraumatic inflammatory reaction]. Unfallchirurg 2005;108:793–803.

157. Hoff WS, Schwab CW. Trauma system development in North America. Clin Orthop Relat Res 2004;422:17–22.

158. Holbrook TL, Anderson JP, Sieber WJ, et al. Outcome after major trauma: 12-month and 18-month follow-up results from the Trauma Recovery Project. J Trauma 1999; 46:765–771.

159. Holbrook TL, Hoyt DB, Anderson JP. The importance of gender on outcome after major trauma: functional and psychologic outcomes in women versus men. J Trauma 2001;50:270–273.

160. Holbrook TL, Hoyt DB, Stein MB, et al. Gender differences in long-term posttraumatic stress disorder outcomes after major trauma: women are at higher risk of adverse outcomes than men. J Trauma 2002;53:882–888.

161. Holcomb JB, Niles SE, Miller CC, et al. Prehospital physiologic data and lifesaving interventions in trauma patients. Milit Med 2005;170:7–13.

162. Holcomb JB, Salinas J, McManus JM, et al. Manual vital signs reliably predict need for life-saving interventions in trauma patients. J Trauma 2005;59:821–828; discussion 828–829.

163. Holmes JHt, Bloch RD, Hall RA, et al. Natural history of traumatic rupture of the thoracic aorta managed nonoperatively: a longitudinal analysis. Ann Thorac Surg 2002; 73-4:1149–1154.

164. Horne G, Schemitsch E. Assessment of the survivors of major trauma accidents. Aust N Z J Surg 1989;59:465–470.

165. Hoth JJ, Scott MJ, Bullock TK, et al. Thoracotomy for blunt trauma: traditional indications may not apply. Am Surg 2003;69-12:1108–1111.

166. Howe HR Jr, Poole GV Jr, Hansen KJ, et al. Salvage of lower extremities following combined orthopedic and vascular trauma. A predictive salvage index. Am Surg 1987; 53:205–208.

167. Hoyt DB, Coimbra R. Trauma systems. Surg Clin North Am 2007;87:21–35.

168. Husum H, Strada G. Injury Severity Score versus New Injury Severity Score for penetrating injuries. Prehosp Disaster Med 2002;17:27–32.

169. Iannelli G, Piscione F, Di Tommaso L, et al. Thoracic aortic emergencies: impact of endovascular surgery. Ann Thorac Surg 2004;77-2:591–596.

170. Iba T, Gando S, Murata A, et al. Predicting the severity of systemic inflammatory response (SIRS)-associated coagulopathy with hemostatic molecular markers and vascular endothelial injury markers. J Trauma 2007;63:1093–1098.

171. Ivarsson BJ, Crandall JR, Okamoto M. Influence of age-related stature on the frequency of body region injury and overall injury severity in child pedestrian casualties. Traffic Inj Prev 2006;7:290–298.

172. Jameson S, Reed MR. Payment by results and coding practice in the National Health Service: the importance for orthopaedic surgeons. J Bone Joint Surg Br 2007;89B: 1427–1430.

173. Jennett B, Snoek J, Bond MR, et al. Disability after severe head injury: observations on the use of the Glasgow Outcome Scale. J Neurol Neurosurg Psychiatry 1981;44: 285–293.

174. Johansen K, Daines M, Howey T, et al. Objective criteria accurately predict amputation following lower extremity trauma. J Trauma 1990;30:568–572.
175. Johnson K, Cadami A, Seibert G. Incidence of ARDS in patients with multiple musculoskeletal injuries: effect of early operative stabilization of fractures. J Trauma 1985;25: 375–384.
176. Jones JH, Murphy MP, Dickson RL, et al. Emergency physician-verified out-of-hospital intubation: miss rates by paramedics. Acad Emerg Med 2004;11:707–709.
177. Joy SA, Lichtig LK, Knauf RA, et al. Identification and categorization of and cost for care of trauma patients: a study of 12 trauma centers and 43,219 state-wide patients. J Trauma 1994;37:303–308.
178. Jurkovich G, Mock C, MacKenzie E, et al. The Sickness Impact Profile as a tool to evaluate functional outcome in trauma patients. J Trauma 1995;39:625–631.
179. Jurkovich GJ, Mock C. Systematic review of trauma system effectiveness based on registry comparisons. J Trauma 1999;47(suppl 3):S46–S55.
180. Kahlke V, Schafmayer C, Schniewind B, et al. Are postoperative complications genetically determined by TNF-beta NcoI gene polymorphism? Surgery 2004;135:365–373.
181. Kallin K, Jensen J, Olsson LL, et al. Why the elderly fall in residential care facilities, and suggested remedies. J Fam Pract 2004;53:41–52.
182. Kanakaris NK, Giannoudis PV. The health economics of the treatment of long-bone nonunions. Injury 2007;38(suppl 2):S77–S84.
183. Kanz KG, Korner M, Linsenmaier U, et al. [Priority-oriented shock trauma room management with the integration of multiple-view spiral computed tomography]. Unfallchirurg 2004;107:937–944.
184. Katsoulis E, Giannoudis PV. Impact of timing of pelvic fixation on functional outcome. Injury 2006;37:1133–1142.
185. Keel M, Trentz O. Pathophysiology of polytrauma. Injury 2005;36:691–709.
186. Kelsey JL, White AA 3rd, Pastides H, Bisbee GE Jr. The impact of musculoskeletal disorders on the population of the United States. J Bone Joint Surg Am 1979;61A: 959–964.
187. Kessel B, Sevi R, Jeroukhimov I, et al. Is routine portable pelvic X-ray in stable multiple trauma patients always justified in a high technology era? Injury 2007;38:559–563.
188. Kim Y, Jung KY, Kim CY, et al. Validation of the International Classification of Diseases 10th Edition-based Injury Severity Score (ICISS). J Trauma 2000;48:280–285.
189. Kinzl L, Gebhard F, Arand M. [Polytrauma and economics]. Unfallchirurgie 1996;22: 179–185.
190. Kirkpatrick AW, Sirois M, Laupland KB, et al. Prospective evaluation of hand-held focused abdominal sonography for trauma (FAST) in blunt abdominal trauma. Can J Surg 2005;48:453–460.
191. Kirkpatrick JR, Youmans RL. Trauma index. An aide in the evaluation of injury victims. J Trauma 1971;11:711–714.
192. Kizer KW, Vassar MJ, Harry RL, Layton KD. Hospitalization charges, costs, and income for firearm-related injuries at a university trauma center. JAMA 1995;273:1768–1773.
193. Knaus WA, Zimmerman JE, Wagner DP, et al. APACHE-acute physiology and chronic health evaluation: a physiologically based classification system. Crit Care Med 1981; 9:591–597.
194. Korner M, Krotz MM, Degenhart C, et al. Current role of emergency US in patients with major trauma. Radiographics 2008;28:225–242.
195. Korosec Jagodic H, Jagodic K, Podbregar M. Long-term outcome and quality of life of patients treated in surgical intensive care: a comparison between sepsis and trauma. Crit Care 2006;10:R134.
196. Krettek C, Schandelmaier P, Rudolf J, Tscherne H. [Current status of surgical technique for unreamed nailing of tibial shaft fractures with the UTN (unreamed tibia nail)]. Unfallchirurg 1994;97:575–599.
197. Kristinsson G, Wall SP, Crain EF. The digital rectal examination in pediatric trauma: a pilot study. J Emerg Med 2007;32:59–62.
198. Krueger PD, Brazil K, Lohfeld LH. Risk factors for falls and injuries in a long-term care facility in Ontario. Can J Public Health 2001;92:117–120.
199. Kuhls DA, Malone DL, McCarter RJ, et al. Predictors of mortality in adult trauma patients: the physiologic trauma score is equivalent to the Trauma and Injury Severity Score. J Am Coll Surg 2002;194:695–704.
200. Kuhne CA, Ruchholtz S, Sauerland S, et al. [Personnel and structural requirements for the shock trauma room management of multiple trauma. A systematic review of the literature]. Unfallchirurg 2004;107:851–861.
201. Kwok PC, Ho KK, Chung TK, et al. Emergency aortic stent grafting for traumatic rupture of the thoracic aorta. Hong Kong Med J 2003;9:435–440.
202. Langanay T, Verhoye JP, Corbineau H, et al. Surgical treatment of acute traumatic rupture of the thoracic aorta: a timing reappraisal? Eur J Cardiothorac Surg 2002;212: 282–287.
203. Lausevic Z, Lausevic M, Trbojevic-Stankovic J, et al. Predicting multiple organ failure in patients with severe trauma. Can J Surg 2008;51:97–102.
204. Lehmann U, Gobiet W, Regel G, et al. [Functional, neuropsychological, and social outcome of polytrauma patients with severe craniocerebral trauma]. Unfallchirurg 1997;100:552–560.
205. Leone M, Boutiere B, Camoin-Jau L, et al. Systemic endothelial activation is greater in septic than in traumatic-hemorrhagic shock but does not correlate with endothelial activation in skin biopsies. Crit Care Med 2002;30:808–814.
206. Liberman M, Branas C, Mulder D. Advanced versus basic life support in the prehospital setting: the controversy between the scoop and run and the stay-and-play approach to the care of the injured patient. Int J Disaster Med 2004;2:1–9.
207. Liberman M, Mulder D, Lavoie A, et al. Multicenter Canadian study of prehospital trauma care. Ann Surg 2003;237:153–160.
208. Liberman M, Mulder DS, Jurkovich GJ, Sampalis JS. The association between trauma system and trauma center components and outcome in a mature regionalized trauma system. Surgery 2005;137:647–658.
209. Liberman M, Mulder DS, Lavoie A, Sampalis JS. Implementation of a trauma care system: evolution through evaluation. J Trauma 2004;56:1330–1335.
210. Lin E, Calvano SE, Lowry SF. Inflammatory cytokines and cell response in surgery. Surgery 2000;127:117–126.
211. Lin WC, Chen YF, Lin CH, et al. Emergent transcatheter arterial embolization in hemodynamically unstable patients with blunt splenic injury. Acad Radiol 2008;15: 201–208.
212. Lindner T, Bail HJ, Manegold S, et al. [Shock trauma room diagnosis: initial diagnosis after blunt abdominal trauma. A review of the literature]. Unfallchirurg 2004;107: 892–902.
213. Liu BC, Ivers R, Norton R, et al. Helmets for preventing injury in motorcycle riders. Cochrane Database Syst Rev 2008;1:CD004333.
214. Lowe PR, Galley HF, Abdel-Fattah A, Webster NR. Influence of interleukin-10 polymorphisms on interleukin-10 expression and survival in critically ill patients. Crit Care Med 2003;31:34–38.
215. MacKenzie EJ, Rivara FP, Jurkovich GJ, et al. A national evaluation of the effect of trauma-center care on mortality. N Engl J Med 2006;354:366–378.
216. MacKenzie EJ, Shapiro S, Moody M, et al. Predicting posttrauma functional disability for individuals without severe brain injury. Med Care 1986;24:377–387.
217. MacKenzie EJ, Steinwachs DM, Shankar B. Classifying trauma severity based on hospital discharge diagnoses. Validation of an ICD-9CM to AIS-85 conversion table. Med Care 1989;27:412–422.
218. MacKenzie EJ. Review of evidence regarding trauma system effectiveness resulting from panel studies. J Trauma 1999;47(suppl 3):S34–S41.
219. Mackersie RC, Tiwary AD, Shackford SR, et al. Intra-abdominal injury following blunt trauma. Identifying the high-risk patient using objective risk factors. Arch Surg 1989; 124:809–813.
220. Maimaris C, Brooks SC. Monitoring progress in major trauma care using TRISS. Arch Emerg Med 1990;7:169–171.
221. Malone DL, Dunne J, Tracy JK, et al. Blood transfusion, independent of shock severity, is associated with worse outcome in trauma. J Trauma 2003;545:898–905.
222. Malone DL, Kuhls D, Napolitano LM, et al. Back to basics: validation of the admission systemic inflammatory response syndrome score in predicting outcome in trauma. J Trauma 2001;51:458–463.
223. Manley GT, Hemphill JC, Morabito D, et al. Cerebral oxygenation during hemorrhagic shock: perils of hyperventilation and the therapeutic potential of hypoventilation. J Trauma 2000;48:1025–1032; discussion 1032–1033.
224. Mann NC, Mullins RJ, MacKenzie EJ, et al. Systematic review of published evidence regarding trauma system effectiveness. J Trauma 1999;47(suppl 3):S25–S33.
225. Markle J, Cayten CG, Byrne DW, et al. Comparison between TRISS and ASCOT methods in controlling for injury severity. J Trauma 1992;33:326–332.
226. Markovchick VJ, Moore EE. Optimal trauma outcome: trauma system design and the trauma team. Emerg Med Clin North Am 2007;25:643–54.
227. Martinowitz U, Halcomb JB, Pusateri AE. Intravenous rFVIIa administered for hemorrhage control in hypothermic coagulopathic swine with grade V liver injuries. J Trauma 2001;50:721–729.
228. McLain RF. Functional outcomes after surgery for spinal fractures: return to work and activity. Spine 2004;29:470–477.
229. McNamara MG, Heckman JD, Corley FG. Severe open fractures of the lower extremity: a retrospective evaluation of the Mangled Extremity Severity Score (MESS). J Orthop Trauma 1994;8:81–87.
230. Meade MO, Cook DJ, Guyatt GH, et al. Ventilation strategy using low tidal volumes, recruitment maneuvers, and high-positive end-expiratory pressure for acute lung injury and acute respiratory distress syndrome: a randomized controlled trial. JAMA 2008; 299:637–645.
231. Meisner M, Adina H, Schmidt J. Correlation of procalcitonin and C-reactive protein to inflammation, complications, and outcome during the intensive care unit course of multiple-trauma patients. Crit Care 2005;10:R1.
232. Melton SM, McGwin G Jr, Abernathy JH 3rd, et al. Motor vehicle crash-related mortality is associated with prehospital and hospital-based resource availability. J Trauma 2003; 54:273–279.
233. Meredith JW, Evans G, Kilgo PD, et al. A comparison of the abilities of nine scoring algorithms in predicting mortality. J Trauma 2002;53:621–628; discussion 628–629.
234. Meregalli A, Oliveira RP, Friedman G. Occult hypoperfusion is associated with increased mortality in hemodynamically stable, high-risk, surgical patients. Crit Care 2004;8:R60–R65.
235. Michaels AJ, Michaels CE, Moon CH, et al. Psychosocial factors limit outcomes after trauma. J Trauma 1998;44:644–648.
236. Miller TR, Lestina DC. Patterns in US medical expenditures and utilization for injury, 1987. Am J Public Health 1996;86:89–92.
237. Miller TR, Levy DT. The effect of regional trauma care systems on costs. Arch Surg 1995;130:188–193.
238. Miltner E, Wiedmann HP, Leutwein B, et al. Technical parameters influencing the severity of injury of front-seat, belt-protected car passengers on the impact side in car-to-car side collisions with the main impact between the front and rear seats (B-pillars). Int J Legal Med 1992;105:11–15.
239. Miranda DR, Gommers D, Papadakos PJ, Lachmann B. Mechanical ventilation affects pulmonary inflammation in cardiac surgery patients: the role of the open-lung concept. J Cardiothorac Vasc Anesth 2007;21:279–284.
240. Mohr AM, Lavery RF, Barone A, et al. Angiographic embolization for liver injuries: low mortality, high morbidity. J Trauma 2003;55:1077–1081; discussion 1081–1082.
241. Moore EE. Hypertonic saline dextran for postinjury resuscitation: experimental background and clinical experience. Aust N Z J Surg 1991;61:732–736.
242. Moore FA, McKinley BA, Moore EE. The next generation in shock resuscitation. Lancet 2004;363:1988–1996.
243. Moore L, Lavoie A, Bergeron E, et al. Modeling probability-based injury severity scores in logistic regression models: the logit transformation should be used. J Trauma 2007; 62:601–605.
244. Moore L, Lavoie A, Le Sage N, et al. Consensus or data-derived anatomic injury severity scoring? J Trauma 2008;64:420–426.
245. Moore L, Lavoie A, Le Sage N, et al. Statistical validation of the Revised Trauma Score. J Trauma 2006;60:305–311.
246. Mueller ME, Allgower M, Schneider R, Willenegger H. Manual of Osteosynthesis. Berlin/Heidelberg/New York: Springer Verlag, 1970.
247. Mulligan ME, Flye CW. Initial experience with Lodox Statscan imaging system for detecting injuries of the pelvis and appendicular skeleton. Emerg Radiol 2006;13: 129–133.
248. Mullins RJ, Mann NC. Population-based research assessing the effectiveness of trauma systems. J Trauma 1999;47(suppl 3):S59–S66.
249. Mullins RJ. A historical perspective of trauma system development in the United States. J Trauma 1999;47(suppl 3):S8–S14.

250. Myers J. Focused assessment with sonography for trauma (FAST): the truth about ultrasound in blunt trauma. J Trauma 2007;62:S28.

251. Nast-Kolb D, Ruchholtz S, Waydhas C, Schweiberer L. [Is maximum management of polytrauma patients financially assured?] Langenbecks Arch Chir Suppl Kongressbd 1996;113:323–325.

252. Nathens AB, Brunet FP, Maier RV. Development of trauma systems and effect on outcomes after injury. Lancet 2004;363:1794–1801.

253. Nathens AB, Jurkovich GJ, Cummings P, et al. The effect of organized systems of trauma care on motor vehicle crash mortality. JAMA 2000;283:1990–1994.

254. Nathens AB, Jurkovich GJ, Rivara FP, et al. Effectiveness of state trauma systems in reducing injury-related mortality: a national evaluation. J Trauma 2000;48:25–30.

255. National Highway Traffic Safety Administration. National occupant protection use survey—1996: Controlled intersection study. Research Note. Washington, DC: US Department of Transportation, 1997.

256. National Highway Traffic Safety Administration. Traffic safety facts. Washington, DC: US Department of Transportation, 1998.

257. National Highway Traffic Safety Administration. Traffic safety facts. Seat belt use in 2007: Use rates in the states and territories. Washington, DC: US Department of Transportation, 2008:1–3.

258. Neuffer MC, McDivitt J, Rose D, et al. Hemostatic dressings for the first responder: a review. Milit Med 2004;169:716–720.

259. Neumaier M, Scherer MA. C-reactive protein levels for early detection of postoperative infection after fracture surgery in 787 patients. Acta Orthop 2008;79:428–432.

260. Newbold D. Caring about the costs. Nurs Stand 2006;20:24–25.

261. Nowotarski PJ, Turen CH, Brumback RJ, Scarboro JM. Conversion of external fixation to intramedullary nailing for fractures of the shaft of the femur in multiply injured patients. J Bone Joint Surg Am 2000;82A:781–788.

262. Nural MS, Yardan T, Guven H, et al. Diagnostic value of ultrasonography in the evaluation of blunt abdominal trauma. Diagn Interv Radiol 2005;11:41–44.

263. O'Kelly TJ, Westaby S. Trauma centres and the efficient use of financial resources. Br J Surg 1990;77:1142–1144.

264. Obaid AK, Barleben A, Porral D, et al. Utility of plain film pelvic radiographs in blunt trauma patients in the emergency department. Am Surg 2006;72:951–954.

265. Obertacke U, Neudeck F, Wihs HJ, Schmit-Neuerburg KP. [Emergency care and treatment costs of polytrauma patients]. Langenbecks Arch Chir Suppl Kongressbd 1996;113:641–645.

266. Oestern HJ, Schwermann T. [Quality and economy: contradictory demands]. Kongressbd Dtsch Ges Chir Kongr 2002;119:937–940.

267. Oestern HJ, Tscherne H. Pathophysiology and classification of soft tissue injuries associated with fractures. In Tscherne H, Gotzen L, eds. Fractures with Soft Tissue Injuries. Berlin: Springer Verlag, 1984:1–9.

268. Oestern HJ. [Management of polytrauma patients in an international comparison]. Unfallchirurg 1999;102:80–91.

269. Office of National Statistics. Personal Social Services Expenditure and Unit Costs: England: 2003–2004. Retrieved April 15, 2009, from http://www.statistics.gov.uk/.

270. Offner PJ, Jurkovich GJ, Gurney J, et al. Revision of TRISS for intubated patients. J Trauma 1992;32:32–35.

271. Oppe S, de Charro FT. The effect of medical care by a helicopter trauma team on the probability of survival and the quality of life of hospitalized victims. Accid Anal Prev 2001;33:129–138.

272. Oppenheim JJ, Yang D. Alarmins: chemotactic activators of immune responses, Curr Opin Immunol 2005;17:359–365.

273. Osler T, Baker SP, Long W. A modification of the injury severity score that both improves accuracy and simplifies scoring. J Trauma 1997;43:922–925.

274. Osterwalder JJ, Riederer M. [Quality assessment of multiple trauma management bu ISS, TRISS or ASCOT?]. Schweiz Med Wochenschr 2000;130:499–504.

275. Osterwalder JJ. Can the "golden hour of shock" safely be extended in blunt polytrauma patients? Prospective cohort study at a level I hospital in eastern Switzerland. Prehosp Disaster Med 2002;17:75–80.

276. Osterwalder JJ. Mortality of blunt polytrauma: a comparison between emergency physicians and emergency medical technicians—prospective cohort study at a level I hospital in eastern Switzerland. J Trauma 2003;55:355–361.

277. Ott R, Holzer U, Spitzenpfeil E, et al. [Quality of life after survival of severe trauma]. Unfallchirurg 1996;99:267–274.

278. Padayachee L, Cooper DJ, Irons S, et al. Cervical spine clearance in unconscious traumatic brain injury patients: dynamic flexion-extension fluoroscopy versus computed tomography with three-dimensional reconstruction. J Trauma 2006;60:341–345.

279. Papadopoulos IN, Kanakaris N, Triantafillidis A, et al. Autopsy findings from 111 deaths in the 1999 Athens earthquake as a basis for auditing the emergency response. Br J Surg 2004;91:1633–1640.

280. Papakostidis C, Kanakaris NK, Kontakis G, Giannoudis P. Pelvic ring disruptions: treatment modalities and analysis of outcomes. Int Orthop 2009;33:329–338.

281. Pape HC, Giannoudis PV, Krettek C, et al. Timing of fixation of major fractures in blunt polytrauma: role of conventional indicators in clinical decision making. J Orthop Trauma 2005;19:551–562.

282. Pape HC, Giannoudis PV, Krettek C. The timing of fracture treatment in polytrauma patients: relevance of damage control orthopaedic surgery. Am J Surg 2002;183: 622–629.

283. Pape HC, Grimme K, van Griensven M, et al. Impact of intramedullary instrumentation versus damage control for femoral fractures on immunoinflammatory parameters: prospective randomized analysis by the EPOFF Study Group. J Trauma 2003;55:7–13.

284. Pape HC, Rixen D, Morley J, et al. Impact of the method of initial stabilization for femoral shaft fractures in patients with multiple injuries at risk for complications (borderline patients). Ann Surg 2007;246:491–499.

285. Pape HC, Stalp M, van Griensven M, et al. [Optimal timing for secondary surgery in polytrauma patients: an evaluation of 4314 serious-injury cases]. Chirurg 1999;70: 1287–1293.

286. Pape HC, van Griensven M, Rice J, et al. Major secondary surgery in blunt trauma patients and perioperative cytokine liberation: determination of the clinical relevance of biochemical markers. J Trauma 2001;50:989–1000.

287. Pape HC, Zelle B, Lohse R, et al. Evaluation and outcome of patients after polytrauma: can patients be recruited for long-term follow-up? Injury 2006;37:1197–1203.

288. Paulozzi LJ. United States pedestrian fatality rates by vehicle type. Inj Prev 2005;11: 232–236.

289. Pitton MB, Herber S, Schmiedt W, et al. Long-term follow-up after endovascular treatment of acute aortic emergencies. Cardiovasc Intervent Radiol 2008;31:23–35.

290. Plotz FB, Slutsky AS, van Vught AJ, Heijnen CJ. Ventilator-induced lung injury and multiple system organ failure: a critical review of facts and hypotheses. Intensive Care Med 2004;30:1865–1872.

291. Polinder S, Meerding WJ, van Baar ME, et al. Cost estimation of injury-related hospital admissions in 10 European countries. J Trauma 2005;59:1283–1290; discussion 1290–1291.

292. Practice guidelines for blood component therapy: a report by the American Society of Anaesthesiologists Task Force on Blood Component Therapy. Anaesthesiology 1996; 84:732–747.

293. Probst C, Hildebrand F, Frink M, et al. [Prehospital treatment of severely injured patients in the field: an update]. Chirurg 2007;78:875–884.

294. Prokop A, Hotte H, Kruger K, et al. [Multislice CT in diagnostic work-up of polytrauma]. Unfallchirurg 2006;109:545–550.

295. Puleo D. Biotherapeutics in orthopaedic medicine: accelerating the healing process? BioDrugs 2003;17:301–314.

296. Rainer TH, Cheung NK, Yeung JH, et al. Do trauma teams make a difference? A single centre registry study. Resuscitation 2007;73:374–381.

297. Rating the severity of tissue damage. I. The Abbreviated Scale. JAMA 1971;215: 277–280.

298. Redl H, Schlag G, Hammerschmidt DE. Quantitative assessment of leukostasis in experimental hypovolemic-traumatic shock, Acta Chir Scand 1984;150:113–117.

299. Regel G, Bayeff-Filloff M. [Diagnosis and immediate therapeutic management of limb injuries. A systematic review of the literature]. Unfallchirurg 2004;107:919–926.

300. Reid CL, Perrey C, Pravica V, et al. Genetic variation in proinflammatory and anti-inflammatory cytokine production in multiple organ dysfunction syndrome. Crit Care Med 2002;30:2216–2221.

301. Rice PL Jr, Rudolph M. Pelvic fractures. Emerg Med Clin North Am 2007;25:795 802, x.

302. Richter ED, Berman T, Friedman L, Ben-David G. Speed, road injury, and public health. Annu Rev Public Health 2006;27:125–152.

303. Richter M, Pape HC, Otte D, Krettek C. Improvements in passive car safety led to decreased injury severity: a comparison between the 1970s and 1990s. Injury 2005; 36:484–488.

304. Ringburg AN, Spanjersberg WR, Frankema SP, et al. Helicopter emergency medical services (HEMS): impact on on-scene times. J Trauma 2007;63:258–262.

305. Riska EB, von Bonsdorff H, Hakkinen S, et al. Primary operative fixation of long bone fractures in patients with multiple injuries. J Trauma 1977;17:111–121.

306. Rivara FP, Thompson DC, Cummings P. Effectiveness of primary and secondary enforced seat belt laws. Am J Prev Med 1999;16(suppl 1):30–39.

307. Rivers EP, Nguyen HB, Huang DT, Donnino M. Early goal-directed therapy. Crit Care Med 2004;32:314–315.

308. Rivers EP. Early goal-directed therapy in severe sepsis and septic shock: converting science to reality. Chest 2006;129:217–218.

309. Rixan D, Siegel JH, Friedman HP. Sepsis/SIRS, physiologic classification, severity stratification, relation to cytokine elaboration, and outcome prediction in posttrauma critical illness. J Trauma 2001;51:458–463.

310. Rizoli SB. Crystalloids and colloids in trauma resuscitation: a brief overview of the current debate. J Trauma 2003;54:S82–S88.

311. Roberts CS, Pape HC, Jones AL, et al. Damage control orthopaedics: evolving concepts in the treatment of patients who have sustained orthopaedic trauma. Instr Course Lect 2005;54:447–462.

312. Rockswold GL, Leonard PR, Nagib MG. Analysis of management in 33 closed head injury patients who "talked and deteriorated." Neurosurgery 1987;21:51–55.

313. Rodenberg H. Effect of aeromedical aircraft on care of trauma patients: evaluation using the Revised Trauma Score. South Med J 1992;85:1065–1071.

314. Rogers FB, Osler TM, Shackford SR, et al. Financial outcome of treating trauma in a rural environment. J Trauma 1997;43:65–72.

315. Roudsari BS, Nathens AB, Cameron P, et al. International comparison of prehospital trauma care systems. Injury 2007;38:993–1000.

316. Rozycki GS, Feliciano DV, Schmidt JA, et al. The role of surgeon-performed ultrasound in patients with possible cardiac wounds. Ann Surg 1996;223:737–744; discussion 744–746.

317. Rozycki GS. Surgeon-performed ultrasound: its use in clinical practice. Ann Surg 1998; 228:16–28.

318. Ruchholtz S, Nast-Kolb D, Waydhas C, et al. [Cost analysis of clinical treatment of polytrauma patients]. Chirurg 1995;66:684–692.

319. Rutledge R, Osler T, Emery S, et al. The end of the Injury Severity Score (ISS) and the Trauma and Injury Severity Score (TRISS): ICISS, an International Classification of Diseases, ninth revision-based prediction tool, outperforms both ISS and TRISS as predictors of trauma patient survival, hospital charges, and hospital length of stay. J Trauma 1998;44:41–49.

320. Sacco WJ, MacKenzie EJ, Champion HR, et al. Comparison of alternative methods for assessing injury severity based on anatomic descriptors. J Trauma 1999;47:441–446; discussion 446–447.

321. Sadri H, Nguyen-Tang T, Stern R, et al. Control of severe hemorrhage using C-clamp and arterial embolization in hemodynamically unstable patients with pelvic ring disruption. Arch Orthop Trauma Surg 2005;125:443–447.

322. Sam A 2nd, Kibbe M, Matsumura J, Eskandari MK. Blunt traumatic aortic transection: endoluminal repair with commercially available aortic cuffs. J Vasc Surg 2003;38: 1132–1135.

323. Sanson G, Di Bartolomeo S, Nardi G, et al. Road traffic accidents with vehicular entrapment: incidence of major injuries and need for advanced life support. Eur J Emerg Med 1999;6:285–291.

324. Sayer NA, Chiros CE, Sigford B, et al. Characteristics and rehabilitation outcomes among patients with blast and other injuries sustained during the Global War on Terror. Arch Phys Med Rehabil 2008;89:163–170.

325. Scalea TM, Boswell SA, Scott JD, et al. External fixation as a bridge to intramedullary nailing for patients with multiple injuries and with femur fractures: damage control orthopaedics. J Trauma 2000;48:613–621.

326. Scalea TM, Rodriguez A, Chiu WC, et al. Focused assessment with sonography for trauma (FAST): results from an international consensus conference. J Trauma 1999; 46:466–472.

327. Schierhout G, Roberts I. Fluid resuscitation with colloid or crystalloid solutions in critically ill patients: a systematic review of randomised trials. BMJ 1998;69:961–964.

328. Schmelz A, Ziegler D, Beck A, et al. [Costs for acute, stationary treatment of polytrauma patients]. Unfallchirurg 2002;105:1043–1048.

329. Schoder M, Prokop M, Lammer J. Traumatic injuries: imaging and intervention of large arterial trauma. Eur Radiol 2002;12:1617–1631.

330. Schonholz CJ, Uflacker R, de Gregorio MA, et al. Stent-graft treatment of trauma to the supra-aortic arteries. A review. J Cardiovasc Surg (Torino) 2007;48:537–549.

331. Schrieber MA, Halcomb JB, Hedner U. The effect of recombinant factor VIIa on coagulopathic pigs with grade V liver injuries. J Trauma 2002;53:252–259.

332. Schroder O, Laun RA, Held B, et al. Association of interleukin-10 promoter polymorphism with the incidence of multiple organ dysfunction following major trauma: results of a prospective pilot study. Shock 2004;21:306–310.

333. Sclafani SJ, Weisberg A, Scalea TM, et al. Blunt splenic injuries: nonsurgical treatment with CT, arteriography, and transcatheter arterial embolization of the splenic artery. Radiology 1991;181:189–196.

334. Sears BW, Luchette FA, Esposito TJ, et al. Old fashion clinical judgment in the era of protocols: is mandatory chest x-ray necessary in injured patients? J Trauma 2005;59: 324–330; discussion 330–332.

335. Seekamp A, Regel G, Bauch S, et al. [Long-term results of therapy of polytrauma patients with special reference to serial fractures of the lower extremity]. Unfallchirurg 1994; 97:57–63.

336. Self ML, Blake AM, Whitley M, et al. The benefit of routine thoracic, abdominal, and pelvic computed tomography to evaluate trauma patients with closed head injuries. Am J Surg 2003;186:609–613; discussion 613–614.

337. Selye, H. The general adaptation syndrome and the diseases of adaptation, Am J Med 1951;10:549–555.

338. Sethi D, Kwan I, Kelly AM, et al. Advanced trauma life support training for ambulance crews. Cochrane Database Syst Rev 2001;2:CD003109.

339. Shackford SR. Effects of small-volume resuscitation on intracranial pressure and related cerebral variables. J Trauma 1997;42:S48–S53.

340. Shafi S, Nathens AB, Elliott AC, et al. Effect of trauma systems on motor vehicle occupant mortality: a comparison between states with and without a formal system. J Trauma 2006;61:1374–1378.

341. Shapiro MB, Jenkins DH, Schwab CW, et al. Damage control: collective review. J Trauma 2000;49:969–978.

342. Shults RA, Elder RW, Sleet DA, et al. Primary enforcement seat belt laws are effective even in the face of rising belt use rates. Accid Anal Prev 2004;36:491–493.

343. Shults RA, Nichols JL, Dinh-Zarr TB, et al. Effectiveness of primary enforcement safety belt laws and enhanced enforcement of safety belt laws: a summary of the Guide to Community Preventive Services systematic reviews. J Safety Res 2004;35:189–196.

344. Siebers C, Stegmaier J, Kirchhoff C, et al. [Analysis of failure modes in multislice computed tomography during primary trauma survey]. Rofo 2008;180:733–739.

345. Siegel JH, Mason-Gonzalez S, Dischinger PC, et al. Causes and costs of injuries in multiple trauma patients requiring extrication from motor vehicle crashes. J Trauma 1993;35:920–931.

346. Sikand M, Williams K, White C, Moran CG. The financial cost of treating polytrauma: implications for tertiary referral centres in the United Kingdom. Injury 2005;36: 733–737.

347. Smith GJ, Kramer GC, Perron P. A comparison of several hypertonic solutions for resuscitation of bled sheep. J Surg Res 1985;39:517–528.

348. Smith HE, Biffl WL, Majercik SD, et al. Splenic artery embolization: have we gone too far? J Trauma 2006;61:541–544.

349. Smith RM, Giannoudis PV. Trauma and the immune response. J R Soc Med 1998;91: 417–420.

350. Soldati G, Testa A, Sher S, et al. Occult traumatic pneumothorax: diagnostic accuracy of lung ultrasonography in the emergency department. Chest 2008;133:204–11.

351. Southard PA. Trauma economics: realities and strategies. Crit Care Nurs Clin North Am 1994;6:435–440.

352. Spence MT, Redmond AD, Edwards JD. Trauma audit: the use of TRISS. Health Trends 1988;20:94–97.

353. Sriussadaporn S, Luengtaviboon K, Benjacholamas V, et al. Significance of a widened mediastinum in blunt chest trauma patients. J Med Assoc Thai 2000;83:1296–1301.

354. Stafford RE, Linn J, Washington L. Incidence and management of occult hemothoraces. Am J Surg 2006;192:722–726.

355. Stalp M, Koch C, Regel G, et al. [Development of a standardized instrument for quantitative and reproducible rehabilitation data assessment after polytrauma (HASPOC)]. Chirurg 2001;72:312–318.

356. Stalp M, Koch C, Ruchholtz S, et al. Standardized outcome evaluation after blunt multiple injuries by scoring systems: a clinical follow-up investigation 2 years after injury. J Trauma 2002;52:1160–1168.

357. Stein DJ, Seedat S, Iversen A, et al. Post-traumatic stress disorder: medicine and politics. Lancet 2007;369:139–144.

358. Stein DM, O'Toole R, Scalea TM. Multidisciplinary approach for patients with pelvic fractures and hemodynamic instability. Scand J Surg 2007;96:272–280.

359. Stephenson SC, Langley JD, Civil ID. Comparing measures of injury severity for use with large databases. J Trauma 2002;53:326–332.

360. Strecker W, Gebhard F, Perl M, et al. Biochemical characterization of individual injury pattern and injury severity. Injury 2003;34-12:879–887.

361. Sturm JA. [Polytrauma and the hospital structure]. Langenbecks Arch Chir Suppl Kongressbd 1997;114:123–129.

362. Sudkamp N, Haas N, Flory PJ, et al. Criteria for amputation, reconstruction and replantation of extremities in multiple trauma patients. Chirurg 1989;60:774–781.

363. Symbas PN, Sherman AJ, Silver JM, et al. Traumatic rupture of the aorta: immediate or delayed repair? Ann Surg 2002;235-6:796–802.

364. Taheri PA, Butz DA, Lottenberg L, et al. The cost of trauma center readiness. Am J Surg 2004;187:7–13.

365. Task Force on Principles for Economic Analysis of Health Care Technology. Economic analysis of health care technology. A report on principles. Ann Intern Med 1995;123: 61–70.

366. Thannheimer A, Woltmann A, Vastmans J, Buhren V. [The unstable patient with pelvic fracture]. Zentralbl Chir 2004;129-1:37–42.

367. The American Association for the Surgery of Trauma. Organ Injury Scale 2000. Retrieved April 15, 2009, from http://www.aast.org.

368. The American College of Surgeons Committee on Trauma Leadership. In: Clark DE, Fantus RJ, eds. National Trauma Data Bank (NTDB) annual report. Chicago: 2007: 1–64.

369. The American College of Surgeons. Advanced Trauma Life Support (ATLS) students manual. 6th edition. Chicago, IL: American College of Surgeons 1997.

370. The Association for the Advancement of Automotive Medicine (AAAM). Retrieved April 15, 2009, from http://www.carcrash.org/index.html.

371. The Trauma Audit and Research Network (TARN). Retrieved April 15, 2009, from https://www.tarn.ac.uk.

372. Thomas SH. Helicopter emergency medical services transport outcomes literature: annotated review of articles published 2000–2003. Prehosp Emerg Care 2004;8: 322–333.

373. Thomason M, Messick J, Rutledge R, et al. Head CT scanning versus urgent exploration in the hypotensive blunt trauma patient. J Trauma 1993;34-1:40–44.

374. Timmermann A, Russo SG, Hollmann MW. Paramedic versus emergency physician emergency medical service: role of the anaesthesiologist and the European versus the Anglo-American concept. Curr Opin Anaesthesiol 2008;21:222–227.

375. Totterman A, Dormagen JB, Madsen JE, et al. A protocol for angiographic embolization in exsanguinating pelvic trauma: a report on 31 patients. Acta Orthop 2006;77: 462–468.

376. Totterman A, Glott T, Soberg HL, et al. Pelvic trauma with displaced sacral fractures: functional outcome at 1 year. Spine 2007;32:1437–1443.

377. Tötterman A, Madsen JE, Skaga NO, Røise O. Extraperitoneal pelvic packing: a salvage procedure to control massive traumatic pelvic hemorrhage. J Trauma 2007;62: 843–852.

378. Tran T, Thordarson D. Functional outcome of multiply injured patients with associated foot injury. Foot Ankle Int 2002;23:340–343.

379. Travis T, Monsky WL, London J, et al. Evaluation of short-term and long-term complications after emergent internal iliac artery embolization in patients with pelvic trauma. J Vasc Interv Radiol 2008;19:840–847.

380. Trentz OL. Polytrauma: pathophysiology, priorities, and management. In Rüedi TP, Buckley RE, Moran CG. AO Principles of Fracture Management. Stuttgart/New York: Thieme, 2007;337–347.

381. Troidl H. Quality of life: definition, conceptualization, and implications: a surgeon's view. Theor Surg 1991;6:138–142.

382. Tscherne H, Oestern HJ, Sturm J. Osteosynthesis of major fractures in polytrauma. World J Surg 1983;7:80–87.

383. Tsoukas A, Andreade A, Zacharogiannis C, et al. Myocardial contusion presented as acute myocardial infarction after chest trauma. Echocardiography 2001;18:167–170.

384. Tuxen DV. Permissive hypercapnic ventilation. Am J Respir Crit Care Med 1994;150: 870–874.

385. Vaslef SN, Knudsen NW, Neligan PJ, Sebastian MW. Massive transfusion exceeding 50 units of blood products in trauma patients. J Trauma 2002;53-2:291–295.

386. Velmahos GC, Theodorou D, Tatevossian R, et al. Radiographic cervical spine evaluation in the alert asymptomatic blunt trauma victim: much ado about nothing. J Trauma 1996;40:768–774.

387. Velmahos GC, Toutouzas KG, Vassiliu P, et al. A prospective study on the safety and efficacy of angiographic embolization for pelvic and visceral injuries. J Trauma 2002; 53:303–308; discussion 308.

388. Voggenreiter G, Eisold C, Sauerland S, et al. [Diagnosis and immediate therapeutic management of chest trauma. A systematic review of the literature]. Unfallchirurg 2004; 107:881–891.

389. Vyrostek SB, Annest JL, Ryan GW. Surveillance for fatal and nonfatal injuries: United States, 2001. MMWR Surveill Summ 2004;53:1–57.

390. Wade CE, Kramer GC, Grady JJ, et al. Efficacy of hypertonic 7.5% saline and 6% dextran-70 in treating trauma: a meta-analysis of controlled clinical studies. Surgery 1997;122:609–616.

391. Wald SL, Shackford SR, Fenwick J. The effect of secondary insults on mortality and long-term disability after severe head injury in a rural region without a trauma system. J Trauma 1993;34-3:377–381.

392. Waller JA, Payne SR, McClallen JM. Trauma centers and DRGs: inherent conflict? J Trauma 1989;29:617–622.

393. Wang H, Ma S. The cytokine storm and factors determining the sequence and severity of organ dysfunction in multiple organ dysfunction syndrome. Am J Emerg Med 2008; 26:711–715.

394. Ward LD, Morandi MM, Pearse M, et al. The immediate treatment of pelvic ring disruption with the pelvic stabilizer. Bull Hosp Jt Dis 1997;56:104–106.

395. Wardrope J. Traumatic deaths in the Sheffield and Barnsley areas. J R Coll Surg Edinb 1989;34:69–73.

396. Ware J Jr, Kosinski M, Keller SD. A 12-Item Short-Form Health Survey: construction of scales and preliminary tests of reliability and validity. Med Care 1996;34:220–233.

397. Watanabe E, Hirasawa H, Oda S, et al. Cytokine-related genotypic differences in peak interleukin-6 blood levels of patients with SIRS and septic complications. J Trauma 2005;59:1181–1189.

398. Waydhas C, Nast-Kolb D, Trupka A, et al. Posttraumatic inflammatory response, secondary operations, and late multiple organ failure. J Trauma 1996;40:624–631.

399. Weiskopf RB, Viele MK, Feiner J. Human cardiovascular and metabolic response to acute, severe isovolaemic haemorrhage. JAMA 1998;279:217–221.

400. Weninger P, Mauritz W, Fridrich P, et al. Emergency room management of patients with blunt major trauma: evaluation of the multislice computed tomography protocol exemplified by an urban trauma center. J Trauma 2007;62:584–591.

401. West TA, Rivara FP, Cummings P, et al. Harborview assessment for risk of mortality: an improved measure of injury severity on the basis of ICD-9-CM. J Trauma 2000;49: 530–540.

402. Williams RF, Fabian TC, Fischer PE, et al. Impact of airbags on a Level I trauma center: injury patterns, infectious morbidity, and hospital costs. J Am Coll Surg 2008;206: 962–968.

403. Wilmink AB, Samra GS, Watson LM, et al. Vehicle entrapment rescue and prehospital trauma care. Injury 1996;27:21–25.

404. Wilson C, Willis C, Hendrikz JK, Bellamy N. Speed enforcement detection devices for preventing road traffic injuries. Cochrane Database Syst Rev 2006;2:CD004607.

405. Winslow JE, Hinshaw JW, Hughes MJ, et al. Quantitative assessment of diagnostic radiation doses in adult blunt trauma patients. Ann Emerg Med 2008;52:93–97.

406. Wintermark M, Poletti PA, Becker CD, et al. Traumatic injuries: organization and ergonomics of imaging in the emergency environment. Eur Radiol 2002;12:959–968.

407. Wisner DH, Victor NS, Holcroft JW. Priorities in the management of multiple trauma: intracranial versus intra-abdominal injury. J Trauma 1993;35:271–276.

408. Wolfl CG, Bouillon B, Lackner CK, et al. [Prehospital Trauma Life Support (PHTLS): an interdisciplinary training in preclinical trauma care]. Unfallchirurg 2008;111:688–694.

409. Wolter TP, Fuchs PC, Horvat N, Pallua N. Is high PEEP low volume ventilation in burn patients beneficial? A retrospective study of 61 patients. Burns 2004;30:368–373.

410. Woltmann A, Buhren V. [Shock trauma room management of spinal injuries in the framework of multiple trauma. A systematic review of the literature]. Unfallchirurg 2004;107:911–918.

411. World Health Organisation (WHO). World health statistics. Retrieved April 15, 2009, from http://www.who.int/whosis/en.

412. Wu JS, Sheng L, Wang SH, et al. The impact of clinical risk factors in the conversion from acute lung injury to acute respiratory distress syndrome in severe multiple trauma patients. J Int Med Res 2008;36:579–586.

413. Zedler S, Faist E. The impact of endogenous triggers on trauma-associated inflammation. Curr Opin Crit Care 2006;12:595–601.

414. Zelle BA, Brown SR, Panzica M, et al. The impact of injuries below the knee joint on the long-term functional outcome following polytrauma. Injury 2005;36:169–177.

415. Zelle BA, Panzica M, Vogt MT, et al. Influence of workers' compensation eligibility upon functional recovery 10 to 28 years after polytrauma. Am J Surg 2005;190:30–36.

416. Zimmerman JE, Kramer AA, McNair DS, et al. Acute Physiology and Chronic Health Evaluation (APACHE) IV: hospital mortality assessment for today's critically ill patients. Crit Care Med 2006;34:1297–1310.

417. Zintl B, Ruchholtz S, Nast-Kolb D, et al. [Quality management in early clinical multiple trauma care. Documentation of treatment and evaluation of critical care quality]. Unfallchirurg 1997;100:811–819.

10

INITIAL MANAGEMENT OF
OPEN FRACTURES

Robert P. Dunbar, Jr, and Michael J. Gardner

INTRODUCTION

Open fractures, previously known as compound fractures, are those in which there is a breach in the soft tissue envelope over or near the fracture such that the underlying bone communicates with the outside environment. Although many closed fractures also may be associated with significant soft tissue injury, they do not have this full thickness break in the soft tissues. Fractures may be classified as either open or closed, with further classification schemes used to specify the severity of the injury.

HISTORICAL PERSPECTIVE

In the ancient world, the Egyptians recognized the need for coverage over fracture wounds to minimize morbidity.[115] Hippocrates (born 460 BCE) recognized that injuries commonly caused local swelling and admonished against occlusive dressing until after swelling had abated. Hippocrates favored operative débridement of purulent material but urged against frequent meddling with wounds that were progressing appropriately.

Galen (129–200 AD), a prominent Roman physician of Greek origin, considered purulence as necessary "laudable pus" and viewed it as essential to the healing process. He and his counterparts actively sought treatments that would lead to a purulent response.[152]

By the time of the Renaissance, Ambroise Paré (c. 1510–1590), a French army surgeon, described the need for opening the wound and the need for the free flow of drainage. He also described the necessity of débridement of all foreign matter and necrotic local tissues. In the same era, Brunschwig and Botello also advocated for operative débridement of necrotic material from nonprogressing wounds. Desault, in the 18th century, reiterated this belief, advising extending open wounds to explore and remove dead tissue. It was he who coined the term *débridement*.[147] Later, the possible effects of the timing of open fracture treatment were appreciated by his pupil, Larrey, which presaged a topic that remains controversial even today.

Still, in the 19th century, prior to aseptic technique and antibiotics, emergency amputation as a lifesaving measure after open fracture was not uncommon. In the American Civil War (1861–1865), the mortality rate for open fractures was 26%. In the Franco-Prussian war (1870–1871), 13,000 amputations were performed to avoid sepsis or death. Nevertheless, even amputation was no guarantor of favorable outcome, as Billroth (1829–1894) reported that 36 of 93 (39%) patients with open fractures of the lower extremities still died.[115]

By World War I, 1914–1918, it became more common to débride, stabilize, and allow open fracture wounds to heal by secondary intent.[70] Sulfonamides, applied topically on wounds, became widely used during World War II (1939–1945).[70] More proper antibiotics became available during the US–Korean War (1950–1954). Gustilo and Anderson described the use of antibiotics and described a classification scheme for open fractures.[66] Small beads of polymethylmethacrylate (PMMA), impregnated with antibiotics, can also be useful in open fracture management. This technique effectively supplements intravenous antibiotic delivery, and occupies "dead space" caused by bone loss, minimizing hematoma formation and bacterial colonization.[75,114]

Some open wounds can be effectively treated definitively with serial wet-to-dry saline gauze dressings. Ideally, uneventful wound healing by secondary intention ensues. However, this technique exposes the wound to the external environment, and inevitable colonization may lead to infection. This is more likely to occur if internal fixation, particularly surface implants, is present, or if fascial defects exist. Advances in plastic surgery techniques in the 1980s and 1990s, specifically the development of microvascular free tissue transfer, aided in the coverage of these wounds. This technique proved useful in both the avoidance and treatment of chronic osteomyelitis and has become a mainstay of treatment of the most severe soft tissue injuries. Unfortunately, the availability of plastic surgeons trained and willing to perform this technique remains limited in certain areas. Further, not all wounds or hosts are compatible candidates for free tissue transfer because of local or systemic vascular disease, injury, or other patient factors.

The use of the negative pressure dressings (Wound VAC, KCI, San Antonio, TX) has also proved to be a useful adjunct in the treatment of these complex injuries. Such dressings provide a closed environment, preventing loss to evaporation, promoting the formulation of granulation tissue, and preparing the wound site for coverage. Although a strong adjunct to the treatment of open fracture wounds, unlike previous thought, it has not decreased the risk of infection when used in a prolonged manner before microvascular free tissue transfer.[15]

As noted above, many of the principles of management of open fracture wounds that are used in civilian settings are the results of lessons learned, forgotten, and repeatedly relearned in the military setting. These include:

1. Application of a sterile dressing over the open wound in anticipation of more formal débridement in a sterile operative setting
2. Immobilization of the extremity
3. Early administration of antibiotics and tetanus (if required)
4. Urgent operative wound débridement and irrigation, with stabilization of the skeletal system either provisionally (e.g., external fixation) or definitively
5. Repeated débridements as indicated and definitive skeletal stabilization and/or soft tissue closure or coverage as soon as prudent

ETIOLOGY AND MECHANISMS OF OPEN FRACTURES

Although it is commonly contended that open fractures are the result of higher energy mechanisms than closed fractures, this is perhaps an oversimplification. Higher energy mechanisms of injury commonly are associated with the energy required to cause open injuries. Nevertheless, depending on the anatomic area involved, some lower energy mechanisms of injury may still result in open fractures. One example is a motor vehicle collision that leads to a femoral shaft fracture, in which one of the fragments tents the intact overlying thigh skin, having traversed the large quadriceps or hamstring musculature of the thigh remains a closed fracture. This may have required significantly more energy than a distal tibial fracture acquired in a soccer game, in which the thin medial soft tissues are compromised in a simple "inside-to-outside" breach, resulting in an open fracture.

In open fractures bacteria from the environment typically contaminate the area of injury,[118] although if an infection develops later, little correlation has been shown between the contaminant and the cultures obtained during treatment of the infection.[96] Higher energy mechanisms typically cause greater soft tissue disruption that leaves the wound more susceptible to infection by contaminating bacteria.[161]

In the setting of open fractures, multiple factors beyond fracture pattern influence prognosis. Local injury variables, such as the presence of copious foreign debris with highly contaminated material, and substantial soft tissue and bone devitalization affect the infection and nonunion rate, and can predispose to a prolonged recovery and a poor outcome. Systemic variables, such as poor host quality, medications taken, and nicotine abuse also influence complication rates. Additional injury and patient specific conditions influencing outcome include the presence or absence of nerve injury and remote fractures and injuries can impact functional prognosis.

PRINCIPLES OF MANAGEMENT

On arrival in the emergency department, the patient should be thoroughly evaluated. The patient should be stabilized according to ATLS protocols.[92] Any life-threatening injuries must be evaluated and treated. Although it is tempting to immediately address the open wound, one must be assured that the patient's airway, breathing, and circulation are in order. Obviously, many processes may be undertaken in parallel rather than in series, but it is important to thoroughly work-up what may be a polytraumatized patient rather than rushing to the operative suite to address the injured extremity.

History

As with any injury, evaluation commences with a thorough history when possible. This should include the site(s) of pain and instability, the mechanism of injury, and changes in sensation or motor function. Any pain in the area of the fracture prior to the traumatic injury may signify a pathologic or stress fracture, as may an unusually low energy mechanism or a report from the patient that he or she sensed that the fracture occurred prior to falling down. Any previous injuries, fractures or surgeries, dermatologic conditions, or radiation therapy in the area in question may also impact treatment or outcome. Obtunded, intubated, or otherwise nonverbal patients may be unable to provide significant history. In these cases witnesses to the accident, family members, and emergency medical providers in the field may provide useful information regarding the mechanism of injury and the patient's medical condition. This may include specifics regarding the injury or vehicle collision, the degree of injury to the vehicle(s); the use or nonuse of seatbelts and other restraints; the extent of injuries to others, including passengers in the vehicle; how far the patient was thrown from the vehicle; the extent of blood loss in the field; or the patient's level of responsiveness prior to arrival in the ED.

All pertinent systemic illnesses, current medications, allergies, and nicotine abuse should be documented.[28,68] Conditions such as nutritional depletion, diabetes mellitus, severe peripheral vascular disease, rheumatoid arthritis (or any condition that requires chronic steroid use) may affect wound and/or fracture healing and may accordingly affect choices for treatment and potential for an optimal outcome. A history of seizures with long term phenytoin use may denote impaired bone quality. Level of activity and weight-bearing status prior to the injury may be a predictor of level of activity posttreatment. History of surgeries, particularly in terms of previous incisions and/or indwelling implants in the vicinity of the open fracture wound, may affect choices for treatment.

Physical Examination

A thorough physical examination is essential. All constricting clothing about the injury should be removed. Visual inspection of the limb is undertaken looking for deformity or bone fragments prominent under the skin or placing the skin at risk, signs of dysvascularity, previous incisions or other scars, gross debris in the wound, burns, abrasions, and degloved soft tissues. Any remaining limb deformity not addressed in the field is corrected. Evaluation for compartment syndrome should not be overlooked, because this may still occur in the setting of open fractures.[40,149]

Open fractures often offer a dramatic presentation, with the fractured end(s) of major fragments often visible in the open wounds or protruding through the wound. In other cases, however, whether a fracture is open or not may not be quite as clear. Any wound in the area of a fracture or even within the same limb segment should be assumed to represent an open fracture until proved otherwise. Full-thickness lacerations, even if a simple poke hole, may represent an open fracture. The wound may be somewhat remote from the fracture if the fragments have telescoped past each other as the fracture shortens, a result of severe axial loading. Persistent oozing of blood from the wound, particularly if fat is noted in the blood, may represent a decompressing fracture hematoma. This is a common, but not constant finding. Even open wounds remote from the fracture site may communicate with the fracture if the skin and subcutaneous tissues have been degloved from the underlying fascia and deeper tissues (Figure 10-1).

A description of the wound should be documented, commenting on its location, length, configuration (linear, stellate or other), orientation (longitudinal, oblique or transverse), condition of the adjacent skin, and associated abrasions or other injuries. In this era of increasingly shared responsibilities for caring for these patients, such documentation cannot be over-emphasized. Additionally, prolonged periods of a joint dislocation or fracture displacement can place excessive tension on the overlying soft tissues, potentially leading to full thickness skin breakdown, effectively converting a closed fracture to an open fracture (Figure 10-2). This may be significant because surgical incisions tend to be longitudinal, and the traumatic wound may affect the surgical plan for approach and access to the fracture. Open fractures in the pelvis may be contaminated from the external environment or internally by rectal, vaginal, or urinary flora. An extremely high index of suspicion should be maintained for an associated open fracture and a thorough examination is imperative, checking for vaginal, perineal, and rectal blood, tears in the soft tissue envelope, or protruding bone fragments. Treatment in these circumstances may include providing fecal diversion via colostomy. In the best of settings and treated appropriately, these fractures are associated with severe morbidity and even mortality. Failure to recognize these injuries as open and contaminated may lead to even more common adverse outcomes.

Examination of neurovascular structures in the area of the fracture and distally is a vital part of the evaluation. Circulation is noted by pulse examination, the warmth and color of the limb, capillary refill, the filling of veins, and ABI testing. Recall that a malaligned limb due to a displaced fracture or unreduced dislocation may demonstrate signs of vascular insufficiency and that realigning the limb to a more appropriate position may provide a return of blood flow to the limb once the vessel is unkinked. If realigning the limb does not improve circulation, then a vascular injury should be suspected and investigated. Never assume that the pulse deficit is caused by vascular spasm. Doing so may lead to catastrophic complications and/or legal ramifications. An expanding hematoma or pulsatile bleeding likely represents an arterial injury.

Neurological examination ensues. The limb should be examined for peripheral nerve function and dermatomal integrity. Typically this begins with evaluation of light touch and pressure sensations. Motor strength testing may be difficult because of splinting, pain, intubation, or chemical sedation or paralysis. It is important to document what can be examined and whether certain parts of the examination remain unknown. It is far better to document that specific portions of the neurological exam could not be determined than to neglect to comment on this information. Secondary survey and reexamination should be undertaken when the patient is able to comply, and any missing portions of the examination documented at that time.

The wound should be covered with moist saline gauze, and the limb splinted with a noncircumferential splint that stabilizes the affected bone and the joints above and below if possible. Compressive dressings may be used sparingly in the setting of a vascular injury. Repeated evaluations of the wound in the emergency department should not be undertaken, because this may predispose to an increased rate of infection. A photograph may be taken of the wound for documentation if the patient or family is agreeable. This is particularly useful in the setting of the mangled extremity. Tetanus status is determined and updated as necessary. Intravenous antibiotics are started as soon as it is obvious that an open fracture is present.

Radiographic Examination

Even in the most obvious of open fractures, appropriate imaging is indicated to provide the information required to appropriately treat the patient. Anteroposterior and lateral radiographs of the entire bone, including adjacent joints, is the minimum required to properly assess long bone injuries. It is routine to include the joint above and below the injury in the imaging plan. Oblique radiographs and comparison views of the contralateral side are utilized only in select cases. A segmental fracture of the diaphysis or a noncontiguous additional fracture extending into a joint proximal or distal to the fracture associated with the open wound is not uncommon in high energy injuries (e.g., distal third tibial shaft fractures with extension into ankle joint). Other information, including the thickness of cortices or the intramed-

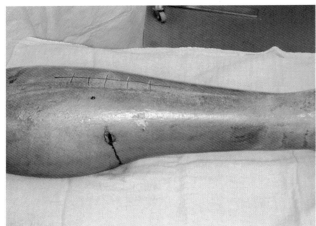

A

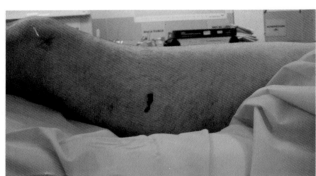

B

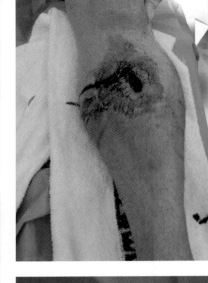

C

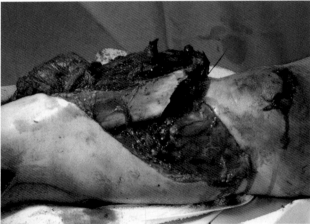

D

FIGURE 10-1 A. Gustilo type I open tibial shaft fracture with wound on the medial face of the tibia. **B.** Gustilo type I open femoral shaft fracture. Note that many surgeons feel that because of the amount of energy required and the amount of soft tissue traversed for this injury to become open, most open femoral shaft fractures should be classified as type III injuries. **C.** Gustilo type II open proximal tibial shaft fracture. **D.** Gustilo type III open tibial fracture prior to débridement, note the associated substantial periosteal stripping and severe muscle injury.

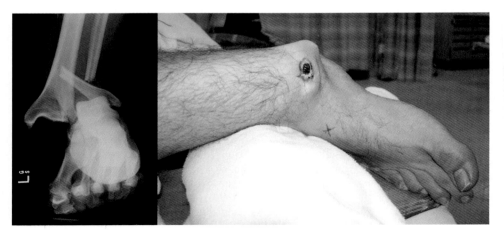

FIGURE 10-2 Closed fracture-dislocation of the ankle with an abrasion and near full thickness skin necrosis. This requires immediate reduction to minimize additional soft tissue injury.

ullary canal, indwelling implants, prior fractures or deformities that may affect the surgical plan, or even bone tumors or other abnormalities are noted and may affect the treatment plan.

Radiographs should be evaluated for foreign debris in the soft tissues and bone loss. The presence of air in the subcutaneous tissues is a common feature of open injuries and may indicate the extent of degloving and or contamination. Recall that such "air," in rare cases may also represent the gas produced by *Clostridium perfringens* or *Escherichia coli*.[6] In the acute setting, however, this usually represents an open fracture.

Knowledge of the patient's comorbidities, the mechanism of injury, the wound, and the radiographs should all be combined to give a sense of the injury personality. For periarticular fractures, particularly those of the distal femur, tibial plateau, tibial pilon, and distal radius, computerized tomography (CT) scanning is commonly performed. This gives valuable information regarding the degree of comminution and or shortening, the orientation of fracture lines, and facilitates preoperative planning. If temporary spanning external fixation of the fracture is planned after débridement, the CT scan may be performed after the fracture has been brought back out to length and reduced, because the information obtained will be more intelligible. MRI scans are not commonly obtained in the acute setting after open fracture.

Associated Injuries and Open Fracture Equivalents

Open joints secondary to traumatic arthrotomies are also treated aggressively. Traumatic arthrotomies may occur with or without fracture. One common traditional diagnostic test used to try to determine whether the knee joint is open is the saline challenge. Saline is injected into the knee and the wound is evaluated for extravasation. A recent study showed that this test is likely insufficient for diagnosing traumatic knee arthrotomies, even when the knee is placed through a range of motion after insertion of the saline.[88] Maintaining a high level of suspicion may be more prudent.

Fractures with Skin at Risk (Impending Open Fractures)

Many unstable fractures can include a soft tissue injury that falls just short of coming through the skin. In some cases the fracture fragments may tent the skin. In other cases the skin is so injured by the injury that it gradually becomes nonviable over the course of several days. Fractures with skin at risk, by virtue of their severe displacement and instability, may place their overlying soft tissue envelope at risk for pressure necrosis. Although certain specific fractures (e.g., medial ankle skin in lateral or posterolateral fractures and fracture dislocations of the ankle) may be predisposed to this issue, almost any fracture that approaches open status will place tension on the overlying soft tissue structures. In some respects this creates an urgency equal to that seen with open fractures, because if the tissues at risk are allowed to die, the patient is left with an open fracture with an uncloseable wound and necrotic tissue. The patient may be at risk of requiring complex microvascular free tissue transfer reconstruction procedures. An amputation may be required if the patient is not a candidate for such a procedure or if such an attempt at soft tissue reconstruction were to fail. As

such, emergent fracture reduction, and sometimes fixation, to resolve soft tissue tension may therefore be required.

The importance of identifying and treating these fractures with skin at risk in a timely manner cannot be overstated. This situation commonly occurs in areas of poor or limited soft tissue coverage. By way of example, certain fractures about the foot and ankle are particularly prone to placing overlying soft tissues at risk. Laterally displaced (fracture-) dislocations of the ankle or tibiotalar joint may place the medial skin overlying the medial malleolus at risk (Figure 10-2). Displaced calcaneal tuberosity fractures may tent or broach the posterior heel skin (Figure 10-3).[60] Talar neck fractures, particularly Hawkins III and IV fractures, and particularly those displaced posteriorly and posteromedially, may cause vascular or nerve injury or place the overlying skin at risk. Similarly, high energy tibial plateau fractures with widely displaced tibial tubercle fragments and highly displaced fractures of the clavicle are other examples of injuries that may require urgent reduction and fixation when fracture fragments are placing undue pressure on their overlying soft tissues.

Classifications

Classification schemes are useful if they convey relevant information, guide treatment, predict outcomes, or assist in research. Various classifications have been developed for the description of open fractures, but the most widely used is that developed by Gustilo and Anderson.[66]

Type I fractures are those with minimal soft tissue injury. Skin lacerations are less than one cm, and are clean, without evidence of deep muscle crushing or foreign debris contamination. Additionally, the underlying fracture pattern must be consistent with a low energy injury. Examples include spiral diaphyseal fractures or rotational periarticular injuries. Higher energy fracture patterns, such as segmental or bending wedge fractures, should be considered as higher grade open fractures. Type II open fractures are those with slightly more soft injury, and with higher energy fracture patterns. Minimal soft tissue degloving and periosteal stripping is present in Type II injuries. Muscle crushing and foreign contamination also must be mild to moderate for Type II designation. Skin lacerations are less than 10 cm in length. The Type III open fractures include higher energy injuries. Substantial soft tissue injury, with periosteal stripping, has occurred, and a crush component is typically present. The fracture pattern, such as segmental comminution, reflects the higher forces imparted. If adequate viable soft tissue and skin is present for coverage, the injury is classified as Type IIIA. If soft tissue reconstruction is required, such as free or rotational muscle flaps, then the designation is Type IIIB. When an arterial injury requiring revascularization is required, Type IIIC classification is invoked (Table 10-1).

Several important caveats exist when classifying open fractures. First, the full extent of the underlying soft tissue injury is often difficult to determine prior to thorough surgical exploration and débridement. Therefore, the utility of assigning a classification upon acute presentation is relatively limited. Next, the length of the skin laceration was emphasized in the original classification description. However, as experience with open fractures has expanded over the last several decades, it has become clear that the underlying muscle and periosteal disruption is more important than the size of the open wound, and this should be accounted for when typing an open fracture. This is most often applied with open femoral shaft fractures, in which

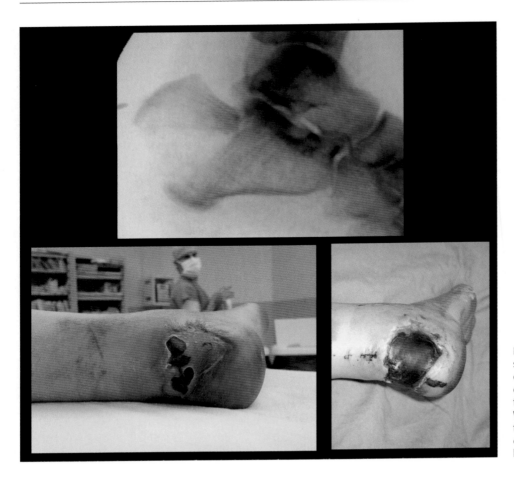

FIGURE 10-3 Deceivingly severe soft tissue injury in this displaced tongue-type calcaneus fracture. Pressure necrosis can convert this closed fracture to an open fracture, leading to significant morbidity. When the thin soft tissue envelope over the posterior hindfoot is at risk, this requires urgent surgical reduction and stabilization.

the skin laceration is small. The high magnitude of force that must be imparted to cause displacement of a fractured femur through the soft tissue envelope and skin mandates a higher energy designation, regardless of the laceration size.

Timing of Treatment

The treatment of open fractures has long been considered an orthopaedic emergency. The rationale has been that it is impera-tive to débride and irrigate the wound to minimize the bacterial load to minimize the risk of infection. There has been much made of the time to débridement as being critical, with 6 hours after injury to débridement considered something of an impor-tant deadline to meet. Certainly it makes little sense to need-lessly delay surgical débridement of these wounds in patients who are physiologically ready for the operative suite. Nonethe-less, some polytraumatized patients may be too physiologically impaired to safely leave the intensive care setting even for the briefest of operative procedures.

The origin of the "6-hour rule" remains somewhat obscure, but the rationale for this appears to have some animal-based evidence. Robson et al. noted that the threshold to sustain an infection was 10^5 organisms.[127] They found that this threshold was reached in 5.17 hours. Cooney et al. noted that with 100,000 organisms per gram of tissue, the immune defenses were overwhelmed and infection ensued.[36]

Several more recent investigations have looked at the risk of infection with delay in treatment after open fracture. Al-Arabi et al. looked at 248 long bone fractures using a cutoff of 6 hours postinjury as a marker. There was no statistical difference between the infection rate of those treated within or beyond the 6 hour cutoff.[3] Other authors also have failed to demonstrate a difference.[5,10,33,41,144]

Nevertheless, once it is determined that the patient with an open fracture is physiologically able to go to the operative suite, preparations for treatment are made. This may include gaining informed consent from the patient or his or her representative, finishing all required preoperative resuscitation and other

TABLE 10-1	Gustilo Classification of Open Fractures
I	Low-energy clean wound <1 cm with minimal soft tissue injury and comminution
II	Wound >1 cm with moderate soft-tissue damage and fracture comminution. Soft tissue component often defined as disruption <10 cm and without periosteal stripping
IIIa	Fracture wound >10 cm with crushed tissue and con-tamination but usually with adequate soft tissue cov-erage
IIIb	Fracture wound >10 cm with crushed tissue and con-tamination having inadequate soft tissue cover associ-ated with periosteal stripping and often requiring trans-fer of vascularized tissue for soft tissue coverage
IIIc	Open fracture associated with a major vascular injury that requires repair for limb salvage

workup, consulting with other specialists for both premorbid and concurrent injuries, early booking of the case with the OR manager, discussing with other surgeons if "bumping" of elective or less urgent nonelective cases is required, and arranging with the operating room staff to have all necessary equipment available. This may include a discussion with the implant company representative if there are any questions about availability or other technical issues regarding anticipated implants. In some cases more than one surgical service may need to work on the patient in the operative suite and arrangements should be made regarding the order of events. This is particularly true in the setting of open fractures with concomitant vascular injury requiring repair.

Antibiotics

Sufficient evidence exists to recommend the use of preoperative prophylactic antibiotics (Table 10-2). The appropriate use of antibiotics has been shown to significantly decrease the rate of surgical site infections.[121] In the setting of an open fracture, intravenous antibiotics are typically given immediately upon arrival in the emergency department. The most common current treatment is for these to be continued for 24 hours and for 24 hours after each subsequent débridement or other surgery rather than continuously throughout the hospital course. There has been little evidence to support giving antibiotics any longer than this in the prophylactic setting.[48]

In spite of this, surgeons must use their best judgment and experience when treating each patient with an open fracture. The individualization of treatment is a cornerstone of treatment. Nevertheless, if a surgeon chooses to pursue treatment that may be considered outside the standard of care, then thorough documentation of rationale should accompany such treatment. It must be recognized that fracture location, type, mechanism, severity, operative treatment, and antibiotic use all play factors in the prevention of infection.

There is no evidence to support keeping a patient on antibiotics as long as drains are in place. There is no evidence to support routine empiric prolongation of prophylactic antibiotic treatment past the initial perioperative period, even if the incision or wound is draining. There is no evidence to support the routine use of prophylactic antibiotics for patients with external fixators (to prevent pin tract infections). Antibiotics are not advised as a substitute for débridement and the aggressive removal of necrotic and/or contaminated material.

Wound Cultures

Although it may seem a reasonable practice to take cultures at the time of initial débridement, there seems to be little correlation of these culture results with likelihood of infection or the specific organism that proves to be the source of the infection. Valenziano et al. investigated the value of cultures taken during the initial débridement of an open fracture. Of the initial cultures, 76% did not demonstrate any growth, and the other 24% only grew skin flora. Of the isolates that grew from the initial cultures, none were the organisms that eventually led to wound infections. They concluded that the use of primary wound cultures in open extremity injuries has no value in the management of patients sustaining long bone open extremity fractures.[150] Lee looked retrospectively at 245 open fractures.[96] He found no difference in the rate of infection in positive or negative predébridement cultures. In cases that did become infected, predébridement cultures grew the infecting organism only 22% of the time and postdébridement cultures grew out the infecting organism only 42% of the time.[96] Merritt similarly showed no correlation between predébridement cultures and the ultimate infecting organism in infected cases, but did show some correlation between the organism that ultimately developed and the last piece of tissue taken in a débridement, so the cultures correlate more with what the patient left the operative suite with than with what they entered the operative suite.[105]

OPERATIVE MANAGEMENT

Patients presenting with gross contamination (leaves, twigs, etc.) in the emergency department should be addressed by removal immediately. The wound is covered with a saline gauze dressing, rather than one soaked in iodine or povidone as has been done widely in the past. There are several reasons for this. Common wound products, such as blood and fat, inactivate the antibacterial activity of povidone-iodine.[165] Systemic toxicity can occur in large wounds or in the setting of impaired renal function.[121] Staining of tissues can make tissue viability during débridement difficult, and tendon desiccation can occur. The effects of povidone-iodine on wound healing at the cellular level remain controversial, but we recommend its avoidance in open wounds due to these other factors. Once it is established that the patient is physiologically ready for the operative treatment of the open fracture, the patient is brought to the operative suite and surrenders to anesthesia. In patients with fractures at risk for associated compartment syndrome rather than general anesthesia, regional blocks that may preclude the ability to examine the patient postoperatively.

Commonly the equipment to be utilized in the débridement of an open fracture is set up separately, often using a separate table or Mayo stand from the equipment to be used in the subsequent stabilization of the fracture. This facilitates transforming the contaminated wound into a clean one and minimizes the chance of implanting contaminated hardware. During the skin and wound prep, any ground-in dirt and other debris may be gently removed with a scrub brush, being mindful of what the soft tissue envelope has already undergone and realiz-

TABLE 10-2	**Common Types of Antibiotic Given for Open Fractures**
Type I	2 g First-generation cephalosporin (if not PCN allergic) Commonly, Cefazolin 2 g every 8 hours
Type II	First-generation cephalosporin
Type III	First-generation cephalosporin plus aminoglycoside Commonly, gentamicin 3–5 mg/kg per day (Varies with renal function) If barnyard or significant soil injury, PCN may be added in type III. Commonly, penicillin 2,000,000 units IV q4 hours If PCN allergic, then vancomycin or clindamycin should be considered

PCN, penicillin

ing that this may not completely cleanse the skin of any organisms, particularly if the patient is treated in a delayed manner.[83] It may be prudent to place a deflated tourniquet on the extremity, if possible, prior to prepping the extremity. This allows for the management of the occasional, otherwise uncontrollable hemorrhage that may ensue when a clot is removed from an unanticipated vascular injury. Another option is to have a sterile tourniquet ready in the operative suite. The tourniquet is typically not inflated otherwise, as the local tissue often has already sustained anoxic significant insult and because this impairs the ability to evaluate muscle viability.

Débridement and Irrigation

Superficial Débridement

Traumatic wounds are extended to facilitate identification and exploration of the entire zone of injury and to gain access to the ends of major bone fragments. The zone of injury is often more extensive than suggested by the open wound. As such, final classification of the fracture should be made at the time of débridement. Wounds that appear small or benign and initially classified as Gustilo type I or II may prove to be better classified as type III injuries if there is significant periosteal stripping involved. The mechanism of injury and the amount of displacement and comminution noted on initial radiographs often provide strong clues to the degree of injury. Similarly, apparent Gustilo type IIIa injuries may initially appear to have enough viable skin for soft tissue coverage. They may need to be reclassified to type IIIb injuries if swelling precludes closure, if débridement of necrotic skin obviates closure, or if a flap with tenuous blood supply dies, leaving the soft tissue envelope uncovered. It is difficult to classify open fractures of the pelvis and because of the potential of both external and internal contamination, diverting colostomy has become a mainstay of treatment in patients with bowel injuries secondary to open pelvic fractures.

Débridement begins in a systematic fashion, typically working from outside to inside. Regardless of original orientation, traumatic wounds are typically transformed to extensile incisions that facilitate visualization of the underlying deep tissues. Another advantage of an extensile (longitudinal) incision, is that as the fracture, which has shortened, is brought back out to length, these wounds are easier to close than transverse wounds that tend to gap when stretched. The incisions may be extended until more normal tissue is encountered, without involving uninjured intact tissues.[113]

Necrotic skin and subcutaneous tissues are sharply excised. Whenever adequate skin is available, excising 1 to 2 mm of contused skin back to viable tissue is reasonable. Nevertheless, excision of skin must be done in a circumspect and prudent manner, because skin may be a previous commodity in certain anatomic areas (tibia, hand, foot) and in patients who are not free flap candidates. Taking care not to leave acute or distally based flaps is essential.[74] Detaching skin and underlying subcutaneous tissue from attached fascia is usually ill advised as this devascularizes the overlying tissues as well as provides another potential space for fluid to accumulate. Clearly nonviable skin should be excised, but any skin that is of marginal viability may be left for later débridement; because skin, unlike necrotic muscle, is not the major generator of infection.

Any nonviable, shredded or contaminated fascia should be excised. Unlike with skin, any marginally viable fascia is excised.

A low threshold should be maintained for fasciotomy. In high energy injuries this is prophylactic against compartment syndrome. In open fractures with a simple rent in the fascia through which the bone fragments traversed, a fasciotomy of the related muscular compartment is advised to gain access to the underlying bone fragments and in anticipation of muscular swelling in response to the initial injury.

Deep Débridement

Although the skeletal injury is typically static and relatively easily assessed, the soft tissue component is not. The extent of injury to the soft tissue envelope, particularly the muscle around an open fracture, is often dynamic and evolving. The overlying wound and even radiographs may underestimate the amount of muscle damage in a given open fracture. Whereas skin tends to tear or puncture, and fascia to split or shred, muscle, because of its high water content, is subject to hydraulic damage by fluid waves when an injuring object strikes the limb. This is particularly true of high energy fractures secondary to indirect rapid loading (e.g., a high-velocity skiing injury resulting in comminution of the tibia or femur), in which the bone literally explodes into many fragments. These fragments travel rapidly outward in the muscle and can cause significant muscle damage even when the outer skin envelope is seemingly undamaged.[27] A small bone fragment may pierce the skin, producing what appears to be a very minor type I open fracture, when in fact there may be considerable deep muscle damage. This occurs because the more rapidly bone is loaded before fracture, the more energy is required to fracture it, and the more energy is released from the fracture when it occurs. Because of this absence of direct physical evidence of trauma, overlooking nonvital muscle is easy because it may not immediately be evident that it has been disturbed or damaged. In muscle débridement, the approach of "when in doubt, take it out" is safest. Necrotic muscle is the major pabulum for bacterial growth and poses a great danger in anaerobic infections. Every effort should be made to remove all nonvital muscle tissue, although this always requires careful judgement.[72,113,148] In type I, II, and IIIA open fractures, this may be taken literally, but in types IIIB and IIIC, débridement of an entire muscle or compartment may be necessary to meet this axiom. If the major arterial supply to a severely damaged muscle has been destroyed, the only recourse is total excision. It has been our experience that if even a small amount of a muscle belly and its attached tendon can be preserved, significant function may be retained. For that reason there may be an indication for leaving marginally viable muscle at the time of initial débridement in severe open fractures, with a plan for returning within 24 to 48 hours for redébridement, at which time the muscle will have better "declared" its viability. Exceptions to this rule include mass casualties (e.g., wartime injuries in austere areas), in which case preservation of life takes precedence over the desire to preserve function.

Judgment of the viability of muscle is challenging. The four tenets of muscle viability are color, consistency, contractility, and capacity to bleed. Scully et al. studied these, trying to confirm the reliability of these factors histologically. They found that muscle consistency and capacity to bleed were the most reliable indicators of muscle viability.[4] We have found that contractility and consistency are more reliably clinically and that color of the muscle and the capacity to bleed are easy to misinterpret. The hypoxemia associated with shock, or the use of a tourniquet, which is discouraged in most open fractures, may make assessing these variables quite difficult.

Further, assessment of muscle viability after fasciotomy for compartment syndrome can be difficult. Muscles in the extremities receive their blood supply from small arteries that run in the epimysial layer. Arterioles branch into the central part of the muscle to supply the deeper muscle. Three zones of postischemic changes that occur in muscle have been described histologically:[143]

1. An inner zone of muscle necrosis in which no swelling occurs
2. A zone of partial ischemic injury with viable muscle that swells substantially
3. An outlying zone of normal muscle in which no swelling occurs

Because of this vascular anatomy, it becomes clear that one may have superficially viable muscle and a substantial amount of deeper necrotic muscle, so the surgeon must look beyond the superficial layers during the débridement. This is done by spreading the muscle in line with the muscle fibers with a hemostat, allowing the surgeon to assess the character of the deeper muscle without substantially injuring the muscle unit.

Tendons, unless injured beyond repair, should be preserved. In open wounds these are subject to desiccation, which can be devastating to function. It is essential to provide coverage or at least to maintain the peritenon. Because maintenance of the peritenon is important, we tend to copiously irrigate this rather than débride it. Consideration should be given at the end of the débridement to try to cover any tendon, and certainly any tendon without peritenon, with muscle, subcutaneous fat, or skin. If this is not a possible, a moist dressing is applied and maintained until more definitive coverage can be procured. Intact arteries and veins and nerves should not be débrided.

Because bone, particularly diaphyseal cortical bone, has a relatively poor blood supply, the bone is largely without defense against infection. It is clear that small bits of bone completely devoid of soft tissue attachments should be removed. Larger cortical segments with limited soft tissue attachments are a more difficult problem. Large bony segments with soft tissue attachments should be retained. In general, cortical fragments without soft tissue attachment ultimately should be removed. These fragments may be useful in determining length, rotation and, alignment and may be utilized provisionally during skeletal stabilization, then removed from the wound after skeletal stabilization. Even when definitive fixation does not occur during the same operative setting, fragments deemed to be important determinants of reduction may be cleansed and retained in a freezer until they can be used and then discarded.[9] Another exception to the strict removal of bone without soft tissue attachment is the rare case in which a significant portion of the articular surface is attached to the loose bony fragment. As the bone in this case is cancellous rather than cortical, and because loss of the articular surface may cause significant functional and reconstructive problems, it is preferred in most cases to retain the fragment, assuming a complete débridement of any gross contaminants can be obtained.[113]

The major bone fragments of long bone fractures are delivered into the wound and their ends and the deep tissues explored for dirt, gravel, grass, clothes, and other foreign debris. The bone ends are cleaned of hematoma with curettes and saline irrigant. Occasionally road debris will be embedded in the bone ends. In this scenario meticulous débridement with dental picks, curettes, and even motorized burrs may be necessary to eliminate the foreign matter.

Irrigation

After thorough meticulous débridement of all foreign debris and necrotic material, irrigation of the wound is performed. Irrigation serves to reduce the bacterial count, float out remaining debris, and cleanse the wound of hematoma to better visualize the remaining tissues. Both high pressure pulsatile lavage and lower pressure gravity irrigation are popular.[120] Some evidence suggests that higher pressure lavage may injure the remaining tissue or even send remaining debris deeper into the wound.[21] A recent randomized prospective study compared lavage with saline to lavage with an antibiotic solution and found no advantage in using the antibiotic solution.[2] No consensus exists regarding the ideal volume of irrigant to be used in open fractures. Many surgeons choose between 6 and 12 liters, but these decisions are not based on high level evidence. Volume should be tailored to the perceived and actual wound contamination with foreign material, as well as the overall energy of the injury and soft tissue damage. Alternatively, some surgeons advocate basing irrigation on a time rather than a specific volume. We generally believe that between 6 and 9 liters is adequate for most open fracture wounds, and use low pressure without additives to the solution. It must again be stressed that irrigation should be performed after thorough tissue débridement.

Skeletal Stabilization

Two vital components of open fracture treatment are restoration of the bony anatomy and skeletal stabilization. Restoring the rotational and angular alignment, and particularly axial length, of diaphyseal and metaphyseal fractures has many benefits for expediting healing of the soft tissue injury. Fracture reduction restores appropriate spatial relationships of arteries, veins, and lymphatic channels, unkinking both large and small caliber conduits, improving perfusion and circulation to the injury zone. Peripheral motor, sympathetic, and parasympathetic nerves function optimally when decompressed, and contribute to initiation of appropriate immune response and healing. Adequate soft tissue tension also substantially facilitates later reconstructive procedures and internal fixation if provisional fixation is selected primarily. Finally, dead space management is most adequately achieved with anatomic myotendinous and fascial plane tension. Minimizing motion of fracture fragments is also important, and decreases persistent soft tissue injury and exaggerated inflammatory mediator release. Both realignment and stabilization allow for immediate vascular inflow, delivering mononuclear and polymorphonuclear cells, as well as antibodies and antibiotics to the compromised tissues (Figure 10-4). Aside from the local benefits, fracture stabilization allows for decreased patient pain, permits mobilization out of recumbency, and minimizes the difficulty with subsequent diagnostic tests.

Acute reduction and fixation of open articular injuries has unique implications in the overall treatment plan and outcome. In two classic studies by Salter et al., the benefits of early joint mobilization for the health and healing of articular cartilage were demonstrated.[129,130] Immediate articular reconstruction

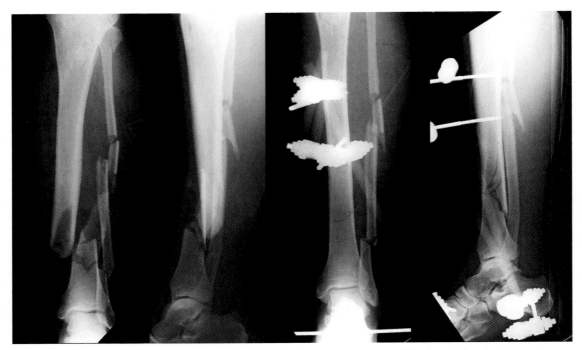

FIGURE 10-4 Example of a high energy Type IIIA open tibial shaft fracture. External fixation and closed reduction was performed acutely following débridement. Appropriate restoration of fracture length and alignment facilitated the early healing response.

that allows joint motion may be beneficial for long term patient outcomes. Acute fracture lines that are visible and accessible directly in the wound at the initial débridement procedure may represent the optimal opportunity for anatomic reduction and fixation.[60] Often reduction and limited screw placement, coupled with spanning external fixation, is an effective initial treatment plan.

Nevertheless, immediate internal fixation must take into account multiple factors. If additional soft tissue dissection is necessary to achieve anatomic articular reduction and fixation, particularly in articular fractures with tenuous soft tissue envelopes (e.g., pilon and tibial plateau), consideration should be given to delayed exposure, reduction, and fixation.[60] If copious contamination is present within the wound and the joint, particularly embedded within the cancellous surfaces of the bone, delay may be prudent. Finally, if the patient's physiologic status is at all in question, articular reconstruction clearly takes a much lower priority than expedient damage control procedures and resuscitation.

Extraosseous Immobilization

Many methods exist for skeletal stabilization, each with its own merits and disadvantages depending on the anatomic region and the clinical severity and situation. On the least invasive end of the spectrum, fracture stabilization is sometimes possible with plaster or fiberglass splints, or skeletal traction. These methods should be employed in carefully selected situations. Low-grade open wounds associated with fractures that would otherwise be treated nonsurgically can be considered for débridement, irrigation, wound closure, and splint immobilization. For example, humeral shaft fractures associated with traumatic lacerations are not necessarily indicated for surgical intervention.[132,133] Minimally displaced Grade 1 open tibial

fractures may be successfully treated with external immobilization.[25] Although plaster splints may provide adequate bony stability, these rarely allow substantial access to the wound or the extremity. Care should be taken to ensure that the traumatic wound is thoroughly débrided and remains benign, and the risks of compartment syndrome are minimal. Skeletal traction is most frequently employed for open pelvic or femoral shaft fractures awaiting more definitive surgical intervention, but is rarely used for definitive treatment. Circumferential casts, even when windowed for wound access, have a very limited role in the acute treatment of open extremity fractures.

External Fixation

External fixation has become a mainstay for temporizing or definitive stabilization of higher grade open fractures. This technique typically involves placing transcutaneous half pins remote from the zone of injury, minimizing additional surgical soft tissue insult. Excellent access to the wound for dressing changes and surveillance is usually possible. These frames may be rapidly applied, and the fracture reduction can be manipulated in multiple planes before clamp tightening. The clamps may later be loosened and the reduction revised after the surgical application in a nonsterile setting. Fracture stabilization following an appropriately placed external fixator is generally adequate to allow for early limb and patient mobilization.

Despite the multiple benefits of external fixation for open fractures, attention to several technical points is necessary to avoid complications. When planning pin placement, the definitive procedure should be carefully considered, and subsequent incisions marked on the extremity. Even without evidence of gross pin site infection, pin tract contamination must be anticipated. If pins are placed within the field of a definitive procedure, the risk of surgical infection may be increased (Figure

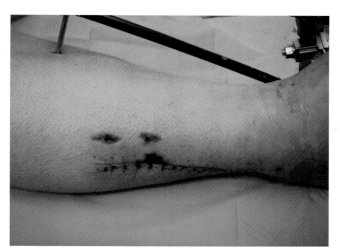

FIGURE 10-5 In this case of an open pilon fracture, the external fixation pins were placed adjacent to the fibular incision, in the zone of the potential definitive incision. The frame was revised and the pin tracts were allowed to defervesce prior to open reduction and internal fixation.

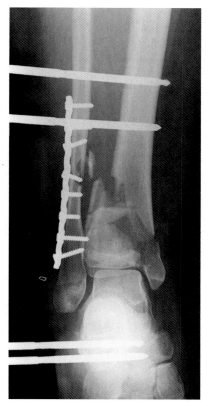

FIGURE 10-6 Tibial external fixator pins placed from lateral to medial, traversing the anterior compartment, have a high loosening and infectious complication rate.

10-5). A second consideration for pin placement is the capsular reflections of adjacent joints. Pins placed in the proximal tibia within 7 cm of the joint line have a higher likelihood of being intraarticular and therefore may cause pyarthrosis.[82] For similar reasons, intra-articular pins, such as in the talus, should be avoided. Finally, pin sites become stable when motion is minimized at the soft tissue interface. Thus pins that are placed through a muscular compartment, such as the anterior compartment of the leg or lateral compartment of the thigh, may be at higher risk for soft tissue instability, infection, and loosening (Figure 10-6).[97] Aside from meticulous pin site placement, the technique for insertion should include predrilling, rather than self-drilling pins, to avoid problems with high temperature generation and bone necrosis.[26]

Recommendations for external fixation pin site postoperative care have been variable and the subject of extensive research.* Pin site infection is problematic and can lead to pin loosening, reduction loss, osteomyelitis, and systemic sepsis, frequently requiring pin removal. Major proposed causes of pin site complications include instability at the soft tissue–pin interface, inappropriate pin insertion sites, and technical errors related to insertion.[93,140,142] Egol et al. randomized 120 fractures around the wrist treated with external fixation, and found that hydrogen peroxide and chlorhexidine pin care regimens did not decrease the infection rate compared with no pin care.[55] Additionally, there was a relatively low incidence of pin tract infections requiring intervention. A recent Cochrane review reported on several randomized trials that evaluated various methods of cleansing, cleansing solutions, and dressings.[97] Based on the evidence in the data studied, no definitive recommendations could be made regarding pin site care. We believe that the vital factor for creation of a stable pin site is immediate immobilization of the surrounding soft tissues. Typically, rolled gauze (or similar foam pad) wrapped around the pin occupies the space between the pin and the bar, allowing for gentle axial compression and stabilization of the skin, achieving this goal.

Definitive treatment of open tibial fractures with external fixation has led to relatively high rates of infection (up to 15%), nonunion (3% to 11%), malunion (up to 36%), and pin tract infection (up to 50%).[7,54,73,78] Because external fixation is currently used much more frequently for provisional fixation than definitive treatment, conversion from external fixation to internal fixation is a critical issue. Several clinical series have indicated that if a tibial pin tract becomes infected, the pin should be removed and the infection treated until granulation occurs. Subsequent intramedullary nailing leads to a low infection rate.[101,156] These data confirm animal studies that indicate that treatment of infected pin sites with débridement and antibiotics can substantially reduce, but not eliminate, subsequent infections.[34] Conversely, other authors have suggested that the history of a pin site infection is a contraindication to subsequent intramedullary nailing.[102] Short periods of provisional external fixation appear to allow safe subsequent conversion to internal fixation.[3,16,111]

Internal Fixation
The primary focus of selection of skeletal fixation methods involves avoiding infection. The implants and insertion techniques utilized should be chosen with this in mind, and should minimize the risk of developing deep infection. For many years the concept of immediate application of internal fixation implants for open fracture stabilization was strongly discouraged.[31] The presence of metal within a wound is a foreign body that is a potential substrate for biofilm formation, with a theoretical increased risk for acute infection.[138,146] Additionally, the

*References 1,2,37,45,49,57,71,99,111,135.

potential bone devitalization required to apply an extramedullary implant was thought to contribute to development of infection. Nevertheless, following thorough wound débridement and irrigation, the benefits of internal skeletal stabilization and appropriate wound closure or coverage may outweigh the inherent infectious risks. Surface implants, such as plates and screws, and intramedullary implants have different implications on blood supply and must be considered separately.

Plates and Screws. Over the past 5 decades, improved metallurgy, surgical techniques, antibiotic therapy, and understanding of the pathophysiology of infection have led to the wide-spread use of immediate internal fixation of open fractures.[37,59,89] Several sentinel works have demonstrated acceptable infection rates.[11,23,31,32,59,84] Gustilo and Anderson, based on their experience of over 1000 fractures, suggested that converting an open fracture into a closed fracture provided the optimal biological environment to prevent contamination and infection.[3] In 1979 Chapman and Mahoney reported on 94 open fractures treated with internal fixation and delayed wound closure.[32] Type I wounds had an infection rate of 1.9%, nearly equivalent to the rate in closed fractures. Type II open fractures had an 8% infection rate, and Type III open wounds had a 41% infection rate. Subsequent studies focusing on ankle fractures[23,59,84] and tibial plateau fractures[11] have also shown low complication rates with protocols that included immediate plate fracture fixation. More recent clinical and in vitro data on locking plates indicates that infection rates in open fractures may be even lower than with standard compression plate devices.[58]

Several important caveats exist for minimizing complications with acute plate fixation of open fractures. First, prior to operative intervention, intravenous antistaphylococcal antibiotics should be administered as soon as possible in the emergency department. The open wound should be covered with a sterile dressing, and the fracture splinted. In the operating room, meticulous débridement should be performed, followed by wound irrigation. Surgical approaches for fracture fixation should be efficient and focused on minimizing periosteal stripping. Finally, the surgeon must ensure that the fracture reduction is anatomic, whether rigid compression fixation or bridge plating techniques are used.

Plates and screws may also be useful as a provisional reduction tool intraoperatively.[53] A central principle in open fracture treatment is exposure of the fracture ends for adequate débridement. After removal of debris, the fracture can be manipulated and reduced by indirect or direct methods, and a compression plate can be placed across the fracture for provisional stabilization. The anteromedial tibial surface is typically conducive to provisional plating and is exposed by the traumatic laceration or surgical extensions. Plates used in this fashion should be placed extraperiosteally to avoid further devascularization of bone (Figure 10-7). Screws should be unicortical (typically 8 to 10 mm in length) to avoid reamer interference. This can greatly facilitate and expedite the fixation portion of the procedure.[53]

Intramedullary Nails. The most common open fractures amenable to intramedullary nailing are tibial shaft fractures, and hence

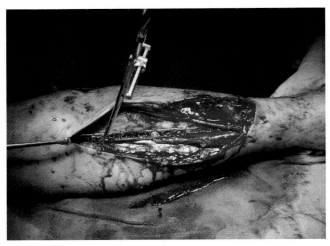

FIGURE 10-7 Example of a small fragment plate placed with unicortical screws for provisional stabilization of an open tibial fracture. The reduction is maintained during reaming and placement of an interlocking intramedullary nail.

they are the most extensively studied. Several decades ago traditional teaching was that intramedullary nailing, particularly with associated reaming, significantly damaged the osseous blood supply, and was ill-advised in open fractures.[9,34] The main concern with intramedullary stabilization of open diaphyseal, and some metaphyseal, fractures is contamination of the medullary canal. Chapman suggested in 1986 that "the vast majority of open fractures of the tibia should be treated with external fixation," based on the observation that infection rates with nailing were as high as 30%.[30] This led Bach and Hansen to randomize 59 high grade open tibial shaft fractures to external fixation or plate fixation.[7] Osteomyelitis occurred in 19% of those treated with plates and in 3% of those treated with external fixation, and these authors concluded that external fixation should be the treatment of choice in these injuries.

On the other hand, since then a plethora of animal and human studies have contributed to changing evidence-based practice patterns. In 1990 Court-Brown et al. reported a 1.6% infection rate in a large series of Type I open tibial shaft fractures treated with locked intramedullary nailing.[38] The same investigators also reported on a series of Type II and III open fractures treated similarly, and concluded that the infectious complication rate was similar for nailing and external fixation; however, less malalignment was noted following nailing.[39] Over the last 2 decades additional studies have directly compared definitive external fixation to locked intramedullary nailing of open tibial shaft fractures.[74,139] In general, external fixation has led to more secondary procedures, more malalignment, lower union rates, and delayed return to function compared to intramedullary nails, and no substantial decrease in infection rates. Currently we favor acute intramedullary nailing with limited reaming in nearly all open tibial shaft fractures, with the exception of those with deep, extensive contamination, vascular injury, or pre-existing deformity.

In addition to the presence of an intramedullary nail, whether reaming is used in the insertion technique has been studied extensively. Because of similar concerns of disseminating wound contamination along the entire diaphysis, unreamed nailing has been favored by some authors.[22] At the time of fracture both the endosteal and periosteal blood supply are injured.[126] In animal models reamed nailing has been shown to decrease cortical perfusion by a significantly greater degree compared with unreamed nailing.[91,137] The endosteal circulation recovers slowly, but a more acute "rebound effect" is seen with upregulation of the periosteal perfusion.[22,65] This effect has not led to healing differences in animal models.[136] With substantial traumatic periosteal stripping at the fracture, however, the endosteal vascular injury with reaming is a theoretical concern.[131] Although early clinical results of unreamed nailing were encouraging,[17,18,85,131] other studies have shown high rates of secondary procedures, malunions, and screw breakage rates.[141,164] "Limited" reaming, which limits cortical perfusion disruption but still allows the mechanical benefits of implant use afforded by reaming, may be an ideal compromise between biology and biomechanics.[64,80,81]

The benefits of reamed nailing for open fracture are several. Stimulation of the periosteal blood supply may enhance fracture healing. A larger diameter nail can be used, with larger interlocking bolts, improving the stability and fatigue characteristics during the prolonged healing time.[57,186] Moreover, reaming of the isthmus allows for a longer segment of nail–bone contact, which further augments mechanical stability and optimizes the ability of the implant to maintain the intraoperative reduction. In one of the first reports of reamed intramedullary nailing for open tibial fractures, Williams et al. reported a low complication rate, with a 2.4% nonunion and infection rate.[160] Thirty-three percent of fractures in this series were Type III. Subsequent prospective studies also showed this treatment method to be efficacious.[86] In a randomized trial of reamed versus unreamed nailing of open tibial fractures, Keating et al. demonstrated that reamed nailing allowed for a larger nail, had fewer hardware failures, and had no difference in union rates, infections, or functional outcomes.[87] These conclusions have been validated by additional data as well.[58,164]

Most recently, a multicenter, randomized trial of 1319 tibial fractures was conducted by the SPRINT study group.[13] Patients were randomized to either reamed or unreamed intramedullary nailing. Of the 406 open fractures, 29% of the reamed group and 24% of the unreamed group underwent a reoperation or had autodynamization in the first year, which was not statistically different ($P = 0.16$).

In open femoral shaft fractures, treatment has been less controversial. In a series of 89 open femur fractures, Brumback et al. reported no infections in Types I, II, or IIIA fractures.[27] Infection rate was 10% in Type IIIB fractures. These results were confirmed by subsequent authors.[8,110,112,128] The robust muscular envelope and vascular supply to the femur likely account for the safety of intramedullary nailing of open femoral shaft fractures.

Wound Closure and Coverage

After thorough débridement, irrigation, and skeletal stabilization of an open fracture, the method and timing of wound closure or coverage must be chosen. Because the most critical factor in achieving a good outcome is a complete mechanical débridement of contamination and necrotic tissue,[51,154] wound treatment should not be determined until after débridement is complete, lest the surgeon be biased during the tissue resection. Open fracture wounds comprise a wide spectrum of injury severity, and as such, the surgeon must be familiar with many different treatment methods.

Wounds without Skin Loss

Historically, delayed wound closure of wounds without skin loss has been espoused to limit the infection risk in open fractures.[11,32] This teaching is mainly derived from war settings, in which highly contaminated fractures led to a high rate of anaerobic infections and gas gangrene.[67,147] More recent support for delayed wound closure is based on a report of 27 patients from four decades ago who developed anaerobic infections.[24] These authors closed all open fracture wounds early, some in the emergency department. Many wounds were severely contaminated, some with fecal matter, and half with contaminated water. During subsequent débridements, abundant organic matter was identified within the wound in several cases because of inadequate initial débridement.

Delayed closure involves placing a sterile, nonadhesive dressing over the wound in the operating room. The wound is then left covered and sterile on the ward, and the patient is returned to the operating room 2 to 5 days later for repeat débridement and wound closure at that time. This prevents immediate sealing of the wound and potential containment of residual contamination or bacteria. The drawbacks of this approach are potential colonization of the wound with nosicomial bacteria skin edge retraction, delay in initiation of the healing response, and an additional anesthesia.[123]

Several studies, both prospective and retrospective in design, have evaluated the timing of closure of open fracture wounds (Table 10-3). In general, the recent trend in the literature indicates that meticulous débridement by an experienced surgeon followed by primary wound closure is safe in many circumstances. Delong et al. analyzed a series of open fractures of varying severity that were treated with primary closure after thorough débridement.[49] Of these, 75% of the Type IIIA fractures were treated with primary closure, and the overall deep infection rate was 7%, which was similar to those treated with delayed closure. Another recent comparative study found no difference in infection rates between open tibial shaft (Types I to IIIA) treated with either delayed or primary closure.[77] Most recently Rajaskeran et al. used strict criteria for primary wound closure and had minimal infectious or healing complications in Type III open fractures.[124]

We currently favor primary wound closure when skin loss is absent and closure is tension free, provided no specific contraindications exist. Reasons to perform delayed wound closure include the following: delayed presentation (>12 hours), delayed administration of intravenous antibiotics (>12 hours), deep seated contamination "ground in" to the bone, high risk of anaerobic contamination (farmyard injuries, fecal contamination, fresh water submersion), substantial neurovascular injuries, patient immunosuppression, or inability to achieve tension-free closure.

Wounds with Skin Loss

In the majority of open fractures, a substantial amount of skin does not need to be resected. Devitalized skin edges should be excised back to bleeding edges. Skin that is avulsed from its underlying subcutaneous tissue layers should be assessed for viability. Nonetheless, the principal risk of inadequate débridement includes retaining necrotic muscle and foreign debris, and

TABLE 10-3	Studies Analyzing the Effect of Wound Closure Timing on Complication Rate				

Study	Years(s)/Design	Fracture Grade (Number/Total)		Wound Closure	Infection Rate (%)	Delayed/Nonunion (%)
Gustilo and Anderson[66]	1961–1968/ Retrospective	III	(16/21)	Primary	7/16 (44)	—
		III	(5/21)	Delayed	1/5(20)	—
Gustilo and Anderson[66]	1969–1973/ Prospective	I	(78/326)	Primary	0	—
		II	(181/326)	Primary	2/181 (1)	—
		III	(67/326)	Delayed	6/67 (9)	—
Caudle and Stern[29]	1979–1983/ Retrospective	IIIA	(11/62)	—	0	3/11 (27)
		IIIB*	(24/62)	Flap in <1 wk	2/24 (8)	5/22 (23)
		IIIB†	(18/62)	Flap >1 wk or secondary intent	10/17 (59)‡	10/13 (77)
		IIIC§	(9/62)	—	4/7 (57)	5/5 (100)
Hope and Cole[79]	1981–1989/ Retrospective‖	I	(22/92)	Primary, 11	0	5/22 (23)
		II	(51/92)	Primary, 35	6/51 (12)	9/51 (18)
		III	(19/92)	Delayed, 14	4/19 (21)	8/19 (42)
Benson et al[12]	1983/Prospective	—¶		Primary, 44	3/44 (7) (all superficial)	—
		—		Delayed, 38	2/38 (5) (all deep)	—
Cullen et al[42]	1983–1993/ Retrospective‖	I	(24/83)	Primary, 20	0	—
		—		Delayed, 4	0	—
		II	(40/83)	Primary, 30	1/30 (3)	—
		—		Delayed, 10	0	—
		III	(19/83)	Primary, 7	1/7 (14)	—
		—		Delayed, 12	0	—
DeLong et al[49]	1984–1987/ Retrospective	I	(25/118)#	Primary, 22	0	1/22 (5)
		—		Delayed, 3	0	0
		II	(43/118)	Primary, 37	2/37 (5)	4/37 (11)
		—		Delayed, 6	0	2/6 (33)
		IIIA	(32/118)	Primary, 24	1/24 (4)	4/24 (17)
		—		Delayed, 8	1/8 (13)	2/8 (25)
		IIIB	(12/118)	Primary, 4	0	1/4 (25)
		—		Delayed, 8	1/8 (13)	3/8 (38)
		IIIC	(6/118)	Delayed, 6**	3/6 (50)	2/6 (33)

Secondary amputation required in *2/24 (85%), †4/17 (24%), §7/9 (78%), and **1/7 (14%).
‡ One patient required early amputation and was excluded from analysis.
‖ Pediatric population
¶ No grading indicated
* One additional patient in this series with a grade IIIc fracture and delayed wound closure had a primary below-knee amputation.
(From Weitz-Marshall AD, Bosse MJ. J Am Acad Orthop Surg 2002;10:379–84, with permission).

excessive skin resection should be avoided. Overzealous skin removal that commits a wound to a soft tissue coverage procedure may be associated with greater morbidity and cost than primary closure.[100] Nevertheless, open fracture wounds that are not able to be closed primarily occur frequently.

In this situation several options exist. The simplest method is for healing by secondary intention. This requires that no bone, tendons, or neurovascular structures are present in the wound bed. When the fascial layer can be closed, the wound can be treated with wet to dry dressings until granulation tissue forms and the wound becomes epithelialized. In wounds in which the fascial layer is incompetent, packing and healing by secondary intention can still be used. Gauze packings should be in place in all wound recesses to drain effluent fluid, but should not be packed tightly to avoid organization of a dead space cavity. As an alternative to wet-to-dry dressings, negative pressure vacuum-foam dressings are also very effective in minimizing wound edema and stimulating granulation tissue formation, which is a necessary first step in secondary intention wound healing.

Although secondary intention generally leads to reliable wound healing, this requires a significant amount of patient compliance and nursing assistance, and may not be feasible in large or deep wounds.

Another option is to perform "releasing," or "relaxing," incisions.[61,125] This technique involves creating a second linear incision to allow adequate mobility of the skin and subcutaneous layers to cover the devitalized and traumatized region. An adequate skin bridge must be maintained to avoid devascularization of the intervening tissue bridge. In anatomic regions with less tissue mobility, such as around the leg and ankle, frequently the "donor" region under the releasing incision requires skin grafting. When larger defects exist in regions of more restricted tissues, fasciocutaneous or rotational flaps should be considered.

Frequently, open wounds are too large or complex for closure or relaxing incisions, and a more reliable immediate postoperative dressing is reliable. Much research has been focused on the efficacy of antibiotic-eluting polymethyl methacrylate

(PMMA) cement or calcium salt-based cements. The concept of antibiotic-impregnated cement beads is that high local tissue concentrations of antibiotics are achieved (~200× that of systemic administration), and systemic levels, and subsequently systemic complications, are minimized.[44,151] Beads may be placed deep in a wound and the skin closed,[60] or alternatively a plastic adhesive may be placed over the beads and the open wound to create a "bead pouch." Antibiotic elution and local concentrations are highest during the initial several days,[20] and gradually decline over the next 1 to 2 months. During the elution period the cement substrate also achieves dead space management. In a defining clinical study, Ostermann et al. reported on 845 open fractures treated with adjunctive PMMA-antibiotic beads and found the method superior to open fractures with systemic antibiotics alone.[114] A report from the same institution concluded that the cost of antibiotic beads is justified when considering the costs of chronic osteomyelitis.[162] Moehring et al.[106] randomized a cohort of patients with open fractures to systemic versus local antibiotic treatment. No statistical difference was found, but the study was likely underpowered to demonstrate a difference in the low incidence outcome of infection. Calcium sulfate[103] and hydroxyapatite[163] have also been described as antibiotic carriers, but their use is mostly applicable in chronic situations with bony defects, with the aim of avoiding a secondary procedure for removal.

One of the most clinically important advances in the management of open fracture wounds has been the refinement and availability of vacuum-foam dressing (VFD) systems (e.g., VAC, KCI, San Antonio, TX). VFDs can be used as wound stabilization until granulation tissue forms and the wound heals by secondary intention, or more commonly, as a bridge between the primary procedure and the definitive soft tissue coverage. When secondary intention is chosen over soft tissue reconstruction, a VFD can stimulate and expedite granulation tissue formation.[76] Wound healing still requires multiple dressing changes and high patient compliance, and this is usually completed using a portable VFD as an outpatient.

The specific features of a wound that demand formal coverage have not been fully defined, and continue to evolve as experience with VFDs expands. DeFranzo et al. described a series of patients with exposed bone in lower extremity wounds.[46] VFD application led to profuse granulation tissue formation over the bone, and coverage was successful in 71 of 75 cases. VFDs have also been useful in cases with exposed orthopaedic implants in the wounds.[46,119]

On the other hand, some wounds may be too complex to allow the VFD to produce a stable granulation bed for secondary intention, and soft tissue coverage procedures are indicated. A VFD is often ideally suited for temporary wound coverage while awaiting definitive reconstruction. Advantages of this method include the ability to minimize dead space within the wound, decrease edema, and seal the wound from the nosocomial microbiology between débridement procedures and before definitive treatment. In most wounds with tissue loss or exposure deep to the fascial layers, we prefer definitive soft tissue reconstruction with free or local muscle coverage. Early plastic surgery consultation during presentation or initial débridement procedures is invaluable. We then typically place a VFD initially, followed by repeat débridement and VFD changes in the operating room every 48 to 72 hours until wounds coverage is performed.

Over the last several decades, beginning with the pioneering work of Godina,[62] the "fix and flap" principle for open lower extremity trauma was disseminated.[63] Many authors argued that definitive soft tissue coverage within 72 hours yielded the most reliable results and fewest complications. With the introduction of VFDs, which provided excellent wound management while awaiting definitive coverage, the next critical question was how interim VFD use affected the time between injury and definitive soft tissue coverage. Dedmond et al. used a temporary VFD in a series of 24 Type IIIB open tibia fractures for an average of 14 days.[45] Infection rate requiring surgery was 29% in this group, and the overall infection rate was similar to historical controls. Nonetheless, the authors did note a substantially lower rate of free tissue transfer than predicted following VFD use. Bhattacharyya et al. reviewed 38 Type IIIB open tibial shaft fractures, all treated with temporary VFD, and found a significantly higher infection rate in patients who had definitive coverage greater than 7 days from injury (57%) compared with those with earlier coverage (13%).[15]

The cellular mechanisms underlying the observed clinical effects of VFDs on wounds continue to be elucidated. Several theories have been proposed that may not be mutually exclusive. First, the subatmospheric pressure creates an environment of soft tissue microdeformation and strain in the range of 5% to 20%.[135] This mechanical milieu is stimulatory for cellular chemotaxis and proliferation, as well as neoangiogenesis, and the subsequent formation of granulation tissue.[94,99,104,107,155] Second, the suction effect is able to actively clear undesirable substances from the local injury zone, including interstitial edema, bacteria, and inflammatory mediators.[90,107,154] By reducing edema, oxygen and nutrient inflow is stimulated, and venous drainage is less impaired.[145] Decreasing the spike of local inflammatory mediator concentration may be a critical mechanism of VFDs. Mediators such as histamine and substance P increase capillary permeability and establish a vicious cycle of persistent edema, impaired microcirculatory perfusion, and ongoing necrosis and potential for infection. This has been termed wound "compartment syndrome," and a VFD may interrupt this sequence and allow for resuscitation of the zone of stasis (Figure 10-8).[108,153]

Additionally, the matrix of the overlying foam component appears to be integral to the VFD's success. If standard gauze is placed in a wound and sealed and connected to continuous subatmospheric pressure, cell apoptosis is greater and migration and proliferation are significantly less than with a reticulated open cell foam dressing.[104] Computer simulation models have determined that reticulated open cell foam leads to a repeated mosaic pattern of strain and microdeformation at the dressing–tissue interface, which may be a particularly important component of VFD systems.[158] As a result, the differences in the structural scaffold through which the suction is applied leads to activation of a divergent pathways of genes.[50]

An important caveat exists to the multitude of successful clinical reports of VFDs. The surgeon must not forget that despite the potential of new VFD technology, the cornerstone of open fracture wound management is still thorough wound exposure, exploration, débridement, and irrigation. Over the last few decades free tissue transfer for open fracture wounds has decreased consistently.[116] This may be due in part to improved understanding of wound care, advancing technology and tech-

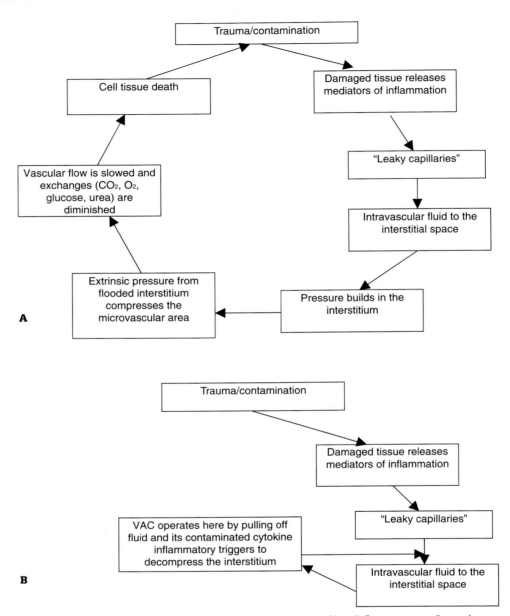

FIGURE 10-8 A. When cells/tissues are damaged, they release cytokines/inflammatory mediators that set in motion a cascade of events which may result in impaired exchange at the microcirculatory level resulting in further tissue necrosis/cellular death. **B.** NPWT/ROCF pulls the fluid from the interstitial space, actively evacuating the edema and its contained cytokines and mediators of inflammation. This decompresses the otherwise compressed interstitial space and thereby decompresses the extrinsic "push" on the microvascular space. The diminution of flow is thereby averted as is the diminution of exchange of O2, CO2, glucose, and urea. Cellular distress and secondary necrosis are thereby minimized. (Adapted from Webb LX, Pape HC. J Orthop Trauma 2008;22:S135–S137, with permission.)

niques, or a decreasing interest level of microvascular reconstructive surgeons.[98]

AUTHORS' PREFERRED TREATMENT

Patients are evaluated in correspondence with the Advanced Trauma Life Support recommendations. Antibiotics and tetanus are given as indicated by the injury and the patient's tetanus status. Awake patients with isolated open fractures

undergo a thorough history, physical, and imaging to guide initial management. Documentation of the examination and what portions could and could not be completed are essential. Limbs not already realigned in the field are realigned in the emergency department. Open wounds are covered and protected in anticipation of an imminent sterile débridement in the operative suite (Table 10-4). Obtunded patients, particularly those in extremis who may not be able to undergo emergent débridement, may undergo wound irrigation under clean conditions, with removal of gross debris, in the emergency department. This is performed only if there is an

TABLE 10-4	**Tenets of Débridement**

1. The wound should be extended until healthy tissue is encountered.

2. Working in a systematized or organized fashion from outside-to-inside and from one region of the wound to another, rather than in a random fashion, will likely ensure a more thorough débridement.

3. Realize that wounds may evolve, particularly in the setting of a dysvascularized limb. Have a low threshold for a repeat débridement if there is concern for further necrosis of tissues. Consider the plan for definitive skeletal fixation, as this may preclude gaining access to portions of the traumatized area. In select cases it may be more prudent to perform a temporizing procedure, such as external fixation, rather than intramedullary nailing to facilitate wound access. External fixation allows inspection of the soft tissues on the "other side" of the bone (e.g., the posterior compartments through an anterior wound), which can be obstructed if intramedullary nailing has been performed. Additionally the bone ends and the medullary canal can be reexamined if external fixation has been performed, which is not possible with a nail in place. After the wound has finished evolving, as determined by repeat débridements, definitive fixation may take place.

4. Fasciotomies should be used liberally. In many cases this will be required simply to visualize the injured muscle and as such is a normal part of the débridement process. Anticipate that edema will ensue from cell death and inflammation. Obtunded patients and those with splints may be difficult or impossible to examine appropriately for compartment syndrome.

5. Always look ahead to the next step. If using temporizing fracture or joint spanning external fixators, place pins remote from anticipated sites of incisions and implants to minimize risk of infection. Marking out these incisions prior to placing external fixator pins may be useful.

6. Because the external fixation pins are placed remote from the ends of major fracture fragments in anticipation of implants placed there, the frame may be somewhat mechanically impaired. Because spanning external fixation is typically a temporizing procedure, in contrast to definitive treatment with an external fixator, the stability provided is typically sufficient until more definitive stabilization can be performed.

7. One of the great benefits of temporary external fixators, sometimes called "travelling traction," is that it allows for re-establishment of appropriate length. Ensuring that this is achieved at the time of initial treatment obviates the need for this later at the time of definitive fixation, when it may be significantly more difficult.

8. Splinting of extremities around external fixators is often still necessary. This helps with out-of-plane (of the external fixator) displacement and provides additional support for the limb. In the case of a tibia that has been externally fixed, remember that some of the muscle bellies in the leg attach to tendon and bones in the foot, which may remain unstabilized and painful if not splinted.

9. If transfer of care is anticipated, speak with the surgeon who will assume responsibility for definitive care prior to any provisional treatment is performed, to ensure that initial treatment facilitates and does not complicate later procedures.

anticipated significant (>24 hour) delay until formal débridement. The surgeon must use his or her best judgment in this setting. The limb is splinted in a noncircumferential manner. If patient transfer prior to definitive treatment in anticipated, the importance of communication with the re-

ceiving surgeon cannot be overemphasized. Specific details of intraoperative findings, the disruption or integrity of specific anatomic structures, and what exactly was done can have significant subsequent treatment implications. Ideally, any additional or more invasive procedures should be discussed with the surgeon who will be devising the definitive treatment plan, to ensure initial procedures are not counterproductive.

COMPLICATIONS

Failure to appreciate and respect the extent of the soft tissue injury is the major cause of complications and poor outcomes for patients with open fractures. Open fractures, because of their exposure to the environment and periosteal stripping, are predisposed to a variety of complications. The management of these complications is complex because there are a multitude of factors that influence acute treatment. Failures of omission such as not recognizing a fracture as open may cause the fracture to be treated or débrided less aggressively, which may favor infection. Although the optimal timing for the treatment of open fractures remains a matter of controversy, timely débridement is still favored by most surgeons. Local factors such as bone or soft issue loss, vascular or nerve injury, or compartment syndrome may all influence the potential to complications.

Systemic factors are may also lead to. complications after open fractures. Open fractures are commonly seen in high energy mechanism and in polytraumatized patients. Such patients may have concomitant head, chest, or abdomen injuries in addition to multiple fractures. Such polytrauma puts the patient as risk for a systemic inflammatory response syndrome (SIRS), which may lead to acute respiratory distress syndrome (ARDS) and/or multisystem organ failure, which may lead to death. Lengthy initial procedures done on such polytraumatized patients may exacerbate this systemic inflammatory response. As such, the concept of damage control orthopaedics has arisen, in which acute interventions are limited to only necessary procedures (fasciotomies, irrigation and débridement, provisional stabilization) to minimize the surgical insult while stabilizing the patient and achieving skeletal stability. Complex and lengthy reconstructive procedures are reserved for days later, when the patient has been resuscitated.

Infectious complications are among those most associated with open fractures. A contamination rate of 65% has been reported, though the infection rate ranges from 0% to 2% for type I fractures, through 10% to 50% for type III fractures.[117] Any acute infection puts the patient at risk for systemic sepsis and/or chronic osteomyelitis. Immunocompromised patients (e.g., diabetic patients, organ transplant patients, those on systemic corticosteroids or with HIV) are also at increased risk for complications, particularly infection, after open fracture.[19] Malnourished patients may also be at risk.

Acute infection after fracture is characterized by pain, but edema and a draining wound is a common but not constant finding. White blood cell count, sedimentation rate and C-reactive protein levels are commonly elevated. Frankly infected wounds are treated with irrigation and débridement. It is generally prudent to obtain radiographs as part of the work up of an infected limb after open fracture. Radiographs may lend insight regarding whether the fixation construct remains stable or whether revision may be necessary. Also, foreign bodies, air, or radiolucencies in the bone may be visible. Fulminant infections that do not respond to irrigation and débridement and lead to sepsis may require amputation as a lifesaving measure. Controversy remains about whether to maintain stability and the existing fracture fixation construct in the face of infection or to remove any hardware that may harbor organisms in hopes of eradicating the infection.[52,95]

Chronic osteomyelitis may develop in 5% or less of open fractures. In this setting the patient may or may not have an elevated WBC and the ESR and C-reactive protein may not be as elevated as in an acute infection. The patient may have vague discomfort and more obvious signs of infection (edema, draining wounds) are commonly not present. Chronic osteomyelitis is typically treated with débridement of any and all infected and necrotic material and may require revision of previously reconstructed fractures. The metallic surfaces of fracture fixation implants may require removal as these offer a site for persistent microorganism colonization.

While urgent treatment of open fractures is the norm, there are instances when immediate treatment may not be indicated. Overly aggressively surgery, treating sick polytraumatized patients and those with poor soft tissues locally may predispose to poor outcomes. Remember that many of these high energy injuries are seen in polytraumatized patients who are not physiologically able to withstand extensive blood loss or time in the operative suite. The concept of damage control orthopaedics has emerged as a strategy for the treating the patient as a whole. Brief procedures that can aid in the patient's resuscitation through minimizing additional insult and decreasing the potential for a devastating systemic inflammatory response are indicated. These include débridements to decrease the load of organisms and necrotic material; external fixation of long bones, periarticular fractures, and unstable joints; and fasciotomies for tight muscle compartments. Performing only brief, safe procedures in the acute phase allows for better resuscitation of the patient as well as time for better preoperative planning of complex injuries.

Open fractures have been identified as a risk factor in the development of nonunion.[14] While the open fracture may have failed to unite due to an underlying infection, nonunion also occurs in the absence of infection and may be due to devascularization at the fracture site or failure to provide adequate mechanical stability at the fracture site. Nevertheless, occult infection should be suspected and investigated as a part of the workup in the treatment of nonunions. Nonunions may be characterized by pain at the fracture site and continued decreased function compared with preinjury.

Less obvious but no less important are the other causes for residual decrease in function after open fracture, which may be considered akin to complications. Soft tissue injury to muscle or tendons may lead to extensive scarring, loss of muscle excursion, and loss of joint motion. Tendon loss may lead to loss of specific joint motion and may be amenable to reconstructive tendon transfers. Similarly, nerve injuries that occur at the time of open fracture—which may be the direct result of a sharp fracture fragment lacerating the nerve or are more often the result of a tension or traction injury—may cause significant morbidity. Loss of sensation, decrease in sensation, change in sensation, or an area of hyperacute sensation may all occur.

Nerve injuries may also lead to significant motor deficits. Loss of protective sensation in the setting of a severe open fracture may influence the decision to amputate or attempt limb salvage in the setting of massive trauma.

Although full length orthogonal images of fractured limb segments are the goal before arrival in the operative suite, in certain cases this may be deferred. Patients with injuries to the abdomen, chest, head, or with dysvascular limbs who require emergent surgical treatment should not have such treatment delayed for extremity radiographs. These may be obtained in the operative suite using either fluoroscopy or portable x-ray machines.

Data and expert opinions have varied somewhat regarding the ideal timing for open fracture surgical treatment. We continue to treat open fractures as emergencies. Bacterial contamination and proliferation continues until surgical débridement is performed. In general, infection risk increases with time, although the development of infection is contingent upon multiple variables. It is left to the surgeon's judgment to determine whether to insist that a polytraumatized patient go to the operating room for emergent débridement, or whether it is more prudent for the patient to undergo further resuscitation prior to such treatment. The energy of the injury, the nature of the open wound, the type of contamination, the overall condition of the patient, underlying medical conditions, and the anticipated length of surgery and blood loss are all factors in this decision.

REFERENCES

1. Al-Arabi YB, Nader M, Hamidian-Jahromi AR, Woods DA. The effect of the timing of antibiotics and surgical treatment on infection rates in open long-bone fractures: a 9-year prospective study from a district general hospital. Injury 2007;38(8):900–905.
2. Anglen JO. Comparison of soap and antibiotic solutions for irrigation of lower-limb open fracture wounds. A prospective, randomized study. J Bone Joint Surg Am 2005l; 87(7):1415–1422.
3. Antich-Adrover P, Marti-Garin D, Murias-Alvarez J, Puente-Alonso C. External fixation and secondary intramedullary nailing of open tibial fractures. A randomised, prospective trial. J Bone Joint Surg Br 1997;79(3):433–437.
4. Artz CP, Sako Y, Scully RE. An evaluation of the surgeon's criteria for determining the viability of muscle during débridement. AMA Arch Surg. 1956;73(6):1031–1035.
5. Ashford RU, Mehta JA, Cripps R. Delayed presentation is no barrier to satisfactory outcome in the management of open tibial fractures. Injury 2004;35(4):411–416.
6. Aufranc OE, Jones WN, Bierbaum BE. Gas gangrene complicating fracture of the tibia. JAMA 1969;209(13):2045–2047.
7. Bach AW, Hansen ST, Jr. Plates versus external fixation in severe open tibial shaft fractures. A randomized trial. Clin Orthop Relat Res 1989 Apr(241):89–94.
8. Baixauli F, Sr., Baixauli EJ, Sanchez-Alepuz E, Baixauli F, Jr. Interlocked intramedullary nailing for treatment of open femoral shaft fractures. Clin Orthop Relat Res 1998 May(350):67–73.
9. Barei DP, Taitsman LA, Beingessner D, et al. Open diaphyseal long bone fractures: a reduction method using devitalized or extruded osseous fragments. J Orthop Trauma 2007;21(8):574–578.
10. Bednar DA, Parikh J. Effect of time delay from injury to primary management on the incidence of deep infection after open fractures of the lower extremities caused by blunt trauma in adults. J Orthop Trauma 1993;7(6):532–535.
11. Benirschke SK, Agnew SG, Mayo KA, et al. Immediate internal fixation of open, complex tibial plateau fractures: treatment by a standard protocol. J Orthop Trauma 1992;6(1): 78–86.
12. Benson DR, Riggins RS, Lawrence RM, et al. Treatment of open fractures: a prospective study. J Trauma 1983;23(1):25–30.
13. Bhandari M, Guyatt G, Tornetta P, 3rd, et al. Randomized trial of reamed and unreamed intramedullary nailing of tibial shaft fractures. J Bone Joint Surg Am 2008;90(12): 2567–2578.
14. Bhandari M, Tornetta P, 3rd, Sprague S, et al. Predictors of reoperation following operative management of fractures of the tibial shaft. J Orthop Trauma 2003;17(5): 353–361.
15. Bhattacharyya T, Mehta P, Smith M, Pomahac B. Routine use of wound vacuum-assisted closure does not allow coverage delay for open tibia fractures. Plast Reconstr Surg 2008;121(4):1263–1266.
16. Blachut PA, Meek RN, O'Brien PJ. External fixation and delayed intramedullary nailing of open fractures of the tibial shaft. A sequential protocol. J Bone Joint Surg Am 1990; 72(5):729–735.
17. Bonatus T, Olson SA, Lee S, Chapman MW. Nonreamed locking intramedullary nailing for open fractures of the tibia. Clin Orthop Relat Res 1997 Jun(339):58–64.
18. Bone LB, Kassman S, Stegemann P, France J. Prospective study of union rate of open

tibial fractures treated with locked, unreamed intramedullary nails. J Orthop Trauma 1994;8(1):45–49.

19. Bowen TR, Widmaier JC. Host classification predicts infection after open fracture. Clin Orthop Relat Res 2005 Apr(433):205–211.

20. Bowyer GW, Cumberland N. Antibiotic release from impregnated pellets and beads. J Trauma 1994;36(3):331–335.

21. Boyd JI, 3rd, Wongworawat MD. High-pressure pulsatile lavage causes soft tissue damage. Clin Orthop Relat Res 2004 Oct(427):13–17.

22. Boynton MD, Schmeling GJ. Nonreamed intramedullary nailing of open tibial fractures. J Am Acad Orthop Surg 1994;2(2):107–114.

23. Bray TJ, Endicott M, Capra SE. Treatment of open ankle fractures. Immediate internal fixation versus closed immobilization and delayed fixation. Clin Orthop Relat Res 1989 Mar(240):47–52.

24. Brown PW, Kinman PB. Gas gangrene in a metropolitan community. J Bone Joint Surg Am 1974;56(7):1445–1451.

25. Brown PW, Urban JG. Early weight-bearing treatment of open fractures of the tibia. An end-result study of 63 cases. J Bone Joint Surg Am 1969;51(1):59–75.

26. Browner BD. Pitfalls in the management of open fractures with Hoffmann external fixation. Ann Chir Gynaecol 1983;72(6):303–307.

27. Brumback RJ, Ellison PS, Jr., Poka A, et al. Intramedullary nailing of open fractures of the femoral shaft. J Bone Joint Surg Am 1989;71(9):1324–1331.

28. Castillo RC, Bosse MJ, MacKenzie EJ, Patterson BM. Impact of smoking on fracture healing and risk of complications in limb-threatening open tibia fractures. J Orthop Trauma 2005;19(3):151–157.

29. Caudle RJ, Stern PJ. Severe open fractures of the tibia. J Bone Joint Surg Am 1987; 69(6):801–807.

30. Chapman MW. The role of intramedullary fixation in open fractures. Clin Orthop Relat Res 1986 Nov(212):26–34.

31. Chapman MW. The use of immediate internal fixation in open fractures. Orthop Clin North Am 1980;11(3):579–591.

32. Chapman MW, Mahoney M. The role of early internal fixation in the management of open fractures. Clin Orthop Relat Res 1979 Jan-Feb(138):120–131.

33. Charalambous CP, Siddique I, Zenios M, et al. Early versus delayed surgical treatment of open tibial fractures: effect on the rates of infection and need of secondary surgical procedures to promote bone union. Injury 2005;36(5):656–661.

34. Clasper JC, Stapley SA, Bowley DM, et al. Spread of infection, in an animal model, after intramedullary nailing of an infected external fixator pin track. J Orthop Res 2001; 19(1):155–159.

35. Coester LM, Nepola JV, Allen J, Marsh JL. The effects of silver coated external fixation pins. Iowa Orthop J 2006;26:48–53.

36. Cooney WP, 3rd, Fitzgerald RH, Jr., Dobyns JH, Washington JA, 2nd. Quantitative wound cultures in upper extremity trauma. J Trauma 1982;22(2):112–117.

37. Copeland CX, Jr., Enneking WF. Incidence of Osteomyelitis in Compound Fractures. Am Surg 1965;31:156–158.

38. Court-Brown CM, Christie J, McQueen MM. Closed intramedullary tibial nailing. Its use in closed and type I open fractures. J Bone Joint Surg Br 1990;72(4):605–611.

39. Court-Brown CM, McQueen MM, Quaba AA, Christie J. Locked intramedullary nailing of open tibial fractures. J Bone Joint Surg Br 1991;73(6):959–964.

40. Cramer KE, Limbird TJ, Green NE. Open fractures of the diaphysis of the lower extremity in children. Treatment, results, and complications. J Bone Joint Surg Am 1992; 74(2):218–232.

41. Crowley DJ, Kanakaris NK, Giannoudis PV. Débridement and wound closure of open fractures: the impact of the time factor on infection rates. Injury 2007;38(8):879–889.

42. Cullen MC, Roy DR, Crawford AH, et al. Open fracture of the tibia in children. J Bone Joint Surg Am 1996;78(7):1039–1047.

43. Davies R, Holt N, Nayagam S. The care of pin sites with external fixation. J Bone Joint Surg Br 2005;87(5):716–719.

44. Decoster TA, Bozorgnia S. Antibiotic beads. J Am Acad Orthop Surg 2008;16(11): 674–678.

45. Dedmond BT, Kortesis B, Punger K, et al. The use of negative-pressure wound therapy (NPWT) in the temporary treatment of soft-tissue injuries associated with high-energy open tibial shaft fractures. J Orthop Trauma 2007;21(1):11–17.

46. DeFranzo AJ, Argenta LC, Marks MW, et al. The use of vacuum-assisted closure therapy for the treatment of lower-extremity wounds with exposed bone. Plast Reconstr Surg 2001;108(5):1184–1191.

47. DeJong ES, DeBerardino TM, Brooks DE, et al. Antimicrobial efficacy of external fixator pins coated with a lipid stabilized hydroxyapatite/chlorhexidine complex to prevent pin tract infection in a goat model. J Trauma 2001;50(6):1008–1014.

48. Dellinger EP, Caplan ES, Weaver LD, et al. Duration of preventive antibiotic administration for open extremity fractures. Arch Surg 1988;123(3):333–339.

49. DeLong WG, Jr., Born CT, Wei SY, et al. Aggressive treatment of 119 open fracture wounds. J Trauma 1999;46(6):1049–1054.

50. Derrick KL, Norbury K, Kieswetter K, et al. Comparative analysis of global gene expression profiles between diabetic rat wounds treated with vacuum-assisted closure therapy, moist wound healing or gauze under suction. Int Wound J 2008;5(5):615–624.

51. Dickson KF, Hoffman WY, Delgado ED, Contreras DM. Unreamed rod with early wound closure for grade IIIA and IIIB open tibial fractures: analysis of 40 consecutive patients. Orthopedics 1998;21(5):531–535.

52. Dunbar RP, Jr. Treatment of infection after fracture fixation. Opinion: retain stable implant and suppress infection until union. J Orthop Trauma 2007;21(7):503–505.

53. Dunbar RP, Nork SE, Barei DP, Mills WJ. Provisional plating of Type III open tibia fractures prior to intramedullary nailing. J Orthop Trauma 2005;19(6):412–414.

54. Edwards CC, Simmons SC, Browner BD, Weigel MC. Severe open tibial fractures. Results treating 202 injuries with external fixation. Clin Orthop Relat Res 1988 May(230):98–115.

55. Egol KA, Paksima N, Puopolo S, et al. Treatment of external fixation pins about the wrist: a prospective, randomized trial. J Bone Joint Surg Am 2006;88(2):349–354.

56. Eijer H, Hauke C, Arens S, et al. PC-Fix and local infection resistance—influence of implant design on postoperative infection development, clinical and experimental results. Injury 2001;32(Suppl 2):B38–43.

57. Fairbank AC, Thomas D, Cunningham B, et al. Stability of reamed and unreamed intramedullary tibial nails: a biomechanical study. Injury 1995;26(7):483–485.

58. Finkemeier CG, Schmidt AH, Kyle RF, et al. A prospective, randomized study of intra-

medullary nails inserted with and without reaming for the treatment of open and closed fractures of the tibial shaft. J Orthop Trauma 2000;14(3):187–193.

59. Franklin JL, Johnson KD, Hansen ST, Jr. Immediate internal fixation of open ankle fractures. Report of 38 cases treated with a standard protocol. J Bone Joint Surg Am 1984;66(9):1349–1356.

60. Gardner MJ, Mehta S, Barei DP, Nork SE. Treatment protocol for open AO/OTA type C3 pilon fractures with segmental bone loss. J Orthop Trauma 2008;22(7):451–457.

61. Ger R. The management of open fracture of the tibia with skin loss. J Trauma 1970; 10(2):112–121.

62. Godina M. Early microsurgical reconstruction of complex trauma of the extremities. Plast Reconstr Surg 1986;78(3):285–292.

63. Gopal S, Majumder S, Batchelor AG, et al. Fix and flap: the radical orthopaedic and plastic treatment of severe open fractures of the tibia. J Bone Joint Surg Br 2000;82(7): 959–966.

64. Grundnes O, Utvag SE, Reikeras O. Effects of graded reaming on fracture healing. Blood flow and healing studied in rat femurs. Acta Orthop Scand 1994;65(1):32–36.

65. Grundnes O, Utvag SE, Reikeras O. Restoration of bone flow following fracture and reaming in rat femora. Acta Orthop Scand 1994;65(2):185–190.

66. Gustilo RB, Anderson JT. Prevention of infection in the treatment of 1025 open fractures of long bones: retrospective and prospective analyses. J Bone Joint Surg Am 1976; 58(4):453–458.

67. Hampton OP, Jr. Basic principles in management of open fractures. J Am Med Assoc 1955;159(5):417–419.

68. Harvey EJ, Agel J, Selznick HS, et al. Deleterious effect of smoking on healing of open tibia-shaft fractures. Am J Orthop 2002;31(9):518–521.

69. Harwood PJ, Giannoudis PV, Probst C, et al. The risk of local infective complications after damage control procedures for femoral shaft fracture. J Orthop Trauma 2006; 20(3):181–189.

70. Hauser CJ, Adams CA, Jr., Eachempati SR. Surgical Infection Society guideline: prophylactic antibiotic use in open fractures: an evidence-based guideline. Surg Infect (Larchmt) 2006;7(4):379–405.

71. Heier KA, Infante AF, Walling AK, Sanders RW. Open fractures of the calcaneus: soft-tissue injury determines outcome. J Bone Joint Surg Am 2003;85-A(12):2276–2282.

72. Heitmann C, Patzakis MJ, Tetsworth KD, Levin LS. Musculoskeletal sepsis: principles of treatment. Instr Course Lect 2003;52:733–743.

73. Henley MB, Chapman JR, Agel J, et al. Treatment of type II, IIIA, and IIIB open fractures of the tibial shaft: a prospective comparison of unreamed interlocking intramedullary nails and half-pin external fixators. J Orthop Trauma 1998;12(1):1–7.

74. Henry AK. Extensile Exposure. Edinburgh: E & S Livingstone, 1952.

75. Henry SL, Ostermann PA, Seligson D. The antibiotic bead pouch technique. The management of severe compound fractures. Clin Orthop Relat Res 1993 Oct(295):54–62.

76. Herscovici D, Jr., Sanders RW, Scaduto JM, et al. Vacuum-assisted wound closure (VAC therapy) for the management of patients with high-energy soft tissue injuries. J Orthop Trauma 2003;17(10):683–638.

77. Hohmann E, Tetsworth K, Radziejowski MJ, Wiesniewski TF. Comparison of delayed and primary wound closure in the treatment of open tibial fractures. Arch Orthop Trauma Surg 2007;127(2):131–136.

78. Holbrook JL, Swiontkowski MF, Sanders R. Treatment of open fractures of the tibial shaft: ender nailing versus external fixation. A randomized, prospective comparison. J Bone Joint Surg Am 1989;71(8):1231–1238.

79. Hope PG, Cole WG. Open fractures of the tibia in children. J Bone Joint Surg Br 1992; 74(4):546–553.

80. Hupel TM, Aksenov SA, Schemitsch EH. Effect of limited and standard reaming on cortical bone blood flow and early strength of union following segmental fracture. J Orthop Trauma 1998;12(6):400–406.

81. Hupel TM, Weinberg JA, Aksenov SA, Schemitsch EH. Effect of unreamed, limited reamed, and standard reamed intramedullary nailing on cortical bone porosity and new bone formation. J Orthop Trauma 2001;15(1):18–27.

82. Hyman J, Moore T. Anatomy of the distal knee joint and pyarthrosis following external fixation. J Orthop Trauma 1999;13(4):241–246.

83. Jeray KJ, Banks DM, Phieffer LS, et al. Evaluation of standard surgical preparation performed on superficial dermal abrasions. J Orthop Trauma 2000;14(3):206–211.

84. Johnson EE, Davlin LB. Open ankle fractures. The indications for immediate open reduction and internal fixation. Clin Orthop Relat Res 1993 Jul(292):118–127.

85. Kakar S, Tornetta P, 3rd. Open fractures of the tibia treated by immediate intramedullary tibial nail insertion without reaming: a prospective study. J Orthop Trauma 2007; 21(3):153–157.

86. Keating JF, O'Brien PI, Blachut PA, et al. Reamed interlocking intramedullary nailing of open fractures of the tibia. Clin Orthop Relat Res 1997 May(338):182–191.

87. Keating JF, O'Brien PJ, Blachut PA, et al. Locking intramedullary nailing with and without reaming for open fractures of the tibial shaft. A prospective, randomized study. J Bone Joint Surg Am 1997;79(3):334–341.

88. Keese GR, Boody AR, Wongworawat MD, Jobe CM. The accuracy of the saline load test in the diagnosis of traumatic knee arthrotomies. J Orthop Trauma 2007;21(7): 442–443.

89. Ketenjian AY, Shelton ML. Primary internal fixation of open fractures: a retrospective study of the use of metallic internal fixation in fresh open fractures. J Trauma 1972; 12(9):756–763.

90. Kilpadi DV, Bower CE, Reade CC, et al. Effect of vacuum-assisted closure therapy on early systemic cytokine levels in a swine model. Wound Repair Regen 2006;14(2): 210–215.

91. Klein MP, Rahn BA, Frigg R, Kessler S, Perren SM. Reaming versus nonreaming in medullary nailing: interference with cortical circulation of the canine tibia. Arch Orthop Trauma Surg 1990;109(6):314–316.

92. Krantz BE. Advanced Trauma Life Support (ATLS) for Doctors. 6th Ed. Chicago: American College of Surgeons, 1997.

93. Kroll JA. The use of the 'fixateur externe' in infected fractures. Arch Chir Neerl 1973; 25(2):137–149.

94. Labler L, Rancan M, Mica L, et al. Vacuum-assisted closure therapy increases local interleukin-8 and vascular endothelial growth factor levels in traumatic wounds. J Trauma 2009;66(3):749–757.

95. Leduc S, Ricci WM. Treatment of infection after fracture fixation. Opinion: two-stage

protocol: treatment of nonunion after treatment of infection. J Orthop Trauma 2007; 21(7):505–506.
96. Lee J. Efficacy of cultures in the management of open fractures. Clin Orthop Relat Res 1997 Jun(339):71–75.
97. Lethaby A, Temple J, Santy J. Pin site care for preventing infections associated with external bone fixators and pins. Cochrane Database Syst Rev 2008(4):CD004551.
98. Levin LS. Early versus delayed closure of open fractures. Injury 2007;38(8):896–899.
99. Li XY, Li WZ, Li YJ, et al. [The influence of vacuum-assisted drainage on the growth of capillaries in the wound produced by explosion in pig]. Zhonghua Shao Shang Za Zhi 2007;23(4):292–295.
100. Marek DJ, Copeland GE, Zlowodzki M, Cole PA. The application of dermatotraction for primary skin closure. Am J Surg 2005;190(1):123–126.
101. Marshall PD, Saleh M, Douglas DL. Risk of deep infection with intramedullary nailing following the use of external fixators. J R Coll Surg Edinb 1991;36(4):268–271.
102. Maurer DJ, Merkow RL, Gustilo RB. Infection after intramedullary nailing of severe open tibial fractures initially treated with external fixation. J Bone Joint Surg Am 1989; 71(6):835–838.
103. McKee MD, Wild LM, Schemitsch EH, Waddell JP. The use of an antibiotic-impregnated, osteoconductive, bioabsorbable bone substitute in the treatment of infected long bone defects: early results of a prospective trial. J Orthop Trauma 2002;16(9):622–627.
104. McNulty AK, Schmidt M, Feeley T, Kieswetter K. Effects of negative pressure wound therapy on fibroblast viability, chemotactic signaling, and proliferation in a provisional wound (fibrin) matrix. Wound Repair Regen 2007;15(6):838–846.
105. Merritt K. Factors increasing the risk of infection in patients with open fractures. J Trauma 1988;28(6):823–827.
106. Moehring HD, Gravel C, Chapman MW, Olson SA. Comparison of antibiotic beads and intravenous antibiotics in open fractures. Clin Orthop Relat Res 2000 Mar(372): 254–261.
107. Morykwas MJ, Argenta LC, Shelton-Brown EI, McGuirt W. Vacuum-assisted closure: a new method for wound control and treatment: animal studies and basic foundation. Ann Plast Surg 1997;38(6):553–562.
108. Morykwas MJ, David LR, Schneider AM, et al. Use of subatmospheric pressure to prevent progression of partial-thickness burns in a swine model. J Burn Care Rehabil 1999;20(1 Pt 1):15–21.
109. Neuhoff D, Thompson RE, Frauchiger VM, et al. Anodic plasma chemical treatment of titanium Schanz screws reduces pin loosening. J Orthop Trauma 2005;19(8):543–550.
110. Noumi T, Yokoyama K, Ohtsuka H, et al. Intramedullary nailing for open fractures of the femoral shaft: evaluation of contributing factors on deep infection and nonunion using multivariate analysis. Injury 2005;36(9):1085–1093.
111. Nowotarski PJ, Turen CH, Brumback RJ, Scarboro JM. Conversion of external fixation to intramedullary nailing for fractures of the shaft of the femur in multiply injured patients. J Bone Joint Surg Am 2000;82(6):781–788.
112. O'Brien PJ, Meek RN, Powell JN, Blachut PA. Primary intramedullary nailing of open femoral shaft fractures. J Trauma 1991;31(1):113–116.
113. Olson SA, Schemitsch EH. Open fractures of the tibial shaft: an update. Instr Course Lect 2003;52:623–631.
114. Ostermann PA, Seligson D, Henry SL. Local antibiotic therapy for severe open fractures. A review of 1085 consecutive cases. J Bone Joint Surg Br 1995;77(1):93–97.
115. Pape HC, Webb LX. History of open wound and fracture treatment. J Orthop Trauma 2008;22(10 Suppl):S133–134.
116. Parrett BM, Matros E, Pribaz JJ, Orgill DP. Lower extremity trauma: trends in the management of soft-tissue reconstruction of open tibia-fibula fractures. Plast Reconstr Surg 2006;117(4):1315–1322; discussion 23–24.
117. Patzakis MJ, Harvey JP, Jr., Ivler D. The role of antibiotics in the management of open fractures. J Bone Joint Surg Am 1974;56(3):532–541.
118. Patzakis MJ, Wilkins J. Factors influencing infection rate in open fracture wounds. Clin Orthop Relat Res 1989 Jun(243):36–40.
119. Pelham FR, Kubiak EN, Sathappan SS, Di Cesare PE. Topical negative pressure in the treatment of infected wounds with exposed orthopaedic implants. J Wound Care 2006; 15(3):111–116.
120. Petrisor B, Jeray K, Schemitsch E, et al. Fluid lavage in patients with open fracture wounds (FLOW): an international survey of 984 surgeons. BMC Musculoskelet Disord 2008;9:7.
121. Pietsch J, Meakins JL. Complications of povidone-iodine absorption in topically treated burn patients. Lancet 1976;1:280–282.
122. Prokuski L. Prophylactic antibiotics in orthopaedic surgery. J Am Acad Orthop Surg 2008;16(5):283–293.
123. Rajasekaran S. Early versus delayed closure of open fractures. Injury 2007;38(8): 890–895.
124. Rajasekaran S, Dheenadhayalan J, Babu JN, et al. Immediate primary skin closure in type-III A and B open fractures: results after a minimum of 5 years. J Bone Joint Surg Br 2009;91(2):217–224.
125. Reckling FW, Roberts MD. Primary closure of open fractures of the tibia and fibula by fibular fixation and relaxing incisions. J Trauma 1970;10(10):853–866.
126. Rhinelander FW. Tibial blood supply in relation to fracture healing. Clin Orthop Relat Res 1974 Nov-Dec(105):34–81.
127. Robson MC, Duke WF, Krizek TJ. Rapid bacterial screening in the treatment of civilian wounds. J Surg Res 1973;14(5):426–430.
128. Rutter JE, de Vries LS, van der Werken C. Intramedullary nailing of open femoral shaft fractures. Injury 1994;25(7):419–422.
129. Salter RB, Field P. The effects of continuous compression on living articular cartilage: an experimental investigation. J Bone Joint Surg Am 1960;42:31–90.
130. Salter RB, Simmonds DF, Malcolm BW, et al. The biological effect of continuous passive motion on the healing of full-thickness defects in articular cartilage. An experimental investigation in the rabbit. J Bone Joint Surg Am 1980;62(8):1232–1251.
131. Sanders R, Jersinovich I, Anglen J, et al. The treatment of open tibial shaft fractures using an interlocked intramedullary nail without reaming. J Orthop Trauma 1994; 8(6):504–510.
132. Sarmiento A, Horowitch A, Aboulafia A, et al. Functional bracing for comminuted extra-articular fractures of the distal third of the humerus. J Bone Joint Surg Br 1990; 72(2):283–287.
133. Sarmiento A, Latta LL. Functional fracture bracing. J Am Acad Orthop Surg 1999;7(1): 66–75.
134. Saw A, Chan CK, Penafort R, Sengupta S. A simple practical protocol for care of metal-skin interface of external fixation. Med J Malaysia 2006;61(Suppl A):62–65.
135. Saxena V, Hwang CW, Huang S, et al. Vacuum-assisted closure: microdeformations of wounds and cell proliferation. Plast Reconstr Surg 2004;114(5):1086–1096; discussion 97–98.
136. Schemitsch EH, Kowalski MJ, Swiontkowski MF, et al. Comparison of the effect of reamed and unreamed locked intramedullary nailing on blood flow in the callus and strength of union following fracture of the sheep tibia. J Orthop Res 1995;13(3): 382–389.
137. Schemitsch EH, Kowalski MJ, Swiontkowski MF, et al. Cortical bone blood flow in reamed and unreamed locked intramedullary nailing: a fractured tibia model in sheep. J Orthop Trauma 1994;8(5):373–382.
138. Schmidt AH, Swiontkowski MF. Pathophysiology of infections after internal fixation of fractures. J Am Acad Orthop Surg 2000;8(5):285–291.
139. Shannon FJ, Mullett H, O'Rourke K. Unreamed intramedullary nail versus external fixation in grade III open tibial fractures. J Trauma 2002;52(4):650–654.
140. Sims M, Saleh M. Protocols for the care of external fixator pin sites. Prof Nurse 1996; 11(4):261–264.
141. Singer RW, Kellam JF. Open tibial diaphyseal fractures. Results of unreamed locked intramedullary nailing. Clin Orthop Relat Res 1995 Jun(315):114–118.
142. Sisk TD. General principles and techniques of external skeletal fixation. Clin Orthop Relat Res 1983 Nov(180):96–100.
143. Skjeldal S, Stromsoe K, Alho A, et al. Acute compartment syndrome: for how long can muscle tolerate increased tissue pressure? Eur J Surg 1992;158(8):437–438.
144. Spencer J, Smith A, Woods D. The effect of time delay on infection in open long-bone fractures: a 5-year prospective audit from a district general hospital. Ann R Coll Surg Engl 2004;86(2):108–112.
145. Tarkin IS. The versatility of negative pressure wound therapy with reticulated open cell foam for soft tissue management after severe musculoskeletal trauma. J Orthop Trauma 2008;22(10 Suppl):S146–151.
146. Trampuz A, Zimmerli W. Diagnosis and treatment of infections associated with fracture-fixation devices. Injury 2006;37(Suppl 2):S59–66.
147. Trueta J. "Closed" treatment of war fractures. Lancet 1939;1:1452–1455.
148. Tscherne H. The Management of Open Fractures. Fractures with Soft Tissue Injuries. New York: Springer-Verlag, 1984.
149. Turen CH, Burgess AR, Vanco B. Skeletal stabilization for tibial fractures associated with acute compartment syndrome. Clin Orthop Relat Res 1995 Jun(315):163–168.
150. Valenziano CP, Chattar-Cora D, O'Neill A, et al. Efficacy of primary wound cultures in long bone open extremity fractures: are they of any value? Arch Orthop Trauma Surg 2002;122(5):259–261.
151. Wahlig H, Dingeldein E, Bergmann R, Reuss K. The release of gentamicin from polymethylmethacrylate beads. An experimental and pharmacokinetic study. J Bone Joint Surg Br 1978;60-B(2):270–275.
152. Wangensteen OH, Wangensteen SD. The Rise of Surgery from Empiric Craft to Scientific Discipline. Minneapolis: University of Minnesota Press, 1978.
153. W-Dahl A, Toksvig-Larsen S. Pin site care in external fixation sodium chloride or chlorhexidine solution as a cleansing agent. Arch Orthop Trauma Surg 2004;124(8): 555–558.
154. W-Dahl A, Toksvig-Larsen S, Lindstrand A. No difference between daily and weekly pin site care: a randomized study of 50 patients with external fixation. Acta Orthop Scand 2003;74(6):704–708.
155. Webb LX, Dedmond B, Schlatterer D, et al. The contaminated high-energy open fracture: a protocol to prevent and treat inflammatory mediator storm-induced soft-tissue compartment syndrome (IMSICS). J Am Acad Orthop Surg 2006;14(10 Spec No.): S82–86.
156. Webb LX, Pape HC. Current thought regarding the mechanism of action of negative pressure wound therapy with reticulated open cell foam. J Orthop Trauma 2008;22(10 Suppl):S135–137.
157. Weitz-Marshall AD, Bosse MJ. Timing of closure of open fractures. J Am Acad Orthop Surg 2002;10(6):379–384.
158. Wheelwright EF, Court-Brown CM. Primary external fixation and secondary intramedullary nailing in the treatment of tibial fractures. Injury 1992;23(6):373–376.
159. Whittle AP, Wester W, Russell TA. Fatigue failure in small diameter tibial nails. Clin Orthop Relat Res 1995 Jun(315):119–128.
160. Wilkes R, Zhao Y, Kieswetter K, et al. Effects of dressing type on 3D tissue microdeformations during negative pressure wound therapy: a computational study. J Biomech Eng 2009;131(3):031012.
161. Wilkins J, Patzakis M. Choice and duration of antibiotics in open fractures. Orthop Clin North Am 1991;22(3):433–437.
162. Williams MM, Askins V, Hinkes EW, et al. Primary reamed intramedullary nailing of open femoral shaft fractures. Clin Orthop Relat Res 1995 Sep(318):182–190.
163. Worlock P. The prevention of infection in open fractures. In: Bunker TD, Colton CL, Webb JK, eds. Frontiers in Fracture Management. Cambridge: Cambridge University Press, 1989.
164. Wright BA, Roberts CS, Seligson D, et al. Cost of antibiotic beads is justified: a study of open fracture wounds and chronic osteomyelitis. J Long Term Eff Med Implants 2007;17(3):181–185.
165. Zamora JL, Price MF, Chuang PI, et al. Inhibition of povidone-iodine's bactericidal activity by common organic substances: an experimental study. Surgery 1985;98: 25–29.
166. Zelken J, Wanich T, Gardner M, et al. PMMA is superior to hydroxyapatite for colony reduction in induced osteomyelitis. Clin Orthop Relat Res 2007;462:190–194.
167. Ziran BH, Darowish M, Klatt BA, et al. Intramedullary nailing in open tibia fractures: a comparison of two techniques. Int Orthop 2004;28(4):235–238.

11

GUNSHOT AND WARTIME INJURIES

Paul J. Dougherty and Soheil Najibi

INTRODUCTION

Gunshot injuries remain a significant part of the workload for some urban trauma centers in the United States and are also common in war-torn regions throughout the world. The purpose of this chapter is to review the epidemiology, pathophysiology, and treatment of gunshot wounds and war injuries. This chapter is intended not only to help those who evaluate gunshot wounds as a major part of their practice but also orthopaedic surgeons who occasionally see patients with such injuries.

NONMILITARY AND MILITARY WEAPONS

Weapons that are used in nonmilitary and military settings differ. Firearms seen in nonmilitary settings include handguns,

rifles, and shotguns.[7,35,83,84,141] Conventional military weapons can be divided into the categories of small arms and explosive munitions. *Small arms* consist of pistols, rifles, and machine guns. *Explosive munitions* consist of artillery, grenades, bombs, mortars, and land mines. Armored vehicle crew casualties represent a special subgroup of injuries seen in those who work and fight in and around armored vehicles.

Small Arms

Small arms are weapons that fire a bullet from a rifled barrel to a target. The bullet is usually contained in a cartridge consisting of powder, a primer, and a cartridge case all in one unit (Fig. 11-1). Handguns and rifles are classified by the diameter (size) of the barrel (9 mm, 0.45 inch, 7.62 mm). Handguns used by the military are the same as used those by civilian police

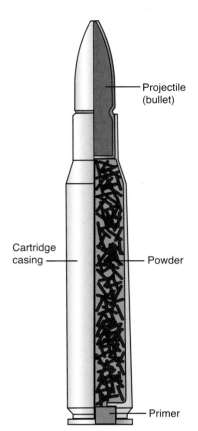

FIGURE 11-1 Schematic drawing of a cartridge. An entire cartridge is made up of the cartridge case, the bullet, a primer, and powder. When struck, the primer initiates powder burning, generating the pressure to propel the bullet in flight.

and others in regard to size, shape, and caliber. They are usually semiautomatic, which means a bullet is fired every time the trigger is pulled and as long as there is ammunition in the weapon's magazine.[7,35,83]

Handguns are the most common firearms associated with nonmilitary injuries. A handgun is intended to be fired over a short range and is small. Two types of handguns are most commonly seen: pistols and revolvers (Fig. 11-2A). A pistol has a magazine that contains cartridges, which are fed (or *cycled*) into the barrel every time the trigger is pulled (Fig. 11-2B). Revolvers contain cylinders with chambers that contain cartridges. The cylinder rotates so that a cartridge is aligned to the barrel when the trigger is pulled.[83,141]

Rifles are shoulder-fired weapons that are intended to strike a target farther away from the shooter than can a handgun or shotgun (Fig. 11-3). In general, the barrel is longer and has rifling to impart a spin on the bullet, lending gyroscopic stability in air. Rifling consists of spiral grooves that line the barrel, engaging the bullet and causing it to spin on the longitudinal axis. The bullets fired from rifles are more aerodynamic in shape than those fired from pistols, leading to more accurate bullet flight. Bullets for nonmilitary rifles may have an open tip or "soft nose" to allow for expansion of the bullet when striking the target. Military bullets have complete metal jacketing to limit deformation or fragmentation, which decreases wound damage. Machine guns are intended to fire in the full automatic mode; this occurs when repeated shots are fired as long as the trigger is held down, as opposed to the semiautomatic fire described earlier. Machine guns generally weigh more than rifles and are installed onto vehicles and aircraft.[130]

Modern military rifles are most often "assault rifles" and have the ability to fire in both fully automatic and semiautomatic modes. In an effort to reduce recoil, cartridges used in these weapons are not the full-powered rifle cartridges seen in civilian hunting rifles or in military weapons of the first half of the twentieth century.[141] For example, the standard Soviet infantry rifle for World Wars I and II was the Mosin Nagant M 91/30, which fired a 7.62-mm, 150-grain bullet at approximately 2800 feet per second (fps). After World War II, the replacement rifle (AK-47) fired a 7.62-mm, 120-grain bullet at 2340 fps. The AK-47 also has the ability to be fired in the fully automatic and semiautomatic modes.

Shotguns are shoulder-fired weapons that have a smooth barrel (Fig. 11-4). Shotguns fire multiple projectiles, called pellets, which vary in size from 0.012 to 0.36 inch. The

A   **B**

FIGURE 11-2 Types of handgun. **A.** A 9-mm Browing P-35 pistol used in several countries as the military handgun. It is also available to the nonmilitary market. This firearm was first produced in the 1930s. **B.** Revolver; the cylinder rotates to align with the barrel for each cartridge.

FIGURE 11-3 M-16 series military rifles (from **top** to **bottom**): M16A1, M-16A2, M-4A1, and M-16A4.

pellets are often contained in a cup or wad that keeps them together and pushes the shot out of the barrel (Fig. 11-5). The pellets begin to spread the farther they move from the barrel.[84] The spread of the pellet shot over a given distance is dependent on the size of the shot, the length of the barrel, and the degree of "choke" on the barrel. Choke is a constriction at the end of the barrel that will cause less spread of the shot over a given distance. A standard measure of choke is the amount of pellets that are put into a circle at 40 yards. A full choke should put 70% of its pellets into the circle, whereas an "improved cylinder" choke should put 50%. When within a few feet of the barrel, the spread of the shot is negligible.

Explosive Munitions

Explosive munitions include artillery, grenades, mortars, land mines, and bombs.[8,9,34,100,120] They are the most common agents for wounding soldiers on a battlefield, starting during the World War I (1914–1918), when artillery became more common on the battlefield, and continuing to be the most common injury mechanism through today. Table 11-1 describes the relative proportion of different types of weapons that generated casualties on the battlefield from various wars during the 20th century.

Explosive munitions wound via one or more of three mechanisms: ballistic, blast, or thermal (Fig. 11-6). *Ballistic injuries* occur from fragments of exploding munitions or from material

Smooth barrel shotgun

Rifled barrel

FIGURE 11-4 Barrel types: smoothbore (shotgun) and rifled. The smoothbore barrel is commonly used for shotguns, whereas a rifled barrel is used in both rifles and handguns.

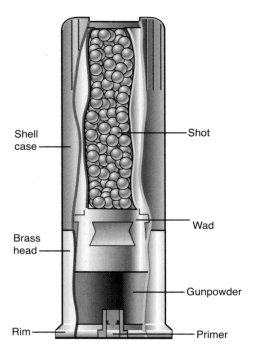

Shell case

Shot

Brass head

Wad

Gunpowder

Rim

Primer

FIGURE 11-5 Shotgun shell. A shotgun shell consists of the primer, powder, wad, and shot. All of this is contained in the shell casing. When powder burning is initiated by the primer, the wadding propels the shot down the barrel and into free flight.

around the explosive device. *Blast injuries* occur because of a transient blast overpressure caused by the exploding munitions. *Thermal injuries* are caused by a transient increase in local temperature as a result of the explosion. Blast and thermal injuries occur relatively close to the exploding munitions, whereas ballistic injuries also can occur farther from the device.[12,34,120] The distances from the munitions that the various effects may be seen (ballistic, blast, thermal) will vary with the type of device and the environment. An explosion in a confined space, for example, will increase the effects of blast overpressure. Someone who is wounded closer to the exploding munitions may have combined ballistic, thermal, and blast effects compared with someone farther away. A typical mortar shell, when detonated

in an open area, might have thermal effects within a few feet of detonation. The blast or pressure wave may cause ear injury within 30 feet. Fragments, however, can still cause injury at greater than 100 yards from detonation.

Artillery includes cannons that fire large projectiles in a range of up to several miles. The projectiles may be antivehicle, contain white phosphorus, or be explosive filled. The diameter of U.S. military artillery cannon barrels ranges in size from 105 mm to 8 inches. The explosive-filled projectiles are most often used against infantry soldiers. When detonated, they produce fragments of varying shape and size, which cause wounds. The fragments produced depend on the casing of the artillery round. Modern artillery casings break up to produce more uniform fragments over a given area. The fragments may range from a few milligrams to several grams in weight. After detonation, fragments may initially travel at several thousand meters per second. This initial velocity rapidly decreases because of the irregular shape of the fragments.[8,12,34,120]

Grenades are small explosive-filled devices that may be thrown or fired from a special launcher (Fig. 11-7). Grenades may produce smoke for signaling or be designed to disable or destroy tanks or to injure soldiers. As with artillery shells, the type of fragments produced is dependent on the composition of the container. Most modern grenades have a notched or pre-fragmented casing that produces fragments of a uniform size when detonated.[8,12,34,120]

Mortars are weapons that have barrels aimed at a high arc to produce indirect fire. Projectiles fired from mortars may produce smoke, white phosphorus, or explosive fragments. These weapons are smaller and are more limited in range compared with the cannon. As with the other weapons described earlier, fragments produced by the explosive shells vary with the composition of the shell's casing.[8,9]

Land mines may be one of two major types: antipersonnel or antivehicle. *Antipersonnel* land mines are those intended to injure individual soldiers. *Antivehicle* land mines are intended to destroy or disable vehicles, such as tanks. Antipersonnel land mines are classified by the U.S. Army as static, bounding, or horizontal spray (Fig. 11-8). Another category, unconventional or improvised devices, will be handled separately in this section. Currently, there is much concern about land mines throughout

		Casualty Generation by Weapon	
TABLE 11-1			
Wounding Agent	World War I	Bougainville Campaign, Solomon Islands (World War II)	Vietnam Conflict (Wound Data and Munitions Effectiveness Team [WDMET])
Bullet	28.06	34	30
Mortar	NR	39.5	19
Booby trap/land mine	NA	1.9	17
Hand grenade	1.21	12.7	11
Artillery	70.4	11	3
RPG*	NA	NA	12

* Vietnam Conflict only.
NA, not available; NR, not reported; RPG, rocket propelled grenade.

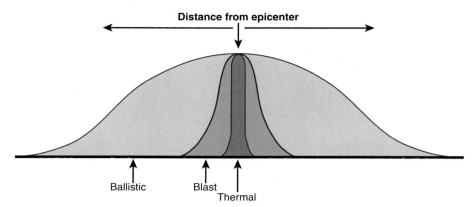

FIGURE 11-6 Mechanisms of injury explosive munition. The three mechanisms of injury are ballistic, blast, and thermal. The ballistic effects take place much farther away from the explosion compared with blast or thermal effects.

the world because of vast land-mined tracts that remain in Asia, Africa, and the Balkans. Estimates vary, but between about 70 to 100 million land mines remain in place, which, until removed, will continue to be a hazard to those living or working in the area (Fig. 11-9).[1,7,8,12,34,112,120]

Static land mines are those that are laid on top of the ground or buried in soil and are detonated when someone steps on the device. They are the most common type of land mine seen throughout the world. They contain a small amount of explosive (100–200 g) and produce a characteristic pattern of injury[112] (Fig. 11-10). Russian surgeons obtained considerable experience with land mines during their war in Afghanistan (1979–1988), which prompted them to conduct both labora-

tory and clinical investigations on the mechanism of injury. Injuries produced by static land mines are primarily to the lower extremity (Fig. 11-11). There are three areas of injury—there is an area of *mangling* or *avulsion (traumatic amputation)*, which occurs at the midfoot or distal tibia. There is a second area in which the *soft tissues are separated* from bone along fascial planes in the leg (brisant). This area is a tidewater area in terms of tissue survival; the tissue is compromised, but it may heal. The area extends from below the knee to the level of "avulsion" injury of the foot or lower leg. Third, more proximally, injuries may occur from *fragments* or *debris* propelled from the land mine but not necessarily from direct effects of the blast itself. The degree of injury is dependent on the size and shape of the

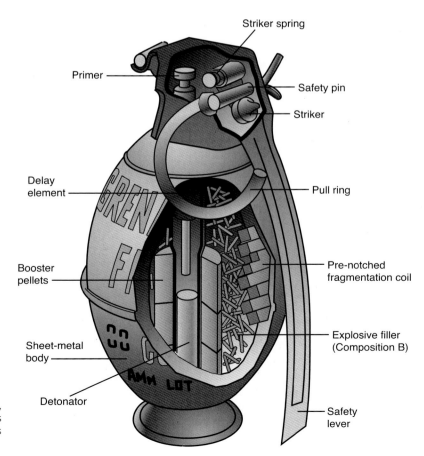

FIGURE 11-7 Grenade. This cutaway illustrates the casing, which is composed of notched wire, producing fragments when detonated. The powder is stored in the casing and is ignited by the detonator.

Static

Bounding

Horizontal spray

FIGURE 11-8 Antipersonnel land mines. This illustrates the types of manufactured antipersonnel land mines seen throughout the world. A static mine is tripped when a person steps on the mine. A bounding mine, when tripped, propels an explosive device to about waist high and then detonates. The horizontal spray mine directs multiple small fragments in one direction when tripped.

FIGURE 11-9 Small static land mine. Note the small size of this land mine compared with a hand. These are usually made of minimal metal components to avoid detection.

individual's limb, the type of footwear and clothing worn, the amount and type of soil overlying the land mine, and the size of the land mine.[1,112]

Bounding mines are land mines that, when tripped, propel a small grenadelike device to about 1 to 2 m in height. The device then explodes, producing multiple small fragment wounds similar in nature to those produced by grenades.[112]

Horizontal spray land mines are mines that, when tripped, fire fragments in one direction. These land mines may be used to protect a perimeter or during an ambush. The U.S. Army's Claymore mine is an example of this type of mine. It fires about 700 steel balls that weigh 10 grains each in one direction. The weapons produce multiple fragment wounds to exposed personnel nearby (Fig. 11-12).[112]

Unconventional or *improvised devices* are another category of land mine. These mines are fabricated out of another piece of

FIGURE 11-10 This photograph is of a foot injured by a small planted land mine. The mine was under the forefoot and the patient had footwear.

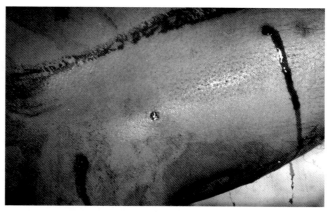

FIGURE 11-12 Claymore mine injury. This photograph illustrates multiple small fragment wounds of a thigh from a patient injured by a Claymore mine.

ordnance, such as a grenade or mortar shell, to detonate when a person steps on the device, a person pulls a tripwire, or the device is triggered remotely by radio or control wires. These devices may be made out of locally available materials as well. They vary in construction from smaller antipersonnel devices to large explosive devices with several kilograms of explosive to disable or destroy vehicles (Fig. 11-13).

The majority of explosive devices used in the Afghanistan and Iraq conflicts are improvised explosive devices. One of the larger antipersonnel mines used against civilians is the *suicide bomber*. This is a term given to an individual who carries a large explosive charge and detonates it in location of a crowd or building to achieve maximum casualties. One of the more common constructs for such a bomb is in the form of a vest containing explosive along with material for fragments. The fragments increase the wounding potential of the device and consist of items such as ball bearings or nails. Large antivehicle land mines have made transportation and troop movements difficult.[1,8,34]

Bombs are explosive devices that are dropped from aircraft. They may consist of one large explosive device or may carry submunitions that are distributed more uniformly over a target area. Cluster bombs are an example of the latter device.[9,12,120]

ARMORED VEHICLE CREW CASUALTIES

Most of the world's armies have tanks, infantry fighting vehicles, and armored reconnaissance vehicles within their inventory.

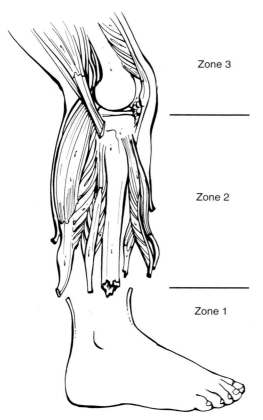

Zone 3

Zone 2

Zone 1

FIGURE 11-11 Small static land mine injury. This illustrates the three areas of injury sustained from a small static land mine. First, there is an area of avulsion or amputation; second, there is an area of soft tissue stripping where tissue may or may not survive. Third, proximal to this area, there may be fragment wounds from debris or the land mine, or injury from the fast translation of being propelled upward from the land mine itself.

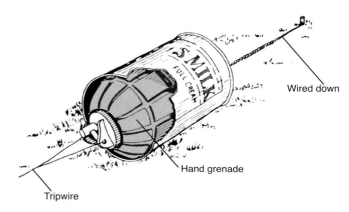

Wired down

Hand grenade

Tripwire

FIGURE 11-13 Improvised explosive device (IED). This illustrates an IED ("booby trap") made from a grenade that is inserted into a can. When the wire is tripped, the grenade explodes. This drawing is taken from a World War II British Commando manual. IEDs are the most common type of land mine or booby trap seen in the Vietnam, Iraq, and Afghanistan conflicts.

FIGURE 11-14 Kinetic energy armor piercing round. This illustration shows the dense metal penetrator shaped like an arrow and the "petals" of the sabot surrounding the penetrator falling away.

Injuries to crewmembers occur both in and around vehicles. Those injured outside of the vehicle have injuries similar to infantrymen. Two types of weapons are used to perforate the armored vehicle's envelope to cause injury to the crewmen (antitank land mines may be considered a third type).

First, there is the kinetic energy round (Fig. 11-14). This consists of a hard piece of metal, such as tungsten or depleted uranium, that is fired out of a cannon at a high velocity. The projectiles used today are long and narrow and cause a high concentration of pressure over a very small cross-sectional area to defeat the armor plate. If the round penetrates to the crew compartment, injuries may be caused by the penetrating round itself, debris knocked off from the inside of the vehicle itself,

or armor debris. Because the penetrating rounds are large, injuries to individuals tend to be catastrophic.[35]

Shaped charges are the other type of weapon seen on the battlefield (Fig. 11-15). They consist of an explosive-filled warhead that is packed around a reverse cone-shaped piece of metal (copper or aluminum). When detonated, the liner collapses and a jet is produced, which travels at up to 10,000 feet per second. The jet produces an area of high temperature and pressure over a very small cross-sectional area. When the jet penetrates the armor, it produces two areas of under armor debris. First, there is the jet of the shaped charge. The jet produces catastrophic wounds when it directly hits one of the crewmen. Second, there is an area of under armor debris called *spall,* which is material knocked off from the inside face of the armored plate itself. Many of today's armored vehicles have liners that do not allow spall debris to form.[35,112]

A variation on the shaped charge is the "explosively formed projectile" (Fig. 11-16). This device has a shallow concavity for the liner and forms a "slug" rather than a fully developed jet to penetrate vehicles. The "slug" is less affected by intermediate targets, such as dirt and debris, than the jet of the shaped charge. Although it is considered to be a new innovation, this technology has been present since at least the 1930s.[2]

EPIDEMIOLOGY

Nonmilitary Gunshot Wounds

Gotsch et al.[56] reported estimates of gunshot injuries in the United States for 1993 through 1998. The authors estimated that during this period, there were approximately 180,533 fatal gunshot wounds and about 411,000 nonfatal gunshot wounds for the 6-year period. There was a decline in the annual nonfatal

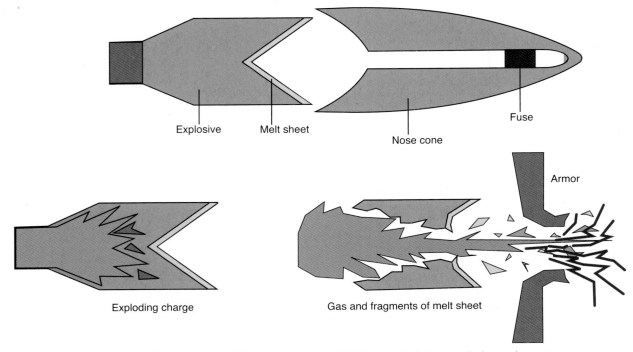

FIGURE 11-15 Shaped charge or high-explosive, antitank (HEAT) round. Explosive is packed around a reverse cone-shaped metal liner called a melt sheet. When detonated, it generates a jet of high temperature and pressure that defeats armor through plastic or elastic deformation.

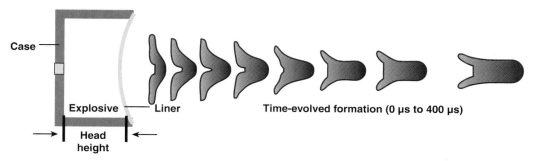

Case

Explosive — **Liner**

Time-evolved formation (0 μs to 400 μs)

Head height

FIGURE 11-16 Explosively formed projectile (EFP). A modification of the shaped charge, the liner has a shallow concavity that propels a "slug" at high velocity. The slug is less likely to be disturbed by intermediate targets or debris compared with the jet of the shaped charge. Antivehicle land mines based on this principal are being used against U.S. and Allied Forces in the Iraqi Conflict.

rate by 40% (from 40.5 to 24 per 100,000 population) and in the fatal rate by 21.1% (from 15.4 to 12.1 per 100,000 population). This decline corresponded with the overall decrease in violent crime of 21%. The stated cause for injury was assault in 57%, self-inflicted in 20%, unintentional for 13%, and unknown for 10%. During the study period, the average number of self-inflicted fatalities exceeded those from assault (18,227 versus 15,371 per year).[56]

From 1998 through 2006, there has been a further decline in violent crime from 566.4 to 473.5 per 100,000 population (16.5%) and in murder from 6.3 to 5.7 per 100,000 population (9.5%).[48] Deaths caused by firearms in the United States also decreased from 35,957 (13.5 per 100,000) to 29,569 (10.5 per 100,000).[26]

Gotsch et al.[56] also found that males were seven times more likely to receive a firearm injury than were females. Black men aged 20 to 24 years had the highest annual firearm-related injury rate for both fatal and nonfatal groups (166.7 and 690 per 100,000 population, respectively). This compared unfavorably to the firearm injury rate of 13.4 per 100,000 (fatal) and 30.1 per 100,000 (nonfatal) for the entire population. These demographics also explain why the concentration of patients with gunshot wounds is higher in trauma centers for cities with a higher black population, such as Detroit, Los Angeles, Philadelphia, Chicago, and New Orleans.[26,48,61]

There is an economic, as well as a human, cost in caring for patients with gunshot wounds.[23,61,153] Hakanson et al.[61] reported that the average cost of treating a gunshot orthopaedic injury is $13,108 per patient. Brown et al.[23] reported on orthopaedic patients treated for gunshot wounds in New Orleans at an inner-city Level I trauma center. They found that patients with gunshot wounds represented 24% of all admissions and 26% of all orthopaedic trauma surgical cases. The most common locations for nonfatal gunshot wounds are in the extremities (Table 11-2). Gotsch et al.[56] reported that extremity wounds represented 46% of nonfatal wounds caused by assault and 71.8% of unintentional wounds. A series from Cordoba, Argentina, found that 63% of gunshot victims had injuries to the upper or lower extremities.[14] A review of records at Henry Ford Hospital in Detroit, MI, from 2001 through 2006 found that 42.4% of all patients admitted with a diagnosis of gunshot wounds had extremity wounds. This figure increases to 50.2% if pelvic and spine injuries are included.

Many patients with gunshot wounds are also treated in emergency departments without admission.[21,56,118] Estimates for the number of patients with gunshot wounds who are treated on an outpatient basis range from 45% to 60%.[26,118] Gotsch et al.[56] reported a ratio of 1:1.2:1 for deaths:hospital admissions and transfers:emergency department treatment and discharge, respectively.

Overview of Battle Casualties

The two best epidemiologic studies concerning battle casualties consist of data from World War II and the Vietnam Conflict.[9,120] A prospective study on battle casualties was conducted during the Bougainville campaign in the Solomon Islands during World War II to assess patient injuries based on the weapon and tactical circumstances.[120] The patients were then followed through their initial surgical care to look at outcome. A second study was performed during the Vietnam Conflict to assess 7964 casualties during an 18-month period during the conflict. The patients in this study (Wound Data and Munitions Effectiveness Team [WDMET]) were evaluated in terms of the tactical situation, the weapons used, the injuries produced, and patient outcome.[9]

The anatomic distribution of wounds among the war injured is relatively constant, probably because wounds produced on the battlefield tend to be a random event (Table 11-3). Between 60% and 70% of wounded patients admitted to a medical treatment facility have wounds to the extremities, and about 21% of those admitted have fractures. Use of body armor to protect soldiers and airmen was studied in World War II and the Korean

TABLE 11-2	Anatomic Distribution of Gunshot Wounds	
	Henry Ford Hospital, Detroit, MI (N = 1505)	Cordoba, Argentina (N = 1326)
Head, ears, eyes, nose, throat	11.7%	12%
Chest	16%	12%
Abdomen/pelvis	24%	13%
Upper extremity	16.2%	18%
Lower extremity	26.2%	45%
Spine	5%	Not reported

TABLE 11-3	Percentage Anatomic Distribution of Wounds (Living Wounded U.S. Soldiers)			
Anatomic Area	U.S. Civil War	World War I	World War II	Bougainville Campaign
Head, face, neck	9.1%	11.4%	16.1%	20.7%
Chest	11.7%	3.6%	9.8%	12.4%
Abdomen	6.0%	3.4%	5.6%	5.7%
Upper extremity	36.6%	36.2%	28.2%	27.4%
Lower extremity	36.6%	45.4%	40.3%	33.8%

Conflict and was found to reduce thoracic and abdominal wounds.[13,73]

The proportion of casualties caused by various weapons from World War I, the Bougainville campaign in World War II, and the Vietnam Conflict is shown in Table 11-1.[9,92,111] The proportion of injuries caused by bullets has been relatively constant from conflict to conflict. Recently, fragment-producing explosive munitions have accounted for an increasing proportion of casualties seen from the battlefield. This trend is expected to continue.

The *lethality* of a weapon is defined as the probability of death from a hit from that weapon (Table 11-4). From both the Bougainville and WDMET data, the lethality of a bullet wound is about 0.33. Fragments from grenades, mortars, and artillery range from 0.05 to 0.10. Death from tripping a land mine is also about 33%.[9,120]

MEDICAL EVACUATION

Wounded soldiers from the battlefield must be simultaneously treated and moved through the evacuation chain (Fig. 11-17). All major armies throughout the world have made some provisions to care for wounded soldiers. The U.S. military (Army, Navy, and Air Force) have similar echelons of care to treat wounded soldiers.[97,98]

The first treatment of a wounded soldier on the battlefield consists of self-care or buddy care. The first step may be to take cover from hostile fire. Treatment for extremity wounds consists of stopping the bleeding, applying a dressing, and splinting.

The next step is care provided by a medic, who evaluates the patient and adjusts the dressings and splint. The medic also has the capability of providing pain relief, administering antibiotics, and arranging for further evacuation.

TABLE 11-4	Lethality by Weapon	
Weapon	Bougainville Campaign	Vietnam Conflict
Bullet	0.32	0.39
Mortar	0.12	0.13
Grenade	0.05	0.13
Artillery	0.11	0.25
Land mine	0.38	0.31

A battalion aid station may be the first physician contact for a wounded soldier. Here, the patient is further evaluated, splints and dressings are adjusted, and the patient is triaged. If the casualty load is light, patients are treated as they arrive. If the casualty load is heavy, patients must be triaged to allocate the resources of evacuation and surgical care. Ideally, the triage takes place along the entire evacuation chain. If a patient's condition worsens, his or her priority may increase.[97,98]

The U.S. Army Medical Company is the next echelon of care in the evacuation scheme. This facility has the capability of providing blood transfusions and has limited radiographic capability. This unit is the first level of care with any bed holding capability. Adjacent to the medical company may be the forward surgical team (FST) that provides the first possible surgical support on the battlefield. The purpose of this unit is to provide surgical care of nontransportable patients, who are those patients whose outcome would be compromised by being evacuated farther for surgical care. Examples of patients who should have surgery at the FST are those with penetrating abdominal wounds who are in shock and those with major traumatic amputations. Because of the mission to treat emergent patients, the FST is staffed with one orthopaedic surgeon and three general surgeons. Having an orthopaedic surgeon is important to make decisions concerning amputations as well as caring for those with multiple injuries. Often those with multiple injuries have major extremity wounds. Because the FST has no bed holding capability, it must be colocated with a medical company to complete its mission. Goals of surgery are to stabilize the patients and prepare them for evacuation. Similar units for the U.S. Navy are the Surgical Company to support the U.S. Marines and the MFST for the U.S. Air Force. While all three are not exactly the same because of the need to meet service-specific requirements, they all function at the same level of care.[97,98]

The U.S. Army's Combat Support Hospital (CSH) is the next echelon of care on the battlefield. The entire unit when assembled has 296 beds and includes intensive care unit capability, six operating rooms, and laboratory capability, and it is staffed by three orthopaedic surgeons in addition to general surgeons, internists, and emergency physicians. This hospital is presently deployed as a modular unit in a 40-bed slice with two operating rooms. There are three general surgeons and one orthopaedic surgeon assigned to the hospital in this configuration. This facility is the first surgical echelon for the majority of battlefield patients, including those with orthopaedic injuries. Goals of care at this hospital are to stabilize the patients and to prepare them for evacuation out of the combat zone. Examples of care for patients arriving at the CSH include the treatment of soft

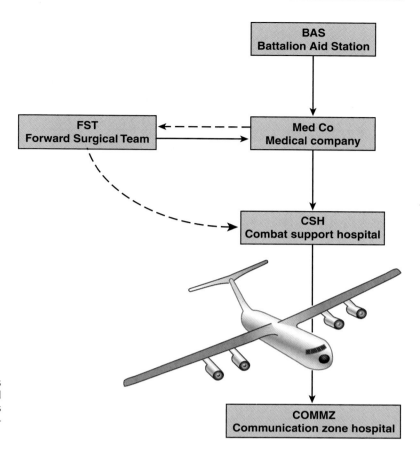

FIGURE 11-17 U.S. military medical evacuation. This shows the present scheme of evacuation for wounded soldiers used by the U.S. Army. Surgical care by orthopaedic surgeons takes place at the forward surgical team (FST), combat support hospital (CSH), or communication zone hospitals.

tissues, fracture stabilization via casting or external fixator application, and treatment of a partial or complete amputation. The CSH is ideally located near an airfield. The equivalent U.S. Navy hospital is the Fleet Hospital, and for the U.S. Air Force, the Expeditionary Medical Support (EMEDS) Hospital, which is a modular system.[97,98]

Patients may be moved to one of the surgical facilities (FST or CSH) directly from the battlefield depending on the severity of the injury and if the tactical situation permits. In more stationary situations, such as during the Vietnam Conflict, this occurs more frequently.[90,91] During the Vietnam Conflict, the U.S. military controlled the airspace and did not have much geographic movement of hospitals or troops, such as occurred during World War II. Because of this, overflight of facilities in the evacuation chain occurred to bring patients promptly to a facility that could provide more care.

WOUND BALLISTICS

Wound ballistics is the science that studies the effects of penetrating projectiles on the body.* Three observable phenomena occur when a bullet strikes tissue. First, tissue is crushed by the projectile as it passes through, leading to a localized area of cell necrosis that is proportional to the size of the projectile.

*References   28,36,37,39,41–43,46–48,57,58,67–70,77–79,88,103, 106,129.

This area of the projectile's path is called the permanent track or permanent cavity (Fig. 11-18).

There is a second area in which elastic tissue is stretched, causing a temporary cavity.[36,37,47,77–79,88,103] The stretch results from a lateral displacement of tissue that occurs after the passage of the projectile. There is a transient increase in pressure of 4 to 6 atmospheres (atm) for a few milliseconds' duration. This transient lateral displacement of tissue, such as skeletal muscle, vessels, and nerves, macroscopically appears as blunt trauma. Inelastic tissue, such as bone, may fracture in this area.

A third component, known as the shock wave, is a pressure wave that travels at the speed of sound preceding the bullet in tissue. This pressure wave is of very short duration, a few microseconds, but it may generate pressures up to 100 atm in magnitude.[43,67,68] The shock wave has not been shown to cause tissue injury.

The two mechanisms of injury (crush and stretch) have differing effects on skin just as with other tissues.[36,37,48,67–70,88,103] When a projectile strikes skin and creates a permanent cavity, it produces a small amount of necrosis that is proportional to the size of the projectile. The temporary cavity splits the skin, which produces a larger opening of tissue. Grundfest et al.[57] used cadaver skin to test threshold velocities for penetration. The skin was stretched over a frame during testing, thus altering the behavior seen in vivo. The authors used steel ball bearings from 1/16 inch to 1/4 inch in size as well as 11/64-inch lead spheres fired from an air rifle. They found that increasing the size of the projectile also required increasing the velocity needed to perforate the skin.

Fackler et al.[46] studied healing of soft tissue using a large

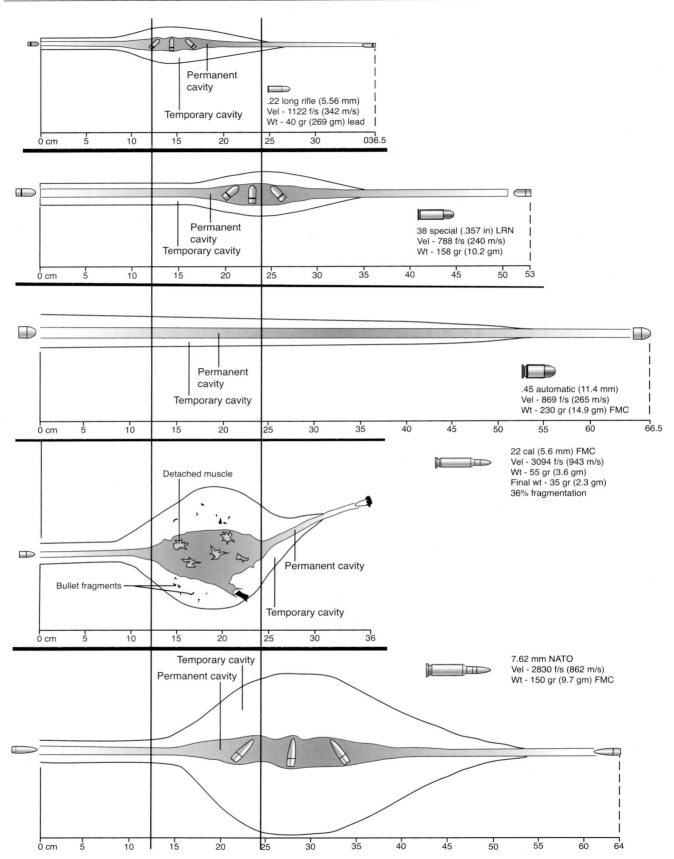

FIGURE 11-18 Projectile tissue interaction. Three areas can be measured in the projectile tissue interaction: the sonic wave, the temporary cavity, and the permanent track. The temporary cavity is caused by a transient lateral displacement of tissue (stretch), whereas the permanent track is made by passage of the projectile, crushing tissue. The sonic wave, although measurable, has not been shown to cause tissue injury.

porcine animal model. These investigators used a solid nonde-forming 5.56-mm bullet and fired it into the thighs of the animals. The authors found larger exit wounds compared with the entrance wounds as a result of splits in the skin caused by the larger temporary cavity produced as the bullet yawed in tissue. The larger wound allowed for better exposure of the wound path and freer drainage of wounds. Also, the authors found skin vasospasm, which produces blanching, soon after wounding. This area did not revascularize for several hours. If the loss of blood supply is a criterion for excision, the transitory nature of the blanching shows that viable tissue would be sacrificed in this area if evaluated soon after wounding.

In another study, Fackler et al.[45] found that projectile shape was important in determining the appearance of a skin wound. The authors fired a solid nondeforming bullet point first and then base first, noting the different appearance of the skin wound in each case. The bullets were fired at over 5000 fps. For the projectile going base first, large skin splits were produced by an early temporary cavity. No such effect was seen with the bullets going point first through the skin.

Injury to skeletal muscle has been studied using animal models by Harvey et al.,[63] Dziemian and Herget,[36] Mendelson and Glover,[103] and Fackler.[43,48] Muscle that is touched by the projectile in the permanent tract has a microscopic rim of tissue that is actually necrotic. This tissue, if the blood supply to the muscle remains intact, can heal over time without surgical intervention. The area of cell death sloughs and, as long as the wound can drain, will heal up spontaneously.

Surrounding the path is an area damaged by the stretch causing the temporary cavity. The stretched area of temporary cavity may split along fascial planes. This area appears grossly as bruised or contused tissue. Bruised skeletal muscle ordinarily heals uneventfully. Microscopically, there are disrupted skeletal muscle fibers and capillaries. After a period, there is leukocyte infiltration followed by inflammation and healing.[36,42,48,69,103]

When a bullet fragments, many permanent paths are formed; thus, the region stretched by the temporary cavity is perforated in multiple places. Tissue weakened by these tiny perforations is often split by the temporary cavity stretch, and pieces between perforations are detached. This often greatly increases the size of the permanent cavity.[48]

If the muzzle of a firearm is in contact with a living body when it is fired, the high-pressure gas that pushes the projectile out of the barrel will pass into the tissues through the hole formed by the projectile—often causing greatly increased tissue displacement and disruption.

Bone injury is common with gunshot wounds to the extremities.[28,58,77–79,106,129] Fractures may occur via two mechanisms, either when the projectile strikes bone or, rarely, indirectly by the temporary cavity. Direct fractures (Fig. 11-19) occur when a projectile strikes the bone. Because of the density and relative inelastic behavior of bone, fracture line propagation may occur well beyond the area crushed by the projectile itself, leading to bone comminution and the production of secondary missiles from the bone itself. Because the secondary missiles of bone disrupt tissue before it is stretched by the temporary cavity, this has the effect of increasing comminution around the bullet path, and might even cause increased soft tissue disruption, reminiscent of the previously mentioned synergism between bullet fragmentation and temporary cavity stretch.

Indirect fractures (Fig. 11-20) may occur when a projectile

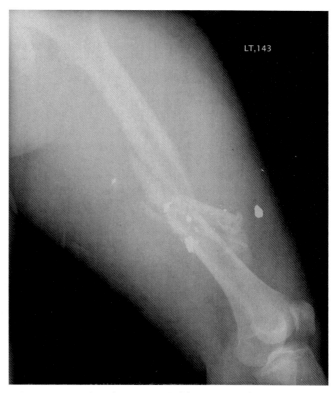

FIGURE 11-19 Direct fracture. Cortical bone is very dense, so when a projectile strikes, fracture lines propagate away from the bullet's path, causing comminution. The temporary cavity may cause further displacement.

passes close to the bone in soft tissue and a strain occurs to such a degree as to cause a fracture. Indirect fractures are almost always simple. Clinically, indirect fractures to bone are rare compared with those formed when bone is struck directly by the projectile.[28,67–70] Figure 11-20 illustrates the shot path 8 mm from the edge of the diaphyseal bone in ordnance gelatin, showing how indirect fractures appear. The bullet path is perpendicular to the page, going away from the reader.

Clasper et al.[28] used sheep femora and hindlimbs to study contamination of both direct and indirect fractures. The authors

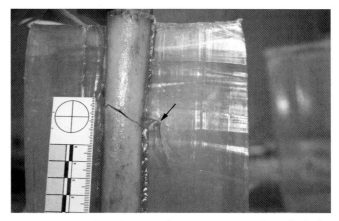

FIGURE 11-20 Indirect fracture. A fracture may occur without the bullet striking the bone. This illustrates a bullet path (*arrow*) adjacent to the bone. A simple fracture occurred from the effects of the temporary cavity.

fired through fluorescein-soaked gauze placed on the surface of the skin to determine the amount of fracture site contamination that occurred with each shot. The authors found massive fluorescein contamination with the direct fractures; however, only 3 of 14 bones with indirect fractures had medullary fluorescein contamination. Periosteal contamination was less with indirect fractures compared with the direct fractures.

Rose et al.[129] proposed a classification of incomplete fractures because of gunshot wounds, describing "drill hole" and "divot" fractures. The "drill hole" fractures are seen with bullet perforation of both cortices yet minimal comminution surrounding the bullet tract. They occur in metaphyseal bone. The "divot" fracture was described as an eccentric perforation of a diaphyseal long bone. More extensive injury may be present than apparent on plain radiographs, and the "divot" injury may be an occult complete fracture of diaphyseal bone. Such fractures should be treated as complete fractures unless other radiographic measures, such as a computed tomography scan, show an incomplete fracture.

There are common misconceptions about wound ballistics.[43] First, some authors have exaggerated the effects of velocity to include it as being the sole criterion for increased injury or as a means to classify gunshot wounds. Velocity is one of several factors involved with the production of the wound. The introduction of the M-16 rifle during the Vietnam Conflict was heralded as producing equivalent wounds or causing equivalent "incapacitation" because of the weapon's higher muzzle velocity of an advertised 3200 fps. The M-193 bullet fired from the M-16A1 rifle was 5.56 mm in diameter and weighed 3.6 g. This compared with the 7.62-mm bullet fired at a velocity of 2700 fps weighing 8 g. Later testing in the laboratory found that the increased severity of wounds sometimes seen with the M-16A1 was the result of bullet fragmentation, not the modest 10% increase in velocity. In fact, the greatest increase in muzzle velocity for military rifles occurred in the late nineteenth century when the armed services of several nations, including the United States, changed to a full metal jacketed bullet from a solid lead one. This resulted in an increase of muzzle velocity from about 1000 fps to 2000 fps.[39] The change in firearms, however, resulted in decreased wound severity because bullet deformation was limited by the jacketing.

A second common misconception[43] is the idea that "kinetic energy" or "energy deposit" is directly proportional to wound severity. Kinetic energy is the amount of potential energy available for work. "Energy deposit" is a description of how much energy is lost or "deposited" in tissue. While one can measure the projectile's velocity and weight as it enters and exits a body or tissue medium, it does not describe how this potential energy is used. The potential energy may be used for the crush or stretch, but it may also be consumed in mechanics that may not cause any tissue injury. Examples where energy may be consumed, but not cause tissue damage, include the shock wave, bullet heating, and bullet deformation.

SOFT TISSUE WOUND MANAGEMENT

Patient Evaluation

Initial evaluation of a patient with any gunshot wound should include a thorough history and physical examination. The extremity should be inspected for both entrance and exit wounds

after all clothing has been removed. The limb should also be inspected for swelling, deformity or shortening, and ecchymosis. The limb should be palpated for crepitus. Examination for distal pulses should be done to assess vascular status. In an awake patient, assessment should also be done to assess the patient's motor and sensory status. If the patient is not able to comply, this fact should be documented with a note to recheck if the patient's condition improves.

Biplanar radiographs should be taken of the injured limb covering the path of the bullet. Standard long bone radiographs, including both the joint above and below, should be done if included in the bullet's path. If a joint wound is suspected, standard views should be taken of the joint.

The most common injuries by gunshot wound are to the soft tissues of skin, subcutaneous fat, and skeletal muscle.

Skin Injuries

Gunshot skin wounds have three general patterns. First, there is a punctate wound about the size of the penetrating bullet (Fig. 11-21). Second, there is a wound that contains splits in the skin but has negligible skin loss and can eventually be closed without resorting to more extensive skin grafting or flap coverage (Fig. 11-22). Third, there is a wound in which there is skin loss, which requires the use of partial-thickness skin grafting or flap coverage (Fig. 11-23).

Perforating nonarticular wounds without a fracture or vascular injury may be candidates for outpatient treatment.[24,120] Under controlled circumstances, simple perforating wounds have been shown to heal uneventfully with simple dressing changes.[49,67,103] Successful treatment with local wound care has been reported by several authors.[24,32,64,101,109,114] Likewise, successful treatment of simple fractures associated with minimal soft tissue disruption have also been treated with local wound care and fracture stabilization in a cast or splint.[54,72,86,92,101,157]

Simple splits in the skin are produced from dilation resulting from the temporary cavity, from a projectile that is traveling sideways and presenting the long axis of the bullet to the skin, or from bone becoming a secondary missile, causing a more extensive wound. The splits produce an exit wound that will allow for free drainage of the wound, preventing the formation of an abscess or a hematoma.

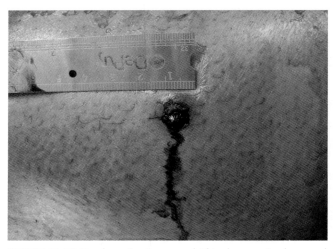

FIGURE 11-21 Simple perforating wound. This shows a simple wound caused by perforation of the bullet.

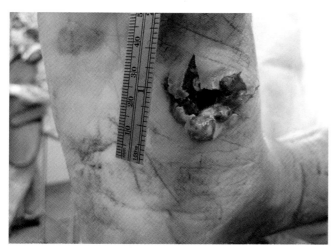

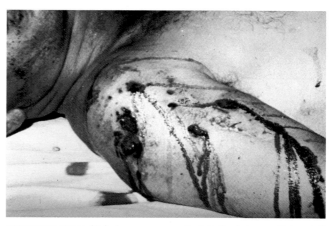

FIGURE 11-24 Multiple fragment wounds. This illustrates multiple small skin wounds that occur with many exploding munitions. They are often of the skin, subcutaneous fat, and skeletal muscle only.

FIGURE 11-22 Skin splits. Splits in the skin may be caused by bone fragments, debris, or the stretch of the temporary cavity.

More extensive wounds with skin loss may be produced from shotgun pellets, bullets, or bone fragmentation. Initial treatment of the more extensive wounds should be done in the operating room. Longitudinal incisions of the skin and underlying fascia to relieve pressure, remove hematoma and debris, and expose the underlying muscle should be done. Surgical removal of skin is rarely indicated for the initial surgery, other than trimming irregular edges. As described earlier, blanching may give a false impression of nonviable skin if seen soon after injury and lead the surgeon to excise viable skin.

In contrast, fragment wounds are the most common types seen in wartime. Injuries range from single fragment wounds to multiple fragment wounds with extensive soft tissue loss (Fig. 11-24). Often, a person has multiple fragment wounds of the extremity skin, subcutaneous fat, and skeletal muscle, yet without significant injury to bone, vascular, or nerve structures.[9,120] In certain controlled circumstances, small fragment wounds may be treated nonoperatively.[17]

The use of negative pressure dressings (vacuum-assisted closure [VAC] dressings) for the initial management of more exten-

sive wounds has been suggested to reduce the size of defect needing coverage, promote local growth factors, and remove debris and nonviable tissue from the wound. A randomized study comparing this method to standard dressing changes is not available in the literature.[91]

An early consultation should be made with a plastic surgeon or a hand surgeon who is skilled in extremity soft tissue coverage. Before soft tissue coverage, the wound should be stable.

Skeletal Muscle Injuries

One of the most controversial aspects in caring for gunshot wounds is the treatment of skeletal muscle. Mendelson and Glover,[103] Dziemian et al.,[37] and Harvey[67] all demonstrated that a relatively minimal margin of necrosis occurs in skeletal muscle if the blood supply remains intact. Excision of tissue has been recommended for skeletal muscle that would not survive, thus acting as a bacteria medium. Recognition of how to identify tissue that needs to be excised is imprecise, at best. Scully et al.[135] evaluated 60 biopsy samples taken from the initial wound excision of 12 war wounds during the Korean Conflict. The surgery took place between 3 and 8 hours from the time of injury. The samples were graded by the surgeon as to the presence of the four "C's": color, consistency, contractility, and circulation (bleeding). The samples were then evaluated by a pathologist who graded the degree of muscle fiber damage. The authors found correlation of microscopic damage to consistency, contractility, and bleeding. Color was not found to correlate to the degree of soft tissue damage. Also, time was not found to be a factor in determining tissue viability.

For wounds in which there is a simple perforation of the limb, there is a small rim of cell death that will heal uneventfully if the wounds are allowed to drain.[46,67,103] For wounds in which there is more extensive skeletal muscle injury, a more formal exploration of the wound is warranted. The wound may be enlarged through the use of longitudinal skin incisions as described earlier. Macroscopic evaluation of skeletal muscle will determine what tissue needs to be removed. A simple analogy for surgeons is, "muscle that looks like hamburger should be excised, muscle that looks like steak should stay."

The term *débridement* is derived from the French verb *débrider*, which means "to unbridle or release."[44,76,93] As noted by Fackler,[44] the original translation of works from the Napoleonic

FIGURE 11-23 Skin defect. A skin defect may occur from secondary missiles created by bone fragments or by multiple fragments or projectiles. This case illustrates a shotgun wound from close range.

Wars by Larrey and Desault showed that incision, to allow for free drainage of the wound and to relieve swelling (compartment pressure), was the technique used by these surgeons for extremity wounds.

Hampton had a similar description: "Debridement of any wound is designed to relieve the area of excessive tension, rid it of dead tissue and massive hematoma and provide excellent drainage. *Perhaps relief of tension is the most important contribution of wound debridement* [authors' emphasis]."[64]

Compartment syndrome occurs when there is swelling inside a relatively closed space, such as the anterior compartment of the leg, which is surrounded by fascia and bone. The swelling occurs because of direct trauma, hemorrhage, or ischemia. A hematoma inside of a compartment may lead to pressure and ischemia of muscle. The diagnosis of compartment syndrome is primarily clinical.

Compartment syndrome associated with gunshot wounds has been reported in the forearm,[38,108] leg,[150] and thigh.[11,52] Forearm compartment syndrome has been well documented and is present in up to 10% of patients.[108] Longitudinal incisions to release pressure within a compartment and to expose tissue has been recommended by military surgeons at least since the time of the Napoleonic Wars.[44]

The amount of swelling present in a compartment after a gunshot wound may range from minimal to that involving the entire compartment. Involvement of the entire compartment is rare, but it does occur when patients have extensive soft tissue injury or vascular injury causing ischemia. With the initial evaluation, patients with a large hematoma, vascular injury, or excess swelling are candidates for more formal operative treatment of the soft tissues.

WOUND INFECTION

Infection has been documented in between 1.5% and 5% for those who sustain gunshot injury. Bullet wounds are contaminated wounds. Bullets themselves, when fired, do not become "sterile" because of the heating and friction encountered in the barrel. LaGarde[89] created contaminated wounds by firing bullets contaminated with anthrax into an animal model. The animals developed an anthrax infection. Dziemian and Herget[36] placed barium sulfate dye on the surface of an ordnance gelatin block. After shooting through the surface into the gelatin, the dye coated the entire path of the projectile's path, showing that surface material is brought into the wound.

Simchen and Sachs[138] evaluated 420 wounded Israeli soldiers following the 1973 October War. They found an overall infection rate of 22% for all wounded. Wounds from explosive munitions have a higher rate of infection than those from gunshot wounds alone. Eight of 20 (40%) soldiers with femur fractures developed infection. In addition to femur fractures, the authors found burns of greater than 25% body surface area and penetrating abdominal wounds of the colon were risk factors.

Simchen et al.[137] further evaluated risk factors in war wounds after the 1982 War in Lebanon. The authors compared 1 month of hospital admissions for wounded Israeli soldiers during the 1973 and 1982 wars. They found the overall infection rates were similar between the two groups (31.5% and 30.4%, respectively). Risk factors for fracture site infections were found to be the presence of open drains, amputations, multisystem injury, and a fractured femur.

The discovery of penicillin in 1929 by Fleming led to its use in caring for the wounded during World War II. Fisher et al.[51] compared 3471 wounded soldiers with 436 soldiers who had wounds "at risk" for the development of gas gangrene (open fractures, more extensive soft tissue injury, long delay to care, wounds to the buttock or thigh). Those with wounds at risk were treated with penicillin, whereas those without at-risk wounds were not. Infection developed in 28 of 3471 (5 with gas gangrene) untreated wounds and in 2 of 436 (0 with gas gangrene) penicillin-treated wounds.

Patzakis et al.[122] divided 310 patients with open fractures (78 because of gunshot wounds) into one of three treatment groups: no antibiotics, penicillin and streptomycin, and cephalothin. Four of 78 wounds (5%) became infected, one with osteomyelitis. The authors attributed the infection to severity of injury in three of the patients who had shotgun wounds with extensive soft tissue damage. A fourth infection occurred in the no-antibiotic group.

Hansraj et al.[65] compared the use of ceftriaxone and cefazolin for gunshot fractures with minimal soft tissue disruption (<1-cm wound) that were treated nonoperatively, with 50 patients in each group. Follow-up was 59%, and the authors reported no infections based on the cultures taken in the emergency department. They concluded that the 1-day ceftriaxone regimen is more cost effective than the 3-day cefazolin regimen.

Knapp et al.[86] reported a prospective study at their institution of 186 patients with 218 gunshot fractures. All fractures were treated nonoperatively and were considered to be "low velocity" based on the appearance of the wound and history. Wounds larger than 1 cm associated with fractures were excluded. The authors compared the use of oral antibiotics (ciprofloxicillin 750 mg twice a day) to the use of intravenous antibiotics (cephapirin sodium 2 g every 4 hours and gentamicin 80 mg every 8 hours). There were two infections reported in each group. All infections were associated with fractures of the distal tibia.

The prevalence of infected gunshot wounds in the nonmilitary setting is low. None of these studies show the superiority of any particular antibiotic regimen; rather, it is the presence of antibiotics versus no antibiotics that helps reduce infection. Infections from war wounds remain higher than those associated with nonmilitary gunshot wounds alone.[95,137,138] Patients with war wounds are usually injured by explosive munitions, which are more debris and dirt ridden, as well as historically having delayed care because of medical evacuation.

AUTHORS' PREFERRED METHOD OF TREATMENT

Antibiotic Recommendations for Nonmilitary Gunshot Wounds

The authors' current antibiotic recommendations (Table 11-5) for nonmilitary gunshot wounds are dependent on injury severity. Isolated perforating wounds of the soft tissue only without vascular injury, or those patients with isolated simple fractures, may be treated initially with a first-generation cephalosporin. This applies to those who are treated as either inpatients or outpatients. Those with more extensive injuries with soft tissue loss may benefit from the addition of an aminoglycocide. For patients who are allergic to penicillin, consider using clindamycin or vancomycin.

TABLE 11-5	Recommended Antibiotic Regimen		
Location	Antibiotic		Dosing
Soft tissue	First-generation cephalosporin		1 g IV in ED, then followed by PO if outpatient
Soft tissue (shotgun) with defect	First-generation cephalosporin; consider aminoglycoside for similar time		Check renal function
Joint	First-generation cephalosporin		1 g IV q8h for 48 hours
Joint with soft tissue defect	First-generation cephalosporin; consider aminoglycoside for similar time		Check renal function
Long fone fracture; minimally displaced with minimal soft tissue injury, outpatient	First-generation cephalosporin or oral fluoroquinolones		1 g IV kefzol followed by cephalexin 500 mg PO TID or ciprofloxicillin 750 mg BID
Long bone fracture with internal fixation	First-generation cephalosporin		1 g IV q8h for 48 hours
Long bone plus extensive soft tissue injury	First-generation cephalosporin; consider aminoglycoside		Check renal function

If cephalosporin or penicillin allergy, consider clindamycin (600 mg IV BID) or vancomycin (dosing per individual patient).

JOINT INJURY

Gunshot injuries of the joint are associated with a high morbidity compared with other gunshot wounds. Intra-articular injuries may result in arthritis secondary to trauma as well as through the degenerative effects of lead itself. While elevated serum lead levels may be present with extra-articular gunshot wounds, the most common reports are with intra-articular wounds.[94,134]

Pathophysiology of Lead Toxicity

Lead is soluble in synovial fluid and has been shown to induce lead synovitis and degenerative arthritis.[15,66,94,96,134] Retained intra-articular bullets not only cause lead synovitis and arthritis but also can cause systemic lead poisoning. Animal studies have demonstrated significant articular degeneration with implantation of lead into rabbit knees compared with controls.[15] Early changes (1–2 weeks) include synovial hyperplasia, mild inflammation, and articular surface slit formation. Late changes (3–6 weeks) include giant cells and foreign particles (lead and bone fragments) in the synovium, focal chondrocyte proliferation, duplication of the tidemark, and chondrocyte columnar disorganization.[15,66] Implantation of lead pellets into rabbit knees induces significantly greater degeneration in the femoral and tibial articular surfaces, medial and lateral meniscus, and synovium at 4, 6, 10, and 14 weeks.[15,66,94,96,134]

Normal blood lead levels for adults is 0 to 19 μg/dL. Nearly 95% of the lead storage in the body occurs in bone. The half-life of lead in the blood stream is less than 2 months compared with 20 to 30 years in the bone.[94]

Principles of Management

Lead is still the major component of both rifle and handgun bullets, and it may be a potential source of lead poisoning. Steel shot has replaced lead in many areas of the world in an attempt to reduce the lead burden on wildlife. Bismuth shot is also being used as a lead replacement in Canada. Modern shotguns therefore may be firing steel rather than lead shot. Regardless of whether the projectile is known to be lead, trauma from a bullet, pellet, or fragment will still have adverse consequences for the joint. Because of this, all intra-articular projectiles should be removed. Through irrigation and debridement of the joint cavity is necessary to remove all the foreign material, including fragments of skin and clothing.

A perforating wound through a joint cavity, even with the absence of fracture, should undergo surgery. Clothing and other debris from the outside may be aspirated into the joint. Also, cartilage damage is common despite the normal radiographic appearance of the joint.[148]

In most cases where articular and periarticular fractures are present, the stabilization of the fractures is carried out initially with spanning external fixation, followed by repeat irrigation and debridement 48 to 72 hours later and definitive internal fixation once adequate debridement has been achieved.

Arthroscopy has been described as a technique for treating patients with intra-articular bullet injures of the shoulder, elbow, hip, and knee. Advantages of this technique include better visualization of the joint surface and the ability to more easily repair osteochondral fragments, ligaments, or knee meniscus. Disadvantages include increased operative and setup time as well as potential compartment syndrome. Care must be taken with using this technique to ensure the equipment is available and the surgeon is familiar with its use.

Shoulder Injuries

Gunshot injury to the entire shoulder region is relatively common, with one series reporting an incidence of 9%.[118] Injuries involving the shoulder joint itself, however, range from 1% to 2% of an overall series.[5,30,111,118,119,145]

Associated injuries are common with penetrating injuries of the shoulder region, including arterial, venous, and nerve injuries. Vascular injury is present in 15% of these cases. The risk of vascular injury in the shoulder is four times higher in patients with a major fracture than in those without a major fracture.[157,160] Nerve injuries are the most important determinant of long-term function of the limb.

Literature supports the use of either arthroscopy or open surgical techniques for removal of the bullet and its fragments from the shoulder joint and the subacromial space.[5,30,111,119,145] In cases where the joint capsule is violated by the bullet and the bullet has traversed the joint, clothing fragments, skin, and other debris could be driven into the joint. In the absence of intra-articular bullet fragments, irrigation and débridement of the joint is warranted.

Fractures that are nondisplaced or easily reducible may be stabilized with arthroscopic techniques. Small and nonviable fragments should be removed.[145] Unstable fractures and those involving the articular surface require open reduction and internal fixation. Large osteochondral fragments can be stabilized with bioabsorbable pins, headless screws such as Herbert screws, Acutrak screws, or a combination of these devices (Fig. 11-25). In the presence of intra-articular fracture displacement, comminution and metaphyseal-diaphyseal dissociation, an open technique with a deltopectoral approach is used to reconstruct the joint surface. Fractures of the surgical neck and shaft can be addressed with internal fixation using a locked plate and screws. Hemiarthroplasty is an option in nonreconstructable fractures.

Brachial plexus and nerve injuries can occur with gunshot wounds to the shoulder region.[144] In a series of 58 patients with penetrating injury to the brachial plexus, there were 6 ulnar nerve injuries, 12 median nerve injuries, 2 radial nerve injuries, 5 musculocutaneous nerve injuries, 1 axillary nerve injury, and 3 suprascapular nerve injuries. In the same cohort, there were 13 C-5, 10 C-6, 10 C-7, 5 C-8, and 10 T-1 root injuries. There were 8 lateral cord, 6 medial cord, and 10 posterior cord injuries. The trunk injuries included seven upper trunk, three middle trunk, and three lower trunk injuries. In this series, 24% of the patients had vascular injuries when brachial plexus injury was present. One or more elements of the plexus were repaired in 36 of the 58 patients in this series. There were 3 good (8%), 23 useful (64%), and 8 (22%) poor results.[144] The main complications include stiffness, infection, and pain.

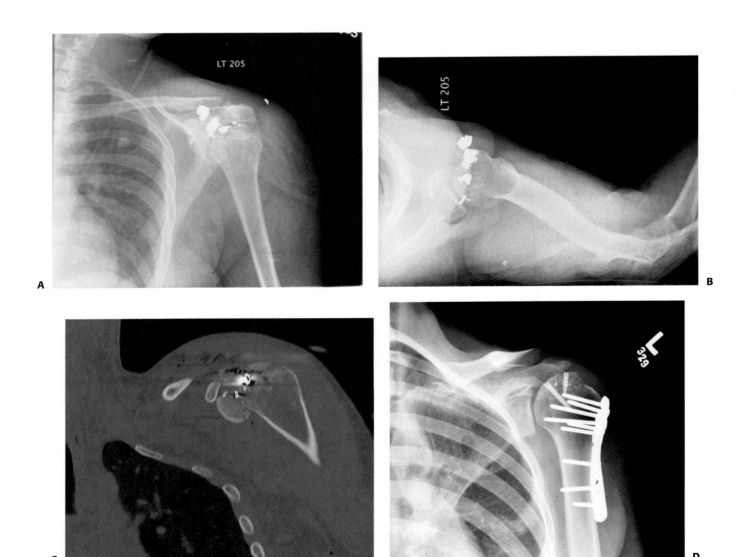

FIGURE 11-25 Preoperative anteroposterior (**A**) and lateral (**B**) radiographs and computed tomography scan (**C**) of the shoulder showing intra-articular injury. **D**. Postoperative radiograph showing reduction with plate and screws. Headless screws were used for the articular fragments.

Elbow Injuries

The incidence of gunshot wounds to the elbow may be underestimated in the literature.[5,18,31,80,102,140] Associated injuries include periarticular fractures, nerve injuries, and arterial and venous injuries.[5,117] In rare cases of an isolated bullet or pellet in the elbow joint, irrigation and débridement and bullet removal can be achieved with the use of the arthroscope.[80]

AUTHORS' PREFERRED METHOD OF TREATMENT

Recommended Treatment for a Suspected Elbow Joint Injury

Recommended treatment for patients with a suspected elbow joint injury is open irrigation and débridement of the joint, and removal of foreign material, bullet fragments, or small loose bone fragments, if present. Initial stabilization of the elbow following a fracture of the distal humerus, the proximal radius, or proximal ulna can be done with a splint. With more comminuted fractures, use of external fixation spanning the elbow can be utilized. After stabilization, computed tomography (CT) will aid in assessment of the fracture and the elbow joint for definitive fracture fixation (Fig. 11-26A–D). In unstable, open fracture-dislocations, urgent internal fixation of the fractures may be necessary, alone or in addition to spanning external fixation of the joint.[18]

Definitive treatment may involve a combination of various techniques, including internal fixation and/or hinged external fixation (Fig. 11-26E–F). Salvage of a severely injured joint may be achieved with compression plate arthrodesis of the elbow[102] or arthroplasty.[31] Young and active patients are not good candidates for elbow arthroplasty. In one study, intermediate-range follow-up of 8 to 12 years post-arthroplasty showed a five of seven (71%) failure rate. In the presence of an arthritic and painful elbow, this subgroup of patients may be considered for arthrodesis.

Complications include stiffness, malunion, nonunion, infection, and nerve injury.[117] In a cohort of 44 patients with elbow gunshot wounds at the author's institution, 4 died of other injuries and 6 were lost to follow-up. Of the remaining 34 patients, 19 (56%) patients had nerve injuries. The nerve injuries included 8 ulnar, 11 radial, and 2 median nerve injuries. Two patients had combined injuries. Two nerves (one radial and one ulnar) were repaired with partial return of function. Two complete radial nerve injuries were treated with tendon transfers. Four patients (12%) had brachial artery injury that required repair. Four patients (12%) developed deep infections requiring irrigation and débridement in the operating room. Three patients required secondary bone grafting to achieve bony union of the fracture.

Hip Injuries

In our series, the prevalence of gunshot wounds to the hip joint is about 2% of all extremity gunshot wounds and 4% of lower extremity gunshot wounds. The prevalence of gunshot wounds to the hip region (femoral neck, peritrochanteric region), with or without joint involvement, with or without fractures is 9% of all extremity gunshot wounds and 17% of lower extremity gunshot wounds.

The diagnosis of hip joint violation is an important step in management of these injuries. The trajectory of the bullet or its fragments can traverse the abdomen, bowel, and/or bladder before violating the hip joint. The projectile may enter the hip capsule without causing a fracture of the acetabulum or the proximal femur, or enter through the acetabulum. In absence of a fracture, the diagnosis of hip joint violation can be difficult.

Diagnosis is based on radiographic and computed tomography scan findings. In the absence of fractures, or when radiographs are inconclusive, a fluoroscopically assisted arthrogram is the most sensitive test to detect joint violation.[20,97] Documentation is important to determine the need for surgery to lavage the joint. A negative arthrogram indicates no joint violation, possibly allowing for nonoperative treatment.

Transabdominal gunshot wounds to the hip joint carry a high risk of infection and should be treated with emergent arthrotomy, irrigation, and débridement. Bowel and bladder injuries should be managed by general surgeons and urologists with either direct repair or diverting colostomy and diversion procedures for the urinary tract respectively.[6,20,33]

Bullet removal can be achieved via arthrotomy or arthroscopy.[55,97,107,139,162] Hip arthroscopy is an available technique for removal of bullet and fragments from the hip joint.* Hip arthroscopy requires special equipment and experience with the technique. The use of a fracture table and fluoroscopy aid in arthroscopy of the hip. Hip arthroscopy carries the risk of intra-abdominal fluid extravasation and abdominal compartment syndrome.[6] In presence of acetabular fractures, extreme care must be taken to measure the arthroscopy fluid inflow and outflow. If the inflow and outflow are mismatched, fluid is likely extravasating into the pelvis and abdomen and can cause cardio-pulmonary arrest.

Recommended treatment of the fractures is by open reduction and internal fixation. For acute fractures of the femoral neck, use of standard techniques such as a compression screw and side plate may be used for fractures with minimal comminution (Fig. 11-27). Comminuted fractures of the femoral neck may be treated by using fixed-angle devices such as a locking plate or blade plate.

Patients with more extensive injury to the articular surface of the femoral head or acetabulum are more difficult clinical problems. Hip arthroplasty or arthrodesis in the acute setting is not recommended.[111,114] These procedures are reserved as elective salvage procedures. In the presence of severe comminution when inadequate bone is available for internal fixation, resection arthroplasty may be performed in the acute setting. Complications of gunshot wounds to the hip include arthrosis, infection, fistula formation,[102,131] nonunion, malunion, and osteonecrosis.

Knee Injuries

Gunshot wounds to the knee region, including the distal femur and proximal tibia, are relatively frequent in all larger series of gunshot wounds.† Perry et al.[123] reported on 67 fractures to the knee: 37 sustained intra-articular fractures and 27 sustained extra-articular fractures. There were 29 femoral, 29 tibial, and 9 patellar fractures. Twenty-three patients had arteriograms for

---

*References 29,97,104,105,107,139,146,162.
†References 5,9,63,121,123,124,125,148.

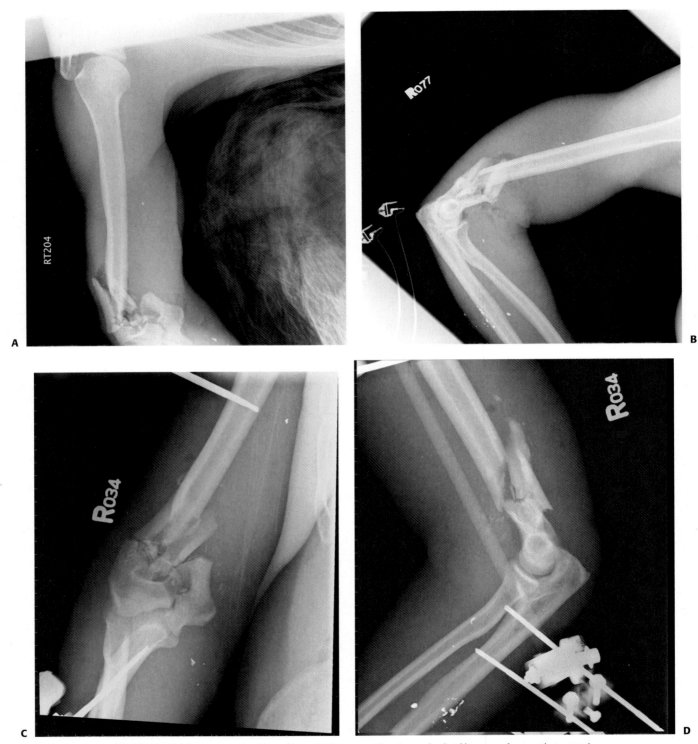

FIGURE 11-26 Anteroposterior (**A**) and lateral (**B**) preoperative views of a distal humerus fracture that extends to the joint. **C–F.** An external fixator was applied and then converted to internal fixation after the swelling of the limb subsided. (*continues*)

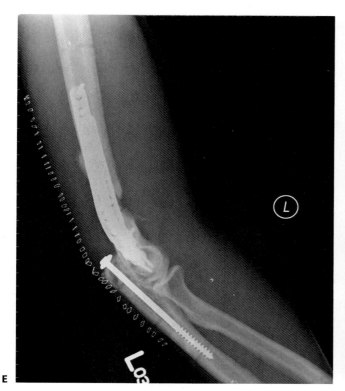

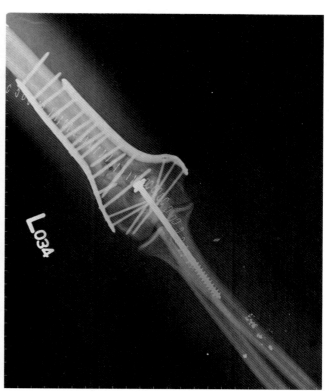

FIGURE 11-26 (*Continued*) The external fixator pins should be used outside the zone of injury.

suspected vascular injury; of these, 6 arteriograms were positive. Five limbs required vascular repair: one each of the common popliteal artery, a branch of the common femoral artery, both the peroneal and posterior tibial arteries, and the superficial femoral artery. Two patients had common peroneal nerve injury. There were also two reported infections: one superficial and one deep.

The diagnosis of an open knee joint injury in the absence of radiographic evidence of intra-articular debris, air, or presence of fractures can be difficult. A saline arthrogram or dye arthrogram can aid in diagnosis if the test is positive. However, these tests have a low sensitivity of around 40% and a negative arthrogram does not rule out an open joint injury.[149]

Goals of initial surgical treatment are to prevent infection and stabilize the limb. In the presence of severely comminuted and unstable fractures, spanning external fixation of the joint is recommended. Delayed reconstruction of the joint may be undertaken once the limb is stable. For larger fractures, an arthrotomy should be used in treating major fractures with open reduction and internal fixation (Fig. 11-28).

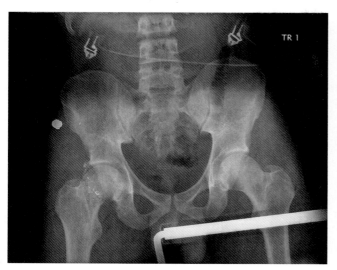

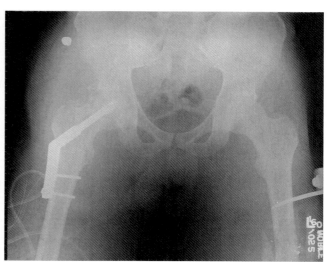

FIGURE 11-27 Anteroposterior preoperative (**A**) and postoperative (**B**) radiographs of a femoral neck fracture sustained by an intra-articular bullet. Femoral neck fractures tend to be comminuted.

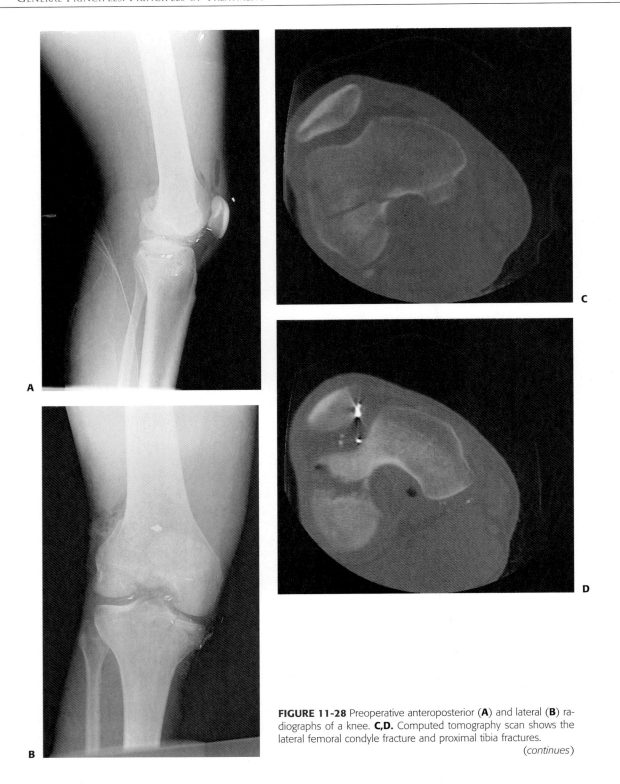

FIGURE 11-28 Preoperative anteroposterior (**A**) and lateral (**B**) radiographs of a knee. **C,D.** Computed tomography scan shows the lateral femoral condyle fracture and proximal tibia fractures.

(continues)

In presence of unstable fractures, or other associated injuries, acute reconstruction of ligaments is not recommended. In these cases, a delayed reconstruction after fracture healing and rehabilitation may be undertaken. Meniscal tears and large osteochondral fragments may be fixed acutely.

The role of arthroscopy in managing gunshot wounds of the knee has been studied by Tornetta and Hue.[148] In a review of 33 gunshot wounds to the knee without radiographic evidence of injury, arthroscopy showed 5 chondral injuries, 14 meniscal

injuries, and 5 knees with debris not seen on radiographs. Based on these findings, diagnostic arthroscopy and arthroscopic-assisted bullet removal and irrigation and débridement are recommended for gunshot wounds through the knee.

Ankle Injuries

In our series, the prevalence of gunshot wounds to the ankle is about 0.5% of those to the lower extremity. Associated injuries

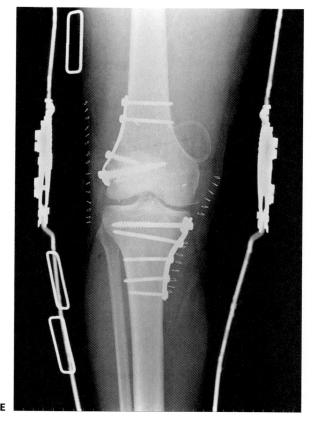

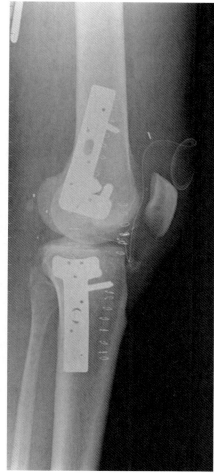

FIGURE 11-28 (*Continued*) **E,F**. This patient was treated with open reduction and internal fixation of both fractures.

include fractures and nerve, vascular, and tendon injuries.[159] Treatment is based on the personality of the fracture, ranging from spanning external fixation and/or internal fixation for a low-velocity injury. For patients with more severe soft tissue or bone injury, arthrodesis or amputation should be considered. Arthroscopy is of limited use because of the confined ankle space, good access through incisions, and the prevalence of fracture necessitating open debridement.

LONG BONE FRACTURES

Long bone fractures caused by gunshot wounds still pose a significant clinical problem for orthopaedic surgeons in war or peace. On the battlefield, caring for patients involves both transportation and treatment. The evacuation of patients may involve long distances, aircraft flight, and delayed definitive care. Initial treatment of gunshot fractures in this setting involves temporary stabilization with subsequent evacuation, followed by definitive fixation once the patient arrives in a stable hospital environment. Temporary stabilization involves the use of an external fixator to span the fracture segment.

In the nonmilitary setting, patients are initially seen and cared for at the same institution without the complexity of patient transportation through multiple echelons of care. Because of this, immediate definitive stabilization for patients with isolated long bone gunshot fractures has become a more common treatment method.

Humerus Fractures

Upper extremity long bone fractures are less prevalent than lower extremity long bone fractures, with gunshot diaphyseal humerus fractures generally being the third most common shaft fracture. Complication such as nerve injuries[59,117,136] are relatively common with patients who sustain gunshot wounds of the humerus. There is an increased prevalence nerve injury associated with the distal humerus compared with more proximal injuries.[*]

Treatment of humeral fractures in either war or peace is controversial. Reported methods of care include fracture brace, external fixation, and internal fixation. There are no prospective studies comparing the various methods of treatment for patients with gunshot wounds.[†]

The fracture brace or coaptation splint is appropriate when there is minimal soft tissue injury and the fracture can be held in alignment by this means. Proximal or very distal fractures are often not amenable to this method of care.[4,130,131]

External fixation has been reported for use in patients with more extensive injuries, such as with military wounds. Zinman et al.[161] reported on 26 Israeli war casualties who had external fixation applied for treatment of open humerus fractures. They applied monolateral external fixators to obtain union in 15 pa-

[*]References 3,4,81,62,82,85,87,130,131,154,161.
[†]References 4,82,85,130,131,154,161.

tients (57.7%). Conversion to compression plates (five patients) or a cast (six patients) was used for the other patients. Five delayed unions were identified, four of which were treated with plating and bone grafting. Fifteen patients had a total of 20 nerve injuries. One of the nerve injuries was caused by a distal, lateral pin placement that injured the radial nerve. There were four brachial and two radial artery repairs. A total of 23 patients had 6.5 years of follow-up after injury. The authors reported excellent results in 14 patients, good results in 4, fair results in 3, and poor results in 2. All fractures did eventually heal. They believed that external fixation was the best means for stabilizing fracture and allowing access to wounds for wound care. For the distal humerus, the authors recommended open pin placement if lateral pins are to be used or placing the pins from a posterior direction. They recommended this as a treatment for patients with severe open injuries secondary to war wounds.

In 1995, the Red Cross evaluated the treatment of refugees who sustained gunshot fractures of the humerus. Keller[85] studied 37 patients who were treated at a Red Cross Hospital on the Sudanese border. Patients were seen an average of 9.5 days after injury, at which time 89% of the wounds were found to be infected. Nerve palsy secondary to injury was present in eight patients in this series. They were treated with external fixation, traction, and a plaster of Paris splint. Twenty-three patients received a functional brace with plaster of Paris and splint, and seven patients received external fixation skeletal traction. Those treated with the splint had an average time of immobilization of 35.8 days, and 90% obtained adequate alignment. The authors also reported eight reoperations on four patients. The seven patients treated with external fixation had the frame applied for an average of 46.3 days, and 60% obtained adequate angulation. The authors also reported a 71.5% nonunion rate and 11 reoperations in five of the patients. Traction was used in seven patients as well, with an average immobilization of 27.7 days, with five patients obtaining union, and six reoperations on three of the patients. Although the best results were obtained in patients who were treated with splinting, the authors reported that those who had external fixation and traction had the more severe injuries.

Hall and Pankovich[62] treated 89 humerus fractures with Ender nails, of which 22 were caused by gunshot wounds (4 shotgun wounds). The authors reported good results with these patients using this technique. We know of no reports using Ender nails since this 1987 report. This technique has been overtaken by conventional intramedullary nailing as for other trauma indications.

For simple fractures with minimal soft tissue disruption, use of a functional brace following a coaptation splint seems to yield acceptable results for both initial and definitive care.[4,130,131] For patients with more extensive injuries, such as a shotgun blast at close range, we recommend the use of a spanning external fixator to provide initial stabilization for the patient.[82,87,154,161] Use of the spanning external fixator is more common with distal fractures. When both the limb and the patient have become stable, planning for fracture stabilization and soft tissue coverage can be done.

Definitive treatment of large bone or soft tissue defects may be challenging. With extensive comminution and soft tissue injury, use of a small pin fixator has been reported with good success.[3,140] For skeletal defects, use of a cage with allograft[3] or a fibular osteoseptocutaneous flap[71] has been described.

Forearm Fractures

There are relatively few reports describing care of gunshot wounds to the forearm.* There is a high reported rate of nerve injury associated with gunshot wounds to this region, and a 10% rate of compartment syndrome.[38,60,108] The goals of fracture care are to restore the length, alignment and bow of the forearm. Care for diaphyseal forearm fractures depends on the severity of the both the soft tissue and bone injury, just as with open forearm fractures not associated with firearms.* Patients with relatively stable fractures of the ulna and associated minimal soft tissue trauma may be treated by application of a cast after appropriate wound treatment. Displaced fractures should be treated with open reduction and internal fixation when soft tissues permit.

For patients with bone loss, initial stabilization with external fixation should be done when both forearm bones are involved.[60] If just the radius or ulna is involved, only splinting may be required. Use of a soft tissue antibiotic-impregnated spacer may be used for initial care of the void.[53] A second, staged procedure to reconstruct bone defects should then be done once the limb is stable. Use of autologous bone graft has been described to fill defects. Use of allograft and bioactive substances, such as bone morphogenetic protein (BMP) or demineralized bone matrix, has yet to be described.

Femur Fractures

Diaphyseal femur fractures are the most common long bone fractures associated with gunshot wounds.† Within the past 50 years, balanced skeletal traction has been the mainstay of care for femur fractures in war or peace.[151] Initial stabilization with this traction is commonly used today as a temporary means of stabilization until more definitive care can be provided.[155]

External fixation has been used for open fractures on the battlefield. Reis et al.[126] reported on 19 femur fractures that were intended to be treated with external fixation to union. Six were converted to cast brace because of pin track infection, and a further five femurs underwent open reduction internal fixation (one for refracture). Fourteen of the femurs were treated with bone grafting. The authors noted that further procedures were not done until the limb was free of obvious infection. Average time to union was 19 weeks.

Recently, external fixation been used for patients who are physiologically unable to undergo a more extensive surgery.[114,132] The concept of using temporary external fixation as a bridge from injury to definitive fracture stabilization has become a popular means to initially stabilize a patient's fracture.

Use of intramedullary nailing for complex femur fractures or malunion, nonunion, and infection associated with gunshot wounds in the United States began after World War II.[19,25]

Holloman and Horowitz[75] reviewed 26 patients who sustained fractures because of "low-velocity" gunshot wounds and were treated with intramedullary nailing an average of 9 days after injury. Nineteen of the patients were followed to union, which occurred at an average of 4.5 months after injury. Two patients had open nailing and the remaining 17 had closed nailing.

---

*References 38,40,53,60,72,127,128,145,158.
†References 10,19,25,74,113,114,116,126,132,147,151,155.

Berman et al.[10] reviewed a series of 65 patients with gunshot femur fractures at Kings County Hospital Center in Brooklyn, New York. The patients were treated with reamed intramedullary nailing an average of 2 days (range, 0–14 days) after injury and were followed an average of 2 years after injury (range, 9.5 months to 6 years). The authors found all fractures healed an average of 18 weeks (range, 13–31 weeks). Two patients had persistent drainage, which resolved with a course of oral antibiotics at 2 and 3 weeks.

Tornetta and Tiburzi[147] reviewed 38 of 55 patients with gunshot femur fractures treated with intramedullary nailing who were followed an average of 2 years (range, 14–36 months). Average time to union was 8.6 weeks (range, 5–22 weeks). Nicholas and McCoy[113] reviewed 12 patients with 14 femur fractures treated with immediate (within 8 hours) intramedullary nailing. Three patients had vascular repairs and two patients had sciatic nerve injuries. Average time to union was 5.5 months (range, 3–8 months). None of the patients had an infection.

Wiss et al.[155] performed a retrospective review of 77 patients who sustained gunshot femur fractures, of which 56 had adequate records for follow-up. The patients were initially treated with skeletal traction for 10 to 14 days, with intramedullary nailing done when the wound tracks healed. No deep wound infections were reported. Average time to union was 23 weeks (range, 14–40 weeks), and average follow-up was 16 months (range, 12–29 months). Five patients had limb length discrepancy of greater than 1 cm, and one patient had angulation of 15 degrees.

This review shows that antegrade intramedullary nails may be safely used for gunshot-induced diaphyseal femur fractures. This procedure may be done immediately or on a delayed basis, depending on the patient's condition and the degree of soft tissue injury. More proximal fractures, such as subtrochanteric fractures, may do best with using reconstruction nails to obtain more proximal fracture stabilization (Fig. 11-29).

Retrograde nailing has become a popular technique in caring for diaphyseal femur fractures, particularly those near the knee. Initially, it was believed that an open fracture would be too great of a risk for knee sepsis to permit using retrograde nails. Our group recently reported on our series of 196 gunshot femur fractures, of which 56 were treated with retrograde nailing (Fig. 11-30). There was no increased infection rate associated with this method of treatment, at either the fracture site or the knee joint. Therefore, use of retrograde nailing for diaphyseal gunshot femur fractures appears to be safe.

Complications

Wiss et al.[155] reported 5 of 56 patients requiring vascular repair in addition to the treatment of the femur fracture. He also reported three associated sciatic nerve injuries, one with return, one with partial return, and one with no return to function. Two patients had peroneal nerve palsies, one with return to function. Infection of patients is infrequent in the nonmilitary setting with gunshot femur fractures. Wiss et al.[155] reported no deep infections with 56 patients at follow-up. Holloman and Horowitz[75] reported no patients with infection after intramedullary nailing. Bergman et al.[10] reported two patients with persistent drainage, and Nicholas and McCoy[113] reported that none of their 14 patients with immediate nailing were infected.

Compartment syndrome is an infrequent complication of femoral shaft fractures. We found the 3 of 102 patients treated for diaphyseal gunshot wounds from 2001 through 2006 at Henry Ford Hospital had the diagnosis of thigh compartment syndrome.

Malunion is infrequent with the use of intramedullary nailing. Wiss et al.[155] reported angulation deformity of 15 degrees for one of 56 patients, rotational deformity reported in one patient, and five patients with a leg length discrepancy of greater than 1 cm.

Use of intramedullary nailing is now routine in many hospitals that treat nonmilitary gunshot wounds on a routine basis. Intramedullary nailing allows for better alignment, less limb length discrepancy, and earlier return to ambulation without an increased rate of infection. The use of temporary external fixation to initially care for patients with more extensive wounds or other severe injuries allows for the patient to be stabilized before undergoing more extensive surgery. Skeletal traction is an option for the short term stabilization of a fracture before more definitive care.

Treatment of femur fractures during the present Iraq and Afghanistan conflicts has been with the staged management of care. For U.S. or Allied soldiers, the fracture is stabilized with an external fixator and the patient transported to a site of definitive care, usually in the Continental United States. Once at a site of definitive care, treatment of the bone by intramedullary nailing may be done if the limb is free of infection and has good soft tissue coverage.

Tibia Fractures

The tibia is the second most frequent long bone fracture because of gunshot wounds, following the femur.[21,22,50] A variety of treatment methods have been reported for fracture care, including the use of cast or fracture brace, external fixation, and intramedullary nailing.

Wischi and Omer[156] reported on the ambulatory treatment in a cast and then fracture brace of 84 patients who sustained tibia fractures secondary to missile injuries. All of the fractures in this series had some comminution. Despite this, the authors reported less than 1 cm of shortening on 48 of 58 patients with isolated injury and an additional three patients with 1 cm of shortening. Seven patients were reported to have osteomyelitis, which prolonged the time to union. Brown and Urban[22] reported on 63 fractures in 60 patients who were also injured by war wounds and were treated in a similar manner. The fractures in this series healed at an average of 19 weeks. Shortening averaged 9 mm, ranging from 2 to 38 mm, compared with the contralateral limb. Twenty-seven of the fractures had no shortening. Four of the 63 patients had persistent drainage. Sarmiento reported on 32 tibia fractures caused by gunshot wounds treated with a fracture brace. The average time to union was 17.5 weeks, with one nonunion.

Leffers and Chandler[90] conducted a retrospective review of 40 patients with 41 tibia fractures caused by gunshot wounds. Thirty-five fractures were treated by casting followed by fracture brace. An additional five fractures were treated with external fixation because of injury severity, followed by functional brace within the first 2 months. One patient had pins and plaster. Those treated by casting healed at an average of 12 weeks, whereas those treated by external fixation healed at an average of 21 weeks. Eight patients had persistent wound drainage, with two undergoing a surgical procedure to care for the wound.

FIGURE 11-29 Anteroposterior preoperative (**A**) and postoperative (**B–D**) views of a subtrochanteric fracture. The patient was treated with a reconstruction nail and had good callus formation in the zone of injury at 6 months. The periosteal sleeve, if left relatively undisturbed, will allow for bone formation.

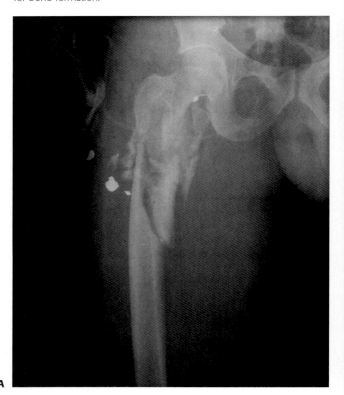

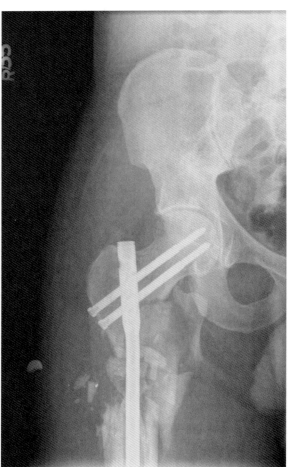

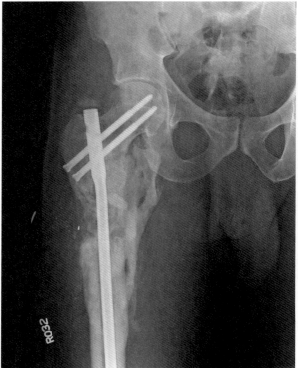

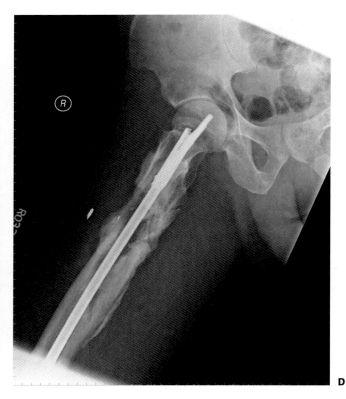

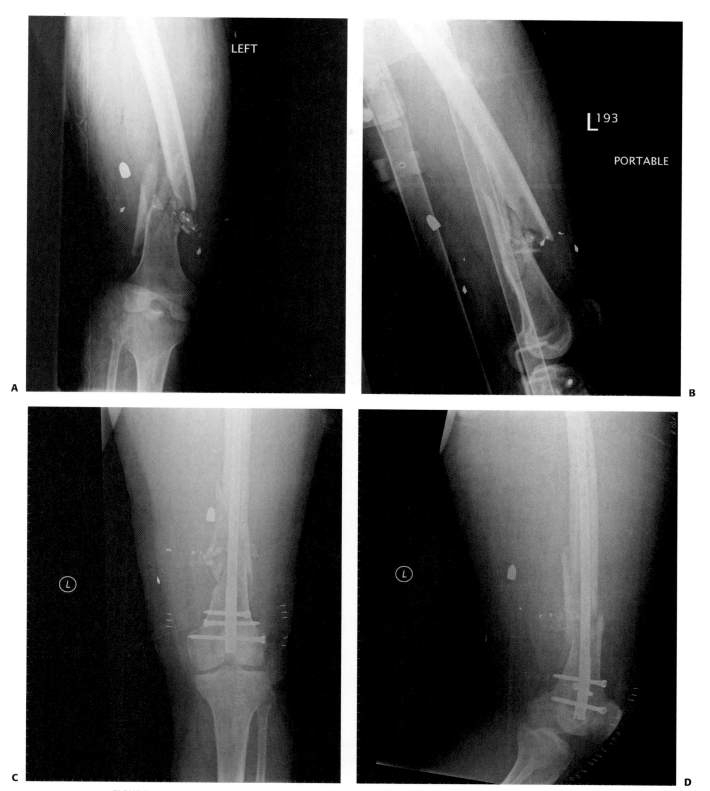

FIGURE 11-30 Preoperative (**A,B**) and postoperative (**C,D**) radiographs of a distal femur fracture. The patient was treated with an immediate retrograde intramedullary nail.

This study was limited in that it reported follow-up of only 27% of the total number of patients seen with this diagnosis at the institution.

Ferraro and Zinar[50] reported a retrospective review of 90 of 133 patients with tibia fractures caused by gunshot wounds treated at Harbor/UCLA medical Center. Fracture stabilization was a long leg cast for 58, external fixation for 17, and unreamed intramedullary nailing for 15 patients. The authors found that fractures classified as Winquist 0, 1, or 2 healed within 12 to 14 weeks and those with Winquist 3, 4, or 5 and treated with intramedullary nailing healed at an average of 18 weeks; those treated with external fixation averaged 27 weeks to union.

Present treatment of gunshot fractures of the tibial shaft depends on the amount of bone comminution and degree of soft tissue injury. Patients with tibia shaft fractures having minimal comminution, soft tissue injury, displacement, and angulation may be successfully treated with local wound care in the emergency department and application of a cast, followed by a functional brace. More comminuted fractures are better cared for with intramedullary nailing. If there is major soft tissue injury requiring a soft tissue transfer, consideration should be given to external fixation until the soft tissues are reconstructed, at which point the fixator may be removed and an intramedullary nail is inserted.

Foot Injuries

Injuries to the foot are infrequent with nonmilitary gunshot wounds. The anatomic location of foot and ankle was 39 of 2277 (1.7%) of all gunshot injuries in 1505 patients seen at Henry Ford Hospital between 2001 and 2006. Gunshot toe and metatarsal injuries vary in the degree of both soft tissue and bone injury. Minimally displaced fractures, particularly when an isolated injury, may be treated without surgical stabilization. After treatment of the soft tissues, a period of using a hard-soled postoperative shoe with dressing changes allows for a good result.

Patients with multiple metatarsal fractures or those with bone loss are candidates for surgical stabilization. Kirschner wires or external fixation may be used for initial surgical stabilization with these patients.[16,152]

Midfoot injuries tend to be more comminuted than metatarsal injuries and as a consequence require surgical stabilization. For acute injuries with bone loss, external fixation to span the area, followed by reconstruction of the bone with plates when the limb is stable, is used. Talus and calcaneus fractures are less likely to require surgical stabilization unless bone loss is present. Treatment for isolated fractures should be dependent on the degree of bone and soft tissue injury. With minimal soft tissue and bone disruption, treatment of the soft tissues followed by casting gives the best results. Infection is more common with foot injuries than other anatomic regions. Boucree reported that 12 of 101 patients with gunshot foot wounds had an infection; this is a higher incidence than reported with other anatomic regions.[16]

Foot injuries in wartime are common injuries, most often resulting from mine explosions. Nikolic et al.[115] reported that 250 of 1860 war casualties (13.4%) treated at the authors' facility in the former Republic of Yugoslavia had foot injuries. Amputations were performed in 76 (26.5%) of the feet.

Severe closed fractures are reported of patients inside vehicles struck by a large mine. This "behind armor blunt trauma" is similar to injuries seen with severe motor vehicle accidents and may be treated with the same definitive care.[112]

CONCLUSIONS

Gunshot injuries remain a major clinical problem in both war and peace. Caring for patients in war-torn regions of the world remains challenging. Patients are often initially managed under austere circumstances before and during transport for definitive care. Gunshot injuries are a significant part of the health care problem for some inner-city hospitals around the world. The orthopaedic surgeon should be knowledgeable about the clinical course and outcome of patients with gunshot wounds to provide the best care within the context of his or her medical system.

REFERENCES

1. Aboutanos MB, Baker SP. Wartime civilian casualties: epidemiology and intervention strategies. J Trauma 1997;43:721–726.
2. Anonymous (GlobalSecurity.org). Improvised explosive devices/booby traps. Available at: http://www.globalsecurity.org/military/intro/ied.htm. Accessed May 6, 2008.
3. Attias N, Lehman R, Bodell L, et al. Surgical management of a long segmental defect of the humerus using a cylindrical titanium mesh cage and plates: a case report. J Orthop Trauma 2005;19:211–216.
4. Balfour GW, Marrero CE. Fracture brace for the treatment of humerus shaft fractures caused by gunshot wounds. Orthop Clin North Am 1995;26:55–63.
5. Ballard A. Wounds of joints. In: Burkhalter WE, ed. Surgery in Vietnam, Orthopaedic Surgery. Washington, DC: Center for Military History; 1994:107–130.
6. Bartlett CS, DiFelice GS, Buly RL, et al. Cardiac arrest as a result of intraabdominal extravasation of fluid during arthroscopic removal of a loose body from the hip joint of a patient with an acetabular fracture. J Orthop Trauma 1998;12:294–299.
7. Bellamy RF, Zajtchuk R. Assessing the effectiveness of conventional weapons. In: Zajtchuk R, ed. Conventional Warfare: Ballistic Blast and Burn Injuries. Washington, DC: Office of the Surgeon General; 1991:53–82.
8. Bellamy RF, Zajtchuk R. The weapons of conventional land warfare. In: Zajtchuk R, ed. Conventional Warfare: Ballistic Blast and Burn Injuries. Washington, DC: Office of the Surgeon General; 1991:1–52.
9. Bellamy RF. Combat trauma overview. In: Anesthesia and Perioperative Care of the Combat Casualty. Washington, DC: Office of the Surgeon General; 1995:1–42.
10. Bergman M, Tornetta P, Kerina M, et al. Femur fractures caused by gunshots: treatment by immediate reamed intramedullary nailing. J Trauma 1993;34:783–785.
11. Best IM, Bumpers HL. Thigh compartment syndrome after acute ischemia. Am Surg 2002;68:996–998.
12. Beyer JC, Arima JK, Johnson DW. Enemy ordnance material. In: Beyer JC, ed. Wound Ballistics. Washington, DC: Office of the Surgeon General; 1962:1–90.
13. Beyer JC, Enos WF, Holmes RH. Personal protective armor. In: Beyer JC, ed. Wound Ballistics. Washington, DC: Office of the Surgeon General; 1962:641–689.
14. Biasutto SN, Moral AL, Bella JA. Firearm-related injuries: clinical considerations on 1326 cases. Int Surg 2006;91:39–43.
15. Bolanos A, Vigorita VJ, Meyerson RI, et al. Intra-articular histologic changes secondary to local lead intoxication in rabbit knee joints. J Trauma 1995;38:668–671.
16. Boucree J, Gabriel R, Lezine-Hanna J. Gunshot wounds to the foot. Orthop Clin North Am 1995;26:191–197.
17. Bowyer GW. Management of small fragment wounds: experience from the Afghan border. J Trauma 1996;40:S170–S172.
18. Brannon JK, Woods C, Chandran RE, et al. Gunshot wounds to the elbow. Orthop Clin North Am 1995;26:75–84.
19. Brav EA. Further evaluation of the use of intramedullary nailing in the treatment of gunshot fractures of the extremities. J Bone Joint Surg Am 1957;39A:513–520.
20. Brien EW, Brien WW, Long WT, et al. Concomitant injuries of the hip joint and abdomen resulting from gunshot wounds. Orthopaedics 1992;15:1317–1319.
21. Brien EW, Long WT, Serocki JH. Management of gunshot wounds to the tibia. Orthop Clin North Am 1995;26:165–180.
22. Brown PW, Urban JG. Early weight-bearing treatment of open fractures of the tibia. J Bone Joint Surg Am 1969;51A:59–75.
23. Brown TD, et al. The impact of gunshot wounds on an orthopaedic surgical service in an urban trauma center. J Orthop Trauma 1997;11:149–153.
24. Byrne A, Curran P. Necessity breeds invention: a study of outpatient management of low-velocity gunshot wounds. Emerg Med J 2006;23:376–378.
25. Carr CR, Turnispeed D. Experiences with intramedullary fixation of compound femoral fractures in war wounds. J Bone Joint Surg Am 1953;35A:153–171.
26. Centers for Disease Control and Prevention. WISQARS fatal injuries: mortality reports. Available at: http://webappa.cdc.gov/sasweb/ncipc/mortrate.html. Accessed January 18, 2008.
27. Chapman JR, Heley MB, Agel J, et al. Randomized prospective study of humeral shaft fracture fixation: intramedullary nails versus plates. J Orthop Trauma 2000;14:162–166.
28. Clasper JC, Hill PF, Watkins PE. Contamination of ballistic fractures: an in vitro model. Injury 2002;33:157–160.

29. Cory JW, Ruch DS. Arthroscopic removal of a .44 caliber bullet from the hip. Arthroscopy 1998;14(6):624–626.
30. Davis GL. Management of open wounds of joints during the Vietnam War. Clin Orthop Relat Res 1970;68:3–9.
31. Demiralp B, Komurcu M, Ozturk C, et al. Total elbow arthroplasty in patients who have elbow fractures by gunshot injuries: 8- to 12-year-follow-up study. Arch Orthop Trauma Surg 2008;128:17–24.
32. DePage A. General considerations as to the treatment of war wounds. Ann Surg 1919; 69:575–588.
33. DiGiacomo JC, Schwab CW, Rotondo MF, et al. Gluteal gunshot wounds: who warrants exploration? J Trauma 1994;37:622–628.
34. Dougherty PJ, Hetz SP, Fackler ML. Weapons and weapons effects. In: Lounsbury DE, ed. Emergency War Surgery Handbook. 4th Am. Ed. Washington, DC: Office of the Surgeon General; 2004.
35. Dougherty PJ. Armored vehicle crew casualties. Milit Med 1991;155:417–420.
36. Dziemian AJ, Herget CM. Physical aspects of primary contamination of bullet wounds. Milit Surg 1950;106:294–299.
37. Dziemian AJ, Mendelson JA, Lindsey D. Comparison of the wounding characteristics of some commonly encountered bullets. J Trauma 1961;1:341–353.
38. Elstrom JA, Pankovich AM, Egwele R. Extra-articular low-velocity gunshot fractures of the radius and ulna. J Bone Joint Surg Am 1978;60A:335–341.
39. Fackler ML, Dougherty PJ. Theodor Kocher and the scientific foundation of wound ballistics. Surg Gynecol Obstet 1991;172:153–160.
40. Fackler ML, Burkhalter WE. Hand and forearm injuries from penetrating projectiles. J Hand Surg 1992;17A:971–975.
41. Fackler ML. Missile-caused wounds. In: Bowen TF, Bellamy RF, eds. Emergency War Surgery. 2nd Am. Rev. Washington, DC: Office of the Surgeon General, Department of the Army; 1988:13–34.
42. Fackler ML, Surinchak JS, Malinowski JA, et al. Wounding potential of the Russian AK-74 Assault Rifle. J Trauma 1984;24:263–266.
43. Fackler ML. Wound ballistics: a review of common misconceptions. JAMA 1988;259: 2730–2736.
44. Fackler ML. Misinterpretations concerning Larrey's methods of wound treatment. Surg Gynecol Obstet 1989;168:280–282.
45. Fackler ML, Bellamy RF, Malinowski JA. A reconsideration of the wounding mechanism of very high-velocity projectiles: importance of projectile shape. J Trauma 1988;28: S63–S67.
46. Fackler ML, Breteau JPL, Courbil LJ, et al. Open wound drainage versus wound excision in treating the modern assault rifle wound. Surgery 1989;105: 576–584.
47. Fackler ML. Bullet fragmentation: a major cause of tissue disruption. J Trauma 1984; 24: 35–39.
48. Federal Bureau of Investigation. Uniformed crime reports. Available at: http://fbi.gov/ucr/ucr.htm. Accessed January 23, 2008.
49. Ferguson LK, Brown RB, Nicholson JT, et al. Observations on the treatment of battle wounds aboard a hospital ship. US Nav Med Bull 1943;41:299–305.
50. Ferraro SP Jr, Zinar DM. Management of gunshot fractures of the tibia. Orthop Clin North Am 1995;26:181.
51. Fisher GH, Florey ME, Grimson TA, et al. Penicillin in clostridial infections. Lancet 1945;March 31:395–309.
52. Foster RD, Albright JA. Acute compartment syndrome of the thigh: case report. J Trauma 1990;30:108–110.
53. Georgiadis GM, DeSilva SP. Reconstruction of skeletal defects in the forearm after trauma: treatment with cement spacer and delayed cancellous bone grafting. J Trauma 1995;38:910–914.
54. Gissler WB, Teasedall RD, Tomasin JD, et al. Management of low-velocity gunshot-induced fractures. J Orthop Trauma 1990;4:39–41.
55. Goldman A, Minkoff J, Price A, et al. A posterior arthroscopic approach to bullet extraction from the hip. J Trauma 1987;27:1294–1300.
56. Gotsch KE, Annest JL, Mercy JA, et al. Surveillance for fatal and nonfatal firearm-related injuries: United States, 1993–1998. Morb Mortal Wkly Rep MMWR 2001;50(SS02): 1–31.
57. Grundfest H, Korr IM, McMillen JH, et al. Ballistics of the Penetration of Human Skin by Small Spheres. Office of Scientific Research and Development; July 6, 1945. Missile Casualty Report No. 11.
58. Grundfest H. Penetration of Steel Spheres Into Bone. Interim report. Office of Scientific Research and Development; July 20, 1945. Missile Casualty Report No. 10.
59. Guo Y, Chiou-Tan F. Radial nerve injuries from gunshot wounds and other trauma: comparison of electrodiagnostic findings. Am J Phys Med Rehabil 2002;81:207–211.
60. Hahn M, Strauss E, Yang E. Gunshot wounds to the forearm. Orthop Clin North Am 1995;26:85–93.
61. Hakanson R, et al. Gunshot fractures: a medical, social, and economic analysis. Orthopedics 1994;17:519–523.
62. Hall RF Jr, Pankovich AM. Ender nailing of acute fractures of the humerus. J. Bone Joint Surg 1987;69A:558–567.
63. Hampton OP. The management of penetrating wounds and suppurative arthritis of the knee joint in the Mediterranean theater of operations. J Bone Joint Surg 1946;28: 659–680.
64. Hampton OP. The indications for debridement of gunshot (bullet) wounds of the extremities in civilian practice. J Trauma 1961;1:368–372.
65. Hansraj KK, Weaver LD, Todd AO, et al. Efficacy of ceftriaxone versus cefazolin in the prophylactic management of extra-articular cortical violation of bone due to low-velocity gunshot wounds. Orthop Clin North Am 1995;26:9–17.
66. Harding NR, Lipton JF, Vigorita VJ, et al. Experimental lead arthropathy: an animal model. J Trauma 1999;47:951–961.
67. Harvey EN. Studies on wound ballistics. In: Andrus EC, Keefer CS, et al., eds. Advances in Military Medicine, vol 1. Boston: Little, Brown, and Co; 1948:191–205.
68. Harvey EN, Butler EG, McMillen JH, et al. Mechanism of wounding. War Med 1945; 8:91–104.
69. Harvey EN, Korr IM, Oster G, et al. Secondary damage in wounding due to pressure changes accompanying the passage of high-velocity missiles. Surgery 1946;21: 218–239.
70. Harvey EN. McMillen JH, Butler EG, et al. Mechanism of Wounding. In: Beyer JC, ed. Wound Ballistics. Washington, DC: Office of the Surgeon General; 1962:143–235.
71. Heitmann C, Erdmann D, Levin LS. Treatment of segmental defects of the humerus with an osteoseptocutaneous fibular transplant. J Bone Jt Surg 2002;84A:2216–2223.
72. Hennessy MJ, Banks HH, Leach RB, et al. Extremity gunshot wound and gunshot fracture in civilian practice. Clin Orthop Rel Res 1976;114:296–303.
73. Herget CM, Coe GB, Beyer JC. Wound ballistics and body armor in Korea. In: Beyer JC, ed. Wound Ballistics. Washington, DC: Office of the Surgeon General; 1962:691–767.
74. Hoegler J, Weir R, Dougherty P, et al. Gunshot wounds of femoral shafts in urban populations: is emergent retrograde intramedullary nailing appropriate? Presented at the Orthopaedic Trauma Association Annual Meeting, Phoenix, AZ, October 2006.
75. Holloman MW, Horowitz M. Femoral fractures secondary- to low-velocity missiles: treatment with delayed intramedullary fixation. J Orthop Trauma 1990;4:64–69.
76. Hoover NW, Ivins JC. Wound debridement. Arch Surg 1959;79:701–710.
77. Huelke DF, Buege LJ, Harger JH. Bone fractures produced by high-velocity impacts. Am J Anat 1967;120:123–132.
78. Huelke DF, Harger JH, Buege LJ, et al. An experimental study in bio-ballistics: femoral fractures produced by projectiles, II: shaft impacts. J Biomech 1968;1:313–321.
79. Huelke DF, Harger JH, Buege LJ, et al. An experimental study in bio-ballistics. J Biomech 1968;1:97–105.
80. Jamdar S, Helm AT, Redfern DR. Arthroscopic removal of a shotgun pellet from the elbow. Arthroscopy 2001;17:1–3.
81. Johnson EC, Strauss E. Recent advances in the treatment of gunshot fractures of the humeral shaft. Clin Orthop 2003;408:126–132.
82. Joshi A, Labbe M, Lindsey RW. Humeral fracture secondary to civilian gunshot injury. Injury 1998;S13–S17.
83. Josserand MH, Stevenson J. Pistols, Revolvers, and Ammunition. New York: Bonanza Books; 1972.
84. Keith E. Shotguns. Harrisburg, PA: Stackpole Books; 1950.
85. Keller A. The management of gunshot fractures of the humerus. Injury 1995;26:93–96.
86. Knapp TP, Patzakis MJ, Lee J, et al. Comparison of intravenous and oral antibiotic therapy in the treatment of fractures caused by low-velocity gunshots. J Bone Joint Surg Am 1996;78A:1167–1171.
87. Komurcu M, Yanmiş I, Ateşalp AS, et al. Treatment results for open comminuted distal humerus fractures with Ilizarov external fixator. Milit Med 2003;168:694–697.
88. Krauss M. Studies in wound ballistics: temporary cavity effects in soft tissues. Milit Med 1957;121:221–231.
89. LaGarde LA. Poisoned wounds by the implements of warfare. JAMA 1903;40: 984–1067.
90. Leffers D, Chandler RW. Tibial fractures associated with civilian gunshot wounds. J Trauma 1985;25:1059–1064.
91. Leininger BE, Rasmussen TE, Smith DL, et al. Experience with wound VAC and delayed primary closure of contaminated soft tissue injuries in Iraq. J Trauma 2006;61: 1207–1211.
92. Lenihan MR, Brien WW, Gellman H, et al. Fractures of the forearm resulting from low-velocity gunshot wounds. J Orthop Trauma 1992;6:32–35.
93. Lewis DD. Debridement. JAMA 1919;73:377–383.
94. Linden MA, Manton WI, Stewart RM, et al. Lead poisoning from retained bullets: pathogenesis, diagnosis, and management. Ann Surg 1982;195: 305–313.
95. Lindberg RB, Wetzler TF, Marshall JD, et al. The bacterial flora of battle wounds at the time of primary debridement. Ann Surg 1955;141:369–374.
96. Leonard MH. The solution of lead by synovial fluid. Clin Orthop 1969;64:255–261.
97. Long WT, Brien EW, Boucree JB, et al. Management of civilian gunshot injuries to the hip. Orthop Clin North Am 1995;26:123–131.
98. Lounsbury DE. Levels of medical care. In: Emergency War Surgery. 4th US Rev. Washington, DC: Borden Institute; 2004:2.1–2.11.
99. Lounsbury DE. Triage. In: Emergency War Surgery. 4th US Rev. Washington, DC: Borden Institute; 2004:3.1–3.17.
100. Love AG. The Medical Department of the United States in the World War. Volume XV, Statistics. Washington, DC: Office of the Surgeon General; 1925:1019.
101. Marcus MA, Blair WF, Shuck JM, et al. Low-velocity gunshot wounds to extremities. J Trauma 1980;20:1061–1064.
102. McAulliffe JA, Burkhalter WE, Ouellette EA, et al. Compression plate arthrodesis of the elbow. J Bone Joint Surg Br 1992;74B:300–304.
103. Mendelson JA, Glover JL. Sphere and shell fragment wounds of soft tissues: experimental study. J Trauma 1967;7:889–914.
104. Meyer NJ, Thiel B, Ninomiya JT. Retrieval of an intact, intra-articular bullet by hip arthroscopy using the lateral approach. J Orthop Trauma 2002;16:51–53.
105. Mineo RC, Gittins ME. Arthroscopic removal of a bullet embedded in the acetabulum. Arthroscopy 2003;19:121–124.
106. Ming L, Yu-Yuan M, Rong-Xiang F, et al. The characteristics of the pressure waves generated in the soft target by impact and its contribution to indirect bone fractures. J Trauma 1988;28:S104–S109.
107. Miric DM, Bumbasirevic MZ, Senohradski KK, et al. Pelvifemoral external fixation for the treatment of open fractures caused by gunshot wounds. Acad Orthop Belg 2002; 58:37–41.
108. Moed BR, Fakhour AJ. Compartment syndrome after low-velocity gunshot wounds to the forearm. J Orthop Trauma 1991;5:134–137.
109. Morgan MM, Spencer AD, Hershey FB. Debridement of civilian gunshot wounds of soft tissue. J Trauma 1961;1:354–360.
110. Morganstern S, Seery W, Borshuk S, et al. Septic arthritis secondary to vesico-acetabular fistula: a case report. J Urol 1976;116:116–117.
111. Najibi S, Dougherty PD, Morandi MM. Management of gunshot wounds to the joints. Tech Orthop 2006;21:200–204.
112. Necchaev EA, Gritsanov AI, Fomin NF, et al. Mine blast trauma. Experience from the war in Afghanistan (Khlunovskaya GP, translator). Stockholm, Sweden: Falths Tryckeri; 1995.
113. Nicholas RM, McCoy GF. Immediate intramedullary nailing of femoral shaft fractures due to gunshots. Injury 1995;26:257–259.
114. Nikolić D, Jovanović Z, Turković G, et al. Subtrochanteric missile fractures of the femur. Injury 1998;29:743–749.
115. Nikolic D, Jovanovic Z, Vulovic R, et al. Primary surgical treatment of war injuries of the foot. Injury 2000;31:193–197.
116. Nowotarski PJ, Turen Ch, Brumback RJ, et al. Conversion of external fixation to intra-

medullary nailing for fractures of the shaft of the femur in multiply injured patients. J. Bone Joint Surg Am 2000;82A:781–788.

117. Omer GE. Injuries to nerves of the upper extremity. J Bone Joint Surg Am 1974;56A: 1615–1624.

118. Ordog GJ, Wasserberger J, Balasubramanium S, et al. Civilian gunshot wounds: outpatient management. J Trauma 1994;36:106–111.

119. Otero F, Cuartas E. Arthroscopic removal of bullet fragments from the subacromial space of the shoulder joint. Arthroscopy 2004;20:754–756.

120. Oughterson AW, Hull HC, Sutherland FA, et al. Study on wound ballistics: Bougainville campaign. In: Beyer JC, ed. Wound Ballistics. Washington, DC: Office of the Surgeon General, Department of the Army; 1962:281–436.

121. Parisien SJ, Esformes I. The role of arthroscopy in management of low-velocity gunshot wounds to the knee joint. Clin Orthop Rel Res 1984;185:207–213.

122. Patzakis MJ, Harvey JP, Ivler D. The role of antibiotics in the management of open fractures. J Bone Joint Surg Am 1974;56A:532–541.

123. Perry DJ, Sanders DP, Nyirenda CD, et al. Gunshot wounds to the knee. Orthop Clin North Am 1995;26:155–163.

124. Petersen W, Beske C, Stein V, et al. Arthroscopic removal of a projectile from the intra-articular cavity of the knee joint. Arch Orthop Trauma Surg 2002;122:235–236.

125. Pool EH, Lee BJ, Dineen PA. Surgery of the soft parts, bones, and joints, at a front hospital. Surg Gynecol Obstet 1919;289–311.

126. Reis ND, Zinman C, Besser MIB, et al. A philosophy of limb salvage in war: use of the fixateur externe. Milit Med 1991;156:505–520.

127. Robert RH. Gunshots to the hand and upper extremity. Clin Orthop 2003;408: 133–144.

128. Rodrigues RL, Sammer DM, Chung KC. Treatment of complex below-the-elbow gunshot wounds. Ann Plast Surg 2006;56:122–127.

129. Rose SC, Fujisaki CK, Moore EE. Incomplete fractures associated with penetrating trauma: etiology, appearance, and natural history. J Trauma 1988;28:106–109.

130. Sarmiento A, Latta L. The evolution of functional bracing of fractures. J Bone Joint Surg Br 2006;88B:141–148.

131. Sarmiento A, Zagorski JB, Zych GA, et al. Functional bracing for the treatment of fractures of the humeral diaphysis. J Bone Joint Surg Am 2000;82A:478–486.

132. Scalea TM, Boswell SA, Scott JD, et al. External fixation as a bridge to intramedullary nailing for patients with multiple injuries and with femur fractures: damage control orthopaedics. J Trauma 2000;48:613–623.

134. Sclafani SJA, Vuletin JC, Twersky J. Lead arthropathy: arthritis caused by retained intra-articular bullets. Radiology 1985;156:299–302.

135. Scully RE, Artiz CP, Sako Y. An evaluation of the surgeon's criteria for determining the viability of muscle during debridement. Arch Surg 1956;72:1031–1035.

136. Shao YC, Harwood P, Grotz MR, et al. Radial nerve palsy associated with fractures of the shaft of the humerus: a systematic review. J Bone Joint Surg Br 2005;87B: 1647–1652.

137. Simchen E, Raz R, Stein H, et al. Risk factors for infection in fracture war wounds (1973 and 1982 Wars, Israel). Milit Med 1991;156:520–527.

138. Simchen E, Sacks T. Infection in war wounds: experience during the 1973 October War in Israel. Ann Surg 1975;182:754–761.

139. Singleton SB, Joshi A, Schwartz MA, et al. Arthroscopic bullet removal from the acetabulum. Arthroscopy 2005;21:360–364.

140. Skaggs DL, Hale DM, Buggay D, et al. Use of a hybrid external fixator for a severely comminuted juxta-articular fracture of the distal humerus. J Orthop Trauma 1998;12: 449–442.

141. Smith WHB. Small Arms of the World. Harrisburg, PA: Stackpole Books; 1983.

142. Smith WS, Ward RM. Septic arthritis of the hip complicating perforation of abdominal organs. JAMA 1966;195:170–173.

143. Stein JS, Strauss E. Gunshot wounds to the upper extremity. Evaluation and management of vascular injuries. Orthop Clin North Am 1995;26:29–36.

144. Stewart MPM, Birch R. Penetrating missile injuries to the brachial plexus. J Bone Joint Surg Br 2001;83B:517–524.

145. Tarkin IS, Hatzidakis A, Hoxie SC, et al. Arthroscopic treatment of gunshot wounds to the shoulder. Arthroscopy 2003;19:85–89.

146. Teloken MA, Schmietd I, Tomlinson DP. Hip arthroscopy: a unique inferomedial approach to bullet removal. Arthroscopy 2002;18:1–3.

147. Tornetta P, Tiburzi D. Anterograde interlocked nailing of distal femoral fractures after gunshot wounds. J Orthop Trauma 1994;8:220–227.

148. Tornetta P, Hue RC. Intraarticular findings after gunshot wounds through the knee. J Orthop Trauma 1997;11:422–424.

149. Tornetta P III, Boes MT, Schepsis AA, et al. How effective is a saline arthrogram for wounds around the knee? Clin Orthop 2008;466:432–435.

150. Turen CH, Burgess AR, Vanco B. Skeletal stabilization for tibial fractures associated with acute compartment syndrome. Clin Orthop 1995;315:163–168.

151. Urist MR, Quigley TB. Use of skeletal traction for mass treatment of compound fractures. Arch Surg 1951;63:834–844.

152. Verheyden C, McLaughlin B, Law C, et al. Through-and-through gunshot wounds to the foot: the "Fearless Fosdick" injury. Ann Plast Surg 2005;55:474–478.

153. Weaver LD, et al. Gunshot wound injuries: frequency and cost analysis in south central Los Angeles. Orthop Clin North Am 1995;26:1–7.

154. Wisniewski TF, Radziejowski MJ. Gunshot fractures of the humeral shaft treated with external fixation. J Orthop Trauma 1996;10:273–278.

155. Wiss DA, Brien WW, Becker V. Interlocking nailing for the treatment of femoral fractures due to gunshot wounds. J Bone Joint Surg Am 1991;73A:598–606.

156. Witschi TH, Omer GE. The treatment of open tibial shaft fractures from Vietnam War. J Trauma 1970;10:105–111.

157. Woloszyn JT, Uitvlugt GM, Castle ME. Management of civilian gunshot fractures of the extremities. Clin Orthop 1988;226:247–250.

158. Wu CD. Low-velocity gunshot fractures of the radius and ulna: report and review of the literature. J Trauma 1995;39:1003–1005.

159. Yildiz CO, Atesalp AS, Demiralp B, et al. High-velocity gunshot wounds of the tibial plafond managed with Ilizarov external fixation. J Orthop Trauma 2003;17:421–429.

160. Zellweger R, et al. An analysis of 124 surgically managed brachial artery injuries. Am J Surg 2004;188:240–245.

161. Zinman C, Norman D, Hamoud K, et al. External fixation for severe open fractures of the humerus caused by missiles. J Orthop Trauma 1997;11:536–539.

162. Zura RD, Bosse MJ. Current treatment of gunshot wounds of the hip and pelvis. Clin Orthop 2003;408:110–114.

12

PRINCIPLES OF MANGLED EXTREMITY MANAGEMENT

Eric S. Moghadamian, Michael J. Bosse, and Ellen J. MacKenzie

INTRODUCTION

The term "mangled extremity" refers to an injury to an extremity so severe that salvage is often questionable and amputation is a possible outcome. This injury is always a result of high-energy trauma caused by some combination of crush, shear, blast, and bending forces. Associated fractures usually verify the high-energy forces of the mechanism of injury by exhibiting extensive comminution patterns. The skin is often degloved with large areas of loss secondary to avulsion or ischemia and the fascial compartments are typically incompletely opened by explosion or tear. Muscle tissues are typically damaged at both local and regional levels by direct as well as indirect injury. Furthermore, soft tissue planes are usually extensively disrupted and, when present, contaminants generally infiltrate all of these planes (Fig. 12-1). Not only are the injury patterns themselves complex, but the medical, psychological, and socioeconomic impacts that these injuries have on the patient make their management a difficult task, even in the most experienced of hands.

Although most of the advances that have taken place in the management of the mangled extremity have occurred during times of war, the majority of limb-threatening injuries seen in practices today are the result of high-speed motor vehicle collisions. Modification of passenger restraints, vehicle safety engineering, and the legislation of seatbelt and air-bag protection appear to be decreasing the mortality rate associated with motor

FIGURE 12-1 A typical example of a limb-threatening injury at presentation.

vehicle crashes. As a result, the incidence of severe lower extremity trauma may be increasing. In the United States, injuries to the lower extremity account for over 250,000 hospital admissions annually for patients 18 to 54 years of age. It is estimated that over half of these admissions result from a high-energy mechanism.[31] Orthopaedic surgeons providing emergency department trauma coverage need to understand the historical concepts surrounding the care for these injuries as well as recent modifications of these concepts based on numerous advances in technology combined with a better understanding of the long-term clinical outcomes of these injury patterns.

HISTORICAL BACKGROUND

From the time of Hippocrates, the management of the limb-threatening lower extremity injury has plagued patients and surgeons alike. Until the implementation of amputation, most severe open fractures resulted in sepsis and these injuries were often fatal.[2] In its infancy, amputation itself usually entailed a very high mortality rate, often from hemorrhage or sepsis. Amputations performed during the Franco-Prussian War and American Civil War carried mortality rates ranging from 26% to as high as 90%.[22,87] As amputation techniques improved, so did our understanding of the concepts of bacterial contamination and infection. By the mid-1880s, through the pioneering works of Pasteur, Koch, and Lister on bacterial contamination and infection, there was a rapid increase in the use of antiseptic agents, soon followed by the introduction of aseptic methods and then mortality rates rapidly declined.[115] Subsequently, topical sulfa agents were introduced just before World War I and systemic antibiotics became available during World War II and the Korean War.[87,89] Through advances in surgical technique, as well as through a better understanding of microbial prophylaxis and treatment, extremity injuries that were once considered to be life threatening have now been rendered, at the very least, survivable.

Despite the relative success of amputation surgery in reducing mortality in the treatment of patients with a life- or limb-threatening injury of the extremity, many patients and physicians have historically perceived amputation as a failure of therapy and have fought aggressively to salvage the mangled limb. Although a pioneer in the field of amputation, Ambrose Paré knowingly risked his own life over limb when he insisted on conservative management of his own open tibia fracture rather than amputation. Not only did he survive the injury, but his documentation of the conservative treatment of a potentially limb- and life-threatening injury serves as one of the first known documented cases of "limb salvage." Nevertheless, for centuries to come, most complex extremity injuries were routinely treated with amputation. After World War II, medical and surgical training became more specialized and numerous developments in the civilian medical arena led to a revolution in the management of limb-threatening battlefield injuries, which dictates our treatment today. Arterial repair and bypass were attempted on a wide scale during the Korean and Vietnam Wars, subsequently reducing the amputation rates in extremities with vascular injuries from 50% to 13%.[51–53,87,96] Over time, similar advances in all aspects of wound and fracture management have improved our ability to reconstruct the severely injured extremity. Limbs that would have required an amputation 20 years ago are now routinely entered into complex reconstruction protocols. The development of second- and third-generation antibiotics and microsurgical tissue transfers[14,62,102,111] and the use of temporary intraluminal vascular shunts,[56] wound irrigation strategies, and tissue-friendly fracture fixation methods have combined to make initial limb salvage, at the very least, feasible in most cases. Furthermore, by using massive autogenous grafts and/or osteoinductive materials,[20,32,40,60,64] as well as through the technique of bone transport,[26,80,92,97] delayed large-segment bone defect reconstruction has become routine. Although limb salvage has become technically feasible, the initial assessment and management of the patient and the injury are paramount in determining whether salvage is advisable.

PRINCIPLES OF MANAGEMENT

Initial Evaluation

Most limb-threatening injuries are very impressive on presentation and can often be distracting to the treating surgeon and medical team. Because these injuries are usually the result of a high-energy mechanism, routine trauma protocols should be followed that first address the patient as a whole and not just the injured extremity, because 10% to 17% of these patients will have an associated life-threatening injury.[16,67] Evaluation should begin by following the principles of Advanced Trauma Life Support (ATLS). Once the patient has been stabilized and the primary and secondary trauma surveys have been completed, a thorough orthopaedic evaluation is mandatory. This should include a determination of the time of injury, mechanism of injury, the age of the patient, and the presence of any other social or medical comorbidities. Prophylactic antibiotics should be administered as soon as possible and tetanus prophylaxis should be administered as indicated. The injured extremity should first be evaluated for adequate perfusion and, if a vascular injury is suspected, vascular surgery consultation should be obtained. The soft tissue wound should be inspected and the pattern of soft tissue injury and contamination should be noted. If possible, a cursory removal of any gross contamination via irrigation should be performed before dressing the wounds and immobilizing the extremity, especially if a fracture reduction or joint reduction is thought to be necessary before transport to the operating room for initial wound débridement. A detailed motor examination and sensory examination should be performed and documented, both before and after any manipulation of the extremity. The presence of an associated compartment syndrome should be entertained and ruled out. Radiographic evaluation should include two orthogonal views of any involved joints or long bones, as well as the joint above and below any confirmed fractures. Photographs of the extremity should be obtained whenever possible. These can provide invaluable documentation of the extent of the initial injury and, during the course of treatment, serve as a visual record of progress to or away from a functional salvaged extremity.[29]

Not only should the orthopaedic examination include the extremity in question, but a comprehensive musculoskeletal examination should be performed to rule out any concomitant musculoskeletal injuries. In the case of a polytrauma patient with a mangled extremity, the initial diagnostic workup and treatment of any life-threatening injuries can often be time consuming and precede the management of the injured limb; therefore, a sterile dressing should be applied to all wounds and the limb immobilized as soon as possible to prevent any ongoing soft tissue damage until proper débridement and stabilization procedures can be performed in the controlled setting of the operating room.

Vascular Assessment

Limb-threatening injuries are often associated with vascular insult. Arterial injuries usually present with either hard or soft signs suggestive of injury. Examples of hard signs that should be documented and investigated include pulsatile bleeding, the presence of a rapidly expanding hematoma, a palpable thrill, or audible bruit, as well as the presence of any of the classic signs of obvious arterial occlusion (pulselessness, pallor, paresthesia, pain, paralysis, poikilothermia). Soft signs of arterial injury include a history of arterial bleeding, a nonexpanding hematoma, a pulse deficit without ischemia, a neurological deficit originating in a nerve adjacent to a named artery, and the proximity of a penetrating wound, fracture, or dislocation near to a named artery.[84] In addition to observing for these hard and soft signs of vascular injury, a formal vascular examination should be conducted. The skin color and time required for capillary refilling of the skin of the distal extremity should be compared with and documented against that of the uninjured contralateral side. The distal extremity should be evaluated for the presence of palpable peripheral pulses and/or Doppler signal. The limb with gross deformity secondary to fracture or dislocation with questionably palpable pulses or reduced Doppler audible flow should undergo immediate gentle reduction of the deformity and immobilization of the reduced limb in an effort to relieve possible kinking or compression of the vascular structures. Subsequently, pulse assessment of the distal extremity should again be performed and documented after any reduction maneuvers. Arterial pressure indices (APIs) should also be obtained in the presence of a history of pulselessness in the extremity or if the vascular status of the distal extremity remains unclear even after reduction attempts have been made to restore reasonable alignment to the extremity. APIs are obtained by first identifying the dorsalis pedis and posterior tibial arteries of the injured extremity using a Doppler probe. Next, a blood pressure cuff is placed proximal to the level of injury and then inflated to a suprasystolic level causing cessation of the normal Doppler signal. The cuff is then slowly deflated and the pressure at which the Doppler signal returns identifies the ankle systolic pressure to the injured limb. This procedure should then be repeated on the contralateral extremity as well as in the arm (brachial pressures). The pressure in the injured extremity is then compared with the pressure in the arm or the unaffected extremity and reported as a ratio of the normal systolic pressure (e.g., if the brachial systolic pressure is equal to 120 mm Hg and the systolic pressure in the injured limb is equal to 90, then API is reported as 0.75). If the API is lower than 0.90 or distal pulses remain absent despite reduction, angiography and/or vascular surgery consultation is indicated.

Once the location of an arterial injury has been identified, treatment should first address restoration of arterial inflow and skeletal stabilization. In the patient with a pulseless but perfused limb, the priority and sequence of vascular and orthopaedic repair depend primarily on the experience and availability of both the orthopaedic and vascular teams. At times, if the fracture is relatively stable and will require little manipulation, immediate arterial repair should precede bony stabilization. However, if the fracture is excessively comminuted, displaced, or shortened, rapid bony stabilization should be performed before any attempts at vascular repair. Not only will this aid in the exposure of the vascular injury, but doing so brings the limb out to its proper resting length, ensuring the vascular repair is of sufficient length to allow for further manipulation and reduction of the extremity with less risk of vascular complications after the repair has been completed.[55]

In the patient who has undergone a period of prolonged ischemia, the restoration of arterial inflow should be the highest priority and consideration should be given to temporary intraluminal vascular shunting of the extremity.[56,57,86] The insertion of an intraluminal shunt can rapidly restore arterial inflow and allow for a more detailed examination to better determine the extent of the injury and whether the limb is indeed salvageable. Because the shunt will hold up to fairly vigorous manipulation, it will also allow for a more thorough débridement and appropriate stabilization of the bone and soft tissues. Once the débridement has been completed and the bony injury temporarily or definitively stabilized, formal vascular repair can then either proceed immediately or in a delayed fashion if the patient remains in extremis.

A compartment syndrome is not uncommon after restoration of arterial inflow to an ischemic and traumatized limb. The diminished arterial inflow during the ischemic period combined with the "reperfusion injury" that occurs after arterial repair can result in interstitial fluid leakage and elevated compartment pressures. Fasciotomies should be performed after any revascularization procedure in the mangled extremity.[67,68,78] While most vascular and general surgeons are adequately trained to perform decompressive fasciotomies, ideally, these should be performed by or under the supervision of the orthopaedic surgeon to ensure adequate compartment decompression as well as appropriate fasciotomy incision placement that will not compromise later bony and soft tissue reconstructive procedures.

Operative Débridement and Stabilization

Once the extremity has been evaluated in the emergency department and photographs have been taken for the medical record, any open wounds should be gently rinsed with a copious amount of normal saline and dressed with sterile gauze.[23] The dressings should be left in place until the patient reaches the operating room for definitive débridement.

In the operating room, a tourniquet should be placed to prevent the possibility of exsanguination, but it should not be inflated unless absolutely necessary to prevent further ischemic injury to the extremity. Once the tourniquet is in place, the splint and dressings can be removed and the extremity again examined for perfusion. Although typically referred to as "irrigation and débridement," the first and most important step is a thorough débridement of the wound. This should be done in a methodical manner to ensure adequate removal of any contaminating material and devitalized tissues. The skin and subcutaneous tissue should be addressed first. While the initial open skin wounds are obvious, the energy imparted at the time of injury typically produces a shock wave that causes stripping of the soft tissues. Acute traumatic injuries to the extremity typically result in so-called zones of injury. A gradient of energy extends peripherally from the site of impact, variably damaging tissues along its path. A central zone of necrotic tissue exists at and around the point of impact and greatest injury. These tissues are typically nonviable regardless of the intervention. Surrounding this area lies a zone of marginal stasis. This ischemic penumbra consists of tissue that is variably injured and may or may not survive despite appropriate intervention. Finally, at the periphery of the injury exists a zone of noninjured or minimally injured tissue that, while not subject to the primary injury, could be at risk from the delayed physiological responses to the primary area of injury.[41,68] To address these zones of injury, the open wounds should be extended or separate extensile incisions should be performed to adequately assess and debride the wound. These incisions should be axially aligned and thoughtfully placed so as not to create "at-risk" flaps or preclude any later reconstructive efforts.

Once the skin wounds have been extended, all necrotic muscle, fat, fascia, skin, and other nonviable tissue within the central zone of injury should be removed. Muscle should be tested for viability based on its contractility, consistency, color, and capillary bleeding (the four Cs), and if it is found to be nonviable, it should be debrided, regardless of the expected functional loss. While the amount of tissue damage seen on the initial débridement can be quite extensive, the quantity of tissue necrosis from the delayed response to the injury within the zone of marginal stasis can far exceed the loss and destruction caused by the initial traumatic injury. Because the exact degree of expected tissue loss and necrosis cannot be determined easily at the time of initial débridement, serial débridements will be required until the identification and removal of all nonviable tissue has been achieved and wound homeostasis obtained.

Skeletal Stabilization

Skeletal stabilization is an extremely important tenant in the initial management of the limb at risk. Stabilization of the bony skeleton prevents ongoing soft tissue damage, promotes wound healing, and is thought to protect against infection. In an animal study, Worlock et al.[124] examined the rate of infection and osteomyelitis associated with stable and unstable skeletal fixation. They reported that the infection rate in the unstable group was nearly double that in the skeletal stabilization group.

The choice of skeletal stabilization is dependent on the location of the bony injury, the degree of soft tissue injury, and the overall condition of the patient at the time of initial operative management. Stabilization options range from splint immobilization or skeletal traction to internal fixation. While no one technique has proved to be superior to all others in all clinical situations, in general, the more severe the injury, the greater is the need for direct skeletal fixation to provide improved access to the traumatic wound. Immediate intramedullary stabilization or plate fixation of type I, II, and IIIA open fractures remains an accepted treatment strategy. However, most limb-threatening injuries present as type IIIB or type IIIC open fractures. These injuries are perhaps most judiciously managed with temporizing external fixation. External fixation in this setting offers many advantages. It can be applied relatively quickly and without the use of fluoroscopy while still providing excellent stability and alignment of the limb until definitive fixation can be performed. External fixation also allows for redisplacement of the fracture fragments for a more thorough evaluation and débridement of the soft tissues during any repeat procedures. Once wound homeostasis has been obtained, conversion to definitive internal fixation can be performed on a delayed basis with good results.[3,103,104] External fixation can also be chosen as the form of definitive fixation for diaphyseal fractures, but multiple studies have found this approach to have slightly higher complication rates and poorer outcomes when directly compared with intramedullary fixation. Henley et al.[46] prospectively compared unreamed intramedullary nailing with external fixation in patients with type II, IIIA, and IIIB open fractures of the tibial shaft. Both groups underwent identical soft tissue management before and after skeletal fixation. Their study showed that those patients in the intramedullary nail fixation group had significantly fewer incidences of malalignment and underwent fewer subsequent procedures than did those in the external fixation group. Tornetta et al.[116] also reported on the early results of a randomized, prospective study comparing external fixation with the use of nonreamed locked nails in type IIIB open tibial fractures. Again, both groups had the same initial management, soft tissue procedures, and early bone grafting. They found that the intramedullary nail treatment group had slightly better knee and ankle motion and less final angulation at the fracture site. They also concluded that that the nailed fractures were consistently easier to manage, especially in terms of soft tissue procedures and bone grafting. Furthermore, they thought the intramedullary nailing was preferred by their patients and that it did not require the same high level of patient compliance as external fixation. Using data obtained through the Lower Extremity Assessment Project (LEAP), Webb et al.[121] reviewed 156 patients with the combination of a fractured tibia in association with a mangled lower extremity. One hundred five patients with 17 type IIIA, 84 type IIIB, and 4 type IIIC tibial fractures had follow-up to 2 years. The authors found that definitive treatment with a nail yielded better outcomes than definitive treatment with external fixation. In their series, the external fixation patients had a significantly increased likelihood of both infection and nonunion.

Hyperbaric Oxygen

Hyperbaric oxygen (HBO) allows patients to breathe 100% oxygen in a chamber under increased barometric pressure. This results in a supraphysiological arterial oxygen saturation level, creating an expanded radius of diffusion for oxygen into the tissues that results in increased oxygen delivery at the periphery of certain wounds. As a result, HBO is thought to enhance oxygen delivery to injured tissues affected by vascular disruption, thrombosis, cytogenic and vasogenic edema, and cellular hypoxia as a result of trauma to the extremity.

This improved oxygen delivery is believed to be most beneficial in the peripheral zone of injury where tissue that is variably injured may or may not survive despite other appropriate interventions. Injured but viable cells in this area have increased oxygen needs at the very time when oxygen delivery is decreased by disruption of the microvascular supply.[54,91] As such, HBO can be applied in an effort to mitigate this process of secondary injury in extremity trauma and minimize the resultant tissue loss at different points in both the pathological and recovery processes.[41]

Most clinical reports on HBO therapy in the treatment of extremity trauma are observational with fairly anecdotal reports on its efficacy. However, in 1996 Bouachour et al.[11] performed a randomized placebo-controlled human trial of HBO as an adjunct to the management of crush injuries to the extremity. Thirty-six patients with crush injuries were assigned in a randomized fashion, within 24 hours after surgery, to treatment with HBO (session of 100% O_2 at 2.5 atmospheres [atm] for 90 minutes, twice daily, over 6 days) or placebo (session of 21% O_2 at 1.1 atm for 90 minutes, twice daily, over 6 days). Both treatment groups (HBO group, n = 18; placebo group, n = 18) were similar in terms of age; risk factors; number, type or location of vascular injuries, neurological injuries, or fractures; and type, location, or timing of surgical procedures. The authors found complete wound healing without tissue necrosis in 17 of the 18 HBO patients and in 10 of the 18 control patients. While two patients in the control group eventually required amputation, no patients in the HBO group went on to amputation. Furthermore, a decreased number of surgical procedures such as skin flaps and grafts, vascular surgery, or eventual amputation were required for patients in the HBO group compared with the placebo group. A subgroup analysis of patients matched for age and severity of injury showed that HBO was especially effective in patients older than 40 with severe soft tissue injury. They concluded that HBO improved wound healing and reduced the number of additional surgical procedures required for treatment of the injury, and that it could be considered a useful adjunct in the management of severe crush injuries of the limbs, especially in patients over 40 years old.

To date, controlled animal experiments, select human case series and a small number of randomized studies seem to suggest a potential benefit of HBO therapy as an adjunct to the management of the severely traumatized limb. However, if efficacious, HBO use in the mangled extremity patient will be selective as many patients are critically ill and are often unable to travel to receive and to tolerate HBO therapy. At this time, more data and stringent clinical investigations are needed to determine the exact indications for, optimal timing of, and appropriate duration and dosage of HBO therapy before it can be recommended in the routine management of complex injuries of the limb.

Soft Tissue Coverage

Wound closure and soft tissue reconstruction are covered in more depth in Chapter 14. However, a few principles are worth discussing here. The first addresses the type of soft tissue coverage selected in the reconstruction pathway. While multiple options for coverage exist, such as skin grafts, local flaps, or free flaps, complications will occur with each. Pollak et al.[94] found that 27% of high-energy tibia injuries requiring soft tissue reconstruction had at least one wound complication within the first 6 months after injury. They also found that the rate of complication differed based on the type of flap coverage. For limbs with the most severe osseous injury (OTA type C fractures), treatment with a rotational flap was 4.3 times more likely to lead to an operative wound complication than was treatment with a free flap. The rate of complications for the limbs with less severe osseous injury did not differ significantly based on soft tissue coverage selection. Based on this information, one should be very cautious when selecting a local flap in the setting of high-energy trauma as the flap, although originally healthy in appearance, may have indeed been included in the initial zone of injury.

A second and perhaps more controversial principle is the timing of the soft tissue reconstructive procedure. The primary argument for early soft tissue reconstruction is to reduce the risk of nosocomial contamination because of repeated exposures of the vulnerable wound to the hospital environment. Some recent data have brought into question the efficacy of early soft tissue reconstruction. When analyzing a subset of patients with open tibial fractures in association with a mangled extremity, Webb et al.[121] failed to observe any advantages related to the performance of early muscle flap wound coverage within the first 72 hours after the injury. In contrast, multiple authors have indeed shown that early reconstruction (within 72 hours) reduces postoperative infection, flap failure, and nonunion rates as well as the risk for the development of osteomyelitis.[33,37,39,47] Others have recommended muscle flap coverage on a more delayed basis (7 to 14 days).[125] Recently, with the advent of negative pressure wound therapy (NPWT) and the decreasing availability of surgeons trained in rotational flaps and free tissue transfer, there seems to be a trend toward increased delays until definitive soft tissue reconstruction procedures are performed. While NPWT can be a very effective tool in the initial soft tissue management of high-energy open fractures, its routine use in open tibia fractures has not been found to reduce the overall infection rates compared with historical controls nor has it been shown to reduce the need for free tissue transfer or rotational muscle flap coverage in these injuries.[28] Bhattacharyya et al.[4] recently evaluated whether the use of NPWT could allow for a delay of flap coverage for open tibia fractures without a subsequent increase in the infection rate. The authors concluded that despite the routine use of NPWT before definitive soft tissue reconstruction in patients with Gustilo type IIIB fractures, patients who underwent definitive soft tissue coverage within 7 days had significantly decreased infection rates compared with those who underwent soft tissue coverage at 7 days or more after injury (12.5% versus 57%).

Despite best efforts, delays in soft tissue reconstruction are often inevitable; however, based on a preponderance of evidence, it still appears that soft tissue coverage should be performed as early as possible once both the patient and the wound bed appear stable enough for such a procedure.

PATIENT ASSESSMENT AND DECISION MAKING

In 1943, U.S. Army Major General N. T. Kirk, a leader at the field of amputation during World War I and World War II, wrote, "Injury, disability, or deformity incompatible with life and function indicates amputation. The surgeon must use his judgment as to whether the amputation is indicated and at what level it can safely be done."[63] Since that time, numerous physicians caring for the patient with a mangled extremity have delineated a multitude of clinical factors to help better guide in the decision-making process in the setting of a potentially salvageable versus an unsalvageable limb injury[66] (Table 12-1). In 2002, factors that influenced the mangled extremity treatment decision process were studied by Swiontkowski and the LEAP Study Group.[112] Orthopaedic and general trauma surgeons caring for the mangled limbs were surveyed to determine the factors they typically used to make a reconstruction or amputation treatment decision. More than 33% of 52 orthopaedic surgeons

TABLE 12-1	Limb Salvage Decision-Making Variables

Patient Variables

Age
Underlying chronic diseases (e.g., diabetes)
Occupational considerations
Patient and family desires

Extremity Variables

Mechanism of injury (soft tissue injury kinetics)
Fracture pattern
Arterial/venous injury (location)
Neurological (anatomic status)
Injury status of ipsilateral foot
Intercalary ischemic zone after revascularization

Associated Variables

Magnitude of associated injury (Injury Severity Score)
Severity and duration of shock
Warm ischemia time

indicated that plantar sensation was the most important determinant for limb salvage. The severity of the soft tissue injury (17%) and limb ischemia (15%) followed in importance. No orthopaedic surgeon ranked the patient's Injury Severity Score (ISS) as a critical factor. In contrast, 33 general trauma surgeons from the same centers ranked the ISS as the most critical determinant (31%), followed by limb ischemia (27%) and plantar sensation (21%). An analysis of the patient, injury, and surgeon characteristics determined that the soft tissue injury (i.e., the extent of muscle injury, deep vein injury, skin defects, and contamination) and the absence of plantar sensation were the factors considered to be most important at the time to predict amputation. Patient characteristics and the experience level of the surgeon did not appear to influence the decision process. Of important note, the orthopaedic surgeon was responsible for the initial treatment decision in all cases. General trauma surgeons participated in the decision-making process 58% of the time and plastic surgeons contributed to the process 26% of the time. While all of these variables play a key role in decision making by the orthopaedic surgeon and the trauma team, a few of these warrant further discussion, as new evidence suggests that we should reconsider the importance of some of these factors.

Survivability

Often, the decision to amputate a severely injured limb can often be a long, drawn-out, and difficult decision for both the patient and the treating surgeon. However, on rare occasions, the decision for amputation can be quite simple. Amputation is generally the only treatment option in cases of a severely injured extremity with an irreparable vascular injury or in the setting of prolonged warm ischemia (longer than 6 hours).[67] In some instances, when the patient's life would be threatened by attempts to save the limb, the dictum of "life over limb" supersedes the feasibility issue of limb salvage, and amputation should be the only option despite the presence of a potentially salvageable limb. Immediate amputation should also be considered in patients critically injured with significant hemodynamic instability, coagulopathy, or an injury constellation that would

preclude the multiple surgeries required for limb salvage.[66,67] In these cases, an immediate guillotine amputation is performed to minimize the soft tissue wound area. This amputation is then revised to a formal closure once the patient's condition is improved.

Plantar Sensation

The origin of the concept that initial plantar sensation is critical to the salvage of an extremity is difficult to trace. Although the LEAP Study Group's[112] decision-making analysis supported the inclusion and perceived importance of plantar sensibility, the fact that this was an established treatment axiom at the time of this study may have driven a self-fulfilling prophesy phenomenon. Because surgeons believed that absent plantar sensation was a reason to amputate a limb, they acted accordingly. Indeed, the literature before 1980 warns of neuropathic ulcers and chronic complications associated with absent plantar sensation. Johansen,[58] Howe,[50] and Russell[99] and their colleagues, however, describe a *confirmed* avulsion or complete transection of the tibial nerve as their definition of absent plantar sensation in their limb salvage algorithms. Lange et al.[67] considered complete tibial nerve disruption in adults to be an absolute indication for amputation.

In most clinical scenarios, however, the assessment of the limb is performed in the emergency department. Once in the operating room, additional dissection of the deep posterior compartment to assess the tibial nerve is usually considered unwise, as surgical exploration of the nerve within the zone of injury is contraindicated because doing so causes additional soft tissue injury. Therefore, in many centers, the absence of initial plantar sensation has been considered the same as a physiological disruption of the nerve. Ischemia, compression, contusion, and stretch can temporarily affect the function of the tibial nerve. Once these factors resolve, nerve function typically returns. In the face of no sensory return, orthopaedic surgeons have successfully demonstrated the ability to care for the insensate foot in other conditions (diabetes or incomplete spine lesions) through education and shoe modifications. Furthermore, the orthopaedic oncology literature has documented cases of limb salvage in the face of tumor with acceptable results after sciatic, peroneal, or tibial nerve resection.[5,12]

In an effort to better understand the true importance of plantar sensation in the mangled extremity, Bosse et al.[10] used the variations in physician practice patterns to explore the outcomes of patients admitted to the LEAP Study with absent plantar sensation. They examined the outcomes of a subset of 55 subjects without plantar foot sensation at the time of initial presentation. The 55 patients were divided into two groups depending on their hospital treatment (i.e., insensate amputation group [n = 26] and insensate salvage group, the study group of primary interest [n = 29]). In addition, a control group was constructed from the parent cohort so that a comparison could also be made to a group of patients in whom plantar sensation was present and whose limbs were reconstructed. The sensate control group consisted of 29 subjects who were matched to the 29 insensate salvage subjects on four limb injury severity characteristics (i.e., severity of muscle, venous, and bony injury as well as the presence of an associated foot injury). Patient and injury characteristics and functional and health-related quality of life outcomes at 12 and 24 months after injury were compared between subjects in the insensate salvage versus the other study groups and considered significant if $p \leq .005$.

The insensate salvage patients did not report or exhibit significantly worse outcomes at 12 or 24 months after injury compared with subjects in the insensate amputation or the sensate control cohort. Among those with a salvaged limb (insensate salvage and sensate control groups), equal proportions (55%) had normal foot sensation at 2 years after injury regardless of whether plantar sensation was reported as intact (sensate control group) or absent (insensate salvage group) on admission. Pain, weight-bearing status, and percentage of patients who had returned to work were similar for subjects in the insensate salvage group compared with subjects in the insensate amputation and the sensate control groups. Furthermore, there were no significant differences noted in the overall, physical, or psychosocial Sickness Impact Profile (SIP) scores between subjects without plantar sensation whose limbs were salvaged (insensate salvage group) and subjects who had undergone amputation (insensate amputation group) or subjects with intact sensation whose limbs were salvaged (sensate control group). More than one half of the patients initially presenting with an insensate foot and treated with limb reconstruction had regained normal sensation at 2 years. At 2 years, only two patients in the insensate salvage group and one patient in the sensate control group had absent plantar sensation. In this cohort, initial plantar sensation was not found to be prognostic of long-term plantar sensory status or functional outcomes. Based on these data, the authors concluded that plantar sensation should not be included as a factor in the decision making for limb salvage in lower extremity trauma.

Decision-Making Protocols and Limb Salvage Scores

Because the decision to amputate or salvage a severely injured lower extremity is difficult, several researchers have attempted to enumerate certain indications for amputation or quantify the severity of the trauma to establish numerical guidelines for the decision to amputate or salvage a limb. These lower extremity injury scoring systems all vary in terms of the factors considered relevant to limb salvage and the relative weights assigned to each element. These scoring systems were validated by the developers and demonstrated a high sensitivity and specificity in predicting limb salvage at the time of their design.

In 1985, Lange et al.[67] proposed a decision-making protocol for primary amputation in type IIIC open tibial fractures. They suggested that the occurrence of one of two absolute indications (complete tibial nerve disruption in an adult or a crush injury with warm ischemia time longer than 6 hours) or at least two of three relative indications (serious associated polytrauma, severe ipsilateral foot trauma, or a projected long course to full recovery) warranted amputation. This protocol, however, presented several limitations in that only a minority of cases can be resolved based on the absolute indications and that the relative indications were quite subjective. Furthermore, this protocol did not address individual patient variables such as age, medical comorbidities, occupational, and other psychosocial factors that can have a significant effect on the overall outcome and no subsequent clinical studies were performed to validate this protocol.

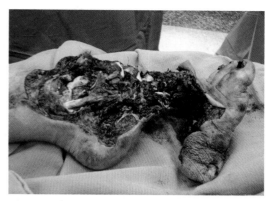

FIGURE 12-2 Another example of a "mangled extremity." Note the extensive degree of both bony and soft tissue injury.

Beginning in 1985, research teams reported attempts to quantify extremity injury severity with scoring systems (Fig. 12-2). Over a 10-year period, six scoring systems were published that valued different injury components as critical to the treatment decision[42,45,50,58,81,99,110] (Table 12-2). These components were assigned arbitrary weights and the summation scores were used to establish "cutoffs" for limb salvage or amputation.

Gregory et al.[42] published the first grading system for the mangled extremity, the Mangled Extremity Syndrome Index (MESI) (Table 12-3). In this study, the authors included 17 patients over a 3-year period who met their criteria of a mangled extremity syndrome (defined by three of four organ/tissue systems—integument, nerve, vessel, bone—injured in the same extremity). These patients' charts were retrospectively reviewed and their injuries classified according to a point system based on the degree of integumentary, nervous, vascular, and osseous injury. Additional scoring schemes were also included to address patient age, the time lag to treatment, preexisting medical comorbidities, and the presence or absence of shock. In their series, they found that 100% of patients with an MESI score of greater than 20 underwent either primary or secondary amputation. From their data, they suggested that if applied prospectively, the MESI could have been used to identify those patients in their series who ultimately underwent amputation and guide

TABLE 12-2	Index Domains		
MESS	**NISSSA/HFS**	**PSI**	**LSI**
Ischemia	Ischemia	Ischemia	Ischemia
Bone/tissue	Bone	Bone	Bone
Shock	Muscle	Muscle	Muscle
Age	Skin	Timing	Skin
	Shock		Nerve
	Age		Vein
	Nerve		

MESS, Mangled Extremity Severity Scoring System; NISSSA/HFS, Nerve injury, Ischemia, Soft tissue injury, Skeletal injury, Shock, and Age of patient/Hanover Fracture Scale; PSI, Predictive Salvage Index; LSI, Limb Salvage Index.

TABLE 12-3 Mangled Extremity Syndrome Index (MESI)

Criterion	Score
Injury Severity Score	
<25	1
25–50	2
>50	3
Integument injury	
Guillotine	1
Crush/burn	2
Avulsion/degloving	3
Nerve injury	
Contusion	1
Transection	2
Avulsion	3
Bone injury	
Simple	1
Segmental	2
Segmental comminuted	3
Bone loss <6 cm	4
Articular	5
Articular with bone loss <6 cm	6
Lag time to operation	
One point is given for each hour over 6 hours	....
Age (yr)	
<40	0
40–50	1
50–60	2
>60	3
Preexisting disease	1
Shock	2

TABLE 12-4 Predictive Salvage Index System (PSI)

Criterion	Score
Level of arterial injury	
Suprapopliteal	1
Popliteal	2
Infrapopliteal	3
Degree of bone injury	
Mild	1
Moderate	2
Severe	3
Degree of muscle injury	
Mild	1
Moderate	2
Severe	3
Interval from injury to operating room	
<6 hr	0
6–12 hr	2
>12 hr	4

In 1990, Johansen et al.[58] and Helfet et al.[45] proposed and reported on the utility of the Mangled Extremity Severity Score (MESS) (Table 12-5). Like the PSI, the MESS system is also based on four clinical criteria (skeletal/soft tissue injury, shock, ischemia, and patient age), and it was developed through the retrospective review of 26 severe lower extremity open fractures with vascular compromise. It was then validated in a prospective trial involving 26 patients at two separate trauma centers. In both the prospective and retrospective studies, all salvaged limbs had had scores of 6 or lower and an MESS score of 7 or greater had a 100% positive predictive value for amputation.

Shortly after the MESS scoring system had been published,

their treatment at the time of initial evaluation. They suggested that their scoring system could help better identify the salvageable versus the unsalvageable extremity. Unfortunately, the MESI had numerous faults. Five of the 17 cases studied were injuries to the upper extremity. The MESI scoring system can also be both cumbersome and somewhat subjective in nature, making it prone to interobserver variability and difficult to apply during the initial evaluation of the patient. These factors prevented its widespread acceptance and application in orthopaedic practice.

The Predictive Salvage Index (PSI)[50] was introduced in 1987 as another scoring system to help predict amputation versus salvage in patients with combined musculoskeletal and vascular injuries of the lower extremity. The PSI ascribes points based on information from four key categories (level of arterial injury, degree of bone injury, degree of muscle injury, and interval from injury to treatment) (Table 12-4). In the initial retrospective analysis, all 12 patients in the salvage group had PSI scores of less than 8, while 7 of 9 in the amputation group had scores of 8 or higher. The authors concluded that the PSI determined the likelihood of amputation with a sensitivity of 78% and a specificity of 100%. Although less complex than the MESI, it still had similar faults in that many of the scores attributed were subjective in nature and thus prone to interobserver variability. And as with the MESI, the information necessary to complete the scoring can be difficult to ascertain readily during the patient's initial evaluation.

TABLE 12-5 Mangled Extremity Severity Scoring System (MESS)

Criterion	Score
Skeletal/soft tissue injury	
Low energy	1
Medium energy	2
High energy	3
Very high energy	4
Limb ischemia	
Pulse reduced or absent but normal perfusion	1*
Pulseless, diminished capillary refill	2*
Cool, paralyzed, insensate, numb	3*
Shock	
SBP always >90 mm Hg	0
SBP transiently <90 mm Hg	1
SBP persistently <90 mm Hg	2
Age (yr)	
<30	0
30–50	1
>50	2

*Double value if duration of ischemia exceeds 6 hours.

TABLE 12-6 Limb Salvage Index (LSI)

Criterion	Score
Arterial injury	
Contusion, intimal tear, partial laceration	0
Occlusion of 2 or more shank vessels, no pedal pulses	1
Occlusion of femoral, popliteal, or three shank vessels	2
Nerve injury	
Contusion, stretch, minimal clean laceration	0
Partial transection or avulsion of sciatic nerve	1
Complete transection or avulsion of sciatic nerve	2
Bone injury	
Closed fracture or open fracture with minimal comminution	0
Open fracture with comminution or large displacement	1
Bone loss >3 cm; type IIIB or IIIC fracture	2
Skin injury	
Clean laceration, primary repair, first-degree burn	0
Contamination, avulsion requiring split-thickness skin graft or flap	1
Muscle injury	
Laceration involving single compartment or tendon	0
Laceration or avulsion of 2 or more tendons	1
Deep vein injury	
Contusion, partial laceration or avulsion	0
Complete laceration or avulsion, or thrombosis	1
Warm ischemia time (hr)	
<6	0
6–9	1
9–12	2
12–15	3
>15	4

TABLE 12-7 NISSSA Scoring System

Criterion	Score
Nerve injury	
Sensate	0
Loss of dorsal sensation	1
Partial plantar sensation	2
Complete loss of plantar sensation	3
Ischemia	
None	0
Mild	1*
Moderate	2*
Severe	3*
Soft tissue injury/contamination	
Low	0
Medium	1
High	2
Severe	3
Skeletal injury	
Low energy	0
Medium energy	1
High energy	2
Very high energy	3
Blood pressure	
Normotensive	0
Transient hypotension	1
Persistent hypotension	2
Age (yr)	
<30	0
30–50	1
>50	2

*Double value if duration of ischemia exceeds 6 hours.

Russel et al.[99] proposed the Limb Salvage Index (LSI) (Table 12-6). In this study, the authors performed a 5-year retrospective review of 70 limbs in 67 patients. Their proposed index was slightly more complex in that it quantified the likelihood of salvage according to the presence and severity of arterial injury, nerve injury, bone injury, skin injury, muscle injury, and venous injury as well as the presence and duration of warm ischemia. They reported that all 59 limbs with an LSI score of less than 6 were able to undergo successful limb salvage, while all 19 patients with an LSI score of 6 or greater had amputations. Criticisms of the LSI are that it is very detailed and requires a thorough operative evaluation to complete the initial scoring. Furthermore, because accurate scoring of the skin category requires a prior knowledge of the treatment and final outcome, the LSI is essentially ineffective during the initial phases of treatment.

In 1994, McNamara et al.[81] modified the MESS by including nerve injury in the scoring system and by separating soft tissue and skeletal injury. Their modification was named the NISSSA (Nerve Injury, Ischemia, Soft tissue Injury, Skeletal Injury, Shock, and Age of patient) scoring system (Table 12-7). Subsequently, the authors applied the MESS and the NISSSA to retrospective data of 24 patients previously treated for limb-threatening injuries. The authors found both the MESS and the NISSSA to be highly accurate in predicting amputation. The NISSSA was also found to be more sensitive (81.8% versus 63.6%) and

more specific (92.3 versus 69.2%) than the MESS in their patient population. Despite the improved statistical outcomes when comparing the NISSSA to the MESS, it inherently retains all the faults of the MESS scoring system while increasing its complexity. The NISSSA has also not been validated in prospective clinical trials.

Although the introduction of the scoring systems has helped highlight certain key factors considered relevant to limb salvage, each system, in and of itself, is not without its own limitations. First, while these scoring systems were validated by the developers and demonstrated a high sensitivity and specificity in predicting limb salvage in their respective studies, the development of the lower-extremity Injury Severity Scores has been flawed by retrospective designs and small sample sizes. In each study, with the exception of the small prospective series in which the MESS system was validated, each proposed classification system was applied retrospectively to patients with known outcomes, rather than prospectively to patients with unknown outcomes. Another important flaw in the development of the scoring systems lies in the fact that component selection and weighting in all of the indices were affected by the clinical bias of the index developers. The NISSSA and LSI include the result of the initial plantar neurological examination. Age, the presence of shock, severity of contamination, and time to treatment are included in some of the other scoring strategies. While each of these factors plays a key role in decision making, strict reliance on certain criteria with disregard to others via strict adherence to a scoring system might lead to premature amputation in an otherwise salvageable situation. As an example, the commonly cited MESS assigns an additional point if the patient is above the age of 29, a point for normal perfusion with a diminished pulse, and points for transient or persistent hypotension without qualifying cause or response to treatment. The suggested MESS threshold score for amputation is 7. Using the MESS, for example, a 30-year-old patient (1 point) with a high-energy open tibia fracture (3 points), with normal perfusion but a diminished pulse secondary to spasm or compression (1 point), who has persistent hypotension before laparotomy related to a spleen injury (2 points) would undergo amputation at the conclusion of the laparotomy despite the fact that the limb perfusion will likely return to normal and splenectomy and appropriate resuscitation will resolve the patient's hypotension.

Since the time of their initial publication, various other authors have attempted to validate several of the proposed scoring systems. Although it was originally devised to assess injuries to the lower limb, Slauterbaeck et al.[107] applied the MESS to the high-energy injuries of the upper extremity. In their series, they retrospectively reviewed the data of 37 patients with 43 mangled upper extremities and found that all 9 upper extremity injuries with an MESS of greater than or equal to 7 were amputated and 34 of 34 with an MESS of less than 7 were successfully salvaged. Based on their findings, they concluded that the MESS system was an accurate predictor of amputation versus salvage when applied to the upper extremity. Conversely, Togawa et al.[114] also retrospectively applied the MESS to patients with severe injuries of the upper extremity with associated arterial involvement. In their series, they successfully salvaged two of three upper extremity injuries with an MESS score of 7 or higher with good functional outcomes. They concluded that because

of the decreased muscle mass in the upper extremity compared with the lower extremity and the increased collateral circulation and tolerance to ischemia seen in the upper extremity, the MESS score was inappropriate for application to the upper limb.

Roessler et al.[98] and Bonanni et al.[6] both attempted to apply the MESI retrospectively to each of their patient populations. Both authors determined that the MESI inaccurately predicted amputation versus salvage. Furthermore, they found that MESI scores were often only approximate at best because many of the variables required surgical intervention for accurate determination of the scores, which negated its usefulness as a prediction tool in the acute phase of assessment and treatment.

Bonanni et al.[6] also evaluated the MESS, LSI, and PSI limb salvage score strategies. They retrospectively applied each limb salvage scoring system to 58 lower limb salvage attempts over a 10-year period. Failure of the reconstruction effort was defined as an amputation or functional failure at 2 years. A limb was considered to be a functional failure based on the ability to walk 150 feet without assistance, climb 12 stairs, or independently transfer. Based on their data, they were not able to support use of any of the three scores to determine limb treatment.

In an attempt to further clarify the clinical utility of any of the limb salvage scores, the LEAP Study prospectively captured all of the elements of the MESS, LSI, PSI, NISSSA, and the Hanover Fracture Scale[110] at the time of each patient's initial assessment and critical decision making.[8] The elements were collected in a fashion so as to not provide the evaluator with a "score" or impact on the decision-making process. The analysis did not validate the clinical utility of any of the lower extremity injury severity scores. The high specificity of the scores did, however, confirm that low scores could be used to predict limb salvage potential. The converse was not true, though, and the low sensitivity of the indices failed to support the validity of the scores as predictors of amputation (Table 12-8). The authors

TABLE 12-8 **Clinical Usefulness of Limb Salvage Scores**			
Score	All Gustilo Type III Fractures (n = 357)*	Gustilo Type IIIB Fractures (n = 214)*	Gustilo Type IIIC Fractures (n = 59)*
MESS			
Sensitivity	0.45 (0.35–0.55)	0.17 (0.10–0.30)	0.78 (0.64–0.89)
Specificity	0.93 (0.90–0.95)	0.94 (0.89–0.97)	0.69 (0.39–0.91)
PSI			
Sensitivity	0.47 (0.37–0.57)	0.35 (0.22–0.51)	0.61 (0.45–0.75)
Specificity	0.84 (0.79–0.88)	0.85 (0.79–0.90)	0.69 (0.39–0.91)
LSI			
Sensitivity	0.51 (0.41–0.61)	0.15 (0.10–0.28)	0.91 (0.79–0.98)
Specificity	0.97 (0.94–0.99)	0.98 (0.95–1.00)	0.69 (0.39–0.91)
NISSSA			
Sensitivity	0.33 (0.24–0.43)	0.13 (0.05–0.25)	0.59 (0.43–0.73)
Specificity	0.98 (0.96–1.00)	1.00 (0.98–1.00)	0.77 (0.46–0.95)
HFS-97			
Sensitivity	0.37 (0.28–0.47)	0.10 (0.04–0.23)	0.67 (0.52–0.81)
Specificity	0.98 (0.95–1.00)	1.00 (0.97–1.00)	0.77 (0.46–0.95)

*95% confidence intervals given in parentheses.
MESS, Mangled Extremity Severity Scoring System; PSI, Predictive Salvage Index; LSI, Limb Salvage Index; NISSSA, Nerve Injury, Ischemia, Soft tissue Injury, Skeletal Injury, Shock, and Age of Patient; HFS-97, Hanover Fracture Scale.

concluded that lower extremity injury severity scores at or above the amputation threshold should be used cautiously by surgeons deciding the fate of a mangled lower extremity.

Ideally, a trauma limb salvage index would be 100% sensitive (all amputated limbs will have scores at or above the threshold) and 100% specific (all salvaged limbs will have scores below the threshold). In the decision to amputate, high specificity is important to ensure that only a small number (ideally, none) of salvageable limbs are incorrectly assigned a score above the amputation decision threshold. A high sensitivity is also important to guard against inappropriate delays in amputation when the limb is ultimately not salvageable. Unfortunately, few clinical scoring systems perform ideally and the limb salvage scoring systems have proved to be no exception.

Concomitant Foot and Ankle Injuries

When discussing the mangled extremity or massive lower extremity trauma, the prototypical injury is the severe open tibial fracture. However, in reality these injuries often occur in conjunction with severe crushing-type injuries to the ankle, hindfoot, and forefoot and this factor should also be carefully considered when opting for salvage versus amputation. Myerson et al.[85] and others[120,122] have shown that despite successful salvage and treatment of crush injuries to the foot, a substantial proportion of these patients will continue to have pain, often neuropathic in nature, and poor functional outcomes.

Turchin et al.[118] also assessed the effect of foot injuries on functional outcomes in the multiply injured patient. They matched 28 multiply injured patients with foot injuries against 28 multiply injured patients without foot injuries and compared their outcomes using the Short Form-36 (SF-36), the Western Ontario and McMaster Universities and Osteoarthritis Index (WOMAC), and the modified Boston Children's Hospital Grading System. They found that the outcome of the multiply injured patients with foot injuries was significantly worse than that of the patients without foot injuries when using any of the three outcome measures. Postinjury evaluation also showed that not only were the physical scores affected in the patients with associated foot injuries, but also the pain and social and emotional health perceptions were dramatically reduced compared with a control population of trauma patients without foot injuries. When using the SF-36, the patients in their study were similar to patients with well-recognized chronic debilitating conditions such as congestive heart failure, ischemic heart disease, or chronic obstructive pulmonary disease. In a similar study, Tran and Thordarson,[117] using validated outcome instruments such as the SF-36, the American Academy of Orthopaedic Surgeons (AAOS) lower limb core questionnaire, and the AAOS foot and ankle questionnaire,[59,90] found that the multiply injured patients with associated foot injuries in their study had had dramatically lower Physical Function (38.9 versus 80.7), Role Physical (a perception of their physical function, 41.1 versus 87.5), Bodily Pain (50.6 versus 81.8), and Social Function (67.9 versus 96.6) compared with the control group of multiply injured patients without associated foot injuries. By use of the AAOS questionnaire, their study also addressed specific lower extremity musculoskeletal endpoints. All five of these scales also showed significantly lower scores for factors such as pain, treatment expectations, satisfaction with symptoms, and shoe comfort in those patients with associated foot injuries.

Armed with this information and the knowledge of the severity of injury to the ipsilateral foot, one should proceed cautiously when recommending salvage in the face of severe crush injuries to the foot. In this situation, a given tibial injury or "mangled" lower limb with concomitant severe injuries to the foot might preclude achieving reasonable limb function despite the feasibility of salvage and amputation may indeed be a better long-term option.

Smoking

Not only is cigarette smoking a marker for potential medical comorbidities such as coronary heart disease and chronic obstructive pulmonary disease in a patient with potentially limb threatening injury, but it also can be used early as a prognostic variable to help inform the patient of potential long-term treatment complications and perhaps better guide treatment recommendations. Both basic science and clinical studies have consistently documented suspected links between cigarette smoking and complications of the fracture healing process. Several studies have provided preliminary evidence of a link between smoking and delayed bone healing and nonunion,* infection,[34,77,113] and osteomyelitis.[34,105] Laboratory studies have also shown that nicotine reduces vascularization at bone healing sites, and this is associated with delayed healing in animal models.[25,49,119] Smoking has also been associated with decreased immune function.[61,69,106]

A concern with many of the current clinical studies has been the presence of many potential confounding variables that may have also affected the outcomes, thus refuting the overall impact of smoking on such negative outcomes as delayed union, nonunion, and infection. Patient age, education, and socioeconomic status have all been shown to have deleterious effects on overall health status, access to treatment, treatment compliance, and other health behaviors, which may have affected the higher complication rates seen in some of the smoking cohorts. In an effort to address these issues, Castillo et al.[15] used data from the LEAP project to determine if cigarette smoking increased the risk of complications in patients with a limb-threatening open tibial fracture, while adjusting for the previously mentioned confounders. They were able to demonstrate that current smoking and even a previous smoking history independently placed the patient at an increased risk for nonunion and infectious complications. Current smokers and previous smokers were 37% and 32%, respectively, less likely to achieve union than nonsmokers. Current smokers were also more than twice as likely to develop an infection and 3.7 times more likely to develop osteomyelitis than were nonsmokers. Furthermore, previous smokers were also 2.8 times more likely to develop osteomyelitis than were patients without a prior history of tobacco use.

Not only has cigarette smoking been shown to correlate with increased bone healing complications in the patient with a limb-threatening injury, but also smoking can significantly threaten the likelihood of success of the soft tissue portion of the reconstructive effort. Smoking is associated with a significant reduction in peripheral blood flow. Sarin et al.[100] have shown that blood flow to the hand is reduced as much as 42% after smoking just one cigarette. Cigarette use has also been shown to nega-

*References 1,9,13,19,21,43,44,65,77,88,101.

tively affect peripheral blood flow in free transverse rectus abdominus flaps.[7] Microsurgeons have reported poor outcomes after digital replantation in smokers. Chang et al.[18] noted that approximately 80% to 90% of cigarette smokers will lose their replanted digits if tobacco use occurred within 2 months before their surgery. Cigarette use has been shown to lead to increased local flap and full-thickness graft necrosis compared with non-smoking status.[38] Smoking has also been shown to adversely affect the success and complication rates associated with microvascular free tissue transfer. Reus et al.[95] studied the incidence of free tissue transfer survival and complications in nonsmokers, active smokers, and patients who had discontinued smoking before surgical intervention. In their series, they found that complications occurred more often in active smokers, with these complications often occurring at the interface between the flap and its bed or an overlying skin graft. They also found that smokers required more secondary surgical procedures at the recipient site to accomplish ultimate wound closure. Lovich and Arnold[70] examined the effect of smoking on various muscle transposition procedures. They performed a retrospective review of 300 pedicled muscle flap procedures and determined that active smokers had a significantly higher complication rate than nonsmokers and smokers who had previously quit. In the smoking group, they noticed a higher incidence of both partial muscle flap necrosis and partial skin graft loss with most of these complications occurring in the immediate postoperative period. Not only is smoking associated with an increased complication rate at the recipient site, but smokers have also been shown to have an increased rate of complications at the donor site.[17]

Clearly, both a history of previous cigarette use and current cigarette smoking places the patient with a limb-threatening injury at increased risk for both osseous and soft tissue complications These factors must be discussed at length and weighed very carefully with the patient before embarking on a prolonged course to salvage a mangled limb.

Patient Selection

Successful treatment of the mangled extremity and the return of the patient to as close to a preinjury level of performance and social interaction as possible are dependent on the interaction of the patient, the patient's environment, the injury, and the treatment course (Fig. 12-3). Understanding the potential impact of elements outside of the surgeon's control—the patient and the patient's environment—is critical to the development of an effective care plan. Through data obtained by the LEAP Study group, Mackenzie et al.[71] were able to characterize and help provide the medical community with a better understanding of the type of patients who face the challenge of amputation versus salvage in the face of a limb-threatening injury. In that study, most of the patients were male (77%), white (72%), and between the ages of 20 and 45 years (71%). These patients were often less educated, as only 70% were high school graduates versus a national rate of 86%. These patients were often impoverished. Significantly more of the patients (25%) lived in households with incomes below the federal poverty line compared with the national rate (16%). This patient cohort also had significantly higher rates of uninsured individuals (38%) and had double the national average of heavy drinkers. Not only do these patients typically present with socioeconomic challenges, but many will have psychological and psychosocial issues, which can make the treatment plan and recovery even more of a challenge. Patients in this study were also found to be slightly more neurotic and extroverted and less open to new experiences compared with the general population. No significant differences were detected between the characteristics of patients entered into the reconstruction or amputation groups.

These findings are important to surgeons planning to care for patients with mangled lower extremities. Compared with the general population, patients with limb-threatening injuries have fewer resources, which can potentially limit their access to rehabilitation services and affect their ability to accommodate to residual disability. These patients are typically employed in more physically demanding jobs, which may impede efforts to return to work, and they have poorer health habits, which may complicate recovery. The personality traits identified in this population could also predispose these patients to a more difficult recovery.

OUTCOMES: AMPUTATION VERSUS LIMB SALVAGE

The clinical challenge faced in every case is deciding, as early as possible, the correct treatment pathway for the patient. The surgeon must weigh the fact that, in most cases, limb reconstruction is possible given the appropriate application of current techniques and counterbalance the expected result of salvage against that which is possible with amputation. Prosthetic bioengineering innovations have significantly improved the function and comfort of lower extremity amputees. Most series reporting on the results of limb salvage or amputation are single center, small, and retrospective. Their conclusions provide a glimpse into the complexity of the clinical decision-making process, but these studies alone should not be used to guide clinical decisions.

Several of these series have supported amputation as the optimal treatment option in the setting of the mangled extremity. Georgiadis et al.[36] retrospectively compared the functional outcomes of 26 patients with successfully reconstructed Grade IIIB open tibia fractures with the outcomes of 18 patients managed with early below-knee amputation. Five patients in the reconstruction group required a late amputation to treat infection complications. The reconstruction patients had more operations, more complications, and longer hospital stays than did patients treated by early amputation. The functional outcomes of the 16 successful reconstructions were compared with the outcomes of the early amputation patients. They found that the reconstruction patients took more time to achieve full weight

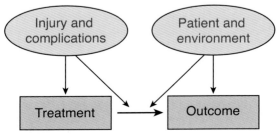

FIGURE 12-3 Factors influencing treatment decision and outcome.

bearing and were less willing or able to return to work. Validated outcomes instruments were used to assess the quality of life for a subset of the patients. Significantly more limb salvage patients considered themselves to be severely disabled and impaired for both occupational and recreational activities. The authors concluded that early below-knee amputation resulted in a quicker recovery with less long-term disability.

Francel et al.,[35] in a retrospective review of 72 acute Grade IIIB open tibia fractures requiring soft tissue reconstruction from 1983 to 1988, also showed that while limb salvage can be successful, over 50% of the patients in the salvage group had severe limitations in the salvaged limb by objective motion measurements, and 48% of the patients in the salvage group at least intermittently required the use of an assistive device for ambulation after complete healing. They also found that in the salvage group, the long-term employment rate was 28% and no patient returned to work after 2 years of unemployment. In contrast, 68% of trauma-related lower extremity amputees from their institution over the same time period returned to work within 2 years.

Based on these studies, proponents of early amputation claim that patients undergoing amputation often have shorter initial hospital stays, decreased initial hospital costs, and a higher likelihood of resuming gainful employment, thus decreasing the financial burden of this life-altering injury.

Hertel et al.[48] also retrospectively compared below-knee amputees with patients receiving complex reconstructions after a Grade IIIB or IIIC open tibial fracture. They also concluded that for the first 4 years after injury, amputation resulted in lower mean annual hospital costs than reconstruction and amputation patients required 3.5 interventions and 12 months of rehabilitation compared with an average of 8 interventions and 30 months of rehabilitation for the reconstruction patients. However, amputation patients were reported as having a higher dollar cost to society, a figure that was inflated by adding the amounts of permanent disability assigned to an amputee compared with a reconstruction patient. Despite this fact, the authors eventually concluded that functional outcome based on pain, range of motion, quadriceps wasting, and walking ability was better in the reconstruction group than in the amputation group and therefore limb reconstruction was advisable (although the data to support this conclusion was soft and no patient-directed outcome measures were used.)

Dagum et al.[27] also touted reconstruction as the preferred option in the management of the mangled extremity. They retrospectively evaluated 55 Grade IIIB and IIIC tibia fractures cared for over a 12-year period. The SF-36 was used as the primary outcomes measure. Although both groups had SF-36 (Physical Component) outcomes scores as low as or lower than those of many serious medical illnesses, successful salvage patients had significantly better physical subscale scores than did amputees. Both groups had psychological subscores similar to a healthy population. Furthermore, 92% of their patients preferred their salvaged leg to an amputation at any stage of their injury, and none would have preferred a primary amputation. Based on their findings, the authors suggested that a below-knee amputation was an inferior option to a successfully reconstructed leg.

While some authors have found that amputation may be less costly in the short term, reconstruction may be more cost effective compared with amputation when lifelong prosthetic costs are taken into account. Smith et al.[108] reviewed hospital and prosthetist records for 15 of 20 patients who survived initial trauma and eventually underwent isolated below-knee amputation from 1980 through 1987. Using the medical record and the billing records of the prosthetist, they calculated the number of prostheses fabricated and the overall prosthetic charges since the initial amputation. They found that during the first 3 years, the mean number of prostheses acquired per patient was 3.4 (range, 1 to 5), with an average total prosthetic charge of $10,829 (range, $2,558 to $15,700). Over the first 5 years, the mean number of prostheses acquired per patient increased to 4.4 (range, 2 to 8), with average total prosthetic charges of $13,945 (range, $6,203 to $20,070). Williams[123] also compared hospital costs and professional fees of 10 patients with Ilizarov limb reconstruction to the hospital costs, professional fees, and prosthetic costs of 3 patients with acute and 3 patients with delayed lower extremity amputation. The average treatment time was higher in the Ilizarov reconstruction group. The hospital costs and professional fees for the amputation group averaged $30,148 without prosthetic costs, while the total cost of the Ilizarov limb reconstruction averaged $59,213. However, with projected lifetime prosthetic costs included, the average long-term cost for the amputee was estimated to be $403,199. Thus, he concluded that Ilizarov limb reconstruction is a more cost-effective treatment option than amputation when long-term prosthetic costs are considered.

The issue of the health care cost of amputation versus limb reconstruction has best been analyzed through information collected via the LEAP Study. MacKenzie et al.[75] compared the 2-year direct health care costs and projected lifetime health care costs associated with both treatment pathways. The calculated patient costs included the initial hospitalization, all rehospitalizations for acute care related to the limb injury, any inpatient rehabilitation, outpatient physician visits, outpatient physical and occupational therapy, and the purchase and maintenance of any prosthetic devices. When the costs associated with rehospitalizations and postacute care were added to the cost of the initial hospitalization, the 2-year costs for reconstruction and amputation were similar. However, when prosthesis-related costs were added, there was a substantial difference between the two groups ($81,316 for patients treated with reconstruction and $91,106 for patients treated with amputation). Furthermore, the projected lifetime health care cost for the patients who had undergone amputation was three times higher than that for those treated with reconstruction ($509,275 and $163,282, respectively). Based on these estimates, they concluded that efforts to improve the rate of successful reconstructions have merit and that not only is reconstruction a reasonable goal, but it may result in lower lifetime costs to the patient.

While most of the conclusions reached in the previous studies offer important insight into the various arguments for amputation or salvage of the mangled extremity, they are also somewhat contradictory, which is likely a result of the retrospective design and small sample sizes in many of the series. The research teams could not adequately assess or control for the injury, treatment, patient, and patient environment variables that could influence the outcome.

The LEAP Study prospectively compared the functional outcomes of a large cohort of patients from eight Level I trauma centers who underwent reconstruction or amputation following an open tibial shaft fracture. The hypothesis was that after controlling for the severity of the limb injury, the presence and severity of other injuries, and patient characteristics, amputation would prove to have a better functional outcome than reconstruction. Detailed patient, patient environment, injury, and treatment (hospital and outpatient) data were collected for each patient.[73] The SIP was used as the primary outcome measurement. The SIP is a multidimensional measure of self-reported health status (scores range from 0 to 100; scores for the general population average 2 to 3, and scores of greater than 10 represent severe disability). Secondary outcomes included the limb status and the presence or absence of a major complication that required rehospitalization. Five hundred sixty-nine patients were followed over 2 years. No significant difference was detected at 2 years in the SIP scores between the amputation and the reconstruction patients. After adjustment for the characteristics of the patients and their injuries, patients who underwent amputation had outcomes that were similar to those who underwent limb reconstruction.[9]

The analysis of all patient, injury, treatment, and environmental variables in the LEAP Study also identified a number of predictors of poorer SIP scores. Negative factors included the rehospitalization of a patient for a major complication, a low education level, nonwhite race, poverty, lack of private health insurance, a poor social support network, a low self-efficacy (the patient's confidence in being able to resume life activities), smoking, and involvement with disability-compensation litigation (Table 12-9). To underscore the combined influence of these multiple factors on outcome, adjusted SIP scores were estimated for two subgroups of patients. A patient with a high school education or less, poor social support, and rehospitalization for a major complication had a mean adjusted SIP score of 15.8. A comparable score for a patient with some college education, strong social support, and an uncomplicated recovery was 8.3 (Table 12-10). Although patients with substantial economic and social resources and no complications could not function at the level of a healthy adult of similar age and gender (SIP typically less than 4), they were still significantly better off than those without such resources.

The study also found that patients who underwent reconstruction were more likely to be rehospitalized than were those who underwent amputation (47.6% versus 33.9%). At 2 years, nonunion was present in 10.9% of the reconstruction patients and 9.4% had developed osteomyelitis. Additional operations were anticipated for 5% of the amputation patients and for 19% of the reconstruction patients. The levels of disability, as measured by the SIP, were high in both groups. More than 40%

TABLE 12-10 | **Adjusted Sickness Impact Profile (SIP) Scores Estimated for Two Patient Subgroups**

Patient-Related Factors	Predicted Outcome*
High school education or less Poor support Low self-efficacy Major complication	Adjusted SIP 15.8
Some college education Strong support High self-efficacy No complications	Adjusted SIP 8.3

*Assuming identical limb injury.

---

of the patients had an SIP score of greater than 10, reflecting severe disability. Except for scores on the psychosocial subscale, there was significant improvement in the scores over time in both treatment groups. Return to work success was disappointing. At 24 months, only 53.0% of the patients who underwent amputation and 49.4% of those who underwent reconstruction had returned to work.

Subsequent to the publication of the original LEAP data, MacKenzie et al.[74] reexamined the outcomes of patients originally enrolled in the study to determine whether their outcomes improved beyond 2 years and whether differences according to the type of treatment emerged. Three hundred ninety-seven of the 569 patients who had originally undergone amputation or reconstruction of the lower extremity were interviewed by telephone at an average of 84 months after the injury. Functional outcomes were assessed with use of the physical and psychosocial subscores of the SIP and were compared with the scores obtained at 24 months. On the average, physical and psychosocial functioning deteriorated between 24 and 84 months after the injury. At 84 months, half of the patients had a physical SIP subscore of 10 or more points, which is indicative of substantial disability, and only 34.5% had a score typical of the general population of similar age and sex. There were few significant differences in the outcomes according to the type of treatment, with two exceptions. Compared with patients treated with reconstruction for a tibial shaft fracture, those with only a severe soft tissue injury of the leg were 3.1 times more likely to have a physical SIP subscore of 5 points and those treated with a through-the-knee amputation were 11.5 times more likely to have a physical subscore of 5 points. There were no significant differences in the psychosocial outcomes according to treatment group. At 7-year follow-up, patient characteristics that were significantly associated with poorer outcomes included older age, female sex, nonwhite race, lower education level, living in a poor household, current or previous smoking, low self-efficacy, poor self-reported health status before the injury, and involvement with the legal system in an effort to obtain disability payments. Except for age, predictors of poor outcome were similar at 24 and 84 months after the injury. These results confirmed the previous conclusion of the LEAP Study that limb reconstruction results in functional outcomes equivalent to those of ampu-

---

TABLE 12-9 | **Predictors of Poor Outcome Found in the LEAP Study after Adjusting for Extent of Injury**

- Major complication
- High school education or less
- Nonwhite
- Low income and no private insurance
- Current smoker
- Low self-efficacy and social support
- Involvement with legal system

tation. The results also showed that regardless of the treatment option, long-term functional outcomes are likely to be poor.

CLINICAL PRACTICE CONSIDERATIONS

Generalization of the findings of the LEAP Study beyond Level I trauma centers must be cautioned against. In the Level 1 trauma center, surgeons should advise their patients with mangled lower limbs that the functional results of reconstruction are equivalent to amputation. The reconstruction process requires more operations and more hospitalizations and is associated with a higher complication rate. At 2 years, both patient groups are significantly disabled, and only 48% are returned to work. Both patient groups show evidence of lingering psychosocial disability. Given the "no outcome difference" at 2 years, patients and surgeons can be comfortable recommending or selecting limb-preservation surgery. Efforts to minimize complications and hastened fracture union might improve the outcome of the reconstruction patients.

The results of the LEAP Study also suggest that major improvements in outcome might require greater emphasis on nonclinical interventions, such as early evaluation by vocational rehabilitation counselors. The study also confirms previous research that found both self-efficacy and social support to be important determinants of outcome.[30,76] Interventions aimed at improving support networks and self-efficacy may benefit patients facing a challenging recovery. Surgeons also need to acknowledge the long-term psychosocial disability associated with the mangled extremity, regardless of the treatment. Posttraumatic stress disorder screening and appropriate referral of patients for therapy may need to become a proactive part of the postoperative treatment plan.[79,82,83,109]

For patients undergoing limb amputation, the LEAP Study also identified a number of clinical issues that can be used by the surgeon in planning amputation level and stump coverage. There were no significant differences between above-knee amputations and below-knee amputations in return to work rates, pain, or SIP scores. Patients with through-knee amputations had SIP scores that were 40% higher than those patients who received either a below-knee amputation or an above-knee amputation. Patients with through-knee amputations also demonstrated significantly lower walking speeds. Physicians were less satisfied with the clinical, cosmetic, and functional recovery of through-knee amputations compared with above-knee and below-knee amputation. Thus, as a generality, in the adult trauma population, a through-knee amputation should be avoided whenever possible.

Atypical wound closures, skin grafts, and flaps did not adversely affect the outcome in this study, suggesting that efforts to preserve the knee are worthwhile.[72] Furthermore, patient outcomes were not affected by the technical sophistication of the prosthesis, although patients with higher-technology prostheses were more satisfied. These findings will challenge the physician who currently fits a patient with a sophisticated (and expensive) prosthesis and the results underscore the need for controlled studies that examine the relationships between the type of prosthetic device, the fit of the device, and its functional outcomes.[24,72]

SUMMARY

The decision to amputate or salvage a severely injured lower extremity is a difficult one, which relies not only on the expertise of the orthopaedic surgeon but also on the input of his subspecialty colleagues (general trauma surgeons, vascular surgeons, and plastic surgeons) as well as the patient. The decision to reconstruct or amputate an extremity cannot depend on limb salvage scores, as all have proved to have little clinical utility. Using current technology and Level I trauma center orthopaedic clinical experience, combined with multispecialty support, current data appear to suggest that the results of limb reconstruction are equal to those of amputation following severe lower extremity trauma, and this observation should encourage the continued efforts to reconstruct severely injured limbs. Ideally, the patient with a mangled extremity should be directed to an experienced limb injury center, where strategies to minimize complications, address related posttraumatic stress disorder, improve the patient's self-efficacy, and target early vocational retraining may improve the long-term outcomes in patients with these life-altering injuries.

REFERENCES

1. Adams CI, Keating JF, Court-Brown CM. Cigarette smoking and open tibial fractures. Injury 2001;32:61–65.
2. Aldea PA, Shaw WW. The evolution of the surgical management of severe lower extremity trauma. Clin Plast Surg 1986;13:549–569.
3. Antich-Adrover P, Marti-Garin D, Murias-Alvarez J, et al. External fixation and secondary intramedullary nailing of open tibial fractures. A randomized, prospective trial. J Bone Joint Surg Br 1997;79:433–437.
4. Bhattacharyya T, Mehta P, Smith M, et al. Routine use of wound vacuum-assisted closure does not allow coverage delay for open tibia fractures. Plast Reconstr Surg 2008;121:1263–1266.
5. Bickels J, Wittig JC, Kollender Y, et al. Sciatic nerve resection: is that truly an indication for amputation? Clin Orthop 2002;399:201–204.
6. Bonanni F, Rhodes M, Lucke JF. The futility of predictive scoring of mangled lower extremities. J Trauma 1993;34:99–104.
7. Booi DI, Debats IB, Boeckx WD, et al. Risk factors and blood flow in the free transverse rectus abdominis (TRAM) flap: smoking and high flap weight impair the free TRAM flap microcirculation. Ann Plast Surg 2007;59:364–371.
8. Bosse MJ, MacKenzie EJ; the LEAP Study Group. A Prospective Evaluation of the Clinical Utility of the Lower-Extremity Injury Severity Scores. J Bone Joint Surg 2001;83:3–14.
9. Bosse MJ, MacKenzie EJ, Kellam JF, et al. An analysis of outcomes of reconstruction or amputation after leg-threatening injuries. N Engl J Med 2002;347:1924–1931.
10. Bosse MJ, McCarthy ML, Jones AL, et al. The insensate foot following severe lower extremity trauma: an indication for amputation? J Bone Joint Surg Am 2005;87A:2601–2608.
11. Bouachour G, Cronier P, Gouello JP, et al. Hyperbaric oxygen therapy in the management of crush injuries: a randomized double-blind placebo-controlled clinical trial. J Trauma 1996;41:333–339.
12. Brooks AD, Gold JS, Graham D, et al. Resection of the sciatic, peroneal, or tibial nerves: assessment of functional status. Ann Surg Oncol 2002;9:41–47.
13. Brown CW, Orme TJ, Richardson HD. The rate of pseudarthrosis (surgical nonunion) in patients who are smokers and patients who are nonsmokers: a comparison study. Spine 1986;11:942–943.
14. Byrd HS, Spicer TE, Cierney G III. Management of open tibial fractures. Plast Reconstr Surg 1985;76:719–730.
15. Castillo RC, Bosse MJ, MacKenzie EJ, et al. Impact of smoking on fracture healing and risk of complications in limb-threatening open tibia fractures. J Orthop Trauma 2005;19:151–157.
16. Caudle RJ, Stern PJ. Severe open fractures of the tibia. J Bone Joint Surg Am 1987;69A:801–807.
17. Chang DW, Reece GP, Wang B, et al. Effect of smoking on complications in patients undergoing free TRAM flap breast reconstruction. Plast Reconstr Surg 2000;105:2374–2380.
18. Chang LD, Buncke G, Slezak S, et al. Cigarette smoking, plastic surgery, and microsurgery. J Reconstr Microsurg 1996;12:467–474.
19. Chen F, Osterman AL, Mahony K. Smoking and bony union after ulna-shortening osteotomy. Am J Orthop 2001;30:486–489.
20. Christian EP, Bosse MJ, Robb G. Reconstruction of large diaphyseal defects, without free fibular transfer, in Grade-IIIB tibial fractures. J Bone Joint Surg Am 1989;71A:994–1004.
21. Cobb TK, Gabrielsen TA, Campbell DC, et al. Cigarette smoking and nonunion after ankle arthrodesis. Foot Ankle Int 1994;15:64–67.
22. Colton C. The history of fracture treatment. In Browner BD, Jupiter JB, Levine AM, Trafton PG, eds. Skeletal trauma. Philadelphia: Saunders;2003:3–28.
23. Crowley DJ, Kanakaris NK, Giannoudis PV. Irrigation of the wounds in open fractures. J Bone Joint Surg Br 2007;89B:580–585.
24. Cyril JK, MacKenzie EJ, Smith DG, et al. Prosthetic device satisfaction among patients with lower extremity amputation due to trauma. Toronto, Ontario, Canada:Orthopaedic Trauma Association 18th Meeting Abstracts 2002.
25. Daftari TK, Whitesides TE Jr, Heller JG, et al. Nicotine on the revascularization of bone graft. An experimental study in rabbits. Spine 1994;19:904–911.

26. Dagher F, Roukoz S. Compound tibial fractures with bone loss treated by the Ilizarov technique. J Bone Joint Surg Br 1991;73B:316–321.
27. Dagum AB, Best AK, Schemitsch EH, et al. Salvage after severe lower-extremity trauma: are the outcomes worth the means? Plast Reconstr Surg 1999;103:1212–1220.
28. Dedmond BT, Kortesis B, Punger K, et al. The use of negative-pressure wound therapy (NPWT) in the temporary treatment of soft-tissue injuries associated with high-energy open tibial shaft fractures. J Orthop Trauma 2007;21:11–17.
29. Dirschl DR, Dahners LE. The mangled extremity: when should it be amputated? J Am Acad Orthop Surg 1996;4:182–190.
30. Ewart CK, Stewart KJ, Gillilan RE, et al. Self-efficacy mediates strength gains during circuit weight training in men with coronary artery disease. Med Sci Sports Exerc 1986; 18:531–540.
31. Finklestein EA, Corso PS, Miller TR, Associates. Incidence and Economic Burden of Injuries in the United States. New York: Oxford University Press; 2006.
32. Finkemeier CG. Bone-grafting and bone-graft substitutes. J Bone Joint Surg Am 2002; 84A:454–464.
33. Fischer MD, Gustilo RB, Varecka TF. The timing of flap coverage, bone-grafting, and intramedullary nailing in patients who have a fracture of the tibial shaft with extensive soft-tissue injury. J Bone Joint Surg Am 1991;73A:1316–1322.
34. Folk JW, Starr AJ, Early JS. Early wound complications of operative treatment of calcaneus fractures: analysis of 190 fractures. J Orthop Trauma 1999;13:369–372.
35. Francel TJ, Vander Kolk CA, Hoopes JE, et al. Microvascular soft-tissue transplantation for reconstruction of acute open tibial fractures: timing of coverage and long-term functional results. Plast Reconstr Surg 1992;89:478–487.
36. Georgiadis GM, Behrens FF, Joyce MJ, et al. Open tibial fractures with severe soft-tissue loss. Limb salvage compared with below-the-knee amputation. J Bone Joint Surg Am 1993;75A:1431–1441.
37. Godina M. Early microsurgical reconstruction of complex trauma of the extremities. Plast Reconstr Surg 1986;78:285–292.
38. Goldminz D, Bennett RG. Cigarette smoking and flap and full-thickness graft necrosis. Arch Dermatol 1991;127:1012–1015.
39. Gopal S, Majumder S, Batchelor AG, et al. Fix and flap: the radical orthopaedic and plastic treatment of severe open fractures of the tibia. J Bone Joint Surg Br 2000;82B: 959–966.
40. Govender S, Csimma C, Genant HK, et al. Recombinant human bone morphogenetic protein-2 for treatment of open tibial fractures. J Bone Joint Surg 2002;84:2123–2134.
41. Greensmith JE. Hyperbaric oxygen therapy in extremity trauma. J Am Acad Orthop Surg 2004;12:376–384.
42. Gregory RT, Gould RJ, Peclet M, et al. The mangled extremity syndrome (M.E.S.): a severity grading system for multisystem injury of the extremity. J Trauma 1985;25: 1147–1150.
43. Hak DJ, Lee SS, Goulet JA. Success of exchange reamed intramedullary nailing for femoral shaft nonunion or delayed union. J Orthop Trauma 2000;14:178–182.
44. Harvey EJ, Agel J, Selznick HS, et al. Deleterious effect of smoking on healing of open tibia-shaft fractures. Am J Orthop 2002;31:518–521.
45. Helfet DL, Howey T, Sanders R, et al. Limb salvage versus amputation. Preliminary results of the Mangled Extremity Severity Score. Clin Orthop Relat Res 1990;80–86.
46. Henley MB, Chapman JR, Agel J, et al. Treatment of type II, IIIA, and IIIB open fractures of the tibial shaft: a prospective comparison of unreamed interlocking intramedullary nails and half-pin external fixators. J Orthop Trauma 1998;12:1–7.
47. Hertel R, Lambert SM, Muller S, et al. On the timing of soft-tissue reconstruction for open fractures of the lower leg. Arch Orthop Trauma Surg 1999;119:7–12.
48. Hertel R, Strebel N, Ganz R. Amputation versus reconstruction in traumatic defects of the leg: outcome and costs. J Orthop Trauma 1996;10:223–229.
49. Hollinger JO, Schmitt JM, Hwang K, et al. Impact of nicotine on bone healing. J Biomed Mater Res 1999;45:294–301.
50. Howe HR Jr, Poole GV Jr, Hansen KJ, et al. Salvage of lower extremities following combined orthopedic and vascular trauma. A predictive salvage index. Am Surg 1987; 53:205–208.
51. Hughes CW. Acute vascular trauma in Korean War casualties; an analysis of 180 cases. Surg Gynecol Obstet 1954;99:91–100.
52. Hughes CW. The primary repair of wounds of major arteries; an analysis of experience in Korea in 1953. Ann Surg 1955;141:297–303.
53. Hughes CW. Arterial repair during the Korean war. Ann Surg 1958;147:555–561.
54. Hunt TK, Pai MP. The effect of varying ambient oxygen tensions on wound metabolism and collagen synthesis. Surg Gynecol Obstet 1972;135:561–567.
55. Iannacone WM, Taffet R, DeLong WG Jr, et al. Early exchange intramedullary nailing of distal femoral fractures with vascular injury initially stabilized with external fixation. J Trauma 1994;37:446–451.
56. Johansen K, Bandyk D, Thiele B, et al. Temporary intraluminal shunts: resolution of a management dilemma in complex vascular injuries. J Trauma 1982;22:395–402.
57. Ding W, Wu X, Li J. Temporary vascular injury: collective review injury. 2008;39 (9): 970–977.
58. Johansen K, Daines M, Howey T, et al. Objective criteria accurately predict amputation following lower extremity trauma. J Trauma 1990;30:568–572.
59. Johanson NA, Liang MH, Daltroy L, et al. American Academy of Orthopaedic Surgeons lower limb outcomes assessment instruments. Reliability, validity, and sensitivity to change. J Bone Joint Surg Am 2004;86A:902–909.
60. Jones AL, Bucholz RW, Bosse MJ, et al. Recombinant human BMP-2 and allograft compared with autogenous bone graft for reconstruction of diaphyseal tibial fractures with cortical defects. A randomized, controlled trial. J Bone Joint Surg Am 2006;88A: 1431–1441.
61. Kalra R, Singh SP, Savage SM, et al. Effects of cigarette smoke on immune response: chronic exposure to cigarette smoke impairs antigen-mediated signaling in T cells and depletes IP3-sensitive Ca(2+) stores. J Pharmacol Exp Ther 2000;293:166–171.
62. Khouri RK, Shaw WW. Reconstruction of the lower extremity with microvascular free flaps: a 10-year experience with 304 consecutive cases. J Trauma 1989;29:1086–1094.
63. Kirk NT. The classic amputations. Clin Orthop Relat Res 1989;3–16.
64. Kobbe P, Tarkin IS, Frink M, et al. [Voluminous bone graft harvesting of the femoral marrow cavity for autologous transplantation: an indication for the "Reamer-Irrigator-Aspirator" (RIA-) technique.] Unfallchirurg 2008;111:469–472.
65. Kyro A, Usenius JP, Aarnio M, et al. Are smokers a risk group for delayed healing of tibial shaft fractures? Ann Chir Gynaecol 1993;82:254–262.
66. Lange RH. Limb reconstruction versus amputation decision making in massive lower extremity trauma. Clin Orthop Relat Res 1989;92–99.
67. Lange RH, Bach AW, Hansen ST Jr, et al. Open tibial fractures with associated vascular injuries: prognosis for limb salvage. J Trauma 1985;25:203–208.
68. Langworthy MJ, Smith JM, Gould M. Treatment of the mangled lower extremity after a terrorist blast injury. Clin Orthop Relat Res 2004;88–96.
69. lister-Sistilli CG, Caggiula AR, Knopf S, et al. The effects of nicotine on the immune system. Psychoneuroendocrinology 1998;23:175–187.
70. Lovich SF, Arnold PG. The effect of smoking on muscle transposition. Plast Reconstr Surg 1994;93:825–828.
71. MacKenzie EJ, Bosse MJ, Kellam JF; LEAP Study Group. Characterization of the patients undergoing amputation versus limb salvage for severe lower extremity trauma. J Orthop Trauma 2000;14:455–466.
72. MacKenzie EJ, Bosse MJ, Castillo RC, et al. Functional outcomes following trauma-related lower-extremity amputation. J Bone Joint Surg Am 2004;86A:1636–1645.
73. MacKenzie EJ, Bosse MJ, Kellam JF, et al. Characterization of patients with high-energy lower extremity trauma. J Orthop Trauma 2000;14:455–466.
74. MacKenzie EJ, Bosse MJ, Pollak AN, et al. Long-term persistence of disability following severe lower-limb trauma. Results of a 7-year follow-up. J Bone Joint Surg Am 2005; 87A:1801–1809.
75. MacKenzie EJ, Jones AS, Bosse MJ, et al. Health-care costs associated with amputation or reconstruction of a limb-threatening injury. J Bone Joint Surg Am 2007;89A: 1685–1692.
76. MacKenzie EJ, Morris JA Jr, Jurkovich GJ, et al. Return to work following injury: the role of economic, social, and job-related factors. Am J Public Health 1998;88: 1630–1637.
77. Marsh DR, Shah S, Elliott J, et al. The Ilizarov method in nonunion, malunion, and infection of fractures. J Bone Joint Surg Br 1997;79B:273–279.
78. McCabe CJ, Ferguson CM, Ottinger LW. Improved limb salvage in popliteal artery injuries. J Trauma 1983;23:982–985.
79. McCarthy ML, MacKenzie EJ, Edwin D, et al. Psychological distress associated with severe lower-limb injury. J Bone Joint Surg Am 2003;85A:1689–1697.
80. McKee MD, Yoo DJ, Zdero R, et al. Combined single-stage osseous and soft tissue reconstruction of the tibia with the Ilizarov method and tissue transfer. J Orthop Trauma 2008;22:183–189.
81. McNamara MG, Heckman JD, Corley FG. Severe open fractures of the lower extremity: a retrospective evaluation of the Mangled Extremity Severity Score (MESS). J Orthop Trauma 1994;8:81–87.
82. Michaels AJ, Michaels CE, Moon CH, et al. Posttraumatic stress disorder after injury: impact on general health outcome and early risk assessment. J Trauma 1999;47: 460–466.
83. Michaels AJ, Michaels CE, Moon CH, et al. Psychosocial factors limit outcomes after trauma. J Trauma 1998;44:644–648.
84. Modrall JG, Weaver FA, Yellin AE. Diagnosis of vascular trauma. Ann Vasc Surg 1995; 9:415–421.
85. Myerson MS, McGarvey WC, Henderson MR, et al. Morbidity after crush injuries to the foot. J Orthop Trauma 1994;8:343–349.
86. Nichols JG, Svoboda JA, Parks SN. Use of temporary intraluminal shunts in selected peripheral arterial injuries. J Trauma 1986;26:1094–1096.
87. Noe A. Extremity injury in war: a brief history. J Am Acad Orthop Surg 2006;14: S1–S6.
88. Nolte PA, van der KA, Patka P, et al. Low-intensity pulsed ultrasound in the treatment of nonunions. J Trauma 2001;51:693–702.
89. Olson SA, Willis MD. Initial management of open fractures. In: Rockwood and Green's Fractures in adults (pp. 390–391), 6th ed. Philadelphia: Lippincott Williams & Wilkins, 2006.
90. Outcomes instruments and information: lower extremity instruments. American Association of Orthopaedic Surgeons web site. Retrieved February 24, 2009, from http://www.aaos.org/research/outcomes/outcomeslower.asp.
91. Pai MP, Hunt TK. Effect of varying oxygen tensions on healing of open wounds. Surg Gynecol Obstet 1972;135:756–758.
92. Paley D, Maar DC. Ilizarov bone transport treatment for tibial defects. J Orthop Trauma 2000;14:76–85.
93. Pare A. Dix Livres de la Chirurgie avec la Magasin des instruments Necessaires a Icelle. 7, Chapter 13. Paris: Jean le Royer, 1564.
94. Pollak AN, McCarthy ML, Burgess AR. Short-term wound complications after application of flaps for coverage of traumatic soft-tissue defects about the tibia. The Lower Extremity Assessment Project (LEAP) Study Group. J Bone Joint Surg Am 2000;82A: 1681–1691.
95. Reus WF III, Colen LB, Straker DJ. Tobacco smoking and complications in elective microsurgery. Plast Reconstr Surg 1992;89:490–494.
96. Rich NM, Baugh JH, Hughes CW. Acute arterial injuries in Vietnam: 1,000 cases. J Trauma 1970;10:359–369.
97. Robert RS, Weitzman AM, Tracey WJ, et al. Simultaneous treatment of tibial bone and soft-tissue defects with the Ilizarov method. J Orthop Trauma 2006;20:197–205.
98. Roessler MS, Wisner DH, Holcroft JW. The mangled extremity. When to amputate? Arch Surg 1991;126:1243–1248.
99. Russell WL, Sailors DM, Whittle TB, et al. Limb salvage versus traumatic amputation. A decision based on a seven-part predictive index. Ann Surg 1991;213:473–480.
100. Sarin CL, Austin JC, Nickel WO. Effects of smoking on digital blood-flow velocity. JAMA 1974;229:1327–1328.
101. Schmitz MA, Finnegan M, Natarajan R, et al. Effect of smoking on tibial shaft fracture healing. Clin Orthop Relat Res 1999;184–200.
102. Seyfer AE, Lower R. Late results of free-muscle flaps and delayed bone grafting in the secondary treatment of open distal tibial fractures. Plast Reconstr Surg 1989;83:77–84.
103. Siebenrock KA, Gerich T, Jakob RP. Sequential intramedullary nailing of open tibial shaft fractures after external fixation. Arch Orthop Trauma Surg 1997;116:32–36.
104. Siebenrock KA, Schillig B, Jakob RP. Treatment of complex tibial shaft fractures. Arguments for early secondary intramedullary nailing. Clin Orthop Relat Res 1993; 269–274.

105. Siegel HJ, Patzakis MJ, Holtom PD, et al. Limb salvage for chronic tibial osteomyelitis: an outcomes study. J Trauma 2000;48:484–489.
106. Singh SP, Kalra R, Puttfarcken P, et al. Acute and chronic nicotine exposures modulate the immune system through different pathways. Toxicol Appl Pharmacol 2000;164: 65–72.
107. Slauterbeck JR, Britton C, Moneim MS, et al. Mangled extremity severity score: an accurate guide to treatment of the severely injured upper extremity. J Orthop Trauma 1994;8:282–285.
108. Smith DG, Horn P, Malchow D, et al. Prosthetic history, prosthetic charges, and functional outcome of the isolated, traumatic below-knee amputee. J Trauma 1995;38: 44–47.
109. Starr AJ, Smith WR, Frawley WH, et al. Symptoms of posttraumatic stress disorder after orthopaedic trauma. J Bone Joint Surg Am 2004;86A:1115–1121.
110. Suedkamp NP, Barbey N, Veuskens A, et al. The incidence of osteitis in open fractures: an analysis of 948 open fractures (a review of the Hannover experience). J Orthop Trauma 1993;7:473–482.
111. Swartz WM, Mears DC. Management of difficult lower extremity fractures and nonunions. Clin Plast Surg 1986;13:633–644.
112. Swiontkowski MF, MacKenzie EJ, Bosse MJ, et al. Factors influencing the decision to amputate or reconstruct after high-energy lower extremity trauma. J Trauma 2002;52: 641–649.
113. Thalgott JS, Cotler HB, Sasso RC, et al. Postoperative infections in spinal implants. Classification and analysis—a multicenter study. Spine 1991;16:981–984.
114. Togawa S, Yamami N, Nakayama H, et al. The validity of the mangled extremity severity score in the assessment of upper limb injuries. J Bone Joint Surg Br 2005;87B: 1516–1519.
115. Toledo-Pereyra LH, Toledo MM. A critical study of Lister's work on antiseptic surgery. Am J Surg 1976;131:736–744.
116. Tornetta P III, Bergman M, Watnik N, et al. Treatment of grade-IIIb open tibial fractures. A prospective randomised comparison of external fixation and nonreamed locked nailing. J Bone Joint Surg Br 1994;76B:13–19.
117. Tran T, Thordarson D. Functional outcome of multiply injured patients with associated foot injury. Foot Ankle Int 2002;23:340–343.
118. Turchin DC, Schemitsch EH, McKee MD, et al. Do foot injuries significantly affect the functional outcome of multiply injured patients? J Orthop Trauma 1999;13:1–4.
119. Ueng SW, Lee SS, Lin SS, et al. Hyperbaric oxygen therapy mitigates the adverse effect of cigarette smoking on the bone healing of tibial lengthening: an experimental study on rabbits. J Trauma 1999;47:752–759.
120. Vora A, Myerson MS. Crush injuries of the foot in the industrial setting. Foot Ankle Clin 2002;7:367–383.
121. Webb LX, Bosse MJ, Castillo RC, et al. Analysis of surgeon-controlled variables in the treatment of limb-threatening type-III open tibial diaphyseal fractures. J Bone Joint Surg Am 2007;89A:923–928.
122. Westphal T, Piatek S, Schubert S, et al. [Quality of life after foot injuries.] Zentralbl Chir 2002;127:238–242.
123. Williams MO. Long-term cost comparison of major limb salvage using the Ilizarov method versus amputation. Clin Orthop Relat Res 1994;156–158.
124. Worlock P, Slack R, Harvey L, et al. The prevention of infection in open fractures: an experimental study of the effect of fracture stability. Injury 1994;25:31–38.
125. Yaremchuk MJ, Brumback RJ, Manson PN, et al. Acute and definitive management of traumatic osteocutaneous defects of the lower extremity. Plast Reconstr Surg 1987;80: 1–14.

13

AMPUTATIONS

William J. J. Ertl

INTRODUCTION

This chapter is written to provide the orthopaedic fracture and trauma surgeon a foundation for amputation surgery. Amputation surgery is one of the oldest known surgical procedures but has, in the past generation of surgeons, been given decreased importance particularly with regard to the proper surgical handling of residual limbs. This may be because of the stigma that is attached to amputations as a procedure of failure, namely failure of vascular reconstruction, joint reconstruction, or limb salvage. Amputation should be regarded as a reconstructive procedure restoring limb function with the prosthesis serving as an extension of the limb, not the limb solely being an attachment site for the prosthesis. It is my hope to instill renewed interest in amputation surgery in the traumatized patient.

HISTORICAL BACKGROUND

Amputation as a surgical technique has its roots in prehistoric times. The earliest known documentation of an amputation as a ritualistic act was noted on cave wall drawings dating back to approximately 5,000 B.C. Archeologists noted that a Neanderthal skeleton found in present-day Iraq provides evidence that the individual had survived an above-elbow amputation.[2] Indications for amputation were extended by Hippocrates and Celsus to include the treatment of infection, a reduction in invalid-

ism, removal of useless limbs, and as a life-saving procedure in selected circumstances. It was not until the ancient surgeons Archigenes and Heliodorus expanded the indications to include traumatic injuries and the use of proximal tight bandages for hemorrhage control, akin to the modern tourniquet.[3] During the 1500s, Paré reintroduced the importance of ligatures for hemorrhage control and Clowes is credited with performing the first successful transfemoral amputation. With the introduction of projectile weaponry in the mid-1300s, battlefield injuries became more severe and maiming, requiring a renewed interest in treating limb injuries with amputation. During the late 1700s and into the early 1800s, the British surgeon George Guthrie and the French surgeon Dominique-Jean Larrey challenged the practice of delaying amputations for battlefield injuries for 3 weeks by advocating rapid primary amputation for these injuries. This change in practice resulted in fewer deaths. Larrey also promoted the rapid transport of wounded soldiers from the field with his "flying ambulance."

The development of amputation techniques has centered on armed conflicts. As a consequence of improvements in armaments, soldiers who survived their injuries often sustained significant limb injuries requiring amputation. Having emphasized expeditious transport and rapid amputation, attention was placed on reconstructive efforts of the residual limb. This was due in part to effective developments in anesthetics, aseptic surgery, antibiotics, an understanding of the basic physiology of the lower extremity, and prosthetic devices. A primary goal of amputation reconstruction was to preserve length and maintain the end-bearing capabilities of the residual limb as emphasized by Chopart and Lisfranc at the mid-foot level and by Pirogoff, Boyd, and Syme at the ankle level. During the late 1800s, Bier attempted osteoplastic reconstruction by placing a bony block between the tibia and the fibula secured with screw fixation. The only transtibial amputation capable of end-bearing was developed by Ertl.[57–59] End-bearing was accomplished by combining the concepts of bony reconstruction (osteoplasty) with soft tissue reconstruction (myoplasty) to create an osteo-myoplastic amputation for the transtibial level. The same concepts of reconstructive surgery have been applied to the trans-metatarsal level and the transfemoral level.[59] Ertl was able to apply his reconstructive techniques to approximately 13,000 patients over the years from World War I through World War II.[59] Mondry and Dederich[14] continued to promote soft tissue stabilization, showing the advantages of restoring normal vascularity to the limb after myoplastic amputation at the transfemoral level. Gottschalk and his colleagues further elucidated the importance of myoplastic reconstruction by characterizing improved alignment and gait at the transfemoral level.[21,22]

With the use of new unique materials and engineering principles, the prosthetic field has rapidly advanced the art and science of prosthetic manufacturing and is now able to fit many patients with poorly performed amputations with a functional prosthesis. As a result, the emphasis on proper surgical technique and focusing on amputation as a reconstructive procedure has slowly faded over time. The remainder of the chapter will serve to reemphasize the need for sound surgical handling of the residual limb and review various surgical approaches and outcomes.

GOALS OF AMPUTATION

The ultimate goal of amputation is to restore and provide function to the patient. Surgery is not and should not be the only focus. The surgeon should be cognizant of the effect that limb loss will have on the patient and be able to provide to the patient all the resources necessary to regain maximum function. This will require a team approach with the patient at the center of attention.[36] The team will include the patient, surgeon, prosthetist, rehabilitation expert, peer support, and family and even psychological support. Burgess[10] believed that the residual limb should function as an end-organ. To this end, the surgeon responsible for the patient should strive for total comprehensive care.

INJURED LIMB SCORING SYSTEMS

As orthopaedic and vascular surgical techniques improved over the past couple of decades, there has been renewed interest in salvaging traumatized limbs. However, our ability to predict which limb can be salvaged and which patients would benefit from early amputation remains very subjective and is quite limited. Gregory and his colleagues[23] first attempted to create a scoring system, the Mangled Extremity Syndrome (MES) Index, in a retrospective review of 60 patients. Using this scoring system, they believed that patients could be identified preoperatively for salvage or amputation. A second scoring system, the

Mangled Extremity Severity Score (MESS) was used by Johansen and colleagues[28] and was thought to be simple and predictive. Helfet et al.[25] then applied this scoring system prospectively and found it to be simple and accurate in determining limbs that could be salvaged and those that should undergo primary amputation. The American College of Surgeons simplified the definition of a mangled limb as one where "high energy transfer or crush causes a combination of injuries to the artery, bone, tendon, nerve, and/or soft tissue."[1] Other scoring systems also have been developed, including the Predictive Salvage Index (PSI),[26] The Limb Salvage Index (LSI),[50] the Nerve injury, Ischemia, Soft-tissue injury, Skeletal injury, Shock and Age of patient (NISSSA) score,[37] and the Hannover Fracture Scale (HFS).[55] Each scoring system placed emphasis on different components of the limb and developed various criteria for amputation or salvage. At this point, the most widely used system in the United States is the MESS.

Although ease and applicability have been touted for each scoring system, questions regarding sensitivity and specificity have arisen. Robertson's[48] review of 152 patients suggested poor sensitivity of the MESS as some patients with scores below the amputation threshold eventually went on to an amputation. Bonanni et al.[4] retrospectively reviewed a 10-year experience of attempted limb salvage on 58 limbs using the Mangled Extremity Severity Index (MESI), MESS, PSI, and LSI. Their review suggested poor predictive utility for limb salvage for all four scoring systems in their patient population. Poole et al.[47] attempted to predict limb salvage of extremities with combined osseous, soft tissue, and vascular injuries independent of a named scoring system. The severity of soft tissue and nerve injury was highly interrelated, but soft tissue injury did not correlate with the severity of the osseous injury. Further, limb salvage or amputation could not be accurately predicted by any variable or group of variables studied. Because of the dynamic changes that can occur in these patients, these authors suggested initial limb salvage to observe the limb and then performance of delayed amputation when indicated.[47] Dirschl and Dahners[15] comprehensively reviewed the MESI, MESS, NISSSA, LSI, and PSI. No scoring system was predictive of salvage or amputation. They proposed that scoring systems be used for documentation and as guides in clinical decision-making, not as absolute indicators for salvage or amputation.[15] Durham et al.[17] assessed the MESI, MESS, PSI, and LSI retrospectively over a 10-year period. Although there was significant variability in predicting amputation versus salvage, no scoring system was able to predict functional outcome.[17] Thuan et al.[53] showed that no injury severity score could predict functional outcome in patients who underwent limb salvage. Bosse et al. (the LEAP Group)[6] prospectively evaluated the use of multiple scoring systems: MESS, LSI, PSI, NISSSA, and the Hannover Fracture Scale-97 (HFS-97). The overall analysis showed that lower scores had specificity for limb salvage potential, but the low sensitivity of these scoring systems did not validate them as predictors of amputation. The authors recommended caution in using these scoring systems at or above the amputation threshold.[6] In comparison, Krettek et al.[29] reevaluated the HFS, naming it the HFS-98, and applied the new scoring system prospectively to 87 open long bone fractures. They concluded that the HFS-98 was a reliable extremity salvage scoring system.[29]

Lower extremity trauma is unique to each individual patient. The spectrum of injury to each organ system, namely the skin and subcutaneous tissue, muscle, neurovascular structures, and bone, is varied. No scoring system has been shown to be predictive of amputation, outcome, or function. Scores that are predictive of salvage may be helpful, but caution is stressed with regard to identifying a specific amputation threshold. Scoring systems may be used as a documentation tool and as a tool to facilitate communication between surgeons. In most cases, initial limb salvage attempts should be instituted first, allowing a complete assessment of the patient, informing the patient of potential surgical options, and allowing the patient to become involved in decision-making regarding salvage versus amputation. Although patients undergoing salvage of a severely injured limb may require frequent rehospitalizations, 2- and 7-year results of amputation compared with limb salvage have demonstrated similar outcomes as measured by the Sickness Impact Profile.[5,34] However, projected lifetime costs for patients having undergone an amputation are estimated to be three times greater than those for limb salvage patients.[35]

CLINICAL ASSESSMENT OF THE PATIENT REQUIRING AMPUTATION

Urgent Evaluation

In the emergent setting, assessment of the traumatized limb and patient begins with as detailed history and as complete a physical examination as possible using the American College of Surgeons Advanced Trauma Life Support ABC algorithm. Once the primary survey is completed and the injury inventory is complete, a secondary survey should be performed and repeated every 4 to 6 hours, especially in the obtunded and/or intubated patient. Additional information can be gained by questioning first responders with regard to the mechanism of injury, the initial presentation of the patient, the time required for extrication, exposure to the elements, the amount of blood loss at the scene, the potential degree of wound contamination, resuscitation efforts, and the total time elapsed from the scene to the hospital. This information may provide a much more comprehensive clinical assessment of the patient, guiding the surgeon in his or her decision-making. Once the patient has been assessed, life-threatening injuries addressed, and resuscitation instituted, a focused examination of the limb can be undertaken. Overall inspection of the limb should take into account its appearance and the presence of any and all open wounds. Closed soft tissue wounds can be quite severe and should be graded using the Tscherne classification[54] and open wounds in association with a fracture should be classified using the Gustilo-Anderson open fracture wound classification system.[24,42] Peripheral pulses should be monitored closely and documented after any reduction maneuver. Dislocations and fractures should be reduced and held reduced with an appropriate splint. Motor and sensory function should also be documented as thoroughly as possible both before and after manipulating the limb. If there are no palpable pulses, a simple Doppler examination of the entire extremity should be performed. A complete Doppler examination may identify occult injuries remote from the main zone of injury that are affecting perfusion and threatening viability of the limb. With diminished or absent distal pulses, an ankle-brachial index (ABI) should be determined. A blood pressure cuff is placed around the calf of the extremity in question. The cuff is inflated until no audible Doppler pulse is appreci-

ated. Then the cuff pressure is slowly released and once a pulse is heard, the systolic blood pressure value is noted. The same is then done for the upper extremity and a ratio of the lower extremity pressure to the upper extremity pressure is created. The ratio obtained should be 0.9 or greater if no vascular injury is present. A value below 0.9 is suggestive of a vascular injury that may require further work-up (e.g., angiography) or intervention. This simple test has shown value in patients with knee dislocation and high-energy tibial plateau fractures.[40,57] Further, simple duplex Doppler examination of the arterial system can be performed before angiography. Angiography should be reserved to determine the exact location of an arterial injury and guide potential intervention, such as intraluminal stenting. If a specific vascular injury is diagnosed, revascularization should be performed to preserve limb viability. If the limb is unstable because of a fracture or ligamentous injury, a simple uniplanar external fixator can be applied quickly to maintain the length and alignment of the limb and provide provisional stability during revascularization.[19]

Elective Evaluation

In patients who present with delayed or nonemergent indications for amputation, a detailed physical examination is imperative. These patients may present with progressive soft tissue necrosis and infection (Fig. 13-1). Overall, inspection of the wounds to determine the extent of potential superficial and/or deep infection is needed as this may determine the ultimate level of amputation. Further, noninvasive vascular assessment should be performed. An ABI of less than 0.45 is suggestive that distal healing is unlikely.[16] However, it has been my experi-

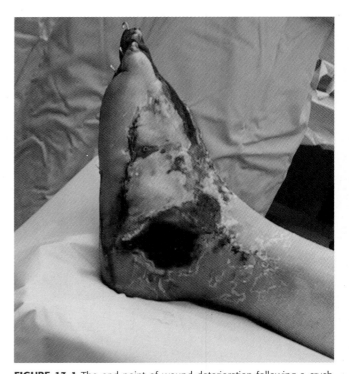

FIGURE 13-1 The end point of wound deterioration following a crush injury to the foot. This patient sustained multiple metatarsal fractures that were treated with percutaneous pin fixation. The foot had a palpable pulse and the wounds were closed; however, the soft tissue envelope did not survive and a transtibial amputation was performed.

ence that, in patients with calcific arteriosclerosis, these values may be falsely high and caution should be used when evaluating this test in these patients. Other useful tests include the duplex Doppler examination of the arterial system and transcutaneous oxygen tension (TcPo$_2$) measurements. Duplex Doppler tests will characterize the arterial anatomy and TcPo$_2$ measurements will aid in determining the healing potential of surgical wounds. TcPo$_2$ values below 20 mm Hg are indicative of nonhealing, and values of 40 mm Hg or greater are indicative of healing. Between these values, the surgeon should take into account the patient's preexisting comorbidities, arterial anatomy, and nutritional status. In my experience, in a patient who has undergone a distal vascular bypass below the knee, a below-knee amputation usually will fail because of the single-vessel dominance of the lower limb. The goal of this workup is to provide both the patient and the surgeon information that can be used to determine the optimal level of amputation to facilitate prosthetic planning and to estimate rehabilitation demands.

SURGICAL TECHNIQUES

Upper Extremity

Temporizing versus Immediate Amputation

Patients who present with a complete amputation of the limb rarely are able to undergo successful reimplantation, usually because the underlying soft tissue injury is so severe compared with the bony injury (Fig. 13-2). Traumatized limbs with segmental injuries, significant vascular injury, significant soft tissue loss, and/or near amputation may be best treated with an immediate open amputation (Fig. 13-3). Traumatized limbs with a nonreconstructible vascular injury will require amputation. The most important factor determining limb salvage versus amputation will be the severity of the soft tissue injury.[33] These patients often have an obvious constellation of nonreconstructible injuries. When immediate amputation is preferred, all viable soft tissue should be maintained as it can be used later for definitive wound closure. Obviously, ischemic, devitalized tissue should be aggressively and thoroughly debrided. Osseous structures

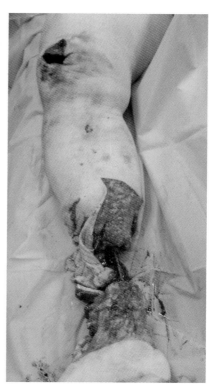

FIGURE 13-3 A motorcyclist sustained limb-threatening injuries to the lower leg. There was segmental bone loss and extensive soft tissue loss, and the foot was pulseless. Vascular reconstruction was not feasible. Injuries such as this one should be treated with staged amputation. An open amputation preserving as much length as possible should be performed first. Following intensive wound care, a definitive amputation is performed when the wound bed seems stable.

should be resected initially to the level of soft tissue resection. Wound care should then be instituted with serial debridements until a stable wound bed is achieved. Negative pressure wound therapy may play an adjunctive role in creating granulation tissue that may aide in wound healing (Fig. 13-4). During this period, patient education and prosthetic consultation should be used to maintain the patient's involvement in his or her treatment course. Further, the clinical evaluation should continue to determine the optimum level of amputation, similar to the patient undergoing nonemergent amputation.

Patients who present with no clear-cut evidence for immediate amputation should undergo early temporizing treatment. This may include the use of temporary external fixation and serial wound debridement procedures. The primary focus of initial temporizing treatment is to obtain and maintain perfusion of the limb before extensive and exhausting reconstructive procedures. If limb viability cannot be maintained or reconstruction/salvage is deemed unfeasible, then an elective amputation should be undertaken.

Below-Elbow Amputation

Preserving a functional elbow joint is vital as this joint acts as a fulcrum to position the hand in space. Maintaining limb length and a functional elbow joint will substantially increase the functional outcome at this level of amputation. If possible, preserving the pronator quadratus allows the patient to maintain two thirds of active forearm rotation. A body-powered prosthesis

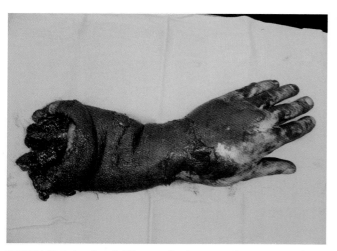

FIGURE 13-2 An oil well driller sustained a traumatic amputation during a drilling operation. Significant soft tissue contamination and extensive degloving precluded reimplantation. The radius and ulna both remained attached to the arm while the hand and forearm soft tissue envelope was completely degloved.

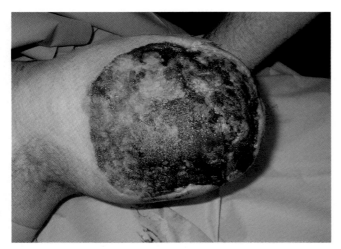

FIGURE 13-4 Negative pressure wound therapy is a powerful adjunctive tool to create healthy granulation tissue in a stable wound bed. In this transhumeral amputation, length was preserved by maintaining soft tissue muscle coverage over the humerus. A split-thickness skin graft was successfully applied and the patient was ultimately fitted with a myoelectric prosthesis.

can be applied to this level. If a myoelectric prosthesis in used, the optimum length will be at the junction of the mid and distal thirds of the forearm. The soft tissue reconstruction must be stable and can be accomplished with myodesis (muscle sutured to bone) or a combination of a myodesis of the deeper layer and myoplasty (antagonistic muscles sutured together) of the superficial layer (using a pants-over-vest technique). This will provide adequate soft tissue coverage distally with volar and dorsal flaps and allow the residual musculature to be active and dynamic, providing a strong myoelectric signal. Although not routinely performed, a Krukenberg procedure splits the radius

and ulna to create a pincers mechanism. It has been recommended for blind patients with bilateral below-elbow amputations or in Third World countries where prosthetic services are limited.[3]

Transhumeral Amputation

If the elbow joint cannot be preserved, then a transhumeral amputation is performed. An amputation through the elbow is a difficult level both for prosthetic fitting and appearance as the prosthetic elbow will be more distal than the contralateral native elbow; therefore, this amputation level is rarely selected. The ideal length of the humerus for a body-powered prosthesis is just proximal to the distal metaphyseal–diaphyseal junction. However, for a myoelectric prosthesis, the humerus will need to be transected at the mid-shaft to allow for adequate fitting of this prosthesis. Soft tissue stabilization again is important to provide distal bony coverage and to provide the residual limb with dynamic muscle function. This can be accomplished by securing the deeper layer via myodesis and the superficial layer with a myoplasty using a pants-over-vest technique.

The rate of overall prosthetic use and satisfaction with upper extremity amputation is much lower than it is for a below-elbow amputation.[16] Recently, targeted nerve reinnervation has shown promise in improving myoelectric prosthetic function.[30,38] This technique uses selective nerve implantation into various muscles to improve myoelectric signaling to the prosthesis. It has been applied to a limited number of patients and continues to evolve, providing hope for improved prosthetic function in the proximal upper extremity amputee.

Lower Extremity

Ankle Disarticulation

Ankle disarticulation was developed as a method to preserve the end-bearing capabilities of the limb. The best known is the Syme amputation (Fig. 13-5), but variations include the Pirogoff

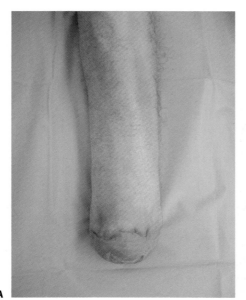

A   **B**

FIGURE 13-5 A. Frontal picture of a patient with a mature Syme amputation demonstrates the regional soft tissue atrophy that can occur over time and the instability of the heal pad that has occurred. The distal tibia has become very prominent and painful in the prosthesis. **B.** The distal end of this Syme amputation demonstrates a hypertrophic callous with fissuring that developed as a result of the unstable heel pad.

amputation involving a calcaneotibial arthrodesis,[46] the Boyd amputation (similar to the Pirogoff),[8] the Lefort-Neff modification of the Pirogoff method,[3] and the Camilleri modification of the Pirogoff method.[11] A requirement for this level of amputation is an intact plantar soft tissue flap that will be able to provide stable coverage and wound closure. This may not be feasible in a patient with compromised soft tissue as the result of an injury. Further, prosthetic fitting may be challenging in this patient and prosthetic options are limited compared with those available for a below-knee amputation. A potential limitation of the Syme's amputation is migration of the heel pad after surgery. This may occur in 7.5% to 45% of patients.[52] Tenodesing the Achilles tendon to the distal tibia with sutures placed through drill holes to stabilize the heel pad was shown to be successful in a series of 10 of 11 patients.[52]

The surgical approach for a Syme amputation is based on the comprehensive description provided by Bowker.[3] An incision is marked out transversely across the anterior ankle joint 1 cm distal to the malleoli and stopping 1 cm anterior to them. Then a vertical incision is carried distally from each malleolus to the plantar aspect of the foot, anterior to the heel pad. The long extensor tendons are transected and the peroneal nerves are isolated, transected and cut, allowing them to retract into the wound bed. The anterior vascular structures should be isolated and controlled with a suture ligature. The foot is then plantarflexed, the collateral ligaments are transected, and the flexor hallucis longus tendon is isolated. The calcaneus is then stripped of its soft tissue attachments and the Achilles tendon is found and carefully detached from the calcaneal tuberosity. Care should be taken to avoid penetration of the posterior soft tissues at the Achilles insertion. The plantar fascia origin is then transected and the foot is disarticulated. The malleoli should be thinned to reduce the potential for a bulbous-shaped distal limb. Closure should be meticulous and the heel pad must be secured to the distal tibia to ensure soft tissue stability. Achilles tendon tenodesis has also been recommended to achieve heel pad stability.[52]

Transtibial Amputation

The most common method of transtibial amputation is with a posterior myocutaneous flap. Historically, this approach was first proposed by Verduyn in 1696 to provide better distal coverage over the residual distal tibia. Bickel is credited with using this amputation in the United States in 1943, and through the educational efforts of Burgess, this technique gained wide acceptance throughout the United States.[3,9] Transtibial amputation has had multiple variations proposed: posterior flap,[9] extended posterior flap,[2] symmetric anterior/posterior flaps,[18] symmetric medial/lateral (sagittal) flaps,[43] skewed sagittal flaps,[49] medial flap,[27] and distal end-bearing via a tibiofibular synostosis.[58,59] With a well-constructed amputation, patients have predictable outcomes with favorable prosthetic use.[51] The selection of amputation level follows guidelines similar to those for the urgent or elective workup, using TcPo$_2$ measurements and characterizing the vascular anatomy with duplex Doppler arterial ultrasonography. Staged treatment of the traumatized limb may be needed to allow a determination of the optimum level of amputation. This may not be possible until the soft tissue envelope has stabilized, which may take several weeks.[2] Preserving the knee joint should always be the goal and many patients can function well with a short residual below-knee stump. Alterna-

tive surgical approaches as listed earlier may need to be used to salvage a below-knee amputation level. Finally, the overall goal is to provide the patient with a cylindrical (not conical) residual limb that has a stable soft tissue envelope and adequate sensation and perfusion, which can then accept and support a prosthesis to maximize function.

After observing the regenerative potential of periosteum in craniofacial reconstruction,[57] Ertl applied the concept of osteoperiosteal flaps to amputation surgery, combining bony reconstruction (osteoplasty [creating a synostosis between the tibia and fibula distally]) with soft tissue reconstruction (myoplasty).[58,59] This effectively created the osteomyoplastic amputation, combining two procedures into one. Essentially, osteoperiosteal flaps are raised from all surfaces of the tibia and fibula distal to the planned level of resection of the tibia and fibula. This may only require up to 3 cm of bone to be resected as the distance from the medial tibial cortex to the lateral fibular cortex is approximately 5 to 6 cm. In primary amputations, the tibial periosteum is quite thick and the surgeon can use only tibial osteoperiosteal flaps to create the synostosis. This will only require up to 6 cm of tissue and not unduly shorten the limb.[1] The tibia and fibula are then transected at the same level, and the anterior cortex of the tibia is beveled to reduce its prominence

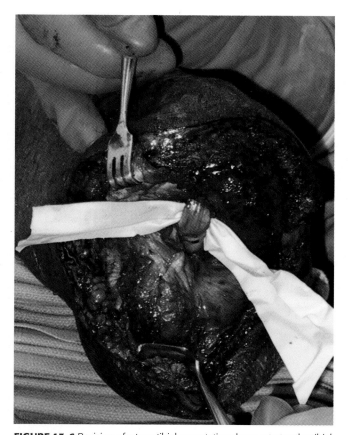

FIGURE 13-6 Revision of a transtibial amputation demonstrates the tibial nerve, which originally was buried directly into the end of the residual tibia. The patient experienced exquisite neurogenic pain with ambulation. Transected nerves should not be buried, placed on traction, or compressed, as doing so will promote the development of a postoperative neuroma. They should simply be transected sharply and allowed to retract into the soft tissues proximally.

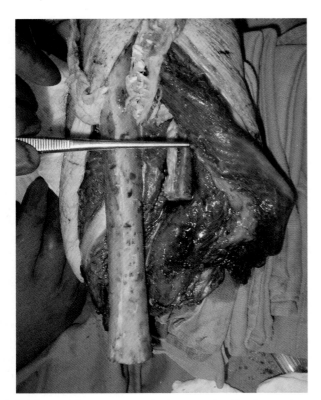

FIGURE 13-7 Primary osteomyoplastic amputation. The forceps demonstrate the level of planned tibial and fibular transection. Note the osteoperiosteal flaps that have been elevated from all surfaces of the tibia. If a portion of the fibula is used, it should be transected about 2.0 to 2.5 cm from the level of the tibial cut. The fibula can then be osteotomized, hinged on its medial periosteal sleeve, and incorporated into the osteoperiosteal flaps that create the synostosis.

anteriorly. The osteoperiosteal flaps are then sewn together to create a synostosis between the tibia and fibula. Over time, this flap regenerates bone, and the bony bridge matures with progressive weight-bearing. Alternative approaches have used a segment of fibula incorporated into the osteoperiosteal sleeve

hinged on its periosteal tissue, a full section of fibula placed between the tibia and fibula, and screw fixation of the fibular graft.[12,41,44,45] Stress shielding is a concern with screw fixation, and removal of the screw has been advocated once the synostosis has formed. Soft tissue stabilization is then performed to provide distal coverage over the residual osseous structures. Nerve handling should be meticulous with care being taken to resect the sural, saphenous, deep and superficial peroneal, and tibial nerves high and allowing them to retract proximally away from any potential compressive force. Burying the nerves places them on tension and may produce a neuroma (Fig. 13-6). A meticulously layered closure is performed, removing any and all redundant tissue and dog-ears. The resultant residual limb then assumes a cylindrical shape[31] (Figs. 13-7 to 13-10).

The posterior flap technique of transtibial amputation relies on the superficial posterior compartment for distal soft tissue coverage (Figs. 13-11 to 13-14). An incision is marked on the limb with an anterior reference point 10 to 15 cm distal to the knee joint. The width of the limb from anterior to posterior is measured. At the level of the anterior third and posterior two thirds of the limb, the posterior flap is drawn extending distally down the leg adding 1 cm for a traditional posterior flap or adding 5 cm for an extended posterior flap technique. At the anterior reference point, a partial transverse incision is made to the line extending distally and then the incision is carried distally to the planned end of the flap. The anterior and lateral compartments are exposed and the muscles are transected. Large vessels should be ligated. Nerves should be resected sharply and allowed to retract proximally. The tibia is transected and the fibula should be transected no higher than 1.5 to 2 cm proximal to the distal tibia. This will ensure maintenance of a cylindrical residual limb. A fibula that is too short in relation to the tibia will result in a conical limb. The interval between the deep and superficial compartments is defined and the deep posterior compartment muscles are transected. The posterior compartment vessels are also controlled with suture ligatures. The plane between the two posterior compartments is developed and the superficial posterior compartment is then resected. Multiple vascular perforators cross from the deep compartment to the superficial compartment, and they may also require su-

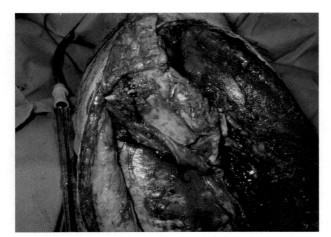

FIGURE 13-8 The bridge is created by suturing the osteoperiosteal flaps to the fibula. The fibular portion can be incorporated into the flap. Cancellous bone can be placed into the created synostosis as an autogenous graft. The cut ends of the osteoperiosteal flaps should be imbricated to prevent exostosis formation from the cambium layer.

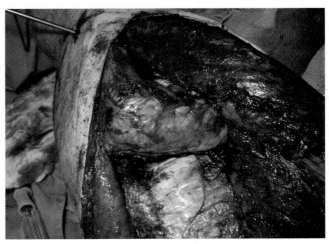

FIGURE 13-9 Completed bridge formation between the tibia and fibula.

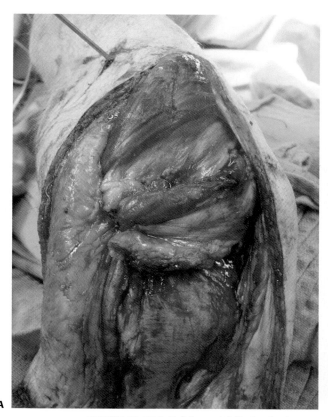
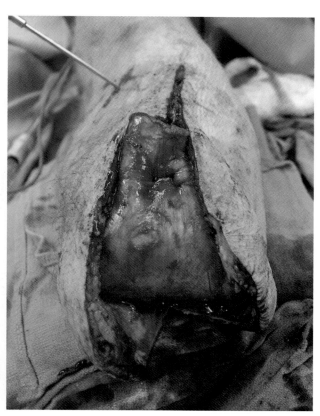

A   B

FIGURE 13-10 A. Soft tissue stabilization for the osteomyoplastic amputation is begun by suturing the anterior and lateral compartments into the deep fascia, providing anterior and distal soft tissue coverage. **B.** After debulking of the deep posterior compartment, the superficial posterior compartment is brought over the end of the residual limb and secured with sutures. Final closure is performed by closing the fascia over the myoplasty, excising redundant skin, and performing a meticulous skin closure.

ture control for hemostasis. The anterior cortex of the tibia should be beveled to avoid any bony prominence. Drill holes are placed in the tibia, and deep soft tissue stabilization of the posterior flap is performed by anchoring its deep fascia with sutures placed through these drill holes. A meticulously layered closure is then performed, taking care to remove any and all redundant tissue to provide a cylindrical shape to the limb. With the extended posterior flap technique, the anterior aspect of the limb will appear substantially bulky but will atrophy over time.

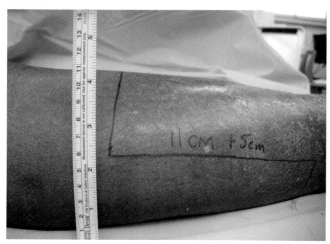

FIGURE 13-11 An extended long posterior flap transtibial amputation. The anterior-posterior width of the limb is measured at the level of tibial transaction and lines are drawn distally to equal the anterior-posterior width (in this case, 11 cm) plus 5 cm.

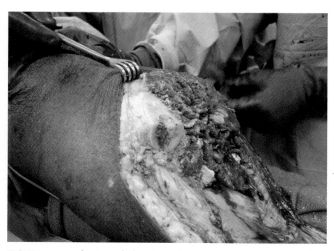

FIGURE 13-12 The extended posterior flap provides an adequate myofasciocutaneous tissue for closure and anterior coverage. The anterior cortex of the tibia should always be beveled.

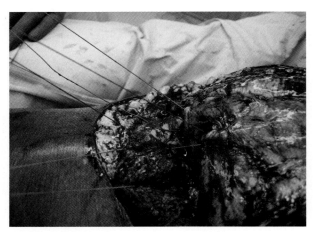

FIGURE 13-13 Drill holes are placed into the anterior tibial cortex such that sutures can be passed through them to anchor the deep fascia of the posterior flap.

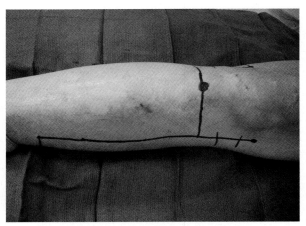

FIGURE 13-15 The basic landmarks for a knee disarticulation with a long posterior flap are the tibial tubercle anteriorly and the medial and lateral epicondyles on either side of the distal femur. The incision should not extend much more proximally than the epicondyles. Doing so will create large dog-ears that will be difficult to control surgically.

Through-Knee

A through-knee amputation or knee disarticulation maintains the end-bearing capabilities of the femur and will maintain mechanical and anatomic alignment of the femur. Knee disarticulation has been indicated for the dysvascular patient, children, bed-bound/nonambulatory patients, and patients with traumatic amputations. In the nonambulatory patient, the long lever arm of the residual limb can be of assistance in transfers. Caution should be used in the traumatic amputee as the functional result with a through-knee amputation is less than that of either the transtibial amputation or the transfemoral amputation.[32]

The surgical approach uses either sagittal flaps as described by Wagner[60] or a long posterior myofasciocutaneous flap.[7] Using the posterior flap technique (Figs. 13-15 to 13-17) at the level of the knee joint, a transverse anterior incision is made to the mid-coronal line medially and laterally. The skin incision is then carried distally to the junction of the conjoined portion of the gastrocnemius and soleus muscles. Anteriorly, dissection is carried down to the tibial plateau and a full-thickness anterior flap is made. The knee joint is entered and the collateral and cruciate ligaments are transected. Posterior dissection then transects the capsule and the medial and lateral hamstrings, exposing the neurovascular structures. The vessels are isolated and controlled with suture ligatures. The tibial and peroneal nerves should be isolated, transected, and allowed to retract proximally into the soft tissue bed. The interval between the gastrocnemius and the deep posterior compartment muscles should be developed and carried distally. Deep vascular perforators may need to be controlled with suture ligatures. A posterior transverse incision distally then allows the lower leg to be removed en bloc. The patella may be retained or removed. Removing the patella creates additional length for the quadriceps, which should be sutured to the remnants of the cruciate ligaments. Both the medial and lateral hamstrings can be sutured to the capsular remnants to maintain their function as hip extensors. The posterior flap is then brought over the distal end of the residual femur in a pants-over-vest fashion. The anterior flap skin can be removed to accommodate the length of the posterior flap. The sural nerve should be identified and transected as high as possible to reduce the risk of postsurgical neuroma formation.

Transfemoral

The key to transfemoral amputation is restoring mechanical and anatomic alignment of the residual femur.[21,22] A long medial flap[20] or equal anterior/posterior flaps can be used, or occasionally in the trauma setting, the surgeon may have to use any viable residual soft tissue uniquely for wound closure (Fig. 13-18). In general, soft tissue flaps should be kept as long as possible to reduce the potential for undue tension at closure and to prevent the need to shorten the femur because of inadequate flap lengths. A proper soft tissue reconstruction creates a dynamic residual extremity, improves the vascularity of the residual limb, and will help to maintain alignment of the residual femur, which in turn improves gait.[13,14,21,22,58,59]

During a primary transfemoral amputation, a knee disarticulation can be performed first. This will preserve soft tissues needed for closure. In the traumatic setting, all viable tissue

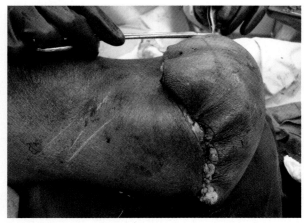

FIGURE 13-14 The remainder of the extended posterior flap is then closed in a layered fashion. This will initially create a bulky appearance to the distal end of the residual limb, but this tissue will atrophy over time, providing adequate soft tissue protection to the anterior tibia.

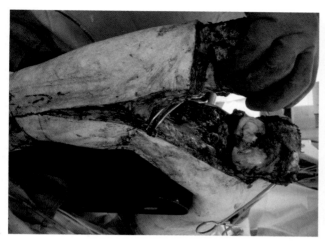

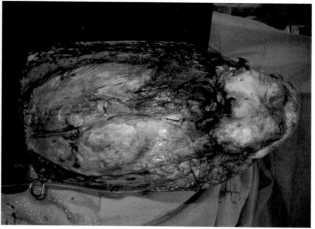

FIGURE 13-16 A. Anterior flap that includes the extensor mechanism has been elevated and the dissection is carried into the knee joint. The cruciate and collateral ligaments are transected, the vessels are ligated, and the nerves are sharply transected. A plane between the gastrocnemius muscle and soleus should be developed as depicted here. This plane should be extended as far distally as possible. **B.** With removal of the distal limb, a long posterior myofasciocutaneous flap is created.

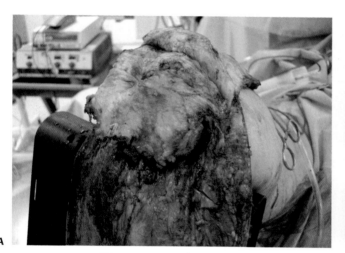

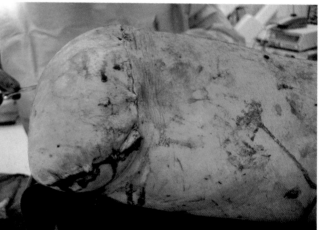

FIGURE 13-17 A. The quadriceps should be anchored with sutures to the remnants of the cruciate ligaments. **B.** Final closure results in an abundant distal soft tissue envelope.

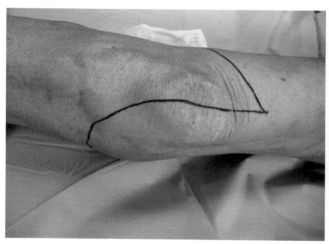

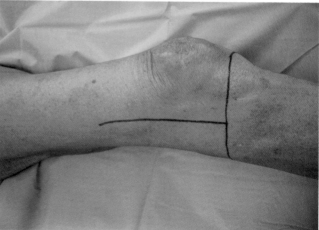

FIGURE 13-18 A. Medial-based flap for a transfemoral amputation as described by Gottschalk.[17] **B.** Equal anterior and posterior flaps for a transfemoral amputation.

should be preserved for wound closure. The three muscle groups (adductors, quadriceps, and hamstrings) are isolated and reflected proximally to expose the distal femur. Vascular structures are isolated and controlled with suture ligatures, preferably double-suture ligatures. The distal femur is then transected to a level that will allow for proper prosthetic fitting. In general, the minimum space required for the prosthetic knee joint to achieve symmetry with the opposite side is 2 inches from the end of the residual limb. Therefore, depending on the technique chosen, the surgeon will need to take into account the amount of space the soft tissue reconstruction will require and add it to the amount of femur removed. The sciatic and obturator nerves should be isolated, transected proximally, and allowed to retract into the soft tissue bed. Nerves should never be buried into bone or tethered for doing so may create tension and neuroma formation. Soft tissue reconstruction begins with securing the medial musculature to the distal end of the femur, typically with sutures passed through drill holes, thus restoring proper anatomic and mechanical alignment of the residual limb. The quadriceps can also be secured distally to the end of femur with the hip in extension with sutures passed through additional drill holes. The hamstrings are secured posteriorly. A meticulous layered closure should then be performed to afford the patient a cylindrical shape to the residual limb.

Ertl described an alternative method of treatment for the femur.[58,59] Osteoperiosteal flaps are elevated off of the femur. After shortening the femur to an appropriate level, the osteoperiosteal flaps are sewn over the end of the femur closing the medullary canal (Figs. 13-19 and 13-20). Soft tissue reconstruction is then performed as described earlier.

FIGURE 13-19 Osteoperiosteal flaps have been elevated for the osteomyoplastic transfemoral amputation.

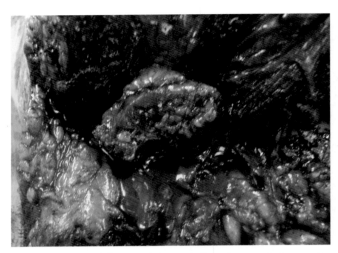

FIGURE 13-20 Medullary canal closure in the osteomyoplastic amputation is accomplished by suturing the osteoperiosteal flaps over the end of the residual femur. The femoral canal can also be packed with cancellous bone graft to augment closure with the osteoperiosteal flaps.

PATIENT-ORIENTED THERAPY

Following amputation, full recovery must include a comprehensive rehabilitation program to provide functional restoration to the patient. The primary goal of a rehabilitation program is to return the patient to a functional status and to return that patient into everyday society. The combination of a sound surgical procedure, proper prosthetic application, and comprehensive rehabilitation is essential. In the acute phase, pain control is paramount and can be accomplished via oral or intravenous narcotics, peripheral nerve blocks, patient-controlled analgesia (PCA), or epidural catheter delivery of analgesic medication. Acute-phase physical therapy includes wound care, basic mobilization, swelling control, joint mobilization, desensitization, upper extremity strengthening, and isometric muscle training of the residual limb.

The patient may want to visit with his prosthetist, if he has not done so before surgery, regarding the prosthesis and develop a timeline for its manufacture and application, usually about 6 weeks after surgery. Once the swelling has decreased and the wounds have healed, the patient is evaluated for socket application. Typically the patient will have a preparatory prosthesis constructed to begin gait training.

It is not simply enough to tell the patient to start walking; rather, a qualified physical therapist is required to teach the patient proper body mechanics and position during gait and how to use a program of core strengthening. Balance training and confidence with balance may be challenging in amputees and vary with the level of amputation and the indication for amputation.[39] After the acute phase, advanced therapy should be instituted to educate the patient beyond basic functions, in preparation to return to work or sport. All patients with a limb amputation will also require in-depth occupational therapy for activities of daily living and the use of assistive technology. Finally, cognitive therapy and psychological support should be considered for all amputees, especially the posttraumatic amputee.

SUMMARY

Amputation resulting from trauma should not be thought of as a failure of intervention. Following severe limb trauma, the surgeon should plan a dynamic, functional amputation level that can accept a prosthesis and improve the functionality and mobility of the patient. Amputation should be reconstructive with a strong emphasis placed on the rehabilitative potential of the patient.

ACKNOWLEDGMENTS

The author would like to acknowledge and thank Janos P. Ertl, MD; Christian W. Ertl, MD; Carol Dionne, PT, PhD, OCS, Cert MDT; and Jonathan Day, CPO, for their insightful suggestions regarding amputee surgery, amputee rehabilitation, and prosthetic application.

REFERENCES

1. American College of Surgeons Committee on Trauma. Advanced Trauma Life Support Courses. Chicago, IL: American College of Surgeons; 1985.
2. Assal M, Blanck R, Smith DG. Extended posterior flap for transtibial amputation. Orthopedics 2005;28:542–546.
3. Smith DG, Michael JW, Bowker JH, Eds. Atlas of amputations and limb deficiencies: surgical, prosthetic, and rehabilitation principles, 3rd ed. Rosemont, IL: American Academy of Orthopaedic Surgeons, 2004.
4. Bonanni F, Rhodes M, Lucke JF. The futility of predictive scoring of mangled lower extremities. J Trauma 1993;34:99–104.
5. Bosse MJ, MacKenzie EJ, Kellam JF, et al. An analysis of outcomes of reconstruction or amputation after leg-threatening injuries. N Engl J Med 2002;347:1906–1907.
6. Bosse MJ, MacKenzie EJ, Kellam JF, et al. A prospective evaluation of the clinical utility of the lower extremity injury-severity scores. J Bone Joint Surg Am 2001;83A:3–14.
7. Bowker JH, San Giovanni TP, Pinzur MS. North American experience with knee disarticulation with use of a posterior myofasciocutaneous flap: healing rate and functional results in 77 patients. J Bone Joint Surg Am 2000;82A:1571–1574.
8. Boyd HB. Amputations of the foot with calcaneotibial arthrodesis. J Bone Joint Surg 1939;21:997–1000.
9. Burgess EM. The below-knee amputation. Bull Prosthet Res 1968;10:19–25.
10. Burgess EM. The stabilization of muscles in lower extremity amputations. J Bone Joint Surg Am 1968;50A:1486–1487.
11. Camilleri A, Anract P, Missenard G, et al. Apurations et désarticulations des membres: Membre inférieur. In Encyclopédie Médico-Chirurgicale. Paris: Editions Scientifiques et Médicales Elsevier, SAS; 2000:6–8.
12. DeCoster TA, Homedan S. Amputation osteoplasty. Iowa Orthop J 2006:26:54–59.
13. Dederich R. Plastic treatment of the muscles and bone in amputation surgery. A method designed to produce physiologic conditions in the stump. J Bone Joint Surg Br 1963; 45B:60–66.
14. Dederich R, Van De Weyer KH. [Arteriographic studies of muscle plastic surgery in amputation stump correction.] [In German] Arztl Wochensch 1959;14:208–211.
15. Dirschl DR, Dahners LE. The mangled extremity: when should it be amputated? J Am Acad Orthop Surg 1996;4:182–190.
16. Dirschl DR, Tornetta P III, Sims SH. Amputations and prosthetics. In Koval KJ, ed. Orthopaedic Knowledge Update. American Academy of Orthopaedic Surgeons; 2002.
17. Durham RM, Mistry BM, Mazuski JE, et al. Outcome and utility of scoring systems in the management of the mangled extremity. Am J Surg 1996;172:569–573.
18. Epps CH. Amputation of the lower limb. In Evarts SM, ed. Surgery of the Musculoskeletal System. New York: Churchill Livingstone; 1990.
19. Ertl W, Henley MB. Provisional external fixation for periarticular fractures of the tibia. Tech Orthop 2002;12;135–144.
20. Gottschalk F. Transfemoral amputation: biomechanics and surgery. Clin Orthop 1999; 361:15–22.
21. Gottschalk FA, Kouroush S. Stills M, et al. Does socket configuration influence the position of the femur in above-knee amputation? J Prosthet Orthot 1989;2:94–102.
22. Gottschalk FA, Stills M. The biomechanics of transfemoral amputation. Prosthet Orthot Int 1994;18:12–17.
23. Gregory RT, Gould RJ, Peclet M, et al. The mangled extremity syndrome (M.E.S.): a severity grading system for multisystem injury of the extremity. J Trauma 1985;25:1147–1150.
24. Gustilo RB, Anderson JT. Prevention of infection in the treatment of 1025 open fractures of long bones. J Bone Joint Surg Am 1976;58A:453–458.
25. Helfet DL, Howey T, Sanders R, Johansen K. Limb salvage versus amputation. Preliminary results of the Mangled Extremity Severity Score. Clin Orthop Relat Res 1990;(256): 80–86.
26. Howe HR Jr, Poole GV Jr, Hansen KJ, et al. Salvage of lower extremities following combined orthopedic and vascular trauma. A predictive salvage index. Am Surg 1987: 53:205–208.
27. Jain AS, Stewart CP, Turner MS. Transtibial amputations using a medially based flap. J R Coll Surg Edinb 1995;40:263–265.
28. Johansen K, Daines M, Howey T, et al. Objective criteria accurately predict amputation following lower extremity trauma. J Trauma 1990;30:568–572.
29. Krettek C, Seekamp A, Köntopp H, et al. Hannover Fracture Scale '98: re-evaluation and new perspectives of an established extremity salvage score. Injury 2001;32:611.
30. Kuiken TA, Dumanian GA, Lipschutz RD, et al. The use of targeted muscle reinnervation for improved myoelectric prosthesis control in a bilateral shoulder disarticulation amputee. Prosthet Orthot Int 2004;28:245–253.
31. Loon HE. Biological and biomechanical principles in amputation surgery. In International Prosthetics Course, Second Proceedings. Committee on Prosthesis, Braces, and Technical Aids; Copenhagen, 1960:41–58.
32. MacKenzie EJ, Bosse MJ, Castillo RC, et al. Functional outcomes following trauma-related lower extremity amputation. J Bone Joint Surg Am 2004;86A:1636–1645.
33. MacKenzie EJ, Bosse MJ, Kellam JF, et al. Factors influencing the decision to amputate or reconstruct after high-energy lower extremity trauma. J Trauma 2002;52:641–649.
34. MacKenzie EJ, Bosse MJ, Pollak AN, et al. Long-term persistence of disability following severe lower-limb trauma. Results of a 7-year follow-up. J Bone Joint Surg Am 2005; 87A:1801–1809.
35. MacKenzie EJ, Jones AS, Bosse MJ, et al. Health-care costs associated with amputation or reconstruction of a limb-threatening injury. J Bone Joint Surg Am 2007;89A:1685–1692.
36. Malone JM, Moore W, Leam JM, et al. Rehabilitation for lower extremity amputation. Arch Surg 1981;116:93–98.
37. McNamara MG, Heckman JD, Corley FG. Severe open fractures of the lower extremity: a retrospective evaluation of the Mangled Extremity Severity Score (MESS). J Orthop Trauma 1994;8:81–87.
38. Miller LA, Stubblefield KA, Lipschutz RD, et al. Improved myoelectric prosthesis control using targeted reinnervation surgery: a case series. IEEE Trans Neural Syst Rehabil Eng 2008;16:4–50.
39. Miller WC, Speechley M, Deathe AB. Balance confidence among people with lower-limb amputations. Phys Ther 2002;82:856–865.
40. Mills WJ, Barei DP, McNair P. The value of the ankle-brachial index for diagnosing arterial injury after knee dislocation: a prospective study. J Trauma 2004;56:1261–1265.
41. Okamoto AM, Guarniero R, Coelho RF, et al. The use of bone bridges in transtibial amputations. Rev Hosp Clin 2000;55:1–13.
42. Oestern HJ, Tscherne HJ. Pathophysiology and classification of soft tissue injuries associated with fractures. In Tscherne H, Gotzen L, eds. Fractures with Soft Tissue Injuries. Berlin: Springer-Verlag; 1984:1–19.
43. Persson BM. Sagittal incision for below-knee amputation in ischaemic gangrene. J Bone Joint Surg Br 1974;56B:110–114.
44. Pinto MA, Harris WW. Fibular segment bone bridging in transtibial amputation. Prosthet Orthot Int 2004;28:220–224.
45. Pinzur MS, Pinto MA, Schon LC, et al. Controversies in amputation surgery. Instr Course Lect 2003;52:445–451.
46. Pirogoff NI. Osteoplastic elongation of the bones of the leg in amputation of the foot. Voyerno Md J 1854;68:83.
47. Poole GV, Agnew SG, Griswold JA, et al. The mangled lower extremity: can salvage be predicted? Am Surg 1994;60:50–55.
48. Robertson PA. Prediction of amputation after severe lower limb trauma. J Bone Joint Surg Br 1991;73B:816–818.
49. Robinson K. Skew flap myoplastic below-knee amputation: a preliminary report. Br J Surg 1982;69:554–557.
50. Russell WL, Sailors DM, Whittle TB, et al. Limb salvage verses traumatic amputation. A decision based on a seven-part predictive index. Ann Surg 1991;213:473–481.
51. Smith DG, Horn P, Malchow D, et al. Prosthetic history, prosthetic charges, and functional outcome of the isolated traumatic below-knee amputation. J Trauma 1995;38: 44–47.
52. Smith DG, Sangeorzan BJ, Hansen ST Jr, et al. Achilles tendon tenodesis to prevent heel pad migration in the Syme amputation. Foot Ankle Int 1994;15:14–17.
53. Thuan VL, Travison TG, Castillo RC, et al., and the LEAP Study Group. Ability of lower extremity injury severity scores to predict functional outcome after limb salvage. J Bone Joint Surg Am 2008;90A:1738–1743.
54. Tscherne H, Gotzen L. Fractures with Soft Tissue Injuries. Berlin: Springer-Verlag; 1984.
55. Tscherne H, Oestern HJ. [A new classification of soft-tissue damage in open and closed fractures]. [In German] Unfallheilkunde 1982;85:111–115.
56. Varnell RM, Coldwell CM, Sangeorzan BJ, et al. Arterial injury complicating knee disruption. Am Surg 1989;55:699–704.
57. Ertl J. Die Chirurgie der Gesichts und Kieferdefekte. Berlin/Wien: Urban & Schwarzenberg; 1918.
58. Ertl J. Regeneration. Ihre Ahnwendung in der Chirurgie. Leipzig: Ambrosius Barth; 1939.
59. Ertl J. Über Amputationstümpfe. Chirurgie 1949;20:21–18.
60. Wagner FW Jr. Management of the diabetic-neuropathic foot. Part II. A classification and treatment program for diabetic, neuropathic, and dysvascular foot problems. Instr Course Lect 1979;28:143–165.

14

BONE AND SOFT TISSUE RECONSTRUCTION

Christopher J. Salgado, Alexander Y. Shin, Samir Mardini, and Steven L. Moran

INTRODUCTION

Open fractures and their associated soft tissue injuries are difficult to treat and often require a multidisciplinary approach for wound management. These wounds place a significant financial burden on the patient and society because of prolonged patient disability. Despite the great diversity among the individuals who sustain open fractures, a majority of these patients are typically young active adults who tend to be injured in automobile or motorcycle accidents or while engaged in sporting activities.[86]

Successful management of these wounds requires treatment of the bone as well as the soft tissue injuries. Advances in microsurgical techniques and our knowledge of the vascular anatomy of the extremities have led to novel advances in wound coverage that can allow for rapid coverage of these wounds and replacement of injured bone, nerve, and muscle. In this chapter, we will review a multidisciplinary approach for the management of bone and soft tissue defects, which includes a combination of orthopaedic surgery and plastic surgery expertise, in addition to providing the reader with a variety of reconstructive options for upper and lower extremity open fracture management.

HISTORY

The problem of open fractures has plagued surgeons since the time of Hippocrates, who described crude attempts at external fixation for the purpose of examination and treatment of open fractures.[4] During the ancient Egyptian period, documents demonstrate that complex fractures were treated expectantly, and open fractures were considered a mortal injury.[8] It was not until the sixteenth century, when Ambroise Paré, the French barber-surgeon, revolutionized surgical management of open extremity injuries by developing amputation techniques which used tourniquet control of blood loss, as well as hemostatic clamps and vascular ligatures.[227] It is only in the eighteenth century, that Percival Pott, a renowned surgeon and educator of the English, introduced the option of limb salvage after open fracture through the use of fracture reduction and wound management.

Within just the past 40 years advances in vascular reconstruction, external and internal fixation and antimicrobial agents have minimized the chances of mortality after an isolated open extremity fracture. Continuing advances in the field of microsurgery, including refinement and development of free tissue transfers, and pedicled and local flaps, as well as a better understanding of wound pathophysiology have improved the surgeons ability to obtain rapid wound coverage, allowing patients to return to ambulation and the workforce; however, many challenges remain and the patient may still succumb to local infection or other soft tissue or bony complications requiring amputation after major limb trauma.

As we become more familiar with the advances in the treatment of bone and soft tissue reconstruction, we have a responsibility to carefully evaluate our results in a sound evidence-based fashion. Comparisons of different types of treatment, and careful evaluation of their outcome, complications, and cost/benefit analysis are essential to providing the optimal treatment for these injuries.

COMPLEX MUSCULOSKELETAL INJURIES

Open fractures by definition are a multisystem injury, and the management of the soft tissue is often as important as the treatment of the fracture itself.[389] Historically, the outcome of the treatment of open fractures was typically determined by the soft tissue defect. In 1966, Carpenter stated that "If the soft tissues overlying the tibia are not preserved, any hope of primary healing of the underlying fracture is lost forever."[58] Although Carpenter was referring to the tibia, the importance the soft tissue envelope to bone healing is real and applicable throughout the body. If soft tissue reconstruction is successful in these injuries,

the bone often becomes the problematic area, and the final outcome depends on the extent of bone devascularization and contamination.[168]

Often the fear of not being able to cover a wound has prevented the orthopaedic surgeon from adequately débriding the soft tissues. This has resulted in the "expectant" management of the soft tissues, an approach that unfortunately still prevails in some surgeons' minds today. Waiting for devitalized tissue to "declare itself" prolongs definitive fracture management, increases the risk of infection, and attenuates the inflammatory response. Pedicled flaps and free tissue transfers are capable of covering large soft tissue defects, thus allowing the surgeon the freedom to perform a wide and thorough débridement. Early collaboration and communication with surgeons skilled in these techniques is crucial for successful outcomes.

Often times, the question arises, "Who should take care of these injuries?" Although each surgical subspecialty may feel that they are the most appropriate ones to care for these injuries, it is important to understand that optimal collaboration is often the best means to treat these highly complex wounds. Even if the primary treating orthopaedic surgeon is not trained in microsurgical techniques, knowledge of the prerequisites, timing, and availability of soft tissue and bone reconstruction will affect the initial treatment plan.[151] A surgeon or group of surgeons highly familiar with the soft tissue as well as bony anatomy, in addition to having microsurgical skills, is optimally best suited to address these injuries.

The basic principle of complex musculoskeletal injury management begins with application of Advanced Trauma Life Support (ATLS) protocols.[1] Once the basics of ATLS are satisfied, a complete assessment of each wound can be made. Understanding the mechanism of injury and the patient's unique medical and social history are imperative. When possible, a discussion of the possible reconstructive options should be discussed with the patient and family.

PATIENT EVALUATION

Once ATLS protocols have been performed and the patient is stabilized, the surgeon begins the detailed evaluation of the open fracture and the associated soft tissue deficit. It is imperative to determine the time of injury, the mechanism of injury, fracture configuration, associated systemic injuries or medical conditions, the degree of soft tissue injury, the vascular, sensory, and motor status of the extremity, and the patient's occupational and leisure time activities. All these factors ultimately influence the decision for limb salvage versus amputation, and must be addressed. Prevention of further injury is paramount. A careful motor, sensory, and vascular examination can determine if a compartment syndrome or dysvascular limb is present. Identification and documentation of nerve injuries and associated injuries as part of the secondary ATLS survey is also performed.

The open wound should be inspected carefully and the wound pattern and any contamination documented. Photographic documentation can be helpful when available. Wounds should not be explored in the emergency department setting, but rather, exploration should be performed whenever possible in the sterile conditions of an operating room. With polytrauma patients, where the work-up of other injuries takes priority over treatment of the open fracture/soft tissue injuries, careful packing of the wound with a sponge moistened with saline and diluted antiseptic solution (Betadine or chlorhexidine) prevents desiccation of the exposed bone and soft tissues until they can be addressed formally in the operating suite.

CLASSIFICATION OF INJURY

Classification of Open Fractures

Most classifications systems of open musculoskeletal injuries have followed the initial attempts of Cauchoix and associates, who were mainly interested in the size of the skin defect, degree of soft tissue crush injury, and complexity of the fracture.[59] Rittmann et al. divided the severity into three groups, focused on the amount of necrotic and contaminated material found in the wounds in addition to the degree of neurovascular injury.[328,329]

In 1976, Gustilo reported on a larger personal series of open fractures and described a classification system that is still in use today with various modifications by multiple authors.[154–157,159,160] In their classic paper, Guistilo and Anderson devised a three-tier classification system: Type 1 fractures have a clean wound smaller than 1 cm in size; type 2 wounds have a soft tissue injury larger than 1 cm and without extensive soft tissue damage; and type 3 wounds are severe soft tissue lacerations with segmental or severely comminuted fractures in high energy trauma.[156,157] In 1982, Gustilo and Mendoza reviewed their expanded experience of 1400 open fractures and noted that there were five factors associated with final outcome: the degree of soft tissue injury, the adequacy of débridement, appropriate use of antibiotics, fracture stability, and early soft tissue coverage.[158] In 1984, Gustilo et al. identified differences within the type III fractures and further subdivided that group into three subgroups based on the soft tissue injuries. The type IIIA injuries are those with large soft tissue injuries or flaps that still had adequate soft tissue coverage of bone. This group also includes fractures with severe comminution or segmental fractures regardless of the size of the soft tissue damage. The type IIIB fractures are those with extensive soft tissue loss and much devascularized bone with massive contamination, and type IIIC fractures are those associated with an arterial injury (Table 14-1).

Classification of Soft Tissue Injury Associated with Closed Fractures

Soft tissue injury may be of several varieties, lacerations, abrasions, contusion, degloving injuries, and burns. In addition, soft

TABLE 14-1	**Gustilo and Anderson Classification of Open Fractures of the Tibia**[156–158]
Type I	Clean wound smaller than 1 cm in size
Type II	Soft tissue injury larger than 1 cm and without extensive soft tissue damage
Type IIIA	Large soft tissue injuries or flaps still with adequate soft tissue coverage of bone
Type IIIB	Extensive soft tissue loss and much devascularized bone with massive contamination
Type IIIC	Fractures associated with an arterial injury

TABLE 14-2	**Tscherne et al.**[389–391] **Classification of Soft Tissue Injury Associated with Closed Fractures**
Grade 0	Minimal soft tissue injury, indirect injury
Grade 1	Injury from within, superficial abrasion/contusion
Grade 2	Direct injury, more extensive soft tissue injury
Grade 3	Severe degloving with destruction of subcutaneous muscle and/or the tissues

tissue damage can occur in absence of frank skin laceration and can result in tissue damage that is even more extensive than that seen in open fractures.[389–391] Closed injuries that are associated with skin contusions, deep abrasions, burns, or frank separation of the dermal layer from the subcutaneous tissues have been classified by Tscherne (Table 14-2).[389–391] Although not critically validated, this classification system has heightened our awareness of the importance of soft tissue injuries associated with closed fractures.

The mechanism of injury will also provide clues as to the severity of the underlying soft tissue injury. Penetrating injury will cause local and immediate surrounding tissue trauma; therefore, the surgical débridement required will typically be limited to the surrounding region of penetration. Blunt force resulting from motor vehicle crashes or falls will lead to more extensive soft tissue trauma and possible associated neurovascular injury with increased muscle contusion, devascularization, and necrosis. A ringer injury or press injury typically carry a poorer prognosis because of the amount of associated tissue damage. Electrical injuries associated with fracture may appear innocuous but will always be associated with significant underlying soft tissue damage.

Wound Healing

To fully appreciate the nature of the soft tissue injury the surgeon must have some understanding of the normal wound healing process. Surgically induced wounds heal in several stages. The wound passes through phases of coagulation, inflammation, matrix synthesis and deposition, angiogenesis, fibroplasia, epithelialization, contraction, and remodeling. These processes have been divided into three main stages: inflammation, fibroplasia, and maturation. Interruption in any of these stages can lead to wound healing complications.[201]

The inflammatory phase of wound healing involves cellular responses to clear the wound of debris and devitalized tissue. Increased capillary permeability and leukocyte infiltration occur secondary to inflammatory mediators and vasoactive substances. Inflammatory cells clean the wound of harmful bacteria and devitalized tissue. Fibronectin and hyaluronate deposition from fibroblasts in the first 24 to 48 hours provides scaffolding for further fibroblast migration.[118,368]

The fibroblast proliferation phase starts within the first 2 to 3 days as large populations of fibroblasts migrate to the wound. Secretion of a variety of substances is necessary for wound healing and includes large quantities of glycosaminoglycans and collagen. Collagen levels rise for approximately 3 weeks corresponding to increasing wound tensile strength. After 3 weeks the rate of degradation equals the rate of deposition. Angiogenesis is an important aspect of the fibroblast proliferation phase, as it helps to support new cells in the healing wound.

The maturation phase starts at around 3 weeks lasting up to 2 years. It is characterized by collagen remodeling and wound strengthening. Collagen is the principal building block of connective tissue and is found in at least 13 different types. Early wounds are comprised of a majority of type III collagen. As the wound matures, type III collagen is replaced by type I collagen. Collagen cross-linking improves tensile strength. There is a rapid increase in strength of the wound by 6 weeks as the wound reaches 70% of the strength of normal tissue. The wound then gradually plateaus to 80% of normal strength, but never returns to preinjury levels.[201]

Wound re-epithelialization occurs as adjacent cells migrate through a sequence of mobilization, migration, mitosis, and cellular differentiation of epithelial cells. Wound contraction starts at about 1 week. It is facilitated by the transformation of certain fibroblasts into myofibroblasts containing α–smooth muscle actin. These cells adhere to the wound margins as well as to each other and effect contraction of the wound. These stages are imperative for proper wound healing, as interruption of these processes results in chronic wound complications.[118,368]

Large wounds, or wounds incapable of primary healing, heal through a process of "secondary wound healing," which is dominated by wound contraction and re-epithelialization. If infection, ischemia, or ongoing trauma inhibit the wound from completing the re-epithelialization process, the wound will then enter into a protracted inflammatory state.[268] In these chronic wounds the wound environment is predominated by neutrophils with the increase production of proteolytic enzymes.[101] In most situations a chronic wound must be converted to a clean acute wound through the process of surgical débridement for healing to occur. Surgical débridement re-establishes a normal healing environment, allowing the wound to heal through primary or secondary intention.

INITIAL MANAGEMENT

During the management of any complex musculoskeletal injury there are several principles one should keep in mind to expedite patient care and maximize patient outcome (Table 14-3).

Principle 1

The first principle is to prevent further injury. After understanding the mechanism of injury, one must determine whether a compartment syndrome[129] may be an issue or if ongoing vascular compromise is present. Any salvage of the extremity is dependent on the prevention of further injury or the neutralization of ongoing injury.

Principle 2

When débridement of injured tissue is undertaken, an aggressive tumor-like débridement of all necrotic and nonviable tissue, including bone, is essential.[133] This is often considered the most important single step in the management of soft tissue trauma and will be further discussed later in this chapter. Often reconstructive plans impede adequate soft tissue débridement, as the surgeon is afraid to lose further soft tissues, which would make the reconstruction more complicated or difficult.

TABLE 14-3	**The Eight General Principles of Management of Soft Tissue Injuries Associated with Fractures**
Principle 1:	Prevent further injury.
Principle 2:	When débridement of injured tissue is undertaken, an aggressive tumor-like débridement of all necrotic and nonviable tissue, including bone, is essential.
Principle 3:	Achieve bone stability.
Principle 4:	Strive for early bone coverage when possible.
Principle 5:	Do not ignore secondary reconstructive needs when addressing initial bone coverage (i.e., plan for future reconstructive procedures).
Principle 6:	Replace damaged tissues with similar tissues when possible (replace like with like).
Principle 7:	Know when a salvage procedure, such as an amputation, may be the better reconstructive option.
Principle 8:	Know when you have taken on too much and seek assistance and advice.

Principle 3

Once adequate débridement of soft tissue and bone has been accomplished, bone stability should be achieved. Bone stability can be achieved with external fixation, internal fixation, or a combination of both. In highly contaminated wounds or wounds that have poor soft tissue coverage, external fixation is often preferred. In wounds that are adequately débrided with good soft tissue coverage of the bone, internal fixation can be used.

Principle 4

When soft tissue coverage is needed, acute coverage should be considered. Use of the reconstructive ladder as described by Levin[244,245] can be helpful in reconstructing the upper extremity (Figure 14-1). When soft tissue coverage is considered, a surgeon should evaluate the simplest type of procedure needed to achieve wound coverage, and increase in complexity as needed. The reconstructive ladder progresses as follows: primary closure, skin grafting, local cutaneous flaps, fasciocutaneous transposition flaps, island fascial or fasciocutaneous flaps, local or distant one-stage muscle or myocutaneous transposition, distant temporary pedicle flaps, and microvascular free tissue transfer. When evaluating the wound for possible coverage options, it is imperative to consider patient factors; defect genesis; the location, size, and depth of the defect; exposed structures; structures needing reconstruction; the degree of contamination; and the quality of the surrounding tissues.

The concept of achieving wound coverage within 72 hours was popularized by Godina.[141] Although the data presented by Godina is compelling, achieving wound coverage within 72 hours can be difficult secondary to both hospital system issues (operating room and surgeon availability) and patient factors. With advances in wound management with vacuum-assisted closure devices and antibiotic bead pouches, wound coverage can occur later than the 72 hours initially recommended without untoward complications.[133]

Reconstructive ladder

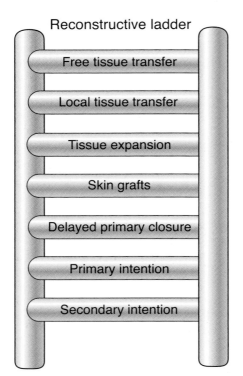

FIGURE 14-1 The reconstructive ladder.

Principle 5

When the initial task at hand is to cover the wound, secondary reconstructive needs are often ignored. It is important to determine these needs before the soft tissue coverage and initial reconstructive procedure. If nerve grafts need to be placed in the future, the vascular pedicle of the free flap should be placed as far away from the nerve graft sites whenever possible. If future bone grafting (vascularized or conventional) or tendon work needs to be performed, planning of the location of the free flap or pedicled flap needs to occur to prevent future injury to the flaps vascular supply of the flap, potentially compromising its survival or soft tissue coverage.

Principle 6

When composite soft tissue loss occurs, composite soft tissue reconstruction should be considered. Composite reconstruction refers to the use of flaps that contain more than one type of tissue. Such an example is an osteocutaneous flap, such as a free fibular graft, which may contain bone, skin, and muscle. This piece of composite tissue can then be used to replace segmental defects of the tibia and replace any overlying skin loss at the same time. The concept of replacing like tissue with like tissue when possible can be applied to upper extremity injuries as well. As a general rule when there is a need for bone, muscle, and skin, one should always consider the possibility of reconstructing the defect with a composite flap.

Principle 7

A salvage procedure, such as an amputation, may be a reasonable solution in selected situations. Although technically feasible, some heroic efforts to reconstruct parts can lead to prolonged

recovery times with loss of gainful employment, psychological problems, and increased morbidity for the patient.

Principle 8

The surgeon should know when he or she has taken on too much and should seek assistance and advice. This is the most humbling of the principles, but can be one of the most important. Collaboration with other surgeons may be extremely helpful in difficult cases. A different perspective can often drastically change the patient's outcome.

Patients with open or closed fractures associated with severe soft tissue injury are typically polytrauma patients with multiple organ systems affected. As such, their fractures and soft tissue injuries must be considered in the context of the polytrauma, recognizing the patient as a whole. Care of these patients and their injuries progresses in three phases: acute stabilization, reconstruction, and rehabilitation. The acute phase includes wound débridement, fracture stabilization, soft tissue reconstruction, and initiating muscle function and joint mobility. The reconstructive phase addresses indirect sequelae of injury, such as nonunions, infections, and malunions. Finally the rehabilitative phase focuses on returning the patient to society.

In the acute phase, treatment includes resuscitation after the ATLS protocols. The injuries are stabilized, wounds are débrided as necessary, antimicrobial measures are taken, and early soft tissue coverage is achieved. Local infection control must be tailored to the clinical situation once adequate tissue cultures have been obtained. There is great debate as to the appropriateness of broad spectrum antibiotic therapy in cases of open fractures and protracted wound closure involving multiple débridements.[80,172,215,308] Level 1 data support the use of a short course of a first-generation cephalosporin beginning immediately after injury, in conjunction with rapid débridement and fracture management.[172]

Débridement

Débridement is the cornerstone of success for the management of any traumatic wound. Adequate débridement requires the complete removal of foreign material and devitalized tissue. Inadequate débridement can promote wound infection, delay surgical healing, and attenuate the inflammatory response.

Careful wound evaluation and wound débridement should take place as soon as possible after the injury, under general anesthesia in the operating room. Débridement performed in the emergency room or on the ward is often inadequate, as it is limited by inadequate lighting and patient analgesia. Débridement in the operating room also allows the surgeon to have on hand the appropriate surgical tools for the removal of devitalized bone and soft tissue and to obtain hemostasis.

For all trauma patients, the surgeon must determine the "zone of injury," which refers to the area throughout which trauma has occurred. The extent of the zone of injury is not always apparent on initial assessment, particularly in degloving, crush, and electrical injuries. If one cannot assure complete excision of all necrotic tissue, soft tissue and bony reconstruction should be postponed and a second débridement planned within 24 hours. The need for fasciotomy should be considered at the first débridement. Injuries sustained in an agricultural setting or in industrial machinery are subject to heavier and deeper contamination. Mechanical roller injuries involving crushing, avulsion, or degloving will also result in more severe tissue damage and have a worse prognosis than blunt trauma or guillotine type injuries.[46,157,160,215] Such injuries should routinely undergo serial débridements over the course of 48 hours to ensure that all devitalized tissue is removed before soft tissue reconstruction.

After sharp débridement all wounds should be irrigated to remove additional loose debris and decrease bacterial contamination. Several different solutions are available for irrigation. Antibiotic solutions (bacitracin, neomycin, and polymyxin) and detergents (Castile soap, benzalkonium chloride) are used by many surgeons in an attempt to minimize infection rates. Although wound irrigation with antibiotic solutions have been effective in some experimental studies,[103,333] there is still a lack of convincing clinical data that it provides a benefit over soap lavage alone. Anglen recently conducted a prospective randomized study of 458 open fractures and concluded that irrigation of open fracture wounds with antibiotic solution offers no advantages over the use of a nonsterile soap solution.[10] Anglen et al. also conducted a series of 10 detailed experiments to investigate the efficacy of soap solution over normal saline irrigation.[11,12] Soap and other detergents work by disrupting the bonds formed between microorganisms and the tissues.[50,383] Anglen found that soap solution removed significantly more bacteria from these wounds than saline irrigation alone.[12] Irrigation of the wound should be performed with more than 4 liters of fluid, ideally under high-pressure flow, as this technique has been shown to remove significantly more bacteria, debris, and clot and lessen the rate of wound infection when compared with small volume low pressure irrigation.[11,330]

High pressure flow, although beneficial for decreasing bacterial counts, should still be used prudently. When using high pressure irrigation, one should avoid driving foreign material further into the wound bed, hydrodissection of uninjured areas, and tissue insufflation.[135,274] High pressure irrigation should be utilized judiciously in the hand, as the water jet can injure or avulse nerves or digital vessels. In such cases, copious amounts of gravity fed irrigation in conjunction with careful débridement will suffice.

Newer débridement devices have been designed to exert variable pressure throughout the débridement process. Devices such as the Versa jet Hydro surgery System (Smith and Nephew, USA) use a controlled fluid jet that allows for precise débridement over tendons in addition to gross débridement of acute and chronic wounds.[56,224,351] In a prospective trial this device has been shown to decrease operative times and allow for increased precision during the débridement process.[146]

Inadequate débridement can often result from the surgeon's concerns over wound closure. If the surgeon is at all concerned about wound closure, early consultation with a plastic surgeon or other wound management specialist should be carried out to allow for a multidisciplinary approach to wound management. Such collaborations will allay concerns and allow for an aggressive initial débridement minimizing late wound complications.

Débridement of Acute Wounds

The first step in any major reconstructive effort is an adequate débridement. With each débridement the surgeon's goal should be to remove all foreign and necrotic tissue. Wound débridement and careful wound evaluation should take place as soon as possible after the injury, under general anesthesia in the oper-

ating room. The débridement process starts with a careful wound scrub using a surgical brush and sterile soap or iodine solution, followed by irrigation with 4 to 8 L of sterile saline, ideally heated to 37°C to avoid excessive cooling of the patient. If there is excessive bleeding, a tourniquet may be inflated before the irrigation process.

Important structures including nerves and vessels should be identified, marked, and protected before sharp débridement of the nonviable soft tissues. Major motor nerves should never be débrided, but rather dissected from necrotic tissue and preserved. Free bony fragments that are completely denuded of soft tissue attachments, and therefore avascular, should be removed from the wound. Avulsed parts can often be used as a source of "spare-parts" for wounds requiring skin grafting or flap closure, and this should always be considered before discarding them.[43] After débridement, the final assessment of tissue viability must be made with the tourniquet deflated.

Skin that is insensate, and does not blanch or bleed at the wound edges should be removed. Clotted venules are a sign of skin devitalization and they should be débrided with the surrounding skin and soft tissue. Healthy muscle is bright red and shiny and will contract when grasped with the forceps. If there is any question regarding muscle viability it may be stimulated with the electrocautery; if there is no evidence of contraction, it should be débrided.

If the surgeon has removed all foreign material and devitalized tissue, immediate reconstruction can be considered. Clean surgical instruments, ideally on a separate operating tray, should be used for any immediate reconstructive procedure, as it has been shown that instruments used for débridement can carry a bacterial concentration in excess of 10^3 organisms.[20] If one cannot assure complete excision of all necrotic tissue, reconstruction should be postponed and a second débridement planned within 24 hours. Débridements should continue at 24- to 48-hour intervals until the wound is clean and ready for reconstruction.

Débridement of Chronic Wounds

As discussed, a chronic wound is a wound that has failed to progress through the normal stages of healing and remains arrested in the inflammatory stage.[20,201] In traumatic cases, such wounds exist because of an infection associated with a retained sequestrum, hardware, or other foreign material. To allow these wounds to heal, all necrotic and infected material must be removed before any attempt at soft tissue reconstruction. Thus, one must turn the chronic wound into an acute wound through the process of thorough débridement. The one caveat to this recommendation is the removal of hardware that is providing critical and stable fracture fixation. If the application of an external fixator is not possible, hardware can be maintained within an infected field until more definitive fixation is possible or bony healing has occurred, providing systemic antibiotics have been administered and the hardware is covered with well-vascularized tissue.[55,325]

Chronic wounds present a greater challenge, as vital structures are often hidden within scar and granulation tissue. Débridement must be extended beyond the zone of injury, into normal tissue, to ensure complete resection of all contaminated tissue. Use of a tourniquet early in the case is important to best visualize and avoid injury to vital structures such as nerves and blood vessels. The tourniquet should be released before closure or dressing application to confirm the removal of all devascularized tissue.

A centripetal approach should be used working from superficial tissues to deep, from the margins to the center of the wound. Every effort is made to preserve nerves and blood vessels crossing the zone of injury. If nerves must be transected, they should be tagged with dyed monofilament suture and documented in the operative records so that they may be more easily identified during later wound débridements or reconstructive efforts. Tissue from the wound should always be sent for bacterial cultures as well as pathologic analysis to rule out the possibility of osteomyelitis, or vasculitis.[20]

Adjuvants to Débridement

Management of the wound between débridements is an issue of some debate. Normal saline wet to dry dressings have been the most common form of wound dressing after surgical débridement. They help to prevent soft tissue desiccation, they obliterate dead space, and the dressing changes provide an opportunity for continuous surveillance of the wound, in addition to providing excellent mechanical wound débridement. One disadvantage is patient discomfort with dressing changes, which may be alleviated by moistening the gauze before removal. Their use is labor intensive. For contaminated wounds, immediately after injury, Dakin's solution or Betadine solution may be used judiciously. Dakin's solution is bacteriostatic and Betadine is bacteriocidal. Their use is controversial, especially if used for more than 3 days, because of their negative effects on wound healing and soft tissue toxicity.[24,229] In cases of established infection, the application of topical antibiotics such as silver sulfadiazine, Sulfamylon (mafenide acetate), and silver nitrate has been shown to reduce bacterial counts.[125,235] For *Pseudomonas* infections, 0.25% acetic acid may be used to reduce surface bacterial counts. Consultation with an infectious disease specialist is recommended in such cases.

The advantage of all these forms of dressing changes is that they ensure consistent monitoring of the wound site. This is in contrast specifically to the use of a vacuum-assisted closure (VAC) device, in which the sponge is commonly not changed for 2 to 4 days, thus preventing wound surveillance by the surgeon who will be performing the reconstruction.

Emollient-type soft tissue coverage with various wound gels, semipermeable films, or even antibiotic impregnated ointments may be used in cases in which there has been avulsion of the dermal surface but without damage to the underlying muscle. The dressings may take the form of a hydrogel, antibiotic impregnated gauze, or simple a semipermeable film. Semipermeable films and semiocclusive hydrogels are impermeable to water and bacteria but permeable to oxygen and water vapor. Occlusive hydrocolloids are impermeable to even water vapor and oxygen. Thus these dressings are not as useful in wounds that require mechanical débridement or wounds that are exudative because of accumulation of fluid under them.

Vessels and nerves that are exposed in the wound should always be covered with a nonadherent gauze or hydrogel dressing to protect them until soft tissue coverage can be obtained. Nerve repairs and blood vessel repairs should be covered with local soft tissue, immediately after repair, to allow for a moist healing environment, as opposed to gauze dressings.

Vacuum-Assisted Closure

If the wound is clean and wound reconstruction is not going to be performed immediately, whether because of concomitant life-threatening injuries or other medical issues, a negative pressure dressing can be used until definitive closure. A wound VAC (Vacuum-Assisted Closure) can help to remove surrounding edema, decrease local metalloproteinases and other inhibitors of wound healing while promoting angiogenesis.[17,293]

The VAC consists of an open polyurethane ether foam sponge, in some cases impregnated with silver for more contaminated cases, sealed by an adhesive drape and attached to suction. All pores in the sponge communicate so that negative pressure applied to the sponge by the suction is applied equally and completely to the entire wound surface. The effects of the VAC on the wound are multiple. The application of negative pressure causes the sponge to collapse toward its center. Traction forces are thus applied to the wound perimeter pulling the wound edges together progressively making the wound smaller. The VAC sponge should be cut to fit inside the wound to maximize these traction forces on the wound edges. The sponge should not overlap intact skin, as skin maceration may occur. In addition, the VAC removes wound edema, and it appears to increase circulation and decrease bacterial counts (Figure 14-2).[293]

The use of the VAC in traumatic lower extremity wounds has been associated with a decreased requirement for skin grafting, free tissue transfers and flap coverage.[94,121] Herscovici reported on 21 patients, 16 of whom had lower extremity wounds because of high-energy trauma. At the time of initial presentation, all wounds "would have required flap coverage"; however, after an average of 19 days of VAC treatment, 12 of the wounds no longer required flap procedures to achieve wound coverage.[180]

Vacuum-assisted therapy must be used with caution over tendons and nerves, as continuous suction can produce desiccation and injury to these structures. When neurovascular structures are exposed, local tissue or flap coverage should be performed in an urgent or emergent manner to prevent desiccation. If wounds remain contaminated despite surgical débridement, wet to dry dressing changes can be performed every 8 hours until the next scheduled surgical débridement or until the wound is clean enough to accept a VAC device.

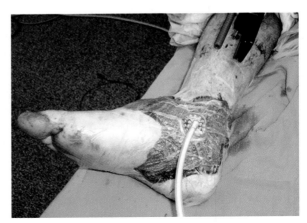

FIGURE 14-2 A vacuum-assisted closure device properly placed on a wound after débridement.

Antibiotic Beads and Spacers

The local use of antibiotics to prevent skeletal infections was incorporated into general practice with the development of joint arthroplasty in Europe in the 1970s. Buchholz et al. reported in a sentinel paper that penicillin, erythromycin, and gentamicin mixed into the polymethyl methacrylate cement used to secure prostheses to bone was found to provide high local concentrations of antibiotics for extended periods of time.[45] Since its original description local antibiotic therapy, through the use of antibiotic-impregnated cement, has been used for prophylaxis in cases of open fractures and to treat chronic osteomyelitis. In 1979, Klemm created gentamicin-impregnated beads and used them to occupy dead space after débridement of infected bone. Klemm reported his experience in more than 100 patients, achieving an infection cure rate of 91.4%.[225]

Local antibiotic delivery may be in the form of beads or spacers. Beads are generally prepared in the operating room from commercially available polymethyl methacrylate (Figure 14-3). If possible the beads and spacers should be covered with local tissue. In wounds with extensive soft tissue damage, closure may not be possible at the time of débridement and coverage may be achieved with an adhesive wound film such as Op-Site. This "bead pouch" should be replaced every 48 to 72 hours under sterile conditions. Final wound closure may then be achieved with primary closure or, in cases with more extensive soft tissue damage, skin grafts and/or flap coverage (Figure 14-4). Alternatively, a spacer may be needed in cases of bone loss to keep an extremity out to length.

The most commonly used antibiotics include gentamicin, tobramycin, and vancomycin. Mixing of more than one antibiotic into bone cement has been shown to have a synergistic effect. Penner et al. demonstrated higher elution rates in vitro when tobramycin and vancomycin were tested together as compared with either one tested alone in saline baths.[310] Thus, not only does a combination of different antibiotics increase the antimicrobial spectrum, it could also lead to increased concentrations of antibiotics in the tissues. Currently, efficient methods of local antibiotic delivery with biodegradable substrates are being investigated.[261]

The most commonly used bone cement is polymethylmethacrylate (PMMA), consisting of a powdered polymer mixed with a liquid monomer to form a solid structure. Currently the after antibiotic-laden PMMA bone cement products are approved by the United States Food and Drug Administration (FDA): Simplex P, which contains 1 g tobramycin (Stryker Howmedica Osteonics, Mahwah, NJ); Palacos G, which contains 0.85 g gentamicin (Zimmer, Warsaw, IN); SmartSet GHV and SmartSet MHV, which contain 1 g gentamicin (DePuy Orthopaedics, Inc., Warsaw, IN); and the PROSTALAC prosthesis (DePuy Orthopaedics, Inc.). Premixed antibiotic PMMA beads are available and widely used in Europe under the name Septopal (Biomet Merck, Dordrecht, The Netherlands) but are not currently approved in the United States.

Despite their popularity, antibiotic bead pouches used for control or prevention of soft tissue infections have not been clearly shown to provide a benefit over intravenous antibiotic therapy in some studies.[281] In addition, concern has been raised over the development of antibiotic resistance because of the prolonged release of antibiotic at subtherapeutic levels.[295] PMMA has the additional undesirable quality of systemic toxicity from the absorbed monomer, a factor shown to cause acute intraoperative hypotension in its use in arthroplasty. Although this has not been a significant clinical problem in the depot delivery of drugs, the theoretical risk remains. Finally, although antibiotic-laden cement serves as an adequate substance for dead-space management, it does not participate in the bone healing process.

Hyperbaric Oxygen Therapy

Hyperbaric oxygen therapy (HBOT) involves the intermittent inhalation of 100% oxygen in specialized chambers at pressures greater than that at sea level (>1 atmosphere absolute, ATA). Typical protocols recommended by the Undersea and Hyperbaric Medical Society (UHMS) for treating wounds expose the patient to pressures of 2 to 2.5 ATA lasting 90 to 120 minutes per session for approximately 40 treatments. The arterial partial pressure of oxygen rises to approximately 1500 mmHg under these hyperbaric conditions; oxygen tensions can approach 500 mmHg in soft tissue and 200 mmHg in bone.[213]

The hypothesis that raising oxygen tension within the soft tissue and bone can enhance the healing of bone stems from lines of evidence similar to those that exist in the many other conditions for which HBOT has been applied. Traumatized and osteomyelitic limbs and bone structures have been shown to be hypoxic, with a partial pressure of 20 to 25 mmHg in animal models, and thus oxygen content can be dramatically raised under hyperbaric conditions.[260] In the presence of infection, the phagocytic and bactericidal abilities of leukocytes parallel the oxygen tension in the tissue. The hypoxic conditions in the diseased bone reduce the ability of neutrophils to generate the reactive oxygen species necessary to kill bacteria, and hyperbaric

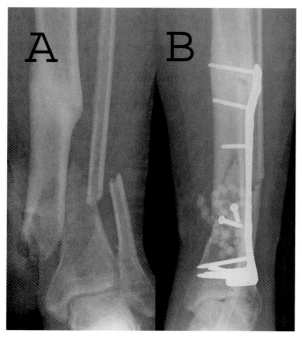

FIGURE 14-3 Use of PMMA antibiotic beads in an open tibia fracture. **A.** Preoperative and (**B**) postoperative views of an open distal tibia fracture with bone loss. The fracture was treated with open reduction, and antibiotic beads were placed. The PMMA beads provide a method for antibiotic delivery as well as dead-space management, but necessitate a future operation for removal.

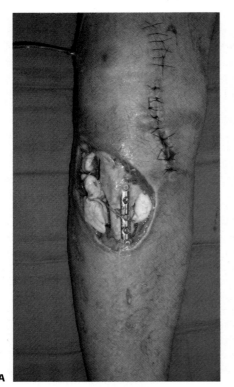 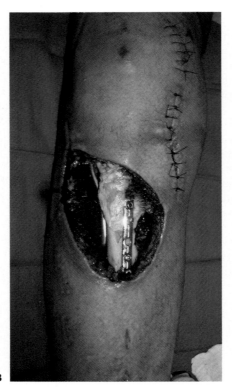 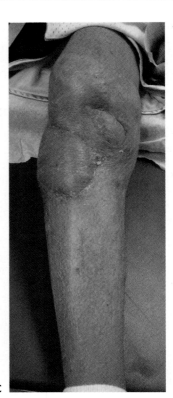

FIGURE 14-4 A. A Grade IIIB contaminated tibial plateau fracture in a 45-year-old smoker with diabetes was treated with an antibiotic bead pouch. **B.** After serial wound débridements a healthy, uninfected bed was ready for coverage with medial and lateral head gastrocnemius muscle flaps and skin graft. **C.** Postoperative appearance.

oxygen (HBO) can enhance this bactericidal activity.[27] The processes of collagen synthesis and osteogenesis are also inhibited in a hypoxic state, and studies have suggested that improved oxygen tension can normalize, if not enhance, these functions.[226] Other efforts have provided evidence of hyperbaric oxygen inducing angiogenesis, suppressing anaerobic organisms, and enhancing antibiotic activity.[27]

A Cochrane review evaluating the literature from 1966 to 2003 for studies on the use of HBOT in fracture healing and nonunion treatment identified 68 references. The review found no level I evidence to support the use of HBOT in acute fracture healing.[31] A recent review performed for the Center of Medicare and Medicaid Services to assess the use of HBOT in treating hypoxic wounds found 57 studies examining the subject published between 1998 and 2001.[405] In this review Wang et al. concluded that these studies as a group suggested HBOT had potential beneficial adjunctive effects for conditions such as chronic nonhealing diabetic wounds, compromised skin grafts, osteoradionecrosis, soft tissue radionecrosis, gas gangrene, and chronic osteomyelitis. One nonrandomized controlled trial and one case series specifically studying chronic osteomyelitis was identified, but these studies were found to be inconsistent in their reported results.[115] Nevertheless, it is notable that in the United States, Medicare currently provides coverage for those patients receiving HBOT as adjunctive therapy for chronic osteomyelitis that is not responding to standard medical and surgical treatment. The definitive value of HBOT remains to be determined through prospective randomized trials.

TIMING OF RECONSTRUCTION

The timing of soft tissue reconstruction in the trauma setting is often debated, and different authors have advocated different time scales including immediate (emergency) closure,[254] early closure (before 5 days),[141] and delayed closure (6 to 21 days).[100] In our opinion the requirements for wound closure should be no different when dealing with primary closure, pedicled flaps, or free tissue transfer; wounds must be free of necrotic tissue and infection. There is experimental and clinical evidence that quantitative bacteriology immediately before wound closure correlates with the likelihood of subsequent infection.[62,84] Breidenbach et al. evaluated 50 free tissue transfers carried out for complex wound closure in the extremities to determine predictors of subsequent infection, and found that quantitative cultures had the highest positive predictive value (89%), negative predictive value (95%), sensitivity, and specificity.[42] Mechanism of injury, type and degree of contamination, wound location and systemic factors such as diabetes, corticosteroid use, immunosuppression, advanced age, and malnutrition also affect the likelihood of clinical infection.[201]

In 1986, Godina published the results of 532 free flaps used for extremity reconstruction. In that study, he was able to reduce the postoperative infection rate in patients with open fractures to 1.5% in a subset of patients undergoing reconstruction within 72 hours.[141] Many subsequent studies support these data, and when free tissue transfer is to be used, reconstruction within 5 days of the injury is a commonly adopted guideline. This approach has been extrapolated into the general practice of trauma reconstruction. "Emergency" free flap reconstruction in the upper limb (within 24 hours of injury) potentially can allow for earlier rehabilitation and a quicker resolution of the inflammatory response after trauma. Several authors have reported successful series of emergency free flaps in the upper extremity.[66,254,297] Nevertheless, no prospective comparative studies have examined the benefits of very early versus later coverage with regard to outcome or functionality. In contrast, studies have shown that flap reconstructions performed beyond the frequently quoted critical interval of 72 hours with or without temporary vacuum-assisted closure coverage yields results similar to those of immediate reconstruction within the first 3 days.[211,370]

Yaremchuk proposed that treatment of the severely injured lower extremity be done in four distinct phases: (i) emergency evaluation, orthopaedic stabilization, and débridement of obviously devitalized structures and tissues; (ii) wound management with serial débridement; (iii) soft tissue coverage; and (iv) delayed bone reconstruction.[427] Soft tissue coverage and bone reconstruction may be performed simultaneously using osteocutaneous flaps. In summation, a wound should be closed when it is clean. The quicker the wound is made clean the sooner reconstruction may occur. If the surgeon is sure all necrotic material has been removed from the wound, then reconstruction should proceed.

AMPUTATION VERSUS LIMB SALVAGE

In complex extremity injuries, the treating physician must make two critical decisions early within the reconstructive process; the first is to determine if it is technically possible to save the injured extremity, and the second is to determine whether salvaging the limb is in the best interest of the patient. An insensate, painful, or chronically unstable leg may provide no benefit over a prosthesis. Many factors have historically come into play when making these decisions, such as patient age, comorbid injuries, and preinjury ambulation status. Several algorithms have been designed to aid the surgeon in this decision-making process.[152,238]

Indications for amputation are total leg amputation in an adult, sciatic nerve transaction in an adult, and irreparable vascular injury. Relative indications for amputation are life-threatening multisystem trauma, a warm ischemia time of greater than 6 hours, an insensate plantar foot, a crushed foot with fracture comminution, extensive bone loss, and multiple joint disruption with multilevel injury, advanced peripheral vascular disease, and rehabilitation concerns.[187,203,275]

Some investigators have suggested that the function of the salvaged extremities is often poorer than after treatment with early amputation and prosthetic fitting.[89,117,126,170] The Lower Extremity Assessment Project (LEAP) was a multicenter prospective study of severe lower extremity trauma in the United States civilian population designed to answer this question. The investigators collected prospective outcome data on patients with Gustilo grade III B and grade IIIC open fractures. Patient outcomes were evaluated through the use of the Sickness Impact Profile, which is a self-reported health status questionnaire. At 2 and 7 years after injury, patients who underwent amputation had functional outcomes that were similar to those who underwent reconstruction. Predictors of poor outcome after recon-

struction included a low education level, nonwhite race, poverty, lack of private health insurance, smoking status, poor social support network, and involvement in disability compensation litigation. Approximately 50% of the patients in each group were able to return to work at 2 years.[39,257]

An additional finding from this study suggests that sensation within the injured extremity has no bearing on long-term outcome. Patients with an insensate extremity at the time of presentation did not demonstrate significantly worse outcomes at 2 years when compared with patients who presented with a sensate foot. Approximately 55% of those with absent or abnormal sensation had recovered normal plantar sensation at 2 years after injury. This study suggests that initial plantar sensation is not a prognostic factor for long-term plantar sensation and should not be used a component of our limb salvage decision algorithm.[40]

Overall the study's findings seem to indicate that outcome is more significantly affected by the patient's economic, social, and personal resources than by the bony injury or level of amputation. Further research is still required to optimize triage decisions to avoid failed reconstructive attempts and examine psychosocial variables, which can be modified to improve outcomes.[52,336] If the patient is still adamant about limb salvage and understands the long-term potential for future surgery, we still remain aggressive in our attempts to salvage the severely injured extremity.

Replantation of severed limbs is beyond the scope of this chapter. However, ideal candidates for lower extremity replantation are young, healthy patients with a guillotine-type amputation at a very distal level.[131] Unfortunately, lower extremity wounds are commonly more severe than upper extremity injuries; lower extremity amputations are often associated with compounding factors such as contamination, crushing, multiple level injury, and the requirement for severe shortening, all if which mitigate against replantation. Before an amputated limb is discarded, however, the salvage of uninjured soft tissues should be considered with the goal of maintaining maximum limb length and functioning joints, because this will minimize energy expenditure during ambulation. For example, the glabrous sole of the foot can provide durable stump coverage and an intact ankle joint can be rotated to simulate a missing knee joint.[210,439] Often these salvaged parts may be transferred without microsurgery if their sensory and vascular supply remains intact.

Fracture Fixation Considerations

The choice of fracture stabilization in the acute setting remains controversial. When wounds are associated with fractures in the acute setting, provisional stabilization should be attempted to maintain soft tissue space, optimize pain control, and minimize bone shortening (Figure 14-5). In blast injuries, large amounts of debris are forced into the wounds with tremendous energy and the level of contamination is typically higher than that seen in most blunt open trauma. In this setting, there is significant potential for widespread osteomyelitis when intramedullary fixation is selected; therefore, external fixation is preferred. In blunt trauma cases despite the degree of soft tissue injury, there is a trend toward immediate and definitive internal fixation, the unreamed nail being the preferred implant for tibial

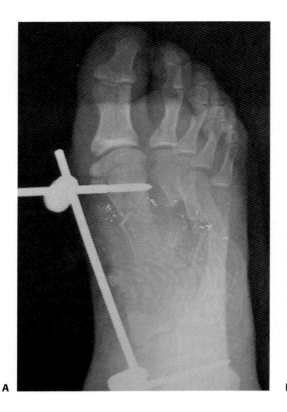

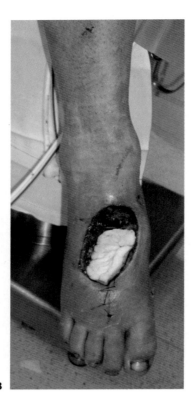

FIGURE 14-5 A. A 17-year-old man sustained a buckshot injury to the foot resulting in severe comminution of the first, second, and third metatarsals with bone loss. Initial stabilization was achieved with an external fixator. **B.** A tobramycin and vancomycin polymethylmethacrylate (PMMA) antibiotic spacer was used to eliminate the dead space and keep the foot out to length before using a free fibular osteocutaneous flap transfer to reconstruct the injured foot.

fractures.[161,231] Intramedullary nailing or plate fixation is only applicable when the fracture is covered or will soon be covered by an adequate soft tissue envelope.[143]

The superiority of external fixation or plate fixation has yet to be determined through prospective randomized trials. Bach's prospective randomized study of 59 patients with Grade II or III tibial fractures found both plating and external fixation to produce good results, but plating was associated with a higher complication rate.[22] Historically, external fixation, especially with the use of transfixion pins, has been associated with frequent complications such as pin tract infection and nonunion.[79]

Several recent studies have noted a two-stage technique with the use of temporary screws, Kirschner wires, and external fixation until the time of soft tissue coverage. Once there is adequate soft tissue coverage, the fixation may be change to definitive internal fixation or plating.[37,362] When the wound has entered a subacute, colonized phase, internal fixation, especially intramedullary nail fixation, becomes hazardous, predisposing to infection.[53] Changing from external to internal fixation should always be timed properly and adequate soft tissue coverage should be present.[427]

WOUND COVERAGE OPTIONS

Once the wound is clean and the decision for limb salvage has been made, bony fixation and wound coverage may proceed. Wound coverage may be obtained by multiple means, including primary closure, local flaps advancement, and free tissue transfer. As our experience and success with free tissue transfer has increased, surgeons have moved away from the classic reconstructive ladder and now opt to reconstruct defects with more complex procedures if they can provide a more rapid and complete reconstructive solution.[267] The most common reconstructive techniques will now be discussed in detail.

Skin Grafting

Skin grafting involves the transfer of the most superficial epidermal and dermal elements of the skin to a new location where the graft is capable of re-establishing blood flow. Skin grafts may be taken as split thickness (including only part of the dermis) or full thickness (including all of the dermis).[273] Full-thickness grafts have greater *primary* contracture rates (the amount the graft rolls or shrinks initially once it is harvested) because of a higher percentage of elastin retained within the graft; however, full-thickness grafts are less likely to contract *secondarily* (after healing has occurred) because of greater preservation of the deep dermal architecture when compared with split-thickness grafts.[348,401] Return of sensation is also superior when compared with split-thickness grafts.[7]

Split-thickness grafts have fewer dermal components and thus undergo less primary contracture but have greater secondary contracture rates. Because of high secondary contracture rates, split-thickness grafts should be avoided over joints (Figure 14-6). Split-thickness grafts are more likely to take over compromised beds as compared with full thickness grafts.[85] The split-thickness graft donor site heals through a process of re-epithelization and contraction as keratinocytes migrate out of retained hair follicles within the donor site.[25,347]

Skin grafts require a well-nourished tissue bed to survive and will not do well in an area of frank infection or on tendon devoid of paratenon, bone, or cartilage. In wounds in which these structures predominate, local, regional, or free tissue transfers are required for successful wound closure. In addition, skin grafting should be avoided in areas that may require sec-

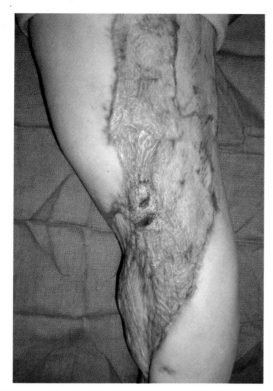

FIGURE 14-6 Late effects of skin grafting over the popliteal fossa. Although the wound is healed, the split-thickness skin graft has not provided durable coverage and is subject to chronic breakdown with knee extension.

ondary surgery for bone or nerve grafting. The greatest risks for graft failure include infection, shearing, motion at the graft site, seroma or hematoma accumulation beneath the graft, and finally poor wound bed vascularity.[273]

Skin grafts survive for the first several days through a process called serum imbibition. During this stage of healing, the graft obtains nutrients from the underlying wound bed through a diffusion process. This commonly occurs in the first 24 to 48 hours. After this point the skin graft undergoes revascularization through an ingrowth of capillary buds primarily from the wound bed.[30,82,83] Clinically most grafts are adherent to the wound bed by the fourth to fifth postoperative day.

Wound Bed Preparation

The wound bed or recipient site must be débrided and clean before attempts at skin grafting. Infection is one of the leading causes of skin graft failure. Because skin grafts are completely dependent on the wound bed they are transplanted to for nutrition, they possess no intrinsic ability to resolve infection.[232]

Operative Technique for Split-thickness Skin Grafting

The patient's position will depend on the location of the graft to be harvested. Most frequently we harvest the skin grafts from the upper thigh of the involved limb so that scarring may be concealed under clothing and only one limb is operated on. The anterior and lateral aspect of the limb is preferred so that the patient is not lying on the donor site when in a supine position and the contralateral limb does not abrade the donor site. With careful planning it is almost never necessary to reposition a patient after skin graft harvest.

Power dermatomes are most commonly used to harvest split-thickness skin grafts.

Procedure

- Ensure that the blade is inserted correctly in the dermatome device. Set and check dermatome thickness (usually 0.010 to 0.15 in) with a No. 15 scalpel blade. The thin, beveled edge of this knife blade is about 0.10 in., whereas the thickest portion of the blade is 0.015 in. thick.
- Clean the donor site to remove any material that will cause the dermatome to stick and apply copious amounts of mineral oil to the donor skin and the dermatome.
- Apply counter-traction to the skin in front of and behind the dermatome blade. Dermatomes, particularly when fitted with larger guards, function much more effectively on flat surfaces.
- The harvested graft is passed through a graft mesher on a dermal carrier (Figure 14-7). This is done to allow for drainage through the graft, make grafts more conformable to the underlying wound bed, and increase the surface area of the graft.
- The perimeter of the skin graft is then fixed to the wound bed with either staples or absorbable sutures. Motion is minimized at the graft site with the use of a tie over bolster or a VAC sponge. A tie over bolster employs silk sutures placed circumferentially around the skin graft and left long to tie over mineral oil–soaked cotton balls wrapped in a nonadherent gauze placed firmly over the graft. The extremity is usually splinted to avoid unnecessary shear or trauma to the skin graft site.

Aftercare and Long-Term Issues

If it is anticipated that hematoma or seroma may accumulate below the graft, the dressings may be removed at 24 hours, otherwise grafts at our institution are left covered for 5 days and then inspected. If the skin graft site develops increasing drainage from the wound site or a foul odor or the patient develops increasing pain or fever the skin graft is inspected immediately to rule out infection.

Donor sites may be covered with nonadherent gauze such as Adaptic (Johnson and Johnson, New Brunswick, NJ) or Tegaderm (3M, St. Paul, MN) as long as care is taken to dry the surrounding skin around the donor site before applying the dressing. The advantage of Tegaderm is decreased pain at the donor site; however, very commonly fluid and serum accumulate under the dressing necessitating puncture and drainage of the dressing if there is a suspicion of infection.[102] Xeroform (Sherwood Medical Industries, Ltd., Markham, Ontario, Canada) for large donor sites is more beneficial and will dry into

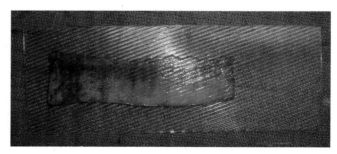

FIGURE 14-7 A split-thickness skin graft with the dermal side up on a dermal carrier that meshes graft at a ratio of 1:1.5.

an eschar when exposed to air. Once dry, it is painless, although the site remains sensitive until the eschar is formed over several days.[347]

Flaps

Classification of Flaps

A flap is tissue transferred from one anatomic location to another. The flap may be based on a random or axial blood supply. Random flaps have no named or defined blood supply. They are raised in a subdermal or subfascial plane and rely on the subdermal vascular plexus of the skin for circulation. To ensure adequate circulation, random flaps should be limited to a length no greater than 2.5 times the width of their base, which is the uncut border of the flap. This ratio may be even more limited in poorly perfused extremities. Varied random pattern flaps include z-plasty, four flap z-plasty, rhomboid flap, banner flap, V-Y advancement flaps, and rotational flaps.

Axial pattern flaps can be pedicled regional flaps or free tissue transfers. The flaps can contain more than one type of tissue. Fasciocutaneous flaps contain skin and the underlying fascia, musculocutaneous flaps contain skin, fascia, and muscle, and osteocutaneous flaps contain bone, fascia, and skin.

Muscle flaps are classified on five patterns of muscle circulation.[269] A muscle for free tissue transfer must be able to survive on one vascular pedicle that is dominant and that will support the entire muscle mass. The classification (with examples) is as follows:

Type I: One vascular pedicle (extensor digitorum brevis or tensor fascia latae)
Type II: One dominant pedicle and minor pedicles (gracilis muscle)
Type III: Two dominant pedicles (rectus abdominis muscle)
Type IV: Segmental vascular pedicles (sternocleidomastoid)
Type V: One dominant and secondary vascular pedicles (latissimus dorsi, pectoralis major)

Animal studies have shown that muscle flaps are able to control a 10-fold higher bacterial count than fasciocutaneous flaps, and improve antibiotic delivery to the wound site.[54] Although the potential antimicrobial advantages of muscle flaps have also been demonstrated clinically, a recent study by Yazar et al. comparing lower limb wounds reconstructed with free fasciocutaneous or free muscle flaps in a total of 177 cases showed no difference in outcomes or infection rates.[429] This highlights the important role of adequate débridement, regardless of the type of flap used.

Free Flaps

The coverage of traumatic wounds within the extremities has historically been accomplished with the use of pedicled, local or distant rotational flaps. However, when defects are very large or encompass multiple structures including nerve, bone, or muscle, the use of composite free tissue transfer provides a reliable and single stage means of reconstruction.

The benefits of free tissue transfer within the extremity includes the transfer of additional vascularized tissue to the injured area, the ability to carry vascularized nerve, bone, skin, and muscle to the injured area in one procedure, and the avoidance of any additional functional deficits to the injured limb that may be incurred with the use of a local or pedicled flap. Free flaps are not tethered at one end, as is the case for pedicled

flaps, and this allows for more freedom in flap positioning and insetting. More recently developed fasciocutaneous and perforator flaps also allow for primary closure of donor sites with minimal sacrifice of donor site muscle. With current microsurgical techniques free flap loss rates range between 1% and 4% for elective free tissue reconstruction.[23,216] The upper extremity is particularly suited for free tissue transfer as the majority of recipient blood vessels utilized for anastomosis are located close to the skin, and are of relatively large caliber.

Major indications for free tissue transfer are for: (i) the primary coverage of large traumatic wounds with exposed bone, joint, and tendons or hardware; (ii) the coverage of complex composite defects requiring bone and soft tissue replacement; (iii) the coverage of soft tissue deficits resulting from the release of contractures or scarring from previous trauma; and (iv) the coverage of extensive burns or electrical injuries.[230,246,247,337,346]

There are few absolute contraindications for free flap transfer within the upper and lower extremities, and in many cases free tissue transfer may be the only option for limb salvage after severe soft tissue loss. Despite this, relative contraindications to free tissue transfer include a history of a hypercoagulable state, a history of a recent upper extremity deep venous thrombosis, and evidence of ongoing infection within the traumatic defect. Other contraindications would include an inadequate recipient vessel for flap anastomosis. Disregarding technical error, the status of the recipient vessel used for flap anastomosis may play the greatest role in flap failure; recipient vessels within the zone of injury are prone to postoperative and intraoperative thrombosis. Recipient vessels for microvascular transfer ideally should be located out of the zone of injury, radiation, or infection. Petechial staining of the adventitia, a ribbon-like appearance of the recipient vessels, and poor flow at the time of arteriotomy are all suggestive of vessel injury, and alternative vessels should be chosen as recipient vessels for microvascular anastomosis. In rare cases, arterial-venous fistulas may be created proximally within the upper extremity or axilla using the cephalic or saphenous vein. These fistulas can be brought into the zone of injury and divided to provide adequate inflow and outflow for a free tissue transfer.[249] Commonly used recipient vessels in the upper extremity are the thoracodorsal, thoracoacromial, circumflex scapular, transverse cervical, brachial, circumflex humeral, superior ulnar collateral, radial collateral, ulnar, radial, and digital vessels.[414] Common recipient vessels in the lower extremity are the superficial femoral, the popliteal, the posterior tibial, and the anterior tibial arteries.[248]

The choice of flap should take into account both functional requirements and the surgeon's experience. Muscle flaps are useful for large three-dimensional defects when soft-tissue bulk is necessary; however, direct coverage of tendons with muscle flaps encourages dense adhesions limiting postoperative tendon excursion. In general, fascial or fasciocutaneous flaps are more useful for coverage of exposed tendons and areas in which a gliding tissue plane needs to be preserved.

SOFT TISSUE RECONSTRUCTIVE ALGORITHMS BY REGION

Lower Extremity Reconstructive Options (Table 14-4)

Lower extremity reconstruction has historically followed an algorithm that is based on the location of the defect. The gastroc-

TABLE 14-4	Reconstructive Options for the Lower Extremity
Pelvis/groin	Rectus abdominis muscle
	Rectus femoris muscle
	Transverse rectus abdominus myocutaneous flap
	Tensor fascia lata
	Free flap
Thigh	Pedicled ALT
	Rectus abdominis muscle
	Rectus femoris muscle
	Tensor facia lata
	Vastus lateralis
	Gracilis
	Sartorius
	Free flap
Knee/per third of tibia	Gastrocnemius muscle
	Reversed ALT
	Anterior tibial perforator flap
	Free flap
Middle third of tibia	Soleus
	Free flap
Lower third tibia/ankle	Free flap
	Sural artery island flap
	Posterior tibial perforator flap
	Posterior tibial flap
	Reverse soleus muscle flap
Foot/dorsum	Free flap
	Sural artery island flap
Foot/plantar	STSG/FTSG
	Free flaps
	Medial plantar island flap
	Abductor hallucis muscle

nemius muscle flap has been used to cover defects around the knee and proximal tibia; the soleus muscle flap has been used to cover defects within the middle third of the tibia, and free flaps have been reserved to cover defects overlying the lower third of the tibia and ankle. Nonetheless, with continuing advancements in microsurgery, there are now several reliable fasciocutaneous flaps and free flaps that may be used for proximal and distal defects in addition to the standard options. An overview of the standard options will be provided with a subsequent explanation of newer approaches for soft tissue coverage.

Upper Thigh, Groin, and Pelvis

Wounds within the pelvis and upper thigh rarely require flap coverage. The bone in this area is covered with enough soft tissue that most defects can be covered with skin grafts. Should the size of the defect prohibit primary closure or skin grafting, the rectus abdominus or the rectus femoris muscle flap may be used in a pedicled fashion to cover most defects in this region. The anterolateral thigh (ALT) flap and tensor fascia lata muscle can also be used to cover wounds surrounding the femur and the greater trochanter.

Anterolateral Thigh Flap. The anterolateral thigh flap is a versatile flap harvested from the anterolateral region of the thigh. It is most often used as a free flap for lower third injuries in the

leg or for reconstruction in the upper extremities, but it may also be pedicled to cover defects in the groin and thigh. Its blood supply is through the descending branch of the lateral femoral circumflex artery. Several branches of this vessel supply the overlying skin. These skin vessels are either septocutaneous or they take a course through the vastus lateralis muscle before supplying the skin.[237] Inclusion of the lateral femoral cutaneous nerve allows for the flap to become sensate. The length of the pedicle is approximately 8 cm, but it can have a longer effective length when the skin paddle is designed so that the perforator is eccentrically located. The flap is easy to design and can be as large as 40 × 20 cm. (Figure 14-8). The skin is relatively pliable and the flap can be thinned to a great degree without compromising the blood supply. This flap can also be used as a flow-through flap that maintains distal blood supply in the extremity,[15] which is particularly useful in extremities that have compromise of one or more vessels.[132,266]

The ALT flap can be dissected to include a variety of tissue components such as muscle (vastus lateralis or rectus femoris), fascia, and skin in a variety of combinations.[70] It has disadvantages such as a color mismatch (when reconstructing defects in distant locations), and the presence of hair in some patients. When large defects are reconstructed, skin grafts are required at the donor site. Donor site morbidity is minimal when the donor site is closed primarily and some residual functional deficit is sometimes noted when a large skin graft is required.[236] If necessary the flap can be thinned down to a 5-mm thickness. This allows for an aesthetically appealing reconstruction while providing a tendon gliding surface when necessary.

The anterolateral thigh flap can also be harvested as an adipofascial flap for areas with adequate skin but a lack of soft tissue. This type of flap can then be buried or skin grafted. When reconstructing lower extremity defects, the flap is designed with a variation in tissue types tailored to the recipient site requirement. Certain areas such as the foot and ankle will require thin cutaneous flaps, whereas other areas will require more tissue bulk. For defects closer to the thigh such as the groin or knee, a pedicled flap can be elevated with the pedicle based proximally or distally. A distally based pedicled anterolateral thigh flap is based on retrograde blood flow from the descending branch of the lateral femoral circumflex artery with the pivot point greater

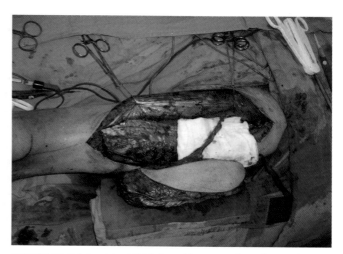

FIGURE 14-8 Anterolateral thigh flap with a vastus lateralis muscle component prior to pedicle division.

than 2 cm above the knee. Longer pedicle length can be achieved by designing the flap more proximally on the upper thigh.

This flap is also extremely useful in lower extremity reconstruction.[303,304,432] Areas such as the foot and ankle, which require a pliable thin flap for defect coverage, can be covered with a cutaneous flap. A strip of fascia lata can be incorporated to reconstruct tendon defects such as an Achilles tendon. Harvested as a myocutaneous flap, it can be used to cover amputation stump defects. A strip of fascia lata can be incorporated with the flap and used for tendon reconstruction.[63] For areas with exposed bone or extensive soft tissue loss, the cutaneous portion is often adequate for reconstruction;[185] however, if necessary, a myocutaneous flap can be used.

Knee and Proximal Third of Tibia

Proximal third tibial injuries around the knee may be covered with the medial or lateral gastrocnemius muscle flap. These muscles may be used in conjunction with each other for large defects. The medial head of the gastrocnemius will cover the *inferior thigh, knee, and proximal tibia* and is more frequently used than the lateral head as it is larger in size. The lateral head may also be used alone or in combination with the medial head for coverage of *lateral knee defects and lateral distal thigh* wounds. The tendinous inferior margin of the gastrocnemius muscle may be used to augment the repair of an injured quadriceps tendon. For coverage of extremely large defects, or in situations in which compromise of the gastrocnemius muscles will hinder ambulation, a free flap can be used for proximal third coverage. Other non-microsurgical options for proximal third coverage include the reverse ALT flap.

Gastrocnemius. The gastrocnemius muscle is located in the superficial posterior compartment and its function is to flex the knee and plantarflex the foot. It has two heads, which lie superficial to the soleus. It is dispensable only if the soleus muscle is intact. Its blood supply is the medial and lateral sural arteries, which are branches from the popliteal artery. This is a type I muscle and the pedicle length is 6 cm. Ideally, only one head of the gastrocnemius is needed for a reconstruction around the knee; however, both heads may be used, depending on the reconstructive requirements. Each head is considered a separate unit for the purpose of flap design. The medial head is longer and its muscular fibers extend more inferiorly. The distal soleus tendon unites with the gastrocnemius to form the Achilles tendon. For defects at the level of the midportion of the tibia, the gastrocnemius may not provide adequate coverage and the soleus muscle is preferred for coverage.

Contraindications to the use of the gastrocnemius muscle flap include active infection and/or significant disruption of the soft tissue and/or vascular pedicle. Additional contraindications for the flap include any procedure or injury that may have traumatized or injured the sural artery, such as a previous repair of a popliteal arterial laceration or repair of a popliteal aneurysm. Occasionally, severe compartment syndromes may render the muscle fibrotic and unusable for transfer.

Although the medial and lateral heads of the gastrocnemius can support a skin paddle, a paddle is not commonly used because of its unreliability and the limitation in size of the skin. The medial gastrocnemius is dissected through a posterior midline incision. The sural nerve and lesser saphenous vein are two

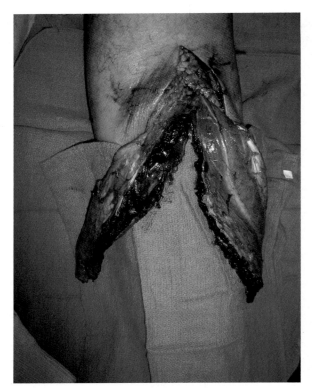

FIGURE 14-9 Gastrocnemius muscle flap after division of the medial and lateral heads along the raphe.

key landmarks that are seen superficial to the muscle belly and preserved. The muscle fascia is split, and the junction between the two heads is incised (Figure 14-9). Blunt dissection in the plane between the gastrocnemius and the soleus is gently done with the finger. The superficial dissection is then performed, and the muscle is transected distally with a cuff of tendon attached for use in fixation to the wound edge. The tunnel through which the muscle is passed should be of adequate size so as to not constrict the blood supply of the flap. To expand the muscle area, the fascia may be incised, with careful attention being paid to not injure the underlying muscle. The flap may be used as an advancement flap to cover part of an amputation stump or upper tibial defects, or as a cross leg flap.

Middle Third of Tibia

Historically the soleus has been the muscle of choice for reconstruction of middle third tibia defects; however we use this flap sparingly, and often opt for free tissue coverage in this area, especially if there is comminution of the bone.[71] There are several factors that may prohibit the successful transfer of the soleus muscle: (i) the size of the defect, (ii) the status of the muscle, and (iii) the status of the surrounding tissue and bone.[240] The standard soleus flap can cover most defects under 75 cm². Large defects occupying the majority of the middle third and lower third of the leg are best covered with a free tissue transfer. The soleus can be used in conjunction with the medial or lateral gastrocnemius muscles for larger defects spanning the upper aspect of the leg, but doing so will compromise active plantar flexion.

Because the soleus muscle is closely adherent to the deep posterior surface of the interosseous membrane, tibia, and fibula, it can often be traumatized after comminuted fractures of the tibia and fibula. Often, during initial wound evaluation and débridement, the muscle can be inspected through the soft tissue defect. If the muscle is extensively lacerated by fracture fragments or contains a significant amount of intramuscular hematoma, one should use another flap for soft tissue coverage. In addition, any associated injury to the popliteal, peroneal, or posterior tibial arteries can adversely affect the survival of the soleus muscle.[240]

Soleus

The soleus muscle is a type II muscle, with dominant pedicles from the posterior tibial, popliteal, and peroneal arteries and minor segmental pedicles from the posterior tibial artery. The muscle originates from the posterior surface of the tibia, the interosseous membrane, and the proximal fibula. It lies in the superficial posterior compartment deep to the plantaris muscle and distally joins the gastrocnemius muscle as the conjoined, Achilles tendon. It is a bipennate muscle with the medial and lateral muscle bellies each receiving an independent neurovascular supply; this allows the lateral and medial portions to be mobilized independently while preserving some function of the remaining soleus muscle. The medial head originates from the tibia and receives the majority of its blood supply from the posterior tibial artery. The lateral head originates from the fibula and receives the majority of its blood supply from the peroneal artery. Typically the soleus muscle is used as a proximally based flap (Figure 14-10). Dividing the muscle longitudinally at the level of the septum allows for the elevation of medial and lateral hemisoleus flaps; however, the proximal dissection is typically more tedious because the distinction between the two heads is often not clear.

In the distal one third of the muscle, the soleus receives segmental arterial perforators from the posterior tibial artery.

These distal perforators may be absent in up to 26% of patients; in these cases distal perfusion to the muscle is provided by axial blood flow from more proximal perforators. The diameter and position of these distal perforators is variable but, if present and of large enough caliber, they can allow for a portion of the muscle to be harvested in a reverse fashion (Figures 14-11).

Knee and ankle motion may begin once the skin graft is adherent to the underlying muscle bed. Weight bearing status is determined by the stability of the underlying fractures. In a study by Hallock of 29 soleus flaps, 24 were used for coverage of high energy impact defects. All of the soleus flaps in this study were based on a proximal pedicle. The complication rate was low (13.8%) and there were no cases of total flap loss.[166] Similar results were found by both Pu and Tobin, when using a proximally based flap.[316,385]

Distal Third of Tibia/Ankle

Free tissue transfer has historically been recommended for lower third tibia coverage; however, other nonmicrosurgical options for soft tissue closure of ankle defects include the reversed soleus flap (described in the preceding) and the sural artery flap.

Sural Artery Flap. The distally based sural artery flap is perfused by reverse flow through the anastomosis between the superficial sural artery and the lowermost perforator of the peroneal artery. This flap has been used for the successful coverage of defects of the posterior and inferior surface of the heel, the Achilles tendon, the middle and distal one third of the leg, the dorsum of the foot, and the medial and lateral malleoli. The flap is contraindicated in patients with destruction of the vascular pedicle or the lowermost perforator of the peroneal artery. Sacrifice of the sural nerve results in hyposensitivity of the lateral border of the foot and a higher rate of complications may be anticipated

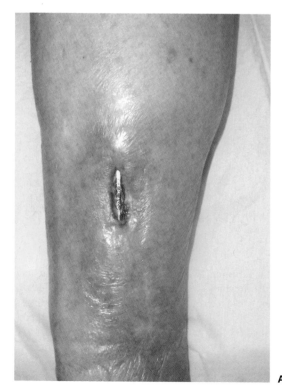
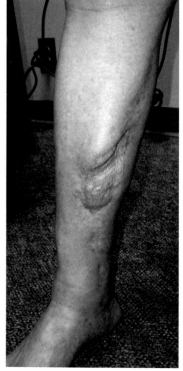

FIGURE 14-10 A medial hemisoleus flap was used to cover this healed infected tibia fracture in a 75-year-old diabetic woman after the hardware was removed. **A.** Preoperative image. **B.** Postoperative view at 6 months. The infection is resolved, and the patient is ambulating without difficulty.

A

B

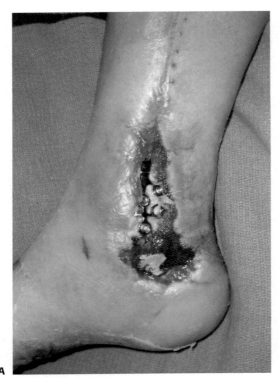

A

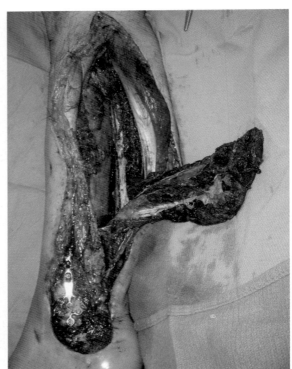

B

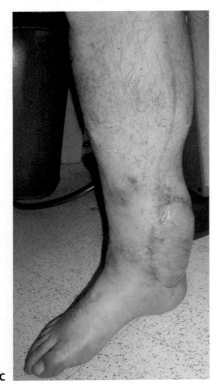

C

FIGURE 14-11 A. An infected Gustillo IIIB distal tibia-fibular fracture after open reduction and internal fixation. **B.** Intraoperative view shows the raised, distally based right hemisoleus flap. Blue markers indicate the distally based perforating vessels from the posterior tibial artery. **C.** One year after surgery, the wound is healed.

in patients with comorbid conditions such as peripheral vascular disease, diabetes mellitus, and venous insufficiency. In this patient population a delay procedure may be performed to increase its survival rate.

Many different methods have been described for flap harvest all in an effort to decrease its main problem of vascular congestion. Our technique is as follows:

- The patient is placed in the prone position

- Markings are an axial line drawn from the superior aspect of the lateral malleolus to the midpoint of the popliteal flexion crease. The skin island, at least 2 to 3 cm. distal to the popliteal flexion crease, is centered on this axis and planned according to defect size.

- The pivot point of the subcutaneous pedicle is at least three finger breadths (4 to 6 cm) superiorly from the superiormost aspect of the lateral malleolus.

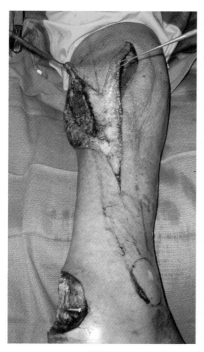
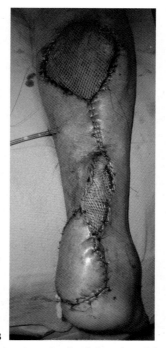
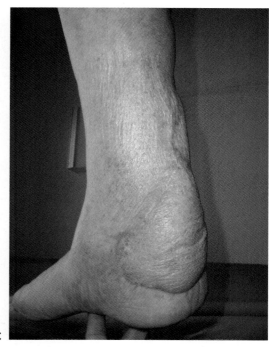

FIGURE 14-12 A. Intraoperative view of a distally based sural flap being raised for coverage of a calcaneal wound. Note the superior skin bridge has not been divided. **B.** Intraoperative view of the distally based sural flap at the time of flap inset with division of the skin bridge over the pedicle and liberal use of skin grafts over the pedicle of the flap and the donor site. **C.** View of the healed distally based sural flap 16 months postoperatively.

- The subcutaneous pedicle should be at least 3 to 4 cm. wide and the skin raised over the subcutaneous pedicle must be very thin so as to not injure the pedicle.
- Dissection is performed in a plane deep to the fascia with an incision isolating the skin paddle and dividing the proximal blood supply if a delay is not planned (Figure 14-12).
- The distally based sural flap is then transferred to the recipient site usually with division of the intervening skin bridge to alleviate any possible compression of the subcutaneous pedicle.
- Skin grafts are used liberally over the flap pedicle and at the donor site of the flap.

Postoperatively, the most important issue is prevention of congestion or compression of the vascular pedicle. This can be achieved either by an adequately elevated position of the leg and/or by the use of conventional splints with a gap over the flap; however, some authors prefer the use of external fixation devices that serve to not only immobilize the limb, but also obviate the need for tight compressive dressings. External fixation also allows the treatment of concomitant fractures and prevents the development of an equinus deformity as well as facilitating elevation of the limb.

Surveillance of flap perfusion in terms of arterial as well as venous flow must be performed regularly during the first several postoperative days. Capillary refill should be tested every several hours in the postoperative period so that interventions may be made to prevent flap loss. A revision procedure should be performed if any signs of poor arterial perfusion or venous congestion are identified. The administration of anticoagulants in the postoperative period after pedicled flap reconstruction remains controversial; however, we commonly will use antico-agulation therapy such as heparin and/or aspirin in mildly congested flaps reserving leech therapy for those with more significant congestion.[69,280] If serious compromise of the flap is evident, the flap may be laid back in the donor site bed as a last resort, in essence creating a delayed flap.

The patient should be at complete bed rest for approximately 4 to 5 days after the procedure with a gradual dangling protocol of the limb to assess tissue tolerance. If signs of significant edema or venous compromise are evident in the flap tissue after 10 to 15 minutes of dangling the extremity, bed rest with elevation should be prolonged for several more days until the flap can tolerate the dependent position. Donor site morbidity is generally low, with the most common finding being sural nerve neuroma and scarring. Neuromas that are painful and significantly distressing to the patient may be resected and the nerve stump buried in the gastrocnemius muscle.

Foot/Dorsum

Most dorsal foot wounds may be treated with a split-thickness skin graft if there is no exposed tendon or bone. Local toe fillet flaps are capable of covering smaller distal defects. Transmetatarsal amputation may be considered if there is extensive concomitant injury to the toes. In such cases, the plantar surface can be advanced to cover the remaining dorsal defect. When tendon or bone is exposed, free tissue transfer provides the most reliable means of durable coverage and preserves the remaining foot function. Smaller defects can be treated with the sural artery flap.

Foot/Plantar

Free flaps are good options for heel wounds as well as defects covering the majority of the plantar surface of the foot. Another

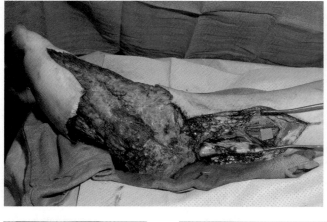
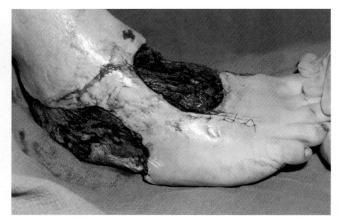
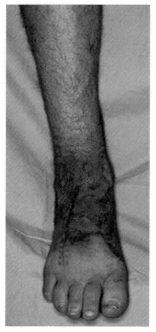
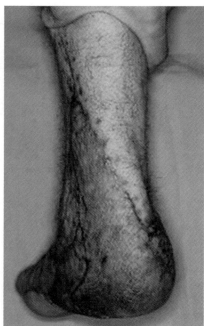
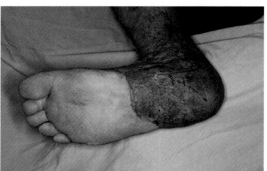

FIGURE 14-13 Small- to moderate-sized foot and ankle defects can be covered with the sural artery flap. **A.** This 55-year-old man has developed wound breakdown following ankle fracture fixation. **B.** The sural artery flap is harvested and pedicled to cover the defect. **C.** The donor site is skin grafted. **D,E.** The flap allows for thin pliable coverage of the area and will eventually allow for normal shoe wear.

option for heel coverage is the medial plantar artery flap, which provides sensate coverage of heel defects without the need for microsurgery. This flap is based on the medial plantar artery. The sural artery flap can also be extended to cover moderate sized heel defects (Figure 14-13).

Free Flaps for Lower Extremity Coverage. We have found that the latissimus dorsi muscle, gracilis muscle, anterolateral thigh and scapular flaps to be the most versatile for lower extremity coverage. For osteocutaneous defects, we most frequently use a free fibular flap or a fibular flap in combination with a latissimus dorsi muscle flap. For moderate-sized ankle defects the gracilis muscle is our flap of choice as it produces minimal donor site morbidity and can be contoured nicely to the malleolar region and will not interfere with normal shoe wear.

Latissimus Dorsi. The latissimus dorsi has proved to be a very reliable muscle for coverage of soft tissue defects for the chest, shoulder, and elbow. The muscle provides a workhorse flap for extremity coverage and is based on the thoracodorsal artery as the major pedicle and on branches of the intercostals and lum-

bar arteries as secondary segmental vessels. It is a Type IV muscle and has a pedicle length of 8 to 12 cm, which can be obtained by dissecting the thoracodorsal vessels proximally toward the axillary artery and vein. Its innervation is the thoracodorsal nerve, which is a direct branch of the brachial plexus, and it enters the muscle 10 cm from the apex of the axilla. It is important to identify the anterior border of the muscle preoperatively by having the patient contract the muscle with the hand supported on the hip in a standing position. Marking of the skin over the posterior superior iliac spine and the scapular tip is helpful also.

The indication for the use of this flap is to cover a large skin and soft tissue defect that cannot be managed with local flaps. Contraindications for flap use include previous injury, or in some cases, axillary lymphadenectomy. Breast cancer surgery, in particular, axillary node dissection, may injure the nerve or arterial supply, rendering the muscle fibrotic and inadequate for transfer.

The latissimus dorsi flap may be harvested as not only a muscle flap but also a musculocutaneous flap. A muscle flap covered with a split-thickness skin graft is often less bulky and

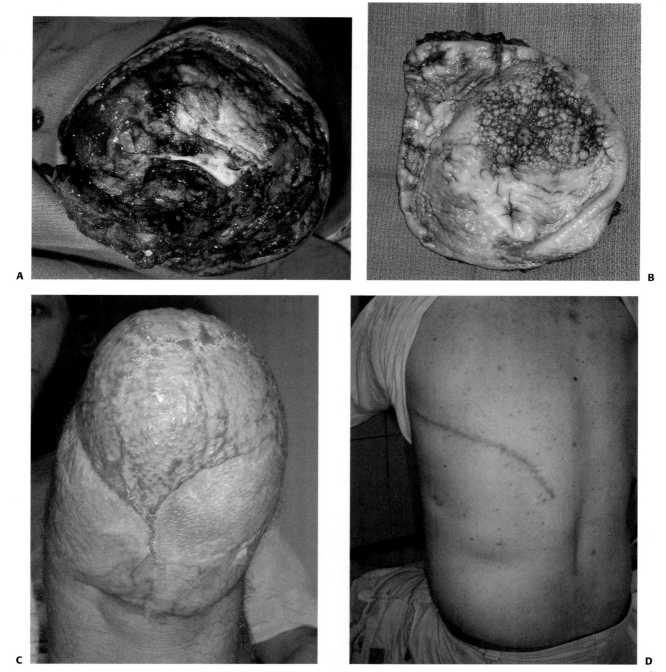

FIGURE 14-14 A. A below-knee amputation stump following resection of poor quality skin. **B.** Thorough débridement of osteomyelitis of the distal tibia. The stump was then covered with a latissimus dorsi muscle flap and split thickness skin graft. **C.** At 6 months postoperatively, the stump has been resurfaced nicely. **D.** The latissimus dorsi flap donor site at 6 months.

can seal deep defects (Figure 14-14), whereas musculocutaneous flaps give better aesthetic reconstruction because the skin paddle can conform to the skin texture of the surrounding tissues, particularly when it is used as a pedicled flap.

Technique. The patient under general anesthesia is placed in a lateral decubitus position with an axillary roll. Dissection is most easily accomplished beginning from the anterior border of the muscle, and this method allows early pedicle identification. If a skin paddle is chosen, then it may be oriented along the muscle

fibers with care being taken to center the paddle on the muscle belly. If no skin paddle is selected, the skin flaps are elevated commonly parallel to the muscle fibers to expose the muscle origins and insertions. The muscle is released from the lumbosacral fascia and iliac crest. The pedicle is identified and the serratus branch is then divided so that the muscle may be reflected toward the axilla. Pedicle dissection should be performed with loupe magnification (2.5× or greater). If performing a functional muscle transfer, marking sutures should be placed along the long axis of the muscle to allow adequate tension adjustment at the recipient site. The muscle can be split longitudinally into halves based on the medial and lateral branches of the thoracodorsal artery, which bifurcate upon entering the muscle.

Upon dissection of the neurovascular pedicle, the insertion of the muscle at the humerus is divided. Additional distal coverage, if it is being used as a pedicled flap for extremity reconstruction, can be obtained by releasing its insertion from the intertubercular groove of the humerus as well. When the latissimus dorsi flap is transferred as a free flap, the vascular pedicle is divided at the juncture with the axillary artery and vein to obtain the maximum pedicle length. Large suction drains should be left beneath the skin flaps and in the axilla to avoid postoperative hematoma or seroma problems. Frequently there is difficulty elevating the flap simultaneously with donor site preparation, particularly when it is used for upper extremity reconstruction. In addition, if used as a musculocutaneous flap it may be excessively thick in obese patients.

Donor site seroma is the most common complication after harvest of a latissimus dorsi flap. Seromas can be relieved with frequent aspiration and compressive garments. Scarring over the donor site is inevitable, and endoscopic harvest can be entertained to minimize subsequent scarring.[251] Total flap necrosis is rare when used as a pedicled flap; however, partial flap necrosis because of an inconsistent blood supply to the lower third of the muscle is not uncommon. Bleeding at the distal edge of the flap should be checked when it is elevated. Kinking and tension on the pedicle can cause a disturbance of flap circulation and must be recognized immediately.

Rectus Abdominis. The rectus abdominis muscle may be harvested with the patient in the supine position. This vertically oriented, Type III muscle (two dominant vascular pedicles), extends between the costal margin and the pubic region and is enclosed by the anterior and posterior rectus sheaths. The superior blood supply is from the superior epigastric artery, which is a continuation of the internal mammary artery. Distally the blood supply is from the inferior epigastric artery, which is a branch of the external iliac artery. The pedicle length is 5 to 7 cm superiorly and 8 to 10 cm inferiorly. Because of the larger size of the inferior epigastric artery and the venae comitantes, it is more commonly used as a free tissue transfer. Large defects of the thigh, where local soft tissues are either not sufficient in area or unusable because of radiation, for example, may be covered with pedicled rectus muscle only or myocutaneous flaps (Figure 14-15).

The motor innervation is supplied by the seventh through twelfth intercostals nerves that enter the deep surface of the muscle at its middle to lateral aspects. The size of the muscle is up to 25×6 cm^2. The skin territory that can be harvested is 21×14 cm^2 and its blood supply is based on musculocutaneous perforators. The donor site created via the fascial incision in the anterior rectus sheath to access a muscle-only flap may be closed primarily with a running or interrupted absorbable or nonabsorbable suture on a tapered needle. When harvesting a myocutaneous flap, a portion of the anterior rectus sheath is taken with the flap and a mesh or biologic implant may be used to reinforce the closure of the abdominal wall fascia to prevent hernia or bulge. Drains are commonly used under the raised skin flaps after muscle harvest. An abdominal wall binder may be used to aid in postoperative recovery in cases of a free tissue transfer. Although the rectus abdominis muscle is considered a work horse flap, its popularity has decreased slightly because of the lower donor site morbidity that other muscle and nonmuscle flaps have to offer.

Gracilis. The gracilis muscle is a very commonly chosen donor site for free tissue transfer to cover foot and ankle soft tissue de-

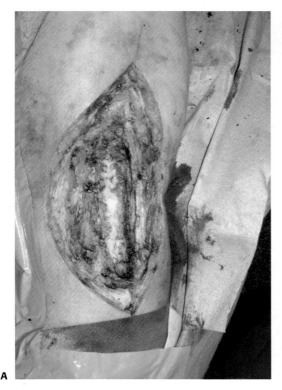
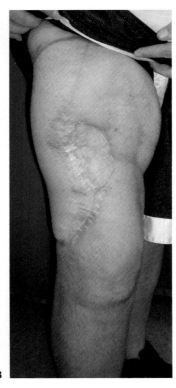

FIGURE 14-15 A. After resection of a recurrent liposarcoma in a radiated field in the thigh, there is extensive exposure of the femur and the scarred wound bed. **B.** Six months after a pedicled vertical rectus abdominis myocutaneous flap for soft tissue coverage. Anteriorly, a skin graft was used over a portion of the flap to minimize size of the skin paddle and facilitate abdominal wall closure.

A

B

fects.[322] Typically, the ipsilateral limb is chosen so that only one limb is immobilized. The blood supply to the muscle is from the medial femoral circumflex artery, which originates from the profunda femoris artery. The major pedicle can be identified 8 to 10 cm inferior to the pubic tubercle. The flap also has a minor arterial pedicle, which enters the muscle at the level of the midthigh. This artery originates from the superficial femoral artery. The muscle receives its innervation from the anterior branch of the obturator nerve. This branch can be harvested with the muscle if there are requirements for a functional muscle transfer.

The muscle is exposed through a medial thigh incision as it lies between the adductor longus medially and the semitendinous muscle inferiorly. It lies superficial to the adductor magnus. The gracilis may be confused with the sartorius and is differentiated from the sartorius and semimembranous by identification of its musculotendinous portion: At the level of the medial femoral condyle the gracilis consists of muscle and tendon, whereas the semimembranous is entirely composed of tendon and the sartorius is entirely muscular.

Once the major pedicle has been identified with loupe magnification and determined to be adequate for a microvascular anastomosis, the secondary pedicle is divided. The origin of the muscle and the branch of the obturator nerve are then divided. The muscle is left to perfuse on its major pedicle until the recipient vessels have been prepared for microvascular anastomosis. Before muscle transfer a final definitive débridement of the defect site is performed and the flap transfer is performed. (Figure 14-16).

Upper Extremity Reconstructive Options (Table 14-5)

Advances in microsurgery have expanded our reconstructive armamentarium over the last 3 decades, and the options for most soft tissue defects are now extensive. As innovations in flap design continue to develop, reconstructive algorithms move away from the traditional reconstructive ladder toward delivering composite flaps to provide the best possible reconstructive solution.[63] Although free flaps are often the preferred method of reconstruction, all surgeons should be familiar with other options for upper limb reconstruction. The major factors determining flap choice are location, size, and tissue involvement.[181]

Skin Grafting

As discussed previously, wounds with exposed muscle and subcutaneous tissue will accept skin grafts; however, exposure of

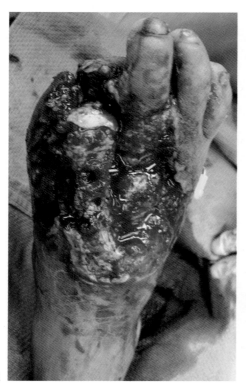

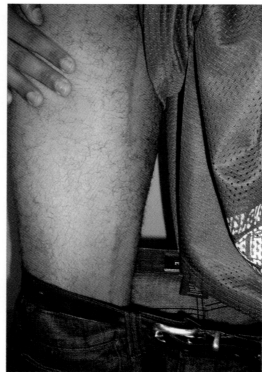

A

B

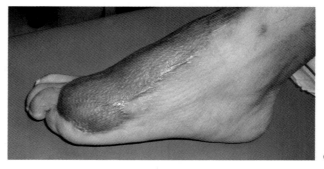

FIGURE 14-16 A. A gunshot wound to the dorsum of the foot with severe comminution of the metatarsals and loss of the hallux and second toe. **B.** The donor site after gracilis muscle harvest using two incisions and preserving a central skin bridge. **C.** One and a half years after gracilis muscle transfer for coverage of the dorsal foot wound.

C

TABLE 14-5	Reconstructive Options for the Upper Extremity
Palm	Radial forearm flap
	Ulnar forearm flap
	Free flap
	Groin flap
Dorsal hand	Radial forearm flap
	Posterior Interosseous flap
	Free flap
	Groin flap
Forearm	Radial forearm flap
	Posterior Interosseous flap
	Free flap
Elbow	Radial forearm flap
	Posterior interosseous flap
	Pedicled latissimus dorsi flap
	Anconeus muscle flap
	Reverse lateral arm flap
	Free flap
Humerus	Pedicled latissimus dorsi flap
	Scapular flap
	Parascapular flap

vital structures such as tendons devoid of paratenon, nerves, vessels, bone, and hardware requires flap coverage. Although a split skin graft (Figure 14-17) *will* typically survive when grafted onto major nerves, vessels, periosteum, and the paratenon large areas of exposed bone need durable coverage, nerves and vessels need robust protection, and the preservation of tendon excursion requires that the overlying tissue is not firmly adherent to the paratenon. Flap coverage is also indicated in situations in which there is a need for the restoration of sensation.

Fasciocutaneous Flaps

Within the upper extremities, fasciocutaneous flaps can be either pedicled or free. The two most common pedicled fasciocutaneous flaps used in the upper extremity are the radial forearm flap and the posterior interosseous flap. Both can be used in an anterograde or retrograde fashion and can provide thin pliable coverage for most defects involving the *dorsum of the hand, the palm, the forearm, and the elbow.*

Radial Forearm Flap. This can be used as local pedicled flap, or as a free flap from the contralateral limb. The radial artery gives off fasciocutaneous perforators along its length, to supply the radial two thirds of the forearm skin, and it also gives branches to the distal half of the radius. A flap measuring up to 15 × 35 cm can be raised as a fascial flap, a fasciocutaneous flap, or an osteocutaneous flap, in an antegrade or retrograde manner.[212] Palmaris longus, flexor carpi radialis, and the lateral and medial antebrachial nerves can also be included.[124,422] The pivot point can be as proximal as the origin of the radial artery, approximately 1 to 4 cm distal to the intercondylar line, or as distal as the wrist crease, allowing it to be used for defects anywhere from the elbow to the dorsum of the hand. The versatility of this flap and the relative ease in flap elevation have made it a workhorse flap for forearm and hand reconstruction.

An adequate collateral circulation to the hand *must* be confirmed before the flap is elevated. The patient should have a normal Allen's test to ensure safe flap harvest. If there is concern about the patency of the ulnar artery during the surgical procedure, the radial artery can be temporarily clamped, before flap division, and perfusion to the hand can be examined. The importance of checking collateral circulation to the hand when raising the flap from the already traumatized forearm cannot be overemphasized (Figure 14-18).

Posterior Interosseous Flap. The posterior interosseous flap was designed in an attempt to find alternatives to the radial forearm flap. The posterior interosseous artery, which this flap is based on, arises from the common interosseous artery in the antecubital fossa and passes dorsally through the interosseous membrane. The descending branch runs in the septum between the extensor carpi ulnaris and extensor digiti minimi, giving rise to several fasciocutaneous perforators to the skin. A fasciocutaneous flap up to 8 cm in width and 12 cm in length can be raised centered over a line drawn from the lateral epicondyle to the distal radioulnar joint.

The posterior interosseous branch of the radial nerve, which also runs in this septum, gives off its branches to the extensor digitorum communis and extensor carpi ulnaris at this level, and these branches are prone to injury when dissecting the flap. The posterior interosseus flap can also be used in a retrograde manner, making use of the collateral flow to the posterior interosseus artery through its distal anastomosis with the anterior interosseous artery. The principal advantages of this flap are as

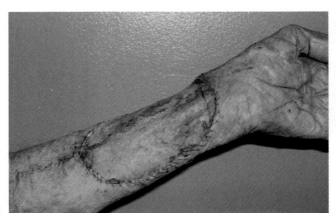

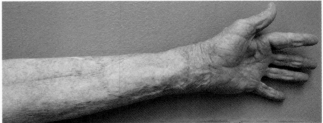

FIGURE 14-17 A split-thickness skin graft on the patient's forearm shown **(A)** 1 week and **(B)** 8 months after surgery.

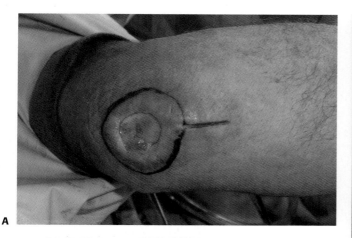

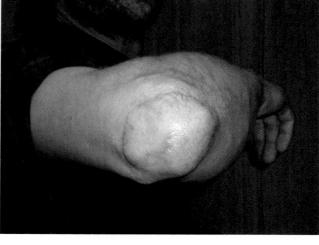

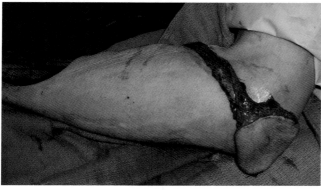

FIGURE 14-18 A. A 34-year-old man with chronic wound of the elbow with osteomyelitis of the olecranon, after a fall from a bike. **B.** Intraoperative view of radial forearm pedicled flap for elbow reconstruction. **C.** Appearance at 6 months postoperatively.

an alternative when the radial or ulnar artery has already been damaged or sacrificed, and when a thin pliable skin flap is needed.[13,272]

Free Fasciocutaneous Flaps

These flaps can be used anywhere throughout the upper extremity. If joints are to be crossed, fasciocutaneous flaps are much preferred as muscle flaps can undergo atrophy and restrict flexion and extension across joints. Some fasciocutaneous free flaps, such as the lateral arm flap and scapular flap, have limitations in size and overall thickness. If a larger skin island is needed, tissue expansion can be performed before flap transfer.

Scapular Flap. The scapular flap provides a large area of fasciocutaneous tissue based on the circumflex scapular branch of the subscapular artery.[374] This is an excellent choice for coverage of large wounds of the forearm. The dissection is relatively easy, and a flap of up to 10 × 25 cm (scapular flap) or 15 × 30 cm (parascapular flap) can be raised and used to reconstruct large defects of the forearm. For defects involving the radius or ulna, the scapular flap can be harvested as an osteocutaneous flap by incorporating the lateral part of the scapula, with very little extra morbidity.[396] Coverage can be extended even further by combining this flap with the latissimus dorsi or serratus anterior muscle flaps on one pedicle.[135,421] Donor sites of up to 7 to 8 cm width can usually be closed directly.

Parascapular Flap. This flap has similar characteristics to the scapular flap but is based on the descending branch of the circumflex scapular artery. Similarly, it provides a large area of pliable and relatively thin tissue for forearm coverage, but the donor site usually requires skin grafting.

Anterolateral Thigh Flap. This flap has been previously discussed. It has recently seen a huge gain in popularity as a free flap, with some authors proclaiming it as the ideal soft tissue flap. Its vascular pedicle is reliably at least 8 cm long and can be lengthened up to 20 cm, the flap is easy to design and can be made up to 40 × 20 cm large. It can be thinned to 3 to 5 mm without compromising its vascularity.[222,319] Some subcutaneous fat can be included to minimize tendon adhesion in the forearm and hand. Wei reviewed a series of 672 flaps with a success rate of over 98%.[408] Its many advantages make it a versatile flap that has been reliably used in upper limb reconstructions including defects of the forearm and elbow (Figure 14-19).[23,63,132,200,406]

Lateral Arm and Reverse Lateral Arm Flaps. The lateral arm flap is a fasciocutaneous flap perfused by the septal perforators of the posterior radial collateral artery, the terminal branch of the profunda brachii. An area of thin, pliable skin can be harvested up to 20 × 14 cm; however, only donor sites of 6 cm width or less can be closed primarily. This flap has a very short vascular leash, and its use as a pedicle flap is therefore limited, with most surgeons preferring to use it as a free flap. The radial recurrent artery provides the retrograde flow when this flap is used as a reversed flap. The reverse lateral arm flap has been used successfully for olecranon and antecubital coverage. As a

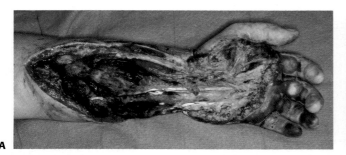

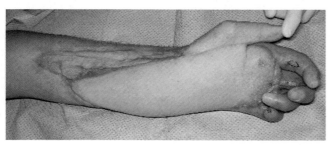

FIGURE 14-19 A. A 48-year-old man had a roller press injury resulting in loss of most of the palmar and forearm skin. **B.** Coverage was obtained with use of an anterolateral thigh flap. **C.** The flap appearance at 3 months, at the time of secondary flexor tendon tenolysis surgery.

free flap, the lateral arm flap is extremely versatile, capable of carrying bone (the humerus) and nerve (the posterior antebrachial nerve). Historically this has been a workhorse flap for upper extremity reconstruction.[18,298,392]

Muscle Flaps

The muscle flaps most commonly used to reconstruct the forearm, elbow, and humerus are the latissimus dorsi muscle, rectus abdominis muscle, serratus anterior muscle, and gracilis muscle. The choice of muscle flap depends on the size of the defect, donor site availability, and donor site morbidity.

Latissimus Dorsi. This is the largest single muscle flap and has a long pedicle (8 to 11 cm), making it one of the most versatile flaps for reconstructing large defects in the upper extremity. Additionally, in the majority of patients, the thoracodorsal trunk has two major divisions, allowing the surgeon to harvest only a portion of the muscle if a narrower flap is needed. Conversely, if a broader flap is required, the serratus muscle (± vascularized rib) can be raised with the flap, taking care to preserve its arterial supply, which arises as a branch from the thoracodorsal artery.

As a pedicle flap it can be transferred as a functional muscle to re-establish lost biceps or triceps function. It can be used in a pedicled fashion for coverage of the elbow, but should not be used for elbow defects extending distal to the olecranon. For such defects the radial forearm flap has been found to provide more reliable coverage.[72,200] Functional morbidity of the donor site is variable, with conflicting reports in the literature. If it is anticipated that a resulting degree of shoulder weakness (adduction, as in patients who crutch-walker and those with paraplegia) would have a major impact on the patient, then an alternative flap should be considered.

Serratus Anterior. The lower three slips of the serratus can be harvested with or without the underlying ribs, based on the thoracodorsal pedicle. This flap is a relatively thin, broad sheet

of muscle but can be very versatile when combined with components of rib or the latissimus dorsi muscle.

Rectus Abdominis. This muscle has a consistent vascular pedicle (5 to 7 cm) arising from the deep inferior epigastric vessels, and can be used for coverage in most situations encountered in forearm trauma. Its main disadvantage is the abdominal wall hernia, which can sometimes occur at the donor site, especially if the fascia is harvested.

Gracilis. This muscle is well suited for small defects requiring muscle coverage. The dominant pedicle is the medial femoral circumflex artery arising from the profunda femoris, and is usually approximately 6 to 7 cm in length. The muscle is unipennate, and has an excursion of approximately 10 cm. The main advantage of this muscle flap in the forearm is its use as a functional motor unit as discussed previously.

Distant Pedicled Flaps

Groin Flap. The workhorse flap before the advent of microsurgery was the groin flap. This flap is based on the superficial femoral circumflex artery, which arises from the femoral artery along with the superficial inferior epigastric artery in the femoral triangle.[290,364] The flap has shown great versatility. It may include the lateral cutaneous branch of the femoral nerve if a neurotized flap is required.[207] The flap may be combined with the abdominohypogastric flap for large defects or it may be expanded before transfer. If bone is required, a portion of the iliac crest may be harvested.[120,323] The flap may also be split longitudinally to cover defects on both aspects of the hand.[363]

The flap can often be divided safely at 3 weeks, especially if the wound is well healed at the flap's distal margin. Any compromise to the arm's vascularity, such as preoperative radiation or electrical injury may prolong the period of revascularization. If there is doubt about the vascularity of the flap prior to division, the pedicle may be occluded with a tourniquet.[420] The disadvantage of the groin flap is the mandatory period of hand

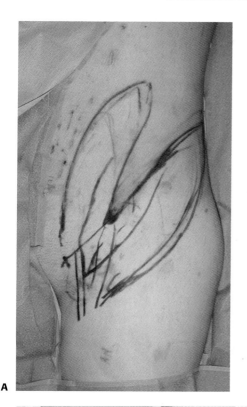

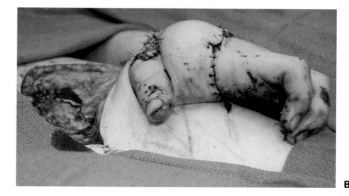

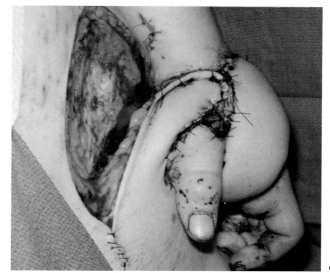

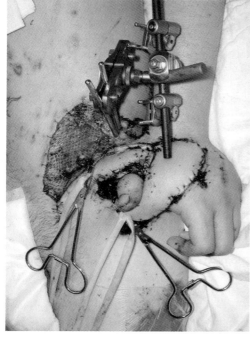

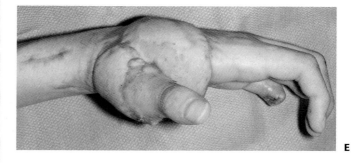

FIGURE 14-20 A. The groin flap can provide versatile coverage of the hand. Here a groin flap was designed with two separate skin paddles to cover both the palmar **(B)** and dorsal **(C)** surfaces of the hand. **D.** The hand was temporarily stabilized to the groin with the use of an external fixator. **E.** The appearance of the hand following flap division and insetting.

immobilization before pedicle division. This can result in hand, elbow, and shoulder stiffness. Despite this the groin flap still remains a reliable means of providing soft tissue coverage for large hand wounds without the need for microvascular experience (Figure 14-20).[290]

Upper Extremity Reconstructive Pearls
For free flap options, our preferred flaps for soft tissue reconstructions of the forearm are the anterolateral thigh flap and the scapular flap. If bone is required, the fibular osteocutaneous flap is a good match for the radius or ulna. Flaps based on the subscapular or thoracodorsal system, taken with rib are also very versatile for the reconstruction of smaller bony defects.*

Musculocutaneous flaps such as the latissimus dorsi and rectus abdominus flaps result in functional loss and donor site morbidity including, particularly in the abdomen, the potential for hernia formation. In addition, in the coverage of joint sur-

*References 23,134,135,169,190,209,230,264,372.

faces, muscle flaps tend to undergo fibrosis and atrophy over time, which may limit joint excursion, particularly when they are placed over the elbow or the dorsum of the hand. Muscle is still indicated for those circumstances involving osteomyelitis or soft tissue contamination.

POSTOPERATIVE CARE AND MONITORING OF PATIENTS AFTER FLAP TRANSFER

Free flap success is not always guaranteed at the completion of the case, as 5% to 25% of transferred flaps require re-exploration for microcirculatory compromise, which can be caused by arterial or venous thrombosis.[47,64,217] Free flaps salvage rates after thrombosis range from 42% to 85%.[64,216,233] Early recognition of vascular compromise has been shown to provide the best chance of successful flap salvage.[64,182,350]

Methods for monitoring free tissue transfers have advanced from clinical observation to implantable Doppler probes. The best method for monitoring has yet to be established. Clinical observation of the nonburied free flap remains the gold standard to which monitoring systems are generally compared.[105] Monitoring devices should ideally be sensitive enough to supersede clinical evidence of vascular thrombosis but specific enough to avoid unnecessary re-exploration. Here we review the current literature regarding monitoring methods and protocols.

Conventional Flap Monitoring Methods

Clinical Observation

In clinical observation, the flap is observed by assessing capillary refill, temperature, swelling, and flap color. Its use is confined to monitoring surface skin flaps and is less reliable in the monitoring of muscle flaps and buried flaps.[105] Capillary refill can be assessed by simply applying deep pressure to the transferred tissue and releasing using one's finger or the flat end of a surgical instrument and then releasing the pressure and evaluating capillary refill time, which is commonly 2 to 3 seconds. With increasing disturbance of the blood supply, a livid bluish discoloration (shortened capillary refill less than 2 seconds) or paleness of the flap (delayed capillary refill greater than 3 seconds) appears in a venous congested or ischemic flap, respectively. When these criteria cannot be reliably assessed or for confirmation, one may then use the pin prick test.

It is important to remember that for clinical observation to be effective, the person performing flap evaluation needs to be educated with regard to the signs of flap failure. Nursing units and young residents require annual in-service education to improve their diagnostic acumen, as these two groups are in constant flux in most medical centers.

Pin Prick Testing

The pin prick test is commonly used on flaps with a cutaneous component. The test is performed by puncturing the cutaneous paddle of the flap with a 24- or 25-gauge needle. The puncture should not be too deep into the tissue, and it should be in a portion of the flap that is not in close proximity to the vascular pedicle and microanastomosis. An indicator of flap viability is a stream of continuous bright red blood upon puncture. A congested flap will produce a continuous stream of dark venous blood. Care should be taken not to perform this test too frequently, particularly in patients on anticoagulants, because repeated puncture trauma may lead to a bruised flap, which may hinder further evaluation of the tissue. This test is certainly the least expensive of the various methods of flap monitoring.

Surface Temperature Monitoring

A difference of greater than 3°C between the surface temperature of the flap and the adjacent skin is associated with arterial compromise and a difference of between 1°C and 2°C is more indicative of venous compromise. A simple liquid crystal temperature probe may be placed on the flap tissue with a second probe placed on the adjacent normal skin. Temperature changes in flaps such as toe flaps placed on an extremity will be more accurate than flaps placed on the trunk, where the flap temperature may be a direct reflection of the body part on which it is placed.

Hand-Held Doppler Ultrasonography

Currently, there is no single adjunctive monitoring technique widely accepted as the method of choice, but the ultrasonography with handheld Doppler (5 to 8 MHz) is the most common technique in use.[204,365,399] Its most important limitation is differentiating between the recipient vessels and the flap's vascular pedicle because of their potential close proximity. A clinician may detect the Doppler signal of the recipient vessels instead of the signal from the flap's vascular pedicle, which may mislead the observer into believing that the flap's pedicle is patent when in reality a thrombosis has occurred. This limitation may be overcome by performing a Doppler ultrasound examination of an arterial signal within the flap tissue intraoperatively and then simultaneously compressing the donor (flap) artery to ensure that this is a true artery within the flap. Upon compression of the donor (flap) artery there should be loss of the arterial ultrasonic signal within the flap.

Handheld Doppler ultrasonography is also an effective method of determining the status of the vein of a flap. The Doppler signal of a vein is detected intraoperatively after flap revascularization and a suture may be placed to mark it. The venous sound is at times difficult to detect but when heard is a clear indication that the vein is patent. When a venous signal is detected, the flap is compressed and a "venous augment" sound should be heard.

Implantable Doppler (Doppler Ultrasonography)

The implantable Doppler device can measure blood flow across a microvascular anastomosis and is an effective tool to monitor flap perfusion and improve salvage rates, especially in buried flaps.[92] Initial research demonstrated a 3% false-positive rate, which led to unnecessary re-explorations, and a 5% false-negative rate when the probe was placed on the artery.[378] Further, up to a 5-hour delay was found between a venous obstruction and the loss of the arterial signal in large muscle flaps.[213] Best results occur if an implantable probe is placed on the vein instead of the artery allowing the detection of venous obstruction immediately followed by detection of arterial thrombosis.

Pulse Oximetry

The pulse oximeter consists of two light-emitting diodes that transmit two separate wavelengths of visible red (660 nm) and infrared (940 nm) light and a photodiode receiver. It can distinguish the difference in light absorption between oxyhemoglobin and reduced hemoglobin and thereby measure oxygen saturation. By the way of photoplethysmography the oximeter can identify pulsatile flow and will therefore provide a continuous display of both the pulse rate and arterial saturation. This is an excellent monitor for replanted and revascularized digits and toe-to-hand transfers.[145]

Laser Doppler

Light from a helium neon laser of uniform wavelength will penetrate 1.5 mm below the surface of the flap, and this light is reflected by the red blood cells moving within the capillaries enclosed within a 1-mm^3 volume of tissue. The frequency shift between the transmitted and reflected light is directly proportional to the velocity of capillary blood flow. This flow value provides an objective measurement of flap perfusion. Laser Doppler interpretation requires experience, as values differ depending on tissue type and patient. Furthermore, perfusion readings may fluctuate for any given patient because of physiologic microcirculation variation or artifacts. Therefore, the observer must monitor the trend rather than the absolute values. This method is limited to monitoring cutaneous circulatory phenomena, as the probe only penetrates 1.5 mm into the flap. Estimated sensitivity and specificity values have been reported at 93% and 94%, respectively, and this technique has been found to be superior to thermometry when used alone for the evaluation of replantations.[186]

 AUTHORS' PREFERRED METHOD

How often and for how long flap monitoring should be performed has been debated, but most series recommending a minimum of hourly monitoring for the first 24 to 48 hours after surgery.[184,234] The majority (greater than 80%) of vascular complications occur within the first 48 to 72 hours postoperatively.[217] Postoperative venous thrombosis is the most common vascular complication.[234] With these factors in mind our current recommendations for flap monitoring include:

1. Placement of an implantable venous Doppler probe when feasible.
2. Flap inspection every hour by experienced nursing staff for first 48 hours, moving to every 2 hours for the next 24 hours.
3. Discontinuation of flap monitoring after day 4, unless there are extenuating circumstances.

Anticoagulation Considerations in Free Flap Surgery

Ninety-six percent of reconstructive surgeons use some type of anticoagulation regimen after free tissue transfer, and in pedicled flap reconstruction the frequency of use is dependent on its vascular supply.[90,140] Unfortunately, there is no consensus on anticoagulation therapy after free tissue transfer, and a full discussion of all pertinent studies pertaining to postoperative anticoagulation is beyond the scope of this chapter. It is sufficient to say that scientific findings are often clouded by anec-

dotal experience. The three most common anticoagulants in use are aspirin, heparin, and dextran.

Aspirin, through its activity on the cyclooxygenase pathway, decreases the production of thromboxane and prostacyclin, both of which are powerful platelet aggregators. Aspirin's effectiveness in decreasing macrovascular graft occlusion has been clearly demonstrated in several studies.[2,21] The effective dose of aspirin to inhibit thromboxane while preserving some of the provasodilatory effects of prostacyclin function is relatively low, within the range of 50 to 100 mg per day.[78,81,412] Despite its use postoperatively to prevent thrombosis, aspirin's most beneficial effect may be when it is given several hours before surgery. The administration of aspirin 10 hours before surgery has been shown to result in a significant increase in vessel patency and a decrease in platelet aggregation.[339]

Heparin has been shown to provide a beneficial effect on anastomotic patency in animal models.[149] Large prospective randomized human trials are not yet in existence. Hematoma formation with the potential for flap loss has been linked to full systemic postoperative anticoagulation. In Pugh's retrospective study, the incidence of hematoma formation after lower-leg reconstruction and systemic anticoagulation with heparin was 66%.[317] The use of subcutaneous heparin or low molecular weight heparin (LMWH) is warranted for prevention of deep venous thrombosis, while also providing a benefit with regard to vessel patency. Khouri et al. found, in the largest multicenter prospective free flap tissue study, that only postoperatively administered subcutaneous heparin had a statistically significant effect on the prevention of postoperative free flap thrombosis.[217]

The combination of subcutaneous heparin and low dose aspirin has been shown to produce no increase in the rate of postoperative hematoma formation.[69] In our opinion, this combination of drugs provides a safe and economical means of providing thrombosis prophylaxis for routine free flap procedures. This combination therapy also provides the benefits of coronary protection and deep venous thrombosis prophylaxis.[77] Subcutaneous heparin does not require monitoring of coagulation factors, and both medications may be given without intravenous access. LMWH also provides the benefits of higher bioavailability, a longer plasma half-life, and a steady dose-response curve and it causes fewer cases of hematoma formation and thrombocytopenia when compared with unfractionated heparin.[19]

Finally, dextran, like heparin, has shown benefit in improving patency rates in the immediate preoperative period when given as a single preoperative bolus;[340,440] however, the effectiveness of prolonged administration is debatable.[315,334,338] An increasing number of reports have noted significant morbidity associated with the use of dextran and have questioned its use in routine microsurgical cases.[171,174] Complications from dextran administration can include renal failure, congestive heart failure, myocardial infarction, pulmonary edema, pleural effusion, and pneumonia.

Because flap failure rates are so small, large prospective randomized multicenter trials will be necessary to definitively decide which anticoagulation therapy is the most effective in preventing postoperative flap thrombosis. *Until that time we feel that a combination of low-dose aspirin and subcutaneous or low-molecular-weight heparin provide adequate flap protection with minimal associated morbidity and little additional cost.*[216]

Hemodynamic Management

Effective medical management of all patients with flaps will improve flap survival and prevent morbidity and mortality. From a cardiac standpoint, surgical patients with coronary artery disease or risk factors for coronary artery disease who undergo tissue transfer surgery should undergo an appropriate evaluation by their cardiologist or internist before surgical intervention. The administration of β-blockade with Atenolol has been shown to have reduced cardiovascular complications and mortality for up to 2 years in this patient population.[265] Hyperglycemia associated with relative insulin resistance or diabetes has been reported to increase the incidence of complications in the surgical patient.[119,287] For this patient population, intensive insulin therapy to maintain blood sugar levels between 80 and 110 mg/dL has been shown to substantially reduce morbidity and mortality from 8% to 4.6%.[400]

Patients must also have adequate intravenous fluid hydration in the perioperative period, and commonly a Foley catheter will be used to record and maintain a urine output of at least 50 cc/hour. In our institution, patients commonly are given nothing by mouth until the morning after surgery in the event reoperation is necessary. Hematocrit levels are kept at greater than 30% in patients with coronary artery disease and greater than 25% in those without it.

Flap Failures and Management

Despite our greatest efforts in reconstructive microsurgery, flap failure will occur. Flap failure can be partial or complete. It is important to recognize the cause of flap failure so it may be reversed or prevented in the next reconstructive attempt. Arterial insufficiency leading to flap complications can be recognized by decreased capillary refill, pallor, reduced temperature, and the absence of bleeding on pin prick testing. The complication can result from arterial spasm, vessel plaque, torsion of the pedicle, pressure on the flap, technical error with injury to the pedicle, a flap harvested that is too large for its blood supply, or small vessel disease secondary to diabetes or smoking. If pharmacologic agents do not relieve spasm at the level of arterial inflow, the vessel anastomosis should be redone.

Venous outflow obstruction can be suspected when the flap has a violaceous color and brisk capillary refill, and dark blood is seen after pin prick. Venous obstruction can occur as a result of flap edema, hematoma, tight closure over the pedicle, or pedicle torsion. Venous compromise will lead to microvascular thrombi, which will then compromise arterial flow if not promptly addressed. Conservative treatment in the acute phase, besides pharmacologic therapy as discussed, may include drainage of an underlying hematoma with suture release to decrease the pressure. Leeches may also be helpful if sufficient venous outflow cannot be established despite a patent venous anastomosis. The leeches work by biting the venous congested tissue and extracting blood via direct suction and injecting *hirudin medicinalis*, a potent anticoagulant present in their saliva. *Aeromonas hydrophilia* is an important microbe present in the leech, and prophylactic antibiotics (usually a second- or third-generation cephalosporin or an aminoglycoside or fluoroquinolone) must be given when patients are undergoing leech therapy.[91,276,413] Because of blood loss from the therapy, it is also important to check serial hemoglobin levels and have the patient typed and crossmatched for blood transfusion at all times.

Nonviable flaps should be débrided promptly as they may serve as a source of infection in an already compromised limb. The timing of removal is dependent on the recipient bed on which it was inset. Scarred, radiated, or dysvascular wound beds only provide minimal blood supply to the overlying flap tissue; therefore, upon flap compromise more flap tissue is lost.[343,411] If a second free flap is considered, obvious errors that led to the original flap compromise need to be recognized and avoided.

SPECIAL CONSIDERATIONS IN BONE AND SOFT TISSUE RECONSTRUCTION

Osteomyelitis

Classification and Radiographic Imaging

Long bone osteomyelitis presents a variety of challenges to the physician. The severity of the disease is staged depending upon the infection's particular features, including its etiology, pathogenesis, the extent of bone involvement, its duration, and host factors particular to the individual patient (infant, child, adult, or immunocompromised). Long bone osteomyelitis may be either hematogenous or caused by a contiguous spread of infection. A single pathogenic organism is almost always recovered from the bone in hematogenous osteomyelitis; *Staphylococcus aureus* is the most common organism isolated. A variety of multidrug resistant organisms (MDROs) continues to be a source of concern in arresting infection. The primary weapons to treat these infections are culture-specific antibiotics, aggressive débridement, muscle flaps, and bone grafts.

Osteomyelitis can be classified by duration (acute or chronic), pathogenesis (trauma, contiguous spread, hematogenous, or surgical), site, extent, or type of patient. Although several classifications of osteomyelitis have been described by different authors, the two most widely used in the medical literature and clinical practice are the classification systems by Waldvogel et al.[404] and Cierny et al.[74] Under the Waldvogel system, osteomyelitis is first described according to duration as either acute or chronic. Secondly, the disease is classified according to source of infection, as hematogenous when it originates from a bacteremia, or as contiguous focus when it originates from an infection in a nearby tissue. A final category of the classification is vascular insufficiency. One of the limitations of the Waldvogel classification system is that it does not consider infection originating from direct penetration of microorganisms into the bone, as may occur after trauma or surgery. In addition, it is an etiologic classification system that does not readily lend itself to guiding surgical or antibiotic therapy. Because of the wide variability in the etiology of osteomyelitis, a classification based upon the pathogenesis of the disease, such as that of the Waldvogel system, has limited value in clinical practice.

The second system is known as the Cierny-Mader classification (Table 14-6). It is a clinical classification based on anatomic, clinical, and radiographic features. It characterizes osteomyelitis as being in one of four anatomic stages. Stage 1, or medullary, osteomyelitis is confined to the medullary cavity of the bone. Stage 2, or superficial, osteomyelitis involves only the cortical bone and most often originates from a direct inoculation or a contiguous focus infection. Stage 3, or localized, osteomyelitis usually involves both cortical and medullary bone. In this stage the bone remains stable, and the infectious process does not

TABLE 14-6	Cierny-Mader Osteomyelitis Staging System

Anatomic Type
Stage 1: Medullary osteomyelitis
Stage 2: Superficial osteomyelitis
Stage 3: Localized osteomyelitis
Stage 4: Diffuse osteomyelitis

Physiologic Class
A Host: Normal host
B Host: Systemic compromise (Bs)*
Local compromise (Bl)*
Systemic and local compromise (Bls)*
C Host: Treatment worse than the disease

involve the entire bone diameter. Stage 4, or diffuse, osteomyelitis involves the entire thickness of the bone, with loss of stability, as in an infected nonunion. The Cierny-Mader system adds a second dimension, characterizing the host as either A, B, or C. The A hosts are patients without systemic or local compromising factors. B hosts are affected by one or more compromising factors. C hosts are patients so severely compromised that the radical treatment necessary would have an unacceptable risk/benefit ratio.

The diagnostic imaging of osteomyelitis can require the combination of diverse imaging techniques for an accurate diagnosis. Conventional radiography should always be the first imaging modality to start with, as it provides an overview of the anatomy and the pathologic conditions of the bone and soft tissues of the region of interest. Sonography is most useful in the diagnosis of fluid collections, periosteal involvement, and surrounding soft tissue abnormalities and may provide guidance for diagnostic or therapeutic aspiration, drainage, or tissue biopsy. Computed tomography (CT) can be a useful method to detect early osseous erosion and document the presence of a sequestrum, foreign body, or gas formation, but generally it is less sensitive than other modalities for the detection of bone infection. Magnetic resonance imaging (MRI) is the most sensitive and specific imaging modality for the detection of osteomyelitis. It provides superb anatomic detail and more accurate information regarding the extent of the infectious process and soft tissues involved. Nuclear medicine imaging is particularly useful in identifying multifocal osseous involvement.

Local and Systemic Antimicrobial Therapy

In the majority of cases, antibiotic treatment will be directed on the basis of cultures or deep bone biopsy, and antibiotic sensitivity tests.[75] After cultures have been obtained, a parenteral course of antibiotics is begun to cover clinically suspected pathogens. When the organism is identified, a specific antibiotic or antibiotics are selected through sensitivity testing. If immediate débridement surgery is required before cultures can be obtained, broad-spectrum antibiotics may be initiated empirically, and the regimen modified when the results of cultures and sensitivity tests are known. Initial antibiotic therapy for long-bone osteomyelitis may consist of either nafcillin or clindamycin (or vancomycin when methicillin-resistant *S. epidermidis* or *S. aureus* [MRSA], or *Enterococcus* sp. are suspected) and ciprofloxacin (except with children, in whom an aminoglycoside should

be used). Levofloxacin has been used, but serum levels often fall below minimum inhibitory concentrations, and at present dosing has failed in both a human and animal osteomyelitis study.[150,360] Bone requires 3 to 4 weeks to revascularize after débridement surgery, and thus antibiotics are used to treat live infected bone and protect it as it undergoes revascularization. After the last major débridement, the patient is treated with 4 to 6 weeks of antimicrobial therapy, and outpatient intravenous therapy may be used.[76,262]

Antibiotic therapy may be directed with regard to the stage of the infection. With Cierny-Mader Stage 1 osteomyelitis, children may be treated with antibiotic therapy alone, because their bones are highly vascular and respond effectively to antibiotics. In adults, a Stage 1 infection is more refractory to therapy and usually is treated with both antibiotics and surgery. With Stage 2 infections, the patient may be treated with a 2-week course of antibiotics after superficial débridement and soft tissue coverage. In these cases, the arrest rate is approximately 80%. In Stages 3 and 4, the patient is treated with 4 to 6 weeks of antimicrobial therapy dated from the last major débridement. At this stage of the disease, most antibiotic regimens will fail without adequate débridement regardless of the duration of therapy. Even after necrotic tissue has been débrided, the remaining bed of tissue must be considered contaminated.

Microbiologists now recognize that a single method, regardless of whether it is conventional or automatic, cannot test all antimicrobial agents against all microorganisms and detect all patterns of resistance.[324] The strategy of using multiple susceptibility testing methods continues to evolve, particularly with regard to Gram-negative organisms. A current issue is the susceptibility testing of the polymyxin class of antimicrobial agents (colistin or polymyxin B and polymyxin B) for the therapy of infections caused by multidrug-resistant isolates of *Pseudomonas aeruginosa* and *Acinetobacter* spp.[369] Guidelines for testing Gram-negative control strains with polymyxin B and colistin have been established for broth microdilution.[206] Currently, however, guidelines do not exist for disc-diffusion testing of polymyxins. Synergy testing represents a shift in the approach by microbiology laboratories driven by the growing challenge of multiresistant bacteria and the need to correlate in vitro tests with in vivo outcomes.

However, the present method of antibiotic sensitivity testing is wholly lacking with respect to biofilm. Clinical microbiologists test antimicrobial efficacy against planktonic and non-biofilm agar based growth cultures. Therefore, the biofilm phenotype and the associated 50- to 500-fold increase in antibiotic resistance (compared with their planktonic counterparts) are often ignored. The result is that antimicrobial therapy is prescribed against a nonbiofilm infection and what is effective against planktonic infections is not always the same as what is effective against a biofilm infection.

Surgical management of osteomyelitis is often challenging. Adequate surgical débridement decreases the bacterial load, removes necrotic tissues, and gives a chance for the host immune system and antibiotics to arrest the infection. Adequate débridement may leave a large bony defect or dead space. Appropriate management of dead space is essential to arrest the disease and maintain the bone's integrity. The objective of dead space management is the replacement of dead bone and scar tissue with durable vascularized tissue. Complete wound closure should be attained whenever possible, and local tissue flaps or free flaps may be used to fill dead space.[262] An alternative technique is to place cancellous bone grafts beneath local or transferred tissues until structural integrity is improved. This technique requires careful preoperative planning to conserve the patient's limited cancellous bone reserves. Open cancellous grafts without soft tissue coverage are useful when free tissue transfer is not an option and local tissue flaps are inadequate. Antibiotic-impregnated acrylic beads or antibiotic-loaded cement also may be used to sterilize and temporarily maintain dead space.[214] The beads are usually removed after 2 to 4 weeks and replaced with a cancellous bone graft. The antibiotics used in the beads are most often vancomycin, tobramycin, and gentamicin.[259] Chronic osteomyelitis of bone with nonunion or bone defects is traditionally treated by a two-stage procedure involving initial débridement and antibiotic delivery, with initial external fixation, and then definitive internal fixation. Antibiotic cement-coated interlocking intramedullary nails can help convert two-stage processes into a single-stage procedure and can be used in patients who are not ideal candidates for external fixation, as well as in patients who do not want to have an external fixator applied.

Considerations in Reconstruction after Eradication

A commonly quoted study regarding muscle flaps and their bacterial fighting potential is by Calderon,[54] which showed that muscle flaps are able to control a 10-fold higher bacterial count than fasciocutaneous flaps and also improve antibiotic delivery to the wound site. What is poorly understood is that this study compared random pattern fasciocutaneous flaps to axial pattern muscle flaps. Therefore this is a flawed comparison because the vascular supply is completely different. In a recent study by Yazar et al. comparing lower limb wounds reconstructed with free fasciocutaneous or free muscle flaps in a total of 177 cases, there was no difference in outcomes or infection rates.[429] This highlights the important role of adequate débridement, regardless of the type of flap used.

Defects smaller than 6 cm can be bridged with conventional autogenous bone grafts such as corticocancellous iliac crest graft.[372,394] Defects greater than 6 cm will likely require distraction osteogenesis with Ilizarov frames.[148] or a vascularized bone graft. Vascularized bone grafts have become an important tool for the reconstructive surgeon dealing with the management of long bone defects or difficult nonunions. They are especially important in the setting of osteomyelitis treatment because they combine the advantages of viable cancellous autografts with the stability of cortical analogues, while leaving the nutrient blood supply intact. Indications for their use include skeletal defects more than 6 cm in length,[252] defects associated with a poor soft tissue envelope, and in cases in which smaller sized nonvascularized bone grafts have failed to incorporate. Vascularized bone grafts incorporate into the recipient site through a different process than avascular grafts. The vascularized grafts bypass the process of creeping substitution, which involves necrosis of the graft, resorption, and new bone formation. They maintain their mass, architecture, and biomechanical strength. Furthermore, the transferred vascularized bone has the ability to hypertrophy, especially in the lower extremity, because of increased mechanical loading. Available donor bones to be used for vascularized bone grafts include the fibula, ilium, scapula, and rib.[430]

The Management of Segmental Bony Defects

When bone defects are present there are three basic reconstruction options: distraction osteogenesis (Ilizarov technique), nonvascularized bone grafting, or vascularized bone grafting. The specific technique employed is dependent on the size of the defect, the quality of the soft tissue envelope, and the location of the defect.

Distraction Osteogenesis (Ilizarov Technique)

Distraction osteogenesis was popularized by Ilizarov, who in the western Siberian city of Kurgan, discovered that normal tissue could be generated under carefully applied tension. [193–196] The effect of the tension-stress effect on bone resulted in neovascularization, increased metabolic activity, and cellular proliferation, similar to but not identical to normal enchondral ossification at the physis. The resulting fibrous tissue in between the distracted bone segments ossifies in an orderly fashion, resulting in structurally sound bone. The soft tissues concomitantly grow linearly in response to the applied tension.[199]

The Ilizarov technique employs a modular system of rings that are held in place by fine wires that are crossed and secured to the ring. The wires are tensioned to between 60 and 130 kg. A series of rings are constructed and bridged together with threaded posts, each with a distraction or compression device that can be adjusted every several hours to effect compression or distraction. Many modifications to this system have been described.

When applied to bone loss, the defect of long bones can be filled with one of two methods: by acutely shortening the bone and then gradually lengthening it to restore the original bone length, or transporting bone either proximal or distal to the bone defect to gradually fill in the defect.[98,99,147,148]

In addition to application of the external ring fixator device, a free tissue transfer can be performed to address complex lower extremity bone injury with significant soft tissue defects. In the acute setting, the external ring fixator or modifications of the fine wire fixators can be applied as the primary management of the fracture. When these devices are applied it is imperative that if soft tissue coverage is required, discussions between the microsurgeon and orthopaedic surgeon occur early in the care of the injured extremity. The fixation can also be used as a means of transporting bone to fill in a segmental defect or a nonunion in chronic cases.

Nonvascularized Bone Grafts

Nonvascularized bone grafts include autograft as well as allograft tissues. They are ideal for small defects and voids and can be obtained from a number of anatomic locations and are typically cancellous or corticocancellous in composition. Autografts are superior in general to allograft material. For most bone defects of less than 6 cm with a well vascularized bed, adequate soft tissue coverage and absence of infection, a conventional cancellous or corticocancellous bone graft is generally recommended.[34] The most common areas for nonvascularized autograft bone harvest include the iliac crest (anterior or posterior), distal radius, and olecranon.[44] Cancellous bone has greater inductive capacity than cortical bone and should be used unless mechanical stability is required.

The process of bone graft incorporation is by "creeping substitution," a process in which vascular ingrowth gradually occurs with resorption and replacement of the necrotic bone graft.[28] Creeping substitution results in rapid revascularization in small cancellous grafts, but is slow and incomplete in cortical bone. As much as 40% to 50% of lamellar bone remains necrotic, and the revascularization process that does occur causes significant mechanical weakening because of bone resorption at 6 to 12 months.[34,49,366] Allografts, like autografts, must also be replaced by living bone. They are replaced more slowly and less completely, and they invoke a local and systemic immune response that diminishes the stimulus of new bone formation. This effect may be diminished by freezing, freeze drying, irradiating or decalcifying the graft, or eliminated with the use of immunosuppressive drugs.* Structural nonvascularized grafts of all types have substantial problems with fatigue fracture, even years after the surgical procedure. Successful grafting requires a well-vascularized bed, adequate immobilization, and protection from excessive stress by rigid internal fixation.[112]

Vascularized Bone Grafts

Unlike conventional bone grafts, the cellular elements of vascularized bone remain alive and dynamic in its new site. Because of its preserved circulation, cell viability is greater than in conventional grafts,[16,32] obviating the need of the gradual creeping substitution of living bone into a "dead" bone.[28,34,49] During healing, extensive osteopenia is not seen with vascularized bone grafts as it is in conventional bone grafts.[88] Vascularized grafts have improved strength, healing and stress response as compared with nonvascularized bone grafts.† The incidence of stress fracture is lower than in massive structural autografts or allografts.[112,169,312,367,410] Finally, union is more rapid, and bone hypertrophy in response to applied stress may occur with time.[130] Bone healing is more likely in difficult circumstances including scarred or irradiated beds, or in an avascular bone bed.[127,128]

In addition to superior cell survival, maintained circulation, and mechanical properties, vascularized grafts have other significant advantages over conventional grafts. These include the possibility to restore longitudinal growth by inclusion of the growth plate,[41,388,436] revascularize necrotic bone,‡ improve local blood flow in scarred soft tissue beds,[314,384] and reconstruct composite tissue loss in one procedure by the inclusion of skin, muscle, tendon, nerve, and other tissues with the bone graft.

Vascularized Bone Graft Indications. Based upon the information reported in the preceding, it would seem that vascularized autografts would be ideal for grafting under most circumstances. Their use as free tissue transfers is technically demanding, however, and pedicle grafts are often more limited in dimension and pedicle length and hence indications. Prolonged operative times and extensive dissection increase the risk of complications, and donor site morbidity may be significant. Therefore, for bone defects less than 6 to 8 cm with normal soft tissues, conventional techniques remain the method of choice under many circumstances.

The principal advantages of a vascularized autogenous graft

are its largely cancellous nature and the large amount of soft tissue that may be raised with the bone as a combined osteomusculocutaneous flap. In such flaps, a more reliable skin flap may be obtained with inclusion of both superficial and deep circumflex iliac vessels. The advantages of the osteocutaneous flap include the ability to: (i) supply vascularized bone to what is frequently a poor recipient bed for a bone graft, (ii) reconstruct both soft tissue and bony defects simultaneously, and (iii) be used in facilities without a capability for microvascular surgery when used as a pedicle flap for the upper extremity.[323] It may also be used for smaller defects.

Segmental Bone Loss. Vascularized transfer is indicated in segmental bone defects larger than 6 to 8 centimeters due to tumor resection,* traumatic bone loss,† osteomyelitis, or infected nonunion.‡

Vascularized transfer in smaller defects is reasonable in cases in which "biologic failure" of bone healing is likely or has already occurred.[288] Examples include persistent nonunion after conventional treatment, poorly vascularized bone and/or its soft tissue bed because of scarring, infection or irradiation, and congenital pseudarthrosis.[9,270,301,312,397,409]

Other indications include osteonecrosis, composite tissue loss requiring complex reconstruction, joint arthrodesis in exceptional circumstances, and the need for longitudinal growth with physeal transfer.

Fibula. The fibula is the most commonly used vascularized bone graft because its structure and shape are appropriate for diaphyseal reconstruction (Figure 14-21). A long, straight segment of 26 to 30 cm in length can be harvested, and osteosynthesis can be securely obtained to the recipient bone. The blood supply to the fibula, as to other long bones, is derived normally from a nutrient artery via radially oriented branches that penetrate the cortex and anastomose with the periosteal vessels. The resulting blood flow is centrifugal from medulla to cortex. This arrangement is the norm for the fibula, which has a single nutrient vessel entering its middle third from the peroneal artery. Additional periosteal branches from the peroneal and anterior tibial artery also supply the diaphysis.[138] The proximal epiphysis is supplied by an arcade of vessels, of which the lateral inferior genicular vessels are the most important.[388] This vessel must be anastomosed if physeal growth is desired after transfer of the fibular head.[41,388]

The vascularized bone may be transferred with a fasciocutaneous skin paddle of up to 10×20 cm. This is possible because of a series of fasciocutaneous or myocutaneous perforators from the peroneal artery that typically pierce the soleus muscle adjacent to the lateral intermuscular septum.[228,434] The location of the perforators may be determined in the operating room prior to skin incision with the use of a Doppler ultrasound stethoscope. Osteomuscular flaps including the flexor hallucis longu or, portions of the soleus or peroneal muscles may also be raised using the same peroneal artery pedicle.[29,67,68] The peroneal pedicle has a length of 6 to 8 cm, and an arterial diameter of 1.5 to 3.0 mm.

---

*References 142,144,198,284,306,307,357,428.
†References 16,32,33,61,107,136,352,353,438,442.
‡References 191,242,263,271,326,356,366,376,393,395,438.

*References 3,108,127,128,137,153,243,263,277,286,300,321,416–418.
†References 35,114,136,169,183,192,263,296,299,313,410,415.
‡References 35,169,178,179,205,208,278,285,321.

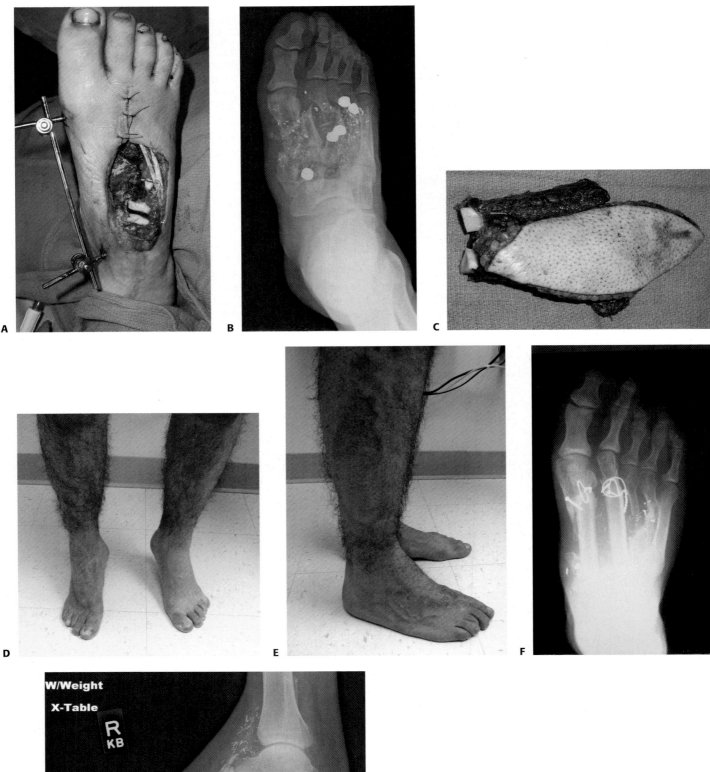

FIGURE 14-21 A,B. Following a gunshot wound to the foot, there was loss of the first and second metatarsals and an extensive dorsal foot wound. **C.** Intraoperative view of the fibular osteocutaneous flap. **D–G.** Clinical photographs and x-rays 16 months following the free fibular osteocutaneous flap for first and second metatarsal ray reconstruction. The patient was able to ambulate without difficulty and to play soccer.

Multiple series have reported the successful salvage of the upper and lower extremities with the use of the free fibula flap in cases of osteomyelitis,[407] pathologic fracture,[128] segmental bone loss of the femur,[407] tibia,[416] radius and ulna,[5,423] humerus,[6] and pelvis (Figure 14-22).[289] The bone is capable of hypertrophying over time through a process of fracture and callous healing.[407] In addition single or multiple osteotomies may be made in the bone as long as one preserves a periosteal sleeve and the nutrient vessel. This then allows for double fibular strut reconstruction in cases of segmental bony injuries.[65,205,407]

The flap is typically harvested under tourniquet control through a lateral approach with the patient in the supine or lateral position. Preoperative vascular studies, although controversial in the literature, have been very useful to us in preoperative planning in cases of posttraumatic reconstruction and in patients with peripheral vascular disease.[104,256] We obtain a CT angiogram in all patients in preparation for free fibular transfer. Unlike a formal angiogram, a CT angiogram adds no additional morbidity while providing information on inflow and outflow vessels in both legs. In 10% of the population the peroneal artery is the dominant arterial supply to the leg, and is referred to as the peroneal arteria magna; in such cases the contralateral leg should be considered for graft harvest.[104,256]

The incision is centered over the posterior margin of the fibula in a line running from the fibular head to the lateral malleolus. We have found it helpful to always include a skin paddle in the flap design; it facilitates closure as well as postoperative flap monitoring. Inclusion of a cuff of soleus muscle or flexor hallucis longus muscle (FHL) can improve the reliability of the skin paddle if skin perforators are small. Dissection is initiated between the plane of the soleus and peroneal muscles. Once the fibula is visualized laterally the peroneal nerve is identified and protected as dissection then continues superficial to the periosteum in a medial direction (Figure 14-23). The interosseous membrane is incised. The bone is then divided proximally and distally with the use of a Gigli saw or sagittal saw, taking care to protect the surrounding neurovascular structures. Six centimeters of the distal fibula must remain intact to stabilize the ankle. In the skeletally immature patients we always perform a syndesmosis at the lateral malleolus after fibula harvest.[291] Six centimeters of fibula bone is also preserved proximally (below the head of the fibula) to preserve the stability of the knee. This is achieved by maintaining the attachment of the tibia to the fibula, and the attachments of the biceps femoris muscle and the fibular collateral ligament to the head of the fibula. The proximal part of the fibula hosts parts of the origins of the peroneus longus, the extensor digitorum longus, the extensor hallucis longus, the soleus, and the tibialis posterior muscles. Minimizing dissection at the level of the fibular head will also help to avoid injury to the peroneal nerve.

Once the bone has been divided, the peroneal artery is identified distally deep to the tibialis posterior muscle and just dorsal to the FHL. The artery is divided and ligated distally. Dissection proceeds proximally to the peroneal–posterior tibial arterial bifurcation. Here the artery is ligated distal to the junction, preserving the posterior tibial artery. The surgeon should always verify the position of the tibial nerve and posterior tibial artery before ligation of the peroneal vessels.

If a skin paddle is taken with the fibular graft, a meshed skin graft is always used to cover the donor site; a tight primary closure can increase the risk of compartment syndrome within the donor leg. Meticulous closure of the donor site, with particular attention to the flexor hallucis longus muscle, is critical to decreasing donor limb morbidity. Patients are typically able to resume pain free weight-bearing ambulation 4 to 6 weeks after fibular harvest.

Bone fixation using a fibular graft needs to be performed with care, as inadvertent screw placement can injure or avulse the pedicle or nutrient vessels. Plates applied to the surface of the fibula should use unicortical screws and ideally the plate and screws should be placed on the lateral surface of the fibula, away from the vascular pedicle. The periosteum at the bone/plate interface should not be stripped and only minimal periosteal stripping should be performed at the points of screw insertion. The bone to bone contact between the fibula and recipient site can be maximized by creating step cuts, or the fibula can be telescoped into the recipient bone when the size is appropriate, such as the femur or humerus. Spanning plates are ideal as they allow for firm fixation above and below the intercalated fibula, yet allow for unicortical purchase of the fibula for stabilization.[381]

Iliac Crest. The iliac crest receives a dual blood supply from the superficial circumflex iliac artery and deep circumflex iliac artery (DCIA).[36] Of the two, the DCIA system is most important.[345] Musculocutaneous perforators penetrating the abdominal wall 1 cm proximal to the iliac crest provide its nutrition. In the experience of several authors, the skin paddle has been less reliable than a standard groin flap, particularly if slightly rotated in relation to the underlying bone.[36,138,344] Its size, when based on the DCIA, is quite variable, ranging from 7 × 10 to 15 × 30 cm. The entire iliac bone, however, is well supplied by the DCIA via multiple perforating arteries at the points of muscle attachment.[302] It remains the pedicle of choice for osteocutaneous flaps, although double-pedicle flaps have been described using both the superficial and deep circumferential iliac vessels and may be desirable.[228]

Although the entire crest may be harvested, it has a practical limit of 10 cm in length as a vascularized graft because of its curved shape. It is relatively less suited for diaphyseal reconstruction than the fibula, as remodeling to tolerate weightbearing is prolonged.[367] Further, osteosynthesis is difficult and weak.

Vascularized Periosteal Grafts. Periosteal grafts have been demonstrated experimentally to produce predictable new bone formation, provided they have adequate vascularity.[223,379] Bone formation after free vascularized transfer of periosteum may be enhanced by enclosing a cancellous bone graft in a periosteal wrap.[332] A variety of donor sites have been identified, including clavicle, fibula, ilium, humerus, tibia and femur, among others.* In the upper extremity, thin corticoperiosteal grafts and small periosteal bone grafts harvested from the supracondylar region of the femur have proved to be of great use, based on either the descending genicular or medial superior genicular artery and vein (Figure 14-24).[357] This graft is elastic and can be readily conformed to the shape of small tubular bones. It has been successfully used for clavicle, humerus, and forearm applica-

*References 87,106,241,311,335,373,435,437,441.

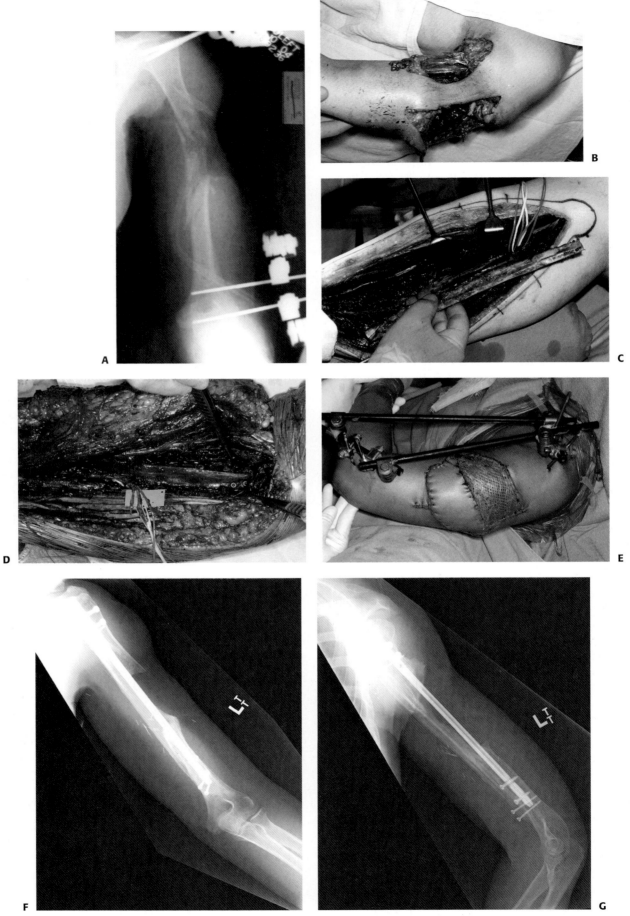

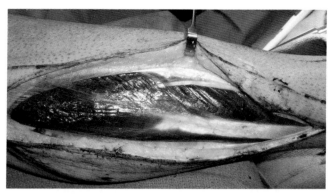

FIGURE 14-23 The superficial peroneal nerve is shown in the lateral compartment of the right leg during free fibula osteoseptocutaneous flap harvest.

tions, including pathologic fractures from radiation necrosis and other recalcitrant nonunions.[106]

Rib Plus Serratus and Latissimus Dorsi.

The rib, although used in early reports,[48,176] is generally not suitable for upper extremity reconstruction because of its membranous, weak structure and curved shape.[299] When based on its anterior internal mammary or supracostal arterial blood supply, only periosteal vessels are supplied.[176] The posterior rib graft, which includes its nutrient artery, requires ligation of the dorsal branch of the posterior intercostal artery.[302] Because this vessel supplies the spinal cord, the potential for causing paraplegia exists. Further, dissection is difficult and usually requires a thoracotomy.

Composite vascularized bone grafts including a muscle flap with vascularized bone graft on a single pedicle have multiple advantages, including the ability to have a vascularized bone graft and then cover it with healthy muscle. One such vascularized bone graft and muscle flap composite graft is the rib, serratus anterior, and latissimus dorsi flap.[219,252,294,309,380,430] Based on the thoracodorsal vessel and its branches to the serratus and latissimus, up to two nonadjacent ribs can be harvested with the overlying serratus muscle which provides the vascularity to the bone. A significant length of rib can be harvested and by making a corticotomy on its concave side, the curved rib can be straightened to be applied to a long bone or long bone defect (Figure 14-25). Hypertrophy of the ribs, in comparison to a fibular graft, does occur with time.

Nerve Injuries Associated with Fractures

Much of our modern understanding of the treatment of acute nerve injuries comes from the works of Seddon, which stemmed from the treatment of World War II patients.[349] Seddon introduced a simple classification of traumatic nerve injuries: neurapraxia, which was minimal injury with localized ischemic demyelination of the nerve; axonotmesis, characterized by interruption of the axons and their myelin sheath with the endoneurial tubes remaining intact; and neurotmesis, which is a completely severed nerve or one that is so seriously disorganized that spontaneous regeneration is impossible. Sunderlund in 1951 proposed a five-level classification that related to the internal structure of the nerve; however, it relied on pathologic examination of the nerve, which is quite impractical in the trauma setting.[377]

The treatment of the injured nerve is dependent on the type of injury to it (neurapraxic, axonotmetic, neurotmetic), the time from the injury, the soft tissue bed quality, the defect size if the nerve is transected, and associated nerve/muscle injuries. In acute fractures with nerve injury, there is tremendous debate on whether to explore or observe. Depending on the energy of the trauma, the decisions may vary. In particular, debate continues regarding treatment of radial nerve injury associated with distal humeral fractures (see Chapter 34).* Generally in acute closed fractures, observation of the nerve injury with serial examination for 3 to 6 months should be undertaken. If no recovery is seen, electrodiagnostic testing should be considered as early as 6 weeks postinjury. If no improvement is observed by 4 to 6 months, exploration with interposition nerve grafting or alternatively nerve transfers should be considered.

In injuries were the nerve is obviously sectioned with a high degree of trauma (i.e., not a sharp laceration) with associated soft tissue injuries, the nerve ends should be tagged and the soft tissue and bone injury addressed. The greatest challenge is the determination of the zone of injury of the nerve.† If acute nerve grafting is to be performed, resecting the injured portion is imperative. Unfortunately, intraoperative assessment by histologic section, touch, or visualization of the injured nerve cannot inform us of the zone of injury. Delay of a few weeks allows the development of intraneural fibrosis, and allows tactile and pathologic visualization of the zone of injury; however, the scarred tissues make the surgical reconstruction more difficult. If acute soft tissue reconstruction is performed, and a delayed nerve reconstruction is planned, the surgeon should consider placing the nerve to be reconstructed in a location where it can be easily accessed. Finally, if more than 6 to 12 months pass between injury and reconstruction, tendon transfers or free

---

*References 93,109–111,123,173,189,197,218,239,255,320,327,354, 359,361.
†References 96,97,116,246,258,386,402.

FIGURE 14-22 A,B. A 44-year-old woman sustained a gunshot wound to the left humerus resulting in a large entrance and exit wound (greater than 15 cm each) with segmental bone loss of the humerus exceeding 10 cm in length. The fractures were temporarily stabilized with external fixation and the soft tissue defect addressed with an ipsilateral free latissimus dorsi flap. **C–E.** Once the soft tissues were stabilized, a free vascularized fibula was used to bridge the bony defect after an intramedullary nail had been placed. **F,G.** The fibula was incorporated into the proximal and distal ends of the humerus by 3 months, resulting in a salvaged and very functional upper extremity.

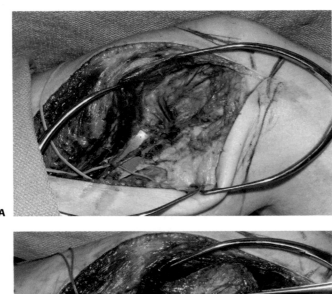

FIGURE 14-24 Medial femoral condyle corticoperiosteal grafts can be used to span shorter defects or be used to wrap around difficult fractures to provide a vascularized bone graft option. After elevating the vastus medialis, the medial femoral condyle is exposed to demonstrate a ring of periosteal vessels based on the descending genicular or medial superior genicular artery and vein **(A)**, a cortico-cancellous graft is elevated **(B)**. **C,D.** The graft is quite flexible and can be molded around bones at the recipient site.

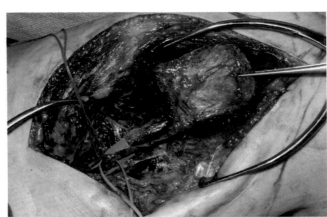

A

B

C

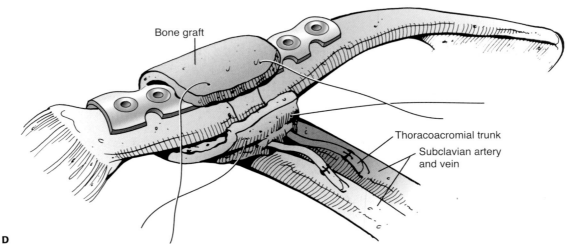

Bone graft

Thoracoacromial trunk

Subclavian artery and vein

D

functioning muscle transfers should be considered as there is a time dependent, irreversible degradation of the motor end-plate that occurs after motor nerve injury.[358]

Brachial Plexus Injuries

Treatment recommendations for complete nerve root avulsions have varied widely over the past 50 years, and the results of treatment have been reported as fair to dismal. After World War II, the standard approach was surgical reconstruction by shoulder fusion, elbow bone block, and finger tenodesis.[177] In the 1960s transhumeral (above elbow) amputation combined with shoulder fusion in slight abduction and flexion was advocated.[122] Yeoman and Seddon noted the tendency for injured

patients to become "one-handed" within 2 years of injury, which led to a dramatic reduction in successful outcomes regardless of the treatment approach.[430] Their retrospective study revealed no good results from the primitive surgical reconstruction of that era, but predominantly good and fair outcomes when amputation plus shoulder fusion were performed within 24 months of injury. They also noted that the loss of glenohumeral motion caused by brachial plexus injuries limited the effectiveness of body-powered prostheses and that manual laborers seemed to accept hook prostheses much more readily than did office workers with similar injuries. Although these observations remain valid today, there have been advances in brachial plexus reconstruction that have yielded outcomes superior to the his-

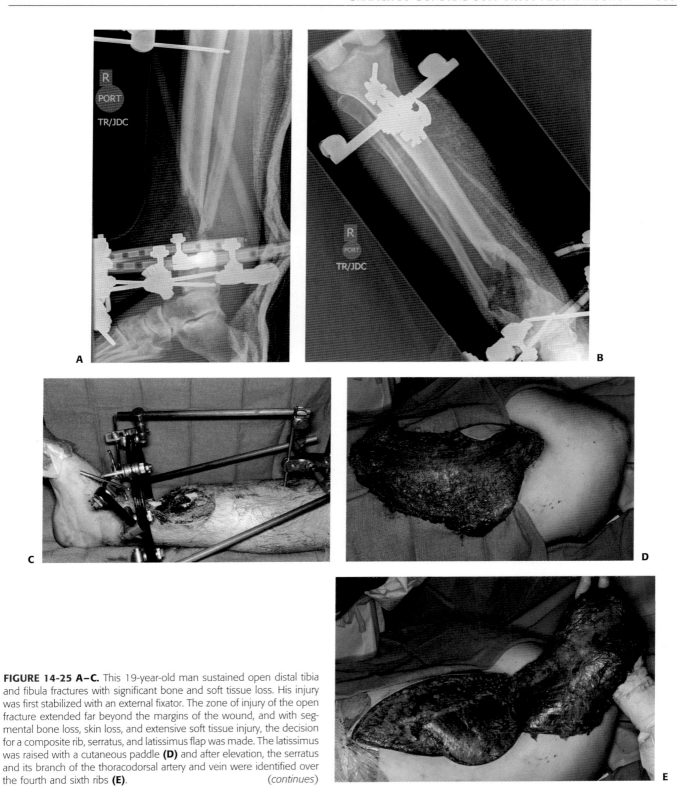

FIGURE 14-25 A–C. This 19-year-old man sustained open distal tibia and fibula fractures with significant bone and soft tissue loss. His injury was first stabilized with an external fixator. The zone of injury of the open fracture extended far beyond the margins of the wound, and with segmental bone loss, skin loss, and extensive soft tissue injury, the decision for a composite rib, serratus, and latissimus flap was made. The latissimus was raised with a cutaneous paddle **(D)** and after elevation, the serratus and its branch of the thoracodorsal artery and vein were identified over the fourth and sixth ribs **(E)**.   (*continues*)

torical results. A better understanding of the pathophysiology of nerve injury and repair, as well as the recent advances in microsurgical techniques, have allowed reliable restoration of elbow flexion and shoulder abduction in addition to useful prehension of the hand in some cases. The specific treatment of these injuries is beyond the scope of this chapter; however, there are multiple modalities, including nerve grafting, nerve

repair, nerve transfers, tendon transfers, and free tissue transfers that can be used to improve function and outcome.[26,57,292,358]

Aesthetic Improvements in Reconstructive Surgery of the Extremities

As with any reconstructive surgical procedure, the goal is to restore form and function. In some areas of the body, the prior-

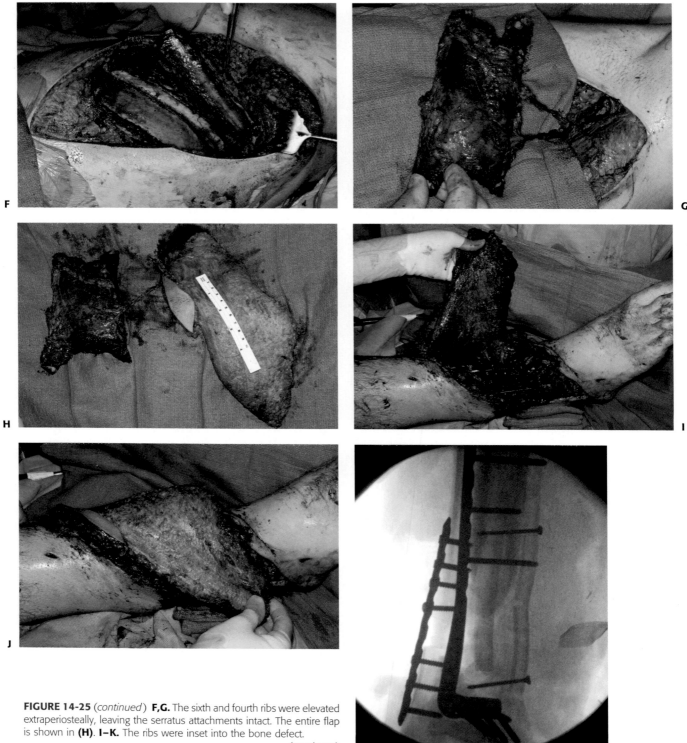

FIGURE 14-25 (*continued*) **F,G.** The sixth and fourth ribs were elevated extraperiosteally, leaving the serratus attachments intact. The entire flap is shown in **(H)**. **I–K.** The ribs were inset into the bone defect.

(*continues*)

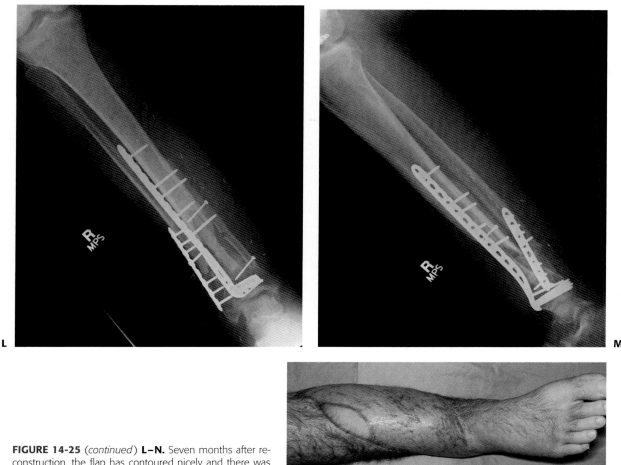

FIGURE 14-25 (*continued*) **L–N.** Seven months after reconstruction, the flap has contoured nicely and there was consolidation of the ribs to the tibia.

ity of improving the aesthetic outcome of the procedure is higher than others. Clearly, when reconstructing a facial defect, this becomes a high focus of the reconstruction. With advancements in the understanding of flap anatomy, major advancements have been seen in the aesthetic refinements that can be achieved when reconstructing defects in the extremities.[318] Improvements in aesthetic outcomes come at two stages in the reconstruction. The first is during the initial reconstructive procedure, when a flap is chosen to meet the functional needs at the recipient site and to achieve a reasonable aesthetic outcome. Choosing a flap that has qualities that match the recipient site, such as color, thickness, and pliability is important. Primary flap thinning can be performed in the operating room to achieve the best aesthetic outcome in the initial setting. The second stage is carried out with the use of additional surgical procedures to refine flap shape; several months after the initial procedure, secondary procedures may be performed, such as flap debulking through direct excision or liposuction[419] or even using the arthroscopic shaver device,[382] flap advancement, and serial excision of the flap.[355] Workhorse flaps in reconstructive surgery that are thin include the radial forearm flap, the lateral arm flap, and many of the discussed perforator flaps. Additionally, depending on the needs at the recipient site, fascia flaps covered with skin grafts often produce aesthetically and functionally good results. These flaps include the temporoparietal fascia flap,[331] the posterior rectus sheath flap,[342] the lateral arm fascia flap,[375] as well as the anterolateral thigh fascia flap.[188]

One of the most significant advancements in limiting donor site morbidity has been the advent of perforator flap surgery. Whereas the muscle was always thought to be a necessary carrier of the blood supply in musculocutaneous flaps, perforator flaps are performed by harvesting the skin and subcutaneous tissue, with a variety of tissue components, while preserving the muscle at the donor site. The skin and subcutaneous tissue are elevated and a large perforator is found. This perforator is then dissected from the surrounding muscle and traced to the mother vessel. The flap is harvested while the muscle is left intact. The remaining muscle is supplied through its secondary blood supply, and innervation of the muscle is maintained by preserving the nerves in the region. Functionally, the patient experiences minimal donor site morbidly. Because the blood supply to the flap is through a perforator that is clearly visualized and its anatomic basis has been studied through anatomic dissections,[398] the surrounding flap can then be trimmed to thin the flap and provide a nicely contoured flap during the initial reconstructive procedure.[63,95] Preoperative planning with the aid of CT and ultrasound to identify perforating blood vessels can improve surgical success.[38,60,139,163] Once the surgeon's skill in microsurgical techniques and flap dissection has reached a high level, one can perform microdissection of a perforator, which allows a detailed visualization of the arterial anatomy of the flap, eventually allowing for aggressive and accurate thinning of the flap.[113,220,221,424]

Commonly used perforator flaps include the deep inferior

epigastric perforator flap based on the deep inferior epigastric artery, the anterolateral thigh flap, the thoracodorsal artery perforator flap,[14] and the gastrocnemius perforator flap.[162] As previously discussed, the most commonly used perforator flaps is the anterolateral thigh perforator flap because of its versatility and the ability to include a variety of structures as well as the ability to thin and tailor the flap to fit the defect.[433]

Another important concept in improving aesthetics in reconstructive surgery is tissue expansion. This tool has been used in both upper and lower extremity reconstruction.[164,165] The flap is expanded before harvest and transfer to the defect site.[167,387] Alternatively tissue expanders can be used to expand the tissue surrounding a defect to provide additional tissue to help in reconstruction, minimizing flap requirements. After acute reconstruction, if the patient is unhappy with the shape or color of the flap, tissue expanders can be placed around the flap, under the normal skin of the extremity, and once expansion is complete the flap can be excised, with the native expanded local skin used to cover the resultant defect. Tissue expansion is associated with complications including infection and implant extrusion, and is usually not recommended in cases of acute reconstruction of contaminated wounds.

Endoscopic harvest and minimally invasive dissection of flaps provides another refinement in reconstructive surgery,[341] the benefit of which has not been fully used at this point. Endoscopic technique now allows for the successful harvested of flaps such as the latissimus dorsi,[279] the rectus abdominis,[253] the gracilis, the temporoparietal fascia flap,[73] and others. It is also used in harvesting vein grafts and nerve grafts which are often used in reconstructive surgery.[250] Comparative studies between open and endoscopically assisted muscle harvest have found patients to have less donor site pain and shorter scar lengths after endoscopic harvest.[251]

Recent Advances in Reconstructive Techniques

Artificial Skin

The role of artificial skin has advanced significantly over the past 15 years; materials are now available which can provide a scaffold for the ingrowth of fibroblasts and blood vessels over avascular or minimal vascularized structures such as tendon and bone. Integra dermal regeneration template (Integra Life sciences, Plainsboro, NJ) was initially developed in the late 1980s as a means of facilitating burn wound management.[51,425,426] More recently, the indications for this material have been extended to include the treatment of acute and chronic traumatic wounds (Figure 14-26).[175,283,403]

The material is bilayered, consisting of a deep layer of collagen glycosaminoglycan biodegradable matrix and a superficial semipermeable silicone layer. The deep layer allows for the ingrowth of native fibroblasts. Fibroblasts can form a "neodermis" upon the collagen scaffold, which is similar in appearance to normal dermis.[282,371] This neodermis can then support a thin split-thickness skin graft. The silicone layer prevents desiccation during the ingrowth period and it is removed before application of a skin graft. Major contraindications to the use of this material include ongoing infection and open fractures exposed within the wound.

Helgeson described the use of Integra in conjunction with skin grafting in 16 combat-related soft tissue wounds. The average wound size was 87 cm². Eleven wounds contained exposed

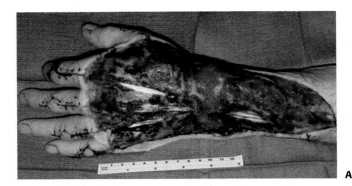

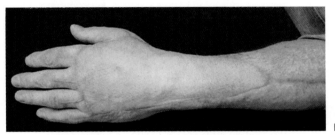

FIGURE 14-26 The application of Integra can allow for skin grafting to be performed over wounds previously requiring flap coverage. **A.** This 32-year-old man sustained an extensive degloving injury to the dorsum of his hand. Integra was applied over the exposed tendons and then VAC therapy was instituted for 14 days. **B.** After the establishment of a neodermis, the Integra was covered with a split-thickness skin graft providing for stable and functional coverage of the hand.

tendon and five wounds had exposed bone devoid of overlying periosteum. Integra application was combined with overlying VAC therapy for an average of 19 days before the application of a split-thickness skin graft to the wounds. Treatment was successful in 83% cases. Failure was associated with the application over cortical bone.[175]

Acceleration of fibroblast ingrowth can be accomplished with the use of fibrin glue for fixation of the Integra and subsequent VAC therapy. In a retrospective review, Jeschke and colleagues found the use of fibrin glue and VAC therapy improved the "take rate" of spit thickness skin grafts from 78% to 98% and shortened the time to skin grafting. Overall hospital stay was also decreased.[202]

The use of the VAC and Integra has led to a decrease in the need for flap coverage for many traumatic wounds.[305] Despite this trend, the surgeon should exercise restraint in trying to apply these technologies to exposed bone, tendon and large defects. Pedicled flaps and free tissue transfer provide reliable solutions to even the largest soft tissue defects, and should be considered the standard of care until formal comparative outcome studies are available to assess functional outcome and long-term consequences of these newer reconstructive technologies.

REFERENCES

1. Advanced Trauma Life Support. American College of Surgeons, 2008.
2. Collaborative overview of randomised trials of antiplatelet therapy—III: Reduction in venous thrombosis and pulmonary embolism by antiplatelet prophylaxis among surgical and medical patients. Antiplatelet Trialists' Collaboration. BMJ 1994:308(6923): 235–246.
3. Aberg M, Rydholm A, Holmberg J, et al. Reconstruction with a free vascularized fibular graft for malignant bone tumor. Acta Orthop Scand 1988;59(4):430–437.

4. Adams F. The genuine works of Hippocrates. New York: Williams Wood, 1891.

5. Adani R, Delcroix L, Innocenti M, et al. Reconstruction of large posttraumatic skeletal defects of the forearm by vascularized free fibular graft. Microsurgery 2004;24: 423–429.

6. Adani R, Delcroix L, Innocenti M, et al. Free fibula flap for humerus segmental reconstruction: report on 13 cases. Chirurgia Degli Organi di Movimento 2008;91(1):21–26.

7. Adeymo O, Wyburn GM. Innervation of skin grafts. Transplant Bull 1957;4:152–153.

8. Aldea PA, Shaw WW. The evolution of the surgical management of severe lower extremity trauma. Clin Plast Surg 1986;13(4):549–569.

9. Allieu Y, Gomis R. Congenital pseudarthrosis of the forearm treated by the fibular graft. J Hand Surg 1981;6:475–481.

10. Anglen JO. Comparison of soap and antibiotic solutions for irrigation of lower-limb open fracture wounds. A prospective, randomized study. J Bone Joint Surg Am 2005; 87(7):1415–1422.

11. Anglen JO. Wound irrigation in musculoskeletal injury. J Am Acad Orthop Surg 2001; 9(4):219–226.

12. Anglen JO, Gainor BJ, Simpson WA, et al. The use of detergent irrigation for musculoskeletal wounds. Int Orthop 2003;27(1):40–46.

13. Angrigiani C, Grilli D, Dominikow D, et al. Posterior interosseous reverse forearm flap: experience with 80 consecutive cases. Plast Reconstr Surg 1993;92:285–293.

14. Angrigiani C, Grilli D, Siebert J. Latissimus dorsi musculocutaneous flap without muscle. Plast Reconstr Surg 1995;96(7):1608–1614.

15. Ao M, Nagase Y, Mae O, Namba Y. Reconstruction of posttraumatic defects of the foot by flow-through anterolateral or anteromedial thigh flaps with preservation of posterior tibial vessels. Ann Plast Surg 1997;38(6):598–603.

16. Arata M, Wood M, Cooney WR. Revascularized segmental diaphyseal bone transfers in the canine. An analysis of viability. J Reconstr Microsurg 1984;1(1):11–19.

17. Argenta LC, Morykwas MJ. Vacuum-assisted closure: a new method for wound control and treatment: clinical experience. Ann Plast Surg 1997;38:563.

18. Arnez ZM, Kersnic M, Smith RW, et al. Free lateral arm osteocutaneous neurosensory flap for thumb reconstruction. J Hand Surg (Br) 1991;16:395–399.

19. Askari M, Fisher BS, Weniger FG, et al. Anticoagulation therapy in microsurgery: a review. J Hand Surg [Am] 2006;31:836.

20. Attinger CE, Janis JE, Steinberg J, et al. Clinical approach to wounds: débridement and wound bed preparation including the use of dressings and wound-healing adjuvants. Plast Reconstr Surg 2006;117:72–109s.

21. Awtry EH, Loscalzo J. Aspirin. Circulation 2000;101:1206.

22. Bach AW, Hansen ST. Plates versus external fixation in severe open tibial shaft fractures. A randomized trial. Clin Orthop Relat Res 1989;241:89–94.

23. Bakri K, Moran SL. Initial assessment and management of complex forearm defects. Hand Clin 2007;23:255–268.

24. Balin AK. Dilute povidone-iodine solutions inhibit human skin fibroblast growth. Dermatol Surg 2002;28(3):210–214.

25. Barnett AB, Ott R, Laub DR. Failure of healing of split skin donor sites in anhidrotic ectodermal dysplasia. Plast Reconstr Surg 1979;64:97–100.

26. Barrie KA, Steinmann SP, Shin AY, et al. Gracilis free muscle transfer for restoration of function after complete brachial plexus avulsion. Neurosurg Focus 2004;15:16(5): E8.

27. Barth E, Sullivan T, Berg E. Animal model for evaluating bone repair with and without adjunctive hyperbaric oxygen therapy (HBO): comparing dose schedules. J Invest Surg 1990;3(4):387–392.

28. Barth H. Histologishe Untersuchungen uber Knochen Transplantation. Beitr Pathol Anat Allg Pathol 1895;17:65–142.

29. Baudet J, Panconi B, Cai P, et al. The composite fibula and soleus transfer. Int J Microsurg 1982;4:10–26.

30. Bellman S, Velander E, Frank HA, Lambert PB. Survival of arteries in experimental full thickness skin autografts. Transplantation 1964;2:167–174.

31. Bennett MH, Stanford R, Turner R. Hyperbaric oxygen therapy for promoting fracture healing and treating fracture non-union. Cochrane Database Syst Rev 2005;(1): CD004712.

32. Berggren A, Weiland AJ, Dorfman A. The effect of prolonged ischemia time on osteocyte and osteoblast survival in composite bone grafts revascularized by microvascular anastomoses. Plast Reconstr Surg 1982;69(1):19–29.

33. Berggren A, Weiland AJ, Dorfman H. Free vascularized bone grafts: factors affecting their survival and ability to heal to recipient bone defects. Plastic Reconst Surg 1982; 69(1):19–29.

34. Bieber EJ, Wood MB. Bone reconstruction. [Review] [73 refs]. Clin Plast Surg 1986; 13(4):645–655.

35. Bishop AT, Wood MB, Sheetz KK. Arthrodesis of the ankle with a free vascularized autogenous bone graft. Reconstruction of segmental loss of bone secondary to osteomyelitis, tumor, or trauma. J Bone Joint Surg Am 1995;77(12):1867–1875.

36. Bitter K, Danai T. The iliac bone or osteocutaneous transplant pedicled to the deep circumflex iliac artery. I. Anatomical and technical considerations. J Maxillofac Surg 1983;11(5):195–200.

37. Blauth M, Bastian L, Krettek C, et al. Surgical options for the treatment of severe tibial pilon fractures: a study of three techniques. J Orthop Trauma 2001;15:153–160.

38. Blondeel PN, Ali SR. Planning of perforator flaps. In: Bolondeel PN, Morris SF, Hallock GG, Neligan PC, eds. Perforator Flaps: Anatomy, Technique, and Clinical Application. 1 ed. St. Louis: QMP, 2006, pp. 109–114.

39. Bosse MJ, MacKenzie EJ, Kellam JF, et al. An analysis of outcomes of reconstruction or amputation of leg threatening injuries. NEJM 2002;347:1924–1931.

40. Bosse MJ, McCarthy ML, Jones AJ, et al. The insensate foot following severe lower extremity trauma: an indication for amputation. J Bone Joint Surg (Am) 2005; 87(2601–2608).

41. Bowen V. Experimental free vascularized epiphyseal transplants. Orthopedics 1986; 9(6):893–898.

42. Breidenbach WC, Trager S. Quantitative culture technique and infection in complex wounds of the extremities closed with free flaps. Plast Reconstr Surg 1995;95(5): 860–865.

43. Brown RE, Wu TY. Use of "spare parts" in mutilated upper extremity injuries. Hand Clin 2003;19(1):73–87, vi.

44. Bruno RJ, Cohen MS, Berzins A, Sumner DR. Bone graft harvesting from the distal radius, olecranon, and iliac crest: a quantitative analysis. J Hand Surg [Am] 2001;26(1): 135–141.

45. Buchholz HW, Engelbrecht H. Depot effects of various antibiotics mixed with Palacos resins. Chirurg 1970;41(11):511–515.

46. Bueno RA Jr, Neumeister MW. Outcomes after mutilating hand injuries: review of the literature and recommendations for assessment. Hand Clin 2003;19(1):193–204.

47. Bui DT, Cordeiro PG, Hu QY, et al. Free flap re-exploration: indications treatment and outcomes in 1193 free flaps. Plast Reconstr Surg 2007;119:2092–2100.

48. Buncke HJ, Furnas DW, Gordon L, Achauer BM. Free osteocutaneous flap from a rib to the tibia. Plast Reconstr Surg 1977;59(6):799–804.

49. Burchardt H. The biology of bone graft repair. Clin Orthop Relat Res 1983;(174): 28–42.

50. Burd T, Christensen GD, Anglen JO, et al. Sequential irrigation with common detergents: a promising new method for decontaminating orthopedic wounds. Am J Orthop 1999;28(3):156–160.

51. Burke JF, Yannas IV, Quinby WC, et al. Successful use of a physiologically acceptable artifical skin in the treatment of extensiveburn injury. Ann Surg 1981;194:413–427.

52. Busse JW, Jacobs CL, Swiontkowski MF, et al. Complex limb salvage of early amputaiton for severe lower-limb injury: a meta-analysis of observational studies. J Orthop Trauma 2006;21:70–76.

53. Byrd HS, Spicer TE, Cierney GD. Management of open tibial fractures. Plast Reconstr Surg 1985;76:719–730.

54. Calderon W, Chang N, Mathes SJ. Comparison of the effect of bacterial inoculation in musculocutaneous and fasciocutaneous flaps. Plast Reconstr Surg 1986;77(5): 785–794.

55. Calvert JW, Kohanzadeh S, Tynan M, Evans GR. Free flap reconstruction for infection of ankle fracture hardware: case report and review of the literature. Surg Infect (Larchmt) 2006;7:315–322.

56. Caputo WJ, Beggs DJ, DeFede JL, et al. A prospective randomised controlled clinical trial comparing hydrosurgery débridement with conventional surgical débridement in lower extremity ulcers. Int Wound J 2008;5:288–294.

57. Carlsen BT, Bishop AT, Shin AY. Late reconstruction for brachial plexus injury. Neurosurg Clin North Am 2009;20(1):51–64, vi.

58. Carpenter EB. Management of fractures of the shaft of the tibia and fibula. J Bone Joint Surg Am 1966;48(8):1640–1646.

59. Cauchoix J, Duparc J, Boulez P. Traitement des fractures ouvertes de jambe. Med Acta Chir 1957;83:811–822.

60. Celik N, Wei FC. Technical tips in perforator flap harvest. Clin Plast Surg 2003;30: 469–472.

61. Chacha PB. Vascularised pedicular bone grafts. Int Orthop 1984;8(2):117–138.

62. Chang N, Mathes SJ. Comparison of the effect of bacterial inoculation in musculocutaneous and random-pattern flaps. Plast Reconstr Surg 1982;70(1):1–10.

63. Chen HC, Tang YB, Mardini S, Tsai BW. Reconstruction of the hand and upper limb with free flaps based on musculocutaneous perforators. Microsurgery 2004;24(4): 270–280.

64. Chen KT, Mardini S, Chuang DC, et al. Timing of presentation of the first signs of vascular compromise dictates the salvage outcome of free flap transfers. Plast Reconstr Surg 2007;120(1):187–195.

65. Chen MC, Chang MC, Chen CM, Chen TH. Double-strut free vascularized fibular grafting for reconstruction of the lower extremities. Injury 2003;34:763–769.

66. Chen SH, Wei FC, Chen HC, et al. Emergency free-flap transfer for reconstruction of acute complex extremity wounds. Plast Reconstr Surg 1992;89(5):882–888; discussion 9–90.

67. Chen ZW, Chen LE, Zhang GJ, Yu HL. Treatment of tibial defect with vascularized osteocutaneous pedicled transfer of fibula. J Reconstr Microsurg 1986;2(3):199–203, 5.

68. Chen ZW, Yan W. The study and clinical application of the osteocutaneous flap of fibula. Microsurgery 1983;4(1):11–16.

69. Chien W, Varvares MA, Hadlock T, et al. Effects of aspirin and low-dose heparin in head and neck reconstruction using microvascular free flaps. Laryngoscope 2005;115(6): 973–976.

70. Chou EK, Ulusal B, Ulusal A, et al. Using the descending branch of the lateral femoral circumflex vessel as a source of two independent flaps. Plast Reconstr Surg 2006; 117(6):2059–2063.

71. Choudry U, Moran S, Karacor Z. Soft tissue coverage and outcome of Gustillo Grade IIIB Midshaft tibia fractures: a 15-year experience. Plast Reconstr Surg 2008;122:479–485.

72. Choudry UH, Moran SL, Li S, Khan S. Soft tissue coverage of the elbow: an outcome analysis and reconstructive algorithm. Plast Reconstr Surg 2007;11:1852–1857.

73. Chung KC, Cederna PS. Endoscopic harvest of temporoparietal fascial free flaps for coverage of hand wounds. J Hand Surg 2002;27A(3):525–533.

74. Cierny 3rd G, Mader JT, Penninck JJ. A clinical staging system for adult osteomyelitis. Clin Orthop 2003;414:7–24.

75. Cierny G, Mader J. Adult chronic osteomyelitis. Orthopedics 1984;7:1557–1564.

76. Cierny G, Mader JT. The surgical Treatment of Adult Osteomyelitis. In: CMC E, ed. London: Churchill Livingstone, 1983, pp. 15–35.

77. Clagett GP, Reisch JS. Prevention of venous thromboembolism in general surgical patients: results of meta-analysis. Ann Surg 1998;208:227.

78. Clarke RJ, Mayo G, Price P, Fitzgerald GA. Suppression of thromboxane A2 but not of systemic prostacyclin by controlled-release aspirin. NEJM 1991;325:1137.

79. Clifford RP, Lyons TJ, Webb JK. Complications of external fixation of open fractures of the tibia. Injury 1987;18:174–176.

80. Cole JD, Ansel LJ, Schwartzberg RA. A sequential protocol for managment of severe open tibial fractures. Clin Orthop 1995;315:84–103.

81. Conrad MH, Adams WP. Pharmacologic optimization of microsurgery in the new millennium. Plast Reconstr Surg 2001;108:2088.

82. Converse JM, Rapaport FT. The vascularization of skin autografts and homografts: an experimental study in man. Ann Surg 1956;143:306–315.

83. Converse JM, Smahel J, Ballantyne DL, Harper AD. Inosculation of vessels of skin graft and host bed: a fortuitous encounter. Br J Plast Surg 1975:274–282.

84. Cooney WP 3rd, Fitzgerald RH Jr, Dobyns JH, Washington JA 2nd. Quantitative wound cultures in upper extremity trauma. J Trauma 1982;22(2):112–117.

85. Corps BVM. The effect of graft thickness, donor site and graft bed on graft shrinkage in the hooded rat. Br J Plast Surg 1969;22:125–133.

86. Court-Brown CM, Rimmer S, Prakash U, McQueen MM. The epidemiology of open long bone fractures. Injury 1998;29(7):529–534.
87. Crock JG, Morrison WA. A vascularised periosteal flap: anatomical study. Br J Plast Surg 1992;45(6):474–478.
88. Cutting CB, McCarthy JG. Comparison of residual osseous mass between vascularized and nonvascularized onlay bone transfers. Plast Reconstr Surg 1983;72(5):672–675.
89. Dagum AB, Best AK, Schemitsch EH, et al. Salvage after severe lower-extremity trauma: are the outcomes worth the means? Plast Reconstr Surg 1999;103(4):1212–1220.
90. Davies DM. A world survey of anticoagulation practice in clinical microvascular surgery. Br J Plast Surg 1982;35:96.
91. de Chalain TMB. Exploring the use of the medicinal leech: a clinical risk-benefit analysis. J Reconstr Microsurg 1996;12:165–172.
92. de la Torre J, Hedden W, Grant JH 3rd, et al. Retrospective review of the internal Doppler probe for intra- and postoperative microvascular surveillance. J Reconstr Microsurg 2003;19(5):287–290.
93. DeFranco MJ, Lawton JN. Radial nerve injuries associated with humeral fractures. J Hand Surg [Am] 2006;31(4):655–663.
94. DeFranzo AJ, Argenta LC, Marks MW, et al. The use of the vacuum-assisted closure therapy for treatment of lower-extremity wound with exposed bone. Plast Reconstr Surg 2001;108:1184.
95. del Piñal F, García-Bernal FJ, Studer A, et al. Super-thinned iliac flap for major defects on the elbow and wrist flexion creases. J Hand Surg [Am] 2008;33(10):1899–1904.
96. Dellon AL. Management of peripheral nerve problems in the upper and lower extremity using quantitative sensory testing. Hand Clin 1999;15(4):697–715, x.
97. Dellon AL. "Think nerve" in upper extremity reconstruction. Clin Plast Surg 1989; 16(3):617–627.
98. Dendrinos GK, Kontos S, Katsenis D, Dalas A. Treatment of high-energy tibial plateau fractures by the Ilizarov circular fixator. J Bone Joint Surg Br 1996;78(5):710–717.
99. Dendrinos GK, Kontos S, Lyritsis E. Use of the Ilizarov technique for treatment of non-union of the tibia associated with infection. J Bone Joint Surg Am 1995;77(6):835–846.
100. Derderian CA, Olivier WA, Baux G, et al. Microvascular free-tissue transfer for traumatic defects of the upper extremity: a 25-year experience. J Reconstr Microsurg 2003;19(7): 455–462.
101. Diegelmann RF, Evans MC. Wound healing: an overview of acute, fibrotic, and delayed healing. Front Biosci 2004;1:283–289.
102. Dinner MI, Peters CR, Sherer J. Use of semipermeable polyurethane membrane as a dressing for split skin graft donor sites. Plast Reconstr Surg 1979;64:112–114.
103. Dirschl DR, Wilson FC. Topical antibiotic irrigation in the prophylaxis of operative wound infections in orthopedic surgery. Orthop Clin North Am 1991;22(3):419–426.
104. Disa JJ, Cordeiro PG. The current role of preoperative arteriography in free fibula flaps. Plast Reconstr Surg 1998;102:1083–1088.
105. Disa JJ, Cordeiro PG, Hidalgo DA. Efficacy of conventional monitoring techniques in free tissue transfer: an 11 year experience in 750 consecutive cases. Plast Reconstr Surg 1999;104(1):97.
106. Doi K, Sakai K. Vascularized periosteal bone graft from the supracondylar region of the femur. Microsurgery 1994;15(5):305–315.
107. Doi K, Tominaga S, Shibata T. Bone grafts with microvascular anastomoses of vascular pedicles: an experimental study in dogs. J Bone Joint Surg Am 1977;59(6):809–815.
108. Dunham WK, Meyer RD. Vascularized bone grafts for reconstruction after tumor surgery. Ala J Med Sci 1984;21(4):407–411.
109. Ekholm R, Ponzer S, Tornkvist H, et al. The Holstein-Lewis humeral shaft fracture: aspects of radial nerve injury, primary treatment, and outcome. J Orthop Trauma 2008; 22(10):693–697.
110. Ekholm R, Ponzer S, Tornkvist H, et al. Primary radial nerve palsy in patients with acute humeral shaft fractures. J Orthop Trauma 2008;22(6):408–414.
111. Elton SG, Rizzo M. Management of radial nerve injury associated with humeral shaft fractures: an evidence-based approach. J Reconstr Microsurg 2008;24(8):569–573.
112. Enneking WF, Eady JL, Burchardt H. Autogenous cortical bone grafts in the reconstruction of segmental skeletal defects. J Bone Joint Surg Am 1980;62(7):1039–1058.
113. Eo S, Kim D, Jones NF. Microdissection thinning of a pedicled deep inferior epigastric perforator flap for burn scar contracture of the groin case report. J Reconstr Microsurg 2005;21(7):447–450; discussion 51–52.
114. Eren S, Klein W, Paar O. [Free, vascularized, folded fibula transplantation]. Handchir Mikrochir Plast Chir 1993;25(1):33–38.
115. Esterhai JL, Pisarello J, Brighton CT, et al. Adjunctive hyperbaric oxygen in the treatment of chronic refractory osteomyelitis. J Trauma 1987;27:763–768.
116. Faibisoff B, Daniel RK. Management of severe forearm injuries. Surg Clin North Am 1981;61(2):287–301.
117. Fairhurst MJ. The function of below-knee amputee versus the patient with salvaged grade III tibial fracture. Clin Orthop 1994;301:227–232.
118. Falanga V. Wound healing and its impairment in the diabetic foot. Lancet 2005; 366(9498):1736–1743.
119. Fietsam R Jr, Bassett J, Glover JL, et al. Complications of coronary artery surgery in diabetic patients. Am Surg 1992;57:551–557.
120. Finseth F, May JW, Smith RJ. Composite groin flap with iliac bone for primary thumb reconstruction. Case report. J Bone Joint Surg Am 1976;58:130–132.
121. Fleischman W, Lang E, Klinzl L. Vacuum-assisted wound closure after dermatofasciotomy of the lower extremity [in German]. Unfallchirurg 1996;99:283.
122. Fletcher I. Traction lesions of the brachial plexus. Hand 1969;1:129–136.
123. Foster RJ, Swiontkowski MF, Bach AW, et al. Radial nerve palsy caused by open humeral shaft fractures. J Hand Surg [Am] 1993;18(1):121–124.
124. Foucher G, van Genechten F, Merle N, et al. A compound radial artery forearm flap in hand surgery: an original modification of the Chinese forearm flap. Br J Plast Surg 1984;37(2):139–148.
125. Fox CL. Silver sulfadiazine, a new topical therapy for *Pseudomonas* in burns. Arch Surg 1968;96:184.
126. Francel TJ. Improving re-employment rates after limb salvage of acute severe tibial fractures by microvascular soft-tissue reconstruction. Plast Reconstr Surg 1994;93: 1028–1034.
127. Friedrich JB, Moran SL, Bishop AT, et al. Free vascularized fibular graft salvage of complications of long-bone allograft after tumor reconstruction. J Bone Joint Surg Am 2008;90(1):93–100.
128. Friedrich JB, Moran SL, Bishop AT, et al. Vascularized fibula flap onlay for salvage of pathologic fracture of the long bones. Plast Reconstr Surg 2008;121(6):2001–2009.
129. Friedrich JB, Shin AY. Management of forearm compartment syndrome. Hand Clin 2007;23(2):245–254, vii.
130. Fujimaki A, Suda H. Experimental study and clinical observations on hypertrophy of vascularized bone grafts. Microsurgery 1994;15(10):726–732.
131. Gayle LB, Lineaweaver WC, Buncke GM, et al. Lower extremity replantation. Clin Plast Surg 1991;18:437–447.
132. Gedebou TM, Wei FC, Lin CH. Clinical experience of 1284 free anterolateral thigh flaps. Handchir Mikrochir Plast Chir 2002;34(4):239–244.
133. Geiger S, McCormick F, Chou R, Wandel AG. War wounds: lessons learned from Operation Iraqi Freedom. Plast Reconstr Surg 2008;122(1):146–153.
134. Georgescu AV, Ivan O. Serratus anterior-rib free flap in limb bone reconstruction. Microsurgery 2003;23(3):217–225.
135. German G, Sherman R, Levin LS. Decision making in reconstructive surgery of the upper extremity. New York: Springer-Verlag; 1999.
136. Gerwin M, Weiland AJ. Vascularized bone grafts to the upper extremity. Indications and technique. Hand Clin 1992;8(3):509–523.
137. Gidumal R, Wood MB, Sim FH, Shives TC. Vascularized bone transfer for limb salvage and reconstruction after resection of aggressive bone lesions. J Reconstr Microsurg 1987;3(3):183–18.
138. Gilbert A. Free vascularized bone grafts. Int Surg 1981;66(1):27–31.
139. Giunta RE, Geisweid A, Feller AM. The value of preoperative Doppler sonography for planning free perforator flaps. Plast Reconstr Surg 2000;105:2381–2386.
140. Glicksman A, Gerder M, Casale P, et al. Fourteen hundred fifty-seven years of microsurgical experience. Plast Reconstr Surg 1997;100(2):355–363.
141. Godina M. Early microsurgical reconstruction of complex trauma of the extremities. Plast Reconstr Surg 1986;78(3):285–292.
142. Goldberg VM, Shaffer JW, Field G, et al. Biology of vascularized bone grafts. Orthop Clin North Am 1987;18(2):197–205.
143. Gopal S, Majumder S, Batchelor AGB, et al. Fix and flap: the radical orthopedic and plastic treatment of severe open fractures of the tibia. J Bone Joint Surg (Br) 2000;82B: 959–966.
144. Gornet MF, Randolph MA, Schofield BH, et al. Immunologic and ultrastructural changes during early rejection of vascularized bone allografts. Plast Reconstr Surg 1991; 88(5):860–868.
145. Graham B, Paulus DA, Caffee HH. Pulse oximetry for vascular monitoring in upper extremity replacement surgery. J Hand Surg [Am] 1986;11A:687.
146. Gravante G, Delogu D, Esposito G, et al. Versajet hydrosurgery versus classic escharectomy for Brun débridement: a prospective randomized trial. J Burn Care Res 2007;28: 720–724.
147. Green SA. Ilizarov method. Clin Orthop Relat Res 1992;(280):2–6.
148. Green SA, Jackson JM, Wall DM, et al. Management of segmental defects by the Ilizarov intercalary bone transport method. Clin Orthop Relat Res 1992;(280):136–142.
149. Greenberg BM, Masem M, May JW. Therapeutic value of intravenous heparin in microvascular surgery: an experimental vascular thrombosis study. Plast Reconstr Surg 1988; 82:463.
150. Greenberg RN, Newman MT, Shariaty S, et al. Ciprofloxacin, lomefloxacin, or levofloxacin as treatment for chronic osteomyelitis. Antimicrob Agents Chemother 2000;44(1): 164–166.
151. Greene TL, Beatty ME. Soft tissue coverage for lower-extremity trauma: current practice and techniques. A review. J Orthop Trauma 1988;2(2):158–173.
152. Gregory RT, Gould RJ, Peclet M, et al. the mangled extremity syndrome (M.E.S.): a severity grading system for multisystem injury of the extremity. J Trauma 1985;25: 1147–1150.
153. Guo F, Ding BF. Vascularized free fibula transfer in the treatment of bone tumours. Report of three cases. Arch Orthop Trauma Surg 1981;98(3):209–215.
154. Gustilo RB. Management of open fractures. An analysis of 673 cases. Minn Med 1971; 54(3):185–19.
155. Gustilo RB. Management of open fractures and complications. Instr Course Lect 1982; 31:64–75.
156. Gustilo RB, Anderson JT. JSBS classics. Prevention of infection in the treatment of 1025 open fractures of long bones. Retrospective and prospective analyses. J Bone Joint Surg Am 2002;84-A(4):682.
157. Gustilo RB, Anderson JT. Prevention of infection in the treatment of 1025 open fractures of long bones: retrospective and prospective analyses. J Bone Joint Surg Am 1976; 58(4):453–458.
158. Gustilo RB, Mendoza RM. Results of treatment of 1400 open fractures. In: Gustilo RB, editor. Management of Open Fractures and Their Complications. Philadelphia: Saunders, 1982; pp. 202–208.
159. Gustilo RB, Merkow RL, Templeman D. The management of open fractures. J Bone Joint Surg Am 1990;72(2):299–304.
160. Gustilo RB, Simpson L, Nixon R, et al. Analysis of 511 open fractures. Clin Orthop Relat Res 1969;66:148–154.
161. Haas N, Krettek C, Schandelmaier P, et al. A new solid unreamed tibial nail for shaft fractures with severe soft tissue injury. Injury 1993;24:49–54.
162. Hallock GG. Anatomic basis of the gastrocnemius perforator based flap. Ann Plast Surg 2001;47(5):517–522.
163. Hallock GG. Doppler sonography and color duplex imaging for planning a perforator flap. Clin Plast Surg 2003;30(3):347–357.
164. Hallock GG. Extremity tissue expansion. Orthop Rev 1987;16(9):606–611.
165. Hallock GG. Free flap donor site refinement using tissue expansion. Ann Plast Surg 1988;20(6):566–572.
166. Hallock GG. Getting the most from the soleus muscle. Ann Plast Surg 1996;36: 139–146.
167. Hallock GG. The pre-expanded anterolateral thigh free flap. Ann Plast Surg 2004;53(2): 170–173.
168. Hallock GG. Severe lower-extremity injury. The rationale for microsurgical reconstruction. Orthop Rev 1986;15(7):465–470.
169. Han CS, Wood MB, Bishop AT, et al. Vascularized bone transfer. J Bone Joint Surg Am 1992;74(10):1441–1449.
170. Hansen ST. The type-IIIC tibial fracture: salvage or amputation. J Bone Joint Surg (Am) 1987;69:799–800.

171. Hardin CK, Kirk WC, Pederson WC. Osmotic complications of low-molecular-weight dextran therapy in free flap surgery. Microsurgery 1992;13:36.
172. Hauser CJ, Adams CA, Eachempati SR. Surgical Infection Society Guideline: prophylactic antibiotic use in open fractures: an evidence-based guideline. Surg Infect 2006;7: 379–405.
173. Heckler MW, Bamberger HB. Humeral shaft fractures and radial nerve palsy: to explore or not to explore...that is the question. Am J Orthop 2008;37(8):415–419.
174. Hein KD, Wechsler ME, Schwartzstein RM, et al. The adult respiratory distress syndrome after dextran infusion as an antithrombotic agent in free TRAM flap breast reconstruction. Plast Reconstr Surg 1999;103:1706.
175. Helgeson MD, Potter BK, Evans KN, et al. Bioartifical dermal substitute: a preliminary report on its use for the management of complex combat-related soft tissue wounds. J Orthop Trauma 2007;21:394–399.
176. Hendel PM, Hattner RS, Rodrigo J, Buncke HJ. The functional vascular anatomy of rib. Plast Reconstr Surg 1982;70(5):578–587.
177. Hendry HAM. The treatment of residual paralysis after brachial plexus lesions. J Bone Joint Surg 1949;31B:42.
178. Hentz VR, Pearl RM. The irreplaceable free flap: Part I. Skeletal reconstruction by microvascular free bone transfer. Ann Plast Surg 1983;10(1):36–42.
179. Hentz VR, Pearl RM. The irreplaceable free flap: part II. Skeletal reconstruction by microvascular free bone transfer. Ann Plast Surg 1983;10(1):43–54.
180. Herscovici D, Sanders RW, Scaduto JM, et al. Vacuum-assisted wound closure (VAC therapy) for management of patients with high-energy soft tissue injuries. J Orthop Trauma 2003;17:683–688.
181. Herter F, Ninkovic M, Ninkovic M. Rational flap selection and timing for coverage of complex upper extremity trauma. J Plast Reconstr Aesthet Surg 2006;60:760–768.
182. Hidalgo DA, Jones CS. The role of emergent exploration in free tissue transfer: a review of 150 consecutive cases. Plast Reconstr Surg 1990;86:492–498.
183. Hierner R, Stock W, Wood MB, Schweiberer L. [Vascularized fibula transfer. A review]. Unfallchirurg 1992;95(3):152–159.
184. Hirigoyen MB, Urken ML, Weinberg H. Free flap monitoring: a review of current practice. Microsurgery 1995;16:723.
185. Hong JP, Shin HW, Kim JJ, et al. The use of anterolateral thigh perforator flaps in chronic osteomyelitis of the lower extremity. Plast Reconstr Surg 2005;115(1): 142–147.
186. Hovius SER, van Adrichem LNA, Mulder HD, et al. Comparison of laser Doppler flowmetry and thermometry in the postoperative monitoring of replantations. J Hand Surg 1995;20:88–93.
187. Howe H, Poole GV, Hansen, KJ, et al. Salvage of lower extremities following combined orthopaedic and vascular trauma: a predictive salvage index. Clin Am 1987;53: 205–208.
188. Hsieh CH, Yang CC, Kuo YR, et al. Free anterolateral thigh adipofascial perforator flap. Plast Reconstr Surg 2003;112(4):976–982.
189. Hugon S, Daubresse F, Depierreux L. Radial nerve entrapment in a humeral fracture callus. Acta Orthop Belg 2008;74(1):118–121.
190. Hui KC, Zhang F, Lineaweaver WC, et al. Serratus anterior-rib composite flap: anatomic studies and clinical application to hand reconstruction. Ann Plast Surg 1999;42(2): 132–136.
191. Hussl H, Sailer R, Daniaux H, Pechlaner S. Revascularization of a partially necrotic talus with a vascularized bone graft from the iliac crest. Arch Orthop Trauma Surg 1989;108(1):27–29.
192. Ikeda K, Tomita K, Hashimoto F, et al. Long-term follow-up of vascularized bone grafts for the reconstruction of tibial nonunion: evaluation with computed tomographic scanning. J Trauma 1992;32(6):693–697.
193. Ilizarov GA. Clinical application of the tension-stress effect for limb lengthening. Clin Orthop Relat Res 1990;Jan(250):8–26.
194. Ilizarov GA. The tension-stress effect on the genesis and growth of tissues. Part I. The influence of stability of fixation and soft-tissue preservation. Clin Orthop Relat Res 1989;Jan(238):249–281.
195. Ilizarov GA. The tension-stress effect on the genesis and growth of tissues: Part II. The influence of the rate and frequency of distraction. Clin Orthop Relat Res 1989;Feb(239): 263–285.
196. Ilizarov GA, Ledyaev VI. The replacement of long tubular bone defects by lengthening distraction osteotomy of one of the fragments. 1969. Clin Orthop Relat Res 1992; Jul(280):7–10.
197. Ilyas AM, Jupiter JB. Treatment of distal humerus fractures. Acta Chir Orthop Traumatol Cech 2008;75(1):6–15.
198. Innis PC, Randolph MA, Paskert JP, et al. Vascularized bone allografts: in vitro assessment of cell-mediated and humoral responses. Plast Reconstr Surg 1991;87(2): 315–325.
199. Ippolito E, Peretti G, Bellocci Met al. Histology and ultrastructure of arteries, veins, and peripheral nerves during limb lengthening. Clin Orthop Relat Res 1994;Nov(308): 54–62.
200. Jensen M, Moran SL. Soft tissue coverage of the elbow: a reconstructive algorithm. Orthop Clin North Am 2008;39:251–264.
201. Jensen MH, Moran SL. Why wounds fail to heal. In: Moran SL, Cooney WP, editors. Soft Tissue Surgery. Baltimore: Lippincott Williams & Wilkins, 2008; pp. 1–10.
202. Jeschke MG, Rose C, Angele P, et al. Development of new reconstructive techniques: Use of Integra in combination with fibrin glue and negative-pressure therapy for reconstruction of acute and chronic wounds. Plast Reconstr Surg 2004;113:525–530.
203. Johansen K, Daines M, Hower T, et al. Objective criteria accurately predict amputation following lower extremity trauma. J Trauma 1990;30:568–573.
204. Jones BM, Greenhalgh RM. The use of the ultrasound Doppler flowmeter in reconstructive microvascular surgery. Br J Plast Surg 1985;36:245.
205. Jones NF, Swartz WM, Mears DC, et al. The "double barrel" free vascularized fibular bone graft. Plast Reconstr Surg 1988;81(3):378–385.
206. Jones RN, Anderegg TR, Swenson JM. Quality control guidelines for testing gram-negative control strains with polymyxin B and colistin (polymyxin E) by standardized methods. J Clin Microbiol 2005;43(2):925–927.
207. Joshi BB. Neural repair for sensory restoration in a groin flap. Hand 1977;9:221–225.
208. Jupiter JB, Bour CJ, May JW Jr. The reconstruction of defects in the femoral shaft with vascularized transfers of fibular bone. J Bone Joint Surg Am 1987;69(3):365–374.
209. Jupiter JB, Gerhard HJ, Guerrero J, et al. Treatment of segmental defects of the radius with use of the vascularized osteoseptocutaneous fibular autogenous graft. J Bone Joint Surg Am 1997;79(4):542–550.
210. Jupiter JB, Tsai TM, Kleinert HE. Salvage replantation of lower limb amputations. Plast 1982;69:1–8.
211. Karanas YL, Nigriny J, Chang J. The timing of microsurgical reconstruction in lower extremity trauma. Microsurgery 2008;28(8):632–634.
212. Kaufman MR, Jones NF. The reverse radial forearm flap for soft tissue reconstruction of the wrist and hand. Tech Hand Up Extrem Surg 2005;9(1):47–51.
213. Kawashima M, Tamura H, Nagayoshi I, et al. Hyperbaric oxygen therapy in orthopedic conditions. Undersea Hyperb Med 2004;31(1):155–162.
214. Kent ME, Rapp RP, Smith KM. Antibiotic beads and osteomyelitis: here today, what's coming tomorrow? Orthopedics 2006;29(7):599–603.
215. Khatod M, Botte MJ, Hoyt DB, et al. Outcomes in open tibial fractures: relationship in delay in treatment and infection. J Trauma 2003;55:951.
216. Khouri RK, Cooley BC, Kunselman AR, et al. A prospective study of microvascular free-flap surgery and outcome. Plast Reconstr Surg 1998;102:711–721.
217. Khouri RK, Cooley BC, Kunselman AR, et al. A prospective study of microvascular free-flap surgery and outcome. Plast Reconstr Surg 1998;102(3):711–721.
218. Kim DH, Kam AC, Chandika P, et al. Surgical management and outcome in patients with radial nerve lesions. J Neurosurg 2001;95(4):573–583.
219. Kim PD, Blackwell KE. Latissimus-serratus-rib free flap for oromandibular and maxillary reconstruction. Arch Otolaryngol Head Neck Surg 2007;133(8):791–795.
220. Kimura N, Saito M, Sumiya Y, Itoh N. Reconstruction of hand skin defects by microdissected mini anterolateral thigh perforator flaps. J Plast Reconstr Aesthet Surg 2008; 61(9):1073–1077.
221. Kimura N, Saitoh M, Okamura T, et al. Concept and anatomical basis of microdissected tailoring method for free flap transfer. Plast Reconstr Surg 2009;123(1):152–162.
222. Kimura N, Satoh K. Consideration of a thin flap as an entity and clinical applications of the thin anterolateral thigh flap. Plast Reconstr Surg 1996;97(5):985–992.
223. King KF. Periosteal pedicle grafting in dogs. J Bone Joint Surg Br 1976;58(1):117–121.
224. Klein MB, Hunter S, Heimbach DM, et al. The VersaJet water dissector: a new tool for tangential excision. Burn Care Rehab 2005;26:483–487.
225. Klemm K. Gentamicin-PMMA-beads in treating bone and soft tissue infections (Author's trans.). Zentralbl Chir 1979;104(14):934–942.
226. Knighton DR, Silver IA, Hunt TK. Regulation of wound-healing angiogenesis: effect of oxygen gradients and inspired oxygen concentration. Surgery 1981;90(2):262–270.
227. Kocher MS. Early limb salvage: open tibia fractures of Ambroise Pare (1510–1590) and Percival Pott (1714–1789). World J Surg 1997;21(1):116–122.
228. Koshima I, Higaki H, Soeda S. Combined vascularized fibula and peroneal composite-flap transfer for severe heat-press injury of the forearm. Plast Reconstr Surg 1991; 88(2):338–341.
229. Kozol RA, Gilles C. Effects of sodium hypochlorite (Dakin's solution) on cells of the wound module. Arch Surg 1988;123(4):420–423.
230. Kremer T, Bickert B, Germann G, et al. Outcome assessment after reconstruction of complex defects of the forearm and hand with osteocutaneous free flaps. Plast Reconstr Surg 2006;118(2):443–454; discussion 55–56.
231. Krettek C, Gluer S, Schandelmaier P, et al. Intramedullary nailing of open fractures. Orthopade 1996;25:223–233.
232. Krizek TJ, Robson MC, Kho E. Bacterial growth and skin graft survival. Surg Forum 1967;18:518–519.
233. Kroll S, Schusterman MA, Reece GP, et al. Timing of pedicle thrombosis and flap loss after free-tissue transfer. Plast Reconstr Surg 1996;98:1230–1233.
234. Kroll SS, Schusterman MA, Reece GP, et al. Timing of pedicle thrombosis and flap loss after free-tissue transfer. Plast Reconstr Surg 1996;98(7):1230–1233.
235. Kucan JO, Robson MC, Heggers JP, et al. Comparison of silver sulfadiazine, povidone-iodine, and physiological saline in the treatment of chronic pressure ulcers. J Am Geriatr Soc 1981;29:232.
236. Kuo YR, Jeng SF, Kuo MH, et al. Free anterolateral thigh flap for extremity reconstruction: clinical experience and functional assessment of donor site. Plast Reconstr Surg 2001;107(7):1766–1771.
237. Kuo YR, Seng-Feng J, Kuo FM, et al. Versatility of the free anterolateral thigh flap for reconstruction of soft-tissue defects: review of 140 cases. Ann Plast Surg 2002;48(2): 161–166.
238. Lange RH. Limb reconstruction versus amputation decision making in massive lower extremity trauma. Clin Orthop 1989;243:92–99.
239. Larsen LB, Barfred T. Radial nerve palsy after simple fracture of the humerus. Scand J Plast Reconstr Surg Hand Surg 2000;34(4):363–366.
240. Lettieri SC, Moran SL. The pedicled soleus muscle flap for coverage of the middle an distal third of the tibia. In: Moran SL, Cooney WPI, eds. Soft Tissue Surgery. Philadelphia: Lippincott Williams & Wilkins, 2008, pp. 345–360.
241. Letts M, Pang E, Yang J, Carpenter B. Periosteal augmentation of the acetabulum. Clin Orthop Relat Res 1998;Sep(354):216–223.
242. Leung PC. Femoral head reconstruction and revascularization. Treatment for ischemic necrosis. Clin Orthop Relat Res 1996;Feb(323):139–145.
243. Leung PC, Hung LK. Bone reconstruction after giant-cell tumor resection at the proximal end of the humerus with vascularized iliac crest graft. A report of three cases. Clin Orthop Relat Res 1989;Oct(247):101–105.
244. Levin LS. The reconstructive ladder. An orthoplastic approach. Orthop Clin North Am. 1993;24(3):393–409.
245. Levin LS, Condit DP. Combined injuries—soft tissue management. Clin Orthop Relat Res 1996;Jun(327):172–181.
246. Levin LS, Erdmann D. Primary and secondary microvascular reconstruction of the upper extremity. Hand Clin 2001;17(3):447–455, ix.
247. Levin LS, Goldner RD, Urbaniak JR, et al. Management of severe musculoskeletal injuries of the upper extremity. J Orthop Trauma 1990;4:432–440.
248. Levin SL, Baumeister S. Lower extremity. In: Wei FC, Mardini S, eds. Flaps and Reconstructive Surgery. London: Elsevier, 1009, pp. 63–70.
249. Lin CH, Mardini S, et al. Sixty-five clinical cases of free tissue transfer using long arteriovenous fistulas or vein grafts. J Trauma 2004;56:1107–1117.
250. Lin CH, Mardini S, Levin SL, et al. Endoscopically assisted sural nerve harvest for upper extremity posttraumatic nerve defects an evaluation of functional outcomes. Plast Reconstr Surg 2007;119(2):616–626.
251. Lin CH, Wei FC, Levin LS, Chen MC. Donor-site morbidity comparison between endo-

scopically assisted and traditional harvest of free latissimus dorsi muscle flap. Plast Reconstr Surg 1999;104:1070–1078.

252. Lin CH, Wei FC, Levin LS, et al. Free composite serratus anterior and rib flaps for tibial composite bone and soft-tissue defect. Plast Reconstr Surg 1997;99(6):1656–1665.

253. Lin CH, Wei FC, Lin YT, Su CI. Endoscopically assisted fascia-saving harvest of rectus abdominis. Plast Reconstr Surg 2001;108(3):713–718.

254. Lister G, Scheker L. Emergency free flaps to the upper extremity. J Hand Surg [Am] 1988;13(1):22–28.

255. Livani B, Belangero WD, Castro de Medeiros R. Fractures of the distal third of the humerus with palsy of the radial nerve: management using minimally-invasive percutaneous plate osteosynthesis. J Bone Joint Surg Br 2006;88(12):1625–1628.

256. Lutz BS, Wei FC, Ng SH, et al. Routine donor leg angiography before vascularized free fibula transplantation is not necessary: a prospective study of 120 clinical cases. Plast Reconstr Surg 1999;103:121–127.

257. MacKenzie EJ, Bosse MJ. Factors influencing outcome following limb threatening lower limb trauma: lessons learned from the Lower Extremity Assessment Project (LEAP). J Am Acad Orthop Surg 2006;14:S205–210.

258. Mackinnon SE, Novak CB. Nerve transfers. New options for reconstruction following nerve injury. Hand Clin 1999;15(4):643–666, ix.

259. Mader J, Calhoun JH. Adult Long Bone Osteomyelitis. In: Mader JHC, ed. Musculoskeletal Infections. New York: Marcel Dekker, 2003, pp. 149–182.

260. Mader JT, Brown GL, Wells CH, et al. A mechanism for the amelioration by hyperbaric oxygen of experimental staphylococcal osteomyelitis in rabbits. J Infect Dis 1980; 142(6):915–922.

261. Mader JT, Calhoun JH, Cobos J. In vitro evaluation of antibiotic diffusion from antibiotic-impregnated biodegradable beads and polymethylmethacrylate beads. Antimicrob Agents Chemother 1997;41(2):415–418.

262. Mader JT, Ortiz M, Calhoun JH. Update on the diagnosis and management of osteomyelitis. Clin Podiatr Med Surg 1996;13(4):701–724.

263. Malizos KN, Quarles LD, Seaber AV, et al. An experimental canine model of osteonecrosis: characterization of the repair process. J Orthop Res 1993;11(3):350–357.

264. Malizos KN, Zalavras CG, Soucacos PN, et al. Free vascularized fibular grafts for reconstruction of skeletal defects. J Am Acad Orthop Surg 2004;12(5):360–369.

265. Mangano DT, Layug EL, Wallace A, Tateo I. Effect of atenolol on mortality and cardiovascular morbidity after noncardiac surgery. NEJM 1996;335(23):1713–1720.

266. Mardini S, Lin LC, Moran SL, et al. Anterolateral thigh flap. In: Wei FC ed. Flaps and Reconstructive Surgery. London: Elsevier, 2009, pp. 93–101.

267. Mardini S, Wei FC, Salgado CJ, Chen HC. Reconstruction of the reconstructive ladder. Plast Reconstr Surg 2005;115(7):2174.

268. Mast BA, Schultz GS. Interaction of cytokines, proteases and growth factors in acute and chronic wounds. Wound Rep Reg 1996;4:411–420.

269. Mathes SJ, Nahai F. Classification of the vascular anatomy of muscles: experimental and clinical correlation. Plast Reconstr Surg 1981;67:177–187.

270. Mathoulin C. Comment on "Scaphoid nonunion: treatment with a pedicled vascularized bone graft based on the 1,2 intercompartmental supraretinacular branch of the radial artery." J Hand Surg [Br] 2003;28(3):281–282; author reply 2.

271. Mazur KU, Bishop AT, Berger RA, editors. Vascularized bone grafting for Kienbock's disease: method and results of retrograde-flow metaphyseal grafts and comparison with cortical graft sites (SS-03). 51st Annual Meeting of the American Society for Surgery of the Hand; 1996; Nashville, TN.

272. Mazzer N, Barbieri CH, Cortez M. The posterior interosseous forearm island flap for skin defects in the hand and elbow. A prospective study of 51 cases. J Hand Surg 1996;21B:237–243.

273. McGregor IA, McGregor AD. Fundamental Techniques of Plastic Surgery, 9th ed. Edinburgh: Churchill-Livingstone, 1995.

274. McKay PL, Nanos G. Initial evaluation and management of complex traumatic wounds. In: Moran SL, Cooney WP, editors. Soft Tissue Surgery. Philadelphia: Lippincott Williams & Wilkins, 2009, pp. 11–37.

275. McNamara MG, Heckman JD, Corley FG. Severe open fracutres of the lower extremity: a retrospective evaluation of the Mangled Extremity Severity Score (MESS). J Orthop Trauma 1994;8:81–87.

276. Mercer N, Beere D, Bornemisza A, Thomas P. Medicinal leeches as sources of wound infection. BMJ 1987;294:937.

277. Metaizeau JP, Olive D. [Conservative treatment of malignant bone tumors by vascularized bone grafts]. Presse Med 1983;12(15):960–961.

278. Minami A, Kaneda K, Itoga H. Treatment of infected segmental defect of long bone with vascularized bone transfer. J Reconstr Microsurg 1992;8(2):75–82.

279. Missana MC, Pomel C. Endoscopic latissimus dorsi flap harvesting. Am J Surg 2007; 194(2):164–169.

280. Miyawaki T, Jackson IT, Elmazar H, et al. The effect of low-molecular-weight heparin in the survival of a rabbit congested skin flap. Plast Reconstr Surg 2002;109(6): 1994–1999.

281. Moehring HD, Gravel C, Chapman MW, et al. Comparison of antibiotic beads and intravenous antibiotics in open fractures. Clin Orthop 2000;372:254–261.

282. Moiemen NS, Staiano JJ, Ojeh NO, et al. Reconstructive surgery with a dermal regeneration template: clinical and histologic study. Plast Reconstr Surg 2001;108:93–103.

283. Molnar JA, Defranzo AJ, Hadaegh A, et al. Acceleration of Integra incorporation in complex tissue defects with subatmospheric pressure. Plast Reconstr Surg 2004;113: 1339–1346.

284. Moore JB, Mazur JM, Zehr D, et al. A biomechanical comparison of vascularized and conventional autogenous bone grafts. Plast Reconstr Surg 1984;73(3):382–386.

285. Moore JR, Weiland AJ. Free vascularized bone and muscle flaps for osteomyelitis. Orthopedics 1986;9(6):819–824.

286. Moore JR, Weiland AJ, Daniel RK. Use of free vascularized bone grafts in the treatment of bone tumors. Clin Orthop Relat Res 1983;May(175):37–44.

287. Moran CG, Wood MB. Vascularized bone autografts. Orthop Rev 1993;22(2):187–197.

288. Moran SL, Salgado CJ. Free tissue transfer in patients with renal disease. Plast Reconstruct Surg 2004;113(7):2006–2011.

289. Moran SL, Bakri K, Mardini S, et al. The use of vascularized fibular grafts for the reconstruction of spinal and sacral defects. Microsurgery 2009;29:393–400.

290. Moran SL, Johnson CH. Skin and soft tissue: pedicled flaps. In: Berger RA, Weiss AP,

eds. Hand Surgery. Philadelphia: Lippincott Williams & Wilkins, 2004, pp. 1131–1160.

291. Moran SL, Shin AY, Bishop AT. the use of massive bone allograft with intramedullary free fibular flap for limb salvage in a pediatric and adolescent population. Plast Reconstr Surg 2006;118:413–419.

292. Moran SL, Steinmann SP, Shin AY. Adult brachial plexus injuries: mechanism, patterns of injury, and physical diagnosis. Hand Clin 2005;21(1):13–24.

293. Morykwas, MJ, Argenta, LC, Shelton-Brown EL, et al. Vacuum-assisted closure: a new method for wound control and treatment: animal studies and basic foundation. Ann Plast 1997;38(6):553–562.

294. Netscher D, Alford EL, Wigoda P, Cohen V. Free composite myo-osseous flap with serratus anterior and rib: indications in head and neck reconstruction. Head Neck 1998;20(2):106–112.

295. Neut D, van de Belt H, van Horn JR, et al. Residual gentamicin-release from antibiotic-loaded polymethylmethacrylate beads after 5 years of implantation. Biomaterials 2003; 24(10):1829–1831.

296. Newington DP, Sykes PJ. The versatility of the free fibula flap in the management of traumatic long bone defects. Injury 1991;22(4):275–281.

297. Ninkovic M, Deetjen H, Ohler K, Anderl H. Emergency free tissue transfer for severe upper extremity injuries. J Hand Surg [Br] 1995;20(1):53–58.

298. Ninkovic M, Harpf C, Schwabegger AH, et al. The lateral arm flap. Clin Plast Surg 2001;28:367–374.

299. Nusbickel FR, Dell PC, McAndrew MP, et al. Vascularized autografts for reconstruction of skeletal defects following lower extremity trauma. A review. Clin Orthop Relat Res 1989;Jun(243):65–70.

300. Okada T, Tsukada S, Obara K, et al. Free vascularized fibular graft for replacement of the radius after excision of giant cell tumor: case report. J Microsurg 1981;3(1):48–53.

301. Ostrowski DM, Eilert RE, Waldstein G. Congenital pseudarthrosis of the ulna: a report of two cases and a review of the literature. J Pediatr Orthop 1985;5(4):463–467.

302. Ostrup LT. Free bone transfers. Some theoretical aspects. Scand J Plast Reconstr Surg Suppl 1982;19:103–104.

303. Ozkan O, Coskunfirat OK, Ozgentas HE. The use of free anterolateral thigh flap for reconstructing soft tissue defects of the lower extremities. Ann Plast Surg 2004;53(5): 455–461.

304. Park JE, Rodriguez ED, Bludbond-Langer R, et al. The anterolateral thigh flap is highly effective for reconstruction of complex lower extremity trauma. J Trauma 2007;62(1): 162–165.

305. Parrett BM, Maros E, Pribaz JJ, et al. Lower extremity trauma: trends in the management of soft-tissue reconstruction of open tibia-fibula fractures. Plast Reconstr Surg 2006; 117:1315–1322.

306. Paskert JP, Yaremchuk MJ, Randolph MA, et al. Prolonging survival in vascularized bone allograft transplantation: developing specific immune unresponsiveness. J Reconstr Microsurg 1987;3(3):253–263.

307. Paskert JP, Yaremchuk MJ, Randolph MA, et al. The role of cyclosporin in prolonging survival in vascularized bone allografts. Plast Reconstr Surg 1987;80(2):240–247.

308. Patzakis M, Wilkins J, Moore TM. Considerations in reducing the infection rate in open tibial fractures. Clin Orthop 1983;178:36–41.

309. Penfold CN, Davies HT, Cole RP, et al. Combined latissimus dorsi-serratus anterior/rib composite free flap in mandibular reconstruction. Int J Oral Maxillofac Surg 1992; 21(2):92–96.

310. Penner MJ, Masri BA, Duncan CP. Elution characteristics of vancomycin and tobramycin combined in acrylic bone-cement. J Arthroplasty 1996;11(8):939–944.

311. Penteado CV, Masquelet AC, Romana MC, et al. Periosteal flaps: anatomical bases of sites of elevation. Surg Radiol Anat 1990;12(1):3–7.

312. Pho RW, Levack B, Satku K, Patradul A. Free vascularised fibular graft in the treatment of congenital pseudarthrosis of the tibia. J Bone Joint Surg Br 1985;67(1):64–70.

313. Pho RW, Vajara R, Satku K. Free vascularized bone transplants in problematic nonunions of fractures. J Trauma 1983;23(4):341–349.

314. Pirela-Cruz MA, DeCoster TA. Vascularized bone grafts. Orthopedics 1994;17(5): 407–412.

315. Pomerance J, Truppa K, Bilos ZJ, et al. Replantation and revascularization of the digits in a community microsurgical practice. J Reconstr Microsurg 1997;13:163.

316. Pu LLQ. Medial hemisoleus muscle flap: a reliable flap for soft tissue reconstruction of the middle third tibial wound. Wound Int 2006;91:194–200.

317. Pugh CM, Dennis RHI, Massac EA. Evaluation of intraoperative anticoagulants in microvascular free-flap surgery. J Natl Med Assoc 1996;88:655.

318. Rainer C, Schwabegger AH, Gardetto A, et al. Aesthetic refinements in reconstructive microsurgery of the lower leg. J Reconstr Microsurg 2004;20(2):123–131.

319. Rajacic N, Gang RK, Krishnan J, et al. Thin anterolateral thigh free flap. Ann Plast Surg 2002;48(3):252–257.

320. Ramachandran M, Birch R, Eastwood DM. Clinical outcome of nerve injuries associated with supracondylar fractures of the humerus in children: the experience of a specialist referral centre. J Bone Joint Surg Br 2006;88(1):90–94.

321. Rasmussen MR, Bishop AT, Wood MB. Arthrodesis of the knee with a vascularized fibular rotatory graft. J Bone Joint Surg Am 1995;77(5):751–759.

322. Redett RJ, Robertson BC, Chang B. Limb salvage in the lower extremity using free gracilis muscle reconstruction. Plast Reconstr Surg 2000;106:1507–1513.

323. Reinisch JF, Winters R, Puckett Cl. The use of the osteocutaneous groin flap in gunshot wounds of the hand. J Hand Surg [Am] 1984;9:12–17.

324. Reller LB, Stratton CW. Serum dilution test for bactericidal activity. II. 1977;136(2): 196–204.

325. Rightmire E, Zurakowski D, Vrahas M. Acute infections after fracture repair: management with hardware in place. Clin Orthop Relat Res 2008;466:466–472.

326. Rindell K, Solonen KA, Lindholm TS. Results of treatment of aseptic necrosis of the femoral head with vascularized bone graft. Ital J Orthop Traumatol 1989;15(2): 145–153.

327. Ring D, Chin K, Jupiter JB. Radial nerve palsy associated with high-energy humeral shaft fractures. J Hand Surg [Am] 2004;29(1):144–147.

328. Rittmann WW, Matter P. Die offene Fraktur. Bern: Hans Huber, Verlag; 1977.

329. Rittmann WW, Matter P, Allgower M. Behandlung offener Frakturen und Infekthaufigkeit. Acta Chir Austriaca, 1970;2:18.

330. Rodheaver GT, Pettry D, Thacker JG, et al. Wound cleansing by high pressure irrigation. Surg Gynecol Obstet 1975;141:357.
331. Rogachefsky RA, Quellette EA, Mendietta CG, et al. Free temporoparietal fascial flap for coverage of a large palmar forearm wound after hand replantation. J Reconstr Microsurg 2001;17(6):421–423.
332. Romana MC, Masquelet AC. Vascularized periosteum associated with cancellous bone graft: an experimental study. Plast Reconstr Surg 1990;85(4):587–592.
333. Rosenstein BD, Wilson FC, Funderburk CH. The use of bacitracin irrigation to prevent infection in postoperative skeletal wounds. An experimental study. J Bone Joint Surg Am 1989 Mar;71(3):427–430.
334. Rothkopf DM, Chu B, Bern S, May JW. The effect of dextran on microvascular thrombosis in an experimental rabbit model. Plast Reconstr Surg 1993;92:511.
335. Rudert M, Wulker N, Wirth CJ. Reconstruction of the lateral ligaments of the ankle using a regional periosteal flap. J Bone Joint Surg Br 1997;79(3):446–451.
336. Saddawi-Konefka D, Kim HM, Chung KC. A systemic review of outcomes and complications of reconstruction and amputation for type IIIB and IIIC fractures of the tibia. Plast Reconstr Surg 2008;122:1796–1805.
337. Saint-Cyr M, Daigle JP. Early free tissue transfer for extremity reconstruction following high-voltage electrical burn injuries. J Reconstr Microsurg 2008;24:259–266.
338. Salemark L, Knudsen F, Dougan P. The effect of dextran 40 on patency following severe trauma in small arteries and veins. Br J Plast Surg 1995;48:121.
339. Salemark L, Wiesland JB, Dougan P, et al. Effects of low and ultralow oral doses of acetylsalicylic acid in microvascular surgery. An experimental study in rabbits. Scand J Plast Reconstr Surg Hand Surg 1991;25:203.
340. Salemark L, Wieslander JB, Dougan P, et al. Studies of the antithrombotic effects of dextran 40 following microarterial trauma. Br J Plast Surg 1991;44:15.
341. Salgado CJ, Orlando GS, Herceg S, et al. Pfannenstiel incision as an alternative approach for harvesting the rectus abdominis muscle for free-tissue transfer. Plast Reconstr Surg 2000;105(4):1330–1333.
342. Salgado CJ, Orlando GS, Serletti JM. Clinical applications of the posterior rectus sheath-peritoneal free flap. Plast Reconstr Surg 2000;106(2):321–326.
343. Salgado CJ, Smith A, Kim S, et al. Effects of late loss of arterial inflow on free flap survival. J Reconstr Microsurg 2002;18(7):579–584.
344. Salibian AH, Anzel SH, Salyer WA. Transfer of vascularized grafts of iliac bone to the extremities. J Bone Joint Surg Am 1987;69(9):1319–1327.
345. Sanders R, Mayou BJ. A new vascularized bone graft transferred by microvascular anastomosis as a free flap. Br J Surg. 1979;66(11):787–788.
346. Sauerbier M, Ofer N, Germann G, et al. Microvascular reconstruction in burn and electrical burn injuries of the severely traumatized upper extremity. Plast Reconstr Surg 2007;119:605–615.
347. Sawhney CP, Subbaraju GV, Chakravarti RN. Healing of donor sites of split skin graft. Br J Plast Surg 1969;22:359–364.
348. Schwanholt C, Greenhalgh DG, Warden GD. A comparison of full-thickness versus split-thickness autografts for the coverage of deep palm burns in the very young pediatric patient. J Burn Care Rehabil 1993;14:20–33.
349. Seddon HJ. Three types of nerve injury. Brain 1943;66:237–238.
350. Serletti JM, Moran SL, Orlando GS, et al. Urokinase protocol for free-flap salvage following prolonged venous thrombosis. Plast Reconstr Surg 1998;102:1947–1953.
351. Shafer DM, Sherman CE, Moran SL. Hydrosurgical tangential excision of partial thickness hand burns. Plast Reconstr Surg 2008;122:96e–97e.
352. Shaffer JW, Field GA, Goldberg VM, et al. Fate of vascularized and nonvascularized autografts. Clin Orthop Relat Res 1985;Jul-Aug(197):32–43.
353. Shaffer JW, Field GA, Wilber RG, Goldberg VM. Experimental vascularized bone grafts: histopathologic correlations with postoperative bone scan: the risk of false-positive results. J Orthop Res 1987;5(3):311–319.
354. Shao YC, Harwood P, Grotz MR, et al. Radial nerve palsy associated with fractures of the shaft of the humerus: a systematic review. J Bone Joint Surg Br 2005;87(12): 1647–1652.
355. Shaw W. Aesthetic reconstructions of the leg after trauma. Clin Plast Surg 1986;13(4): 723–733.
356. Sheetz KK, Bishop AT, Berger RA. The arterial blood supply of the distal radius and its potential use in vascularized pedicled bone grafts. J Hand Surg 1995;20A:902–914.
357. Shigetomi M, Doi K, Kuwata N, et al. Experimental study on vascularized bone allografts for reconstruction of massive bone defects. Microsurgery 1994;15(9):663–670.
358. Shin AY, Spinner RJ, Steinmann SP, et al. Adult traumatic brachial plexus injuries. J Am Acad Orthop Surg 2005;13(6):382–396.
359. Shin R, Ring D. The ulnar nerve in elbow trauma. J Bone Joint Surg Am 2007;89(5): 1108–1116.
360. Shirtliff ME, Calhoun JH, Mader JT. Comparative evaluation of oral levofloxacin and parenteral nafcillin in the treatment of experimental methicillin-susceptible *Staphylococcus aureus* osteomyelitis in rabbits. J Antimicrob Chemother 2001;48(2):253–258.
361. Shivarathre DG, Dheerendra SK, Bari A, et al. Management of clinical radial nerve palsy with closed fracture shaft of humerus—a postal questionnaire survey. Surgeon 2008; 6(2):76–78.
362. Sirkin M, Sanders R, DiPasquale T, et al. A staged protocol for soft tissue management in the treatment of complex pilon fractures. J Orthop Trauma 2004;18:s32–38.
363. Smith PJ. The Y-shaped hypogastric-groin flap. Hand 1982;14:263–270.
364. Smith PJ FB, McGregor IA, Jackson IT. The anatomical basis of the groin flap. Plast Reconstr Surg 1972;49:41–47.
365. Solomon GA, Yaremchuk MJ, Manson PN. Doppler ultrasound surface monitoring of both arterial and venous flow in clinical free tissue transfers. J Reconstr Microsurg 1986;3:39.
366. Solonen KA, Rindell K, Paavilainen T. Vascularized pedicled bone graft into the femoral head—treatment of aseptic necrosis of the femoral head. Arch Orthop Trauma Surg 1990;109(3):160–163.
367. Sowa DT, Weiland AJ. Clinical applications of vascularized bone autografts. Orthop Clin North Am 1987;18(2):257–273.
368. Stadelmann WK, Digenis AG, Tobin GR. Impediments to wound healing. Am J Surg 1998;176(2, Suppl 1):39S–47S.
369. Stein A, Raoult D. Colistin: an antimicrobial for the 21st century? Clin Infect Dis 2002; 35(7):901–902.
370. Steirt AE, Gohritz A. Delayed flap coverage of open extremity fractures after previous vacuum-assisted closure (VAC) therapy—worse or worth? J Plast Reconstr Aesthet Surg 2008;62(5):675–683.
371. Stern R, McPherson M, Longaker MT. Histologic study of artificial skin used in the treatment of full-thickness thermal injury. J Burn Care Rehabil 1990;11:7–13.
372. Stevanovic M, Gutow AP, Sharpe F. The management of bone defects of the forearm after trauma. Hand Clin 1999;15(2):299–318.
373. Stock W, Hierner R, Dielert E, et al. The iliac crest region: donor site for vascularized bone periosteal and soft tissue flaps. Ann Plast Surg 1991;26(1):105–109.
374. Strauch B, Yu H-L. Atlas of Microvascular Surgery. Anatomy and Operative Approach. 2nd ed. New York: Thieme, 2006.
375. Summers AN, Sanger JR, Matloub HS. Lateral arm fascial flap microarterial anatomy and potential J Reconstr Microsurg 2000;16(4):279–286.
376. Sunagawa T, Bishop AT, Muramatsu K. Role of conventional and vascularized bone grafts in scaphoid nonunion with avascular necrosis: a canine experimental study [in proc cit]. J Hand Surg 2000;25A(5):849–859 [MEDLINE record in process].
377. Sunderland S. A classification of peripheral nerve injuries producing loss of function. Brain 1951;74:491–516.
378. Swartz WM, Izquierdo R, Miller MJ. Implantable venous Doppler microvascular monitoring. Plast Reconstr Surg 1994;93:152–163.
379. Takato T, Harii K, Nakatsuka T, et al. Vascularized periosteal grafts: an experimental study using two different forms of tibial periosteum in rabbits. Plast Reconstr Surg 1986;78(4):489–497.
380. Takayanagi S, Ohtsuka M, Tsukie T. Use of the latissimus dorsi and the serratus anterior muscles as a combined flap. Ann Plast Surg 1988;20(4):333–339.
381. Tan CH. Reconstruction of the bones and joints of the upper extremity by vascularized free fibular graft: report of 46 cases. J Reconstr Microsurg 1992;8:285–292.
382. Tan NC, Cigna E, Varkey P, et al. Debulking of free myocutaneous flaps for head and neck reconstruction using an arthroscopic shaver. Int J Oral Maxillofac Surg 2007; 36(5):450–452.
383. Tarbox BB, Conroy BP, Malicky ES, et al. Benzalkonium chloride. A potential disinfecting irrigation solution for orthopaedic wounds. Clin Orthop Relat Res 1998;Jan(346): 255–261.
384. Taylor GI. The current status of free vascularized bone grafts. Clin Plast Surg 1983; 10(1):185–209.
385. Tobin GR. Hemisoleus and reversed hemisoleus flaps. Plast Reconstr Surg 1985;76: 87–96.
386. Trumble TE, McCallister WV. Repair of peripheral nerve defects in the upper extremity. Hand Clin 2000;16(1):37–52.
387. Tsai FC. A new method perforator-based tissue expansion for a preexpanded free cutaneous perforator flap. Burns 2003;29(8):845–848.
388. Tsai TM, Ludwig L, Tonkin M. Vascularized fibular epiphyseal transfer. A clinical study. Clin Orthop Relat Res 1986;Sep(210):228–234.
389. Tscherne H. The management of open fractures. In: Tscherne H, Gotzen L, eds. Fractures with Soft Tissue Injuries. New York: Springer Verlag, 1984, pp. 10–32.
390. Tscherne H, Gotzen L. Fractures with Soft Tissue Injuries. Berlin: Springer-Verlag, 1984.
391. Tscherne H, Oestern HJ. Die Klassifizierung des Weichteilschadens bei offenen und geschlossenen Frakturen. Unfallheilkunde 1982;85:111–115.
392. Tung TC, Wang KC, Fang CM, et al. Reverse pedicle lateral arm flap for reconstruction of posterior soft-tissue defects of the elbow. Ann Plast Surg 1997;38:635–641.
393. Uchida Y, Sugioka Y. Effects of vascularized bone graft on surrounding necrotic bone: an experimental study. J Reconstr Microsurg 1990;6(2):101–107; discussion 9, 11.
394. Ueng SW, Wei FC, Shih CH. Management of femoral diaphyseal infected nonunion with antibiotic beads, local therapy, external skeletal fixation, and staged bone grafting. J Trauma 1999;46:97–103.
395. Urbaniak JR, Coogan PG, Gunneson EB, et al. Treatment of osteonecrosis of the femoral head with free vascularized fibular grafting. A long-term follow-up study of one hundred and three hips. J Bone Joint Surg Am 1995;77(5):681–694.
396. Urken ML, Bridger AG, Zur KB, Genden EM. The scapular osteofasciocutaneous flap: a 12-year experience. Arch Otolaryngol Head Neck Surg 2001;127(7):862–869.
397. Usami F, Iketani M, Hirukawa M, et al. Treatment of congenital pseudoarthrosis of the tibia by a free vascularized fibular graft: case report. J Microsurg 1981;3(1):40–47.
398. Uysal AC, Lu F, Mizuno H, et al. Defining vascular supply and territory of thinned perforator flaps: Part I. Anterolateral thigh perforator flap. Plast Reconstr Surg 2006; 118(1):288–289.
399. Van Beek AL, Link WJ, Bennet JE, Glover JL. Ultrasound evaluation of microanastomosis. Arch Surg 1975;110:945.
400. Van Den Berghe G, Wouers P, Weekers F, et al. Intensive insulin therapy in critically ill patients. NEJM 2001;345(19):1359–1366.
401. Vande Berg JS, Rudolph R. Immunohistochemistry of fibronectin and actin in ungrafted wound and wounds covered with full-thickness and split-thickness skin grafts. Plast Reconstr Surg 1993;91:684–692.
402. Varitimidis SE, Sotereanos DG. Partial nerve injuries in the upper extremity. Hand Clin 2000;16(1):141–149.
403. Violas P, Abid A, Darodes P, et al. Integra artificial skin in the management of severe tissue defects, including bone exposure, in injured children. J Pediatr Orthop 2005; 14:381–384.
404. Waldvogel FA, Medoff G, Swartz MN. Osteomyelitis: a review of clinical features, therapeutic considerations, and unusual aspects. 1970;282(6):316–322.
405. Wang C, Schwaitzberg S, Berliner E, et al. Hyperbaric oxygen for treating wounds: a systematic review of the literature. Arch Surg 2003;138:272–279.
406. Wang HT, Erdmann D, Fletcher JW, et al. Anterolateral thigh flap technique in hand and upper extremity reconstruction. Tech Hand Up Extrem Surg 2004;8(4):257–261.
407. Wei FC, El-Gammal TA, Lin CH, Ueng WN. Free fibular osteoseptocutaneous graft for reconstruction of segmental femoral shaft defects. J Trauma 1997;43:784–792.
408. Wei FC, Jain V, Celik N, et al. Have we found an ideal soft-tissue flap? An experience with 672 anterolateral thigh flaps. Plast Reconstr Surg 2002;109(7):2219–2226; discussion 27–30.
409. Weiland AJ. Vascularized bone transfers. Instr Course Lect 1984;33:446–460.
410. Weiland AJ, Moore JR, Daniel RK. Vascularized bone autografts. Experience with 41 cases. Clin Orthop Relat Res 1983;Apr(174):87–95.
411. Weinzweig N, Gonzalez M. Free tissue failure is not an all-or-none phenomenon. Plast Reconstr Surg 1995;96(3):648–660.

412. Weksler BB, Pett SB, Alonso D, et al. Differential inhibition by aspirin of vascular and platelet prostaglandin synthesis in atherosclerotic patients. NEJM 1983;308(14): 800–805.

413. Whitlock MR, O'Hare PM, Sanders R, et al. The medicinal leech and its use in plastic surgery: a possible cause of infection. Br J Plast Surg 1983;36:240–244.

414. Winograd JM, Guo L. Upper extremity. In: Wei FC, Mardini S, eds. Flaps and Reconstructive Surgery. London: Elsevier, 2009, pp. 51–61.

415. Wood MB. Femoral reconstruction by vascularized bone transfer. Microsurgery 1990; 11(1):74–79.

416. Wood MB. Free vascularized bone transfers for nonunions, segmental gaps, and following tumor resection. Orthopedics 1986;9(6):810–816.

417. Wood MB. Upper extremity reconstruction by vascularized bone transfers: results and complications. J Hand Surg [Am] 1987;12(3):422–427.

418. Wood MB, Cooney WP 3rd, Irons GB Jr. Skeletal reconstruction by vascularized bone transfer: indications and results. Mayo Clin Proc 1985;60(11):729–734.

419. Wooden WA, Shestak KC, Newton ED, et al. Liposuction-assisted revision and recontouring of free microvascular tissue transfers. Aesthetic Plast Surg 1993;17(2): 103–107.

420. Wray RC, Wise DM, Young VL, et al. The groin flap in severe hand injuries. Ann Plast Surg 1982;9:459–462.

421. Wu WC, Chang YP, So YC, et al. The combined use of flaps based on the subscapular vascular system for limb reconstruction. Br J Plast Surg 1997;50(2):73–80.

422. Yajima H, Inada Y, Shono M, et al. Radical forearm flap with vascularized tendons for hand reconstruction. Plast Reconstr Surg 1996;98(2):328–333.

423. Yajima H, Tamai S, Ono H, et al. Free vascularized fibular grafts in surgery of the upper limb. J Reconstr Microsurg 1999;15:515–521.

424. Yang WG, Chiang YC, Wei FC, et al. Thin anterolateral thigh perforator flap using a modified perforator microdissection technique and its clinical application for foot resurfacing. Plast Reconstr Surg 2006;117(3):1004–1008.

425. Yannas IV, Burke JF. Design of an artifiical skin. I. basic design principles. J Biomed Mater Res 1980;14:65–81.

426. Yannas IV, Burke JF, Gordon PL, et al. Design of an artificial skin. II. Control of chemical composition. J Biomed Mater Res 1980;14:107–131.

427. Yaremchuk MJ. Acute management of severe soft-tissue damage accompanying open fractures of the lower extremity. Clin Plast Surg 1986;13:621–629.

428. Yaremchuk MJ, Nettelblad H, Randolph MA, et al. Vascularized bone allograft transplantation in a genetically defined rat model. Plast Reconstr Surg 1985;75(3):355–362.

429. Yazar S, Lin CH, Lin YT, et al. Outcome comparison between free muscle and free fasciocutaneous flaps for reconstruction of distal third and ankle traumatic open tibial fractures. Plast Reconstr Surg 2006;117(7):2468–2475; discussion 76–77.

430. Yazar S, Lin CH, Wei FC. One-stage reconstruction of composite bone and soft-tissue defects in traumatic lower extremities. Plast Reconstr Surg 2004;114(6):1457–1466.

431. Yeoman PM, Seddon HJ. Brachial plexus injuries: treatment of the flail arm. J Bone Joint Surg 1961;43B:493–500.

432. Yildirim S, Giderolu K, Aköz T. Anterolateral thigh flap: ideal free flap choice for lower extremity soft-tissue reconstruction. J Reconstr Microsurg 2003;19(4):225–233.

433. Yildirim S, Gideroğlu K, Aköz T. Anterolateral thigh flap ideal free flap choice for lower extremity soft-tissue reconstruction. J Reconstr Microsurg 2003;19(4):225–233.

434. Yoshimura M, Shimamura K, Iwai Y, et al. Free vascularized fibular transplant. A new method for monitoring circulation of the grafted fibula. J Bone Joint Surg Am 1983; 65(9):1295–1301.

435. Yoshimura Y, Kondoh T. Treatment of chylous fistula with fibrin glue and clavicular periosteal flap. Br J Oral Maxillofac Surg 2002;40(2):138–139.

436. Yoshizaki K. [Experimental study of vascularized fibular grafting including the epiphyseal growth plate—autogenous orthotopic grafting]. Nippon Seikeigeka Gakkai Zasshi 1984;58(8):813–828.

437. Yu AX, Chen ZG, Yu GR. [Repair of humeral fracture and non-union with transfer of vascularized periosteal flap]. Zhongguo Xiu Fu Chong Jian Wai Ke Za Zhi 2001;15(5): 310–311.

438. Zaidemberg C, Siebert JW, Angrigiani C. A new vascularized bone graft for scaphoid nonunion. J Hand Surg 1991;16A(3):474–478.

439. Zeng BF, Chen YF, Zhang ZR, et al. Emergency rotationplasty of ankle to knee. Plast 1998;101:1608–1615.

440. Zhang BM, Wieslander JB. Dextrin's antithrombotic properties in small arteries are not altered by low-molecular-weight heparin or the fibrinolytic inhibitor tranexamic acid: an experimental study. Microsurgery 1993;14:289.

441. Zhang F, Liu J, Zhong G. [Applied anatomy of osteo-periosteal flap pedicled with superior malleolar branch of anterior tibial artery]. Zhongguo Xiu Fu Chong Jian Wai Ke Za Zhi 1997;11(5):312–314.

442. Zinberg EM, Wood MB, Brown ML. Vascularized bone transfer: evaluation of viability by postoperative bone scan. J Reconstr Microsurg 1985;2(1):13–19.

15

OUTCOME STUDIES IN TRAUMA

Mohit Bhandari

INTRODUCTION

The "outcomes" movement in orthopaedic surgery involves careful attention to the design, statistical analysis, and critical appraisal of clinical research. The delineation between "outcomes" research and "evidence-based medicine" is vague. Because the term evidence-based medicine (EBM) was coined first at McMaster University, orthopaedic surgeons and researchers have adopted their own style of critical appraisal, often coined as "evidence-based orthopaedics" (EBO). EBO entails using a clear delineation of relevant clinical questions, a thorough search of the literature relating to the questions, a critical appraisal of available evidence and its applicability to the clinical situation, and a balanced application of the conclusions to the clinical problem.[27,47,48]

The balanced application of the evidence (the clinical decision-making) is the central point of practicing EBO and involves, according to EBM principles, integration of our clinical expertise and judgment, patients' perceptions and societal values, and the best available research evidence.[2,19]

EBO involves a hierarchy of evidence, from meta-analyses of high-quality randomized trials showing definitive results directly applicable to an individual patient, to relying on physiologic rationale or previous experience with a small number of similar patients. The hallmark of the evidence-based surgeon is that, for particular clinical decisions, he or she knows the strength of the evidence, and therefore the degree of uncertainty.

In the process of adopting EBO strategies, surgeons must avoid common misconceptions about EBO. Critics have mistakenly suggested that evidence can be derived only from the results of randomized trials or that statistical significance automatically means clinical relevance. These things are not true. This chapter provides an evaluation of all study designs with recommendations to their appropriate use in orthopaedic clinical research.

HIERARCHY OF EVIDENCE

Among various study designs, there exists a hierarchy of evidence with randomized controlled trials (RCTs) at the top, controlled observational studies in the middle, and uncontrolled studies and opinion at the bottom (Fig. 15-1).[17,19,20,47] Understanding the association between study design and level of evidence is important. The *Journal of Bone and Joint Surgery* (JBJS), as of January 2003, has published the level of evidence associated with each published scientific article to provide readers with a gauge of the validity of the study results. Based upon a review of several existing evidence ratings, the JBJS uses five levels for each of the four different study types (therapeutic, prognostic, diagnostic, and economic or decision-modeling studies) (Table 15-1).[52] Level 1 studies may be deemed appropriate for the application to patient care, whereas Level 4 studies should be interpreted with caution. For example, readers should be more confident about the results of a high-quality multicenter randomized trial of arthroplasty versus internal fixation on revision rates and mortality (Level 1 study) than two separate case series evaluating either arthroplasty or internal fixation on the same outcomes (Level 4 studies).

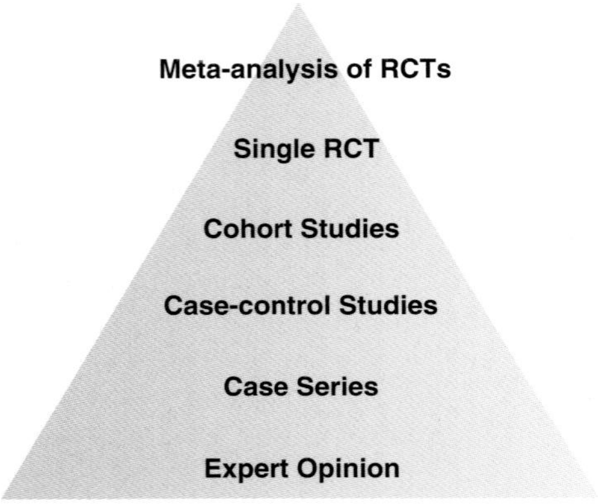

Bhandari et al.[14] have evaluated the interobserver agreement among reviewers with varying levels of epidemiology training in categorizing clinical studies published in the JBJS into levels of evidence. Among 51 included articles, the majority were studies of therapy (68.6%) constituting Level 4 evidence (56.9%). Overall, agreement among reviewers for the study type, level of evidence, and subcategory within each level was substantial (range: 0.61–0.75). Epidemiology trained reviewers demonstrated greater agreement (range: 0.99–1.0) across all aspects of the classification system when compared with nonepidemiology trained reviewers (range: 0.60–0.75). The findings suggested that epidemiology and nonepidemiology trained reviewers can apply the levels of evidence guide to published studies with acceptable interobserver agreement. Although reliable, it remains unknown whether this system is valid.[14]

The hierarchy of evidence bases its classification on the validity of the study design. Thus, those designs that limit bias to the greatest extent find themselves at the top of the pyramid and those inherently biased designs are at the bottom (see Fig. 15-1). Application of the levels of evidence also requires a fundamental understanding of various study designs.

Sackett et al.[47] proposed a grading system that categorizes the hierarchy of research designs as levels of evidence. Each level (from 1–5) is associated with a corresponding grade of recommendation: (i) grade A—consistent Level 1 studies, (ii) grade B—consistent Level 2 or Level 3 studies, (iii) grade C—Level 4 studies, and (iv) grade D—Level 5 studies.[17,19,20,47]

More recently, the GRADE working group suggested that, when making a recommendation for treatment, four areas should be considered (Table 15-2)[3-5]: (i) What are the benefits versus the harms? Are there clear benefits to an intervention or are there more harms than good?; (ii) What is the quality of the evidence? (iii) Are there modifying factors affecting the clinical setting such as the proximity of qualified persons able to carry out the intervention? (iv) What is the baseline risk for the potential population being treated?

STUDY DESIGNS

The types of study designs used in clinical research can be classified broadly according to whether the study focuses on describing the distributions or characteristics of a disease or on elucidating its determinants (Fig. 15-2).[20] *Descriptive studies* describe the distribution of a disease, particularly what type of people have the disease, in what locations, and when. Cross

FIGURE 15-1 The hierarchy of evidence with high-quality randomized trials at the top and expert opinion at the bottom.

Meta-analysis of RCTs

Single RCT

Cohort Studies

Case-control Studies

Case Series

Expert Opinion

| TABLE 15-1 | **Levels of Evidence** | | | |

	Types of Studies			
	Therapeutic Studies—Investigating the Results of Treatment	**Prognostic Studies—Investigating the Outcome of Disease**	**Diagnostic Studies—Investigating a Diagnostic Test**	**Economic and Decision Analyses—Developing an Economic or Decision Model**

Level I	1. Randomized Trial
	  a. Statistically significant difference
	  b. No statistically significant difference but narrow CIs
	2. Systematic Review[†] of Level I RCTs (and studies were homogenous)
		1. Prospective study*
		2. Systematic review[†] of Level I studies
			1. Testing of previously developed diagnostic criteria on consecutive patients (with universally applied reference criterion standard)
			2. Systematic review[†] of Level I studies
				1. Clinically sensible costs and alternatives; values obtained from many studies; with multiway sensitivity analyses
				2. Systematic review[†] of Level I studies

Level II	1. Prospective cohort study[‡]
	2. Poor quality RCT (e.g., < 80% follow-up)
	3. Systematic review[†]
	  a. Level II studies
	  b. Nonhomogeneous Level 1 studies
		1. Retrospective** study
		2. Untreated controls from a RCT
		3. Systematic review[†] of Level II studies
			1. Development of diagnostic criteria on consecutive patients (with universally applied reference criterion standard)
			2. Systematic review[†] of Level II studies
				1. Clinically sensible costs and alternatives; values obtained from limited studies; with multiway sensitivity analyses
				2. Systematic review[†] of Level II studies

Level III	1. Case control study[††] 2. Retrospective** cohort study 3. Systematic review[†] of Level III studies		1. Study of nonconsecutive patients; without consistently applied reference criterion standard 2. Systematic review[†] of Level III studies	1. Analyses based on limited alternatives and costs and poor estimates 2. Systematic review[†] of Level III studies
Level IV	Case series (no, or historical, control group)	Case series	1. Case-control study 2. Poor reference standard	Analyses with no sensitivity analyses
Level V	Expert opinion	Expert opinion	Expert opinion	Expert opinion

*Study was started before the first patient enrolled.
[†]A combination of results from two or more prior studies.
[‡]Patients treated one way (e.g., with cemented hip arthroplasty) compared with patients treated another way (e.g., with cementless hip arthroplasty) at the same institution.
**Study was started after the first patient enrolled.
[††]Patients identified for the study on the basis of their outcome (e.g., failed total hip arthroplasty), called "cases," are compared with those who did not have the outcome (e.g., had a successful total hip arthroplasty), called "controls."
Adapted from JBJS Guidelines. Available online at http://www2.ejbs.org/misc/instrux.dtl#levels.

sectional studies, case reports, and case series represent types of descriptive studies. *Analytic studies* focus on determinants of a disease by testing a hypothesis with the ultimate goal of judging whether a particular exposure causes or prevents disease. Analytic design strategies are broken into two types: observational studies, such as case-control and cohort studies, and experimental studies, also called clinical trials. The difference between the two types of analytic studies is the role that the investigator plays in each of the studies. In the observational study, the investigator simply observes the natural course of events. In the trial, the investigator assigns the intervention or treatment.

Bhandari et al.[16] reviewed each type of study to highlight methodological issues inherent in their design (Table 15-3).

Meta-Analysis (Level 1 Evidence; Grade A Recommendation)

Although not considered to be a primary study design, meta-analysis deserves mention because it is frequently utilized in

the surgical literature. A meta-analysis is a systematic review that combines the results of multiple studies (of small sample size) to answer a focused clinical question. Meta-analyses are retrospective in nature. The main advantage of meta-analysis is the ability to increase the "total sample size" of the study by combining the results of many smaller studies. When well-designed studies are available on a particular question of interest, a meta-analysis can provide important information to guide clinical practice. Consider the following example. Several small randomized trials have attempted to resolve the issue of whether operative repair of acute Achilles tendon ruptures in younger patients reduces the risk of rerupture compared with conservative treatment. Of five randomized trials (ranging in sample size from 27 to 111 patients), four found nonsignificant differences in rerupture rates. These studies were underpowered. Using meta-analytic techniques, the results of these small studies were combined (n = 336 patients) to produce a summary estimate of 3.6% surgery versus 10.6% conservative (relative risk =

TABLE 15-2	**Criteria for Assessing Grade of Evidence**

Type of Evidence
Randomized trial = high quality
Quasi-randomized = moderate quality
Observational study = low quality
Any other evidence = very low quality

Decrease Grade(s) if:
Serious (−1) or very serious (−2) limitation to study quality
Important inconsistency (−1)
Some (−1) or major (−2) uncertainty about directness
Imprecise or sparse data (−1)
High probability of reporting bias (−1)

Increase Grade(s) if:
Strong evidence of association—significant relative risk greater than 2 (<0.5) based on consistent evidence from two or more observational studies, with no plausible confounders (+1)
Very strong evidence of association—significant relative risk greater than 5 (<0.2) based on direct evidence with no major threats to validity (+2)
Evidence of a dose response gradient (+1)
All plausible confounders would have reduced the effect (+1)

0.41; 95% confidence interval [CI], 0.17%–0.99%; $p = 0.05$) of adequate study power (>80%) to help guide patient care.[9]

Another benefit of meta-analysis is the increased impact over traditional reviews (i.e., narrative or nonsystematic reviews). Rigorous systematic reviews received over twice the number of mean citations compared with other systematic or narrative reviews (13.8 vs. 6.0, $p = 0.008$).[12]

Authors of meta-analyses can be limited to summarizing the outcomes available and not necessarily the outcomes of interest. There is often a trade off between pooling data from many studies on common and sometimes less relevant outcomes (i.e., nonunion) versus fewer studies reporting less common outcomes of interest (i.e., avascular necrosis). Thus, the definition

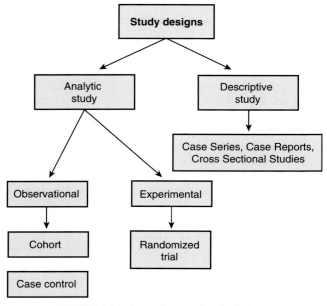

FIGURE 15-2 Categorization of study designs.

eligibility criteria for the studies to be included is an important step in the conduct of a meta-analysis.

Meta-analysis of high-quality randomized trials represents the current standard in the translation of evidence to practice. While meta-analysis can be a powerful tool, its value is diminished when poor quality studies (i.e., case series) are included in the pooling. Pooled analyses of nonrandomized studies are prone to bias and have limited validity. Surgeons should be aware of these limitations when extrapolating such data to their particular clinical settings.

Randomized Trial (Level 1 Evidence; Grade A Recommendation)

When considering a single study, the randomized trial is the single most important design to limit bias in clinical research.[11] While it may seem elementary to explain the term "randomization," most surgeons are unfamiliar with the rationale for random allocation of patients in a trial. Orthopaedic treatment studies attempt to determine the impact of an intervention on events such as nonunions, infections, or death—occurrences that we call the trial's target outcomes or target events. Patients' age, the underlying severity of fracture, the presence of comorbid conditions, health habits, and a host of other factors typically determine the frequency with which a trial's target outcome occurs (prognostic factors). Randomization gives a patient entering a clinical trial an equal probability (or chance) of being allocated to alternative treatments. Patients can be randomized to alternative treatments by random number tables or computerized randomization systems. Randomization is the only method for controlling for known and unknown prognostic factors between two comparison groups. For instance, in a study comparing plates and intramedullary nails for the treatment of tibial shaft fractures in patients with concomitant head injury, investigators reported imbalance in acetabular fractures between treatment groups. Readers will agree that differences in patient function or mortality may not be attributed to treatment groups, but rather differences in the proportion of patients with acetabular fractures. Realizing this imbalance due to lack of randomization, the investigators employed a less attractive strategy to deal with the imbalance—statistical adjustment for differences between groups. By controlling for the difference in the number of acetabular fractures between groups, the effect of plates versus nails in patients was determined.

Equally important is the concept of "concealment" (not to be confused with blinding).[11] Concealed randomization ensures that surgeons are unable to predict the treatment to which their next patient will be allocated. The safest manner in which to limit this occurrence is a remote 24-hour telephone randomization service. Historically, treatment allocations in surgical trials have been placed within envelopes; while seemingly concealed, envelopes are prone to tampering.

While it is believed that surgical trials cannot be double-blinded due to the relative impossibility of blinding surgeons, Devereaux and colleagues[24] have recently challenged the "classic" definition of double-blinding. In a survey of 91 internists and researchers, 17 unique definitions of "double-blinding" were obtained. Moreover, randomized trials in five high-profile medical journals (*New England Journal of Medicine*, *The Lancet*, *British Medical Journal*, *Annals of Internal Medicine*, and *Journal of the American Medical Association*) revealed considerable

TABLE 15-3 **Study Designs and Common Errors**

Study Design	Summary	Common Errors
Meta-analysis	High quality studies addressing a focused clinical question are critically reviewed and their results statistically combined.	Major differences between pooled studies (heterogeneity) Poor quality studies pooled = less valid results
Randomized Trial	Patients are randomized to receive alternative treatments (i.e., cast versus intramedullary nail for tibial shaft fracture). Outcomes (i.e., infection rates) are measured prospectively.	Type II (beta) errors: insufficient sample size Type I (alpha) error: overuse of statistical tests and multiple outcomes Lack of blinding Lack of concealed randomization
Prospective Cohort (with Comparison Group)	Patients who receive two different treatments are followed forward in time. Choice of treatment is not randomly assigned (i.e., surgeon preference, patient preference). Comparison group is identified and followed at the same time as the treatment group (i.e., concurrent comparison group). Outcomes (i.e., infection rates) are measured prospectively.	Type II (beta) errors: insufficient sample size Type I (alpha) error: overuse of statistical tests and multiple outcomes Lack of adjustment for differences in characteristics between treatment and comparison groups
Prospective Case Series (without Comparison Group)	Patients who receive a particular treatment are followed forward in time (i.e., intramedullary nailing of tibial fractures). No concurrent comparison group is utilized.	Lack of independent or blinded assessment of outcomes Lack of follow-up
Case-Control Study	Patients with an outcome of interest (i.e., infection) are compared backward in time (retrospective) to similar patients without the outcome of interest (i.e., no infection). Risk factors for a particular outcome can be determined between cases and controls.	Type II (beta) errors: insufficient sample size Type I (alpha) error: overuse of statistical tests and multiple outcomes Problems in ascertainment of cases and controls
Retrospective Case Series (with Comparison Group)	Patients with a particular treatment are identified backward in time (i.e., retrospectively). Comparison patients are also identified retrospectively.	Type II (beta) errors: insufficient sample size Type I (alpha) error: overuse of statistical tests and multiple outcomes Incomplete reporting in patient charts

variability in the reporting of blinding terminology. Common sources of blinding in a randomized trial include: physicians, patients, outcome assessors, and data analysts. Current recommendations for reporting randomized trials include explicit statements about who was blinded in the study rather than using the term "double-blinded." Surgical trials can always blind the data analyst, almost always blind the outcome assessor, occasionally blind the patient, and never blind the surgeon. In a review of orthopaedic trials, outcome assessors were blinded only 44% of the time and data analysts were never blinded. However, at least two thirds of surgical trials could have achieved double-blinding by blinding the outcome assessors, patients, or data analysts.[13]

The principle of attributing all patients to the group to which they were randomized results is an *intention-to-treat* principle (Fig. 15-3).[11] This strategy preserves the value of randomization: prognostic factors that we know about and those we don't know about will be, on average, equally distributed in the two groups, and the effect we see will be just that due to the treatment assigned. When reviewing a report of a randomized trial, one should look for evidence that the investigators analyzed all patients in the groups to which they were randomized. Some suggest that an intention-to-treat approach is too conservative and more susceptible to type II error due to increased biologic

variability. Their argument is that an intention-to-treat analysis is less likely to show a positive treatment effect, especially for those studies that randomized patients who had little or no chance of benefiting from the intervention.

An alternative approach, referred to as a *per protocol* analysis,

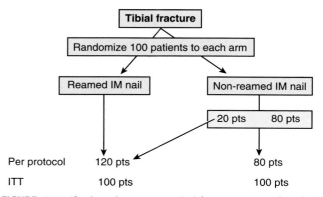

FIGURE 15-3 The intention to treat principle: a per protocol analysis analyzes patient outcomes to the treatment they "actually received" whereas intention to treat analysis evaluates outcomes based upon the treatment to which patients were originally randomized.

reports outcomes on the treatments patients actually received regardless of the number of crossovers from one treatment to another. This approach is often utilized to determine whether imbalances in baseline factors actually affect the final result. It may be particularly important when patients who are randomized to one treatment (i.e., reamed or unreamed tibial nail) but never receive either treatment. For example, in a trial of reamed versus unreamed tibial nailing, a patient randomized to a reamed tibial nail who ultimately receives an external fixator due to an intraoperative surgical decision will be excluded from in per protocol analysis; however, recall that this same patient would be included in the reamed tibial nail group in an intention-to-treat analysis.

The overall quality of a randomized trial can be evaluated with a simple checklist (Table 15-4). This checklist provides guides to the assessment of the methodological rigor of a trial.

Randomized Trial (Expertise-Based Design)

In conventional surgical hip fracture trials, all surgeons involved in the trial have performed both total hip arthroplasties (THA) and hemiarthroplasties. Surgeons performing arthroplasty are frequently less experienced (or expert) in one or both surgical alternatives. This trial aims to limit this differential expertise across treatment alternatives. In our proposed expertise-based design, we will randomize patients to receive THA (by surgeons who are experienced and committed to performing only THA) or to hemiarthroplasty (by surgeons with expertise in hemiarthroplasty who are committed to performing only hemiarthroplasty). Devereaux and colleagues[23] have outlined the ad-

vantages of this trial design, which include the following: (i) elimination of differential expertise bias where, in conventional designs, a larger proportion of surgeons are expert in one procedure under investigation than the other; (ii) differential performance, cointervention, data collection, and outcome assessment are less likely than in conventional RCTs; (iii) procedural crossovers are less likely because surgeons are committed and experienced in their procedures; and (iv) ethical concerns are reduced because all surgeries are conducted by surgeons with expertise and conviction concerning the procedure.[23]

Observational Study (Cohort, Case Series)

Studies in which randomization is not employed can be referred to as nonrandomized, or *observational*, study designs. The role of observational comparative studies in evaluating treatments is an area of continued debate: deliberate choice of the treatment for each patient implies that observed outcomes may be caused by differences among people being given the two treatments, rather than the treatments alone.[10] Unrecognized confounding factors can interfere with attempts to correct for identified differences between groups. There has been considerable debate about whether the results of nonrandomized studies are consistent with the results of RCTs.[7,22,29,33] Nonrandomized studies have been reported to overestimate or underestimate treatment effects.[29,33]

One example of the pitfalls of nonrandomized studies was reported in a study comparing study designs that addressed the general topic of comparison of arthroplasty and internal fixation for hip fracture.[17] Mortality data was available in 13 nonran-

TABLE 15-4 **Checklist for Assessing Quality of Reporting**			
Randomization	1 Yes	1 Partly	0 No
Were the patients assigned randomly?	2 Yes		0 No
Randomization adequately described?	1 Yes		0 No
Was treatment group concealed to investigator?			
Total/4			
Description of outcome measurement adequate?	1 Yes	1 Partly	0 No
Outcome measurements objective?	2 Yes		0 No
Were the assessors blind to treatment?	1 Yes		0 No
Total/4			
Were inclusion/exclusion criteria well defined?	2 Yes	1 Partly	0 No
Number of patients excluded and reason?	2 Yes	1 Partly	0 No
Total/4			
Was the therapy fully described for the treatment group?	2 Yes	1 Partly	0 No
Was the therapy fully described for the controls?	2 Yes	1 Partly	0 No
Total/4			
Statistics	1 Yes	1 Partial	0 No
Was the test stated and was there a p value?	2 Yes		0 No
Was the statistical analysis appropriate?	1 Yes		0 No
Is the trial was negative, were confidence intervals of post hoc power calculations performed?	1 Yes		0 No
Sample size calculation before the study?			
Total/4 (if positive trial) Total/5 (negative trial)			

Total Score: 20 points (if positive trial)
　　　　　　21 points (if negative trial)

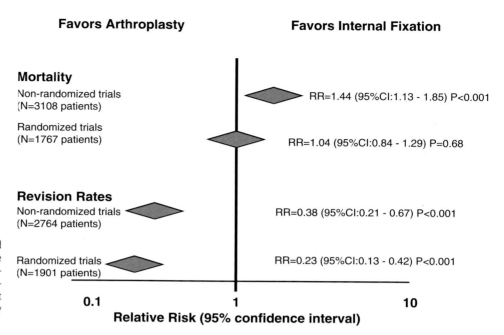

FIGURE 15-4 Estimates from randomized trials tend to provide a more conservative estimate of a treatment effect when compared to nonrandomized studies. Nonrandomized studies overestimate the benefit of internal fixation regarding mortality by 40%.

domized studies (n = 3108 patients) and in 12 randomized studies (n = 1767 patients). Nonrandomized studies overestimated the risk of mortality by 40% when compared with the results of randomized trials (relative risk: 1.44 vs. 1.04, respectively) (Fig. 15-4). If we believe the data from the nonrandomized trials, then no surgeon would offer a patient a hemiarthroplasty for a displaced hip fracture given the significant risk of mortality. However, in practice, arthroplasty is generally favored over internal fixation in the treatment of displaced femoral neck fractures. Thus, surgeons believe the randomized trials that report no significant differences in mortality and significant reductions in revisions with arthroplasty.

Important contradictory examples of observational and RCT results can be found in the surgical literature. An observational study of extracranial-to-intracranial bypass surgery suggested a "dramatic improvement in the symptomatology of virtually all patients" undergoing the procedure.[56] However, a subsequent large RCT demonstrated a 14% relative increase in the risk of fatal and nonfatal stroke in patients undergoing this procedure compared to medical management.[1] These considerations have supported a hierarchy of evidence, with RCTs at the top, controlled observational studies in the middle, and uncontrolled studies and opinion at the bottom. However, these findings have not been supported in two publications in the *New England Journal of Medicine* that identified nonsignificant differences in results between RCTs and observational studies.[7,22]

Although randomized trials, when available, represent the most valid evidence, information from nonrandomized studies can provide invaluable data to generate hypotheses for future studies.

Prospective Observational Study (Level 2 Evidence; Grade B Recommendation)

A prospective observational study identifies a group of patients at a similar point in time and follows them forward in time. Outcomes are determined prior to the start of the study and evaluated at regular time intervals until the conclusion of the

study. A comparison group (controls) may also be identified concurrently and followed for the same time period.

While comparison groups are helpful when comparing outcomes of two surgical alternatives, a prospective evaluation of a single group of patients with complex injuries can provide information on the frequency of success (radiographic and functional outcomes) and expected complications. This information is most useful when the data collected remains consistent over time, the data collected includes important baseline patient characteristics and patient outcomes, and efforts are made to ensure patients are followed over time. Professor Joel Matta's acetabular fracture database is one striking example of a carefully designed single-surgeon, prospective database that has consistently collected data on patients for more than 20 years (personal communication). With over 1000 patients with acetabular fractures included in this database, the current limits of technique, results, and complications can be reported to serve as a benchmark for future studies. In addition, these types of studies can assist surgeons in discussing the expected risk and outcomes of surgery with their patients during the informed consent process.

Case-Control Study (Level 3 Evidence; Grade B Recommendation)

If the outcome of interest is rare (i.e., mortality or infection), conducting a prospective cohort study may be cost-prohibitive. A case-control study is a useful strategy in such circumstances.[20] Cases with the outcome of interest are identified retrospectively from a group of patients (i.e., databases) and matched (i.e., by age, gender, severity of injury) with control patients who do not have the outcome of interest. Both groups can be compared for differences in "risk" factors.[10] One control may be matched for each case that is identified (1:1 matching). Alternatively, multiple controls may be matched to each case (i.e., 3:1 or 4:1 matching). The validity of results from case-control studies depends upon the accuracy of the reporting of the outcomes of interest. For example, investigators conducted a study to determine risk factors for hip fracture among elderly women.[28]

To accomplish this, they identified 159 women with their first hip fracture and 159 controls (1:1 matching) matched for gender, age, and residence. Risk factors included perceived safety of the residence, psychotropic drug use, and tendency to fall. Comparison of these factors between the hip fracture and control groups revealed an increased risk of perceived safety (odds ratio = 5.8), psychotropic drug use (odds ratio = 2.6), and tendency to fall (odds ratio = 2.3) among patients who sustained a fracture compared to those who did not.

Retrospective Case Series (Level 4 Evidence; Grade C Recommendation)

The retrospective study design, while less costly and less time consuming, is often limited by bias in the ascertainment of cases and the evaluation of outcomes. Comparison groups can be identified during the same time period as the treatment group (concurrent controls). However, controls from a different period of time can also be utilized (historical controls). Patient follow-up may be conducted passively (via patient records) or actively (patient follow-up appointment and examination). When patient charts have formed the basis for the outcome evaluation, readers should be convinced that the outcomes were objective measures accurately obtained from patient records. For example, in-hospital mortality data is an objective outcome that is likely to have been well documented in patient charts; however, patient satisfaction or functional outcome is subjective and far less likely to have been recorded with any standardization or consistency.

A case series can provide initial useful information about the safety and complication profile of a new surgical technique or implant. This information is most valid when eligibility criteria for patient inclusion are clearly defined, consecutive patients are screened for eligibility, surgery and perioperative care is consistent, outcomes are objective and independently assessed, and follow-up is complete. Unfortunately, the validity of the results can be compromised by inadequate and incomplete reporting of patient characteristics and outcomes in patient charts.

Case Study: The Study to Prospectively Evaluate Reamed Intramedullary Nails in Tibial Fractures Trial (Level 1 Study)

The debate of reamed versus nonreamed insertion of tibial intramedullary nails was largely fueled decades ago by case series (Level IV evidence). Case series eventually led to prospective cohort comparison of reamed and unreamed nailing techniques (Level II). Realizing the biases inherent in nonrandomized designs, a number of investigators conducted randomized trials ranging in sample size from 50–136 patients.[57] Despite a strong design, these trials were limited by small sample sizes, imprecise treatment effects, lack of outcome assessment blinding, and unconcealed allocation of patients to treatment groups.

The Study to Prospectively evaluate Reamed Intramedullary Nails in Tibial fractures (SPRINT) trial was designed to compare the effects of reamed and nonreamed intramedullary nailing approaches.[58] To overcome limitations of previous studies, the design involved concealed central randomization, blind adjudication of outcomes, and disallowing reoperation before 6 months.

SPRINT enrolled 1339 patients from July 2000 to September 2005 across 29 clinical sites in Canada, the United States, and the Netherlands. The final follow-up occurred in September 2006 and final outcomes adjudication was completed in January 2007. Participating investigators randomized patients by accessing a 24-hour toll-free remote telephone randomization system that ensured concealment. Randomization was stratified by center and severity of soft tissue injury (open, closed, or both open and closed) in randomly permuted blocks of 2 and 4. Patients and clinicians were unaware of block sizes. Patients were allocated to fracture fixation with an intramedullary nail following reaming of the intramedullary canal (Reamed Group) or with an intramedullary nail without prior reaming (Nonreamed Group).

All patients received postoperative care according to the same protocol. SPRINT investigators hypothesized that the benefits of reamed nails suggested by previous literature may have been due to a lower threshold for early reoperation in patients with nonreamed nails. Therefore, reoperations were disallowed within the first 6 months following surgery. Exceptions to the 6-month rule included reoperations for infections, fracture gaps, nail breakage, bone loss, or malalignment. Patients, outcome assessors, and data analysts were blinded to treatment allocation. Reoperation rates were monitored at hospital discharge, 2 weeks postdischarge, 6 weeks postsurgery, and 3, 6, 9, and 12 months postsurgery.

The SPRINT trial set a number of important benchmarks in study methodology including: (i) a sample size 10-fold greater than the largest previous tibial fracture trial; (ii) a modern trial organization including an independent blinded adjudication and data safety monitoring committee; (iii) use of innovative trial infrastructure for randomization and data management; and (iv) large scale multimillion collaborative funding from the National Institutes of Health and the Canadian Institutes of Health proving that orthopaedic surgical trials belong in the same arena as the large cardiovascular and osteoporosis trials.

UNDERSTANDING STATISTICS IN TRAUMA OUTCOME STUDIES

Hypothesis Testing

The essential paradigm for statistical inference in the medical literature has been that of hypothesis testing. The investigator starts with what is called a *null hypothesis* that the statistical test is designed to consider and possibly disprove. Typically, the null hypothesis is that there is no difference between treatments being compared. In a randomized trial in which investigators compare an experimental treatment with a placebo control, one can state the null hypothesis as follows: the true difference in effect on the outcome of interest between the experimental and control treatments is zero. We start with the assumption that the treatments are equally effective, and we adhere to this position unless data make it untenable.

In this hypothesis-testing framework, the statistical analysis addresses the question of whether the observed data are consistent with the null hypothesis. The logic of the approach is as follows: Even if the treatment truly has no positive or negative impact on the outcome (that is, the effect size is zero), the results observed will seldom show exact equivalence; that is, no difference at all will be observed between the experimental and control groups. As the results diverge further from the finding of "no difference," the null hypothesis that there is no difference between treatment effects becomes less and less credible. If the difference between results of the treatment and control groups becomes large enough, clinicians must abandon belief in the null hypothesis. We will further develop the underlying logic by describing the role of chance in clinical research.

Let us conduct a hypothetical experiment in which the suspected coin is tossed 10 times and, on all 10 occasions, the result is heads.[2] How likely is this to have occurred if the coin was indeed unbiased? Most people would conclude that it is highly unlikely that chance could explain this extreme result. We would therefore be ready to reject the hypothesis that the coin is unbiased (the null hypothesis) and conclude that the coin is biased. Statistical methods allow us to be more precise by ascertaining just how unlikely the result is to have occurred simply as a result of chance if the null hypothesis is true. The law of multiplicative probabilities for independent events (where one event in no way influences the other) tells us that the probability of 10 consecutive heads can be found by multiplying the probability of a single head (1/2) 10 times over; that is, $1/2 \times 1/2 \times 1/2$, and so on.[2] The probability of getting 10 consecutive heads is slightly less than 1 in 1000. In a journal article, one would likely see this probability expressed as a p value, such as $p < 0.001$.

What Is the p Value?

What is the precise meaning of this p value? Statistical convention calls results that fall beyond this boundary (that is, p value <0.05) *statistically significant*. The meaning of statistically significant, therefore, is that it is "sufficiently unlikely to be due to chance alone that we are ready to reject the null hypothesis." In other words, the p value is defined as the probability, under the assumption of no difference (null hypothesis), of obtaining a result equal to or more extreme than what was actually observed. Let us use the example of a study that reports the following: patient function scores following tibial intramedullary nailing were significantly greater than those patients treated with plates (75 points vs. 60 points, $p < 0.05$). This may be interpreted as the probability that the difference of 15 points observed in the study was due to chance is less than 5% (or 1 in 20).

The 95% Confidence Interval

Investigators usually (though arbitrarily) use the 95% CI when reporting the precision around a proportion. One can consider the 95% CI as defining the range that includes the true difference 95% of the time.[11] In other words, if the investigators repeated their study 100 times, it would be expected that the point estimate of their result would lie within the CI 95 of those 100 times. The true point estimate will lie beyond these extremes only 5% of the time, a property of the CI that relates closely to the conventional level of statistical significance of p <0.05. For example, if a study reports that nails reduced the risk of infection by 50% compared to plates in patients with tibial shaft fractures (95% CI: 25%–75%), one may interpret the results consistent with as little as a 25% risk reduction or as much as a 75% risk reduction. In other words, the true risk reduction of infection with nails lies somewhere between 25% and 75% (95% of the time).

Measures of Central Tendency and Spread

Investigators will often provide a general summary of data from a clinical or experimental study. A number of measures can be utilized. These include measures of central tendency (mean, median, and mode) and measures of spread (standard deviation, range). The sample mean is equal to the sum of the measurements divided by the number of observations. The median of a set of measurements is the number that falls in the middle. The mode, however, is the most frequently occurring number in a set of measurements. Continuous variables (such as blood pressure or body weight) can be summarized with a mean if the data is normally distributed. If the data is not normally distributed, then the median may be a better summary statistic. Categorical variables (pain grade: 0, 1, 2, 3, 4, or 5) can be summarized with a median.

Along with measures of central tendency, investigators will often include a measure of spread. The standard deviation is derived from the square root of the sample variance. One standard deviation away from the mean accounts for somewhere around 68% of the observations. Two standard deviations away from the mean account for roughly 95% of the observations and three standard deviations account for about 99% of the observations.

The variance is calculated as the average of the squares of the deviations of the measurements about their mean. The range of a dataset reflects the smallest value and largest value.

Measures of Treatment Effect (Dichotomous Variables)

Information comparing the outcomes (dichotomous: mortality, reoperation) of two procedures can be presented to patients as an odds ratio, a relative risk, a relative risk reduction, an absolute risk reduction, and the number needed to treat. Both reduction in relative risk and reduction in absolute risk have been reported to have the strongest influences on patient decision-making.[15]

Common Statistical Tests

Common statistical tests include those that examine differences between two or more means, differences between proportions, and associations between two or more variables (Table 15-5).[26]

Comparing Two Independent Means

When we wish to test the null hypothesis that the means of two independent samples of normally distributed continuous data are the same, the appropriate test statistic is called t, hence the t-test. The author of the original article describing the distribution of the t-statistic used the pseudonym *Student* leading to the common attribution Student's t-test.[59] When the data is nonnormally distributed, a nonparametric test such as the Mann Whitney U or Wilcoxon rank sum test can be utilized. If the means are paired, such as left and right knees, a paired t-test is most appropriate. The nonparametric correlate of this test is the Wilcoxon signed rank test.

Comparing Multiple Independent Means

When three or more different means have to be compared (i.e., hospital stay among three tibial fracture treatment groups: plate fixation, intramedullary nail, and external fixation), single factor

TABLE 15-5	**Common Statistical Tests***			
		Data Type and Distribution		
Samples		Categorical	Ordered Categorical or Continuous and Nonnormal	Continuous and Normal
Two samples	Different individuals	x^2 test Fisher's exact test	Mann-Whitney U test Wilcoxon rank sum test	Unpaired t-test
	Related or matched samples	McNemar's test	Wilcoxon signed rank test	Paired t-test
Three or more samples	Different individuals	x^2 test Fisher's exact test	Kruskal-Wallis statistic	ANOVA
	Related samples	Cochran Q-test	Friedman statistic	Repeated measures ANOVA

*Consult a statistician when planning an analysis or planning a study.
Adapted from Griffin D, Audige L. Common statistical methods in orthopaedic clinical studies. Clin Orthop Relat Res 2003;413: 70–79.

analysis of variance is a test of choice. If the test yields statistical significance, investigators can conduct post hoc comparison tests (usually a series of pairwise comparisons using t-tests) to determine where the differences lie. It should be recalled that the p value (alpha level) should be adjusted for multiple post hoc tests. One rather conservative method is the Bonferroni correction factor that simply divides the alpha level ($p = 0.05$) by the number of tests performed.

Comparing Two Proportions

A common situation in the orthopaedic literature is that two proportions are compared. For example, these may be the proportion of patients in each of two treatment groups who experience an infection. The Chi-square (χ^2) test is a simple method of determining whether the proportions are really different. When samples are small, the χ^2 test becomes rather approximate because the data is discrete but the χ^2 distribution from which the p-value is calculated is continuous. A "Yates' correction" is a device that is sometimes used to account for this, but when cell counts in the contingency table become very low (say, less than five), the χ^2 test becomes unreliable and a Fisher's exact test is the test of choice.

Determining Association between One or More Variables against One Continuous Variable

When two variables have been shown to be associated, it may be logical to try to use one variable to predict the other. The variable to be predicted is called the dependent variable and is to be used for prediction is the independent variable. For such a linear relationship, the equation $y = a + bx$ is defined as the regression equation. *A* is a constant and *b* the regression coefficient. Fitting the regression equation, generally using a software package, is the process of calculating values for *a* and *b*, which allows the regression line represented by this equation to best fit the observed data. The p value reflects the result of a hypothesis test that x and y are in fact unrelated, or in this case that b is equal to zero.

Correlation

The strength of the relationship between two variables (i.e., age versus hospital stay in patients with ankle fractures) can be summarized in a single number: the *correlation coefficient*. The correlation coefficient, which is denoted by the letter r, can range from -1.0 (representing the strongest possible negative relationship in which the person who scores the highest on variable scores the lowest on the other variable) to 1.0 (representing the strongest possible positive relationship in which the person who is older also has the longest hospital stay). A correlation coefficient of zero denotes no relationship between the two variables.

COMMON ERRORS IN THE DESIGN OF ORTHOPAEDIC STUDIES

Any study that compares two or more treatments (i.e., comparative study: randomized trial, observational study with control group, case-control) can be subject to errors in hypothesis testing. For example, when investigators conduct studies to determine whether two treatments have different outcomes, there are four potential outcomes (Fig. 15-5)[47]: (i) a true positive result (i.e., the study correctly identifies a true difference between treatments); (ii) a true negative result (i.e., the study correctly identifies no difference between treatment); (iii) a false negative result—Type II (beta) error (i.e., the study incorrectly concludes no difference between treatments when a difference really exists); and (iv) a false positive result—Type I (alpha) error (i.e., the study incorrectly concludes a difference between treatments when no difference exists).

		Difference	No difference
Results of the study	Difference	Correct conclusion (1-β)	False positive (α error or Type I error)
	No difference	False negative (β error or Type II error)	Correct conclusion (1-α)

FIGURE 15-5 Errors in hypothesis testing: type I and type II errors are presented along with the power of a study (1-β).

Type II Errors (Beta Error)

It is perceived that trials of surgical therapies may be sufficiently undersized to have a meaningful impact on clinical practice. Such trials of small sample size are subject to beta errors (Type II errors): the probability of concluding that no difference between treatment groups exists, when, in fact, there is a difference (Fig. 15-6). Typically, investigators will accept a beta error rate of 20% (β = 0.20), which corresponds with a study power of 80%. Most investigators agree that beta error rates greater than 20% (study power less than 80%) are subject to unacceptably high risks of false negative results.

In an effort to quantify the extent to which orthopaedic trauma trials were underpowered, Lochner et al.[34] reviewed 117 randomized trials in trauma for type II error rates. The mean overall study power was 24.65% (range 2%–99%). The potential type II error rate for primary outcomes was 91%. For example, one study demonstrated "no difference" between reamed and nonreamed tibial intramedullary nailing; however, this study was underpowered for this conclusion (study power = 32%). Thus, these conclusions should be interpreted with caution.

Type I Error (Alpha Error)

Most surgeons are less familiar with the concept of concluding that the results of a particular study are true, when, in fact, they are really due to chance (or random sampling error). This erroneous false positive conclusion is designated as a type I or α-error (see Fig. 15-6).[18] By convention, most studies in orthopaedics adopt an α-error rate of 0.05. Thus, investigators can expect a false positive error about 5% of the time. Ideally, a type I error rate is based on one comparison between alternative treatment groups usually designated as the primary outcome measure. In situations where no primary outcome variable has been determined, there is a risk of conducting multiple tests of significance on multiple outcomes measures. This form of data dredging by investigators risks spurious false positive findings. Several techniques are available to adjust for multiple comparisons, such as the Bonferroni correction.

Most readers are intuitively skeptical when 1 in a list of 20 outcomes measured by an investigator is significant ($p < 0.05$) between two treatment groups. This situation typically occurs when investigators are not sure what they are looking for and therefore test several hypotheses hoping that one may be true. Statistical aspects of the multiple testing issues are straightforward. If n independent associations are examined for statistical significance, the probability that at least one of them will be found statistically significant is $1-(1-\alpha)^n$ if all n of the individual null hypotheses are true. Therefore, it is argued that studies that generate a large number of measures of association have markedly greater probability of generating some false-positive results because of random error than does the stated alpha level for individual comparisons.

Bhandari and colleagues[18] conducted a review of recently published randomized trials (within the last 2 years) to determine the risk of type I errors among surgical trials that did not explicitly state a primary outcome. One study examining outcomes in two different uncemented total knee arthroplasty designs evaluated 21 different outcome measures and found 13 outcomes that were significantly different between groups. As there was no clear statement about a designated primary outcome measure, the risk of a false-positive result was 66%.[18]

The Misuse of Subgroup Analyses in Orthopaedic Outcome Studies

Subgroup analyses can be defined as treatment outcome comparisons for patients subdivided by baseline characteristics.[43,53] For instance, in a study of operative versus nonoperative management of calcaneal fractures, investigators may report no difference in the overall outcome (patient function) but subsequently conduct a series of comparisons across different patient subgroups (gender, disability status, or comorbidities). Subgroup analyses are frequently post hoc analyses that risk false-positive results (type I error) in which ineffective (or even harmful) treatments may be deemed beneficial in a subgroup. Conducting multiple statistical tests risks spurious false-positive findings. Alternatively, false-negative results may occur because negative subgroup analyses are often underpowered.

Bhandari et al.[8] identified important errors in surgical RCTs related to subgroup analyses. The majority of authors did not report whether subgroup analyses were planned a priori, and these analyses often formed the basis of the RCT conclusions. Inferences from such RCTs may be misleading and their application to clinical practice unwarranted.[43,53]

In a review of 72 RCTs published in orthopaedics and other surgical subspecialties, 27 (38%) RCTs reported a total of 54 subgroup analyses with a minimum of 1 and maximum of 32

FIGURE 15-6 The current conceptual framework for evidence-based practice encompassing research findings, patients' values and preferences, clinical circumstances, and expertise.

subgroup analyses per study.[8] The majority of subgroup analyses 49 (91%) were performed post hoc and not stated to be preplanned at the outset of the study nor included in the hypothesis. The majority of investigators inappropriately used tests of significance when comparing outcomes between subgroups of patients (41 subgroup analyses, 76%); however, only three of the analyses were performed using statistical tests for interaction. Investigators reported differences between subgroups in 31 (57%) of the analyses, all of which were featured in the summary or conclusion of the published paper.

Subgroup analyses should be undertaken and interpreted with caution. The validity of a subgroup analysis can be improved by defining a few important (and biologically plausible) subgroups prior to conducting a study and conducting statistical tests of interaction. When faced with a subgroup analysis in a published scientific paper, readers should ask the following questions: Is the subgroup difference suggested by comparisons within rather than between studies? Did the hypothesis precede rather than follow the analysis? Was the subgroup effect one of a small number of hypothesized effects tested? Is the magnitude of the effect large? Was the effect statistically significant? Is the effect consistent across studies? Is there indirect evidence that supports the hypothesized subgroup effect?

Statistical versus Clinical Significance

Statistically significant differences between two treatments may not necessarily reflect a clinically important difference. Although it is well known that orthopaedic studies with small sample sizes risk underpowered false negative conclusions (beta errors), statistically significant findings in small trials can occur at the consequence of very large differences between treatments (treatment effect). It is not uncommon for randomized trials to report relative risk reductions larger than 50% when comparing one treatment with another.

Sung et al.[51] conducted a comprehensive search for all RCTs between January 1, 1995, and December 31, 2004. Eligible studies included those that focused upon orthopaedic trauma. Baseline characteristics and treatment effects were abstracted by two reviewers. Briefly, for continuous outcome measures (i.e., functional scores), effect sizes (mean difference/standard deviation) were calculated. Dichotomous variables (i.e., infection, nonunion) were summarized as absolute risk differences and relative risk reductions (RRR). Effect sizes >0.80 and RRRs greater than 50% were defined as large effects.

These investigators identified 433 RCTs, of which 76 RCTs had statistically significant findings on 184 outcomes (122 continuous/62 dichotomous outcomes). The average study reported large reductions (>50% RRR) in the risk of an adverse outcome event versus a comparative treatment; however, almost 1 in 2 study outcomes (47%) had RRRs less than 50%, and over 1 in 5 (23%) had RRRs less than 20%.

Study Power and Sample Size Calculation

The power of a study is the probability of concluding a difference between two treatments when one actually exists. Power (1-β) is simply the complement of the type II error (β). Thus, if we accept a 20% chance of an incorrect study conclusion (β = 0.20), we are also accepting that we will come to the correct conclusion 80% of the time. Study power can be used before the start of a clinical trial to assist with sample size determination, or following the completion of study to determine if the negative findings were true (or due to chance).

The power of a statistical test is typically a function of the magnitude of the treatment effect, the designated type I error rate (α), and the sample size (n). When designing a trial, investigators can decide upon the desired study power (1-β) and calculate the necessary sample to achieve this goal.[26] Numerous free sample size calculators are available on the internet and use the same principles and formulae estimating sample size in clinical trials.

Comparing Two Continuous Variables

A continuous variable is one with a scale (i.e., blood pressure, functional outcome score, time to healing). For example, in planning a trial of alternate strategies for the treatment of humeral shaft fractures, an investigator may identify a systematic review of the literature that reports that time to fracture healing with Treatment A is 110 ± 45 days, while time to healing with Treatment B (control group) can be expected to be up to 130 ± 40 days. The expected treatment difference is 20 days and the effect size (mean difference/standard deviation) is 0.5 (20/40). Effect sizes can be categorized as small (0.10), medium (0.30), and large (0.50). The anticipated sample size for this continuous outcome measure is determined by a standard equation.

A particular study will require approximately 63 patients in total to have sufficient power to identify a difference of 20 days between treatments, if it occurs. An investigator may then audit his or her center's previous year and decide if enough patients will present to the center to meet the sample size requirements. Table 15-6 provides additional scenarios and the sample size requirements for varying differences in healing times between treatment and control groups. As the difference between treatments diminishes, the sample size requirements increase (see Table 15-6).

Let us consider another study that aims to compare functional outcome scores in patients with ankle fractures treated operatively versus nonoperatively. Previous studies using the functional outcome score have reported standard deviations for operative and nonoperative cases of 12 points, respectively. Based upon previous studies, we want to be able to detect a difference of 5 points on this functional outcome score between treatments.

From the equation in the Appendix at the end of this chapter, our proposed study will require 90 patients per treatment arm to have adequate study power.

TABLE 15-6	**Sample Size Requirements for Continuous Outcome (Time to Fracture Healing)**		
Time to Healing (Control Group)	Time to Healing (Treatment Group)	% Reduction in Time to Healing	Number of Patients Needed per Group
150 Days	120	20%	16
150 Days	135	10%	63
150 Days	143	5%	289

Reworking the above equation, the study power can be calculated for any given sample size by transforming the above formula and calculating the z-score:

$$z_{1-\beta} = (n_1(\Delta^2)/2(\sigma^2))^{1/2} - z_{1-\alpha/2}$$

The actual study power that corresponds to the calculated z-score can be looked up in readily available statistical literature[17] or on the internet (keyword: "z-table").[20,52] From the above example, the z-score will be 0.84 for a sample size of 90 patients. The corresponding study power for a z-score of 0.84 is 80%.

When the Outcome Measure Is Dichotomous (Proportion)

A dichotomous variable is typically one that has one of two options (i.e., infection or not, nonunion or not, alive or dead). Let's assume that this same investigator chooses nonunion as the primary outcome instead of time to union. Based upon the previous literature, he or she believes that Treatment A will result in a 95% union rate and Treatment B (control group) will result in a 90% union rate. Eight hundred and sixty-nine patients are required for the study to identify a 5% difference in nonunion rates between treatments. An investigator may realize that this number is sufficiently large enough to prohibit the trial being conducted at one center and may elect to gain support at multiple sites for this trial. For example, in a proposed trial using pulmonary embolus risk as the primary outcome, the number of patients required may be prohibitive (Table 15-7).

Returning to our example of ankle fractures, let us now assume that we wish to change our outcome measure to differences in secondary surgical procedures between operative and nonoperatively treated ankle fractures. A clinically important difference is considered to be 5%. Based upon the previous literature, it is estimated that the secondary surgical rates in operative and nonoperative treated ankles will be 5% and 10%, respectively. The number of patients required for our study can now be calculated from the equation presented in the Appendix.

Thus, we need 433 patients per treatment arm to have adequate study power for our proposed trial.

Reworking the above equation, the study power can be calculated for any given sample size by transforming the above formula and calculating the z-score:

$$z_{1-\beta} = ((n (\Delta^2))^{1/2} - (2p_m q_m)^{1/2} z_{1-\alpha/2}) / (p_1 q_1 + p_2 q_2)^{1/2}$$

TABLE 15-7 **Sample Size Requirements for Difference Baseline Risks of Pulmonary Embolus**

Pulmonary Embolus Rate Control Group	Pulmonary Embolus Rate Treatment Group	% Reduction in Pulmonary Embolus Risk	Number of Patients Needed Per Group
10%	8%	20%	3213
1%	0.80%	20%	35,001
0.10%	0.08%	20%	352,881

From the above example, the z-score will be 0.84 for a sample size of 433 patients. The corresponding study power for a z-score of 0.84 is 80%.

MEASURING PATIENT HEALTH AND FUNCTION

The basis of the "outcomes movement" in trauma is the move toward identifying patient relevant and clinically important measures to evaluate the success (or failure) of surgical interventions. Common to any outcome measure that gains widespread use should be its reliability and validity. Reliability refers to the extent to which an instrument yields the same results in repeated applications in a population with stable health. In other words, reliability represents the extent to which the instrument is free of random error. Validity is an estimation of the extent to which an instrument measures what it was intended to measure. The process of validating an instrument involves accumulating evidence that indicates the degree to which the measure represents what it was intended to represent. Some of these methods include face, content, and construct validity.[6,30]

What Is Health-Related Quality of Life?

The World Health Organization defines health as "a state of complete physical, mental, and social well-being." Thus, when measuring health in a clinical or research setting, questioning a patient's well-being within each of these domains is necessary to comprehensively represent the concept of health. Instruments that measure aspects of this broad concept of health are often referred to as health-related quality of life (HRQOL) measures. These measures encompass a broad spectrum of items including those associated with activities of daily life, such as work, recreation, household management, and relationships with family, friends, and social groups. HRQOL considers not only the ability to function within these roles, but also the degree of satisfaction derived from performing them.

A generic instrument is one that measures general health status inclusive of physical symptoms, function, and emotional dimensions of health. A disadvantage of generic instruments, however, is that they may not be sensitive enough to be able to detect small but important changes.[26]

Disease-specific measures, on the other hand, are tailored to inquire about the specific physical, mental, and social aspects of health affected by the disease in question, allowing them to detect small, important changes.[30] Therefore, in order to provide the most comprehensive evaluation of treatment effects, no matter the disease or intervention, investigators often include both a disease-specific and generic health measure. In fact, many granting agencies and ethics boards insist that a generic instrument be included in the design of proposed clinical studies.

Often, the combination of objective endpoints in a surgical study (i.e., quality of fracture reduction) and validated measures of patient function and quality of life is an ideal combination. While an intra-articular step off in a tibial plafond fracture may be viewed as a less than satisfactory radiograph outcome, there may be no detectable effect on patient function or quality of life.[35]

Another factor to consider is the ability of the outcome measure to discriminate between patients across a spectrum of the injury in question. Questionnaires may sometimes exhibit ceiling and floor effects. Ceiling effects occur when the instrument is too easy and all respondents score the highest possible score. Alternatively, floor effects can occur if the instrument is very difficult or tapping into rare issues associated with the disease. Most patients will score the lowest possible score. Miranda et al.,[39] in a study of 80 patients with pelvic fractures, found that the severity of pelvic fracture did not alter Short Form-36 and Iowa pelvic scores.

Despite increasing severity of the pelvic injury, functional outcomes remained equally poor. This was likely related to the associated soft tissue injuries that created a "floor effect" limiting the ability to discriminate between the orthopaedic injuries.

Common Outcome Instruments Used in Trauma

Beaton and Schemitsch[6] have reported commonly used measures of outcome in orthopaedics (Table 15-8). These include both generic and disease-specific instruments. Properties of these instruments follow.

EQ-5D/EuroQOL

The EQ-5D, formally described as the EuroQOL, is a five-item scale that is designed to allow people to describe their health state across five dimensions.[17] There are three response categories that combine for a total of 243 possible health states. The preference weight allows a single numeric score from slightly less than zero (theoretically worse than death) to one (best health state). EQ-5D scores are used in economic appraisals (such as cost utility analyses) in the construction of quality-adjusted life years for the calculation of cost per quality of life year gained and its comparison across interventions.

Short Form-36

The Short Form 36 (SF-36) is a generic measure of health status. It is probably one of the most widely used measures. The SF-36 has 35 items that fit into one of 8 subscales. One additional item is not used in the scores. In 1994, the developers, led by John Ware,[60] produced two summary scores for the SF-36: - the physical component score (more heavily weights dimensions of pain, physical function, and role function physical) and the mental component score (more weight given to mental health, vitality, etc). The two physical component scores are standardized, so the general population (based on a U.S. sample) will score 50 on average, with a standard deviation of 10. The subscale scores, often presented as a profile graph, are scored on a scale of 0–100 where 100 is a good health state.

Short Musculoskeletal Function Assessment Form

The short musculoskeletal function assessment form (S-MFA) is a 46-item questionnaire that is a shortened version of Swionkowski's full Musculoskeletal Functional Assessment.[61] The S-MFA has two main scores: the function index (items 1–34) and the bothersome index (items 35–46). The functional index is subdivided into 4 subscales (daily activities, emotional status, arm and hand function, and mobility). The S-MFA has been tested in patients with musculoskeletal disorders, as this is the target population. The psychometric properties are high, suggesting that it can be used for monitoring individual patients. The S-MFA was designed to describe the various levels of function in people with musculoskeletal disorders, as well as monitor change over time. The SMFA correlates highly with the

SF-36 and use of both instruments in the same patient population is likely redundant.

Disabilities of the Arm, Shoulder, and Hand Form

The Disabilities of the Arm, Shoulder, and Hand Form (DASH) is a 30-item questionnaire designed to measure physical function and disability in any or all disorders of the upper limb. It is therefore designed to be sensitive to disability and change in disability in the hand as well as in the shoulder. In one study, it was directly compared to a shoulder and a wrist measure, and had similar levels of construct validity, responsiveness, and reliability. Another study showed slightly lower properties in the DASH as compared to a wrist specific measure in patients with wrist fracture. Like the S-MFA, the measurement properties of the DASH are quite high (internal consistency 0.96, test-retest 0.95, good validity and responsiveness) suggesting it could also be used in individual patients in a clinical setting.

Western Ontario McMaster Osteoarthritis Index

The Western Ontario McMaster Osteoarthritis Index (WOMAC) is a 24-item scale divided into three dimensions: function, pain, and stiffness. The most commonly used response scale is a five-point Likert; however, there is a visual analogue scale version. It has been widely used and tested in the field of osteoarthritis and rheumatoid arthritis and a review of its psychometric properties was summarized by McConnell et al.[37] in 2001. The WOMAC is the most commonly used and endorsed patient-based outcome after hip or knee arthroplasty.

Hip Rating Questionnaire

The Hip Rating Questionnaire (HRQ) is a patient-administered, 14-item questionnaire that uses a 100-point summated rating scale. A higher score suggests better health status. Equal weight is given to the domains of the overall impact of arthritis, pain, walking, and function. This questionnaire is designed to assess outcomes after total hip replacement surgery. According to Johanson et al.,[32] 2-week test-retest administrations produced a weighted Kappa score of 0.70, and the sensitivity to change was deemed to be excellent.

Harris Hip Score

The Harris Hip Score (HHS) is a patient- and clinician-administered questionnaire designed to assess patients with traumatic arthritis of the hip.[44] It is a 10-item questionnaire that uses a 100-point summated rating scale and takes approximately 15 to 30 minutes to administer. There are four domains: the pain domain contributes 44 points; function, 47; range of motion; 5; and absence of deformity, 4. The function domain is divided into gait and activities, while deformity considers hip flexion, adduction, internal rotation, and limb-length discrepancy and range of motion measures.[44] A higher score suggests better health status. The HHS is the most commonly used scoring system for evaluating hip arthroplasty. Its responsiveness has been found to be comparable to and, in some cases, better than the WOMAC pain and function subscales.[44]

The Hospital for Joint Diseases Hip Fracture Recovery Score (Functional Recovery Score)

The Hospital for Joint Diseases Hip Fracture Recovery Score (FRS) is an interviewer-administered questionnaire with 11

TABLE 15-8 **Commonly Used Outcome Measures**

Type	Measure	Domains/Scales	Number Items	Response Categories	Target Population	Measurement Properties					Comments
						Internal Consistency	Test-Retest Reliability	Construct Validity	Responsiveness		
Utility	EQ-5D	Mobility Self care Usual activities Anxiety/ depression Pain	1 1 1 1 1 total: 5	3	All	NA	Y	YY	Y		Describes health state that is transcribed into utility using UK data. Indirect measure of utility.
Generic	SF-36 version 2	Physical function Bodily pain Role function– physical Role function– emotional Mental health Vitality Social functioning General health	10 2 4 3 5 4 2 5 total = 35 + 1 item	3–6	All	YY	Y	YY	YY		Version 2 now in use. Uses improved scaling for role functioning, and clearer wording. Reliability is lower than desired for individual level of interpretation, fine for group.
Region	S-MFA	Daily activities Emotional status Arm/hand function Mobility Above combined for functional index Bothersome index	10 7 8 9 34 12	5 point	Musculoskeletal	YY	YY	YY	YY		Normative data now available.[70] Only measure designed for any musculoskeletal problem.
	DASH	Physical function, symptoms (one scale)	30	5	All upper limb musculoskeletal disorders	YY	YY	Y	YY		Normative data now available.[70] Manual available.
	TESS	Physical function in surgical oncology	30	5	Lower limb sarcoma	YY	YY	Y	YY		Developed in oncology; used in hip fractures.

(continues)

TABLE 15-8   Commonly Used Outcome Measures (*Continued*)

Type	Measure	Domains/Scales	Number Items	Response Categories	Target Population	Internal Consistency	Test-Retest Reliability	Construct Validity	Responsiveness	Comments
Specific	WOMAC	Physical function Pain Stiffness	17 5 2	5 or VAS	Osteoarthritis of knee, hip	YY	YY	YY	YY	Adopted as key outcome for evaluating knee arthroplasty.
	Roland and Morris	Physical function due to low back pain	24	2 (Yes/No)	Low back pain	Y	YY	YY	YY	Excellent review and comparison with Oswestry in Roland and Fairbanks.[45]
	Oswestry	Pain Personal care Lifting Walking Sitting Standing Sleeping Sex life Social life Traveling	1 each	6 points	Low back pain	YY	YY	YY	YY	Excellent review and comparison with Roland in Roland and Fairbanks.[45]
	Simple Shoulder Test (SST)	Function-8 Pain Sleep position	8 1 1 2	2 (Yes difficult Yes/No)	Shoulder disorders	Y	YY	YY	YY	Developers suggest reporting % with difficulty in each item, not a summative score. Some psychometrics done using sum of items.
	Neck disability index	Pain Personal care Lifting Reading Headaches Concentration Work Driving Sleeping Recreation	1 each	6 point	Whiplash disorders	Y	Y	Y	Y	Neck pain has few instruments that have been evaluated for psychometrics. This is most tested.
Patient specific	—	—	—	—	—	—	—	—	—	No patient-specific measure found in literature reviewed.

NA, not available; Y, one or two articles found *in support* of this attribute; YY, multiple articles supporting this attribute.
From Beaton DE, Schemitsch E. Measures of health-related quality of life and physical function. Clin Orthop Relat Res 2003;413:90–105.

items comprising three main components: basic activities of daily living assessed by four items and contributing 44 points, instrumental activities of daily living assessed by six items and contributing 33 points, and mobility assessed by one item and contributing 33 points. Therefore, complete independence in basic and instrumental activities of daily living and mobility will give a score of 100 points.[54,55] It is a patient-oriented outcomes measure that is designed to assess functional recovery for ambulatory hip fracture patients.[54,55] Use of the FRS can provide the means of assessing the recovery of prefracture function.[54,55] The FRS has been found to be responsive to change, reliable, and has predictive validity as well as discriminant validity.[55]

Get-Up-and-Go Test

The Get-Up-and-Go Test (GUG) was developed as a clinical measure of balance in elderly people and is an in-person assessment. The GUG test measures the time a person takes to get up from a chair and walk 15.2 m (50 ft) as fast as possible along a level and unobstructed corridor. Thus, this performance-based measure of physical function requires the patient to be able to rise from a seated position, walk, and maintain his or her balance.[42] The scoring of this instrument is based on balance function, which is scored on a 5-point scale, with 1 indicating normal and 5 indicating severely abnormal. A patient with a score of 3 or more is at risk for falling. Mathias et al.[36] found that when patients underwent laboratory tests of balance and gait, there was good correlation between the laboratory tests and the objective assessment.

Merle d'Aubigné-Postel Score

The Merle d'Aubigné-Postel Score (MDP) contains three domains: pain, mobility and walking ability. These three domains have the same impact. The scores for pain and walking ability can be added and subsequently classified into the grades very good, good, medium, fair, and poor. These grades are then adjusted down by 1–2 grades to account for the mobility score, which results in the final clinical grade. The modified MDP is slightly different from the original in terms of language and grading, as the modified version is calculated a scale of 0–6 (as opposed to 1–6) and does not combine the scores to obtain a total score.[41]

Knee Injury and Osteoarthritis Outcome Score

The Knee Injury and Osteoarthritis Outcome Score (KOOS) is designed to assess short- and long-term patient relevant outcomes after knee injury.[46] The KOOS was designed based on the WOMAC, literature review, and an expert panel and has been statistically validated for content validity, construct validity, reliability, and responsiveness. The questionnaire is composed of 42 items that are scored on a Likert scale. A higher score indicates better health status. Subscales include pain, symptoms, activities of daily living, sport and recreation, and knee-related quality of life.[46]

Lower Extremity Measure

The Lower Extremity Measure is a patient-administered instrument designed to assess physical function.[31] This questionnaire is a modification of the Toronto Extremity Salvage Score and has been statistically confirmed for reliability, validity, and responsiveness. The Lower Extremity Measure is composed of 29 items on a Likert scale and administration takes approximately 5 minutes. This questionnaire has been designed for an elderly population, with 10 points indicating significant clinical change.[31]

Olerud and Molander Scoring System

The Olerud and Molander Scoring System is a patient-administered questionnaire designed to assess symptoms after ankle fracture.[40] It is composed of 9 items on a summated rating scale and has been compared to the visual analog scale (VAS), range of motion, osteoarthritis, and dislocation for statistical validation. A higher score indicates better health status.[40]

American Shoulder and Elbow Surgeons Assessment Form

The American Shoulder and Elbow Surgeons (ASES) Assessment Form is designed to assess the shoulder and elbow and is patient- and clinician-administered.[38] There is no cost to obtain this instrument. Subscales include shoulder score index pain, instability, activities of daily living, range of motion, signs, and strength. A higher score indicates better health status. The instrument is a combination of VAS and Yes/No scaled questions. Administration by the patient takes approximately 3 minutes.[38]

American Orthopedic Foot and Ankle Scale

The American Orthopedic Foot and Ankle Scale was designed for use among patients with foot or ankle dysfunction. It contains four region-specific scales, including ankle-hindfoot, midfoot, hallux metatarsophalangeal, and lesser metatarsophalangeal–interphalangeal scales. Patients self report information about pain and function in each region. This scale also incorporates physical examination results recorded by the clinician. Although the American Orthopedic Foot and Ankle Scale has been widely used in studies of foot and ankle surgical outcomes, limitations have also been reported.[49,50]

UTILIZING OUTCOME STUDIES IN DECISION-MAKING (EVIDENCE-BASED ORTHOPAEDICS)

What Is Evidence-Based Orthopaedics?

The term EBM first appeared in the Fall of 1990 in a document for applicants to the Internal Medicine residency program at McMaster University in Ontario, Canada, which described EBM as an attitude of enlightened skepticism toward the application of diagnostic, therapeutic, and prognostic technologies. As outlined in the text *Clinical Epidemiology* and first described in the literature in the *ACP Journal Club* in 1991, the EBM approach to practicing medicine relies on an awareness of the evidence upon which a clinician's practice is based and the strength of inference permitted by that evidence.[27] The most sophisticated practice of EBM requires, in turn, a clear delineation of relevant clinical questions, a thorough search of the literature relating to the questions, a critical appraisal of available evidence and its applicability to the clinical situation, and a balanced application of the conclusions to the clinical problem. The balanced application of the evidence (i.e., the clinical decision-making) is the central point of practicing evidence-based medicine and involves, according to EBM principles, integration of our clinical expertise and judgment with patients' preferences and societal values and with the best available research evidence (see Fig. 15-6). The EBM working group at McMaster University has proposed a working model for evidence-based clinical practice that encompasses current research evidence, patient preferences, clinical circumstances, and clinical expertise. EBM is commonly misunderstood as removing clinical expertise as a factor in patient decision-making. This is not so. The common thread that weaves the relationships between patients, circumstances, and research is the experience and skill of the surgeon.

Finding Current Evidence in Trauma

To be effective EBM practitioners, surgeons must acquire the necessary skills to find the "best" evidence available to answer clinically important questions. Reading a few articles published in common orthopedic journals each month is insufficient preparation for answering the questions that emerge in daily practice. There are at least 100 orthopaedic journals indexed by MEDLINE.[2] For surgeons whose principal interest is orthopaedic traumatology, the list is even larger. Given their large clinical demands, surgeons' evidence searches must be time-efficient. Evidence summaries (such as those published in the *Journal of Orthopaedic Trauma*) and systematic reviews (comprehensive literature reviews) are useful resources for surgeons (Table 15-9). The most efficient way to find them is by electronic searching of databases and/or the internet. With time at a premium, it is important to know where to look and how to develop a search strategy, or filter, in order to identify the evidence most efficiently and effectively.

User's Guide to Evaluate an Orthopaedic Intervention

Most surgical interventions have inherent benefits and associated risks. Before implementing a new therapy, one should as-

certain the benefits and risks of the therapy, and be assured that the resources consumed in the intervention will not be exorbitant. A simple three-step approach can be used when reading an article from the orthopaedic literature (Table 15-10). It is prudent to ask whether the study can provide valid results (internal validity), to review the results, and to consider how the results can be applied to patient care (generalizability). Lack of randomization, no concealment of treatment allocation, lack of blinding, and incomplete follow-up are serious threats to the validity of a published randomized trial. The user's guide focuses the assessment on assuring that investigators have considered these issues in the conduct of their study. Understanding the language of EBM is also important. Table 15-11 provides a summary of common terms used when considering the results of a clinical paper. While randomized trials sit atop the hierarchy of an intervention, not all orthopaedic research questions are suitable for randomized trials. For example, observational studies (prospective cohorts) are more suitable designs when evaluating prognosis (or risk factors) for outcome following a surgical procedure. However, common problems with alternative (and accepted) surgical treatments argue strongly in favor of randomized trials. Complex problems with nonconsensus in surgical technique or lack of acceptance of one approach argue in favor of observational studies to further elucidate the technique as well as understand the indications for alternative approaches prior to embarking on an randomized trial.

Incorporating Evidence-Based Orthopaedics into Daily Trauma Practice

EBM is becoming an accepted educational paradigm in medical education at a variety of levels. An analysis of the literature related to journal clubs in residency programs in specialties

---

TABLE 15-9   **Finding Current Evidence: Resources**

Publications
EBM
Using the Medical Literature
  Journal of American Medical Association User's Guides
  Canadian Medical Association Journal User's Guides
  Journal of Bone and Joint Surgery User's Guides
  Canadian Journal of Surgery User's Guides

Databases
Best Evidence
Cochrane Library and Cochrane Randomized Trials Register (www.update-software.com/cochrane/)
Database of Abstracts and Reviews of Effectiveness (DARE)
Internet Database of Evidence-based Abstracts and Articles (IDEA)
Medline/PubMED (www.ncbi.nlm.nih.gov/entrez/query.fcgi)
EMBASE (European equivalent of Medline)
Clinical Evidence (www.clinicalevidence.org/)
SUMsearch (www.sumsearch.uthscsa.edu)
TRIP database (www.tripdatabase.com/)

Electronic Publications
ACP Journal Club (American College of Physicians) (www.acpjc.org/)
Bandolier: Evidence-based healthcare
EBM
National Guideline Clearinghouse (Agency of Health Care Policy and Research [AHCPR]; www.guidelines.gov)

Internet Resources
Healthweb: Evidence-Based Health Care (www.healthweb.org)
EBM from McMaster University (www.hiru.hiru net.mcmaster.ca)
Center for Evidence-Based Medicine (www.cebm.net)
Critically Appraised Topics (CAT) databank (www.cebm.net/toolbox.asp)
New York Academy of Medicine EBM resource center (www.ebmny.org)
University of Alberta EBM (cebm.med.ualberta.ca/ebm/ebm.htm)
Trauma Links—Edinburgh Orthopaedic Trauma Unit (http://www.trauma.co.uk/traumalinks.htm)

TABLE 15-10 **User's Guide to Orthopaedic Randomized Trials**

Validity
Did experimental and control groups begin the study with a similar prognosis?
Were patients randomized?
   Was randomization concealed?
   Were patients analyzed in the groups to which they were randomized?
   Were patients in the treatment and control groups similar with respect to known prognostic factors?
Did experimental and control groups retain a similar prognosis after the study started?

Blinding
Did investigators avoid effects of patient awareness of allocation—were patients blinded?
Were aspects of care that affect prognosis similar in the two groups—were clinicians blinded?
Was outcome assessed in a uniform way in experimental and control groups—were those assessing outcome blinded?
Was follow-up complete?

Results
How large was the treatment effect?
How precise was the estimate of the treatment effect?

Applicability
Can the results be applied to my patient?
Were all patient-important outcomes considered?
Are the likely treatment benefits worth the potential harms and costs?

other than orthopaedic surgery reveals that the three most common goals were to teach critical appraisal skills (67%), to have an impact on clinical practice (59%), and to keep up with the current literature (56%).[25] The implementation of the structured article review checklist has been found to increase resident satisfaction and improve the perceived educational value of the journal club without increasing resident workload or decreasing attendance at the conference.

Structured review instruments have been applied in a number of orthopaedic training programs; assessments of the outcomes and effectiveness of this format for journal club are ongoing. One example of one structured review instrument for use in orthopaedic training programs is provided in Fig. 15-7.

TABLE 15-11 **Presentation of Results**

	Infection	No Infection
Treatment Group	10	90
	A	**B**
Control Group	50	50
	C	**D**

Treatment Event Rate (TER): A/A+B = 10/100 = 10%
   The incidence of infection in the treatment group

Control Event Rate (CER): C/C+D = 50/100 = 50%
   The incidence of infection in the control group

Relative Risk: TER/CER = 10/50 = 0.2
   The relative risk of infection in the treatment group relative to the control group

RRR: 1−RR = 1−0.2 = 0.8 or 80%
   Treatment reduces the risk of infection by 80% compared to controls

Absolute Risk Reduction (ARR): CER−TER = 50%−10%
                                              = 40%
   The actual numerical difference in infection rates between treatment and controls

Number Needed to Treat: 1/ARR = 1/0.40 = 2.5
   For every 2.5 patients who received the treatment, 1 infection can be prevented

Odds Ratio: AD/BC = (10)(50)/(90)(50) = 500/4500 = 0.11
   The odds of infection in treatment compared to controls is 0.11

THE FUTURE OF OUTCOME STUDIES IN ORTHOPAEDIC TRAUMA

Over the past 50 years, there has been a vast proliferation of randomized trials. While the strength of evidence is most persuasive in large, randomized trials with small CIs around their treatment effect, this is not always feasible for many clinical problems in orthopaedics. Indeed, only 3% (72 of 2498 studies) of studies published in orthopaedics reflect randomized trial methodology.[13] The design, conduct, and analysis of orthopaedic research has gained widespread appreciation in surgery, particularly in orthopaedic surgery. Still, only 14% of the original contributions in JBJS represent Level I evidence.[14] When randomization is either not feasible or unethical, prospective observational studies represent the best evidence. Approximately 1 in 5 scientific articles published in JBJS represent this Level II evidence.[14] In a more recent review of the literature, Chan et al.[21] identified 87 randomized trials in orthopaedic surgical procedures, representing 14% of the published studies. JBJS contributed 4.1% of the published randomized trials in this report.

Future studies can provide high-quality data on which to base practice if we conduct RCTs whenever feasible, ensure adequate sample size, involve biostatisticians and methodologists, collect data meticulously, and accurately report our results using sensible outcomes and measures of treatment effect. Limiting type II errors (beta errors) will need multicenter initiatives.

1. Study Design
Randomized Trial or Meta-Analysis (MA) of Randomized Trial   12
Prospective Observational Study with a Comparison group or MA   10
Retrospective Observational Study with a Comparison group or MA   8
Prospective Observational Study with no Comparison group or MA   6
Retrospective Observational Study with no Comparison group or MA   4
Cross-Sectional (Single point in time)/Survey   2
Not Reported/Unable to Discern   0   **/12**

2. Eligibility Criteria
Eligibility criteria defined   3
Eligibility criteria partially defined   2
Eligibility criteria not reported   0   **/3**

Ineligible or excluded patients reported   3
Ineligible or excluded patients partially reported   2
Ineligible patients or excluded not reported   0   **/3**

3. Similarity of Comparison Groups at beginning of study
Groups similar due to randomization   8
Groups similar by matching cases to controls or p values shown   6
Groups not similar but statistical tests utilized to correct for imbalances   4
Authors report groups similar but with no supporting information   2
Groups not similar , Single Group Only or Not Reported   0   **/8**

4. Similarity of Comparison Groups at completion of study (omit, if MA)
Groups remained similar (no crossovers occurred)   4
Groups dissimilar (crossovers occurred)   2
Single Group Only or Unsure / Not Reported/Not applicable   0   **/4**

5. Outcomes assessment
Main outcomes are objective (ie. don't require major judgement-mortality)   3
Main outcomes are not objective   1   **/3**

Outcome assessors independent or blinded   3
Outcome assessors not independent or not blinded   0
Unsure   0   **/3**

6. Follow Up
90% or greater follow up achieved (prospective, active)   6
80-89% follow up (prospective, active)   4
70-79% follow up (prospective, active)   2
Less than 70% follow up achieved   1
Not reported or Unsure or Not applicable or Passive Follow Up   0   **/6**

7. Sample Size
Pre-study sample size or Power calculation reported   4
Post-study power calculation reported   2
Pre-study sample size or Power calculation not reported   0   **/4**

8. Statistical Tests
p-Value and Confidence interval(s) Reported   4
p-Value or Confidence intervals(s) Reported   2
No statistics reported   0   **/4**

Total Score   **/50**
If meta-analysis   /46

FIGURE 15-7 A checklist to assess the quality of surgical therapies.

These larger trials have the advantage of increased generalizability of the results and the potential for large scale and efficient recruitment (1000 patients or more). Single center trials that may have taken a decade to recruit enough patients can now be completed in a few years with collaborative research trials. The obvious drawback with multicenter initiatives is the relative complexity of the design and the cost. It is reasonable to expect that a trial of over 1000 patients will cost more than \$3–4 million to conduct.

CONCLUSION

The purpose of the "outcomes movement" and EBM is to provide healthcare practitioners and decision-makers (physicians, nurses, administrators, regulators) with tools that allow them to gather, access, interpret, and summarize the evidence required to inform their decisions and to explicitly integrate this evidence with the values of patients. In this sense, EBM is not an end in itself, but rather a set of principles and tools that help clinicians distinguish ignorance of evidence from real scientific uncertainty, distinguish evidence from unsubstantiated opinions, and ultimately provide better patient care.

APPENDIX: SAMPLE SIZE CALCULATIONS

1. Continuous Variables

The number of patients required per treatment arm to obtain 80% study power ($\beta = 0.20$) at a 0.05 alpha level of significance is as follows:

$$n_1 = n_2 = 2(\sigma^2)(z_{1-\alpha/2} + z_{1-\beta})^2 / \Delta^2$$

where

n_1 = sample size of group one

n_2 = sample size of group two

Δ = difference of outcome parameter between groups (5 points)

σ = sample standard deviations (12)

$z_{1-\alpha/2} = z_{0.975} = 1.96$ (for $\alpha = 0.05$)

$z_{1-\beta} = z_{0.80} = 0.84$ (for $\beta = 0.2$)

2. Dichotomous Variables

The number of patients required per treatment arm to obtain 80% study power ($\beta = 0.20$) at a 0.05 alpha level of significance is as follows:

$$n_1 = n_2 = [(2p_m q_m)^{1/2} z_{1-\alpha/2} + (p_1 q_1 + p_2 q_2)^{1/2} z_{1-\beta}]^2 / \Delta^2$$

where

n_1 = sample size of group one

n_2 = sample size of group two

p_1, p_2 = sample probabilities (5% and 10%)

q_1, q_2 = $1 - p_1$, $1 - p_2$ (95% and 90%)

$p_m = (p_1 + p_2)/2$ (7.5%)

$q_m = 1 - p_m$ (92.5%)

Δ = difference = $p_2 - p_1$ (5%)

$z_{1-\alpha/2} = z_{0.975} = 1.96$ (for $\alpha = 0.05$)

$z_{1-\beta} = z_{0.80} = 0.84$ (for $\beta = 0.2$)

REFERENCES

1. American Medical Association. User's guides to the medical literature: a manual for evidence-based clinical practice. In Guyatt GH, Rennie D, eds. 2nd ed. Chicago: American Medical Association Press, 2001.
2. Atkins D, Best D, Briss PA, et al. Grading quality of evidence and strength of recommendations. BMJ 2004;328(7454):1490.
3. Atkins D, Briss PA, Eccles M, et al. Systems for grading the quality of evidence and the strength of recommendations II: pilot study of a new system. BMC Health Serv Res 2005;5(1):25.
4. Atkins D, Eccles M, Flottorp S, et al. Systems for grading the quality of evidence and the strength of recommendations I: critical appraisal of existing approaches. The GRADE Working Group. BMC Health Serv Res 2004;4:38.
5. Beaton DE, Schemitsch E. Measures of health-related quality of life and physical function. Clin Orthop 2003;413:90–105.
6. Benson K, Hartz AJ. A comparison of observational studies and randomized, controlled trials. N Engl J Med 2000;342:1878–1886.
7. Bhandari M, Devereaux PJ, Li P, et al. The misuse of baseline comparison tests and subgroup analyses in surgical randomized controlled trials. Clin Orthop Relat Res 2006; 447:247–251.
8. Bhandari M, Guyatt GH, Siddiqui F, et al. Operative versus nonoperative treatment of achilles tendon rupture—a systematic overview and meta-analysis. Clin Orthop Relat Res 2002:400:190–200.
9. Bhandari M, Guyatt GH, Swiontkowski MF. User's guide to the orthopaedic literature: how to use an article about a prognosis. J Bone Joint Surg 2001;83A:1555–1564.
10. Bhandari M, Guyatt GH, Swiontkowski MF. User's guide to the orthopaedic literature: how to use an article about a surgical therapy. J Bone Joint Surg 2001;83A:916–926.
11. Bhandari M, Montori VM, Devereaux PJ, et al. Doubling the impact: publication of systematic review articles in orthopaedic journals. J Bone Joint Surg Am 2004;86: 1012–1016.
12. Bhandari M, Richards R, Schemitsch EH. The quality of randomized trials in Journal of Bone and Joint Surgery from 1988–2000. J Bone Joint Surg 2002;84A:388–396.
13. Bhandari M, Swiontkowski MF, Einhorn TA, et al. Interobserver agreement in the application of levels of evidence to scientific papers in the American volume of the Journal of Bone and Joint Surgery. J Bone Joint Surg Am 2004;86A:1717–1720.
14. Bhandari M, Tornetta P III. Communicating the risks of surgery to patients. European J Trauma 2004;30:177–180.
15. Bhandari M, Tornetta P III. Issues in the hierarchy of study design, hypothesis testing, and presentation of results. Tech Orthop 2004;19:57–65.
16. Bhandari M, Tornetta P III, Ellis T, et al. Hierarchy of evidence: differences in results between nonrandomized studies and randomized trials in patients with femoral neck fractures. Arch Orthop Trauma Surg 2004;124(1):10–16.
17. Bhandari M, Whang W, Kuo JC, et al. The risk of false-positive results in orthopaedic surgical trials. Clin Orthop 2003;413:63–69.
18. Bhandari M, Zlowodzki M, Cole PA. From eminence-based practice to evidence-based practice: a paradigm shift. Minn Med 2004;4:51–54.
19. Brighton B, Bhandari M, Tornetta P III, et al. Hierarchy of evidence: from case reports to randomized controlled trials. Clin Orthop 2003;413:19–24.
20. Chan S, Bhandari M. The quality of reporting of orthopaedic randomized trials with use of a checklist for nonpharmacological therapies. J Bone Joint Surg Am 2007;89: 1970–1978.
21. Concato J, Shah N, Horwitz RI. Randomized, controlled trials, observational studies, and the hierarchy of research designs. N Engl J Med 2000;342:1887–1894.
22. Devereaux PJ, Bhandari M, Clarke M, et al. Need for expertise-based randomized controlled trials. BMJ 2005;330(7482):88.
23. Devereaux PJ, Manns BJ, Ghali W, et al. In the dark: physician interpretations and textbook definitions of blinding terminology in randomized controlled trials. JAMA 2001;285:2000–2003.
24. Dirschl DR, Tornetta P III, Bhandari M. Designing, conducting, and evaluating journal clubs in orthopaedic surgery. Clin Orthop 2003;413:146–157.
25. The EC/IC Bypass Study Group. Failure of extracranial–intracranial arterial bypass to reduce the risk of ischemic stroke: results of an international randomized trial. N Engl J Med 1985;313:1191–1200.
26. Griffin D, Audige L. Common statistical methods in orthopaedic clinical studies. Clin Orthop 2003;413:70–79.
27. Guyatt GH. Evidence-based medicine. ACP J Club 1991;114:A16.
28. Haentjens P, Autier P, Boonen S. Clinical risk factors for hip fracture in elderly women: a case-control study. J Orthop Trauma 2002;6:379–385.
29. Ioannidis JP, Haidich AB, Pappa M, et al. Comparison of evidence of treatment effects in randomized and nonrandomized studies. JAMA 2001;286:821–830.
30. Jackowski D, Guyatt G. A guide to health measurement. Clin Orthop 2003;413:80–89.
31. Jaglal S, Lakhani Z, Schatzker J. Reliability, validity, and responsiveness of the lower extremity measure for patients with a hip fracture. J Bone Joint Surg Am 2000;82-A: 955–962.
32. Johanson NA, Charlson ME, Szatrowske TP, et al. A self-administered hip-rating questionnaire for the assessment of outcome after total hip replacement. J Bone Joint Surg Am 1992;74:587–597.
33. Kunz R, Oxman AD. The unpredictability paradox: review of empirical comparisons of randomized and nonrandomized clinical trials. BMJ 1998;317:1185–1190.
34. Lochner H, Bhandari M, Tornetta P III. Type II error rates (beta errors) in randomized trials in orthopaedic trauma. J Bone Joint Surg 2002;83A:1650–1655.
35. Marsh JL, Weigel DP, Dirschl DR. Tibial plafond fractures. How do these ankles function over time? J Bone Joint Surg Am 2003;85A:287–295.
36. Mathias S, Nayak USL, Isaacs B. Balance in the elderly patients: the "get-up-and-go" test. Arch Phys Med Rehab 1986;67:387–389.

37. McConnell S, Kolopack P, Davis AM. The Western Ontario and McMaster Universities Osteoarthritis Index (WOMAC): a review of its utility and measurement properties. Arthritis Rheum 2001;45:453–461.

38. Michener LA, McClure PW, Sennett BJ. American Shoulder and Elbow Surgeons Standardized Shoulder Assessment Form patient self-report section: reliability, validity, and responsiveness. J Shoulder Elbow Surg 2002;11:587–594.

39. Miranda MA, Riemer BL, Butterfield SL, et al. Pelvic ring injuries. A long-term functional outcome study. Clin Orthop Relat Res 1996;329:152–159.

40. Olerud C, Molander H. A scoring scale for symptom evaluation after ankle fracture. Arch Orthop Trauma Surg 1984;103:190–194.

41. Øvre S, Sandvik L, Madsen JE, et al. Comparison of distribution, agreement, and correlation between the original and modified Merle d'Aubigné-Postel Score and the Harris Hip Score after acetabular fracture treatment: moderate-agreement, high-ceiling effect and excellent correlation in 450 patients. Acta Orthop Scand 2005;76:796–802.

42. Piva SR, Fitzgerald GK, Irrgang JJ, et al. Get-up-and-go test in patients with knee osteoarthritis. Arch Phys Med Rehabil 2004;85:284–289.

43. Pocock S, Assman S, Enos L, et al. Subgroup analysis, covariate adjustment, and baseline comparisons in clinical trial reporting: current practice and problems. Stats Med 2002;21:2917–2930.

44. Rogers JC, Irrgang JJ. Measures of adult lower extremity function. Arthitis Rheum 2003;49:S67–S84.

45. Roland M, Fairbank J. The Roland-Morris disability questionnaire and the Oswestry disability questionnaire. Spine 2000;25:3115–3124.

46. Roos EM, Toksvig-Larsen S. Knee injury and Osteoarthritis Outcome Score (KOOS)—validation and comparison to the WOMAC in total knee replacement. Health Qual Life Outcomes 2003;1:17.

47. Sackett DL, Haynes RB, Guyatt GH, et al. Clinical Epidemiology: A Basic Science for Clinical Medicine. Boston: Little Brown, 1991.

48. Sackett DL, Richardson WS, Rosenberg WM, et al. Evidence-Based Medicine: How to Practice and Teach EBM. New York: Churchill Livingstone, 1997

49. Saltzman CL, Domsic RT, Baumhauer JF. Foot and ankle research priority: report from the Research Council of the American Orthopaedic Foot and Ankle Society. Foot Ankle Int 1997;18:447–448.

50. SooHoo NF, Shuler M, Fleming LL. Evaluation of the validity of the AOFAS Clinical Rating Systems by correlation to the SF-36. Foot Ankle Int 2003;24:50–55.

51. Sung J, Siegel J, Tornetta P III et al. The orthopaedic trauma literature: an evaluation of statistically significant findings in orthopaedic trauma randomized trials. BMC Musculoskelet Disord 2008;29(9):14.

52. Wright JG, Swiontkowski MF, Heckman JD. Introducing levels of evidence to the journal. J Bone Joint Surg Am 2003;85A:1–3.

53. Yusuf S, Wittes J, Probstfield J, et al. Analysis and interpretation of treatment effects in subgroups of patients in randomized clinical trials. JAMA 1991;266:93–98.

54. Zuckerman JD, Koval KJ, Aharonoff GB, et al. A functional recovery score for elderly hip patients: I. Development. J Orthop Trauma 2000:14:20–25.

55. Zuckerman JD, Koval KJ, Aharonoff GB, et al. A functional recovery score for elderly hip patients: II. Validity and reliability. J Orthop Trauma 2000:14:26–30.

56. Haynes RB, Mukherjee J, Sackett D, et al. Functional status changes following medical or surgical treatment for cerebral ischemia: results in the EC/IC, Bypass Study. JAMA 1987;257:2043-2046.

57. SPRINT Investigators, Bhandari M, Guyatt G, et al. Study to prospectively evaluate reamed intramedullary nails in patients with tibial fractures (SPRINT): study rationale and design. BMC Musculoskeletal Discord 2008;9:91.

58. SPRINT Investigators, Bhandari M, Guyatt G, et al. Randomized trial of reamed and unreamed intramedullary nailing of tibial shaft fractures. J Bone Joint Surg Am 2008;90:2567-2578.

59. Box JF, Guinness, Gosset, Fisher, and small samples. Statistical Science 1987;2:45-52.

60. Ware J. Available online at http://www.qualitymetric.com. Accessed September 10, 2009.

61. SMFA Swionkowski. Available online at http://www.med.umn.edu/ortho/research.html. Accessed September 10, 2009.

16

IMAGING CONSIDERATIONS IN ORTHOPAEDIC TRAUMA

Andrew H. Schmidt and Kerry M. Kallas

GENERAL CONSIDERATIONS

Medical imaging in the setting of acute musculoskeletal trauma contributes greatly to the initial diagnosis and subsequent management of orthopaedic injuries. In many instances, patients are able to provide details of the injury, and imaging studies often confirm or exclude diagnoses already suggested by the clinical history, mechanism of injury, and physical examination findings. Imaging plays a critical role in the management of multitrauma patients who arrive obtunded or unconscious or are intubated and therefore unable to localize symptoms or cooperate during the physical examination. Multitrauma patients may also have coexisting neurological and visceral injury, and in this setting orthopaedic imaging is often deferred for other imaging studies and surgical triage for life-threatening injuries. However, plain radiographs must be made of all potential musculoskeletal injuries as soon as possible so that appropriate early treatment decisions are made.

A wide variety of imaging examinations are available in clinical practice today, and use of a particular modality may be influenced by multiple factors, such as availability, image resolution, invasiveness, cost-effectiveness, patient risk, and re-

quirements for special handling of the trauma patient. Many imaging studies are routinely ordered for specific indications and need no justification; for example, conventional radiographs are used to evaluate acute bony trauma of the extremities. Particularly with regard to more advanced imaging techniques, however, clinicians must often consider these tradeoffs in deciding whether to pursue additional imaging.

Availability

Although there is widespread availability of conventional radiography in both clinical and hospital settings, there is more variable access to advanced imaging modalities, particularly in rural communities and after hours. Although data are lacking, it has been previously estimated that only 10% of hospitals offer full radiology coverage to emergency departments 24 hours per day.[83,163] Many emergency departments do have continuous access to computed tomography (CT) scanners, but access to more advanced imaging modalities, such as ultrasound (US), nuclear medicine (NM), and magnetic resonance imaging (MRI), varies significantly among hospitals and communities and may be available only on an "on-call" basis or not available at all after hours.

Fortunately, all that is needed to evaluate the orthopedic trauma patient in the immediate setting are plain radiographs, which provide information sufficient to diagnose any fracture or dislocation. The primary exception to this is in the evaluation of the spine, especially in the comatose patient and in the setting of specific injury patterns, where both CT and MRI have well-defined roles.[56,70,72] However, controversy continues over the relative merits of CT versus MRI in the evaluation of spine trauma, with one group considering that MRI is the new standard for the evaluation of blunt cervical spine trauma.[132] Although MRI has the added benefit of more clearly demonstrating soft tissue injuries in general, and disc herniation in the spine in particular, the inconsistent after-hours availability of MRI, as well as the obvious logistic problems of transporting and monitoring a trauma patient within an MRI unit, means that CT will remain the most common method of imaging the spine in the early evaluation of the trauma patient.[173]

The recent introduction of digital radiography (DR) and teleradiology provides a means to obtain after-hours interpretation of images by trained radiologists.[54,126,154,178] Although this is most often done in the management of acute neurological emergencies and in the assessment of cross-sectional imaging of the abdomen and chest, such technology will no doubt benefit musculoskeletal trauma patients as well. In a recent report describing the benefits of a nighttime teleradiology service for emergencies, 43 of 75 studies were musculoskeletal.[54]

Image Resolution

The choice of a particular imaging examination may, in part, be influenced by spatial resolution and contrast resolution. The ability of an imaging modality to resolve small objects of high subject contrast (e.g., bone–muscle interface) as distinct entities is referred to as spatial resolution, which is typically measured in line pairs per millimeter (lp/mm); higher values of lp/mm indicate greater resolution. For comparison, the limiting spatial resolution of the human eye is approximately 30 lp/mm. Resolution may also be expressed in millimeters, whereby smaller values represent greater spatial resolution. Table 16-1 lists representative values of limiting spatial resolution for common imaging modalities. Conventional radiographs have considerably better spatial resolution than cross-sectional imaging techniques, although overlapping bony structures often complicate evaluation of osseous anatomy. CT has better spatial resolution than MRI and is more commonly performed for evaluating finer bony abnormalities, such as avulsion fractures and calcification within tumor matrix.

Contrast resolution refers to the ability to resolve two tissues of similar subject contrast. Conventional radiographs typically have poor soft tissue contrast resolution, whereas CT and MRI, in particular, have much better contrast resolution, in part related to their tomographic nature. For example, on conventional radiographs, subcutaneous fat may be discerned from the underlying muscle groups, although the intermuscular fascial planes cannot be visualized. CT and MRI better demonstrate the subcutaneous fat and intermuscular fascial planes, although MRI shows superior soft tissue contrast resolution compared with CT.

Invasiveness

Most medical imaging procedures are noninvasive, or may require minimally invasive procedures, such as placement of intravenous access for contrast administration. Some imaging techniques are more invasive, however, such as peripheral angiography for vascular assessment in the trauma patient, and not

TABLE 16-1	**The Limiting Spatial Resolutions of Various Medical Imaging Modalities: The Resolution Levels Achieved in _Typical_ Clinical Usage of the Modality**		

| Modality | Resolution | | Comments |
	lp/mm	mm	
Screen film radiography	6	0.08	Limited by focal spot and detector resolution
Digital radiography	3	0.17	Limited by size of detector elements
Fluoroscopy	4	0.125	Limited by detector and focal spot
CT	1	0.4	About ½-mm pixels
NM: planar imaging	<0.1	7	Spatial resolution degrades substantially with distance from detector
SPECT	<0.1	7	Spatial resolution worst toward the center of cross-sectional image slice
PET	0.1	5	Better spatial resolution than other nuclear medicine imaging modalities
MRI	0.5	1.0	Resolution can be improved at higher magnetic fields
US	1.7	0.3 (5 MHz)	Limited by wavelength of sound

CT, computed tomography; MRI, magnetic resonance imaging; NM, nuclear medicine; PET, positron emission tomography; SPECT, single-photon emission computed tomography; US, ultrasound.
Modified and reprinted with permission from Brushberg JT, Seibert JA, Leidholt EM Jr, et al. The essential physics of medical imaging, 2nd ed. Philadelphia: Lippincott Williams & Wilkins, 2002.

only carry more inherent risk to the patient but also require greater resources and coordination on an emergent basis. When used appropriately, the diagnostic and therapeutic advantages of these procedures can contribute substantially to the patient's management.

Cost-Effectiveness

With increasing pressures on cost containment, studies have been performed to address the cost-effectiveness of algorithms incorporating conventional radiography in the diagnosis and follow-up of musculoskeletal trauma.[6] Significant costs may be incurred at receiving hospitals as a result of repeating radiographic workups for patients who have been transferred from referring facilities along with their original radiographs.[171] Several recent studies have shown the benefits of "rules" in deciding when to order radiographs for knee and ankle trauma, resulting in fewer radiographs ordered and reduced cost without increased incidence of missed fractures.* Additional studies have also shown the ability to reduce postoperative and follow-up radiographs in treatment of ankle fractures.[78,125] Similar studies have addressed the cost-effectiveness of routine pelvic radiography in the setting of blunt trauma, although with mixed results.[49,89] Study of pediatric torus fractures has shown that postcasting radiographs are unnecessary and follow-up radiographs do not change fracture management, with the implication of significant cost-savings as a result of decreased radiography.[59]

Given the increases in health care costs each year in the United States, an area of particular concern is the perceived expense of advanced musculoskeletal imaging techniques such as MRI. According to one estimate, the use of musculoskeletal MRI has grown nearly 14 times faster than overall musculoskeletal imaging during the period 1996–2005 (353% increase versus 26% increase).[142] Parker et al.[142] explored the possible cost-savings that could be realized if ultrasound was used instead of MRI for the diagnosis of musculoskeletal disorders.[142] According to their review of 3621 musculoskeletal MRI reports, 45.4% of primary diagnoses and 30.6% of all diagnoses could have been made with US instead.[142] By extrapolating these data into the future, Parker et al.[142] predict that the substitution of musculoskeletal US for MRI in appropriate cases could save more than $6.9 billion in the period 2006–2020 and lead to large cost-savings for Medicare.[142]

Other studies have shown that advanced imaging can be very cost-effective to the degree that such imaging improves initial diagnostic accuracy and avoids delays in treatment that can contribute to increased morbidity to the patient or delay to return to work. For example, several studies have shown that early MRI in cases of wrist trauma can be cost-effective by providing accurate diagnosis of scaphoid fractures in cases where initial conventional radiography was normal.[25,46,117] MRI also proved superior to follow-up radiography for diagnosis of occult fractures, resulting in a change in management in up to 89% of cases.[152] Cost was found to be similar or reduced in all studies comparing early MRI with more traditional algorithms of casting and radiographic follow-up.[25,46,160] Two studies showed cost benefits associated with earlier rather than later MRI scanning.[25,152] Similar studies have shown the cost-effectiveness of

early limited MRI in the diagnosis and management of occult hip fractures.[110]

Patient Risk

As a rule, imaging procedures used in evaluating orthopaedic trauma contribute very little increased risk to the patient. However, potential risks include patient handling, ionizing radiation, and contrast reactions.

Handling trauma patients requires special attention and care, especially when transferring patients from gurneys onto imaging equipment. Many trauma patients have potential spine injuries, necessitating the use of spinal precautions and special radiographic views during imaging procedures. Likewise, fractured limbs may be very painful when moved, and there may be changes in fracture reduction or redislocation of an injured joint during manipulation of an extremity for radiographs. Because of pain and disorientation, patients may be unable to lie still during imaging examinations and may require analgesia and sedation. Sometimes, mechanical ventilation and multiple lines as well as catheters must be managed. Life support equipment and external fixation devices may also be incompatible with or limit the usefulness of certain examinations, such as conventional radiography and MRI.

Cancer risks associated with ionizing radiation vary with modality; CT generates considerably higher radiation does compared to conventional radiography, while US and MRI do not involve ionizing radiation. Radiation doses also vary considerably among CT protocols and between manufacturers.[155] One study showed a 61% to 71% decrease in radiation dose between standard-dose and low-dose multidetector CT in cervical spine trauma.[133] It has been estimated that as many as 1.5% to 2.0% of all cancers in the U.S. patients may be attributable to radiation from CT studies.[24,38] CT is often used to evaluate to evaluate the multiply-injured and unconscious patient. These patients typically undergo head and body CT for evaluation of intracranial and body trauma, and the use of CT to clear the cervical spine, in lieu of conventional radiography, may be increasing. Body CT generates the greatest radiation dose. In the cervical region, the greatest risk of ionizing radiation is induction of thyroid malignancy. One study suggests that use of CT to clear the cervical spine in unconscious major trauma patients is justified given the relatively minor concern for inducing thyroid malignancy. However, in those patients who are conscious or with a Glasgow Coma Scale score between 9 and 12, clinical evaluation is more likely to be helpful, and the risk of thyroid malignancy in a young cohort does not justify the use of CT to clear the entire cervical spine.[155]

Intravenous administration of iodinated contrast medium carries a small risk of adverse events, which may be categorized as mild, moderate, severe, and end organ.[3] With traditional high-osmolality ionic contrast media, most adverse reactions are mild to moderate and occur in 5% to 12% of all patients. This incidence is significantly decreased with use of the newer low-osmolality nonionic contrast agents. The occurrence of severe contrast reactions is approximately 1 to 2 per 1000 patients receiving high-osmolality contrast agents, whereas this number decreases to approximately 1 to 2 per 10,000 patients receiving low-osmolality contrast media.[4] Examples of end-organ adverse events include thrombophlebitis related to the injection site, nephrotoxicity, pulseless electrical activity, seizures, and pul-

*References 6,9,26,55,93,104,105,136,168.

monary edema.[3] Peripheral angiography carries a low risk of complications, including bleeding and further vascular injury, although these problems may be minimized with experience and careful technique.

SPECIFIC IMAGING MODALITIES

Radiography

Technical Considerations

Conventional Radiography. Conventional radiography (screen film radiography, plain film radiography) involves the use of x-rays, which are high-energy electromagnetic radiation with wavelengths smaller than ultraviolet light but longer than gamma rays. X-rays are produced using an x-ray tube, whereby electrons are emitted from a heated tungsten filament and accelerated across a voltage potential to strike an opposing tungsten target. The flow of electrons from filament to the target results in a tube current, and its interaction with the tungsten target generates a spectrum of x-rays and heat. Before leaving the x-ray tube, the x-rays are filtered and collimated into a useable beam. Factors that are set by the technologist to vary the quality and/or quantity of the x-ray beam include the voltage potential (measured in peak kilovoltage [kVp]), tube current (milliamperes [mA]), and exposure time (seconds). The output of the x-ray tube is expressed in mAs, calculated by multiplying the tube current (mA) by the exposure time (s). These factors are routinely recorded on digital radiographs, whereas they may be handwritten on portable radiographs for use with future examinations.

After leaving the x-ray tube, the x-ray beam is directed through the patient and onto a screen/film cassette. The x-ray beam is attenuated as it passes through the patient, primarily via two processes: the photoelectric effect and Compton scatter. After passing through the patient and before reaching the screen/film cassette, the transmitted radiation may be further collimated using a lead grid to remove the scatted radiation. Scatter increases with increasing patient thickness and larger fields of view and is a significant source of image degradation. Scatter may be negligible with extremities, in part related to their smaller size and greater proximity to the cassette; hence, grids may not be required.

Screen/film cassettes are used to capture the transmitted radiation and create the latent image. Intensifying screens absorb x-ray photons and subsequently emit a greater number of light photons, which are then absorbed by the film. The film consists of a base, which is covered on one or both sides by an emulsion containing silver grains. Absorbed light photons result in liberation of free electrons within the emulsion, which subsequently reduce the silver atoms. When the film is developed, the reduced silver atoms are amplified and appear black on the film. Most screen/film cassettes use a dual-screen and dual-emulsion film combination, which is enclosed in a light-tight cassette and ensures good contact between the screens and film. To improve bone detail, a single-screen, single emulsion system may be used.

Portable Radiography. Portable radiography is frequently used to evaluate acute trauma patients, and its use may be complicated by several factors not encountered in the radiology department's controlled environment. Trauma patients frequently are immobile and require special handling precautions, which may make it difficult to obtain routine anteroposterior (AP) and lateral projections. Appropriate placement and alignment of the screen/film cassette may be especially challenging, and if placed behind a backboard or beneath the patient's cart, it may introduce artifacts into the radiograph and obscure anatomy of interest. Objects outside of the patient's body related to his or her resuscitation, including endotracheal tubes, nasogastric tubes, chest tubes, and intravenous access, frequently project onto the radiograph. Casts, splints, and other external fixation devices may also project onto extremity radiographs and limit visualization of underlying bony detail.

Technical factors, such as levels of kilovoltage peak (kVp) and mA, also need modification with portable radiography. Portable examinations are often performed with higher kVp settings, which provide for a wider margin of error in selecting other technical factors. Higher kVp values will result in greater scattered radiation, however, and may necessitate the use of a grid with the screen/film cassette. Precise alignment of the grid and cassette to the central beam of the portable x-ray tube is also more difficult because each of the components are not fixed in space, and malalignment results in significant obscuration of the image and degradation in image quality.

Conventional Tomography. Tomography is a specialized application of conventional radiography, where the objective is to image a specific plane of tissue within the body. Historically, its primary use in orthopedic trauma was the imaging of suspected fracture nonunion. Once commonly practiced, plain tomography has been largely replaced by more advanced cross-sectional imaging techniques such as CT and MRI. The use of these advanced technologies has led to a decline in availability of tomography equipment in most imaging departments and a corresponding decrease in technologist experience in performing such examinations. However, it remains a viable low-cost and low-risk alternative to CT in those centers where conventional tomography is still available.

Conventional tomography is accomplished by a specialized radiography system whereby the patient is kept stationary while the x-ray tube and film cassette move about the patient, usually in a linear fashion but in opposite directions. Structures within the focal plane of interest are imaged in the same relative location on the film during tube and cassette translations, whereas images of structures located in front or behind the desired plane are blurred out by spreading their images over the entire film. The disadvantages of tomography include long examination times and potential for significant radiation exposure to the patient with larger numbers of images.

Digital Radiography. Several digital technologies for acquiring radiographs are in use and continue to be refined. In all DR systems, the creation of x-rays and attenuation of the x-ray beam as it passes through the patient are similar to conventional radiography systems. What differentiates DR systems is the type of image receptor that interacts with the attenuated x-ray beam to create a medical image.

Computed radiography (CR) was first introduced in the late 1970s and has gained wide popularity in radiology departments within the last decade. With CR, the screen/film cassette is replaced by a cassette containing a photostimulatable phosphor deposited onto a substrate. When this type of phosphor interacts with x-rays, electrons are elevated to and trapped at higher energy levels within the phosphor. The amount of electron trapping is proportional to the incident x-rays and results in the creation of a latent image, which can later be read using a specialized CR cassette reader. The reader scans the phosphor plate using a laser, which releases the electrons from their higher energy states, and results in emission of light as they drop down to lower energy states. The emitted light is captured by a photomultiplier tube, which converts the light into an electrical signal, which is subsequently digitized and stored. This process is done on a point-by-point basis throughout the entire phosphor plate to create a digital image.

Relatively recent advances in flat panel detectors have led to a new digital imaging technology that has been referred to as direct capture radiography, or alternatively, indirect and direct DR. Each of these systems uses flat panel detectors that incorporate a large array of individual detector elements; each one corresponds to a pixel in the final image. In indirect DR, the detector elements are sensitive to light; hence, an x-ray intensifying screen is used to convert the incident x-rays into light, which is then captured by the individual detector elements and stored as a net negative charge. In direct DR, the individual detector elements are coated with a photoconductive material (selenium is commonly used). On exposure to x-rays, electrons are liberated from the photoconductor and are captured by the underlying detector elements, resulting in a net negative charge within each detector element. With both systems, the negative charges within the array of detector elements are read out electronically, digitized, and stored to create the final image.

Currently, the spatial resolution of conventional radiography is greater than for DR systems. CR and DR, however, offer significant advantages over conventional radiography, including the ability to manipulate digital images and alter image contrast, decreased radiation dose to the patient and radiological personnel, and greater ease of storage and transmission of radiographs both within and beyond the imaging department. DR systems are expensive to implement, as they require replacement of the entire radiography suite. CR systems are much more economical to implement, as they only require replacement of the screen/film cassettes and purchase of a CR reader. Both digital systems, though, offer ongoing cost savings as a result of decreased numbers of retakes and reduction in film costs. Although DR is likely the future of radiography, it currently does not match conventional radiography for fracture assessment in terms of spatial resolution (Table 16-1).

Applications

Conventional radiography remains the primary diagnostic modality for assessing fractures and dislocations. Orthogonal views, occasionally supplemented by additional specific projections, are sufficient to identify and manage most fractures. Orthopaedic surgeons' immediate interpretation of conventional radiographs of simple fractures has been shown to be timely, accurate, and inexpensive and contributes to patient care, whereas formal interpretation of the same studies by a radiologist typically occurs after care is rendered, may be inaccurate, adds expense, and does not contribute to patient management.[21]

For many injuries, including those in the spine, specific measurements have been reported that may characterize a given injury.[18] In addition to delineating the fracture pattern, conventional radiographs are useful for assessing limb length and alignment and are the primary means by which fracture healing is monitored. Numerous examples of the use of conventional radiographs are found throughout this text. In many cases, more subtle indications of injury apparent on conventional radiographs can suggest the need for further diagnostic imaging or intervention. Examples of such cases would be the identification of a posterior fat pad sign in a pediatric elbow, indicating an occult elbow injury, a joint effusion, or the finding of a fat-fluid level in the knee joint capsule indicating osteochondral fracture. Surrounding soft tissues may also be evaluated for and show additional evidence of trauma, including swelling, foreign bodies, and gas. Although conventional radiographs are universally used for assessing fracture healing, one recent report noted that there is very poor interobserver agreement regarding the determination of fracture healing after internal fixation.[40]

DR has largely replaced conventional radiography and has provided a platform on which to develop new methods of musculoskeletal imaging. Digital imaging facilitates computer processing of images, which may improve their diagnostic value. Botser and colleagues[22] studied a series of nondisplaced proximal femoral fractures and found that digital enhancement with the use of specific filter techniques improved fracture diagnosis. One recent advance is a full body scanner that can take rapid digital images of the entire body in one or multiple planes (Statscan Critical Imaging System; Lodox Systems Ltd., South Africa). The use of Statscan in the evaluation of multiple trauma patients and pediatric patients has been reported.[57,134,147] The primary advantages are the rapid detection of injuries and less time needed for resuscitation. In one study, 96% of fractures were identified on the initial Statscan.[147] In another study focusing on 37 consecutive pelvic injuries, findings on Statscan images were compared to those seen with CR and CT.[134] Of 73 abnormalities noted in these patients, 18 were not identifiable on the Statscan, although only one of the missed findings was considered significant for the initial management of the patient.[134] Although many patients initially evaluated with Statscan still need formal CT, such studies can be more limited and result in less overall radiation exposure to the patient than conventional imaging algorithms.[57]

Fluoroscopy

Technical Considerations

Conventional Fluoroscopy. Fluoroscopy involves the use of low-dose x-rays to image patient anatomy at high temporal resolutions—that is, in real time. Typical components of a fluoroscopy system include an x-ray tube, filters, and a collimator, similar to that used in conventional radiography. The x-ray tube is energized continuously using a low exposure rate, and the x-ray beam is directed through the patient onto an image intensifier. The image intensifier is responsible for converting the attenuated x-ray beam into a visible light image, which is frequently coupled to a closed-circuit television camera to produce a "live" image on a video monitor. An optical coupling system, using high-resolution lenses and mirrors, may also be used to direct the light image to recording devices, such as video recorders and photospot cameras.

The components of the image intensifier are housed in a glass vacuum tube and include a large input phosphor, a photocathode, a series of electrostatic lenses, an anode, and a smaller output phosphor. Incident x-rays are directed onto the input phosphor and are converted into light photons, similar to a radiographic intensifying screen. The light photons are channeled by the phosphor to the adjacent photocathode as a result of the linear crystalline structure of the phosphor matrix. The photocathode is composed of a thin metal layer, containing cesium and antimony, applied to the posterior surface of the input phosphor, which interacts with the light photons and results in emission of electrons. The electrons are then accelerated from the photocathode to the anode by an applied voltage approximating 25,000 V. During the acceleration process, the electrons emitted across the entire cross-sectional area of the photocathode are kept in relative alignment by a series of electrostatic lenses, such that the spatial information they contain is preserved. The electrons are subsequently focused onto the output phosphor, which results in light emission and creation of an image.

Fluoroscopy systems vary in configuration, from permanently installed biplane angiography suites to mobile C-arm designs. Mini C-arm units have become increasingly popular for outpatient clinics. Image intensifiers are produced in different sizes, and measurements refer to the size of the input phosphor. Typical diameters range from 4 to 16 inches (10 to 40 cm), and various sizes may be better suited or standardized to specific applications. Many fluoroscopy systems offer additional magnification modes, which use a smaller area of the input phosphor to create the magnified image. The theoretical resolution of an image intensifier is approximately 4 to 5 lp/mm, with somewhat better resolution obtained in magnification modes (Table 16-1). This is achievable only when the images are output to film. The image intensifier output is usually coupled to a video monitor for real-time viewing, which results in degradation of the resolution achievable by the image intensifier. Resolution of such closed-circuit television systems is typically 1 to 2 lp/mm.

Digital Fluoroscopy. Advances in digital technology have led to the development of digital fluoroscopy systems, which are now common in clinical practice. The output of the image intensifier may be coupled to a high-resolution video camera with subsequently digitized output, or directed onto a charge-coupled device (CCD). A CCD is a small plate containing a large array of photosensitive elements, each of which corresponds to a single pixel in the final digital image. Each element stores charge in proportion to the amount of absorbed light, which is then read out electronically and digitized to produce a pixel value. The matrix of pixel values is then used to create the final digital image. The resolution of a CCD depends on the size of each of its array elements; CCDs with a 1024 × 1024 matrix may achieve a resolution of 10 lp/mm. The digital nature of the image lends itself to computer postprocessing, including digital subtraction techniques, which improves image contrast. More recent advances in flat panel detector technology using thin film transistor (TFT) arrays may allow replacement of the image intensifier and video camera by TFT panels, resulting in even greater improvement in image contrast.

Applications
Intraoperative Imaging. Intraoperative radiography and fluoroscopy are almost universally used during the operative care of fractures. Imaging techniques are needed during surgery to verify the reduction of fractures, identify the starting portals for intramedullary nails, target cannulated or interlocking screws, and verify implant position (Fig. 16-1). Fluoroscopic assessment of tibial plateau fracture reduction leads to results as good as or better than those obtained with arthroscopy-assisted reduction.[111] Norris et al.[137] used intraoperative fluoroscopy during the repair of acetabular fractures and found it as effective as postoperative radiographs to assess fracture reduction and comparable to postoperative CT to evaluate for intra-articular extension of hardware. Recent advances in "minimally invasive" fracture fixation rely even more on the interpretation of fluoroscopic images[99] (Fig. 16-2).

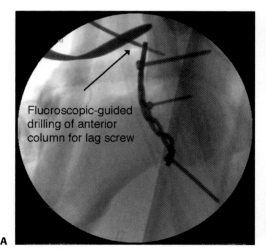 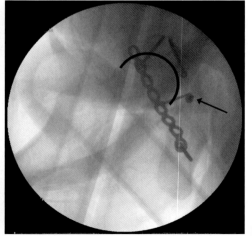

Fluoroscopic-guided drilling of anterior column for lag screw

A **B**

FIGURE 16-1 A. Intraoperative fluoroscopic anteroposterior view of the pelvis used to evaluate fracture reduction and guide placement of fixation hardware. Here, intraoperative fluoroscopy is used to target drilling of a lag screw across the anterior column component of an associated transverse and posterior wall fracture repaired from a posterior approach. **B.** Intraoperative imaging is also useful for ensuring that hardware is not within the joint does not extend into the joint space. Multiple views are taken with the C-arm in different positions until the screw of interest is seen "head-on." With this view, it can then be determined whether the screw penetrates the joint surface. The screw can then be compared with the joint space in profile to evaluate for intra-articular extension. In this case, the screw (*arrow*) is clearly outside of the joint.

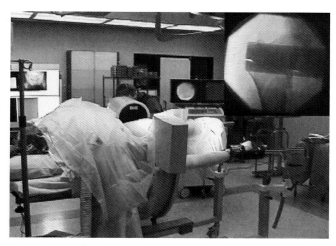

FIGURE 16-2 This intraoperative photograph of a patient in the lateral position for femoral nailing on a fracture table demonstrates the use of fluoroscopy to evaluate fracture reduction and, later, to guide implant positioning. *Top right,* corresponding fluoroscopic image.

Despite the benefits of intraoperative fluoroscopy, most surgeons insist on obtaining conventional radiographs at the completion of surgery. Although this practice requires further radiation exposure and adds time and expense, it is important for both clinical and medicolegal documentation. Fluoroscopic images have limited field-of-view and may not demonstrate the full extent of hardware fixation (as in the case of an intramedullary nail) or overall limb alignment as well as conventional radiographs. Finally, it may be difficult to compare intraoperative fluoroscopic images to later conventional radiographs, so the immediate postoperative radiograph represents an important baseline reference for future comparisons.

Several studies have examined the amount of ionizing radiation that operating room personnel are exposed to during the care of fractures when fluoroscopy is used.[15,87,170] Fortunately, with modern fluoroscopic systems, measurable radiation exposure is limited to the surgeon's hands,[15,87] although he or she needs to limit excessive use of the fluoroscope during surgical procedures. Recently, Matthews et al.[122] showed that during surgery, repetitive fluoroscopic scout imaging is performed to reproduce a specific desired image. In a simulated test-rig, an average of seven scout images were required to reproduce a given C-arm position.[122] In contrast, these investigators showed that the use of navigation-assisted repositioning using a standard, commercially available image-guided surgical navigation system did not require a single additional scout image, with comparable positioning times.[122]

A recent advance in intraoperative fluoroscopy is the ability to generate a cross-sectional, computer-reconstructed axial image in real-time.[8,30,90,91,176] C-arms that are adapted for this purpose incorporate a motor that rotates the x-ray tube and image intensifier around the patient while taking hundreds of images. Immediate computer processing generates a reconstructed cross-sectional image that is similar to an axial CT image. The ability to obtain immediate cross-sectional images during surgery can help the surgeon assess reduction during the repair of certain intra-articular fractures when direct visualization of the articular surface is not possible.[30] Cross-sectional intraoperative imaging may also be of benefit in situations when

hardware placement requires precision, such the insertion of pedicle screws or iliosacral screws. In cadaver models of calcaneal fracture[90] and acetabular fracture,[91] three-dimensional (3D) fluoroscopy was superior to standard two-dimensional (2D) fluoroscopy and comparable to CT for the detection of intra-articular hardware and intermediate between the other modalities in demonstrating articular impaction of acetabular fracture[91] or the articular reduction or medial screw protrusion in calcaneal fractures.[90] In a clinical series of articular fractures, information obtained via intraoperative 3D fluoroscopy led to a decision to revise the fracture and/or fixation in 11% of cases.[8] In another series of patients undergoing surgery for foot and ankle trauma, 39% of cases with adequate conventional C-arm images were revised intraoperatively after 3D fluoroscopy was performed.[156] However, it is important to note that no one has documented that the use of 3D fluoroscopy improves outcomes, so for now this technology remains mostly investigational.

Surgical Navigation. Although computer-assisted surgical navigation techniques may be performed with cross-sectional imaging data obtained from preoperative CT, fluoroscopy is commonly used for surgical navigation because of its flexibility, convenience, low radiation exposure, and low cost. Although the field of surgical navigation is in its infancy, computer-assisted surgical navigation has already been applied to cervical and thoracic spine fracture fixation,[7] placement of percutaneous iliosacral and anterior column screws in the pelvis,[39,73,131] and intramedullary nailing (see Chapter 17).[88,94,169]

Fluoroscopic surgical navigation requires a specialized computer-based system, which tracks the position of a hand-held tool in space. It is necessary to "register" the patient's bone within the computer based on preoperative CT data or the use of a generic dataset. Fluoroscopic views need be taken only once; thereafter, all movements of the tool are recorded against the registered bone image and may be displayed in different planes simultaneously, superimposed on the static images by the computer system. This dramatically reduces the need for repeated intraoperative imaging, decreasing the time of surgery and the radiation exposure of the patient and surgical team. However, intraoperative changes in the patient's position or in the dimensions of the registered bone (such as might occur during fracture reduction) decrease the accuracy of image registration. Surgical navigation has been used for hip fractures[33,109] and placement of iliosacral screws.[131] During intramedullary nailing of the femur, surgical navigation facilitates accurate entry-point location, fracture reduction, and insertion of interlocking and blocking screws and assists with determination of nail and screw length.[65,94,180] Weil et al.[180] used a cadaveric femur model to demonstrate that computerized navigation may increase the precision of fracture reduction, while at the same time lessening requirements for intraoperative fluoroscopy. In another cadaveric model, navigated distal interlocking was found to lead to less rotational deformity (2 degrees) compared with freehand distal interlocking (7 degrees).[65]

Although this technology has been proved to be feasible, the clinical importance and cost-effectiveness of surgical navigation remain undetermined. Collinge et al.[36] compared the safety and efficiency of standard multiplanar fluoroscopy with those of virtual fluoroscopy for use in the percutaneous insertion of iliosacral screws in 29 cadaver specimens. Interestingly, both methods were equally accurate; one screw was incorrectly inserted in each group, and both groups contained examples of screws with minor deviations in trajectory. Although the actual time for screw insertion was less with virtual fluoroscopy (3.5 minutes versus 7.1 minutes), this was offset by the increased time needed to set up and calibrate the image-guided system.[36] Liebergall et al.[109] showed improved screw parallelism and screw spread when navigation was used during repair of femoral neck fractures, and this correlated with fewer reoperations and overall complications in the navigated group.

Computed Tomography

Technical Considerations

CT has had the greatest clinical impact of any of the radiographic imaging modalities; its inventors (Godfrey Houndsfield and Allan Cormack) received the Nobel Prize for Medicine in 1979. Since its inception in the early 1970s, advances in technology and computer science have guided the development of several new generations of CT scanners, each capable of greater throughput and improved resolution. Although a more detailed review of the history of CT scanners is beyond the scope of this section, a brief description of current concepts in CT scanner technology is presented.

Helical (spiral) CT scanners were developed in the late 1980s and are so named because of the helical path the x-ray beam takes through the patient. The development of "slip ring" technology allowed the gantry (x-ray tube and detectors) to rotate continuously around the patient, whereas with previous-generation scanners, gantry rotation was constrained by electrical cables, which needed to be unwound in between slice acquisitions. With nonhelical scanners, table position was incrementally advanced in between slice acquisitions; with slip ring technology, the table position is advanced continuously while the gantry rotates, resulting in a helical x-ray beam path.

The first dual-slice helical scanner was demonstrated in 1992, with 4- and 16-slice models appearing in 1998 and 2001. On the whole, multislice scanners are similar to single-slice helical scanners in many respects. Instead of a single row of detectors, however, multiple rows of detectors are present within the gantry and are designed to allow acquisition of multiple slices at the same time. Now 64-slice CT scanners are clinically available, and 256-slice scanners are currently under development.

With these new technologies, scanning algorithms needed to be modified, which resulted in new terminology and imaging parameters to adjust. For single-slice helical scanners (and older-generation scanners as well), slice thickness is determined by x-ray beam collimation, whereas, for multislice scanners, it is determined by detector width. For single-slice scanners, pitch is defined as the ratio of table movement (mm) per 360-degree rotation to slice thickness (mm). A pitch of 1.0 is comparable to older-generation scanners where the table movement increment was the same as the slice thickness. A pitch of less than 1.0 results in overlapping of the x-ray beam and higher patient radiation dose; a pitch greater than 1.0 results in increased coverage through the patient and decreased radiation dose. In practice, pitch is generally limited to 1.5 to 2.0, although protocols vary. For multislice scanners, the definition of pitch changes to incorporate the detector array width rather than the single slice width and is referred to as *detector pitch*.

The data sets from single-slice and multislice scanners are both helical in nature, and individual slices must be interpolated from the data set. Minimum slice thickness is set by the original x-ray beam collimation (single-slice scanners) or detector width (multislice scanners). Any number of slices may be reconstructed at any position along the long axis of the patient, and in any thickness equal to or greater than the minimal slice thickness. This allows reconstruction of overcontiguous slices (with typically 50% overlap), which increases the sensitivity for detecting small lesions that may otherwise be averaged between adjacent slices. This also results in twice as many images, although with no increase in scan time or additional radiation dose to the patient.

Multiplanar reconstructions (MPRs) and 3D reconstructions are also routinely performed with both single-slice and multislice helical scanners. This, in part, is related to the fact that today's CT examinations routinely produce hundreds of images, and MPR and 3D reformatting assist in interpreting these data. Advances in detector technology have allowed slice thickness to decrease such that slice thicknesses of 0.5 mm are routinely achieved clinically and allow acquisition of isotropic voxels. A voxel is the 3D equivalent of a pixel and represents the volume of tissue represented by a single pixel; isotropic voxels have uniform thickness in all directions (e.g. 0.5 mm $\times$ 0.5 mm $\times$ 0.5 mm). Acquisition of images with isotropic voxels results in multiplanar (nonaxial) reconstructions that have in-plane resolutions equal to those of the original axial image. Additionally, the use of overcontiguous images is useful in 3D reconstructions to eliminate stair-step artifact.

Orthopaedic hardware results in metallic streak artifact on standard CT images, which frequently obscures surrounding bone and soft tissue detail. This streak artifact is propagated on multiplanar reformatted images as well. Fortunately, volume-rendering of a multidetector CT axial database can dramatically reduce streak artifact associated with hardware.[60]

Overall, the advantages of multislice helical scanners include faster scan times and patient throughput, reduced motion artifacts, reduced intravenous contrast requirements, improved lesion detection, and improved multiplanar and 3D reconstructions. Disadvantages include the potential for decreased resolution along the long axis of the patient (related to increased pitch) and a large number of images, resulting in increased reconstruction time and storage requirements. Another disadvantage of CT in general is the high radiation dose associated with this modality. However, radiation doses can be reduced by using low-dose, rather than standard-dose, scanning algorithms without differences in subjective image quality evaluation.[133]

Applications

Complex Fractures. CT remains the imaging modality of choice for evaluating complex fractures as well as ruling out injury to the spine. In addition to high-resolution axial images, multiplanar reconstructions are commonly performed (Fig. 16-3). Such information provides critical data about the displacement of fracture fragments, including assessment of intra-articular displacement, articular surface depression, and bone loss. Three-dimensional reconstructions using surface rendering techniques are often less helpful in fracture management compared with multiplanar reconstructions. With 3D imaging techniques, fracture planes are frequently obscured by overlying fracture fragments and underestimate the true degree of commi-

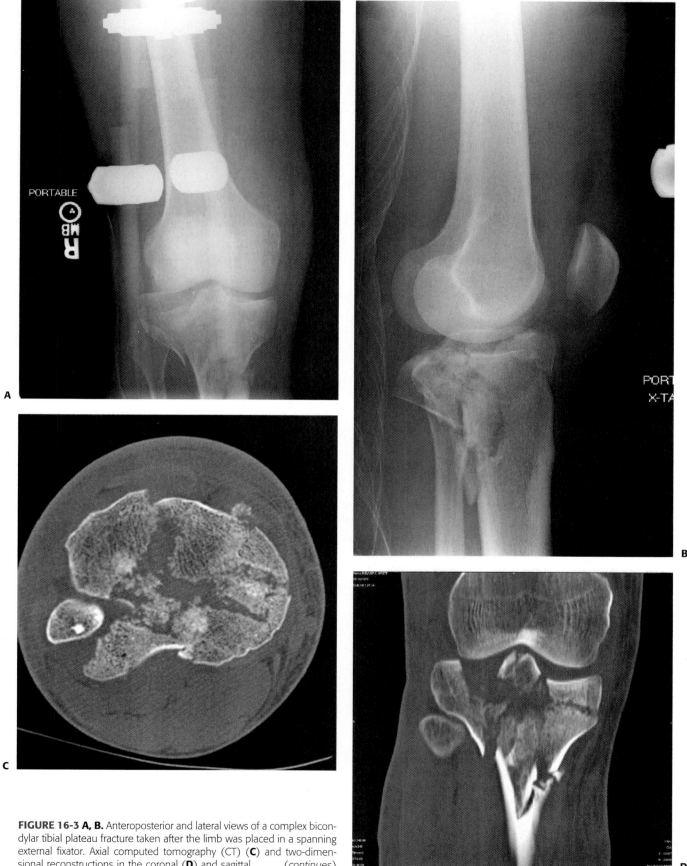

FIGURE 16-3 A, B. Anteroposterior and lateral views of a complex bicondylar tibial plateau fracture taken after the limb was placed in a spanning external fixator. Axial computed tomography (CT) (**C**) and two-dimensional reconstructions in the coronal (**D**) and sagittal   (*continues*)

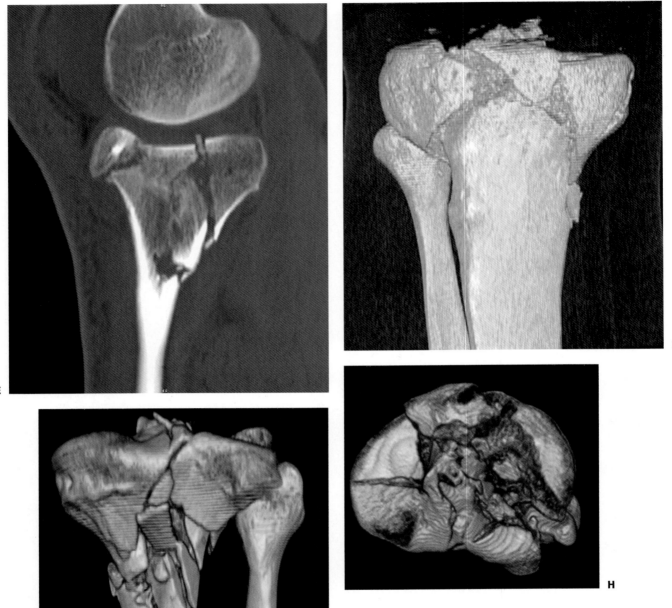

FIGURE 16-3 (*continued*) (**E**) planes better demonstrate the extent of comminution. With high-resolution three-dimensional reconstruction (**F, G**), a very good appreciation of the fracture pattern is possible. Finally, the tibial plateau can be viewed from "above" by digitally subtracting the femur and patella and rotating the image (**H**). For complex fractures such as this, advanced CT scanning is unparalleled.

nution; however, they may be helpful in evaluating angulation and displacement of fracture fragments, in addition to depression of articular surfaces. With previous-generation CT scanners, evaluation of fracture planes parallel to the scan plane was suboptimal because of volume averaging of the fracture plane with adjacent intact bone. With newer helical scanners, image data are obtained as a volume rather than as individual slices, and multiplanar reconstructions typically have resolution equal to the axial images. For this reason, detection of transversely oriented fracture planes is significantly enhanced. Typical indi-

cations for CT include fractures of the proximal humerus, scapula, spine, pelvis, tibial plateau, tibial plafond, calcaneus, and midfoot.

In the spine, helical CT has become the imaging modality of choice. A variety of measurements that incorporate CT data have been described that are useful in the assessment of the cervical spine following injury, including cervical translation and vertebral body height loss, canal compromise, spinal cord compression, and facet fracture and/or subluxation.[18] Despite its greater initial expense, CT has been shown to have sensitivity and specificity of 96%, both greater than for conventional plain radiography.[72] Grogan et al.[72] present a decision analysis emphasizing cost minimization and conclude that helical CT is the preferred initial screening test for detecting cervical spine injury in moderate- to high-risk trauma patients.

In the upper extremity, CT is commonly performed to evaluate fractures of the proximal humerus and scapula.[74,124] Multiplanar reconstructions of complex proximal humeral and scapular fractures assist in surgical planning. For proximal humeral fractures, simple axial images provide important information about the glenohumeral relationship, demonstrate glenoid rim fractures, and reveal whether the tuberosities of the humerus are fractured. Occult fractures of the coracoid process and lesser tuberosity are readily seen.[74] Despite the valuable information that CT provides (with or without multiplanar reconstructions), several studies have shown that the interobserver assessment of proximal humeral and scapular neck fractures was not improved with the addition of CT.[124] For distal radial fractures that mandate surgical reconstruction, CT is more accurate than conventional radiography in demonstrating involvement of the distal radioulnar joint, the extent of articular surface depression, and the amount of comminution.[35,150] Three-dimensional CT was found to further improve the accuracy of fracture classification and to influence treatment decisions compared to standard 2D CT in a series of 30 intra-articular distal radius fractures.[76]

CT is routinely used in evaluating pelvic fractures. A CT-based classification of acetabular fractures has been proposed.[77] For the assessment of acetabular fractures, CT is better than conventional plain radiography at identifying intra-articular step-offs and gaps and is considered an essential part of the preoperative evaluation.[19] Reformatted images can be obtained in oblique planes to simulate standard Judet radiographs[66] (Fig. 16-4). Use of CT-reformatting avoids the pain and risk of fracture displacement or hip redislocation that might occur while repositioning the patient 45 degrees on each side for Judet views. A potential disadvantage is the slight loss of information resulting from volume averaging and computer reconstruction that could affect interpretation of the images. In an unpublished study, 60 orthopedic trauma surgeons randomly reviewed sets of pelvic radiographs from 11 patients and were asked to classify each according to the Judet-Letournal system; each patient had 2 sets of images (one with traditional Judet radiographs and one with reformatted CT scans). For 10 of the 11 cases there were no differences in classification; in the final case of a T-type fracture, classification was more consistent when the CT-reformatted images were viewed (personal communication, Rena Stewart, MD). Postoperative CT after acetabular fracture repair identifies residual articular defects or incongruities better than plain radiographs.[20] CT demonstrates intra-articular debris in a significant number of patients after hip dislocation,[82] and CT should be performed in any patient whose conventional plain radiographs show an incongruent reduction. Because small intra-articular bodies may not be visible on radiographs, one should consider obtaining CT images in all patients who sustain a hip dislocation, even when conventional plain radiographs appear to be normal.

The impact of CT on tibial plateau fracture management is well described[32] (Fig. 16-3). In one study, when using just

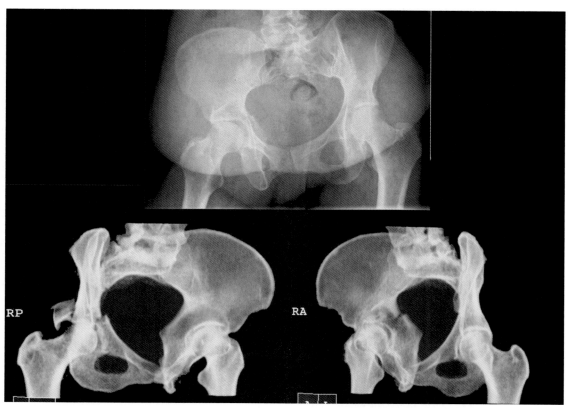

FIGURE 16-4 Computed tomography of the pelvis reformatted in 45-degree right and left oblique planes (*bottom*) to simulate the traditional plain film Judet views of the pelvis. The corresponding anteroposterior view is shown above. (Courtesy of Dr. Rena Stewart.)

conventional radiographs for formulating a treatment plan, the mean interobserver kappa coefficient was 0.58, which increased to 0.71 after adding CT. The mean intraobserver kappa coefficient for fracture classification using radiographs was 0.70, which increased to 0.80 with addition of CT. The mean intraobserver kappa coefficient for treatment plan based on radiographs alone was 0.62, which increased to 0.82 after adding CT. With the addition of CT, the fracture classification was changed in 12% of cases, whereas the treatment plan was altered 26% of the time.[32] In another study, Wicky et al.[183] compared helical CT with 3D reconstructions to conventional radiography in patients with tibial plateau fractures and found that, for the purpose of classification, fractures were underestimated in 43% of cases by radiographs. Among a smaller subset of patients in whom operative plans were formulated with and without CT, the same investigators found that the addition of helical CT 3D reconstructions led to modifications in the surgical plan in more than half the cases.[183]

Tornetta and Gorup[174] evaluated the use of preoperative CT in the management of tibial pilon fractures. Twenty-two patients were studied with both conventional radiographs and CT. The fracture pattern, number of fragments, degree of comminution, presence of articular impaction, and location of the major fracture line were recorded. CT revealed more fragments in 12 patients, increased impaction in 6 patients, and more severe comminution in 11 patients. The operative plan was changed in 14 (64%) patients, and additional information was gained in 18 (82%) patients.[174]

CT is valuable for assessing fractures of the hindfoot. CT reveals bone debris in the subtalar joint of patients with lateral process fractures of the talus.[53] In children with Tillaux fractures of the anterolateral distal tibia, CT is better than conventional radiography in detecting displacement of more than 2 mm, which is considered an indication for surgery[81] (Fig. 16-5). Helical CT is valuable for the preoperative planning of calcaneal fractures.[61] Axial images of the calcaneus best show hindfoot deformity, whereas multiplanar reconstructions (including 3D imaging with dislocation of the joint) best reveal intra-articular involvement.[61]

Postoperative Evaluation of Fracture Reduction. CT is also useful for postoperative assessment of complex fractures. Moed et al.[127] compared the functional outcome of 67 patients with posterior wall acetabular fractures with the findings on postoperative CT. In this study, postoperative CT more accurately revealed the degree of residual fracture displacement compared with conventional radiographs, and the accuracy of surgical reduction seen on postoperative CT was highly predictive of the clinical outcome.[127] Vasarhelyi et al.[175] found side-to-side torsional differences of greater than 10 degrees in one-quarter of 61 patients undergoing fixation of distal fibula fractures.[175] Kurozumi et al.[102] correlated postoperative radiographs and CT with functional outcomes in 67 patients with intra-articular calcaneal fractures and found that better reduction of the calcaneocuboid joint and posterior facet of the subtalar joint correlated with improved outcome.

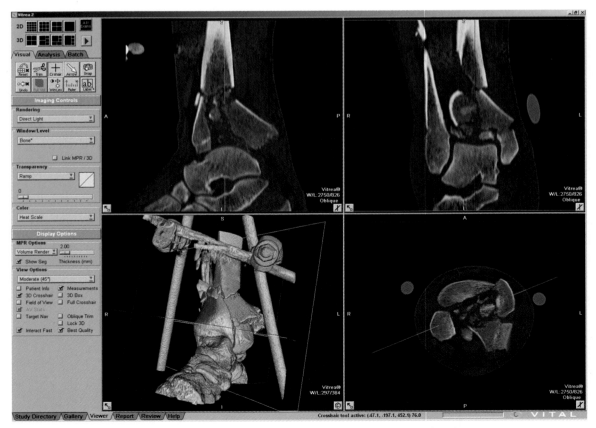

FIGURE 16-5 Computed tomography of a triplane fracture as viewed on a digital workstation. Users can visualize axial and reconstructed coronal and sagittal images simultaneously.

Healing of Fractures. Conventional radiographs are often limited in demonstrating persistent fracture lines, and such nonunions are more readily demonstrated on CT[13] (Fig. 16-6). CT has replaced conventional tomography in most centers for the identification of fracture nonunions. Multiplanar CT reconstructions may be needed if the fracture pattern is complex. Assessing partially united fractures can also be difficult, even with CT. The accuracy of CT in detecting tibial nonunion was evaluated. Bhattacharyya et al.[13] studied 35 patients with suspected tibial nonunion and equivocal plain radiograph findings. In this series, the sensitivity of CT for detecting nonunion was 100%, but its accuracy was limited by a low specificity of 62%, because three patients who were diagnosed as having tibial nonunion by CT were found to have a healed fracture at surgery.[13]

A more interesting role for CT is evaluation of early fracture healing. CT reveals external callus formation earlier than conventional radiography and allows for more complete and detailed visualization of fracture healing, which may be obscured by overlying casts and/or fixation hardware on radiographs.[71] Lynch et al.[116] developed a means of measuring changes in CT density at fracture sites by quantifying the formation of mineralized tissue within fracture gaps, while ignoring loss of bone mineral caused by disuse osteoporosis. In a preliminary study of seven patients with distal radial fractures, this technique demonstrated increased CT density 2 weeks postfracture that correlated with the visual appearance of sclerosis and blurring of the fracture line on conventional radiographs.[116] It is not yet known whether such information will be predictive of fracture healing complications.

Magnetic Resonance Imaging

Technical Considerations

MRI does not use ionizing radiation. Rather, MRI uses radiofrequency (RF) waves, in the presence of a strong magnetic field, to interact with the patient's hydrogen atoms (protons) to create images of superb soft tissue contrast. Although the physics of MRI is complex and too detailed to review in this section, the more practical aspects of MRI relevant to the evaluation of orthopaedic imaging will be discussed.

Present-day MRI scanners may be classified according to field strength. The basic unit of measurement of magnetic field strength is the Gauss (G); the earth's magnetic field measures approximately 0.5 G. Field strengths for MRI are much greater and are measured in Tesla (T), which is defined as 10,000 G. Low–field-strength scanners are typically 0.2 to 0.3 T and are commonly used in outpatient settings as "extremity" or "open" scanners. High–field-strength scanners are generally those greater than 1.0 T, with 1.5-T scanners dominating the market and representing more than 90% of installed scanners worldwide. The 3.0-T scanners have also become clinically available, although their acceptance has been limited because of the higher cost of these systems and relatively limited selection of receiver coils. Advantages to higher–field-strength scanners include increased capability, increased resolution and image quality, and decreased scan time.

The RF coils are an important element of any MRI system. RF coils are used to transmit RF waves into the patient, as well as receive RF signals ("echoes") from the patient during the course of the examination. A standard "body" coil is incorporated into scanners as a default coil from which to both send and receive RF signals. The body coil is located within the housing of the magnet and, as a result, is located some distance from the patient. This distance factor decreases the strength of the RF signal received from the patient, although this is not a problem for imaging larger body parts such as the abdomen and pelvis. For smaller body parts, such as extremities in orthopaedic imaging, specialized RF coils are available and are widely used to increase the quality of MRI studies. These coils are usually "receive only" coils, meaning the body coil transmits the RF pulse; some specialty coils, however, incorporate both transmit and receive functions. These smaller coils are placed around or over the body part to be scanned, which decreases the distance from the patient's anatomy to the coil and results in greater signal return from the underlying tissue. This increases the signal-to-noise ratio (SNR) of the resulting images and produces images of greater contrast resolution and higher image quality, which may be used to improve image quality, increase spatial resolution, or decrease scan time.

Advances in RF coil technology have led to a wide variety of RF coil designs available today. Volume coils encircle the anatomy of interest and provide increased signal homogeneity. Surface coils are placed over the anatomy of interest and significantly improve near-field signal strength returning from the underlying anatomy. Quadrature and phased-array coil designs incorporate multiple coil elements with electronic coupling to increase signal strength and SNR. Specialized coils are available for orthopaedic imaging and include dedicated phased-array coils, as well as various sizes of flexible surface coils.

MR images are generated using a series of pulse sequences. The term *pulse sequence* refers to sequence of radiofrequency pulses that are applied in concert with a series of magnetic gradients. These pulses are applied in a particular order and with a particular timing scheme, with the RF coils listening for the resulting "echoes" at specific time intervals. Pulse sequences determine the type of image contrast produced. During each pulse sequence, magnetic gradients are applied to the main magnetic field to achieve spatial localization. A magnetic gradient along the long axis of the bore of the magnet (and patient) is used for slice selection, whereas gradients along the transverse plane are responsible for frequency and phase encoding, which result in localization within the transverse plane. Most MRI examinations are particularly loud as a result of rapidly switching the gradients on and off, which necessitates use of earplugs or headphones during the test study. Inherent in all pulse sequences are specifications for parameters such as geometry (imaging plane, field of view, number of slices), resolution (number of frequency and phase encoding steps, slice thickness), and image contrast (repetition time [TR], echo delay time [TE]). A collection of multiple pulse sequences used for a particular examination is often referred to as a *protocol*.

Common sequences used in orthopaedic imaging include spin-echo (SE) and gradient-echo (gradient recalled echo [GRE]) imaging. Spin-echo sequences are most frequently used in conjunction with a fast imaging technique, termed *fast* spin-echo (FSE) or *turbo* spin-echo (TSE) imaging, depending on the manufacturer. Spin-echo sequences provide T1-weighted (T1W), proton density (PD), and T2-weighted (T2W) image contrast based on selection of the parameters TR and TE. T1W images tend to depict anatomy well and are sensitive, but not specific, for pathology. T2W images are fluid-sensitive images and tend to depict pathology well. PD images are neither T1W

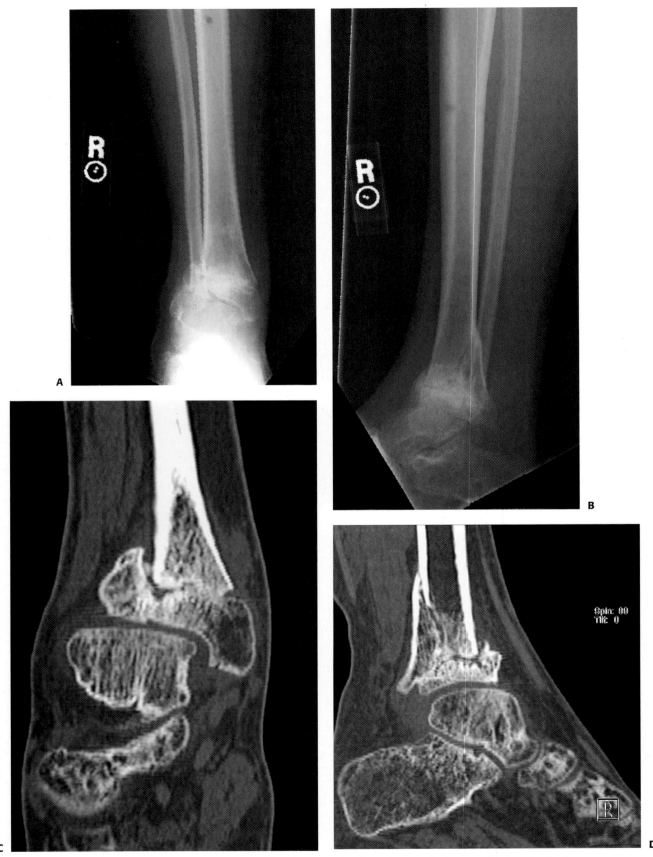

FIGURE 16-6 A, B. Anteroposterior and lateral radiographs of a patient who had external fixation of a distal tibia fracture with progressive deformity. **C, D.** Computed tomography of the nonunion with two-dimensional reconstructions in the coronal and sagittal planes provides unambiguous evidence of fracture nonunion.

nor T2W, and contrast is derived from differences in proton density within the tissues. PD images are commonly used in orthopaedic imaging, as they result in high SNR images and depict anatomy and pathology well. PD images are often acquired in conjunction with T2W images during the same pulse sequence; in this case, the PD image is referred to as the *first echo*, and the T2W image is called the *second echo*. This combination may also be referred to as a *double echo* (DE, 2E) sequence.

One consequence of FSE/TSE techniques is that fat, like fluid, is relatively bright on PD and T2W sequences. Fat suppression (FS) techniques are necessary to evaluate for edema or fluid with fat-containing tissues, such as bone marrow. Two techniques are commonly used: short TI inversion recovery (STIR) and chemical saturation ("fat-sat," spectral saturation, frequency-selective presaturation). STIR is a distinctive spin-echo pulse sequence that results in suppression of a particular tissue based on the choice of an additional parameter, TI. A relatively short TI value of 150 ms results in suppression of fat-containing tissues. This sequence tends to be relatively low in SNR and, as a consequence, is often performed at lower resolution. The sequence is less affected by variations in magnetic field homogeneity, however, and results in fairly uniform fat suppression throughout the image. Chemical saturation is a frequency-selective RF pulse, which is applied before the normal RF pulse, and effectively eliminates the signal from fat-containing tissues. This may be applied to any of the spin-echo sequences (T1W, PD, T2W); T1W FS sequences are typically used after contrast (gadolinium) enhancement, whereas PD FS and T2W FS sequences are used in evaluating a variety of tissues, including bone marrow and articular cartilage. Chemical saturation is often used in conjunction with lower-resolution FSE sequences, as the technique decreases SNR as a result of eliminating fat signal, resulting in "grainier" images at higher resolutions. Chemical saturation is also sensitive to inhomogeneities in the external magnetic field, which may result in nonuniform fat suppression across the field of view. This is particularly a problem with extremities positioned off-center with the bore of the magnet, such as the elbow, where the magnetic field is not as uniform compared with isocenter. When uniformity of fat suppression is a problem, STIR images may be substituted. STIR images are not sensitive to gadolinium and cannot be used to evaluate gadolinium-contrast enhancement, and hence are less useful for MR arthrography or intravenous contrast studies.

Developing orthopaedic imaging protocols is a challenging task that involves balancing tradeoffs in signal (SNR), spatial resolution, contrast resolution, and image acquisition time. Low SNR images tend to be "noisy" or "grainy" and unpleasant to view. Higher-resolution techniques result in both lower SNR and longer acquisition times and may not be practical for all patients; for this reason, lower resolution techniques may be required. Many patients are unable to tolerate long scan times because of pain and limitations on movement during the examination, and, motion artifact may become a problem. MR artifacts (wrap around, motion artifact, pulsation artifact, metallic artifact) represent additional sources of image degradation and can be difficult at times to eliminate. Newer modifications of existing pulse sequences are available on high-field MR scanners to reduce metallic artifacts associated with orthopaedic implants. When difficulties arise during an MRI examination, pulse sequences often need to be modified to obtain the information needed from the examination.

Applications

MRI is frequently performed in evaluating both osseous and soft tissue injury after trauma. It is capable of defining fractures that are radiographically occult, pediatric articular fractures, and associated soft tissue injuries that may not be suspected or evaluable after physical examination and plain radiography. Although MR angiography is a well-established technique for noninvasive evaluation of the arterial system, it may be impractical for evaluating the multitrauma patient. Evaluation of vascular trauma is accomplished much more rapidly with CTA or conventional angiography, which also allows for interventional procedures (e.g., embolization of arterial bleeding). A more controversial application is MR venography (MRV) to detect deep venous thrombosis (DVT) of the proximal thigh and pelvic veins. In a recent review of the imaging of deep vein thrombosis, Orbell et al.[138] note that MRV has many advantages, including lack of exposure to ionizing radiation and avoidance of any need for vein cannulation and injection of contrast (for nonenhanced studies). MRV is as sensitive and specific for proximal leg DVT as ultrasonography (US) or venography[29] and is reported to be more accurate in the detection of isolated pelvic thrombi.[129] Unfortunately, the cost and logistical problems of MRI have limited its usefulness in the imaging of DVT.

MRI has been advocated to be the gold standard for imaging of the cervical spine following trauma,[132] and faster imaging protocols certainly make the use of MRI much more feasible in the acutely injured patient.[56] However, the practicality of using MRI in trauma patients may be limited by difficulties associated with transporting patients to the MRI suite, as well as MRI incompatibilities with various life-support equipment and patient implants. MRI scan times are also much longer than with CT and other imaging modalities and may not be tolerated by potentially unstable patients or those in considerable pain. Thus, for practical reasons, MRI continues to have only a limited role in the immediate management of the trauma patient.

Osseous Injury. Recent advances in MRI have made it possible to quantitatively assess bone structure and function, so that MRI may someday supplant bone densitometry as a tool to assess fracture risk caused by osteoporosis as well as the response to treatment.[179] It is now well known that bone marrow edema (bone bruise, bone marrow contusion) is frequently identified on MRI after extremity trauma. Histologically, these imaging findings correlate with cancellous bone microfractures as well as edema and hemorrhage within the fatty marrow.[153] The long-term sequelae of these radiographically occult lesions have not been well defined. Roemer and Bohndorf[159] evaluated 176 consecutive patients with acute knee injuries and found that nearly three fourths had bone marrow abnormalities. The majority of lesions (69%) involved the lateral compartment of the knee; 29% were medial, and 2% were patellofemoral. Many of the lesions resembled edema of the subchondral bone, without other osseous or cartilage injury, while nearly one fourth represented subchondral impaction fractures and one third comprised osteochondral or chondral lesions. Forty-nine of these patients had repeat MR studies conducted at least 2 years after their injury. In these patients, only 7 of 49 (14%) had persistent signal changes within the marrow space. The extent of signal abnormality was less than originally seen, and none of the patients developed degenerative changes, regardless of the injury type that was initially present. No cases of posttraumatic osteonecrosis were found. Therefore, one must be careful to avoid interpreting marrow signal abnormalities alone on MRI as evidence of a true fracture, as this may lead to overtreatment. This distinction is especially problematic in the assessment of hip pain after a fall, where trochanteric bone marrow edema might be interpreted as a fracture, leading to a decision to perform internal fixation.

MRI is very useful in the evaluation of radiographically occult fractures. Fracture lines are distinctly visualized on PD or T2W images as linear, lower-signal intensity abnormalities silhouetted by higher-signal intensity marrow fat. Fracture lines can also be seen on STIR and PD/T2W FS images, which also show the degree of surrounding reactive marrow edema. Care is needed in interpreting T1W images; however, images as fracture lines may be obscured by surrounding marrow edema, both of which are hypointense in signal intensity on T1W images.[67]

MRI has become the imaging modality of choice for identifying occult fractures for which correct early diagnosis is essential, such as femoral neck fractures[110,115] (Fig. 16-7), scaphoid fractures,[46,100,152,160] and pediatric elbow injuries.[151] In elderly patients with hip pain after a fall, early MRI when radiographs are normal can avoid delays in diagnosis and treatment of hip fractures. In one study, 25 patients with hip pain were evaluated for occult fracture with conventional radiographs, scintigraphy, CT, or a combination of studies.[148] A final diagnosis was ultimately determined from repeat radiographs in 10 patients and by scintigraphy in 15 patients. The time to final diagnosis averaged 9.6 days when the diagnosis was made by serial radiographs and averaged 5.3 days when the diagnosis was made by scintigraphy. Given the delay in diagnosis associated with using more conventional methods of imaging, the authors point out that use of immediate MRI instead can dramatically decrease the number of imaging examinations performed and the time to diagnosis, resulting in decreased costs of care and possibly reduced complications.[148] In a more recent study, six elderly patients with hip pain after a fall had both MRI and CT, while seven others had MRI alone.[115] In the first group, four of the six CT studies were inaccurate, while all MRI studies correctly defined the pathology.[115] In cases of occult hip fracture, the fracture pattern can be delineated using MRI, which may be of therapeutic importance. Occult fractures of the femoral neck that frequently are treated with screw fixation may be distinguished on MRI from occult intertrochanteric fractures, greater trochanter fractures, or pubic rami fractures that do not require surgical stabilization. Finally, if the MRI does not demonstrate fracture, it often does indicate another finding that explains a given patient's symptoms.[62] Clinicians may be more apt to rely on MRI alone than on NM studies; in one report, clinicians always requested additional imaging for cases in which the bone scan was positive.[43] MRI may also identify additional comorbid conditions such as preexisting osteonecrosis or metastatic disease.[75]

MRI is similarly advantageous in the assessment of pediatric elbow injuries. In one series, seven of nine pediatric patients with an elbow effusion after injury were found to have a radiographically occult fracture.[151] In the same series, MRI provided further useful diagnostic information in 16 other patients despite the presence of a visible fracture and/or dislocation of the elbow on plain radiographs.[151]

Although CT with multiplanar reformatting remains the modality of choice for imaging complex fractures, recent studies indicate that MRI may be valuable in the assessing such injuries as well. In one such study, the impact of MRI on the treatment of tibial plateau fractures was assessed.[187] Patients presenting with tibial plateau fracture were assessed with conventional radiography, CT, and MRI. Three sets of images were prepared for each injury: radiographs alone, radiographs with CT, and radiographs with MRI. Three surgeons were asked to determine the fracture classification and suggest a treatment plan based on each set of images. The investigators found that the best interobserver variability for both fracture classification and fracture management was seen with the combination of conventional radiographs and MRI. The Schatzker classification of tibial plateau fractures based on conventional radiographs changed an average of 6% with the addition of the CT and 21% with the addition of MRI. MRI changed the treatment plan in 23% of cases. Holt et al.[80] studied 21 consecutive patients with tibial plateau fractures who were evaluated with both conventional radiography and MRI before treatment. MRI was more accurate in determining fracture classification, in revealing occult fracture lines, and in measuring the displacement and depression of fragments. The MRI findings resulted in a change in the classification of 10 fractures (48%) and a change in the management of four patients (19%). MRI also allowed diagnosis of associated intra-articular and periarticular soft tissue injuries preoperatively.

The role of CT is well recognized in the assessment of spinal trauma, but MRI is increasingly being used to evaluate for associated injuries such as herniated discs with cervical spine injuries and possible spinal cord injury associated with thoracolumbar spine fracture/dislocations. Green and Saifuddin[70] have shown that 77% of patients with spine injury have a secondary injury level identified by whole spine MRI. Most commonly, these secondary injuries were bone marrow contusions, but 34% of patients had noncontiguous compression or burst fractures diagnosed by MRI.

Soft Tissue Injury. Because of its superb soft tissue contrast resolution and good spatial resolution, MRI provides an accurate means to assess soft tissue injury. MRI of the shoulder and knee is commonly ordered for evaluation of tendons, ligaments, and cartilage after trauma, frequently related to athletic injuries. Common indications for shoulder MRI following trauma include evaluation of the rotator cuff tendons for tearing, the superior glenoid labrum for superior labral anterior-posterior (SLAP) tears, and the anteroinferior labral-ligamentous complex after glenohumeral joint dislocation.[11,37,172] Standard indications for knee MRI following trauma include evaluation of the cruciate and posterolateral corner ligaments for sprain or disruption, the menisci for tears, and the articular cartilage for osteochondral injury.[50,63,182,184] Lonner et al.[112] compared MRI findings to examination under anesthesia in 10 patients with acute knee dislocations who had later surgical intervention, at which time the pathology was defined. Although the investigators considered MRI to be useful for defining the presence of ligamentous injuries in knee dislocations, the clinical examination under anesthesia was more accurate in this series when correlated with findings at surgery.[112]

MR arthrography is a potentially valuable technique for assessing intra-articular derangement in many joints. Common indications include distinguishing partial- from full-thickness rotator cuff tears and evaluating labral-ligamentous pathology

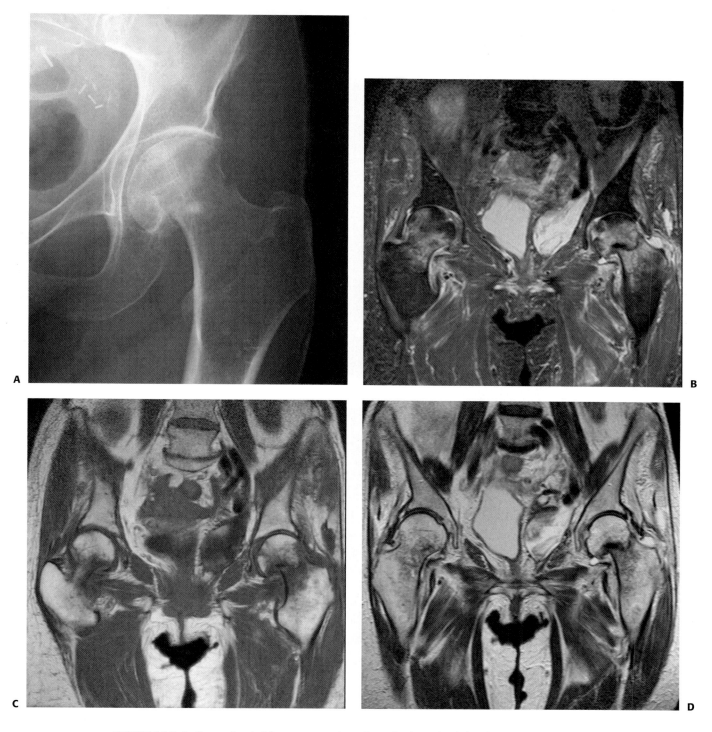

FIGURE 16-7 A. Conventional plain anteroposterior radiograph of a patient's hip demonstrates a femoral neck fracture. Although the fracture can be seen on routine radiographs, the patient was at risk for osteonecrosis because of corticosteroid use related to a kidney transplant. Some apparent changes are seen in the bone density of the femoral head. Magnetic resonance imaging of the pelvis confirms the presence of an acute left hip fracture and demonstrates that there was no osteonecrosis. Incidentally noted is a small developing fracture with surrounding stress reaction in the right femoral neck medially: (**B**) STIR, (**C**) T1-weighted, and (**D**) T2-weighted images. Higher-resolution images of the left hip fracture demonstrating mild impaction at the fracture site without significant angulation. *(continues)*

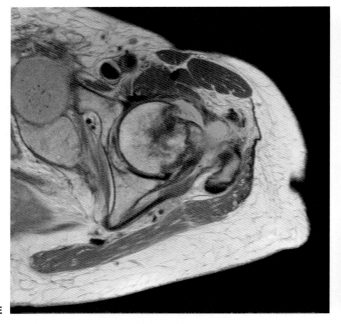

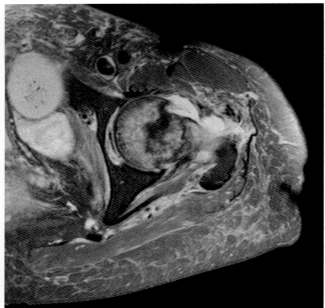

E

F

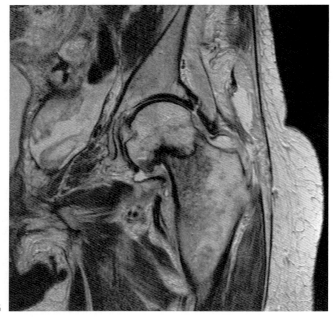

G

FIGURE 16-7 (*continued*) Axial proton density (**E**), axial fat-suppressed proton density (**F**), and coronal T2-weighted (**G**) images. Note inferior pole of kidney transplant in the lower left pelvis with surrounding complex fluid collection.

in the shoulder, evaluating the collateral ligaments in the elbow and the intercarpal ligaments in the wrist, demonstrating labral tears in the hip, evaluating postoperative menisci in the knee, assessing stability of osteochondral lesions, and delineating intra-articular bodies.[167] Direct MR arthrography is performed by intra-articular injection of a dilute gadolinium solution, resulting in distention of the joint capsule and improved delineation of intra-articular structures. Indirect MR arthrography is performed using intravenous injection of gadolinium, with a delay before scanning during which mild exercise may be performed. The indirect technique is based on recognition that the intravenous gadolinium diffuses from the highly vascular synovium into the joint space. The indirect technique does not produce controlled joint distention, however, and is best applied in smaller joints such as the elbow, wrist, ankle, and shoulder.[12]

Orthopaedic Hardware. Orthopaedic hardware presents a challenge in MRI because metal distorts the magnetic field and results in large areas of signal void, which frequently obscures adjacent anatomy. Modifications of traditional MR pulse sequences have been developed on high-field MR scanners to reduce artifact associated with orthopaedic implants. FSE (turbo) sequences are used, which inherently decrease metallic artifact compared with routine SE and GRE sequences. Modifications to FSE sequences include increasing receiver readout bandwidths, decreasing interecho spacing and reducing effective echo times to maintain SNRs.[165] These protocols are now commonly found in the sequence libraries of many newer MR scanners. Protocols based on modification of receiver bandwidth have been shown to reduce metallic artifact by an average of 60%, whereas additional experimental protocols (not commercially available) using a combination of several susceptibility artifact reduction techniques further reduce metallic artifact by an average of 79%.[98] The degree of artifact is also dependent on the metallic composition of the orthopaedic hardware, with titanium generally exhibiting the least amount of artifact. Applications for these sequences include evaluation of painful joint replacements, particularly knee and hip prostheses,[149,164,165] and osteonecrosis of the femoral head after pinning femoral neck fractures (Fig. 16-8).

Ferromagnetic material placed within a magnetic field may experience linear force, torque, and heating. In general, most contemporary orthopaedic implants are not ferromagnetic and are MRI compatible in terms of heating and migration. Most fracture implants are made of 316L stainless steel, titanium, or titanium alloy; none of these materials contain delta ferrite, so they are not magnetic.[44] MRI can be safely performed about plates, screws, and total joint implants, although artifacts may degrade the image as described earlier. In contrast, some external fixator components, especially clamps, contain strongly ferromagnetic materials and can be potentially unsafe in an MRI scanner.[41,101] Davison and colleagues[41] studied 10 sets of commercially available tibial external fixators that they applied to sawbone tibia. The external fixators were tested for magnetic attraction using a hand-held magnet while positioned 30 cm outside the entry portal of a 1.5-Tesla scanner, at the level of the entry portal, and 30 cm inside the MRI tube. The EBI Dynafix with Ankle Clamp, EBI Dynafix, and EBI Dynafix Hybrid, along with the Hoffman II, Hoffman II Hybrid, Ilizarov with stainless steel rings, and Synthes Hybrid, all had more than 1 kg of magnetic attraction at all three locations, which is a significant enough force to cause potential movement of implant and pain. These devices were not scanned. Three devices—the Ilizarov fixator with carbon fiber rings, Richards Hex-Fix, and Large Synthes External Fixator—had less than 1 kg of magnetic attrac-

tion at all three locations and were scanned for 30 minutes while temperature measurements were obtained with a digital thermometer and thermocouple. No component of these three fixators experienced more than 2°F of temperature elevation during a 30-minute MRI scan. Davison et al.[41] conclude that many commercially available external fixators have components that have significant magnetic attraction to the MRI scanner. Fixators that have less than 1 kg of attraction do not experience significant heating during MRI.

The American Society for Testing and Materials (ASTM) has established standards for MRI compatibility of implants.[186] Many orthopedic manufacturers have redesigned their implants to make them MRI compatible; Luechinger et al.[107] recently studied new MRI-compatible large external fixator clamps made by Synthes and found dramatic reductions in forces experienced in a 3-T field compared with older devices. All orthopedic surgeons should check with the manufacturer and be aware of the MRI compatibility of their particular external fixator inventory.

Arthrography

Technical Considerations
Conventional Arthrography. Arthrography involves distention of a joint capsule using positive or negative contrast agents. Water-soluble, iodinated contrast media is typically used to provide positive contrast, whereas air has been historically used to produce negative contrast. Double-contrast examinations may also be performed using both agents simultaneously, although these techniques are largely of historical interest, as advances in cross-sectional imaging have supplanted double-contrast arthrography techniques.

Injection technique involves placement of a needle into the joint capsule, usually under fluoroscopic or CT guidance. Typi-

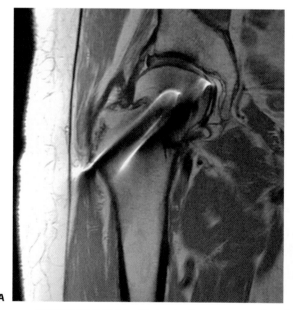
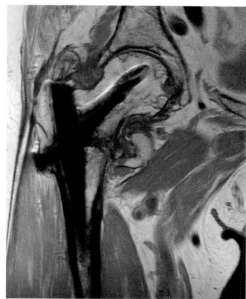

FIGURE 16-8 Metal artifact reduction sequences. **A.** A femoral neck fracture after pinning with four screws demonstrates nonunion. Magnetic resonance imaging using metal artifact reduction sequences shows no evidence of avascular necrosis of the femoral head. **B.** An additional case of nonunion of an intertrochanteric fracture that demonstrates avascular necrosis of the femoral head without subchondral fracture or collapse. The intramedullary rod and screw are titanium, which results in fewer artifacts than stainless steel or other alloys.

cally, a 22-gauge needle is used for larger joints, including the shoulder, hip, and knee, and a 25-gauge needle is used for smaller joints, such as the elbow, wrist, ankle, and smaller joints of the hands and feet. The anatomic approach varies according to each joint; for example, a lateral approach into the radiocapitellar joint space is frequently used for the elbow, and anterior approaches are typically used for the shoulder, hip, and tibiotalar joint. Table 16-2 lists technical considerations for arthrography of selected joints. After needle placement, small amounts of contrast are injected until the intra-articular location of the needle tip is confirmed. Contrast is then injected with subsequent distention of the joint capsule; the amount also varies by joint.

Frequently, the injection is performed under fluoroscopy, and sequential spot films are obtained before and during the injection to evaluate the flow of contrast. Pathology is inferred by abnormal communication of contrast with extracapsular structures. Passive and active range of motion are often required to demonstrate pathology, as abnormalities may only be shown after contrast is allowed to work its way through defects in the capsule and into the surrounding soft tissues. Contrast extravasation through capsular abnormalities can be fairly rapid and may occur during passive or active range of motion. Extravasation may also occur during periods when the fluoroscope is not energized. In addition, the fluoroscope only provides 2D views of bony anatomy, and it is extremely limited in its evaluation of surrounding soft tissues. Consequently, localizing the site of extravasation during conventional arthrography can be quite challenging. Care is also needed to avoid overdistention of the joint capsule, as extravasation through the capsule can occur, leading to subsequent decompression of intra-articular contrast and possible false-positive interpretations.

Complications of arthrography are uncommon but may include bleeding and infection at the injection site, in addition to allergic reactions related to iodinated contrast media. A small number of patients experience postprocedural pain, possibly related to a mild synovial inflammatory response to the contrast media. Although patients are generally apprehensive about the procedure, they generally tolerate the procedure with less discomfort than expected.[158]

Digital Subtraction Arthrography. With the advent of digital imaging, digital subtraction techniques have been developed for fluoroscopy. Typically, a preliminary scout film serves as a "mask," which is subsequently subtracted from images following contrast injection. This significantly improves contrast resolution of the fluoroscopic spot films and enables visualization of contrast that would otherwise be inapparent when adjacent to similar high-density objects, such as joint prostheses. Digital subtraction arthrography (DSA) also allows sequential injection and evaluation of adjacent joint compartments, as a new mask is obtained after injection of the first compartment, which is subsequently subtracted from images acquired during injection of the second compartment. DSA techniques are sensitive to patient motion, however, which produces misregistration artifact as a result of misalignment of the mask and subsequent images. DSA also requires specialized equipment, which may not be available outside of radiology departments.

CT and MR Arthrography. Cross-sectional techniques, such as CT and MRI, have largely replaced conventional arthrography for evaluating internal derangement, but these imaging modalities may be combined with arthrography using appropriate contrast agents for each modality.[58,167] For CT arthrography (CTA), an arthrogram is first obtained using a contrast solution containing saline and water-soluble, iodinated contrast media, typically in a 1:1 dilution. Thin-section CT is then performed through the joint, and images in orthogonal planes are reconstructed. For MR arthrography, a very dilute gadolinium solution (typically 1:200 dilution) is injected into the joint, and MRI is subsequently performed. In addition to routine sequences, fat-suppressed T1W images are used to visualize the injected contrast. With both imaging modalities, evaluation is aided not only by silhouetting intra-articular structures by relatively bright contrast but also by distention of the joint capsule. This results in separation of intra-articular ligaments and capsular structures and allows more precise evaluation of complex anatomy (Fig. 16-9). Bony and soft tissue abnormalities are directly visualized with these cross-sectional techniques, compared to conventional arthrography, whereby pathology is inferred based

TABLE 16-2	**Arthrographic Techniques of Selected Joints**		
Joint	Injection Approach	Needle Size	Volume of Contrast[167]
Shoulder	Anterior glenohumeral joint space	22-gauge 3½-inch spinal needle	15 mL
Elbow	Lateral radiocapitellar joint space	25-gauge 1½-inch needle	10 mL
Wrist	Dorsal radioscaphoid joint space	25-gauge 1½-inch needle	4 mL
Hip	Anterior femoral head/neck junction	22-gauge 3½-inch needle	15 mL
Knee	Medial or lateral patellofemoral joint space	22-gauge 1½-inch needle	40 mL
Ankle	Anterior tibiotalar joint space	22-gauge 3½-inch spinal needle	10–12 mL

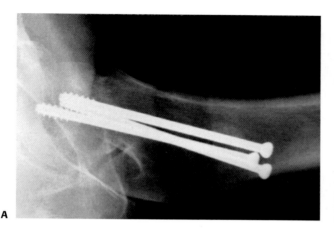

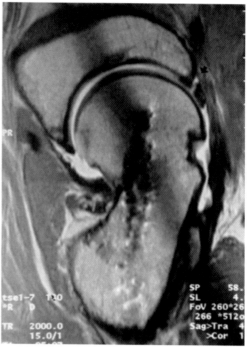

FIGURE 16-9 A. Lateral radiograph of the proximal femur after fixation of a femoral neck fracture, showing malunion with retroversion of the femoral neck. **B.** The patient had persistent hip pain, and magnetic resonance arthrography revealed a tear of the anterior acetabular labrum. Note angular deformity at the site of fracture malunion and residual micrometallic artifact related to insertion of prior screws. (Reprinted with permission from Eijer H, Myers SR, Ganz R. Anterior femoroacetabular impingement after femoral neck fractures. J Orthop Trauma 2001;15:475–481.)

on the appearance of the contrast collection in relation to the bony landmarks.

Applications

Before advanced cross-sectional imaging techniques, arthrography was traditionally used for assessing periarticular soft tissue injuries associated with trauma. Today, there are more limited indications for arthrography, although it is frequently performed in combination with CT and MRI to increase the sensitivity and specificity for internal derangement.

Arthrography may be substituted in patients with contraindications to MRI, such as pacemakers or intracranial aneurysm clips. CTA is preferred, however, as advances in CT scanner technology have led to marked improvements in resolution and scan time, resulting in high spatial resolution images and multiplanar reconstructions of intra-articular structures.

Upper Extremity. In the upper extremity, shoulder arthrography may be performed to evaluate for full-thickness rotator cuff tears. Extravasation of contrast into the subacromial/subdeltoid bursa is diagnostic of a full-thickness tear. Even with careful fluoroscopic observation during the injection process, it is frequently impossible to delineate the site or extent of the tear, as contrast medium may accumulate in the bursa without visualization of an obvious tract through the torn tendon. Occasionally, no extravasation is seen after completing the injection; however, after passively and/or actively exercising the shoulder, subsequent fluoroscopy reveals contrast flooding the bursa as a result of the medium working itself through a full-thickness tear. Special care is needed in interpreting arthrography of the postoperative rotator cuff, because intact cuff repairs may continue to leak contrast into the bursa.

The value of three-compartment arthrography has been documented in the setting of acute wrist trauma,[68,69] as has the value of digital subtraction techniques in wrist arthrogra-

phy.[42,188] Arthrography has historically been applied to the evaluation of ulnar collateral ligament injuries of the thumb ("gamekeeper's thumb"). Recent literature has shown MR arthrography to be more accurate in detecting ulnar collateral ligament injuries and in evaluating displacement of the torn ligament.[1]

Lower Extremity. In the lower extremity, arthrography alone is rarely performed for trauma but may be combined with CT or MRI for evaluating osteochondral abnormalities[113] (Fig. 16-9). A recent study comparing CTA with MR arthrography suggests that CTA may be more accurate in evaluating cartilage lesions of the ankle joint.[161]

Arthrography may also be useful in the evaluation of pain after treating calcaneal fractures with intra-articular extension.[121] Matsui et al.[121] performed posterior subtalar joint arthrography at a mean of 6 months postinjury in 22 patients; 15 had undergone surgical repair and 7 had been treated nonoperatively. The patients were separated into four groups based on arthrographic findings: normal, narrow, irregular, and ankylosis. Clinical follow-up performed at a mean of 23 months postinjury correlated very well with the earlier arthrographic findings, suggesting that subtalar arthrosis is responsible for much of the symptoms that develop after calcaneal fracture.

Pediatric Injuries. Arthrography is valuable in assessing pediatric physeal injuries (especially the elbow)[2,14,48,106,119] that are not visible on conventional radiographs. It is also used intraoperatively to assist with the reduction of pediatric radial head fractures.[86] The use of arthrography to assess pediatric injuries has been largely supplanted by MRI (when available), although in the pediatric population both procedures may require sedation.

Dynamic Imaging. Arthrography remains the investigation of choice when dynamic imaging is necessary. In German literature, Klein et al.[96] compared MRI with arthrography and CTA for the diagnosis of wrist pain in 346 patients. Imaging findings were correlated with surgical findings in 78 of these patients and with the clinical course in the remainder. Because of its ability to perform functional imaging, arthrography was the best method for evaluating scapholunate ligament tears and defects of the ulnolunate and ulnotriquetral ligaments.

Ultrasonography

Technical Considerations

Conventional Ultrasonography. US refers to the spectrum of sound waves with frequencies greater than 20 kHz (20,000 Hz), which are beyond the audible range of the human ear. Typical frequencies used in medical diagnostic US range from 2.0 to 12 MHz, although frequencies of 20 MHz and higher are in clinical use for more specialized applications involving very small regions of anatomy. Lower frequencies within this range (2 to 5 MHz) allow deeper penetration of the US beam for evaluation of thicker body parts, although at lower spatial resolutions. Higher-frequency US beams (10 to 12 MHz) provide greater spatial resolution and are frequently used in evaluating superficial anatomy, such as tendons.

US beams are generated by transducers, which make use of piezoelectric materials to convert electrical energy into mechanical energy (sound waves). Today's transducer designs are complex and may incorporate hundreds of individual piezoelectric elements, each of which is energized in turn or in combination, such that the individual sound waves combine into an US beam. The US beam propagates into the underlying tissues and is partially reflected back at tissue boundaries because of differences in acoustic impedance between tissues. Acoustic impedance is defined as the product of tissue density and the speed of sound, both of which vary among tissues. Small differences in acoustic impedance will produce smaller reflections of sound waves, whereas large differences in acoustic impedances will result in larger reflections. The reflected echoes travel back to the transducer, where the transducer elements convert the sound waves into electrical signals, which are then used to create the US image.

An US image is composed of an array of pixels, each corresponding to a tissue element at a particular depth and location. Echoes returning from underlying soft tissue elements are generated from reflections of the US beam at tissue interfaces of different acoustic impedance. In addition, smaller cellular elements within tissues can also act as individual "scatterers." Each of these scatterers reflects a small portion of the US beam in all directions. A portion of these scattered echoes are reflected back toward the transducer and are displayed in the image as background "echogenicity" that is characteristic for that tissue. Echoes returning from superficial soft tissues have shorter round trip distances to travel back to the transducer and are detected earlier than those for deeper soft tissues. For this reason, the depth of a tissue element can be calculated using the return time of its corresponding echo. The amplitude of the returning echo determines the brightness, or echogenicity, of a tissue element. As the US beam travels deeper within the soft tissues, it progressively loses energy and subsequent echoes from deeper tissue elements are smaller in amplitude. A correction factor, termed *time gain compensation*, is applied to deeper soft tissues to account for this drop off in echo amplitude. Thus,

differences in echogenicity in the resulting US image will be less dependent on tissue depth and more related to differences in acoustic impedance and scattering.

During a single cycle, the transducer sends a short burst of US waves (the US pulse) into the underlying tissues, and then listens for the returning echoes. The time spent sending out the US pulse is a tiny fraction of the listening time, typically about 0.5% of the total cycle time. The pulse repetition frequency determines how many pulses are sent into the underlying tissue over time, and typically ranges between 2000 and 4000 cycles/ s (2 to 4 kHz). During routine scanning, the transducer is constantly steering and refocusing the US beam within the underlying tissue to generate echoes that will correspond to each pixel in the US image. The two-dimensional US image that is generated is typically referred to as B-mode ("brightness" mode) *imaging*. The designs of current transducers are quite complex and rely on advanced electronics and scanning algorithms, but have resulted in greater spatial resolution and more advanced feature sets, including 3D, four-dimensional, and Doppler imaging.

Echogenicity is a term used to describe the relative brightness of echoes returning from tissues or tissue interfaces. Tissues may be described as *hypoechoic* or *hyperechoic* with regard to a reference tissue, in addition to *isoechoic* if two distinct soft tissues share the same level of echogenicity. The descriptor *anechoic* refers to a tissue or medium that produces no reflected echoes and is black on the corresponding US image. Water is the best example of an anechoic medium, because all of the sound waves are transmitted through the medium without any reflections. In such situations, the energy within the US beam will be greater as it reaches the tissues on the far side of the medium and the distal tissues will appear brighter; this is referred to as *increased through transmission*. Conversely, any tissue or medium that blocks transmission of all sound waves will appear highly echogenic at its proximal interface with the US beam and will exhibit "distal acoustic shadowing," whereby the more distal tissues appear black, resembling a shadow. Cortical bone and air are examples where the large differences in acoustic impedance result in marked attenuation of the US beam, producing distal acoustic shadowing.

US examinations are highly operator dependent, and the quality of the examination can be influenced by the sonographer's training, experience performing certain examinations, and understanding of normal anatomy and disease states. US is a real-time examination, and although images that represent the underlying anatomy are saved, these two-dimensional images cannot provide the depth of understanding that real-time visualization provides. For this reason, it may be necessary for the interpreting physician to be present or to image the patient to interpret complex examinations.

Doppler US. Doppler US is used to evaluate moving tissues, such as blood flow within vessels. Velocity measurements and directions of flow may be ascertained based on frequency shifts of the returning echoes. When the US beam is reflected from a tissue moving toward the transducer, the returning echoes undergo a slight increase in frequency. Similarly, when interacting with a tissue moving away from the transducer, the US beam will be reflected such that the returning echoes will incur a slight decrease in their frequency. These frequency shifts are used to calculate the speed of the moving tissue, whereas the direction of frequency shift (positive versus negative) is used to determine the direction of motion relative to the transducer.

Various modes of Doppler operation are available on today's scanners and are frequently used for vascular evaluation. Duplex Doppler imaging combines 2D B-mode imaging with pulsed Doppler imaging; the 2D B-mode image provides an anatomical map to identify vessels for subsequent Doppler interrogation. Color Doppler combines B-mode grayscale imaging with color flow superimposed over vessels, as determined by Doppler imaging. Shades of red and blue are assigned to the vessels based on their velocities and directions and represent flow toward and away from the transducer, respectively. Power Doppler imaging is a signal-processing algorithm that uses the total amplitude of the Doppler signal to generate maps of flow, which are then superimposed on B-mode grayscale images. The corresponding images demonstrate greater sensitivity to slow flow, although no directional information is available.

Applications

US is a simple, noninvasive, relatively inexpensive imaging modality that is now widely available in most hospitals and in many clinics. Diagnostic US has an established role in the immediate diagnosis of trauma patients according to the ATLS protocol, where it is used in the "Focused Abdominal Sonography for Trauma" examination for intra-abdominal injury. US also has applications in evaluation of fractures, fracture healing, soft tissue trauma including ligamentous injury, and venous thromboembolism.

Fractures. US has potential in the assessment of fractures, and may be under-used in this regard.[142] US compares favorably to conventional radiography in the assessment of occult scaphoid fracture in patients with wrist pain.[79] Durston et al.[52] used US to assess the reduction of pediatric forearm fractures in the emergency department, thereby avoiding multiple trips to the radiology suite while gaining much more rapid assessment of the quality of fracture reduction. In some centers, US is used to rule out intra-articular elbow fractures.[92] Assessing pediatric elbow injuries is notoriously difficult because of the complex joint anatomy and the multiplicity of its ossification centers, many of which are relatively unossified in childhood. US has proved to be valuable in evaluating lateral condylar fractures, in that it is able to assess the extent of the fracture line through the unossified capitellum and trochlea, to distinguish unstable intra-articular fractures from their stable extra-articular counterparts.[177]

US may also be clinically useful in evaluating fractures in settings where conventional radiography may not be readily available, such as in military or aerospace settings.[95] Dulchavsky et al.[51] prospectively evaluated 158 injured extremities by US. Nonphysician cast technicians, who had received limited training and were blinded to the patient's radiographic diagnoses, performed the US evaluations. Examinations only required an average of 4 minutes and accurately diagnosed injury in 94% of patients with no false-positive results. Injuries that were diagnosed by US included fractures in the upper arm, forearm, femur, tibia/fibula, hand, and foot.

Fracture Healing. US is a useful method to monitor fracture healing. Moed et al.[128] performed sonographic evaluation of patients 6 and 12 weeks after unreamed tibial nailing and found that persistent nail visualization indicated poor callus formation and predicted later healing complications. Color Doppler sonography has been shown to demonstrate progressive vascularization of fracture callus and predict delayed callus formation in another study of patients with tibial fractures.[31]

Soft Tissue Trauma. US is also well suited for diagnosing musculoskeletal soft tissue injuries and is of proven value in the assessment of many tendon injuries, such as those of the tendo-achilles, rotator cuff, and ankle.[16,28,34,157] US has been used to assess muscle injury, depicted as a tear or hematoma and subsequent complications such as fibrosis, cystic lesions, or heterotopic ossification.[144] US is valuable in localizing foreign bodies within soft tissues; an advantage over conventional radiography is that foreign objects do not need to be radiopaque to visualize them.[108]

Venous Thromboembolism. US has come to play a very important role in managing venous thromboembolism in trauma patients.[189] All trauma patients are at risk for developing deep vein thrombosis (DVT), and venous US has become the most widely used imaging modality for DVT diagnosis. In fact, the Intersocietal Commission for the Accreditation of Vascular Laboratories now mandates duplex Doppler US as the primary instrument for peripheral venous testing.[85] Venous scanning performed by skilled operators is the most practical and cost-effective method for assessing DVT of the proximal and distal lower extremity veins. Several US modalities are used to evaluate DVT, including B-mode for real-time visualization of compression of larger veins.

Duplex Doppler for evaluating waveforms and velocities and color Doppler for depicting patency of veins are particularly useful in the calf and iliac veins.[189] The diagnostic accuracy of US is well documented, and the sensitivity and specificity of venous US (including all types) for the diagnosis of symptomatic proximal DVT is 97% and 94%, respectively.[189] The high specificity of venous US is sufficient to initiate treatment of DVT without further confirmation, and the high sensitivity for proximal DVT makes it possible to withhold treatment if the examination is negative.[189] When US examinations cannot be performed (e.g., uncooperative patient, presence of bandages, casts), an alternative diagnostic procedure, such as contrast venography, may be needed. More advanced imaging modalities, such as CT or MR venography are also available. US is less accurate in the diagnosis of proximal DVT involving the pelvis; MR venography has been suggested as a more accurate modality for detecting intrapelvic DVT.[129]

Nuclear Medicine Imaging

Technical Considerations

Nuclear scintigraphy involves intravenous injection of a radiopharmaceutical with subsequent imaging using a gamma scintillation camera. The radiopharmaceutical is typically composed of two moieties: a radionuclide and a pharmaceutical compound. The pharmaceutical is responsible for localization of the molecule in the body, and the radionuclide allows imaging of the pharmaceutical distribution.

Radionuclides are radioactive isotopes that undergo spontaneous decay, which results in the emission of photons. Photons that are generated in the nucleus of the atom are gamma rays, whereas photons generated by electron transitions within their orbital shells are x-rays. Either may be used for imaging, although the particular choice of a radionuclide predetermines the types and energies of photons that are emitted. In many NM imaging applications, technetium (^{99m}Tc) is commonly used as the radionuclide because of its favorable imaging properties (140 keV gamma energy), clinically suitable half-life (6 hours), availability (^{99}Mo/^{99m}Tc generator) and ease in labeling of pharmaceuticals. Other radionuclides used in orthopaedic imaging include gallium (^{67}Ga) and indium (^{111}In) and are discussed later in this section.

Pharmaceuticals are metabolically active molecules that are designed to localize to target tissues once injected intravenously. There are many different mechanisms of localization, but for orthopaedic imaging, regional blood flow is important for all administered radiopharmaceuticals. Specific radiopharmaceuticals for orthopaedic imaging and their method of localization are discussed later in this section.

Gamma scintillation cameras are specialized detectors that capture photons within a large flat crystal, commonly made of sodium iodide activated with thallium. Photons interact with the scintillation crystal and are converted to visible light, which is then captured by photomultiplier tubes (PMTs) coupled to the crystal. The PMT converts the light photon into an electrical signal, which is subsequently amplified and electronically processed. This process results in a single "count" in the final NM image corresponding to a single radioactive decay in the patient.

NM images are formed by placing the gamma scintillation camera over the anatomy of interest and accumulating counts for a specific amount of time or for a minimum number of counts, typically on the order of hundreds of thousands of counts. Imaging is often performed after a delay to allow localization and/or uptake of the radiopharmaceutical within the target tissues. Delayed imaging demonstrates characteristic patterns of distribution throughout the body for a particular radiopharmaceutical, in addition to abnormal accumulation or absence of activity corresponding to disease states. Consequently, nuclear imaging studies are based on visualization of metabolic function, rather than anatomy. Anatomic features are frequently visualized on NM images, although spatial resolution is typically quite poor compared with other imaging modalities (Table 16-1).

During routine acquisition of NM images, the gamma scintillation camera is left stationary in a single projection, resulting in a planar image. Single-photon emission computed tomography (SPECT) is an extension of planar imaging, whereby the gamma camera rotates around the patient, stopping at predefined intervals, to acquire multiple static planar images. Using techniques similar to those in CT, these planar data sets are then processed by computers. Images are typically created in orthogonal tomographic planes (axial, coronal, sagittal), in addition to 3D volumes. Although the main advantage of SPECT over planar images is the improved image contrast resolution as a result of eliminating radioactivity from overlapping anatomy, spatial resolution is similar or slightly decreased compared to planar imaging (Table 16-1).

Indwelling orthopaedic hardware may affect image quality by introducing artifacts into the diagnostic image. Hardware can shield the gamma camera from photons arising behind the hardware, resulting in a photopenic defect. Knowledge of indwelling hardware and their characteristic photopenic appearances alleviates misinterpretation of these defects. Multiple projections are also frequently performed during a single examination, which allows evaluation of the activity on multiple sides of the hardware.

NM techniques relevant to trauma and orthopaedics are described in the sections to follow.

Skeletal Scintigraphy. Skeletal scintigraphy, commonly referred to as a *bone scan*, is the most commonly performed NM study with respect to the skeletal system. The radiopharmaceutical used is typically a ^{99m}Tc-labeled diphosphonate, which localizes to bone based on chemiadsorption of the phosphorus compound to the mineral phase of bone, particularly at sites of increased osteoblastic activity. Regional blood flow is also important for tracer distribution, as areas of increased regional blood flow deliver greater tracer to the adjacent skeleton, and result in greater uptake. The term *bone scan* typically refers to images obtained after a 2- to 4-hour delay, to allow localization of the diphosphonate compound. *Three-phase bone scans* incorporate additional dynamic and immediate imaging phases. A radionuclide angiogram (first phase) is obtained during transit of radiopharmaceutical through the arterial system. Immediate static images are then obtained for an additional 5 minutes (second phase) and represent "blood pool" or "tissue phase" images. Both of these earlier imaging phases are used to evaluate for regional hyperemia, as evidenced by both increased blood flow and increased surrounding soft tissue uptake.

Normal bone scan images show a characteristic appearance of the skeleton, with slightly greater uptake in the axial skeleton (spine, pelvis) than the extremities. In skeletally immature individuals, there is normal avid uptake in the growth plates, resulting in symmetrically increased bands of activity occurring adjacent to joints and apophyses. Many diseases are characterized by both increased osteoblastic and osteoclastic activity within the bone, in addition to regional hyperemia, and result in greater tracer uptake ("hot" lesions) than normal bone. These abnormalities may be solitary or multiple, and focal or diffuse in nature. Some pathological processes, particularly permeative processes (small round cell tumors) or those that elicit little surrounding bone reaction, result in regions of decreased tracer uptake, or "cold" lesions. These lesions may be difficult to detect on routine bone scans. Bone scans are highly sensitive for disease processes, although specificity is poor. A normal bone scan may rule out underlying skeletal abnormality, but a positive bone scan necessitates further workup of the underlying abnormality.

Marrow Imaging. Marrow imaging is performed using ^{99m}Tc-labeled sulfur colloid. The sulfur colloid is composed of particles measuring between 0.1 and 2.0 μm, which are taken up by the reticuloendothelial cells within the liver (85%), spleen (10%), and bone marrow (5%). Uptake is rapid (half-life is 2 to 3 minutes), and imaging is performed after a 20-minute delay. Current indications for marrow imaging are limited but include evaluation of osteomyelitis in conjunction with ^{111}In-labeled white blood cell imaging.

Gallium Imaging. Gallium-67 citrate is a radiopharmaceutical that was originally developed as a bone-imaging agent but was later found to be useful in imaging infection and inflammation. After intravenous injection, gallium binds to transferrin and circulates in the bloodstream. At sites of inflammation or infection, increased regional blood flow and increased vascular permeability result in greater accumulation of gallium. In addition, neutrophils release large amounts of lactoferrin as a part of their inflammatory response; gallium has a higher binding affinity for lactoferrin than transferrin and localizes at the site of inflammation. Gallium is a relatively poor imaging agent, as its photons are not optimum for imaging with present-day gamma cameras, and total body clearance is slow with considerable background activity. Imaging is typically performed at 48 hours, which contributes to delays in diagnosis.

Gallium scans are often interpreted with bone scans for evaluation of osteomyelitis. Gallium activity that is greater than, or in different distribution than, corresponding activity on the bone scan is diagnostic for osteomyelitis.

White Blood Cell Imaging.

There are several approaches for using labeled white blood cells (WBCs) for diagnosing infection and/or inflammatory processes. Of these, ^{111}In oxine– and ^{99m}Tc-labeled hexamethylpropyleneamine (HMPAO)–labeled WBCs are discussed briefly.

Indium-111 is complexed with oxine, which results in a lipid-soluble complex that readily crosses the cell membranes. Approximately 50 mL of blood must be withdrawn and the leukocytes need to be separated from the plasma and red cells. Labeling is accomplished by incubating the leukocytes with the ^{111}In oxine complex for 30 minutes. The leukocytes are then resuspended in plasma and reinjected into the patient within a total of 2 to 4 hours. Imaging is typically performed at 24 hours to allow for leukocyte localization and clearance from the blood pool.

[99m]Tc HMPAO is a cerebral perfusion agent that also crosses cell membranes and may be used to label WBCs, preferentially granulocytes. Approximately 50 to 75 mL of blood is withdrawn and incubated with the radiopharmaceutical; however, the labeling process is performed in plasma, and cell separation is not needed. The labeled cells are then reinjected, and imaging is performed at 4 hours for the peripheral skeleton.

Labeled WBC studies should be interpreted in combination with sulfur colloid marrow studies for evaluation of osteomyelitis and infected joint replacements. When used alone, labeled white cell studies may result in false-positive results, because labeled WBCs normally distribute to the bone marrow, in addition to the liver and spleen, after reinjection. The sulfur colloid marrow study is used to map out areas of normal residual marrow activity. Congruent activity is seen within the bone marrow on both examinations. Osteomyelitis results in replacement of marrow activity on the sulfur colloid study, resulting in a photopenic defect, whereas there is significantly increased activity on the corresponding labeled WBC study.

Applications

NM imaging is frequently used for further evaluation when conventional radiographs are normal or to evaluate the significance of abnormalities seen on radiographs. Although typically highly sensitive for disease processes, its poor specificity makes it necessary to correlate the findings with additional clinical history, laboratory evaluation, or imaging examinations. Applications of NM to orthopaedic trauma include evaluation of fractures, osteomyelitis, and osteonecrosis.

Fractures. Bone scans are highly sensitive for acute fractures. Matin et al.[120] demonstrated positive scans in 80% of fractures at 24 hours, and in 95% by 72 hours. Advanced age and debilitation contributed to nonvisualization of fractures beyond this time frame. The minimum time to return to normal was 5 months, and 90% of fractures returned to normal by 2 years. Because of its poor specificity, scintigraphy can lead to false-positive diagnoses of fracture. Garcia-Morales et al.[64] reported five cases of false-positive scans for hip fracture because of collar osteophytes; subsequent MRI in these patients was negative.

Radiographically negative stress fractures and insufficiency fractures are also well delineated on bone scintigraphy as focal areas of increased radiotracer uptake. Characteristic sites of stress fractures depend on the activity that produced them, although there is considerable overlap. Some fracture patterns show characteristic appearances on scintigraphy. For example, in elderly patients with chronic low back or hip pain, sacral insufficiency fractures reveal a classic "H" pattern of uptake, known as the "Honda" sign.[143] Not uncommonly, several focal areas of increased tracer uptake are seen in the skeleton, which presumably represent a combination of acute and more chronic findings. In these cases, three-phase scintigraphy can provide additional information regarding hyperemia and may help to differentiate acute from chronic injuries. Typically, hyperemia resolves within 4 to 8 weeks after initial injury, with the blood flow, then the blood pool, images normalizing.

Scintigraphy may be useful in the early identification of fracture healing complications. Barros et al.[10] performed scintigraphy at 6, 12, and 24 weeks with 25 mCi of MDP-^{99m}Tc in 40 patients with tibial shaft fractures that were treated nonsurgically. Using the normal leg as a control, an activity index (the ratio of the uptake counts of the injured leg to the normal leg) was calculated. All fractures in this series healed within 20 weeks and the activity ratio index progressively decreased at the three evaluations.[10] The investigators speculate that a persistently increased activity index would indicate future development of healing complications, such as delayed union or nonunion, although they did not have any such healing complications in their series.[10]

Bone scintigraphy may also be used in evaluating a child with nonaccidental trauma. In a study from Australia, studies of 30 children who were the victims of suspected child abuse and who had both skeletal surveys and bone scintigraphy were retrospectively reviewed.[118] Excluding rib fractures, there were 64 bony injuries, of which 33% were seen on both imaging modalities, 44% were seen on skeletal survey only, and 25% of the injuries were seen on bone scans alone. Metaphyseal lesions typical of child abuse were found in 20 cases (31%) on skeletal survey; only 35% of these were identified on bone scan. The investigators believed that both skeletal survey and bone scintigraphy should be performed in cases of suspected child abuse.

Infection. Osteomyelitis may result from hematogenous spread of microorganisms to bone, from direct extension from areas of adjacent soft tissue infection, or as a result of open fractures and/or surgery. Persistent pain or delayed healing after surgery can be difficult to evaluate with regard to infection, as conventional radiographs may show only more advanced destructive changes and MRI may be very difficult to interpret in light of recent surgery.

Radionuclide imaging has evolved over time with respect to imaging orthopaedic infections. In addition to three-phase bone scans, dual gallium/bone scintigraphy and labeled WBC studies, including combination leukocyte/bone and leukocyte/marrow studies, are valuable in diagnosing both acute and chronic osteomyelitis as well as infected joint replacements. No one study is equally applicable to all clinical situations, however.[141]

Although three-phase bone scans have excellent accuracy for detecting osteomyelitis in normal underlying bone, the specificity of this test is markedly reduced in the presence of underlying bone disease.

Dual gallium (^{67}Ga)/bone scintigraphy has been used to evaluate osteomyelitis. Gallium scintigraphy demonstrates greater accuracy (86%) in diagnosing spinal osteomyelitis compared with ^{111}In-labeled WBCs (66%).[140] A recent evaluation of imaging techniques in spinal osteomyelitis and surrounding soft tissue infections has recommended SPECT ^{67}Ga as the radionuclide study of choice when MRI is unavailable or as an adjunct in patients with possible spinal infection in whom the diagnosis remains uncertain.[114] Gallium is also better suited for imaging of chronic osteomyelitis compared with ^{99m}Tc HMPAO–labeled WBCs, which are better for imaging acute infections.[146]

^{99m}Tc HMPAO–labeled WBC scintigraphy exhibits high sensitivity (97.7%) and specificity (96.8%) for acute osteomyelitis, although its sensitivity for chronic osteomyelitis is slightly decreased.[185] ^{99m}Tc HMPAO–labeled WBC scintigraphy is preferred for evaluating children because the radiation dose to the spleen is smaller and less blood is needed for labeling.[162] ^{99m}Tc HMPAO–labeled WBC scintigraphy is superior to ^{99m}Tc bone scintigraphy for children younger than 6 months because of the poor sensitivity of bone scintigraphy at this age.[146] ^{111}In-labeled WBC scintigraphy is preferred in evaluating chronic osteomyelitis, as dual ^{111}In WBC/^{99m}Tc SC studies result in improved accuracy for diagnosis of osteomyelitis in regions containing active bone marrow.[146,162] In more complex regions with overlapping bone and soft tissues, such as the skull and hips, simultaneous ^{111}In WBC/^{99m}Tc bone SPECT imaging has been recommended.[162]

Dual ^{111}In WBC/^{99m}Tc bone scans have been used to evaluate for osteomyelitis at sites of delayed union or nonunion.[135] The sensitivity, specificity, positive and negative predictive values, and accuracy of this approach were 86%, 84%, 69%, 94%, and 82%, respectively.

Recently, a meta-analysis of ^{99m}Tc-radiolabeled antigranulocyte monoclonal antibodies has shown a sensitivity of 81% and specificity of 77% in the diagnosis of osteomyelitis. The authors conclude that antigranulocyte scintigraphy can be used as a major diagnostic method in patients with suspected osteomyelitis but cannot replace traditional methods such as histological examination and cell culture.[139]

Osteonecrosis. Because scintigraphy is able to demonstrate the vascularity of bone, it is often used to try to assess the risk of osteonecrosis after an injury. Although largely supplanted by MRI, bone scanning can be used to identify osteonecrosis of the femoral head before it is apparent on conventional radiographs[17] (Fig. 16-10). Studies by Drane and Rudd[47] and Mortensson et al.[130] have shown that bone scintigraphy cannot predict the risk of osteonecrosis after femoral neck fracture. Subsequent work has suggested that SPECT imaging may be more accurate in assessing vascularity of the femoral head in fractures of the femoral neck.[27]

Angiography

Technical Considerations

Conventional Angiography. Techniques in conventional angiography are well established and involve cannulation of a vessel, commonly a major artery, for subsequent diagnostic and therapeutic interventions. Typically, the right common femoral artery is accessed, although less common access sites include the left common femoral artery, the axillary and brachial arteries, and translumbar aortic approaches, the selection of which depend on the clinical situation and goal of angiography. The Seldinger technique, the standard procedure for cannulating the common femoral artery, involves placing an 18-gauge needle into the artery at the level of the midfemoral head under fluoroscopic guidance. A double wall puncture is preferred, whereby the needle is advanced through both the anterior and posterior arterial walls until contact is made with the femoral head. The needle tip is pulled back slowly until it is within the arterial lumen and pulsatile flow is observed from the needle hub. A guidewire is then passed through the needle and into the vessel

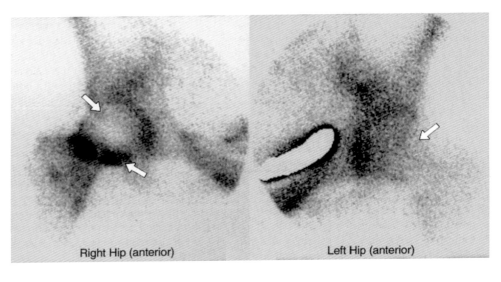

Right Hip (anterior)   **Left Hip (anterior)**

FIGURE 16-10 Pinhole bone scintigraphy (anteroposterior views) showing a photon-deficient area centrally in the right femoral head and increased uptake in the femoral neck and subcapital area compared with normal left hip findings. (Reprinted with permission from Yoon TR, Rowe SM, Song EK, et al. Unusual osteonecrosis of the femoral head misdiagnosed as a stress fracture. J Orthop Trauma 2004;18:43–47.)

lumen, and the needle is then exchanged over the guidewire for a catheter or sheath. Selective catheterization of individual vessels involves advancing the guidewire into the arterial tree, with subsequent advancement of the catheter over the guidewire.

Diagnostic angiography is performed by positioning the catheter tip proximal within the artery of interest and rapidly injecting nonionic iodinated contrast medium, the rate and volume of which are proportional to the size of and flow within the vessel lumen. Rapid fluoroscopic spot filming is timed to coincide with contrast opacification of the arterial tree and documents progressive filling and washout of the vessels. Venous return may also be demonstrated with appropriate delays in filming. Abnormal findings associated with vascular trauma include transection, laceration, dissection, arteriovenous fistula, pseudoaneurysm, mural hematoma, intimal tears, and vasospasm.

Digital subtraction angiography (DSA) is a commonly used technique, whereby a preliminary fluoroscopic spot film (the "mask") is taken before contrast injection and is subsequently subtracted from dynamic images obtained during contrast injection. The background tissues (bones, soft tissues) are removed from the dynamic arterial images, resulting in greater image contrast resolution. The concentration of iodinated contrast may be reduced using this technique, resulting in a lower total volume of injected contrast medium. Disadvantages of this technique include lower spatial resolution and misregistration artifact, which occurs as a result of patient motion after the mask image has been performed and results in misalignment of the mask during subtraction.

Therapeutic interventions may be performed during angiography and, for trauma patients, most commonly include embolization of bleeding arterial vessels in association with both visceral and bony fractures. Superselective catheterization of the bleeding vessel is first performed, with subsequent occlusion of the vessel using agents administered through the catheter. Temporary and permanent embolic agents are available, and their use is directed by the clinical situation and therapeutic goal. Temporary agents include autologous blood clots and Gelfoam pledgets, whereas permanent agents include microcoils and macrocoils, detachable balloons, polyvinyl alcohol, as well as various tissue adhesives and glues. Preembolization and postembolization angiograms are performed not only to document occlusion of the bleeding vessel but also to evaluate for collateral flow around the occluded vessel.

Complications of angiography include puncture site complications (e.g., groin hematoma, arteriovenous fistula, pseudoaneurysm), contrast complications (e.g., anaphylactoid reactions, renal failure), catheter-related complications (e.g., vessel wall dissection, thromboembolism), and therapy-related complications (e.g., tissue necrosis distal to embolization). Complications may be reduced with experience and careful technique by the angiographer.

Computed Tomography Angiography.

CT angiography (CTA) is a relatively new application of multislice helical CT technology. Intravenous nonionic iodinated contrast medium is injected, usually through an antecubital vein, using a volume of 120 to 150 mL at a rate of approximately 3 to 4 mL/s. Scanning is performed after an appropriate delay to ensure passage of contrast through the lungs and heart and into the arterial tree,

so that imaging occurs during peak intravascular enhancement throughout the arterial segment of interest. Technical factors such as beam collimation and pitch are adjusted to ensure adequate coverage and acceptable scanning times, while preserving high resolution of the study. Images are typically reconstructed from the helical dataset at 1.0-mm slice thicknesses with a 50% overlap. Because a typical CTA study generates hundreds to thousands of images, evaluation of the data is performed using 3D workstations, whereby the images may be viewed using cine modes, multiplanar reconstructions, and interactive real-time volume-rendering techniques. In addition to arterial injury, concomitant complex fractures are well evaluated on the same study.

Applications

Vascular Trauma.

Conventional angiography and, more recently, CTA are important diagnostic and therapeutic modalities in trauma patients with hemodynamic instability because of severe abdominal and pelvic trauma or extremity injuries with vascular damage (Fig. 16-11). Although management of a hemodynamically unstable patient with a pelvic fracture remains controversial, many experts suggest emergent angiography in these situations.[45] The yield in terms of identifiable arterial injury is low; however, when vascular injury is present, embolization using interventional techniques can be life saving. If necessary, pelvic angiography can be performed concomitantly with external fixation of the pelvis in patients with severe "open-book" injuries of the pelvic ring (Fig. 16-11).

More recently, CT angiography (CTA) has emerged as a simple and effective means of assessing possible vascular injury of the pelvis and extremities. CTA of the pelvis can be easily and successfully incorporated into standard CT evaluation protocols in patients with blunt trauma and is capable of differentiating active arterial and venous bleeding that can be useful information in guiding further care.[5] In a study of 48 trauma patients, contrast-enhanced CT was compared to formal angiography in detecting pelvic bleeding; CT had 94.1% sensitivity and 97.6% negative predictive value for the detection of active hemorrhage, and 92.6% sensitivity and 91.2% negative predictive value for predicting need for surgical or endovascular intervention.[123]

One traditional indication for angiography has been in the assessment of popliteal artery injury in the patient with definite or suspected knee dislocation. Recently, several studies have clarified the role of angiography in such patients, showing that urgent angiography is not needed unless there are deficits in distal pulses, ideally quantified by determination of the ankle-brachial index.[97,166]

CT angiography has significant advantages for the assessment of potential vascular injury in the lower extremity because of its noninvasiveness and immediate availability. At some trauma centers, CTA has supplanted arteriography for initial radiographic evaluation of peripheral vascular injuries.[145] Inaba et al.[84] used multislice CTA in 59 patients who underwent a total of 63 studies. In their series, multislice CTA was both 100% sensitive and 100% specific for detecting clinically significant arterial injury.[84] A recent study by LeBus and Collinge[103] suggests that routine use of CTA in the evaluation of patients with high-energy tibial plafond injuries may be beneficial. Twenty-five consecutive patients were treated with a standard protocol that included preoperative CT (and CTA). In 13 of the patients (52%), notable arterial injury was identified, most involving

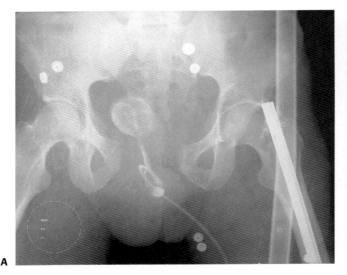

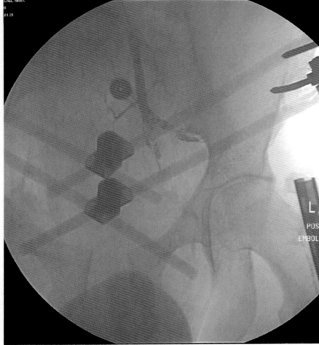

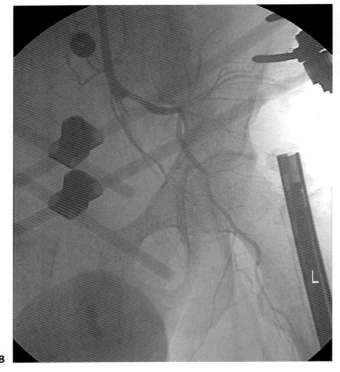

FIGURE 16-11 Pelvic angiography in a hemodynamically unstable trauma patient with a pelvic ring injury. **A.** The anteroposterior pelvic radiograph shows wide diastasis of the pubic symphysis. After emergent application of an anterior pelvic external fixator, the patient underwent selective embolization of both right and left internal iliac arteries. **B.** Spot film of the left internal iliac artery demonstrates dissection and nonfilling of multiple medial branches. Contrast fills the left internal iliac artery and its branches before embolization. **C.** Postembolization spot film demonstrates no flow of contrast distal to the embolization coils.

the anterior tibial artery. The authors thought that information about associated vascular injury allowed them to make better decisions about surgical tactics to be used for a given procedure, including whether to use traditional open or minimally invasive approaches, as well as in choices about placement of incisions.[103]

MANAGEMENT OF IMAGING DATA

Advances in digital imaging modalities have necessarily been paralleled by advances in distributing, viewing, and storing imaging data. In many instances, the traditional light box has been replaced by digital workstations, the file room has been upgraded with digital archives, and the transport of films has been replaced by digital transmission of images across networks to remote workstations. Many of these changes have evolved in response to the increasing size of digital imaging studies, in addition to the need to use and distribute this information more efficiently within the health care environment. All of these changes have relied on continued improvements in computer networks, workstations, storage devices, and display media, in addition to implementation of standards, to support the evolving digital imaging infrastructure. Although a thorough discussion of digital image management is beyond the scope of this section, a brief review of some of the more common concepts and standards will be presented.

Distribution of Imaging Information

Distribution of medical images is influenced by several factors, including size and volume of imaging studies, computer network infrastructure, and clinical needs by interpreting and referring physicians. Current trends in digital imaging technology have resulted in greater image resolution and greater numbers of images, both of which substantially contribute to increasing sizes of imaging studies. For example, a typical 256 × 256 matrix image, using 2 bytes of storage for each pixel, requires approximately 125 KB of storage per image, whereas a 512 × 512 matrix image requires approximately 500 KB, or four times as much as its lower-resolution counterpart. CT and MRI studies routinely contain 100 to 200 images, resulting in storage requirements of 12 MB to 100 MB per study. Newer 64-slice and 256-slice CT scanners may result in data files of up to 2.5 and 10 GB, respectively, per study.

Media for distribution include printed films, CD-ROMs, and networks for remote viewing or processing on workstations (Fig. 16-5). Although many imaging departments are transitioning to filmless environments, sheet films are commonly printed and may be necessary outside of the imaging department, such as in private clinics and offices, in addition to the operating room. In particular, hardcopy CT scans and specific radiographic views must remain available to the orthopaedic trauma surgeon to use in the operating room when dealing with complex injuries such as intra-articular fractures and pelvic ring or acetabular fractures. CD-ROM products are increasing in popularity, although computer access is necessary to read them and a greater level of sophistication is needed to use these products. Patients referred for trauma care from other institutions now often arrive with all of their imaging studies archived onto a CD-ROM. A frustrating problem for clinicians is the numerous proprietary software programs that have evolved for viewing images on a CD-ROM. All too often, the "viewer" embedded within a CD will not open on a given computer, and even when it does, the user is often not familiar with the software and can have problems viewing the images. Images stored on a CD-ROM are highly compressed and are of poor quality when enlarged to standard viewing size on a monitor. Institutions with available resources can scan such images into their picture archive and communications system (PACS) so that they are available to all, but the inability to do this in a timely fashion, especially outside normal working hours, can compromise patient care and require studies to be repeated at the receiving hospital.

Many imaging devices are connected to networks for transmitting image data to remote locations for image viewing and storage, to which the term *teleradiology* applies. There is a wide variety of network configurations, with descriptors such as local or wide area networks (LAN, WAN), intranets, and the Internet. Speed of transmission across networks depends on the various types of communication links within the network (modem, ISDN, DSL, cable modem, T1, T3, fiberoptic cable), as well as the level of network traffic. Data compression is used to decrease the size of imaging studies before electronic transmission, and compression schemes are categorized as "lossless" (no loss of original data, typically 3:1 compression) or "lossy" (some loss of data in original image, typically 15:1 or greater compression). Use of the Internet to transmit imaging studies is growing, although patient confidentiality and security issues have received considerable attention.

Imaging studies sent to interpreting physicians are commonly viewed on workstations, which are able to display images at full resolution using specific formats ("hanging protocols") and provide advanced capabilities for image processing (Fig.

16-5). Such workstations allow 3D images to be manipulated and reviewed in real-time; some can save movie files of the 3D image onto a disk. Of course, such capabilities are of limited value if they are not available to the orthopaedic trauma surgeon in a timely manner. Current, high-end workstations are expensive and are usually not available outside of the radiology department; normally, less-sophisticated viewing stations provide basic access to images outside of the imaging department. In certain environments, use of hardcopy images will remain necessary. Examples of this situation include the operating room, where multiple images of different imaging modalities need to be viewed together by a surgeon in sterile operating garb, and in the clinic, where the viewing of multiple studies in chronological order is necessary to observe fracture healing or changes in fracture alignment.

Picture Archive and Communications Systems

A PACS represents a network of mechanisms used to acquire, view, and store digital images and at its most basic level includes devices used to acquire digital images (e.g., CT and MRI scanners), workstations whereby images may be viewed and manipulated for diagnostic interpretations, and archives where digital images are stored for later retrieval. PACS may also include viewing stations for departments outside of the radiology department (e.g., emergency department, intensive care unit), and may be contained within their own LAN or exist as a part of a larger WAN. PACS may also communicate with Radiology Information Systems and Hospital Information Systems to share and/or modify patient information.

There are many advantages of PACS, including prompt access to clinical images, postprocessing of image data (window levels, multiplanar and 3D reconstructions, measurement and annotations tools), the ability of more than one user to simultaneously view the same images, and reduced filming costs and lost films. On the other hand, significant disadvantages include initial and recurring expenses related to installing and maintaining PACS, massive storage requirements for image archival, and the necessity of support personnel to maintain the network and its components. One study showed that LCD personal computer monitors and PACS workstations did not differ significantly in the diagnostic quality of cervical spine fracture radiographs, suggesting that LCD personal computer monitors are sufficient for fast, accurate diagnosis in the emergency department for evaluation of cervical spine injuries at considerably reduced cost.[23]

Digital Imaging and Communications in Medicine Standards

In 1983, the American College of Radiology (ACR) and the National Electrical Manufacturers Association (NEMA) formed a joint committee to develop a standard by which users could retrieve images and associated information from digital imaging equipment in a form that would be compatible across all manufacturers. Two years later, the first version of the ACR-NEMA standard was published, and in 1988, an updated second version was published, which corrected errors and inconsistencies and added new data elements. The first two versions relied on point-to-point connections between equipment, and by 1988, the growing implementation of networks and PACS necessitated a complete rewriting of the standard, which is currently known as Digital Imaging and Communications in Medicine (DICOM) Version 3.0.

The DICOM standard sets forth a uniform set of rules for communication of medical images and associated information, which are complex but practical and adaptable. The standard is flexible enough to accommodate a variety of images and image information across a broad range of medical imaging platforms. Conformance with the standard is voluntary, and manufacturers of medical imaging equipment or software who support the standard must provide conformance statements describing their particular implementation of the standard. This does not guarantee that two DICOM-compliant devices will communicate properly with one another; rather, the conformance statement serves as a guide to rule out obvious incompatibilities between equipment.

Digital Imaging and Teleradiology in Orthopaedics

Digital Imaging

Digital imaging is the future of radiology and has definite advantages and disadvantages in the management of musculoskeletal injuries. In a recent review, Wade et al.[178] noted the many potential advantages of digital imaging: reduction of foot traffic between clinics, wards, and the radiology department; increased availability of investigations; increase in the speed of availability; the virtual elimination of missing studies; less radiation exposure; fewer wasted films, and reduction in retrieval times. However, there are logistical problems associated with the adoption and use of filmless systems in an emergency department setting that must be overcome.[181] In addition, DR remains inferior to conventional radiography in terms of image spatial resolution (Table 16-1). Work is progressing in digital detector technology that may eventually provide spatial resolution equal to or exceeding that of conventional radiography. Miller et al.[126] describe the medical application of total-body DR for screening trauma patients, using a C-arm–based system initially developed in South Africa to detect theft by diamond miners. Full implementation of DR and PACS can be expensive and subject to the nuisances of technological failure and requires technical support skills that may not be universally available. Traditional printed images will continue to have a role in the operating room, in the clinic, and in other venues where access to the PACS system is not available or appropriate.

Teleradiology

Teleradiology can affect the practice of fracture management in many ways. Teleradiology allows emergency physicians and/or house staff to send digital images of radiographs or clinical photographs to off-site attending orthopaedic staff. There is potential application for community-based orthopaedists to obtain second opinions about fracture management from specialists at tertiary care centers. Traditionally, such consultation required the referring orthopaedic surgeon to obtain, duplicate, and mail hardcopies of radiographs to the consulting surgeon, who has then had to communicate his or her opinion to the referring surgeon by telephone. Using teleradiology, the transmission of patient information, imaging studies, and the consultant's evaluation can all be accomplished with greater convenience and less cost.

Ricci and Borrelli[154] demonstrated that teleradiology improved clinical decision making in the management of acute fractures. A series of 123 consecutive fractures was studied; in all cases, a junior orthopaedic resident performed the initial orthopaedic evaluation. All radiographs were digitized and electronically sent to the attending orthopaedist. Treatment plans were formulated and documented at three different times: after verbal communication of the patient's history and injuries, after the digitized radiographs were viewed, and after the original hardcopy radiographs were viewed. The investigators recognized two different types of changes that were made to the initial plan of management: acute treatment changes and changes in the definitive management of the fracture. Overall, the viewing of digitized radiographs resulted in a change of management in 21% of the fractures. No further changes in management were decided on after review of the original radiographs. The investigators concluded that the routine use of digitized radiographs improves fracture management.[154]

REFERENCES

1. Ahn JM, Sartoris DJ, Kang HS, et al. Gamekeeper thumb: comparison of MR arthrography with conventional arthrography and MR imaging in cadavers. Radiology 1998; 206:737–744.
2. Akbarnia BA, Silberstein MJ, Rende RJ, et al. Arthrography in the diagnosis of fractures of the distal end of the humerus in infants. J Bone Joint Surg Am 1986;68A:599–602.
3. American College of Radiology Committee on Drugs and Contrast Media. Manual on contrast media, Version 5.0. Reston, VA: American College of Radiology, 2004:7–10.
4. American College of Radiology Committee on Drugs and Contrast Media. Manual on contrast media, Version 5.0. Reston, VA: American College of Radiology, 2004:13.
5. Anderson SW, Soto JA, Lucey BC, et al. Blunt trauma: feasibility and clinical utility of pelvic CT angiography performed with 64-detector row CT. Radiology 2008;246: 410–419.
6. Anis AH, Stiell IG, Stewart DG, et al. Cost-effectiveness analysis of the Ottawa Ankle Rules. Ann Emerg Med 1995;26:422–428.
7. Arand M, Hartwig E, Kinzl L, et al. Spinal navigation in cervical fractures: a preliminary clinical study on Judet-osteosynthesis of the axis. Comput Aided Surg 2001;6:170–175.
8. Atesok K, Finkelstein J, Khoury A, et al. The use of intraoperative three-dimensional imaging (ISO-C-3D) in fixation of intraarticular fractures. Injury 2007;38:1163–1169.
9. Bachmann LM, Haberzeth S, Steurer J, et al. The accuracy of the Ottawa Knee Rule to rule out knee fractures: a systematic review. Ann Intern Med 2004;140:121–124.
10. Barros JW, Barbieri CH, Fernandes CD. Scintigraphic evaluation of tibial shaft fracture healing. Injury 2000;31:51–54.
11. Bencardino JT, Garcia AI, Palmer WE. Magnetic resonance imaging of the shoulder: rotator cuff. Top Magn Reson Imag 2003;14:51–67.
12. Bergin D, Schweitzer ME. Indirect magnetic resonance arthrography. Skeletal Radiol 2003;32:551–558.
13. Bhattacharyya T, Bouchard KA, Phadke A, et al. The accuracy of computed tomography for the diagnosis of tibial nonunion. J Bone Joint Surg Am 2006;88A:692–697.
14. Blane CE, Kling TF Jr, Andrews JC, et al. Arthrography in the posttraumatic elbow in children. AJR Am J Roentgenol 1984;143:17–21.
15. Blattert TR, Fill UA, Kunz E, et al. Skill dependence of radiation exposure for the orthopaedic surgeon during interlocking nailing of long-bone shaft fractures: a clinical study. Arch Orthop Trauma Surg 2004;124:659–664.
16. Bleakney RR, Tallon C, Wong JK, et al. Long-term ultrasonographic features of the Achilles tendon after rupture. Clin J Sport Med 2002;12:273–278.
17. Bonnarens F, Hernandez A, D'Ambrosia R. Bone scintigraphic changes in osteonecrosis of the femoral head. Orthop Clin North Am 1985;16:697–703.
18. Bono CM, Vaccaro AR, Fehlings M, et al. Measurement techniques for lower cervical spine injuries. Consensus statement of the Spine Trauma Study Group. Spine 2006; 31:603–609.
19. Borrelli J Jr, Goldfarb C, Catalano L, et al. Assessment of articular fragment displacement in acetabular fractures: a comparison of computerized tomography and plain radiographs. J Orthop Trauma 2002;16:449–456.
20. Borrelli J, Ricci WM, Steger-May K, et al. Postoperative radiographic assessment of acetabular fractures: a comparison of plain radiographs and CT scans. J Orthop Trauma 2005;19:299–304.
21. Bosse MJ, Brumback RJ, Hash C. Medical cost containment: analysis of dual orthopedic/radiology interpretation of X-rays in the trauma patient. J Trauma 1995;38:220–222.
22. Botser IB, Herman A, Nathaniel R, et al. Digital image enhancement improves diagnosis of nondisplaced proximal femur fractures. Clin Orthop Rel Res. 2009;467:246–253.
23. Brem MH, Böhner C, Brenning A, et al. Evaluation of low-cost computer monitors for the detection of cervical spine injuries in the emergency room: an observer confidence-based study. Emerg Med J 2006;23:850–853.
24. Bremer DJ, Hall EJ. Computed tomography: an increasing source of radiation exposure. N Engl J Med 2007;357:2277–2284.
25. Brooks S, Cicuttini FM, Lim S, et al. Cost effectiveness of adding magnetic resonance imaging to the usual management of suspected scaphoid fractures. Br J Sports Med 2005;39:75–79.
26. Bulloch B, Neto G, Plint A, et al. Validation of the Ottawa Knee Rule in children: a multicenter study. Ann Emerg Med 2003;42:48–55.

27. Calder SJ, McCaskie AW, Belton IP, et al. Single-photon-emission computerised tomography compared with planar bone scan to assess femoral head vascularity. J Bone Joint Surg Br 1995;77B:637–639.
28. Campbell DG, Menz A, Isaacs J. Dynamic ankle ultrasonography: a new imaging technique for acute ankle ligament injuries. Am J Sports Med 1994;22:855–858.
29. Cantwell CP, Cradock A, Bruzzi J, et al. MR venography with true fast imaging with steady-state precession for suspected lower-limb deep vein thrombosis. J Vasc Interv Radiol 2006;17:1763–1769.
30. Carelsen B, Haverlag R, Ubbink DTh, et al. Does intraoperative fluoroscopic 3D imaging provide extra information for fracture surgery? Arch Orthop Trauma Surg 2008;128: 1419–1424.
31. Caruso G, Lagalla R, Derchi L, et al. Monitoring of fracture calluses with color Doppler sonography. J Clin Ultrasound 2000;28:20–27.
32. Chan PS, Klimkiewicz JJ, Luchetti WT, et al. Impact of CT scan on treatment plan and fracture classification of tibial plateau fractures. J Orthop Trauma 1997;11:484–489.
33. Chong KW, Wong MK, Rikhraj IS, et al. The use of computer navigation in performing minimally invasive surgery for intertrochanteric hip fractures: the experience in Singapore. Injury 2006;37:755–762.
34. Churchill RS, Fehringer EV, Dubinsky TJ, et al. Rotator cuff ultrasonography: diagnostic capabilities. J Am Acad Orthop Surg 2004;12:6–11.
35. Cole RJ, Bindra RR, Evanoff BA, et al. Radiographic evaluation of osseous displacement following intra-articular fractures of the distal radius: reliability of plain radiography versus computed tomography. J Hand Surg Am 1997;22:792–800.
36. Collinge CA, Coons D, Tornetta P, et al. Standard multiplanar fluoroscopy versus a fluoroscopically based navigation system for the percutaneous insertion of iliosacral screws: a cadaver model. J Orthop Trauma 2005; 19:254–258.
37. Connell DA, Potter HG. Magnetic resonance evaluation of the labral capsular ligamentous complex: a pictorial review. Australas Radiol 1999;43:419–426.
38. Correspondence. Computed tomography and radiation exposure. N Engl J Med 2008; 358:850–853.
39. Crowl AC, Kahler DM. Closed reduction and percutaneous fixation of anterior column acetabular fractures. Comput Aided Surg 2002;7:169–178.
40. Davis BJ, Roberts PJ, Moorcroft CI, et al. Reliability of radiographs in defining union of internally fixed fractures. Injury 2004;35:557–561.
41. Davison BL, Cantu RV, Van Woerkom S. The magnetic attraction of lower extremity external fixators in an MRI suite. J Orthop Trauma 2004;18:24–27.
42. Delcoigne L, Durant H, Kunnen M, et al. Digital subtraction in multicompartment arthrography of the wrist. J Belg Radiol 1993;76:7–10.
43. Deutsch AL, Mink JH, Waxman AD. Occult fractures of the proximal femur: MR imaging. Radiology 1989;170:113–116.
44. Disegi JA. Magnetic resonance imaging of AO/ASIF stainless steel and titanium implants. Injury 1992;23(suppl 2):1–4.
45. Dondelinger RF, Trotteur G, Ghaye B, et al. Traumatic injuries: radiological hemostatic intervention at admission. Eur Radiol 2002;12:979–993.
46. Dorsay TA, Major NM, Helms CA. Cost-effectiveness of immediate MR imaging versus traditional follow-up for revealing radiographically occult scaphoid fractures. AJR Am J Roentgenol 2001;177:1257–1263.
47. Drane WE, Rudd TG. Femoral head viability following hip fracture. Prognostic role of radionuclide bone imaging. Clin Nucl Med 1985;10:141–146.
48. Drvaric DM, Rooks MD. Anterior sleeve fracture of the capitellum. J Orthop Trauma 1990;4:188–192.
49. Duane TM, Cole FJ Jr, Weireter LJ Jr, et al. Blunt trauma and the role of routine pelvic radiographs. Am Surg 2001;67:849–852.
50. Duc SR, Pfirrmann CW, Schmid MR, et al. Articular cartilage defects detected with 3D water excitation true FISP: prospective comparison with sequences commonly used for knee imaging. Radiology 2007; 245:216–223.
51. Dulchavsky SA, Henry SE, Moed BR, et al. Advanced ultrasonic diagnosis of extremity trauma: the FASTER examination. J Trauma 2002;53:28–32.
52. Durston W, Swartzentruber R. Ultrasound-guided reduction of pediatric forearm fractures in the ED. Am J Emerg Med 2000;18:72–77.
53. Ebraheim NA, Skie MC, Podeszwa DA, et al. Evaluation of process fractures of the talus using computed tomography. J Orthop Trauma 1994;8:332–337.
54. Eklof H, Radecka E, Liss P. Teleradiology Uppsala-Sydney for nighttime emergencies: preliminary experience. Acta Radiol 2007;48:851–853.
55. Emparanza JI, Aginaga JR. Validation of the Ottawa Knee Rules. Ann Emerg Med 2001; 38:364–368.
56. Eustace S, Adams J, Assaf A. Emergency MR imaging of orthopaedic trauma. Current and future directions. Radiol Clin North Am 1999;37:975–994.
57. Exadaktylos AK, Benneker LM, Jeger V, et al. Total-body digital X-ray in trauma. An experience report on the first operational full body scanner in Europe and its possible role in ATLS. Injury 2008;39:525–529.
58. Farber JM. CT arthrography and postoperative musculoskeletal imaging with multichannel computed tomography. Semin Musculoskelet Radiol 2004;8:157–166.
59. Farbman KS, Vinci RJ, Cranley WR, et al. The role of serial radiographs in the management of pediatric torus fractures. Arch Pediatr Adolesc Med 1999;153:923–925.
60. Fayad LM, Bluemke DA, Fishman EK. Musculoskeletal imaging with computed tomography and magnetic resonance imaging: when is computed tomography the study of choice? Curr Probl Diagn Radiol 2005;34:220–237.
61. Freund M, Thomsen M, Hohendorf B, et al. Optimized preoperative planning of calcaneal fractures using spiral computed tomography. Eur Radiol 1999;9:901–906.
62. Frihagen F, Nordsletten L Tariq R, et al. MRI diagnosis of occult hip fractures. Acta Orthop 2005;76:524–530.
63. Fritz RC. MR imaging of meniscal and cruciate ligament injuries. Magn Reson Imaging Clin North Am 2003;11:283–293.
64. Garcia-Morales F, Seo GS, et al. Collar osteophytes: a cause of false-positive findings in bone scans for hip fractures. AJR Am J Roentgenol 2003;181:191–194.
65. Gardner MJ, Citak M, Kendoff D, et al. Femoral fracture malrotation caused by freehand versus navigated distal interlocking. Injury 2008;39:176–180.
66. Geijer M, El-Khoury GY. Imaging of the acetabulum in the era of multidetector computed tomography. Emerg Radiol 2007;14:271–287.
67. Grangier C, Garcia J, Howarth NR, et al. Role of MRI in the diagnosis of insufficiency fractures of the sacrum and acetabular roof. Skeletal Radiol 1997;26:517–524.
68. Grechenig W, Fellinger M, Seibert FJ, et al. Die arthrography des handgelenks beim frischen trauma [Arthrography of the wrist joint in acute trauma]. Unfallchirurg 1996; 99:260–266.
69. Grechenig W, Peicha G, Fellinger M, et al. Wrist arthrography after acute trauma to the distal radius: diagnostic accuracy, technique, and sources of diagnostic errors. Invest Radiol 1998;33:273–278.
70. Green RAR, Saifuddin A. Whole spine MRI in the assessment of acute vertebral body trauma. Skeletal Radiol 2004;33:129–135.
71. Grigoryan M, Lynch JA, Fierlinger AL, et al. Quantitative and qualitative assessment of closed fracture healing using computed tomography and conventional radiography. Acad Radiol 2003;10:1267–1273.
72. Grogan EL, Morris JA Jr, Dittus RS, et al. Cervical spine evaluation in urban trauma centers: lowering institutional costs and complications through helical CT scan. J Am Coll Surg 2005;200:160–165.
73. Grutzner PA, Rose E, Vock B, et al. Computer-assistierte perkutane Verschraubung des hinteren Beckenrings. Erste Erfahrungen mit einem Bildwandler basierten optoelektronischen Navigationssystem. [Computer-assisted screw osteosynthesis of the posterior pelvic ring. Initial experiences with an image reconstruction based optoelectronic navigation system.] Unfallchirurg 2002;105:254–260.
74. Haapamaki VV, Kiuru MJ, Koskinen SK. Multidetector CT in shoulder fractures. Emerg Radiol 2004;11:89–94.
75. Haramati N, Staron RB, Barax C, et al. Magnetic resonance imaging of occult fractures of the proximal femur. Skeletal Radiol 1994;23:19–22.
76. Harness NG, Ring D, Zurakowski D, et al. The influence of three-dimensional computed tomography reconstructions on the characterization and treatment of distal radial fractures. J Bone Joint Surg Am 2006:88A:1315–1323.
77. Harris JH, Coupe KJ, Lee JS, et al. Acetabular fractures revisited: Part 2, A new CT-based classification. AJR Am J Roentgenol 2004;182:1367.
78. Harish S, Vince AS, Patel AD. Routine radiography following ankle fracture fixation: a case for limiting its use. Injury 1999;30:699–701.
79. Herneth AM, Siegmeth A, Bader TR, et al. Scaphoid fractures: evaluation with high-spatial-resolution US initial results. Radiology 2001;220:231–235.
80. Holt MD, Williams LA, Dent CM. MRI in the management of tibial plateau fractures. Injury 1995;26:595–599.
81. Horn BD, Crisci K, Krug M, et al. Radiologic evaluation of juvenile Tillaux fractures of the distal tibia. J Pediatr Orthop 2001;21:162–164.
82. Hougaard K, Lindequist S, Nielsen LB. Computerised tomography after posterior dislocation of the hip. J Bone Joint Surg Br 1987;69B:556–557.
83. Hunter TB, Taljanovic MS, Krupinski E, et al. Academic radiologists' on-call and late-evening duties. J Am Coll Radiol 2007;4:716–719.
84. Inaba K, Potzman J, Munera F, et al. Multi-slice CT angiography for arterial evaluation in the injured lower extremity. J Trauma 2006;60:502–506.
85. Intersocietal Accreditation Commission. ICAVL: Essentials and standards for accreditation in noninvasive vascular testing. Part II. Vascular laboratory operations: Peripheral venous testing. 2000:1–8. Retrieved June 15, 2004, from www.intersocietal.org/intersocietal.htm.
86. Javed A, Guichet JM. Arthrography for reduction of a fracture of the radial neck in a child with a nonossified radial epiphysis. J Bone Joint Surg Br 2001;83B:542–543.
87. Jones DG, Stoddart J. Radiation use in the orthopaedic theatre: a prospective audit. Aust N Z J Surg 1998;68:782–784.
88. Kahler DM. Virtual fluoroscopy: a tool for decreasing radiation exposure during femoral intramedullary nailing. Stud Health Technol Inform 2001;81:225–228.
89. Kaneriya PP, Schweitzer ME, Spettell C, et al. The cost-effectiveness of routine pelvic radiography in the evaluation of blunt trauma patients. Skeletal Radiol 1999;28: 271–273.
90. Kendoff D, Citak M, Gardner M, et al. Three-dimensional fluoroscopy for evaluation of articular reduction and screw placement in calcaneal fractures. Foot Ankle Int 2007; 28:1165–1171.
91. Kendoff D, Gardner MJ, Citak M, et al. Value of 3D fluoroscopic imaging of acetabular fractures. Comparison to 2D fluoroscopy and CT imaging. Arch Orthop Trauma Surg 2008;128:599–605.
92. Kessler T, Winkler H, Weiss C, et al. Sonographie des Ellenbogengelenks bei der Radiuskopfchenfraktur [Ultrasound diagnosis of the elbow joint in fracture of the head of the radius]. Orthopade 2002;31:268–270.
93. Ketelslegers E, Collard X, Vande Berg B, et al. Validation of the Ottawa Knee Rules in an emergency teaching centre. Eur Radiol 2002;12:1218–1220.
94. Khoury A, Liebergall M, Weil Y, et al. Computerized fluoroscopic-based navigation-assisted intramedullary nailing. Am J Orthop 2007;36:582–585.
95. Kirkpatrick AW, Brown R, Diebel LN, et al. Rapid diagnosis of an ulnar fracture with portable hand-held ultrasound. Milit Med 2003;168:312–313.
96. Klein HM, Vrsalovic V, Balas R, et al. Bildgebende Diagnostik des Handgelenkes: MRT und Arthrographie/Arthro-CT [Imaging diagnostics of the wrist: MRI and arthrography/arthro-CT]. Rofo Fortschr Geb Rontgenstr Neuen Bildgeb Verfahr 2002;174:177–182.
97. Klineberg EO, Crites BM, Flinn WR, et al. The role of arteriography in assessing popliteal artery injury in knee dislocations. J Trauma 2004;56:786–790.
98. Kolind SH, MacKay AL, Munk PL, et al. Quantitative evaluation of metal artifact reduction techniques. J Magn Reson Imaging 2004;20:487–495.
99. Krettek C, Miclau T, Grun O, et al. Intraoperative control of axes, rotation, and length in femoral and tibial fractures. Technical note. Injury 1998;29(suppl 3):C29–C39.
100. Kukla C, Gaebler C, Breitenseher MJ, et al. Occult fractures of the scaphoid. The diagnostic usefulness and indirect economic repercussions of radiography versus magnetic resonance scanning. J Hand Surg Br 1997;22:810–813.
101. Kumar R, Lerski RA, Gandy S, et al. Safety of orthopedic implants in magnetic resonance imaging: an experimental verification. J Orthop Res 2006;24:1799–1802.
102. Kurozumi T, Jinno Y, Sato T, et al. Open reduction for intra-articular calcaneal fractures: evaluation using computed tomography. Foot Ankle Int 2003;24:942–948.
103. LeBus GF, Collinge C. Vascular abnormalities as assessed with CT angiography in high-energy tibial plafond fractures. J Orthop Trauma 2008; 22:16–22.
104. Leddy JJ, Smolinski RJ, Lawrence J, et al. Prospective evaluation of the Ottawa Ankle Rules in a university sports medicine center. With a modification to increase specificity for identifying malleolar fractures. Am J Sports Med 1998;26:158–165.
105. Leddy JJ, Kesari A, Smolinski RJ. Implementation of the Ottawa Ankle Rule in a university sports medicine center. Med Sci Sports Exerc 2002;34:57–62.

106. Leet AI, Young C, Hoffer MM. Medial condyle fractures of the humerus in children. J Pediatr Orthop 2002;22:2–7.

107. Luechinger R, Boesiger P, Disegi JA. Safety evaluation of large external fixation clamps and frames in a magnetic resonance environment. J Biomed Mater Res B 2007;82:17–22.

108. Levy AD, Harcke HT. Handheld ultrasound device for detection of nonopaque and semi-opaque foreign bodies in soft tissues. J Clin Ultrasound 2003;31:183–188.

109. Liebergall M, Ben-David D, Weil Y, et al. Computerized navigation for the internal fixation of femoral neck fractures. J Bone Joint Surg Am 2006;88A:1748–1754.

110. Lim KB, Eng AK, Chng SM, et al. Limited magnetic resonance imaging (MRI) and the occult hip fracture. Ann Acad Med Singapore 2002;31:607–610.

111. Lobenhoffer P, Schulze M, Gerich T, et al. Closed reduction/percutaneous fixation of tibial plateau fractures: arthroscopic versus fluoroscopic control of reduction. J Orthop Trauma 1999;13:426–431.

112. Lonner JH, Dupuy DE, Siliski JM. Comparison of magnetic resonance imaging with operative findings in acute traumatic dislocations of the adult knee. J Orthop Trauma 2000;14:183–186.

113. Loredo R, Sanders TG. Imaging of osteochondral injuries. Clin Sports Med 2001;20:249–278.

114. Love C, Patel M, Lonner BS, et al. Diagnosing spinal osteomyelitis: a comparison of bone and Ga-67 scintigraphy and magnetic resonance imaging. Clin Nucl Med 2000;25:963–977.

115. Lubovsky O, Liebergall M, Mattan Y, et al. Early diagnosis of occult hip fractures MRI versus CT scan. Injury 2005;36:788–792.

116. Lynch JA, Grigoryan M, Fierlinger A, et al. Measurement of changes in trabecular bone at fracture sites using X-ray CT and automated image registration and processing. J Orthop Res 2004;22:362–367.

117. Mack MG, Keim S, Balzer JO, et al. Clinical impact of MRI in acute wrist fractures. Eur Radiol 2003;13:612–617.

118. Mandelstam SA, Cook D, Fitzgerald M, et al. Complementary use of radiological skeletal survey and bone scintigraphy in detection of bony injuries in suspected child abuse. Arch Dis Child 2003;88:387–390.

119. Marzo JM, d'Amato C, Strong M, et al. Usefulness and accuracy of arthrography in management of lateral humeral condyle fractures in children. J Pediatr Orthop 1990;10:317–321.

120. Matin P. The appearance of bone scans following fractures, including immediate and long-term studies. J Nucl Med 1979;20:1227–1231.

121. Matsui Y, Myoui A, Nakahara H, et al. Prognostic significance of posterior subtalar joint arthrography following fractures of the calcaneus. Arch Orthop Trauma Surg 1995;114:257–259.

122. Matthews F, Hoigne DJ, Weiser M, et al. Navigating the fluoroscope's C-arm back into position: an accurate and practicable solution to cut radiation and optimize intraoperative workflow. J Orthop Trauma 2007;21:687–692.

123. Maturen KE, Adusumilli S, Blane CE, et al. Contrast-enhanced CT accurately detects hemorrhage in torso trauma: direct comparison with angiography. J Trauma 2007;62:740–745.

124. McAdams TR, Blevins FT, Martin TP, et al. The role of plain films and computed tomography in the evaluation of scapular neck fractures. J Orthop Trauma 2002;16:7–11.

125. Michelson JD, Ahn U, Magid D. Economic analysis of roentgenogram use in the closed treatment of stable ankle fractures. J Trauma 1995;39:1119–1122.

126. Miller LA, Mirvis SE, Harris L, et al. Total-body digital radiography for trauma screening: initial experience. Appl Radiol 2004;33:8–14.

127. Moed BR, Carr SE, Gruson KI, et al. Computed tomographic assessment of fractures of the posterior wall of the acetabulum after operative treatment. J Bone Joint Surg Am 2003;85A:512–522.

128. Moed BR, Subramanian S, van Holsbeeck M, et al. Ultrasound for the early diagnosis of tibial fracture healing after static interlocked nailing without reaming: clinical results. J Orthop Trauma 1998;12:206–213.

129. Montgomery KD, Potter HG, Helfet DL. Magnetic resonance venography to evaluate the deep venous system of the pelvis in patients who have an acetabular fracture. J Bone Joint Surg Am 1995;77A:1639–1649.

130. Mortensson W, Rosenborg M, Gretzer H. The role of bone scintigraphy in predicting femoral head collapse following cervical fractures in children. Acta Radiol 1990;31:291–292.

131. Mosheiff R, Khoury A, Weil Y, et al. First generation computerized fluoroscopic navigation in percutaneous pelvic surgery. J Orthop Trauma 2004;18:106–111.

132. Muchow RD, Resnick DK, Abdel MP, et al. Magnetic resonance imaging (MRI) in the clearance of the cervical spine in blunt trauma: a meta-analysis. J Trauma 2008;64:179–189.

133. Mulkens TH, Marchal P, Daineffe S, et al. Comparison of low-dose with standard-dose multidetector CT in cervical spine trauma. AJNR Am J Neuroradiol 2007;28:1444–1450.

134. Mulligan ME, Flye CW. Initial experience with Lodox Statscan imaging system for detecting injuries of the pelvis and appendicular skeleton. Emerg Radiol 2006;13:129–133.

135. Nepola JV, Seabold JE, Marsh JL, et al. Diagnosis of infection in ununited fractures. Combined imaging with indium-111-labeled leukocytes and technetium-99m methylene diphosphonate. J Bone Joint Surg Am 1993;75-A:1816–1822.

136. Nichol G, Stiell IG, Wells GA, et al. An economic analysis of the Ottawa Knee Rule. Ann Emerg Med 1999;34:438–447.

137. Norris BL, Hahn DH, Bosse MJ, et al. Intraoperative fluoroscopy to evaluate fracture reduction and hardware placement during acetabular surgery. J Orthop Trauma 1999;13:414–417.

138. Orbell JH, Smith A, Burnand KG, et al. Imaging of deep vein thrombosis. Br J Surg 2008;95:137–146.

139. Pakos EE, Koumoulis HD, Fotopoulos AD, et al. Osteomyelitis: antigranulocyte scintigraphy with 99mTc radiolabeled monoclonal antibodies for diagnosis: meta-analysis. Radiology 2007;245:732–741.

140. Palestro CJ. The current role of gallium imaging in infection. Semin Nucl Med 1994;24:128–141.

141. Palestro CJ, Torres MA. Radionuclide imaging in orthopedic infections. Semin Nucl Med 1997;27:334–345.

142. Parker L, Nazarian LN, Carrino JA, et al. Musculoskeletal imaging: Medicare use, costs, and potential for cost substitution. J Am Coll Radiol 2008;5:182–188.

143. Peh WC, Khong PL, Yin Y, et al. Imaging of pelvic insufficiency fractures. Radiographics 1996;16:335–348.

144. Peetrons P. Ultrasound of muscles. Eur Radiol 2002;12:35–43.

145. Peng PD, Spain DA, Tataria M, et al. CT angiography effectively evaluates extremity vascular trauma. Am Surg 2008;74:103–107.

146. Peters AM The utility of [99mTc]HMPAO-leukocytes for imaging infection. Semin Nucl Med 1994;24:110–127.

147. Pitcher RD, van As AB, Sanders V, et al. A pilot study evaluating the "STATSCAN" digital X-ray machine in paediatric polytrauma. Emerg Radiol 2008;15:35–42.

148. Pool FJ, Crabbe JP. Occult femoral neck fractures in the elderly: optimisation of investigation. N Z Med J 1996;109:235–237.

149. Potter HG, Nestor BJ, Sofka CM, et al. Magnetic resonance imaging after total hip arthroplasty: evaluation of periprosthetic soft tissue. J Bone Joint Surg Am 2004;86A:1947–1954.

150. Pruitt DL, Gilula LA, Manske PR, et al. Computed tomography scanning with image reconstruction in evaluation of distal radius fractures. J Hand Surg Am 1994;19:720–727.

151. Pudas T, Hurme T, Mattila K, et al. Magnetic resonance imaging in pediatric elbow fractures. Acta Radiol 2005;46:636–644.

152. Raby N. Magnetic resonance imaging of suspected scaphoid fractures using a low field dedicated extremity MR system. Clin Radiol 2001;56:316–320.

153. Rangger C, Kathrein A, Freund MC, et al. Bone bruise of the knee: histology and cryosections in 5 cases. Acta Orthop Scand 1998;69:291–294.

154. Ricci WM, Borrelli J. Teleradiology in orthopaedic surgery: impact on clinical decision making for acute fracture management. J Orthop Trauma 2002;16:1–6.

155. Richards PJ, Summerfield R, George J, et al. Major trauma and cervical clearance radiation doses and cancer induction. Injury 2008;39:347–356.

156. Richter M, Geerling J, Zech S, et al. Intraoperative three-dimensional imaging with a motorized mobile C-arm (SIREMOBIL ISO-C-3D) in foot and ankle trauma care: a preliminary report. J Orthop Trauma 2005;19:259–266.

157. Roberts CS, Beck DJ, Heinsen J, et al. Review article: diagnostic ultrasonography: applications in orthopaedic surgery. Clin Orthop 2002;401:248–264.

158. Robbins MI, Anzilotti KF, Katz LD, et al. Patient perception of magnetic resonance arthrography. Skeletal Radiol 2000;29:265–269.

159. Roemer FW, Bohndorf K. Long-term osseous sequelae after acute trauma of the knee joint evaluated by MRI. Skeletal Radiol 2002;31:615–623.

160. Saxena P, McDonald R, Gull S, et al. Diagnostic scanning for suspected scaphoid fractures: an economic evaluation based on cost-minimisation models. Injury 2003;34:503–511.

161. Schmid MR, Pfirrmann CW, Hodler J, et al. Cartilage lesions in the ankle joint: comparison of MR arthrography and CT arthrography. Skeletal Radiol 2003;32:259–265.

162. Seabold JE, Nepola JV. Imaging techniques for evaluation of postoperative orthopaedic infections. Q J Nucl Med 1999;43:21–28.

163. Smith R. Giving emergency radiology its due. Decisions in Imaging Economics, August 2001. Retrieved October 15, 2004, from http://www.imagingeconomics.com/library/200108-08.asp.

164. Sofka CM, Potter HG. MR imaging of joint arthroplasty. Semin Musculoskelet Radiol 2002;6:79–85.

165. Sofka CM, Potter HG, Figgie M, et al. Magnetic resonance imaging of total knee arthroplasty. Clin Orthop 2003;406:129–135.

166. Stannard JP, Sheils TM, Lopez-Ben RR, et al. Vascular injuries in knee dislocations: the role of physical examination in determining the need for arteriography. J Bone Joint Surg Am 2004;86A:910–915.

167. Steinbach LS, Palmer WE, Schweitzer ME. Special focus session. MR arthrography. Radiographics 2002;22:1223–1246.

168. Stiell I, Wells G, Laupacis A, et al. Multicentre trial to introduce the Ottawa ankle rules for use of radiography in acute ankle injuries. Multicentre Ankle Rule Study Group. Br Med J 1995;311:594–597.

169. Suhm N, Jacob AL, Nolte LP, et al. Surgical navigation based on fluoroscopy: clinical application for computer-assisted distal locking of intramedullary implants. Comput Aided Surg 2000;5:391–400.

170. Theocharopoulos N, Damilakis J, Perisinakis K, et al. Image-guided reconstruction of femoral fractures: is the staff progeny safe? Clin Orthop 2005;430:182–188.

171. Thomas SH, Orf J, Peterson C, et al. Frequency and costs of laboratory and radiograph repetition in trauma patients undergoing interfacility transfer. Am J Emerg Med 2000;18:156–158.

172. Tirman PF, Smith ED, Stoller DW, et al. Shoulder imaging in athletes. Semin Musculoskelet Radiol 2004;8:29–40.

173. Tomycz ND, Chew BG, Chang Y-F, et al. MRI is unnecessary to clear the cervical spine in obtunded/comatose trauma patients: the 4-year experience of a Level I Trauma Center. J Trauma 2008; 64:1258–1263.

174. Tornetta P, Gorup J. Axial computed tomography of pilon fractures. Clin Orthop 1996;323:273–276.

175. Vasarhelyi A, Lubitz J, Gierer P, et al. Detection of fibular torsional deformities after surgery for ankle fractures with a novel CT method. Foot Ankle Int 2006;27:1115–1121.

176. Verlaan JJ, van de Kraats EB, Dhert WJ, et al. The role of 3-D rotational x-ray imaging in spinal trauma. Injury 2005;36(suppl 2):B98–B103.

177. Vocke-Hell AK, Schmid A. Sonographic differentiation of stable and unstable lateral condyle fractures of the humerus in children. J Pediatr Orthop B 2001;10:138–141.

178. Wade FA, Oliver CW, McBride K. Digital imaging in trauma and orthopaedic surgery. Is it worth it? J Bone Joint Surg Br 2000;82B:791–794.

179. Wehrli FW, Song HK, Saha PK, et al. Quantitative MRI for the assessment of bone structure and function. NMR Biomed 2006;19:731–764.

180. Weil YA, Gardner MJ, Helfet DL, et al. Computer navigation allows for accurate reduction of femoral fractures. Clin Orthop 2007 460;185–191.

181. White FA, Zwemer FL, Beach C, et al. Emergency department digital radiology: moving from photos to pixels. Acad Emerg Med 2004;11:1213–1222.

182. White LM, Miniaci A. Cruciate and posterolateral corner injuries in the athlete: clinical and magnetic resonance imaging features. Semin Musculoskelet Radiol 2004;8:111–131.

183. Wicky S, Blaser PF, Blanc CH, et al. Comparison between standard radiography and spiral CT with 3D reconstruction in the evaluation, classification, and management of tibial plateau fractures. Eur Radiol 2000;10:1227–1232.

184. Winalski CS, Gupta KB. Magnetic resonance imaging of focal articular cartilage lesions. Top Magn Reson Imaging 2003;14:131–144.

185. Wolf G, Aigner RM, Schwarz T. Diagnosis of bone infection using 99m Tc-HMPAO labelled leukocytes. Nucl Med Commun 2001;22:1201–1206.

186. Wood TO. MRI safety and compatibility of implants and medical devices. In: Stainless Steels for Medical and Surgical Applications, ASTM STP 1438, G.L. Winters and M.J. Nutt, Eds,. ASTM International, West Conshohocken, PA 2003.

187. Yacoubian SV, Nevins RT, Sallis JG, et al. Impact of MRI on treatment plan and fracture classification of tibial plateau fractures. J Orthop Trauma 2002;16:632–637.

188. Yin Y, Wilson AJ, Gilula LA. Three-compartment wrist arthrography: direct comparison of digital subtraction with nonsubtraction images. Radiology 1995;197:287–290.

189. Zierler BK. Ultrasonography and diagnosis of venous thromboembolism. Circulation 2004;109(suppl I):I-9–I-14.

17

COMPUTER-AIDED ORTHOPAEDIC SURGERY IN SKELETAL TRAUMA

Meir Liebergall, Rami Mosheiff, and Leo Joskowicz

INTRODUCTION

Computers are becoming pervasive in all fields of human endeavor, and medicine is no exception. Starting with the advent of computed tomography (CT) in the 1970s, computer-based systems have become the standard of care in many clinical fields, most notably in radiology, radiation therapy, neurosurgery, and orthopaedics. These systems assist the surgeon in planning, executing, and evaluating the surgery, often improving existing procedures and at times enabling new procedures that could not have been realized without them.

The first computer-based systems for surgery were developed in the mid 1980s for neurosurgery. The key characteristic of these systems was an *integration of preoperative information with intraoperative execution*. Traditionally, preoperative film radiograph, CT, and magnetic resonance images (MRIs) showing the patient's condition and the planned approach are brought into the operating room to guide the surgeon. However, when performing surgical actions, it is not possible to determine exactly where the surgical tools and implants are with respect to these images, especially when direct line-of-sight is limited, such as in keyhole, minimally invasive, and percutaneous surgery. Often, intraoperative images, such as fluoroscopic radiographs, are acquired to monitor the location of tools, implants, and anatomy. The surgeon must then mentally recreate the spatiotemporal situation from these images and decide on a course of action. This integration is qualitative and imprecise, as is the surgeon's hand–eye coordination, which requires significant skill, experience, and judgment and varies from surgeon to surgeon.

Computer-aided surgery (CAS) systems perform this integration automatically and accurately, thereby providing the surgeon with a precise, more complete, and up-to-date view of the intraoperative situation.[44] By incorporating real-time tracking of the location of instruments and anatomy, and their precise relation to preoperative and intraoperative images, the systems create a new modality akin to continuous imaging. In this sense, CAS systems are like navigators based on global positioning systems (GPSs), currently found in cars which help drivers find their way to a desired destination. During driving, the system shows the exact location of the car at all times on a computerized map and provides turn-by-turn directions ahead of time.

In orthopaedics, the first CT-based navigation commercial systems were introduced in the mid 1990s for spinal surgery.[28] Several years later, fluoroscopic radiography–based systems were developed for total hip and total knee replacement.[37] Today, a variety of image-free and image-based systems exist for planning and executing a variety of orthopaedic procedures, including primary and revision total hip and total knee replacement, anterior cruciate ligament reconstruction, spinal pedicle screw insertion, and trauma.[15,20,30,36,37]

CAS has already become an integral part of the orthopaedic trauma surgery setup. The rapid development in the use of computers in this field provides many feasible options at all stages of treatment of the orthopaedic trauma patient, from preoperative planning to postoperative evaluation. The role of computerization in the treatment of trauma patients is not only to enhance the surgical options in the preplanning stage but also to shorten surgery, an advantage that could be crucial for patient morbidity in a trauma setup. Although computerized imaging equipment can be moved into the admitting area and/or the trauma unit of the emergency department, this may involve adaptation of an existing setup, requiring administrative changes and incurring high costs. Another option is the use of comprehensive imaging provided by the improvement of conventional image intensifiers in achieving accurate three-dimensional (3D) information in a minimal period of time inside the operating room such as can be achieved with the SireMobil Iso-C 3D (Siemens Medical Solutions, Erlangen, Germany).

Recently, computerized navigation has made a breakthrough in expanding the use of CAS from the preplanning to the intraoperative stage. This integrates well with the current tendency toward minimal invasive surgery. CAS technology brings important digitized information into the operating room, enabling the accomplishment of two main goals: minimal invasive surgery and maximal accuracy. Moreover, both surgeon and patient enjoy a significant reduction in the amount of radiation exposure usually associated with orthopaedic trauma surgery. The main modality, which is currently in various stages of application and has been adapted to trauma surgery, is fluoroscopy-based navigation. While this technology might be viewed by some as only improved fluoroscopy, it is undoubtedly this feature that has allowed computer-based navigation systems to become a pioneer in the process of CAS integration in the orthopaedic trauma operating room.

TECHNICAL ELEMENTS

Computer-aided orthopaedic surgery in skeletal trauma (CAOS-ST) systems consist of preoperative planning (when available and feasible) and intraoperative navigation. We next describe the technical principles of each and the existing types of navigation systems.

Computerized Preoperative Planning and Model Construction

Preoperative planning for skeletal trauma surgery has traditionally been accomplished using film radiographs and film CT. The drawbacks of this current practice are that anatomic measurements either are approximate or cannot be obtained; that fixation plates and implant templates are usually not available; that the fixation plate's and/or implant's size, position, and orientation can be only approximately determined; and that spatial views are unavailable. Consequently, only a few alternatives can be explored.

Digital radiographic and CT data have improved significantly and allow better planning. Digital radiographic images can be correlated, and anatomic measurements, such as anteversion angle and leg length, can be performed on them. Digital templates of fixation and implant devices can be superimposed onto the radiographic images to explore a variety of alternatives. Computer-aided planning packages allow surgeons to select digital templates of fixation devices, position them, and take appropriate measurements. This computerized support allows for greater accuracy, versatility, and simplicity compared with traditional analog templating and measuring techniques.[4,35] Figure 17-1A shows a screen shot of a preoperative planning session for internal fixation of a fractured tibia.

For CT data, preoperative planning allows for 3D measurements and spatial visualization of complex structures and fractures. It allows the construction of computer *models*, such as bone *surface mesh*, anatomic axes, and osteotomy planes. Bone fragment models and implants can be visualized in three dimensions and manipulated to analyze several possible scenarios. The resulting fixation can be evaluated in three dimensions and with a simulated postoperative radiograph, known as a digitally reconstructed radiograph, obtained from the preoperative CT and the fixation hardware. Figures 17-1B–C illustrate the concepts of preoperative planning of reduction and fixation of a pelvic fracture.

An increasing number of computer programs have been developed enabling the performance of virtually all steps of the real surgical procedure.[3,6] This ability to exercise a virtual surgical procedure marks out safe zones; allows for precise planning of screw dimensions and pathways; and enables prechecking of the percutaneous option as an alternative to the open approach.

Principles of Navigation and Guidance

The goal of *navigation* is to provide precise, real-time visual feedback of the spatial location of surgical instruments and anatomic structures that cannot be directly observed. In current practice, this information is obtained by repeated use of fluoroscopic radiography, which produces a time-frozen two-dimensional (2D) view, is not updated in real time, and results in cumulative radiation to the surgeon, staff, and patient. The goal of *guidance* is to indicate to the surgeon in real time, via images, graphics, or sound, the best course of action during surgery.

Navigation systems show the current location of surgical instruments with respect to images of the anatomy using either preoperative CT or intraoperative fluoroscopic radiography images and continuously update the image as the instruments and bone structures move. The resulting display, called *navigation images*, is equivalent to continuous intraoperative imaging without radiation.

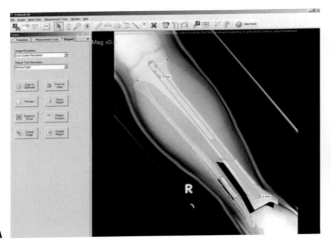

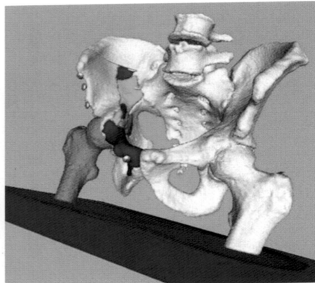

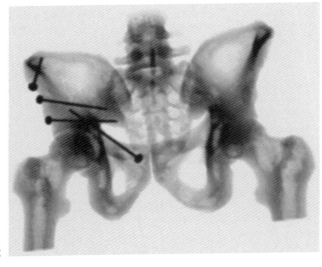

FIGURE 17-1 Preoperative planning. **A.** Preplanning for internal fixation of a distal tibia and fibula fracture using an intramedullary nail and fibular plate. Interlocking screw sizes are estimated, using a ruler tool. **B.** Preplanning for reduction and fixation of an acetabular fracture: three-dimensional visualization of the pelvis and fragment (each fragment is indicated in a different color) with planned fixation screws; **(C)** Simulated postoperative radiography image. (**A,** Image from TraumaCad, courtesy OrtoCRAT Ltd., Israel. **B, C,** Images property of the authors.)

Navigation requires *tracking, registration, visualization,* and *validation.* Tracking determines in real time the location of moving objects in space. Registration establishes a common reference frame between the moving objects and the images. Visualization creates navigation images showing the location of moving objects with respect to the anatomy. Validation ensures that the updated images match the clinical intraoperative situation.

The key advantage of navigation is that it obviates the need for repeated fluoroscopic radiography. However, it requires additional procedures, including setting up the navigation system and attaching trackers to both instruments and bone structures of interest, as well as additional surgical training.

System Components and Mode of Operation

A navigation system consists of a computer unit, a tracking unit, and tracker mounting hardware. Figure 17-2 shows the equipment setup in the operating room. A rolling cart usually holds the computer unit and the *tracking base unit.* The cart is placed next to the patient, so that the surgeon can conveniently see the display. Tracking requires a *position sensor* and one or

more *trackers.* The position sensor determines the spatial location of the trackers at any given moment in time. By attaching trackers to surgical tools and bone structures, their relative spatial position can continuously be followed and updated in the computer display. Trackers are rigidly mounted on tools and bones with *tracker mounting jigs,* which are mechanical jigs similar to screws and clamps. Because the trackers and their mounting jigs come in contact with the patient, they must be sterilized. The position sensor is either mounted on the cart, part of a separate unit, or attached to the ceiling or to a wall. It is aimed at the surgical field so that the expected tracker motions are within its working area throughout surgery. The position sensor's location can be changed during surgery as needed. When fluoroscopic radiography images are used for navigation, the computer unit is also connected to a C-arm and imports images acquired with it. The C-arm is usually fitted with its own tracker to determine its relative location with respect to the tracked objects and imaged anatomy.

The tracking base unit receives and integrates the signals from the position sensor and the trackers. The computer integrates the signals from the base unit with fluoroscopic radiogra-

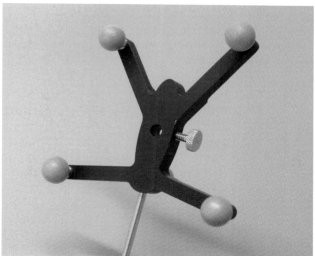

FIGURE 17-2 Equipment setup in the operating room. A navigation system consists of a computer unit, tracker unit, and tracker mounting hardware. The computer unit consists of a computer, keyboard, mouse, and display monitor or touch screen. The tracking unit consists of a tracking base unit, position sensor, one or more trackers, and a tool calibration unit (optional). (Image property of authors.)

phy or CT images and instrument models (registration), and creates one or more views for display (visualization). The navigated images are updated in real time by the computer as the instruments and anatomy move. The *tool calibration unit* is used to obtain geometric data of surgical tools fitted with trackers, such as the tool tip's offset. These geometric data are used to create the instrument model for display.

Tracking

A tracking system obtains the position and orientation of trackers by measuring spatially dependent physical properties, which can be optical, magnetic, acoustic, or mechanical. Currently, two types of tracking technologies are available for medical applications: optical and magnetic, with optical being by far the most commonly used (Fig. 17-3).

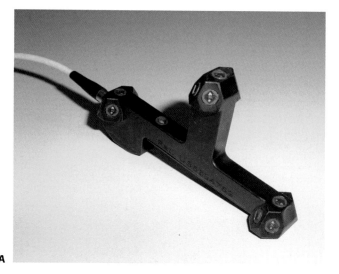

A

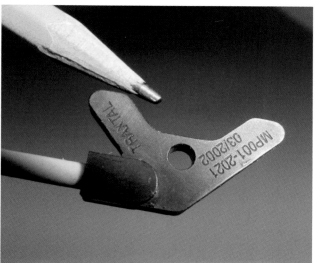

C

B

FIGURE 17-3 Trackers. **A.** Active optical tracker. **B.** Passive optical tracker. **C.** Magnetic tracker. (Courtesy of Traxtal Technologies, Toronto, Canada.)

Optical Tracking. In optical tracking, the position sensor consists of two or more *optical cameras* that detect light emitted or reflected by *markers*. Each camera measures the distance of the markers from the camera. Because the base distance between the optical cameras is known, the position of the marker with respect to the camera's base line can be computed by a method known as triangulation. A *tracker* consists of three or more markers mounted on a rigid base (Fig. 17-3A). The tracker's position and orientation are determined by the markers' positions relative to each other and by their sensed position with respect to the position sensor. A key requirement is the maintenance of an unobstructed *line-of-sight* between the position sensor and the trackers. Optical tracking systems can be *active*, *passive*, or *hybrid*.

Active Tracking. Active tracking uses active markers, which are light-emitting diodes (LEDs) that are strobbed (turned on and off) in tandem by the base unit. LEDs emit infrared light that is detected by the cameras. The cameras' capture is synchronized with the LED strobbing so that the identity of the lighting marker is known. Active trackers consist of three or more wired LEDs mounted onto a rigid base and connected by a cable or by a wireless link (tetherless communication) to the tracking base unit. Each active tracker has a unique identifier. Active trackers are built so that they can be sterilized many times.

Passive Tracking. Passive tracking uses passive markers, which can be reflective spheres or printed patterns (Fig. 17-3B). Reflective spheres reflect the infrared light generated by the position sensor, which is then detected by the cameras. Unlike the active markers, passive markers are not controlled by the tracking base unit and are "seen" simultaneously by the cameras. Passive trackers consist of three or more passive markers. The identity of the passive tracker is determined by the configuration of the markers on the rigid mounting base. Consequently, no two passive trackers can have the same marker configuration. The tracking base unit must know the tracker configuration. Because the markers lose their reflectance with sterilization and touch, they must be replaced after several uses.

Hybrid Tracking. Hybrid tracking incorporates both active and passive tracking. Hybrid tracking systems simultaneously track both passive and active trackers, thus providing the advantages of both technologies. Table 17-1 summarizes the advantages and disadvantages of active (wired and tetherless) and passive trackers. Because neither technology is always superior to the other in all categories, the anatomy, the surgical instruments, and the clinical situation determine the best choice of trackers.

In terms of physical characteristics, trackers are comparable. Passive trackers are lightest, while tetherless active trackers are heaviest because of the battery required to activate the circuitry and the LEDs. Passive trackers are more rugged than active ones because they have no electronics. Tetherless trackers are more convenient because there are no cables to get in the way. In terms of functionality, active trackers have the advantage that they indicate, on the tracker itself (via a light indicator), when the line-of-sight is maintained, while passive tracker obstruction can only be shown on the display. Active trackers are automatically recognized as soon as they are plugged in. Passive trackers

	Optical			
TABLE 17-1 **Comparison of Tracking Technologies**				
Characteristic	Active wired	Active tetherless	Passive	Magnetic
Physical				
Size	0	0	0	+
Weight	0	−	+	+
Ruggedness	0	−	+	+
Ergonomics	−	0	+	−
Functional				
Activation indicator	+	+	NA	+
Integrated switch	+	+	NA	+
Tool recognition	+	+	NA	+
Reliability	0	−	+	0
Performance				
Orientation dependency	−	−	+	−
Accuracy	+	+	0	
Cost				
Upfront cost	0	−	+	+
Running cost	+	−	0	+
Amortized cost	0	−	+	+

Scores (+, 0, −) are relative: + indicates most favorable; 0, neutral; and −, least favorable. NA, feature is not available.

are the most reliable, because there are no electric connections; tetherless active trackers are the least reliable because of possible communication interferences and their short battery life (LEDs require substantial power for illumination). In terms of performance, active trackers are somewhat more accurate than passive trackers but they are also more sensitive to their orientation with respect to the cameras. In terms of cost, it is highest for active tetherless tracking because of the additional electronics and lowest for passive trackers, which have no electronics at all. The running cost of active wired tracking is lowest, because there are no batteries or reflective spheres to replace. The amortized cost over time of the wired active trackers represents a significant improvement.

Magnetic Tracking.

Magnetic tracking works by measuring variations of generated magnetic fields. The position sensor consists of a magnet that generates a uniform magnetic field and a sensor that measures its phase and intensity variations. Trackers consist of one or more miniature coils mounted on a rigid base that generate a local magnetic field from an electric current, either alternating or pulsed direct (Fig. 17-3C). Both the position sensor and the trackers are connected to the tracking base unit. The tracker magnetic field modifies the sensor's magnetic field characteristics according to its position in space. The location of the tracker is computed from the relative variations of the sensor's intensity and its phase magnetic field. A key requirement is the maintenance of a uniform magnetic field, which is altered by the vicinity of magnetic fields from other electronic devices and by nearby ferromagnetic objects.

Magnetic trackers are usually much smaller, lighter, and cheaper than optical trackers and their functionality is similar to that of active optical trackers (Table 17-1). However, the accuracy of existing magnetic tracking systems is less than that of optical tracking systems. Their main advantages are that they are small and do not require a direct line-of-sight, and therefore they are useful in percutaneous procedures. However, they do require careful control of the environment in which they operate, because the nearby presence of ferrous objects and electrical instruments in the operating room can influence their measurements.

Tracking: Technical Issues.

The best way to visualize a tracking system is as a 3D measurement instrument, also known as a *coordinate measuring machine*. A 3D measurement instrument provides a stream of spatial location measurements in a given range, accuracy, and rate (frequency). It measures the *location* of an object (a tracker) with respect to a fixed coordinate frame centered at the position sensor's origin. The location of an object in space, its position and orientation, is uniquely determined by six parameters: three translational (vertical, horizontal, and depth) and three rotational (roll, yaw, and pitch).

Tracking systems measure the position of markers in a predefined volume in space, called the *tracking work volume*. Its shape is usually simple, such as a sphere, pyramid, or cube, depending on the type of position sensor technology used. The distance between the position sensor and the tracking work volume center is fixed.

Accuracy is defined as the measure of an instrument's capability to approach a true or absolute value. Accuracy is a function

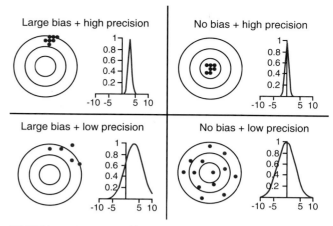

FIGURE 17-4 Accuracy and bias. Accuracy is a combination of precision and bias. High accuracy requires no bias and high precision (top right). The concentric circles represent the distance from the true value (the common center of the circles); dots represent actual measurements. (Image property of authors.)

of both *bias* and *precision* (Fig. 17-4). Bias is a measure of how closely the mean value in a series of replicated measurements approaches the true value. Precision is a measure of how closely the values within a series of replicated measurements agree with each other. It has no units and indicates the relative degree of repeatability. *Repeatability* is a measure of *resolution* and *stability*. Resolution is the smallest discernible difference between two measurements. Stability refers to making identical measurements at a steady state and over a sufficiently long period. *Frequency* is the number of overall measurements per second. Static accuracy refers to measurements obtained when the trackers are at rest, while dynamic accuracy refers to measurements obtained as the trackers move.

The factors influencing tracking accuracy are as follows:

- *Position sensor accuracy:* For optical tracking, the number of cameras, the distance between them, and their resolution. For magnetic tracking, the intensity of the magnetic field and the resolution of the magnetic sensor.
- *Marker accuracy:* For optical tracking, the type of LEDs or sphere size and reflectance. For magnetic tracking, the strength of the coil magnetic field.
- *Tracker accuracy:* Depends on the marker accuracy, number of markers, their configuration, and the distance between them.
- *Tracking system accuracy:* Depends on all of the above, and on the relative position and orientation of the position sensor with respect to the trackers.

It should be noted that accuracy is not uniform within the tracking work volume. It is usually highest at the center, with decay toward the boundaries of the tracking work volume. Therefore, the position sensor should always be placed as close as possible to the center of the expected operating volume. It is often useful to distinguish between position and orientation accuracy. Statistics on accuracy include average, minimum, maximum, and root-mean-square (RMS) error. Table 17-2 summarizes the typical characteristics of current tracking systems.

Tool and Bone Tracking.

Tool and bone tracking are achieved by rigidly attaching trackers to them with mounting hardware

TABLE 17-2	**Typical Characteristics of Commercial Tracking Systems**		
	Optical		
Characteristic	Active	Passive	Magnetic
Work volume	Sphere 1-m³ diameter	Sphere 1-m³ diameter	Cube 0.5 × 0.5 × 0.5 m³
Distance from center	2.25 m	1 m	0.55 m
Accuracy (root-mean-square)	0.1–0.35 mm	0.35 mm	1–2 mm 0.8–1.7 degrees
Frequency	60–450 Hz	60–250 Hz	20–45 Hz
Interferences	Line-of-sight	Line-of-sight	Ferrous objects Magnetic fields
Number of tools	3	6	3

(Fig. 17-5). To track a surgical tool, a tracker can be added to it or the tool can be custom designed, with markers integrated within the tool. To track the C-arm, a ring with several dozen markers is attached to its image intensifier. It is very important that the trackers do not move with respect to the tracked body during surgery, because relative movement cannot be detected and measured and will increase system error.

Registration

Registration is the process of establishing a common reference frame between objects and images. It is a prerequisite for creating a reliable image of the intraoperative situation, accurately showing the relative locations of the anatomy and the surgical tools of interest with respect to the preoperative and/or intraoperative images.[13] Registration is achieved by *transformations* between the objects' *coordinate frames* at all times.

A coordinate frame serves as a reference within which the spatial locations (position and orientation) of objects can be described. Each object of interest has its own coordinate frame. The relative location of objects is described by a transformation T_B^A, describing the location of B's coordinate frame with respect to A. A transformation is a matrix describing the relationship between the three rotational and three translational parameters of the objects. The transformation is *static* (constant) when the relative locations of A and B do not change or *dynamic* $T_B^A(t)$ (a function of time t) when one or both of the objects move. The relative locations of objects are obtained by *chaining* (composing) transformations. Thus, the location of C with respect to A is obtained from the location of B with respect to A and the location of C with respect to B,

$$T_C^A = T_B^A \bullet T_C^B$$

The goal is to compute the location of the surgical tools with respect to the displayed images $T_{tool}^{display}(t)$, as illustrated in Figure 17-6. This registration involves four types of transformations: (1) tracker transformations, (2) tool transformations, (3) image transformations, and (4) display transformations.

1. *Tracking transformations*: Tracking transformations $T_{tracker}^{sensor}(t)$ indicate the location of each tracker with respect to the position sensor coordinate system. They are provided in real time by the tracking system and can be static or dynamic,

depending on whether the objects attached to the tracker move or do not move. The relative location of one tracker with respect to the other is obtained by chaining their transformations:

$$T_{tracker1}^{tracker2}(t) = T_{sensor}^{tracker1}(t) \bullet T_{tracker2}^{sensor}(t)$$

where $T_{sensor}^{tracker1}(t) = [T_{tracker1}^{sensor}(t)]^{-1}$ is the inverse transformation.

2. *Tool transformations*: Tool transformations $T_{tool}^{t\_tracker}$ indicate the location of the tool coordinate frame with respect to the tracker. Because the tracker is rigidly attached to the tool, the transformations are static. They are provided at shipping time when the tracker and the tool come from the same manufacturer (i.e., precalibrated tools). Alternatively, they are computed shortly before surgery with a *tool calibration* procedure, which typically consists of attaching the tool to a tracked calibration object and computing with custom calibration software the transformation and the tool's geometric features, such as its main axis and tip position.

3. *Image transformations*: Image transformations T_{images}^{sensor} indicate the location of the images with respect to the position sensor. There are two types of transformations, T_{CT}^{sensor} and $(T_{x-ray}^{sensor})_i$, depending on the type of images used: one preoperative CT or several intraoperative fluoroscopic radiography images. The transformation between the position sensor and the CT image T_{CT}^{sensor} is static and unknown and must be computed with a *CT registration procedure*. The transformation between the position sensor and fluoroscopic radiography images $(T_{x-ray}^{sensor})_i$, where i indicates each C-arm viewpoint, is computed from the transformation $(T_{i\_tracker}^{sensor})_i$ of the ring tracker attached to the C-arm image intensifier transformation and $(T_{x-ray}^{t\_tracker})_i$ the C-arm internal imaging transformation:

$$(T_{x-ray}^{sensor})_i = (T_{i\_tracker}^{sensor}) \bullet (T_{x-ray}^{t\_tracker})$$

In older fluoroscopic units, this internal transformation is orientation dependent and thus must be computed for each C-arm viewpoint i.[31]

4. *Display transformations*: Display transformations $T_{CT}^{display}$ and $(T_{x-ray}^{display})_i$ indicate the location of the CT and fluoroscopic radiography images with respect to the display shown to the surgeon, respectively. The transformations are determined by the viewpoint shown to the surgeon. Note that the trans-

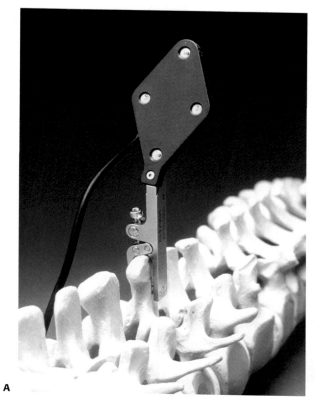

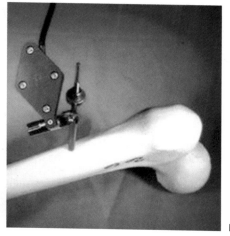

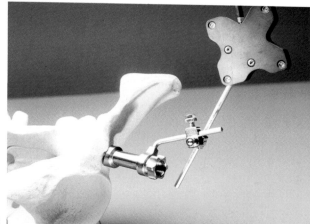

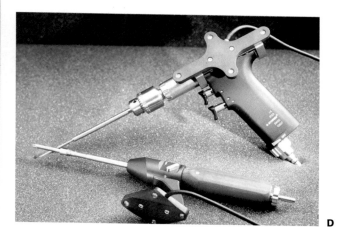

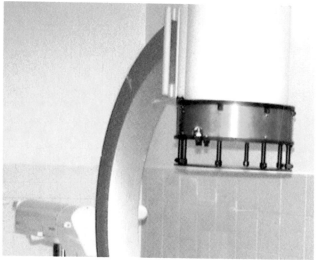

FIGURE 17-5 Trackers and mounting hardware. **A.** Bone clamp attached to spinous process. **B.** Bone screw attached to femur. **C.** Bone screw and extender attached to pelvis. **D.** Trackers on surgical drill and screwdriver. **E.** Ring tracker on C-arm image intensifier. (Photographs **A,B,D** courtesy of Traxtal Technologies, Toronto, Canada; **C,** courtesy of MedVision, Unna, Germany; **E,** property of authors.)

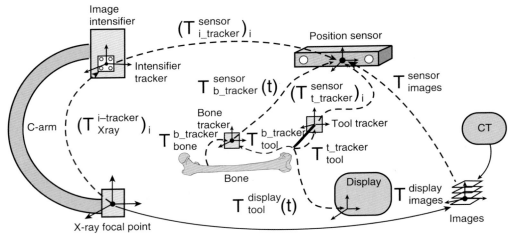

FIGURE 17-6 Coordinate frames and transformations between objects. The goal is to compute the location of the surgical tools with respect to the displayed images $T_{tool}^{display}$. (Image property of authors.)

formation between the bone and the tracker $T_{bone}^{b\_tracker}$ is unknown and cannot be computed, because the exact location of the tracker mounting jig with respect to the bone is not known. Instead, the relative location of the tool with respect to the tracker is used:

$$T_{tool}^{b\_tracker}(t) = T_{sensor}^{b\_tracker}(t) \cdot T_{t\_tracker}^{sensor}(t) \cdot T_{tool}^{t\_tracker}$$

In effect, the bone tracker becomes the reference coordinate frame and therefore is also called the *dynamic reference frame*.

The registration between the tool coordinate frame and the display coordinate frame $T_{tool}^{display}(t)$ is computed by chaining the transformations:

$$T_{tool}^{display}(t) = T_{image}^{display} \cdot T_{sensor}^{image} \cdot T_{t\_tracker}^{sensor} \cdot T_{tool}^{t\_tracker}$$

For fluoroscopic radiography images, there is one transformation $(T_{x\text{-}ray}^{sensor})_i$ and $(T_{tool}^{display})_i(t)$ for every C-arm viewpoint i.

Registration Accuracy. The accuracy of the registration depends on the accuracy of each transformation and on the cumulative effect of transformation chaining. Because the transformation includes rotation, the translational error is amplified as the distance from the reference frame increases (Fig. 17-7).

Tracking transformation accuracy depends on the accuracy of the tracking system and on the location of the tracker with respect to the center of the position sensor working volume. Tool transformation accuracy depends on the accuracy of the tool calibration procedure and on the relative location of the tracker with respect to the tool tip. Image transformation accuracy depends on the accuracy of the imaging modality used and on the tracking system's accuracy. For CT images, it depends on the resolution (slice spacing and pixel size) of the CT scan and on the accuracy of the CT registration procedure. For fluoroscopic radiography images, it depends on the C-arm calibration and on distortion correction procedures. Display transformation accuracy is very high, as it only involves numerical computations.

Note that any accidental shift in the location of the bone tracker with respect to the bone will introduce an error in the registration. It is therefore essential that the bone tracker remain rigidly secured to the bone at all times during navigation.

Visualization

Visualization creates updated images that show the location of moving objects with respect to the anatomy. The navigation

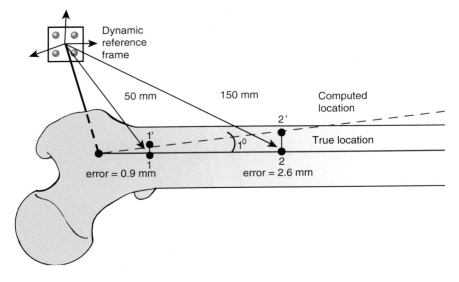

FIGURE 17-7 Influence of the angular error on the translational offset. A dynamic reference frame is attached to the proximal femur. With an angular transformation error of only 1 degree, a nearby target (**1**) 50 mm from the origin of the bone coordinate frame will be offset by 0.9 mm (**1'**), which is acceptable in most situations. However, a farther target (**2**) 150 mm away will be offset by 2.6 mm (**2'**), which may not be acceptable. (Image property of authors.)

images are created by merging the preoperative and intraoperative images with the tools and bone location information. The navigation images can be augmented with relevant procedure-dependent data, such as anteversion angle and distance from a predefined safe zone.

The type of navigation images created depends on the preoperative and intraoperative images that are used, on the surgical tools, and on the surgical procedure. In fluoroscopic-based navigation systems, the navigation images consist of fluoroscopic radiography images from the C-arm typically used in conventional surgical procedure poses (anterior-posterior, lateral, oblique) with the surgical tool silhouette at its present location superimposed onto them. For example, when the tool is a long cylinder (e.g., drill, pointer, or screwdriver), the tool's location and its prolongation are displayed in two different colors, to indicate what would be the tool's location if the current direction were followed. The number of images, tool silhouette, and additional navigation information are procedure dependent.

In CT-based navigation systems, the navigation images typically consist of sagittal, coronal, and transverse CT cross sections, and a spatial view with the preoperative plan (e.g., fixation screws, fixation plate at their desired location), with the surgical tool's silhouette at its current location superimposed onto them. Typically, the tool tip corresponds to the crosshair location in the CT cross sections.

Visualization software usually provides the surgeon with various image processing, viewpoint selection, and information display features such as contrast enhancement, viewpoint rotation and translation, window selection, and tool silhouette thickness and color control.

Validation

Validation is the task of verifying that the images and data used for intraoperative navigation closely correspond to the clinical situation. It is essential to verify and quantify the correlation; otherwise the data can mislead the surgeon and yield unwanted results. Validation is an integral part of the navigation surgical protocol. It is performed both before the surgery starts and at key points during the surgery.

There are three main types of verification:

1. *Tool calibration verification*: Verifies that the tool's geometric information is accurate. Sources of inaccuracy include deformations in the tool as a result of high-temperature sterilization, bending, wear and tear, tracker relative motion, and marker drift.
2. *Dynamic reference frame verification*: Verifies that the bone tracker has not moved with respect to the bone to which it is attached.
3. *Registration accuracy verification*: Verifies that the tool, implant, and bone fragment locations are indeed where they are shown in the navigation images. Over time, registration accuracy depends on variations in the tool's calibration accuracy; on the dynamic reference frame's relative location with respect to the bone to which it is attached; on the tracking system's drift over time; and on the accumulation of small computational numerical errors.

The validation procedure depends on the type of surgery, the navigated surgical tools, and the images used. Tool calibration verification usually consists of verifying with a calibration jig that the tool tip is at its computed location. Dynamic reference frame and registration accuracy verification usually consist of verifying that the tracked bones and tools are indeed where the navigated images indicate. This is done by acquiring one or more fluoroscopic radiography images and comparing them with the navigation images. Alternatively, it is done by touching with the tip of a surgical tool the known anatomic landmarks and verifying that the tool tip appears close to the landmark in the navigated image. Registration accuracy is quantified by measuring the drift between the actual and the computed location of tools and anatomic landmarks. When registration accuracy is inadequate, the surgeon must repeat the registration process.

NAVIGATION SYSTEMS

There are currently two types of navigation systems for CAS in skeletal trauma: fluoroscopy-based and CT-based navigation systems.

Fluoroscopy-Based Systems

Fluoroscopy-based systems create navigation images by superimposing the surgical tool silhouette onto conventional fluoroscopic images and updating its location in real time, thereby creating the impression of continuous fluoroscopy without the ensuing radiation. The resulting effect is called *virtual fluoroscopy*. Fluoroscopy-based systems are thus closest to the current practice of conventional fluoroscopy because the navigation images are in close proximity to the familiar fluoroscopic images, with the advantage being that only a dozen fluoroscopic radiography images are used, instead of tens or even hundreds.

There are two types of fluoroscopy-based navigation systems: systems that use conventional C-arm fluoroscopy and those that use new 3D fluoroscopy, such as the Siemens Iso-C 3D C-arm. Virtually any C-arm can be used, provided that the images are corrected for geometric distortion and the C-arm imaging properties are calibrated. The correction is usually done with an online C-arm calibration procedure that relies on imaged patterns of metallic spheres mounted on the C-arm ring tracker (the spheres appear as a grid of black circles in the images). Newer conventional and 3D C-arms do not require calibration.

Conventional C-Arm Fluoroscopy

The surgical protocol is as follows: shortly before surgery, the rolling cart with the display, computer unit, and tracking base unit is positioned in the operating room so that the display can be easily seen by the surgeon. The position sensor is positioned so that it does not get in the way and its working volume is roughly at the center of where the surgical actions will take place. Next, the ring tracker is mounted on the C-arm's image intensifier and covered with a transparent plastic for sterility. The patient is then brought into the operating room and surgical preparations proceed as usual. Next, the surgeon validates the tool calibration and installs the dynamic reference frame with tracker mounting hardware. Touching known anatomic landmarks with the tip of a surgical tool and verifying that the tool tip appears close to the landmark in the navigated image validates the registration. Once registration validation is successful, the navigated surgery begins. At key points during surgery, such as before drilling a pilot hole or inserting a fixation screw, one or more validation fluoroscopic radiography images can be taken to verify that the navigated images correspond to the actual situation. The navigation procedure can be repeated with other tools and implants. At any time during the procedure, the navigation system can be stopped and the procedure can continue in a conventional manner.

Three-Dimensional Fluoroscopy

Three-dimensional fluoroscopy is a new imaging modality that allows for the acquisition of CT-like images during surgery by taking about 100 fluoroscopic radiography images at 1-degree intervals with a motorized isocentric C-arm. It can also be used as a conventional C-arm, with the added advantage that CT and fluoroscopic radiography images acquired with it are already registered. Although these images are not of as high a quality as those obtained with a preoperative CT, and can be used only to image limbs, the radiation dose is about half of the dose of a regular CT and accurately reflects the actual intraoperative situation. The navigation images consist of both CT images and fluoroscopic radiography images. The advantages are that complex fractures can be better visualized and that CT images can be taken before and after reduction. In addition, CT images present an entrée for better intraoperative planning and thus might advantageously blur the distinction between preoperative and intraoperative planning. The surgical protocol is very similar to that of conventional fluoroscopy, with the additional step of acquiring the intraoperative CT images during surgery when necessary.[9,12] Figure 17-8 shows an example of navigation with 3D fluoroscopy.

Computed Tomography–Based Systems

CT-based systems create navigation images by superimposing the surgical tool silhouette onto preoperative CT cross-sectional and spatial images and updating its location in real time. This type of navigation is only feasible when a CT data set is available.

The surgical protocol is as follows: any time between a few hours to a day before surgery, a CT scan is acquired and transferred to the computer, within which the planning will be performed by the surgeon. With the help of preoperative planning and model construction software, the surgeon visualizes the clinical situation, takes measurements, and plans the target location of implants and fixation screws for navigation. The plan is then saved for use during surgery. Shortly before surgery, the rolling cart with the display, computer unit, and tracking base unit is positioned in the operating room so that the surgeon can easily see the display. The position sensor is positioned so that it does not get in the way and its working area is roughly placed at the center of where the surgical actions will take place. The preoperative plan is loaded into the computer unit. The patient is then brought into the operating room and surgical preparations proceed as usual. Next, the surgeon validates the tool calibration and installs the dynamic reference frame with tracker mounting hardware. Prior to the beginning of surgery, the preoperative CT is registered to the actual intraoperative anatomic site with a *CT registration procedure*. Touching known anatomic landmarks with the tip of a surgical tool and verifying that the tool tip appears close to the landmark in the navigated image validate the registration. Once registration validation is successful, the navigated surgery begins. At key points during surgery, such as before drilling a pilot hole or inserting a fixation screw, one or more validation fluoroscopic radiography images are taken to verify that the navigated images correspond to the actual situation. The navigation procedure can be repeated with other tools and implants. At any time during the procedure, the navigation system can be stopped and the procedure can continue in a conventional manner. Figure 17-9 shows images of a typical CT-based navigation system.[22,23]

A key step in the protocol is the CT registration procedure. The relationship between the CT and the intraoperative situation is established by automatically matching a set of points on the surface of the bone region to the corresponding points on the CT surface model. The intraoperative point set is obtained by touching the surface of the bone region of interest with a precalibrated tracked pointer and recording the location of a few dozen of these points by pressing on a foot pedal. The point set is then matched to a corresponding point set, automatically extracted from the CT surface model of the same bone region. The points must be a representative sample of the bone surface; that is, they must be as far apart as is possible and cover the entire region of interest.

Comparison of Fluoroscopy- and Computed Tomography–Based Systems

Table 17-3 summarizes the advantages and disadvantages of navigation systems. Only CT-based systems allow for preoperative planning. Spatial visualization is only available with a CT data set and thus is only available in CT-based and 3D fluoroscopy–based systems. No additional registration procedure is necessary for intraoperative imaging, as the position sensor provides a common reference frame for trackers and images. All navigation systems require additional setup procedures, which is a drawback compared with conventional practice. CT-based systems are not suitable for fracture reduction, as there is no way to determine bone fragment locations during and after reduction. The 3D fluoroscopy–based systems can be used before and after, but not during, reduction, provided that two before

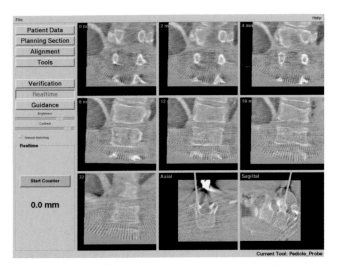

FIGURE 17-8 Pedicle screw insertion with three-dimensional fluoroscopy. Screen view of three-dimensional fluoroscopy navigation during pedicle screw insertion in a fractured thoracic vertebra with the SireMobil Iso-C 3D (Siemens Medical Solutions, Erlangen, Germany). (Image courtesy of Prof. F. Gebhard.)

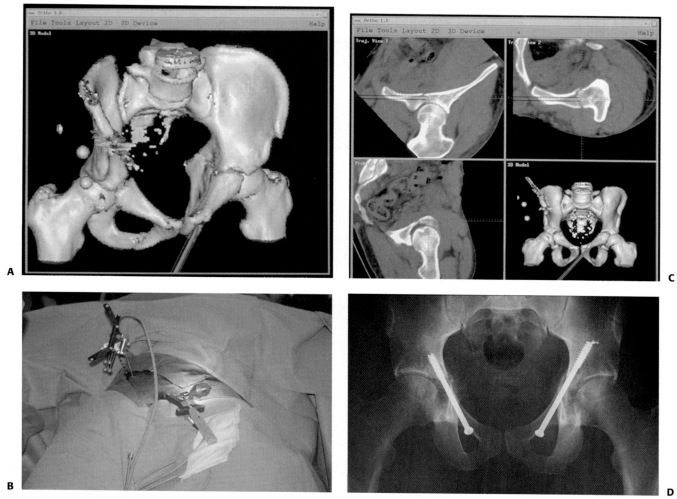

FIGURE 17-9 Retrograde anterior column screw. **A.** Three-dimensional model of the patient's pelvis built on the computer-guided surgery workstation (StealthStation; Sofamor-Danek, Memphis, TN). The position of a virtual drill guide for placement of a retrograde anterior column screw has been added to the virtual image. **B.** Intraoperative photograph taken during placement of the right retrograde anterior column screw (view from the foot of the bed). The reference frame attached to the external fixator is visible at the top left. Also visible are the navigated drill guide, chuck, and guidewire. **C.** The two top images show a preoperative plan for placement of the left-sided retrograde anterior column screw. Two customized orthogonal planes relative to the drilling path are depicted, with a planned trajectory diameter of 7.0 mm. There is a small safe zone available between the planned position of the implant and the pelvic brim, as well as the articular surface of the acetabulum. The implant path is perpendicular to the fracture line, allowing lag screw reduction and fracture fixation. **D.** Anteroposterior pelvis image at 6 weeks postfixation shows accurate implant placement and early fracture healing without displacement. (Images courtesy of Dr. D. Kahler.)

and after images are acquired. In fluoroscopy-based systems, reduction navigation is feasible when the bone fragments have trackers attached to them and new images are acquired at key points during reduction. Currently, CT-based navigation requires the surgeon to touch the surface of the bone; therefore, it cannot be used for percutaneous procedures. In terms of radiation, the best option for the patient and the surgeon is fluoroscopy-based navigation. The indications for fluoroscopy-based systems present the most options, while 3D fluoroscopy–based and CT-based systems are best used with complex situations requiring spatial visualization. Currently, CT-based systems are mostly used for pelvic fracture fixation, while fluoroscopy-based systems are used for intramedullary nailing and fixation screw insertion.

SURGICAL TECHNIQUES

Clinical Considerations

The concept of combining computer-aided procedures in the treatment of trauma patients should take into account available innovative technologies together with the clinical situation, as part of the decision-making process. The main goals of CAS are minimal invasiveness and maximal accuracy in surgical procedures. Recent experience has shown that, if used appropriately, this combination has added value. While the first generation of CAS uses computerized technology for current surgical concepts, it is clear that in the future the surgeon will be able to develop new ways of approaching surgical conditions.

There is no doubt that the timing and duration of procedures

TABLE 17-3 Comparison between the Conventional Technique and Fluoroscopy-Based and Computed Tomography (CT)-Based Navigation Systems

Characteristics	No Computerized Navigation	Fluoroscopy–Based		CT–Based
		Conventional Technique	Three-dimensional Fluoroscopy	
Preoperative planning	No (−)	No (−)	No (−)	Yes (+)
Three-dimensional views	No (−)	No (−)	Yes (+)	Yes (+)
Registration	No (+)	No (+)	No (+)	Yes (−)
Additional operating room setup	None (+)	Yes (−)	Yes (−)	Yes (−)
Reduction	Yes (+)	Yes (+)	Limited (−)	No (−)
Percutaneous	Yes (+)	Yes (+)	Yes (+)	No (−)
Radiation to surgeon	Yes (−)	Very limited (+)	Very limited (+)	None (+)
Radiation to patient	Yes (−)	Very limited (+)	Yes (−)	Yes (−)
Indications	Current practice	Wide range of procedures	Complex anatomy	CT available; partially open
Current use	All of trauma	Intramedullary nailing; screw fixation	Just beginning	Pedicle screw insertion

+, An advantage; −, a disadvantage.

are of major concern in trauma management. Damage control principles are considered the leading guidelines in the treatment of the severely injured patient. Alternatively, isolated skeletal trauma may be treated in a semielective fashion. Adding computer-assisted procedures to the trauma armamentarium is definitely influenced by, and affects, time-related factors. This is relevant to all stages of trauma patients' treatment, beginning with the preplanning stage and up to the end of the surgery itself.

Currently, most surgeons believe that CAS is a time-consuming and cumbersome procedure. The system's set-up time and registration process prolong the preparation phase and might not suit acute trauma management considerations. Moreover, experienced surgeons believe that most surgical tasks can be easily, sufficiently, and accurately carried out, without the use of computer-related technologies. This conservative approach is well known in medical history, whenever a new technology emerges. For example, many years elapsed from the introduction of laparoscopic procedures until surgeons were ready to routinely use them.

Although computer-aided technology has been available for several years, it appears that we are still in the learning phase for CAS systems, and therefore indications for their use are still being selected. Further assimilation of these promising technologies requires them to become easier to use (i.e., more user friendly). The set-up time for the computerized system will definitely be reduced in the modern surgical suite, when it is built directly into the operating theatre environment, as presently available in several pioneering institutions. Furthermore, the execution of some surgical tasks is faster and more accurate with CAS equipment and will, in the future, allow for procedures that are currently considered almost unfeasible. For example, the placement of a sacroiliac screw in the fixation of pelvic and acetabular fractures becomes a fast and accurate procedure with minimal radiation by using a navigation system.[7,8,22]

An additional example is retrograde percutaneous posterior column screw placement, which previously had been considered an almost impossible task to perform and now is an available option with computer assistance.[32,41] The solutions may be categorized into "enablers" and "improvers." While enablers refer to procedures that are not possible without CAS (i.e., the introduction of a new concept or ability rather than a translation of a current technique into CAS), improvers mainly yield improved accuracy and not a new concept. A simple but extremely important example of improvement is the significant reduction in radiation exposure that can be achieved with CAS. As more orthopaedic procedures are found to be suitable for CAS applications and as younger surgeons, born into the era of information technologies, enter the operating theatre, the adoption of CAS will become more natural and routine in the operating rooms.

The simple indications for using CAOS-ST systems in trauma care are percutaneous surgical procedures in which added imaging can provide essential information that will contribute to reducing invasiveness and increasing accuracy.[24,29] Clearly, the fixation of nondisplaced fractures is most suitably carried out with navigation systems, although often the indication for internal fixation is questionable. Alternatively, because available systems can only follow one or two tracked bony fragments, they are not suitable for treating displaced multiple fragment fractures such as comminuted articular fractures, where careful anatomic reduction is required.

In general, navigation systems function better in static or stable situations. For example, using a fracture reduction table or an external fixator eliminates movement between fragments and creates a temporary situation in which there is little or no movement at the fracture site. Moreover, it has been shown that in such "stable" situations, the reference frame can be attached to the fracture table, avoiding additional harm to the patient while maintaining acceptable accuracy.[19] Following fracture reduction, a guidewire or fixation tool can be inserted using the navigation system according to specific clinical guidelines.

Required accuracy is a key factor for deciding whether to use a CAOS-ST system. For example, the accuracy needed for pedicular screw insertion is by far greater than that needed for hip fracture fixation with cannulated screws. Accuracy is directly influenced by the cost of inaccuracy (e.g., the cost of inaccuracy in spinal surgery is much greater than in intramedullary nailing).

Computerized navigation has been shown to increase placement accuracy and reduce variability compared with manual placement. In a recent study, the accuracy of cannulated screw placement in hip fracture fixation was evaluated.[29] After verifying stable reduction on a fracture table, the reference tracker was attached to the anterior superior iliac crest. The reference frame was not attached to the affected bone so as to improve working convenience during the procedure and minimize morbidity. It was found that the accuracy of the procedure was much better than that of nonnavigated procedures. The navigation system enabled the surgeon to place screws with optimal alignment including configuration, parallelism, and scattering. This experience demonstrates that stable reduction creates a stable situation for navigation systems and that the reference tracked frame may be fixed, on such occasions, to an adjacent bone as well as to an external fixator or to the operating table, as mentioned earlier.[19]

Preparation for Surgery

Before surgery, the decision as to whether the procedure is suitable for CAOS-ST is determined by the surgeon's knowledge and capabilities. In most trauma cases, fluoroscopy-based navigation (2D or 3D) is the method of choice.

It is very important to plan and prepare the operating room to create a surgeon-friendly environment and to enable proper tracking without interference (Fig. 17-10). Adding CAOS-ST equipment (computer, monitor, position sensor, and trackers) to an already crowded room requires careful planning. The computer screen should be positioned so that the surgeon can see it without any effort, because, as in arthroscopic procedures, most of the time the surgeon will watch the screen rather than the operative site. Easy access to the computer's control panel is also important and is usually realized with a sterile touch screen. When using optical tracking, maintaining an unobstructed line-of-sight between the position sensor and the trackers is very important. Thus, the location of the position sensor with respect to the surgeon, nurses, and patient must be carefully examined.

Inherent to the implementation of a new technique is the learning curve. In CAS, the learning curve affects all members of the surgical team. It affects surgeons performing the operation, nurses having to cope with new tools, anesthetists who need to adjust the anesthesia time to the expected operation time, and x-ray technicians who sometimes need to operate fluoroscopy-based navigation. The entire team should be aware that there is a "new partner" in the operating theater (i.e., the computer), and sometimes a computer technician will also need to be part of the team.

During the initial phase, the minimal required free field of vision is determined by the location of the ring tracker attached to the C-arm, the reference frame tracker attached to the pa-

tient's anatomy, and by the optical camera. During the navigation phase, tracked surgical instruments replace the ring tracker and the tracking space changes accordingly. Continuous tracking of the patient's anatomy and of the surgical instrument is required. Verification and validation are extremely important at every stage, to achieve optimal accuracy. Tracking the surgical instrument is more simple and precise, whereas tracking anatomy, especially in trauma surgery, is more problematic, such as in those cases where two fragments are simultaneously tracked, as in the fracture reduction process.

Registration and tracking of the patient's anatomy are usually the main cause of inaccuracy. The first obstacle is attaching the rigid frame to the patient. The problem of inserting a stable screw into the bone fragment is well known from the use of external fixation. Screw or pin grip depends on their design and on bone quality. For each procedure, the location needs to be selected according to local morbidity (soft tissue access and crucial anatomic structures), convenience during the procedure (line-of-sight and free surgical site), and stability of anatomic frame fixation. The stability of the screw holding the anatomically referenced tracked frames depends on bone quality and soft tissue interference. Subcutaneous locations such as the iliac crest or the medial aspect of the tibia are preferable. The site of frame fixation should also take into account the surgical task (e.g., avoiding the medullary canal in long bone fracture reduction).

Newly designed frames contain more than one screw as well as several soft tissue adaptors and are able to detach from the frame during the nonnavigational steps of the procedure. Improvement of bone tracking technology, as well as the ability to track more than one or two large bone fragments, will significantly enhance the surgeon's surgical performance in the treatment of fractures.

Basic Procedures under Navigation

The clinical situations in which computerized navigation is recommended are now presented. For each clinical application, both the rationale and the contribution of these systems will be discussed. The aim of this section is to expose the reader to the first generations of computerized navigation systems. The specific indication for each surgical procedure is beyond the scope of this discussion. All the surgical procedures discussed are based on optical infrared tracking.

When using fluoroscopy-based navigation, the first step is to mount the ring tracker on the C-arm and drape it for sterility. Next, a reference frame (either one or two) is attached to the patient's anatomy and several essential fluoroscopic images are acquired—typically, between one and four for 2D navigation or computerized controlled imaging for 3D navigation using Iso-C technology. The optimal images are stored in the computer and activated during the navigation process. It should be noted, that for all of the clinical examples to be discussed, the preliminary fluoroscopic views can be taken while the operating team stands at a distance of 2 m or more from the radiation source, thus almost eliminating the team's radiation exposure.

The next stage relates to the activation of the designated surgical tool (i.e., wires, awls, drill-bits, etc.), which is to be attached to a tracker, commonly referred to as the *instrument tracker*. The contour of the instrument in its current location is displayed on the previously activated fluoroscopic images,

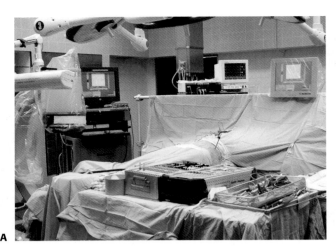

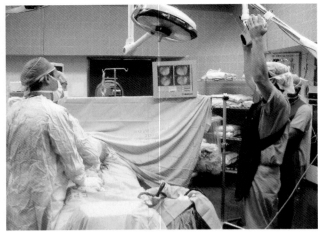

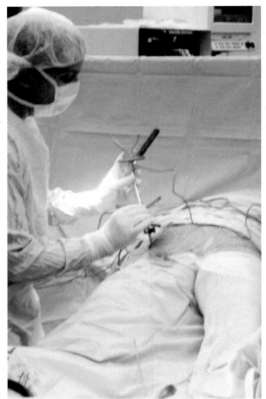

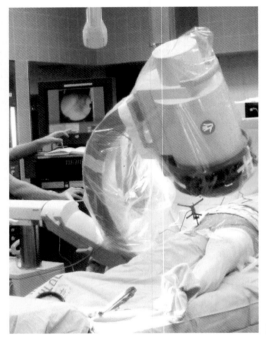

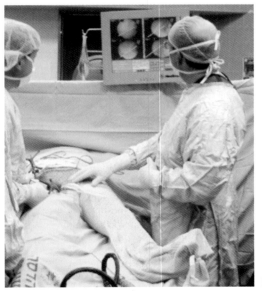

FIGURE 17-10 Operating room setup. **A.** View of the operating room showing locations of the computer unit, position sensor, and bone-mounted reference frame. **B.** Reorientation of the position sensor during surgery. **C.** Surgical tool calibration. **D.** Acquisition of fluoroscopic images. **E.** Navigation with fluoroscopy-based system. (Images property of authors.)

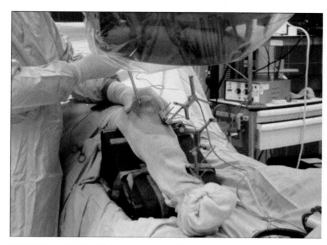

FIGURE 17-11 Tibial intramedullary nailing using fracture reduction software with two frames attached to the two bone fragments. (Image property of authors.)

thereby creating the effect of virtual fluoroscopy. Similar concepts may be used for tracking fracture reduction—in this case, instead of following the relationship between the tracked instrument and the tracked bone, we track the relationship between the two tracked bone fragments (Fig. 17-11).

Currently available procedures are as follows:

- Trajectory navigation—drill guide applications (hip and pelvic fractures)
- Fracture reduction
- Intra-articular fracture fixation
- Novel uses of navigation: localization of bone lesions or removal of surgical hardware and shrapnel

Trajectory Navigation—Drill Guide Applications (Hip and Pelvic Fractures)

Insertion of straight surgical fixation implants such as nails and screws is a common task in orthopaedic traumatology. This procedure can often be performed percutaneously and thereby fit the CAS philosophy of minimal invasiveness with high accuracy. Navigated 2D fluoroscopy provides a natural computerized enhancement for this surgical application. Thus, the most common current indication for the use of CAOS-ST systems is the insertion of cannulated screws. This surgical procedure requires high accuracy and unusually large radiation exposure for the surgeon and for the patient. Both issues can be successfully addressed with fluoroscopy-based navigation.

Percutaneous pelvic and acetabulum fractures and internal fixation of slipped capital femoral epiphysis are procedures that can greatly benefit from computerized navigation. The use of computerized navigation turns the procedure into a simple task to perform, while using minimal radiation.[24] Internal fixation of intracapsular fractures of the femoral neck is considered straightforward, although accurate performance requires high proficiency on the one hand and large exposure to radiation on the other. Recently, a prospective comparison between patients who underwent internal fixation of intracapsular fracture of the femoral neck by means of cannulated screws, with and without the assistance of a navigation system, was performed.[29] This study revealed that computerized navigation increased the accuracy of screw placements in all measured parameters. Having

acquired proficiency with the computerized system, the surgeon is ready to move on to the next level, which includes percutaneous fixation of pelvic and acetabular fractures.

Internal pelvic fracture fixation is a challenging task for the orthopaedic trauma surgeon. The pelvis is a complex 3D structure that contains important anatomic structures in a confined environment. Therefore, surgical fixation of displaced traumatic fractures should be meticulously performed under strict visual control, because the "safe zones" are narrow. In many cases, closed reduction and percutaneous fixation is feasible and provides enough stability to allow for immediate patient mobilization. The conventional image intensifier is most frequently used in percutaneous pelvic fixation. However, it provides only a 2D image and requires multiple images in different projections to determine the correct point of entry and the direction of the screw. Furthermore, the use of conventional fluoroscopy makes the procedure long and tedious and exposes both the patient and the medical team to prolonged radiation.[8,22,23] Fluoroscopy-based navigation systems (2D and 3D) have the potential to significantly reduce radiation exposure and operative time, while allowing the surgeon to achieve maximum accuracy.[8,29,38,46]

The indications for percutaneous pelvic and acetabular surgery are controversial and are not discussed here. At this stage, a selected population with traumatic pelvic and acetabular fractures can be treated percutaneously under three conditions: (i) cases with minimally displaced pelvic and acetabular fractures, (ii) displaced fractures with feasible closed reduction, and (iii) in cases of open pelvic surgery when the insertion of several screws is very challenging and demands the assistance of guiding systems such as fluoroscopy or navigated fluoroscopy following appropriate open reduction.

It is important to note that the percutaneous approach to fracture fixation of the pelvis is still evolving and is undergoing many improvements and developments in which computerized technology may be of great assistance. For example, in preplanning, the use of standard axial CT data to create computer-reconstructed 3D images and/or models may replace the standard radiographic assessment of pelvic and acetabular fractures.[5,11,16,38] Similarly, 3D fluoroscopy technology allows the surgeon to obtain immediate and accurate 3D reconstructions in the operating room. By integrating these images into navigation systems, preplanning becomes easier and more accurate and allows for direct, truly spatial surgical navigation. It also enables the precise evaluation of closed reduction (using a fracture table, external fixator and/or other fixation instruments) before the insertion of the navigated screws.

Surgical Technique. For both acetabular and pelvic surgery, the dynamic reference frame can rigidly be attached to the patient's iliac crest. Several appropriate fluoroscopic images of the pelvis are acquired and saved in the system's computer. No further fluoroscopic imaging is necessary, except for verification fluoroscopy prior to the insertion of the cannulated screw, or in the case of reduced fracture, the crossing of the fracture site.

During surgery, following the activation of the fluoroscopic images, the surgeon can accurately determine the entry point and direction of each screw. At the same time, by means of a virtual trajectory line, the correct length and diameter of the screw can be calculated (Fig. 17-12). After satisfactory virtual alignment and length have been achieved, the conventional

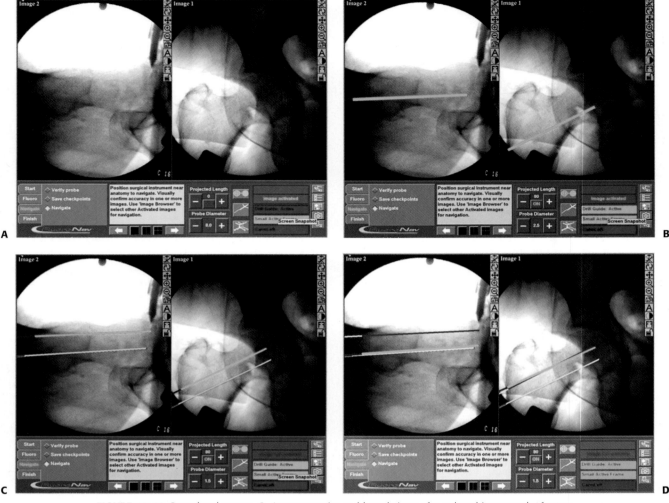

FIGURE 17-12 Cannulated screws. **A.** Anteroposterior and lateral views of a reduced intracapsular fracture of the femoral neck displayed on the computer's screen. **B–D.** Insertion of the three guidewires without additional radiation.   (*continues*)

guidewire pertaining to the cannulated screw system is driven through the drill guide. Before insertion of a self-drilled cannulated screw, the position of the guidewire should be verified by fluoroscopy. When the insertion of several screws in the same area is required, such as in the fixation of fractures or dislocations in the sacroiliac zone, the acquired fluoroscopic views can be used for the insertion of more than one screw (Figs. 17-13 and 17-14).

In pelvic surgery, serious complications might arise from the surgical procedure and intervention, rather than from the initial injury. Therefore, it is only natural that percutaneous minimal surgical approaches are sought, to overcome the difficulties that arise in relation to fractures in the complex anatomy of the pelvis and acetabulum.

Figure 17-9 illustrates the placement of a retrograde anterior column screw with a CT-based navigation system.

Fracture Reduction
Intramedullary nailing is the preferred surgical option in many long bone fracture cases. Although it is a routine procedure, performed by most trauma surgeons, it is not devoid of technical pitfalls and complications. Achieving accurate and successful

results with conventional techniques involves exposure to significant amounts of radiation for both patients and the surgical team.

Fluoroscopy-based navigation can be helpful in closed intramedullary nailing by increasing precision, minimizing soft tissue damage, and significantly decreasing radiation exposure.[14,21,25] Several surgical goals can be achieved by using computerized navigation systems. The insertion of instruments based on real-time information becomes possible and significantly increases the accuracy of nail placement. Determining the exact point of entry of the nail is critical because it is one of the main sources of morbidity in intramedullary nailing as well as a reason for malalignment. As previously discussed, computerized navigation systems help to precisely locate the nail entry point by means of trajectory navigation, thus minimizing soft tissue dissection. This is particularly helpful in special cases such as with obese patients where anatomic landmarks are obscured. Working with several images simultaneously can also decrease unnecessary drill holes, tissue damage, and cartilage perforation, because all targeting is done virtually, before the introduction of the actual instrument. The insertion of locking screws into certain nails can be a potential hazard for neurovas-

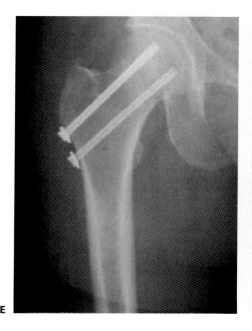

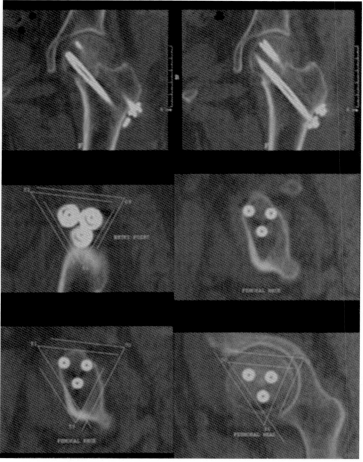

FIGURE 17-12 *(Continued)* **E,F.** Radiograph and CT scan showing the precise scattering of the three screws in a spatial configuration of an inverted triangle. (Images property of authors.)

cular structures.[26,40,43] Additional improvement in nailing techniques is achieved by the facilitation of Poller screw insertion. When precisely placed, better angular correction of metaphyseal fractures is achieved. The most important future contribution of the new generation of navigation technology will be to allow for the tracking and aligning of two fragments, thus enabling fracture reduction without radiation and reduction wire insertion and, more important, its ability to provide the surgeon with information to restore alignment, including length and rotation.[17,26,34] The precision of length measurement may also decrease the rate of complications associated with nailing such as protrusion of the nail or screw ends.

Surgical Technique. The use of a fluoroscopy-based surgical navigation system can be implemented, either for the entire task, at different stages of intramedullary nailing, including the nail's entry point, nail and screw measurements, freehand locking, or placement of auxiliary screws, or for the reduction task. The procedure will be presented according to its different stages. Navigation of the entrance point and the locking procedure is performed by using straight-line trajectory. The reference frame should be attached to the tracked bone fragment, either proximal or distal, depending on the specific task.

1. *Nail entry point:* The actual point of entry is determined by the use of simultaneous virtual fluoroscopic views, these usually being anteroposterior (AP) and lateral views. Before incision, the tracked drill guide is drawn next to the skin. Its position is adjusted by viewing its virtual trajectory superimposed on the activated fluoroscopic images so as to minimize the surgical exposure. The entry point location is established, while moving the tracked drill guide to an optimal position (Fig. 17-15A). No further fluoroscopy is required and a verification fluoroscopic image is taken only after insertion of the guidewire. After this task is performed, a cannulated awl or a larger cannulated drill is inserted, according to the manufacturer's instructions, through this guide, to open the medullary canal.[26]

2. *Freehand locking:* This technique is relatively easy to perform and involves minimal radiation exposure. The bone tracker is fixed closed to the location of the locking screws. Using the "perfect circle" technique, an AP or a lateral of the locking hole, in which the holes almost resemble circles, is acquired. An additional AP or lateral view may be taken to determine the screw length measurement. The tracked drill guide is then drawn toward the locking screw area and is navigated until a circle appears within the hole on the computer screen (Figs. 17-15B–C). This is followed by drilling through the tracked drill guide and inserting the locking screw. Sometimes, such as in the case of the tibial nail, the same AP and lateral views can be used for insertion of two or even three adjacent locking screws.[40,43]

3. *Placement of other screws:* Poller screws are important tools for correcting bone alignment while nailing metaphyseal fractures. Precise placement of these screws can now be performed using a technique similar to that of locking screws.

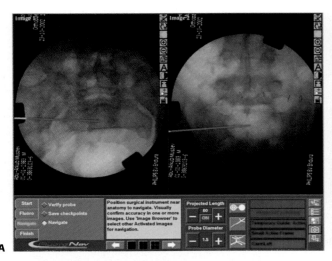
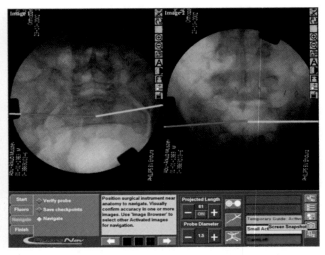

A   **B**

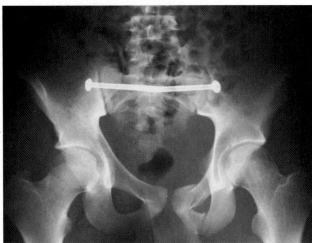

C

FIGURE 17-13 Bilateral sacroiliac screws. **A,B.** Typical intraoperative display of computer screen during bilateral insertion of two sacroiliac screws. The live spatial position of the drill guide is simultaneously presented on two views (inlet and outlet) with a virtual continuation representing the track of the guidewire. **C.** Postoperative verification radiograph showing the accurate real position of the two sacroiliac screws after the navigation process. (Images property of authors.)

Virtual fluoroscopy based on AP and lateral images enables easy and precise positioning of Poller screws. For "miss-a-nail" screws, additional AP and lateral images of the proximal femur are obtained following the insertion of the intramedullary nail. The goal is then to insert the cross-neck screw without interfering with the intramedullary nail. The navigation system enables the surgeon to determine the precise position of the "miss-a-nail" cross-neck screws and to safely navigate through the narrow safe zone[26] (Fig. 17-16).

Fracture Reduction. New software is available for the entire fracture reduction procedure. This became possible because of the ability to simultaneously track two reference frames. The frames are attached to the distal and proximal long bone fragments. Several AP and lateral views are acquired, enabling visualization of the entire bone. Usually, six views (three AP and three lateral) are needed to visualize the proximal fragment, the fracture site, and the distal fragment in two planes. It is possible to virtually define each segment on the computer display and to track each fragment by navigation as already described. The special location of each fragment in relationship to the other enables actual fracture reduction and insertion of the reduction wire. The procedure resembles the fluoroscopic process of fracture reduction surgery with two major advantages: no radiation

and simultaneous two-plane tracking. The ability to track and visualize the entire bone enables the taking of several measurements including length and rotation. Preliminary data indicate that this technology is feasible in the clinical setup and may significantly contribute to the clinical outcome of long bone fracture reduction (Fig. 17-17). Recently, several software packages have been developed that also enable the tracking of implants, particularly fixation plates. Thus, it is possible to track the position of the implant in relationship to the bone. This technique overcomes some of the drawbacks of the first generation of computer navigation systems. In the future, customized tracked instruments based on these principles will further improve and facilitate computer-aided intramedullary nailing.[10,17,26,34,38,47]

Intra-articular Fracture Fixation

Intra-articular fracture fixation presents unique technical difficulties. In many cases, the fracture is comminuted and has complex geometry that is difficult to evaluate on conventional CT slices or fluoroscopic radiography images. Recently introduced 3D intraoperative imaging, such as Iso C-arm imaging, is a useful tool for this visualization. However, it also has limitations, as it can be used only once or twice during surgery because of radiation exposure and because it is a static view. Other difficul-

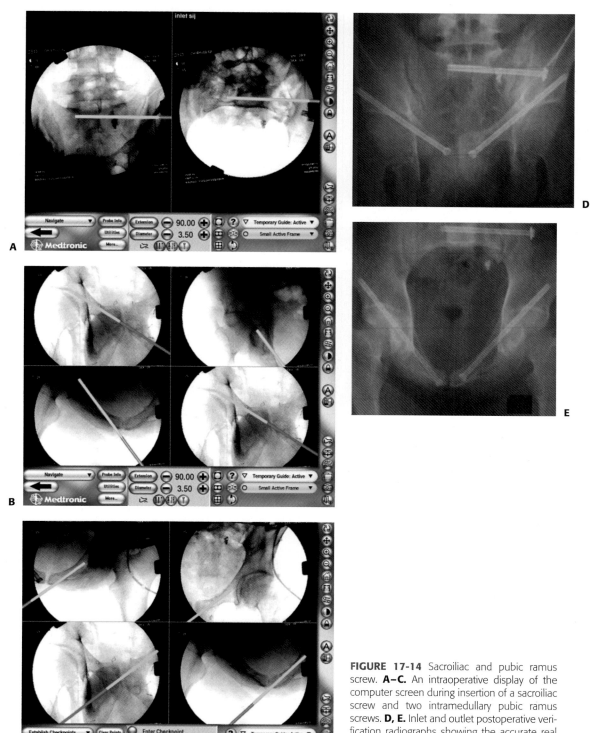

FIGURE 17-14 Sacroiliac and pubic ramus screw. **A–C.** An intraoperative display of the computer screen during insertion of a sacroiliac screw and two intramedullary pubic ramus screws. **D, E.** Inlet and outlet postoperative verification radiographs showing the accurate real placement of the three screws. (Images property of authors.)

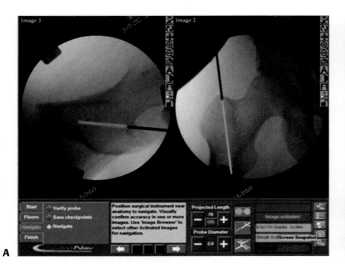

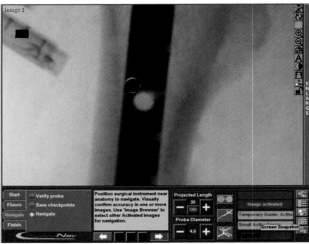

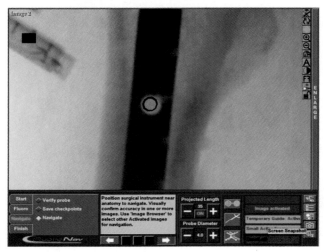

FIGURE 17-15 Intramedullary nailing. **A.** Typical computer display used during antegrade femoral intramedullary nailing consisting of simultaneous anteroposterior and lateral views, where the pink line represents the guide's insertion point at the precise entry point in the piriformis fossa and the green line represents the nail's direction. **B,C.** Proximal locking hole in the retrograde femoral nail. Note the hole as a perfect circle enabling precise aiming of the locking screw. (Images property of authors.)

ties include tracking of small bone fragments and possible fragment motion during fixation.

Intraoperative Control. Intraoperative rather than postoperative confirmation of the reduction and fixation of intra-articular fractures can save patients and surgeons from uncertainty relating to the quality of reduction. Recent developments have yielded new options for intraoperative 3D imaging. The SireMobil Iso-C 3D (Siemens Medical Solutions), for example, combines the capabilities of routine intraoperative C-arm fluoroscopy with resultant 3D images. The 3D imaging equipment has the ability to automatically revolve around a fixed surgical target (isocentric) acquiring up to 100 images. Of these images, axial cuts, 2D and 3D reformations can be generated that are comparable to CT images. Using this unique imaging modality can help the surgeon to intraoperatively assess fracture anatomy, including in the vicinity of the acetabulum and the posterior pelvic ring. The performance of the Iso-C 3D has already been described in several studies for intraoperative demonstration of high-contrast skeletal objects, with encouraging results.[1,2] The persisting disadvantages of 3D fluoroscopes is a limited image size of 12.5 cm^3, which is sufficient for the sacroiliac joint but not for the entire posterior pelvic ring, and relatively inferior image quality. Modifications of the isocentric C-arm have recently been introduced, to offer superior image quality, in-

creased field of view, higher spatial resolution, and soft tissue visibility, as well as the elimination of the need to rotate around a fixed point (isocentricity).

Fracture Fixation. An improved method for image guidance in intra-articular fracture fixation is 3D fluoroscopy–based navigation. Of the intraoperative axial cuts, 2D and 3D reformations can be generated and the data can be transferred to the navigation system. With inherent registration, the navigation procedure can be performed, similar to CT navigation, but without any registration procedure.[42]

New developments integrating a second-generation 3D fluoroscope (e.g., the Arcadis Orbic; Siemens AG, Erlangen, Germany) and a multifunctional navigation system onto one common trolley will markedly improve data transfer and system handling. Thus, the indications for image guidance in intra-articular fractures, including pelvic surgery, will be expanded to include reduced open procedures (Fig. 17-18).

Novel Uses of Navigation: Localization of Bone Lesions or Removal of Surgical Hardware and Shrapnel

The simplest indication for using CAOS-ST systems is a situation in which a foreign body is retained in bone or soft tissue, such as surgical hardware or penetrating injuries with retained metals (e.g., shrapnel, nuts, and bolts) that need to be removed.

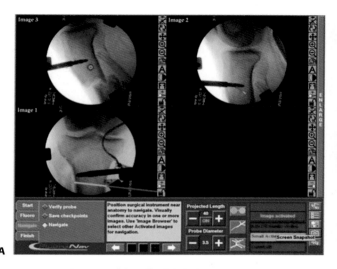

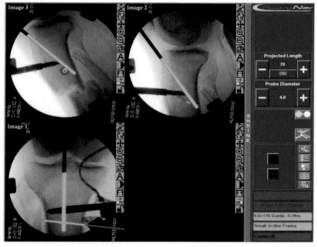

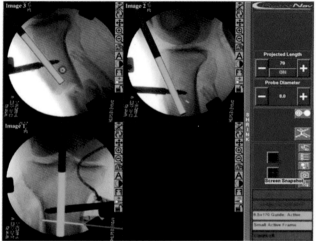

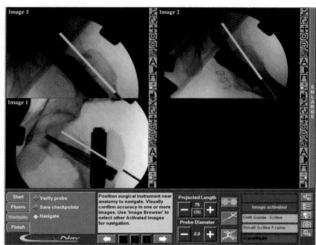

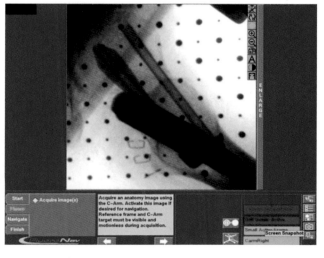

FIGURE 17-16 Intramedullary nailing: Poller and "miss-a-nail." **A.** Poller screw planning for reduction of a proximal tibial fracture. The red circle depicts the planned position of the Poller screw. The green line is the virtual nail. The surgeon can predict the relationship between the two. **B,C.** Poller screw insertion process. **D,E.** "Miss-a-nail" screw through a femoral neck fracture after insertion of a femoral nail with a spiral blade. **D.** Planning the "miss-a-nail" route with the navigation system displayed as a green line. **E.** Fluoroscopic image after nail insertion. Note the parallelism between the planned and real route of the nail. (Images property of authors.)

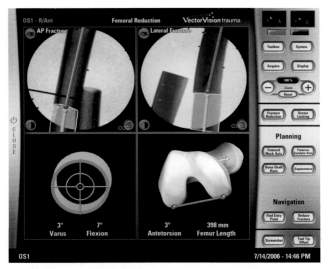

FIGURE 17-17 Fracture reduction. The navigation process of two fragments. The software enables simultaneous tracking of the two fragments, with information regarding length, angulation, and rotation. (Images courtesy of Dr. Y. Weil.)

It is not necessary to track foreign bodies, as they usually remain in place and do not drift. They can be reached with a navigated tool by following the tool's location with respect to them, in the activated fluoroscopic images. Given the simplicity of the procedure, we recommend that this be the first surgical procedure using computerized navigation systems to be performed by inexperienced surgeons.[29]

The main indication for metal/hardware removal is local discomfort, although other indications include infection or risk of toxicity. The removal of missiles retained in an inaccessible location poses a major problem for the trauma surgeon, because they can be hazardous to the integrity of adjacent internal structures.

Fluoroscopy-based navigation is the method of choice for these situations. Unlike CT-based systems, it requires very short preoperative preparation, making it appropriate in emergency situations as well, where its effectiveness has already been proved, even during the urgent stages of treatment. Thanks to the high accuracy of fluoroscopy-based navigation, its use in complex and dangerous situations where a foreign body is located in the proximity of structures such as blood vessels and/or nerves is promising. In comparison to other conventional techniques, the use of fluoroscopy-based navigation has allowed orthopaedic surgeons to minimize soft tissue dissection. The same principle can be use for guided bone biopsy.

Surgical Technique. Tracked reference frames are rigidly attached to the patient's adjacent bone and to a calibrated pointer. Several fluoroscopic images of the required anatomic site are acquired and stored in the computer, or 3D information using Iso-C technology is acquired. The accurate spatial location of the foreign object can be seen in the images displayed on the computer's screen (Fig. 17-19). The surgeon then plans the most accurate and safest minimal surgical approach toward the foreign body that needs to be removed. Once the fluoroscopic images have been activated, the location of the guided probe with respect to the patient's anatomy is continuously displayed and updated on all of the fluoroscopic images. This enables accurate determination of the entry point and spatial advancement of the probe toward the foreign body.[33]

COMPLICATIONS AND CONTROVERSIES

The most frequent clinical and technical complications that lead to navigation errors and failure are listed.

1. *Loss of line-of-sight* An unobstructed view between the optical camera and the trackers at all times is the basic requirement of optical navigation. Loss of line-of-sight occurs when the view between the optical camera and one or more of the trackers is obstructed by the surgeon or another member of

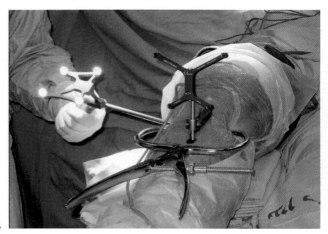

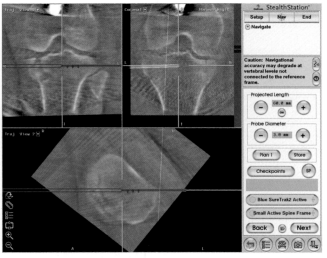

FIGURE 17-18 Using SireMobil Iso-C 3D (Siemens Medical Solutions, Erlangen, Germany) for fracture reduction. **A.** Percutaneous reduction of a tibial plateau fracture using reduction instruments with application of a reference frame. **B.** Three images displayed on the system's screen (coronal and sagittal), showing the location of the surgical tool (blue) and allowing for real-time tracking with the virtual green line, which assists in determining the direction of the surgical tool in a three-dimensional environment. (Images property of authors.)

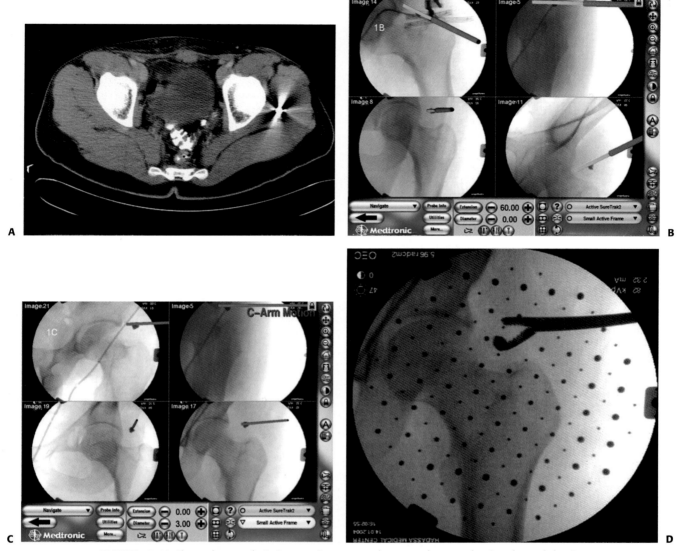

FIGURE 17-19 Shrapnel removal. **A.** Preoperative computed tomography scan showing shrapnel that is intended to be removed because of its proximity to the left hip joint. **B.** Four acquired images displayed on the system's screen, showing the location of the missile and allowing for immediate presurgical planning of the percutaneous surgical approach. The pink line represents the surgical tool and the virtual green line assists in determining the point of entry and direction of the surgical tool. **C.** The surgical tool, represented by the pink line, arrives at the missile. **D.** Verification fluoroscopy followed by removal of the missile. (Images property of authors.)

the surgical team, the patient's body, the fluoroscopy C-arm, the overhead lamps, or any other object in the vicinity of the surgical field. When there is no line-of-sight, the tracker, which is not seen, either disappears from the display or the entire display freezes. Navigation resumes as soon as the obstruction disappears.

Loss of line-of-sight can be remedied by moving the object causing the interference, by repositioning the optical camera, or by changing the surgical team's location around the patient. In some situations, because of the surgical approach, it is not possible to see all of the trackers at once. In this case, partial navigation is possible with the visible trackers. In some surgical situations, maintenance of the line-of-sight is not possible and therefore navigation should be avoided. As previously discussed, the surgeon can control some of the obstacles by appropriate placement of the track-

ers and the camera. Practically, this step should be considered as an integral part of the preplanning stage of CAOS-ST.

2. *Shift of the dynamic reference frame rigid bone mounting* Maintaining a rigid attachment between the bone tracker and the bone throughout surgery is essential in order to guarantee registration accuracy. Shifting is usually the result of bone fixation loosening, poor jig fixation, or unintentionally pushing or hitting the tracker and its mounting jig. An undetected shift will result in inaccurate navigation images that might mislead the surgeon and lead to undesired results and complications. To avoid this situation, the surgeon should ensure that the tracker mounting jig is securely fixated to the bone structure.

The only way to detect dynamic reference frame motion is by validation. Validation is preformed either by acquiring one or more fluoroscopic radiography images and comparing them with the navigation images, or by touching with the tip of a surgical tool known anatomic landmarks and verifying that the tool tip appears close to the landmark in the navigated image. Validation should be performed at key points during surgery and always when in doubt.

3. *Tool decalibration* Tool decalibration occurs when the geometric data of the tracked tool do not match its actual geometry. Tool decalibration is caused by tool wear and tear (e.g., tip bending, frame deformation because of repeated sterilization or tool tracker shift). To avoid these situations, the surgeon should verify tool calibration before surgery, at key points during the surgery, and always when in doubt. Tool decalibration cannot be detected automatically. The surgeon must perform a tool calibration verification procedure, which usually involves the use of custom calibration software and hardware.

4. *Navigation image inaccuracy* Inaccuracy of navigation images is the mismatch between the displayed images and the intraoperative situation. The inaccuracy is the result of errors in the registration chain. The main causes of the errors include the shift of the dynamic reference frame, tool decalibration, and the shift of the C-arm tracker ring. Secondary causes include tracking system drift over time and navigation at the edge of the position sensor working volume. Other causes are related to the images themselves. In CT images, they include poor contrast, low slice resolution, insufficient radiation dose, large spacing between slices, patient motion during the CT scan, and blooming artifacts as a result of the presence of metallic objects. In fluoroscopic radiography images, they include poor image resolution, poor contrast because of insufficient or excessive radiation, inappropriate viewpoints, and patient motion during image acquisition.

   The surgeon must realize that the acquired images serve as the basis for the entire navigated surgical procedure.[18,20,39] Therefore, optimization of these images (contrast, field, viewing angle, etc.) is crucial and should be done during the image acquisition stage, before surgery begins. Note that navigation image inaccuracy can be observed by the surgeon but cannot automatically be detected. It requires performing validation tests for C-arm ring and dynamic reference frame shift, tool decalibration, restarting of the tracking system, repositioning of the position sensor, and the acquisition of new images.[27]

5. *System robustness issues* Robustness is the ability of a system to perform its intended tasks with a minimum number of failures over time. The more robust the system, the more acceptable it will be to the surgeon. Robustness depends on both software and hardware components. Software failures include flaws in the computer operating system, in the custom-designed software, and in the tracking base unit controller. At best, software flaws can be temporarily overcome by restarting the system. At worst, they require preempting navigation and reporting the flaw to the company. Hardware failures include failure of the computer unit, poor cable connections, and failure of the tracking unit.

6. *Verification of surgical tool and implant spatial position* The surgeon should always remember to make a distinction between the virtual and nonvirtual situations displayed on the computer screen. This is of great importance, especially in trauma surgery, because the surgeon is used to working under fluoroscopic guidance that provides a true view of the surgical site as opposed to the virtual display in CAOS-ST procedures. For example, a perfect virtual position of a guidewire may be a false presentation of the real situation, because during insertion of the real guidewire, it may slip or bend and point to a wrong position, without being detected or shown on the augmented image. There are several ways to tackle this critical obstacle. The best is to use to use rigid guidewires to prevent bending. Moreover, the first obstacle is penetrating the cortical bone in the right location. Experience and/or the use of rigid drills can usually overcome this problem. In addition, it is also very important to perform real-time fluoroscopic verification at critical or questionable time points during the surgical procedure.

7. *Adaptation to different surgical techniques* The main addition to computer-assisted navigation compared with conventional fluoroscopic trauma surgery is the bone-mounted reference frame. The significant ramifications of the loosening of the reference frame have been previously described. The actual location of this frame can interfere during the surgical procedure. For example, while inserting the reference frame screw into the bone diaphysis during intramedullary nailing, it should not penetrate the medullary canal. In addition, during the insertion of a locking screw, the reference frame might be in the way and prevent either an accurate line-of-sight or the proper positioning of certain surgical instruments (e.g., drills). The surgeon must choose between placing the frame close to the operative site, to increase accuracy of the procedure and to improve triangulation, and placing the frame where it establishes a convenient working distance.

PERSPECTIVES

Technical and Economic Perspectives

Navigation systems are limited by technical elements. Currently, their main limitations, in decreasing order of importance, and perspectives for improvements are as follows:

1. *Support for implants and instrumentation* Navigation systems are designed to be used with specific tools, implants, and hardware from specific manufacturers. The choice of supported instruments and implants depends on decisions made by the navigation and instrument companies, which are primarily dictated by commercial interests. Often, the software module only accepts models from one manufacturer. In some cases, tools from other manufacturers can be incorporated following a tool calibration procedure. Currently, only a handful of instruments and implants are supported.

2. *Support for surgical procedures* Navigation systems require software modules (software surgical protocols) that implement the surgical protocol for navigation for specific procedures. Without the custom software module for the surgical procedure, the navigation system cannot be used, although in principle it is technically feasible in procedures other than those for which they were designed. Currently, only a handful of procedures are supported.

3. *Improvements in tracking technology* Current optical tracking technology has several drawbacks, including line-of-sight, size of trackers, cables, number of trackers, accuracy, and cost. Magnetic tracking offers a variety of potential advantages, including no line-of-sight requirement, reduced tracker size, and reduced cost. Although the technology is

not as yet ready for routine clinical use, it is likely that some of the obstacles will be overcome in the near future, offering the possibility of tracking bone fragments and easing tracker fixation to the bone, thus significantly reducing or eliminating dynamic reference frame shift and opening the door for navigation during reduction.

4. *Image-based CT registration* Current CT-based navigation systems require the surgeon to acquire points on the surface of the anatomy of interest to perform the registration between the CT data set and the intraoperative situation. This precludes its use in percutaneous procedures because it is time consuming and error prone and produces suboptimal registration results. An alternative is to use fluoroscopic radiography images instead of points harvested from the bone surface. This type of registration, called anatomy-based CT to fluoroscopic radiography registration, has been demonstrated in the laboratory and will be available in navigation systems.

5. *Planning* Current intraoperative planning is either nonexistent or limited at best. Intraoperative definition of goals, such as screw path safety zone and insertion axis, can greatly help the surgeon perform the surgery. The blurring of the distinction between preoperative and intraoperative planning opens the door for better, more adaptive planning and consequently better and more consistent results.

6. *Spatial visualization without CT* A drawback of fluoroscopy-based navigation systems is that they do not show spatial views of the intraoperative situation, which can only be produced when CT data are available. Isometric fluoroscopic technology (Iso-C) overcomes this obstacle; however, it provides a relatively small visual field. Newly design technology is now available with better quality and a larger view. Another way to overcome this limitation has been proposed—to acquire several fluoroscopic radiography images and adapt a closely related CT or generic anatomic model so as to match the patient-specific fluoroscopic radiography images. This approach, called *atlas-based matching*, is currently under investigation.

7. *Ergonometric factors* Most operating rooms were not designed with new technology in mind in terms of size; placement of the computer, computer screen, and cables; and so on. A surgeon experienced with CAS can appreciate the advanced ease of use in newer generations of navigation systems. However, the insertion of a navigation system into the operating room still warrants special consideration. The machine occupies space. Its positioning is dictated by lines-of-sight between the tracker sensor and the markers.

These obvious technical and economic factors need to be taken into account along with the human factors.

Clinical Perspectives

The use of computerized navigation systems in orthopaedic trauma surgery is rather new. The four main contributions to trauma surgery are as follows:

1. Facilitates minimal invasive surgery (MIS) by reducing soft tissue damage, thus shortening the postoperative rehabilitation process

2. Improves the accuracy of fracture reduction and implant placement compared with that obtained with conventional methods and reduces outcome variability

3. Significantly reduces radiation exposure to both the patient and the surgeon

4. Creates a powerful educational and quality control tool

Most of the contributions achieved to date are in the preplanning stage. If we take, for instance, the imaging field, it is clear that computerized imaging supplies a better 3D understanding that may influence the planning of the surgical procedure. Undoubtedly, this new technology can and should change our way of thinking in relation to other stages of surgical treatment.

It is quite obvious that computerized navigation systems are continuously advancing and offer additional possibilities. Although these systems are taking their first steps, it appears that they have already managed to change the setting in several trauma centers. The CT suite can be transformed into an operating room or, alternatively, the modern hi-tech fluoroscope can now be altered to produce 3D images. These modern available technologies, on the one hand, and surgeons' preferences and compliance, on the other, will in the future determine the setup of the operating room, where it will be situated and so forth. Future generations of computerized navigation systems will be characterized not only by improved accuracy but also in diminishing the robustness and improving working convenience in the computerized environment. When these changes finally take place, it is expected that computerized technology will be of assistance not only in navigation but also in the execution of the surgical procedure by means of robots.[45] If the trauma surgeon can overcome the difficulties entailed in integrating the new technology, we may experience a revolution in surgical approaches and education.

GLOSSARY

General

CAOS (computer-aided orthopaedic surgery) Planning and execution of an orthopaedic surgery with the help of a computer system.

CAOS-ST (computer-aided orthopaedic surgery for skeletal trauma) Planning and execution of a skeletal trauma orthopaedic surgery with the help of a computer system.

CAS (computer-aided surgery) Planning and execution of an orthopaedic surgery with the help of a computer system. Synonyms: *computer-assisted surgery, computer-integrated surgery (CIS), image-guided surgery (IGS), surgical navigation*

Planning

Model Computer representation of the relevant characteristics (e.g., shape, location, main axis) of an object of interest (e.g., a bone, bone fragment, surgical instrument, implant, fixation plate, cutting plane). Synonym: *digital template*

Preoperative planning Process of creating a computerized plan for the purposes of surgery.

Surface mesh Geometric description of a bone surface consisting of a collection of interconnected points, usually extracted from CT data. Synonym: *surface model*

Navigation

CT-based navigation Navigation with images created by superimposing onto preoperative CT cross section and spatial images the surgical tool silhouette and updating its location in real time.

Fluoroscopy-based navigation Navigation using images created by superimposing onto conventional fluoroscopic images the surgical tool silhouette and updating its location in real time, thereby creating the impression of continuous fluoroscopy without the ensuing radiation. Synonyms: *virtual fluoroscopy, augmented fluoroscopy*

Guidance Process of indicating in real time to the surgeon, via images, graphics, or sound, the best course of action during surgery.

Navigation Process of determining the spatial location of surgical instruments and anatomic structures in real time for the purposes of guiding surgical gestures during surgery.

Navigation images Images created by a navigation system for the purposes of navigation. Synonyms: *active display, navigation display, real-time visualization*

Navigation system System that shows the current location of surgical instruments with respect to images of the anatomy and continuously updates this image as the instruments and bone structures move. It requires tracking, registration, visualization, and validation. Synonyms: *surgical navigator, guidance system*

Tracking

Line-of-sight Basic requirement of optical tracking systems in which there must be no occluding objects between the position sensor and the trackers..

Marker Basic element recognized by the position sensor; can be an LED or a reflective sphere. Synonyms: *infrared light-emitting diode (IRED)*

Position sensor System that determines the spatial location of the trackers at any moment in time. It is an **optical camera** for optical systems and a **magnetic field generator** for magnetic systems. Synonym: *localizer*

Tracked pointer Pointer with a tracker used for pointing and probing during navigation. Synonym: *digitizing probe*

Tracker Rigid body with markers that are recognized by the position sensor. Synonyms: *optical localizer, 3D localizer, sensor, marker carrier*

Tracker mounting jigs Mechanical jigs, such as screws and clamps, used to rigidly attach trackers to surgical instruments and bone structures and whose purpose is to mechanically fix their positional relationship. Synonym: *attachment*

Tracking Process of determining in real time the spatial location of moving objects. Synonym: *localization*

Tracking base unit Unit that controls and processes the information from the position sensor and the trackers. Synonym: *tracking data acquisition unit*

Tracking system System that obtains the position and orientation of trackers by measuring spatially dependent physical properties, such as optical and magnetic properties. Synonym: *localization system*

Tracking technology Physical means by which the location of trackers is measured. Tracking technology is optical or magnetic. Optical tracking is active (light-emitting diodes), passive (reflective spheres), or hybrid (both active and passive), and is called semiactive. Synonym: *localization technology*

Tracking work volume Volume of space covered by the position sensor in which measurements can be made. Synonym: *measurement volume*

Accuracy

Accuracy Measure of an instrument's capability to approach a true or absolute value. Static accuracy refers to measurements that do not change over time, while dynamic accuracy refers to time-varying measurements. Accuracy is a function of both bias and precision.

Bias Measure of how closely the mean value in a series of replicate measurements approaches the true value.

Frequency Number of overall measurements per second. Static accuracy refers to measurements obtained when the trackers are at rest, while dynamic accuracy refers to measurements obtained as the trackers move. Synonyms: *rate, frame rate, display rate*

Precision Measure of how closely the values within a series of replicate measurements agree with each other.

Repeatability Measure of resolution and stability. Resolution is the smallest discernible difference between two measurements. Stability refers to measurements made at steady state and over a sufficiently long period of time.

Registration

Coordinate frame Fixed reference within which the spatial locations of objects can be described. Each object of interest has its own coordinate frame. Synonym: *coordinate system (COS)*

CT registration Process of establishing a common reference frame between the preoperative CT images and the intraoperative situation. Synonyms: *point registration, surface registration, contact registration*

Dynamic reference frame Tracker attached to the bone used to track the bone motions to determine the relative location of the bone with respect to the tool. Synonyms: *reference, reference base, dynamic reference base (DRB), dynamic referencing*

Location Six parameters determining the position and orientation of an object in space. Synonyms: *placement, degrees of freedom (DOF)*

Registration Process of establishing a common reference frame between objects and images. Synonym: *alignment*

Registration chain Series of transformations that relate the locations of objects in space.

Tool calibration Process of computing the transformation and the tool's geometric features, such as its main axis and its tip position. Tool calibration verification is the process of comparing the actual and computed calibration. The tool calibration unit is the device used for calibrating tools.

Transformation: Mathematical description of the relationship between the locations of two objects. Transformations are static (constant) when the relative locations of the objects do not change, dynamic otherwise. There are four types of transformations: tracking transformations, tools transformations, image transformations, and display transformations.

Visualization

Silhouette Projection of the contours of a 3D object onto a plane.

Viewpoint Location from which navigation images are created.

Visualization Process of creating, manipulating, and displaying images showing the location of objects in space.

Validation

Validation Process of verifying that the navigation images match the clinical intraoperative situation. There are three types of validation: tool calibration validation, dynamic reference frame validation, and registration accuracy validation. Synonym: *verification*

REFERENCES

1. Atesok K, Finkelstein J, Khoury A, et al. CT (ISO-C-3D) image-based computer-assisted navigation in trauma surgery: a preliminary report. Injury 2008;39:39–43.
2. Atesok K, Finkelstein J, Khoury A, et al. The use of intraoperative three-dimensional imaging (ISO-C-3D) in fixation of intraarticular fractures. Injury 2007;38:1163–1169.
3. Attias N, Lindsey RW, Starr AJ, et al. The use of a virtual three-dimensional model to evaluate the intraosseous space available for percutaneous screw fixation of acetabular fractures. J Bone Joint Surg Br 2005;87B:1520–1523.
4. Bono JV. Digital templating in total hip arthroplasty. J Bone Joint Surg Am 2004;86A: 118–122.
5. Borrelli J, Peele M, Ricci WM, et al. Validation of CT-reconstructed images for the evaluation of acetabular fractures. Proceedings of the American Academy of Orthopedic Surgery, 2004, San Francisco: 610.
6. Cimerman M, Kristan A. Preoperative planning in pelvic and acetabular surgery: the value of advanced computerized planning modules. Injury 2007;38:442–449.
7. Citak M, Hüfner T, Geerling J, et al. Navigated percutaneous pelvic sacroiliac screw fixation: experimental comparison of accuracy between fluoroscopy and Iso-C 3D navigation. Comput Aided Surg 2006;11:209–213.
8. Crowl AC, Kahler DM. Closed reduction and percutaneous fixation of anterior column acetabular fractures. Comput Aided Surg 2002;7:169–178.
9. Euler E, Heining T, Fischer T, et al. Initial clinical experiences with the SIREMOBIL Iso-3D. Electromedica 2002;70:48–51.
10. Gardner MJ, Citak M, Kendoff D, et al. Femoral fracture malrotation caused by freehand versus navigated distal interlocking. Injury 2008;39:176–180.
11. Gautier E, Bachler R, Heini PF, et al. Accuracy of computer-guided screw fixation of the sacroiliac joint. Clin Orthop 2001;393:310–317.
12. Grutzner PA, Hebecker A, Waelti H, et al. Clinical study for registration-free 3D navigation with the SIREMOBIL Iso-3D mobile C-arm. Electromedica 2003;71:6–15.
13. Hajnal J, Hill D, Hawkes D. Medical Image Registration. Boca Raton: CRC Press, 2001.
14. Hazan E. Computer aided orthopaedic surgery: special issue. Techn Orthop 2003;18.
15. Hazan E, Joskowicz L. Computer-assisted image-guided intramedullary nailing of femoral shaft fractures. Techn Orthop 2003;18:191–201.
16. Hinsche AF, Giannoudis PV, Smith RM. Fluoroscopy based multiplanar image guidance for insertion of sacroiliac screws. Clin Orthop 2002;395:135–144.
17. Hofstetter R, Slomczykowski M, Krettek C, et al. Computer-assisted fluoroscopy-based reduction of femoral fractures and anteversion correction. Comput Aided Surg 2000;5: 311–325.
18. Hufner T, Pohlemann T, Tarte S, et al. Computer-assisted fracture reduction of pelvic ring fractures: an in vitro study. Clin Orthop 2002;399:231–239.
19. Ilsar I, Weil YA, Joskowicz L, et al. Fracture-table-mounted versus bone-mounted dynamic reference frame tracking accuracy using computer-assisted orthopaedic surgery: a comparative study. Comput Aided Surg 2007;12:125–130.
20. Jaramaz B, Eckman K. Virtual reality simulation of fluoroscopic navigation. Clin Orthop Relat Res 2006;442:30–34.
21. Joskowicz L, Milgrom C, Simkin A, et al. FRACAS: a system for computer-aided image-guided long bone fracture surgery. Comput Aided Surg 1999;3:271–288.
22. Kahler DM. Computer-assisted closed techniques of reduction and fixation. In: Tile M, Helfet D, Kellam J, eds. Surgery of the Pelvis and Acetabulum. Philadelphia: Lippincott Williams & Wilkins, 2003:604–615.
23. Kahler DM. Computer-assisted fixation of acetabular fractures and pelvic ring disruptions. Techn Orthop 2000;10:20–24.
24. Kahler DM. Image guidance: fluoroscopic navigation. Clin Orthop Relat Res 2004;421: 70–76.
25. Kahler DM. Virtual fluoroscopy: a tool for decreasing radiation exposure during femoral intramedullary nailing. Stud Health Technol Inform 2001;81:225–228.
26. Khoury A, Liebergall M, Weil Y, et al. Computerized fluoroscopic-based navigation-assisted intramedullary nailing. Am J Orthop 2007;36:582–585.
27. Langlotz F. Potential pitfalls of computer aided orthopedic surgery. Injury 2004;35(suppl 1):17–23.
28. Lavallee S, Sautot P, Troccaz J, et al. Computer-assisted spine surgery: a technique for accurate transpedicular screw fixation using CT data and a 3D optical localizer. Comput Aided Surg (formerly J Image Guid Surg) 1995;1:65–73.
29. Liebergall M, Ben-David D, Weil Y, et al. Computerized navigation for the internal fixation of femoral neck fractures. J Bone Joint Surg Am 2006;88A:1748–1754.
30. Liebergall M, Mosheiff R, Segal D. Navigation in orthopaedic trauma. Oper Techn Orthop 2003;13:64–72.
31. Livyatan H, Yaniv Z, Joskowicz L. Robust automatic C-arm calibration for fluoroscopy-based navigation: a practical approach. Proceedings of the Fifth International Conference on Medical Computing and Computer-Aided Intervention. Lecture Notes in Computer Science 2488, Springer Verlag 2002;2:60–68.
32. Mosheiff R, Khoury A, Weil Y, et al. First generation of fluoroscopic navigation in percutaneous pelvic surgery. J Orthop Trauma 2004;18:106–111.
33. Mosheiff R, Weil Y, Khoury A, et al. The use of computerized navigation in the treatment of gunshot and shrapnel injury. Comput Aided Surg 2004;9:39–43.
34. Mosheiff R, Weil Y, Peleg E, et al. Computerized navigation for closed reduction during femoral intramedullary nailing. Injury 2005;36:866–870.
35. Reddix RN, Webb LX. Computed-assisted preoperative planning in the surgical treatment of acetabular fractures. J Surg Orthop Adv 2007;16:138–143.
36. Nolte L, Beutler T. Basic principles of CAOS. Injury 2004;35(suppl 1):6–16.
37. Nolte LP, Ganz R. Computer-Assisted Orthopaedic Surgery. Bern: Hogrefe and Huber Publishers, 1999.
38. Schep NW, Haverlag R, van Vugt AB. Computer-assisted versus conventional surgery for insertion of 96 cannulated iliosacral screws in patients with postpartum pelvic pain. J Trauma 2004;57:1299–1302.
39. Schmucki D, Gebhard F, Grutzner P, et al. Computer-aided reduction and imaging. Injury 2004;35(suppl 1):96–104.
40. Slomczykowski MA, Hofstetter R, Sati M, et al. Novel computer-assisted fluoroscopy system for intraoperative guidance: feasibility study for distal locking of femoral nails. J Orthop Trauma 2001;15:122–131.
41. Stockle U, Krettek C, Pohlemann T, et al. Clinical applications: pelvis. Injury 2004; 35(suppl 1):46–56.
42. Stockle U, Schaser K, Konig B. Image guidance in pelvic and acetabular surgery: expectations, success, and limitations. Injury 2007;38:450–462.
43. Suhm N, Jacob AL, Nolte LP, et al. Surgical navigation based on fluoroscopy: clinical application for computer-assisted distal locking of intramedullary implants. Comput Aided Surg 2000;5:391–400.
44. Taylor R, Lavallee S, Burdea C, et al. Computer-Integrated Surgery: Technology and Clinical Applications. Boston: The MIT Press, 1995.
45. Taylor RH. Medical robotics. IEEE Trans Robot Automat 2003;Special Issue:19.
46. Weil Y, Liebergall M, Khoury A, et al. The use of computerized fluoroscopic navigation for removal of pelvic screws. Am J Orthop 2004;33:384–385.
47. Weil YA, Gardner MJ, Helfet DL, et al. Computer navigation allows for accurate reduction of femoral fractures. Clin Orthop Relat Res 2007;460:185–191.
48. Weil YA, Liebergall M, Mosheiff R, et al. Long bone fracture reduction using a fluoroscopy-based navigation system: a feasibility and accuracy study. Comput Aided Surg 2007;12:295–302.

18

PRINCIPLES OF OSTEOPOROSIS AND FRAGILITY FRACTURES

Magnus K. Karlsson and Per Olof Josefsson

EPIDEMIOLOGY

Osteoporosis was first observed in Egypt in 990 BC,[63] but the definition of osteoporosis has changed. The most commonly used definition, as defined by the World Health Organization (WHO), is a bone mineral density (BMD) of 2.5 standard deviations (SDs) or more below the young normal mean[311] (Table 18-1). But this definition only includes postmenopausal women evaluated by the total body dual-energy X-ray absorptiometry (DXA) scanning technique. No similar definition exists for young women or men. Using the WHO definition, a quarter of all postmenopausal white Americans, a total of 26 million people, are osteoporotic.[198] Furthermore, the number of fragility fractures, those of the proximal humerus, distal forearm, vertebrae, pelvis, hip, and the tibial condyles, have risen exponentially during the same period,[15,135,220] even if some reports indicate that the increased incidence during the last few years has leveled off or even declined[136,199] (Fig. 18-1). These fractures show a number of common epidemiologic features. The incidence is higher in women than in men and increases exponentially with age (Fig. 18-2). The fractures also occur at sites where there is a large proportion of trabecular bone.[15,201,220] The rea-

TABLE 18-1	World Health Organization Definition of Normal Bone Mineral Density (BMD), Osteopenia, Osteoporosis, and Established Osteoporosis	
Diagnostic Category	Definition	BMD T-score
Normal bone mass	BMD >1 standard deviation below the average young and adult value	>−1
Osteopenia	BMD 1 to 2.5 standard deviations below the average young adult value	−1 to −2.5
Osteoporosis	BMD >2.5 standard deviations below the average young adult value	<−2.5
Severe osteoporosis or established osteoporosis	BMD >2.5 standard deviations below the average young adult value and at least one osteoporotic fractures	<−2.5

World Health Organization. Assessment of fracture risk and its application to screening for postmenopausal osteoporosis. Report of a WHO Study Group. World Health Organ Tech Rep Ser 1994;843:1–129.

son for the increase in incidence is not fully understood. The changes in population demographics, particularly the high incidence of elderly in the population, as well as changes in bone mineral density (BMD) and other risk factors, have all influenced the incidence of osteoporotic fractures.

One of the commonest risk factors associated with fracture is a fall.[99,286,290] In fact, some researchers have suggested that we should change our interest from the prevention of osteoporosis to the prevention of falls.[127] Approximately one third of community dwellers aged 65 years or older and 50% to 60% of residents of nursing homes and "old people's homes" fall each year, with women falling more often than men.[183,263,285,290] Fractures, dislocations, or serious soft tissue injuries result from about 10% to 15% of falls in patients living in the community[213,285,290] and from about 15% to 20% of falls in institutionalized patients.[213,285,288] Fractures occur in 3% to 12% of falls in the elderly and are more common in women than in men.[286] Hip fractures occur in fewer than 1% of falls.[101,183,213,263,285,288,290] The annual prevalence of hip fractures in those with a tendency to fall is 7% but is 14% among frequent fallers. In the United States, falls are responsible for the second highest injury-related cost to the economy.[252] Unintentional falling is an important cause of mortality in the elderly. Twenty-three percent of injury-related deaths in patients over 65 years of age and 34% in those over 85 years of age occur as a result of a fall.[77] It is therefore obvious that a major goal must be to reduce the frequency of falls.[127] Fragility fractures also impose an enormous cost on society. Hip fracture is a major cause of hospital admission in the elderly, and in the United States the direct cost of hip fractures was more than $7 billion per year in 1992.[238] It was estimated in the United Kingdom to be £750 million per year in 1994.[224] In addition, the cost of nursing home care for patients who had hip fractures in the United States in 1992 was estimated to be $1.5 billion.[238] The costs and outcome of hip fractures are often closely monitored because this fracture is usually regarded as the most significant osteoporotic fracture. The mortality attributable to osteoporosis is most obviously associated with hip fractures with the highest incidence occurring in the first 6 months after fracture.[305] Hip fractures are also associated with up to 20% reduction in expected survival[54] with the highest mortality occurring in men,[271] older patients.[146] and nonwhites.[146] Also, many patients become permanently disabled after hip fracture, with the proportion who cannot walk rising from 20% to 50% after the fracture.[119] One third of patients become totally dependent and require institutional care.[28]

The highest incidence of hip fractures has been reported in whites living in northern Europe, followed by whites living in North America and by Asians, with the lowest incidence being recorded in the African American population.[301] The female-to-male ratio is 3:1 in whites but is 1:1 in Chinese and the Bantu.[301] The incidence is age dependent in both men and women, rising from 2 per 100,000 person-years among white women younger than 35 years to 3032 per 100,000 person-years in women at least 85 years old[44,258] (Fig. 18-2). The incidence of hip fracture has also increased during the past 40 years,[15,220] even if recent data suggest either a leveling off or a slight downturn in North America and Europe[136,199] (Fig. 18-1). In contrast, the incidence of hip fractures in developing Asian countries has rapidly increased during the past decades, so that by 2050, it is estimated that 6.3 million hip fractures will occur globally with more than half of these in occurring in Asia[43] (Fig. 18-3).

The prevalence of vertebral fractures also varies in different ethnic groups, being higher in Scandinavian, American, and Hong Kong Chinese females than in eastern European females. The rates in male Hong Kong Chinese and male white Americans are lower than in male Europeans.[112,163,200,219] The female-to-male ratio is 2:1 in whites, and the incidence is age dependent in both men and women. In North America, this rises from fewer than 20 per 100,000 person-years in men and women under 45 years of age to 1200 per 100,000 person-years in both men and women at least 85 years of age.[112,219] According to Swedish data, the incidence of vertebral fracture has increased from 1950 to 1983,[15] but this trend has not been confirmed in Denmark[106] or in Rochester, New York.[212] Mortality following a vertebral fracture is increased in men and women, although it is less than after hip fracture.[110,111] Patients with vertebral frac-

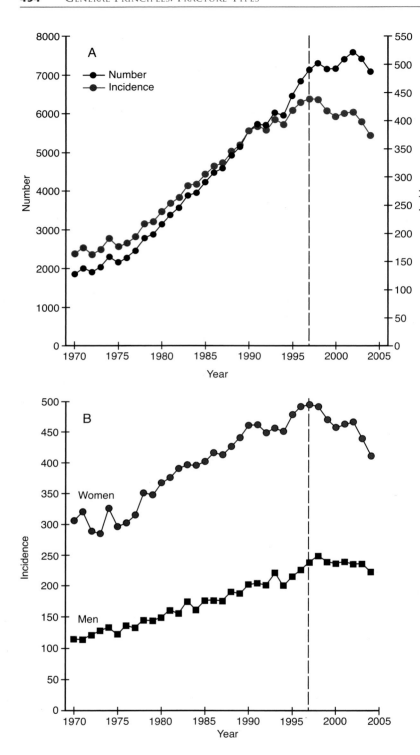

FIGURE 18-1 Hip fractures in Finland in people 50 years or older between 1970 and 2004. **A.** Number and crude incidence (per 100,000 persons). **B.** Age-adjusted incidence (per 100,000 persons). The latest year of the original report or 1997 is indicated with a dotted vertical line. (Reprinted with permission from Kannus P, Niemi S, Parkkari J, et al. Nationwide decline in incidence of hip fracture. J Bone Miner Res 2006; 21:1836–1838.)

tures also experience a reduction in quality of life, usually as a result of back pain. In addition, they also have functional limitation, loss of height, depression, and disability.[71,72]

PATHOGENESIS OF OSTEOPOROSIS

During the first decades of life, there is an increase in skeletal size, a process called *modeling,* and accrual of BMD.[9,281] The BMD at age 18 to 30 years is described as the peak bone mass, being the highest BMD that the individual will reach in life. It occurs in different skeletal regions at different ages, possibly as early as 18 years in the hip and as late as 35 years in the distal forearm.[4,151,178,281] The factors that determine BMD are poorly understood, but studies in twins indicate that 60% to 80% of the BMD is determined by heredity.[269] Other important factors are environmental factors such as exercise and nutrition as well as any diseases that interfere with normal growth and sex and growth hormones.[140,179,197,269] It is also likely that both anabolic and catabolic environmental factors have the greatest impact on bone during skeletal growth. For example, the skeletal

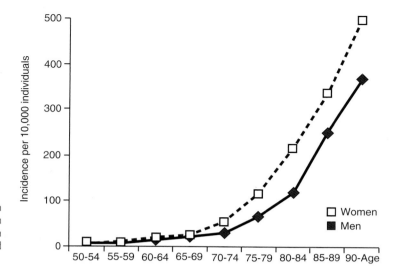

FIGURE 18-2 Incidence of hip fractures per 10,000 inhabitants in Malmo, Sweden, 1992–1995. (Reprinted with permission from Rogmark C, Sernbo I, Johnell O, et al. Incidence of hip fractures in Malmo, Sweden, 1992–1995. A trend-break. Acta Orthop Scand 1999;70:19–22.)

response to exercise is most pronounced during the prepubertal and early pubertal years, this being the period of fastest growth and the highest accrual of BMD[9,133,281] (Fig. 18-4).

Once peak bone mass is reached, the BMD is virtually stable or shows a slight decrease until menopause. At the menopause, the levels of estradiol and estrone drop to about 25% and 50% of their premenopausal values. At this time, they are mainly produced by extraglandular conversion of androgen precursors in muscles and adipose tissues. Because the female sex hormones are the most important hormones regulating BMD in both men and women, an accelerated loss of BMD naturally

occurs during the 5 to 10 years after the menopause.[4,174] At this time, the increase in the number of sites undergoing active remodeling leads to BMD loss,[4,174] trabecular perforation,[227] and an increased risk of fracture.[174] The processes that lead to age-related bone loss are probably multifactorial. With increasing age, calcium absorption is impaired, which may lead to secondary hyperparathyroidism and accelerated bone loss. There is also a reduced production of active vitamin D due to thinning of the skin and reduced exposure to sunlight.[254] This process is exacerbated by estrogen deficiency in both elderly men and women.[254] The main difference between osteoporotic

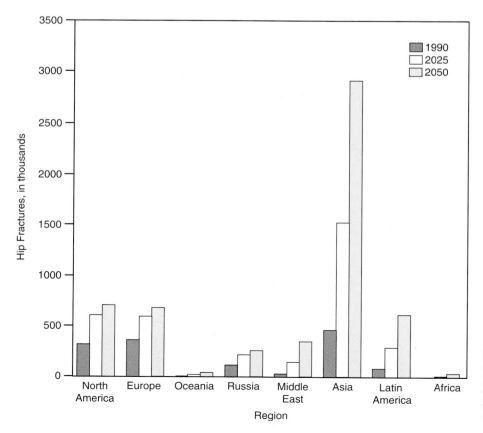

FIGURE 18-3 Estimated numbers of hip fractures in eight geographic regions in 1990, 2025, and 2050. (Reprinted with permission from Cooper C, Campion G, Melton LJ 3rd. Hip fractures in the elderly: a worldwide projection. Osteoporos Int 1992;2:285–289.)

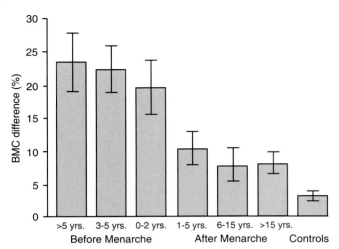

FIGURE 18-4 The mean (95% confidence interval) playing-to-nonplaying arm difference in bone mineral content of humeral shaft in 105 female tennis and squash players and their 50 controls according to biological age at which training was started (i.e., starting age of playing relative to age at menarche). (Reprinted with permission from Kannus P, Haapasalo H, Sankelo M, et al. Effect of starting age of physical activity on bone mass in the dominant arm of tennis and squash players. Ann Intern Med 1995; 123:27–31.)

individuals and their nonosteoporotic peers seems to be related to defective bone formation. Bone turnover in osteoporotic individuals may be elevated, normal, or reduced, but the imbalance between resorption and formation always seems to be present.[69] In addition, with aging, collagen synthesis and the secretion of other osteotropic factors decline, a fact that also could influence skeletal strength.[144]

As there is no demonstrable underlying medical cause for osteoporosis in 80% of women and 50% of men who present with fragility fractures, a diagnosis of primary involutional osteoporosis is often made.[255] Riggs and Melton[255] subdivided primary osteoporosis into type I and type II osteoporosis, type I being related to the loss of ovarian function after the meno-

pause and type II being an exaggeration of the normal aging process. A recent study has emphasized the importance of estrogen in bone loss in both men and women and proposed a link between type I and type II osteoporosis.[254] Nowadays, the expression "primary or idiopathic osteoporosis" is more commonly used than "type I or type II osteoporosis." Despite this, it is important to realize that involutional osteoporosis is multifactorial and that the roles of each specific fracture are still poorly understood. If there is a cause for osteoporosis such as an endocrine, metabolic, gastrointestinal, renal, or hematologic disorder in addition to certain hereditary diseases and drug treatment, the diagnosis is that of secondary osteoporosis (Table 18-2). The higher proportion of secondary osteoporosis in men than in women is usually attributed to alcoholism, malignant disease, long-term corticosteroid treatment, and hypogonadism[295] (Table 18-2).

ASSESSMENT OF BONE MINERAL DENSITY

The ability to measure BMD has been one of the most significant advances in the investigation and treatment of osteoporosis because BMD strongly correlates with bone strength. Variation in the level of BMD accounts for 60% to 80% of bone strength, but it is important to realize that bone strength depends not only on the amount of mineral measured by current techniques but also on the structural characteristics of the skeleton such as size, shape, and three-dimensional architecture.[4] Up until now, the prediction of bone strength and risk of fracture has mainly been based on densitometric measurements, but current research evaluating the macrogeometric and microgeometric structure of bone will probably improve the prediction of bone strength and the risk of fracture in the future.[4,13,85]

Single-Photon Absorptiometry and Dual-Photon Absorptiometry

The first specific bone scanning method to be developed, the single-photon absorptiometry technique (SPA), used a single

TABLE 18-2	Diseases and Conditions Associated with Secondary Osteoporosis

Hormonal
Hypogonadism
Cushing syndrome
Addison disease
Hyperthyroidism
Hyperparathyroidism
Acromegaly

Nutritional
Severe malnutrition (e.g., anorexia nervosa)
Malabsorption (e.g., postgastrectomy)
Severe liver disease

Hereditary
Osteogenesis imperfecta
Ehler-Danlos syndrome
Homocystinuria
Congenital porphyria
Hypophosphatasia

Rheumatologic
Rheumatoid arthritis and related diseases
Ankylosing spondylitis

Hematologic
Multiple myeloma and related diseases
Hemochromatomatosis
Hemophilia
Mastocytosis
Thalassemia
Leukemia and lymphoma

Other
Paralysis or total immobilization
Chronic obstructive lung disease
Diffuse metastatic carcinoma
Hypercalcemia of malignancy

TABLE 18-3	Methods for Bone Mineral Measurement	
Ionizing Radiation		Nonionizing Radiation
Gamma-radiation	**X-ray**	
Single-photon absorptiometry (SPA)	Radiogrammetry	
Dual-photon absorptiometry (DPA)	Single x-ray absorptiometry (SXA)	Ultrasound
Neutron activation analysis (NAA)	Dual x-ray absorptiometry (DXA)	Magnetic resonance tomography (MRT)
Compton scattering technique	Quantitative computed tomography (QCT)	

energy radionuclide.[4] The technique of photon absorptiometry relies on the relationship between bone mineral content and the ease with which photons pass through skeletal tissue (Table 18-3). The denser the skeleton, the more photons are absorbed by the bone tissue. This method can only be used in regions with minimal soft tissue, usually the distal radius or the calcaneus, because the scan cannot differentiate between absorption in soft tissue and bone.* Dual-photon absorptiometry (DPA), which uses two different photon energies, was developed to separately evaluate the absorption in soft tissue and bone so that skeletal structures surrounded by soft tissues could be evaluated. However, because of low precision relative to the rate of change of BMD, DPA is not suitable for monitoring longitudinal changes.[216]

Dual-Energy X-ray Absorptiometry

Dual x-ray absorptiometry (DXA) was introduced in 1987.[148,216] This method uses x-rays as the photon source, avoiding the problems of isotope source decay and replacement. The scan time is reduced to minutes with markedly improved scan image quality and resolution. However, the most important advance was that precision was markedly improved compared with the DPA technique, making the technique adequate for longitudinal monitoring of BMD. DXA is currently the most used scanning technique for predicting the risk of fractures, establishing or confirming the diagnosis of osteoporosis, selecting patients for therapy, and monitoring the effectiveness of therapy[192] (Table 18-3). Fan-beam DXA technology offers semiautomatic vertebral morphometry (MXA) for screening vertebral deformities with scanning in the lateral projection.[278] Thus far, fan-beam DXA technology has been used in research to screen for the presence of fractures, but in the future this technique may be used to improve fracture prediction. When deciding treatment strategies for osteoporosis, most clinicians currently use the hip scan, or occasionally the spine scan in younger patients, as the gold standard. Newer and smaller DXA equip-

ment that measure the radius or the calcaneus is promising because of lower cost and because the machines are portable. However, further studies must be undertaken before these machines can be recommended in general screening programs.

Quantitative Ultrasound

Quantitative ultrasound (QUS) transmits a signal through the bone in the range of 100 kHz up to 2 MHz. It started in 1984 with the introduction of parameter broadband ultrasound attenuation (BUA)[161] (Table 18-3). This parameter evaluated the attenuation in the bone, this being mainly caused by scattering but also by absorption.[161] Attenuation seems to reflect not only the amount of mineral in the bone but also the bone structure, elasticity, and strength. Bone microstructure and material properties have both been shown to affect QUS parameters, and studies have supported the view that QUS can predict fractures independent of the BMD value estimated by DXA scan.[13,89] It has been suggested that BUA is not only influenced by BMD but also by the microarchitecture of bone, whereas the speed of sound (SOS) may vary with the elasticity of bone.[13,89] Therefore, QUS approaches may provide a better insight into skeletal status because it relates to mechanical strength (Table 18-3). The two parameters BUA and SOS are often combined in weighted averages, most commonly presented as "stiffness," quantitative ultrasound index (QUI), or "soundness." However, none of the indices reflects biomechanical stiffness, nor do they supply additional information over those provided by BUA and SOS. They are, however, practical to use because they summarize BUA and SOS and have a lower precision error, which probably makes stiffness more suitable for monitoring.

The main use of QUS is in the assessment of fracture risk. Two large prospective studies with sample sizes of 6500 to 10,000 women showed that QUS measured at the calcaneus can be used to predict future hip fracture risk equally as well as DXA measurements.[13,105] Typically, the risk of fracture increases by approximately a factor of 2 if a QUS value is reduced by 1 SD, but this varies between devices and QUS parameters as well as between different types of fractures.[13,105] The use of QUS in monitoring and diagnosis requires further study.

Quantified Computer Tomography

Quantified computer tomography (QCT) is a technique that measures the density of different tissues.[85] Standard CT scanners can be adapted to provide qualitative bone density measurements. QCT is a densitometric technique that measures the actual volumetric bone density. Other ionizing techniques measure the amount of mineral within the scanned area.[85,216] This is done with QCT by selecting a region in the central portion of the vertebral body, or any other specified area, and measuring the true density of trabecular bone. It is also possible to specifically select cortical bone and estimate bone size and shape. In recent years, smaller peripheral QCT (pQCT) units have been manufactured that are capable of measuring BMD in the forearm and the lower leg. The previous problems of high radiation exposure and poor reproducibility compared with DXA have been minimized with the new versions of pQCT software. Although promising, this method has thus far been mainly used for research purposes, and currently there is no consensus regarding the role of pQCT for fracture prediction. There are a number of other techniques using ionizing and nonionizing

*References 4,13,69,85,144,174,216,227,254,255,295.

sources in the evaluation of BMD, but these methods are not used in clinical practice (Table 18-3).

ASSESSMENT OF BONE METABOLISM BY BIOCHEMICAL BONE MARKERS

Bone Formation

Bone contains hydroxyapatite crystals, which are present in the matrix, consisting of about 90% type 1 collagen and 10% non-collagenous proteins including osteocalcin, the dominant non-collagenous protein in bone. The basic structure of collagen is a triple helix consisting of two α-1 chains and one α-2 chain with a high content of glycine, proline, and hydroxyproline. Procollagen is formed in the osteoclasts, and after secretion to the extracellular space, the procollagen I extension peptides are split at the amino (N) terminals (P1NP) and carboxyl (C) terminals (P1CP) before final fibril formation. These extension peptides are a marker of bone formation and can be measured in blood.[262] However, type 1 collagen is present in many tissues, particularly the skin, and the relative contribution from these sites to circulating P1CP and P1NP influences the estimation of bone formation. In addition, during bone formation, the bone cells secrete noncollagenous small proteins that become incorporated into the matrix. One of these, osteocalcin (BGP), can be measured in blood as a marker of bone formation.[189,262] Alkaline phosphatase (ASP) and bone-specific alkaline phosphatase (BSAP), an enzyme involved in the mineralization of bone, are also used as markers of bone formation[189,262,314] (Table 18-4).

Bone Resorption

Urinary hydroxyproline (OHP) is widely used to estimate the degradation of bone collagen and as such is a marker of bone resorption. However, because this marker is present in all types of collagen and the excretion is largely dependent on collagen-rich food, the clinical interpretation of OHP is difficult.[262] The collagen molecules aggregate to fibrils that are stabilized by covalent cross-links. The pyridinium cross-links comprise pryidinoline (Pyr) and deoxypryidinoline (D-Pyr), which are present in all mature collagen except skin. Because D-Pyr is only present in significant amounts in bone, it is considered to be more bone specific than Pyr. The pyridinium cross-links are measured as total pryidinolines, free pryidinolines, and telopeptides, the peptide cross-link fragments at the N terminals (NTx) and C terminals (CTx), in serum as markers of bone resorption.[154,189,262,314] During bone resorption, osteoclasts also secrete tartrate-resistant acid phosphatase isoenzymes (TRACP), and the serum concentration of this enzyme has sometimes been used as a marker of bone resorption.[86,206] However, the enzyme is not specific to bone, and it is difficult to separate from isoenzymes derived from other tissues such as platelets and erythrocytes. Another collagen degradation product used to estimate bone resorption is C-terminal cross-linking telopeptide of type 1 collagen, which is found in both serum and urine (Table 18-4).

As most of the bone metabolic markers are affected by underlying factors such as diurnal rhythm, day-to-day variations, seasonal variations, menstrual variations, age, sex, diet, alcohol intake, systemic diseases, medication, and physical activity,[98,313] the interpretation of bone markers must be undertaken with care. Markers have proved to be useful in epidemiologic and interventional studies in which groups of patients are studied and in patients with metabolic diseases associated with high bone turnover such as Paget disease. However, guidelines for classifying and evaluating individual patients with osteoporosis are less well defined. For example, it is not possible to separate a large skeleton with a low turnover from a small skeleton with a high turnover. Nevertheless, some studies have shown that measurement of a marker of bone turnover or a combination of markers can identify groups of patients with low BMD or fast bone loss.[124] Whether a single measurement can predict low BMD or a future fracture in an isolated patient remains under debate.[245] Biochemical markers of bone turnover may also have a role in short-term monitoring of treatment.[107] It remains to be proved if measurements of bone markers will add to the predictive values obtained by BMD measurement.

RISK FACTORS FOR OSTEOPOROSIS AND FRAGILITY FRACTURES

Risk factors for fragility fractures can be divided into two main types—those related to trauma, such as a tendency to fall, and those related to bone strength, such as BMD, skeletal architecture, and bone size[4,13,56] (Table 18-5). However, several risk factors, such as immobility and aging, may operate through both skeletal and extraskeletal routes. For example, fracture risk increases with age partly due to increased bone loss and partly due to the fact that older patients are at greater risk of fracture than are younger patients, independent of their BMD level. Clinically, it is important to determine all risk factors, because women with multiple risk factors and low BMD are at an especially high risk of fracture[56] (Table 18-5, Fig. 18-5).

TABLE 18-4 **Measurements of Bone Turnover, Evaluating Bone Formation and Resorption, by Bone Metabolic Markers**

Markers of Bone Formation

Serum
Osteocalcin (OC)
Bone-specific alkaline phosphatase (BALP)
Total alkaline phosphatase (ALP)
Procollagen I C-terminal extension peptide (PICP)
Procollagen I N-terminal extension peptide (PINP)

Markers of Bone Resorption

Serum
Tartrate-resistant acid phosphatase (TRACP)
Tartrate-resistant acid phosphatase 5b (TRACP 5b)
C-terminal cross-linking telopeptide of type I collagen (CTX)
N-terminal cross-linking telopeptide of type I collagen (NTX)
C-terminal cross-linking telopeptide of type I collagen (ICTP)

Urine
Deoxypyridinoline (DPD)
Pyridinoline (PYD)
Hydroxyproline (Hyp)
C-terminal cross-linking telopeptide of type I collagen (CTX)

TABLE 18-5	Risk Factors for Osteoporosis, Falls, and Fracture		
Risk Factor	**Osteoporosis**	**Fall**	**Fracture**
Low bone mineral density			+
High age	+	+	+
Female sex	+	+	+
Primary or secondary amenorrhea	+		+
Primary or secondary hypogonadism in men	+		+
Premature menopause	+		+
Postmenopausal status	+	+	+
Tallness		+	+
Low body weight	+		+
Long hip axis length			+
Previous fragility fracture	+	+	+
Family history of fracture			+
White or Asian ethnic origin			+
Immobility/low physical activity	+	+	+
Current smoking	+	+	+
High caffeine intake			+
Alcohol abuse	+	+	+
High bone turnover	+		+
Osteomalacia/vitamin D deficiency	+	+	+
Low dietary calcium intake	+		+
Chronic illnesses	+	+	+
Glucocorticoid therapy	+		+
Sedative medications		+	+
Visual impairment		+	+
Cognitive impairment		+	+
Neurologic diseases		+	+
Lower limb disability	+	+	+
Hyperthyroidism	+		+
Hyperparathyroidism	+		+
Malabsorption	+		+
Celiac disease	+		+
Gastrectomy	+		+
Chronic arthritides	+	+	+
Chronic renal/liver diseases	+		+
Cushing syndrome	+		+
Malignancies	+		+
Organ transplantations	+		+
Nursing home resident		+	+

Bone Mineral Density

At present, BMD is probably the best surrogate measure of the breaking strength of bone. Furthermore, the diagnosis of osteoporosis is only defined by BMD measurement using the DXA technique and only in women[311] (Table 18-1). BMD was not originally designed to be used as a criterion for therapeutic intervention but to identify the proportion of the population at increased risk of fracture. Using this criterion, 30% of the American postmenopausal female population is now recognized as having osteoporosis.[176] The definition of osteopenia (Table 18-1) as a BMD between −1 and −2.5 SDs below the young normal mean was meant to describe a group of individuals at increased risk of developing osteoporosis but still not having a particularly high risk of fracture. The classification of established osteoporosis adds the risk factor of previous fracture to the treatment protocol in an individual patient.[259,311] Clinicians must understand that the risk of fracture increases exponentially with decreasing BMD.[158] No specific BMD level signifies a "fracture threshold." The definition is arbitrary. A decreased BMD of 1 SD is thought to increase the fracture risk by about 1.5 times but it may be up to 2.5 times according to the region[51,188] (Table 18-6). One study that followed 8134 non−African American women over 65 years of age found that the age-adjusted relative risk of hip fracture was 1.6 for each 1-SD decrease in BMD in the lumbar spine and 2.6 for each 1-SD decrease in BMD in the femoral neck[51,188] (Table 18-6). It has also been shown that peripheral measurements of the radius and calcaneus can predict future fractures.[121,259]

Data also suggest that the QUS of the calcaneus will independently predict the risk of hip fracture in elderly women as well as a DXA scan.[13,105] In the EPIDOS study, 5662 elderly women with a mean age of 80.4 years were assessed with calcaneal ultrasound and femoral neck DXA. The relative risk of hip fracture for a 1-SD reduction was 2.0 for ultrasound broadband attenuation, 1.7 for SOS, and 1.9 for femoral BMD measured by the DXA technique.[13,105] More prospective validation using studies of perimenopausal and early postmenopausal women is needed before bone ultrasound can be recommended for fracture risk assessment in these groups.

Even if BMD is an excellent screening tool for fractures, population screening for osteoporosis is not recommended.[277] It is recommended that patients are selected for bone densitometry on the basis of significant risk factors. There are several well-established risk factors related to secondary osteoporosis, and further diagnosis by BMD is indicated in these patients even if they are asymptomatic (Table 18-5). Similarly, the diagnosis of osteoporosis may be confirmed with bone densitometry in patients with previous low-trauma fractures or a vertebral deformity.

Skeletal Geometry

The geometry of the femoral neck probably plays an important part in the risk of sustaining a hip fracture. The length of the femoral neck, the hip axis length (HAL), measured between the external border of the greater trochanter and the inner pelvic rim has been shown to be an independent predictor of hip fracture.[74] A new algorithm was developed by Yoshikawa et al.[317] and Beck et al.[14] using the principles of single-plane engineering. This estimates femoral neck mechanical strength from an anteroposterior DXA scan, a so-called hip strength analysis

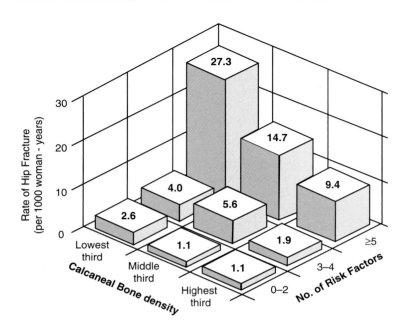

FIGURE 18-5 Annual risk of hip fracture according to the number of risk factors and the age-specific calcaneal bone density. (Reprinted with permission from Cummings SR, Nevitt MC, Browner WS, et al. Risk factors for hip fracture in white women. Study of Osteoporotic Fractures Research Group. N Engl J Med 1995;332: 767–773.)

(HSA). A similar geometric approach for the prediction of fractures has also been undertaken from forearm bone scans.[4] Preliminary data indicate that the inclusion of geometric analyses in the estimate of risk factors could improve fracture prediction.[4,46]

Heredity

Twin and family studies have demonstrated that 60% to 80% of bone mass is determined by genetic factors.[269] This is probably true during both growth and aging. Daughters of mothers with osteoporosis have a relatively low BMD compared with age-matched daughters of mothers without osteoporosis.[269] The risk of sustaining a hip fracture in women with a maternal history of hip fracture is about twice that of women without such a history, independent of BMD.[56] One of the first groups to report a relationship between genetic polymorphism and bone mass was Kelly et al.,[147] even though the paper was later withdrawn. Subsequent studies have only implied a minor association between BMD and a vitamin D receptor. However, further studies have indicated the importance of genetic polymorphism in a variety of candidate genes. As an example, it is likely that there is an association between a specific polymorphism in the

type I collagen,[95] transforming growth factor-β (TGFβ),[160] the estrogen receptor,[153] the type I collagen gene (*COLIA1*),[297] the interleukin 1 and 6 gene,[280] low-density lipoprotein receptor–related protein 5,[300] and low BMD. It is probable that new associations between genetic polymorphism and BMD will be made, but because osteoporosis is a polygenic disease, it is also probable that no single gene will provide sufficient information to predict the risk of fracture.[241,242] However, a combination of a number of genes, perhaps in conjunction with BMD measurements and other risk factors, could facilitate prediction of individuals at high risk of fracture.[241,242]

History of Previous Fracture

Fractures caused by a fall from a standing height are often related to osteoporosis, and it is estimated that osteoporosis plays a role in up to 75% of fractures in people aged 45 years or older.[45] Women who have had either vertebral fractures or non-spine fractures have an increased risk of sustaining new vertebral fractures,[259] and women who have had wrist fractures have an increased risk of sustaining a hip fracture[185] independent of the BMD. In a study of osteoporotic fractures (SOS) that included 9516 white women of 65 years or older, it was found

TABLE 18-6	**Age-Adjusted Relative Increase in Risk of Fractures**			
Site of Measurement	Forearm Fracture	Hip Fracture	Vertebral Fracture	All Fractures
Distal radius	1.7 (1.4 to 2.0)	1.8 (1.4 to 2.2)	1.7 (1.4 to 2.1)	1.4 (1.3 to 1.6)
Femoral neck	1.4 (1.4 to 1.6)	2.6 (2.0 to 3.5)	1.8 (1.1 to 2.7)	1.6 (1.4 to 1.8)
Lumbar spine	1.5 (1.3 to 1 to 8)	1.6 (1.2 to 2.2)	2.3 (1.9 to 2.8)	1.5 (1.4 to 1.7)

In women, for every one standard deviation decrease in bone mineral density (absorptiometry) below the mean value for age (95% confidence interval).
From Marshall D, Johnell O, Wedel H. Meta-analysis of how well measures of bone mineral density predict occurrence of osteoporotic fractures. Br Med J 1996;312:1254–1259.

that a history of fracture increased the risk of hip fracture by 50% independent of the BMD.[56] In addition, any type of fracture sustained since the age of 15 years increases the risk of having subsequent fractures by 70% in perimenopausal women aged 47 to 56 years independent of BMD.[122] Because the risk is independent of BMD, a history of fractures may indicate an increased tendency to fall, the existence of extraskeletal risk factors, or a defect in bone strength other than a low BMD.

Falls

One third of the elderly population fall annually, and the incidence of falls that cause injury increases with age.[263] The incidence is higher in the institutionalized elderly compared with elderly patients living at home.[183] Frequent falling is also one of the most common risk factors for fractures, and virtually the same risk factors for falls also account for fractures[99,201, 286,287,290] (Table 18-5). Intrinsic risk factors for falls include the following[99,101,201,285–288,290]:

- Old age
- Female gender
- Low body mass
- Medical comorbidities
- Musculoskeletal diseases
- Cognitive impairment
- Gait and balance disorders
- Sensory impairments
- Postural hypotension
- History of previous falls
- Use of certain medications
  - Benzodiazepines
  - Sedative-hypnotic drugs
  - Antidepressants
  - Antihypertensive medication
  - Antiarrhythmic drugs
  - Diuretics
  - Antiseizure medications

In contrast, environmental hazards such as rugs, slippery and uneven floor surfaces, poor lighting, electrical cords, foot stools without handrails, slippery top surfaces, and unsuitable footwear are often classified as extrinsic risk factors.[99,101,201, 232,285–288,290] Extrinsic factors play a progressively smaller role in falls as age advances largely because it is the intrinsic factors that assume a much more important role as chronic illness becomes a more significant problem.[232]

Age

Most risk factors associated with fractures become more prevalent with advancing age, the risk of sustaining a hip fracture increasing 1.5 to 2 times every 5 years.[225] During the perimenopausal years, the risk of fracture is increased in perimenopausal women compared with premenopausal women independent of BMD,[158] indicating that risk factors other than BMD account for the increase.[13]

Gender

Females are at greater risk of osteoporotic fractures. Lower peak BMD, faster bone loss, smaller bone size, and the higher prevalence of falls in women may account for this. Mechanical properties of bone are not only dependent on BMD but also on size,

geometry, and architecture. Gender differences and the recurrence of fracture may be explained in part by the larger cross-sectional area of bones in men and differences in subperiosteal bone apposition with aging.[4,261]

Weight

Low body weight is associated with low BMD[159] and increased fracture incidence.[102] Gaining weight after the age of 25 years provides protection against hip fracture,[56] while, in contrast, losing weight increases the risk of osteoporotic fractures.[68] The Framingham study reported that the relative risk of fracture was found to be 0.63 in individuals 114% to 123% overweight and 0.33 in individuals more than 138% overweight.[149] Obesity may protect the skeleton in several ways. These are increased extraglandular production of estrone in the fat tissue, improved vitamin D status due to storage of vitamin D in fatty tissues, the provision of a local cushioning effect at the hip when falling, and a denser and stronger skeleton due to increased skeletal loading in obese people.

Body Length

Tall individuals seem to have an increased risk of having a hip fracture.[56,205] The reason could be that tall individuals fall farther, thus hitting the ground with greater force,[114] or because tall individuals have a longer hip axis length.[74]

Calcium Intake

Studies evaluating the relationship between dietary calcium intake and hip fracture risk have given conflicting results.[129,225,312] Errors in the measurement of dietary calcium intake and slow changes in BMD may explain this, but it appears that increased dietary calcium partially prevents bone loss, although the effect in populations with high calcium is small.[61]

Smoking

Studies suggest that current smokers have a low BMD and more fractures than nonsmokers.[58] A recent meta-analysis supported this view reporting that smoking is a risk factor for osteoporotic fractures, independent of BMD, in postmenopausal women.[168] This could be due to the fact that smokers, in comparison with nonsmokers, have an earlier menopause, are slimmer, have a reduced extraglandular production of estrogens, and have an increased metabolic clearance rate of estrogens and that smoking inhibits the function of osteoclasts.

Caffeine

Studies report that a high caffeine intake in the elderly is associated with an increased fracture risk.[56,150] In contrast, high caffeine consumption does not appear to be associated with an increased risk of fracture in perimenopausal women.[117,122,293] Thus, the adverse effects of caffeine on bone may be only important in the elderly.

Alcohol

Individuals who abuse alcohol have an increasing risk of sustaining fractures partly due to poor balance, associated illnesses, frequent falls, and accidents but also due to the adverse effect of alcohol on bone metabolism.[117] Alcohol exerts a direct toxic effect on bone cells. It affects osteoblast proliferation in vitro and reduces matrix protein synthesis in vivo.[214] In contrast, moderate alcohol consumption does not appear to be a risk factor for osteoporosis or fracture.[150]

Immobility

Osteoclasts are sensitive to mechanical loading and the reduced loading that occurs in immobile patients leads to increased BMD loss.[90] Immobility also contributes to decreased muscle strength, this being a major risk factor for falls.[91,156,159] Decreased muscle strength may also have a direct negative influence on BMD.[91,156,159] Increased hip fracture risk has been reported to be linked with poor quadriceps strength associated with immobility independent of the BMD.[213] Several studies have confirmed this showing that mobile women have a lower risk of hip fracture compared with less mobile women.[56,140] However, it is not known whether the adverse effects of physical inactivity and immobility are mediated by a decreased BMD, coexisting illnesses, and increased risk of falls or all of these factors.

Medical Conditions

Impaired health and chronic illnesses predispose to fractures by impairing BMD, bone quality, and muscle function. They also tend to decrease physical activity and to increase the likelihood of falling. Diseases and conditions that have been found to increase the risk of sustaining fractures include the following[56,59,90,101,131]:

- Hyperthyroidism
- Decreased visual acuity
- Poor depth perception
- Mental impairment or dementia
- Impaired neuromuscular function (e.g., the inability to rise from a chair without using the arms)
- Hypercorticalism
- Hypergonadism
- Hyperparathyroidism
- Osteomalacia
- Renal and hepatic diseases
- Certain malignancies
- Rheumatoid arthritis
- Paget disease
- Gastrectomy and organ transplantations

Many of these conditions are considered to be associated with fall-related risk factors rather than BMD-related factors.[210,286]

Drug Treatment

A variety of drugs are related to an increased risk of hip fracture independent of the BMD.[56] Studies have reported that treatment with corticosteroids, long-acting benzodiazepines, anticonvulsant drugs (especially phenytoin), gonadotrophin-releasing hormone agonists, tamoxifen, long-term treatment with heparin, cytotoxic drugs, and lithium are associated with an increased risk of sustaining a fracture.[56,131] This association remains after adjusting for BMD, suggesting that the associated illnesses, impaired health, and increased likelihood of falls affect the risk of fracture.[56,131]

Modification of Risk Factors

Several risk factors can be modified. It is possible to influence BMD and the likelihood of falling,[239,289] but prevention requires a multifaceted strategy including environmental changes, the provision of adequate calcium intake, supporting physical activity, improving functional ability, correcting or treating health disorders, and avoiding polypharmacy.[239,289] In individuals with risk factors other than low BMD, these factors should be addressed.

Other risk factors cannot be modified. These risk factors, together with the modifiable risk factors, can be used to identify at-risk groups suitable for bone densitometry and amenable to different treatment strategies. In the Study of Osteoporotic Fractures, white women older than 65 years were classified according to their calcaneal BMD and the number of clinical risk factors for hip fracture.[56] The relationship between BMD and fracture risk was least apparent with fewer clinical risk factors. Thus, women with a higher calcaneal BMD with more than four clinical risk factors had a higher risk of sustaining a hip fracture than did women with lower BMDs but few other risk fractures (Fig. 18-5). The highest risk for hip fractures was found in women with the lowest BMDs who had more than four clinical risk factors.

PREVENTION OF OSTEOPOROTIC FRACTURES

Half of all women and one third of all men will sustain a fragility fracture during their lifetime.[43]

Increased morbidity and mortality and the high costs associated with the rising incidence of osteoporotic fractures make it imperative to implement prevention strategies in the community.[42,236] Hip and vertebral fractures in women are most commonly discussed, but other fragility fractures are also associated with significant problems.[246] In addition, the number of fractures in men and children has increased and we must also discuss these groups.[32,133,267] However, general screening to detect low BMD is not considered to be cost effective because a modest deficit in BMD is associated with a low absolute risk of sustaining a fracture. The use of drug treatment in these groups would mean a considerable therapeutic investment to save a relatively small number of fractures. Furthermore, studies show that it is only individuals with osteoporosis or osteopenia with fractures in whom drugs will reduce the incidence of fractures. It is unclear whether individuals with a more modest deficit in BMD benefit from drug treatment* (Table 18-6). If the aim of health care is to reduce the fracture rate in the community widely accessible, inexpensive intervention programs with no adverse effects are required.

Nonpharmacological Prevention of Osteoporotic Fractures

Nutrition

Normal skeletal health is dependent on a balanced diet with an adequate intake of energy, minerals, vitamins, and proteins. Calcium is the most important nutrient for attaining adequate peak bone mass, but there is no universal consensus about the

---

*References 22,34,35,52,70,108,186,195,223,248,260.

daily requirement. The 1994 consensus conference discussing the optimum calcium intake recommended a daily intake of 1200 to 1500 mg for adolescents, 1000 mg for adults up to 65 years of age, and 1500 mg for postmenopausal women not receiving estrogen and for elderly individuals.[7] Although the results of most studies indicate a beneficial effect from calcium supplements, especially in individuals with a low intake, the long-term effect of a high dietary calcium on BMD is unclear. Calcium also seems to work as a threshold nutritional element with about 400 mg per day as a limit. Below this level, increasing calcium intake seems beneficial and necessary.[190] The positive correlation between dietary calcium and BMD has been shown in children,[169] adolescents,[123] and young women,[284] indicating that higher calcium intake results in a higher BMD. It has been calculated that variations in calcium nutrition early in life may account for as much as 5% to 10% difference in peak adult bone mass, which would contribute to more than 50% of the difference in the rates of hip fracture in later life.[191]

Calcium absorption is also dependent on the vitamin D level and serum concentrations of 25-hydroxy vitamin D decline with age. The current recommendation is that the daily intake of vitamin D should be about 400 to 800 IU if exposure to sunlight is low, especially in the elderly, who have decreased ability to activate precursors in the skin, decreased ability to hydroxylate vitamin D in the kidney and liver, reduced dietary intake, and diminished absorption from food. Another problem in frail elderly individuals is achieving an adequate intake of protein, total energy, and a variety of other nutritional components such as phosphorus, magnesium, zinc, copper, iron, fluoride, sodium, and vitamins D, A, C, and K, all of which are required for normal bone health.

Physical Activity

Bone tissue seems to be most adaptive to mechanical load during periods of rapid skeletal change as in the late prepubertal and early pubertal period. Mechanical loading increases BMD but also improves bone structure, geometry, architecture, and possibly material properties such as strength, stiffness, and its energy-absorbing capacity.[133,139,171,172] The biological purpose of this adaptation is to achieve a skeleton that is more resistant to load but still as light as possible to facilitate mobility.[139] Data have unequivocally shown that physical activity may increase BMD, skeletal geometry, and bone strength by up to 30% to 50%[133,139,140] in those individuals in whom training is initiated before puberty[133,140,171,172] (Fig. 18-4). The reason for this can be explained by the fact that the adolescent growth spurt is the only time in life when bone is added in substantial amounts to both sides of the bone cortex by endosteal and periosteal apposition.[228] The importance of regarding exercise during growth as a prevention strategy for fragility fractures in old age originates from the data that relate exercise to increased peak bone mass and show that 60% to 70% of the variance in BMD at 65 years of age is attributed to achieved peak bone mass.[269] Bone tissue is also able to respond to exercise in adulthood although to a lesser extent than during growth. During adulthood physical activity should be regarded more as bone preserving rather than bone building because most studies show a 1% to 3% increase in BMD with exercise.[12,115] This has also been shown in Cochrane Database Systematic Reviews.[27,272]

Nevertheless, the exercise-induced bone-preserving effect in adulthood may be of great importance in maintaining bone

strength and preventing age-related fractures because only a small increase in BMD is associated with a significant reduction in the risk of fracture.[51] Furthermore, exercise may cause a reduction in the incidence of fracture through nonskeletal effects.[100,128] In the postmenopausal period, physical activity may prevent age-related bone loss.[57,116] Brisk walking, climbing up and down stairs, dancing, and callisthenics are the most suitable activities for older people since they are easily available and are inexpensive and safe.[128] It also appears that exercise should be lifelong if bone strength is to be maintained because cessation of exercise is followed by a rapid decline of the exercise-achieved BMD.[142,217,299] Regular impact loading activities that create high-magnitude strains and versatile strain distributions throughout the bone structure best improve bone strength.[115,116,139,140,142,162] Squash, tennis, badminton, aerobics, step exercises, volleyball, basketball, soccer, gymnastics, weight and power training, and similar sports may best fulfill these demands.[139,140] In contrast, endurance training such as long distance running, swimming, and cycling has not proved as effective in increasing BMD.[140]

The best proof that exercise could be used to prevent fractures would be gained from studies that had the incidence of fracture as their outcome criterion. Unfortunately, no such randomized controlled trials (RCTs) exist. Instead, we have to rely on prospective and retrospective observational and case-control studies. These types of studies consistently show that both past and current physical activity is associated with a reduced risk of hip fracture in women and men, the risk reduction being up to 50%.[100,128] Several studies also report a dose-response relationship that further supports the probability of a link. It seems that vigorous activity during youth followed by more moderate activity during adulthood is the best combination to prevent hip fracture because vigorous activity in old age may actually increase the incidence of falls that cause injury.[126,276] Studies focusing on physical activity and fractures other than hip fractures are few and present contradictory results. If anything, these studies suggest that lifetime physical activity protects against all types of fractures, although it must be appreciated that vigorous activity in the elderly may increase the risk of falls and therefore fractures.[57,100,128,184,276] Activity programs for the elderly must therefore be designed specifically for each individual and be based on the physical abilities of that person. They should be undertaken with caution and after proper training.[276] It would seem that promotion of lifelong physical activities is probably one of the most important goals in public health programs of the new millennium.[184,276]

Prevention of Falls

Prospective RCTs have shown that exercise can reduce the risk of falling in elderly and frail individuals.[29,83,87,239] Exercise, including balance training, improves balance and decreases the risk of falling. The greatest effect was seen in those who were most compliant with the program.[177,275,316] In several recent studies, Tai Chi has been shown to be an effective intervention reducing falls by almost 50%.[315] The effectiveness of modifying other risk factors has not been demonstrated in controlled studies. However, it makes sense to modify the home environment to eliminate as many elements as possible that could lead to falls. Because previous falls are an independent risk factor for future falls, it is especially important to evaluate each elderly person who has fallen for any risk factors in the home environment. This has been successfully used in the PROFET study (Prevention of Falls in the Elderly Trial), in which intervention decreased the risk of falls by 70% in patients who had presented to emergency departments with fall-related injuries.[39] The key elements of such programs of risk reduction are as follows:

1. Individual management so that factors relevant to a particular patient are addressed
2. Reduction of environmental hazards
3. Appropriate reduction of medication
4. Education of the individual in behavior strategies
5. Education techniques for getting up after falls
6. Exercise programs to improve strength, balance, and aerobic capacity

Hip Protectors

More than 90% of hip fractures are related to direct impact on the hip.[134] Falls directly on the hip increase the odds ratio for a hip fracture by about 20-fold.[114] In nursing home patients who fall on their hips, the risk of fracture is 25% in women and 33% in men.[167] Energy absorption in the soft tissue surrounding the hip has been shown to protect against hip fractures,[165,180] and as much as 75% of the energy in a fall can be absorbed.[165] This partly explains why being overweight protects against hip fractures.[164] Based on these facts, various hip padding systems have been developed. There are a number of different types, including an energy-shunting type (horseshoe) system,[113] a crash helmet type,[166,230] an energy-absorptive type,[270] and an airbag type,[36] designed to reduce the impact of the skeleton in a fall[55,114,137,138,167] (Fig. 18-6). Randomized controlled trials, including nursing home residents and those frail elderly living at home, have shown a protective effect of 34% by hip protectors when using pooled data.[67,137,138,167] Based on a subgroup analysis in a previously reported nursing home study, the compliance in the use of hip protectors was 24%.[126] In a more recent community-based study, an initial acceptance rate of 57% decreasing to 40% after 2 years[118] was found. The effectiveness of hip protectors is verified in one Cochrane Database Systematic Review including 13 RCTs of a total of 4316 patients.[229] So far, no studies have shown that hip protectors have a general protective effect in people living at home and

the cost-effectiveness remains unclear.[229] The most significant problem with this type of prevention strategy appears to be compliance.[229]

Pharmacological Prevention of Osteoporotic Fractures

Calcium and Vitamin D

Calcium supplements, generally prescribed as 500 to 1000 mg daily, are known to slow the rate of bone loss in the elderly and in individuals with a low calcium intake.[123,169,284] There are also studies that suggest that calcium supplements may reduce the incidence of fractures, but usually calcium supplementation is regarded as an adjunctive treatment for osteoporosis rather than as a single treatment.[60,247,250] This view is supported in a meta-analysis of 15 trials including 1806 individuals[274] and in a Cochrane Database Systematic Review.[273] Calcium supplements are safe, although mild gastrointestinal disturbances such as constipation have been reported. The risk of kidney stones related to increased urinary calcium excretion does not appear to be a problem.

There is evidence that vitamin D is also useful in the treatment of osteoporosis. A French study including 3270 elderly women who lived in long-term care facilities and who were treated daily for 3 years with 1200 IU calcium and 800 IU vitamin D showed a 29% reduction in the incidence of hip fracture and a 24% reduction in the incidence of nonvertebral fracture compared with a placebo group[34,35] (Table 18-7). Another study reported a similar trend with a 50% reduction in nonvertebral fractures in patients whose daily diet was supplemented with calcium and vitamin D.[61] A British study, including 2686 men and women living in their own homes, reported that calcium and vitamin D treatment over a 5-year period reduced the risk of fracture by 22% and the risk of fractures in the hip, forearm, or spine by 33%.[296] This study implied that calcium and vitamin D treatment might decrease fracture risk in nursing home residents who did not have a deficient calcium intake. In contrast, a study of 2578 elderly healthy Dutch women with a high calcium intake who were treated daily with 400 IU vitamin D over 3.5 years showed no effect on the risk of hip fracture,[175] and a study including 36,282 postmenopausal women aged 50 to 79 years and followed for an average of 7 years showed no evidence of a reduced hip fracture risk.[125] One published meta-analysis reported that vitamin D treatment alone did not reduce the risk of fractures.[88] However, in combination with calcium, the risk of hip fractures was reduced by 26% in elderly care home residents, although in healthy individuals living in their own home, there was no reduction in the incidence of hip fracture, although the risk of sustaining vertebral fractures was reduced by 54%.[88] Similar results were published in another meta-analysis of 8124 individuals.[226] Thus, the literature, including a Cochrane Systematic Database Review,[8] suggests that calcium and vitamin D should be used routinely in elderly individuals living in old people's homes because of a high prevalence of vitamin D deficiency as a result of low intake, low exposure to sunlight, and impaired vitamin D synthesis in the skin. In these cohorts, including seven trials and 10,376 participants, the treatment led to 21% fewer hip and 13% fewer other nonvertebral fractures.[8] In this analysis, there was no effect on vertebral fracture risk.

The effectiveness of vitamin D alone in fracture prevention is unclear.[8,94] One meta-analysis including 5292 individuals

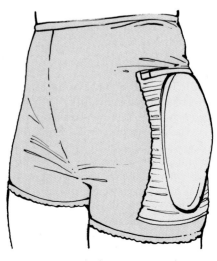

FIGURE 18-6 The hip protector underwear.

TABLE 18-7 Randomized Controlled Trials with Incidence of Vertebral and Hip Fractures over 3 Years[a]

Drug	Study	Risk Profile of Patients at Baseline	Sex	Mean Age (yr)	No. of Patients Included	Placebo	Drug	Relative Risk (95% CI or p value)
Vertebral Fracture Drug								
HRT	WHI[260]	Healthy postmenopausal women	Women	63	16,608	0.74%	0.48%	0.66 (0.44 to 0.98)
Raloxifen 60 mg	MORE-1[70]	No vertebral fracture	Women	65	3012	5%	2%	0.50 (0.4 to 0.8)
Raloxifene 60 mg	MORE-2[70]	Vertebral fractures	Women	68	1539	21%	15%	0.70 (0.6 to 0.9)
Alendronate 5 and 10 mg	FIT-1[22]	Vertebral fractures	Women	71	2027	15%	8%	0.53 (0.41 to 0.68)
Alendronate 5 and 10 mg	FIT-2[52]	No vertebral fractures Subgroup T-score <−2.5	Women Women	68 ...	4432 1631	3% 4%	2% 2%	0.56 (0.39 to 0.8) 0.50 (0.31 to 0.82)
Alendronate	Orwoll et al.[223]	FN T-score <−2 or >−1 and a fragility fracture	Men	63	241	7.1%	0.8%	0.11 (p = 0.02)
Risedronate 5 mg	VERT-US[108]	Vertebral fractures	Women	69	1628	16%	11%	0.51 (0.36 to 0.73)
Risedronate 5 mg	VERT-MN[248]	Vertebral fractures	Women	71	815	29%	18%	0.59 (0.43 to 0.82)
Calcitonin 200 IU	PROOF[37]	Vertebral fractures	Women	69	557	16%	11%	0.67 (0.47 to 0.97)
Rh(1−34) PTH 20 μg	Neer et al.[211]	Vertebral fractures	Women	69	892	14%	5%	0.35 (0.22 to 0.55)
Strontium 2 g	Menuire et al.[202]	T-score <−2.5 and vertebral fracture	Women	69	1649	24.4%	17.7%	0.59 (0.48 to 0.73)
Hip Fracture Drug								
Calcium 1.2 g/vitamin D 800 IU	Chapuy[34]	Living in care home	Women	84	3270	4.2%	2.4%	0.73 (p = 0.043)
HRT	WHI[260]	Healthy postmenopausal women	Women	63	16,608	0.77%	0.52%	0.66 (0.45 to 0.98)
Raloxifen 60 and 120 mg	MORE[70]	Osteoporosis (T-score <−2.5) with or without vertebral fractures	Women	67	7705	0.7%	0.8%	1.1 (0.6 to 1.9)
Alendronate 5 and 10 mg	FIT-1[22]	Vertebral fractures	Women	71	2027	2.2%	1.1%	0.49 (0.23 to 0.99)
Alendronate 5 and 10 mg	FIT-2[52]	T-score <−2.5 T-score <−1.6	Women Women	... 68	1631 4432	1.6% 0.8%	0.72% 0.65%	0.44 (0.18 to 0.97) 0.79 (0.43 to 1.44)
Risedronate 5 mg	VERT-US[108]	Vertebral fractures	Women	69	1628	1.8%	1.4%	NA
Risedronate 5 mg	VERT-MN[248]	Vertebral fractures	Women	71	815	2.7%	2.2%	NA
Risodronate 2.5 and 5 mg	HIP[196]	70 to 80 years with osteoporosis Subgroup prevalent vertebral fracture >80 years with or without osteoporosis	Women Women Women	74 ... 83	5445 ... 3886	3.2% 5.7% 5.1%	1.9 2.3% 4.2%	0.6 (0.4 to 0.9) 0.4 (0.2 to 0.8) 0.8 (0.6 to 1.2)
Calcitonin 200 IU	PROOF[37]	Vertebral fractures	Women	69	557	1.8%	1.2%	0.5 (0.2 to 1.6)
Rh(1−34) PTH 20 μm	Neer et al.[211]	Vertebral fractures	Women	69	892	0.74%	0.0037%	NA

[a]If not specifically presented otherwise, with percent of patients and relative risk (95% confidence interval or p value) in trials done with calcium and vitamin D, hormone replacement therapy (HRT), raloxifen, alendronate, risedronate, nasal calcitonin, 1−34 fragment of recombinant human parathyroid hormone (Rh 1−34 PTH), and strontium ranelate in the treatment of postmenopausal osteoporosis.
Follow-up period when calculating incidence and relative risk: WHI, 5.2 years; FIT-2, 2.4 years extrapolated to 3 years; PROOF, 5 years data extrapolated to 3 years; Chapuy et al, 18 months; Trivedi et al., 5 years; Neer et al, data 21 months.
NA, not available.

older than 70 years and a second meta-analysis including 3324 women older than 70 years concluded that the fracture reduction effect in the previously mobile elderly is questionable. However, other reports including 9294 women, aged at least 60 years, in five different trials suggest that in ambulatory women the prevalence of hip fracture declines if they are given a dose of 700 to 800 IU/day.[20] Vitamin D in this dosage is safe and does not require monitoring. When compliance is low, 150,000 to 300,000 IU can be given intramuscularly twice a year. Calcium and vitamin D also reduce cortisone-induced bone loss. As has already been described, there is still controversy regarding whether calcium and vitamin D supplementation in healthy elderly people with an adequate intake of dairy products influences the risk of fracture.[20,88,94,226,237,296]

Hormone Replacement Therapy

Estrogen reduces bone loss in postmenopausal women by inhibiting bone resorption resulting in, at best, a 5% increase in BMD over 1 to 3 years.[174,231] Additional calcium supplementation seems to further enhance the beneficial effects of hormone replacement therapy (HRT) treatment.[215] Recent data also suggest that smaller doses of HRT than those often used in early postmenopausal women—in the range of 0.5 to 1 mg of oral 17-estradiol, 25 mg of transdermal 17-estradiol, or 0.3 mg of conjugated equine estrogens—have a similar beneficial skeletal effect. Estrogen influences BMD loss for as long as the drug is given.[3] When HRT is stopped, bone loss mimics bone loss after the menopause.[38,75,173] Fracture data from the Million Women Study, a prospective observational study including 138,737 postmenopausal women followed for 1.9 to 3.9 years, support this finding.[10]

There are also data to support the theory that fracture risk is reduced by estrogen treatment. Case-control and cohort studies suggest that HRT decreases the risk of hip fracture by about 30%.[149] Two controlled studies of osteoporotic women indicate a 50% reduction in the risk of fractures of the spine.[174,182] Another meta-analysis of controlled trials supports this reporting a 33% reduction of vertebral fractures with HRT.[292] Another study including 22 randomized trials shows a 27% reduction in nonvertebral fractures and specifically a 40% reduction in both hip and wrist fractures.[291] The study that finally supported the theory that estrogen in combination with a gestagen drug reduces the risk of fracture was the Women's Health Initiative Study (WHI). This study included 161,809 healthy postmenopausal women including 16,608 involved in fracture evaluation over a 5.2-year period.[186,260] After this period, the planned 8-year follow-up study was cancelled when the adverse negative effects outweighed the positive effects. The study reported that estrogen reduced hip fracture incidence by 34%, vertebral fractures by 34%, fragility fractures by 23%, and all fractures by 24%[260] (Table 18-7). One recently published meta-analysis including more than 20,000 women followed for an average of 4.9 years supported the WHI study results, reporting that the general fracture risk was reduced by 28%.[16]

The downside of HRT is that it has many serious adverse effects including vaginal bleeding, breast tenderness, deep vein thrombosis and pulmonary embolism, stroke, heart disease, gall bladder disease, and an increased risk of breast, endometrial, and ovarian cancer after long-term use.[18,41,103,186,260] Women who have had a hysterectomy can be given estrogen alone, but in others estrogen and a progestogen should be given cyclically or in a combined continuous regimen to reduce the risk of endometrial cancer.[17] Readers should also be aware that the WHI study evaluated younger postmenopausal women, not only elderly women with osteoporosis, this being the important group. Whether estrogen influences steroid-induced bone loss is unclear. In most countries, estrogen is not recommended as the primary preventative agent for osteoporosis.

Selective Estrogen Receptor Modulator

In contrast to HRT, which has multiple target organs leading to a number of adverse effects, selective estrogen receptor modulators (SERMs) act as estrogen agonists or antagonists depending on the target tissue. Raloxifene acts as an antagonist of estrogen in the breast and the endometrium but acts as an agonist on bone and lipid metabolism. Raloxifene has been shown to prevent menopausal bone loss, decrease bone turnover to premenopausal levels, and reduce the incidence of fracture. The evaluation of fracture incidence is based on a large RCT, the MORE study (Multiple Outcomes of Raloxifene Evaluation) involving 7705 women with osteoporosis (Table 18-7). This study reported a 30% reduction of vertebral fractures in women who did not have a previous vertebral fracture and a 50% reduction in women who had a previous vertebral fracture.[70] No effects were found on nonvertebral fractures.[70] Raloxifene also lowers the frequency of breast cancer by 70%[31,53] but increases the incidence of venous thrombosis and pulmonary embolism at a similar rate to HRT.[11] The RUTH study (Raloxifene Use for The Heart Trial) will provide more data regarding the effects of raloxifene. Because new SERMs are now in phase III trials, it is likely that the number of these drugs available for use will increase in the future.

Tibolone is a synthetic steroid that has been used for the prevention of osteoporosis. It acts on estrogen, progesterone, and androgen receptors either directly or indirectly through metabolites and has different effects from different target tissues. Tibolone prevents bone loss in postmenopausal women,[21] but so far there are no data regarding fractures. The ongoing Long Term Intervention on Fractures with Tibolone (LIFT) study will provide data.

Bisphosphonates

Bisphosphonates are stable analogues of pyrophosphates characterized by a phosphorous–carbon–phosphorous bond that strongly binds to the hydroxyapatite crystal with a half-life in bone of several years. The drug inhibits bone resorption by reducing the recruitment and activity of osteoclasts and by increasing their apoptosis.[78] Because food, calcium, iron, coffee, tea, and orange juice reduce the absorption of bisphosphonates, the drug should be taken orally while fasting. However, nowadays the drug can also be administered intravenously. There are mild adverse effects including dyspepsia, abdominal pain, and diarrhea in addition to esophagitis that may force a patient to stop the medication.[62] This problem is reduced if the drug is taken in a weekly or monthly dose compared with daily administration.[265] If taken intravenously, short-term adverse effects mimicking influenza are commonly seen for a few days, especially after the first injection.[23]

Etidronate was the first bisphosphonate used for the treatment of low BMD. A dose of 400 mg per day was given for 2 weeks and then repeated every 3 months. The increase in BMD was reported to be about 4% and results showed a reduction of the rate of vertebral fractures after 2 years of treatment.[279,304] A long-term study showed no fracture reduction after 3 years of treatment.[109] One meta-analysis, including 13 RCTs of etidronate with more than a 1-year follow-up, reported that the risk of sustaining vertebral fractures was reduced by 40%, whereas there was no effect on any other fracture.[47] A Cochrane Database Systematic Review including 1248 patients in 11 controlled trials verified that a daily dose of 400 mg reduced the risk of vertebral fractures as a secondary prevention by 41%, while there was no reduction in hip or nonvertebral fractures.[310] There was no prevention of fractures when used as primary prevention.[310] Etidronate seems to reduce steroid-induced bone loss, but any effect on fracture incidence is as yet unclear.[47]

Alendronate is a bisphosphonate that prevents postmenopausal bone loss.[120,195] In 2027 osteoporotic women with at least one previous vertebral fracture, a 5-mg daily dose for 2 years followed by 10 mg daily for a third year was associated with a reduction of about 47% in vertebral, wrist, and hip fractures compared with a placebo[22] (Table 18-7). A 4-year study of the use of alendronate in women with low BMD, but without a pre-existing vertebral fracture, supported these results by finding a nonsignificant decrease in the frequency of fractures ($p = 0.07$) and a 45% reduction in new vertebral fractures[52] (Table 18-7). When the data from these two studies were pooled and only women with osteoporosis were included, it was found that alendronate did reduce the risk of fracture with 12 to 18 months of treatment.[22,25,52] Another placebo-controlled study using 10 mg of alendronate daily in 1908 postmenopausal women with a BMD T-score below −2 SDs reported a 47% reduced risk of nonvertebral fracture after 1 year.[235] The incidence of radiologically confirmed vertebral fracture was also reduced by 89% in men with 2 years of treatment with alendronate[223] (Table 18-7). A meta-analysis including 11 RCTs of the use of alendronate with more than a 1-year follow-up reported that the risk of sustaining vertebral fractures was reduced by 48%, whereas in those who were treated with 10 mg of alendronate daily, there was also a 49% risk reduction in sustaining nonvertebral fractures.[50] A Cochrane Database Systematic Review including 12,068 patients in 11 controlled trials verified that a daily dose of 10 mg reduced the risk of vertebral fractures in secondary prevention by 45%, nonvertebral fractures by 23%, hip fractures by 53%, and wrist fractures by 50%.[309] There was also a reduction of 45% for vertebral fractures when used as primary prevention.[309,216] Alendronate seems to reduce steroid-induced bone loss, but whether there is any effect on fracture incidence has not been fully evaluated.

Risedronate is another bisphosphonate that prevents postmenopausal bone loss.[208] A study of 2400 women who had had previous vertebral fractures and were given 5 mg of risedronate per day showed that this reduced the incidence of new vertebral fractures by 65% after the first year and by 41% over 3 years[108] (Table 18-7). Risedronate treatment over 3 years also reduced the incidence of vertebral fractures by 49% in another study that included 1226 patients who had at least two previous vertebral fractures[248] (Table 18-7). The overall incidence of nonvertebral fractures in the two studies was reduced by 30% to 40%.[108,249] However, the data supporting the reduction in the incidence of hip fracture by risedronate are less clear. Risedronate treatment in 5445 osteoporotic women aged 70 to 79 years showed a 40% reduction in hip fracture over 3 years, reaching 60% in those with a previous vertebral fracture.[196] In contrast, the same treatment in 3896 women older than 80 years who had clinical risk factors for falls, but without BMD assessment in most cases, had no effect on the rate of hip fractures.[196] A meta-analysis of the effect of risedronate contained five studies that included vertebral fractures and seven studies with nonvertebral fractures. This meta-analysis reported that risedronate reduced the risk of vertebral fractures by 36% and of nonvertebral fractures by 27%.[48] A Cochrane Database Systematic Review including 14,049 patients in seven controlled trials verified that a daily dose of 5 mg reduced the risk of vertebral fractures in secondary prevention by 39%, nonvertebral fractures by 20%, and hip fractures by 26%.[308] There was no prevention of fractures when used as primary prevention.[308]

One bisphosphonate is now available that has been shown to reduce the incidence of fractures if it is given intravenously once a year.[23] A single infusion of 5 mg zoledronic acid given to 3889 postmenopausal women in an RCT for 3 years was shown to reduce the risk of sustaining a vertebral fracture by 70%, a nonvertebral fracture by 25%, a hip fracture by 41%, and a clinical fracture by 33%.[23]

There are also other bisphosphonates that probably reduce the incidence of fractures, but their use has not been as well documented as the bisphosphonates already discussed. A dose of 800 mg daily of clodronate seems to reduce the number of vertebral fractures by 46%.[194] This was confirmed in a later publication.[193] Ibandronate, in a dose of 2.5 mg daily, seems to reduce the vertebral fracture risk by 62% and by 50% if given in a dose of 20 mg monthly.[240] Tiludronate is used for the treatment of Paget's disease of bone but cannot be recommended for the treatment of osteoporosis because of an absence of relevant data. Orally administered daily pamidronate may be effective in osteoporosis but has a high incidence of upper gastrointestinal symptoms, reducing its clinical usefulness.[181] In contrast, intravenous infusion of pamidronate is commonly used in malignant bone disease and in Paget disease of bone with only minor side effects.[251]

Calcitonin

Calcitonin is produced by the thyroid C cells. It reduces bone absorption by osteoclast inhibition. The treatment can be provided by subcutaneous or intramuscular injection. Side effects include nausea, facial flushes, and diarrhea. This compares unfavorably with the intranasal administration of salmon calcitonin in which 200 IU daily provides treatment that has no such side effects. The PROOF study (Prevent Recurrence Of Osteoporotic Fractures), a 5-year controlled trial of 1255 postmenopausal women with osteoporosis, reported that 200 IU of intranasal salmon calcitonin per day reduced vertebral fracture risk by 31% while no effects was found on peripheral fractures[37] (Table 18-7). However, this study must be interpreted with care because 60% of individuals were lost to follow-up. Doses of 100 and 400 IU had no effect, and no consistent effect on BMD and bone turnover markers was noted.[37] A meta-analysis of 30 RCTs provided evidence that calcitonin reduces the risk of vertebral fractures by 54%.[49] Whether calcitonin influences steroid-induced bone loss is as yet unclear.

Parathyroid Hormone

Continuous treatment by parathyroid hormone (PTH) results in increased bone resorption and bone loss. By contrast, intermittent PTH treatment in individuals with osteoporosis stimulates bone formation, increases BMD, and reduces the risk of fractures.[211,268] In one RCT including 1637 postmenopausal women with a previous vertebral fracture, 20 μg of subcutaneous recombinant human PTH administered daily for a median of 19 months reduced the incidence of new vertebral fractures by 65% and 40 μg reduced the incidence by 69%[211] (Table 18-7). The reduction in the incidence of nonvertebral fragility fractures was 53% with both doses during the same period, while BMD increased by 9% and 13% in the spine and by 3% and 6%, respectively, in the femoral neck with the two doses after 21 months of treatment. Injection with PTH has adverse effects, mainly nausea and headache. Another RCT following 2532 postmenopausal women for 18 months reported that treatment with 100 mg human parathyroid hormone led to a 58% reduction of the risk of sustaining a vertebral fracture.[97]

Strontium

Strontium ranelate treatment is also associated with reduced bone resorption and possibly with increased bone formation.[187] A rise in BMD and a reduction in vertebral fracture incidence have been suggested,[204] and results of an RCT suggest that strontium reduces fractures.[202] This study included 1649 postmenopausal women with osteoporosis and at least one previous vertebral fracture. Two grams of strontium ranelate per day, administered for 3 years, increased BMD and reduced the risk of sustaining new vertebral fractures by 49% during the first year and by 41% during the entire 3-year period (Table 18-7). In addition, there were no more adverse effects in the treatment group than in the placebo group. A Cochrane Database Systematic Review including four controlled trials verified that a daily dose of 2.0 g/day for 3 years reduced the risk of vertebral fractures by 37% and of nonvertebral fractures by 14%.[218]

Fluoride

Fluoride is a mineral that is incorporated into the hydroxyapatite crystal of bone. It stimulates osteoblast recruitment and activity and increases BMD in the spine but less so in the hip.[203,253] However, controlled trials have failed to show that fluoride reduces fractures. If anything, it seems as though the incidence of nonvertebral fractures might increase. A Cochrane Database Systematic Review including 1429 individuals in 11 trials verifies this view, reporting that fluoride does not result in a reduction of fractures.[104] Currently, fluoride cannot be recommended for the treatment of osteoporosis.

Other Drugs

Several other drugs have been used in the treatment of osteoporosis. Studies report an increase in BMD with their use, but none provide adequate data about fractures. Alfacalcidol and calcitriol are vitamin D analogues occasionally used as treatment for osteoporosis. Studies show a small increase in spine BMD, but because there are inadequate data regarding fracture treatment with these drugs, they cannot be regarded as having the potential to reduce fractures.[81,82,222] Treatment with menatetrenone, a vitamin K_2 compound, has shown improved BMD.[221]

Vitamin K has also been suggested as a treatment for osteoporosis, and it has been reported that a low intake of vitamin K is associated with an increased risk of hip fracture.[76] One meta-analysis of menaquinone-4 treatment (oral vitamin K) in Japanese patients showed a reduction of 60% in vertebral fractures, of 77% in hip fractures, and of 81% in nonvertebral fractures,[40]

but currently there are no RCTs with an adequate sample size evaluating the effect of vitamin K on fractures. Growth hormone is another drug used in the treatment of osteoporosis because it theoretically could increase muscle strength and BMD. However, there is no proof that it prevents bone loss and reduces fracture risk in postmenopausal women.

Ipriflavone, a synthetic compound belonging to the family of isoflavones, may prevent bone loss, but it does not seem to reduce the incidence of fractures in osteoporotic women.[6] Finally, statins have been shown to increase BMD in animal studies,[209] but further information is required about their effects in humans before it can be recommended for the prevention of fragility fractures.

SPECIFIC SURGICAL CONSIDERATIONS FOR TREATING FRACTURES IN AN OSTEOPOROTIC BONE

If an older patient with osteoporosis sustains a fracture, there are several important age-related factors to consider when planning treatment. The functional demands in the elderly are different from those of young healthy people and long-term immobilization in bed must be avoided. Delaying fracture treatment by more than 1 day has been reported to increase mortality in the elderly.[30,66] Thus, it is probably even more important in the elderly to achieve stable fracture fixation that will reduce pain and facilitate mobilization. Reduced bone mass, increased bone brittleness, and structural changes such as medullary expansion must be taken into account in the osteoporotic patient when deciding on the type of surgical method to be used. It must also be understood, when making a decision regarding treatment, that the osteoporotic patient usually has low physical demands and a reduced life expectancy. For example, long-term complications following arthroplasty will not occur in the majority of elderly patients. Thus, joint replacement surgery is a good option after displaced femoral neck fractures because the stability provided by the implant permits immediate weight bearing and mobilization.[257] The major problem in osteoporotic fracture treatment is fixation of the device to the bone because bone failure is much more common than implant breakage. Internal fixation devices such as sliding nail plates, intramedullary nails, and tension band constructs that permit skeletal loading minimize stress at the implant–bone interface. Some osteoporotic fractures are also associated with bone loss. If this occurs, it is important to achieve bone contact between the two main fragments even if this results in shortening of the extremity. Good bone contact will improve the chance of healing, reduce the healing period, and reduce strains on the fixation device. If plates are used, these should ideally be used as tension bands, which require cortical contact opposite the plates. In addition, long plates, where the spacing of the screws is more important than the number of screws, should be used because they will distribute the forces over a larger area, reducing the risk of bone failure.[294]

Several types of fragility fractures, such as fractures of the humerus and distal radius and closed fractures of the tibial diaphysis, can be mobilized in a sling, cast, or brace.[264] Immobilization in casts has the disadvantage of immobilizing the joints adjacent to the fracture often leading to joint stiffness. Furthermore, a cast does not control fracture shortening, which is often seen in osteoporotic bone, and if the subcutaneous tissue is very mobile, as it often is in the elderly, cast fixation will not provide adequate fracture fixation. External fixators can be used, but the main problem with external fixation in osteoporotic bone is the same as for screw fixation—namely, loss of fixation. Loosening of the device is often followed by pin infection and local bone resorption, sometimes leading to a secondary fracture at the pin site.[5] The introduction of hydroxyapatite-coated pins has reduced this complication because fixation is improved compared with when using titanium-coated and standard pins.[207] Another method used to improve internal fixation and to avoid bone resorption is to anchor the pins or screws with polymethylmethacrylate bone cement. This can be inserted into the bone and allowed to harden before drilling, or it can be inserted into the screw holes just before the screws are inserted. The screws can then be tightened after the cement hardens (Fig. 18-7). If this method is used, it is important that the cement does not penetrate the fracture so as to interfere with fracture healing.

The introduction of screws locked into the plate increases the strength of the fixation. Threaded screw holes in the plates create angular stability between the screws and the plates. For example, the locking compression plates (LCP) provide 3 times greater stability than a standard lateral condylar buttress plate and about 2.5 times greater stability than a 95-degree condylar plate in axial loading.[157] This strength is increased if the screws are fixed at multiple angles.[266] The use of these multiple screws in fixed angle devices is particularly useful in the metaphyseal region (Fig. 18-8). A particular problem that often prevents the use of screws and plates in osteoporotic bone is the peri-

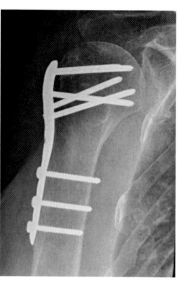

FIGURE 18-8 A proximal humerus fracture primarily treated by open reduction and open fixation with a locking plate.

prosthetic fracture. These can be treated with plates using wires for fixation around the femoral shaft (Fig. 18-9). Periprosthetic fractures and their treatment are discussed further in Chapter 21.

Intramedullary nailing is a popular treatment for osteoporotic long-bone fractures. It is biomechanically more favorable than plates and screws and will usually permit immediate

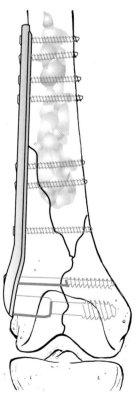

FIGURE 18-7 A displaced distal femur fracture primarily treated by open reduction and open fixation with an angle plate with augmentation of the screw fixation in the bone by polymethylmethacrylate.

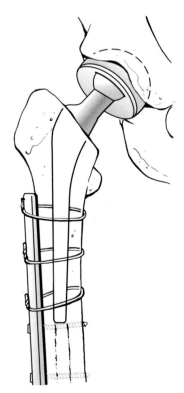

FIGURE 18-9 A periprosthetic femur fracture primarily treated by open reduction and open fixation with a plate using wires for fixation around the femoral shaft and screws distal to the implant. Excellent screw fixation is achieved through the cement distal to the prosthesis.

weight bearing. With the introduction of interlocking nails, it is also possible to nail fractures that are close to the metaphyseal regions in long bones. The fixation can be improved by the use of several interlocking screws in different directions or by augmentation of the screws with bone cement. It is also important to realize that because osteoporosis causes the diameter of the intramedullary canal to increase,[2,4] larger-diameter nails must often be used in older patients. Even if osteoporosis does not impair fracture healing, the diminished bone mass will reduce the amount of callus formation and increase the time taken to restore adequate bone strength. There are some experimental studies that show a reduced rate of healing in estrogen-deficient animals.[303] Because fracture fixation is reduced in osteoporotic bone, it would be advantageous to accelerate the healing process. Therefore, autogenous cancellous bone graft is often recommended to enhance fracture healing because the osteoconductive bone matrix, osteoinductive growth factors, and mesenchymal stem cells present in this type of graft are often thought to stimulate the healing process. However, in patients with osteoporosis, the amount of cancellous bone available for grafting is reduced, often necessitating the use of allografts, which are biologically inferior to autografts and carry the additional risk of disease transmission. To overcome these problems, growth factors are available to induce new bone formation. There are also biodegradable synthetic products such as calcium phosphate cement that fill defects in osteoporotic bone. These have mainly been used in the treatment of distal radial fractures[33,84,145,155] and proximal tibial fractures[307] (Fig. 18-10).

Vertebroplasty and Kyphoplasty

The treatment of osteoporotic vertebral compression fractures has usually been nonoperative, with the amount of disability directly relating to the number of fractured vertebrae. However, within the past few years, vertebroplasty and kyphoplasty have been introduced as new treatment modalities, although they have not yet been fully evaluated. So far there are no RCTs

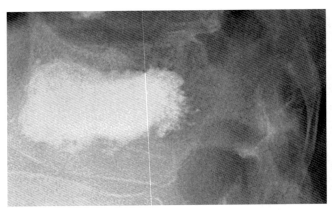

FIGURE 18-11 Vertebroplasty performed in the lumbar spine.

published that evaluate these methods. In both techniques, the crushed vertebrae are filled with material, usually polymethylmethacrylate bone cement, to avoid further compression. Kyphoplasty also aims to reduce fracture compression before the bone cement is injected. The operative techniques for these procedures have been described elsewhere[243] and will therefore only be reviewed briefly in this chapter.

Vertebroplasty was initially described in 1987.[80] Kyphoplasty has evolved from vertebroplasty in the last few years. Both procedures can usually be undertaken under local anaesthetic. The patient is positioned prone on bolsters in an attempt to reduce the Kyphosis, and a trochar and cannula are inserted through the pedicle into the posterior or central areas of the vertebral body. Radiopaque bone cement is then injected under fluoroscopic guidance into the vertebral body (Fig. 18-11). Care must be taken not to inject the cement outside the vertebral body and particularly not to inject it into the spinal canal. In kyphoplasty, the patient is placed in the same position, but once the cannula has been inserted, an inflated balloon is introduced into the vertebral body under manometric control. The objective is to partially or fully reduce the compressed vertebral body. After this has been done, the balloon is removed and the operation proceeds as for vertebroplasty (Fig. 18-12). There has been considerable interest in these two techniques, but unfortunately the methods have not been evaluated in RCTs. Despite this, the impression is that both procedures are associated with good pain relief. A retrospective study of 500 patients showed

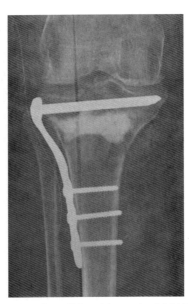

FIGURE 18-10 A metaphyseal bicondylar proximal tibial fracture primarily treated by open reduction and internal fixation with a locking plate augmented with calcium phosphate cement.

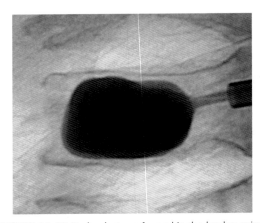

FIGURE 18-12 Kyphoplasty performed in the lumbar spine.

that vertebroplasty was associated with significant pain reduction and an improvement in functional status in 50% of the patients 7 months after the procedure. The results were obtained regardless of the number of vertebral fractures that were treated.[73] Another study has indicated that there is significant relief from symptoms and improvement in function within 24 hours of the procedure.[65] However, 6 to 12 months after the procedure, there was no evidence of any difference between the groups of patients. The weakness of this study is that the controls comprised the individuals who declined vertebroplasty. One nonrandomized controlled study including 126 patients reported that vertebroplasty was associated with 60% improvement in pain, 29% improvement in physical functioning, and 43% reduction in hospital bed-days occupied in the short term.[64] However, 12 and 24 months after the intervention, there was no differences between the surgical and conservatively treated groups.[64] One review including 1136 interventions in 793 patients showed that the procedure was associated with a 60% immediate pain relief.[234] One RCT including only 32 patients supported this view reporting that vertebroplasty was associated with immediate pain relief and improvement of mobility and function.[302] However, these patients were followed for only 2 weeks. Ongoing RCTs such as the INVEST study (Investigational Vertebroplasty Efficacy and Safety Trial)[96] and the VERTOS II study (Percutaneous Vertebroplasty Versus Conservative Therapy in Patients With Osteoporotic Vertebral Compression Fractures)[152] will provide us with a higher level of evidence regarding the efficacy of the procedure. However, it appears that while the technique produces short-term pain relief, the long-term results are less clear.

The results of kyphoplasty also tend to be short-term evaluations of the technique. A number of studies report that between 20% and 50% of patients showed no restoration of vertebral body height after the procedure,[170,233] while others report mean reduction in the kyphosis of about 10 degrees.[233] Most studies indicate good pain relief immediately after the procedure, but there is conflicting evidence about the long-term results.[170,233] A retrospective controlled study comparing kyphoplasty patients with nonoperated control subjects showed that the procedure was associated with immediate pain relief and functional improvement compared with the patients' status before surgery and with the control group.[306] Hospital stay was also longer in the nonoperatively treated group. One prospective nonrandomized controlled trial supports this view when reporting 12% increased vertebral height as well as reduced pain and improved mobility in patients after kyphoplasty.[143] However, the patients selected their own treatment in this study, which increases the risk of selection bias. The favorable outcome was maintained after 6 months[143] and 12 months.[93] Finally, one study including 75 prospective controlled and uncontrolled studies of both vertebroplasty and kyphoplasty concluded that surgery was superior to conservative treatment in management of symptomatic osteoporotic vertebral compression fractures.[282,283]

Theoretically, the technique of kyphoplasty should minimize cement leakage into the surrounding tissue. However, there are as yet no studies that directly compare vertebroplasty and kyphoplasty, although observational studies report an incidence of at least 10% cement leakage in patients treated with kyphoplasty which is similar to the incidence noted after vertebroplasty.[170,233,306] More serious adverse events have been reported: extravasation into segmental veins,[306] leakage into the

spinal canal with associated neurologic disturbance, and perioperative pulmonary edema with myocardial infarction and rib fractures.[170,233] There is also the additional potential problem of a surgical procedure altering the biomechanical forces in the spine and resulting in new vertebral fractures. One paper described 12% of patients with new vertebral fractures within 2 years of a vertebroplasty, most being adjacent to the operated vertebrae.[298] It is likely, however, that the complication rate is higher because this study only included symptomatic vertebral fractures and the follow-up was restricted to only 16% of the operated patients.

AUTHORS' PREFERRED METHOD OF TREATMENT
Osteoporosis and Osteoporotic Fractures Prevention Strategies

There are a number of pharmacologic and nonpharmacologic agents that have been proved to reduce the incidence of osteoporotic fractures. It can no longer be regarded as acceptable clinical practice to avoid investigating or treating patients with osteoporosis who present with low-energy fractures. One fragility fracture indicates further fractures, and it should be borne in mind that BMD measurement has a better predictive ability for future fractures than blood pressure has for a future stroke. The evaluation of the patient must include a history of risk factors and, in many cases, a BMD scan. Prevention strategies may involve both pharmacologic and nonpharmacologic approaches.

Increased physical activity is the first recommendation we make to virtually all patients with a fragility fracture, independent of age. There is good evidence in the literature that physical activity is beneficial for BMD and reduces the incidence of fracture, especially in postmenopausal women.[57,100] We believe that the recommendation to increase physical activity is advantageous not only from the point of view of reducing the risk of future fracture but also for other sound biological reasons. There is good evidence that calcium and vitamin D supplementation can reduce the risk of sustaining a hip fracture in elderly institutionalized patients.[35] At the moment, there is no evidence that any other nutritional supplement has the same effect. The fact that hip fracture patients are considerably thinner than age-matched individuals without a fracture[141] suggests that increased nutritional intake including calcium, vitamin D, and protein may also provide protection from future fractures. We therefore recommend a well-balanced diet in patients presenting with a low-energy fracture.

The use of hip protectors in the frail elderly has been shown to reduce the incidence of hip fracture in a number of RCTs.[137,138,167] Currently, we recommend hip protectors mainly to institutionalized individuals partly because of the low compliance and lack of data showing benefit to the elderly living in their own homes. Pharmacologic prevention is based on several double-blinded prospective RCTs showing that drug treatment reduces the incidence of fracture. Calcium and vitamin D given together in sufficient dosage have been shown to reduce the incidence of fracture particularly in institutionalized patients.[35,61,92] We believe that 500 to 1000 mg calcium and 400 to 800 IU of vitamin D should be provided to all elderly individuals. These doses do not give rise to significant side effects except for occasional gastrointestinal discomfort.

In individuals with osteoporosis who require further treatment, we believe that bisphosphonates are usually the drug of choice. Studies indicate that bisphosphonates have been proved to reduce the risk of fracture compared with no treatment.[22,108] Because of the possibility of gastrointestinal disturbances, particularly esophagitis, we prescribe a weekly or monthly dose that has been proves to reduce these effects[23,240,265] in preference to an annual bisphosphonate injection. SERMs can also be recommended for fracture prevention because they have been shown to be successful in RCTs.[70] However, the relative effect of bisphosphonates and the fact that they have increased side effects such as thromboembolism[11] mean that SERMs are our second choice for pharmacologic prevention. Subcutaneous parathyroid hormone (PTH) has been documented to reduce fractures.[24,26, 97,211] However, because of its expense, the requirement for daily injections, and the incidence of potential side effects, we only use this drug in the most severe cases of osteoporosis or in those patients who have severe adverse effects with other drugs. We try to avoid giving PTH to younger patients with osteoporosis because of the lack of long-term data. There are data indicating that estrogen reduces fracture incidence in postmenopausal women[186,260]; however, because of the serious side effects that were discussed earlier in this chapter, we currently do not use estrogen as a first-line treatment option in osteoporosis.

Surgical Strategies

In the old, fragile, and osteoporotic patient, it is important to assess the functional demands of the patients before we select a treatment strategy. We must look beyond the simple assessment of the severity and location of the fracture. In general, we treat low-energy fractures in the upper and lower limbs slightly differently. Most fractures of the upper limb are treated nonoperatively because these fractures usually do not immobilize the patients in bed and because the results of a nonsurgical approach are generally good. In addition, the difficulties of internally fixing many of these fractures and the lower functional demands in the older osteoporotic patient mean that nonoperative management is often satisfactory. The different spectrum of surgery in upper and lower limb fractures in the elderly is discussed further in Chapter 6. Open reduction and internal fixation, hemiarthroplasty of the shoulder, arthroplasty of the elbow, and closed reduction and external fixation of the wrist are usually reserved for more complex fractures.[5,79,155,256,318]

In the lower limb, we aim to achieve stable fixation that allows immediate weight bearing and early mobilization.[30,66] Some fractures, such as osteoporotic acetabular fractures, can often be managed nonoperatively with a period of non–weight-bearing mobilization, although primary arthroplasty is considered for selected patients. Other major fractures in the lower extremities are treated in the same way as in patients who do not have osteoporosis, with operative fixation and mobilization, with full weight bearing being allowed several weeks after the surgical procedure.[145,244]

Vertebroplasty and kyphoplasty are promising new operative treatments for osteoporotic vertebral fractures. However, we caution surgeons that clinical studies must indicate that these new techniques are useful before they can be widely recommended.

FUTURE PERSPECTIVE

Few physicians see as many patients with osteoporosis as orthopaedic surgeons. The diagnosis is often made in the orthopaedic wards or in the outpatient clinic after a low-energy fracture has occurred. Orthopaedic surgeons must be careful that they do not just concentrate on the technical aspects of fracture fixation and that they appreciate the considerable consequences of osteoporosis. Identification of subjects at high risk of future fracture constitutes the most rational approach to fracture prevention. We believe that it is the responsibility of the orthopaedic surgeon to arrange for patients who present with low-energy fractures to be properly advised and investigated for osteoporosis. It is also the responsibility of every orthopaedic surgeon to be aware of the different treatment modalities that exist and to appropriately advise the patient.

The investigation and treatment of osteoporosis are not necessarily the province of the orthopaedic surgeon. Referral to an appropriate physician interested in the investigation and treatment of osteoporosis is, however, the responsibility of the orthopaedic surgeon. We believe it likely that the prediction of the risk of future fractures will determine treatment strategy. Table 18-8 shows the 10-year fracture probability for the common

TABLE 18-8	Ten-Year Probability of Fracture (%) According to Age and Risk Relative to the Average Population[a]			
	Age (yr)			
Relative risk	50	60	70	80
Hip fracture (men)				
1	0.84	1.26	3.68	9.53
2	1.68	2.50	7.21	17.89
3	2.58	3.73	10.59	25.26
4	3.33	4.94	13.83	31.75
Hip fracture (women)				
1	0.57	2.40	7.87	18.0
2	1.14	4.75	15.1	32.0
3	1.71	7.04	21.7	42.9
4	2.27	9.27	27.7	51.6
Hip, clinical spine, humeral, Colles fracture (men)				
1	3.3	4.7	7.0	12.6
2	6.5	9.1	13.5	23.1
3	9.6	13.3	19.4	23.9
4	12.6	17.3	24.9	39.3
Hip, clinical spine, humeral, Colles fracture (women)				
1	5.8	9.6	16.1	21.5
2	11.3	18.2	29.4	37.4
3	16.5	26.0	40.0	49.2
4	21.4	33.1	49.5	58.1

[a]In Sweden.
From Kanis JA, Oden A, Johnell O, et al. The burden of osteoporotic fractures: a method for setting intervention thresholds. Osteoporos Int 2001;12:417–427.

osteoporotic fractures in Sweden according to the population at risk.[132] Similar calculations such as the WHO Fracture Assessment Tool (FRAX) that provide an assessment of the 10-year probability of fracture are now available on the Internet as an aid to selecting which patients require preventative treatment (http://www.shef.ac.uk/FRAX). Similar tables can help provide country-specific estimates of the risk of fracture from the relative risk estimates that are acquired from bone scans and the investigation of risk factors (Table 18-5). When a hip fracture alone is considered, a 10-year probability of 10% or greater provides a cost-effective threshold for treating women.[130] Because the aim of the assessment of fracture risk is to target cost-effective treatment interventions to those at the highest risk, we hope it can be decided more easily who to treat.

REFERENCES

1. Adams CI, Robinson CM, Court-Brown CM, et al. Prospective randomized controlled trial of an intramedullary nail versus dynamic screw and plate for intertrochanteric fractures of the femur. J Orthop Trauma 2001;15:394–400.
2. Ahlborg HG, Johnell O, Karlsson MK. An age-related medullary expansion can have implications for the long-term fixation of hip prostheses. Acta Orthop Scand 2004;75:154–159.
3. Ahlborg HG, Johnell O, Karlsson MK. Long-term effects of oestrogen therapy on bone loss in postmenopausal women: a 23-year prospective study. BJOG 2004;111:335–339.
4. Ahlborg HG, Johnell O, Turner CH, et al. Bone loss and bone size after menopause. N Engl J Med 2003;349:327–334.
5. Ahlborg HG, Josefsson PO. Pin-tract complications in external fixation of fractures of the distal radius. Acta Orthop Scand 1999;70:116–118.
6. Alexandersen P, Toussaint A, Christiansen C, et al. Ipriflavone in the treatment of postmenopausal osteoporosis: a randomized controlled trial. JAMA 2001;285:1482–1488.
7. Anon. NIH consensus development panel on optimal calcium intag. JAMA 1994;272:1942–1948.
8. Avenell A, Gillespie WJ, Gillespie LD, et al. Vitamin D and vitamin D analogues for preventing fractures associated with involutional and postmenopausal osteoporosis. Cochrane Database Syst Rev 2005:CD000227.
9. Bailey DA, McKay HA, Mirwald RL, et al. A 6-year longitudinal study of the relationship of physical activity to bone mineral accrual in growing children: the University of Saskatchewan Bone Mineral Accrual Study. J Bone Miner Res 1999;14:1672–1679.
10. Banks E, Beral V, Reeves G, et al. Fracture incidence in relation to the pattern of use of hormone therapy in postmenopausal women. JAMA 2004;291:2212–2220.
11. Barrett-Connor E, Grady D, et al. Raloxifene and cardiovascular events in osteoporotic postmenopausal women: 4-year results from the MORE (Multiple Outcomes of Raloxifene Evaluation) randomized trial. JAMA 2002;287:847–857.
12. Bassey EJ, Ramsdale SJ. Increase in femoral bone density in young women following high-impact exercise. Osteoporos Int 1994;4:72–75.
13. Bauer DC, Gluer CC, Cauley JA, et al. Broadband ultrasound attenuation predicts fractures strongly and independently of densitometry in older women. A prospective study. Study of Osteoporotic Fractures Research Group. Arch Intern Med 1997;157:629–634.
14. Beck TJ, Ruff CB, Warden KE, et al. Predicting femoral neck strength from bone mineral data. A structural approach. Invest Radiol 1990;25:6–18.
15. Bengner U. Epidemiological changes over 30 years in an urban population. Thesis, Lund University, Lund, Sweden, 1987.
16. Beral V, Banks E, Reeves G. Evidence from randomised trials on the long-term effects of hormone replacement therapy. Lancet 2002;360:942–944.
17. Beresford SA, Weiss NS, Voigt LF, et al. Risk of endometrial cancer in relation to use of oestrogen combined with cyclic progestagen therapy in postmenopausal women. Lancet 1997;349:458–461.
18. Bergkvist L, Persson I. Hormone replacement therapy and breast cancer. A review of current knowledge. Drug Saf 1996;15:360–370.
19. Bhandari M, Devereaux PJ, Swiontkowski MF, et al. Internal fixation compared with arthroplasty for displaced fractures of the femoral neck. A meta-analysis. J Bone Joint Surg Am 2003;85A:1673–1681.
20. Bischoff-Ferrari HA, Willett WC, Wong JB, et al. Fracture prevention with vitamin D supplementation: a meta-analysis of randomized controlled trials. JAMA 2005;293:2257–2264.
21. Bjarnason NH, Bjarnason K, Haarbo J, et al. Tibolone: prevention of bone loss in late postmenopausal women. J Clin Endocrinol Metab 1996;81:2419–2422.
22. Black DM, Cummings SR, Karpf DB, et al. Randomised trial of effect of alendronate on risk of fracture in women with existing vertebral fractures. Fracture Intervention Trial Research Group. Lancet 1996;348:1535–1541.
23. Black DM, Delmas PD, Eastell R, et al. Once-yearly zoledronic acid for treatment of postmenopausal osteoporosis. N Engl J Med 2007;356:1809–1822.
24. Black DM, Greenspan SL, Ensrud KE, et al. The effects of parathyroid hormone and alendronate alone or in combination in postmenopausal osteoporosis. N Engl J Med 2003;349:1207–1215.
25. Black DM, Thompson DE, Bauer DC, et al. Fracture risk reduction with alendronate in women with osteoporosis: the Fracture Intervention Trial. FIT Research Group. J Clin Endocrinol Metab 2000;85:4118–4124.
26. Body JJ, Gaich GA, Scheele WH, et al. A randomized double-blind trial to compare the efficacy of teriparatide [recombinant human parathyroid hormone (1-34)] with alendronate in postmenopausal women with osteoporosis. J Clin Endocrinol Metab 2002;87:4528–4535.
27. Bonaiuti D, Shea B, Iovine R, et al. Exercise for preventing and treating osteoporosis in postmenopausal women. Cochrane Database Syst Rev 2002:CD000333.
28. Bonar SK, Tinetti ME, Speechley M, et al. Factors associated with short- versus long-term skilled nursing facility placement among community-living hip fracture patients. J Am Geriatr Soc 1990;38:1139–1144.
29. Campbell AJ, Robertson MC, Gardner MM, et al. Falls prevention over 2 years: a randomized controlled trial in women 80 years and older. Age Ageing 1999;28:513–518.
30. Casaletto JA, Gatt R. Post-operative mortality related to waiting time for hip fracture surgery. Injury 2004;35:114–120.
31. Cauley JA, Norton L, Lippman ME, et al. Continued breast cancer risk reduction in postmenopausal women treated with raloxifene: 4-year results from the MORE trial. Multiple outcomes of raloxifene evaluation. Breast Cancer Res Treat 2001;65:125–134.
32. Center JR, Nguyen TV, Schneider D, et al. Mortality after all major types of osteoporotic fracture in men and women: an observational study. Lancet 1999;353:878–882.
33. Chapman MW, Bucholz R, Cornell C. Treatment of acute fractures with a collagen-calcium phosphate graft material. A randomized clinical trial. J Bone Joint Surg Am 1997;79:495–502.
34. Chapuy MC, Arlot ME, Delmas PD, et al. Effect of calcium and cholecalciferol treatment for three years on hip fractures in elderly women. BMJ (Clin Res) 1994;308:1081–1082.
35. Chapuy MC, Arlot ME, Duboeuf F, et al. Vitamin D3 and calcium to prevent hip fractures in the elderly women. N Engl J Med 1992;327:1637–1642.
36. Charpentier P. A hip protector based on airbag technology. Bone 1996;18:S117.
37. Chesnut CH 3rd, Silverman S, Andriano K, et al. A randomized trial of nasal spray salmon calcitonin in postmenopausal women with established osteoporosis: the prevent recurrence of osteoporotic fractures study. PROOF Study Group. Am J Med 2000;109:267–276.
38. Christiansen C, Christensen MS, Transbol I. Bone mass in postmenopausal women after withdrawal of oestrogen/gestagen replacement therapy. Lancet 1981;1:459–461.
39. Close J, Ellis M, Hooper R, et al. Prevention of falls in the elderly trial (PROFET): a randomised controlled trial. Lancet 1999;353:93–97.
40. Cockayne S, Adamson J, Lanham-New S, et al. Vitamin K and the prevention of fractures: systematic review and meta-analysis of randomized controlled trials. Arch Intern Med 2006;166:1256–1261.
41. Colditz GA, Hankinson SE, Hunter DJ, et al. The use of estrogens and progestins and the risk of breast cancer in postmenopausal women. N Engl J Med 1995;332:1589–1593.
42. Cooper C, Atkinson EJ, Jacobsen SJ, et al. Population-based study of survival after osteoporotic fractures. Am J Epidemiol 1993;137:1001–1005.
43. Cooper C, Campion G, Melton LJ 3rd. Hip fractures in the elderly: a worldwide projection. Osteoporos Int 1992;2:285–289.
44. Cooper C, Melton LJ 3rd. Epidemiology of osteoporosis. Trends Endocrinol Metab 1992;314:224–229.
45. Cooper C, Melton LJ 3rd. Magnitude and impact of osteoporosis and fractures. In: Press A, ed. Osteoporosis. San Diego, CA; 1996:419–434.
46. Crabtree N, Adams J, Pols H, et al. Age, gender, and geographical effects on hip geometry and bone mineral distribution: The EPOS study. Osteoporos Int 1997;7:291.
47. Cranney A, Guyatt G, Krolicki N, et al. A meta-analysis of etidronate for the treatment of postmenopausal osteoporosis. Osteoporos Int 2001;12:140–151.
48. Cranney A, Tugwell P, Adachi J, et al. Meta-analyses of therapies for postmenopausal osteoporosis. III. Meta-analysis of risedronate for the treatment of postmenopausal osteoporosis. Endocrine Rev 2002;23:517–523.
49. Cranney A, Tugwell P, Zytaruk N, et al. Meta-analyses of therapies for postmenopausal osteoporosis. VI. Meta-analysis of calcitonin for the treatment of postmenopausal osteoporosis. Endocrine Rev 2002;23:540–551.
50. Cranney A, Wells G, Willan A, et al. Meta-analyses of therapies for postmenopausal osteoporosis. II. Meta-analysis of alendronate for the treatment of postmenopausal women. Endocrine Rev 2002;23:508–516.
51. Cummings SR, Black DM, Nevitt MC, et al. Bone density at various sites for prediction of hip fractures. The Study of Osteoporotic Fractures Research Group. Lancet 1993;341:72–75.
52. Cummings SR, Black DM, Thompson DE, et al. Effect of alendronate on risk of fracture in women with low bone density but without vertebral fractures: results from the Fracture Intervention Trial. JAMA 1998;280:2077–2082.
53. Cummings SR, Eckert S, Krueger KA, et al. The effect of raloxifene on risk of breast cancer in postmenopausal women: results from the MORE randomized trial. Multiple Outcomes of Raloxifene Evaluation. JAMA 1999;281:2189–2197.
54. Cummings SR, Kelsey JL, Nevitt MC, et al. Epidemiology of osteoporosis and osteoporotic fractures. Epidemiol Rev 1985;7:178–208.
55. Cummings SR, Nevitt MC. A hypothesis: the causes of hip fractures. J Gerontol 1989;44:M107–M111.
56. Cummings SR, Nevitt MC, Browner WS, et al. Risk factors for hip fracture in white women. Study of Osteoporotic Fractures Research Group. N Engl J Med 1995;332:767–73.
57. Dalsky GP, Stocke KS, Ehsani AA, et al. Weight-bearing exercise training and lumbar bone mineral content in postmenopausal women. Ann Intern Med 1988;108:824–828.
58. Daniell HW. Osteoporosis of the slender smoker. Vertebral compression fractures and loss of metacarpal cortex in relation to postmenopausal cigarette smoking and lack of obesity. Arch Intern Med 1976;136:298–304.
59. Dargent-Molina P, Favier F, Grandjean H, et al. Fall-related factors and risk of hip fracture: the EPIDOS prospective study. Lancet 1996;348:145–149.
60. Dawson-Hughes B, Dallal GE, Krall EA, et al. A controlled trial of the effect of calcium supplementation on bone density in postmenopausal women. N Engl J Med 1990;323:878–883.
61. Dawson-Hughes B, Harris SS, Krall EA, et al. Effect of calcium and vitamin D supplementation on bone density in men and women 65 years of age or older. N Engl J Med 1997;337:670–676.
62. de Groen PC, Lubbe DF, Hirsch LJ, et al. Esophagitis associated with the use of alendronate. N Engl J Med 1996;335:1016–1021.

63. Dequeker J, Ortner DJ, Stix AI, et al. Hip fracture and osteoporosis in a XIIth Dynasty female skeleton from Lisht, upper Egypt. J Bone Miner Res 1997;12:881–888.

64. Diamond TH, Bryant C, Browne L, et al. Clinical outcomes after acute osteoporotic vertebral fractures: a 2-year nonrandomized trial comparing percutaneous vertebroplasty with conservative therapy. Med J Austral 2006;184:113–117.

65. Diamond TH, Champion B, Clark WA. Management of acute osteoporotic vertebral fractures: a nonrandomized trial comparing percutaneous vertebroplasty with conservative therapy. Am J Med 2003;114:257–265.

66. Dorotka R, Schoechtner H, Buchinger W. The influence of immediate surgical treatment of proximal femoral fractures on mortality and quality of life. Operation within 6 hours of the fracture versus later than 6 hours. J Bone Joint Surg Br 2003;85:1107–1113.

67. Ekman A, Mallmin H, Michaelsson K, et al. External hip protectors to prevent osteoporotic hip fractures. Lancet 1997;350:563–564.

68. Ensrud KE, Cauley J, Lipschutz R, et al. Weight change and fractures in older women. Study of Osteoporotic Fractures Research Group. Arch Intern Med 1997;157:857–863.

69. Eriksen EF, Hodgson SF, Eastell R, et al. Cancellous bone remodeling in type I postmenopausal osteoporosis: quantitative assessment of rates of formation, resorption, and bone loss at tissue and cellular levels. J Bone Miner Res 1990;5:311–319.

70. Ettinger B, Black DM, Mitlak BH, et al. Reduction of vertebral fracture risk in postmenopausal women with osteoporosis treated with raloxifene: results from a 3-year randomized clinical trial. Multiple Outcomes of Raloxifene Evaluation (MORE) Investigators. JAMA 1999;282:637–645.

71. Ettinger B, Black DM, Nevitt MC, et al. Contribution of vertebral deformities to chronic back pain and disability. The Study of Osteoporotic Fractures Research Group. J Bone Miner Res 1992;7:449–456.

72. Ettinger B, Block JE, Smith R, et al. An examination of the association between vertebral deformities, physical disabilities, and psychosocial problems. Maturitas 1988;10: 283–296.

73. Evans AJ, Jensen ME, Kip KE, et al. Vertebral compression fractures: pain reduction and improvement in functional mobility after percutaneous polymethylmethacrylate vertebroplasty retrospective report of 245 cases. Radiology 2003;226:366–372.

74. Faulkner KG, Cummings SR, Black D, et al. Simple measurement of femoral geometry predicts hip fracture: the study of osteoporotic fractures. J Bone Miner Res 1993;8: 1211–1217.

75. Felson DT, Zhang Y, Hannan MT, et al. The effect of postmenopausal estrogen therapy on bone density in elderly women. N Engl J Med 1993;329:1141–1146.

76. Feskanich D, Weber P, Willett WC, et al. Vitamin K intake and hip fractures in women: a prospective study. Am J Clin Nutr 1999;69:74–79.

77. Fingerhut L, Warner M. Injury Chartbook, Health, United States, 1996–1997, Statistics. Hyattsville, MD: National Centre for Health and Statistics, 1997.

78. Fleisch H. Bisphosphonates in Bone Disease: From the Laboratory to the Patient. 4th ed. San Diego: Academic Press, 2000.

79. Frankle MA, Herscovici D Jr, DiPasquale TG, et al. A comparison of open reduction and internal fixation and primary total elbow arthroplasty in the treatment of intraarticular distal humerus fractures in women older than age 65. J Orthop Trauma 2003;17: 473–480.

80. Galibert P, Deramond H, Rosat P, et al. [Preliminary note on the treatment of vertebral angioma by percutaneous acrylic vertebroplasty]. Neurochirurgie 1987;33:166–168.

81. Gallagher JC, Goldgar D. Treatment of postmenopausal osteoporosis with high doses of synthetic calcitriol. A randomized controlled study. Ann Intern Med 1990;113: 649–655.

82. Gallagher JC, Riggs BL, Recker RR, et al. The effect of calcitriol on patients with postmenopausal osteoporosis with special reference to fracture frequency. Proc Soc Exp Biol Med 1989;191:287–292.

83. Gardner MM, Robertson MC, Campbell AJ. Exercise in preventing falls and fall-related injuries in older people: a review of randomised controlled trials. Br J Sports Med 2000;34:7–17.

84. Gazdag AR, Lane JM, Glaser D, et al. Alternatives to autogenous bone graft: efficacy and indications. J Am Acad Orthop Surg 1995;3:1–8.

85. Genant HK, Cann CE, Ettinger B, et al. Quantitative computed tomography of vertebral spongiosa: a sensitive method for detecting early bone loss after oophorectomy. Ann Intern Med 1982;97:699–705.

86. Gerdhem P, Ivaska KK, Alatalo SL, et al. Biochemical markers of bone metabolism and prediction of fracture in elderly women. J Bone Miner Res 2004;19:386–393. Epub 2003 Dec 22.

87. Gillespie LD, Gillespie WJ, Robertson MC, et al. Interventions for preventing falls in elderly people. Cochrane Database Syst Rev 2003:CD000340.

88. Gillespie WJ, Avenell A, Henry DA, et al. Vitamin D and vitamin D analogues for preventing fractures associated with involutional and postmenopausal osteoporosis. Cochrane Database Syst Rev 2001:CD000227.

89. Gluer CC. Quantitative ultrasound techniques for the assessment of osteoporosis: expert agreement on current status. The International Quantitative Ultrasound Consensus Group. J Bone Miner Res 1997;12:1280–1288.

90. Graafmans WC, Ooms ME, Bezemer PD, et al. Different risk profiles for hip fractures and distal forearm fractures: a prospective study. Osteoporos Int 1996;6:427–431.

91. Graafmans WC, Ooms ME, Hofstee HM, et al. Falls in the elderly: a prospective study of risk factors and risk profiles. Am J Epidemiol 1996;143:1129–1136.

92. Grados F, Brazier M, Kamel S, et al. Effects on bone mineral density of calcium and vitamin D supplementation in elderly women with vitamin D deficiency. Joint Bone Spine 2003;70:203–208.

93. Grafe IA, Da Fonseca K, Hillmeier J, et al. Reduction of pain and fracture incidence after kyphoplasty: 1-year outcomes of a prospective controlled trial of patients with primary osteoporosis. Osteoporos Int 2005;16:2005–2012.

94. Grant AM, Avenell A, Campbell MK, et al. Oral vitamin D3 and calcium for secondary prevention of low-trauma fractures in elderly people (Randomised Evaluation of Calcium Or vitamin D, RECORD): a randomised placebo-controlled trial. Lancet 2005; 365:1621–1628.

95. Grant SF, Reid DM, Blake G, et al. Reduced bone density and osteoporosis associated with a polymorphic Sp1 binding site in the collagen type I alpha 1 gene. Nat Genet 1996;14:203–205.

96. Gray LA, Jarvik JG, Heagerty PJ, et al. INvestigational Vertebroplasty Efficacy and Safety Trial (INVEST): a randomized controlled trial of percutaneous vertebroplasty. BMC musculoskeletal disorders 2007;8:126.

97. Greenspan SL, Bone HG, Ettinger MP, et al. Effect of recombinant human parathyroid hormone(1–84) on vertebral fracture and bone mineral density in postmenopausal women with osteoporosis: a randomized trial. Ann Intern Med 2007;146:326–339.

98. Greenspan SL, Dresner-Pollak R, Parker RA, et al. Diurnal variation of bone mineral turnover in elderly men and women. Calcif Tissue Int 1997;60:419–423.

99. Greenspan SL, Myers ER, Maitland LA, et al. Fall severity and bone mineral density as risk factors for hip fracture in ambulatory elderly. JAMA 1994;271:128–133.

100. Gregg EW, Cauley JA, Seeley DG, et al. Physical activity and osteoporotic fracture risk in older women. Study of Osteoporotic Fractures Research Group. Ann Intern Med 1998;129:81–88.

101. Grisso JA, Kelsey JL, Strom BL, et al. Risk factors for falls as a cause of hip fracture in women. The Northeast Hip Fracture Study Group. N Engl J Med 1991;324:1326–1331.

102. Grisso JA, Schwarz DF, Wolfson V, et al. The impact of falls in an inner-city elderly African American population. J Am Geriatr Soc 1992;40:673–678.

103. Grodstein F, Stampfer MJ, Goldhaber SZ, et al. Prospective study of exogenous hormones and risk of pulmonary embolism in women. Lancet 1996;348:983–987.

104. Haguenauer D, Welch V, Shea B, et al. Fluoride for treating postmenopausal osteoporosis. Cochrane Database Syst Rev 2000:CD002825.

105. Hans D, Dargent-Molina P, Schott AM, et al. Ultrasonographic heel measurements to predict hip fracture in elderly women: the EPIDOS prospective study. Lancet 1996; 348:511–514.

106. Hansen M, Overgaard K, Christiansen C. Does the Prevalence of Vertebral Fractures Increase? Osteoporosis 1990. Copenhagen; 1990. p. 95.

107. Harris ST, Gertz BJ, Genant HK, et al. The effect of short-term treatment with alendronate on vertebral density and biochemical markers of bone remodeling in early postmenopausal women. J Clin Endocrinol Metab 1993;76:1399–1406.

108. Harris ST, Watts NB, Genant HK, et al. Effects of risedronate treatment on vertebral and nonvertebral fractures in women with postmenopausal osteoporosis: a randomized controlled trial. Vertebral Efficacy With Risedronate Therapy (VERT) Study Group. JAMA 1999;282:1344–1352.

109. Harris ST, Watts NB, Jackson RD, et al. Four-year study of intermittent cyclic etidronate treatment of postmenopausal osteoporosis: 3 years of blinded therapy followed by one year of open therapy. Am J Med 1993;95:557–567.

110. Hasserius R, Karlsson MK, Jonsson B, et al. Long-term morbidity and mortality after a clinically diagnosed vertebral fracture in the elderly: a 12- and 22-year follow-up of 257 patients. Calcif Tissue Int 2005;76:235–242.

111. Hasserius R, Karlsson MK, Nilsson BE, et al. Prevalent vertebral deformities predict increased mortality and increased fracture rate in both men and women: a 10-year population-based study of 598 individuals from the Swedish cohort in the European Vertebral Osteoporosis Study. Osteoporos Int 2003;14:61–68.

112. Hasserius R, Redlund-Johnell I, Mellstrom D, et al. Vertebral deformation in urban Swedish men and women: prevalence based on 797 subjects. Acta Orthop Scand 2001; 72:273–278.

113. Hayes WC. Bone Fracture Prevention Garment and Method. Washington, DC: Patent and Trademark Office; 1992.

114. Hayes WC, Myers ER, Morris JN, et al. Impact near the hip dominates fracture risk in elderly nursing home residents who fall. Calcif Tissue Int 1993;52:192–198.

115. Heinonen A, Kannus P, Sievanen H, et al. Randomised controlled trial of effect of high-impact exercise on selected risk factors for osteoporotic fractures. Lancet 1996;348: 1343–1347.

116. Heinonen A, Oja P, Sievanen H, et al. Effect of two training regimens on bone mineral density in healthy perimenopausal women: a randomized controlled trial. J Bone Miner Res 1998;13:483–490.

117. Hernandez-Avila M, Colditz GA, Stampfer MJ, et al. Caffeine, moderate alcohol intake, and risk of fractures of the hip and forearm in middle-aged women. Am J Clin Nutr 1991;54:157–163.

118. Hindso K. Behavioral attitude toward hip protectors in elderly orthopedic patients. Osteoporosis International 1998;8:119.

119. Holbrook T, Grazier K, Kelsey J, Stauffer R. The Frequency of Occurrence, Impact, and Cost of Selected Musculoskeletal Conditions in the United States. Chicago: American Academy of Orthopaedic Surgeons, 1984.

120. Hosking D, Chilvers CE, Christiansen C, et al. Prevention of bone loss with alendronate in postmenopausal women under 60 years of age. Early Postmenopausal Intervention Cohort Study Group. N Engl J Med 1998;338:485–492.

121. Hui SL, Slemenda CW, Johnston CC Jr. Baseline measurement of bone mass predicts fracture in white women. Ann Intern Med 1989;111:355–361.

122. Huopio J, Kröger H, Honkanen R, et al. Risk factors for perimenopausal fractures. A prospective population-based study. Osteoporosis International 1998;8(suppl 3):6.

123. Ilich JZ, Skugor M, Hangartner T, et al. Relation of nutrition, body composition, and physical activity to skeletal development: a cross-sectional study in preadolescent females. J Am Coll Nutr 1998;17:136–147.

124. Ivaska KK, Lenora J, Gerdhem P, et al. Serial assessment of serum bone metabolism markers identifies women with the highest rate of bone loss and osteoporosis risk. J Clin Endocrinol Metab 2008;May 6.

125. Jackson RD, LaCroix AZ, Gass M, et al. Calcium plus vitamin D supplementation and the risk of fractures. N Engl J Med 2006;354:669–683.

126. Jaglal SB, Kreiger N, Darlington G. Past and recent physical activity and risk of hip fracture. Am J Epidemiol 1993;138:107–118.

127. Jarvinen TL, Sievanen H, Khan KM, et al. Shifting the focus in fracture prevention from osteoporosis to falls. BMJ.Clinical research ed 2008;336:124–126.

128. Joakimsen RM, Magnus JH, Fonnebo V. Physical activity and predisposition for hip fractures: a review. Osteoporos Int 1997;7:503–513.

129. Johnell O, Gullberg B, Kanis JA, et al. Risk factors for hip fracture in European women: the MEDOS Study. Mediterranean Osteoporosis Study. J Bone Miner Res 1995;10: 1802–1815.

130. Kanis JA, Dawson A, Oden A, et al. Cost-effectiveness of preventing hip fracture in the general female population. Osteoporos Int 2001;12:356–361.

131. Kanis JA, Delmas P, Burckhardt P, et al. Guidelines for diagnosis and management of osteoporosis. The European Foundation for Osteoporosis and Bone Disease. Osteoporos Int 1997;7:390–406.

132. Kanis JA, Oden A, Johnell O, et al. The burden of osteoporotic fractures: a method for setting intervention thresholds. Osteoporos Int 2001;12:417–427.

133. Kannus P, Haapasalo H, Sankelo M, et al. Effect of starting age of physical activity on

bone mass in the dominant arm of tennis and squash players. Ann Intern Med 1995; 123:27–31.
134. Kannus P, Leiponen P, Parkkari J, et al. A sideways fall and hip fracture. Bone 2006; 39:383–384.
135. Kannus P, Niemi S, Parkkari J, et al. Hip fractures in Finland between 1970 and 1997 and predictions for the future. Lancet 1999;353:802–805.
136. Kannus P, Niemi S, Parkkari J, et al. Nationwide decline in incidence of hip fracture. J Bone Miner Res 2006;21:1836–1838.
137. Kannus P, Parkkari J. Hip protectors for preventing hip fracture. JAMA 2007;298: 454–455.
138. Kannus P, Parkkari J, Niemi S, et al. Prevention of hip fracture in elderly people with use of a hip protector. N Engl J Med 2000;343:1506–1513.
139. Kannus P, Sievanen H, Vuori I. Physical loading, exercise, and bone. Bone 1996;18 (1 suppl):1S–3S.
140. Karlsson M, Bass S, Seeman E. The evidence that exercise during growth or adulthood reduces the risk of fragility fractures is weak. Best Pract Res Clin Rheumatol 2001;15: 429–450.
141. Karlsson MK, Johnell O, Nilsson BE, et al. Bone mineral mass in hip fracture patients. Bone 1993;14:161–165.
142. Karlsson MK, Linden C, Karlsson C, et al. Exercise during growth and bone mineral density and fractures in old age. Lancet 2000;355:469–470.
143. Kasperk C, Hillmeier J, Noldge G, et al. Treatment of painful vertebral fractures by kyphoplasty in patients with primary osteoporosis: a prospective nonrandomized controlled study. J Bone Miner Res 2005;20:604–612.
144. Kassem M, Ankersen L, Eriksen EF, et al. Demonstration of cellular aging and senescence in serially passaged long-term cultures of human trabecular osteoblasts. Osteoporos Int 1997;7:514–524.
145. Keating JF. Tibial plateau fractures in the older patient. Bull Hosp Jt Dis 1999;58: 19–23.
146. Kellie SE, Brody JA. Sex-specific and race-specific hip fracture rates. Am J Public Health 1990;80:326–328.
147. Kelly PJ, Morrison N, Sambrook PN, et al. Genetics and osteoporosis: role of the vitamin D receptor gene. Agents Actions 1994;42:i–ii.
148. Kelly TL, Slovik DM, Schoenfeld DA, et al. Quantitative digital radiography versus dual photon absorptiometry of the lumbar spine. J Clin Endocrinol Metab 1988;67: 839–844.
149. Kiel DP, Felson DT, Anderson JJ, et al. Hip fracture and the use of estrogens in postmenopausal women. The Framingham Study. N Engl J Med 1987;317:1169–1174.
150. Kiel DP, Felson DT, Hannan MT, et al. Caffeine and the risk of hip fracture: the Framingham Study. Am J Epidemiol 1990;132:675–684.
151. Kindblom JM, Lorentzon M, Norjavaara E, et al. Pubertal timing predicts previous fractures and BMD in young adult men: the GOOD study. J Bone Miner Res 2006;21: 790–795.
152. Klazen C, Verhaar H, Lampmann L, et al. VERTOS II: Percutaneous vertebroplasty versus conservative therapy in patients with painful osteoporotic vertebral compression fractures; rationale, objectives and design of a multicenter randomized controlled trial. Trials 2007;8:33.
153. Kobayashi S, Inoue S, Hosoi T, et al. Association of bone mineral density with polymorphism of the estrogen receptor gene. J Bone Miner Res 1996;11:306–311.
154. Kollerup G, Thamsborg G, Bhatia H, et al. Quantitation of urinary hydroxypyridinium cross-links from collagen by high-performance liquid chromatography. Scand J Clin Lab Invest 1992;52:657–662.
155. Kopylov P, Runnqvist K, Jonsson K, et al. Norian SRS versus external fixation in redisplaced distal radial fractures. A randomized study in 40 patients. Acta Orthop Scand 1999;70:1–5.
156. Koski K, Luukinen H, Laippala P, et al. Physiological factors and medications as predictors of injurious falls by elderly people: a prospective population-based study. Age Ageing 1996;25:29–38.
157. Koval KJ, Hoehl JJ, Kummer FJ, et al. Distal femoral fixation: a biomechanical comparison of the standard condylar buttress plate, a locked buttress plate, and the 95-degree blade plate. J Orthop Trauma 1997;11:521–524.
158. Kroger H, Huopio J, Honkanen R, et al. Prediction of fracture risk using axial bone mineral density in a perimenopausal population: a prospective study. J Bone Miner Res 1995;10:302–306.
159. Kroger H, Tuppurainen M, Honkanen R, et al. Bone mineral density and risk factors for osteoporosis: a population-based study of 1600 perimenopausal women. Calcif Tissue Int 1994;55:1–7.
160. Langdahl BL, Knudsen JY, Jensen HK, et al. A sequence variation: 713-8delC in the transforming growth factor-beta 1 gene has higher prevalence in osteoporotic women than in normal women and is associated with very low bone mass in osteoporotic women and increased bone turnover in both osteoporotic and normal women. Bone 1997;20:289–294.
161. Langton CM, Palmer SB, Porter RW. The measurement of broadband ultrasonic attenuation in cancellous bone. Eng Med 1984;13:89–91.
162. Lanyon LE. Using functional loading to influence bone mass and architecture: objectives, mechanisms, and relationship with estrogen of the mechanically adaptive process in bone. Bone 1996;18(1 suppl):37S–43S.
163. Lau EM, Chan HH, Woo J, et al. Normal ranges for vertebral height ratios and prevalence of vertebral fracture in Hong Kong Chinese: a comparison with American Caucasians. J Bone Miner Res 1996;11:1364–1368.
164. Lauritzen JB. Body fat distribution and hip fractures. Acta Orthop Scand 1992;63:S89.
165. Lauritzen JB. Estimate of hip fracture threshold adjusted for energy absorption in soft tissue. J Nucl Med 1994;21:S48.
166. Lauritzen JB. Impacts in patients with hip fractures and in vitro study of the padding effect: introduction of a hip protector. Acta Orthop Scand 1990;61:S239.
167. Lauritzen JB, Petersen MM, Lund B. Effect of external hip protectors on hip fractures. Lancet 1993;341:11–13.
168. Law MR, Hackshaw AK. A meta-analysis of cigarette smoking, bone mineral density, and risk of hip fracture: recognition of a major effect. BMJ (Clin Res) 1997;315: 841–846.
169. Lee WT, Leung SS, Ng MY, et al. Bone mineral content of two populations of Chinese children with different calcium intakes. Bone Miner 1993;23:195–206.
170. Lieberman IH, Dudeney S, Reinhardt MK, et al. Initial outcome and efficacy of "kyphoplasty" in the treatment of painful osteoporotic vertebral compression fractures. Spine 2001;26:1631–1638.
171. Linden C, Ahlborg HG, Besjakov J, et al. A school curriculum-based exercise program increases bone mineral accrual and bone size in prepubertal girls: two-year data from the Pediatric Osteoporosis Prevention (POP) study. J Bone Miner Res 2006;21: 829–835.
172. Linden C, Alwis G, Ahlborg H, et al. Exercise, bone mass, and bone size in prepubertal boys: one-year data from the pediatric osteoporosis prevention study. Scand J Med Sci Sports 2007;17:340–347.
173. Lindsay R, Hart DM, Fogelman I. Bone mass after withdrawal of oestrogen replacement. Lancet 1981;1:729.
174. Lindsay R, Hart DM, Forrest C, et al. Prevention of spinal osteoporosis in oophorectomised women. Lancet 1980;2:1151–1154.
175. Lips P, Graafmans WC, Ooms ME, et al. Vitamin D supplementation and fracture incidence in elderly persons. A randomized, placebo-controlled clinical trial. Ann Intern Med 1996;124:400–406.
176. Looker AC, Wahner HW, Dunn WL, et al. Proximal femur bone mineral levels of US adults. Osteoporos Int 1995;5:389–409.
177. Lord SR, Ward JA, Williams P, et al. The effect of a 12-month exercise trial on balance, strength, and falls in older women: a randomized controlled trial. J Am Geriatr Soc 1995;43:1198–1206.
178. Lorentzon M, Mellstrom D, Ohlsson C. Age of attainment of peak bone mass is site specific in Swedish men: the GOOD study. J Bone Miner Res 2005;20:1223–1227.
179. Lorentzon M, Swanson C, Andersson N, et al. Free testosterone is a positive, whereas free estradiol is a negative, predictor of cortical bone size in young Swedish men: the GOOD study. J Bone Miner Res 2005;20:1334–1341.
180. Lotz JC, Hayes WC. The use of quantitative computed tomography to estimate risk of fracture of the hip from falls. J Bone Joint Surg Am 1990;72:689–700.
181. Lufkin EG, Argueta R, Whitaker MD, et al. Pamidronate: an unrecognized problem in gastrointestinal tolerability. Osteoporos Int 1994;4:320–322.
182. Lufkin EG, Wahner HW, O'Fallon WM, et al. Treatment of postmenopausal osteoporosis with transdermal estrogen. Ann Intern Med 1992;117:1–9.
183. Luukinen H, Koski K, Honkanen R, et al. Incidence of injury-causing falls among older adults by place of residence: a population-based study. J Am Geriatr Soc 1995;43: 871–876.
184. Mallmin H, Ljunghall S, Persson I, et al. Risk factors for fractures of the distal forearm: a population-based case-control study. Osteoporos Int 1994;4:298–304.
185. Mallmin H, Ljunghall S, Persson I, et al. Fracture of the distal forearm as a forecaster of subsequent hip fracture: a population-based cohort study with 24 years of follow-up. Calcif Tissue Int 1993;52:269–272.
186. Manson JE, Hsia J, Johnson KC, et al. Estrogen plus progestin and the risk of coronary heart disease. N Engl J Med 2003;349:523–534.
187. Marie PJ, Hott M, Modrowski D, et al. An uncoupling agent containing strontium prevents bone loss by depressing bone resorption and maintaining bone formation in estrogen-deficient rats. J Bone Miner Res 1993;8:607–615.
188. Marshall D, Johnell O, Wedel H. Meta-analysis of how well measures of bone mineral density predict occurrence of osteoporotic fractures. BMJ.Clinical research ed 1996; 312:1254–1259.
189. Masters PW, Jones RG, Purves DA, et al. Commercial assays for serum osteocalcin give clinically discordant results. Clin Chem 1994;40:358–363.
190. Matkovic V, Heaney RP. Calcium balance during human growth: evidence for threshold behavior. Am J Clin Nutr 1992;55:992–996.
191. Matkovic V, Kostial K, Simonovic I, et al. Bone status and fracture rates in two regions of Yugoslavia. Am J Clin Nutr 1979;32:540–549.
192. Mazess RB, Barden HS, Bisek JP, et al. Dual-energy x-ray absorptiometry for total-body and regional bone-mineral and soft-tissue composition. Am J Clin Nutr 1990; 51:1106–1112.
193. McCloskey E, Selby P, Davies M, et al. Clodronate reduces vertebral fracture risk in women with postmenopausal or secondary osteoporosis: results of a double-blind, placebo-controlled 3-year study. J Bone Miner Res 2004;19:728–736.
194. McCloskey E, Selby P, de Takats D, et al. Effects of clodronate on vertebral fracture risk in osteoporosis: a 1-year interim analysis. Bone 2001;28:310–315.
195. McClung M, Clemmesen B, Daifotis A, et al. Alendronate prevents postmenopausal bone loss in women without osteoporosis. A double-blind, randomized, controlled trial. Alendronate Osteoporosis Prevention Study Group. Ann Intern Med 1998;128: 253–261.
196. McClung MR, Geusens P, Miller PD, et al. Effect of risedronate on the risk of hip fracture in elderly women. Hip Intervention Program Study Group. N Engl J Med 2001; 344:333–340.
197. Mellstrom D, Johnell O, Ljunggren O, et al. Free testosterone is an independent predictor of BMD and prevalent fractures in elderly men: MrOS Sweden. J Bone Miner Res 2006;21:529–535.
198. Melton LJ 3rd. How many women have osteoporosis now? J Bone Miner Res 1995; 10:175–177.
199. Melton LJ 3rd, Atkinson EJ, Madhok R. Downturn in hip fracture incidence. Public Health Rep 1996;111:146–151.
200. Melton LJ 3rd, Lane AW, Cooper C, et al. Prevalence and incidence of vertebral deformities. Osteoporos Int 1993;3:113–119.
201. Melton LJ 3rd, Riggs BL. Risk factors for injury after a fall. Clin Geriatr Med 1985;1: 525–539.
202. Meunier PJ, Roux C, Seeman E, et al. The effects of strontium ranelate on the risk of vertebral fracture in women with postmenopausal osteoporosis. N Engl J Med 2004; 350:459–468.
203. Meunier PJ, Sebert JL, Reginster JY, et al. Fluoride salts are no better at preventing new vertebral fractures than calcium-vitamin D in postmenopausal osteoporosis: the FAVO Study. Osteoporos Int 1998;8:4–12.
204. Meunier PJ, Slosman DO, Delmas PD, et al. Strontium ranelate: dose-dependent effects in established postmenopausal vertebral osteoporosis: a 2-year randomized placebo controlled trial. J Clin Endocrinol Metab 2002;87:2060–2066.
205. Meyer HE, Tverdal A, Falch JA. Risk factors for hip fracture in middle-aged Norwegian women and men. Am J Epidemiol 1993;137:1203–1211.
206. Minkin C. Bone acid phosphatase: tartrate-resistant acid phosphatase as a marker of osteoclast function. Calcif Tissue Int 1982;34:285–290.

207. Moroni A, Toksvig-Larsen S, Maltarello MC, et al. A comparison of hydroxyapatite-coated, titanium-coated, and uncoated tapered external-fixation pins. An in vivo study in sheep. J Bone Joint Surg Am 1998;80:547–554.

208. Mortensen L, Charles P, Bekker PJ, et al. Risedronate increases bone mass in an early postmenopausal population: two years of treatment plus one year of follow-up. J Clin Endocrinol Metab 1998;83:396–402.

209. Mundy G, Garrett R, Harris S, et al. Stimulation of bone formation in vitro and in rodents by statins. Science 1999;286:1946–1949.

210. Myers AH, Baker SP, Van Natta ML, et al. Risk factors associated with falls and injuries among elderly institutionalized persons. Am J Epidemiol 1991;133:1179–1190.

211. Neer RM, Arnaud CD, Zanchetta JR, et al. Effect of parathyroid hormone (1–34) on fractures and bone mineral density in postmenopausal women with osteoporosis. N Engl J Med 2001;344:1434–1441.

212. Nevitt MC, Cummings SR. Type of fall and risk of hip and wrist fractures: the study of osteoporotic fractures. The Study of Osteoporotic Fractures Research Group. J Am Geriatr Soc 1993;41:1226–1234.

213. Nguyen T, Sambrook P, Kelly P, et al. Prediction of osteoporotic fractures by postural instability and bone density. BMJ (Clin Res) 1993;307:1111–1115.

214. Nielsen HK, Lundby L, Rasmussen K, et al. Alcohol decreases serum osteocalcin in a dose-dependent way in normal subjects. Calcif Tissue Int 1990;46:173–178.

215. Nieves JW, Komar L, Cosman F, et al. Calcium potentiates the effect of estrogen and calcitonin on bone mass: review and analysis. Am J Clin Nutr 1998;67:18–24.

216. Nilsson BE, Johnell O, Petersson C. In vivo bone-mineral measurement. How and why: a review. Acta Orthop Scand 1990;61:275–281.

217. Nordstrom A, Karlsson C, Nyquist F, et al. Bone loss and fracture risk after reduced physical activity. J Bone Miner Res 2005;20:202–207.

218. O'Donnell S, Cranney A, Wells GA, et al. Strontium ranelate for preventing and treating postmenopausal osteoporosis. Cochrane Database Syst Rev 2006:CD005326.

219. O'Neill TW, Felsenberg D, Varlow J, et al. The prevalence of vertebral deformity in european men and women: the European Vertebral Osteoporosis Study. J Bone Miner Res 1996;11:1010–1018.

220. Obrant KJ, Bengner U, Johnell O, et al. Increasing age-adjusted risk of fragility fractures: a sign of increasing osteoporosis in successive generations? Calcif Tissue Int 1989;44:157–167.

221. Orimo H, Shiraki M. Clinical evaluation of menatetrenone in the treatment of involutional osteoporosis. IVth International Symposium on Osteoporosis, Hong Kong, 1993.

222. Orimo H, Shiraki M, Hayashi T, Nakamura T. Reduced occurrence of vertebral crush fractures in senile osteoporosis treated with 1 alpha (OH)-vitamin D3. Bone Miner 1987;3:47–52.

223. Orwoll E, Ettinger M, Weiss S, et al. Alendronate for the treatment of osteoporosis in men. N Engl J Med 2000;343:604–610.

224. Osteoporosis Ago. Report. London: Department of Health, 1994.

225. Paganini-Hill A, Chao A, Ross RK, et al. Exercise and other factors in the prevention of hip fracture: the Leisure World study. Epidemiology 1991;2:16–25.

226. Papadimitropoulos E, Wells G, Shea B, et al. Meta-analyses of therapies for postmenopausal osteoporosis. VIII: Meta-analysis of the efficacy of vitamin D treatment in preventing osteoporosis in postmenopausal women. Endocrine reviews 2002;23:560–569.

227. Parfitt AM. Age-related structural changes in trabecular and cortical bone: cellular mechanisms and biomechanical consequences. Calcif Tissue Int 1984;36(suppl 1):S123–S128.

228. Parfitt AM. The two faces of growth: benefits and risks to bone integrity. Osteoporos Int 1994;4:382–398.

229. Parker MJ, Gillespie LD, Gillespie WJ. Hip protectors for preventing hip fractures in the elderly. Cochrane Database Syst Rev 2004:CD001255.

230. Parkkari J, Kannus P, Heikkila J, et al. Energy-shunting external hip protector attenuates the peak femoral impact force below the theoretical fracture threshold: an in vitro biomechanical study under falling conditions of the elderly. J Bone Miner Res 1995;10:1437–1442.

231. PEPI Writing Group. Effects of hormone therapy on bone mineral density: results from the Postmenopausal Estrogen/Progestin Interventions (PEPI) trial. The Writing Group for the PEPI. JAMA 1996;276:1389–1396.

232. Perry BC. Falls among the elderly: a review of the methods and conclusions of epidemiologic studies. J Am Geriatr Soc 1982;30:367–371.

233. Phillips FM, Ho E, Campbell-Hupp M, et al. Early radiographic and clinical results of balloon kyphoplasty for the treatment of osteoporotic vertebral compression fractures. Spine 2003;28:2260–2267.

234. Ploeg WT, Veldhuizen AG, The B, et al. Percutaneous vertebroplasty as a treatment for osteoporotic vertebral compression fractures: a systematic review. Eur Spine J 2006;15:1749–1758.

235. Pols HA, Felsenberg D, Hanley DA, et al. Multinational, placebo-controlled, randomized trial of the effects of alendronate on bone density and fracture risk in postmenopausal women with low bone mass: results of the FOSIT study. Foxamax International Trial Study Group. Osteoporos Int 1999;9:461–468.

236. Poor G, Atkinson EJ, O'Fallon WM, et al. Determinants of reduced survival following hip fractures in men. Clin Orthop 1995 Oct:260–265.

237. Porthouse J, Cockayne S, King C, et al. Randomised controlled trial of calcium and supplementation with cholecalciferol (vitamin D3) for prevention of fractures in primary care. BMJ (Clin Res) 2005;330:1003.

238. Praemer A, Furner S, Rice D. Musculoskeletal Condition in the United States. Park Ridge, IL: American Academy of Orthopaedic Surgeons, 1992.

239. Province MA, Hadley EC, Hornbrook MC, et al. The effects of exercise on falls in elderly patients. A preplanned meta-analysis of the FICSIT Trials. Frailty and Injuries: Cooperative Studies of Intervention Techniques. JAMA 1995;273:1341–1347.

240. Pyon EY. Once-monthly ibandronate for postmenopausal osteoporosis: review of a new dosing regimen. Clinical therapeutics 2006;28:475–490.

241. Ralston SH. Genetic determinants of osteoporosis. Curr Opin Rheumatol 2005;17:475–479.

242. Ralston SH. Genetics of osteoporosis. Proc Nutr Soc 2007;66:158–165.

243. Rao RD, Singrakhia MD. Painful osteoporotic vertebral fracture. Pathogenesis, evaluation, and roles of vertebroplasty and kyphoplasty in its management. J Bone Joint Surg Am 2003;85A:2010–2022.

244. Rasmussen PS. Tibial condylar fractures. Impairment of knee joint stability as an indication for surgical treatment. J Bone Joint Surg Am 1973;55:1331–1350.

245. Ravn P, Fledelius C, Rosenquist C, et al. High bone turnover is associated with low bone mass in both pre- and postmenopausal women. Bone 1996;19:291–298.

246. Ray NF, Chan JK, Thamer M, et al. Medical expenditures for the treatment of osteoporotic fractures in the United States in 1995: report from the National Osteoporosis Foundation. J Bone Miner Res 1997;12:24–35.

247. Recker RR, Hinders S, Davies KM, et al. Correcting calcium nutritional deficiency prevents spine fractures in elderly women. J Bone Miner Res 1996;11:1961–1966.

248. Reginster J, Minne HW, Sorensen OH, et al. Randomized trial of the effects of risedronate on vertebral fractures in women with established postmenopausal osteoporosis. Vertebral Efficacy with Risedronate Therapy (VERT) Study Group. Osteoporos Int 2000;11:83–91.

249. Reginster JY, Wilson KM, Dumont E, et al. Monthly oral ibandronate is well tolerated and efficacious in postmenopausal women: results from the monthly oral pilot study. J Clin Endocrinol Metab 2005;90:5018–5024.

250. Reid IR, Ames RW, Evans MC, et al. Long-term effects of calcium supplementation on bone loss and fractures in postmenopausal women: a randomized controlled trial. Am J Med 1995;98:331–335.

251. Reid IR, Wattie DJ, Evans MC, et al. Continuous therapy with pamidronate, a potent bisphosphonate, in postmenopausal osteoporosis. J Clin Endocrinol Metab 1994;79:1595–1599.

252. Rice D, MacKenzie E, Associates. Cost of Injury in the United States: A report to Congress. San Francisco: University of California, 1989.

253. Riggs BL, Hodgson SF, O'Fallon WM, et al. Effect of fluoride treatment on the fracture rate in postmenopausal women with osteoporosis. N Engl J Med 1990;322:802–809.

254. Riggs BL, Khosla S, Melton LJ 3rd. A unitary model for involutional osteoporosis: estrogen deficiency causes both type I and type II osteoporosis in postmenopausal women and contributes to bone loss in aging men. J Bone Miner Res 1998;13:763–773.

255. Riggs BL, Melton LJ 3rd. Clinical review 8: Clinical heterogeneity of involutional osteoporosis: implications for preventive therapy. J Clin Endocrinol Metab 1990;70:1229–1232.

256. Robinson CM, Page RS, Hill RM, et al. Primary hemiarthroplasty for treatment of proximal humeral fractures. J Bone Joint Surg Am 2003;85A:1215–1223.

257. Rogmark C, Carlsson A, Johnell O, et al. A prospective randomised trial of internal fixation versus arthroplasty for displaced fractures of the neck of the femur. Functional outcome for 450 patients at 2 years. J Bone Joint Surg Br 2002;84B:183–188.

258. Rogmark C, Sernbo I, Johnell O, et al. Incidence of hip fractures in Malmo, Sweden, 1992–1995. A trend-break. Acta Orthop Scand 1999;70:19–22.

259. Ross PD, Davis JW, Epstein RS, et al. Pre-existing fractures and bone mass predict vertebral fracture incidence in women. Ann Intern Med 1991;114:919–923.

260. Rossouw JE, Anderson GL, Prentice RL, et al. Risks and benefits of estrogen plus progestin in healthy postmenopausal women: principal results From the Women's Health Initiative randomized controlled trial. JAMA 2002;288:321–333.

261. Ruff CB, Hayes WC. Sex differences in age-related remodeling of the femur and tibia. J Orthop Res 1988;6:886–896.

262. Russell RG. The assessment of bone metabolism in vivo using biochemical approaches. Horm Metab Res 1997;29:138–144.

263. Ryynanen OP, Kivela SL, Honkanen R, et al. Incidence of falling injuries leading to medical treatment in the elderly. Public Health 1991;105:373–386.

264. Sarmiento A, Sharpe FE, Ebramzadeh E, et al. Factors influencing the outcome of closed tibial fractures treated with functional bracing. Clin Orthop 1995:8–24.

265. Schnitzer T, Bone HG, Crepaldi G, et al. Therapeutic equivalence of alendronate 70 mg once-weekly and alendronate 10 mg daily in the treatment of osteoporosis. Alendronate Once-Weekly Study Group. Aging (Milano) 2000;12:1–12.

266. Schutz M, Sudkamp NP. Revolution in plate osteosynthesis: new internal fixator systems. J Orthop Sci 2003;8:252–258.

267. Seeman E. The dilemma of osteoporosis in men. Am J Med 1995;98(2A):76S–88S.

268. Seeman E, Delmas PD. Reconstructing the skeleton with intermittent parathyroid hormone. Trends Endocrinol Metab 2001;12:281–283.

269. Seeman E, Tsalamandris C, Formica C, et al. Reduced femoral neck bone density in the daughters of women with hip fractures: the role of low-peak bone density in the pathogenesis of osteoporosis. J Bone Miner Res 1994;9:739–743.

270. Sellberg M. The development of a passive protective device for the elderly to prevent hip fractures from accidental falls. Adv Bioeng 1992;22:505–208.

271. Sexson SB, Lehner JT. Factors affecting hip fracture mortality. J Orthop Trauma 1987;1:298–305.

272. Shea B, Bonaiuti D, Iovine R, et al. Cochrane Review on exercise for preventing and treating osteoporosis in postmenopausal women. Eur Medicophys 2004;40:199–209.

273. Shea B, Wells G, Cranney A, et al. Calcium supplementation on bone loss in postmenopausal women. Cochrane Database Syst Rev 2004:CD004526.

274. Shea B, Wells G, Cranney A, et al. Meta-analyses of therapies for postmenopausal osteoporosis. VII. Meta-analysis of calcium supplementation for the prevention of postmenopausal osteoporosis. Endocrine Rev 2002;23:552–559.

275. Shumway-Cook A, Gruber W, Baldwin M, et al. The effect of multidimensional exercises on balance, mobility, and fall risk in community-dwelling older adults. Phys Ther 1997;77:46–57.

276. Slemenda C. Prevention of hip fractures: risk factor modification. Am J Med 1997;103(2A):65S–71S; discussion S-3S.

277. Statement CD. Consensus Development Statement. Who are candidates for prevention and treatment for osteoporosis? Osteoporos Int 1997;7:1–6.

278. Steiger P, Cummings SR, Genant HK, et al. Morphometric X-ray absorptiometry of the spine: correlation in vivo with morphometric radiography. Study of Osteoporotic Fractures Research Group. Osteoporos Int 1994;4:238–244.

279. Storm T, Thamsborg G, Steiniche T, et al. Effect of intermittent cyclical etidronate therapy on bone mass and fracture rate in women with postmenopausal osteoporosis. N Engl J Med 1990;322:1265–1271.

280. Strandberg L, Mellstrom D, Ljunggren O, et al. IL6 and IL1B polymorphisms are associated with fat mass in older men: the MrOS Study Sweden. Obesity (Silver Spring) 2008;16:710–713.

281. Sundberg M. Skeletal growth and effects of physical activity during adolescence. Thesis, Lunds University, Lund, Sweden, 2001.

282. Taylor RS, Fritzell P, Taylor RJ. Balloon kyphoplasty in the management of vertebral compression fractures: an updated systematic review and meta-analysis. Eur Spine J 2007;16:1085–1100.

283. Taylor RS, Taylor RJ, Fritzell P. Balloon kyphoplasty and vertebroplasty for vertebral compression fractures: a comparative systematic review of efficacy and safety. Spine 2006;31:2747–2755.

284. Teegarden D, Lyle RM, McCabe GP, et al. Dietary calcium, protein, and phosphorus are related to bone mineral density and content in young women. Am J Clin Nutr 1998;68:749–754.

285. Tinetti ME. Factors associated with serious injury during falls by ambulatory nursing home residents. J Am Geriatr Soc 1987;35:644–648.

286. Tinetti ME, Doucette J, Claus E, et al. Risk factors for serious injury during falls by older persons in the community. J Am Geriatr Soc 1995;43:1214–1221.

287. Tinetti ME, Doucette JT, Claus EB. The contribution of predisposing and situational risk factors to serious fall injuries. J Am Geriatr Soc 1995;43:1207–1213.

288. Tinetti ME, Liu WL, Ginter SF. Mechanical restraint use and fall-related injuries among residents of skilled nursing facilities. Ann Intern Med 1992;116:369–374.

289. Tinetti ME, McAvay G, Claus E. Does multiple risk factor reduction explain the reduction in fall rate in the Yale FICSIT Trial? Frailty and Injuries Cooperative Studies of Intervention Techniques. Am J Epidemiol 1996;144:389–399.

290. Tinetti ME, Speechley M, Ginter SF. Risk factors for falls among elderly persons living in the community. N Engl J Med 1988;319:1701–1707.

291. Torgerson DJ, Bell-Syer SE. Hormone replacement therapy and prevention of nonvertebral fractures: a meta-analysis of randomized trials. JAMA 2001;285:2891–2897.

292. Torgerson DJ, Bell-Syer SE. Hormone replacement therapy and prevention of vertebral fractures: a meta-analysis of randomised trials. BMC musculoskeletal disorders 2001; 2:7.

293. Torgerson DJ, Campbell MK, Thomas RE, et al. Prediction of perimenopausal fractures by bone mineral density and other risk factors. J Bone Miner Res 1996;11:293–297.

294. Tornkvist H, Hearn TC, Schatzker J. The strength of plate fixation in relation to the number and spacing of bone screws. J Orthop Trauma 1996;10:204–208.

295. Toussirot E, Royet O, Wendling D. [Aetiologic features of osteoporosis in male patients aged less than 50 years: study of 28 cases with a comparative series of 30 patients over the age of 50.] Rev Med Interne 1998;19:479–485.

296. Trivedi DP, Doll R, Khaw KT. Effect of four monthly oral vitamin D3.cholecalciferol supplementation on fractures and mortality in men and women living in the community: randomised double blind controlled trial. BMJ (Clin Res) 2003;326:469.

297. Uitterlinden AG, Burger H, Huang Q, et al. Relation of alleles of the collagen type Ialpha1 gene to bone density and the risk of osteoporotic fractures in postmenopausal women. N Engl J Med 1998;338:1016–1021.

298. Uppin AA, Hirsch JA, Centenera LV, et al. Occurrence of new vertebral body fracture after percutaneous vertebroplasty in patients with osteoporosis. Radiology 2003;226: 119–124.

299. Valdimarsson O, Alborg HG, Duppe H, et al. Reduced training is associated with increased loss of BMD. J Bone Miner Res 2005;20:906–912.

300. van Meurs JB, Trikalinos TA, Ralston SH, et al. Large-scale analysis of association between LRP5 and LRP6 variants and osteoporosis. JAMA 2008;299:1277–1290.

301. Villa M, Nelson L. Race, ethnicity, and osteoporosis. California: Academic Press, 1996. pp. 435–447.

302. Voormolen MH, Måli WP, Lohle PN, et al. Percutaneous vertebroplasty compared with optimal pain medication treatment: short-term clinical outcome of patients with subacute or chronic painful osteoporotic vertebral compression fractures. The VERTOS study. AJNR 2007;28:555–560.

303. Walsh WR, Sherman P, Howlett CR, et al. Fracture healing in a rat osteopenia model. Clin Orthop 1997:218–227.

304. Watts NB, Harris ST, Genant HK, et al. Intermittent cyclical etidronate treatment of postmenopausal osteoporosis. N Engl J Med 1990;323:73–79.

305. Weiss NS, Liff JM, Ure CL, et al. Mortality in women following hip fracture. J Chronic Dis 1983;36:879–882.

306. Weisskopf M, Herlein S, Birnbaum K, et al. [Kyphoplasty—a new minimally invasive treatment for repositioning and stabilising vertebral bodies.] Z Orthop Ihre Grenzgeb 2003;141:406–411.

307. Welch RD, Zhang H, Bronson DG. Experimental tibial plateau fractures augmented with calcium phosphate cement or autologous bone graft. J Bone Joint Surg Am 2003; 85A:222–231.

308. Wells G, Cranney A, Peterson J, et al. Risedronate for the primary and secondary prevention of osteoporotic fractures in postmenopausal women. Cochrane Database Syst Rev 2008:CD004523.

309. Wells GA, Cranney A, Peterson J, et al. Alendronate for the primary and secondary prevention of osteoporotic fractures in postmenopausal women. Cochrane Database Syst Rev 2008:CD001155.

310. Wells GA, Cranney A, Peterson J, et al. Etidronate for the primary and secondary prevention of osteoporotic fractures in postmenopausal women. Cochrane Database Syst Rev 2008:CD003376.

311. WHO. Assessment of fracture risk and its application to screening for postmenopausal osteoporosis. Report of a WHO Study Group. World Health Organ Tech Rep Ser 1994; 843:1–129.

312. Wickham CA, Walsh K, Cooper C, et al. Dietary calcium, physical activity, and risk of hip fracture: a prospective study. BMJ (Clin Res) 1989;299:889–892.

313. Woitge HW, Scheidt-Nave C, Kissling C, et al. Seasonal variation of biochemical indexes of bone turnover: results of a population-based study. J Clin Endocrinol Metab 1998; 83:68–75.

314. Woitge HW, Seibel MJ, Ziegler R. Comparison of total and bone-specific alkaline phosphatase in patients with nonskeletal disorder or metabolic bone diseases. Clin Chem 1996;42:1796–804.

315. Wolf SIL, Barnhart HX, Ellison GL, et al. The effect of Tai Chi Quan and computerized balance training on postural stability in older subjects. Atlanta FICSIT Group. Frailty and Injuries: Cooperative Studies on Intervention Techniques. Phys Ther 1997;77: 371–381; discussion 82–84.

316. Wolfson L, Whipple R, Derby C, et al. Balance and strength training in older adults: intervention gains and Tai Chi maintenance. J Am Geriatr Soc 1996;44:498–506.

317. Yoshikawa T, Turner CH, Peacock M, et al. Geometric structure of the femoral neck measured using dual-energy x-ray absorptiometry. J Bone Miner Res 1994;9: 1053–1064.

318. Zyto K. Nonoperative treatment of comminuted fractures of the proximal humerus in elderly patients. Injury 1998;29:349–352.

19

STRESS FRACTURES

David C. Teague

INTRODUCTION

Much has changed in our understanding of stress fractures since the likely initial description by Breithaupt in 1855 of a syndrome of painful swollen feet among marching Prussian soldiers.[27] It took until 1956 for the first report of the condition in athletes.[58] Originally the domain of military recruits and military physicians, recreational and competitive athletes with stress fractures now commonly present to civilian practitioners. Athletic populations involved in team and individual sports increasingly develop overuse injuries, and stress fractures have been reported in most bones in the body.

Stress fracture incidences evade precise determination in athletic populations because of a variability in training programs and a lack of standardized reporting.[166] Track and field teams have shown incidences ranging from 10% to 31%, with lesser but substantial numbers noted for participants in gymnastics, ballet, figure skating, basketball, crew, soccer, and lacrosse.[18,93] U.S. military recruits develop lower extremity stress fractures at a gender-dependent rate of up to 4% in men and 7% in women.[4,80,95,103]

By convention, stress fractures occur in normal bone when that bone is subjected to abnormal or unaccustomed stresses. This condition is distinct from insufficiency fractures, wherein normal stresses applied to abnormal bone produce fracture.

PRINCIPLES OF MANAGEMENT

Pathophysiology of Injury

Various forces exert loads on bone during all physical activities. Ground and joint reaction forces as well as muscle forces stress the bone by application of force across unit areas of bone. These stresses yield local deformation or change in length, termed *strain*. Therefore, stress, a measure of the load applied, produces strain or bone deformation in a given direction.[42]

According to Wolff law, normal loads delivered to normal bone produce normal bone remodeling.[44] This remodeling response to cyclic loading entails initial osteoclastic bone resorption followed by osteoblastic new bone formation within cortical bone as well as on the trabeculae of cancellous bone.[33,39] The resorption process peaks at 3 weeks, but it takes 3 months to adequately create the new bone to complete the remodeling cycle.[70,96,158,176] When optimally loaded and with sufficient time for remodeling, bone mass remains static, no stress fracture or injury ensues, and the bone becomes stronger.[70,71,110,158,186] However, repetitive loading, which outstrips the bone's ability to create new bone in the resorption tunnels and pits, engenders a resorption-dominated accelerated remodeling process that actually weakens the bone.[41,71,96,110,120] Then, with continued repetitive loading, a positive feedback mechanism develops in which increased mechanical usage stimulates bone turnover, resulting in focally increased remodeling porosity and decreased bone mass. This weakened site is thus more susceptible to further microdamage, which will incite additional resorption. Ultimately, stress fracture can result from continued loading superimposed onto the focally decreased bone mass generated by progressively larger resorption sites.[162]

Signs and Symptoms

A careful history of load-related pain often points to the likely diagnosis of stress fracture. Most athletes can accurately characterize their symptom progression and relate the gradual onset of vague pain over a period of weeks during training. Symptoms are initially described as mild and present only during the stress or activity.[110] The symptoms very often occur during the first few weeks after an increase in training volume or intensity, a change in technique or surface, or an alteration of footwear. Any change in a previously regimented training program may be the inciting historical event.[42,83,120] For nonathletes, a recent unusual uptick in activity, like a vacation with a great deal more walking than usual or a new aerobic exercise program, may be described.[62] If left unchecked, the process may progress to persistent pain after training, pain at rest, and even night pain. Pertinent historical questions relate to potential risk factors. History of previous stress fractures or other painful sites and the presence of eating disorders, leg length discrepancy, or muscle imbalance should be evaluated. In the female patient, age of menarche and presence of menstrual irregularities must be considered. For athletes, training regimen alterations are usually the root cause of the pain. For runners, the most common training change is a significant increase in the distance run during a brief period of training.[150] Furthermore, the potential impact to the patient must be assessed. For example, a scholarship athlete may wish to make different treatment choices than a weekend runner.

The hallmark physical finding is focal bone pain with palpation and stressing, but findings vary depending on the location of the stress fracture and the time from injury onset to presentation. When the site is accessible, local swelling may be noted. Percussion of the bone typically produces pain, but passive and active ranges of motion of adjacent joints do not. The anatomic location of the pain can help in the diagnosis. For example, femoral diaphyseal stress fractures occur typically in the medial cortex, so lateral thigh pain is not likely to be correlated with a stress fracture.[62] Inaccessible sites require indirect physical tests for diagnosis. For example, back pain produced by hip extension while standing on the opposite leg may implicate stress fractures of the pars interarticularis.[29]

Risk Factors

In general, the predominant risk factor for the development of a stress fracture is an increase in training frequency and intensity. However, work based on the concepts of Grimston and Frost allows analysis of the factors that may lead to bone's failure to successfully adapt to the mechanical loads to which it is exposed.[13,69,85] Mechanical competence of bone depends on properties like bone density and geometry, all related to cellular activity. The theoretical mechanosensory system of bone, classically considered to be Wolff law, can be understood as a mechanostat that senses strain, compares it to a given threshold, and initiates an adaptive cellular response. Physiologic, mechanical, and pharmacologic factors generate mechanostat responses by providing functional stimuli to the bone. Systemic constraints on bone health such as genetics or eating disorders may impede the bone's ability to respond despite messages from the mechanostat.

In contrast to elderly patients with osteoporosis and bone density measurements predictive of fragility fracture risks, the majority of young active individuals have normal bone density.[15] Little work points to any significant connection between bone density and risk of stress fracture in men. Studies of male soldiers and runners typically find no difference in tibial bone density between those with and those without stress fractures.[17,52,77] While not clearly causally related, low bone density may be a risk factor for women.[12] A multivariate analysis showed a strong association between low femoral neck bone density and risk of stress fracture in female military recruits.[111] An 8% lower bone density at the tibia was identified in a subgroup of female track athletes who developed tibial stress fractures.[17] However, the bone density measures for these women were still higher than those for similar less active nonathletes, perhaps suggesting that the bone density required by athletes may be greater than that needed by the general population. In summary, bone density measurement does not appear to be a useful screening tool for stress fractures.[12]

Smaller bone size appears to predispose to stress fracture.[13] In a prospective evaluation of more than 600 military recruits, an up to 10% smaller tibial width and cross-sectional area was found among those who developed stress fractures.[10] Similar results for male runners are reported.[52] Although bone geometry likely affects stress fracture development, no practical imaging system yet allows this variable to be used as a screening tool.

Activity that produces repetitive loading clearly can lead to stress fracture development. Multiple factors influence the clinical responses to bone loading.[13] Most studies support the notion that poor baseline physical fitness predisposes to stress fracture development when a significant increase in activity occurs.[49,165,192] However, well-conditioned athletes also develop stress fractures, so other factors must be considered. Load magnitude and rate appear to present the most significant stimulation of bone cellular dynamics, so the training regimen of soldiers and athletes often merits scrutiny.[13] Training modifications including rest periods,[164,193] banning concrete as a training surface,[83,151] use of running shoes,[83,149] and restricting high-impact activities[143,164,179] can reduce the incidence of stress fractures in military recruits. Shock-absorbing boot inserts may lead to fewer stress injuries in recruits, but comfort and compliance issues prevent strong conclusions.[155] Surveys of athletes relate changes in training in more than 80% of them before the onset of a stress fracture. Increased training volume is related to higher stress fracture risks in ballet dancers and runners.[38,98]

The role of flexibility, either too much or not enough, cannot be conclusively documented to contribute to stress fracture development.[13] Many investigators have evaluated factors including joint mobility and laxity, and muscle length. Only limited ankle dorsiflexion and increased hip external rotation have been somewhat implicated in stress fracture development.[77,78,91] Similarly, the contribution of foot structure to stress fracture risk is controversial.[7,122,169] For example, some studies support an association in male military recruits between high midfoot arch and greater risk of stress fracture.[79,169] This correlation does not appear in all studies.[130] The stress fracture–foot type relationship is likely variable depending on which bone is involved. Leg length discrepancy actually appears to increase the chance of stress fracture for military and athletic individuals, but the risk is not specific to either the shorter or the longer limb.[17,38,68] The second metatarsal and second toe lengths do not correlate to risk of second metatarsal base stress fracture in dancers.[55]

Impact attenuation during training should alter the functional stimuli transmitted to the bone. Conventionally, the training surface is considered a factor in the development of stress fracture. Most advise athletes to avoid training on hard, uneven surfaces, but no clear scientific data support or refute this recommendation.[13,109] Although ground reaction forces decrease with more compliant running surfaces, these same surfaces may result in more or earlier muscle fatigue.[124,175]

No study demonstrates a correlation between a host of body size and composition factors and the incidence of stress fractures.[13] Height, weight, body mass index, body girth and width, as well as many other variables, have been investigated.[8,17,98,116] Even in military recruits, who display more variability in body size than typical groups of similar athletes, no consistent associations between stress fractures and body size and composition can be demonstrated.[49,77,179,192]

While skeletal homeostasis is affected by multiple endogenous hormones, sex hormones, primarily in women, appear to have substantial impact on the stress fracture risks. No relationship between lowered testosterone levels and stress fractures exists for male athletes.[170] Even when testosterone levels are decreased, they are typically within the range of normal for healthy adult men.[88,117,171] Conversely, female athletes with menstrual irregularities uniformly are found to have an increased risk for the development of stress fractures. These women with menstrual disturbances present a two to four times higher relative risk for stress fractures than eumenorrheic athletes.[12] Also, amenorrheic athletes are at a higher risk of developing multiple stress fractures.[8] Yet use of oral contraceptives does not conclusively reduce the risk of stress fractures in these athletes.[51,104] Lifetime menstrual history similarly yields information regarding the risk of stress fracture, with the historically regular athletes reporting a 20% less risk than those with very irregular menstrual cycles.

The mechanism that produces increased stress fracture risk with menstrual disturbance is unclear and most certainly multifactorial. Nevertheless, the association is unassailable and frequently found presenting together with eating disorders and osteopenia. This combination, known as the *female athlete triad,* mandates attention be directed to all facets of the patient's condition.[12,64,141] Eating disorders occur more commonly in female athletes than males.[94,144] Even active duty female soldiers admit to an 8% prevalence of eating disorders.[112] Disordered eating patterns appear to increase the risk of stress fractures in ballet dancers and young adult female track athletes.[16,72] Indeed, extreme weight-control behavior in college athletes doubles the risk of stress fracture.[132] Lower dietary calcium intake may well be an independent risk factor, particularly for female runners with irregular menses.[51,104]

Stress fractures occur in people of all ages. The peak incidence appears in late adolescence and early adulthood among military recruits, competitive and recreational athletes, and dancers.[14,19,81,92,95,122] Age is an important factor in determining the location of stress fractures, but age does not appear to be an important factor in their etiology.[92]

Imaging Modalities

The diagnosis of a stress fracture often requires no imaging studies, especially when a careful history and a classic physical exam combine to make the diagnosis with certainty. However, several radiographic modalities are at the disposal of the cli-

cian for definitive documentation and differential evaluations. Plain radiographs, bone scintigraphs, computed tomography (CT) scans, and magnetic resonance (MR) images are now the routine studies used to evaluate and diagnose stress fractures.

Plain Radiographs

Radiographs obtained very early in the stress fracture process typically are not effective in demonstrating an abnormality. Seldom do radiographic findings appear before 2 to 3 weeks from the onset of symptoms. New periosteal bone formation, the classic radiographic marker of a healing response, often does not appear until 3 months from symptom onset. Radiographic changes never appear for some stress fractures in some patients.[46] When changes are evident, several findings confirm the presence of a stress fracture, rendering this modality poorly sensitive but highly specific. Only 20% of bone scan foci positive for stress fractures correlate with positive plain radiographic findings.[127,196] The false-negative rate for radiographs approaches 100% for early Grade I bone scan–positive lesions but drops to 24% for Grade III lesions, demonstrating that stress fractures later in their course have more ability to remodel and respond to the altered stresses, and the later response often is apparent on plain radiographs.

Associated findings may include periosteal bone formation, horizontal or oblique linear patterns of sclerosis, endosteal callus, and a frank fracture line. The initial radiographic sign of a progressing stress fracture is the so-called gray cortex, which corresponds to a low-density cortical area affected by increased osteoclastic bone resorption activity[42] (Fig. 19-1). As the process evolves in long bones, the stress fracture undergoes marginal resorption and may yield an ovoid lucency within a thickened area of cortical hyperostosis.[29] A late-stage stress fracture in cortical bone appears as a radiolucent line with extension partially or completely across the cortex. Similar-stage stress fractures in cancellous bone demonstrate a fracture lucency oriented perpendicular to the trabeculae. Healing is denoted by focal sclerosis in areas of cancellous bone, while diaphyseal healing involves both periosteal and endosteal cortical thickening.[29] Plain films are most likely to present positive findings in the fibula and metatarsals. The x-ray beam should be centered over the painful, suspected bone. Plain films typically are not helpful in discerning stress injuries to the pars interarticularis. Some authors contend that plain films are unlikely to yield positive results when investigating possible tibial stress fractures, while others state the femur, pars interarticularis, and tarsal bones are least likely to yield remarkable findings on initial plain film investigation.[29,46]

Scintigraphy

When radiographic findings are conclusive, additional studies are not required. If multiple sites of stress fracture are possible based on history and physical exam, or if plain films do not support the presumptive diagnosis of stress fracture, three-phase bone scintigraphy has been the study of choice. Bone scan has long been considered the most sensitive test for stress fracture, with sensitivity approaching 100%.[42,46] However, the sensitivity is not coupled with high specificity, so clinical features must be correlated.

Isotopes are atoms with identical atomic numbers but different atomic weights, while a nuclide is the nucleus of a given isotope. Nuclides or isotopes with differences in numbers of

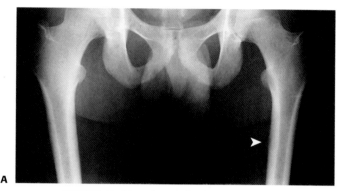
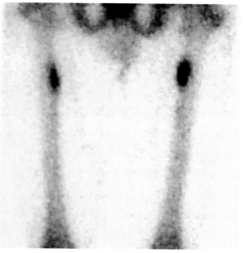

FIGURE 19-1 Imaging studies for a 20-year-old distance runner with bilateral proximal activity-related thigh pain. **A.** A plain radiograph demonstrates the gray cortex on the left femur (arrow) with minimal changes on the right. **B.** Delayed spot image scintigraphic study shows Grade 3 increased activity at the left proximal femur, while the right side demonstrates a slightly less intense increased signal.

protons and neutrons are unstable and give off particles or electromagnetic radiation in their transition to stability; this is known as *radioactive decay*. These materials are synonymously termed radionuclides or radioisotopes. When used for diagnostic purposes, the materials are termed radiopharmaceuticals and radiotracers.[163]

Technetium-99m methylene diphosphonate (^{99m}Tc MDP) is the radioisotope usually used for bone scans. Gamma radiation is emitted, and the whole body dose for a bone scan is about 0.13 to 0.19 rad. The bladder dose, where the radioactivity is concentrated in the urine, is 2.62 to 3.90 rads—hence, the need for frequent voiding during and after the scanning period.

[99m]Tc MDP is available in good supply at low cost, has a 6-hour half-life, and emits gamma energy at an ideal frequency for gamma cameras used in diagnostic imaging.[163]

The radioisotope is administered as a bolus intravenously. The mechanism of uptake in bone is not precisely elucidated, but blood flow to the bone is a fundamental requirement. In normal bone, uptake is in proportion to blood flow to the bone. However, in abnormal situations like stress fractures that are accompanied by high bone vascularity, factors other than bone blood flow play a larger role in radiotracer uptake. New bone formation proves to be the most important factor in the uptake, whereas bone destruction without new bone formation yields no increase in uptake.[29,163]

Bone scintigraphy is performed in three phases—two early and one delayed. The initial images acquired immediately after radiotracer injection are representative of blood perfusion to bone and soft tissue and correspond roughly to contrast angiography. The second set of images, obtained approximately 2 to 5 minutes after injection and termed the *blood pool scans*, demonstrate radionuclide location in the soft tissues or extravascular space. These images reflect the extent of hyperemia and capillary permeability and generally correspond to the acuity and severity of the injury. At 2 to 4 hours after injection, the delayed images document radionuclide accumulation in the skeleton and, to a lesser extent, the soft tissue. Over this time, 50% of the diphosphonate tracer is postulated to be adsorbed on the hydroxyapatite matrix of bone, with special affinity for new bone formation sites.[46]

Given a correlating history and physical exam, the scintigraphic diagnosis of stress fracture is made by focal increased uptake on the third-phase images. Stress fractures are positive on all three phases, but periostitis develops positive foci only on the delayed images.[5,29,157] Other soft tissue injuries are positive only in the first two phases, allowing some differentiation between bony and soft tissue pathology. However, the lack of specificity remains a disadvantage of this modality.[29,46] The typical list of conditions producing similar localized uptake includes osteoid osteoma, other bony tumors, osteomyelitis, bony infarct, and bony dysplasias. Due to its improved ability to differentiate many of these conditions, MR imaging may be the diagnostic method of choice in certain settings.

Radionuclide scans can be positive within hours of a bone injury.[29] Acute stress fractures are positive on all three phases. As bony healing proceeds, the initial phase perfusion scan normalizes first. Within the ensuing few weeks, the blood pool second phase images return to normal. Since bony remodeling continues for an extended period, focal uptake on the delayed images resolves last. Uptake gradually diminishes in intensity over a three to six month period, but some increased uptake can last up to a year, even in uncomplicated stress fractures with uneventful healing.[5] Bone scans are not therefore particularly useful for monitoring healing and do not merit frequent repeating.

A grading system, based on the scintigraphic appearance, allows classification into milder or more severe stress fractures, recognizing that these stress injuries occur along a continuum of bony involvement[196] (Table 19-1). The minimally symptomatic Grade 1 or Grade 2 stress fractures typically resolve more quickly and completely. The grading system can assist in prescribing the requisite rest and rehabilitation intervals[29] (Fig. 19-1).

Single-photon emission computed tomography (SPECT) is used when lumbosacral stress fractures are suspected. The cam-

TABLE 19-1		**Bone Scintigraphy and Magnetic Resonance Imaging Grading Scale**

Grade	Bone Scan	Magnetic Resonance Imaging
1	Small, ill-defined cortical area of mildly increased activity	Periosteal edema: mild to moderate on fat-suppressed T2 or STIR images Marrow: normal on T1 and fat-suppressed T2 or STIR images
2	Better-defined cortical area of moderately increased activity	Periosteal edema: moderate to severe on fat-suppressed T2 or STIR images Marrow edema on fat-suppressed T2 or STIR images
3	Wide to fusiform, cortical medullary area of highly increased activity	Periosteal edema: moderate to severe on fat-suppressed T2 or STIR images Marrow edema on T1 and fat-suppressed T2 or STIR images
4	Transcortical area of intensely increased activity	Periosteal edema: moderate to severe on fat-suppressed T2 or STIR images Marrow edema on T1 and fat-suppressed T2 or STIR images Fracture line clearly visible

STIR, short tau inversion recovery.
Adapted from Fredericson M, Bergman G, Hoffman KL, et al. Tibial stress reaction in runners: correlation of clinical symptoms and scintigraphy with a new magnetic resonance imaging grading system. Am J Sports Med 1995;23:472–481.

era rotates about the patient, generating three-dimensional images of radioisotope uptake. This modality is particularly useful for investigating suspected pars interarticularis and sacral stress fractures.[29,42]

Magnetic Resonance Imaging

MR images provide identical sensitivity and superior specificity compared with bone scintigraphy for the evaluation of stress fractures.[100,152] The improved specificity derives from the comprehensive anatomic visualization provided from this modality, allowing for precise localization of the injury and differentiation from other possible conditions. The bony tissue, with comparatively few mobile protons, is not represented in significant detail. Instead, MR imaging accentuates reactive edema in the soft tissues and marrow surrounding a stress injury. This soft tissue response is seen best in edema-sensitive sequences like fat-suppressed T2-weighted and short tau inversion recovery (STIR) scans. Areas of edema appear as high signal intensity sites on these sequences.[29,57]

A grading system that corresponds to the scintigraphic grading system addresses the typical progression of stress injury documented on MR images[66] (Table 19-1). Earliest injuries demonstrate increased signal intensity first in the periosteum, then also in the marrow on STIR and T2-weighted images, while the T1 scans are normal. In Grade 3 injuries, decreased marrow signal occurs with the T1 sequence, while the STIR and T2 sequences yield even higher intensity marrow changes. Grade 4 stress fractures feature a low signal fracture line on both sequences continuous with the cortex and medullary space[57,66] (Fig. 19-2).

Although plain radiographs and bone scintigraphs accurately diagnose stress fractures in most patients, MR images are increasingly advocated as the study of choice.[29,46,81] MR imaging

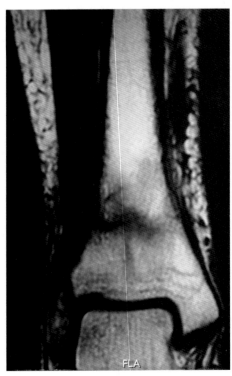

FIGURE 19-2 Coronal T1-weighted magnetic resonance image of a Grade 4 distal tibia stress fracture with visible fracture line and surrounding marrow edema.

involves no exposure to ionizing radiation and requires much shorter imaging times than bone scintigraphy. The specificity of MR images significantly exceeds that of scintigraphs.[168] Thus, straightforward cases can be investigated reliably without MR imaging, but more difficult diagnostic dilemmas or problematic cases warrant MR imaging, which is now regarded as the overall best technique for assessment.[67,75,172]

Computed Tomography

CT scans provide excellent bony anatomic detail. The delineation of fracture line orientation is assisted with three-dimensional CT information, which may improve treatment decisions for certain bones such as the tarsal navicular.[107,108] Longitudinal fracture lines in diaphyseal locations can also be elucidated. Pars and sacral stress fractures are well characterized with CT scans as well.[42]

Rationale of Initial Management

The fundamental principle of initial management is modified rest to allow the bone remodeling process to equilibrate. The inciting strain must be eliminated to break the cycle of accelerated resorption, allowing new bone formation to catch up and adequately repair the focus of stress fracture.[42,150] Earlier initiation of rest, when the resorption–formation mismatch is minimal, allows a brief period of activity restriction to suffice.[126] For athletes, alternative training should continue provided regimens can be devised that unload the area of stress fracture.[22] For nonathletes, a brief period of rest is usually well tolerated and adequate to reverse the process.

Different stress fracture sites mandate certain specific management approaches, but the overarching message of activity modification and rest applies to every site.[60,99] During this first phase of treatment, remediable risk factors should be addressed. The training errors or changes that precipitated the stress fracture should be identified and corrected.[110] Braces or other forms of immobilization are seldom needed. No controlled study strongly supports adjunctive measures like external electrical stimulation or ultrasound.[9,11,26,122,153] For high-level athletes, early pool running programs prove highly successful at maintaining baseline fitness during the rest phase.[28,76]

Second-phase rehabilitation begins when pain is substantially diminished or absent.[42,150] For lower extremity injuries, this timeframe is roughly 2 weeks after painless walking is resumed.[66,110] The training program emphasizes progressive aerobic conditioning with specified rest times to permit bone compensation for the slowly increasing strains.[28,164] Provided the progression does not reproduce the patient's pain, activity reintroduction proceeds steadily. Cross-training is advisable to reduce the likelihood of recurrence.[28] Surgery is seldom contemplated or required for the management of most stress fractures. No study proves or disproves an adverse link between healing of stress fractures and use of nonsteroidal anti-inflammatory drugs.[189] A trial of prophylactic treatment with risedronate failed to demonstrate a reduction in stress fracture risk among infantry recruits.[125]

CURRENT TREATMENT OPTIONS

Lower Extremity

Femoral Neck

Early recognition of femoral neck stress fractures prevents catastrophic consequences. Younger patients typically present with

inferior or medial neck lesions, commonly known as compression-side stress fractures. Older patients are prone to superior, tension-side fractures, and these are more likely to fail and displace with continued activity.[34,73,74] With either lesion, patients complain of activity-related diffuse groin or anterior hip pain and have pain at the limits of hip rotation on exam. MR images may be more accurate than scintigraphy in this region and provide differential information for other causes of hip pain like tendonitis, bone cysts, or avascular necrosis of the femoral head.[168]

Stage 1 or 2 injuries without a cortical crack are treated with a modified rest protocol beginning with an initial period of non–weight bearing until pain resolves. Stage 3 compression side injuries, demonstrating a nondisplaced cortical crack, are still stable and can be managed nonoperatively[73,145] (Fig. 19-3). Tension-sided stage 3 injuries, with a nondisplaced crack, can be managed similarly with complete unloading and frequent clinical and radiographic follow-up to document healing.[50,73] However, because of the long-term functional consequences of a displaced femoral neck fracture, some authors support stabilization with cannulated screw fixation for this injury.[61] Stage 4 injuries demonstrate widening of the cortical crack or even frank displacement of the completed fracture. These injuries demand operative stabilization. Nondisplaced complete fractures are stabilized with multiple screws. Fluoroscopy-guided curettage of the tension side fracture site has been advocated. In young people with displaced fractures, emergent open reduction with internal fixation (ORIF) is mandatory.[73,188] A recent series of displaced femoral neck stress fractures in military recruits identified an association between delayed surgery and varus malreduction and an increased risk of both avascular necrosis and poor function.[114] In older patients, consideration can be given to hip arthroplasty depending on the individual situation.

Femoral Shaft

In most athletes, femoral diaphyseal stress fractures occur proximally in the medial or posteromedial cortex[87,93] (Fig. 19-1).

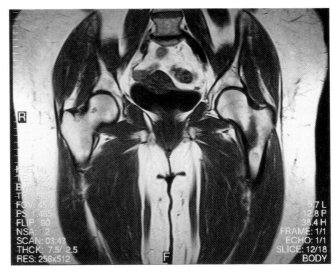

FIGURE 19-3 Coronal T1-weighted pelvis magnetic resonance image of a 50-year-old female runner demonstrates a Grade 3 left compression-side femoral neck stress fracture. The darker marrow signal represents edema.

Vague activity-related anterior thigh pain is the typical complaint, and vigorous stressing on physical exam can reproduce the pain.[34] Some longitudinal stress fractures, parallel to the cortex, appear best in MR images.[182] Other sites including the distal femoral supracondylar region are also susceptible to stress fractures.[159] Femoral shaft lesions occur in sites of compressive stress, are stable, and heal with modified rest protocols. Only catastrophic complete failures require reamed intramedullary stabilization.

Tibia

Tibial stress fractures are the most commonly reported among the many lower extremity stress fractures.[122] Other overuse injuries may simultaneously present or require elimination from the differential diagnosis. Inflammation of the aponeurotic tenoperiosteal origins of the tibialis posterior and soleus muscles and of the fascial attachments to the posterior medial border of the tibia produces pain previously termed shin splints and now characterized as medial tibial stress syndrome.[6,177] Pain from this inflammatory situation typically occurs along the medial border of the tibia, improves after warm-up, and is worse in the morning. Exertional compartment syndromes of the anterior or deep posterior compartments present with muscle aching and subjective tightness that increase shortly after exercise begins. No bony tenderness usually accompanies this condition. Tibial stress fracture pain is progressive, with a gradual onset exacerbated by exercise and made worse with impact, ultimately occurring while simply walking, or even at rest or at night. Tenderness is localized and bony.[31]

The majority of tibial stress fractures are posteromedial compression injuries and occur usually in the proximal or distal thirds.[21,31] When a fracture has developed, a transverse orientation is typical (Fig. 19-2), but longitudinal stress fractures also are reported.[102] These fractures respond well to cessation of the repetitive loading activity, which almost always is distance running, along with complete leg rest using crutches until the pain subsides.[31] Some work suggests adjunctive treatment with a pneumatic brace may facilitate earlier functional return to activity by accelerating the initial time to pain-free walking, but other investigators have not demonstrated a benefit.[3,155,178,190] Pulsed ultrasound and capacitively coupled electrical stimulation treatments do not significantly reduce the healing time.[9,156] Surgery is not required for this condition, but return to activity can take up to 3 months.[150]

The more unusual but significantly more vexing tibial stress fracture appears in the middle third of the anterior cortex. This tension-side injury results from repetitive stress of jumping or leaping, as seen in basketball players and ballet dancers. Bone pain is easily demonstrated, and palpable periosteal thickening may be present if the process is chronic. These fractures frequently progress to nonunion, and complete fractures are also reported.[21,84] In chronic cases, a transverse, wedge-shaped defect in the anterior cortex, dubbed the *dreaded black line,* is often seen in conjunction with cortical hypertrophy[150] (Fig. 19-4). Tissue obtained from these sites demonstrates limited healing potential, consistent with a pseudarthrosis.[138,154]

Initial conservative treatment requires prolonged modified rest, with or without cast or brace immobilization.[180] However, even over 4 to 6 months, many of these fractures with chronic changes and anterior fissures or cracks will remain symptomatic and nonunited. Some authors have shown healing benefits from

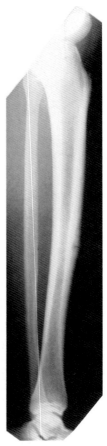

FIGURE 19-4 Lateral radiograph of the left tibia of a collegiate track athlete demonstrates anterior cortical hypertrophy and the dreaded black line of an anterior tension-side stress fracture.

adjunctive electrical stimulation or ultrasound in nonoperative protocols,[11,26,153] while others demonstrate no benefits from these modalities.[84] Transverse drilling of the nonunion sites reportedly stimulates healing and speeds time to return to activity.[110,138,150] Reamed intramedullary nailing works well for recalcitrant cases and now has some support as the initial treatment of choice for the anterior cortical stress fracture nonunion.[45,146,187] Following nail fixation, return to sport within 4 months is typical, although failure to unite and knee problems are reported.[142,187] A small series touts anterior tension band plating for this lesion in elite female athletes, with return to full activity at 10 weeks.[23]

Medial Malleolus

Participants in repetitive running and jumping activities are at risk for the development of medial malleolus stress fractures characterized by bony tenderness and ankle effusion. The typically vertically oriented fracture line originates at the junction between the malleolus and plafond directly above the medial border of the talus, which is postulated to be the cyclic force transmitter.[21,167] For grade 1 and 2 injuries, impact avoidance in a cast or pneumatic brace achieves return to function in 6 to 8 weeks. For grade 3 and 4 stress fractures, similar conservative measures are appropriate, but healing may take 4 to 5 months. More aggressive intervention is also supported depending on the injury chronicity and the demands of the patient. Drilling may enhance healing.[139] Screw fixation for displaced fractures, nonunion, and chronic cases and in elite performers allows early motion and may promote earlier return to activity.[21,31]

Tarsal Navicular

Repetitive running and jumping activity places sprinters, hurdlers, middle-distance runners, football players, basketball players, ballet dancers, and other athletes at risk for tarsal navicular stress fracture.[36,122] The insidious onset of vague medial arch pain usually accompanies dorsal navicular tenderness to palpation.[30] The stress fracture occurs in the sagittal plane in the relatively avascular central third of the bone, originating at the proximal dorsal articular surface and extending in a plantar distal direction.[21,184] Plain radiography often fails to demonstrate the navicular stress fracture.[106] Although bone scintigraphy is sensitive, CT or MR imaging provides specific information regarding fracture completeness and orientation[21] (Fig. 19-5).

Among patients with an early diagnosis, 6 weeks of non–weight-bearing cast immobilization yields high union rates.[107,184] Conversely, less than 25% of patients treated with weight-bearing immobilization heal, and the risk of delayed union and recurrence is also much higher.[40,59,65,107,115,137,184] Following the initial period of strict non–weight bearing, graduated return to activity is pursued provided the physical exam reveals no navicular tenderness.[30] In cases of displaced frac-

tures, delayed unions, and nonunions, surgical stabilization is undertaken.[21] Regardless of chronicity, some authors recommend ORIF when imaging confirms extension of the stress fracture into the body of the navicular.[161] Compression screw fixation alone usually provides adequate stability. Often the dorsal cortex is not visibly disrupted, so placing supplemental bone graft may require more extensive dissection except in cases of complete, displaced stress fractures or nonunions.[65,115] Non–weight bearing after fixation is advised. Surgical and conservative management leads to good results, but most patients note slight long-term pain and functional loss even after return to activity.[148]

Metatarsals

Metatarsal stress fractures are common in distance runners and ballet dancers.[30] The second metatarsal neck is the most likely site for stress fracture, but all metatarsals are susceptible. Gradually worsening forefoot pain exacerbated by running or dancing herald the diagnosis, especially when accompanied by focal bony tenderness. For short-lived complaints, initiation of modified rest without imaging studies usually leads to symptom resolution. For uncertain diagnoses or chronic complaints, imaging modalities provide clarification. A second metatarsal plantar base stress fracture previously recognized only in female ballet dancers appears to be secondary to the *en pointe* position and responds to rest and activity modification.[82,136] This stress fracture site has now been reported in nondancer athletes, and 50% of the patients in those small series required surgery for nonunion.[47,160]

Stress fracture of the proximal diaphysis of the fifth metatarsal, common in basketball players, often are slow to heal, and can demonstrate high recurrence rates.[97,183] The problematic site is in the proximal 1.5 cm of the diaphysis, where cortical hypertrophy commonly occurs in running and jumping athletes, rendering the zone relatively avascular with a narrow medullary canal.[54] Treatment choices are predicated on the stage of the lesion as described by Torg and colleagues.[183,185] Patients with acute fractures often acknowledge a 2- to 3-week prodromal history of activity-related lateral foot pain. These acute injuries show clear fracture lines with no medullary sclerosis and little or no cortical hypertrophy. Healing in most acute fractures ensues with a 6- to 8-week course of non–weight-bearing cast immobilization.[1,48,185,195] Closed treatment with full weight bearing appears to predispose to nonunion and refracture.[97] Surgical management of acute stress fractures, especially in athletes, is recommended by some to avoid prolonged healing. Sliding bone graft procedures[53,86,194] and intramedullary compression screw fixation[56,101] techniques usually result in satisfactory healing within 3 months.[128]

Patients with a history of previous injury and recurrent symptoms will have radiographic evidence of delayed union or nonunion. Delayed unions demonstrate a wider fracture completely through the medial and lateral cortices with some medullary sclerosis (Fig. 19-6). A very wide gap with periosteal new bone formation and complete medullary sclerosis characterizes the appearance of established nonunions.[183,185] Delayed unions may heal with prolonged non–weight-bearing cast immobilization, but functional recovery often requires 6 months.[185,195] Most active patients with delayed union and virtually all with an established nonunion recover faster with surgical management. Torg[185] advises sclerotic bone débridement and inlay bone

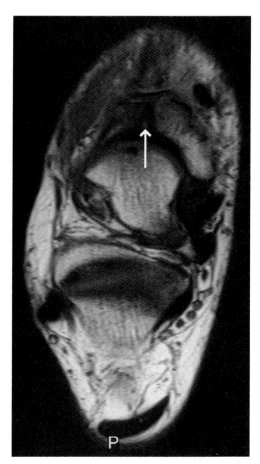

FIGURE 19-5 T1-weighted magnetic resonance image of the right ankle of a collegiate basketball player shows a navicular stress fracture (arrow) originating at the talonavicular joint surface.

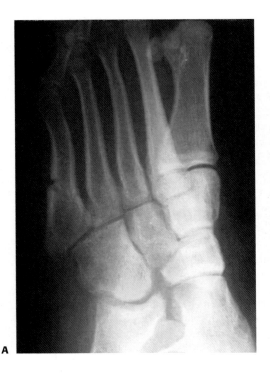

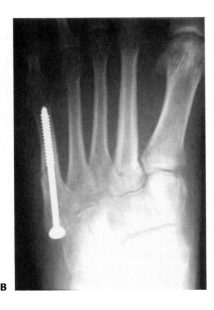

FIGURE 19-6 Middle-aged recreational runner with several-month history of worsening activity-related lateral foot pain. **A.** Intermediate delayed union fifth metatarsal stress fracture with a complete fracture, some widening of the cortical gap, and moderate medullary sclerosis. **B.** Radiographic appearance 3 months following medullary drilling, bone grafting, compression screw stabilization, and initial period of non–weight bearing.

grafting. Others propose a sliding bone graft[53] or compression screw fixation[56,113,147] (Fig. 19-6). For those averse to surgery, electrical stimulation has been shown to be effective.[90]

Other Sites

Stress fractures are reported in most of the remaining bones in the lower extremity. Rare patellar stress fractures, usually transverse but occasionally longitudinal, respond to extension immobilization for 4 weeks followed by progressive rehabilitation.[31,121,181] Runners and jumpers are susceptible to this injury. Failure to improve and acute displacement are indications for open management with tension band stabilization.[140] Fibular stress fractures occur typically in runners 1 to 2 inches above the ankle joint line, are much less common than tibial injuries, and usually respond to modified rest protocols.[110,129] Talar neck and body stress fractures are rare, but talar head stress lesions appear in military recruits.[173] Nonoperative management produces healing with only mild residual symptoms. Stress fractures of the lateral process of the talus are encountered on occasion, and a 6-week period of non–weight-bearing produces control of symptoms.[30,110] Surgical stabilization or excision may be considered for recalcitrant or displaced cases.[20,24] Calcaneal stress fractures typically occur transversely through the tuberosity in soldiers, runners, ballet dancers, and jumpers.[30,174] Conservative treatment measures are always sufficient. Similarly, a few reports of cuboid and cuneiform stress fractures describe successful modified rest treatment protocols.[105,119] Some calcaneal stress fractures occur in isolation, but most calcaneal and other tarsal stress fractures are associated with at least one other foot stress injury best diagnosed by MR imaging.[133,174]

Upper Extremity

Stress fractures in non–weight-bearing bones result from repetitive strains associated with recurrent loading activities like rowing, swimming, and throwing. The possibility of stress fracture should be considered in athletes primarily involved in upper extremity sports who complain of the gradual onset bony pain associated with the activity. Physical examination typically reveals bony tenderness to palpation and stressing. Imaging modalities are useful for clarifying the diagnosis. Modified rest and training technique corrections or alterations almost always result in early healing and return to activity.[37]

Stress fractures of the ribs occur not uncommonly in competitive rowers, typically anterolaterally between the fourth and ninth ribs.[59] Most humerus stress fractures occur in baseball pitchers, although other reports detail occurrence in athletes ranging from tennis players to weight lifters.[37] All of these athletes can be managed with modified rest and gradual resumption of activity. One report describes progression of humerus stress fractures to spontaneous shaft fractures in men in a baseball league.[25] The risk factors for complete fracture include age over 30 years, a prolonged layoff from pitching before resumption of participation, no regular exercise program, and prodromal arm pain.

In older adolescents and young adults involved in throwing sports or gymnastics, the presentation of gradually increasing elbow pain with activity mandates consideration of an olecranon stress fracture.[37] Some patients who complain less of prodromal symptoms and more of acute elbow pain related to a particularly strong throwing effort may have tip avulsion fractures involving up to the proximal third of the olecranon. Surgical excision of the fractured tip allows early return to sport.[135] Patients with classical stress fractures complain of longer duration pain that recurs when throwing resumes. These fractures are usually transverse and in the middle third of the olecranon. Among baseball players, the olecranon is the most common site for stress fracture. Adolescent gymnasts can also develop this stress fracture.[118] For nondisplaced fractures, immobilization and progressive return to activity are recommended. When displaced or delayed in healing, tension band fixation is effective.[118,135,191]

Stress fractures of the ulna may occur in baseball and softball pitchers, tennis players, weight-lifters, and volleyball players. Repetitive strains from underhanded softball pitching and two-handed tennis backhand strokes are representative of the typical inciting stresses. The athletes complain of bony pain with activity and even after the activity. Depending on the stage of injury, radiographs may demonstrate periosteal bone formation or a small cortical fracture. All reports document healing with modified rest for 4 to 6 weeks and progressive resumption of activity.[35,37]

Stress injuries to the distal radial physis are common in young gymnasts,[43] but radial shaft stress fractures in young adults are less common. Bilateral radial shaft stress fractures have been seen in a gymnast who doubled her weekly training time.[2] Athletes in any sport who begin a high-stress weight program are at risk for developing a radial stress reaction. The typical modified rest protocol should be instituted for the radius. If weight training is the inciting stress but the athlete's primary sport does not repetitively load the radius, continued participation in the sport usually presents no additional risk.

Repetitive strains to the metacarpals, particularly the second and fifth, can lead to stress fracture.[134] Patients describe a change in training volume and technique. Tennis players may be susceptible at the second metacarpal because the racquet provides a fulcrum.[131] Rest from the activity will yield healing and return to sport within 4 weeks, provided technique errors and training overload are altered.

Pelvis

Stress fractures of the pubic rami occur not uncommonly in female distance runners, most of whom have associated risk factors, as well as female military recruits.[89] When present, groin pain prevents further training, and single leg stance reproduces the pain. Deep palpation of the bone in these characteristically thin individuals typically elicits significant pain. Plain films and bone scintigraphs are usually diagnostic. An 8- to 12-week modified training regimen allows graduated return to activity.[134]

Sacral stress fractures predominantly develop in female distance runners but are also reported in their male counterparts. Female military conscripts show dramatically increased risks for this site.[123] Most have prodromal low back and buttock pain. Physical exam demonstrates localized tenderness to palpation and stress of the sacroiliac region. SPECT scanning has been the investigation of choice, but MR imaging now provides more specificity. Implementation of initial protected weight bearing followed by a progressive activity regimen reliably leads to uneventful healing.[32,63]

Grade 3 or grade 4 tension-side femoral neck stress fractures should be stabilized with multiple screw fixation to promote healing and prevent displacement. Because the patients who develop this injury are usually runners, care must be taken to place the screws in good position and avoid lateral entry points below the midportion of the level of the lesser trochanter to minimize the risk of iatrogenic subtrochanteric fracture from stress risers. Acutely displaced femoral neck stress fractures require urgent ORIF in the typical younger, active population.

Anterior tibial stress fractures with an established transverse cortical lucency have limited healing potential even with activity modification. For patients who fail the rest and rehabilitation protocol, or for those unwilling or unable to modify their activities for perhaps as long as 1 year, reamed intramedullary nailing predictably leads to healing of the stress fracture in a shorter time course. Inadequate data make prediction of long-term functional outcomes following nailing uncertain with regard to return to unrestricted sport or military activity.

For acute tarsal navicular stress fractures, an initial 6-week period of non–weight-bearing cast immobilization is the treatment of choice. For patients with delayed diagnosis or delayed union, compression screw stabilization provides high union rates. Displaced fractures and established sclerotic nonunions require ORIF and supplemental bone graft.

Acute fifth metatarsal stress fractures treated with strict non–weight-bearing cast immobilization seldom require further intervention. Many high-demand athletes may prefer cannulated screw fixation for these acute fractures to speed return to activity. The intermediate delayed union injury is preferentially managed with intramedullary compression screw placement after the medullary canal at the fracture site has been adequately drilled to remove fibrous tissue and sclerotic bone (Fig. 19-6). The established nonunion requires open débridement of the fracture gap with placement of graft, combined with intramedullary screw placement, although a recent report encourages use of a cannulated 4.5-mm screw without exposure of the nonunion site and with an accelerated rehabilitation program of progressive early loading and use of a semirigid full-length shoe insert.[147]

ACKNOWLEDGMENTS

The author thanks Doug Beall, MD, and Weyton Tam, MD, for providing the figures in this chapter, and Sheila M. Algan, MD; W. Bentley Edmonds, MD; Don McGinnis, MD; and Brock Schnebel, MD, for providing cases and sports medicine expertise.

AUTHORS' PREFERRED METHOD OF TREATMENT

Stress Fractures

A modified rest protocol successfully addresses the majority of stress fractures, and this initial conservative approach should be considered for all stress fractures and implemented for most. However, patients with certain high-risk or problematic stress fractures may benefit from early surgical intervention.

REFERENCES

1. Acker JH, Drez D Jr. Nonoperative treatment of stress fractures of the proximal shaft of the fifth metatarsal (Jones fracture). Foot Ankle 1986;7:152–155.
2. Ahluwalia R, Datz FL, Morton KA, et al. Bilateral fatigue fractures of the radial shaft in a gymnast. Clin Nucl Med 1994;19:665–667.
3. Allen CS, Flynn TW, Kardouni JR, et al. The use of a pneumatic leg brace in soldiers with tibial stress fractures: a randomized clinical trial. Milit Med 2004;169:880–884.
4. Almeida SA, Williams KM, Shaffer RA, et al. Epidemiological patterns of musculoskeletal injuries and physical training. Med Sci Sports Exerc 1999;31:1176–1182.
5. Ammann W, Matheson GO. Radionuclide bone imaging in the detection of stress fractures. Clin J Sports Med 1991;1:115–122.

6. Aoki Y, Yasuda K, Tohyama H, et al. Magnetic resonance imaging in stress fractures and shin splints. Clin Orthop Relat Res 2004;421:260–267.

7. Barnes A, Wheat J, Milner C. Association between foot type and tibial stress injuries: a systematic review. Br J Sports Med 2008;42:93–98.

8. Barrow GW, Saha S. Menstrual irregularity and stress fractures in collegiate female distance runners. Am J Sports Med 1988;16:209–216.

9. Beck BR, Matheson GO, Bergman G, et al. Do capacitively coupled electric fields accelerate tibial stress fracture healing? A randomized controlled trial. Am J Sports Med 2008;36:545–553.

10. Beck TJ, Ruff CB, Mourtada FA, et al. Dual-energy x-ray absorptiometry derived structural geometry for stress fracture prediction in male U.S. Marine Corps recruits. J Bone Miner Res 1996;11:645–653.

11. Benazzo F, Mosconi M, Beccarisi G, et al. Use of capacitive coupled electric fields in stress fracture in athletes. Clin Orthop 1995;310:145–149.

12. Bennell K, Grimston S. Factors associated with the development of stress fractures in women. In: Burr DB, Milgrom C, eds. Musculoskeletal Fatigue and Stress Fractures. Boca Raton: CRC Press, 2001:35–54.

13. Bennell K, Grimston S. Risk factors for developing stress fractures. In: Burr DB, Milgrom C, eds. Musculoskeletal Fatigue and Stress Fractures. Boca Raton: CRC Press, 2001:15–33.

14. Bennell KL, Brukner PD. Epidemiology and site specificity of stress fractures. Clin Sports Med 1997;16:179–196.

15. Bennell KL, Malcolm SA, Khan KM, et al. Bone mass and bone turnover in power athletes, endurance athletes, and controls: a 12-month longitudinal study. Bone 1997;20:477–484.

16. Bennell KL, Malcolm SA, Thomas SA, et al. Risk factors for stress fractures in female track-and-field athletes: a retrospective analysis. Clin J Sports Med 1995;5:229–235.

17. Bennell KL, Malcolm SA, Thomas SA, et al. Risk factors for stress fractures in track and field athletes: a 12-month prospective study. Am J Sports Med 1996;24:810–818.

18. Bennell KL, Malcolm SA, Thomas SA, et al. The incidence and distribution of stress fractures in competitive track and field athletes. A 12-month prospective study. Am J Sports Med 1996;24:211–217.

19. Bennell KL, Matheson GO, Meeuwisse W, et al. Risk factors for stress fractures. Sports Med 1999;28:91–122.

20. Black KP, Ehlert KJ. A stress fracture of the lateral process of the talus in a runner. J Bone Joint Surg 1994;76:441–443.

21. Boden BP, Osbahr DC. High-risk stress fractures: evaluation and treatment. J Am Acad Orthop Surg 2000;8:344–353.

22. Bolin D, Kemper A, Brolinson PG. Current concepts in the evaluation and management of stress fractures. Curr Sports Med Rep 2005;4:295–300.

23. Borens O, Sen MK, Huang PC, et al. Anterior tension band plating for anterior tibial stress fractures in high-performance female athletes: a report of four cases. J Orthop Trauma 2006;20:425–430.

24. Bradshaw C, Khan K, Brukner P. Stress fracture of the body of the talus in athletes demonstrated with computer tomography. Clin J Sports Med 1996;6:48–51.

25. Branch T, Partin C, Chamberland P, et al. Spontaneous fractures of the humerus during pitching: a series of 12 cases. Am J Sports Med 1992;20:468–470.

26. Brand JC Jr, Brindle T, Nyland J, et al. Does pulsed low intensity ultrasound allow early return to normal activities when treating stress fractures? A review of one tarsal navicular and eight tibial stress fractures. Iowa Orthop J 1999;19:26–30.

27. Briethaupt MD. Fur pathologie des menschlichen fusses. Medizinische Zeitung 1855;24:169–177.

28. Brukner P, Bennell K, Matheson G. Diagnosis of stress fractures II. In: Stress Fractures. Victoria: Blackwell Science, 1999:97–105.

29. Brukner P, Bennell K, Matheson G. Diagnosis of stress fractures I. In: Stress Fractures. Victoria: Blackwell Science, 1999:83–96.

30. Brukner P, Bennell K, Matheson G. Stress fractures of the foot and ankle. In: Stress Fractures. Victoria: Blackwell Science, 1999:163–186.

31. Brukner P, Bennell K, Matheson G. Stress fractures of the lower leg. In: Stress Fractures. Victoria: Blackwell Science, 1999:147–161.

32. Brukner P, Bennell K, Matheson G. Stress fractures of the trunk. In: Stress Fractures. Victoria: Blackwell Science, 1999:119–138.

33. Brukner P, Bennell K, Matheson G. The pathophysiology of stress fractures. In: Stress Fractures. Victoria: Blackwell Science, 1999:1–13.

34. Brukner P, Bennell K. Matheson G. Stress fractures of the pelvis and thigh. In: Stress Fractures. Victoria: Blackwell Science, 1999:139–146.

35. Brukner P, Bennell K. Matheson G. Stress fractures of the upper limb. In: Stress Fractures. Victoria: Blackwell Science, 1999:107–117.

36. Brukner P, Bradshaw C, Khan K, et al. Stress fractures: a review of 180 cases. Clin J Sports Med 1996;6:85–89.

37. Brukner P. Stress fractures of the upper limb. Sports Med 1998;26:415–424.

38. Brunet ME, Cook SD, Brinker MR, et al. A survey of running injuries in 1505 competitive and recreational runners. J Sports Med Phys Fitness 1990;30:307–315.

39. Buckwalter JA, Glimcher MJ, Cooper RR, et al. Bone biology. J Bone Joint Surg Am 1995;77A:1256–1275.

40. Burne, SG, Mahoney CM, Forster BB, et al. Tarsal navicular stress injury: long-term outcome and clinicoradiological correlation using both CT and MRI. Am J Sports Med 2005;33:1875–1881.

41. Burr DB. Remodeling and the repair of fatigue damage. Calcif Tissue Int 1993;53(suppl 1):S75–S81.

42. Carpenter RD, Matheson GO, Carter DR. Stress fractures and stress injuries in bone. In: Garrick JG, ed. Orthopaedic Knowledge Update: Sports Medicine. 3rd ed. Rosemont, IL: American Academy of Orthopaedic Surgeons, 2004:273–283.

43. Carter SR, Aldridge MJ. Stress injury of the distal radial growth plate. J Bone Joint Surg 1988;70:834–836.

44. Chamay A, Tschants P. Mechanical influence in bone remodeling: experimental research on Wolff law. J Biomech 1972;2:173–180.

45. Chang PS, Harris RM. Intramedullary nailing for chronic tibial stress fractures: a review of five cases. Am J Sports Med 1996;24:688–692.

46. Chisin R. The role of various imaging modalities in diagnosing stress fractures. In: Burr DB, Milgrom C, eds. Musculoskeletal Fatigue and Stress Fractures. Boca Raton: CRC Press, 2001:279–293.

47. Chuckpaiwong B, Cook C, Nunley JA. Stress fractures of the second metatarsal base occur in nondancers. Clin Orthop Relat Res 2007;461:197–202.

48. Clapper MF, O'Brien TJ, Lyons PM. Fractures of the fifth metatarsal: analysis of a fracture registry. Clin Orthop Relat Res 1995;315:238–241.

49. Cline AD, Jansen GR, Melby CL. Stress fractures in female army recruits: implications of bone density, calcium intake, and exercise. J Am Coll Nutr 1998;17:128–135.

50. Clough TM. Femoral neck stress fracture: the importance of clinical suspicion and early review. Br J Sports Med 2002;36:308–309.

51. Cobb KL, Bachrach LK, Sowers M, et al. The effect of oral contraceptives on bone mass and stress fractures in female runners. Med Sci Sports Exerc 2007;39:1464–1473.

52. Crossley K, Bennell KL, Wrigley T, et al. Ground reaction forces, bone characteristics, and tibial stress fracture in male runners. Med Sci Sports Exerc 1999;31:1088–1093.

53. Dameron TB Jr. Fractures and anatomical variations of the proximal portion of the fifth metatarsal. J Bone Joint Surg Am 1975;57A:788–792.

54. Dameron TB Jr. Fractures of the proximal fifth metatarsal: selecting the best treatment option. J Am Acad Orthop Surg 1995;3:110–114.

55. Davidson G, Pizzari T, Mayes S. The influence of second toe and metatarsal length on stress fractures at the base of the second metatarsal in classical dancers. Foot Ankle Int 2007;28:1082–1086.

56. DeLee JC, Evans JP, Julian J. Stress fracture of the fifth metatarsal. Am J Sports Med 1983;11:349–353.

57. Deutsch AL, Coel MN, Mink JH. Imaging of stress injuries to bone: radiography, scintigraphy, and MR imaging. Clin Sports Med 1997;16:275–290.

58. Devas MB, Sweetnam R. Stress fractures of the fibula: a review of 50 cases in athletes. J Bone Joint Surg Br 1956;38B:818–829.

59. Dragoni S, Giombini A, Di Cesare A, et al. Stress fractures of the ribs in elite competitive rowers: a report of nine cases. Skeletal Radiol 2007;36:951–954.

60. Dugan SA, Weber KM. Stress fractures and rehabilitation. Phys Med Rehab Clin N Am 2007;18:401–416.

61. Egol KA, Frankel VH. Problematic stress fractures. In: Burr DB, Milgrom C, eds. Musculoskeletal Fatigue and Stress Fractures. Boca Raton: CRC Press, 2001:305–319.

62. Ekenman I. Physical diagnosis of stress fractures. In: Burr DB, Milgrom C, eds. Musculoskeletal Fatigue and Stress Fractures. Boca Raton: CRC Press, 2001:271–278.

63. Eller DJ, Katz DS, Bergman AG, et al. Sacral stress fractures in long-distance runners. Clin J Sport Med 1997;7:222–225.

64. Feingold D, Hame SL. Female athlete triad and stress fractures. Orthop Clin N Am 2006;37:575–583.

65. Fitch KD, Blackwell JB, Gilmour WN. Operation for nonunion of stress fracture of the tarsal navicular. J Bone Joint Surg Br 1989;71B:105–110.

66. Fredericson M, Bergman AG, Hoffman KL, et al. Tibial stress reaction in runners: correlation of clinical symptoms and scintigraphy with a new magnetic resonance imaging grading system. Am J Sports Med 1995;23:472–481.

67. Fredericson M, Jennings F, Beaulieu C, et al. Stress fractures in athletes. Top Magn Reson Imaging 2006;17:309–325.

68. Friberg O. Leg length asymmetry in stress fractures. A clinical and radiological study. J Sports Med 1982;22:485–488.

69. Frost HM. Skeletal structural adaptations to mechanical usage (SATMU): redefining Wolff law. Anat Rec 1990;226:403–413.

70. Frost HM. Some ABCs of skeletal pathophysiology vs. microdamage physiology. Calcif Tissue Int 1991;49:229–231.

71. Frost HM. Wolff law and bone's structural adaptation to mechanical usage: an overview for clinicians. Angle Orthod 1994;64:175–188.

72. Frusztajer NT, Dhuper S, Warren MP, et al. Nutrition and the incidence of stress fractures in ballet dancers. Am J Clin Nutr 1990;51:779–783.

73. Fullerton LR, Snowdy HA. Femoral neck stress fractures. Am J Sports Med 1988;16:365–377.

74. Fullerton LR. Femoral neck stress fractures. Sports Med 1990;9:192–197

75. Gaeta M, Minutoli F, Scribano E, et al. CT and MR imaging findings in athletes with early tibial stress injuries: comparison with bone scintigraphy findings and emphasis on cortical abnormalities. Radiology 2005;235:553–61.

76. Gehring MM, Keller BA, Brehm BA. Water running with and without a flotation vest in competitive and recreational runners. Med Sci Sports Exerc 1997;29:1374–1378.

77. Giladi M, Milgrom C, Simkin A, et al. Stress fractures: identifiable risk factors. Am J Sports Med 1991;19:647–652.

78. Giladi M, Milgrom C, Stein M, et al. External rotation of the hip. A predictor of risk for stress fractures. Clin Orthop Relat Res 1987;216:131–134.

79. Giladi M, Milgrom C, Stein M, et al. The low arch, a protective factor in stress fractures. A prospective study of 295 military recruits. Orthop Rev 1985;14:709–712.

80. Gilbert RS, Johnson HA. Stress fractures in military recruits: a review of 12 years' experience. Milit Med 1966;131:716–721.

81. Goldberg B, Pecora C. Stress fractures: a risk of increased training in freshmen. Phys Sportsmed 1994;22:68–74.

82. Goulart M, O'Malley MJ, Hodgkins CW, et al. Foot and ankle fractures in dancers. Clin in Sports Med 2008;27:295–304.

83. Greaney RB, Gerber FH, Laughlin RL, et al. Distribution and natural history of stress fractures in US Marine recruits. Radiology 1983;146:339–346.

84. Green NE, Rogers RA, Lipscomb AB. Nonunions of stress fractures of the tibia. Am J Sports Med 1985;13:171–176.

85. Grimston SK. An application of mechanostat theory to research design: a theoretical model. Med Sci Sports Exerc 1993;25:1293–1297.

86. Hens J, Martens M. Surgical treatment of Jones fractures. Orthop Trauma Surg 1990;109:277–279.

87. Hershman EB, Lombardo J, Bergfeld JA. Femoral shaft stress fractures in athletes. Clin Sports Med 1990;9:111–119.

88. Hetland ML, Haarbo J, Christiansen C. Low bone mass and high bone turnover in male long-distance runners. J Clin Endocrinol Metab 1993;77:770–775.

89. Hod N, Ashkenazi I, Levi Y, et al. Characteristics of skeletal stress fractures in female military recruits of the Israel defense forces on bone scintigraphy. Clin Nucl Med 2006;31:742–749.

90. Holmes GB Jr. Treatment of delayed unions and nonunions of the proximal fifth metatarsal with pulsed electromagnetic fields. Foot Ankle 1994;15:552–556.

91. Hughes LY. Biomechanical analysis of the foot and ankle for predisposition to developing stress fractures. J Orthop Sports Phys Ther 1985;7:96–101.

92. Hulkko A, Orava S. The role of age in the development of stress and fatigue fractures. In: Burr DB, Milgrom C, eds. Musculoskeletal Fatigue and Stress Fractures. Boca Raton: CRC Press, 2001:55–71.
93. Johnson AW, Weiss CB Jr, Wheeler, DL. Stress fractures of the femoral shaft in athletes: more common than expected. A new clinical test. Am J Sports Med 1994;22:248–256.
94. Johnson C, Powers PS, Dick R. Athletes and eating disorders: the National Collegiate Athletic Association study. Int J Eating Disorders 1999;26:179–188.
95. Jones BH, Cowan DN, Tomlinson JP, et al. Epidemiology of injuries associated with physical training among young men in the army. Med Sci Sports Exerc 1993;25: 197–203.
96. Jones BH, Harris J, Vinh TN, et al. Exercise-induced stress fractures and reactions of bone. Epidemiology, etiology, and classification. Exerc Sports Sci Rev 1989;17: 379–422.
97. Josefsson PO, Karlsson M, Redlund-Johnell I, et al. Closed treatment of Jones fracture: good results in 40 cases after 11–26 years. Acta Orthop Scand 1994;65:545–547.
98. Kadel NJ, Teitz CC, Kronmal RA. Stress fractures in ballet dancers. Am J Sports Med 1992;20:445–449.
99. Kaeding CC, Yu JR, Wright R, et al. Management and return to play of stress fractures. Clin J Sports Med 2005;15:442–447.
100. Kaplan PA, Helms CA, Dussault R, et al. Osseous trauma. In: Musculoskeletal MRI. Philadelphia: WB Saunders, 2001:151–167.
101. Kavanaugh JH, Brower TD, Mann RV. The Jones fracture revisited. J Bone Joint Surg Am 1978;60A:776–782.
102. Keating JF, Beggs I, Thorpe GW. Three cases of longitudinal stress fracture of the tibia. Acta Orthop Scand 1995;66:41–42.
103. Kelly EW, Jonson SR, Cohen ME, et al. Stress fractures of the pelvis in female navy recruits: an analysis of possible mechanisms of injury. Milit Med 2000;165:142–146.
104. Kelsey JL, Bachrach LK, Procter-Gray E, et al. Risk factors for stress fracture among young female cross-country runners. Med Sci Sports Exerc 2007;39:1457–1463.
105. Khan KM, Brukner PD, Bradshaw C. Stress fracture of the medial cuneiform bone in a runner. Clin J Sports Med 1993;3:262–264.
106. Khan KM, Brukner PD, Kearney C, et al. Tarsal navicular stress fractures in athletes. Sports Med 1994;17:65–76.
107. Khan KM, Fuller PJ, Brukner PD, et al. Outcome of conservative and surgical management of navicular stress fracture in athletes. Am J Sports Med 1992;20:657–666.
108. Kiss ZA, Khan KM, Fuller PJ. Stress fractures of the tarsal navicular bone: CT findings in 55 cases. AJR Am J Roentgenol 1993;160:111–115.
109. Laker SR, Saint-Phard D, Tyburski M, et al. Stress fractures in elite cross-country athletes. Orthopedics 2007;30:313–315.
110. Lassus J, Tulikoura I, Konttinen Y, et al: Bone stress injuries of the lower extremity: a review. Acta Orthop Scan 2002;73:359–368.
111. Lauder TD, Dixit S, Pezzin LE, et al. The relation between stress fractures and bone mineral density: evidence from active-duty army women. Arch Phys Med Rehab 2000; 81:73–79.
112. Lauder TD, et al. Abnormal eating behaviors in military women. Med Sci Sports Exerc 1999;31:1265–1271.
113. Lawrence SJ, Botte MJ. Jones' fractures and related fractures of the proximal fifth metatarsal. Foot Ankle 1993;14:358–365.
114. Lee CH, Huang GS, Chao KH, et al. Surgical treatment of displaced stress fractures of the femoral neck in military recruits: a report of 42 cases. Arch Orthop Trauma Surg 2003;123:527–533.
115. Lee S, Anderson RB. Stress fractures of the tarsal navicular. Foot Ankle Clin 2004;9: 85–104.
116. Lloyd T, Triantafyllou SJ, Baker ER, et al. Women athletes with menstrual irregularity have increased musculoskeletal injuries. Med Sci Sports Exerc 1986;18:374–379.
117. MacDougall JD, Webber CE, Martin J, et al. Relationship among running mileage, bone density, and serum testosterone in male runners. J Appl Physiol 1992;73:1165–1170.
118. Maffulli N, Chan D, Aldridge MJ. Overuse injuries of the olecranon in young gymnasts. J Bone Joint Surg 1992;74:305–308.
119. Mahler P, Fricker P. Case report: cuboid stress fracture. Excel 1992;8:147–148.
120. Maitra RS, Johnson DL. Stress fractures. Clinical history and physical examination. Clin Sports Med 1997;16:259–274.
121. Mata SG, Grande MM, Ovejero AH. Transverse stress fracture of the patella. Clin J Sports Med 1996;6:259–261.
122. Matheson GO, Clement DB, McKenzie JE, et al. Stress fractures in athletes. A study of 320 cases. Am J Sports Med 1987;15:46–58.
123. Mattila VM, Niva M, Kiuru M, Pihlajamaki H. Risk factors for bone stress injuries: a follow-up study of 102,515 person-years. Med Sci Sports Exerc 2007;39:1061–1066.
124. McMahon TA, Greene PR. The influence of track compliance on running. J Biomech 1979;12:893–904.
125. Milgrom C, Finestone A, Novack V, et al. The effect of prophylactic treatment with risedronate on stress fracture incidence among infantry recruits. Bone 2004;35: 418–424.
126. Milgrom C, Friedman E. Early diagnosis and clinical treatment of stress fractures. In: Burr DB, Milgrom C, eds. Musculoskeletal Fatigue and Stress Fractures. Boca Raton: CRC Press, 2001:295–303.
127. Milgrom C, Giladi M, Stein M, et al. Stress fractures in military recruits. J Bone Joint Surg 1985;67B:732–735.
128. Mindrebo N, Shelbourne D, van Meter CD, et al. Outpatient percutaneous screw fixation of the acute Jones fracture. Am J Sports Med 1993;21:720–723.
129. Monteleone GP Jr. Stress fractures in the athlete. Sports Med 1995;26:423–432.
130. Montgomery LC, Nelson FR, Norton JP, et al. Orthopedic history and examination in the etiology of overuse injuries. Med Sci Sports Exerc 1989;21:237–243.
131. Murakami Y. Stress fracture of the metacarpal in an adolescent tennis player. Am J Sports Med 1988;16:419–420.
132. Nattiv A, Puffer JC, Green GA. Lifestyles and health risks of collegiate athletes: a multicenter study. Clin J Sports Med 1997;7:262–272.
133. Niva MH, Sormaala MJ, Kiuru MJ, et al. Bone stress injuries of the ankle and foot: an 86-month MRI-based study of physically active young adults. Am J Sports Med 2007; 35:643–649.
134. Noakes TD, Smith JA, Lindenberg G, et al. Pelvic stress fractures in long distance runners. Am J Sports Med 1985;13:120–123.
135. Nuber GW, Diment MT. Olecranon stress fractures in throwers: a report of two cases and a review of the literature. Clin Orthop 1992;278:58–61.
136. O'Malley MJ, Hamilton WG, Munyak J, et al. Stress fractures at the base of the second metatarsal in ballet dancers. Foot Ankle Int 1996;17:89–94.
137. Orava S, Hulkko A. Delayed unions and nonunions of stress fractures in athletes. Am J Sports Med 1988;16:378–382.
138. Orava S, Karpakka J, Hulkko A, et al. Diagnosis and treatment of stress fractures located at the midtibial shaft in athletes. Int J Sports Med 1991;12:419–422.
139. Orava S, Karpakka J, Taimela S, et al. Stress fracture of the medial malleolus. J Bone Joint Surg Am 1995;77A:362–365.
140. Orava S, Taimela S, Kvist M, et al. Diagnosis and treatment of stress fracture of the patella in athletes. Knee Surg Sports Trauma Arthrosc 1996;4:206–211.
141. Otis CL, et al. American College of Sports Medicine position stand. The female athlete triad. Med Sci Sports Exerc 1997;29:i–ix.
142. Pandya NK, Webner D, Sennett B, et al. Recurrent fracture after operative treatment for a tibial stress fracture. Clin Orthop Relat Res 2006;456:254–258.
143. Pester S, Smith PC. Stress fractures in the lower extremities of soldiers in basic training. Orthop Rev 1992;21:297–303.
144. Picard CL. The level of competition as a factor for the development of eating disorders in female collegiate athletes. J Youth Adolesc 1999;28:583–595.
145. Pihlajamaki HK, Ruohola JP, Weckstrom M, et al. Long-term outcome of undisplaced fatigue fractures of the femoral neck in young male adults. J Bone Joint Surg Br 2006; 88B:1574–1579.
146. Plasschaert VF, Johansson CG, Micheli LJ. Anterior tibial stress fracture treated with intramedullary nailing: a case report. Clin J Sports Med 1995;5:58–62.
147. Porter DA, Duncan M, Meyer SJ. Fifth metatarsal Jones fracture fixation with a 4.5-mm cannulated stainless steel screw in the competitive and recreational athlete: a clinical and radiographic evaluation. Am J Sports Med 2005;33:726–733.
148. Potter NJ, Brukner PD, Makdissi M, et al. Navicular stress fractures: outcomes of surgical and conservative management. Br J Sports Med 2006;40:692–695.
149. Proztman RR. Physiologic performance of women compared to men. Am J Sports Med 1979;7:191–195.
150. Reeder MT, Dick BH, Atkins JK, et al. Stress fractures: current concepts of diagnosis and treatment. Sports Med 1996;22:198–212.
151. Reinker KA, Ozburne, SA. A comparison of male and female orthopaedic pathology in basic training. Milit Med 1979;144:532–536.
152. Resnick D, Goergen TG. Physical injury: concepts and terminology. In: Resnick D, Kransdorf MJ, eds. Bone and Joint Imaging, 3rd ed. Philadelphia: Elsevier Saunders, 2005:789–830.
153. Rettig AC, Shelbourne KD, McCarroll JR, et al. The natural history and treatment of delayed union stress fractures of the anterior cortex of the tibia. Am J Sports Med 1988;16:250–255.
154. Rolf C, Ekenman I, Tornqvist H, et al. The anterior stress fracture of the tibia: an atrophic pseudoarthrosis. Scand J Med Sci Sports 1997;7:249–252.
155. Rome K, Handoll HH, Ashford R. Interventions for preventing and treating stress fractures and stress reactions of bone of the lower limbs in young adults. Cochrane Database Syst Rev 2005;CD000450.
156. Rue JP, Armstrong DW 3rd, Frassica FJ, et al. The effect of pulsed ultrasound in the treatment of tibial stress fractures. Orthopedics 2004;27:1192–1195.
157. Rupani HD, Holder LE, Espinola DA, et al. Three-phase radionuclide bone imaging in sports medicine. Radiology 1985;156:187–196.
158. Sallis RE, Jones K. Stress fractures in athletes: how to spot this underdiagnosed injury. Post Grad Med 1991;89:185–192.
159. Salminen ST, Bostman OM, Kiuru MJ, et al. Bilateral femoral fatigue fracture. An unusual fracture in a military recruit. Clin Orthop Relat Res 2006;456:259–263.
160. Sarimo J, Orava S, Alanen J. Operative treatment of stress fractures of the proximal second metatarsal. Scand J Med Sci Sports 2007;17:383–386.
161. Saxena A, Fullem B. Navicular stress fractures: a prospective study on athletes. Foot Ankle Int 2006;27:917–921.
162. Schaffler MB. Bone fatigue and remodeling in the development of stress fractures. In: Burr DB, Milgrom C, eds. Musculoskeletal Fatigue and Stress Fractures. Boca Raton: CRC Press, 2001:161–182.
163. Schneider R. Radionuclide techniques. In: Resnick D, Kransdorf MJ, eds. Bone and Joint Imaging, 3rd ed. Philadelphia: Elsevier Saunders, 2005:86–117.
164. Scully TJ, Besterman, G. Stress fracture: a preventable training injury. Milit Med 1982; 147:285–287.
165. Shaffer RA, Brodine SK, Almeida SA, et al. Use of simple measures of physical activity to predict stress fractures in young men undergoing a rigorous physical training program. Am J Epidemiol 1999;149:236–242.
166. Shaffer RA. Incidence and prevalence of stress fractures in military and athletic populations. In: Burr DB, Milgrom C, eds. Musculoskeletal Fatigue and Stress Fractures. Boca Raton: CRC Press, 2001:1–14.
167. Shelbourne KD, Fisher DA, Rettig AC, et al. Stress fractures of the medial malleolus. Am J Sports Med 1988;16:60–63.
168. Shin AY, Morin WD, Gorman JD, et al. The superiority of magnetic resonance imaging in differentiating the cause of hip pain in endurance athletes. Am J Sports Med 1996; 24:168–176.
169. Simkin A, Leichter I, Giladi M, et al. Combined effect of foot arch structure and an orthotic device on stress fractures. Foot Ankle 1989;10:25–29.
170. Skarda ST, Burge MR. Prospective evaluation of risk factors for exercise-induced hypogonadism in male runners. West J Med 1998;169:9–13.
171. Smith R, Rutherford OM. Spine and total body bone mineral density and serum testosterone levels in male athletes. Eur J Appl Physiol 1993;67:330–334.
172. Sofka CM. Imaging of stress fractures. Clin Sports Med 2006;25:53–62.
173. Sormaala MJ, Niva MH, Kiuru MJ, et al. Outcomes of stress fractures of the talus. Am J Sports Med 2006;34:1809–1814.
174. Sormaala MJ, Niva MH, Kiuru MJ, et al. Stress injuries of the calcaneus detected with magnetic resonance imaging in military recruits. J Bone Joint Surg Am 2006;88A: 2237–2242.
175. Steele JR, Milburn PD. Effect of different synthetic sport surfaces on ground reaction forces at landing in netball. Int J Sport Biomech 1988;4:130–145.
176. Sterling JC, Edelstein DW, Calvo RD, et al. Stress fractures in the athlete: diagnosis and management. Sports Med 1992;14:336–346.

177. Story J, Cymet TC. Shin splints: painful to have and to treat. Comprehensive Ther 2006;32:192–195.

178. Swenson EJ, DeHaven KE, Sebastienelli WJ, et al. The effect of a pneumatic leg brace on return to play in athletes with tibial stress fractures. Am J Sports Med 1997;25: 322–328.

179. Taimela S, Kujala UM, Osterman K. Stress injury proneness: a prospective study during a physical training program. Int J Sports Med 1990;11:162–165.

180. Taube RR, Wadsworth LT. Managing tibial stress fractures. Phys Sports Med 1993;21: 123–128.

181. Teitz CC, Harrington RM. Patellar stress fracture. Am J Sports Med 1992;20:761–765.

182. Theodorou SJ, Theodorou DJ, Resnick D. Imaging findings in symptomatic patients with femoral diaphyseal stress injuries. Acta Radiol 2006;47:377–384.

183. Torg JS, Balduini FC, Zelko RR, et al. Fractures of the base of the fifth metatarsal distal to the tuberosity: classification and guidelines for nonsurgical and surgical management. J Bone Joint Surg Am 1984;66A:209–214.

184. Torg JS, Pavlov H, Cooley LH, et al. Stress fractures of the tarsal navicular: a retrospective review of 21 cases. J Bone Joint Surg Am 1982;64A:700–712.

185. Torg JS. Fractures of the base of the fifth metatarsal distal to the tuberosity: a review. Contemp Orthop 1989;19:497–505.

186. Uhthoff HK, Jaworski ZG. Periosteal stress-induced reactions resembling stress fractures: a radiologic and histologic study in dogs. Clin Orthop Relat Res 1985;199: 284–291.

187. Varner KE, Younas SA, Lintner DM, et al. Chronic anterior midtibial stress fractures in athletes treated with reamed intramedullary nailing. Am J Sports Med 2005;33: 1071–1076.

188. Visuri T, Vara A, Meurman KO. Displaced stress fractures of the femoral neck in young male adults: a report of 12 operative cases. J Trauma 1988;28:1562–1569.

189. Wheeler P, Batt ME. Do nonsteroidal anti-inflammatory drugs adversely affect stress fracture healing? A short review. Br J Sports Med 2005;39:65–69.

190. Whitelaw GP, Wetzler MJ, Levy AS, et al. A pneumatic leg brace for the treatment of tibial stress fractures. Clin Orthop Relat Res 1991;270:302–305.

191. Wilkerson RD, Johns JC. Nonunion of an olecranon stress fracture in an adolescent gymnast: a case report. Am J Sports Med 1990;18:432–434.

192. Winfield AC, Moore J, Bracker M, et al. Risk factors associated with stress reactions in female marines. Milit Med 1997;162:698–702.

193. Worthen BM, Yanklowitz BA. The pathophysiology and treatment of stress fractures in military personnel. J Am Podiatr Med Assoc 1978;68:317–325.

194. Zelko RR, Torg JS, Rachun A. Proximal diaphyseal fractures of the fifth metatarsal: treatment of the fractures and their complications in athletes. Am J Sports Med 1979; 7:95–101.

195. Zogby RG, Baker BE. A review of nonoperative treatment of Jones fracture. Am J Sports Med 1987;15:304–307.

196. Zwas TS, Elkanovitch R, Frank G. Interpretation and classification of bone scintigraphic findings in stress fractures. J Nucl Med 1987;28:452–457.

20

PATHOLOGIC FRACTURES

Kristy L. Weber

INTRODUCTION

Pathologic fractures occur in abnormal bone. Weakened bone predisposes the patient for failure during normal activity or after minor trauma. Failure (pathologic fracture) of bone under these circumstances should alert the orthopaedic surgeon to the presence of an underlying condition. Successful management of the patient requires recognition, diagnosis, and treatment of the condition affecting the bone. The management of the fracture may be dramatically altered by the associated pathologic condition, and failure to recognize a condition such as osteoporosis or metastatic bone disease may be detrimental to the patient's life or limb.

When planning the management of patients with a pathologic fracture and systemic, nonneoplastic skeletal disease, it is best to separate the underlying problem into correctable and uncorrectable conditions. Correctable conditions include renal osteodystrophy, hyperparathyroidism, osteomalacia, and disuse osteoporosis. Uncorrectable conditions include osteogenesis imperfecta, polyostotic fibrous dysplasia, postmenopausal os-

teoporosis, Paget's disease, and osteopetrosis. All of these disorders involve bones that are weak and predisposed to fracture or plastic deformation. The fracture callus may not form normally, and healing often occurs slowly. Many of these patients have an increased incidence of fracture, delayed union, and nonunion.

If the underlying process is correctable, appropriate treatment should be initiated. If the underlying process cannot be corrected, the condition of the remainder of the skeleton must be considered when planning treatment of the fracture. In the management of patients with systemic skeletal disease, it is important to try and prevent disuse osteoporosis, which may lead to additional pathologic fractures.

Osteoporosis is the most common condition associated with pathologic fractures, and the management of patients with this condition may only require minor modifications of typical fracture care. In contrast, the treatment of patients with metastatic bone disease who have actual or impending pathologic fractures necessitates a multidisciplinary approach with different principles applied to fracture fixation.

This chapter will primarily focus on the evaluation and treatment of patients with metastatic bone disease and actual or impending pathologic fractures. It will briefly cover the management of pathologic fractures in patients with primary benign or malignant bone tumors. Treatment of patients with metabolic abnormalities and decreased bone density unrelated to malignancy will be addressed in a less comprehensive fashion. The majority of patients with pathologic fractures are treated by general orthopaedic surgeons. It is important that all orthopaedic surgeons have a basic understanding of the principles involved in the care of these patients so that appropriate treatment is initiated.

Demographics

Currently, an estimated 10 million Americans have osteoporosis, while another 34 million have osteomalacia and are at risk for developing osteoporosis.[31] It is a major public health concern for 55% of people who are 50 years or older. Eighty percent of those affected by osteoporosis are women. Approximately 2 million people sustain a pathologic fracture related to osteoporosis each year.[31] Of patients over 50 years of age, 24% who sustain a hip fracture die within 1 year.[31] One of every two women will have an osteoporosis-related fracture in her lifetime.[16] Other skeletal conditions such as Paget disease affect an estimated 1 million people in the United States, while approximately 20,000 to 50,000 Americans have osteogenesis imperfecta.[31]

The American Cancer Society predicts over 1.4 million new cancer cases will be diagnosed in 2009, and nearly 50% of these tumors can metastasize to the skeleton.[48] With improved medical treatment of many cancers, especially those originating in the breast and prostate, patients are living longer. There is an increased prevalence of bone metastasis in this population, which increases the chances that these patients will develop a pathologic fracture. The vast majority of bone metastasis originate from cancers of the breast, lung, and prostate, thyroid, and kidney.[83] The most common sites of metastasis in the skeleton include the spine, pelvis, ribs, skull, and proximal long bones.[94]

EVALUATION OF THE PATIENT WITH AN IMPENDING OR ACTUAL PATHOLOGIC FRACTURE

Clinical

History

A comprehensive evaluation of a patient with a lytic bone lesion or pathologic fracture is essential (Table 20-1).[77,94] A thorough history must be obtained to understand the circumstances surrounding the current injury. Certain symptoms should alert the orthopaedic surgeon to the possibility of an associated pathologic process (Table 20-2). The degree of trauma required to cause the fracture and presence of pain before the injury may provide information about the underlying bone strength. Pain is the most common presenting symptom before fracture, ranging from a dull constant ache to an intense pain exacerbated by weight bearing. Patients must be asked specifically about previously diagnosed or treated cancer; otherwise, they may consider themselves cured and not volunteer this information. A history of radiation is important. Standard review of systems questions

---

TABLE 20-1	Comprehensive Evaluation of a Patient with a Lytic Bone Lesion

1. *History:* thyroid, breast, or prostate nodule
2. *Review of systems:* gastrointestinal symptoms, weight loss, flank pain, hematuria
3. *Physical examination:* lymph nodes, thyroid, breast, lungs, abdomen, prostate, testicles, rectum
4. *Plain x-rays:* chest, affected bone (additional sites as directed by bone scan findings)
5. *99mTc total body bone scan* (FDG-PET scan in selected cases such as lymphoma)
6. *CT scan with contrast:* chest, abdomen, pelvis
7. *Laboratory:* complete blood count, erythrocyte sedimentation rate, calcium, phosphate, urinalysis, prostate specific antigen, immunoelectrophoresis, and alkaline phosphatase
8. *Biopsy:* needle versus open

FDG, fluorine-18 deoxyglucose; PET, positron emission tomography; CT, computed tomography.

---

about recent weight loss, fevers, night sweats, and fatigue are important. Questions about relevant risk factors such as smoking, dietary habits, and toxic exposures should be asked.

Physical Examination

The physical examination should include a thorough evaluation of the affected skeletal region. Palpation of a mass, identification of an obvious deformity, and a detailed neurologic examination of the extremities are essential. All extremities and the entire spine should be evaluated for additional lesions or lymphadenopathy, as patients can have multiple sites of involvement with bone metastasis, lymphoma, multiple myeloma, or osteoporosis. A physical examination should include careful evaluation of all possible primary sites (breast, prostate, lung, thyroid) and a stool guiac test.[94]

Laboratory Studies

Laboratory tests will not often make the diagnosis, especially in cases of cancer, but they are supporting data relevant to the

---

TABLE 20-2	Factors Suggesting a Pathologic Fracture

- Spontaneous fracture
- Fracture after minor trauma
- Pain at the site before the fracture
- Multiple recent fractures
- Unusual fracture pattern ("banana fracture")*
- Patient older than 45 years
- History of primary malignancy

*A "banana fracture" is a transverse fracture after minimal trauma through an abnormal area of bone. It is a frequent pattern in pathologic situations and has the appearance of breaking a segment off of a banana.

TABLE 20-3 **Disorders Producing Osteopenia**				
	Laboratory Value			
Disorder	Serum Calcium	Serum Phosphorus	Serum Alkaline Phosphatase	Urine
Osteoporosis	Normal	Normal	Normal	Normal calcium
Osteomalacia	Normal	Normal	Normal	Low calcium
Hyperparathyroidism	Normal to high	Normal to low	Normal	High calcium
Renal osteodystrophy	Low	High	High	
Paget disease	Normal	Normal	Very high	Hydroxyproline
Myeloma*	Normal	Normal	Normal	Protein

*Abnormal serum or urine immunoelectrophoresis.

overall patient evaluation. A baseline laboratory profile should include a complete blood count with manual differential, erythrocyte sedimentation rate, serum chemistries, blood urea nitrogen (BUN), serum glucose, liver function tests, protein, albumin, calcium, phosphorus, and alkaline phosphatase. Patients with widespread bone metastasis may exhibit anemia of chronic disease, hypercalcemia, and increased alkaline phosphatase. The hemoglobin is also often low in patients with multiple myeloma. A standard urinalysis is necessary to look for microscopic hematuria which suggests renal cell carcinoma, and a 24-hour urine collection is necessary for a complete metabolic evaluation. Serum and urine protein electrophoreses are important to exclude multiple myeloma. Thyroid function tests, carcinoembryonic antigen (CEA), CA125, and prostate specific antigen (PSA) are serum markers for specific tumors. N-telopeptide and C-telopeptide are new biomechanical markers of bone collagen breakdown that can be measured in the serum and urine. These markers are used to confirm increased destruction caused by bone metastasis, measure the overall extent of bone involvement, and assess the response of the bone to bisphosphonates.[20]

Patients with osteoporosis have normal values for the aforementioned laboratory tests, whereas patients with osteomalacia have low serum calcium and phosphorus, high serum alkaline phosphatase, high urinary phosphorus, and high urinary hydroxyproline values (Table 20-3). Patients with primary hyperparathyroidism have high serum calcium, alkaline phosphatase, and parathyroid hormone with low serum phosphorus. They also have high urinary calcium, phosphorus, and hydroxyproline. Patients with renal osteodystrophy have low serum calcium with high serum phosphorus, alkaline phosphatase, and BUN. When secondary hyperparathyroidism develops in these patients, the serum calcium increases to normal or elevated values with elevated parathyroid hormone levels. Urine values are difficult to assess in patients with secondary hyperparathyroidism caused by abnormal glomerular filtration. Patients with Paget disease have normal values for serum calcium and phosphorus but markedly elevated levels of alkaline phosphatase and urinary hydroxyproline. Prostate specific antigen is a sensitive measurement of prostate cancer. A value less than 10 ng/mL essentially excludes the presence of bone metastasis. Remember that serum calcium is a measurement of unbound calcium in the serum and, therefore, determination of serum protein is neces-

sary to interpret the calcium level. If the serum protein is lower than normal, the normal range of serum calcium is lowered.

Associated Medical Problems

The clinical problems encountered by patients with metastatic bone disease are substantial. Patients often have marked pain or pathologic fractures that leave them unable to ambulate or perform their activities of daily living (ADLs). Patients with spinal fractures may develop neurologic deficits that lead to paralysis. Patients with impending or actual extremity fractures may be forced to remain at bedrest for prolonged periods of time, predisposing them to hypercalcemia. Anemia is a common hematologic abnormality in these patients. The most encompassing and tragic concern of patients with pathologic fractures from metastatic disease is the general loss in their quality of life.

Approximately 40% of the 75,000 cases of hypercalcemia diagnosed in the United States each year are related to hypercalcemia of malignancy, most commonly associated with cancers of the lung, breast, kidney, and genitourinary tract.[74] The remainder is caused by primary hyperparathyroidism. Rarely, the two causes occur simultaneously. The orthopaedic surgeon managing a patient with metastatic carcinoma to bone must be aware of the risks, symptoms, and management of hypercalcemia as it can be lethal if untreated (Table 20-4).

Hypercalcemia is not usually the presenting sign of malignancy, but it portends a poor prognosis for the patient. As many as 60% of patients with hypercalcemia will survive less than 3 months, and only 20% will be alive at 1 year. Often the symp-

TABLE 20-4 **Signs and Symptoms of Hypercalcemia**
• *Neurologic:* headache, confusion, irritability, blurred vision
• *Gastrointestinal:* anorexia, nausea, vomiting, abdominal pain, constipation, weight loss
• *Musculoskeletal:* fatigue, weakness, joint and bone pain, unsteady gait
• *Urinary:* nocturia, polydypsia, polyuria, urinary tract infections

toms are nonspecific, so it is easiest to diagnose the problem by measuring the serum calcium. There is not a reliable correlation between the severity of the hypercalcemia and the degree of metastatic bone disease. Patients with lung cancer often develop hypercalcemia without obvious bone metastases, whereas hypercalcemia in multiple myeloma or breast carcinoma correlates with the extent of bone metastases.[74] Diffuse osteoclastic activity associated with clinical hypercalcemia can be seen histologically without the presence of metastasis in the bone.

A treatment plan for the patient with hypercalcemia often requires inpatient care. Vigorous volume repletion is a temporizing measure, so treatment must focus on reducing the degree of bone resorption. This can be accomplished by treating the primary tumor directly or by using bisphosphonates to reduce osteoclastic activity.[64] Correction of any electrolyte imbalance or hypercalcemia should ideally be done before surgery.

Radiographic Workup

Plain Radiographs. The first and most important imaging study used to evaluate a patient with a destructive bone lesion or pathologic fracture is a plain radiograph in two planes.[94] The radiographs should be carefully reviewed with attention to specific lesions and overall bone quality. Specifically they should be examined for diagnostic clues such as generalized osteopenia, periosteal reaction, cortical thinning, Looser's lines, and abnormal soft tissue shadows. A series of questions to assist in determining the underlying process was popularized by W. Enneking, M.D., and can be reviewed in Table 20-5. The entire affected bone should be imaged to identify all possible lesions, and it must be remembered that referred pain to distal sites may be caused by a more proximal lesion.

Osteopenia is the radiographic term used to indicate inadequate bone (osteoporosis) or inadequately mineralized bone (osteomalacia). These two disorders cannot be definitively distinguished on plain radiographs, but there are some suggestive differential clues. Looser's lines (compression-side radiolucent lines), calcification of small vessels, and phalangeal periosteal reaction are features of osteomalacia or hyperparathyroidism.

Thin cortices and loss of the normal trabecular pattern without other abnormalities are more suggestive of osteoporosis.

When an osteolytic or osteoblastic lesion is noted in otherwise normal bone, the process is most likely neoplastic. It is important to determine whether the lesion is inactive, active, or aggressive. Small osteolytic lesions surrounded by a rim of reactive bone without endosteal or periosteal reaction are usually inactive or minimally active benign bone tumors. Lesions that erode the cortex but are contained by periosteum are usually active benign or low-grade malignant bone tumors. Large lesions that destroy the cortex are usually aggressive, malignant lesions that can be primary or metastatic. A permeative or "moth-eaten" pattern of cortical destruction is highly suggestive of malignancy. Most destructive bone lesions in patients over 40 years of age are caused by metastatic carcinoma followed by multiple myeloma and lymphoma; however, a solitary bone lesion should be fully evaluated to rule out a primary bone tumor such as a chondrosarcoma, malignant fibrous histiocytoma, or osteosarcoma.[94]

The radiographic appearance of bone metastasis can be osteolytic, osteoblastic, or mixed. Osteolytic destruction is most common and occurs in metastases from cancers of the lung, thyroid, kidney, and colon (Fig. 20-1). An osteoblastic appearance with sclerosis of the bone is common in metastatic prostate cancer. Metastatic breast cancer often has a mixed osteolytic and osteoblastic appearance in the bone (Fig. 20-2). The radiographic appearance is determined by the balance of bone destruction by osteoclasts and bone production by osteoblasts. Tumor cells secrete factors that interact with host cells in the bone microenvironment and affect the cycle of normal bone turnover.[21,75,90,93] An isolated avulsion of the lesser trochanter is almost always pathologic, and this specific injury should arouse suspicion of occult metastatic disease and an imminent femoral neck fracture (Fig. 20-3).[8] A cortical lesion in an adult is usually a metastasis, most commonly from lung cancer.[34]

Nuclear Medicine Studies

When a bone metastasis is diagnosed or suspected, the remainder of the skeleton should be evaluated for additional bony sites

---

TABLE 20-5 Evaluation of Plain Radiographs

Question	Option	Interpretation
1. Where is the lesion?	Epiphysis vs. metaphysis vs. diaphysis Cortex vs. medullary canal Long bone (femur, humerus) vs. flat bone (pelvis, scapula)	
2. What is the lesion doing to the bone?	Bone destruction (osteolysis) • Total • Diffuse • Minimal	
3. What is the bone doing to the lesion?	Well-defined reactive rim Intact but abundant periosteal reaction Periosteal reaction that cannot keep up with tumor (Codman triangle)	Benign or slow growing Aggressive Highly malignant
4. What are the clues to the tissue type within the lesion?	Calcification Ossification Ground-glass appearance	Bone infarct/cartilage tumor Osteosarcoma/osteoblastoma Fibrous dysplasia

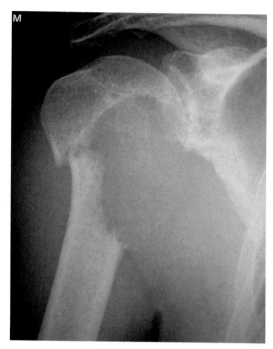

FIGURE 20-1 Anteroposterior radiograph of the right shoulder in a 55-year-old man with metastatic renal cell carcinoma. He had pain for 6 weeks before sustaining a minor injury to the right shoulder. Note the purely lytic lesion with a pathologic fracture through the surgical neck of the humerus.

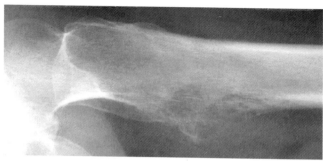

FIGURE 20-3 Lateral radiograph of the left hip reveals an osteolytic lesion in the lesser trochanter. This is a classic worrisome sign that suggests an impending fracture of the femoral neck.

of disease. Technetium bone scintigraphy is helpful in determining the extent of metastatic disease to the skeleton, as it detects osteoblastic activity and is quite sensitive. Multiple myeloma is falsely negative on a bone scan as are occasional cases of metastatic renal cell carcinoma because of the decreased osteoblastic response to the tumor. More recently, positron emission tomography (PET) scanning has been available but the indications are not clear for staging patients with metastatic bone disease.[70] It has been useful in staging patients with lymphoma and monitoring response to lymphoma treatment.[54] In a recent study, PET/computed tomography (CT) scanning had higher sensitivity and specificity than PET scanning alone for detection of malignant bone lesions.[26]

Additional Staging and Three-Dimensional Studies

Further imaging studies are necessary to search for a primary lesion when metastatic carcinoma to the skeleton is suspected.[77] The recommended radiographic staging study is a CT scan of the chest, abdomen, and pelvis. A mammogram should also be done if breast cancer is suspected. If multiple myeloma is considered, a skeletal survey including skull films is recommended.

Magnetic resonance imaging (MRI) is not generally used to evaluate metastatic lesions in the extremity, but it is useful in the evaluation of patients with spinal metastasis to define the relationship of tumor to the underlying neurologic structures. A standard angiogram is still useful when embolizing feeding tumor vessels in vascular lesions such as metastatic renal cell carcinoma or multiple myeloma as definitive treatment or before surgery.

When and How to Perform a Biopsy

A thorough history and physical examination with appropriate imaging studies often leads to the correct diagnosis, particularly in the case of widespread metastatic bone disease. However, a solitary bone lesion in a patient with or without a history of cancer should be biopsied to obtain an accurate diagnosis. Presuming a solitary lesion is a bone metastasis in an older patient may lead you to perform the wrong operation, thereby potentially compromising the life and limb of the patient if the lesion is actually a primary sarcoma of bone.

If a tissue diagnosis is necessary, a biopsy must be performed. Either a needle or open incisional biopsy is reasonable depending on the availability of expert musculoskeletal radiologists and pathologists.[91] A needle biopsy is usually definitive when

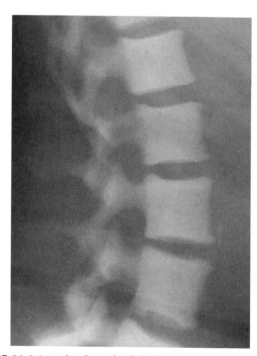

FIGURE 20-2 Lateral radiograph of the thoracic vertebral bodies in a 56-year-old woman with metastatic breast cancer. Note their osteoblastic appearance caused by an imbalance in bone production over bone destruction.

differentiating a carcinoma from a sarcoma. Specific immunohistochemical staining may allow determination of the primary site of origin of a carcinoma, most commonly from the lung, breast, thyroid, or prostate. When there is a pathologic fracture through a lytic lesion, the biopsy can be complicated due to bleeding and early fracture callus. The fracture should be stabilized initially with traction or a cast to allow preliminary staging studies to be completed, which may allow the diagnosis to be made on imaging alone, or there may be a different lesion more amenable to biopsy.

If a needle biopsy is nondiagnostic or unable to be done, a careful incisional biopsy should be performed using oncologic principles so as not to preclude subsequent surgical treatment.[65] When possible, the tissue should be obtained from a site near but unaffected by the fracture. The biopsy should be as small as possible, in a longitudinal fashion in line with the extremity, and with excellent hemostasis. Tissues contaminated by a post-biopsy hematoma must be considered contaminated by tumor cells. Cultures should always be sent at the time of biopsy to rule out infection, which can be confused radiographically with a tumor. If a definitive diagnosis of metastatic disease can be made on an intraoperative frozen section, surgical treatment of the pathologic fracture can be performed at the same operative setting. If the frozen section is not diagnostic, it is best to wait for the permanent sections before definitively treating the tumor and fracture.

IMPENDING PATHOLOGIC FRACTURES

Bone metastases are painful even without an associated fracture. Treatment options for known skeletal metastasis include (a) prophylactic surgical stabilization before radiation therapy or (b) radiation and/or chemotherapy without prophylactic fixation.[47,94] The term *impending fracture* is used throughout the literature on metastatic disease, but there are no clear guidelines supported by prospective clinical studies to define this term. Retrospective studies have formed the basis to guide the indications for prophylactic fixation, but they are often limited by the use of plain radiographs, subjective patient information, and an inadequate understanding of the biomechanical factors involved in the bone affected by a neoplastic process.[28,68,82] Although experienced orthopaedic oncologists may have an intuitive

sense for which lesions are at high risk for fracture, there is considerable controversy about what constitutes an impending fracture and little reliable data to guide treatment.

Classification Systems

Factors necessary for the assessment of fracture risk include the radiographic appearance of the lesion and the patient's symptoms. Fidler[28] assessed preoperative and postoperative pain in patients with impending fractures and found that, among patients with 50% to 75% cortical involvement, all had moderate to severe pain preoperatively and none or minimal pain after prophylactic internal fixation. Commonly, a lesion is considered to be at risk for fracture if it is painful and larger than 2.5 cm and involves over 50% of the cortex.[82] In an attempt to quantify this risk, Mirels[67] developed a scoring system based on the presence or absence of pain and the size, location, and radiographic appearance of the lesion. Each of the four variables is assigned from 1 to 3 points (Table 20-6). Mirels analyzed 78 lesions previously irradiated without prophylactic surgical fixation. Over a 6-month period, 27 lesions (35 %) fractured and 51 remained stable. A mean score of 7 in the nonfracture group and 10 in the fracture group was calculated. The author concluded that lesions scoring 7 or lower can be safely irradiated, while lesions scoring 8 or higher require prophylactic internal fixation before radiation.[67]

Subsequently, investigators have attempted to quantify the risk of pathologic fracture in patients with metastatic bone disease. *Fracture risk* is defined as the load-bearing requirement of the bone divided by its load-bearing capacity. The load-bearing requirement depends on the patient's age, weight, activity level, and ability to protect the site. The load-bearing capacity depends on the amount of bone loss, modulus of the remaining bone, and location of the defect with respect to the type of load applied.[68] A biomechanical study of simulated lytic defects in whale vertebral bodies demonstrated that relative fracture risk in vivo could be predicted by a structural rigidity analysis using cross-sectional imaging data.[44] Although this system provides a comprehensive method to determine the risk of pathologic fracture, it is not yet routinely used in the clinical setting.

Patients treated by prophylactic stabilization of an impending fracture versus those treated after an actual fracture have the following outcomes: shorter hospitalization (average 2 days),

TABLE 20-6	**Mirels Criteria for Risk of Fracture**		
	Number Assigned		
Variable	1	2	3
Site	Upper extremity	Lower extremity	Peritrochanteric
Pain	Mild	Moderate	Severe
Lesion*	Blastic	Mixed	Lytic
Size	<$\frac{1}{3}$ diameter of the bone	$\frac{1}{3}$–$\frac{2}{3}$ diameter of the bone	>$\frac{2}{3}$ diameter of the bone

Each patient's situation is assessed by assigning a number (1, 2, or 3) to each aspect of his or her presentation (site, pain, lesion, and size) and then adding the numbers to obtain a total number to indicate the patient's risk for fracture. Mirel's data suggest that those patients whose total number is 7 or less can be observed, but those with a number of 8 or more should have prophylactic internal fixation.
*By radiography.

discharge to home more likely (40%), more immediate pain relief, faster and less complicated surgery, less blood loss, quicker return to premorbid function, improved survival, and fewer hardware complications.[12,51] Elective stabilization also allows the medical oncologist and surgeon to coordinate operative treatment and systemic chemotherapy. One critical caveat when treating patients with impending pathologic fractures is that fracture risk is greatest during the surgical positioning, preparation, and draping. When patients are anesthetized, they cannot protect the affected extremity and must rely on the surgical team to proceed carefully. Low energy fractures will occur after very minor trauma or a twisting movement. If a pathologic fracture occurs, damage to the surrounding soft tissues is minimal compared to traumatic fractures in healthy bone.

The goals of surgical treatment in a patient with an impending pathologic fracture are to alleviate pain, reduce narcotic utilization, restore skeletal stability, and regain functional independence.[47,94] However, the decision to proceed with operative intervention is multifactorial and must be individualized. Factors included in the decision making are (a) life expectancy of the patient, (b) patient comorbidities, (c) extent of the disease, (d) tumor histology, (e) anticipated future oncologic treatments, and (f) degree of pain. Patients with a life expectancy of less than 6 weeks may not gain significant benefit from major reconstructive surgery. However, an accurate prognosis is not always possible, and the decision of whether to proceed with surgery should be discussed with the multidisciplinary team, the patient, and the patient's family.

TREATMENT OPTIONS FOR PATIENTS WITH METASTATIC OR SYSTEMIC DISEASE

General Considerations

As stated earlier in this chapter, the most common pathologic fracture is caused by osteoporosis. In most situations, these fractures should be managed in a standard fashion as recommended in the accompanying chapters of this text. Modifications such as the addition of methylmethacrylate or locking plate fixation may be necessary because of the weakened bone.[5] Pathologic fractures caused by metastatic bone disease demand special considerations, which will be discussed in further detail.

Patients with cancer are living longer. More patients are living with bone metastasis. Because of the advances in systemic treatment, pain control, and local modalities including radiation and surgery, the philosophy has changed from one of palliation for immediate demise to aggressive care to improve the quality of remaining life. The local bone lesion can be treated with nonsurgical management (radiation, functional bracing, and bisphosphonates) or surgical stabilization with or without resection. Medical treatment with bisphosphonates has decreased the incidence of pathologic fractures because of inhibition of osteoclast-mediated bone destruction.[40,61,62] Patients with small bone lesions, especially in non–weight-bearing bones, are often candidates for radiation therapy rather than surgical stabilization. Surgical intervention is usually employed for large lytic lesions at risk for fracture or for existing pathologic fractures. Postoperatively, external beam radiation is used as an adjuvant local treatment for the entire operative field and implant unless the metastatic lesion is completely resected.[88,94]

Patients who present with a pathologic fracture are often medically debilitated and require multidisciplinary care. In addition to an orthopaedic surgeon, the comprehensive team includes medical oncologists, radiation oncologists, endocrinologists, radiologists, pathologists, pain specialists, nutritionists, physical therapists, and psychologist/psychiatrists. Nutrition is of particular concern; serum prealbumin should be measured and improved if it is low. This may require the addition of enteral or parenteral hyperalimentation perioperatively. Patients may have relative bone marrow suppression and will require adequate replacement of blood products. Perioperative antibiotic coverage, prophylaxis for embolic events, aggressive postoperative pulmonary toilet, and early mobilization are all instituted as standard treatment.

Nonoperative Treatment

Bracing an impending or actual pathologic fracture is indicated if the patient is not a surgical candidate. Nonsurgical candidates are those with limited life expectancies, severe comorbidities, small lesions, or radiosensitive tumors.[94] The use of a fracture brace works well for lesions in the upper extremity. Patients should limit weight bearing on the affected extremity. A braced lesion may heal with or without radiation therapy. Lesions most amenable to bracing are those in the humeral diaphysis, forearm, and occasionally the tibia. Patients with proximal humeral lesions can be treated with a sling, and those with distal humeral lesions can be immobilized in a posterior elbow splint with or without a hinge. If a patient has multiple lesions requiring the use of all extremities to ambulate, surgical stabilization will provide better support than a brace.

After treatment for a pathologic fracture, the bone may or may not heal. The factors that influence whether healing will occur include location of the lesion, extent of bony destruction, tumor histology, type of treatment, and length of patient survival. Gainor et al.[30] determined the most important factor affecting union was length of patient survival. Of 129 pathologic long bone fractures, the overall rate of fracture healing was 34%; however, it was 74% in the group of patients who survived greater than 6 months. Among different tumor histologies, fractures secondary to multiple myeloma were most likely to heal.[30]

Operative Treatment

Surgical treatment of metastatic bone disease uses the most current internal fixation devices and prosthetic replacements. The ideal reconstruction allows immediate weight bearing and is durable enough to last for the increased total life span of patients with metastatic bone disease.[47,94] It should be assumed that the fixation device used will be load-bearing, as only 30% to 40% of pathologic fractures unite even after radiation treatment.[11,30]

Depending on the external forces, bone quality, and likelihood of tumor progression, standard internal fixation may be contraindicated. An intramedullary device or modular prosthesis provides more definitive stability. Polymethylmethacrylate (PMMA) is often used to increase the strength of the fixation, but it should not be used alone to replace a segment of bone. PMMA improves the bending strength of a fixation construct and the outcome of fixation in both animal and human studies.[39,81] It does not affect the use of therapeutic radiation, nor are the properties of the PMMA affected adversely by the radiation.[25] Autogenous bone graft is not generally used in the treatment of extremity fractures from metastatic bone disease. Segmental allografts are also rarely indicated, as they require a prolonged healing time.

The most expedient reconstruction with the least risk of complication or failure should be used for patients with metastatic bone disease. In the vast majority of cases, this requires metal and PMMA. When a prosthesis is used to replace a joint affected by a metastatic lesion or a pathologic fracture, it should be cemented into the host bone. The goal is to have the patient allowed to bear weight as tolerated after the surgical procedure. Another guideline when treating patients with metastatic disease is to prophylactically stabilize as much of the affected bone as possible. When an intramedullary device is indicated, the entire femur, humerus or tibia should be treated with a statically locked nail.[96,101] For femoral lesions, a reconstruction nail is used to stabilize the femoral neck even if no lesion is present there at the time of surgery. Patients with metastatic disease often develop subsequent lesions and the reconstruction nail is helpful in preventing a future pathologic femoral neck fracture.

Some carcinomas are relatively resistant to chemotherapy and radiation therapy when they spread to the skeleton. Renal cell carcinoma (RCC) is a notable example. Surgical treatment is often indicated for even small RCC lesions, as they tend to progress despite standard medical treatment and external beam radiation.[49,84] Depending on the patient's expected lifespan and location of the lesion, open treatment with thorough curettage of metastatic RCC followed by intramedullary fixation and PMMA will decrease the tumor burden.[60] Postoperative radiation is often used to prevent growth of the residual microscopic disease.[88] When complete resection and joint replacement is performed for metastatic disease, the chances of progressive bone destruction from recurrent tumor are decreased.[49,84]

Hypervascular metastases put the patient at risk for life-threatening intraoperative hemorrhage without adequate precautions. Metastatic RCC is the most likely lesion to cause excessive blood loss, but metastatic thyroid cancer and multiple myeloma are also hypervascular. When possible, a tourniquet should be used during surgery. However, most metastasis occur in the proximal extremities, precluding use of a tourniquet. Excessive blood loss can often be avoided if preoperative embolization is performed by an interventional radiologist within 36 hours of the surgical procedure.[14] Patients with metastatic RCC often have only one functioning kidney, so a careful evaluation of their renal status should be performed before injecting nephrotoxic dye for angiography.

Upper Extremity Fractures

Twenty percent of osseous metastases occur in the upper extremity with approximately 50% occurring in the humerus. Upper extremity metastases can result in substantial functional impairment by hindering personal hygiene, independent ambulation, meal management, ability to use external aids, and general ADLs.[94] When making decisions about treatment of upper extremity metastasis, the benefits to quality of life should outweigh the risks of potential surgery. Contractures of the shoulder and elbow are common with or without surgical treatment, and these joints should be kept moving. Gentle pendulum exercises can maintain motion in the shoulder and, with appropriate precautions against using torsion, are safe for most proximal and mid-humeral impending fractures. Gravity-assisted elbow flexion and extension exercises can also be performed safely by most patients.

Scapula/Clavicle. Metastatic lesions to the clavicle and scapula are generally treated nonoperatively with shoulder immobilization, radiation, and/or medical management. Occasionally a large, destructive metastasis will occur in the inferior body or articular portion (glenoid) of the scapula. As pain dictates, these areas of the scapula can be resected.

Proximal Humerus. Pathologic fractures involving the humeral head or neck are treated with a proximal humeral replacement or intramedullary fixation. If enough bone is available in the proximal humerus, an intramedullary locked device with multiple proximal screws is acceptable and maintains shoulder range of motion.[101] PMMA may be required to supplement the fixation. When there is extensive destruction of the proximal humerus or a fracture leaving minimal bone for adequate fixation, resection of the lesion and reconstruction with a cemented proximal humeral endoprosthesis are indicated.[52] This modular construct replaces a variable amount of proximal humerus and has a long cemented stem to protect the remainder of the bone (Fig. 20-4). In the face of distal disease progression, it can be modified to a total humeral prosthesis. Involvement of the glenoid is rare, so replacement of this articular surface is generally not necessary. The goal of a proximal humeral replacement is pain relief and local control of the tumor; shoulder range of motion and stability are often compromised because of poor soft tissue attachments to the metal construct. A synthetic vascular graft or mesh sutured to the glenoid labrum and around the prosthetic humeral head can offer some stability. Postoperative radiation therapy is used for patients when intralesional treatment is performed.

Humeral Diaphysis. Humeral diaphyseal lesions of fractures can be surgically treated with locked intramedullary fixation or an intercalary metal spacer.[17,18,101] Locked intramedullary humeral nails span the entire humerus and provide mechanical and rotational stability (Fig. 20-5). As previously mentioned, PMMA improves implant stability and supplements poor bone quality when used with surgical stabilization.[39] Intercalary spacers offer a modular reconstructive option after resection of large diaphyseal lesions.[18] They are used in segmental defects and cases of failed fixation caused by progressive disease. Intercalary spacers can be used for reconstruction after complete resection of a metastatic lesion in the humeral diaphysis, minimizing blood loss in hypervascular lesions and often alleviating the need for postoperative radiation. Damron et al. reported that intercalary spacers provide immediate stable fixation, excellent pain relief, and early return of function.[18,42] Plate fixation produces good to excellent functional results in nonpathologic humeral fractures; however, drawbacks for their use in metastatic disease include the need for extensive exposure of the humerus and the inability to protect the entire bone. With disease progression, there is risk of hardware failure when plate fixation is used.

Distal Humerus. Distal humeral lesions or fractures are treated with flexible intramedullary nails, bicondylar plate fixation, or resection with modular distal humeral reconstruction. Flexible

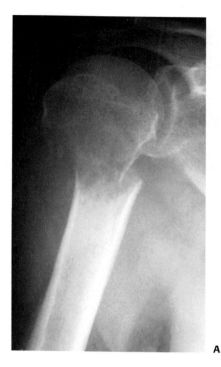
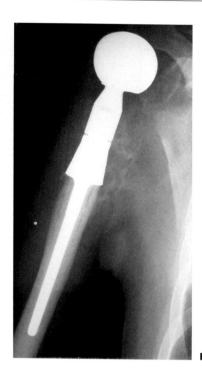

FIGURE 20-4 A. Anteroposterior radiograph of the right proximal humerus in a 54-year-old man with multiple myeloma. He has a displaced fracture through the humeral neck with a large lytic lesion filling the proximal humerus. **B.** Postoperative radiograph after resection of the proximal humerus and modular prosthetic replacement. The stem is cemented into the native humerus. Excellent pain control was achieved with this reconstruction.

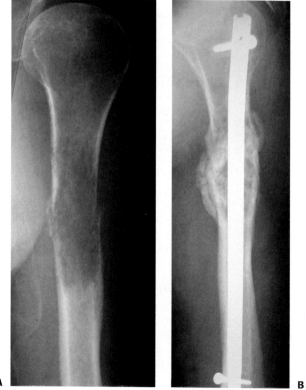

FIGURE 20-5 A. Anteroposterior radiograph of the left humerus in a 58-year-old man with multiple myeloma. This minimally displaced fracture was the presenting feature of his disease. **B.** Postoperative radiograph 6 months after closed intramedullary humeral nail placement. With systemic chemotherapy and external beam radiation to the left humerus, the fracture and lesion have healed.

nails, inserted in a retrograde manner through small medial and lateral incisions, offer ease of insertion, the ability to span the entire humerus, excellent functional recovery, and preservation of the native elbow joint. Curettage of the distal humeral lesion allows an open reduction in the case of a fracture and the opportunity to use PMMA in the lesion to gain rotational stability (Fig. 20-6). Orthogonal plate fixation is similar to nonpathologic fracture care but, when combined with PMMA, it can provide a stable construct about the elbow. This method of fixation does not protect the proximal humerus against a future metastatic lesion or fracture. A distal humeral resection and modular endoprosthetic reconstruction of the elbow is the best option for massive bone loss involving the condyles.[95]

Forearm/Hand. Metastases distal to the elbow are unusual, and the most common are from the lung, breast and kidney.[57] Metastatic lesions to the radius and ulna can be treated with flexible rods or rigid plate fixation. Pathologic fractures of the radial head can be treated with resection. Intralesional surgery is preferred for hand metastasis with curettage, internal fixation, and cementation. If the lesion is distal or extensive, amputation may be the best option.

Pelvic/Acetabular Fractures

Many bone metastasis or pathologic fractures in the bony pelvis do not affect weight-bearing functions; consequently, they do not require surgical intervention. Lesions of the iliac wing, superior/inferior pubic rami, or sacroiliac region fit into this category. Insufficiency fractures caused by osteoporosis frequently occur in these locations and are managed with protected weightbearing until the pain diminishes followed by assessment of bone density and appropriate medical treatment.[10,69]

Periacetabular lesions or fractures, however, affect ambulatory status and often present a difficult surgical problem.[38,53,66,85] The situation is magnified if there is protrusion of the

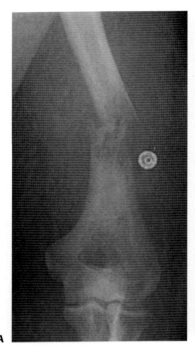

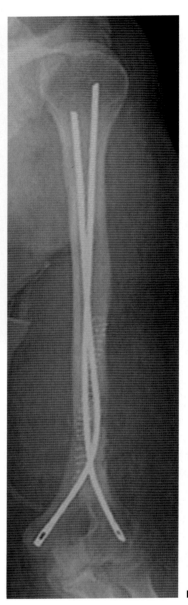

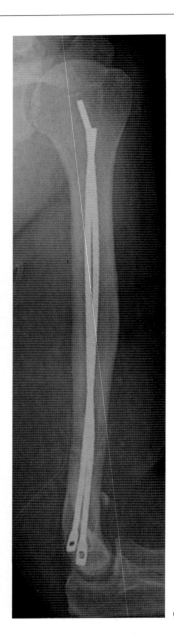

FIGURE 20-6 A. Anteroposterior radiograph of the left distal humerus in a 53-year-old-man with metastatic thyroid carcinoma. The osteolytic lesion was considered too distal for stabilization with an anterograde intramedullary nail. Internal fixation with dual plates is an option but would leave the remainder of the proximal humerus unprotected if future lesions occur. Anteroposterior (**B**) and lateral (**C**) postoperative radiographs demonstrate the reconstruction with flexible pins extending the length of the humerus. Curettage of the lesion was performed via a posterior approach, the humerus was intentionally shortened slightly for increased cortical contact, and methylmethacrylate was used to fill the defect after the fixation was placed.

femoral head through a pathologic acetabular fracture (Fig. 20-7). All pathologic fractures or defects in this location should be assessed with CT scans with three-dimensional reconstruction. There are several classification systems for acetabular defects, but various modifications of the Harrington classification are used for assessing metastatic disease. This system classifies the location and extent of the defect and guides the technical considerations of fixation.[38] The modification often used describes Class I lesions as minor acetabular defects with maintenance of the lateral cortices, superior and medial walls. A conventional cemented acetabular component provides sufficient support. Class II lesions are major acetabular defects with a deficient medial wall and superior dome. An antiprotrusion device and/or medial mesh is necessary (Fig. 20-7). Class III lesions are massive defects with deficient lateral cortices and superior dome. There is no substantial peripheral rim for fixation of a metal component; therefore, weight-bearing stresses must be transmitted from the acetabular component into bone

unaffected by the tumor, usually near the sacroiliac joint. An acetabular cage should be used with long screw fixation into any remaining pubis, ischium, and ilium. The massive bony defect is filled with PMMA to provide immediate stability after long screws and threaded $\frac{5}{16}$-inch Steinman pins anchor the construct. A polyethylene cup is then cemented into the acetabular cage in the correct orientation (Fig. 20-8). Class IV lesions involve pelvic discontinuity and can be treated expediently with resection and reconstruction using a saddle prosthesis or a resection arthroplasty depending on patient factors and expected life span.[1] With these techniques, satisfactory pain relief and function can be achieved in 70% to 75% of patients. Complications are common and occur in 20% to 30% of cases.[1,2,38,53,66,85] Extensive blood loss can be anticipated with massive lytic defects. This demanding surgery is best done by surgeons with extensive experience treating this type of lesion. The trabecular metal tantalum provides new options for acetabular fixation by allowing early bone ingrowth. It can be used in combination with a cemented acetabular cage.[76]

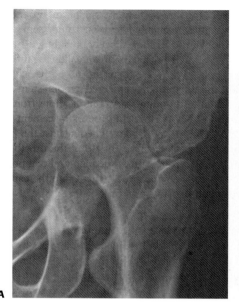
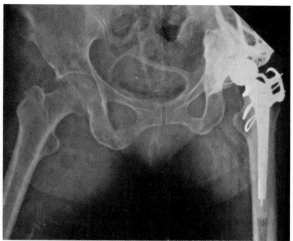

FIGURE 20-7 A. Anteroposterior radiograph of the left hip in a 61-year-old woman with metastatic breast cancer. Note the femoral head protrusion into the pelvis through a pathologic acetabular fracture. It is important to try and identify metastatic lesions before they fracture so that prophylactic fixation can be performed. Note the extensive bone loss in the superior dome and medial wall. This would be categorized as a Class II lesion. **B.** Postoperative radiograph after acetabular reconstruction with an antiprotrusion cage, multiple screws, and PMMA.

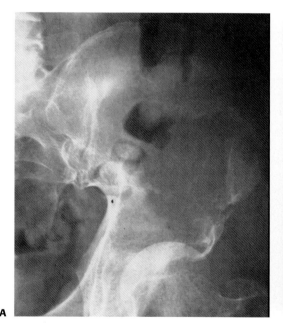
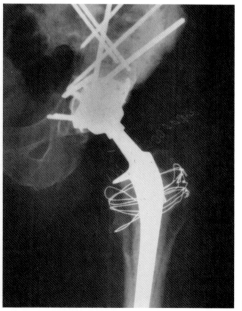

FIGURE 20-8 A. Anteroposterior radiograph of the left acetabulum in a 49-year-old woman with metastatic renal cell carcinoma and a Class III acetabular lesion. Note the massive bone destruction of the periacetabular region, precluding peripheral rim fixation. Arterial embolization of the tumor to decrease intraoperative bleeding is recommended. **B.** Postoperative radiograph after reconstruction using a cemented acetabular cage with long Steinman pins transmitting stress into the sacroiliac region.

Lower Extremity Fractures

The femur is the most common long bone to be affected by metastasis.[96] The proximal third is involved in 50% of cases, with the intertrochanteric region accounting for 20% of cases. Metastatic disease to the femur is the most painful of the bone metastasis, likely because of the high weight-bearing stresses through the proximal region. Pathologic fractures of the femur suddenly alter the quality of a patient's life and threaten an individual's level of independence. Without proper surgical attention, the patient with a pathologic fracture of the femur will be confined to bed, a situation that is medically and psychologically devastating.

Painful destructive lesions in the proximal femur should be prophylactically stabilized whenever possible because of the high incidence of subsequent fracture and the comparative ease of the operation. The development of bone metastasis is a continuous process, so it is important to stabilize as much of the femur as possible to avoid future peri-implant failure.[96] At a minimum, it is recommended that the tip of the chosen fixation device should bypass a given lesion by at least twice the diameter of the femur.

Femoral Neck. Pathologic fractures of the femoral head and neck rarely heal, and the neoplastic process tends to progress.[56] Accordingly, there is a high incidence of failure if traditional fracture fixation devices are used. The procedure of choice for patients with metastatic disease to the femoral head or neck is a cemented replacement prosthesis[56,71] (Fig. 20-9). The decision to use a hemiarthroplasty versus a total hip replacement depends on the presence of acetabular involvement. This must be carefully scrutinized as acetabular disease can go unrecognized. All tumor tissue should be curetted from the femoral canal before implanting the prosthesis. When there are adjacent lesions in the subtrochanteric region or proximal diaphysis, a long-stemmed cemented femoral component should be used for prophylactic fixation distally, avoiding a future pathologic fracture through a distal lesion and allowing full weight bearing postoperatively. When there are no additional lesions in the femur, the length of the cemented femoral stem is controversial. The risk of cardiopulmonary complications from monomer embolization after pressurizing the extra cement and long stem within the canal must be weighed against the potential risk of future metastasis distal to the tip of the prosthesis if a shorter stem is used.[94] If long-stemmed femoral components are used, it is important to inject the cement into the canal while still in a fairly liquid state.[6,15]

Intertrochanteric Region. Traditional fixation of an intertrochanteric fracture with screw and side-plate fixation has a high rate of failure when used in the setting of metastatic bone disease, even when supplemented with adjuvant PMMA and postoperative radiation. The standard of care is intramedullary fixation or prosthetic replacement.[96] The choice of fixation in this region of the femur depends on the extent of the lesion and whether it is radiosensitive. If bone with sufficient strength remains in the femoral head and neck and local control is likely to be achieved with postoperative external beam radiation, an intramedullary reconstruction device is recommended, which will allow the highest level of function. A cephalomedullary nail protects the femoral neck and is used for all metastatic lesions or pathologic fractures of the femur when an intramedullary device is indicated. If the destruction is more extensive, a cemented calcar-replacing prosthesis is required (Fig. 20-9). The same issues arise related to the length of the femoral stem as discussed in the previous section.

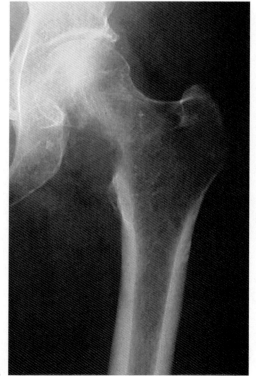

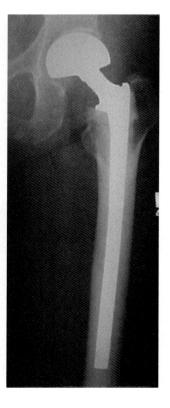

FIGURE 20-9 A. Anteroposterior radiograph of the left hip in a 52-year-old woman with metastatic lung carcinoma. There is an impending fracture caused by an osteolytic lesion in the medial aspect of the femoral neck. **B.** Postoperative radiograph after placement of a cemented medium-length, calcar-replacing, bipolar hemiarthroplasty.

A   **B**

Subtrochanteric Region. Using plate and screw internal fixation for subtrochanteric fractures in patients with metastatic bone disease will usually end in failure. This region of the femur is subjected to forces of up to four to six times body weight. Statically locked intramedullary fixation with or without PMMA will stabilize the area and provide weight-bearing support.[97] Even impending fractures should be statically locked as the lesion can fracture later causing shortening of the femur. A modular proximal femoral prosthesis is reserved for cases with extensive bone destruction or used as a salvage device for failed internal fixation (Fig. 20-10).[71] It can also be used when a wide resection is necessary for a pathologic fracture through a primary bone sarcoma. There is an increased risk of dislocation and abductor mechanism weakness with a megaprosthesis, but this should not prevent its use in patients with radioresistant or locally aggressive tumors. A bipolar head is used to provide more stability if the acetabulum is not involved with metastatic disease. Excellent pain relief and local tumor control can be obtained after tumor resection and prosthetic reconstruction.

Femoral Diaphysis. Pathologic fractures of the femoral diaphysis are treated most effectively with a statically locked cephalomedullary nail, with or without PMMA[96,101] (Fig. 20-11). Plate fixation, although more rigid, will not protect a large enough segment of bone and is prone to failure with disease progression. Cephalomedullary nail fixation protects the entire bone and is technically simple, especially when performed prophylactically. A trochanteric or piriformis entry point can be used, and the canal is slowly overreamed 1.0 to 1.5 mm to avoid high impaction forces during rod placement.[6] Because the device will be load bearing if the fracture does not unite, a nail with the largest possible diameter should be used. The fields for postoperative radiation should encompass the entire implant.

Supracondylar Femur. The choice of fixation for pathologic supracondylar femur fractures depends on the extent of local bone destruction and the presence of additional lesions in the proximal femur. The distal lesions can be a treatment challenge caused by frequent comminution and poor bone stock, especially in older patients. Options include lateral locking plate fixation supplemented with PMMA or a modular distal femoral prosthesis.[91] A retrograde nail has the drawback of potentially seeding the knee joint with tumor while failing to provide fixation to the femoral neck region. The locking plate provides stable fixation after curettage and cementation of the metastatic lesion. The modular endoprosthesis is the optimal choice for local control when there is massive destruction of the femoral condyles, as it allows the lesion to be resected en bloc.[24]

Tibia. Metastases distal to the knee are uncommon but, for proximal tibial lesions, similar principles should be used as for lesions in the supracondylar femoral area. A locking plate with PMMA after thorough curettage of the lesion is generally sufficient. Extensive lesions may require a modular proximal tibial prosthesis. Tibial diaphyseal lesions and fractures should be managed with a locked intramedullary device. Various techniques can be employed for pathologic fractures of the distal

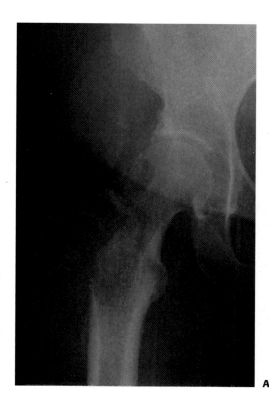

FIGURE 20-10 A. Anteroposterior radiograph of the right proximal femur in a 52-year-old woman with metastatic adrenocortical carcinoma affecting the right greater trochanter and femoral neck. There is a visible lateral soft tissue mass. **B.** Postoperative radiograph after resection of the proximal femur and reconstruction with a cemented, modular proximal femoral replacement and bipolar cup.

A   B

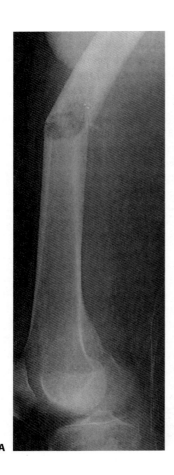

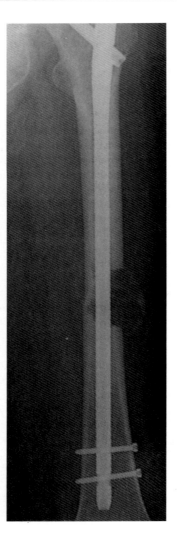

FIGURE 20-11 A. Anteroposterior radiograph of the left femur in a 65-year-old man with metastatic renal cell carcinoma. He has a pathologic fracture through a small, osteolytic lesion in a high-stress area. **B.** Postoperative radiograph after stabilization of the fracture with a statically locked cephalomedullary femoral nail. Preoperative embolization was performed to minimize blood loss. Open curettage of the lesion was not performed because of its small size and the limited (less than 3 months) life span of the patient.

tibia, but standard internal fixation methods are generally advised with generous use of PMMA to augment the construct.[19,57] The treatment of foot and ankle lesions must be individualized to maintain maximal function.[41]

Spinal Fractures

Between 5% and 10% of patients who die of metastatic carcinoma will have microscopic disease in their spine. The metastases most commonly involve the vertebral body rather than the posterior elements. The majority of these patients will not have clinically significant spine disease during their lifetime and will not need treatment specific to this location. The lesions are often discovered incidentally on a bone scan during a routine metastatic workup in a patient with known cancer. However, if the disease progresses, it can cause moderate to severe pain persisting for months before the onset of focal neurologic deficits. Occasionally, the onset of pain is sudden following a pathologic compression fracture.

When the patient does not have a history of cancer, it must be decided whether a compression fracture is secondary to osteoporosis or a bone metastasis. If the patient has a history of cancer or if the patient's current symptoms, physical examination, laboratory studies, or imaging suggests a primary carcinoma or myeloma, the patient should be evaluated for a compression fracture caused by metastatic disease. It is imperative to consider spinal metastasis in any cancer patient with back pain. A delay in diagnosis can allow progression and possible neurologic compromise, leading to permanent functional deficits. Patients with a suspected malignancy should have a biopsy, but others should be treated symptomatically. If a patient treated for an osteoporotic compression fracture does not respond to the treatment or if there is progressive destruction of bone, a biopsy should be performed. Percutaneous CT-guided needle biopsy of vertebral lesions can be performed with local anesthesia and intravenous sedation.

The classic plain radiographic finding in metastatic involvement of the spine is loss of a pedicle on an anteroposterior view. MRI can be used to differentiate an osteoporotic compression fracture from one caused by a malignant lesion.[102] When there is complete replacement of the vertebral segment, multiple vertebral body lesions, pedicle involvement, and an intact intervertebral disk, metastatic disease is most likely (Fig. 20-12). Some patients with myeloma, lymphoma, or leukemia may present with osteopenia of the vertebra. To determine if the patient has a hematologic malignancy, a bone marrow aspirate should be considered. Most of these patients will have systemic findings (e.g., weight loss, fatigue, fever). If a metastatic lesion in the spine is identified, the patient is at risk of having additional skeletal lesions.

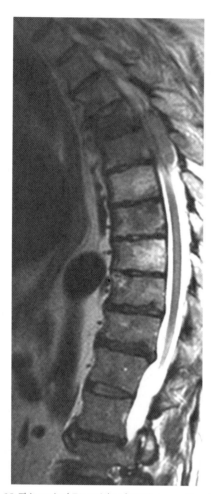

FIGURE 20-12 This sagittal T2-weighted MR image without fat suppression in a 57-year-old man with multiple myeloma shows a thoracic vertebral compression fracture with marrow replacement in multiple vertebral bodies and an associated large epidural lesion.

Treatment options for patients with symptomatic metastatic disease to the spine include nonoperative management with radiation, corticosteroids, and/or bracing; minimally invasive techniques such as kyphoplasty and vertebroplasty; and surgical treatment with adjuvant radiation.[3,22,27,35,37,63,80] Scoring systems for the evaluation of patients with vertebral metastasis have been reported, but no system has been universally adopted to guide treatment.[58,86] Quality of life must be considered as these are painful lesions, but surgical treatment is often a major undertaking that may require a prolonged recovery.[45]

Generally, symptoms from a vertebral compression fracture caused by osteoporosis are minor and can be successfully controlled with temporarily decreased activity or bracing. If the patient has asymptomatic vertebral metastases that are not at risk for pathologic fracture, systemic treatment can be used to address the primary and metastatic disease. Regular imaging of the spine should be performed to ensure that any disease progression is identified quickly. Often, early recognition of a spinal metastasis allows pain relief with nonoperative management. If the patient has pain but no neurologic compromise or risk of impending fracture, radiation treatment is indicated. Radiation is also used for radiation-sensitive tumors such as lymphoma or myeloma even when they present with neurologic compromise. The tumor response is usually sufficiently rapid

such that the risk of permanent neurologic loss is no higher than that seen after surgical decompression. When there is minimal or no bone destruction but cord compression is caused by tumor extension, emergent radiation is recommended.[73] The patient should also be treated with a short course of high-dose corticosteroids to reduce edema surrounding the tumor that contributes to compression and neurologic damage. Other indications for radiation of vertebral metastasis include patients with medical comorbidities precluding surgery, patients with 6 weeks or less to live, and those with multilevel disease. Radiation should be added preoperatively or postoperatively to improve local disease control when patients are treated with surgery.[88] More recently, cyberknife radiosurgery has provided effective pain relief in patients with spinal metastases. It can be used in patients who have had prior external beam radiation as it focuses small beams of radiation into the tumor from many different directions via a robotic arm. This minimizes radiation exposure to the surrounding tissues. Cyberknife is a computer-assisted, minimally invasive procedure that can be performed as an outpatient in only one to three sessions and serves as another alternative to major surgery.[32]

Indications for surgical treatment of vertebral metastasis include progression of disease after radiation, neurologic compromise caused by bony impingement or radioresistant tumor within the spinal canal, an impending fracture, or spinal instability caused by a pathologic fracture or progressive deformity. The goals of surgery are to maintain or restore neurologic function and spinal stability.

When surgical treatment is necessary to relieve compression of the spinal cord, decompression and stabilization are required. Before surgery, MRI is used to verify the level of the lesion and rule out the possibility of compression at additional levels. A preoperative angiogram with embolization of feeder vessels should be considered in patients with highly vascular metastasis, such as RCC, to reduce intraoperative blood loss.[14] Relief of symptoms can often be accomplished via a posterior decompression and fusion using instrumentation.[3] When there is anterior collapse of the vertebrae and anterior compression of the spinal cord resulting in kyphosis, the patient is also treated with an anterior decompression and stabilization.[27,37,50,63] When the posterior elements are involved with tumor and the cord is compressed anteriorly, the patient should have an anterior decompression with posterior stabilization and fusion (Fig. 20-13).[86] Internal fixation is indicated to provide immediate stability for all but the most limited decompressions. In recent years, there has been considerable improvement in the available implants to manage structural deficiency of the spine, including pedicle screws, cages, and more sophisticated plates and rods. Specific techniques for anterior and posterior decompression and stabilization, including the use of modern instrumentation systems, are described in the literature.[27,86] Surgical implants made of titanium allow easier assessment of recurrent disease on MRI. As patients live longer with their metastatic disease, aggressive surgical treatment of spinal lesions can enhance quality of life. However, the magnitude of the operative procedure should not exceed the patient's chance of surviving the surgery or the surgeon's level of competence.

Kyphoplasty/Vertebroplasty. Minimally invasive treatments for metastatic disease to the spine have been used to control pain in patients who have developed compression fractures.[22,80] Ver-

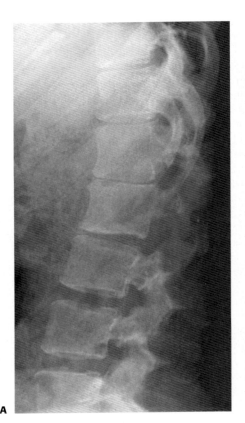

A

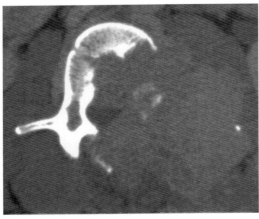

B

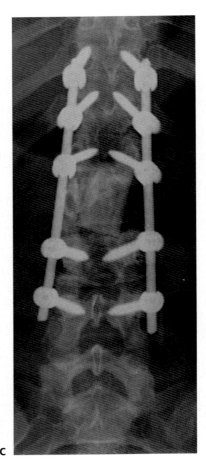

C

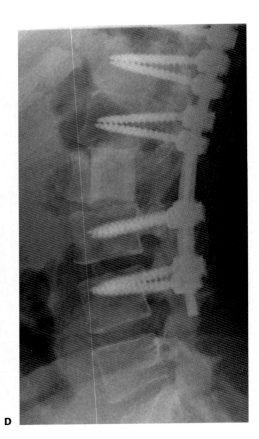

D

FIGURE 20-13 A. Lateral lumbar spine radiograph in a 27-year-old woman with metastatic thyroid cancer reveals destruction of the posterior portion of the L2 vertebral body. **B.** Axial CT scan through L2 reveals extensive destruction of the bone with soft tissue extension posterolaterally into the spinal canal. The patient presented with L2 nerve root symptoms. Anteroposterior (**C**) and lateral (**D**) postoperative radiographs after L2 anterior corpectomy, posterior spinal decompression, and segmental instrumentation and fusion from T11 to L4. She also had anterior reconstruction and fusion from L1 to L3 using humeral allograft.

tebroplasty or kyphoplasty can be used for pathologic vertebral body fractures caused by osteoporosis, metastatic carcinoma, or multiple myeloma. The literature suggests that the results are similar in patients with malignancy versus osteoporosis, although these procedures have not been directly compared. Indications include patients with stable compression fractures who have normal neurologic function but persistent pain. One technique, vertebroplasty, involves percutaneous direct injection of PMMA through the pedicle to maintain vertebral height. Kyphoplasty is a way of regaining vertebral body height by expanding the compression fracture with a balloon before injecting the PMMA (Fig. 20-14). Reported complications include extrusion of cement around the neurologic structures, so this procedure

should only be performed after careful consideration of the risks.

Complications

Because patients with pathologic fractures are often older with multiple associated medical problems, the chance of perioperative complications is increased. These patients have the same risks as those with nonpathologic fractures when they consent to surgical treatment, but some complications are more likely in patients with widespread cancer. Two of the most concerning problems are tumor progression with resultant hardware failure and cardiopulmonary compromise.

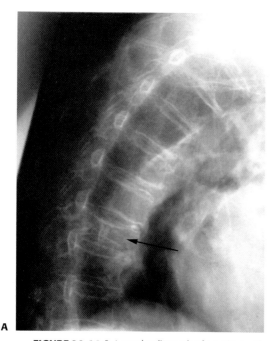
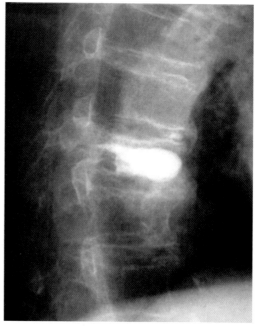

FIGURE 20-14 A. Lateral radiograph of a patient with senile osteoporosis and a thoracic compression fracture. **B.** Lateral radiograph after treatment with kyphoplasty to regain vertebral height and relieve pain. Note that the methylmethacrylate is relatively well contained. The fracture reduction is minimal but she had complete pain relief 2 weeks after the procedure.

Bone metastases that are unresponsive to chemotherapy and radiation will continue to destroy bone so that the existing hardware or prosthesis is load bearing rather than load sharing. Using the principles of surgical treatment outlined in this chapter will minimize the risk of hardware failure, but inevitably some constructs will fail. The salvage of failed reconstructions must be individualized, but modular endoprostheses can frequently be used to salvage failed intramedullary fixation.[47] Again, the patient's life span and general health must be favorable before they are indicated for a prolonged procedure.

Cardiopulmonary compromise is a noted risk in patients with bone metastasis. First, many of these patients have pulmonary metastasis or primary lung tumors that make ventilation more difficult. Some patients will have a surgical procedure to stabilize a pathologic fracture and fail postoperative attempts at extubation, remaining in an intensive care setting for a prolonged time. Second, the placement of long-stemmed cemented femoral prostheses or prophylactic femoral or humeral nails must be done carefully to avoid embolic events. Careful suction of the canal and slow reaming are tips to decrease this complication.[6,15] It is unclear from the available literature whether the actual incidence of fat emboli is increased during placement of intramedullary rods or long cemented femoral stems in patients with malignancy compared to those without cancer. However, patients with cancer are more hypercoagulable and are likely less able to compensate for fat emboli to the lung than are patients without cancer, especially if they have primary or metastatic pulmonary disease.

Role of Adjuvant Radiation and Medical Treatment

External Beam Radiation

External beam radiation is used to treat pain secondary to bone metastases, halt the progression of bony destruction, and allow healing of an impending pathologic fracture. It is a reasonable alternative to surgical treatment for certain lesions. When the endpoint is pain relief, local radiation therapy typically results in partial relief in over 80% of patients with bone metastasis and complete pain relief in 50% to 60% of cases.[94] Variability in response rates depends on multiple factors including the histology and location of the lesion.[99] The onset of symptomatic relief usually occurs in the first 1 to 2 weeks, but maximal relief may take several months. Radiation is used in the postoperative setting to increase local tumor control after surgical stabilization. Retrospective data have shown that postoperative radiation improves limb function and decreases the rates of second orthopedic procedures.[88] The majority of patients in this study had the entire prosthesis or internal fixation device included in the treatment field. Radiation can usually begin 2 weeks after the surgical procedure if there are no wound complications.

Systemic Radionucleotides

Systemic therapy for bone metastasis using radioactive bone-seeking agents provides palliation of bone pain. It may be appropriate for widespread bone metastases when more traditional forms of radiation have reached their limit or when standard radiation techniques are not feasible because of surrounding normal tissue tolerances. Strontium-89 is used clinically and preferentially taken up at sites of active bone mineral turnover, similar to bisphosphonates. There is a greater uptake of the radionucleotides in metastatic lesions than in normal bone. A systematic review of the published literature on palliation of painful bone metastasis with radiopharmaceuticals revealed better pain relief with fewer sites of disease using strontium-89 compared to placebo or local radiation therapy.[7]

Bisphosphonates

Bisphosphonates bind preferentially to the bone matrix and inhibit osteoclastic bone resorption. They decrease the depth of resorption cavities at osteoclastic binding sites, inhibit osteoclastic function, alter the morphology of the osteoclast ruffled border, and inhibit maturation and recruitment of osteoclasts from the monocyte/macrophage cell line. They promote osteoclast apoptosis, and there are some data to suggest direct effects on tumor cells. Intravenous bisphosphonates have been used with success to treat bone pain and hypercalcemia in breast cancer, and they are most commonly used as an adjunct to other systemic therapies.[62]

There have been multiple, well-organized studies that document a decrease in the time to skeletal-related events as well as a decrease in the rate of these events in patients with bone metastasis treated with various bisphosphonates.[40,61,62]

Controversies and Future Directions

Two of the main controversies in the management of patients with metastatic bone disease are (a) the ideal length of a cemented femoral stem in patients with metastatic disease about the hip and (b) the specific characteristics that define an impending fracture. These topics were discussed previously.

There is also continued debate as to the surgical treatment of patients with a solitary metastasis. There is literature to suggest that wide resection of a solitary RCC metastasis leads to increased survival.[49,84] However, it has not been shown that these data are applicable to metastatic disease from other primary sites. The study recommending resection of solitary RCC metastasis was conducted before widespread use of PET scanning, which allows discovery of smaller foci of active disease. It is likely that many patients presumed to have solitary metastasis would have additional sites of disease if screened with PET imaging. However, a patient with a solitary metastasis from any origin who has been tumor free for several years should be theoretically considered a candidate for a resection. RCC and follicular thyroid carcinoma are the two tumor types most likely to produce isolated bone metastasis years after treatment of the primary tumor.

Future directions in the surgical treatment of patients with metastatic bone disease of the spine and extremities will likely include continued use and new applications for trabecular metal.[59] The tantalum acetabular components allow excellent bone ingrowth and are being used more routinely in revision joint arthroplasty to reconstruct large acetabular defects.[47,76] Further advances in this type of metal fixation may allow improvement in the attachment of soft tissues to megaprostheses after tumor resection. Endoprostheses made of porous tantalum have been used in limb-sparing surgery in patients with lower extremity sarcomas with short-term follow-up.[43]

Interventional radiologists are working more closely with orthopaedic surgeons to manage patients with bone metastasis. Radiofrequency ablation (RFA) and cryotherapy are now being used routinely for palliative treatment of painful metastatic lesions. These techniques provide an alternative to external beam radiation or surgery.[33] A recent study of patients with pelvic and sacral metastasis treated with RFA showed a clinical benefit with significant pain relief in 95% of patients.[33] Most of these patients had failed to respond to prior treatment or were considered to be poor candidates for narcotic medication or radiation. Another new procedure termed acetabuloplasty is similar to vertebroplasty in that PMMA is injected percutaneously into an acetabular defect to provide pain relief and possibly avoid a major surgical reconstruction.[47,98]

TREATMENT OPTIONS FOR PATIENTS WITH PATHOLOGIC FRACTURES THROUGH PRIMARY BONE TUMORS

Benign Bone Tumors

Benign bone tumors occur most commonly in children and young adults. Most tumors gradually enlarge until the patient reaches skeletal maturity and then resolve or become inactive. Inactive lesions do not require surgical treatment. Active or aggressive benign lesions often require intralesional curettage with or without bone grafting to remove the tumor and allow healing of the underlying bone. A pathologic fracture through a benign bone tumor may change the course of treatment. Because of the age and activity level of patients who have benign bone tumors, pathologic fractures are not uncommon.

In general, the treatment of a pathologic fracture through a benign bone lesion depends on the activity of the underlying lesion. Most can be treated nonoperatively in a cast until the fracture heals. At that time, treatment of the benign tumor can be addressed. Indications for surgical treatment of the fracture include unacceptable deformity in a cast, open fracture, fracture nonunion, or an association with active or aggressive lesions such as giant cell tumor or aneurysmal bone cyst. The treatment of pathologic fractures in the context of specific benign bone tumors is discussed next. The reader is referred to comprehensive musculoskeletal oncology textbooks to learn more about the diagnosis and treatment of individual tumors.

Unicameral Bone Cyst

A pathologic fracture is the presenting complaint in two-thirds of patients with a unicameral bone cyst (UBC).[13] The majority of these lytic lesions are located in the proximal humerus or proximal femur (Fig. 20-15). A humeral fracture should be allowed to heal in a satisfactory position as the fracture occasionally stimulates healing of the cyst. If the cyst does not heal spontaneously after the fracture callus remodels, corticosteroid injection into the cyst is recommended. A displaced fracture through a proximal femoral UBC in a child usually requires open reduction, bone grafting of the cyst, and internal fixation due to weight-bearing requirements.

Aneurysmal Bone Cyst

An aneurysmal bone cyst (ABC) is an active benign lesion that can grow rapidly in the metaphysis of a young patient, simulating a malignancy.[13] Despite its occasional aggressive growth pattern, pathologic fractures are uncommon. Approximately 15% to 20% of lesions occur in the posterior elements of the spine and can cause neurologic compromise. The standard treatment of an ABC with or without a fracture is intralesional curettage and bone grafting. Depending on the age of the patient and location of the ABC, a pathologic fracture might require internal fixation at the time of curettage.

Eosinophilic Granuloma

An eosinophilic granuloma is a solitary lesion in the spectrum of disease known as Langerhans cell histiocytosis. It is a benign bone tumor, and affected patients present with pain. This tumor

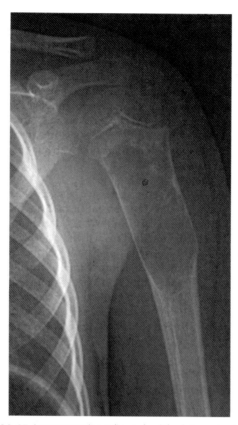

FIGURE 20-15 Anteroposterior radiograph of the left proximal humerus in a 5-year-old girl with a unicameral bone cyst. Note the centrally located, osteolytic lesion. She previously had a pathologic fracture through the lesion and subsequently had an intralesional steroid injection. The cyst does not affect the proximal humeral growth plate.

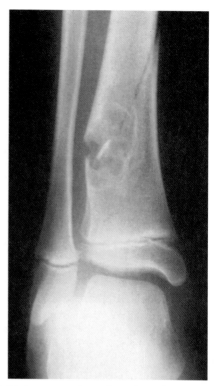

FIGURE 20-16 Anteroposterior radiograph of the distal tibia of a 10-year-old boy. The well-developed reactive rim of bone around the eccentric, metaphyseal, radiolucent lesion is virtually diagnostic of a nonossifying fibroma (NOF). The patient had no symptoms until he slid into second base and caught his foot, twisting his lower leg. He heard a crack and had acute pain. The fracture was treated in a cast and healed, but the NOF remained 2 more years before healing completely.

can cause collapse of a vertebral body (vertebra plana) and neurologic symptoms. Patients with symptomatic vertebra plana are braced, and eventually the vertebral height is restored without surgery.[72] For extremity lesions that do not spontaneously resolve, the standard of care is an intralesional corticosteroid injection. Open curettage is reserved for selected lesions that fail to respond or are unsuitable for steroid injection because of the size, location, or aggressiveness of the lesion.[100] A pathologic fracture should be allowed to heal before performing a needle biopsy and injection, so the fracture callus does not confuse the histologic picture.

Nonossifying Fibroma

Nonossifying fibromas are extremely common lytic lesions in young patients. They spontaneously resolve after skeletal maturity. They are asymptomatic, but large lesions can fracture. Common pathologic fracture locations include the distal tibia, distal femur, and proximal tibia (Fig. 20-16). Patients with multiple lesions have a higher risk of fracture. Pathologic fractures can be treated successfully in the majority of cases with closed reduction and cast immobilization.[23] If the lesion persists after fracture consolidation, curettage and bone grafting can be performed if necessary. If a fracture is unstable and cannot be reduced in a closed fashion, curettage and bone grafting is combined with internal fixation.

Enchondroma

Enchondromas are benign cartilage tumors that are asymptomatic unless associated with a pathologic fracture.[78] The lesions in long bones rarely fracture. Those most prone to pathologic fractures and pain occur in the small bones of the hand (Fig. 20-17). Some advocate nonsurgical treatment of these lesions, as the fracture occasionally stimulates resolution of the enchondroma. Most agree that surgical intervention, if performed, should be delayed until the fracture has healed.[87] Surgical treatment of the enchondroma eliminates the future risk of pathologic fracture and avoids progressive deformity. Whether to perform a bone graft to the defect after curettage remains controversial. Multiple enchondromas with frequent hand fractures and deformities occur in Ollier disease and Mafucci syndrome.

Fibrous Dysplasia

Fibrous dysplasia is defined as a developmental abnormality rather than a true neoplasm and occurs in both monostotic and polyostotic forms.[36] Most solitary lesions of fibrous dysplasia are asymptomatic, but patients can present with a painful pathologic fracture or bowed extremity. In the polyostotic form, lesions involve multiple areas of a single bone or multiple bones in one extremity, and fractures occur in 85% of these patients. The structural bone strength is decreased in fibrous dysplasia, and sequential fractures can result in progressive deformity pro-

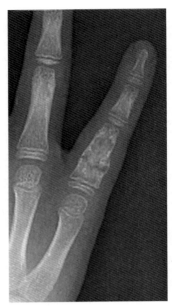

FIGURE 20-17 Anteroposterior radiograph of the right fifth finger in a 9-year-old boy with a proximal phalanx pathologic fracture. The fracture is through an enchondroma and is minimally displaced. It healed with immobilization and no treatment was necessary for the asymptomatic benign bone lesion.

ducing the classic Shepherd's crook varus appearance of the proximal femur. The fractures are rarely displaced and heal well.

Pathologic fractures or symptomatic lesions in the upper extremity and spine can be treated nonoperatively, whereas lower extremity fractures usually require internal fixation.[36] Extensive areas of fibrous dysplasia in high-stress weight-bearing areas are treated with prophylactic internal fixation. The lesion should be biopsied at the time of surgery to confirm the diagnosis before proceeding with intramedullary fixation to stabilize long bones. The goal is to strengthen and straighten the bone, not to resect the lesion. If bone graft is used, it should be allograft, as autograft has the same genetic abnormality as the dysplastic bone and may not heal properly. Internal fixation does not alter the disease process but provides mechanical support and pain relief. Another option is medical treatment with bisphosphonates alone or in combination with surgery.[55]

Giant Cell Tumor

Giant cell tumor (GCT) is an aggressive benign bone tumor that occurs in young adults. Ten percent of patients present with a pathologic fracture. In patients whose adjacent joint can be preserved, the GCT should be treated with thorough curettage and bone grafting or cementation.[89] Internal fixation is often necessary after a pathologic fracture as there is usually extensive bone loss and deformity (Fig. 20-18). Adjuvant treatment with phenol or cryosurgery should be used with caution in patients when a pathologic fracture exposes adjacent soft tissues. Primary wide resection and reconstruction is only necessary when the associated joint is destroyed.

Malignant Bone Tumors

Primary malignant bone tumors are treated with a combination of surgery, chemotherapy, and/or radiation. Multiple myeloma is a primary malignant bone tumor with a systemic presentation that occurs in older patients. Pathologic fractures in patients with myeloma, lymphoma, and metastatic carcinoma can be treated with fixation through the tumor as they are systemic diseases treated primarily with chemotherapy and radiation. The overall survival of these patients is not compromised by palliative surgical stabilization.

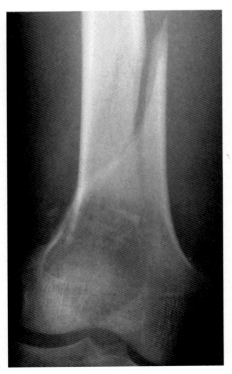

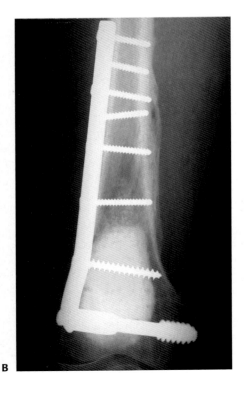

A **B**

FIGURE 20-18 A. Anteroposterior radiograph of a 37-year-old man with a giant cell tumor in the right distal femur (lateral femoral condyle). Note the lack of a sclerotic rim and extension to the subchondral bone. There is a spiral pathologic displaced fracture through the lesion. **B.** Postoperative radiograph after curettage and cementation of the giant cell tumor. The fracture was reduced and internally fixed and healed uneventfully.

Primary malignant bone tumors such as osteosarcoma, Ewing's sarcoma, and chondrosarcoma are treated much differently than systemic neoplastic disease.[92] These tumors grow initially in the bone and can metastasize to the lungs. Local control of the primary lesion is achieved by complete surgical resection. A pathologic fracture through the lesion theoretically decreases the chance of local control, because tumor cells spread throughout the hematoma. Amputation should be discussed as a potential surgical option for patients with a pathologic fracture through primary malignant bone tumors. The literature is controversial on whether a pathologic fracture through an osteosarcoma compromises the chance for local control. To some degree this depends on the amount of fracture displacement, histology of the tumor, and response to chemotherapy.

Before initiating treatment for a patient with a pathologic fracture through a presumed primary bone sarcoma, the patient should be staged and a biopsy performed. An appropriate staging workup includes a CT scan of the chest for all patients, and a bone marrow biopsy when Ewing sarcoma is suspected. The biopsy of a presumed bone sarcoma is especially difficult in the setting of an associated pathologic fracture. The fracture hematoma and healing process alters the histology and may confuse the pathologist. Whenever possible, the biopsy should be performed away from the fracture. When there is an extraosseous soft tissue mass associated with the tumor, an image-guided needle biopsy is usually adequate. When the lesion is intraosseous and fracture callus is present, an open biopsy may be necessary. The surgeon who will eventually perform the definitive surgical treatment of the lesion should be the one who orders or performs the diagnostic biopsy.

Internal fixation of a pathologic fracture through a primary sarcoma may compromise the limb and life of the patient. If the patient will be treated with preoperative chemotherapy, cast immobilization of the fracture is preferred. The fracture usually heals during systemic treatment, and a cast avoids potential pin tract infections in neutropenic patients stabilized with an external fixator.

Patients with a pathologic fracture through a primary malignancy of bone require a coordinated multidisciplinary team that includes a medical oncologist, radiation oncologist, musculoskeletal pathologist, radiologist, physical therapist, and orthopaedic oncologist; only with the full complement of care can these patients achieve the best quality of life and maximum overall survival.

Osteosarcoma/Ewing Sarcoma

These are the two most common primary malignant bone tumors in children. Approximately 10% of patients present with a pathologic fracture. Closed treatment of the fracture in a cast is indicated after a needle or open biopsy is performed. When staging is complete, preoperative chemotherapy is used for patients with osteosarcoma or Ewing sarcoma. After 3 to 4 months of systemic therapy, a decision is made about local control of the primary tumor. For patients with osteosarcoma, surgical resection is indicated. If patients have a clinical and radiographic response to chemotherapy, a limb salvage procedure is generally preferred. Articles have shown no difference in overall survival for patients with osteosarcoma and a pathologic fracture that are treated with limb salvage compared to amputation.[4,79] Close follow-up is necessary to identify a possible local recurrence.

Local control in Ewing sarcoma can be achieved with surgical resection, radiation, or both. In reconstructable sites, most patients are treated with limb salvage surgery to remove all chemotherapy-resistant clones and avoid the risks of radiation in a growing child. However, in patients with a pathologic fracture treated with surgical resection, consideration should be given to adding radiation as a postoperative adjuvant to improve the chance of local control and avoid amputation.[29]

Chondrosarcoma

Chondrosarcoma occurs in middle-aged and older adults.[9] The pelvis is a common site, but displaced pathologic fractures are rare in this location. The most common location of a pathologic fracture through a chondrosarcoma is in the proximal femur (Fig. 20-19). A serious mistake is to assume the fracture is secondary to metastatic carcinoma and place an intramedullary rod through the lesion. This act generally precludes any safe limb salvage option for the patient. An older patient with a solitary lytic lesion should be staged appropriately with a biopsy to confirm the diagnosis before any surgical treatment.

The treatment of a patient with a pathologic fracture through a chondrosarcoma is wide resection by an orthopaedic oncologist. Chemotherapy and radiation are not effective for this tumor. A pathologic fracture greatly compromises the local area, as any stray tumor cells not resected will likely grow into a locally recurrent lesion. A displaced fracture through a chondrosarcoma is a reason to consider amputation, especially if wide resection cannot be achieved with a limb salvage procedure.

SUMMARY AND KEY POINTS

- Any process that reduces bone strength predisposes a patient to a pathologic fracture during normal activity or after minimal trauma. It must be recognized as a pathologic fracture if the patient is to be treated properly.
- The most common cause for a pathologic fracture is osteoporosis or osteomalacia.
- Patients with osteoporosis or osteomalacia require evaluation and management of the underlying disorder.
- Patients over 40 years of age with a pathologic fracture through a discrete bone lesion are much more likely to have metastatic bone disease than a primary bone tumor.
- The prognosis for patients with metastatic bone disease is improving because of early recognition and better adjuvant treatment; therefore, many patients will live longer than 2 years.
- Do not immediately assume that a lytic lesion or pathologic fracture is from metastatic disease. A thorough workup and possible biopsy are required.
- Prophylactic fixation for impending (versus actual) fractures from metastatic disease is technically easier for the surgeon and allows a quicker patient recovery.
- The Mirels scoring system is available to guide the treatment of an impending fracture from metastatic bone disease.
- Femoral neck fractures caused by metastatic bone disease require a cemented hip prosthesis, as internal fixation has a high rate of failure with disease progression.
- When surgery is required for metastatic disease to the spine, decompression and stabilization with internal fixation are generally necessary.

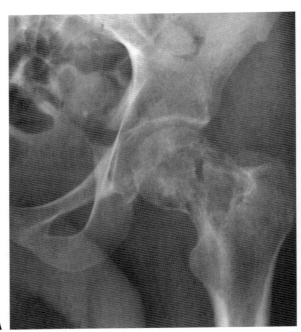
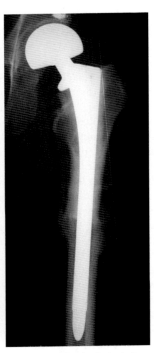

A **B**

FIGURE 20-19 A. Anteroposterior radiograph of the left hip in a 24-year-old man with a pathologic fracture of the femoral neck. He had pain for 6 months prior sustaining the fracture after minimal trauma. This history in a young healthy patient should raise suspicion of an underlying process in the bone. There is matrix production within the lesion, and an open biopsy revealed a grade 2 chondrosarcoma. **B.** Postoperative radiograph after resection of the proximal femur and hip capsule and reconstruction with an allograft-prosthetic composite. The prosthesis is cemented into the allograft and press-fit into the host bone. The patient was free of local recurrence when he died of metastatic disease 2 years later.

- Surgical reconstruction for pathologic fractures should be durable enough to allow immediate weight bearing and last the patient's expected lifespan.
- A pathologic fracture through a primary malignant bone tumor is treated much differently than a fracture through a metastatic lesion.
- Treatment of patients with pathologic fractures requires the presence of a multidisciplinary team comprised of orthopaedic surgeons, medical oncologists, radiation oncologists, endocrinologists, radiologists, pathologists, pain specialists, nutritionists, physical therapists, and psychologist/psychiatrists.

REFERENCES

1. Aboulafia AJ, Buch R, Mathews J, et al. Reconstruction using the saddle prosthesis following excision of primary and metastatic periacetabular tumors. Clin Orthop 1995; May:203–213.
2. Abudu A, Grimer RJ, Cannon SR, et al. Reconstruction of the hemipelvis after the excision of malignant tumors. Complications and functional outcome of prostheses. J Bone Joint Surg Br 1997;79:773–779.
3. Akeyson EW, McCutcheon IE. Single-stage posterior vertebrectomy and replacement combined with posterior instrumentation for spinal metastasis. J Neurosurg 1996;85: 211–220.
4. Bacci G, Ferrari S, Longhi A, et al. Nonmetastatic osteosarcoma of the extremity with pathologic fracture at presentation: local and systemic control by amputation or limb salvage after preoperative chemotherapy. Acta Orthop Scand 2003;74:449–454.
5. Bartucci EJ, Gonzalez MH, Cooperman DR, et al. The effect of adjunctive methylmethacrylate on failures of fixation and function in patients with intertrochanteric fractures and osteoporosis. J Bone Joint Surg 1985;67:1094–1107.
6. Barwood SA, Wilson JL, Molnar RR, et al. The incidence of acute cardiorespiratory and vascular dysfunction following intramedullary nail fixation of femoral metastasis. Acta Orthop Scand 2000;71:147–152.
7. Bauman G, Charette M, Reid R, et al. Radiopharmaceuticals for the palliation of painful bone metastasis: a systemic review. Radiother Oncol 2005;75:258–270.
8. Bertin KC, Horstman J, Coleman SS. Isolated fractures of the lesser trochanter in adults: an initial manifestation of metastatic malignant disease. J Bone Joint Surg 1984;66: 770–773.
9. Bjornsson J, McLeod RA, Unni KK, et al. Primary chondrosarcoma of long bones and limb girdles. Cancer 1998;15;83:2105–2119.
10. Brahme SK, Cervilla V, Vinct V, et al. Magnetic resonance appearance of sacral insufficiency fractures. Skeletal Radiol 1990;19:489–493.
11. Brown RK, Pelker RR, Friedlaender GE, et al. Postfracture radiation effects on the biomechanical and histologic parameters of fracture healing. J Orthop Res 1991;9: 876–882.
12. Bunting RW, Boublik M, Blevins FT, et al. Functional outcome of pathologic fracture secondary to malignant diseases in a rehabilitation hospital. Cancer 1992;69:98–102.
13. Campanacci M, Capanna R, Picci P. Unicameral and aneurysmal bone cysts. Clin Orthop 1986;204:25–36.
14. Chatziioannou AN, Johnson ME, Penumaticos SG, et al. Preoperative embolization of bone metastases from renal cell carcinoma. Eur J Radiol 2000;10:593–596.
15. Churchill DL, Incavo SJ, Uroskie JA, et al. Femoral stem insertion generates high bone cement pressurization. Clin Orthop 2001;Dec:335–344.
16. Cummings SR, Melton LJ. Epidemiology and outcomes of osteoporotic fractures. Lancet 2002;359:1761–1767.
17. Damron TA, Rock MG, Choudhury SN, et al. Biomechanical analysis of prophylactic fixation for middle third humeral impending pathologic fractures. Clin Orthop 1999; 363:240–248.
18. Damron TA, Sim FH, Shives TC, et al. Intercalary spacers in the treatment of segmentally destructive diaphyseal humeral lesions in disseminated malignancies. Clin Orthop 1996;324:233–243.
19. De Geeter K, Reynders P, Samson I, et al. Metastatic fractures of the tibia. Acta Orthop Belg 2001;67:54–59.
20. Demers LM, Costa L, Lipton A. Biochemical markers and skeletal metastases. Clin Orthop 2003;S415:S138–S147.
21. Dougall WC, Chaisson M. The RANK/RANKL/OPG triad in cancer-induced bone disease. Cancer Metast Rev 2006;25:541–549.
22. Dudeney S, Lieberman IH, Reinhardt MK, et al. Kyphoplasty in the treatment of osteolytic vertebral compression fractures as a result of multiple myeloma. J Clin Oncol 2002;20:2382–2387.
23. Easley ME, Kneisl JS. Pathologic fractures through nonossifying fibromas: is prophylactic treatment warranted? J Pediatr Orthop 1997;17:808–813.
24. Eckardt JJ, Kabo M, Kelly CM, et al. Endoprosthetic reconstruction for bone metastases. Clin Orthop 2003;S254–S262.
25. Eftekhar NS, Thurston CW. Effect of radiation on acrylic cement with special reference to fixation of pathological fractures. J Biomech 1975;8:53–56.
26. Even-Sapir E, Metser U, Flusser G, et al. Assessment of malignant skeletal disease: initial experience with 18F-fluoride PET/CT and comparison between 18F-Fluoride PET and 18F-fluoride PET/CT. J Nucl Med 2004;45:272–278.

27. Feiz-Erfan I, Rhines LD, Weinberg JS. The role of surgery in the management of metastatic spinal tumors. Semin Oncol 2008;35:108–117.

28. Fidler M. Prophylactic internal fixation of secondary neoplastic deposits in long bones. BMJ 1973;1:341–343.

29. Fuchs B, Valenzuela RG, Sim FH. Pathologic fracture as a complication in the treatment of Ewing sarcoma. Clin Orthop 2003:25–30.

30. Gainor BJ, Buchert P. Fracture healing in metastatic bone disease. Clin Orthop 1983; 178:297–302.

31. Gass M, Dawson-Hughes B. Preventing osteoporosis-related fractures: an overview. Am J Med 2006;119(4 suppl 1):S3–S11.

32. Gerszten PC, Welch WC. Cyberknife radiosurgery for metastatic spine tumors. Neurosurg Clin N Am 2004;15:491–501.

33. Goetz MP, Callstrom MR, Charboneau JW, et al. Percutaneous image-guided radiofrequency ablation of painful metastases involving bone: a multicenter study. J Clin Oncol 2004;22:300–306.

34. Greenspan A, Norman A. Osteolytic cortical destruction: an unusual pattern of skeletal metastases. Skeletal Radiol 1988;17:402–406.

35. Gronemeyer DH, Schirp S, Gevargez A. Image-guided radiofrequency ablation of spinal tumors: preliminary experience with an expandable array electrode. Cancer J 2002;8: 33–39.

36. Guille JT, Jumar SJ, MacEwin GD. Fibrous dysplasia of the proximal part of the femur. Long-term results of curettage and bone-grafting and mechanical realignment. J Bone Joint Surg 1998;80:648–658.

37. Harrington KD. Anterior decompression and stabilization of the spine as a treatment for vertebral collapse and spinal cord compression from metastatic malignancy. Clin Orthop 1988;233:177–197.

38. Harrington KD. The management of acetabular insufficiency secondary to metastatic malignant disease. J Bone Joint Surg 1981;63:653–664.

39. Harrington KD, Sim FH, Enis JE, et al. Methylmethacrylate as an adjunct in internal fixation of pathologic fractures. J Bone Joint Surg 1976;58:1047–1055.

40. Hatoum HT, Lin SJ, Smith MR, et al. Zoledronic acid and skeletal complications in patients with solid tumors and bone metastases: analysis of a national medical claims database. Cancer 2008;113:1438–1445.

41. Hattrup SJ, Amadio PC, Sim FH, et al. Metastatic tumors of the foot and ankle. Foot Ankle 1988;8:243–247.

42. Henry JC, Damron TA, Weiner MM, et al. Biomechanical analysis of humeral diaphyseal segmental defect fixation. Clin Orthop 2002:231–239.

43. Holt GE, Christie MJ, Schwartz HS. Trabecular Metal Endoprosthetic Limb Salvage Reconstruction of the Lower Limb. J Arthroplasty 2008;Sept 30 (epub ahead of print).

44. Hong J, Cabe GD, Tedrow JR, et al. Failure of trabecular bone with simulated lytic defects can be predicted noninvasively by structural analysis. J Orthop Res 2004;22: 479–486.

45. Ibrahim A, Crockard A, Antonietti P, et al. Does spinal surgery improve the quality of life for those with extradural (spinal) osseous metastases? An international multicenter prospective observational study of 223 patients. Invited submission from the Joint Section Meeting on Disorders of the Spine and Peripheral Nerves, March 2007. J Neurosurg Spine 2008;8:271–278.

46. Itala A, Heijink A, Leerapun T, et al. Successful canine patellar tendon reattachment to porous tantalum. Clin Orthop Relat Res 2007;463:202–207.

47. Jacofsky DJ, Papagelopoulos PJ, Sim FH. Advances and challenges in the surgical treatment of metastatic bone disease. Clin Orthop 2003;(415 suppl):S14–S18.

48. Jemal A, Siegel R, Ward E, et al. Cancer statistics, 2008. CA Cancer J Clin 2008;58: 71–96.

49. Jung ST, Ghert MA, Harrelson JM, et al. Treatment of osseous metastases in patients with renal cell carcinoma. Clin Orthop 2003;Apr:223–231.

50. Kanayama M, Ng JT, Cunningham BW, et al. Biomechanical analysis of anterior versus circumferential spinal reconstruction for various anatomic stages of tumor lesions. Spine 1999;24:445–450.

51. Katzer A, Meenen NM, Grabbe F, et al. Surgery of skeletal metastases. Arch Orthop Trauma Surg 2002;122:251–258.

52. Kumar D, Grimer RJ, Abudu A, et al. Endoprosthetic replacement of the proximal humerus. Long-term results. J Bone Joint Surg Br 2003;85:717–722.

53. Kunisada T, Choong PF. Major reconstruction for periacetabular metastasis: early complications and outcome following surgical treatment in 40 hips. Acta Orthop Scand 2000;71:585–590.

54. Kwee TC, Kwee RM, Nievelstein RA: Imaging in staging of malignant lymphoma: a systematic review. Blood 2008;111:504–516.

55. Lane JM, Khan SN, O'Connor WJ, et al. Bisphosphonate therapy in fibrous dysplasia. Clin Orthop 2001;382:6–12.

56. Lane JM, Sculco TP, Zolan S. Treatment of pathological fractures of the hip by endoprosthetic replacement. J Bone Joint Surg 1980;62:954–959.

57. Leeson MC, Makley JT, Carter JR. Metastatic skeletal disease distal to the elbow and knee. Clin Orthop 1986;206:94–99.

58. Leithner A, Radl R, Gruber G, et al. Predictive value of seven preoperative prognostic scoring systems for spinal metastases. Eur Spine J 2008;17:1488–1495.

59. Levine BR, Sporer S, Poggie RA, et al. Experimental and clinical performance of porous tantalum in orthopaedic surgery. Biomaterials 2006;27:4671–4681.

60. Lin PP, Mirza AN, Lewis VO, et al. Patient survival after surgery for osseous metastases from renal cell carcinoma. J Bone Joint Surg Am 2007;89:1794–1801.

61. Lipton A. Efficacy and safety of intravenous bisphosphonates in patients with bone metastases caused by metastatic breast cancer. Clin Breast Cancer 2007;7(suppl 1): S14–S20.

62. Lipton A. Treatment of bone metastasis and bone pain with bisphosphonates. Support Cancer Ther 2007;4:92–100.

63. Liu JK, Apfelbau RI, Chiles BW III, et al. Cervical spinal metastasis: anterior reconstruction and stabilization techniques after tumor resection. Neurosurg Focus 2003;15:E2.

64. Major P, Lortholary A, Hon J, et al. Zoledronic acid is superior to pamidronate in the treatment of hypercalcemia of malignancy: a pooled analysis of two randomized, controlled clinical trials. J Clin Oncol 2001;19:558–567.

65. Mankin HJ, Mankin CJ, Simon MA. The hazards of the biopsy, revisited. Members of the Musculoskeletal Tumor Society. J Bone Joint Surg 1996;78:656–663.

66. Marco RA, Sheth DS, Boland PJ, et al. Functional and oncological outcome of acetabular reconstruction for the treatment of metastatic disease. J Bone Joint Surg 2000;82: 642–651.

67. Mirels H. Metastatic disease in long bones: a proposed scoring system for diagnosing impending pathological fractures. Clin Orthop 1989;249:256–265.

68. Nazarian A, von Stechow D, Zurakowski D, et al. Bone volume fraction explains the variation in strength and stiffness of cancellous bone affected by metastatic cancer and osteoporosis. Calcif Tissue Int 2008;Oct 23.

69. Newhouse KE, El-Khoury GY, Buckwalter JA. Occult sacral fractures in osteopenic patients. J Bone Joint Surg 1992;74:1472–1477.

70. Ohta M, Tokuda Y, Suzuki Y, et al. Whole body PET for the evaluation for bony metastases in patients with breast cancer: comparison with 99Tcm-MDP bone scintigraphy. Nucl Med Commun 2001;22:875–879.

71. Papagelopoulos PJ, Galanis EC, Greipp PR, et al. Prosthetic hip replacement for pathologic or impending pathologic fractures in myeloma. Clin Orthop 1997:192–205.

72. Raab P, Hohmann F, Kuhl J. et al. Vertebral remodeling in eosinophilic granuloma of the spine. A long-term follow-up. Spine 1998;23:1351–1354.

73. Rades D, Blach M, Nerreter V, et al. Metastatic spinal cord compression. Influence of time between onset of motoric deficits and start of radiation on therapeutic effect. Strahlenther Onkol 1999;175:378–381.

74. Ralston S, Fogelman I, Gardner MD, et al. Hypercalcemia and metastatic bone disease: is there a causal link? Lancet 1982;2:903–905.

75. Roodman GD. Biology of osteoclast activation in cancer. J Clin Oncol 2001;19: 3562–3571.

76. Rose PS, Halasy M, Trousdale RT, et al. Preliminary results of tantalum acetabular components for THA after pelvic radiation. Clin Orthop Relat Res 2006;453:195–198.

77. Rougraff BT. Evaluation of the patient with carcinoma of unknown primary origin metastatic to bone. Clin Orthop Relat Res 2003;415:S105–S109.

78. Scarborough M, Moreau G. Benign cartilage tumors. Orthop Clin N Am 1996;27: 683–589.

79. Scully SP, Ghert MA, Zurakowski D, et al. Pathologic fracture in osteosarcoma: prognostic importance and treatment implications. J Bone Joint Surg Am 2002;84A:49–57.

80. Siemionow K, Lieberman IH: Vertebral augmentation in osteoporosis and bone metastasis. Curr Opin Support Palliat Care 2007;1:323–327.

81. Sim FH, Daugherty TW, Ivins JC. The adjunctive use of methylmethacrylate in fixation of pathological fractures. J Bone Joint Surg 1974;56:40–48.

82. Snell W, Beals RL. Femoral metastases and fractures from breast carcinoma. Surg Gynecol Obstet 1964;119:22–24.

83. Sugiura H, Yamada K, Sugiura T, et al. Predictors of survival in patients with bone metastasis of lung cancer. Clin Orthop Relat Res 2008;466:729–736.

84. Swanson DA. Surgery for metastases of renal cell carcinoma. Scand J Surg 2004;93: 150–155.

85. Tillman RM, Myers GJ, Abudu AT, et al. The three-pin modified "Harrington" procedure for advanced metastatic destruction of the acetabulum. J Bone Joint Surg Br 2008; 90B:84–87.

86. Tomita K, Kawahara N, Kobayashi T, et al. Surgical strategy for spinal metastasis. Spine 2001;26:298.

87. Tordai P, Lugnegard H. Is the treatment of enchondroma in the hand by simple curettage a rewarding method? J Hand Surg 1990;15B:331–334.

88. Townsend P, Smalley S, Cozad S. Role of postoperative radiation therapy after stabilization of fractures caused by metastatic disease. Int J Radiat Oncol Biol Phys 1995;31:43.

89. Turcotte RE, Wunder JS, Isler MH, et al. Giant cell tumor of long bone: a Canadian Sarcoma Group study. Clin Orthop Relat Res 2002:248–258.

90. Virk MS, Petrigliano FA, Liu NQ, et al. Influence of simultaneous targeting of the bone morphogenetic protein pathway and RANK/RANKL axis in osteolytic prostate cancer lesion in bone. Bone 2008;Sept 26.

91. Weber KL. Specialty update: what's new in musculoskeletal oncology. J Bone Joint Surg 2007;86:1104–1109.

92. Weber K, Damron TA, Frassica FJ, et al. Malignant bone tumors. Instr Course Lect 2008;57:673–688.

93. Weber KL, Gebhardt MC. Specialty update: what's new in musculoskeletal oncology. J Bone Joint Surg 2003;85:761–767.

94. Weber KL, Lewis VO, Randall L, et al. An approach to the management of the patient with metastatic bone disease. Instr Course Lect Ser 2004;53:663–676.

95. Weber KL, Lin PP, Yasko AW. Complex segmental elbow reconstruction after tumor resection. Clin Orthop 2003;415:31–44.

96. Weber KL, O'Connor MI. Operative treatment of long bone metastases: focus on the femur. Clin Orthop 2003;S276–S278.

97. Weikert DR, Schwartz HS. Intramedullary nailing for impending pathological subtrochanteric fractures. J Bone Joint Surg Br 1991;73B:668–670.

98. Weill A, Kobaiter H, Chiras J: Acetabulum malignancies: technique and impact on pain of percutaneous injection of acrylic surgical cement. Eur Radiol 1998;8:123–129.

99. Wu J, Wong R, Johnston M, et al. Meta-analysis of dose-fractionation radiotherapy trials for the palliation of painful bone metastases. Int J Radiat Oncol Biol Phys 2003; 55:594.

100. Yasko AW, Fanning CV, Ayala AG, et al. Percutaneous techniques for the diagnosis and treatment of localized Langerhans-cell histiocytosis (eosinophilic granuloma of bone). J Bone Joint Surg 1998;80:219–228.

101. Yazawa Y, Frassica FJ, Chao EY, et al. Metastatic bone disease: a study of the surgical treatment of 166 pathologic humeral and femoral fractures. Clin Orthop 1990;251: 213–219.

102. Yuh WTC, Zacharck CK, Barloon TJ, et al. Vertebral compression fractures: distinction between benign and malignant causes with MR imaging. Radiology 1989;172:215–218.

21

PERIPROSTHETIC FRACTURES

William M. Ricci and George J. Haidukewych

INTRODUCTION

Periprosthetic fractures continue to increase in frequency. This is due, in part, to the increasing number of primary and revision arthroplasties performed annually and also to the increasing age and fragility of patients with such implants. All types of periprosthetic fractures can present unique and substantial treatment challenges. In each situation, the presence of an arthroplasty component either obviates the use of, or increases the difficulty of, standard fixation techniques. Additionally, these fractures often occur in elderly patients with osteoporotic bone, making stable fixation even more problematic.

The difficulty in management of periprosthetic fractures, regardless of location, is evidenced by the array of treatment options described in the literature without a clear consensus emerging on the most appropriate method.[73,84,125–127] Most recently, treatment of the most common periprosthetic fractures, those of the femoral shaft and the femoral supracondylar region, has focused on open reduction with internal fixation (ORIF) or revision arthroplasty procedures with or without supplementary autologous or allogeneic bone grafting.[22,54,121] Successful application of these strategies can be extrapolated to other locations but must also consider the fracture location relative to the arthroplasty component, the implant stability, the quality of the surrounding bone, and the medical and functional status of the patient.[34]

PRINCIPLES OF PERIPROSTHETIC FRACTURE MANAGEMENT

Mechanisms of Injury, Etiology, and Injuries Associated with Periprosthetic Fractures

Low-energy falls are the mechanism of injury in most patients with periprosthetic fractures of both the upper and lower extremity.[42,78,89,126] Lower extremity fractures tend to occur postoperatively and a relatively larger proportion of upper extremity periprosthetic fractures, especially those about humeral shoulder arthroplasty stems, occur intraoperatively. Postoperative low-energy falls account for greater than 75% of all periprosthetic femur fractures from the Swedish registry database,[89] whereas a majority, up to 76% of humeral fractures, have been reported to occur intraoperatively.[19,148] Spontaneous fracture has been noted to be more common after revision arthroplasty than after primary arthroplasty. This is likely due to the reduced bone stock often present after revision.[89] High-energy trauma accounts for only a small percentage of periprosthetic fractures

and these types are usually associated with a more comminuted fracture pattern than seen with low-energy fractures.[6] Intraoperative fractures of both the upper and lower extremities occur more commonly during revision procedures and with implantation of large noncemented stems.[102,132] The risk increases when there is mismatch of the shape of long prosthetic stems and the shape of the bone.[178] Given the predominance of low-energy injury mechanisms, associated injuries are relatively uncommon. Of course, vigilance is required to avoid missing the occasional associated injury.

History and Physical Exam for Periprosthetic Fractures

When evaluating patients with obvious or even suspected periprosthetic fractures, the history should include a detailed account of the status of the arthroplasty, including as much detail as possible on the date of implantation, the specific prosthesis used, the index diagnosis for implantation, and the relevant history related to the associated arthroplasty. Additional secondary procedures should be carefully cataloged as well as other complications, such as prior infection. The baseline functional status specific to the involved joint as well as to the patient as a whole, such as handedness, occupation, ambulatory status, and any need for assist devices, are a standard part of the history. The time course of any recent change in status or symptoms related to the arthroplasty can be a clue to heighten suspicion of a subtle periprosthetic fracture or prefracture implant loosening.

The standard comprehensive orthopaedic exam is warranted with specific attention to prior surgical wounds about the joint in question; the presence or absence of associated lesions, such as venous stasis or diabetic ulcers of the ipsilateral or contralateral limbs; limb length evaluation; as well as strength and neurologic evaluation. Obviously, in cases of displaced fracture, many of these parameters will be abnormal and not represent the patient's baseline status. However, it is still important to obtain a comprehensive history, as clues to potential etiologic factors to the acute fracture such as implant loosening, osteolysis, and infection may need to be addressed during the course of fracture repair.

Direct observation of periprosthetic fractures occurs when the fracture happens intraoperatively. A pitch change during malleting a trial or final prosthesis alerts the surgeon to the possibility of fracture and should prompt an appropriate investigation starting with direct observation. Similarly, an abrupt easing of insertion resistance can be a subtle sign of fracture or perforation.

Imaging for Periprosthetic Fractures

The diagnosis of a postoperative periprosthetic fracture, rather than an intraoperative fracture, is usually obvious. The patient typically has an abrupt onset of pain and deformity associated with trauma. However, more subtle fractures can occur, especially when associated with significant osteopenia or osteolysis. In these cases, a clinical suspicion is necessary to instigate a specific radiographic evaluation to rule out fracture. The standard radiographic evaluation should include plain radiographic anteroposterior (AP) and lateral views to include the joint in question and full-length radiographs of the bones above and below the joint. Attention should be paid not only to fracture specifics but also to an evaluation of the prosthesis relative to the fracture, as well as the prosthesis relative to the native bone to which it is secured. It is useful to assess for prosthetic loosening, presence of osteolysis, and prosthetic and limb alignment. Prefracture radiographs, when available, can provide insight to the time course of any existing or impending prosthetic failure, specifically osteolysis, progression of cortical erosions, and presence of any cortical penetrations or notching.

Diagnosis of intraoperative fracture can be from direct observation or indirectly based on suspicion from auditory changes in the pitch of sounds coming from mallet blows of a broach or implant. In such circumstances, intraoperative radiographs should be obtained to define the extent of the fracture, which can be more extensive than seen under direct vision.

Cross sectional imaging is not routinely required to evaluate periprosthetic fractures. However, significant advances have been made to reduce metal artifact of both computed tomography scans and magnetic resonance imaging scans, which may help in evaluating subtle fractures or in evaluation of available bone stock for fracture repair.[109,111,166]

Goals of Treatment for Periprosthetic Fractures

In the most general sense, the goals of periprosthetic fracture care are no different than the goals of treatment of any other periarticular fracture. These goals include timely and uncomplicated fracture union, restoration of alignment, and return to preinjury level of pain and function. By definition, periprosthetic fractures are not associated with normal joints. Therefore, baseline painless normal joint function and normal anatomic alignment cannot be assumed nor can return to normal function be the defacto goal. Instead, an accurate history of prefracture function should be elicited to help guide goals and prognosis. In the setting of a poorly functioning loose prosthesis, return of the patient to a better functional level after fracture fixation and revision arthroplasty may be a reasonable goal. If prefracture malalignment existed, a careful determination must be made whether restoring baseline alignment or normal alignment should be the goal. This decision is often predicated on the alignment of the prosthesis relative to the bone on the nonfractured side of the joint, which may provide an inherent compensatory alignment. A unique consideration when treating periprosthetic rather than native periarticular fractures is consideration of prosthesis stability and the potential need for future revision arthroplasty. The additional goal here is to assure stability of the prosthesis and restoration of adequate bone stock to maximize the potential success of any such subsequent procedures.

PERIPROSTHETIC FEMORAL SHAFT FRACTURES ABOUT HIP ARTHROPLASTY STEMS

Incidence and Risk Factors for Periprosthetic Femoral Shaft Fractures About Hip Arthroplasty Stems

Periprosthetic femoral shaft fractures have increased in frequency due to the increasing number of patients with hip arthroplasties. The incidence of periprosthetic femur fracture after primary hip arthroplasty has been generally considered to be less than 1%[68,84] but has been reported to be as high as 2.3%.[7,43,46,84] A recent survivorship analysis on 6458 primary cemented femoral hip prostheses revealed a fracture incidence of 0.8% at 5 years and 3.5% at 10 years.[26] After revision arthroplasty, the incidence climbs to between 1.5% and 7.8%.[7,68,84,105] The risk further increases after an increasing number of revision surgeries.[42] The lapsed time period from an index primary hip arthroplasty to periprosthetic femur fracture averages 6.3 to 7.4 years[26,89] and is reduced to an interval of 2.3 years after a third revision procedure.[89]

Risk factors for periprosthetic femoral shaft fractures about hip arthroplasty femoral stems are related to the age of the patient, gender, index diagnosis, presence or absence of osteolysis, presence or absence of aseptic loosening, primary or revision status, the specific type of implant, and whether cemented or noncemented technique was utilized. Identifying risk factors can both improve patient counseling and potentially improve efforts at fracture prevention. Furthermore, patients with periprosthetic femur fractures have increased mortality.[42] In a recent series, 11% of patients with periprosthetic fractures died within 1 year following surgical treatment.[9] This mortality rate approached that of hip fracture patients (16.5%) treated during the same time period and was significantly lower than the mortality of patients undergoing primary joint replacement (2.9%).

Age, although commonly cited as a risk fracture for periprosthetic femur fracture, is not clearly an independent risk factor. Coexisting medical comorbidities such as osteoporosis,[174] increased activity level,[138] and fall risk also contribute. Furthermore, the number of years after arthroplasty must be considered as each year after arthroplasty has been associated with a 1.01 additional risk ratio per year.[42]

Although a higher proportion of periprosthetic femur fractures among female patients (52% to 70%) has been reported in many series,[6,8,65,167] associated osteoporosis and a higher percentage of procedures being performed in female patients makes gender less clear as an independent risk factor. Accordingly, reports that account for such biases report no increased,[88,139] or even reduced, risk for females.[42]

The index diagnosis may also be a risk factor with rheumatoid arthritis and arthroplasty for hip fracture each being identified as having increased risk ratios.[42,139] Rheumatoid arthritis (RA) having an increased ratio of 1.56 to 2.1[42,139] and hip fracture having a reported risk ratio of 4.4.[139]

Osteolysis, especially near the tip of a loose femoral stem, represents an impending pathologic fracture, a growing problem in arthroplasty, and a complex reconstructive problem. Fracture, deficient bone stock, a loose implant, and an inciting particle generator may each need to be addressed during fracture repair and reconstruction.

Reports vary as to whether periprosthetic femur fracture is most often associated with a loose prosthesis, with some data indicating that the presence of a loose stem represents a risk factor for subsequent fracture[63,160] and other data showing no such association.[89,157]

Intraoperative fracture has a unique subset of associated risk factors. During primary total hip or hemiarthroplasty, implantation of a cementless femoral component presents a reported 3% to 5.4% risk of intraoperative fracture compared to 0% to 1.2% for a cemented stem.[7,41,143,154] Impaction grafting for revision of a femoral hip component carries up to a 22.4% perioperative risk for fracture.[37,102,132] Most of these fractures, many incidental perforations, have been found to occur with cement removal rather than the reconstructive procedure.[37] Revision with large porus-coated diaphyseal stems has been reported to be associated with a nearly 30% risk,[100] and long straight revision stems have an intermediate reported fracture occurrence of 18% with an additional 55% of cases thought to be at increased potential subsequent risk due to impingement of the distal stem tip on the anterior femoral cortex.[178]

Classification of Periprosthetic Femoral Shaft Fractures About Hip Arthroplasty Stems

Postoperative Fracture Classification

The Vancouver classification is most useful to direct communication about and treatment of periprosthetic femoral shaft fractures about hip arthroplasty stems.[34] Its reliability and validity has been confirmed and therefore it represents the current standard for assessing and reporting these fractures.[14,34] It considers the location of the fracture relative to the stem, the stability of the implant, and associated bone loss (Fig. 21-1). Type A fractures are in the trochanteric region, type B fractures involve the tip of the stem, and type C fractures are distant to the tip of the stem such that their treatment is considered independent of the hip prosthesis. Type A fractures are subdivided into fractures of the greater trochanter, A_G, which are frequently associated with osteolysis and remain stable, and those about the lesser trochanter, A_L, which are more likely to be associated with eventual implant loosening. Type B fractures are also further subdivided: B1 fractures are associated with a stable implant, B2 fractures are associated with an unstable implant, and B3 fractures are associated with bone loss and usually also a loose implant (Table 21-1).

Intraoperative Fracture Classification

The original Vancouver classification was developed to describe postoperative fractures, but has been expanded to address intraoperative periprosthetic fractures.[96] Similar to the original, the intraoperative Vancouver classification divides fractures into three zones: type A being of the proximal metaphysis without extension to the diaphysis, type B are diaphyseal about the tip of the stem, and type C fractures extend beyond the longest revision stem and include fractures of the distal metaphysis. The subclassification of each type distinguishes the intraoperative from the postoperative classification and reflects fracture stability: subtype 1 represents a simple cortical perforation, subtype 2 is a nondisplaced linear cortical crack, and subtype 3 is a displaced or otherwise unstable fracture (Table 21-2). The treatment options for fractures occurring intraoperatively varies somewhat based on when the fracture was detected. Intraoperative identification, in general, leads to more surgical interventions than identification in the recovery room or later (see Table 21-2).

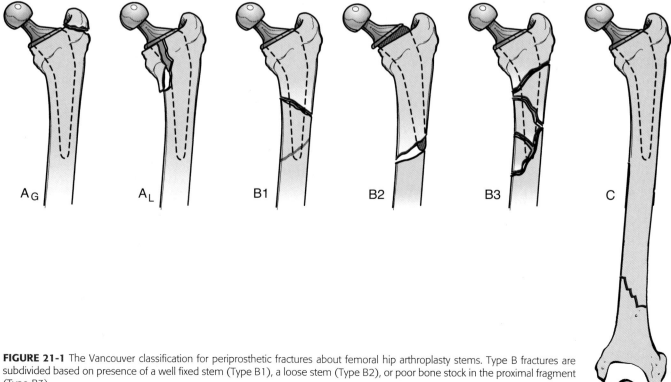

FIGURE 21-1 The Vancouver classification for periprosthetic fractures about femoral hip arthroplasty stems. Type B fractures are subdivided based on presence of a well fixed stem (Type B1), a loose stem (Type B2), or poor bone stock in the proximal fragment (Type B3).

TABLE 21-1 **Vancouver Postoperative Classification Scheme and Treatment Options**

Classification	Trochanteric		Diaphyseal			Distal to Stem
	A_L	A_G	B1	B2	B3	C
Bone stock	Good	Good	Good	Good	Poor	Good
Stem fixation	Well-fixed	Well-fixed	Well-fixed	Loose	Loose	Well-fixed
Authors' preferred treatment options	Symptomatic treatment unless substantial medial cortex is involved	Symptomatic treatment or ORIF with claw plate to treat pain, weakness, limp, or instability	Lateral plate applied with biologic fracture reduction techniques Consider extending plate to include lateral femoral condyle	Uncemented revision long stem with or without lateral plate	Long stem revision with allograft with or without a lateral plate or revision to a tumor prosthesis	Distal femoral locking plate extending proximal to overlap the femoral stem

Treatment Options and Results for Periprosthetic Femoral Shaft Fractures About Hip Arthroplasty Stems

Trochanteric Fractures (Vancouver Type A)

The majority of periprosthetic fractures of the greater trochanter, Type A_G, are stable. They are usually non- or minimally displaced and are stabilized by the opposite pull and continuity of the soft tissue sleeve connecting the abductors and the vastus lateralis.[162] Such stable fractures, when occurring postoperatively, can be managed nonoperatively with symptomatic treatment. Weight bearing to tolerance is generally allowed. Intraoperative stable fractures of the greater trochanter can be managed

similarly, especially when recognized after wound closure. When recognized intraoperatively, internal fixation may be considered. Widely displaced, or otherwise unstable, fractures of the greater trochanter, especially when associated with substantial pain, weakness, or limp, are generally treated operatively with ORIF, typically with a claw plate that engages the soft tissue attachment of the gluteus medius as well as the bone of the greater trochanter. Results with these modern plates represent an improvement over earlier wiring techniques.[89,90] Distal fixation of these claw plates is with cables around the zone of the femoral stem. There is usually no requirement to extend the plate beyond the tip of the femoral prosthesis. However, very short plates have been associated with fixation failure.[90]

TABLE 21-2 **Vancouver Intraoperative Classification Scheme and Treatment Options**

Classification	Metaphyseal			Diaphyseal			Distal to Stem		
	A1	A2	A3	B1	B2	B3	C1	C2	C3
Fracture morphology	Cortical perforation	Undisplaced crack	Displaced or unstable	Cortical perforation	Undisplaced crack	Displaced or unstable	Cortical perforation	Undisplaced crack	Displaced or unstable
Authors' preferred treatment options									
Recognized fractures	Protected weight bearing or bone graft	Protected weight bearing or cerclage cables	ORIF with claw plate with conversion to long stem if implant unstable	Cortical strut with or without conversion to long stem	Lateral plate with conversion to long stem if implant unstable	Lateral plate with conversion to long stem if implant unstable	Cortical strut	Lateral plate	Lateral plate
Unrecognized fractures	Protected weight bearing	Protected weight bearing	ORIF with claw plate with revision to long stem if implant unstable	Cortical strut	Lateral plate with revision to long stem if implant unstable	Lateral plate with revision to long stem if implant unstable	Cortical strut	Protected weight bearing or lateral plate	Lateral plate

Of course, the stability of the arthroplasty components are considered and when loose they are revised. When these fractures are associated with substantial osteolysis, bone grafting is indicated with care to maintain the soft tissue stabilizers.[162] There is very little in the way of published modern series of acute Vancouver Type A_G fractures to guide treatment and establish expected outcomes. Much of the available information includes or is exclusively related to treatment of greater trochanteric osteotomies or nonunions.[52,87,89,90] In a recent series of 31 cases of claw plate fixation of the greater trochanter, only 8 were for acute fracture.[90] Results for these patients were not distinguished. Overall, union occurred in 28 of 31 patients with 3 having fibrous union of the trochanter. Other complications included painful bursitis requiring plate removal in 3 patients and deep infection in one. In the setting of greater trochanteric nonunion, adjunctive vertically oriented wires have resulted in better osseous contact and union.[166]

Shaft Fractures (Vancouver Type B)

The difficulty in management of periprosthetic femoral shaft fractures is evidenced by the array of treatment options described without a clear consensus emerging on the most appropriate method.[73,84] Most recently, treatment of these femur fractures has focused on ORIF or revision arthroplasty procedures with or without supplementary autologous or allogeneic bone grafting.[22,54,121] Successful application of these techniques must consider the fracture location relative to the femoral component, the implant stability, the quality of the surrounding bone, and the medical and functional status of the patient.[34] In the context of femoral shaft fractures about well-fixed implants (Vancouver Type B1 fractures), stabilization using ORIF techniques with plates and screws or cortical onlay allografts or a combination of both has been advocated.[13,53,157,170] Newer indirect fracture reduction techniques have favorable biologic features that minimize soft tissue disruption, preserve the vascular supply to bone, enhance healing, and decrease the incidence of nonunion for many fractures,[61] often obviating the need for supplemental bone grafting.[124] There is little role for revision arthroplasty for B1 fractures given the stable prosthesis. Types B2 and B3 fractures are amendable to femoral component revision with or without adjuvant plate and/or allograft strut fixation.

Internal Fixation. The results of traditional plate and screw fixation for periprosthetic femoral shaft fractures using older direct reduction techniques have been varied.[17,28,40,47,101,103,104,152, 157,164,180] Failure of traditional cable-plate constructs with cable fixation in zone of intramedullary implant and nonlocked screws distally is likely related, at least in part, to older direct reduction techniques and not necessarily to the construct being inappropriate (Fig. 21-2). Soft tissue stripping associated with direct reduction can delay healing, which eventually manifests as implant failure. The addition of strut grafts 90 degrees to a lateral plate offers prolonged construct stability and improved results when these older direct reduction techniques are utilized (Fig. 21-3). In a report on 40 patients, Haddad et al. concluded that cortical allografts should be used routinely to augment fixation and healing of periprosthetic femoral fracture around well fixed implants.[53] Treatment methods varied in this study and included either cortical onlay strut allograft alone, a plate and one cortical strut, or a plate and two struts. The nonstandardized use of adjuvant bone grafting materials in this study further increased the heterogeneity of the treatment methods: 8 patients received autograft, 29 received morselized allograft and 15 received demineralized bone matrix. Based on 100% healing, it

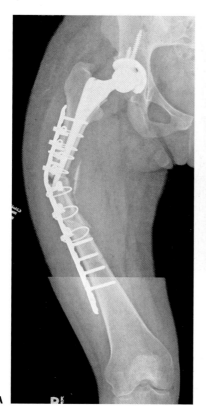

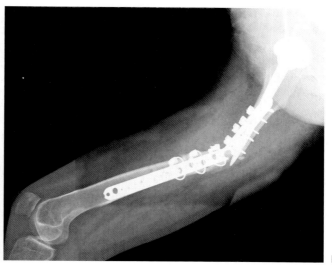

FIGURE 21-2 A,B: High failure rates have been associated with lateral plate fixation when older direct, nonbiologically friendly reduction techniques are utilized.

FIGURE 21-3 An intraoperative clinical photograph showing lateral plate fixation augmented with an anterior femoral strut allograft.

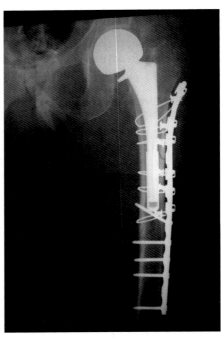

FIGURE 21-4 AP view of the traditional Ogden type construct with cable fixation proximally and nonlocked screw fixation distally.

is logical to conclude that the use of strut allografts plus adjuvant bone graft and/or lateral plate fixation can achieve good results. However, it may be overstated to conclude from this study that allograft is a requirement for treatment of Vancouver B1 fractures. Newer biologic plating techniques that maximally preserve the soft tissue attachments about a fracture have been shown to be successful without adjuvant bone grafting for fractures in other anatomic areas that traditionally were treated with adjuvant bone grafts.

Ricci et al. and Abhaykumar et al. were among the first to apply these methods to Vancouver Type B1 periprosthetic femoral shaft fractures.[2,124] Indirect fracture reduction and a single, laterally applied plate without the use of structural allograft nor any other substitute was uniformly utilized in the series of Ricci et al.[124] Union occurred after the index procedure in all of the 41 patients who lived beyond the perioperative period. The average time required for healing was relatively short, 11 weeks, and was very homogenous with the standard deviation being only ± 4 weeks. All patients healed in satisfactory alignment (less than 5 degrees of malalignment). Although minor implant related complications, such as cable fracture, occurred in 3 patients, this did not appear to complicate the healing process. Each of these three fractures healed at between 10 and 12 weeks in satisfactory alignment and without the need for further operation. Care in preserving the soft tissue envelope around the fracture was attributed to the consistent healing. These results compare favorably to treatment of similar fractures using cortical onlay grafts alone,[21,22,53,170] where nonunion requiring revision surgery has been reported in 8% to 10% of cases[21,22,170] and where angular malunion has been reported to occur in 5% to 10% of cases.[21,53] The reason for the higher malunion rate seen when allograft strut fixation is used alone may be because these struts cannot be bent or contoured as can plates. Fracture alignment, therefore, cannot be adjusted with struts as precisely as with the use of plates.

A host of biomechanical studies exist to define the characteristics of various plate constructs used for Vancouver Type B fractures.[16,32,33,45,153,179] The Ogden type construct (Fig. 21-4), cables proximally and standard nonlocked screws distally, is the typical control construct. Prior to the advent of locking

plates, cortical allograft struts either in place of or in addition to the Ogden concept were the focus of testing.[32,33] More recently, proximal unicortical locking screws either in lieu of or in addition to cables have been investigated.[45,153,179] In each of these studies, the stiffness of various experimental constructs was greater than the Ogden construct, but the fatigue characteristics were not investigated in the majority of studies, limiting the clinical applicability of these investigations.[32,33,45,179] The recent clinical series utilizing modern biologic plating techniques have shown good results with slight modification of the Ogden construct: addition of unicortical locked screws in the proximal segment to augment (but not replace) cables, or bicortical locked screws in the distal segment to augment nonlocked screws in the presence of osteoporotic bone (Fig. 21-5).[2,124] Unicortical locked screws alone, without cables; have not been shown to provide adequate fixation for these fractures. This is primarily due to the poor rotational stability of such short unicortical screws. Therefore, locked screws should be used as an adjuvant but not as a substitute for cable fixation in the zone of the hip prosthesis. Any long-term detrimental effect of unicortical screws inserted into a cement mantle remains unknown.

Several considerations go into distal fixation details. Minimum plate length is to obtain satisfactory distal fixation, usually at least six plate holes with near and far holes to the fracture filled with four or more screws. Locked screws should be considered when osteoporotic bone is present. Longer plates that extend to the lateral femoral condyle have recently been advocated to protect the entire femur (see Fig. 21-5) and reduce risk of subsequent peri-implant fracture at the distal margin of the plate (Fig. 21-6).[126] This strategy is at the expense of a likely increased risk of plate-related pain over the subcutaneously located condylar extent of the plate.

The specific type of plate utilized for fixation of peripros-

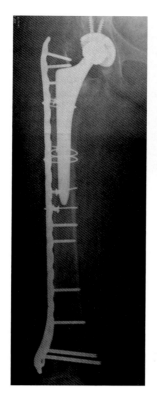

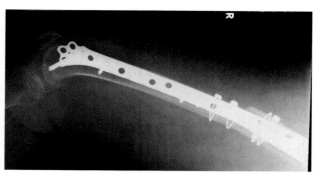

FIGURE 21-5 AP view of a modern modification of the Ogden construct with a long distal femoral plate to protect the entire femur and with locked screws to augment fixation.

thetic femoral shaft fractures is probably less important than the technique utilized for its implantation. A number of designs that employ various mechanisms for attachment of cables through or around the plate are available (Fig. 21-7). However, good results have been achieved with standard plates.[2,53,124,125] A plate that is bowed in the sagittal plane to match the anterior

femoral bow makes sense to assist in obtaining an anatomic reduction in this plane (Fig. 21-8).

Revision Hip Arthroplasty. For fractures around a loose implant (Vancouver Types B2 and B3), revision of the femoral component is typically recommended (Fig. 21-9). This strategy ad-

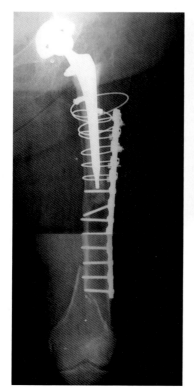

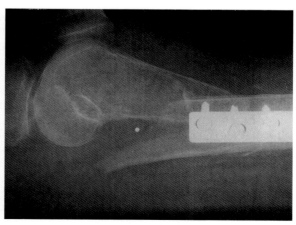

FIGURE 21-6 A Vancouver Type B femur fracture treated successfully with a lateral plate until fracture occurred at the distal tip of the plate. Constructs that span the entire femur (see Figure 21-5) avoid such complications.

FIGURE 21-7 Grommet for stabilization of a cable about a plate. The grommets theoretically prevent slippage of the cable along the plate and reduce fretting of the cable.

dresses both the loose component and the fracture and provides intramedullary stability by virtue of long femoral stems used for revision. Fracture fixation with a lateral plate or reconstitution of bone stock with allograft strut or sometimes a combination of both plates and struts are utilized in addition to femoral component revision. In more severe cases of bone loss, an allograft prosthesis composite, impaction bone grafting technique, or proximal femoral replacement may be considered.[80,106] The overall functional outcome based on the Oxford hip score for revision arthroplasty in the setting of periprosthetic fracture have been found, in a large comparative analysis (n = 232 revisions for fracture), to be worse than when revision is for aseptic loosening.[175] Further, this study demonstrated an eight-fold higher mortality rate (7.3%) seen in the periprosthetic fracture patients. This data is consistent with the high mortality rates (11%) seen in patients treated with ORIF for periprosthetic femur fractures[153] and together paint a sobering picture of the seriousness of these injuries.

Knowledge of specific revision techniques is necessary to effectively handle these challenging cases. In addition to the aforementioned radiographic evaluation of the fracture and femoral stem stability, quality orthogonal radiographs are also mandatory to evaluate the fixation status of the acetabular component and remaining acetabular and femoral bone stock. If possible, the operative note from the original arthroplasty should be obtained to determine the manufacturer of the components, so that new acetabular liners, if needed, can be available. The presence of prefracture hip symptoms, such as thigh or groin pain, can alert the surgeon to potential component loosening, if the radiographs are equivocal. Serologies such as sedimentation rate and C-reactive protein are of unknown benefit in the presence of an acute fracture. If there is any concern for infection, a preoperative hip aspiration should be considered.

The specific revision strategy chosen depends on the quality of the remaining bone stock, the diameter of the femoral canal distal to the fracture, and patient factors such as age and baseline functional status. Through the fracture, cement and cement re-

strictors can be removed. If necessary, the proximal fracture fragment can be split coronally to allow excellent access for stem removal and direct visualization of the distal canal to allow accurate reaming.[149] The acetabular component is typically exposed after the femoral component is removed. The liner is removed if modular, and the acetabular component is manually tested for stability. If it is loose, acetabular revision is performed. If it is well fixed, the liner is typically exchanged, and the head size increased, if possible, to allow improved hip stability.

Several strategies can be used for the femur, but all rely on obtaining secure distal fixation. Only rarely is cemented long stem revision considered. This can be useful in very osteopenic bone with capacious canals.[67] If the fracture is anatomically reduced and fixed with cerclage cables and if the cement is not vigorously pressurized, cement extravasation will not typically occur. After cementation, intraoperative radiographs are recommended to determine if any problematic cement extravasation has occurred. It should be emphasized that cemented reconstructions are rarely useful in the setting of periprosthetic fractures. The most effective strategies include noncemented distal fixation techniques.

Preoperative radiographic findings can help guide the selection of the appropriate uncemented reconstruction. These include the endosteal diameter and morphology of the distal fragment. If the distal fragment demonstrates parallel endosteal cortices with 5 cm or more of tubular diaphysis (usually with a diameter of less than 18 mm), then extensively coated uncemented long stem prosthesis with or without lateral plate augmentation is appropriate (see Fig. 21-9). The distal canal is reamed and a trial stem is potted into the distal fragment. The proximal fragments can then be reduced using the trial implant as a template. Cerclage cables are applied, and a trial reduction is performed. Once leg length and stability are acceptable, the trial is removed and the femoral component is impacted. The cerclage cables are then retensioned, crimped, and cut. The appropriate femoral head length is selected, and the reconstruction completed. These types of stems have demonstrated excellent long-term survivorship in the revision setting and for periprosthetic fracture situations.[73,84,107,110] Union occurs reliably and functional outcome is, as expected for complex revision arthroplasty, modest. At a mean follow-up of 10.8 years, 17 of 22 patients treated with an extensively porous-coated implant had a satisfactory functional result with delayed union occurring in only 1.[110] Concomitant acetabular revision was required in 19 patients. Another similarly treated group of 24 patients had an average Harris hip score of 69 with 91% of fractures uniting uneventfully.[107]

If the distal diaphysis demonstrates divergent endosteal morphology, or large diameters (typically over 18 mm), fluted titanium tapered modular stems can be used effectively. These stems are commercially available in diameters up to 30 millimeters and can be useful in capacious canals. Reaming under fluo-

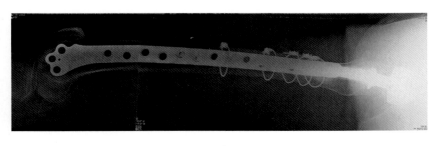

FIGURE 21-8 Fixation of midshaft femur fractures with a bowed plate helps preserve anatomic alignment in the sagittal plane.

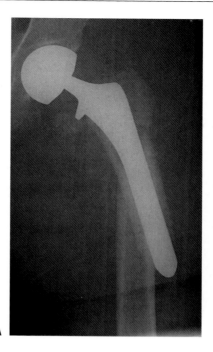 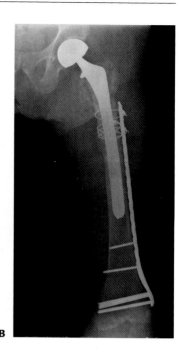

FIGURE 21-9 Treatment of a periprosthetic femoral shaft fracture **(A)** with a porus-coated long stem prosthesis with an adjunctive lateral plate that spanned the entire remaining femur **(B)**.

roscopic control and "by hand," especially in osteopenic bone, can help to avoid anterior femoral cortical perforation. When axial stability is obtained by diaphyseal reaming, the implant is impacted into place. It is wise to place a prophylactic cable at the mouth of the distal fragment prior to stem impaction. The proximal bodies of the modular implants are then chosen to restore appropriate leg length, offset, and hip stability. After trialing, the components are assembled and the hip reduced. The proximal fragments are then reduced and cerclaged around the body of the implant. The authors find this strategy effective for Vancouver type B2 and even some B3 fractures; however, concerns remain about the durability of the modular junction of such stems without proximal bony support.

Rarely, the proximal bone is so deficient that either a modular proximal femoral replacement (so called "tumor prosthesis"),[72,176] proximal femoral allograft,[70,97] or impaction grafting with plate fixation[159,161] is appropriate. The former two methods are typically used in very osteopenic bone; therefore, cemented distal fixation is recommended. Preserving a sleeve of remaining proximal bone, albeit deficient, provides some soft tissue attachment and assists in maintaining a stable hip. A coronal split (Wagner type) of the proximal bone can facilitate stem removal. The new implant is cemented into the distal fragment, and then the proximal sleeve of remaining bone and soft tissue can be cerclaged around the body of the proximal femoral replacing prosthesis or the proximal femoral allograft/revision stem composite with cable or heavy braided suture (Fig. 21-10). Results of these extreme revision scenarios are not as good as seen with the less complex revisions associated with type B1 fractures. Patients should be counseled that neither bone healing nor function are predictably good, but that both can be satisfactory. Twenty-three of 24 patients treated with such an allograft/implant composite for Vancouver type B3 fractures were able to walk, but 15 required a walker.[70,97] Osseous union of the allograft to host femur occurred in 80% and union of the greater trochanter occurred in 68%. At a mean follow-up of 5.1 years, 16% had required a repeat revision. In a series of 21 similar fractures treated with a proximal femoral replacement and fol-

lowed for 3.2 years, all but one was able to walk.[72] Despite a relatively high complication rate (2 wound drainage problems, 2 dislocations, 1 refracture distal to the femoral stem, 1 acetabular cage failure), the authors concluded this was a viable option for patients with a severe problem. When impaction grafting technique is chosen, better results have been demonstrated with use of a long stem femoral component that bypasses the fracture then with a short stem.[161] It is important to note that if the abductors are deficient, any of these constructs should include a constrained acetabular liner to minimize the risk of postoperative dislocation. If the acetabular component is of sufficient diameter and a compatible constrained liner is not available, some surgeons have recommended cementing a constrained liner into a well-fixed acetabular component. Good containment of the locked liner by the acetabular component is required, and cup position should be acceptable. Contouring the backside of the liner to be cemented is recommended (if it is smooth) to allow cement interdigitation.

Distal Fractures (*Vancouver Type C*)

In the initial description of the Vancouver Classification, type C, fractures were described as those "well distal" to the stem.[34] It has been inferred that fixation of these fractures is independent of the femoral prosthesis. This, however, is an oversimplification of the typical situation. Distal shaft fractures in the absence of a hip prosthesis are typically treated with intramedullary nails (either antegrade or retrograde), and supracondylar or intercondylar fractures are treated with either a lateral plate or retrograde nail. Vancouver type C fractures, by virtue of the femoral stem, obviate standard nail treatment options, and attempts to insert retrograde nails in this short segment are ill-advised due to inadequate fixation within the proximal fragment (Fig. 21-11). Ending the plate at (Fig. 21-12) or just distal to the femoral stem should also be avoided to minimize the stress rise effect. Additional principles and results of treating these distal femoral shaft and metaphyseal fractures are presented in Chapters 50 and 51.

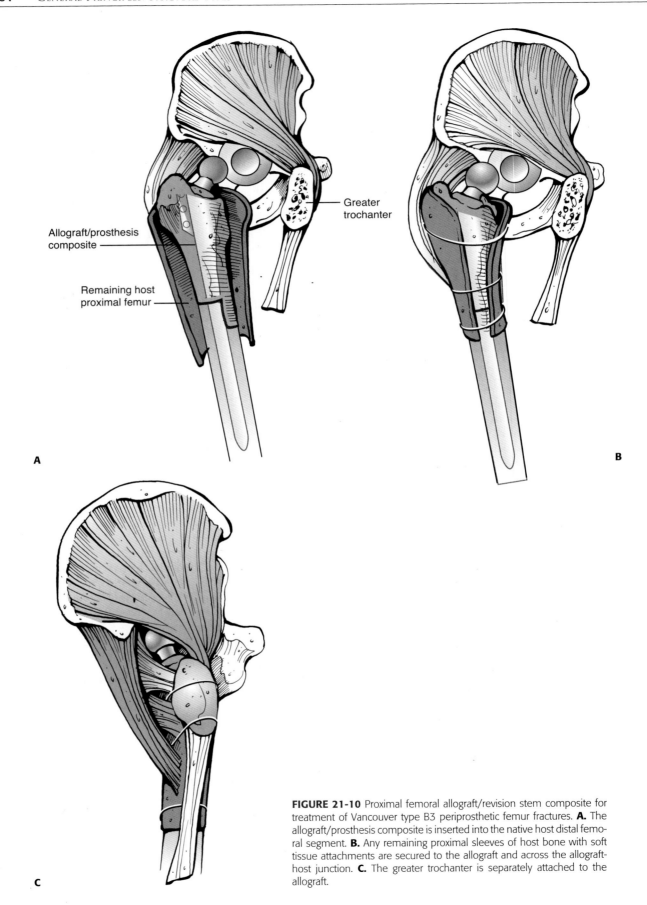

Allograft/prosthesis composite

Remaining host proximal femur

Greater trochanter

A

B

C

FIGURE 21-10 Proximal femoral allograft/revision stem composite for treatment of Vancouver type B3 periprosthetic femur fractures. **A.** The allograft/prosthesis composite is inserted into the native host distal femoral segment. **B.** Any remaining proximal sleeves of host bone with soft tissue attachments are secured to the allograft and across the allograft-host junction. **C.** The greater trochanter is separately attached to the allograft.

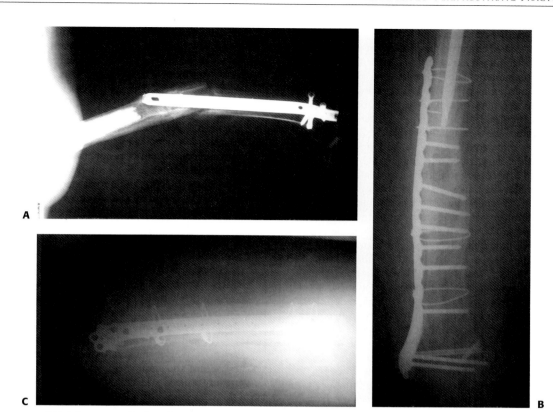

FIGURE 21-11 A. Ill-advised treatment of a Vancouver type C femur fracture distal to a hip arthroplasty stem. The nail eroded through the anterior cortex and the fracture developed nonunion. This was treated with nail removal, ORIF with a lateral plate, autologus bone graft to stimulate nonunion healing, and an anterior strut graft to restore bone stock **(B,C)**.

 AUTHORS' PREFERRED TREATMENT

Periprosthetic Femoral Fractures About Hip Arthroplasty Stems

Vancouver Type A Fractures

Non- and minimally displaced periprosthetic trochanteric fractures are generally treated nonoperatively with a limited period of protected weight bearing. Assist devices are encouraged to preserve mobility and balance and to help avoid subsequent falls. When fractures of the medical calcar are noted intraoperatively, radiographs are obtained to delineate the extent of fracture, as occasionally these splits can spiral down toward the stem tip. Limited, nondisplaced medial cracks noted intraoperatively are treated with one or two cerclage cables. When propagation is present, a lateral plate is used to bypass the distal extent of the fracture. Displaced fractures of either the lesser or greater trochanter are treated operatively with an anatomic ORIF. Limited sized lesser trochanteric fractures are cabled. Claw plates are used for fixation of greater trochanteric fractures. The tines of the claw are placed through the tendinous insertion of the gluteus medius and impacted into the tip of the trochanter, thereby gaining soft tissue and boney purchase. A plate long enough to bypass the apex of the fracture by long enough to apply three well spaced (approximately 2 cm apart) cables. A vertically applied cable is recommended to augment the claw fixation proximally. Initial protected weight bearing with use of a walker is encouraged with weight bearing advanced thereafter as tolerated.

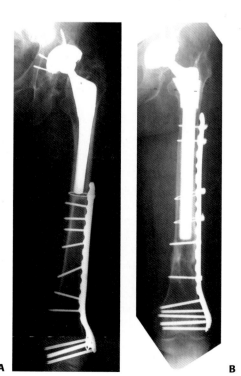

FIGURE 21-12 A. Ill-advised treatment of a Vancouver type C fracture with a plate that is too short because it creates an unnecessary additional stress riser at the tip of the arthroplasty stem. **B.** More optimal plate constructs span the entire unprotected zone of the femur.

Vancouver Type B Fractures

The authors' preferred construct for Vancouver type B1 fractures includes a lateral plate contoured proximally to accommodate the trochanteric flare. Distally, the plate should either have a minimum of 6–8 holes covering the native femur distal to the stem or extend to the condylar region (where a distal femoral plate design is utilized). A bowed plate to accommodate the sagittal bow of the femur is preferred. Three or more equally spaced cables are used proximally between the lesser trochanter and the tip of the stem. We do not find it necessary to use devices to attach or hold cables to the plate, the cables are simply passed around the plate with the crimping connection purposely positioned either just anterior or just posterior to the plate to minimize prominence and to allow easy access for locking the cable. The cables are sequentially tightened and provisionally secured then retightened sequentially akin to the method of tightening lug nuts on a car wheel. This assures that tightening one cable does not result in loosening of an adjacent cable. Locked screws are placed in the trochanteric region after all cables are tensioned. Distal plate fixation is with screws. Two screws are placed immediately distal to the prosthesis through the cement mantle, if present. The distal extent of the plate is secured with two additional screws. If the fracture pattern is amendable, lag screws are placed through the plate. The most critical screws are those nearest and farthest from the fracture, so between holes can be left empty. If the diaphyseal bone is osteoporotic, as it is in many cases of periprosthetic fractures, locked screws are indicated. Locked screws should be placed after nonlocked screws and appear to be most advantageous near to the fracture.

Strut allografts are reserved for situations with associated bone loss (Vancouver B3 fractures). The strut is secured anteriorly with cables independent of an associated plate (cables over the strut and under the plate) and with cables around both the plate and strut.

When postoperative fractures occur around loose implants, revision strategies should rely on diaphyseal, not proximal, fixation. The diameter, geometry, and bone quality of the diaphyseal bone will determine whether an extensively coated cylindrical stem or a tapered modular stem is appropriate. Extensively coated cylindrical stems are appropriate in smaller canals (<18 mm), simple fracture patterns, and in situations where 5 cm of parallel diaphyseal endosteum is available for fixation. This situation is rare; therefore, the authors generally prefer to osteotomize the proximal femur, utilizing existing fracture lines if possible for direct access to the diaphysis, and then obtain distal fixation with a tapered modular stem. Modular trials are used to restore leg length and hip stability. After the assembly of the implant, the proximal fragments are stabilized with cerclage, typically utilizing cables, using the intramedullary stem as an "endoskeleton." Rarely, the proximal bone is so deficient that proximal femoral replacement with a modular megaprosthesis is necessary. An effort should be made to preserve the proximal femoral muscular attachments. The authors prefer to "wrap" any residual bony fragments around the megaprosthesis with cerclage in an attempt to improve construct stability. Obviously, if there are any acetabular component issues, they can be addressed simultaneously, either with modular liner exchange, or cup revision as indicated.

Postoperatively, early rehabilitation is concentrated on mobilization and knee range of motion with weight bearing being protected for approximately 6 to 8 weeks. Patients are mobilized postoperatively typically with 50% weight bearing initially followed by full weight bearing at 6 to 8 weeks to allow some healing of the proximal fragments. A brace to avoid hyperflexion and adduction is used if necessary to protect trochanteric and other proximal fragments.

Vancouver Type C Fractures

Vancouver type C fractures are defined as being "well distal" to the femoral stem. These are usually in the supracondylar femur region and are occasionally intercondylar. Although the fracture fixation is not entirely dictated by the presence of the femoral stem, the femoral stem must be considered. We do not recommend use of retrograde nails for treatment of these distal femur fractures. There is almost always not enough proximal shaft bone to allow stable fixation of a retrograde nail. The mainstay of treatment of distal femur fractures in the presence of a femoral stem is ORIF with lateral plates. We prefer locked plates to provide fixed angle stability of the end segment and improved fixation in an osteoporotic shaft segment. General principles are anatomic reduction and fixation of any intra-articular component. The articular block is then reduced and fixed to the shaft restoring anatomic length alignment and rotation. Great care is taken to preserve the soft tissue envelope in the zone of the fracture and indirect fracture reduction techniques are generally utilized. The main deviation from standard fixation of these fractures due to the presence of the hip arthroplasty stem comes with fixation proximally. It is rarely the case that a lateral plate to provide stable fixation of the distal femur fracture is short enough to avoid a stress riser effect between the top of the plate and the hip arthroplasty femoral stem. Therefore, we recommend that plates utilized for Vancouver type C fractures belong enough to overlap the femoral stem. Fixation in the proximal fragment is with multiple screws distal to the stem into the native shaft fragment and is supplemented with two cables around the plate in the zone of the femoral prosthesis. This construct provides satisfactory stability for fixation of the distal femur fracture and protects the entire femur from future fracture.

PERIPROSTHETIC ACETABULAR FRACTURES

Incidence and Risk Factors for Periprosthetic Acetabular Fractures

Periprosthetic acetabular fractures are very uncommon. They may occur intraoperatively or postoperatively. Intraoperative fractures are most commonly associated with insertion of noncemented components.[55,145] The incidence of intraoperative fracture was found to be 0.3% in a series of 7121 primary total hip arthroplasties (THAs) performed at the Mayo Clinic between 1990 and 2000.[55] All 21 fractures occurred during insertion of a noncemented component resulting in a fracture incidence of 0.4% for noncemented components and 0% for cemented components. The fracture occurrence was most common during impaction of the final component (16/21) but fracture was also noted to occur during reaming (3/21) and during initial dislocation (2/21). This study also demonstrated that elliptical designs had a significantly higher rate of fracture (0.7%) compared to hemispherical designs (0.09%). This increased risk of fracture with elliptical designs was largely related to the association with a monoblock design, one with the liner bound to the shell such that visualization of implant seating through screw holes is not possible. Monoblock elliptical components had a 3.5% incidence of fracture, whereas modular elliptical components had a 0.3% incidence. There was no statistical difference in fracture between the modular elliptical and hemispherical designs supporting the theory that the reduced feedback from the monoblock design may be a greater contributing factor than the elliptical shape.

Postoperative periprosthetic acetabular fractures have an exceedingly low rate of occurrence. In another large cohort study from the Mayo Clinic (23,850 patients), the incidence of postoperative acetabular fracture was 0.07%.[119] A number of factors have been implicated to be associated with periprosthetic acetabular fracture. Although low-energy trauma, most notably falls from a standing height, is the most common mechanism,[119] fractures may also be seen without antecedent trauma or on occasion from high-energy trauma. In some of these occult cases, especially those diagnosed soon after arthroplasty, a missed intraoperative fracture may be causative. De novo fractures in the postoperative period that are not associated with trauma are normally associated with reduced bone quality, quantity, or both. Osteolytic lesions clearly reduce bone stock and, not surprisingly, fractures through such lesions have been reported.[136] Based on indirect evidence, usually in the form of a disproportionately high ratio of females, many authors have implicated osteoporosis as a risk factor.[55,145,147] Weakening of the pelvic bone stock associated with reaming required to obtain a secure fit of a large diameter hemispherical component for revision resulted in a 1.2% incidence of transverse acetabular fracture without associated trauma.[147] Stress fracture has also been reported in association with revision arthroplasty and should be considered with acute pain onset associated with abrupt increased activity level.[4] The prudent clinician should consider periprosthetic acetabular fracture whenever there is acute onset of pain associated with total hip arthroplasty, especially in situations with compromised bone stock.

Classification of Periprosthetic Acetabular Fractures

Peterson and Lewallen distinguished three types of periprosthetic acetabular fractures based on the stability of the acetabular component.[119] Type 1 fractures are associated with a radiographically stable component, one where there was no change in the position of the component compared with that seen on radiographs made before the fracture (if available) and where gentle passive range of motion of hip caused little or no pain. Fractures were considered type 2 if the acetabular component was obviously displaced or radiographically loose and there was notable pain with any motion of the hip. This classification scheme does not account for the morphology of the fracture nor does it include the relative location of the fracture. A modification of the acetabular fracture classification system of Letournel (see Chapter 45) that includes a category for fractures of the medial wall of the acetabulum, a location that is common when these fractures occur postoperatively, provides more insight into the fracture pattern and location. In Peterson's series of postoperative fractures occurring at an average of 6.2 years after the index procedure, there were eight type 1 fractures and three type 2 fractures.[119] The medial wall was the most common pattern (5 of the 11 cases) followed by posterior column in three, transverse in two, and anterior column in one patient. Given the need to consider both the stability of the component

and the fracture location and pattern to determine a treatment plan, it seems that neither classification system is sufficient without consideration of the other.

Treatment Options and Results for Periprosthetic Acetabular Fractures

Treatment of periprosthetic acetabular fractures requires consideration of many factors. In addition to the obvious consideration of patient factors such as medical condition and functional demands, the timing of the fracture (intraoperative or postoperative), the displacement, the location, and the stability of the component should be accounted for in the decision algorithm. The overall goals are union of the fracture and return of the patient to their prefracture functional level with a stable acetabular component. Avoidance of fracture may be the first step. To this end, the degree of reaming is of paramount importance. Too much reaming, especially in the revision setting where bone stock is already compromised or in the presence of serve osteoporosis, should be avoided. Careful reaming without violation of the acetabular walls, including the medial wall, will reduce risk for fracture and also provide the necessary foundation for component stability.[31] The degree of reaming relative to the size of an uncemented implant is also critical. Underreaming of the acetabulum more than 2 mm is ill-advised unless the component is unusually large. Care must also be exercised during insertion of the component. Excessive force should be avoided and failure of the component to seat properly with successive mallet blows should be an indication for increased caution and possibly additional reaming.

Intraoperative Fractures

Treatment of intraoperative acetabular fractures begins with the evaluation of the acetabular component stability and defining the fracture location and displacement. Intraoperative radiographs including AP and obturator and iliac oblique views will help define the location and degree of displacement. Small fractures of either the anterior or posterior walls may not affect the stability of the implant and can be treated without any further surgery. If the component is relegated unstable by a large wall fracture or a fracture that traverses one of the acetabular columns, then additional steps are required to insure component stability that may involve adjunctive fracture fixation. When the fracture is nondisplaced, screw fixation through holes in the acetabular component may be sufficient to provide component stability. However, if a column is involved, there should be a low threshold for independent fracture reduction and plate and screw fixation of the acetabular fracture, especially if the fracture is displaced. Bone grafting of the fracture site with reamings or morselized femoral head may be beneficial to speed fracture healing.[145] After plate and screw fixation of the acetabulum, the acetabulum should be reamed line-to-line for a new multihole component that is carefully impacted and then stabilized with multiple screws. Weight bearing is typically restricted for at least 6 weeks based on radiographic and clinical evidence of fracture healing unless the fracture is of the acetabular wall and is very small.

Sharkey et al. identified nine intraoperative fractures.[145] Two were small posterior wall fractures that did not compromise component stability and therefore had no additional treatment and were allowed immediate weight bearing. One similar fracture had no additional intraoperative treatment but had restricted postoperative weight bearing. The other six were managed with screws either through the component or placed peripherally outside the cup and in four of these autograft was packed into the fracture site. Other than one patient who required resection arthroplasty due to infection, all fractures healed and no patient required revision at an average follow-up of 42 months. Haidukewych et al. identified 21 intraoperative fractures occurring during primary arthroplasty.[55] Seventeen were judged not to compromise component stability and received no additional intraoperative treatment. In 4 of their 21 patients, the component was found to be unstable necessitating a change in component to one that provided supplemental screw fixation. No adjunctive plates or screws outside the component were used. All patients were treated with protected weight bearing. All fractures healed and no patient required revision for loosening at an average follow-up of 44 months.

Postoperative Fractures

Postoperative periprosthetic acetabular fractures are very different than those occurring intraoperatively. Intraoperative fractures are usually minimally displaced, most commonly involve the acetabular walls rather than columns, generally require minimally additional surgical management, and are generally associated with good results. Postoperative fractures, on the other hand, are usually more complex, require a greater degree of surgical intervention, and in general have poorer results. Before treatment can be instituted, etiologic factors should be considered, the stability of the cup determined, and the available bone stock quantified.

Fractures About Stable Components. Fractures about stable components (type 1 fractures) with good bone stock can be expected to have a high union rate with nonoperative management consisting of protected weight bearing for 6 to 12 weeks. Despite union and in distinction from similar intraoperative fractures, the fate of the component is dubious. These components have a high likelihood of loosening. In the series of Peterson et al., 75% of patients treated nonoperatively for a type 1 fracture (stable component) eventually required revision of their acetabular component.[119] Of the eight fractures, six healed but four eventually required revision of their acetabular component for loosening. The other 2 patients developed delayed or nonunion and both eventually required revision. The 2 patients without their revision healed and had no requirement for subsequent revision. All 8 patients had a stable prosthesis at a mean of 36 months after their latest revision procedure. Clearly, these results are far inferior to those seen for type 1 fractures occurring intraoperatively. Immediate surgical treatment for fractures with stable components in the absence of osteolysis may be indicated for widely displaced fractures. Component revision should be considered to accompany reduction and fixation of the fracture in such instances; however, there is little in the way of published results to guide this decision making. Springer et al. reported seven displaced transverse periprosthetic acetabular fractures after uncemented acetabular revision about well-fixed components.[147] Two were identified on routine radiographs, were asymptomatic, treated nonoperatively with the period of protective weight bearing, and healed. Of the 5 symptomatic patients, all were treated operatively. Four patients where the component was well fixed to the superior portion of the ileum were treated with ORIF of the posterior column of the acetabulum without

revision of the acetabular component. In one case where the cup was fixed to the inferior, ischial segment, treatment was with a reconstruction cage. Of the 5 operatively treated patients, 1 went on to nonunion and the other 4 healed and at the latest follow-up had a stable, well-fixed cup.

Fractures About Loose Components. Fractures that are associated with a loose acetabular component, type 2 fractures, generally require revision of the acetabular component and supplemental fracture fixation with plates and screws. The type of component revision is highly dependent upon the available bone stock. In cases with severe osteolysis or pelvic discontinuity, reconstruction typically requires bone grafting, a reconstruction cage, or both. After removal of the acetabular component, the fracture is fixed with plates and screws based on the fracture pattern in order to restore, to the extent possible, the integrity of the acetabular columns. Bone grafts, either morselized or structural depending upon the size and location of the defect, are used to reestablish any residual structural deficiencies. A large multihole cup with screws or a cage are used to complete the reconstruction. There is little published data to guide subtle variations in treatment or to establish prognosis. Two patients in the series of Peterson et al. with type 2 fractures had immediate revision of the acetabular component without adjuvant plate and screw fixation of the fracture.[119] In one, a cemented component was utilized and the fracture healed. The other was revised with a noncemented component with screw fixation through the shell. This patient went onto nonunion and required repeat revision with a cemented acetabular component and plate and screw plate fixation of the acetabular nonunion.

Fractures Associated with Osteolysis. Periprosthetic acetabular fractures in association with osteolysis have been the subject of case reports.[23,136] Regardless of the healing potential of the fracture, which in most cases is nondisplaced, surgical management is indicated for the underlying osteolytic process as well to deal with the loose component that in most instances accompany these fractures. Treatment is primarily directed to management of the osteolytic lesions with bone graft. Revision of the acetabular component is usually required even if stable so that adequate access to the lesions for bone grafting can be accomplished.

 AUTHORS' PREFERRED TREATMENT

Periprosthetic Acetabular Fractures

Treatment of intraoperative acetabular fractures associated with implantation of noncemented acetabular components starts with identification of these fractures. Any change in pitch upon implantation of these components or sudden loosening of a component should alert the surgeon to the possible presence of such a fracture. Direct observation usually identifies these fractures but if any doubt remains, intraoperative plain film radiographs are recommended. When fractures are occult and the cup remains stable, we generally supplement cup fixation with multiple screws without formal plate fixation of the periprosthetic acetabular fracture especially if the fracture is small and of a wall. However, when fracture gaps exist, displacement is wide, or the acetabular component is loose, we have a low threshold to perform ORIF with plates and screws to first stabilize the fracture.

Bone graft from reamings or from the removed femoral head can be used to fill any residual gaps. The acetabulum is reamed to a slightly larger size and a new cup is gently inserted and fixed with multiple screws. When possible, we prefer to have screws on either side of the fracture.

Postoperative minimally displaced fractures, type I fractures, are generally treated nonoperatively with a period of approximately 6 weeks of protected weight bearing. Patients that sustain this type of fracture are monitored carefully at regular intervals thereafter for any evidence of early loosening. Postoperative fractures associated with osteolysis or a loose implant are treated with revision. In these situations, the fracture is typically of minimal consequence relative to the osteolytic process and therefore principles of revision arthroplasty in the setting of osteolysis prevail. As always, when revising one side of a total joint arthroplasty, contingencies should be made in case intraoperative factors indicate the other side requires revision also.

PERIPROSTHETIC SUPRACONDYLAR FEMUR FRACTURES ABOUT TOTAL KNEE ARTHROPLASTY

Incidence and Risk Factors for Periprosthetic Supracondylar Femur Fractures About Total Knee Arthroplasty

Approximately 300,000 primary knee arthroplasties are performed annually in the United States, and this number continues to increase. It is estimated that 0.3% to 2.5% of patients will sustain a periprosthetic fracture as a complication of primary total knee arthroplasty (TKA).[5,30,103] The prevalence of these fractures is substantially higher, up to 38%, after revision TKA.[114] Patient-specific risk factors such as RA, osteolysis, osteopenic bone, frequent falls common in the elderly population, and technique-specific risk factors such as anterior femoral cortical notching have all been implicated as potential causes of periprosthetic fractures.

Osteopenia, from a multitude of potential causes, is a major contributing factor to periprosthetic fractures in total knee arthroplasty.[1,17,28,101] Bone mineral density (BMD) in the distal femur has been shown to decrease between 19% and 44% 1 year after TKA compared to initial value.[117] Progressive loss in BMD has been reported in a follow-up study 2 years after surgery.[118] The authors suggested that stress shielding in the anterior distal femur is responsible and that these decreases in BMD may be an important determinant of periprosthetic fracture. Neurologic disorders have been implicated as etiologic factors,[28,83] but this too may be related to osteopenia from associated disuse or neuroleptic medications.

Stress fractures in the femur and tibia associated with a sudden increase in activity soon after TKA have been described and may be related to relative disuse osteopenia occurring with extended periods of inactivity prior to TKA.[36] In the femur, these fractures may occur at any location and may present a diagnostic challenge in a patient that complains of sudden onset of pain without antecedent trauma and without signs of infection.[27,56,79,83,113,123] Repeat plain radiographs a period of weeks after the onset of symptoms may reveal the previously occult stress fracture or a bone scan may be diagnostic earlier. With an index of suspicion, protected weight bearing is prudent until stress fracture is ruled out. When ruled in, protected weight bearing for approximately 6 weeks followed by gradual advancements is usually a successful treatment plan.

With or without associated osteopenia, several local factors may further contribute to the occurrence of periprosthetic fractures above TKAs. Fractures through an osteolytic lesion about TKAs are much less common than their occurrence about femoral hip components, but these certainly may occur.[116] Anterior femoral notching has been implicated as another risk factor for subsequent periprosthetic supracondylar femur fracture. Biomechanical evaluations in human cadaveric bone indicate that anterior notching significantly reduces load to failure compared to matched pairs without notching.[82] When loaded in bending, notched femurs failed with a short oblique fracture originating at the cortical defect while unnotched femora sustained a midshaft fracture. No difference in failure mode was noted with loading in torsion. The force to failure was significantly less for notched femurs than unnotched: 18% less in bending and 39% less than torsion. Finite element analysis has also yielded results that indicate notching reduces the fracture threshold.[177] Larger notches, sharper notches, and proximity to the prosthesis each lead to increased local stresses. Despite commonsense and laboratory investigations indicating notching as a risk factor for periprosthetic supracondylar femur fractures, clinical data remains unconvincing. The lack of statistical association between notching and fracture are likely due to underpowered studies and extremely small number of observed fractures. Lesh et al. reviewed 164 supracondylar periprosthetic femur fractures reported in the literature and noted more than 30% were associated with notching.[82] Many of these patients, however, were noted to have other risk factors for fracture. Ritter et al., in two separate studies, failed to find an association between notching and fracture.[130,131] However, with only two fractures in each of these cohorts, statistical association would be difficult to determine. In the first study, one fracture occurred from a group of 490 TKAs without notching and one from a group of 180 TKAs with notching.[130] In the second study, there were no fractures from a group of 325 with notching and two fractures from a group of 764 without notching.[131]

Prosthetic designs with a posterior stabilized femoral component that removes bone from the intercondylar region has been noted to increase risk for intraoperative fracture.[134] Fracture, typically of the medial femoral condyle, is more likely to occur if the component is not centered between the condyles. A relatively new potential risk factor has been described in a case report of periprosthetic supracondylar femur fractures through a navigation pin hole.[86] With the increasing popularity of surgical navigation for TKA, this complication should be considered when choosing a location for navigation instruments.

Classification of Periprosthetic Supracondylar Femur Fractures About Total Knee Arthroplasty

The Lewis and Rorabeck classification scheme for periprosthetic femur fractures about TKAs accounts for fracture displacement and prosthesis stability (Fig. 21-13).[85,133] Type I are stable fractures essentially nondisplaced and the bone/prosthesis interface remains intact. Type II fractures are displaced with an intact

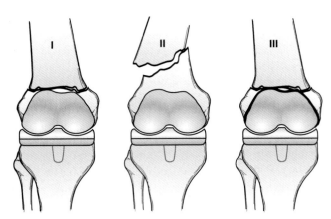

FIGURE 21-13 Classification scheme for periprosthetic fractures about the femoral component of the knee. Type I fractures are minimally displaced with an intact prosthesis bone interface, type II fractures are displaced but maintain an intact bone prosthesis interface, and type III fractures may be displaced or nondisplaced, but have a loose femoral component. (Modified from Lewis PL, Rorabeck CH. Periprosthetic fractures. In: Engh GA, Roabeck CH, eds. Revision total knee arthroplasty. Baltimore: Williams & Wilkins, 1997:275–295).

interface and type III fractures have a loose or failing prosthesis regardless of the fracture displacement.

The shortfall of this classification is it does not account for the fracture location relative to the prosthesis, a factor that has the potential to dictate treatment. The classification scheme of Su et al. is useful in this vein where fractures are divided into three types according to the fracture location relative to the proximal border of the femoral component.[151] Type I fractures are proximal to the femoral component, type II originate at the proximal end of the component and extend proximally, and type III extend distal to the proximal border of the femoral component (Fig. 21-14).

Treatment Options and Results for Periprosthetic Supracondylar Femur Fractures About Total Knee Arthroplasty

Treatment of patients with supracondylar femur fractures associated with TKA prostheses present unique challenges. Nonop-

erative treatment has been associated with poor results for displaced fractures, especially relative to results of operative fixation.[17,28,40,47,101,104] The presence of a TKA prosthesis can complicate operative treatment of these fractures by interfering with or precluding the use of standard fixation methods. A TKA prosthesis with a narrow or closed intracondylar space either limits the diameter for a retrograde nail or completely obviates its use.[93] Traditional plate fixation is prone to varus collapse,[30] while blade plates or condylar screws have limited applicability for very distal fractures or when associated with a TKA prosthesis that has a deep intracondylar box. New locked plate devices offer many theoretic advantages for these patients. The multiple locked distal screws provide both a fixed angle to prevent varus collapse, and the ability to address distal fractures even when associated with a deep intracondylar box. The provision for locked screw insertion into the diaphyseal fragment theoretically improves fixation in the often associated osteoporotic bone. These devices can also be inserted with relative ease and familiarity. The results of locked plate fixation for treatment of periprosthetic supracondylar femur fractures above a TKA have been investigated by several authors.[59,120,125,127,155] Intramedullary nailing represents another slightly more limited but efficacious option for these fractures.[3,48,59,168] Distal femoral replacement, although with limited longevity,[74,104] has a role in certain subsets of patients. Patients with loose TKA prostheses and in those where internal fixation is undesirable should be considered for distal femoral replacement.

Internal Fixation

Older methods of internal fixation, namely plate fixation of supracondylar femur fractures with traditional condylar buttress type plates, are prone to complications. When comminution is present, these nonfixed-angle implants are especially prone to varus collapse. Davison reported more than 5 degrees of collapse to occur in 11 of 26 (42%) such comminuted distal femur fractures.[30] These problems can be magnified in patients with fractures associated with a TKA as these patients are often elderly with osteoporotic bone making stable internal fixation even more unreliable. This is confounded by the reduced ability to gain bicondylar screw purchase due to interference of the TKA prosthesis. Figgie et al. reported failure of internal fixation in 5 of 10 patients with periprosthetic femur fractures above a

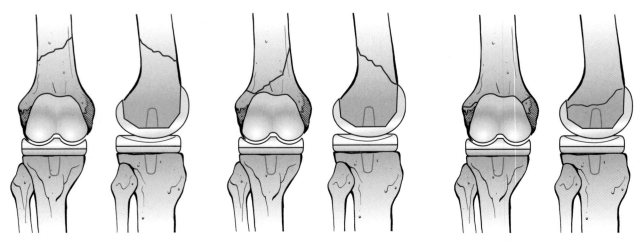

FIGURE 21-14 The Su classification of periprosthetic distal femur fractures accounts for location of the fracture relative to the femoral TKA component.

TKA treated with traditional plating methods[40] and Merkel and Johnson reported satisfactory results in only 3 of 5 such patients.[101] Traditional fixed angle plate constructs, such as 95-degree condylar plates and blade plates, reduce the risk for varus collapse, but have limited application for fractures about a TKA prosthesis due to interference of the femoral component. More modern methods of fixation, locked plating and retrograde nailing, have recently been shown in a systematic review of 415 cases to provide superior results to conventional treatment options for distal femur fractures above TKAs.[59] The overall nonunion rate was 9%, fixation failure rate 4%, infection rate 3%, and revision surgery rate 13%. Retrograde nailing was found to offer relative risk reduction in nonunion (87%) and revision surgery (70%) compared to traditional nonlocked plating. Locked plating showed nonsignificant trends toward similar risk reductions (57% for nonunions, 43% for revision surgery).

Plates designed for placement along the distal lateral femur with the capacity for locking screws have potential advantages for the fixation of supracondylar femur fractures associated with TKA (Fig. 21-15). In contrast to traditional 95-degree plate devices, locking plates offer multiple, rather than single, distal fixed angle screw options. Ricci et al. showed that at least two such locked screws were typically able to be placed across to the medial condyle despite the presence of a TKA femoral component.[127] When the TKA blocked bicondylar screw fixation, unicondylar locked screws were utilized. This combination of bicondylar and unicondylar locked screw fixation provided excellent distal fixation as no distal fixation failures occured in Ricci's series. These results are consistent with those of other locking plate devices used for fixation of native distal femur fractures.[140,142] With such secure distal fixation, repetitive stresses have led to plate failure over the zone of fracture or to screw failure in the proximal fragment in up to 33% of cases.[59,120,127] Of note, three of the four proximal screw failures

occurred when exclusively nonlocking screws were used in the shaft fragment. This study was the first to describe modern "hybrid" locked fixation, where nonlocked and locked screws were used in the same construct. The authors pointed out that inserting nonlocked screws prior to locked screws in any given fragment allows the plate to be used as a reduction aid where the contour of the plate helps dictate the reduction in the coronal plane. Malreductions using this technique were present in only 2 of 22 cases (9%). This compares favorably with the reduction (6% to 20% malreductions) reported with internal fixator systems where exclusive use of locked screws makes reduction independent of plate contour.[75,94,140,142] Only one such failure occurred among the 14 cases where locking screws supplemented nonlocked fixation in the shaft, this being a patient with diabetes and obesity who developed an aseptic nonunion. Biomechanical investigations suggest that locked screws in the diaphysis may protect from this type of screw failure, especially in osteoporotic bone.[35,115] The 3 patients with healing complications in this series were at exceedingly high risk for complications. All had insulin dependent diabetes mellitus, neuropathy, and obesity as associated comorbidities.

Retrograde intramedullary nailing has evolved as a satisfactory treatment option for fixation of supracondylar femur fractures that are not associated with TKA. This fixation method is advantageous because of the indirect nature of the fracture reduction and associated minimization of soft tissue disruption about the fracture. However, problems obtaining stable fixation with intramedullary nails in patients with wide metaphyseal areas, with osteopenia, or both can lead to loss of fixation and malalignment (Fig. 21-16A–C).[3] When a TKA is present, the potential difficulties of retrograde nailing of supracondylar femur fractures are also increased. Some TKA designs, because of a closed or narrow intercondylar notch, preclude the use of retrograde nails or limit their maximum diameter, respectively. Furthermore, the specific prosthesis type may be unknown at

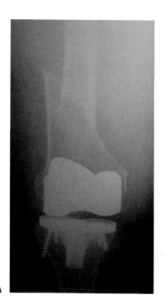
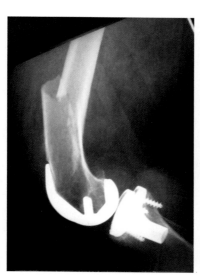
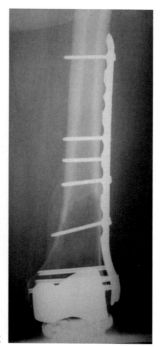
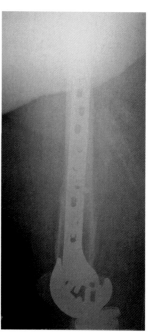

A   **B**   **C**   **D**

FIGURE 21-15 Treatment of a periprosthetic distal femur fracture (**A,B**) with a lateral locking plate (**C,D**).

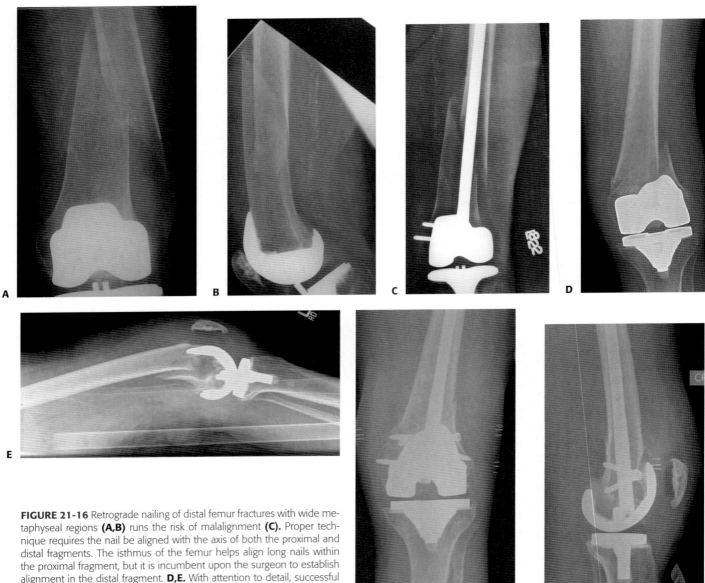

FIGURE 21-16 Retrograde nailing of distal femur fractures with wide metaphyseal regions **(A,B)** runs the risk of malalignment **(C).** Proper technique requires the nail be aligned with the axis of both the proximal and distal fragments. The isthmus of the femur helps align long nails within the proximal fragment, but it is incumbent upon the surgeon to establish alignment in the distal fragment. **D,E.** With attention to detail, successful alignment can be accomplished even with distal fractures. **F,G.** Nails with multiple distal locking options are recommended. (D–G courtesy of P. Tornetta, III, MD.)

the time of fracture fixation. In these cases, the choice of an anterior surgical approach used for retrograde nailing may need to be aborted in favor of a lateral approach for plate fixation if a nonaccommodating prosthesis is encountered. Despite these potential pitfalls, retrograde intramedullary nailing can be successfully applied to periprosthetic supracondylar femur fractures that have adequate distal bone stock and is the preferred method of treatment by some authors (see Fig. 21-16).[48] Wick et al. found comparable results for retrograde nailing and locked plating of these fractures in a small comparative series of nine fractures each.[168] They noted that locked plates were preferred in cases with osteoporotic bone. Another small series of 10 periprosthetic supracondylar femur fractures treated with retrograde nailing resulted in 100% union.[48] The one major complication was malunion in 35 degrees of valgus requiring revision to a stemmed TKA. This may be related to the use of a short nail which, because they do not benefit from the stability and

alignment control that comes from passing the nail across the femoral isthmus, are not generally recommended any longer for treatment of distal femur fractures. Recent advances in nail design that provide multiple locked interlocks at multiple angles may provide improved fixation of the distal segment and may therefore expand the indications for this technique.

Revision Knee Arthroplasty

For patients with loose implants associated with a supracondylar fracture, revision is typically considered. Bony defects, areas of osteolysis, osteopenia, and short periarticular fragments all pose challenges to a successful revision arthroplasty in this setting. In elderly patients, distal femoral replacement megaprostheses are often required to reconstruct massive bony defects. Attention to specific technical details is necessary for a successful result, and the surgeon undertaking such reconstructions should be experienced in both arthroplasty and fracture management techniques. In patients with a loose implant or a history of prefracture knee pain, the routine preoperative evaluation of these patients should include a complete blood count with manual differential, sedimentation rate, C-reactive protein serologies, and a knee aspiration to exclude occult infection.

If available, the operative note from the original arthroplasty should be obtained. This is especially important if isolated component revision is contemplated. Older implant designs may not offer varying degrees of constraint, augmentations, or polyethylene insert sizes, and thus compatibility issues may necessitate complete arthroplasty revision. Previous incisions and the status of the soft tissues should be circumferentially evaluated and the neurovascular status of the limb should be carefully documented.

The need for revision TKA secondary to periprosthetic fracture has become less common in the authors' practices with the advent of improved internal fixation devices such as locked plates. Typically, revision arthroplasty is reserved for fractures around a loose prosthesis, fractures with inadequate bone stock to allow for stable internal fixation, or for recalcitrant supracondylar nonunions that require resection and megaprosthesis implantation. Surgeons who treat periprosthetic fractures around TKA must have the expertise and technical support to be able to perform either long-stemmed revision TKA or revision to a megaprosthesis, as one is often unable to determine which reconstructive option is necessary until the fracture has been exposed in the operating room. Bony defects secondary to comminution, multiple previous procedures, the presence of broken hardware, and the presence of deformity all may present technical challenges to a successful outcome.

Revision TKA with intramedullary femoral stems that engage the diaphysis and simultaneously stabilize the fracture can be used. Cemented stems may be used, but care must be taken to prevent extrusion of cement into the fracture site. Allograft struts with cerclage wiring can be used to reinforce the stability provided by a long stem prosthesis. It is very unusual, however,

to have distal femoral bone stock that is inadequate for internal fixation yet adequate for formal revision. The ideal indication for long stem revision TKA would be the presence of adequate bone stock in the face of a supracondylar fracture with a grossly loose femoral component.[5,36] Most of the clinical data evaluating the outcomes of a simultaneous revision arthroplasty with intramedullary stem fixation of a supracondylar fracture have been gathered from the treatment of distal femoral nonunion. Kress et al.[76] reported a small series of nonunions about the knee treated successfully with revision and uncemented femoral stems with bone grafting. They used uncemented femoral stems and bone grafting and achieved union in 6 months.

Distal femoral replacement megaprostheses have been used for salvage of failed internal fixation of supracondylar periprosthetic femur fractures. The long-term results of the kinematic rotating hinge prosthesis for oncologic resections about the knee have been good, with a 10-year survivorship of approximately 90%. As their success becomes more predictable, the indications for megaprostheses are expanding. Elderly patients with refractory periprosthetic supracondylar nonunions (Fig. 21-17) or those with acute fractures with bone stock inadequate for internal fixation are reasonable candidates for megaprostheses. Davila et al. have reported a small series of supracondylar distal femoral nonunions treated with a megaprostheses in elderly patients.[29] They have shown that a cemented megaprosthesis in this patient population permits early ambulation and return to activities of daily living. Freedman performed distal femoral replacement in 5 elderly patients with acute fractures and reported four good results and one poor result secondary to infection.[44] The 4 patients with good results regained ambulation in less than 1 month and had an average arc of motion of 99 degrees. All patients had some degree of extension lag.

For a younger, active patient, an allograft prosthetic composite may be a better alternative. Distal femoral reconstruction with an allograft prosthetic composite, providing a biologic interface, can help restore bone stock and potentially make future

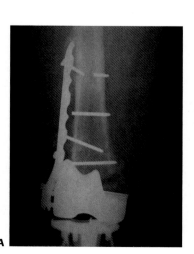
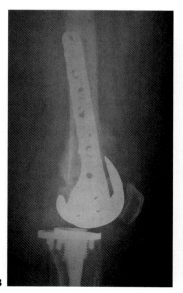
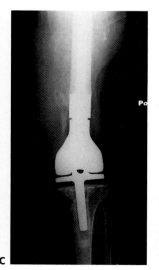
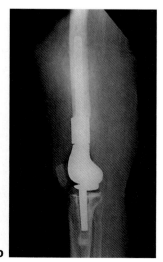

A   B   C   D

FIGURE 21-17 A periprosthetic distal femoral nonunion after ORIF **(A,B)** treated with a distal femoral replacement **(C,D)**.

revision easier.[25,36] Kraay et al. have reported a series of allograft prosthetic reconstructions for the treatment of supracondylar fractures in patients with TKAs.[74] At a minimum 2 year follow-up, the mean Knee Society score was 71 and the mean arc of motion was 96 degrees. All femoral components were well fixed at follow-up. Results of this study indicate that large segmental distal femoral allograft prosthetic composites can be a reasonable treatment method in this setting.

AUTHORS' PREFERRED TREATMENT

Periprosthetic Supracondylar Femur Fractures About Total Knee Arthroplasty

The vast majority of periprosthetic supracondylar femur fractures about TKA are in the presence of a stable femoral component. Therefore, ORIF is generally performed in this scenario. For fractures that are at the diaphyseal-metaphyseal junction, retrograde intramedullary nailing is usually our treatment of choice. Of course, it is incumbent upon the surgeon to clearly identify the femoral component type and to assure that retrograde nailing through the intercondylar box is possible. If so, standard retrograde nailing technique is utilized. A critical aspect of this procedure is the trajectory of the starting point in the distal fragment. This trajectory must be collinear with a long axis to the femur in both the sagittal and coronal planes to assure proper alignment. Given the often coexistent osteopenic bone and wide metaphyseal areas in this patient population, an initial opening reamer passed in an ideal trajectory will not necessarily guarantee that subsequent reamers and the retrograde nail will follow the same path. Therefore, a surgeon must be prepared to utilize supplementary techniques to assure that the nail is aligned properly with the distal fragment. We prefer the use of blocking screws. These screws are place anterior to posterior to control varus-valgus alignment and from lateral to medial to control flexion-extension alignment. The blocking screws should be placed relatively near the fracture to optimally affect alignment. Additional technical details of blocking screw placement can be found in multi-

ple chapters throughout this book including Chapter 7, Chapter 51, and Chapter 55.

Fractures that are distal to the diaphyseal/metaphyseal junction are treated with ORIF with locked plates, even when fracture extension is extremely distal. We have found that locked plating constructs offer satisfactory fixation distally even in these short segments (Fig. 21-18). An important principle for plate fixation of these fractures is the use of biologically friendly, indirect, fracture reduction techniques. A lateral plate is applied and fixed distally first with non-locked then with locked screws. Proximally, fixation is with nonlocked or locked screws depending on the presence of osteoporosis.

A unique situation that is becoming more and more common is periprosthetic fracture between a TKA and THA, the so-called interprosthetic fracture.[92] These fractures have been found to be in the supracondylar region above the TKA about two times more frequently than in the shaft about the THA stem. Treatment of these interprosthetic fractures should follow the principles of the individual type of fracture encountered and simultaneously protect against future fracture. This situation almost universally lends to plate fixation with a long distal femoral locking plate that spans from the distal femur to overlap with the region of the femoral stem (Fig. 21-19) as described for treatment of Vancouver type C fractures taking into account the issues of distal fixation in the presence of the TKA femoral component discussed in this section.

Revision arthroplasty is typically chosen for fractures around loose implants and fractures of the distal femur with distal fragments that offer no reasonable opportunity for internal fixation. Revision of femoral components typically requires metal augmentation due to the inevitable bone deficiency associated with component removal. Stems should be used routinely, and it is recommended that the stems engage the femoral diaphysis both for alignment and fixation reasons. Commercially available metaphyseal sleeves and trabecular metal cones can be useful for managing capacious metaphyseal defects. It should be noted that implants with increased varus-valgus constraint and hinged implants

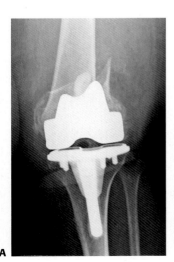
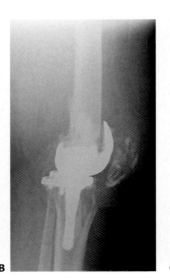
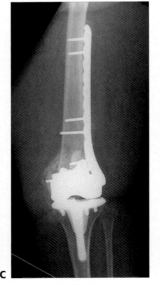
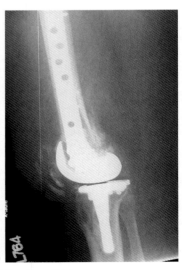

A   **B**   **C**   **D**

FIGURE 21-18 An extreme distal periprosthetic fracture above a TKA **(A,B)** treated successfully with a distal lateral femoral locking plate **(C,D)**.

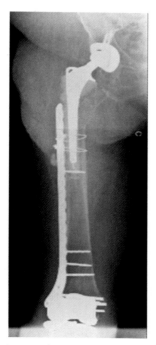

FIGURE 21-19 An interprosthetic fracture located in the distal femur is treated with a long distal lateral femoral locking plate that protects the entire femur by overlapping with the hip arthroplasty stem.

should be available, since ligamentous insufficiency is common in this setting. More commonly, with a distal femoral fracture above a loose implant, there is simply not enough bone to support a traditional revision, even with the use of diaphyseal engaging stems. This situation is not uncommon in the elderly, low demand patient. In these cases, a modular megaprosthesis (distal femoral replacement) is performed. Careful dissection of the residual distal femoral bone is performed to avoid vascular injury. Various modular segments are available to manage metaphyseal bone loss due to fracture comminution, yet still allow restoration of appropriate leg length, limb alignment, and knee stability. Cement fixation is typically used in this setting.

PERIPROSTHETIC TIBIA AND PATELLA FRACTURES ABOUT TOTAL KNEE ARTHROPLASTY

Incidence and Risk Factors for Periprosthetic Tibia and Patella Fractures About Total Knee Arthroplasty

The frequency of periprosthetic tibia and patella fractures about TKA is substantially less than that for fracture on the femoral side of these prostheses. An analysis of fractures about TKAs from the Mayo Clinic joint registry published in 1999 indicated that postoperative fracture after primary TKA occurred with an incidence of 0.4% in the tibia, 0.7% in the patella, and 0.9% in the femur. In our unpublished collective experience, however, periprosthetic fractures above a TKA are much more than twice as common as those below, and in several published series, the frequency of all three of these fractures is substantially higher,

with distal femur fractures occurring in up to 38% and patella fractures occurring in up to 21% of revision TKAs.[5,30,114,128,158]

Etiologic factors related to periprosthetic tibia and patella fractures may be either systemic or local. Systemic risk factors are not unique to these anatomic locations and are therefore similar to those for other types of periprosthetic fractures and primarily includes osteopenia from a variety of causes. Patients with RA, especially those taking corticosteroids, are at a particularly high risk for fracture about a TKA.[10,17,60] BMD in the tibia below the tibial component has been shown to progressively decrease at 3 years follow-up after arthroplasty.[118,165] Wang et. al found that alendronate taken for 6 months postoperatively improves BMD.[165]

Patella

Patellar fracture is the second most frequent periprosthetic fracture around the knee joint, and given the critical nature of the extensor mechanism for knee function, these fractures are significant to the ultimate arthroplasty success. Fractures of the patella generally occur postoperatively and may occur with either unresurfaced or resurfaced cases.[20,146] Chalidi et al.,[20] in a literature review, found that only 11.68% of 539 reported fractures were directly associated with trauma. The remaining occurred spontaneously and most fractures occurred during the first 2 years after arthroplasty. Etiologic factors specific to the patella are component design, excessive resection of bone, limb and prosthesis alignment, and presence or absence of a lateral release.[15,18,39,49,58] Intraoperative fractures, although uncommon, can occur with aggressive clamping of the patella component, bone resection leaving less than 10 to 15 mm of bone, and in the setting of revision arthroplasty in cases with poor remaining bone stock. Devascularization of the patella from lateral retinacular release may be a risk factor for subsequent fracture as well as for failure of subsequent fracture management. Tria et al. reported that all 18 patella fractures in a series of 504 primary TKAs were associated with a prior lateral release.[158] In this series, 4% of those with lateral release (n = 413) had subsequent fracture of the patella compared to 0% of those without lateral release (n = 91). The association of lateral release and fracture was significant. However, opposite results were found in another study by Ritter and Campbell.[128] In this series, unlike Tria's series, a vast majority of the 555 patients did not have a lateral release (n = 471). Fractures occurred in 1.2% of cases with and 3.6% of those without lateral release. These conflicting reports, both from large series, make it difficult to determine if lateral release should be considered an independent risk factor for patella fracture.

Tibia

Local risk factors for periprosthetic tibia and patella fractures may be related to technique as well as to implant design. Osteotomy of the tibial tubercle facilitates exposure for the very stiff knee but it reduces the structural integrity of the proximal tibia. In a small series of nine TKAs with tibial tubercle osteotomy, Ritter et. al reported two proximal tibia fractures.[129] Both cases occurred soon after surgery (within 2 months) and each healed with nonoperative management. Any prior bony defects, such as from bone-patellar tendon-bone donor sites or tunnels from anterior cruciate ligament reconstructions, are additional potential risk factors for fracture of either the patella or the tibia. Also,

TABLE 21-3	Ortiguera and Berry Classification for Periprosthetic Patella Fractures[112]			
Classification	Type I	Type II	Type IIIa	Type IIIb
Extensor mechanism	Intact	Disrupted	Intact	Intact
Implant fixation	Well-fixed	Well-fixed or loose	Loose	Loose
Bone stock	Unspecified	Unspecified	Reasonable	Poor

prior fracture malunion and holes from prior fixation devices for high tibial osteotomy or tibial plateau fracture fixation pose stress risers.

Fracture associated with uncemented insertion of the low contact stress knee system tibial component has been reported.[156] The technique used for implantation, reaming a conical hole for the tibial stem without impaction and absence of trialing, rather than the implant itself, may have been causative.

Unicompartmental knee arthroplasty represents a potential new situation related to periprosthetic fractures about knee arthroplasty. A small number of these fractures have been reported including both intraoperative and postoperative fractures.[77,163] Surgical technique was held responsible for the three intraoperative fractures reported by Van Loon et al.[163] All cases ended up being treated with revision to a TKA.

Classification of Periprosthetic Tibia and Patella Fractures About Total Knee Arthroplasty

Patella

There are many classification schemes utilized for periprosthetic patellar fractures.[49,62,112] In an extensive literature review, Chalidid et al.[20] found that the classification scheme of Ortiguera and Berry[112] was utilized most frequently in the available literature. This classification takes into account the integrity of the extensor mechanism, the status of the patellar component (well-fixed or loose), and the amount of available bone stock (Table 21-3). Type I fractures have an intact extensor mechanism and a stable implant, type II have disruption of the extensor mechanism with or without a stable implant, and type III an intact extensor mechanism and a loose implant. Type III subtype A has reasonable remaining bone stock, and subtype B poor bone stock. Among 265 fractures in the literature classified using this system, approximately 50% were type III with the rest almost equally divided between types I and II.[20]

Tibia

Location of the fracture, stability of the implant, and timing of the fracture (intra- or postoperative) are incorporated into the classification of periprosthetic tibia fractures according to Felix et al.[38,150] Type I fractures occur in the tibial plateau, type II adjacent to the stem tip, type III distal to the prosthesis, and type IV involve the tibial tubercle. Subtype A have a well fixed implant, subtype B a loose implant, and subtype C occur intraoperatively (Table 21-4 and Fig. 21-20).

Treatment Options and Results for Periprosthetic Tibia and Patella Fractures About Total Knee Arthroplasty

Patella

A number of factors guide treatment of periprosthetic patellar fractures. The integrity and tracking of the extensor mechanism, locations and displacement of the fracture, stability of the implant, and the available remaining bone stock must all be considered. As with management of other periprosthetic fractures, the determination of the optimal method can be complex and fracture management can be difficult. A clear vision of the ultimate management goals, typically restoration of the extensor mechanism and at least return to baseline function and pain levels, helps define the optimal individual management scheme. Treatment options include a range from nonoperative management, ORIF, component resection, and patellectomy (partial or complete). Nonoperative management is usually appropriate in a majority of patients. When the extensor mechanism is intact and even sometimes when it is not, nonoperative management is recommended. Surgical management is usually reserved for disturbance of the extensor mechanism integrity, a loose patellar component, and patellar maltracking. The results of surgical management is, however, marginal. ORIF with tension band technique or cerclage wiring results in nonunion in a very large

TABLE 21-4	Classification for Periprosthetic Tibia Fractures[38,151]			
Classification	Type I	Type II	Type III	Type IV
Fracture location	Tibial plateau	Adjacent to stem	Distal to prosthesis	Tibial tubercle
Subtype				
A	Prosthesis well-fixed	Prosthesis well-fixed	Prosthesis well-fixed	Prosthesis well-fixed
B	Prosthesis loose	Prosthesis loose	Prosthesis loose	Prosthesis loose
C	Intraoperative	Intraoperative	Intraoperative	Intraoperative

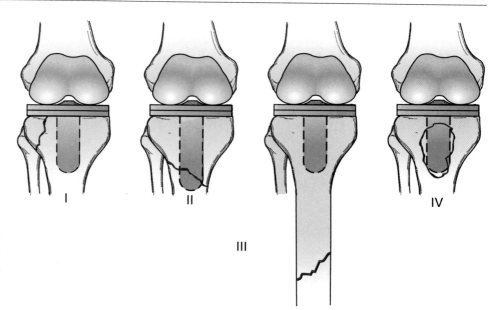

FIGURE 21-20 Classification scheme for periprosthetic tibia fractures about a TKA: type I fractures involve only a small portion of the tibial plateau, type II fractures are about the stem, type III fractures are distal to the stem, and type IV fractures are of the tibial tubercle. The subtypes are described in Table 21-4.

proportion of patients in many reports, with an overall average nonunion rate of 92%.[15,20,24,50,62,69,112,144] Although fibrous union can on occasion restore painless extensor mechanism function, in general poor results in the face of nonunion can be expected. The relatively small and avascular fracture fragments have limited healing potential, which can be negatively influenced by surgical dissection, potentially leading to nonunion and infection. Therefore, nonoperative management is not an unreasonable consideration even in the face of a disrupted extensor mechanism. The presence of fracture and a loose implant is understandably associated with high complication rates regardless of treatment method. These situations usually leads to surgery for either removal or revision of the component. When there is adequate bone stock (more than 10 mm), revision of the patellar component is reasonable. Severe bone deficiency, however, mandates patellar resection arthroplasty with partial or complete patellectomy. Knee function among all patients treated for periprosthetic patella fracture reveals an extensor lag of no more than 10 degrees and a limitation of approximately 20 to 30 degrees of flexion in most patients.[20] However, function is highly variable and related to the ultimate status of the extensor mechanism.

Tibia

Periprosthetic fractures of the tibia associated with TKA are extremely uncommon, and the tibial component is almost always loose. Tibial fractures associated with loose components are best treated with revision arthroplasty, frequently utilizing a long stem to bypass the fracture.[5,36,38] It is wise to have an entire revision system available because often the femoral component will need to be revised as well for sizing, constraint, exposure, or gap balancing reasons. Often, these fractures are associated with extensive osteolysis and therefore may require structural or morselized bone grafting, the use of metal wedges, or in the most severe cases proximal tibial megaprosthesis or allograft prosthetic composites. Maximizing host bone support is critical for a good result. General principles include the use of stem extensions with either metaphyseal cementation or longer, diaphyseal press-fit strategies. More contemporary techniques utilize metaphyseal filling sleeves that provide rotational and axial stability; however, long-term data on such reconstructions is lacking. The largest series

of periprosthetic tibial fractures around loose prostheses was reported by Rand and Coventry.[122] They reported that all 15 knees had varus axial malalignment when compared to a control group. Similar studies have confirmed that varus malalignment may be a potential risk factor for periprosthetic tibial fracture.[91,169] Specific technical considerations include careful soft tissue dissection and retraction to minimize soft tissue trauma to the already compromised skin flaps. It is important that the surgeon undertaking these reconstructions be experienced in revision arthroplasty techniques and fracture management techniques to achieve a successful outcome.

On the occasion where periprosthetic tibia fracture is associated with a well-fixed component, nonoperative management with a cast or brace is indicated for nondisplaced fractures and ORIF is indicated for displaced fractures. If cast management is chosen, great care should be taken to monitor for pressure sores especially in patients with RA and those with diabetes. Maintenance of limb alignment is important, therefore frequent, usually weekly, radiographic surveillance is advisable with conversion to ORIF considered for failure to maintain satisfactory alignment. As with any other immobilized joint, arthrofibrosis is a potential risk factor. ORIF is advisable for displaced fractures involving the metaphyseal-diaphyseal junction (Fig. 21-21) and those more distal (Fig. 21-22). Plate and screw constructs are limited by the available bone proximally to pass bicortical screws. This is highly dependent upon the prosthesis design with regard to the degree of metaphyseal filling. The inability to pass multiple screws across the proximal fragment calls for adjunctive fixation with unicortical locked screws, cables, secondary posterior-medial plates, or some combination thereof.

AUTHORS' PREFERRED TREATMENT

Periprosthetic Tibia and Patella Fractures About Total Knee Arthroplasty

Patella

Patellar fractures are among the most difficult periprosthetic fractures to manage. Operative management is associated with relatively high nonunion and infection rates, and non-

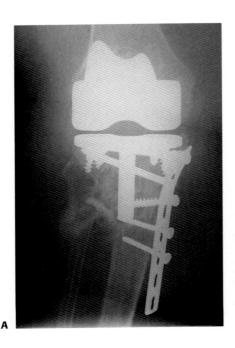

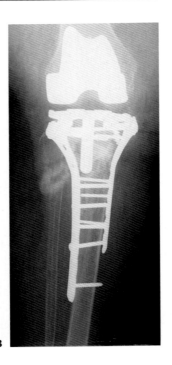

FIGURE 21-21 A proximal tibial periprosthetic nonunion **(A)** is treated with a combination of lateral locked plating, posterior medial locked plating, bone grafting, and adjuvant BMP **(B)**.

operative management may require prolonged immobilization and does not address loose components. We tend to lean toward nonoperative management for these fractures unless displacement is severe or the component so loose that is it may dislodge. A staged management protocol that treats a periprosthetic patellar fracture associated with a loose com-

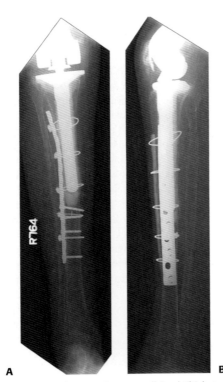

FIGURE 21-22 A,B: A fracture about a well-fixed tibial stemmed tibial component of a TKA had a previously untreated perforation near the tip of the stem. This was managed with a lateral plate and an anterior medial strut allograft.

ponent sequentially rather than simultaneously is sometimes prudent to avoid major complications. Nonoperative fracture management to healing followed by surgical management of a loose component, if symptomatic, is a strategy that takes longer to complete but may ultimately result in fewer complications. When acute operative management is undertaken in the face of a stable component, we have a low threshold for excision of small- to moderate-sized superior or inferior pole fragments with suture repair of the associated tendon to the remaining bone. Patellectomy is our operative treatment of choice for cases with loose prosthesis and poor bone stock.

Tibia

Fortunately, periprosthetic tibia fractures around TKAs are relatively uncommon. When they do occur, most often they are associated with a loose tibial component; therefore, revision is preferred in these situations. Tibial revision for periprosthetic fracture requires the routine use of stems and augments and metaphyseal filling metal implants can be useful for managing bone deficiencies. The tibial base trays have often subsided into varus, and anticipating medial and central defects is wise. The surgeon should be aware that isolated tibial component revision is rare, and commonly, one should be prepared to revise the entire arthroplasty.

On the occasion that the arthroplasty component is stable, our preferred method of treatment is with locked plates. Although there is scant literature supporting this practice, it is our feeling that locked plates are invaluable for these fractures. The amount and quality of bone proximally is usually marginal, where nonlocked screws rarely obtain adequate fixation purchase. Locked screws proximally and either locked or nonlocked screws distally through a lateral plate provide sufficient stability. We, however, have a low threshold to supplement a lateral plate with a posterior medial plate (see Fig. 21-21). It is critical that these exposures be through separate incisions so as to maximally preserve the soft tissue envelope. Even in the presence of a midline incision from the TKA, separate lateral and medial incisions can provide an adequate skin bridge in all but the thinnest of patients.

PERIPROSTHETIC HUMERAL SHAFT FRACTURES ABOUT SHOULDER ARTHROPLASTY

Incidence and Risk Factors for Periprosthetic Humeral Shaft Fractures About Total Shoulder Arthroplasty

Fractures of the humerus associated with total shoulder arthroplasty or hemiarthroplasty occur with intermediate frequency relative to other periprosthetic fractures. Among series that focus exclusively on fractures that occurred postoperatively, the incidence has been remarkably consistent at between 0.6% and 2.3%.[12,78,172,173] With only limited data to rely on, the incidence of intraoperative fracture may be substantially higher. Two studies that distinguish between intraoperative and postoperative fractures both found two times more fractures occurred intraoperatively.[19,51] Many risk factors for fracture have been postulated, but the limited number of fractures in most series, usually less than 10, make scientific analysis impossible. It is logical, however, that conditions that further weaken a bone that already has a stress riser would put that patient at a particularly high risk of fracture after even minor trauma.

RA has been implicated as a significant risk factor. In Boyd's series of seven postoperative fractures, 5 patients had RA. The incidence of fracture among those treated with their initial arthroplasty due to RA (1.8%), however, was only slightly higher than for those treated for other diagnoses (1.5%). Studies from the Mayo clinic, where a large proportion of patients had a primary diagnosis of RA, have shown higher incidences of fracture among patients with RA. Wright and Cofield reported on nine postoperative fractures from a cohort of 499, 144 of whom had RA.[173] The incidence of fracture was 3.4% among those with RA and 1.1% among the rest. A more recent study from the Mayo clinic that included a larger cohort of patients found a relatively low overall incidence of postoperative fracture (0.6%). Nineteen fractures among 3091 patients.[78] The proportion of fractures that occurred in patients with RA was high (31%) but the relative numbers of patients in the entire cohort who had RA was not reported, so evaluation of RA as a risk factor is impossible.

Osteopenia or severe cortical thinning has been cited as a risk factor for fracture, especially among patients with revision arthroplasty stems.[19,51,148] It should be noted, however, that such statement has been made without sufficient data in some series.[19,51] Campbell et al. quantified the degree of osteopenia as the ratio of the combined width of the middiaphyseal cortices to the diameter of the diaphysis.[19] Normal bone was considered to have a ratio of greater than 50%, mild osteopenia was a ratio of between 25% and 50%, and severe osteopenia less than 25%. The validity of these criteria and definitions, it should be noted, are unsubstantiated. Using this criteria, 25% of their 20 patients with a fracture had normal bone, 45% mild osteopenia, and 30% severe osteopenia. It is useful to note that their 75% preva-

lence of osteopenia in this cohort is very high; however, without data on the bone quality of those without fracture, it is inaccurate to conclude that this truly represents a risk factor for fracture. Kumar et al. utilized this system to grade bone quality and found all of their patients with fracture had osteopenia (44% severe).[78] The presence or degree of osteopenia has not been correlated with a particular injury mechanism, outcome, nor a particular treatment strategy. It seems intuitive, however, that any treatment algorithm in a patient with severely compromised bone stock should include consideration of minimizing the presence of stress risers in the final fracture treatment construct in order to avoid subsequent additional fractures.

Other implicated risk factors for postoperative fracture, advanced age and female gender,[98] are also subject to limitations of a general lack of data for patients without fracture. When such data is available, age in particular does not appear to be substantially different in those with and without fracture. The average age of all 3091 patients who had undergone shoulder arthroplasty at the Mayo Clinic between 1976 and 2001 was 63 years and the age of those who sustained a fracture was also 63 years.[78] The female to male ratio was slightly higher in those with fracture (63%) compared to the entire group (56%).

A number of technical issues may relate to intraoperative fracture. Most notably to manipulations of the humerus during surgical exposure or to preparation of the canal with reamers or an oversized broach.[19,51] Excessive external rotation required to provide exposure in patients with large muscles or scars was causative for half of all intraoperative fractures in one series.[19] In half of these, associated overreaming of the diaphysis caused notching of the endosteum resulting in a stress riser for spiral fracture formation during subsequent external rotation. Hoop stresses associated with an oversized broach or prosthesis can cause transverse or oblique fractures.[19,51] Fracture during revision shoulder arthroplasty may be intentional[19] as a less destructive method to remove a stem. Unintentional fracture may occur during explantation of the prosthesis, removal of associated cement, or during implantation of the revision prosthesis.

Classification Periprosthetic Humeral Shaft Fractures About Total Shoulder Arthroplasty

Several classification schemes have been reported for periprosthetic humeral shaft fractures about shoulder arthroplasty stems. Most distinguish fractures by their location relative to the tip of the stem,[19,51,173] and a smaller subset account for fractures of the tuberocities or the stability of the stem.[172] None are universally accepted. Wright and Cofield described three fracture patterns occurring in their series of nine postoperative fractures: type A centered at the tip of the stem and extending proximally more than one-third the length of the stem, type B also centered at the tip of the stem but with less proximal extension, and type C involving the distal humeral diaphysis, distal to the tip of the stem, and extending into the metaphysis (Fig. 21-23).[173] Campbell et al. categorized fractures into one of four regions (Fig. 21-24).[19] Region 1 included the greater or lesser tuberosities, region 2 the proximal metaphysis, region 3 the proximal humeral diaphysis, and region 4 the mid- and distal diaphysis. They classified their 21 fractures based on the distal most fracture extent. Groh et al., like Wright and Cofield, classified fractures of the shaft into three types (Fig. 21-25).[51] Type I occur proximal to the tip of the prosthesis, Type II fractures originate proximal to the tip and extend distal to it, and Type

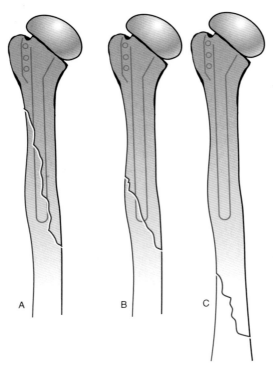

FIGURE 21-23 The Wright and Cofield classification of periprosthetic humeral fractures.[173]

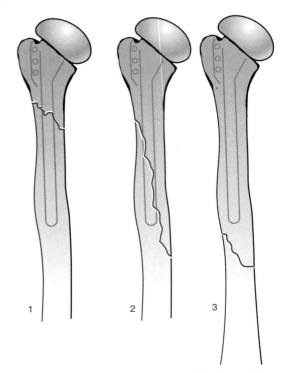

FIGURE 21-25 Groh classification of periprosthetic humeral fractures.[51]

III fractures originate below the tip. Worland et al. considered each fracture location, fracture obliquity, and implant stability (Fig. 21-26).[172] They also made treatment recommendations based on the fracture classification. Types A, B, and C were designated by the location of the fracture: A about the tuberosities, B around the stem, and C well distal to the stem. Type B fractures were subdivided. B1 fractures were spiral with a stable stem, B2 transverse or short oblique with a stable stem, and B3 were any fracture associated with a loose stem. Their recommended treatment was very general, with conservative management or ORIF recommended for all but B2 and B3 types where long stem revision was recommended.

Treatment Options and Results for Periprosthetic Humeral Shaft Fractures About Shoulder Arthroplasty

Treatment of periprosthetic humeral shaft fractures, as much as any other periprosthetic fracture, starts with prevention of intraoperative fracture. Steps include detailed preoperative

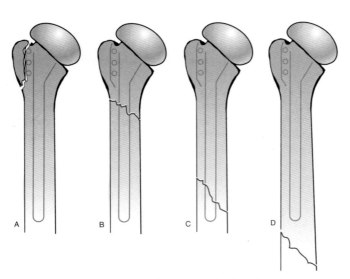

FIGURE 21-24 The Campbell classification of periprosthetic humeral fractures.[19]

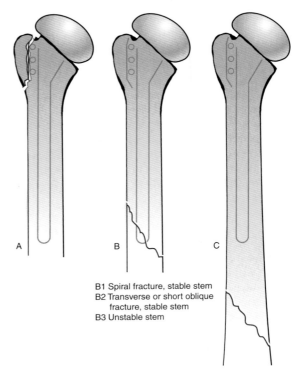

B1 Spiral fracture, stable stem
B2 Transverse or short oblique fracture, stable stem
B3 Unstable stem

FIGURE 21-26 Worland classification of periprosthetic humeral fractures.[172]

planning particularly with regard to templating stem diameter. This requires good quality preoperative radiographs taking into account magnification. Substantive soft tissue releases reduce risk of fracture by reducing stresses that accompany arm manipulations during arthroplasty. Capsular contractures as well as scar formations in the subacromial and subdeltoid spaces should be addressed to allow gentle delivery of the bone so stress free preparation and implantation can occur. Proper sizing of the implant and meticulous care to be colinear with the long axis of the bone during canal preparation will help to avoid perforation. Small perforations that are diagnosed intraoperatively can easily be treated with a stem that bypasses the defect by two or more bone diameters. There should be a low threshold for intraoperative radiographs to assure a split that propagated distally did not accompany the perforation, as this might require additional treatment to stabilize the distal extent of such a fracture. Non- or minimally displaced fractures of the lesser tuberosity can occur with some frequency during placement of the trial component. Treatment of these is generally with suture repair using heavy nonabsorbable sutures placed through the subscapularis tendon and either through or around the lesser tuberosity then into the adjacent intact bone on the other side of the fracture. Similarly, cracks about the greater tuberosity are stabilized with sutures to assure displacement does not ensue.

Displaced humeral shaft fractures are treated with goals of uneventful fracture healing and implant stability. This can be accomplished by a variety of means. Intraoperative fractures of the shaft are carefully examined with intraoperative radiographs. A long stemmed noncemented prosthesis with adjunctive cerclage cables are useful for these spiral fractures. More transverse intraoperative fractures that are not amenable to cable stabilization are more appropriately treated with a long stemmed prostheses and either plate or strut stabilization. When there is compromised bone stock, strut allografts are utilized.

Fractures that occur postoperatively can be treated nonoperatively if the implant is stable and the fracture is otherwise amenable to bracing (Fig. 21-27). This usually means the fracture is middiaphyseal, spiral, or short oblique (not transverse), and there is not drastic displacement, where interposed muscle may inhibit fracture healing. The results of treating these fractures nonoperatively is mixed in the literature and some advocate ORIF in this setting (Fig. 21-28).[11,12,19,51,71,78,98,148,172,173] Kumar et al. treated 11 postoperative periprosthetic humeral shaft fractures nonoperatively.[78] Six healed uneventfully but five required eventual operative intervention: three had ORIF with bone grafting and two underwent revision arthroplasty with a long stem for associated loosening. Failure of nonoperative management in this series may be related to the presence of loose implants. Immediate ORIF was performed in only 2 patients with stable prostheses: both had uneventful union. Similarly, marginal results were reported by Boyd et al. in a small series where nonunion occurred in 4 of 7 patients treated nonoperatively and radial nerve palsy occurred in another 2.[12] To the contrary, Groh et al. reported union in all five postoperative fractures treated nonoperatively.[51] Nonunion after nonoperative treatment is typically managed with a combination of bone grafting, ORIF, and revision to a long stemmed arthroplasty.[78,173]

In the setting of a loose prosthesis with or without osteolysis, revision arthroplasty is indicated. A revision stem that crosses the fracture provides intramedullary stabilization and is usually accompanied by plate fixation in the absence of bone loss. Strut grafts (Fig. 21-29), with or without plates are used to restore

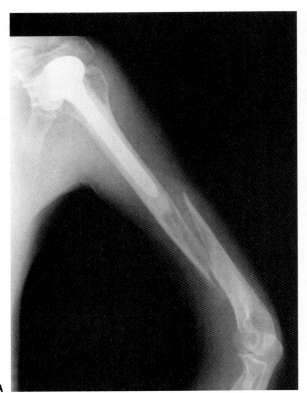
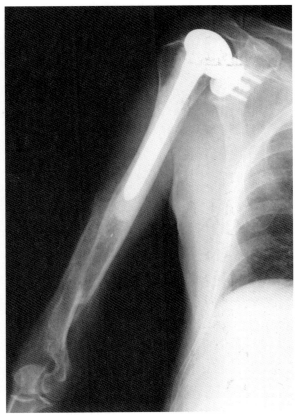

A   **B**

FIGURE 21-27 A humeral shaft fracture distal to a humeral prosthesis **(A)** treated nonoperatively to union **(B)**.

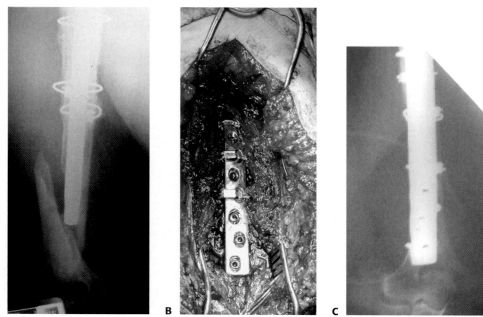

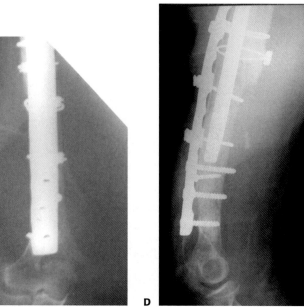

FIGURE 21-28 A. A periprosthetic humeral shaft fracture distal to a revision humeral component. The proximal allograft was used previously during the revision arthroplasty. The acute periprosthetic fracture was treated via the posterior approach using biologic reduction techniques seen in an intraoperative photograph **(B)** that preserved the majority of the soft tissue attachments. **C,D.** A posterior plate with cables proximally and screws distally were used for fixation.

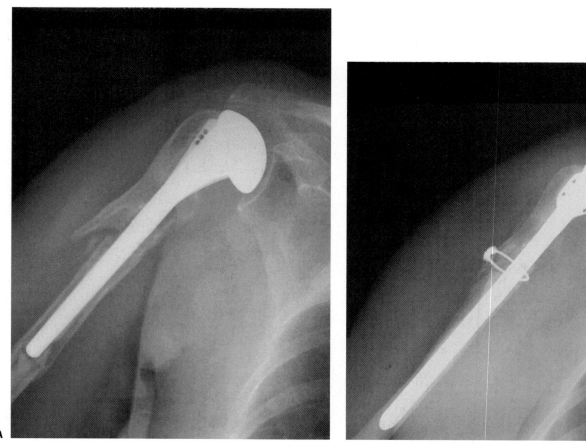

FIGURE 21-29 Treatment of a periprosthetic humeral shaft fracture associated with a loose prosthesis **(A)** with a long stem revision, allograft, and a cerclage cable **(B)**.

any associated deficient bone stock. Kumar et al.[78] treated five periprosthetic humeral fractures or nonunions after nonoperative treatment with revision arthroplasty (three with adjuvant allograft). One of the patients with nonunion had persistent nonunion after revision arthroplasty and ultimately required free fibular transfer, further demonstrating the complexity of treating periprosthetic nonunions.

AUTHORS' PREFERRED TREATMENT

Periprosthetic Humeral Shaft Fractures About Shoulder Arthroplasty

For displaced periprosthetic humeral shaft fractures associated with a stable implant, we recommend ORIF (see Fig. 21-28). Our preferred exposure is through a posterior approach. This is extensile and allows visualization of the entire shaft of the humerus. Furthermore, this exposure allows clear identification and protection of the radial nerve during reduction, plating, and most importantly cable fixation in the zone of the prosthesis. Applying cables through an anterior exposure is dangerous with regard to potential injury and entrapment of the radial nerve and in our opinion should be avoided. On occasion, the non- or minimally displaced fracture, especially in elderly patients that are otherwise poor candidates for surgery, are treated nonoperatively with a fracture brace. Consideration is given to the timing of the fracture relative to the arthroplasty. When the fracture occurs shortly after joint replacement, surgical fixation offers better capability to perform shoulder rehabilitation and therefore we tend to treat these fractures operatively.

With fractures associated with a loose prosthesis, a long stem revision component that bypasses the fracture is used. We prefer to use noncemented technique whenever there is good quality bone to provide a reasonably tight fit. We also have a low threshold for supplemental plate fixation applied using the technique described above. If either of the fragments has poor quality bone, cemented technique can be utilized in that fragment (usually the distal fragment) and noncemented technique in the other. When osteolysis is severe, either impaction bone grafting technique, an allograft prosthesis composite, or a tumor prosthesis is utilized. These are extremely technically demanding cases that are individualized based on secondary factors and should be undertaken by surgeons and in centers familiar with and stocked with appropriate equipment, respectively.

Periprosthetic Glenoid Fractures About Shoulder Arthroplasty

Periprosthetic fractures of the glenoid most commonly occur intraoperatively and are related to retraction. A retractor that is on the posterior glenoid margin to retract the humerus posteriorly during preparation of the glenoid articular surface can cause fracture. Patients undergoing revision surgery and those with severe osteopenia are at a particularly high risk. Due to the relative rarity of these fractures and absence of large series dealing with them, no generally accepted fracture classification exists. Large fragments may be treated with screws or plates. However, commonly, the fragments are small and comminuted and are not amenable to screw fixa-

tion. With inadequate bone support, glenoid resurfacing should be abandoned and the defect bone grafted. After fracture healing, conversion of the hemiarthroplasty to a total shoulder arthroplasty can be contemplated if symptoms require.

Periprosthetic Humeral and Ulna Fractures About Total Elbow Arthroplasty

Incidence and Risk Factors for Periprosthetic Humeral and Ulna Fractures About Total Elbow Arthroplasty

There are few large scale evaluations of periprosthetic fractures about total elbow prostheses. One notable exception is the Mayo Clinic experience with 1072 linked Coonrad-Morrey procedures performed between 1983 and 2003. Periprosthetic fractures occurred with 9% of primary and 23% of revision procedures. These were equally distributed between fractures of the humerus and those of the ulna (Table 21-5). Specific risk factors have not been clearly elucidated due to the relative paucity of published data related to this topic. However, it is probably safe to consider that systemic or local conditions that reduce or weaken the bone stock in the proximity to total elbow arthroplasty (TEAs) would predispose to periprosthetic fracture.

Classification of Periprosthetic Fractures About Total Elbow Arthroplasty

O'Driscoll and Morrey classified humeral and ulna periprosthetic fractures according to fracture location, component fixation, and bone quality (Fig. 21-30). Type I fractures are metaphyseal, type II are of the shaft and in the zone of the stem, and type III are beyond the stem. As popularized by the Vancouver Classification of periprosthetic femur fractures, periprosthetic elbow fractures are further subdivided by the status of the stem fixation. Subtype A fractures are well-fixed, and B fractures are associated with a loose implant.

Treatment Options and Results for Periprosthetic Fractures About Total Elbow Arthroplasty

Treatment of periprosthetic fractures about total elbow arthroplasties depends upon the location and displacement of the fracture, the time of occurrence (intra- or postoperative), the status of the implant (well-fixed or loose), and the type of

| TABLE 21-5 | **Frequency of Periprosthetic Fractures About Total Elbow Arthroplasty by Anatomic Location** |

Fracture Occurrence by Procedure Type

	Primary (748) No/%	Revision (324) No/%	Total
Humerus	39/5%	32/10%	71/1072 (7)
Ulna	29/4%	41/13%	70/1072 (7)
Total	**68/9%**	**73/23%**	**141/1072 (14)**

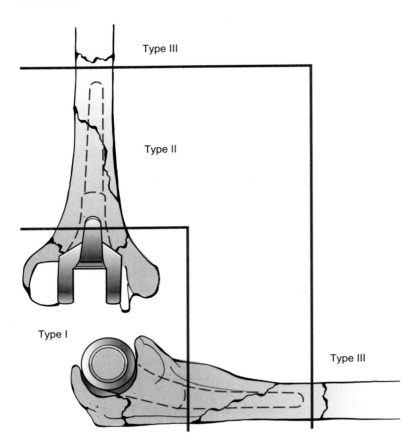

FIGURE 21-30 The Mayo classification of periprosthetic fractures about total elbow arthroplasty. Type I fractures are metaphyseal, type II involve bone occupied by the implant, and type III fractures extend beyond the stem. The subdivisions of these fractures is presented in the text.

prosthesis (constrained or unconstrained). Subtype A fractures are typically treated by either nonoperative means if non- or minimally displaced, otherwise they are treated with ORIF. Type B fractures, those with a loose prosthesis, merit revision arthroplasty.

Type I Fractures

Type I Humerus. Type I fractures of the humerus represent condylar fractures and may occur intraoperatively or postoperatively. Intraoperative fractures are associated with implant preparation in the metaphyseal region. Avulsion fracture of either the medial or lateral condyle can occur with stressing the collateral ligaments, especially if bone resection was generous. This weakened area may be subject to spontaneous postoperative fracture or with minor trauma. Treatment of these fractures depends upon the prosthesis being used. A linked prosthesis such as the Coonrad-Morray device does not rely upon the collateral ligaments for stability; therefore, these fractures with this implant type have little implications regarding prognosis. Nonoperative management is the mainstay so long as displacement is not so great to compromise eventual union as nonunion may cause pain. In the setting of prostheses that rely upon the collateral ligaments for elbow stability, surgical fixation of these fractures is indicated. Peer reviewed data for results of these fractures is lacking.

Type I Ulna. Type I ulna fractures are either of the olecranon or coronoid. Coronoid fractures are very uncommon and usually occur intraoperatively. If the fragment is large, extends towards the diaphysis, or compromises ulnar stem fixation, then cable

or wire fixation is performed. Type I fractures involving the olecranon are more likely to affect function as these fractures may disrupt the extensor mechanism. Thinning of the olecranon either due to systemic disease such as from RA or from intraoperative bone resection predisposes to fracture, and in these instances extreme care must be taken to avoid critical stress on the olecranon, particularly during intraoperative forearm manipulation. Postoperative fracture can, of course, be related to direct trauma but may also occur spontaneously due to the force generated by triceps muscle contraction when there is compromised bone. Treatment is generally with ORIF utilizing a tension band technique for intraoperative fractures. Postoperative fractures are typically treated nonoperatively unless displacement is greater than approximately 2 cm. Nonunion has been reported in up to 50% of these fractures, but fibrous union and lack of displacement of more than 1 cm has been attributed to the generally good results despite lack of healing.[95]

Type II Fractures

Type IIA fractures of the humerus and of the ulna are very uncommon. They can theoretically occur at the time of implantation, especially if a long humeral component is inserted into an excessively bowed humerus. Fractures around the stem of the implant are more likely to occur postoperatively and be associated with osteolysis (type IIB) or with relatively high-energy trauma. Treatment of these fractures should provide fracture stabilization, restoration of bone stock, and a stable prosthesis. The treatment principles follow that for the much more common and extensively studied Vancouver Type B femoral fractures. In the absence of a loose prosthesis, ORIF with a strut allograft or plate can provide the required stability. When the prosthesis is loose, implant revision with a long stem that bypasses the fracture provides intramedullary stability. Unlike the femur where canal filling fully porous-coated stems is mainstream, long humeral stems do not reliably provide such stabilization. Therefore, plate or strut fixation is used. When bone deficiencies are present, strut allografts are indicated with or without an adjunctive plate. Results of strut fixation of 11 humeral and 22 ulnar fractures revealed approximately 99% success at 3 to 5 years of both anatomic sites.[66,137]

Type III Fractures

Fractures of the humerus or ulna distant to the stem tip are relatively uncommon and are usually associated with trauma and a loose stem. By definition, these fractures of the humerus are relatively proximal and may be difficult to control with splints or braces. Control of such fractures of the ulna is generally easier by closed means. Operative treatment is indicated for displaced fractures and those associated with a loose prosthesis (Fig. 21-31). Goals are to obtain stable fixation, adequate bone stock, and a stable prosthesis. When revision is indicated, a long stem is inserted across the fracture if practical. Regardless of stem position, ORIF with plates and struts are relied on to provide fracture stability.

AUTHORS' PREFERRED TREATMENT

Periprosthetic Fractures About Total Elbow Arthroplasty

Fractures of the humeral shaft about stable elbow arthroplasties are generally treated with ORIF with a plate and cable construct applied through a posterior approach. The critical aspects of this procedure are identification and protection of the ulnar nerve distally and the radial nerve proximally.

Formal exposure of the median nerve is generally not necessary as long as great care is taken to pass cables around the anterior aspect of the distal humerus adjacent to the anterior surface of the bone. Proximal fixation is with standard screws or, if the bone is osteoporotic, locked screws. We generally choose a plate long enough to extend proximal to the radial neurovascular bundle. The plate is gently slid beneath the bundle and fixed to the proximal fragment above and below the bundle. Historically, large fragment broad plates have been advocated for plating humeral fractures. However, with utilization of modern biologic fracture reduction techniques, the strength and associated bulk of these implants is somewhat excessive. We now use narrow large fragment plates. Occasionally, fractures about the stem of the humeral component are non- or minimally displaced or the patient is otherwise not a candidate for surgery. In these cases, nonoperative treatment of the periprosthetic shaft fracture follows standard means with a fracture brace. In cases with associated bone loss, strut allografts can be utilized in lieu of or as an adjunct to a posteriorly applied plate. We prefer using a strut directly over the zone of bone deficiency and a plate adjacent to the strut. For periprosthetic ulna fractures, the strategy is similar. Plates are preferred if there is a stable implant with no associated bone loss. However, if there is significantly diminished bone stock, a strut allograft with or without supplemental plate is typically utilized. Revision arthroplasty is indicated when there is a loose prosthesis on either side of the joint, osteolysis, or both.

PERIPROSTHETIC FRACTURES ABOUT TOTAL ANKLE ARTHROPLASTY

Incidence and Risk Factors for Periprosthetic Fractures About Total Ankle Arthroplasty

There have been a number of reports of malleolar fractures complicating total ankle arthroplasty (TAA), but no large series have been published to date clearly elucidating specific etiological factors or classification schemes.[57,81,99,108,135,141,171] One risk factor, however, seems to be clear. Multiple studies have demonstrated that fracture of the malleoli decrease with increasing surgeon experience with the procedure. Lee et al.[81] and Myerson and Mroczak[108] each compared results of their first 25 cases to their next 25. Both showed substantial reduction in intraoperative malleolar fractures with experience: Lee et al. had 4 fractures among the first 25 cases (16%) and 1 in the subsequent 25 (4%), and Myerson and Mroczak had 5 from the initial group (20%) and 2 from the second group (8%). These results are similar to those of several other authors. Haskell and Mann[57] found a reduction in intraoperative fracture from 12% in the initial 50 cases to 9% in the subsequent 137 cases, and Schuberth et al.[141] reported 19 intraoperative fractures from 50 cases (38%) and noted that this complication decreased with experience.

The medial malleolus is the most common site of intraoperative fracture, occurring approximately twice as frequently as lateral malleolus fractures.[57,99,135,171] The vast majority of periprosthetic fractures about TAAs occur intraoperatively; however, postoperative malleolar fracture has been reported.[57,99,171] Wood and Deakin[171] had 10 postoperative fractures occur between 3 days and 23 months in their series of 200 TAAs. Two of the 10 were associated with implant loosening.

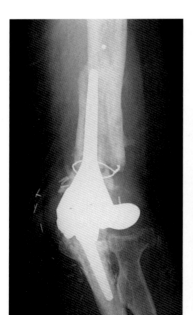
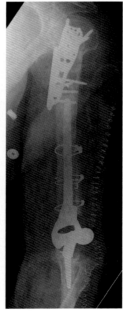

FIGURE 21-31 A periprosthetic humerus fracture about the humeral component of a total elbow arthroplasty **(A)** treated with ORIF **(B)**.

Treatment Options and Results of Periprosthetic Fractures About Total Ankle Arthroplasty

There is no accepted standard for treatment of periprosthetic fractures about TAA. However, the general principles of management of other periprosthetic fractures can be applied. Fracture union, implant stability, and re-establishment of any associated loss of bone stock are general goals of management with the hope of restoring baseline function. Several authors describe internal fixation for intraoperative malleolar fractures that compromised implant stability,[57,99] and yet others treated many of these fractures nonoperatively.[81,108,171] Nonunion occurred after intraoperative fracture in 1 of 6 nonoperatively treated from one study[57] and in 1 of 5 treated with ORIF from another.[99] Most postoperative fractures are also of the malleolus and are typically treated nonoperatively unless associated with implant loosening or osteolysis.[57,99,171]

COMPLICATIONS OF PERIPROSTHETIC FRACTURES

The complications of periprosthetic fractures is a compilation of the typical complication seen after acute fracture through native bone and the complications associated with joint arthroplasty. Such complications can occur in isolation or in combination. Clearly, treatment must consider both the implications relative to the periprosthetic fracture and the implication with regard to arthroplasty stability and function. It is sometimes useful to prioritize the goals of treatment and decide if outcome for the periprosthetic fracture is paramount or if preservation of the arthroplasty function is the primary goal. These are sometimes conflicting goals.

Nonunion

Nonunion is perhaps the most common complication associated with periprosthetic fractures. Nonunion rates for periprosthetic fracture fixation is generally higher than the rate for treatment of the same fracture in the absence of a prosthesis. It has been postulated that damage to the endosteal blood supply related to the intramedullary implant could alter the healing response to fracture, but this remains theory. A more influential cause of higher nonunion rates is the potentially compromised fixation caused by the prosthesis inhibiting optimal fixation. Cable fixation is the mainstay for plate or strut fixation around the zone of prostheses and has inferior strength compared to bicortical screws. However, advances in surgical technique and implant technologies have led to recent improvement in union rates. These advancements include biologic reduction techniques and locked plates where locking screws augment cable fixation in the zone of the implant and also augment fixation when osteopenic bone is encountered. Treatment of nonunion can be extremely challenging. Results of nonunion repair of periprosthetic fracture are marginal. A multimodal approach is required.[64] Correction of any systemic processes that could inhibit fracture healing is done prior to nonunion repair. This consists of smoking cessation, discontinuation of nonsteroidal anti-inflammatory drugs, strict control of diabetes, and discontinuation of any other dispensable medications that could alter bone metabolism. Operative strategies include utilization of long stem prostheses in conjunction with extramedullary strut and plate fixation. Generous use of osteogenic and osteoinductive grafts and graft substitutes are imperative. Autologous iliac crest bone graft remains the criterion standard, but supplementation with BMP is a growing part of the armamentarium for these difficult cases. It goes without saying that restoration of anatomic limb alignment is another critical step.

Neurologic Injury

Neurologic injury associated with periprosthetic fractures is reported in a number of series especially with fixation of humeral fractures. One partial radial and two partial ulnar nerve pulses were reported in a series of 11 periprosthetic humeral shaft fractures.[137] The proximity of the radial and ulnar nerves to the fracture, the fixation devices, and securing cerclage cables put these structures at particular risk for injury. The best strategy for dealing with neurologic injury is one based on prevention. Appropriate choice of surgical approach is the first step. We prefer to directly expose any and all nerves that are potentially compromised. Therefore, the posterior approach is preferred for access to the humeral shaft. This way, the radial nerve is precisely located and can be protected throughout the procedure. Gentle soft tissue handling is also important with avoidance of forceful or prolonged retraction of nerves. Passing cerclage cables can be a harrowing experience. There is no substitute for knowledge of nerve location and direct protection during passage of cables.

Infection

Infection can complicate any surgical procedure, but when infection is associated with periprosthetic fracture it can be particularly devastating. Not only is fracture healing compromised but also the survivorship of the associated arthroplasty. Relatively aggressive early surgical treatment with irrigation and débridement and parental organism specific antibiotics followed by long-term oral suppression has a potential to spare the fracture fixation and arthroplasty implants. Failure to control infection can have serious results including resection arthroplasty or amputation at or above the involved joint.

Joint Stiffness

Treatment of any periarticular fracture can result in temporary or permanent stiffness of the involved joint due to contracture and scar of the surrounding soft tissues from the original injury as well as from the trauma of surgery. Immobilization of the joint as part of fracture care can compound the tendency for stiffness. These issues are also relevant to the treatment of periprosthetic fractures. Fortunately, by nature most periprosthetic fractures are at some distance from the involved joint and by definition are not intraarticular. Nevertheless, every effort should be made to obtain stable enough fixation to minimize the requirement for joint immobilization and to allow as early as possible range of motion exercises.

REFERENCES

1. Aaron RK, Scott R. Supracondylar fracture of the femur after total knee arthroplasty. Clin Orthop Relat Res 1987;136–139.
2. Abhaykumar S, Elliott DS. Percutaneous plate fixation for periprosthetic femoral fractures—a preliminary report. Injury 2000;31:627–630.
3. Althausen PL, Lee MA, Finkemeier CG, et al. Operative stabilization of supracondylar

femur fractures above total knee arthroplasty: a comparison of four treatment methods. J Arthroplasty 2003;18:834–839.

4. Andrews P, Barrack RL, Harris WH. Stress fracture of the medial wall of the acetabulum adjacent to a cementless acetabular component. J Arthroplasty 2002;17:117–120.

5. Ayers DC. Supracondylar fracture of the distal femur proximal to a total knee replacement. Instr Course Lect 1997;46:197–203.

6. Beals RK, Tower SS. Periprosthetic fractures of the femur. An analysis of 93 fractures. Clin Orthop Relat Res 1996;238–246.

7. Berry DJ Epidemiology: hip and knee. Orthop Clin North Am 1999;30:183–190.

8. Bethea JS, III, DeAndrade JR, Fleming LL, et al. Proximal femoral fractures following total hip arthroplasty. Clin Orthop Relat Res 1982;95–106.

9. Bhattacharyya T, Chang D, Meigs JB, et al. Mortality after periprosthetic fracture of the femur. J Bone Joint Surg Am 2007;89:2658–2662.

10. Bogoch E, Hastings D, Gross A, et al. Supracondylar fractures of the femur adjacent to resurfacing and MacIntosh arthroplasties of the knee in patients with rheumatoid arthritis. Clin Orthop Relat Res 1988;213–220.

11. Bonutti PM, Hawkins RJ. Fracture of the humeral shaft associated with total replacement arthroplasty of the shoulder. A case report. J Bone Joint Surg Am 1992;74:617–618.

12. Boyd AD, Jr., Thornhill TS, Barnes CL. Fractures adjacent to humeral prostheses. J Bone Joint Surg Am 1992;74:1498–1504.

13. Brady OH, Garbuz DS, Masri BA. et al. The treatment of periprosthetic fractures of the femur using cortical onlay allograft struts. Orthop Clin North Am 1999;30:249–257.

14. Brady OH, Garbuz DS, Masri BA, et al. The reliability and validity of the Vancouver classification of femoral fractures after hip replacement. J Arthroplasty 2000;15:59–62.

15. Brick GW, Scott RD. The patellofemoral component of total knee arthroplasty. Clin Orthop Relat Res 1988;163–178.

16. Buttaro MA, Farfalli G, Paredes NM, et al. Locking compression plate fixation of Vancouver type-B1 periprosthetic femoral fractures. J Bone Joint Surg Am 2007;89:1964–1969.

17. Cain PR, Rubash HE, Wissinger HA, et al. Periprosthetic femoral fractures following total knee arthroplasty. Clin Orthop Relat Res 1986;205–214.

18. Cameron HU, Jung YB. Noncemented stem tibial component in total knee replacement: the 2- to 6-year results. Can J Surg 1993;36:555–559.

19. Campbell JT, Moore RS, Iannotti JP, et al. Periprosthetic humeral fractures: mechanisms of fracture and treatment options. J Shoulder Elbow Surg 1998;7:406–413.

20. Chalidis BE, Tsiridis E, Tragas AA, et al. Management of periprosthetic patellar fractures. A systematic review of literature. Injury 2007;38:714–724.

21. Chandler HP, King D, Limbird R, et al. The use of cortical allograft struts for fixation of fractures associated with well-fixed total joint prostheses. Semin Arthroplasty 1993;4:99–107.

22. Chandler HP, Tigges RG. The role of allografts in the treatment of periprosthetic femoral fractures. Instr Course Lect 1998;47:257–264.

23. Chatoo M, Parfitt J, Pearse MF: Periprosthetic acetabular fracture associated with extensive osteolysis. J Arthroplasty 1998;13:843–845.

24. Chun KA, Ohashi K, Bennett DL, et al. Patellar fractures after total knee replacement. Am J Roentgenol 2005;185:655–660.

25. Clatworthy MG, Ballance J, Brick GW, et al. The use of structural allograft for uncontained defects in revision total knee arthroplasty. A minimum five-year review. J Bone Joint Surg Am 2001;83-A:404–411.

26. Cook RE, Jenkins PJ, Walmsley PJ, et al. Risk factors for periprosthetic fractures of the hip: a survivorship analysis. Clin Orthop Relat Res 2008;466:1652–1656.

27. Cracchiolo A. Stress fractures of the pelvis as a cause of hip pain following total hip and knee arthroplasty. Arthritis Rheum 1981;24:740–742.

28. Culp RW, Schmidt RG, Hanks G, et al. Supracondylar fracture of the femur following prosthetic knee arthroplasty. Clin Orthop Relat Res 1987;212–222.

29. Davila J, Malkani A, Paiso JM. Supracondylar distal femoral nonunions treated with a megaprosthesis in elderly patients: a report of two cases. J Orthop Trauma 2001;15:574–578.

30. Davison BL. Varus collapse of comminuted distal femur fractures after open reduction and internal fixation with a lateral condylar buttress plate. Am J Orthop 2003;32:27–30.

31. Della Valle CJ, Momberger NG, Paprosky WG. Periprosthetic fractures of the acetabulum associated with a total hip arthroplasty. Instr Course Lect 2003;52:281–290.

32. Dennis MG, Simon JA, Kummer FJ, et al. Fixation of periprosthetic femoral shaft fractures: a biomechanical comparison of two techniques. J Orthop Trauma 2001;15:177–180.

33. Dennis MG, Simon JA, Kummer FJ, et al. Fixation of periprosthetic femoral shaft fractures occurring at the tip of the stem: a biomechanical study of 5 techniques. J Arthroplasty 2000;15:523–528.

34. Duncan CP, Masri BA. Fractures of the femur after hip replacement. Instr Course Lect 1995; 44:293–304.

35. Egol KA, Kubiak EN, Fulkerson E, et al. Biomechanics of locked plates and screws. J Orthop Trauma 2004;18:488–493.

36. Engh GA, Ammeen DJ. Periprosthetic fractures adjacent to total knee implants: treatment and clinical results. Instr Course Lect 1998;47:437–448.

37. Farfalli GL, Buttaro MA, Piccaluga F. Femoral fractures in revision hip surgeries with impacted bone allograft. Clin Orthop Relat Res 2007;462:130–136.

38. Felix NA, Stuart MJ, Hanssen AD. Periprosthetic fractures of the tibia associated with total knee arthroplasty. Clin Orthop Relat Res 1997;113–124.

39. Figgie HE, III, Goldberg VM, Figgie MP, et al. The effect of alignment of the implant on fractures of the patella after condylar total knee arthroplasty. J Bone Joint Surg Am 1989;71:1031–1039.

40. Figgie MP, Goldberg VM, Figgie HE, III, et al. The results of treatment of supracondylar fracture above total knee arthroplasty. J Arthroplasty 1990;5:267–276.

41. Foster AP, Thompson NW, Wong J, et al. Periprosthetic femoral fractures—a comparison between cemented and uncemented hemiarthroplasties. Injury 2005;36:424–429.

42. Franklin J, Malchau H. Risk factors for periprosthetic femoral fracture. Injury 2007;38:655–660.

43. Fredin HO, Lindberg H, Carlsson AS. Femoral fracture following hip arthroplasty. Acta Orthop Scand 1987;58:20–22.

44. Freedman EL, Hak DJ, Johnson EE, et al. Total knee replacement including a modular distal femoral component in elderly patients with acute fracture or nonunion. J Orthop Trauma 1995;9:231–237.

45. Fulkerson E, Koval K, Preston CF, et al. Fixation of periprosthetic femoral shaft fractures associated with cemented femoral stems: a biomechanical comparison of locked plating and conventional cable plates. J Orthop Trauma 2006;20:89–93.

46. Garcia-Cimbrelo E, Munuera L, Gil-Garay E. Femoral shaft fractures after cemented total hip arthroplasty. Int Orthop 1992;16:97–100.

47. Garnavos C, Rafiq M, Henry AP. Treatment of femoral fracture above a knee prosthesis. 18 cases followed 0.5–14 years. Acta Orthop Scand 1994;65:610–614.

48. Gliatis J, Megas P, Panagiotopoulos E, et al. Midterm results of treatment with a retrograde nail for supracondylar periprosthetic fractures of the femur following total knee arthroplasty. J Orthop Trauma 2005;19:164–170.

49. Goldberg VM, Figgie HE III, Inglis AE, et al. Patellar fracture type and prognosis in condylar total knee arthroplasty. Clin Orthop Relat Res 1988;115–122.

50. Grace JN, Sim FH. Fracture of the patella after total knee arthroplasty. Clin Orthop Relat Res 1988;168–175.

51. Groh GI, Heckman MM, Wirth MA, et al. Treatment of fractures adjacent to humeral prostheses. J Shoulder Elbow Surg 2008;17:85–89.

52. Guidera KJ, Borrelli JJ, Raney E, et al. Orthopaedic manifestations of Rett syndrome. J Pediatr Orthop 1991;11:204–208.

53. Haddad FS, Duncan CP, Berry DJ, et al. Periprosthetic femoral fractures around well-fixed implants: use of cortical onlay allografts with or without a plate. J Bone Joint Surg Am 2002;84-A:945–950.

54. Haddad FS, Marston RA, Muirhead-Allwood SK. The Dall-Miles cable and plate system for periprosthetic femoral fractures. Injury 1997;28:445–447.

55. Haidukewych GJ, Jacofsky DJ, Hanssen AD, et al. Intraoperative fractures of the acetabulum during primary total hip arthroplasty. J Bone Joint Surg Am 2006;88:1952–1956.

56. Hardy DC, Delince PE, Yasik E, et al. Stress fracture of the hip. An unusual complication of total knee arthroplasty. Clin Orthop Relat Res 1992;140–144.

57. Haskell A, Mann RA. Perioperative complication rate of total ankle replacement is reduced by surgeon experience. Foot Ankle Int 2004;25:283–289.

58. Healy WL, Wasilewski SA, Takei R, et al. Patellofemoral complications following total knee arthroplasty. Correlation with implant design and patient risk factors. J Arthroplasty 1995;10:197–201.

59. Herrera DA, Kregor PJ, Cole PA, et al. Treatment of acute distal femur fractures above a total knee arthroplasty: systematic review of 415 cases (1981–2006). Acta Orthop 2008;79:22–27.

60. Hirsh DM, Bhalla S, Roffman M. Supracondylar fracture of the femur following total knee replacement. Report of four cases. J Bone Joint Surg Am 1981;63:162–163.

61. Holden CE. The role of blood supply to soft tissue in the healing of diaphyseal fractures. An experimental study. J Bone Joint Surg Am 1972;54:993–1000.

62. Hozack WJ, Goll SR, Lotke PA, et al. The treatment of patellar fractures after total knee arthroplasty. Clin Orthop Relat Res 1988;123–127.

63. Incavo SJ, Beard DM, Pupparo F, et al. One-stage revision of periprosthetic fractures around loose cemented total hip arthroplasty. Am J Orthop 1998;27:35–41.

64. Jani MM, Ricci WM, Borrelli J Jr, et al. A protocol for treatment of unstable ankle fractures using transarticular fixation in patients with diabetes mellitus and loss of protective sensibility. Foot Ankle Int 2003;24:838–844.

65. Johansson JE, McBroom R, Barrington TW, et al. Fracture of the ipsilateral femur in patients wih total hip replacement. J Bone Joint Surg Am 1981;63:1435–1442.

66. Kamineni S, Morrey BF. Proximal ulnar reconstruction with strut allograft in revision total elbow arthroplasty. J Bone Joint Surg Am 2004;86-A:1223–1229.

67. Katzer A, Ince A, Wodtke J, et al. Component exchange in treatment of periprosthetic femoral fractures. J Arthroplasty 2006;21:572–579.

68. Kavanagh BF. Femoral fractures associated with total hip arthroplasty. Orthop Clin North Am 1992;23:249–257.

69. Keating EM, Haas G, Meding JB. Patella fracture after post total knee replacements. Clin.Orthop Relat Res 2003;93–97.

70. Kellett CF, Boscainos PJ, Maury AC, et al. Proximal femoral allograft treatment of Vancouver type-B3 periprosthetic femoral fractures after total hip arthroplasty. Surgical technique. J Bone Joint Surg Am 2007;89(Suppl 2 Pt1):68–79.

71. Kim DH, Clavert P, Warner JJ. Displaced periprosthetic humeral fracture treated with functional bracing: a report of two cases. J Shoulder Elbow Surg 2005;14:221–223.

72. Klein GR, Parvizi J, Rapuri V, et al. Proximal femoral replacement for the treatment of periprosthetic fractures. J Bone Joint Surg Am 2005;87:1777–1781.

73. Kolstad K. Revision THR after periprosthetic femoral fractures. An analysis of 23 cases. Acta Orthop Scand 1994;65:505–508.

74. Kraay MJ, Goldberg VM, Figgie MP, et al. Distal femoral replacement with allograft/prosthetic reconstruction for treatment of supracondylar fractures in patients with total knee arthroplasty. J Arthroplasty 1992;7:7–16.

75. Kregor PJ, Stannard JA, Zlowodzki M, et al. Treatment of distal femur fractures using the less invasive stabilization system: surgical experience and early clinical results in 103 fractures. J Orthop Trauma 2004;18:509–520.

76. Kress KJ, Scuderi GR, Windsor RE, et al. Treatment of Nonunions About the Knee Utilizing Custom Total Knee Arthroplasty With Press-fit Intramedullary Stems. J Arthroplasty 1995;8(1):49–55.

77. Kumar A, Chambers I, Wong P. Periprosthetic fracture of the proximal tibia after lateral unicompartmental knee arthroplasty. J Arthroplasty 2008;23:615–618.

78. Kumar S, Sperling JW, Haidukewych GH, et al. Periprosthetic humeral fractures after shoulder arthroplasty. J Bone Joint Surg Am 2004;86-A:680–689.

79. Kumm DA, Rack C, Rutt J. Subtrochanteric stress fracture of the femur following total knee arthroplasty. J Arthroplasty 1997;12:580–583.

80. Lee GC, Nelson CL, Virmani S, et al. Management of periprosthetic femur fractures with severe bone loss using impaction bone grafting technique. J Arthroplasty 2009.

81. Lee KB, Cho SG, Hur CI, et al. Perioperative complications of HINTEGRA total ankle replacement: our initial 50 cases. Foot Ankle Int 2008;29:978–984.

82. Lesh ML, Schneider DJ, Deol G, et al. The consequences of anterior femoral notching in total knee arthroplasty. A biomechanical study. J Bone Joint Surg Am 2000;82-A:1096–1101.

83. Lesniewski PJ, Testa NN. Stress fracture of the hip as a complication of total knee replacement. Case report. J Bone Joint Surg Am 1982;64:304–306.

84. Lewallen DG, Berry DJ. Periprosthetic fracture of the femur after total hip arthroplasty: treatment and results to date. Instr Course Lect 1998;47:243–249.

85. Lewis PL, Rorabeck CH. Periprosthetic Fractures. In: Engh GA, Rorabeck CH, Eds. Revision total knee arthroplasty. Baltimore: Williams & Wilkins; 2007:275–295.

86. Li CH, Chen TH, Su YP, et al. Periprosthetic femoral supracondylar fracture after total knee arthroplasty with navigation system. J Arthroplasty 2008;23:304–307.

87. Lindahl H. Epidemiology of periprosthetic femur fracture around a total hip arthroplasty. Injury 2007;38:651–654.

88. Lindahl H, Garellick G, Regner H, et al. Three hundred and twenty-one periprosthetic femoral fractures. J Bone Joint Surg Am 2006;88:1215–1222.

89. Lindahl H, Malchau H, Herberts P, et al. Periprosthetic femoral fractures classification and demographics of 1049 periprosthetic femoral fractures from the Swedish National Hip Arthroplasty Register. J Arthroplasty 2005;20:857–865.

90. Lindahl H, Oden A, Garellick G, et al. The excess mortality due to periprosthetic femur fracture. A study from the Swedish national hip arthroplasty register. Bone 2007;40: 1294–1298.

91. Lotke PA, Ecker ML. Influence of positioning of prosthesis in total knee replacement. J Bone Joint Surg Am 1977;59:77–79.

92. Mamczak CN, Gardner MJ, Bolhofner B, et al. Interprosthetic Femur Fractures. 2009 OTA Annual Meeting 2009 (Abstract).

93. Maniar RN, Umlas ME, Rodriguez JA, et al. Supracondylar femoral fracture above a PFC posterior cruciate—substituting total knee arthroplasty treated with supracondylar nailing. A unique technical problem. J Arthroplasty 1996;11:637–639.

94. Markmiller M, Konrad G, Sudkamp N. Femur–LISS and distal femoral nail for fixation of distal femoral fractures: are there differences in outcome and complications? Clin Orthop Relat Res 2004;252–257.

95. Marra G, Morrey BF, Gallay SH, et al. Fracture and nonunion of the olecranon in total elbow arthroplasty. J Shoulder Elbow Surg 2006;15:486–494.

96. Masri BA, Meek RM, Duncan CP. Periprosthetic fractures evaluation and treatment. Clin Orthop Relat Res 2004;80–95.

97. Maury AC, Pressman A, Cayen B, et al. Proximal femoral allograft treatment of Vancouver type-B3 periprosthetic femoral fractures after total hip arthroplasty. J Bone Joint Surg Am 2006;88:953–958.

98. McDonough EB, Crosby LA. Periprosthetic fractures of the humerus. Am J Orthop 2005;34:586–591.

99. McGarvey WC, Clanton TO, Lunz D. Malleolar fracture after total ankle arthroplasty: a comparison of two designs. Clin Orthop Relat Res 2004;104–110.

100. Meek RM, Garbuz DS, Masri BA, et al. Intraoperative fracture of the femur in revision total hip arthroplasty with a diaphyseal fitting stem. J Bone Joint Surg Am 2004;86-A:480–485.

101. Merkel KD, Johnson EW Jr. Supracondylar fracture of the femur after total knee arthroplasty. J Bone Joint Surg Am 1986;68:29–43.

102. Mikhail WE, Wretenberg PF, Weidenhielm LR, et al. Complex cemented revision using polished stem and morselized allograft.Minimum 5-years' follow-up. Arch Orthop Trauma Surg 1999;119:288–291.

103. Mont MA, Maar DC. Fractures of the ipsilateral femur after hip arthroplasty. A statistical analysis of outcome based on 487 patients. J Arthroplasty 1994;9:511–519.

104. Moran MC, Brick GW, Sledge CB, et al. Supracondylar femoral fracture following total knee arthroplasty. Clin Orthop Relat Res 1996;196–209.

105. Morrey BF, Kavanagh BF. Complications with revision of the femoral component of total hip arthroplasty. Comparison between cemented and uncemented techniques. J Arthroplasty 1992;7:71–79.

106. Mukundan C, Rayan F, Kheir E, Macdonald D. Management of late periprosthetic femur fractures: a retrospective cohort of 72 patients. Int Orthop 2009.

107. Mulay S, Hassan T, Birtwistle S, et al. Management of types B2 and B3 femoral periprosthetic fractures by a tapered, fluted, and distally fixed stem. J Arthroplasty 2005;20: 751–756.

108. Myerson MS, Mroczek K. Perioperative complications of total ankle arthroplasty. Foot Ankle Int 2003;24:17–21.

109. Naraghi AM, White LM. Magnetic resonance imaging of joint replacements. Semin Musculoskelet Radiol 2006;10:98–106.

110. O'Shea K, Quinlan JF, Kutty S, et al. The use of uncemented extensively porous-coated femoral components in the management of Vancouver B2 and B3 periprosthetic femoral fractures. J Bone Joint Surg Br 2005;87:1617–1621.

111. Olsen RV, Munk PL, Lee MJ, et al. Metal artifact reduction sequence: early clinical applications. Radiographics 2000;20:699–712.

112. Ortiguera CJ, Berry DJ. Patellar fracture after total knee arthroplasty. J Bone Joint Surg Am 2002;84-A:532–540.

113. Palance MD, Albareda J, Seral F. Subcapital stress fracture of the femoral neck after total knee arthroplasty. Int Orthop 1994;18:308–309.

114. Parvizi J, Jain N, Schmidt AH. Periprosthetic knee fractures. J Orthop Trauma 2008; 22:663–671.

115. Perren SM, Linke B, Schwieger K, et al. Aspects of internal fixation of fractures in porotic bone. Principles, technologies and procedures using locked plate screws. Acta Chir Orthop Traumatol Cech 2005;72:89–97.

116. Peters CL, Hennessey R, Barden RM, et al. Revision total knee arthroplasty with a cemented posterior—stabilized or constrained condylar prosthesis: a minimum 3-year and average 5-year follow-up study. J Arthroplasty 1997;12:896–903.

117. Petersen MM, Lauritzen JB, Pedersen JG, et al. Decreased bone density of the distal femur after uncemented knee arthroplasty. A 1-year follow-up of 29 knees. Acta Orthop Scand 1996;67:339–344.

118. Petersen MM, Olsen C, Lauritzen JB, et al. Changes in bone mineral density of the distal femur following uncemented total knee arthroplasty. J Arthroplasty 1995;10: 7–11.

119. Peterson CA, Lewallen DG. Periprosthetic fracture of the acetabulum after total hip arthroplasty. J Bone Joint Surg Am 1996;78:1206–1213.

120. Pressmar J, Macholz F, Merkert W, et al. [Results and complications in the treatment of periprosthetic femur fractures with a locked plate system.] Unfallchirurg 2009.

121. Radcliffe SN, Smith DN. The Mennen plate in periprosthetic hip fractures. Injury 1996; 27:27–30.

122. Rand JA, Coventry MB. Stress fractures after total knee arthroplasty. J Bone Joint Surg Am1980;62:226–233.

123. Rawes ML, Patsalis T, Gregg PJ. Subcapital stress fractures of the hip complicating total knee replacement. Injury 1995;26:421–423.

124. Ricci WM, Bolhofner BR, Loftus T, et al. Indirect reduction and plate fixation, without grafting, for periprosthetic femoral shaft fractures about a stable intramedullary implant. J Bone Joint Surg Am 2005;87:2240–2245.

125. Ricci WM, Borrelli J Jr. Operative management of periprosthetic femur fractures in the elderly using biological fracture reduction and fixation techniques. Injury 2007; 38(Suppl 3):S53–58.

126. Ricci WM, Haidukewych GJ. Periprosthetic femoral fractures. Instr Course Lect 2009; 58:105–115.

127. Ricci WM, Loftus T, Cox C, et al. Locked plates combined with minimally invasive insertion technique for the treatment of periprosthetic supracondylar femur fractures above a total knee arthroplasty. J Orthop Trauma 2006;20:190–196.

128. Ritter MA, Campbell ED. Postoperative patellar complications with or without lateral release during total knee arthroplasty. Clin Orthop Relat Res 1987;163–168.

129. Ritter MA, Carr K, Keating EM, Faris PM, Meding JB. Tibial shaft fracture following tibial tubercle osteotomy. J Arthroplasty 1996;11:117–119.

130. Ritter MA, Faris PM, Keating EM. Anterior femoral notching and ipsilateral supracondylar femur fracture in total knee arthroplasty. J Arthroplasty 1988;3:185–187.

131. Ritter MA, Thong AE, Keating EM, et al. The effect of femoral notching during total knee arthroplasty on the prevalence of postoperative femoral fractures and on clinical outcome. J Bone Joint Surg Am 2005;87:2411–2414.

132. Robinson DE, Lee MB, Smith EJ, et al. Femoral impaction grafting in revision hip arthroplasty with irradiated bone. J Arthroplasty 2002;17:834–840.

133. Rorabeck CH, Taylor JW. Classification of periprosthetic fractures complicating total knee arthroplasty. Orthop Clin North Am 1999;30:209–214.

134. Rorabeck CH, Taylor JW. Periprosthetic fractures of the femur complicating total knee arthroplasty. Orthop Clin North Am 1999;30:265–277.

135. Saltzman CL, Amendola A, Anderson R, et al. Surgeon training and complications in total ankle arthroplasty. Foot Ankle Int 2003;24:514–518.

136. Sanchez-Sotelo J, McGrory BJ, Berry DJ. Acute periprosthetic fracture of the acetabulum associated with osteolytic pelvic lesions: a report of 3 cases. J Arthroplasty 2000;15: 126–130.

137. Sanchez-Sotelo J, O'Driscoll S, Morrey BF. Periprosthetic humeral fractures after total elbow arthroplasty: treatment with implant revision and strut allograft augmentation. J Bone Joint Surg Am 2002;84-A:1642–1650.

138. Sarvilinna R, Huhtala H, Pajamaki J. Young age and wedge stem design are risk factors for periprosthetic fracture after arthroplasty due to hip fracture. A case–control study. Acta Orthop 2005;76:56–60.

139. Sarvilinna R, Huhtala HS, Sovelius RT, et al. Factors predisposing to periprosthetic fracture after hip arthroplasty: a case (n = 31)–control study. Acta Orthop Scand 2004;75:16–20.

140. Schandelmaier P, Partenheimer A, Koenemann B, et al. Distal femoral fractures and LISS stabilization. Injury 2001;32(Suppl 3):SC55–63.

141. Schuberth JM, Patel S, Zarutsky E. Perioperative complications of the Agility total ankle replacement in 50 initial, consecutive cases. J Foot Ankle Surg 2006;45:139–146.

142. Schutz M, Muller M, Krettek C, et al. Minimally invasive fracture stabilization of distal femoral fractures with the LISS: a prospective multicenter study. Results of a clinical study with special emphasis on difficult cases. Injury 2001;32(Suppl 3):SC48–54.

143. Schwartz JT Jr, Mayer JG, Engh CA. Femoral fracture during non–cemented total hip arthroplasty. J Bone Joint Surg Am 1989;71:1135–1142.

144. Scott RD, Turoff N, Ewald FC. Stress fracture of the patella following duopatellar total knee arthroplasty with patellar resurfacing. Clin Orthop Relat Res 1982;147–151.

145. Sharkey PF, Hozack WJ, Callaghan JJ, et al. Acetabular fracture associated with cementless acetabular component insertion: a report of 13 cases. J Arthroplasty 1999; 14:426–431.

146. Sheth NP, Pedowitz DI, Lonner JH. Periprosthetic patellar fractures. J Bone Joint Surg Am 2007;89:2285–2296.

147. Springer BD, Berry DJ, Cabanela ME, et al. Early postoperative transverse pelvic fracture: a new complication related to revision arthroplasty with an uncemented cup. J Bone Joint Surg Am 2005;87:2626–2631.

148. Steinmann SP, Cheung EV. Treatment of periprosthetic humerus fractures associated with shoulder arthroplasty. J Am Acad Orthop Surg 2008;16:199–207.

149. Stiehl JB. Extended osteotomy for periprosthetic femoral fractures in total hip arthroplasty. Am J Orthop 2006;35:20–23.

150. Stuart MJ, Hanssen AD. Total knee arthroplasty: periprosthetic tibial fractures. Orthop Clin North Am 1999;30:279–286.

151. Su ET, DeWal H, Di Cesare PE. Periprosthetic femoral fractures above total knee replacements. J Am Acad Orthop Surg 2004;12:12–20.

152. Tadross TS, Nanu AM, Buchanan MJ, et al. Dall-Miles plating for periprosthetic B1 fractures of the femur. J Arthroplasty 2000;15(1):47–51.

153. Talbot M, Zdero R, Schemitsch EH. Cyclic loading of periprosthetic fracture fixation constructs. J Trauma 2008;64:1308–1312.

154. Taylor MM, Meyers MH, Harvey JP Jr. Intraoperative femur fractures during total hip replacement. Clin Orthop Relat Res 1978;96–103.

155. Tharani R, Nakasone C, Vince KG. Periprosthetic fractures after total knee arthroplasty. J Arthroplasty 2005;20:27–32.

156. Thompson NW, McAlinden MG, Breslin E, et al. Periprosthetic tibial fractures after cementless low contact stress total knee arthroplasty. J Arthroplasty 2001;16:984–990.

157. Tower SS, Beals RK. Fractures of the femur after hip replacement: the Oregon experience. Orthop Clin North Am 1999;30:235–247.

158. Tria AJ Jr, Harwood DA, Alicea JA, et al. Patellar fractures in posterior stabilized knee arthroplasties. Clin Orthop Relat Res 1994;131–138.

159. Tsiridis E, Amin MS, Charity J, et al. Impaction allografting revision for B3 periprosthetic femoral fractures using a Mennen plate to contain the graft: a technical report. Acta Orthop Belg 2007;73:332–338.

160. Tsiridis E, Haddad FS, Gie GA. The management of periprosthetic femoral fractures around hip replacements. Injury 2003;34:95–105.

161. Tsiridis E, Narvani AA, Haddad FS, et al. Impaction femoral allografting and cemented revision for periprosthetic femoral fractures. J Bone Joint Surg Br 2004;86:1124–1132.

162. Tsiridis E, Spence G, Gamie Z, et al. Grafting for periprosthetic femoral fractures: strut, impaction or femoral replacement. Injury 2007;38:688–697.

163. Van Loon P, de Munnynck B, Bellemans J. Periprosthetic fracture of the tibial plateau after unicompartmental knee arthroplasty. Acta Orthop Belg 2006;72:369–374.

164. Venu KM, Koka R, Garikipati R, et al. Dall-Miles cable and plate fixation for the treatment of peri-prosthetic femoral fractures—analysis of results in 13 cases. Injury 2001; 32:395–400.

165. Wang CJ, Wang JW, Weng LH, et al. The effect of alendronate on bone mineral density in the distal part of the femur and proximal part of the tibia after total knee arthroplasty. J Bone Joint Surg Am 2003;85-A:2121–2126.

166. White LM, Kim JK, Mehta M, et al. Complications of total hip arthroplasty: MR imaging–initial experience. Radiology 2000;215:254–262.

167. Whittaker RP, Sotos LN, Ralston EL. Fractures of the femur about femoral endoprostheses. J Trauma 1974;14:675–694.

168. Wick M, Muller EJ, Kutscha-Lissberg F, et al. [Periprosthetic supracondylar femoral fractures: LISS or retrograde intramedullary nailing? Problems with the use of minimally invasive technique]. Unfallchirurg 2004;107:181–188.

169. Wilson FC, Venters GC. Results of knee replacement with the Walldius prosthesis: an interim report. Clin Orthop Relat Res 1976;39–46.

170. Wong P, Gross AE. The use of structural allografts for treating periprosthetic fractures about the hip and knee. Orthop Clin North Am 1999;30:259–264.

171. Wood PL, Deakin S. Total ankle replacement. The results in 200 ankles. J Bone Joint Surg Br 2003;85:334–341.

172. Worland RL, Kim DY, Arredondo J. Periprosthetic humeral fractures: management and classification. J Shoulder Elbow Surg 1999;8:590–594.

173. Wright TW, Cofield RH. Humeral fractures after shoulder arthroplasty. J Bone Joint Surg Am 1995;77:1340–1346.

174. Wu CC, Au MK, Wu SS, et al. Risk factors for postoperative femoral fracture in cementless hip arthroplasty. J Formos Med Assoc 1999;98:190–194.

175. Young SW, Walker CG, Pitto RP. Functional outcome of femoral peri prosthetic fracture and revision hip arthroplasty: a matched–pair study from the New Zealand Registry. Acta Orthop 2008;79:483–488.

176. Zaki SH, Sadiq S, Purbach B, et al. Periprosthetic femoral fractures treated with a modular distally cemented stem. J Orthop Surg (Hong Kong) 2007;15:163–166.

177. Zalzal P, Backstein D, Gross AE, et al. Notching of the anterior femoral cortex during total knee arthroplasty characteristics that increase local stresses. J Arthroplasty 2006; 21:737–743.

178. Zalzal P, Gandhi R, Petruccelli D, et al. Fractures at the tip of long-stem prostheses used for revision hip arthroplasty. J Arthroplasty 2003;18:741–745.

179. Zdero R, Walker R, Waddell JP, et al. Biomechanical evaluation of periprosthetic femoral fracture fixation. J Bone Joint Surg Am 2008;90:1068–1077.

180. Zenni EJ Jr, Pomeroy DL, Caudle RJ Ogden plate and other fixations for fractures complicating femoral endoprostheses. Clin Orthop 1988;83–90.

22

SYSTEMIC COMPLICATIONS

Tim White and Adam Watts

INTRODUCTION

The systemic complications of trauma have their origins in the stress response, which is initiated at the time of injury. The early resuscitation of injured patients, aiming primarily to save life, then to save limb and thirdly to restore function, has been covered in Chapter 9. This chapter aims to describe the stress response and its later consequences in greater detail and to address the associated issues of rhabdomyolysis, venous thromboembolism, and postoperative pyrexia.

THE SYSTEMIC RESPONSE TO TRAUMA

The systemic response to trauma begins at the time of injury and is often well advanced by the time a patient is brought to the emergency department. The response not only continues to evolve throughout the process of resuscitation and definitive management, but is influenced by this process. Where the response is excessive, a cycle of events develops leading to multiple organ dysfunction and death. Our current understanding of this complex process is incomplete, and this is an area of considerable controversy, interest, and exciting potential. In order to influence this process effectively in the future we need to:

1. Understand more fully the natural history of the systemic response to major trauma.
2. Be able to identify *soon after presentation* those patients who are at risk of developing complications later in their management.
3. Develop an intervention, targeted at this group of patients, which will allow this excessive response to be attenuated or avoided.

Pathophysiology

The systemic response is a summation of a number of pathophysiologic processes including fat embolism, inflammatory hyperstimulation, coagulation activation, and neuroendocrine stimulation (Fig. 22-1).

Fat Embolism and Fat Embolus Syndrome

Ninety percent of all fractures are associated with measurable pulmonary fat embolism,[53,133] but only a small proportion of these patients will go on to develop the clinical features of fat embolus syndrome (FES). Fat emboli arise from intravasation of fat and bone marrow from the medullary cavity of bone. There are at least 130 mL of liquid fat in the adult human tibia or femur[113] and the sudden pressure wave at the time of fracture

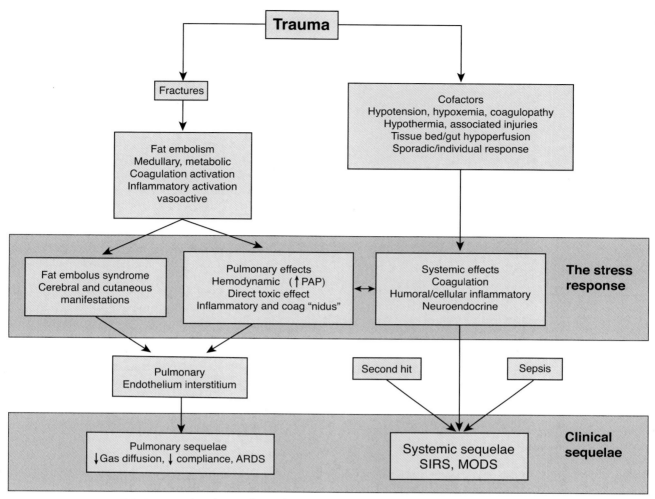

FIGURE 22-1 Flow chart to show schematic representation of the stress response to trauma.

forces fat out of the medullary cavity and into the venous circulation. Bone fracture is not necessarily required: several cases of fatal fat embolism have been reported after bone contusion.[8] Fat emboli also form from the destabilization of serum lipids (under the influence of C-reactive protein), and from the formation of fat de novo from depot precursors (following neuroendocrine activation).[6,118] Continued movement of unstabilized fractures and surgical instrumentation of the medullary canal causes further intravasation.[152] Fat travels through the right side of the heart and embolizes in the lungs, which act as a filter. Neutral fats from the bone marrow are chemically innocuous, but over the course of 12 to 72 hours undergo hydrolysis in the lungs to form fatty acids.[8,42,64] These are exceptionally toxic to pulmonary tissue, causing disruption of the alveolar capillary membrane and the development of hemorrhagic pulmonary edema, accompanied by reduced surfactant activity.

Just 20 mL of fat, if broken down uniformly, would yield 40 billion microemboli, 10 μm in diameter, which would be sufficient to block every capillary in the lung[8] were it not for the opening up of arteriovenous connections. This "shunting" allows fat to enter the left-sided (systemic) circulation, where it eventually embolizes in peripheral vascular beds including the brain, skin, and kidney. However, shunting also results in deoxygenated blood passing directly back into the right-sided circulation, resulting in hypoxemia.

If sufficiently severe, this process results in the clinically recognized features of FES (Table 22-1). The diagnostic criteria of Gurd and Wilson[57] are widely quoted and represent an early attempt to understand and describe this process. The criteria are largely empirical, and alternatives have been proposed.[43,63,76] Clinically, most patients spontaneously improve from Fat Embolism Syndrome and return to normal after about 5 days,[118] but there is an associated mortality of between 10%[43,124] and 20%.[42]

Inflammation

It has become increasingly clear that this simple mechanistic interpretation of fat embolism and posttraumatic respiratory failure is insufficient to explain the range of responses encountered after trauma, and the inflammatory system is implicated as an important and complex component of the response. The fracture itself causes a localized inflammatory reaction: monocytes, macrophages, neutrophils, and endothelial cells all release cytokines at the fracture site,[91] and these enter the venous circulation along with the fat and are carried to the lungs and then to the systemic circulation.

Cytokines can be classified as either proinflammatory or anti-inflammatory, and certain cytokines such as interleukin-6 (Il-6) have been shown to exhibit pleiotropism, displaying either proinflammatory or anti-inflammatory effects depending upon

TABLE 22-1	**Fat Embolus Syndrome: Gurd and Wilson's Diagnostic Criteria**
Major	Respiratory symptoms and signs (hypoxemia); radiographic changes
	Cerebral signs unrelated to head injury or other conditions
	Petechial rash
Minor	Tachycardia over 110 beats per minute
	Pyrexia >38.5°C
	Retinal changes of fat or petechiae
	Renal changes
	Jaundice
	Laboratory:
	Acute fall in hemoglobin
	Sudden thrombocytopenia
	High erythrocyte sedimentation rate
	Fat macroglobulinemia

One major and four minor criteria and fat macroglobulinemia are required for diagnosis.[58]

the circumstances.[71] Proinflammatory cytokines include tumour necrosis factor α (TNFα), Il-6, and Il-8, which serve to initiate inflammatory activity and the release of other cytokines, and to stimulate the hepatic acute phase response. Anti-inflammatory cytokines (including Il-4, Il-10, and Il-13) suppress this inflammatory activity.

The release of inflammatory cytokines initiates a defined sequence of neutrophil chemotaxis and recruitment. This process requires the expression of specific adhesion molecules by both the neutrophil (CD11-b) and endothelial cell (intercellular adhesion molecules [ICAM] and selectins) and is stimulated by the local secretion of Il-8.[50,97] Endothelial permeability is increased, and the neutrophil gains access to the interstitial space by diapedesis, and then degranulates with the release of further cytokines, reactive oxygen metabolites, and proteases.[20] These substances cause the local disruption of cell membranes and connective tissue. In the lung, the parenchyma becomes edematous, reducing oxygen diffusion from the alveoli, impairing respiratory compliance, and generating the typical radiographic appearance of acute lung injury: diffuse pulmonary infiltration (Table 22-2).

TABLE 22-2	**Criteria Stipulated by the American-European Consensus Document for the Diagnosis of Adult Respiratory Distress Syndrome**[10,11]
Partial pressure of oxygen in arterial blood/Fraction of inspired oxygen	<26.7 kilopascal
Radiology (P:F ratio)	Bilateral infiltrates on frontal chest radiograph
Pulmonary artery wedge pressure	<18 mm Hg or no clinical evidence of left atrial hypertension

Coagulation

The coagulation system is also intimately involved in the stress response to trauma. The extrinsic pathway of the coagulation system is activated after injury by tissue hypoxia[24] and the exposure of fat and subendothelial tissue factor, resulting in thrombin and fibrin formation. This activation is further promoted by the inflammatory response in two ways: (i) circulating TNFα, Il-1, and Il-6 stimulate the expression of tissue factor and up-regulate fibrinogen production, resulting in a procoagulant response, and (ii) the same cytokines also stimulate increased levels of plasminogen activator inhibitor (PAI-1), which leads to inhibition of fibrinolysis, resulting in an antifibrinolytic response.[70,127] After injury, this locally serves to promote hemostasis. However, systemic activation causes a shift in the dynamic equilibrium between the stimulation and suppression of coagulation, and results in net systemic coagulation (demonstrated by elevated prothrombin fragment and fibrinogen levels), platelet activation (elevated β-thromboglobulin levels), and fibrinolysis (elevated D-dimers).[121]

Intravascular fibrin microthrombi are generated and embolize in distal vascular beds (causing tissue ischemia and cell death), and the consumption of clotting factors and platelets results in a prolonged prothrombin time or even disseminated intravascular coagulation.[47] With the transendothelial exudation of edema fluid, coagulation factors, and cytokines, fibrin and fibrinogen deposition also occurs in the extravascular space. As a result, platelets levels fall over the 24 hours after injury, while fibrinogen levels and prothrombin time rise gradually over the first 4 days.[47] Such coagulopathy during this period increases the risk of hemorrhage and is an independent predictor of mortality after trauma.[81]

Neuroendocrine Response

Although the current evidence derives principally from animal studies and the clinical implications are unclear, the perception (or anticipation) of nociceptive stimuli is likely to be an important component of the stress response.[152]. However, ameliorating pain (aside from a clear humanitarian requirement) probably also contributes to the control of the stress response.

Respiratory Failure and Adult Respiratory Distress Syndrome

Respiratory insufficiency is common after trauma.[90] It is a key determinant of morbidity and mortality, and often precedes the systemic manifestations of multisystem dysfunction.[43,118] The clinical signs of hypoxemia are well recognized: agitated or obtunded sensorium, tachypnea, tachycardia, and cyanosis. These signs are easily confirmed by measurements of hemoglobin saturation and arterial oxygen tension, which should be routinely monitored after major trauma. A discrete underlying cause may be apparent on clinical assessment (Table 22-3).

However, in a proportion of patients, a severe respiratory failure develops, which is refractory to oxygen therapy and is not due solely to these treatable causes. The resulting hypoxemic state has been variously termed FES, shock lung, neurogenic pulmonary edema,[122] acute lung injury, and acute respiratory distress syndrome (ARDS). These terms have been applied inconsistently and often interchangeably, and in some instances probably reflect recognition of the same pathologic and clinical process by those in disparate branches of medicine. The pre-

TABLE 22-3	Causes of Hypoxemia after Trauma

Type 1 Respiratory Failure: Inadequate Oxygenation
(resulting in hypoxemia[79,154])
Upper airway obstruction
    Foreign body or misplaced endotracheal tube
Thoracic injury
    Flail chest, pneumothorax, pulmonary contusion, aspiration pneumonitis
Circulatory failure
    Hypovolemia, cardiac tamponade, cardiac failure (including fluid overload)

Type 2 Respiratory Failure: Inadequate Ventilation
(resulting in hypoxemia and hypercapnia >6.1 kilopascal[79,154])
Head Injury
Drug Toxicity
    Prescribed or nonprescribed drugs including alcohol taken prior to injury
    Drugs given during resuscitation including analgesics and anaesthetic agents

ferred definitions for this hypoxic state are provided by the American-European Consensus Criteria, which distinguish acute lung injury and ARDS according to degree of severity (see Table 22-2). Management of ARDS, once developed, is currently entirely supportive with use of high-inspired oxygen fractions and ventilator settings to counter the poor compliance and reduced diffusion capabilities of the stiff, heavy lung tissue[26]; however, a number of treatment modalities have been tried (and rejected) in the past. The administration of steroids (methylprednisolone) as "membrane stabilizers" was initially promising, but sepsis proved to be a significant complication, and subsequent modern studies have not supported its use.[1,12,75,86,138] Heparin transiently enjoyed widespread clinical use,[8,123] despite the dangers of hemorrhage and rapid lipolysis, but its current role remains to be defined.[74] Ethanol, which decreases lipolysis, and dextrose, which decreases free fatty acid mobilization, have also been used empirically.[53,133,138]

Recent advances in many fields, particularly the immunology of sepsis, have suggested more focussed possible treatments, including (in animal models) specific receptor antagonists to Il-1,[95] antibodies to adhesion proteins CD 11 and ICAM, and cyclo-oxygenase inhibitors.[30] Tissue plasminogen activator and antithrombin III also reduce lung injury in animal models of ARDS.[7] Activated protein C (APC) has been shown to reduce mortality in septic human patients, an effect which may be due to its promotion of fibrinolysis or its direct inhibition of Il-1, Il-6, and TNFα expression.[64] Although APC increased the risk of significant hemorrhage (which limits its applicability in trauma), the success of this immunologic therapy raises the prospect of more specific drug treatments in the future.

Mortality from ARDS is in the region of 30% to 50%. The aim of the orthopaedic traumatologist should be to prevent the development of ARDS wherever possible, by identifying patients who are at risk, monitoring them closely, and ensuring that unstable fractures of the pelvis and femur are stabilized promptly. The issues of how to identify these patients accurately, and what constitutes their optimal initial management, remain unclear.

Who Is at Risk?

Patients at risk of developing respiratory insufficiency are at present most satisfactorily identified by their injury profile.[125,152] However, while this approach has reasonable sensitivity, it has poor positive predictive value.[50] Analysis of the Il-8 concentrations within bronchioalveolar lavage fluid taken at the time of presentation has been shown to be indicative of the risk of the later development of ARDS, but is invasive and requires additional expertise in the emergency department.[38] Urinary albumin excretion rate 8 hours after admission following trauma has been shown to offer a high positive and negative predictive value for the later development of ARDS and respiratory insufficiency, but is not so discriminatory at the time of admission.[97,98] It has been proposed that laboratory measurements of humoral inflammatory and coagulation markers at the time of admission may allow more convenient and precise identification of patients at increased risk.[48,120]

Il-6 and Il-8 are markedly raised in the systemic circulation after trauma, tending to peak between 7 and 24 hours, usually returning to normal after 3 to 4 days.[51,93,110] The degree of elevation of Il-6 is associated with the severity of trauma:[108,110] There is no increase in Il-6 after ankle fracture compared with normal levels (around 10 pg/mL^{-1}), but levels increase to 50 pg/mL^{-1} after an isolated femoral fracture and nearly 600 pg mL^{-1} after multiple trauma with femoral fracture.[108] Although Il-6 levels as high as 700 pg/mL^{-1} are observed in patients not suffering complications,[108] there is accumulating circumstantial evidence that the degree of elevation of these cytokines after injury correlates with the likelihood of subsequent adverse outcome.[93] Serum levels of Il-6, Il-8, and elastase are significantly higher among those developing multiple organ dysfunction syndrome (MODS), and levels are higher again in those dying of MODS[93]: Nast-Kolb[93] reported that trauma patients developing MODS had a mean Il-6 at admission of over 700 pg/mL^{-1}, compared with a mean level of less than 200 pg/mL^{-1} at admission for those patients not developing complications. Pape[107,109] reported that Il-6 concentrations in excess of 500 pg/mL^{-1} were associated with the development of MODS.

Markers of neutrophil activation and adhesion are also raised after trauma. ICAM, L-selectin, CD-11 integrin,[50,81] and elastase[149] levels are all raised at the time of admission. Increases in markers of coagulation system activation are also reported after trauma, and the degree of elevation is also associated with the development of complications.[46,64,93,120] Patients developing respiratory insufficiency have been shown to have significantly greater perturbations in coagulation times, platelet consumption, and the levels of β-thromboglobulins, prothrombin fragments, and D-dimers than those that do not.[120]

Measurements of cytokines and markers of coagulation activation are therefore attractive as surrogate outcome measurements after trauma, and the identification of a discrete test or tests that would correlate with clinical outcome would be highly desirable.[48] However, the sensitivity, specificity, and relationship with clinical complications remains undefined for analyses of this highly complex system of cascades. Most importantly, cytokine levels have not been shown to be of independent (or even additional) predictive importance beyond standard clinical data at the time of admission. There is insufficient experience with these techniques to base judgements or management decisions on plasma cytokine assays, and these measurements remain research tools at present.

Genetic Predisposition

Patients with unexceptional injuries have been noted to suffer exaggerated systemic responses to injury, and a genetic basis for such sporadic complications has been proposed.[51] A few polymorphisms have been identified as important after injury. For example, a single base-pair (4G/5G) polymorphism exists for the gene that governs plasma concentrations of PAI-1 and influences inflammation. In a striking study of 61 comparable trauma patients, it was shown that the homozygous 4G/4G genotype resulted in increased levels of PAI-1, with a mortality of 51%, whereas the mortality of the heterozygous 4G/5G genotype was only 28% and of the 5G/5G genotype, only 15%.[88]

Many more genetic polymorphisms have been identified that are procoagulant and antifibrinolytic,[127,132] and several proinflammatory polymorphisms have been identified in relation to autoimmune, inflammatory, and neoplastic disease; these may also have an influence in the posttraumatic state.[49,116,135,154]

Timing of Surgery

Numerous simultaneous improvements in the management of trauma patients have resulted in a marked fall in the incidence of respiratory insufficiency from as much as 22% of trauma admissions in the 1960s and 1970s, when much of the published work on FES was produced,[119] to below 5% in recent studies. Many factors are likely to be of importance in this falling incidence, including better prehospital care, more rapid (and aggressive) resuscitation protocols, and improved intensive medical supportive therapy. Major advances in fracture management have also occurred over the past 4 decades, from a conservative approach involving traction and plaster cast immobilization, to an interventional strategy involving operative internal stabilization and early patient rehabilitation.

It was established in the 1970s and 1980s that the early stabilization of long bone (principally femoral) fractures reduces mortality. Early and delayed stabilization were directly compared in several retrospective reviews[9,18,28,33,68,86,115,123,131,141,143] and a small prospective study.[78] The risk of ARDS was demonstrated to be around five times higher in patients who had stabilization delayed beyond 24 hours. The influential prospective randomized study by Bone et al.[17] confirmed a decreased risk of ARDS, FES, pulmonary emboli, and pneumonia in those patients with multiple injuries undergoing stabilization of all long bone fractures within 24 hours of injury, and the concept of early surgical stabilization of major fractures has now been widely accepted. There is strong biologic support for this concept: delayed stabilization of fractures results in prolonged activation of the coagulation and complement responses, which then rapidly decrease towards normal following surgical stabilization.[130]

Selecting the Type of Surgery and the "Second Hit" Phenomenon

The injury that initiates the systemic stress response is termed the "first hit." In addition to this direct response, the first hit also results in neutrophil "priming." A primed neutrophil generates a more intense reaction to a subsequent stimulus,[20,21,97,111,157] termed the "second hit." This priming response may persist for more than 24 hours after the first hit.[21]

Surgery, as well as persistent physiologic instability, is a potent potential second hit and intensifies the inflammatory response.[51,109] The nailing of femoral fractures in particular causes an increase in circulating levels of elastase and Il-6.[51] The magnitude of this secondary response is related to the extent of the first hit[109] and thus is more marked in severely injured patients and those with persisting physiologic instability.[59] In comparisons of surgical strategies in physiologically stable patients, immediate intramedullary nailing raised Il-6 levels from 55 to 250 pg/mL^{-1}, while primary external fixation resulted in no such increase.[105]

Although the intramedullary stabilization of fractures reduces the incidence of posttraumatic respiratory insufficiency, nailing also theoretically provides the circumstances for the exacerbation of the stress response and lung injury. Refinements in the technique of nailing have been sought in order to minimize this second hit. Animal and surrogate end-point studies have suggested that the use of unreamed intramedullary nails,[51,107] altered reamer design,[102] faster reamer revolutions with slower introduction of the reamer,[92] and venting of the distal fragment[83] may result in less severe pulmonary injury. However, no advantage has been substantiated by clinical studies, and much interest centers on whether there is an association between this second hit response detected using surrogate outcome measurements and clinically relevant respiratory insufficiency, and whether such complications can be diminished by pharmacologic therapy or by reducing the severity of the second hit.

"Damage Control Orthopaedics": Polytrauma, Thoracic Injuries, and Head Injuries

A small, discrete group of multiply injured patients who remain physiologically unstable despite initial resuscitation are unsuitable for prolonged or extensive immediate surgery. Scalea and his coauthors[128] first proposed that these patients should undergo "damage control orthopaedic surgery" (DCO): a rapid, minimally invasive stabilization procedure (effectively, the external fixation of femoral shaft fractures and mechanically unstable pelvic fractures) followed by a period of resuscitation and physiologic stabilization in the intensive therapy unit, before undergoing later conversion to internal fixation. These proposed patients include those with head and thoracic injuries, and the "lethal triad" of hypoxemia, hypothermia, and coagulopathy.[105,106,114] It has not been possible to establish clear, evidenced-based criteria for the use of damage control techniques. Moreover, there are a number of potential disadvantages, including the requirement for two operative procedures, and the morbidity often resulting from definitive external fixation of femoral fractures in those who do not undergo conversion. Proposed applications of DCO include the following:

- **Physiologic instability:** An empirical categorization of patients into four categories has been proposed: stable, borderline, unstable, and in extremis. The precise definition of each category, particularly that of the borderline patient, has tended to vary in the literature (Table 22-4). A detailed description based on the grades of shock identified by advanced trauma life support and elements of the lethal triad measured in the resuscitation room has been proposed (Table 22-5).[104] This paradigm proposes the use of standard

| TABLE 22-4 | **Characteristics of the Borderline Trauma Patient[104]** |

Polytrauma with injury severity score >40

Polytrauma with injury severity score >20 *plus* thoracic injury (abbreviated injury scale >3)

Polytrauma *plus* abdominal/pelvic injury *plus* systolic blood pressure <90 mm Hg

Pulmonary artery pressure exceeding 30 mm Hg

Pulmonary artery pressure rise exceeding 6 mm Hg during nailing of femur

internal fixation for stable patients and the use of DCO techniques (external fixation) for patients who are unstable or are in extremis. The management of the "borderline" patient is with standard techniques if the patient is stable on review during resuscitation or with DCO techniques if their response is uncertain. A retrospective study has suggested that use of these techniques may result in improved outcomes, but this has not been confirmed elsewhere and the issue remains contentious.[85,100,106]

- **Thoracic injury:** Of particular interest has been the potential application of DCO techniques in the management of patients with femoral fractures in association with significant thoracic injuries. A direct thoracic injury is three times more likely to be associated with respiratory failure than is a long bone fracture.[120] After a femoral fracture, an additional thoracic injury imparts a greater risk of pulmonary complications.[101,103] Interest has centered on the converse question: whether a patient with thoracic injury is at any additional risk when this injury is accompanied by a femoral fracture.[101] Contused, atelectatic, or collapsed regions of lung are hemorrhagic and edematous and have a reduced capillary bed perfusion. Therefore, in the presence of lung injury, the pulmonary blood flow may be directed to a smaller volume of parenchyma, delivering a greater concentration of fat, thrombus, and inflammatory cytokines, and thus a long bone injury might be expected to exacerbate a thoracic injury. However, the majority of studies[15,17,19,22,32,145,146] and a meta-analysis[120] report that the additional femoral fracture (however treated) is inconsequential in precipitating respiratory insufficiency, and it is the thoracic injury rather than the femoral fracture which determines overall risk.

- **Head injury:** Head injuries represent a similar potential exacerbating injury. The concept of secondary brain injury as a result of systemic hypotension or hypoxia is well established, and these patients might be expected to benefit from the application of DCO principles. However, the available evidence does not confirm this concept. Again, it appears that the head injury itself defines prognosis, and that the addition of a femoral fracture (however treated) does not influence outcome.[14,84]

Summary of the Systemic Response to Trauma

Severe injury results in a complex stress response that commences with the release of fat, thrombus, and cytokines from the site of injury to the systemic circulation and a neuroendocrine response. Respiratory insufficiency is an early and prognostically important consequence. It is largely accepted that multiply injured patients should undergo rapid resuscitation followed by early immobilization of major injuries, particularly pelvic and femoral fractures, within 12 to 24 hours. Although DCO is an attractive, rational concept and is probably as safe as definitive femoral nailing,[142] there is as yet no clinical evidence that it confers any advantage in terms of survival or outcome, and there are several inherent disadvantages. There remains a requirement for a large-scale prospective randomized clinical trial.

| TABLE 22-5 | **Clinical Parameters Influencing Management after Major Trauma** |

Element of the Lethal Triad	Parameter	Patient's Response to Resuscitation			
		Stable	Borderline	Unstable	In Extremis
Shock	Advanced trauma life support grade	I	II,III	III,IV	IV
	Blood pressure (mm Hg)	>100	80–100	60–90	<60
	Lactate	Normal	2.5	>2.5	Severe acidosis
	Base deficit (mmol/L^{-1})	Normal	No data	No data	>6
	Urine output (mL/hr^{-1})	>150	50–150	<100	<50
Coagulation	Platelet count	>100,000	90,000–110,000	<90,000	<70,000
Temperature	°C	>35	33–35	30–32	<30
Severity of associated injuries	Oxygen exchange (Partial pressure of oxygen in arterial blood: Fraction of inspired oxygen)	>350	300	200–300	<200
	AIS thorax	1	2–3	2–3	>3
	AIS extremity	1	2–3	3–4	Crush
Surgical strategy		Definitive surgery	Definitive surgery if stable, DCO if uncertain.	DCO	DCO

From Pape HC, Giannoudis PV, Krettek C, et al. Timing of fixation of major fractures in blunt polytrauma: role of conventional indicators in clinical decision making. J Orthop Trauma 2005;19:551–562.

Multiply injured patients should be managed by an orthopaedic trauma surgeon in a facility equipped and familiar with contemporary orthopaedic trauma management. The majority of injuries should be treated in the first 24 hours after injury, with long bone fractures of the lower limbs being stabilized with locked intramedullary nails. Where there is on-going physiologic instability during resuscitation, as measured by persistent grade III shock, coagulopathy, and hypothermia (the lethal triad), consideration should be given to rapid stabilization of femoral fractures and unstable pelvic fractures with an external fixator (DCO) to allow for further resuscitation in the intensive care setting. Definitive fixation is then provided once these elements of instability have been resolved.

CRUSH INJURIES AND RENAL FAILURE

Injury to muscle tissue may result from direct traumatic crush injury, compartment syndrome, vascular occlusion, or unprotected immobilization resulting in prolonged muscle compression. These factors, and injury sustained from reperfusion of ischemic tissue, may result in "crush syndrome," a systemic complication characterized by tense, edematous, painful muscles, dark-tea–colored urine, shock, and acidosis.[30] The history and a positive urine dipstick test, indicating the presence of hemoglobin in the absence of red blood cells on microscopy, should raise the suspicion of irreversible muscle injury (rhabdomyolysis), which can be confirmed by elevated plasma creatine kinase (CK) levels. Muscle can tolerate short periods (up to 2 hours) of complete ischemia, but after longer periods rhabdomyolysis occurs.[58] Partial ischemia may be more injurious and produce more severe systemic complications due to the constant leakage of metabolic by-products of injured myocytes. In a limb with total vascular occlusion, the systemic injury occurs at the time of reperfusion. After 3 hours of ischemic time, reperfusion results in a localized inflammatory response and edema due to increased capillary permeability. Calcium-mediated local cellular injury results in the release of myoglobin and potassium into the systemic circulation. Patients with rhabdomyolysis are at risk of acute renal failure (ARF) for the following reasons: intravascular hypovolemia as a result of localized intramuscular sequestration of plasma, precipitation of myoglobin in glomerular filtrate resulting in tubular obstruction, and renal ischemia due to the release of potent vasoconstrictors.

Sixty-five percent of patients with rhabdomyolysis develop renal failure. Prediction of patients at risk of ARF as a result of rhabdomyolysis is difficult. Admission serum CK concentrations cannot be used to predict who will develop renal failure after crush injury. Despite evidence that the mean CK level in this group is significantly higher, no suitable cut-off has been identified[36]; however, laboratory measurement of serum bicarbonate levels has been shown to be accurate in predicting who will develop renal failure especially in the presence of myoglobinuria. If the admission bicarbonate level is less than 17 mml/L, then the risk of developing renal failure is high.[93]

Prevention of crush syndrome can be divided into prevention of muscle injury and prevention of ARF. Restoration of blood flow to muscle compartments by treatment of the causative factor must be prompt (ischemia of longer than 6 hours is associated with a less favorable outcome).[89] Direct vascular injury may require emergency repair or bypass, and skeletal injuries must be stabilized. Fasciotomy may be indicated for compartment syndrome, although there is debate concerning the wisdom of reperfusion following prolonged ischemia.[13,45] Amputation may be indicated to protect the patient from the systemic injury of reperfusion. The Mangled Extremity Severity Score may help identify nonsalvageable extremities.[67]

The essential treatment following significant muscle injury to prevent ARF is effective fluid resuscitation to correct the hypotensive renal ischemia. After significant crush injury, serum myoglobin levels fall exponentially following removal of the causative factor even in the absence of renal function or hemodialysis.[149] High-volume diuresis by crystalloid infusion is indicated in these patients and central venous pressure recording may be required in those with cardiac impairment to avoid overload. An initial bolus of 1 L of normal saline followed by an infusion of normal saline at 200 to 700 mL/hr has been proposed.[125] Other measures include the use of mannitol to create an osmotic diuresis[78] and alkalinization of the urine with sodium bicarbonate to prevent tubular cast formation; however, the value of these additional interventions has been questioned, with no apparent benefit seen in one retrospective review of intensive care unit patients.[27] High-volume crystalloid infusion alone may suffice. If renal failure develops, renal dialysis or hemofiltration may be required. Mortality from crush syndrome is threefold higher (59%) in those who develop ARF.[36]

VENOUS THROMBOEMBOLISM

Virchow[147] identified the triad of factors responsible for venous thrombosis in 1856: venous stasis, vascular damage, and hypercoagulability. All three are frequently encountered following trauma, especially following high-energy injuries (Fig. 22-2).

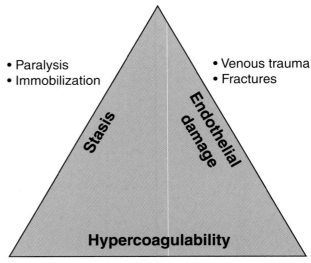

FIGURE 22-2 Virchow triad.

Orthopaedic trauma patients, in particular those requiring hospital admission, are often at risk of venous thrombosis and pulmonary embolism.[5] The estimate of that risk varies considerably and is dependent on the definition, mode of identification, and the nature of the study population's injuries. Most studies employ the outcome measure of deep vein thrombosis (DVT) identified on venography, duplex ultrasound, radioisotope uptake, or plethysmography as a surrogate for clinical DVT, placing the incidence between 6% and 60%. The incidence of symptomatic venous thromboembolism (VTE) following hip fracture from recent studies using chemical prophylaxis is 1% to 2%.[4,40] Fatal pulmonary embolism occurs in approximately 0.3% of hip fracture patients undergoing modern treatment including early mobilization and chemical thromboprophylaxis.

Among orthopaedic trauma patients, the risk of developing VTE is increased in those with spinal cord injury, fractures of the femur or tibia, those requiring surgery or a blood transfusion, and with increasing age.[48] Immobilization for more than 3 days has also been shown to increase the risk of VTE,[72] but it is not clear whether the factors outlined above are independent of this. Inheritance of a genetic predisposition to thrombus formation (thrombophilia) may increase the risk for an individual but cost-benefit analysis does not support trauma population screening.[25]

Surgeons should inquire about past history and a family history of venous thrombosis and consider postoperative anticoagulation for those with a positive history, although the latter has been shown to be a poor predictor of the presence of thrombophilia.[129] Approximately 10% of patients with hip fractures will have evidence of asymptomatic DVT using surrogate measures on admission to hospital. If admission is delayed by more than 48 hours from the time of the injury, then the incidence of DVT has been reported to be as high as 55%.[61] Importantly, the incidence of DVT for hospitalized patients with a delay greater than 48 hours between injury and surgery is associated with a similarly high (62%) incidence of DVT on ascending venography despite chemical prophylaxis with unfractionated heparin initiated on admission.[156]

The diagnosis of DVT or pulmonary embolism (PE) is made using a combination of history, clinical signs, clinical probability assessment, and imaging techniques. Assessment tools such as the Wells scoring system rely on factors including calf or thigh swelling, localized tenderness along the distribution of the deep venous system, unilateral pitting edema, recent history of surgery or immobilization, and personal or family history of VTE.[151] Fibrin D-dimer testing has been employed to exclude the diagnosis of VTE in ambulatory patients in whom the diagnosis is suspected; however, in the seriously injured patient or postoperative period, the sensitivity and specificity have been shown to be too low to guide diagnosis.[148]

Ultrasonography is nearly equivalent to venography, which is regarded as the criterion standard, in diagnosis of DVT proximal to the popliteal region and has the advantage of being noninvasive and repeatable.[73,144] Computed tomography (CT) venography has been shown to be less accurate than ultrasonography for the diagnosis of DVT.

The clinical symptoms of PE include transient dyspnea, chest pain and hemoptysis, with right-sided heart failure, syncope, and hypotension if the embolus is very large. Electrocardiogram findings are abnormal but nonspecific in 70% of patients with PE, the most common finding being a sinus tachycardia. Chest radiographs and blood gas analysis help to exclude alternative causes of dyspnea. Pulmonary angiography is the criterion standard in the diagnosis of PE. CT pulmonary angiography has been shown to be superior to ventilation-perfusion lung scanning[2] and is now the most widely used imaging modality with a specificity of 96% and sensitivity of 83%, which can be increased by the addition of venous phase imaging.[138] There are concerns about the clinical significance of some smaller lesions identified on modern high-resolution scanners.

PE is often a fatal complication with two thirds of patients surviving only 20 minutes from the onset of symptoms, which is why efforts are aimed at thromboembolic prophylaxis.

Measures employed to prevent VTE include early mobilization, avoiding hemoconcentration by maintaining adequate hydration, and chemical and physical prophylaxis. Numerous investigators have studied the effectiveness of chemical prophylaxis at reducing the incidence of VTE following hip fracture surgery using surrogate asymptomatic DVT as the primary outcome measure but the picture remains unclear. Level 1 placebo-controlled studies have shown the use of low-molecular-weight heparin (LMWH) to be effective in reducing the surrogate DVT rate up to 9 days following surgery.[69] Fondaparinux sodium has been found to be more effective than LMWH in reducing the asymptomatic VTE rate but at the cost of higher significant postoperative bleeding.[40] The addition of mechanical prophylaxis may reduce the rate of DVT further for those on LMWH.[136] A large randomized study has demonstrated significant reduction in the incidence of symptomatic VTE with the use of aspirin for chemoprophylaxis when compared to placebo.[4] Concerns have been raised about this study, in particular over the use of other chemoprophylactic agents for some patients enrolled in the trial. No study has yet shown evidence of a significant reduction in fatal PE with any prophylactic regime, and in many studies there are no significant differences in symptomatic VTE events.

A common concern with much of the literature on VTE prophylaxis is that the end-point is selected during the initial inpatient stay, typically day 7 to 10, whereas there is some evidence that the risk to the patient may be greatest in the period between discharge and 3 months. The concept of a rebound thrombophilia on cessation of chemoprophylaxis at discharge has prompted investigators to look at the effect of extended prophylaxis. One level 1 study has shown significant reduction in asymptomatic and symptomatic VTE events with fondaparinux sodium continued up to 23 days compared to only inpatient fondaparinux prophylaxis[41] after hip fracture surgery. Again, there was a trend toward an increase in major bleeding. Mechanical devices, including foot or calf compression devices and inferior vena cava filters, avoid the risk of anticoagulation and can be used when chemical prophylaxis is contraindicated (e.g., patients with head injury or abdominal injury). Few studies demonstrate any significant differences in VTE rate with mechanical prophylaxis compared to chemical prophylaxis, but they may be associated with a significant reduction in asymptomatic events when used in combination.[46] Inferior vena cava filters do not eliminate the risk of PE and may increase the risk of recurrent DVT and VTE[37]; however, no pulmonary embolic events were reported in a retrospective study of 56 orthopaedic patients with removable caval filters.[140] Graded venous compression stockings have not been shown to reduce the DVT rate when used as an adjunct to chemical prophylaxis,[34] and patient compliance is poor. Most clinicians treat DVT and PE with oral adjusted dose warfarin for a minimum of 3 months; alternatively, DVT can be treated with appropriate doses of LMWH.

Practice regarding ambulatory trauma patients (e.g., patients with ankle fractures with cast immobilization) varies widely. Recent evidence suggests that the risk is low, with 5 of 100 patients with stable ankle fractures treated in below-knee plaster cast having DVT diagnosed on color Doppler duplex ultrasound.[132] Two were proximal to the calf and none were symptomatic. Chemical prophylaxis has not been shown to reduce the risk of DVT in this ambulatory group.[74]

The subject of venous thrombosis is full of conflicting evidence and institutions' recommendations vary considerably. In attempts to harmonize practice, many groups have published guidelines based on scientific critique of the literature. Unfortunately, some of these recommendations have added to the controversy.

 AUTHORS' PREFERRED MANAGEMENT OF VENOUS THROMBOEMBOLISM

The ideal regime for DVT prophylaxis following trauma remains contentious. While guidelines help to standardize management and improve prescribing compliance, each patient should be assessed individually. This assessment should include consideration of the individual's preinjury risk factors (increased risk with increasing age, obesity, oral contraceptive pill, malignancy), injury sustained (increased risk with spinal cord injury, femur/tibial fracture, the need for surgery or transfusion), and postoperative rehabilitation (increased risk with immobilization greater than 3 days). Equal weight should be given to the risk to the patient of chemical thromboprophylaxis. Patients with an increased bleeding risk should be managed with mechanical prophylaxis devices. Those patients considered to have a high risk of venous thrombosis and a low risk of bleeding should be managed with mechanical prophylaxis and chemical prophylaxis which should be continued until 4 weeks after surgery or until the patient is ambulant, whichever is longer.

A patient suspected of having a venous thrombotic event should be investigated with duplex ultrasound for DVT or CT pulmonary angiography with venous phase imaging for PE depending on the clinical picture. Where venous thrombosis is demonstrated, the patient should be commenced on therapeutic warfarin for a minimum of 3 months.

POSTOPERATIVE PYREXIA

Normal body temperature is maintained at around 36.8°C (+/− 0.4°C). There is diurnal variation in body temperature with a peak in the late afternoon and trough in the early morning.[80] Fever, which is typically defined as a core body temperature greater than 38.0°C, is a normal physiologic adaptation in response to cytokine and prostaglandin-mediated stimuli. The hypothalamus is responsible for thermoregulation, controlling heat loss in response to metabolic heat production, and the surrounding ambient environment. It has no contact with circulating pathogens or inflammatory factors because of the blood brain barrier, but receives prostaglandin E_2 mediated signals from the circumventricular organ system that is in contact with the systemic circulation. While fever is clearly an adaptive response that presumably affords some survival advantage, there is uncertainty as to what these benefits might be. Indirect evidence suggests that it may enhance the immunologic response to infection or impede replication of some microorganisms.[39] Fever is most commonly triggered in response to an infectious pathogen or its toxins; however, in the perioperative period, there are a number of other factors that may produce a rise in core body temperature.

The major cause of low-grade pyrexia in the immediate postoperative period is cytokine release due to tissue trauma.[56] Other causes are listed in Table 22-6 and include blood transfusion, hematoma, and pulmonary atelectasis. Administration of antipyrogens for patient comfort should suffice, and the fever will usually settle within a few days. Fever developing around day 5 is often as a result of infectious pathogen. Catheter-associated urinary tract infection is the most common cause, responsible for over 40% of all acquired infections in the postoperative phase. Infecting organisms are introduced at the time of catheter insertion or ascend from the perineum adjacent to the catheter, and most originate from the patient's own cutaneous flora or from the hands of healthcare workers. Avoidance or prompt removal of in-dwelling urinary and vascular catheters can prevent nosocomial infection. Pyrexia developing 5 to 7 days after surgery may suggest a surgical site infection. A mandatory survey of surgical site infection in England carried out between October 1997 and December 2003 found that the rate of infection following hip hemiarthroplasty was 4.9% (95% confidence interval [CI] 4.6 to 5.3) and following open reduction of a fracture was 3.8% (95% CI 3.3 to 4.3).[60]

Determination of cause is the first step in the management of a patient with postoperative pyrexia. A thorough clinical ex-

TABLE 22-6	**Causes of Perioperative Pyrexia**

Noninfectious Causes

Major tissue trauma
Transfused blood products
Postoperative atelectasis
Hematoma
VTE
Acute myocardial infarct
Intracranial pathology
Pancreatitis
Alcohol withdrawal
Medications

Infectious Causes

Catheter-associated urinary tract infection
Lower respiratory tract infection
Wound infection
Intravascular catheter-associated infection
Primary Gram-negative septicemia
Abdominal sepsis
Clostridium difficile colitis
Fungal infection

amination, including chest auscultation, may suggest a cause. Plain chest radiography, culture of urinary specimens, and blood cultures may aid the diagnosis and identify the infecting organism to guide treatment. In addition, elevated serum levels of C-reactive protein and the erythrocyte sedimentation rate may support the diagnosis or at least provide a baseline to monitor progress. There is some evidence that persistently elevated serum Il-6[44] levels may be more specific for infection in the early postoperative phase, but this test is not widely available. The value of wound swabs when surgical site infection is suspected has been questioned (see Chapter 24).[23] In noncatheterized patients, a count of 10^5 organisms per mL of urine is used as the criterion for the diagnosis of a urinary tract infection. In catheterized patients, it has been shown that a count of 10^3 microorganisms per mL is a sensitive cut-off.[137]

Nosocomial pneumonia is the second most common infective cause of postoperative pyrexia. Adults at greatest risk are those over 65 years, those with serious comorbidities, immunosuppression, depressed sensorium, malnutrition, and those subject to thoracoabdominal trauma or surgery. Those receiving mechanical ventilation make up a small proportion of patients with nosocomial pneumonia but are at high risk, and the development of ventilator-associated pneumonia is a poor prognostic marker with mortality rates up to 10 times greater for this group than ventilated patients without pneumonia.[117] Ventilator-associated pneumonia also typically occurs 4 to 5 days after intubation. Most bacterial infections occur secondary to aspiration of pathogens that colonise the oropharynx or upper gastrointestinal tract and are frequently polymicrobial with Gram-negative bacilli as the predominant organism. The diagnosis is made on the basis of pyrexia, cough, and purulent sputum with the presence of radiographic evidence of new or progressive pulmonary infiltrate. Sputum cultures, tracheal aspirate, pleural aspiration, and blood cultures may help to identify the responsible organisms to guide treatment. Preventative measures include decreasing aspiration by the patient, hand washing by healthcare workers, appropriate decontamination of ventilatory devices, and use of available vaccines.

QUALITY OF LIFE AFTER SEVERE TRAUMA

Survival after trauma does not equate to returning to a preinjury level of function. Patients are often restricted in their level of mechanical or social function, cognitive ability, and ability to care for and provide for themselves and their families. With the more frequent use of patient-centered outcome measurements, it has become possible to measure the long-term sequelae of major trauma more easily.

Cognitive Defects

Direct brain or spinal cord injury has major implications for subsequent physical, cognitive, psychologic, and social function, and the specialty of rehabilitation medicine has developed to provide for the requirements of this group of patients.[95] More generally, survivors of critical illness, particularly ARDS, are also known to suffer from depression and psychologic morbidity.[35] However, it is also clear that secondary brain injury resulting from purely orthopaedic injuries can have substantial long-term cognitive consequences, particularly where these deficits are

sought. Recent case reports and retrospective reviews have detailed deficits in working memory, executive functioning, verbal fluency, and mental processing speed, along with anxiety, depression, and posttraumatic stress disorder occurring after trauma in the absence of head injury.[55,66]

Neuromuscular Weakness

In addition to specific regional weakness resulting from local injuries to nerve or muscle, a profound and persisting weakness can occur after trauma, termed critical illness polyneuropathy. This condition may operate at the level of the nerve, motor end plate, or muscle, with proposed etiologies including compression, disuse atrophy, inflammation, and pharmacologic neuromuscular blockade, and may persist indefinitely despite extensive rehabilitation, resulting in loss of function and independence.[3,62]

REFERENCES

1. Alho, A. Fat embolism syndrome: etiology, pathogenesis, and treatment. Acta Chir Scand.Suppl1980;499:75–85.
2. Anderson DR, Kahn SR, Rodger MA, et al. Computed tomographic pulmonary angiography vs. ventilation-perfusion lung scanning in patients with suspected pulmonary embolism: a randomized controlled trial. JAMA 2007;298:2743–2753.
3. Angel MJ, Bril V, Shannon P, et al. Neuromuscular function in survivors of the acute respiratory distress syndrome. Can J Neurol Sci 2007;34:427–432.
4. Anonymous. Prevention of pulmonary embolism and deep vein thrombosis with low-dose aspirin: Pulmonary Embolism Prevention (PEP) trial. Lancet 2000;355: 1295–1302.
5. Anonymous. Risk of and prophylaxis for venous thromboembolism in hospital patients. Thromboembolic Risk Factors (THRIFT) Consensus Group. BMJ 1992;305:567–574.
6. Baker PL, Pazell JA, Peltier LF. Free fatty acids, catecholamines, and arterial hypoxia in patients with fat embolism. J Trauma 1971;11:1026–1030.
7. Balk RA, Jacobs RF, Tryka AF, et al. Effects of ibuprofen on neutrophil function and acute lung injury in canine endotoxin shock. Crit Care Med 1988;16:1121–1127.
8. Beck JP, Collins JA. Theoretical and clinical aspects of posttraumatic fat embolism syndrome. Instr Course Lect 1973;38–87.
9. Behrman SW, Fabian TC, Kudsk KA, et al. Improved outcome with femur fractures: early vs. delayed fixation. J Trauma 1990;30:792–797.
10. Bernard GR, Artigas A, Brigham KL. The American-European Consensus Conference on ARDS; definitions, mechanisms, relevant outcomes, and clinical trial coordination. Am J Resp Crit Care Med 1994;149:818–824.
11. Bernard GR, Artigas A, Brigham KL, et al. Report of the American-European Consensus conference on acute respiratory distress syndrome: definitions, mechanisms, relevant outcomes, and clinical trial coordination. Consensus Committee. J Crit Care 1994;9: 72–81.
12. Bernard GR, Luce JM, Sprung CL, et al. High-dose corticosteroids in patients with the adult respiratory distress syndrome. N Engl J Med 1987;317:1565–1570.
13. Better OS, Stein JH. Early management of shock and prophylaxis of acute renal failure in traumatic rhabdomyolysis. N Engl J Med 1990;322:825–829.
14. Bhandari M, Guyatt GH, Khera V, et al. Operative management of lower extremity fractures in patients with head injuries. Clin Orthop Relat Res 2003;407:187–198.
15. Bone LB, Anders MJ, Rohrbacher BJ. Treatment of femoral fractures in the multiply injured patient with thoracic injury. Clin Orthop Relat Res 1998;347:57–61.
16. Bone LB, Babikian G, Stegemann PM. Femoral canal reaming in the polytrauma patient with chest injury. A clinical perspective. Clin Orthop Relat Res 1995;318:91–94.
17. Bone LB, Johnson KD, Weigelt J, et al. Early versus delayed stabilization of femoral fractures. A prospective randomized study. J Bone Joint Surg Am 1989;71:336–340.
18. Bone LB, McNamara K, Shine B, et al. Mortality in multiple trauma patients with fractures. J Trauma 1994;37:262–264.
19. Bosse MJ, MacKenzie EJ, Riemer BL, et al. Adult respiratory distress syndrome, pneumonia, and mortality following thoracic injury and a femoral fracture treated either with intramedullary nailing with reaming or with a plate. A comparative study. J Bone Joint Surg Am 1997;79:799–809.
20. Botha AJ, Moore FA, Moore EE, et al. Early neutrophil sequestration after injury: a pathogenic mechanism for multiple organ failure. J Trauma 1995;39:411–417.
21. Botha AJ, Moore FA, Moore EE, et al. Postinjury neutrophil priming and activation: an early vulnerable window. Surgery 1995;118:358–364.
22. Boulanger BR, Stephen D, Brenneman FD. Thoracic trauma and early intramedullary nailing of femur fractures: are we doing harm? J Trauma 1997;43:24–28.
23. Bowler PG, Duerden BI, Armstrong DG. Wound microbiology and associated approaches to wound management. Clin Microbiol Rev 2001;14:244–269.
24. Brohi K, Cohen MJ, Davenport RA. Acute coagulopathy of trauma: mechanism, identification, and effect. Curr Opin Crit Care 2007;13:680–685.
25. Brouwer JL, Veeger NJ, Kluin-Nelemans HC, et al. The pathogenesis of venous thromboembolism: evidence for multiple interrelated causes. Ann Intern Med 2006;145: 807–815.
26. Brower RG, Lanken PN, MacIntyre N, et al. Higher-versus lower-positive end-expiratory pressures in patients with the acute respiratory distress syndrome. N Engl J Med 2004;351:327–336.

27. Brown CV, Rhee P, Chan L, et al. Preventing renal failure in patients with rhabdomyolysis: do bicarbonate and mannitol make a difference? J Trauma 2004;56:1191–1196.

28. Brundage SI, McGhan R, Jurkovich GJ, et al. Timing of femur fracture fixation: effect on outcome in patients with thoracic and head injuries. J Trauma 2002;52:299–307.

29. Burhop KE, Selig WM, Beeler DA, et al. Effect of heparin on increased pulmonary microvascular permeability after bone marrow embolism in awake sheep. Am Rev Respir Dis 1987;136:134–141.

30. Bywaters EG, Delory GE, Rimington C, et al. Myohaemoglobin in the urine of air raid casualties with crushing injury. Biochem J 1941;35:1164–1168.

31. Carey PD, Leeper-Woodford SK, Walsh CJ, et al. Delayed cyclo-oxygenase blockade reduces the neutrophil respiratory burst and plasma tumor necrosis factor levels in sepsis-induced acute lung injury. J Trauma 1991;31:733–740.

32. Carlson DW, Rodman GH Jr, Kaehr D, et al. Femur fractures in chest-injured patients: is reaming contraindicated? J Orthop Trauma 1998;12:164–168.

33. Charash WE, Fabian TC, Croce MA. Delayed surgical fixation of femur fractures is a risk factor for pulmonary failure independent of thoracic trauma. J Trauma 1994;37:667–672.

34. Cohen AT, Skinner JA, Warwick D, et al. The use of graduated compression stockings in association with fondaparinux in surgery of the hip. A multicenter, multinational, randomized, open-label, parallel-group comparative study. J Bone Joint Surg Br 2007;89:887–892.

35. Davidson TA, Caldwell ES, Curtis JR, et al. Reduced quality of life in survivors of acute respiratory distress syndrome compared with critically ill control patients. JAMA 1999;281:354–360.

36. de Meijer AR, Fikkers BG, de Keijzer MH., et al. Serum creatine kinase as predictor of clinical course in rhabdomyolysis: a 5-year intensive care survey. Intensive Care Med 2003;29:1121–1125.

37. Decousus H, Leizorovicz A, Parent F, et al. A clinical trial of vena caval filters in the prevention of pulmonary embolism in patients with proximal deep-vein thrombosis. Prevention du Risque d'Embolie Pulmonaire par Interruption Cave Study Group. N Engl J Med 1998;338:409–415.

38. Donnelly SC, Strieter RM, Kunkel SL, et al. Interleukin-8 and development of adult respiratory distress syndrome in at-risk patient groups. Lancet 1993;341:643–647.

39. Duff GW. Is fever beneficial to the host: a clinical perspective. Yale J Biol Med 1986;59:125–130.

40. Eriksson BI, Bauer KA, Lassen MR, et al. Fondaparinux compared with enoxaparin for the prevention of venous thromboembolism after hip-fracture surgery. N Engl J Med 2001;345:1298–1304.

41. Eriksson BI, Lassen MR. Duration of prophylaxis against venous thromboembolism with fondaparinux after hip fracture surgery: a multicenter, randomized, placebo-controlled, double-blind study. Arch Intern Med 2003;163:1337–1342.

42. Fabian TC. Unravelling the fat embolism syndrome. N Engl J Med 1993;329:961–963.

43. Fabian TC, Hoots AV, Stanford DS, et al. Fat embolism syndrome: prospective evaluation in 92 fracture patients. Crit Care Med 1990;18:42–46.

44. Fassbender K, Pargger H, Muller W, et al. Interleukin-6 and acute-phase protein concentrations in surgical intensive care unit patients: diagnostic signs in nosocomial infection. Crit Care Med 1993;21:1175–1180.

45. Finkelstein JA, Hunter GA, Hu RW. Lower limb compartment syndrome: course after delayed fasciotomy. J Trauma 1996;40:342–344.

46. Fuchs S, Heyse T, Rudofsky G, et al. Continuous passive motion in the prevention of deep-vein thrombosis: a randomized comparison in trauma patients. J Bone Joint Surg Br 2005;87:1117–1122.

47. Gando S. Disseminated intravascular coagulation in trauma patients. Semin Thromb Hemost 2001;27:585–592.

48. Geerts WH, Code KI, Jay RM, et al. A prospective study of venous thromboembolism after major trauma. N Engl J Med 1994;331:1601–1606.

49. Giannoudis PV, Hildebrand F, Pape HC. Inflammatory serum markers in patients with multiple trauma. Can they predict outcome? J Bone Joint Surg Br 2004;86:313–323.

50. Giannoudis PV, Perry S, Smith RM. Systemic response to trauma. Current Orthopaedics 2001;15:176–183.

51. Giannoudis PV, Smith RM, Bellamy MC, et al. Stimulation of the inflammatory system by reamed and unreamed nailing of femoral fractures. An analysis of the second hit. J Bone Joint Surg Br 1999;81:356–361.

52. Giannoudis PV, Smith RM, Windsor AC, et al. Monocyte human leukocyte antigen-DR expression correlates with intrapulmonary shunting after major trauma. Am J Surg 1999;177:454–459.

53. Gitin TA, Seidel T, Cera PJ, et al. Pulmonary microvascular fat: the significance? Crit Care Med 1993;21:673–677.

54. Goris RJ, Gimbrere JS, van Niekerk JL, et al. Early osteosynthesis and prophylactic mechanical ventilation in the multitrauma patient. J Trauma 1982;22:895–903.

55. Gray AC, Torrens L, White TO, et al. The cognitive effects of fat embolus syndrome following an isolated femoral shaft fracture. A case report. J Bone Joint Surg Am 2007;89:1092–1096.

56. Guinn S, Castro FP Jr, Garcia R, et al. Fever following total knee arthroplasty. Am J Knee Surg 1999;12:161–164.

57. Gurd AR, Wilson RI. The fat embolism syndrome. J Bone Joint Surg Br 1974;56B:408–416.

58. Harris K, Walker PM, Mickle DA, et al. Metabolic response of skeletal muscle to ischemia. Am J Physiol 1986;250:H213–H220.

59. Harwood PJ, Giannoudis PV, van Griensven M, et al. Alterations in the systemic inflammatory response after early total care and damage control procedures for femoral shaft fracture in severely injured patients. J Trauma 2005;58:446–452.

60. Health Protection Agency. Surgical site surveillance in England. CDR Weekly 2004;14:1–5.

61. Hefley FG Jr, Nelson CL, Puskarich-May CL. Effect of delayed admission to the hospital on the preoperative prevalence of deep-vein thrombosis associated with fractures about the hip. J Bone Joint Surg Am 1996;78:581–583.

62. Herridge MS, Cheung AM, Tansey CM, et al. One-year outcomes in survivors of the acute respiratory distress syndrome. N Engl J Med 2003;348:683–693.

63. Hulman, G. The pathogenesis of fat embolism. J Pathol 1995;176:3–9.

64. Hulman G. Pathogenesis of nontraumatic fat embolism. Lancet 1988;1:1366–1367.

65. Idell S. Coagulation, fibrinolysis, and fibrin deposition in acute lung injury. Crit Care Med 2003;31:S213–S220.

66. Jackson JC, Hart RP, Gordon SM, et al. Six-month neuropsychological outcome of medical intensive care unit patients. Crit Care Med 2003;31:1226–1234.

67. Johansen K, Daines M, Howey T, et al. Objective criteria accurately predict amputation following lower extremity trauma. J Trauma 1990;30:568–572.

68. Johnson KD, Cadambi A, Seibert GB. Incidence of adult respiratory distress syndrome in patients with multiple musculoskeletal injuries: effect of early operative stabilization of fractures. J Trauma 1985;25:375–384.

69. Jørgensen PS, Knudsen JB, Broeng L, et al. The thromboprophylactic effect of a low-molecular-weight heparin (Fragmin) in hip fracture surgery. A placebo-controlled study. Clin Orthop Relat Res 1992;278:95–100.

70. Kerr R, Stirling D, Ludlam C. A. Interleukin 6 and haemostasis. Br J Haematol 2001;115:3–12.

71. Kim PK, Deutschman CS. Inflammatory responses and mediators. Surg Clin North Am 2000;80:885–894.

72. Knudson MM, Ikossi DG. Venous thromboembolism after trauma. Curr Opin Crit Care 2004;10:539–548.

73. Lapidus LJ, de Bri E, Ponzer S, et al. High sensitivity with color duplex sonography in thrombosis screening after ankle fracture surgery. J Thromb Haemost 2006;4:807–812.

74. Lapidus LJ, Ponzer S, Elvin A, et al. Prolonged thromboprophylaxis with Dalteparin during immobilization after ankle fracture surgery: a randomized, placebo-controlled, double-blind study. Acta Orthop 2007;78:528–35.

75. Laterre PF, Wittebole X, Dhainaut JF. Anticoagulant therapy in acute lung injury. Crit Care Med 2003;31:S329–S336.

76. Lindeque BG, Schoeman HS, Dommisse GF, et al. Fat embolism and the fat embolism syndrome. A double-blind therapeutic study. J Bone Joint Surg Br 1987;69:128–131.

77. Lozman J, Deno DC, Feustel PJ, et al. Pulmonary and cardiovascular consequences of immediate fixation or conservative management of long-bone fractures. Arch Surg 1986;121:992–999.

78. Luke RG, Linton AL, Briggs JD, et al. Mannitol therapy in acute renal failure. Lancet 1965;1:980–982.

79. Lumb AB. Nunn's Applied Respiratory Physiology. 5th ed. Philadelphia: Butterworth-Heinemann, 2000.

80. Mackowiak PA, Wasserman SS, Levine MM. A critical appraisal of 98.6°F, the upper limit of the normal body temperature, and other legacies of Carl Reinhold August Wunderlich. JAMA 1992;268:1578–1580.

81. MacLeod JB, Lynn M, McKenney MG, et al. Early coagulopathy predicts mortality in trauma. J Trauma 2003;55:39–44.

82. Maekawa K, Futami S, Nishida M, et al. Effects of trauma and sepsis on soluble L-selectin and cell surface expression of L-selectin and CD11b. J Trauma 1998;44:460–468.

83. Martin R, Leighton RK, Petrie D, et al. Effect of proximal and distal venting during intramedullary nailing. Clin Orthop Relat Res 1996;332:80–89.

84. McKee MD, Schemitsch EH, Vincent LO, et al. The effect of a femoral fracture on concomitant closed head injury in patients with multiple injuries. J Trauma 1997;42:1041–1045.

85. Meek RN. The John Border Memorial Lecture: delaying emergency fracture surgery—fact or fad. J Orthop Trauma 2006;20:337–340.

86. Meek RN, Vivoda EE, Pirani S. Comparison of mortality of patients with multiple injuries according to type of fracture treatment—a retrospective age- and injury-matched series. Injury 1986;17:2–4.

87. Mellor A, Soni N. Fat embolism. Anaesthesia 2001;56:145–154.

88. Menges T, Hermans PW, Little SG, et al. Plasminogen-activator-inhibitor-1 4G/5G promoter polymorphism and prognosis of severely injured patients. Lancet 2001;357:1096–1097.

89. Miller HH, Welch CS. Quantitative studies on the time factor in arterial injuries. Ann Surg 1949;130:428–438.

90. Moed BR, Boyd DW, Andring RE. Clinically inapparent hypoxemia after skeletal injury. The use of the pulse oximeter as a screening method. Clin Orthop Relat Res 1993;293:269–273.

91. Morley JR, Smith RM, Pape HC, et al. Stimulation of the local femoral inflammatory response to fracture and intramedullary reaming: a preliminary study of the source of the second-hit phenomenon. J Bone Joint Surg Br 2008;90:393–399.

92. Mousavi M, David R, Schwendenwein I, et al. Influence of controlled reaming on fat intravasation after femoral osteotomy in sheep. Clin Orthop Relat Res 2002;394:263–270.

93. Muckart DJ, Moodley M, Naidu AG, et al. Prediction of acute renal failure following soft-tissue injury using the venous bicarbonate concentration. J Trauma 1992;33:813–817.

94. Nast-Kolb D, Waydhas C, Gippner-Steppert C, et al. Indicators of the posttraumatic inflammatory response correlate with organ failure in patients with multiple injuries. J Trauma 1997;42:446–454.

95. Nyein K, Thu A, Turner-Stokes L. Complex specialized rehabilitation following severe brain injury: a UK perspective. J Head Trauma Rehabil 2007;22:239–247.

96. Ohlsson K, Bjork P, Bergenfeldt M, et al Interleukin-1 receptor antagonist reduces mortality from endotoxin shock. Nature 1990;348:550–552.

97. Pallister I, Dent C, Topley N. Increased neutrophil migratory activity after major trauma: a factor in the etiology of acute respiratory distress syndrome? Crit Care Med 2002;30:1717–1721.

98. Pallister I, Dent C, Wise CC, et al. Early posttraumatic acute respiratory distress syndrome and albumin excretion rate: a prospective evaluation of a "point-of-care" predictive test. Injury 2001;32:177–181.

99. Pallister I, Gosling P, Alpar K, et al. Prediction of posttraumatic adult respiratory distress syndrome by albumin excretion rate 8 hours after admission. J Trauma 1997;42:1056–1061.

100. Pape HC. John Border Memorial Lecture controversy comment. Fracture lines—the newsletter of the Orthopaedic Trauma Association. 2006;2.

101. Pape HC, Auf'm'Kolk M, Paffrath T, et al. Primary intramedullary femur fixation in multiple trauma patients with associated lung contusion—a cause of posttraumatic ARDS? J Trauma 1993;34:540–547.

102. Pape HC, Dwenger A, Grotz M, et al. Does the reamer type influence the degree of lung dysfunction after femoral nailing following severe trauma? An animal study. J Orthop Trauma 1994;8:300–309.

103. Pape HC, Giannoudis PV, Krettek C, et al. Timing of fixation of major fractures in

blunt polytrauma: role of conventional indicators in clinical decision making. J Orthop Trauma 2005;19:551–562.

104. Pape HC, Giannoudis P, Krettek C. The timing of fracture treatment in polytrauma patients: relevance of damage-control orthopedic surgery. Am J Surg 2002;183: 622–629.

105. Pape HC, Grimme K, van Griensven M, et al. Impact of intramedullary instrumentation versus damage control for femoral fractures on immunoinflammatory parameters: prospective randomized analysis by the EPOFF Study Group. J Trauma 2003;55:7–13.

106. Pape HC, Hildebrand F, Pertschy S, et al. Changes in the management of femoral shaft fractures in polytrauma patients: from early total care to damage-control orthopedic surgery. J Trauma 2002;53:452–461.

107. Pape HC, Regel G, Dwenger A, et al. Influences of different methods of intramedullary femoral nailing on lung function in patients with multiple trauma. J Trauma 1993;35: 709–716.

108. Pape HC, Remmers D, Grotz M, et al. Levels of antibodies to endotoxin and cytokine release in patients with severe trauma: does posttraumatic dysergy contribute to organ failure? J Trauma 1999;46:907–913.

109. Pape HC, Schmidt RE, Rice J, et al. Biochemical changes after trauma and skeletal surgery of the lower extremity: quantification of the operative burden. Crit Care Med 2000;28:3441–3448.

110. Pape HC, van Griensven M, Rice J, et al. Major secondary surgery in blunt trauma patients and perioperative cytokine liberation: determination of the clinical relevance of biochemical markers. J Trauma 2001;50:989–1000.

111. Partrick DA, Moore FA, Moore EE, et al. Barney Resident Research Award winner. The inflammatory profile of interleukin-6, interleukin-8, and soluble intercellular adhesion molecule-1 in postinjury multiple organ failure. Am J Surg 1996;172:425–429.

112. Patil S, Gandhi J, Curzon I, et al Incidence of deep-vein thrombosis in patients with fractures of the ankle treated in a plaster cast. J Bone Joint Surg Br 2007;89:1340–1343.

113. Peltier LF. Fat embolism. An appraisal of the problem. Clin Orthop Relat Res 1984; 187:3–17.

114. Phillips TF, Contreras DM. Timing of operative treatment of fractures in patients who have multiple injuries. J Bone Joint Surg Am 1990;72:784–788.

115. Pinney SJ, Keating JF, Meek RN. Fat embolism syndrome in isolated femoral fractures: does timing of nailing influence incidence? Injury 1998;29:131–133.

116. Rasmussen TE, Hallett JW Jr, Metzger RL, et al. Genetic risk factors in inflammatory abdominal aortic aneurysms: polymorphic residue 70 in the HLA-DR B1 gene as a key genetic element. J Vasc Surg 1997;25:356–364.

117. Rello J, Paiva JA, Baraibar J, et al. International Conference for the Development of Consensus on the Diagnosis and Treatment of Ventilator-Associated Pneumonia. Chest 2001;120:955–970.

118. Riseborough EJ, Herndon JH. Alterations in pulmonary function, coagulation, and fat metabolism in patients with fractures of the lower limbs. Clin Orthop Relat Res 1976; 115:248–267.

119. Riska EB, von Bonsdorff H, Hakkinen S, et al. Prevention of fat embolism by early internal fixation of fractures in patients with multiple injuries. Injury 1976;8:110–116.

120. Robinson CM. Current concepts of respiratory insufficiency syndromes after fracture. J Bone Joint Surg 2001;83-B:781–791.

121. Robinson CM, Ludlam CA, Ray DC, et al. The coagulative and cardiorespiratory responses to reamed intramedullary nailing of isolated fractures. J Bone Joint Surg Br 2001;83:963–973.

122. Rogers FB, Shackford SR, Trevisani GT, et al. Neurogenic pulmonary edema in fatal and nonfatal head injuries. J Trauma 1995;39:860–866.

123. Rogers FB, Shackford SR, Vane DW, et al. Prompt fixation of isolated femur fractures in a rural trauma center: a study examining the timing of fixation and resource allocation. J Trauma 1994;36:774–777.

124. Rokkanen P, Lahdensuu M, Kataja J, et al. The syndrome of fat embolism: analysis of 30 consecutive cases compared to trauma patients with similar injuries. J Trauma 1970; 10:299–306.

125. Ron D, Taitelman U, Michaelson M, et al. Prevention of acute renal failure in traumatic rhabdomyolysis. Arch Intern Med 1984;144:277–280.

126. Roumen RM, Hendriks T, van der Ven-Jongekrijg J, et al. Cytokine patterns in patients after major vascular surgery, hemorrhagic shock, and severe blunt trauma. Relation with subsequent adult respiratory distress syndrome and multiple organ failure. Ann Surg 1993;218:769–776.

127. Russell JA. Genetics of coagulation factors in acute lung injury. Crit Care Med 2003; 31:S243–S247.

128. Scalea TM, Boswell SA, Scott JD, et al. External fixation as a bridge to intramedullary

nailing for patients with multiple injuries and with femur fractures: damage-control orthopedics. J Trauma 2000;48:613–621.

129. Schambeck CM, Schwender S, Haubitz I, et al. Selective screening for the Factor V Leiden mutation: is it advisable prior to the prescription of oral contraceptives? Thromb Haemost 1997;78:1480–1483.

130. Schoffel U, Bonnaire F, van Specht BU, et al. Monitoring the response to injury. Injury 1991;22:377–382.

131. Seibel R, LaDuca J, Hassett JM, et al. Blunt multiple trauma (ISS 36), femur traction, and the pulmonary failure-septic state. Ann Surg 1985;202:283–295.

132. Seligsohn U, Lubetsky A. Genetic susceptibility to venous thrombosis. N Engl J Med 2001;344:1222–1231.

133. Sevitt S. Fat Embolism. London: Butterworth & Co., 1959.

134. Shier MR, Wilson RF, James RE, et al. Fat embolism prophylaxis: a study of four treatment modalities. J Trauma 1977;17:621–629.

135. Skoog T, van't Hooft FM, Kallin B, et al. A common functional polymorphism (C–>A substitution at position -863) in the promoter region of the tumour necrosis factor-alpha (TNF-alpha) gene associated with reduced circulating levels of TNF-alpha. Hum Mol Genet 1999;8:1443–1449.

136. Stannard JP, Lopez B, Volgas DA, et al. Prophylaxis against deep-vein thrombosis following trauma: a prospective, randomized comparison of mechanical and pharmacologic prophylaxis. J Bone Joint Surg Am 2006;88:261–266.

137. Stark RP, Maki DG. Bacteriuria in the catheterized patient. What quantitative level of bacteriuria is relevant? N Engl J Med 1984;311:560–564.

138. Stein PD, Fowler SE, Goodman LR, et al. Multidetector computed tomography for acute pulmonary embolism. N Engl J Med 2006;354:2317–2327.

139. Stoltenberg JJ, Gustilo RB. The use of methylprednisolone and hypertonic glucose in the prophylaxis of fat embolism syndrome. Clin Orthop Relat Res 1979;143:211–221.

140. Strauss EJ, Egol KA, Alaia M, et al. The use of retrievable inferior vena cava filters in orthopaedic patients. J Bone Joint Surg Br 2008;90:662–667.

141. Svenningsen S, Nesse O, Finsen V, et al. Prevention of fat embolism syndrome in patients with femoral fractures—immediate or delayed operative fixation? Ann Chir Gynaecol 1987;76:163–166.

142. Taeger G, Ruchholtz S, Waydhas C, et al. Damage-control orthopedics in patients with multiple injuries is effective, time saving, and safe. J Trauma 2005;59:409–416.

143. Talucci RC, Manning J, Lampard S, et al. Early intramedullary nailing of femoral shaft fractures: a cause of fat embolism syndrome. Am J Surg 1983;146:107–111.

144. Terao M, Ozaki T, Sato T. Diagnosis of deep vein thrombosis after operation for fracture of the proximal femur: comparative study of ultrasonography and venography. J Orthop Sci 2006;11:146–153.

145. van der Made WJ, Smit EJ, van Luyt PA, et al. Intramedullary femoral osteosynthesis: an additional cause of ARDS in multiply injured patients? Injury 1996;27:391–393.

146. van Os JP, Roumen RM, Schoots FJ, et al. Is early osteosynthesis safe in multiple trauma patients with severe thoracic trauma and pulmonary contusion? J Trauma 1994;36: 495–498.

147. Virchow R. Cellular pathology. New York: RM DE Witt; 1860.

148. Wahl WL, Ahrns KS, Zajkowski PJ, et al. Normal D-dimer levels do not exclude thrombotic complications in trauma patients. Surgery 2003;134:529–532.

149. Wakabayashi Y, Kikuno T, Ohwada T, et al. Rapid fall in blood myoglobin in massive rhabdomyolysis and acute renal failure. Intensive Care Med 1994;20:109–112.

150. Waydhas C, Nast-Kolb D, Trupka A, et al. Posttraumatic inflammatory response, secondary operations, and late multiple organ failure. J Trauma 1996;40:624–630.

151. Wells PS, Hirsh J, Anderson DR, et al. A simple clinical model for the diagnosis of deep-vein thrombosis combined with impedance plethysmography: potential for an improvement in the diagnostic process. J Intern Med 1998;243:15–23.

152. White TO, Clutton RE, Salter D, et al. The early response to major trauma and intramedullary nailing. J Bone Joint Surg Br 2006;88:823–827.

153. White TO, Jenkins PJ, Smith RD, et al. The epidemiology of posttraumatic adult respiratory distress syndrome. J Bone Joint Surg Am 2004;86-A:2366–2376.

154. Woo P. Cytokine polymorphisms and inflammation. Clin Exp Rheumatol 2000;18: 767–771.

155. Yentis SM, Hirsch NP, Smith GB. Anaesthesia and Intensive Care A–Z: An Encyclopaedia of Principles and Practice. Philadelphia: Butterworth-Heinemann, 2000.

156. Zahn HR, Skinner JA, Porteous MJ. The preoperative prevalence of deep vein thrombosis in patients with femoral neck fractures and delayed operation. Injury 1999;30: 605–607.

157. Zallen G, Moore EE, Johnson JL, et al. Circulating postinjury neutrophils are primed for the release of proinflammatory cytokines. J Trauma 1999;46:42–48.

23

PRINCIPLES OF COMPLEX REGIONAL PAIN SYNDROME

Roger M. Atkins

INTRODUCTION

During the American Civil War, Silas Weir Mitchell described a syndrome that occurred in patients who had suffered gunshot injuries to major nerves.[120] Noting that a leading feature was burning pain, he called the condition *causalgia*. At the beginning of the 20th century, Paul Südeck, a clinician in Hamburg, Germany, used the newly invented technique of roentgenology to investigate patients with severe pain after injury.[145,146] He described a posttraumatic pain syndrome with edema, trophic changes, and osteoporosis. In 1979, the AO group advocated open reduction and rigid internal fixation to prevent fracture disease, which was defined as a combination of circulatory disturbance, inflammation, and pain as a result of dysfunction of joints and muscles.[121] In an intriguing vignette, Channon and Lloyd[32] noted that finger stiffness after Colles fracture could be either simple or associated with swelling and changes in hand temperature. In the latter case, it did not respond well to physiotherapy. The modern term for the syndrome described in different circumstances by these researchers is *complex regional pain syndrome*, usually abbreviated as CRPS.

CRPS consists of abnormal pain, swelling, vasomotor and sudomotor dysfunction, contracture, and osteoporosis. It used to be considered a rare, devastating complication of injury, caused by abnormalities in the sympathetic nervous system (SNS) and seen mainly in psychologically abnormal patients. Modern research is altering this view radically. This review will specifically examine CRPS within the context of orthopaedic trauma surgery. For this reason, the emphasis, descriptions, and concepts differ slightly from those routinely found in publications from the International Association for the Study of Pain (IASP). It is important to appreciate that these apparent differences are merely counterpoints. The theme is identical.

SOME IMPORTANT DEFINITIONS

A cardinal feature of CRPS is abnormalities of pain perception, which are mainly foreign to orthopaedic surgeons. They have been codified by Merskey and Bogduk[119] and because they will be used throughout this text, they are described here.

- *Allodynia* (literally "other pain") is a painful perception of a stimulus that should not usually be painful. Thus, for example, a patient will find gentle stroking of the affected part painful. Allodynia differs from referred pain, but allodynic pain can occur in areas other than the one stimulated. There are several forms of allodynia:
  - *Mechanical* (or *tactile*) *allodynia* implies pain in response to touch. It may be further subdivided into *static mechanical allodynia*, implying pain in response to light touch or pressure, and *dynamic mechanical allodynia*, where the pain occurs as a result of brushing.[107]
  - In *thermal* (*hot or cold*) *allodynia*, the pain is caused by mild changes in skin temperature in the affected area.
- *Hyperalgesia* is an increased sensitivity to pain, which may be caused by damage to nociceptors or peripheral nerves. Thus, the patient finds gentle touching with a pin unbearably painful. Hyperalgesia is usually experienced in focal, discrete areas, typically associated with injury. Focal hyperalgesia may be divided into two subtypes:
  - *Primary hyperalgesia* describes pain sensitivity that occurs directly in the damaged tissues.
  - *Secondary hyperalgesia* describes pain sensitivity that occurs in surrounding undamaged tissues.

  Rarely, hyperalgesia is seen in a more diffuse, bodywide form.
- *Hyperpathia* is a temporal and spatial summation of an allodynic or hyperalgesic response. Thus, the patient finds gentle touching painful, but repetitive touching either on the same spot or on another part of the affected limb becomes increasingly unbearable and the pain continues for a period (up to 30 minutes) after the stimulus has been withdrawn. In severe cases, the pain may be accentuated by unusual and extraneous things such as the sudden noise of a door shutting or a draft of cold air.

It is important for the orthopaedic surgeon to realize that these patients are not malingering or mad. These are absolutely real perceptions of pain.

A HISTORIC VIEW OF TAXONOMY

A historic review of nomenclature will help to elucidate much confusion that surrounds this condition. In the past, CRPS was diagnosed using a variety of nonstandardized and idiosyncratic diagnostic systems derived solely from the authors' clinical experiences, none of which achieved wide acceptance. The condition was given a number of synonyms (Table 23-1) reflecting site affected, cause and clinical features. During the American Civil War, Mitchell et al.[120] noted the burning nature of pain following nerve trauma and described this as *causalgia* (from the Greek "burning pain"). In contrast, in the 1900s, Südeck[145,146] investigated conditions characterized by severe osteoporosis, including some cases of CRPS. The condition was named *Südeck's atrophy* by Nonne in 1901.[123] Leriche[99,100] demonstrated that sympathectomy could alter the clinical features associated with *posttraumatic osteoporosis*, and De Takats[38] first suggested *reflex dystrophy* in 1937. Evans[46] introduced the term *reflex sympathetic dystrophy*, based on the theory (following Leriche's observations) that sympathetic hyperactivity was involved in the pathophysiology, and this term was popularized by Bonica.[18] In 1940, Homans[85] proposed *minor causalgia* to imply a relationship between Mitchell et al.'s causalgia, renamed *major cau-*

TABLE 23-1	Synonyms for Complex Regional Pain Syndrome

- Complex regional pain syndrome
- Reflex sympathetic dystrophy
- Südeck's atrophy
- Causalgia
- Minor causalgia
- Mimo-causalgia
- Algodystrophy
- Algoneurodystrophy
- Post-traumatic pain syndrome
- Painful post-traumatic dystrophy
- Painful post-traumatic osteoporosis
- Transient migratory osteoporosis

salgia, and similar conditions arising without direct nerve injury. *Causalgic state*[37] and *mimo causalgia*[126] followed to add to the confusion. Today the term *causalgia* is reserved for Mitchell et al.'s original use, in which a major nerve injury produces burning pain.[141]

Steinbrocker[143] introduced the term *shoulder hand syndrome* for a condition that may be separate from true CRPS, and *algoneurodystrophy* was suggested by Glik and Helal.[69] *Algodystrophy*, from the Greek meaning "painful disuse," was introduced by French rheumatologists in the late 1970s.[44]

Sympathetically maintained pain consists of pain, hyperpathia, and allodynia, which are relieved by selective sympathetic blockade. The relationship between CRPS and sympathetically maintained pain is disputed.[141] In CRPS a proportion of the pain is usually sympathetically maintained and is therefore relieved by sympathetic blockade. However, in CRPS a process is also taking place that leads to initial tissue edema followed by severe contracture. This is not an inevitable part of sympathetically maintained pain.[91] Sympathetically maintained pain is not a particularly helpful concept for the orthopaedic surgeon; however, it will be explored further when the etiology of CRPS is considered.

MODERN TAXONOMY AND DIAGNOSIS

Fortunately, all the above confusion is now of historic interest. The International Association for the Study of Pain (IASP) has undertaken a major work in analyzing the features of CRPS and reclassifying the condition.[119] A brief history of this work will help to understand the current position. The name of the condition was changed to complex regional pain syndrome (CRPS) at a consensus workshop in Orlando, Florida, in 1994,[16,141] and a new set of standardized diagnostic criteria was established[119] (Table 23-2). To complement the diagnostic criteria, a broad description of CRPS was offered later[22,80]:

> CRPS describes an array of painful conditions that are characterized by a continuing (spontaneous and/or evoked) regional pain that is seemingly disproportionate in time or degree to the usual course of any known trauma or other lesion. The pain is regional

TABLE 23-2	**The Original International Association for the Study of Pain Diagnostic Criteria for Complex Regional Pain Syndrome (CRPS)**

1. The presence of an initiating noxious event, or a cause of immobilization (not required for diagnosis; 5%–10% of patients will not have this)

2. Continuing pain, allodynia, or hyperalgesia in which the pain is disproportionate to any known inciting event

3. Evidence at some time of edema, changes in skin blood flow, or abnormal sudomotor activity in the region of pain (can be sign or symptom)

4. This diagnosis is excluded by the existence of other conditions that would otherwise account for the degree of pain and dysfunction.

If the condition occurs in the absence of "major nerve damage," the diagnosis is CRPS type 1.

If "major nerve damage" is present, the diagnosis is CRPS type 2.

Adapted from Merskey and Bogduk.[119]

that occurs without any precipitating noxious stimulus, and spontaneous or burning pain, hyperalgesia, allodynia, and hyperpathia are common but not universal features.[119] Pain is unremitting (although sleep is often unaffected), worsening and radiating with time. The pain may be increased by dependency of the limb, physical contact, emotional upset, or even by extraneous factors such as a sudden loud noise or a blast of cold air.

Early Phase of Complex Regional Pain Syndrome

Vasomotor instability (VMI) and edema dominate the early phase (Fig. 23-1), although this is less marked with more proximal CRPS. The classic description of the temporal evolution of the condition divides the early phase of CRPS into two stages depending on the type of the vasomotor instability.[44] In this description, initially the limb is dry, hot, and pink (vasodilated, Stage 1) but after a variable period of days to weeks, it becomes blue, cold, and sweaty (vasoconstricted, Stage 2). As noted, this classic evolution is rarely seen. Most commonly, especially in more mild cases, the vasomotor instability is an increase in temperature sensitivity, with variable abnormality of sweating. Alternatively, some patients remain substantially vasodilated,

(not in a specific nerve territory or dermatome) and usually has a distal predominance of abnormal sensory, motor, sudomotor, vasomotor, and/or trophic findings, including osteoporosis. The syndrome shows variable progression over time.

CRPS was arbitrarily divided into CRPS2 type 2, where the cause was believed to be damage to a major nerve, and CRPS type 1, where it was not.

Clinical Features

Because the etiology of CRPS is obscure, the diagnosis must be clinical and therefore precise descriptions of symptoms and signs acquire great importance. Classic descriptions of the condition describe three stages occurring sequentially.[17,38,44,68,137,138] Modern evidence, however, suggests that CRPS does not invariably pass through these stages[13,157,173,174] and supports the clinical impression that this evolution is seen in more severe cases (as might be expected from historic series). Nevertheless, the classic descriptions provide the greatest information concerning the clinical features, and the description that follows draws on these and will therefore refer to the staging system where it is helpful to the description.

Regardless of whether a particular patient will pass through the three classic stages, it is essential to grasp the concept that CRPS is a biphasic condition with early swelling and vasomotor instability giving way over a variable timescale to late contracture and joint stiffness.[44] The hand and foot are most frequently involved, although involvement of the knee is increasingly recognized.[35,36,93] The elbow is rarely affected, whereas shoulder disease is common and some cases of frozen shoulder are probably CRPS.[143] The hip is affected in transient osteoporosis of pregnancy.

CRPS usually begins up to a month after the precipitating trauma, although the delay may be greater. Antecedent trauma is not essential but within an orthopaedic context it is almost invariable.[44] As the direct effects of injury subside, a new diffuse, unpleasant, neuropathic pain arises.[168] Neuropathic pain is pain

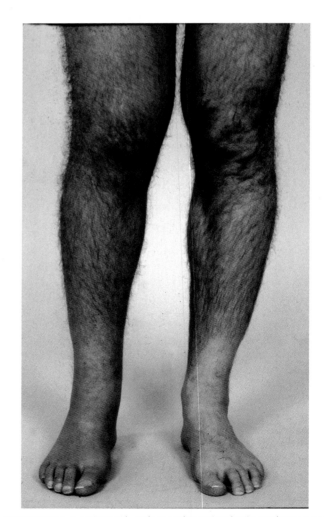

FIGURE 23-1 A patient with early complex regional pain syndrome type 1 affecting the leg. Note the swelling of the leg and the discoloration of the shin.

while others are vasoconstricted with no history of vasodilatation.[13,21,157,175]

In the early phase of CRPS, edema is marked, particularly where the distal part of the limb is affected. Initially, the edema is simple tissue swelling and may be overcome by physical therapy and elevation, if the patient will permit. With time, however (in the classic description, passing from stage 1 to stage 2), the edema becomes more fixed and indurated with coalescence of tissue planes and structures.

Initially, in the early phase of CRPS, loss of joint mobility is caused by swelling and pain combined with an apparent inability to initiate movement or state of neglect or denial with respect to the limb.[27–29,61,62] Weakness, dystonia, spasms, tremor, and myoclonus have also been reported[15,56,106,137]; however, these are not usually prominent within an orthopaedic context. As the early phase progresses, loss of joint mobility will increasingly be the result of the development of contracture. Only if the disease can be halted in the early phase before fixed contracture has occurred can complete resolution occur.

Late Phase of Complex Regional Pain Syndrome

Passing into the late phase, VMI recedes, edema resolves, and atrophy of the limb occurs (Fig. 23-2), which affects every tissue. The skin is thinned and joint creases and subcutaneous fat disappear. Hairs become fragile, uneven, and curled, while nails are pitted, ridged, brittle, and discolored brown. Palmar and plantar fascias thicken and contract simulating Dupuytren disease.[106] Tendon sheaths become constricted, causing triggering and increased resistance to movement. Muscle contracture combined with tendon adherence leads to reduced tendon excursion. Joint capsules and collateral ligaments become shortened, thickened, and adherent, causing joint contracture.

It is important to restate that the progression of CRPS is very variable. Within orthopaedic practice, the large majority of patients who demonstrate the features of the early phase of CRPS after trauma will not go on to develop severe late phase

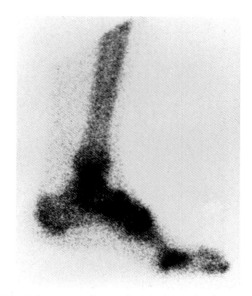

FIGURE 23-3 Bone scan changes in complex regional pain syndrome (CRPS). The delayed phase of a bone scan of a patient with early CRPS type 1 of the lower leg. There is increased uptake throughout the affected region. The bone scan will usually revert to normal after 6 months.

contracture, although a significant proportion will show chronic subclinical contracture.[106]

Bone Changes

Bone involvement is universal with increased uptake on bone scanning in early CRPS (Fig. 23-3). This was originally thought to be periarticular, suggesting arthralgia[84,97,110]; however, CRPS does not cause arthritis and more recent studies have shown generalized hyperfixation,[5,34,40] confirming the view of Doury et al.[44] Increased uptake is not invariable in children.[167] Later, the bone scan returns to normal and there are radiographic features of rapid bone loss: visible demineralization with patchy,

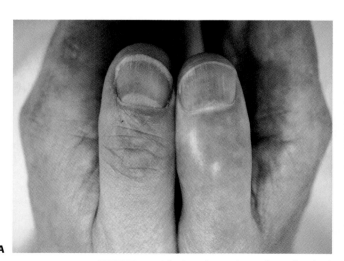

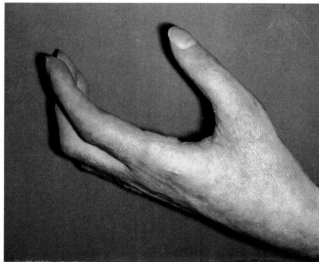

A **B**

FIGURE 23-2 The late phase of complex regional pain syndrome (CRPS). **A.** Detail of the thumbs of a patient with late CRPS type 1 of the right hand. There is spindling of the digit particularly distally. The nail is excessively ridged and is discolored. **B.** The hand of a patient with late CRPS type 1. The patient is trying to make a fist. Note the digital spindling and extension contractures with loss of joint creases

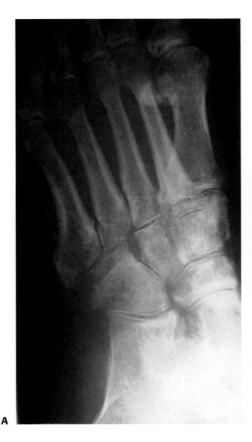

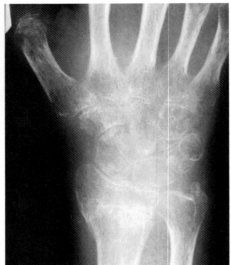

FIGURE 23-4 Radiographic features of complex regional pain syndrome (CRPS). **A.** Oblique radiograph of a patient with CRPS type 1 of the foot. There is patchy osteoporosis with accentuation of the osteoporosis beneath the joints. **B.** Profound osteoporosis in a patient with late severe CRPS type 1 affecting the hand.

subchondral or subperiosteal osteoporosis, metaphyseal banding, and profound bone loss[98] (Fig. 23-4). Despite the osteoporosis, fracture is uncommon, presumably because the patients protect the painful limb very effectively.

INCIDENCE

It is the common experience of orthopaedic surgeons that patients, such as the case shown in Figure 23-2, are extremely rare. Thus, severe, chronic CRPS associated with severe contracture is uncommon with a reported prevalence of less than 2% in retrospective series.[8,75,102,108,129] In contrast, prospective studies designed to look specifically for the early features of CRPS show that they occur after 30% to 40% of every fracture and surgical trauma (e.g., total knee replacement),[2,3,7,13,14,51,81,135,139] where the features of CRPS have been actively sought. Furthermore, statistically, the features tend to occur together.[3] These common early cases of CRPS are usually not specifically diagnosed.[139] They resolve substantially either spontaneously or with standard treatment by physical therapy and analgesia within 1 year.[13,14,105,139] Some features, particularly stiffness, may remain, suggesting that CRPS may be responsible for significant long-term morbidity even when mild.[5,18] The truly intriguing question is, if CRPS is so common, why is it not a universal finding after trauma or orthopaedic surgery?

ETIOLOGY

CRPS may occur after any particular trauma while an identical stimulus in a different limb does not cause it. The incidence is not changed by treatment method and open anatomic reduction and rigid internal fixation does not abolish it.[135] It is unclear whether injury severity or quality of fracture reduction alters the incidence.[3,14] There is, however, an association with excessively tight casts[55] and there may be a genetic predilection.[41,94,96,111,112] The following etiologies have been proposed:

Psychological Abnormalities

A psychological cause for chronic pain was first suggested by Freud,[19] and historically, it has been suggested that CRPS may be purely a psychological problem.[33] Most orthopaedic clinicians immediately recognize a "Sudecky" patient—that is, broadly speaking, a patient who appears to the clinician to be somebody who is likely to fare poorly after surgical intervention or trauma, perhaps because of to their inability to cooperate fully with physical therapy. In fact, the literature fails to identify this sort of patient and the evidence does not support the notion that CRPS is primarily psychological.[25] Studies of premorbid personality show no consistent abnormality.[122,172] Most patients are psychologically normal,[158] although emotional lability, low pain threshold,[39] hysteria,[127] and depression[144] have been reported. There is an association with antecedent psychological stress,[20,25,63–65,156] which probably exacerbates pain in CRPS, as in other diseases.[23] It seems likely that the severe chronic pain of CRPS causes depression and that a "Sudecky" type of patient who develops CRPS is at risk of a poor outcome because they will not mobilize in the face of pain.

Abnormal (Neuropathic) Pain

CRPS is characterized by excessive and abnormal pain. Pain is usually caused when an intense noxious stimulus activates high-threshold nociceptors, thus preventing tissue damage. Neuropathic pain in CRPS occurs without appropriate stimulus and has no protective function. However, injured peripheral nerve fibers undergo cellular changes, which cause usually innocuous tactile inputs to stimulate the dorsal horn cells via A-β fibers from low-threshold mechanoreceptors, causing allodynia in CRPS 2.[92,167] Similar C-nociceptor dysfunction explains causalgia. Furthermore, axonal injury prevents nerve growth factor transport, which is essential for normal nerve function.[104,168] In CRPS 1, covert nerve lesions with artificial synapses have been postulated.[43] These "ephases" have not been demonstrated and are unnecessary since inflammatory mediators released by the initial trauma (and possibly retained due to a failure of free radical clearance), can sensitize nociceptors to respond to normally innocuous stimuli.[168]

Sympathetic Nervous System Abnormalities

That CRPS is associated with apparent abnormalities in the SNS is obvious—hence, the popularity of the eponym *reflex sympathetic dystrophy*. Furthermore, since Leriche's early studies,[99,100] generations of therapists have treated CRPS with sympathetic manipulation, noting an acute change in the clinical features,[31,70,76–78,86] although recent studies cast some doubt on whether sympathetic manipulation improves the long-term outcome of the condition.[87,105]

The features of CRPS that suggest SNS dysfunction include abnormalities in skin blood flow, temperature regulation and sweating, and edema. However, SNS activity is not usually painful.[88,89] In CRPS, however, some pain (termed *sympathetically maintained pain* [SMP][141]) is SNS dependent. This accounts for spontaneous pain and allodynia, which may therefore be relieved by stellate ganglion blockade[130] and then restored by noradrenalin injection.[1,148] Furthermore, there is an abnormal difference in cutaneous sensory threshold between the limbs, which is reversed by sympathetic blockade,[54,57,131,132] while increasing sympathetic activity worsens pain.[90]

What, then, is the cause of SMP in CRPS? It is due to the body's reaction to injury. After partial nerve division, injured and uninjured somatic axons express α-adrenergic receptors[30] and sympathetic axons come to surround sensory neuron cell bodies in dorsal root ganglia.[117,161,168] These changes, which may be temporary,[148,159,160] make the somatic sensory nervous system sensitive to circulating catecholamines and norepinephrine released from postganglionic sympathetic terminals.

Abnormal Inflammation

Superficially, CRPS resembles an inflammatory state leading to gross scarring. For this reason, the major differential diagnoses within an orthopaedic context are occult causes of inflammation such as soft tissue infection or stress fracture. Indeed, CRPS is associated with inflammatory changes including macromolecule extravasation[125] and reduced oxygen consumption.[71,149] In animals, infusion of free radical donors causes a CRPS-like state,[150] and amputated human specimens with CRPS show basement-membrane thickening consistent with overexposure to free radicals.[151] These considerations suggest that CRPS is an exaggerated local inflammatory response to injury.[72,73] In other words, on this hypothesis, CRPS represents a local form of the systemic free radical disease that causes adult respiratory distress syndrome and multiple organ failure after severe trauma. This concept is supported by evidence that the free radical scavenger vitamin C is effective prophylaxis against post-traumatic CRPS.[170,171]

An alternative explanation for the apparent inflammatory changes in early CRPS is a primary capillary imbalance causing stasis, extravasation, and consequent local tissue anoxia.[48,49,114,134]

Failure to Use the Affected Limb

The popular French term for CRPS, *algodystrophy,* means "painful disuse."[44] It is a common clinical observation that patients who appear to be at risk of developing CRPS are unable or unwilling to cooperate with physical therapy to mobilize their limb after trauma or orthopaedic surgery. Indeed, undue immobilization has traditionally been believed to be at least an important contributory factor in the generation of CRPS or even the sole cause.[9,47,121,163]

CRPS obviously involves a significant abnormality of afferent sensory perception but only recently has the possibility of abnormal efferent motor function been systematically explored. Classically, it was believed that the "immobile RSD limb" was guarded by the patient to prevent inadvertent painful movement or sensory contact.[44,60] In fact, CRPS is associated with an abnormality of motor function that is often overlooked partially because of patient embarrassment and partly because in the past it has been labeled as "hysterical."[33,152] In 1990, Schwartzman and Kerrigan[137] reported a subgroup of CRPS patients with a variety of motor disorders and a minority of patients with CRPS demonstrate obvious dystonia or spasms.[10,45,110,113] A prospective study of 829 CRPS patients showed that abnormalities of motor function were reported by 95%, varying from weakness to incoordination and tremor.[30] Objective testing in small numbers of patients shows that CRPS patients have impaired grip force coordination, target reaching, and grasping.[136,164]

Interviews with patients suggest further possible reasons for the lack of movement in CRPS. Patients demonstrate evidence of "neglect" of the affected limb, similar to that seen after parietal lobe stroke. When asked about moving the limb, statements are made such as "my limb feels disconnected from my body" and "I need to focus all my mental attention and look at the limb in order for it to move the way I want. . . ."[59] Another study revealed bizarre perceptions about a body part including a desperate desire for amputation. There was a mismatch between limb sensation and appearance with mental erasure of the affected part. These authors suggested the term "body perception disturbance" rather than "neglect" to describe this phenomenon.[101] There appears to be a central sensory confusion, in that when a nonnoxious stimulus is provided that the patient finds painful due to allodynia, the patient is unable to determine whether it is truly painful, and by impairing integration between sensory input and motor output, movement is impaired.[83,115]

Overall, in CRPS, patients tend to ignore their affected limb and find it difficult to initiate or accurately direct movement and there is a mismatch between sensation, perception, and movement.[29,60,152] Failure to use the limb appears to relate to this rather than the traditional view of learned pain avoidance behavior in response to allodynia. Whatever the exact cause, failure of mobilization may be central to the etiology of CRPS because all the features of phase 1 CRPS, except pain, are produced in volunteers after a period of cast immobilization.[27–29] This may be explained by the fact that activity-dependent gene function is common in the nervous system.[168] and normal tactile and proprioceptive input are necessary for correct central nerve signal processing.[103]

A study of the treatment with mirror visual feedback (MVF) supports the central role of movement disorder in CRPS.[116] The rationale for MVF is restoration of the congruence between sensory and motor information, and it was originally used for the treatment of phantom limb pain.[133] The patients are instructed to exercise both the unaffected and the affected limb. However, a mirror is placed so that they cannot see the affected limb, and when they think they are looking at it, they are actually observing the mirror image of their normal limb. As might be expected, MVF resulted in improvement in range of movement; however, in addition in early CRPS, MVF also abolished or substantially improved pain and vasomotor instability.[150]

MAKING A DIAGNOSIS

Considerable confusion has been generated by a failure to understand the recent work from the IASP. In 1994, when the IASP produced the new diagnostic entity of CRPS, it was descriptive, and general and based on a consensus.[119] Deliberately, it did not imply any etiology or pathology (including any direct role for the SNS). The intention was to provide an officially endorsed set of standardized diagnostic criteria to improve clinical communication and facilitate research.[118] In other words, this was intended as a starting point from which individual researchers could move forward. It was not thought of as a mature clinical diagnostic device.

Since their original publication, the diagnostic criteria have been validated, refined, and developed. The validation studies suggest that the original criteria are adequately sensitive *within the context of a pain clinic* (i.e., they rarely miss a case of actual CRPS); however, the criteria cause problems of overdiagnosis because of poor specificity.[58,80] Comparison of CRPS patients to other proved pain states, such as chronic diabetic patients with ascending symmetric pain, whose neuropathy is confirmed by nerve conduction studies, also show that the criteria are very sensitive but have low specificity, so that a diagnosis of CRPS may be erroneous in up to 60% of cases.[22]

Other problems are evident. For example, the criteria assume that any sign or symptom of vasomotor, sudomotor, and edema-related change is sufficient to justify the diagnosis and there is no possibility of providing greater diagnostic or prognostic accuracy by observing more than one of these features. An additional weakness is the failure to include motor or trophic signs and symptoms. Numerous studies have described various signs of motor dysfunction (e.g., dystonia, tremor) as important characteristics of this disorder, and trophic changes have frequently been mentioned in historical clinical descriptions.[26,28] These differentiate CRPS from other pain syndromes.[58,138] Finally, the wording of the criteria permits diagnosis based solely on patient-reported historical symptoms. This may be inappropriate in the context of litigation.

Factor analysis of 123 CRPS patients has indicated that the features cluster into four statistically distinct subgroups.[80]

1. A set of signs and symptoms indicating abnormalities in pain processing (e.g., allodynia, hyperalgesia, hyperpathia)
2. Skin color and temperature changes, indicating vasomotor dysfunction
3. Edema and abnormalities of sweating
4. Motor and trophic signs and symptoms

The statistical separation of edema and sudomotor dysfunction from vasomotor instability and the finding of motor and trophic abnormalities are at variance with the original IASP criteria, which were therefore modified[22,58,80] (Table 23-3). The important changes are inclusion of clinical signs, their separation from symptoms, and the inclusion of features of motor abnormalities and trophic changes. Intriguingly, these subgroups are virtually identical to those suggested by our group a decade earlier.[3]

Statistical analysis has been undertaken to investigate sensitivity and specificity of decision rules for diagnosis of CRPS compared to neuropathic pain of a proved non-CRPS cause using these criteria[22] (Table 23-4). These propose different diagnostic criteria depending on the clinical circumstances. Thus, for purely clinical diagnosis, the criteria provide a sensitivity of 0.85 and a specificity of 0.69, whereas for research diagnosis, the criteria provide a sensitivity of 0.70 and specificity of 0.94, because, in the former circumstance, one wishes to avoid failing to offer treatment to a possible candidate while in the latter situation one is more concerned to be investigating a homogeneous group in whom the diagnosis cannot be in doubt.

It is critical to understand that the Bruehl modification of the original IASP criteria[24] given in Table 23-3 apply to the diagnosis of CRPS *within a pain clinic setting* and are therefore intended to differentiate CRPS from other causes of chronic pain within that setting. They do not apply directly to the diagnosis of CRPS within the context of an orthopaedic practice. The reason for this apparent conundrum is that the precise nature of CRPS remains unclear and it is therefore a diagnosis of exclusion. Conditions from which CRPS must be distinguished in a pain clinic (e.g., neuropathic pain in association with diabetic neuropathy) are different from those which apply in an orthopaedic or fracture clinic (e.g., soft tissue infection or stress fracture). Therefore, the diagnostic criteria must be slightly different, just as slightly different criteria are required within a pain clinic for diagnosis of CRPS depending on whether the diagnosis is being made for clinical or research purposes.

Atkins et al.[2-4] proposed a set of diagnostic criteria for CRPS specifically in an orthopaedic context (Table 23-5). These were derived empirically from a less formal but similar process to the IASP consensus approach. The criteria were designed as far as possible to be objective, but the patient's veracity was assumed, so no attempt was made to separate reports of vasomotor or sudomotor abnormalities from observation of them. A number of the criteria are quantifiable,[2,3,51] which allows their powerful use to investigate treatment.[53,54,105] The original criteria were developed in the context of CRPS of the hand following Colles' fracture of the wrist, but they have subsequently been generalized for use in the diagnosis of CRPS in other orthopaedic scenarios and in the lower limb.[13,135] Diagnosis by these criteria, when used after Colles' fracture, maps virtually exactly with the Bruehl criteria, suggesting their reliability.[147]

Clinical Diagnosis in an Orthopaedic Setting

1. **Pain**

   A history of excessive pain is elicited. Abnormalities of pain perception are examined in comparison with the opposite normal side. Excessive tenderness is found by squeezing digits in the affected part between thumb and fingers. This may be quantitated using dolorimetry but this is usually a research tool.[4,6] Allodynia is demonstrated by fine touch and hyperalgesia using a pin. Hyperpathia is examined by serial fine touch or pin prick.

TABLE 23-3 **Modified International Association for the Study of Pain Diagnostic Criteria for Complex Regional Pain Syndrome (CRPS)**

General definition of the syndrome

CRPS describes an array of painful conditions that are characterized by a continuing (spontaneous and/or evoked) regional pain that is seemingly disproportionate in time or degree to the usual course of any known trauma or other lesion. The pain is regional (not in a specific nerve territory or dermatome) and usually has a distal predominance of abnormal sensory, motor, sudomotor, vasomotor, and/or trophic findings. The syndrome shows variable progression over time.

To make the *clinical* diagnosis, the following criteria must be met (sensitivity of 0.85 specificity of 0.69)

1. Continuing pain, which is disproportionate to any inciting event

2. Must report at least one symptom in *three of the four* following categories:
   Sensory
       Reports of hyperesthesia and/or allodynia
   Vasomotor
       Reports of temperature asymmetry and/or skin color changes and/or skin color asymmetry
   Sudomotor/edema
       Reports of edema and/or sweating changes and/or sweating asymmetry
   Motor/trophic
       Reports of decreased range of motion and/or motor dysfunction (weakness, tremor, dystonia) and/or trophic changes (hair, nail, skin)

3. Must display at least one sign **at time of evaluation** in *two or more* of the following categories:
   Sensory
       Evidence of hyperalgesia (to pinprick) and/or allodynia (to light touch and/or temperature sensation and/or deep somatic pressure and/or joint movement)
   Vasomotor
       Evidence of temperature asymmetry ($>1°$ C) and/or skin color changes and/or asymmetry
   Sudomotor/edema
       Evidence of oedema and/or sweating changes and/or sweating asymmetry
   Motor/trophic
       Evidence of decreased range of motion and/or motor dysfunction (weakness, tremor, dystonia) and/or trophic changes (hair, nail, skin)

4. There is no other diagnosis that better explains the signs and symptoms.

For *research* **purposes**, diagnostic decision rule should be at least one symptom *in all four* symptom categories and at least one sign (observed at evaluation) in two or more sign categories (sensitivity of 0.70, specificity of 0.94).

From Bruehl et al.[22] and Harden et al.[80]

2a. Vasomotor instability

Vasomotor instability is often transitory and so it may not be present at the time of examination. If the patient is reliable, then a history confirms its presence. Visual inspection is the usual means of diagnosis.

Thermography can be used to quantitate temperature difference between the limbs. This is greater in CRPS than other pain syndromes,[128,162] and this can be used to distinguish CRPS from other causes of neuropathic pain. However, thermography has not been validated within an orthopaedic context and must therefore be used with caution. It is not usually used in an orthopaedic context.

2b. Abnormal sweating

Whether this feature should be considered with vasomotor instability as proposed by Atkins et al.[3,6] or should be with edema as suggested recently by Harden et al.[80] is not yet clear. As for vasomotor instability, the feature is inconstant and it may be necessary to rely on history. Excessive sweat-

ing is usually clinically obvious. In a doubtful case, the resistance to a biro or pencil gently stroked across the limb is useful. The extent of sweating can be quantified by iontophoresis but this is rarely undertaken.

3. Edema and swelling

This is usually obvious on inspection. In the hand, it may be quantified by hand volume measurement. Similarly, skinfold thickness and digital circumference may be measured.[3,6]

4. Loss of joint mobility and atrophy

Loss of joint mobility is usually diagnosed by standard clinical examination. The range of finger joint movement may be accurately quantified.[3,6,51] As outlined here, atrophy will affect every tissue within the limb.

5. Bone changes

Radiographic appearances and bone scans are discussed earlier. CRPS does not cause arthritis and joint space is preserved. Sudeck's technique of assessing bone density by radiographing two extremities on one plate[120,145] remains

TABLE 23-4 Diagnostic Sensitivity and Specificity for the International Association for the Study of Pain Modified Criteria (see Table 23-3) in Distinguishing Patients with Complex Regional Pain Syndrome (CRPS) from Patients with Neuropathic Pain from a Documented Non-CRPS Cause

Decision rule	Sensitivity	Specificity
2+ sign categories and 2+ symptom categories	0.94	0.36
2+ sign categories and 3+ symptom categories	0.85	0.69
2+ sign categories and 4 symptom categories	0.70	0.94
3+ sign categories and 2+ symptom categories	0.76	0.81
3+ sign categories and 3+ symptom categories	0.70	0.83
3+ sign categories and 4 symptom categories	0.86	0.75

From Bruehl et al.[22]

useful but densitometry is not usually helpful.[156] A normal bone scan without radiographic osteoporosis virtually excludes adult CRPS.

Other Clinical Examinations

Making a diagnosis of "neglect"-like phenomena is relatively easy clinically but may not as yet be useful. Sensory neglect can be elucidated either by history or direct sensory examination with the patient watching or looking away from the affected limb. Motor neglect is examined by asking the patient to undertake a simple task initially while looking away and then while watching the limb. In the upper limb, this can be repetitively opening the closing the fingers or, in the lower limb, tapping the foot. If there is a significant improvement when the patient is watching the limb, a degree of motor neglect is present.[61]

TABLE 23-5 Suggested Criteria for the Diagnosis of Complex Regional Pain Syndrome (CRPS) within an Orthopaedic Setting

The diagnosis is made clinically by the finding of the following associated sets of abnormalities:
1. Neuropathic pain. Nondermatomal, without cause, burning, with associated allodynia and hyperpathia
2. Vasomotor instability and abnormalities of sweating. Warm red and dry, cool blue, and clammy or an increase in temperature sensitivity. Associated with an abnormal temperature difference between the limbs
3. Swelling
4. Loss of joint mobility with associated joint and soft tissue contracture, including skin thinning and hair and nail dystrophy

These clinical findings are backed up by
1. Increased uptake on delayed bone scintigraphy early in CRPS
2. Radiographic evidence of osteoporosis after 3 months

The diagnosis is excluded by the existence of conditions that would otherwise account for the degree of dysfunction.

Modified from Atkins et al.[2,3]

Investigations

CRPS is a clinical diagnosis and there is no single diagnostic test. The classic case is obvious and direct effects of trauma, fracture, cellulitis, arthritis, and malignancy are common alternative diagnoses. The patient is systemically well with normal general clinical examination, biochemical markers, and infection indices.

Magnetic resonance imaging (MRI) shows early bone and soft tissue edema with late atrophy and fibrosis but is not diagnostic. However, in CRPS 2, MRI may be useful to demonstrate nerve thinning with poststenotic dilatation caused by compression and may even demonstrate a fibrous band causing the compression. It may also demonstrate neuroma formation, although many neuromas are too small to be adequately shown.

Computed tomography (CT) scanning may also be useful in demonstrating a bony compressing lesion. Electromyographic and nerve conduction studies are normal in CRPS 1 but may demonstrate a nerve lesion in CRPS 2.

Differential Diagnosis

Pain, swelling, and vasomotor instability are common associations of trauma and orthopaedic surgery. The following are common differential diagnoses.

1. *Soft tissue infection.* The clinical features are usually clear. The patient is systemically unwell with raised inflammatory markers.
2. *"Mechanical" problems.* Classic examples are incorrect sizing of a total knee replacement causing pain, swelling, and stiffness; overlong screws impinging on a joint; or malreduction of an intra-articular fracture (Fig. 23-5). In accordance with category 4 of the original IASP criteria for CRPS, all mechanical causes for the symptoms and signs must be excluded before making a diagnosis of CRPS. However, it must be borne in mind that the chronic pain of a mechanical problem can itself be the precipitating cause of CRPS.
3. *Conscious exaggeration of symptoms.* This is usually seen in the context of litigation, but the secondary gain from exaggeration may also relate to complex and pathological interpersonal relationships. This problem has been accidentally made more acute and severe by the IASP criteria for CRPS

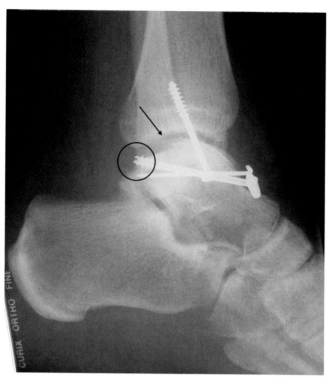

FIGURE 23-5 A patient referred with a diagnosis of CRPS. This patient with severe pain in his foot was referred some years after internal fixation of a talar body fracture. He has severe pain and dysfunction. The lateral radiograph shows no evidence of significant osteoporosis, which is inconsistent with the diagnosis. The talar body fracture is not reduced (*arrow*), which renders the ankle and subtalar joints incongruous. Furthermore, the screws are overlong (*circle*) and impinge on the ankle joint. This patient does not have CRPS; he has a mechanical cause for his severe pain, which was resolved by talar osteotomy, anatomic reduction, and refixation. It is important to exclude mechanical causes for pain before invoking the diagnosis of CRPS.

diagnosis. The original criteria (Table 23-2) are readily mimicked by a patient determined to deceive the examining clinician. Unfortunately, the modified criteria may also provide a diagnosis of CRPS in a deceitful patient. Categories 1 and 2 are simple. The patient merely has to report these problems. Category 3 refers to objective criteria. However, sensory abnormalities rely on the patient's subjective response to stimulus. Skin color change can be caused by deliberate dependency and immobility of the limb. Loss of joint range of movement can be caused by conscious resistant to movement, and dystonia, tremor, and weakness can likewise be produced artifactually. The rise of the Internet means that any reasonably determined patient can have very great knowledge of the features of CRPS and the diagnostic criteria. The solution to this problem is to remember that the IASP criteria are designed to differentiate CRPS from other chronically painful conditions. They are not intended to deal with a patient whose veracity is open to question. CRPS is a condition that inevitably leads to dystrophy,[21,44,58,138] and in a patient who has suffered from significant CRPS for any significant length, objective features of dystrophy, such as nail or hair dystrophy, skin and subcutaneous tissue atrophy, fixed joint contracture, and radiographic features of significant osteoporosis with abnormalities of bone scanning,

should be present. If the patient's veracity is in doubt, the astute clinician will give only limited or no credence to those features that can be mimicked and look for incontrovertible physical signs.

4. *Psychiatric disease.* Separate from the conscious exaggeration described earlier, psychiatric disease may cause a patient unconsciously to exaggerate the level or impact of physical disease. Somatoform disorders describe conditions in which patients unconsciously exaggerate physical symptoms, and conversion disorders refer to unconscious exaggeration of physical signs. These patients are often psychologically fragile, they may have a history of an unusually severe reaction to multiple minor medical problems, and they may show a tendency to "catastrophize" life events. In addition to this direct influence on a diagnosis of CRPS, patients with CRPS may be depressed because of chronic pain and psychiatric disease may play an indirect part in the condition. It is often very useful to obtain formal psychiatric or psychological opinion and treatment.[156]

5. *Neuropathic pain.* This has been defined and discussed. Neuropathic pain is part of CRPS, but a patient may have neuropathic pain without having CRPS. However, neuropathic pain may give rise to CRPS.

6. *Chronic pain state.* Patients with long-lasting and unremitting pain may become depressed, particularly when there is a neuropathic element. They learn to avoid activities that cause pain, and their relatives and carers act to protect them from perceived injury. This generates a complex psychosocial situation that may require psychological, psychiatric, pain therapeutic, and orthopaedic combined management.

Management

A bewildering array of treatments have been proposed, but proper scientifically constructed prospectively randomized blinded studies are few,[95] and uncontrolled investigations are particularly unreliable in CRPS because of the variety of symptoms and the trend toward self-resolution in the majority of cases. This is well illustrated by a series of publications investigating the treatment of early CRPS after Colles' fracture with intravenous regional guanethidine blockade (IVRGB). An initial investigation showed that IVRGB caused improvement in objective criteria of CRPS severity.[54] A subsequent pilot study appeared to confirm the immediate improvement induced by IVRGB was associated with sustained symptomatic improvement.[53] However, a full prospectively randomized double-blind controlled study demonstrated that IVRGB actually seemed to worsen the condition.[105] The lesson is that these potentially fragile patients must be approached with caution.

This chapter has presented evidence that CRPS is very common in orthopaedic trauma practice. Most sufferers are sensible people, concerned about the development of inexplicable pain, but the occasional "Sudecky" patient fares poorly and should be treated vigorously. Early treatment, begun before contractures occur, gives optimal results, so a high index of clinical suspicion must be maintained. It is not reprehensible to have caused a case of CRPS through surgery or nonoperative management of injury. However, delay in diagnosis and treatment may contribute to a poor outcome.

Modern CRPS treatment emphasizes functional rehabilitation of the limb to break the vicious cycle of disuse,[79,82,141] rather than SNS manipulation.[26] Initial treatment from the orthopaedic surgeon is with reassurance, excellent analgesia, and intensive, careful physical therapy avoiding exacerbation of pain.[66] Nonsteroidal anti-inflammatory drugs may give better pain relief than opiates, and a centrally acting analgesic such as amitriptyline is often useful even at this early stage. Immobilization and splintage should generally be avoided but, if used, joints must be placed in a safe position and splintage is a temporary adjunct to mobilization. It seems sensible to give the patients vitamin C in view of the early evidence of its efficacy.[170,171]

Abnormalities of pain sensation will often respond to desensitization. The patient is asked to stroke the area of allodynia, where stroking is painful. They are reminded that simple stroking cannot by definition be painful and they are instructed to stroke the affected part repetitively while looking at it and repeatedly saying "this does not hurt, it is merely a gentle touch." The earlier this is begun, the more effective it is. A similar attitude can be taken with early loss of joint mobility due to perceived pain rather than contracture.

The use of mirror virtual therapy is an exciting new concept that is as yet unproved in an orthopaedic context.[116,133]

If the patient does not respond rapidly, a pain specialist should be involved and treatment continued on a shared basis. Psychological or psychiatric input may be important.[25] Second-line treatment is often unsuccessful and many patients are left with pain and disability. Further treatments include centrally acting analgesic medications such as amitriptyline, gabapentin, or carbamazepine; regional anesthesia; calcitonin; the use of membrane-stabilizing drugs such as mexilitene; sympathetic blockade and manipulation; desensitization of peripheral nerve receptors with capsaicin; or transcutaneous nerve stimulation or an implanted dorsal column stimulator.[109,124,142] Behavioral therapy may be necessary in children.[165–167] Where the knee is affected, epidural anesthesia and continuous passive motion may be appropriate.[35,36]

The role of surgery is limited and hazardous. While there is debate within pain therapy circles as to the utility of separating CRPS type 1 from type 2 (although there is evidence that they are symptomatically different[21]), within orthopaedic practice, it is extremely useful. The wording of the IASP criteria is not surgically precise (Table 23-2). However, if one substitutes surgically correctable nerve lesion, in cases of CRPS type 2, treatment should be directed at curing the nerve lesion. Occult nerve compression should be sought and dealt with. For example, decompression of a median nerve at the wrist that is causing CRPS of the hand may abort the CRPS and should be undertaken cautiously in the presence of active disease.

Surgery is rarely indicated to treat fixed contractures, which usually involve all of the soft tissues. Surgical release must therefore be radical and expectations limited. Surgery for contracture should be delayed until the active phase of CRPS has completely passed, and ideally there should be a gap of at least 1 year since the patient last experienced pain and swelling.

Amputation of a limb affected by severe CRPS should be approached with great caution. Dielissen et al.[42] reported a series of 28 patients who underwent 34 amputations in 31 limbs. Surgery was usually performed for recurrent infection or to improve residual function. Pain relief was rare and unpredictable, and neither was infection always cured nor function universally improved. CRPS often recurred in the stump, especially if the

amputation level was symptomatic at the time of surgery. For this reason, only two patients wore a prosthesis.

Generally, surgery represents a painful stimulus that may exacerbate CRPS or precipitate a new attack. This risk must be balanced carefully against the proposed benefit. The risk of surgically precipitated recurrence is greatest when the same site is operated on in a patient with abnormal psychology in the presence of active disease and lowest when these conditions do not apply. Surgery must be performed carefully with minimal trauma with excellent and complete postoperative analgesia. The surgery may be covered by gabapentin. Ideally, the anesthetist will have a particular interest in the treatment of CRPS.

CONCLUSION

This chapter has presented the proposal that CRPS in a mild form, which is often not formally diagnosed, is very common but not universal in an orthopaedic trauma practice. Although the majority of cases will resolve with simple management, CRPS is responsible for significant acute disability and may cause long-term problems.

REFERENCES

1. Ali Z, Raja SN, Wesselmann U, et al. Intradermal injection of norepinephrine evokes pain in patients with sympathetically maintained pain. Pain 2000;88:161–168.
2. Atkins RM, Duckworth T, Kanis JA. Algodystrophy following Colles' fracture. J Hand Surg [Br] 1989;14:161–164.
3. Atkins RM, Duckworth T, Kanis JA. Features of algodystrophy after Colles' fracture. J Bone Joint Surg Br 1990;72:105–110.
4. Atkins RM, Kanis JA. The use of dolorimetry in the assessment of posttraumatic algodystrophy of the hand. Br J Rheumatol 1989;28:404–409.
5. Atkins RM, Tindale W, Bickerstaff D, et al. Quantitative bone scintigraphy in reflex sympathetic dystrophy. Br J Rheumatol 1993;32:41–45.
6. Atkins RM. Algodystrophy. Oxford: University of Oxford, 1989.
7. Aubert PG. Etude sur le risque algodystrophique. [These pour le doctorat en medecin diplome d'etat.] Paris: University of Paris, Val de Marne, 1980.
8. Bacorn R, Kurtz J. Colles' fracture: a study of 2000 cases from the New York State Workmen's Compensation Board. J Bone Joint Surg Am 1953;35A:643–658.
9. Bernstein BH, Singsen BH, Kent JT, et al. Reflex neurovascular dystrophy in childhood. J Pediatr 1978;93:211–215.
10. Bhatia KP, Bhatt MH, Marsden CD. The causalgia-dystonia syndrome. Brain 1993;116:843–851.
11. Bhatia KP, Marsden CD. Reflex sympathetic dystrophy may be accompanied by involuntary movements. BMJ 1995;311:811–812.
12. Bickerstaff DR, Charlesworth D, Kanis JA. Changes in cortical and trabecular bone in algodystrophy. Br J Rheumatol 1993;32:46–51.
13. Bickerstaff DR, Kanis JA. Algodystrophy: an underrecognized complication of minor trauma. Br J Rheumatol 1994;33:240–248.
14. Bickerstaff DR. The Natural History of Posttraumatic Algodystrophy. Sheffield, UK: University of Sheffield, 1990.
15. Birklein F, Riedl B, Sieweke N, et al. Neurological findings in complex regional pain syndromes—analysis of 145 cases. Acta Neurol Scand 2000;101:262–269.
16. Boas R. Complex regional pain syndromes: symptoms, signs, and differential diagnosis. In: Janig W, Stanton-Hicks M, eds. Reflex Sympathetic Dystrophy: A Deappraisal. Seattle, WA: IASP Press, 1996:79–92.
17. Bonica JJ. Causalgia and other reflex sympathetic dystrophies. In: Bonica JJ, ed. Management of Pain. Philadelphia: Lea & Febiger, 1990:220–243.
18. Bonica JJ. The management of pain. Philadelphia: Lea & Febiger; 1953.
19. Breuer J, Freud S. Studies in Hysteria. Translated and edited by J. Strachey with the collaboration of A. Freud. New York: Basic Books, 1982.
20. Bruehl S. Do psychological factors play a role in the onset and maintenance of CRPS-1? In: Harden RN, Baron R, et al, eds. Complex Regional Pain Syndrome. Seattle, WA: IASP Press, 2001.
21. Bruehl S. Psychological interventions. In: Wilson P, Stanton-Hicks M, Harden RN, eds. CRPS: Current Diagnosis and Therapy. Seattle, WA: IASP Press, 2005:201–216.
22. Bruehl S, Carlson CR. Predisposing psychological factors in the development of reflex sympathetic dystrophy. A review of the empirical evidence. Clin J Pain 1992;8:287–299.
23. Bruehl S, Harden RN, Galer BS, et al. Complex regional pain syndrome: are there distinct subtypes and sequential stages of the syndrome? Pain 2002;95:119–124.
24. Bruehl S, Harden RN, Galer BS, et al. External validation of IASP diagnostic criteria for complex regional pain syndrome and proposed research diagnostic criteria. International Association for the Study of Pain. Pain 1999;81:147–154.
25. Bruehl S, Husfeldt B, Lubenow TR, et al. Psychological differences between reflex sympathetic dystrophy and non-RSD chronic pain patients. Pain 1996;67:107–114.
26. Burton AW, Lubenow TR, Prithvi Raj P. Traditional interventional therapies. In: Wilson

P, Stanton-Hicks M, Harden RN, eds. CRPS: Current Diagnosis and Treatment. Seattle, WA: IASP Press, 2005:217–233.
27. Butler SH. Disuse and CRPS. In: Harden RN, Baron R, Janig W, eds. Complex Regional Pain Syndrome. Seattle, WA: IASP Press, 2001:141–150.
28. Butler SH, Galer BS, Benirsche S. Disuse as a cause of signs and symptoms of CRPS. Abstracts: 8th World Congress on Pain. Seattle, WA: IASP Press; 1996:401.
29. Butler SH, Nyman M, Gordh T, editors. Immobility in volunteers produces signs and symptoms of CRPS and a neglect-like state. Abstracts: 9th World Congress on Pain; 1999. Seattle, WA: IASP Press.
30. Campbell J, Raga S, Meyer R. Painful sequelae of nerve injury. In: Dubner R, Gebhart G, Bond M, eds. Proceedings of the 5th World Congress on Pain. Amsterdam: Elsevier Science Publishers; 1988:135–143.
31. Casale R, Glynn CJ, Buonocore M. Autonomic variations after stellate ganglion block: are they evidence of an autonomic afference? Funct Neurol 1990;5:245–246.
32. Channon GN, Lloyd GJ. The investigation of hand stiffness using Doppler ultrasound, radionuclide scanning and thermography. J Bone Joint Surg Br 1979;61B:519.
33. Charcot JM. Two cases of hysterical contracture of traumatic origin (Lectures VII and VIII). Lectures on Diseases of the Nervous System. Nijmegen: Arts and Boeve; 1889: 84–106.
34. Constantinesco A, Brunot B, Demangeat JL, et al. Three-phase bone scanning as an aid to early diagnosis in reflex sympathetic dystrophy of the hand. A study of 89 cases. Ann Chir Main 1986;5:93–104.
35. Cooper DE, DeLee JC. Reflex sympathetic dystrophy of the knee. J Am Acad Orthop Surg 1994;2:79–86.
36. Cooper DE, DeLee JC, Ramamurthy S. Reflex sympathetic dystrophy of the knee. Treatment using continuous epidural anesthesia. J Bone Joint Surg Am 1989;71A:365–369.
37. De Takats G. Causalgic states in peace and war. JAMA 1945;128:699–704.
38. De Takats G. The nature of painful vasodilatation in causalgic states. Arch Neurol 1943; 53:318–326.
39. De Takats G. Reflex dystrophy of the extremities. Arch Surg 1937;34:939–956.
40. Demangeat JL, Constantinesco A, Brunot B, et al. Three-phase bone scanning in reflex sympathetic dystrophy of the hand. J Nucl Med 1988;29:26–32.
41. Devor M, Raber P. Heritability of symptoms in an experimental model of neuropathic pain. Pain 1990;42:51–67.
42. Dielissen PW, Claassen AT, Veldman PH, et al. Amputation for reflex sympathetic dystrophy. J Bone Joint Surg Br 1995;77B:270–273.
43. Doupe J, Cullen C, Chance G. Posttraumatic pain and causalgic syndrome. J Neurol Neurosurg Psychiatry 1944;7:33–35.
44. Doury P, Dirheimer Y, Pattin S. Algodystrophy: Diagnosis and Therapy of a Frequent Disease of the Locomotor Apparatus. Berlin: Springer Verlag, 1981.
45. Dressler D, Thompson PD, Gledhill RF, et al. The syndrome of painful legs and moving toes. Mov Disord 1994;9:13–21.
46. Evans JA. Reflex sympathetic dystrophy. Surg Clin N Am 1946;26:780–790.
47. Fam AG, Stein J. Disappearance of chondrocalcinosis following reflex sympathetic dystrophy syndrome. Arthritis Rheum 1981;24:747–749.
48. Ficat P, Arlet J, Lartigue G, et al. [Postinjury reflex algodystrophies. Hemodynamic and anatomopathological study]. Rev Chir Orthop Reparatrice Appar Mot 1973;59: 401–414.
49. Ficat P, Arlet J, Pujol M, et al. [Injury, reflex dystrophy, and osteonecrosis of the femoral head]. Ann Chir 1971;25:911–917.
50. Field J. Measurement of finger stiffness in algodystrophy. Hand Clin 2003;19:511–515.
51. Field J, Atkins RM. Algodystrophy is an early complication of Colles' fracture. What are the implications? J Hand Surg [Br] 1997;22:178–182.
52. Field J, Atkins RM. Effect of guanethidine on the natural history of posttraumatic algodystrophy. Ann Rheum Dis 1993;52:467–469.
53. Field J, Gardner FV. Psychological distress associated with algodystrophy. J Hand Surg [Br] 1997;22:100–101.
54. Field J, Monk C, Atkins RM. Objective improvements in algodystrophy following regional intravenous guanethidine. J Hand Surg [Br] 1993;18:339–342.
55. Field J, Protheroe DL, Atkins RM. Algodystrophy after Colles fractures is associated with secondary tightness of casts. J Bone Joint Surg Br 1994;76B:901–905.
56. Field J, Warwick D, Bannister GC. Features of algodystrophy 10 years after Colles' fracture. J Hand Surg [Br] 1992;17:318–320.
57. Francini F, Zoppi M, Maresca M, et al. Skin potential and EMG changes induced by electrical stimulation. 1. Normal man in arousing and nonarousing environment. Appl Neurophysiol 1979;42:113–124.
58. Galer BS, Bruehl S, Harden RN. IASP diagnostic criteria for complex regional pain syndrome: a preliminary empirical validation study. International Association for the Study of Pain. Clin J Pain 1998;14:48–54.
59. Galer BS, Butler S, Jensen MP. Case reports and hypothesis: a neglect-like syndrome may be responsible for the motor disturbance in reflex sympathetic dystrophy (complex regional pain syndrome-1). J Pain Symptom Manage 1995;10:385–391.
60. Galer BS, Harden N. Motor abnormalities in CRPS: a neglected but key component. In: Harden N, Baron R, et al, eds. Complex Regional Pain Syndrome. Seattle, WA: IASP Press, 2001.
61. Galer BS, Harden RN. Motor abnormalities in CRPS: a neglected but key component. In: Harden RN, Baron R, Janig W, editors. Complex Regional Pain Syndrome. Seattle, WA: IASP Press, 2001:135–140.
62. Galer BS, Jensen M. Neglect-like symptoms in Complex Regional Pain Syndrome: results of a self-administered survey. J Pain Symptom Manage 1999;18:213–217.
63. Geertzen JH, de Bruijn H, de Bruijn-Kofman AT, et al. Reflex sympathetic dystrophy: early treatment and psychological aspects. Arch Phys Med Rehabil 1994;75:442–446.
64. Geertzen JH, de Bruijn-Kofman AT, de Bruijn HP, et al. Stressful life events and psychological dysfunction in complex regional pain syndrome type I. Clin J Pain 1998;14: 143–147.
65. Geertzen JH, Dijkstra PU, Groothoff JW, et al. Reflex sympathetic dystrophy of the upper extremity—a 5.5-year follow-up. Part II. Social life events, general health, and changes in occupation. Acta Orthop Scand Suppl 1998;279:19–23.
66. Geertzen JH, Harden RN. Physical and occupational therapies. In: Wilson P, Stanton-Hicks M, Harden RN, eds. CRPS: Current Diagnosis and Therapy. Seattle, WA: IASP Press, 2005:173–179.
67. Gibbons JJ, Wilson PR. RSD score: criteria for the diagnosis of reflex sympathetic dystrophy and causalgia. Clin J Pain 1992;8:260–263.
68. Glick EN. Reflex dystrophy (algoneurodystrophy): results of treatment by corticosteroids. Rheumatol Rehabil 1973;12:84.
69. Glick EN, Helal B. Posttraumatic neurodystrophy. Treatment by corticosteroids. Hand 1976;8:45–47.
70. Glynn CJ, Basedow RW, Walsh JA. Pain relief following postganglionic sympathetic blockade with I.V. guanethidine. Br J Anaesth 1981;53:1297–1302.
71. Goris RJ. Conditions associated with impaired oxygen extraction. In: Gutierrez G, Vincent JL, eds. Tissue Oxygen Utilisation. Berlin: Springer Verlag, 1991:350–369.
72. Goris RJ. Treatment of reflex sympathetic dystrophy with hydroxyl radical scavengers. Unfallchirurg 1985;88:330–332.
73. Goris RJ, Dongen LM, Winters HA. Are toxic oxygen radicals involved in the pathogenesis of reflex sympathetic dystrophy? Free Radic Res Commun 1987;3:13–18.
74. Green JT, Gay FH. Colles' fracture residual disability. Am J Surg 1956;91:636–646.
75. Hannington-Kiff JG. Hyperadrenergic-effected limb causalgia: relief by IV pharmacologic norepinephrine blockade. Am Heart J 1982;103:152–153.
76. Hannington-Kiff JG. Pharmacological target blocks in hand surgery and rehabilitation. J Hand Surg [Br] 1984;9:29–36.
77. Hannington-Kiff JG. Relief of causalgia in limbs by regional intravenous guanethidine. Br Med J 1979;2:367–368.
78. Hannington-Kiff JG. Relief of Sudeck's atrophy by regional intravenous guanethidine. Lancet 1977;1(8022):1132–1133.
79. Harden RN. The rationale for integrated functional restoration. In: Wilson P, Stanton-Hicks M, Harden RN, eds. CRPS: Current Diagnosis and Therapy. Seattle, WA: IASP Press, 2005:163–171.
80. Harden RN, Bruehl S, Galer BS, et al. Complex regional pain syndrome: are the IASP diagnostic criteria valid and sufficiently comprehensive? Pain 1999;83:211–219.
81. Harden RN, Bruehl S, Stanos S, et al. Prospective examination of pain-related and psychological predictors of CRPS-like phenomena following total knee arthroplasty: a preliminary study. Pain 2003;106:393–400.
82. Harden RN, Swan M, King A, et al. Treatment of complex regional pain syndrome: functional restoration. Clin J Pain 2006;22:420–424.
83. Harris AJ. Cortical origin of pathological pain. Lancet 1999;354:1464–1466.
84. Holder LE, Mackinnon SE. Reflex sympathetic dystrophy in the hands: clinical and scintigraphic criteria. Radiology 1984;152:517–522.
85. Homans J. Minor causalgia. A hyperaesthetic neurovascular syndrome. N Engl J Med 1940;222:870–874.
86. Jacquemoud G, Chamay A. Treatment of algodystrophy using intravenous guanethidine regional block. Ann Chir Main 1982;1:57–64.
87. Jadad AR, Carroll D, Glynn CJ, et al. Intravenous regional sympathetic blockade for pain relief in reflex sympathetic dystrophy: a systematic review and a randomized, double-blind crossover study. J Pain Symptom Manage 1995;10:13–20.
88. Janig W, Koltzenburg M. Possible ways of sympathetic afferent interaction. In: Janig W, Schmidt RF, eds. Reflex Sympathetic Dystrophy: Pathophysiological Mechanisms and Clinical Implications. New York: VCH Verlagsgesellschaft, 1992:213–243.
89. Janig W, Koltzenburg M. What is the interaction between the sympathetic terminal and the primary afferent fibre? In: Basbaum AI, et al, eds. Towards a new pharmacology of pain. Chichester: John Wiley and Sons; 1991:331–352.
90. Janig W. CRPS 1 and CRPS 2: A strategic view. In: Harden RN, Baron R, Janig W, eds. Complex Regional Pain Syndrome. Seattle, WA: IASP Press, 2p. 3–15.
91. Janig W. The sympathetic nervous system in pain: physiology and pathophysiology. In: Stanton-Hicks M, editor. Pain in the Sympathetic Nervous System. Massachussetts: Kluwer Academic Publishers, 1990:17–89.
92. Jensen TS, Baron R. Translation of symptoms and signs into mechanisms in neuropathic pain. Pain 2003;102:1–8.
93. Katz MM, Hungerford DS. Reflex sympathetic dystrophy affecting the knee. J Bone Joint Surg Br 1987;69B:797–803.
94. Kimura T, Komatsu T, Hosoda R, et al. Angiotensin-converting enzyme gene polymorphism in patients with neuropathic pain. In: Devor M, Rowbotham M, Wiesenfeld-Hallin D, eds. Proceedings of the 9th World Conference on Pain. Seattle, WA: IASP Press; 2000:471–476.
95. Kingery WS. A critical review of controlled clinical trials for peripheral neuropathic pain and complex regional pain syndromes. Pain 1997;73:123–139.
96. Knepper R. [Pathogenic evaluation of pain]. Med Welt 1967;35:1994–1996.
97. Kozin F, Genant HK, Bekerman C, et al. The reflex sympathetic dystrophy syndrome. II. Roentgenographic and scintigraphic evidence of bilaterality and of periarticular accentuation. Am J Med 1976;60:332–338.
98. Kozin F, McCarty DJ, Sims J, et al. The reflex sympathetic dystrophy syndrome. I. Clinical and histologic studies: evidence for bilaterality, response to corticosteroids, and articular involvement. Am J Med 1976;60:321–331.
99. Leriche R. Oedeme dur aigu post-traumatique de la main avec impotence fonctionelle complete. Transformation soudaine cinq heures apres sympathectomie humerale. Lyon Chir 1923;20:814–818.
100. Leriche R. Traitement par la sympathectomie periarterielle des osteoporoses traumatiques. Bull Mem Soc Chir Paris 1926;52:247–251.
101. Lewis JS, Kersten P, McCabe CS, et al. Body perception disturbance: a contribution to pain in complex regional pain syndrome (CRPS). Pain 2007;133:111–119.
102. Lidström A. Fractures of the distal end of radius. A clinical and statistical study of end results. Acta Orthop Scand 1959;suppl 41.
103. Liepert J, Tegenthoff M, Malin JP. Changes of cortical motor area size during immobilization. Electroencephalogr Clin Neurophysiol 1995;97:382–386.
104. Lindsay RM, Harmar AJ. Nerve growth factor regulates expression of neuropeptide genes in adult sensory neurons. Nature 1989;337:362–364.
105. Livingstone JA, Atkins RM. Intravenous regional guanethidine blockade in the treatment of posttraumatic complex regional pain syndrome type 1 (algodystrophy) of the hand. J Bone Joint Surg Br 2002;84B:380–386.
106. Livingstone JA, Field J. Algodystrophy and its association with Dupuytren disease. J Hand Surg [Br] 1999;24:199–202.
107. LoPinto C, Young WB, Ashkenazi A. Comparison of dynamic (brush) and static (pressure) mechanical allodynia in migraine. Cephalalgia 2006;26:852–856.
108. Louyot P, Gaucher A, Montet Y, et al. [Algodystrophy of the lower extremity]. Rev Rhum Mal Osteoartic 1967;34:733–737.
109. Lubenow TR, Buvanendran A, Stanton-Hicks M. Implanted Therapies. In: Wilson P,

Stanton-Hicks M, Harden RN, eds. CRPS: Current Diagnosis and Therapy. Seattle, WA: IASP Press, 2005:235–253.

110. Mackinnon SE, Holder LE. The use of three-phase radionuclide bone scanning in the diagnosis of reflex sympathetic dystrophy. J Hand Surg [Am] 1984;9:556–563.

111. Mailis A, Wade J. Profile of Caucasian women with possible genetic predisposition to reflex sympathetic dystrophy: a pilot study. Clin J Pain 1994;10:210–217.

112. Mailis A, Wade JA. Genetic considerations in CRPS. In: Harden RN, Baron R, Janig W, eds. Complex Regional Pain Syndrome. IASP Press; 2001:227–238.

113. Marsden CD, Obeso JA, Traub MM, et al. Muscle spasms associated with Sudeck's atrophy after injury. Br Med J (Clin Res Ed) 1984;288:173–176.

114. Matsumura H, Jimbo Y, Watanabe K. Haemodynamic changes in early phase reflex sympathetic dystrophy. Scand J Plast Reconstr Surg Hand Surg 1996;30:133–138.

115. McCabe CS, Haigh RC, Halligan PW, et al. Referred sensations in patients with complex regional pain syndrome type 1. Rheumatology (Oxford) 2003;42:1067–1073.

116. McCabe CS, Haigh RC, Ring EF, et al. A controlled pilot study of the utility of mirror visual feedback in the treatment of complex regional pain syndrome (type 1). Rheumatology (Oxford) 2003;42:97–101.

117. McLachlan EM, Janig W, Devor M, et al. Peripheral nerve injury triggers noradrenergic sprouting within dorsal root ganglia. Nature 1993;363:543–546.

118. Merskey H. Essence, investigation, and management of "neuropathic" pains: hopes from acknowledgment of chaos. Muscle Nerve 1995;18:455–456; author reply 8–62.

119. Merskey H, Bogduk N. Classification of Chronic Pain: Descriptions of Chronic Pain Syndromes and Definitions of Pain Terms. 2nd ed. Seattle, WA: IASP Press, 1994.

120. Mitchell SW, Morehouse GG, Keen WW. Gunshot Wounds and Other Injuries of Nerves. Philadelphia: JB Lippincott, 1864.

121. Muller ME, Allgower M, Schneider R, et al. Manual of internal fixation. Techniques recommended by the AO group. 2nd ed. London/New York: Springer Verlag; 1979.

122. Nelson DV, Novy DM. Psychological characteristics of reflex sympathetic dystrophy versus myofascial pain syndromes. Reg Anesth 1996;21:202–208.

123. Nonne N. Über die Radiographische nachweisbare akute und kronische "Knochena-trophie" (Südeck bie Nerven-Erkrankungen). Fortschr Geb Röntgenstr 1901;5: 293–297.

124. Oaklander AL. Evidence-based pharmacotherapy for CRPS and related conditions. In: Wilson P, Stanton-Hicks M, Harden RN, eds. CRPS: Current Diagnosis and Therapy. Seattle, WA: IASP Press, 2005:181–200.

125. Oyen WJ, Arntz IE, Claessens RM, et al. Reflex sympathetic dystrophy of the hand: an excessive inflammatory response? Pain 1993;55:151–157.

126. Patman RD, Thompson JE, Persson AV. Management of posttraumatic pain syndromes: report of 113 cases. Ann Surg 1973;177:780–787.

127. Pelissier J, Touchon J, Besset A, et al. La personnalite du sujet souffrant d'algodystrophie sympathique reflexe. Etudes Psychometrques par le test MMPI. Rheumatologie 1981; 23:351–354.

128. Perelman RB, Adler D, Humphreys M. Reflex sympathetic dystrophy: electronic thermography as an aid in diagnosis. Orthop Rev 1987;16:561–566.

129. Plewes LW. Sudek's atrophy of the hand. J Bone Joint Surg Br 1956;38B:195–203.

130. Price DD, Long S, Wilsey B, Rafii A. Analysis of peak magnitude and duration of analgesia produced by local anesthetics injected into sympathetic ganglia of complex regional pain syndrome patients. Clin J Pain 1998;14:216–226.

131. Procacci P, Francini F, Maresca M, et al. Skin potential and EMG changes induced by cutaneous electrical stimulation. II. Subjects with reflex sympathetic dystrophies. Appl Neurophysiol 1979;42:125–134.

132. Procacci P, Francini F, Zoppi M, et al. Cutaneous pain threshold changes after sympathetic block in reflex dystrophies. Pain 1975;1:167–175.

133. Ramachandran VS, Roger-Ramachandran D. Synaesthesia in phantom limbs induced with mirrors. Proc R Soc Lond B Biol Sci 1996;263:377–386.

134. Renier JC, Moreau R, Bernat M, et al. [Contribution of dynamic isotopic tests in the study of algodystrophies]. Rev Rhum Mal Osteoartic 1979;46:235–241.

135. Sarangi PP, Ward AJ, Smith EJ, et al. Algodystrophy and osteoporosis after tibial fractures. J Bone Joint Surg Br 1993;75B:450–452.

136. Schattschneider J, Wenzelburger R, Deuschl G, et al. Kinematic analysis of the upper extremity in CRPS. In: Harden RN, Baron R, Janig W, eds. Complex Regional Pain Syndrome. Seattle, WA: IASP Press, 2001:119–128.

137. Schwartzman RJ, Kerrigan J. The movement disorder of reflex sympathetic dystrophy. Neurology 1990;40:57–61.

138. Schwartzman RJ, McLellan TL. Reflex sympathetic dystrophy. A review. Arch Neurol 1987;44:555–561.

139. Stanos SP, Harden RN, Wagner-Raphael L, et al. A prospective clinical model for investigating the development of CRPS. In: Harden RN, Baron R, Janig W, eds. Complex Regional Pain Syndrome. Seattle, WA: IASP Press, 2001:151–164.

140. Stanton-Hicks M, Baron R, Boas R, et al. Complex regional pain syndromes: guidelines for therapy. Clin J Pain 1998;14:155–166.

141. Stanton-Hicks M, Janig W, Hassenbusch S, et al. Reflex sympathetic dystrophy: changing concepts and taxonomy. Pain 1995;63:127–133.

142. Stanton-Hicks M, Rauck R, Hendrickson M, et al. Miscellaneous and experimental therapies. In: Wilson P, Stanton-Hicks M, Harden RN, eds. CRPS: Current Diagnosis and Therapy. Seattle, WA: IASP Press, 2005:255–274.

143. Steinbrocker O. The shoulder-hand syndrome: present perspective. Arch Phys Med Rehabil 1968;49:388–395.

144. Subbarao J, Stillwell GK. Reflex sympathetic dystrophy syndrome of the upper extremity: analysis of total outcome of management of 125 cases. Arch Phys Med Rehabil 1981;62:549–554.

145. Südeck P. Über die akute (reflektorische) Knochenatrophie nach Entzündungen und Verletzungen in den Extremitäten und ihre klinischen Erscheinungen. Fortschr Geb Rontgenstr 1901;5:227–293.

146. Südeck P. Über die Akute (reflektorische) Knochenatrophie. Arch Klin Chir 1900;762: 147–156.

147. Thomson McBride AR, Barnett AJ, Livingstone JA, et al. Complex regional pain syndrome (type 1): a comparison of 2 diagnostic criteria methods. Clin J Pain 2008;24: 637–640.

148. Torebjork E, Wahren L, Wallin G, et al. Noradrenaline-evoked pain in neuralgia. Pain 1995;63:11–20.

149. van der Laan L, Goris RJ. Reflex sympathetic dystrophy. An exaggerated regional inflammatory response? Hand Clin 1997;13:373–385.

150. van der Laan L, Kapitein P, Verhofstad A, et al. Clinical signs and symptoms of acute reflex sympathetic dystrophy in one hindlimb of the rat, induced by infusion of a free-radical donor. Acta Orthop Belg 1998;64:210–217.

151. van der Laan L, ter Laak HJ, Gabreels-Festen A, et al. Complex regional pain syndrome type I (RSD): pathology of skeletal muscle and peripheral nerve. Neurology 1998;51: 20–25.

152. Van Hilten JJ, Blumberg H, Schwartzman R. Factor IV: movement disorders and dystrophy. pathophysiology and measurement. In: Wilson P, Stanton-Hicks M, Harden RN, eds. CRPS: Current Diagnosis and Therapy. Seattle, WA: IASP Press, 2005:119–137.

153. van Hilten JJ, van de Beek WJ, Vein AA, et al. Clinical aspects of multifocal or generalized tonic dystonia in reflex sympathetic dystrophy. Neurology 200126;56:1762–1765.

154. Van Houdenhove B, Vasquez G, Onghena P, et al. Etiopathogenesis of reflex sympathetic dystrophy: a review and biopsychosocial hypothesis. Clin J Pain 1992;8: 300–306.

155. Van Houdenhove B. Neuro-algodystrophy: a psychiatrist's view. Clin Rheumatol 1986; 5:399–406.

156. Van Houdenhove B, Vasquez G. Is there a relationship between reflex sympathetic dystrophy and helplessness? Case reports and a hypothesis. Gen Hosp Psychiatry 1993; 15:325–329

157. Veldman PH, Reynen HM, Arntz IE, et al. Signs and symptoms of reflex sympathetic dystrophy: prospective study of 829 patients. Lancet 1993;342:1012–1016.

158. Vincent G, Ernst J, Henniaux M, et al. [Attempt at a psychological approach in algoneurodystrophy]. Rev Rhum Mal Osteoartic 1982;49:767–769.

159. Wahren LK, Gordh TJ, Torebjork E. Effects of regional intravenous guanethidine in patients with neuralgia in the hand; a follow-up study over a decade. Pain 1995;62: 379–385.

160. Wall PD. Noradrenaline-evoked pain in neuralgia. Pain 1995;63:1.

161. Wall PD, Devor M. Sensory afferent impulses originate from dorsal root ganglia as well as from the periphery in normal and nerve injured rats. Pain 1983;17:321–339.

162. Wasner G, Schattschneider J, Baron R. Skin temperature side differences—a diagnostic tool for CRPS? Pain 2002;98:19–26.

163. Watson Jones SR. Fractures and Joint Injuries. 4th ed. Edinburgh, London: ES Livingstone, 1952.

164. Wenzelburger R, Schattschneider J, Wasner G, et al. Grip force coordination in CRPS. In: Harden RN, Baron R, Janig W, eds. Complex Regional Pain Syndrome. Seattle, WA: IASP Press, 2001:129–134.

165. Wilder R, Olsson GL. Management of pediatric patients with CRPS. In: Wilson P, Stanton-Hicks M, Harden RN, eds. CRPS: Current Diagnosis and Therapy. Seattle, WA: IASP Press, 2005:275–289.

166. Wilder RT. Management of pediatric patients with complex regional pain syndrome. Clin J Pain 2006;22:443–448.

167. Wilder RT, Berde CB, Wolohan M, et al. Reflex sympathetic dystrophy in children. Clinical characteristics and follow-up of 70 patients. J Bone Joint Surg Am 1992;74A: 910–919.

168. Woolf CJ, Mannion RJ. Neuropathic pain: aetiology, symptoms, mechanisms, and management. Lancet 1999;353:1959–1964.

169. Woolf CJ, Salter MW. Neuronal plasticity: increasing the gain in pain. Science 2000; 288:1765–1768.

170. Zollinger PE, Tuinebreijer WE, Breederveld RS, et al. Can vitamin C prevent complex regional pain syndrome in patients with wrist fractures? A randomized, controlled, multicenter dose-response study. J Bone Joint Surg Am 2007;89A:1424–1431.

171. Zollinger PE, Tuinebreijer WE, Kreis RW, et al. Effect of vitamin C on frequency of reflex sympathetic dystrophy in wrist fractures: a randomised trial. Lancet 1999;354: 2025–2028.

172. Zucchini M, Alberti G, Moretti MP. Algodystrophy and related psychological features. Funct Neurol 1989 Apr-Jun;4:153–156.

173. Zyluk A. [The three-staged evolution of the posttraumatic algodystrophy]. Chir Narzadow Ruchu Ortop Pol 1998;63:479–486.

174. Zyluk A. Results of the treatment of posttraumatic reflex sympathetic dystrophy of the upper extremity with regional intravenous blocks of methylprednisolone and lidocaine. Acta Orthop Belg 1998;64:452–456.

175. Zyluk A. The natural history of posttraumatic reflex sympathetic dystrophy. J Hand Surg [Br] 1998;23:20–23.

24

ORTHOPAEDIC INFECTIONS
AND OSTEOMYELITIS

Bruce H. Ziran, Wade Smith, and Nalini Rao

INTRODUCTION

The first descriptions of infections date back to the early Sumerian carvings, when the tenets of treatment were irrigation, immobilization, and bandaging.[82] In these early times, the practice of infection and wound care was essentially an art and there was very little science applied to it. Treatment included the use of honey, wine, and donkey feces, and there were a number of philosophies regarding the value of purulence. Dominant personalities had a significant influence over medical practice and the value of purulence persisted because of the writings of Galen of Pergamum (120–201 A.D.). It was not until the latter third of the second millennium that the concept of the value of purulence would be challenged.[82]

In the past three centuries, the treatment of infection has involved the use of local ointments or salves and the maintenance of an open wound that permitted purulence to exit the body. Some important terms were adopted into medical parlance. A *sequestrum* was defined as "a fragment of dead bone separated from the body." The word *sequestrum* is derived from

the Latin words *sequester* meaning "depositary" and *sequestrate* meaning "to give up for safe keeping." The word *sequestrum* is used to describe a detached piece of bone lying within a cavity formed by necrosis. The term *involucrum* derives from the Latin word *involucrum* meaning "enveloping sheath or envelope." This term describes the effects of the body's inflammatory response when trying to envelope and isolate the sequestrum from the host. The natural history of osteomyelitis was seen as the process of isolation of the infective material followed by a slow attempted resorption of the material by the immune system. However, the term *osteomyelitis* was not coined until the mid-1800s, when it was adopted by Nelaton.[98]

In his book *The Story of Orthopaedics,* Mercer Rang describes the three pivotal discoveries that allowed orthopaedic surgery to be successful:[98] anesthesia, antisepsis, and radiography. The first two were important in all surgical specialties. Anesthesia made surgery tolerable, but there was still considerable morbidity secondary to infection. It was not until the mid-1800s that progress with antisepsis permitted infection control and more effective surgical intervention. As a result of this, infection issues became an integral part of medicine and were studied in a more formal basis. However, descriptions of the first sequestrectomies of the tibia had been illustrated as early as 1593 by Scultetus.[98]

Prior to anesthesia, most operative procedures were performed using forced immobility and inebriation. Operating rooms were created because procedures undertaken in the wards horrified patients who witnessed them and the screams of agony did nothing to encourage other patients to seek surgical treatment. Thus, the patients were isolated from the rest of the ward. In the same era, many modern drugs were developed, including morphine, heroin, nitrous oxide, and ether. Ether was in fact serendipitously identified as an anesthetic agent during one of the drug parties that were common at this time. However, it was first used for anesthesia in Massachusetts General Hospital in 1846 by William T. G. Morton, and its use quickly caught on around the world. This increased the incentive to undertake surgical procedures. The ensuing increase in the number of surgical procedures, together with the lack of antisepsis, meant that the morbidity and mortality of surgery also increased.[98] Pasteur and Lister are most commonly credited as being the forerunners of antisepsis, but the most notable achievement in demonstrating the efficacy of bacterial transmission is the work of Semmelweiss, who, in 1848, demonstrated that hand washing between obstetric deliveries reduced maternal mortality from 18% to about 1%. Lister read Pasteur's work on fermentation and likened tissue putrefaction to the same process. He subsequently developed carbolic acid, which reduced mortality from amputation from 43% in an untreated cohort of patients to 15% in a treated cohort. Despite this significant discovery, his findings were resisted for decades. Even when his concepts were adopted, the remaining pieces of the puzzle required for successful aseptic surgery did not come together for another 100 years.

The initial use of antibiotics was just as serendipitous as the use of anesthesia and antisepsis. Some antibacterial treatments were introduced, but it was not until the discovery of penicillin by Alexander Fleming in 1928 that the proven usefulness of antibiotics became understood. Even Fleming did not vigorously pursue his discovery. However, when Florey and Chain read Fleming's initial report, they pursued and found the true impact of penicillin, which was effective against streptococci. Since then, many antibiotics have been developed, but the number of resistant bacteria has also increased. Hand washing, gloves, hats, enclosed rooms, aseptic techniques, and early antibiotics all slightly decreased the incidence of surgical infection. However, the operating theaters in the early 1900s still admitted observers who coughed, did not use masks, and wore street clothes. It was not until the mid–20th century that surgeons began to integrate all the controllable aspects of patient exposure to infectious agents by attempting to standardize the contributive effects of the environment, patient, surgeon, wound, antisepsis, antibiotics, and surgical techniques. It is likely, though, that many of the answers to the problem of infection remain undiscovered, and it seems likely that at the moment we do not fully understand the complex symbiosis between bacteria and humans.

This chapter will concentrate on the description, etiology, diagnosis, and management of orthopaedic infections but will have a specific focus on posttraumatic conditions. Historically, the treatment of orthopaedic infection was either ablative, when an amputation was performed, or temporizing with treatment of a chronic wound or sinus. There was little chance of limb salvage as we know it today, and infections that were not adequately treated would occasionally become systemic and fatal.

Certainly the high mortality of open gunshot wounds to the femur in the American Civil War and World War I were largely due to sepsis. In every war, the science of surgery and medicine advances, and this is particularly true for trauma surgery and extremity injuries, which still account for approximately 65% of all war-related injuries.[83] Thus, many advances in infection treatment and extremity injuries have ironically come about as a result of war.

To treat orthopaedic infection, one must first understand the basics of the interdependence of humans and bacteria. Bacteria are a necessary part of our existence and normal flora live in abundance on our bodies. It is worth considering that an individual's skin can contain up to 180 different types of bacteria at any given time.[45] There are up to 10 colony-forming units (CFUs) of bacteria in the mouth and perineum. Nearly 95% of bacteria found in the hands exist under the fingernails. The average human is composed of 100 trillion cells, but it is thought that we harbor over a 1000 trillion bacteria in or on our bodies. Our blood is constantly infiltrated with bacteria from breaks in the skin, translocation across mucous membranes, and other roots. However, nearly all of these bacteria are quickly and efficiently eradicated by our host defense mechanisms. It is the disruption of our own homeostasis that provides an opportunity for either external contaminant or opportunistic host bacteria to become pathogenic and cause infection. While colonization necessarily precedes infection, the presence of bacteria by itself does not constitute infection. This is highlighted by the findings of one study of hardware removal in which 50% of cultures were positive in patients with no signs of symptoms or infection.[80] Thus, there is an important distinction between colonization and infection. Understanding the factors that have changed the local or systemic environment with resultant bacterial infection is the key to effective prophylaxis, treatment, and improved outcomes in orthopaedic surgery.

CLASSIFICATION

Historically, osteomyelitis was classified as either acute or chronic depending on the duration of symptoms. Kelly documented a classification system based on the etiology of the osteomyelitis.[61] There were four types with type I being hematogenous osteomyelitis. Type II was osteomyelitis associated with fracture union, while type III was osteomyelitis without fracture union and type IV was postoperative or posttraumatic osteomyelitis without a fracture. Weiland et al.[123] in 1984 suggested another classification scheme based on the nature of the bony involvement. In this classification system, there were three types, with type I being characterized by open exposed bone without evidence of osseous infection but with evidence of soft tissue infection. In type II fractures, there was circumferential cortical and endosteal infection, and in type III fractures, the cortical and endosteal infection was associated with a segmental defect.

In 1989, May et al.[71] proposed another classification scheme for osteomyelitis focusing on the tibia. This system was based on the nature of the bone following soft tissue and bony débridement. They proposed that there were five different categories.

Type I posttraumatic tibial osteomyelitis was defined as being present when the intact tibia and fibula were able to withstand functional loads and no reconstruction was required. In type II osteomyelitis, the intact tibia was unable to withstand functional loading and required bone grafting. In type III osteomyelitis, there was an intact fibula but a tibial defect that measured no more than 6 cm. The tibial defect required cancellous bone grafting, tibiofibular synostosis, or distraction histogenesis. Type IV osteomyelitis was characterized by an intact fibula but with a defect of more than 6 cm in length, which required distraction osteogenesis, tibiofibular synostosis, or a vascularized bone graft. Type V osteomyelitis was characterized by a tibial defect of more than 6 cm without an intact fibula, which often required amputation.

The Waldvogel classification[121] categorized osteomyelitis into three primary etiologies—hematogenous, contiguous (from an adjacent root such as an open fracture or a seeded implant), or chronic, this being a longstanding osteomyelitis with mature host reaction.

These various classification systems were predicated on the beliefs and treatment options of the times, and they have all become less relevant with current diagnostic and treatment modalities. However, each classification represented an important effort to categorize the pathophysiology of bone infection to facilitate the choice of an effective treatment.

The currently accepted classification remains the Cierny-Mader classification,[21] which not only describes the pathology in the bone but, more importantly, also classifies the host or patient (Tables 24-1 and 24-2). The usefulness of the Cierny-Mader system is its applicability to clinical practice and the wealth of experience and data gleaned from a single surgeon's practice with meticulous records. The hallmark of Cierny's approach is the use of oncologic principles for treatment. In fact, osteomyelitis behaves very similarly to a benign bone tumor in that it is rarely lethal but has a tendency to return without complete eradiation. Interestingly, the outcome data reported by Cierny et al.[21] indicate that once appropriate surgical treatment is undertaken, the host may be the most important variable affecting treatment and outcome.

A novel aspect of the Cierny-Mader classification is its analysis of the physiologic state of the patient or host. The host is classified by the number of systemic and local comorbidities. An A host has a healthy physiology and limb with little systemic or local compromise. The B host is further divided into one with local compromise (B local), systemic compromise (B systemic), or both (B systemic/local systemic compromise, which includes any immunocompromised condition, poor nutrition, diabetes, old age, multiple trauma, chronic hypoxia, vascular disease, malignancy, or organ failure such as renal insufficiency or liver failure). Local compromise includes conditions such as previous surgery or trauma, cellulitis, radiation fibrosis, scarring from burns or trauma, local manifestations of vascular disease, lymphoedema, or zone-of-injury issues. We believe that a new variable of compromise can be identified in the trauma patient where systemic compromise is due to multiple organ damage and the consequent systemic response to trauma and local compromise is defined by the zone-of-injury effects on local tissues.

The C host is a patient in whom the morbidity of treatment is greater than the morbidity of disease because of multiple and severe comorbid conditions that cannot be treated safely. In these patients, the risks of curative treatment such as extensive surgery, as might be used with free flaps, or prolonged reconstruction with bone transport would be greater than that caused by the infective condition itself. Type C hosts are often better treated with limited nonablative surgery and suppression or, if appropriate, by an amputation.

In the Cierny-Mader classification[21], the bone lesion is classified by the extent of involvement and stability. Type I is a medullary or endosteal infection without penetration through cortex. This is the type of infection that occurs after intramedullary nailing. Type II is a superficial osteomyelitis that involves only the outer cortex and is frequently contiguous with a pressure ulcer or adjacent abscess. Type III is permeative in that there is involvement of both cortical and medullary bone but, importantly, there is no loss of axial stability of the bone. Type IV also involves cortical and medullary bone but in a segmental fashion such that axial stability is lost. Types III and IV would be typical infections related to open fractures. In type IV lesions, the segmental resection that is required necessitates reconstruction of the bone, whereas in type III lesions, additional stabilization may not be required (Tables 24-1 and 24-2).

The pairing of the four types of osteomyelitis with the three host classes allows for the development of practical treatment strategies. Cierny et al.[21] proposed a detailed treatment regimen defining optimal treatment modalities for each stage. They achieved an overall clinical 2-year success rate of 91% for all states. As one would expect, when their results were broken down by class of host and type of lesion. Class A hosts fared the best. In class A hosts, success rates of 98% were achieved even with type IV osteomyelitis. The compromised class B host success rates were far lower, ranging from 79% to 92% depending on anatomic type. In his series Cierny found that the host class seemed to be more important than the type of infection. A cumulative success rate of greater than 90% was achieved with most of the failures being in B hosts. C hosts were recommended for amputation or suppressive treatment.[22] The lessons that stem from their findings are that it is important not just to treat the disease but also the host and that the patient's physiologic condition should be optimized. Thus, a B systemic-local host who has had a previous open fracture but also smokes and has uncontrolled diabetes, renal insufficiency, and malnutrition should have all of these problems treated together with the bone disease. Improving host status would appear to be a fruitful endeavor when one considers Cierny et al.'s[21,22] findings.

It should be noted that Cierny et al.'s[21,22] results used outcome criteria that were commonly used at that time. Current outcome studies focus more on subjective patient-based assessments than on surgeon-based assessments. We do not have much data on the functional outcomes in the scenarios described by Cierny and colleagues, and it is possible that some of the patients whom they salvaged would have fared better with prosthetic replacement and vice versa. The findings of the LEAP study for acute limb salvage have raised new questions about the true nature of outcome and success.[65]

PATHOGENESIS

Before a discussion of diagnosis and treatment, it is vital to understand the mechanisms by which infections occur. Most infections encountered in orthopaedics are related to biofilm-

TABLE 24-1	**Cierny-Mader Classification of Bone**	
	Osseous location	Involvement

Type I—Medullary
Infection is limited to the medullary canal. Typically seen after intramedullary nailing.

Medullary

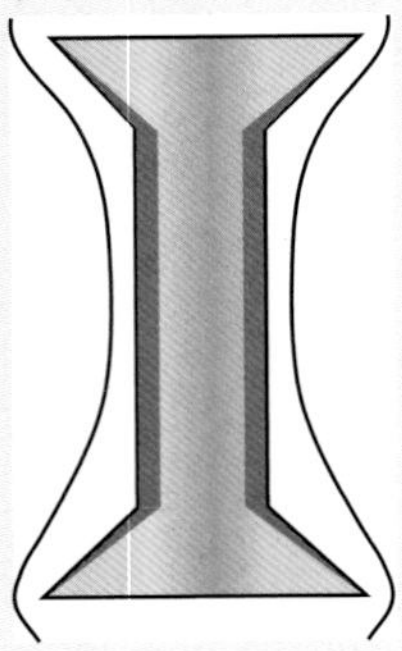

Type II—Superficial
Infection is limited to the exterior of the bone and does not penetrate the cortex. Typically seen from pressure ulcers.

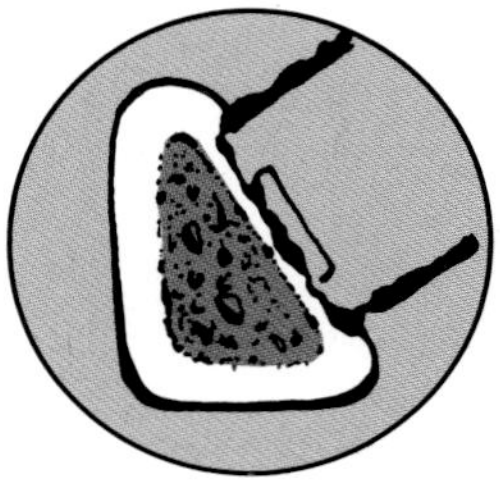

Superficial

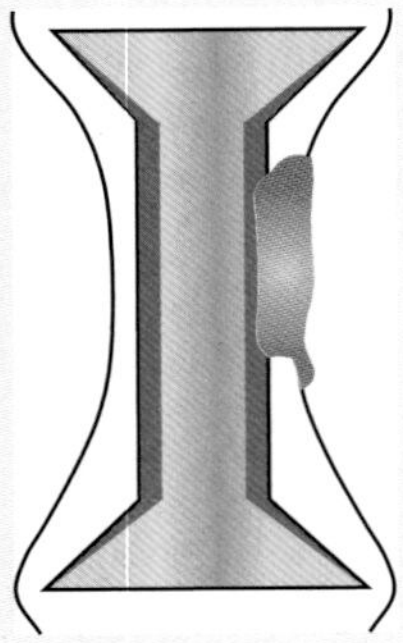

Type III—Permeative/Stable
Infection penetrates cortex but bone is axially stable and generally will not require supplemental stabilization. Typically seen after internal fixation with plates.

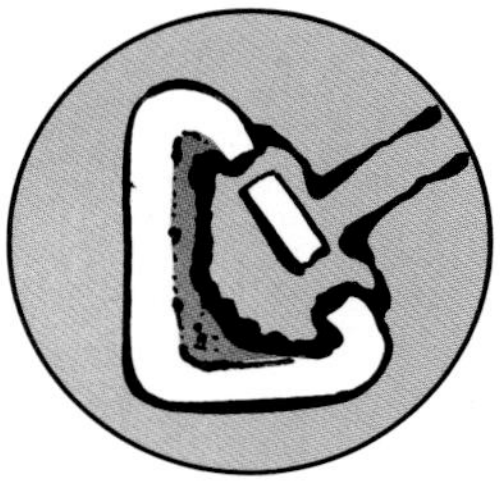

Localized

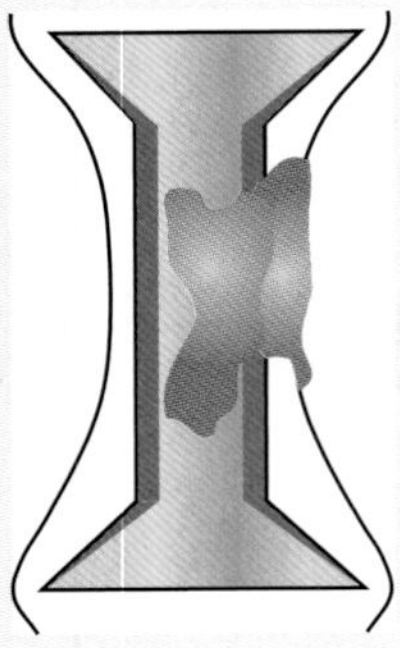

Type IV—Permeative/Unstable
Infection is throughout the bone in segmental fashion and results in axial instability. Typically seen in extensive infections or after aggressive débridement of type III infections that results in loss of axial stability.

Diffuse

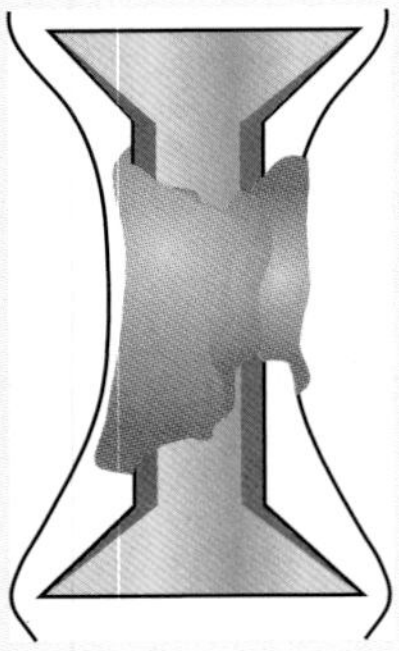

forming bacteria. Much of our understanding of biofilm bacteria has come from the Centre for Biofilm Engineering in Bozeman, Montana. Biofilm bacteria are also important in the oil, food processing, naval, paper manufacturing, and water processing industries.

Biofilm bacteria exist in one of two states—the planktonic state or the stationary state (Fig. 24-1). Planktonic state bacteria are free floating in the extracellular matrix and are isolated and relatively small in quantity. In this state, the body host defenses can easily eradicate the organism through the usual immuno-logic mechanisms. It is rare for planktonic bacteria to survive long in the extracellular matrix despite numerous and repeated occurrences of entry. However, if the bacterial load is large and sustained, they can overwhelm the host defenses and escape the effects of antibiotics. They can then invade tissue and blood, leading to septicemia and death. Planktonic bacteria are also metabolically active and reproductive. This is an important consideration for antibiotic treatments that work by either interfering with cell wall or protein synthesis or with reproduction.

If planktonic bacteria encounter a suitable inert surface such

TABLE 24-2	Cierny-Mader Classification of the Host
Host Class	**Description**
A host	Healthy physiology and limb
B host: systemic	Diabetes, stable multiple organ disease, nicotine use, substance abuse, immunologic deficiency, malnutrition, malignancy, old age, vascular disease **Trauma context:** Multiple injuries
B host: local	Previous trauma, burns, previous surgery, vascular disease, cellulitis, scarring, previous radiation treatment, lymphedema **Trauma context:** Zone of injury
B host: systemic/ local	Combinations of systemic and local conditions
C host	Multiple uncorrectable comorbidities. Unable to tolerate extent of surgical reconstruction required. Treatment of the disease is worse than the disease itself

In the early stages of colonization, sessile bacteria can be killed or neutralized by the host defenses. However, some of these bacteria may escape destruction and potentially act as a nidus for future infection. Transition from colonization to infection usually requires other conditions to exist. This might occur if there was an inoculum that was larger than threshold levels, impaired host immune defense mechanisms, traumatized or necrotic tissues, foreign body, or an acellular or inanimate surface such as dead bone, cartilage, or biomaterials.

As previously discussed, the first step in the transition from colonization to infection requires bacterial adhesion, which will usually not occur on viable tissue surfaces. Thus, when foreign material or dead tissue is found in the body, a "race for the surface" begins. Host cells will attempt to incorporate nonliving material or sequester nonviable tissue via encapsulation so that a well-incorporated biomaterial implant that has such a tissue-integrated neocapsule will be resistant to bacterial adhesion. Furthermore, the same tissue integration can often isolate bacteria that have become sessile on an implant surface by sequestering the bacteria from necessary nutrients until host mechanisms can act.

However, if bacteria encounter the surface and develop mature colonies, tissue integration by the host may be impaired and the process of infection may proceed. Damaged bone, being relatively acellular, acts as a suitable surface for bacterial adhesion and colonization.[69] Devitalized bone devoid of normal periosteum presents a collagen matrix to which bacteria can bind. Moreover, it has been suggested that bone sialoprotein can act as a ligand for bacterial binding to bone.[69] Biomaterials and other foreign bodies are usually inert and susceptible to bacterial colonization because they are inanimate. Regardless of how inert a metal is, it may still modulate molecular events on its surfaces, these being receptor–ligand interactions, covalent bonding, and thermodynamic interactions.[44,50] The most important feature of any particular method is the interaction between its outer surface atomic layer and the glycoproteins of prokaryotic and eukaryotic cells. Stainless steel and cobalt-chromium and titanium alloys are resistant to corrosion because of several mechanisms including surface oxide passivates. These surface oxides form a reactive interface with bacteria that can promote colony formation. There is therefore a balance between implanting devices with surface structures that lower corrosion rates but

as dead or necrotic tissue, foreign bodies, or any avascular body part by either direct contamination, contiguous spreading, or hematogenous seeding, they can attach and begin the process of colonization. Juxtaposition of the bacteria with a surface or biomaterial is accomplished by Van der Waals forces, which allow bacteria to develop irreversible cross-links with the surface (adhesion–receptor interaction).[27] Adhesion is based on time-dependent specific protein adhesion–receptor interactions, as well as carbohydrate polymer synthesis in addition to charge and physical forces.[61] Following adhesion to a surface, bacteria begin to create a mucopolysaccharide layer called *biofilm* or *slime*. They then develop into colonies. These colonies exhibit remarkably resilient behavior. Figure 24-2 illustrates mature biofilm colonies where pillars of a mature biofilm are visible distributed on top of a monolayer of surface-associated cells. In addition to fixed cells, there are motile cells, which maintain their association with the biofilm for long periods, swimming between pillars of biofilm-associated bacteria.[122] The interaction of the colonies and bacteria demonstrates complex communication via proteins or markers that can alter bacterial behavior.

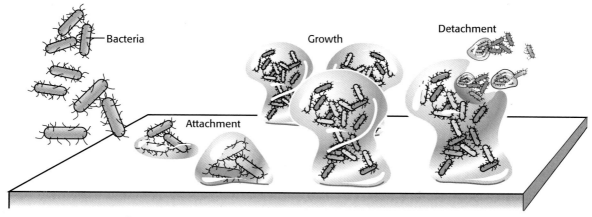

FIGURE 24-1 Illustration of bacterial attachment to a surface followed by colonization and detachment. (Redrawn with permission after P. Dirckx, MSU Center for Biofilm Engineering, Bozeman, MT.)

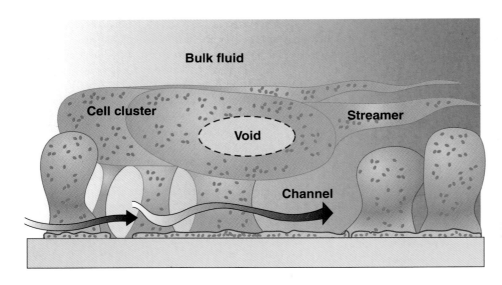

FIGURE 24-2 Mature biofilm colonies showing potential intercolony communication. (Redrawn with permission after P. Dirckx, MSU Center for Biofilm Engineering, Bozeman, MT.)

might increase the likelihood of surface binding by bacteria. Thus, a large surface area and bacteria inoculum, combined with local tissue damage and a compromised or insufficient host response, can collectively create the necessary conditions for infection.

Following bacterial adherence and colonization, the resistance to antibiotics appears to increase.[84,86] This resistance is dependent on the type of surface to which the organisms are attached. Organisms that adhere to hydrocarbon polymers are extremely resistant to antibiotics. These same organisms, when attached to metals, do not resist antibiotic therapy to the same extent. Bacterial colonies can undergo phenotypic changes and appear to hibernate. They can survive in a dormant state without causing infection, and this can explain the recovery of bacteria from asymptomatic hardware removal.[80] So while colonization is a necessary antecedent for infection, colonization alone does not necessarily lead to infection.

Two characteristics of colonized bacteria may help understand and explain this pseudo-resistance. Because the passage of antibiotics through tissues is based on a diffusion gradient, colonized bacteria are insulated with a natural barrier of glycocalyx, often referred to as a *slime*, through which the circulating antibiotic must diffuse before arriving at the bacterial cell wall (Fig. 24-3). The antibiotic molecules must then diffuse into the

bacterial cell or be transported by metabolically active bacterial cell membranes. Because it is theorized that bacteria within biofilms have a decreased metabolic rate and undergo phenotypic changes, active processes such as cell membrane formation, which are targeted by antibiotics, would be similarly decreased (Fig. 24-3).[116] Consequently, antibiotic concentrations of 1500 times normal may be required to penetrate both the biofilm and the bacterial cell wall. Even then, most antimicrobials work via interference with cell wall synthesis or cellular reproduction, and they therefore require metabolically active bacteria to be effective. Thus, bacteria in the biofilm may be dormant and appear to be pseudoresistant. The more metabolically inactive the bacteria, the less bactericidal will be the antibiotic therapy, which is why mature or chronic infections can rarely be cured with antibiotics alone. Table 24-3 outlines the major antibiotic classes and their mechanisms of action, all of which may be limited by the bacterial state in biofilm.

Once colonization occurs, body defenses continue to identify bacteria as foreign. There may be chemotactic mechanisms that keep immune cells active. The subsequent collection of inflammatory cells brought in to wall off the bacteria via chemotaxis manifests as *purulence*, which is a symptom of the host's attempt to isolate and destroy the infection. The acute inflammatory cells will also release a spectrum of oxidative and enzymatic

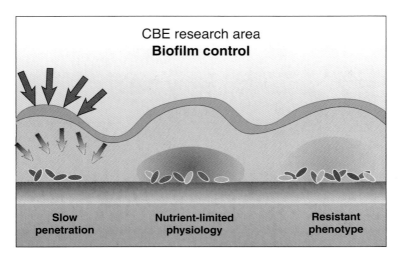

FIGURE 24-3 Biofilm creates a diffusion barrier that interferes with the ability of antibiotics to reach bacterial organisms. Biofilm bacteria are metabolically inactive and therefore not subject to the mechanism of action of most antibiotics. They appear as "pseudoresistant." (Redrawn with permission after P. Dirckx, MSU Center for Biofilm Engineering, Bozeman, MT.)

TABLE 24-3	Major Antibiotic Classes and Their Mechanism of Action
Inhibition of cell wall synthesis/development	Penicillin, cephalosporins, vancomycin, bacitracin, chlorhexidine
Inhibition of protein synthesis	Chloramphenicol, macrolides, lincosamides, tetracyclines
Inhibition of RNA synthesis	Rifampin
Inhibition of DNA synthesis	Quinolones, macrolides
Inhibition of enzymatic/metabolic activity	Trimethoprim–sulfamethoxazole (blocks folic acid production)

Source: www.sigmaaldrich.com/Area_of_Interest/Biochemicals/Antibiotic_Explorer/Mechanism_of_Action.html.

products in an attempt to penetrate the glycocalyx. These mediators and enzymes are nonspecific and may be toxic to host tissue. Increased host tissue damage can lead to more surface substrate for local bacteria, creating a cycle of tissue damage, host response, and exacerbation of infection (Fig. 24-4). The host tissues will eventually react to limit the spread of infection macroscopically as well as microscopically. The clinical manifestation of a sequestered infection is an abscess or involucrum.

Alternatively, if the infection grows and reaches the skin or an internal epithelial surface, a sinus tract forms as a route to dispel detritus. While the appearance of a sinus tract is a manifestation of a locally devastating disease process and indicates severe underlying infection, it should be remembered that it may also prevent the accumulation of internal fixation, which can lead to bacteremia and septicemia.

Eventually, an equilibrium may exist in the form of a chronic

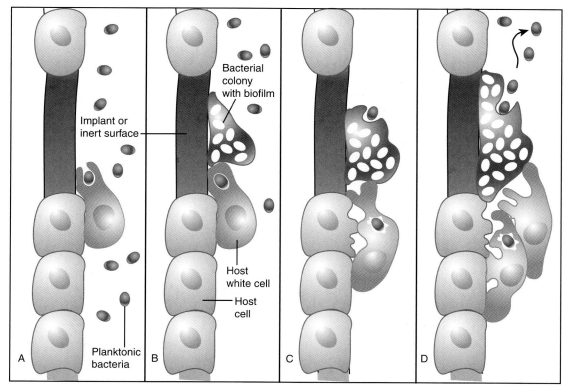

FIGURE 24-4 Autoinjury mechanism of host white cells in response to biofilm bacteria. **A.** Host white cell engulfs planktonic bacteria and then **B.** moves to engulf a bacterial colony that has developed but is unable to do so. **C.** Host white cell's next response to engulfed bacteria is to release oxidative enzymes, but those enzymes also cause damage to local host cells. **D.** Unsuccessful eradication of bacteria and colony growth attracts more host white cells, resulting in increased damage to host tissue.

infection, which is what many surgeons see in practice. There is usually a history of intermittent symptoms and drainage that has responded to some type of antibiotic regimen. What this probably represents is the inhibition of colony expansion at the borders of the infectious site. Clinically harmful manifestations of infection are generally caused by the release of bacteria into the bloodstream that are metabolically active and release toxins in addition to the release of oxidative enzymes by the host cell. Although the bacteria remain susceptible to the body's host defenses and to antibiotics, their numbers and continued release into the bloodstream represent a chronic debilitating disease. Any acute stress on the host environment from trauma, disease, or immunosuppression can allow the infection to strengthen and spread. Thus, longstanding infections that were tolerated by young healthy individuals may suddenly become limb or life threatening as the individual's age.

New developments stemming from the work of the Bozeman group provide novel opportunities to treat bacterial infection of orthopaedic implants. These include surface coatings, agents that inhibit colonization or promote dissolution of colonies, small electric fields, and low pH and acidic and negatively charged surfaces that are resistant to biofilms. Surface properties of implants or local or systemic drugs may help decrease the risk to infection, particularly in the elderly population, who have decreased immune system activity.[17]

INFECTION AFTER FRACTURE

Infection after fracture is most likely to be associated with open fractures or invasive surgical procedures. Few closed fractures treated nonoperatively develop osteomyelitis. To improve the diagnosis of posttraumatic bone infection, it is necessary to understand the mechanisms of infection, particularly for open fractures.

Approximately 60% to 70% of open fractures are contaminated by bacteria, but a much small percentage develop infection. The risk of infection correlates significantly with the degree of soft tissue injury.[117] If one remembers that merely the presence of bacteria in an open wound is not sufficient to cause infection, it is important to recognize that a severely contaminated fracture can rarely be débrided to the point of achieving a sterile or bacteria-free tissue bed. We believe that next to removing the majority of bacteria from the contaminated tissue bed, the second major goal of a wide and aggressive débridement is to leave behind a viable tissue bed with minimal necrotic or inert surfaces for the remaining bacteria to colonize. By minimizing the bacterial contamination by eliminating adhesions and nutrition, the host gains an opportunity to eradicate any remaining contaminants in the zone of injury. Figure 24-5 demonstrates the concept of open fracture débridement where a contaminated wound is débrided until the remaining wound looks as if it is created surgically, with residual tissue being healthy with little evidence of contamination. It is important to remember that contamination can penetrate into tissue planes or locations that are not obvious in the initial wound. The use of pulsatile irrigation before surgical exploration and débridement may in fact push the initial contaminants deeper into the tissues and result in contaminants being left behind in a locally compromised tissue bed. This will increase the likelihood of both acute and delayed infection.

An important fact that is often unrecognized is that the bacteria recovered from clinical infections are not necessarily the bacteria found acutely in the contaminated tissue bed. Several studies have found that routine cultures of open fractures are not useful because the predominant organism recovered from acute cultures is frequently not the organism recovered if and when an infection occurs. Antibiotic treatment based on the acute culture, whether before or after débridement, may be det-

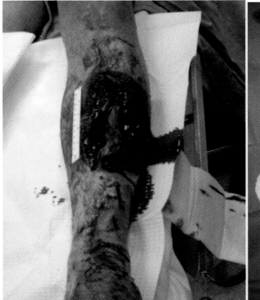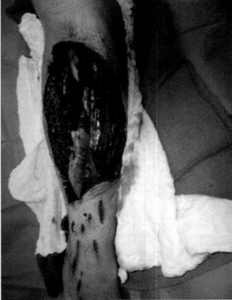

A   B

FIGURE 24-5 Operative photographs of a severe open fracture. **A.** The appearance before surgical débridement. **B.** The appearance after surgical débridement. Note that after débridement, the tissues and wound appear as if they were surgically created. While it is unlikely that all bacteria have been removed, a thorough exploration and débridement leaving behind only viable tissues will minimize the risk of subsequent infection.

rimental because the antibiotic that is chosen may not be specifically indicated and has the potential to promote changes and overgrowth in the bacterial flora. In the worst case scenario, routine antibiotic treatment based on initial wound cultures may promote the development of resistant bacterial strains.[63,92,118]

Many of the organisms responsible for eventual osteomyelitis are often hospital-acquired pathogens such as resistant *Staphylococcus aureus* or gram-negative bacilli, including *Pseudomonas aeruginosa*,[51,67] which are not initially present in a traumatic wound. This does not mean that other bacteria should not be considered and these may depend on the environment. *Clostridium perfringens* must be considered if there is soil contamination and *Pseudomonas*, and *Aeromonas hydrophila* may be present following a freshwater injury. *Vibrio* and *Erysipelothrix* may be present in saltwater injuries. One possible explanation for the lack of correlation between acute cultures and the eventual infection may be that the initial contaminants are of low virulence and easily neutralized by a combination of débridement and antibiotics but that the locally and, in polytrauma, the systemically, compromised tissue bed is susceptible to the more aggressive nosocomial organisms.

ACUTE POSTTRAUMATIC OSTEOMYELITIS

Acute posttraumatic osteomyelitis is a bone infection that results in traumatic injury that allows pathogenic organisms to make contact with damaged bone and soft tissues, with a proliferation and expression of infection.[74] In a patient with traumatic injuries, additional factors that contribute to the subsequent development of osteomyelitis are the presence of hypotension, inadequate débridement of the fracture site, malnutrition, sustained intensive care unit hospitalization, alcoholism, and smoking.[42,115] Trauma may lead to interference with the host response to infection. Tissue injury or the presence of bacteria triggers activation of the complement cascade that leads to local vasodilatation, tissue edema, migration of polymorphonuclear leukocytes (PMNs) to the site of the injury, and enhanced ability to phagocytes to ingest bacteria.[56] Trauma has been reported to delay the inflammatory response to bacteria as well as to depress cell-mediated immunity and to impair the function of PMNs, including chemotaxis, superoxide production, and microbial killing.[56] The commonly used system of Cierny-Mader[21] has been shown to have a close correlation with the general condition of the patient rather than the specifics of bone involvement.

CHRONIC OSTEOMYELITIS

This condition is often the result of an acute osteomyelitis that is inadequately treated. General factors that may predispose to chronic osteomyelitis include the degree of bone necrosis, poor nutrition, the infecting organism, the age of the patient, the presence of comorbidities, and drug abuse.[26] The infecting organism generally varies with the cause of the chronic osteomyelitis. Chronic osteomyelitis results from acute osteomyelitis and is frequently caused by *S. aureus*, although chronic osteomyelitis that occurs after a fracture can be polymicrobial or gram negative. Intravenous drug users are commonly found to have *Pseudomonas* as well as *S. aureus* infections. Gram-negative organisms are now seen in up to 50% of all cases of chronic osteomyelitis, and this may be due to variables such as surgical intervention, chronic antibiotics, nosocomial causes, or changes in the bacterial flora of the tissue bed.[26] The fundamental problem in chronic osteomyelitis is a slow progressive revascularization of bone that leaves protected pockets of necrotic material to support bacterial growth that are relatively protected from systemic antibiotic therapy. This collection of necrotic tissue, bone, and bacteria is what becomes termed a *sequestrum*, and the body's attempt to wall off the offending material with reactive inflammatory tissue, whether this is bone or soft tissue, is termed the *involucrum*. The involucrum can be highly vascular and may be viable and structural, and this should be taken into consideration during surgical débridement.

FUNGAL OSTEOMYELITIS

Fungal osteoarticular infections are caused by two groups of fungi. The dimorphic fungi, which include *Blastomyces dermatitidis*, *Ciccidioides* sp., *Histoplasma capsulatum,* and *Sporothrix schenckii*, typically cause infections in healthy hosts in endemic regions, while *Candida* sp., *Cryptococcus,* and *Aspergillus* cause infections in immunocompromised hosts. Infection is introduced by direct trauma or injury but may be associated with a penetrating foreign body or hematogenous spread.

Candida sp. is the most common fungus seen in osteomyelitis. It affects both native and prosthetic joints, vertebrae, and long bones. Risk factors include loss of skin integrity, diabetes, malnutrition, immunosuppressive therapy, intravenous drug use, hyperalimentation, the use of central venous catheters, intra-articular steroid injections, and the use of broad-spectrum antibiotics. A combined approach to therapy using medical and surgical modalities is necessary for optimal results. Azole antifungals and lipid preparations of Amphotericin B have expanded the therapeutic options in fungal osteomyelitis as there is reduced toxicity associated with long-term therapy.[74]

CLINICAL AND LABORATORY DIAGNOSTIC TESTS

A history of infection or intercurrent illness as well as of remote surgery or trauma should raise the clinical suspicion of osteomyelitis. Normal signs of inflammation may be absent and thus the diagnosis of infection may be difficult. Patients may have a history of infection at another site, such as the lungs, bladder, or skin in conjunction with a history of trauma. They usually complain of pain in the affected area and feel generally unwell. Moreover, reduced activity, malaise, anorexia, fever, tachycardia, and listlessness may be present. Local findings include swelling and warmth, occasional erythema, tenderness to palpation, drainage, and restricted range of motion in adjacent joints.

Aspects of the clinical history that should alert the surgeon to look for infection include a history of open fracture, severe soft tissue injury, a history of substance abuse and smoking, inadequate previous treatment, or an immunocompromised state. These are all factors that contribute to a B host. Factors affecting treatment that need to be assessed include the time of onset of the infection, the status of the soft tissues, the viability of the bone, the status of fracture healing, implant stability, the condition of the host, and the neurovascular examination (Fig. 24-6).

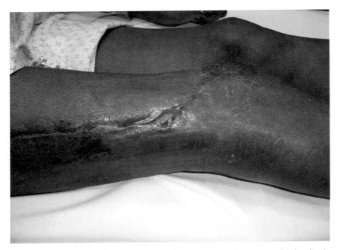

FIGURE 24-6 Typical appearance of a postoperative wound. The limb looks relatively benign. This patient had an extensive type III infection and had been treated with attempted débridement on several occasions before referral. Poor nutrition and nicotine use together with her previous multiple surgeries made her a B systemic/local host.

Routine blood cultures are of little help unless patients show manifestations of systemic disease, but they may be positive in up to 50% to 75% of cases where there is concomitant bacteremia or septicemia.[124] Blood cultures that yield coagulase-negative staphylococci, a common contaminant and pathogen, must be correlated with other clinical findings before attribution of clinical significance. Blood results that are suggestive of infection include an elevation of the white blood cell (WBC) count and elevations in the C-reactive protein (CRP) and erythrocyte sedimentation rate (ESR) levels. The ESR may be normal in the first 48 hours but rises to levels about 100 mm/hr and may remain elevated for several weeks. It is, however, a nonspecific marker.[124] Combination of the ESR with the CRP improves specificity such that if both are negative, the specificity is 90% to 95% for acute osteomyelitis. In other words, a negative CRP and ESR makes osteomyelitis unlikely. Their values are also age dependent, and there is a steady increase in normal values with aging. In one recent study, the ESR and CRP were found to be useful diagnostic tools for the detection of an infected arthroplasty. While they had low sensitivities and positive predictive values and therefore were of little value for screening, they had high specificity and negative predictive value and therefore were useful for treatment decisions.[49] These studies and other diagnostic studies may not be as useful in acute postoperative and chronic infections. In the acute setting, the ESR and CRP are expected to be elevated due to local and systemic inflammation from the surgical procedure. In chronic infections, the host has had time to adapt to the offending condition and thus may not mount the response required to trigger an elevation in these tests. Once osteomyelitis treatment is initiated, the CRP and ESR are useful in following the response to treatment. We use the ESR and CRP to establish a baseline value before débridement and initiation of antibiotic therapy and to monitor the subsequent response to treatment.

Radiographic Imaging

Radiologic findings in the initial presentation of acute osteomyelitis are often normal. The most common radiographic signs of bone infection are rarefaction, which represents diffuse demineralization secondary to inflammatory hyperemia; soft tissue swelling with obliteration of tissue planes; trabecular destruction; lysis; cortical permeation; periosteal reaction; and involucrum formation. Radiologically detectable demineralization may not be seen for at least 10 days after the onset of acute osteomyelitis.[124] When present, mineralization usually signifies trabecular bone destruction. If the infection spreads to the cortex, usually within 3 to 6 weeks, a periosteal reaction may be seen on radiographs. One study reported that in cases of proven osteomyelitis, 5% of radiographs were abnormal initially, 33% were abnormal by 1 week, and 90% were abnormal by 4 weeks.[6] In trauma and fracture treatment, the nature of callus formation and the obfuscation of bone by hardware may make radiologic changes difficult to recognize in the early or middle states of infection. Often it is not until there is a clear sequestrum, sinus, or involucrum that parallels the clinical findings that specific radiographic changes are recognized (Fig. 24-7).

Bone Scintigraphy

Scintigraphy has been widely used and remains a very useful diagnostic tool. There are numerous types of scintigraphy, but three scan types are commonly used to diagnose musculoskeletal infection. These are the bone scan, which uses tagged red cells; the leukocyte scan, which uses tagged white cells; and the bone marrow scan, which investigates marrow cell activity. Recently, positron emission tomography (PET) has shown promise and is undergoing increased investigation and use.

Technetium-99m is the principal radioisotope used in most whole body red cell bone scans.[28,32,43] Technetium is formed as a metastable intermediate during the decay of molybdenum-99. It has a 6-hour half-life and is relatively inexpensive and

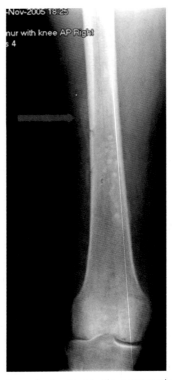

FIGURE 24-7 Radiograph of patient in Figure 24-6. The arrow points to periosteal reaction.

readily available.[28] After intravenous injection, there is a rapid distribution of this agent throughout the extracellular fluid. Within several hours, more than half the dose will accumulate in bone, while the remainder is excreted in the urine. Technetium phosphates bind to both the organic and inorganic matrix. However, the key characteristic that makes technetium scanning useful is that there is preferential incorporation into metabolically active bone. Bone images are usually acquired 2 to 4 hours following intravenous injection of the isotope. A triple-phase bone scan is one that is useful for examining general inflammation and related processes. Following the initial injection, dynamic images are captured over the specified region. These are followed by static images at later time points. The first phase represents the blood flow phase, the second phase immediately postinjection represents the bone pooling phase, and the third phase is a delayed image made at 3 hours when there is decreased soft tissue activity. Classically, osteomyelitis presents as a region of increased blood flow, and it should appear "hot" in all phases with focal uptake in the third phase (Fig. 24-8). Other processes such as healing fractures, loose prostheses, and degenerative change do not appear hot in the early phase despite a hot appearance in the delayed phase. Reported sensitivities of bone scintigraphy for the detection of osteomyelitis vary considerably from 32% to 100%. Reported specificities have ranged from 0% to 100%.[103,120]

Gallium-67 citrate binds rapidly to serum proteins, particularly Transferrin.[10,100] There is also uptake in the blood, especially by leukocytes. Gallium has been used in conjunction with technetium-99 to increase the specificity of the bone scanning.[40,52] Several mechanisms have been postulated to explain the increased activity at sites of inflammation. Enhanced blood flow and increased capillary permeability cause enhanced delivery. Bacteria have high iron requirements and thus take up gallium. Gallium is strongly bound to bacterial siderophores and leukocyte lactoferrins. In regions of inflammation, these proteins are available extracellularly and can bind with gallium avidly. Chemotaxis also acts to localize gallium-labeled WBCs at the sites of infection. In a typical study, gallium is injected intravenously and delayed images are acquired at 48 to 72 hours. The hallmark of osteomyelitis is the focal increased uptake of gallium. Unfortunately, gallium's nonspecific bone uptake can be problematic because any processes causing reactive new bone formation will appear hot. In patients with fractures or a prosthesis, osteomyelitis cannot be easily diagnosed with gallium alone. Gallium images are usually interpreted in conjunction with a technetium bone scan. Gallium activity is interpreted as abnormal either if it is incongruous with the bone scan activity or if there is a matching pattern with gallium activity. Reported sensitivities and specificities for the diagnosis of osteomyelitis range from 22% to 100% and 0% to 100%, respectively.[2,52,76,103] Despite its lower-than-optimal diagnostic value, gallium still has some advantages. It is easily administered and it is the agent of choice in chronic soft tissue injection, although it is less effective in bone infections. It has also proved useful in following the resolution of an inflammatory process by showing a progressive decline in activity.

An indium-111 or 99mTc-hexamethylpropyleneamine osime (99mTc-HMPAO) (Ceretec; GE Healthcare) -labeled leukocyte scan is the most common scan used in conjunction with a standard bone scan. The labeled leukocytes migrate to the region of active infection resulting in a hot white cell scan over the area of active inflammation. The use of a combined red cell and white cell scan significantly increases both the sensitivity and specificity and now represents the gold standard of radionuclide testing for infection.[68] Because of the variable accuracy of both technetium and gallium scans most laboratories routinely use 111In-labeled leukocytes.[100,102,106,119] Indium WBC preparations require the withdrawal of approximately 50 mL of autologous whole blood with a leukocyte count at least 5000 cells/mm[3]. The leukocytes are labeled with 1 mCi of indium oxine and then reinjected. They redistribute in the intravascular space. Immediate images show activity in the lungs, liver, spleen, and blood pool. The half-life is about 7 hours. After 24 hours, only the liver, spleen, and bone marrow show activity. Wounds that heal normally and fully treated infections show no increase in uptake. Leukocytes that migrate to an area of active bone infection will show increased uptake (Fig. 24-9). Most results show improved sensitivity (80% to 100%) and specificity (50% to 100%) for the diagnosis of ostemyelitis.[29–31,54,58] Indium-labeled WBC scans are generally superior to bone scans and gallium scans in the detection of infection. McCarthy et al.[72] reported on the use of indium scans in 39 patients who had suspected osteomyelitis confirmed by bone biopsy. They found indium scans to be 97% sensitive and 82% specific for osteomyelitis. The few false-positive results occurred in patients who had overlying soft tissue infections. An accompanying bone scan can help to differentiate bone infection from soft tissue infection. In these situations, the indium scan should be performed before the bone scan to avoid false-positive results. With both tests, the sensitivities and specificities are in excess of 90%.

Until recently, a clinician investigating the site of infectious foci using nuclear medicine had a choice between 67Ga-citrate

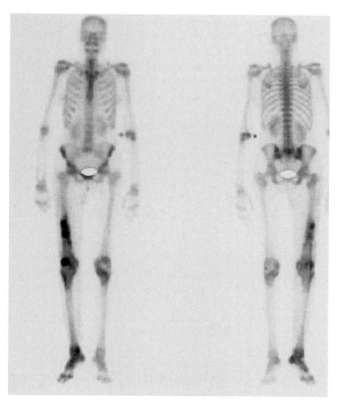

FIGURE 24-8 Red cell scan of patient in Figure 24-6 demonstrating increased activity in distal femur.

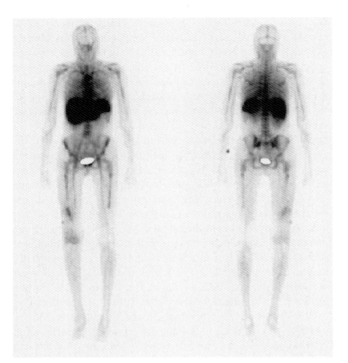

FIGURE 24-9 White cell scan of patient in Figure 24-6 demonstrating increased accumulation of tracer in distal femur.

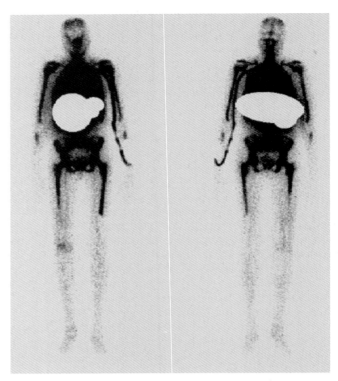

FIGURE 24-10 Marrow scan of patient in Figure 24-6 demonstrating relative suppression of marrow in distal femur.

imaging and 111In-oxine leukocyte imaging.[29] Scientific advances, especially in nuclear medicine, have increased these choices considerably. Several techniques in nuclear medicine have significantly aided the diagnosis of infection including imaging with 99mTc-HMPAO and 99mTc-stannous fluoride colloid-labeled leukocytes.[58] The principal clinical indications for 99mTc-HMPAO leukocytes include osteomyelitis and soft tissue sepsis. Chronic osteomyelitis, including infected joint prostheses, is better diagnosed with 111In-labeled leukocytes.[91] The use of 99mTc-HMPAO leukocyte scintigraphy in patients with symptomatic total hip or knee arthroplasty has shown improved diagnostic accuracy through the use of semiquantitative evaluation.[123]

Sulfur colloid bone scanning is a newer modality that is being increasingly used for diagnosis of infection. The scan evaluates the bone marrow activity in an area where infection is suspected. The marrow may be reactive in several conditions that are not infected and is generally suppressed when infection is present. With the use of microcolloid bone marrow scans, more information is available to increase the specificity of diagnosis. There is the possibility of leukocyte accumulation with certain inflammatory conditions that could result in a false-positive indium scan. An infection will tend to suppress marrow activity and thus render the marrow scan cold, while the white cell scan may still be hot (Fig. 24-10). If the white cell scan is as hot as the marrow scan, it is possible that an infection may not be present. Segura et al.[109] examined technetium-labeled white cell scans (Tc-HMPAO) *and* technetium microcolloid marrow scans in total joint replacements. They found that in 77 patients, the white cell scans by themselves had a sensitivity of 96% and a specificity of 30%. When the colloid scan was added, the sensitivity decreased to 93% but the specificity increased to 98%. The addition of a regular red cell scan was not helpful.[109] In

another study by Palestro et al.,[90] an indium-labeled white cell scan was compared with technetium sulfur colloid scans to differentiate infection from Charçot arthropathy. They found that white cell scans were positive in 4 of 20 cases, of which 3 were infected. In the 16 negative white cell scans, the marrow scan was also negative. However, in the 4 positive cases, the marrow scan was positive in 2 cases that were confirmed to be infected. They concluded that white cell scans can be positive in hematopoietically active bones, which can occur in the absence of infection, and that marrow scans should be used to confirm the diagnosis.

Various combinations of the aforementioned scintigraphic test remain the gold standard diagnostic method in posttraumatic infection. This is especially true because the presence of metallic implants limits the usefulness of magnetic resonance imaging (MRI) scanning. Classically, a combination of red cell bone scan and a labeled leukocyte scan has been used. Because standard bone scan agents and gallium are usually both positive at fracture sites, they have limited value in the detection of infection following a fracture. With no discernible uptake in reactive bone, indium-labeled WBC scans are superior in the detection of infection following fracture. In a prospective study of 20 patients with suspected osteomyelitis together with delayed union, Esterhai et al.[41] reported 100% accuracy of indium-labeled WBC scans. Seabold et al.[107] have shown that the use of indium-labeled WBC scans and bone scans, to differentiate between soft tissue infections, can be 97% specific for osteomyelitis. In chronic or recurrent osteomyelitis, bone scans by themselves are of less value since they show increased uptake for 2 years following the successful treatment and resolution of infection.[48] Although gallium scans have historically been shown to be successful in following the resolution of chronic osteomyelitis, indium-labeled WBC scans appear to be superior. Merkel et al.[75] compared indium-labeled WBC and gallium scans in a prospective study of 50 patients. They found that indium-labeled WBC scans had an accuracy of 83% compared with 57% for gallium scans in the detection of osteomyelitis. However, it is important to remember that all clinical data, including a detailed clinical history, a characterization of the host, appropriate laboratory studies, clinical examination, and radiographic studies, are important in determining the likelihood and extent of infection.

Recently, it was suggested that the sulfur colloid marrow scan should be added to the combination of red cell and white cell scans to increase the accuracy of scintigraphy. We have investigated the usefulness of these three scans read by a nuclear medicine specialist in a blinded fashion using receiver operating curves. We did not find any particular scan combinations that provided a reliable screening tool (sensitivity), but we did find that certain combinations provided good treatment decisions (specificity). Furthermore, the combination of white cell and marrow scans was equivalent to the combination of all three scans and better than the combination of red and white cell scans, which implies that the red cell scan may be of limited value. While the sensitivities of all of these tests and combinations were low, the specificities remained at about 90% and the conclusion was that standard red cell scanning may not be necessary for the diagnosis of posttraumatic infection. Furthermore, we corroborated the findings of Segura et al.[109] and found that the red cell scan added little. Unfortunately, surgeons often continue to base their suspicion of infection on a simple bone scan. Table 24-4 illustrates the matrix as a guide to assist the interpretation of bone scan combinations.[24]

Other Scintigraphic Methods

In general, the accumulation of radiolabeled compounds and infectious conditions occurs via several routes. The labeled agents can bind to activate endothelium (anti–E-selectin). They can also enhance the influx of leukocytes or related by products (autologous leukocytes, antigranulocyte antibodies, or cytokines), and they can enhance glucose uptake by activated leukocytes ([18F]-fluorodeoxyglucose [FDG]). In addition, they bind directly to microorganisms (radiolabeled ciprofloxacin or antimicrobial peptides). Labeling of polyclonal immunoglobin is a newer technique to investigate infection. It uses antigranulocyte antibodies, radiolabeled nonspecific human immunoglobin (IgG), interleukins, and antimicrobial peptides.[9] The nonspecific polyclonal IgG prepared from human serum gamma globulin can be labeled with various agents, including indium, gallium, or technetium, and can be used for the detection of osteomyelitis.[9,95,102] Unlike labeled leukocyte scans, the immunoglobulin agent is easily prepared with short blood half-lives of about 24 hours. The primary uptake occurs in the liver with less bone marrow uptake.[74]

Indium IgG scintigraphy is useful for the detection of musculoskeletal infection in patients in whom sterile inflammatory events stimulate infectious processes.[78] However, despite its usefulness, this modality has not yet found its way into common clinical practice. PET with FDG has been shown to delineate various infective and inflammatory disorders with a high sensitivity. The FDG-PET scan enables noninvasive detection and demonstration of the extent of chronic osteomyelitis with 97% accuracy.[33] PET scanning is especially accurate in the central skeleton within active bone marrow.[32] Although not yet in widespread use, it may well prove to be the single most useful test in specifically diagnosing bone infection. In one study, the overall accuracy of FDG-PET in evaluating infection involving orthopaedic hardware was 96.2% for hip prostheses, 81% for knee prostheses, and 100% in 15 additional patients with other orthopaedic implants. In patients with chronic osteomyelitis, the accuracy is 91%.[19] FDG-PET scanning appears to be a sensitive and specific method for the detection of infective foci due to metallic implants, which makes it useful in patients with trauma. Sensitivity, specificity, and accuracy were 100%, 93.3%, and 97%, respectively, for all PET data. The figures were 100%, 100%, and 100% for the central skeleton and 100%, 87.5%, and 95%, respectively, for the peripheral skeleton.[104]

Magnetic Resonance Imaging

MRI continues to play an important role in the evaluation of musculoskeletal infection.[77,97,111] The sensitivity and specificity of MRI scans for osteomyelitis range from 60% to 100% and from 50% to 90%, respectively. MRI has the spatial resolution necessary to accurately evaluate the extent of infection in preparation for surgical treatment and particularly to localize abscess cavities. T1- and T2-weighted imaging is usually sufficient; fat suppression and short tau inversion recovery (STIR) sequences may be added to improve the imaging of bone marrow and soft tissue abnormalities. MRI also has the ability to differentiate between infected bone and involved adjacent soft tissue structures. Images can be acquired in any orientation and there is no radiation exposure. Occasionally a sinus tract can be identified (Fig. 24-11). Gadolinium enhancement should be obtained in the postoperative population to better differentiate postsurgical artifact from infection-related bone marrow edema patterns. Gadolinium may differentiate abscess formation from diffuse inflammatory changes and noninfectious fluid collections.

Active osteomyelitis characteristically displays a decreased signal in T1-weighted images and appears bright in T2-weighted images. The process presents the replacement of marrow fat with water from edema, exudates, hyperemia, and ischemia. However, the MRI signal characteristics that reflect osteomyelitis are intrinsically nonspecific, and tumors and fractures can also increase the marrow water content. In patients without prior complications, MRI has been found to be sensitive, but not specific, for osteomyelitis. When a fracture or prior surgery is evident, MRI is less specific in the diagnosis of infection. Furthermore, in the presence of metallic implants, artifacts make it difficult to comment on areas of interest that are near the implant. Certain external fixators are not compatible with

| TABLE 24-4 | **Matrix of Scintigraphic Combinations and Potential for Infection** |

	Scan results (activity)			
Bone scan	Cold	Hot	Hot	Hot
White cell scan	Cold	Cold	Hot	Hot
Marrow scan	Cold	Cold	Cold	Hot
Infection present?	No	Unlikely	Probably	Maybe

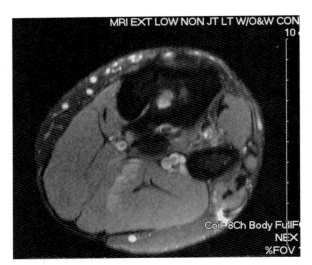

FIGURE 24-11 Magnetic resonance image of infected tibia with sinus tract leading to central sequestrum (white area in medullary canal).

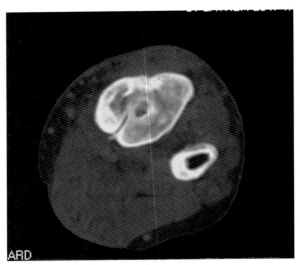

FIGURE 24-12 Same patient as Figure 24-11 but demonstrating appearance of sinus on computed tomography scan.

MRI and thus will preclude its use. We have found that the best use of MRI is helping to determine the extent of the infection for preoperative planning. Our experience has been that using MRI to plan the degree of bone resection or débridement is helpful but that MRI may lead to an overestimation of the extent of the infection due to the detection of adjacent edema.

Computed Tomography

Computed tomography (CT) has assumed a lesser role in the evaluation of osteomyelitis with the widespread use of MRI.[32] However, CT remains unsurpassed in the imaging of cortical bone. It is especially useful in delineating the cortical details in chronic osteomyelitis.[112] CT is also useful in evaluating the adequacy of cortical débridement in the staged treatment of chronic osteomyelitis. Thus, it can help differentiate between type III and type IV infections. With modern equipment, CT scanning around fracture implants has improved and it can help evaluate both bone pathology and the extent of bone union. CT is also valuable in the treatment of extensive osteomyelitis in that it can determine the extent of bony involvement. In chronic cases, with some remodeling of both host and pathologic bone, it can often differentiate and identify sequestra or sclerosed diseased bone. It may often demonstrate useful pathologic findings (Fig. 24-12).

Cultures and Biopsy

Identification of an organism and determination of antibiotic resistance patterns are crucial to a successful outcome in the management of osteomyelitis. With regard to open fractures, the issue of culturing the predébridement or postdébridement tissue bed is often discussed among surgeons and infectious disease specialists. In civilian wounds, gram-positive bacteria usually predominate at the time of injury but frequently change to gram-negative bacteria, which are often the cause of late infections. In one study, 119 of 225 open fractures had positive wound cultures with only 8% of predébridement cultures correctly identifying the infecting organism, while 7% of those with negative predébridement cultures also developed infection. In only 22% did the postdébridement cultures correlate with the ultimate infecting organism. These data are clinically relevant because treating the wrong bacteria can promote overgrowth of the true infecting bacteria or add to the development of resistant organisms. In recent war experience, military surgeons have noted different bacteria flora causing infection, but the same principles still apply to their treatment.[15,52,83,118] While cultures of the sinus tract can be helpful, they should not be the sole guide for antibiotic treatment.[41] A study by Moussa et al.[81] found that 88.7% of sinus tract isolates were identical to operative specimens in 55 patients with chronic bone infection. However, other researchers have reported a concordance rate of between 25% and 45%.[66] The ability to obtain true deep cultures of the sinus improves concordance, but it is still not helpful. One study concluded that nonbone specimens had a worse concordance than bone specimens and were associated with 52% false negatives and 36% false positives.[128] It is important to recognize not only that superficial cultures of sinus tracts, open wounds, and fractures are unhelpful but also that an error in bacterial identification may lead to inappropriate antibiotic selection and ultimately compromise patient outcome. Bone biopsy remains the preferred diagnostic procedure in chronic osteomyelitis. Multiple specimens should be obtained if possible, not only to minimize sampling error but also to increase specificity and sensitivity. Histologic and microbiological evaluation of percutaneous biopsy samples should be combined in cases of suspected osteomyelitis. The sensitivity of culture in the diagnosis of osteomyelitis can be improved from 42% to 84% by the addition of histologic evaluation.

Molecular Diagnostics

Identification procedures based on molecular analysis and RNA or DNA typing are currently in development to facilitate diagnosis in osteomyelitis. These techniques offer a precise method of organism identification in cases in which standard techniques do not identify a pathogen despite the clinical presence of infection. This scenario is not uncommon in patients who have been treated with antibiotics shortly before sample collection. These methods target specific macromolecules unique to the infecting pathogens that are absent in the host cells.[39,116] They have the potential to provide rapid results with high accuracy.[57] The most commonly used method for the diagnosis of orthopaedic infections is the polymerase chain reaction (PCR).[57] This has been used to identify microremnants of bacteria by identifying their nuclear contents. Sequences within bacterial 16S ribosomal RNA have served as targets for amplification and detection.[57] Unfortunately, PCR cannot easily delineate between nuclear materials from living or dead bacteria. This increases the likelihood of false positive studies. Further investigations are required before these techniques can be widely used as currently they lack sufficient sensitivity and specificity. However, their use remains promising. There have been recent reports of real-time testing that also appear more reliable and rapid, which could be very useful when deciding whether there is ongoing infection before undertaking a procedure requiring the implantation of orthopaedic hardware.[113]

MANAGEMENT AND TREATMENT

In orthopaedic surgery and particularly in the treatment of fractures, postoperative infection is an unfortunate reality. The important questions to be posed are "Is there an infection?" and then "What do I do now?" The challenge is the difficulty in being certain whether an infection exists because we do not have an absolutely reliable method of determining the necessary elements of true postoperative or posttraumatic infection. As previously discussed, the establishment of colonization followed by an opportunistic bacteria, in a compromised host or environment, is necessary to allow an infection to occur. Furthermore, the accuracy and reliability of available diagnostic tests are not 100% and therefore experience and clinical judgment are vital and could be more considered more important than the tests that are currently available.

As has already been noted, treatment must follow basic principles but also must be tailored to the reality of the individual clinical scenario. It would be naive to assume that an inflamed and draining postoperative wound in a polytraumatized patient (B systemic) with significant fracture treatment (B local) that responds to a short course of antibiotics has no chance of recurrence. In such a case, sufficient treatment might have been provided so the balance would tip to favor the host defense mechanism. However, what probably occurred was that the threshold level for infection was exceeded and the body manifested a response in the form of inflammation and drainage. With the use of antibiotic treatment, the bacterial counts were reduced so that the host was able to take over and sequester the infection effectively. Thus, an initial positive response to antibiotic therapy does not necessarily mean that the infection was eradicated. It simply means that it was suppressed and possibly sequestered. Using an oncologic analogy, the infection may have been forced into remission, possibly for an indefinite period, but many of these patients present later with signs of infection in the same limb. Unfortunately, by this time the patient may be older, in poorer health, and less able or willing to tolerate an aggressive ablative procedure, thus lowering the potential for cure. In the long run, early suppression may cause the patient more physical and psychological harm than early aggressive measures to achieve complete eradication. On the other hand, an overaggressive approach may require extensive reconstructive efforts that lead to other problems. Thus, in a world seeking clear black-

and-white answers, osteomyelitis usually presents as a shade of gray!

The principles of osteomyelitis management rely on a multidisciplinary approach that begins with diagnosis and optimization in the form of medicine and radiology and then combines débridement, soft tissue coverage, antimicrobial therapy using orthopaedic surgery, microvascular surgery, and infectious disease. This gives the best chance of a cure.[38,70] Initially, the infection needs to be diagnosed and the host optimized. This involves treating any comorbidities and optimizing the physiologic condition of the host. Interventions involving nutrition, the use of nicotine, diabetes, vascular disease, and improvement of tissue oxygenation will increase the chances of successful treatment. Second, the osteomyelitis needs to be classified and staged. It is then important to identify the organism to determine appropriate antimicrobial treatment. This can be done independently with a bone biopsy or deep culture or, more commonly, it is done at the time of surgery. Identification will also give an idea of the potential virulence of the causative organism, which may influence decisions regarding treatment. We recommend that if the risk of sepsis or amputation is low, then a period of time off all antibiotics may improve bacterial identification. This may be more important in longstanding cases where the usual organisms may have been replaced by other, more exotic species.

Once the extent of the disease plus the nature of the host and the infecting organism are understood, determination should be made regarding one of several general treatment algorithms. Available treatment options include attempted ablation and cure of the infection, or, in selective cases such as C hosts who are not suitable for surgery, some type of suppressive treatment may be undertaken. Attempted ablation and complete cure have numerous issues and decision-making steps and will often require the oncologic equivalent of a wide resection with clean margins. While a surgically clean bed with extensive resection is desirable, all efforts should be made to maintain skeletal axial stability where possible. Thus, retention of a well-vascularized but affected involucrum or a viable segment of bone adjacent to infection may be preferable to a segmental resection that would add a level of complexity to the treatment regime. If an adequate resection would result in an overextensive reconstruction that is unsuitable for the host's function or desire, an amputation is the best option and it should not be considered a failure. In some cases of life- or limb-threatening infection, debulking of the infection may be a suitable first step followed by chronic suppression. In these circumstances, identification of the infecting bacteria is required to allow use of a specific antibiotic. Otherwise, broad-spectrum antibiotics are required.

We have embraced a collaborative approach with our infectious disease colleagues. Modern antimicrobials have become so numerous and complex that their expert involvement is likely to increase the chances of successful treatment. Increasingly, in many hospitals bone infection mandates an infectious disease consult because of the risk of inadvertently creating resistance pathogens, the efficacy of combined antibiotic protocols, patient safety issues, and the cost of new treatment regimens. However, it is still important that the orthopaedist has an understanding of antimicrobial treatment since it is the orthopaedist who will initiate the treatment before consulting his or her infectious disease colleagues. We also recommend that orthopaedic surgeons recognize that not all infectious disease practices are evidence based and not all specialists have a specific interest and training in bone infections. Therefore, it is vital that the orthopaedist initiates an open and collegial partnership with the infectious diseases specialists in his or her community to work on behalf of the patient. Both the orthopaedic surgeon and the infectious diseases physicians should work together to employ a consistent strategy of surgical and chemotherapeutic treatment predicated on the best evidence and logic available. Ziran et al.[126] showed that a dedicated team approach can enhance the outcomes of treatment, providing higher cure and successful suppression rates. The subsequent sections in this chapter will briefly review both systemic and local antimicrobial agents as well as discuss the techniques and implants used during treatment. Specific scenarios and algorithms will then be reviewed.

Novel techniques under development include the use of compounds that promote detachment of stationary colonized bacteria into the planktonic state, where they are easier to eradicate. The techniques include surface treatments that inhibit colonization and the use of a light-activated dye that destroys certain bacteria in wounds. In this latter technique, indocyanine green, which is a harmless dye, is placed into the wound and activated with near infrared light. The light results in the dye-releasing molecules that are toxic to the methicillin-resistant *S. aureus* (MRSA) bacteria. The mechanism of action is so varied and unlike standard antibiotics that the development of resistance may be unlikely. These and other methods under development may provide novel adjunctive treatments to help treat osteomyelitis.

Antimicrobial Therapy

Ideally, antibiotics should be nontoxic, convenient to administer, affordable, and based on the in vitro susceptibilities of the microorganisms. Regimens for the initial treatment of osteomyelitis by common bacteria are outlined in Table 24-5. Since bone represents a unique compartment of the body, the antimicrobial that is used should have reliable bone penetration. Serum and bone concentrations associated with the use of commonly used antibiotics are given in Table 24-6. The duration of antibiotic therapy for osteomyelitis varies. Some researchers have recommended as little as 2 weeks, whereas others have suggested longer therapy. There is no general consensus. Short-term therapy may be used in otherwise healthy patients when total débridement is combined with healthy host tissue. Long-term antibiotic therapy is based on the knowledge of how biofilms function and is usually used in patients with virulent or long-standing infections in whom the initial débridement will be followed later by staged reconstruction or in the presence of

---

TABLE 24-5   Common Bacteria-Specific Antibiotic Regimens

Organism	First-Line Antibiotic(s)	Alternative Antibiotic(s)
Staphylococcus aureus or coagulase-negative staphylococci (methicillin-sensitive), MSSA	Oxacillin 2 g IV q6h Clindamycin 600 mg IV q8h	First-generation cephalosporin, vancomycin, daptomycin, tigecycline
S. aureus or coagulase-negative staphylococci (methicillin-resistant), MRSA	Vancomycin 1 g IV q12h ± Rifampin 300 mg PO BID	Linezolid, trimethoprim-sulfamethoxazole or minocycline + rifampin, daptomycin, tigecycline
Penicillin-sensitive *Streptococcus pneumoniae*, varied streptococci (groups A and B β-hemolytic organisms)	Penicillin G, 4 million units IV q6h Ceftriaxone 2 g IV QD Cefazolin 1 g IV q8h	Clindamycin, erythromycin, vancomycin
Intermediate penicillin-resistant *S. pneumoniae*	Ceftriaxone 2 g IV q24h	Erythromycin, clindamycin, or fluoroquinolone
Penicillin-resistant *S. pneumoniae*	Vancomycin 1 g IV q12h	Fluoroquinolone
Enterococcus spp.	Penicillin G, 4 million units IV q6h Ampicillin 2 g IV q6h + Gentamicin 3–5 mg/kg/day Vancomycin 1 g IV q12h	Ampicillin–sulbactam, linezolid, daptomycin, tigecycline + gentamicin
Pseudomonas spp., *Serratia* spp., or *Enterobacter* spp.	Cefepime 2 g IV q12h ± Fluoroquinolone (see Table 24-7) Meropenem 1 g IV q8h	Fluoroquinolone, ertapenem
Enteric gram-negative rods	Ceftriaxone 2 g IV q24h Fluoroquinolone (see later)	Third-generation cephalosporin
Anaerobes	Clindamycin 600 mg IV q8h Metronidazole 500 mg PO q4	For gram-negative anaerobes: amoxicillin–clavulanate or metronidazole
Mixed aerobic and anaerobic organisms	Amoxicillin-clavulanate 3 g IV q6h	Ertapenem

Fluoroquinolones: ciprofloxacin 750 mg PO BID, levofloxacin 500 mg PO QD, moxifloxacin 400 mg PO QD.
Note that use of fluoroquinolones has been associated with altered bone healing in animal models and increased risk of tendon rupture in humans.
Note that many antibiotics may result in development of severe colitis.

TABLE 24-6	Serum and Bone Concentrations after Antibiotic Administration			
Antibiotic		**Serum**	**Bone**	**% Serum**
Clindamycin (7 mg/kg)		2.1 ± 0.6	1.9 ± 1.9	98.3
Vancomycin (30 mg/kg)		36.4 ± 4.6	5.3 ± 0.8	14.5
Nafcillin (40 mg/kg)		21.8 ± 4.6	2.1 ± 0.3	9.6
Moxalactam (40 mg/kg)		65.2 ± 5.2	6.2 ± 0.7	9.5
Tobramycin (5 mg/kg)		14.3 ± 1.3	1.3 ± 0.1	9.1
Cefazolin (15 mg/kg)		7.2 ± 2.6	4.1 ± 0.7	6.1
Cefazolin (5 mg/kg)		45.6 ± 3.2	2.6 ± 0.2	5.7
Cephalothin (40 mg/kg)		34.8 ± 2.8	1.3 ± 0.2	3.7

From Mader JT, Calhoun JH. Osteomyelitis. In Mandell GL, Douglas RG, Bennett JE, eds. Principles and Practice of Infectious Diseases. New York: Churchill Livingstone, 1995:1039–1051.

retained implants. If the patient requires grafting or reconstruction following the successful débridement of osteomyelitis, antibiotics will often be administered for 6 to 8 weeks. This is followed by a period of antibiotics with observation of the CRP and ESR levels and possible repeat biopsy. If there are no ongoing indicators of infection, reconstruction can safely be performed in possible cases without additional long-term antibiotic treatment. One caveat of this approach is that it can only be done if there are no adverse effects from the use of antibiotics. There are reports of immunosuppression, allergic reaction, poor tolerance, compliance, and financial hardship that must also be considered when deciding on long-term antibiotic administration. To increase patient compliance, the antibiotic agents that are selected should be the least toxic and the least expensive possible and preferably require administration once or twice daily. Antibiotics with excellent oral bioavailability are listed in Table 24-7. These antibiotics may be substituted for intravenous agents whenever possible provided that the microorganism is susceptible to these agents and bone penetration is adequate.

Because of the increased incidences of vancomycin-resistant *Enterococcus*, especially in intensive care units, and vancomycin-resistant *S. aureus* (VRSA), vancomycin should be used only if there is a high institutional incidence of MRSA or methicillin-resistant *Staphylococcus epidermidis* (MRSE). A single dose of vancomycin administered before surgery followed by two or three doses postoperatively should provide adequate perioperative prophylaxis in high-risk cases. Vancomycin should only be used with type I hypersensitivity to cephalosporins in patients with urticaria, laryngeal edema, and bronchospasm without cardiovascular shock. Clindamycin is considered the substitute of choice when cephalosporins are contraindicated.

We have identified several common paradigms of antibiotic use that merit discussion. Routine prophylaxis is indicated for most orthopaedic procedures.

Prophylaxis

On the basis that prevention is always better than cure, prophylactic antibiotics have an important role in the treatment of closed fractures. The prophylactic use of appropriate antibiotics for closed fractures and elective cases will reduce the incidence of postoperative osteomyelitis. Antibiotic administration is not a substitute for proper aseptic technique, but it is a validated additional measure to reduce postoperative infection.

The use of prophylactic antibiotics was demonstrated in a Dutch trauma trial that found, in 2195 cases of closed fracture surgery, a single preoperative dose of ceftriaxone resulted in an infection rate of 3.6% in comparison to a placebo group infection rate of 8.3% ($P < .001$).[12] Furthermore, the trial also found that there was a lower incidence of nosocomial urinary tract and respiratory tract infections in the first 30 postoperative days (2.3% versus 10.2%, $P < .001$). In another retrospective study of 2847 surgical cases, the timing of antibiotic administration was also found to be an important factor. If the antibiotics were given more than 2 hours before or 3 hours after the incision,

TABLE 24-7	Selected Oral Antimicrobial Agents with Excellent Oral Bioavailability Commonly Used to Treat Osteomyelitis	
	Antimicrobial Agents	
Fluoroquinolones	Ciprofloxacin 750 mg q12h Levofloxacin 500 mg q12h Moxifloxacin 400 mg q12h	
Mixed	Metronidazole 500 mg q8h Linezolid 600 mg q12h Rifampin 300 mg q12h (not to be used alone) Trimethoprim–sulfamethoxazole 1 DS QD Minocycline–doxycycline 100 mg q12h	
Azoles (antifungal)	Fluconazole 400 mg q24h Itraconazole 200 mg q12h	

there was a sixfold increase in the rate of surgical site infection.[23] The current recommendation is that antibiotics should be administered 30 to 60 minutes before the incision is made, except when using vancomycin, where a longer delay permits appropriate infusion rates.[46,105] For routine uncomplicated closed fracture surgery, prophylaxis should not be administered for greater than 24 hours, and many surgeons believe that only a single dose is necessary. Gillespie and Walenkamp performed a meta-analysis of 8307 patients undergoing surgical treatment of hip and long bone fractures, to determine whether antibiotic prophylaxis reduced the incidence of wound infection. A total of 22 studies were analyzed. Single doses of antibiotic prophylaxis were found to significantly reduce the incidence of wound infection (relative risk, 0.4; 95% confidence interval, 0.24–0.67).[46] Controversy exists regarding the appropriate prophylaxis for orthopedic surgical patients in hospitals with high rates of MRSA. Traditional first-generation cephalosporins may not provide adequate coverage, and given the increasing prevalence of MRSA infections in Europe and North America, further studies are needed to understand the risk/benefit ratio of using routine vancomycin as a prophylaxis agent. The disadvantages of potential nephrotoxicity and an increase in the emergence of VRSA must be weighed against the risk of increased postoperative infection rates. Currently, neither vancomycin nor clindamycin is routinely used except in cases of known penicillin or cephalosporin allergy. In cases of reported penicillin allergy, patients can be given a small test dose of a cephalosporin after anesthesia induction to determine if there is any cross-reactivity.

Open Fractures

Historically, the teaching in open fractures has been to use a first-generation cephalosporin followed by the addition of an aminoglycoside for more contaminated wounds using supplementary penicillin if there is any soil contamination. It is perhaps surprising to realize that this recommendation is more than 30 years old and is not supported by any newer, high-level evidence-based studies. This practice was primarily an empirical and theoretical recommendation. Since the incidence of infection is so low that any treatment will also have a small statistical effect size, it may not be possible to undertake a sufficiently powered study to adequate test the success of this antibiotic regimen. A Cochrane review undertaken in 2004 clearly identified the usefulness of some antibiotics for the treatment of open fractures.[47] The EAST practice management guidelines also concluded that antibiotics were useful but that their use required more scientific study.[64] The most recent review by the Surgical Infection Society found that the current standard antibiotic prophylaxis is based on very limited data.[55]

Another question that remains unanswered concerns the true requirement for aminoglycosides at the time of injury. Given that the initial organism is often a staphylococcus but that the eventual infective organism is a resistant gram-negative organism, it begs the question of whether early aminoglycoside administration, which is often given in adequate doses, will promote the development of a resistant organism. In two studies, a cephalosporin alone performed as well as the combination of a cephalosporin and penicillin or the combination of a cephalosporin and an aminoglycoside.[92] Another study examining the use of broad-spectrum antibiotics proposed that their use could result in the development of resistant bacteria.

Increasingly at the authors' institutions, quinolones are replacing aminoglycosides for the treatment of open fractures, particularly in patients in the intensive care unit. This view is supported by an assessment of the U.S. military experience with high-energy open fractures, which has shown that there is sufficient level I data to support the use of a cephalosporin but that the use of aminoglycosides, even for grade III open fractures, may be deleterious. These recommendations are based on timely and adequate surgical débridement. If there is a delay to treatment whereby bacterial colonization may have begun and matured or if the wound is such that gram-negative or anaerobic conditions exist, then supplementation with appropriate antibiotics, in addition to a more aggressive initial débridement, may be useful. Because there is little scientific evidence about the subject, much current surgical practice is anecdotal. The authors believe that the initial débridement is the most important principle of open fracture treatment as well as in the management of acute or chronic infection. Minimalist approaches to the removal of devitalized tissue, in the hopes of preventing extensive later reconstructive surgery, are usually doomed to failure. By the surgeon taking less initially, the patient is often condemned to lose more later because of ongoing infection and diffuse tissue destruction.

With regard to the timing and duration of antibiotic treatment, there is again little good science and little chance of undertaking a well-performed scientific study because of the sample size that would be required. In the classic retrospective study of over 2800 patients, surgical site infections were increased sixfold if antibiotics were given too early (<2 hours before incision) or too late (>3 hours after incision).[23] A study on over 2000 fracture fixation patients that compared ceftriaxone to a placebo clearly identified the usefulness of prophylactic antibiotics.[12] The duration of antibiotic use in open fractures has also been poorly studied, but the current recommendation is to use antibiotics for 1 to 3 days following wound closure or coverage with ongoing treatment based on a reassessment of the injury zone. However, the current practice of continuing the use of antibiotics until definitive wound closure has occurred has no scientific basis. In fact, the literature suggests that the long duration of empirical or prophylactic antibiotic use may breed resistant organisms. The current recommendation is to use antibiotics for an extended period only if this is supported by the condition of the wound which will show signs of infection.[82] The authors' institutions summarized the available literature and concluded that open fractures should be treated with antibiotics for 24 hours following definitive wound closure. These are also the recommendations being developed in new guidelines by the U.S. Centers for Disease Control and Prevention (CDC).[18] Recently, a journal supplement focusing on military injuries has examined and summarized the current thinking on extremity infection in war time injury.[82,83]

Established Infection

There are also little data with regard to the use and duration of antibiotics to establish infection. The most common practice is to begin with a 2- to 6-week course of a species-specific, bioavailable agent.[62] Such an agent may be used until adequate revascularization occurs. With the advent of many new and expensive oral agents, it may be possible to reduce the morbidity associated with intravenous use with an early stepdown program converting to an oral agent. Obviously, this regimen may be less successful, with resistant organisms. Thus, to date there have been few recommendations for the duration of antibiotics in established osteomyelitis.

A common clinical scenario is the partially treated infection. Patients who may have been suppressed but incompletely treated may present with an acutely inflamed, limb-threatening condition. Our approach has been to continue the use of antibiotics during the diagnostic and staging period when the necessary tests are undertaken and the host is optimized. However, we believe that as long as there are no signs of impending sepsis or limb loss, it is worthwhile stopping antibiotic treatment 1 to 2 weeks before surgical intervention so that more precise and reliable bacterial identification is possible. Begin an empirical course of antibiotics intraoperatively after all the cultures have been taken and continue until the culture results are available. In chronic cases, we will cover both gram-negative and MRSA and collaborate with our infectious diseases colleagues regarding final antibiotic selection and management.

Irrigation Solutions

The original use of pulsatile irrigation was based on early studies on infections that recommended that colonized bacteria are adherent to tissue and needed to be moved from the surface. Although such mechanical cleansing may work, acutely mature colonies of bacteria are not easily eradicated with this method. Furthermore, there is evidence that the velocity of the fluid stream may be deleterious to both bone and soft tissue cells.[3,8,13,53,110] So while high-pressure flow has been shown to remove more bacteria and debris and to lower the rate of wound infection compared with low-pressure irrigation, recent in vitro and animal studies suggest that pressure irrigation may damage bone or push bacteria even deeper into the wound.[8,13,53] Damage to bone and soft tissue may result in necrosis and create a new iatrogenic surface for bacterial colonization. In short, pulsatile flow has not been demonstrated to increase efficacy.

Irrigation with saline alone has been shown in animal studies to reduce colony counts by about 50% in contaminated wounds.[7] However, conflicting studies have shown no beneficial effect of the use of saline.[16,25] In one study, tap water was compared with sterile saline irrigation and no difference was found in infection rates.[79] The effect of adding bacteriocidal agents to irrigation solutions to aid with both bacterial removal and destruction has also been studied in an adherent staphylococci model.[8] These studies have shown that while solutions such as Betadine and hydrogen peroxide are effective in eliminating bacteria, they are also toxic to osteoblasts. Also, the addition of antibiotics to irrigation solutions has had mixed results, and overall it appears to have little benefit but there is a significant increase in cost. Their use as an adjunct to irrigation solutions is questionable at best.[4,35,94] The authors do not add any supplementary chemicals or antibiotics to irrigation solutions, and we do not recommend the use of full-strength Betadine placed directly into an open wound.

Given the minimal effects of antibiotics in irrigation fluids, detergent-type compounds or surfactant solutions have been recently investigated as a way of disrupting the hydrophobic or electrostatic forces that drive the initial stages of bacterial surface adhesion. A sequential surfactant-irrigation protocol was developed and shown to be effective in polymicrobial wounds associated with an established infection.[5,36,81] Detergents, or soaps,

have been shown to be the only irrigation solutions that remove additional bacteria beyond the effect of mechanical irrigation alone.[8] Moreover, soap solutions have been found to have minimal effects on bone formation and osteoblast numbers in vitro.[7] The proposed mechanism of their effect is based on the formation of micelles that overcome the strength of the interaction between the organisms and bone. Castille soap has recently been reported to be useful in this situation.[5,80]

Antibiotic Depot Devices and Techniques

The concept of local antibiotic therapy in the form of antibiotics impregnated in bone cement to reduce infected arthroplasties was introduced in the 1970s[14]. As a result of the success of this work, interest developed in using antibiotic-impregnated bone cement as treatment for osteomyelitis.[99] Keating et al.[60] reported a 4% infection rate in 53 open tibial fractures with tobramycin-impregnated beads. Ostermann et al.[89] reported a significant difference in infection rates with grade IIIB fractures treated with aminoglycoside beads together with parenteral antibiotics compared with patients who only received parenteral antibiotics. They reported a 6.9% infection rate in 112 patients with combined therapy compared with a 40.7% infection rate in 27 patients who only had parenteral antibiotics. The use of antibiotic depots allows for high local concentrations of antibiotic with little systemic absorption. Antibiotic release is biphasic with most occurring during the first few days to weeks after implantation. However, elution of the antibiotic persists for several weeks. Occasionally, antibiotics can be recovered after several years, but because the elution is based on a diffusion gradient, only the outer 1 cm or so of large-volume depots will elute antibiotic. The core of such large-volume depots will often contain antibiotic but it will not be useful.[62,108]

The key issue of the polymethylmethacrylate (PMMA) antibiotic depot is the need for a heat-stable antibiotic agent, because during the cement-hardening process, the exothermic reaction can render heat-labile antibiotics ineffective. Some of the antibiotics that have been tried with PMMA include clindamycin, which elutes well but is not available as a pharmaceutical grade power. Fluoroquinolones have been reported to have suitable elution, but clinical reports of their success are lacking.[34] Erythromycin was used in some earlier studies, but a subsequent study showed inadequate elution of erythromycin from Palacos cement. Mactolides and azalides are unavailable, and tetracycline and polymyxin E (Colistin) fail to elute from the Palacos cement in clinically useful quantities. Another issue with PMMA depot systems is that they require removal. If they are left for a prolonged period, the PMMA spaces can become encased in scar and may be difficult to remove. After antibiotics have eluted from the outer surface of the cement mass, the surface is rendered unprotected and may provide a suitable surface for secondary colonization. When used acutely for open fractures or for a short period, removal is not generally problematic and may even be undertaken percutaneously. There are entire issues of *Clinical Orthopaedics and Related Research* (Numbers 295 and 427) dedicated to the use of PMMA antibiotic depot methods to which the reader is referred for more in-depth information.[1,2] The authors' formulation for PMMA antibiotic-laden beads uses vancomycin and tobramycin. While up to 4 g of vancomycin and 4.8 g of tobramycin can be mixed per 40-g bag of cement, the cement may become difficult to manage. Other PMMA for-

FIGURE 24-13 Antibiotic balls placed on stainless steel wire to form beads. One ball has been flattened to form a disc.

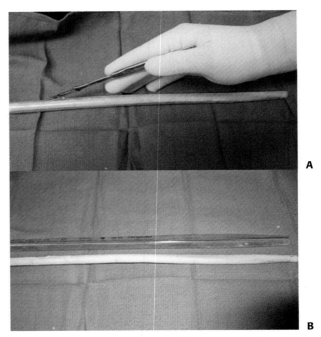

FIGURE 24-15 Manufacture of an antibiotic-impregnated cement rod. **A.** The thoracostomy tube filled with antibiotic cement is cut to allow removal of antibiotic intramedullary rod (bottom). **B.** The antibiotic-impregnated cement rod.

mulations such as Cranioplast do not tolerate even small amounts of antibiotic powder. For routine use, we place between 1 and 2 g of vancomycin and 1.2 to 2.4 g of tobramycin per bag. Depending on the clinical situation, we have developed a method to create three forms of antibiotic beads. We first cut a length of 18-gauge steel wire and loop one end. As the bowl becomes doughy, we roll multiple cement balls of about 1 to 2 cm in diameter. The wire is then moistened with water and the bead is allowed to slide and drop on the wire. The adherent cement is cleaned off the wire to allow subsequent beads to slide down. After the beads are placed, they can be left to cure as balls or they may be checked into oblong sausage-shaped beads by rolling them like dough. Alternatively, they can be shaped into discs by simply pressing each bead flat on the wire. We prefer the use of discs because they fit better between tissue planes and are less likely to have local compressive effects on the tissues (Figs. 24-13 and 24-14).

Recently, intramedullary antibiotic cement rods have been used. These are fashioned by using a large 36 French thoracostomy tube and placing an 18- to 20-gauge wire inside. After

the tube has been cut to discard the vent holes, bone wax or a Kelly clamp can be used to obstruct the thin end. The antibiotic–cement mixture is then injected into the tube in a liquid state. Once the cement cures, the thoracostomy tube is cut off with a scalpel and the rod can then be used. It is important to ensure that both canal diameter and rod length have been measured (Fig. 24-15).

Most of the antibiotic cement used in the United States has been off-label use by the surgeon, and despite encouraging results from several studies, their approval by the U.S. Food and Drug Administration has been discouragingly slow. There are a number of commercial antibiotic-impregnated PMMA cements becoming available in the United States, and of course they have been available for some time in other parts of the world. We believe that the use of an aminoglycoside in antibiotic-impregnated cement does not provide the versatility that we need because vancomycin should be considered when there is a chance of resistant staphylococcal organisms. Thus, commercially produced antibiotic-laden cement may best be suited as prophylaxis during cemented arthroplasty.

There are also newer types of material available for local delivery of antibiotics that are resorbable and do not require removal. Surgical-grade calcium sulfate has been used recently, and its use is reported in both open fractures and infections.[73] Although calcium sulfate products have been promoted as a bone graft substitute, there are little data in human fractures and infections demonstrating the efficacy of this dual function of depot and graft. Calcium sulfates and carbonate will absorb or dissolve independently of bone formation, whereas calcium phosphates tend to be replaced very slowly with bone. Furthermore, large volumes of calcium sulfate can cause an osmotic effect that results in fluid accumulation and the potential for

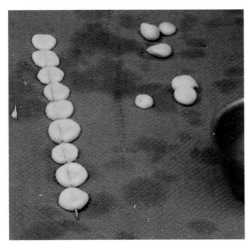

FIGURE 24-14 The final appearance of antibiotic discs. We believe that they produce less local tissue pressure and ischemia than antibiotic balls.

seroma formation and wound drainage. When mixed with fluid and blood, the calcium drainage looks like bloody pus and may prompt extra surgical treatments resulting in unacceptable complication rates.[11,127] In one study, the use of a calcium sulfate–DBM mixture (Allomatrix; Wright Medical, Memphis, TN) resulted in an unacceptably high rate of drainage, infection, and failure. We have heard of numerous anecdotal reports concerning the drainage problem of calcium sulfate and we do not recommend its use as a bone graft substitute. However, we have found it useful as an antibiotic depot. To minimize the drainage problem, we do not recommend placing a large amount of calcium sulfate beads into a cavity, but if this is unavoidable, a multiple-level water-tight closure is essential. We have not found any problems with drainage when the beads are interspersed in small spaces and tissue planes. Another feature to note is that the addition of tobramycin to calcium sulfate greatly prolongs the setting time, which may be 30 to 45 minutes. Vancomycin greatly shortens the setting time, which may be as fast as 2 minutes, and for this reason the agent may be impractical. We routinely use both vancomycin and tobramycin for high-risk infections and find that the effect of tobramycin dominates the settling profile. Thus, despite a seemingly novel concept and marketing claims, such products should be used with caution and experience.

The use of impregnated hydroxyapatite ceramic beads may simulate a bone graft by serving as an osteoconductive matrix, but they are resorbed slowly and after elution may behave as a foreign body with potential reinfection as may occur with PMMA beads. Gentamicin-impregnated polylactide-polyglycolide copolymer implants are biodegradable and may not need removal once they have been implanted. However, there is little clinical experience, and it is possible that they elicit an inflammatory response that may mimic acute infection.

Débridement Techniques

If surgical treatment is chosen, the hallmark of treatment is débridement. All nonviable and inert structures should be débrided to remove infected material and debris without destabilizing the bony structure. The goal is to convert a necrotic, hypoxic, infected wound to a viable wound. The critical judgment for the surgeon occurs when there is potentially infected bone, which might be partially vascularized, which is needed to maintain the structural stability of the bone. Sinus tracts that are present for longer than 1 year should be excised and sent for pathologic examination to rule out an occult carcinoma.[101] Soft tissue retraction should be minimal and flaps should not be created. There is a balance between leaving behind infection, which may result in recurrence, and resection and subsequent destabilization, which might necessitate extensive surgical reconstruction with its associated risks. The risk/benefit ratio must be evaluated in each case and should form the basis of thorough informed consent. Meticulous débridement is one of the most important initial steps in the treatment of infected bone and soft tissue. The limits of débridement have classically been determined by the "paprika sign," which is characterized by punctuate cortical or cancellous bleeding (Fig. 24-16). Efforts should be made to limit any periosteal stripping that may further devitalize the bone. Reactive new bone surrounding an area of chronic inflammation is living and sometimes does not require débridement.[20] Any sequestrated dead bone needs to be identi-

FIGURE 24-16 A close up of the paprika sign demonstrating bone vascularity.

fied and removed, whereas live bone may be preserved (Fig. 24-17). Rapid débridement can be achieved with a high speed burr but used with continuous irrigation to limit thermal necrosis. Laser Doppler flowmetry may facilitate accurate assessment of the microvascular status of bone, thereby identifying it for removal.[37] However, we have found this technique to have little benefit compared with visual inspection. Laser Doppler flowmetry is the only nondestructive in vivo method of blood flow determination that provides instantaneous determination of perfusion.

When the medullary canal is infected, intramedullary reaming is an effective method of débridement that preserves cortical stability. In general, one should overream the medullary canal by 2 mm. Excessive reaming may cause cortical necrosis and exacerbate infection by increasing the surface area of dead bone. Lavage can be performed from the reaming entry portal with the canal irrigator tips used in arthroplasty, with egress being provided through a vent or previous locking screw holes. Dull reamers and the generation of head should be avoided to prevent further cortical necrosis.

Intramedullary reaming of the medullary canal as a débridement technique has shown favorable results in the treatment of medullary osteomyelitis. In a cohort of 32 patients who had

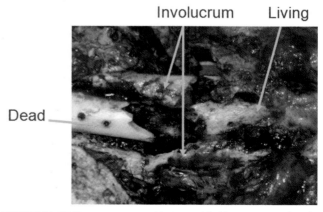

FIGURE 24-17 The appearance of bone at débridement. Note that the living bone has a pinkish hue and a petechial appearance indicating vascularity. The surrounding bone is involucrum and is also vascular. Resection of the involucrum should be at the judgment of the surgeon. The dead bone is clearly avascular and requires resection.

had an average of 3.2 surgical operations for osteomyelitis, Pape et al.[91] found that reaming of the medullary canal was successful in that 84% of patients were able to return to their previous profession and 97% were pain free. Evidence for the treatment of an infected intramedullary nail has been largely derived from observational data. Pommer et al.[96] found that reaming of an infected intramedullary canal resulted in eradication of infection in all patients when the infection occurred after primary intramedullary nailing compared with 62% of those with multiple operations before reaming and nailing. In another series, 25 patients with posttraumatic osteomyelitis, of whom 22 were treated with intramedullary reaming, were followed for at least 6 months.[87] Twenty-one of the 22 patients were free of any recurrent infection after an average period of 26 months. In a more recent study, 40 patients with chronic osteomyelitis were treated with intramedullary reaming, with only 4 patients having a recurrent infection.[88] If the medullary infection is too proximal or distal for a tight reamer fit, saucerization must be undertaken with the trough being created to débride the canal directly. Biomechanically, the most desirable shape for the trough is an oval with this shape resulting in minimal diminution of the bone's torsional strength. If segmental resection is undertaken or there is more than 30% loss of circumferential cortical contact, stabilization is required.

AUTHORS' PREFERRED METHODS

Initial Evaluation

The authors assume that any patient with a history of surgical fracture treatment, subsequent drainage, wound dehiscence, antibiotic treatment, or unplanned surgery may potentially have osteomyelitis. Many of these patients present with a paucity of medical records and other details, and often their own recollection of events is poor. Therefore, we presume infection until we have strong evidence to the contrary, particularly if symptoms occur in conjunction with fracture nonunion.

The host is classified first and efforts are made to optimize the host status. Improving nutrition and tissue oxygenation is important before embarking on surgical treatment. Occasionally, hyperbaric oxygen is helpful if it is available and can be tolerated by the patient. Ideally, the patient should stop smoking, but this is generally difficult to accomplish. However, we encourage patients to limit nicotine use because it is thought that nicotine causes local microvascular effects. Therefore, nicotine patches and gum, while useful for smoking cessation programs, may not be useful for local tissue optimization. Consultation with a primary care physician will help stabilize chronic medical conditions in many patients.

The limb is also evaluated for its ability to tolerate surgical intervention. Multiply operated limbs are B local by definition and heavily scarred and immobilized tissues may present risks for subsequent wound healing. Some patients may not be candidates or may not tolerate the extensive surgery that is required, and therefore compromises in treatment and patient expectations may be necessary. Many surgeons are now opting to treat exposed bone with a vacuum-assisted closure device. While this can often produce healthy granulating tissue bed, it should be remembered that the underlying bone is compromised and has a higher risk of nonunion

and infection. Another problem is that the soft tissue envelope tends to be adherent layer of scar over the bone, which may not tolerate secondary surgery well. Secondary surgery under these circumstances may well result in further infection. For this reason, we still advocate the use of healthy muscle or fascial flaps that not only help being an external blood supply to the surface of the bone but can better tolerate subsequent surgical procedures.

Diagnostic Evaluation

Initially, laboratory testing including assessment of the WBC, ESR, and CRP is undertaken. If these tests are negative and there is no further reason to suspect infection, then we treat the patient as having an aseptic nonunion but we will pay attention to our intraoperative findings. If there is any indication of infection despite normal laboratory findings, we obtain intraoperative cultures or undertake a biopsy and await results. One common scenario is a presumed aseptic case where routine cultures end up growing a few colonies of bacteria. The issue is whether the culture results represent a real infection or contamination. In these cases, we discuss the surgical findings with the infectious diseases specialist who explains their assessment of the validity of the cultures. If we believe that the risk of infection is low, we may cover the patient with a short course of culture-specific oral antibiotics. However, if we believe that the risk is high, we use a longer course of antibiotic treatment. We have found that even when there is little diagnostic and operative evidence of infection, patients may still develop later infection. We have no way of knowing if the subsequent infection was a resurgence of an old occult infection or a secondary infection from the recent surgical intervention.

In cases in which we suspect infection but do not know the organism, we will often remove the initial hardware and then take numerous cultures and biopsy samples of bone and soft tissue. We will then temporarily stabilize the bone in the least invasive manner using a cast, brace, or monolateral external fixator. Sometimes it is helpful to obtain two different sets of cultures. One set of cultures is obtained from the most suspicious areas during the initial part of the surgical procedure. The second set of cultures is obtained after débridement from the margins of the tissue bed. If this methodology is used, one can assess whether the débridement was adequate, especially if the initial cultures were positive. If we remain uncertain about the extent of the infection, we will attempt to use MRI with contrast to determine the intramedullary and soft tissue extent of the infection and then plan our treatment accordingly. Unfortunately, in a majority of cases, there is implanted metal, which makes the use of MRI less applicable. When possible, we use scintigraphic studies preoperatively despite their limitations. We have anecdotally noted significant variations in the accuracy of the readings between various radiologists and encourage working with a few radiologists who are interested and experienced with musculoskeletal infection. Because of our own findings and those in the literature, we now depend less on scintigraphy than on other signs and generally no longer use the red cell scan. The initial findings of PET scanning are encouraging.

Treatment

Once infection has been confirmed, an organism is identified, and the extent of the infection is delineated, we decide whether the goal is to cure the infection, suppress the infection, or recommend amputation. In compromised hosts, cure can usually only be achieved by complete excision of all the infected tissue, which often means that amputation is required. In healthier hosts, marginal resection leaving some bacteria behind or even intra-lesional resections when the infection is periarticular can lead to cure with appropriate antibiotic therapy. Generally speaking, our preference is to advise the patient that resection with a clean margin has the best chance of cure.

If bone resection and limb salvage are chosen, we follow the general principles that bone defects of 6 cm or greater require bone transport with distraction osteogenesis, whereas smaller defects can often undergo bone grafting. In the tibia, we prefer the posterolateral tibia-pro-fibula technique, but in some cases we will undertake central bone grafting. We try to avoid the exclusive use of demineralized bone matrix (DBM) and allograft because we have found a relatively low incidence of bone union. The low success rates using DBM products may be due to the poor vascularity found in such tissue beds and patients. Anecdotally, we have noted cases where patients present years after failed DBM grafting of the distal tibia, and during reoperation the original DBM material appears to be unchanged. This indicates failure of angiogenesis.

Bone morphogenetic proteins (BMPs) show significant promise. We have found that appropriate use of BMP as an inductor together with a common void filler such as allograft, tricalcium phosphate (TCP), or autograft has greatly enhanced the success of limb salvage in complex cases and is associated with little morbidity. The newer technique of graft harvest with the reamer-irrigator-aspirator (RIA) also holds promise for the treatment of large defects and our initial experience has been positive.[85] Further study on these techniques is required.

In general, the mainstay of reconstruction for complex infection remains the bone transport techniques described by Ilizarov. These are described in detail in Chapter 14. While this technique is not simple for either patient or surgeon, there are notable advantages compared with grafting techniques. These include the early development of regenerate bone soon after bone resection. If bone grafting is used, one must wait 8 weeks or longer as part of a staged reconstruction plan. Also, the effects of corticotomy include increasing blood flow in the limb for 4 to 6 weeks, and this may have a positive effect in infection cases. Most important, function is improved. The patient is encouraged to weight bear and to resume most activities of daily living. In many cases, patients can return to work, participate in recreational activities, and even swim. In cases where transport takes a considerable period or where transport has finished but one has to wait for maturation of regenerate, we have used long percutaneously inserted locked plates as an internal fixator that spans and protects maturing regenerate bone. This allows for early removal of the ring fixator (Fig. 24-18). Alternatively, some cases are amenable to transport over a nail (Fig. 24-19). We encourage surgeons who wish to treat bone infection to be familiar with Ilizarov's method and to seek out appropriate training.

A key component in the management of infection is functional rehabilitation. Often the patients are extremely debilitated from years of disability due to their condition. Treatments that permit early weight bearing and encourage range

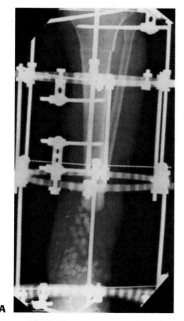 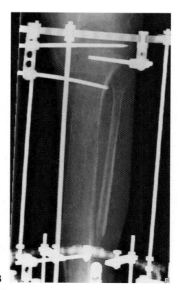 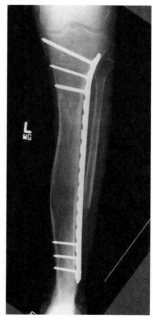

FIGURE 24-18 Conversion of external to internal fixation. **A.** A ring fixator has been used to stabilize the tibia after excision of infected bone. Antibiotic beads have been placed in the defect and a proximal corticotomy has been undertaken. **B.** Bone transport was successful but the regenerate was slow to mature. **C.** A locking plate was applied as an "internal fixator" using proximally and distally locked screws.

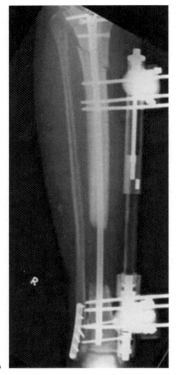
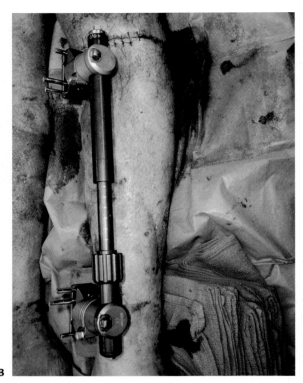
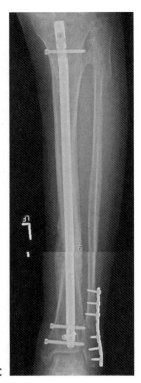

A   **B**   **C**

FIGURE 24-19 Bone transport over an intramedullary nail. **A.** A nail has been used to stabilize a tibia after resection of infected bone. A proximal corticotomy has been undertaken. **B.** The tibia/nail construct has been stabilized with an adjustable, dynamic monolateral external fixator. **C.** After successful bone transport, bone graft was used at the docking site to facilitate bone union. The nail supports the regenerate bone during maturation.

of motion in adjacent joints promote physical and psychological well-being. It is unusual for treatment to fail because patients have been walking on their limb. Usually failure is due to inadequate resection, inadequate stability, and inadequate biology.

It is also important to treat these patients in collaboration with colleagues. We depend heavily on the expertise of our colleagues in infectious disease, psychiatry, medicine, microvascular surgery, social work, and physical and occupational therapy. However, even with access to these experts and appropriate surgery, the success rate for the treatment of osteomyelitis is still significantly less than 100%. There is no doubt that prevention remains the best overall strategy.

ACKNOWLEDGMENTS

The authors acknowledge the efforts of Gabrielle M. Peacher, Research Coordinator, at the Denver Health Medical Center.

REFERENCES

1. Clin Orthop Relat Res. 1993;295.
2. Clin Orthop Relat Res. 2004;420.
3. Anglen JO. Comparison of soap and antibiotic solutions for irrigation of lower-limb open fracture wounds. A prospective, randomized study. J Bone Joint Surg Am 2005; 87A:1415–1422.
4. Anglen JO. Wound irrigation in musculoskeletal injury. J Am Acad Orthop Surg 2001; 9:219–226.
5. Anglen JO, Apostoles S, Christensen G, et al. The efficacy of various irrigation solutions in removing slime-producing *Staphylococcus*. J Orthop Trauma 1994;8:390–396.
6. Ash JM, Gilday DL. The futility of bone scanning in neonatal osteomyelitis: concise communication. J Nucl Med 1980;21:417–420.
7. Benjamin JB, Volz RG. Efficacy of a topical antibiotic irrigant in decreasing or eliminating bacterial contamination in surgical wounds. Clin Orthop Relat Res 1984:114–117.
8. Bhandari M, Schemitsch EH, Adili A, et al. High- and low-pressure pulsatile lavage of contaminated tibial fractures: an in vitro study of bacterial adherence and bone damage. J Orthop Trauma 1999;13:526–533.
9. Boerman OC, Rennen H, Oyen WJ, et al. Radiopharmaceuticals to image infection and inflammation. Semin Nucl Med 2001;31:286–295.
10. Borman TR, Johnson RA, Sherman FC. Gallium scintigraphy for diagnosis of septic arthritis and osteomyelitis in children. J Pediatr Orthop 1986;6:317–325.
11. Borrelli JJ, Prickett WD, Ricci WM. Treatment of nonunions and osseous defects with bone graft and calcium sulfate. Clin Orthop Relat Res 2003;411:245–254.
12. Boxma H, Broekhuizen T, Patka P, et al. Randomized controlled trial of single-dose antibiotic prophylaxis in surgical treatment of closed fractures: the Dutch Trauma Trial. Lancet 1996;347:1133–1137.
13. Boyd JI 3rd, Wongworawat MD. High-pressure pulsatile lavage causes soft tissue damage. Clin Orthop Relat Res 2004:13–17.
14. Bucholz HW, Engelbrecht H. Depot effects of various antibiotics mixed with palaces resins. Chirurg 1970;41:511–515.
15. Carsenti-Etesse H, Doyon F, Desplaces N, et al. Epidemiology of bacterial infection during management of open leg fractures. Eur J Clin Microbiol Infect Dis 1999;18: 315–323.
16. Casten DF, Nach RJ, Spinzia J. An experimental and clinical study of the effectiveness of antibiotic wound irrigation in preventing infection. Surg Gynecol Obstet 1964;118: 783–787.
17. Costerton JW. Introduction to biofilm. Int J Antimicrob Agents 1999;11:217–221.
18. Mangram AJ, Horan TC, Pearson ML, et al. Guideline for prevention of surgical site infection, 1999. Hospital Infection Control Practices Advisory Committee. Infect Control Hosp Epidemiol 1999;20:250–278.
19. Chacko TK, Zhuang H, Nakhoda KZ, et al. Applications of fluorodeoxyglucose positron emission tomography in the diagnosis of infection. Nucl Med Commun 2003;24: 615–624.
20. Cierny G. Treating chronic osteomyelitis: evolving our antibiotic protocols. Paper presented at Musculoskeletal Infection Society, August 2000.
21. Cierny G 3rd, Mader JT, Penninck JJ. A clinical staging system for adult osteomyelitis. Clin Orthop Relat Res 2003;7–24.
22. Cierny G, Mader JT, Pennick JJ. A clinical staging system for adult osteomyelitis. Contemp Orthop 1985;10:17–37.
23. Classen DC, Evans RS, Pestotnik SL, et al. The timing of prophylactic administration of antibiotics and the risk of surgical-wound infection. N Engl J Med 1992;326:281–286.
24. Collier BD. Personal communication.

25. Condie JD, Fergerson DJ. Experimental wound infections: contamination versus surgical technique. Surgery 1961;50:367.
26. Cunha B, Klein N. Bone and Joint Infections. In: Dee R, Hurst LC, Gruber MA, Kottmeier SA, eds. Principles of Orthopaedic Practice. 2nd ed. New York: McGraw-Hill, 1997:317–344.
27. Dankert J, Hogt AH, Feijen J. Biomedical polymers: bacterial adhesion, colonization, and infection. CRC Crit Rev Biocompat 1986;2:219–301.
28. Datz FL. Minutes in Nuclear Medicine. 2nd ed. New York: Appleton Century Crofts, 1983:82–85.
29. Datz FL. Infection imaging. Semin Nucl Med 1994;24:89–91.
30. Datz FL. Abdominal abscess detection: gallium, 111In-, and 99mTc-labeled leukocytes, and polyclonal and monoclonal antibodies. Semin Nucl Med 1996;26:51–64.
31. Datz FL, Seabold JE, Brown ML, et al. Procedure guideline for technetium-99m-HMPAO-labeled leukocyte scintigraphy for suspected infection/inflammation. Society of Nuclear Medicine. J Nucl Med 1997;38:987–990.
32. David R, Barron BJ, Madewell JE. Osteomyelitis, acute and chronic. Radiol Clin North Am 1987;25:1171–1201.
33. Dich VQ, Nelson JD, Haltalin KC. Osteomyelitis in infants and children. A review of 163 cases. Am J Dis Child 1975;129:1273–1278.
34. DiMaio FR, O'Halloran JJ, Quale JM. In vitro elution of ciprofloxacin from polymethylmethacrylate cement beads. J Orthop Res 1994;12:79–82.
35. Dirschl DR, Duff GP, Dahners LE, et al. High-pressure pulsatile lavage irrigation of intraarticular fractures: effects on fracture healing. J Orthop Trauma 1998;12:460–463.
36. Dirschl DR, Wilson FC. Topical antibiotic irrigation in the prophylaxis of operative wound infections in orthopedic surgery. Orthop Clin North Am 1991;22:419–426.
37. Duwelius PJ, Schmidt AH. Assessment of bone viability in patients with osteomyelitis: preliminary clinical experience with laser Doppler flowmetry. J Orthop Trauma 1992; 6:327–332.
38. Eckardt JJ, Wirganowicz PZ, Mar T. An aggressive surgical approach to the management of chronic osteomyelitis. Clin Orthop Relat Res 1994:229–239.
39. Eisenstein BI. The polymerase chain reaction. A new method of using molecular genetics for medical diagnosis. N Engl J Med 1990;322:178–183.
40. Esterhai J, Alavi A, Mandell GA, et al. Sequential technetium-99m/gallium-67 scintigraphic evaluation of subclinical osteomyelitis complicating fracture nonunion. J Orthop Res 1985;3:219–225.
41. Esterhai JL Jr, Goll SR, McCarthy KE, et al. Indium-111 leukocyte scintigraphic detection of subclinical osteomyelitis complicating delayed and nonunion long bone fractures: a prospective study. J Orthop Res 1987;5:1–6.
42. Evans RP, Nelson CL, Harrison BH. The effect of wound environment on the incidence of acute osteomyelitis. Clin Orthop Relat Res 1993:289–297.
43. Fink-Bennett D, Balon HR, Irwin R. Sequential technetium-99m sulfur colloid/indium-111 white blood cell imaging in macroglobulinemia of Waldenstrom. Clin Nucl Med 1990;15:389–391.
44. Fischer B, Vaudaux P, Magnin M, et al. Novel animal model for studying the molecular mechanisms of bacterial adhesion to bone-implanted metallic devices: role of fibronectin in *Staphylococcus aureus* adhesion. J Orthop Res 1996;14:914–920.
45. Gao Z, Tseng CH, Pei Z, et al. Molecular analysis of human forearm superficial skin bacterial biota. Proc Natl Acad Sci U S A 2007;104:2927–2932.
46. Gillespie WJ, Walenkamp G. Antibiotic prophylaxis for surgery for proximal femoral and other closed long bone fractures. Cochrane Database Syst Rev 2001;1(CD000244).
47. Gosselin RA, Roberts I, Gillespie WJ. Antibiotics for preventing infection in open limb fractures. Cochrane Database Syst Rev 2004(CD003764).
48. Graham GD, Lundy MM, Frederick RJ, et al. Predicting the cure of osteomyelitis under treatment: concise communication. J Nucl Med 1983;24:110–113.
49. Greidanus NV, Masri BA, Garbuz DS, et al. Use of erythrocyte sedimentation rate and C-reactive protein level to diagnose infection before revision total knee arthroplasty. A prospective evaluation. J Bone Joint Surg Am 2007;89A:1409–1416.
50. Gristina AG, Barth E, Webb LX. Microbial adhesion and the pathogenesis of biomaterial-centered infections. In: Gustilo RB, Tsukayama DT, eds. *Orthopaedic Infection*. Philadelphia: WB Saunders, 1989:3–25.
51. Haas DW, McAndrew MP. Bacterial osteomyelitis in adults: evolving considerations in diagnosis and treatment. Am J Med 1996;101:550–561.
52. Hartshorne MF, Graham G, Lancaster J, et al. Gallium-67/technetium-99m methylene diphosphonate ratio imaging: early rabbit osteomyelitis and fracture. J Nucl Med 1985; 26:272–277.
53. Hassinger SM, Harding G, Wongworawat MD. High-pressure pulsatile lavage propagates bacteria into soft tissue. Clin Orthop Relat Res 2005;439:27–31.
54. Hauet JR, Barge ML, Fajon O, et al. Sternal infection and retrosternal abscess shown on Tc-99m HMPAO-labeled leukocyte scintigraphy. Clin Nucl Med 2004;29:194–195.
55. Hauser CJ, Adams CA Jr, Eachempati SR. Surgical Infection Society guideline: prophylactic antibiotic use in open fractures: an evidence-based guideline. Surg Infect (Larchmt 2006;7:379–405.
56. Hoch RC, Rodriguez R, Manning T, et al. Effects of accidental trauma on cytokine and endotoxin production. Crit Care Med 1993;21:839–845.
57. Hoeffel DP, Hinrichs SH, Garvin KL. Molecular diagnostics for the detection of musculoskeletal infection. Clin Orthop Relat Res 1999:37–46.
58. Hughes DK. Nuclear medicine and infection detection: the relative effectiveness of imaging with ^{111}In-oxine-, ^{99m}Tc-HMPAO-, and ^{99m}Tc-stannous fluoride colloid-labeled leukocytes and with ^{67}Ga-citrate. J Nucl Med Technol 2003;31:196–201; quiz 203–194.
59. Jefferson KK. What drives bacteria to produce a biofilm? FEMS Microbiol Lett 2004; 236:163–173.
60. Keating JF, Blachut PA, O'Brien PJ, et al. Reamed nailing of open tibial fractures: does the antibiotic bead pouch reduce the deep infection rate? J Orthop Trauma 1996;10: 298–303.
61. Kelly PJ. Infected nonunion of the femur and tibia. Orthop Clin North Am 1984;15: 481–490.
62. Law HT, Flemming RH, Gilmore MF, et al. In vitro measurement and computer modelling of the diffusion of antibiotic in bone cement. J Biomed Eng 1986;8:149–155.
63. Lee J. Efficacy of cultures in the management of open fractures. Clin Orthop Relat Res 1997:71–75.
64. Luchette FA, Bone LB, Born CT, et al. EAST Practice Management Guidelines Work Group: practice management guidelines for prophylactic antibiotic use in open fractures. 2000.
65. Mackenzie EJ, Bosse MJ. Factors influencing outcome following limb-threatening lower limb trauma: lessons learned from the Lower Extremity Assessment Project (LEAP). J Am Acad Orthop Surg 2006;14(10 suppl):S205–S210.
66. Mackowiak PA, Jones SR, Smith JW. Diagnostic value of sinus-tract cultures in chronic osteomyelitis. JAMA 1978;239:2772–2775.
67. Mader JT, Calhoun J. Long-bone osteomyelitis diagnosis and management. Hosp Pract (Off Ed) 1994;29:71–76, 79, 83 passim.
68. Magnuson JE, Brown ML, Hauser MF, et al. In-111-labeled leukocyte scintigraphy in suspected orthopedic prosthesis infection: comparison with other imaging modalities. Radiology 1988;168:235–239.
69. Mann S. Molecular recognition in biomineralization. Nature 1988;332:119–124.
70. Marsh JL, Prokuski L, Biermann JS. Chronic infected tibial nonunions with bone loss. Conventional techniques versus bone transport. Clin Orthop Relat Res 1994:139–146.
71. May JW Jr, Jupiter JB, Weiland AJ, et al. Clinical classification of posttraumatic tibial osteomyelitis. J Bone Joint Surg Am 1989;71A:1422–1428.
72. McCarthy K, Velchik MG, Alavi A, et al. Indium-111-labeled white blood cells in the detection of osteomyelitis complicated by a pre-existing condition. J Nucl Med 1988; 29:1015–1021.
73. McKee MD, Wild LM, Schemitsch EH, et al. The use of an antibiotic-impregnated, osteoconductive, bioabsorbable bone substitute in the treatment of infected long bone defects: early results of a prospective trial. J Orthop Trauma 2002;16:622–627.
74. Meadows SE, Zuckerman JD, Koval KJ. Posttraumatic tibial osteomyelitis: diagnosis, classification, and treatment. Bull Hosp Jt Dis 1993;52:11–16.
75. Merkel KD, Brown ML, Dewanjee MK, et al. Comparison of indium-labeled-leukocyte imaging with sequential technetium-gallium scanning in the diagnosis of low-grade musculoskeletal sepsis. A prospective study. J Bone Joint Surg Am 1985;67A:465–476.
76. Merkel KD, Brown ML, Fitzgerald RH Jr. Sequential technetium-99m HMDP-gallium-67 citrate imaging for the evaluation of infection in the painful prosthesis. J Nucl Med 1986;27:1413–1417.
77. Modic MT, Feiglin DH, Piraino DW, et al. Vertebral osteomyelitis: assessment using MR. Radiology 1985;157:157–166.
78. Molina-Murphy IL, Palmer EL, Scott JA, et al. Polyclonal, nonspecific ^{111}In-IgG scintigraphy in the evaluation of complicated osteomyelitis and septic arthritis. Q J Nucl Med 1999;43:29–37.
79. Moscati RM, Mayrose J, Reardon RF, et al. A multicenter comparison of tap water versus sterile saline for wound irrigation. Acad Emerg Med 2007;14:404–409.
80. Moussa FW, Anglen JO, Gehrke JC, et al. The significance of positive cultures from orthopedic fixation devices in the absence of clinical infection. Am J Orthop 1997;26: 617–620.
81. Moussa FW, Gainor BJ, Anglen JO, et al. Disinfecting agents for removing adherent bacteria from orthopaedic hardware. Clin Orthop Relat Res 1996:255–262.
82. Murray CK, Hinkle MK, Yun HC. History of infections associated with combat-related injuries. J Trauma 2008;64(3 suppl):S221–231.
83. Murray CK, Hsu JR, Solomkin JS, et al. Prevention and management of infections associated with combat-related extremity injuries. J Trauma 2008;64(3 suppl):S239–251.
84. Naylor P, Jennings R, Myrvik Q. Antibiotic sensitivity of biomaterial-adherent *Staphylococcus epidermidis*. Orthop Trans 1988;12:524–525.
85. Newman JT, Stahel PF, Smith WR, et al. A new minimally invasive technique for large volume bone graft harvest for treatment of fracture nonunions. Orthopedics 2008;31: 257–261.
86. Nichols WW, Dorrington SM, Slack MP, et al. Inhibition of tobramycin diffusion by binding to alginate. Antimicrob Agents Chemother 1988;32:518–523.
87. Oschner PE, Gösele A, Buess P. The value of intramedulary reaming in the treatment of chronic osteomyelitis of long bones. Arch Orthop Trauma 1990;190:341–347.
88. Ochsner PE, Brunazzi MG. Intramedullary reaming and soft tissue procedures in treatment of chronic osteomyelitis of long bones. Orthopedics 1994;17:433–440.
89. Ostermann PA, Henry SL, Seligson D. [Value of adjuvant local antibiotic administration in therapy of open fractures. A comparative analysis of 704 consecutive cases.] Langenbecks Arch Chir 1993;378:32–36.
90. Palestro CJ, Mehta HH, Patel M, et al. Marrow versus infection in the Charcot joint: indium-111 leukocyte and technetium-99m sulfur colloid scintigraphy. J Nucl Med 1998;39:346–350.
91. Pape HC, Zwipp H, Regel G, et al. [Chronic treatment refractory osteomyelitis of long tubular bones—possibilities and risks of intramedullary boring.] Unfallchirurg 1995; 98:139–144.
92. Patzakis MJ, Wilkins J. Factors influencing infection rate in open fracture wounds. Clin Orthop Relat Res 1989:36–40.
93. Peters AM. The utility of [99mTc]HMPAO-leukocytes for imaging infection. Semin Nucl Med 1994;24:110–127.
94. Petrisor B, Jeray K, Schemitsch E, et al. Fluid lavage in patients with open fracture wounds (FLOW): an international survey of 984 surgeons. BMC Musculoskelet Disord 2008;23:7.
95. Poirier JY, Garin E, Derrien C, et al. Diagnosis of osteomyelitis in the diabetic foot with a 99mTc-HMPAO leucocyte scintigraphy combined with a 99mTc-MDP bone scintigraphy. Diabetes Metab 2002;28(6 Pt 1):485–490.
96. Pommer A, David A, Richter J, et al. [Intramedullary boring in infected intramedullary nail osteosyntheses of the tibia and femur.] Unfallchirurg 1998;101:628–633.
97. Quinn SF, Murray W, Clark RA, et al. MR imaging of chronic osteomyelitis. J Comput Assist Tomogr 1988;12:113–117.
98. Rang M. The Story of Orthopaedics. Philadelphia: WB Saunders, 2000.
99. Rosenstein BD, Wilson FC, Funderburk CH. The use of bacitracin irrigation to prevent infection in postoperative skeletal wounds. An experimental study. J Bone Joint Surg Am 1989;71A:427–430.
100. Rubin RH, Fischman AJ, Needleman M, et al. Radio-labeled, nonspecific, polyclonal human immunoglobulin in the detection of focal inflammation by scintigraphy: comparison with gallium-67 citrate and technetium-99m-labeled albumin. J Nucl Med 1989;30:385–389.
101. Sankaran-Kutty M, Corea JR, Ali MS, et al. Squamous cell carcinoma in chronic osteomyelitis. Report of a case and review of the literature. Clin Orthop Relat Res 1985: 264–267.

102. Schauwecker DS. Osteomyelitis: diagnosis with In-111-labeled leukocytes. Radiology 1989;171:141–146.

103. Schauwecker DS, Braunstein EM, Wheat LJ. Diagnostic imaging of osteomyelitis. Infect Dis Clin North Am 1990;4:441–463.

104. Schiesser M, Stumpe KD, Trentz O, et al. Detection of metallic implant-associated infections with FDG PET in patients with trauma: correlation with microbiologic results. Radiology 2003;226:391–398.

105. Schmidt AH, Swiontkowski MF. Pathophysiology of infections after internal fixation of fractures. J Am Acad Orthop Surg 2000;8:285–291.

106. Seabold JE, Flickinger FW, Kao SC, et al. Indium-111-leukocyte/technetium-99m-MDP bone and magnetic resonance imaging: difficulty of diagnosing osteomyelitis in patients with neuropathic osteoarthropathy. J Nucl Med 1990;31:549–556.

107. Seabold JE, Nepola JV, Conrad GR, et al. Detection of osteomyelitis at fracture nonunion sites: comparison of two scintigraphic methods. AJR Am J Roentgenol 1989;152:1021–1027.

108. Seeley SK, Seeley JV, Telehowski P, et al. Volume and surface area study of tobramycin-polymethacrylate beads. Clin Orthop Relat Res 2004:298–303.

109. Segura AB, Munoz A, Brulles YR, et al. What is the role of bone scintigraphy in the diagnosis of infected joint prostheses? Nucl Med Commun 2004;25:527–532.

110. Svoboda SJ, Bice TG, Gooden HA, et al. Comparison of bulb syringe and pulsed lavage irrigation with use of a bioluminescent musculoskletal wound model. J Bone Joint Surg Am 2006;88A:2167–2174.

111. Tang JS, Gold RH, Bassett LW, et al. Musculoskeletal infection of the extremities: evaluation with MR imaging. Radiology 1988;166(1 Pt 1):205–209.

112. Tehranzadeh J, Wang F, Mesgarzadeh M. Magnetic resonance imaging of osteomyelitis. Crit Rev Diagn Imaging 1992;33:495–534.

113. Thomas LC, Gidding HF, Ginn AN, et al. Development of a real-time *Staphylococcus aureus* and MRSA (SAM-) PCR for routine blood culture. J Microbiol Methods 2007; 68:296–302.

114. Toguchi A, Siano M, Burkart M, et al. Genetics of swarming motility in *Salmonella enterica serovar typhimurium*: critical role for lipopolysaccharide. J Bacteriol 2000;182:6308–6321.

115. Toh CL, Jupiter JB. The infected nonunion of the tibia. Clin Orthop Relat Res 1995:176–191.

116. Tompkins LS. The use of molecular methods in infectious diseases. N Engl J Med 1992;327:1290–1297.

117. Tsukayama DT. Pathophysiology of posttraumatic osteomyelitis. Clin Orthop Relat Res 1999:22–29.

118. Valenziano CP, Chattar-Cora D, O'Neill A, et al. Efficacy of primary wound cultures in long bone open extremity fractures: are they of any value? Arch Orthop Trauma Surg 2002;122:259–261.

119. Van Nostrand D, Abreu SH, Callaghan JJ. et al. In-111-labeled white blood cell uptake in noninfected closed fracture in humans: prospective study. Radiology 1988;167:495–498.

120. Wald ER, Mirro R, Gartner JC. Pitfalls on the diagnosis of acute osteomyelitis by bone scan. Clin Pediatr (Phila) 1980;19:597–601.

121. Waldvogel FA, Medoff G, Swartz MN. Osteomyelitis: a review of clinical features, therapeutic considerations, and unusual aspects. N Engl J Med 1970;282:198–206.

122. Watnick P, Kolter R. Biofilm, city of microbes. J Bacteriol 2000;182:2675–2679.

123. Weiland AJ, Moore JR, Daniel RK. The efficacy of free tissue transfer in the treatment of osteomyelitis. J Bone Joint Surg Am 1984;66A:181–193.

124. Wheat J. Diagnostic strategies in osteomyelitis. Am J Med 1985;78:218–224.

125. Wolf G, Aigner RM, Schwarz T. Diagnosis of bone infection using 99m Tc-HMPAO labelled leukocytes. Nucl Med Commun 2001;22:1201–1206.

126. Ziran BH, Rao N, Hall RA. A dedicated team approach enhances outcomes of osteomyelitis treatment. Clin Orthop Relat Res 2003;414:31–36.

127. Ziran BH, Smith WR, Morgan SJ. Use of calcium-based demineralized bone matrix/allograft for nonunions and posttraumatic reconstruction of the appendicular skeleton: preliminary results and complications. J Trauma 2007;63:1324–1328.

128. Zuluaga AF, Galvis W, Jaimes F, et al. Lack of microbiological concordance between bone and nonbone specimens in chronic osteomyelitis: an observational study. BMC Infect Dis 2002;2:8.

25

PRINCIPLES OF NONUNION TREATMENT

Brett R. Bolhofner and William M. Ricci

INTRODUCTION

Bone healing is a simple but endlessly complex biologic phenomenon. Bone begets bone. Most other tissues in the human body can only manage to heal with scar, but bone heals by forming new bone. Bone healing may be affected or interrupted in many ways. Most simply put, nonunion occurs when a fracture has failed to heal in the expected time. Delayed union occurs when a fracture has not completely healed in the time expected. While this may seem self evident, identifying when healing occurs can be elusive. Establishment of a nonunion can be defined based on a lack of complete bone healing in a specified time frame, commonly 6 to 8 months, but this is arbitrary.[114] In a more general sense, nonunion occurs when further progress in healing will not occur without intervention.[16,18,82]

In delayed union, clinical and radiographic evidence of healing is lagging behind what would ordinarily be present in a similar fracture in the same bone. This, of course, will further depend on not only the particular bone involved, but also the anatomic region, the fracture pattern, and the method of treatment. Comparison to healing times reported in the literature for similar fractures along with clinical experience is necessary to identify a delayed union. The potential inconsistencies in this analysis are confounded by the mere fact that attempts to define a cellular process by reviewing radiographic data is inherently inaccurate. It has been suggested that cessation of the periosteal and not the endosteal healing response prior to fracture bridging may define delayed union at the cellular level.[84]

Nonunion, while often obvious in retrospect, is often difficult to define and diagnose in real time. The time for distal radial metaphyseal bone to be considered nonunited will be different than the hard diaphyseal bone of the tibial shaft. Both clinical and radiographic findings are necessary for the diagnosis of nonunion, but these signs may not be evident as primary and secondary healing may be occurring simultaneously. On a cellular level, nonunion occurs when there is cessation of a reparative process antecedent to bony union.[49,133]

Operative treatment may further complicate the diagnosis and definition due to failure of hardware or the lack thereof in the presence of nonunion. While hardware failure may make the diagnosis obvious, with newer implants and techniques (locked nails and plates) a paucity of clinical symptoms and radiographic findings may persist long after progress in healing has ceased.

PATHOPHYSIOLOGY AND ETIOLOGY OF NONUNION

Failure of an acute fracture to progress to timely union may be caused by a myriad of factors leading to an estimated prevalence of 2.5%.[127] Some of these factors are and some are not within the surgeon's control. The risk for nonunion increases with increasing energy of injury with the incidence of nonunion approaching 20% in the presence of open fractures and extensive soft tissue injury.[127] The characteristics of the original injury, the patients ability (or inability) to generate a normal healing response to the particular injury, the mechanical and biological environment created by the chosen treatment method, and the presence or absence of associated infection are among the factors that can influence the rate and the likelihood of uncomplicated and timely fracture healing.

Fracture Specific Factors Related to Nonunion

The involved bone and the specific location of the fracture influence the innate ability for fracture healing. This is related, in large part, to the associated vascular supply to the fracture region. The talar neck, the metaphyseal-diaphyseal junction of the fifth metatarsal, the femoral neck, and the scaphoid are examples of anatomic sites that have relatively limited or watershed vascular supplies that are potentially cut off by fracture. Hence, fractures in these sites have a propensity for healing complications or the development of osteonecrosis. On the other hand, the metaphyseal regions of most other long bones as well as the pelvic bones and scapula have a robust vascular supply, and in the absence of other complicating factors, usually heal reliably. The diaphyseal regions of long bones, especially the tibia, fall between these extremes. The diaphyseal region of bone has a relatively limited blood supply, and therefore diaphyseal fractures usually require longer periods of time to achieve union than metaphyseal fractures.

Independent of the anatomic location of the fracture, the degree of bone and surrounding soft tissue injury influences the healing potential. High-energy fractures cause devascularization of the fractured bone in the form of periosteal stripping or disruption of the endosteal blood supply or both. This is clearly evident with open fractures (Fig. 25-1), but internal soft tissue stripping can occur equally in closed fractures. In addition, severe high-energy injuries can leave the bone ends nonviable either from immediate cell death or via the process of apoptosis.[15] Bone loss, either traumatically associated with an open fracture or the result of surgical débridement, is a potential precursor of nonunion. Another reason nonunion is associated with open fractures is by virtue of providing a source of bacterial contamination and potential for infection.

Host Factors Related to Nonunion

Host factors play a major role in the potential for alterations in fracture healing. Specific conditions that are most notably considered to affect fracture healing are diabetes mellitus and smoking.[46,89] It is postulated that the microvascular disease and perhaps reduced immunocompetence and neuropathy associated with the diabetic condition leads to alterations in bone metabolism leading to delayed fracture healing.[104] Diabetes also poses greater risks for soft tissue healing complications as well as an increased risk for infection after surgical fracture manage-

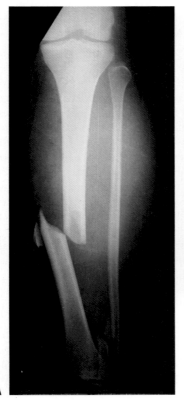

FIGURE 25-1 Anteroposterior radiograph **(A)** of an open tibial shaft fracture with associated periosteal stripping seen in the clinical photograph **(B)**.

ment.[69] Smoking has been associated with altered acute fracture healing as well as failure of nonunion treatment.[23,80,89] Evidence suggests that the vasoconstrictive properties of nicotine inhibit tissue differentiation and the normal angiogenic responses in the early stages of fracture healing and that nicotine directly interferes with osteoblast function.[31,137,150] Nicotine supplementation as part of a smoking cessation program, therefore, should also be considered detrimental to bone healing.

Other chronic health conditions, although not directly shown to negatively impact fracture healing, empirically can lead to altered healing responses. Any state leading to malnutrition or immunosuppression, including steroid use, rheumatoid disease, and malignancy, can negatively impact the body's healing response, including fracture healing. Nonsteroidal anti-inflammatory medications, once used ubiquitously to control postfracture pain, have been implicated in inducing fracture nonunion through inhibition of angiogenesis.[91] These medications are now used much more sparingly in the setting of acute fracture or nonunion repair, especially in the initial weeks after injury, a time corresponding to the inflammatory phase of fracture healing. Previously irradiated bone or bone actively infiltrates with tumor also are at high risk for delayed or nonunion. Although children have higher healing potential than adults, whether advanced age (once physeal closure has occurred) is an independent risk factor for nonunion is unclear.[54] Advanced age was found to be an independent risk factor for nonunion in patients with acute clavicle fracture,[112] but many other prognostic studies have failed to identify age as a risk factor for nonunion in other anatomic locations.[10,30]

Treatment Factors Related to Nonunion

Adequate mechanical stability is required to create an environment conducive to fracture healing. Unfortunately, the adequacy of stability is very difficult to define and even more difficult to quantify. In fact, adequate stability depends, to a great extent, on the chosen method of stabilization. The natural process of bone healing, commonly referred to as secondary bone healing, through the formation of callus accommodates for some motion at the fracture site. In nature, fractures can heal with no immobilization, but nonunion can also result. It is clear, however, that fractures heal more reliably when immobilized.

Indeed, most fractures heal with the relatively limited stability provided by cast immobilization. Rigid internal fixation, as provided by compression plating techniques, represents the other end of the stability spectrum associated with fracture care. Such fractures heal without callus via primary bone healing, a relatively unnatural, yet often successful, strategy.

Regardless of whether the chosen treatment method relies on primary or secondary bone healing, improper technique can lead to inadequate bone healing. A poorly applied cast or one applied to a severely lipomatous extremity, for instance, may provide inadequate stability resulting in excessive fracture site motion permitting the development of a nonunion. Relatively rigid internal fixation techniques that fail to achieve bone-to-bone contact and compression (i.e., ones with gaps across the fracture) do not support the primary bone healing process, which relies upon direct remodeling of bone via cutting cones that traverse the fracture, and can also lead to nonunion (Fig. 25-2). Whereas modern surgical techniques emphasize biologically friendly tissue handling, older techniques that included anatomic reduction of individual fracture fragments often required soft tissue stripping from about the fracture site and led to a suboptimal environment for fracture healing. Whether fracture reduction is direct or indirect, or the fixation construct is relatively stable or rigid, minimizing soft tissue disruption is paramount to maximizing the healing potential and minimizing other complications that relate to devitalization of bone, namely infection.

Infection as a Factor Related to Nonunion

Fractures can heal in the face of infection; however, controlled infection may slow the healing process and uncontrolled osteomyelitis can inhibit normal fracture healing altogether. The inflammatory process in response to infection may inhibit fracture healing by causing excessive remodeling and osteolysis.[45] Tissue necrosis may be accelerated by infection but histologic evidence indicates that soft tissue disruption caused by the initial trauma and surgical insult are the primary events leading to bone necrosis in cases of osteomyelitis associated with fracture.[97] Loose dead bone and bone pieces demarcated by osteoclastic activity are eventually transformed into sequestra.[97] Infection not only predisposes to nonunion, but makes nonunion repair substan-

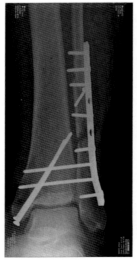 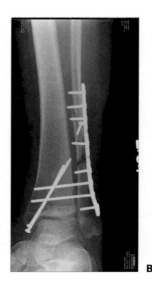 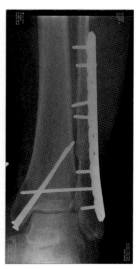

FIGURE 25-2 A. Postoperative radiograph showing a fibular gap. **B.** At 3 months postoperative, the gap persists. **C.** Repair of the atrophic nonunion with bone graft yielded union.

A   B   C

tially more complex, often requiring multistaged treatment protocols.

CLASSIFICATION OF NONUNION

Nonunions may be divided into septic and aseptic groups. Septic nonunion implies that there is an infectious process at the site while aseptic nonunion occurs in the absence of infection. Further classification of nonunion is an attempt to relate the radiographic picture to the biologic occurrences, or lack thereof, at the fracture site. Both septic and aseptic nonunions may be further classified as atrophic, oligotrophic, and hypertrophic as well as a frank pseudarthrosis.

Atrophic nonunion, also referred to as avascular, nonviable, or avital indicates a poor healing response with little or no bone forming cells.[87,90] This is typically manifested radiographically by absence of any bone reaction (see Fig. 25-2). This lack of healing response may be due to the injury (e.g., an open fracture), subsequent surgical treatment (e.g., significant surgical

stripping of soft tissues about the fracture site), or host issues (e.g., diabetes or smoking).[122] Strategies for the treatment of atrophic nonunions generally include a method to provide a biologic stimulus to the fracture site.

At the other end of the spectrum of abnormal healing responses is the hypertrophic nonunion, also referred to as a hypervascular, viable, or vital nonunion. Associated is an adequate healing response and good vascularity.[87,90] These fractures lack adequate immobilization or stability to progress to union. The viable healing fibrocartilage cannot mineralize due to unfavorable mechanical factors (strain/stress) at the fracture site.[122] This is manifested radiographically by callus formation, usually abundant, with an interceding area of fibrocartilage lacking mineral and thus appearing dark on standard radiographs. Successful treatment of hypertrophic nonunions utilizes methods to provide the stability required for the adequate biologic response to come to completion. Unlike atrophic nonunions, biologic stimulus is not a treatment necessity (Fig. 25-3).

Oligotrophic nonunions probably represent a condition somewhere between atrophic and hypertrophic. They are viable,

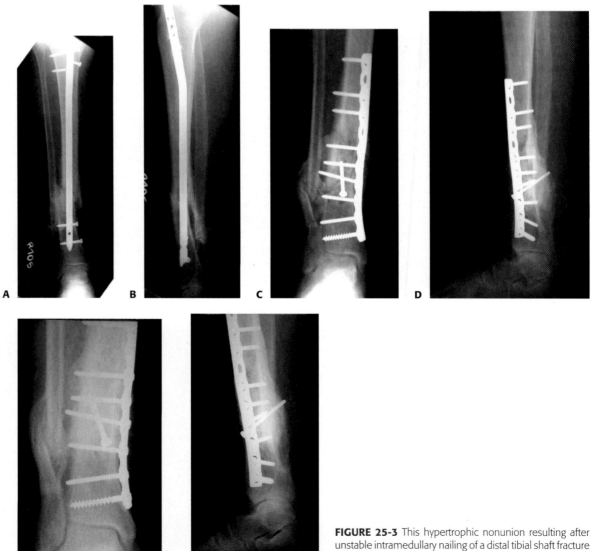

FIGURE 25-3 This hypertrophic nonunion resulting after unstable intramedullary nailing of a distal tibial shaft fracture **(A,B)** was treated simply with plate and screw fixation **(C,D)** and healed without the need for bone graft **(E,F)**.

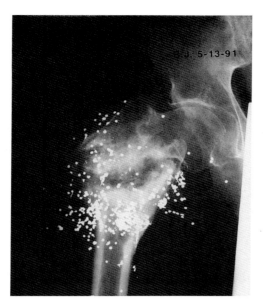

FIGURE 25-4 A pseudarthrosis 20 years after shotgun injury and nonoperative treatment.

but usually manifest a minimal radiographic healing reaction (callus) often due to inadequate approximation of the fracture surfaces. A bone scan may be necessary to distinguish this type of nonunion from a frankly atrophic one. The oligotrophic situation will manifest increased uptake whereas the atrophic nonunion would be relative cold.[129]

Pseudarthrosis (Fig. 25-4) has properties of a hypertrophic nonunion due to excessive and chronic motion, and a synovial lined cavity containing synovial fluid much like an actual joint may be present. The medullary ends are usually sealed and an interceding cold cleft can be seen on bone scan.

EVALUATION AND DIAGNOSIS OF NONUNION

The diagnosis of nonunion is an inexact science even when ignoring the temporal issues of defining when a fracture should or should not yet be considered a nonunion. At any given point, determining if a fracture is united rather than if it is not is a straightforward but not a simple task. Bone healing is a progressive process wherein the strength of the reparative process, under usual circumstances, gradually increases over a long period of time. Clinical attempts to define union are hampered by utilizing indirect means to evaluate the strength of the healing process. Furthermore, even if the integrity of the healing bone could be accurately evaluated, neither the baseline strength or stiffness of the uninjured bone nor the fraction of that value required to define union are known. Given these limitations, indirect means are required in the evaluation of fracture healing and in determining if union has occurred.

Depending on the diagnostic modality being used, the diagnosis of a nonunion may be one of inclusion or exclusion. That is, when evidence of union exists, nonunion is ruled out. Some diagnostic modalities such as a bone scan may directly identify nonunion by a positive test result. In usual clinical practice, the information gathered from many modalities, such as history, physical exam, radiographs, and other special tests, is used in concert to determine the presence or absence of fracture union.

History and Physical Examination

History and physical examination are critically important to both the initial evaluation of the patient being scrutinized to determine the presence or absence of fracture union after an acute fracture, as well as in the assessment of a patient with an established nonunion. The history of the events surrounding the index injury provides insight into any deviations from the expected course of fracture healing for the particular fracture being evaluated. This information may heighten the index of suspicion not only for nonunion but also for associated problems such as infection. A particularly high-energy injury may portend a higher risk for healing complications. Similarly, the nature of the associated soft tissue injury maybe prognostic for delayed bone healing. If the fracture was open, delayed fracture healing is expected and infection becomes more common.

The details of prior treatments and subsequent recovery complete the history of the problem at hand. It is critical to uncover the type and timing of the initial treatments and any subsequent interventions. The indication for, the specific details of, and the result of any additional procedures should be identified. Specifically, it is critical to know if secondary débridement procedures were done as planned prophylactic procedures or for the treatment of a documented infection. Causative organisms, antibiotic susceptibilities, and details of antibiotic treatments should be elucidated. The clinical response to such treatments can provide valuable insight into future responses to similar treatment. The nature of prior surgical procedures aimed at augmenting fracture healing provides useful information regarding the diagnosis and helps direct future treatments. It is important to distinguish prior hardware removal performed for pain from similar procedures done to promote fracture healing such as nail dynamization. With a history of prior bone grafting, it should be clarified if the graft was autologous or from another source. If autologous, the prior harvest site should be confirmed by physical examination so that if a future graft harvest is contemplated, a different site can be prepared. If there was treatment with a bone growth stimulator, such devices may be incorporated in future treatments with little or no additional patient expense.

Of critical importance to the diagnosis of a nonunion and the potential need for, and utility of, additional operative intervention is the patient's individual response to prior treatment, their current level of disability, time constraints for future weight-bearing restrictions, and occupational needs. With all other factors being equal, the patient with a progressive increase in pain and disability from a nonunited fracture is more likely to benefit from surgical intervention than a patient with minimal or improving symptoms. Conversely, the patient with clear radiographic signs of nonunion but with limited pain and marginal functional disability may be more suited for less invasive treatment means such as external bone growth stimulation especially if operative management would provide untimely loss of employment (Fig. 25-5).

The typical signs and symptoms of nonunion are a combination of pain, tenderness, and detectible motion at the site of fracture. It should be noted that symptoms of nonunion can be masked in patients with relatively stable or rigid fixation such

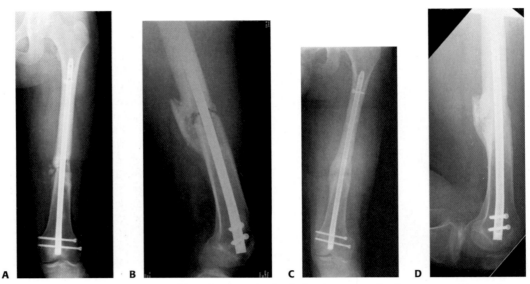

FIGURE 25-5 Anteroposterior and lateral radiographs **(A,B)** showing a nonunion in a 27-year-old man 6 months after IM nailing of a middiaphyseal femur fracture. At this point, the patient was fully weight bearing with minimal pain and an ultrasound external bone stimulator was applied 20 minutes daily. Six months later and without further surgical intervention, the nonunion is healed **(C,D)**.

as is seen with locked plate constructs. It is not uncommon for such patients to present with an acute onset of pain and disability after a long time period associated with full weight bearing with no or a relative paucity of symptoms (Fig. 25-6). In these circumstances, acute failure of the hardware is often the cause of the new symptoms.

Plain Radiographic Diagnosis of Nonunion

Plain radiographs are used ubiquitously in the evaluation of fractures as they provide a timely, accurate, and inexpensive means to diagnose an acute fracture. The utility of plain radio-

graphs in evaluating fracture union is less clear. Using plain radiographs, the diagnosis of nonunion is very often arrived at by excluding union.

The diagnosis of fracture union by plain radiographs is typically defined by the presence of bridging callus across the fracture. Whether circumferential bridging, as evidenced by bridging across all four cortices seen on orthogonal radiographs, is required to accurately diagnosis union is unclear. The orthopaedic literature is conflicted with regard to this requirement. Many studies define union as healing across only 2 or 3, rather than 4, cortices on the two orthogonal views. Although identifying the

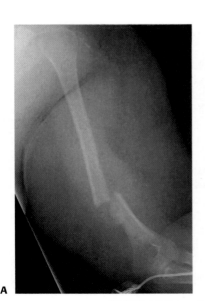 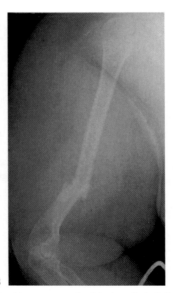 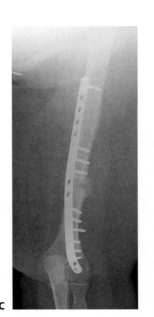 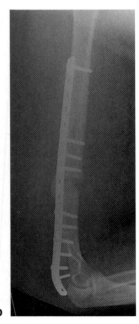

FIGURE 25-6 A patient with an open distal humeral shaft fracture **(A,B)** was treated with irrigation and débridement and plate fixation **(C,D)**.   (*continues*)

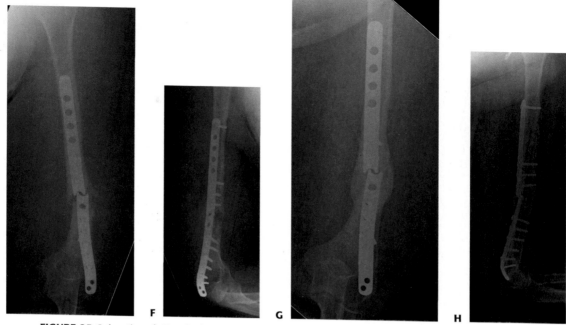

FIGURE 25-6 (*continued*) Despite having a nonunion at 6 months, she was functioning well and without pain due to the stability provided by the plate. An acute increase in pain occurred as a result of fracture of the plate **(E,F)**. With immobilization, this fracture healed in slight varus without further surgery **(G,H)**.

number of healed cortices may seem straightforward, in practice this is a very subjective and imprecise exercise especially in the presence of implants that obscure visualization. Furthermore, it is often difficult to know if the radiograph and fracture are coplanar. When not, fracture gaps may be disguised by overlying bone (Fig. 25-7). Minor variances in the angle of the radiograph can completely disguise a nonunion (Fig. 25-8).

The location and type of fracture and the relative stability of the fixation method creates great variations in the expected biologic healing response and therefore the radiographic ap-

pearance of union. Simple diaphyseal fractures fixed anatomically with rigid compression plate techniques that promote primary bone healing without fracture callus may look nearly identical at healing as they did immediately after fixation (Fig. 25-9). Under these circumstances, accurate diagnosis of union may be difficult, but lack of union may be directly or indirectly evident. Direct evidence is a fracture gap seen on a radiograph taken coplanar with the fracture (see Figs. 25-7B and 25-8B). In the absence of direct evidence of nonunion, plain radiographs should be carefully scrutinized for indirect evidence of a lack

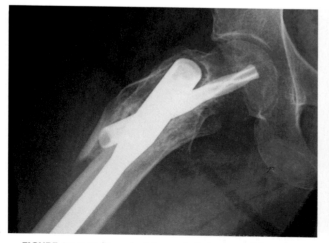
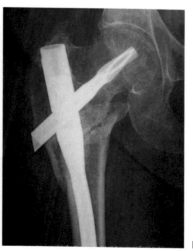

FIGURE 25-7 Radiographs taken out of plane may fail to identify a nonunion. Six months after IM nailing of a reverse obliquity intertrochanteric femur fracture, a lateral radiograph **(A)** reveals no persistent fracture line because the x-ray beam is not coplanar with the nonunion. The anteroposterior radiograph **(B)** is coplanar with the fracture and clearly demonstrates the nonunion. Indirect evidence of nonunion is evident on the lateral view **(A)** in the form of motion artifact around the nail.

of healing. Progressively loosened or broken implants indicate persistent motion at the fracture site. More subtle findings are motion artifacts seen in bone at or around the margin of seemingly stable implants or fractured screws without complete loss of fixation (Fig. 25-10). Judicious utilization of other imaging methods helps to confirm the diagnosis of nonunion when only indirect evidence is present using plain radiographs.

Computed Tomography Scans to Diagnose Nonunion

Computed tomography (CT) offers an opportunity to more accurately delineate bony anatomy at the site of a suspected nonunion. Modern CT scans can be reformatted in high quality in any plane. This allows an image orientation precisely optimized to evaluate the potential lack of bridging bone, eliminating the major shortcoming of plain radiography. CT scans have been shown to be highly sensitive (100%) for detecting tibial nonunion.[11] The limitation of CT, however, is the relative lack of specificity (62%), that can lead to surgery in patients who actually have healed fractures (Fig. 25-11).[11] CT may be useful in providing a quantitative evaluation of fracture healing and stability. In one study, patients with less than 25% bridging of the circumference of bone were found to be at high risk (37.5%) for clinical failure of fracture union, whereas those with greater than 25% bridging had only 9.7% failure.[29]

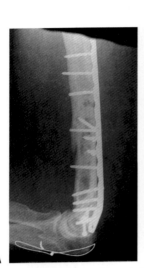
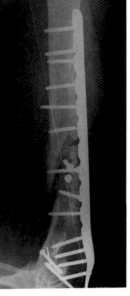

FIGURE 25-8 A lateral radiograph **(A)** fails to clearly identify a nonunion 8 months after open reduction and internal fixation of a distal humeral shaft fracture, whereas a slightly oblique projection **(B)** shows the nonunion clearly.

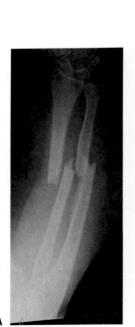
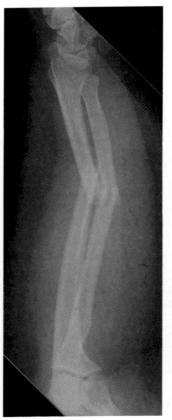
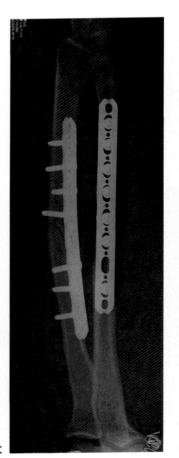
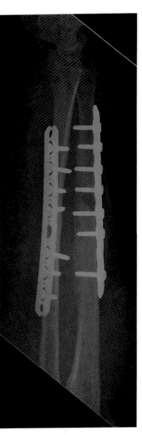

FIGURE 25-9 A patient with open radius and ulna shaft fractures **(A,B)** was treated with open reduction and internal fixation of both fractures **(C,D)**.

(continues)

Various other types of scans, individually or in combination, have been used in attempts to differentiate simple nonunion from those that are complicated by infection. Increased blood flow and blood pool as demonstrated during the first and second phases of a three-phase bone scan are consistent with the inflammatory reaction seen with infection but are not pathognomonic for infection. The combined use of a Tc-99m and gallium-67 scans has produced inconsistent results for accurately detecting infection at the site of nonunion.[36,121] In contrast to other forms of nonunion, a synovial pseudoarthrosis correlates with the presence of a cold cleft between two intense areas of uptake on scintigraphy.[37]

TREATMENT OF NONUNIONS

Nonoperative Treatment

Nonoperative interventions may accelerate the existing healing process or promote additional healing that would otherwise not have taken place. Such strategies may be most successful for promoting a delayed union to proceed to union, but healing of established nonunion has also been reported for some nonoperative treatments. The attractiveness of nonoperative treatment is essentially the absence of surgical complications.

Nonoperative treatment can be divided into direct and indirect intervention. Direct intervention implies application of treatment directly to the nonunited bone. Examples include electrical stimulation and ultrasound. Indirect intervention implies institution of treatment directed more towards the patient as a whole. Examples of indirect intervention would include maximizing nutrition, alteration of certain medications, and smoking cessation (Table 25-1).

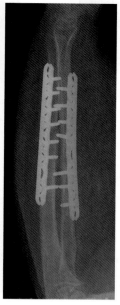

FIGURE 25-9 (*continued*) **E,F.** The simple ulnar fracture was treated with compression plating technique and healed without callus formation.

Bone Scan to Detect Nonunion

Technetium-99m methylene diphosphonate (Tc-99m) bone scintigraphy can be used to help diagnose nonunion, but a positive result can be relatively nonspecific. On the bone scan, the vast majority of nonunions show intense tracer uptake at the fracture site, as do fractures undergoing normal healing.[121]

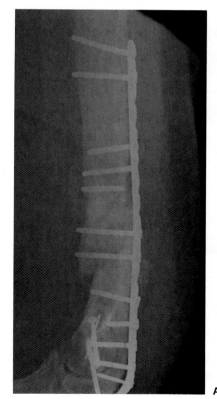
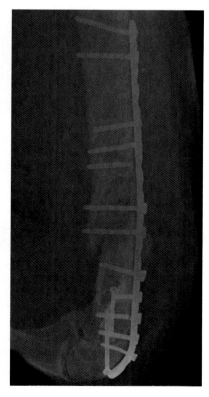

FIGURE 25-10 Fractured or loose screws can be indirect evidence of nonunion. **A.** Four months after repair of the distal humerus nonunion depicted in Figure 25-8, the lateral radiograph reveals fracture of a distal locking screw. **B.** Two months later, multiple additional screws are fractured consistent with the diagnosis of a persistent nonunion.

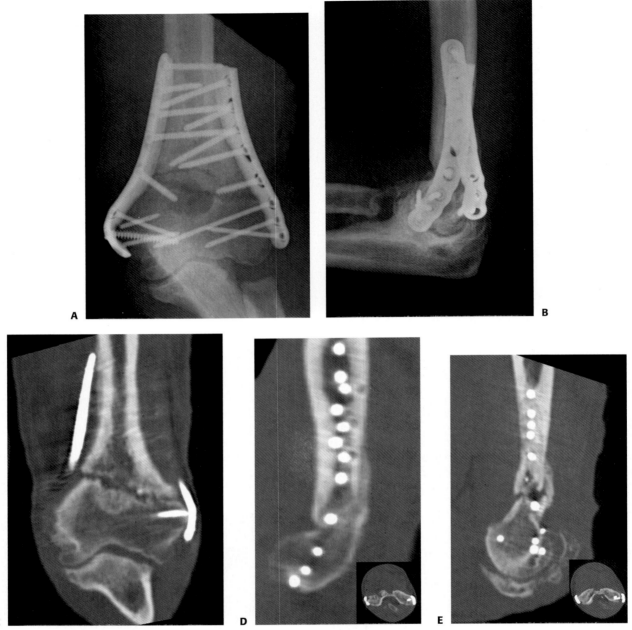

FIGURE 25-11 Lack of specificity of CT in the diagnosis of nonunion. **A,B.** Anteroposterior and lateral radiographs 6 months after repair of a distal humeral nonunion show equivocal healing. **C.** The coronal CT scan demonstrates a lucent line consistent with the diagnosis of nonunion. Revision nonunion repair was undertaken but solid healing, rather than nonunion, was encountered. Further scrutiny of the CT scan in retrospect reveals healing of both the posterior cortices of the medial **(D)** and lateral **(E)** columns.

Indirect Interventions

Adequate nutrition is probably the most obvious and necessary ingredient for healing of all tissues, including bone. Adequate caloric intake, vitamins, and protein are necessary to optimize healing.[55,113,130] Smoking is probably the most commonly studied patient comorbidity. Therefore, it would seem cessation of smoking would be very important as a nonoperative intervention to encourage fracture union. Higher rates of delayed and nonunion have been reported in smokers and the increased rates are probably related to the number of cigarettes smoked.[78,124] The mechanism, although not completely under-

stood, likely relates to diminished osteoblast function and decreased local vascularity.[31,38]

Medical conditions such as diabetes also affect bone healing and increase the risk of nonunion. Diabetic patients with one or more comorbidities are at increased risk for the development of nonunion.[71] Diet modification and controlled blood sugar levels may minimize the negative effect of diabetes on fracture healing.[5]

Other metabolic and endocrine abnormalities may also play a role in nonunion in some patients. Although a direct cause or role is not completely defined, it is certainly suspected. Con-

TABLE 25-1	**Nonoperative Treatment of Nonunions**

Indirect Intervention

Smoking cessation

Optimizing nutrition

Correction of endocrine and metabolic disorders

Elimination or reduction of certain medications

Direct Intervention

Weight bearing

External immobilization or support (e.g., cast or orthosis)

Electrical Stimulation

Ultrasound

ditions like calcium imbalance, hypogonadism, and thyroid and parathyroid disorders should be addressed medically by the appropriate specialist.[20]

In addition to nicotine, other drugs and medications including steroids, phenytoin, chemotherapeutic agents, nonsteroidal anti-inflammatory drugs, and some antibiotics (fluoroquinolones) can negatively affect bone healing.[21,51,102]

Adequate medical treatment of systemic infection, including human immunodeficiency virus, is desirable in the face of fracture and probably absolutely necessary in the treatment of an established nonunion.[61]

There appears to be no clinical evidence at this time to support the use of hyperbaric oxygen for the treatment of nonunion.[8]

Direct Intervention

Probably the simplest and most long standing direct intervention for a nonunion would be application of weight bearing in a functional brace. This, however, is only reasonably practical for the tibia. The mechanism for the success of this treatment is said to be stimulation of osteoblastic activity by mechanical loading.[105,120]

Various forms of electrical stimulation including capacitive coupling, direct current, and inductive coupling have been used for several decades and are felt to be helpful in bone healing. The mechanism of action is alteration of the electrical potential at the fracture site.[43,103,126] Requisite conditions of alignment and bone edge proximity are important. Although results comparable to operative treatment have been reported,[53] some degree of skepticism probably still exists due to the lack of well-designed clinical trials. In the only perspective double blind trial of electrical stimulation, published in 1994, the placebo group which had no treatment had a 0% healing rate compared to 60% in the treated group.[126] The series, however, was small with only 21 patients enrolled.[126] Risk factors and relative contraindications for electrical stimulation are considered to be prolonged nonunion, prior bone graft surgery, prior electrical stimulation which failed, open fractures, active osteomyelitis, extensive comminution. and atrophic nonunion.[17] Electrical stimulation at this time can probably be considered to be a generally reasonable, acceptable nonoperative form of treatment

for nonunion. Additional large double blind trials offering Level I evidence can probably not be expected due to the necessity of the control group having no treatment for the nonunion for a prolonged period of time.

Low-intensity ultrasound has been shown to accelerate the time to union in fresh fractures. Appropriate studies and trials have been conducted which demonstrate shorter healing times for fresh fractures using low-intensity ultrasound.[62,77] The mechanism is believed to be in part related to the actual mechanical phenomenon created by the ultrasound. Ultrasound is a form of low mechanical energy which may be stimulative to bone healing. The three phases of healing (inflammation, repair, and remodeling) are each probably influenced as well as angiogenesis, chondrogenesis, and osteoblastic activity.[3,107,116,148]

High-quality, double-blind, placebo-controlled clinical trials for the use of ultrasound in the treatment of nonunions, however, do not exist and will probably not be done. Once again, there is an ethical consideration as the control group would essentially need to have no treatment for their nonunions for a long period of time. There are, however, studies supporting its use (primarily self-pared controls for nonunion cases) with healing rates approaching 90% and healing times ranging from approximately 100 to 180 days.[41,48,95]

Nonoperative treatment of nonunions has few, if any, complications with the only downside being the length of time that may be required to achieve union when compared with operative methods. A contraindication to nonoperative treatment is malalignment at the nonunion site which, should the nonunion heal, would still leave the patient with a functional deficit due to the residual deformity.

Operative Treatment of Nonunion

Although a common goal of surgical treatment of nonunion is bone healing, there is a wide range of methods available for achieving this. Whereas a single treatment option is often clearly superior for an acute fracture (e.g., intramedullary [IM] nailing for a closed middiaphyseal tibia fracture), several options may be equally suited for treatment of a nonunion of the same injury (e.g., exchange nailing, dynamization, plate osteosynthesis, circular external fixation, and external bone stimulation for a middiaphyseal tibial nonunion). The vast array of options can usually be refined with consideration of the integrity of the soft tissue envelope and coexisting conditions. For instance, nonunion in the face of associated infection makes repair with plates less and external fixation more attractive. Malaligned nonunions are not well suited for interventions that do not address the deformity such as external stimulation or dynamization. Further refinement of the most desired treatment method considers surgeon experience and skill with, the relative risks and benefits of, as well as patient tolerance for, the remaining treatment methods.

Soft Tissue Management Associated with Nonunion

In many cases, the soft tissues are compromised by the original injury or subsequent surgeries. In nonunion cases where operative treatment is planned, it may be necessary to acquire soft tissue coverage by local rotational or free tissue flaps. Of the myriad of flaps available, only free tissue transfer brings something new to the local environment in terms of vascularity and oxygen.[25,39,40,86] Particular attention should be paid to the soft tissue on the concave side of the deformity when angular correction of a malaligned nonunion is planned. A perfect osseous procedure may be planned and carried out only to have insufficient tissue to allow tension-free closure to occur at the conclusion of the case. When soft tissue coverage is lacking and flap coverage is not practical, deficient soft tissues can be dealt with using an external fixation technique or through primary shortening by other means. Purposeful shortening and bone deformation to allow soft tissue closure without tension followed by gradual correction of alignment and distraction osteogenesis has been described utilizing the Taylor Spatial Frame device.[94] Another successful strategy is primary shortening during nonunion repair, followed by secondary lengthening after union has occurred.[81,100]

General Principles of Surgical Nonunion Treatment

Regardless of the chosen method for operative nonunion repair, there are some common principles. As with most medical conditions, accurately identifying the diagnosis is a critical first step to designing a rational treatment plan. This is especially important when dealing with nonunions. Classifying the nonunion as hypertrophic, oligotrophic, atrophic, or pseudoarthrosis, identifying whether it is septic or aseptic, and recognizing associated deformity are each critical to formulation of the complete diagnosis. The classification of the nonunion dictates whether a formal takedown is required and if adjuvant bone grafting is indicated. Hypertrophic nonunions, by definition, have inherent biologic capacity but lack sufficient mechanical stability required for completion of union. Treatment for this diagnosis is therefore focused upon increasing, and often maximizing, mechanical stability. More rigid forms of fixation such as plate fixation or a snug fitting nail in a diaphyseal region are generally preferred to less rigid means such as braces or loose fitting nails in metaphyseal regions. Because hypertrophic nonunions have the biologic potential to heal, débridement of the nonunion site and bone grafting is not an absolute requirement (see Fig. 25-3).

Despite atrophic nonunions being considered avital whereas pseudoarthroses are vital, atrophic nonunions and pseudoarthroses have in common the need for débridement of the nonunion site. The basic principle of atrophic nonunion management calls for débridement of the nonviable bone ends back to healthy bleeding bone. Both of these classes of nonunions also typically require bone grafting. The relative paucity of healing potential of an atrophic nonunion calls for a graft with osteoinductive or osteogenic properties. A pseudoarthrosis, once débrided, has viable vascular ends, and, technically speaking, may therefore not require a bone graft. However, in the absence of bone transport or purposeful shortening, graft is usually used to fill the gap that is invariably left by débriding the synovial tissue in and around the pseudoarthrosis. Oligotrophic nonunions are intermediate in their biologic capacity. It can be difficult to establish whether failure to unite was related to a primary problem of biology or of mechanics or a combination of both. It is therefore prudent to aim treatment at improving both.

Control, and preferably eradication, of any associated infection is another general principle of nonunion treatment. Even severe and complex nonunions can be successfully treated in the absence of infection while simple nonunions can be recalcitrant in the presence of infection. If infection is diagnosed prior to nonunion treatment, then dealing with infection becomes a priority. Removal of associated implants with serial débridement of necrotic soft tissues and bone until a stable healthy environment is achieved is a typical first step. Stabilization by means that are conducive to eradication of infection often calls for external fixation that spares the zone of infection from implants. Internal fixation is generally avoided with the notable exception of antibiotic coated IM nails, which have recently been shown to be successful in this scenario.[99,106,136] Infection treatment continues with organism-specific antibiotics, usually delivered for 6 weeks parentally. Once clinical and laboratory data indicate there is infection control, definitive treatment of the nonunion ensues. If conversion of external to internal fixation is planned, then a staged protocol consisting of removal of the external fixator and cast application (when cast application is reasonably appropriate) allows pin site healing prior to the definitive nonunion surgery. On occasion, union can be accomplished concurrent with the antibiotic phase of treatment, but infection treatment should not be compromised toward this goal.

Positive intraoperative cultures obtained at the time of nonunion repair when preoperative clinical or laboratory evidence of infection was otherwise absent is occasionally encountered. Internal fixation and bone grafts in such a clinically noninfected but culture positive nonunion site can be successfully left in situ, but appropriate antibiotic therapy should be continued until union occurs. However, internal fixation and bone grafting in the face of known infection should be avoided whenever possible.

In the presence of a malaligned nonunion, correction of any associated deformity is paramount to not only the restoration of normal anatomy, but is also critical to establishing appropriate mechanics as the site of nonunion to maximally promote healing.

Plate Fixation for Nonunion Repair

Nonunion repair with plate and screw constructs is applicable to most anatomic locations (Fig. 25-12). The universality of plate constructs extends from almost any particular bone to almost any location within a given bone. That is, plates are applicable to repair of diaphyseal as well as end segment nonunions.[7] Whereas IM nailing is almost universally considered the treatment of choice for acute middiaphyseal fractures of the femur and tibia, and by some the humerus, plate fixation is applicable and may be preferred for repair of ununited fractures in these locations.[7,65,142] Whether the tibia, femur, or humerus is involved, a pre-existing IM nail is, in most circumstances, removed at the time of nonunion repair with plates. However, successful locked plate fixation without nail removal has been reported using eccentric positioning of the plate that allows bicortical screw fixation around the nail to augment unicortical locked screws.[92]

Nonunion repair with plates is limited most by its relative invasiveness, most notably with regard to the potential compromise of an already marginal soft tissue envelope that is often encountered. In the absence of soft tissue concerns, where the local soft tissues can accommodate the bulk of the implant and the dissection required for insertion, nonunion repair with plate constructs is a very powerful method that can be used successfully for any class of nonunion (i.e., atrophic or hypertrophic)

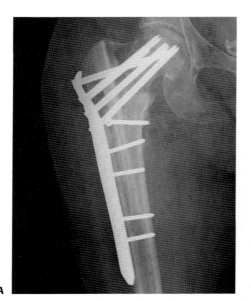
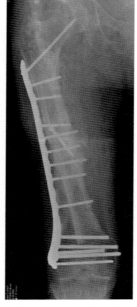
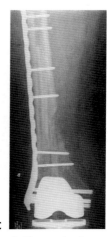

FIGURE 25-12 Plates can be used to treat nonunions at almost any part of any long bone. **A.** The proximal femur nonunion shown in Figure 25-7 was repaired with a proximal femoral locking plate with iliac crest bone graft and an intramedullary fibular strut. Nonunions of the midshaft and distal ends of the femur can be repaired with a straight lateral plate **(B)** and a distal femoral locking plate **(C)**, respectively.

by providing the stability, alignment control, and, when appropriate, the compression required for successful treatment.

Aftercare specific to plate-repaired nonunions must consider the soft tissue envelope. These procedures are often extensive, and postoperative swelling can be substantial and lead to blistering, unforeseen wound issues, and even compartment syndrome. Therefore, efforts to minimizing limb swelling are paramount. A well-padded splint, one without proximal occlusiveness, is often used even if not required to protect the mechanical integrity of the repair. Elevation of the limb above the heart level and cold therapy are mainstays of the initial postoperative regimen. Careful and timely observation of wounds is a practice that can identify and potentially minimize or avoid impending problems.

Intramedullary Nailing of Nonunions

IM nail fixation of nonunions and delayed unions can take three forms: primary nailing of a nonunion in the absence of a pre-existing nail, exchange nailing, and dynamization. Regardless which of these three situations is present, nail treatment is most applicable to diaphyseal nonunion locations. Success is most often reported for the tibia and femur, with exchange nailing of humeral nonunions being less consistent unless supplemental bone graft is utilized.[19,57,76,139,144] Nailing metaphyseal nonunions has been associated with mixed results and is dependent upon the specific region being treated with success most notably being reported for the distal femur and distal tibia.[109,145]

Exchange nailing, the practice of removing a pre-existing nail in favor of a new nail, is most applicable to situations where deficiencies of the pre-existing nail can be overcome with a new, larger reamed nail. Such deficiencies can include lack of rotational control because of absence or fracture of interlocking screws and lack of adequate stability caused by an undersized

nail. The reaming associated with an exchange nailing procedure can provide deposition of small amounts of local bone graft, but these deposits cannot be expected to fill defects of any substantial size. Therefore, exchange nailing is most applicable to situations without bone loss, unless adjuvant open bone grafting accompanies the procedure. Also, exchange nailing is best considered when angular alignment is satisfactory. The new nail will tend to follow the pre-existing intramedullary path of the prior nail and, therefore, angular malalignments tend to persist after exchange nailing when specific efforts are not taken to correct them (Fig. 25-13). Alterations of angular alignment can be made during exchange nailing, but this adds substantial technical challenges to the procedure as correction of malalignment needs to occur prior to reaming. This requires mobility of the nonunion, either at baseline or by surgical means. External devices, such as a femoral distractor, are invaluable tools to help obtain and maintain alignment during the procedure. When multiplanar deformities are present, the simultaneous use of two distractors can be helpful: one in the sagittal plane and one in the coronal plane. All distractor pins should be placed in locations that will not interfere with nailing. Union rates for exchange nailing of femoral and tibial diaphyseal nonunions have ranged substantially, from less than 50% to over 90%.[19,57,98,141,144,146] The degree of overreaming required for effective application of exchange nailing is somewhat controversial. Newer evidence suggests that 1 mm of overreaming is sufficient rather than the historic recommendations for at least 2 mm of overreaming.[144] It should be clear that a minimum requirement for exchange nailing is the ability to insert a large enough nail to provide mechanical strength to the repair. When considering exchange nailing for the tibia, an associated fibular osteotomy to allow fracture compression during repair has been considered an integral part of the procedure, but recent evidence suggests this is not essential.[66]

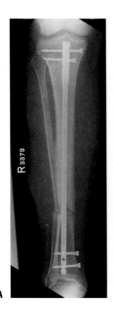
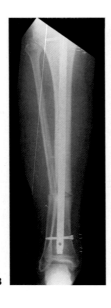
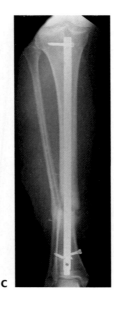

FIGURE 25-13 Exchange nailing of a malaligned tibia nonunion. **A.** An undersized nail was used to treat an open tibial shaft fracture leading to an atrophic nonunion in slight valgus alignment. **B.** Exchange nailing was performed without specific consideration of the malalignment resulting in almost identical valgus. **C.** Persistent nonunion, although now oligotrophic, with fractured interlocking screws results.

Dynamization, the practice of removing interlocking screws at one end of a nail to allow axial shortening with weight bearing, is a method advocated to promote healing of delayed unions or nonunions when small gaps are present at the fracture site. Such gaps may be present due to bone loss, osteoclastic bone resorption, or as a result of prior static locked nailing with distraction at the fracture site. Dynamization with modern nails that provide a dynamic interlocking slot can take two forms. Removal of static screws with retention or addition of a dynamic screw has the advantage of maintaining rotational control, but limits the amount of shortening to the amount of excursion of the dynamic screw within the oval dynamic slot in the nail, usually just a few millimeters with most nail designs. This limit may be advantageous to avoid excessive shortening, or on the other hand, it may be detrimental by preventing sufficient compression at the fracture to achieve union. The other form of dynamization is removal of all interlocking screws from one end of the nail. This allows more freedom for shortening at the expense of a lack of any axial or rotational control inherent to the nail construct. The ideal situation for this form of dynamization is when the fracture pattern itself will result in limited shortening. The compression allowed by dynamization will also provide increasing rotational stability.

Several considerations should go into the decision for which end of a nail should be dynamized. Stability is maximized if screws near the fracture are retained and those on the opposite side of the isthmus relative to the nonunion site are removed. Another consideration relates to which end should be allowed to telescope over the nail. As the bone shortens, the nail will become more prominent on the side of the nail with removed screws, though predicting the degree of shortening can be imprecise. Therefore, screws should not be removed if this result is undesirable. In the case of a retrograde femoral nail, removal of distal screws, those near the knee, is a notable example. In this scenario, the driving end of the nail, if devoid of interlocking screws, can theoretically extend into the knee joint and cause devastating damage to the patellar articular cartilage.

The practice of dynamization, given its relatively simplicity and minimal patient morbidity, was at one time commonplace

and even became a routine planned staged procedure prior to establishment of a healing problem after femoral nailing. This practice occurred despite a lack of clinical evidence to support its use. Good results after routine dynamization of acute femur fractures was a justification for the practice.[73,135] Later evidence revealed that high union rates could be expected with static nailing without secondary dynamization.[22] In the case of an established nonunion, dynamization is successful in promoting union in only approximately 50% of cases.[143,146]

External Fixation for Nonunion Treatment

Of the many different types of external fixation frames and techniques used to treat fractures, circular ring fixators utilizing thin wires and the concepts of Ilizarov are the mainstays for treatment of nonunions by external fixation. The general principles of these techniques are presented in Chapter 8. The applicability of thin wire fixators to nonunions extends to almost any location within any long bone as well as to the hand, foot, and even to the clavicle.[24,66,72,75,79,136] Other advantages of Ilizarov's techniques are the relative paucity of soft tissue trauma imparted by the repair method and the ability to slowly correct associated deformities. The latter also protects the soft tissues from stretching that can accompany acute deformity correction. Other advantages include the ability to fine tune correction and the potential for early weight bearing. A limitation to treatment of end segment nonunions with ring fixators is the proximity of thin wires to the involved joint.[132] Wires that puncture the joint capsule incur the risk of joint sepsis if pin site infection develops. Computer guided treatment with the Taylor Spatial Frame is a recent advance that has considerably simplified Ilizarov type correction of any malalignment, even complex multiplanar deformities.[35,115] The Taylor Spatial Frame differs from traditional Ilizarov fixators by utilizing adjustable struts that are oriented in a hexapod configuration. In conjunction with special web-based software programs, six axes of deformity can be corrected simultaneously and accurately (Fig. 25-14).

During decision-making for nonunion treatment with ring fixators, the surgeon must consider if adjuvant open bone grafting is prudent either at the initial nonunion procedure or in a

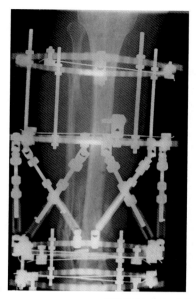
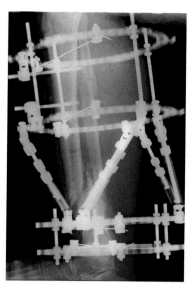
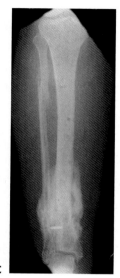
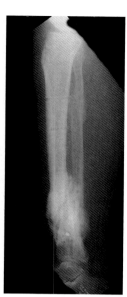

FIGURE 25-14 A,B. An infected hypertrophic nonunion with varus, shortening, posterior translation, and apex anterior angulation seen immediately after application of the Taylor Spatial Frame. **C,D.** After gradual correction using computer software guidance, union and substantial correction of the deformity has been achieved.

planned staged manner. The characteristics of the nonunion dictate this aspect of the strategy, with stiff nonunions being differentiated from mobile nonunions. Radiographic evaluation of the stiff nonunion usually reveals hypertrophic callus formation, and upon physical examination stress across the nonunion site is accompanied by pain with resistance to deformation. In contrast, the mobile nonunion is characterized by either atrophic features on radiographic examination or by features of a synovial pseudoarthrosis. On physical examination, the mobile nonunion moves easily with stress, often without substantial pain. The stiff nonunions have inherent biologic activity and therefore usually respond favorably to closed external fixation methods that utilize compression, distraction, or a combination of both.[24,68,72,75] According to the principles of distraction osteogenesis, gradual distraction of the hypertrophic nonunion stimulates new bone formation and eventual union. The nonunion acts similarly to the regenerated bone seen with lengthening or transport procedures. Modest lengthening, of up to approximately 1.5 cm, can typically be accomplished through a hypertrophic nonunion. If more length is required, a distant osteotomy and lengthening at that site can be performed. Before distraction, a short period of compression, typically 7 to 14 days, may be helpful to prime the site for the osteogenic process. In certain circumstances, when there exists a transverse nonunion site where external compression will result in compression of the fracture fragments, union can be accomplished with pure compression. Clearly, an advantage of such gradual treatment, especially when associated with deformity correction, is the preservation of the often compromised soft tissue envelope.

Treatment of mobile nonunions with ring fixators usually requires opening the nonunion site surgically to convert the nonviable atrophic nonunion to fresh viable bone ends, or in the case of pseudoarthrosis to resect the synovium, pseudocapsule, and fibrocartilage covering the bone ends. In either case, the medullary canal is opened and the site typically bone grafted. Adherents to the Ilizarov principles may, instead of bone grafting, utilize a corticotomy of the involved bone at a site with healthy soft tissues and then transport the intercalary segment with eventual healing being achieved by compression at the nonunion site and regenerate bone formation at the corticotomy site, respectively. This technique is technically much more demanding, potentially more time consuming, relies on healing at two sites rather than one site, and has the potential complications inherent to bone transport, but despite this, it is a powerful strategy in experienced hands especially when lengthening of more than 2 cm is required.

Aftercare specific to nonunion treatment with circular frames requires management of pin sites. Pin site infection near a joint has the potential for joint sepsis, and in these cases careful pin site care and close observation can avoid disastrous consequences. The accepted strategies for pin site care are many, but at least one should be chosen and clearly outlined to the patient and caregivers. Signs and symptoms of infection should prompt more aggressive treatment, such as initiation of antibiotic therapy or wire removal or exchange. The potential for safe and early weight bearing is an advantage of nonunion treatment with ring fixators. Once any associated deformities are corrected and any soft tissue deficiencies are healed, some degree of weight bearing in the frame is generally permitted in all but the most extreme cases.

Arthroplasty for Nonunion Treatment

There are limited circumstances that make arthroplasty a viable option for the treatment of nonunion. However, when circumstances are appropriate, arthroplasty can result in rapid and profound symptomatic and functional improvement. Several factors determine the appropriateness for arthroplasty. A minimum requirement is a nonunion located in a periarticular location that has an associated arthroplasty option that can accommodate the bone resection required to eliminate the nonunion. Standard hip and shoulder arthroplasty (either hemi- or total as dictated by other factors such as the condition of the joint and patient demand) are options for nonunions of the femoral neck and intertrochanteric region and the surgical neck of the humerus, respectively.[56,149] Depending upon other factors, arthroplasty for these indications can either be an excellent first choice, an option of last resort, or contraindicated. In the elderly, especially with associated joint arthritis which may be in the form of pre-existing arthritis, posttraumatic arthritis, joint destruction from prior implants, or osteonecrosis, arthroplasty is preferred to other methods of nonunion treatment. In these circumstances, arthroplasty usually offers the advantages of immediate weight bearing and concomitant treatment of the associated arthritis, two things that are not accomplished with nonunion repair. In physiologically younger patients, arthroplasty becomes less advantageous due to limited longevity of the implants. In the absence of substantial and debilitating arthritis in this patient population, periarticular nonunions are usually best managed with repair. Regardless of patient age, active infection at the site of nonunion is a contraindication to total joint arthroplasty. Strategies for arthroplasty after eradication of infection, often accompanied with antibiotic spacer placement, are not unreasonable but are associated with a substantial risk of persistent infection.

One of the most suitable metaphyseal nonunion locations that is amenable to arthroplasty is the distal femur. Here, a total knee arthroplasty that includes distal femoral replacement is relatively mainstream, technically of moderate but not extreme complexity, and due to a lack of critical soft tissue attachments on the distal femur, is generally associated with good functional outcomes.[1,13,57,96] Analogous are nonunions of the distal humerus where even standard total elbow replacements are commonly sufficient.[119] This is because of a combination of the high frequency of juxta-articular fractures of the distal humerus, potential problems with fixation of very distal fractures in this region, and the common coexistence of osteoporosis. When nonunions are more proximal, a distal humeral replacing total elbow prosthesis can be used.[27] In contrast to the distal metaphyseal ends of the femur and humerus, metaphyseal nonunions of the proximal ends of these bones are somewhat less ideal for arthroplasty. The common reason is related to the tendon insertions onto the greater trochanter of the femur and the greater and lesser tuberosities of the humerus, respectively. These tendon attachments must be preserved to maintain normal function and therefore proximal replacing arthroplasty in these regions should only be considered in extreme circumstances where other options are of equal or greater disfavor.[108]

Arthroplasty for nonunion of the proximal tibia, due to the critical importance of the integrity of the tibial tubercle, is typically avoided even in the presence of knee arthritis in favor of staged knee arthroplasty after nonunion repair. Critical soft tissue attachments do not limit the applicability of total ankle replacement for nonunion of the distal tibia but the lack of prostheses that accommodate bone loss in this location do.

Once the technical aspects of arthroplasty have been considered, the presence or absence of associated joint arthritis will increase or decrease the threshold for selecting arthroplasty, respectively. Similarly, the functional demands and age of the patient are considered, with physiologically younger patients typically undergoing nonunion repair rather than arthroplasty. Any documented history, or even suggestive history, of infection must be identified and considered. Active infection is a contraindication to arthroplasty. Arthroplasty can be considered after

aggressive treatment of an infected nonunion. This typically involves relatively radical débridement of the involved bone, internal implantation of antibiotic-impregnated cement spacers, and prolonged administration of organism-specific parental antibiotics. Whether an infection-free period of time off antibiotics prior to arthroplasty, aimed to demonstrate eradication of the infection, or whether arthroplasty should be accompanied by long-term oral suppression is unclear, and this decision is typically individualized and made in concert with consultant infectious disease specialists. More distant history of infection presents a similar quandary. Biopsy or joint aspiration prior to arthroplasty can be useful to guide decision-making.

Amputation for Nonunion Treatment

Amputation as definitive treatment for nonunions is often dictated by associated comorbid conditions and by patient preference rather than a technical inability to eventually achieve union. Psychologic and psychosocial factors specific to each individual patient are important to recognize, discuss, and consider before making a decision for amputation in the setting of nonunion. The invested time and effort in prior treatments makes some patients reluctant to consider amputation and eager for fresh ideas and strategies for repair whereas the same investments in prior failures may leave other patients frustrated, worn out, and ready to proceed with a definitive procedure such as amputation. Candid assessments for potential success with additional attempts at nonunion repair, the required investment of time and energy of the patient, and the relative functional, cosmetic, and neurologic (i.e., pain, neuralgia) outcomes of success versus failure of nonunion repair should be discussed and used to guide treatment decisions. The chronic pain from nonunion that will dissipate with bone healing needs to be differentiated from neurogenic pain which is likely to linger. If such neurogenic pain is chronically disabling, then efforts at nonunion repair may be misguided and amputation deserves serious consideration. Also, a contingency plan for what follows if a future nonunion repair fails is useful. A plan for amputation if failure occurs with the next intervention may make it much easier for some patients to select a course of treatment.

ADJUNCTS TO NONUNION REPAIR

Autogenous Bone Graft

Autogenous bone graft remains the clinical standard graft substance. It has the best and longest documentation and experience. For instance, autograft from the iliac crest used in the treatment of tibial and femoral nonunion typically results in union rates exceeding 90%.[6,14,26,42,117] Autogenous bone graft supplies osteogenic and osteoconductive materials. Osteogenic cells, including stroma cells, are also present in the graft material. It provides an excellent osteoconductive scaffold by way of cancellous bone spicules. There is probably little to no bone morphogenic protein in autogenous graft so that it probably cannot be considered truly osteoinductive.[123]

Iliac crest is the most commonly used site for large volume grafts, but other sites such as the greater trochanter and the femoral and tibial condyles can be used for small amounts. It is estimated that 15% of the osteocytes or osteoblasts survive the bone graft procedure.[34] Autogenous bone grafting leads to concomitant bone formation and resorption.

The disadvantage of autogenous bone grafting is the limited amount which can be harvested. Additionally, the quality of the autogenous graft will be dependent on host health issues such as osteoporosis. Donor site morbidity (25% to 40%) includes infection, pain (acute and chronic), secondary fracture, and hematoma formation.[2] Autogenous bone grafting is used in atrophic and some oligotrophic nonunions and to repair some pseudarthroses. Effective application requires decortication of the bone in the recipient bed in most instances for success.

Recently, a less invasive technique for harvesting autogenous graft from the femoral canal has been proposed using the Reamer-Irrigator-Aspirator (Synthes, Paoli, PA) (Fig. 25-15).[93] This device was originally designed as a one-pass reamer for IM nailing to minimize embolic phenomenon. Using this device, the reamings are evacuated via suction and subsequently can be collected and used as bone graft. A reamer that is 1 to 4 mm greater than the narrowest part of the femoral canal as measured on preoperative and/or intraoperative images is selected. The starting point is the same as for IM nailing and maybe a piriformis or trochanteric entry site. This is identified intraoperatively by fluoroscopy. The technique is limited to femoral canals which are between 10 mm and 16 mm in diameter. This is due to the currently limited reamer sizes available for the device. Using standard IM nailing technique, a guidewire is inserted into the canal of the femur with image control, and a one-time pass reamer is gently used to ream the femoral canal with an in and out motion so as not to advance too aggressively. A trap is used to collect the reamings. Typically, 60 to 80 mL of graft can be harvested with experience. In the relatively limited experiences reported so far, minimal complications have occurred (mechanical malfunction, femur fracture, embolism, excessive blood loss), but the potential certainly exists.[93,131] Reamings in general have been shown in in vitro analysis to contain pluripotential stem cells with the possibility of dedifferentiation into osteoblasts. Specifically quantitative assessment has demonstrated the presence of growth factors using the irrigant/aspirate technique.[123] An animal study has additionally suggested that

a superior quality of callus may result from reimplantation of graft material harvested in this way.[59] Randomized trials comparing this method of graft harvest to standard iliac crest grafts are needed.

Vascularized Grafts

Vascularized grafts are most commonly used to treat segmental defects. They are advantageous in this situation as they provide a live bone graft that also has structural properties, something that is not provided by standard iliac crest cancellous autograft. The fibula is the most commonly harvested bone, although other sites such as the iliac crest[118] and rib[140] have been used. They typically must undergo some degree of hypertrophy for ultimate success in addition to healing to the host tissue at each end.[67] Double vascularized grafts (fibula) combined with cancellous grafts have been proposed to gain additional and more rapid stability.[4] It is, however, a technically demanding procedure requiring microvascular anastomoses. Complications include recurrent graft fractures and donor site morbidity.[60]

Bone Graft Substitutes

Autologous bone graft has recently been challenged as the criterion standard bone graft substance for nonunions.[127] Alternatives to autologous bone graft, including demineralized bone matrix, bone marrow aspirate, platelet-rich plasma, allograft, and ceramics, have been developed and utilized for nonunion treatment with varying degrees of success. New advances in bioengineering based on an enhanced understanding of the cellular and molecular aspects of fracture healing have led to the development and clinical use of growth factors, such as bone morphogenetic proteins (BMPs), that augment fracture healing. The details of the basic science and mechanism of action of these alternatives is presented in Chapter 5. Advantages of these substitutes in the treatment of nonunion include reduced or eliminated patient morbidity and increased or unlimited supply relative to autologous bone graft. The ideal graft substitute for

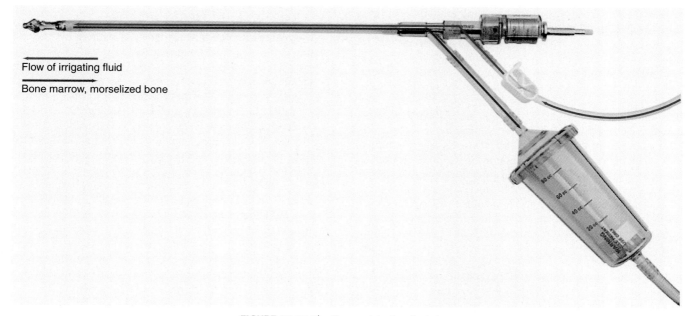

Flow of irrigating fluid

Bone marrow, morselized bone

FIGURE 25-15 The Reamer-Irrigation-Aspirator.

nonunion treatment would be inexpensive, of unlimited supply, easy to prepare and handle, easy to implant, without adverse reactions, and 100% efficacious.

Each of the aforementioned graft substitutes has some of these attributes, but none have all. Nonunion healing rates with use of these substitutes has been reported but there is little in the way of direct comparison to autologous bone grafting.[12,28,50,52,65,76,83,128] Recombinant human osteogenic protein-1 (rhOP-1) was directly compared to autograft in the treatment of 124 tibial nonunions in a prospective randomized study.[44] At 9 months after repair using an IM nail, 81% of the rhOP-1 and 85% of the autograft treated nonunions healed clinically. Radiographic healing in the rhOP-1 group was 75%, while it remained essentially unchanged from clinical healing in the autologous group (84%). The main advantage of rhOP-1 was elimination of the donor site pain, which occurred in 20% of the patients receiving autograft.

One randomized controlled study exists comparing rhBMP-2 and allograft to autogenous bone graft for reconstruction of diaphyseal tibial fractures with cortical defects.[70] Thirteen patients in the rhBMP-2 group had results comparable to 10 patients in the autograft group. These tibial defects were not nonunions but with an average of 4 cm in size, they were certainly unlikely to heal without intervention.

Demineralized bone matrix (DBM) used as an adjunct to locked compression plating of osteoporotic humeral shaft nonunions resulted in union in 11 out of 13 patients.[110] Both patients with DBM failure united after a secondary iliac crest bone grafting. By comparison, all 12 treated with autograft from the same retrospective study healed without further intervention. Noncomparative data has shown good healing rates, 89% to 92%, with rhBMP-7 (rhOP-1) in the treatment of various upper and lower extremity nonunions.[33,88] A disadvantage of recombinant BMPs is the cost, although recent data suggests using BMPs could actually reduce costs when treating complex or recalcitrant nonunions by reducing the number of procedures and number of hospital days.[32]

Bone marrow aspirate, primarily from the iliac crest, has been shown to contain osteoprogenitor cells and has both osteogenic and osteoinductive properties.[9] The generally low concentration of such cells ($612/cm^3$) and the variability between patients (12 to $1224/cm^3$) has led to the development of improved aspiration techniques with specialized aspiration needles and cell concentration systems aimed at increasing both the number and the density of the progenitor cells[63] without concentration; some evidence suggests that the number of cells in marrow aspirates is suboptimal for nonunion treatment.[64] Furthermore, some controversy exists as to whether concentrated cells should be injected directly and percutaneously into nonunion sites or if application with an osteoconductive carrier after open débridement of the nonunion is required for optimal results.[127] The actual efficiency of direct marrow injection is difficult to interpret in the face of associated interventions including cast immobilization and IM nailing that have accompanied the injection in series reporting 75% to 90% union rates.[28,47,52] Platelet-rich plasma (PRP) is harvested as the thin layer between clear plasma and red blood cells in centrifuged peripheral blood. This fluid contains concentrated platelets (300%–600%) which are believed to promote osteoblast proliferation and differentiation.[137] However, to date no clinical evidence exits to support the use of PRP in the treatment of nonunions.

Other graft substitute materials such as ceramics (calcium sulfate, calcium phosphates, beta tricalcium phosphate, and hydroxyapatite) and allograft that lack osteoinductive or osteogenic properties have little role in promoting bone healing in the setting of nonunion. These materials are primarily osteoconductive and function best as graft extenders or carriers for osteoinductive compounds.

AUTHORS' PREFERRED TREATMENT

Nonoperative Nonunion Treatment

Among our patients who smoke, we have experienced a persistent inability to achieve smoking cessation even in the face of potential limb loss. However, hope is not lost and new treatments may provide some improved results for these patients.

External stimulation alone is reserved for patients who are minimally symptomatic from their nonunion and who are not candidates for surgery or additional procedures (see Fig. 25-5). Both electrical and ultrasound stimulation are used in conjunction with operative treatment in high-risk patients such as smokers and diabetics.

Operative Treatment of Nonunions

Exchange nailing is used almost exclusively for well-aligned tibial diaphyseal nonunions with reasonable success, but much less favorable results have accompanied exchange nailing for nonunions of the femur shaft. Nevertheless, in a well aligned isthmal femoral diaphyseal nonunion which is hypertrophic or oligotrophic, exchange nailing is still attempted in some cases.[7]

Most often, however, as the nonunion approaches the articular segment, a plate and bone graft technique is used. Hypertrophic nonunions are simply stabilized and, when possible, compressed (Fig. 25-16), while oligotrophic and atrophic nonunions are also grafted with autogenous cancellous bone. As experience has been gained with the Reamer-Irrigator-Aspirator (Synthes, Paoli, PA), the graft volume and quality as well as the favorable healing reaction with decreased morbidity compared to iliac crest harvest have been impressive (Fig. 25-17).

For segmental loss, the technique of Masquelet or primary shortening followed by lengthening is favored. In this technique, the area of segmental loss is filled with polymethylmethacrylate cement. At 4 to 6 weeks, when an osteogenic membrane has formed around the cement, the membrane is surgically reopened and the cement is removed and generous cancellous bone grafting is carried out (see Fig. 25-17). Recorticalization generally occurs slowly but usually by 3 to 6 months. This, is done in conjunction with internal stabilization most frequently using a locked intramedullary rod for diaphyseal defects or locked plates for metaphyseal defects.[85] The initial role of the spacer is to maintain limb lengthening and a space for future grafting by avoiding fibrous tissue ingrowth. The secondary role of the spacer is the induction of a membrane formation. This membrane is synovial-like with few inflammatory cells.[101] The membrane itself serves to contain the graft, prevent fibrous invasion, and provide growth factors. Immunochemistry has shown that the membrane produces growth factors and inductive factors including BMP-2, which is probably maximal at around 4 weeks.[101] In his original article, Masquelet[85] reported successful use of this two

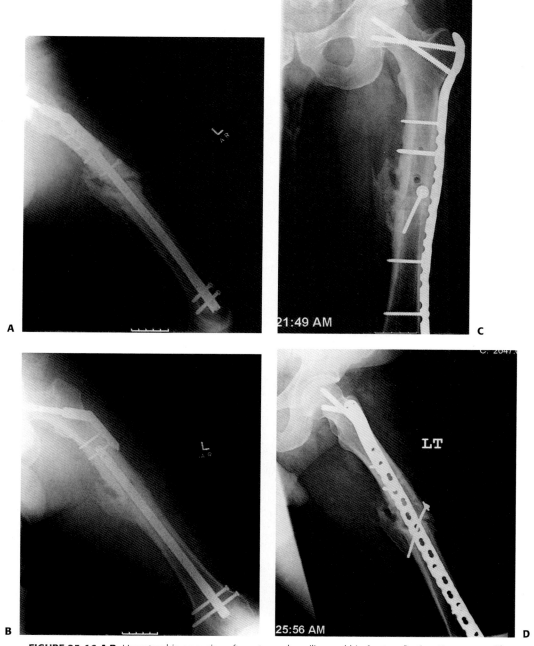

FIGURE 25-16 A,B. Hypertrophic nonunion after retrograde nailing and hip fracture fixation. Treatment with compression plating **(C,D)** resulted in healing of the diaphyseal nonunion.

stage technique in 35 cases with defects ranging from 4 to 25 cm. Other authors have had similar success with this staged membrane-induced technique.[111,125] The underlying mechanism of the membrane formation is not well understood, but cases when the membrane itself has generated enough bone so that secondary grafting is not necessary have been observed in our practices. It is unclear whether this membrane can form with substances other than methylmethacrylate, and this technique requires an excellent soft tissue envelope.[85]

When soft tissues are poor or deficient and free tissue transfer is not possible, primary shortening over an IM rod followed by full weight bearing with an elevated shoe is preferred. Once healing has occurred, the limb is then length-

ened with either an internal skeletal distraction nail (ISKD Orthofix Inc, McKinney, TX) (Fig. 25-18) or the Ilizarov technique. In some cases with less than 3 or 4 cm of shortening, patients are often satisfied with the result and do not desire the lengthening procedure. The internal skeletal distraction nail seems to be better tolerated than the skinny wire external fixator techniques. It is, however, no faster. Complications similar to those with other distraction or transport techniques still exist including too fast or too slow distraction, failure of or delay in regenerate formation, adjacent joint problems, need for exchange nailing, and failure of the distraction device itself.

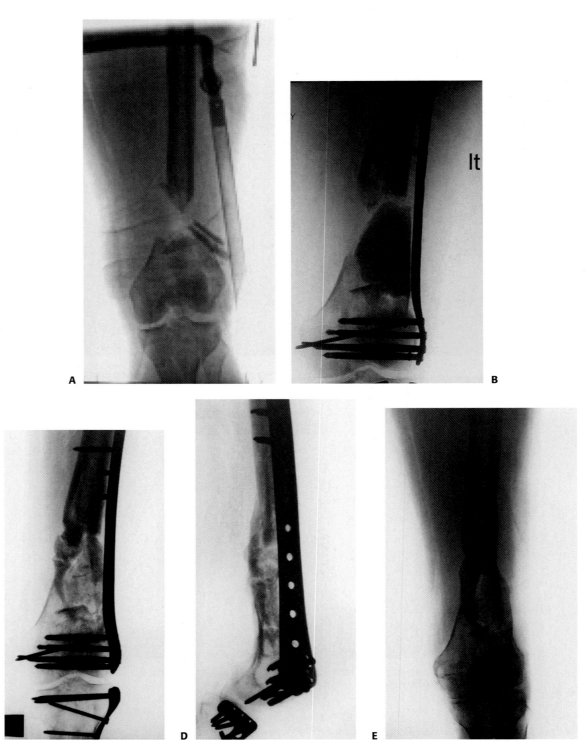

FIGURE 25-17 A. Grade IIIB comminuted open distal femur fracture with bone loss. **B.** Bridging plate with cement spacer. **C,D.** Anteroposterior and lateral views after Reamer-Irrigation-Aspirator grafting. **E.** Anteroposterior view after hardware removal. (Courtesy of Dr. Timothy Weber, Orthoindy Indianapolis, IN.)

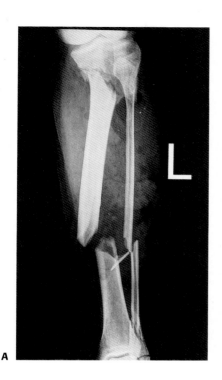

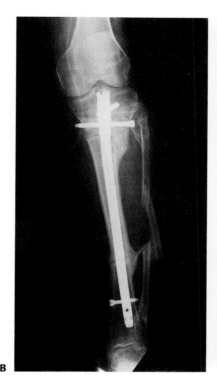

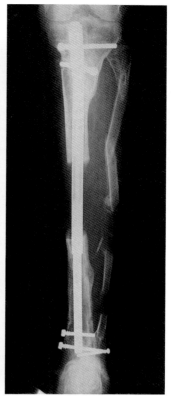

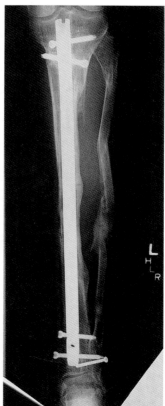

FIGURE 25-18 A. A 40-year-old woman with a grade IIIB open tibia. The central fragment was completely stripped of soft tissue. She was not a candidate for free tissue transfer. **B.** After resection of significant bone, the leg was shortened and the fracture was treated with a locked rod. The fracture healed with full weight-bearing ambulation in a built up shoe. Note the overlapping fibula. Only her local tissues, which were adequate in volume after shortening, were used for coverage. **C.** Subsequent lengthening was then achieved with an internal skeletal distraction nail. **D.** After exchange nailing, the regenerate was mature at about 6 months.

REFERENCES

1. Appleton P, Moran M, Houshian S, et al. Distal femoral fractures treated by hinged total knee replacement in elderly patients. J Bone Joint Surg Br 2006;88:1065–1070.
2. Arrington ED, Smith WJ, Chambers HG, et al. Complications of iliac crest bone graft harvesting. Clin Orthop Relat Res 1996;329:300–309.
3. Azuma Y, Ito M, Harada Y, et al. Low-intensity pulsed ultrasound accelerates rat femoral fracture healing by acting on the various cellular reactions in the fracture callus. J Bone Miner Res 2001;16:671–680.
4. Banic A, Hertel R. Double vascularized fibulas for reconstruction of large tibial defects. J Reconstr Microsurg 1993;9:421–428.
5. Beam HA, Parsons JR, Lin SS. The effects of blood glucose control upon fracture healing in the BB Wistar rat with diabetes mellitus. J Orthop Res 2002;20:1210–1216.
6. Bellabarba C, Ricci WM, Bolhofner BR. Indirect reduction and plating of distal femoral nonunions. J Orthop Trauma 2002;16:287–296.
7. Bellabarba C, Ricci WM, Bolhofner BR. Results of indirect reduction and plating of femoral shaft nonunions after intramedullary nailing. J Orthop Trauma 2001;15: 254–263.
8. Bennett MH, Stanford R, Turner R. Hyperbaric oxygen therapy for promoting fracture healing and treating fracture nonunion. Cochrane Database Syst Rev 2005;1: CD004712.
9. Beresford JN. Osteogenic stem cells and the stromal system of bone and marrow. Clin Orthop Relat Res 1989;240:270–280.
10. Bhandari M, Tornetta P III, Sprague S, et al. Predictors of reoperation following operative management of fractures of the tibial shaft. J Orthop Trauma 2003;17:353–361.
11. Bhattacharyya T, Bouchard KA, Phadke A, et al. The accuracy of computed tomography for the diagnosis of tibial nonunion. J Bone Joint Surg Am 2006;88:692–697.
12. Bielecki T, Gazdzik TS, Szczepanski T. Benefit of percutaneous injection of autologous platelet-leukocyte-rich gel in patients with delayed union and nonunion. Eur Surg Res 2008;40:289–296.
13. Boileau P, Trojani C, Walch G, et al. Shoulder arthroplasty for the treatment of the sequelae of fractures of the proximal humerus. J Shoulder Elbow Surg 2001;10: 299–308.
14. Borrelli J Jr, Prickett WD, Ricci WM. Treatment of nonunions and osseous defects with bone graft and calcium sulfate. Clin Orthop Relat Res 2003;411:245–254.
15. Borrelli J Jr, Tinsley K, Ricci WM, et al. Induction of chondrocyte apoptosis following impact load. J Orthop Trauma 2003;17:635–641.
16. Brashear HR. Treatment of ununited fractures of the long bones; diagnosis and prevention of nonunion. J Bone Joint Surg Am 1965;47:174–178.
17. Brighton CT, Shaman P, Heppenstall RB, et al. Tibial nonunion treated with direct current, capacitive coupling, or bone graft. Clin Orthop Relat Res 1995;321;223–234.
18. Brinker MR. Nonunions. In: Browner BD, Jupiter J, Levine A, et al., eds. Skeletal Trauma. Philadelphia: Saunders, 2003:507–604.
19. Brinker MR, O'Connor DP. Exchange nailing of ununited fractures. J Bone Joint Surg Am 2007;89:177–188.
20. Brinker MR, O'Connor DP, Monla YT, et al. Metabolic and endocrine abnormalities in patients with nonunions. J Orthop Trauma 2007;21:557–570.
21. Brown KM, Saunders MM, Kirsch T, et al. Effect of COX-2-specific inhibition on fracture-healing in the rat femur. J Bone Joint Surg Am 2004;86-A:116–123.
22. Brumback RJ. Intramedullary nailing of femoral shaft fractures. Part II: fracture-healing with static interlocking fixation. J Bone Joint Surg Am 1988;70:1453–1462.
23. Castillo RC, Bosse MJ, MacKenzie EJ, et al. Impact of smoking on fracture healing and risk of complications in limb-threatening open tibia fractures. J Orthop Trauma 2005; 19:151–157.
24. Catagni MA, Guerreschi F, Holman JA, et al. Distraction osteogenesis in the treatment of stiff hypertrophic nonunions using the Ilizarov apparatus. Clin Orthop Relat Res 1994;301:159–163.
25. Chang N, Mathes SJ. Comparison of the effect of bacterial inoculation in musculocutaneous and random-pattern flaps. Plast Reconstr Surg 1982;70:1–10.
26. Chapman MW, Finkemeier CG. Treatment of supracondylar nonunions of the femur with plate fixation and bone graft. J Bone Joint Surg Am 1999;81:1217–1228.
27. Cil A, Veillette CJ, Sanchez-Sotelo J, et al. Linked elbow replacement: a salvage procedure for distal humeral nonunion. J Bone Joint Surg Am 2008;90:1939–1950.
28. Connolly JF, Guse R, Tiedeman J, et al. Autologous marrow injection as a substitute for operative grafting of tibial nonunions. Clin Orthop Relat Res 1991;266:259–270.
29. Costelloe CM, Dickson K, Cody DD, et al. Computed tomography reformation in evaluation of fracture healing with metallic fixation: correlation with clinical outcome. J Trauma 2008;65:1421–1424.
30. Court-Brown CM, McQueen MM. Nonunions of the proximal humerus: their prevalence and functional outcome. J Trauma 2008;64:1517–1521.
31. Daftari TK, Whitesides TE Jr, Heller JG, et al. Nicotine on the revascularization of bone graft. An experimental study in rabbits. Spine 1994;19:904–911.
32. Dahabreh Z, Dimitriou R, Giannoudis PV. Health economics: a cost analysis of treatment of persistent fracture nonunions using bone morphogenetic protein-7. Injury 2007;38:371–377.
33. Dimitriou R, Dahabreh Z, Katsoulis E, et al. Application of recombinant BMP-7 on persistent upper and lower limb non-unions. Injury 2005;36(Suppl 4):S51–S59.
34. Ebraheim NA, Elgafy H, Xu R. Bone-graft harvesting from iliac and fibular donor sites: techniques and complications. J Am Acad Orthop Surg 2001;9:210–218.
35. Elbatrawy Y, Fayed M. Deformity correction with an external fixator: ease of use and accuracy? Orthopedics 2009;32(2):82.
36. Esterhai J, Alavi A, Mandell GA, et al. Sequential technetium-99m/gallium-67 scintigraphic evaluation of subclinical osteomyelitis complicating fracture nonunion. J Orthop Res 1985;3:219–225.
37. Esterhai JL Jr, Brighton CT, Heppenstall RB, et al. Detection of synovial pseudarthrosis by 99mTc scintigraphy: application to treatment of traumatic nonunion with constant direct current. Clin Orthop Relat Res 1981;161:15–23.
38. Fang MA, Frost PJ, Iida-Klein A, et al. Effects of nicotine on cellular function in UMR 106-01 osteoblast-like cells. Bone 1991;12:283–286.
39. Feng LJ, Price DC, Mathes SJ, et al. Dynamic properties of blood flow and leukocyte mobilization in infected flaps. World J Surg 1990;14:796–803.
40. Fisher J, Wood MB. Experimental comparison of bone revascularization by musculocutaneous and cutaneous flaps. Plast Reconstr Surg 1987;79:81–90.
41. Frankel VH. Results of prescription use of pulse ultrasound therapy in fracture management. Surg Technol Int 1998;VII:389–393.
42. Freeland AE, Mutz SB. Posterior bone-grafting for infected ununited fracture of the tibia. J Bone Joint Surg Am 1976;58:653–657.
43. Friedenberg ZB, Brighton CT. Bioelectric potentials in bone. J Bone Joint Surg Am 1966;48:915–923.
44. Friedlaender GE, Perry CR, Cole JD, et al. Osteogenic protein-1 (bone morphogenetic protein-7) in the treatment of tibial nonunions. J Bone Joint Surg Am 2001;83-A(Suppl 1):S151–S158.
45. Friedrich B, Klaue P. Mechanical stability and posttraumatic osteitis: an experimental evaluation of the relation between infection of bone and internal fixation. Injury 1977; 9:23–29.
46. Gandhi A, Liporace F, Azad V, et al. Diabetic fracture healing. Foot Ankle Clin 2006; 11:805–824.
47. Garg NK, Gaur S, Sharma S. Percutaneous autogenous bone marrow grafting in 20 cases of ununited fracture. Acta Orthop Scand 1993;64:671–672.
48. Gebauer D, Mayr E, Orthner E. Nonunions treated by pulsed low-intensity ultrasound. J Orthop Trauma 2000;14:154.
49. Gerstenfeld LC, Cullinane DM, Barnes GL, et al. Fracture healing as a postnatal developmental process: molecular, spatial, and temporal aspects of its regulation. J Cell Biochem 2003;88:873–884.
50. Giannoudis PV, Kanakaris NK, Dimitriou R, et al. The synergistic effect of autograft and BMP-7 in the treatment of atrophic nonunions. Clin Orthop Relat Res 2009 (epub ahead of print).
51. Giannoudis,PV, MacDonald DA, Matthews SJ, et al. Nonunion of the femoral diaphysis. The influence of reaming and nonsteroidal anti-inflammatory drugs. J Bone Joint Surg Br 2000;82:655–658.
52. Goel A, Sangwan SS, Siwach RC, et al. Percutaneous bone marrow grafting for the treatment of tibial nonunion. Injury 2005;36:203–206.
53. Gossling HR, Bernstein RA, Abbott J. Treatment of ununited tibial fractures: a comparison of surgery and pulsed electromagnetic fields (PEMF). Orthopedics 1992;15: 711–719.
54. Gruber R, Koch H, Doll BA, et al. Fracture healing in the elderly patient. Exp Gerontol 2006;41:1080–1093.
55. Guarniero R, Barros Filho TE, Tannuri U, et al. Study of fracture healing in protein malnutrition. Rev Paul Med 1992;110:63–68.
56. Haidukewych GJ. Salvage of failed treatment of femoral neck fractures. Instr Course Lect 2009;58:83–90.
57. Haidukewych GJ, Springer BD, Jacofsky DJ, et al. Total knee arthroplasty for salvage of failed internal fixation or nonunion of the distal femur. J Arthroplasty 2005;20: 344–349.
58. Hak DJ, Lee SS, Goulet JA. Success of exchange reamed intramedullary nailing for femoral shaft nonunion or delayed union. J Orthop Trauma 2000;14:178–182.
59. Hammer TO, Wieling R, Green JM, et al. Effect of reimplanted particles from intramedullary reaming on mechanical properties and callus formation. A laboratory study. J Bone Joint Surg Br 2007;89:1534–1538.
60. Han CS, Wood MB, Bishop AT, et al. Vascularized bone transfer. J Bone Joint Surg Am 1992;74:1441–1449.
61. Harrison WJ, Lewis CP, Lavy CB. Open fractures of the tibia in HIV positive patients: a prospective controlled single-blind study. Injury 2004;35:852–856.
62. Heckman JD, Ryaby JP, McCabe J, et al. Acceleration of tibial fracture-healing by non-invasive, low-intensity pulsed ultrasound. J Bone Joint Surg Am 1994;76:26–34.
63. Hernigou P, Mathieu G, Poignard A, et al. Percutaneous autologous bone-marrow grafting for nonunions. Surgical technique. J Bone Joint Surg Am 2006;88(Suppl 1 Pt 2):322–327.
64. Hernigou P, Poignard A, Beaujean F, et al. Percutaneous autologous bone-marrow grafting for nonunions. Influence of the number and concentration of progenitor cells. J Bone Joint Surg Am 2005;87:1430–1437.
65. Hierholzer C, Sama D, Toro JB, et al. Plate fixation of ununited humeral shaft fractures: effect of type of bone graft on healing. J Bone Joint Surg Am 2006;88:1442–1447.
66. Hsiao CW, Wu CC, Su CY, et al. Exchange nailing for aseptic tibial shaft nonunion: emphasis on the influence of a concomitant fibulotomy. Chang Gung Med J 2006;29: 283–290.
67. Ikeda K, Tomita K, Hashimoto F, et al. Long-term follow-up of vascularized bone grafts for the reconstruction of tibial nonunion: evaluation with computed tomographic scanning. J Trauma 1992;32:693–697.
68. Inan M, Karaoglu S, Cilli F, et al. Treatment of femoral nonunions by using cyclic compression and distraction. Clin Orthop Relat Res 2005;436:222–228.
69. Jani MM, Ricci WM, Borrelli J Jr, et al. A protocol for treatment of unstable ankle fractures using transarticular fixation in patients with diabetes mellitus and loss of protective sensibility. Foot Ankle Int 2003;24:838–844.
70. Jones AL, Bucholz RW, Bosse MJ, et al. Recombinant human BMP-2 and allograft compared with autogenous bone graft for reconstruction of diaphyseal tibial fractures with cortical defects. A randomized, controlled trial. J Bone Joint Surg Am 2006;88: 1431–1441.
71. Jones KB, Maiers-Yelden KA, Marsh JL, et al. Ankle fractures in patients with diabetes mellitus. J Bone Joint Surg Br 2005;87:489–495.
72. Kabata T, Tsuchiya H, Sakurakichi K, et al. Reconstruction with distraction osteogenesis for juxta-articular nonunions with bone loss. J Trauma 2005;58:1213–1222.
73. Kellam JF. Early results of the Sunnybrook experience with locked intramedullary nailing. Orthopedics 1985;8:1387–1388.
74. Kettunen J, Makela EA, Turunen V, et al. Percutaneous bone grafting in the treatment of the delayed union and non-union of tibial fractures. Injury 2002;33:239–245.
75. Kocaoglu M, Eralp L, Sen C, et al. Management of stiff hypertrophic nonunions by distraction osteogenesis: a report of 16 cases. J Orthop Trauma 2003;17:543–548.
76. Kontakis GM, Papadokostakis GM, Alpantaki K, et al. Intramedullary nailing for non-union of the humeral diaphysis: a review. Injury 2006;37:953–960.
77. Kristiansen TK, Ryaby JP, McCabe J, et al. Accelerated healing of distal radial fractures with the use of specific, low-intensity ultrasound. A multicenter, prospective, randomized, double-blind, placebo-controlled study. J Bone Joint Surg Am 1997;79:961–973.

78. Kyro A, Usenius JP, Aarnio M, et al. Are smokers a risk group for delayed healing of tibial shaft fractures? Ann Chir Gynaecol 1993;82:254–262.

79. Lammens J, Bauduin G, Driesen R, et al. Treatment of nonunion of the humerus using the Ilizarov external fixator. Clin Orthop Relat Res 1998;353:223–230.

80. Lynch JR, Taitsman LA, Barei DP, et al. Femoral nonunion: risk factors and treatment options. J Am Acad Orthop Surg 2008;16:88–97.

81. Mahaluxmivala J, Nadarajah R, Allen PW, et al. Ilizarov external fixator: acute shortening and lengthening versus bone transport in the management of tibial nonunions. Injury 2005;36:662–668.

82. Mandt PR, Gershuni DH. Treatment of nonunion of fractures in the epiphyseal-metaphyseal region of long bones. J Orthop Trauma 1987;1:141–151.

83. Mariconda M, Cozzolino F, Cozzolino A, et al. Platelet gel supplementation in long bone nonunions treated by external fixation. J Orthop Trauma 2008;22:342–345.

84. Marsh D. Concepts of fracture union, delayed union, and nonunion. Clin Orthop Relat Res 1998;335 Suppl:S22–S30.

85. Masquelet AC, Fitoussi F, Begue T, et al. [Reconstruction of the long bones by the induced membrane and spongy autograft]. Ann Chir Plast Esthet 2000;45:346–353.

86. Mathes SJ, Alpert BS, Chang N. Use of the muscle flap in chronic osteomyelitis: experimental and clinical correlation. Plast Reconstr Surg 1982;69:815–829.

87. McKee M. Aseptic nonunion. In: Ruedi TP, Murphy W, eds. AO Principles of Fracture Management. Stuttgart: Thieme Vercal, 2000:748–762.

88. McKee MD. Recombinant human bone morphogenic protein-7: applications for clinical trauma. J Orthop Trauma 2005;19:S26–S28.

89. McKee MD, DiPasquale DJ, Wild LM, et al. The effect of smoking on clinical outcome and complication rates following Ilizarov reconstruction. J Orthop Trauma 2003;17:663–667.

90. Megas P. Classification of nonunion. Injury 2005;36(Suppl 4):S30–S37.

91. Murnaghan M, Li G, Marsh DR. Nonsteroidal anti-inflammatory drug-induced fracture nonunion: an inhibition of angiogenesis? J Bone Joint Surg Am 2006;88(Suppl 3):140–147.

92. Nadkarni B, Srivastav S, Mittal V, et al. Use of locking compression plates for long bone nonunions without removing existing intramedullary nail: review of literature and our experience. J Trauma 2008;65:482–486.

93. Newman JT, Stahel PF, Smith WR, et al. A new minimally invasive technique for large volume bone graft harvest for treatment of fracture nonunions. Orthopedics 2008;31:257.

94. Nho SJ, Helfet DL, Rozbruch SR. Temporary intentional leg shortening and deformation to facilitate wound closure using the Ilizarov/Taylor spatial frame. J Orthop Trauma 2006;20:419–424.

95. Nolte PA, van der Krans A, Patka P, et al. Low-intensity pulsed ultrasound in the treatment of nonunions. J Trauma 2001;51:693–702.

96. Norris TR, Green A, McGuigan FX. Late prosthetic shoulder arthroplasty for displaced proximal humerus fractures. J Shoulder Elbow Surg 1995;4:271–280.

97. Ochsner PE, Hailemariam S. Histology of osteosynthesis associated bone infection. Injury 2006;37(Suppl 2):S49–S58.

98. Oh JK, Bae JH, Oh CW, et al. Treatment of femoral and tibial diaphyseal nonunions using reamed intramedullary nailing without bone graft. Injury 2008;39:952–959

99. Ohtsuka H, Yokoyama K, Higashi K, et al. Use of antibiotic-impregnated bone cement nail to treat septic nonunion after open tibial fracture. J Trauma 2002;52:364–366.

100. Paley D, Catagni MA, Argnani F, et al. Ilizarov treatment of tibial nonunions with bone loss. Clin Orthop Relat Res 1989;241:146–165.

101. Pelissier P, Masquelet AC, Bareille R, et al. Induced membranes secrete growth factors including vascular and osteoinductive factors and could stimulate bone regeneration. J Orthop Res 2004;22:73–79.

102. Perry AC, Prpa B, Rouse MS, et al. Levofloxacin and trovafloxacin inhibition of experimental fracture-healing. Clin Orthop Relat Res 2003;414:95–100.

103. Perry CR. Bone repair techniques, bone graft, and bone graft substitutes. Clin Orthop Relat Res 1999;360:71–86.

104. Piepkorn B, Kann P, Forst T, et al. Bone mineral density and bone metabolism in diabetes mellitus. Horm Metab Res 1997;29:584–591.

105. Polyzois VD, Papakostas I, Stamatis ED, et al. Current concepts in delayed bone union and nonunion. Clin Podiatr Med Surg 2006;23:445–453, viii.

106. Qiang Z, Jun PZ, Jie XJ, et al. Use of antibiotic cement rod to treat intramedullary infection after nailing: preliminary study in 19 patients. Arch Orthop Trauma Surg 2007;127:945–951.

107. Rawool NM, Goldberg BB, Forsberg F, et al. Power Doppler assessment of vascular changes during fracture treatment with low-intensity ultrasound. J Ultrasound Med 2003;22:145–153.

108. Ricci WM, Haidukewych GJ. Periprosthetic femoral fractures. Instr Course Lect 2009;58:105–115.

109. Richmond J, Colleran K, Borens O, et al. Nonunions of the distal tibia treated by reamed intramedullary nailing. J Orthop Trauma 2004;18:603–610.

110. Ring D, Kloen P, Kadzielski J, et al. Locking compression plates for osteoporotic nonunions of the diaphyseal humerus. Clin Orthop Relat Res 2004;425:50–54.

111. Ristiniemi J, Lakovaara M, Flinkkila T, et al. Staged method using antibiotic beads and subsequent autografting for large traumatic tibial bone loss: 22 of 23 fractures healed after 5 to 20 months. Acta Orthop 2007;78:520–527.

112. Robinson CM, Court-Brown CM, McQueen MM, et al. Estimating the risk of nonunion following nonoperative treatment of a clavicular fracture. J Bone Joint Surg Am 2004;86-A:1359–1365.

113. Rosen H. Nonunion and malunion. In Browner BD, Levine AM, Jupiter JB, eds. Skeletal Trauma. Philadelphia: WB Saunders, 1998:501–541.

114. Rosen H. Treatment of nonunion. In Chapman W, ed. Operative Orthopedics. Philadelphia: Lippincott-Raven, 1988:489–509.

115. Rozbruch SR, Pugsley JS, Fragomen AT, et al. Repair of tibial nonunions and bone defects with the Taylor Spatial Frame. J Orthop Trauma 2008;22:88–95.

116. Ryaby JJ, Bachner EJ, Bendo JA, et al. Low-intensity pulsed ultrasound increases calcium incorporation in both differentiating cartilage and bone cell cultures. Trans Orthop Res Soc 1989;14:15.

117. Ryzewicz M, Morgan SJ, Linford E, et al. Central bone grafting for nonunion of fractures of the tibia: a retrospective series. J Bone Joint Surg Br 2009;91:522–529.

118. Salibian AH, Anzel SH, Salyer WA. Transfer of vascularized grafts of iliac bone to the extremities. J Bone Joint Surg Am 1987;69:1319–1327.

119. Sanchez-Sotelo J. Distal humeral nonunion. Instr Course Lect 2009;58:541–548.

120. Sarmiento A, Burkhalter WE, Latta LL. Functional bracing in the treatment of delayed union and nonunion of the tibia. Int Orthop 2003;27:26–29.

121. Schelstraete K, Daneels F, Obrie E. Technetium-99m-diphosphonate, gallium-67 and labeled leukocyte scanning techniques in tibial nonunion. Acta Orthop Belg 1992;58(Suppl 1):168–172.

122. Schenk RK. Histology of Fracture Repair and Nonunion. Bulletin of the Swiss Association for Study of Internal Fixation. Bern, Switzerland: Association for Study of Internal Fixation, 1978.

123. Schmidmaier G, Herrmann S, Green J, et al. Quantitative assessment of growth factors in reaming aspirate, iliac crest, and platelet preparation. Bone 2006;39:1156–1163.

124. Schmitz MA, Finnegan M, Natarajan R, et al. Effect of smoking on tibial shaft fracture healing. Clin Orthop Relat Res 1999;365:184–200.

125. Schottle PB, Werner CM, Dumont CE. Two-stage reconstruction with free vascularized soft tissue transfer and conventional bone graft for infected nonunions of the tibia: 6 patients followed for 1.5 to 5 years. Acta Orthop 2005;76:878–883.

126. Scott G, King JB. A prospective, double-blind trial of electrical capacitive coupling in the treatment of nonunion of long bones. J Bone Joint Surg Am 1994;76:820–826.

127. Sen MK, Miclau T. Autologous iliac crest bone graft: should it still be the gold standard for treating nonunions? Injury 2007;38(Suppl 1):S75–S80.

128. Sim R, Liang TS, Tay BK. Autologous marrow injection in the treatment of delayed and non-union in long bones. Singapore Med J 1993;34:412–417.

129. Smith MA, Jones EA, Strachan RK, et al. Prediction of fracture healing in the tibia by quantitative radionuclide imaging. J Bone Joint Surg Br 1987;69:441–447.

130. Smith TK. Prevention of complications in orthopedic surgery secondary to nutritional depletion. Clin Orthop Relat Res 1987;222:91–97.

131. Stafford P, Norris B. Reamer-Irrigator-Aspirator as a bone graft harvester. Techniques in Foot & Ankle Surgery 2007;6:100–107.

132. Stavlas P, Polyzois D. Septic arthritis of the major joints of the lower limb after periarticular external fixation application: are conventional safe corridors enough to prevent it? Injury 2005;36:239–247.

133. Taylor J. Delayed union and nonunion of fractures. In: Crenshaw A, ed. Campbell's Operative Orthopedics. St. Louis: Mosby, 1992:1287–1345.

134. Thonse R, Conway J. Antibiotic cement-coated interlocking nail for the treatment of infected nonunions and segmental bone defects. J Orthop Trauma 2007;21:258–268.

135. Thoresen BO, Alho A, Ekeland A, et al. Interlocking intramedullary nailing in femoral shaft fractures. A report of 48 cases. J Bone Joint Surg Am 1985;67:1313–1320.

136. Tomic S, Bumbasirevic M, Lesic A, et al. Modification of the Ilizarov external fixator for aseptic hypertrophic nonunion of the clavicle: an option for treatment. J Orthop Trauma 2006;20:122–128.

137. Ueng SW, Lin SS, Wang CR, et al. Bone healing of tibial lengthening is delayed by cigarette smoking: study of bone mineral density and torsional strength on rabbits. J Trauma 1999;46:110–115.

138. Veillette CJ, McKee MD. Growth factors—BMPs, DBMs, and buffy coat products: are there any proven differences amongst them? Injury 2007;38(Suppl 1):S38–S48.

139. Verbruggen JP, Stapert JW. Failure of reamed nailing in humeral nonunion: an analysis of 26 patients. Injury 2005;36:430–438.

140. Weiland AJ. Current concepts review: vascularized free bone transplants. J Bone Joint Surg Am 1981;63:166–169.

141. Weresh MJ, Hakanson R, Stover MD, et al. Failure of exchange reamed intramedullary nails for ununited femoral shaft fractures. J Orthop Trauma 2000;14:335–338.

142. Wiss DA, Johnson DL, Miao M. Compression plating for nonunion after failed external fixation of open tibial fractures. J Bone Joint Surg Am 1992;74:1279–1285.

143. Wu CC. The effect of dynamization on slowing the healing of femur shaft fractures after interlocking nailing. J Trauma 1997;43:263–267.

144. Wu CC. Exchange nailing for aseptic nonunion of femoral shaft: a retrospective cohort study for effect of reaming size. J Trauma 2007;63:859–865.

145. Wu CC. Retrograde dynamic locked nailing for femoral supracondylar nonunions after plating. J Trauma 2009;66:195–199.

146. Wu CC, Shih CH. Effect of dynamization of a static interlocking nail on fracture healing. Can J Surg 1993;36:302–306.

147. Wu CC, Shih CH, Chen WJ, et al. High success rate with exchange nailing to treat a tibial shaft aseptic nonunion. J Orthop Trauma 1999;13:33–38.

148. Yang KH, Parvizi J, Wang SJ, et al. Exposure to low-intensity ultrasound increases aggrecan gene expression in a rat femur fracture model. J Orthop Res 1996;14:802–809.

149. Zhang B, Chiu KY, Wang M. Hip arthroplasty for failed internal fixation of intertrochanteric fractures. J Arthroplasty 2004;19:329–333.

150. Zheng LW, Ma L, Cheung LK. Changes in blood perfusion and bone healing induced by nicotine during distraction osteogenesis. Bone 2008;43:355–361.

26

PRINCIPLES OF MALUNIONS

Mark R. Brinker and Daniel P. O'Connor

EVALUATION

Each malunited fracture presents a unique set of bony deformities. Deformities are described in terms of abnormalities of length, angulation, rotation, and translation. The location, magnitude, and direction of the deformity complete the characterization of the malunion. Proper evaluation allows the surgeon to determine an effective treatment plan for deformity correction.

Clinical

Evaluation begins with a medical history and a review of all available medical records, including the date and mechanism of injury of the initial fracture and all subsequent operative and nonoperative interventions. The history should also include descriptions of prior wound and bone infections, and prior culture reports should be obtained. All preinjury medical problems, disabilities, or associated injuries should be noted. The patient's current level of pain and functional limitations as well as medication use should be documented.

Following the history, a physical examination is performed. The skin and soft tissues in the injury zone should be inspected. The presence of active drainage or sinus formation should be noted.

The malunion site should be manually stressed to rule out motion and assess pain. In a solidly healed fracture with deformity, manual stressing should not elicit pain. If pain is elicited on manual stressing, the orthopaedic surgeon should consider the possibility that the patient has an ununited fracture.

A neurovascular examination of the limb and evaluation of active and passive motion of the joints proximal and distal to the malunion site should be performed. Reduced motion in a joint adjacent to a malunion site may alter both the treatment plan and the expectations for the ultimate functional outcome. Patients who have a periarticular malunion may also have a compensatory fixed deformity at an adjacent joint, which must be recognized to include its correction in the treatment plan. Correction of the malunion without addressing a compensatory joint deformity results in a straight bone with a maloriented joint, thus producing a disabled limb. The limb may appear aligned in these cases, but x-ray evaluation will reveal the joint deformity. If the patient cannot place the joint into the position that parallels the deformity at the malunion site (e.g., evert the subtalar joint into valgus in the presence of a tibial valgus malunion), the joint deformity is fixed and requires correction (Fig. 26-1).

Radiographic

The plain radiographs from the original fracture show the type and severity of the initial bony injury. Subsequent plain radiographs show the status of orthopaedic hardware (e.g., loose, broken, undersized) as well as document the timing of removal or insertion. The evolution of deformity—gradual versus sudden, for example—should be evaluated.

The current radiographs are evaluated next. Anteroposterior (AP) and lateral radiographs of the involved bone, including the proximal and distal joints, are used to evaluate the axes of the involved bone; manual measurement of standard radiographs or computer-assisted measurement of digital radiographs may be used with equivalent accuracy.[88,92,99] Bilateral

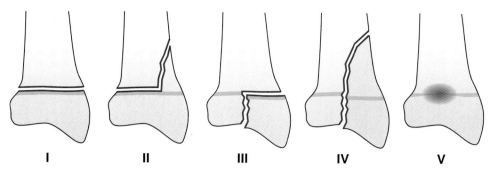

FIGURE 26-1 Angular deformity near a joint can result in a compensatory deformity through a neighboring joint. For example, frontal plane deformities of the distal tibia can result in a compensatory frontal plane deformity of the subtalar joint. The deformity of the subtalar joint is fixed **(A)** if the patient's foot cannot be positioned to parallel the deformity of the distal tibia or flexible **(B)** if the foot can be positioned parallel to the deformity of the distal tibia.

AP and lateral 51-inch alignment radiographs are obtained for lower extremity deformities to evaluate limb alignment (Fig. 26-2). Flexion/extension lateral radiographs may be useful to determine the arc of motion of the surrounding joints.

The current radiographs are used to describe the following characteristics: limb alignment, joint orientation, anatomic axes, mechanical axes, and center of rotation of angulation (CORA). Normative values for the relations among these various parameters[10,72] are used to assess deformities.

Limb Alignment

Evaluation of limb alignment involves assessment of the frontal plane mechanical axis of the entire limb rather than single bones.[35,45,47,77,78,90] In the lower extremity, the frontal plane mechanical axis of the entire limb is evaluated using the weight-bearing AP 51-inch alignment radiograph with the feet pointed forward (neutral rotation).[41,49,82] Mechanical axis deviation (MAD) is measured as the distance from the knee joint center to the line connecting the joint centers of the hip and ankle. The hip joint center is located at the center of the femoral head. The knee joint center is half the distance from the nadir between the tibial spines to the apex of the intercondylar notch on the femur. The ankle joint center is the center of the tibial plafond.

Normally, the mechanical axis of the lower extremity lies 1 mm to 15 mm medial to the knee joint center (Fig. 26-3). If the limb mechanical axis is outside this range, the deformity is described as MAD (see Fig. 26-3). MAD greater than 15 mm medial to the knee midpoint is varus malalignment; any MAD lateral to the knee midpoint is valgus malalignment.

Anatomic Axes

The anatomic and mechanical axes of each of the long bones are assessed in both the frontal plane (AP radiographs) and sagittal plane (lateral radiographs). The anatomic axes are defined as the line that passes through the center of the diaphysis along the length of the bone. To identify the anatomic axis of a long bone, the center of the transverse diameter of the diaphysis is identified at several points along the bone. The line that

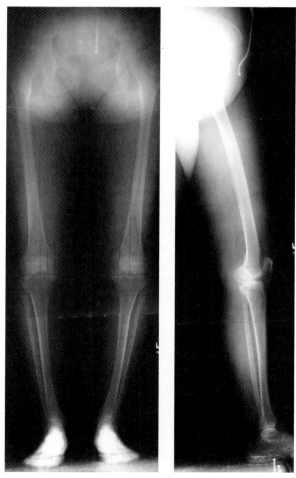

FIGURE 26-2 A. Bilateral weight-bearing 51-inch AP alignment radiograph and **(B)** a 51-inch lateral alignment radiograph, which are used to evaluate lower extremity limb alignment.

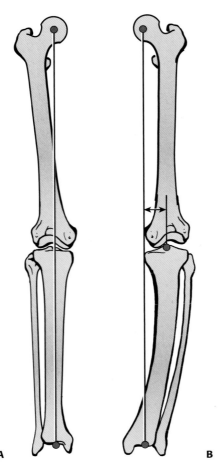

FIGURE 26-3 A. Mechanical axis of the lower extremity, which normally lies 1 mm to 15 mm medial to the knee joint center. **B.** Medial mechanical axis deviation, in which the mechanical axis of the lower extremity lies more than 15 mm medial to the knee joint center.

passes through these points represents the anatomic axis (Fig. 26-4).

In a normal bone, the anatomic axis is a single straight line. In a malunited bone with angulation, each bony segment can be defined by its own anatomic axis with a line through the center of the diameter of the diaphysis of each bone segment representing the respective anatomic axis for that segment (Fig. 26-5). In bones with multiapical or combined deformities, there may be multiple anatomic axes in the same plane.

Mechanical Axes
The mechanical axis of a long bone is defined as the line that passes through the joint centers of the proximal and distal joints. To identify the mechanical axis in a long bone, the joint centers are connected by a line (Fig. 26-6). The mechanical axis of the entire lower extremity was described above under the heading "Limb Alignment."

Joint Orientation Lines
Joint orientation describes the relation of a joint to the respective anatomic and mechanical axes of a long bone. Joint orientation lines are drawn on the AP and lateral radiographs in the frontal and sagittal planes, respectively.

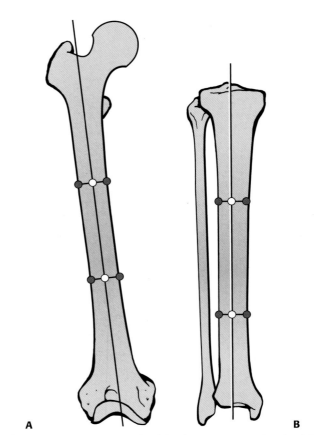

FIGURE 26-4 A. Anatomic axis of the femur. **B.** Anatomic axis of the tibia.

Hip orientation may be assessed in two ways in the frontal plane. The trochanter-head line connects the tip of the greater trochanter with center of the hip joint (the center of the femoral head). The femoral neck line connects the hip joint center with a series of points which bisect the diameter of the femoral neck.

Knee orientation is represented in the frontal plane by joint orientation lines at the distal femur and the proximal tibia. The distal femur joint orientation line is drawn tangential to the most distal points of the femoral condyles. The proximal tibial joint orientation line is drawn tangential to the subchondral lines of the medial and lateral tibial plateaus. The angle between these two knee joint orientation lines is called the joint line congruence angle (JLCA), which normally varies from 0 degrees to 2 degrees medial JLCA (i.e., slight knee joint varus). A lateral JLCA represents valgus malorientation of the knee, and a medial JLCA of 3 degrees or greater represents varus malorientation of the knee.

Knee orientation is represented in the sagittal plane by joint orientation lines at the distal femur and the proximal tibia. The sagittal distal femur joint orientation line is drawn through the anterior and posterior junctions of the femoral condyles and the metaphysis. The sagittal proximal tibial joint orientation line is drawn tangential to the subchondral lines of the tibial plateaus.

Malorientation of the knee joint produces malalignment, but limb malalignment (MAD outside the normal range) is not necessarily due to knee joint malorientation.

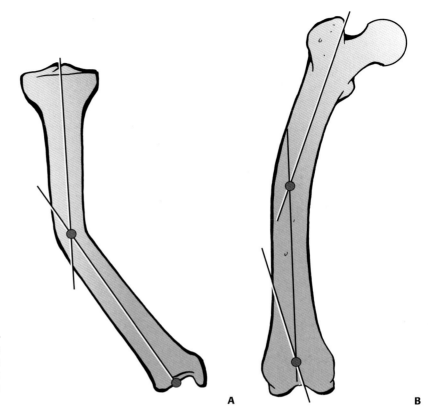

FIGURE 26-5 A. A malunited tibia fracture with angulation showing the anatomic axis for each bony segment as a line through the center of the diameter of the respective diaphyseal segments. **B.** A malunited femur fracture with a multiapical deformity, showing multiple anatomical axes in the same plane.

A   **B**

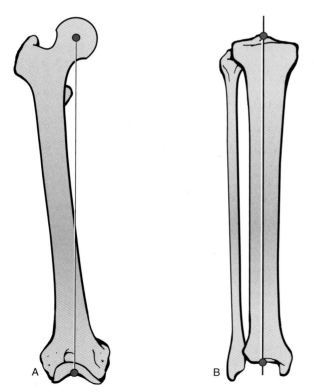

FIGURE 26-6 The mechanical axis of a long bone is defined as the line that passes through the joint centers of the proximal and distal joints. **A.** The mechanical axis of the femur. **B.** The mechanical axis of the tibia.

Ankle orientation is represented in the frontal plane by a line drawn through the subchondral line of the tibial plafond. Ankle orientation is represented in the sagittal plane by a line drawn through the most distal points of the anterior and posterior distal tibia.

Joint Orientation Angles

The relation between the anatomic axes or the mechanical axes and the joint orientation lines can be referred to as joint orientation angles described using standard nomenclature (Table 26-1 and Fig. 26-7).

In order to draw a joint orientation angle in the lower extremity, begin by drawing a joint orientation line. Next, identify the joint center, as the joint center will always lie on the mechanical axis and the joint orientation line. The mechanical axis line of the segment near the joint can be drawn using one of three methods: (i) using the population mean value for that particular joint orientation angle; (ii) using the joint orientation angle of the contralateral extremity, assuming it is normal; or (iii) by extending the mechanical axis of the neighboring bone.

For example, in order to draw the mechanical lateral distal femoral angle (mLDFA) in a femur with a frontal plane deformity, the steps would be as follows. Step 1: Draw the distal femoral joint orientation line. Step 2: Start at the joint center and draw an 88-degree mLDFA (population normal mean value), which will define the mechanical axis of the distal femoral segment, or draw the mLDFA which mimics the contralateral distal femur (if normal), or extend the mechanical axis of the tibia proximally (if normal) to define the distal femoral mechanical axis.

TABLE 26-1	**Normal Values for Joint Orientation Angles in the Lower Extremity**			
Bone—Plane		Components	Mean Value (in degrees)	Normal Range (in degrees)
Femur—Frontal				
Anatomic medial proximal femoral angle	Anatomic axis	Trochanter-head line	84	80–89
Mechanical lateral proximal femoral angle	Mechanical axis	Trochanter-head line	90	85–95
Neck shaft angle	Anatomic axis	Femoral neck line	130	124–136
Anatomic lateral distal femoral angle	Anatomic axis	Distal femoral joint orientation line	81	79–83
Mechanical lateral distal femoral angle	Mechanical axis	Distal femoral joint orientation line	88	85–90
Femur—Sagittal				
Anatomic posterior distal femoral angle	Middiaphyseal line	Sagittal distal femoral joint orientation line	83	79–87
Tibial—Frontal				
Mechanical medial proximal tibial angle	Mechanical axis	Proximal tibial joint orientation line	87	85–90
Mechanical lateral distal tibial angle	Mechanical axis	Distal tibial joint orientation line	89	88–92
Tibial—Sagittal				
Anatomic posterior proximal tibial angle	Middiaphyseal line	Sagittal proximal tibial joint orientation line	81	77–84
Anatomic anterior distal tibial angle	Middiaphyseal line	Sagittal distal tibial joint orientation line	80	78–82

Center of Rotation of Angulation (CORA)

The intersection of the proximal axis and distal axis of a deformed bone is called the CORA (Fig. 26-8), which is the point about which a deformity may be rotated to achieve correction.[22,30,34,46,72,73,76–78,89] The angle formed by the two axes at the CORA is a measure of angular deformity in that plane. Either the anatomic or mechanical axes may be used to identify the CORA, but these axes cannot be mixed. For diaphyseal malunions, the anatomic axes are most convenient. For juxta-articular (metaphyseal, epiphyseal) deformities, the axis line of the short segment is constructed using one of the three methods described above.

To define the CORA, the proximal axis and distal axis of the bone are identified, and then the orientations of the proximal and distal joints are assessed. If the intersection of the proximal and distal axes lies at the point of obvious deformity in the bone and the joint orientations are normal, the intersection point is the CORA and the deformity is uniapical (in the respective plane). If their intersection lies outside the point of obvious deformity or either joint orientation is abnormal, either a second CORA exists in that plane and the deformity is multiapical or a translational deformity exists in that plane, which is usually obvious on the radiograph.

The CORA is used to plan the operative correction of angular deformities. Correction of angulation by rotating the bone around a point on the line that bisects the angle of the CORA (the "bisector") ensures realignment of the anatomic and mechanical axes without introducing an iatrogenic translational deformity.[34] The bisector is a line that passes through the CORA and bisects the angle formed by the proximal and distal axes (see Fig. 26-8).[72] Angular correction along the bisector results in complete deformity correction without the introduction of a translational deformity.[10,73,75,77,78] All points that lie on the bisector can be considered to be CORAs because angulation about these points will result in realignment of the deformed bone (see "Treatment—Osteotomies").

Note that the proximal half of the mechanical axis for the femur normally lies outside the bone, so the CORA identified using the mechanical axis of the femur may lie outside the bone as well. By contrast, if the CORA identified using the anatomic axis of the femur or either axis of the tibia lies outside the bone, then a multiapical deformity exists (see Fig. 26-8).

Evaluation of the Various Deformity Types

Length

Deformities involving length include shortening and overdistraction and are characterized by their direction and magnitude. They are measured from joint center to joint center in centimeters on plain radiographs and compared to the contralateral normal extremity, using an x-ray marker to correct for magnification (Fig. 26-9).[91] Shortening after an injury may result from bone loss (from the injury or débridement) or overriding of the healed fracture fragments. Overdistraction at the time of fracture fixation may result in a healed fracture with overlengthening of the bone.

Angulation

Deformities involving angulation are characterized by their magnitude and the direction of the apex of angulation. Angulation deformity of the diaphysis is often associated with limb malalignment (MAD), as described above. Angulation deformities of the metaphysis and epiphysis (juxta-articular deformities) can be difficult to characterize. In particular, the angle formed by the intersection of a joint orientation line and the anatomic or mechanical axis of the deformed bone should be measured. When the angle formed differs markedly from the contralateral normal limb (or normal values when the contralateral limb is abnormal), a juxta-articular deformity is present.[10,75,78] The identification of the CORA is key in characterizing angular deformities and planning their correction.

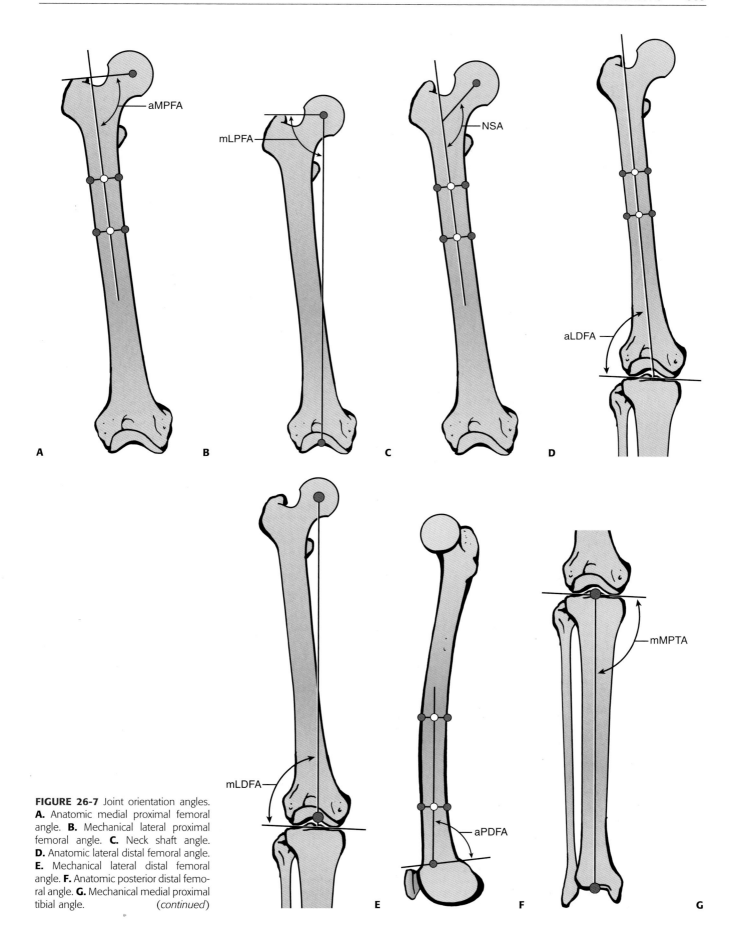

FIGURE 26-7 Joint orientation angles. **A.** Anatomic medial proximal femoral angle. **B.** Mechanical lateral proximal femoral angle. **C.** Neck shaft angle. **D.** Anatomic lateral distal femoral angle. **E.** Mechanical lateral distal femoral angle. **F.** Anatomic posterior distal femoral angle. **G.** Mechanical medial proximal tibial angle. *(continued)*

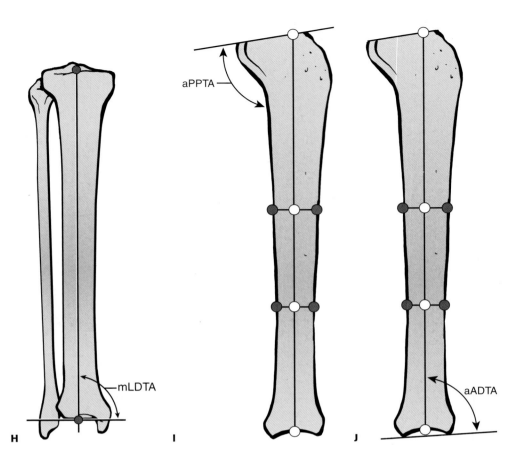

FIGURE 26-7 (*continued*) **H.** Mechanical lateral distal tibial angle. **I.** Anatomic posterior proximal tibial angle. **J.** Anatomic anterior distal tibial angle.

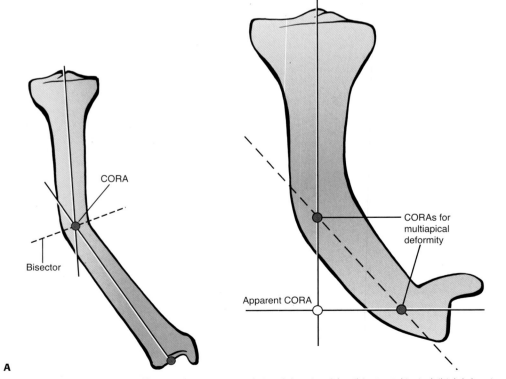

FIGURE 26-8 A. CORA and bisector for a varus angulation deformity of the tibia. **B.** Multiapical tibial deformity showing that the apparent CORA joining the proximal and distal anatomic axes (*solid lines*) lies outside of the bone. A third anatomic axis for the middle segment (*dashed line*) shows two CORAs for this multiapical deformity that both lie within the bone.

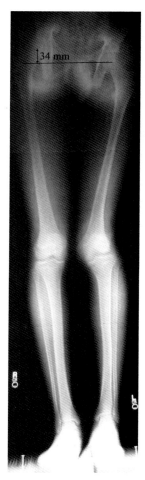

FIGURE 26-9 Bilateral standing 51-inch AP alignment radiograph reveals a 34-mm leg length inequality.

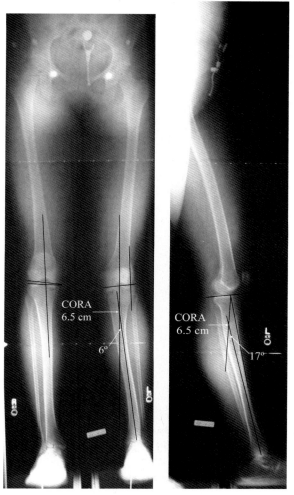

FIGURE 26-10 A 28-year-old woman presented with complaints of her leg "going out" and her knee hyperextending. **A.** 51-inch AP alignment radiograph reveals a 6-degree apex medial deformity with the CORA 6.5 cm distal to the proximal tibial joint orientation line. **B.** The lateral alignment radiograph shows a 17-degree apex posterior angulation with a CORA 6.5 cm distal to the proximal tibial joint orientation line. This patient has an oblique plane angular deformity without translation.

Pure frontal or sagittal plane deformities are simple to characterize; the angular deformity appears only on the AP or lateral radiograph, respectively. If, however, the AP and lateral radiographs both appear to have angulation with CORAs at the same level on both views, the orientation of the angulation deformity is in an oblique plane (Fig. 26-10). Characterization of the magnitude and direction of oblique plane deformities can be computed from the AP and lateral x-ray measures using either the trigonometric or graphic method.[18,37,72] Using the trigonometric method, the magnitude of an oblique plane angular deformity is

$$\text{oblique magnitude} = \tan^{-1}\sqrt{\tan^2 (\text{frontal magnitude}) + \tan^2 (\text{sagittal magnitude})},$$

and the orientation (relative to the frontal plane) of an oblique plane deformity is

$$\text{oblique orientation} = \tan^{-1}\left[\frac{\tan (\text{sagittal magnitude})}{\tan (\text{frontal magnitude})}\right].$$

Using the graphic method, the magnitude of an oblique plane angular deformity is

$$\text{oblique magnitude} = \sqrt{(\text{frontal magnitude})^2 + (\text{sagittal magnitude})^2},$$

and the orientation (relative to the frontal plane) of an oblique plane deformity is

$$\text{oblique orientation} = \tan^{-1}\left(\frac{\text{sagittal magnitude}}{\text{frontal magnitude}}\right).$$

The graphic method, based on the Pythagorean Theorem, approximates the exact trigonometric method. The error of approximation for angular deformities using the graphic method is less than 4 degrees unless the frontal and sagittal plane magnitudes are both greater than 45 degrees.[10,46,72,75,77,78]

In the case that the CORA is at a different level on the AP and lateral radiographs, a translational deformity is present in addition to an angulation deformity (Fig. 26-11).

A multiapical deformity is defined by the presence of more than one CORA on either the AP or lateral radiograph (or both). In a multiapical deformity without translation, one of the joints will appear maloriented relative to the anatomic axis of the respective segment. For multiapical deformity, the anatomic

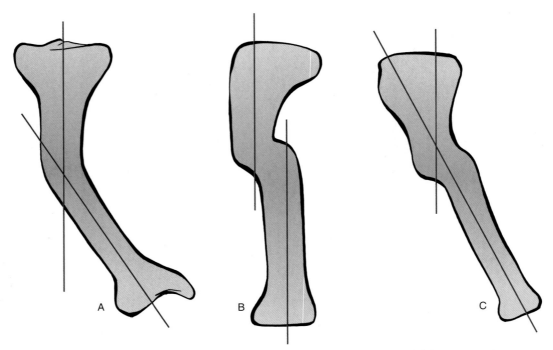

FIGURE 26-11 A. Frontal and **B.** sagittal views of a tibia with an angulation-translational deformity. Note that the angulation deformity is evident only on the frontal view and the translational deformity is evident only on the sagittal view. **C.** The oblique view showing both deformities.

axis of the segment that has the joint malorientation provides a third line that crosses both of the existing lines. These intersections are the sites of the multiple CORAs (see Fig. 26-8B).

Rotation

A rotational deformity occurs about the longitudinal axis of the bone. Rotational deformities are described in terms of their magnitude and the position (internal or external rotation) of the distal segment relative to the proximal segment. Identification of a rotational deformity and quantification of the magnitude can be done using clinical measurements,[101] axial computed tomography (Fig. 26-12),[12] or AP and lateral radiographs with either trigonometric calculation or graphical approximation.[72] While axial computed tomography and radiographic methods allow for more precise measurement of rotational deformities, clinical examination often results in measures of sufficient accuracy to allow for adequate correction.[101]

To measure tibial malrotation using clinical examination, the position of the foot axis, as indicated by a line running from the second toe through the center of the calcaneus, is compared to the projection of either the femoral or the tibial anatomic axis. To use the femoral axis, the patient is positioned prone or sits with the knee flexed to 90 degrees. The examiner measures the deviation of the foot axis from the line of the femoral axis; any deviation is considered to represent tibial malrotation. To use the tibial axis, the patient stands with the patella facing anteriorly (i.e., aligned in the frontal plane). To measure tibial malrotation, the examiner measures the deviation of the foot axis from the anterior projection of the tibial anatomic axis in the sagittal plane; any deviation of the foot axis from the tibial anatomic axis is considered to represent tibial malrotation.

To measure a femoral rotational deformity using clinical examination, the patient is positioned prone with the knee flexed

to 90 degrees and the femoral condyles parallel to the examination table. The femur is passively rotated internally and externally by the examiner, and the respective angular excursions of the tibia are measured. Asymmetry of rotation in comparison to the opposite side indicates a femoral rotational deformity. If the patient also has a tibial angulation deformity, the tibia will not be perpendicular to the examination table when the femoral condyles are so positioned; tibial angulation deformity will cause an apparent asymmetry in femoral rotation. In this case, the rotational excursions of the tibia must be adjusted for the magnitude of the tibial angular deformity to avoid an incorrect assessment of femoral rotation.

Translation

Translational deformities may result from malunion following either a fracture or an osteotomy. Translational deformities are characterized by their plane, direction, magnitude, and level. The direction of translational deformities is described in terms of the position of the distal segment relative to the proximal segment (medial, lateral, anterior, posterior), except for the femoral and humeral heads where the description is the position of the head relative to the shaft. Translational deformities may occur in an oblique plane, and trigonometric or graphical methods similar to those described for characterizing angulation deformities may be used to identify the plane and direction of the deformity.[18,37,72] Magnitude of translation is measured as the horizontal distance from the proximal segment's anatomic axis to the distal segment's anatomic axis at the level of the proximal end of the distal segment (Fig. 26-13).

TREATMENT

The clinical and radiographic evaluation of the deformity provides the information needed to develop a treatment plan. Fol-

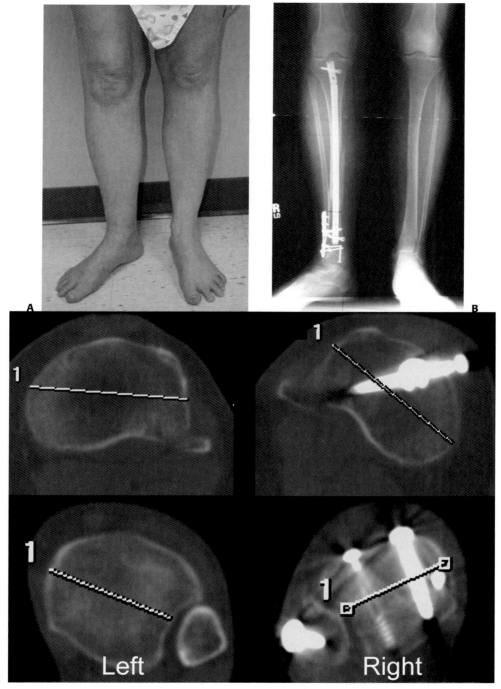

FIGURE 26-12 A. Clinical photograph of a 38-year-old woman who presented 9 months after nail fixation of a tibial fracture. She complained of her right foot "pointing outward." **B.** Plain radiographs show what appears to be a healed fracture following tibial nailing. Comparison of the proximal and distal tibias bilaterally was consistent with malrotation of the right distal tibia. **C.** Computed tomography scans of both proximal and distal tibias show asymmetric external rotation of the right distal tibia that measures 42 degrees. The computed tomography scan also confirmed solid bony union at the fracture site.

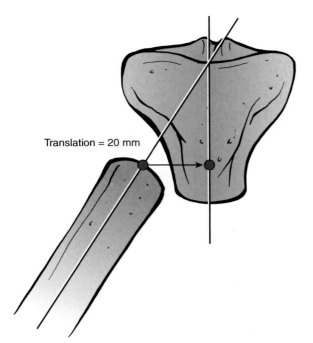

Translation = 20 mm

FIGURE 26-13 Method for measuring the magnitude of translational deformities. In this example, with both angulation and translation, the magnitude of the translational deformity is the horizontal distance from the proximal segment's anatomic axis to the distal segment's anatomic axis at the level of the proximal end of the distal segment.

lowing evaluation, the deformity is characterized by its type (length, angulation, rotational, translational, or combined), the direction of the apex (anterior, lateral, posterolateral, etc.), the orientation plane, its magnitude, and the level of the CORA.

The status of the soft tissues may impact the surgical treatment of a bony deformity. Preoperative planning should include an evaluation of overlying soft tissue free flaps and skin grafts. In addition, scarring, tethering of neurovascular bundles, and infection may require modifications to the treatment plan in order to address these concomitant conditions in addition to correcting the malunion. Furthermore, if neurovascular structures lie on the concave side of an angular deformity, acute correction may lead to a traction injury to them with temporary or permanent complications. In such cases, gradual deformity correction may be preferable and allow for gradual accommodation of the nerves or vasculature and thus avoid complications.

Osteotomies

An osteotomy is used to separate the deformed bone segments to allow realignment of the anatomic and mechanical axes. The ability of an osteotomy to restore alignment depends on the location of the CORA, the axis about which correction is performed (the correction axis), and the location of the osteotomy. While the CORA is defined by the type, direction, and magnitude of the deformity, the correction axis depends on the location and type of the osteotomy, the soft tissues, and the choice of fixation technique. The relation of these three factors to one another determines the final position of the bone segments. Reduction following osteotomy produces one of three possible results: (i) realignment through angulation alone; (ii) realign-

ment through angulation and translation; and (iii) realignment through angulation and translation with an iatrogenic residual translational abnormality (Fig. 26-14).

When the CORA, correction axis, and osteotomy lie at the same location, the bone will realign through angulation alone, without translation. When the CORA and correction axis are at the same location but the osteotomy is made proximal or distal to that location, the bone will realign through both angulation and translation. When the CORA is at a location different than the correction axis and osteotomy, correction of angulation aligns the proximal and distal axes in parallel but excess translation occurs and results in an iatrogenic translational deformity (see Fig. 26-14).

Osteotomies can be classified by cut (straight or dome [understand that these osteotomies are not truly shaped like a dome, they are cylindrical]) and type (opening, closing, neutral). A straight cut, such as a transverse or wedge osteotomy, is made such that the opposing bone ends have flat surfaces. A dome osteotomy is made such that the opposing bone ends have congruent convex and concave cylindrical surfaces. The type describes the rotation of the bone segments relative to one another at the osteotomy site.

Selection of the osteotomy type depends on the type, magnitude, and direction of deformity, the proximity of the deformity to a joint, the location and its effect on the soft tissues, and the type of fixation selected. In certain cases, a small iatrogenic deformity may be acceptable if it is expected to have no effect on the patient's final functional outcome. This situation may be preferable to attempting an unfamiliar fixation method or using a fixation technique that the patient may tolerate poorly.

Wedge Osteotomy

The type of wedge osteotomy is determined by the location of the osteotomy relative to the locations of the CORA and the correction axis. When the CORA and correction axis are in the same location (to avoid translational deformity), they may lie on the cortex on the convex side of the deformity, on the cortex on the concave side of the deformity, or in the middle of the bone (Fig. 26-15).

When the CORA and correction axis lie on the convex cortex of the deformity, the correction will result in an opening wedge osteotomy (see Fig. 26-15). In an opening wedge osteotomy, the cortex on the concave side of the deformity is distracted to restore alignment, opening an empty wedge that traverses the diameter of the bone. An opening wedge osteotomy also increases bone length.

When the CORA and correction axis lie in the middle of the bone, the correction distracts the concave side cortex and compresses the convex side cortex. A bone wedge is removed from only the convex side to allow realignment. This neutral wedge osteotomy (see Fig. 26-15) has no effect on bone length.

When the CORA and correction axis lie on the concave cortex of the deformity, the correction will result in a closing wedge osteotomy (see Fig. 26-15). In a closing wedge osteotomy, the cortex on the convex side of the deformity is compressed to restore alignment; this requires removal of a bone wedge across the entire bone diameter. A closing wedge osteotomy also decreases bone length (resulting in shortening).

These principles of osteotomy also hold true when the osteotomy is located proximal or distal to the mutual site of the CORA and correction axis. As stated above, realignment in these

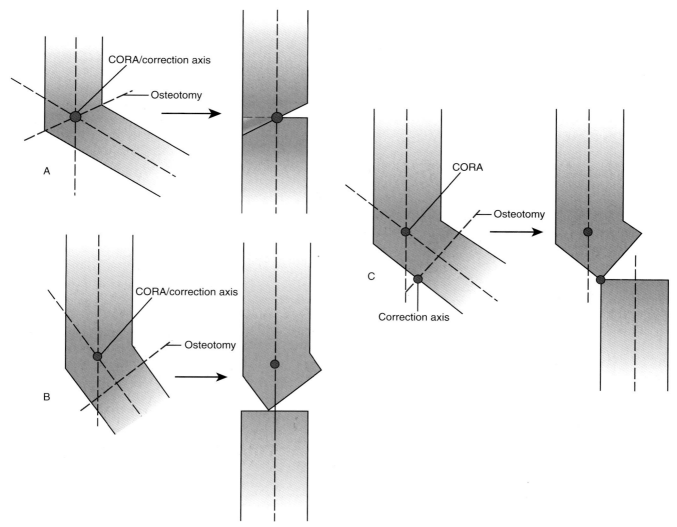

FIGURE 26-14 Possible results when using osteotomy for correction of deformity. **A.** The CORA, the correction axis, and the osteotomy all lie at the same location; the bone realigns through angulation alone, without translation. **B.** The CORA and the correction axis lie in the same location, but the osteotomy is proximal or distal to that location; the bone realigns through both angulation and translation. **C.** The CORA lies at one location and the correction axis and the osteotomy lie in a different location; correction of angulation results in an iatrogenic translational deformity.

cases occurs via angulation and translation. When the CORA and correction axis are not at the same point and the osteotomy is proximal or distal to the CORA, the correction maneuver results in excess translation and an iatrogenic translational deformity.

Dome Osteotomy

The type of dome osteotomy is also determined by the location of the CORA and the correction axis relative to the osteotomy. In contrast to a wedge osteotomy, however, the osteotomy site can never pass through the mutual CORA-correction axis (Fig. 26-16). Thus, translation will always occur with deformity correction using a dome osteotomy.

Ideally, the CORA and correction axis are mutually located such that the angulation and obligatory translation that occurs at the osteotomy site results in realignment. Attempts at realignment when the CORA and correction axis are not mutually located results in a translational deformity (see Fig. 26-16). Sim-

ilar to wedge osteotomy, the CORA and correction axis may lie on the cortex on the convex side of the deformity, on the cortex on the concave side of the deformity, or in the middle of the bone.

The principles guiding wedge osteotomies are also true for dome osteotomies. When the CORA and correction axis lie on the convex cortex of the deformity, the correction will result in an opening dome osteotomy (Fig. 26-17). The translation that occurs in an opening dome osteotomy increases final bone length. When the CORA and correction axis lie in the middle of the bone, the correction will result in a neutral dome osteotomy. A neutral dome osteotomy has no effect on bone length. When the CORA and correction axis lie on the concave cortex of the deformity, the correction will result in a closing dome osteotomy. The translation that occurs in a closing dome osteotomy decreases final bone length. Unlike wedge osteotomies, the movement of one bone segment on the other is rarely impeded, so removal of bone is not typically required unless the final

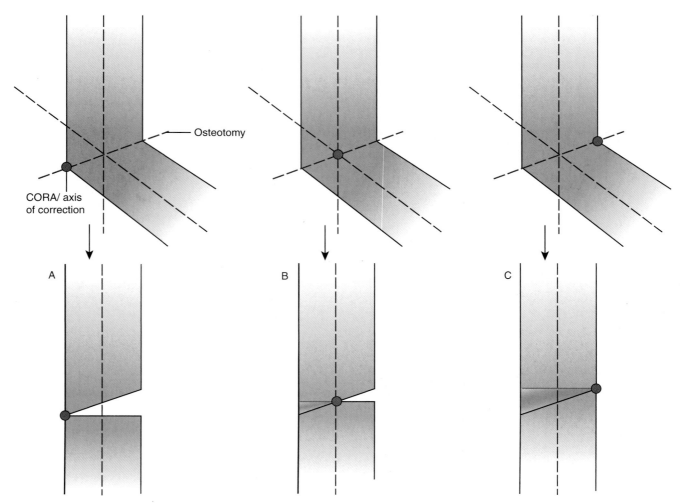

FIGURE 26-15 Wedge osteotomies; the osteotomy is made at the level of the CORA and correction axis in all of these examples. **A.** Opening wedge osteotomy. The CORA and correction axis lie on the cortex on the convex side of the deformity. The cortex on the concave side of the deformity is distracted to restore alignment, opening an empty wedge that traverses the diameter of the bone. Opening wedge osteotomy increases final bone length. **B.** Neutral wedge osteotomy. The CORA and correction axis lie in the middle of the bone. The concave side cortex is distracted and the convex side cortex is compressed. A bone wedge is removed from the convex side. Neutral wedge osteotomy has no effect on final bone length. **C.** Closing wedge osteotomy. The CORA and correction axis lie on the concave cortex of the deformity. The cortex on the convex side of the deformity is compressed to restore alignment, requiring removal of a bone wedge across the entire bone diameter. A closing wedge osteotomy decreases final bone length.

configuration results in significant overhang of the bone beyond the aligned bone column.

Treatment by Deformity Type

Length

Acute distraction or compression methods obtain immediate correction of limb length by acute lengthening with bone grafting or acute shortening, respectively. The extent of acute lengthening or shortening that is possible is limited by the soft tissues (soft tissue compliance, surgical and open wounds, and neurovascular structures).

Acute distraction treatment methods involve distracting the bone ends to the appropriate length, applying a bone graft, and stabilizing the construct to allow incorporation of the graft. Options for treating length deformities include the use of: (i) autogenous cancellous or cortical bone grafts; (ii) vascularized autografts; (iii) bulk or strut cortical allografts; (iv) mesh cage-bone graft constructs; and (v) synostosis techniques. A variety of internal and external fixation treatment methods may be used to stabilize the construct during graft incorporation.[9] The amount of shortening that requires lengthening correction is uncertain.[38,65,102] In the upper extremity, up to 3 to 4 cm of shortening is generally well tolerated, and restoring length when shortening exceeds this value have been reported to improve function.[1,19,59,71,81,96,104,107] In the lower extremity, up to 2 cm of shortening may be treated with a shoe lift; tolerance for a 2 to 4 cm shoe lift is poor for most patients, and most patients with shortening of greater than 4 cm will benefit from restoration of length.[7,8,31,64,102,109]

Acute compression methods are used to correct overdistraction by first resecting the appropriate length of bone and then stabilizing the approximated bone ends under compression. For the paired bones of the forearm and leg, the unaffected bone

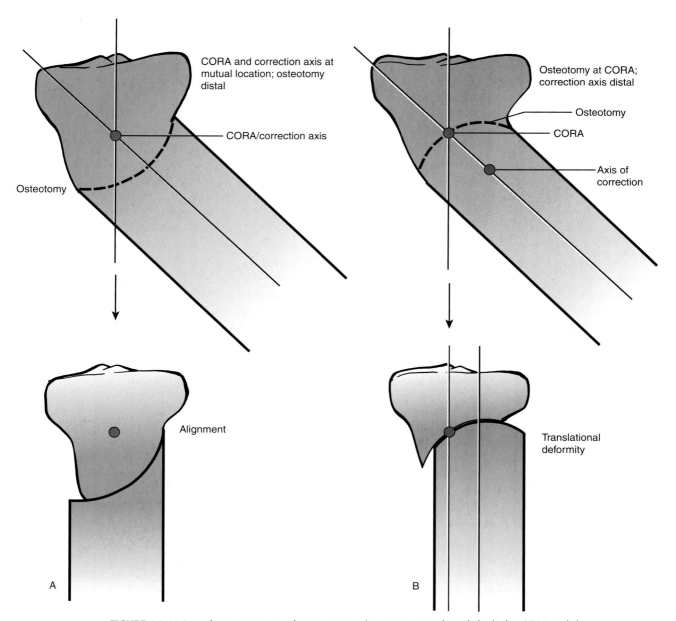

FIGURE 26-16 In a dome osteotomy, the osteotomy site cannot pass through both the CORA and the correction axis. Thus, translation will always occur when using a dome osteotomy. **A.** Ideally, the CORA and correction axis are mutually located with the osteotomy proximal or distal to that location such that the angulation and obligatory translation that occurs at the osteotomy site results in realignment of the bone axis. **B.** When the CORA and correction axis are not mutually located, a dome osteotomy through the CORA location results in a translational deformity.

requires partial excision to allow shortening and compression of the affected bone. For example, partial excision of the intact fibula is necessary to allow shortening and compression of the tibia.

Gradual correction techniques for length deformities typically use tensioned-wire (Ilizarov) external fixation,[3,16,50,59,60, 62,74,102,104,107] although gradual lengthening using conventional monolateral external fixation has been described,[70,93,94] and an intramedullary nail that provides a continuous lengthening force has recently been developed.[17,43,44] The most common form of gradual correction is gradual distraction to correct limb shortening. Gradual correction methods for length deformities

can also be used to correct associated angular, translational, or rotational deformities simultaneously while restoring length.

Gradual distraction involves the creation of a corticotomy (usually metaphyseal) and distraction of the bone segments at a rate of 1 mm per day using a rhythm of 0.25 mm of distraction repeated four times per day. The bone formed at the distraction site is formed through the process of distraction osteogenesis, as discussed below in the "Ilizarov Techniques" section.

Angulation

Correction of angulation deformities involves making an osteotomy, obtaining realignment of the bone segments, and securing

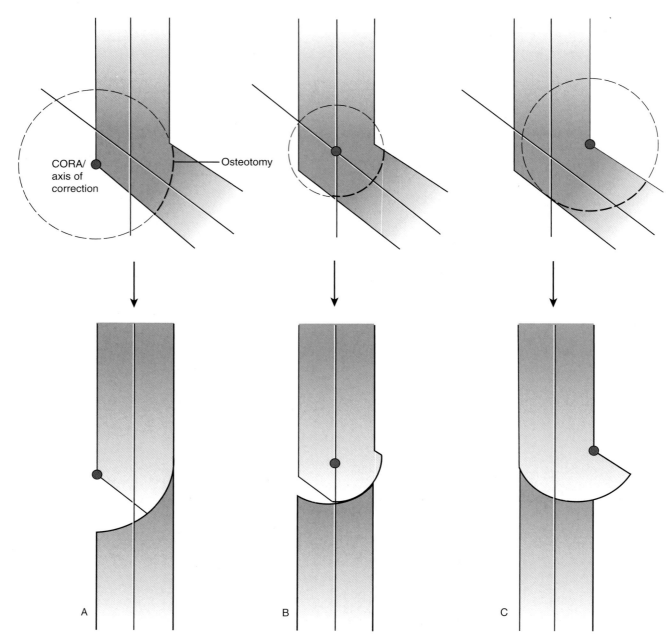

FIGURE 26-17 Dome osteotomies; the CORA and correction axis are mutually located with the osteotomy distal to that location in all of these examples. **A.** Opening dome osteotomy. The CORA and correction axis lie on the cortex on the convex side of the deformity. Opening dome osteotomy increases final bone length. **B.** Neutral dome osteotomy. The CORA and correction axis lie in the middle of the bone. Neutral dome osteotomy has no effect on final bone length. **C.** Closing dome osteotomy. The CORA and correction axis lie on the concave cortex of the deformity. A closing dome osteotomy decreases final bone length and can result in significant overhang of bone that may require resection.

fixation during healing. The correction may be made acutely and then stabilized using a number of internal or external fixation methods.[28,39] Alternatively, the correction may be made gradually using external fixation to both restore alignment and provide stabilization during healing.[28,105]

Angulation deformities in the diaphysis are most amenable to correction using a wedge osteotomy at the same level as the correction axis and the CORA. For juxta-articular angulation deformities, however, the correction axis and the CORA may be located too close to the respective joint to permit a wedge osteotomy. Thus, juxta-articular angulation deformities may require a dome osteotomy with location of the osteotomy proximal or distal to the level of the correction axis and the CORA.

Rotation

Correction of a rotational deformity requires an osteotomy and rotational realignment followed by stabilization. Stabilization may be accomplished using internal or external fixation following acute correction, or external fixation may be used to gradually correct the deformity. The level for the osteotomy, however, can be difficult to determine. While the level of the deformity is obvious in the case of an angulated malunion, the level of deformity in rotational limb deformities is often difficult to determine. Consequently, other factors, including muscle and tendon line of pull, neurovascular structures, and soft tissues, are usually considered to determine the level of deformity and level of osteotomy for correction of a rotational deformity.[32,56,57,72,80,100]

Translation

Translational deformities may be corrected in one of three ways. First, a single transverse osteotomy may be made to restore alignment through pure translation without angulation; the transverse osteotomy does not have to be made at the level of the deformity (Fig. 26-18). Second, a single oblique osteotomy may be made at the level of the deformity to restore alignment and gain length. Third, a translational deformity can be represented as two angulations with identical magnitudes but opposite directions. Therefore, two wedge osteotomies at the level of the respective CORAs and angular corrections of equal magnitudes in opposite directions may be used to correct a translational deformity. It should be noted that the osteotomy types

used in this third method (opening, closing, or neutral) will affect final bone length. Internal or external fixation may be used to provide stabilization following acute correction of translational deformities, or gradual correction may be carried out using external fixation.

Combined Deformities

Combined deformities are characterized by the presence of two or more types of deformity in a single bone.[37,40] Treatment planning begins with identifying and characterizing each deformity independent from the other deformities. Once all deformities have been characterized, they are assessed to determine which require correction to restore function. Correction of all of the deformities may be unnecessary; for example, small translational deformities or angulation deformities in the sagittal plane may not interfere with limb function and may remain untreated. Once those deformities requiring correction are identified, the treatment plan outlines the order and method of correction for each deformity.

In many instances, a single osteotomy can be used to correct two deformities. For example, a combined angulation-translational deformity can be corrected using a single osteotomy at

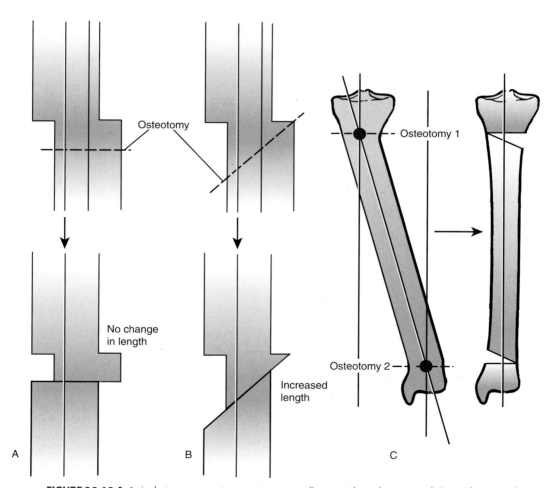

FIGURE 26-18 A. A single transverse osteotomy to restore alignment through pure translation without angulation. **B.** A single oblique osteotomy at the level of the deformity to restore alignment and gain length. **C.** A translational deformity represented as two angulations with identical magnitudes but opposite directions causing malalignment of the mechanical axis of the lower extremity. Two wedge osteotomies of equal magnitudes in opposite directions at the levels of the respective CORAs may be used to correct a translational deformity and restore alignment of the mechanical axis of the lower extremity.

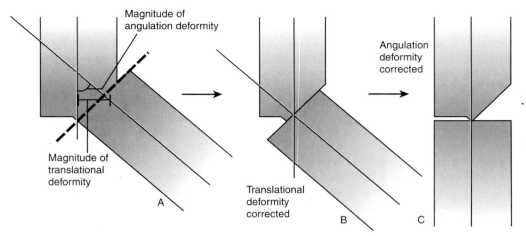

FIGURE 26-19 A single osteotomy to correct an angulation-translational deformity. **A.** A single osteotomy is made to allow correction of both deformities. **B.** Correction of the translational deformity, followed by **C.** correction of the angulation deformity, resulting in realignment.

the level of the apex of the angulation deformity. This method restores alignment and congruency of the medullary canals and cortices of the respective bone segments (Fig. 26-19). The deformities are then reduced one at a time—reducing translation and then angulation, for instance. Consequently, stabilization can be achieved using an intramedullary nail, as well as a number of other internal fixation and external fixation methods.

Combined angulation-translation deformities can also be treated as multiapical angulation deformities with an osteotomy through either or both CORAs in the frontal and sagittal planes.

While this method restores alignment of the bone's mechanical axis, it can also result in incomplete bone-to-bone contact and incongruence of the bone segments' medullary canals and cortices. As a result, stabilization cannot be achieved using an intramedullary nail and other internal fixation and external fixation methods are required to stabilize the bone segments.

A combined angulation-rotational deformity can be corrected by a single rotation of the distal segment around an oblique axis that represents the resolutions of both the component angulation axis and rotation axis (Fig. 26-20).[66] The direc-

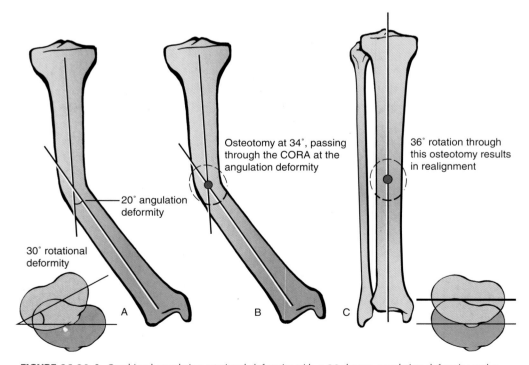

FIGURE 26-20 A. Combined angulation-rotational deformity with a 20-degree angulation deformity and a 30-degree rotational deformity. Calculations of the correction axis (see text for formula) show an inclination of 56 degrees, which corresponds to an osteotomy inclination of 34 degrees. **B.** The 34-degree osteotomy is made such that it passes through the CORA of the angulation deformity. **C.** Rotation of 36 degrees about the correction axis in the plane of the osteotomy results in realignment by simultaneous correction of both deformities.

tion and magnitude of the combined angulation-rotational deformity are both characterized in this oblique axis. The angle of the oblique correction axis, which is perpendicular to the plane of the necessary osteotomy, can be approximated using trigonometry (axis angle = arctan[rotation/angulation]; orientation of plane of osteotomy = 90– axis angle).

This single osteotomy is made at a location such that it passes through the level of the CORA of the angulation deformity (i.e., the bisector of the axes of the proximal and distal segments). Rotation of the distal segment about this CORA in the plane of the osteotomy results in realignment; opening and closing wedge corrections can also be achieved by using the CORA located on the respective cortex. Rotation of the distal segment in the plane of the osteotomy but not about a CORA will lead to a secondary translational deformity. This secondary deformity can be corrected by reducing the translation after rotation is completed. Locating the level of the osteotomy distal to the level of the CORA and correcting the secondary translational deformity can be used to correct a combined deformity if locating the osteotomy at the level of the CORA is impractical, such as would occur if the osteotomy would violate a growth plate or place soft tissues or neurovascular structures at risk.

Treatment by Deformity Location

The bone involved and the specific bone region or regions (e.g., epiphysis, metaphysis, diaphysis) define the anatomic location. While a bone-by-bone discussion is beyond the scope of this chapter, we will address the influence of anatomic region on the treatment of malunions in general terms.

Shaft

Diaphyseal deformities involve primarily cortical bone in the central section of long bones. Characterizing deformities is straightforward, as angulation and translational deformities are usually obvious on plain radiographs. In addition, the use of wedge osteotomies through the CORA for deformity correction is generally achievable, thus allowing reduction of the deformity without concerns about inducing secondary translational deformities. By virtue of their relatively homogenous morphology, diaphyseal deformities are amenable to a wide array of fixation methods following correction. Intramedullary nail fixation is preferable when practical (Fig. 26-21).

Periarticular

Periarticular deformities located in the metaphysis and epiphysis are more difficult to identify, characterize, and treat. In addition to the juxta-articular deformities of length, angulation, rotation, and translation and the presence of joint malorientation, there may also be malreduction of articular surfaces and compensatory joint deformities, such as soft tissue contractures and fixed joint subluxation or dislocation. Identification, characterization, and prioritization of each component of the deformity are critical to forming a successful treatment plan.

Acute correction of periarticular deformities is most often accomplished using plate and screw fixation or external fixation. Gradual correction may be accomplished using external fixation (Fig. 26-22).

Treatment by Method

Plate and Screw Fixation

The advantages of plate and screw fixation include rigidity of fixation, versatility for various anatomic locations and situations (e.g., periarticular deformities), correction of deformities under direct visualization, and safety following failed or temporary external fixation. Disadvantages of the method include extensive soft tissue dissection, limitation of early weight bearing and

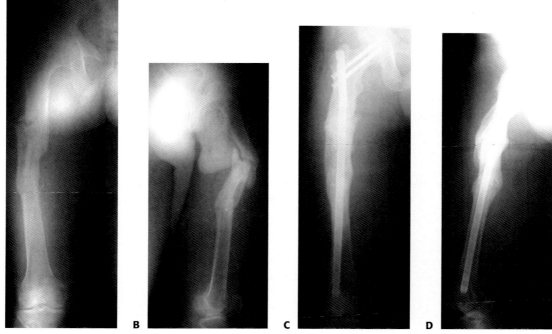

FIGURE 26-21 A,B. AP and lateral radiographs on presentation. **C,D.** AP and lateral radiographs following deformity correction with closed antegrade femoral nailing.

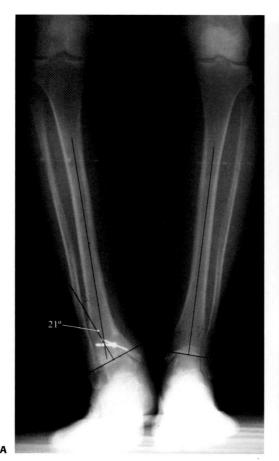

21°

A

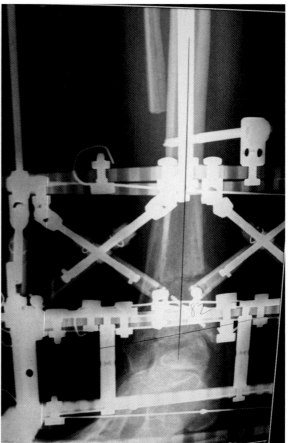

B

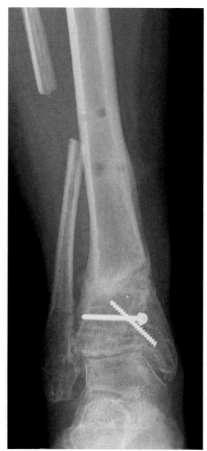

C

FIGURE 26-22 A. Presenting AP radiograph of a 45-year-old woman with a malunited distal tibial fracture. This pure frontal plane deformity measured 21 degrees of varus with a CORA located 21 mm proximal to the distal tibial joint orientation line. **B.** AP radiograph following transverse osteotomy during gradual deformity correction (differential lengthening) using a Taylor Spatial Frame. **C.** Final AP radiograph following deformity correction and bony consolidation.

FIGURE 26-23 A,B. AP and lateral 51-inch alignment radiographs of a 52-year-old woman with a painful total knee arthroplasty. This patient had severe arthrofibrosis, severe pain, and had failed revision total knee arthroplasty. She was referred for a knee fusion but was noted to have an oblique plane angular malunion of her proximal femur from a prior fracture, as indicated by the white lines superimposed on the femur. It was felt that without correction of this femoral malunion, passage of the knee fusion nail through the angled femoral diaphysis would have been difficult, and the final clinical and functional results would likely have been suboptimal due to malalignment of the mechanical axis of the lower extremity. **C,D.** Follow-up radiographs 5 months after operative treatment with resection of the total knee arthroplasty, percutaneous corticotomy of the proximal femur to correct the deformity, and percutaneous antegrade femoral nailing to stabilize the corticotomy site and stabilize the knee fusion site.

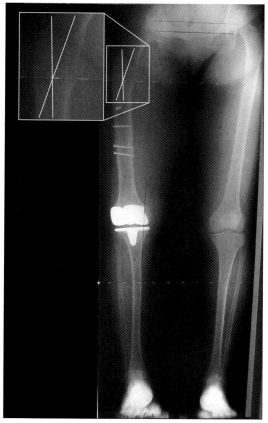

A

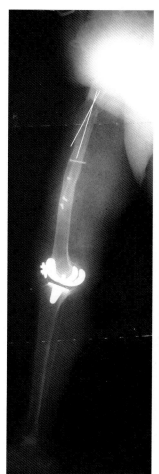

B

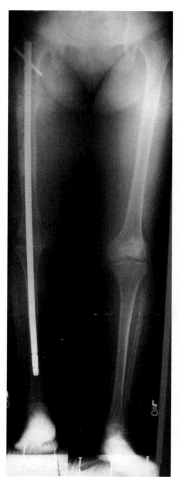

C

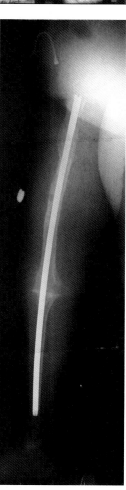

D

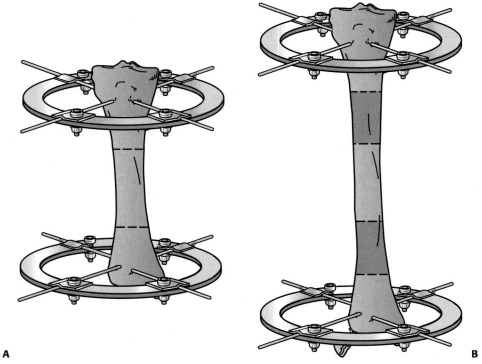

A   **B**

FIGURE 26-24 Bifocal lengthening. **A.** Tibia with length deformity showing two corticotomy sites. **B.** Tibia following distraction osteogenesis at both corticotomy sites showing restoration of length.

function, and inability to correct significant shortening deformity. A variety of plate types and techniques is available, and these are presented in the chapters covering specific fracture types. In cases of deformity correction with poor bone-to-bone contact following reduction, however, other methods of skeletal stabilization should be considered.

Locking plates have screws with threads that lock into threaded holes on the corresponding plate. This locking effect creates a fixed-angle device, or "single-beam" construct, because no motion occurs between the screws and the plate.[15,24,42] In contrast to traditional plate-and-screw constructs, the locked screws resist bending moments and the construct distributes axial load across all of the screw-bone interfaces.[24,42] As compared to compression plating where healing is by direct osteonal bridging, locked plating performed without compression results in healing via callus formation.[24,48,79,95,110] Due to the inherent axial and rotational stability with locked devices, obtaining contact between the plate and the bone is not necessary; the construct can be thought of as an external fixator placed within the body. Consequently, periosteal damage and microvascular compromise are minimal. Locking plates are considerably more expensive than traditional plates and should be used in deformity cases that are not amenable to traditional plate-and-screw fixation.[15]

Intramedullary Nail

Intramedullary nail fixation is particularly useful in the lower extremity because of the strength and load-sharing characteristics of intramedullary nails. This method of fixation is ideal for cases where diaphyseal deformities are being corrected (Fig. 26-23). The method may also be useful for deformities at the metaphyseal-diaphyseal junction. Intramedullary implants are excellent for osteopenic bone where screw purchase may be poor.

Ilizarov Techniques

Ilizarov techniques* have many advantages, including that they: (i) are primarily percutaneous, minimally invasive, and typically requires only minimal soft tissue dissection; (ii) can promote the generation of osseous tissue; (iii) are versatile; (iv) can be used in the presence of acute or chronic infection; (v) allow for stabilization of small intra-articular or periarticular bone fragments; (vi) allow simultaneous deformity correction and enhancement of bone healing;[3–5,9,13,36,54,55] (vii) allow immediate weight bearing and early joint function; (viii) allow augmentation or modification of the treatment as needed through frame adjustment; and (ix) resist shear and rotational forces while the tensioned wires allow the "trampoline effect" (axial loading-unloading) during weight-bearing activities.

The Ilizarov external fixator can be used to reduce and stabilize virtually any type of deformity, including complex combined deformities, and restore limb length in cases of limb foreshortening. A variety of treatment modes can be employed using the Ilizarov external fixator, including distraction-lengthening, and multiple sites in a single bone can be treated simultaneously. Monofocal lengthening involves a single site undergoing distraction. Bifocal lengthening denotes that two lengthening sites exist (Fig. 26-24).

Distraction-Lengthening. The bone formed at the corticotomy site in distraction-lengthening Ilizarov treatment occurs by dis-

*References 3–6,11,12,14,21,23,26,33,36,39,46,50–54,61,73,74,81, 84,85,104,105.

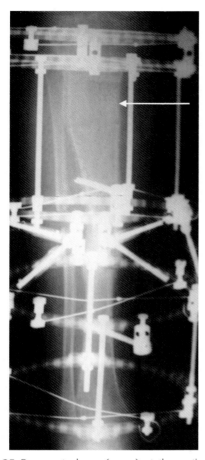

FIGURE 26-25 Regenerate bone (*arrow*) at the corticotomy site is formed via distraction osteogenesis.

traction osteogenesis (Fig. 26-25).[5,6,20,50,67] Distraction produces a tension-stress effect that causes neovascularity and cellular proliferation in many tissues, including bone regeneration primarily through intramembranous bone formation. Corticotomy and distraction osteogenesis result in profound biological stimulation, similar to bone grafting. For example, Aronson[4] reported a nearly ten-fold increase in blood flow following corticotomy and lengthening at the proximal tibia distraction site relative to the control limb in dogs as well as increased blood flow in the distal tibia.

A variety of mechanical and biologic factors affect distraction osteogenesis. First, the corticotomy or osteotomy must be performed using a low-energy technique to minimize necrosis. Second, distraction of the metaphyseal or metaphyseal-diaphyseal regions has superior potential for regenerate bone formation relative to diaphyseal sites. Third, the external fixator construct must be very stable. Fourth, a latency period of 7 to 14 days following the corticotomy and prior to beginning distraction is recommended. Fifth, since the formation of the bony regenerate is slower in some patients, the treating physician should monitor the progression of the regenerate on plain radiographs and adjust the rate and rhythm of distraction accordingly. Sixth, a consolidation phase in which external fixation continues in a static mode following restoration of length that generally lasts 2 to 3 times as long as the distraction phase is required to allow maturation and hypertrophy of the regenerate.

Complex Combined Deformities. All bone deformities can be characterized by describing the position of one bone segment relative to another in terms of angular rotations in each of three planes and linear displacements in each of three axes. Using the methods described above, complex deformities can be characterized using magnitudes for each of these six parameters. Directions of the rotations or displacements are defined as positive and negative relative to the anatomic position. Anterior, right, and superior displacements are defined as positive values. Positive rotation is defined by the right-hand rule: with the thumb pointed in the positive direction along the respective axis (defined identically to the displacement descriptions), the curled fingers indicate the direction of positive rotation (Fig. 26-26). For example, angulation in the frontal plane is rotation about an AP axis. With anterior defined as the positive direction for this axis, counterclockwise rotation (to an examiner who is face to face with the patient) is positive and clockwise rotation is negative.

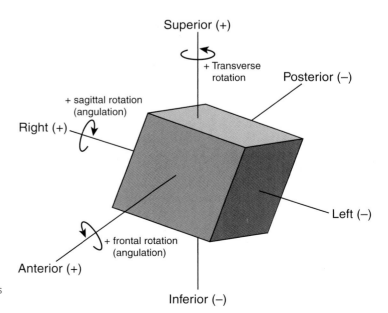

FIGURE 26-26 Definitions used to characterize complex deformities using three angular rotations and three linear displacements.

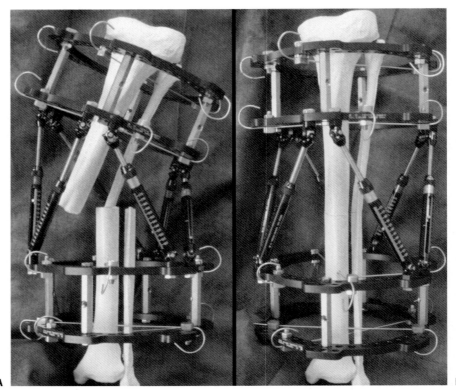

FIGURE 26-27 A. Taylor Spatial Frame with rings placed obliquely to one another and in parallel with the position of the tibial angular-translation deformity. **B.** Taylor Spatial Frame following correction of the deformity by adjusting the six struts to attain neutral frame height (i.e., rings in parallel).

Complex combined deformities often require gradual correction to allow adaptation of not only the bone but also surrounding soft tissues and neurovascular structures. The modern Ilizarov hardware system uses different components (hinges, threaded rods, rotation-translation boxes) to achieve correction of multiple deformity types in a single bone. Alternatively, the Taylor Spatial Frame (Fig. 26-27), which uses six telescopic struts, can be used to correct complex combined deformities.[2,25–27,29,58,62,63,68,69,83–87,97,98,103,106,108,111,112] A computer program is used in treatment planning to determine strut lengths for the original frame construction. The rings of the external fixator frame are attached perpendicular to the respective bone segments and the struts are gradually adjusted to attain neutral frame height (i.e., rings in parallel). Any residual deformity is then corrected by further adjusting the struts.

Correction can be simultaneous, in which all deformities are corrected at the same time, or sequential, in which some deformities (e.g., angulation-rotation) are corrected before others (e.g., translations). The rate at which correction occurs must be determined on a patient-by-patient basis and depends on the type and magnitude of deformity, the potential effects on the soft tissues, the health and healing potential of the patient, and the balance between premature consolidation and inadequate regenerate formation.

REFERENCES

1. Abe M, Shirai H, Okamoto M, Onomura T. Lengthening of the forearm by callus distraction. J Hand Surg [Br] 1996 Apr;21(2):151–163.
2. Al-Sayyad MJ. Taylor Spatial Frame in the treatment of pediatric and adolescent tibial shaft fractures. J Pediatr Orthop 2006;26(2):164–170.
3. Aronson J. Limb-lengthening, skeletal reconstruction, and bone transport with the Ilizarov method. J Bone Joint Surg 1997;79(8):1243–1258.
4. Aronson J. Temporal and spatial increases in blood flow during distraction osteogenesis. Clin Orthop Relat Res 1994;301:124–131.
5. Aronson J, Good B, Stewart C, et al. Preliminary studies of mineralization during distraction osteogenesis. Clin Orthop Relat Res 1990;250:43–49.
6. Aronson J, Harrison B, Boyd CM, et al. Mechanical induction of osteogenesis: preliminary studies. Ann Clin Lab Sci 1988;18(3):195–203.
7. Bhave A, Paley D, Herzenberg JE. Improvement in gait parameters after lengthening for the treatment of limb-length discrepancy. J Bone Joint Surg 1999 Apr;81(4):529–534.
8. Brady RJ, Dean JB, Skinner TM, et al. Limb length inequality: clinical implications for assessment and intervention. J Orthop Sports Phys Ther 2003;33(5):221–234.
9. Brinker MR. Nonunions: evaluation and treatment. In: Browner BD, Levine AM, Jupiter JB, et al, eds. Skeletal Trauma: Basic Science, Management, and Reconstruction. 3rd ed. Philadelphia: W.B. Saunders, 2003:507–604.
10. Brinker MR. Principles of fractures. In: Brinker MR, ed. Review of Orthopaedic Trauma. Philadelphia: W.B. Saunders, 2001:24–41.
11. Brinker MR, Gugenheim JJ. The treatment of complex traumatic problems of the forearm using Ilizarov external fixation. Atlas of the Hand Clinics 2000;5(1):103–116.
12. Brinker MR, Gugenheim JJ, O'Connor DP, et al. Ilizarov correction of malrotated femoral shaft fracture initially treated with an intramedullary nail: a case report. Am J Orthop 2004;33(10):489–493.
13. Brinker MR, O'Connor DP. Basic sciences. In: Miller MD, ed. Review of Orthopaedics. 4th ed. Philadelphia: W.B. Saunders, 2004:1–153.
14. Brinker MR, O'Connor DP. Ilizarov compression over a nail for aseptic femoral nonunions that have failed exchange nailing: a report of five cases. J Orthop Trauma 2003; 17(10):668–676.
15. Cantu RV, Koval KJ. The use of locking plates in fracture care. J Am Acad Orthop Surg 2006;14(3):183–190.
16. Cattaneo R, Catagni M, Johnson EE. The treatment of infected nonunions and segmental defects of the tibia by the methods of Ilizarov. Clin Orthop Relat Res 1992;280: 143–152.
17. Cole JD, Justin D, Kasparis T, et al. The intramedullary skeletal kinetic distractor (ISKD): first clinical results of a new intramedullary nail for lengthening of the femur and tibia. Injury 2001;32(Suppl 4):SD129–139.
18. Dahl MT. Preoperative planning in deformity correction and limb lengthening surgery. Instr Course Lect 2000;49:503–509.
19. Damsin JP, Ghanem I. Upper limb lengthening. Hand Clin 2000;16(4):685–701.
20. Delloye C, Delefortrie G, Coutelier L, et al. Bone regenerate formation in cortical bone during distraction lengthening: an experimental study. Clin Orthop Relat Res 1990; 250:34–42.
21. DiPasquale D, Ochsner MG, Kelly AM, et al. The Ilizarov method for complex fracture nonunions. J Trauma 1994;37(4):629–634.
22. Dismukes DI, Fox DB, Tomlinson JL, et al. Use of radiographic measures and three-

dimensional computed tomographic imaging in surgical correction of an antebrachial deformity in a dog. J Am Vet Med Assoc 2008;232(1):68–73.

23. Ebraheim NA, Skie MC, Jackson WT. The treatment of tibial nonunion with angular deformity using an Ilizarov device. J Trauma 1995;38(1):111–117.

24. Egol KA, Kubiak EN, Fulkerson E, et al. Biomechanics of locked plates and screws. J Orthop Trauma 2004;18(8):488–493.

25. Eidelman M, Bialik V, Katzman A. Correction of deformities in children using the Taylor spatial frame. J Pediatr Orthop B 2006 Nov;15(6):387–395.

26. Fadel M, Hosny G. The Taylor spatial frame for deformity correction in the lower limbs. Int Orthop 2005;29(2):125–129.

27. Feldman DS, Madan SS, Koval KJ, et al. Correction of tibia vara with six-axis deformity analysis and the Taylor Spatial Frame. J Pediatr Orthop 2003;23(3):387–391.

28. Feldman DS, Madan SS, Ruchelsman DE, et al. Accuracy of correction of tibia vara: acute versus gradual correction. J Pediatr Orthop 2006;26(6):794–798.

29. Feldman DS, Shin SS, Madan S, et al. Correction of tibial malunion and nonunion with six-axis analysis deformity correction using the Taylor Spatial Frame. J Orthop Trauma 2003;17(8):549–554.

30. Fox DB, Tomlinson JL, Cook JL, et al. Principles of uniapical and biapical radial deformity correction using dome osteotomies and the center of rotation of angulation methodology in dogs. Vet Surg 2006;35(1):67–77.

31. Friend L, Widmann RF. Advances in management of limb length discrepancy and lower limb deformity. Curr Opin Pediatr 2008;20(1):46–51.

32. Fujimoto M, Kato H, Minami A. Rotational osteotomy at the diaphysis of the radius in the treatment of congenital radioulnar synostosis. J Pediatr Orthop 2005;25(5):676–679.

33. Gardner TN, Evans M, Simpson H, et al. Force-displacement behaviour of biological tissue during distraction osteogenesis. Med Eng Phys 1998;20(9):708–715.

34. Gladbach B, Heijens E, Pfeil J, et al. Calculation and correction of secondary translation deformities and secondary length deformities. Orthopedics 2004;27(7):760–766.

35. Goker B, Block JA. Improved precision in quantifying knee alignment angle. Clin Orthop Relat Res 2007;458:145–149.

36. Green SA. The Ilizarov method. In: Browner BD, Levine AM, Jupiter JB, eds. Skeletal Trauma: Fractures, Dislocations, Ligamentous Injuries. 2nd ed. Philadelphia: W.B. Saunders, 1998:661–701.

37. Green SA, Gibbs P. The relationship of angulation to translation in fracture deformities. J Bone Joint Surg 1994;76(3):390–397.

38. Gross RH. Leg length discrepancy: how much is too much? Orthopedics 1978;1(4):307–310.

39. Gugenheim JJ Jr, Brinker MR. Bone realignment with use of temporary external fixation for distal femoral valgus and varus deformities. J Bone Joint Surg 2003;85-A(7):1229–1237.

40. Gugenheim JJ, Probe RA, Brinker MR. The effects of femoral shaft malrotation on lower extremity anatomy. J Orthop Trauma 2004;18(10):658–664.

41. Guichet JM, Javed A, Russell J, et al. Effect of the foot on the mechanical alignment of the lower limbs. Clin Orthop Relat Res 2003;415(415):193–201.

42. Haidukewych GJ. Innovations in locking plate technology. J Am Acad Orthop Surg 2004;12(4):205–212.

43. Hankemeier S, Gosling T, Pape HC, et al. Limb lengthening with the Intramedullary Skeletal Kinetic Distractor (ISKD). Operative Orthopadie und Traumatologie 2005;17(1):79–101.

44. Hankemeier S, Pape HC, Gosling T, et al. Improved comfort in lower limb lengthening with the intramedullary skeletal kinetic distractor. Principles and preliminary clinical experiences. Arch Orthop Trauma Surg 2004;124(2):129–133.

45. Heijens E, Gladbach B, Pfeil J. Definition, quantification, and correction of translation deformities using long leg, frontal plane radiography. J Pediatr Orthop B 1999;8(4):285–291.

46. Herzenberg JE, Smith JD, Paley D. Correcting tibial deformities with Ilizarov's apparatus. Clin Orthop Relat Res 1994;302:36–41.

47. Hinman RS, May RL, Crossley KM. Is there an alternative to the full-leg radiograph for determining knee joint alignment in osteoarthritis? Arthritis Rheum 2006;55(2):306–313.

48. Hofer HP, Wildburger R, Szyszkowitz R. Observations concerning different patterns of bone healing using the Point Contact Fixator (PC-Fix) as a new technique for fracture fixation. Injury 2001;32(Suppl 2):B15–25.

49. Hunt MA, Fowler PJ, Birmingham TB, et al. Foot rotational effects on radiographic measures of lower limb alignment. Can J Surg 2006;49(6):401–406.

50. Ilizarov GA. Clinical application of the tension-stress effect for limb lengthening. Clin Orthop Relat Res 1990;250:8–26.

51. Ilizarov GA. The principles of the Ilizarov method. Bull Hosp Jt Dis Orthop Inst 1988;48:1–11.

52. Ilizarov GA. The tension-stress effect on the genesis and growth of tissues. Part I. The influence of stability of fixation and soft-tissue preservation. Clin Orthop Relat Res 1989;238:249–281.

53. Ilizarov GA. The tension-stress effect on the genesis and growth of tissues. Part II. The influence of the rate and frequency of distraction. Clin Orthop Relat Res 1989;239:263–85.

54. Ilizarov GA. Transosseous Osteosynthesis. Theoretical and Clinical Aspects of the Regeneration and Growth of Tissue. Berlin: Springer-Verlag, 1992.

55. Ilizarov GA, Kaplunov AG, Degtiarev VE, et al. Treatment of pseudarthroses and ununited fractures, complicated by purulent infection, by the method of compression-distraction osteosynthesis. Ortop Travmatol Protez 1972;33(11):10–14.

56. Inan M, Ferri-de Baros F, Chan G, et al. Correction of rotational deformity of the tibia in cerebral palsy by percutaneous supramalleolar osteotomy. J Bone Joint Surg Br 2005;87(10):1411–1415.

57. Krengel WF 3rd, Staheli LT. Tibial rotational osteotomy for idiopathic torsion. A comparison of the proximal and distal osteotomy levels. Clin Orthop Relat Res 1992;283(283):285–289.

58. Kristiansen LP, Steen H, Reikeras O. No difference in tibial lengthening index by use of Taylor spatial frame or Ilizarov external fixator. Acta Orthop 2006;77(5):772–777.

59. Maffuli N, Fixsen JA. Distraction osteogenesis in congenital limb length discrepancy: a review. J R Coll Surg Edinb 1996;41(4):258–264.

60. Mahaluxmivala J, Nadarajah R, Allen PW, et al. Ilizarov external fixator: acute shorten-

ing and lengthening versus bone transport in the management of tibial non-unions. Injury 2005;36(5):662–668.

61. Marsh DR, Shah S, Elliott J, et al. The Ilizarov method in nonunion, malunion, and infection of fractures. J Bone Joint Surg Br 1997;79(2):273–279.

62. Matsubara H, Tsuchiya H, Sakurakichi K, et al. Deformity correction and lengthening of lower legs with an external fixator. Int Orthop 2006;30(6):550–554.

63. Matsubara H, Tsuchiya H, Takato K, et al. Correction of ankle ankylosis with deformity using the taylor spatial frame: a report of three cases. Foot Ankle Int 2007;28(12):1290–1294.

64. McCarthy JJ, MacEwen GD. Management of leg length inequality. J South Orthop Assoc 2001;10(2):73–85.

65. McCaw ST, Bates BT. Biomechanical implications of mild leg length inequality. Br J Sports Med 1991;25(1):10–13.

66. Meyer DC, Siebenrock KA, Schiele B, et al. A new methodology for the planning of single-cut corrective osteotomies of malaligned long bones. Clin Biomech (Bristol, Avon) 2005;20(2):223–227.

67. Murray JH, Fitch RD. Distraction histiogenesis: principles and indications. J Am Acad Orthop Surg 1996;4(6):317–327.

68. Nakase T, Ohzono K, Shimizu N, et al. Correction of severe posttraumatic deformities in the distal femur by distraction osteogenesis using Taylor Spatial Frame: a case report. Arch Orthop Trauma Surg 2006;126(1):66–69.

69. Nho SJ, Helfet DL, Rozbruch SR. Temporary intentional leg shortening and deformation to facilitate wound closure using the Ilizarov/Taylor spatial frame. J Orthop Trauma 2006;20(6):419–424.

70. Noonan KJ, Leyes M, Forriol F, et al. Distraction osteogenesis of the lower extremity with use of monolateral external fixation. A study of 261 femora and tibiae. J Bone Joint Surg 1998;80(6):793–806.

71. Pajardi G, Campiglio GL, Candiani P. Bone lengthening in malformed upper limbs: a 4-year experience. Acta Chir Plast 1994;36(1):3–6.

72. Paley D. Principles of Deformity Correction. Berlin: Springer-Verlag; 2002.

73. Paley D, Chaudray M, Pirone AM, et al. Treatment of malunions and malnonunions of the femur and tibia by detailed preoperative planning and the Ilizarov techniques. Orthop Clin North Am 1990;21(4):667–691.

74. Paley D, Herzenberg JE, Paremain G, et al. Femoral lengthening over an intramedullary nail. A matched-case comparison with Ilizarov femoral lengthening. J Bone Joint Surg 1997;79(10):1464–1480.

75. Paley D, Herzenberg JE, Tetsworth K, eds. Program Manual: Annual Baltimore Limb Deformity Course. Baltimore: Maryland Center for Limb Lengthening, 2000.

76. Paley D, Herzenberg JE, Tetsworth K, et al. Deformity planning for frontal and sagittal plane corrective osteotomies. Orthop Clin North Am 1994;25(3):425–465.

77. Paley D, Tetsworth K. Mechanical axis deviation of the lower limbs. Preoperative planning of multiapical frontal plane angular and bowing deformities of the femur and tibia. Clin Orthop Relat Res 1992;280:65–71.

78. Paley D, Tetsworth K. Mechanical axis deviation of the lower limbs. Preoperative planning of uniapical angular deformities of the tibia or femur. Clin Orthop Relat Res 1992;280:48–64.

79. Perren SM. Evolution of the internal fixation of long bone fractures. The scientific basis of biological internal fixation: choosing a new balance between stability and biology. J Bone Joint Surg Br 2002;84(8):1093–1110.

80. Pirpiris M, Trivett A, Baker R, et al. Femoral derotation osteotomy in spastic diplegia. Proximal or distal? J Bone Joint Surg Br 2003;85(2):265–272.

81. Raimondo RA, Skaggs DL, Rosenwasser MP, et al. Lengthening of pediatric forearm deformities using the Ilizarov technique: functional and cosmetic results. J Hand Surg [Am] 1999;24(2):331–338.

82. Rauh MA, Boyle J, Mihalko WM, et al. Reliability of measuring long-standing lower extremity radiographs. Orthopedics 2007;30(4):299–303.

83. Rogers MJ, McFadyen I, Livingstone JA, et al. Computer hexapod assisted orthopaedic surgery (CHAOS) in the correction of long bone fracture and deformity. J Orthop Trauma 2007;21(5):337–342.

84. Rozbruch SR, Fragomen AT, Ilizarov S. Correction of tibial deformity with use of the Ilizarov-Taylor spatial frame. J Bone Joint Surg 2006;88(Suppl 4):156–174.

85. Rozbruch SR, Helfet DL, Blyakher A. Distraction of hypertrophic nonunion of tibia with deformity using Ilizarov/Taylor Spatial Frame. Report of two cases. Arch Orthop Trauma Surg 2002;122(5):295–298.

86. Rozbruch SR, Pugsley JS, Fragomen AT, et al. Repair of tibial nonunions and bone defects with the Taylor Spatial Frame. J Orthop Trauma 2008;22(2):88–95.

87. Rozbruch SR, Weitzman AM, Watson JT, et al. Simultaneous treatment of tibial bone and soft-tissue defects with the Ilizarov method. J Orthop Trauma 2006;20(3):197–205.

88. Rozzanigo U, Pizzoli A, Minari C, et al. Alignment and articular orientation of lower limbs: manual vs computer-aided measurements on digital radiograms. Radiol Med (Torino) 2005;109(3):234–238.

89. Sabharwal S, Lee J Jr, Zhao C. Multiplanar deformity analysis of untreated Blount disease. J Pediatr Orthop 2007;27(3):260–265.

90. Sabharwal S, Zhao C. Assessment of lower limb alignment: supine fluoroscopy compared with a standing full-length radiograph. J Bone Joint Surg 2008;90(1):43–51.

91. Sabharwal S, Zhao C, McKeon JJ, et al. Computed radiographic measurement of limb-length discrepancy. Full-length standing anteroposterior radiograph compared with scanogram. J Bone Joint Surg 2006;88(10):2243–2251.

92. Sailer J, Scharitzer M, Peloschek P, et al. Quantification of axial alignment of the lower extremity on conventional and digital total leg radiographs. Eur Radiol 2005;15(1):170–173.

93. Sangkaew C. Distraction osteogenesis with conventional external fixator for tibial bone loss. Int Orthop 2004;28(3):171–175.

94. Sangkaew C. Distraction osteogenesis of the femur using conventional monolateral external fixator. Arch Orthop Trauma Surg 2008;128(9):889–899.

95. Schutz M, Sudkamp NP. Revolution in plate osteosynthesis: new internal fixator systems. J Orthop Sci 2003;8(2):252–258.

96. Seitz WH Jr, Froimson AI. Callotasis lengthening in the upper extremity: indications, techniques, and pitfalls. J Hand Surg [Am] 1991;16(5):932–939.

97. Siapkara A, Nordin L, Hill RA. Spatial frame correction of anterior growth arrest of the proximal tibia: report of three cases. J Pediatr Orthop B 2008;17(2):61–64.

98. Sluga M, Pfeiffer M, Kotz R, et al. Lower limb deformities in children: two-stage correction using the Taylor spatial frame. J Pediatr Orthop B 2003;12(2):123–128.

99. Specogna AV, Birmingham TB, DaSilva JJ, et al. Reliability of lower limb frontal plane alignment measurements using plain radiographs and digitized images. J Knee Surg 2004;17(4):203–210.

100. Staheli LT. Torsion—treatment indications. Clin Orthop Relat Res 1989;(247):61–66.

101. Staheli LT, Corbett M, Wyss C, et al. Lower-extremity rotational problems in children. Normal values to guide management. J Bone Joint Surg 1985;67(1):39–47.

102. Stanitski DF. Limb-length inequality: assessment and treatment options. J Am Acad Orthop Surg 1999;7(3):143–153.

103. Taylor JC. Perioperative planning for two- and three-plane deformities. Foot Ankle Clin 2008;13(1):69–121, vi.

104. Tetsworth K, Krome J, Paley D. Lengthening and deformity correction of the upper extremity by the Ilizarov technique. Orthop Clin North Am 1991;22(4):689–713.

105. Tetsworth KD, Paley D. Accuracy of correction of complex lower-extremity deformities by the Ilizarov method. Clin Orthop Relat Res 1994;301(301):102–110.

106. Tsaridis E, Sarikloglou S, Papasoulis E, et al. Correction of tibial deformity in Paget disease using the Taylor spatial frame. J Bone Joint Surg Br 2008;90(2):243–244.

107. Villa A, Paley D, Catagni MA, et al. Lengthening of the forearm by the Ilizarov technique. Clin Orthop Relat Res 1990;250(250):125–137.

108. Viskontas DG, MacLeod MD, Sanders DW. High tibial osteotomy with use of the Taylor Spatial Frame external fixator for osteoarthritis of the knee. Can J Surg 2006;49(4):245–250.

109. Vitale MA, Choe JC, Sesko AM, et al. The effect of limb length discrepancy on health-related quality of life: is the "2-cm rule" appropriate? J Pediatr Orthop B 2006;15(1):1–5.

110. Wagner M, Frenk A, Frigg R. New concepts for bone fracture treatment and the locking compression plate. Surg Technol Int 2004;12:271–277.

111. Watanabe K, Tsuchiya H, Matsubara H, et al. Revision high tibial osteotomy with the Taylor spatial frame for failed opening-wedge high tibial osteotomy. J Orthop Sci 2008;13(2):145–149.

112. Watanabe K, Tsuchiya H, Sakurakichi K, et al. Double-level correction with the Taylor Spatial Frame for shepherd's crook deformity in fibrous dysplasia. J Orthop Sci 2007;12(4):390–394.

27

ACUTE COMPARTMENT SYNDROME

Margaret M. McQueen

INTRODUCTION

Acute compartment syndrome occurs when pressure rises within a confined space in the body, resulting in a critical reduction of the blood flow to the tissues contained within the space. Without urgent decompression, tissue ischemia, necrosis, and functional impairment occur. The acute compartment syndrome should be differentiated from other related conditions.

Awareness of the different definitions associated with a compartment syndrome is important. Acute compartment syndrome is defined as an elevation of intracompartmental pressure to a level and for a duration that without decompression will cause tissue ischemia and necrosis.

Exertional compartment syndrome is elevation of intercompartmental pressure during exercise, causing ischemia, pain, and rarely neurological symptoms and signs. It is characterized by resolution of symptoms with rest but may proceed to acute compartment syndrome if exercise continues.

Volkmann's ischemic contracture is the end stage of neglected acute compartment syndrome with irreversible muscle necrosis leading to ischemic contractures.

The crush syndrome is the systemic result of muscle necrosis commonly caused by prolonged external compression of an extremity. In crush syndrome muscle necrosis is established by the time of presentation, but intracompartmental pressure may rise as a result of intracompartmental edema, causing a superimposed acute compartment syndrome.

HISTORY

Well over a century has passed since the first description of ischemic muscle contractures was published in the medical literature. The first report of the condition was attributed to Hamilton in 1850 by Hildebrand[61] but Hamilton's original description has never been found. The credit for the first full description belongs to Richard Von Volkmann[148] who published a summary of his views in 1881. He stated that paralysis and contractures appeared after too tight bandaging of the forearm and hand, were ischemic in nature, and were caused by prolonged blocking of arterial blood. He recognized that muscle cannot survive longer than 6 hours with complete interruption of its blood flow and that 12 hours or less of too tight bandaging were enough to result in "dismal permanent crippling." In 1888 Peterson recognized that ischemic contracture could occur in the absence of bandaging but did not postulate a cause.[115]

The first major reports appeared in the English speaking literature in the early twentieth century. At this time it was suggested that swelling after removal of tight bandaging might contribute to the contracture and that the contracture was caused by "fibrous-tissue forming elements" or a myositic process.[28,125,150] By the early part of the twentieth century published accounts of the sequence of events in acute compartment syndrome were remarkably similar to what is known today, with differentiation between acute ischemia caused by major vessel rupture, acute ischemia caused by "subfascial tension," the late stage of ischemic contracture, and the separate concept of nerve involvement.[9] This paper was the first description of fasciotomy to relieve the pressure. The importance of early fasciotomy was suggested at this time[9,107] and confirmed by prevention of the development of contractures in animal experiments.[68]

During the Second World War attention was directed away from these sound conclusions. A belief arose that ischemic contracture was caused by arterial injury and spasm with reflex collateral spasm. Successful results from excision of the damaged artery[34,44] were undoubtedly owing to the fasciotomy carried out as part of the exposure for the surgery. An unfortunate legacy of this belief persists today in the dangerously mistaken view that an acute compartment syndrome cannot exist in the presence of normal peripheral pulses.

The arterial injury theory was challenged by Seddon in 1966.[128] He noted that in all cases of ischemic contracture there was early and gross swelling requiring prompt fasciotomy, and that 50% of his cases had palpable peripheral pulses. He was unable to explain muscle infarcts at the same level as the injury on the basis of arterial damage. He recommended early fasciotomy.

In their classic paper McQuillan and Nolan reported on fifteen cases complicated by "local ischemia."[85] They described the vicious circle of increasing tension in an enclosed compartment causing venous obstruction and subsequent reduction in arterial inflow. Their most important conclusion was that delay in performing a fasciotomy was the single cause of failure of treatment.

EPIDEMIOLOGY

Knowledge of the epidemiology of acute compartment syndrome is important in defining the patient at risk of developing acute compartment syndrome. The epidemiology of acute compartment syndrome has been described in a cohort of 164 patients drawn from a defined population in the United Kingdom.[84] From adolescence, younger patients are at more risk of compartment syndrome.

The incidence of acute compartment syndrome in a westernized population is 3.1 per 100,000 of the population per annum.[84] The annual incidence for males is 7.3 per 100,000

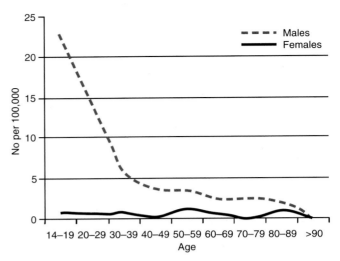

FIGURE 27-1 The annual age and gender specific incidence of acute compartment syndrome.

compared with 0.7 per 100,000 for females, a tenfold increase in risk for males. The age and gender-specific incidences are illustrated in Fig. 27-1, showing a Type B pattern (see Chapter 3) or the L-shaped pattern described by Buhr and Cooke.[18] The mean age for the whole group was 32 years; the median age for males was 30 years and for females 44 years.

The underlying condition causing acute compartment syndrome was most commonly a fracture (69% of cases) (Table 27-1). Similar figures have been reported in children, with 76% of cases caused by fracture, predominantly tibial diaphyseal, distal radius, and forearm.[8] The most common fracture associated with acute compartment syndrome in adults is tibial diaphyseal fracture. The prevalence of acute compartment syn-

TABLE 27-1	Conditions Associated with Injury Causing Acute Compartment Syndrome Presenting to an Orthopaedic Trauma Unit	
Underlying Condition		**% of Cases**
Tibial diaphyseal fracture		36
Soft tissue injury		23.2
Distal radius fracture		9.8
Crush syndrome		7.9
Diaphyseal fracture forearm		7.9
Femoral diaphyseal fracture		3.0
Tibial plateau fracture		3.0
Hand fracture(s)		2.5
Tibial pilon fractures		2.5
Foot fracture(s)		1.8
Ankle fracture		0.6
Elbow fracture dislocation		0.6
Pelvic fracture		0.6
Humeral diaphyseal fracture		0.6

TABLE 27-2	**Less Common Causes of Acute Compartment Syndrome**

Conditions Increasing the Volume of Compartment Contents

Fracture

Soft tissue injury

Crush syndrome (including use of the lithotomy position)[90]

Revascularization

Exercise[79]

Fluid infusion (including arthroscopy)[10,129]

Arterial puncture[130]

Ruptured ganglia/cysts[29]

Osteotomy[43]

Snake bite[145]

Nephrotic syndrome[139]

Leukemic infiltration[144]

Viral myositis[76]

Acute hematogenous osteomyelitis[137]

Conditions Reducing Compartment Volume

Burns

Repair of muscle hernia[4]

Medical Comorbidity

Diabetes[20]

Hypothyroidism[65]

Bleeding diathesis/anticoagulants[63]

---

drome in tibial diaphyseal fractures is reported as 2.7% to 15%,* with the differences in prevalences likely to be because of different diagnostic techniques and selection of patients.

The second most common cause of acute compartment syndrome is soft tissue injury, which added to tibial diaphyseal fracture makes up almost two thirds of the cases. The second most common fracture to be complicated by acute compartment syndrome is the distal radius fracture, which occurs in approximately 0.25% of cases. Forearm diaphyseal fractures are complicated by acute compartment syndrome in 3% of cases. The prevalence of acute compartment syndrome in other anatomic locations is rarely reported. Other less common causes of acute compartment syndrome are listed in Table 27-2.

As mentioned, from adolescence younger patients are at more risk of compartment syndrome. In tibial diaphyseal fracture the prevalence of acute compartment syndrome was reported as being three times greater in the under 35-year-old age group, and in distal radial fractures the prevalence is 35 times less in the older age group.[84] Adolescents have been recognized as having a high rate (8.3%) of compartment syndrome after tibial fracture.[23] Analysis of 1403 tibial diaphyseal fractures presenting to the Edinburgh Orthopaedic Trauma Unit over the period from 1995 to 2007 shows that there were 160 cases of

acute compartment syndrome (11.4%). Using univariate analysis, significant risk factors for the development of acute compartment syndrome were youth (*P* <0.001), and male gender. Males were almost six times more likely to develop acute compartment syndrome if aged between 20 and 29 years compared with those aged over 40 years. Youth, regardless of gender, is therefore a significant risk factor for the development of acute compartment syndrome after tibial fracture. The only exception to youth being a risk factor in acute compartment syndrome is in cases with soft tissue injury only. These patients have an average age of 36 years and are significantly older than those with a fracture.[63]

High energy injury is generally believed to increase the risks of developing an acute compartment syndrome. Nevertheless, in tibial diaphyseal fracture complicated by acute compartment syndrome the proportion of high and low energy injury shows a slight preponderance of low energy injury (59%).[84] In the same population there is an equal number of high energy and low energy injury in tibial diaphyseal fractures uncomplicated by acute compartment syndrome.[24] In the larger Edinburgh series there was an increased risk of acute compartment syndrome in closed compared with open fractures (*P* <0.05). This suggests acute compartment syndrome may be more prevalent after low energy injury, possibly because in low energy injury the compartment boundaries are less likely to be disrupted and an "autodecompression" effect is avoided. The concept of patients with lower energy injury being at higher risk is supported by the distribution of severe open fractures in each group. In those complicated by acute compartment syndrome, 20% are Gustilo Type III [84]; in the whole population of tibial fractures, 60% were Type III.[24] It is important to note that open tibial diaphyseal fractures remain at risk of acute compartment syndrome, which occurs in approximately 3%,[84] but it appears that the lower Gustilo types are at more risk, again possibly because of the lack of disruption of the compartment boundaries.

Distal radial and forearm diaphyseal fractures associated with high energy injury are more likely to be complicated by acute compartment syndrome, probably because of the high preponderance of young males who sustained these types of injury. This is illustrated by a comparison of the age and gender related incidence of distal radius fractures complicated by acute compartment syndrome (Fig. 27-2). The likely explanation for the

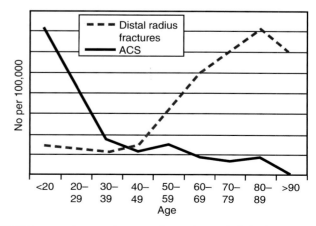

FIGURE 27-2 The annual age specific incidence of all distal radius fractures compared with the annual age specific incidence of acute compartment syndrome in distal radial fractures.

*References 3,16,23,32,83,84,106,155.

TABLE 27-3	Risk Factors for Development or Late Diagnosis of Acute Compartment Syndrome	
Demographic		Altered pain perception
Youth		Altered conscious level
Tibial fracture		Regional anesthesia
High energy forearm fracture		Patient controlled analgesia
High energy femoral diaphyseal fracture		Children
Bleeding diathesis/anticoagulants		Associated nerve injury
Polytrauma with high base deficit, lactate levels, and transfusion requirement		

preponderance of young males with acute compartment syndrome is that young men have relatively large muscle volumes, whereas their compartment size does note change after growth is complete. Thus young men may have less space for swelling of the muscle after injury. Presumably the older person has smaller hypotrophic muscles allowing more space for swelling. There may also be a protective effect of hypertension in the older patient.

The second most common type of acute compartment syndrome is that arising in the absence of fractures. The majority of these arise subsequent to soft tissue injury, particularly a crushing type injury, but some arise with no preceding history of trauma.[63] In children 61% of cases of acute compartment syndrome in the absence of fracture are reported as being iatrogenic.[117] Patients with acute compartment syndrome without fracture tend to be older and have more medical comorbidities than those with a fracture. They are more evenly distributed between the genders with a male to female ratio of five to one. The use of anticoagulants seems also to be a risk factor for the development of acute compartment syndrome.

Patients with polytrauma are at particular risk of delay in the diagnosis of their acute compartment syndrome so identification of at risk factors in this group is of particular importance.[35] Kosir and his coauthors examined risk factors for lower limb acute compartment syndrome in 45 critically ill trauma patients with the institution of an aggressive screening protocol.[73] The prevalence of acute compartment syndrome was 20%. High base deficits, lactate levels, and transfusion requirements were significant risk factors in this group.

The possible risk factors for the development or late diagnosis of acute compartment syndrome are listed in Table 27-3. As well as demographic risk factors, altered pain perception can delay diagnosis. This can occur if the patient has an altered conscious state or with certain types of anesthesia or analgesia.[52, 87,105]

PATHOGENESIS

There remains uncertainty about the exact physiological mechanism of the reduction in blood flow in the acute compartment syndrome, although it is generally accepted that the effect is at small vessel level, either arteriolar, capillary, or venous levels.

The critical closing pressure theory states that there is a critical closing pressure in the small vessels when the transmural pressure (the difference between intravascular pressure and tissue pressure) drops.[19] Transmural pressure (TM) is balanced by a constricting force (TC) consisting of active and elastic tension derived from smooth muscle action in the vessel walls. The equilibrium between expanding and contracting forces is expressed in a derivation of Laplace's law:

$$TM = TC \div r$$

where r is the radius of the vessel.

If, because of increasing tissue pressure, the transmural pressure drops to a level such that elastic fibers in the vessel wall are no longer stretched and therefore cannot contribute any elastic tension, then there will be no further automatic decrease in the radius. TC ÷ r then becomes greater than TM and active closure of the vessel will occur. This concept has been verified in both animal and human local vascular beds.[6,112,121,160] Ashton was the first to relate these findings to acute compartment syndrome and concluded that whatever the cause of the raised tissue pressure, blood flow will be decreased and may temporarily cease altogether as a result of a combination of active arteriolar closure and passive capillary compression, depending on vasomotor tone and the height of the total tissue pressure.[7] Critics of this theory doubt the possibility of maintaining arteriolar closure in the presence of ischemia, which is a strong local stimulus for vasodilatation.[91] Ashton noted that flow resumes after 30 to 60 seconds of maintained tissue pressure and attributes this to vessel re-opening possibly because of an accumulation of vasodilator metabolites.[6]

A second theory is the arteriovenous gradient theory.[91,98] According to this theory the increases in local tissue pressure reduce the local arteriovenous pressure gradient and thus reduce blood flow. When flow diminishes to less than the metabolic demands of the tissues (not necessarily to zero), then functional abnormalities result. The relationship between arteriovenous (AV) gradient and the local blood flow (LBF) is summarized in the equation:

$$LBF = Pa - Pv \div R$$

where Pa is the local arterial pressure, Pv is the local venous pressure, and R is the local vascular resistance. Veins are collapsible tubes and the pressure within them can never be less than the local tissue pressure. If tissue pressure rises as in the acute compartment syndrome, then the Pv must rise also, thus reducing the AV gradient (Pa − Pv) and therefore the local blood flow. At low AV gradients compensation from local vascular resistance (R) is relatively ineffective[59] and local blood flow is primarily determined by the AV gradient. Matsen and his colleagues presented results on human subjects demonstrating reduction of the AV gradient with elevation of the limb in the presence of raised tissue pressure.[98] This theory has been supported by recent work that demonstrated that with external pressure applied, simulating acute compartment syndrome, venous and capillary flow ceased but arterioles were still capable of carrying flow.[147] This disproves the critical closing theory but supports the hypothesis of reduced arteriovenous gradient as the mechanism of reducing blood flow.

A third theory, the microvascular occlusion theory postulates that capillary occlusion is the main mechanism reducing blood flow in acute compartment syndrome.[49] Measurement of capillary pressure in dogs with normal tissue pressures revealed a mean level of 25 mm Hg. Hargens and his colleagues suggest that a tissue pressure of similar value is sufficient to reduce capillary blood flow.[49] Resultant muscle ischemia leads to increased capillary membrane permeability to plasma proteins, increasing edema and obstruction of lymphatic by the raised tissue pressure. Nonetheless, the authors admit that reactive hyperemia and vasodilatation both tend to raise the critical pressure level for microvascular occlusion. Note, however, that this work was done in the presence of normal tissue pressures, and it has also been pointed out that capillaries are collapsible tubes[91] and their intravascular pressure ought to rise in the presence of raised tissue pressure. Hargens' theory[49] is supported by more recent work demonstrating reduction of the number of perfused capillaries per unit area with raised tissue pressures.[54]

Effects of Raised Tissue Pressure on Muscle

Regardless of the mechanism of vessel closure, reduction in blood flow in the acute compartment syndrome has a profound effect on muscle tissue. Skeletal muscle is the tissue in the extremities most vulnerable to ischemia and is therefore the most important tissue to be considered in acute compartment syndrome. Both the magnitude and duration of pressure elevation have been shown experimentally to be important influences in the extent of muscle damage.

There is now universal agreement that rising tissue pressure leads to a reduction in muscle blood flow. A number of experimental studies have highlighted the importance of perfusion pressure as well as tissue pressure in the reduction of muscle blood flow. MR measurements of cellular metabolic derangement (PH, tissue oxygenation, and energy stores) and histological studies, including electron microscopy and videomicroscopy studies of capillary blood flow, have shown that critical tissue pressure thresholds are 10 to 20 mm Hg below diastolic blood pressure or 25 to 30 mm Hg below mean arterial pressure.[54,57,60,89] Increased vulnerability in previously traumatized or ischemic muscle has been demonstrated when the critical threshold may occur at tissue pressures more than 30 mm Hg below mean arterial pressure.[11]

The ultimate result of reduced blood flow to skeletal muscle is ischemia followed by necrosis, with general agreement that increasing periods of complete ischemia produce increasing irreversible changes.[56,75,116] Evidence indicates that muscle necrosis is present in its greatest extent in the central position of the muscle, and that external evaluation of the degree of muscle necrosis is unreliable. The duration of muscle ischemia dictates the amount of necrosis, although some muscle fibers are more vulnerable than others to ischemia. For example, the muscles of the anterior compartment of the leg contain Type 1 fibers or red slow twitch fibers, whereas the gastrocnemius contains mainly Type 2 or white fast twitch fibers. Type 1 fibers depend on oxidative metabolism of triglycerides for their energy source and are more vulnerable to oxygen depletion than Type 2 fibers whose metabolism is primarily anaerobic.[77] This may explain the particular vulnerability of the anterior compartment to raised intracompartmental pressure.

Effects of Raised Tissue Pressure on Nerve

There is little dispute about the effects of raised tissue pressure on neurological function. All investigators note a loss of neuro-

muscular function with raised tissue pressures but at varying pressure thresholds and duration.[40,51,93,134] In a study on human neurological function, Matsen et al. found considerable variation of pressure tolerance that could not be attributed to differences in systemic pressure.[95]

The mechanism of damage to nerve is as yet uncertain and could result from ischemia, ischemia plus compression, toxic effects, or the effects of acidosis.

Effects of Raised Tissue Pressure on Bone

Nonunion is now recognized as a complication of acute compartment syndrome.[25,26,69,82,100] It was first suggested by Nario in 1938 that "Volkmann's disease" caused obliteration of the "musculodiaphyseal" vessels and caused frequent pseudarthrosis.[110] McQueen observed a reduction in bone blood flow and bone union in rabbit tibiae after an experimentally induced acute compartment syndrome.[80] It is likely that muscle ischemia reduces the capacity for development of the extraosseous blood supply on which long bones depend for healing.

Reperfusion Injury

The reperfusion syndrome is a group of complications following reestablishment of blood flow to the ischemic tissues and can occur after fasciotomy and restoration of muscle blood flow in the acute compartment syndrome. Reperfusion is followed by an inflammatory response in the ischemic tissue that can cause further tissue damage. The trigger for the inflammatory response is probably the breakdown products of muscle.[15] Some breakdown products are procoagulants that activate the intrinsic clotting system. This results in increasing microvascular thrombosis, which in turn increases the extent of muscle damage.

If there is a large amount of muscle involved in the ischemic process, the inflammatory response may become systemic. In acute compartment syndrome this is most likely to occur in the crush syndrome. Procoagulants escape into the systemic circulation and produce systemic coagulopathy with parallel activation of inflammatory mediators. These then damage vascular endothelium, leading to increased permeability and subsequent multiple organ failure. Systemic clotting and the breakdown products of dead and dying cells also lead to activation of white blood cells, with the release of additional inflammatory mediators such as histamine, interleukin, oxygen free radicals, thromboxane, and many others.[15] This is the basis for the use of agents such as antioxidants, antithromboxanes, antileukotrienes, and anti–platelet-activating factors that modify the inflammatory process. Some of these agents have been shown in the laboratory to be capable of reducing muscle injury.[1,70,71,149]

DIAGNOSIS OF ACUTE COMPARTMENT SYNDROME

Prompt diagnosis of acute compartment syndrome is the key to a successful outcome. Delay in diagnosis has long been recognized as the single cause of failure of the treatment of acute compartment syndrome.[85,92,122,124] Delay in diagnosis may be because of inexperience and lack of awareness of the possibility of acute compartment syndrome, an indefinite and confusing clinical presentation,[99,143] or to anesthetic or analgesic techniques that mask the clinical signs.[52,87,105]

Delay in treatment of the acute compartment syndrome can be catastrophic, leading to serious complications such as permanent sensory and motor deficits, contractures, infection and at times, amputation of the limb.[106,117,124] In serious cases there may be systemic injury from the reperfusion syndrome. A clear understanding of the clinical techniques necessary to make an early diagnosis is therefore essential to any physician treating acute compartment syndrome in order to avoid such complications. As well as improving outcome, early recognition and treatment of acute compartment syndrome is associated with decreased indemnity risk in potential malpractice claims.[14]

CLINICAL DIAGNOSIS

Pain is considered to be the first symptom of acute compartment syndrome. The pain experienced by the patient is by nature ischemic, and usually severe and out of proportion to the clinical situation. Pain may, however, be an unreliable indication of the presence of acute compartment syndrome because it can be variable in its intensity.[30,94,153] Pain may be absent in acute compartment syndrome associated with nerve injury[62,159] or minimal in the deep posterior compartment syndrome.[92,94] Pain is present in most cases because of the index injury but cannot be elicited in the unconscious patient. Kosir and his coauthors abandoned clinical examination as part of their screening protocol for critically ill trauma patients because of the difficulty in eliciting reliable symptoms and signs in this group.[73] Children may not be able to express the severity of their pain, so restlessness, agitation, and anxiety with increasing analgesic requirements should raise the suspicion of the presence of an acute compartment syndrome.[8] Both Shereff[135] and Myerson[108] state that clinical diagnosis of acute compartment syndrome in the foot is so unreliable that other methods should be used.

Pain has been shown to have a sensitivity of only 19% and a specificity of 97% in the diagnosis of acute compartment syndrome (i.e., a high proportion of false negative or missed cases but a low proportion of false positive cases).[143] There is general agreement, however, that pain if present is a relatively early symptom of acute compartment syndrome in the awake alert patient.[143]

Pain with passive stretch of the muscles involved is recognized as a symptom of acute compartment syndrome. Thus pain is increased for example in an anterior compartment syndrome when the toes or foot are plantarflexed. This symptom is no more reliable than rest pain, because the reasons for unreliability quoted above apply equally to pain on passive stretch. The sensitivity and specificity of pain on passive stretch are similar to those for rest pain.[143]

Paraesthesia and hypoesthesia may occur in the territory of the nerves traversing the affected compartment and are usually the first signs of nerve ischemia, although sensory abnormality may be the result of concomitant nerve injury.[155,159] Ulmer reports a sensitivity of 13% and specificity of 98% for the clinical finding of paraesthesia in acute compartment syndrome, a false negative rate that precludes this symptom from being a useful diagnostic tool.[143]

Paralysis of muscle groups affected by the acute compartment syndrome is recognized as being a late sign.[143] This sign has equally low sensitivity as others in predicting the presence of acute compartment syndrome, probably because of the difficulty of interpreting the underlying cause of the weakness, which could be inhibition by pain, direct injury to muscle, or associated nerve injury. If a motor deficit develops, full recovery is rare.[17,26,122,127,157] Bradley[17] reported full recovery in only 13% of patients with paralysis as a sign of their acute compartment syndrome.[143]

Palpable swelling in the compartment affected may be a further sign of compartment syndrome; although the degree of swelling is difficult to assess accurately, making this sign very subjective. Casts or dressings often obscure compartments at risk and prevent assessment of swelling.[73] Some compartments such as the deep posterior compartment of the leg are completely buried under the muscle compartments, obscuring any swelling.

Peripheral pulses and capillary return are always intact in acute compartment syndrome unless there is major arterial injury or disease or in the very late stages of acute compartment syndrome when amputation is inevitable. If acute compartment syndrome is suspected and pulses are absent, then arteriography is indicated. Conversely, it is dangerous to exclude the diagnosis of acute compartment syndrome because distal pulses are present.

Using a combination of clinical symptoms and signs increases their sensitivity as diagnostic tools.[143] To achieve a probability of over 90% of acute compartment syndrome being present, however, three clinical findings must be noted. The third clinical finding is paresis; thus to achieve an accurate clinical diagnosis of acute compartment syndrome the condition must be allowed to progress until a late stage. This is clearly unacceptable and has led to a search for earlier, more reliable methods of diagnosis.

COMPARTMENT PRESSURE MONITORING

Several techniques were developed to measure intracompartmental pressure (ICP) once it was appreciated that acute compartment syndrome was caused by increased tissue pressure within the affected compartment. Because raised tissue pressure is the primary event in acute compartment syndrome, changes in ICP will precede the clinical symptoms and signs.[83]

There are a number of methods available to measure ICP. One of the first to be used was the needle manometer method, using a needle introduced into the compartment and connected to a column filled partly with saline and partly with air.[153] A syringe filled with air is attached to this column, as is a pressure manometer or transducer. The ICP is the pressure that is required to inject air into the tubing and flatten the meniscus between the saline and the air. This method was modified by Matsen and his colleagues to allow infusion of saline into the compartment.[96,97] The ICP is the pressure resistance to infusion of saline. These methods, although simple and inexpensive have some drawbacks. A danger exists of too large a volume being infused, possibly inducing acute compartment syndrome. It is probably the least accurate of the measurement techniques available, with falsely high values having been recorded in comparison with other techniques[101] and falsely low values in cases of very high ICP.[138] A needle with only one perforation at its tip also can become easily blocked.

The wick catheter was first described for use in acute compartment syndrome by Mubarak and his coauthors.[102] This is a modification of the needle technique, in which fibrils protrude from the bore of the catheter assembly. This allows a large surface area for measurement and prevents obstruction of the needle; it is ideal for continuous measurement. A disadvantage of this technique is the possibility of a blood clot blocking the tip or air in the column of fluid between the catheter and the transducer, which will dampen the response and give falsely low readings. There is a theoretical risk of retention of wick material in the tissues.

The slit catheter was first described by Rorabeck and his associates.[123] This operates on the same principal as the wick catheter in that it is designed to increase the surface area at the tip of the catheter by means of being cut axially at the end of the catheter (Fig. 27-3). The interstitial pressure is measured through a column of saline attached to a transducer. Patency can be confirmed by gentle pressure over the catheter tip; an immediate rise in the pressure should be seen. Care must be taken to avoid the presence of air bubbles in the system as this can, like the wick catheter, result in falsely low readings. The slit catheter is more accurate than the continuous infusion method[101] and is as accurate as the wick catheter.[133]

Attempts to improve the reliability of ICP measurement led to the placement of the pressure transducer directly into the compartment by siting it within the lumen of a catheter. The solid state transducer intracompartmental catheter (STIC) was described in 1984 and measurements were correlated with conventional pressure monitoring systems.[78] This device is now commercially available and widely used, although to retain patency of the catheter for continuous monitoring. an infusion must be used with its attendant problems. The alternative is intermittent pressure measurements, which is likely to cause significant discomfort to patients and is more labor intensive. Newer systems with the transducer placed at the tip of the catheter do not depend on a column of fluid and therefore avoid the problems of patency.[158] These systems are more expensive, however, and are a potential problem for resterilization.

All the methods above measure ICP, which is an indirect way of measuring muscle blood flow and oxygenation. Near infrared spectroscopy measures tissue oxygen saturation noninvasively by means of a probe placed on the skin. This has proved to correlate to tissue pressures experimentally[5] and in human volunteers.[41] It has also been used to demonstrate the hyperemic response to injury in tibial fracture.[136] The technique has promise but requires further validation in humans subjected to injury.[64]

FIGURE 27-3 The tip of a slit catheter, which can be made easily from standard equipment by cutting two slits in the tip of the catheter.

TABLE 27-4	Recommended Catheter Placements for Compartmental Pressure Monitoring
Anatomic Area	**Catheter Placement**
Thigh	Anterior compartment
Leg	Anterior compartment
	Deep posterior if clinically suspected
Foot	Interosseous compartments
	Consider calcaneal compartment in hindfoot injuries
Forearm	Flexor compartment
Hand	Interosseous compartment

ICP is usually monitored in the anterior compartment because this is most commonly involved in acute compartment syndrome and is easily accessible.[82] There is a risk of missing an acute compartment syndrome in the deep posterior compartments and some authors recommend measurement of both,[58] but measuring two compartments is much more cumbersome. If the anterior compartment alone is monitored, the surgeon must be aware of the small chance of deep posterior acute compartment syndrome and measure the deep posterior compartment pressures if there are unexplained symptoms in the presence of anterior compartment pressures with a safe difference between the perfusion pressure and the tissue pressure (ΔP). It is important to measure the peak pressure within the limb, which usually occurs within 5 cm of the level of the fracture.[58] Recommended catheter placement for each of the anatomic areas is summarized in Table 27-4.

THRESHOLD FOR DECOMPRESSION IN ACUTE COMPARTMENT SYNDROME

Much debate has occurred about the critical pressure threshold, beyond which decompression of acute compartment syndrome is required. After appreciation of the nature of acute compartment syndrome being raised pressure, debate centered around the use of tissue pressure alone as indication of the need for decompression. One level believed to be critical was 30 mm Hg of ICP because this is a value close to capillary blood pressure.[50,104] Some authors felt that 40 mm Hg of tissue pressure should be the threshold for decompression,[47,78,96,127] although some recognized a significant individual variation between individuals in their tolerance of raised ICP.[47,98] In a series of patients with tibial fractures, a tissue pressure of 50 mm Hg was recommended as a pressure threshold for decompression in normotensive patients.[48]

It is now recognized that apparent variation between individuals in their tolerance of raised ICP is because of variations in systemic blood pressure. Whitesides and his coauthors were the first to suggest the importance of the difference between the diastolic blood pressure and tissue pressure or ΔP.[153] They stated that there is inadequate perfusion and relative ischemia when the tissue pressure rises to within 10 to 30 mm Hg of the diastolic pressure. There is now good evidence from experimental work to support this concept[57,89] or the similar concept that the difference between mean arterial pressure and tissue pressure should not be less than 30 mm Hg in normal muscle or 40 mm Hg in muscle subject to trauma[60] or antecedent ischemia.[11]

This concept was tested in a clinical study designed to test the hypothesis of the differential pressure as a threshold for decompression.[83] One hundred and sixteen patients with tibial diaphyseal fractures underwent continuous intracompartmental pressure monitoring both perioperatively and for at least 24 hours postoperatively. The differential pressure between the diastolic blood pressure and the ICP was recorded. Mean pressures over a 12-hour period were calculated to include the duration of elevated pressure in the analysis. Three patients had ΔP of less than 30 mm Hg and underwent fasciotomy. Of the remaining patients, all maintained a ΔP greater than 30 mm Hg despite a number with ICP greater than 40 mm Hg. None of these patients underwent fasciotomy and none had any sequelae of acute compartment syndrome at final review. The authors concluded that a ΔP of 30 mm Hg is a safe threshold for decompression in acute compartment syndrome. This has recently been validated by the same group who examined the outcome in terms of muscle power and return to function in two groups of patients with tibial fractures.[154] The first group of patients all had an ICP of greater than 30 mm Hg and the second all had an ICP less than 30 mm Hg. Both groups had maintained a ΔP of greater than 30 mm Hg. There were no differences in the outcomes between the two groups. The concept of the use of ΔP is also supported by Ovre et al., who found an unacceptably high rate of fasciotomies (29%) using an ICP of 30 mm Hg as a threshold for decompression.[114]

All of the work quoted above was performed in adults and with reference to leg compartment syndrome. The threshold may differ for children who have a low diastolic pressure and are therefore more likely to have a ΔP less than 30 mm Hg. Mars and Hadley recommend the use of the mean arterial pressure rather than the diastolic pressure to obviate this problem.[88] It has been assumed that these pressure thresholds apply equally to anatomic areas other than the leg, although this has not been formally examined.

TIMING

Time factors are also important in making the decision to proceed to fasciotomy. It is well established experimentally and clinically that both the duration and severity of the pressure elevation influence the development of muscle necrosis.* Continuous pressure monitoring allows a clear record of the trend of the tissue pressure measurements. In situations where the ΔP drops below 30 mm Hg if the ICP is dropping and the ΔP is rising, then it is safe to observe the patient in anticipation of the ΔP returning within a short time to safe levels. If the ICP is rising, the ΔP is dropping and less than 30 mm Hg, and this trend has been consistent for a period of 1 to 2 hours, then fasciotomy should be performed. Fasciotomy should not be performed based on a single pressure reading except in extreme

*References 75,77,82,89,116,117,163.

cases. Using this protocol, delay to fasciotomy and the sequelae of acute compartment syndrome are reduced without unnecessary fasciotomies being performed.[82]

Overtreatment has been cited as a problem with continuous monitoring,[67] but this study did not consider the importance of the duration of raised ICP in the diagnosis of acute compartment syndrome. Some authors have found compartment pressure monitoring less useful but used clinical symptoms and signs as their indication for fasciotomy with pressure monitoring only as an adjunct.[3,53] For ICP monitoring to be most effective in reducing delay, it must be used as the primary indication for fasciotomy.

SURGICAL AND APPLIED ANATOMY

Thigh

The thigh is divided into three main compartments, both of which are bounded by the fascia lata and separated by the medial and lateral intermuscular septa (Fig. 27-4). Their contents and the clinical signs of compartment syndrome in each compartment are summarized in Table 27-5. Involvement of the adductor compartment is rare.

Leg

There are four compartments in the leg—anterior, lateral, superficial posterior and deep posterior (Fig. 27-5).

The anterior compartment is enclosed anteriorly by skin and fascia, laterally by the intermuscular septum, posteriorly by the fibula and interosseous membrane, and medially by the tibia. Its contents and the clinical signs of acute compartment syndrome are listed in Table 27-6.

The lateral compartment is enclosed laterally by skin and fascia, posteriorly by the posterior intermuscular septum, medi-

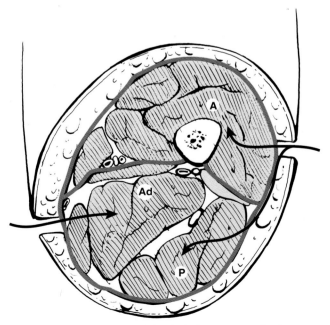

FIGURE 27-4 A cross section of the thigh demonstrating the three compartments and the access to them. A, anterior; Ad, adductor; P, posterior.

TABLE 27-5 **Compartments of the Thigh, Their Contents, and Signs of Acute Compartment Syndrome**

Compartment	Contents	Signs
Anterior	Quadriceps muscles Sartorius Femoral nerve	Pain on passive knee flexion Numbness—medial leg/foot Weakness—knee extension
Posterior	Hamstring muscles Sciatic Nerve	Pain on passive knee extension Sensory changes rare Weakness—knee flexion
Adductor	Adductor muscles Obturator nerve	Pain on passive hip abduction Sensory changes rare Weakness—hip adduction

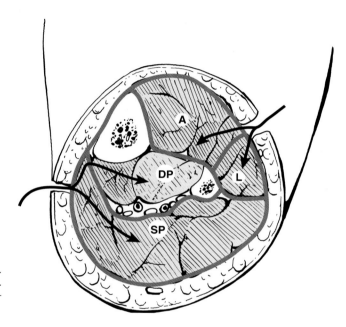

FIGURE 27-5 A cross section of the leg showing the four compartments. The *arrows* show the routes for double incision four compartment fasciotomy. A, anterior compartment; DP, deep posterior compartment; L, lateral compartment; SP, superficial posterior compartment.

TABLE 27-6 **Compartments of the Leg with Their Contents and Clinical Signs of Acute Compartment Syndrome in Each**

Compartment	Contents	Signs
Anterior	Tibialis anterior Extensor digitorum longus Extensor hallucis longus Peroneus tertius Deep peroneal (anterior tibial) nerve and vessels	Pain on passive flexion—ankle/toes Numbness—1st web space Weakness—ankle/toe flexion
Lateral	Peroneus longus Peroneus brevis Superficial peroneal nerve	Pain on passive foot inversion Numbness—dorsum of foot Weakness of eversion
Superficial posterior	Gastrocnemius Soleus Plantaris Sural nerve	Pain on passive ankle extension Numbness—dorsolateral foot Weakness—plantar flexion
Deep posterior	Tibialis posterior Flexor digitorum longus Flexor hallucis longus Posterior tibial nerve	Pain on passive ankle/toe extension/foot eversion Numbness—sole of foot Weakness—toe/ankle flexion, foot inversion

ally by the fibula, and anteriorly by the anterior intermuscular septum. Its contents and the clinical signs of involvement in acute compartment syndrome are detailed in Table 27-6. The deep peroneal nerve may rarely be affected as it passes through the lateral compartment en route to the anterior compartment.

The superficial posterior compartment is bounded anteriorly by the intermuscular septum between the superficial and deep compartments and posteriorly by skin and fascia. Its contents and the clinical signs of acute compartment syndrome are summarized in Table 27-6.

The deep posterior compartment is limited anteriorly by the tibia and interosseous membrane, laterally by the fibula, posteriorly by the intermuscular septum separating it from the superficial posterior compartment, and medially by skin and fascia in the distal part of the leg. Table 27-6 lists the contents of the deep posterior compartment and the likely clinical signs in acute compartment syndrome.

Foot

Until recently most authorities believed that there were four compartments in the foot—medial, lateral, central, and interosseous (Fig. 27-6). The medial compartment lies on the plantar surface of the hallux, the lateral compartment is on the plantar surface of the fifth metatarsal, and the central compartment lies on the plantar surface of the foot. The interosseous compartment lies dorsal to the others between the metatarsals. Their contents are shown in Table 27-7.

Manoli and Weber challenged the concept of four compartments using cadaver infusion techniques.[86] They believe that there are nine compartments in the foot, with two central compartments, one superficial containing flexor digitorum brevis, and one deep (the calcaneal compartment) (Fig. 27-7) containing quadratus plantae, which communicates with the deep posterior compartment of the leg. They demonstrated that each of the four interosseous muscles and adductor hallucis lie in separate compartments, thus increasing the number of compartments to nine. The clinical importance of these anatomic findings has been challenged after the finding that the barrier between the superficial and calcaneal compartments becomes incompetent at a pressure of 10 mm Hg, much lower than that

required to produce an acute compartment syndrome.[46] The clinical diagnosis of acute compartment syndrome should be suspected in the presence of severe swelling, but differentiating the affected compartments is extremely difficult.

Arm

There are two compartments in the arm: anterior and posterior (Fig. 27-8). The anterior compartment is bounded by the humerus posteriorly, the lateral and medial intermuscular septa, and the brachial fascia anteriorly. Its contents and the clinical signs of acute compartment syndrome are detailed in Table 27-8. In late cases paralysis of the muscles innervated by the median, ulna, and radial nerves is seen.

The posterior compartment has the same boundaries as the anterior but lies posterior to the humerus. Its contents and the

TABLE 27-7	Compartments of the Foot and Their Contents
Compartment	Contents
Medial	Intrinsic muscles of the great toe
Lateral	Flexor digiti minimi Abductor digiti minimi
Central —Superficial —Deep (calcaneal)	Flexor digitorum brevis Quadratus plantae
Adductor hallucis	Adductor hallucis
Interosseous × 4	Interosseous muscles Digital nerves

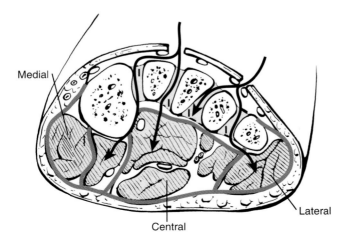

FIGURE 27-6 A cross section of the foot showing access from the dorsum of the foot to the compartments. I, interosseous.

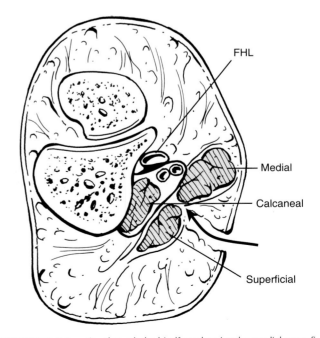

FIGURE 27-7 A section through the hindfoot showing the medial, superficial, and deep central (calcaneal) compartments. The medial approach for release of the calcaneal compartment is shown. FHL, flexor hallucis longus.

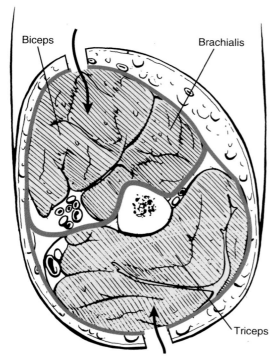

FIGURE 27-8 A cross section of the arm showing the anterior compartment containing biceps(B) and brachialis(Br), and the posterior compartment containing triceps(T).

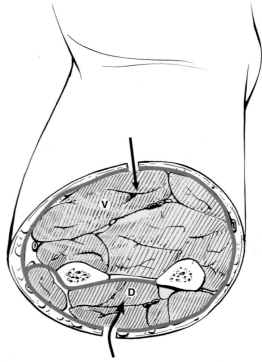

FIGURE 27-9 A cross section of the midforearm. The pronator quadratus compartment is not shown as it lies in the distal forearm. D, dorsal; V, volar.

clinical signs of acute compartment syndrome are listed in Table 27-8.

Forearm

The forearm contains three compartments: volar, dorsal, and "the mobile wad" (Fig. 27-9). The volar compartment has the ulna, radius, and interosseous membrane as its posterior limit and the antebrachial fascia as its anterior limit. Table 27-9 lists the contents and clinical signs of acute compartment syndrome in the volar compartment of the forearm. A suggestion has been made that the volar compartment of the forearm contains three

spaces, the superficial volar, deep volar, and pronator quadratus spaces,[38] but in practice it is not usually necessary to distinguish between these at fasciotomy.[21]

The dorsal compartment of the forearm lies dorsal to the radius, ulna, and interosseous membrane and contains the finger and thumb extensors, abductor pollicis longus, and extensor carpi ulnaris. Its contents and the clinical signs of acute compartment syndrome are summarized in Table 27-9.

Hand

General agreement exists that the hand has ten muscle compartments: one thenar, one hypothenar, one adductor pollicis, four

TABLE 27-8	Compartments of the Arm, Their Contents, and Clinical Signs of Acute Compartment Syndrome	
Compartment	Contents	Signs
Anterior	Biceps	Pain on passive elbow extension
	Brachialis	Numbness—median/ulnar distribution
	Coracobrachialis	Numbness—volar/lateral distal forearm
	Median nerve	Weakness—elbow flexion
	Ulnar nerve	Weakness—median/ulnar motor function
	Musculocutaneous nerve	
	Lateral cutaneous nerve	
	Antebrachial nerve	
	Radial nerve (distal third)	
Posterior	Triceps	Pain on passive elbow flexion
	Radial nerve	Numbness—ulnar/radial distribution
	Ulnar nerve (distally)	Weakness—elbow extension
		Weakness—radial/ulnar motor function

TABLE 27-9	Compartments of The Forearm, Their Contents, and Signs of Acute Compartment Syndrome	
Compartment	Contents	Signs
Volar	Flexor carpi radialis longus and brevis Flexor digitorum superficialis and profundus Pronator teres Pronator quadratus Median nerve Ulnar nerve	Pain on passive wrist/finger extension Numbness—median/ulnar distribution Weakness—wrist/finger flexion Weakness—median/ulnar motor function in hand
Dorsal	Extensor digitorum Extensor pollicis longus Abductor pollicis longus Extensor carpi ulnaris	Pain—passive wrist/finger flexion Weakness—wrist/finger flexion
Mobile wad	Brachioradialis Extensor carpi radialis	Pain on passive wrist flexion/elbow extension Weakness—wrist extension/elbow flexion

dorsal interosseous, and three volar interosseous compartments (Fig. 27-10). The thenar compartment is surrounded by the thenar fascia, the thenar septum, and the first metacarpal. The hypothenar compartment is contained by the hypothenar fascia and septum and the fifth metacarpal. The dorsal interosseous compartments lie between the metacarpals and are bounded by them laterally and the interosseous fascia anteriorly and posteriorly. The volar interosseous compartments lie on the volar aspect of the metacarpals, but it is unlikely that these are functionally separate from the dorsal interosseous compartments because the tissue barrier between the two cannot withstand pressures of more than 15 mm Hg.[45] The contents of the hand compartments are detailed in Table 27-10.

TREATMENT

The single most effective treatment for acute compartment syndrome is fasciotomy, which if delayed can cause devastating

complications. Nevertheless, other preliminary measures should be taken in cases of impending acute compartment syndrome. The process may on occasion be aborted by release of external limiting envelopes such as dressings or plaster casts, including the padding under the cast. Splitting and spreading a cast has been shown to reduce ICP as has release of dressings.[36] The split and spread cast is the only method that can accommodate increasing limb swelling.[161] The limb should not be elevated above the height of the heart as this reduces the arteriovenous gradient.[98] Hypotension should be corrected, because this will reduce perfusion pressure. Oxygen therapy should be instituted to ensure maximum oxygen saturation.

Fasciotomy

The basic principle of fasciotomy of any compartment is full and adequate decompression. Skin incisions must be made along the full length of the affected compartment. There is no place for limited or subcutaneous fasciotomy in acute compartment syndrome. It is essential to visualize all contained muscles in their entirety (Fig. 27-11) in order to assess their viability and any muscle necrosis must be thoroughly débrided to avoid infection.

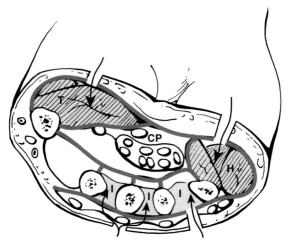

FIGURE 27-10 A cross section of the hand showing the muscle compartments. The adductor pollicis lies more distally. CP, central palmar; H, hypothenar; I, interosseous; T, thenar.

TABLE 27-10	The Compartments of The Hand and Their Contents	
Compartment		Contents
Thenar		Abductor pollicis brevis Flexor pollicis brevis Opponens pollicis
Hypothenar		Abductor digiti minimi Flexor digiti minimi Opponens digiti minimi
Dorsal interosseous × 4		Dorsal interossei
Volar interossei × 3		Volar interossei
Adductor pollicis		Adductor pollicis

FIGURE 27-11 Fasciotomy of the anterior and lateral compartments of the leg. Note that the incision extends the whole length of the muscle compartment allowing inspection of all muscle groups.

Subcutaneous fasciotomy is contraindicated for these reasons and also because the skin may act as a limiting boundary.[37]

In the leg, all four compartments should be released. One of the most commonly used techniques is the double incision four-compartment fasciotomy.[103] The anterior and lateral compartments are released through a lateral skin incision over the intermuscular septum between the compartments (see Figure 27-5). The skin may then be retracted to allow fascial incisions over both compartments. Care must be taken not to injure the superficial peroneal nerve that pierces the fascia and lies superficial to it in the distal third of the leg (see Figure 27-11). There is considerable variation in its course, with approximately three quarters of the nerve remaining in the lateral compartment before its exit through the deep fascia and one quarter passing into the anterior compartment.[2] The two posterior compartments are accessed through a skin incision 2 cm from the medial edge of the tibia (see Figure 27-5). This allows a generous skin bridge to the lateral incision but is anterior to the posterior tibial artery, especially in open fractures, to protect perforating vessels that supply local fasciocutaneous flaps.[120] The superficial posterior compartment is easily exposed by skin retraction. The deep posterior compartment is exposed by posterior retraction of the superficial compartment and is most easily identified in the distal third of the leg (Fig. 27-12). It is sometimes necessary to elevate the superficial compartment muscles from the tibia for a short distance to allow release of the deep posterior compartment along its length. Care must be taken to protect

the saphenous vein and nerve in this area and to protect the posterior tibial vessels and nerves.[118]

Single incision fasciotomy of all four compartments was first described using excision of the fibula,[72] but this is unnecessarily destructive and risks damage to the common peroneal nerve. Single incision four-compartment fasciotomy without fibulectomy can be performed through a lateral incision that affords easy access to the anterior and lateral compartments.[22] Anterior retraction of the peroneal muscles allows exposure of the posterior intermuscular septum overlying the superficial posterior compartment. The deep posterior compartment is entered by an incision immediately posterior to the posterolateral border of the fibula.

Double incision fasciotomy is faster and probably safer than single incision methods because the fascial incisions are all superficial. Using the single incision method, it can be difficult to visualize the full extent of the deep posterior compartment. Both methods seem to be equally effective at reducing ICP.[103,146]

In the thigh and gluteal regions decompression is simple and the compartments easily visualized. Both thigh compartments can be approached through a single lateral skin incision (Fig. 27-13),[140] although a medial incision can be used over the adductors if considered necessary (see Figure 27-4).

In the foot there are a number of compartments to decompress, and a sound knowledge of the anatomy is essential. Dorsal incisions overlying the second and fourth metacarpals allow sufficient access to the interosseous compartments and the central compartment that lies deep to the interosseous compartments (see Figure 27-6). The medial and lateral compartments can be accessed around the deep surfaces of the first and fifth metatarsal, respectively. Such a decompression is usually sufficient in cases of forefoot injury, but when a hindfoot injury, especially a calcaneal fracture, is present a separate medial incision may be required to decompress the calcaneal compartment (see Figure 27-7).[109,126]

Fasciotomy of the arm is performed through anterior and posterior incisions (see Figure 27-8) when the compartments are easily visualized. On rare occasions the deltoid muscle should also be decompressed.[27]

In the forearm both volar and dorsal fasciotomies may be performed. In most cases the volar compartment is approached first through an incision extending from the biceps tendon at the elbow to the palm of the hand, to allow carpal tunnel de-

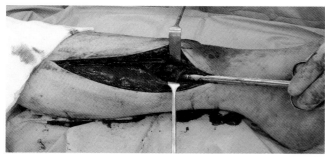

FIGURE 27-12 Decompression of the medial side of the leg. The superficial posterior compartment is being retracted to display the deep compartment. The scissors are deep to the fascia overlying the deep posterior compartment.

FIGURE 27-13 Fasciotomy of the thigh through a single lateral incision.

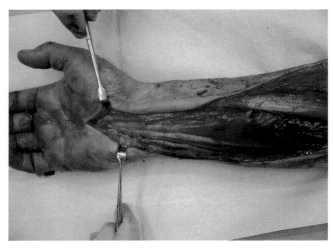

FIGURE 27-14 Fasciotomy of the forearm in a case of crush syndrome. There is necrosis of the forearm flexors proximally. The carpal tunnel has been decompressed.

compression that is usually necessary (Fig. 27-14). Fascial incision then allows direct access to the compartment (see Figure 27-9). The deep flexors must be carefully inspected after fascial incision. Separate exposure and decompression of pronator quadratus may be necessary.[21] Often volar fasciotomy is sufficient to decompress the forearm, but if ICP remains elevated in the dorsal compartment perioperatively, then dorsal compression is easily performed through a straight dorsal incision (see Figure 27-9).

Decompression of the hand can usually be adequately achieved using two dorsal incisions that allow access to the interosseous compartments (see Figure 27-10). This may often be sufficient, but if there is clinical suspicion or raised ICP on measurement then incisions may be made over the thenar and hypothenar eminences, allowing fasciotomy of these compartments.

Management of Fasciotomy Wounds

Fasciotomy incisions must never be closed primarily because this may result in persistent elevation of ICP.[55] The wounds should be left open and dressed, and approximately 48 hours after fasciotomy a "second look" procedure should be undertaken to ensure viability of all muscle groups. Skin closure or cover should not be attempted unless all muscle groups are viable.

The wounds may then be closed by delayed primary closure if possible, although this must be without tension on the skin edges. Commonly in the leg this technique is possible in the medial but not the lateral wound. If delayed primary closure cannot be achieved, then the wound may be closed using either dermatotraction techniques or split skin grafting. Dermatotraction or gradual closure techniques have the advantage of avoiding the cosmetic problems of split skin grafting but may cause skin edge necrosis.[66] A further disadvantage is the prolonged time required to achieve closure, which may be up to 10 days.[12,66]

Split skin grafting although offering immediate skin cover has the disadvantage of a high rate of long-term morbidity.[33] The recent introduction of vacuum assisted closure (VAC) systems is likely to be a significant advantage in this area and may

reduce the need for split skin grafting with a low complication rate.[151]

Management of Associated Fractures

As is now generally accepted, fractures, especially of the long bones, should be stabilized in the presence of acute compartment syndrome treated by fasciotomy.[39,42,122,142] In reality the treatment of the fracture should not be altered by the presence of an acute compartment syndrome, although cast management of a tibial fracture is contraindicated in the presence of acute compartment syndrome. Fasciotomy should be performed prior to fracture stabilization in order to eliminate any unnecessary delay in decompression. Stabilization of the fracture allows easy access to the soft tissues and protects the soft tissues, allowing them to heal.

Reamed intramedullary nailing of the tibia confers excellent stabilization of a diaphyseal fracture and is now probably the treatment of choice in most centers for tibial diaphyseal fracture. Some authors, however, have implicated reaming as a possible cause of acute compartment syndrome.[74,100] This was refuted by other studies examining intercompartmental pressures during and after tibial nailing. McQueen and coauthors studying reamed intramedullary nailing,[81] and Tornetta and French studying unreamed intramedullary nailing[141] agreed that the ICP increased perioperatively and dissipated postoperatively, and that nailing did not increase the likelihood of acute compartment syndrome. Nassif and his coauthors found no differences in ICP between reamed and unreamed nailing.[111]

Several factors may raise ICP during stabilization of tibial fractures. These include traction, which raises pressure in the deep posterior compartment by approximately 6% per kilogram of weight applied.[132] Counter-traction using a thigh bar can cause external calf compression if the bar is wrongly positioned and can also decrease arterial flow and venous return, making the leg more vulnerable to ischemia. Elevation of the leg as in the 90-90 position decreases the tolerance of the limb to ischemia.[95] Thus excessive traction, poor positioning of the thigh bar and high elevation of the leg should be avoided in patients at risk of acute compartment syndrome.

COMPLICATIONS OF ACUTE COMPARTMENT SYNDROME

Complications of acute compartment syndrome are unusual if the condition has been treated expeditiously. Delay in diagnosis has been cited as the single reason for failure in the management of acute compartment syndrome.[85] Delay to fasciotomy of more than 6 hours is likely to cause significant sequelae,[124] including muscle contractures, muscle weakness, sensory loss, infection, and nonunion of fractures.* In severe cases amputation may be necessary because of infection or lack of function.[31]

Late Diagnosis

There is some debate about the place of decompression when the diagnosis is made late and muscle necrosis is inevitable, whether because of a missed acute compartment syndrome or the crush syndrome. Little can be gained in exploring a closed

*References 25,26,40,51, 56,69,77,82,93,95,100,134.

crush syndrome when complete muscle necrosis is inevitable, except in circumstances where there are severe or potentially severe systemic effects wherein amputation may be necessary. Increased sepsis rates with potentially serious consequences have been reported when these cases have been explored.[119] Nonetheless, if partial muscle necrosis is suspected and compartment monitoring reveals pressures above the threshold for decompression, there may be an indication for fasciotomy to salvage remaining viable muscle. In these circumstances debridement of necrotic muscle must be thorough to reduce the chances of infection. In rare cases the ICP may be high enough to occlude major vessels. This is a further indication for fasciotomy to salvage the distal part of the limb.[119]

It is recommended that if there is no likelihood of any surviving muscle and compartment pressures are low, then fasciotomy should be withheld. If there is any possibility of any remaining viable muscle or if compartment pressures are above critical levels, fasciotomy should be performed to preserve any viable muscle. In any circumstances a thorough débridement of necrotic muscle is mandatory.

 AUTHORS' PREFERRED METHOD OF MANAGEMENT

Early diagnosis of acute compartment syndrome is essential, and it is important to be aware of the patients at risk of developing acute compartment syndrome. Good clinical examination techniques in the alert patient will help to identify the compartments at risk. Compartment monitoring should be used in all "at risk" patients as defined in Table 27-3. In practice this means that all tibial fractures should be monitored, but if resources to do so are limited, then younger patients should be selected for monitoring. The anterior compartment should be monitored, but in rare cases where symptoms are present that cannot be explained by the tissue pressures in the anterior compartment, the posterior compartment should also be monitored.

Fasciotomy is performed on the basis of a persistent differential pressure of less than 30 mm Hg. If the ΔP is less than 30 mm Hg but the tissue pressure is dropping, as can happen for instance for a short time after tibial nailing, then the pressure may be observed for a short period in anticipation of the ΔP rising. On the other hand, if the ΔP remains less than 30 mm Hg or is reducing, then immediate fasciotomy is indicated. Delay and complications are minimized by making the decision to perform a fasciotomy primarily on the level of ΔP, with clinical symptoms and signs being used as an adjunct to diagnosis.

I prefer four-compartment fasciotomy in the leg because it is simpler and gives an excellent view of all compartments. At this stage if a fracture is present, it should be stabilized if this has not been done previously. Closure is with a suction type of dressing, followed at 48 hours with either direct closure or split skin grafting. There is no indication to prolong closure beyond this unless there is residual muscle necrosis.

FUTURE DIRECTIONS

Acute compartment syndrome remains a potentially devastating complication of fracture that continues to be a significant cause of disability and successful litigation.[14] Delay to diagnosis was cited as the single cause of a poor outcome more than 40 years ago, yet there remains a remarkable lack of consistency in the methods used to diagnose the condition.[152,156] Universally acceptable, clear, clinical guidelines are required to improve speed of diagnosis in all units managing trauma and would likely be the single biggest advance in the management of the condition.

Other future developments are likely to center on methods of measuring blood flow directly rather than indirectly by ICP measurement. Noninvasive methods of diagnosing acute compartment syndrome are being examined.[131] One such example is near infrared spectroscopy, which measures the amount of oxygenated hemoglobin in muscle tissues transcutaneously.[5,52,64,136]

Methods of reducing the effects of acute compartment syndrome are also likely to play a part in the future. Some basic science research has already been published on the effects of antioxidants on the outcome of acute compartment syndrome with promising results.[70] This work should be extended to human studies in an attempt to reduce the effects of acute compartment syndrome in the clinical situation.

Prevention of acute compartment syndrome is the ultimate goal in its management. Attempts have been made to reduce ICP with the administration of hypertonic fluids intravenously,[13] but these have never been successful clinically. Nevertheless, an experiment on human subjects using tissue ultrafiltration to remove fluid from the compartment has been shown to reduce ICP.[113] Whether this technique can be useful clinically remains to be seen.

REFERENCES

1. Adams JG, Dhar A, Shukla SD, Silver D. Effect of pentoxifylline on tissue injury and platelet-activating factor production during ischemia-reperfusion injury. J Vasc Surg 1995;21:742–748.
2. Adkison DP, Bosse MJ, Gaccione DR, Gabriel KR. Anatomical variations in the course of the superficial peroneal nerve. J Bone Joint Surg (Am);73A:112–114.
3. Al-Dadah OQ, Darrah C, Cooper A, et al. Continuous compartment pressure monitoring vs clinical monitoring in tibial diaphyseal fractures. Injury 2008;39:1204–1209.
4. Almdahl SM, Due J, Samdal FA. Compartment syndrome with muscle necrosis following repair of hernia of tibialis anterior. Case report. Acta Chir Scand 1987;153: 695–697.
5. Arbabi S, Brundage SI, Gentilello LM. Near-infrared spectroscopy: a potential method for continuous transcutaneous monitoring for compartmental syndrome in critically injured patients. J Trauma 1999;47:829–833.
6. Ashton H. Critical closing pressure in human peripheral vascular beds. Clin Sci 1962; 22:79–87.
7. Ashton H. The effect of increased tissue pressure on blood flow. Clin Orthop 1975; 113:15–26.
8. Bae DS, Kadiyala RK, Waters PM. Acute compartment syndrome in children: contemporary diagnosis, treatment and outcome. J Paed Orthop 2001;21:680–688.
9. Bardenheuer L. Die Anlang und Behandlung der ischaemische Muskellahmungen und Kontrakturen. Samml Klin Vorträge 1911;122:437.
10. Belanger M, Fadale P. Compartment syndrome of the leg after arthroscopic examination of a tibial plateau fracture. Case report and review of the literature. Arthroscopy 1997; 13:646–651.
11. Bernot M, Gupta R, Dobrasz J, et al. The effect of antecedent ischemia on the tolerance of skeletal muscle to increased interstitial pressure. J Orthop Trauma 1996;10:555–559.
12. Berman SS, Schilling JD, McIntyre KE, et al. Shoelace technique for delayed primary closure of fasciotomies. Am J Surg 1994;169:435–436.
13. Better OS, Zinman C, Reis DN, et al. Hypertonic mannitol ameliorates intracompartmental tamponade in a model compartment syndrome in the dog. Nephron 1991;58: 344–346.
14. Bhattacharyya T, Vrahas M. The medicolegal aspects of compartment syndrome. J Bone Joint Surg (Am) 2004;86A:864–868.
15. Blaisdell FW. The pathophysiology of skeletal muscle ischemia and the reperfusion syndrome: a review. Cardiovasc Surg 2002;10:620–630.
16. Blick SS, Brumback PJ, Poka A, et al. Compartment syndrome in open tibial fractures. J Bone Joint Surg Am 1986;68:1348–1353.
17. Bradley EL. The anterior tibial compartment syndrome. Surg Gynecol Obstet 1973; 136:289–297.
18. Buhr AJ, Cooke AM. Fracture patterns. Lancet 1959;1:531–536.
19. Burton A. On the physical equilibrium of small blood vessels. J Biomechanics 1971; 4:155–158.

20. Chautems RC, Irmay F, Magnin M, et al. Spontaneous anterior and lateral tibial compartment syndrome in a Type 1 diabetic patient: Case report. J Trauma 1997;43:140–141.
21. Chan PS, Steinberg DR, Pepe MD, Beredjiklian PK. The significance of the three volar spaces in forearm compartment syndrome: a clinical and cadaveric correlation. J Hand Surg (Am) 1998;23:1077–1081.
22. Cooper GG. A method of single incision four compartment fasciotomy of the leg. Eur J Vasc Surg 1992;6:659–661.
23. Court-Brown CM, Byrnes T, McLaughlin G. Intramedullary nailing of tibial diaphyseal fractures in children with open physes. Injury 2003;34:781–785.
24. Court-Brown CM, McBirnie J. The epidemiology of tibial fractures. J Bone Joint Surg Br 1995;77:417–421.
25. Court-Brown CM, McQueen MM. Compartment syndrome delays tibial union. Acta Orthop Scand 1987;58:249–252.
26. Delee JC, Stiehl JB. Open tibia fracture with compartment syndrome. Clin Orthop 1981;160:175–184.
27. Diminick M, Shapiro G, Cornell C. Acute compartment syndrome of the triceps and deltoid. J Orthop Trauma 1999;13:225–227.
28, Dudgeon LS. Volkmann's contracture. Lancet 1902;1:78–85.
29. Dunlop D, Parker PJ, Keating JF. Ruptured Baker's cyst causing posterior compartment syndrome. Injury 1997;28:561–562.
30. Eaton RG, Green WT. Volkmann's ischemia: a volar compartment syndrome of the forearm. Clin Orthop 1975;113:58–64.
31. Finkelstein JA, Hunter GA, Hu RW. Lower limb compartment syndrome: course after delayed fasciotomy. J Trauma 1996;40:342–344.
32. Finkemeier CG, Schmidt AH, Kyle RF, et al. A prospective randomized study of intramedullary nails inserted with and without reaming for the treatment of open and closed fractures of the tibial shaft. J Orthop Trauma 2000;14:187–193.
33. Fitzgerald AM, Gaston P, Wilson Y, et al. Long-term sequelae of fasciotomy wounds. Br J Plast Surg 2000;53:690–693.
34. Foisie PS. Volkmann's ischemic contracture. N Eng J Med 1942;226:671–679.
35. Frink M, Kalus AK, Kuther G, et al. Long-term results of compartment syndrome of the lower limb in polytraumatised patients. Injury 2007;38:607–613.
36. Garfin SR, Mubarak SJ, Evans KL, et al. Quantification of intracompartmental pressure and volume under plaster casts. J Bone Joint Surg (Am) 1981;63A:449–453.
37. Gaspard DJ, Kohl RD. Compartmental syndromes in which skin is the limiting boundary. Clin Orthop 1975;113:65–68.
38. Gerber A, Masquelet AC. Anatomy and intracompartmental pressure measurement technique of the pronator quadratus compartment. J Hand Surg Am 2001;26:1129–1134
39. Gelberman RH. Upper extremity compartment syndromes. In: Mubarak SJ, Hargens AR, eds. Compartment Syndromes and Volkmann's Contracture. Philadelphia: WB Saunders, 1981.
40. Gelberman RH, Szabo RM, Williamson RV, et al. Tissue pressure threshold for peripheral nerve viability. Clin Orthop 1983;178:285–291.
41. Gentilello LM, Sanzone A, Wang L, et al. Near-infrared spectroscopy versus compartment pressure for the diagnosis of lower extremity compartmental syndrome using electromyelography-determined measurements of neuromuscular function. J Trauma 2001;51:1–8.
42. Gershuni DH, Mubarak SJ, Yani NC, et al. Fracture of the tibia complicated by acute compartment syndrome. Clin Orthop 1987;217:221–227.
43. Gibson MJ, Barnes MR, Allen MJ, et al. Weakness of foot dorsiflexion and changes in compartment pressures after tibial osteotomy. J Bone Joint Surg Br 1986;68:471–475.
44. Griffiths DL. Volkmann's ischemic contracture. Br J Surg 1940; 28: 239–260.
45. Guyton GP, Shearman CM, Saltzman CL. Compartmental divisions of the hand revisited. Rethinking the validity of cadaver infusion experiments. J Bone Joint Surg Br 2001;83:241–244.
46. Guyton GP, Shearman CM, Saltzman CL. The compartments of the foot revisited. Rethinking the validity of cadaver infusion experiments. J Bone Joint Surg Br 2001; 83:245–249.
47. Halpern AA, Nagel DA. Compartment syndrome of the forearm: early recognition using tissue pressure measurement. J Hand Surg Am 1979;4:258–263.
48. Halpern AA, Nagel DA. Anterior compartment pressure in patients with tibial fracture. J Trauma 1980; 20:786–790.
49. Hargens AR, Akeson WH, Mubarak SJ, et al. Fluid balance within the canine anterolateral compartment and its relationship to compartment syndromes. J Bone Joint Surg Am 1978;60:499–505.
50. Hargens AR, Akeson WH, Mubarak SJ, et al. Kappa Delta Award paper: tissue fluid pressures: from basic research tools to clinical applications. J Orthop Res 1989;7:902–909.
51. Hargens AR, Romine JS, Sipe JC, et al. Peripheral nerve conduction block by high muscle compartment pressure. J Bone Joint Surg Am 1979;61:192–200.
52. Harrington P, Bunola J, Jennings AJ, et al. Acute compartment syndrome masked by intravenous morphine from a patient-controlled analgesia pump. Injury 2000;31; 387–389.
53. Harris IA, Kadir A, Donald G. Continuous compartment pressure monitoring for tibia fractures: does it influence outcome? J Trauma 2006;60:1330–1335.
54. Hartsock LA, O'Farrell D, Seaber AV, et al. Effect of increased compartment pressure on the microcirculation of skeletal muscle. Microsurgery 1998;18:67–71.
55. Havig MT, Leversedge FJ, Seiler JG. Forearm compartment pressures: an in vitro analysis of open and endoscopic fasciotomy. J Hand Surg Am 1999;24:1289–1297.
56. Hayes G, Liauw S, Romaschin AD, et al. Separation of reperfusion injury from ischemia induced necrosis. Surg Forum 1988;39:306–308.
57. Heckman MM, Whitesides TE, Greive SR, et al. Compartment pressure in association with closed tibial fractures. The relationship between tissue pressure, compartment and the distance from the site of the fracture. J Bone Joint Surg Am 1994;76:1285–1292.
58. Heckman MM, Whitesides TE, Greve SR, et al. Histologic determination of the ischemic threshold of muscle in the canine compartment syndrome model. J Orth Trauma 1993; 7:199–210.
59. Henriksen O. Orthostatic changes of blood flow in subcutaneous tissue in patients with arterial insufficiency of the legs. Scand J Clin Lab Invest 1974;34:103–109.
60. Heppenstall RB, Sapega AA, Scott R, et al. The compartment syndrome. An experimental and clinical study of muscular energy metabolism using phosphorus nuclear magnetic resonance spectroscopy. Clin Orthop 1988;226:138–155.
61. Hildebrand O. Die Lehre von den ischämischen Muskellahmungen und Kontrakturen. Zeitschrift für Chirurgie 1906;108:44–201.
62. Holden CEA. The pathology and prevention of Volkmann's ischemic contracture. J Bone Joint Surg Br 1979;61:296–300.
63. Hope MJ, McQueen MM. Acute compartment syndrome in the absence of fracture. J Orthop Trauma 2004;18:220–224.
64. Hope MJ, Simpson H, McQueen MM. Noninvasive acute compartment syndrome monitoring. The influence of haematoma on near-infrared spectroscopy. Proc AAOS 2003; 4:514.
65. Hsu SI, Thadhani RI, Daniels GH. Acute compartment syndrome in a hypothyroid patient. Thyroid 1995;5:305–308.
66. Janzing H, Broos P. Dermotraction: an effective technique for the closure of fasciotomy: a preliminary report of 15 patients. J Orthop Trauma 2001;15:438–441.
67. Janzing HMJ, Broos PLO. Routine monitoring of compartment pressure in patients with tibial fractures: beware of overtreatment! Injury 2001;32:415–421.
68. Jepson PN. Ischemic contracture: experimental study. Ann Surg 1926;84:785–795.
69. Karlstrom G, Lonnerholm T, Olerud S. Cavus deformity of the foot after fracture of the tibial shaft. J Bone Joint Surg Am 1975;57:893–900.
70. Kearns SR, Daly AF, Sheehan K, et al. Oral vitamin C reduces the injury to skeletal muscle caused by compartment syndrome. J Bone Joint Surg Br 2004;86:906–911.
71. Kearns SR, Moneley D, Murray P, et al. Oral vitamin C attenuates acute ischemia-reperfusion injury in skeletal muscle. J Bone Joint Surg Br 2001;83:1202–1206.
72. Kelly RP, Whitesides TE. Transfibular route for fasciotomy of the leg. J Bone Joint Surg Am 1967;49:1022–1023.
73. Kosir R, Moore FA, Selby JH, et al. Acute lower extremity compartment syndrome (ALECS) screening protocol in critically ill trauma patients. J Trauma 2007;63: 268–275.
74. Koval KJ, Clapper MF, Brumback RJ, et al. Complications of reamed intramedullary nailing of the tibia. J Orthop Trauma 1991;5:184–189.
75. Labbe R, Lindsay T, Walker PM. The extent and distribution of skeletal muscle necrosis after graded periods of complete ischemia. J Vasc Surg 1987;6:152–157.
76. Lam R, Lin PH, Alankar S, et al. Acute limb ischemia secondary to myositis-induced compartment syndrome in a patient with human immunodeficiency virus infection. J Vasc Surg 2003;37:1103–1105.
77. Lindsay TF, Liauw S, Rouraschin AD, et al. The effect of ischemia/reperfusion on adenosine nucleotide metabolism and xanthine oxidase production in skeletal muscle. J Vasc Surg 1990;12:8–15.
78. McDermott AGP, Marble AE, Yabsley RH. Monitoring acute compartment pressures with the STIC catheter. Clin Orthop 1984;190:192–198.
79. McKee MD, Jupiter JB. Acute exercise-induced bilateral anterolateral leg compartment syndrome in a healthy young man. Am J Orthop 1995;24:862–864
80. McQueen MM. The effect of acute compartment syndrome on bone blood flow and bone union. MD Thesis, University of Edinburgh, 1995.
81. McQueen MM, Christie J, Court-Brown CM. Acute compartment syndrome in tibial diaphyseal fractures. J Bone Joint Surg Br 1996;78:95–98.
82. McQueen MM, Court-Brown CM. Compartment monitoring in tibial fractures. The pressure threshold for decompression. J Bone Joint Surg Br 1996;78:99–104.
83. McQueen MM, Christie J, Court-Brown CM. Compartment pressures after intramedullary nailing of the tibia. J Bone Joint Surg Br 1990;72:95–98.
84. McQueen MM, Gaston P, Court-Brown CM. Acute compartment syndrome: who is at risk? J Bone Joint Surg Br 2000; 82:200–203.
85. McQuillan WM, Nolan B. Ischemia complicating injury. J Bone Joint Surg Br 1968; 50:482–492.
86. Manoli A, Weber TG. Fasciotomy of the foot: an anatomical study with special reference to release of the calcaneal compartment. Foot Ankle 1990;10:267–275.
87. Mar GJ, Barrington MJ, McGuirk BR. Acute compartment syndrome of the lower limb and the effect of postoperative analgesia on diagnosis. Br J Anaesth 2009;102:3–11.
88. Mars M, Hadley GP. Raised compartmental pressure in children: a basis for management. Injury 1998;29:183–185.
89. Matava MS, Whitesides TE, Seiler JG, et al. Determination of the compartment pressure threshold of muscle ischemia in a canine model. J Trauma 1994;37;50–58.
90. Mathews PV, Perry JJ, Murray PC. Compartment syndrome of the well leg as a result of the hemilithotomy position: a report of two cases and review of literature. J Orthop Trauma 2001;15:580–583.
91. Matsen FA. In: Compartmental Syndromes. New York: Grune & Stratton, 1980.
92. Matsen FA, Clawson DK. The deep posterior compartmental syndrome of the leg. J Bone Joint Surg Am 1975;57:34–39.
93. Matsen FA, King RV, Krugmire RB, et al. Physiological effects of increased tissue pressure. Int Orthop 1979;3:237–244
94. Matsen FA, Krugmire RB. Compartmental syndromes. Surg Gynaecol Obstet 1978; 147:943–949.
95. Matsen FA, Mayo KA, Krugmire RB, et al. A model compartment syndrome in man with particular reference to the quantification of nerve function. J Bone Joint Surg Am 1978;59:648–653.
96. Matsen FA, Mayo KY, Sheridan GW, et al. Monitoring of intramuscular pressure. Surgery 1976;79:702–709.
97. Matsen FA, Winquist RA, Krugmire RB. Diagnosis and management of compartmental syndromes. J Bone Joint Surg Am 1980;62:286–291.
98. Matsen FA, Wyss CR, Krugmire RB, et al. The effect of limb elevation and dependency on local arteriovenous gradients in normal human limbs with particular reference to limbs with increased tissue pressure. Clin Orthop 1980;150:187–195.
99. Mithoefer K, Llhowe DW, Vrahas MS, et al. Functional outcome after acute compartment syndrome of the thigh. J Bone Joint Surg Am 2006;88:729–737.
100. Moed BR, Strom DE. Compartment syndrome after closed intramedullary nailing of the tibia: a canine model and report of two cases. J Orthop Trauma 1991;5:71–77.
101. Moed BR, Thorderson PK. Measurement of ICP: a comparison of the slit catheter, side-ported needle, and simple needle. J Bone Joint Surg Am 1993;75:231–235.
102. Mubarak SJ, Hargens AR, Owen CA, et al. The wick catheter technique for measurement of intramuscular pressure. J Bone Joint Surg Am 1976;58:1016–1020.
103. Mubarak SJ, Owen CA. Double incision fasciotomy of the leg for decompression in compartment syndromes. J Bone Joint Surg Am 1977;59:184–187.

104. Mubarak SJ, Owen CA, Hargens AR, et al. Acute compartment syndromes: diagnosis and treatment with the aid of the wick catheter. J Bone Joint Surg Am 1978;60: 1091–1095.

105. Mubarak SJ, Wilton NCT. Compartment syndromes and epidural analgesia. J Paed Orthop 1997;17:282–284.

106. Mullett H, Al-Abed K, Prasad C, et al. Outcome of compartment syndrome following intramedullary nailing of tibial diaphyseal fractures. Injury 2001;32:411–413.

107. Murphy JB. Myositis. JAMA 1914;63(15):1249–1255.

108. Myerson MS. Management of compartment syndromes of the foot. Clin Orthop 1991; 271:239–248.

109. Myerson M, Manoli A. Compartment syndromes of the foot after calcaneal fractures. Clin Orthop 1993;290:142–150.

110. Nario CV. La enfermedad de Volkman experimental. Ann Fac Med Montivideo 1938; 10:87–128.

111. Nassif JM, Gorczyca JT, Cole JK, et al. Effect of acute reamed versus unreamed intramedullary nailing on compartment pressure when treating closed tibial shaft fractures: a randomized prospective study. J Orthop Trauma 2000;14:554–558.

112. Nichol J, Girling F, Jerrard W, et al. Fundamental instability of the small blood vessels and critical closing pressures in vascular beds. Am J Physiol 1951;164:330–344.

113. Odland R, Schmidt AH, Hunter B, et al. Use of tissue ultrafiltration for treatment of compartment syndrome: a pilot study using porcine hindlimbs. J Orthop Trauma 2005; 19:267–275.

114. Ovre S, Hvaal K, Holm I, et al. Compartment pressure in nailed tibial fractures. A threshold of 30 mm Hg for decompression gives 29% fasciotomies. Arch Orthop Trauma Surg 1998;118:29–31.

115. Peterson F. Über ischämische Muskellahmung. Arch Klin Chir 1888;37:675–677.

116. Petrasek PF, Homer-Vanmasinkam S, Walker PM. Determinants of ischemic injury to skeletal muscle. J Vasc Surg 1994;19:623–631.

117. Prasarn ML, Ouellette EA, Livingstone A, et al. Acute pediatric upper extremity compartment syndrome in the absence of fracture. J Pediatr Orthop 2009;29:263–268.

118. Pyne D, Jawad ASM, Padhiar N. Saphenous nerve injury after fasciotomy for compartment syndrome. Br J Sports Med 2003;37:541–542.

119. Reis ND, Michaelson M. Crush injury to the lower limbs. Treatment of the local injury. J Bone Joint Surg Am 1986;68:414–418.

120. Report by the British Orthopaedic Association/British Association of Plastic Surgeons working party on the management of open tibial fractures. Br J Plast Surg 1997;50: 570–583.

121. Roddie IC, Shepherd JT. Evidence for critical closure of digital resistance vessels with reduced transmural pressure and passive vasodilation with increased venous pressure. J Physiol 1957;136:498–506.

122. Rorabeck CH. The treatment of compartment syndromes of the leg. J Bone Joint Surg Br 1984;66:93–97.

123. Rorabeck CH, Castle GSP, Hardie R, et al. Compartmental pressure measurements: an experimental investigation using the slit catheter. J Trauma 1981;21:446–449.

124. Rorabeck CH, Macnab L. Anterior tibial compartment syndrome complicating fractures of the shaft of the tibia. J Bone Joint Surg Am 1976;58:549–550.

125. Rowlands RP. A case of Volkmann's contracture treated by shortening the radius and ulna. Lancet 1905;2:1168–1171.

126. Sanders R. Displaced intra-articular fractures of the calcaneus. J Bone Joint Surg Am 2000;82:225–250.

127. Schwartz JT, Brumback RJ, Lakatos R, et al. Acute compartment syndrome of the thigh: a spectrum of injury. J Bone Joint Surg Am 1989;71:392–400.

128. Seddon HJ. Volkmann's ischemia in the lower limb. J Bone Joint Surg Br 1966;48: 627–636.

129. Seiler JG, Valadie AL, Frederick RW, et al. Perioperative compartment syndrome. A report of four cases. J Bone Joint Surg Am 1996;78:600–602.

130. Shabat S, Carmel A, Cohen Y, et al. Iatrogenic forearm compartment syndrome in a cardiac intensive care unit induced by brachial artery puncture and acute anticoagulation. J Interv Cardiol 2002;15:107–109.

131. Shadgan B, Menon M, O'Brien P, et al. Diagnostic techniques in acute compartment syndrome of the leg. J Orthop Trauma 2008;22:581–587.

132. Shakespeare DT, Henderson NJ. Compartmental pressure changes during calcaneal traction in tibial fractures. J Bone Joint Surg Br1982;64:498–499.

133. Shakespeare DT, Henderson NJ, Clough G. The slit catheter: a comparison with the wick catheter in the measurement of compartment pressure. Injury 1982;13:404–408.

134. Sheridan GW, Matsen FA, Krugmire RB. Further investigations on the pathophysiology of the compartmental syndrome. Clin Orthop 1977;123:266–270.

135. Sheref MJ. Compartment syndromes of the foot. Instr Course Lect 1990;39:127–132.

136. Shuler MS, Reisman WM, Whitesides TE Jr, et al. Near infrared spectroscopy in lower extremity trauma. J Bone Joint Surg Am 2009;91:1360–1368.

137. Stott NS, Zionts LE, Holtom PD, et al. Acute hematogenous osteomyelitis. An unusual case of compartment syndrome in a child. Clin Orthop 1995;317:210–222.

138. Styf JR, Crenshaw A, Hargens AR. Intramuscular pressures during exercise. Comparison of measurements with and without infusion. Acta Orthop Scand 1989;60:593–596.

139. Sweeney HE, O'Brien F. Bilateral anterior tibial compartment syndrome in association with the nephritic syndrome; report of a case. Arch Intern Med 1965;116:487–488.

140. Tarlow SD, Achterman CA, Hayhurst J, et al. Acute compartment syndrome in the thigh complicating fracture of the femur. A report of three cases. J Bone Joint Surg Am 1986;68:1439–1443.

141. Tornetta P, French BG. Compartment pressures during nonreamed tibial nailing without traction. J Orthop Trauma 1997;11:24–27.

142. Turen CH, Burgess AR, Vanco B. Skeletal stabilization for tibial fractures associated with acute compartment syndrome. Clin Orthop 1995;315:163–168.

143. Ulmer T. The clinical diagnosis of compartment syndrome of the lower leg: are clinical findings predictive of the disorder? J Orthop Trauma 2002;16:572–577.

144. Veeragandham RS, Paz IB, Nadeemanee A. Compartment syndrome of the leg secondary to leukemic infiltration: a case report and review of the literature. J Surg Oncol 1994;55:198–200.

145. Vigasio A, Battiston B, De Filippo G, et al. Compartmental syndrome due to viper bite. Arch Orthop Trauma Surg 1991;110:175–177.

146. Vitale GC, Richardson JD, George SM, et al. Fasciotomy for severe blunt and penetrating trauma of the extremity. Surg Gynaecol Obstet 1988;166:397–401.

147. Vollmar B, Westermann S, Menzer M. Microvascular response to compartment syndrome-like external pressure elevation: an in vivo fluorescence microscopic study in the hamster striated muscle. J Trauma 1999;46:91–96.

148. Von Volkmann R. Die ischämischen Muskellahmungen und Kontrakturen. Centralb f Chir 1881;51–801.

149. Walker PM, Lindsay TF, Labbe R, et al. Salvage of skeletal muscle with free radical scavengers. J Vasc Surg 1987;5:68–75.

150. Wallis FC. Treatment of paralysis and muscular atrophy after the prolonged use of splints or of an Esmarch's cord. The Practitioner 1907;67:429–436.

151. Webb LX. New techniques in wound management: vacuum-assisted wound closure. J Am Acad Orth Surg 2002;10:303–311.

152. Wall CJ, Richardson MD, Lowe AJ, et al. Survey of management of acute traumatic compartment syndrome of the leg in Australia. ANZ J Surg 2007;77:733–737.

153. Whitesides TE, Haney TC, Morimoto K, et al. Tissue pressure measurements as a determinant for the need of fasciotomy. Clin Orthop 1975;113:43–51.

154. White TO, Howell GED, Will EM, et al. Elevated intramuscular compartment pressures do not influence outcome after tibial fracture. J Trauma 2003;55:1133–1138.

155. Williams J, Gibbons M, Trindle H, et al. Complications of nailing in closed tibial fractures. J Orthop Trauma 1995;9:476–481.

156. Williams PR, Russell ID, Mintowt-Czyz WJ. Compartment pressure monitoring—current UK orthopaedic practice. Injury 1998;29:229–232.

157. Willis RB, Rorabeck CH. Treatment of compartment syndrome in children. Orthop Clin N Am 1990;21:401–412.

158. Willy C, Gerngross H, Sterk J. Measurement of intracompartmental pressure with use of a new electronic transducer-tipped catheter system. J Bone Joint Surg Am 1999;81: 158–168.

159. Wright JG, Bogoch ER, Hastings DE. The "occult" compartment syndrome. J Trauma 1989;29:133–134.

160. Yamada S. Effects of positive tissue pressure on blood flow of the finger. J Appl Physiol 1954;6:495–500.

161. Younger ASE, Curran P, McQueen MM. Backslabs and plaster casts: which will best accommodate increasing intracompartmental pressures? Injury 1990;21:178–181.

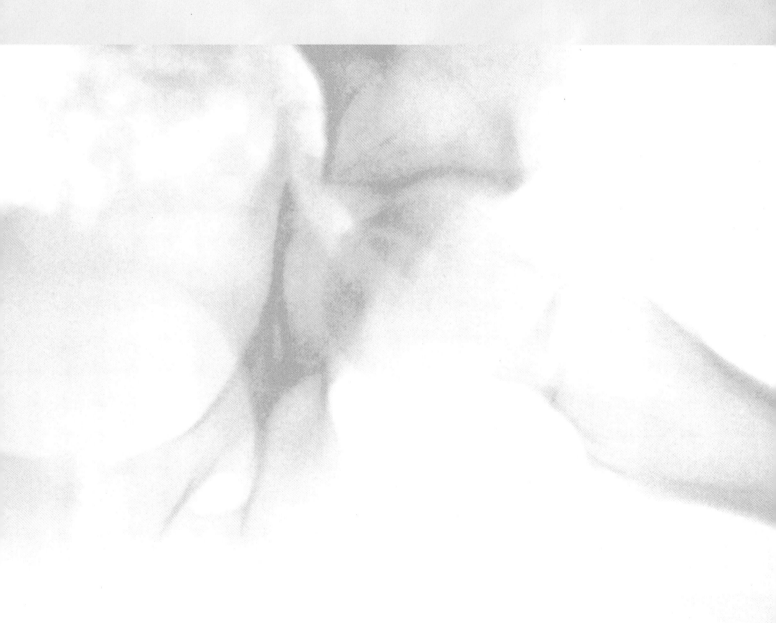

TWO

UPPER EXTREMITY

28

HAND FRACTURES AND DISLOCATIONS

Mark H. Henry

INTRODUCTION

Fractures and dislocations of the hand are some of the most frequently encountered musculoskeletal injuries. In Canada, the annual incidence was found to be 29 per 10,000 in people older than 20 years of age, and 61 per 10,000 in people younger than 20 years of age.[48] Males had a 2.08 times greater risk until after age 65, when females become at greater risk.[48,145] The 1998 U.S. National Hospital Ambulatory Medical Care Survey found phalangeal (23%) and metacarpal (18%) fractures to be the second and third most common fractures below the elbow, peaking in the third decade for men and the second decade for women.[25] Another series of 1358 fractures reported the distribution as 57.4% for proximal phalanx, 30.4% for middle phalanx, and 12.2% for metacarpal.[86] Of 502 phalangeal fractures, 192 were at the proximal phalanx (P1), 195 were at the middle phalanx (P2), and 115 were at the distal phalanx (P3).[165] The small finger axis is the most commonly injured, constituting as high as 37% of total hand fractures.[145]

The potential for functional loss is often underappreciated and difficult to measure. No statistically significant correlation could be drawn in a study comparing the American Medical Association impairment rating with the Disability of the Arm, Shoulder, and Hand (DASH) questionnaire.[166] In a series of 924 hand fractures, overall results were excellent or good in 90% of thumbs but only 59% to 76% of fingers, citing comminution and open or multiple fractures as poor prognostic indicators.[86] The most common complication is stiffness. Intra-articular extension appears to confer a worse prognosis with total active motion (TAM) of 169 degrees compared with a TAM of 213 degrees in fractures without intra-articular extension.[62] Only a few patterns of dislocation lead to residual instability. Fractures, however, can easily result in malunion. Some practitioners perceive a direct tradeoff between stiffness and either residual instability or malunion. This is not necessarily the case. As the understanding of these difficult injuries improves along with new surgical techniques, it is becoming increasingly possible to achieve good hand function while avoiding complications for most isolated fractures and dislocations. Major hand trauma is another matter.

PRINCIPLES OF MANAGEMENT

One of the most fundamental principles of management is that the negative effects of surgery on the tissues should not exceed the negative effects of the original injury. Accordingly, nonoperative treatment plays a significant role in the management of fractures and dislocations of the hand. A corollary to this principle is that even though fractures and dislocations are fundamentally skeletal injuries, most of the difficult decision-making centers on management of the soft tissues. The injured part must not be considered in isolation. The multiple joints of the hand are maintained in a delicate balance by the intrinsic and extrinsic tendon systems such that a disturbance in one set of tissues will often significantly affect others.

Mechanism of Injury

The history of the mechanism of injury should reveal the magnitude, direction, point of application, and type of force that caused the injury. A high degree of variation in mechanism of injury accounts for the broad spectrum of patterns seen in skeletal trauma sustained by the hand. Axial load or "jamming" injuries are frequently sustained during ball sports or sudden reaches made during everyday activities such as to catch a falling object. Patterns frequently resulting from this mechanism are shearing articular fractures or metaphyseal compression fractures. Axial loading along the upper extremity must also make one suspicious of associated injuries to the carpus, forearm, elbow, and shoulder girdle. Diaphyseal fractures and joint dislocations usually require a bending component in the mechanism of injury, which can occur during ball-handling sports or when the hand is trapped by an object and unable to move with the rest of the arm. Individual digits can easily be caught in clothing, furniture, or workplace equipment to sustain torsional mechanisms of injury, resulting in spiral fractures or more complex dislocation patterns. Industrial settings or other environments with heavy objects and high forces lead to crushing mechanisms that combine bending, shearing, and torsion to produce unique patterns of skeletal injury and significant associated soft tissue damage.

Fracture Reduction

Reduction maneuvers should not cause added tissue trauma. If the injury is reducible at all, gentle manipulation will accomplish the reduction far more successfully than forceful longitudinal traction. The principle is relaxation of deforming forces through proximal joint positioning such as metacarpophalangeal (MP) joint flexion to relax the intrinsics or wrist flexion to relax the digital flexor tendons. Often, a gentle back-and-forth rotatory maneuver is necessary to free a bony prominence from soft tissue entrapment. The mobile distal part is then reduced to the stable proximal part.

Splinting

Splints should immobilize the minimum number of joints possible and allow unrestricted motion of all other joints. One controversial point concerns the need to immobilize the wrist. Setting appropriate length–tension relationships in the extrinsic motors (in cases where they are deforming forces) is most easily accomplished through immobilization of the wrist in 25 to 35 degrees of extension. This is extremely helpful in patients with low pain tolerance who tend to place the hand in a characteristic dysfunctional posture of wrist flexion–MP joint extension–interphalangeal (IP) joint flexion (the "wounded paw" position). Other patients who are capable of avoiding this position on their own often do not need wrist immobilization. A simple splint that is useful for injuries ranging from the carpometacarpal (CMC) joints proximally to P1 fractures distally consists of a single slab of plaster or fiberglass applied dorsally. With a foundation at the forearm, the splint runs out to the level of the proximal interphalangeal (PIP) joints distally with the wrist extended and the MP joints fully flexed. Full motion of the IP joints should be encouraged throughout the healing process. The total duration of immobilization should rarely exceed 3 to 4 weeks. Hand fractures are stable enough by this time to tolerate active range of motion (AROM) with further remodeling by 8 to 10 weeks.[15]

Signs and Symptoms

Symptoms associated with a fracture or dislocation of the hand include pain, swelling, stiffness, weakness, deformity, and loss of coordination. Numbness and tingling signify associated nerve involvement (either direct injury to the nerve or as a secondary effect of swelling). Signs include tenderness, swelling, ecchymosis, deformity, crepitus, and instability. A better skeletal examination can often be obtained with the aid of anesthesia applied directly at the injury site or regionally. Isolated MP joint dislocations and metacarpal fractures can be treated with direct injection of anesthetic into the injury site. More distal injuries are easily anesthetized with a digital block. More global pain relief can be obtained through nerve blocks performed at the wrist to include the median nerve, ulnar nerve, and dorsal cutaneous branches of the radial and ulnar nerves. The time following administration of the anesthetic can be used to cleanse any superficial wounds and to prepare splinting supplies. Pain-free demonstration of tendon excursion and fracture and ligament stability can then be performed. At the conclusion of the anesthetized skeletal exam, the injury can be promptly reduced and splinted.

An important factor in many treatment algorithms is the presence of rotational deformity. The examiner must understand the appropriate method of assessment. The bones of the hand are short tubular structures. Malrotation at one bone segment is best represented by the alignment of the next more distal segment. This alignment is best demonstrated when the intervening joint is flexed to 90 degrees. Comparing nail plate alignment is an inadequate method of evaluating rotation. Other unique physical examination findings will be discussed in association with specific injuries.

Associated Injuries

Open Injuries

The integument is easily damaged, and open fractures are common. Open wounds should not be probed in the emergency department; doing so only drives surface contaminants deeper and rarely yields useful information. The need for prophylactic antibiotics in open hand fractures is controversial. The previous standard administration of Ancef no longer appears applicable with methicillin-resistant *Staphylococcus aureus* (MRSA) dominating most community-acquired infection profiles. Clindamycin, vancomycin, Bactrim, and the quinolones are useful agents against MRSA. Aminoglycosides are added for contaminated wounds, and penicillin for soil or farm environments. No hard evidence exists to support continuation of antibiotics beyond the initial 24 hours. The exception to this may be bite wounds, whose potential for osteomyelitis is significant if the tooth directly penetrates the cortex, allowing the saliva into the cancellous structure. Aggressive and early surgical debridement is needed for all bite wounds.

The distal phalanx directly supports the nail matrix. With substantial displacement of the dorsal cortex, nail matrix disruption should be expected and direct repair planned. Reconstruction of residual open wounds overlying skeletal injury sites requires the use of flaps. Frequently transposition flaps will suffice. Less frequently, pedicle or free flaps will prove necessary.[75,76] The greatest challenge in the hand, and particularly the digit, is to achieve both thin and supple tissue coverage. A fascial flap covered with a split-thickness skin graft provides this combination of features, except at the volar pulp,

where a directly innervated glabrous cutaneous flap is needed (Fig. 28-1).

Tendons

Closed extensor tendon ruptures near insertion points may accompany dislocations. Prime examples are terminal tendon ruptures sustained in association with distal interphalangeal (DIP) joint injuries and central slip ruptures sustained in association with PIP joint injuries. Initial examination of the traumatized hand must include a survey that inventories each potential tendon injury. Apart from these, tendon damage usually only occurs with an associated laceration or in open combined injuries.

Nerves and Vessels

Apart from open combined injuries, these tissues are rarely injured as part of simple fractures and dislocations of the hand. In major open hand trauma, there is usually a significant zone of injury. Appropriate treatment includes excision of the devitalized tissues in the zone of injury including nerve and vessel tissues followed by reconstruction with autogenous grafts or adjacent transfers.

Combined Injuries

The term combined refers to the association of a hand fracture with injury to at least one of the soft tissues listed above. These are most often open injuries with the soft tissue component of greatest significance being the injury to flexor tendons, extensor tendons, or both. The occurrence of this combined pattern of injury directly impacts the treatment strategy for the fracture itself. Many fracture patterns presenting as an isolated injury would be best cared for nonoperatively or with closed reduction and internal fixation (CRIF) using smooth stainless steel Kirschner wires (K-wires). The open wound leading to the fracture site automatically changes the surgical approach to open reduction, usually with internal fixation (ORIF). The presence of an adjacent tendon repair site necessitates achieving skeletal stability sufficient to withstand the forces of an immediate tendon glide rehabilitation program. This often means the use of rigid internal fixation (Fig. 28-2). In a study limited to ORIF of intra-articular fractures, comminution and an initial open injury were identified as independent variables leading to a worse prognosis.[154] Only 6 of 16 patients in another study of comminuted phalangeal fractures and associated soft tissue injuries achieved greater than 180 degrees of TAM.[29] The remainder of this chapter describes the most appropriate techniques for managing fractures and dislocations of the hand as isolated injuries. The term *combined injuries* will be found associated with the more stable fixation options as part of the "Indications for Treatment" tables listed throughout the chapter.

Massive Hand Trauma

The comprehensive planning required for treatment of massive hand trauma merits a textbook in its own right and is beyond the scope of this chapter. The majority of the complex decision-making in these injuries occurs with respect to the strategy chosen for the soft tissues (Fig. 28-3). With true degloving injuries and exposed bone and tendon, either pedicle or free flaps are required for coverage.[75,76] Pedicle flaps are simpler and faster but are limited in size and reach and are associated with

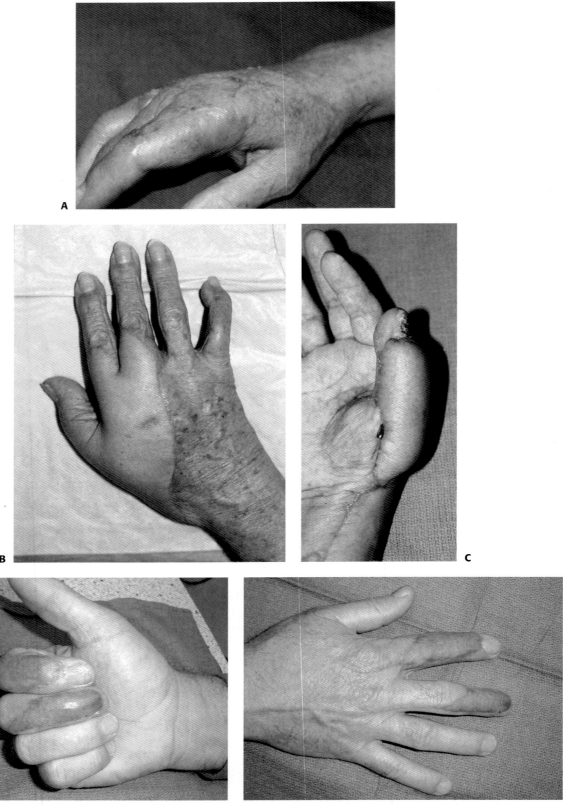

FIGURE 28-1 Thin supple coverage of open hand trauma wounds can be accomplished with (**A**) thinner fascial flaps covered with a split-thickness skin graft or (**B**) bulkier cutaneous or fasciocutaneous flaps. **C.** Fasciocutaneous flaps at the digital level may demonstrate an even more substantial difference compared with the thinness and flexibility of a grafted fascial flap (**D,E**).

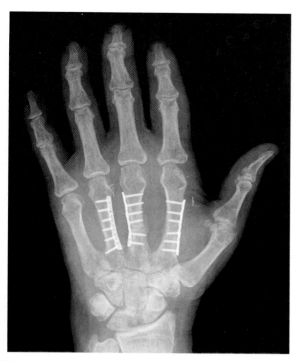

FIGURE 28-2 Major open hand trauma frequently requires the most stable forms of fixation to facilitate an aggressive early motion rehabilitation program focusing on tendon gliding.

a higher complication rate than thin fascial free flaps that can cover a defect of any size and shape.[75,76] Clinical evaluation of these injuries is quite difficult because the patient is often unable or unwilling to do very much with respect to an interactive examination. Much of the determination regarding the extent of injury is made intraoperatively. Good-quality radiographs are rarely obtained initially and usually consist of semioblique views of the hand with a high degree of bone overlap. Every effort should be made within the scope of total patient management to obtain additional radiographic views that can be set up properly so that associated injuries are not missed. More often than not, the opportunity for these views first presents itself in the operating room. A very easy pitfall is to draw attention to the most obvious radiographic findings without taking the time to search for more subtle injuries. Radiographic evidence of foreign matter embedded in the hand should be sought as well as its absence at the conclusion of the debridement.

The Gustilo classification of open fractures has been modified for the hand by reducing the 10-cm wound length threshold to 2 cm. The validity of the classification is supported by 62.5% normal hand function found after type I injuries compared with 21% following type III fractures.[111] Another series found 92% poor results associated with grade III B and C injuries.[39] From a series of 200 open hand fractures, Swanson[151] differentiated type II wounds from type I wounds by three criteria: contamination at initial presentation, open for more than 24 hours before treatment, or in patients with systemic illness. Type II wounds are not recommended for primary closure.

Both internal and external fixation may be appropriate in massive hand injuries. Standard indications for external fixation include gross contamination of the original wound, segmental bone loss or comminution, or the lack of availability of good

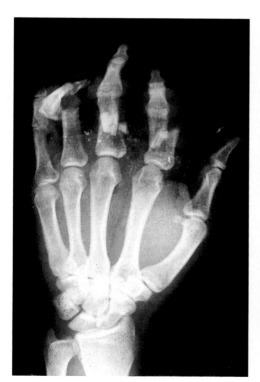

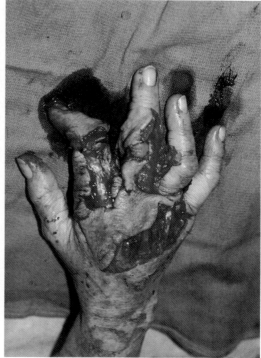

FIGURE 28-3 Massive crushing trauma to the hand usually causes its most devastating effects, not to the skeletal elements themselves, but rather diffusely through devitalization of the soft tissues covering the bone.

soft tissue coverage.[37] The biomechanics of external fixation in the hand are the same as elsewhere in the body with pin diameter constituting the chief determinant of fixator stiffness. Four pins, two proximally and two distally, are sufficient for most hand applications. A given hand injury may best be fixed by all internal, all external, or a combination of the two methods of fixation. An improved understanding and a wider array of elegant soft tissue coverage techniques have overcome previous concerns regarding exposure of hardware with internal fixation.[75,76]

Whenever the injury involves the first web space (especially with crush injuries), the thumb and index metacarpals should be pinned into abduction to prevent a first web space contracture. No matter how the injury is managed, the strategy should plan for rehabilitation to begin, unobstructed by bulky external dressings, by 72 hours after surgery. In one series, 72 metacarpal and phalangeal fractures with severe associated soft tissue injury were treated with plates and screws yielding 46% good, 32% fair, and 22% poor results by the American Society for Surgery of the Hand (ASSH) criteria of total active motion.[21] The overall results for treatment of these severe injuries are most closely related to the soft tissue component rather than the status of the skeletal injury.[65] In 245 open injuries studied prospectively, extensor tendon injury alone had 50% poor results, but flexor tendon or multiple soft tissue injuries produced 80% poor results.[24] A series of 140 open fractures demonstrated better results at the metacarpal compared with the phalangeal level with the worst outcomes occurring for injuries at the P1 and PIP level, especially when associated with an overlying tendon injury.[39]

Bone Loss

Segmental bone loss is a frequent finding in massive hand injuries. Once the wound has been rendered clean through either a single or multiple débridements, bone grafting is appropriate using corticocancellous iliac crest, shaped and sized to match the curvature of the missing segment. If only mild comminution is present without loss of structural stability, cancellous graft alone is sufficient. Stable fixation is achieved with either internal plate (Fig. 28-4) or external fixator application. With proper débridement, immediate primary bone grafting is safe. A series of 12 patients with type III open fractures and another 20 patients with low-velocity gunshot phalangeal fractures both demonstrated 0% infection rates with the use of an immediate autograft.[62,133] If delayed bone grafting is planned, a temporary spacer may be used to preserve the volume that will later be occupied by the graft (Fig. 28-5). Bone loss that includes the articular surface represents an entirely different and much more complex problem. Strategies that have been advocated include autografts of metatarsal head, second, and third CMC joints; immediate Silastic prosthetic replacement; osteoarticular allografts; primary arthrodesis; and free vascularized composite whole toe joint transfer.[87]

Rationale

The fundamental rationale for treatment in fractures and dislocations of the hand is to achieve sufficient stability of the bone or joint injury to permit early motion rehabilitation without resulting in malunions for fractures or residual instability for dislocations. The correct treatment option is the least invasive technique that can accomplish these goals. When multiple injuries are present, one must determine treatment for the primary injury upon which the management of the other injuries will be based. There are essentially five major treatment alternatives: immediate motion, temporary splinting, CRIF, ORIF, and immediate reconstruction.[91,97,146,154,156] The general advantages of entirely nonoperative treatment are assumed to be lower cost and avoidance of the risks and complications associated with surgery and anesthesia. The generally presumed disadvantage is that stability is less ensured than with some form of operative fixation. CRIF is expected to prevent overt deformity but not to achieve an anatomically perfect reduction. Pin tract infection is the prime complication that should be mentioned to patients in association with CRIF. Open treatments are considered to add the morbidity of surgical tissue trauma, titrated against the presumed advantages of achieving the most anatomic and stable reduction.

Treatment Selection

Critical elements in selecting between nonoperative and operative treatment are the assessments of rotational malalignment and stability (Fig. 28-6). If carefully sought, rotational discrepancy is relatively easy to determine.[140] Defining stability is somewhat more difficult. Some authors have used what seems to be the very reasonable criterion of maintenance of fracture reduction when the adjacent joints are taken through at least 30% of their normal motion.[24] Contraction of soft tissues begins approximately 72 hours following injury. Motion should be instituted by this time for all joints stable enough to tolerate rehabilitation.[28] Elevation and elastic compression promote edema control.[109] The more aggressive the surgeon's management of the injury has been, the more aggressive must be the rehabilitation. Low-energy isolated injuries have far less risk of stiffness than those created by high-energy trauma with large zones of injury.

Diagnosis and Classification

The diagnosis of a fracture or dislocation of the hand should be made in accordance with the fundamental principles of patient evaluation and management. A well-taken history should be followed by a thorough examination that is followed by imaging studies. The set of combined information from these three sources creates a profile of the individual patient's unique problem that then leads to all subsequent management decisions. The history should include a description of the environment where the injury occurred. If the injury is open, expected contaminants from different environments would dictate different choices for prophylactic antibiotics. A clear history of the mechanism of injury should be obtained. The patient should be questioned regarding visible deformity immediately following injury and whether any immediate reduction maneuvers were performed at the site of injury or subsequently in an emergency department. The degree and duration of swelling should be described with specific reference to exact location. The patient's current symptoms and chief complaint are essential and often the best clues to uncovering associated injury patterns. Physical examination includes assessment of all tissue layers beginning with the integument and including flexor and extensor tendons, nerves, vessels, and, ultimately, the skeletal structure.

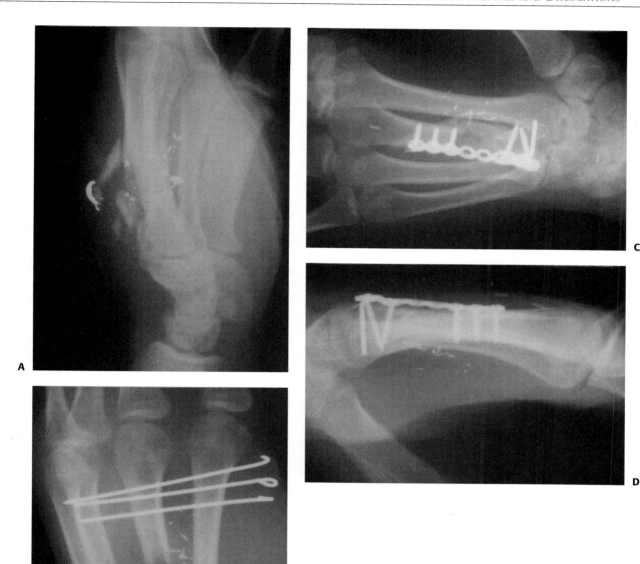

FIGURE 28-4 When segmental bone loss occurs (**A**), shortening may be prevented by temporary stabilization (**B**). Subsequent internal fixation (**C, D**) and bone grafting can restore the original anatomic parameters of the skeletal unit.

Imaging

Plain radiographic evaluation includes at least two projections with the beam centered at the level of interest. A third oblique view is often quite instructive, revealing displacement not evident on the standard posteroanterior (PA) or lateral. Rarely are other imaging studies necessary in evaluating fractures and dislocations of the hand. In complex periarticular fractures, such as "pilon" fractures at the base of P2, computed tomography (CT) scans assist some surgeons with operative planning. Foreign bodies may not always be detected by standard radio-

graphic projections. Glass or gravel is best seen with soft tissue technique. CT scans may detect plastic, glass, and wood. Ultrasound can detect objects that lack radiopacity. Magnetic resonance imaging (MRI) remains a more expensive backup for all types of foreign materials.

Classification

Unfortunately, the literature regarding these injuries has not been written in accordance with any defined classification scheme, and true comparisons are difficult to make. Descrip-

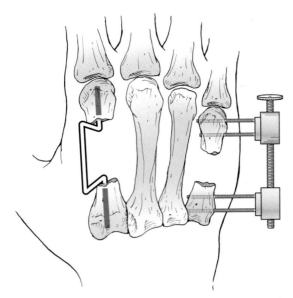

FIGURE 28-5 When extensive contamination precludes the use of internal fixation or when bone reconstruction is to be done at a later date, the use of spacer wires or the application of an external fixator with distraction and compression capabilities can be useful.

tions of fractures have been based largely on the location within the bone (head, neck, shaft, base) and further modified by the direction of the fracture plane (transverse, spiral, oblique, comminuted) and the measurable degree of displacement. Dislocations have been described by the direction the distal segment travels (dorsal, volar, rotatory) and further modified by the capacity (simple) or incapacity (complex) for closed reduction. In the sections that follow regarding each injury, it will be assumed that the above-stated designations are in effect unless specific exceptions are noted.

DISTAL PHALANX (P3) FRACTURES

As the terminal point of contact with the environment, the distal phalanx experiences stress loading with nearly every use of the

hand. The soft tissue coverage is limited and local signs of fracture can usually be detected at the surface. When fractures accompany a nail bed injury, hematoma can be seen beneath the nail plate. When the seal between the nail plate and the hyponychium is also broken, the fracture is open and should be treated as such. The mechanism of injury often involves crushing, and the soft tissue injury is frequently of greater significance for long-term prognosis than the fracture. When one is suspicious of a distal phalanx fracture, radiographs should be taken as isolated views of the injured digit.

Surgical and Applied Anatomy

Unique features of the distal phalanx include the ligaments that pass from the distal margin of the widened lateral base to the expanded proximal margins of the tuft. Small branches of the proper digital artery that supply the dorsal arcade just proximal to the nail fold pass under these ligaments very close to the base of the shaft of the distal phalanx. The tuft is an anchoring point for the specialized architecture of the digital pulp, a honeycomb structure of fibrous septae that contain pockets of fat in each compartment. The proximal part of the pulp is thicker and more mobile than the distal pulp. The proximal portion of a tuft fracture may become entrapped in the septae of the pulp and prove irreducible.[5] The dorsal surface of the distal phalanx is the direct support for the germinal matrix and sterile matrix of the nail. The bone volarly and the nail plate dorsally create a three-layer sandwich with the matrix in the middle (Fig. 28-7).

Fractures in the distal phalanx can be conceived of as occurring in three primary regions: the tuft, the shaft, and the base (Fig. 28-8). The two mechanisms of injury experienced most frequently are a sudden axial load (as in ball-handling sports) or crush injuries. Crush fractures of the tuft are often stable injuries held in place by the fibrous network of the pulp volarly and the splinting effect of the nail plate dorsally. Proximally, the digital flexor and terminal extensor tendons insert on the volar and dorsal bases of the distal phalanx. Since these are the last tendon attachments in the digit, all fracture planes occurring distal to these tendon insertions have been separated from any internal deforming forces. In contrast, volar and dorsal base fractures are unstable, with the entire force of a tendon pulling

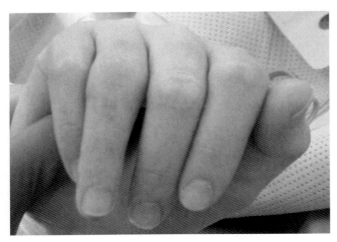

FIGURE 28-6 Pronation of the ring finger proximal phalanx is easily demonstrated by the angular discrepancy of the middle phalanges viewed with the proximal interphalangeal joints flexed 90 degrees.

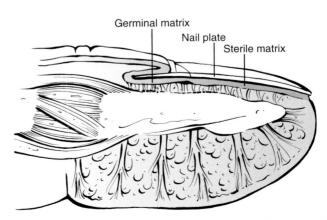

FIGURE 28-7 An intimate relationship exists between the three layers of the dorsal cortex of the distal phalanx, the nail matrix (both germinal and sterile), and the nail plate.

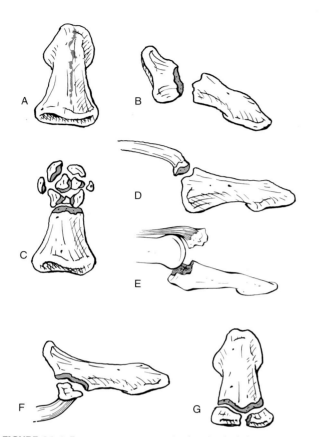

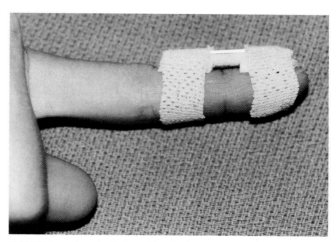

FIGURE 28-9 Dorsal splinting of the distal phalanx and the distal interphalangeal joint is easily accomplished with an aluminum and foam splint. Cutting out the foam over the dorsal nail fold skin relieves direct pressure where the skin is at greatest risk for ischemic necrosis.

FIGURE 28-8 Fracture patterns seen in the distal phalanx include (**A**) longitudinal shaft, (**B**) transverse shaft, (**C**) tuft, (**D**) dorsal base avulsion, (**E**) dorsal base shear, (**F**) volar base, and (**G**) complete articular.

the small base fragment away from the remainder of the bone. Controlling rotation in these small pieces may be particularly difficult. Dorsal base intra-articular fractures because of the shearing component of an axial load injury should be distinguished from avulsion fractures occurring under tension from the terminal tendon. The latter are smaller fragments with the fracture line perpendicular to the line of tensile force in the tendon, whereas the former are larger fragments comprising a significant (greater than 20%) portion of the articular surface with the fracture line being perpendicular to the articular surface. These are very different injuries with different treatment requirements.[104] In a similar fashion, the majority of bone flakes at the volar base of P3 are really flexor digitorum profundus (FDP) tendon ruptures occurring through bone. A small percentage of volar base fractures, especially when large in size, are not FDP avulsions but rather shearing fractures that are amenable to extension block splinting.

Current Treatment Options

Many distal phalanx fractures can be treated with digital splints (Fig. 28-9). The splint should leave the PIP joint free but usually needs to cross the DIP joint simply to gain enough foundation to provide adequate stability. The splint may be removed daily to perform active DIP joint-blocking exercises. Aluminum and foam splints or plaster of Paris are common materials chosen. The significance of lingering symptoms with fractures of the distal phalanx remains underappreciated (Table 28-1).

Tuft Fractures

If the dorsal surface of the distal portion of the phalanx that supports the nail matrix has a significant step-off, especially with a concomitant nail plate avulsion, the fracture should be restored to a level surface and pinned to render support to the surgical repair of the nail matrix. Conversely, if the nail plate has maintained its seal at the hyponychium and the dorsal surface of the distal phalanx is level, formal removal of the plate to perform a nail matrix repair is not necessary despite any measured percentage of hematoma occupying the area under the nail. Matrix defects should be split-thickness grafted from the adjacent or a distant nail bed. Following repair, the dorsal nail fold should be stented to prevent adherence to the matrix but still allow fluid drainage. The patient should be warned of the potential for nail deformity and the time required (4 to 5 months) for regrowth.

Shaft Fractures

Most shaft fractures have limited enough displacement that nonoperative management is appropriate. Active motion of the DIP joint can be pursued from the outset since the forces of the flexor digitorum profundus and the terminal extensor tendon are not acting across the fracture site. Only externally applied forces such as pinch will deform the fracture. Shaft fractures with wide displacement are headed for a nonunion without closer approximation of the fragments. CRIF is usually sufficient for these fractures unless there is interposed tissue blocking the reduction (Fig. 28-10). Kirschner wire fixation may also be preferable (0 of 5 malunions) compared with splinting (3 of 18 flexion malunions) when the fracture is transverse, extra-articular, and located at the base of the distal phalanx.[4]

Dorsal Base Fractures—CRIF

CRIF is the treatment of choice for true displaced dorsal base fractures, comprising over 25% of the articular surface (Fig. 28-11). A variety of closed pinning techniques are possible, but the mainstay is extension block pinning[80,123] (Figs. 28-12 and 28-13). Twenty-three patients treated with extension block pinning for fragments comprising an average of 40% of the joint

TABLE 28-1	**Distal Phalanx Fractures**	
Treatment Option	Pros	Cons
Splinting	Minimal treatment-related complications; this is, the maximum treatment needed for minimally displaced tuft fractures with a level dorsal cortex under the nail matrix	Not precise enough to control an angulated shaft fracture, displaced articular fracture, or widely displaced large fragment tuft fracture
CRIF	Capable of maintaining the dorsal cortex level to support the nail, extension block pinning for dorsal base fractures restores articular congruence	Pin tract infection rate is significant owing to distal location in hand and retention of pins for at least 4 weeks
ORIF	Part of open fracture management	High rate of complications related to hardware and wound healing with generally unsatisfactory results

CRIF, closed reduction and internal fixation; ORIF, open reduction and internal fixation.

surface had mean flexion of 77 degrees with a four-degree extensor lag and two losses of reduction.[80] The difficulty in comparing the published outcomes for these injuries is that the literature has usually failed to distinguish between dorsal fractures that are merely bony variants of terminal tendon injuries and those that are the more significant intra-articular fractures discussed in this section.

Dorsal Base Fractures—ORIF

Dorsal base fractures may rarely require ORIF. Although subluxation has been cited as a reason to perform ORIF, a biomechanical study showed that subluxation was not seen whenever the smaller fragment carried less than 43% of the articular surface.[84] Thirty-three patients with K-wire ORIF had a mean arc of 4 to 67 degrees of final motion.[153] As an alternative method of ORIF, nine patients were treated with a custom "hook plate" formed by cutting a 1.3-mm modular straight plate and achieved an average of 64 degrees of ROM at the DIP joint with no extensor lag.[155] One method of avoiding the complications potentially associated with open DIP joint surgery (0 of 19) might be the 5 weeks of external fixation employed in 19 patients resulting in 70 degrees of flexion with a two-degree average extensor lag.[88]

Volar Base Fractures

ORIF is the treatment of choice for highly displaced volar base fractures that have a large intra-articular fragment and loss of

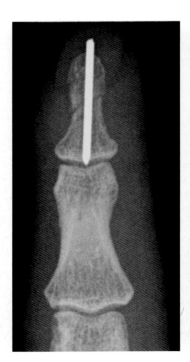
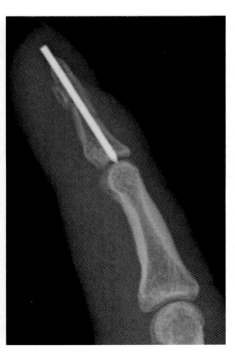

FIGURE 28-10 Shaft fractures should first be axially compressed then stabilized with a longitudinal K-wire that is drilled just short of the subchondral bone plate then axially tapped into the subchondral bone without spinning the wire.

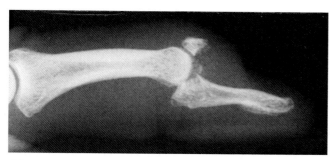

FIGURE 28-11 Dorsal base fractures from axial impaction with shearing rather than a traction avulsion injury may demonstrate subluxation of the volar fragment with rotation into extension of the smaller dorsal fragment. These features are consistent with operative management of the injury.

FDP functional integrity. If the volar FDP fragment is large enough, it may be fixed with a compression screw. Extension block pinning is another rarely used alternative. The remainder of small bone flakes located at the volar base of the distal phalanx are tendon avulsions and should be treated in accordance with modern principles of flexor tendon reinsertion.

Rehabilitation

Healing at this level of the digit is often prolonged. Transverse shaft fractures may take 3 to 4 months before being able to resist maximum pinch force. For stable tuft and longitudinal fractures, splints may be removed and functional use of the hand instituted as soon as tolerated. Dorsal base fractures usually have the Kirschner wires removed by 4 weeks with continued external protection for 2 to 3 more weeks when using traditional pinning techniques. The dorsal base extension block method works through the institution of passive extension exercises beginning at 4 weeks and coinciding with wire removal. The more distal the injury is in the digit, the more hypersensitivity to surface contact the patient is likely to have. Desensitization through progressively more stimulating contact is the earliest component of the rehabilitation program, with the goal of reincorporating the fingertip into as many activities of daily living as possible.

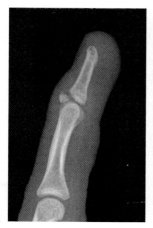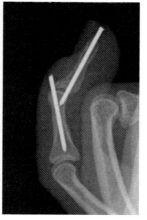

FIGURE 28-12 Dorsal base shearing articular fractures (**A**) can be stabilized by the extension block pinning technique (**B**) using two 0.045-inch K-wires.

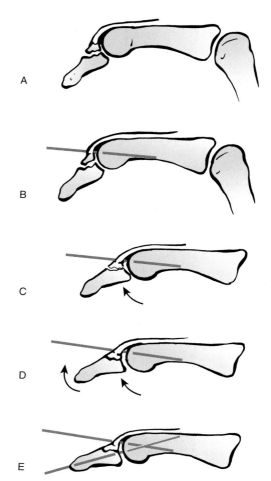

FIGURE 28-13 The steps of the extension block pinning method begin with (**A**) hyperflexion of the distal interphalangeal joint to draw the smaller dorsal fragment volarly where it is (**B**) blocked from returning into further extension by the first 0.045-inch K-wire. The larger volar fragment is then reduced (**C**) first at the articular surface to meet the dorsal fragment followed by (**D**) extension of the shaft to approximate the metaphysis, and maintained by the second K-wire (**E**).

AUTHORS' PREFERRED METHOD OF TREATMENT
Tuft, Shaft, and Base Fractures

Tuft Fractures

Many tuft fractures can be splinted in a simple aluminum and foam splint for a duration determined by the patient's symptoms alone. The time course for healing of the associated soft tissue injury may well determine the total duration of disability far more than that of the fracture itself. When the seal of the nail plate with the hyponychium has been broken and the tuft fracture is displaced, this represents an open fracture that should be treated on the day of injury with direct nail bed repair. If the distal fragment is of substantial size, the dorsal cortex of the distal phalanx that supports the nail bed will provide a more level surface if pinned with one or more 0.035-inch K-wires for 4 to 6 weeks.

Shaft Fractures

Longitudinal sagittal plane shaft fractures of the distal phalanx can be treated entirely nonoperatively if minimally displaced with CRIF with oblique 0.028- to 0.035-inch K-wires being used for the rare displaced fracture. For unstable transverse shaft fractures, the surrounding tissues usually impart enough rotational stability that a single axial wire is sufficient. Depending on the size of the phalanx, either a 0.045- or 0.035-inch Kirschner wire is appropriate. Care should be taken to avoid penetration of the nail matrix tissues with the wire. If the fracture is at mid-shaft level or more distal, the wire will provide enough stability if driven to the subchondral base of the distal phalanx only. Fractures occurring at the metadiaphyseal junction may need to have the wire passed across the DIP joint to achieve sufficient stability. Distraction at the shaft fracture site can easily occur and should be avoided to diminish the possibility of nonunion. One way to overcome this is with axial compression provided by a variable pitch headless screw now offered in a micro size (Fig. 28-14). This same technique can be used percutaneously to treat a fibrous nonunion of a previous shaft fracture. The old standard had been to leave pins emerging from the hyponychium for ease of removal later in the office, but in the MRSA era, cutting them below the skin surface guards against pin tract infection. The distal phalanx heals slowly, often taking up to 8 weeks or longer. Fortunately, DIP joint rehabilitation may proceed since the fracture is only deformed by external application of pinch forces.

Dorsal Base Fractures

Dorsal base intra-articular shear fractures produce a triangular dorsal fragment that is extended and translated by the pull of the terminal tendon. With proper collateral ligament damage, the larger articular fragment that is in continuity with the remainder of the phalanx may sublux volarly. ORIF adds excessive surgical trauma to this delicate set of tissues and the dorsal fragment is usually too small to accommodate fixation devices passing directly through it without experiencing comminution. The injury is best addressed by extension block pinning. The DIP joint is hyperflexed, drawing the dorsal fragment volarly to reach its natural position in relation to the head of the middle phalanx. A 0.045-inch K-wire is then inserted at the dorsal margin of the fragment (but not through the fragment) to block it from returning to the retracted position under the influence of the terminal extensor tendon (see Fig. 28-13). The remainder of the distal

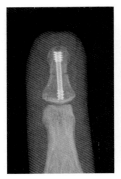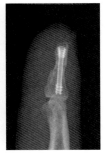

FIGURE 28-14 Shaft fractures can be axially compressed to avoid nonunion resulting from distraction by using a variable pitch headless compression microsized screw placed over a guidewire.

phalanx consisting of the volar articular fragment and shaft is then extended to meet the blocked smaller fragment and restore articular congruity. A second 0.045-inch K-wire is passed from P3 across the DIP joint into the middle phalanx. The wires are retained for 4 weeks. Upon removal, passive extension exercises further compress the two fragments and assist in the final stages of cancellous bone healing. The treatment can still be executed up to 4 to 5 weeks after the initial injury, but the early callus that has formed between the two fragments must be dispersed or satisfactory approximation will not be achieved.

Pearls and Pitfalls

The volar pulp space adjacent to distal phalanx fractures represents a tense three-dimensional hydrodynamic unit that will tend to expand when injured and forcibly distract fracture fragments from each other resulting in nonunion frequently seen at this level. The most common direction of displacement is in distraction. Smooth sided K-wires are the most common fixation devices used for P3 fracture fixation but they can allow the fracture fragments to slide along the surface of the wires. The best way to defeat this is to place the wires as obliquely as possible and to use converging and diverging patterns (Fig. 28-15). When performing the extension block pinning technique for dorsal base fractures, achieving a truly congruent joint is difficult. There are two typical problems: rotation of the smaller fragment into extension under the influence of the terminal extensor tendon and cantilevering of the volar articular-shaft fragment. A method to overcome the first problem is to insert another K-wire percutaneously to hold pressure on the dorsal cortex of the small fragment while placing the extension block wire. The flat side of the wire rather than the sharp tip should be used for this reduction maneuver. The surgeon holding the distal phalanx shaft fragment manually and applying the extension force for reduction creates the second problem. Instead of achieving a congruent joint reduction, the larger fragment cantilevers and reduces at the metaphyseal level but leaves an incongruent articular gap. Placing an instrument handle, such as a Freer elevator, transversely across the volar base just distal to the flexion crease and using the instrument to apply the extension force directly at the level of the joint can overcome this second problem. The reduction will first occur congruently at the joint and then secondarily at the metaphysis.

Nail Matrix.. Matrix tissue may fold into any dorsal opening of a fracture site, particularly at the base of the germinal matrix. If reduction of a distal phalanx fracture with a visible dorsal cortical gap on the lateral radiograph is not forthcoming, this possibility must be considered and matrix extrication performed to prevent both nonunion and nail deformity. Suturing the nail matrix can be difficult. Friable nail matrix tissue is easily torn as the needle is pushed rather than rolled along its axis during repair, a problem that is compounded by the needle tip's tendency to catch on the dorsal cortex during the bottom of the stroke. These problems are overcome by using a special 7-0 chromic suture with a spatula tipped needle that can be passed with a rolling motion of the fingers when loaded on a Castro-Viejo needle driver.

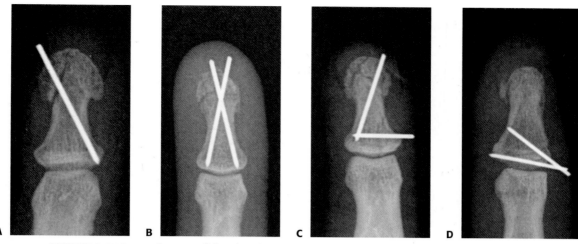

FIGURE 28-15 Fracture fragment sliding along the smooth shaft of the K-wire is prevented by (**A**) maximum oblique placement from one lateral edge of the tuft to the opposite far lateral corner of the base, (**B**) two wires targeting the lateral corners of the base, (**C**) converging wire patterns, or (**D**) diverging wire patterns.

DISTAL INTERPHALANGEAL AND THUMB INTERPHALANGEAL JOINT DISLOCATIONS

Dislocations at the DIP/IP joint suffer from underappreciation and late presentation. Injuries are considered chronic after 3 weeks. Pure dislocations without tendon rupture are rare, usually result from ball-catching sports, are primarily dorsal in direction, and may occur in association with PIP joint dislocations (Fig. 28-16). Transverse open wounds in the volar skin crease are frequent (Fig. 28-17). Injury to a single collateral ligament or to the volar plate alone at the DIP joint is rare.

Surgical and Applied Anatomy

The DIP/IP joint is a bicondylar ginglymus joint stabilized on each side by proper and accessory collateral ligaments and the volar plate (Fig. 28-18). The proper collateral ligaments insert on the lateral tubercles at the base of P3, which also serve as the origin for the lateral ligaments to the tuft. The accessory collateral ligaments attach distally to the lateral margins of the volar plate. The volar plate of the DIP joint has a proximal attachment weakly confluent with the distal extent of the flexor digitorum superficialis (FDS) tendon but has no strong check-rein ligaments like those at the PIP joint. This is in keeping with the clinical observation of proximal volar plate detachment with dorsal dislocation. The joint is inherently stable owing to articular congruity and the dynamic balance of flexor and extensor tendons. However, the DIP/IP joint is not as intrinsically stable as the PIP joint and depends to a greater degree on its ligaments.

The DIP joints have complex motion patterns involving axial rotation that are different for each finger and designed to ensure conformity when the hand surrounds an object. The capacity for passive DIP hyperextension is unique to modern humans, but the role this plays in the etiology of dislocation is unclear. Irreducible dorsal dislocations are thought to occur through a variety of different anatomic circumstances (Fig. 28-19). Reasons include a trapped volar plate, the FDP being trapped behind a single condyle of the middle phalanx (marked lateral displacement), the middle phalanx buttonholed through the volar plate or through a rent in the FDP. Volar dislocations may

FIGURE 28-16 Dislocations of the distal interphalangeal joint are nearly always dorsal.

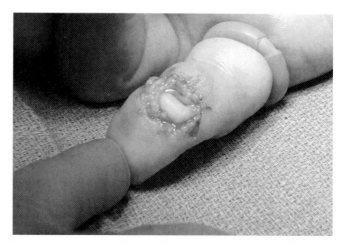

FIGURE 28-17 Dorsal distal interphalangeal dislocations are often open with a transverse rent in the flexion crease from tearing rather than direct laceration. The wound should be débrided before reduction if possible.

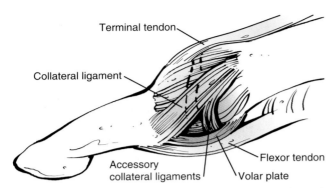

FIGURE 28-18 The balanced forces of the terminal extensor tendon and the long flexor tendon dynamically stabilize the distal interphalangeal joint. The proper and accessory collateral ligaments and the volar plate provide static stability.

also be irreducible with the extensor tendon displaced around the head of the middle phalanx. Thumb sesamoids or the volar plate may render an IP joint dislocation irreducible.[46,131]

Current Treatment Options

Nonoperative Management

Reduced dislocations that are stable may begin immediate AROM. The rare unstable dorsal dislocation should be immobilized in 20 degrees of flexion for up to 3 weeks before instituting AROM. The duration of the immobilization should be in direct proportion to the surgeon's assessment of joint stability following reduction. Complete collateral ligament injuries should be protected from lateral stress for at least 4 weeks. When splinting at the level of the DIP/IP joint, extreme caution must be exercised with regard to the vascularity of the dorsal skin between the extension skin crease and the dorsal nail fold. It is not only direct pressure but merely the angle of hyperextension that can "wash out" the blood supply to this skin, potentially resulting in full-thickness necrosis. This complication is thought to occur at an angle representing 50% of the available passive hyperextension of the DIP joint and can be identified by blanching of the skin (Table 28-2).

CRIF

It is possible that the degree of postreduction instability is great enough to require a brief period (3 to 4 weeks) of 0.045-inch K-wire stabilization across the joint (Fig. 28-20). The need for added stabilization occurs primarily when aggressive rehabilitation is required for adjacent hand injuries.

Open Reduction

Delayed presentation (more than 3 weeks) of a subluxated joint may require open reduction to resect scar tissue and permit a congruent reduction, but can result in additional postoperative stiffness. In one study, 10 patients with chronic dorsal fracture-dislocations of the DIP and IP joints (average, 8 weeks) underwent a volar plate arthroplasty with 4 weeks of K-wire fixation yielding a 42-degree average arc of motion for finger DIP joints and 51 degrees for thumb IP joints with an average flexion contracture of 12 degrees.[126] Open dislocations require thor-

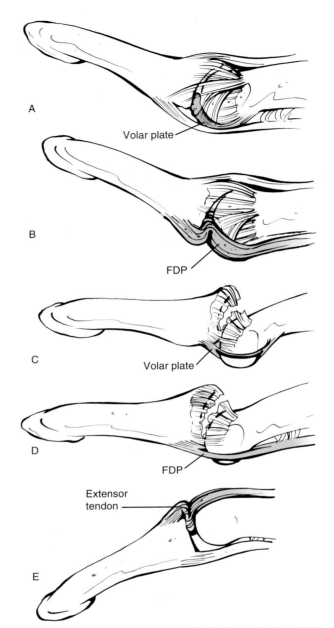

FIGURE 28-19 Irreducible dislocations of the distal interphalangeal joint occur due to (**A**) volar plate entrapment, (**B**) the flexor digitorum profundus being trapped behind a single condyle of the middle phalanx, (**C**) the middle phalanx being buttonholed through the volar plate, (**D**) the middle phalanx being buttonholed through a rent in the flexor digitorum profundus, and (**E**) the extensor tendon being displaced around the head of the middle phalanx.

ough débridement to prevent infection. The need for fixation with a K-wire should be based on the assessment of stability and fixation is not necessarily required for all open dislocations. The wire may be placed either longitudinally or on an oblique path. The duration of pinning should not be longer than 4 weeks. The advantage of longitudinal pinning is the absence of any lateral wire protrusion to contact adjacent digits. The advantage of oblique pinning is the ability to remove both sections of the wire should breakage across the joint occur. When open reduction of the joint is required, a transverse dorsal inci-

TABLE 28-2	Distal Interphalangeal Joint and Thumb Interphalangeal Joint Dislocations		
Treatment Option	**Pros**		**Cons**
Reduction and splinting	Minimizes treatment-related complications		In a noncompliant patient will not prevent redislocation
CRIF	Prevents redislocation during early collateral ligament healing		Pin tract infection and stiffness
ORIF	Part of open dislocation management, and essential for irreducible dislocations		Introduces wound healing complications, and stiffness may be a more significant problem

CRIF, closed reduction and internal fixation; ORIF, open reduction and internal fixation.

sion at the distal joint crease from midaxial line to midaxial line provides ample exposure. Should additional exposure be required, midaxial proximal extensions can be made.

AUTHORS' PREFERRED METHOD OF TREATMENT

Distal Interphalangeal and Thumb Interphalangeal Joint Dislocations

Closed reduction and splinting is the preferred treatment for most injuries. Should added pin stabilization prove necessary because of recurrent instability, a single longitudinal 0.045-inch K-wire is sufficient. Closed reduction may seem to be impossible. Interposed tissue is usually the cause and may include volar plate, collateral ligament, or tendon. Longitudinal traction rarely is successful in overcoming the blockade. Instead, proximal joint positioning to relax the involved tendons and gentle rotation may allow the interposed tissue to slip out of the joint.

Open Reduction

My preferred incision for the DIP/IP joint is dorsal and transverse (Fig. 28-21). The most distal of the major extensor creases corresponds to the joint level. Proximal extensions of 5 mm made in the midaxial lines create a small trapdoor effect that gives ample exposure for any procedure. The terminal extensor tendon or extensor pollicis longus should be protected. Using a single-prong skin hook is a gentle method to control the tendon without grasping and crushing its fibers with forceps while working to achieve reduction. One must search for small chondral or osteochondral injuries primarily for the purpose of removing the fragments from the joint to prevent subsequent third body wear.

Pearls and Pitfalls

Two primary complications of open surgery in this region are impaired wound healing and hypersensitivity. Dissecting and preserving longitudinal venous channels during the surgery facilitates venous drainage of the narrow skin flap between the wound and the dorsal nail fold. There is usually one major group of veins directly in the midline overlying the extensor tendon and one major group at each dorsolateral corner. The lateral venous groups are accompanied by the distal branches of the dorsal digital nerves. Transection of these small nerve branches with the subsequent formation of small neuromas adherent to the wound may be one

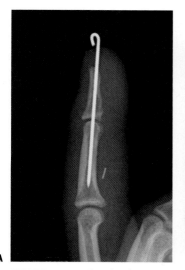
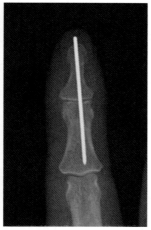

A   **B**

FIGURE 28-20 Closed reduction and internal fixation of the distal interphalangeal joint should ensure (**A**) a congruent articulation in neutral on the lateral view and (**B**) neutral pin placement on the anteroposterior view.

FIGURE 28-21 The safest surgical approach to the distal interphalangeal joint with respect to skin blood supply is transverse in the distal extensor crease with midaxial proximal extensions as needed not exceeding 5 mm.

reason for the high incidence of hypersensitivity in this region. The initial surgical incision should be just through dermis only, followed by careful longitudinal dissection of these neurovascular structures under magnification before proceeding with the remainder of the surgery. An additional nonoperative pitfall is the development of imbalance following splinting, perhaps as a result of failure to monitor the physical examination at each time point during healing.

MIDDLE PHALANX FRACTURES

This section is intentionally biased to concentrate on the intra-articular fractures that occur at the base of the middle phalanx. These are perhaps the most functionally devastating of all fractures, and dislocations of the hand and the most technically difficult to treat. Many other fracture patterns that occur in the middle phalanx are the same as those patterns seen in the proximal phalanx. The literature rarely distinguishes between P1 and the middle phalanx when reporting on the phalangeal fractures, and the majority of the published data on this subject is covered in the section on proximal phalanx fractures later in the chapter.

Surgical and Applied Anatomy

Fractures of the middle phalanx can be grouped by the anatomic regions of head, neck, shaft, and base (Fig. 28-22). Tendon insertions that play a role in fracture deformation include the central slip at the dorsal base and the terminal tendon acting through the DIP joint. The flexor digitorum superficialis has a long insertion along the volar lateral margins of the shaft of the middle phalanx from the proximal fourth to the distal fourth. Fractures at the neck of the middle phalanx will usually angulate apex volar as the proximal fragment is flexed by the FDS and the distal fragment is extended by the terminal tendon (Fig. 28-23). Those at the base will usually angulate apex dorsal as the distal fragment is flexed by the FDS and the proximal fragment is extended by the central slip. Despite the theoretical resolution of these force vectors, actual P2 are less predictable and subject to any variety of displacement patterns. Axial loading patterns of injury may produce unicondylar or bicondylar fractures of the head or intra-articular fractures of the base. Base fractures can be divided into partial articular fractures of the dorsal base, volar base, and lateral base or complete articular fractures that are usually comminuted and often referred to as "pilon" frac-

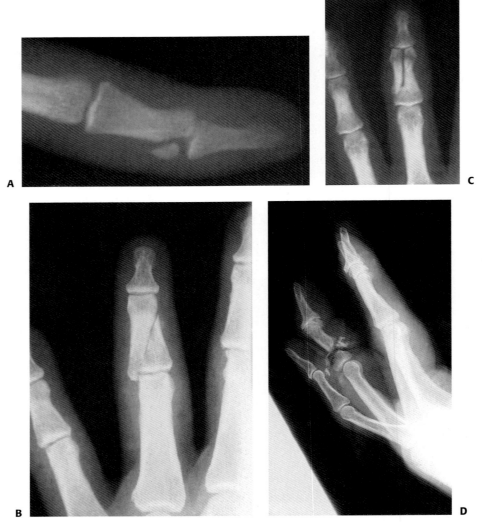

FIGURE 28-22 Fracture patterns of the middle phalanx other than the specific base patterns discussed later include (**A**) intra-articular fractures of the head, (**B**) oblique shaft fractures, (**C**) longitudinal shaft fractures, and (**D**) transverse shaft fractures.

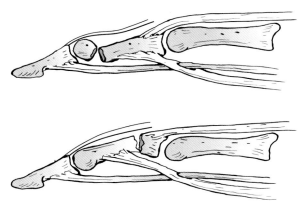

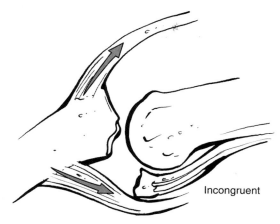

Incongruent

FIGURE 28-23 The insertions of the flexor digitorum superficialis, the flexor digitorum profundus, and the components of the extensor apparatus typically cause fractures in the distal fourth of the middle phalanx to angulate apex volar and those in the proximal fourth of the middle phalanx to angulate apex dorsal.

FIGURE 28-25 The central slip of the extensor tendon and the flexor digitorum superficialis serve as prime deforming forces for dorsal subluxation in volar base P2 fractures.

tures. "Pilon" fractures are unstable in every direction including axially.

Although the complete articular fractures are the most challenging ones in which to restore function, the force vectors of volar base fractures are perhaps more interesting. Fractures at the volar base of the middle phalanx can be particularly unstable in direct relation to the percentage of articular surface involved. When the volar fragment constitutes greater than around 40% of the articular surface, this fragment carries the majority of the proper collateral ligament insertion in addition to the accessory ligament and volar plate insertions (Fig. 28-24). The dorsal fragment and remainder of the middle phalanx will thus sublux proximally and dorsally with displacement being driven by the pull of the FDS and the central slip (Fig. 28-25). The joint then hinges rather than glides, pivoting on the fracture margin of the dorsal fragment and destroying articular cartilage on the head of P1.

Current Treatment Options

Static Splinting
Many P2 fractures can be effectively managed entirely nonoperatively (Tables 28-3 to 28-5). The presence of

comminution alone does not necessitate surgery. When crushing is the mechanism of injury, the periosteal envelope may remain relatively intact as long as fracture displacement is not significant. Degree of displacement is more related to inherent stability than the direction or number of fracture planes. Nevertheless, certain patterns are more stable than others. Transverse fractures are more stable than long oblique or spiral fractures, both of which tend to shorten and either laterally deviate or rotate to cause interference patterns with neighboring digits. Splinting is confined to the digit alone with dorsally applied aluminum and foam or custom orthoplast splints. Motion rehabilitation should be initiated by 3 weeks postinjury with interim splinting until clinical signs of healing are present (but not longer than 6 weeks).[20] Side strapping to an adjacent digit usually provides sufficient protection from external forces after the first 3 weeks.

Dynamic Extension Block Splinting
A nonoperative technique used specifically for volar base fractures is extension block splinting. Fractures at the volar base of the middle phalanx that involve less than 40% of the articular surface can usually be managed effectively with extension block splinting. The key to success with this treatment is absolute maintenance of a congruent reduction, avoiding the hinge motion that occurs with dorsal and proximal subluxation of the major fragment. Correct application of a dorsal extension block splint requires maintenance of contact between the dorsum of the proximal phalangeal segment and the splint. If the digit is allowed to "pull away" from the splint volarly, the PIP joint can extend beyond the safe range, subluxate, and negate the desired effect of the splint. Once the splint is in place, weekly follow-up with a true lateral radiograph of the PIP joint is mandatory to monitor the advancement of extension at a rate of around 10 degrees per week (see later for details of extension block splinting).

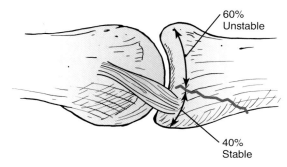

60%
Unstable

40%
Stable

FIGURE 28-24 When the volar fragment of the base of the middle phalanx comprises more than 40% of the joint surface, the collateral ligaments attach to the volar, rather than the dorsal, fragment rendering the dorsal fragment with the shaft unstable in extension.

Condylar Fractures of the Head
Displaced unicondylar or bicondylar fractures of the head of the middle phalanx require a transverse wire to be placed across

TABLE 28-3 **Middle Phalanx Fractures Not Involving the Proximal Interphalangeal Joint**

Treatment Option	Pros	Cons
Splinting	Simple	Only effective in fractures with inherent stability and minimal displacement
CRIF	Treatment of choice for most unstable head, neck, and shaft fractures	Pin tract infection
ORIF with screws only	Compression achieved between condyles in fractures of the head; controls rotation effectively	Stiffness; extensor lag of distal interphalangeal joint; not effective in the presence of comminution
ORIF with plates and screws	Necessary in open fractures and for internal fixation with bone loss or a high degree of comminution	Stiffness, extensor lag of distal interphalangeal joint, need for hardware removal

CRIF, closed reduction and internal fixation; ORIF, open reduction and internal fixation.

the condyles to maintain a level distal articular surface at the DIP joint. A second wire passed obliquely to the diaphysis of the opposite cortex will prevent lateral migration of the condylar fragment along the smooth shaft of the first wire, which would create an articular gap (Figs. 28-26 and 28-27). This second wire also controls the rotation of the fragment in the sagittal plane that can occur with single-wire fixation alone. If the patient presents late or soft tissue lies interposed in the fracture plane between condyles, achieving an accurate closed reduction is unlikely and open reduction may be required. Once opened, the opportunity for threaded lag screw fixation exists as opposed to smooth K-wire fixation. If the condylar fragment does not have a diaphyseal extension, then the location for lag screw placement is directly through the collateral ligament, which may

negate the screw's theoretical advantage over two diverging K-wires in terms of early motion.

Unstable Shaft Fractures

CRIF is usually accomplished with 0.035-inch K-wires depending on patient size (Fig. 28-28). Kirschner wires that cross in the middle of the shaft produce a less stable pattern of fixation particularly if the fracture is located at the level where the wires cross. For transverse or short oblique patterns, K-wire placement other than the crossing pattern may be difficult to achieve without violating either the DIP or PIP joint or directly penetrating a tendon (Fig. 28-29). Long oblique or spiral shaft fractures are amenable to relatively transverse placement of K-wires without joint or tendon penetration. When rotational alignment cannot be effec-

TABLE 28-4 **Volar Base Fracture Dislocations of the Middle Phalanx at the Proximal Interphalangeal Joint**

Treatment Option	Pros	Cons
Extension block splinting	Treatment of choice for most less-than-40% articular surface volar base fractures	Requires careful assessment of congruence and follow-up, not effective in most greater-than-40% articular surface volar base fractures
Extension block pinning	Specific strategy for dorsal base fractures and select volar base fractures that reduce spontaneously with proximal interphalangeal joint flexion	Useful only in these specific patterns Pin tract infection
Volar plate arthroplasty	Specific strategy for the subset of volar base fractures involving between 30% and 60% of articular surface that are not candidates for a hemihamate autograft reconstruction	Numerous specific anatomic requirements must be met for procedure to be effective; surface is not hyaline cartilage
Osteochondral reconstruction	Bone-to-bone healing; true hyaline cartilage restoration; recreates volar lip buttress effectively	Technically complex; subsequent graft resorption and collapse are possible

TABLE 28-5	"Pilon" Complete Articular Fractures of the Base of the Middle Phalanx		
Treatment Option	Pros		Cons
Splinting	No hardware-related complications		Only effective for minimally displaced, inherently stable fractures
CRIF	No added stiffness of open procedure		Pin tract infection; no early motion if pinned across the joint; if not pinned across the joint, congruent reduction may not be controlled
ORIF	Most precise reduction of articular surface; no pin tracts		Even with a condylar blade plate, the method may still not control metaphyseal collapse or maintain joint congruence; hardware-related complications; technically most difficult option
Dynamic traction	Maintains joint congruence, protects against metaphyseal collapse, and permits early active motion		Requires multiple adjustments to ensure precisely congruent tracking with motion Pin tract infection

CRIF, closed reduction and internal fixation; ORIF, open reduction and internal fixation.

tively restored by closed means, interfragmentary lag screw fixation is usually quite effective for spiral fractures. When comminution or axial instability is present, a limited number of P2 fractures may actually be most appropriately treated with plate and screw fixation (Fig. 28-30).

Temporary Transarticular Pinning for Partial Articular Base Fractures

Extension block pinning is an effective strategy for dorsal and volar base fractures (Figs. 28-31 and 28-32). An average PIP joint ROM of 91 degrees was achieved following CRIF of dorsal base fractures despite an extensor lag of over 10 degrees in 5 of 9 patients.[127] Extension block pinning for 3 weeks or even longer to treat volar base fractures has been used with success in limited numbers of patients.[162,167] Ten patients with 16-year follow-up of transarticular pins for 3 weeks with 2 additional weeks of extension block splinting achieved an average 85-degree arc of motion with an 8-degree flexion contracture and no severe degenerative changes.[115] Another study compared transarticular fixation (eight patients) to ORIF with lag screws (six patients) or ORIF with cerclage wires (five patients). At 7-year mean follow-up, cerclage wires produced the smallest arc of motion (median, 48 degrees) compared with pinning

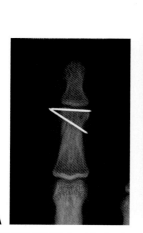
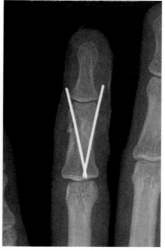

A   **B**

FIGURE 28-26 Condylar fractures at the head of the middle phalanx tend to slide along the pin interface producing an articular gap and/or step-off. **A.** Unicondylar fractures require diverging wires to prevent fragment separation. **B.** In bicondylar fractures, converging wires are used to prevent fragment separation.

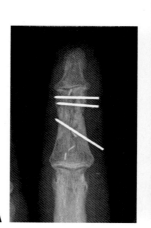
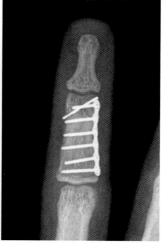

A   **B**

FIGURE 28-27 More complex bicondylar fractures can be stabilized by either (**A**) multiple wires in different planes or (**B**) a lateral plate and screws.

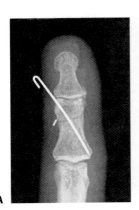
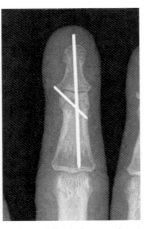

FIGURE 28-28 Fractures of the neck of the middle phalanx can be pinned with (**A**) a single oblique pin only when local soft tissues and the geometry of the fracture itself add some inherent stability. Correct placement is from the collateral recess distally to the opposite corner of the metaphyseal base. **B.** If there is a concomitant zone II extensor tendon repair needing protection, pinning can include the distal interphalangeal joint with an oblique wire in the middle phalanx to prevent axial rotation.

(median, 75 degrees). Eleven of the 19 total patients healed with some degree of incongruence or frank subluxation.[2]

Volar Base Fractures

A closed fixation strategy uniquely designed for volar base fractures is a force couple device that works to dynamically reduce the tendency for dorsal subluxation of the middle phalanx [17] (see Table 28-4). Acute volar base fractures involving more than 40% of the joint surface and those with subacute or chronic residual subluxation can be treated with volar plate arthroplasty.[36] Seventeen patients followed at 11.5 years demonstrated a TAM of 85 degrees when operated on within 4 weeks of injury and 61 degrees when operated on later than 4 weeks from injury.[36] A series of 56 patients with volar base fracture-dislocations treated by either volar plate arthroplasty (23 of 56) or ORIF (33 of 56) yielded at 46-month follow-up minimal pain in 83% but radiographic evidence of degenerative changes in 96%.[34]

Lag screw fixation is an excellent option for large volar fragments without comminution (Fig. 28-33). Seven patients undergoing lag screw fixation within 2 weeks of injury achieved an average PIP joint ROM of 100 degrees with a similar group of seven patients operated after 2 weeks achieving an average of 86 degrees.[66] Another 12 digits followed-for an average of 8.7 months after lag screw ORIF demonstrated combined PIP

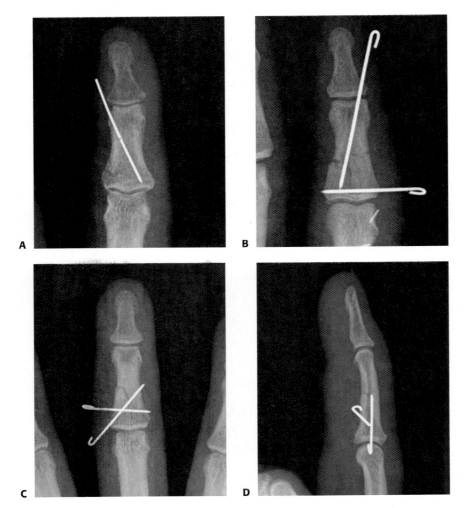

FIGURE 28-29 Shaft fractures of the middle phalanx can be stabilized with (**A**) a single oblique pin from the collateral recess to the opposite base if relatively stable upon reduction, (**B**) converging wires in different planes when added stability is needed, or (**C,D**) diverging wires.

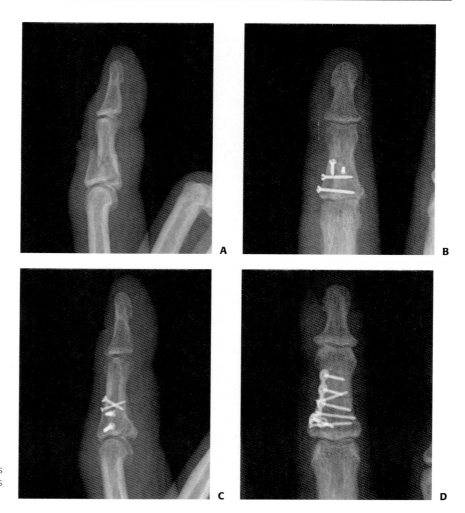

FIGURE 28-30 More complex shaft fractures (**A**) can be stabilized by (**B,C**) multiple lag screws or (**D**) a lateral plate and screws.

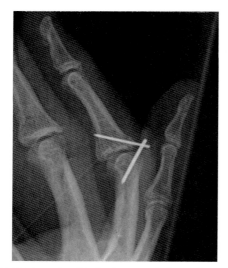

FIGURE 28-31 Extension block pinning includes at least one K-wire placed into the intercondylar notch of the proximal phalanx to prevent dorsal displacement of the base of the middle phalanx and a second interfragmentary wire may be added in the base of the middle phalanx itself.

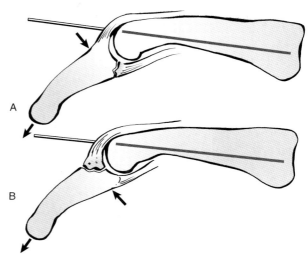

FIGURE 28-32 Extension block pinning is a closed strategy for managing (**A**) volar base fractures of the middle phalanx and (**B**) dorsal base fractures of the middle phalanx.

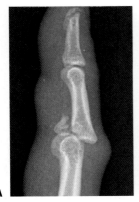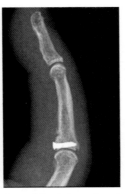

FIGURE 28-33 Volar base fractures of the middle phalanx allow the shaft and dorsal base fragment to (**A**) sublux dorsally and proximally resulting in hinge, rather than gliding, motion. Fixation of the volar base fragment must (**B**) restore the volar lip buttress against subluxation and recreate a congruent articulation.

and DIP motion arcs that averaged 132 degrees.[96] When followed at an average of 42 months from surgery, 9 similar patients demonstrated an average PIP range of 70 degrees with a 14-degree flexion contracture.[68] Even displaced fractures more than 5 weeks from injury can be carefully corrected at the articular surface and supported by bone graft using the volar "shotgun" exposure.[32] An interesting alternative procedure offered by Weiss[172] and performed through the same "shotgun" volar exposure is that of cerclage wiring of the base of the middle

phalanx, which resulted in an average PIP ROM of 89 degrees for 12 patients. When comminution is excessive, restoration of the volar buttress with true hyaline cartilage is possible using a hemi-hamate osteochondral autograft. Thirteen patients treated with this strategy at an average of 45 days postinjury for comminution of the volar 60% of the the middle phalanx base had an average PIP 85-degree arc of motion at 16-month follow-up.[175]

"Pilon" Fractures

The most functionally devastating injuries to the PIP joint are "pilon" fractures that involve the complete articular surface combined with metaphyseal compaction (Table 28-5). These are highly unstable injuries refractory to standard surgical techniques. Although other adverse events such as pin tract infection may intercede, the primary complication is stiffness. Unique forms of treatment have been devised for these injury patterns involving "dynamic traction."[8,42,106,129,134,152,157] An alternative design uses a dorsal spring mechanism.[45] The general principle is to establish a foundation at the center of rotation in the head of P1. From this foundation, traction (adjustable or elastic) is applied along the axis of the middle phalanx to hold the metaphyseal component of the fracture out to length while allowing early motion to remodel the articular surface (Fig. 28-34). Dynamic traction with pins and rubber bands in 14 patients followed for 2.5 years produced average PIP motion of 74 degrees and a TAM of 196 degrees.[106] Dynamic fixation with wires but not elasticity in eight patients yielded a final average motion of 12 to 88 degrees following wire removal at 6 weeks.[85] Ideally, the patient should begin treatment acutely compared with de-

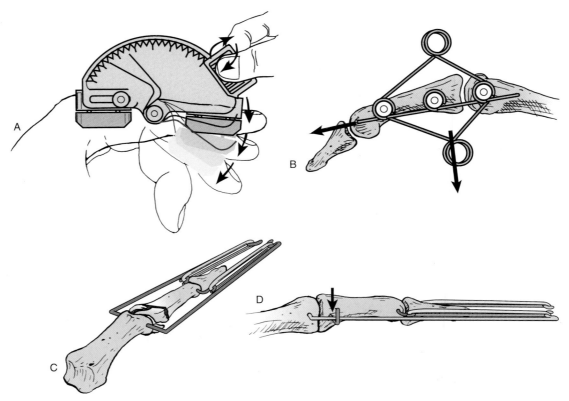

FIGURE 28-34 Strategies for managing "pilon" fractures at the base of the middle phalanx include (**A**) an adjustable unilateral hinged external fixator with distraction capabilities, (**B**) a wire spring construct, (**C**) the original configuration of pins and rubber bands, and (**D**) the same foundation augmented with an additional transverse wire across the metaphyseal base of the middle phalanx to resist dorsal subluxation.

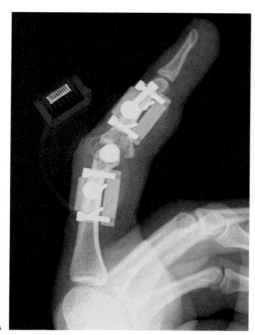 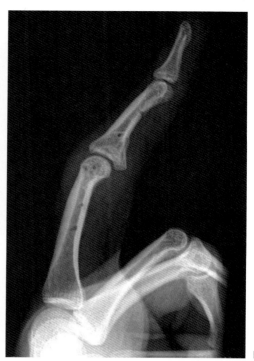

FIGURE 28-35 A hinged external fixator can be used to control "pilon" fractures beginning with (**A**) the placement of a transverse K-wire through the center of proximal interphalangeal rotation in the head of the proximal phalanx, followed by assembly of the device around that foundation wire. If performed correctly, the result will be (**B**) a congruent joint when healed.

layed application of the device.[23] Many types of device constructs are possible (Fig. 28-35). The simplest constructs involve only K-wires and rubber bands. Thirty-four patients from the armed services achieved a final average arc of motion at the PIP joint of 88 degrees and the DIP joint of 60 degrees using such a device with eight pin tract infections.[129] Another group of nonmilitary personnel achieved average PIP arcs of 64 degrees and DIP arcs of 52 degrees.[157] With the traction left in place for only 3.5 weeks on average, an average PIP arc of 94 degrees and thumb IP arc of 62.5 degrees was achieved in six total patients.[134] Another six patients having the device removed between 3 and 4 weeks achieved average PIP range from 5 degrees to 89 degrees with two pin tract infections.[8] In another series, by an average of 26 months postoperatively, five of eight patients already demonstrated step-off deformities or arthritis.[42]

AUTHORS' PREFERRED METHOD OF TREATMENT

Stable fractures are preferably treated by limited digital splints for 3 weeks or less and protected early motion thereafter with side strapping to an adjacent digit until clinically healed. Unstable but not comminuted fractures of the shaft can be treated well by temporary (3 weeks) closed pinning (Fig. 28-36). There are a few spiral fractures for which closed reduction will not achieve satisfactory control of rotation such that lag screw fixation with 1.2-mm screws is preferable to closed pinning techniques. These treatment strategies are

also used in proximal phalanx fractures and more detail may be found in that subsequent section of the chapter.

Dorsal Base Fractures

When a dorsal base fracture presents early, extension block pinning is an excellent treatment. The principles are all the same as described above for extension block pinning of dorsal base fractures in the distal phalanx. At the base of the middle phalanx, the larger dorsal fragment (compared with the base of P3) is easier to work with and manipulate, but the PIP joint (compared with the DIP joint) imposes greater demands for a perfectly congruent joint reduction because of its more important role in overall digital function. The volar articular and shaft fragment is almost always sublux-

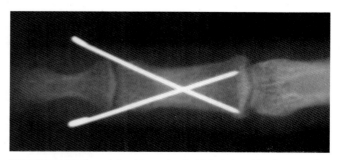

FIGURE 28-36 The relative biomechanical inferiority of K-wires crossing at the midshaft of the phalanx is offset by the lesser demands placed on the middle phalanx during rehabilitation than on the proximal phalanx and the advantage of avoiding articular penetration to achieve a closed pinning.

ated proximally and volarly. When more than 10 to 14 days have passed since injury, it can be quite difficult (because of early soft tissue contracture) to achieve a closed reduction of this fragment relative to the head of P1. It is for these reasons that late presenting dorsal base fractures are often better managed with ORIF to ensure the clearance of consolidating hematoma from between the fragments and exact approximation of the articular reduction (Fig. 28-37). In this setting, fixation with two 1.2-mm lag screws affords enough stability to pursue early motion. Use of the countersink tap is important to minimize dorsal prominence of the screw heads and to avoid pressure concentration that might comminute the still relatively small dorsal fragment. Even though the surgical procedure occurs distal to extensor zone IV, a priority still must be placed on active extensor tendon excursion during rehabilitation to avoid a long-term extensor lag. Intraoperative assessment of the stability of the fixation will guide the progression of rehabilitation to ensure against fixation failure, recognizing the small size of the thread purchase in cancellous rather than cortical bone at the metaphyseal base of the middle phalanx.

Volar Base Fractures—Closed Treatment

Volar base fractures constituting less than 25% to 30% of the joint surface rarely require surgery unless presenting late with an incongruent joint. When seen acutely, these fractures are well managed with extension block splinting that begins at around 40 degrees and advances 10 to 15 degrees per week for the first 3 weeks. If the extension block splint cannot be eliminated in 3 weeks' time, this treatment strategy may not

be appropriate. Fractures constituting more than 25% but less than 40% of the joint surface pose a difficulty in treatment planning as they constitute an intermediate group where the disadvantages of the two primary options are relatively well matched. It is difficult to predict in advance how the disadvantages will play out over the course of treatment for an individual patient. The disadvantage of extension block splinting or pinning is that with a greater amount of joint surface involved, the blocking must begin at a higher angle and it will take longer to achieve full extension. A permanent fixed flexion contracture is the consequence to be avoided. This must be compared with the overall tendency for loss of joint motion associated with ORIF or open reconstruction.

Volar Base Fractures—ORIF

When the volar fragment(s) constitute greater than 40% of the joint surface, an open procedure offers the greatest assurance of achieving a congruent joint as a final result. The distinction between ORIF for one or two relatively large fragments or open reconstruction for highly comminuted multiple fragments cannot often be made until the time of surgery. One should always be prepared for both possibilities in the preoperative planning discussions with the patient. Dorsal base fractures usually provide a single fragment of reasonable size for direct lag screw fixation. Volar base fractures are not so easy. One or two large fragments that facilitate lag screw fixation are the exception rather than the rule. In this case, two 1.2-mm lag screws are appropriate. Placement is side by side with one screw in the radial half of the base fragment

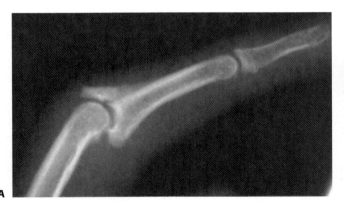

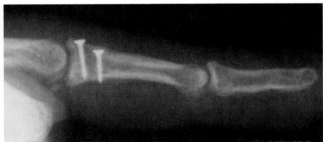

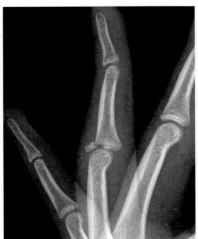

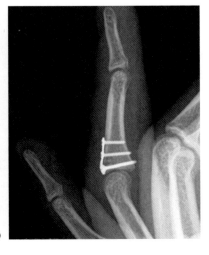

FIGURE 28-37 Dorsal base fractures allow (**A**) the volar articular fragment and the attached shaft of the middle phalanx to sublux volarly and proximally. (**B**) A congruent joint is restored with sufficient stability to initiate early rehabilitation by lag screw fixation. An alternative fixation strategy is (**C,D**) a small custom-cut hook plate.

and other in the ulnar half. If two separate radial and ulnar volar base fragments are found, this strategy is still acceptable provided that the fragment diameter is at least three times the screw diameter and compression can be achieved without causing fragment comminution. The countersink tap is useful in this regard. The operative approach is the same as described for reconstruction of a collection of comminuted fragments.

Volar Base Fractures—Osteochondral Reconstruction

A Bruner incision is made using one limb over P1 and a second over the middle phalanx. The flexor tendon sheath is reflected as a single rectangular flap hinging on its lateral margin between the distal margin of the A2 pulley and the proximal margin of the A4 pulley. The FDS and FDP are retracted laterally, one to either side, and the collateral ligament origins are dissected as a sleeve from the lateral surfaces of the head of P1. Release of the volar plate allows complete hyperextension of the PIP joint and presentation of both joint surfaces toward the surgeon. This is the so-called "shotgun" approach, and its variations center on the management of the volar plate. This approach is also used for volar plate arthroplasty and ORIF. In the former procedure, the volar plate is released distally so that it may be advanced to replace the defect in the volar articular surface. In the latter, it should remain attached to the fragments as an important source of blood supply. When performing a reconstruction of irreparable comminution, the volar plate may be released along its distal margin. The defect in the volar articular surface may range anywhere from 40% up to almost 90%, often with irregular margins. A small saw or burr should be used to straighten the irregular margins into sharp orthogonal cuts that define a clear bed of cancellous bone in the metaphysis that can be accurately measured for reconstruction. The articular surface at the base of the middle phalanx has a sagittally oriented ridge that interdigitates with the recession between the two condyles at the head of P1. This relationship is important not only for preserving joint congruence but for maintaining stability in the setting of the collateral ligament releases. An excellent geometric match has been found in the distal articular surface of the hamate at the ridge that separates the ring from the small finger CMC joints. The measurements taken from the defect at the base of the middle phalanx are transposed to the hamate and a small saw and osteotomes are used to remove the osteochondral graft from its donor site. The graft is then exactly trimmed to match the defect and secured with two 1.2-mm lag screws (Fig. 28-38). The joint is checked clinically and radiographically for maintenance of congruence through a full ROM. The flexor sheath is reapproximated with 6-0 monofilament sutures and the PIP joint splinted for protection. Immediate active motion rehabilitation is begun within days of surgery.

Open Reduction with Internal and External Fixation of "Pilon" Fractures

Complete articular fractures of the base of the middle phalanx may be treated by entirely closed reduction and stabilization. If significant metaphyseal bone loss is present or if the articular fragments at the base of the middle phalanx do not reduce sufficiently with traction alone, a small incision can be made through which cancellous bone graft can be added to fill the metaphyseal void and to assist in supporting

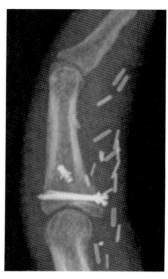

FIGURE 28-38 Volar base fractures with comminution of a substantial portion of the articular surface and subluxation can be reconstructed with an osteochondral graft from the hamate with particular emphasis placed on recreating the volar lip buttress and a truly congruent reproduction of the radius of curvature.

a reduction of the articular fragments. Transverse 0.035-inch K-wires may be placed at the subchondral level to maintain the articular relationships. The fracture must then be reduced at the metaphyseal level and undergo stabilization sufficient to withstand the rigors of early motion that must accompany the rehabilitation of articular fractures. It is at this point that the significant variations in technique arise along with different devices available for stabilization. My preference is for an off-the-shelf unilateral hinged external fixator with a manual adjustment for longitudinal traction. The device itself allows either free AROM with a gear disengaged or passive range of motion (PROM) with the gear engaged (see Fig. 28-35). Active motion with the device in place should be checked with fluoroscopy to ensure that congruent motion rather than hinge motion is occurring at the PIP joint. For this reason, these cases should be done under digital block, and the need for AROM by the patient should be explained before the procedure. Motion rehabilitation is initiated immediately and continued until final healing. The patient's performance of hourly motion exercises often causes significant pin irritation to the point of necessitating an early removal before the planned 4 weeks. Any external fixator device for a "pilon" fracture is not well appreciated by the patient. Some "pilon" fractures are amenable to ORIF, and this is a well-received option by patients provided that stable fixation is achieved and the result maintained during the stress of therapy (Fig. 28-39).

Pearls and Pitfalls

Volar Base Fracture Dislocations. There are two critical steps in performing volar base osteochondral graft reconstructions. The first is to establish sharp and flat borders in the metaphyseal defect to receive and inset the graft stably with broad cancellous surfaces for rapid bone healing. The second critical step is trimming the

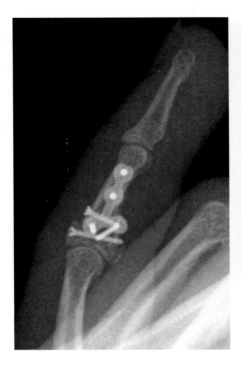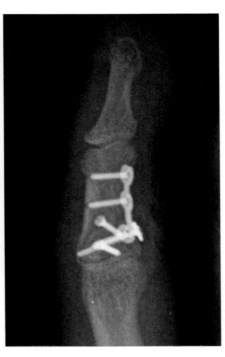

FIGURE 28-39 Some "pilon" fractures are amenable to open reduction and internal fixation, which then avoids the complications of pin tract infection associated with the dynamic traction strategies.

graft to fit this bed. The common pitfall is to set the graft's articular surface perpendicular to the neutral axis of the bone. This fails to reestablish the volar buttress and a truly congruent joint surface. If the graft is cut correctly, once inset it should replicate the buttressing function of the native volar base and prevent dorsal dislocation.

"Pilon" Fractures.. When fixing a "pilon" fracture with the unilateral hinged fixator, repeated checks on orientation of the device as a whole are needed to prevent progression to malunion. The majority of the mistakes cause the hinge on the device to rotate along a different axis than the joint itself.

Common errors are to have the device translated farther from the neutral axis of the bone at the P1 level than the the middle phalanx level or to have the pins entering the phalanges obliquely rather than in the true mid-axial plane. Above all, the surgery should be performed under a local anesthetic with the patient demonstrating true active PIP joint motion under fluoroscopy to judge the maintenance of congruence throughout the ROM. Finally, there must be no tension in the skin around the pins, as the hourly motion performed in rehabilitation will promote pin tract infections.

PROXIMAL INTERPHALANGEAL JOINT DISLOCATIONS

Dislocations of the PIP joint have a high rate of missed diagnoses that are passed off as "sprains." Although a large number of incomplete injuries occur (especially in ball-handling sports), complete disruptions of the collateral ligaments and the volar plate are also frequent. Since dramatic swelling is often present even with minor injuries to the PIP joint, this sign may often get dismissed by initial examiners of the patient. Careful palpation for localized tenderness may direct attention to one of the collateral ligaments, the volar plate, or the insertion of the central slip. The capacity for active PIP extension against resistance from a starting position of PIP flexion confirms the integrity of the central slip. Limitation of passive DIP flexion while the PIP joint is held in extension may appear several weeks following the initial injury and signify a developing boutonnière deformity. Congruence on the lateral radiograph is the key to detecting residual subluxation. Correct axial rotational alignment is demonstrated when both P1 and the middle phalanx are seen in a true lateral projection on the same film.

Residual instability is quite rare in pure dislocations as opposed to fracture-dislocations where it is the chief issue at stake. It manifests as hyperextension laxity following volar plate injuries managed with an inadequate initial degree of extension blocking. Correction of hyperextension instability can be performed with either delayed reattachment of the volar plate or a capsulotenodesis reconstruction. In pure dislocations, stiffness is the primary concern. Stiffness can occur following any injury pattern and responds best at the late stage to complete collateral ligament excision.[33,100] Chronic missed dislocations require open reduction with a predictable amount of subsequent stiffness. Patients should be counseled to expect permanent residual enlargement of the joint and for the final resolution of stiffness and aching to take as long as 12 to 18 months.

Surgical and Applied Anatomy

The head of P1 is quite different from that of the metacarpal. There is no cam effect. The head is bicondylar, and the collateral

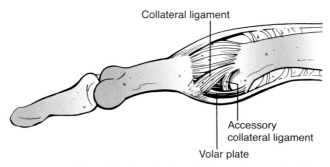

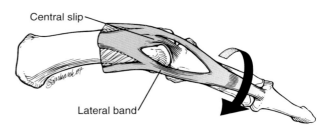

FIGURE 28-40 The proximal interphalangeal joint receives static stability from the proper and accessory collateral ligaments and the volar plate, supplemented by the dynamic stability of the dorsal plate and other balanced tendon forces acting across the joint.

FIGURE 28-42 In volar rotatory dislocations, the head of the proximal phalanx protrudes between the intact central slip and one lateral band, which create a noose effect, preventing reduction, especially if longitudinal traction is applied.

ligaments originate from the center axis of joint rotation. Nevertheless, the accessory collateral ligaments and volar plate are lax in flexion and will become contracted if immobilized in that position. At the volar base of the middle phalanx, there are tubercles for the confluence of the proper and accessory collateral ligaments with the volar plate. This junction is referred to as the "critical corner." This three-sided box design provides excellent inherent joint stability (Fig. 28-40). The volar plate anatomy is unique at the PIP joint with the presence of strong check-rein ligaments that originate inside the margins of the A2 pulley confluent with the C1 pulley fibers and the oblique retinacular ligament. The distal insertion of the volar plate is strong only at its lateral margins. The undersurface of the central slip has an articulating fibrocartilage that may aid in stabilization, prevent central slip attenuation, and increase the extensor moment arm. Although primarily a hinge, the PIP joint accommodates 7 to 10 degrees of lateral deviation and slight axial rotation. The normal ROM may be up to 120 degrees of flexion. In contrast to the other small joints of the hand, PIP joint volar plate disruptions usually occur distally. The proper collateral ligaments are the primary stabilizers to lateral stress, and a

greater than 20-degree opening signifies complete disruption. Collateral ligament disruption is usually proximal, but the fibers traditionally stay positioned over their anatomic origin for subsequent healing.

Recognized patterns of dislocation other than complete collateral ligament injury are dorsal dislocation, pure volar dislocation, and rotatory volar dislocation (Fig. 28-41). Dorsal dislocations involve volar plate injury (usually distally, with or without a small flake of bone). For pure volar dislocations the pathologic findings are consistently damage to the volar plate, at least one collateral ligament, and the central slip. Rotatory volar dislocation occurs as the head of P1 passes between the central slip and the lateral bands, which can form a noose effect and prevent reduction (Fig. 28-42). Irreducible dislocations obstructed by the volar plate or flexor tendons are uncommon injuries.

Current Treatment Options

Dorsal Dislocations—Nonoperative Management
Isolated volar plate injuries can be managed with only 7 to 10 days of splinting followed by 6 weeks of "buddy taped"

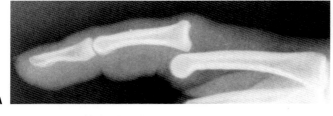

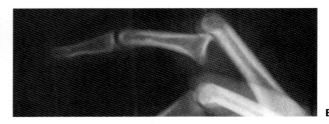

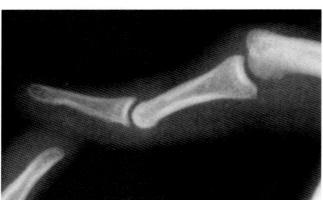

FIGURE 28-41 Three variants of proximal interphalangeal dislocation are seen. **A.** The most common, dorsal, (**B**) pure volar with central slip disruption, and (**C**) volar rotatory (note that the middle phalanx is seen as a true lateral, whereas the proximal phalanx is seen in oblique profile).

TABLE 28-6	Proximal Interphalangeal Joint Dislocations	
Treatment Option	Pros	Cons
Splinting/early motion	Least stiffness	Requires patient cooperation
CRIF	Reliably maintains reduction	Rarely indicated; pin tract infection; stiffness
ORIF	Part of open dislocation management; required for irreducible dislocations	Added stiffness

CRIF, closed reduction and internal fixation; ORIF, open reduction and internal fixation.

(strapped to an adjacent digit) AROM (Table 28-6). Fortunately, the majority of hyperextension injuries remain congruent even at full extension and do not require extension block splinting. However, one must consider that the distal volar plate is poorly vascularized, and a lack of early healing may lead to chronic hyperextension laxity. Lower-profile digitally based splints or buddy taping may effectively prevent the full extension that could threaten sound volar plate healing. When formal extension block splinting is chosen (usually only in the situation of fracture-subluxation), the rate of progression each week is determined by the severity of the initial injury but should reach full extension no later than 4 weeks from injury.

Pure Volar Dislocations—Nonoperative Management

With pure volar dislocations, central slip disruption occurs and will result in a boutonnière deformity if not treated properly. Careful examination consisting of PIP extension against resistance from a starting position of full flexion will prevent missing the diagnosis of a central slip disruption. Limitation of passive DIP flexion is an early sign of a developing boutonnière deformity. Even when identified late, the treatment of choice is extension splinting at the PIP joint with immediate active DIP blocking exercises. Active DIP flexion pulls the whole extensor mechanism (including the ruptured central slip) distally through the intact lateral bands. The duration of PIP extension splinting is usually 4 to 6 weeks with a transitional period of night splinting for several additional weeks.

Rotatory Volar Dislocations—Nonoperative Management

Rotatory volar dislocations where the head of P1 is trapped between the central slip and lateral band may be difficult to reduce owing to the noose effect exerted by these two soft tissue structures. The key to closed reduction (if it is possible at all) is to relax both structures. Wrist extension relaxes the extrinsic component, and full metacarpophalangeal joint flexion relaxes the intrinsic component. A gentle rotating maneuver that avoids excessive longitudinal traction stands the highest chance of success. A few of these dislocations remain irreducible even in the most skilled hands. When a reduction can be achieved, early mobilization is then instituted with buddy taping to an adjacent digit (usually the more radial) in an attempt to prevent stiffness.

Open Reduction

There are two indications for open treatment of PIP joint injuries: an open injury or an irreducible dislocation.[118] Lateral dislocations may also be irreducible because of interposition of a torn collateral ligament (Fig. 28-43). A midaxial (or dual midaxial) incision allows for management of both dorsal and volar dislocations. Controversy remains as to the need for direct repair of complete collateral ligament ruptures and volar plate injuries. Direct repair is probably only functionally necessary in the long term for the radial collateral ligament of the index finger. Chronic reconstruction of collateral ligament deficiency is an even more technically demanding procedure with a high pro-

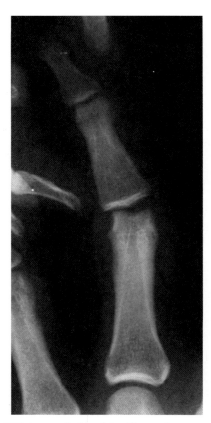

FIGURE 28-43 Entrapment of a collateral ligament can prevent reduction of the proximal interphalangeal joint; lateral stress examination demonstrates the high degree of instability in this situation.

pensity for generating stiffness but may be accomplished by a variety of techniques.

AUTHORS' PREFERRED METHOD OF TREATMENT

Proximal Interphalangeal Joint Dislocations

Once reduced, rotatory volar dislocations, isolated collateral ligament ruptures, and dorsal dislocations congruent in full extension on the lateral radiograph can all begin immediate AROM with adjacent digit strapping. Dorsal dislocations that are subluxated on the extension lateral radiograph require a few weeks of extension block splinting before progressing (however, this is an almost unheard of situation with pure dislocation and no fracture component). Volar dislocations with central slip disruptions require 4 to 6 weeks of PIP extension splinting followed by nighttime static extension splinting for 2 additional weeks. The DIP joint should be unsplinted and actively flexed throughout the entire recovery period.

Open dorsal dislocations usually have a transverse rent in the skin at the flexion crease. Debridement of this wound should precede reduction of the dislocation. Any joint debris should be cleared out to prevent third body wear. The "critical corner" warrants particular attention. For closed irreducible joints, unilateral or bilateral midaxial incisions allow excellent access to both volar and dorsal structures without violating the extensor mechanism. Postoperative management follows the same time courses stated earlier for nonoperative management based on the injury pattern and severity.

Pearls and Pitfalls

Straight longitudinal traction is almost never the answer to accomplishing a reduction and certainly is the surest way to fail at the PIP joint. Relaxation of the most powerful tendon forces acting across the joint is the key to facilitating a smooth reduction that does not cause additional hyaline cartilage damage. Postreduction clinical and radiographic assessment is crucial with an emphasis on the lateral radiograph in full extension to assess congruence. The patient should be able to move the finger through a near full ROM under the influence of the digital block used to accomplish the reduction. Open dislocations should be taken seriously for their potentially high rate of complications and debrided before reduction.

PROXIMAL PHALANX FRACTURES

Types of proximal phalanx fractures that have been recognized include intra-articular fractures of the head, extra-articular fractures of the neck and shaft, and both extra-articular and intra-articular fractures of the base (Fig. 28-44). Further describing the pattern of the fracture as transverse, short oblique, long oblique, or spiral for shaft fractures and partial or complete articular for intra-articular fractures (along with the degree and direction of displacement) provides the necessary information on which to base treatment decisions. A specific fracture pattern that risks extreme PIP limitation is that of the neck of the proximal phalanx, where a volar spike of bone from the proximal fracture fragment impinges into the subcapital recess volar to the neck of P1 (Fig. 28-44B). If the fracture heals in this position,

full PIP flexion is prevented by obstruction of the space for volar plate in-folding. This pattern is best identified on an individual digital lateral radiograph and warrants operative treatment to prevent a functionally disabling malunion.

Surgical and Applied Anatomy

Local Soft Tissue Relationships

Fracture of the proximal phalanx may well be one of the most frustrating hand injuries to manage.[91,97] The prime reason is the local soft tissue anatomy. While the metacarpal has only a cordlike extensor tendon running well dorsal to it, the proximal phalanx is closely invested by a sheetlike extensor mechanism with a complex array of decussating collagen fibers (Fig. 28-45). Surgical disturbance of the fine balance between these fibers can permanently alter the long-term function of the digit. The operative approach to P1 can be either dorsal or lateral. The dorsal approach may be technically simpler but transgresses the extensor mechanism. The lateral midaxial approach allows the fracture to be fully exposed and hardware placed in its proper lateral position (if hardware is indicated) without directly violating the extensor mechanism.[73] If prominent hardware is to be placed, the intrinsic tendon on that side (usually ulnar) may be resected. The proximal phalanx is not a cylinder but rather highly elliptical (in fact, tunnel shaped) in cross section, with a thicker dorsal cortex.

Deforming Forces

At the proximal phalangeal level, both intrinsic and extrinsic tendon forces deform the fracture. They result in a predictable apex volar deformity for transverse and short oblique fractures. These forces can be used with benefit during rehabilitation. If the MP joints are maximally flexed (the intrinsic plus position), the intrinsic muscle forces acting through the extensor mechanism overlying P1 create a tension band effect that helps to maintain fracture reduction (Fig. 28-46). Active PIP joint motion will heighten this effect and forms the basis for nonoperative fracture management. Spiral and long oblique fractures tend to shorten and rotate rather than angulate. These fractures also have more complex patterns of deformity that are not so easily controlled through the joint positioning just described.

One can expect 12 degrees of extensor lag at the PIP joint for each millimeter of shortening and 1.5 degrees of extensor lag for each degree of apex palmar fracture angulation.[163]

Biomechanics of Fixation

Transverse and short oblique proximal phalanx shaft fractures deform through apex volar bending. Laboratory investigation has shown the biomechanical inefficiency of dorsally applied plates in an apex volar bending model that correlated with the clinical forces experienced at the P1 level.[103] Even with plate fixation, the soft tissue envelope has been shown to add stability under load application.[120] This is particularly true in the most proximal 6 to 9 mm at the base of P1.[174] The most valuable foundation in a fixation paradigm is a well placed lag screw across a noncomminuted fracture interface, although some surgeons have bypassed the step of lagging the screw in favor of less labor intensive bicortical screws.[128] Long oblique and spiral proximal phalanx fractures demonstrate less angular deformity than transverse fractures, instead shortening and axially rotating.

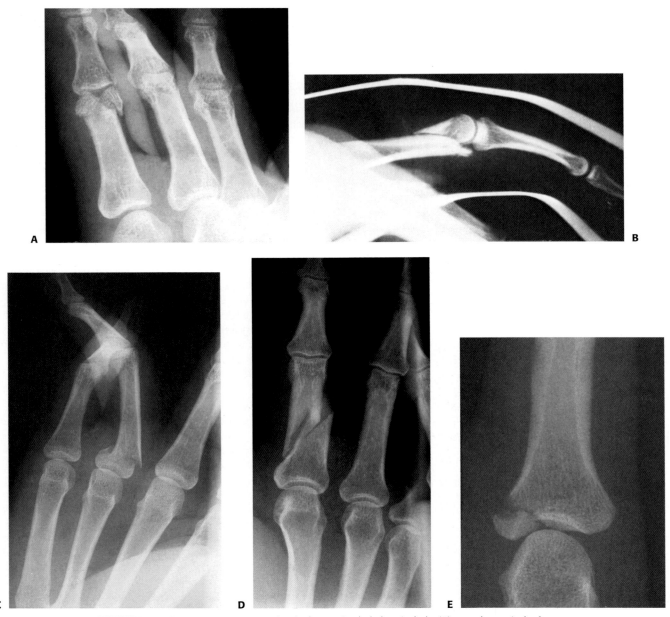

FIGURE 28-44 Fracture patterns appearing in the proximal phalanx include (**A**) complete articular fractures of the head, (**B**) subcapital fractures with impingement in the volar plate recess, (**C**) transverse fractures of the shaft or base, (**D**) oblique fractures of the shaft, and (**E**) articular fractures of the base.

Current Treatment Options

Nonoperative Management

This is the preferred treatment for many phalangeal fractures that are either minimally displaced or easily rendered stable by reduction (Table 28-7). Transverse fracture patterns will generally prove to be stable after reduction compared with oblique, spiral, or comminuted fractures. Stable proximal phalangeal fractures are ideal candidates for dorsal splinting with the MP joint in flexion. Only 4 of 45 patients treated in intrinsic plus splints failed to achieve full motion by 6 weeks.[41] The splint should be able to be discontinued at 3 weeks and followed by AROM exercises without resistance. Stable, nondisplaced fractures may even be treated by a program of immediate AROM, protected only with adjacent digit strapping. The take-home message for nonoperative management is that a carefully formed splint and/or adjacent digit strapping can effectively maintain an existing and reasonably stable reduction. What splints and strapping cannot accomplish is a reduction in their own right. In case this fact is not appreciated at the initial encounter, all patients undergoing nonoperative management should be seen back in the office at a week to verify maintenance of reduction radiographically.

Closed Reduction Internal Fixation

This is the treatment of choice for the category of reducible but unstable isolated fractures, both extra-articular and some intra-articular. A higher degree of care must be exercised when pursuing CRIF in the phalanges compared with the metacarpals be-

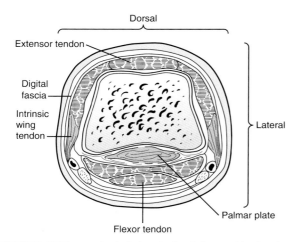

FIGURE 28-45 The proximal phalanx is closely invested by the sheet of the zone IV extensor tendon dorsally, the blending of the intrinsic wing tendons laterally and volarly, and the flexor tendons and flexor sheath direct volarly.

cause of the close investment by the broad extensor mechanism. Pin entry sites should be chosen carefully to minimize tethering of the extensor mechanism. In the proximal two thirds of P1, this is virtually impossible. As one approaches the distal third, a direct lateral approach can be made volar to the interosseous tendon. For long oblique and spiral fractures, three K-wires (0.045 or 0.035 inch) are placed perpendicular to the fracture plane (Fig. 28-47). For neck fractures, retrograde pinning may be necessary (Fig. 28-48). For short oblique and transverse fractures, longitudinal K-wires (0.045-inch) are placed through the MP joint (Fig. 28-49). Twelve patients achieved an average TAM of 265 degrees with two longitudinal pins placed across the MP joint and down the shaft of the proximal phalanx.[81] Trocar-tipped K-wires rather than diamond-tipped or surgeon-cut wires should be used. The wire should be passed through the soft tissues and down to bone before activating the wire driver. Pins should be cut just below the skin surface to prevent pin tract infection or left protruding for ease of removal at the surgeon's discretion. Absolute parallelism of the K-wires for oblique fractures risks the fracture displacing as it slides along the wires. Some degree of convergence or divergence of the wires will help to prevent this consequence of using smooth

wires. The procedure of CRIF is made more difficult than it may initially appear by the challenge of obtaining a truly accurate reduction by closed means. Commercially available devices have been specially designed for closed intramedullary rodding of the phalanx (Fig. 28-50). Routinely, pins should be removed by 3 weeks. When this is done, any final limitations of motion are most likely because of the injury itself rather than the pins. In 35 fractures of the proximal phalanx treated by percutaneous pinning, 32% developed a PIP flexion contracture averaging 18 degrees.[43] A slight variation on the theme is "intrafocal" pinning used in five patients to achieve an average PIP range of 90 degrees.[27]

Open Reduction and Internal Fixation

ORIF is the technique of choice for severe open fractures with multiple associated soft tissue injuries and for patients with multiple fractures (within the same hand or polytrauma patients). It is also the technique of choice for intra-articular fractures with displacement in P1. In a series of 38 distal unicondylar fractures of P1, five of seven initially nondisplaced and unfixed fractures and four of ten fixed with a single K-wire went on to displace.[173] Displaced fractures at the intra-articular base of P1 with more than 20% articular involvement should be internally fixed. Using a volar A1 pulley approach, 10 patients had fixation of lateral base fractures with full motion recovery, good stability, and over 90% contralateral grip strength.[92] The role of ORIF for an isolated, noncomminuted, extra-articular fracture of the phalanx is clearly defined only for the rare irreducible fracture. Spiral fractures may benefit from ORIF with lag screws to achieve precise control over rotation, provided that surgeons experienced in this specific technique can minimize soft tissue disruption. Most surgeons will be more comfortable with CRIF for those fractures that can be reduced. The 40-month follow-up of 32 patients prospectively randomized to percutaneous pinning versus lag screw fixation for long oblique and spiral shaft fractures found no differences in function, pain scores, ROM, or grip strength, but with a mean loss of active extension of 8 degrees in the pinning group and 27 degrees in the screw fixation group.[82] Surgical technique was such that there were 8 malunions of the 15 lag screw patients using screws as large as 2.0 mm. Three of the 17 K-wire patients required subsequent formal extensor tenolysis for tethering but none of the lag screw patients did.[82] ORIF with screws and/or plates is

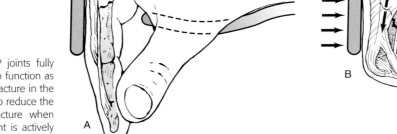

FIGURE 28-46 Flexing the MP joints fully causes the extensor apparatus to function as a tension band to a transverse fracture in the proximal phalanx shaft, helping to reduce the deformity and stabilize the fracture when the proximal interphalangeal joint is actively flexed.

TABLE 28-7 **Proximal Phalanx Fractures**

Treatment Option	Pros	Cons
Splinting	Treatment of choice for stable and minimally displaced fractures, no added surgical stiffness	Does not effectively control rotation; may fail in noncompliant patients with unstable fractures
CRIF	Very effective for simple two-part fractures especially transverse and short oblique	Pin tract infection, may not control the rotation of spiral fractures effectively
ORIF: lag screws	Controls rotation accurately for spiral fractures	Potential for added postoperative stiffness especially at proximal interphalangeal joint and extensor lag
ORIF: plates and screws	Necessary for comminution or bone loss	Added hardware bulk may necessitate removal with stiffness proportionate to the extent of surgical dissection
ORIF: composite wiring	Simple supplies are easily obtained. Does not require special knowledge of small screw surgical techniques	K-wires protrude to interfere with tendons; need for hardware removal; not effective in presence of segmental bone loss

CRIF, closed reduction and internal fixation; ORIF, open reduction and internal fixation.

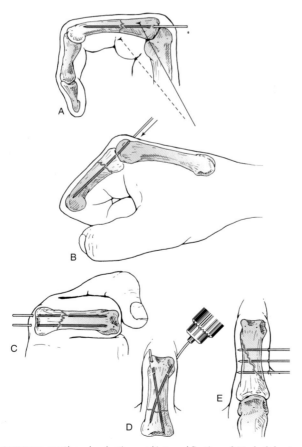

FIGURE 28-47 Closed reduction and internal fixation of P1 shaft fractures can be accomplished (**A**) longitudinally through the metacarpophalangeal joint but not the metacarpal head, (**B**) or through the metacarpal head, (**C**) with the wires for either of these options running parallel in the phalanx, or (**D**) entering at the collateral recess and crossing, or (**E**) passing transversely.

considerably more technically demanding than in the metacarpal for a number of reasons including the proximity of the extensor mechanism, the origins of the fibro-osseous flexor tendon sheath, and the size and consistency of the bone. More than just the technical complexity of ORIF is the problem of the postoperative response of the surrounding soft tissues to the surgical dissection and the presence of hardware.

Options for ORIF include intraosseous wiring, composite wiring, screw-only fixation, or screw and plate fixation [22,29,58,62,72,73,74,132,133,150] (Figs. 28-51 and 28-52). The familiarity of the surgeon with the specific technique is probably the most important factor in the selection of a method. Of 30 patients followed for 2.3 years after tension band wiring, 17 had a TAM of over 195 degrees and 13 had a TAM of between 130 and 195 degrees.[132] More recently, attention has increasingly turned to the use of screw and plate technology (Figs. 28-53 and 28-54). The relative bulkiness of plates at the phalangeal level compared with the metacarpals can result in the need for their removal even with initially excellent results. The results of internal fixation are intimately related to the associated injuries present. The gravest danger, however, occurs when the surgeon elects ORIF but is then unable to secure rigid fixation of the fracture. In this situation, the patient has been subjected to the "worst of both worlds," and a poor outcome can be reliably predicted.

Intra-articular Fractures

Two intra-articular patterns are seen distally at the phalangeal head, unicondylar (partial articular fracture), or bicondylar (complete articular fracture). The condylar fragments usually are extremely small, can be fragile, and receive their blood supply from the attached collateral ligament. Fixation of a single condyle is most rigid when accomplished with a compression screw placed transversely, entering near the collateral ligament origin (Fig. 28-55). This can be quite challenging technically, and the bone stock may only tolerate K-wire or composite wiring techniques (Fig. 28-56). When the unicondylar fragment has a solid extension to the shaft level cannulated microsized headless compression screws can be used.[58] Triplane fractures of the head of the proximal phalanx are

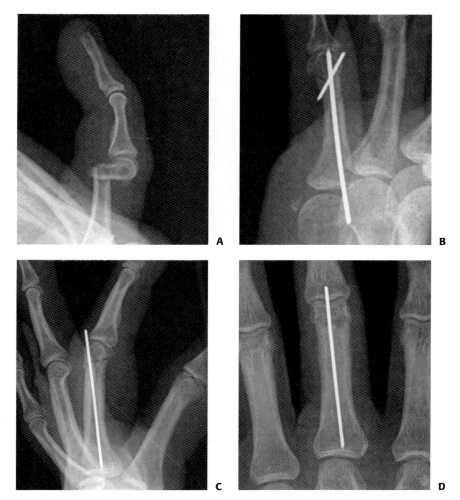

A

B

C

D

FIGURE 28-48 Fractures of the proximal phalangeal neck that are angulated apex volarly (**A**), can be stabilized by (**B**) antegrade pinning with a rotational control cross wire if the fracture is sufficiently proximal, but very distal fractures (**C,D**) usually require retrograde pinning.

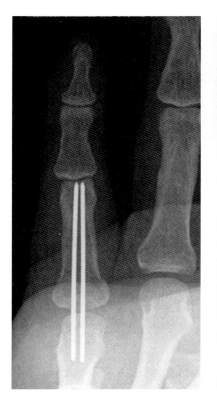

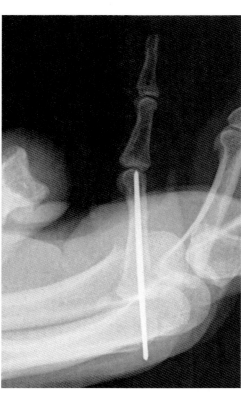

FIGURE 28-49 Transverse shaft fractures of the proximal phalanx are best stabilized by 0.045-inch K-wires passed longitudinally through the metacarpal head and removed at 3 weeks.

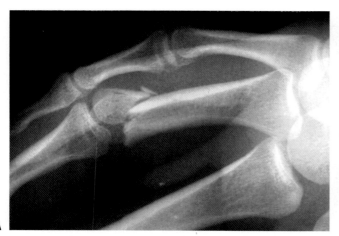
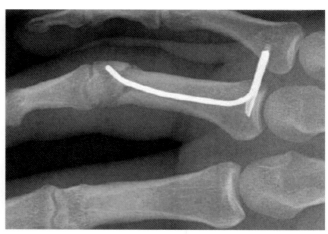

FIGURE 28-50 A. Proximal phalanx fractures can be stabilized by closed placement of a specially designed device that achieves (**B**) three-point fixation with a rotational locking sleeve proximally.

well managed with 1.2-mm lag screws (Fig. 28-57).[22] Complete articular fractures can be fixed with screws only if one of the two condyles has an extended spike. If not, minicondylar or locking plate fixation may be necessary to achieve excellent rigidity. Again, the bone stock may not tolerate the application of this device, and wiring techniques remain an alternative strategy.

The final group of articular fractures are those seen at the lateral corner of the phalangeal base, which are particularly amenable to the technique of tension band wiring (see Fig. 51C). An alternative is a volar approach to lateral base P1 fractures using a single lag screw for fixation to achieve full motion by 3 weeks.[137] Comminuted intra-articular fractures of the proximal phalangeal base can be stabilized by a small volar plate placed

through the A1 pulley approach.[72] A specific subset of proximal phalangeal base fractures that are purely impactions by nature may be treated by supporting the impacted fragments with packed cancellous bone only; in one series of 10 patients followed for 32 months, there was no secondary displacement and an average PIP joint flexion of 88 degrees was achieved.[150]

Rehabilitation

Nonoperative management should restrict splinting to 3 weeks followed by AROM that can include adjacent digit strapping if necessary. Similarly, CRIF should allow for pin removal at 3 weeks, with AROM beginning no later than this time. If ORIF is chosen, AROM should begin within 72 hours of surgery and edema control should be foremost in the treatment plan using cohesive elastic bandages.[53] AROM alone

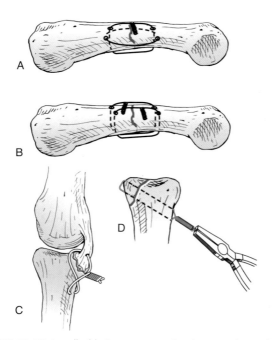

FIGURE 28-51 A malleable intraosseous wire alone can be applied in its strongest configuration of (**A**) two loops at 90 degrees to each other, (**B**) two parallel loops, (**C**) a figure-of-eight tension band, and (**D**) a single loop to compress a smaller fragment against the larger fragment.

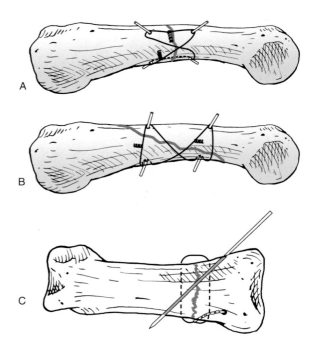

FIGURE 28-52 Composite wiring techniques may involve any configuration or combination of nonflexible fixation with a malleable wire that is twisted to achieve compression across the fracture site.

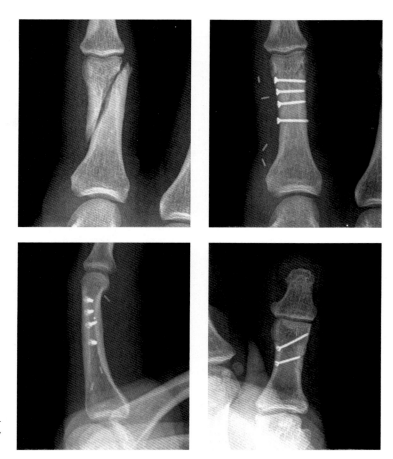

FIGURE 28-53 In long oblique fractures of the shaft with shortening, an exact reduction and stability sufficient to withstand early motion can be achieved through lag screw fixation only.

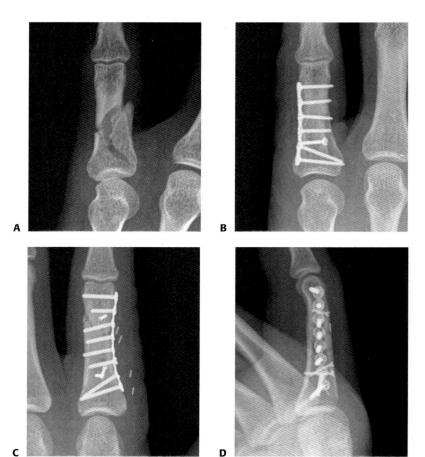

FIGURE 28-54 More complex fractures of the shaft (**A**) can be well stabilized by (**B**) lateral plating. Specific care should be taken to (**C**) contour the plate meticulously to fit the cortex and to place the hardware in (**D**) the true midlateral position.

743

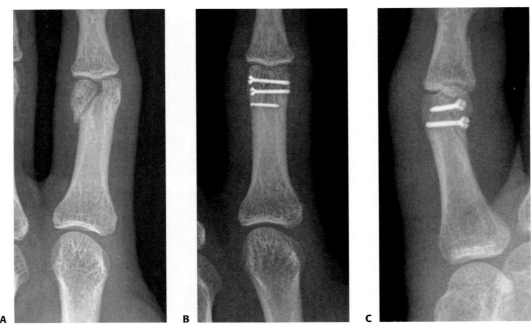

A   **B**   **C**

FIGURE 28-55 A. Unicondylar fractures of the head of the proximal phalanx benefit from compression between the articular fragments through (**B,C**) lag screw fixation.

may be insufficient to counteract extensor lag at the joint distal to the site of fixation. Rapidly accelerating the extensor tendon concentrically without resistance best limits local adhesion formation[77] (Fig. 28-58). These exercises can be supplemented with the use of electrical muscle stimulation during outpatient therapy sessions. Night splinting with the PIP joint in extension can be helpful but will not in and of itself overcome an extensor lag.

 AUTHORS' PREFERRED METHOD OF TREATMENT

Proximal Phalanx Fractures

Closed Reduction Internal Fixation

CRIF is my preferred treatment for all isolated, closed transverse and short oblique fractures of the proximal phalanx (Fig.

28-59). Longitudinal pinning with two K-wires passing through the metacarpal head with the MP joint flexed 80 to 90 degrees has yielded reliable results.[74] In larger patients, two 0.045-inch K-wires can both be fit through the medullary canal. In smaller patients, one 0.045-inch and one 0.035-inch wire may be more compatible. When rotational interlock is felt between the fragments, one wire can be used. The wires are placed one each on either side of the thick central extensor tendon dorsal to the MP joint, thus passing through the sagittal band fibers. The wires are then passed through the base fragment, across the fracture site, and down the distal shaft of the phalanx to the head. Care must be taken to not power drill the wires through the subchondral bone of the phalangeal head, creating a pin tract into the PIP joint. If such a passage exists, the wire may migrate distally into the PIP joint during early rehabilitation and cause hyaline cartilage damage to the

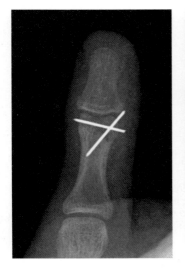 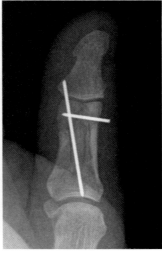

FIGURE 28-56 When a unicondylar fracture of the head of the proximal phalanx has a proximal shaft extension on the smaller fragment, K-wire fixation in a diverging pattern can prevent migration of the fragment that would otherwise occur with a single smooth K-wire as the only fixation.

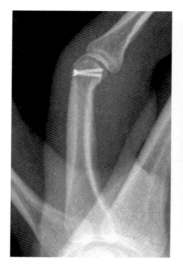
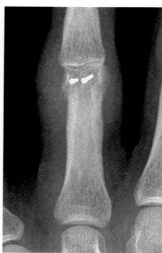

FIGURE 28-57 Triplane fractures of the proximal phalangeal head can be well stabilized by two small lag screws (1.2-mm to 1.5-mm).

base of the middle phalanx. Instead, the wire should be drilled up to but not into the subchondral bone. After cutting the wires dorsally, they may be manually impacted a few millimeters further into the subchondral bone, conferring an added degree of stability.

Closed pinning is also a valuable technique for nondisplaced fractures at the head of P1. Both a transverse pin

connecting the two condyles and an oblique pin from the condyle to the opposite diaphyseal cortex should be used for a unicondylar fracture. For bicondylar fractures, two oblique pins are needed. The oblique pins are best cut for retrieval proximally rather than distally as their passage through the periarticular soft tissues will interfere with PIP joint motion. Closed pinning also represents a reasonable treatment option

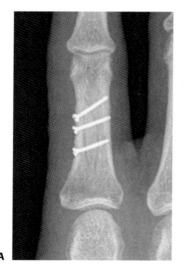

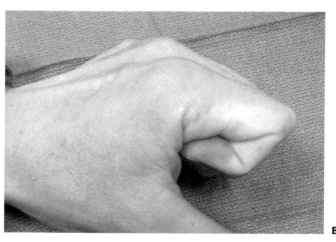

FIGURE 28-58 Following (**A**) lag screw fixation of a shaft fracture in the proximal phalanx, (**B**) complete proximal interphalangeal joint flexion and (**C**) proximal interphalangeal joint hyperextension are achievable with an aggressive special therapy program of resisted zone IV extensor tendon preload followed by sudden release with follow-through.

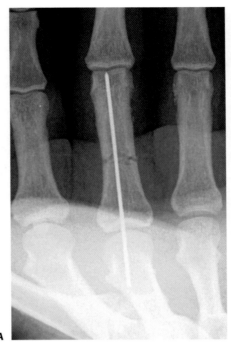
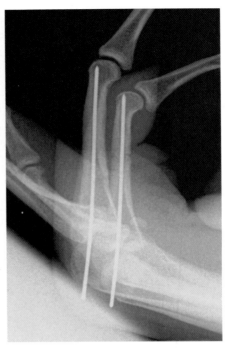

A   B

FIGURE 28-59 A. Transverse proximal phalanx fractures without comminution should achieve sufficient inter-fragmentary stability to have axial rotational control with a single wire alone that targets the (**A**) intercondylar notch and extending (**B**) all the way to the subchondral bone.

for nondisplaced long oblique or spiral fractures that are suspected of subsequent displacement when subjected to the stress of motion rehabilitation. However, practically I have not found this fracture pattern to exist. I see either truly nondisplaced fractures that I expect to remain stable, and I treat them nonoperatively, or displaced long oblique and spiral fractures that I prefer to treat with open reduction.

Open Reduction and Internal Fixation with Lag Screws

This is my preferred treatment for long oblique and spiral fractures of the shaft and displaced partial articular fractures (Fig. 28-60). I have found it difficult through closed means alone to correct all the shortening and rotation of long oblique and spiral fractures. There is a natural tradeoff between the undeniable added surgical trauma of an open approach and the benefits of an anatomically precise reduction. When lag screws alone are used for fixation, full motion rehabilitation can begin immediately.[73, 77] This is not the case with K-wires that tether soft tissues, limiting motion and risking pin tract infection. Performing the open fixation gently and precisely to minimize soft tissue trauma is more easily described than executed. The first principle is to carefully evaluate fracture geometry. In a simple two-fragment diaphyseal fracture, there will be inherent stability between the bone edges once the fracture has been reduced. The role of internal fixation is then to exploit this inherent stability by further compressing the fracture line. Fixation involving the use of lag screws achieves the maximum compression possible. One must always heed the ground rules for screw-only fixation: fracture length is at least two times the bone diameter, and fragment width is at least three times the screw

diameter. For all of the above techniques, adherence to strict principles is mandatory; multiple drill bit passes are not well tolerated by the phalanx. Screws of 1.2- to 1.5-mm diameters are appropriate for P1. Biomechanically, it is desirable to have at least one screw placed perpendicular to the neutral axis of the bone. The remaining screws should be perpendicular to the fracture plane. In a spiral fracture, one screw can satisfy both of these requirements simultaneously and is termed the "ideal" screw. In an oblique fracture, this will not be the case.

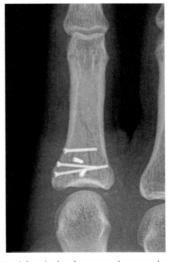

FIGURE 28-60 Partial articular fractures that can be rendered stable by interfragmentary compression are excellent candidates for lag screw fixation.

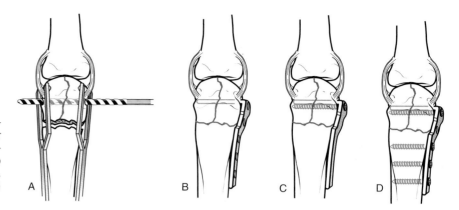

FIGURE 28-61 After reduction of the condylar fragments to each other and the shaft, (**A**) the hole for the condylar blade is drilled and its depth is measured. **B.** The blade is cut to size and inserted to evaluate the accuracy of the plate contouring. **C.** The condylar screw is inserted, along with (**D**) the shaft screws.

Plates at the Phalangeal Level

Plates at the phalangeal level are not desirable because of their bulk and propensity for tendon adherence, and I avoid using them whenever possible. This is my treatment of choice for fractures with comminution and bone loss and complete articular fractures of the phalangeal head that are unstable (Fig. 28-61). Since the biomechanics of P1 fractures create an apex palmar sagittal plane deformity, the plate would (impossibly so) have to be applied to the volar surface of the bone to have its optimum tension band effect. Lateral placement is then the next most desirable option, and this corresponds well to the surgical access that is least harmful to the soft tissues.[73] A midaxial incision is carried volar to the margin of the extensor mechanism, straight through periosteum and the entire soft tissue sleeve is elevated as a single unit, avoiding any dissection of planes surrounding the extensor tendon.[73] When plates are used, one should attempt to place screws as perpendicular to the surface of the plate as possible (Fig. 28-62). The heads of obliquely placed screws have a prominent edge.

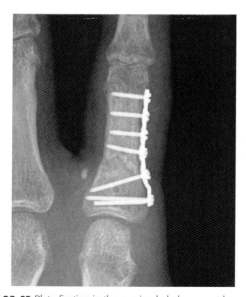

FIGURE 28-62 Plate fixation in the proximal phalanx must be contoured meticulously to restore the normal anatomic shape of the bone. The condylar blade plate can also be used at the metaphyseal base of a proximal phalanx. An oblique screw is often advantageous to achieve an extra point of compression in the metaphyseal fragment.

Plates should also be painstakingly contoured to ensure both the lowest profile as well as proper biomechanical function (preload, dynamic compression, and a buttress effect). If more than 50% of the cross-sectional area of the bone is comminuted or lost, bone graft will be required.

Pearls and Pitfalls

The pearls of CRIF are captured in the author's preferred treatment section. The details of the difficult open fixation procedures at the proximal phalanx level will be covered here. I prefer to operate on closed fractures around postinjury day 3 to 5 when even adult periosteum will thicken dramatically in response to injury and can be surgically manipulated as a tissue flap. Posttraumatic swelling will have begun to subside by this time. A true midaxial incision is in the neutral tension lines of the skin and brings the approach down to the volar leading edge of the intrinsic wing tendon. One of the most important principles in open fixation of a P1 fracture is to not create planes of surgical dissection either superficial or deep to the zone IV extensor tendon (Fig. 28-63). The only dissection that should occur at the subcutaneous level is to identify dorsal cutaneous nerve branches passing obliquely from the proper digital nerves and to mobilize them effectively to avoid neuromas. Other than this, the approach should create a single tissue flap from skin through periosteum to bone.[73] A sharp blade is needed to carefully preserve the periosteum for later repair using fine monofilament resorbable sutures. This creates an additional gliding layer of protection for the extensor mechanism. A fine-tipped curette must be used to clear the fracture interface of all clot and soft tissue or a truly anatomic interdigitated reduction will not be possible. Although provisional fixation of the fracture with K-wires has been recommended by others, I have found that the absoluteness of a perfect reduction is not well maintained by smooth wires, which invariably allow the reduction to slip a little bit. This ensures that the drill path will not be exactly in the desired location and that final placement of the screw or plate will thus be imperfect. I prefer to hold the reduction manually with either a bone clamp specialized for the short tubular bones of the hand or with Brown-Adson forceps. Caution must be used to drill at lower speeds as high speeds can introduce an eccentric "whip" to the tip of these small drill bits, resulting in a larger drill path than desired. I strongly prefer a "pencil grip" microdrill over a "pistol grip" driver for the sake of accuracy in drilling a straight path.

The steps for screw-only fixation after reduction and provisional stabilization are core drilling followed by countersinking the near bone surface (Fig. 28-64). Countersinking not only recesses the

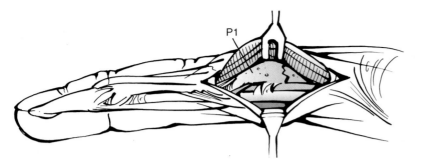

FIGURE 28-63 The lateral approach to the proximal phalanx should not create layers of dissection around the extensor tendon but rather pass volar to the leading edge of the intrinsic wing tendon and through periosteum to bone, leaving skin, extensor tendon, and periosteum as a single tissue flap for retraction.

screw head but also distributes the force of compression, lessening the chance of propagating a new fracture line. Measuring for screw length is done next, and the time for the scrub technician to procure the correct screw can be used to drill the gliding hole. Self-tapping screws are a little difficult to start into bone as some axial load is necessary to get them to bite, but application of this load off the true axis will toggle the screw. A fine touch must be learned over the course of many cases using these implants. Screws are tightened with a "chuck" pinch on the screwdriver using three fingers, not with the more forceful key pinch that may shear the head off the shaft of the screw. All plates must be meti-

culously and often painstakingly contoured before application (Fig. 28-65). One must not hesitate to remove a plate and recontour it after the first two screws have been placed if it is clear that the shape is not correct. Application of an incorrectly contoured plate guarantees an imperfect fracture reduction. A common error is with plates ending near the metaphyseal flare that must have a small bend at the last hole to accommodate the curvature of the bone at this level. Since the last edition of this text, locking plate technology has found its way down to the size range for the small bones of the hand. This is a huge advantage over the sole previously available implant that offered fixed angle stability, the mini-

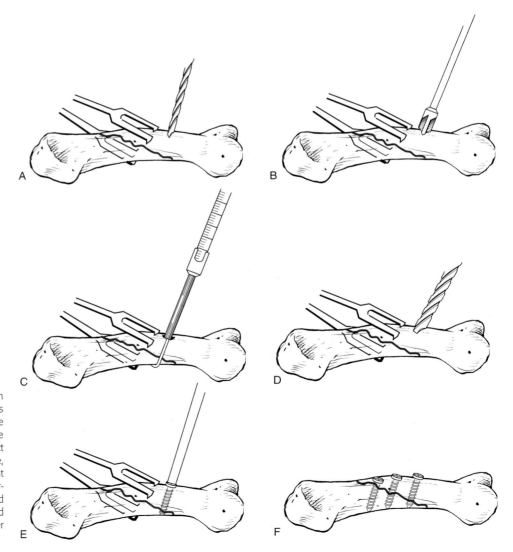

FIGURE 28-64 After stabilized reduction of a shaft fracture, lag screw fixation is accomplished by (**A**) drilling with the smaller core bit, (**B**) countersinking the near cortex, (**C**) measuring the correct length, (**D**) drilling the gliding hole, (**E**) tightening the lag screw with light three finger tip pressure, and (**F**) ensuring all distances between screws and fracture edges are sufficient to avoid propagation of new fracture lines under the pressure of screw tightening.

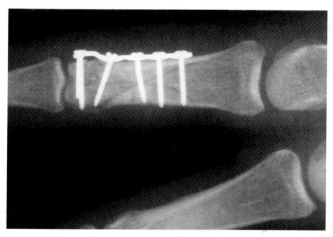
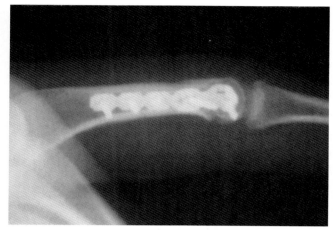

A

B

FIGURE 28-65 Comminuted fractures involving the head and shaft of the proximal phalanx (**A**) can be stabilized for early motion with a condylar blade plate (**B**) placed laterally in the midaxial plane.

condylar plate. The minicondylar plate could not be fully contoured to the bone surface before placing the blade; a locking plate can.

METACARPOPHALANGEAL JOINT DISLOCATIONS

Dorsal MP joint dislocations are the most common. Simple dislocations are reducible and present with a hyperextension posture. They are really subluxations, as some contact remains between the base of P1 and the metacarpal head (Fig. 28-66). The volar plate stays volar or distal to the metacarpal head. Reduction should be achieved with simple flexion of the joint; excessive longitudinal traction on the finger should be avoided. Wrist flexion to relax the flexor tendons may assist reduction. The other variety of MP joint dislocation is a complex dislocation,

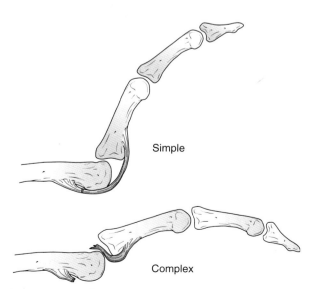

Simple

Complex

FIGURE 28-66 Simple metacarpophalangeal joint dislocations are spontaneously reducible and usually present in an extended posture with the articular surface of the proximal phalanx sitting on the dorsum of the metacarpal head. Complex dislocations have bayonet apposition with volar plate interposition that prevents reduction.

which is by definition irreducible, most often because of volar plate interposition (Figs. 28-66B and 28-67). Complex dislocations occur most frequently in the index finger. Longitudinal traction can convert a simple into a complex dislocation. A pathognomonic radiographic sign of complex dislocation is the appearance of a sesamoid in the joint space. Concomitant injuries include small chip fractures on the dorsum of the metacarpal head that have been sheared off in complex dislocations by the volar base of P1.[67,79] Other difficult fractures to detect are bony collateral ligament avulsions.

Most dorsal dislocations will be stable following reduction and do not need surgical repair of the ligaments or volar plate. Volar dislocations are rare but particularly unstable. Volar dislocations risk late instability and should have repair of the ligaments.[113] Obstructions to reducing volar dislocations include the volar plate, collateral ligament, and dorsal capsule. Open dislocations may be either reducible or irreducible. Small fracture fragments at the collateral insertions (base of P1 or metacarpal head) need special consideration as such injuries share the features of ligament instability and the consequences of an intra-articular fracture.[135,137,138] Isolated collateral ligament injuries are more common on the radial aspect of the small finger followed by the index finger. A differential diagnosis to consider with posttraumatic swelling at the MP joint level is rupture of the sagittal bands (confirmed by visible or palpable ulnar subluxation of the zone 5 extensor tendon), which requires protection in extension for 4 weeks. A rare variant injury to the MP joint is a dorsal capsular tear (Boxer's knuckle) that can prove persistently symptomatic. In a series of 16 patients that included extensor tendon dislocation in 7, surgical closure of the rent found in the dorsal capsule or extensor hood was reported to be successful in all cases.[6]

Thumb Metacarpophalangeal Joint Ligament Injuries

Complete rupture of the ulnar collateral ligament (UCL) of the thumb MP joint is a common injury that less frequently may accompany a full MP joint dislocation (Fig. 28-68). Circumferential palpation of the MP joint can often localize pain to the UCL, radial collateral ligament (RCL), volar plate, or combinations of these. Following joint injection with local anesthetic,

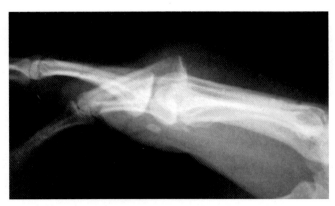

FIGURE 28-67 The typical complex dorsal dislocation of the metacarpophalangeal joint presents with complete overriding of the phalanx on the metacarpal.

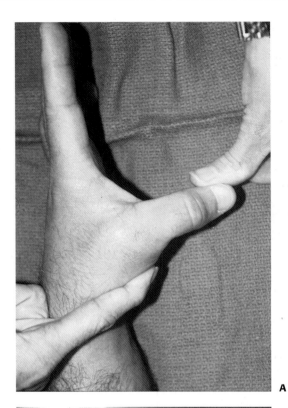

stress testing in full extension and 30 degrees of flexion (eliminates the false-negative conclusion of stability in the setting of a ruptured proper collateral ligament but an intact volar plate) should reveal any instability (Fig. 28-69A). If clinical uncertainty remains, stress radiography may also be performed (Fig. 28-69B). Finding a consistent role for MRI in the diagnosis of the Stener lesion (a distally ruptured ulnar collateral ligament blocked from healing by the interposed adductor aponeurosis) has yet to occur.[78] In a series of 24 patients, a palpable tender mass on the ulnar side of the MP joint was used as the sole diagnostic criterion for the Stener lesion. Operative treatment was performed for those thought to have the lesion and nonoperative management for those who did not, resulting in only a single case of long-term instability.[1]

The term *gamekeeper's thumb*, which more appropriately applies to chronic attrition injuries, has largely been supplanted by *skier's thumb* owing to the prominent role played by this

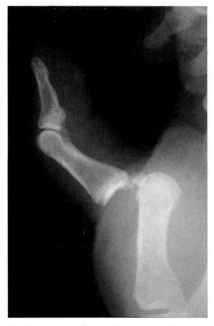

FIGURE 28-68 Metacarpophalangeal joint dislocation in the thumb, like the fingers, is typically dorsal.

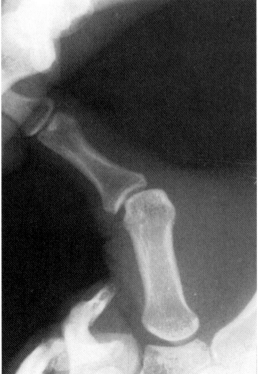

FIGURE 28-69 A. Clinical stress testing of the ulnar collateral ligament in 30 degrees of flexion prevents reaching a false-negative conclusion when an intact volar plate obscures the instability of a complete proper ulnar collateral ligament rupture. **B.** Radiographic stress testing is also useful when there is clinical uncertainty.

sport in the etiology of acute UCL injuries. The interaction between the thumb and first web space with ski pole grips has been blamed for the association of UCL ruptures in this sport. Not all fracture fragments seen on the ulnar aspect of the MP joint represent the anatomic insertion of the UCL. Some of these fragments may be attached to the volar plate insertion, separate from the collateral ligament. The differential diagnosis of sesamoid fracture must also be considered when volar tenderness is present. Oblique radiographs may be helpful in this respect when considering the frequent incomplete ossification of the sesamoids. Special mention should be made of irreducible dislocations. Irreducible volar dislocations have been reported with the radial condyle of the metacarpal trapped in a rent dorsal to the accessory collateral–volar plate complex.[79] Other causes of volar trapping may involve the extensor pollicis longus and brevis. The flexor pollicis longus may block reduction of a dorsal dislocation.[83]

Surgical and Applied Anatomy

The anatomy of the MP joint is like the same three-sided box previously presented for the PIP joint, composed of the proper collateral ligaments, the accessory collateral ligaments, and the volar plate (Fig. 28-70). The radial and ulnar proper collateral ligaments are the primary stabilizers to motion in all planes, including distraction, dorsopalmar translation, abduction-adduction, and supination-pronation. The accessory collateral ligaments supplement adduction-abduction stability. The volar plates are connected to each other by the deep transverse intermetacarpal ligament. The MP collateral ligaments have an origin dorsal to the center axis of joint rotation. This feature combines with two others (a greater width of the metacarpal head volarly and a greater distance from the center of rotation to the volar articular surface than the distal articular surface) to maximize tension in the true collateral portion of the ligament when the joint is in full flexion. Consequently, stress testing to determine the presence of instability must be performed in full flexion.

Access for open reduction of complex dislocations is a topic of great controversy. Central MP joints can be approached either dorsally or volarly. Although the volar plate is the most commonly noted structure in the prevention of reduction, the flexor tendons, lumbricals, deep transverse intermetacarpal ligaments, juncturae tendinae, and dorsal capsule have all been implicated.[122] In a series of 10 operatively treated ligament ruptures, most were distal with the ligament occasionally trapped between the intrinsic tendon and the sagittal band, including two associated dorsal interosseous ruptures at the phalangeal insertion.[31]

Thumb Metacarpophalangeal Joint

The thumb MP joint, in addition to its primary plane of flexion and extension, allows abduction-adduction and a slight amount of rotation (pronation with flexion). The range of flexion and extension has a wide natural variation that may be related to the flatness of the metacarpal head and may also play a role in predisposition to injury for those with less motion. With a one-sided collateral ligament injury, the phalanx tends to subluxate volarly in a rotatory fashion, pivoting around the opposite intact collateral ligament. The ulnar collateral ligament may have a two-level injury consisting of a fracture of the ulnar base of P1 with the ligament also rupturing off the fracture fragment.[59] Of particular importance is the proximal edge of the adductor aponeurosis that forms the anatomic basis of the Stener lesion. The torn UCL stump comes to lie dorsal to the aponeurosis and is thus prevented from healing to its anatomic insertion on the volar, ulnar base of the proximal phalanx (Fig. 28-71). The true incidence of the Stener lesion remains unknown because of widely disparate reports. The abductor pollicis brevis also sends fibers to the extensor mechanism, but a discrete edge capable of preventing healing of the radial collateral ligament does not

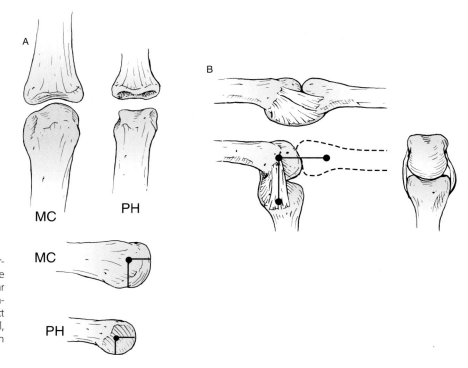

FIGURE 28-70 A. The anatomy of the metacarpophalangeal (MP) joint differs from that of the proximal interphalangeal joint in the unicondylar head of the metacarpal (MC) versus the bicondylar head of the phalanx (PH), the cam effect in the sagittal plane unique to the metacarpal, and (**B**) the collateral origin offset dorsally from the center of rotation in the metacarpal.

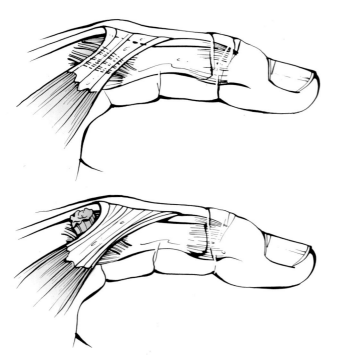

FIGURE 28-71 The Stener lesion. The proximal edge of the adductor aponeurosis functions as a shelf that blocks the distal phalangeal insertion of the ruptured ulnar collateral ligament of the thumb metacarpophalangeal joint from returning to its natural location for healing after it comes to lie on top of the aponeurosis.

exist; therefore, there is no correlate to a Stener lesion on this side of the joint. Radial collateral ligaments injuries have been found to occur at the phalangeal insertion in 13 of 38 cases and at the metacarpal origin in 25 of 38.[26]

Current Treatment Options

Nonoperative Management —Fingers

For reducible dorsal dislocations and collateral ligament injuries, nonoperative management is the treatment of choice (Table 28-8). Collateral ligament injuries should be immobilized in incomplete flexion (50 degrees) for 3 weeks followed by AROM while the digit is strapped to an adjacent digit to resist lateral de-

viation stress. Even with fracture fragments constituting up to 25% of the width of the phalangeal base, early active mobilization using side strap protection led to normal motion and grip strength in 6 of 7 patients with a mean DASH score of 3.1.[135] Dorsal dislocations will normally prove stable during early AROM. Only in an exceptional case would the use of extension block splinting of 20 degrees or so for 2 to 3 weeks be required. In a high-demand patient the radial collateral ligament of the index MP joint should be considered for operative repair.

Nonoperative Management—Thumb

Nonoperative management is the mainstay of treatment for thumb MP joint injuries. Only the complete UCL injury with a Stener lesion and volar dislocations require more aggressive treatment. The standard treatment consists of 4 weeks of static MP joint immobilization with the IP joint left free. Management in the presence of a fracture at the ulnar base of P1 is more controversial. Nine patients with less than 2-mm displacement of such a fragment treated nonoperatively all had chronic pain with pinch strength rated at 36% of normal. Following operative treatment, pinch improved to 89% of normal with symptom resolution.[35] Conversely, 28 patients with ulnar base fractures but with a joint clinically assessed as stable to stress testing were managed nonoperatively resulting in equivalent grip and pinch strengths to the contralateral side and 93% were pain free despite a 60% rate of fibrous union.[142] Radial collateral ligament disruptions and pure dorsal dislocations can be successfully managed by a 4-week period of MP joint immobilization. Sesamoid fractures also are managed primarily by 3 to 4 weeks of immobilization in partial flexion.

Open Reduction—Fingers

Volar dislocations, complex dorsal dislocations, and collateral ligament disruptions associated with large bone fragments should be treated with open reduction and repair (Fig. 28-72). Radial collateral ligament injuries repaired late risk a higher incidence of pinch weakness and should be attended to promptly. Open repair or reconstruction with a free tendon graft may also be required in chronic cases with persistent symptoms following initial nonoperative management. Of 33 patients with MP collateral ligament avulsion fractures from the base of the proximal phalanx, the eight who were treated nonoperatively

TABLE 28-8	**Metacarpophalangeal Joint Dislocations**	
Treatment Option	Pros	Cons
Splinting	No added surgical stiffness	Does not guarantee anatomic ligament healing at critical locations
Open ligament repair	Restores stability in cases treated early Important for Stener lesion and possibly for torn radial collateral of the index finger	Added surgical stiffness
Open ligament reconstruction	Restores stability in cases treated late when functional instability is a clinical problem	Surgical stiffness may be greater following reconstruction compared with repair in some cases

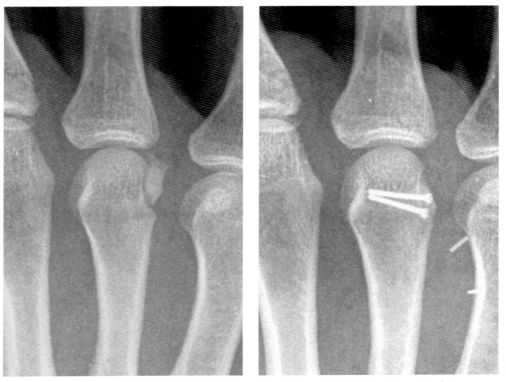

FIGURE 28-72 Collateral ligament injuries that (**A**) avulse a large bone fragment at the metacarpal head can be stabilized by direct bone fixation (**B**).

initially all went on to symptomatic nonunion requiring subsequent surgery.[137] In a similar series of 19 patients with the avulsion occurring at the metacarpal head, successful results occurred in the 11 displaced fragments internally fixed through a dorsal approach but 3 of 7 initially nondisplaced fragments went on to symptomatic nonunion requiring surgery.[138] Volar MP dislocations should have repair of the collateral ligaments and volar plate to prevent late instability. Either a dorsal or a volar approach is acceptable, and the one that provides access to the major pathology should be chosen based on the individual patient's preoperative findings. Dorsally, a midline longitudinal incision provides good access to manage any associated osteochondral fractures. One may have to split the volar plate longitudinally and draw it around the sides of the metacarpal head to accomplish a reduction. The volar approach avoids splitting the volar plate but risks injury to digital nerves which are tented over the deformity and lying directly under the dermis. Volarly, the volar plate can be pulled back out of the joint and reduced without splitting it.

The duration of immobilization should be in direct proportion to the surgeon's assessment of instability following reduction. While most patients may begin AROM immediately, those injuries that demonstrate an extra degree of instability during the postreduction assessment should be immobilized in partial flexion for 3 weeks. Whether simple or complex, the dislocations should be immobilized in only partial (50-degree) flexion to allow ligament healing under appropriate tension. After 3 weeks, AROM is progressed until 6 weeks, when full passive motion including hyperextension is allowed.

Open Reduction—Thumb

Surgical management of thumb MP joint injuries is largely limited to UCL disruptions with a Stener lesion and volar or irredu-cible MP dislocations.[83] The results of acute repair of the *radial* collateral ligament equal those of chronic reconstructions. This makes a very weak case for early operative repair considering that no Stener lesion exists on the radial side of the joint. Determining the presence of a Stener lesion on the ulnar side of the joint remains an inexact science; therefore, open management can be argued to be the treatment of choice for all widely unstable ulnar-sided disruptions. Pure ligamentous midsubstance ruptures can be repaired by direct suture. The usual site of disruption is distally at the phalangeal insertion where bone anchors can be used for ligament reinsertion. Thirty-six patients with suture anchor repairs healed with loss of 10 degrees of MP joint motion and 15 degrees of IP joint motion.[170] Overtensioning should be avoided as insertion sites malpositioned volarly or distally on the proximal phalanx will cause loss of motion.[9] Arthroscopic reduction of the Stener lesion has been reported in eight patients.[130] With bony avulsion fragments, tension band wiring, intraosseous wiring, or fragment excision with ligament anchorage may all be used at the surgeon's discretion.

Ligament Reconstruction

Cases presenting late with residual instability (after degeneration of the tendon substance has occurred) may require reconstructive methods.[47] Twenty-six patients with tendon reconstruction for the thumb UCL followed for 4.5 years had 85% normal ROM and key pinch strength equal to the opposite side at 20 pounds.[60] High-grade radial collateral ligament tears that are widely unstable may benefit from direct soft tissue advancement and repair with 38 patients at 10-month follow-up achieving 92% of normal pinch and 87% were symptom free.[26]

Associated Osteochondral Injuries to the Metacarpal Head or a Base of P1 Fracture

Careful inspection of the dorsal aspect of the metacarpal head should identify any chondral or osteochondral fractures. There are three strategies to manage these fractures. If the fragment is small and extremely unstable, it should be excised. If the fragment has a large subchondral bone base, it can be fixed with a countersunk screw. If fixation is not possible but the fragment can be stably trapped in its bed by the congruent opposing joint surface, it can be further restrained with fine resorbable sutures. For collateral ligament injuries associated with bone fragments, there are two options. If the bone fragment is both large and solid enough to receive definitive fixation, ORIF may be performed with a tension band wire or lag screw. Twenty-five patients with base of P1 ligament avulsion injuries were reported to have recovered full motion by 3 weeks following volar approach single lag screw fixation.[137] If the bone fragment is too small or too comminuted, the bone can be excised and the end of the ligament reinserted to the cancellous bed of either the metacarpal head or the base of the proximal phalanx. This can be accomplished with a mini-bone anchor (many models are currently available) or by transosseous suture. Surgery may not always be necessary to achieve grip and key pinch strength in avulsion fractures of the lateral base of P1. For example, 27 of 30 nonoperatively treated patients achieved clinical stability despite a 25% incidence of radiographic nonunion, but with only 19 of 30 reporting no pain.[95]

AUTHORS' PREFERRED METHOD OF TREATMENT

Metacarpophalangeal Joint Dislocations

Careful review of the published literature regarding both finger and thumb MP joint ligament injuries indicates that the clinical assessment of instability is paramount in planning subsequent treatment. Local anesthetic injection into the MP joint allows vigorous stress testing of the ligament to be performed without fighting the patient or causing undue pain. Testing in both extension and flexion reveals the absolute value of deviation as well as the discrepancy compared with the uninjured side. The feel at the end point is also a significant piece of information. A greater than 15-degree difference side to side and a soft end point are stronger indicators of complete ligament disruption than the absolute value of the joint angle when stressed. The integrity of the volar plate should be assessed along with the appearance of rotatory subluxation. I use a combination of the clinical degree of instability and the presence of a palpable Stener lesion to choose direct repair of the thumb UCL, the index RCL, and large bony avulsion injuries. Thumb radial collateral ligament and other finger MP joint injuries are managed nonoperatively. Volar dislocations risk late instability if not surgically repaired. When the patient presents late following a complete ligament rupture, direct repair is rarely possible. The simplest reconstruction is then to create a proximally based flap of retracted ligament and advance it back to the anatomic insertion at the volar base of the proximal phalanx. This tissue is not always of sufficient quality. When that is the case, a free tendon graft (plantaris or palmaris longus) can be placed through drill holes to reconstruct the ligament. With appropriate rehabilitation, these patients can still achieve near normal motion.

Open Reduction of Finger Metacarpophalangeal Dislocations

The border digits, the index and small fingers, can easily be approached with a midaxial incision that offers all the advantages that are proposed for both volar and dorsal approaches. Cartilage injuries on the metacarpal head can be well visualized, the digital nerves are easily protected, and the volar plate can be guided back into its correct position. For the long and ring fingers, I prefer a transverse incision made at the level of the distal portion of the metacarpal head. This level can reliably be found at the dorsal apex of the sloping V shape of the web commissure. The sagittal bands do not need to be divided but rather they can be retracted distally to access the joint. The volar plate can be reduced without dividing it through a combination of wrist flexion to relax the extrinsic flexor tendons and MP hyperextension. A Freer elevator then guides the volar plate to the distal surface of the metacarpal head before attempting to reduce the joint itself. For the radial collateral ligament of the index, an absorbable 1.3-mm bone anchor can be used for repair of insertional ruptures and a 4-0 absorbable monofilament suture for midsubstance ruptures. Pinning of the joint is not necessary in fingers as adjacent digit strapping provides enough restraint to excessive coronal plane deviation to protect the healing repair. The exception to this is the rare high energy volar dislocation that is so unstable as to require 3 weeks of transarticular pin fixation.

Thumb Metacarpophalangeal Collateral Ligament Repair

The operative technique consists of a chevron incision over the ulnar aspect of the MP joint ensuring adequate volar exposure at the base of the proximal phalanx. Care must be taken with the superficial branches of the radial nerve to avoid neuroma formation. There is usually one large branch passing through the surgical field that is best mobilized dorsally. An incision in the adductor aponeurosis is made just ulnar to the extensor pollicis longus tendon with a cuff being left for repair. Reflection of this layer reveals the joint capsule and torn collateral ligament (Fig. 28-73). While all patterns of disruption have been reported, the most frequent is that of distal avulsion from the base of the proximal phalanx. Often there is a transverse rent in the dorsal capsule and

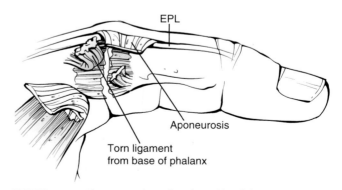

FIGURE 28-73 The approach to the ulnar side of the MP joint must protect dorsal digital nerve branches, leave a cuff for aponeurosis repair to the extensor pollicis longus (EPL), and provide adequate exposure to reach the true volar location of the tubercle at the base of the phalanx that represents the anatomic point of proper collateral ligament insertion or the "critical corner."

evidence of volar plate injury as well. Direct repair is easiest with an absorbable 1.3-mm bone anchor placed at the true insertion site on the volar lateral tubercle to restore normal anatomy and reduce the rotatory subluxation of the joint. The repair may include a suture through the volar plate margin to recreate the "critical corner." The joint is pinned with a 0.045-inch K-wire before tying the anchor sutures to prevent inadvertent radial deviation and early rupture of the repair during the first 4 weeks postoperatively. A large bone fragment carrying the point of ligament insertion can be stabilized with one or two lag screws (Fig. 28-74). The IP joint should be left free for motion at all times. Motion at the MP joint can begin in a protected fashion at 4 weeks following pin removal and then in an unprotected fashion by 6 weeks. Power pinch activities that stress the ligament in the coronal plane of the thumb should be avoided for up to 3 months after repair.

Free Tendon Graft Reconstruction of the Thumb UCL

The approach to the ulnar base of the thumb is the same as for simple repair. The correct anatomic sites of ligament origin at the metacarpal head and insertion at the phalangeal base should be easily discernable, having remnants of the original ligament fibers. Drill tunnels are made from each of these points obliquely directed away from the joint with a 2.5-mm bit. Free tendon graft may be harvested by conventional methods from either the palmaris longus (within the operative field) or the plantaris (a more appropriate size match). The tendon is passed through each of the drill holes and out the opposite cortex where it may be grasped for tensioning of the reconstruction (Fig. 28-75). The joint is pinned with a 0.045-inch K-wire before setting the final tension. The graft tension may be secured in any number of ways, but a simple method involves the use of two absorbable 1.3-mm bone anchors. One anchor is drilled adjacent to each bone tunnel, further away from the joint. The tendon graft is captured by the sutures from the anchor at the margin of the bone tunnel, thus fixing the tension in the graft between these two points.

Pearls and Pitfalls

Hypersensitivity and small cutaneous neuroma formation are often considered the banes of hand surgery. Although never to-

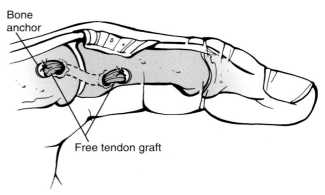

FIGURE 28-75 Free tendon graft reconstruction of the thumb metacarpophalangeal ulnar collateral ligament uses the same surgical approach as for direct ligament repair. Drill holes are made obliquely through the metacarpal and the phalanx from the points of anatomic ligament attachment so that a free tendon graft can be passed and tensioned. The graft may be secured by bone anchors adjacent to the bone tunnels.

tally avoidable, these unwanted complications can be minimized by a thorough knowledge of the branching patterns of the cutaneous nerves and meticulous attention to detail at the time of surgery. The dorsal digital nerve along the ulnar side the thumb MP joint is at high risk of injury. It should be mobilized dorsally for the procedure and checked each time before drilling. Perhaps the greatest risk is during closure of the adductor aponeurosis along the margin of the extensor pollicis longus tendon. It is quite easy to simply capture the nerve branch with one of these sutures if it is not visualized to be clear with each suture pass.

First web space contracture can easily occur following immobilization of any hand injury and especially when the injury is located in the first web space. Since the first web is located at the level of the MP joint, all positioning forces designed to prevent contracture act on the proximal phalanx and across the MP joint. The value of pinning the thumb MP joint with a 0.045-inch K-wire during the 4-week period of immobilization in a thumb spica splint is that the splint may be appropriately molded to abduct the thumb and avoid web space contracture.

METACARPAL FRACTURES

Fracture patterns may be broken down into those of the metacarpal head, neck, and shaft. Intra-articular fractures of the metacarpal base are covered in the next section on CMC joint fracture-dislocations. Metacarpal head fractures present in a variety of patterns requiring different treatment strategies aimed at restoring a smooth congruent joint surface. Transverse metacarpal neck and shaft fractures will typically demonstrate apex dorsal angulation. The normal anatomic neck to shaft angle of 15 degrees should be recalled when assessing the amount of angulation in subcapital fractures radiographically. Radiographic assessment of apex dorsal angulation has a high interobserver and intraobserver variability.[99] Pseudoclawing is a term used to describe a dynamic imbalance manifested as a hyperextension deformity of the MP joint and a flexion deformity of the PIP joint (Fig. 28-76). This occurs as a compensatory response to the apex dorsal angulation of the metacarpal fracture (usually at the neck) and represents a clinical indication for correcting the fracture angulation. Oblique and spiral fractures

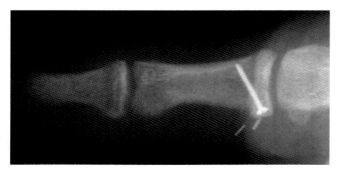

FIGURE 28-74 When a substantial bone fragment accompanies an ulnar collateral ligament injury to the MP joint, lag screw compression provides excellent stability through direct bone healing provided that there is not a multilevel injury of the ligament separating it from the bone fragment as well.

FIGURE 28-76 Pseudoclawing is an imbalance of compensatory metacarpophalangeal joint hyperextension and proximal interphalangeal joint flexion that occurs on attempted digital extension in proportion to the degree of apex dorsal angulation at the metacarpal fracture site and represents one indication for surgery.

tend to shorten and rotate more than angulate (Fig. 28-77). As with all hand fractures, evaluation of rotation remains one of the most critical assessments to make in order to avoid a functionally disabling malunion. Ten degrees of malrotation (which risks as much as 2 cm of overlap at the digital tip) should represent the upper tolerable limit. The problem of overlapping bone shadows has led to the development of a number of specialized radiographic views (Fig. 28-78). The Brewerton and Mehara views may show otherwise occult fractures at the metacarpal bases. The reverse oblique projection allows a more accurate estimation of angulation at the second metacarpal neck. The skyline view may show vertical impaction fractures of the metacarpal head not appreciable in any other projection.

Surgical and Applied Anatomy

The metacarpals are the key skeletal elements participating in the formation of the three arches of the hand (Fig. 28-79). There are two transverse arches that exist at the CMC and MP joint levels. The metacarpals themselves are longitudinally arched with a fairly broad convex dorsal surface. Intramedullary geometry is highly variable but with a consistently 20% thicker

volar cortex. Surgical access to the metacarpals is easily achieved through incisions placed over the intermetacarpal valleys and curved distally to avoid entering the digital web commissures.

The metacarpals are held tightly bound to each other by strong interosseous ligaments at their bases and by the deep transverse intermetacarpal ligaments distally. These connections help to maintain the transverse arches of the hand, but flattening can occur with multiple metacarpal fractures or crushing injuries. Shortening of individual metacarpal fractures is limited by these same ligaments (more effectively for the central metacarpals than for the border metacarpals). For each 2 mm of metacarpal shortening, 7 degrees of extensor lag can be expected.[148] One of the weakest points in the metacarpal is the volar aspect of the neck, where comminution is often present (Fig. 28-80). In the sagittal plane the primary deforming forces are the intrinsic muscles, which can be counteracted through MP joint flexion, an important component of the reduction maneuver for metacarpal fractures. Correction of apex dorsal angulation and rotational control is achieved indirectly by grasping the finger to exert control over the distal metacarpal fragment. Flexion of the PIP joint for reduction, as has been long recommended, is an unnecessary maneuver that actually encumbers the reduction process by tensioning the intrinsics (Fig. 28-81).

The biomechanics of fixation for metacarpal fractures has spawned a large body of literature.[11,49,50,110,124,125] The majority consists of cadaver studies evaluating different fixation constructs in materials testing machines using transverse or oblique osteotomies, cantilever, torsion, three- or four-point bending, and producing load-displacement data. The inherent flaw in this whole approach is that the stiffness of the implant is not the important factor for the surgeon to consider. More important is the implant's fatigue failure properties in response to cyclic stress. Nevertheless, the conclusions reached by nearly all the authors support the following: (a) The interfragmentary lag screw is, biomechanically, one of the most effective tools available to the surgeon. When applied alone or with a plate, it can even resist nearly the same failure loads as intact bone. (b) Self-tapping screws are as strong as standard screws that require a separate step of advance tapping. (c) Plates function most effectively as tension bands (which dictates dorsal placement for metacarpal fractures). (d) Intraosseous wire constructs placed in orthogonal planes (90 degrees/90 degrees) are not improved with the addition of K-wires and are the only intraosseous wire constructs that can compete with plates and screws. (e) All other intraosseous wire designs are less rigid than screws and/or plates but stronger than K-wires alone, which tend to slide through bone and loosen. Modern plating systems tolerate applied loads in cadaver specimens sufficient for immediate full active motion rehabilitation.[141] Locking intramedullary nails can be used in special cases such as following gunshot wounds.[7] External fixation has been reported even for closed fractures.[108]

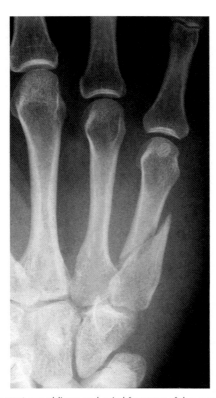

FIGURE 28-77 Long oblique and spiral fractures of the metacarpal shaft tend to shorten and rotate more than angulate.

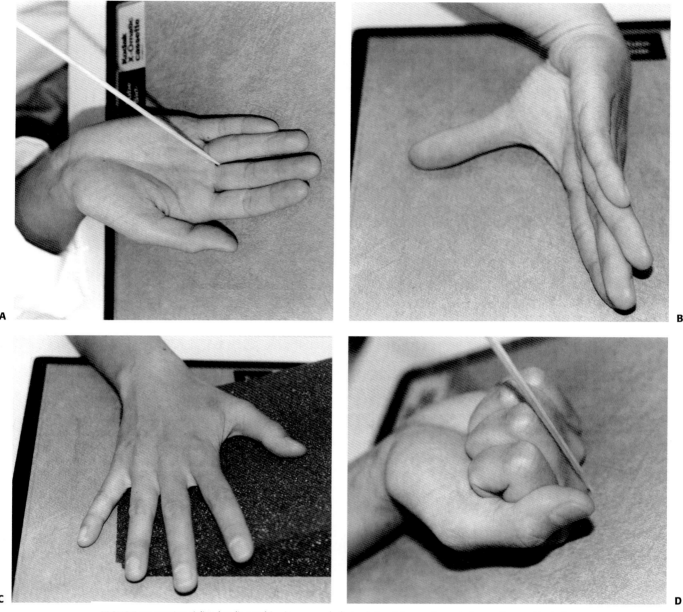

FIGURE 28-78 Specialized radiographic views may help to define injury patterns in the metacarpal including (**A**) the Brewerton view for the metacarpal bases, (**B**) the Mehara view for the index carpometacarpal relationships, (**C**) the reverse oblique view for angulation in the index metacarpal neck, and (**D**) the skyline view for vertical impaction fractures of the metacarpal head.

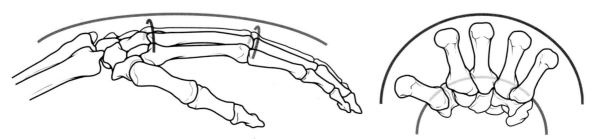

FIGURE 28-79 The three arches of the hand are the longitudinal arch and two transverse arches (one at the metacarpal bases and the other at the metacarpal neck level).

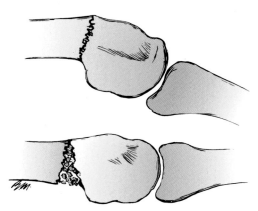

FIGURE 28-80 Fractures of the metacarpal neck frequently experience volar comminution and lack the inherent stability to resist apex dorsal angulation.

Current Treatment Options

Nonoperative Management

Many metacarpal neck and shaft fractures can be treated nonoperatively (Table 28-9). Twenty-seven small finger metacarpal fractures with initial angulation of 40 degrees were reduced and treated in a short hand cast for 4 weeks with only 3 patients losing reduction beyond 15 degrees.[30] Intra-articular fractures of the head and base may also be treated nonoperatively provided the fracture plane is both stable and minimally displaced. Metacarpal fractures with significant rotation or shortening cannot be effectively controlled through entirely nonoperative means. An externally applied splint exerts indirect (but not direct) control over fracture position through positioning and reduction of myotendinous deforming forces. A splint is able to

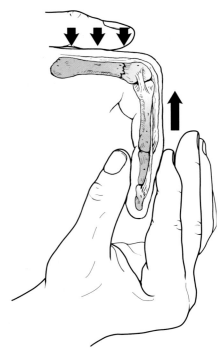

FIGURE 28-81 Reduction of metacarpal fractures can be accomplished by using the digit to control the distal fragment but the proximal interphalangeal joint should be extended rather than flexed.

preserve a fracture position that is inherently stable but is not capable of reducing and maintaining an unstable position. The stability of a metacarpal fracture is determined primarily by the adjacent structures (periosteum, adjacent metacarpals, deep transverse intermetacarpal, and proximal interosseous ligaments) as well as the degrees of initial displacement and comminution. Splinting should be directed at pain control and neutralization of deforming forces. Surface contact should be as broad as possible with an appropriate amount of padding. The splint may be discontinued as soon as the patient can comfortably perform ROM with the hand and not later than 3 weeks. Interphalangeal joint motion should begin immediately following injury. A dorsal splint in full MP joint flexion meets the patient's needs well but may be more than is required. Even less restrictive methods of functional bracing have been advocated. Compared to simple adjacent digit strapping in 73 patients, a molded metacarpal brace for less than 40-degree angulated fractures of the small finger metacarpal neck yielded similar clinical results with less pain.[70] Extending this concept, some have advocated functional mobilization for metacarpal fractures without splinting at all.[14] Defining the acceptable limits of deformity for each injury location is the subject of much controversy. Functionally, pseudoclawing is unacceptable. Also, the patient may be troubled by the appearance of a dorsal prominence at the fracture site or a shift in the metacarpal head from its dorsally visible position toward the palm. Only rarely will the shift toward the palm create a functional problem. Each patient may have different degrees of deformity that he or she is willing to tolerate. A correlation between deformity and symptoms has not been clearly established. Greater degrees of angulation are tolerable in neck fractures than in shaft fractures. Greater angulation is tolerable in the ring and small metacarpals than in the index and long metacarpals because of the increased mobility of the ulnar-sided CMC joints. Biomechanically significant decay in flexor tendon efficiency because of slack in the flexor digiti minimi and third volar interosseous occurs with angulations over 30 degrees in the fifth metacarpal neck, the site of greatest allowable angulation.[3,12]

Closed Reduction and Internal Fixation

CRIF is the mainstay of treatment for isolated metacarpal fractures not meeting the criteria for nonoperative treatment (Fig. 28-82). Twenty-five patients with small finger metacarpal fractures achieved excellent functional results following stabilization with 3 transverse K-wires and demonstrated no shortening, appreciable angulation, or complications.[56] A comparison between transverse and intramedullary K-wires in 59 patients failed to show any differences in outcome with no complications in either group.[176] CRIF may be used for both extra-articular and intra-articular fractures provided that the fracture is anatomically reducible and stable to the stress of motion with only K-wire fixation (Fig. 28-83). CRIF is the minimum treatment necessary for metacarpal base fractures that cannot be held reduced by nonoperative means.

Intramedullary Fixation

Intramedullary fixation strategies are best matched with transverse and short oblique fracture patterns and include a single large-diameter rod such as a Steinmann pin, an expandable intramedullary device, multiple prebent K-wires, or specially manufactured devices inserted at the metacarpal base designed

TABLE 28-9 **Metacarpal Fractures Not Involving the CMC Joints**

Treatment Options	Pros	Cons
Splinting	No added surgical stiffness	Will not maintain reduction of an inherently unstable fracture Limited control of rotation
CRIF	Treatment of choice for most single metacarpal fractures	Transverse method cannot be used for adjacent fractures at the same level in one column
Intramedullary fixation	Can be used for multiple adjacent fractures without opening the fracture site	Rotational control is not exact Tendon irritation proximally
ORIF with screws only	Effective control of rotation for spiral fractures Independent of adjacent fracture patterns	Not effective in the presence of comminution or segmental bone loss
ORIF with plates and screws	Bridges segmental bone loss or comminution	Hardware related complications Added surgical stiffness

CRIF, closed reduction and internal fixation; ORIF, open reduction and internal fixation.

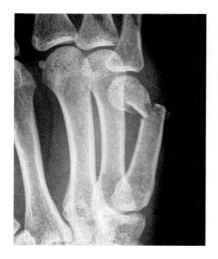
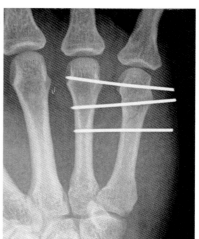

FIGURE 28-82 Closed reduction and internal fixation is effective for metacarpal neck fractures despite the smaller size of the head fragment and the need to achieve separation of the two wires that pass through it for control of fragment rotation in the sagittal plane.

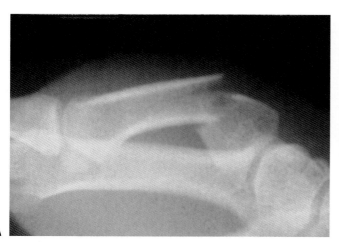
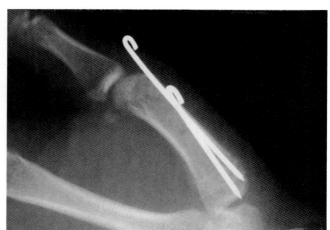

A   B

FIGURE 28-83 Extra-articular fractures of the thumb metacarpal (**A**) can be effective managed by (**B**) retrograde longitudinal pinning across the fracture into the base fragment.

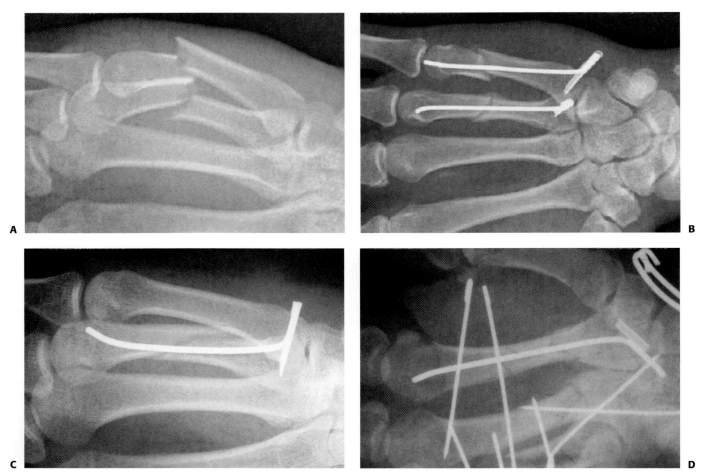

FIGURE 28-84 Fractures of the metacarpal at the same level that cannot be treated by transverse pinning (**A**) can be stabilized by (**B**) a specially manufactured device shaped for three-point fixation and closed intramedullary application with a rotational locking sleeve used proximally. This device is also effective (**C**) in oblique fracture patterns and (**D**) fractures near the base.

to achieve three-point intramedullary fixation[52,63,64,102,107,116] (Fig. 28-84). A single Steinmann pin may be inserted open through the fracture site with the two fragments then impacted over it. Rotational control is achieved by fracture fragment interlock, and motion can be started immediately. The strategy of multiple, stacked prebent wires has received broader acceptance than the other two strategies, perhaps owing to the closed technique used for introduction.[52,64,102,107] The wires are to be prebent such that three-point contact is obtained dorsally at the proximal and distal ends of the metacarpal and volarly at the mid-diaphysis (Fig. 28-85). This bow opposes the natural dorsal convexity of the metacarpal and is the basis for the apparently secure fixation achieved with this technique. The pins are to be stacked into the canal, filling it and imparting improved rotational control; as many as three to five 0.045-inch K-wires may be required. Excellent results with multiple wires have been reported primarily for fractures at the metacarpal neck level.[52,107] One series of 20 patients with 5-year follow-up reported essentially no complications.[107] Another series of 66 patients with 4.5-year follow-up noted eight incomplete reductions (average 18-degree deformity) and 12 patients with MP joint extensor lags of 10 to 15 degrees.[52]

Open Reduction and Internal Fixation

ORIF is the treatment of choice for intra-articular fractures that cannot be reduced and held by closed means. Internal fixation is also required for multiple fractures without inherent stability and for open fractures especially when associated with tendon disruptions.[54] Internal fixation can be accomplished with intraosseous wiring, composite wiring, screws only, or screws and

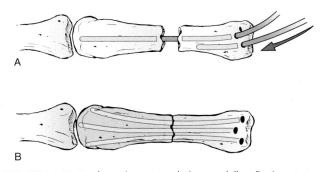

FIGURE 28-85 An alternative antegrade intramedullary fixation strategy includes multiple prebent 0.045-inch K-wires "stacked" into the canal in an attempt to achieve both rotational and angular control over the fracture.

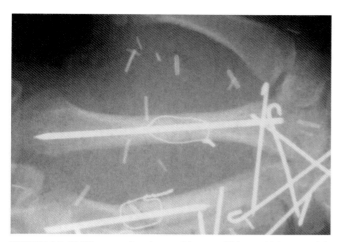

FIGURE 28-86 When rotational control is not sufficient with intramedullary fixation alone, composite wiring is useful and also adds a compressive force across the fracture site.

plates (Fig. 28-86). Wiring techniques have traditionally held the advantage over plate and screw application in terms of technical ease and availability of materials. However, with the modular plating systems now available specifically for use in hand surgery, lower profile fixation can be achieved with greater rigidity (Fig. 28-87). The most important consideration is that the surgeon should choose the method of internal fixation with which he or she is the most comfortable.

Metacarpal Head Fractures

For partial articular metacarpal head fractures, screw-only fixation is the treatment of choice. If sufficient interlock of

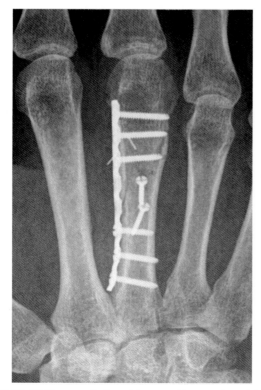

FIGURE 28-87 Plates are indicated for use with comminuted fractures lacking inherent stability and open fractures with associated soft tissue injury requiring immediate aggressive rehabilitation.

bone spicules occurs, a single 1.2- to 1.5-mm countersunk screw can control rotation of the fragment. If interlock is not effective, two screws are preferred even if this means downsizing the screw diameter to accommodate both of them in the fragment without causing comminution (Fig. 28-88). For complete articular head fractures, the condylar blade plate used to be required, but it is the most technically demanding plate to apply. It is applied laterally with the blade dorsal and the condylar screw hole volar. The drill hole for the blade is round but the blade is rectangular in cross-sectional area. This makes manual insertion of the blade into its hole difficult, and a fine touch is required to not further comminute the metacarpal head. More importantly, the exact angle of the drill path for the blade must be determined in advance relative to the cortical surface of the more proximal shaft against which the plate will be applied. The condylar screw hole of the plate usually needs to be bent to avoid prominence on its volar edge. Since the last edition of this text, locking plate technology has become available in the size range for small hand fracture plates. This allows fixed angle support of comminuted periarticular fractures with the ability to contour the plate first and avoid the complexity associated with inserting the blade plate (Fig. 28-89).

Rehabilitation

The importance of early motion must be considered in direct proportion to the magnitude of the injury or the surgical procedure performed.[112] The more tissue damage that is present, the more aggressive must be the motion program. One frequently overlooked factor that greatly confounds progress in therapy is edema control. External compression wraps to the zone of injury with cohesive elastic bandages work to minimize the presence of edema from the outset. When internal fixation has been required, one must anticipate the development of an extensor lag at the MP joint. Specific attention should be given to extensor tendon gliding in zone VI to overcome a developing lag. Rapid tendon activation has been successful in breaking free developing adhesions between the peritendinous tissues and their surroundings[77] (Fig. 28-90). Patients should be allowed to use the hand for light activities throughout the healing period. Light resistance activities can begin at 6 weeks. Extremely forceful use patterns should be deferred until 3 months.[15]

AUTHORS' PREFERRED METHOD OF TREATMENT
Metacarpal Fractures

Nonoperative Management

Many extra-articular and some intra-articular fractures, which are categorized as stable by virtue of having over 30% normal ROM without motion at the fracture site, can be managed with entirely nonoperative means using temporary splinting. Patients with entirely nondisplaced fractures that have excellent inherent stability do not require any external immobilization at all and can begin immediate AROM, usually with the added protection of adjacent digit strapping. Patients with stable metacarpal shaft fractures can be returned to nearly all light activities in a hand-based splint that is continued for a maximum of 3 weeks. Stable neck and intra-articular head fractures are more effectively protected by support that covers from the PIP level to the fore-

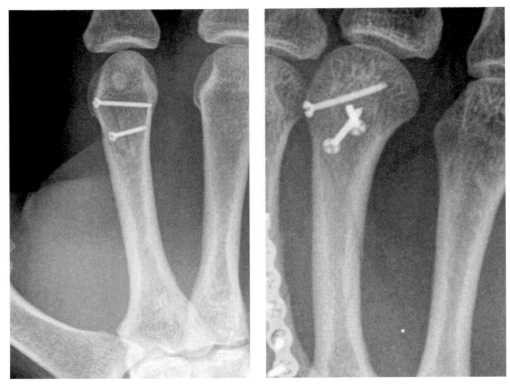

FIGURE 28-88 Metacarpal head fractures consisting of only a few fragments are best stabilized by countersunk small lag screws.

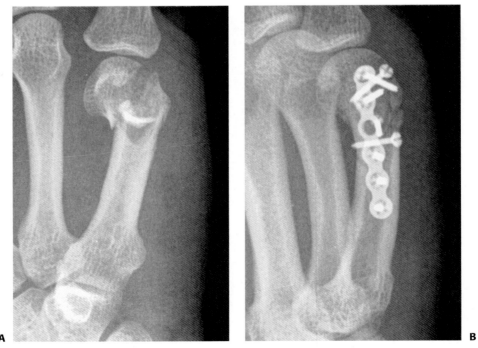

A

B

FIGURE 28-89 Metacarpal head fractures with (**A**) high degrees of comminution and inherent instability may require (**B**) plate stabilization to avoid collapse.

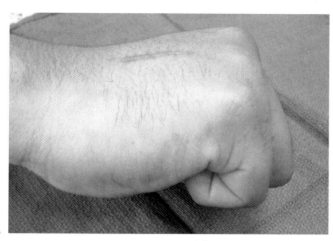
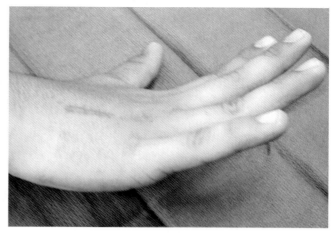

FIGURE 28-90 Even following open reduction and internal fixation, when a properly designed rehabilitation program is administered, (**A**) complete flexion and (**B**) hyperextension are possible.

arm with the MP joints in full flexion. At least one adjacent digit is included with the affected ray. Interphalangeal joint motion should begin immediately with all strategies.

Closed Reduction and Internal Fixation

Transverse pinning to adjacent metacarpals is my treatment of choice for all unstable closed metacarpal fractures except multiple adjacent fractures at the same level that include a border digit (Fig. 28-91). The biomechanics of the transverse pinning strategy is that of external fixation. Four points of

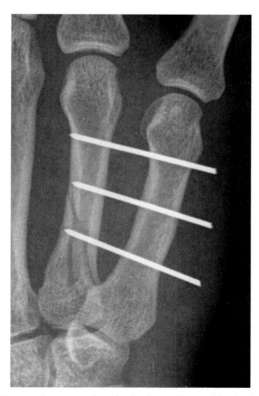

FIGURE 28-91 Transverse closed reduction and internal fixation functions under the same biomechanical principles as external fixation. Note the distal wire is placed just proximal to the collateral recess of both bones and has also avoided tethering the sagittal bands.

control are needed. The two points closest to the fracture site on either side should be as close together as possible. The two farthest from the fracture site should be as far apart as possible. The proximal intermetacarpal and CMC ligaments are stout enough to qualify as the most proximal point of fixation such that only one 0.045-inch K-wire is required proximal to the fracture site. The distal most pin should avoid transgression of the sagittal bands if at all possible. This must be titrated clinically against the goal of placing the point of fixation as far from the fracture site as possible. The transverse pinning strategy works equally well for central (long and ring) and border (index and small) metacarpals. If the four finger metacarpals are conceived of as occurring in two columns (a radial column for index and long and an ulnar column for ring and small), then most combinations of multiple metacarpal fractures can still be fixed with this strategy, and it can always be used if there is only one fracture per column. If both metacarpals in the column are fractured, but at different levels, they can be used to reciprocally stabilize each other (Fig. 28-92). The specific requirement for reciprocal stabilization to be effective is that there is a zone in the diaphysis of both bones where two pins can be placed with adequate spacing from each other (distal to one fracture site and proximal to the other). At the conclusion of the procedure, one has the choice of leaving the pins protruding through the skin or cutting them off beneath the skin. In previous editions of this chapter I had advocated allowing pins of less than 4 weeks' duration to be left outside the skin for ease of removal, but I now cut nearly all pins below the skin level given the prevalence of MRSA in the community. The hand is initially splinted in full MP flexion to resist the development of contractures. Early motion can proceed while the pins are still in place.

Open Reduction and Internal Fixation

ORIF is my treatment of choice for open fractures and multiple fractures not meeting the criteria for reciprocal transverse stabilization. When fracture plane interlock between bone spicules is present, intraosseous wiring, composite wiring, screw-only, or screw and plate fixation may all be considered. I prefer lag screw fixation for long-oblique or spiral

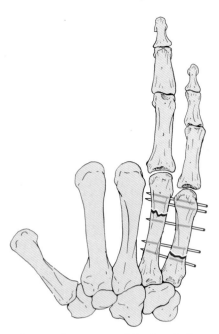

FIGURE 28-92 Reciprocal transverse stabilization of adjacent metacarpal fractures is possible when the levels of the two fractures are separated enough to be able to place two pins that fall distal to the first fracture and proximal to the second such that the first metacarpal is sufficiently stabilized to in turn provide stability to the other metacarpal.

fractures since CRIF cannot control the reduction of these patterns nearly as well as transverse fractures (Fig. 28-93). To select screw-only fixation, the ratio of the length of the oblique or spiral fracture plane to the bone diameter must be at least 2:1. Furthermore, to avoid comminution, the screws must pass through an area in the bone spike where the screw outer diameter is less than one-third the width of the spike. The screw sizes most appropriate for a metacarpal are 1.5 and 1.7 mm. Multiple open transverse or short oblique fractures of the mid-diaphysis from open crushing injuries are nicely managed with intramedullary pins. Rotational control can be supplemented with a composite wire loop. When interfragmentary compression cannot be achieved owing to the presence of comminution or bone loss, plates and screws are indicated.

As with all techniques of internal fixation, it is essential to cover the hardware with periosteal closure to provide a separate gliding layer. I prefer to operate 3 to 5 days following injury so that the periosteum will have thickened in response to injury and both can be dissected as a discrete tissue flap and closed with solid suture purchase. Unlike over the proximal phalanx, the extensor tendons at this level are discrete cords, and placement of the hardware away from them should be possible in most cases. Placement of the plate dorsally puts it on the tension cortex of the bone, but in this position it interferes most directly with the extensor tendons. Placement of the plate in a true lateral position allows sagittal plane forces to be resisted by the width of the plate rather than its thickness, and doing so is almost always possible, just technically more difficult. This is my choice for plate placement unless extenuating circumstances dictate dorsal placement. One such circumstance is fracture comminution extending all the way to the base of the metacarpal. All the technical comments made in the section on proximal phalangeal fractures apply equally here.

Pearls and Pitfalls

The metacarpal is the most proximal bone in the ray. Rotational malunions here will be the most obvious and functionally disabling. In large part, the management of metacarpal fractures is all about ensuring that rotation is correct. Length and angulation are, of course, not to be forgotten. The assessment of rotation both preoperatively and intraoperatively merits discussion. In both cases, the examiner should not touch the digit during the assessment. The awake, preoperative patient may require an anesthetic block to relieve enough pain so that he or she is capable of flexing sufficiently to demonstrate the rotational status of the digit. In the anesthetized patient, tenodesis driven by full-range wrist motion produces sufficient flexion and extension of the digit that rotational alignment can be accurately judged.

When performing transverse pinning of metacarpals, intraoperative imaging will effectively demonstrate depth of pin penetration and coronal plane fracture orientation. Metacarpal overlap obscures any individual metacarpal lateral view. Ensuring that the pins have penetrated both cortices of both metacarpals cannot be judged radiographically and must be determined by feel at the time of placement. If the reduction is difficult to obtain closed or tends to slip as the pins are driven, the case does not have to be converted to a full open reduction. A small instrument such as a

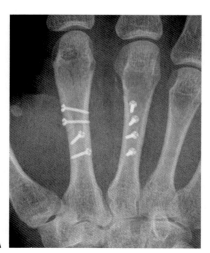

A

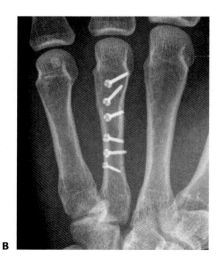

B

FIGURE 28-93 Interfragmentary lag screws allow stable fixation of (**A**) adjacent metacarpals and (**B**) three fragment fractures with an intermediate butterfly fragment sufficient to permit full, immediate motion rehabilitation.

dental pick or microelevator can be placed percutaneously at the fracture site to directly control reduction while the surgeon proceeds with the otherwise entirely closed pinning. Compared with plating of phalangeal fractures, there is even greater risk of inducing an iatrogenic rotational malunion when tightening down the screws. If a metacarpal plate has not been axially contoured correctly, when the screws are tightened, the plate will actually rotate the distal fragment out of an otherwise previously correct reduction. For this reason, no matter how many times the reduction has already been clinically evaluated, it must be evaluated at least one more time upon final placement of all fixation.

CARPOMETACARPAL JOINT DISLOCATIONS AND FRACTURE-DISLOCATIONS

Dislocations and fracture-dislocations at the finger CMC joints are usually high-energy injuries with involvement of associated structures, often neurovascular (Fig. 28-94). Particular care must be given to the examination of ulnar nerve function, especially motor, because of its close proximity to the fifth CMC joint. Frequently, the pattern is one of fracture-dislocation involving the metacarpal bases, the distal carpal bones, or both.[93] Overlap on the lateral radiograph obscures accurate depiction of the injury pattern, and most authors recommend at least one variant of an oblique view.[177] The Brewerton view may be helpful in this respect, profiling individual metacarpal bases. Another special view has been described for the second metacarpal base.[240] When fracture-dislocations include the dorsal cortex of the hamate, CT or polytomography may be necessary to fully evaluate the pathoanatomy. Another pattern to recognize is dislocation of one CMC joint with fracture of an adjacent metacarpal base. Shortening can be evaluated by noting a disruption in the normal cascade seen distally at the MP joints. Volar CMC dislocations are rare.

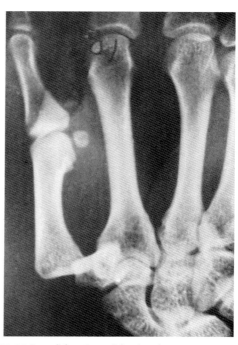

FIGURE 28-95 Pure dislocations of the thumb carpometacarpal joint are rare injuries and typically occur dorsoradially.

Pure Thumb Carpometacarpal Dislocations

Most thumb CMC dislocations are dorsal and are thought to occur through axial loading of a partially flexed thumb (Fig. 28-95). Motorcyclists may be uniquely prone to sustaining this rare injury and to having the injury missed on initial evaluation. The injury will often be reduced before being seen by the surgeon. Clinical diagnosis is then based on identifying the residual instability. Differentiating complete from incomplete ligament rupture is essential, as initial operative treatment is appropriate

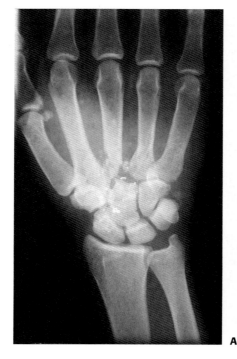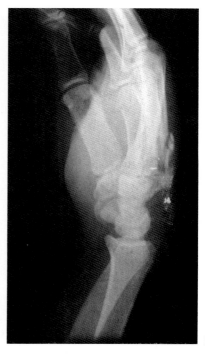

FIGURE 28-94 Fractures of carpometacarpal joints (**A**) are typically high-energy injuries with (**B**) comminution of both the metacarpal base and the distal carpal row.

only for complete disruptions. Instillation of local anesthetic into the joint may be required to allow an unimpeded examination. Manual stress testing compared with the contralateral side should allow diagnosis in most cases.

Thumb Carpometacarpal Fracture-Dislocations

The majority of thumb metacarpal base fractures are intra-articular (Fig. 28-96). The majority of thumb CMC joint injuries are fracture-dislocations rather than pure dislocations. The smaller fracture fragment at the thumb metacarpal volar base is deeply placed and not palpable. Eponyms associated with these fracture-dislocations are Bennett (partial articular), and Rolando (complete articular) fractures. Specific radiographs must be obtained in the true AP and lateral planes of the thumb (not a series of hand radiographs) if injuries along this axis are to be correctly identified (Fig. 28-97).

Surgical and Applied Anatomy

Finger Carpometacarpal Joints

Stability at the finger CMC joints is provided by a system of four ligaments. There is a high degree of variation with dorsal, multiple palmar, and two sets of interosseous ligaments (only one between the long and ring metacarpals).[40,114] The interosseous ligaments are the strongest and have a V-configuration with the base of the V oriented toward the fourth metacarpal. Range of motion of the index and long CMC joints is limited to less than 5 degrees, with 15 degrees at the ring, and up to 25 to 30 degrees at the small finger. Small finger CMC motion is reduced 28% to 40% when the ring finger is immobilized.[44] The axis of motion is located near the base of the metacarpal. The index metacarpal has a particularly stable configuration through its wedge-shaped articulation with the trapezoid. The small finger CMC joint is the only joint not having a gliding configuration but instead is a modified saddle-shaped joint. The increased mobility on the ulnar side of the hand may predispose to its greater frequency of injury. Critical soft tissue relationships to appreciate during treatment of injuries to the CMC joints are the positions of the motor branch of the ulnar nerve directly in front of the fifth CMC joint and the deep palmar arch in front of the third CMC joint. Of all hand fractures and dislocations, injury at the CMC level requires the highest degree of vigilance regarding associated neurologic injury. The high-energy mechanism of these injuries and profound degrees of swelling may lead to worsened outcomes through residual long-term nerve compression.

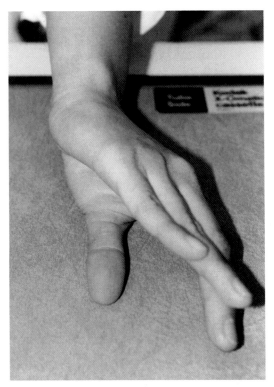

FIGURE 28-97 The thumb does not reside in the same plane as the rest of the hand. A true AP view of the thumb can be obtained with the Robert view.

Thumb Carpometacarpal Joints

Branches of both the lateral antebrachial cutaneous and superficial radial nerve ramify throughout the region of the thumb base on the radial side. Three tendons pass through this region: the abductor pollicis longus (APL), extensor pollicis brevis (EPB), and extensor pollicis longus (EPL). The radial artery passes beneath the APL and EPB on its course to the first web space and lies just proximal to the CMC joint. The joint anatomy includes reciprocal saddle-shaped surfaces of the distal trapezium and proximal metacarpal. The axis of this concavoconvex joint is then itself curved in a third plane with the convexity lateral. The normal ROM at the thumb CMC joint is around 50 degrees of flexion-extension, 40 degrees of abduction-adduction, and 15 degrees of pronation-supination. There is consensus as to which ligaments are anatomically present at the trapeziometacarpal joint (Fig. 28-98). They are the superficial

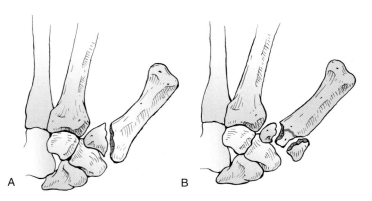

A   B

FIGURE 28-96 The most recognized patterns of thumb metacarpal base intra-articular fractures are (**A**) the partial articular Bennett fracture and (**B**) the complete articular Rolando fracture.

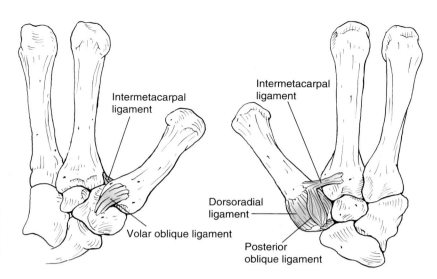

FIGURE 28-98 The primary stabilizing ligaments of the thumb carpometacarpal joint include the deep anterior oblique, dorsoradial, posterior oblique, and intermetacarpal ligaments. The superficial anterior oblique and ulnar collateral ligaments are not primary stabilizers.

anterior oblique, deep anterior oblique (beak), ulnar collateral, intermetacarpal, posterior oblique, and dorsoradial ligaments.[10] A point of confluence exists at the palmar ulnar tubercle of the first metacarpal base. There was a period of disagreement regarding the primary stabilizing ligament in preventing dislocation between the deep anterior oblique and the dorsoradial ligament. Although the deep anterior oblique was previously considered the primary stabilizer, more recent research has effectively demonstrated that the dorsoradial ligament is the prime restraint to dislocation. The dorsoradial ligament is the shortest ligament in the group and the first to become taut with dorsal or dorsoradial subluxation.[10] Selective ligament sectioning showed that deficiency of the dorsoradial ligament led to the greatest degree of subluxation.[164] Dorsal dislocation usually occurs through rupture of the dorsal ligaments with a sleeve-type avulsion of the anterior oblique ligament as it peels off the volar surface of the first metacarpal.[148] Supination may also play a significant role in the mechanism of this injury. Deformation of fractures at the base of the thumb metacarpal occurs with a complex motion (Fig. 28-99). The distal metacarpal is adducted and supinated by the adductor pollicis. At the same time, the APL pulls the metacarpal radially and proximally. Reduction maneuvers must attempt to counteract each of these forces. Probably the most difficult aspect of the reduction to maintain through splinting is the radial displacement of the base.

Current Treatment Options

Nonoperative Management

Closed reduction is usually possible early but may be difficult later following injury (Table 28-10). Dorsal finger CMC fracture-dislocations usually cannot be held effectively by external means alone. Although usually acceptable as the least invasive method of treatment for most injuries, entirely nonoperative management of pure thumb CMC dislocations does not provide sufficient stability for accurate healing of the ligaments. It is not possible through external means to completely maintain control over the reduction of a widely displaced intra-articular fracture-dislocation at the base of the thumb throughout the entire period of healing. However, the need to achieve anatomic union in these fractures has been questioned. Although no one study

is definitive, the risk of significant malunion when managing an initially widely displaced intra-articular fracture is too great to warrant entirely nonoperative management.

Finger Carpometacarpal Dislocations and Fracture Dislocations—Operative Management

For those injuries that can be accurately reduced, CRIF is the treatment of choice. The technique involves restoration of anatomic length to the shortened and dislocated metacarpals through the combined application of traction and direct pressure at the metacarpal bases. Manual reduction is then followed by placement of 0.045-inch K-wires across the metacarpal shaft and into either the carpal bones or into adjacent stable metacarpals (Fig. 28-100). Adequacy of reduction as well as stability should be evaluated both radiographically and clinically. Pins should remain for 6 weeks. Unlike most other hand fractures, residual instability rather than stiffness is the risk with this in-

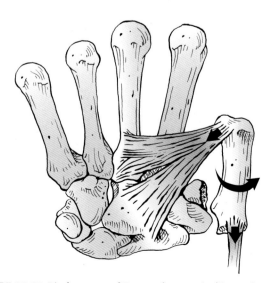

FIGURE 28-99 Displacement of Bennett fractures is driven primarily by the abductor pollicis longus (proximal migration) and the adductor pollicis (adduction and supination).

TABLE 28-10	Carpometacarpal Joint Dislocations and Fracture Dislocations		
Treatment Options	**Pros**		**Cons**
Splinting	Avoidance of surgical complications		Only capable of maintaining reduction of inherently stable, minimally displaced fractures and fracture-dislocations
CRIF	Avoids open surgical tissue trauma Able to maintain reduction of those injuries that can be accurately reduced closed		Many carpometacarpal fracture dislocation patterns cannot be accurately reduced closed Poor results for pure thumb carpometacarpal dislocations
ORIF	Allows direct control and visualization of reduction; direct ligament repair for pure thumb carpometacarpal dislocations		Added surgical tissue trauma

CRIF, closed reduction and internal fixation; ORIF, open reduction and internal fixation.

jury. Initially open fractures and those with tissue interposition preventing reduction will require ORIF. Open reduction is much more likely to be required in cases presenting late and may be accomplished as long as three months after the initial injury (Fig. 28-101). The stabilization strategy is the same as for CRIF with the open part of the procedure being used strictly for reduction purposes.[51,136] Excellent long-term stability without pain is achieved in the majority of cases. In more severe cases, immediate arthrodesis of the CMC joints may be required.[69]

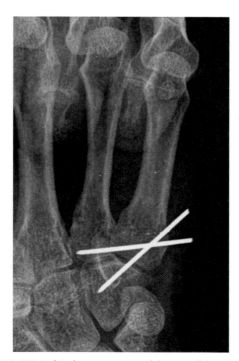

FIGURE 28-100 Isolated carpometacarpal fracture dislocations can be reduced and pinned closed to a stable adjacent metacarpal and to the distal carpal row.

Thumb Carpometacarpal Pure Dislocations—Operative Management

Surprisingly, even the results of CRIF have not been sufficient to consistently prevent long-term symptoms of instability and arthritis in pure thumb CMC dislocations. In a series of eight dislocations pinned for 6 weeks and immobilized for a total of 7.4 weeks, four required ligament reconstruction (three for symptomatic instability and one for progression of early post-traumatic arthritis).[139] Based on these poor results, the same authors subsequently treated the next nine patients with early ligament reconstruction, resulting in no late symptoms, full motion, and normal grip strength[139] (Fig. 28-102).

Thumb Carpometacarpal Fracture Dislocations—Operative Management

Closed reduction and internal K-wire (0.045-inch) stabilization is the treatment of choice for nearly all Bennett fractures and some Rolando fractures (Fig. 28-103). A series of 32 patients followed for 7 years with intra-articular step-offs of less than 1 mm found no difference between closed pinning and ORIF for Bennett's fractures with the exception of a higher incidence of adduction contracture in the pinning group.[105] Advocates of internal fixation may choose to manage less comminuted Rolando's fractures and some Bennett's fractures with ORIF.[101] When there are reasonably large fragments that will support purchase of at least one solid screw per fragment, one may consider plate and screw stabilization of a Rolando fracture (Fig. 28-104). However, ORIF of a Rolando fracture is not for the occasional hand surgeon. Comminution is the rule rather than the exception, and restoration of normal anatomy is quite difficult. The combination of limited internal fixation and external fixation to support the length and unload the articular reduction may be helpful in complex Rolando's fractures. A series of ten patients managed this way and followed at 35 months showed 88% key pinch strength compared with the contralateral side with 9 of 10 patients having good or fair overall satisfaction.[19] While some series have deemphasized the role of anatomic reduction in improving long-term results, others have stressed its

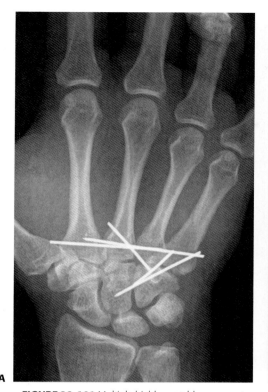
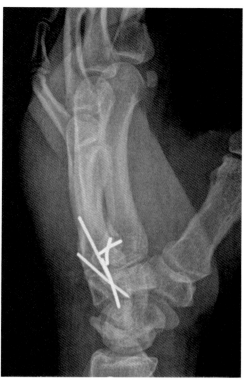

FIGURE 28-101 Multiple highly unstable carpometacarpal dislocations are at high risk of incomplete reduction and require (**A**) multiple points of fixation and (**B**) a careful check on the lateral radiograph to identify any residual dorsal subluxation.

role. Eighteen patients followed to 10.7 years showed a clear correlation between the quality of reduction and posttraumatic arthritis.[159] A similar series with over 7-year follow-up demonstrated a clear correlation between radiographic post-traumatic arthritis and greater than 1-mm step-off in the final reduction.[158] Twenty-one patients achieved 80% of normal grip strength despite radiographic signs of degeneration in 16 that did not correlate to clinical outcome.[16] Thirty-one patients followed at 7.3 years demonstrated a correlation of both radiographic signs of osteoarthritis and (more important) symptoms of pain with the final residual displacement when healing occurred with more than a 2-mm articular step-off.[90]

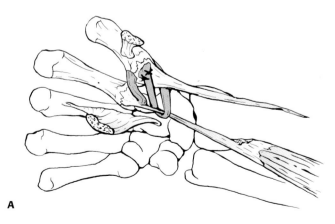
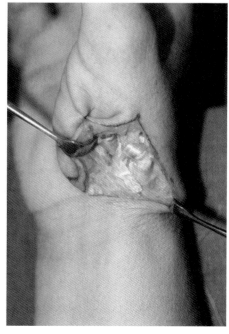

FIGURE 28-102 Reconstruction of the thumb carpometacarpal ligaments can be performed with (**A**) a split flexor carpi radialis graft woven through a bone tunnel in the thumb metacarpal base, exiting the dorsal cortex, passing deep to the abductor pollicis longus, around the intact remaining flexor carpi radialis, and back to the volar radial aspect of the metacarpal base. **B.** This procedure is accomplished through a traditional Wagner approach.

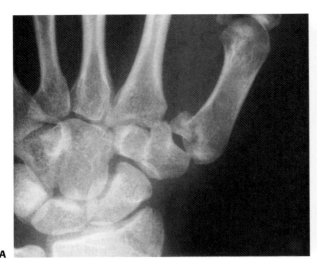

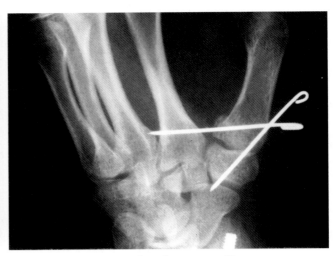

A **B**

FIGURE 28-103 A. Bennett fractures can be stabilized with (**B**) closed pinning to the index metacarpal base and across the carpometacarpal joint into the trapezium.

Rehabilitation

Immobilization should last from 6 to 8 weeks in an orthoplast splint. The primary problem with finger CMC joint injuries is residual instability, not joint stiffness. The MP joints should be left free throughout the aftercare period with attention paid to excursion of the common digital extensor tendons. For thumb CMC joint injuries, immobilization is continued for 6 weeks in a thumb spica splint. The IP joint should be left free throughout the postoperative period. Following cast removal the patient undergoes a standard progression of ROM exercises that graduates as tolerated into functional use by 8 to 10 weeks. Forceful pinch loading is avoided for 3 months after surgery.

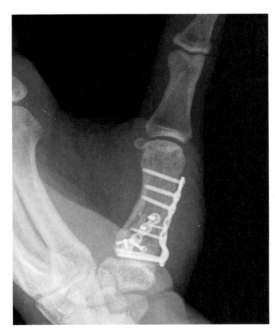

FIGURE 28-104 Rolando fractures are highly unstable and require techniques such as fixed angle plates adjacent to the subchondral bone to resist collapse and sometimes even a smaller second plate placed at 90 degrees to the primary plate.

▶▶ AUTHORS' PREFERRED METHOD OF TREATMENT

Carpometacarpal Joint Dislocations and Fracture-Dislocations

Finger Carpometacarpal Joint Pure Dislocations

Pure dislocations rarely occur without fracture of either the metacarpal bases or carpal bones of the distal row. However, the absence of such fractures creates an opportunity for successful management by CRIF. The metacarpal bases must both be felt to engage their articulations fully and demonstrate complete congruence on radiographs. This is one injury pattern where the added time invested in obtaining true radiographs rather than fluoroscopy alone is worthwhile to assure this congruence. Only when the x-ray beam passes tangentially through the joint can an accurate assessment be made. It is practical to use the fluoroscope to determine the angle of projection that best demonstrates the reduction and then try to reproduce the shot with the plain radiograph. K-wires are retained for 6 weeks outside the skin with an additional 2 weeks of splint protection before initiating wrist and CMC rehabilitation. All other joints remain mobile throughout the postoperative period.

Finger Carpometacarpal Joint Fracture-Dislocations

If an accurate closed reduction can be achieved, CRIF is an excellent choice. Cases seen many days after injury or those with tissue interposition will likely require ORIF to achieve accurate reduction. The approach may be dictated by the presence of an open traumatic wound. Otherwise, a dorsal transverse incision at the level of the joint is best. Branches of the superficial radial nerve and dorsal cutaneous branch of the ulnar nerve must be identified and protected not only from the surgical approach to reach the injury site but also during pin placement. The common extensor tendons overlie the central metacarpal bases, and the wrist extensor tendons insert on the border metacarpals. Incision of the extensor retinaculum increases the lateral mobility of these tendons, allowing the surgeon to work around them. Bone and cartilage fragments too small for fixation but large enough to create third body wear in the joint should be removed. Fixation is founded upon 0.045-inch K-wire passage from the metacarpal bases across the CMC joints into the distal carpal row. If adjacent metacarpals are stable without CMC joint injury, transverse stabilization between metacarpal bases is an excellent addition. Evaluation of the dorsal cortices of the hamate and capitate should be performed on each case as these are often also fractured. Large bone fragments should be restored to their cancellous beds and fixed with countersunk compression screws. Small bone fragments should be excised. Index or long finger CMC joints with extensive articular cartilage damage are good candidates for primary arthrodesis. Motion in the ring and small finger CMC joints should be preserved if possible but arthrodesis remains an acceptable method of management as a last resort.

Thumb Carpometacarpal Joint Pure Dislocations

The literature simply does not support CRIF as a valid treatment for this injury despite basic principles that should allow this method to produce satisfactory results. Although some articles suggest that one needs to perform immediate free tendon graft reconstruction of complete thumb CMC dislocations, this has not been my experience. I have consistently found open ligament repair to produce stable and pain-free motion. The reproducible surgical findings are a sleevelike avulsion of the deep anterior oblique ligament from the volar surface of the metacarpal and a rupture of the dorsoradial and posterior oblique ligaments. The rupture has usually been distally from the metacarpal insertion. The procedure is easily accomplished by inserting a series of 1.3-mm bone anchors around the margin of the metacarpal base and using the sutures for anatomic repair of the dorsal ligaments. The joint should be pinned in a reduced position before tying down the dorsal ligaments. The deep anterior oblique ligament comes to lie flush with the metacarpal surface when the joint is reduced and stabilized. Pins are retained for 6 weeks with thumb CMC joint motion being instituted at that time. Light pinch is also allowed with progression to power pinch by 3 months postoperatively.

Thumb Carpometacarpal Joint Fracture-Dislocations

The majority of these can be treated with CRIF, most of the remainder augmented with small openings to control small articular fragments or pack bone graft into the metaphysis, and the final minority with full ORIF. The soft tissue anatomy of this region should be taken into account when placing pins. The drill should not be activated until the pin is solidly placed down to bone. Bennett fractures can be stabilized with either one or two pins. The primary pin reduces and stabilizes the shaft of the metacarpal to the trapezium. An alternative to trapezium pinning is to pin the thumb to the index metacarpal or to both. A second pin may be placed across the two fragments to prevent the development of an articular step-off, but this pin will not hold the fracture surfaces opposed. Many surgeons do not even use this second pin.

The goals of treatment in a Rolando fracture are different. The primary aim is to provide distraction to allow healing through the often-comminuted metaphyseal zone. This is best accomplished by pinning the thumb metacarpal (with two 0.062-inch K-wires) to the index metacarpal rather than

to the trapezium. It is in the complete articular cases with comminution that making a small opening to place an elevator into the metaphysis may prove useful. The articular fragments can be molded against the distal surface of the trapezium and kept there by either packing bone graft in behind them or with additional smaller-caliber (0.035-inch) pins placed transversely at the subchondral level to maintain articular congruity. The advantage of plate and screw stabilization of an intra-articular fracture in general is usually to allow early motion of the joint for the sake of cartilage nutrition and preservation of long-term ROM. The small fragments at the base of the thumb metacarpal are more at risk of devascularization with a widely open procedure that includes periosteal stripping to place a small titanium plate. I have not experienced that long-term loss of motion is a problem at the trapeziometacarpal joint following 6 weeks of pin immobilization for these fractures. I have observed that the presence of the plate results in adherence of the extensor pollicis longus and brevis tendons and can cause long-term loss of motion of both the MP and IP joint, which is a clinically relevant problem.

If ORIF is chosen for a select case, a Wagner incision along the glabrous/nonglabrous border of the thumb base may be curved in a volar and transverse direction to expose the thenar muscle group (Fig. 28-102B). Reflection of these muscles reveals the joint capsule volar to the insertion of the APL. Arthrotomy reveals the intra-articular fracture, and subperiosteal dissection along the shaft allows for placement of a plate. Stable internal fixation of Rolando's fractures is only possible when the fragments are large enough to accept the purchase of individual screws. My current fixation of choice in this situation is a titanium locking condylar plate (either 1.7-mm or 2.3-mm depending on the size of the patient). Eccentric drilling of the condylar holes can add transverse compression between the articular base fragments. If ORIF is chosen for a Bennett's fracture, a smaller version of the same approach is used to allow sufficient access to compress the reduction and place an interfragmentary lag screw from dorsal to volar. Recently, micro-sized variable pitch headless screws have become available and are well suited to the fragment sizes seen in a Bennett's fracture.

Pearls and Pitfalls

Treatment of both finger and thumb CMC joint injuries provides ample opportunity for the occurrence of two complications frequent in hand surgery: injury to cutaneous nerves and pin tract infections. The injury to cutaneous nerves is likely to occur by a pin rather than during dissection and particularly when approaching the radial side of the thumb base. Pins are retained longer here (6 weeks) than for stabilization of metacarpal (removed by 4 weeks) or phalangeal (removed by 3 weeks) fractures. There is thus more time for a pin tract infection to develop. The pearls and pitfalls for finger CMC joint fracture-dislocations are contained in two statements: Be sure the joint is fully reduced, and do not miss associated carpal bone fractures of significant size. Although most isolated single ray CMC fracture-dislocations occur in the small finger axis, there is a reproducible pattern that will occasionally be seen for the index ray where the articular base is split into two good quality fragments very amenable to a percutaneous headless compression screw fixation (Fig. 28-105).

Comminuted fractures of the thumb CMC joint are indeed

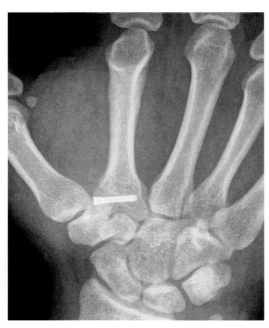

FIGURE 28-105 An isolated index metacarpal carpometacarpal fracture-dislocation can be percutaneously reduced and stably fixed with a headless variable pitch compression screw.

difficult injuries to treat but are made much simpler by approaching their management as follows: Conceive of where the shaft of the thumb metacarpal lies when in a correct functional position relative to the rest of the hand and pin it there (to the index metacarpal) with two 0.062-inch K-wires. Then make the articular surface of the metacarpal base congruent with supportive bone graft and/or small subchondral wires through a limited opening. What originally appeared as an impossible undertaking now becomes a relatively simple two-step process.

COMPLICATIONS

Published complication rates associated with rigid internal fixation are high and often attributable to the complex nature of the injuries for which this treatment method is selected. In a series of 41 metacarpal and 27 phalangeal fractures, complications related to hardware (45%), extensor lag (19%), and infection (12%) were seen.[119] Another series of 37 phalangeal fractures reported a 92% complication rate including 60% extensor lag, and 38% fixed flexion contracture.[121] Increased complication rates were associated with intra-articular/periarticular locations with extension to the shaft, open injuries, associated soft tissue injury, and the need for bone graft. As long as 18 months may be required for soreness and stiffness to abate following small joint dislocations. In 490 severe phalangeal fractures, there were 31 (6%) nonunions, 44 (9%) malunions, and 8 (2%) infections.[166]

In 200 open hand fractures, there were 9 deep infections, 18 malunions, 17 delayed unions or nonunions, 23 fixation-related complications, and two late amputations.[151] These complications were usually associated with Swanson type II wounds (14% compared with 1.4% in type I wounds) but not with the use of internal fixation, high-energy injury, large wound size, or associated soft tissue injury.

Infection

Despite the excellent vascularity of the hand, infection still occurs with open fractures.[18] An 11% infection rate occurred in 146 open hand fractures, all in Gustilo type II or III injuries, and in association with a crushing component.[13] Preoperative wound cultures were of no help, and *S. aureus* was the most commonly isolated species. In current practice, MRSA is the most commonly isolated species. The role of antibiotics in reducing the infection rate in noncontaminated open wounds with intact vessels has not been supported. When 198 patients were randomized in a double-blind placebo-controlled study with flucloxacillin for open distal phalangeal fractures, there were seven superficial and no deep infections (three with antibiotic, four without).[147]

Stiffness

Perhaps the most feared complication and certainly one of the most common following a fracture or dislocation of the hand is stiffness. Twenty-two of 54 patients failed to achieve TAM over 180 degrees following plate fixation of phalangeal fractures.[94] Stiffness is a product of the magnitude of the original trauma, the age and genetic composition of the patient, the duration of immobilization, the position of immobilization, and the invasiveness of any surgical intervention. The primary factors influencing stiffness are the associated soft tissue injury and the age of the patient.[24,173] Too often the position of immobilization violates the fundamental principles of splinting ligaments at full length and balancing tendon forces that act across the fracture site.[53] First web space contractures are common and can be minimized by pinning or splinting the thumb metacarpal in maximum abduction. Active versus passive motion discrepancies most commonly appear in the form of an extensor lag. The overlying extensor tendon becomes adherent to the fracture site and its subsequent failure of excursion produces an extensor lag at the next most distal joint. This is most common at the PIP joint following fractures of P1 with adherence of the flat and broad extensor tendon in zone IV. Only 11% of phalangeal fractures fixed with plates had a TAM of greater than 220 degrees.[121] A focused rehabilitation technique that uses the differential viscoelastic properties of tendon and scar tissue can be used to maximize extensor excursion over both phalangeal and metacarpal fractures.[77] Once a fixed contracture has been established by the time of tissue homeostasis following the initial trauma, tenocapsulolysis is required if the patient desires to improve motion.[100] One of the chief concerns with operative management of thumb MP ligament disruptions has been the loss of motion. Loss of motion may be more significant in patients undergoing late reconstructions as occurred in 21 patients from a series of 70 after free tendon graft.[95]

Hypersensitivity

The size and structure of the hand provide for very little padding between the surface and a complex array of small-caliber nerve branches. There are very few locations for either surgical incisions or percutaneous pins where small nerve branches are more than 1 cm away. Hypersensitivity is a frequently seen consequence of the mechanism of injury itself. Crush injuries are almost invariably accompanied by some degree of hypersensitivity. When surgical management is performed soon after the injury, the procedure itself is often erroneously blamed for caus-

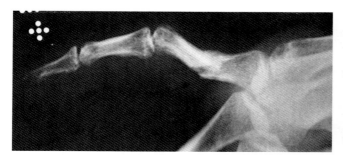

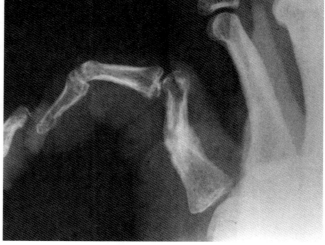

FIGURE 28-106 Malunion of proximal phalanx fractures is typically apex volar with a compensatory loss of extension at the proximal interphalangeal joint correctable only with osteotomy.

ing the hypersensitivity. Some areas are at higher risk than others. Neuroma formation through direct injury or nerve encasement in postoperative scar should be guarded against when one is operating along the ulnar side of the thumb MP joint with its high concentration of small dorsal digital nerve branches and at the radial side of the wrist near the superficial radial nerve. Treatment is based on a combination of specific medications designed to reduce nerve pain such as gabapentin, amitriptyline, or pregabalin and a progressive contact desensitization therapy program. Gentle surface contact essentially trains the sensitive nerve fibers to tolerate that level of stimulation before then progressing to more intense stimulation. Eventually, the patient works his or her way up to normal use of the hand over a period of weeks. In the meantime, overstimulation of the nerve pain by traction and motion must be avoided even if this means slower progress in the motion program. Failure to heed this principle will result in progression from straightforward hypersensitivity to complex regional pain syndromes and a downward spiral of worsening pain and function that far exceeds the simple early reduction in motion.

Malunion and Deformity

Malunion is a frequently encountered complication in hand fractures owing to a lack of understanding regarding hand biomechanics, to an unfounded belief that all hand fractures do well with nonoperative treatment, or to a noncompliant patient. Malunions are managed with corrective osteotomy. Each aspect of the deformity must be well understood from angular to rotational to length considerations. The decision is whether to place the osteotomy at the site of original deformity or to make a compensatory osteotomy that produces reciprocal deformities. Fundamentally, it is best to make the correction at the site of the original deformity. The problem is hardware interference with soft tissues. The plate and screws usually necessary to stabilize the correction may not fit well at the site of original deformity. Another consideration is the healing potential of metaphyseal as compared with diaphyseal regions particularly if the diaphyseal bone has been stripped of its blood supply during prior procedures. A popular location for rotational corrections in particular is the metacarpal base for the above reasons.

Sagittal plane malunion of the proximal phalanx with the apex volar usually occurs because of failure to splint the hand in the position of full MP flexion that will correct the dynamic imbalance across the fracture site (Fig. 28-106). Rotational malunion is usually the result of improper choice of nonoperative treatment when direct fixation was needed to control rotation. Spiral fractures are difficult to correctly reduce closed, and rotational malunions can easily result from CRIF especially at the level of the proximal phalanx. Using nail plate alignment is an inadequate method of assessing rotation, which should be judged by parallelism of the short tubular bone segment distal to the injured one with the intervening joint flexed to 90 degrees. Corrective osteotomy is more successful at the metacarpal level than the phalangeal level[61] (Fig. 28-107). Correction of a sagittal plane or multidirectional malunion is best accomplished at the site of the original fracture.[98,161] Significant stiffness often accompanies the malunion. A concomitant tenocapsulolysis can be performed if rigid fixation of the osteotomy is achieved. The alternative is to break the solution down into two parts: stage 1 achieves correction of the skeletal deformity through osteotomy, and stage 2 improves motion through tenocapsulolysis. These patients achieve the greatest gains in motion even though the measured final range may be less than that of other patients with less severe injuries.[18,159] Tenolysis alone improves extensor lag, but when a dorsal capsulotomy is required to regain flexion, the lag may actually increase. For mild to moderate malunions, a realistic assessment regarding the expected improvement in function must be weighed carefully against the predicted degree of digital stiffness created by the osteotomy procedure itself and the hardware used.[163,178] Intra-articular osteotomy is an extremely demanding undertaking and should be restricted to carefully selected patients (Fig. 28-108). Five patients undergoing extra-articular osteotomy for malunited unicondylar fractures of the proximal phalanx saw an increase in average PIP motion from 40 degrees preoperative to 86 degrees postoperative.[71] Surgery may be performed as late as several months after the initial injury through the original fracture plane.

Malunion of a metacarpal fracture usually presents as an apex dorsal sagittal plane deformity. Patients may complain of the cosmetic deformity, pain at the dorsal prominence, or grip

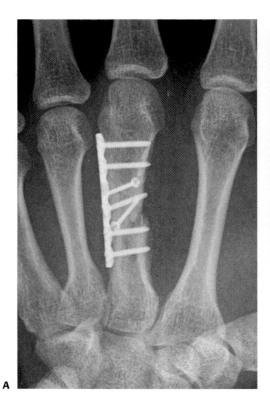

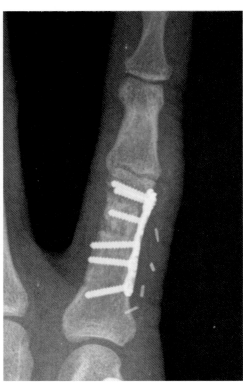

A

B

FIGURE 28-107 Corrective osteotomy often requires prolonged healing and bone graft and is best supported by a laterally placed locking plate at both the (**A**) metacarpal and (**B**) phalangeal level.

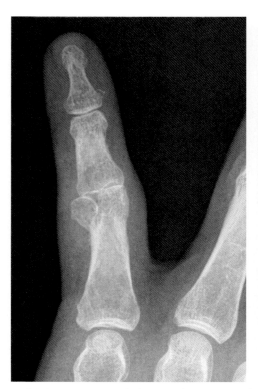

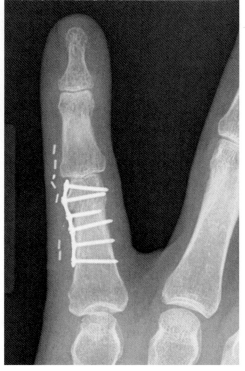

FIGURE 28-108 Intra-articular corrective osteotomy is a demanding undertaking but can produce excellent results when precise attention is given to restoring articular congruence.

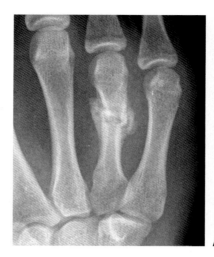
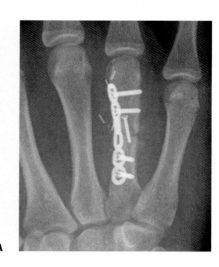

FIGURE 28-109 Nascent malunions that have healed by callus but where the original fracture plane can be cut with an osteotome by hand rather than a saw (**A**) are excellent opportunities to achieve a true anatomic restoration as opposed to a close approximation (**B**).

discomfort with a prominent metacarpal head in the palm. Patients should be counseled to evaluate their deformity and decide if their dissatisfaction is sufficient to warrant undergoing corrective osteotomy. The osteotomy should be delayed until tissue homeostasis has been achieved unless an opportunity for early intervention (less than 6 weeks) exists (Fig. 28-109). Correction is best achieved through the site of the original fracture with rigid internal fixation followed by immediate motion. In choosing between opening wedge, closing wedge, pivot osteotomy, or oblique osteotomy, the exact pattern of deformity needs to be assessed and the osteotomy designed to most closely restore normal anatomy. This will demand a different cut for each patient, but the simpler the intended osteotomy, the more likely it is that the surgeon can achieve a good result. Shortening must be considered if a closing wedge is planned. An extensor lag at the MP joint of 7 degrees can be predicted for every 2 mm of shortening.[148] Rotational malunion in a metacarpal may also occur, causing digital overlap. Osteotomy can be performed at the site of original injury or at the metacarpal base. Rotational osteotomy performed at the base of the metacarpal offers broader cancellous surfaces for healing and can correct up to 25 to 30 degrees of rotation. If the plane of deformity is more complex than pure rotation, it may be wiser to attempt multiplanar correction through the original fracture site.

Intra-articular osteotomy at the metacarpal head has infrequent indications, as correction of an intra-articular malunion is extremely difficult. In long-term follow-up, intra-articular malunion at the metacarpal base leads to osteoarthritis (65%), decreased grip (49%), and pain (38%).[89] Arthrodesis is the preferred solution for these problems, even for the fifth metacarpal. It reliably improves grip strength with the elimination of pain. Compensatory triquetrohamate motion may alleviate the effect of arthrodesis on the mobility of the ulnar side of the hand.

Nonunion

Nonunion is a rare complication in hand fractures with the exception of distal phalanx fractures, when CRIF has caused distraction, or in fractures treated with ORIF where excessive periosteal stripping has occurred. Nonunions are treated no differently than anywhere else in the body. Hypertrophic nonunions may be addressed by compression alone using a dynamic compression plate. Nonunions with bone loss or inadequate vascular supply require supplementary bone grafting in addition to stable fixation. Tuft fractures of the distal phalanx rarely achieve osseous union, going on instead to fibrous union. Transverse shaft fractures of the distal phalanx left without support too early may result in an apex volar malunion or nonunion after being repeatedly subjected to pinch forces. Microsized headless variable pitch compression screws are now available to treat P3 shaft nonunions, but caution is still required in assessing the relationship of the screw to the sagittal plane dimension of P3, risking both fracture extension and damage to the overlying nail apparatus[171] (Fig. 28-110). Four nonunions were seen in a series of 52 unstable hand fractures, of which 61.5% were open.[24] A treatment for phalangeal nonunion consisting of a Herbert screw placed through the distal joint has been proposed based on the results in four patients.[171] If no bone loss is present, simple compression across a hypertrophic nonunion site with a short plate should be sufficient to achieve healing. If bone loss is present, a longer plate and corticocancellous or cancellous bone graft may be required. Osteonecrosis of the metacarpal head remains a concern in periarticular fractures that may lack an independent blood supply.

Residual Instability

Residual instability following dislocation is rare distally but more common proximally. All five carpometacarpal joints are quite subject to recurrent instability particularly with pure dislocation patterns rather than fracture-dislocations. The reason is that in pure dislocation, all the ligaments are ruptured and require ligament-to-bone or ligament-to-ligament healing. Fracture-dislocations usually occur with one or more key stabilizing ligaments remaining attached to the smaller fragment that remains at the joint while the larger articular fragment dislocates. If properly reduced and stabilized, bone-to-bone healing will restore joint stability. In one series, redislocation occurred in 6 of 56 dorsal fracture-dislocations of the PIP joint.[34] Chronic instability following closed treatment of a complete MP joint radial collateral ligament injury may need to be treated surgically. A small population of patients exists with chronic hyperextension laxity at the thumb MP joint that may be either passive (volar plate only) or active (involving the intrinsics) and may in a few instances require surgical advancement of the volar

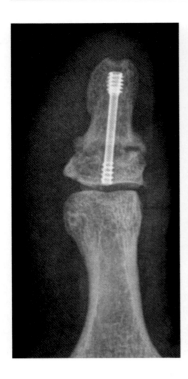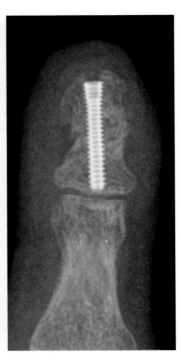

FIGURE 28-110 Nonunions of the distal phalanx shaft can be managed by adding compression across the nonunion site with a headless variable-pitch cannulated microscrew; healing is prolonged.

plate for reconstruction and restoration of stability. Late symptomatic (painful) instability after finger CMC fracture-dislocation can be evaluated with lidocaine injection into the joint. If relief is provided, arthrodesis is a reliable way to eliminate the pain. The fifth CMC joint may be fused in 20 to 30 degrees of flexion with little long-term loss of hand motion, apparently through increased compensatory triquetrohamate motion. Thumb CMC painful residual instability is treated by ligament reconstruction rather than arthrodesis.

Posttraumatic Arthritis

As in other locations throughout the body, intra-articular fractures and residual joint instability may cause accelerated hyaline cartilage wear and lead to posttraumatic arthritis. A poor correlation exists between the radiographic appearance of posttraumatic arthritis and clinical loss of function and pain. Patients should be managed for the arthritis on the basis of clinical deficits and not based on radiographic abnormality. Posttraumatic arthritis of the thumb MP joint can be successfully managed by arthrodesis with excellent overall hand function. Few other joints in the hand can be fused with so little impact on function (index and long finger CMC joints). Finger MP and PIP joint fusions result in tremendous loss of function.

Hardware Complications

Kirschner wires are appropriate tools for performing internal fixation of hand fractures and occasionally for stabilizing dislocations, but they can demonstrate complication rates as high as 15%.[144] Pin tract infections are the most common complication seen. Infections used to be rare when pins were left in for less than 4 weeks and usually responded well to removal of the pin and administration of oral antibiotics. With the increasing prevalence of MRSA in the community, that no longer seems to be true, and pins may be more safely cut below the skin level. Another hardware complication is simply irritation of adjacent

tissues such as overlying tendons by the presence of prominent hardware. Given the delicate and thin tissues of the hand, even implants measuring several millimeters thick are enough to produce persistent symptoms for many patients. In one series, 7 of 57 patients required plate removal.[117] Another series reported a complication rate of 82% following plate fixation for phalangeal fractures compared with 31% for metacarpal plates.[160] A unique concern with plates, however, is the potential for delayed or nonunion in transverse metacarpal fractures (30%) as opposed to fracture sites with a broader interface (7%).[55]

Tendon Rupture

Tendon ruptures can occur in association with dislocations of the joint adjacent to the site of tendon insertion. Failure to recognize this associated injury may occur with an inadequate examination. The consequence is usually a deformity posture such as mallet finger at the DIP joint or a Boutonniere deformity at the PIP joint. Open reconstructions of chronic terminal tendon ruptures with either local tissues or free tendon grafts have not proven particularly successful. For disabling terminal tendon deficiencies in a high angle of flexion, arthrodesis of the DIP joint is a permanent and durable solution to the problem. The loss of motion associated with arthrodesis is not as well tolerated at the PIP joint where every effort should be made to restore active extension. Mild deformities especially when identified reasonably early may respond to a program of PIP extension splinting and DIP joint flexion exercises. Success is dependent on the natural tendency of collagen-based scar to contract. For more substantial deficiencies, surgical reconstruction with local tissues or a free tendon graft may be required once passive motion has first been regained through either rehabilitation or a previously staged surgical capsulectomy.

Nail Matrix

Nail deformities can occur when a crush mechanism of injury includes the zone of the nail or when fixation hardware damages the delicate matrix tissues. Temporary or permanent passage of fixation devices through the region of the germinal matrix should be avoided, and sterile matrix penetration should be either temporary or by suture material. A rare but troublesome complication is entrapment of the germinal matrix in a transverse fracture gap (which can occur with a reasonably normal external appearance of the digit) that both prevents fracture healing and results in permanent nail deformity.

CONTROVERSIES AND FUTURE DIRECTIONS

Decision Making

There is not a great deal of controversy surrounding the technical methods of reduction and fixation for fractures and dislocations of the hand. Controversy is much greater when it comes to deciding how specific fractures and dislocations should be managed. Most surgeons understand and accept the basic principle that the least invasive method should be used that will result in stable, anatomically correct healing and still permit enough motion rehabilitation to achieve a useful and functional final result. The problem lies in the fact that the data simply do not exist anywhere in the published literature to definitively link specific treatment strategies to the many different fracture patterns that exist. Each of the various small bones in the hand (P3, P2, P1, metacarpal) responds to treatment differently. There are numerous varieties of just the fracture pattern alone in each of these bones, not to mention the associated soft tissue injuries that impact final outcome substantially. No study has used rigorous enough statistics to separate all the groups and stratify the results. The same holds true for dislocations.

The area where decision-making becomes particularly difficult is that of coordinating more complex reconstructions that involve multiple tissues. When the original management of skeletal trauma to the hand yields unsatisfactory results, secondary surgery may be required. The timing and order of events are very much a matter of individual surgeon experience and preference. The foundation for good hand function is a stable inner skeletal structure and a well-vascularized and supple outer envelope of integument. These are the first steps to be accomplished in any reconstruction. The next step is to ensure passively supple joints that are also stable. This infrastructure is then powered by three groups of tendons responsible for active motion in the hand: the extrinsic extensors, the extrinsic flexors, and the intrinsics. Good motion facilitates interaction with the environment, a function that also requires sensibility. Reconstructive surgery of nerves is well timed to coincide with tendon procedures. Three stages have been outlined here, but this does not necessarily mean that three distinct surgical procedures are required. Judging which combinations of procedures will yield the best results is the province of an experienced revision hand surgeon. In general, procedures that require the same type of rehabilitation may be combined, whereas those that have disparate therapy goals should be separated as distinct surgical events. When a series of surgical procedures is staged, tissue homeostasis after the former procedure should be achieved before executing the subsequent procedure.

Posttraumatic Arthritis

The only alternative to arthrodesis apart from microvascular whole joint transfer was previously implantation of a Swanson-type one piece silicone prosthesis with the attendant high rates of prosthetic fracture and generation of silicone debris leading to osteolysis. Since earlier editions of this text, new prosthetic implants have become available for total joint replacement of the MP and PIP joints. There are models with metal on polyethylene bearing surfaces as well as pyrolytic carbon-bearing surfaces. Rates of loosening, osteolysis from debris, and prosthetic breakage will determine if these models offer a new opportunity for improved hand motion and function to those with posttraumatic arthritis in the MP and PIP joints.

Managing Skeletal Loss

Skeletal loss can occur at either periarticular locations or in the diaphysis. Diaphyseal loss is by far the more straightforward issue. Current controversies relate to the choice of purely cancellous graft with bridge plating as opposed to corticocancellous grafts. Additional controversy exists regarding the timing of bone grafting for open fractures. The traditions have been corticocancellous grafts with delay. New trends are for immediate grafting after extensive debridement and using purely cancellous graft.[144] Osteoarticular defects can be replaced with nonvascularized osteoarticular autografts as long as the defect only involves at most one half of a joint.[87] Partial toe joint osteochondral grafts to the PIP joint of the hand resulted in significant motion loss in three of five cases and resorption in one.[57] The most common sites requiring partial osteoarticular grafts are single condyles at the head of P1 and the volar base of the middle phalanx. Toe PIP joints provide well-matched condyle donor sites. The dorsal portion of the hamate provides an excellent donor site for the volar base of the middle phalanx. Nonvascularized whole joint transfers have been unsuccessful. If an entire joint requires autogenous replacement, a vascularized whole joint transfer from the foot is required. Unique cases offer the opportunity to create a pedicled, vascularized whole joint transfer from one unsalvageable digit to an adjacent digit.

Associated Wounds

Achieving stable wound coverage is a prerequisite to any other reconstruction. It is often performed at the same time as skeletal reconstruction and should be performed before most other reconstructions except first-stage tendon grafting. Methods of wound reconstruction include primary closure, secondary closure, split- or full-thickness skin grafts, transposition flaps, pedicle flaps, and free flaps. The simplest strategy that provides for optimum gliding of subjacent structures without contracture formation should be chosen. The challenge for more complex wounds that require flap reconstruction in the hand is finding tissue that is both supple and thin. Current trends are for earlier applications (within 72 hours) of increasingly thinner flaps. A useful strategy involves fascial flaps that are covered with split-thickness skin grafts. The lateral arm flap inverted to orient the muscular surface to receive the skin graft has performed particularly well in this respect.[76] The fascia overlying the serratus anterior is thin with a reliable, large, and long pedicle. One criticism of skin-grafted fascial flaps is that they are slightly more difficult to operate through at the time of further revision compared with cutaneous flaps. The current trend in microsurgery for perforator flaps has spawned a number of cutaneous flaps thin enough for use around the hand, wrist, and forearm but not the digits.

Bioabsorbable Implants

A polylactic acid plate and screw system tested in vitro showed maintenance of strength for 8 weeks comparable to titanium but then degraded with loss of strength over 12 weeks under four-point bending stress.[13] Testing in 112 fresh-frozen cadavers of 2-mm poly-L/DL-lactide plates demonstrated an overall stability comparable to that of 1.7-mm titanium plates. There have been studies such as these in the literature,[168,169] but the regular use of bioabsorbable implants in the hand simply has not caught on clinically. One concern may be reports of sterile abscess formation around implants of the same materials used in other orthopaedic applications. The soft tissues of the hand have little tolerance for any process that might cause additional inflammation at the site of skeletal trauma.[38] At the same time, there is no doubt that the physical presence of a plate (even when 1.3 to 2.0 mm in thickness) along the surface of a short tubular bone can create significant problems for tendon adherence and obstructed motion. Since the last edition of this text, there has been no apparent advance toward greater use of bioabsorbable implants for hand fractures.

SUMMARY

Fractures and dislocations of the hand represent a diverse group of injuries that share a common theme in management. The hand is a delicate organ that requires both stability and flexibility; function follows form. Although rough guidelines can be drawn from the published literature, it remains the responsibility of individual surgeons to judge which fractures and dislocations can be managed by each of the various methods discussed in this chapter. There are three basic treatment options for most fractures and dislocations of the hand: splinting, CRIF, and ORIF. Many fractures and the majority of dislocations of the hand have enough inherent stability to be managed nonoperatively. Testing for inherent stability in the office setting using active motion under the protection of injectable anesthetics should demonstrate those fractures and dislocations that can safely be managed without surgery. Malrotated, multiple, high-energy, and open fractures are usually treated operatively. CMC dislocations and fracture-dislocations (unlike MP and PIP joint injuries) are usually treated operatively. The majority of operatively treated hand fractures and dislocations are closed and isolated injuries for which CRIF is usually an appropriate method. The exceptions to this are noted throughout the chapter. A few select injury patterns such as intra-articular P2 base fractures have specific and unique treatments that must be remembered and used according to the indications described. Once underway with treatment, one should stay focused on edema control and promoting early motion. The final steps to a successful outcome lie in avoiding complications such as nerve hypersensitivity and pin tract infections. When complications do occur, the key is in planning a well-thought-out correction in terms of risk-benefit analysis and staging. Finally, patients should be counseled regarding expectations, which are that fractures and dislocations of the hand produce swelling, stiffness, and aching that frequently takes more than 1 year to overcome.

REFERENCES

1. Abrahamson S-O, Sollerman C, Lundborg G, et al. Diagnosis of displaced ulnar collateral ligament of the metacarpophalangeal joint of the thumb. J Hand Surg 1990;15A:457–460.
2. Aladin A, Davis TRC. Dorsal fracture-dislocation of the proximal interphalangeal joint: a comparative study of percutaneous Kirschner wire fixation versus open reduction and internal fixation. J Hand Surg 2005;30B:120–128.
3. Ali A, Hamman J, Mass DP. The biomechanical effects of angulated boxer's fractures. J Hand Surg 1999;24:835–844.
4. Al-Qattan. Extra-articular transverse fractures of the base of the distal phalanx (Seymour's fracture) in children and adults. J Hand Surg 2001;26B:201–206.
5. Al-Qattan MM, Hashem F, Helmi A. Irreducible tuft fractures of the distal phalanx. J Hand Surg 2003;28B:18–20.
6. Arai K, Toh S, Nakahara K, et al. Treatment of soft tissue injuries to the dorsum of the metacarpophalangeal joint (Boxer's knuckle). J Hand Surg 2002;27B:90–95.
7. Bach HG, Gonzales MH, Hall Jr RF. Locked intramedullary nailing of metacarpal fractures secondary to gunshot wounds. J Hand Surg 2006;31A:1083–1087.
8. Badia A, Riano F, Ravikoff J, et al. Dynamic intradigital external fixation for proximal interphalangeal joint fracture dislocations. J Hand Surg 2005;30A:154–160.
9. Bean CHG, Tencer AF, Trumble TE. The effect of thumb metacarpophalangeal ulnar collateral ligament attachment site on joint range of motion: an in vitro study. J Hand Surg 1999;24:283–287.
10. Bettinger PC, Linscheid RL, Berger RA, et al. An anatomic study of the stabilizing ligaments of the trapezium and trapeziometacarpal joint. J Hand Surg 1999;24:786–798.
11. Bickley BT, Hanel DP. Self-tapping versus standard tapped titanium screw fixation in the upper extremity. J Hand Surg 1998;23A:308–311.
12. Birndorf MS, Daley R, Greenwald DP. Metacarpal fracture angulation decreases flexor mechanical efficiency in human hands. Plast Reconstr Surg 1997;99:1079–1083.
13. Bozic KJ, Perez LE, Wilson DR, et al. Mechanical testing of bioresorbable implants for use in metacarpal fracture fixation. J Hand Surg 2001;26:755–761.
14. Braakman M. Functional taping of fractures of the fifth metacarpal results in a quicker recovery. Injury 1998;29:5–9.
15. Brennwald J. Fracture healing in the hand. A brief update. Clin Orthop 1996;327:9–11.
16. Bruske J, Bednarski M, Niedzwiedz Z, et al. The results of operative treatment of fractures of the thumb metacarpal base. Acta Orthop Belg 2001;67:368–373.
17. Buchanan RT. Mechanical requirements for application and modification of the dynamic force couple method. Hand Clin 1994;10:221–228.
18. Buchler U, Gupta A, Ruf S. Corrective osteotomy for posttraumatic malunion of the phalanges of the hand. J Hand Surg 1996;21B:33–42.
19. Buchler U, McCollam SM, Oppikofer C. Comminuted fractures of the basilar joint of thumb: combined treatment by external fixation, limited internal fixation, and bone grafting. J Hand Surg 1991;16A:556–560.
20. Cannon NM. Rehabilitation approaches for distal and middle phalanx fractures of the hand. J Hand Ther 2003;16:105–116.
21. Chen SH, Wei FC, Chen HC, et al. Miniature plates and screws in acute complex hand injury. J Trauma 1994;37:237–242.
22. Chin KR, Jupiter JB. Treatment of triplane fractures of the head of the proximal phalanx. J Hand Surg 1999;24:1263–1268.
23. Chinchalkar SJ, Gan BS. Management of proximal interphalangeal joint fractures and dislocations. J Hand Ther 2003;16:117–128.
24. Chow SP, Pun WK, So YC, et al. A prospective study of 245 open digital fractures of the hand. J Hand Surg 1991;16B:137–140.
25. Chung KC, Spilson SV. The frequency and epidemiology of hand and forearm fractures in the United States. J Hand Surg 2001;26:908–915.
26. Coyle MP. Grade III radial collateral ligament injuries of the thumb metacarpophalangeal joint: treatment by soft tissue advancement and bony reattachment. J Hand Surg 2003;28:14–20.
27. Crofoot CD, Saing M, Raphael J. Intrafocal pinning for juxta-articular phalanx fractures. Tech Hand Up Extrem Surg 2005;9:169–171.
28. Crosby CA, Wehbe MA. Early motion protocols in hand and wrist rehabilitation. Hand Clin 1996;12:31–41.
29. Curtin CM, Chung KC. Use of eight-hole titanium miniplates for unstable phalangeal fractures. Ann Plast Surg 2002;49:580–586.
30. Debnath UK, Nassab RS, Oni JA, et al. A prospective study of the treatment of fractures of the little finger metacarpal shaft with a short hand cast. J Hand Surg 2004;29B:214–217.
31. Delaere OP, Suttor PM, Degolla R, et al. Early surgical treatment for collateral ligament rupture of metacarpophalangeal joints of the fingers. J Hand Surg 2003;28:309–315.
32. Del Pinal F, Garcia-Bernal FJ, Delgado J, et al. Results of osteotomy, open reduction, and internal fixation for late-presenting malunited intra-articular fractures of the base of the middle phalanx. J Hand Surg 2005;30A:1039e1–e14.
33. Diao E, Eaton RG. Total collateral ligament excision for contractures of the proximal interphalangeal joint. J Hand Surg 1993;18A:395–402.
34. Dietch MA, Kiefhaber TR, Comisar R, et al. Dorsal fracture dislocations of the proximal interphalangeal joint: surgical complications and long-term results. J Hand Surg 1999;24:914–923.
35. Dinowitz M, Trumble T, Hanel D, et al. Failure of cast immobilization for thumb ulnar collateral ligament avulsion fractures. J Hand Surg 1997;22A:1057–1063.
36. Dionysian E, Eaton RG. The long-term outcome of volar plate arthroplasty of the proximal interphalangeal joint. J Hand Surg 2000;25:429–437.
37. Drenth DJ, Klasen HJ. External fixation for phalangeal and metacarpal fractures. J Bone Joint Surg 1998;80B:227–230.
38. Dumont C, Fuchs M, Burchhardt H, et al. Clinical results of absorbable plates for displaced metacarpal fractures. J Hand Surg 2007;32A:491–496.
39. Duncan RW, Freeland AE, Jabaley ME, et al. Open hand fractures: an analysis of the recovery of active motion and of complications. J Hand Surg 1993;18A:387–394.
40. Dzwierzynski WW, Matloub HS, Yan J-G, et al. Anatomy of the intermetacarpal ligaments of the carpometacarpal joints of the fingers. J Hand Surg 1997;22:931–934.

41. Ebinger T, Erhard N, Kinzl L, et al. Dynamic treatment of displaced proximal phalangeal fractures. J Hand Surg 1999;24:1254–1262.
42. Ellis SJ, Cheng R, Prokopis P, et al. Treatment of proximal interphalangeal dorsal fracture-dislocation injuries with dynamic external fixation: a pins and rubber band system. J Hand Surg 2007;32A:1242–1250.
43. Elmaraghy MW, Elmaraghy AW, Richards RS, et al. Transmetacarpal intramedullary K-wire fixation of proximal phalangeal fractures. Ann Plast Surg 1998;41:125–130.
44. El-shennawy M, Nakamura K, Patterson RM, et al. Three-dimensional kinematic analysis of the second through fifth carpometacarpal joints. J Hand Surg 2001;26: 1030–1035.
45. Fahmy N, Khan W. The S-Quattro in the management of acute intra-articular phalangeal fractures of the hand. J Hand Surg 2006;31:79–92.
46. Failla JM. Irreducible thumb interphalangeal joint dislocation due to a sesamoid and palmar plate: a case report. J Hand Surg 1995;20:490–491.
47. Fairhurst M, Hansen L. Treatment of "gamekeeper's thumb" by reconstruction of the ulnar collateral ligament. J Hand Surg 2003;27B:542–545.
48. Feehan LM, Sheps SB. Incidence and demographics of hand fractures in British Columbia, Canada: a population-based study. J Hand Surg 2006;31A:1068–1074.
49. Firoozbakhsh KK, Moneim MS, Howey T, et al. Comparative fatigue strengths and stabilities of metacarpal internal fixation techniques. J Hand Surg 1993;18A: 1059–1068.
50. Fischer KJ, Bastidas JA, Provenzano DA, et al. Low-profile versus conventional metacarpal plating systems: a comparison of construct stiffness and strength. J Hand Surg 1999;24:928–934.
51. Foster RJ. Stabilization of ulnar CMC dislocations or fracture-dislocations. Clin Orthop 1996;327:94–97.
52. Foucher G. "Bouquet" osteosynthesis in metacarpal neck fractures: a series of 66 patients. J Hand Surg 1995;20A:s86–s90.
53. Freeland AE, Hardy MA, Singletary S. Rehabilitation for proximal phalangeal fractures. J Hand Ther 2003;16:129–142.
54. Freeland AE, Lineaweaver WC, Lindley SG. Fracture fixation in the mutilated hand. Hand Clin 2003;19:51–61.
55. Fusetti C, Della Santa DR. Influence of fracture pattern on consolidation after metacarpal plate fixation. Chir Main 2004;23:32–36.
56. Galanakis I, Aliquizakis A, Katonis P, et al. Treatment of closed unstable metacarpal fractures using percutaneous transverse fixation with Kirschner wires. J Trauma 2003; 55:509–513.
57. Gaul JS. Articular fractures of the proximal interphalangeal joint with missing elements: repair with partial toe joint osteochondral autografts. J Hand Surg 1999;24:78–85.
58. Geissler WB. Cannulated percutaneous fixation of intra-articular hand fractures. Hand Clin 2006;22:297–305.
59. Giele H, Martin J. The two-level ulnar collateral ligament injury of the metacarpophalangeal joint of the thumb. J Hand Surg 2003;28B:92–93.
60. Glickel SZ, Malerich M, Pearce SM, et al. Ligament replacement for chronic instability of the ulnar collateral ligament of the metacarpophalangeal joint of the thumb. J Hand Surg 1993;18A:930–941.
61. Gollamudi S, Jones WA. Corrective osteotomy of malunited fractures of phalanges and metacarpals. J Hand Surg 2000;25B:439–441.
62. Gonzales MH, Hall M, Hall RF Jr. Low-velocity gunshot wounds of the proximal phalanx: treatment by early stable fixation. J Hand Surg 1998;23A:142–149.
63. Gonzalez MH, Ingram CM, Hall RF. Flexible intramedullary nailing for metacarpal fractures. J Hand Surg 1995;20:382–387.
64. Gonzales MH. Intramedullary fixation of metacarpal and proximal phalangeal fractures of the hand. Clin Orthop 1996;327:47–54.
65. Graham TJ. The exploded hand syndrome: logical evaluation and comprehensive treatment of the severely crushed hand. J Hand Surg 2006;31A:1012–1023.
66. Grant I, Berger AC, Tham SK. Internal fixation of unstable fracture dislocations of the proximal interphalangeal joint. J Hand Surg 2005;30:492–498.
67. Hamada Y, Sairyo K, Tonogai I, et al. Irreducible fracture dislocation of a finger metacarpophalangeal joint: A case report. Hand 2008;3:76–78.
68. Hamilton SC, Stern PJ, Fassler PR, et al. Miniscrew fixation for the treatment of proximal interphalangeal joint dorsal fracture-dislocations. J Hand Surg 2006;31A: 1349–1354.
69. Hanel DP. Primary fusion of fracture dislocations of central carpometacarpal joints. Clin Orthop 1996;327:85–93.
70. Harding IJ, Parry D, Barrington RL. The use of a moulded metacarpal brace versus neighbour strapping for fractures of the finger metacarpal neck. J Hand Surg 2001; 26B:261–263.
71. Harness NG, Chen A, Jupiter JB. Extra-articular osteotomy for malunited unicondylar fractures of the proximal phalanx. J Hand Surg 2005;30A: 566–572.
72. Hattori Y, Doi K, Sakamoto S, et al. Volar plating for intra-articular fracture of the base of the proximal phalanx. J Hand Surg 2007;32A:1299–1303.
73. Henry MH. Soft tissue sleeve approach to open reduction and internal fixation of proximal phalangeal fractures. Tech Hand Up Extr Surg 2008;12.
74. Henry MH. Fractures of the proximal phalanx and metacarpals in the hand: preferred methods of stabilization. J Am Acad Orthop Surg 2008;16.
75. Henry MH. Specific complications associated with different types of intrinsic pedicle flaps of the hand. J Reconstr Microsurg 2008;24.
76. Henry MH. Degloving combined with structural trauma at the digital level: functional coverage with fascial free flaps. J Reconstr Microsurg 2007;23:59–62.
77. Henry MH, Stutz C, Brown H. Technique for extensor tendon acceleration. J Hand Ther 2006;19:421–424.
78. Hinke DH, Erickson SJ, Chamoy L, et al. Ulnar collateral ligament of the thumb: MR findings in cadavers, volunteers, and patients with ligamentous injury (gamekeeper's thumb). AJR Am J Roentgenol 1994;163:1431–1434.
79. Hirata H, Tsujii M, Nakao E. Locking of the metacarpophalangeal joint of the thumb caused by a fracture fragment of the radial condyle of the metacarpal head after dorsal dislocation. J Hand Surg 2006;31B:635–636.
80. Hofmeister EP, Mazurek MT, Shin AY, et al. Extension block pinning for large mallet fractures. J Hand Surg 2003;28:453–459.
81. Hornbach EE, Cohen MS. Closed reduction and percutaneous pinning of fractures of the proximal phalanx. J Hand Surg 2003;26B:45–49.
82. Horton TC, Hatton M, Davis TRC. A prospective randomized controlled study of fixation of long oblique and spiral shaft fractures of the proximal phalanx: closed reduction and percutaneous Kirschner wiring versus open reduction and lag screw fixation. J Hand Surg 2003;28B:5–9.
83. Hughes LA, Freiberg A. Irreducible MP joint dislocation due to entrapment of FPL. J Hand Surg 1993;18B:708–709.
84. Husain SN, Dietz JF, Kalainov DM, et al. A biomechanical study of distal interphalangeal joint subluxation after mallet fracture injury. J Hand Surg 2008;33:26–30.
85. Hynes MC, Giddins GEB. Dynamic external fixation for pilon fractures of the interphalangeal joints. J Hand Surg 2001;26B:122–124.
86. Ip WY, Ng KH, Chow SP. A prospective study of 924 digital fractures of the hand. Injury 1996;27:279–285.
87. Ishida O, Ikuta Y, Kuroki H. Ipsilateral osteochondral grafting for finger joint repair. J Hand Surg 1994;19:372–377.
88. Kaleli T, Ozturk C, Ersozlu S. External fixation for surgical treatment of a mallet finger. J Hand Surg 2003;28B:228–230.
89. Kjaer-Peterson K, Jurik AG, Peterson LK. Intraarticular fractures at the base of the fifth metacarpal. A clinical and radiographic study of 64 cases. J Hand Surg 1992;17B: 144–147.
90. Kjaer-Peterson K, Langoff O, Andersen K. Bennett fracture. J Hand Surg 1990;15B: 58–61.
91. Kozin SH, Thoder JJ, Lieberman G. Operative treatment of metacarpal and phalangeal shaft fractures. J Am Acad Orthop Surg 2000;8:111–121.
92. Kuhn KM, Khiem DD, Shin AY. Volar A1 pulley approach for the fixation of avulsion fractures of the base of the proximal phalanx. J Hand Surg 2001;26:762–771.
93. Kumar R, Malhotra R. Divergent fracture-dislocation of the second carpometacarpal joint and the three ulnar carpometacarpal joints. J Hand Surg 2001;26:123–129.
94. Kurzen P, Fusetti C, Bonaccio M, et al. Complications after plate fixation of phalangeal fractures. J Trauma 2006;60:841–384.
95. Kuz JE, Husband JB, Tokar N, et al. Outcome of avulsion fractures of the ulnar base of the proximal phalanx of the thumb treated nonsurgically. J Hand Surg 1999;24: 275–282.
96. Lee JYL, Teoh LC. Dorsal fracture dislocations of the proximal interphalangeal joint treated by open reduction and interfragmentary screw fixation: indications, approaches, and results. J Hand Surg 2006;31B:138–146.
97. Lee SG, Jupiter JB. Phalangeal and metacarpal fractures of the hand. Hand Clin 2000; 16:323–332.
98. Lester B, Mallik A. Impending malunions of the hand. Treatment of subacute, malaligned fractures. Clin Orthop 1996;327:55–62.
99. Leung YL, Beredjiklian PK, Monaghan BA, Bozentka DJ. Radiographic assessment of small finger metacarpal neck fractures. J Hand Surg 2002;27:443–448.
100. Levaro F, Henry MH. Management of the stiff proximal interphalangeal joint. J Am Soc Surg Hand 2003;3:78–87.
101. Liebovic SJ. Treatment of Bennett and Rolando fractures. Tech Hand Upper Ext Surg 1998;2:36–46.
102. Liew KH, Chan BK, Low CO. Metacarpal and proximal phalangeal fractures-fixation with multiple intramedullary Kirschner wires. Hand Surg 2000;5:125–130.
103. Lins RE. A comparative mechanical analysis of plate fixation in a proximal phalanx fracture model. J Hand Surg 1996;21A:1059–1064.
104. Lubahn JD, Hood JM. Fractures of the distal interphalangeal joint. Clin Orthop 1996; 327:12–20.
105. Lutz M, Sailer R, Zimmerman R, et al. Closed reduction transarticular Kirshner wire fixation versus open reduction internal fixation in the treatment of Bennett fracture dislocation. J Hand Surg 2003;28B:142–147.
106. Majumder S, Peck F, Watson JS, et al. Lessons learned from the management of complex intra-articular fractures at the base of the middle phalanges of fingers. J Hand Surg 2003;28B:559–565.
107. Manueddu CA, Della-Santa D. Fasciculated intramedullary pinning of metacarpal fractures. J Hand Surg 1996;21B:230–236.
108. Margic K. External fixation of closed metacarpal and phalangeal fractures of digits. A prospective study of 100 consecutive patients. J Hand Surg 2006;31B:30–40.
109. Margles SW. Early motion in the treatment of fractures and dislocations in the hand and wrist. Hand Clin 1996;12:65–72.
110. Matloub HS, Jensen PL, Sanger JR, et al. Spiral fracture fixation techniques. A biomechanical study. J Hand Surg 1993;18B:515–519.
111. McLain RF, Steyers C, Stoddard M. Infections in open fractures of the hand. J Hand Surg 1991;16A:108–112.
112. McNemar TB, Howell JW, Chang E. Management of metacarpal fractures. J Hand Ther 2003;16:143–151.
113. Murase T, Morimoto H, Yoshikawa H. Palmar dislocation of the metacarpophalangeal joint of the finger. J Hand Surg 2004;29B: 90–93.
114. Nakamura K, Patterson RM, Viegas SF. The ligament and skeletal anatomy of the second through fifth carpometacarpal joints and adjacent structures. J Hand Surg 2001;26: 1016–1029.
115. Newington DP, Davis TRC, Barton NJ. The treatment of dorsal fracture-dislocation of the proximal interphalangeal joint by closed reduction and Kirschner wire fixation: a 16-year follow up. J Hand Surg 2002;27B:537–540.
116. Orbay JL, Indriago I, Gonzales E, et al. Percutaneous fixation of metacarpal fractures. Oper Tech Plast Reconstr Surg 2002;9:138–142.
117. O'Sullivan ST, Limantzakis G, Kay SP. The role of low-profile titanium miniplates in emergency and elective hand surgery. J Hand Surg 1999;24B:347–349.
118. Otani K, Fukuda K, Hamanishi C. An unusual dorsal fracture-dislocation of the proximal interphalangeal joint. J Hand Surg 2007;32E:193–194.
119. Ouellette EA. Use of the minicondylar plate in metacarpal and phalangeal fractures. Clin Orthop 1996;327:38–46.
120. Ouellette EA, Dennis JJ, Latta LL, et al. The role of soft tissues in plate fixation of proximal phalanx fractures. Clin Orthop 2004;418:213–218.
121. Page SM, Stern PJ. Complications and range of motion following plate fixation of metacarpal and phalangeal fractures. J Hand Surg 1998;23A:827–832.
122. Patel MR, Bassini L. Irreducible palmar Metacarpophalangeal joint dislocation due to juncture tendinum interposition: a case report and review of the literature. J Hand Surg 2000;25:166–172.
123. Pegoli L, Toh S, Arai K, et al. The Ishiguro extension block technique for the treatment of mallet finger fracture: indications and clinical results. J Hand Surg 2003;28B:15–17.

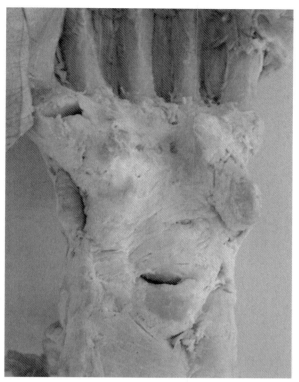

FIGURE 29-2 It is difficult to distinguish the extrinsic ligaments from the fibrous capsule; however, they are quite prominent from the intra-articular aspect of the joint.

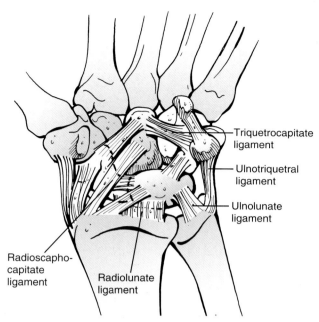

FIGURE 29-3 The palmar capsule consists of two major ligamentous inclusions: the RL ligament is the deeper of the two, which proceeds to the triquetrum and composes in effect the radiolunotriquetral ligament. The more distal and superficial component is often referred to as the arcuate ligament or distal V. The radial component of this ligament is the radioscaphocapitate ligament. The ulnar component of the arcuate ligament is the triquetrocapitate ligament.

(Fig. 29-3). The proximal limb consists of the radiolunatotriquetral and radioscaphoid ligaments laterally and the ulnolunate und ulnotriquetral ligaments medially.

The radioscaphoid ligament that inserts into the tuberosity of the scaphoid is the radial expansion of the radioscaphocapitate ligament, which courses over the palmar concavity of the scaphoid proximal to the tuberosity before inserting on the palmar aspect of the keel and neck of the capitate.[39] It appears to act as a sling across the waist of the scaphoid over which the scaphoid rotates, and it usually does not have a ligamentous insertion into the scaphoid itself.

The distal portions of the radiocapitate and ulnocapitate ligaments do not attach to the head of the capitate, but form a support sling commonly referred to as the "arcuate ligament." Between these two rows of ligaments is a thinned area called the space of Poirier.[144] This area expands when the wrist is dorsiflexed and disappears in palmarflexion. A rent develops during dorsal dislocations, and it is through this interval that the lunate displaces into the carpal canal.

The extrinsic palmar radiolunate (RL) ligaments have been subdivided into short and long RL ligaments. The radioscapholunate ligament originates from the palmar aspect of the ridge between the scaphoid and lunate fossae and inserts into the scapholunate interosseus ligament.[102,178] The radioscapholunate ligament acts as a neurovascular supply to the scapholunate interosseus membrane and it is not a true extrinsic ligament of the wrist.

Dorsal Wrist Ligaments. The dorsal ligaments of importance are the radiotriquetral and scaphotriquetral (dorsal intercarpal)

ligaments, which describe a V-shape from the dorsal aspect of the distal radius near Lister's tubercle to the triquetrum and then back to the dorsal scaphoid rim. The radial capsule is thickened and fused with the radioscaphoid ligament, while the ulnodorsal capsule is augmented by the floors of the fifth and sixth dorsal compartments. There are no true collateral ligaments.[39]

Another group of extrinsic ligaments support the midcarpal joint and couple the distal carpal bones to each other. On the radial side of the wrist, a V-shaped scaphotrapezial ligament extends from the scaphoid tuberosity to the palmar tubercle of the trapezium. Adjacent to it medially are the scaphocapitate and palmar capitotrapezial ligaments and the capitotrapezoidal ligament. On the ulnar side of the wrist, the triquetrocapitate and the triquetrohamate ligaments are a continuation of the ulnotriquetral ligament.[39]

Intrinsic Ligaments

The intrinsic ligaments interconnect individual carpal bones particularly the scaphoid, lunate, and triquetrum. They are collections of relatively short fibers that bind the bones of either the proximal or distal rows to each other.[108,121,173] In the proximal carpal row, the ligaments are intra-articular, connecting the scaphoid to the lunate and the lunate to the triquetrum (Fig. 29-4). There is a contiguous blending of the interosseous ligaments with the joint articular cartilage.

Laterally, the strong scapholunate interosseous ligament (SLIL) has been shown to consist of three components: palmar, central, and dorsal. The scapholunate (SL) ligament has an important role in carpal stability. The dorsal SL ligament is the key SL joint stabilizer. It is formed by a thick collection of fibers

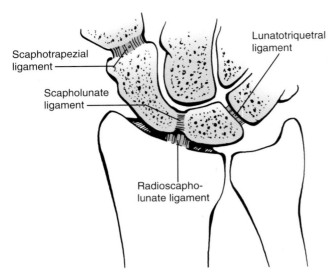

FIGURE 29-4 The intra-articular intrinsic ligaments connect adjacent carpal bones.

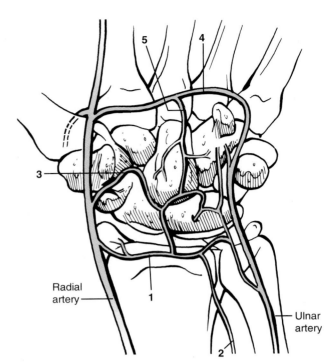

FIGURE 29-5 Schematic drawing of the arterial supply of the palmar aspect of the carpus. Circulation of the wrist is obtained through the radial, ulnar, and anterior interosseous arteries and the deep palmar arch. 1, palmar radiocarpal arch; 2, palmar branch of anterior interosseous artery; 3, palmar intercarpal arch; 4, deep palmar arch; 5, recurrent artery.

and is transversely oriented, linking the dorsomedial edge of the scaphoid to the dorsolateral rim of the lunate. The palmar SL ligament, a secondary SL stabilizer, is formed by longer, more obliquely oriented fibers. The long fibers of the palmar portion of the SL interosseous membrane allow the scaphoid flexibility as it rotates on the lunate. The dorsal third of the ligament is the strongest, while the palmar ligament has more laxity. The central third appears to be a fibrocartilaginous membrane which blends with the adjacent cartilage of scaphoid and lunate. The membrane is thicker palmarly, as it incorporates a richly vascularized expansion from the radioscapholunate ligament.[17,19,39,115,121]

The lunatotriquetral interosseous ligament (LTIL) is similarly formed from two interosseous ligaments (palmar and dorsal) connecting the proximal edges of triquetrum and lunate. It interdigitates with the dorsal radiotriquetral ligament and palmar ulnotriquetral, ulnolunate, and radiolunatotriquetral insertions. The palmar third of the lunatotriquetral (LT) ligament is stronger than the dorsal third being supported by strong palmar ulnocarpal ligaments. Its fibers are tighter through all ranges of motion than the SL ligaments, making for a closer kinematic relationship.[39,121,173]

Neurovascular Anatomy

The innervation and blood supply of the wrist and carpus come from the regional nerves and vessels. Circulation of the wrist is obtained through the radial, ulnar, and anterior interosseous arteries and the deep palmar arch. The extraosseous arterial pattern is formed by an anastomotic network of three dorsal and three palmar arches connected longitudinally at their medial and lateral borders by the radial and ulnar arteries (Fig. 29-5). In addition to transverse and longitudinal anastomoses, there are dorsal to palmar interconnections between the dorsal and palmar branches of the anterior interosseous artery.[73,137,172]

The intrinsic blood supply to the carpal bones is an important factor in the incidence of avascular necrosis (AVN) after trauma.[172] Studies[75,73,137] show three patterns of intraosseous vascularization:

1. The scaphoid, capitate, and about 20% of all lunates are supplied by a single vessel and thus are at risk for avascular necrosis.
2. The trapezium, triquetrum, pisiform, and 80% of lunates receive nutrient arteries through two nonarticular surfaces and have consistent intraosseous anastomoses. AVN is therefore rare.
3. The trapezoid and hamate lack an intraosseous anastomosis and, after fracture, can have avascular fragments.

These observations extend previous work, which showed that the blood supply to most carpal bones enters the distal half, leaving the proximal half at risk. There is no interval, for example, by which the scaphoid can be approached without endangering some of the branches that supply its circulation. The lunate blood supply is constantly endangered by common dorsal approaches to the wrist, but the blood supply from the palmar radiocarpal arch is usually sufficient to maintain its blood supply. With fracture–dislocations of the wrist, the palmar radiocarpal arch usually remains intact, because the dislocation is distal through the space of Poirier.

MECHANISM OF INJURY

The most common mechanism of injury is an axial compression force applied with the wrist in hyperextension, in which the palmar ligaments are placed under tension and the dorsal joint surfaces are compressed and subject to shear stresses.[39,111,113] Depending on the degree of radial or ulnar deviation, a ligament, bone injury, or a combination of both will result. A scaphoid fracture appears to occur when the wrist is dorsiflexed past 97

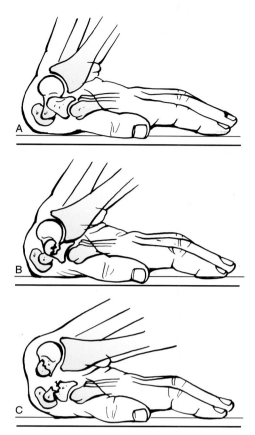

FIGURE 29-6 The most common mechanism of injury is an axial compressive force applied with the wrist in hyperextension. **A–C.** The drawings show the fracture mechanism of the scaphoid where the proximal pole of the scaphoid is trapped between the radius and the tense palmar extrinsic ligaments; the full force is concentrated at the waist of the scaphoid.

degrees and radially deviated by 10 degrees. In this position, the proximal pole of the scaphoid is securely held by the radius and the proximal radioscaphocapitate ligament while the distal pole of the bone is carried dorsally by the trapeziocapitate complex (Fig. 29-6). The radioscaphoid ligament is relaxed by the radial deviation and cannot alleviate the tensile stresses accumulating on the radiopalmar aspect of the scaphoid. The fracture then propagates dorsally and can be transverse, oblique, or comminuted depending on the direction of the applied loads.[198]

The most common injury is a fall on the outstretched hand when an individual straightens the arm for protection and the body weight and exterior forces are concentrated across the wrist. Other mechanisms include palmarflexion, as occurs in an over-the-handlebars motorcycle accident, or twisting injuries in sports where the hand is forcefully rotated against the stationary body. Ligament tears involve more substantial force to the hand. High-energy forces result in carpal bone fractures or ligamentous disruptions of both intrinsic and extrinsic ligaments and perilunate dislocations. The majority of these injuries occur around the lunate, which as the carpal keystone is held most securely to the distal radius. Several authors[39,122] have shown that many injuries to the wrist appear to be sequential variants of perilunate dislocation. Minor injuries, such as sprains, result from low-energy forces.

Kinematics

The global motion of the wrist is composed of flexion–extension, radioulnar deviation at the radiocarpal joint, and axial rotation around the distal radioulnar joint (DRUJ).[110] The radiocarpal articulation acts as a universal joint allowing a small degree of intercarpal motion around the longitudinal axis related to the rotation of individual carpal bones. The forearm accounts for about 140 degrees of rotation. Radiocarpal joint motion is primarily flexion–extension of nearly equal proportions (70 degrees), and radial and ulnar deviation of 20 and 40 degrees, respectively. This amount of motion is possible as a result of complex arrangements between the two carpal rows. During flexion and extension, each carpal row angulates in the same direction with nearly equal amplitude and in a synchronous fashion (Fig. 29-7).[29,53,110,124] Much of the wrist's versatility, however, is due to the intercalated three-bone system of the proximal carpal row. During radioulnar deviation, the proximal row exhibits a secondary angulation in the sagittal plane to the synchronous motion occurring in the coronal plane. Radial deviation induces flexion of the obliquely situated scaphoid as the trapezium approaches the radius. Through the dorsal aspect of the SL ligament, this motion is transmitted sequentially to the lunate and triquetrum, which flex approximately 25 degrees.[39,110,115] As the carpus moves back to neutral and onto full ulnar deviation, the proximal row extends and supinates with respect to the radius.

The scaphoid can be observed to extend with ulnar deviation, but it is the proximal migration of the hamate that forces the triquetrum to displace palmarly and extend, bringing the lunate with it. This rotation, by varying the length and contour of the proximal carpal row, allows for extensive excursion of the wrist while maintaining stability around a longitudinal axis. This has been described as the "variable geometry" of the proximal carpal row. When this mechanism is disrupted by fracture or ligamentous injury, the wrist becomes destabilized. The usual arcs of motion are no longer synchronous, and the intercarpal contact patterns change. A snap, catch, or clunk can be appreciated with motion of the wrist, particularly when under compressive load. Instability leads, in time, to degenerative changes as a consequence of increased shear forces and abnormal contact between individual carpal bones.

Normally, in the coronal plane, the center of rotation of the wrist is located within a small area in the capitate neck. A line drawn through the axis of rotation parallel with the anatomic axis of the forearm will, with the hand in neutral position, pass through the head and base of the third metacarpal, the capitate, the radial aspect of the lunate, and the center of the lunate fossa of the radius.[124] In the sagittal plane with the wrist in neutral flexion–extension, a line passing through the longitudinal axis of the capitate, lunate, and radius will show these to be nearly superimposed or colinear. The scaphoid axis lies at 45 degrees to this line and passes between the lunate and capitate in a fashion that provides optimal stability to the midcarpal joint. The scaphoid acts as a stabilizing strut or column to support the central column. By virtue of its obliquity, the scaphoid will flex when under compression and exerts a similar force on the lunate. The lunate, however, is also under the influence of the triquetrum, which inherently prefers to extend. For this reason, the lunate may be thought of being in a state of dynamic balance between two antagonists. It tends to lie in the position of least mechanical potential energy.[39]

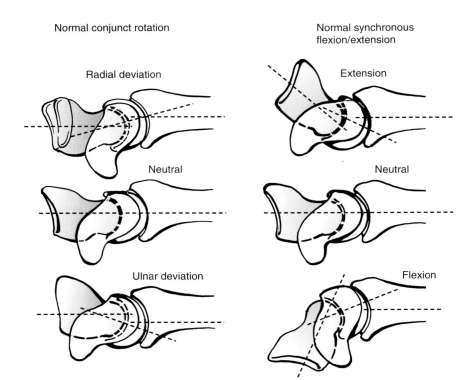

Normal conjunct rotation

Radial deviation

Neutral

Ulnar deviation

Normal synchronous
flexion/extension

Extension

Neutral

Flexion

FIGURE 29-7 Conjunct rotation of the entire proximal row occurs in flexion during radial deviation (upper left). The axes of the radius and carpal rows are collinear in neutral (middle left), and the proximal row extends with ulnar deviation (lower left). Angulatory excursions of the proximal and distal rows are essentially equal in amplitude and direction during extension (upper right) and flexion (lower right). This has been described as synchronous angulation.

Volar Intercalated Segment Instability and Dorsal Intercalated Segment Instability

When the dynamic balance is interrupted, the lunate will tend to flex with loss of ulnar support from the triquetrum (Fig. 29-8). When the lunate slips into a statically fixed position of flexion of more than 15 degrees, volar intercalated segment instability (VISI) is present. VISI is typical of LT dissociation (LTD), nondissociative carpal instability, and a carpal instability complex in which associated instabilities are also present.

When the lunate slips into fixed extension of more than 10 degrees, dorsal intercalated segment instability (DISI) is present. The relative alignment of the scaphoid to the lunate, which is usually about 45 degrees, is important. When this exceeds 70 degrees, the ligamentous linkage between the scaphoid and lunate is usually inoperative. The lunate then generally adopts an extended position (i.e., DISI) and maintains this position even during radial deviation, thus interrupting the normal rotation and the spatial adaptability of the proximal row. The same is true when the lunate is fixed in flexion in a VISI deformity. The wrist will not extend even during ulnar deviation. A DISI deformity is rarely seen in acute scaphoid fractures, where it indicates gross carpal instability. It is more often seen in association with scaphoid pseudarthrosis and scapholunate dissociation, where it indicates the degree of carpal collapse deformity that has occurred. In advanced cases, the capitolunate joint becomes subluxed and may show signs of degenerative arthritis.[85]

IMAGING OF THE CARPUS

Radiographic Examination

It is not easy to differentiate clinically if a fall on the outstretched hand led to an injury of the wrist or to an injury of the carpus.

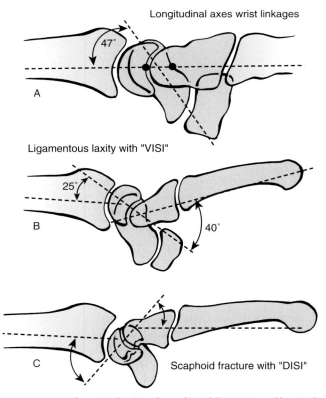

Longitudinal axes wrist linkages

47°

A

Ligamentous laxity with "VISI"

25°

40°

B

C

Scaphoid fracture with "DISI"

FIGURE 29-8 Schematic drawing of carpal instability. **A.** Normal longitudinal alignment of the carpal bones with the scaphoid axis at a 47-degree angle to the axes of the capitate, lunate, and radius. **B.** VISI deformity is usually associated with disruption of the LT ligament. **C.** DISI deformity is associated with SL ligament disruption or a displaced scaphoid fracture.

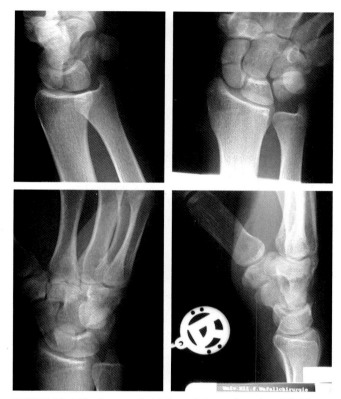

FIGURE 29-9 The four scaphoid views (AP, true lateral, radial oblique, ulnar oblique) detect most of carpal fractures. A fisted AP view can be helpful in detecting scaphoid fractures

TABLE 29-1	Radiologic Views for Detection and Assessment of Scaphoid Fractures
Radiologic View	Advantages/Disadvantages
Neutral AP	Can be misleading because of tubercle overhang
Ulnar-deviated AP	Especially useful for proximal pole fractures
Ulnar-deviated AP with 20-degree tube angulation to the elbow	Good for waist fractures as beam at right angles to long axis; patterns oblique to beam poorly visualised
45-degree oblique (semi-pronated) AP	Best for oblique sulcal fractures but also shows waist and tubercle fractures; shows displacement particularly of waist fractures
45-degree oblique (semisupinated) AP	Best for proximal pole fractures
Lateral	Poor for fracture detection. Used for assessment of alignment, mainly demonstration of carpal collapse.

The four standard views to diagnose an injury are the anteroposterior (AP) and lateral radiographs, each taken in the exactly neutral position, and the radial oblique (supinated AP) and ulnar oblique views (Fig. 29-9). These four standard views detect most carpal injuries,[67] but the neutral AP view is probably the most misleading as the tubercle overhangs the waist of the scaphoid in this view and can obscure a fracture.[36] If there is the suspicion of carpal instability, additional views in maximal radial and ulnar deviation are recommended. Although most scaphoid fractures will be detected by the four standard views, further views should be taken if there is strong clinical suspicion of the presence of an undetected fracture. Useful views are summarized in Table 29-1.[36]

In the normal carpus, with the wrist in neutral position, the longitudinal axes of the long finger metacarpal, capitate, lunate, and the radius all fall in the same line. The longitudinal axis of the scaphoid can be drawn through the midpoints of its proximal and distal poles. Using these axes, it is possible to measure angles that define the positions of the carpal bones. For example, the scapholunate angle averages 45 degrees, and ranges from 30 to 60 degrees in normal wrists. An angle greater than 70 degrees suggests instability, and one greater than 80 degrees is almost certain proof of carpal instability or displacement. A capitolunate angle of more than 20 degrees is also strongly suggestive of carpal instability.

Gilula's lines (three smooth radiographic arcs) should be examined on the AP view. Disruption of these arcs indicates ligamentous instability.[77] The assessment of Gilula's line continuity should be a standard in the evaluation of all AP wrist radiographs to prevent a missed diagnosis of a perilunate dislocation (Fig. 29-10).

DISI and VISI patterns are diagnosed easily by lateral radiographs. The DISI pattern is most commonly observed with displaced scaphoid fractures and scapholunate dissociation (SLD), while the VISI pattern is more likely to be associated with LTD.

SLD and LTD are diagnosed by AP views. The normal radiograph should show a constant space between scaphoid, lunate, and triquetrum, which is maintained throughout the range of motion. The joint space between scaphoid and lunate is usually 1 to 2 mm. With SLD, an increasing gap appears which may in time be wide enough to accept proximal migration of the entire capitate head. A spread of more than 3 mm is considered abnormal, and a gap greater than 5 mm is confirmatory of an SL injury. In addition, the scaphoid flexes palmarward which gives it less of an elongated profile on the AP view and projects the cortical waist of the scaphoid as an overlapping ring of bone inside the scaphoid projection, also known as the "the cortical ring sign." The lunate also moves into a DISI position, which can be visualized on the AP view by the increasing overlap of the capitate silhouette by a lunate horn producing a wedge shape (Fig 29-10B). With LTD, a gap between the two bones is not usually evident, but a break in the normal carpal arc of the proximal carpal row can be seen.

Carpal height ratio, which is carpal height divided by the length of the third metacarpal, is used to quantify carpal collapse. One method of measuring carpal height is to determine the distance between the base of the third metacarpal and the articular surface of the distal radius using a line bisecting the middle of the radius and metacarpal. The carpal height ratio, however, is of little significance in assessing ligament damage in wrist hyperextension injuries.

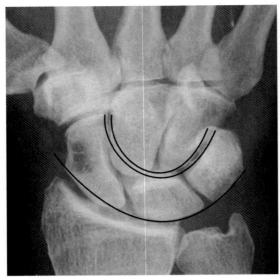
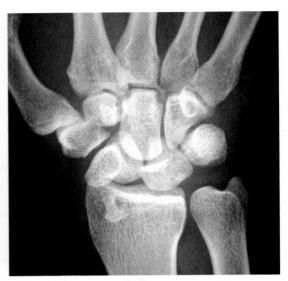

A **B**

FIGURE 29-10 Gilula's lines. **A.** AP views show three smooth Gilula arcs in a normal wrist. These arcs outline proximal and distal surfaces of the proximal carpal row and the proximal cortical margins of capitate and hamate. **B.** Arc I is broken, which indicates an abnormal lunotriquetral joint due to a perilunate dislocation. Additional findings are the cortical ring sign produced by the cortical outline of the distal pole of the scaphoid and a trapezoidal shape of the lunate.

Special Imaging Techniques

Arthrography, magnetic resonance (MR) wrist arthrography, videoradiography, and arthroscopy can assist in the diagnosis of carpal ligament injuries.[25,39] Computed tomography (CT) scans are helpful in evaluating carpal fractures, malunion, nonunion, and bone loss. Three-dimensional imaging is of use in planning reconstructive procedures for malunions and nonunions. Macroradiography does not show any advantage in diagnosing carpal fractures, particularly scaphoid fractures compared to normal radiographs.[50]

Bone scans can be helpful in confirming occult fractures and avulsion injury.[179,180] However, MR imaging (MRI) scans are more sensitive in detecting occult fractures and AVN of the carpal bones[64,65] as well as in detecting soft tissue injuries, including ruptures of the SL ligament and TFCC injuries.

Pearls and Pitfalls

- Standard scaphoid views detect most carpal injuries.
- A DISI pattern is most commonly observed with displaced scaphoid fractures and SLD.
- A VISI pattern is more likely to be associated with LTD.
- MRI scans are useful in detecting occult fractures, AVN of the carpal bones, and ligamentous injuries.
- Perilunate dislocations are easily missed if the continuity of Gilula's line is not assessed.

SCAPHOID FRACTURES

Acute fractures of the scaphoid were first recognized in 1889 by Cousin and Destot before the discovery of radiographs. They were also well described by Mouchet and Jeanne in 1919. The position of the scaphoid on the radial side of the wrist, as the proximal extension of the thumb ray, makes it vulnerable to injury.

From the data presented in Chapter 3, the annual incidence of carpal fractures is 39.7 per 100,000 of the population per year in the United Kingdom. Scaphoid fractures account for 2.9% of all fractures and for 69% of all carpal injuries (see Table 3-18). Scaphoid fractures are common among young men with a male to female ratio of 71:29 and an average age of 35 years. The average time for healing of a nondisplaced scaphoid fracture in a cast is 8 to 12 weeks, accounting for a considerable loss of time and productivity in this young and active population.[14,39,65,121,144,152,173,184]

Anatomy

The scaphoid is one of the smallest bones of the human body. It is an irregularly shaped tubular bone, twisted, and bent into an S-shape (Fig. 29-11). It resembles a deformed peanut or a boat (in Greek, skaphos means boat). It lies entirely within the wrist joint, with more than 80% of its surface being covered by articular cartilage,[69] which reduces its capacity for periosteal healing and increases its tendency to delayed union and nonunion. The scaphoid is located in a 45-degree plane to the longitudinal and horizontal axis of the wrist.

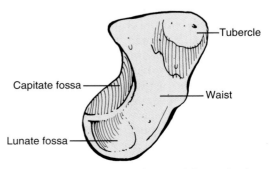

FIGURE 29-11 Schematic drawing of the scaphoid.

The scaphoid is concave on its ulnar surface where it articulates like a socket with the spherical head of the capitate. Proximally, there is a small, semilunar facet for articulation with the lunate. The proximal third of the radial surface is convex and articulates with the radius. Distal to this articulation is the waist, grooved on its palmar surface by the radioscaphocapitate ligament which acts as a sling across the waist of the scaphoid although it has no connection to the bone itself. Taleisnik[174] suggested that the radioscaphocapitate ligament provided a fulcrum for the scaphoid. The scaphoid is ridged across its nonarticular dorsoradial surface, along which the critical dorsal ridge vessels traverse. The ridge acts as an insertion point for both the dorsal component of the SLIL,[17] as well as the intercarpal ligament.[129] The distal pole is pronated, flexed, and ulnarly angulated with respect to the proximal pole and presents separate articular surfaces to the trapezium and trapezoid distally.[173]

The stability of the scaphoid depends to a great extent on the short intrinsic ligaments (see Fig. 29-4) that attach it to the lunate and distally to the trapezium and trapezoid. Motion in these joints is restricted by the strong ligaments, which permit a degree of rotation proximally and a degree of gliding distally.[85] These ligaments merge with the extrinsic ligaments and capsule, which are loose enough to allow free motion of the scaphoid within the wrist. Otherwise, the scaphoid has no ligamentous or tendinous attachments and acts with the rest of the proximal carpal row as an "intercalated segment."

Biomechanics

The scaphoid acts as a link across the midcarpal joint, connecting the proximal and distal carpal rows. Any shear strain that occurs across the midcarpal joint is transferred through the scaphoid and may cause fractures and dislocations. Through its stout proximal and distal ligamentous connections, the scaphoid serves to coordinate and smooth the motions of the proximal and distal rows, and it has been likened to a slider-crank mechanism that stabilizes an inherently unstable dual link system as the midcarpal joint tends to assume a lunate-extended posture unless constrained by an intact scaphoid.[113,207] The kinematic effect of an unstable scaphoid fracture is a dissociation of the proximal and distal carpal rows that permits the natural tendency of the two carpal rows to fail by collapsing. This is demonstrated clinically by the collapse pattern seen with chronic scaphoid nonunion, a condition called "scaphoid nonunion advanced collapse" appearing as DISI.[56,165,207] Under axial load, the two halves of the scaphoid collapse into a flexed or "humpback" posture.[6,154]

Vascularity

The scaphoid receives most of its blood supply from two major vascular pedicles.[74,137] One enters the scaphoid tubercle and supplies its distal 20% to 30% and the other arises from the dorsal scaphoid branch of the radial artery (Fig. 29-12). The dorsal ridge vessels enter through numerous small foramina along the spiral groove and dorsal ridge. This source accounts for about 80% of the blood supply. Several studies have shown no vascular supply or only a single perforator proximal to the waist of the scaphoid.[74,134] Because of its unusual retrograde vascular supply, the scaphoid has a high risk of nonunion and AVN after fracture. Temporary interruption of the blood supply to the proximal fragment is virtually certain with proximal pole

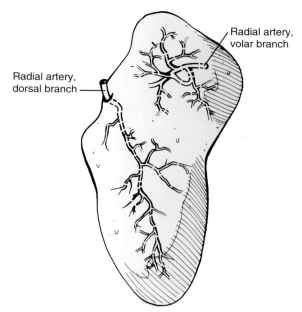

FIGURE 29-12 The vascular supply of the scaphoid is provided by two vascular pedicles.

fractures but, if stabilized, the proximal pole has the capacity to revascularize and heal.[76,118,207]

Fracture Mechanism and Functional Anatomy

Further analysis of the data presented in Chapter 3 reveals that scaphoid fractures are common in young men due to falls (40.7%) and sporting injuries (32.8%). High-energy injury is much less common, occurring in just over 10% of cases.

The mechanism of fracture is usually considered to be bending with compression dorsally and tension on the palmar surface, due to forced dorsiflexion of the wrist. When the wrist is extended beyond 95 degrees, the proximal pole of the scaphoid is tightly held between the capitate, the dorsal lip of the radius, and the taut palmar capsule. Fracture of the scaphoid occurs at the waist which is exposed to the maximal bending movement.[198] However, scaphoid fractures can be caused by several other mechanisms.[14] The force must be sufficient to produce at least a transient subluxation of the joint. This is only one step away from the classic transscaphoid perilunate fracture–dislocation that results from more severe trauma. Thus, there must be a subtle difference between the degree of force required to produce an occult fracture, a complete but stable fracture, or an unstable fracture of the scaphoid. Herbert[85] stated that since the line of the midcarpal joint crosses the proximal pole in radial deviation and the distal pole in ulnar deviation, the wrist deviation at the time of injury might determine the line of fracture. Fractures of the waist are usually the result of shear forces across the scaphoid. Fractures of the tubercle, like radial styloid fractures, appear to be caused by either compression or avulsion.[56,144] Compson[36] suggested that the size of a proximal pole fracture depends on the level of the proximal extent of the joint facet with the capitate, which is the most variable aspect of scaphoid anatomy and accounts for the variation in the size of proximal pole fracture. Smaller

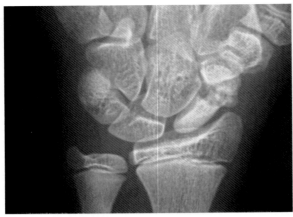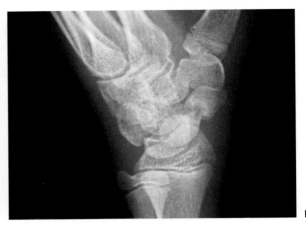

FIGURE 29-13 A,B. Symptomatic scaphoid nonunion in a 12-year-old boy because of a fall 2 months prior.

proximal pole fractures can also be caused by an avulsion of the attachment of the SL ligament.

Scaphoid fractures in children are uncommon because the physis of the distal radius usually fails first. However, scaphoid fractures can occur in children, and radiographs are mandatory to diagnose this injury (Fig. 29-13A,B). Concomitant fractures of the distal radius and scaphoid have been reported. Most fractures heal with cast at an average of 6 to 8 weeks; however, nonunion and AVN can occur.[50,80,187] In the elderly, the distal radial metaphysis usually fractures before the scaphoid.

Fractures of the scaphoid result in significant functional disability as well as time off work, loss of earnings, and interference with recreational activities. A common problem with the fractured scaphoid is diagnosis,[65] and posttraumatic complications include pain, dysfunction, malunion, delayed union, and nonunion.

Malunion occurs because the distal pole of the fractured scaphoid tends to flex and the proximal scaphoid extends with the proximal carpal row, initially causing a dorsal fracture gap followed by the humpback deformity (Fig. 29-14).[56] Despite the lack of direct tendon attachments, joint compressive forces, trapezium-scaphoid shear stress, and capitolunate rotation mo-

ments all act on the fractured scaphoid. The scaphoid often assumes an anteverted position, the lunate and triquetrum subluxate forward and rotate dorsally, and the capitate and hamate subluxate dorsally and proximally, producing the DISI deformity (see Fig. 29-8C).[69] As a consequence of these mechanical factors, as well as the critical vascularity of the scaphoid bone, scaphoid fractures have a high tendency to delayed union and nonunion. Nonunion of the scaphoid is a severe problem, causing arthritis secondary to abnormal loading on the articular surfaces of the midcarpal joint, pain, and weakness.

Signs and Symptoms

Patients with scaphoid injuries usually complain of wrist pain after a fall on the outstretched hand. The diagnosis of a scaphoid fracture is made from the clinical history with about 90% of patients recalling a hyperextension injury, the clinical examination where the index of suspicion is raised, and by proper radiographic examination which confirms the diagnosis. The importance of obtaining an accurate history cannot be overestimated because both treatment and prognosis depend on the type of fracture and fracture mechanism.[85] It is important to inquire carefully about previous trauma and not to treat a nonunion as

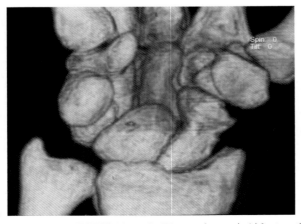
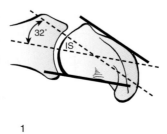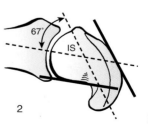

FIGURE 29-14 A. CT scan of a scaphoid fracture that has healed with a humpback deformity. **B.** Schematic drawing of scaphoid: (1) normal scaphoid, (2) humpback deformity. The normal intrascaphoid angle (IS) is 30 degrees ± 5 degrees. The humpback deformity angle measure 67 degrees and the normal scaphoid 32 degrees.

if it was an acute fracture. Although tenderness in the anatomic snuffbox has been described as a classic finding in scaphoid fractures, it is an overly sensitive test that is notoriously inaccurate when used in isolation.[62,141] Swelling and pain are usually apparent in acute fractures; however, these symptoms can be minimal. After 24 hours, there is often diffuse pain and swelling. Pain in the anatomic snuff box may be elicited with longitudinal thumb compression, on either radial or ulnar deviation with pronation, and using the Kirk-Watson test (see below).

The difficulty in making a clinical diagnosis is that no one symptom or sign is sufficiently sensitive or specific (Table 29-2). Parvizi et al.[144] found that any the use of one clinical tests in isolation was inadequate but that a combination of snuffbox tenderness, scaphoid tubercle tenderness, and pain with axial compression yielded a sensitivity of 100% and a specificity of 74%. However, their findings were only valid in the first 24 hours after fracture.

Loss of wrist extension is a typical finding in ununited scaphoid fractures associated with carpal collapse deformity and palmar capsular contracture. Missed diagnosis is not uncommon and often results in additional morbidity from secondary changes, including nonunion, collapse deformity, and degenerative arthritis.

Radiographic Examination

Because of the inconsistency of clinical signs, the diagnosis of scaphoid fracture is usually made by radiograph. Radiographic diagnosis of a scaphoid fracture requires four radiographs: an AP view with the hand in a fist to extend the scaphoid, a lateral view, a radial oblique (supinated AP) view, and an ulnar oblique view (see Fig. 29-9). These four views detect most scaphoid fractures.[26,67,85,184] Comparative views of the opposite uninjured wrist are often helpful. It is difficult to diagnose scaphoid fractures on the lateral radiograph, although this radiograph is essential to diagnose perilunate fracture–dislocations and to evaluate the overall alignment of the carpus.

Barton[14] described three common reasons as to why scaphoid fractures are incorrectly diagnosed:

1. A dark line may be formed by the dorsal lip of the radius overlapping the scaphoid.
2. The presence of a white line formed by the proximal end of the scaphoid tuberosity
3. The dorsal ridge of the scaphoid may appear bent on the semisupinated view.

Motion views of the wrist (flexion–extension and radioulnar deviation) may demonstrate fracture displacement, which indicates an unstable scaphoid fracture. Since the scaphoid flexes in radial deviation and extends in ulnar deviation, the length of bone should be assessed by comparing ulnar and radial deviation views in both wrists. Assuming that the two views are identical, any difference in length must indicate a scaphoid deformity resulting from either a fracture or ligament injury.[85] When instability of the scaphoid is suspected, careful analysis of the lateral radiograph for intrascaphoid angulation or a dorsally tilted lunate is recommended.

It is a well-known fact that undisplaced scaphoid fractures may not be visible on the initial set of radiographs, although it has been shown that this is rarely the case if they are evaluated by experienced observers.[14,67] Clinical studies[7] have shown that scaphoid and pronator fat stripe signs are poor predictors of the presence or absence of underlying occult fractures. If there is clinical suspicion but radiographs are negative, a scaphoid cast is applied and another set of scaphoid views is performed after 10 days (Fig. 29-15).[67] As most of the patients with suspected scaphoid fractures are young and active, early diagnosis is important. Macroradiography[66] and ultrasound[132] have a sensitivity of less than 50% in detecting occult scaphoid fractures. MRI scans are the most effective way of diagnosing scaphoid fractures (Fig. 29-16).[27,65] It has been shown that an MRI performed as early as 48 hours after the injury has a sensitivity and specificity approaching 100% and may have the potential to save as much as $7200 per 100,000 inhabitants by avoiding loss of productivity due to unnecessary cast immobilization.[65] Technetium-99m bone scans[28,180] also have a high sensitivity in diagnosing occult fractures of the carpus. CT scans have the advantage of speed and can produce high resolution fine-cut

---

TABLE 29-2	**Reliability of the Clinical Signs of Scaphoid Fracture**			
Clinical Sign	Sensitivity (%)	Positive Predictive Value (%)	Specificity (%)	Negative Predictive Value (%)
ASB tenderness	100	30	19	100
Scaphoid tubercle tenderness	100	34	30	100
Longitudinal thumb compression	100	40	48	100
Reduced thumb movement	66	41	66	85
ASB swelling	61	50	52	58
ASB pain in ulnar deviation/pronation	83	44	17	56
ASB pain in radial deviation/pronation	70	45	31	56
Pain on thumb/index pinch	48	44	31	41
Scaphoid shift test	66	49	31	69

ASB, anatomic snuff box.

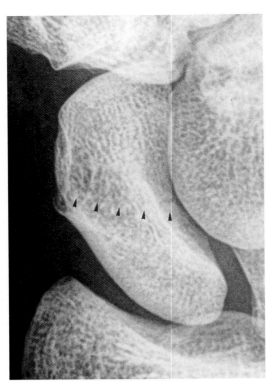

FIGURE 29-15 An occult fracture was detected 10 days after a fall on the outstretched hand. This fracture was not visible on the initial set of radiographs

images of the scaphoid in multiple planes.[150] Three-dimensional reconstructions of these scans can be helpful for planning operative procedures of scaphoid reconstruction.

Differentiation between an acute scaphoid fracture and a scaphoid nonunion is important for planning treatment, and good radiographs should distinguish between the two,[39] although an MRI scan may be helpful. Not uncommonly, a second injury will draw attention to a minimally symptomatic nonunion which has been aggravated by the recent event. The acute scaphoid fracture is represented by a single line through the bone, occasionally with dorsoradial comminution and dorsal angulation. Late presentation of a fracture or an established

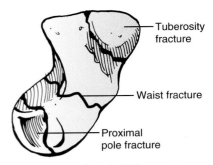

FIGURE 29-17 Classification of scaphoid fractures by anatomic location.

nonunion may show resorption at the fracture site, subchondral sclerosis, and displacement on both the AP and lateral radiographs. The longer the time since injury, the greater the cystic resorption, the denser the sclerosis, the more prominent the shortening of the scaphoid, and the greater the loss of carpal height.[85] Secondary degenerative changes are usually present by 10 to 15 years.

Associated Injuries

Fractures of the distal radius are not uncommon and injuries such as perilunate dislocation and transscaphoid perilunate fracture–dislocations may occur. Whatever the mechanism of scaphoid fracture, it is important to remember that a radiograph never reveals the true degree of joint and ligament damage that inevitably accompanies this injury.[85]

Classification

Classification by anatomic location has many proponents, some of whom attempt to correlate fracture union rate with the site of injury (Fig. 29-17). Waist fractures account for 65% of scaphoid fractures, with a further 26% being in the proximal pole with 9% either in the tuberosity or distal articular fractures. Herbert and Fisher[68] proposed a classification intended to identify those fractures most applicable for operative fixation (Table 29-3 and Fig. 29-18). They recommended early operative management of all acute fractures of the scaphoid waist or proximal pole because of the incidence of displacement or nonunion.

The blood supply of the scaphoid is critical in regard to

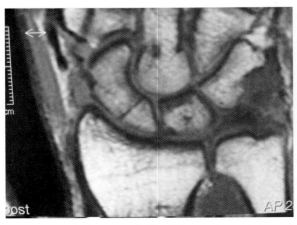
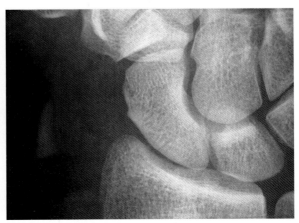

FIGURE 29-16 A. The MRI scan demonstrates a clear fracture line of the scaphoid (proximal pole). **B.** It is difficult to identify the proximal fracture by native radiographs.

TABLE 29-3	**Classification of Scaphoid Fractures**

Type A: Stable Acute Fractures

Features:
- Fracture appears incomplete (only one cortex involved)
- Union normally rapid
- Minimal treatment required

Type A1: Fracture of Tuberosity
Type A2: Incomplete Fracture through Waist

Type B: Unstable Acute Fractures

Features:
- Fracture likely to displace in plaster
- Delayed union common
- Internal fixation is the treatment of choice

Type B1: Distal Oblique Fracture
Type B2: Complete Fracture of Waist
Type B3: Proximal Pole Fracture
Type B4: Transscaphoid-Perilunate Fracture–Dislocation of Carpus
Type B5: Comminuted Fractures

Type C: Delayed Union

Features:
- Widening of the fracture line
- Development of cysts adjacent to the fracture
- Relative density of the proximal fragment

Type D: Established Nonunion

Type D1: Fibrous Union
Features:
- Common after conservative treatment
  Relatively stable
- Little or no deformity
- Variable cystic change
- Likely to progress to pseudarthrosis in time
- Surgery is normally required

Type D2: Pseudarthrosis
Features:
- Usually unstable
- Progressive deformity
- Leads to development of osteoarthritis
- May result following untreated fibrous union (type D)
- Surgery is normally required

---

different fracture types ranges from 4 to 6 weeks for tuberosity fractures, 6 to 8 weeks for occult and stable fractures, 10 to 12 weeks for distal third and waist fractures, and 12 to 20 weeks for comminuted and proximal pole fractures.

Occult Scaphoid Fractures

Undisplaced fissures and fractures of the scaphoid might not be visible on the initial set of radiographs. Patients with wrist injuries are usually seen in the emergency department by less experienced doctors who are aware of the dangers of missing a scaphoid fracture and who know that up to 30% of all scaphoid fractures might not be detected on initial radiographs.[14,67,133] Knowledge of the poor outcome of undiagnosed and untreated scaphoid fractures ending in pseudarthrosis of the scaphoid and severe radiocarpal arthritis leads to a tendency to overtreatment. To avoid missing a few occult fractures of the scaphoid, some patients are immobilized for prolonged periods of time without a diagnosis being made before being seen by a senior surgeon.[16,146]

Diagnosis of Occult Scaphoid Fractures

It has been demonstrated that radionuclide[28,180] and MRI scans[65,95] are reliable methods of diagnosing occult fractures of the scaphoid. MRI has a higher sensitivity and specificity in the diagnosis of occult fractures of the scaphoid compared to other methods of diagnosis and might even be more cost effective than repeated clinical examinations and radiographs.[65] However, most countries do not have the facilities to refer patients with supposedly minor injuries for an MRI scan. The literature states that there is low inter- and intraobserver reliability in diagnosing occult scaphoid fractures on plain radiographs.[179,180] Scaphoid fractures and other injuries to the wrist might not be very painful initially, although persisting pain clearly indicates an injury. The diagnosis is usually made by a combination of clinical and radiologic findings,[85] which means that the evaluation of radiographs even by experienced radiologists can lead to poor diagnostic results.[179] If an occult fracture of the scaphoid or severe concomitant wrist injury is suspected but not visible on initial radiographs, the wrist should be immobilized for 10 days in a forearm cast or splint, and the patient should be seen by an experienced surgeon and a repeat scaphoid series should be obtained. However, a prospective study has shown that 70% of all occult scaphoid fractures and 60% of avulsion fractures are visible on the initial set of radiographs.[67] There is little doubt that MRI scans are the most reliable method of diagnosing occult carpal and wrist fractures at an early stage.[27,65] However, it has been shown that that repeated clinical examinations and radiographs can also detect occult fractures of the scaphoid and associated wrist injuries in a reasonable time.[67] N'Dow et al.[133] showed that patients with suspected injuries to the scaphoid and wrist were often seen for months by junior staff and unnecessarily immobilized for the same time. It is therefore advised that a protocol be adopted where senior members of staff see these patients at the first follow-up and at least once again after 6 weeks.

Because of its high sensitivity and specificity, MRI is the criterion standard in the diagnosis of occult fractures of the wrist. However, if MRI is not available, adequate clinical follow-up and radiography should lead to the correct diagnosis. It is important to include the radius and proximal aspects of the

---

fracture location. Gelberman's work[74,75,137] confirmed earlier studies by demonstrating that the major blood supply comes from the scaphoid branches of the radial artery which enter the dorsal ridge and supply 70% to 80% of the bone, including the proximal pole. The second major group of vessels enters the scaphoid tubercle, perfusing only the distal 20% to 30% of the bone. In fractures through the waist and proximal third, revascularization will occur only with fracture healing. One can reasonably assume that, with proper treatment, nearly 100% of tuberosity and distal third scaphoid fractures will heal, as will 80% to 90% of waist fractures, but only 60% to 70% of proximal pole fractures will heal.[39,85] Similarly, union in oblique or shear fractures has been shown to be delayed in comparison to horizontal fractures. Comminuted or distracted osteochondral fractures have the poorest rate of union. The healing time for these

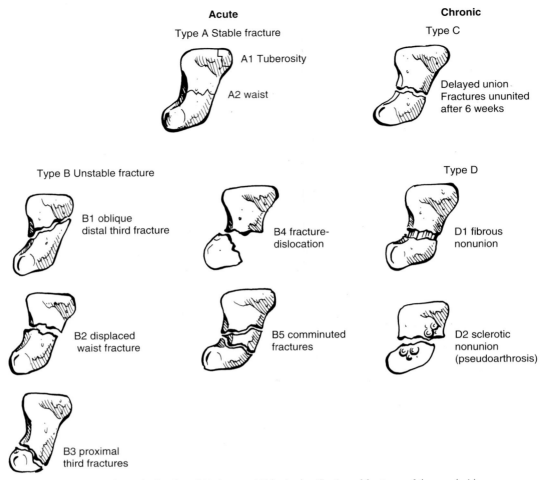

Acute

Type A Stable fracture

A1 Tuberosity

A2 waist

Chronic

Type C

Delayed union
Fractures ununited
after 6 weeks

Type B Unstable fracture

B1 oblique
distal third fracture

B4 fracture-
dislocation

Type D

D1 fibrous
nonunion

B2 displaced
waist fracture

B5 comminuted
fractures

D2 sclerotic
nonunion
(pseudoarthrosis)

B3 proximal
third fractures

FIGURE 29-18 Schematic drawing of Herbert and Fisher's classification of fractures of the scaphoid.

metacarpals in the scaphoid series to evaluate possible injuries to these bones. Fractures of the radius, ulna, and the metacarpals occur in 13% of all cases.[67]

Only 30% of all scaphoid fractures are truly occult, but 85% of all other carpal fractures are true occult fractures.[67] About 66% of carpal avulsion fractures and distal radial fractures are detectable on the initial set of scaphoid views.[67] A few more might be diagnosed by more views, but up to 16 radiographs, as suggested by Trojan,[184] would seem to be potentially harmful and an unnecessary waste of time and money. The literature suggests that there may be up to 34% of other wrist injuries where an occult scaphoid fracture is initially suspected.[86,169] However, Gaebler et al.[67] found a higher rate of these injuries. Of all the injuries detected, only 25% were scaphoid fractures. The other 75% consisted of carpal fractures other than the scaphoid (13%), avulsion fractures of extrinsic ligaments (12.5%), fractures of the distal radius (12%), bone bruises (10%), other fractures (26.5%), and soft tissue injuries (26%).

MRI is cost effective compared to repeated clinical and radiographic follow-up examinations.[65] However, many countries provide MRI scans only for emergency situations or do not have MRI facilities at all. The results of a prospective study showed that repeat clinical and radiographic examinations are adequate.[67] They will reveal occult fractures of the scaphoid and other occult fractures of the wrist but have the disadvantage that soft tissue injury remains undetected except for ruptures of the SL ligament resulting in SLD.

Current Treatment Options

Occult Fractures

Early diagnosis of an occult scaphoid fracture is important. If MRI proves the diagnosis, cast immobilization should be used. Above-elbow casts and scaphoid casts are not required, and a simple Colles forearm cast should be used for 4 to 6 weeks. Check radiographs should be obtained at the time of cast removal. If there are still clinical and radiologic signs of a scaphoid fracture, another cast is applied for an additional 2 weeks.

If MRI is not available and there is clinical suspicion of an occult fracture of the scaphoid, a Colles cast should be applied. Most nonunions are caused by the patient or surgeon suspecting a simple wrist sprain and undertaking no further diagnosis or treatment. The solution is a simple clinic policy. Patients with a suspected occult scaphoid fracture and negative radiographs are treated by the application of a Colles cast for 10 to 14 days. After this time, the cast is removed and a further scaphoid series undertaken. In most cases, a correct diagnosis is then made and appropriate treatment commenced.

Fractures of the Tubercle (Type A1)

These are benign fractures and represent an avulsion injury. Although some authors suggest that splinting is adequate, we prefer cast immobilization for 4 weeks. This injury represents a soft tissue injury and requires time to heal properly. Radiographs can show persistent displacement and fibrous union causing no disability, although these findings are more commonly seen in fractures treated without immobilization.

Undisplaced Scaphoid Fractures (Type A2)

Conservative Treatment. Undisplaced scaphoid fractures are usually stable. However, it is not always easy to decide whether this is the case. Thus, radiologic follow-up is mandatory and surgery may be necessary if the fracture displaces. If there is doubt about the fracture type and the presence of displacement, a CT scan is recommended with the treatment being based on the findings.

Most authors suggest that cast immobilization is the method of choice for the primary treatment for undisplaced fractures of the scaphoid; the important questions to be answered are which joints should be immobilized and what type of cast should be applied.

Above-Elbow Casts. Some authors still advocate the use of above-elbow casts in scaphoid fractures citing union rates of 95%. However, studies have shown no advantage to the use of above-elbow casts.[4,14] In fact, Kuhlmann et al.,[103] in a prospective study, found the above-elbow cast harmful as it blocked the normal rotation of forearm bones and transferred any rotational movement to the radiocarpal joint where it caused movement at the fracture.

Scaphoid Casts. Prior to 1942, Böhler[22] proposed the use of an unpadded dorsal backslab, but in 1942 he changed the cast to include the proximal phalanx of the thumb. This method of treatment quickly became accepted and is still used in many hospitals. However, Trojan,[184] one of Böhler's pupils, assessed most of the patients treated by Böhler and found no advantage in the use of the scaphoid cast and advocated its use only for highly unstable and proximal pole fractures.

Colles Casts. Yanni et al.[211] found that, provided the wrist was not ulnar deviated or extended, the position of the thumb had no influence on the fracture gap. Clay and coworkers,[34] in a large prospective study, showed that there was no difference in union rates whether the thumb was immobilized or not. For this reason, the use of Colles or forearm casts, rather than scaphoid casts, is advocated.

There is a general consensus that most stable scaphoid fractures unite in 6 to 8 weeks with cast immobilization. However, bone consolidation can take 12 to 16 weeks and some fractures will not have healed even after this time. Apart from the fact that vertical and proximal fractures have a worse prognosis than other scaphoid fractures, there is unfortunately no reliable way of predicting the outcome in undisplaced fractures.[14]

Operative Treatment. Herbert and Fisher[86] believed the incidence of nonunion to be about 50%, and they advocated internal fixation of scaphoid fractures with a newly designed screw. However, the idea of internal fixation was not new. McLaughlin[123] published the first results of primary open reduction and internal fixation of scaphoid fractures in 1954, followed by

Streli[169] in 1970. More recently, McQueen et al.[125] showed in a randomized study that percutaneous screw fixation of undisplaced fractures gives significantly better results and a significantly lower rate of nonunion together with shorter times to return to work and sports when compared to conservative treatment. These findings have been corroborated by other surgeons.[64,140,212]

Percutaneous Fixation. Percutaneous fixation of the acute undisplaced or minimally displaced fractures of the scaphoid has become increasingly popular since the advent of cannulated screw fixation.[64,125,146,147,208] The technique is simple and can be performed through either a volar or dorsal approach. The dorsal approach requires a small open incision as there is a likely risk to tendons or nerves,[1] and the wrist must be in flexion which may displace the fracture and makes imaging more challenging. With the use of the volar approach, a potential disadvantage is an increased prevalence of later scaphotrapezial osteoarthrosis which is usually asymptomatic and has no impact on the final function.[191] Neither approach has been shown to have an advantage in terms of outcome, although the dorsal approach may improve fixation in proximal pole fractures.[81]

There have now been a number of randomized controlled trials of percutaneous fixation and cast management in undisplaced or minimally displaced acute scaphoid waist fractures.[3,12,23,125] These show advantages with percutaneous fixation in a more rapid union rate by 4 to 5 weeks,[12,23,125] a more rapid return to work and sport, and a more rapid improvement in functional tests.[3,12,125] Arora and his colleagues[3] also demonstrated a cost benefit of percutaneous fixation, although this was not statistically significant. However, Davis et al.[42] argued compellingly on cost benefit grounds for the surgical treatment of undisplaced fractures even with open reduction and internal fixation, which might be expected to be more expensive than percutaneous fixation.

Open Reduction and Internal Fixation. With the advent and success of percutaneous fixation of the scaphoid, open reduction and internal fixation is usually reserved for displaced scaphoid fractures which are irreducible closed. A displaced fracture is defined as one with more than 1 mm of step-off or more than 60 degrees of SL or 15 degrees of lunatocapitate angulation as observed on either plain radiographs or CT scans.

Open reduction and internal fixation have been compared with cast management in two randomized controlled trials. The first[156] did not define whether the fractures studied were displaced or not but found no differences in union times or complications except for an increased prevalence of asymptomatic osteoarthrosis of the scaphotrapezial joint in the operatively managed cases. Return to function was faster in the operated group and the authors concluded that open reduction and internal fixation should be comsidered as an alternative to a cast. The second study[46] randomized treatment between open reduction and internal fixation and cast management in undisplaced or minimally displaced fractures of the scaphoid waist. There were advantages in the operated group in early return of movement, better early patient-orientated outcome measures, and a maintained improvement in grip strength throughout the period of review. Ten patients in the cast group developed nonunion compared to none in the operated group. The disadvantage of open reduction and internal fixation were minor problems with the scar. Despite these findings, the authors concluded that scaphoid waist fractures should be treated in a cast.

AUTHORS' PREFERRED TREATMENT: UNDISPLACED SCAPHOID FRACTURES (TYPE A2)

Cast Immobilization

We recommend a Colles cast for nondisplaced stable scaphoid fractures in low-demand patients, with the wrist in neutral deviation and neutral flexion–extension for 6 to 12 weeks until there is radiographic union. If there is doubt about the presence of displacement, a CT scan will confirm the position of the fracture. Careful clinical and radiographic follow-up examinations at the time of cast removal are essential. It is recommended that the patient be reviewed 6 weeks after cast removal for clinical and radiologic examination and then every 3 months until the outcome is clear.

Percutaneous Screw Fixation

In all other patients with acute scaphoid fractures, we prefer percutaneous screw fixation. This includes the majority of young high-demand patients. The method is relatively easy and, if the patient is compliant, it allows postoperative treatment without cast immobilization. The advantage of this minimally invasive method is early return to sports and work in a population which is usually young and active.[82,121] No serious complications are expected when the surgical procedure is performed carefully. Of all the screws available, the authors prefer the Acutrak screw (Acumed, Inc., Beaverton, OR), which has some key features that make it different from other cannulated screws (Fig 29-19J). It was developed to produce interfragmentary compression with a headless screw. The thread pitch varies at a constant rate along the length of the screw. This accumulation of pitch differentials results in gradual compression at the fracture site. The taper on the outer profile of the screw causes the threads to constantly purchase new bone. This minimizes thread damage and improves pull-out strength. Biomechanic studies

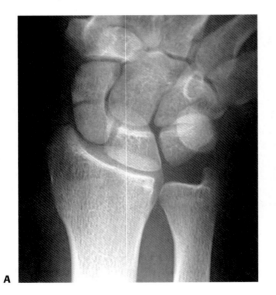

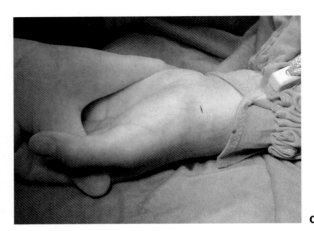

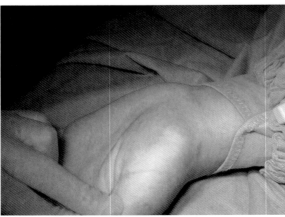

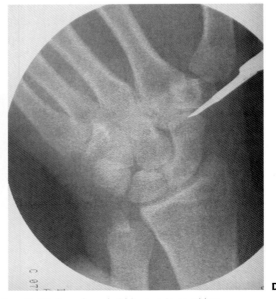

FIGURE 29-19 Percutaneous stabilization of scaphoid fracture. **A.** AP view of scaphoid fracture in an athlete. **B.** The wrist should be dorsiflexed prior to insertion of the K-wire. **C.** A 4 to 5 mm incision is sufficient for insertion of the screw. The incision should be placed in skin crease to avoid visible scars. **D.** The joint space between scaphoid and trapezium is opened under flouroscopy.   (*continues*)

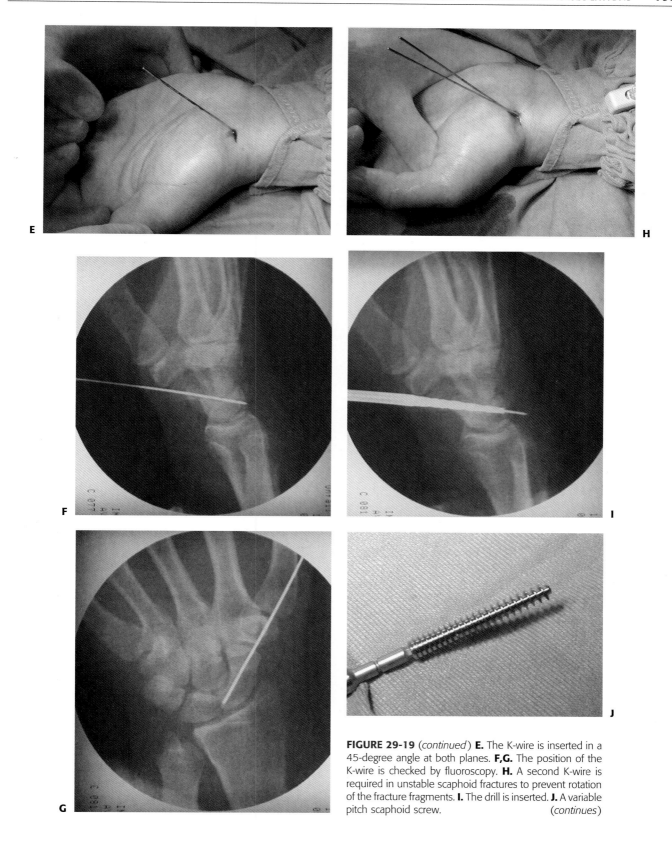

FIGURE 29-19 (*continued*) **E.** The K-wire is inserted in a 45-degree angle at both planes. **F,G.** The position of the K-wire is checked by fluoroscopy. **H.** A second K-wire is required in unstable scaphoid fractures to prevent rotation of the fracture fragments. **I.** The drill is inserted. **J.** A variable pitch scaphoid screw.   (*continues*)

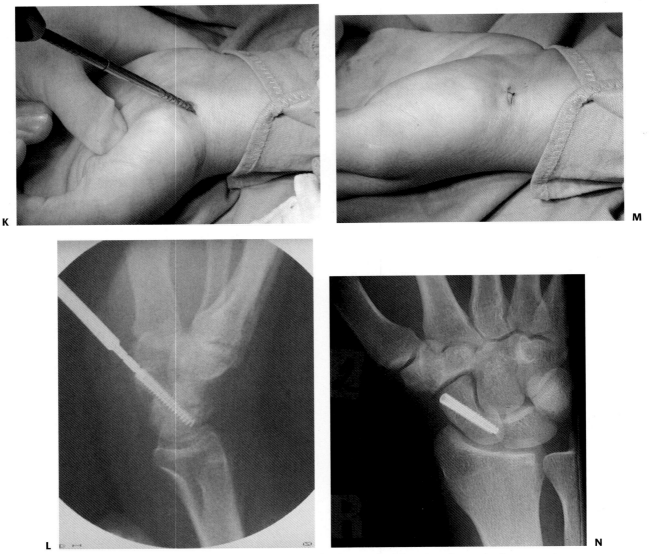

FIGURE 29-19 (*continued*) **K.** Insertion of scaphoid screw. **L.** Check insertion of screw by flouroscopy to avoid rotation of fracture fragments. **M.** Closure of wound with one suture. **N.** Postoperative radiograph shows a good compression of the fragments; the fracture gap is no longer visible.

have shown that the Acutrak variable pitch, tapered, headless, compression screw performed significantly better and provided superior fixation than did the Herbert compression screw, and it was often better than the AO lag screw.[16,68,93,181,202]

The operative procedure is simple and fast, but a good three-dimensional understanding of the anatomy of the scaphoid is required (Fig. 29-19). There are no major vessels, nerves, or tendons endangered by the minimal invasive approach to the scaphoid. The hand is placed on a radiolucent table with the shoulder abducted and the forearm in supination. The wrist is extended over a roll. The correct placement of the guide wire is crucial to the success of the procedure. It helps to remember that the scaphoid lies in a 45-degree plane to both the longitudinal and horizontal axes of the wrist. A 4 to 5 mm skin incision is made about 1 cm distal and radial to the scaphoid tubercle and the tip of the guidewire placed on the scaphoid tubercle. The correct entry point

is one that will allow central placement of the screw in the scaphoid in both the AP and lateral planes. In a few cases with an overhanging trapezium, it may be necessary to insert the guidewire through the trapezium, which does not seem to result in added morbidity.[126] The guidewire is inserted at a 45-degree angle in both planes, visualizing the AP plane with a fluoroscope. Unstable scaphoid fractures have a tendency to rotate when the screw is inserted. If so, a second wire is inserted to support the fracture site and avoid rotational deformity. The length of the screw is then measured and approximately 3 mm subtracted from the length to avoid prominence at either end. The Acutrak screw, which is self-drilling and self-tapping, is then inserted. Screw progress should be monitored with the fluoroscope to ensure that no rotation or distraction occurs at the fracture site. If distraction occurs, the screw should be removed and the track drilled. A central position of the screw without joint penetration at the radiocarpal joint or prominence at the scaphotrapezial joint should be confirmed with AP, lateral, and supinated and pronated views of the wrist. Postoperatively, a bandage is applied with no cast being required. Noncontact sports are allowed immediately. Contact sports, heavy lifting, or weight bearing through the wrist are allowed 6 weeks after surgery.

Unstable and Displaced Fractures (Type B2)

Displaced fractures of the scaphoid as well as proximal pole and oblique fractures require different treatment from that of nondisplaced fractures. Unstable or displaced fractures of the scaphoid have a high incidence of delayed union and nonunion, and the routine use of cast immobilization is not generally recommended. However, there are a few indications for closed reduction and cast management of displaced scaphoid fracture. Patients who undergo conservative treatment have to be carefully selected and will include patients with metabolic diseases, noncompliant patients, and those patients with significant medical comorbidities. Closed reduction involves three-point pressure on the tubercle of the distal scaphoid in a palmar direction combined with dorsal pressure over the capitate and dorsal support of the distal radius, which helps reduce and maintain the dorsolunate angulation. An acceptable reduction includes alignment with less than 1 mm of displacement and a SL angle of not more than 60 degrees.

Herbert[85] questioned the efficacy of closed treatment as he was convinced, as are most orthopaedic surgeons, that for sound bone union to take place, the fracture fragments must be in close apposition so that soft tissue interposition or synovial fluid cannot affect healing. He believed that if closed treatment is used for complete fractures, osseous union may be the result more of luck than skill.[85]

AUTHORS' PREFERRED TREATMENT: UNSTABLE AND DISPLACED FRACTURES (TYPE B2)

As most of these fractures occur in a young, healthy, active population, proper stabilization should be performed. We prefer percutaneous screw fixation as described above (see Fig. 29-19). If reduction cannot be achieved, two pins should be inserted, one in each fragment, and these pins are used as joysticks to reduce the fracture. A temporary Kirschner-wire (K-wire) can be inserted to maintain the reduction, and the guidewire for the screw is then introduced. For acute displaced fractures that cannot be reduced percutaneously, we recommend open reduction and compression screw fixation of the scaphoid as soft tissue interposition is not uncommon and often results in fibrous instead of osseous union.[85,104,135,205] If there is a humpback deformity as a result of comminution, then bone grafting is required. K-wire fixation alone is not advisable as the rate of nonunion is high. Cast immobilization is not usually required unless there is associated ligamentous injury.

Proximal Pole Fractures (Type B3)

Proximal pole fractures (Type B3) should be treated operatively as they rarely unite without surgery.

AUTHORS' PREFERRED TREATMENT: PROXIMAL POLE FRACTURES (TYPE B3)

The authors stabilize these fractures percutaneously using either a dorsal approach (Fig. 29-20) or a volar approach, driving the guidewire through the proximal pole and inserting the screw from the dorsal aspect. With this technique, it is much easier to get a proper purchase on the small proximal fragment.[162]

An open technique is required for the exposure of displaced small proximal pole fractures, nonunions of the proximal pole, and for exposure of injuries to the SL ligament. We prefer a straight 3 to 4 cm incision centered over the back of the wrist after checking the level of the SL junction with the fluoroscope. The extensor pollicis longus tendon is mobilized radially after incision of the retinaculum. The dorsal capsule is then incised and the scaphoid exposed. Care is taken to avoid injury to the dorsal ridge vasculature during the approach. The fragments are reduced manually or with the assistance of K-wire joysticks. Bone grafting may be used to stimulate union. A compression screw is then used after inserting a temporary K-wire to prevent rotation. The dorsal wrist capsule should always be repaired. The use of postoperative immobilization depends on the screw purchase in bone and the stability of the fragment after fixation.

Scaphoid Nonunion

Nonunion of the scaphoid occurs in around 10% of nonoperatively managed scaphoid fractures,[14,45,125] but the risk is probably greater in unstable fractures and correspondingly less in stable fractures. The natural history of a scaphoid nonunion depends on the stability of the nonunion with progressive degenerative changes correlating with increasing displacement of the nonunion.[118]

Patients with nonunion of the scaphoid have either not been immobilized at all or only for a week or two[14,106] or develop nonunion after a prolonged period of cast immobilization. A

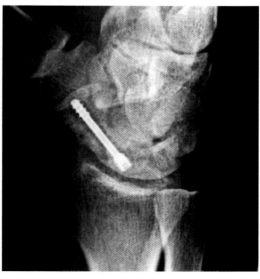

FIGURE 29-20 Healed proximal pole fracture 6 months after dorsal approach.

few will have had percutaneous fixation of their fracture. If initial nonoperative treatment is chosen for the stable undisplaced fracture, careful clinical and radiologic follow-up is required to identify a developing nonunion. If there are no signs of union after 12 weeks, operative intervention should be considered. If conservative treatment is continued and there are still no signs of union after 16 weeks, the patient has to understand that union is unlikely.

Stable Nonunions (Herbert Type D1)

It is essential to differentiate between stable and unstable scaphoid nonunions. The stable scaphoid nonunion is characterized by a firm fibrous nonunion that prevents deformity from occurring. The length and shape of the scaphoid remain well preserved, and the risk of osteoarthritis is small. Radiographs show an indistinct fracture line with variable cystic changes affecting the adjacent bone fragments. The patients are usually relatively symptom-free unless the wrist is subjected to further trauma, which often leads to an unstable nonunion with all of the associated problems of carpal collapse, osteoarthritis, pain, and weakness.[85] Although there are patients who seem to have an asymptomatic, stable nonunion of the scaphoid for many years, most patients will become symptomatic if the stable nonunion progresses to an unstable one and osteoarthritis occurs. This has been reported as occurring in the majority of cases,[118] but it must be appreciated that studies relate to symptomatic nonunion as asymptomatic cases do not present frequently to the orthopaedic surgeon.

The indication to treat patients with a stable nonunion is to prevent progression to an unstable nonunion and the development of degenerative changes. Treating fibrous nonunions is usually straightforward and gives good results, whereas patients with unstable nonunions often have persistent postoperative problems due to the osteoarthritic changes of the radiocarpal joint. The earlier the surgery, the lower the incidence of secondary osteoarthritis. The standard palmar approach should be used for all reconstructions, except those involving small proximal pole fractures.[85]

Slade and coworkers[163] reported a series of stable scaphoid nonunions that were treated by percutaneous screw fixation with good results. Their indications were nonunions that were well aligned and without extensive sclerosis or bone resorption at the nonunion site. It seems that selected nonunions might require only rigid fixation, preferably undertaken percutaneously to minimize devascularization.

AUTHORS' PREFERRED TREATMENT: STABLE NON-UNIONS (HERBERT TYPE D1)

We prefer an open palmar approach using a straight incision as opposed to the curved incision described by Russe.[153] The incision is based over or radial to the flexor carpi radialis from the scaphoid tubercle to the distal radius. The sheath of the flexor carpi radialis tendon is incised and the tendon retracted ulnarly. Directly beneath the tendon lies the palmar capsule of the wrist, just above the scaphoid. The capsule should be incised longitudinally. There are no neurovascular structures at risk as the radial neurovascular bundle lies radially. The superficial palmar branch of the radial artery is distal at the end of incision and needs to be ligated in cases

of wider exposure of the distal scaphoid. It is important to prepare the nonunion surfaces by removing any fibrous tissue and sclerotic bone. We usually leave the dorsal cartilage in place. This provides a hinge and facilitates assessment of scaphoid length. In most cases of stable nonunion, cancellous bone graft from the distal radius usually provides sufficient volume, although iliac crest bone graft can be used if necessary. Screw fixation of the scaphoid is then used. Immobilization in a cast or splint is not required postoperatively except in occasional cases for pain relief.

Unstable Nonunions (Herbert Type D2)

The unstable scaphoid nonunion is characterized by sclerotic bone surfaces, with synovial erosion, fibrous cysts, and continuous bone wear at the fracture leading to a marked discrepancy between the sizes of the two bone fragments. Unstable scaphoid nonunion leads to instability and progressive collapse and deformity.[56,57,118,152] Fisk[56] was the first to describe the humpback deformity of the scaphoid that results from established nonunion where the proximal scaphoid rotates dorsally into extension and the distal part faces downward in flexion. Impingement between the palmarflexed distal pole of the scaphoid and the styloid process of the radius results in radiocarpal osteoarthritis.[195] At the same time, the unsupported carpus collapses into a DISI deformity with increasing subluxation and secondary arthritis of the midcarpal joint.[85] Techniques of palmar and radiopalmar bone grafting have been developed to correct scaphoid malalignment and to restore normal scaphoid length. Failure to correct the humpback deformity results in intraoperative problems because the screw cannot be adequately placed and will cut out, leaving residual instability. Even if the nonunion heals, the malunited scaphoid has a twofold increase in degenerative arthritis compared with a scaphoid that has healed with correct alignment.[185]

The prognosis following surgery in D1 fractures is usually excellent whereas in D2 fractures the result depends on the viability of the bone fragments and the extent to which secondary changes have developed. The quoted success rates of achieving union with internal fixation and bone grafting range from 60% to 95%.[48,183] The differing rates may be explained by differences in the type of fractures, differences in the demographics of the patients, or the acknowledged difficulty in defining union. Recently, smoking has been implicated as a reason for failure of nonunion surgery.[48,114]

The aim of treatment is to achieve union and thereby relieve pain, increase function, and prevent the development or progression of osteoarthritis. In the treatment of nonunion of the scaphoid, it is essential to maintain the important principles of fracture healing and at the same time secure correct scaphoid alignment. The major principles to follow are early diagnosis, complete resection of the nonunion, correction of deformity secondary to carpal collapse and carpal instability, preservation of blood supply, bone apposition by an inlay graft, and screw fixation for fracture stability.

Preoperative Planning. Careful preoperative planning is required to determine the degree of correction that one may expect to achieve. Radiographs should be compared with films of the opposite uninjured wrist. Sagittal images from CT scans provide the best method of evaluating the location of the nonunion and the degree of collapse. The lateral intrascaphoid angle[6] and the height-to-length ratio of the bone help identify angulation and collapse of the scaphoid.[185] The lateral intrascaphoid angle is formed by the intersection of the perpendicular lines to the diameters of the proximal and distal poles. An angle of more than 35 degrees has been shown to be associated with an increased incidence of arthrosis even in fractures that went on to unite.[7] The collapse of the scaphoid in the sagittal plane causes DISI pathology and increases the chances of wrist arthrosis even if the scaphoid finally heals.[6] Restoration of normal scaphoid anatomy in the treatment of nonunion therefore aims to reduce or postpone the incidence of osteoarthritis and to improve the function of the wrist.[55]

Although AVN of the proximal fragment can affect the healing potential of a scaphoid, diminished vascularity of the proximal scaphoid is not a contraindication to a palmar inlay bone graft.[39] If fracture union can be achieved, the relative avascularity will improve. It is advantageous to confirm AVN of proximal pole fragments to determine the prognosis for successful treatment. Methods of assessing AVN include bone scan, CT scans, and MRI. The latter technique is undoubtedly the most sensitive and is preferred. However, the only definitive test for confirming AVN is the observation at surgery of the presence or absence of bleeding from bone. Green[78] reported that the number of punctuate bleeding points is a good indicator of vascularity of the bone. When the proximal pole was completely avascular, the likelihood of successful healing with a graft was virtually nil and an alternative procedure such as intercarpal fusion, excision of the proximal scaphoid, interposition arthroplasty, proximal row carpectomy, or scaphoid allograft should be considered. Herbert[85] stated that carpal collapse and secondary arthritis are rarely associated with proximal pole nonunion. He therefore argued against the use of interposition bone grafts and suggested screw fixation by a dorsal approach, with or without cancellous bone grafting, depending on the findings at the time of surgery. Although the fracture may not unite, the patient's own bone should be better than any implant. Another alternative is a vascularized bone graft.

The standard palmar approach should be used for most reconstructions of unstable scaphoid nonunions to avoid damaging the dorsal blood supply. Scaphoid nonunions might not be visible macroscopically and often need sharp division with the knife. It is useful to check the site of a nonunion as fusion of the proximal pole of the scaphoid with the lunate has been undertaken assuming that this joint was the site of nonunion!

There are a number of methods of bone grafting in use but none has been shown to be superior in terms of achieving union.[15,183] Prior to the introduction of modern fixation methods the Russe inlay graft[130] was used in the treatment of scaphoid nonunion (Fig. 29-21), but this technique does not usually correct volar shortening. Anterior wedge grafting procedures are now in common use as humpback deformities can be corrected with this technique.[51,182] Initial reduction of the lunate and temporary pin fixation to the radius can facilitate accurate reduction.[182]

AUTHORS' PREFERRED TREATMENT: UNSTABLE NONUNIONS (HERBERT TYPE D2)

A volar approach is necessary to correct a humpback deformity. The nonunion gap is exposed and débrided, and the fracture fragments are mobilized. It is best to leave a cartilage hinge posteriorly to provide a fulcrum around which the fragments may be hinged open although this is often not possible in older, unstable scaphoid fractures. If the hinge is released in an effort to regain all of the scaphoid length, the fracture fragments will become extremely unstable and difficult to align. Furthermore, the gap between the two fragments may be too great for the scaphoid to revascularize the proximal pole.[185]

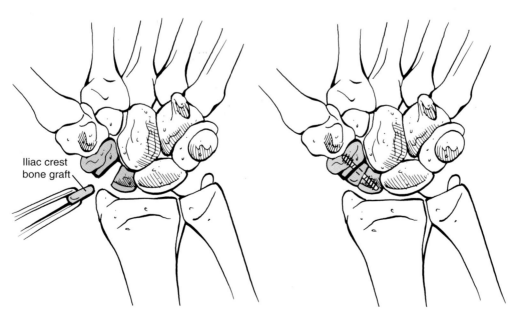

Iliac crest bone graft

FIGURE 29-21 Standard Russe[153] bone graft (top). His technique relied on packing a corticocancellous bone graft into a trough curretted through the volar cortex of both fragments. Because the volar cortex is often foreshortened by erosion of the fragments, loss of length is difficult to correct without introducing a cortical graft (center). Modified Russe winged graft that is impacted into a volar trough to lengthen the scaphoid (bottom).

The wrist is extended and the two fragments gently distracted with small spreaders. This maneuver usually achieves adequate correction of the carpal deformity and a satisfactory improvement in wrist extension. Provided that reasonable correction is achieved and that the wrist extends to at least 45 degrees, most patients achieve satisfactory clinical results.[69] The fracture surfaces are excised with a small osteotome, burr, or curette. We prefer a corticocancellous wedge graft from the iliac crest. This is an interposition graft, which is inserted on the palmar surface and serves to bridge the fracture gap and correct any displacement or angulation of the scaphoid that has occurred. To correct angular deformity and restore normal scaphoid length, the amount of resection and size of the graft can be calculated preoperatively by CT scans. The indications for interposition grafting include gross motion at the nonunion site, scaphoid resorption, and loss of carpal height. Most commonly, the operative procedure involves an anterior interposition bone graft, with the size based on comparative scaphoid views of the opposite wrist and intraoperative measurements.

The width and depth of the defect is measured and a graft of the exact size is removed from the iliac crest with an osteotome. Oscillating saws should not be used, as thermal necrosis of the graft can occur. With the wedge graft in place and the scaphoid reduced and held with a K-wire, a compression screw is inserted (Fig. 29-22). Internal fixation with K-wires alone is usually not successful as compression is required to achieve union. However, if the graft shows a tendency to rotate, additional fixation with a K-wire may be required. If there is a severe or longstanding DISI deformity with a RL angle greater than 20 degrees, additional pinning of the lunate to radius for 6 to 8 weeks is advised.[55] It may be difficult to completely correct carpal instability in longstanding cases, and these patients may be better served by various salvage procedures.

With stable fixation, postoperative immobilization is usually not required but a Colles cast can be used if there is doubt about stability or pins have been used across the radiocarpal joint.

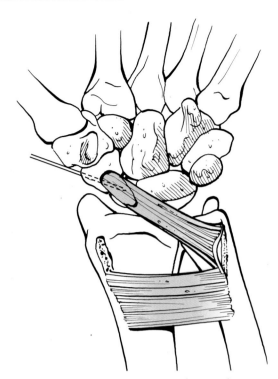

FIGURE 29-23 Pronator quadratus graft.

Vascularized bone grafts from the distal radius (radial artery) or distal ulna (ulnar artery) have also been described.[168] We prefer the pronator quadratus graft (Fig. 29-23).

A partial radial styloidectomy (Fig. 29-24) can be performed in patients with radiologic signs of stage I radioscaphoid arthritis, this being arthritis that is limited to the scaphoid and radial styloid. This is undertaken to relieve pain arising from arthritic joints or osteophyte impingement. If there are no radiologic signs of arthritis, a styloidectomy should not be undertaken at the same time as a scaphoid reconstruction often relieves symptoms.

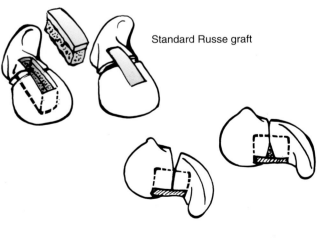

Standard Russe graft

Winged graft

FIGURE 29-22 Insertion of an iliac crest bone graft and stabilization with a screw for treatment of scaphoid nonunions. The bone graft is wedged to correct the angulation deformity that often occurs.

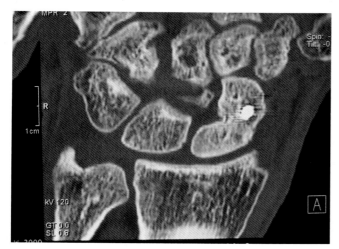

FIGURE 29-24 Radial styloidectomy for pain relief in a patient who showed arthritic changes due to scaphoid nonunion.

Salvage Procedures for Scaphoid Nonunion

Excision of Part or all of the Scaphoid. A very small fragment can be excised with impunity. However, most surgeons are aware that if it is more than 8 mm long, the results are poor and the wrist feels weak.[14]

Wrist Denervation. Wrist denervation[30] is often helpful as it is combined with significant pain relief. However, pain relief can be temporary.

Proximal Row Carpectomy. The results of excising the scaphoid, lunate, and triquetrum have been disappointing in some series,[85] which is why we prefer wrist arthrodesis in cases of panscaphoid arthritis and severe pain.

Scaphoid Prosthesis. In selected patients with panscaphoid osteoarthritis, total replacement of the scaphoid is worth considering.[189] If the scaphoid must be excised, it seems reasonable to replace it with something! Silicone implants induced progressive silicone arthritis in many cases,[84] and the technique was abandoned 20 years ago. Other methods of replacement such as cadaveric bones and titanium implants are currently in clinical trials. However, unless the midcarpal joint is stable and painless, this procedure should be combined with a fusion across the midcarpal joint.[85] Without this fusion, progressive carpal subluxation is likely to occur. The fusion is unlikely to trouble patients as most have long-standing carpal collapse deformity with secondary osteoarthritis. It is important to correct the midcarpal subluxation as much as possible in order to improve the range of dorsiflexion. Unless at least 30 degrees of extension is maintained after surgery, the patient will almost certainly continue to experience pain when the wrist is loaded.[85] Young and active patients are likely to complain of continued pain after this procedure, and wrist arthrodesis is therefore preferable in these patients.

Wrist Arthrodesis. Unstable nonunion of the scaphoid can lead to increasing midcarpal and radiocarpal osteoarthritis secondary to increasing carpus collapse. If this is not treated, there is increasing pain and weakness, and wrist motion becomes re-

stricted to the extent that reconstructive surgery is no longer feasible and wrist fusion is required. Pain is the main factor to be taken into consideration when deciding for or against wrist arthrodesis. Arthrodesis is an accepted surgical treatment option for patients with markedly restricted and painful wrist motion. Instability and deformity of the wrist affect hand function significantly but pain diminishes both strength and dexterity. Wrist arthrodesis achieves good pain relief,[85,92] especially in younger patients with high functional demands. It can be difficult to convince patients with severe pain but good wrist movement that the optimal treatment might be a wrist fusion. However, the pain relief associated with a successful fusion results in significant improvement of hand function and grip strength. Preoperatively, it is easy to supply the patient with a dorsal splint to simulate arthrodesis to see if this helps wrist function and symptoms.

Scaphoid Malunion

Fractured scaphoids are prone to triplane angulation due to the joint compressive forces at the scaphotrapezial and radioscaphoid joints. The proximal fragment has a tendency to extend, deviate radially, and supinate relative to the distal fragment. The collapse of the scaphoid in the sagittal plane causes DISI pathology and increases the chances of wrist arthrosis even if the scaphoid finally heals.[6]

Although the malunited scaphoid fracture is a recognized entity that causes altered carpal kinematics and abnormal load distribution which may cause premature wrist arthrosis, the reported number of patients treated with early osteotomy is surprisingly small. Indications for osteotomy are pain, weakness, limited range of motion, and deformity of the scaphoid detected on radiographs and evaluated by CT scans. Restoration of normal scaphoid anatomy in malunion aims to reduce or postpone the incidence of osteoarthritis and to improve function of the wrist.[52,55] Lynch et al.[117] reported a technique of corrective osteotomy that corrects the intrascaphoid angles, restores palmar length to the scaphoid, and reduces DISI deformity of the carpus. This method seems to have a role in the prevention or slowing of the onset of arthritis in young patients with high functional demands.[117]

Avascular Necrosis of the Scaphoid

AVN of the scaphoid can occur as a late complication of scaphoid fractures, especially those involving the proximal pole. Occasionally, AVN may occur without a fracture, either as a complication of SL ligament injury or as an idiopathic condition known as Preiser's disease.[143] The term Preiser disease is associated with AVN of the scaphoid without fracture or trauma, although it should be noted that the AVN described by Preiser probably occurred in fractured scaphoids as all of his patients had a well-documented history of trauma. The typical symptoms of AVN are increasing pain and stiffness of the wrist. Radiographs usually show a small, deformed proximal pole fragment with cystic changes and areas of sclerosis. It is mandatory in all cases of scaphoid nonunion to exclude AVN by MRI scans before surgery is undertaken as the diagnosis of AVN alters the treatment options.

If AVN is present, a vascularized bone graft is often recommended.[139,193] The bone graft can be harvested dorsally through the second dorsal compartment of the distal radius, anteriorly in the form of a pronator quadratus graft, or from the second metacarpal. It is important to adhere to the basic principles of nonunion treatment with meticulous preparation and stabilization of the nonunion site.

Pearls and Pitfalls

- Occult scaphoid fractures are easily detected by MRI scans.
- Percutaneous stabilization of scaphoid fractures significantly reduces time lost from work and sports and increases the rate of union.
- Proximal pole fractures can also be stabilized percutaneously by a dorsal approach.
- Malalignment of scaphoid fractures is often undiagnosed. CT scans are helpful.
- Conservative treatment often ends in delayed healing. An aggressive operative approach is recommended.

LUNATE FRACTURES

Lunate fractures are rare, making up less than 1% of all carpal fractures (see Table 3-18). Isolated fractures of the lunate are often unrecognized,[33] and some authors believe that unrecognized and untreated fractures of the lunate lead to Kienböck disease. This opinion was based on the work of Verdan,[190] who applied strong forces to cadaver bones and observed that the resulting fractures were not visible on standard radiographs but only on histology. A major argument against this hypothesis are the MRI findings of Schiltenwolf et al.,[157] who postulated that early venous congestion of the lunate was responsible for the pathogenesis of Kienböck disease but found no fractures. The lunate necrosis after perilunate dislocation is probably due to impairment of the arterial vasculature.[160]

Kienböck disease is an eponym for idiopathic avascular osteonecrosis of the lunate. It usually has an insidious onset without a history of injury; however, diagnosis is sometimes made after a simple fall that fractures the necrotic bone (Fig. 29-25). Osteonecrosis may be the result of interruption of the vascular supply to the lunate,[157] which shows no radiographic evidence of injury until sclerosis and osteochondral collapse are seen. The condition is more common in patients with an ulnar minus variant.

Anatomy

The lunate sits like a keystone in the proximal carpal row in the well-protected concavity of the lunate fossa of the radius, anchored on either side by the interosseous ligaments to the scaphoid and triquetrum with which it articulates. Distally, the convex capitate head fits into the concavity of the lunate. The joint reaction force from the capitate and radius squeezes the lunate ulnarly. The proximal pole of the hamate has a variable articular facet on the distal ulnar surface of the lunate, and ulnar deviation increases the degree of contact of these two bones. The vascular supply of the lunate is primarily through the proximal carpal arcade both dorsally and palmarly. However, the literature suggests that 7% to 26% of lunates may have a single volar or dorsal blood supply and are therefore vulnerable to AVN because of disruption of extraosseous blood supply.[58] Several authors.[39,75,137] have shown the intralunate anastomoses to be of three main types. The degree of cross flow between the systems is variable.

Mechanisms of Injury

Most patients with fractures of the lunate have a history of a hyperextension injury such as a fall on the outstretched hand. Occasionally, repetitive stresses of the wrist or a strenuous push will give rise to a "snap" in the wrist.[39] In extension, the lunate is displaced onto the palmar aspect of the lunate fossa and rotated dorsally. The capitate drives against the palmar aspect of the lunate and at the same time pushes it in an ulnar direction. This is resisted by the RL ligament, which exerts tension at its lunate insertion. If there is an ulnar minus variant, the support offered by the TFCC and ulnar head will be minimal, and even less when the hand is pronated. The compressive stresses over the proximal convexity of the lunate shift dramatically at the interface between the TFCC and radial articular surface. The lack of ulnar support may also allow proximal displacement of the triquetrum placing further tensile stress on the lunate surface through the LT ligament. This appears to provide a reasonable scenario for the transverse fractures that occur in the sagittal plane.

Avulsions of the dorsal pole are more likely due to tension that develops in the SL ligament, because these are frequently seen with SLD. Avulsion fractures of the ulnar aspect of the palmar pole are usually associated with a perilunate dislocation. It is also possible that sufficient stress develops, where the arteries penetrate the bone, to induce devascularization. In this situation, avascularity would precede fracture, rather than vice versa. Indeed, there is considerable evidence that both mechanisms can be responsible for Kienböck disease and that several contributing factors such as trauma, ulnar variance, and impaired vascularity interact to produce Kienböck disease.

Classification

Lunate fractures can be difficult to describe and part of the difficulty is that the fragmentation that occurs in Kienböck disease can be confused with fractures (Fig. 29-25A). However, acute fractures of the lunate are classified into five groups[177]:

1. Frontal fractures of the palmar pole with involvement of the palmar nutrient arteries.
2. Osteochondral fractures of the proximal articular surface without substantial damage to the nutrient vessels.
3. Frontal fractures of the dorsal pole.
4. Transverse fractures of the body.
5. Transarticular frontal fractures of the body of the lunate.

Fresh fractures of the lunate include dorsal and palmar horn avulsion fractures that occur more often in the radial corner than in the ulnar corner. Fractures of the body are usually transverse in the coronal plane. The more common of these is between the middle and palmar thirds of the body.

Radiographic Findings

Lunate fractures may be difficult to visualize early because a nondisplaced crack is often obscured by superimposed structures. The best example of this problem is the palmar cortical line of the radial styloid which is aligned with the division between the dorsal and palmar thirds of the lunate where a transverse fracture often occurs.[39] The AP view of this is in a plane almost perpendicular to the fracture, which is overlapped by the rims of the distal radius and is therefore not apparent. The palmar horn of the lunate may also be hidden by the pisiform

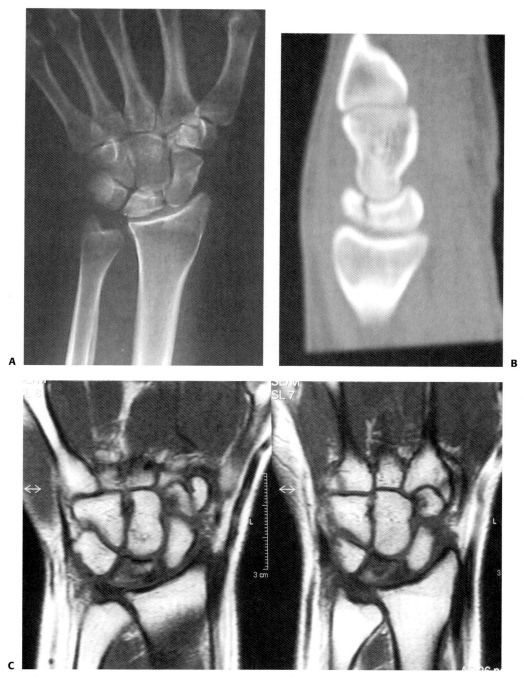

FIGURE 29-25 A. AP radiograph of a 25-year-old woman after a skiing accident. It shows a sclerotic lunate and an ulnar negative variance. **B.** A CT scan demonstrates a fracture of the sclerotic lunate. **C.** An MRI scan demonstrates decreased vascularity of the lunate.

and scaphoid shadows. For these reasons, clinical suspicion must take precedence over the findings on plain films. A technetium-99m bone scan will be positive within 24 hours of injury. Oblique films sometimes help to visualise fracture lines, but CT scans provide more precise detail. Osteonecrotic changes are also more easily seen on CT scans than on radiographs, and it is also often possible to differentiate the primary fracture from the secondary fractures associated with fragmentation.

MRI is an excellent tool to assess vascularity, diagnose the early stages of lunate AVN, and to demonstrate revascularization as well as healing. MRI will show evidence of diminished vascu-

larity before changes are apparent on radiograph, and this modality is now the imaging procedure of choice for early evaluation of Kienböck's disease. Gadolinium enhancement allows a more accurate assessment of lunate vascularity and revascularization. Arthroscopic examination permits a direct assessment of the articular surfaces and the integrity of the intrinsic ligaments.

Treatment

Most fractures of the lunate can be treated by cast immobilization for 4 weeks. Healing of nondisplaced lunate fractures, especially of avulsion injuries of the dorsal or palmar horns, is relatively good. A transverse fracture of the body will heal if it remains nondisplaced, particularly in adolescents. However, it is important to recognize that, especially with high-energy injury, a lunate fracture may be associated with carpal dislocation or subluxation and the fracture may progress to carpal instability, nonunion, or AVN.[39] Indications for open reduction and internal fixation include displacement or associated carpal instability. Imaging can be very helpful and ideally should include MRI scans. If there is evidence of separation of the lunate fragments by the capitate, union will not occur and the risk of AVN is markedly increased. Although the efficacy of internal fixation of the lunate is unproven and the obstacles to successful reduction and fixation are substantial, the consequences of inaction are quite predictable. Distraction with an external fixator may facilitate reduction of the lunate fragments.[39]

Nonunion of a lunate body fracture is rare, because most progress to Kienböck disease. If this occurs, the treatment includes radial shortening, radial wedge osteotomy, or ulnar lengthening in the early stages and carpal arthodeses if the condition is advanced.

FRACTURES OF THE OTHER CARPAL BONES

Triquetrum

The triquetrum is the carpal bone that is most commonly fractured after the scaphoid (see Table 3-18). Most fractures of the triquetrum are avulsion injuries that may be associated with ligament damage.[43] The triquetrum may sustain a transverse fracture in a perilunate dislocation, but it usually displaces dorsally with the distal carpal row away from the lunate. The most common triquetral fracture is probably the impingement shear fracture of the ulnar styloid against the dorsal triquetrum which occurs with the wrist in extension and ulnar deviation, particularly when a long ulnar styloid is present.[70] Shear impingement by the hamate against the posteroradial projection of the triquetrum, the triquetrohamate impaction syndrome, occurs through compression of the wrist, when the body weight is supported by the hand placed in forced dorsal and ulnar extension while the forearm is pronated.[112] The triquetrum is rarely dislocated alone because of its strong ligamentous connections.

Diagnosis

The clinical signs and symptoms are pain and tenderness localized to the appropriate area. Dorsal chip fractures of the triquetrum are easily overlooked on the AP radiograph because of the normal superimposition of the dorsal lip on the lunate. Such fractures are usually seen in one of the views of the normal scaphoid series. If not, a slightly oblique, pronated lateral radiograph will project the triquetrum even more dorsal to the lunate. Transverse fractures of the triquetral body are usually easily identified on the standard AP view. CT scans may be required to detect the extent of injury. If occult fractures are suspected, MRI scans should be considered.[65,67]

Treatment

Close treatment in a cast or splint for 2 to 3 weeks until symptoms subside is sufficient for avulsion injuries. Triquetral body

fractures in association with carpal disruption require internal fixation.

Pisiform

Fractures of the pisiform are rare (see Table 3-18). The pisiform is generally injured during a fall on the dorsiflexed, outstretched hand. Most fractures are sports-related and easily missed.[105] A direct blow while the pisiform is held firmly against the triquetrum under tension from the flexor carpi ulnaris leads to either avulsion of its distal portion with a vertical fracture or an osteochondral compression fracture at the pisotriquetral joint. Based on the findings of Arner and Hagberg,[11] the fractured bone should be excised.[148,160] This avoids pisotriquetral incongruity. The type of fracture pattern is therefore irrelevant as excision eliminates any impact of fracture pattern on clinical outcome. The small amount of loss of grip strength associated with excision is not of functional significance.[160] However, absence of the pisiform exposes the ulnar artery and nerve to more trauma and may increase the possibility of hammer syndrome and neuropathy. We prefer conservative therapy primarily and undertake secondary resection if there are any problems with nonunion and incongruity.

Diagnosis

Clinically, there is pain in the area of the pisiform, although some patients may present with ulnar nerve symptoms as the nerve divides into its terminal branches beside the pisiform bone. Special views are required to see pisiform injuries. A lateral view of the wrist with the forearm in 20 to 45 degrees supination and carpal tunnel views are useful. If subluxation of the pisotriquetral joint is suspected, the diagnosis is made when one or more of the following are present: a joint space of less than 4 mm in width, loss of parallelism of the joint surfaces greater than 20 degrees, and proximal or distal overriding of the pisiform amounting to more than 15% of the width of the joint surfaces.[39]

Treatment

Cast treatment for a few weeks until symptoms subside is usually sufficient. Rarely painful nonunion may occur when excision of the pisiform is usually effective.

Trapezium

Fractures of the trapezium comprise almost 4% of all carpal bone fractures (see Table 3-18). About 60% of the reported cases have an unsatisfactory outcome.[40] The majority of trapezial fractures are ridge avulsion fractures or vertical fractures of the body. Fracture through the articular surface of the trapezium is produced by the base of the first metacarpal being driven into the articular surface of the trapezium by the adducted thumb. There might also be an anvil mechanism related to the radial styloid. These fractures may be associated with dislocation of the first carpometacarpal joint. Avulsion fractures caused by the capsular ligaments can occur during forceful deviation, traction, or rotation. Direct blows to the palmar arch area or forceful distraction of the proximal palmar arch may result in avulsion of the ridge of the trapezium by the transverse carpal ligament.[39] Fractures of the tuberosity of the trapezium may be associated with fractures of the hook of the hamate or with dislocation of the hamate because the flexor retinaculum is fixed to the ridges of both bones.[160]

Standard scaphoid views are usually enough to detect a fracture of the trapezium. Fractures of the tuberosity are projected by carpal tunnel views.

Treatment

Treatment in a cast including the thumb is usually sufficient for undisplaced fractures. If displacement or dislocation is present, open reduction and internal fixation is indicated in most cases. Painful nonunion sometimes occurs with trapezial ridge fractures when excision is usually successful in eliminating symptoms.

Trapezoid

Isolated fractures of the trapezoid are extremely rare (see Table 3-18) as are isolated trapezoid dislocations, although palmar dislocations have been reported. The trapezoid is located between the first and second ray, which might explain why this bone may be exposed to fewer forces able to cause fracture or dislocation.[160] Injury to the trapezoid is generally associated with forces applied through the second metacarpal. Ligamentous instability produced by a similar injury or osteochondral injuries to the trapezoid-second metacarpal, capitate-third metacarpal, or metacarpohamate joints often escape detection.

Diagnosis

Patients complain of pain at the base of the second metacarpal. A trapezoid dislocation or fracture–dislocation is seen on the AP radiograph as a loss of the normal relationship between the second metacarpal base and the trapezoid. The trapezoid may be superimposed over the trapezium or the capitate, and the second metacarpal may be proximally displaced. Oblique views and CT scans may be helpful.

Treatment

Because of their rarity, there is no standard treatment for trapezoid fractures. Displacement of up to 2 mm has been treated successfully nonoperatively. Open reduction and internal fixation or excision of smaller fragments can be used for displaced fractures.[155]

Capitate

There is an ongoing debate in the literature as to whether capitate fractures are rare or frequent. It is likely that capitate fractures are more common than was previously thought.[31,65,67] However, diagnosis may be difficult without an MRI scan, and the capitate obviously heals even without immobilization, as nonunion is rare.

Three injury mechanisms are postulated:

1. Direct blow or crushing injuries. These are usually associated with injuries to the metacarpals and other carpal bones.
2. The scaphocapitate syndrome, described by Fenton,[54] in which a violent blow directed to the radial styloid would first fracture the scaphoid and then the capitate but produce no dislocation. However, because fractures of the scaphoid and the capitate are only stage 1 or stage 2 of the spectrum of injury that culminates in a transscaphoid, transcapitate, or perilunate dislocation of the carpus, it is not surprising

that the capitate fragment can be frequently rotated 90 to 180 degrees with the articular surface displaced anteriorly or facing the fracture surface of the capitate neck.[188] Without reduction, AVN will result.

3. A fall with the wrist in dorsiflexion, forcing the capitate onto the dorsal rim of the radius. The dorsal border of the radius will impinge on the capitate and cause a fracture through its waist. This is the anvil mechanism theory.

Diagnosis

Fractures of the capitate can usually be identified on standard scaphoid views, although motion studies are recommended to look for displacement. A lucent line through the neck of the capitate may be isolated or may be combined with other fractures or fracture–dislocations. In such instances, the head of the capitate should be identified on the lateral view to determine if it has been rotated or displaced. Nonunion of the capitate can occur[63] and is diagnosed by CT scans. CT scans and MRI may be necessary to detect occult capitate fractures. MRI provides further information regarding the vascularity of the proximal capitate.

Treatment

Cast management is appropriate for the undisplaced fracture. Open reduction and internal fixation with screws or plates should be used in cases with displacement.

Hamate

Hamate fractures are quite rare (see Table 3-18).[65,67,160] The most common are probably fractures of the hook of the hamate.[60,125] They may also be dorsoulnar flake fractures[213] or fractures of the body, which have been most commonly described as coronal fractures.[201] Many fractures of the hamate are associated with fifth or, occasionally, fourth metacarpal fractures or axial fracture–dislocations.

Hook fractures of the hamate are usually sports-related injuries, resulting from direct blows to the palm of the hand. They mainly in sports requiring the use of a racket, baseball bat, or golf club (Fig. 29-26).[160] The fracture generally occurs at the base of the hook although avulsion fractures of the tip also may be seen. Symptoms are often minimal, leading the patient to downplay the injury until persistent pain and nonunion of the hamate are present.[24,196] Nonunion is relatively common and can induce ruptures of the little finger flexor tendon.

Coronal fractures of the hamate are usually caused by a punch injury and occur most commonly in young men.[201] They are often associated with subluxation or dislocation of the bases of the fourth or fifth metacarpals.

Flake or avulsion fractures may be more common than previously appreciated because of missed diagnosis, with 50% being missed on first presentation.[213] They occur in mostly young men either as a result of a direct blow or a fall on the outstretched hand. These are benign injuries in which symptoms usually resolve with immobilisation for a few weeks.

Diagnosis

The usual clinical signs and symptoms are pain and tenderness in the area of the hook of the hamate, although some patients may present with the symptoms of ulnar nerve entrapment as the deep branch of the ulnar nerve nerves winds around the

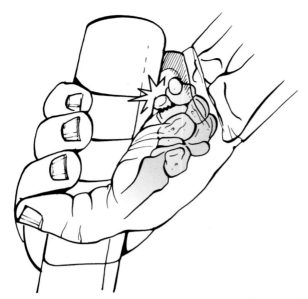

FIGURE 29-26 Fractures of the hamate usually occur in those who play sports requiring to hold a racket, making them susceptible to a direct blow to the hook of the bone.

hook of the hamate. Fractures and dislocations of the hamate are usually identified on standard scaphoid views. A dislocation usually results in some rotation that alters the contour of the bone and the normal oval appearance of the hook. Fracture of the hook of the hamate is best visualized on the carpal tunnel view. CT scans will confirm the fracture. The hook of the hamate may ossify independently and occasionally may fail to fuse with the body of the hamate. This separate bone, known as the os hamulus proprium, can be mistaken for a fracture. MRI scans are helpful to differentiate acute injuries from this developmental anomaly.

Treatment

Fractures of the hook of the hamate can be treated conservatively. Excision might be required in case of nonunion and entrapment of the ulnar nerve,[166] although bone grafting has been advocated to preserve the pulley effect on the flexor tendons.[196] If ulnar nerve entrapment occurs, it is important to decompress Guyon canal as the weakness in the hand may be considerable, because the hypothenar muscle group, the medial

two lumbricales, all seven interossei, the adductor pollicis, and the flexor pollicis brevis are involved.[160]

In hamate body fractures with displacement, subluxation, or dislocation, open reduction and internal fixation is required. Undisplaced fractures can be treated with splintage or casting. The outcome of promptly treated fractures is good.[201]

CARPAL INSTABILITIES

Classification

There are a number of ways of classifying acute carpal ligament injury. Three of those are shown in Table 29-4. Instability may also be adaptive secondary to malalignment outwith the carpus such as in distal radius malunion. There may also be complex combinations of different types of instability.

Dissociative Instabilities of the Carpus

These include ligament disruptions between two connected bones or bone disruption such as a scaphoid fracture. The perilunate dislocation pattern provides a whole spectrum of wrist sprains, fractures, dislocations, and instabilities. This injury pattern usually begins radially and proceeds either through the body of the scaphoid or through the SL interval resulting in SLD. Further destabilization passes distally between the capitate and lunate, either through the space of Poirier between the proximal and distal palmar V-ligaments or through the capitate, resulting in a transcapitate fracture, and then ulnar to the lunate, either through the hamate and triquetrum or through the lunatotriquentral interval. This type of perilunate dislocation usually results in a DISI collapse pattern because the stabilizing influence of the scaphoid is lost. A similar pattern of destabilization can begin ulnarly and propagate radially around the lunate, such that the lunate is first dissociated from the triquetrum.[39] The lunate may retain sufficient connection to the scaphoid that the residual collapse pattern is VISI. Both of these collapse patterns are dissociative because there is disruption of the ligament bond or the bone structure between the lunate and one or both of the adjacent carpal bones.

Nondissociative Instabilities of the Carpal Row

These include subluxations or incomplete dislocations of the entire carpus that may be purely ligamentous but more commonly include a fragment of the distal radius. These dislocations

TABLE 29-4	**Classifications of Carpal Instability**	
Classification	Types	Description
Linscheid[113]	DISI	Lunate extended (>15 degrees capitolunate, >60 degrees SL)
		Dorsal subluxation of capitate
	VISI	Lunate flexed (>30 degrees capitolunate, <30 degrees SL)
Taleisnik[174]	Static	Standard radiographs show malalignment of carpus
	Dynamic	Abnormal alignment only when carpus is stressed
Dissociative/nondissociative	Dissociative	Disruption of normal kinematics within a carpal row
	Nondissociative	Disruption between carpal rows

are either a palmar Barton or a dorsal Barton fracture–dislocation or a radial styloid fracture–dislocation, known as a chauffeur's fracture. Associated VISI or DISI instabilities are possible. These may be either dissociative or nondissociative depending on the degree of damage to the ligamentous connections of the proximal carpal row.

There are three other radiocarpal instabilities.[39] These are ulnar translation of the entire carpus, dorsal translation instabilities, and occasionally palmar translation instabilities. Combinations of these instabilities may occur, although one deformity pattern is usually predominant. The basic patterns are similar in instability dislocations and fracture–dislocations, suggesting that there is a spectrum of problems that occur in the linkage system within the carpus. Using these concepts, it is possible to group all known injuries that result in carpal instability into interrelated categories.

Signs and Symptoms

The most constant and dependable sign of carpal injury is well-localized tenderness.[39] Fractures of the scaphoid, for example, are most tender to pressure in the anatomic snuffbox. SL and lunate injuries cause tenderness just distal to Lister tubercle. Triquetral, LT, and triquetrohamate ligament injuries result in tenderness over the dorsal margin of the appropriate bone, usually a fingerbreadth distal to the ulnar head. Other clinical findings are highly variable and depend on the extent of carpal disruption, with more traumatic carpal disruption seen in perilunate dislocations.

Tenderness and swelling are general rather than localized. There may be swelling that is severe and generalized or discrete and barely detectable. Changes in alignment of the hand, wrist, and forearm may be clinically evident on inspection of the extremity. Swelling over the proximal carpal row is suggestive of a ligament avulsion with or without an associated fracture. Marked prominence of the entire carpus dorsally is suggestive of a perilunate dislocation. Compressive stresses applied actively or passively may produce pain at the site of damage and result in snaps, clicks, shifts, and thuds, which are palpable and audible.

Provocative Stress Tests

There are a number of specific tests for ligamentous disruption in the carpus[39]:

1. **The scaphoid shift test.**[194] Pressure is applied to the scaphoid tubercle while the wrist is brought from radial to ulnar deviation. In a positive finding, there is a "clunk" as the scaphoid subluxes dorsally out of the scaphoid fossa. The diagnosis is SL disruption.
2. **The midcarpal shift test.**[109] Pressure is applied to the dorsum of the capitate as the wrist is moved from radial to ulnar deviation. A positive finding is a "clunk" as the lunate reduces from the palmarflexed position. The diagnosis is midcarpal instability.
3. **LT ballottement.**[145] The lunate is fixed with the thumb and index finger of one hand while the triquetrum is displaced palmarly and dorsally with the thumb of the other hand. A positive finding is pain. The diagnosis is LT instability or arthritis.
4. **Scaphoid lift test.** This is a reproduction of pain with dorsopalmar translation of the scaphoid.

All of these tests must be interpreted with care as there are a number of false positive and false negative results. It is useful to test the opposite wrist as there is a range of ligamentous laxity in normal individuals. This may be associated with the ability to subluxate the midcarpal joint by displacing the carpometacarpal unit on the distal radius. Tendon displacements with audible snaps are easily produced by some persons but are seldom symptomatic. Distraction can be a good clue to a "lax wrist" or a damaged area, particularly when viewed under fluoroscopic imaging with static traction of approximately 25 pounds applied. Stress-loading the wrist with compression and motion from radial to ulnar deviation may simulate midcarpal instability (MCI) and produce a "catch-up clunk" as the proximal row of carpal bones snap from a flexion to extension.

RADIOCARPAL INSTABILITY

The most common injuries at the radiocarpal joint are fracture–dislocations of the distal radius and carpus: palmar and dorsal Barton fracture–dislocations, radial styloid fracture–dislocations, and die-punch fracture–dislocations. Less common are the pure ligamentous radiocarpal injuries (Fig. 29-27), which may cause the wrist to translate in an ulnar, dorsal, or palmar direction. True dislocations without fracture of the bony margins are rare, and they may sometimes spontaneously reduce, making it even more difficult to demonstrate them. However, they are occasionally seen unreduced with the carpus lying dorsal, palmar, or ulnar to the radius.[39]

Diagnosis of these injuries is made from a history of appropriate trauma followed by the usual initial findings of swelling, deformity, tenderness, and pain. Swelling and tenderness are most noticeable dorsally at the radiocarpal level and are aggravated by wrist motion. Deformity may be an ulnar, dorsal, or palmar shift of the carpus.

Radiocarpal dislocation has been classified into two groups.[49] Type I are radiocarpal dislocations with no fracture

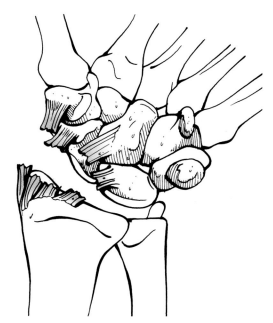

FIGURE 29-27 Radiocarpal dislocation with torn radiocarpal ligaments. This injury requires K-wire stabilization and direct repair of the radiocarpal ligaments.

or a fracture of the tip of the radial styloid when it is assumed that the radiocarpal ligaments are avulsed from the radius. Type II have a fracture of the radial styloid involving more than one third of the scaphoid fossa when it is assumed that the radiocarpal ligaments remain attached to the styloid process. Moneim[128] also classified these injuries into two groups, but his classification is dependent on the presence or absence of intercarpal ligament injury. Type I have intact intercarpal ligaments, while Type II have a combination of radiocarpal and intercarpal dislocation.

These injuries occur predominantly in young males and are severe injuries, with the majority of patients having associated injuries.[49,131] A common association is injury to the ipsilateral distal radioulnar joint.

Radiologic examination should include standard radiographs, although provocative stress tests may be required to demonstrate dynamic radiocarpal instability.[39] Ulnar translation is the most frequent radiocarpal instability.[39] It may occur acutely, develop gradually, or be observed as a late sequela of a perilunate dislocation. It may occur after an injury at the radiocarpal level, where the radiocarpal ligaments are avulsed from their origins, or after perilunate injury. Clinically, the carpus and hand are offset in an ulnar direction. The radiographic appearance is often dramatic, with the lunate positioned just distal to the ulna and a large space between the radial styloid and the scaphoid. If perilunate destabilization is also involved, the lunate and triquetrum slide ulnarly, opening a gap between scaphoid and lunate. In some cases, the ulnar shift is subtle, and a decrease in the ulnocarpal index may provide the only clue to diagnosis. Ulnar translation is also commonly seen in diseases such as rheumatoid arthritis and in developmental deformities such as Madelung deformity. It may occur with an increase in the radial to ulnar slope of the distal radius.

Dorsal translation of the carpus together with ulnar translation can be seen in two modes: one a true instability secondary to ligament damage, the other an apparent instability due to a carpal shift in response to a change in position of the distal radial articular surface. Pure dorsal translation usually occurs after a loss of the normal palmar slope of the distal radius from a flexion angle to an extension angle. The latter is a common problem after collapse of a distal radius fracture.[39]

Treatment of Radiocarpal Instability

Dislocations of the radiocarpal joint require immediate reduction because the associated deformity may compromise adjacent neurovascular structures. Although reduction is usually possible, maintaining it is often difficult. Open treatment should be considered in most carpal dislocations. In Dumontier type I injuries, the volar radiocarpal ligaments should be repaired, often using anchor sutures to prevent secondary ulnar or volar translation.[49] Where there is a substantial fracture fragment, the volar ligaments are likely to be attached to it. Open reduction and internal fixation of the fragment should be used. Added stabilization of the radiocarpal joint is recommended using percutaneous K-wires or external fixation to prevent late carpal translation, especially in type I injuries.[49,94] Concomitant intercarpal ligament injuries should also be repaired.[128] Limitation of wrist movement of 30% to 40% of normal should be expected following radiocarpal dislocation.[49,131]

Late identification of ulnar translation deformity or dorsal or palmar translation deformity has responded poorly to ligamentous repair. The most certain method of controlling possible recurrence of deformity is to carry out a partial or total radiocarpal arthrodesis. RL fusion is an appropriate technique for this situation, although the variation of joint damage may indicate radioscaphoid fusion in some cases and radioscapholunate fusion in others. The latter is usually indicated in the combination of radiocarpal and perilunate instability.[39]

SCAPHOLUNATE DISSOCIATION

SLD or rotatory subluxation of the scaphoid is the most frequent pattern of carpal instability. It may occur alone or in association with wrist fractures.[13,35,39,108,130,159,176] Most injuries result from excessive wrist extension and ulnar deviation with intracarpal supination such as occurs with a fall onto the outstretched pronated hand. SLD includes a spectrum of injuries ranging from grade I sprains through all grades of ligament destabilization of a single SLIL to injuries of multiple ligaments up to scaphoid dislocation (SLD, SL-instability, rotatory subluxation of scaphoid, DISI). A variety of ligament injuries are associated with SLD. The involved ligaments include the SLIL, the radioscapholunate ligament, the radioscaphocapitate ligament, the scaphotrapezial ligament complex, the dorsal radiocarpal ligament, and the dorsal intercarpal ligament. Disruption of the SLIL results in separation of the motion between the scaphoid and lunate in the acute phase and the development of persisting widening of the SL joint as a late clinical consequence (Fig. 29-28).[175]

The clinical consequences of the injury depend on the tightness or laxity of the capsuloligamentous system of the wrist and the presence of any associated palmar radiocarpal or midcarpal ligament damage. Without treatment, this injury leads to advanced SL collapse and progressive, painful arthritis of the wrist (see Fig. 29-28). SL injuries in children are rare[9] and should be treated operatively.

History and Clinical Signs

The diagnosis may be made from the clinical history which is usually consistent with a dorsiflexion ulnar deviation injury with stress loading of the extended carpus. This combination of position and axial compression causes injury to the SLIL

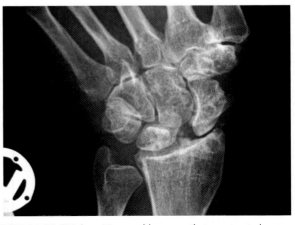

FIGURE 29-28 SLD in a 60-year-old woman that was treated conservatively resulting in progressive carpal collapse and painful arthritis.

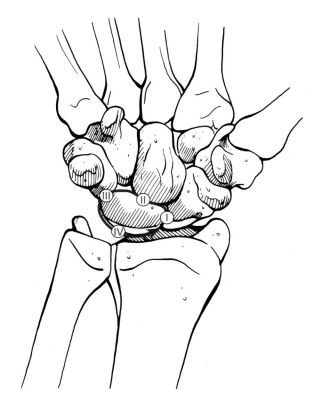

FIGURE 29-29 The Mayfield stages of progressive perilunate instability. Stage I results in SL instability. Stages II–IV result in progressively worse perilunate instability.

and palmar wrist ligaments.[19,130] Particularly vulnerable are the radioscaphocapitate and RL ligaments, which are under maximum tension in dorsiflexion and ulnar deviation. In Mayfield's classification, this injury is stage I (Fig. 29-29). Prior or repetitive injury or the presence of acute or chronic synovitis modifies the degree of stress required to the point that the index event may be fairly trivial, such as slamming a car door or catching a basketball.[39]

The clinical symptoms are swelling and tenderness over the SL area. Associated radial styloid fractures may cause pain over the radial styloid. A neurovascular examination is imperative, as acute carpal tunnel syndrome can occur with carpal fractures and dislocations.[130] The degree of associated stability may be such that only provocative stress will reveal the classic findings. An easy provocative maneuver is a vigorous grasp that induces pain; another indication is decreasing repetitive grip strength. The patient may also demonstrate pain during flexion–extension or radioulnar deviation.

Provocative stress is often accompanied by a click in the region of the proximal scaphoid and sometimes by a visible deformity dorsally. A positive Watson test is highly suggestive of SL instability (Fig. 29-30A). This test is not absolutely specific for SLD, because it may reposition the entire proximal carpal row if the row, rather than the individual scaphoid, is unstable. In addition, in individuals with lax ligaments, there may be false-positive signs of dorsal subluxation of the scaphoid that are not pathologic. Generalized ligamentous laxity may be present, as many wrists with an SL injury have some form of pre-existing ligamentous laxity.[39,120,130,174]

Imaging

The four standard views of the carpus are mandatory in the diagnosis of SL instability. SL injuries may be associated with fractures of the radius or carpus, especially in younger patients. Radiographs of patients with fractures of the distal radius should be evaluated closely for evidence of ligamentous injury. A greater arc injury is associated with radial styloid fractures and SL ligament disruption.[130] Gilula lines should be examined to evaluate ligamentous instability (see Fig. 29-10A). The appearance of the lunate should also be assessed. The lunate projects as a quadrilateral shape on the AP radiograph in normal wrists. Malrotation of the lunate makes it appear more triangular, this being commonly seen in perilunate dislocations.

A scapholunate gap greater than 3 mm suggests and a gap greater than 5 mm confirms SLD if there is a positive cortical ring sign (see Fig. 29-10B). An AP view with the fist clenched can be helpful as it accentuates the SL gap. This increased space between scaphoid and lunate has been named the Terry Thomas sign[61] after the gap-toothed smile of the British comedian (Fig. 29-30B). However, the techniques used to measure the diastasis have not been uniform (Fig. 29-30C). Generally, it is suggested that the SL gap should be compared to the uninjured opposite extremity.[32,174] SL diastasis without a dorsiflexed lunate is most likely nontraumatic.[134] Similar findings may be apparent on views of the contralateral extremity.

The SL angle is an angle created by the longitudinal axes of the scaphoid and the lunate. The long axis of the scaphoid is determined by a line tangential to the palmar convex surfaces of the proximal and distal poles of the scaphoid. The longitudinal axis of the lunate is a line perpendicular to the line connecting the dorsal and palmar lips of the lunate (Fig. 29-30D). Normal SL angles range from 30 to 60 degrees. The lateral radiographic appearance of a SL angle greater 60 degrees suggests SL instability, and if the angle is greater than 80 degrees, the radiographic appearance confirms SL instability.[40,78,89,114,134] The RL angle describes the tilt of the lunate with respect to the radius. A capitolunate or RL angle greater than 15 degrees is suspect, but if greater than 20 degrees, it confirms SL instability. Carpal height ratio (Fig. 29-30E), which is carpal height divided by the length of the third metacarpal, is used to quantify carpal collapse. A DISI deformity with a dorsally angulated lunate and a flexed position of the scaphoid is a typical consequence of SLD. Another sign suggestive of SL instability is the cortical ring sign (see Fig. 29-10B), which suggests that the scaphoid is flexed. The distal tubercle of the scaphoid is seen end-on on an AP projection of the wrist.[32,174]

If these findings are not present, the provocative maneuvers discussed earlier may cause them to appear. If SL instability cannot be seen with clenched-fist views or radioulnar stress radiographs, then fluoroscopy or cineradiography using standard and provocative stress motions should be performed. Arthrography has a high rate of false-positive and false-negative results and is therefore not recommended. Arthroscopy can be used to determine the extent of ligament disruption and the presence of radioscaphoid arthritis, as well as to classify and treat SL injuries.[72,91] MRI is helpful in discriminating the extent of ligament injury.

Classification

The classification of SL instability considers whether the injury is acute or chronic and whether it is static or dynamic this

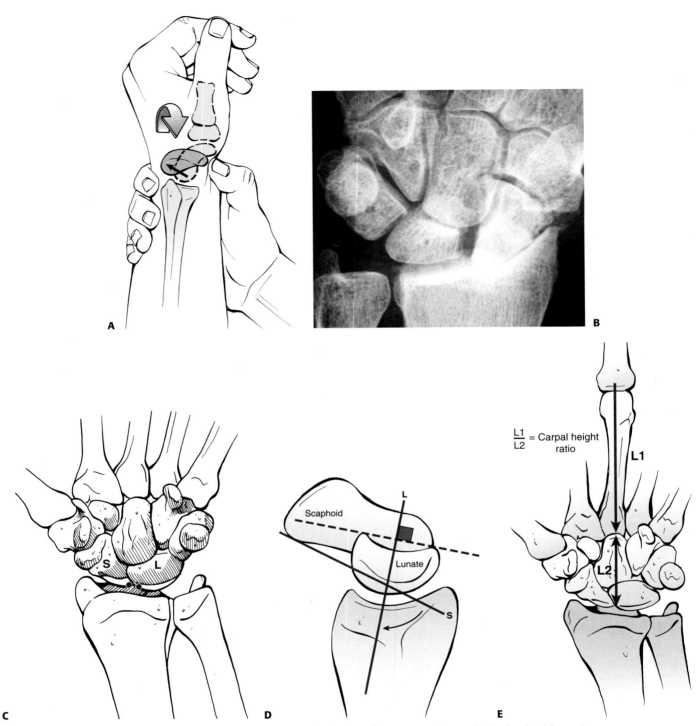

FIGURE 29-30 A. Watson test: pressure applied to the palmar aspect of the scaphoid tubercle while moving the wrist from an ulnar to radial deviation. A positive test elicits a combination of pain and a palpable clunk or snapping. **B.** Radiograph of patient with old SL instability, Terry Thomas sign, and progressive arthritic deformation of the radiocarpal joint. **C.** Measurement of the SL gap from the proximal ulnar corner of the scaphoid to the proximal radial corner of the lunate. **D.** The SL angle is created by the long axis of the scaphoid and a line perpendicular to the capitolunate joint. **E.** Carpal–height ratio.

being helpful for planning further treatment procedures. Static deformity does not occur with isolated injury to the dorsal SL ligament.[17] Static instability, which means that the injury can be identified on plain AP and lateral radiographs, occurs when the dorsal SLIL is injured along with the palmar ligaments, particularly the RL ligaments and the radioscaphocapitate ligament. Dynamic instability, which cannot be determined with plain radiographs, but may be apparent on stress radiographs or fluoroscopy, is thought to result from isolated injury to the dorsal SLIL.[130,151]

Geissler and his coauthors[72] identified four grades of ligament injury arthroscopically. In grade I injury, attenuation or hemorrhage of the ligament is seen from the midcarpal space but the bones are congruent. In grade II injury, there is incongruency between the carpal bones when viewed from the midcarpal space. In grade III and IV injuries, there is a gap between the carpal bones allowing entry of a 1-mm probe in grade III and a 2.7-mm arthroscope in grade IV.

Current Treatment Options

Different treatment options need to be considered based on the duration of injury, extent of ligamentous involvement, and the presence of associated carpal instabilities. The patient with an injury fewer than 4 weeks old is considered to have an acute tear. If the injury occurred less than 4 weeks but few than 24 weeks prior, it is a subacute tear. If it is greater than 6 months from injury, the tear is chronic and may be reducible or irreducible. Depending on the mechanism of injury and amount of force across the wrist, the SL ligament may be accompanied by injuries to the palmar radiocarpal and LT ligament or the TFCC.

Acute Scapholunate Dissociation

Patients with ligament sprain (Geissler grade I) without carpal instability may be treated conservatively with cast immobilization. Cast immobilization is ineffective in unstable cases[176] because the scaphoid requires wrist extension to maintain reduction and the lunate requires wrist flexion.

In patients with partial ligament tears and incongruence identified arthroscopically (Geissler grade II), percutaneous K-wires in combination with cast immobilization for 8 weeks can be used. Such injuries, even if not initially associated with obvious instability, can progress to SL collapse.[192] One K-wire

is placed from the scaphoid to the lunate and another from the scaphoid to the capitate. Pins can be placed into the scaphoid and lunate and used as joysticks to reduce the SL joint. Whipple[203] reported an 85% success rate in maintaining SL reduction in patients with an SL interval that was greater than the unaffected wrist by 3 mm or less and whose injuries were less than 3 months old. Results were less satisfactory in patients with a wrist injury that was older than 3 months.

Open ligament repair and pin fixation is recommended in all acute SL injuries unless the carpus is easily reduced anatomically by closed techniques and remains reduced in sequential radiographs without carpal malalignment. An increasing SL angle exceeding 60 degrees, a lunatocapitate angle exceeding 15 degrees, or an increasing scapholunate gap greater than 3 mm are indications for operative intervention. Anatomic restoration of the SL complex by open ligament repair is a realistic goal when the patient presents early. Soft tissue repair and reconstruction are popular because they attempt to restore the normal kinematics of the wrist. Arthroscopy of the wrist can assist in confirming the diagnosis and determining the location and extent of ligamentous damage. The technique of repair changed considerably with the introduction of intraosseous suture retaining anchors allowing ligament attachment directly to the bone (Fig. 29-31).[204,210]

The primary goals of the treatment of SLD are stabilization of the carpal bones in their proper alignment and the maintenance of wrist mobility. The earlier ligament repair takes place, the easier it is to perform a direct repair. The results of direct ligament repair are superior to ligament reconstruction.[65] Experimental studies have shown that reduction of the displaced SL joint is essential to the recovery of wrist kinematics after SLD.[175]

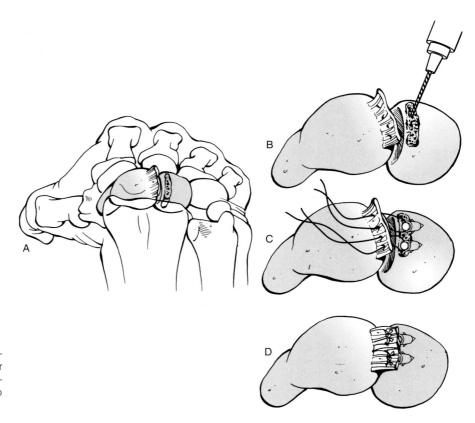

FIGURE 29-31 A-D. Ligament reapir for SL instability. Anchors are placed into the lunate (or scaphoid, depending on where the SLIL has ruptured), and the ligament is sutured back into position.

Results of primary open ligament repair by a dorsal approach are very good, although not universally so.[20,107] Bickert and his coauthors[20] reported on the outcome of 12 patients at an average of 19 months. In 10 patients, there was maintenance of a normal SL angle. The average range of motion was 78%, and the average grip strength was 81% of normal. Eight patients had excellent or good results. However, there was no correlation between functional and radiologic results although one of the two poor results was associated with lunate necrosis. Longer term outcomes are uncertain.

SL injuries occurring in combination with distal radius fractures should be operatively treated as the results of conservative treatment are unacceptably poor.[210] An ulnar positive variance of more than 2 mm in nonosteoporotic patients with intra-articular fracture of the distal radius has been shown to be predictive of severe SL injury.[58]

AUTHORS' PREFERRED TREATMENT: ACUTE SCAPHOLUNATE DISSOCIATION

We recommend primary repair and pin fixation for acute SLD using a dorsal approach. The approach is centered over Lister's tubercle, reflecting the dorsal wrist capsule to preserve the dorsal intercarpal and dorsal radiotriquetral ligaments, using a radial-based capsular flap. The radial capsule is reflected from the scaphoid to its waist. The open technique allows direct visualization of the injured ligament, reduction, and ligament repair. Most often, the SL ligament is found to be torn off the scaphoid and still attached to the lunate. In rare cases, avulsion from the lunate or an oblique tear will be seen.

Reduction of the lunate and scaphoid is performed with K-wire joysticks inserted in a dorsal to palmar direction. The rim of the proximal scaphoid is freshened to subcortical bone with a fine rongeur to facilitate ligament healing. Ideally, high-speed burrs should be avoided as thermal necrosis may occur. When the ligament remains attached to the lunate, intraosseous anchors are inserted into the waist of the scaphoid. The anchors are placed in such a position that the suture lies in a slightly oblique direction in order to resist the rotational forces between scaphoid and lunate (see Fig. 29-31).[20] The sutures attached to the anchors are placed in the SL ligament in a palmar to dorsal direction. If anchors are not available, drill holes in the scaphoid are required to allow direct attachment of the ligament onto the scaphoid. When the sutures are positioned, the scaphoid and lunate are reduced with joysticks and held in the reduced position with K-wires. One K-wire is placed from the scaphoid to the lunate and another from the scaphoid to the capitate. The sutures are tied and the capsule repaired. A forearm cast is applied and retained for 12 weeks, when the K wires are removed.

Subacute Ligament Tear

For subacute SL ligament tears, the addition of local tissue may be necessary if the SL ligament has retracted or is deficient.[39] Blatt's technique[21] (Fig. 29-32) reflects a proximally based dorsal capsular flap onto the SL interspace, and this is sutured tautly to the dorsal scaphoid to act as a tether to the proximal

pole. This flap can be added to the ligament repair process described earlier by placing nonabsorbable sutures from the lunate ligament remnant into the capsular tissue and then out through the scaphoid. An alternative method is to use a strip of tendon from the radial wrist extensors (extensor carpi radialis longus or extensor carpi radialis brevis), but tendon tissue is not an ideal ligament replacement, and capsular tissue is preferred.[39]

In both subacute and severe acute SL tears, palmar extrinsic ligament attenuation may be found.[39] Use of the arthroscope intraoperatively helps to identify these conditions and plan appropriate incisions.[203] A palmar approach with direct ligament repair by nonabsorbable sutures can be performed. If there is deficient tissue in the subacute case, part of the flexor carpi radialis can be used to augment the repair process by placing drill holes through the proximal scaphoid and radial half of the lunate and passing one half of the flexor carpi radialis tendon in a circular fashion to reinforce the dorsal and palmar ligaments. The radioscaphocapitate and RL ligaments may be advanced into the gap. With a large, complete SL ligament tear associated with a wide SL gap of 5 mm or more, palmar ligament repair is usually needed.[39] A carpal tunnel incision extended slightly radially is performed, and the damaged area is identified with a probe inserted from a separate dorsal incision. The interval between the radioscaphocapitate ligament and long RL ligament is developed. Sutures may then be placed with intraosseous anchors into the scaphoid proximal pole or remnants of the interosseous membrane, which are then used to pull the RL ligament against the proximal pole to hold the overreduction of the proximal scaphoid, which is stabilized by K-wires. The purpose of this palmar repair is to bring the dorsally subluxed and rotated proximal scaphoid in apposition with the palmar intracapsular ligaments.

Whether the approach is dorsal or palmar or combined, tight repair of the capsular structures is required for subacute dissociation. Internal fixation for a period of 12 weeks is preferred, supplemented with a supportive Colles cast. After cast removal, an orthoplast splint is worn as muscle strength and joint motion are restored. Return to work or sports is best delayed for a minimum of 6 months, with continued protection being used during sports activities.

Chronic Scapholunate Instability

The major concerns with chronic SL instability are whether the ligaments can be directly repaired, whether any residual carpal dislocation is reducible, and whether the joint has developed arthritis. When possible, restoration of normal carpal anatomy by repair and reconstruction of the support ligaments of the wrist remains the preferred treatment. This requires sufficient local tissue for a repair and a correctable carpal instability. When the patient presents with a fixed carpal deformity and the rotational subluxation of the scaphoid or dorsal angulated lunate (DISI) cannot be reduced, or when local degenerative changes or work demands that require heavy lifting or repetitive stress loading are present, the alternative of partial or complete fusion of the wrist may be preferred.[39] There are many techniques described to treat chronic SL instability.[21,39,158,171] Weiss et al.[200] showed that, in patients with a suspected intercarpal ligament tear and normal radiographs, arthroscopy was useful for both diagnosis and treatment. Current techniques for ligament reconstruction include repair with the dorsal capsular flap pro-

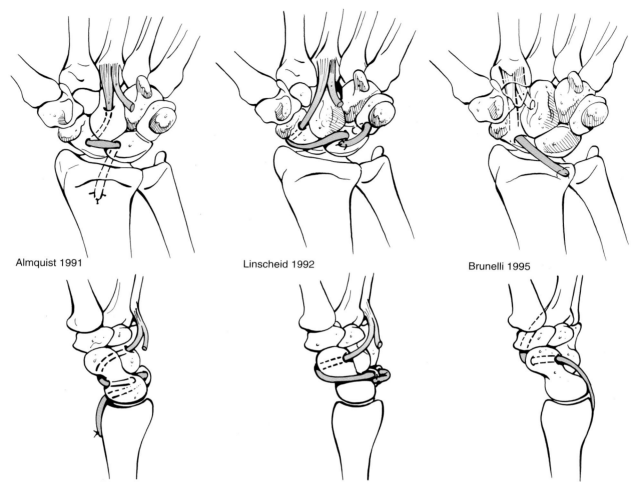

Almquist 1991   Linscheid 1992   Brunelli 1995

FIGURE 29-32 Tendon weaves and reconstructions proposed by various authors.

cedure, a palmar ligament reefing procedure, and combined dorsal and palmar procedures that add flexor or extensor tendon tissue to the repair site. The goal of each of these repair techniques involves the addition of local tissue to provide a collagen framework for future stability.[21,39,171] Soft tissue reconstructions have several theoretical advantages that make them attractive alternatives to other procedures. In contrast to arthrodeses, soft tissue reconstructions preserve more intercarpal motion.[171]

Several procedures have been designed to restrict rotatory subluxation of the scaphoid by creating a dorsal tether (Fig. 29-33).[21,116,164,171] A commonly used method of dorsal capsu-

lodesis is the Blatt type of capsular reconstruction.[21] Results of Blatt capsulodesis are acceptable,[21] although some clinical series have not reported favorable outcomes which might be related to patient selection.[44] Slater and Szabo.[164,171] described the dorsal intercarpal ligament capsulodesis, which is a soft tissue reconstruction procedure based on the dorsal intercarpal ligament of the wrist. The theoretical advantage of this method is that it avoids a tether between the distal radius and scaphoid. This keeps the proximal carpal row linked as a functional unit. Clinical results seem to be encouraging.[171]

Wyrick et al.[210] evaluated SL ligament repair and dorsal capsulodesis for static SLD and found that no patients were free of pain at follow-up. The experience of Wyrick and others suggests that dorsal capsulodesis is more suited for patients with dynamic instability than for those with static instability.[13] Dynamic instability is characterized by normal radiographs of the unloaded wrist, but a typical step-off between scaphoid and lunate when evaluated arthroscopically. Axial loading of the wrist can produce a widening of the SL gap in dynamic instability. Static instability is characterized by a widening of the SL gap in an unloaded wrist and an SL angle greater than 60 degrees. Arthroscopy in such a case is grossly abnormal and there is usually a communication between the radiocarpal and midcarpal joints. Static instability requires an intercarpal arthrodesis.

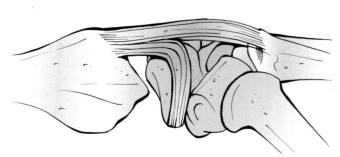

FIGURE 29-33 Blatt type of dorsal capsulodesis: The scaphoid is reduced and the capsular flap is secured to the distal pole with an anchor.

Tendon weave procedures and tenodeses (Fig. 29-32) have been attempted with variable success. Wrist extensor or flexor tendon augmentation procedures require placement of drill holes in bone. In this procedure, drill holes are carefully placed in a dorsal-to-palmar direction through the scaphoid and lunate. Tendon strips are then passed through these holes to attempt a reconstruction of the SLIL. The large holes required to pass tendon grafts often lead to carpal fractures. An alternative technique is to take part of an extensor or flexor tendon and pass it through the capitate, scaphoid, lunate, and distal radius.[5] Another technique is the reconstruction of the dorsal part of the SL ligament using a bone–ligament–bone autograft. However, clinical results are not particularly convincing.[98]

The palmar approach for SL ligament repair (Conyers' technique) is performed through a carpal tunnel incision.[39] A probe or needle passed dorsal to palmar is helpful in locating the ligament tear and palmar ligament intervals. Flaps of radio-scaphocapitate and long RL ligaments are reflected laterally and medially. The cartilage surfaces of the scaphoid and lunate are denuded to subchondral bone to encourage a strong syndesmosis. The scaphoid and lunate are then reduced and pinned with threaded wires that are left in place for at least 8 weeks. The palmar ligaments are carefully repaired. Motion is delayed 10 to 12 weeks to encourage adequate strength of the syndesmosis.

AUTHORS' PREFERRED METHOD OF TREATMENT: CHRONIC SCAPHOLUNATE INSTABILITY

We prefer the Blatt technique of capsule reconstruction,[21] using dorsal capsulodesis for the treatment of chronic SLD (see Fig. 29-33). For the Blatt type of capsule reconstruction, a long rectangular flap, about 1.5 cm wide, based on the dorsal aspect of the distal radius, is used. The distal edge of capsule is sutured to the distal pole of the scaphoid once the scaphoid is placed in a reduced position. A K-wire can be passed into the dorsum of the lunate to be used as a joystick to reduce any DISI. The scaphoid is reduced by pressure on the scaphoid tubercle and then transfixed to the capitate by another K-wire. The dorsal surface of the scaphoid is roughened with a fine rongeur just distal to the center of rotation. The dorsal flap of wrist capsule is sutured under tension with intraosseous anchors distal to the scaphoid center of rotation so that it tethers the proximal pole in the scaphoid fossa. The flap is sutured to reinforce the local tissue of the SL interval. For a distally-based flap, one can raise a rectangular capsular flap, leaving the distal end of the flap attached to the scaphoid.[87]

After SL ligament reconstruction, immobilization in a Colles cast is recommended for 8 weeks. The K-wires are removed at 8 weeks. Splint immobilization for an additional 4 weeks is suggested to allow for tissue healing with gradual stress loading. Supporting splints are best worn intermittently for 6 months to prevent sudden stress to the wrist and to allow further collagen maturation.[39]

Scaphotrapeziotrapezoidal Fusion

The decision regarding the need for intercarpal fusion for SLD is based on the length of time from the original injury, the degree of ligament disruption, and the ability to reduce the carpal instability. The expectations of the patient are also important. The presence of radiocarpal and midcarpal arthritis should influence the decision toward intercarpal fusion. Arthroscopic examination of both midcarpal and radiocarpal joints may determine the extent of SL ligament and articular cartilage damage and therefore assist in determining treatment.[91] Of the partial wrist fusions performed for wrist instability, the scaphotrapezio-trapezoidal (STT) fusion has had the widest clinical application.[39,41,127] The purpose of this procedure is to stabilize the distal scaphoid and thereby hold the proximal pole more securely within the scaphoid fossa of the distal radius.[195] This operation can be performed through a transverse incision centered over the STT joint or through the universal longitudinal incision.

If either STT fusion or the equivalent scaphocapitate fusion are undertaken, it is important to reduce the palmarflexed scaphoid, close the SL interval, and maintain carpal height. Radiograph control is recommended. The ideal flexion angle of the scaphoid is 45 degrees. Fixation of the STT or scaphocapitate joints is performed with K-wires, screws, or staples. Bone graft from the distal radius or iliac crest is placed between the decorticated distal scaphold and the proximal surfaces of the trapezium and trapezoid (STT fusion) or between the medial articular surface of the scaphoid and the lateral surface of the capitate (scaphocapitate fusion). Once scaphoid alignment is achieved, cancellous bone graft is inserted and K-wires are placed to support the fusion area. Prereduction placement of K-wires into the scaphoid facilitates correct orientation after reduction.[39] Clinical studies have shown that STT fusion is reliable and effective, giving pain relief and reasonable functional results.[127] However, in the longer term, degenerative changes in adjacent joints may be a problem.[59]

Immobilization after intercarpal fusion is usually for 8 weeks in a scaphoid cast, followed by a support splint for 4 to 6 weeks. CT scans of the wrist can help determine the degree of consolidation at the fusion site.

Four-Corner Fusion

Young active patients with chronic SL instability and severe arthritis can be treated with excision of the scaphoid and a four-corner fusion with arthrodesis of the capitate, lunate, hamate, and triquetrum.

PERILUNATE DISLOCATIONS AND FRACTURE–DISLOCATIONS

Of all wrist dislocations, the perilunate is the most common. Most patients are usually young males as the bone stock of the distal radius and the scaphoid needs to be strong enough to resist the amount of torque that is involved in these dislocations. Perilunate dislocations are characterized by a progressive disruption of most capsular and ligamentous connections of the lunate to the adjacent carpal bones and radius. Ligament disruption typically begins radially and propagates around or through the lunate to the ulnar side of the carpus (Fig. 29-34). Ligament disruption may be associated with different carpal fractures around the lunate. The distal row dislocates in a dorsal or dorsoradial direction followed by the entire scaphoid and triquetrum in pure perilunate dislocations or just by the distal portion of these bones in perilunate fracture–dislocations. SLD or LTD

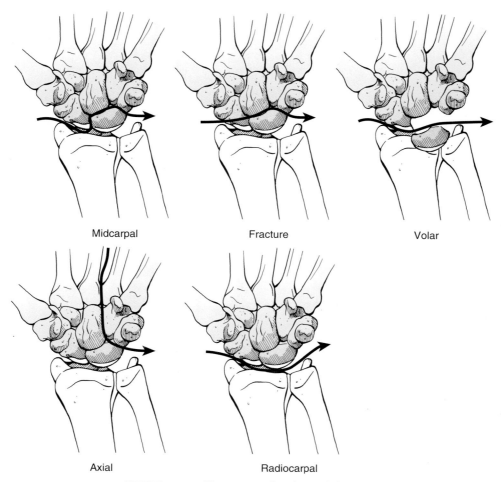

FIGURE 29-34 Different types of perilunate dislocations.

often persists even after relocation of the perilunate injury. Recurrence of carpal instability is common whether the injury involves the lesser arc injury through ligamentous tissue, the greater arc injury through bone, or some combination of the two. The most common pattern of perilunate instability is the transscaphoid perilunate fracture–dislocation.[37,39,71,88,181]

Pathomechanics

Most dorsal perilunate injuries occur as a consequence of a fall from a height on the outstretched hand or from motor vehicle accidents. At the time of impact, the hand is typically extended and ulnarly deviated.[122] The axial compressive load twists the joint beyond the limits of extension and ulnar deviation, adding a progressive midcarpal supination stress that induces the progressive perilunate dissociation. Differences in bone stock, direction, and magnitude of the deforming forces or position of the wrist at the time of impact explain the different types of injuries that occur. These injuries are associated with marked carpal instability.[71,83,119–120,138] There are also rare cases of reversed perilunate instability, when the wrist is pronated at the time that of impact thus adding an external force to the hypothenar region, forcing the wrist into extension and radial deviation. In such cases, the LTD occurs first followed by LTD and then SLD.[71,145]

Signs and Symptoms

The diagnosis is established by a history of a hyperextension injury and persistent pain, swelling, and deformity often after a fall from a height or a motor vehicle accident. These high-energy injuries produce significant deformity and soft tissue damage. Commonly, the clinical presentation includes median nerve injury, but ulnar neuropathy, arterial injury, and tendon damage may also be seen. The pattern of skeletal deformity is variable. The hand and distal carpal row usually remain intact, but the disruption pattern between distal and proximal carpal rows is quite variable. In the transscaphoid fracture–dislocation, the distal scaphoid dislocates with the distal row leaving the proximal scaphoid and lunate in near-normal relationship to the forearm. When the perilunate ligaments rupture, the lunate usually remains within the radiocarpal joint and the remainder of the carpus dislocates, usually dorsally but occasionally in a volar direction. Occasionally, the lunate is displaced and rotated palmarly and the remainder of the carpus settles into a semi-normal alignment with the distal radius. Rarely, even the palmar attachment of lunate is torn, allowing extrusion into the forearm or through the skin.

Radiographic Examination

The diagnosis is based on careful examination of the radiographs (Fig. 29-35A–C). The basic pattern can be discerned on stan-

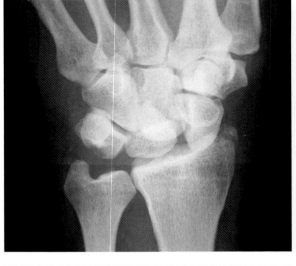

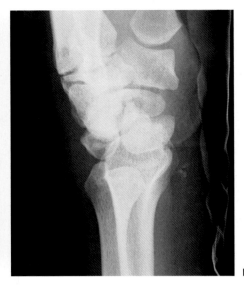

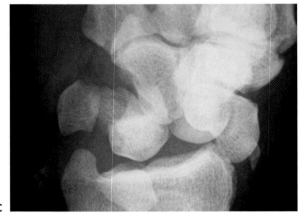

FIGURE 29-35 Typical radiologic signs of perilunate fracture–dislocation. **A.** Gilula arcs show an obvious discontinuity. The dorsally dislocated distal carpal row creates an abnormal overlapping of bones across the midcarpal joint. The lunate appears triangularly shaped. Additionally, there is a typical injury of the radial styloid. **B.** The lateral view shows that the distal concavity of the lunate no longer contains the proximal convexity of the capitate. **C.** The oblique view demonstrates the gross dislocation.

dard AP and lateral radiographs. The typical radiographic appearances of a perilunate dislocation are:

- The proximal and distal outlines of the proximal carpal rows (Gilula lines) (see Fig. 29-10) present with a discontinuity that indicates a grossly altered intercarpal relationship.
- The more the lunate is rotated the more it appears triangularly shaped.
- On the lateral view, the lunate no longer articulates with the head of the capitate, but appears palmarly rotated, the so-called "spilled teapot sign."

Approximately 20% of perilunate dislocations are misinterpreted on the initial radiographs,[60] leading to late treatment which is difficult and frequently less successful. It is usually the lesser arc dislocation that is missed because of the lack of an obvious osseous pathology and inexperience of the initial observer. Additional useful studies include tomography, CT scanning, and MRI. Arthrography and arthroscopy may have a useful role in determining the exact injury.

Classification

Mayfield et al.[120,122] showed that the disruption of ligaments due to perilunate dislocation is not random but follows the progressive perilunate instability (PLI) pattern of joint derangement (see Fig. 29-29). Four stages of PLI have been identified.[122]

Stage I—Scaphoid Fracture, Scapholunate Dissociation, or Both

As the distal carpal row is violently extended, supinated, and ulnarly deviated, the STT and scaphocapitate ligaments are tightened causing the scaphoid to extend. As the scaphoid extends, the SL ligaments transmit the forces to the lunate, which cannot rotate as much as the scaphoid, because it is constrained by the palmarly located RL and ulnolunate ligaments. As a consequence, a scaphoid fracture or a progressive tearing of the SL ligaments may occur, eventually leading to a complete SLD.

Stage II—Lunatocapitate Dislocation

If the extension–supination force on the wrist persists once the proximal carpal row has been dislocated, the capitate may displace and eventually may dislocate dorsally. It is followed by the rest of the distal carpal row and the radial-most portion of the dislocated proximal carpal row. This may be the complete scaphoid or just its distal fragment.

Stage III—Lunatocapitate Disruption

If the extension–supination force to the wrist persists, once the capitate is displaced dorsally an LTD or triquetrum–hamate–capitate ligament disruption may occur. LTDs are more common. Stage III is complete when the palmar LT ligament, including the medial expansions of the long RL ligament, is completely disrupted, and the joint has displaced.

Stage IV—Perilunate Dislocation

If the extension–supination force to the wrist persists and the dorsally displaced capitate is pulled proximally, pressure is applied onto the dorsal aspect of the lunate, forcing it to dislocation in a palmar direction. Because the palmar ligaments are much stronger than the dorsal capsule, such a dislocation seldom involves a pure palmar displacement of the lunate, but rather a variable degree of palmar rotation of the bone into the carpal tunnel, using the intact palmar ligaments as a hinge. Lunate dislocation is the end stage of progressive perilunate dislocation.

Perilunate dislocations can be further subdivided into two subgroups[96]:

1. Lesser-arc perilunate dislocations, which are characterized by pure ligamentous injuries around the lunate.
2. Greater-arc perilunate dislocations, which are characterized by a fracture of one or more of the bones around the lunate.

According to Witvoet and Allieu,[206] the lunate may appear normally aligned (grade I), rotated palmarly less than 90 degrees (grade II), rotated palmarly more than 90 degrees but still attached to the radius by its palmar ligaments (grade III), or totally enucleated without any connection to the radius (grade IV).

In clinical practice, the prefix *trans* is used to refer to fractures, whereas the prefix *peri* is used to describe a dislocation.[71] Based on this terminology, the amount of osseous and ligamentous injury as well as the amount of dislocation can be described exactly; thus a transscaphoid, transcapitate dorsal perilunate dislocation grade IV implies the existence of a displaced fracture of the scaphoid and the capitate, with their distal fragments being dislocated dorsally together with the rest of the distal carpal row. The lunate is rotated and totally enucleated without any connection to the radius

Treatment

Lesser-Arc Injuries

These injuries are divided into (a) acute and reducible perilunate dislocations, (b) acute and irreducible perilunate dislocations, and (c) chronic perilunate dislocations.

Acute and Reducible Perilunate Dislocations. There are reductions that are so stable that it is difficult to determine whether a full perilunate-type dislocation took place, and there are others that reduce and can be maintained in near-normal alignment in casts and splints. Ideally, reduction should be undertaken in the emergency room. The most commonly used method of closed reduction is the Tavernier maneuver, which was discussed by Watson-Jones.[197] It consists of locking the capitate into the distal concavity of the lunate by combined axial traction and flexion of the distal row, followed by reduction of the capitate–lunate unit onto the radius by an extension movement, while externally applying a localized dorsally directed force to the lunate to help reposition it.[71] The earlier reduction is performed, the easier it is. Complete relaxation under general or regional anesthesia is required. Local anesthesia is not sufficient. Successful closed reduction requires adequate imaging with good, standardized AP and lateral radiographs of the wrist or special imaging techniques. An SL angle that is greater than 80 degrees, an asymmetric SL gap, or both indicates poor reduction and a poor prognosis if not corrected. It is also important to

confirm ligamentous stability with stress-test imaging, MRI, arthroscopy, or open exploration.

The rare injuries that reduce to a normal alignment by closed reduction can be treated with a scaphoid cast with the wrist placed in neutral. They require monitoring on a daily basis for the first week and on a weekly basis thereafter. Cast immobilization of 12 weeks is required. However, the results of closed reduction and cast immobilization are unpredictable with loss of reduction with cast loosening being common.[39] It is now generally agreed that the risk of late deformity after successful reduction and cast management alone is unacceptably high.[2,10]

The use of percutaneous K-wire fixation to stabilize the carpus after closed reduction is now recommended. This reduces the incidence of later loss of reduction and enhances the healing capability of the intrinsic ligaments by maintaining complete immobility.[71] If possible, pin fixation should be performed using arthroscopy. Perilunate dislocations that are stable after reduction require only two pins for fixation. One transverse pin is placed from the scaphoid into the lunate (this can also be pinned through the radius into the lunate to neutralize the RL alignment), and a second pin is placed from the scaphoid into the capitate. The pins are usually removed at 8 weeks, but wrist immobilization in a scaphoid cast should be maintained for a total of 12 weeks after reduction.[71]

Acute and Irreducible Perilunate Dislocations. The majority of perilunate injuries fall into the irreducible or unstable group. If reduction is not optimal or reduction cannot be achieved at all, then open exploration and repair is indicated.[79] We believe that open reduction should be undertaken in all cases where there is the slightest doubt about reduction or stability. Significantly better results have been reported after open reduction and ligament repair compared to closed reduction and percutaneous pinning.[71,89] However, the prognosis is guarded even with successful reduction and maintenance of intercarpal relationships. Trumble and Verheyden[186] reported on 22 patients with perilunate dislocations treated with open reduction, cerclage wire fixation, and ligament repair with an average review period of over 4 years from injury. Patient satisfaction was high for 15 patients but only 10 patients returned to the same type of employment as before their injury. Range of movement was 87% and grip strength 77% of the contralateral wrist.

Median nerve dysfunction is reported to occur in 16% of cases of perilunate dislocation but the majority of patients experience resolution of their symptoms after closed reduction.[2] Immediate median nerve decompression is not usually required but should be performed where there is no resolution of symptoms or where late symptoms develop.[47]

AUTHORS' PREFERRED TREATMENT: ACUTE AND IRREDUCIBLE PERILUNATE DISLOCATIONS

We prefer a dorsal approach because it gives good exposure of the proximal carpal row and midcarpal joint (Fig. 29-36A–C). If there are neurovascular problems, an additional palmar approach allows access for median nerve decompression, vascular repair if required, and repair of the damaged palmar carpal ligaments. This allows both intra-articular and extra-articular damage to be assessed and treated adequately.[39,71,167] The surgery is similar to that for treatment

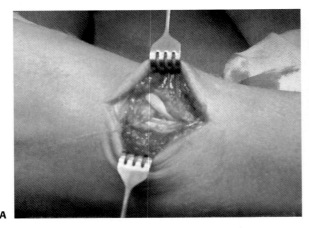

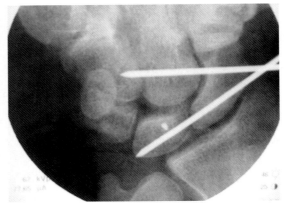

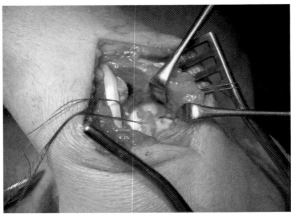

FIGURE 29-36 A. The dorsal capsule is exposed through a longitudinal incision that is centered on the Lister tubercle, dividing the extensor retinaculum between the second and third extensor compartments. The fourth compartment is opened by sectioning the septum between the third and fourth compartment. **B.** A ligament splitting capsulotomy is performed exposing the dorsal structures. **C.** Reduction and percutaneous pinning is performed under direct control Additional K-wires can be inserted into scaphoid and lunate to help with the reduction. The dorsal SLIL and LT interosseous ligament are repaired then by using anchors and sutures.

of SLD, except that an extended carpal tunnel release is performed. The palmar capsule should be examined either along its attachments to the radial rim or through the frequently damaged space of Poirier. The dorsal capsule is usually opened along its origin from the dorsal radial rim, as well as longitudinally in the space between the second and fourth extensor compartments, and the proximal carpal row is examined. If a scaphoid fracture is present, it can be reduced through the dorsal approach, temporarily stabilized with K-wires, and fixed with a cannulated screw. After the scaphoid is reduced, the lunate is reduced to the neutral position using a K-wire as a joystick. The normal SL relationship is restored, while a K-wire is placed through the scaphoid percutaneously, from radial to ulnar, to stabilize the SL joint. A second wire is placed through the scaphoid into the capitate. The LT relationship is restored next and stabilized with another K-wire from ulnar to radial. Torn ligaments can be repaired through the palmar and dorsal incisions. Intraosseous bone anchors are used to repair the SL and lunotriquetral ligaments.

It is important to assess all elements of the injury, restore the normal bony anatomy, and repair soft tissue damage. Reduction and K-wire fixation should be centered on the lunate. The lunate must be aligned and pinned first to the distal radius to neutralize the RL alignment. The LT joint is then reduced and fixed by a second K-wire. Ligaments are repaired as needed. The capitolunate joint alignment is then evaluated and correct colinear alignment is assessed. Lastly, the SL joint is reduced and held with K-wires. Many of the

patients have an associated radial styloid fracture, which should be reduced anatomically and stabilized with K-wires or a compression screw.

Chronic Perilunate Dislocations. The literature suggests that 16% to 25% of perilunate dislocations are missed initially.[54, 71,88] This results in pain, reduced wrist motion, and considerable dysfunction. Several clinical studies have shown that delay between injury and treatment worsens the prognosis with neglected cases resulting in pain, weakness, stiffness, posttraumatic osteoarthritis, and carpal tunnel syndrome.[88,89] Those injuries seen within 3 to 6 months are still potentially treatable by open reduction as long as no cartilage degeneration has already occurred, although treatment at this stage is often more difficult because of articular changes and capsular contracture. A good clue to the potential success of late reduction is gained by examining radiographs of the carpus under 25 to 30 pounds of traction. An attempt at open reduction (by palmar and dorsal approaches), repair, and internal fixation should be offered if carpal bone realignment is feasible, because even in late cases results can be surprisingly good.[39,167]

Untreated perilunate dislocations are rare, but they may be seen months or years after the initial injury. The patient is more likely to present because of increasing nerve symptoms or tendon rupture than because of wrist deformity to which the patient has often become accustomed. These very late problems nearly always require some type of salvage operation, usually a proximal row carpectomy or a total wrist arthrodesis.[39]

Another group of chronic perilunate-type injuries includes those where prior treatment has not been completely successful. Depending on the time of presentation from injury and the extent and type of any surgery that has already been undertaken, the options for treatment are identical to those of acute treatment. When a bone or bone fragment has been removed such as a proximal scaphoid or capitate fragment, the alternatives are to rehabilitate the limb and assess the functional level or to consider a salvage procedure such as radiocarpal fusion or proximal row carpectomy.[39]

Greater-Arc Injuries

Most perilunate fracture–dislocations combine ligament ruptures, bone avulsions, and various types of fractures, the most common being the transscaphoid perilunate fracture–dislocation. In a series of 166 perilunate displocations and fracture–dislocations, fracture–dislocations were twice as common as pure dislocation. Sixty-one percent of the whole series were dorsal transscaphoid perilunate fracture–dislocations.[89] Displaced transverse fractures of the neck of the capitate and sagittal fractures of the triquetrum are also quite frequent.[9,54,71,88,170,173] The capitate fragment is frequently rotated through 180 degrees so that its articular surface faces the raw cancellous surface of the major capitate fragment. Both capitate and scaphoid fragments are devascularized by displacement. This is known as the scaphocapitate syndrome. It is important to define any associated ligamentous injuries such as lunatotriquetral or SL disruption to prevent late carpal collapse.[101]

Treatment is by immediate closed reduction to reduce any pressure on the median nerve,[90] followed by open reduction and internal fixation which is the best method of achieving anatomic reduction of the fracture fragments. This also allows repair of associated ligament injury[37,54] or primary bone grafting where the scaphoid is comminuted.[205] Cases can be performed through either a dorsal or a volar approach, although a combined approach may be necessary especially if the dislocation is irreducible closed.[89] Some authors use a combined approach in all cases in order to repair the palmar capsule.[90] Minimal invasive techniques of fixation and repair have also been used with satisfactory results.[214] Arthroscopically assisted techniques have also been described.[199]

Most series report acceptable radiologic results, although the majority of cases have radiographic arthritis at longer term review.[89,90] Restoration of function is rarely complete with residual wrist stiffness and weakness of grip strength.[89,90,101] Patient-rated evaluation reflects loss of function.[89,90,101]

 AUTHORS' PREFERRED TREATMENT: GREATER-ARC INJURIES

We prefer urgent closed reduction followed by open reduction and internal fixation of the scaphoid fracture. The use of autogenous bone graft to restore scaphoid length may be required. Ligamentous structures are assessed and repaired and reinforced with K-wires in a similar fashion to the treatment of lesser arc injuries. Soft tissue damage is common in these high-energy lesions, and it may be obvious that a severe neuropathy or vascular compromise has occurred. When these are present, open treatment and evaluation of the structures at risk is essential. Treatment of vascular and nerve injuries should proceed once the fractures are stabilized. Se-

vere or increasing median or ulnar neuropathy is an indication for surgical exploration.

LUNATOTRIQUETRAL DISSOCIATION

The LT joint is an important component of the proximal carpal row. Ligament tears between the lunate and triquetrum are approximately one sixth as common as those between the scaphoid and lunate.[35] The LT ligament is much thinner than its SL counterpart, and these two bones are much more tightly coupled during wrist motion. LTD involves sprains as well as partial or complete tears of the interosseous ligaments between the lunate and triquetrum. It may present as an isolated injury, as part of the spectrum of perilunate dislocation, or in association with ulnocarpal impingement and TFCC injuries.[39] Clinical signs are often diffuse and fall into the broad category of ulnar-sided wrist pain.

The pathomechanics of LT injuries that accompany perilunate dislocation are well known but the mechanism of isolated injury requires further study. Because the LT joint is more stable than the SL joint, it seems apparent that associated ligament damage, particularly to the dorsal radiotriquetral ligament or palmar ulnocarpal ligaments, must be present before severe, fixed deformities can occur.[39] One of the problems with LT disorders is that many patients have a normal radiograph. Although LTD is not associated with the development of degenerative changes in the carpus, it can have a devastating effect on carpal mechanics, especially if it advances to a stage of VISI. Even without this progression, the patient with chronic ulnar-sided pain experiences significant ongoing disability.[18]

Anatomy

The LT joint is part of the proximal carpal row forming the articulation between the medial surface of the lunate and the lateral surface of the triquetrum. The LT joint is also under the influence of the radiocarpal and midcarpal joints. The radiocarpal joint is a hybrid articulation between the proximal surfaces of the lunate and the triquetrum which articulates with the lunate fossa of the distal radius and the TFCC. Under normal circumstances, no more than 50% of the lunate articulates with the TFCC.[18]

The most critical aspect of the LT ligament complex is the LTIL. The LTIL is C-shaped and interdigitates with the dorsal radiotriquetral ligament and palmar ulnotriquetral, ulnolunate, and radiolunatotriquetral insertions. The palmar third of the LTIL is stronger than the dorsal third, being supported by strong palmar ulnocarpal ligaments. Dorsal extrinsic ligaments of importance are the radiotriquetral and scaphotriquetral (dorsal intercarpal) ligaments, which describe a V-shape from the dorsal aspect of the distal radius near Lister's tubercle to the triquetrum and then back to the dorsal scaphoid rim. On the ulnar side of the wrist, the triquetrocapitate and the triquetrohamate ligaments are a continuation of the ulnotriquetral ligament.

The extrinsic palmar RL ligaments have been subdivided into short and long RL ligaments. The radioscapholunate ligament originates from the palmar aspect of the ridge between the scaphoid and lunate fossae and inserts into the SLIL. Another important ligament is the ulnolunate ligament, which arises from the palmar radioulnar ligament to attach to the ulnar half of the palmar cortex of the lunate. The ulnotriquetral ligament arises proximally from the palmar radioulnar ligament and the ulnar styloid process. Palmar and superficial to the ulnolunate and ulnotriquetral ligament is the ulnocapitate ligament, which reinforces both ligaments. Distally, there are two strong midcarpal ligaments that arise from the distal edge of the triquetrum: the triquetrocapitate and triquetrohamate ligaments.[18,39,102,122,174,178]

Mechanism of Injury

LT injuries commonly result from a sudden axial load, such as a fall. There is a consensus that a true LTD is part of a spectrum of progressive ligament disruption associated with a lunate or perilunate dislocation. Mayfield et al.[120,122] determined that there are two general patterns of damage in progressive perilunate instability: damage to the greater and lesser arcs. Greater-arc perilunate dislocations involve fracture–dislocations of the radial styloid process, scaphoid, capitate, hamate, triquetrum, and ulnar styloid process. Lesser-arc injuries involve only ligaments with no associated fractures. The typical pattern of progressive perilunate instability begins with disruption of the SLIL. The disruption continues distally and ulnarly. Owing to the strength of the short and long RL ligaments, the lunate typically remains associated with the radius, but the radial half of the carpus begins to dislocate dorsally away form the radius and lunate. The soft tissue disruption propagates proximally, disrupting the LTIL, and often extending proximally into the palmar radioulnar ligament of the TFCC. This dissociates the triquetrum from the lunate.[18,54,111,113,120,122]

Diagnosis

Diagnosis of LTD involves a history of specific injury with ulnar-sided wrist pain aggravated by activity. Tenderness is present directly over the LT joint, and ballottement of the unstable triquetrum may be possible. Many patients even state that they sense a "clunk" in their wrist with radial–ulnar deviation.[18] Stress loading of the LT joint (compression, ballottement, or shear) helps to confirm the diagnosis.[39] The most sensitive test to diagnose LTD is the LT shear test. This is performed by applying a dorsally directed pressure to the pisiform (which is directly palmar to the triquetrum) and a palmarly directed pressure to the lunate (just distal to the palpable dorsoulnar corner of the distal radius). This maneuver results in a shearing vector across the lunotriquetral joint and results in crepitation or clicking, reproducing the patient's pain.

Radiographic diagnosis is more difficult than the diagnosis of SLD because the findings are subtle and provocative; stress-induced deformity is less frequent.[39] As in all conditions of the wrist, imaging studies should be considered as confirmatory rather than diagnostic.[18] True LTD may result in a disruption of Gilula's lines. A static VISI deformity implies an injury to the LT ligament because there is dissociation between lunate and triquetrum, and the usual pattern is for the lunate to follow the scaphoid into flexion while the triquetrum extends.[39] Wrist arthrography is not a reliable diagnostic tool, but videofluoroscopy can be helpful. Arthroscopy has become the most important diagnostic tool for confirming the presence and degree of LTD. Radiocarpal and midcarpal arthroscopy allows visualization of the scaphoid–trapezoid–trapezium joint, midcarpal extrinsic ligaments, the capitohamate joint, and the articular sur-

faces of the carpal bones. Arthroscopic staging is applicable to SLD, LTD, and all other ligamentous dissociations.[91]

Treatment

Acute LTD with minimal deformity is ideally treated with a well-molded Colles cast using closed reduction and percutaneous internal fixation of the lunate to the triquetrum if there is displacement. If conservative measures fail, surgical intervention can be considered.[18]

LTD with angular deformity or following unsatisfactory results from previous treatment may need open treatment, particularly in the subacute or acute phase.[39] Arthroscopy can be helpful in acute injuries to guide closed reduction and percutaneous pinning.[136] It is suggested that the arthroscope be placed in the radial midcarpal portal for this procedure because the alignment of the LT joint is much easier to evaluate from this perspective.[18]

Open reduction, repair of lax or damaged ligaments, and temporary internal fixation with percutaneous wires across the triquetrum and lunate left in place for 6 to 8 weeks is recommended for isolated LT ligament tears if arthroscopy fails. All ligaments that seem to be concerned with LT stability should be reattached. An open repair should be attempted only when there are sufficiently strong ligament remnants present, when the ligament remnants have a reasonable healing potential, and when the LT relationship is easily reduced. These criteria limit the application of open repair techniques to acute injuries.[18]

The interosseous ligament repair is usually done through a dorsal approach. Care should be taken to avoid injury to the dorsal sensory branch of the ulnar nerve or to branches of the superficial radial nerve. The fifth extensor compartment is opened and an ulnar-based retinacular flap is elevated. The ligament is more likely to be stripped from the triquetrum. Intraosseous bone anchors with attached sutures are used for reconstruction. Capsular flaps are useful for reinforcing the dorsal portion of such a repair or augmenting the dorsal radiotriquetral and dorsal scaphotriquetral ligaments. For late presentations with complete ligament disruption and no tissue for repair, ligament reconstruction using part of the extensor carpi ulnaris tendon is recommended.[39]

If it appears that soft tissue repair cannot control the tendency to recurrent deformity, LT fusion may be indicated. It is mandatory to correct the VISI deformity. Treatment of the painful wrist may be accompanied with denervation procedures. Concomitant ulnar shortening procedures should be considered (especially with ulnar plus variance) to tighten the palmar ulnocarpal ligaments in addition to LT fusion or ligament reconstruction.[39] More aggressive treatments are proximal row carpectomy and total wrist arthrodesis in patients with radiologic signs of arthrosis.

MIDCARPAL INSTABILITY

Anatomy and Kinematics

The midcarpal joint can be regarded as a combination of three different types of articulations[149]:

1. Radially, there is a universal joint that is composed of the distal surface of the scaphoid and the concavity that is formed by the trapezium, the trapezoid, and the radial aspect of the capitate.

2. In the center, there is a ball-and-socket type of joint, with the socket lying proximally being formed by the distal surfaces of the scaphoid and lunate. The ball lies distally being formed by the head of the capitate and, variably, the proximal pole of the hamate.

3. Finally, on the ulnar side of the midcarpal joint, the triquetrohamate articulation is helicoid, or screw-shaped, in configuration. A helicoid facet represents a surface that is generated by the rotation of a plane or a twisted curve about a fixed line, so that each point of the curve traces a circular helix with the fixed line as the axis. The surfaces of the triquetrohamate joint are only in full contact when the wrist is ulnarly deviated.

The kinematics of the midcarpal joint are controlled by several anatomic structures including the bones and the intrinsic and extrinsic ligaments. The intrinsic ligaments are not always well differentiated and seem to form a continuous palmar capsule that spans the entire width of the midcarpal joint space. However, it is possible to discern two V-shaped ligamentous bands that converge centrally towards the capitate. These bands are formed by the intrinsic palmar midcarpal ligaments, the extrinsic radiocarpal and ulnocarpal ligaments, the radioscaphocapitate ligament, and the short and long RL ligaments. The extrinsic dorsal intercarpal ligament originates from the dorsal aspect of the triquetrum, crosses the midcarpal joint almost transversely in a radial direction, and inserts mainly onto the waist of the scaphoid, the trapezium, and the trapezoid. Despite the fact that there are no attachments to the capitate or hamate, the dorsal intercarpal ligament is capable of holding the head of the capitate and proximal pole of the hamate in position during wrist flexion. The palmar distal V-shaped ligament, consisting of the radiocapitate and ulnocapitate ligaments, also does not attach to the head of the capitate, but forms a support sling commonly referred to as the arcuate ligament. Together, these bands allow for maximum range of motion at the level of the midcarpal joint with maximum midcarpal stability.[39,134,149]

Pathology

MCI does not refer to one specific pathology, but to a number of conditions.[8,134] MCI is characterized by a loss of normal alignment between the bones in the proximal and distal carpal rows when they are placed under physiologic and pathologic loads, due to ligament injuries of the wrist. Carpal instabilities have been classified as dissociative and nondissociative (CIND), which have already been discussed in the section dealing with carpal instabilities. MCI is a form of CIND and is difficult to diagnose.

There are four types of MCI.[149]

Midcarpal Instability Type I

The so-called palmar MCI is secondary to an injury to the palmar midcarpal ligaments. This includes the scaphotrapeziotrapezoid ligaments, the triquetrohamate and triquetrocapitate ligaments, or both. The direction of subluxation is palmar.

Midcarpal Instability Type II

The so-called dorsal MCI is a type I MCI in combination with an injury to the radioscaphocapitate ligament. The direction of subluxation is dorsal.

Midcarpal Instability Type III

This is characterized by hyperlaxity of the midcarpal and radiocarpal (dorsal and palmar) ligaments. The direction of subluxation is dorsal or palmar.

Midcarpal Instability Type IV

The so-called extrinsic MCI is due to a malunited radius with dorsal (less commonly palmar) angulation with adaptive deformity of the carpus inducing progressive stretching of the radiocapitate ligaments, thus reproducing the typical symptoms of a dorsal MCI. The direction of subluxation is dorsal (rarely palmar).

Diagnosis

The history and the physical findings differ little between radiocarpal and midcarpal types of CIND. Some patients recall a history of recent hyperextension injury and a localized area of tenderness. However, many patients do not recall a significant trauma. Frequently, MCI is associated with congenital ligamentous laxity and a hypermobile wrist. Either VISI or DISI deformity or alternating patterns may occur at either level. In the early stages, these patterns of deformity may be so subtle that they are difficult to detect. Nearly all patients with MCI present with painful clunking on the ulnar side of the wrist during activities that involve active ulnar deviation. Many of these patients have had asymptomatic wrist clunking for many years.

The diagnosis is made by the midcarpal stress test. A painful and characteristic clunk (catch-up clunk) can be produced by applying an axial load to a pronated and slightly flexed wrist, which is then brought into ulnar deviation. The "catching-up" occurs when the smooth transition during ulnar deviation lags behind until late in ulnar deviation, when the proximal row suddenly clunks into a reduced extended posture.[35,149] The contralateral wrist should be examined in similar fashion, as 50% of patients with MCI may also have a contralateral clunk that is not yet symptomatic.[209]

As MCI is a dynamic condition, plain radiographs are often normal. However, they can show a moderate or even severe VISI deformity (type I MCI) or a DISI deformity (type II MCI). An extrinsic MCI (type IV) shows significant angulatory malunion with an adaptive Z-shaped deformity of the carpus.[149] Videofluoroscopy, while moving the compressed carpus through the normal range of motion and applying ulnar deviation to the pronated wrist, shows a dramatic and sudden shift at the midcarpal joint, when the proximal row suddenly clunks into a reduced extended posture.[39,149]

Imaging findings are also almost identical for radiocarpal or midcarpal CIND and drawing a careful distinction between these uncommon and unusual injuries is difficult. Comparison of video motion patterns of the symptomatic wrist to the normal contralateral wrist is often useful.[39] These difficulties are compounded by the fact that ligament insufficiency, which is usually posttraumatic but occasionally congenital,[209] may be present at both radiocarpal and midcarpal levels. Visualizing both joints and the intervening proximal carpal row by arthroscopy[75] or surgery gives the final opportunity to decide where the instability is most noticeable. Inflammatory synovitis and clear ligament laxity are the diagnostic signs. Even then, one may have to judge from subtle deviations from the norm because the attenuation may not be obvious.[39]

Treatment

Conservative treatment is usually used initially as many patients with MCI, especially the milder variety, respond well to nonoperative management. Many of these wrist problems occur in individuals with congenitally or posttraumatically lax wrists who can control the subluxation tendency to some degree by muscle contraction. In such instances, external support to limit the provocative wrist motion together with musculotendinous training may suffice. Additionally, patients may be treated with nonsteroidal anti-inflammatory drugs or steroid injections or modification of their employment may be suggested.[39,149]

For those with relatively normal joint surfaces but in whom conservative treatment has failed, surgery aims to prevent pathologic motion at the midcarpal joint and to stabilize the proximal carpal row. If a specific lesion can be identified, such as damage to radial arcuate (radioscaphocapitate) ligament, the ulnar palmar arcuate (triquetrocapitate) ligament, or the scaphotrapeziotrapezoidal ligament, direct soft tissue reconstruction is indicated with temporary percutaneous fixation.[39,149]

In type I MCI with VISI instability, four quadrant fusion (lunate–capitate–triquetrum–hamate) is the criterion standard.[149] In type II MCI, the interligamentous sulcus between the radioscaphocapitate and the long RL ligaments is closed with strong sutures constructing a radiocarpal tether between radius and proximal carpal row that limits proximal row excursion. If manual reduction is incomplete or there is rapid recurrence after reduction, localized fusion of the midcarpal joint is the best treatment.[39,95,149] In type III MCI, radiocarpal fusion is more likely to control the unstable proximal carpal row but proximal row carpectomy is a satisfactory salvage procedure.

In type IV MCI, a corrective open-wedge osteotomy and bone grafting in combination with plate fixation of the radius is the treatment of choice. If there is associated instability of the distal ulna, DRUJ problems, or fixed deformity of the carpus, then further surgical alternatives, such as ulnar shortening, DRUJ stabilization, or midcarpal joint fusion, may need to be undertaken at the same time.[39,149]

Axial Instabilities

Axial (longitudinal) instabilities are a type of carpal instability in which the injury affects longitudinal support or alignment of the wrist rather than transverse alignment of the proximal and distal carpal rows. Crush injuries that flatten the hand cause this "axial" instability. Axial instabilities have been separately categorized from other carpal injuries (Fig. 29-37). They represent longitudinal fracture–dislocations of the wrist and, for the most part, are caused by high-energy injuries. Traumatic causes have included an exploding truck tire, crushing under heavy objects, and high-pressure machine compression. The basic pathophysiology is collapse of the carpal arch, often with tearing or avulsion of the bony origins of the transverse carpal ligament. The focus of this injury is usually in the distal carpus and adjacent metacarpals, occasionally extending either distally into the intermetacarpal area or proximally through the proximal carpal row.[39] The most common pattern is separation of either radial or ulnar "columns" of the carpus with their metacarpal rays from the central carpus. From a review of the more common patterns, a proposed nomenclature is axial-radial, axial-ulnar, or a combination of the two fracture–dislocations. The carpal elements involved are usually indicated by the term *peri* if the

discontinuity is primarily ligamentous, as in peritrapezial or peritrapezoidal-trapezial. If the discontinuity is through bone, the term *trans* is employed, as in transtrapezial or transtrapeziotrapezoidal. The accompanying soft tissue disruption is often of more importance than the bone and joint disruption. Neurovascular injury is frequent, sometimes to the point of nonviability of the digits.[39]

Diagnosis is established by the history of a force propagating in the sagittal plane, with a dorsal to palmar crush, often with evidence of severe soft tissue damage, swelling, and open wounds. Standard radiographs should confirm the diagnosis, although the carpal malalignment may be subtle and escape notice. A high index of suspicion is needed. Provocative stress radiographs, CT scanning, or MRI should be obtained preoperatively. Evidence of neurologic, vascular, musculotendinous, and ligamentous damage is usually present, often to a severe degree. Instances of median neuropathy are less than expected, probably because the carpal tunnel is usually decompressed by the injury.[39]

Treatment

A complete assessment is needed in these injuries for planning of both soft tissue and joint repair. Urgent surgical intervention is often indicated to salvage neurovascular function and restore skeletal alignment. Massive swelling may necessitate decompression of compartments not already decompressed by the injury. Traction can help reduce the axial displacement. Fractures and dislocations, once reduced, can be maintained by K-wires and lag screws. Transcarpal or metacarpal K-wire fixation is usually necessary to prevent redisplacement. Early active motion of the hand helps prevent adhesions of the flexor and extensor tendons. Rehabilitation is often prolonged, and the prognosis depends mainly on the severity of soft tissue damage.[39]

Pearls and Pitfalls

- Dissociative instability involves disruption of the ligaments or bone structure between the lunate and an adjacent carpal bone.
- Nondissociative instabilities include subluxations or incomplete dislocations of the entire carpus with or without a distal radial fracture.
- Perilunate dislocation patterns include a considerable spectrum of sprains, fracture–dislocations, and instabilities.
- SLD is the most common pattern of carpal instability.
- A capitolunate or RL angle greater than 20 degrees confirms SL instability.
- LT dissocation may result in disruption of Gilula lines on radiograph.
- There are four types of MCI and the direction of subluxation may be palmar or dorsal.
- A SLD without a dorsiflexed lunate is probably not traumatic.
- In SLD, the results of K-wire treatment are unpredictable. Ligamentous repair should be undertaken if closed reduction is unsuccessful on serial radiographs.
- In chronic SL instability, partial or complete wrist fusion may be needed.
- Sixteen to 25% of perilunate dislocations are missed initially.
- Open repair of the LT ligament is only possible in acute injury.
- Radiographs in MCI may be normal or may show a VISI or DISI deformity.

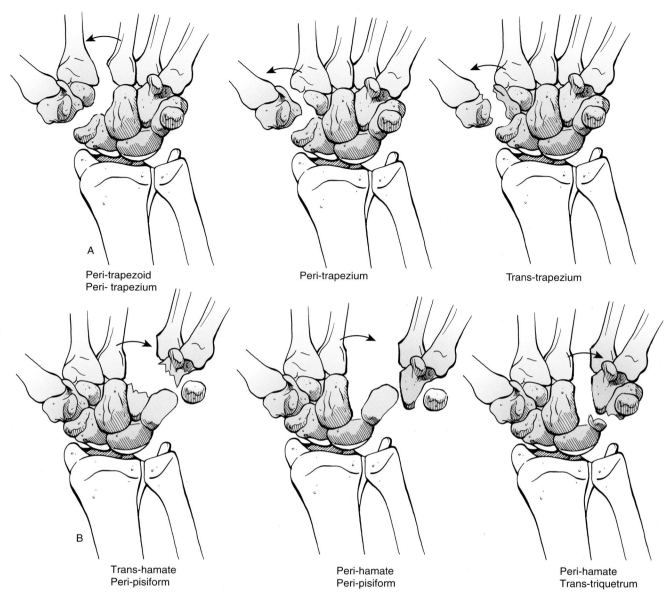

A

Peri-trapezoid
Peri- trapezium

Peri-trapezium

Trans-trapezium

B

Trans-hamate
Peri-pisiform

Peri-hamate
Peri-pisiform

Peri-hamate
Trans-triquetrum

FIGURE 29-37 Axial disruptions of the carpus. **A.** Axial radial disruptions of the carpus. **B.** Axial ulnar disruptions.

FUTURE DIRECTIONS

Significant progress has been made in the understanding and detection of carpal fractures and instabilities in the last decade, mainly because of better imaging techniques. Unfortunately, the dissemination of knowledge has lagged behind, and it is important that surgeons appreciate the importance of early diagnosis and treatment of these relatively common injuries.

Hopefully, improved imaging and surgery will allow better prediction of the evolution of individual carpal instabilities and therefore determine the requirement for operative treatment at an earlier stage. It is likely that improved surgical methods will be devised to treat these problems. The use of closed, fluoroscopically controlled and arthroscopically controlled techniques, especially in the scaphoid, should increase and the results of treatment should improve. It is interesting to speculate whether an increasingly aging society will affect the diagnosis and management of carpal problems. Currently, they mainly occur in younger patients, but with altering patient demographics, this may not continue and a new set of challenges may emerge.

REFERENCES

1. Adamany DC, Mikola EA, Fraser BJ. Percutaneous fixation of the scaphoid through a dorsal approach: an anatomic study. J Hand Surg Am 2008;33:327–331.
2. Adkison JW, Chapman MW. Treatment of acute lunate and perilunate dislocations. Clin Orthop 1982;164:199–207.
3. Adolfsson L, Lindau T, Arner M. Acutrak screw fixation versus cast immobilization for undisplaced scaphoid fractures. J Hand Surg Br 2001;26:192–195.
4. Alho A, Kankaanpaa U. Management of fractured scaphoid bone: a prospective study of 100 fractures. Acta Orthop Scand 1975;46:737–743.
5. Almquist EE, Bach AW, Sack JT et al. Four-bone ligament reconstruction for treatment of chronic complete scapholunate separation. J Hand Surg 1991;16-A:322–327.
6. Amadio PC, Berquist TH, Smith DK, et al. Scaphoid malunion. J Hand Surg 1989;14-A:679–687.

7. Annamalai G, Raby N. Scaphoid and pronator fat stripes are unreliable soft tissue signs in the detection of radiographically occult fractures. Clin Radiol 2003;58:798–800.
8. Apergis EP. The unstable capitolunate and radiolunate joints as a source of wrist pain in young women. J Hand Surg 1996;21B(4):501–506.
9. Apergis EP, Darmanis S, Kastanis G, et al. Does the term scaphocapitate syndrome need to be revised? A report of 6 cases. J Hand Surg 2001;26B(5):441–445.
10. Apergis E, Maris J, Theodoratos G, et al. Perilunate dislocations and fracture-dislocations. Closed and early open reduction compared in 28 cases. Acta Orthop Scand Suppl 1997;275:55–59.
11. Arner M, Hagberg L. Wrist flexion strength after excision of the pisiform bone. Scand J Plast Reconstr Surg 1984;18:241–245.
12. Arora R, Gschwentner M, Krappinger D, et al. Fixation of nondisplaced scaphoid fractures: making treatment cost effective. Prospective controlled trial. Arch Orthop Trauma Surg 2007;127:39–46.
13. Baratz ME, Dunn MJ. Ligament injuries and instability of the carpus: scapholunate joint. In: Berger RA, Weiss APC, eds. Hand Surgery. Vol. 1. Philadelphia: Lippincott Williams & Wilkins, 2004:460–479.
14. Barton NJ. Twenty questions about scaphoid fractures. J Hand Surg 1992;17-B: 289–310.
15. Barton NJ. Experience with scaphoid grafting. J Hand Surg Br 1997;22:153–160.
16. Beadel GP, Ferreira L, Johnson JA, et al. Interfragmentary compression across a simulated scaphoid fracture—analysis of 3 screws. J Hand Surg 2004;29A:273–278.
17. Berger RA. The gross and histologic anatomy of the scapholunate interosseous ligament. J Hand Surg 1996;21-A:170–178.
18. Berger RA. Lunotriquetral joint. In: Berger RA, Weiss APC, eds. Hand Surgery. Vol. 1. Philadelphia: Lippincott Williams & Wilkins, 2004:495–509.
19. Berger RA, Blair WF, Crowninshied RD, et al. The scapholunate ligament. J Hand Surg 1982;7-A:87–91.
20. Bickert B, Sauerbier M, Germann G. Scapholunate ligament repair using the Mitek bone anchor. J Hand Surg Br 2000;25(2):188–192.
21. Blatt G. Capsulodesis in reconstructive hand surgery: dorsal capsulodesis for the unstable scaphoid and volar capsulodesis following excision of the distal ulna. Hand Clin 1987;3:81–102.
22. Bohler L, Trojan E, Jahna H. The results of treatment of 734 fresh, simple fractures of the scaphoid. J Hand Surg Br 2003;28:319–331.
23. Bond CD, Shin AJ, McBride MT, et al. Percutaneous screw fixation or cast immobilization for nondisplaced scaphoid fractures. J Bone Joint Surg Am 2001;83:483–488.
24. Boulas HJ, Milek MA. Hook of the hamate fractures. Diagnosis, treatment, and complications. Orthop Rev 1990;19:518–529.
25. Braun H, Krenn W, Schneider S, Graf M, et al. Arthrographie des Handgelenkes–Wertigkeit im Nachweis von Komplett-und Partialdefekten der intrinsischen Ligamente und des TFCC im Vergleich zur Arthroskopie. Fortschr Röntgenstr 2003;175: 1515–1524.
26. Breitenseher MJ, Gaebler C. Trauma of the wrist. Eur J Radiol 1997;25:129–139.
27. Breitenseher MJ, Metz VM, Gilula LA, et al. Radiographically occult scaphoid fractures: value of MR imaging in detection. Radiology 1997;203:245–250.
28. Brismar J. Skeletal scintigraphy of the wrist in suggested scaphoid fracture. Acta Radiol 1988;29:101–107.
29. Brumbaugh RB, Crowninschield RD, Blair WF, et al. An in-vivo study of normal wrist kinematics. J Biomech Eng 1982;104:176–181.
30. Buck-Gramcko D. Denervation of the wrist joint. J Hand Surg 1977;2:54–61.
31. Calandruccio JH, Duncan SF. Isolated nondisplaced capitate waist fracture diagnosed by magnetic resonance imaging. J Hand Surg 1999;24-A:856–859.
32. Cautilli GP, Wehbe MA. Sacpholunate distance and cortical ring sign. J Hand Surg 1991;16-A:501–503.
33. Cetti R, Christensen SE, Reuther K. Fracture of the lunate bone. Hand 1982;14:80–84.
34. Clay NR, Dias JJ, Costigan PS, et al. Need the thumb be immobilized in scaphoid fractures? A randomized prospective trial. J Bone Joint Surg 1991;73B:828–832.
35. Cohen MS. Ligamentous injuries of the wrist in the athlete. Clin Sports Med 1998;17: 533–552.
36. Compson JP. The anatomy of acute scaphoid fractures. A three-dimensional analysis of patterns. J Bone Joint Surg Br 1998;80:218–224.
37. Cooney WP, Bussey R, Dobyns JH, et al. Difficult wrist fractures. Perilunate fracture-dislocations of the wrist. Clin Orthop Relat Res 1987;214:136–147.
38. Cooney WP, Garcia-Elias M, Dobyns JH, et al. Anatomy and mechanics of carpal instability. Surg Rounds Orthop 1989;1:15–24.
39. Cooney WP, Linscheid RL, Dobyns JH. Fractures and dislocations of the wrist. In: Rockwood CA, Green DP, Bucholz RW, et al, eds. Rockwood and Greens Fractures in Adults. Philadelphia: Lippincott Williams & Wilkins, 1996:745–867.
40. Cordrey LJ, Ferrer-Torrels M. Management of fractures of the greater multangular. J Bone Joint Surg 1969;42-A:1111–1118.
41. Crosby EB, Linscheid RL, Dobyns JH. Scaphotrapezial trapezoidal arthrosis. J Hand Surg 1978;3:223–234.
42. Davis EN, Chung KC, Kotsis SV, et al. A cost/utility analysis of open reduction and internal fixation versus cast management for acute nondisplaced midwaist scaphoid fractures. Plast Reconstr Surg 2006;117:1223–1235.
43. De Beer JD, Hudson DA. Fractures of the triquetrum. J Hand Surg 1987;12-B:52–53.
44. Deshmukh SC, Givissis D, Belloso D, et al. Blatt's capsulodesis for chronic scapholunate dissociation. J Hand Surg 1999;24B(2):215–220.
45. Dias JJ, Brenkel IJ, Finlay DB. Patterns of union in fractures of the waist of the scaphoid. J Bone Joint Surg Br 1989;71:307–310.
46. Dias JJ, Wildin CJ, Bhowal B, et al. Should acute scaphoid fractures be fixed? A randomised controlled trial. J Bone Joint Surg Am 2005;87:2160–2168.
47. DiGiovanni B, Shaffer J. Treatment of perilunate and transscaphoid perilunate dislocations of the wrist. Am J Orthop 1995;24:818–826.
48. Dinah AF, Vickers RH. Smoking increases failure rate of operation for established nonunion of the scaphoid bone. Int Orthop 2007;31:503–505.
49. Dumontier C, Meyer zu Reckendorf G, Sautet A, et al. Radiocarpal dislocations: classification and proposal for treatment. A review of 27 cases. J Bone Joint Surg Am 2001; 83:212–218.
50. Duteille F, Dautel G. Nonunion fractures of the scaphoid and carpal bones in children: surgical treatment. J Ped Orthop 2004;13(1):34–38.
51. Eggli S, Fernandez DL, Beck T. Unstable scaphoid fracture nonunion: a medium-term study of anterior wedge grafting procedures. J Hand Surg 2002;27B(1):36–41.
52. El-Karef EA. Corrective osteotomy for symptomatic scaphoid malunion. Injury 2005; 36:1440–1448.
53. Erdman AG, Mayfield JK, Dorman F, et al. Kinematic and kinetic analysis of the human wrist by stereoscopic instrumentation. J Biomech Eng 1979;101:124–133.
54. Fenton RL. The naviculo-capitate syndrome: J Bone Joint Surg 1956;38-A:681–684.
55. Fernandez DL, Eggli S. Scaphoid nonunion and malunion. How to correct deformity. Hand Clinics 2001;17:631–646.
56. Fisk GR. Carpal instability and the fractured scaphoid. Ann R Coll Surg Engl 1970; 46:63–76.
57. Fisk GR. The wrist. J Bone Joint Surg 1984;66:396–407.
58. Forward DP, Lindau T, Melsom D. Intercarpal ligament injuries associated with fractures of the distal part of the radius. J Bone Joint Surg Am 2007;89:2334–2340.
59. Fortin PT, Louis DS. Long-term follow-up of scaphoid-trapezium-trapezoid arthrodesis. J Hand Surg Am 1993;18:576–681.
60. Foucher G, Schuind F, Merle M, et al. Fractures of the hook of the hamate. J Hand Surg 1985;10-B:205–210.
61. Frankel VH. The Terry-Thomas sign. Clin Orthop Relat Res 1986;20:50–56.
62. Freeland P. Scaphoid tubercle tenderness: a better indicator of scaphoid fractures? Arch Emerg Med 1989;6:46–50.
63. Freeman BH, Hay EL. Nonunion of the capitate: a case report. J Hand Surg 1985;10-A:187–190.
64. Gaebler C, Kukla C, Breitenseher MJ, et al. Die diagnostische Sicherheit von 0,2 Tesla dedizierten MRT Niederfeldgeräten in der Traumatologie. Swiss Surgery 1998;4: 175–179.
65. Gaebler C, Kukla C, Breitenseher M, et al. Magnetic resonance imaging of occult scaphoid fractures. J Trauma 1996;41:73–76.
66. Gaebler C, Kukla C, Breitenseher MJ, et al. Limited diagnostic value of macroradiography in scaphoid fractures. Acta Orthop Scand 1998;69:401–403.
67. Gaebler CH, Kukla CH, Breitenseher MJ, et al. Diagnosis of occult scaphoid fractures and other wrist injuries: Are repeated clinical examinations and plain radiographs still state of the art. Langenbeck's Archives of Surgery 2001;386:150–154.
68. Galladay GJ, Jebson PJL, Louis DS. The versatility of a new variable pitch screw system in hand, wrist and elbow surgery. Minneapolis, MN: Annual Meeting American Society of Hand Surgery 1998.
69. Garcia-Elias M. Carpal bone fractures (excluding scaphoid fractures). In: Watson HK, Weinberg J, eds. The Wrist. Philadelphia: Lippincott Williams & Wilkins, 2001: 173–186.
70. Garcia-Elias M. Dorsal fractures of the triquetrum. Avulsion or compression fractures? J Hand Surg 1987;12-A:266–268.
71. Garcia-Elias M. Perilunate injuries including fracture dislocations. In: Berger RA, Weiss APC, eds. Hand Surgery. Vol. 1. Philadelphia: Lippincott Williams & Wilkins, 2004: 511–523.
72. Geissler WB, Freeland AE, Savoie FH, et al. Intracarpal soft-tissue lesions associated with an intra-articular fracture of the distal end of the radius. J Bone Joint Surg Am 1996;78:357–65.
73. Gelberman RH, Gross MS. The vascularity of the wrist. Identification of arterial patterns at risk. Clin Orthop Relat Res 1986;202:40–49.
74. Gelberman RH, Menon J. The vascularity of the scaphoid bone. J Hand Surg 1980;5: 508–513.
75. Gelberman RH, Panagis JS, Taleisnik J, et al. The arterial anatomy of the human carpus: part I. The extraosseous vascularity. J Hand Surg 1983;8-A:367–376.
76. Gelberman RH, Wolock BS, Siegel DB. Fractures and nonunions of the carpal scaphoid. J Bone Joint Surg 1989;71-A:1560–1565.
77. Gilula LA, Weeks PM. Posttraumatic ligamentous instabilities of the wrist. Radiology 1978;129:641–651.
78. Green DP. The effect of avascular necrosis on Russe bone grafting for scaphoid nonunion. J Hand Surg 1985;10-A:597–605.
79. Green DP, O'Brian ET. Open reduction of carpal dislocations: indications and operative techniques. J Hand Surg 1978;3A:250–265.
80. Günal Ý, Öztuna V, Özcelik A, et al. Medium-term results of trapezio-lunate external fixation of scaphoid fractures. J Hand Surg 2002;27B(5):410–412.
81. Gutow AP. Percutaneous fixation of scaphoid fractures. J Am Acad Orthop Surg 2007; 15:474–485.
82. Haddad FS, Goddard NJ. Acute percutaneous scaphoid fixation. A pilot study. J Bone Joint Surg 1998;80B:95–99.
83. Harrington P, Quinlan WB. Palmar lunate transscaphoid, transtriquetral fracture-dislocation. J Hand Surg 1999;24B(4):493–496.
84. Haussmann P. Long-term results after silicone prosthesis replacement of the proximal pole of the scaphoid bone in advanced scaphoid nonunion. J Hand Surg 2002;27B(5): 417–423.
85. Herbert TJ. The Fractured Scaphoid. St. Louis: Quality Medical Publishing, 1990.
86. Herbert TJ, Fisher WE. Management of the fractured scaphoid using a new bone screw. J Bone Joint Surg 1984;66B:114–123.
87. Herbert TJ, Hargreaves IC, Clarke AM. A new surgical technique for treating rotatory instability of the scaphoid. J Hand Surg1996;21-B:75–77.
88. Hertzberg G, Comtet JJ, Linscheid RL, et al. Perilunate dislocations and fracture dislocations: a multicenter study. J Hand Surg 1993;18-A:768–779.
89. Herzberg G, Forissier D. Acute dorsal transscaphoid perilunate fracture-dislocations: medium-term results. J Hand Surg 2002;27B(6):498–502.
90. Hildebrand KA, Ross DC, Patterson SD, et al. Dorsal perilunate dislocations and fracture-dislocations: questionnaire, clinical and radiographic evaluation. J Hand Surg Am 2000;25:1069–1079.
91. Hofmeister EP, Dao KD, Glowacki KA, et al. The role of midcarpal arthroscopy in the diagnosis of disorders of the wrist. J Hand Surg 2001;26A:407–414.
92. Houshian S, Schröder HA. Wrist arthrodesis with the AO titanium wrist fusion plate: a consecutive series of 42 cases. J Hand Surg 2001;26B(4):355–359.
93. Hoy G, Powell G. Scaphoid fixation using the Acutrak screw. Presented at the Australian/New Zealand Hand Surgery Meeting; Cairns, Australia; September 25, 1996.
94. Ilyas AM, Mudgal CS. Radiocarpal fracture-dislocations. J Am Acad Orthop Surg 2008; 16:647–655.

95. Imaeda T, Nakamura R, Miura T, et al. Magnetic resonance imaging in scaphoid fracture. J Hand Surg 1992;17-B;20–27.
96. Johnson RP. The acutely injured wrist and its residuals. Clin Orthop Relat Res 1980; 149:33–44.
97. Johnson RP, Carrera GF. Chronic capitolunate instability. J Bone Joint Surg 1986;68-A:1164–1176.
98. Kalb K, Markert S. Erste Erfahrungen mit der Osteoligamentoplastik und Kapsulodese nach Cuénod zur Behandlung der chronischen skapholunären Dissoziation. Handchir Mikrochir Plast Chir 2003;35:310–316.
99. Kauer JMG. Functional anatomy of the wrist. Clin Orthop Relat Res 1980;149:9–20.
100. Kauer JMG. The mechanism of carpal joint. Clin Orthop Relat Res 1986;202:16–26.
101. Knoll VD, Allan C, Trumble TE. Transscaphoid perilunate fracture dislocations: results of screw fixation of the scaphoid and lunatotriquetral repair with the dorsal approach. J Hand Surg Am 2005;30:1145–1152.
102. Kuenz CL. Les geodes du semi-lunaire (Thesis). Lyon, France; 1923
103. Kuhlmann JN, Boabighi A, Kirsch JM, et al. An experimental study of plaster immobilization for fractures of the carpal scaphoid. A clinical investigation. French J Orthop Surg 1987;1:43–50.
104. Kujala S, Raatikinen T, Kaarela O, et al. Successful treatment of scaphoid fractures and nonunions using bioabsorbable screws: report of six cases. J Hand Surg 2004;29A: 68–73.
105. Lacey JD, Hodge JC. Pisiform and hamulus fractures: easily missed wrist fractures diagnosed on a reverse oblique radiograph. J Emer Medicine 1998;16:445–452.
106. Langhoff O, Andersen JL. Consequences of late immobilization of scaphoid fractures. J Hand Surg 1988;13-B:77–79.
107. Lavernia CJ, Cohen MS, Taleisnik J. Treatment of scapho-lunate dissociation by ligamentous repair and capsulodesis. J Hand Surg 1992;17-A:354–359.
108. Lewis DM, Osterman AL. Scapholunate instability in athletes. Clin Sports Med 2001; 20:131–139.
109. Lichtman DM, Schneider JR, Swafford AR, et al. Ulnar midcarpal instability-clinical and laboratory analysis. J Hand Surg Am 1981;6:515–523.
110. Linscheid RL. Kinematic considerations of the wrist. Clin. Orthop Relat Res 1986;202: 27–39.
111. Linscheid RL, Dobyns JH. The unified concept of carpal injuries. Ann Chir Main Memb Super 1984;3:35–44.
112. Linscheid RL, Dobyns JH. Wrist sprains. In: Tubiana R, ed. The Hand. Vol. 2. Philadelphia: WB Saunders, 1985:970–985.
113. Linscheid RL, Dobyns JH, Beabout JW, et al. Traumatic instability of the wrist: diagnosis, classification, and pathomechanics. J Bone Joint Surg 1972;54-A:1612–1632.
114. Little CP, Burston BJ, Hopkinson-Woolley J, et al. Failure of surgery for scaphoid nonunion is associated with smoking. J Hand Surg Br 2006;31:252–255.
115. Logan SE, Nowak MD, Gould PL, et al. Biomechanical behaviour of the scapholunate ligament. Biomed Sci Instrum 1986;22:81–85.
116. Lutz M, Kralinger F, Goldhahn J, et al. Dorsal scapholunate ligament reconstruction using a periostal flap of the iliac crest. Arch Orthop Trauma Surg 2004; 124: 197–202.
117. Lynch NM, Linscheid RL. Corrective osteotomy for scaphoid malunion: technique and long-term follow-up evaluation. J Hand Surg 1997;22A:35–43.
118. Mack GR, Bosse MJ, Gelbermannh RH, et al. The natural history of scaphoid nonunion. J Bone Joint Surg 1984;66A:504–509.
119. Masmejean EH, Romano SJ, Saffar PH. Palmar perilunate fracture-dislocation of the carpus. J Hand Surg 1998;23B(2):264–265.
120. Mayfield JK. Pattern of injury to carpal ligaments: a spectrum. Clin Orthop Relat Res 1984;187:36–42.
121. Mayfield JK, Johnson RP, Kilcoyne RK. The ligaments of the human wrist and their functional significance. Anat Rec 1976;186:417–428.
122. Mayfield JK, Kilcoyne RK, Johnson RP. Carpal dislocations: Pathomechanics and progressive perilunate instability. J Hand Surg 1980;5:226–241.
123. McLaughlin HL. Fracture of the carpal navicular (scaphoid) bone. Some observations based on treatment by open reduction and internal fixation. J Bone Joint Surg 1954; 36A:765–774.
124. McMurtry RY, Youm Y, Flatt AE, et al. Kinematics of the wrist: II. Clinical Applications. J Bone Joint Surg 1978;60-A:955–961.
125. McQueen MM, Gelbke MK, Wakefield A, et al. Percutaneous screw fixation versus conservative treatment for fractures of the waist of the scaphoid. A prospective randomised study. J Bone Joint Surg Br 2008;90:66–71.
126. Meermans G, Verstreken F. Percutaneous transtrapezial fixation of scaphoid fractures. J Hand Surg Eur 2008;33:791–795.
127. Meier R, Prommersberger KJ, Krimmer H. Teil-arthrodesen von skaphoid, trapezium und trapezoideum (STT-Fusion). Handchir Mikrochir Plast Chir 2003;35:323–327.
128. Moneim MS, Bolger JT, Omer GE. Radiocarpal dislocation–classification and rationale for management. Clin Orthop Relat Res 1985;192:199–209.
129. Moritomo H, Viegas SF, Nakamura K, et al. The scaphotrapezio-trapezoidal joint. Part I: An anatomic and radiographic study. J Hand Surg 1999;25-A:899–910.
130. Mudgal CS, Jones WA. Scapho-lunate diastasis: a component of fractures of the distal radius. J Hand Surg 1990;15-B:503–505.
131. Mudgal CS, Psenica J, Jupiter JB. Radiocarpal fracture dislocation. J Hand Surg Br 1999; 24:92–98.
132. Munk B, Bolvig L, Kroner K, et al. Ultrasound for diagnosis of scaphoid fractures. J Hand Surg 2000;25-B:369–371.
133. N'Dow J, N'Dow K, Maffulli N, et al. The suspected scaphoid fracture. How useful is a unit policy? Bull H J Diseases 1998;57:93–95.
134. Ono H, Gilula LA, Evanoff BA, et al. Midcarpal instability: is capitolunate instability pattern a clinical condition? J Hand Surg 1996;21B(2):197–201.
135. Osterman AL, Mikulics M. Scaphoid nonunion. Hand Clin 1988;4:437–455.
136. Osterman AL, Seidman GD. The role of arthroscopy in the treatment of lunatotriquetral ligament injuries. Hand Clin 1995;11:41–50.
137. Panagis JM, Gelberman RH, Taleisnik J, et al. The arterial anatomy of the human carpus II. The intraosseous vascularity. J Hand Surg 1983;8:375–382.
138. Pandit R. Proximal and palmar dislocation of the lunate and proximal scaphoid as a unit in a case of scaphocapitate syndrome–a 32-month follow-up. J Hand Surg 1998; 23B(2):266–268.
139. Pao VS, Chang J. Scaphoid nonunion: diagnosis and treatment. Plast Reconstr Surg 2003;112:1666–1675.
140. Papaloizos MY, Fusetti C, Christen T, et al. Minimally invasive fixation versus conservative treatment of undisplaced scaphoid fractures: a cost-effectiveness study. J Hand Surg 2004;29B(2):116–119.
141. Parvizi J, Wayman J, Kelly P, et al. Combining the clinical signs improves diagnosis of scaphoid fractures. A prospective study with follow-up. J Hand Surg 1998;23-B: 324–327.
142. Poirier P, Charpy A. Traite d'Anatomie Humaine (Arthrologie). Paris: Masson et Cie, 1897.
143. Preiser G. Zu einer typischen posttraumatischen und zur Spontanfraktur führenden Osteitis des Naviculare Carpi. Fortschr Roentgenstr 1910;15:189.
144. Prosser AJ, Brenkel IJ, Irvine GB. Articular fractures of the distal scaphoid. J Hand Surg 1988;19B:87–91.
145. Reagan DS, Linscheid RL, Dobyns JH. Lunotriquetral sprains. J Hand Surg Am 1984; 9:502–514.
146. Rettig AC. Elbow, forearm, and wrist injuries in the athlete. Sports Med 1998;25: 115–130.
147. Rettig AC, Weidenbener EJ, Gloyeske R. Alternative management of midthird scaphoid fractures in the athlete. Am J Sports Med 1994:22:711–714.
148. Rettig ME, Dassa GL, Raskin KB, et al. Wrist fractures in the athlete. Distal radius and carpal fractures. Clin Sports Med 1998;17:469–489.
149. Ritt MJPF. Midcarpal instability. In: Berger RA, Weiss APC, eds. Hand Surgery. Vol. 1. Philadelphia: Lippincott Williams & Wilkins, 2004;525–532.
150. Roolker W, Tiel-van-Buul MM, Ritt MJ, et al. Experimental evaluation of scaphoid X-series, carpal box radiographs, planar tomography, computed tomography, and magnetic resonance imaging in the diagnosis of scaphoid fracture. J Trauma 1997;42: 247–253.
151. Ruby LK. Carpal instability. J Bone Joint Surg 1995;77-A:476–487.
152. Ruby LK, Stinson J, Belsky MR. The natural history of scaphoid nonunion: a review of 50 cases. J Bone Joint Surg 1985;67A:428–432.
153. Russe O. Fracture of the carpal navicular: diagnosis, nonoperative treatment, and operative treatment. J Bone Joint Surg 1960;42A:759–765.
154. Sanders WE. Evaluation of the humpback scaphoid by computed tomography in the longitudinal axial plane of the scaphoid. J Hand Surg 1988;13-A:182–187.
155. Sadowski RM, Montilla RD. Rare isolated trapeziod fracture: a case report. Hand 2008; 3:372–374.
156. Saeden B, Tornkvist H, Ponzer S, et al. Fracture of the carpal scaphoid. A prospective randomised 12-year follow-up comparing conservative and operative treatment. J Bone Join Surg Br 2001;83:230–234.
157. Schiltenwolf M, Martini AK, Eversheim S, et al. Die bedeutung des intraossären druckes für die pathogenese des morbus kienböck. Handchir Mikrochir Plast Chir 1996;28: 215–219.
158. Schweizer A, Steiger R. Long-term results after repair and augmentation ligamentoplasty of rotatory subluxation of the scaphoid. J Hand Surg 2002;27A:674–684.
159. Schwendenwein E, Wozasek GE, Hajdu S, et al. Okkulte skapholunäre Dissoziation bei distaler Radiusfraktur. Wiener Klin Wochenschr 2003;115:580–583.
160. Sennwald GR. Carpal bone fractures other than the scaphoid. In: Berger RA, Weiss APC, eds. Hand Surgery. Vol. 1. Philadelphia: Lippincott Williams & Wilkins, 2004: 409–423.
161. Siegert JJ, Frassica FJ, Amadio PC. Treatment of chronic perilunate dislocations. J Hand Surg Am 1988;13:206–212.
162. Slade JF, Jaskwhich D. Percutaneous fixation of scaphoid fractures. Hand Clinics 2001; 17:553–574.
163. Slade JF, Geissler WB, Gutow AP, et al. Percutaneous internal fixation of selected scaphoid nonunions with an arthroscopically assisted dorsal approach. J Bone Joint Surg 2003;86-A(Suppl 4):20–32.
164. Slater RR, Szabo RM, Bay BK, et al. Dorsal intercarpal ligament capsulodesis for scapholunate association: biomechanical analysis in a cadaver model. J Hand Surg 1999;24A: 232–239.
165. Smith BS, Cooney WP. Revision of failed bone grafting for nonunion of the scaphoid. Treatment options and results. Clin Orthop Relat Res 1996;327:98–109.
166. Smith P 3rd, Wright TW, Wallace PF, et al. Excision of the hook of the hamate: a retrospective survey and review of the literature. J Hand Surg Am 1988;13:612–615.
167. Sotereanos DG, Mitsionis GJ, Giannakopoulos PN, et al. Perilunate dislocation and fracture dislocation: a critical analysis of the volar-dorsal approach. J Hand Surg 1997; 22A:49–56.
168. Steinmann SP, Bishop AT. A vascularized bone graft for repair of scaphoid nonunion. Hand Clinics 2001;17:647–653.
169. Streli R. Perkutane verschraubung des handkahnbeines mit bohrdrahtkompressionsschraube. Zentralbl Chir 1970;95:1060–1078.
170. Strohm PC, Laier P, Müller CA, et al. Erstbeschreibung des beidseitigen auftretens einer seltenen verletzung. Unfallchirurg 2003;106:339–342.
171. Szabo RM, Slater RR, Palumbo CF, et al. Dorsal intercarpal ligament capsulodesis for chronic, static scapholunate dissociation: clinical results. J Hand Surg 2002;27A: 978–984.
172. Taleisnik J, Kelly PJ. Extraosseous and intraosseous blood supply of the scaphoid bone. J Bone Joint Surg 1966;48-A:1125–1137.
173. Taleisnik J. Fractures of the scaphoid. In: Taleisnik J, ed. The Wrist. New York: Churchill Livingstone, 1985:105–148.
174. Taleisnik J. The ligaments of the wrist. J Hand Surg 1976;1:110–118.
175. Tang JB, Ryu J, Omokawa S, et al. Wrist kinetics after scapholunate dissociation: the effect of scapholunate interosseous ligament injury and persistent scapholunate gaps. J Orthop Res 2002;20:215–221.
176. Tang JB, Shi D, Gu YQ, et al. Can cast immobilization successfully treat scapholunate dissociation associated with distal radius fractures? J Hand Surg 1996;21A:583–590.
177. Teisen H, Hjarback J. Classification of fresh fractures of the lunate. J Hand Surg 1989; 13-B:458–462.
178. Testut L, Latarget A. Traite d'Anatomie Humaine. Paris: Doin; 1949.
179. Tiel-van-Buul MMC, vanBeek EJR, Borm JJJ, et al. Radiography and scintigraphy of suspected scaphoid fracture. A long-term study in 160 patients. J Bone Joint Surg 1993; 75-B:61–65.
180. Tiel-van-Buul MMC, vanBeek EJR, Borm JJJ, et al. The value of radiographs and bone scintigraphy in suspected scaphoid fracture. A statistical analysis. J Hand Surg 1993; 18-B:403–406.

181. Toby EB, Butler TE, McCormack TJ, et al. A comparison of fixation screws for the scaphoid during application of cyclical bending loads. J Bone Joint Surg 1997;79A: 1190–1197.

182. Tomaino MM, King J, Pizillo M. Correction of lunate malalignment when bone grafting scaphoid nonunion with humpback deformity: rationale and results of a technique revisited. J Hand Surg Am 2000;25:322–329.

183. Trezies AJH, Davis TRC, Barton NJ. Factors influencing the outcome of bone grafting surgery for scaphoid fracture nonunion. Injury 2000;31:605–607.

184. Trojan E. Der Kahnbeinbruch der Hand, Habilitationsschrift, Eigenverlag. Austria: Druck Brüder Hollinek, 1961.

185. Trumble T, Nyland W. Scaphoid nonunions–pitfalls and pearls. Hand Clinics 2001; 17:611–624.

186. Trumble T, Verheyden J. Treatment of isolated perilunate and lunate dislocations with combined dorsal and volar approach and interosseous cerclage wire. J Hand Surg Am 2004;29:412–417.

187. Vahvanen V, Westerlund M. Fracture of the carpal scaphoid in children. A clinical and roentgenological study of 108 cases. Acta Orthop Scand 1980;51:909–913.

188. Vance RM, Gelberman RH, Evans EF. Scaphocapitate fractures. J Bone Joint Surg 1980; 62-A:271–276.

189. Vender MI, Watson HK, Black DM, et al. Acute scaphoid fracture with scapholunate gap. J Hand Surg 1989;14A:1004–1007.

190. Verdan C. Les fractures ignorèes du semi-lunaire. Ann Chir Main 1982;1:248–249.

191. Vinnars B, Pietreanu M, Bodestedt A, et al. Nonoperative compared with operative treatment of acute scaphoid fractures. A randomized controlled trial. J Bone Joint Surg Am 2008;90:1176–1185.

192. Walsh JJ, Berger RA, Cooney WP. Current status of scapholunate interosseous ligament injuries. J Am Acad Orthop Surg 2002;10:32–42.

193. Waters PM, Stewart SL. Surgical treatment of nonunion and avascular necrosis of the proximal part of the scaphoid in adolescents. J Bone Joint Surg 2002;84-A(6):915–920.

194. Watson HK, Ashmead D 4th, Makhlouf MV. Examination of the scaphoid. J Hand Surg Am 1988;13(5):657–660.

195. Watson HK, Ryu J, DiBella A. An approach to Keinbock disease: triscaphe arthrodesis. J Hand Surg Am 1985;10:179–187.

196. Watson HK, Rogers WD. Nonunion of the hook of the hamate: an argument for bone grafting the nonunion. J Hand Surg 1989;14:486–490.

197. Watson-Jones R. Fractures and Joint Injuries. 3rd ed. Edinburgh: Churchill Livingstone, 1943:568–577.

198. Weber ER, Chao EY. An experimental approach to the mechanism of scaphoid waist fractures. J Hand Surg 1978;3:142–148.

199. Weil W, Slade JF, Trumble T. Open and arthroscopic treatment of perilunate injuries. Clin Orthop 2006;445:120–132.

200. Weiss AP, Sachar K, Glowacki KA. Arthroscopic debridement alone for intercarpal tears. J Hand Surg 1997;22-A:344–349.

201. Wharton D, Casaletto JA, Choa R, et al. Outcome following coronal fractures of the hamate. J Hand Surg Eur 2009 Mar 12. [Epub ahead of print]

202. Wheeler DL, McLoughlin SW. Biomechanical assessment of compression screws. Clin Orthop Relat Res 1998;350:237–245.

203. Whipple TL. The role of arthroscopy in the treatment of scapholunate instability. Hand Clin 1995;11:37–40.

204. Wilhelm K, Kettler M, Strassmair MSL. Bandrekonstruktion mit mitek-fadenankerdübeln. Erste klinische ergebnisse. Unfallchirurg 2001;104:127–130.

205. Wilton TJ. Soft tissue interposition as a possible cause of scaphoid nonunion. J Hand Surg 1987;12B:50–51.

206. Witvoet J, Allieu Y. Lesions traumatiques fraiches. Rev Chir Orthop 1973;59 Suppl: 98–125.

207. Wolfe SW. Fractures of the carpus: scaphoid fractures. In: Berger RA, Weiss APC, eds. Hand Surgery. Vol. 1. Philadelphia: Lippincott Williams & Wilkins, 2004;381–408.

208. Wozasek GE, Moser KD. Percutaneous screw fixation for fractures of the scaphoid. J Bone Joint Surg 1991;73B:138–142.

209. Wright TW, Dobyns JH, Linscheid RL, et al. Carpal instabilities nondissociative. J Hand Surg 1994;19-A:763–773.

210. Wyrick JD, Youse BD, Kiefhaber TR. Scapholunate ligament repair and capsulodesis for the treatment of static scapholunate dissociation. J Hand Surg 1998;23-B:776–780.

211. Yanni D, Lieppins P, Laurence M. Fractures of the carpal scaphoid. A critical study of the standard splint. J Bone Joint Surg 1991;73B:600–602.

212. Yip HSF, Wu WC, Chang RYP, et al. Percutaneous cannulated screw fixation of acute scpahoid wrist fracture. J Hand Surg 2002;27B(1):42–46.

213. Zoltie N. Fractures of the body of the hamate. Injury 1991;22:459–462.

214. Wong TC, Ip FK. Minimally invasive management of trans-scaphoid perilunate fracture-dislocations. Hand Surg 2008;13:159–165.

30

DISTAL RADIUS AND ULNA FRACTURES

David S. Ruch and Margaret M. McQueen

HISTORICAL PERSPECTIVE

The management of fractures of the distal radius has undergone an extraordinary evolution over the preceding twenty years. Universal cast treatment gave way to neutralization with a bridging external fixator, which in turn was replaced by dorsal buttress plating. The technical advance of palmar locked plating has again changed the management of this fracture in a real and seemingly permanent way. The advance has also resulted in a growing understanding that many techniques may result in satisfactory long term clinical outcomes but have real short term advantages for patients. The significance of these short term advantages for the patient must now be weighed against the financial impact of routine operative intervention has cost. In addition, with an aging society with greater longevity, previously held dictums of cast treatment for geriatric patients are being challenged both by surgeons and society. Although some patients still seem to confirm Abraham Colles' famous remarks that the casted wrist "will at some remote period again enjoy perfect freedom in all of its motions and be completely exempt from pain,"[52] an increasing preponderance of published studies support the need for operative intervention in this aging population.[204] Finally, and perhaps most importantly, it is becoming increasingly apparent that operative intervention needs to be customized to the patient and the fracture as well as the expertise of the surgeon. Prospective randomized trials that group these factors may not result in answers to the critical questions that surgeons wish to answer.

In addition to apparent discrepancies regarding surgical interventions, there are other equally disparate studies regarding multiple facets of this fracture. Conflicting data exist regarding the long term relationship between radiographic parameters and patient reported outcomes. Fernandez, Trumble, and others have reported that as little as 1 mm of articular incongruity is associated with a worse functional outcome.[75,256] Catalano et al. have indicated that although there is a correlation between articular incongruity and radiographic arthrosis, there is not a correlation with self reported function.[42] Age is also a confounding variable in determining the need for operative management. Young and Rayan indicated that in elderly patients (mean age 72 years) the radiographic outcome did not correlate with functional outcome despite significant collapse and incongruity.[272] By contrast, Madhok indicated that 26% of elderly patients still experience functional impairment following nonoperative management at 1 year following closed treatment.[181] Current data confirm that patients over the age of 65 with extra-articular fractures are more likely to be satisfied with closed treatment than younger patients, but that there are still some geriatric patients who will not accept shortening and angulation. Which patients are likely to be pleased with nonoperative management in this age group remains difficult to identify.[96] Even when operative intervention is clearly indicated, controversy still exists over the use of external fixation versus one of the growing number of internal fixation devices. Although initial studies indicated that there may be advantages of external fixation versus internal fixation, more recent studies are concluding that the restoration of normal anatomy is more important than the technique that is used. The perception that internal fixation allows immediate range of motion, and therefore an improved functional arc of motion at the end of treatment, has been questioned. Immediate motion may not change the outcome as much as the other factors associated with patient demographics and fracture reduction.[16] The perceived differences between the techniques are short term, and patient perception of outcomes may equalize between 6 months and 1 year regardless of the operative technique used.[11,97,101,219,227,249] Perhaps more interesting is that the outcomes may be more related to fracture severity, with superiority of internal fixation being seen in the lower energy fractures.[156] This chapter will examine the presumably known variables including the epidemiology, mechanism of injury, and classification systems as well as the current trends in nonoperative and operative management, and the complications and pitfalls of each.

EPIDEMIOLOGY

Fractures of the distal radius represent approximately 16% of all fractures treated by orthopaedic surgeons (Table 3-4). Data extracted from the National Hospital Ambulatory Medical Care Survey indicate that in 1998 there were approximately 644,985 fractures of the distal radius treated in the United States. The incidence of this injury appears to be both gender and age specific.[100] There are three main peaks of fracture distribution: one in children age 5–14, the second in males under age 50, and the third in females over the age of 40 years.[56] There seems to be a growing incidence of these fractures in all three groups, with the sharpest increase seen in both elderly females and younger adult males.[192,245,250] More importantly, these studies suggest that the difference in the two peak incidences indicates that these fractures represent two very different injuries: one, an insufficiency fracture in elderly patients and the other a traumatic injury in younger males. The differences in these injuries and corresponding groups may in some way account for some of the discrepancies noted in the literature. Current data suggest that distal radius fractures in the elderly may represent an insufficiency fracture associated with all of the risk factors for osteoporosis.[192] The age-adjusted incidence rates of distal radius fractures for women were 165 in 1986 and 211 in 1995, indicating a steady rise over ten years.[100] In females the incidence rises sharply after the age of 40 from approximately 36.8/10,000 to 115/10,000 at age 70 years.[182,202] In males aged 35 years and over the incidence is approximately 9/10,000 and remains constant until a slight rise at age 70 years.[182,202] The data also indicate that this is the most common osteoporotic fracture,[56] with a strong correlation with femoral neck bone mineral density.[200] The sharpest increase in incidence occurs in elderly females, and has been linked to estrogen withdrawal and reduced bone mineral density.[187,192] Recent attention has focused on the incidence of osteoporosis in males as well as females. In one study from Ireland the incidence of osteoporosis in male patients with forearm fractures was found to be 27%, with a high association of vitamin D deficiency as well as endocrine abnormalities.[270] Further, just as studies have indicated an increased mortality associated with hip and vertebral fractures, there is evidence to suggest a higher mortality rate following distal radius fractures, particularly in elderly males.[225]

Although there is also a growing incidence of wrist fractures in males under the age of 49 years, epidemiologic studies suggest that the injury in younger adults is not as strongly related to gender, but occurs more equally between the sexes.[100,163] Further, the injury in this population is related to higher energy injuries (21% of all fractures) rather than to simple falls. These data suggest that one should regard distal radius fractures in this population differently from those in elderly patients.[57,163] The majority of fractures in the elderly are extra-articular, whereas there is a much higher incidence of intra-articular fractures in younger patients.[235] There is also a difference in the mechanism of injury between the groups. The majority of osteoporotic fractures occur as the result of a fall, whereas the majority of injuries in the younger patients are secondary to motor vehicle accidents and sports.[2,57,194] This may also explain the growing trend seen in hospital admissions for this injury in younger patients, as these patients particularly are being treated increasingly with operative intervention.

Risk factors for fractures of the distal radius in the elderly have been studied extensively. Decreased bone mineral density, female gender, ethnicity, heredity, and early menopause have all been demonstrated to be risk factors for this injury.[154,183,184,192] Although the relationship between bone density and risk of distal radius fracture is not as powerful as is seen with hip and spine fractures, it is clearly evident in the epidemiologic literature.[116,192] Furthermore, late onset of menopause and estrogen replacement may help protect against injury in this group.

DIAGNOSIS

Physical Examination

The majority of the external physical findings seen with displaced fractures of the distal radius may be related to the fact that the fractured radius has shortened relative to the intact strut of the ulna and has tilted in either a dorsal or a volar direction. This relationship accounts for the radially deviated and dorsally prominent distal forearm described by Goyrand[94] and Colles.[52] The degree of dorsal angulation and the presence of the prominent palmar proximal fragment result in significant displacement of the median nerve. This displacement of the nerve and the associated hematoma in the carpal tunnel may result in symptoms of an acute carpal tunnel syndrome. The acute shortening of the radius relative to the ulna may manifest as an open wound palmarly and ulnarly where the intact ulna buttonholes through the skin. Finally, the degree of radial shortening accounts for the significant distal radioulnar joint injuries seen with the fractured radius. A cadaveric study demonstrated that shortening of the radius relative to the intact ulna of over 5 mm must result in disruption of the distal radioulnar joint (DRUJ) ligaments.[2]

After injury, in addition to examination of the radius a thorough examination of the affected ipsilateral shoulder and elbow is required to identify associated fractures, especially of the proximal humerus in the elderly. Associated injuries have significant implications regarding (1) the higher degree of energy imparted to the fracture in younger patients and (2) rehabilitation challenges with injuries to both the elbow and the wrist. Ipsilateral radial head and distal radial fractures may indicate that sufficient energy has been imparted to result in an Essex–Lopresti lesion.[240] An effort should also be made to identify an ipsilateral scaphoid fracture, which may direct the surgeon to consider operative versus nonoperative management. Although there are no prospective studies in the literature, there may be a benefit to rigid internal fixation of the scaphoid to permit early motion of both injuries.[111,255]

Attention should then be directed to soft tissue considerations. Open fractures typically result in soft tissue injury palmarly and ulnarly where the distal ulna emerges as the radius displaces dorsally. Direct blows and rotational injuries may result in dorsal soft tissue injuries. A thorough evaluation of the extrinsic flexor and extensors is indicated. Particular attention should be directed to the extensor pollicis longus, which may be injured acutely at Lister's tubercle or may present with a late spontaneous rupture. Finally, attention is directed to the neurologic complications. Median nerve injury—either acute or chronic—is a common cause of functional impairment and chronic pain secondary to complex regional pain syndrome. Examination should include both a subjective evaluation of the

patient's pain and an objective assessment of median nerve function. Subjectively, the patient should be monitored for pain out of proportion to the injury and also for "burning pain," which is often associated with nerve injury. Reduction of the fracture and elevation of the limb typically will improve this type of pain. Objectively, sensibility in the median innervated digits must be assessed and monitored before and after reduction and immobilization. Abnormal sensory examination despite reduction and immobilization may be secondary to (1) direct contusion, (2) mechanical deformation of the nerve, or (3) abnormal pressure within the carpal tunnel. Neurapraxia is typically present at presentation and is associated with only moderate pain with gradual improvement over time. Mechanical deformation of the nerve typically improves with reduction and limb elevation. Symptoms caused by increased pressure within the carpal canal however may not improve and require more aggressive treatment. This diagnosis is similar to a compartment syndrome involving the median nerve and urgent treatment may be required to avoid long term dystrophic symptoms. If fracture reduction and immobilization does not improve symptoms, with patients continuing to report worsening pain and if the degree of neurologic impairment does not improve objectively, early decompression of the carpal canal is indicated.

 AUTHORS' PREFERRED TREATMENT

Before reduction and immobilization, the patient's pain is quantified numerically and the two point sensation is assessed in both the median and the ulnar nerve distributions. After satisfactory radiographic and clinical reduction of the deformity, the examination is again performed to provide a baseline for subsequent serial examinations. The upper extremity is elevated above the level of the heart and oral narcotics are administered. Any worsening of the patient's symptoms from this point on requires repeat pain measurements and assessment of sensory and motor function. The immobilization is loosened down to the skin and ice packs may be applied. If no relief is seen within 6 hours, then an immediate carpal tunnel release should be performed. We prefer a longitudinal incision, which permits proximal identification of the median nerve and subsequent release of the antebrachial fascia and transverse carpal ligament. It should be noted that the bony deformity, hematoma, and edema make visualization difficult, and an extensile approach may be necessary to avoid iatrogenic nerve injury. Any hematoma is evacuated, and a silastic drain may be necessary to avoid reaccumulation. In general, it is not necessary to release Guyon's canal at this time. The exception to this rule occurs when there is obvious extrusion of the palmar lunate facet which may impinge on the ulnar nerve. Finally, if there is clinical evidence of a compartment syndrome of the hand, then the compartment pressures in the adductor and dorsal interosseous muscles must be checked and the compartments decompressed when elevated pressures are found.

Imaging Studies

The standard series of PA, lateral, and oblique x-ray views is useful to visualize a suspected fracture of the distal radius. Additional views may be obtained as needed to assess for displacement or additional injuries.

A number of radiological measurements quantifying the orientation of the distal radius are in common use, and it is important to understand these in order to reduce interobserver error. Significant discrepancy regarding intra- and interobserver reliability has been demonstrated in the measurement of standard radiographic criteria in the management of these fractures. For extra-articular fractures the mean standard deviation between surgeons was 3.2 degrees for radial angle, 3.6 degrees for palmar tilt in a true lateral view, and 2.1 degrees for palmar tilt in 15 degrees of rotation from the true lateral view.[127]

Dorsal/Palmar Tilt

On a true lateral view a line is drawn connecting the most distal points of the volar and dorsal lips of the radius. The dorsal or palmar tilt is the angle created with a line drawn along the longitudinal axis of the radius (Fig. 30-1A).

Radial Length

Radial length is measured on the PA radiograph. It is the distance in millimeters between a line drawn perpendicular to the long axis of the radius and tangential to the most distal point of the ulnar head and a line drawn perpendicular to the long axis of the radius and at the level of the tip of the radial styloid (Fig. 30-1B).

Ulnar Variance

This is a measure of radial shortening and should not be confused with measurement of radial length. Ulnar variance is the vertical distance between a line parallel to the medial corner of the articular surface of the radius and a line parallel to the most distal point of the articular surface of the ulnar head, both of which are perpendicular to the long axis of the radius (Fig. 30-1B).

Radial Inclination

On the PA view the radius inclines towards the ulna. This is measured by the angle betwee a line drawn from the tip of the radial styloid to the medial corner of the articular surface of the radius and a line drawn perpendicular to the long axis of the radius (Fig. 30-1B).

Carpal Malalignment

Two types of carpal malalignment are associated with fracture of the distal radius. The most common is malalignment that compensates for the tilt of the distal radius which is extrinsic to the carpus.[253] On a lateral view one line is drawn along the long axis of the capitate and one down the long axis of the radius. If the carpus is aligned, the lines will intersect within the carpus. If not, they will intersect outwith the carpus (Fig. 30-1A). Carpal malalignment can also be caused by associated carpal ligament disruption. The radiological diagnosis of this condition is detailed in Chapter 28. Specific features should be assessed on each view of the distal radius as follows:

PA View

For extra-articular fractures: assess (a) radial length/ulnar variance, (b) extent of metaphyseal comminution, and (c) ulnar styloid fracture location (tip/waist/base). For intra-articular fractures: assess (a) depression of the lunate facet, (b) gap between scaphoid and lunate facet, (c) central impaction fragments, and (d) interruption of the proximal carpal row.

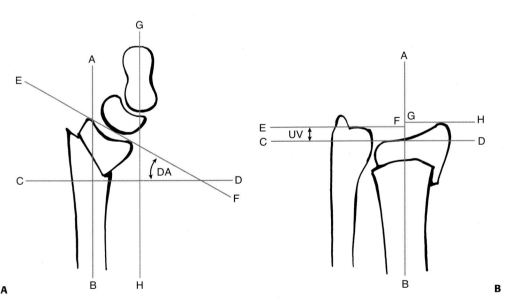

FIGURE 30-1 A. The dorsal angle (DA) is measured by finding the angle between a line (CD) perpendicular to the long axis of the radius (AB) and a line joining the dorsal and volar extremities of the radiocarpal joint (EF). Carpal alignment is assessed by the point of intersection of the line parallel to the long axis of the radius (AB) and a line parallel to the long axis of the capitate (GH). If these intersect outwith the carpus or do no intersect as in this illustration, then the carpus is malaligned. **B.** Ulnar variance (UV) is the distance between two lines perpendicular to the long axis of the radius (AB). The first is tangential to the ulnar corner of the radius (CD) and the second tangential to the ulnar head (EF). Radial length is the distance between line EF and a line tangential to the radial styloid (GH). (From Court-Brown C, McQueen M, Tornetta P. Orthopaedic Surgery Essentials: Trauma. Philadelphia: Lippincott Williams & Wilkins, 2006, with permission.)

Lateral View

For extra-articular fractures: assess (a) dorsal/palmar tilt, (b) extent of metaphyseal comminution, (c) carpal alignment, (d) displacement of the volar cortex, and (e) position of the DRUJ. For intra-articular fractures: assess (a) depression of the palmar lunate facet, (b) depression of the central fragment, and (c) gap between palmar and dorsal fragments.

It is important that measurements of dorsal and volar tilt are made on a true lateral view of the distal radius, because malposition with rotation of the radial styloid in relation to the shaft has a significant effect on the apparent alignment, with an increase in palmar tilt with supination and a decrease with pronation.[40] Johnson and Szabo found that rotation of the radius on the lateral view resulted in a change in the apparent palmar tilt. A 5-degree rotational change produces a 1.6-degree change in palmar tilt on the conventional lateral view and a 1-degree change on the 15-degree lateral view.[127]

Oblique View

For extraarticular fractures, assess radial comminution. For intraarticular fractures, assess (a) the radial styloid for split or depression and (b) depression of the dorsal lunate facet.

Tilted Lateral View

The tilted lateral view is a lateral view taken with a pad under the hand to incline the radius 20 degrees toward the beam.[169] It eliminates the shadow of the radial styloid and provides a clear tangential view of the lunate facet. It is useful to assess (a) residual depression of the palmar lunate facet and (b) possible hardware penetration into the articular surface.

Traction Views (AP and Lateral)

These views are taken with manual traction or finger traps applied after reduction. They indicate whether external fixation may reduce the fracture sufficiently or whether direct reduction will be required. A traction view also helps to identify fracture fragments that may be obscured by the displacement of the fracture. Furthermore, examination of the proximal carpal row may indicate the presence of incongruity consistent with interosseous ligament injury.

Contralateral Wrist (AP and Lateral)

These radiographs may be indicated before surgery to assess the patient's normal ulnar variance and scapholunate angle, both of which vary between patients.

Other Studies

In 1986 Knirk and Jupiter correlated patient outcome with residual intraarticular incongruity. They found a 91% incidence of radiographically apparent arthrosis with any measurable intraarticular step-off and a 100% incidence with over 2 mm of articular step-off.[142] Subsequent authors also emphasized the relationship of as little a 1 mm or more of articular incongruity with a worse clinical outcome.[91,144] Although these studies indicate the importance of restoring articular congruity, other authors question the ability of plain radiographs to consistently demonstrate incongruity of less than 2 mm. Data on healed fractures indicate that clinicians measuring step and gap deformity on a random x-ray film will differ by more than 3 mm at least 10% of the time. Repeat step or gap measurements by the same observer are also expected to differ by more than 2 mm at least 10% of the time.[145]

In an effort to improve the accuracy of measurement of articular congruity, some authors have proposed the use of computerized tomography (CT) to assess intraarticular fractures. Clinical data suggests that CT demonstrates intraarticular extension more accurately than plain radiographs[126] and it has been shown to be superior in defining step-off and gaps in the articular surface of the distal radius when compared with plain radiographs. Cole et al. found that there was greater reproducibility of measurements with CT and a poor correlation between radiographic measurements and CT measurements.[51] CT also allows more accurate measurement of gap formation between palmar and dorsal fragments and has also been documented to be superior for imaging the sigmoid notch. In one study comparing plain radiographs to CT the authors found that in 20 consecutive fractures, plain radiographs documented notch involvement in only 35% of the fractures compared with 65% found on CT. Finally, CT may improve the reliability of classification of these fractures by accurately determining the presence of articular involvement.[80] More recently three-dimensional computerized tomography has been used to characterize these fractures. The use of this technique has increased the perceived need for open exposure of displaced articular segments when compared with conventional CT.[104] Although it seems that plain radiographs do not reliably permit measurements at the level of 1 mm, the clinical significance of these studies remains unknown. The majority of clinical outcome studies have relied on plain radiographs to assess both the injury and the treatment outcomes.

CLASSIFICATION

Perhaps no other fracture in the orthopedic literature has garnered so many eponyms over time than fractures of the distal radius. Classifications of fractures as "Colle's," "Pouteau's," "Barton's," "Smith's," "Chauffeur's," and "Reverse Barton's" continue to be presented despite the authors' failure to read the original descriptions. The resultant conflicting understanding of each eponym creates difficulty in assessing outcomes following treatment.

To remedy this, several classification systems have been proposed. To present a complete record of each would be exhaustive and probably inadequate. Some proposed classifications seem to be more of an attempt to stress the significance of some feature of the fracture rather than to provide a more global approach. There are, however, some classification patterns that have stood the test of time and continue to be useful in understanding these fractures.

Gartland and Werley proposed a classification system that assessed the three basic components of these injuries: (1) metaphyseal comminution, (2) intra-articular extension, and (3) displacement of the fragments.[87] Their classification system (which follows) has been accompanied by one of the first clinically useful outcomes scores (Fig. 30-2).

Group I: Simple Colles' fracture with no involvement of the radial articular surfaces

Group II: Comminuted Colles' fractures with intra-articular extension without displacement

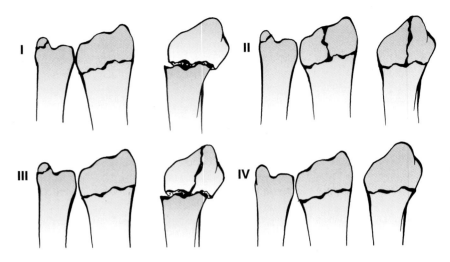

FIGURE 30-2 Gartland and Werley Classification System.

Group III: Comminuted Colles' fractures with intra-articular extension with displacement

Group IV: Extra-articular, undisplaced

Frykman established a classification that incorporated individual involvement of the radiocarpal and radioulnar joints (Fig. 30-3)[85]:

Type I: Extra-articular fracture

Type II: Extra-articular fracture with ulnar styloid fracture

Type III: Radiocarpal articular involvement

Type IV: Radiocarpal involvement with ulnar styloid fracture

Type V: Radioulnar involvement

Type VI: Radioulnar involvement with ulnar styloid fracture

Type VII: Radioulnar and radiocarpal involvement

Type VIII: Radioulnar and radiocarpal involvement with ulnar styloid fracture

Melone emphasized the effect of the impaction of the lunate on the radial articular surface to create four characteristic fracture fragments (Fig. 30-4).[191]

- Type I: Stable fracture without displacement. This pattern has characteristic fragments of the radial styloid and a palmar and dorsal lunate facet.
- Type II: Unstable "die punch" with displacement of the characteristic fragments and comminution of the anterior and posterior cortices
  - Type IIA: Reducible
  - Type IIB: Irreducible (central impaction fracture)
- Type III: "Spike" fracture. Unstable. Displacement of the articular surface and also of the proximal spike of the radius
- Type IV: "Split" fracture. Unstable medial complex that is severely comminuted with separation and or rotation of the distal and palmar fragments
- Type V: Explosion injury

The OTA/AO classification emphasizes the increasing severity of the bony injury (Fig. 30-5).

- Type A: Extraarticular fracture. Subgroups are based on direction of displacement and comminution.
- Type B: Partial articular fracture. Subgroups are based on lateral (radial styloid) palmar or dorsal fragments.

- Type C: Complete articular. Subgroups are based on the degree of comminution of the articular surface and the metaphysis.

These classifications are based on the location of the fracture line(s), the displacement of the distal fragment, the extent of articular involvement, and the presence of an ulnar styloid fracture. Critics point out that the simple classification systems group fractures of differing severity and prognosis, whereas the more complex systems have poor reproducibility. Anderson et al. compared intra- and interobserver reliability for the AO, Frykman, Melone, and Mayo classification systems, which emphasized fracture stability. They found that interrater reliability was moderate for the Mayo system and only fair for the AO, Frykman, and Melone classifications. This apparent lack of interobserver reliability was not as evident with more experienced surgeons, but was still present in evaluating the fractures using the subgroups of the AO classification.[8] Despite the plethora of classification systems, there continue to be perceived deficits in our ability to classify these fractures consistently and accurately in a manner that provides both prognosis and treatment guidance. It has also become increasingly apparent that outcome following these fractures may also be dependent on the degree of soft tissue injury, including interosseous ligament injury and DRUJ instability.[128]

In 1993 Fernandez proposed a mechanism-based classification system that would address the potential for ligamentous injury and thereby assist in treatment recommendations (Fig. 30-6)[70]:

- Type I: Metaphyseal bending fractures with the inherent problems of loss of palmar tilt and radial shortening relative to the ulna (DRUJ injuries)
- Type II: Shearing fractures requiring reduction and often buttressing of the articular segment
- Type III: Compression of the articular surface *without the characteristic fragmentation*; also the potential for significant interosseous ligament injury
- Type IV: Avulsion fractures or radiocarpal fracture dislocations
- Type V: Combined injuries with significant soft tissue involvement because of the high energy nature of these fractures

There is also a separate grouping of the possible associated distal radioulnar joint lesions.[77]

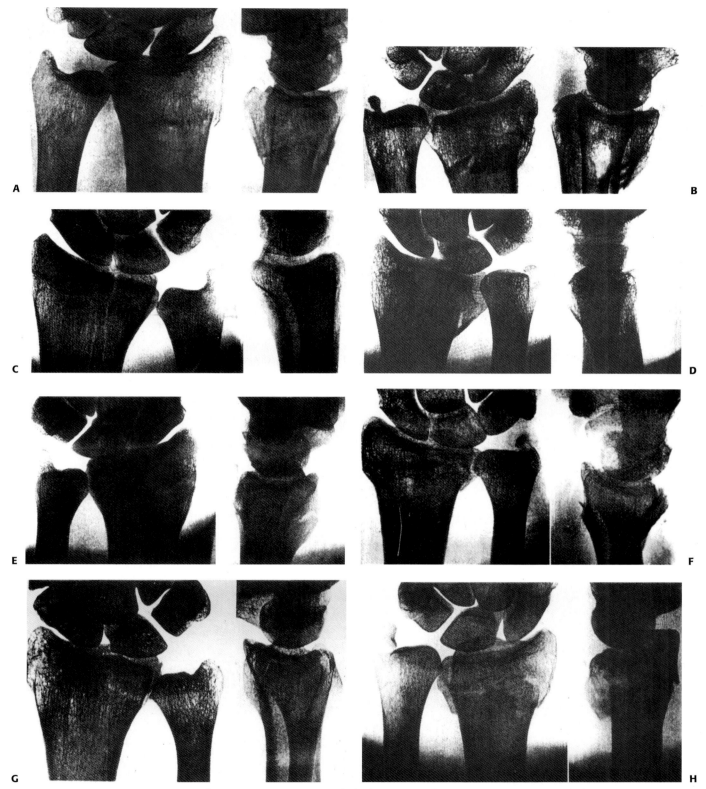

FIGURE 30-3 A. Frykman Fracture Type I: Extra-articular fracture. **B.** Frykman Fracture Type II: Extra-articular fracture with ulnar styloid fracture. **C.** Frykman Fracture Type III: Radiocarpal articular involvement. **D.** Frykman Fracture Type IV: Radiocarpal involvement with ulnar styloid fracture. **E.** Frykman Fracture Type V: Radioulnar involvement. **F.** Frykman Fracture Type VI: Radioulnar involvement with ulnar styloid fracture. **G.** Frykman Fracture Type VII: Radioulnar and radiocarpal involvement. **H.** Frykman Fracture Type VIII: Radioulnar and radiocarpal involvement with ulnar styloid fracture.

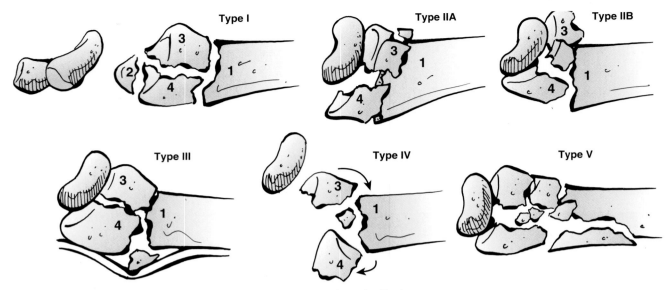

FIGURE 30-4 Melone classification.

RATIONALE FOR TREATMENT

The goal of treatment of these fractures is a wrist that provides sufficient pain-free motion and stability to permit vocational and avocational activities in all age groups without the propensity for future degenerative changes in the young. Although this goal may be easily accepted, there is very little consistency regarding the radiographic features that will afford this result.

Palmar Tilt

Clinical studies have implicated the loss of the normal 11 degrees to 12 degrees of palmar tilt as having a significant effect on functional outcome. Gartland and Werley concluded that residual dorsal tilt has a more direct effect on outcome than residual radial deviation, radial shortening, or loss of integrity of the radioulnar joint.[87] In a retrospective review Kopylov found that loss of as little as 12 degrees from the normal tilt resulted in an 80% increased risk of radiographically apparent arthritis.[144] McQueen examined 30 patients with extraarticular fractures and found that loss of 12 degrees or more of the normal palmar tilt resulted in functional impairment when compared with those fractures which healed at neutral or with a positive palmar tilt.[173] Porter felt that loss of function did not occur until at least 20 degrees of palmar tilt was lost.[208] Why the loss

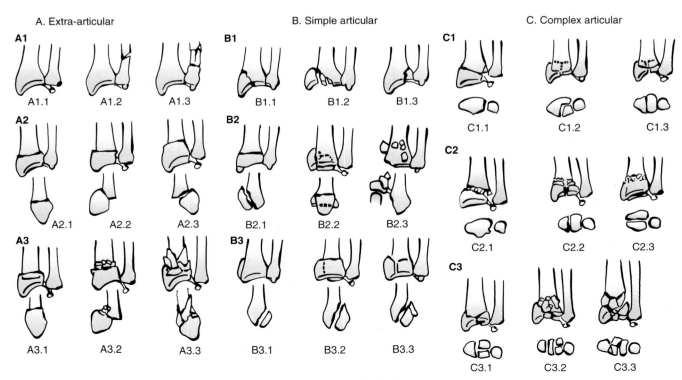

FIGURE 30-5 AO classification.

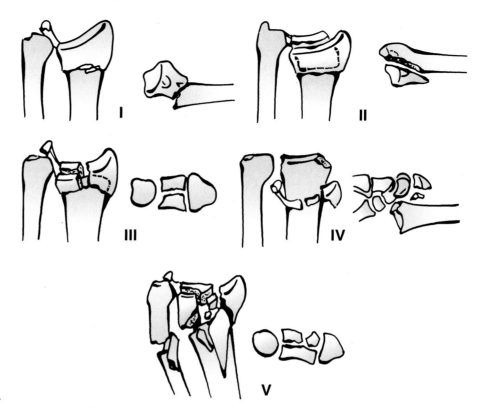

FIGURE 30-6 Fernandez classification.

of palmar tilt results in functional impairment is not entirely clear. McQueen concluded that angulation of the distal radius resulted in carpal malalignment, which correlated more closely with functional outcome than measurement of the dorsal tilt, possibly because of the inaccuracy of measurements.[61] Taleisnik indicated that the dorsal shift of the proximal carpal row results in a clinically apparent midcarpal instability with ulnar deviation. The symptoms of instability resolved with corrective osteotomy of the radius.[253]

The reason for the loss of function is probably multifactorial; however, cadaveric data have provided some potential explanations. The changes in palmar tilt affect not only radiocarpal mechanics, but also radioulnar mechanics. Short et al. found that as little as a 10-degree loss of palmar tilt causes the area of maximum load on the radius to become more concentrated and to shift dorsally. This change in load concentration may explain the clinical findings relating dorsal tilt to radiographically apparent degenerative changes at long-term follow-up.[239] In addition, the change in palmar tilt increases the tension on the palmar and dorsal radioulnar ligaments, resulting in an increased load required for forearm rotation.[140]

Radial Length/Ulnar Variance

Although collapse of the lunate facet results in radiocarpal incongruity, collapse of the radial metaphysis results in radioulnar incongruity. In a series of cadaver studies Adams found that positive ulnar variance resulted in the most significant changes in the kinematics of the radioulnar joint when compared with loss of radial inclination and palmar tilt.[2] Clinical studies have also indicated a strong correlation between radial length and loss of strength. McQueen found that over 2 mm of positive ulnar variance resulted in symptomatic loss of strength.[173] Jen-

kins found that not only was shortening of over 4 mm associated with loss of strength, but it also correlated with pain.[125] Solgaard retrospectively analyzed a series of 269 fractures and concluded that reduction of the distal radius should primarily aim at the correction of radial length.[243] Their findings were corroborated by Batra and Gupta who noted that the most important factor affecting functional outcome was radial length followed by palmar tilt.[23]

Radial Inclination

Cadaver data indicate that the carpus shifts ulnarly in response to loss of radial inclination, thereby resulting in increased load on the triangular fibrocartilage complex (TFCC) and the ulna. Although this effect is not as severe as other deformities, clinical studies demonstrate a correlation between decreased radial inclination and decreased grip strength.[125] In addition, long term follow up indicates that this increases the risk of degenerative changes by 90%.[144]

Significantly, these deformities frequently do not occur in isolation.[259] The typical malunion is a three-dimensional deformity, which is visualized using two-dimensional plain radiographs. Although the radius is shortened with an apparent loss of palmar tilt, there is also a rotational component, which is typically not visualized and may prove to be significant. It is difficult, therefore, to separate out the effect of one of these deformities from the others when assessing their impact on outcome.

Carpal Malalignment

Carpal malalignment after distal radius fracture is usually an adaptive process in response to dorsal or excessive palmar tilt of the distal radius. The lunate tilts in the same direction as the distal radius and the carpus adapts to this at the midcarpal joint with flexion of the midcarpal joint in dorsal tilt and extension in volar tilt in order to realign the hand on the forearm. This deformity is therefore extrinsic to the carpus and occurs without any disruption of the carpal ligaments. Taleisnik and Watson demonstrated relief of symptoms when carpal malalignment was corrected by radial osteotomy.[253] Since then carpal malalignment has been shown to correlate with poorer grip strength and rotation [174] and with fewer good results.[23] Bickerstaff and Bell found that the degree of carpal malalignment at 1 year after fracture was the most significant indicator of a poor result.[28]

The role of ligamentous injuries or intrinsic malalignment in subsequent outcomes is only recently becoming apparent as studies document significant associated ligament injuries during arthroscopically assisted treatment. [93,162,215,228]

Although some degree of widening of the lateral scapholunate angle caused by palmar flexion of the scaphoid may be acceptable, it appears that a dorsiflexed lunate (a static DISI deformity) is associated with a worse outcome.[23,254] The critical shift is in the radiolunate angle, as it indicates a shift of contact forces dorsally on the radius in the intermediate column. There is as yet no defined threshold for this angle; however, more than 25 degrees has been correlated with a worse outcome.[23]

Intra-articular Incongruity

Radiocarpal articular congruity remains the most clinically significant radiographic parameter in younger patients with regard to both functional outcome and future degenerative changes. The threshold for acceptable amounts of radiographic congruity remains somewhat controversial. Knirk and Jupiter retrospectively evaluated 43 young adults at 6.7 years and found that any degree of articular incongruity was associated with radiographically apparent arthritis. If 2 mm of incongruity was present, there was a 100% incidence of degenerative changes on plain radiographs.[142] Trumble et al. evaluated 52 intra-articular fractures in patients with an average age of 37 years and found that the strongest indicator of outcome was articular congruity.[256] Note that both these studies documented the significance of residual depression of the lunate facet following lunate impaction (die punch) fractures as being the cause of residual articular incongruity. Cadaver studies using pressure sensitive film document increases in contact stresses with step-offs as small as 1 mm (Fig. 30-7).[265]

Although these authors and others have noted the radiographic changes seen following incomplete reduction of articular congruity, their functional significance is debated.[91,144] Catalano et al. examined 26 operatively treated intra-articular fractures in young adults at a mean of 7.1 years. The authors found that despite radiographically apparent arthrosis, there was no correlation between residual articular congruity and the functional outcome. They also found that step-off in the articular surface is more significant than gapping between fragments of the same height.[142] Similarly with extra-articular fractures, Tsukazaki et al. examined 83 consecutive patients and found poor correlation between final angulation and functional outcome at 2 years.[258] The discrepancy in these data combined with limitations in the ability to visualize step-offs of less than 2 mm on plain radiographs makes definitive recommendations difficult to mandate.[145] As a result of these studies, the parameters presented in Table 30-1 are currently considered to be

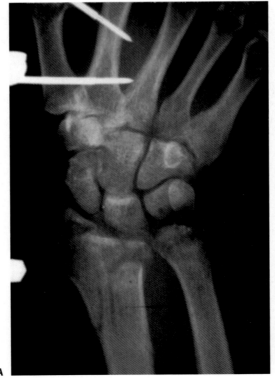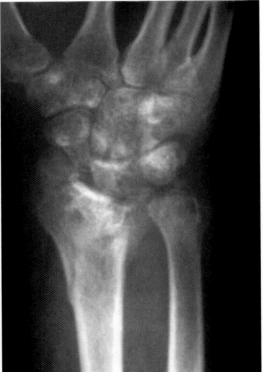

A   B

FIGURE 30-7 There is incongruity of the radiocarpal joint despite attempted external fixation of the radius **(A)**. The radiographic result **(B)** is significant arthrosis at 2 years, necessitating a fusion of the wrist.

TABLE 30-1	Acceptable Radiographic Parameters for Healed Radius Fracture in an Active, Healthy Patient
Radial length	Within 2–3 mm of the contralateral wrist
Palmar tilt	Neutral tilt (0 degrees)
Intra articular step-off	<2 mm
Radial angle	<5 degrees loss
Carpal malalignment	Absent

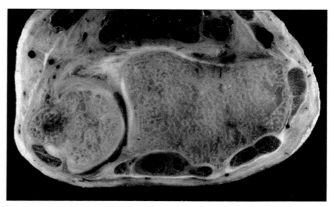

FIGURE 30-9 The cross-sectional anatomy of the radius immediately below the radiocarpal joint. Note that the radial styloid angles palmarly. Note that the extensor tendons are in immediate contact with the bone, whereas palmarly a layer of fat protects the flexors from the bone.

acceptable radiographic parameters for a healed radius fracture in an active, healthy patient.

SURGICAL AND APPLIED ANATOMY

Although the surgical anatomy of the distal radius remains relatively significant, pitfalls lie in interpretation of the bony architecture using two-dimensional imaging, including fluoroscopy. In addition, the complex ligamentous anatomy of both the extrinsic and intrinsic aspects of the radiocarpal and distal radioulnar joints compounds the challenge.

Bony Anatomy

The distal radius consists of the (1) metaphysis, (2) scaphoid facet, (3) lunate facet, and (4) sigmoid notch. The metaphysis is flared distally in both the AP and the lateral planes with thinner cortical bone lying dorsally and radially (Fig. 30-8). The significance of the thinness of these cortices is that the fractures typically collapse dorsoradially. In addition, the bone with the greatest trabecular density lies in the palmar ulnar cortex.[89] The fact that this bone is thicker even in osteoporotic cadaver specimens may explain the success of internal fixation techniques, which take advantage of this superior bone.[203] Distally the radius has a somewhat trapezoidal shape. The radial styloid rotates palmarly 15 degrees off the axis of the radius, which makes capture difficult from a dorsal approach (Figs. 30-9 and 30-10).

In the anteroposterior plane the strongest bone is found under the lunate facet of the radius. The line of force passes down the long finger axis through the capitolunate articulation

and contacts the radius at this location. The "palmar ulnar corner" is often referred to as the keystone of the radius. It serves as the attachment for the palmar distal radioulnar ligaments and also for the stout radiolunate ligament. Displacement of this fragment is associated with palmar displacement of the carpus and also with loss of forearm rotation.[10] Fig. 30-11 demonstrates residual depression of the lunate facet. The result is loss of rotation as well as a step-off in the articular surface.

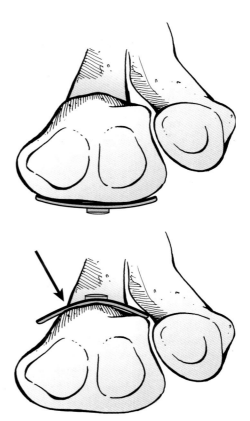

FIGURE 30-10 Cross-sectional anatomy of the radial metaphysis. Note that the dorsal surface is much more irregular than the palmar surface. The V-shape dorsally caused by Lister's tubercle (*arrow*) makes it difficult to contour a plate to fit the dorsum of the radius. (From Papadonikolakis A, with permission.)

FIGURE 30-8 The cross-sectional anatomy of the radius with comminution dorsally and radially. Note the tendency to dorsal collapse is the result of dorsal comminution and the collapse at the midcarpal joint.

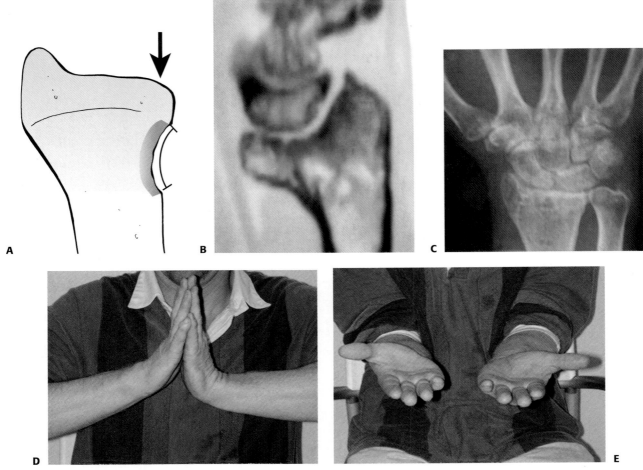

FIGURE 30-11 A. Disruption of the critical corner of the radius results in depression of the lunate facet.
B–E. The radiographic and clinical effects are demonstrated.

Ligamentous Anatomy

The extrinsic ligaments of the wrist play a major role in the use of indirect reduction techniques. The palmar extrinsic ligaments are attached to the distal radius, and it is these ligaments that are relied on to reduce the components of a fracture using closed methods. There are two factors about these ligaments that make them significant for reduction: First the orientation of the extrinsic ligaments from the radial styloid is oblique relative to the more vertical orientation of the ligaments attached to the lunate facet. Figures 30-12 and 30-13 demonstrate the palmar and dorsal extrinsic ligamentous anatomy in the wrist.

The second significance of the ligamentous anatomy is because of the relative strengths of the thicker palmar ligaments when compared to the thinner dorsal ligaments. In addition, the dorsal ligaments are oriented in a relative "z" orientation, which allows them to lengthen with less force than the more vertically oriented palmar ligaments. The significance is that distraction will result in the palmar ligaments becoming taut before the dorsal ligaments. Thus the palmar cortex is brought out to length before the dorsal cortex. It is for this reason that it is difficult to achieve reduction of the normal 12 degrees of palmar tilt using distraction alone (Fig. 30-13).

Applied Anatomy

Jakob and his co-authors interpreted the wrist as consisting of three distinct columns, each of which is subjected to different forces and thus must be addressed as discrete elements.[121] Figure 30-14 demonstrates the "columnar" approach to management of intra-articular fractures of the radius.

The *radial column* consists of the scaphoid fossa and the radial styloid. Because of the radial inclination of 22 degrees, impaction of the scaphoid on the articular surface results in a shear moment on the radial styloid causing failure laterally at the radial cortex. The radial column, therefore, is best stabilized by buttressing the lateral cortex.

The *intermediate column* consists of the lunate fossa and the sigmoid notch of the radius. The intermediate column may be considered the cornerstone of the radius because it is critical for both articular congruity and distal radioulnar function. Failure of the intermediate column occurs as a result of impaction of the lunate on the articular surface with dorsal comminution. The column is stabilized by a direct buttress of the dorsal ulnar aspect of the radius.

The *ulnar column* consists of the ulna styloid but also should include the TFCC and the ulnocarpal ligaments.

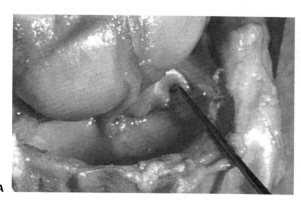
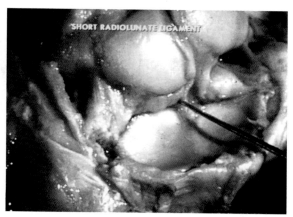

FIGURE 30-12 These images show the thick palmar radial extrinsic ligaments when viewed from the back. Note that these ligaments are oriented obliquely off the radial styloid **(A)** and vertically off the lunate facet **(B)**. Application of ulnar deviation to restore radial length with cast immobilization or external fixation results in a distraction of the radial styloid but does little to reduce the lunate facet.

CURRENT TREATMENT OPTIONS

Nonoperative Management

Closed reduction and cast immobilization has historically been the mainstay of treatment for these fractures. The difficulty in treating patients with immobilization lies in the ability to accurately predict the position of the fracture at final union. Cast immobilization is indicated in (1) stable fractures in which the expected radiographic outcome achieves the goals of treatment outlined above, and (2) low demand elderly patients in whom future functional impairment is less of a priority than immediate health concerns and/or operative risks.[27]

Stable Fractures

In order to understand the definition of stability, it is useful to consider the mechanical loads that caused the bone to fail and present with the initial radiographic images (prereduction x-rays). A fall on the outstretched hand may result in (1) a metaphyseal bending fracture, (2) a lunate impaction fracture,

or (3) an articular shear fracture. The stability of the avulsion fractures is based on the prognosis of the ligamentous injury, and combined injuries are generally too unstable to be treated with cast immobilization.

A metaphyseal bending fracture that failed under tension must be able to resist (a) axial load and (b) dorsal displacement. A cast with a dorsal mold may prevent dorsal displacement; however, a cast does not resist collapse caused by an axial load. Resistance to collapse is dependent on an intact palmar buttress. Several authors have documented that when comminution extends into the palmar buttress, collapse occurs even in the face of cast immobilization.[81,274] The critical degree to which the comminution extends from the dorsal cortex to the palmar cortex as viewed on the lateral radiograph lies somewhere between two thirds and three quarters of the radial metaphysis (Fig. 30-15).[274] Lunate impaction fractures typically result secondary to axial load. Although cast immobilization prevents dorsal dis-

FIGURE 30-13 The dorsal ligaments of the wrist have a "z" configuration that allows for elongation. Compared with the palmar ligaments, the dorsal ligaments must stretch further to achieve reduction of the palmar tilt.

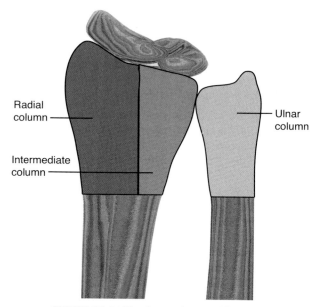

FIGURE 30-14 The three columns of the wrist.

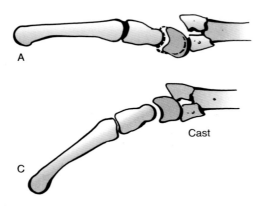

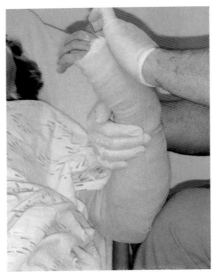

FIGURE 30-15 The fate of the lunate facet with attempted closed treatment of an intra-articular fracture **(A)**. Palmar flexion **(B)**, which is used to restore palmar tilt, results in depression of the volar lunate facet **(C)**.

placement, it does not resist axial loads, and as such cannot resist redisplacement of the lunate facet over time.

Prediction of Instability

Several factors have been associated with redisplacement following closed manipulation of a distal radius fracture:

1) The age of the patient. Patients over 80 years of age with a displaced fracture of the distal radius are three times more likely to have instability than those less than 30 years of age. This is even more striking in patients with minimally or undisplaced fractures when the risk of instability increases tenfold in older patients.[180] Fractures in elderly patients with osteopenic bones may also displace at a later stage.
2) The initial displacement of the fracture.[122,243,251] The greater the degree of initial displacement (particularly radial shortening), the more energy is imparted to the fracture resulting in a higher likelihood that closed treatment will be unsuccessful.
3) The extent of metaphyseal comminution (the metaphyseal defect) as evidenced by either plain radiographs or computerized tomography.[122,180]
4) Finally, displacement following closed treatment is a predictor of instability, and repeat manipulation is unlikely to result in a successful radiographic outcome.[83,155,174,175]

Mackenney and his coauthors examined the natural history of over 3500 distal radius fractures and detailed the independently significant predictors of early instability (redisplacement before 2 weeks), late instability (redisplacement between 2 weeks and fracture union), and malunion for both undisplaced and displaced fractures.[180] Mathematical formulae were constructed to give a percentage chance of redisplacement or malunion for individual patients. The authors give an example of an independent 85 year old lady with a dorsally displaced fracture of the distal radius with metaphyseal comminution and a positive ulnar variance of 2 mm. The calculated probability of malunion is 82%. Clinical application of these formulae is likely to encourage early treatment in appropriate cases and reduce the prevalence of malunion.

Patient Considerations

The decision regarding cast treatment versus operative management of a comminuted unstable fracture must also incorporate host factors including physical demands, health status, independent lifestyle, vocation, avocation, and comorbidities. With the use of regional anesthesia and the results of several cohort series of elderly patients having a favorable outcome with surgery, it has become more difficult to identify those patients in whom nonoperative treatment is indicated.

The literature reflects the controversy regarding nonoperative management. Young et al. reported that at seven years there was overall good function with nonoperative management and no apparent advantage seen with external fixation.[271] Young and Rayan indicated that in low demand patients over the age of 60, radiographic appearance at union had a poor correlation with patient reported outcomes.[5,209] Other authors noted persistent disability after nonoperative management and have proposed more aggressive treatment in elderly patients to avoid collapse.[11,131] Although it is clear that restoration of normal anatomy is the goal, it appears that the effect of "malalignment" of extra-articular fractures may be mitigated in patients older than age 65, possibly because of reducing demands.[96] Future prospective randomized studies will need to address whether patient needs and expectations should affect the operative indications.

Technique of Closed Reduction

Successful reduction of a displaced fracture requires adequate pain relief to overcome muscle spasm. Hematoma block with supplemental IV sedation or Bier block provides adequate anesthesia in most settings although there is some evidence that haematoma block provides poorer anesthesia and therefore a poorer reduction than regional block.[1,50] The use of finger traps may prove useful in the management of completely displaced fractures and assist in the application of a cast or splint.

Manipulation starts with longitudinal traction, and then direct pressure is applied on the displaced radial metaphyseal fragment. Great care must be taken to avoid tearing of the skin, particularly in elderly patients with parchment-like skin. Reduction may be confirmed using sonography, fluoroscopy, or with plain radiographs after the maneuver.[44]

The position of immobilization of the radius is critical following reduction. The splint or cast should provide a dorsal buttress to prevent collapse, but excessive palmar flexion of the radius should be avoided. Palmar flexion of an uninjured wrist to 60 degrees has been demonstrated to cause a significant elevation of pressure in the carpal tunnel. When palmar flexion is combined with the swelling seen with a distal radius fracture, the elevation of pressure may result in an acute carpal tunnel syndrome.[266] The exact amount of palmar flexion of the wrist that places the median nerve at risk is dependent on the degree of swelling, any pre-existing carpal tunnel syndrome, and the presence of an associated hematoma. It appears likely that a position of the wrist at greater than 30 degrees of palmar flexion places the patient at an increased risk of an acute carpal tunnel syndrome.[34] Agee has indicated that not only does the palmarly flexed position of the wrist predispose the patient to median nerve symptoms, but it also places tension on the extrinsic extensor tendons, thereby preventing complete digital flexion.[4] One study has shown no benefit to placing the wrist in flexion compared to the neural position or even dorsiflexion.[98]

The optimal position of immobilization of the radioulnar joint is controversial, although immobilization in supination has been proposed.[244] This position restores stability to the distal radioulnar joint and theoretically allows the injured DRUJ complex to heal in the appropriate position. Nonetheless, randomized studies showed no benefit in immobilisation of forearm rotation, implying that the injury pattern determines the outcome.[207,247,259]

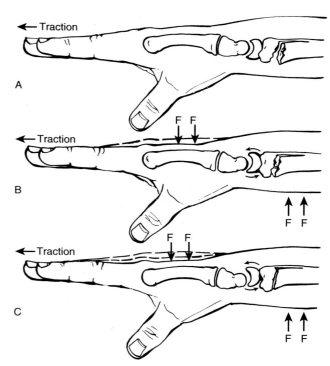

FIGURE 30-16 To apply the Agee maneuver, traction is first applied either manually or with finger traps **(A)**. A volar translation force (F) is applied to the distal fragment of the radius **(B)**. The lunate translates on the distal radius, causing the distal fragment to tilt in a volar direction **(C)**. (From Court-Brown C, McQueen M, Tornetta P. Orthopaedic Surgery Essentials: Trauma. Philadelphia: Lippincott Williams & Wilkins, 2006, with permission.)

AUTHORS' PREFERRED TREATMENT

A careful examination of the patient is performed with particular attention to (1) skin quality and integrity, (2) median and ulnar nerve function as measured by 2-point discrimination, and (3) continuity of the extrinsic digital flexor and extensor tendons, most importantly those to the thumb.

Reduction of the distal metaphysis is reduced by increasing the degree of the deformity and then applying longitudinal traction. Only when sufficient traction has been applied can the distal metaphyseal fragment be reduced on the shaft. The initial goal is to reapproximate the palmar cortex. When the palmar cortex is re-established then the cast has only to resist dorsal angulation Finally, palmar tilt is restored using gentle pressure on the distal fragment. In recalcitrant cases Agee's technique of palmar translation of the hand relative to the forearm may be successful in restoring volar tilt (Fig. 30-16).[3] Care is taken to avoid excessive palmar flexion of the radiocarpal joint, which can result in an acute carpal tunnel syndrome. We find it useful to have a portable fluoroscopy unit present to verify the reduction. Although some surgeons prefer long arm casts, the literature does not support their use and a forearm cast is sufficient.[207,247]

Postreduction radiographs are obtained at 7, 14, and 21 days. The postreduction radiographs must be compared with the initial postreduction radiographs to exclude re-displacement.

The optimum length of time of cast immobilisation is

controversial. Traditionally, distal radius fractures have been placed in a cast for 5 to 6 weeks, but there is evidence that the less severe fractures can be safely immobilised for 3 weeks.[170,261] It may be unnecessary to use a cast at all in undisplaced fractures with outcomes shown to be better with a simple bandage.[59]

Operative Treatment

The indications for operative treatment of distal radius fractures are summarised in Table 30-2 with the first two being the most common.

TABLE 30-2	**Indications for Operative Intervention**
Predicted or established metaphyseal instability	
Comminuted displaced intra-articular fracture	
Open fractures	
Associated carpal fractures	
Associated neurovascular injury/tendon injury	
Bilateral fractures	
Impaired contralateral extremity	

Timing

The optimal timing of the surgical intervention is dependent on the associated soft tissue factors and the proposed surgical procedure. As in all operative treatment of fractures, optimally one should provide adequate soft tissue coverage of the implants and all vital soft tissue structures. In the case of acute fractures the fracture should be reduced by closed means as soon as possible to minimize complications, and then operative stabilization should be performed acutely in most cases. One exception is arthroscopically assisted reduction and stabilization in which operative treatment is delayed for at least 3 to 5 days to avoid significant extravasation of irrigation fluid into the surrounding soft tissue.[228]

Percutaneous Pinning

The addition of percutaneous pins to provide additional stability is one of the earliest forms of internal fixation. This technique can be used for both metaphyseal instability and intra-articular displacement. It is minimally invasive and inexpensive. It relies on the ability to reduce the distal segment and to maintain the reduction while the pins are applied. For the larger fragments, 0.62-inch K-wires (Kirschner wires) may be used, whereas 0.45-inch K-wires may be used to fix the intermediate column and for subchondral fragment support. The radial styloid is pinned to the proximal shaft in a reduced position. Once the lateral cortex is reconstituted, then the intermediate column (lunate facet) is pinned from dorsal ulnar to proximal radial (Fig. 30-17). Finally, any central impaction fragments can be supported using subchondral transverse wires.

Kapandji described a technique of trapping the major fragment by buttressing to prevent displacement. The wires are inserted both radially and dorsally directly into the fracture site. The wires are then levered up and directed into the proximal intact opposite cortex. The fragments are thus buttressed from displacing dorsally or proximally. In addition to being relatively simple and inexpensive, this technique can be very effective (Fig. 30-18).[221,231,257,264] A difficulty with this technique is the tendency to translate the distal fragment in the opposite direction of the pin. This is particularly problematic if the pins are placed dorsally resulting in palmar displacement of the distal fragment, thereby preventing the palmar cortex from reducing anatomically.

Outcome studies reveal that management of extra-articular and simple articular fractures in younger patients with less comminuted fractures can be successful using percutaneous pinning.[5,257,264] The major disadvantage of this technique is in older patients with osteoporotic bone where randomized studies have shown no significant advantage with the use of percutane-

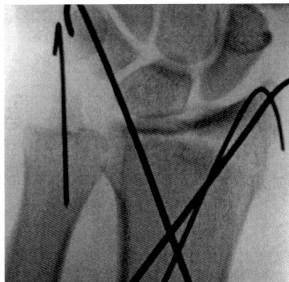

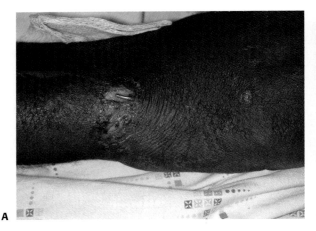

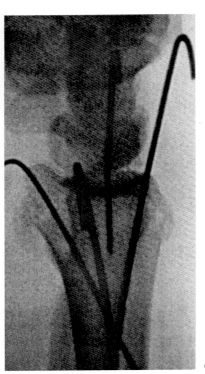

FIGURE 30-17 A–C. Comminuted radius fracture in a poly trauma patient treated with percutaneous pinning technique.

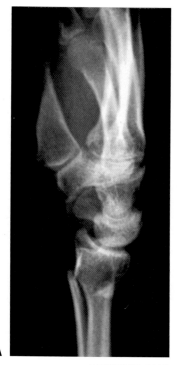
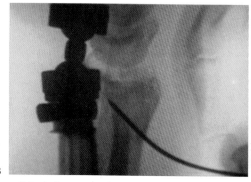
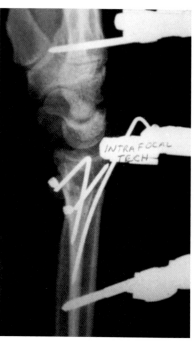

A   **B**   **C**

FIGURE 30-18 The Kapandji Technique: metaphyseal fracture with redisplacement after reduction **(A)**. A pin is inserted into the fracture site, manipulated to elevate the fragment distally **(B)**, and then driven into the opposite cortex **(C)**. The fragments are thus trapped and prevented from dorsal displacement.

ous pins compared to cast management.[18,248] Biomechanically, percutaneous pinning relies on fixation to the proximal shaft. This results in an oblique orientation of the pins that does little to prevent collapse of the fragments. A further disadvantage lies in the need for associated cast immobilization to neutralize the flexion-extension moments at the wrist, because the fixation using this technique alone is often insufficient to prevent displacement. Thus the technique does not eliminate the causes of so called fracture disease that leads to digital swelling and stiffness. In addition, the pins may become superficially infected as pin care is difficult with the cast in place.[268]

External Fixation

Although percutaneous pinning, plaster immobilization, and Kapandji pinning remain effective techniques for extra-articular fractures in younger patients, they are still unable to neutralize the axial forces caused by the physiologic tension of the extrinsic flexors and extensors. External fixation neutralizes the axial load imparted by physiologic load of the forearm musculature. External fixation may be performed in a "bridging" technique in which the fixation crosses the radiocarpal joint or in a "nonbridging technique" in which the distal fixation pins are placed in the subchondral bone and radiocarpal motion is permitted.

Bridging External Fixation.

Bridging external fixation allows distraction across the radiocarpal joint and directly neutralizes axial load. Initially external fixation was felt to provide "ligamentotaxis" to the fracture fragments. The philosophy was that the intact wrist capsule and ligamentous structures would "indirectly" reduce both the metaphyseal displacement and any impacted articular fragments, and open reduction would not be

necessary. Multiple cohort series of patients have documented the efficacy of this technique.[66,76,115] Several studies have compared external fixation to cast immobilization. Although there is some conflicting data, it appears that external fixation provides superior radiographic parameters when compared to cast treatment.[22,47,114,124,174]

Several detailed studies have documented that external fixation alone may not be sufficiently rigid to prevent some degree of collapse and some loss of palmar tilt during the course of healing,[43,54,88,172,174] with some degree of collapse being seen in up to 50% of patients and significant collapse in up to 10% of patients. Cadaver studies further document the difficulty in utilizing external fixation alone to obtain palmar tilt and that even augmented external fixation may not be as stable as internal fixation.[21,113]

Adjunctive Fixation. *Supplemental Graft:* In an effort to allow the fixator to be removed earlier and to prevent collapse of the fracture, many authors have advocated the use of supplemental bone graft or a bone graft substitute within the fracture site.[39,107,159] Leung et al. retrospectively reviewed 72 cases in which the metaphyseal defect was packed with cancellous autograft and the external fixator was removed at 3 weeks, with the initiation of early range of motion. Only five patients demonstrated radiographic evidence of collapse and 70 of 72 regained an average of 137 degrees of flexion-extension at only 6 months.[158] The additional morbidity of obtaining cancellous autograft, however, prompted the use of other substrates to fill the void; and cancellous allograft has proved to be a useful adjunct to external fixation, particularly in the elderly patient population (Fig. 30-19).

As in other fractures there has been a myriad of other sub-

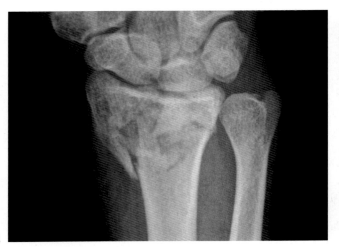

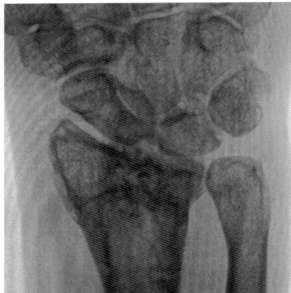

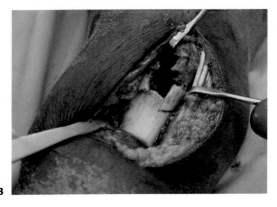

FIGURE 30-19 A,B. A large metaphyseal defect is seen in a young adult with a comminuted fracture. The defect was filled with cancellous autograft and the fracture was stabilized with a dorsal plate. Note the appearance of the metaphysis after healing and plate removal **(C)**.

strates, both bone inductive and conductive, which have been proposed to fill the metaphysis and prevent fracture collapse. Of particular interest in distal radius fractures is the potential for percutaneous application of a liquid substrate that could harden and prevent articular collapse. Cassidy and coauthors performed a prospective randomized study comparing closed manipulation and percutaneous introduction of a calcium-phosphate bone cement to treatment with external fixation or cast application. Although significant clinical differences were seen at 6 and 8 weeks postoperatively, there were no substantial differences at 3 months. The radiographic results demonstrated superior maintenance of radial length in the cement group. The authors concluded that use of this material may allow for a more accelerated rehabilitation, compared with external fixation or cast treatment.[41] Their results corroborate a previous study comparing cement with cast treatment alone (Fig. 30-20).[232]

Adjunctive K-Wire Fixation. The use of adjunctive percutaneous pins has also been introduced to improve the stability of external fixation and prevent loss of reduction. Cadaver studies have demonstrated that supplemental wires increase the stability of the construct to nearly that of dorsal plating.[64] The use of crossed wires engaging the contralateral cortex substantially further increases the rigidity of the construct. The major complication seen with the use of pins is with iatrogenic injury to the superficial radial nerve. The nerve emerges proximally through the brachioradialis and arborizes distally. This risk of injury may be lessened by making a small 5-mm incision and spreading with a hemostat down to bone. Several authors have documented the clinical effi-

cacy of this technique in preventing loss of reduction and achieving excellent clinical outcomes (Fig. 30-21).[91,237]

Nonbridging External Fixation. The first recorded use of nonbridging external fixation in the wrist was reported by Ombrédanne who used a nonbridging technique for fractures and osteotomies of the forearm in children in 1929. Ombrédanne concluded that "temporary osteosynthesis with external connection allows a mathematical adjustment of the surgical correction . . . and guarantees further retention with ample and sufficient precision."[74]

For about 60 years this sensible conclusion was largely ignored after the introduction of bridging external fixation by Anderson and O'Neil.[9] They introduced bridging external fixation for severely comminuted intra-articular fractures of the distal radius in young men in whom nonbridging external fixation may not have been an option. Interest in the nonbridging technique was stimulated in the 1990s by the realization that bridging external fixation was not an ideal option for the increasing numbers of fitter, elderly patients with low-energy extra-articular or minimal articular fractures who, unlike previous generations, were not prepared to accept malunion and possible functional deficit.

Nonbridging external fixation is indicated for extra-articular or minimal intra-articular dorsally displaced fractures with metaphyseal instability and it is applicable to most of these fractures.[106] The technique is not suitable for the treatment of volar displaced fractures. Fewer cases with displaced articular extensions are suitable for nonbridging ex fix, as after fixation of the

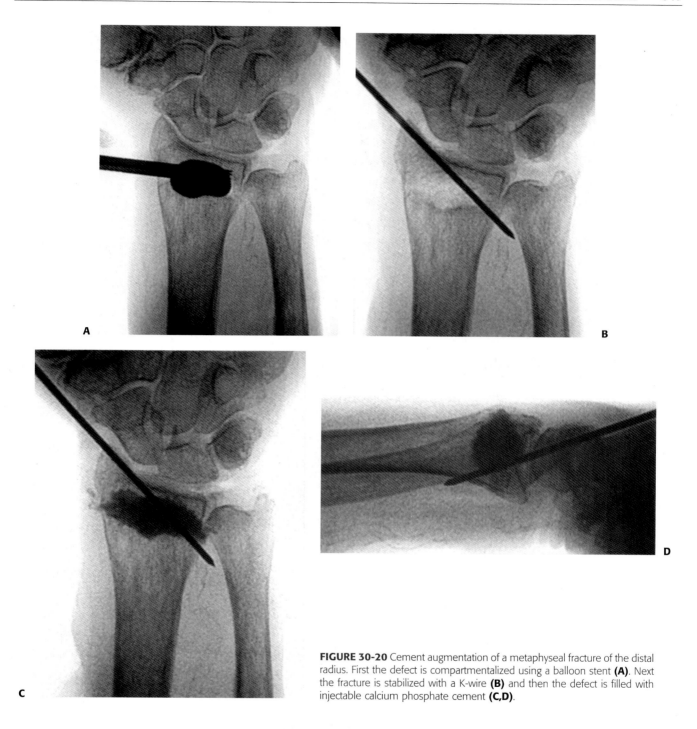

FIGURE 30-20 Cement augmentation of a metaphyseal fracture of the distal radius. First the defect is compartmentalized using a balloon stent **(A)**. Next the fracture is stabilized with a K-wire **(B)** and then the defect is filled with injectable calcium phosphate cement **(C,D)**.

joint surface they may lack the necessary space in the distal fragment for the distal pins. Nevertheless, the use of multiplanar wires both to reduce and hold the articular fragments and to hold the metaphyseal alignment in a hybrid type construct of nonbridging external fixation has been reported as a good treatment option for articular fractures.[95]

The main contraindication for the technique of nonbridging external fixation is lack of space for pins in the distal fragment: approximately 1cm of intact volar cortex is required to give purchase for the pins. Neither dorsal metaphyseal comminution nor osteoporosis is a contraindication for the technique, because the pins achieve their grip on the volar cortex and fixation failure is rare.[25,79,106,172,174,176] As with any external fixation technique

insertion of pins through areas of possible skin infection is contraindicated.

Radiological outcomes of nonbridging external fixation for extra-articular or minimal articular fractures are uniformly good.* The first report of nonbridging external fixation with anatomic results was a comparison of plaster and nonbridging external fixation in patients under 60 with displaced distal radial fractures. The quality of the reduction was good in both groups, but the reduced position was maintained better ($P < 0.01$) by the external fixation group.[123]

*References 83,95,106,123,148,149,172,174,176,178.

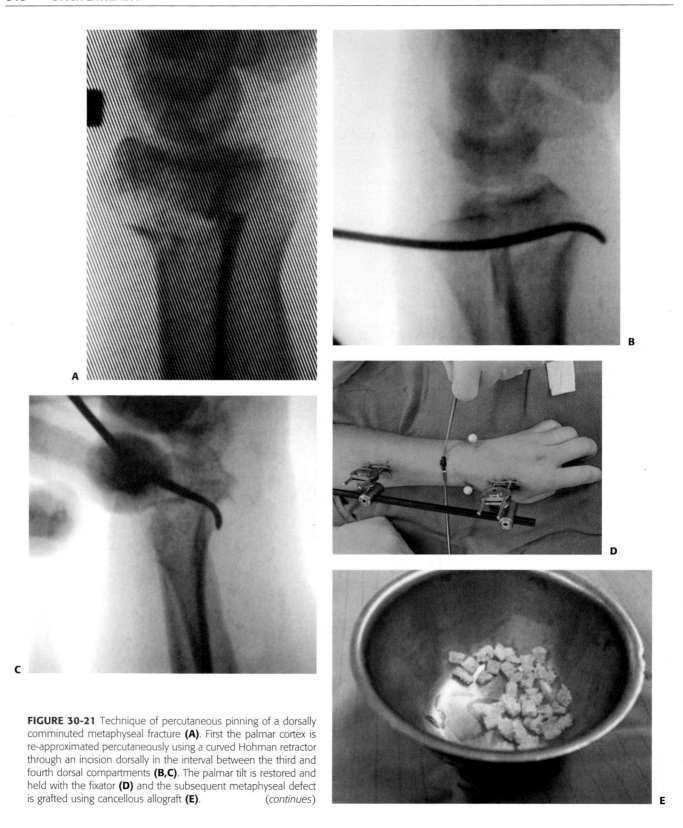

FIGURE 30-21 Technique of percutaneous pinning of a dorsally comminuted metaphyseal fracture **(A)**. First the palmar cortex is re-approximated percutaneously using a curved Hohman retractor through an incision dorsally in the interval between the third and fourth dorsal compartments **(B,C)**. The palmar tilt is restored and held with the fixator **(D)** and the subsequent metaphyseal defect is grafted using cancellous allograft **(E)**.   (*continues*)

The first randomized study of nonbridging external fixation was a comparison with bridging external fixation. Sixty patients with an average age of 61 years and redisplaced distal radial fractures were studied. Nonbridging external fixation showed statistically significant improvement in both dorsal angle and radial shortening compared with bridging external fixation at all stages of review, with no loss of volar tilt until final review at one year.[172] There were no malunions in the nonbridging group in this study.

The main radiological advantage of nonbridging external fixation is therefore restoration and maintenance of the normal volar tilt of the distal radius. In bridging external fixation, reduc-

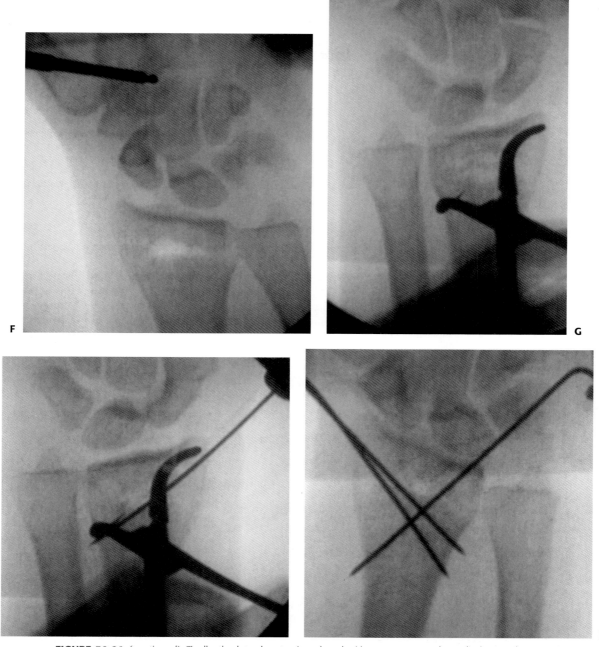

FIGURE 30-21 (*continued*) Finally, the lateral cortex is reduced with a percutaneously applied tenaculum clamp and crossed pins are inserted **(F–H)**. The stability of the construct may be improved with the use of an additional pin applied radially **(I)**.

tion of the fracture depends on ligamentotaxis. Volar tilt may not be restored, because the volar ligaments are shorter and stronger than the dorsal ligaments and prevent full reduction.[21] With nonbridging external fixation the reduction is performed using the distal pins as a joystick, allowing the surgeon direct control of the distal fragment and obviating the need for ligamentotaxis (Fig. 30-22).

Superior functional outcomes are also reported in nonbridging external fixation for acute fractures of the distal radius compared with bridging techniques.[172] In this study the average grip strength in the nonbridging group was restored to 87% of the opposite normal side, allowing for dominance. Other indices

of function also showed superior results in the nonbridging group. Nevertheless, when the technique is used for severe articular fractures this difference disappears, probably because the severity of the injury dictates the outcome,[148,149] although with the use of smaller distal pins inserted orthogonally to the intermediate and the radial column this technique has been demonstrated to be useful in simple impaction fractures with articular extension (Fig. 30-23).

Surgical Technique. The mainstay of preoperative imaging for nonbridging external fixation is a good series of preoperative films with true anteroposterior and lateral views of the wrist to

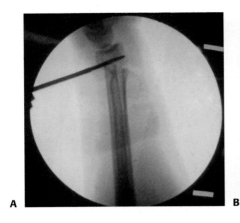

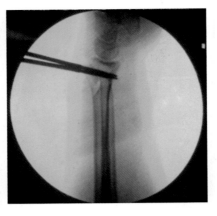

FIGURE 30-22 A. A fluoroscopic view of the distal pins for a nonbridging external fixator. The fracture is unreduced and the pins have been inserted parallel to the radiocarpal joint, between the fracture and the joint and engaging the volar cortex. **B.** The fracture has been reduced into palmar tilt using the pins as a "joystick." Note the defect in the dorsal cortex from dorsal comminution.

assess the size of the distal fragment. On the lateral view the volar cortex should be seen clearly: 1 cm of intact volar cortex is required. The PA view also allows assessment of the size of the fragment particularly on the ulnar side. Some distal fragments narrow towards the distal radioulnar joint on the AP view. This configuration may not allow sufficient purchase for an ulnar sided pin. More advanced imaging usually is not necessary unless the nonbridging technique is to be used for severe articular fractures, when CT scanning may be required to visualise the articular fracture pattern and to plan placement of hybrid type pins.

Axillary or supraclavicular regional block is recommended as some evidence shows that the use of this technique reduces the incidence of complex regional pain syndrome type I.[214] The patient is placed supine with the arm extended on the hand table and the wrist in neutral rotation. A tourniquet is applied

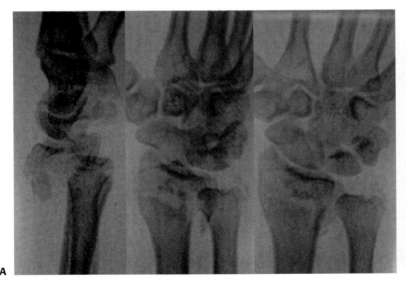

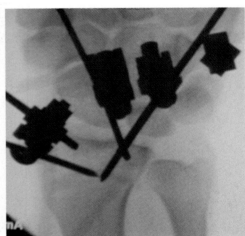

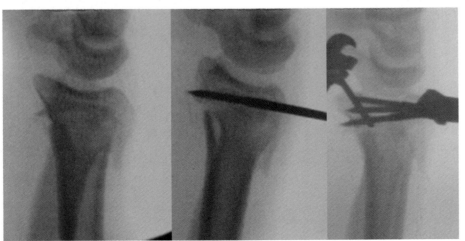

FIGURE 30-23 A. A three-part distal intra-articular fracture. **B.** Placement of shanz pins in the distal fragments through the palmar cortex allowing control of palmar tilt. **C.** Note that these distal pins control both the radial and the intermediate column separately and that these fragments are locked into the construct

to the upper arm. The surgeon is seated on the cephalic side of the arm table and the C-arm is positioned on the opposite side. Fracture reduction prior to insertion of the pins is not necessary.

The distal pins are inserted first from dorsal to volar, midway between the fracture site and the radiocarpal joint and on either side of Lister's tubercle (Fig. 30-22A). If there is an undisplaced sagittal articular fracture, pins should be placed on both the radial and ulnar sides of the articular extension. A marker is placed on the skin and its position in relation to the entry point on bone confirmed with the C-arm. A 1-cm longitudinal incision is made at this point and the extensor retinaculum exposed. A longitudinal incision is made in the extensor retinaculum under direct vision, with care taken to protect the underlying tendons, and the bone is exposed. A fixator pin is placed on the bone and its position confirmed on the C-arm. The angle of the pin is then adjusted so that its projected course is parallel to the radiocarpal joint on the lateral view. The pin is then inserted by hand without predrilling until its tip penetrates the volar cortex. Further pins may then be inserted using the same technique with the spacing and relationship of the pins being determined by the fixator used.

Pins are then placed in the radial diaphysis proximal to the fracture utilising open pin placement to avoid damage to the dorsal branch of the radial nerve. A longitudinal skin incision is made over the dorsum of the radius, followed by blunt dissection to expose the tendons of extensor carpi radialis longus and extensor carpi radialis brevis. The natural interval between these tendons is developed to expose the radius. The proximal pins are then inserted by hand with or without predrilling and should engage both cortices of the radius. The fixator should then be assembled but not tightened. Reduction of the fracture is then achieved using the distal pins as "joysticks," which requires little force in an acute fracture (Fig. 30-22B). Where reduction has been delayed, forcible reduction should not be attempted because this may cause pin loosening. In late cases reduction using the pins should be gentle and gradual. A good reduction is usually possible up to approximately 3 weeks after fracture. Should reduction not be possible without undue force, a small incision should be made over the dorsum of the fracture and a lever inserted to reduce the fracture directly. The fixator is then tightened and the reduction confirmed using the C-arm.

There are few perioperative pitfalls. The most frequent is overreduction of the fracture (Fig. 30-24), especially where there is overlap of the volar cortex. This should be preventable as it is easily recognised radiologically. If the insertion of distal pins proves unsuccessful because of insufficient intact volar cortex, it is simple to convert the construct to a bridging construct with or without augmentation.

Hybrid External Fixation

Several authors have documented improved mechanical stability and control over palmar tilt with the insertion of pins into the distal metaphyseal fragment and attachment of them directly to a bridging external fixator.[35,63,186,269] As with nonbridging external fixation, direct control over the distal fragment may eliminate some of the loss of reduction seen with external fixators, including the loss of palmar tilt and radial collapse (Fig. 30-23). Nonetheless, the use of this technique has limited application because this can be achieved with nonbridging external

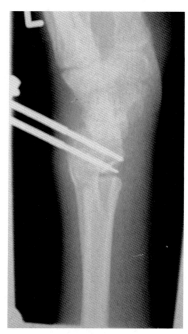

FIGURE 30-24 The fracture has been overreduced with excessive palmar tilt. This can be prevented by use of the fluoroscope and adjustment of the external fixator.

fixation without any disadvantages and without sacrificing early wrist motion.

Combined Open Reduction and Internal Fixation with External Fixation

This technique has been demonstrated to be effective when the articular fragments are felt to be too small and too numerous for internal fixation with plate-screw constructs, and yet the fracture does not reduce anatomically with standard techniques. It has been used primarily for high-energy injuries with comminution both dorsally and palmarly. The technique permits internal fixation of the comminuted fragments palmarly, and the use of the external fixation device prevents collapse on the side opposite the plate. Several cohort series have documented success with this technique.[22,212,217] The underlying principle is to create an intact palmar buttress using a plate and then to prevent dorsal collapse by tensioning across it using an external fixator. The technique was felt to obviate the need for combined plate fixation and the extensive soft tissue stripping that goes with it.[230]

Operative Technique. The technique is most often used when external fixation has been performed and persistent incongruity of the palmar lunate facet is demonstrated. It is critical to reduce and stabilize this facet to obtain both articular congruity and distal radioulnar joint stability. A 5-cm skin incision is made ulnar to the flexor tendons, which are gently retracted to expose the intermediate column. The lunate facet is elevated and then held in position with a palmar plate. Once the plate is fixed proximally it creates an intact palmar buttress, across which tension can be applied (Fig. 30-25).

Once the dorsal cortex is out to length, then the distal screws may be placed. The radial column may be stabilized with either

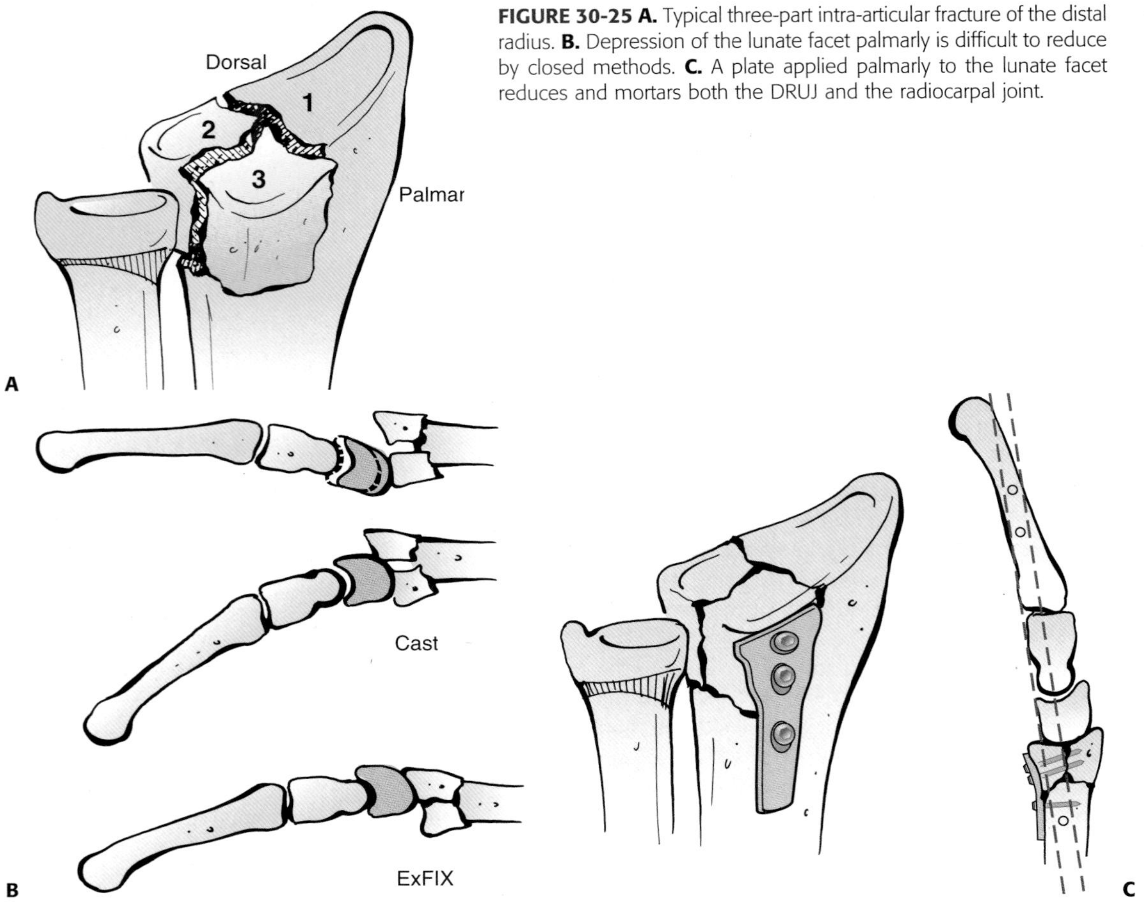

FIGURE 30-25 A. Typical three-part intra-articular fracture of the distal radius. **B.** Depression of the lunate facet palmarly is difficult to reduce by closed methods. **C.** A plate applied palmarly to the lunate facet reduces and mortars both the DRUJ and the radiocarpal joint.

the radial limb of the plate or with percutaneously applied K-wires.

Arthroscopically Assisted Reduction and External Fixation of Intra-articular Fractures

Although many authors have documented the importance of articular congruity in the outcome following distal radius fractures, concern remains whether we can adequately visualize the articular surface intraoperatively.[70,73,90,142,256] Despite the reported significance of a residual step-off of 1 mm or more, several authors have documented difficulty in the reliable measurement of articular step-offs of 1 mm using conventional radiographs or intra operative fluoroscopy.[65,145] Arthroscopy has demonstrated residual displacement of articular fragments in 33% to 71% of fractures following reduction under fluoroscopy.[17,65] The technique has also been extremely useful in documenting a wide variety of chondral lesions, interosseous ligament injuries, and avulsions of the triangular fibrocartilage.[93,160-162,215] The incidence of interosseous ligament injuries associated with intra-articular fractures appears to be approximately 50% for scapholunate ligament injuries and 20% for lunotriquetral injuries.[71] Triangular fibrocartilage injuries occur in approximately 40% of fractures and direct chondral injury in up to 30% of fractures.[161]

Although arthroscopy has been invaluable in enhancing existing knowledge of associated soft tissue lesions in distal radius fractures, there is still some question whether the technique provides outcomes superior to conventional techniques. Kazut-

eru et al. performed a prospective randomized study comparing the results of 34 patients treated using arthroscopically guided reduction, with 48 patients treated with open reduction and internal fixation.[138] The results indicated superior radiographic and functional outcomes with the arthroscopically guided procedure. A second matched control study comparing arthroscopically assisted external fixation with fluoroscopically assisted external fixation, however, documented no significant differences between groups with the exception of forearm rotation and ulnar sided symptoms.[228] The authors concluded that although arthroscopy provides superior imaging of the articular surface, external fixation permits some collapse during fracture union, which may detract from the subsequent radiographic outcome measurements. One alternative is to make use of arthroscopic assistance to assess reduction while using volar plate fixation to stabilize the fracture. This approach has been shown to accurately more assess the magnitude of step and gap in the articular surface following fixation, using a palmar approach and fluoroscopic assistance in reduction. A perceived difficulty with this approach is that arthroscopy is used to assess the reduction only after the hardware is in place, thereby precluding improving the reduction without removing the fixation. Alternatively, direct control of the articular surface using smaller pins that lock into the external fixator may allow the surgeon to directly mimimize the step and gap under arthroscopic control prior to fixation with a volar plate.

Operative Technique. The decision regarding which fractures would benefit most from arthroscopically assisted reduction and external fixation is controversial. Generally speaking, fractures with extensive metaphyseal comminution might be best managed with formal open reduction and internal fixation to prevent subsequent collapse. In patients with a large ulnar styloid fracture fragment and distal radioulnar instability, open reduction and internal fixation of the ulnar styloid fragment may be required, and arthroscopy may not add substantially to the care. Those fractures that may benefit most from adjunctive arthroscopy are (1) complex articular fractures without metaphyseal comminution, particularly those with central impaction fragments, and (2) fractures with evidence of substantial interosseous ligament or TFCC injury without a large ulnar styloid fragment (a fracture at the base of the styloid).

Timing. Ideally, the procedure is performed between 5 and 15 days postinjury. When fragments are significantly displaced, associated palmar and dorsal rents in the capsule may exist. This situation permits extravasation of irrigation fluid into the surrounding soft tissue, which is exacerbated with the use of a pump. Waiting 5 to 7 days minimizes this complication.

The external fixator may be applied before or after reduction of the articular surface; however, there are advantages to having the fixator in place prior to the arthroscopy. First the extra-articular portion is reduced and out to length, thereby providing a template for elevation of the depressed segments of the articular surface. Second, the external fixator provides excellent distraction of the joint for the arthroscopy.

After the external fixator has been placed, the metaphyseal defect must be addressed. Through a small 2-cm incision, the dorsal metaphyseal comminution may be exposed and the defect may be partially filled with graft. One should avoid interposing graft between the major fragments of the articular surface. The window is left exposed to allow for manipulation during the arthroscopy. A provisional reduction is obtained and verified fluoroscopically. Additionally, prepositioned K-wires in the major fragments are useful to facilitate stabilization once the reduction has been effected.

The first step of the procedure is to irrigate the clot and other debris from the joint and perform a diagnostic arthroscopy through the 3-4 portal. This portal is best utilized for the purposes of instrumentation, whereas the 6-R or 6-U portals permit superior visualization of the fracture.[228] Careful inspection of the scapholunate and lunotriquetral ligaments as well as the TFCC is performed, both for prognostic and therapeutic purposes. Any disruptions of the interosseous ligaments may require further inspection through the midcarpal portals. Pathology is addressed from the radial side, proceeding ulnarly. Incomplete ligament injuries may be stable, and debridement can be performed if indicated. Subluxations from complete ligament injuries are reduced and pinned using Kirschner wires. Next the articular surface is reduced and pinned. It is critical to have a landmark for length and tilt in order to reduce the articular surface correctly. Kirschner wires are placed in each of the major fragments and their depth of penetration is verified at the end to avoid over penetration palmarly. Ulnarly the lunotriquetral interosseous ligament (LTIO) is treated with pinning or debridement. Finally, the TFCC may be repaired back to the extrinsic carpi ulnaris (ECU) subsheath. If distal radioulnar joint instability has been treated surgically, the forearm is placed in

30 degrees of supination for a total of 3.5 weeks, after which range of motion is initiated (Fig. 30-26).

Complications of External Fixation. Reported complication rates for the use of external fixation to treat distal radius fractures range from 6% to 60% depending on how "major" and "minor" complications are reported.[216,217,233] Although many complications of distal radius fractures are seen regardless of the treatment, some are directly related to treatment with an external fixator and or supplemental pins.[119]

Overdistraction. Overdistraction during bridging external fixation has been implicated in producing worse digital motion, worse functional outcomes, and worse strength and pain scores following fracture treatment.[132] Although there is no threshold limit for distraction, it appears that there is a correlation between increasing carpal height index and worse functional outcomes.[133] The fact that there is no threshold for overdistraction makes it difficult to demonstrate a strict causal relationship, as evidenced by one study that documented distraction of 5 to 8 mm across the radiocarpal and midcarpal joints without a negative outcome.[30] Overdistraction of the wrist, particularly if it is combined with palmar flexion, results in relative lengthening of the extrinsic extensor tendons and may prevent full active and passive digital motion. Prolonged loss of full flexion combined with the swelling following a wrist fracture can result in permanent loss of metacarpophalangeal motion. Therefore it is critical to look for this complication following completion of the procedure. The diagnosis is suspected when there is a gap across the midcarpal joint on fluoroscopic assessment during the procedure, and confirmed when full passive digital motion is difficult to achieve.

Usually overdistraction is attributable to a failure to recognize the limitations of external fixation alone in the management of highly comminuted fractures. In extra-articular fractures, external fixation in isolation does not typically restore the physiologic 12 degrees of palmar tilt. Cadaver studies indicate that the thicker and vertically oriented palmar ligaments become taut before the thinner and "Z" configured ligaments dorsally. Pure distraction results in the palmar ligaments tightening before the dorsal ligaments and a failure to achieve palmar tilt.[21,55] Clinical studies also indicate that loss of palmar tilt is common following external fixation alone without supplemental grafting or pinning.[35,54,55,58,172,174] In addition, external fixation in isolation may not elevate a displaced intra-articular fracture. Central impaction fragments have no capsuloligamentous attachments; therefore distraction alone will not elevate these fragments. The palmar lunate facet may not reduce with distraction alone, and ulnar deviation actually allows the lunate to settle relative to the radial styloid because of the oblique orientation of the extrinsic radial ligaments. This complication may be avoided by recognizing the limitations of the technique and making use of more direct reduction tools to achieve a congruent articular surface and physiologic palmar tilt.

Cutaneous Nerve Injury. Injury to the superficial radial nerve may be seen following open pin insertion, percutaneous half pin insertion, or with the use of supplemental K-wires. The incidence varies; however, several series report transient dysethesias in 16% to 21% of cases.[38,113,150] In an effort to lessen this

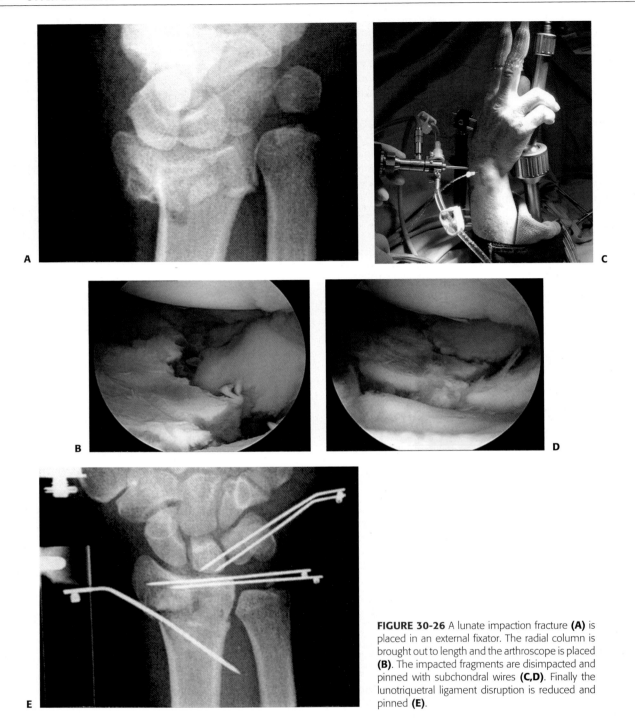

FIGURE 30-26 A lunate impaction fracture **(A)** is placed in an external fixator. The radial column is brought out to length and the arthroscope is placed **(B)**. The impacted fragments are disimpacted and pinned with subchondral wires **(C,D)**. Finally the lunotriquetral ligament disruption is reduced and pinned **(E)**.

complication several authors have recommended open rather than percutaneous half pin insertion.[54,67,105]

The use of adjunctive Kirschner wires offers increased rigidity but may also result in the increased likelihood of injury associated soft tissue structures, particularly branches of the superficial radial nerve. These smaller branches have been shown to be at risk with percutaneous introduction of pins in the distal radius or the carpus.[99] These injuries tend to be transient, with resolution by 6 months, but they may also precipitate a complex regional pain syndrome. Biomechanically, the pins are best placed radially; however, the more dorsal the pin placement the safer they are from iatrogenic cutaneous nerve injury (Fig. 30-27).

Pin Tract Infections. The true incidence of pin tract infections is unknown, in part because of failure to define whether such an entity is a transient cellulitis or a deeper infection with or without bony involvement. For K-wires the incidence ranges from 6% to as high as 33%.[103] For external fixation pins the incidence has been reported to range from 1% to 8%.[54,67,118] Because the instance of pin tract infection is relatively low, studies comparing predrilling with direct drilling of the pins are generally underpowered, and the relationship of predrilling to the infection rate has not been established.[118] Egol et al. performed a prospective randomized trial evaluating the use of hydrogen peroxide wound care and chlorhexidine impregnated dressings and found no statistical difference in pin site infections

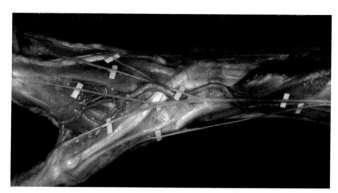

FIGURE 30-27 The anatomy of the superficial radial nerve at the distal radius. Note that the majority of the branches lie palmar to the second dorsal compartment.

in these groups when compared to sterile dry dressings.[68] In general, pin tract infections will resolve with the use of oral antibiotics and increased frequency of dressings. It is rare for pin tract infections to affect the final outcome.

Open Reduction and Internal Fixation

During the interval from 1950 to 1985 over 450 articles were published on distal radius fractures. Of these, 60 dealt with internal fixation of the fracture. By contrast, the last 15 years have produced over 2000 articles on distal radius fractures, 400 of which focused on internal fixation.[226] Internal fixation of periarticular fractures has many potential advantages including direct fixation of articular fragments, early range of motion of the joint, and avoidance of constrictive dressings or casts. In a recent prospective randomized trial of 144 intra-articular fractures, internal fixation was found to have superior results to bridging external fixation supplemented by percutaneous pinning radiographically and using the Gartland and Werley outcome score, especially for C2 fractures.[156] On the other hand, an earlier study showed significant benefit with external fixation and percutaneous pinning compared with open reduction and internal fixation, provided the indirect reduction succeeded using the Musculoskeletal Functional Assessment as the primary outcome.[147] Open reduction and internal fixation of intra-articular fractures has been considered technically difficult, and a number of soft tissue complications have been noted with the use of plate fixation.[236]

Dorsal Plating. Internal fixation using a dorsal plate has several theoretical advantages. Technically familiar to most surgeons, the approach avoids the neurovascular structures on the palmar side. Further, the fixation is on the compression side of most distal radius fractures and provides a buttress against collapse. Initial reports of the technique demonstrated successful outcomes with the theoretical advantages of earlier return of function and better restoration of radial anatomy than was seen with external fixation.[102,108,121,143,218,223]

Despite the initial success with the technique, there were increasing reports of extensor tendon ruptures because of prominent hardware, particularly at Lister tubercle.[166,168,223,236,273] The more distally the plate is applied on the dorsum of the wrist, the more proximally the distal screws need to be directed

to avoid articular penetration. This oblique orientation of the screws allows the distal fragment to displace palmarly. The palmar displacement of the fragment is particularly problematic because it results in (1) incongruity at the distal radioulnar joint and (2) prominence of the hardware dorsally with the tendency for extensor tenosynovitis or tendon rupture (Fig. 32-28).

More proximal fractures with larger distal fragments allow superior purchase in the distal fragment while permitting screw placement from proximal to distal, thereby engaging the palmar fragment and preventing it from collapsing palmarly. Although reports of successful outcomes with dorsal plate fixation have been reported, several retrospective studies indicate that there may be a higher incidence of complications associated with the routine use of this approach when compared with the palmar approach.[213,227] In general most authors agree that the decision of palmar versus dorsal plate application should be determined by the fracture fragment displacement rather than routine use of one approach versus another.

Operative Technique. A longitudinal incision is centered over the fracture in line with the ulnar aspect of Lister tubercle. The extensor retinaculum is incised in a z-plasty manner that allows for one limb to be placed over the plate and the second limb to be repaired over the extensor tendons to prevent bowstringing of the tendons with wrist extension. The extensor pollicis longus tendon is dislocated from its position at the tubercle and subperiosteal dissection is performed radially and ulnarly. Care should be taken to preserve all of the dorsal fragments for re-establishment of radial length. Traction is then applied by either an assistant or by the use of finger traps with weights suspended off the end of the table. Care should be taken to ensure that the hand is not pronated relative to the forearm. The metaphyseal void can then be filled with graft and the articular surface assessed. In the case of residual incongruity of the articular surface, the joint may be directly assessed by extending the periosteal dissection distally, but care must be taken to avoid injury to the scapholunate interosseous ligament. Skin hooks can be placed under the capsular flaps and the articular surface can be visualized and reduced. Generally speaking, it is preferable to achieve the reduction by supporting the articular surface with supplemental graft and preventing subsequent displacement with screws placed through the distal aspect of the plate. If an arthrotomy is not performed, then the articular surface should be visualized using a 20-degree inclined fluoroscopy view to assess for palmar displacement of the lunate facet and screw penetration into the articular surface. It is critical to ascertain whether the palmar cortex is aligned and does not displace palmarly with plate application. It is also advantageous to position the plate such that the screws are oriented perpendicular to the radial shaft, rather than directed from distal to proximal (Fig. 30-28C–F). In cases when there is extensive palmar comminution, supplemental fixation may be necessary. The addition of K-wires or a screw through the radial styloid to engage the proximal cortex of the radius is helpful to prevent palmar collapse.

Palmar Plating. Because of concerns over extensor tendon rupture from prominent dorsal hardware, a number of authors have proposed using palmar plating, originally reserved for palmar displaced fractures (Figs. 30-29 and 30-30), for the stabilization of dorsally displaced fractures through a palmar approach (Fig. 30-33).[53,61,134,153,157] This technique has gained widespread ac-

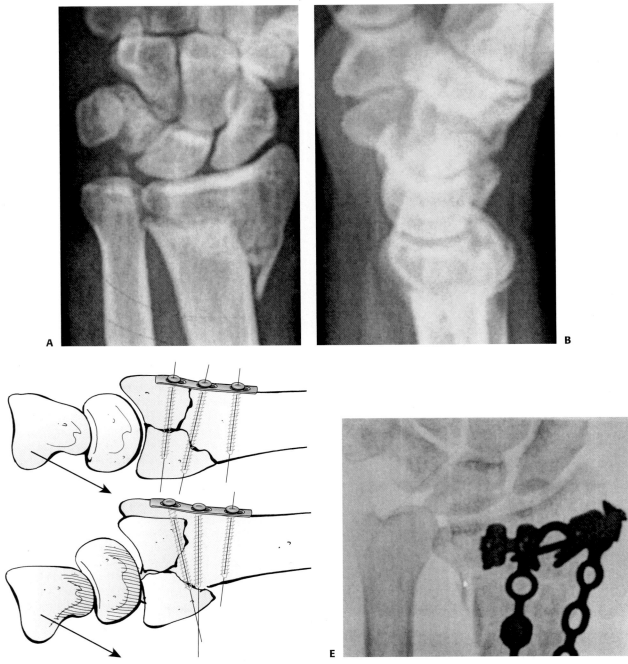

FIGURE 30-28 Fracture with both palmar and dorsal comminution **(A,B)**. Dorsal plate application permits palmar collapse of the fragment in the absence of an intact palmar buttress **(C,D)**. The palmar displacement of the metaphyseal fragment relative to the distal ulna results in radioulnar incongruity and loss of rotation **(E–G)**.   (*continues*)

ceptance; however, there is a paucity of well controlled prospective trials documenting clear superiority of this technique. Although the position of the plate on the side opposite the displacement does not permit a direct buttress against dorsal displacement, the screw position in the distal fragment directly buttresses collapse. The addition of locking fixation of the screws in the distal fragment further prevents dorsal displacement of the distal fragment. One concern over these locking plates is the potential for articular penetration with distal plate position on the palmar surface of the radius. The more

distal the plate placement on the radius, the more the screws need to angle back proximally to avoid penetration into the lunate fossa (Fig. 30-31).

Collapse of the fracture also can lead to joint penetration by the distal screws. This is reported to occur in up to 57% of cases and is a particular risk in osteopenic patients.[12,13,61,224] A further complication that has been reported with locked plates is tendon irritation or rupture in up to 38% of cases,[6,12,13,61,199,224] which is similar to rates of tendon problems with dorsal plating. Extensor tendon problems can be caused by penetra-

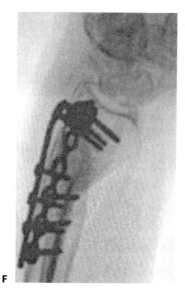

F

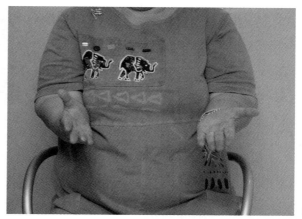

G

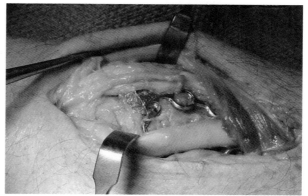

FIGURE 30-28 (*continued*) Furthermore, hardware is now more prominent relative to the extensor tendons, resulting in extensor tenosynovitis and tendon rupture **(H)**.

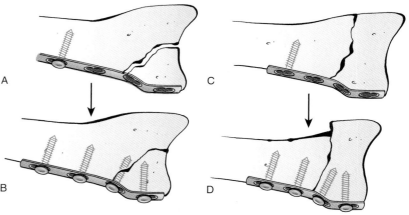

H

tion of the screws through the dorsal cortex especially in the third dorsal compartment, bony spurs, or excessive gapping at the fracture site.[26] The former cause can be prevented by reducing the measured size of the central distal screws. Too distal plate placement beyond the "watershed" has been cited as a reason for flexor tendon damage.[12]

Operative Technique. Palmar plates may be applied through either a flexor carpi radialis (FCR)/radial artery interval or through a midline flexor tendon/ulnar neurovascular bundle interval. The FCR/radial artery approach is preferable for (1) fixation of dorsally displaced fractures with dorsal comminution and (2) fixation of partial articular fractures (articular shear frac-

tures). The skin incision is centered over the FCR, with care being taken to avoid injury to the palmar cutaneous branch of the median nerve that lies ulnar to the tendon. The radial artery is mobilized, and dissection is carried radially by releasing the brachioradialis tendon from the radial styloid. Using this approach, the comminution on the dorsum of the radius can be visualized and graft can be placed. Articular depression can also be seen by pronation of the radius away from the rest of the articular surface. The depressed articular surface may be visualized from within the fracture site. This allows for subarticular graft placement. The pronator quadratus muscle is released from its radial attachment and should be preserved to place over the plate at the conclusion of the case. The main limitation of this

FIGURE 30-29 Palmar plating. The use of a palmar plate was originally reserved for articular shear fractures. Here use of a palmarly applied undercontoured plate allows compression of the volar lip back to the intact dorsal buttress **(A,B)**. In the absence of an intact dorsal buttress, undercontouring of the plate will result in dorsal displacement of the entire articular surface as shown in **C** and **D**.

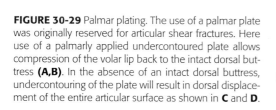

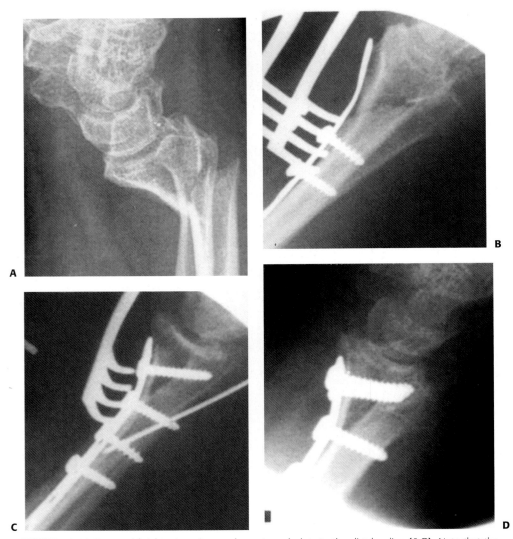

FIGURE 30-30 Sequential tightening of an undercontoured plate to the distal radius **(A,B)**. Note that the technique requires an intact dorsal cortex, otherwise the technique will push the distal radius dorsally. To prevent this, a temporary pin may be placed to provide a dorsal buttress while the plate is applied. The pin is then removed after the screws have been tightened **(C,D)**.

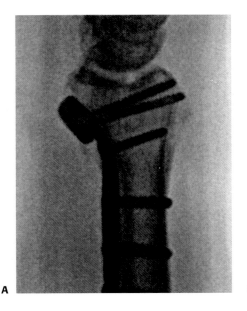
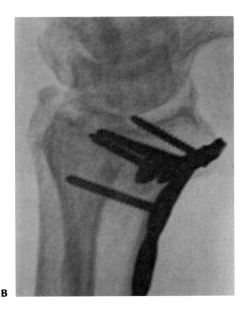

FIGURE 30-31 A,B. Palmar plate fixation of a distal radius fracture. Note the anatomy of the volar lip of the radius distally. The more distal the placement of the plate, the more likely is the screw to penetrate the articular surface.

approach is in the visualization of the palmar ulnar corner of the radius.

The second surgical approach to the palmar radius is the flexor tendon/ulnar neurovascular bundle interval. The skin incision is centered over the ulnar border of the palmaris longus, the flexor tendons are mobilized radially, and the ulnar neurovascular bundle is taken ulnarly. With this approach the pronator quadratus is released from the ulna. The incision may be extended distally to release the transverse carpal ligament, particularly if the patient had any median nerve symptoms preoperatively. This incision is preferred when the majority of the comminution is at the palmar lunate facet. Note that the location of the skin incision does not preclude the surgeon from developing the interval between the FCR and the radial artery through the same incision. This incision permits the development of both intervals if there is any question of the adequacy of the reduction.

Once the approach has been performed, the next step is to obtain an anatomic reduction. In extra-articular fractures with dorsal displacement, this can be achieved using the plate. Screws are placed distally in the plate parallel to the joint surface in the lateral view, taking care not to penetrate the dorsal cortex. Pronated and supinated oblique views are useful at this stage to ensure that the distal screws have not penetrated the radiocarpal or distal radioulnar joints. The plate is then lying off the shaft of the radius (Fig. 30-32A). The proximal limb of the plate is then gently pushed on to the shaft, the so-called lift technique[242] and fixed in place (Fig. 30-32B). This usually reduces the distal fragment in a similar manner to the joystick effect of nonbridging external fixation (Fig. 30-22B).

In articular fractures both the radial and the intermediate columns must be reduced. The first column to reduce is the one in which the cortex can be anatomically reduced and fixed using a K-wire. Once the columns have been aligned, the fracture may be fixed to the palmar plate. First the plate is temporarily fixed to the shaft, preferably with either a unicortical screw or a screw in a sliding hole in the plate. The lateral view is useful to determine if screws placed through the plate are going to penetrate the articular surface. A combination of traction and palmar flexion usually

reduces the metaphyseal fragment to the plate and then the remaining screws may be placed (Figs. 30-33 and 30-34). At this stage, pronated and supinated oblique views must be obtained to verify that the screws have not penetrated the radiocarpal joint (Fig. 30-34).

AUTHORS' PREFERRED TREATMENT

As has been noted throughout this chapter, there are a wide variety of techniques that may be applied successfully to nearly every fracture. A dogmatic approach is not appropriate and cannot be supported by the literature. Evidence that compares different options indicates that the most important aspect of outcome is to achieve the radiographic measures of a successful outcome in the least invasive method possible.

Metaphyseal Bending Fractures

Metaphyseal bending fractures typically arise as the result of a fall on the outstretched hand. The fracture is usually a lower energy injury and may be considered as either a stable or an unstable fracture. Stable fractures are characterized by (i) minimal metaphyseal void with no palmar comminution, (ii) an intact palmar cortex after reduction, and (iii) good quality bone stock without osteoporosis or osteopenia secondary to advanced age or metabolic bone disease.

Unstable fractures create two long term problems: (i) shortening of the radius relative to the intact ulna and (ii) loss of palmar tilt at the radiocarpal joint. Shortening of the radius relative to the ulna during the injury disrupts the distal radioulnar joint ligaments. Adams demonstrated that shortening of the radius relative to the intact ulna of more than 5 mm must by definition disrupt the TFCC or cause avulsion of the ulnar styloid.[2] The resultant distal radioulnar joint instability may thus be responsible for the ulnar sided pain noted in follow-up by several authors.[92,160] Further, the residual shortening results in long-term ulnar impaction syndrome with resultant pain with

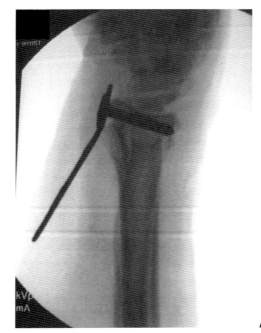

FIGURE 30-32 A. A volar plate has been applied to the distal fragment only, with the fracture unreduced. **B.** The "lift" technique. The plate has been pushed gently on to the shaft of the radius, reducing the fracture.

A

B

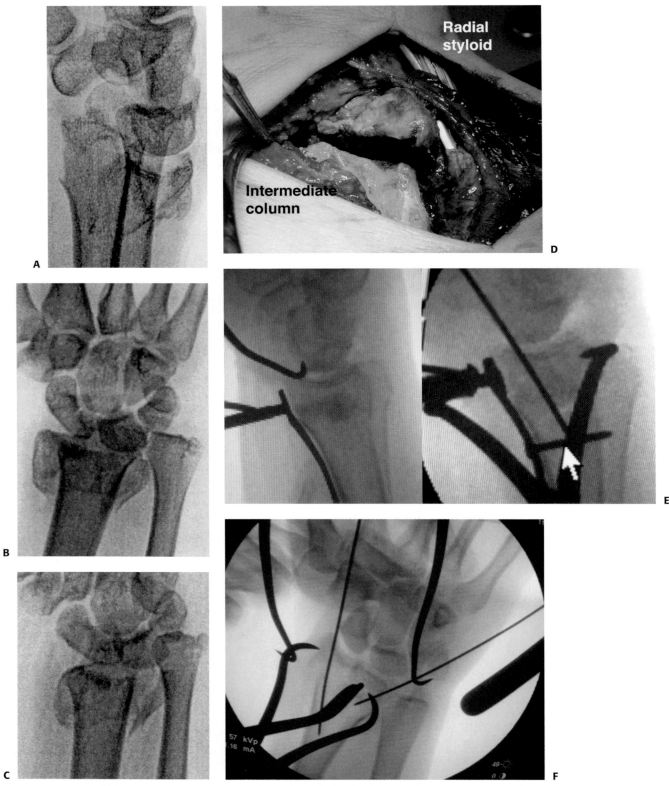

FIGURE 30-33 A comminuted dorsally angulated distal radius fracture with an associated nondisplaced scaphoid fracture **(A–C)**. The flexor carpi radialis/radial artery interval is used, and the radial and the intermediate columns are reduced and pinned **(D)**. The plate is first applied to the shaft with one screw placed though the sliding hole. Then the correct proximal/distal location of the plate is determined on the lateral x-ray view. Once the palmar cortex has been reestablished with the plate, then tension and traction will restore palmar tilt. Alternatively, a tenaculum may assist in reestablishing palmar tilt. Gapping between the intermediate and radial columns may be reduced by use of a tenaculum clamp and provisional pinning **(E,F)**.

ulnar deviation and strong grip. The ability to predict which fracture will be unstable has been studied extensively. The most consistent predictors of instability are (1) patient age, (2) degree of metaphyseal comminution, and (3) the degree of radial shortening (ulnar variance) at presentation. These factors may be used in an effort to assess the risk of early and late instability and may prove useful in counselling of patients regarding surgical versus nonoperative management.[179,180]

Unstable bending fractures of the distal radius can be treated with either nonbridging external fixation or open reduction and internal fixation with a palmar locked plate. Bridging external fixation with augmentation with K-wires can be used where the distal fragment is too small to accommodate either fixator pins or screws, which is unusual in older patients.[106] Nonbridging external fixation is less invasive than palmar locked plating and its most common complication (minor pin tract infection) rarely compromises the final outcome. However nonbridging external fixation is less useful if the fracture is irreducible closed. This can occur if there is marked radial shortening with overlap of the volar cortex or if the surgery is delayed and early healing has occurred. In this situation locked volar plating is preferred, with care taken to avoid tendon impingement. In cases with

severe osteoporosis and a large metaphyseal defect, added support with a bone substitute or autograft is required to prevent collapse around the plate.

Palmar Articular Shear Fractures

The optimal management of articular shear fractures is one of the few accepted treatment modalities. Like most partial articular fractures, the emphasis is on anatomic reduction of the articular surface and compression across the fracture site to assist in primary bone healing. Fixation should be sufficiently stable to allow early range of motion. The ideal fixation is with a palmar buttress plate that is slightly undercontoured relative to the degree of palmar flexion of the radius (Fig. 30-34). This plate not only prevents axial displacement of the palmar fragment, but also compresses the fragment against the intact dorsal cortex (Fig. 30-29).

The results of operative treatment of partial articular fractures with this technique are excellent; however, there are two potential pitfalls. One is that these fractures represent an impaction of both the scaphoid and the lunate on the volar lip of the radius. As such, there may be a nondisplaced fracture line between the scaphoid and the lunate facets. The implant must

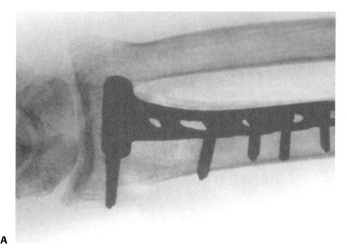

A

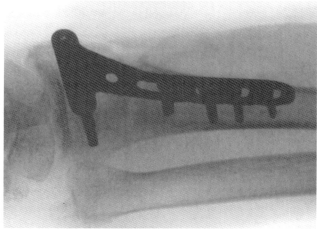

B

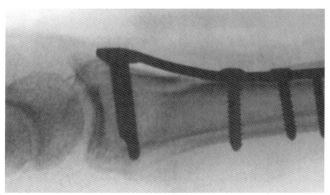

C

D

FIGURE 30-34 It is important to ensure that dorsal cortex and intra-articular screw penetration is avoided with application of a palmar plate. **A.** Pronation of 60 degrees demonstrates the intermediate column. **B–D.** The forearm is elevated 20 degrees off the table to obtain a true lateral of the radiocarpal joint. This shows a tangential tangential view of the intermediate column.

extend sufficiently ulnarly to stabilize the lunate facet and prevent it from late collapse. The second pitfall lies in the potential for a nondisplaced fracture across the dorsum of the radius. Undercontouring of the plate in this fracture can result in displacement of the entire articular surface dorsally (Fig. 30-30).[130,139]

Compression Fractures of the Articular Surface

The optimal management of lunate impaction fractures is one of the most controversial topics in wrist fracture surgery. The most critical point in treating these injuries is to understand the mechanism of the injury and recognize the fragments. Melone emphasized the role of the lunate in the creation of intraarticular fractures.[190] As the lunate impacts on the articular surface, it splits the lunate fossa into two characteristic fragments with the potential for a third "central impaction" fracture. The scaphoid impacts on the radial styloid and results in a shearing force that typically does not split the styloid into a palmar and a dorsal fragment. When faced with these fractures, the surgeon is required to identify each fragment and assess for displacement. Once the fragments have been identified, the decision must be made whether to stabilize the displaced fragments based on the fragment size and the degree of the displacement.

In general terms there are two methods for stabilizing displaced articular fragments: external fixation and internal fixation. The decision over which technique to use may be based in part on whether direct reduction of the fragments is necessary and feasible through a closed or percutaneous technique employed with external fixation. In general, depressions on the palmar articular surface are difficult to reduce in a closed fashion and often require open reduction. In this case internal fixation may be preferred as the surgeon already has the exposure necessary for internal fixation. Each technique has its advantages and its complications. In an attempt to directly compare each technique, one group of investigators prospectively randomized patients between internal and external fixation. The external fixation group demonstrated superior outcomes provided that they were able to achieve satisfactory radiographic parameters at the end of treatment. The authors concluded that the goal should be to achieve satisfactory radiographic parameters using the least invasive technique possible.[147] In general terms it can be concluded that each individual surgeon will have a level of comfort for which one technique or the other may be preferable.

External fixation is an exceedingly useful technique for treating a variety of radius fractures; however, it is critical to understand that certain fracture patterns will require more invasive techniques. In the case of lunate impaction fractures, the lunate must be assessed prior to obtaining patient consent. If the lunate facet is split into a palmar and a dorsal fragment, traction alone may not reduce the critical volar ulnar corner. The surgeon and the patient must understand that if indirect reduction of this fragment does not occur with traction, then direct reduction will be required.

In one study of 132 patients treated with external fixation, 15 (11%) required limited open techniques to achieve reduction.[120] Direct reduction may be performed either through a limited open or an extensile approach. Smaller fragments may be fixed with wires, whereas fragments that extend more proximally may require plate stabilization. Because volar plating may actually address all the components of the fracture, the surgeon may elect to use a locked volar plate only and forego external fixation. Because of the multitude of variables, extensive preoperative planning and templating is critical.

The first step is application of a bridging external fixator. The preferred method of anesthesia is axillary block; a tourniquet is used. A 3-cm dorsoradial skin incision is made at the distal third of the radius. Careful dissection is performed to avoid injury to the dorsal sensory portion of the radial nerve that emerges from under the brachioradialis tendon 7.5 to 11.0 cm proximal to the tip of the radial styloid (Fig. 30-35).

The drill holes are placed in the interval between the extensor carpi radialis brevis and longus. This position places the extensor carpi radialis longus (ECRL) between the pin and the sensory branch of the radial nerve. Predrilling and hand placement of the pins may prevent overheating of the cortical bone and subsequent pin site problems. To avoid interference with thumb retroflexion, the distal pins should be placed 45 degrees off the sagittal plane at the adductor tubercle of the index metacarpals. The fracture is then reduced manually in the following sequence: (1) longitudinal traction is applied to achieve radial length and the fracture is assessed for the presence of a metaphyseal defect, (2) palmar translation (not palmar flexion) of the carpus, and finally (3) ulnar deviation. If there is evidence of significant radioulnar instability, the fracture is reduced in supination to avoid displacing the radial metaphysis palmar to the distal ulna as ulnar deviation is applied. The most critical ele-

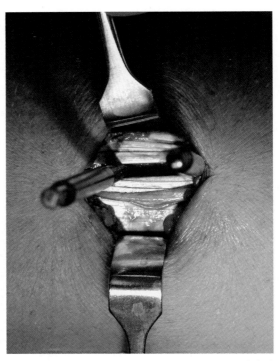

FIGURE 30-35 Pin position between the extensor carpi radialis longus and brevis. Note the proximity of the dorsal sensory branch of the radial nerve. Iatrogenic injury to this nerve is a frequent cause of neurogenic pain after external fixation and may be minimized by open rather than percutaneous pin insertion.

ment to this technique is to align the palmar cortex anatomically on the lateral view. It is especially useful to incline the radius 15 degrees to 20 degrees to the fluoroscopy beam to check the alignment. In order to prevent collapse during healing and permit early removal of the external fixator, the metaphyseal void may be filled with a bone graft or a bone graft substitute at this time. It may be useful to temporarily overdistract the fracture to enlarge the defect. The majority of graft substitutes do not permit complete packing of the defect and thus some temporary over distraction will allow better filling of the void. As traction is decreased, the material will be compacted. The metaphyseal comminution permits "opening" of the fracture through a 2-cm wound dorsally immediately proximal to the fracture. Small right angle retractors may facilitate exposure of the thin metaphyseal dorsal cortical fragments. One or more of these fragments may be removed after marking its distal aspect with a marking pen to indicate its correct orientation for reinsertion. This opens the fracture and exposes the metaphyseal defect to allow irrigation of the clot from the fracture site. For extra-articular fractures the graft is packed radially and distally, with care being taken to avoid displacement of the palmar cortex.

Supplemental support with autograft or a bone substitute is critical in external fixation of most compression fractures, particularly those with a central impaction component. After irrigating out the clot, a tamp can be used to gently elevate the compressed segments. Start palmarly and work dorsally. It is theoretically useful to elevate some of the native cancellous bone up with the fragments to create a uniform subchondral surface for the intermediate column. The supplemental graft can then be packed in the resultant defect. The dorsal cortical "window" can then be replaced, with care being taken to create a smooth surface for the extensor tendons.

Intra-articular Fractures

Following reduction of the radial metaphysis, it is critical to evaluate the lunate facet on the inclined lateral view with traction in place. If traction fails to reduce the palmar facet, then direct reduction will be required through an open rather than a percutaneous approach.

Two-Part Intra-articular Fractures

In the case of a two-part intra-articular fracture, the radial column may be reduced with longitudinal traction and slight ulnar deviation. The radial column is stabilized using two percutaneously placed 0.45- or 0.62-inch Kirschner wires. Once the radial column is out to length, the lunate fossa may be pinned in a reduced position. If there is minimal comminution, a large tenaculum clamp may be placed percutaneously between the dorsal ulnar corner and the newly fixed radial column. In some cases where there is residual depression of the lunate, percutaneous elevation may be required. After verifying that the lunate fossa is out to length and that there is no step-off between the scaphoid and the lunate facets, transverse wires may be placed under the subchondral surface.

Three-Part Intra-articular Fractures

In the case of three-part intra-articular fractures, the radial column again is reduced first. The lunate fossa should then be assessed on a tilted lateral view. If the palmar lunate facet is reduced following grafting and application of traction, trans-

verse subchondral wires may again be placed, with care being taken to direct at least one of the wires to support the palmar lunate facet.

When radiographs reveal that the palmar lunate facet is still depressed after application of traction and placement of graft material, a direct reduction is performed. A skin incision is placed longitudinally at the ulnar aspect of flexor tendons but radial to the ulnar neurovascular bundle. The flexor tendons are retracted radially and the ulnar neurovascular bundle is retracted ulnarly to expose the critical palmar ulnar fragment. If the fracture lies distally and does not involve the thick cortical support of the lunate facet, then the fragment may be fixed with two Kirschner wires, leaving the wire emerging dorsally for later removal. The more common fracture pattern results in extension below the level of the sigmoid notch. The proximal extension typically results in a triangular shaped fragment of cortical bone that will require buttress fixation using a plate-screw construct. If the surgeon plans to leave the external fixation in place and the radial column is well stabilized, then a small 2.0- or 2.4-mm plate may be applied to the intermediate column.

It is critical when applying this plate to make sure that the dorsal lunate facet is out to length when the distal screws are placed. Failure to reduce the dorsal lunate facet will result in an intra-articular step-off as the distal screws are placed. Once the intermediate column is fixed, then the radial side is reassessed to make sure that there is no step-off. The radial pins may need to be readjusted to reflect the reduced position to the intermediate column (Fig. 30-33).

Four-Part Fractures

When the articular surface is comminuted into four parts or greater, it becomes even more critical to support the articular surface with bone graft or a bone graft substitute. Placing the graft from the dorsum may result in the ability to restore a relatively congruous articular surface from below.

Once the graft has been placed, it is important to evaluate for displacement of the palmar radial and ulnar facets. The central impaction fragment may be reduced percutaneously from the dorsal side using the subchondral graft and wires, although the palmar articular facets remain a problem. If tilted radiographs reveal displacement palmarly, then the surgeon should make a limited or an extensile palmar approach. After stabilization of the intermediate column with a small buttress plate, lateral radiographs may still reveal some articular step-off palmarly, which reflects the split in the radial styloid. The radial column is visible through the midline incision, but it may not be stabilized by a smaller 2.0- or 2.4-mm plate buttressing the lunate facet. At this time the surgeon can either apply a more conventional "T" plate or maintain the reduction with percutaneously applied K-wires exiting radially.

Supplemental Fixation

In an effort to fix the fractured segments directly and avoid the loss of palmar tilt and radial length following external fixation, several authors have recommended supplemental fixation with or without the use of adjunctive bone graft.[64,237] On completion of the fixation it is critical to evaluate the tension in the extrinsic extensor tendons by assessing passive metacarpophalangeal motion. Overdistraction results in excessive tension on the digital extensors. The metacarpal phalangeal joints may be passively flexible, but with excessive tension the digits "spring" back into extension when the digit is released. If there is any doubt, the traction can be let off and the passive motion reassessed. If the motion is improved after releasing some distraction, fixation should be secured in this position.

Internal Fixation of Intra-articular Fractures

The approach to internal fixation of intra-articular fractures is determined by the location and degree of displacement of the intra-articular component and the degree of comminution. In general terms, for fractures that are primarily comminuted either palmarly or dorsally, the most direct approach may be performed. When the comminution involves both the palmar and the dorsal cortices, the use of a palmar locked plate is preferred. Rarely comminution extends very distally on the dorsal margin of the distal radius fracture. In this case the purchase of the locking screws applied from the volar surface may not provide adequate purchase, particularly in the dorsal lunate facet. In this case the surgeon may need to stabilize this fragment with an external fixator or one of the smaller plates, which may be applied through a separate incision between the fifth and sixth dorsal compartments.

It is useful to have both the injury film and the postreduction films to determine the approach and the implant selection. AP, lateral, and oblique radiographs following reduction should be viewed to determine any displacement of the radial styloid and the palmar and dorsal lunate facets. Any uncertainty about central impaction is assessed with computerized tomography. Typically the intermediate column is assessed for residual displacement first. Residual displacement of the palmar lunate cortex should be addressed with palmar plate. Comminution of the intermediate column should be addressed first and then the displaced palmar lunate cortex should be approached through the flexor tendon/ulnar neurovascular bundle interval (Fig. 30-36A,B). Residual displacement of the radial styloid should be addressed with a separate plate or with percutaneous wires (Fig. 30-36C–F). For residual dorsal displacement with the palmar cortex reduced, a dorsal approach to the intermediate column should be used, with an incision between third and fourth compartments (Fig. 30-37A,B). Separate fixation of the radial column may be needed to avoid dorsal impingement at the Lister tubercle (Fig. 30-37C–E).

Associated Injuries
Radial styloid fractures, isolated volar or dorsal lip fractures, and ulnar styloid fractures serve as markers of high energy ligament injuries about the wrist.

Radial Styloid Fractures

Depressed radial styloid fractures are associated with a high incidence of scapholunate ligament injuries in younger patients; the scaphoid displaces relative to the lunate. A shear injury between the two bones ruptures the scapholunate interosseous ligament. Treatment should be geared toward the ligamentous injury and include stabilization of the radial styloid. For acute injuries, a dorsal ligament repair with reattachment of the dorsal extrinsic ligaments may be performed. A cannulated screw or K-wires may be used to stabilize the fracture.

Volar Lip Injuries

The management of volar lip injuries is dependent on the size of the fragment relative to the remaining portion of the lunate facet. Smaller ulnar sided fragments are indicative of a distal radioulnar joint injury, and treatment may be geared toward reduction and stabilization of the distal radioulnar joint. Larger fragments are indicative of true palmar radiocarpal instability and should be assessed for residual palmar displacement of the lunate relative to the radiocarpal joint.[46,198,241,252] Stabilization of these fragments may be difficult. Smaller fragments may be neutralized by placing a wire through the fragment and through a drill hole in the radius. The fragments are then sutured to the radius. Larger fragments may be fixed with a plate screw construct. As these fragments represent the insertions of the volar extrinsic ligaments, there is a growing trend to repair, rather than excise, these fragments. External fixation may be required to stabilize the radiocarpal joint.

Dorsal Lip Injuries

Avulsion injuries of the dorsal lip of the radius are indicators of a variety of ligamentous injuries. In one review of 20 fractures of the dorsal articular margin the authors confirmed that these injuries result in substantial injury to the volar extrinsic ligaments and frequently include avulsion fractures of the volar lip of the radius. In addition, there is frequently a component of impaction with these injuries, and computerized tomography may prove of benefit to assess for impaction of the articular surface before operative management.[167]

Generally speaking, if the injury arises from the dorsum of the radius, then both the radiocarpal joint and the scaphoid should be assessed for stability. External fixation may be used to stabilize the radiocarpal joint and percutaneous pinning may be used to fix the intercarpal instability.

Ulnar Styloid Fractures

Fractures of the ulnar styloid occur in approximately 60% to 70% of distal radius fractures.[45,69,188,201,238] It is well accepted that the distal ulna is a common source of symptoms after injury. The disability that arises directly from the fracture versus the associated injury to the triangular fibrocartilage complex remains controversial.[92,136,222] Adams documented in cadaver studies that displacement of the radius relative to the ulna of 5 mm or more must result in a fracture of the ulna styloid or a disruption of the TFCC.[2] The disruption may occur at the base of the ulnar styloid, the ulnar insertion of the distal radioulnar ligaments, or the radial insertion of the TFCC complex.

The indications for treatment of these injuries remain controversial. Although it is accepted that displacement of the radius results in acute disruption of the joint, whether these injuries require treatment is unknown. Lindau documented that persistent radioulnar instability was a risk factor for a poor outcome independent of radiographic appearance. Clinically apparent instability was present in 26 of 76 patients at 1 year postinjury. Instability of the distal radioulnar joint was associated with a worse wrist score and doubled the score on the visual analog pain scale.[164] Although fixation of the ulnar styloid and or repair of the TFCC has been reported to have good outcomes, it is uncertain as to which injuries require acute repair.[229,238] The indications for treatment of ulnar styloid fractures is evolving.

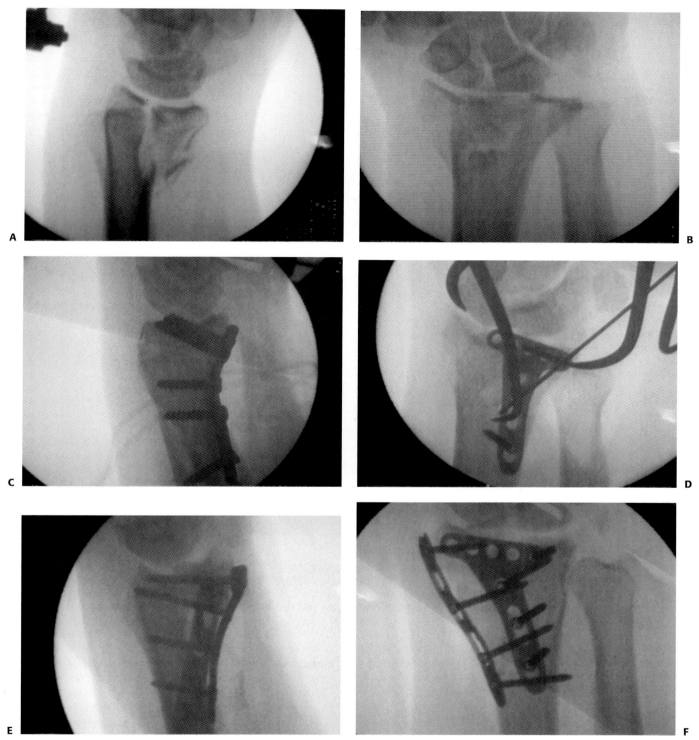

FIGURE 30-36 Lateral and PA fluoroscopy views **(A,B)** after reduction in traction of a highly comminuted intra-articular fracture. Note that the dorsal cortex comes out to length whereas the palmar cortex remains displaced. Following application of a palmar plate, there still remains some residual comminution of the radial styloid **(C,D)**. The radial styloid (particularly distally) may require adjunctive fixation with either a second plate or K-wires. For this case a separate radial column plate was used to create the final construct **(E,F)**.

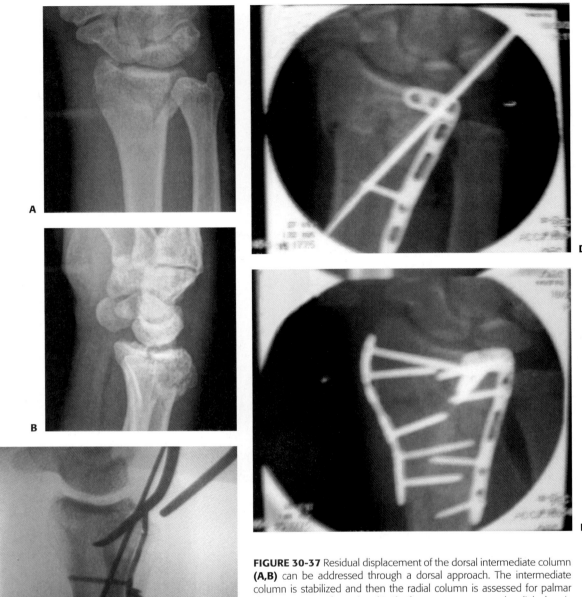

FIGURE 30-37 Residual displacement of the dorsal intermediate column **(A,B)** can be addressed through a dorsal approach. The intermediate column is stabilized and then the radial column is assessed for palmar displacement and rotation **(C,D)**. If necessary, a second radial plate is applied **(E)**.

Currently a fracture at the base of the ulnar styloid with both significant displacement and gross palmar dorsal translation of the radius relative to the ulna represents an indication for treatment.

One special circumstance is a large displaced ulnar styloid fragment that may appear to be lined up in the AP plane; however, when the lateral view is examined, the styloid fragment is actually displaced palmarly in relation to the distal ulna. Often this problem is only recognized late when the patient has difficulty achieving wrist supination either actively or passively. The treatment for such a displaced fragment both acutely and subacutely is reattachment of the styloid to the distal ulna.

The distal ulna is approached through a longitudinal incision over the extensor carpi ulnaris. Transverse branches of the ulnar nerve are preserved. Often the extensor carpi ulnaris subsheath is still attached to the fragment. The fragment typically will reduce with supination of the wrist and will displace with pro-

nation. It is helpful to maintain the wrist in supination while repairing the styloid to the distal ulna. For large fragments the simplest and most secure fixation may be with a cannulated headless screw. For smaller fragments, 0.28-inch K-wires and a 24-gauge tension band may be applied. Care must be taken to bury the hardware, as it is often prominent in this region and may require removal later.

Geissler has documented that significant TFCC injuries may occur with ulnar styloid fractures.[93] Reattachment of the ulnar styloid alone may not result in restoration of stability in this situation. Therefore it is critical to reassess the stability of the DRUJ following repair of the styloid.

An alternative to internal fixation is to reduce the distal radioulnar joint by supinating the forearm. Immobilization of the wrist in supination allows the soft tissue to heal in a reduced position and may prevent late instability of the radioulnar joint (Fig. 30-38).

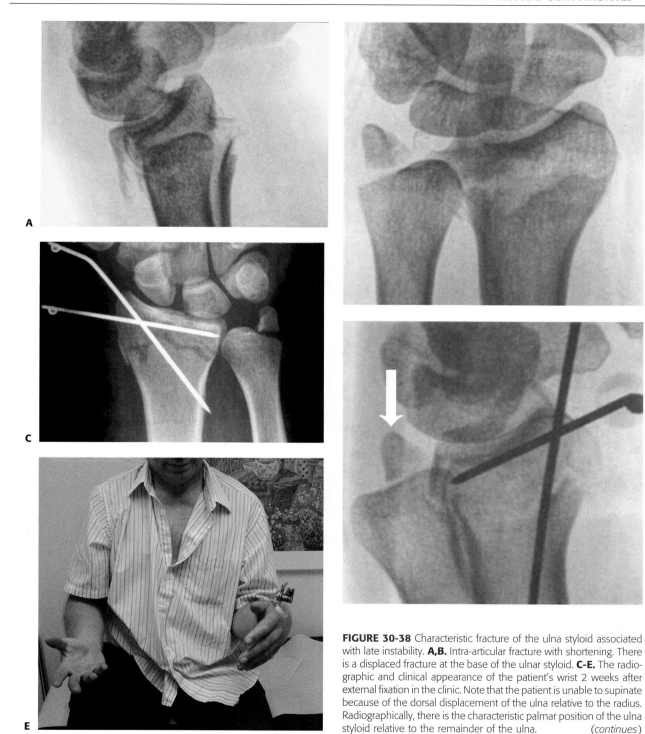

FIGURE 30-38 Characteristic fracture of the ulna styloid associated with late instability. **A,B.** Intra-articular fracture with shortening. There is a displaced fracture at the base of the ulnar styloid. **C-E.** The radiographic and clinical appearance of the patient's wrist 2 weeks after external fixation in the clinic. Note that the patient is unable to supinate because of the dorsal displacement of the ulna relative to the radius. Radiographically, there is the characteristic palmar position of the ulna styloid relative to the remainder of the ulna. (*continues*)

Fractures of the distal ulnar metaphysis occur much less commonly.[31] In one report of 320 fractures the distal ulnar metaphysis was fractured in 7% of cases, with the most common fracture pattern being an extra-articular fracture of the ulna metaphysis. Although nonoperative management may be successful, care should be taken to immobilize the radioulnar joint in a reduced position and look for radiographic evidence of impingement. Late heterotopic bone formation is common and will result in significant loss of rotation with this fracture pattern.

Combined (High-Energy) Injuries

Combined injuries represent those fractures with components of several of the other fracture types. These injuries characteristically (1) are high energy, (2) have significant comminution often with proximal extension, and (3) may have significant soft tissue injuries. The management of these injuries is often complex and may require several steps. It is useful to manage them in a stepwise fashion by first achieving rigid skeletal stabilization and then addressing the soft tissue injuries.

Simple articular fractures with diaphyseal extension are best

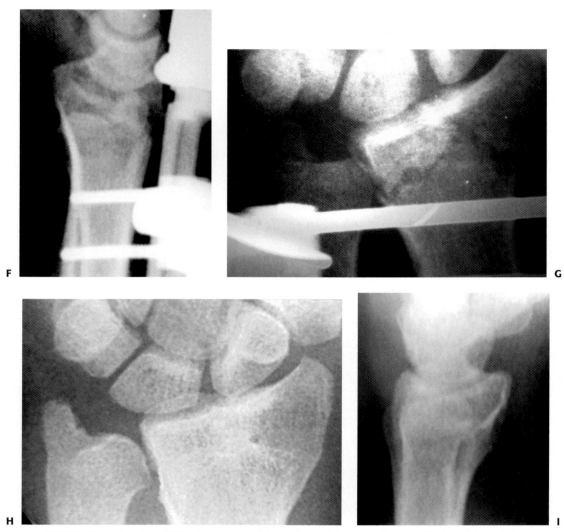

FIGURE 30-38 (*continued*) **F,G.** Appearance of the radius and the ulna after repositioning of the wrist in supination and maintaining it in this position. **H,I.** Final radiographic appearance at 2-year follow-up. The patient regained full pronation and supination.

managed with a palmar plate. Using external fixation for the diaphyseal component will result in significant collapse prior to fracture union. Dorsal plates often will impinge where they intersect, thus a palmar locking plate is preferred. When there is also extensive distal comminution, then hybrid fixation may be necessary. In this case a palmar plate is applied, and a dorsal external fixator may be used to neutralize the displacement through the distal comminution. Extensive grafting may be necessary in order to prevent late collapse.

When an open dislocation of the distal radioulnar joint has occurred, it is generally the result of extreme shortening of the fractured radius relative to the intact ulna. In these cases exploration reveals that the ulna has been stripped of the insertion of the DRUJ ligaments and the ulnocarpal ligaments. In some cases with an associated large ulnar styloid base fracture, those ligaments may still be attached to the base of the ulnar styloid. Stability may be restored by repairing the ulnar styloid base back to the shaft of the ulna, fixing it with either a headless

screw or a tension band wire construct. In cases in which there is no associated ulnar styloid base fracture, the ligaments may reapproximate to the ulna provided that the DRUJ is reduced. For this reason, in patients with obvious DRUJ instability and no large ulnar styloid fracture, the patient should be immobilized in supination to reduce the DRUJ for 4 weeks before permitting forearm rotation.

ASSOCIATED INJURIES

Soft Tissue Injuries

Adjunctive arthroscopy has demonstrated that significant interosseous and distal radioulnar ligament injuries occur in association with both metaphyseal bending and intra-articular fractures.

Interosseous Ligament Injuries

Injury to the interosseous ligaments occurs in roughly 50% of all intra-articular distal radius fractures in younger patients and varies by fracture pattern.[93,162] Geissler graded these injuries as follows: Grade I injuries have attenuation or hemorrhage of the ligament. Grade II injuries have incongruity of the ligament from the midcarpal portal, and the probe may be inserted between the bones. Grade III injuries show an incongruity from both the midcarpal and the radiocarpal portals, and the probe may be passed all the way through the articulation. Grade IV injuries have gross instability with manipulation, and the arthroscope (2.7-mm) may be passed from the radiocarpal to the midcarpal joints.

Scapholunate ligament injuries have been documented to occur approximately twice as frequently as lunotriquetral injuries.[93,162] They are seen most frequently in fractures that result in significant displacement of the lunate facet from the radial styloid (Fig. 30-39).

Although several studies examine the incidence of these injuries, the natural history of these soft tissue lesions remains controversial. In one study of 51 patients with distal radius fractures, there were a total of 10 grade III scapholunate ligament injuries. The authors found at 1-year follow-up that 6 patients

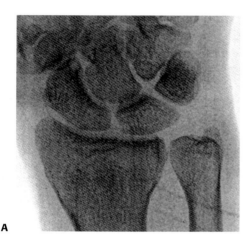

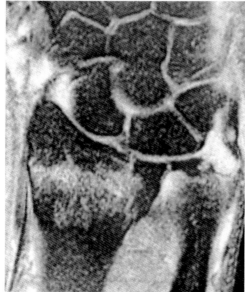

FIGURE 30-39 A,B. Minimally displaced lunate impaction fracture with disruption of both the scapholunate interosseous ligament and the triangular fibrocartilage complex.

had radiographic evidence of dissociation and an increased scapholunate angle and that this may be associated with SL pain at follow-up.[84] In a second study examining 76 patients following fracture, radiographically apparent scapholunate instability was not associated with either pain or functional impairment.[164] In a purely radiographic study of 95 fractures, dissociative ligamentous lesions were seen in 40 patients, of which 24 were noted to progress at 1-year follow-up. The results of this study again found no correlation between radiographic evidence of instability and symptoms at 1 year.[152]

Triangular Fibrocartilage (TFCC) Injuries

Lesions of the TFCC occur in roughly 40% to 70% of intraarticular fractures of the distal radius in young patients.[93,160,215] The majority of these lesions are peripheral avulsions, generally from the ulnar insertion compared with fewer central perforations. These lesions may occur with or without fracture of the ulnar styloid. In contrast to the interosseous ligament injuries, peripheral avulsions of the TFCC appear to be more likely to be symptomatic at short term follow-up. Lindau documented that 10 of 11 peripheral avulsions of the TFCC had DRUJ instability and worse outcome scores than other ligamentous injuries at 1-year follow-up.[164] Repair of these injuries acutely has been documented to restore stability and provide excellent results, yet the indications for acute repair have yet to be elucidated.[229]

OUTCOMES

Distal radius fractures remain one of the few areas in orthopedics where excellent prospective randomized studies have been performed.* Although these important studies remain excellent examples of outcome studies designed to answer a significant clinical question, they have also raised several important questions regarding the outcome of these fractures. Recent data suggests that patient related outcomes may vary markedly from physician related scores. Catalano et al reported on a significant discrepancy between radiographic appearance of the radiocarpal joint and patients' self reported outcomes at 7 years following operative intervention.[42] Several studies have indicated that perhaps one explanation may lie in the soft tissue injuries to the intrinsic ligaments of the carpus, with a resultant shift in carpal alignment or to associated trauma to the TFCC.[102,160,162,164]

A significant shift in the nature of outcome studies has been appreciated over the past 5 years. Recent evidence indicates that patient factors that are not associated with the injury or its treatment play a significant role in patient related outcome scores. In one comprehensive review of patients with successful volar plate surgery, the only variables associated with patient related scores were age and income.[48] Perhaps most significantly, the impact of patient's underlying psychological diagnoses may play a significant role in patient related outcome scores. Symptoms such as depression, anxiety, and pain correlate strongly with self reported outcome scores, thereby further confounding outcome studies.

*References 32,146,147,156,172,174,178,193,263.

COMPLICATIONS

The complications seen following the management of fractures of the distal radius often are difficult to assess as to whether the complication was a sequela of the fracture or a complication of the technique employed to treat the fracture. Certainly there are complications that may be associated with a given technique, such as pin tract infections associated with external fixation, but other complications such as complex regional pain syndrome (CRPS) or stiffness of the wrist or digits may be difficult to ascribe to one technique versus another. With the recent enthusiasm for palmar plates there is an effort being made to define the complications associated with one technique versus another. In addition, one study indicated that although palmar plating had a lower incidence of hardware related complications than dorsal plates, there may be a higher incidence of hardware collapse.[224]

Malunion

Malunion following treatment of distal radius fractures continues to be a significant complication following nonoperative management. In addition, as the number of operatively treated cases increases, so too does the incidence of collapse and malunion seen in previously treated fractures. The effect of radial malunion has to be taken into consideration when considering treatment options. Malunion of the radius results in alterations to (1) the radiocarpal joint, (2) the midcarpal joint, and (3) the radioulnar joint. The effect of these changes can be significant with regard to both immediate functional impairment and the development of late degenerative changes.

Radial malunion can have two potential effects on radiocarpal mechanics. First, the loss of palmar tilt shifts the carpus distally on the radius, thereby increasing contact stress on the dorsal lip of the radius. In addition, the loss of radial inclination results in increased stress at the radiolunate articulation.[206, 208,210] The increased contact stresses result in a higher likelihood of degenerative changes.[144] Functionally, the shortening may account for the loss of grip strength that has been observed after malunion.[210] There is also evidence that there is a functionally significant loss of motion at the radiocarpal joint after malunited extra-articular fractures.[137] Finally, the extended position of the lunate and the scaphoid may result in a compensatory collapse at the midcarpal joint (see Fig. 30-8).[195]

Intra-articular incongruity similarly causes a significant change in contact stresses at the radiocarpal joint. Note that depression of the lunate facet results in significant increases in the contact forces at the radioscaphoid articulation. Clinical studies indicate that 2 millimeters of lunate depression results in degenerative changes and worse functional outcomes.[142,144,196]

The impact of radial malunion on radioulnar mechanics has received significant attention. Dorsal angulation results in increased strain on the radioulnar ligaments.[19,37,62,109,197,234] Because of this increased strain, increased force is required to achieve full rotation of the forearm. Loss of rotation in these cases seems to occur at approximately 30 degrees loss of palmar tilt. By contrast, in cases of severe angulation with significant shortening, the same loss of rotation is not seen. One explanation offered for this contradiction is that in cases of severe deformity, there are no longer any attachments of the distal radioul-

nar ligaments to constrain the joint. Unconstrained by soft tissue attachments, the joint enjoys its full mobility.[19,37,62,109,197,234]

Corrective Osteotomy

The exact indications for osteotomy remains unknown. Cadaver studies have not examined the additive effects of radial shortening and loss of tilt and associated ligamentous injuries. Most surgeons perform corrective osteotomy for symptomatic malunion, with the commonest symptoms being DRUJ pain with or without contracture, midcarpal pain, carpal tunnel syndrome, or weakness of grip.[177] In one review of 23 intrarticular malunions treated with corrective osteotomy, the indications were (1) dorsal or palmar subluxation of the radiocarpal joint or (2) articular incongruity of greater than 2 mm on the AP radiograph,[211] although in general terms it is difficult to recommend surgical treatment of an asymptomatic deformity. Likewise, correction of the deformity has to offer a high likelihood of alleviating the patient symptoms.

In general terms, the osteotomy may be performed as early as the surgeon and the patient agree that there is a plateau in the patient's improvement. At one time there was a feeling that the osteotomy should be delayed until the fracture callus had completely incorporated. This practice is probably not necessary, because taking down the callus and internal fixation may be technically easier and not require bone graft when done before the fracture is healed.[129]

Although it is accepted that the deformity is a three-dimensional one, standard PA and lateral radiographs of both wrists are considered adequate for planning the osteotomy. The contralateral view is critical for assessing the radial length, radial inclination, palmar tilt, and carpal alignment. Special attention must be paid to the distal radioulnar joint to assess for congruency of the distal radioulnar joint and for potential arthritis of the distal ulna, which may require an associated resection.

Generally speaking, an opening wedge osteotomy is preferred when the distal radioulnar joint can be salvaged, and a closing wedge osteotomy is preferred with an associated hemiresection of the ulna when the DRUJ cannot be reconstructed. For an intra-articular osteotomy, computerized tomography with three-dimensional reconstructions may be necessary to determine the location of the intra articular step-off in both planes. Finally, computerized tomography with superimposition of the proximal forearm may also be useful for the correction of rotational deformity.

The typical deformity of the distal radius malunion has three components: (1) loss of radial inclination, (2) loss of palmar tilt, and (3) pronation of the fracture fragment. The surgical technique is dependent on the location of and the degree of the deformity.

Dorsal Displacement with Loss of Radial Inclination

The osteotomy is best performed at the site of the deformity. Typically an opening wedge osteotomy is performed and a corticocancellous graft is placed. It is notable that with the use of more rigid implants, it may be satisfactory to use cancellous graft alone.[72] Stabilization of the osteotomy has been described using K-wires, dorsal plates, palmar plates, and external fixators.* Regardless of the method of stabilization, the goal is to

---

*References 7,14,20,33,36,71,82,151,177,189,260,262,267.

correct the deformity and achieve early union. In general, a trapezoidal defect is created after the osteotomy and correction of both the palmar tilt and the radial inclination. The void is filled and the bone is stabilized. Rotation is verified before fixation of the osteotomy.

Palmar Displacement of the Distal Fragment

Palmar displacement (apex volar angulation) is best approached via a palmar approach. An associated carpal tunnel release should be strongly considered if lengthening is to be achieved. The osteotomy is again done at the previous fracture line. If radial inclination has been lost then the FCR/radial artery approach allows opening of the radial column and release of the contracted brachioradialis tendon. A corticocancellous graft is inserted and a palmar plate is applied. It is critical to recognize that an apex palmar angulation is often associated with dorsal displacement of the ulna relative to the radius, leading to loss of rotation. Restoration of rotation must be assessed before finalizing the position of the distal fragment relative to the proximal diaphysis. The results of osteotomy to correct palmar angulation have been reported, with restoration of rotation being better than the restoration of extension (Fig. 30-40).[165]

AUTHORS' PREFERRED TREATMENT

In planning an osteotomy it is important to consider what the patient is seeking from the procedure from both a symptomatic and a functional perspective. It is important to note the preoperative range of motion, as some loss of the total arc of motion may be expected. Because extension is typically more critical than flexion, the surgeon may wish to template the wrist to a neutral palmar tilt rather than to an anatomic 12 degrees of palmar tilt.

A second preoperative consideration is the distal radioulnar joint. It is important to note the presence of significant deformity or loss of articular cartilage on the distal ulna, which may preclude salvage of a reasonably functioning radioulnar joint. Computerized tomography may be indicated to assess the potential for salvage of the distal radioulnar joint.

A third consideration is the need for bone graft or substitute to fill the defect after the deformity is corrected. Options include autograft, allograft, or a variety of substiutes. In general, the use of fixed angle devices through a palmar ap-

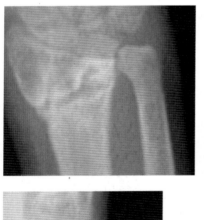
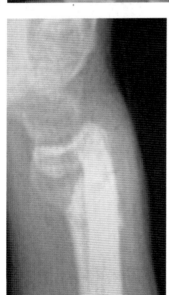
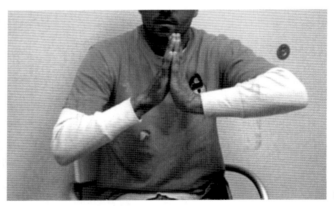
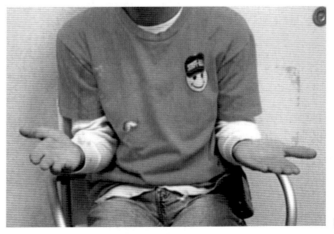

FIGURE 30-40 Palmar malunion following dorsal plating and collapse **(A,B)**. Note the position of the ulna relative to the radius in the lateral plane. Although dorsiflexion was limited, the patient's chief complaint was loss of supination **(C,D)**.

proach is perceived as sufficiently stable to permit the use of allograft or substitutes, whereas prior studies espoused the use of autograft. If the distal radioulnar joint is not salvageable in frail elderly patients, consideration should be given to using the distal ulna as a graft to avoid the need to harvest one from the iliac crest. If salvage of the DRUJ is precluded, then complete restoration of radial length may not be as important as correction of the tilt in the sagittal plane. Restoration of palmar tilt requires a triangular graft, whereas restoration of overall radial length may require a trapezoidal graft.

Finally, the surgeon must decide if there are any adjunctive procedures that may be required in order to achieve a satisfactory outcome. Carpal tunnel symptoms preoperatively may be exacerbated by an acute change in the length of the radius or by swelling in the carpal canal.[34] Although an opening wedge osteotomy may actually alleviate the deformity that causes the carpal tunnel symptoms, it is critical to consider whether the patient will tolerate the acute swelling and lengthening of the nerve associated with an osteotomy.[151] Decompression of the nerve associated with correction of the deformity may prevent an acute carpal tunnel syndrome.

These considerations must be taken during discussion with the patient preoperatively. In templating the deformity, we are increasingly relying on tomography to assess the deformity in multiple planes. These deformities are three-dimensional, and the surgeon should have a low threshold for obtaining CT scans with reformatted images to look for significant rotational deformity and the presence of significant arthritis in the distal radioulnar joint. (Fig. 30-41)

Operative Approach: Plating

Typically the deformity is approached from the collapsed side, which is dorsal in most cases. A longitudinal approach is performed and the extensor retinaculum is preserved to permit later coverage of the plate. In cases of long-standing deformity or when significant shortening has occurred, it is critical to release the brachioradialis from its insertion on the distal radius. A z-plasty can be performed if preoperative templating reveals the need for hardware distally over the styloid; however, this is usually unnecessary and the tendon may be left to heal back to the styloid. It is also helpful to visualize the dorsal ulnar corner of the radius and assess the distal radioulnar joint directly for articular changes that could preclude salvage or require further DRUJ procedures.[86]

Under C-arm guidance on the lateral view, a pin is inserted proximal (preferably proximal to the proximal extent of the plate) and perpendicular to the radial shaft. A second pin is placed distally in the radial metaphysis parallel to the articular surface. In the case of severe or long term deformity, it is helpful to use terminally threaded pins from a small external fixator. Once the osteotomy has been performed, the fixator can be

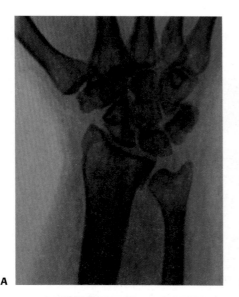

A

B

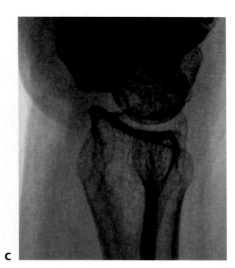

C

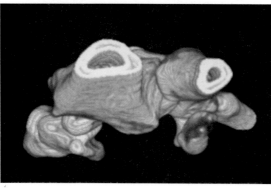

D

FIGURE 30-41 A–C. Typical malunion of the distal radius. The radius is collapsed dorsally. **D.** CT reconstruction demonstrates that the ulna is subluxated dorsally.

used to maintain the radius in the reduced position while the bone graft and/or the plate is applied. An oscillating saw is then used to cut the bone. It is significant here again to assess whether correction should be limited to palmar tilt or should include correction of radial length and inclination as well. If the correction is for palmar tilt, then it is easier to leave the palmar cortex intact and hinge the distal fragment on the cortex. If correction of length is to be achieved, then the osteotomy must be completed. In this situation the addition of the external fixator is particularly helpful. The graft material is harvested, preferably from the iliac crest graft, particularly when radial length is required. In elderly patients or when the distal radioulnar joint is not salvageable, the ulnar head may be harvested and inserted in the defect; however, it is generally not sufficient for complex deformities. Preoperative templating may now be confirmed visually by directly measuring the defect when the pins are made parallel on the lateral plane. The iliac crest graft is harvested with an oscillating saw, matching as precisely as possible the measurements of the defect.

Once the graft has been inserted, the plate can be applied. In the case of a trapezoidal graft to correct radial length, it may be helpful to maintain its position with crossed wires to prevent displacing the distal fragment proximally when the plate is applied. Once the plate has been applied and the position confirmed radiographically, the retinaculum may be closed over the plate and the wounds closed. The length of immobilization is determined by the stability of the construct and the distal radioulnar joint (Fig. 30-42).

A second alternative is to make use of the more rigid volar locking plates to stabilize the osteotomy. The technique is similar, with placement of pins to verify the correction of the deformity. An extensile FCR radial artery approach may be used, which allows the osteotomy to be performed from the radial column to the intermediate column. Alternatively, a 2.5-cm incision may be made dorsally at the osteotomy site and the saw may be used to cut the bone, leaving an intact palmar hinge. The void may then be filled with cancellous graft. Case cohort series indicate that this technique may obviate the need for tricortical graft because of the perceived strength of the palmar locked plates.[185]

Nonbridging external fixation has been used for corrective osteotomy with excellent functional results.[177] This technique had the advantage of being minimally invasive with a short transverse dorsal skin incision and of obviating the need for hardware removal. Corticocancellous graft is used to allow removal of the fixator after 6 weeks. This technique achieves excellent correction of the deformity and improvement in all functional indices except extension.[177]

For volar collapse a palmar approach is used. The interval that is followed is generally the FCR radial artery approach. The incision is taken down to the volar carpal branch of the radial artery. The pronator quadratus is detached and preserved to lie back down over the plate. A pin may be placed perpendicular to the articular surface and a second pin perpendicular to the proximal shaft. The osteotomy may then be performed and the articular surface may be manipulated back to the appropriate degree of tilt. In general, a small corticocancellous graft enhances the stability, but is not always necessary. A palmar plate is applied (Fig. 30-43).

Distal Radioulnar Joint Complications Associated with Malunions

Some fractures of the distal radius resulting in incongruity at the distal radioulnar joint may not be amenable to an osteotomy of the distal radius or demonstrate residual radial shortening after corrective osteotomy. In these cases the treatment is directed at the distal ulna in an effort to either restore congruity (i.e., an ulnar shortening osteotomy) or to salvage function (i.e., arthroplasty).

Ulnar Shortening Osteotomy

In cases when the radius has shortened without significant loss of palmar tilt or radiocarpal incongruity, it is preferable to perform an ulnar shortening osteotomy rather than a radial lengthening.[86] The procedure, performed through a longitudinal approach to the ulna and fixed with a dynamic compression plate, has been extensively reported for ulnar abutment syndrome (Fig. 30-44).[86,117,205,220] Contraindications to the procedure are: (1) ulnar translation of the radial metaphysis in association with the deformity, as shortening of the ulna results in excessive contact at the distal radioulnar joint; and (2) excessive *palmar* tilt of the radius, as shortening of the ulna will still leave the ulna dorsally displaced relative to the radius. In cases where the radial length has been restored but there remains DRUJ contracture or pain, an excisional arthroplasty (Bower procedure) of the DRUJ can be successful.[86]

Neurologic Injuries

Complications associated with the neurovascular structures at the wrist may be classified as those injuries that occurred at the time of the fracture and those that arise late as a result of swelling, scarring, or deformity.

Median Nerve

Acute carpal tunnel syndrome may be seen with either intra- or extra-articular fractures.[171] Risk factors are bleeding dyscrasias, open fractures, compressive dressings, excessive wrist flexion maintained in a cast and a prolonged period between injury and reduction. The pressure within the canal following a closed fracture treated conservatively has been shown to be at its highest during reduction and then to fall gradually during the following 12 hours.[60] Chronic compressive neuropathy of the median nerve occurs in approximately 5% of conservatively treated fractures of the distal radius.[24,112] Acute carpal tunnel syndrome that does not resolve rapidly after reduction is an indication for decompression.

Ulnar nerve

Ulnar nerve injuries occur far less commonly than median nerve injuries.[24,112] This nerve may have more excursion and is located at an increased distance from the displacement of the radius.[49] Acute injuries may be seen with displacement of the palmar lunate facet or with a palmar distal radioulnar joint dislocation and are often open. In a series of five cases the authors reported that these represent neurapraxic injury to the ulnar nerve, and that decompression should be limited to open wounds or associated acute carpal tunnel syndrome.[246] Late progressive ulnar nerve palsy has been reported caused by open distal radioulnar joint injuries.[49]

Complex Regional Pain Syndrome

Complex regional pain syndrome (CRPS) occurs in its early stages in up to 40% of fractures of the distal radius[15,29,78] al-

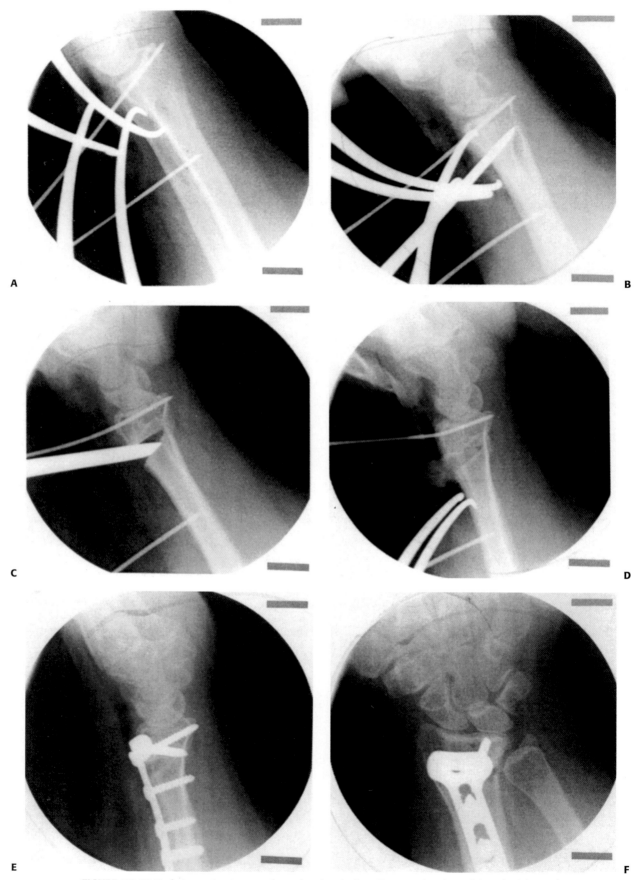

FIGURE 30-42 Technique of osteotomy for a dorsal malunion. Pins are placed parallel to the joint and perpendicular to the shaft **(A)**. An oscillating saw is used to cut the dorsal cortex **(B)**, whereas the palmar cortex is left intact. The fragment is levered into position **(C)**, and the bone graft is placed **(D)** and a dorsal plate is applied **(E,F)**.

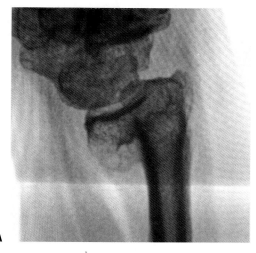

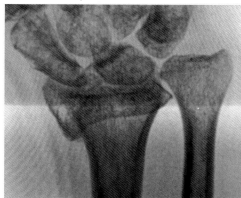

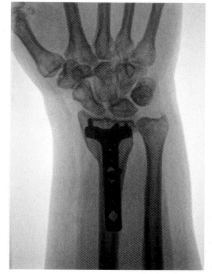

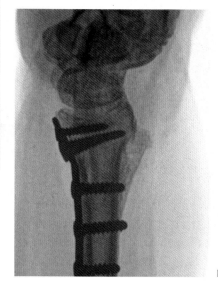

FIGURE 30-43 Palmar displacement of the distal fragment **(A,B)**. This deformity is common with collapse following dorsal plating. There is a profound effect on supination as the ulna becomes in essence "dislocated" dorsally because of the palmar displacement of the radius. The osteotomy is performed through a palmar approach and stabilized with a palmar plate **(C,D)**.

though severe chronic cases with serious and sometimes devastating disability are fortunately less common, occurring in less than 2% of cases. CRPS type 2 occurs in association with damage to a peripheral nerve and CRPS type 1 in the absence of nerve pathology.

Early recognition of CRPS is critical in order to institute early treatment, and surgeons dealing with distal radius fractures must maintain a high index of suspicion for CRPS. The cardinal features are abnormal or neuropathic pain, temperature changes, abnormal sweating, swelling, joint stiffness and atrophy, and bone changes. Diagnosis in an orthopaedic setting is dealt with in detail in Chapter 23.

The mainstay of treatment is multidisciplinary, with effective analgesia often with the advice of a pain specialist and intensive physical therapy. Surgery should be avoided unless there is good evidence of peripheral nerve compression, mostly commonly a carpal tunnel syndrome. Other treatment modalities include intravenous guanethidine blockade, Vitamin C, and desensitisation. These are discussed in detail in Chapter 23.

Tendon Injuries

The majority of flexor tendon injuries associated with distal radius fractures occur as a result of penetrating trauma and direct laceration. Closed ruptures, particularly of the extensor pollicis longus, have been extensively reported; however, rupture appears to be relatively uncommon in other tendons. These injuries may occur either acutely as a result of the initial trauma or late and be related to either increased pressure within the compartment or because of attrition from either callus or hardware.

Late extensor pollicis longus rupture occurs in roughly 0.3% of distal radius fractures.[110] Interestingly, these ruptures occur most frequently in minimally displaced fractures treated nonoperatively. The rupture is usually painless and occurs late at 6 weeks to 3 months after injury. Treatment is directed first at mobilizing the wrist and then performing an appropriate transfer.

In closed fractures flexor tendon ruptures may occur either as a result of a rotational injury at the time of fracture or in a

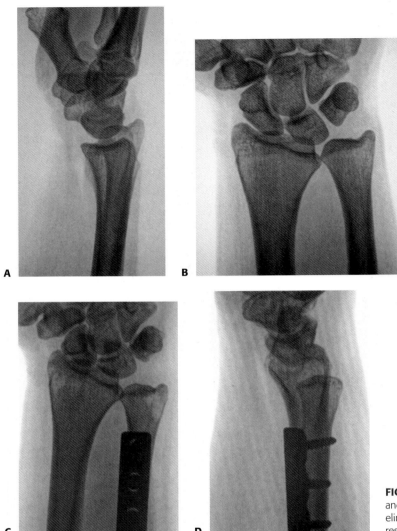

FIGURE 30-44 Malunion of the radius with loss of radial length and loss of forearm rotation **(A,B)**. An ulnar shortening osteotomy eliminated the symptoms of impaction **(C,D)**, and full rotation was restored.

delayed fashion because of attrition.[135] Late ruptures caused by hardware impingement have been described, particularly secondary to attrition of the flexor pollicis on prominent hardware.[141,153] More recently with increased use of volar locking plates, extensor tendon injury has been reported caused by dor-

sal penetration of locking screws at the distal dorsal margin of the radius.[6] Care must be taken intraoperatively to assess tangential views of the radial and intermediate columns, to avoid dorsal screw penetration and subsequent attritional tendon rupture (Fig. 30-45).

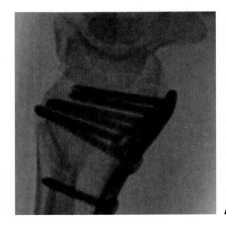

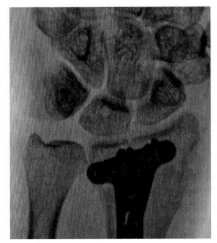

FIGURE 30-45 A,B. A patient with an extensor pollicis longus tendon rupture following palmar plate application. Note that on the initial lateral view from the OR   (continues)

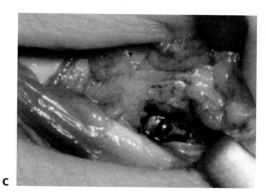

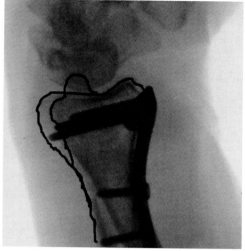

C

D

FIGURE 30-45 (*continued*) **(A)**, the screws appear to be well contained by the dorsal cortex. However, the Lister tubercle is the outline dorsally on the lateral view **(C,D)** and does not protect against dorsal cortical penetration either radially or ulnarly.

REFERENCES

1. Abbaszadegan H, Jonsson U. Regional anesthesia preferable for Colles' fracture. Controlled comparison with local anesthesia. Acta Orthop Scand 1990;61:348–349.
2. Adams BD. Effects of radial deformity on distal radioulnar joint mechanics. J Hand Surg Am 1993;18:492–498.
3. Agee JM. Distal radius fracture: Multiplanar ligamentotaxis. Hand Clin 1993;9:577–586.
4. Agee JM, Szabo RM, Chidgey LK, et al. Treatment of comminuted distal radius fractures: an approach based on pathomechanics. Orthopedics 1994;17:1115–1122.
5. Allain J, le Guilloux P, Le Mouel S, et al. Trans-styloid fixation of fractures of the distal radius. A prospective randomized comparison between 6- and 1-week postoperative immobilization in 60 fractures. Acta Orthop Scand 1999;70:119–123.
6. Al-Rashid M, Theivendran K, Craigen MA. Delayed ruptures of the extensor tendon secondary to the use of volar locking compression plates for distal radial fractures. J Bone Joint Surg Br 2006;88:1610–1612.
7. Amadio PC, Botte MJ. Treatment of malunion of the distal radius. Hand Clin 1987;3:541–561.
8. Andersen DJ, Blair WF, Steyers CM, Jr., et al. Classification of distal radius fractures: an analysis of interobserver reliability and intraobserver reproducibility. J Hand Surg Am 1996;21:574–582.
9. Anderson R, O'Neil G. Comminuted fractures of the distal end of the radius. Surg Gynaecol Obstet 1944;78:434–440.
10. Apergis E, Darmanis S, Theodoratos G, Maris J. Beware of the ulno-palmar distal radial fragment. J Hand Surg Br 2002;27:139–145.
11. Ark J, Jupiter JB. The rationale for precise management of distal radius fractures. Orthop Clin North Am 1993;24:205–210.
12. Arora R, Lutz M, Fritz D, et al. Palmar locking plate for treatment of unstable dorsal dislocated distal radius fractures. Arch Orthop Trauma 2005;125:399–404.
13. Arora R, Lutz M, Hennerbichler A, et al. Complications following internal fixation of unstable distal radius fracture with a palmar locking plate. J Orthop Trauma 2007;21:316–322.
14. Arslan H, Subasi M, Kesemenli C, et al. Distraction osteotomy for malunion of the distal end of the radius with radial shortening. Acta Orthop Belg 2003;69:23–28.
15. Atkins RM, Duckworth T, Kanis JA. Algodystrophy following Colles' fracture. J Hand Surg Br 1989;14:161–164.
16. Atroshi I, Brogren E, Larsson GU, et al. Wrist-bridging versus non-bridging external fixation for displaced distal radius fractures: a randomized assessor-blind clinical trial of 38 patients followed for 1 year. Acta Orthop 2006;77:445–531.
17. Auge WK, Velazquez PA. The application of indirect reduction techniques in the distal radius: the role of adjuvant arthroscopy. Arthroscopy 2000;16:830–835.
18. Azzopardi T, Ehrendorfer S, Coulton T, et al. Unstable extra-articular fractures of the distal radius: a prospective, randomised study of immobilisation in a cast versus supplementary percutaneous pinning. J Bone Joint Surg Br 2005;87:837–840.
19. Bade H, Lobeck F. Behaviour of the joint surface of the distal radio-ulnar joint in malposition of the distal radius. Unfallchirurgie 1991;17:213–217.
20. Baillon R, Gris M, Tollet P, Schuind F, Burny F.[Corrective osteotomy using Hoffmann II external fixators for extra-articular malunion of the distal radius]. Acta Orthop Belg 2001;67:500–504.
21. Bartosh RA, Saldana MJ. Intra-articular fractures of the distal radius: a cadaveric study to determine if ligamentotaxis restores radiopalmar tilt. J Hand Surg Am 1990;15:18–21.
22. Bass RL, Blair WF, Hubbard PP. Results of combined internal and external fixation for the treatment of severe AO-C3 fractures of the distal radius. J Hand Surg Am 1995;20:373–381.
23. Batra S, Gupta A. The effect of fracture-related factors on the functional outcome at 1 year in distal radius fractures. Injury 2002;33:499–502.
24. Bauman TD, Gelberman RH, Mubarak SJ, et al. The acute carpal tunnel syndrome. Clin Orthop 1981;156:151–156.
25. Bednar DA, Al-Harran H. Non-bridging external fixation for fractures of the distal radius. Can J Surg 2004;47:426–430.
26. Benson EC, DeCarvalho A, Mikola EA, et al. Two potential causes of EPL rupture after distal radius volar plate fixation. Clin Orthop 2006;451:218–222.
27. Beumer A, McQueen MM. Fractures of the distal radius in low demand elderly patients: closed reduction is of no value in 53 of 60 wrists. Acta Orthop Scand 2003; 74:98–100.
28. Bickerstaff DR, Bell MJ. Carpal malalignment in Colles' fractures. J Hand Surg Br 1989; 14:155–160.
29. Bickerstaff, DR, Kanis JA. Algodystrophy: an under-recognized complication of minor trauma. Br J Rheumatol 1994;33:240–248.
30. Biyani A. Over-distraction of the radio-carpal and mid-carpal joints following external fixation of comminuted distal radial fractures. J Hand Surg Br 1993;18:506–510.
31. Biyani A, Simison AJ, Klenerman L. Fractures of the distal radius and ulna. J Hand Surg Br 1995;20:357–364.
32. Bong MR, Egol KA, Leibman M, et al. A comparison of immediate post-reduction splinting constructs for controlling initial displacement of fractures of the distal radius: a prospective randomized study of long-arm versus short-arm splinting. J Hand Surg Am 2006;31:766–770.
33. Bora FW, Jr., Osterman AL, Zielinski CJ. Osteotomy of the distal radius with a biplanar iliac bone graft for malunion. Bull Hosp Jt Dis 1984;44:122–131.
34. Bourrel P, Ferro RM. Nerve complications in closed fractures of the lower end of the radius. Ann Chir Main 1982;1:119–126.
35. Braun RM, Gellman H. Dorsal pin placement and external fixation for correction of dorsal tilt in fractures of the distal radius. J Hand Surg Am 1994;19:653–655.
36. Brown JN, Bell MJ. Distal radial osteotomy for malunion of wrist fractures in young patients. J Hand Surg Br 1994;19:589–593.
37. Bronstein AJ, Trumble TE, Tencer AF. The effects of distal radius fracture malalignment on forearm rotation: a cadaveric study. J Hand Surg Am 1997;22:258–262.
38. Bruske J, Niedzwiedz Z, Bednarski M, et al. [Acute carpal tunnel syndrome after distal radius fractures—long term results of surgical treatment with decompression and external fixator application]. Chir Narzadow Ruchu Ortop Pol 2002;67:47–53.
39. Cannegieter DM, Juttmann JW. Cancellous grafting and external fixation for unstable Colles' fractures. J Bone Joint Surg Br 1997;79:428–432.
40. Capo JT, Accousti K, Jacob G, et al. The effect of rotational malalignment on X-rays of the wrist. J Hand Surg Eur 2009;34:166–172.
41. Cassidy C, Jupiter JB, Cohen M, et al. Norian SRS cement compared with conventional fixation in distal radial fractures. A randomized study. J Bone Joint Surg Am 2003;85:2127–2137.
42. Catalano LW, Cole RJ, Gelberman RH, et al. Displaced intra-articular fractures of the distal aspect of the radius. Long-term results in young adults after open reduction and internal fixation. J Bone and Joint Am1997;79:1290–3102.
43. Chan BK, Leong LC, Low CO, et al. The use of the external fixator in the treatment of intra-articular fractures of the distal radius. Singapore Med J 1999;40:420–424.
44. Chern TC, Jou IM, Lai KA, et al. Sonography for monitoring closed reduction of displaced extra-articular distal radial fractures. J Bone Joint Surg Am 2002;84:194–203.
45. Chidgey LK. Treatment of acute and chronic instability of the distal radio-ulnar joint. Hand Clin 1998;14:297–303.
46. Chin KR, Jupiter JB. Wire-loop fixation of volar displaced osteochondral fractures of the distal radius. J Hand Surg Am 1999 ;24:525–533.
47. Christensen OM, Christiansen TC, Krasheninnikoff M, et al. Plaster cast compared with bridging external fixation for distal radius fractures of the Colles' type. Int Orthop 2001;24:358–360.

48. Chung KC, Kotsis SV, Kim HM. Predictors of functional outcomes after surgical treatment of distal radius fractures. J Hand Surg Am 2007;32:76–83.
49. Clarke AC, Spencer RF. Ulnar nerve palsy following fractures of the distal radius: clinical and anatomical studies. J Hand Surg Br 1991;16:438–440.
50. Cobb AG, Houghton GR. Local anaesthetic infiltration versus Bier's block for Colles' fractures.Br Med J 1985;291:1683–1684.
51. Cole RJ, Bindra RR, Evanoff BA, et al. Radiographic evaluation of osseous displacement following intra-articular fractures of the distal radius: reliability of plain radiography versus computed tomography. J Hand Surg Am 1997;22:792–800.
52. Colles A. On the fracture of the carpal extremity of the radius. Edinburgh Med Surg 1814;10:182–186.
53. Constantine KJ, Clawson MC, Stern PJ. Volar neutralization plate fixation of dorsally displaced distal radius fractures. Orthopedics 2002;25:125–128.
54. Cooney WP. External fixation of distal radial fractures. Clin Orthop 1983;180:44–49.
55. Combalia A. Over-distraction of the radiocarpal and midcarpal joints with external fixation of comminuted distal radial fractures. J Hand Surg Br 1996;21:289.
56. Court-Brown CM, Caesar B. Epidemiology of adult fractures: a review. Injury 2006; 37:691–697.
57. Cuenca J, Martinez AA, Herrera A, Domingo J. The incidence of distal forearm fractures in Zaragoza (Spain). Chir Main 2003;22:211–215.
58. Dee W, Klein W, Rieger H. Reduction techniques in distal radius fractures. Injury 2000;31(Suppl 1):48–55.
59. Dias JJ, Wray CC, Jones JM, Gregg PJ. The value of early mobilisation in the treatment of Colles' fractures. J Bone Joint Surg Br 1987;69:463–467.
60. Dresing K, Peterson T, Schmit-Neuerburg KP. Compartment pressure in the carpal tunnel in distal fractures of the radius. A prospective study. Arch Orthop Trauma Surg 1994;113:285–289.
61. Drobetz H, Kutscha-Lissberg E. Osteosynthesis of distal radial fractures with a volar locking screw plate system. Int Orthop 2003;27:1–6.
62. Dumont CE, Thalmann R, Macy JC. The effect of rotational malunion of the radius and the ulna on supination and pronation. J Bone Joint Surg Br 2002;84:1070–1074.
63. Dunning CE, Lindsay CS, Bicknell RT, et al. Ilizarov hybrid external fixation for fractures of the distal radius: Part II. Internal fixation versus Ilizarov hybrid external fixation: stability as assessed by cadaveric simulated motion testing. J Hand Surg Am 2001; 26:218–227.
64. Dunning CE, Lindsay CS, Bicknell RT, et al. Supplemental pinning improves the stability of external fixation in distal radius fractures during simulated finger and forearm motion. J Hand Surg Am 1999;24:992–1000.
65. Edwards CC, Haraszti CJ, McGillivary GR, Gutow AP. Intra-articular distal radius fractures: arthroscopic assessment of radiographically assisted reduction. J Hand Surg Am 2001;26:1036–1041.
66. Edwards GS, Jr. Intra-articular fractures of the distal part of the radius treated with the small AO external fixator. J Bone Joint Surg Am 1991;73:1241–1250.
67. Eglseder WA, Hay M. Open half-pin insertion for distal radial fractures. Mil Med 1993; 158:708–711.
68. Egol KA, Paksima N, Puopolo S, et al. Treatment of external fixation pins about the wrist: a prospective, randomized trial. J Bone Joint Surg Am. 2006;88(2):349–354.
69. Faierman E, Jupiter J. The management of acute fractures involving the distal radioulnar joint and distal ulna. Hand Clin 1998;14:213–229.
70. Fernandez DL. Fractures of the distal radius: operative treatment. Instr Course Lect 1993;42:73–88.
71. Fernandez DL. Malunion of the distal radius: current approach to management. Instr Course Lect 1993;42:99–113.
72. Fernandez DL. Reconstructive procedures for malunion and traumatic arthritis. Orthop Clin North Am 1993;24:341–363.
73. Fernandez DL. Should anatomic reduction be pursued in distal radial fractures? J Hand Surg Br 2000;25:523–527.
74. Fernandez DL, Fleming MC. History, evolution and biomechanics of external fixation of the wrist joint. Injury 1994;25(Suppl 4):S-D-1–13.
75. Fernandez DL, Geissler WB. Treatment of displaced articular fractures of the radius. J Hand Surg Am 1991;16:375–384.
76. Fernandez DL, Jakob RP, Buchler U. External fixation of the wrist. Current indications and technique. Ann Chir Gynaecol 1983;72:298–302.
77. Fernandez DL, Jupiter JB. Fractures of the Distal Radius. 2nd Ed. New York: Springer-Verlag. 2002.
78. Field J, Atkins RM. Algodystrophy is an early complication of Colles' fracture. What are the implications? J Hand Surg Br 1997;22:178–82.
79. Fischer T, Koch P, Saager C, Kohut GN. The radio-radial external fixator in the treatment of fractures of the distal radius. J Hand Surg Br 1999;24:604–609.
80. Flinkkila T, Nikkola-Sihto A, Kaaela O, et al. Poor interobserver reliability of AO classification of fractures of the distal radius. J Bone Joint Surg Br 1998;80:670–672.
81. Flinkkila T, Nikkola-Sihto A, Raatikainen T, et al. Role of metaphyseal cancellous bone defect size in secondary displacement in Colles' fracture. Arch Orthop Trauma Surg 1999;119:319–323.
82. Flinkkila T, Raatikainen T, Kaarela O, et al. Corrective osteotomy for malunion of the distal radius. Arch Orthop Trauma Surg 2000;120:23–26.
83. Flinkkilä T, Ristiniemi J, Hyvönen P, et al. Nonbridging external fixation in the treatment of unstable fractures of the distal forearm. Arch Orthop Trauma Surg 2003;123: 349–352.
84. Forward DP, Lindau TR, Melsom DS. Intercarpal ligament injuries associated with fractures of the distal part of the radius. J Bone Joint Surg Am 2007;89:2334–2340.
85. Frykman GK. Fractures of the distal radius including sequelae-shoulder-hand-finger syndrome, disturbance in the distal radio-ulnar joint and impairment of nerve function. Acta Orthop Scand 1967:Suppl 108:7–153.
86. Gaebler C, McQueen MM. Ulnar procedures for post-traumatic disorders of the distal radioulnar joint. Injury 2003;34:47–59.
87. Gartland J, Werley C. Evaluation of healed Colles' fractures. J Bone and Joint Surg Am 1951;33:895–907.
88. Gausepohl T, Pennig D, Mader K. Principles of external fixation and supplementary techniques in distal radius fractures. Injury 2000;31(Suppl 1):56–70.
89. Gausepohl T, Worner S, Pennig D, et al. Extraarticular external fixation in distal radius fractures pinplacement in osteoporotic bone. Injury 2001;32(Suppl 4):SD79–SD85.
90. Geissler WB, Fernandes D. Percutaneous and limited open reduction of intra-articular distal radial fractures. Hand Surg 2000;5:85–92.
91. Geissler WB, Fernandez DL. Percutaneous and limited open reduction of the articular surface of the distal radius. J Orthop Trauma 1991;5:255–264.
92. Geissler WB, Fernandez DL, Lamey DM. Distal radioulnar joint injuries associated with fractures of the distal radius. Clin Orthop1996;327:135–146.
93. Geissler WB, Freeland AE, Savoie FH, et al. Intracarpal soft-tissue lesions associated with an intra-articular fracture of the distal end of the radius. J Bone Joint Surg Am 1996;78:357–365.
94. Goyrand G. Memoire sur les fractures de l'extremite inferieure du radius qui simulent les luxations du poignet. Gaz Med 1832;3:664–667.
95. Gradl G, Jupiter JB, Gierer P, Mittlmeier T. Fractures of the distal radius treated with a nonbridging external fixation technique using multiplanar k-wires. J Hand Surg Am 2005;30:960–968.
96. Grewal R, MacDermid JC. The risk of adverse outcomes in extra-articular distal radius fractures is increased with malalignment in patients of all ages but mitigated in older patients. J Hand Surg Am 2007;32:962–970.
97. Grewal R, Perey B, Wilmink M, Stothers K. A randomized prospective study on the treatment of intra-articular distal radius fractures: open reduction and internal fixation with dorsal plating versus mini open reduction, percutaneous fixation, and external fixation. J Hand Surg Am 2005;30:764–772.
98. Gupta A. The treatment of Colles' fracture. Immobilisation with the wrist dorsiflexed. J Bone Joint Surg Br 1991;73:312–315.
99. Habernek H, Weinstabl R, Schmid L. [Anatomic studies of percutaneous bore wire osteosynthesis of the distal radius]. Unfallchirurgie 1993;19:49–53.
100. Hagino H, Yamamoto K, Ohshiro H, et al. Changing incidence of hip, distal radius, and proximal humerus fractures in Tottori Prefecture, Japan. Bone 1999;24:265–270.
101. Hanel DP, Jones MD, Trumble TE. Wrist fractures. Orthop Clin North Am 2002;33: 35–57.
102. Hahnloser D, Platz A, Amgwerd M, Trentz O. Internal fixation of distal radius fractures with dorsal dislocation: pi-plate or two 1/4 tube plates? A prospective randomized study. J Trauma 1999;47:760–765.
103. Hargreaves DG, Drew SJ, Eckersley R. Kirschner wire pin tract infection rates: a randomized controlled trial between percutaneous and buried wires. J Hand Surg Br2004; 29:374–376.
104. Harness NG, Ring D, Zurakowski D, et al. The influence of three-dimensional computed tomography reconstructions on the characterization and treatment of distal radial fractures. J Bone Joint Surg Am 2006;88:1315–1323.
105. Hassan DM, Johnston GH. Safety of the limited open technique of bone-transfixing threaded-pin placement for external fixation of distal radial fractures: a cadaver study. Can J Surg 1999;42:363–365.
106. Hayes AJ, Duffy PJ, McQueen MM. Bridging and non-bridging external fixation in the treatment of unstable fractures of the distal radius: a retrospective study of 588 cases. Acta Orthop 2008;79:540–547.
107. Herrera M, Chapman CB, Roh M, et al. Treatment of unstable distal radius fractures with cancellous allograft and external fixation. J Hand Surg Am 1999;24:1269–1278.
108. Herron M, Faraj A, Craigen MA. Dorsal plating for displaced intra-articular fractures of the distal radius. Injury 2003;34:497–502.
109. Hirahara H, Neale PG, Lin YT, et al. Kinematic and torque-related effects of dorsally angulated distal radius fractures. J Hand Surg Am 2003;28:614–621.
110. Hove LM. Delayed rupture of the thumb extensor tendon. A 5-year study of 18 consecutive cases. Acta Orthop Scand 1994;65:199–203.
111. Hove LM. Simultaneous scaphoid and distal radial fractures. J Hand Surg Br 1994;19: 384–388.
112. Hove LM. Nerve entrapment and reflex sympathetic dystrophy after fractures of the distal radius. Scand J Plast Reconstr Surg Hand Surg 1995;29:53–58.
113. Hove LM, Furnes O, Nilsen PT, et al. Closed reduction and external fixation of unstable fractures of the distal radius. Scand J Plast Reconstr Surg Hand Surg 1997;31:159–164.
114. Howard P, Stewart H, Hind R, Burke F. External fixation or plaster for severely displaced comminuted Colles' fractures? A prospective study of anatomical and functional results. J Bone Joint Surg Br 1989;71(1):68–73.
115. Huch K, Hunerbein M, Meeder PJ. External fixation of intra-articular fracture of the distal radius in young and old adults. Arch Orthop Trauma Surg 1996;115:38–42.
116. Hui SL, Slemenda CW, Johnston CC, Jr. Age and bone mass as predictors of fracture in a prospective study. J Clin Invest 1988;81:1804–1809.
117. Hunt TR, Hastings H, II, Graham T. A systematic approach to handling the distal radioulnar joint in cases of malunited distal radius fractures. Hand Clin 1998;14: 239–249.
118. Hutchinson DT, Bachus KN, Higgenbotham T. External fixation of the distal radius: to predrill or not to predrill. J Hand Surg Am 2000;25:1064–1068.
119. Hutchinson DT, Strenz GO, Cautilli RA. Pins and plaster vs external fixation in the treatment of unstable distal radial fractures. A randomized prospective study. J Hand Surg Br 1995;20:365–372.
120. Jakim I, Pieterse HS, Sweet MB. External fixation for intra-articular fractures of the distal radius. J Bone Joint Surg Br 1991;73:302–306.
121. Jakob M, Rikli DA, Regazzoni P. Fractures of the distal radius treated by internal fixation and early function. A prospective study of 73 consecutive patients. J Bone Joint Surg Br 2000;82:340–344.
122. Jenkins NH. The unstable Colles' fracture. J Hand Surg 1989;14:149–154.
123. Jenkins NH, Jones DG, Johnson SR, Mintowt-Czyz WJ. External fixation of Colles' fractures. An anatomical study. J Bone Joint Surg Br. 1987;69:207–211.
124. Jenkins N, Jones D, Mintowt-Czyz. External fixation and recovery of function following fractures of the distal radius in young adults. Injury 1988;19:235–238.
125. Jenkins NH, Mintowt-Czyz WJ. Mal-union and dysfunction in Colles' fracture. J Hand Surg Br 1988;13:291–293.
126. Johnston GH, Friedman L, Kriegler JC. Computerized tomographic evaluation of acute distal radial fractures. J Hand Surg Am 1992;17:738–744.
127. Johnson PG, Szabo RM. Angle Measurements of the Distal Radius: a Cadaver Study. Skeletal Radiology 1993;22:243–246.
128. Jupiter J, Fernandez DL. Comparative classification for fractures of the distal end of the radius. J Hand Surg Am 1997;22:563–571.
129. Jupiter JB, Fernandez DL. Complications Following Distal Radial Fractures. J Bone Joint Surg Am 2001;83:1244–1265.

124. Prevel CD. Comparative biomechanical stability of titanium bone fixation systems in metacarpal fractures. Ann Plast Surg 1995;35:6–14.
125. Prevel CD, Eppley BL, Jackson JR, et al. Mini- and micro-plating of phalangeal and metacarpal fractures: a biomechanical study. J Hand Surg 1995;20:44–49.
126. Rettig ME, Dassa G, Raskin KB. Volar plate arthroplasty of the distal interphalanageal joint. J Hand Surg 2001;26A:940–944.
127. Rosenstadt BE, Glickel SZ, Lane LB, et al. Palmar fracture dislocation of the proximal interphalangeal joint. J Hand Surg 1998;23A:811–820.
128. Roth JJ, Auerbach DM. Fixation of hand fractures with bicortical screws. J Hand Surg 2005;30:151–153.
129. Ruland RT, Hogan CJ, Cannon DL, et al. Use of dynamic distraction external fixation for unstable fracture-dislocations of the proximal interphalangeal joint. J Hand Surg 2008;33:19–25.
130. Ryu J, Fagan R. Arthroscopic treatment of acute complete thumb metacarpophalangeal ulnar collateral ligament tears. J Hand Surg 1995;20A:1037–1042.
131. Sabapathy SR, Bose VC, Rex C. Irreducible dislocation of the interphalangeal joint of the thumb due to sesamoid bone interposition: a case report. J Hand Surg 1995;20:487–489.
132. Safoury Y. Treatment of phalangeal fractures by tension band wiring. J Hand Surg 2001;26B:50–52.
133. Saint-Cyr M, Miranda D, Gonzalez R, et al. Immediate corticocancellous bone autografting in segmental bone defects of the hand. J Hand Surg 2006;31B:168–177.
134. Sarris I, Goitz RJ, Sotereanos DG. Dynamic traction and minimal internal fixation for thumb and digital pilon fractures. J Hand Surg 2004;29A:39–43.
135. Sawant N, Kulikov Y, Giddins GEB. Outcome following conservative treatment of metacarpophalangeal collateral ligament avulsion fractures of the finger. J Hand Surg 2007;32B:102–104.
136. Schortinghuis J, Klasen HJ. Open reduction and internal fixation of combined fourth and fifth carpometacarpal fracture dislocations. J Trauma 1997;42:1052–1055.
137. Shewring DJ, Thomas RH. Avulsion fractures from the base of the proximal phalanges of the fingers. J Hand Surg 2003;28B:10–14.
138. Shewring DJ, Thomas RH. Collateral ligament avulsion fractures from the heads of the metacarpals of the fingers. J Hand Surg 2006;31B:537–541.
139. Simonian PT, Trumble TE. Traumatic dislocation of the thumb carpometacarpal joint: early ligamentous reconstruction versus closed reduction and pinning. J Hand Surg 1996;21A:802–806.
140. Smith NC, Moncrieff NJ, Hartnell N, et al. Pseudorotation of the little finger metacarpal. J Hand Surg 2003;28B:395–398.
141. Sohn RC, Jahng KH, Curtiss SB, et al. Comparison of metacarpal plating methods. J Hand Surg 2008;33A:316–321.
142. Sorene ED, Goodwin DR. Nonoperative treatment of displaced avulsion fractures of the ulnar base of the proximal phalanx of the thumb. Scand J Plast Reconstr Surg Hand Surg 2003;37:225–227.
143. Stahl S, Lerner A, Kaufman T. Immediate autografting of bone in open fractures with bone loss of the hand: a preliminary report. Case reports. Scand J Plast Reconstr Surg Hand Surg 1999;33:117–122.
144. Stahl S, Schwartz O. Complications of K-wire fixation of fractures and dislocations in the hand and wrist. Arch Orthop Trauma Surg 2001;121:527–530.
145. Stanton JS, Dias JJ, Burke FD. Fractures of the tubular bones of the hand. J Hand Surg 2007;32E:626–636.
146. Stern PJ. Management of fractures of the hand over the last 25 years. J Hand Surg 2000;25A:817–823.
147. Stevenson J, McNaughton G, Riley J. The use of prophylactic flucloxacillin in treatment of open fractures of the distal phalanx within an accident and emergency department: a double-blind randomized placebo-controlled trial. J Hand Surg 2003;28B:388–394.
148. Strauch RJ, Behrman MJ, Rosenwasser MP. Acute dislocation of the carpometacarpal joint of the thumb: an anatomic and cadaver study. J Hand Surg 1994;19:93–98.
149. Strauch RJ, Rosenwasser MP, Lunt JG. Metacarpal shaft fractures: the effect of shortening on the extensor tendon mechanism. J Hand Surg 1998;23:519–523.
150. Strickler M, Nagy L, Buchler U. Rigid internal fixation of basilar fractures of the proximal phalanges by cancellous bone grafting only. J Hand Surg 2001;26B:455–458.
151. Swanson TV, Szabo RM, Anderson DD. Open hand fractures: prognosis and classification. J Hand Surg 1991;16A:101–107.
152. Syed AA, Agarwal M, Boome R. Dynamic external fixation for pilon fractures of the proximal interphalangeal joints: a simple fixator for a complex fracture. J Hand Surg 2003;28B:137–141.
153. Takami H, Takahashi S, Ando M. Operative treatment of mallet finger due to intra-articular fracture of the distal phalanx. Arch Orthop Trauma Surg 2000;120:9–13.
154. Tan V, Beredjiklian PK, Weiland AJ. Intra-articular fractures of the hand: treatment by open reduction and internal fixation. J Orthop Trauma 2005;19:518–523.
155. Teoh LC, Lee JYL. Mallet fractures: a novel approach to internal fixation using a hook plate. J Hand Surg 2007;32B:24–30.
156. Teoh LC, Tan PL, Tan SH, Cheong EC. Cerclage wiring–assisted fixation of difficult hand fractures. J Hand Surg 2006;31B:637–642.
157. Theivendran K, Pollock J, Rajaratnam V. Proximal interphalangeal joint fractures of the hand: treatment with an external dynamic traction device. Ann Plast Surg 2007;58:625–629.
158. Thurston AJ, Dempsey SM. Bennett fracture: a medium- to long-term review. Aust NZ J Surg 1993;63:120–123.
159. Timmenga EJF, Blokhuis TJ, Maas M, et al. Long-term evaluation of Bennett. A comparison between open and closed reduction. J Hand Surg 1994;19B:373–377.
160. Trevisan C, Morganti A, Casiraghi A, et al. Low-severity metacarpal and phalangeal fractures treated with miniature plates and screws. Arch Orthop Trauma Surg 2004;124:675–680.
161. Trumble T, Gilbert M. In situ osteotomy for extra-articular malunion of the proximal phalanx. J Hand Surg 1998;23A:821–826.
162. Twyman RS, David HG. The doorstop procedure. A technique for treating unstable fracture dislocations of the proximal interphalangeal joint. J Hand Surg 1993;18B:714–715.
163. Vahey JW, Wegner DA, Hastings H II. Effect of proximal phalangeal fracture deformity on extensor tendon function. J Hand Surg 1998;23A:673–681.
164. Van Brenk B, Richards RR, Mackay MB, et al. A biomechanical assessment of ligaments preventing dorsoradial subluxation of the trapeziometacarpal joint. J Hand Surg 1998;23:607–611.
165. Van Onselen EBH, Karim RB, Hage JJ, et al. Prevalence and distribution of hand fractures. J Hand Surg 2003;28B:491–495.
166. Van Oosterom FJT, Brete GJV, Ozdemir C. Treatment of phalangeal fractures in severely injured hands. J Hand Surg 2001;26B:108–111.
167. Viegas SF. Extension block pinning for proximal interphalangeal joint fracture dislocations: preliminary report of a new technique. J Hand Surg 1992;17A:896–901.
168. Waris E, Ashammakhi N, Happonen H, et al. Bioabsorbable miniplating versus metallic fixation for metacarpal fractures. Clin Orthop 2003;410:310–319.
169. Waris E, Ashammakhi N, Raatikainen T, et al. Self-reinforced bioabsorbable versus metallic fixation systems for metacarpal and phalangeal fractures: a biomechanical study. J Hand Surg 2002;27:902–909.
170. Weiland AJ, Berner SH, Hotchkiss RN, et al. Repair of acute ulnar collateral ligament injuries of the thumb metacarpophalangeal joint with an intraosseous suture anchor. J Hand Surg 1997;22A:585–591.
171. Weiss APC. Cerclage fixation for fracture dislocation of the PIP joint. Clin Orthop 1996;327:21–28.
172. Weiss APC. Intramedullary Herbert screws for treatment of phalangeal nonunion. Tech Hand Upper Ext Surg 1997;1:41–47.
173. Weiss APC, Hastings H II. Distal unicondylar fractures of the proximal phalanx. J Hand Surg 1993;18A:594–599.
174. Widgerow AD, Ladas CS. Anatomical attachments to the proximal phalangeal base: a case for stability. Scand J Plast Reconstr Surg Hand Surg 2001;35:85–90.
175. Williams RMM, Kiefhaber TR, Sommerkamp TG, et al. Treatment of unstable dorsal proximal interphalangeal fracture/dislocations using a hemi-hamate autograft. J Hand Surg 2003;28:856–865.
176. Wong T-C, Ip FK, Yeung SH. Comparison between percutaneous transverse fixation and intramedullary K-wires in treating closed fractures of the metacarpal neck of the little finger. J Hand Surg 2006;31B:61–65.
177. Yoshida R, Shah MA, Patterson RM, et al. Anatomy and pathomechanics of ring and small finger carpometacarpal joint injuries. J Hand Surg 2003;28:1035–1043.
178. Yong FC, Tan SH, Tow BPB, et al. Trapezoid rotational bone graft osteotomy for metacarpal and phalangeal fracture malunion. J Hand Surg 2007;32B:282–288.

29

CARPUS FRACTURES AND DISLOCATIONS

Christian Gaebler and Margaret M. McQueen

130. Jupiter JB, Fernandez DL, Toh CL, et al. Operative treatment of volar intra-articular fractures of the distal end of the radius. J Bone Joint Surg Am 1996;78:1817–1828.
131. Jupiter JB, Ring D, Weitzel PP. Surgical treatment of redisplaced fractures of the distal radius in patients older than 60 years. J Hand Surg Am 2002;27:714–723.
132. Kaempffe FA. External fixation for distal radius fractures: adverse effects of excess distraction. Am J Orthop 1996;25:205–209.
133. Kaempffe FA, Walker KM. External fixation for distal radius fractures: effect of distraction on outcome. Clin Orthop 2000;380:220–225.
134. Kamano M, Honda Y, Kazuki K, Yasuda M. Palmar plating for dorsally displaced fractures of the distal radius. Clin Orthop 2002;397:403–408.
135. Kato N, Nemoto K, Arino H, et al. Ruptures of flexor tendons at the wrist as a complication of fracture of the distal radius. Scand J Plast Reconstr Surg Hand Surg 2002;36: 245–248.
136. Kaukonen JP, Karaharju EO, Porras M, et al. Functional recovery after fractures of the distal forearm. Analysis of radiographic and other factors affecting the outcome. Ann Chir Gynaecol 1988;77:27–31.
137. Kazuki K, Kusunoki M, Yamada J, et al. Cineradiographic study of wrist motion after fracture of the distal radius. J Hand Surg Am 1993;18:41–46.
138. Kazuteru D, Hattori Y, Otsuka K, et al. Intraarticular fractures of the distal aspect of the radius: Arthroscopically assisted reduction compared with open reduction and internal fixation. J Bone Joint Surg Am 1999;81:1093–1110.
139. Keating JF, Court-Brown CM, McQueen MM. Internal fixation of volar-displaced distal radial fractures. J Bone Joint Surg Br 1994;76:401–405.
140. Kihara H, Palmer AK, Werner F, et al. The effect of dorsally angulated distal radius fractures on distal radiolunar joint congruency and forearm rotation. J Hand Surg Am 1996;21:40–47.
141. Klug RA, Press CM, Gonzalez MH. Rupture of the flexor pollicis longus tendon after volar fixed-angle plating of a distal radius fracture: a case report. J Hand Surg Am 2007;32:984–988.
142. Knirk JL, Jupiter JB. Intra-articular fractures of the distal end of the radius in young adults. J Bone Joint Surg Am 1986;68:647–659.
143. Konrath GA, Bahler S. Open reduction and internal fixation of unstable distal radius fractures: results using the trimed fixation system. J Orthop Trauma 2002;16:578–585.
144. Kopylov P, Johnell O, Redlund-Johnell I, et al. Fractures of the distal end of the radius in young adults: a 30-year follow-up. J Hand Surg Br 1993;18:45–49.
145. Kreder HJ, Hanel DP, McKee M, et al. X-ray film measurements for healed distal radius fractures. J Hand Surg Am 1996;21:31–39.
146. Kreder HJ, Agel J, McKee MD, et al. A randomized, controlled trial of distal radius fractures with metaphyseal displacement but without joint incongruity: closed reduction and casting versus closed reduction, spanning external fixation, and optional percutaneous K-wires. J Orthop Trauma 2006;20:115–121.
147. Kreder HJ, Hanel DP, Agel J, et al. Indirect reduction and percutaneous fixation versus open reduction and internal fixation for displaced intra-articular fractures of the distal radius: a randomised, controlled trial. J Bone Joint Surg Br 2005;87:829–836.
148. Krishnan J, Chipchase LS, Slavotinek J. Intraarticular fractures of the distal radius treated with metaphyseal external fixation. Early clinical results. J Hand Surg Br 1998; 23:396–399.
149. Krishnan J, Wigg AER, Walker RW, et al. Intra-articular fractures of the distal radius: a prospective randomised controlled trial comparing static bridging and dynamic non-bridging external fixation. J Hand Surg Br 2003; 28:417–421.
150. Kuner EH, Mellios K, Berwarth H. Treatment of complicated fracture of the distal radius with external fixator. Follow-up—complications—outcomes. Unfallchirurg 2002;105: 199–207.
151. Kwasny O, Fuchs M, Schabus R. Opening wedge osteotomy for malunion of the distal radius with neuropathy. 13 cases followed for 6 (1–11) years. Acta Orthop Scand 1994;65:207–208.
152. Laulan J, Bismuth JP. Intracarpal ligamentous lesions associated with fractures of the distal radius: outcome at one year. A prospective study of 95 cases. Acta Orthop Belg 1999;65:418–423.
153. Lee HC, Wong YS, Chan BK, et al. Fixation of distal radius fractures using AO titanium volar distal radius plate. Hand Surg 2003;8:7–15.
154. Lester GE, Anderson JJ, Tylavsky FA, et al. Update on the use of distal radial bone density measurements in prediction of hip and Colles' fracture risk. J Orthop Res 1990; 8:220–226.
155. Leung F, Ozkan M, Chow SP. Conservative treatment of intra-articular fractures of the distal radius—factors affecting functional outcome. Hand Surg 2000;5:145–153.
156. Leung F, Tu YK, Chew WY, et al. Comparison of external and percutaneous pin fixation with plate fixation for intra-articular distal radial fractures. A randomized study. J Bone Joint Surg Am 2008;90:16–22.
157. Leung F, Zhu L, Ho H. Palmar plate fixation of AO type C2 fracture of distal radius using a locking compression plate—a biomechanical study in a cadaveric model. J Hand Surg Br 2003;28:263–266.
158. Leung KS, Shen W, Leung P, et al. Ligamentotaxis and bone grafting for comminuted fractures of the distal radius. J Bone Joint Surg Br 1989;71:838–842.
159. Leung KS, So W, Chiu V, et al. Ligamentotaxis for comminuted distal radial fractures modified by primary cancellous grafting and functional bracing: long-term results. J Orthop Trauma 1991;5:265–271.
160. Lindau T, Adlercreutz C, Aspenberg P. Peripheral tears of the triangular fibrocartilage complex cause distal radioulnar joint instability after distal radial fractures. J Hand Surg Am 2000;25:464–468.
161. Lindau T, Adlercreutz C, Aspenberg P. Cartilage injuries in distal radial fractures. Acta Orthop Scand 2003;74:327–331.
162. Lindau T, Arner M, Hagberg L. Intraarticular lesions in distal fractures of the radius in young adults. A descriptive arthroscopic study in 50 patients. J Hand Surg Br 1997; 22:638–643.
163. Lindau TR, Aspenberg P, Arner M, et al. Fractures of the distal forearm in young adults. An epidemiologic description of 341 patients. Acta Orthop Scand 1999;70:124–128.
164. Lindau T, Hagberg L, Adlercreutz C, et al. Distal radioulnar instability is an independent worsening factor in distal radial fractures. Clin Orthop 2000;376:229–235.
165. Linder L, Stattin J. Malunited fractures of the distal radius with volar angulation: corrective osteotomy in 6 cases using the volar approach. Acta Orthop Scand 1996;67: 179–181.
166. Lowry KJ, Gainor BJ, Hoskins JS. Extensor tendon rupture secondary to the AO/ASIF titanium distal radius plate without associated plate failure: a case report. Am J Orthop 2000;29:789–791.
167. Lozano-Calderon SA, Doornberg J, Ring D. Fractures of the dorsal articular margin of the distal part of the radius with dorsal radiocarpal subluxation. J Bone Joint Surg Am 2006;88:1486–1493.
168. Lucas GL, Fejfar ST. Complications in internal fixation of the distal radius. J Hand Surg Am 1998;23:1117.
169. Lundy D, Quisling S, Lourie G, et al. Tilted lateral radiographs in the evaluation of intra-articular distal radius fractures. J Hand Surg Am 1999;24:249–256.
170. McAuliffe TB, Hilliar KM, Coates CJ, et al. Early mobilisation of Colles' fractures. A prospective trial. J Bone Joint Surg Br 1987;69:727–729.
171. McClain EJ, Wissinger HA. The acute carpal tunnel syndrome: nine case reports. J Trauma 1976;16:75–78.
172. McQueen MM. Redisplaced fractures of the distal radius. A randomised prospective study of bridging versus non-bridging external fixation. J Bone Joint Surg Br 1998;80; 665–669.
173. McQueen M, Caspers J. Colles' Fracture: Does the anatomical result afftect the final function? J Bone Joint Surg Br 1988;70:649–651.
174. McQueen MM, Hajducka C, Court-Brown C. Redisplaced unstable fractures of the distal radius: A randomised, prospective study of bridging versus non-bridging external fixation. J Bone Joint Surg Br 1996;78:404–409.
175. McQueen MM, Maclaren A, Chalmers J. The value of remanipulating Colles' fractures. J Bone Joint Surg Br1986;68:232–233.
176. McQueen MM, Simpson D, Court-Brown CM. Metaphyseal external fixation of redisplaced unstable distal radial fractures. Use of the Hoffman 2 compact external fixator. J Orthop Trauma 1999;13:501–505.
177. McQueen MM, Wakefield A. Distal radial osteotomy for malunion using non-bridging external fixation: good results in 23 patients.Acta Orthop 2008;79:390–395.
178. Maciel JS, Taylor NF, McIlveen C. A randomised clinical trial of activity-focussed physiotherapy on patients with distal radius fractures. Arch Orthop Trauma Surg 2005; 125:515–520.
179. Mackenney PJ. Re: An evaluation of two scoring systems to predict instability in fractures of the distal radius. J Trauma 2005;59:1535.
180. Mackenney PJ, McQueen MM, Elton R. Prediction of instability in distal radial fractures. J Bone Joint Surg Am 2006;88:1944–1951.
181. Madhok R, Green S. Longer term functional outcome and societal implications of upper limb fractures in the elderly. J R Soc Health 1993;113:179–180.
182. Mallmin H, Ljunghall S. Incidence of Colles' fracture in Uppsala. A prospective study of a quarter-million population. Acta Orthop Scand 1992;63:213–215.
183. Mallmin H, Ljunghall S, Naessen T. Colles' fracture associated with reduced bone mineral content. Photon densitometry in 74 patients with matched controls. Acta Orthop Scand 1992;63:552–554.
184. Mallmin H, Ljunghall S, Persson I, et al. Risk factors for fractures of the distal forearm: a population-based case-control study. Osteoporos Int 1994;4:298–304.
185. Malone KJ, Magnell TD, Freeman DC, et al. Surgical correction of dorsally angulated distal radius malunions with fixed angle volar plating: a case series. J Hand Surg Am 2006;31:366–372.
186. Markiewitz AD, Gellman H. Five-pin external fixation and early range of motion for distal radius fractures. Orthop Clin North Am 2001;32:329–335.
187. Masud T, Jordan D, Hosking DJ. Distal forearm fracture history in an older community-dwelling population: the Nottingham Community Osteoporosis (NOCOS) study. Age Ageing 2001;30:255–258.
188. May MM, Lawton JN, Blazar PE. Ulnar styloid fractures associated with distal radius fractures: incidence and implications for distal radioulnar joint instability. J Hand Surg Am 2002;27:965–971.
189. Melendez EM. Opening-wedge osteotomy, bone graft, and external fixation for correction of radius malunion. J Hand Surg Am 1997;22:785–791.
190. Melone CP, Melone C. Open treatment for displaced articular fractures of the distal radius. Clin Orthop 1986;202:103–111.
191. Melone CP. Distal radius fractures: Patterns of articular fragmentation. Orthop Clin North Am 1993;24:239–253.
192. Mensforth RP, Latimer BM. Hamann-Todd Collection aging studies: osteoporosis fracture syndrome. Am J Phys Anthropol 1989;80:461–479.
193. Miller BS, Taylor B, Widmann RF, et al. Cast immobilization versus percutaneous pin fixation of displaced distal radius fractures in children: a prospective, randomized study. J Pediatr Orthop 2005;25:490–494.
194. Miller SW, Evans JG. Fractures of the distal forearm in Newcastle: an epidemiological survey. Age Ageing 1985;14:155–158.
195. Minami A, Ogino T. Midcarpal instability following malunion of a fracture of the distal radius. A case report. Ital J Orthop Traumatol 1986;12:473–477.
196. Missakian M, Cooney W, Amadio P, et al. Open reduction and internal fixation for distal radius fractures. J Hand Surg Am 1992;17:745–755.
197. Moore DC, Hogan KA, Crisco JJ, III, et al. Three-dimensional in vivo kinematics of the distal radioulnar joint in malunited distal radius fractures. J Hand Surg Am 2002; 27:233–242.
198. Mudgal CS, Psenica J, Jupiter JB. Radiocarpal fracture-dislocation. J Hand Surg Br 1999; 24:92–98.
199. Musgrave DS, Idler RS. Volar fixation of dorsally displaced distal radius fractures using the 2.4mm locking compression plates. J Hand Surg Am 2005;30:743–749.
200. Nguyen TV, Center JR, Sambrook PN, et al. Risk factors for proximal humerus, forearm, and wrist fractures in elderly men and women: the Dubbo Osteoporosis Epidemiology Study. Am J Epidemiol 2001;153:587–595.
201. Nicolaidis SC, Hildreth DH, Lichtman DM. Acute injuries of the distal radioulnar joint. Hand Clin 2000;16:449–459.
202. O'Neill TW, Cooper C, Finn JD, et al.Incidence of distal forearm fracture in British men and women.Osteoporos Int 2001;12:555–558.
203. Orbay JL, Fernandez DL. Volar fixation for dorsally displaced fractures of the distal radius: a preliminary report. J Hand Surg Am 2002;27:205–215.
204. Oshige T, Sakai A, Zenke Y, et al. A comparative study of clinical and radiological outcomes of dorsally angulated, unstable distal radius fractures in elderly patients: intrafocal pinning versus volar locking plating. J Hand Surg Am 2007;32:1385–1392.
205. Oskam J, Kingma J, Klasen HJ. Ulnar-shortening osteotomy after fracture of the distal radius. Arch Orthop Trauma Surg 1993;112:198–200.

206. Pogue DJ, Viegas SF, Patterson RM, et al. Effects of distal radius fracture malunion on wrist joint mechanics. J Hand Surg Am 1990;15:721–727.

207. Pool C. Colles's fracture. A prospective study of treatment. J Bone Joint Surg Br 1973; 55:540–544.

208. Porter M, Stockley I. Fractures of the distal radius. Intermediate and end results in relation to radiologic parameters. Clin Orthop 1987;220:241–252.

209. Prokop A, Swol-Ben J, Rehm KE. Treatment methods for geriatric patients at the Traumatology Clinic at the University of Cologne—retrospective studies. Chir Narzadow Ruchu Ortop Pol 1996;61:315–318.

210. Prommersberger KJ, Lanz U. [Biomechanical aspects of malunited distal radius fracture. A review of the literature.] Handchir Mikrochir Plast Chir 1999;31:221–226.

211. Prommersberger KJ, Ring D, del Pino JG, et al. Corrective osteotomy for intra-articular malunion of the distal part of the radius. Surgical technique. J Bone Joint Surg Am 2006;88(Suppl 1, Pt 2):202–211.

212. Putnam MD, Fischer MD. Treatment of unstable distal radius fractures: methods and comparison of external distraction and ORIF versus external distraction-ORIF neutralization. J Hand Surg Am 1997;22:238–251.

213. Rein S, Schikore H, Schneiders W, et al. Results of dorsal or volar plate fixation of AO type C3 distal radius fractures: a retrospective study. J Hand Surg Am 2007;32: 954–961.

214. Reuben SS, Pristas R, Dixon D, et al. The incidence of CRPS after fasciectomy for Dupuytren's contracture: a prospective observational study of from anaesthetic techniques. Anaesth Analg 2006;102:499–503.

215. Richards RS, Bennett JD, Roth JH, et al. Arthroscopic diagnosis of intra-articular soft tissue injuries associated with distal radial fractures. J Hand Surg Am 1997;22: 772–776.

216. Riis J, Fruensgaard S. Treatment of unstable Colles' fractures by external fixation. J Hand Surg Br 1989;14:145–148.

217. Rikli DA, Kupfer K, Bodoky A. Long-term results of the external fixation of distal radius fractures. J Trauma 1998;44:970–976.

218. Ring D, Jupiter JB, Brennwald J, et al. Prospective multicenter trial of a plate for dorsal fixation of distal radius fractures. J Hand Surg Am 1997;22:777–784.

219. Ring D, Kadzielski J, Fabian L, et al. Self-reported upper extremity health status correlates with depression. J Bone Joint Surg Am 2006;88:1983–1988.

220. Rodriguez Merchan EC, de la Corte H. Injuries of the distal radioulnar joint. Contemp Orthop 1994;29:193–200.

221. Rosenthal AH, Chung KC. Intrafocal pinning of distal radius fractures: a simplified approach. Ann Plast Surg 2002;48:593–599.

222. Roysam GS. The distal radio-ulnar joint in Colles' fractures. J Bone Joint Surg Br 1993; 75:58–60.

223. Rozental TD, Beredjiklian PK, Bozentka DJ. Functional outcome and complications following two types of dorsal plating for unstable fractures of the distal part of the radius. J Bone Joint Surg Am 2003;85:1956–1960.

224. Rozental TD, Blazar PE. Functional outcome and complications after volar plating for dorsally displaced, unstable fractures of the distal radius. J Hand Surg Am 2006;31: 359–365.

225. Rozental TD, Branas CC, Bozentka DJ, et al. Survival among elderly patients after fractures of the distal radius. J Hand Surg Am 2002;27:948–952.

226. Ruch DS, Ginn TA. Open reduction and internal fixation of distal radius fractures. Operative Techniques in Orthopaedics 2003;13:138–143.

227. Ruch DS, Papadonikolakis A. Volar versus dorsal plating in the management of intra-articular distal radius fractures. J Hand Surg Am 2006;31:9–16.

228. Ruch DS, Vallee J, Poehling GG, et al. Arthroscopic reduction versus fluoroscopic reduction in the management of intra-articular distal radius fractures. Arthroscopy 2004;20:225–230.

229. Ruch DS, Yang CC, Smith BP. Results of acute arthroscopically repaired triangular fibrocartilage complex injuries associated with intra-articular distal radius fractures. Arthroscopy 2003;19:511–516.

230. Ruch DS, Yang C, Smith BP. Results of palmar plating of the lunate facet combined with external fixation for the treatment of high-energy compression fractures of the distal radius. J Orthop Trauma 2004;18:28–33.

231. Saeki Y, Hashizume H, Nagoshi M, et al. Mechanical strength of intramedullary pinning and transfragmental Kirschner wire fixation for Colles' fractures. J Hand Surg Br 2001; 26:550–555.

232. Sanchez-Sotelo J, Munuera L, Madero R. Treatment of fractures of the distal radius with a remodellable bone cement. J Bone Joint Surg Br 2000;82:856–863.

233. Sanders RA, Keppel FL, Waldrop JI. External fixation of distal radial fractures: results and complications. J Hand Surg Am 1991;16:385–391.

234. Sato S. Load transmission through the wrist joint: a biomechanical study comparing the normal and pathological wrist. Nippon Seikeigeka Gakkai Zasshi 1995;69:470–483.

235. Schmalholz A. Epidemiology of distal radius fracture in Stockholm 1981–82. Acta Orthop Scand 1988;59:701–703.

236. Schnur DP, Chang B. Extensor tendon rupture after internal fixation of a distal radius fracture using a dorsally placed AO/ASIF titanium pi plate. Ann Plast Surg 2000;44: 564–566.

237. Seitz WH, Jr., Froimson AI, Leb R, Shapiro JD. Augmented external fixation of unstable distal radius fractures. J Hand Surg Am 1991;16:1010–1016.

238. Shaw JA, Bruno A, Paul EM. Ulnar styloid fixation in the treatment of posttraumatic instability of the radioulnar joint: a biomechanical study with clinical correlation. J Hand Surg Am 1990;15:712–720.

239. Short WH, Palmer AK, Werner FW, et al. A biomechanical study of distal radial fractures. J Hand Surg Am1987;12A:529–534.

240. Smith AM, Castle JA, Ruch DS. Arthroscopic resection of the common extensor origin: anatomic considerations. J Shoulder Elbow Surg 2003;12:375–379.

241. Smith RS, Crick JC, Alonso J, et al. Open reduction and internal fixation of volar lip fractures of the distal radius. J Orthop Trauma 1988;2:181–187.

242. Smith DW., Henry MH. Volar Fixed angle plating of the distal radius. J Am Acad Orth Surg 2005;13:28–36

243. Solgaard S. Function after distal radius fracture. Acta Orthop Scand 1988;59:39–42.

244. Solgaard S, Bunger C, Sllund K. Displaced distal radius fractures. A comparative study of early results following external fixation, functional bracing in supination, or dorsal plaster immobilization. Arch Orthop Trauma Surg 1990;109:34–38.

245. Solgaard S, Petersen VS. Epidemiology of distal radius fractures. Acta Orthop Scand 1985;56:391–393.

246. Soong M, Ring D. Ulnar nerve palsy associated with fracture of the distal radius. J Orthop Trauma 2007;21:113–116.

247. Stewart HD, Innes AR, Burke FD. Functional cast-bracing for Colles' fractures. A comparison between cast-bracing and conventional plaster casts. J Bone Joint Surg Br 1984; 66:749–753.

248. Stoffelen DV, Broos PL. Closed reduction versus Kapandji-pinning for extra-articular distal radial fractures. J Hand Surg Br 1999;24:89–91.

249. Strauss EJ, Banerjee D, Kummer FJ, Tejwani NC. Evaluation of a novel, nonspanning external fixator for treatment of unstable extra-articular fractures of the distal radius: biomechanical comparison with a volar locking plate. J Trauma 2008;64:975–981.

250. Swiontkowski MF. Increasing rates of forearm fractures in children. JAMA 2003 24; 290:3193.

251. Szabo RM. Extra-articular fractures of the distal radius. Orthop Clin North Am 1993; 24:229–237.

252. Takami H, Takahashi S, Ando M. Comminuted intra-articular fracture of the distal radius with rotation of the palmar medial articular fragment: case reports. J Trauma 1992;32:404–407.

253. Taleisnik J, Watson HK. Midcarpal instability caused by malunited fractures of the distal radius. J Hand Surg Am 1984;9:350–357.

254. Tang JB, Shi D, Gu YQ, et al. Can cast immobilization successfully treat scapholunate dissociation associated with distal radius fractures? J Hand Surg Am 1996;21:583–590.

255. Trumble TE, Benirschke SK, Vedder NB. Ipsilateral fractures of the scaphoid and radius. J Hand Surg Am 1993;18:8–14.

256. Trumble TE, Schmitt S, Vedder NB. Factors affecting functional outcome of displaced intra-articular distal radius fractures. J Hand Surg Am 1994;19:325–340.

257. Trumble TE, Wagner W, Hanel DP, et al. Intrafocal (Kapandji) pinning of distal radius fractures with and without external fixation. J Hand Surg Am 1998;23:381–394.

258. Tsukazaki T, Takagi K, Iwasaki K. Poor correlation between functional results and radiographic findings in Colles' fracture. J Hand Surg Br 1993;18:588–591.

259. van der Linden W, Ericson R. Colles' fracture. How should its displacement be measured and how should it be immobilized? J Bone Joint Surg Am 1981;63:1285–1288.

260. Van Cauwelaert de Wyels J, De Smet L. Corrective osteotomy for malunion of the distal radius in young and middle-aged patients: an outcome study. Chir Main 2003;22: 84–89.

261. Vang Hansen F, Staunstrup H, Mikkelsen S. A comparison of 3 and 5 weeks immobilization for older type 1 and 2 Colles' fractures. J Hand Surg Br 1998 23:400–401.

262. Viso R, Wegener EE, Freeland AE. Use of a closing wedge osteotomy to correct malunion of dorsally displaced extra-articular distal radius fractures. Orthopedics 2000; 23:721–724.

263. Wakefield A, McQueen MM. The role of physiotherapy and clinical predictors of outcome after distal radial fracture. J Bone Joint Surg 2000;82:972–976.

264. Walton NP, Brammar TJ, Hutchinson J, et al. Treatment of unstable distal radial fractures by intrafocal, intramedullary K-wires. Injury 2001;32:383–389.

265. Wagner WF, Tencer AF, Kiser P. Effects of intra-articular distal radius depression on wrist joint contact characteristics. J Hand Surg Am 1996;21:554–560.

266. Waters PM, Kolettis GJ, Schwend R. Acute median neuropathy following physeal fractures of the distal radius. J Pediatr Orthop 1994;14:173–177.

267. Watson HK, Castle TH, Jr. Trapezoidal osteotomy of the distal radius for unacceptable articular angulation after Colles' fracture. J Hand Surg Am 1988;13:837–843.

268. Weber SC, Szabo RM. Severely comminuted distal radial fracture as an unsolved problem: complications associated with external fixation and pins and plaster techniques. J Hand Surg Am 1986;11:157–165.

269. Werber KD, Raeder F, Brauer RB, et al. External fixation of distal radial fractures: four compared with five pins: a randomized prospective study. J Bone Joint Surg Am 2003; 85:660–666.

270. Wright S, Beringer T, Taggart H, et al. A study of male patients with forearm fracture in Northern Ireland. Clin Rheumatol 2007;26:191–195.

271. Young CF, Nanu AM, Checketts RG. Seven-year outcome following Colles' type distal radial fracture. A comparison of two treatment methods. J Hand Surg Br 2003;28: 422–426.

272. Young BT, Rayan GM. Outcome following nonoperative treatment of displaced distal radius fractures in low-demand patients older than 60 years. J Hand Surg 2000;25: 19–28.

273. Zemel NP. The prevention and treatment of complications from fractures of the distal radius and ulna. Hand Clin 1987;3:1–11.

274. Zmurko MG, Eglseder WA, Jr., Belkoff SM. Biomechanical evaluation of distal radius fracture stability. J Orthop Trauma 1998 ;12:46–50.

RADIAL AND ULNAR SHAFT FRACTURES

Shew-Ping Chow and Frankie Leung

INTRODUCTION

The human forearm is adapted more for mobility than stability. In fish, amphibians, and birds, the forearm skeletons are rigid in order to provide stability. In reptiles and some mammals, the huge pisiform contributes to a three-bone forearm skeleton articulating with the carpal bones and thus allowing only side-to-side movement. The appearance of bipedalism in evolution freed the upper extremity from the requirements of support, placing greater emphasis on increasing mobility rather than stability.[2] The recession of the pisiform from the forearm and the appearance of the synovial distal radioulnar joint (DRUJ) were the crucial steps in the development of pronation and supination, which greatly increased the mobility of the forearm and the wrist.

The human forearm serves an important role in upper extremity function, facilitating placement of the hand in space thus helping to provide the upper extremity with its unique mobility. The presence of the proximal and distal radioulnar joints allows pronation and supination, and such movements are important to all of us in the usual activities of daily living. Moreover, the forearm serves as the origin for muscles inserting on the hand. Therefore, fractures involving the bones of the forearm present unique problems not encountered with fractures of other long bones and may significantly affect the function of the upper limb.

Anatomic reduction and internal fixation of forearm fractures can facilitate restoration of function and is now the standard for treatment of fractures of the shaft of the forearm. This is supported by the good results of rigid plate fixation in many studies. Dynamic compression plating has been used in the past. In an attempt to preserve vascularity of the bone, new plates with limited contact between the plate and the bone have been devised. A new locking screw concept has also been introduced in plate fixation of forearm fractures.

This chapter includes a discussion of fractures of the shafts of forearm, fracture-dislocations involving fractures of the radius associated with DRUJ injury (Galeazzi fracture), and fractures of the ulna associated with proximal radioulnar joint injury

(Monteggia fracture). A description of the Essex-Lopresti injury is also included.

PRINCIPLES OF MANAGEMENT

Mechanisms of Injury

Various mechanisms of injury are involved in fractures of the radius and ulna. Common to all, a significant energy of trauma must be present before the forearm bones can be broken. Most forearm diaphyseal fractures are caused by a fall from standing height, a direct blow, or a road traffic accident. Causes of direct blow injuries include fights in which the victim is struck on the forearm with a hard object. By instinct, the victim lifts up the forearm to defend against an attacker and to protect his or her head. The forearm is then the recipient of the violence. An isolated fracture of the ulna shaft resulting from such a direct blow, known as a nightstick fracture, can occur at any site along the ulnar length. It is often more stable than other forearm fractures, especially if the displacement is less than 50% when there is less injury to the interosseous membrane.[22]

Open fractures of the forearm may result in significant disability with damage to associated tendons and nerves. A common cause of open fractures is gunshot injury. Besides nerve or soft tissue injuries, there is frequently significant bone loss, leading to delay in healing and the necessity for additional surgery.

History and Physical Examination

Fractures of the shaft of the radius and ulna are often displaced. This is usually due to the significant force causing the fracture in adults and also the fact that the pull of the fracture fragments by the forearm muscle tends to accentuate the displacement. As a result of the displacement and the instability, the diagnosis can easily be made from the signs and symptoms, including pain, deformity, and loss of function. In nightstick fractures, palpation along the subcutaneous border of the ulna usually elicits tenderness at the level of the fracture. Some degree of swelling is almost always present and is usually related to both the force causing the injury and the time since the injury.

Physical examination should include a careful neurologic evaluation of the motor and sensory functions of the radial, median, and ulnar nerves, especially in open fractures with penetrating injury which are commonly associated with nerve and major blood vessel injury. If the forearm is swollen and tense, a compartment syndrome may be present or may be developing. In such cases, pain on passive stretch as well as neurologic deficit should be sought. Compartment pressures should then be measured and immediate treatment by fasciotomy is required when a compartment syndrome is diagnosed (see Chapter 27).

In forearm fractures due to high-energy trauma, associated injuries to the soft tissues, particularly the ligaments of the elbow and the wrist, are often seen. There are three such lesions that are associated with forearm fractures: the Monteggia, Galeazzi, and Essex-Lopresti lesions. Prompt recognition of these injuries is important, since the correct treatment should consist of both adequate fracture stabilization and accurate restoration of the normal wrist and elbow articulation. In order to achieve this, soft tissue repair and reconstruction is sometimes needed. These three injuries are described in the following section.

Monteggia Fracture–Dislocation

Fractures of the proximal ulna with a concomitant dislocation of the radial head are uncommon injuries that comprise less than 5% of all forearm fractures. This injury was first described by Monteggia in 1814.

Typically, a patient with a Monteggia fracture dislocation will complain of pain about the elbow and a mechanical block to elbow flexion and forearm rotation. Depending on the type of Monteggia injury, the radial head may be palpable over the anterior or posterior aspect of the elbow.

It is important to perform a careful examination of the nerves, especially the posterior interosseous nerve with a reported incidence as high as 17%.[11] The cause of the injury is often due to stretching of the nerve by a dislocated radial head. According to the reports by Spinner[95] and later Boyd and Boals,[9] all of these nerve palsies recover spontaneously. However, entrapment of the posterior interosseous nerve causing a Monteggia lesion to be irreducible has occasionally been reported.[75,94,105] In these rare situations, an open exploration of the nerve should be performed. Even with successful closed reduction of the radioulnar articulation, if there is no return of function by 8 weeks, a surgical exploration and decompression of the nerve is advocated.[54] Injuries of other nerves, including the anterior interosseous nerve,[26] median nerve, and ulnar nerve can also occur.

Galeazzi Fracture–Dislocation

Fracture of the radius at the junction of the middle and distal thirds commonly occurs in association with a dislocation of the DRUJ (Fig. 31-1). This lesion, reported by Galeazzi[30] in 1934, is characterized by its unstable nature and the need for open reduction and internal fixation to achieve a satisfactory functional outcome. A high index of suspicion should be maintained by the surgeon, especially when the radiographs show a widened gap between the distal radius and the ulna and a relative shortening of the radius. Any instability of the DRUJ must be detected by careful ballottement after the radius fracture has been surgically stabilized.

The instability of this fracture–dislocation complex results from the large force that caused the radial shaft fracture and was then transmitted via the interosseous membrane to the ulna. The ulnar head is dislocated and tearing of the triangular fibrocartilage complex occurs, rendering the entire DRUJ complex unstable. The ulnar styloid may be fractured. A special type of Galeazzi injury with both the radial and ulnar shaft fractured[71] can also occur, and sometimes disruption of the distal radioulnar joint may be overlooked.

Essex-Lopresti Injury

This lesion was described by Essex-Lopresti[27] in 1951 and is a rare complex injury of the forearm that may be best described as a radioulnar dissociation. It usually occurs after a fall on the outstretched hand, resulting in a fracture of the head of the radius and disruption of both the interosseous membrane and the DRUJ leading to proximal migration of the radius. It is often missed because of the attention directed to the radial head fracture to the exclusion of the rest of the forearm. The pathomechanics of the proximal migration of the radius was shown by Hotchkiss et al.[50] to be a result of the large force causing the fracture and concomitant disruption of the DRUJ together with the interosseous membrane. Besides radial head fractures, such

It is important to detect disruption of the elbow and wrist joints as they have significant implications for prognosis and treatment. In cases where there is uncertainty about the integrity of the proximal or DRUJs, an oblique view can also be taken. In any of the projections of the proximal forearm, a line drawn through the proximal radial shaft and the center of the radial head should pass through the center of the capitellum,[69] as shown in Figure 31-2.

With possible DRUJ disruption, there is widening of the DRUJ space and shortening of the radius in relation to the distal

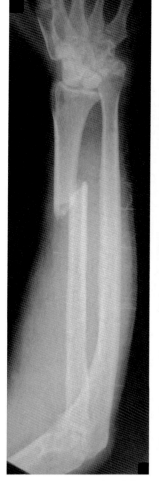
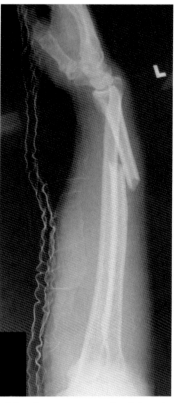

A   **B**

FIGURE 31-1 A Galeazzi fracture dislocation. Anteroposterior **(A)** and lateral **(B)** views.

proximal migration of radius and disruption of DRUJ joint has also been associated with Galeazzi fracture,[58] radial shaft fracture,[24] and elbow dislocation.[7]

The clinical features at the elbow are similar to those of radial head fractures. Hence, Essex-Lopresti injuries can easily be overlooked or the correct diagnosis is delayed unless a careful history is taken to elicit symptoms of wrist pain and examination of the forearm and wrist is performed. All patients with comminuted radial head fractures should have radiographs of their wrists to assess radial length.

Radiographic Findings

Conventional anteroposterior and lateral radiographs of the forearm are usually sufficient to diagnose a forearm fracture. The elbow and wrist must be included in order to exclude associated articular fractures or fracture–dislocations and especially any Monteggia, Galeazzi, or Essex-Lopresti lesions. Computed tomography scan or magnetic resonance imaging is rarely required. The configuration of shaft fractures of the radius and ulna varies depending on the mechanism of injury and the degree of violence involved. Low-energy fractures are often not comminuted and of short oblique or transverse type, whereas high-energy injuries often cause comminuted or segmental fractures.

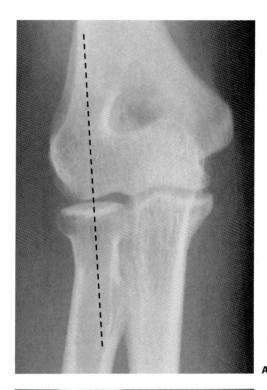

A

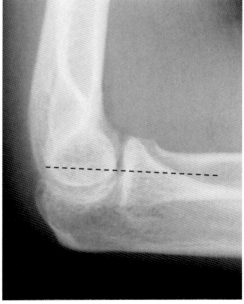

B

FIGURE 31-2 On normal radiographs, a line drawn through the proximal radial shaft **(A)** and the center of the radial head **(B)** should pass through the center of the capitellum.

ulna on an anteroposterior radiograph. On a true lateral projection, the distal ulna may also be dorsally displaced. There may also be a fracture of the ulnar styloid at its base. Ring et al.[84] defined injury of the DRUJ as more than 5 mm of ulnar-positive variance on radiographs taken before any manipulative or surgical reduction. Ultrasound examination can be used to detect interosseous membrane tears.[29]

Classification and Epidemiology

Fractures of both bones of the forearm are usually described according to the level of fracture, the pattern of the fracture,

the degree of displacement, the presence or absence of comminution or segmental bone loss, and whether they are open or closed. For descriptive purposes, it is also useful to divide the entire length of the radius and ulna into upper, middle, and lower thirds.

The most comprehensive classification of forearm fractures presently available is the AO classification,[76] which has also been adopted by the Orthopaedic Trauma Association (OTA) (Fig. 31-3). Type A fractures are the unifocal simple fracture with A1 being isolated ulnar fractures, A2 radial fractures, and A3 fractures in both bones. In the A1 and A2 fractures, the

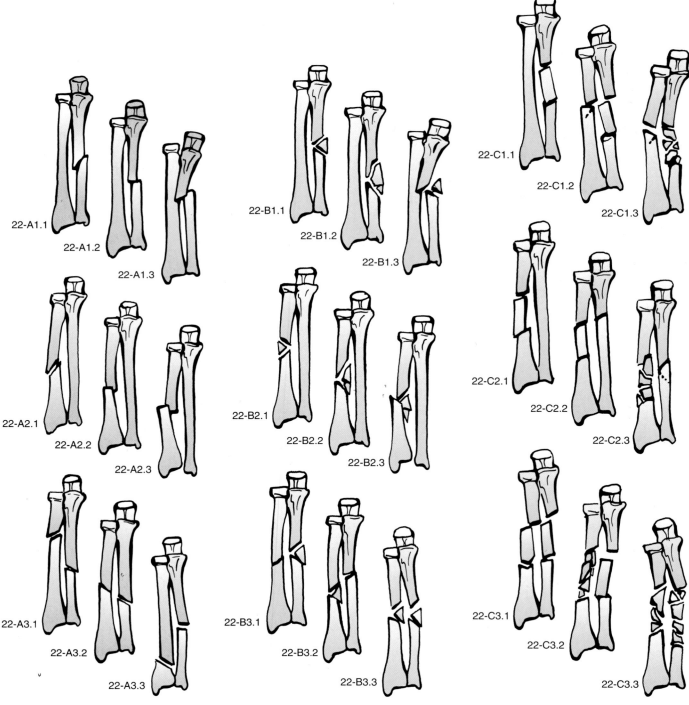

FIGURE 31-3 AO/OTA classification.

suffixes refer to the morphology of the fracture and the presence of a proximal or distal dislocation of the radioulnar joint. The A1.1 and A2.1 fractures are oblique and the A1.2 and A2.2 fractures are transverse. The suffix .3 indicates either a Monteggia fracture (A1.3) or a Galeazzi fracture (A2.3). In A3 fractures, the suffix relates to the position of the radial fracture with A3.1 being in the proximal third of the radius, A3.2 in the middle third, and A3.3 in the distal third.

Type B fractures are wedge fractures. The classification of is similar to type A fractures although it also differentiates between an intact or a fragmented wedge. In B1 and B2 fractures, the suffix .1 signifies an intact wedge, .2 a fragmented wedge, and .3 a fracture–dislocation. B1.3 fractures are Monteggia lesions and B2.3 are Galeazzi fractures. B3 fractures are both bone fractures with the suffix signifying different combinations of simple and wedge fractures (see Fig. 31-3).

Type C fractures are complex fractures. C1 fractures are complex ulnar fractures with (C1.2) or without (C1.1) a simple radial fracture. C1.3 is a Monteggia fracture with a complex ulnar fracture and simple radial fracture. C2 fractures are similar with the complex fracture being radial and the C2.3 being a Galeazzi fracture. C3 fractures are complex fractures involving both bones with the complexity increasing from C3.1 to C3.3.

Forearm fractures account for around 1% of all fractures. Their epidemiology is shown in Table 31-1. This data is extracted from the data presented in Chapter 3.

Fracture of the proximal ulna with a concomitant dislocation of the radial head was first described by Monteggia in 1814. In 1967, Bado[3] reported a series of such injuries, and he classified the injury into four distinct types (Fig. 31-4):

Type I: Fracture of the ulnar diaphysis at any level with anterior angulation at the fracture site and an associated anterior dislocation of the radial head (Fig. 31-5A).

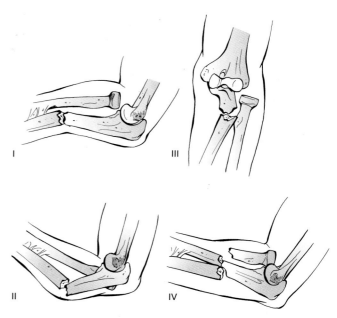

FIGURE 31-4 Bado classification of Monteggia fracture dislocation.

Type II: Fracture of the ulnar diaphysis with posterior angulation at the fracture site and a posterolateral dislocation of the radial head.

Type III: Fracture of the ulnar metaphysis with a lateral or anterolateral dislocation of the radial head (Fig. 31-5B).

Type IV: Fracture of the proximal third of both the radius and ulna at the same level with an anterior dislocation of the radial head.

Bado[3] also described several Monteggia equivalents possessing similar characteristics to his types 1 and 2 (Table 31-2). There were no equivalents for types 3 and 4.

Bado type 2 fractures have been subdivided into four types by Jupiter and his colleagues.[56] In type 2a, the fracture of the ulna involves the distal part of the olecranon and the coronoid process. In type 2b, the fracture is at the metaphyseal–diaphyseal junction distal to the coronoid, and in type 2c, the fracture is diaphyseal. The fourth subtype, type 2d, extends into the proximal half of the diaphysis of the ulna. A complex variation of the type 2 Monteggia with associated ulnohumeral dislocation has also been reported.[79]

Monteggia fractures constitute 5% to 10% of all forearm fractures. In adult patients, the Bado type 2 injury is the most common, being reported in 59% to 79% of cases.[60,82] In these reports, type 1 injuries occur in 15% to 30%, with types 3 and 4 occurring in very few cases. Males and females were equally represented, and the average age was 52 years. Sixty percent of cases were low-energy injuries. However, when the Bado types 1 and 2 injuries were compared there was a preponderance of middle-aged to elderly women with Bado type 2 fractures, with much higher prevalences of coronoid and radial head fractures.[82]

A Galeazzi fracture is a fracture of the diaphysis of the radius with a dislocation of the DRUJ. These injuries account for 3% of forearm fractures (see Chapter 3) and are more common in

TABLE 31-1	The Epidemiology of Forearm Fractures	
Proportion of all fractures		0.9%
Average age		40.1 years
Male/female		73/27
Distribution		Type D (Table 3-2)
Incidence		11.7/10^5/year
Open fractures		11.7%
Most common causes		
Fall		28.3%
Direct blow/assault		21.6%
Sport		18.3%
Motor vehicle accident		13.3%
OTA(AO) classification		
Type A		86.4%
Type B		11.9%
Type C		1.7%
Most common subgroups		
A1.2		25%
A1.1		25%
A1.3		6.7%
A2.2		6.7%
B1.1		6.7%

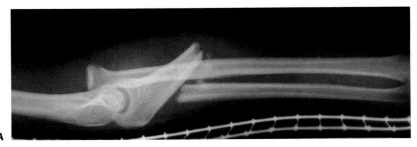

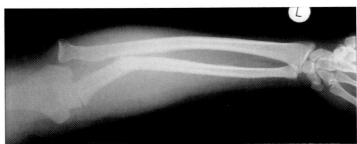

FIGURE 31-5 A. A type I Monteggia fracture dislocation. **B.** A type III lesion

males.[71,74] They can be separated into two types: type 1 in which the radial fracture is in the distal third within 7.5 cm of the distal radial articular surface and type 2 in which the radial fracture is in the middle third of the radius and more than 7.5 cm from the articular surface of the distal radius.[80] Type 2 fractures are more likely to have DRUJ instability with a reported prevalence of 55% compared to 6% in type 1 fractures.[80]

In Essex-Lopresti injuries, there is a preponderance of high-energy injury occurring in patients ranging in age from youth to middle age. Edwards and Jupiter[24] classified the injury depending on the type of radial head fracture. Type 1 fractures were large displaced radial head fractures. Type 2 fractures were severely comminuted radial head fractures, and type 3 were old injuries with irreducible proximal migration of the radius.

TABLE 31-2	Monteggia Equivalents Described by Bado[4]

Type 1

Anterior dislocation of the radial head (in children, the "pulled elbow")

Fracture of the ulnar shaft with fracture of the proximal third or neck of the radius

Fracture of the neck of the radius

Fracture of the ulnar diaphysis and olecranon with anterior dislocation of the radial head

Posterior dislocation of the elbow; fracture of the ulnar shaft with or without proximal radius fracture

Fracture of the proximal radius

Type 2

Dislocation of the radial head with an epiphyseal fracture

Radial neck fracture

SURGICAL AND APPLIED ANATOMY AND COMMON SURGICAL APPROACHES

Surgical and Applied Anatomy

The entire forearm has a complex structure, consisting of muscles, tendons, bones, and joints. A coordinated function of all these structures is responsible for arm and hand movement, including rotation.

The radius and ulna function as a unit but come into contact with each other only at the two ends. During rotational movements, the radius rotates around the relatively immobile ulna. Besides coordinated muscle exertion, these movements also rely on the normal function of five articulations (Fig. 31-6). At the elbow, the two bones articulate directly with the humerus to form the ulnohumeral and the radiocapitellar joints. At the wrist, only the radius articulates directly with the carpal bones to form the radiocarpal joint. The two bones also articulate with each other proximally and distally at the proximal and distal radioulnar joints. The two bones are bound proximally by the capsule of the elbow joint and the annular ligament and distally by the capsule of the wrist joint, the dorsal and volar radioulnar ligaments, and the triangular fibrocartilage complex. The interosseous membrane is frequently referred to as a separate joint of the forearm bones, and its disruption or contracture can lead to instability or stiffness.

In order for the rotational movement to proceed smoothly, the ulna has a relatively straight form, but the radius has a more pronounced curve. Sage[87] measured the curves in cadaveric radii and found that the proximal curvature averaged 13.1 degrees apex medial and 13.1 degrees apex anterior in the coronal and sagittal planes, respectively. The distal curvature averaged 9.3 degrees apex lateral and 6.4 degrees apex posterior in the coronal and sagittal planes, respectively. He[87] pointed out the importance of maintaining these curves, especially the lateral bow of the radius. A study by Schemitsch and Richards[90] confirmed the importance of restoration of the radial bow for forearm function after fracture. They described a method of quanti-

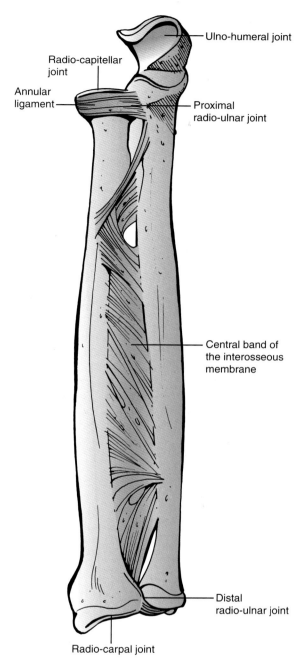

Ulno-humeral joint

Radio-capitellar joint

Annular ligament

Proximal radio-ulnar joint

Central band of the interosseous membrane

Distal radio-ulnar joint

Radio-carpal joint

FIGURE 31-6 The two bones are connected by ligaments at the proximal and distal radioulnar joints and in their midportions by the interosseous membrane that transmits any force at the wrist from the radius to the ulna. The central part of the interosseous membrane is thickened to form the central band. There are five articulations, namely the radiohumeral, the ulnohumeral, radiocarpal, and the proximal and distal radioulnar joints.

fying the amount and location of the radial bow (Fig. 31-7) and correlated restoration of the radial bow with forearm function. They found that restoration of function was significantly better in cases in which the radial bow was restored to a mean of less than 1.5-mm difference and to within 9% for the location compared to the opposite side.

The ulna also has a slight bow that must also be taken into consideration during fixation of an ulnar fracture. There is an apex posterior bow along the entire length of ulna that can be

visualized on a lateral radiograph. The posterior border of the ulna is subcutaneous and easily palpable throughout its length.

In the midportion of the forearm, the radius and the ulna are both triangular in cross section with their interosseous apices representing the attachment of the interosseous membrane. The fibers of the interosseous membrane run obliquely across the interosseous space from the proximal radius at the level of the pronator quadratus to the junction of the middle and distal thirds of the ulna. It consists of a thin membranous part and a thick ligamentous part called the central band, which measures about 3.5 cm in width and is 2 or 3 times as thick as the membranous part (see Fig. 31-6). Experimental studies by Hotchkiss et al.[50] showed that incision of the triangular fibrocartilage complex alone decreased relative stability by 8%. Incision of the triangular fibrocartilage complex and interosseous membrane proximal to the central band decreased stability by only 11%. Incision of the central band, however, reduced stability by 71%. The thickened central band of the interosseous membrane is a constant structure and is the second principal stabilizer of the radius, particularly when the radial head is injured and requires resection. Proximal migration of the radius may occur following radial head resection resulting in painful ulnocarpal impingement.

On the anterior aspect of the forearm, there are two groups of muscles: the mobile wad and the flexor pronator group. The mobile wad consists of brachioradialis, extensor carpi radialis longus (ECRL), and extensor carpi radialis brevis (ECRB). They lie on the lateral side of the forearm and are innervated by the radial nerve. The flexor-pronator group lies on the medial aspect and has three layers:

1. Superficial—pronator teres, flexor carpi radialis (FCR), palmaris longus, and flexor carpi ulnaris (FCU), in order from lateral to medial
2. Middle—flexor digitorum superficialis (FDS)
3. Deep—flexor digitorum profundus (FDP), flexor pollicis longus (FPL), and pronator quadratus

This group is innervated by the median and ulnar nerves.

The mobile wad lies laterally on the dorsum of the forearm. The superficial extensors (extensor digitorum communis [EDC], extensor digiti minimi and extensor carpi ulnaris [ECU]) and anconeus lie on the ulnar aspect. The extensors are supplied by the posterior interosseous nerve while the anconeus has its own branch of the radial nerve arising proximal to the elbow.

Complex muscle groups act across the forearm exerting forces on different parts of the bones, and these forces can cause displacement if the bones of the forearm are fractured. There are three muscles which join the radius and the ulna: the supinator, pronator teres, and pronator quadratus. When there is a fracture, these muscles tend to approximate the radius and ulna and decrease the interosseous space. In addition, the forearm muscles that take origin on the ulnar aspect of the forearm and insert on the radial side of the wrist or hand, such as the pronator teres, pronator quadratus, and the flexor carpi radialis, tend to exert a pronating force.[87] In a similar manner, muscles such as the abductor pollicis longus (APL) and brevis and the extensor pollicis longus (EPL), which have their origins on the ulna and interosseous membrane on the dorsal side and are inserted on the radial side of the dorsum of the wrist, tend to exert a supinating force.

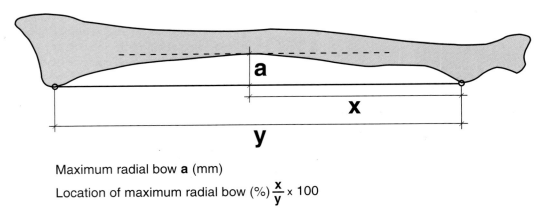

Maximum radial bow **a** (mm)

Location of maximum radial bow (%) $\frac{x}{y} \times 100$

FIGURE 31-7 The method of Schemitsch et al.[90] for quantifying the maximum radial bow and its location relative to the length of the entire radius.

In addition to the supinator muscle itself, the biceps brachii is a powerful supinator of the radius. In fractures of the upper radius below the insertion of the supinator and above the insertion of the pronator teres, two strong muscles (the biceps and the supinator) exert an unopposed force that supinates the proximal radial fragment (Fig 31-8A). In fractures of the radius located distal to the pronator teres, the combined force of the biceps and supinator is somewhat neutralized. In these frac-tures, the proximal fragment of the radius is usually in a slightly supinated or neutral position (Fig. 31-8B). In performing reduction of forearm fractures, the location of the fracture of the radius helps to determine the degree of supination of the distal fragment needed to correct rotational alignment. Failure to correct this will lead to rotational malunion and a resultant loss of rotation. It is therefore crucial that an anatomic reduction should be achieved, usually by open surgery.

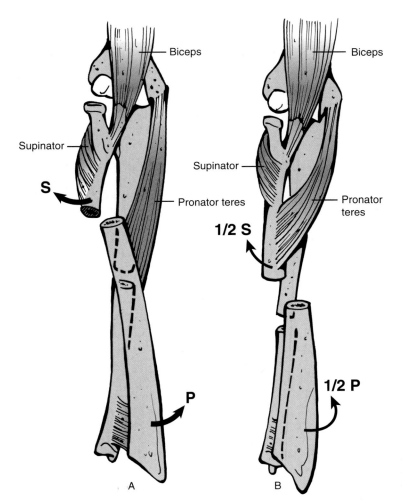

FIGURE 31-8 A. In fractures proximal to the pronator teres insertion onto the radius, biceps, and supinator supinate the proximal fragment. **B.** When the fracture is distal to the pronator teres insertion, the proximal fragment is either slightly supinated or in the neutral position.

It is important that the surgeon is aware of the location of the three nerves in the forearm: ulnar, median, and radial. The ulnar nerve enters the forearm under the fascial band of the origin of FCU and then runs between FCU and FDS incorporated into the epimysium of FDP, lying lateral to the tendon of FCU distally. Its superficial branch crosses the distal end of the ulna from volar to dorsal and is at risk in the exposure of the distal third of the ulna. The median nerve enters the forearm in the cubital fossa and passes between the heads of pronator teres. It then runs between FDS and FDP. The anterior interosseous nerve arises proximal to the elbow and is a distinct branch running on the interosseous membrane between FPL and FDP, ending in the pronator quadratus. The radial nerve has two branches in the forearm: its superficial branch and the posterior interosseous nerve. The superficial branch runs on the undersurface of brachioradialis and crosses from volar to dorsal over the distal third of the radius where it is vulnerable to injury. The posterior interosseous nerve lies between the two heads of supinator at the arcade of Frohse and is usually separated from the radial neck by the deep head of supinator. The surgeon should be aware that in some cases the nerve is directly applied to the neck of the radius where it is at risk of iatrogenic injury.

The radial artery passes medial to the biceps tendon and lies on the supinator muscle. It then runs distally on the undersurface of brachioradialis with the superficial radial nerve. At the wrist, it lies on the radial side of FCR. The ulnar artery runs deep to pronator teres and FDS proximally and then superficial to FDP between FDS and FCU with the ulnar nerve.

Common Surgical Approaches

Surgical Approaches to the Radius
Anterior or Henry Approach.[45] The patient is positioned supine on the operating table with the arm abducted on a hand table. The arm is then prepped and draped to just above the elbow. A tourniquet is used unless there has been a vascular injury. The arm is held in supination. The medial edge of the mobile wad forms the course of the planned incision.

The incision is deepened to the fascial layer taking care to preserve, if possible, the superficial veins. The fascia is split at the edge of the brachioradialis muscle. The dissection is then extended between the flexor-pronator mass on the ulnar side and the radial artery and the mobile wad on the radial side (Fig. 31-9). Small branches of the radial artery should be carefully ligated to facilitate retraction of the mobile wad. Care should be taken not to damage the superficial radial nerve, which is situated underneath the brachioradialis and is retracted laterally with the mobile wad. The radial artery is exposed and retracted medially.

For access to the proximal third of the radius, the supinator must be detached from the bone. The forearm should be supinated to expose the insertion of the supinator and displace the posterior interosseous nerve laterally and posteriorly. The muscle can then be elevated subperiosteally (Fig. 31-10). It must always be handled with care to reduce any traction on the nerve.

For access to the middle third of the radius, the forearm is pronated allowing release of the insertion of the pronator teres from the radial aspect of the radius from proximal to distal. FPL, pronator quadratus, and supinator can also be elevated if required.

In the distal third of the radius, retraction of the FCR tendon to the ulnar side exposes the transverse fibres of pronator quadratus which should be elevated subperiosteally from the radial side of the radius to expose the bone.

Thompson Approach. The Thompson approach allows access to the dorsal surface of the radius. This approach utilizes the internervous plane between the mobile wad of Henry (brachioradialis, ECRL, and ECRB), which is innervated by radial nerve and the extrinsic hand extensor muscles on the back of the forearm.

The patient is positioned supine on the operating table with the arm abducted and the forearm pronated on a hand table. The skin incision lies on a line from the lateral epicondyle of the humerus, along the ulnar border of the mobile wad dorsally and finishing at Lister's tubercle. The underlying fascia is divided in the same line. The approach then follows the interval between EDC and ECRB from the midpart of the forearm distally to where APL and EPB cross the field. These muscles may have to be released extraperiosteally from the radius and mobilized proximally and distally. Proximally, the common origin of ECRL

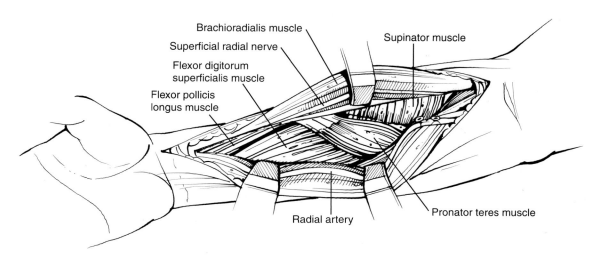

FIGURE 31-9 After the interval between brachioradialis and FCR is exposed and the radial artery retracted medially, supinator, pronator teres, FPL, and FDS can be seen.

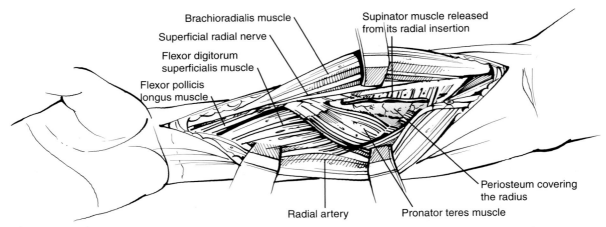

FIGURE 31-10 The insertion of supinator should be released with the patient's arm held in supination. The posterior interosseous nerve should be left within the muscle.

and ECRB is split to reveal the supinator muscle. At this stage, it is important to identify and protect the posterior interosseous nerve which is most easily found as it exits supinator. If necessary, the course of the nerve can be followed through supinator. The forearm is then supinated to expose the anterior insertion of supinator which is detached extraperiosteally to expose the proximal radius (Fig 31-11). Distally, the dorsum of the radius is exposed by developing the interval between ECRB and EPL.

Thompson's approach has the disadvantage of not being extensile. Proximal and distal exposure is more difficult than with Henry's approach. The posterior interosseous nerve must be protected in the proximal third of both approaches.

Surgical Approach to the Ulna

Since the ulna is located subcutaneously in its entire length and there are no major neurovascular structures between the skin and the bone, surgical exposure of the ulna is relatively straightforward. Access is usually achieved with the arm abducted and the elbow flexed. The ulna can also be exposed with the arm across the chest or with the patient in the lateral decubitus position with the arm on an arm rest. The latter is only suitable for isolated ulnar fractures as it restricts access to the anterior forearm. The fascia is incised in the same line as the skin inci-

sion, exposing the plane between extensor and flexor carpi ulnaris. This plane is developed to expose the underlying bone. Distally, the dorsal branch of the ulnar nerve is encountered and should be protected as it passes dorsally over ECU. Anteriorly, the ulnar nerve and artery run deep to FCU, which should therefore be retracted with care.

CURRENT TREATMENT OPTIONS

Fractures of the forearm must be adequately treated in order to avoid any loss of function. Bony union is not the only goal of treatment. The fracture must be reduced precisely, restoring the length and axial and rotational alignment of the forearm. Anatomic reduction of the proximal and DRUJs is essential to allow full recovery of supination and pronation. If full and speedy functional recovery is to be achieved, the fracture must be stabilized rigidly and range of motion exercise should be started shortly after the surgery.

Nonoperative Treatment

Conservative treatment of displaced forearm shaft fractures usually results in a poor functional outcome because of the impor-

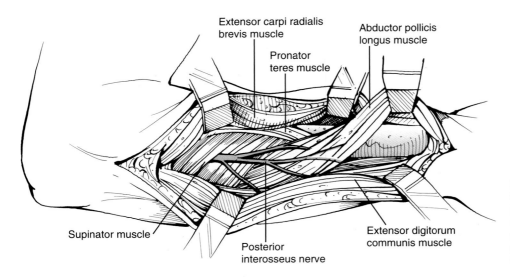

FIGURE 31-11 Development of the interval between ECRB and EPL reveals the radius distal to EPB. Proximally, the nerve can be mobilized where it exits the supinator if required. The posterior interosseous nerve should be identified and protected throughout the whole procedure.

tance of the anatomic relationship of the radius and ulna and the difficulty in obtaining and maintaining an acceptable reduction. Treatment by closed reduction and cast immobilization risks a poor functional outcome with unsatisfactory results reported in up to 92% of cases,[15,51,59] usually caused by malunion, nonunion, or synostosis. Most series of conservatively treated displaced both bone fractures of the forearm were published before 1960, indicating that closed reduction and cast treatment for both bone fractures of the forearm has been effectively abandoned with the advent of modern plating systems.

The results of functional bracing have been reported by Sarmiento et al.[88] in cases of both bone fractures of the forearm. Thirteen of their 44 cases were both bone fractures treated with closed manipulation and initial plaster cast followed by functional bracing applied an average of 15 days after fracture. At final review, there was an average of 12 degrees loss of pronation and 19 degrees loss of supination. Union time was an average of 15 weeks with a range from 9 to 33 weeks.

In contrast, isolated ulnar shaft fracture, or nightstick fracture, can be successfully treated in a cast. The fracture is more stable probably due to the splinting effect of the intact radius. Dymond[22] showed that if the fracture displacement is less than 50% of the width of the bone, then the interosseous membrane is largely intact and the fracture can be immobilized by a below-elbow cast. De Boeck et al.[18] showed that in their 46 patients with isolated distal ulnar shaft fractures, treatment with a below-elbow cast can yield satisfactory results in 89% of patients. Gebuhr et al.[36] reported a randomized trial and found that patients treated with a prefabricated functional brace had significantly better wrist function and were more satisfied than those treated with a long-arm cast. The Cochrane Review attempted to assess the effects of various forms of treatment for isolated fractures of the ulnar shaft, but no conclusion could be drawn from the data obtained so far.[42]

In general, if the displacement is less than 50% of the width of the bone[22] and the angulation less than 10 degrees,[18] no closed reduction or manipulation is needed and the fracture can be treated by cast immobilization or functional bracing.[66] In such cases, Sarmiento et al.[88] reported a union rate of 99% and good to excellent function in 96% of cases. In addition, when nonunion of the ulnar shaft occurs, its prevalence has not been shown to be reduced by early fixation.[10] In our opinion, if the fracture displacement is more significant or if an early return of function is necessary, operative treatment with open reduction and compression plating should be performed.

Operative Treatment

It is generally accepted that anatomic reconstruction of both radius and ulna is absolutely essential in order to restore full functional recovery. The indications for surgery are summarized in Table 31-3.

Timing of Surgery

In general, internal fixation of closed forearm fractures is best performed as early as possible after injury. In most circumstances, there is no need to wait for the soft tissue swelling to subside. Prolonged delay in fixation may increase the difficulty of the reduction of the fracture as well as the surgical dissection leading to devascularization of the bone fragments. In open fractures, an urgent débridement followed by external or internal fixation should be done.

TABLE 31-3	**Indications for Surgical Treatment of Forearm Fractures in Adults**

1. Displaced fractures of both radius and ulna
2. Isolated fracture of either bone with translational, rotational, or angulated displacement; a simple, nondisplaced shaft fracture may be treated by nonoperative means (i.e., with a brace)
3. Monteggia, Galeazzi, and Essex-Lopresti type fracture dislocations
4. All open fractures

If the patient is polytraumatized and in a poor general condition with major visceral injuries or other significant fractures such as pelvis or femoral shaft, then it is acceptable to delay the surgery until the patient is stabilized. If there is delay in admission to the hospital and the patient presents with compromised soft tissues with fracture blisters or infected wounds near the intended incision sites, it is also advisable to delay fixation until the soft tissue conditions improve.

Plate Fixation

Open reduction and plate fixation is the most common method of treatment of forearm fractures. In 1975, Anderson et al.[3] reported on 258 adults treated with compression plating for diaphyseal fractures of the radius and ulna. There were 193 radial fractures and 137 ulnar fractures with rates of union of 98% for fractures of the radius and 96% for fractures of the ulna. Autologous bone grafting was used in 26% but did not increase the union rates compared to those treated without grafting. An excellent or satisfactory result was achieved in 86% of their patients. Despite the passage of several decades, there has been no significant change in the reported outcomes in more recent papers.[17,41,46]

The most recent of these studies is from Hertel and his coauthors.[46] They reported on a retrospective review of 132 fractures treated with compression plating with a mean review period of 10 years. Uneventful union within 6 months was reported in 96% of fractures. There was a superficial infection in 1 patient but no deep infections.

In an attempt to reduce the damage to vascularity of the bone and the risk of infection by minimizing the contact on bone, the limited contact dynamic compression plate (LC-DCP) and the point contact fixator (PC-Fix) were developed.[25,78] This has been termed *biologic fixation*. We have reported our results of a randomized study of plate fixation using the PC-Fix and the LC-DCP.[63] There were 92 patients with 125 forearm fractures. Five of 66 fractures in the LC-DCP group and 4 of the 59 treated with the PC-Fix went on to delayed union. There were no nonunions. One deep infection and one refracture occurred in each group. Using the original criteria of Anderson[3] to determine the range of motion, all patients in both PC-Fix and LC-DCP groups achieved a full or nearly full range of motion. The study also showed that the pattern of bone healing was affected by the quality of fracture reduction rather than the type of implant used. When anatomic reduction was achieved in either group, there was minimal callus formation and primary bone healing was found. Despite the fact that the PC-Fix and the LC-DCP use different concepts of fixation,[48] both implants were shown to be highly effective in the treatment of diaphyseal forearm fractures.

These results are similar to those reported in 387 fractures in 272 patients[40] treated with the PC-Fix. In this study, there was a 96% union rate and a deep infection rate of 0.6% in closed fractures.

We have also reported on the results of 45 forearm fractures treated with open reduction and internal fixation using the locking compression plate (LCP) as the fixation method.[64] This plate allows a combination of compression and a stable construct conferred by the locking screws. There were two delayed unions and no deep infections. All patients had full or nearly full range of motion. Although the LCP (Fig. 31-12) represents the latest development in plate development, its usage in fractures with simple configuration and its superiority over conventional plating systems (e.g., LC-DCP) has yet to be proven.

Intramedullary Nailing of Forearm Fractures

Historical reports on intramedullary nailing used Kirschner-wires, Steinman pins, Rush pins,[93] or the Sage nail.[87] The former paper reported on 338 patients with 555 fractures.[93] The results were disappointing with a high rate of nonunion (20%) and a poor final range of rotation. This paper was the stimulus for the development of the Sage nail, a prebent, triangular intramedullary nail. In the latter report, Sage[87] described the rationale for and the design of his intramedullary forearm nail with improved results. He reported a non- or delayed union rate of 11%.

Recently, there have been a few reports on the use of newer designs of intramedullary nails. Gao et al.[31] studied 18 patients with 32 diaphyseal forearm fractures treated with the ForeSight (Smith & Nephew, Memphis, TN) forearm interlocking nail which has a diameter of 4 to 5 mm (Fig. 31-13). Compared

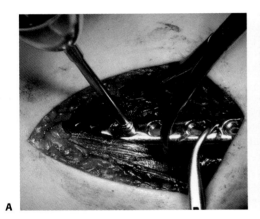

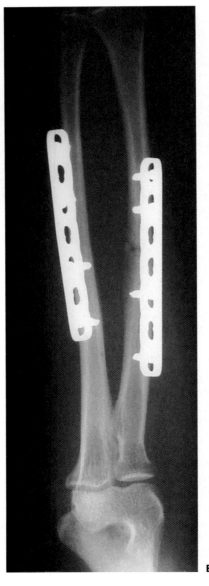

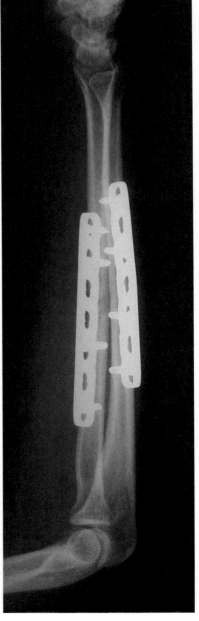

FIGURE 31-12 Fracture of the forearm treated with a locking compression plate. **A.** The application of locking screw. Good alignment and uneventful healing was seen in the anteroposterior **(B)** and lateral **(C)** follow-up radiographs at 6 months.

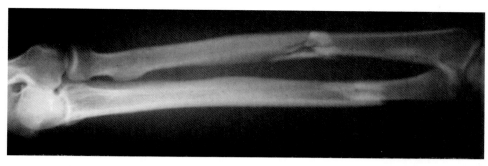

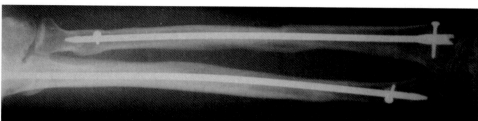

FIGURE 31-13 A. A 51-year-old man sustained a closed displaced diaphyseal forearm fracture (AO type B3) in a traffic accident. **B.** Fractures were reduced and fixed with interlocking intramedullary nail (ForeSight nail) using a closed technique. Radiographs taken 12 months after the injury showed satisfactory union and alignment. (Courtesy of Dr. Gao Hong, MD, Department of Orthopaedics, The Sixth Affiliated People's Hospital of Jiaotong University, Shanghai, PR of China.)

with the normal arm, the mean loss of rotation of the forearm was 32 degrees. There was mild to moderate impairment demonstrated with the Disabilities of the Arm, Shoulder, and Hand (DASH) score. The overall infection rate was 12.5% but all were superficial. Weckbach et al.[107] reported a series of 33 forearm fractures treated with intramedullary ForeSight nails. They found the surgical technique demanding but still satisfactory despite a nonunion rate of 8% and loss of rotation in 12% of patients. Intramedullary nailing using multiple Kirschner-wires in 288 forearm fractures in 184 patients was recently reported from a developing country.[1] The authors reported a delayed or nonunion rate of 12%, a deep infection rate of 2%, and cross union in 2% of forearms. Twenty-three percent of patients had unsatisfactory results but the authors pointed out that the method is cheap and required minimal expertise. They concluded that Kirschner wiring remains acceptable for use in developing countries.

Intramedullary nailing has also been used to treat nonunion of forearm fractures. Hong et al.[49] reported a series of 15 patients with nonunion of diaphyseal forearm fractures treated with intramedullary nailing and bone grafting. Forty-seven percent of patients had unsatisfactory or poor results. The authors concluded that interlocking intramedullary nailing of nonunions of the diaphysis of the radius or ulna with an open reaming technique should not be considered an adequate alternative to plate fixation of these injuries.

In our opinion, the intramedullary devices currently available cannot fulfil the surgical goals of restoration of normal bowing, adequate rotational stability, and early mobilization. We do not advocate their use for displaced forearm fractures in adults where plating is possible.

External Fixation

External fixation of forearm fractures should only be regarded as an alternative management of open forearm fractures when there is significant soft tissue or bone loss.[108] Schuind et al.[91] advocated external fixation of both closed and open diaphyseal fractures of the radius and ulna. However, the reported malunion rate was 16.5% and the delayed or nonunion rate was

8.5%. Restoration of forearm rotation was disappointing. External fixation of the forearm is also associated with pin track infection.[92]

The stability achieved by external fixation is much less than internal fixation and hence the length of the bones and the normal bowing are usually poorly restored. Its use should be temporary, and a sequential exchange to internal fixation is mandatory once the soft tissue condition improves or when soft tissue cover is achieved.[44] External fixation of the forearm can also be employed in severely injured patients for damage control surgery (see Chapter 22) and can be useful in combat situations.[43]

For temporary external fixation, the pins should be placed in the ulna. The whole subcutaneous border of the ulna can be palpated and offers a safe site for pin placement. Caution should be exercised at the proximal and distal part of the ulna where the ulnar nerve lies in close proximity to the bone.

External fixation of the radius is seldom necessary and it also requires a sound knowledge of the anatomy of the forearm.[34] In order to avoid inadvertent nerve and blood vessel damage, an open pin insertion technique should be used. When a pin is placed in the proximal radius, care must be taken not to damage the posterior interosseous nerve. When a pin is placed in the radial aspect of the shaft of the radius, care must also be taken not to damage the sensory branch of the radial nerve. Simple unilateral fixators usually suffice as an exchange to internal fixation and should be done once the soft tissue condition has stabilized.

Management of Monteggia Fracture Dislocation

The goal of treatment of a Monteggia injury is anatomic relocation of the dislocated radial head, together with reduction and fixation of the ulna.[81] Any residual angulation of the ulnar fracture predisposes to subsequent redislocation or subluxation of the radial head.[89] In the adult patient, open reduction and internal fixation should be used.

A direct incision over the posterior border of the ulna should be made for open reduction and plate fixation of the ulna. After fixation of the ulna, the reduction of the radial head must be confirmed with image intensification. A line along the proximal radial shaft and the center of the radial head should pass through the center of the capitellum in any position of the elbow, confirmed with two radiographic views (see Fig. 31-2).[68]

In rare cases where the radial head does not reduce after accurate reduction of the ulna, a small separate anterolateral (Kocher) incision should be made and the radial head inspected for interposition of the annular ligament. In young adults, the annular ligament may remain intact with the radial head having slipped out due to axial traction. In these cases, it may be necessary to divide the annular ligament, reduce the radial head, and then repair the ligament.

Historically, the results of the treatment of Monteggia fractures were poor. Watson-Jones stated in 1943 that, "no fracture presents so many problems; no injury is beset with greater difficulty; no treatment is characterised by more general failure."[106] He reported that 95% of Monteggia fractures had permanent disability.[106] In 1974, Bruce et al.[11] reported the results of the treatment of 21 adults with Monteggia fractures, 5 by closed reduction and cast immobilization, and the remaining 16 were treated with either an intramedullary rod or compression plating. There were no excellent results and only 24% had good results. There was a high rate of complications including iatrogenic nerve palsies in 2 patients and nonunion in 8.

However, modern methods of fixation have improved the outcome of management of these injuries. In a series of 48 adult patients with Monteggia injuries treated with open reduction and rigid internal fixation,[82] there were 83% excellent or good results, though this was achieved after a number of reoperations and reconstructive surgery. The majority of the poorer results resulted from Bado type 2 injuries; all had a radial head fracture and half of the cases had a coronoid fracture. More recently Konrad and his coauthors[60] reported on the outcome of 47 adult patients who had sustained a Monteggia fracture and were treated with open reduction and internal fixation. There was a similar preponderance of women in the Bado type 2 group although with a younger average age than in the series by Ring et al.[84] Seventy-three percent had excellent or good results at an average review period of 8.4 years. The authors correlated Bado type 2 fractures, Jupiter type 2a fractures, radial head fracture, coronoid fracture, and complications requiring reoperation with a poorer prognosis. Associated ulnohumeral instability has also been noted as a poor prognostic factor.[98]

Management of Galeazzi Fracture Dislocation
Treatment in adults is surgical, and both bone and soft tissue injuries should be addressed.

The goal of surgery should be relocation of the DRUJ, together with a precise reduction of the radial fracture which is rigidly fixed. An anterior (Henry) approach is used to expose the fracture, and a plate is applied to the volar aspect of the distal radial shaft. Reduction of the DRUJ must then be confirmed with image intensification in two planes and by passive rotation of the forearm. If the joint is stable throughout the entire range of rotation and is well aligned on the image intensifier views, there is no need for additional postoperative immobilization and early range of motion exercises should be started.

Most cases of instability of the DRUJ can be diagnosed easily with a combination of clinical and radiologic examination. However, a number of features should raise suspicion of instability. These are listed in Table 31-4.

TABLE 31-4	**Indications of Possible Distal Radioulnar Joint Instability[7,12]**

Requirement for forceful reduction

A "mushy" feel to the reduction

Fracture of the base of the ulnar styloid

Persistent incongruity of the distal ulna on a true lateral radiograph

Shortening (>5 mm) of the radius

Widening of the DRUJ on an anteroposterior radiograph

If the DRUJ can be reduced but there is still residual instability on forearm rotation, the distal ulna can be transfixed to the radius using two Kirschner wires with the forearm in supination.[67,80] An above-elbow splint with the forearm in supination is then applied. The wires are removed at 6 weeks.

If the DRUJ is irreducible, there may be interposition of the ECU between the radius and the ulna[13] or the ECU tendon may be displaced in an ulnar and volar direction preventing reduction of the distal ulna.[12] Other tendons such as extensor digiti minimi or extensor digitorum communis have been implicated.[52,53] Frequently, there is an associated ulnar styloid fracture. If the DRUJ is irreducible, an open reduction through a small separate incision should be performed, any interposed tissue removed, and the soft tissue defect repaired with tight sutures (Fig. 31-14). If the ulnar styloid fracture is of sufficient size, it should be reduced and internally fixed.

There are few reports of the outcome of Galeazzi fractures, but it is clear that anatomic reduction is mandatory. Any residual shortening of the radial fracture predisposes to subsequent problems with the DRUJ.[100] In this series of 19 patients with long-term follow-up, those patients with radiographic evidence of anatomic fracture reduction had minimal deficit and better functional results than patients with imperfect reduction. Moore and his coauthors[74] reported on 36 closed Galeazzi fractures treated using compression plating. The average restoration of grip strength was 71%, and only one patient failed to return to employment. Loss of grip strength was more severe in seven patients with significant restriction of wrist and forearm movement.

Complication rates are relatively high. Moore et al.[74] reported a complication rate of 39%, including nonunion, malunion, infection, refracture after plate removal, and instability of the DRUJ. Nerve injury was the most common with seven injuries to the radial nerve and six to the dorsal branch. One to the dorsal interosseous branch was attributed to retraction.

Management of Essex-Lopresti Injury
The goals of treatment of Essex-Lopresti injuries are restoration of the length of the radius and stabilization of the DRUJ. If the radial head is fractured with large fragments (type 1), open reduction and internal fixation with small Herbert screws, mini-AO screws, or miniplates should be performed. If the fracture fragments of the radial head are comminuted and not amenable to internal fixation (type 2), a radial head prosthesis should be inserted to maintain the length of the radius.[66a,101] All concomitant injuries, including radial shaft fracture and ligamentous injuries around the elbow should be dealt with in order to treat all components of this complex injury (Fig. 31-15).

FIGURE 31-14 A. A patient with a variant of Galeazzi injury with a segmental radius fracture and an ulnar shaft fracture. She complained of burning sensation along the distribution of the superficial branch of radial nerve. Intraoperatively, there was pressure on the nerve from a sharp piece of bone at the fracture (*white arrow*). **B.** The DRUJ was also irreducible on closed manipulation. **C.** A separate incision for open reduction was made. The ECU tendon was found trapped beneath the ulnar head.

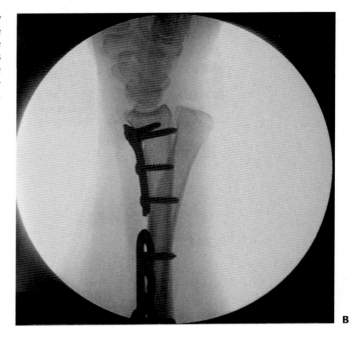

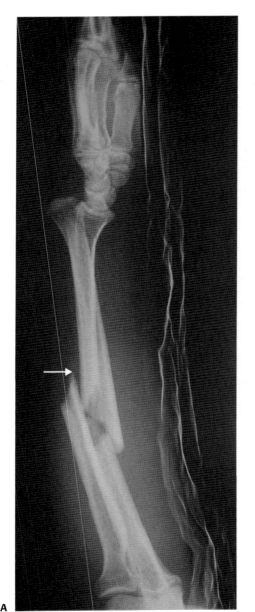

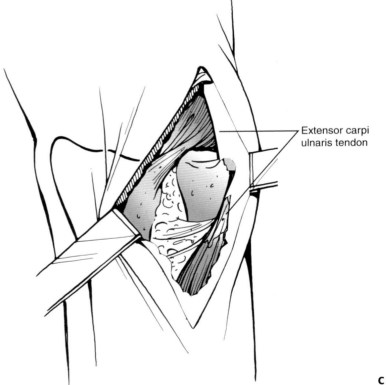

Extensor carpi ulnaris tendon

The stability of the DRUJ should be tested intraoperatively. If the joint is reduced and stable, external immobilization in supination should be maintained for 3 weeks. If the ulnar head is not stable after reduction, a radioulnar pin can be inserted with the forearm in supination and maintained for 3 to 4 weeks.

When the Essex-Lopresti injury is diagnosed late, accurate realignment of the radius and ulna is necessary and usually requires radial head replacement. Distal ulnar procedures such as ulnar shortening or a Sauve-Kapandji procedure are frequently required. Recently, a technique of reconstruction of the central band of the interosseous membrane was described by Chloros et al.[16] by rerouting of the pronator teres tendon and using it as a graft. Although all the components of the Essex-Lopresti injury are addressed, the efficacy of this procedure has yet to be confirmed.

Early detection and treatment seems to improve the outcome of this complex injury. Edwards and Jupiter[23] reported three excellent results in seven cases. All three were treated within 1 week of injury. The remaining four had treatment delayed by 4 weeks or more.

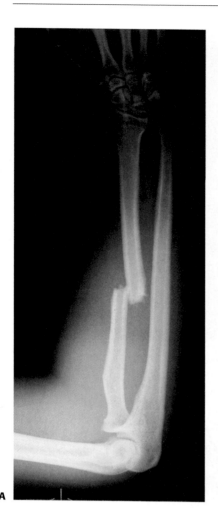

A

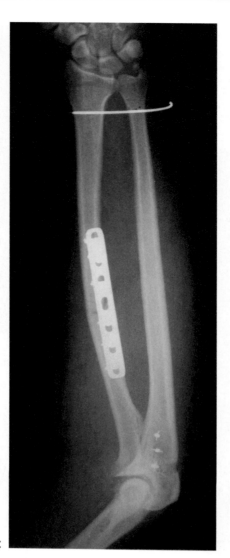

C

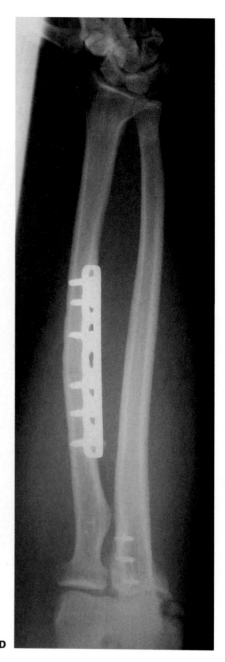

D

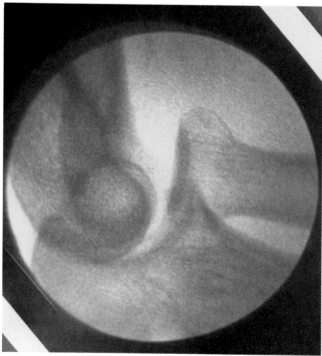

B

FIGURE 31-15 A. A young man fell from a horse and sustained a fracture of the radial shaft. The DRUJ was also disrupted. **B.** Intraoperative screening showed a dislocation of the radial head as well. **C.** Plate fixation of the radial shaft fracture, repair of annular ligament, and percutaneous ulnoradial pinning were performed. **D.** Follow-up at 1 year showing both normal elbow and wrist joint articulations. The patient had nearly full functional recovery.

Management of Open Fractures of the Forearm

As in open fractures of other long bones, the most important initial management of open fractures of the forearm is thorough irrigation and débridement (see Chapter 10). Following débridement, the method of stabilization of the fracture must be considered. In earlier series, primary plate fixation was not favored,[3] fearing that it might lead to increased risk of infection. More recently, however, authors have recommended immediate internal fixation of such fractures. Moed et al.[73] in a series of 50 patients with open forearm fractures including 11 Gustilo type 3 injuries, found a 4% incidence of deep infection and 12% incidence of nonunion. The functional results were excellent or good in 85% of the series. Chapman[14] reported only a 2% incidence of infection after primary plate fixation of open forearm fractures. Duncan et al.[21] reported a series of 103 open forearm fractures treated with immediate internal fixation within 24 hours. They recommended that immediate plating can be done in grade I, II, and IIIA open forearm fractures. Lenihan et al.[62] reported a series of seven forearm fractures from low-velocity gunshot wounds treated with open reduction and internal fixation and found no cases of infection. Jones[55] reported 18 patients with grade III open forearm injuries treated with immediate plate fixation in conjunction with aggressive soft tissue management, including eight IIIB and three IIIC open fractures. He reported good or excellent results in 12 patients and only one deep infection, which was managed successfully with subsequent surgeries.

Open fractures of the forearm should be treated with immediate internal fixation with plating following a thorough débridement. If possible, the implant should be covered with muscles or other soft tissues but the skin should be left open. Redébridement should be done at 24 to 48 hour intervals until the wound is suitably healthy to allow secondary closure or soft tissue cover.

In situations where there is severe comminution or bone loss, a bridging plate should be used taking care to restore the axial and rotational alignment and the length of the radius. Bone grafting is usually employed as a secondary procedure after healing of all soft tissue wounds, usually at 8 to 10 weeks postoperatively.[55]

If there is doubt about the feasibility of soft tissue coverage or the wound is severely contaminated, a temporary external fixator can be applied to stabilize the fracture followed by secondary internal fixation when the soft tissues are stabilized.

AUTHORS' PREFERRED TREATMENT

Open Reduction and Plate Fixation

Preoperative Planning

Preoperative planning is of the utmost importance and often determines the success or failure of the internal fixation.[68] It should provide the surgeon a full picture of the surgical procedure and the possible problems that may be encountered during the surgery. A number of factors should be considered before embarking on surgery. These are listed in Table 31-5.

It is of paramount importance that before the surgery, the surgeon studies the radiographs thoroughly and decides the type of plate fixation to be used. In general, the OTA classification of diaphyseal fractures can serve as a guide. All

| TABLE 31-5 | **Checklist before Performing Plate Fixation of Forearm Fracture** |

- Properly taken radiographs
- Correct diagnosis of the fracture including classification
- Goal of surgical fixation: compression plating or bridge plating
- Patient positioning
- Use of tourniquet
- Reduction tools: pointed reduction clips and reduction bone clamps
- Which implants and sets: 3.5-mm implants and 2.7-mm screws
- Length of plate and the number of screws to be engaged in the cortices
- Need for lag screw or prebent plating
- Kind of approach
- Need for bone graft
- Closure technique
- Plan of postoperative rehabilitation

simple fractures (group A) can be fixed with compression plating or lag screws with plating. Almost all wedge fractures (group B) can be fixed with interfragmentary lag screws with neutralization plating. Complex (group C) fractures can be fixed with either compression plating or bridge plating. If the fracture is bifocal, with each of the fractures being of a simple configuration, then compression plating can be applied. In the presence of increasing comminution with smaller fracture fragments that are not amenable to lag screw fixation, bridge plating should be used.

Surgical Exposure

The surgical approach should be chosen with reference to the type of fracture and associated soft tissue injury. Routinely, the Henry approach is used for the radius, but the Thompson approach may be required for specific reasons such as a dorsal soft tissue injury requiring débridement. The authors prefer extraperiosteal dissection (Fig. 31-16). If periosteal stripping is necessary to achieve a precise anatomic reduction, it should be limited to 1 to 2 mm at the fracture ends. Stripping of the periosteum along the length of the plate is contraindicated since this may lead to delay in healing and increased risk of infection. In particular, modern locking plates are applied with minimal contact between the plate and the bone allowing preservation of the periosteum.

Reduction and Fixation

In order to preserve the vascularity of the bone and its surrounding soft tissues, indirect reduction techniques involving continuous longitudinal traction applied through an external fixation device or directly through an applied plate using a plate-tensioning device have been advocated.

However, we do not use this method as a routine, except in AO type C fractures with significant comminution.

In simple transverse or spiral fractures or in wedge fractures with large bone fragments, we recommend using direct

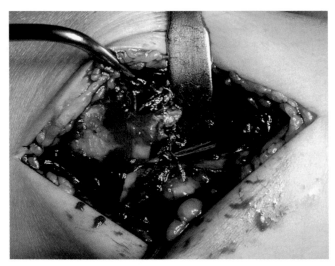

FIGURE 31-16 Preservation of soft tissue surrounding the fracture, exposing bare bone only if necessary. After the fracture is exposed, a Hohmann retractor is put under the fracture to retract the surrounding soft tissues and to support the fracture

reduction methods to achieve anatomic reduction. With the size of the forearm bones, most fracture fragments can be held and manipulated with ease using small pointed reduction forceps (Fig. 31-17). The reduction is performed under longitudinal traction and direct vision. Depending on the fracture configuration, the reduction may require traction or a rotational maneuver. The relatively sharp edge of the interosseous border of the bones should also be matched on both sides of the fracture and used as a landmark for precise reduction of rotational alignment. In the case of a transverse fracture, lag screw application is not necessary and interfragmentary compression is achieved by the dynamic compression screw mechanism.

In spiral or oblique fractures, once the reduction is achieved, a third pair of pointed reduction forceps is applied to close the fracture gap completely and hold the fracture temporarily to allow lag screw fixation. In our experience, the use of 2.7-mm screws is very helpful in fixing smaller bone fragments that cannot accommodate a 3.5-mm screw. A neutralization plate is then applied to provide stability to the whole bone–implant construct.

If the fracture is more comminuted and the fracture fragments are too small for lag screw fixation, excessive soft tissue dissection in order to reduce each fracture fragment anatomically should be avoided. If indirect reduction is used, the fracture site is not exposed and remains covered by the surrounding soft tissues with maximal preservation of the biology surrounding the bone fragments. The aim of the reduction is to restore the length and curvature of the forearm bones. It is therefore essential to confirm the physiologic bowing of the forearm bones and the normal articulation of the proximal and distal radioulnar joints on image intensification during surgery.

Choice of Implant

The good results of compression plating achieved by Anderson et al.[3] and Chapman et al.[14] have set the standard of plate fixation of forearm fractures. The length of the plate is intimately related to the extent of the fracture. It is generally accepted that three cortical screws engaging in at least six to seven cortices in each main fragment are recommended to secure the fixation.[76] The number may be decreased due to anatomic reasons (metaphyseal/epiphyseal regions) or increased because of bone quality (osteoporosis).

Different plate designs have been shown to be effective, including dynamic compression plate, limited contact dynamic compression plate, PC-Fix, and LCP. In general, the authors prefer to use the locking compression plate, which offers the flexibility of being used as a compression plate, as a bridging fixator, or as a system combining both techniques. The LCP also offers better fixation in osteoporotic

FIGURE 31-17 A. Pointed reduction clips are applied to the main fracture fragments. **B.** Longitudinal traction was applied. **C.** The fracture is reduced under direct vision.

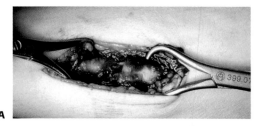

A

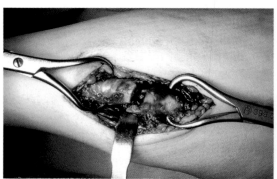

B

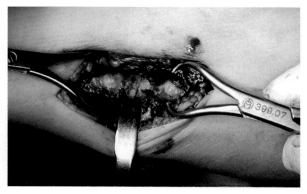

C

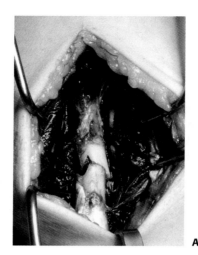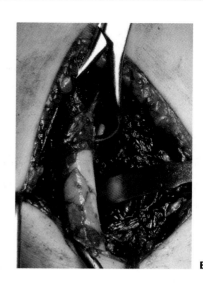

FIGURE 31-18 A. In fracture with a small wedge fragment, the two main fracture fragments can be reduced first. **B.** The small bony piece is placed in the cortical defect. Interfragmentary compression is then applied, and no bone graft is needed.

A

B

bone and the cancellous bone of metaphyseal region. Each screw hole, or "combination hole," can allow the insertion of a conventional screw or a locking head screw as the hole has features of both a smooth sliding compression hole and a threaded locking hole.[104]

However, there has not been any rigid guideline as to the type and number of locking screws to be inserted. Gautier and Sommer[35] suggested that from a mechanical perspective, at least two monocortical screws on each main fragment are required, but in clinical practice, it is advisable to insert more screws. We feel that if the locking screws are inserted properly and engaging in strong cortical bone, then fixation in only four cortices is necessary in each fracture fragment. This can be in form of two bicortical screws or one bicortical with two monocortical screws. If the fracture fixation is in osteoporotic bone or in the metaphysis, then only bicortical screws should be inserted as monocortical screws can easily pull out from the thin cortex.

Closure and Aftercare

Wound closure should be done with utmost care, avoiding undue tension at the wound edges that might lead to necrosis and wound breakdown. In general, there is no need to suture the fascial layer, as this will increase the compartment pressure of the forearm. Instead, the skin wound should be closed and the bone and metal implants should be covered by soft tissues. In cases of severe swelling which makes primary closure inappropriate or impossible, it is acceptable to leave the wound open over the radius, which is usually covered by the forearm muscles. Secondary skin closure or split skin grafting can be done once the swelling reduces.

If the plate fixation is done correctly and the desired stability is achieved, it is not necessary to apply any splints or casts postoperatively. The patient is instructed to keep the arm elevated and early active movement of the wrist and elbow can be started as early as the first postoperative day. Normal daily activities can be resumed after 2 to 3 weeks, while the patient should refrain from any manual work or sports activities involving the injured arm until bony union has occurred, which may take 12 to 16 weeks.

Pearls and Pitfalls

Which Bone First?

Usually, the authors will fix the fracture with the less comminution first, so as to achieve a more anatomic initial reduction and to have a better chance of restoring the normal length and rotation. If both the radius and ulna have the same degree of comminution, then the radius is usually fixed first, as it is easier to operate first on the volar aspect of the supinated forearm. Afterward, the elbow can be flexed to allow access to the ulna.

Need for Bone Graft

There have been controversies over the use of bone graft in comminuted fractures of the forearm. Anderson et al.[3] recommended bone grafting in the presence of comminution more than one third of the circumference of the bone. However, Ring et al.[83] reported that the use of bone graft was not associated with a higher union rate.

Under normal circumstances, we do not find primary autologous bone grafting necessary (Fig. 31-18). The only exception is the case of a comminuted fracture with several small devascularized cortical fragments that are not amenable to lag screw fixation and preclude a good interfragmentary compression between the two main fragments. In that case, one should restore the normal length and curvature of the bone with bridge plate fixation. The bone defect is then filled with cancellous bone graft obtained from the ipsilateral olecranon or the iliac crest. It is of utmost importance that such bone grafts should not be placed in the interosseous space so as to prevent radioulnar synostosis.

COMPLICATIONS OF FOREARM FRACTURES

Compartment Syndrome

Although compartment syndrome is relatively uncommon in the upper limbs, it is a potentially serious complication. Risk factors include crush injury and other high-energy trauma that cause the forearm fracture.[10a] Moed and Fakouri[72] reported a 10% incidence of compartment syndrome in 131 cases of forearm gunshot wounds with or without fractures. Fracture location was the only significant risk factor and the majority of compartment syndromes they reported occurred in gunshot fractures of the proximal third of the forearm. Young men with associated fracture of the distal end of the radius have also been found to be at risk of compartment syndrome.[70]

A high level of suspicion and frequent physical examination are of paramount importance in making a correct diagnosis of compartment syndrome. Excruciating pain that is disproportional to the clinical picture, severe pain on passive stretching of the fingers, and reduced hand sensibility or paresthesiae are cardinal features of compartment syndrome.[37] Intracompartmental pressure should be measured and, where differential pressures are below 30mm Hg for any length of time, forearm fasciotomy is indicated (see Chapter 27).

Usually, volar compartment decompression through a single curvilinear incision is sufficient.[38] When indicated, an additional straight dorsal incision may be used. The postfasciotomy compartment pressure can be determined intraoperatively to assess the adequacy of the surgical release.

Since median nerve compression is common in acute compartment syndrome of the forearm,[12] the incision should continue in the midline distally and cross the wrist crease to release the carpal tunnel. If the compartment syndrome progresses to include symptoms or signs of ulnar nerve involvement, it should also be released.

Neurovascular Injury

The forearm and the hand are supplied by both the radial and ulnar arteries, which form the superficial and the deep palmar arches. The collateral circulation is usually sufficient to maintain adequate perfusion of the hand. As a result, revascularization is usually unnecessary in the face of a single artery injury. Vascular repair of the blood vessels of the forearm would be indicated in severely crushed forearm or traumatic amputation and should be done after the fracture is stabilized by plate fixation or an external fixator (see Chapter 12).

Nerve injuries involving the median, ulnar, and radial nerves have all been associated with forearm fractures.[32,54,101a] However, the posterior interosseous nerve is by far the most common nerve injury, especially in association with a Monteggia fracture dislocation. In general, most of these injuries are neurapraxias, and nerve exploration is only indicated if there are no signs of recovery at 2 to 4 months.[54,77] However, where there is a deteriorating neurologic status, an arterial injury, an open wound, or an irreducible fracture, earlier exploration is indicated. This does not usually require added surgery as most cases are treated surgically in any case.

Iatrogenic nerve injury can also occur as a result of operative treatment of the forearm fractures. The posterior interosseous nerve is particularly at risk of injury when the proximal radial shaft is exposed. In order to prevent its damage during a Henry approach, the bone must be exposed subperiosteally, with the forearm in maximal supination. Careful retraction of the muscle after the nerve is identified is advisable when the proximal radius is exposed surgically via a dorsal (Thompson) approach.

The superficial branch of the radial nerve can be injured in forearm fractures as a result of impingement by a bone fragment (see Fig. 31-14A) or damage during operative fixation or plate removal.[61] When the anterior or Henry approach is used to expose the radius, the nerve is usually retracted laterally along with the brachioradialis muscle. Care must be taken to use only blunt and broad retractors for this muscle and to avoid prolonged impingement on the nerve by a retractor.

Infection

Despite earlier fears of introducing infection with plating, perioperative antibiotic prophylaxis, good surgical techniques, and modern implants that preserve more blood supply to the bone have resulted in a low incidence of infection after plate fixation of forearm fractures.[14,63,64] Immediate plate fixation of open forearm fractures carries an acceptable risk of infection even in open fractures and is the method of choice along with adequate and appropriate soft tissue management.[15,55,73] If infection does occur, adequate débridement with copious irrigation is recommended, followed by an appropriate antibiotic treatment, which should be based on the results of bacteriologic studies (see Chapter 24). Implant removal is not advised in the presence of infection provided the bone fragments are vascularized and the fixation is stable. Maintenance of stable internal fixation aids wound care, maintains alignment, facilitates bone union, and allows early function.

Nonunion

Failure of fracture union is often due to either inadequate stability or compromise of the vascularity of the bone. Intramedullary nailing of forearm fractures offers less stability than plate fixation and hence carries a higher chance of nonunion.[93,99] Rigidity of the internal fixation device has been reported to have a significant effect on the healing process when rigid and nonrigid devices were compared.[65] However, some flexibility has also been shown to be beneficial. In a biomechanical study of the locked internal fixator, Stoffel et al.[97] examined a simple fracture with a small interfragmentary gap of less than 2 mm. They suggested that the placement of screws in one or even two plate holes near the fracture gap should be omitted to retain some physiologic flexibility of the construct, so as to stimulate bone healing.

With proper plating techniques and an appropriate choice between compression plating and bridge plating, diaphyseal nonunions of forearm fractures are unusual. The current reported incidence of nonunion in forearm fractures treated with plate fixation is less than 2%.[14,63,64] With modern techniques, nonunions can often be ascribed to technical errors. The common pitfalls include the use of inappropriate implants (e.g., one third tubular plates) or plates of inadequate length (Fig. 31-19). Failure to achieve precise reduction of simple or wedge fracture configurations will also lead to compromise in the rigidity of the fixation and a higher risk of a poor result.[61a] Open fracture with significant bone loss is also a common cause of delay in union.

With established diaphyseal nonunions of the radius and ulna, Ring et al.[81] reported successful treatment with autogenous cancellous bone grafting in bone defects of 1 to 6 cm. They reported a high rate of union and improved upper limb function. The prerequisites are stable plate fixation and a healthy and vascular soft tissue envelope.

Malunion

The radius, the ulna, and the interosseous membrane form the integral parts of forearm movement, especially supination and pronation. If the surgeon fails to restore the normal anatomic radial and ulnar bows, bony union will take place in the presence of narrowing of the interosseous space and subsequent contracture of the interosseous membrane. Such malunion will result in significant loss of function, especially in forearm rotation.

Malunion is more common with intramedullary nailing or closed reduction and cast management which remains in com-

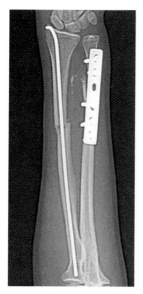

FIGURE 31-19 Poor fixation technique, as in this example of intramedullary pinning, can cause nonunion.

mon usage in pediatric fractures. This is due to failure to restore and maintain the normal bowing of bone and rotational alignment. With the plate fixation that requires a precise reduction, malunion as a complication is rarely reported.

Malunion that causes functional deficit should be treated with osteotomy and rigid plate fixation. Schemitsch and Richards[90] re-

ported 55 patients with malunion and found that good functional results were associated with restoration of the normal amount and location of the radial bow. Trousdale and Linscheid[102] reported a series of 27 cases of malunion of forearm fractures with limitation of motion treated with corrective osteotomy. They suggested that early correction may have a greater improvement in motion than late correction after 1 year of original injury.

Refracture

Removal of plates in the forearm has been associated with a risk of refracture as high as 30%.[47] Before embarking on this surgery, union should be confirmed as an increased risk of refractures has been found in cases in which there are factors which might predispose to nonunion. These include high-energy, crush, or open injuries, failure of reduction or compression, and persistent radiolucency at the fracture site.[19]

Refracture can occur through the original fracture site or through an old screw track. The use of excessively large screws and early removal of plates before 1 year are both associated with higher risk of refracture.[14,85,86] The use of monocortical screws does not reduce the risk of refracture. Leung and Chow[63] compared the use of PC-Fix using monocortical screws versus LC-DCP using bicortical screws and reported the same risk of refracture of 4%. All refractures occurred through the old screw track, even when the original screw engaged in one cortex only. Equally, the advent of new implants such as the LCP does not decrease the risk of refracture. Leung and Chow[63] also reported two cases of refracture (9%) after removal of forearm LCP, both at the original fracture site (Fig. 31-20). Both original fractures

FIGURE 31-20 Radiographs of a 26-year-old man showing **(A)** bone union after implant removal at 12 months. Both the radius and ulna refractured after a fall **(B)** and were fixed with a plate that was longer than the original plate **(C)**.

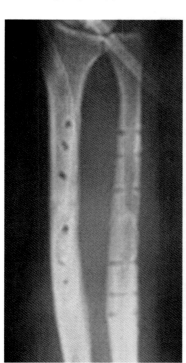

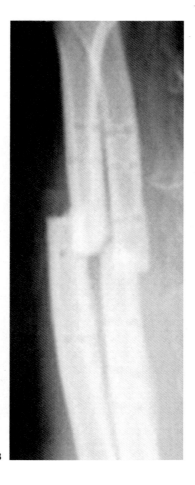

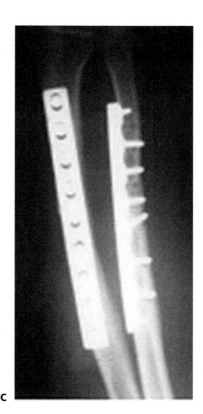

A   B   C

were of simple transverse configuration and demonstrated primary bone union with no callus. Removal was undertaken at 11 and 12 months after the initial fixation, which were earlier than the average 16 months for the series. The authors postulated that the combination of interfragmentary compression with a superimposed locking internal fixator can produce a very stable construct, though it may not be conducive to sound fracture healing, including callus formation.

With a substantial risk of refracture[6] or injury to the superficial branch of the radial nerve,[6] we believe that elective plate removal is contraindicated in the asymptomatic patient. Plate removal should only be considered if there is pain or another symptom resulting from hardware irritation to the soft tissues. It should be delayed for at least 18 months after the initial fixation.

Radioulnar Synostosis

This complication can occur after nonoperative or operative treatment of forearm fractures. Although radioulnar synostosis is more common with fractures of the both the radius and ulna, especially if they are at the same level or in the proximal third of the forearm, it can still occur when only one bone is fractured and the other bone is intact. The incidence of synostosis after plate fixation reported in the literature ranges from 2% to 9%.[5,96,103]

Bauer et al.[5] reported an increased risk using a single incision to approach both bones and advised the use of two separate incisions. Botting[8] reported a series of 10 cases of radioulnar synostosis in which seven were associated with a delay in fixation. Vince and Miller[103] suggested that severe local trauma and delayed open reduction may predispose to synostosis. Bone fragments left in the interosseous space and bone screws that breached the opposite part of the cortex extending into the interosseous space were common findings in their reported cases. A further risk factor is forearm fracture in patients with head injuries.[33]

Prevention of this complication is very important. During the initial fixation of fractures of both the radius and ulna, a separate incision should be used for each bone. Surgical dissection near the interosseous membrane should be limited and narrowing of the interosseous space must be avoided. In cases of proximal forearm fracture, the two bones lie in close vicinity and the surgeon must take care not to penetrate the other bone with a drill during plate application. When the use of bone graft is necessary in comminuted fractures, it should not be placed near the interosseous space.

Since this condition is very disabling to the patient with complete loss of forearm rotation, surgical excision of the synostosis is recommended (Fig. 31-21). A computed tomography scan is

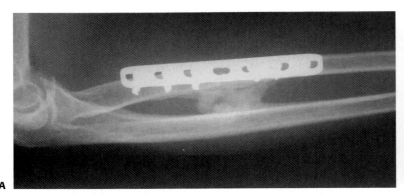

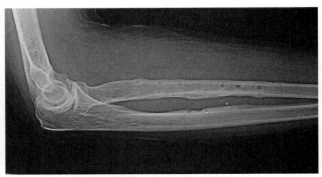

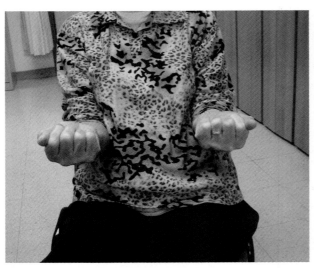

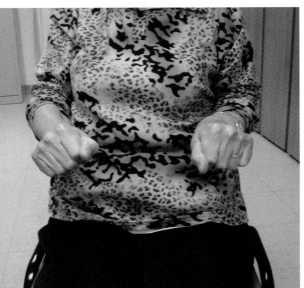

FIGURE 31-21 A. A 61-year-old lady developed radioulnar synostosis after plate fixation of a radial shaft fracture. **B.** Excision was done at 9 months after the initial fixation. **C,D.** The patient had good range of motion afterward.

very helpful to delineate the extent and the location of the bone block, especially when it occurs in the proximal forearm.

Following excision, the tourniquet should be released and hemostasis ensured. Interposition of free fat tissue in the interosseous space helps to prevent recurrence.[57] The patient should be given adequate analgesics in the postoperative period and early range-of-motion exercises should be encouraged. As in heterotopic ossification occurring in other parts of the body, indomethacin should be prescribed to decrease chance of recurrence. We do not adopt the use of postoperative irradiation as a prophylaxis.

Results of excision of a forearm synostosis can be very rewarding but the risk of recurrence is about 30%.[28,103,109]

OUTCOMES

Up to the present time, open reduction and plate fixation has been the standard in management of forearm fractures with very satisfactory results in terms of alignment and union. Few studies have attempted to assess patient orientated outcomes. Goldfarb et al.[39] analyzed the DASH and the musculoskeletal functional assessment (MFA) after fractures of both bones of forearm in 23 patients. The mean DASH score was 12 and the mean MFA score was 19. Significant reduction in pronation (mean difference 10 degrees) and grip strength (mean difference 6 Kg) were found compared to the contralateral forearm. Decreased range of rotation and wrist movement correlated with poorer subjective scores. Droll et al.[20] investigated the DASH and SF-36 as patient-based functional outcomes and measured strength following plate fixation of fractures of both bones of forearm in a cohort of 30 patients. They reported an average loss of 30% strength, although it should be noted that there was a high proportion of high-energy or open injuries. The main determinant of the final DASH score was pain, and the authors suggested that perceived disability was determined by pain more than by objective physical impairment.

FUTURE DIRECTIONS

If normal form and function of the forearm is the aim of our surgical treatment, then a large part of this goal has been achieved by the modern method of plate fixation of forearm fractures. The introduction of locking implants will add the further benefit of stronger fixation in osteoporotic bones. The technique of minimally invasive plate osteosynthesis has gained much popularity recently, and we feel that the ulna fractures may be suitable for this technique. However, with its many muscles attachment and a deeper position in the forearm, the radius is not ideal for this technique.

While stabilization with plate fixation of both bones of forearm restores nearly normal anatomy and motion, there is still room for improvement in terms of patient-based outcome. We suggest that measuring bony union and motion after treatment of forearm fractures is not sufficient. All future studies on this fracture should include a patient-assessed outcome measurement to evaluate the effectiveness of the treatment methods.

REFERENCES

1. Abalo A, Dossim A, Assiobo A, et al. Intramedullary fixation using multiple Kirschner wires for forearm fractures: a developing country perspective. J Orthop Surg 2007;15: 319–322.
2. Almquist EE. Evolution of the distal radioulnar joint. Clin Orthop Relat Res 1992;275: 5–13.
3. Anderson LD, Sisk D, Tooms RE, et al. Compression-plate fixation in acute diaphyseal fractures of the radius and ulna. J Bone Joint Surg Am 1975;57(3):287.
4. Bado JL. The Monteggia lesion. Clin Orthop Relat Res 1967;50:71–86.
5. Bauer G, Arand M, Mutschler W. Posttraumatic radioulnar synostosis after forearm fracture osteosynthesis. Arch Orthop Trauma Surg 1991;110(3):142–145.
6. Bednar DA, Grandwilewski W. Complications of forearm plate removal. Can J Surg 1992;35(4):428–431.
7. Bock GW, Cohen MS, Resnick D. Fracture-dislocation of the elbow with inferior radio-ulnar dislocation: a variant of the Essex-Lopresti injury. Skeletal Radiol 1992;21(5): 315–317.
8. Botting TD. Posttraumatic radioulna cross union. J Trauma 1970;10(1):16–24.
9. Boyd HB, Boals JC. The Monteggia lesion. A review of 159 cases. Clin Orthop Relat Res 1969;66:94–100.
10. Brakenbury PH, Corea JR, Blakemore ME. Nonunion of the isolated fracture of the ulnar shaft in adults. Injury 1981;12(5):371–375.
10a. Broström LA, Stark A, Svartengren G. Acute compartment syndrome in forearm fractures. Acta Orthop Scand 1990;61(1):50–53.
11. Bruce HE, Harvey JP, Wilson JC Jr. Monteggia fractures. J Bone Joint Surg Am 1974; 56(8):1563–1576.
12. Bruckner JD, Lichtman DM, Alexander AH. Complex dislocations of the distal radioulnar joint. Clin Orthop Relat Res 1992;275:90–103.
13. Cetti NE. An unusual cause of blocked reduction of the Galeazzi injury. Injury 1977; 9:59.
14. Chapman MW, Gordon JE, Zissimos AG. Compression-plate fixation of acute fractures of the diaphyses of the radius and ulna. J Bone Joint Surg Am 1989;71(2):159–169.
15. Charnley J. Closed Treatment of Common Fractures. 3rd ed. Edinburgh: Livingstone, 1961.
16. Chloros GD, Wiesler ER, Stabile KJ, et al. Reconstruction of Essex-Lopresti injury of the forearm: technical note. J Hand Surg Am 2008;33(1):124–130.
17. Corea JR, Brakenbury PH, Blakemore ME. The treatment of isolated fractures of the ulnar shaft in adults. Injury 1981;12(5):365–370.
18. De Boeck H, Haentjens P, Handelberg F, et al. Treatment of isolated distal ulnar shaft fractures with below-elbow plaster cast. A prospective study. Arch Orthop Trauma Surg 1996;115(6):316–320.
19. DeLuca PE, Lindsay RW, Ruwe PA. Refracture of bones of the forearm after the removal of compression plate. J Bone Joint Surg Am 1988;70(9):1372–1376.
20. Droll KP, Perna P, Potter J, et al. Outcomes following plate fixation of fractures of both bones of the forearm in adults. J Bone Joint Surg Am 2007;89(12):2619–2624.
21. Duncan R, Geissler W, Freeland AE, et al. Immediate internal fixation of open fractures of the diaphysis of the forearm. J Orthop Trauma 1992;6(1):25–31.
22. Dymond IW. The treatment of isolated fractures of the distal ulna. J Bone Joint Surg Br 1984;66(3):408–410.
23. Edwards GS Jr, Jupiter JB. Radial head fractures with acute distal radioulnar dislocation. Essex-Lopresti revisited. Clin Orthop Relat Res 1988;234:61–69.
24. Eglseder WA, Hay M. Combined Essex-Lopresti and radial shaft fractures: case report. J Trauma 1993;34(2):310–312.
25. Eijer H, Hauke C, Arens S, et al. PC-Fix and local infection resistance—influence of implant design on postoperative infection development, clinical, and experimental results. Injury 2001;32(Suppl 2):B38–B43.
26. Engber WD, Keene JS. Anterior interosseous nerve palsy associated with a Monteggia fracture. A case report. Clin Orthop Relat Res 1983;174:133–137.
27. Essex-Lopresti P. Fractures of the radial head with distal radioulnar dislocation; report of two cases. J Bone Joint Surg Br 1951;33B(2):244–247.
28. Failla JM, Amadio PC, Morrey BF. Posttraumatic proximal radioulnar synostosis. Results of surgical treatment. J Bone Joint Surg Am 1989;71(8):1208–1213.
29. Failla JM, Jacobson J, van Holsbeeck M. Ultrasound diagnosis and surgical pathology of the torn interosseous membrane in forearm fractures/dislocations. J Hand Surg Am 1999;24:257–266.
30. Galeazzi R. Ueber ein besonderes syndrom bei verletzungen im Bereich der unterarm-knocken. Arch. Orthop Unfallchir 1934;35:557–562.
31. Gao H, Luo CF, Zhang CQ, et al. Internal fixation of diaphyseal fractures of the forearm by interlocking intramedullary nail: short-term results in eighteen patients. J Orthop Trauma 2005;19(6):384–391.
32. Garg M, Kumar S. Entrapment and transection of the median nerve associated with minimally displaced fractures of the forearm: case report and review of the literature. Arch Orthop Trauma Surg 2001;121(9):544–545.
33. Garland DE, Dowling V. Forearm fractures in the head-injured adult. Clin Orthop Relat Res 1983;176:190–196.
34. Gausepohl T, Koebke J, Pennig D, et al. The anatomical base of unilateral external fixation in the upper limb. Injury 2000;31(Suppl 1):11–20.
35. Gautier E, Sommer C. Guidelines for the clinical application of the LCP. Injury 2003: 34(Suppl 2):63–76.
36. Gebuhr P, Holmich P, Orsnes T, et al. Isolated ulnar shaft fractures. Comparison of treatment by a functional brace and long-arm cast. J Bone Joint Surg Br 1992;74(5): 757–759.
37. Gelberman RH, Garfin SR, Hergenroeder PT, et al. Compartment syndromes of the forearm: diagnosis and treatment. Clin Orthop Relat Res 1981;161:252–261.
38. Gelberman RH, Zakaib GS, Mubarak SJ, et al. Decompression of forearm compartment syndromes. Clin Orthop Relat Res 1978;134:225–229.
39. Goldfarb CA, Ricci WM, Tull F, et al. Functional outcome after fracture of both bones of the forearm. J Bone Joint Surg Br 2005;87(3):374–379.
40. Haas N, Hauke C, Schutz M, et al. Treatment of diaphyseal fractures of the forearm using the Point Contact Fixator (PC-Fix): results of 387 fractures of a prospective multicentric study. Injury 2001;32(Suppl 2):B51–B62.
41. Hadden WA, Reschauer R, Seggl W. Results of AO plate fixation of forearm shaft fractures in adults. Injury 1983;15:44–52.
42. Handoll HH, Pearce PK. Interventions for isolated diaphyseal fractures of the ulna in adults. Cochrane Database Syst Rev 2004;2:CD000523.
43. Has B, Jovanovic S, Wetheimer B, et al. External fixation as a primary and definitive treatment of open limb fractures. Injury 1995;26:245–248.
44. Helber MU, Ulrich C. External fixation in forearm shaft fractures. Injury 2000;31(Suppl 1):45–47.

45. Henry AK. Exposure of the long bones and other surgical methods. Bristol: Wright, 1927.

46. Hertel R, Pisan M, Lambert S, et al. Plate osteosynthesis of diaphyseal fractures of the radius and ulna. Injury 1996;27:545–548.

47. Hidaka S, Gustilo RB. Refracture of bones of the forearm after plate removal. J Bone Joint Surg Am 1984;66A(8):1241–1242.

48. Hofer HP, Wildburger R, Szyszkowitz R. Observations concerning different patterns of bone healing using the Point Contact Fixator (PC-Fix) as a new technique for fracture fixation. Injury 2001;32(Suppl 2):B15–B25.

49. Hong G, Cong-Feng L, Hui-Peng S, et al. Treatment of diaphyseal forearm nonunions with interlocking intramedullary nails. Clin Orthop Relat Res 2006;450:186–192.

50. Hotchkiss RN, An KN, Sowa DT, et al. An anatomic and mechanical study of the interosseous membrane of the forearm: pathomechanics of proximal migration of the radius. J Hand Surg Am 1989;14(2 Pt 1):256–261.

51. Hughston JD. Fractures of the distal radial shaft, mistakes in management. J Bone Joint Surg Am 1957;39:249–264.

52. Itoh Y, Horiuchi Y, Takahashi M, et al. Extensor tendon involvement in Smith's and Galeazzi's fractures. J Hand Surg Am 1987;12:535–540.

53. Jenkins NH, Mintowt-Cyz WJ, Fairclough JA. Irreducible dislocation of the distal radioulnar joint. Injury 1987;18:40–43.

54. Jessing P. Monteggia lesions and their complicating nerve damage. Acta Orthop Scand 1975;46(4):601–609.

55. Jones JA. Immediate internal fixation of high-energy open forearm fractures. J Orthop Trauma 1991;5(3):272–279.

56. Jupiter JB, Leibovic SJ, Ribbans W, et al. The posterior Monteggia lesion. J Orthop Trauma 1991;5:395–402.

57. Jupiter JB, Ring D. Operative treatment of post-traumatic proximal radioulnar synostosis. J Bone Joint Surg Am 1998;80(2):248–257.

58. Khurana JS, Kattapuram SV, Becker S, et al. Galeazzi injury with an associated fracture of the radial head. Clin Orthop Relat Res 1988;234:70–71.

59. Knight RA, Purvis GD. Fractures of both bones of the forearm in adults. J Bone Joint Surg Am 1949;31:755–764.

60. Konrad GG, Kundel K, Kreuz PC, et al. Monteggia frcatures in adults. J Bone Joint Surg Br 2007;89:354–360.

61. Langkamer VG, Ackroyd CE. Removal of forearm plates. A review of the complications. J Bone Joint Surg Br 1990;72:601–604.

61a. Langkamer VG, Ackroyd CE. Internal fixation of forearm fractures in the 1980s: lessons to be learnt. Injury 1991;22(2):97–102.

62. Lenihan MR, Brien WW, Gellman H, et al. Fractures of the forearm resulting from low-velocity gunshot wounds. J Orthop Trauma 1992;6(1):32–35.

63. Leung F, Chow SP. A prospective, randomized trial comparing the limited contact dynamic compression plate with the point contact fixator for forearm fractures. J Bone Joint Surg Am 2003;85-A(12):2343–2348.

64. Leung F, Chow SP. Locking compression plate in the treatment of forearm fractures: a prospective study. J Orthop Surg (Hong Kong) 2006;14(3):291–294.

65. Lyritis G, Ioannidis TH, Hartofylakidis-Garofalidis G. The influence of timing and rigidity of internal fixation on bony union of fractures of the forearm. Injury 1981;15:53–56.

66. Mackay D, Wood L, Rangan A. The treatment of isolated ulnar fractures in adults: a systematic review. Injury 2000;31(8):565–570.

66a. Mackay I, Fitzgerald B, Miller JH. Silastic replacement of the head of the radius in trauma. J Bone Joint Surg Br 1979;61-B(4):494–497.

67. Macule Beneyto F, Arandes Renu JM, et al. Treatment of Galeazzi fracture-dislocations. J Trauma 1994;36(3):352–355.

68. Mast J, Jakob R, Ganz R. Planning and Reduction Techniques in Fracture Surgery. Berlin: Springer-Verlag, 1989.

69. McLaughlin HL. Trauma. Philiadelphia: Saunders, 1959.

70. McQueen MM, Gaston P, Court-Brown CM. Acute compartment syndrome. Who is at risk? 2000;82(2):200–203.

71. Mikic ZD. Galeazzi fracture-dislocations. J Bone Joint Surg Am 1975;57(8):1071–1080.

72. Moed BR, Fakhouri AJ. Compartment syndrome after low-velocity gunshot wounds to the forearm. J Orthop Trauma 1991;5(2):134–137.

73. Moed BR, Kellam JF, Foster RJ, et al. Immediate internal fixation of open fractures of the diaphysis of the forearm. J Bone Joint Surg 1986;68:1008–1017.

74. Moore TM, Klein JP, Patzakis MJ, et al. Results of compression-plating of closed Galeazzi fractures. J Bone Joint Surg Am 1985;67(7):1015–1021.

75. Morris AH. Irreducible Monteggia lesion with radial-nerve entrapment. A case report. J Bone Joint Surg Am 1974;56(8):1744–1746.

76. Muller ME, ed. The Comprehensive Classification of Fractures of Long Bones. Berlin: Springer-Verlag, 1990.

77. Omer GE Jr. Results of untreated peripheral nerve injuries. Clin Orthop Relat Res 1982;163:15–19.

78. Perren SM. The concept of biological plating using the limited contact-dynamic compression plate (LC-DCP). Scientific background, design and application. Injury 1991;22(Suppl 1):1–41.

79. Preston CF, Chen AL, Wolinsky PR, et al. Posterior dislocation of the elbow with concomitant fractures of the proximal ulnar diaphysis and radial head: a complex variant of the posterior Monteggia lesion. J Orthop Trauma 2003;17:530–533.

80. Rettig ME, Raskin KB. Galeazzi fracture-dislocation: a new treatment oriented classification. J Hand Surg Am 2001;26(2):228–235.

81. Ring D, Allende C, Jafarnia K, et al. Ununited diaphyseal forearm fractures with segmental defects: plate fixation and autogenous cancellous bone-grafting. J Bone Joint Surg Am 2004;86-A(11):2440–2445.

82. Ring D, Jupiter JB, Simpson NS. Monteggia fractures in adults. J Bone Joint Surg Am 1998;80:1733–1744.

83. Ring D, Rhim R, Carpenter C, et al. Comminuted diaphyseal fractures of the radius and ulna: does bone grafting affect nonunion rate? J Trauma 2005;59(2):438–441.

84. Ring D, Rhim R, Carpenter C, et al. Isolated radial shaft fractures are more common than Galeazzi fractures. J Hand Surg Am 2006;31(1):17–21.

85. Rosson JW, Shearer JR. Refracture after the removal of plates from the forearm—an avoidable complication. J Bone Joint Surg Br 1991;73:415–417.

86. Rumball K, Finnegan M. Refractures after forearm plate removal. J Orthop Trauma 1990;4(2):124–129.

87. Sage FP. Medullary fixation of fractures of the forearm. A study of the medullary canal of the radius and a report of 50 fractures of the radius treated with a prebent triangular nail. J Bone Joint Surg Am 1959;41-A:1489–1516.

88. Sarmiento A, Cooper JS, Sinclair WF. Forearm fractures. Early functional bracing—a preliminary report. J Bone Joint Surg Am 1975;57(3):297–304.

89. Sarmiento A, Latta LL, Zych G, et al. Isolated ulnar shaft fractures treated with functional braces. J Orthop Trauma 1998;12:420–423.

90. Schemitsch EH, Richards RR. The effect of malunion on functional outcome after plate fixation of fractures of both bones of the forearm in adults. J Bone Joint Surg Am 1992;74(7):1068–1078.

91. Schuind F, Andrianne Y, Burny F. Treatment of forearm fractures by Hoffman external fixation. A study of 93 patients. Clin Orthop Relat Res 1991;266:197–204.

92. Smith DK, Cooney WP. External fixation of high-energy upper extremity injuries. J Orthop Trauma 1990;4:7–18.

93. Smith H, Sage FP. Medullary fixation of forearm fractures. J Bone Joint Surg Am 1957;39-A(1):91–98.

94. Spar I. A neurologic complication following Monteggia fracture. Clin Orthop Relat Res 197;122:207–209.

95. Spinner M, Freundlich BD, Teicher J. Posterior interosseous nerve palsy as a complication of Monteggia fractures in children. Clin Orthop Relat Res 1968;58:141–145.

96. Stern PJ, Drury WJ. Complications of plate fixation of forearm fractures. Clin Orthop Relat Res 1983;175:25–29.

97. Stoffel K, Dieter U, Stachowiak G, et al. Biomechanical testing of the LCP—how can stability in locked internal fixators be controlled? Injury 2003;34(Suppl 2):B11–B19.

98. Strauss EJ, Tejwani NC, Preston CF, et al. The posterior Monteggia lesion with associated ulnohumeral instability. J Bone Joint Surg Br 2006;88:84–89.

99. Street DM. Intramedullary forearm nailing. Clin Orthop Relat Res 1986;212:219–230.

100. Strehle J, Gerber C. Distal radioulnar joint function after Galeazzi fracture-dislocations treated by open reduction and internal plate fixation. Clin. Orthop Relat Res 1993;293:240–245.

101. Swanson AB, Jaeger SH, La Rochelle D. Comminuted fractures of the radial head. The role of silicone-implant replacement arthroplasty. J Bone Joint Surg Am 1981;63(7):1039–1049.

101a. Torpey BM, Pess GM, Kircher MT, et al. Ulnar nerve laceration in a closed both bone forearm fracture. J Orthop Trauma 1996;10(2):131–134.

102. Trousdale RT, Linscheid RL. Operative treatment of malunited fractures of the forearm. J Bone Joint Surg Am 1995;77(6):894–901.

103. Vince KG, Miller JE. Cross-union complicating fracture of the forearm. Part I: adults. J Bone Joint Surg Am 1987;69(5):640–653.

104. Wagner M. General principles for the clinical use of the LCP. Injury 2003;34(Suppl 2):31–42.

105. Watson JA, Singer GC. Irreducible Monteggia fracture: beware nerve entrapment. Injury 1994;25(5):325–327.

106. Watson-Jones R. Fractures and Joint Injuries. 3rd ed. Baltimore: Williams and Wilkins, 1943.

107. Weckbach A, Blattert TR, Weisser CH. Interlocking nailing of forearm fractures. Arch Orthop Trauma Surg 2006;126(5):309–315.

108. Wild JJ Jr, Hanson GW, Bennett JB, et al. External fixation use in the management of massive upper extremity trauma. Clin Orthop Relat Res 1982;164:172–176.

109. Yong-Hing K, Tchang SP. Traumatic radioulnar synostosis treated by excision and a free fat transplant. A report of two cases. J Bone Joint Surg Br 1983;65(4):433–435.

32

ELBOW FRACTURES AND DISLOCATIONS

David Ring

INTRODUCTION

Trauma to the adult elbow can be challenging to treat by virtue of the complex articular structure, complex capsuloligamentous and musculotendinous arrangements, and the proximity of neurovascular structures. An increasing understanding of elbow injuries has led to a rapid evolution in treatment concepts.[90]

Awareness of the patterns of injury and the pitfalls of each can lead to restoration of a functional elbow in most patients. The majority of complications can be addressed with secondary surgery, but certain key structures—such as the ulnotrochlear relationship—must be reconstructed and protected by the initial treatment or salvage measures will become necessary.

ANATOMY

Anatomy of Stability

The elbow is an inherently stable joint. The nearly 180-degree capture of the trochlea in the trochlear notch is tilted somewhat posterior, thereby increasing the anterior buttress of the coronoid process (Fig. 32-1A). The trochlea is wide and has a central groove that interdigitates with a ridge in the center of the trochlear notch (Fig. 32-1B). The contacts between (i) the anteromedial coronoid facet and the medial lip of the trochlea and (ii) the radial head and capitellum represent the most important stabilizing columns of the elbow. In the absence of a radial head or capitellum, the contact between the lateral lip of the trochlea and the lateral portion of the coronoid becomes more important.

This inherent bony stability is reinforced by capsuloligamentous structures (Fig. 32-2). The medial collateral ligament (MCL) has been singled out as the most important stabilizer of the elbow,[83,84] but this is only true in athletes who throw.[53] The importance of the MCL may also have been overstated because of the fact that its contribution to elbow stability is much easier to isolate in cadavers.[16,83] Injury to the lateral collateral ligament (LCL) is a consistent feature of traumatic elbow instability and inadequate treatment of the LCL is the source of a large proportion of the cases of posttraumatic elbow instability.[86,89,92] The LCL and MCL are often referred to as complexes to emphasize that their contributions to elbow stability are enhanced by adjacent capsuloligamentous, fascial, and musculotendinous structures.[16] The anterior capsule also makes a substantial contribution to elbow stability.[83]

Dynamic forces from the muscles that cross the elbow joint provide an important element of stability when other stabilizing structures have been injured.[24,26]

Anatomy of Mobility

Flexion of the elbow is enhanced by the anterior translation of the trochlea with respect to the humeral shaft and the coronoid and radial fossae above the trochlea on the anterior surface of the distal humerus[62] (Fig. 32-1C). Extension of the elbow is enhanced by the olecranon fossa above the trochlea posteriorly (Fig. 32-1D). The elbow has a predilection for stiffness after trauma as a result of capsular scarring and formation of fibrous tissue in the fossae and heterotopic ossification. Loss of the anterior translation of the trochlea and articular malalignment, incongruity, and arthrosis will also limit motion.

Pathoanatomy of Injury

Elbow injuries occur in specific patterns. Recognition of these patterns can help the surgeon anticipate associated fractures and ligament injuries, better predict the prognosis of the injury, and plan and execute operative treatment.[106,109,111,112] For example, the capsuloligamentous injury in an elbow dislocation progresses from lateral to medial with a posterolateral rotatory mechanism.[91] As the elbow dislocates posteriorly, the radial head and/or the coronoid process can fracture as they collide with the distal humerus. The last structure to be injured is the anterior band of the MCL[91] (Fig. 32-3). On the other hand, the elbow can be destabilized by a distinct injury pattern that in-

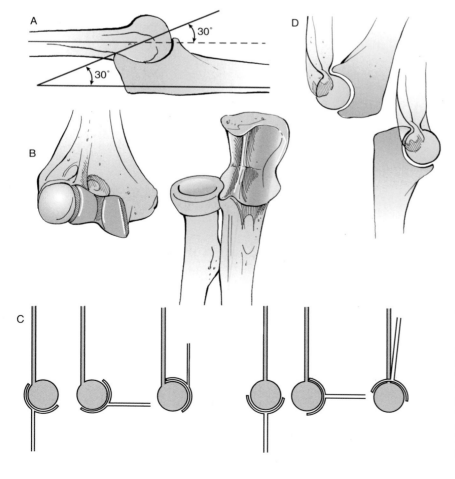

FIGURE 32-1 The elbow is an inherently stable joint. **A.** The trochlear notch of the ulna provides a nearly 180-degree capture of the trochlea, which tilts posteriorly approximately 30 degrees. **B.** The ridge in the center of the trochlear notch interdigitates with a groove on the trochlea, further enhancing stability. **C.** Flexion of the elbow is enhanced by the anterior translation of the trochlea with respect to the humeral shaft as well as the coronoid and radial fossae on the anterior surface of the humerus that accept the coronoid process and radial head respectively. **D.** Posteriorly, the olecranon fossa enhances extension by accommodating the olecranon process.

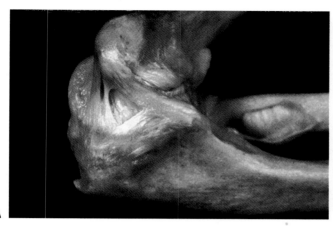
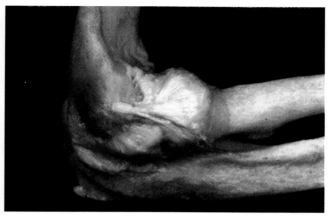

A   **B**

FIGURE 32-2 The medial and lateral collateral ligament complexes of the elbow. **A.** The medial collateral ligament is described as having anterior, posterior, and transverse bundles, but the most important part is the anterior bundle, which originates on the undersurface of the medial epicondyle and inserts at the base of the coronoid process. **B.** The lateral collateral ligament originates from the inferior point of a small tubercle in the center of the lateral epicondyle, converges with the annular ligament and inserts onto the lateral aspect of the ulna at the crista supinatoris. (Courtesy of David Ruch, MD.)

volves a varus posteromedial rotational injury force.[90] This is characterized by a fracture of the anteromedial facet of the coronoid process with either a LCL injury, a fracture of the olecranon, or both. The anatomy of specific injury patterns is described in greater detail for each specific injury later.

The LCL and the MCL typically fail by avulsion of their origins from the epicondyles along with a variable amount of the common extensor or flexor musculature.[73] This facilitates identification and repair of the injury. The MCL originates from the anteroinferior portion of the medial epicondyle (Fig. 32-2A).

The LCL originates at the inferior portion of a small tubercle on the lateral epicondyle, which represents the center of rotation of the elbow (Fig. 32-2B).

The anterior band of the MCL inserts on the base of the coronoid process[8] (Fig. 32-4). Consequently, the anterior band of the MCL is likely to be intact in complex fractures associated with large fractures of the coronoid base or anteromedial coro-

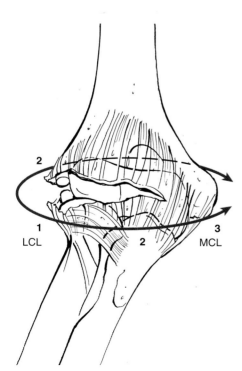

FIGURE 32-3 The capsuloligamentous structures of the elbow are injured in a lateral to medial progression during a dislocation of the elbow. The elbow can dislocate with the anterior band of the medial collateral ligament (MCL) remaining intact.

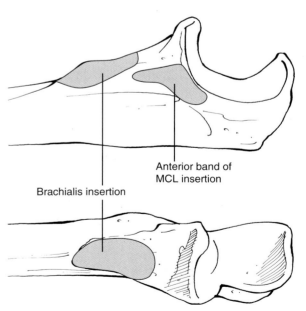

FIGURE 32-4 The soft tissue attachments to the coronoid process. The anterior band of the medial collateral ligament (MCL) inserts at the base of the coronoid process. Consequently, if there is a large coronoid fracture, or a coronoid fracture that involves the anteromedial facet of the coronoid, the medial collateral ligament usually remains intact, the failure having occurred through bone rather than ligament. Although the anterior capsule inserts several millimeters below the tip of the coronoid process, tip fractures nearly always include the capsular insertion. The brachialis insertion is broad and extends distally and its function is rarely disrupted by a fracture of the coronoid.

noid fractures, with its function disrupted by the bony injury and restored with stable internal fixation. The brachialis has a broad insertion that extends distal to the coronoid process[8] (Fig. 32-4). Even with large coronoid fractures, a substantial portion of the brachialis insertion usually remains on the ulnar shaft. The anterior capsule inserts a few millimeters below the tip of the olecranon process.[8] This has been interpreted to mean that a very small coronoid fracture involving the very tip of the coronoid process (type 1 according to Regan and Morrey) may represent intra-articular free fragments; however, operative treatment of small coronoid fractures discloses that coronoid tip fractures are much larger on exposure than might be guessed based on the radiographs and that they always include the capsular insertion.[101,109,110,112,117]

The junction of the olecranon process with the proximal ulnar metaphysis occurs at the transverse groove of the olecranon, which is a nonarticular area with consequently less subchondral bone, and it is also a relatively narrow area in the sagittal plane (Fig. 32-1B). These factors may increase the susceptibility to fracture at this site.[77]

Operative Anatomy

Some general principles are common to all elbow surgery. The robust blood supply of the skin of the upper extremity increases the safety of elevating skin flaps even in the face of posttraumatic swelling, blistering, and contusion. As a result, elbow surgeons often prefer to make a single, long posterior skin incision, through which all aspects of the elbow can be exposed, including the anterior structures.[94] Separate medial and lateral incisions can also be used, although care must be taken to protect the medial antebrachial cutaneous nerve on the medial side of the elbow as it is prone to develop a painful neuroma when injured.[23]

The ulnar nerve passes through the narrow and constrictive cubital tunnel at the medial epicondyle and is held tightly by Osbourne fascia for several centimeters distal to the elbow. Consequently, it is no surprise that ulnar nerve dysfunction is common after elbow injury in either the acute, subacute, or chronic setting. In many cases, mobilization and transposition of the ulnar nerve facilitate internal fixation of the medial epicondyle or the coronoid process. An in situ release may be considered for any major elbow trauma, particularly those associated with elbow instability, in an attempt to help limit ulnar nerve–related sequelae.

The other neurovascular structures are relatively safe with careful dissection and retractor placement. The radial nerve is most often injured by retraction. The safety of retraction is improved by a more extensive release of the common extensor and radial wrist extensor muscles from the lateral condyle. One must also take care to protect the posterior interosseous nerve when implants are applied to the neck of the radius. The brachialis muscle usually provides protection for the median nerve and brachial artery.

Several muscle intervals are used routinely on the medial and lateral aspects of the elbow. These are not necessarily internervous intervals, but since they are developed for only a few centimeters, the nerve supply to the muscles is usually safe. On the medial aspect, the flexor pronator mass can be split in half,[49] the split of the flexor carpi ulnaris where the ulnar nerve runs can be developed,[90,112] the entire flexor pronator mass can

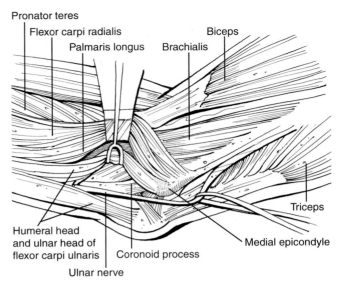

Pronator teres
Flexor carpi radialis
Palmaris longus
Biceps
Brachialis
Triceps
Medial epicondyle
Humeral head and ulnar head of flexor carpi ulnaris
Coronoid process
Ulnar nerve

FIGURE 32-5 Medial exposures of the coronoid and elbow joint. From posterior to anterior, the intervals that can be used are elevation of the entire flexor pronator mass off of the medial ulna, development of the split in the flexor carpi ulnaris where the ulnar nerve runs, or splitting the flexor pronator mass anteriorly.

be elevated off of the ulna from posterior to anterior,[94,127] or the flexor pronator mass can be detached and reflected distally (Fig. 32-5). On the lateral aspect of the elbow, essentially any interval can be developed. The most commonly used intervals are between the extensor carpi radialis longus and brevis (or between the extensor carpi radialis brevis and the extensor digitorum communis)[48,81]; between the anconeus and extensor carpi ulnaris (the Kocher approach)[63]; or reflecting the entire common extensor mass with the ruptured LCL origin or lateral epicondyle fracture fragment[33,43,44,106] (Fig. 32-6).

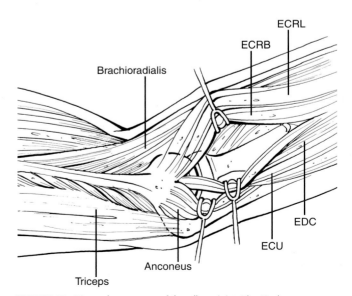

ECRL
ECRB
Brachioradialis
EDC
ECU
Anconeus
Triceps

FIGURE 32-6 Lateral exposures of the elbow joint. The Kocher exposure (between the anconeus and extensor carpi ulnaris) is a commonly used exposure, but a more anterior exposure (splitting the common extensor muscles) can help protect the lateral collateral ligament complex and provide better access to the coronoid.

Anatomy of Internal and External Fixation

Elbow implants must respect articular surfaces, fossae, and neurovascular structures. The posterior interosseous nerve crosses over the radial neck and may be in direct contact with the bone. Pronation helps to protect the nerve during a lateral approach to the radial head[19] and supination helps to protect it during an anterior approach.[45]

The radial head has very little nonarticular surface for the placement of implants. The nonarticular area can be determined as a roughly 90-degree arc with its midpoint directly laterally with the forearm in neutral rotation, with a slightly greater margin anteriorly.[124] It can be more straightforward to define a safe area intraoperatively by applying a plate as posteriorly as possible with the forearm in full supination[125] or as the area on the proximal radius that corresponds to the area between Lister's tubercle and the radial styloid on the distal radius[9] (Fig. 32-7).

The anatomy of the radial head is difficult to replicate with a prosthesis.[128] It has a slightly elliptical cross section and interdigitates precisely with both the lesser sigmoid notch and the lateral lip of the trochlea, as well as the capitellar articular surface.[62] The slight angulation of the proximal radius with respect to the shaft further complicates attempts to reconstruct or replace the radius.

The triceps has a very broad and thick insertion onto the posterior and proximal aspects of the olecranon. This is notable during the application of a plate that contours around this portion of the bone—if the center of the triceps insertion is not split and elevated from the bone, the proximal aspect of the plate will rest well off the bone. For complex olecranon fractures, this compromise may sometimes be preferable to additional dissection of the soft tissue attachments.

GENERAL FEATURES OF ELBOW INJURIES

Several features of elbow injuries are similar for very different injury types and are best considered in general before reviewing the specific injury types.

Mechanism of Injury

Elbow injuries occur in identifiable patterns that are determined by the injury forces or mechanism, the energy of the injury, and the quality of the underlying bone. Recognition of the injury pattern helps with management of the injury and counseling of the patient.

Signs and Symptoms

Patients with fractures and dislocations of the elbow present with varying degrees of pain, swelling, and ecchymosis. In many cases, there is also instability, crepitation, and deformity.

Associated Injuries

Relatively few of these injuries are associated with open wounds or acute neurovascular injury. Most elbow injuries occur in isolation with ipsilateral skeletal injuries and polytrauma being much less common.

Rationale of the Treatment of Elbow Injuries

The key element in the treatment of elbow injuries is restoration of a congruent articular reduction. Malaligned articular surfaces or instability will restrict motion and cause arthrosis that is difficult to salvage.[111,119] In contrast, a stiff but congruent elbow joint can often be restored to good function with secondary surgeries even when there is extensive heterotopic bone, an ununited fracture, or ulnar neuropathy.[15,60,66,108] While the majority of elbow injuries benefit from early active use and exercise, with complex articular fractures and very unstable elbows it can be better to err on the side of achieving a healed and congruent but stiff elbow by delaying mobilization or even—in rare instances—by cross-pinning the joint.

Recognition of the injury pattern leads directly to an understanding of the injury components. Appropriate treatment of each injury component will help avoid pitfalls and provide the best opportunity for recovery.

Rehabilitation

The hand is typically swollen and ecchymotic after an elbow injury and can become permanently stiff if confident active exercises are not encouraged.

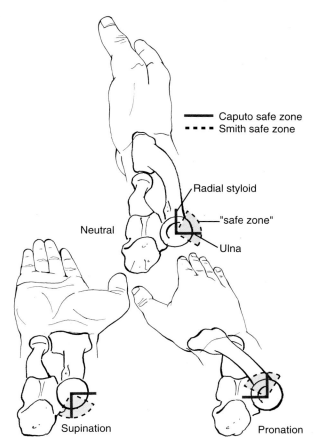

FIGURE 32-7 The nonarticular area of the radial head—or the so-called safe zone for the application of internal fixation devices—has been defined in various ways. Smith and Hotchkiss defined it based on lines bisecting the radial head made in full supination, full pronation, and neutral. Implants can be placed as far as halfway between the middle and posterior lines and a few millimeters beyond halfway between the middle and anterior lines. Caputo and colleagues recommend using the radial styloid and Lister's tubercle as intraoperative guides to this safe zone, but this describes a slightly different zone.

Active exercises and gentle functional use of the arm for daily activities are usually initiated within a few days, most often the morning after surgery. The patient is encouraged to use the other hand, gravity, and pushing against other objects to help assist with elbow mobilization.

Passive manipulation by a therapist or family member is discouraged. There is a long-standing belief that this will contribute to heterotopic bone formation. It may also be more likely to loosen implants or impede healing. Finally, the patient must learn how to mobilize his or her own upper extremity if the exercise program is to be effective.

In the treatment of traumatic elbow instability, slight sagging or subluxation of an otherwise concentrically reduced joint noted radiographically can usually be addressed by encouraging confident active motion of the elbow.[26,55] This adds a dynamic muscular component of stability, which overcomes what is likely a form of pseudosubluxation of the joint. More substantial subluxations should be treated operatively as they risk damage to the articular surface. Given the useful dynamic component of stability, combined with the fact that the elbow can dislocated in a cast when unstable, the value of casts or braces for enhancing elbow stability must be questioned—I personally do not use them. The idea of an extension block brace is also common but probably not usually necessary because patients then usually struggle to regain extension.

When a LCL injury or an anteromedial facet coronoid fracture is repaired, it is useful to avoid shoulder abduction for a few weeks—"varus stress precautions."[26]

The use of continuous passive elbow motion (using various devices) with or without continuous anesthesia via a brachial plexus catheter is gaining in popularity despite the lack of evidence that it improves elbow motion. It is not clear that the additional risk and cost are justified. I believe that active elbow motion is the key and that motivated patients will do better—I therefore shy away from passive treatments.

Complications

Stiffness and Heterotopic Ossification

Stiffness is a complication that is common to all elbow injuries.[49] Some permanent loss of elbow motion is to be expected for all but the simplest injuries; usually it is a loss of extension. Severe loss of motion is often associated with heterotopic ossification, joint incongruity, ulnar neuropathy, or arthrosis. In the absence of these associated problems, a program of active-assisted exercises supplemented by static progressive or dynamic elbow splints can improve motion to a functional range in a large percentage of patients.[34,37] With complex or unresponsive stiffness, operative release of the contracted capsule, the constricted ulnar nerve, heterotopic bone, and osteophytes can often improve motion.[49] Passive manipulation of the elbow in an attempt to regain motion is generally discouraged for fear of causing heterotopic ossification, inhibiting healing, or fracturing the arm.

The formation of heterotopic ossification can be reduced by the administration of a single local 700-Gy dose of radiation[70] and, to some degree, by nonsteroidal anti-inflammatory drugs.[132] Both of these interventions may also inhibit fracture healing. Radiation also has a potential cancer risk that must be respected. It is still recommended that these prophylactic measures be used selectively. Patients with head injuries, high-energy fracture-dislocations, and repeat surgery during the first few weeks are at the highest risk for substantial heterotopic ossification.

Ulnar Neuropathy

The ulnar nerve is vulnerable to constriction because it runs beneath the cubital tunnel fascia and Osbourne fascia. Cubital tunnel syndrome—a gradually developing, chronic ulnar neuropathy—is quite common after elbow trauma.[72] It is likely because of the swelling, bleeding, tissue injury and distortion, scar formation and tissue contracture, heterotopic ossification, and arthrosis that develop after injury. Consideration has been given to routine in situ decompression of the ulnar nerve for some fractures that seem to be particularly at risk, such as fracture-dislocations of the elbow.

An ulnar neuropathy that develops after treatment of the injury can contribute to stiffness and pain in addition to affecting hand function.[29] It is important to be aware of the importance of the ulnar nerve and always evaluate the patient for symptoms and signs of ulnar nerve dysfunction, being particularly suspicious when stiffness or pain is greater than might otherwise be expected.

Acute ulnar nerve dysfunction with an intact nerve (caused by either the injury or handling of the nerve during surgery) usually, but not always, recovers. It can take a very long time, in some cases more than 1 year or longer, to recover. Serial clinical examination and nerve conduction studies and electromyography can help determine if surgical intervention is worthwhile. Operative treatment is considered if serial neurophysiological testing does not demonstrate improvement or if there is obvious worsening of the deficit on exam.

Instability

Truly unstable or flail elbows are usually related to bone loss or nonunion.[114] Instability after a fracture-dislocation usually is related to residual malalignment and incongruity of the elbow.[107,111] This will lead to arthrosis and must be addressed as soon as possible. Even a few weeks of elbow motion and use in a malaligned position can permanently damage the articular surfaces. At that point, only a interpositional arthroplasty or total joint arthroplasty can be considered—neither are great options in young, active individuals.

If the elbow articulation remains malaligned after operative treatment, additional surgery is necessary as soon as possible, even though early reoperation increases the risk of extensive heterotopic ossification. Operative treatment of persistent elbow malalignment consists of restoration of the stabilizing anatomy of the elbow (radial head, coronoid, collateral ligaments) and hinged external fixation to maintain a concentric reduction during the initial treatment period.[107,111,119] While this is fortunately uncommon, it is my impression that patients in whom the trochlear notch is relatively spared do better than those with instability associated with large and complex coronoid fractures.

Nonunion

The metaphyseal bone around the elbow is well vascularized and nonunions are relatively uncommon overall; however, several specific injuries are more prone to nonunions than others and require specific attention in treatment.

Whereas nonunion of the olecranon is very unusual, fractures of the proximal ulna with extensive metaphyseal comminution have been more problematic.[93,113] Much of this seems to relate to inadequate fixation of the proximal, metaphyseal fragment, particularly with osteoporotic bone. In the treatment of both fresh fractures and nonunions, it seems better to apply a long plate on the dorsal surface of the ulna that wraps around the olecranon process, thereby providing additional screw fixation.[113,116,119] It is also important not to remove the muscular and periosteal attachments to the comminuted fragments in the metaphysis but rather to bridge this area with a long plate and use the fragments as vascularized bone grafts, rather than depending on them for stability. In the setting of nonunion, debriding the fracture site of sclerotic, inflammatory, and devitalized tissues and applying a nonstructural cancellous bone graft has been very successful in our experience.[115,116]

Nonunion of the radial head may be more common than previously recognized.[14,43,104,120] Minimally displaced fractures involving the radial neck may fail to heal.[14,104] We do not know the true incidence of nonunion because it rarely causes symptoms; we do not usually reevaluate the elbow radiographically; and ununited fractures of the radial head may eventually heal without additional intervention if followed for longer than 2 years.[14,120]

Complex fractures of the radial head that are repaired with a plate and screws are also prone to early failure and nonunion.[43,120] In this case, usually the reconstructed radial head has served well as a stabilizer of the elbow and, with the ligaments now healed, it can safely be resected without replacing it.

Infection

Infections are fortunately very uncommon after the operative treatment of elbow fractures. They are usually related to complex open injuries, devitalized fracture fragments, and immunocompromised patients. These infections are usually treated with serial débridement, retention of implants, and parenteral antibiotics, particularly when the fracture is complex. Healing of the fractures can usually be achieved with this regimen. Eventually, complete eradication of the infection usually requires implant removal. Elbow mobility is typically allowed during treatment of infection. It can be assisted with external fixation or hinged external fixation when there is associated elbow instability or an unsupported fracture or nonunion.

Wound Problems

Wound problems are also very uncommon, because of the excellent blood supply. Most patients with wound edge necrosis or slight wound separation can be treated with dressing changes, but patients with exposed implants or an underlying total elbow arthroplasty should be treated operatively to obtain better skin cover. This can often be accomplished with local rotational flaps, pedicled flaps (such as a radial forearm flap), or, on occasion, a free microvascular tissue transfer.[122,126] I follow the so-called reconstructive stepladder (see Chapter 14), using the simplest procedure that will address the problem.

Arthrosis

Despite sometimes-dramatic claims made by nutritional supplement and pharmaceutical companies, there is no cure for posttraumatic arthrosis. Patients must adapt to and live with the arthrosis or consider reconstructive procedures, none of which are perfect. Débridement of osteophytes and loose bodies and

capsulectomy can be useful in the short term and may be best used in conjunction with ulnar nerve release because ulnar neuropathy is a commonly associated problem.[1]

Patients with severe articular damage or incongruity must consider interpositional arthroplasty[12,30] or total elbow arthroplasty.[82] Total elbow arthroplasty has a finite life span (with each revision becoming increasingly more difficult), is more prone to infection and major complications than knee or hip arthroplasty, requires strict activity limitations (a 5-kg lifting limit), and is only suitable for older, low-demand patients. Fascial interpositional arthroplasty is better suited for younger, more active patients. The material used for interposition has traditionally been the cutis layer of skin or the fascia lata, but more recently allograft Achilles tendon has been used. Interpositional arthroplasty does not eliminate elbow pain and leaves the elbow somewhat unstable. Thus, it is best suited for patients with severe stiffness related to arthrosis.[12,30]

RADIAL HEAD FRACTURES

Mechanism of Injury

The radial head fractures when it collides with the capitellum. This can occur with a pure axial load (the most extreme example of which is the Essex-Lopresti injury[28]), with a posterolateral rotatory (elbow dislocation) type of load, or as the radial head dislocates posteriorly as part of a posterior Monteggia injury or posterior olecranon fracture-dislocation. The vast majority of these injuries are the result of a fall onto the outstretched hand, with the higher energy injuries representing falls from a height or during sports.

Signs and Symptoms

Even relatively minor fractures of the radial head (radiographically occult fractures, for instance) can be quite painful because the elbow joint is usually distended with blood. There is a variable amount of swelling and ecchymosis, which may correspond with the degree of associated ligament injury. The distal radioulnar joint, the interosseous space, and the medial side of the elbow should be examined for signs of associated ligament injury. There is often crepitation of the radial head with forearm rotation, and occasionally a fracture fragment will block forearm rotation.

Associated Injuries

Isolated radial head fractures are straightforward to treat. One of the keys to successful management is to identify and address associated injuries. This is particularly important for very displaced fractures and fractures that involve the entire head of the radius. In the study by Davidson and colleagues, all 11 patients with a fracture involving the entire radial head had an associated injury to the elbow or forearm.[17] In my experience, complex fractures of the entire head do occur without associated ligament damage on occasion—particularly in older patients—but I believe that one should assume there is an associated injury until it has been proved otherwise. In fact, a markedly displaced partial radial head fracture should raise similar concerns.

There are several patterns of complex injury that include a fracture of the radial head. Identification of these injury patterns can help guide treatment. These patterns include (i) fracture of the radial head associated with rupture of the MCL, (ii) concomitant fractures of the radial head and capitellum, (iii) posterior dislocation of the elbow with fracture of the radial head, (iv) posterior dislocation of the elbow with fracture of the radial head and the coronoid process (the so-called terrible triad of the elbow), (v) posterior Monteggia fractures including posterior olecranon fracture-dislocations, and (vi) Essex-Lopresti lesions and variants.

Radiographic evaluation alone may not disclose associated ligament injury. In particular, intraoperative examination after removal of the radial head is important to avoid missing injury to the interosseous ligament of the forearm. After removing the radial head fragments, the surgeon should push and pull on the radius. If the radial neck is very mobile and collides with the capitellum, the surgeon should assume that the interosseous ligament of the forearm is injured.[123]

Rationale of Treatment of Fracture of the Radial Head

The goals of treatment of fracture of the radial head include (i) correction of any hindrance of forearm rotation by the fracture, (ii) restoration of elbow and forearm motion by early initiation of an adequate exercise program, (iii) achieving stability of the forearm and elbow, (iv) limitation of the potential for ulnohumeral and radiocapitellar arthrosis, although the latter seems to be an uncommon problem, and (v) avoidance of injury-related complications and complications related to operative intervention, including nonunion, avascular necrosis, an expanded or incongruous radial head that restricts motion, restriction of motion by plates and screws, radioulnar synostosis, posterolateral rotatory instability, and a prominent radial head prosthesis leading to capitellar wear.

Diagnosis and Classification

In combination with the evaluation of the signs and symptoms described earlier, radiographs of the elbow and wrist will disclose most associated injuries. For isolated partial fractures of the radial head, the ability of the patient to fully pronate and supinate the forearm will influence treatment. Pain can make this very difficult to evaluate during the first few days after injury. If the radiographs reveal a fracture that may restrict forearm rotation and operative treatment is being considered, it may be useful to aspirate some of the blood from the elbow joint and instill some local anesthetic (usually lidocaine). This can be done at the anatomic soft-spot (roughly at the center of a triangle formed by the dorsal point of the olecranon, the radial head, and the lateral epicondyle) on the lateral side of the elbow. Alternatively, if the patient returns to the office a few days to a week after injury, he or she is likely to feel much better and be capable of demonstrating forearm rotation. A true block to forearm rotation is uncommon, so either injection or delayed serial examination or both are important steps in decision making.

Operative treatment of widely displaced fractures of the radial head typically reveals a more complex fracture than was apparent on radiographs. While two-dimensional and three-dimensional computed tomography scans will depict these aspects in greater detail and thereby facilitate planning of the operation, it is not necessary to obtain these studies provided that the surgeon is prepared for all possible treatment options including repair with plates and/or screws or excision of the fractured radial head with insertion of a metal prosthesis if there is an associated forearm or elbow injury.

Mason[67] classified fractures of the radial head at a time when they were either excised or treated nonoperatively. He distinguished nondisplaced fractures that did well with nonoperative treatment (type 1), comminuted fractures of the entire head of the radius (type 3) that were best treated by excision, and displaced fractures involving part of the radial head (type 2), which presented a treatment dilemma in that the majority of the head was intact, but some of these fractures had poor results. His classification did not include radial neck fractures, did not account for associated injuries, and did not quantify displacement.

Morrey[80] modified Mason's classification to (i) include fractures of the radial neck, (ii) provide a quantitative definition of displacement (a fragment involving 30% or more of the articular surface that is displaced more than 2 mm), and (iii) incorporate fracture-dislocations of the elbow as suggested by Johnston[54] as a Mason type 4 fracture. The inclusion of radial neck fractures is not useful because these fractures have different management issues and should be considered separately. The inclusion of dislocations is also not useful because fractures of the radial head are associated with a variety of complex injury patterns and, regardless of which injury pattern is present, it is still important to characterize the fracture of the radial head. Finally, there are little data to support the quantitative definition of displacement that is offered in this system.

Hotchkiss' modification of Mason's classification directly reflects current treatment options: type 1 fractures are minimally displaced fractures that do well with nonoperative treatment; type 2 fractures are displaced partial head fractures that block forearm rotation and fractures involving the entire head that are repairable; and type 3 fractures are irreparable fractures that require excision with or without prosthetic replacement.[48] This classification is useful conceptually, but the means for distinguishing repairable from unrepairable fractures are incompletely defined.

The Comprehensive Classification of Fractures[85] mixes fractures of the proximal radius and ulna in a way that is not useful for patient management; however, one useful aspect of this system is a modifier that distinguished fractures with greater than three fragments from those with two or three major fragments. The presence of greater than three fragments has been associated with a much higher risk of early failure of internal fixation, nonunion, and loss of forearm rotation.[120]

Other factors that may have an important influence on treatment, but are not well accounted for in current classification systems, include (i) lost fragments—a very common occurrence with displaced fractures, (ii) fragments that are too small to be repaired and must be discarded, (iii) fragments with little or no subchondral bone, (iv) fragments with osteoporotic bone, (v) impaction and deformation of the fracture fragments, and (vi) metaphyseal bone loss (Fig. 32-8). Partial resection of the radial head has long been associated with inferior results[11] and was one factor associated with problems in our study of operative treatment.[106] Therefore, when fragments are lost, are too small to fix, or have inadequate or poor quality bone and must be discarded, the surgeon probably ought to err toward resection of the radial head with or without prosthetic replacement depending on the presence or absence of associated injuries. Im-

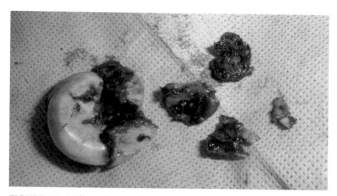

FIGURE 32-8 These fracture fragments demonstrate impaction and deformation of the head in the largest fragment (*left*), metaphyseal fragmentation and small unrepairable articular fragments (*right*).

pacted fractures may be less suitable for operative fixation because enlargement and deformation of the radial head have been observed in long-term follow-up and seem to hinder forearm rotation. Metaphyseal bone loss and impaction are observed even with partial radial head fractures and plate fixation may be superior to screws alone in this circumstance (Fig. 32-9).

Current Treatment Options

Nonoperative Treatment

The vast majority of isolated fractures of the radial head are treated nonoperatively. The major problem that patients encounter after an isolated fracture of the radial head is elbow stiffness. Only one study has noted fracture displacement with immediate active motion,[102] and it seems to be a very unusual problem. Nonunion occurs on occasion but is usually asymptomatic.[14,104]

There are no radiographic criteria that have been consistently associated with a poor result with nonoperative treatment.[46,75,133] The only absolute indication for internal fixation of an isolated displaced Mason type 2 fracture is restriction of forearm rotation because of the fracture fragment. In one recent study from Malmo, Sweden, at least 74% of patients with a fracture involving greater than 30% of the head and displaced greater than 2 mm had good or excellent results decades after the fracture using a very strict rating system.[46]

Nonoperative treatment can also be considered for some fracture-dislocations of the elbow. Two series have documented good results in terms of stability, but this approach is associated with a high rate of reoperation to address problems related to the fractured radial head.[6,56] Extreme caution is advised in the presence of an associated fracture of the coronoid as these so-called terrible triad injuries can be very unstable.[56,117]

Resection of the Radial Head

Resection of the radial head without prosthetic replacement is still a very good treatment option in select patients—usually older patients with complex isolated fractures, but also for the occasional fracture-dislocation without a fracture of the coronoid. The surgeon, however, should always be prepared to place a prosthesis in case a careful intraoperative evaluation discloses forearm instability or an associated coronoid fracture.

Open Reduction and Internal Fixation

Open reduction and internal fixation are best considered according to the various fracture types.

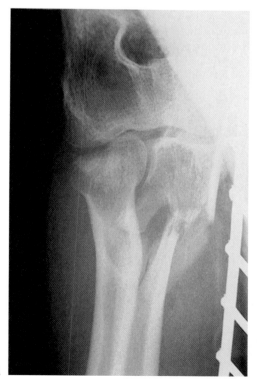
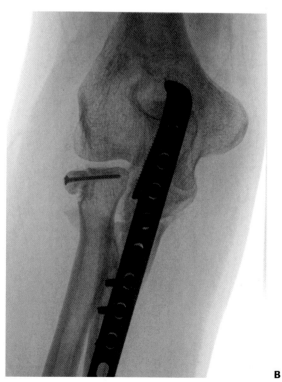

A **B**

FIGURE 32-9 Substantially displaced partial head fractures (Mason 2) may benefit from plate fixation. **A.** This fracture is part of a posterior Monteggia injury. **B.** Fixation with screws was complicated by delayed union and settling of the fracture. The metaphyseal bone loss is evident.

Isolated Partial Radial Head Fractures. The one accepted indication for operative treatment of a displaced partial radial head fracture (Mason type 2) is a block to motion. A relative indication is displacement of greater than 2 mm without a block to motion.

A Kocher[63] or Kaplan[81] exposure is developed, taking care to protect the uninjured LCL complex. The anterolateral aspect of the radial head is usually involved and is readily exposed through these intervals. The fracture is usually only slightly displaced. In fact, it is usually impacted into a stable position. The periosteum is usually intact over the metaphyseal fracture line. An attempt should be made to preserve this inherent stability by using a bone tamp to reposition the fragment. After the fragment has been realigned, one or two small screws are used to secure it (Fig. 32-10).

Partial Radial Head Fracture as Part of a Complex Injury.
The treatment of partial radial head fractures that are part of a complex injury pattern must also consider the important role of the radial head in elbow stability. Even a relatively small fracture can make an important contribution to the stability of the elbow and forearm. Partial head fragments that are part of a complex injury are often displaced and unstable with little or no soft tissue attachments. Occasionally some fragments are lost in the soft tissues.

While partial head fractures are usually considered good candidates for open reduction and internal fixation (ORIF), widely displaced fractures associated with complex injuries can be very challenging to treat because of fragmentation, the small size of the fragments, lost fragments, poor bone quality, limited subchondral bone on the fracture fragments, and metaphyseal comminution and bone loss (Fig. 32-9).

ORIF is performed when stable, reliable fixation can be achieved. Discarding the unrepairable fragments (partial radial head resection) has been documented to have poor results in older series,[11] but a recent report on the operative treatment of terrible triad injuries reported partial head resection in several patients with no apparent problems related to it.[101]

Because small fragments can make important contributions to elbow stability,[3] for a very unstable elbow or forearm injury, it may be preferable to resect the remaining intact radial head and replace it with a metal prosthesis, to enhance stability.

Fractures Involving the Entire Head of the Radius.
When treating a fracture-dislocation of the forearm or elbow with an associated fracture involving the entire head of the radius, ORIF should only be considered a viable option if stable, reliable fixation can be achieved. There is a risk of early failure that can contribute to recurrent instability.[120] Many patients who develop a chronic Essex-Lopresti lesion (longitudinal instability of the forearm) had failed internal fixation of a radial head fracture. Other factors, such as loss offragments, metaphyseal bone loss, impaction and deformity of fragments,[17] and the size and quality of the fracture fragments, may make ORIF a less predictable choice. In particular, if there are more than three articular fragments, the rates of early failure, nonunion, and poor forearm rotation may be unacceptable[120] (Fig. 32-11).

The optimal fracture for ORIF will have three or fewer articular fragments without impaction or deformity. Each should be of sufficient size and bone quality to accept screw fixation, and there should be little or no metaphyseal bone loss. Excellent exposure is required, and the surgeon should not hesitate to release the origin of the LCL complex to improve exposure in the unusual situation where it is not injured (Fig. 32-12). In many cases, it will prove useful to remove the fracture fragments from the wound and reassemble them outside the body (on the "back table"). Sacrificing any small residual capsular attachments to do this seems to be an acceptable tradeoff to achieve the goal of stable, anatomic fixation. The reconstructed radial head is then secured to the radial neck with a plate. Consideration should be given to applying bone graft to metaphyseal

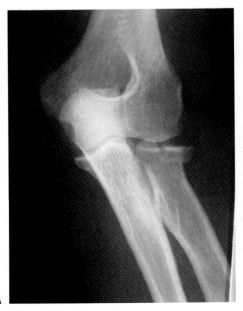
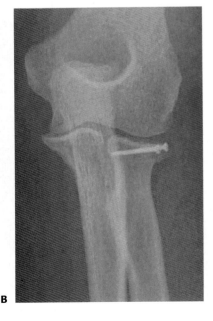

A   **B**

FIGURE 32-10 The majority of isolated partial head fractures (Mason type 2) are impacted but not widely displaced. **A.** This fragment blocked forearm rotation. **B.** A bone tamp was used to realign the fragment and it was secured with two screws.

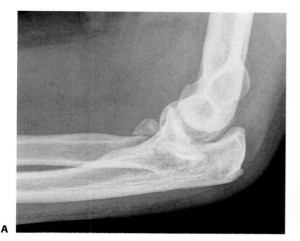

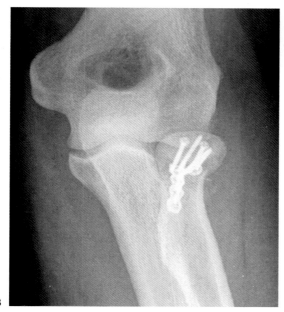

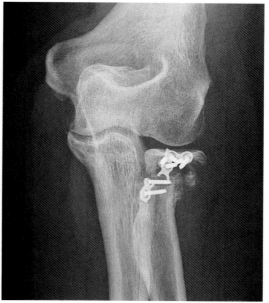

FIGURE 32-11 Early failure and nonunion are common after open reduction an internal fixation of fractures that involve the entire radial head (Mason type 3), particularly those fractures that create more than three articular fragments. **A.** This displaced fracture was part of a fracture-dislocation. **B.** Stable internal fixation was achieved initially. **C.** Six months later, the plate was broken and the radial neck remained unhealed.

defects—sufficient bone can often be obtained from the lateral epicondyle or proximal ulna.

Prosthetic Replacement

The silicone rubber prostheses that were popular during the past three decades of the twentieth century did not provide much stability and often caused a destructive synovitis.[10,36,130] Metal prostheses, which have been used for years in some centers,[21,38,39,76] are now more widely available. Some prostheses have intentionally smooth stems that lie somewhat loose in the radial neck, serving as a spacer rather than a fixed prosthesis.[21,38,39,76] Others are either press fit or cemented. Some designs have a mobile head.[58]

The major problem with a metal radial head prosthesis is "overstuffing" the joint.[129] A radial head prosthesis that lies more than 1 mm proximal to the lateral edge of the coronoid process (unpublished computed tomography–based measurements from our research group) may hinge the elbow open on the lateral side and lead to capitellar wear, arthrosis, and synovitis (Fig. 32-13).

> **AUTHORS' PREFERRED METHOD OF TREATMENT**
>
> ### Nondisplaced Fractures and Isolated Displaced Partial Head Fractures
>
> I treat all nondisplaced fractures and most isolated displaced partial head fractures nonoperatively, preferring to use no more than a sling for comfort if possible, with immediate initiation of active motion.
>
> Isolated fractures that block motion, selected partial head fractures that are displaced more than 2 mm, and repairable fractures associated with fracture-dislocations of the forearm and elbow are treated with ORIF.
>
> Fractures that are difficult or impossible to repair (leading to a tenuous repair) are excised. A metal prosthesis is inserted when there is elbow or forearm instability, and in most young, active patients (Table 32-1).

Operative Exposures

The most popular interval for the exposure of fractures of the radial head is between the anconeus and extensor carpi ulnaris

FIGURE 32-12 In this patient with lateral collateral ligament avulsion from the lateral epicondyle, excellent exposure of the radial head has been obtained to facilitate plate application.

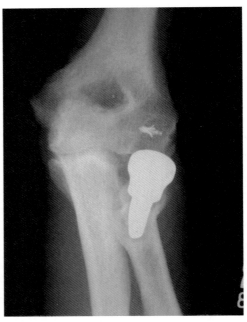

FIGURE 32-13 The major pitfall with a metallic radial head prosthesis is implantation of a prosthesis that is too long. This radiograph shows gaping open on the lateral side of the ulnohumeral joint and a large cyst in the capitellum.

TABLE 32-1 Pitfalls and Pearls for Fractures of the Radial Head	
Pitfalls	Pearls
• Resection of the radial head contributing to elbow or forearm instability	• Beware of complex injury patterns associated with fracture of the radial head. • Do not use radial head resection for terrible triad and Essex-Lopresti injuries. • Only use resection when the radius pull test is normal.
• Early failure of radial head fixation	• Do not repair the radial head if the fracture is too complex. More than three articular fragments, lost fragments, metaphyseal comminution, and impaction/deformation of radial head fragments should make the surgeon less enthusiastic about operative fixation. • Do not accept tenuous fixation for injury patterns with a high potential for instability (e.g., terrible triad and Essex-Lopresti).
• Impingement of implants in proximal radio-ulnar joint blocking motion	• Respect the safe zones for internal fixation. • Countersink all implants outside the safe zone.
• Overstuffing of the radiocapitellar joint with a metal prosthesis leading to malalignment of the ulnohumeral joint and painful capitellar erosions	• The proximal articular surface of the radial head should protrude no more than 1 millimeter more than the lateral edge of the coronoid process.

(Kocher exposure)[63,81] (Fig. 32-6). This interval is fairly easy to define intraoperatively. It represents the most posterior interval and provides good access to fragments of the radial head that displace posteriorly. It also provides greater protection for the posterior interosseous nerve. On the other hand, attention must be paid to protecting the LCL complex. The anconeus should not be elevated posteriorly and the elbow capsule and annular ligament should be incised diagonally, in line with the posterior margin of the extensor carpi ulnaris.[16]

A more anterior interval protects the LCL complex but places the posterior interosseous nerve at greater risk.[48] Some authors recommend identifying the nerve if dissection onto the radial neck is required.[48] Kaplan[81] described an interval between the extensor carpi radialis brevis and the extensor digitorum communis, whereas Hotchkiss[48] recommends going directly through the extensor digitorum communis muscle. I find these intervals difficult to define precisely based on intraoperative observations. A useful technique for choosing a good interval and protecting the LCL complex was described by Hotchkiss[48]: starting at the supracondylar ridge of the distal humerus, if one incises the origin of the extensor carpi radialis, elevates it, and incises the underlying elbow capsule, it is then possible to see the capitellum and radial head. The interval for more distal dissection should be just anterior to a line bisecting the radial head in the anteroposterior plane.

In my practice, the vast majority of fractures of the radial head that merit operative treatment are associated with fracture-dislocations of the elbow. In this context, exposure is greatly facilitated by the associated capsuloligamentous and muscle injury.[73,109,120] When the elbow has dislocated, the LCL has ruptured and the injury always occurs (or nearly always according to some authors[73]) as an avulsion from the lateral epicondyle. Along with a variable amount of muscle avulsion from the lateral epicondyle,[27,55,57,73,112] these injuries leave a relatively bare epicondyle. There is often a split in the common extensor muscle that can be developed more distally.

In the setting of a posterior olecranon fracture-dislocation or posterior Monteggia fracture, the radial head often displaces posteriorly through capsule and muscle. Accentuation of the injury deformity usually brings the radial head up into the wound (Fig. 32-14). In some cases, the surgeon will extend the posterior muscle injury to mobilize the olecranon fracture

FIGURE 32-14 When treating a posterior olecranon fracture-dislocation or posterior Monteggia injury, the radial head can often be addressed through the posterior traumatic interval.

proximally to expose and manipulate the coronoid fracture through the elbow articulation. Slight additional dissection between the radius and the ulna is acceptable given the usually extensive injury in this region, but extensive new dissection in this area has been implicated in an increased risk of proximal radioulnar synostosis.[2,131]

When treating a complex fracture of the radial head with the LCL complex intact (for instance, an Essex-Lopresti injury), it may be difficult to gain adequate exposure without releasing the LCL complex from the lateral epicondyle. This can be done either by directly incising the origin of the LCL complex from bone or by performing an osteotomy of the lateral epicondyle.[32,33,43,44,94] In either case, a secure repair and avoidance of varus stress in the early postoperative period are important.

Excision

The fragments are excised and the neck smoothed off. In the setting of an olecranon fracture-dislocation or posterior Monteggia injury, it may be useful to seal the end of the radius with bone wax. The LCL complex should be reattached to the lateral epicondyle if avulsed.

Open Reduction and Internal Fixation

Increased enthusiasm for ORIF of the radial head paralleled the development of small screws (2.7, 2.0, and 1.5 mm) and the techniques for using them.[44] At the same time, small, headless, variable pitch compression screws (such as the Herbert screw) were developed, allowing for fixation of entirely articular fragments.[7,69,96] Standard screws can be used in this way as well, countersinking the head below the articular surface, although they are prone to backing out into the joint with the slightest amount of settling at the fracture site.

Some small fragments can only be repaired with small Kirschner wires. Threaded wires are usually used because of the tendency for smooth wires to migrate and travel to various parts of the body.[65] Absorbable pins and screws are being developed for similar uses[47,97] but are still somewhat brittle and sometimes associated with an inflammatory response.

Small plates are available for fractures that involve the entire head. Plate types include T- and L-shaped plates with standard screws, small (condylar) blade plates, and new plates designed specifically for the radial head (many of which incorporate angular stable screws—screws that thread directly into the plate). The use of plates that are placed within the radial head or countersunk into the articular surface has also been described.[32]

Prosthetic Replacement

When preparing for prosthetic replacement, if some of the radial head is still attached to the neck, it is separated at the point on the radial neck where the flare of the head begins. I prefer to use a prosthesis with a smooth stem that serves as a loose spacer.[21,38] The laxity in the neck facilitates insertion and removal of the prosthesis and accommodates some of the nonanatomic features of the prosthesis compared to the native radial head. I use a neck diameter one size less than the reamer that can be passed with slight effort. I use a head size slightly smaller in diameter than the native head. I almost never add more length through the head. It is important to realize that the prosthesis will sit on the most prominent portion of the radial neck; therefore, one should be careful to choose a head thickness based upon the thinnest portion of the radial head. I smooth off but do not evenly plane the remaining radial neck. It is important to check the level of the radial head with respect to the lateral edge of the coronoid process—it should be no more than 1 mm more proximal.

In the unusual patient in whom the comminution extends into the neck, a prosthetic head of greater thickness can be used. In cases of extreme neck comminution, the prosthesis can be cemented in the neck.

Complications

Laceration or permanent injury to the posterior interosseous nerve during ORIF of a radial head fracture is unusual. Most commonly, this complication is experienced as a palsy related to retraction or exposure that resolves over weeks to months. To limit the potential for this complication, retractors should not be placed around the radial neck, the forearm should be pronated during exposure of the radial neck, and consideration should be given to identifying and protecting the nerve when more distal dissection and internal fixation are needed, particularly when a more anterior muscle interval is used for exposure.

Early failure of fixation and later nonunion are not infrequent, particularly after ORIF of complex fractures involving the entire head. In a recent series, 3 of 14 fractures involving the entire radial head and creating greater than three articular fragments had failure of fixation within the first month.[120] Because this situation can contribute to instability of the forearm or elbow, unstable or unpredictable fixation is undesirable and such fractures should probably be treated with prosthetic replacement. Among fractures of the entire radial head, 6 of 11 fractures in one series[43] and 8 of 26 fractures in another series[120] (including 2 of 12 fractures with three or fewer fragments and 6 of 14 fractures with greater than three articular fragments) had nonunion.

Delayed resection of the radial head has usually been performed to improved forearm rotation, and not for painful arthrosis of the radiocapitellar joint.[5,35] Incongruity of the proximal radioulnar joint presents as stiffness rather than pain or arthrosis and incongruity of the radiocapitellar joint inconsistently and unpredictably leads to radiocapitellar arthrosis, which seems to be an uncommon problem.

A radial head prosthesis that is too large can cause malalignment of the elbow, capitellar wear, and synovitis and usually needs to be removed. Removal of a metal radial head prosthesis can be very difficult. Given the alternative of releasing the origin of the LCL complex to subluxate the elbow, in most patients, I prefer to excise a portion of the radial neck so that I can pry out the prosthesis. The difficulty encountered in removing these prostheses is one reason I prefer to use one with a slightly loose-fitting stem.

Controversies and Future Directions

Several new plates are in development, including plates with screws that lock to the plate. Prostheses also continue to evolve. It remains unclear how appropriately sized prostheses will function over the long term. If they continue to perform as well as they have in published studies, surgeons will likely gradually become more confident with prosthetic replacement and less accepting of tenuous internal fixation.

TRAUMATIC ELBOW INSTABILITY

Traumatic elbow instability occurs in three basic forms: posterolateral rotatory instability (elbow dislocations with or without associated fractures), varus posteromedial rotational instability (anteromedial coronoid facet fractures), and olecranon fracture-dislocations. Identification of the specific pattern of traumatic elbow instability will indicate which structures are likely to be injured, the morphology of the injuries, and the prognosis, all of which will help to guide management.

Mechanism of Injury

Posterolateral rotatory instability results in dislocation of the elbow with or without fractures of the radial head and coronoid. Posterolateral rotatory injuries occur during a fall on to the outstretched arm that create a valgus, axial, and posterolateral rotatory force. The ulna and the forearm supinate away from the humerus and dislocate posteriorly. Sometimes this results in injury to the radial head or coronoid. The soft tissue injury proceeds from lateral to medial, with the anterior band of the MCL being the last structure injured[91] (Fig. 32-3). It is possible to dislocate the elbow with the anterior band of the MCL remaining intact.

Varus, posteromedial rotational instability occurs with a fall onto the outstretched arm that creates a varus stress, axial load, and posteromedial rotational force to the elbow.[90] This results in fracture of the anteromedial facet of the coronoid process and either (i) injury to the LCL, (ii) fracture of the olecranon, or (iii) an additional fracture of the coronoid at its base.[20,22,105] When the fracture of the anteromedial facet is very small (more or less a capsular avulsion) and the elbow completely dislocates, this may represent an alternative mechanism for elbow dislocation in contrast to the posterolateral rotatory mechanism. I suspect that dislocations that occur via a varus, posteromedial rotational mechanism may be less stable and more likely to require operative treatment.[25]

Anterior olecranon fracture-dislocations are the result of a direct blow to the flexed elbow, but the mechanism of posterior olecranon fracture-dislocations is more speculative with some authors suggesting they may result from the same mechanism that usually creates elbow dislocations, particularly in older osteopenic individuals.[95,98]

Signs and Symptoms

In the majority of patients with traumatic elbow instability, the problem is evident. In some patients the dislocation has reduced, either spontaneously or with assistance. Pain, ecchymosis, and swelling are present along with deformity if the elbow is still dislocated. The point of the olecranon process and the medial and lateral epicondyles should form a triangle in the coronal plane with the elbow flexed 90 degrees. If the point of the olecranon is well posterior to the epicondyles, the elbow is likely dislocated.

Associated Injuries

Acute neurovascular injuries are uncommon, but the ulnar and median nerves are most commonly involved. The brachial artery may also be injured, particularly with an open dislocation, which is also unusual.

Rationale of Treatment of Fracture-Dislocations of the Elbow

The treatment of fracture-dislocations of the elbow is intended to restore the inherent bony stability of the elbow that allows treatment of the most simple elbow dislocations with immediate active motion with a high degree of success. Critical to achieving this is restoration of the trochlear notch of the ulna, particularly the coronoid process. Anatomic alignment of anteromedial and basal coronoid fractures is necessary for elbow stability and function. Radiocapitellar contact is also very important to the stability of the injured elbow. The LCL is far more important than the MCL in the setting of most cases of traumatic elbow instability. The trochlear notch (coronoid and olecranon), radial head, and LCL are repaired or reconstructed, but the MCL rarely needs to be repaired. Some surgeons are still becoming comfortable with the idea that MCL repair is not necessary for most fracture-dislocations.[118] If the elbow is stable, or can be made stable with surgery on the lateral side, the MCL will heal properly with active motion and its repair is not necessary to achieve stability.[101]

Diagnosis and Classification

The majority of elbow dislocations and fracture-dislocations result in injury to all of the capsuloligamentous stabilizers of the elbow joint.[27,56,57,91] The exceptions include fracture-dislocations of the olecranon and other injuries with fractures of the coronoid involving nearly the entire coronoid process.[90,109,115,116]

The capsuloligamentous injury progresses from lateral to medial and the elbow can completely dislocate with the anterior band of the MCL remaining intact.[91] There is also a variable degree of injury to the common flexor and extensor musculature.[27,55,57,71]

One recent study notes that the LCL complex fails by avulsion from the lateral epicondyle in over 75% of patients with elbow dislocations.[73] In my personal observations treating over 60 fracture-dislocations of the elbow, I have found that the LCL is always avulsed from the lateral epicondyle. In many patients, there are small pieces of the ligament or other long strands of musculotendinous tissue, which may lead the surgeon to misinterpret the situation (Fig. 32-15). Defined practically, reattachment of the soft tissue sleeve to the lateral epicondyle is nearly always sufficient.

O'Driscoll[91] has described several stages of posterolateral rotatory elbow instability (Fig. 32-16). Stage 1 involves partial or complete disruption of the LCL, which may result in slight posterior subluxation of the radial head with respect to the capitellum. Stage 2 involves an incomplete posterior dislocation with disruption of the lateral ligamentous complex and further injury to the osseous or ligamentous supporting structures anteriorly and/or posteriorly. The medial edge of the ulna may be found to rest on the trochlea. This gives the appearance of the

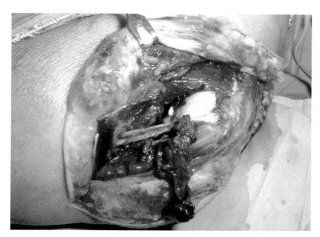

FIGURE 32-15 The lateral collateral ligament nearly always fails via avulsion of its lateral epicondylar origin. The remaining tissue attached to the epicondyle is the remnant of the common extensor musculature, much of which has been torn more distally.

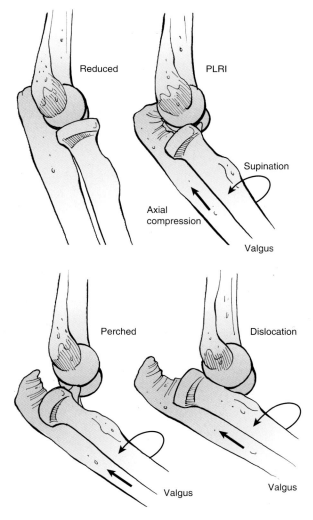

FIGURE 32-16 Posterolateral rotatory instability (PLRI) occurs in several stages. Elbow dislocation is the final stage.

coronoid being perched on the trochlea on a lateral radio-graph.[91] Stage 3 is divided into three subgroups (A, B, and C). Stage 3A involves injury to all the soft tissue support except the anterior band of the MCL. The elbow dislocates in a postero-lateral direction, rotating about the intact anterior MCL. Stage 3B involves injury to the entire medial ligamentous complex, resulting in varus, valgus, and rotary instability. Stage 3C injuries are very unstable because of complete soft tissue disruption from the distal humerus, with the elbow having the ability to dislocate even when immobilized in a cast.[90]

Elbow dislocations that are associated with one or more intra-articular fractures are at greater risk for recurrent or chronic instability.[41,56,109] Fracture-dislocations of the elbow usually occur in one of several distinct, recognizable injury patterns: (i) posterior dislocation with fracture of the radial head, (ii) posterior dislocation with fractures of the radial head and coronoid process—the so-called terrible triad injury (Fig. 32-17), (iii) varus posteromedial rotational instability pattern injuries (Fig. 32-18), (iv) anterior olecranon fracture-dislocations (Fig. 32-19), and (v) posterior olecranon fracture-dislocations (Fig. 32-20). Each of these patterns is associated with character-istic injury components and fracture morphologies, the knowl-edge of which can help guide effective management.

Most varus posteromedial rotational instability pattern inju-ries and olecranon fracture-dislocations are not true dislocations in that apposition of the articular surfaces is not lost (Figs. 32-18 through 32-20). Rather, they are usually fracture-subluxation injuries where the major problem is disruption of the trochlear notch.

Recent reports on elbow instability have emphasized the im-portance of the coronoid process.[90,109,117] The injuries that give surgeons the most trouble are the terrible triad, varus postero-medial, and olecranon fracture-dislocations with associated cor-onoid fractures.[90] In each case, the fracture of the coronoid is the most important and challenging part of the injury.

Regan and Morrey[103] classified coronoid fractures based on the size of the fragment: type I, avulsion of the tip of the coro-noid process; type II, a single or comminuted fragment involv-ing 50% of the process or less; and type III, a single or commi-nuted fragment involving more than 50% of the process.[103] They also included a modifier to indicate the presence (type B) or absence (type A) of an elbow dislocation. However, it has become clear that the pattern of the overall injury and morphol-ogy of the fracture may be equally or more important than the size of the fragment and the presence or absence of dislocation.

O'Driscoll[90] proposed a new classification system for coro-noid fractures based on the anatomic location of the fracture. Fractures may involve the tip, the anteromedial facet, or the basal aspect of the coronoid. The three groups are further di-vided into subtypes based on the severity of coronoid involve-

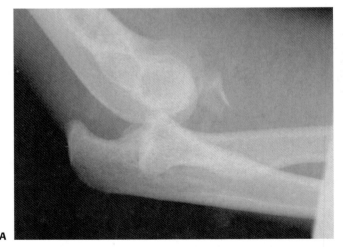

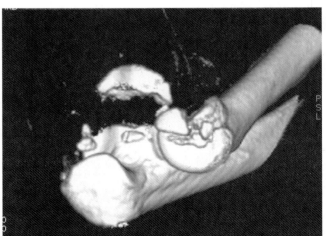

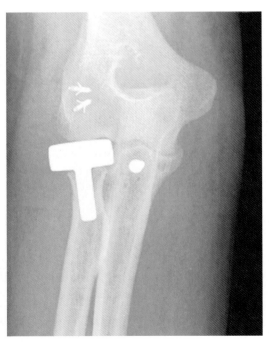

FIGURE 32-17 The so-called terrible triad of the elbow consists of dislocation of the elbow with fractures of the coronoid and radial head. **A.** The coronoid fragment is the triangular fragment anterior to the trochlea. After manipula-tive reduction, this elbow could not be kept reduced de-spite cast immobilization. **B.** The coronoid fracture is a transverse fracture of the tip as seen on this three-dimen-sional computed tomography reconstruction. **C.** Operative fixation of the coronoid, replacement of the radial head, and reattachment of the lateral collateral ligament complex to the lateral epicondyle restored good elbow function.

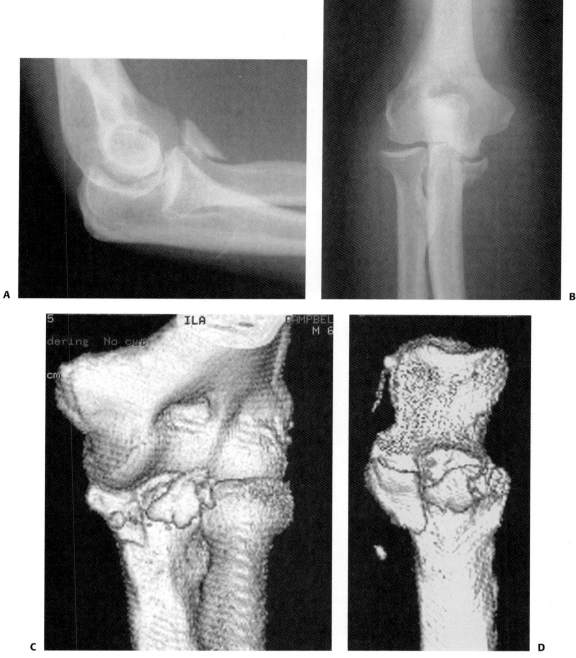

FIGURE 32-18 Small coronoid fractures are often problematic. **A.** This appears to be a small isolated fracture of the coronoid. **B.** On the anteroposterior view, it is clear that the anteromedial facet of the coronoid process is fractured. There is varus subluxation and opening of the joint on the lateral side betraying the associated lateral collateral ligament injury. **C.** Three-dimensional computed tomography depicts external rotation of the distal humerus with respect to the forearm as the trochlea rotates forward into the coronoid defect. **D.** There are separate coronoid tip and anteromedial facet fracture fragments. *(continues)*

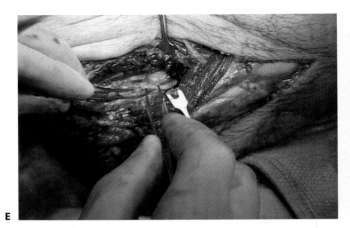

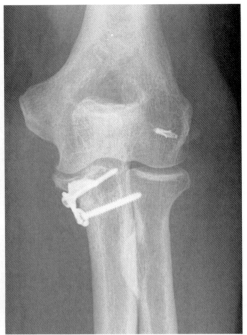

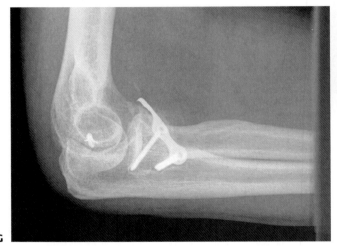

FIGURE 32-18 (*Continued*) **E.** Exposure is obtained by transposing the ulnar nerve anteriorly and elevating the anterior portion of the flexor-pronator muscles off of the medial collateral ligament and the coronoid process. **F.** The coronoid fractures were secured with a buttress plate and the lateral collateral ligament origin was reattached to the lateral epicondyle with a suture anchor. **G.** A concentric reduction and good elbow function resulted.

ment. His system considers the mechanism of injury along with the associated fractures and soft tissue injuries and helps to dictate treatment (Fig. 32-21).

The first group of coronoid fractures involves the tip but does not extend medially past the sublime tubercle or into the body. Tip, subtype 1 fractures involve less than 2 mm of the coronoid and may be found in isolation or with a fracture-dislocation. Tip, subtype 2 fractures involve greater than 2 mm and are largely associated with terrible triad injuries. In my experience, all of these fracture fragments contain the insertion of the anterior capsule and the 2-mm distinction between subtypes 1 and 2 is arbitrary and does not influence treatment.

The second group of coronoid fractures involves the anteromedial aspect of the coronoid. Anteromedial subtype 1 fractures extend from just medial to the tip of the coronoid to the anterior half of the sublime tubercle (the insertion of the anterior band of the MCL). Anteromedial subtype 2 fractures are subtype 1 injuries with extension of the fracture line into the tip. Anteromedial subtype 3 fractures involve the anteromedial rim and the entire sublime tubercle with or without involvement of the tip of the coronoid. The mechanism of injury is usually a varus/posteromedial rotation injury with axial loading. The LCL complex is generally disrupted unless the olecranon is also fractured. Radial head fractures may be seen in higher-energy, subtype 3 injuries. Anteromedial coronoid fractures cause incongruent articulation of the ulnohumeral joint, which may lead to an earlier onset of posttraumatic arthritis.

Basal coronoid fractures make up the third category and involve at least 50% of the height of the coronoid. Basal subtype 1 fractures involve the coronoid alone, while subtype 2 fractures are associated with fractures of the olecranon. In general, these fractures have less soft tissue disruption than those that involve only the tip of the coronoid.

The following observations may be useful in guiding treatment: (i) Terrible triad injuries nearly always have a small transverse fracture of the tip of the coronoid including the anterior capsular attachment (Fig. 32-17B). Much less commonly, the coronoid fracture is either very large or involves the anteromedial facet of the coronoid preferentially. (ii) Varus posteromedial rotational instability pattern injuries are defined by a fracture of the anteromedial facet of the coronoid process (Fig. 32-18). (iii) In the setting of an olecranon fracture-dislocation, the coronoid fracture can be one simple large fragment; it can be fragmented into two or three large pieces (anteromedial facet, central, and lesser sigmoid notch) with or without a tip fragment as well, or it can be more comminuted.

Intraoperative Testing of Elbow Stability

Intraoperative testing of elbow stability is important. Substantial subluxation or redislocation of the elbow is challenging to treat and the elbow can be unstable despite cast immobilization. Therefore, it is very important not to leave the operating room until adequate stability has been achieved. Morrey[78] recom-

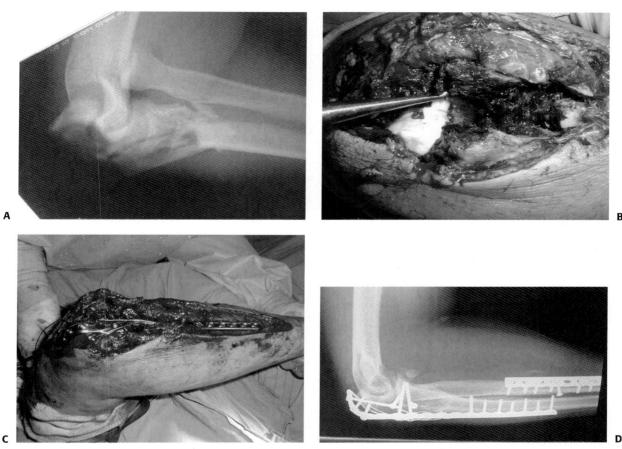

A

B

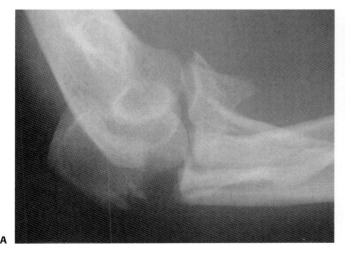

C

D

FIGURE 32-19 Anterior (or trans olecranon) olecranon fracture-dislocations are relatively uncommon injuries that are characterized by anterior translation of the forearm, an intact radial head, and fracture of the proximal ulna. **A.** This very complex proximal ulna fracture involves the coronoid process. **B.** The coronoid is split in the sagittal plane and can be repaired with interfragmentary compression screws. **C.** The metaphyseal and diaphyseal fragmentation is bridged with a long plate, contoured to wrap around the dorsal surface of the ulna. Tension wires are used to enhance fixation of the small proximal fragments. **D.** Six months later, the fracture is healed and good elbow function has been restored.

A

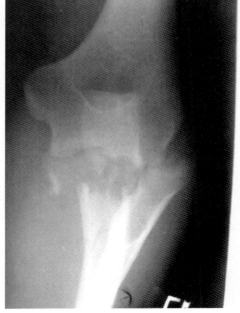

B

FIGURE 32-20 Posterior olecranon fracture-dislocations can be very complex injuries. **A.** In this patient, the coronoid and radial head are fractured. **B.** The coronoid is split into three fragments.   (*continues*)

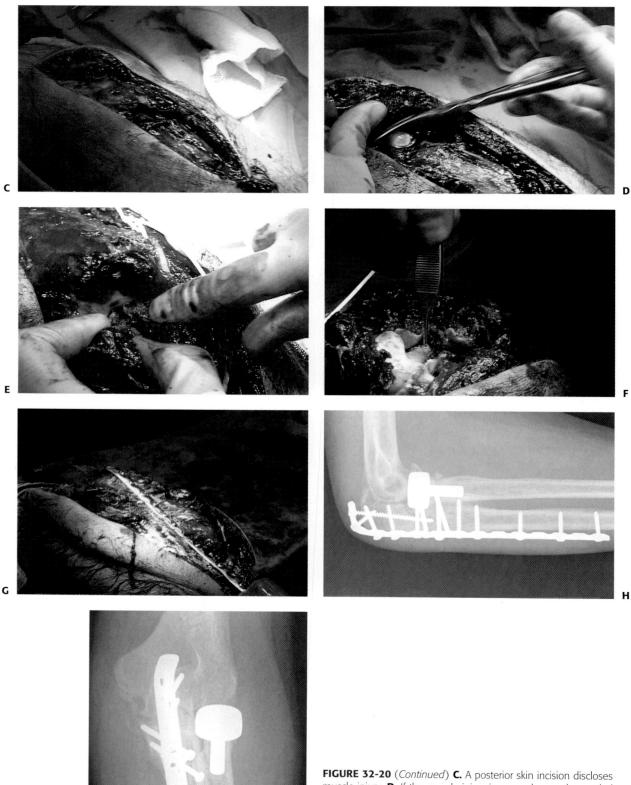

FIGURE 32-20 (*Continued*) **C.** A posterior skin incision discloses muscle injury. **D.** If the muscle injury is opened up and extended somewhat, the olecranon fragment can be translated proximally like an olecranon osteotomy, exposing the elbow articulation. **E.** An additional medial exposure with transposition of the ulnar nerve helps with manipulation of the anteromedial fracture fragment. **F.** The coronoid is split into three large fragments: anteromedial, central, and lesser sigmoid notch. **G.** A long dorsal plate is applied, bridging the comminution and securing the coronoid. **H.** The radial head is replaced. **I.** The anteromedial portion of the coronoid is secured with screws. Healing occured and good elbow function was restored.

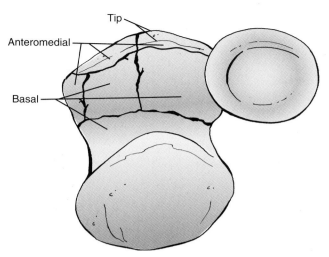

FIGURE 32-21 O'Driscoll has described the common fracture fragments seen with coronoid fractures. The tip fragment is seen most often with varus posteromedial injuries and terrible triad injuries, but can also be seen in comminuted basal injuries. The anteromedial facet fracture is seen in varus posteromedial rotatory instability as well as with posterior olecranon fracture-dislocations. Basal fractures are usually associated with olecranon fracture-dislocations.

mended that the elbow should not redislocate before reaching 45 degrees of flexion from a fully flexed position, and Jupiter[109] and I recommended that the elbow should be able to go to 30 degrees before substantial subluxation or dislocation occurs. These are relatively arbitrary numbers.

My current practice is to test stability in gravity extension with the forearm in neutral rotation (Fig. 32-22). In other words, I support the upper arm or humerus, straighten the elbow, and let gravity apply a stress to the extended elbow. I then gently flex the elbow and feel for any clunk or crepitation. I repeat the maneuver under image intensification. In most cases, the elbow is stable with this maneuver and no more than slight subluxation is seen radiographically. If greater subluxation occurs, I consider additional treatment such as the use of hinged external fixation.

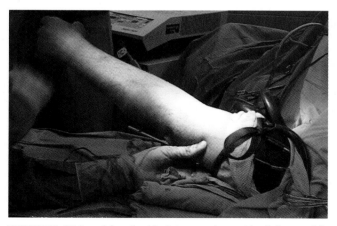

FIGURE 32-22 A useful method for intraoperative testing of elbow stability is to place the arm in gravity extension with the forearm in neutral. After this maneuver is performed, the elbow is gently flexed and palpated for recurrence of any subluxation or dislocation. It is also useful to monitor this maneuver on an image intensifier.

SIMPLE ELBOW DISLOCATIONS

Rationale of Treatment of Simple Elbow Dislocations

Most simple elbow dislocations are stable after manipulative reduction. Acute redislocations and chronic recurrent dislocations are uncommon.[25] Mobilization of the elbow within 2 weeks results in less stiffness and pain.[74,100] Simple elbow dislocations that redislocate after manipulative reduction seem to be related to a greater degree of soft tissue avulsion from the distal humerus and are typically observed in frail older patients and younger patients with very high-energy dislocations.[25,71]

Diagnosis and Classification

Radiographs taken before and after manipulative reduction will help to ensure there are no associated fractures. Even very small fractures of the coronoid and radial head can be important and potentially problematic.[117] These can be better characterized with two- and three-dimensional computed tomography scans.

Anterior dislocations of the elbow without associated fractures are exceedingly uncommon. Medial and lateral dislocations are likely to be incompletely reduced posterior dislocations. Consequently, classification of simple elbow dislocations into anterior, medial, lateral, and posterior is not very useful.

A dislocation in which the olecranon comes to lie in a posterolateral position may be more likely than a posteromedial dislocation to have torn the anterior band of the MCL.[87,91]

Current Treatment Options

Nonoperative Treatment

Manipulative reduction is usually performed with conscious sedation. The basic technique for manipulative reduction is to line up the olecranon and the distal humerus in the medial-lateral plane, apply traction across the elbow with the elbow flexed at 90 degrees, and lever the olecranon over the distal humerus with direct pressure. It can sometimes be helpful to supinate the forearm. Reduction is usually easy, but it can take some force if the anterior band of the MCL is intact. Successful reduction can be confirmed by checking for a smooth, unrestricted arc of elbow motion and realignment of the relationship between the point of the olecranon and the medial and lateral epicondyles in the same plane.

The stability of the reduction is checked by having the patient move the elbow through as complete an arc of motion as pain will allow. In the unusual elbow that redislocates with this maneuver, some authors have suggested attempting range of motion with the forearm pronated and, if successful, applying a cast brace that allows elbow motion with the forearm held in this position. It is interesting to check varus and valgus stability to note that in some patients valgus stability is preserved, but this examination does not usually alter treatment.

A posterior splint immobilizing the elbow in 90 degrees of flexion and the forearm in neutral rotation is applied for comfort and discarded within 2 weeks of injury. Active elbow motion is encouraged as soon as the patient can tolerate it. Specific exercises to regain terminal elbow extension and flexion are often helpful and can be taught by the physician or a therapist.

Treatment of Persistent Subluxation

Patients with persistent elbow subluxation have been treated with a cast brace with the forearm held in pronation.[64] An

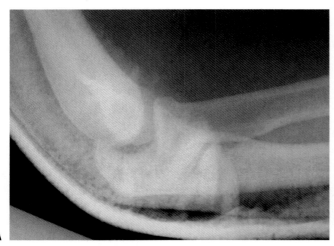
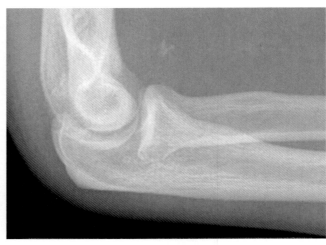

A   **B**

FIGURE 32-23 Residual subluxation of the elbow after a simple elbow dislocation can be effectively treated with active elbow exercises in most patients. **A.** This is attempted when the subluxation is more of a pseudosubluxation, as seen here, and not when the trochlea is perched on the coronoid. **B.** A radiograph taken after confident active mobilization of the elbow shows a concentric reduction.

alternative is to forego the brace or cast and encourage confident active motion of the elbow.[26] Patients with persistent subluxation of the elbow resemble patients with so-called pseudosubluxation of the shoulder from pain-related inhibition of the shoulder muscles. Active elbow mobilization provides additional dynamic muscular contribution to elbow stability. This should only be attempted in patients with slight subluxation or opening of the joint and not in patients with "perched" dislocations in which the trochlea is resting on and scraping against the coronoid process (Fig. 32-23).

Treatment of Unstable Dislocations

When the elbow cannot be held in a concentrically reduced position, redislocates before a postreduction radiograph is obtained, or dislocates later on despite splint immobilization the dislocation is deemed unstable and operative treatment is required. There are three general approaches to this problem: (i) open relocation and repair of soft tissues back to the distal humerus (Fig. 32-24), (ii) hinged external fixation and (iii) cross-pinning of the joint.

AUTHORS' PREFERRED METHOD OF TREATMENT

Simple Elbow Dislocations

After closed manipulative reduction, I prefer to avoid a splint if possible and start immediate active mobilization of the elbow. I do not immobilize the elbow longer than 1 week. Slight subluxations nearly always recover with confident elbow exercises, and I have used this technique following reduction as late as 6 weeks after a simple elbow dislocation (Table 32-2).

In my opinion, neither persistent subluxation nor unstable elbow dislocations benefit from cast immobilization. Persistent subluxation may be exacerbated by additional weight on a relaxed elbow and the elbow also becomes very stiff. Unstable elbows can dislocate despite cast or brace immobilization and the patient may not be aware of it.[117]

I believe that persistent subluxation or dislocation of the elbow after manipulative reduction and active elbow exercises requires operative treatment. In older patients, it is often sufficient to repair the lateral soft tissues back to the lateral epicondyle. In younger patients with high-energy injuries, I have found that repair of both the medial and lateral soft tissue structures back to the distal humerus may not completely stabilize the elbow, and stability may be enhanced by reattachment of the anterior capsule to the coronoid process. I try to limit operative dissection using either cross-pinning alone or LCL repair combined with hinged external fixation. I have performed hinged external fixation without ligament repair and found it did not provide adequate stability to initiate elbow motion. In older, infirm patients, cross-pinning of the ulnohumeral joint is adequate and can be accomplished with sedation and local anesthesia. The pins are protected in an above elbow cast and removed 3 weeks after surgery.

Surgical Procedure: Soft Tissue Repair

A midline posterior incision is created and a lateral skin flap elevated. The extent of the soft tissue injury may not be apparent until the overlying fascia is incised. The avulsed LCL origin and common extensor musculature are reattached to the lateral epicondyle with suture anchors or sutures passed through drill holes in bone. I place one anchor or drill hole at the origin of the LCL and one more proximally if necessary for repair of the avulsed or detached radial wrist extensor muscle origins (Fig. 32-25). This lateral soft tissue repair is often sufficient in older patients, but a medial sided repair will be necessary in most young patients with high-energy injuries (Fig. 32-24).

If the elbow redislocates with gravity extension, a medial flap is elevated and the ulnar nerve is released from where it passes through the medial intermuscular septum proximally through Osbourne's fascia distally and transposed into the subcutaneous tissues anteriorly. The anterior capsule is reattached to the coronoid using sutures passed through drill holes in the coronoid (entering from the dorsal surface of the ulna) and the MCL and com-

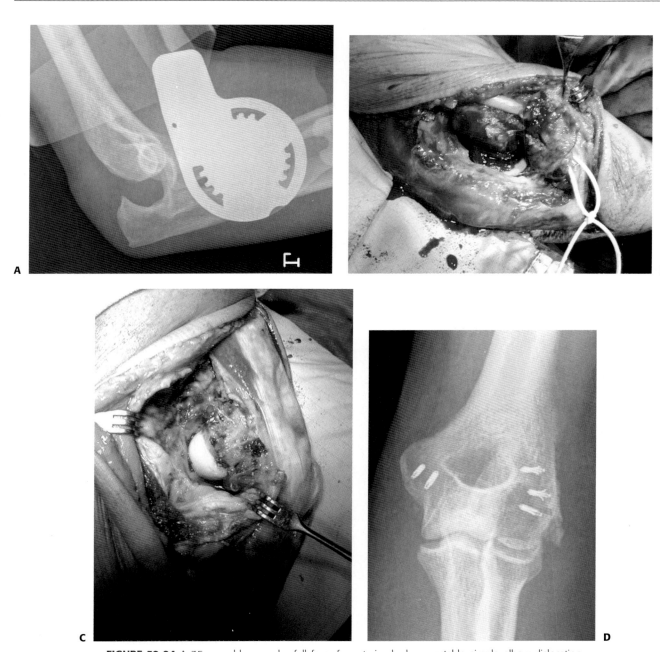

FIGURE 32-24 A 35-year-old man who fell from four stories had an unstable simple elbow dislocation. **A.** Despite a hinged brace, the trochlea is perched on the coronoid process. **B.** The medial collateral ligament and common flexor muscles were avulsed from the medial epicondyle. **C.** The lateral collateral ligament and common extensor muscles were stripped off of the lateral epicondyle. **D.** Anteroposterior radiograph after reattachment of the soft tissues to the epicondyles shows concentric reduction.

mon flexor origins are then repaired back to the medial epicondyle using suture anchors or sutures passed through drill holes in bone. If the elbow dislocates in gravity extension, hinged external fixation or cross-pinning of the elbow should be considered. If stability is restored with soft tissue repair alone, the elbow can be mobilized within a few days of surgery, but I usually splint the elbow until suture removal about 10 days later and then initiate active elbow exercises.

Surgical Procedure: Hinged External Fixation
The elbow joint is reduced and held in a reduced position with temporary cross pinning of the joint using smooth $^5/_{64}$-inch Steinmann pins and a hinged external fixator is applied. There

are several varieties of hinged external fixators including unilateral (lateral) fixators, fixators with transfixation pins, and fixators based on an Ilizarov-type frame—the specific instructions for application should be followed (Fig. 32-26).

Active mobilization is allowed the morning after surgery. Some fixators include a mechanism for applying a static progressive stretch to the elbow, and this can be instituted immediately. The fixator is removed 4 weeks after surgery and the exercises are continued.

Surgical Procedure: Cross-Pinning
Under sedation, the skin over the olecranon is infiltrated with local anesthesia. The elbow is manipulated and two $^5/_{64}$-inch

TABLE 32-2 *Pitfalls and Pearls for Simple Elbow Dislocations*

Pitfalls	Pearls
• Stiffness of the elbow	• Immobilize the elbow for comfort only. Initiate active exercises within 2 weeks of injury.
• Continued casting or operative treatment to treat slight subluxation after elbow relocation	• The majority of elbows with slight subluxation (or pseudosubluxation) after dislocation will improve with active motion.
• Unrecognized redislocation	• Beware of the potential for a simple elbow dislocation to be unstable in (i) elderly patients and (ii) younger patients after high-energy injuries.

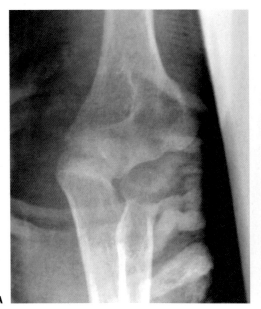

A

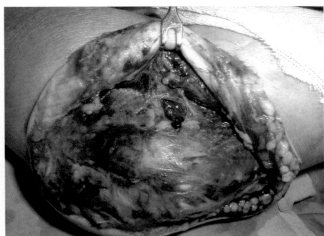

B

C

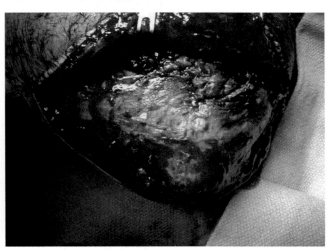

D

FIGURE 32-25 A 65-year-old woman had an unstable simple elbow dislocation. **A.** The elbow seems to be hinging open on some intact medial soft tissues. **B.** After elevating a lateral skin flap, there is very little damage evident. **C.** After incision of the overlying fascia, the injury to the lateral collateral ligament and common extensors is apparent. The remaining tissue on the lateral epicondyle is tendon and not ligament. **D.** Repair of the lateral sided soft tissue injury restored stability.

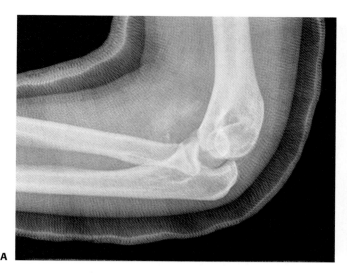

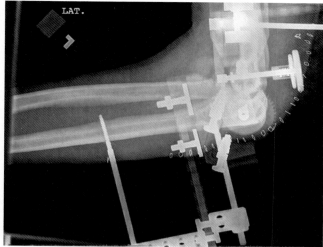

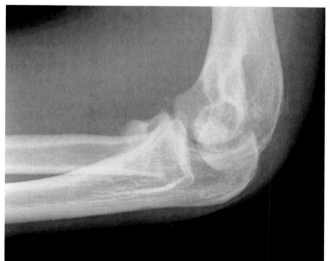

FIGURE 32-26 A 30-year-old man injured in a fall from a height had an unstable simple elbow dislocation. **A.** The trochlea remains perched on the coronoid process despite cast immobilization. **B.** An open reduction, reattachment of the lateral collateral ligament to the lateral epicondyle and application of hinged external fixation were performed. **C.** A second procedure to remove anterior heterotopic bone was performed and a stable elbow with near normal elbow motion was obtained.

Kirschner wires are drilled across the ulnohumeral joint. Usually one axially directed wire and one obliquely directed wire (starting lateral to avoid the ulnar nerve) are adequate (Fig. 32-27). The wires are aimed somewhat posteriorly to account for the anterior translation of the trochlea with respect to the humeral shaft. The adequacy of the reduction is confirmed radiographically, the wires are trimmed and bent above the skin and a well-padded cast is applied. The cast and pins are removed 3 or 4 weeks later and active exercises are initiated. Some surgeons who use cross-pinning prefer to use screws because they are worried about breakage of the pins, but I have not found this desirable or necessary.

Complications

Varus, valgus, and posterolateral rotatory instability is very uncommon after elbow dislocation. Persistent subluxation and dislocation can destroy the ulnohumeral articulation if not promptly identified and treated as the joint surfaces scrape against one another. Slight subluxation with relative congruence of the articular surfaces can be treated with active exercises as described earlier. Wide dislocation is actually preferred over subluxation with abnormal contact of the articular surfaces, because the articular surfaces are less likely to be damaged. We

have had success treating a chronic simple elbow dislocation with relocation and 6 weeks of hinged external fixation without ligament repair or reconstruction, likely because the articular surfaces have been relatively well preserved.[61]

ELBOW FRACTURE-DISLOCATIONS AND CORONOID FRACTURES

Posterior Dislocation and Fracture of the Radial Head

The simplest pattern of elbow fracture-dislocation is posterior dislocation of the elbow with fracture of the radial head. This injury is identical to a simple elbow dislocation with the addition of a fracture of the radial head as it collides with the capitellum during dislocation.

Rationale of Treatment

Loss of support between the radial head and capitellum as a result of fracture of the radial head creates an additional measure of instability, but this injury pattern is not as problematic as when the coronoid process is fractured as well. Broberg and Morrey[6] and Josefson and colleagues[56] documented good re-

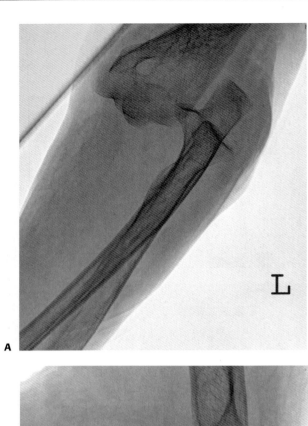

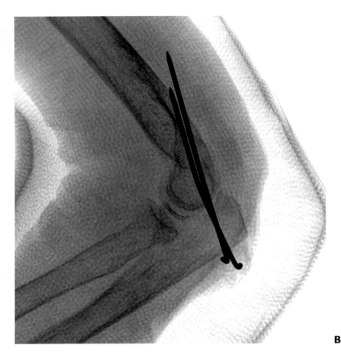

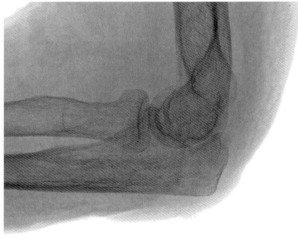

FIGURE 32-27 An 80-year-old woman had an unstable simple elbow dislocation after a fall. **A.** The radiograph of the initial injury. **B.** The elbow was stabilized with two smooth Kirschner wires under sedation and local anesthesia and a long arm cast was applied. The pins and cast were removed 4 weeks later. **C.** A stable concentric reduction with near normal motion was obtained.

sults treating these injuries with or without radial head resection and 1 month of cast immobilization with two caveats: (i) patients with associated coronoid fractures redislocated in the cast and (ii) patients treated nonoperatively often needed secondary procedures to address restriction of forearm rotation because of the fracture of the radial head. While the radial head may not be necessary to keep the elbow concentrically reduced in this injury pattern, some authors have suggested that preservation of the stabilizing influence of radiocapitellar contact may delay the onset of ulnohumeral arthrosis.[121]

Current Treatment Options
Nonoperative Treatment. Some patients are wary of operative treatment. Whereas avoidance of operative treatment might be unwise when the elbow dislocation is associated with both coro-

noid and radial head fractures, it is a reasonable treatment option in patients with dislocation and fracture of the radial head only. A computed tomography scan may be necessary to be certain that the coronoid is not fractured. Patients who elect nonoperative treatment need to be aware of the slight potential for instability and the substantial potential for restriction of motion or arthrosis from the radial head fracture. The literature documents the results after one month of cast immobilization,[6,56] but under close supervision, it is reasonable to remove the splint and begin active motion at the patient's first visit to the office, typically about 1 week after injury.

Operative Treatment: Radial Head Resection, Repair, or Replacement and Lateral Collateral Ligament Repair. When the fracture of the radial head cannot be repaired with confidence, it is reasonable to resect it (without prosthetic replacement). Good results with this treatment have been reported, provided that there is no coronoid fracture.[6,56] The experience reported in the literature does not include collateral ligament repair. We now understand the importance of the LCL to elbow stability, and it is helpful to reattach this ligament to the lateral epicondyle.[101]

When feasible, repair of the radial head restores the native anatomy and contributes to the immediate and long-term stability of the elbow. The injured LCL facilitates exposure of the radial head.

If the radial head cannot be repaired, resection and replacement with a metal prosthesis will enhance immediate and long-term stability but also expose the patient to its potential complications.

When the LCL is repaired, immediate active motion is usually possible (particularly if radiocapitellar contact has also been restored), but up to 10 days of immobilization is reasonable.[101]

AUTHORS' PREFERRED METHOD OF TREATMENT

Elbow Fracture-Dislocations and Coronoid Fractures

I usually recommend operative treatment, but I have treated a few very motivated and informed patients nonoperatively and have been delightfully surprised with the results (Fig. 32-28). Most patients will benefit from treatment of the radial head fracture. I repair the radial head only when all the fragments are present, the bone quality is adequate, and secure fixation can be accomplished. Otherwise, I resect the radial head and replace it with a metal prosthesis. I have treated a few lower-demand patients who did not want a prosthesis (again, well informed and motivated) with resection and LCL repair alone, also with good results. Operative treatment of the radial head fracture and collateral ligament injury are described earlier.

Complications

Acute redislocation, recurrent dislocation, and chronic instability are very uncommon with this injury pattern. Untreated or inadequately treated fractures of the radial head can contribute to loss of forearm motion and arthrosis and are treated with a second operation to excise the radial head. An oversized radial head prosthesis can cause painful radiocapitellar wear and arthrosis.

Controversies and Future Directions

The idea that preservation of radiocapitellar contact delays the progression of ulnohumeral arthrosis is unproved, but a patient without a radial head probably could not be a baseball pitcher. The potential enhancement of stability that a radial head prosthesis can provide in a young athlete or laborer must be balanced with the potential short- and long-term risks of a metal prosthesis, which remain incompletely defined.

Terrible Triad Fracture-Dislocations

Rationale of Treatment

The addition of a coronoid fracture, no matter how small, to a dislocation of the elbow and fracture of the radial head, dramatically increases the instability and the potential for problems.[56,101,117] As a result, the term "terrible triad of the elbow" has been coined by Hotchkiss[50] to refer to this injury pattern. Not all terrible triad injuries will be unstable, but it can be difficult to predict which injuries will be unstable. Recurrent subluxation or dislocation can destroy the elbow articulation, particularly if it is not recognized and abnormal contact of the articular surface persists.

Diagnosis and Classification

There is often confusion about whether the fracture fragments come from the radial head or coronoid. The coronoid fracture is usually quite easily distinguished as a small triangular fragment anterior to the trochlea in a dislocated position and in the coronoid fossa after reduction (Fig. 32-17A). The coronoid process

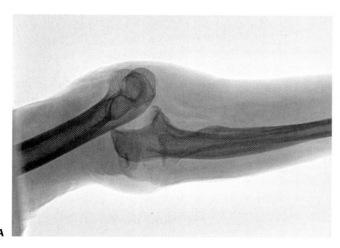

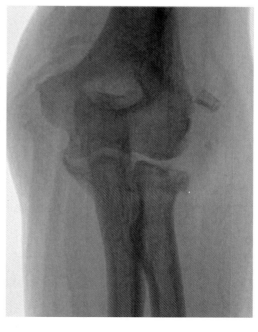

FIGURE 32-28 A fracture-dislocation of the elbow without a coronoid fracture can be treated nonoperatively in some patients. **A.** A 55-year-old patient with an elbow dislocation and radial head fracture had manipulative reduction and splinting. **B.** Despite a complex fracture of the radial head, the patient declined operative treatment. Concentric reduction was maintained and his eventual functional result was excellent.

should be evaluated for a defect. Given the important influence of an associated coronoid fracture, a computed tomography scan should be obtained if there is any doubt. The coronoid fracture is nearly always a small transverse fracture of the tip with the capsule attached (Fig. 32-17B). On rare occasions, the fracture will involve the anteromedial facet.

Current Treatment Options

Nonoperative treatment is risky because the elbow can dislocate in a cast, unknown to the patient. Radial head resection without prosthetic replacement is unwise as recurrent dislocation of the elbow is common.[117] Good results have been documented with repair of the coronoid or anterior capsule, repair or replacement of the radial head, and LCL repair.[101] Doing so restores stability in most cases, but in some patients MCL repair or hinged external fixation is also necessary. The use of cross-pinning of the ulnohumeral joint has been presented at a national meeting (K. Cramer and colleagues, presented at the 1999 annual meeting of the Orthopaedic Trauma Association, Charlotte, NC) with reasonably good results but has not yet been published in a peer-reviewed journal. With specific treatment of each of the injury components, this step should rarely be necessary.[101]

AUTHORS' PREFERRED METHOD OF TREATMENT

Terrible Triad Fracture-Dislocations

Nonoperative treatment is risky but can be successful. I have used it in very motivated patients with concentric reductions who were capable of confident active motion of the elbow. In particular, when a patient presents more than 1 week after injury with a comfortable and stable 80- to 100-degree arc of ulnohumeral motion, unrestricted forearm motion, and a concentric reduction on radiographs, it is difficult to justify operative treatment.

It might be possible to restore stability with radial head repair or replacement and LCL repair only in many patients; however, if doing so results in inadequate stability, these repairs must be taken down to restore access to the coronoid. Respecting that these injuries are infamously problematic, I prefer to repair the coronoid fracture, the radial head and the LCL working from inside out. This nearly always restores good stability in gravity extension of the elbow without the need for MCL repair, hinged external fixation, or cross-pinning of the joint.

Surgical Procedure

Internal Fixation of the Coronoid. Exposure and fixation of the small transverse fractures of the coronoid that are usually associated with a terrible triad injury pattern can be accomplished through a lateral exposure. The unusual anteromedial coronoid fracture will require a separate medial exposure.

I prefer to use a single midline posterior longitudinal incision, elevating a lateral skin flap. This provides access to the dorsal ulna for passing the coronoid sutures and to the medial side of the elbow in case the ulnar nerve or MCL needs to be addressed or a hinged external fixator will be applied.

If there is a traumatic rent in the fascia, it can be developed proximally and distally (Fig. 32-29A), but usually the overlying fascia is intact. In such cases, I identify the supracondylar ridge of the humerus and incise and elevate the radial wrist extensors off of the ridge anteriorly. As one works distally, it will become apparent that the LCL and some or all of the common extensor musculature has been avulsed from the lateral epicondyle. An interval in the common extensors is selected based upon what is injured and it is developed distally. This interval should be anterior to the midline of the radial head and neck. The supinator is spread bluntly over the radial neck, but it is rarely necessary to dissect very far distally where the posterior interosseous nerve would be placed at risk.

Removal of the radial head fragments from the wound, elevation of the radial wrist extensors from the supracondylar ridge, slight splitting of the supinator distally, and subluxation of the elbow all help to expose the coronoid fracture in the depths of the wound.

The coronoid is repaired with sutures passed through drill holes in the ulna. Creation of the drill holes can be facilitated with a drill guide such as that used to assist with repair of the anterior cruciate ligament of the knee or they can be made free hand. Two drill holes, one medial and one lateral, are created in the bed of the coronoid fracture. A simple method for passing the sutures is to put a suture loop on a Keith needle, pass the needle and loop into the drill holes and pull the suture loop from the coronoid base out into the wound. A suture can then be easily passed through the loop and pulled through the ulna. Suture passers can also be used, but they require passing the suture deep in the confined space of the wound. The suture is passed through drill holes in the coronoid fragment for larger fragments (Fig. 32-29B) and around the fragment and through the anterior capsular attachment in small or comminuted coronoid fragments. It is then passed through the other hole in the ulna. Precise anatomic alignment is not crucial—the goal is to restore the anterior capsular insertion and create an anterior bony buttress (Fig. 32-29C). This suture is not tied until the radial head has been treated as subluxation of the joint facilitates treatment of the radial head.

The radial head is either repaired or replaced as described in the section on radial head fractures. The LCL is repaired as described earlier (Fig. 32-29D). The coronoid suture is then tensioned and tied followed by tying of the LCL repair sutures. Stability in gravity extension is tested. If there is substantial subluxation or dislocation of the elbow in gravity extension, consideration is given to repairing the MCL. Alternatively, a hinged external fixator is applied. If the elbow remains unstable after the surgeon has done everything within their skill and resources to stabilize it, it is reasonable to cross-pin the elbow.

Complications

Instability, arthrosis, heterotopic ossification, and ulnar neuropathy are all relatively more frequent after terrible triad injuries than simple dislocations and dislocation with fracture of the radial head.[101,117]

Controversies and Future Directions

It can be debated whether repair of the coronoid is always necessary for these injuries. We have data showing that nonoperative treatment and radial head resection without prosthetic replacement risks redislocation[117] and data that fixation of the coronoid can restore stability in most cases,[101] but we do not have data regarding the efficacy of treatment of the radial head and collateral ligaments alone.

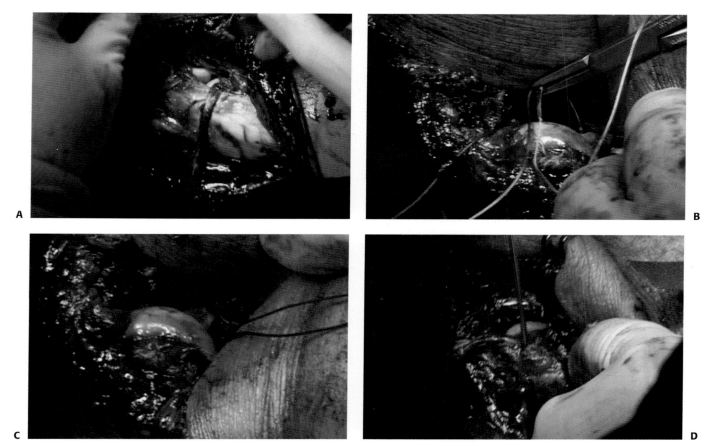

FIGURE 32-29 Operative treatment of a terrible triad elbow fracture-dislocation. **A.** A traumatic rent in the common extensors was developed distally. The strand of tissue still attached to the lateral epicondyle is musculoteninous, not ligament. **B.** Sutures passed through drill holes in the ulna are passed through drill holes in the large coronoid fragment. **C.** The coronoid is reduced, restoring an anterior buttress and the function of the anterior capsule. **D.** The lateral collateral ligament complex is reattached to the lateral epicondyle using a suture anchor. The radial head has been replaced with a prosthesis.

The role of MCL repair is debatable. I, and others, find that it is rarely necessary when all of the lateral structures and the coronoid have been repaired.[101] In fact, it is my impression that in the rare patient in whom treatment of the coronoid, radial head, and LCL do not restore stability, then repair of the MCL will not add much and one should be prepared to proceed to hinged external fixation or cross-pinning of the joint.

The use of cross-pinning of the joint is very controversial. I would point out that a stiff elbow with preserved articular surface is easier to treat than an elbow with a damaged articular surface because of chronic subluxation and abnormal wear. Recognizing the expense, skill, and resources needed to apply a hinged fixator successfully, I think cross-pinning has a useful role for the very unstable elbow.

Varus Posteromedial Rotational Instability Injuries

Signs and Symptoms

With this injury, the elbow is swollen and painful as expected, but the patient is often capable of substantial active motion. In fact, given the small size of the associated coronoid fracture in most cases, the surgeon may be tempted to treat the injury with

early active motion to avoid instability (Table 32-3). Patients will often report clunking or giving way of the elbow when this is attempted—evidence of the underlying instability.

Rationale of Treatment

This is an unstable injury that can lead to chronic subluxation and arthrosis of the elbow. It has only recently been recognized and it is relatively uncommon, so our knowledge of the results of nonoperative treatment is limited. Early experience would suggest that these injuries benefit from operative treatment.[90]

Diagnosis and Classification

This injury is underrecognized. The key element of this injury is a displaced fracture of the anteromedial facet of the coronoid process (Fig. 32-30A), reflecting the varus injury mechanism. Associated injuries include one of the following: (i) injury to the LCL (Fig. 32-30B), (ii) fracture of the olecranon (Fig. 32-30C), or (iii) an additional fracture of the coronoid at its base (Fig. 32-30D–F). It is rare to have more than one of these associated injuries.

When the olecranon is not fractured, a varus stress radiograph may be necessary to appreciate the LCL injury (Fig. 32-30A–B). Computed tomography, particularly three-dimen-

TABLE 32-3	*Pitfalls and Pearls for Elbow Fracture-Dislocations and Coronoid Fractures*
Pitfalls	**Pearls**
• Failure to recognize a complex injury pattern	• The majority of small coronoid fractures are part of a potentially troublesome complex injury pattern. • In the setting of a dislocation with fracture of the radial head, a small triangular fragment in front of the trochlea or in the coronoid fossa is a coronoid fragment. When in doubt, use computed tomography. • Anteromedial coronoid facet fractures are associated with varus instability—beware of associated lateral collateral ligament or olecranon injury.
• Recurrent instability	• Never resect the radial head without replacing it with a prosthesis in the setting of a terrible triad injury. • Identify the injury pattern and treat each of the components of the injury. • Do not trust a cast to maintain reduction.
• Arthrosis caused by persistent subluxation	• Check the elbow frequently for the first 6 weeks after injury and surgery. • When substantial subluxation (perching of the trochlea on the coronoid) is identified, the surgeon should intervene before articular damage occurs.
• Underestimation of the importance of a small coronoid fracture with resultant instability	• Become comfortable with operative fixation of coronoid fractures or refer patients to surgeons who are comfortable with these techniques.

sional reconstructions, is useful to plan treatment of the coronoid fracture. The coronoid fracture usually involves anteromedial facet and tip fragments and occasionally extends to the base of the coronoid process.

AUTHORS' PREFERRED METHOD OF TREATMENT

Varus Posteromedial Rotational Instability Injuries

This injury is treated with operative repair of all injured structures. The LCL and/or olecranon fracture is repaired, and the coronoid is repaired through a medial exposure using some combination of wires, plates, and screws. A buttress plate is particularly useful.

Surgical Procedure: Anteromedial Coronoid Facet Fracture. A medial skin flap is elevated with care taken to protect the medial antebrachial cutaneous nerve and the ulnar nerve. We prefer to mobilize the ulnar nerve from the cubital tunnel, allowing it to remain anteriorly transposed in the subcutaneous tissues at the end of the procedure (Fig. 32-18E). From the medial side, the coronoid can be exposed directly medially—between the heads of the flexor carpi ulnaris where the ulnar nerve usually lies—or superiorly through the over-the-top approach described by Hotchkiss[49] for contracture release (Fig. 32-5). Taylor and Scram[127] described elevation of the entire flexor-pronator mass, but this requires far more dissection than elevation from within the split in the flexor carpi ulnaris. It is useful for very large fragments.

The dissection on the medial side should remain superficial to the anterior band of the MCL. In addition, capsular attachments to the tip of the coronoid should be preserved. Through this exposure a small T-plate or a plate designed specifically for internal fixation of the coronoid can be applied.

Complications

An extensive dissection, transposition, and retraction of the ulnar nerve is needed to perform a medial repair and ulnar nerve palsies sometimes occur. Large tapes and tapes with hemostats should not be used for retraction as they may lead to excessive traction on the nerve. A means for providing adequate retraction of the nerve without prolonged pressure needs to be devised. I have sutured the skin to the forearm fascia to hold the transposed nerve anteriorly as I work on the coronoid.

Subluxation of the elbow can occur with rotation of the humerus into the coronoid defect leading to arthrosis.[90] Heterotopic bone formation is uncommon after this injury.

Controversies and Future Directions

This injury has only recently been recognized, and our understanding of it and the best treatment methods for it are evolving.

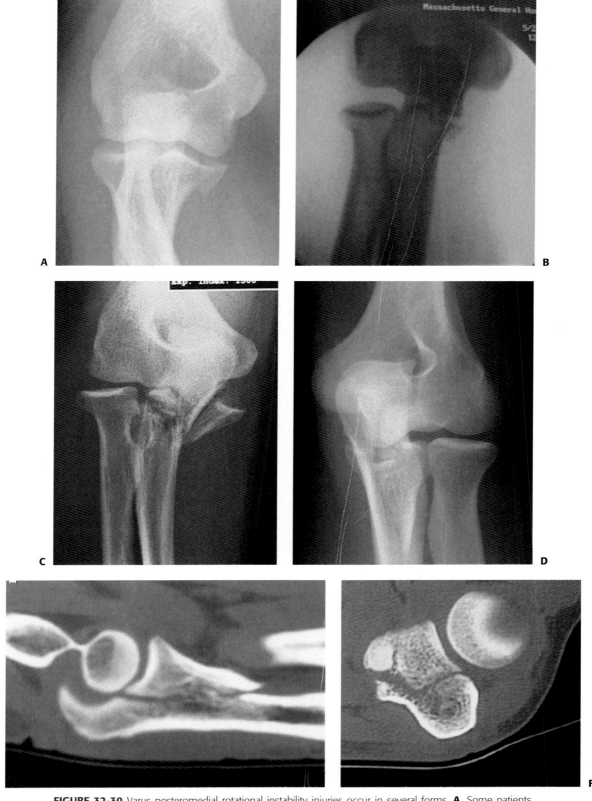

FIGURE 32-30 Varus posteromedial rotational instability injuries occur in several forms. **A.** Some patients present with small isolated anteromedial facet coronoid fractures. **B.** Stress radiographs reveal injury to the lateral collateral ligament. **C.** Alternatively, there may be a fracture of the olecranon, in which case there is usually not a lateral collateral ligament injury. **D–F.** Finally, some patients with anteromedial coronoid facet fractures may have a fracture of the coronoid at its base.

Improved exposure and plating techniques for the medial coronoid will most likely be developed with increasing experience with this injury pattern.

OLECRANON AND PROXIMAL ULNA FRACTURES

Rationale of Treatment of Fracture of the Proximal Ulna

The key element in the treatment of a fracture of the proximal ulna, no matter how complex, is to restore the contour and dimensions of the trochlear notch of the ulna. Small articular incongruities and comminution in the relatively nonarticular transverse groove will be of little consequence provided that stable realignment of the coronoid and olecranon facets is achieved.[90,115,116] These fractures often occur in patients with poor bone quality.[116] Careful technique and an understanding of how to achieve reliable internal fixation are important. Restoration of the trochlear notch is the key to restoring elbow stability. Also important are repair or replacement of the radial head and repair of the LCL complex when they are injured. Stable fixation will allow immediate mobilization, thereby diminishing the risk of stiffness and heterotopic ossification (Table 32-4).

Diagnosis and Classification

The initial radiographs obtained after the injury are often of limited quality because of the deformity and pain in the limb. Nevertheless, it is usually possible to discern the overall pattern of the injury, which in turn leads one to suspect other injury components that may not be immediately obvious. For example,

a posterior olecranon fracture-dislocation is often associated with fractures of the radial head and coronoid process as well as injury to the LCL complex,[116] whereas an anterior fracture-dislocation rarely involves injury to the radial head or collateral ligaments.[115]

Radiographs obtained after manipulative reduction and splint immobilization of the limb (when appropriate) may provide better views of the elbow and additional information about the injury. When additional information about fractures of the radial head or coronoid may influence decision making, computed tomography is useful. In particular, three-dimensional reconstructions with the distal humerus removed can provide a very accurate characterization of the injury. Using such images, preoperative planning will be more accurate.

Additional information regarding the character of the injury can be obtained by viewing the elbow under the image intensifier once the patient is anesthetized. For some complex injuries, complete characterization of the injury pattern—and therefore a final treatment plan—can only be made based on operative exposure. Thus, the surgeon must be comfortable with extensile exposures providing adequate access to the injury components.

Posterior Olecranon Fracture-Dislocations

The Bado type 2 or posterior Monteggia lesion has long been recognized as a distinct injury that is usually associated with fracture of the radial head and often occurs in the setting of osteoporosis[59,95,98] (see Chapter 31). There is a spectrum of posterior Monteggia injuries with similar features that vary according to the location of the ulnar fracture.[59] These have been subclassified as type A when the fracture is at the level of the trochlear notch (involving the olecranon and often the coronoid processes); type B, in the metaphysis just distal to the trochlear

| **TABLE 32-4** | *Pitfalls and Pearls for Olecranon and Proximal Ulna Fractures* |

Pitfalls	Pearls
• Use of tension band wiring for complex injury patterns	• Recognize anterior and posterior olecranon fracture-dislocations and use plate and screw fixation.
• Failure to restore alignment of a large coronoid fracture	• Recognize complex injury patterns. • Be prepared for large coronoid fractures. • Be prepared for complex comminution. • Become familiar with the techniques of exposure and internal fixation of large coronoid fractures as part of an olecranon fracture-dislocation or refer the patient to a surgeon who is familiar.
• Postoperative dislocation of the ulnohumeral joint	• Be aware of the potential for ulnohumeral instability with posterior olecranon fracture-dislocations. • Restore radiocapitellar contact, realign the ulna including the coronoid, and repair the lateral collateral ligament.
• Early loss of fixation and nonunion	• Use a long plate that follows the contour of the olecranon, preferably on the dorsal surface. This provides for a greater number of screws and screws in orthogonal directions. • Be aware of the likelihood of osteoporosis, particularly with posterior olecranon fracture-dislocations after low-energy injuries.

notch; and type C, in the diaphysis. Type D fractures are multi-fragmented fractures that involve more than one region.[59] These fractures are inherently unstable by virtue of the associated capsuloligamentous damage, fracture and dislocation of the radial head, and the morphology of the ulnar fracture, which often involves a triangular or quadrangular fragment of the ulna that includes the anterior ulnar cortex and sometimes the coronoid process.

Olecranon Fractures

The Mayo classification of olecranon fractures distinguishes three factors that have a direct influence on treatment: (i) fracture displacement, (ii) comminution, and (iii) ulnohumeral instability[79] (Fig. 32-31). Type 1 fractures that are nondisplaced or minimally displaced are either noncomminuted (type 1A) or comminuted (type 1B) and are treated nonoperatively. Type II fractures feature displacement of the proximal fragment without elbow instability—these fractures require operative treatment. Type IIA fractures, which are noncomminuted, are well treated by tension band wire fixation. When the fracture is oblique, an ancillary interfragmentary compression screw can be added. Type IIB fractures are comminuted and require plate fixation. Type III fractures feature instability of the ulnohumeral joint and require surgical treatment.

Olecranon Fracture-Dislocations

Fractures of the proximal ulna can appear extremely complex, and identification of basic injury patterns can facilitate manage-

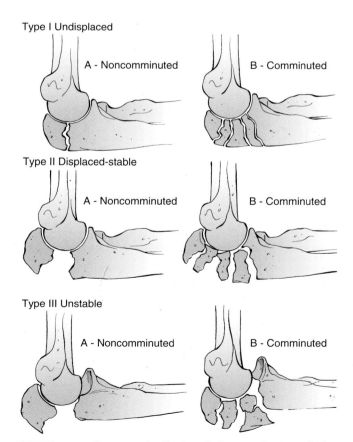

Type I Undisplaced

A - Noncomminuted

B - Comminuted

Type II Displaced-stable

A - Noncomminuted

B - Comminuted

Type III Unstable

A - Noncomminuted

B - Comminuted

FIGURE 32-31 The Mayo classification of olecranon fractures divides fractures according to displacement, comminution, and subluxation/dislocation.

ment. Even a simple fracture pattern of the olecranon can have associated injuries, which the surgeon must be careful not to miss.

Varus posteromedial rotational instability pattern injuries have only recently been recognized and described. The central element of this injury is a fracture of the anteromedial facet of the coronoid process, resulting in varus instability.[112] There is an associated injury, either an avulsion of the LCL complex from the lateral epicondyle or a fracture of the olecranon—but rarely both. The radial head is rarely fractured.

The majority of olecranon fracture-dislocations occur in either an anterior or a posterior direction.[115,116] Anterior olecranon fracture-dislocations have been described as transolecranon fracture dislocations because the trochlea of the distal humerus implodes through the trochlear notch of the ulna as the forearm translates anteriorly[4,115] (Fig. 32-19). This pattern can be confused with posterior fracture-dislocations with a similar appearance, so the term *anterior olecranon fracture-dislocation* may be preferable. Anterior fracture-dislocations are injuries to the ulnohumeral articulation with the radioulnar relationship being relatively preserved and the radial head rarely injured. The fracture of the proximal ulna can be a simple oblique fracture, but it is often very complex, including fragmentation of the olecranon, fragmentation extending into the ulnar diaphysis, and fracture of the coronoid. Associated collateral ligament injury is unusual.[4,115]

It is useful to consider posterior fracture-dislocations of the olecranon as the most proximal type of a posterior Monteggia injury.[59] Common factors of posterior Monteggia injuries include an apex posterior fracture of the ulna, posterior translation of the radial head with respect to the capitellum, fracture of the radial head, and frequent injury to the LCL complex. With posterior olecranon fracture-dislocations (or type A posterior Monteggia fractures, according to Jupiter and colleagues[59]), the fracture of the ulna occurs at the level of the olecranon and is nearly always associated with a fracture of the coronoid process. When a complex olecranon fracture-dislocation is identified as being posterior in direction, fractures of the radial head and coronoid and injury to the LCL should be suspected (Fig. 32-20).

The fracture of the coronoid varies somewhat with each specific type of olecranon fracture-dislocation. Those associated with a varus posteromedial mechanism will involve the anteromedial facet and the tip and the radial head will not be fractured. The fracture of the coronoid that occurs with an anterior olecranon fracture-dislocation is usually a single, large fragment involving nearly the entire coronoid, but it is occasionally split once or twice in the sagittal plane. The fractures of the coronoid associated with posterior olecranon fracture-dislocations are more variable including the occasional fracture of the tip, a single large fragment, comminution into three fragments (anteromedial, central, and sigmoid notch), and more extensive comminution (Fig. 32-19).

Current Treatment Options

Nonoperative Treatment

The unusual fracture of the olecranon that is minimally displaced and does not displace further with the arm placed in 90 degrees of flexion can be treated nonoperatively. The elbow is splinted for 3 to 4 weeks in 90 degrees of flexion, and then gentle active motion is started gradually progressing to active assisted motion.

Excision and Triceps Advancement

The olecranon process is rarely so fragmented that it cannot be repaired. Tension band wiring techniques can gain fixation of the soft tissue attachments until healing occurs. As a result, excision of the olecranon and triceps advancement are used sparingly for primary treatment of fractures of the olecranon and occasionally for treatment of secondary complications. As primary treatment, excision of the olecranon is best suited to infirmed older patients with limited functional demands.[18,31] The surgeon must be certain that the collateral ligaments, radial head, and coronoid process are intact.

Tension Band Wiring

Tension band wiring is appropriate for relatively simple fractures at the level of the transverse groove of the trochlear notch, without associated ligament injuries or fracture of the coronoid or radial head (Fig. 32-32). Tension band wire techniques have been described using screws or Kirschner wires.

Plate and Screws Fixation

A plate and screws is used for comminuted olecranon fractures, Monteggia fractures, and olecranon fracture-dislocations (Fig. 32-33). In addition to standard plates, there are several precontoured plates for the proximal ulna now available.

AUTHOR'S PREFERRED METHOD OF TREATMENT

Olecranon and Proximal Ulna Fractures

I use cast immobilization on occasion for a stable, nondisplaced fracture of the olecranon but prefer to repair the majority of these fractures to start confident active motion exercises and functional use of the limb.

For simple, noncomminuted fractures without associated ligament injuries, I use tension band wiring with Kirschner wires rather than a screw. For comminuted fractures and fracture dislocations, I use a dorsal plate and screws contoured to wrap around the proximal ulna.[109,115,116] For some complex fractures, I place the proximal aspect of the plate over the triceps insertion. Otherwise, I elevate the triceps insertion and place the plate directly on bone. When the proximal olecranon fragment is small, fragmented, or osteopenic, I also use a tension band wire that engages the triceps insertion (Fig. 32-33).

For fractures of the coronoid that involve the anteromedial facet, I use a medial plate unless the fragments are large enough to be reliably repaired with screws.[112] For unreconstructable or very complex fractures of the coronoid, I use 4 to 8 weeks of hinged external fixation to maintain a concentric ulnohumeral reduction and protect the healing coronoid.

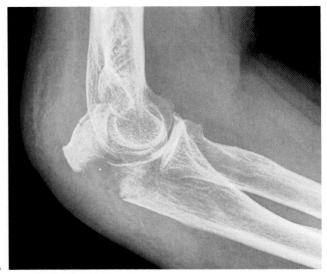

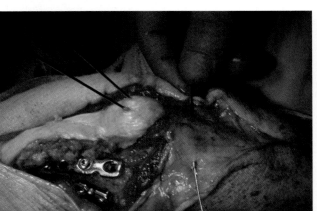

FIGURE 32-32 Tension band wiring is useful for simple isolated fractures of the olecranon. **A.** Lateral radiograph demonstrates a transverse fracture of the olecranon. **B.** The fracture is realigned and secured with two 0.045-inch Kirschner wires drilled obliquely so that they engage the anterior ulnar cortex distal to the coronoid. **C.** Two 22-gauge stainless steel wires are passed through drill holes in the ulna distal to the fracture. **D.** The wires are passed underneath the triceps insertion adjacent to the Kirschner wires. *(continues)*

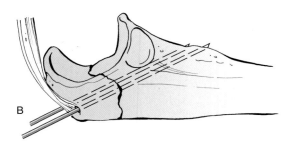

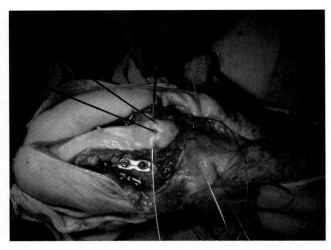

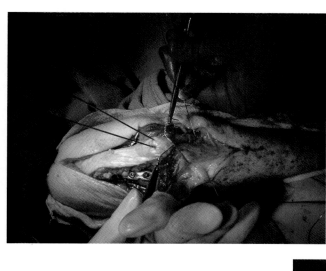

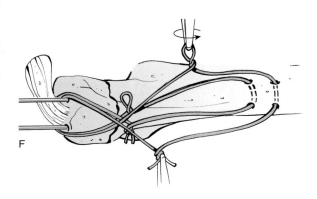

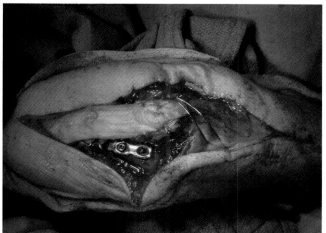

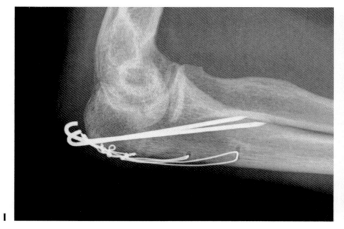

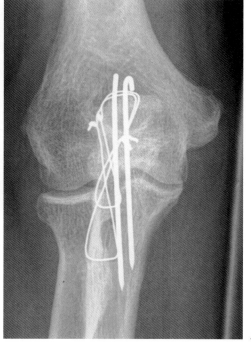

FIGURE 32-32 (*Continued*) **E,F.** The wires are then tensioned both medially and laterally. **G.** The Kirschner wires are then bent 180 degrees and impacted into the olecranon beneath the triceps insertion. **H.** The wires are bent into the adjacent soft tissues so that the entire construct has a very low profile. **I.** Postoperative lateral radiograph. **J.** Postoperative anteroposterior radiograph.

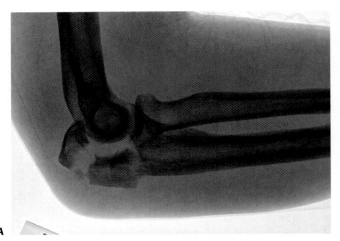
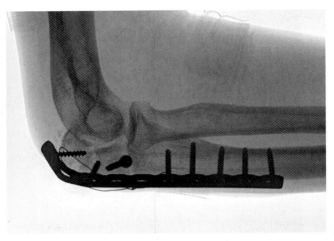

A

B

FIGURE 32-33 Comminuted olecranon fractures require plate and screw fixation. **A.** This injury created a small olecranon fragment. **B.** In addition to the plate and screws used to maintain alignment of the trochlear notch, a tension band wire is used to gain hold of the small proximal fragment.

Operative Techniques

Skin Incision. A midline posterior skin incision is used for all complex fractures of the proximal ulna. Traumatic wounds are incorporated. Some surgeons prefer that the incision not pass directly over the olecranon, and curve it slightly.[81] A direct midline incision may cut fewer cutaneous nerves.[23]

Operative Technique

Excision of Fracture Fragments and Triceps Advancement. The fragments of the olecranon are excised. Drill holes are made starting from immediately adjacent to the articular margin of the remaining olecranon and exiting the dorsal surface of the ulna. Stout sutures are placed in the triceps using one of a variety of techniques designed to gain hold over a broad portion of the tendon. These are then passed through the drill holes in the ulna, tensioned and tied. The elbow is immobilized for 4 weeks and active motion is allowed thereafter. In low-demand individuals, formal therapy is not necessary.

Operative Technique

Tension Band Wiring. The fracture is opened and the hematoma removed to be sure that comminution and articular involvement are limited. Periosteum and muscular attachments are elevated minimally—just enough to ensure accurate reduction of the fragments. A large tenaculum clamp can be used to maintain reduction of the olecranon. A drill hole made in the dorsal surface of the ulna can provide a good anchor point for the distal tine of the clamp.

Kirschner Wire Tension Bond Technique. Two parallel Kirschner wires are drilled across the osteotomy site. The majority of surgeons use 0.062-inch wires, but we use 0.045-inch wires with few problems. The wires are often drilled parallel to the ulnar diaphysis, but we and others favor drilling the wires obliquely so that they pass through the anterior ulnar cortex, just distal to the coronoid process.[13,99] This is intended to limit the potential for wire migration. After exiting the anterior cortex, the wires are retracted between 5 and 10 mm, anticipating subsequent impaction of the wires into the olecranon process proximally.

The extensor carpi ulnaris and flexor carpi ulnaris muscles are partly elevated from the apex of the ulna distal to the fracture site to expose the cortex. The appropriate distance between the fracture and the transverse ulnar drill hole(s) has been commented on based on mechanical calculations, but the location is determined more practically by the transition from the flat proximal ulna to the apex posterior triangular shape of the diaphysis. Likewise, the placement of the drill holes in the anteroposterior plane is not critical except that they should not be so dorsal as to risk breaking out of the ulna. Large drill holes (2.5 mm) facilitate wire passage.

Many surgeons use a single 18-gauge stainless steel wire for the tension wire, but we prefer to use two 22-gauge stainless steel wires, each passed through its own drill hole distally (Fig. 32-32). The smaller wires are less prominent.

The tension band wires are placed in a figure-of eight configuration over the dorsal ulna. The proximal end of each wire is passed deep to the Kirschner wires, through the insertion of the triceps using a large-gauge needle. The tension band wires are then tensioned on both the medial and lateral sides of the ulna until they rest flush with the ulna. Some surgeons prefer to twist the wires until they are very tight, but this cannot be done with smaller gauge wires—they will break. The wire does not need to be tight; it is only important to take up all of the slack in the wires. This is done by twisting each wire until it starts to bend over itself. The twisted ends are trimmed and bent into the adjacent soft tissues to limit prominence.

The proximal ends of the Kirschner wires are bent 180 degrees and trimmed. The triceps insertion is then incised, and these bent ends are impacted into the proximal olecranon using a bone tamp and mallet. The strength of the fixation can be tested by completely flexing the elbow—the fracture should not separate.

Screw Tension Bond Technique. Some surgeons prefer to use screws instead of Kirschner wires. Some recommend using a very long screw that engages the medullary canal of the ulnar diaphysis distally.[51] Others recommend aiming the screw anteriorly to engage the anterior ulnar cortex. An oblique screw is particularly well suited to an oblique fracture. The remaining portion of the technique is as described for the Kirschner wire technique.

Plate and Screw Fixation

When a plate is applied to the proximal ulna, it should be contoured to wrap around the proximal aspect of the ulna (Fig. 32-33). A straight plate will only have two or three screws in metaphyseal bone proximal to the fracture. Many patients with complex proximal ulna fractures have osteopenic bone, which further compromises the strength of plate and screw fixation. Bending the plate around the proximal aspect of the olecranon provides for additional screws to be placed in the proximal fragment. In addition, the most proximal screws are oriented orthogonal to the more distal screws. Finally, the most proximal screws can be very long, crossing the fracture line into the distal fragment. In some cases, these screws can be directed to engage one of the cortices of the distal fragment, such as the anterior ulnar cortex.

A plate applied to the dorsal surface of the proximal ulna also has several advantages over plates applied to the medial or lateral aspects of the ulna. Placing the plate along the flat dorsal surface can assist in obtaining and monitoring reduction. The dorsal surface is in the plane of the forces generated by active elbow motion so that the plate functions to a certain extent as a tension band. Finally, dorsal plate placement requires very limited soft tissue stripping.

Exposure of the ulna should preserve periosteal and muscle attachments. A plate contoured to wrap around the proximal ulna can be placed on top of the triceps insertion with few problems. This is particularly useful when the olecranon fragment is small or fragmented. Alternatively, the triceps insertion can be incised longitudinally and partially elevated medially and laterally to allow direct plate contact with bone.

Distally, a dorsal plate will lie directly on the apex of the ulnar diaphysis. This might seem unsettling to some surgeons, but has not been a problem in our hands. One advantage of this situation is that the muscle need only be split sufficiently to gain access to this apex—there is no need to elevate the muscle or periosteum off either the medial or lateral flat aspect of the ulna. No attempt is made to precisely realign intervening fragmentation—once the relationship of the coronoid and olecranon facets is restored and the overall alignment is restored, the remaining fragments are bridged, leaving their soft tissue attachments intact. Despite extensive fragmentation, bone grafts[52] are rarely necessary if the soft tissue attachments are preserved.[115,116]

Fracture-Dislocations

Fractures of the radial head and coronoid process can be evaluated and often definitively treated through the exposure provided by the fracture of the olecranon process. With little additional dissection, the olecranon fragment can be mobilized proximally, providing exposure of the coronoid through the ulnohumeral joint. If the exposure of the radial head through the posterior injury is inadequate, a separate muscle interval (e.g., Kocher or Kaplan intervals[81])—accessed by the elevation of a broad lateral skin flap can be used.

If the exposure of the coronoid is inadequate through the straight dorsal skin incision, a separate medial or lateral exposure can be developed. Posterior olecranon fracture-dislocations often require a lateral exposure to address a fracture of the radial head or coronoid, or to repair the LCL. When the LCL is injured it is usually avulsed from the lateral epicondyle. This injury facilitates both exposure and repair. The LCL origin and common extensor musculature can be included in an anterior or a posterior flap, or mobilized distally.

Improved exposure of the coronoid can be obtained by releasing the origins of the radial wrist extensors from the lateral supracondylar ridge and elevating the brachialis from the anterior humerus, and by excising the fractured radial head.[110,112] A medial exposure, developed between the two heads of the flexor carpi ulnaris, or by splitting the flexor-pronator mass more anteriorly, may be needed to address a complex fracture of the coronoid, particularly one that involves the anteromedial facet of the coronoid process.

The fracture of the coronoid can often be reduced directly through the elbow joint using the limited access provided by the olecranon fracture.[41,42,88] Provisional fixation can be obtained using Kirschner wires to attach the fragments to either the metaphyseal or diaphyseal fragments of the ulna or to the trochlea of the distal humerus when there is extensive fragmentation of the proximal ulna.[40,68] An alternative to keep in mind when there is extensive fragmentation of the proximal ulna is the use of a skeletal distractor (a temporary external fixator).[68,115] External fixation applied between a wire driven through the olecranon fragment and up into the trochlea and a second wire in the distal ulnar diaphysis can often obtain reduction indirectly when distraction is applied between the pins. Definitive fixation can usually be obtained with screws applied under image intensifier guidance. The screws are placed through the plate when there is extensive fragmentation of the proximal ulna. If the coronoid fracture is very comminuted and cannot be securely repaired, the ulnohumeral joint should be protected with temporary hinged or static external fixation, or temporary pin fixation of the ulnohumeral joint, depending on the equipment and expertise available.

A long plate is contoured to wrap around the proximal olecranon. A very long plate should be considered (between 12 or 16 holes), particularly when there is extensive fragmentation or the bone quality is poor. When the olecranon is fragmented or osteoporotic, a plate and screws alone may not provide reliable fixation. In this situation, it has proved useful to use ancillary tension band wire fixation to control the olecranon fragments through the triceps insertion.

Complications

Tension band wire constructs can fail when used for complex fractures or fracture-dislocations, but rarely fail when used for simple fractures unless the patient returns to forceful activity too soon. Plate loosening is most common in older patients with fracture-dislocations when a noncontoured plate has been placed on either the medial or lateral side of the proximal ulna (Fig. 32-34). Failed internal fixation can be salvaged with realignment and repeat internal fixation using a dorsal contoured plate and screws. If there is a bone defect or delayed union, autogenous cancellous bone graft can be applied to the fracture site.

Nonunion after simple olecranon fractures is very unusual.[93] Proximal ulnar nonunion usually occurs after a fracture-dislocation of the proximal ulna. Union can usually be achieved with contoured dorsal plate fixation and autogenous bone grafting.[93,113]

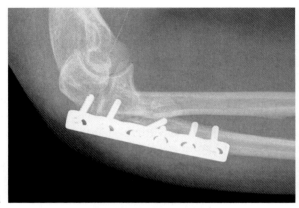
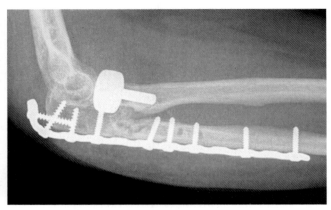

FIGURE 32-34 Medial and lateral plates seem prone to failure when treating posterior Monteggia injuries. **A.** This plate only has two screws in the proximal, osteoporotic metaphyseal fragment and it is therefore not surprising that it loosened. **B.** A much more secure plate applied to the dorsal surface and contoured to wrap around the olecranon process has four screws in the proximal fragment with orthogonal interlocking of the most proximal screws.

Ulnohumeral instability is sometimes a surprise to the surgeon when treating a complex proximal ulna fracture. It is usually the result of some combination of fixation of the proximal ulna with apex dorsal deformity, as well as inadequate treatment of an injury to the coronoid, radial head and for LCL complex. This instability can often be salvaged by secondary surgery, often including the use of hinged external fixation.[71,107,111,119]

Both the elbow and the forearm can become stiff with these injuries, particularly posterior olecranon-fracture dislocations. Proximal radioulnar synostosis occurs fairly frequently with these injuries.

Controversies and Future Directions

Many surgeons are starting to use plate and screw fixation for even relatively simple fractures of the olecranon. In some ways, the tension band wire is a more reliable way to fix these relatively small fracture fragments. Additional data are needed to understand the relative advantages and disadvantages of each technique.

Our understanding of complex fractures of the proximal ulna and olecranon fracture-dislocations continues to evolve and improve. In particular, the handling of a complex comminuted basal coronoid fracture still represents a substantial challenge.

REFERENCES

1. Antuna SA, Morrey BF, Adams RA, et al. Ulnohumeral arthroplasty for primary degenerative arthritis of the elbow: long-term outcome and complications. J Bone Joint Surg Am 2002;84A:2168–2173.
2. Bauer G, Worsdorfer O, Braun K. [Radio-ulnar bridge callus following osteosynthesis of forearm fractures.] Aktuelle Traumatol 1990;20:194–198.
3. Beingessner DM, Dunning CE, Beingessner CJ, et al. The effect of radial head fracture size on radiocapitellar joint stability. Clin Biomech 2003;18:677–681.
4. Biga N, Thomine JM. La luxation transolecranienne du coude. Rev Chir Orthop 1974;60:557–567.
5. Broberg MA, Morrey BF. Results of delayed excision of the radial head after fracture. J Bone Joint Surg Am 1986;68A:669–674.
6. Broberg MA, Morrey BF. Results of treatment of fracture-dislocations of the elbow. Clin Orthop 1987;216:109–119.
7. Bunker TD, Newman LH. The Herbert differential pitch bone screw in displaced radial head fractures. Injury 1987;16:621–624.
8. Cage DJN, Abrams RA, Callahan JJ, et al. Soft tissue attachments of the ulnar coronoid process. Clin Orthop 1995;320:154–158.
9. Caputo AE, Mazzocca AD, Santoro VM. The nonarticulating portion of the radial head: anatomic and clinical correlations for internal fixation. J Hand Surg 1998;23A:1082–1090.
10. Carn RM, Medige J, Curtain D, et al. Silicone rubber replacement of the severely fractured radial head. Clin Orthop 1986;209:259–269.
11. Carstam N. Operative treatment of fractures of the upper end of the radius. Acta Orthop Scan 1950;19:502–526.
12. Cheng SL, Morrey BF. Treatment of the mobile, painful arthritic elbow by distraction interposition arthroplasty. J Bone Joint Surg Br 2000;82B:233–238.
13. Chin KR, Ring D, Jupiter JB. Double tension-band fixation of the olecranon. Tech Shoulder Elbow Surg 2000;1:61–66.
14. Cobb TK, Beckenbaugh RD. Nonunion of the radial head and neck. Orthopaedics 1998;21:364–368.
15. Cohen MS, Hastings H. Posttraumatic contracture of the elbow: operative release using a lateral collateral ligament sparing approach. J Bone Joint Surg 1998;80B:805–812.
16. Cohen MS, Hastings H. Rotatory instability of the elbow: the anatomy and role of the lateral stabilizers. J Bone Joint Surg Am 1997;79A:225–233.
17. Davidson PA, Moseley JB, Tullos HS. Radial head fracture. A potentially complex injury. Clin Orthop 1993;297:224–130.
18. Didonna ML, Fernandez JJ, Lim TH, et al. Partial olecranon excision: the relationship between triceps insertion site and extension strength of the elbow. J Hand Surg Am 2003;28A:117–122.
19. Diliberti T, Botte MJ, Abrams RA. Anatomical considerations regarding the posterior interosseous nerve during posterolateral approaches to the proximal part of the radius. J Bone Joint Surg Am 2000;82A:809–813.
20. Doornberg JN, de Jong IM, Lindenhovius AL, et al. The anteromedial facet of the coronoid process of the ulna. J Shoulder Elbow Surg 2007;16:667–670.
21. Doornberg JN, Parisien R, van Duijn PJ, et al. Radial head arthroplasty with a modular metal spacer to treat acute traumatic elbow instability. J Bone Joint Surg Am 2007;89:1075–1080.
22. Doornberg JN, Ring DC. Fracture of the anteromedial facet of the coronoid process. J Bone Joint Surg Am 2006;88:2216–2224.
23. Dowdy PA, Bain GI, King GJW, et al. The midline posterior elbow incision. J Bone Joint Surg Br 1995;77B:696–699.
24. Duckworth AD, Kulijdian A, McKee MD, et al. Residual subluxation of the elbow after dislocation or fracture-dislocation: treatment with active elbow exercises and avoidance of varus stress. J Shoulder Elbow Surg 2007;Dec 24.
25. Duckworth AD, Ring D, Kulijdian A, et al. Unstable elbow dislocations. J Shoulder Elbow Surg 2007;Dec 7.
26. Dunning CE, Zarzour ZD, Patterson SD, et al. Muscle forces and pronation stabilize the lateral ligament deficient elbow. Clin Orthop 2001;388:118–124.
27. Dürig M, Müller W, Rüedi TP, et al. The operative treatment of elbow dislocation in the adult. J Bone Joint Surg Am 1979;61A:239–244.
28. Essex-Lopresti P. Fractures of the radial head with distal radioulnar dislocation. J Bone Joint Surg Br 1951;33B:244–247.
29. Faierman E, Wang J, Jupiter JB. Secondary ulnar nerve palsy in adults after elbow trauma: a report of two cases. J Hand Surg 2001;26A:675–678.
30. Froimson AI, Silva JE, Richey DG. Cutis arthroplasty of the elbow joint. J Bone Joint Surg Am 1976;58A:863–865.
31. Gartsman GM, Scales JC, Otis JC. Operative treatment of olecranon fractures. J Bone Joint Surg Am 1981;63A:718–721.
32. Geel C. Fractures of the radial head. In: McQueen MM, Jupiter JB, eds. Radius and Ulna. Oxford: Butterworth-Heinemann, 1999:159–168.
33. Geel CW, Palmer AK, Rüedi T, et al. Internal fixation of proximal radial head fractures. J Orthop Trauma 1990;4:270–274.
34. Gelinas JJ, Faber KJ, Patterson SD, et al. The effectiveness of turnbuckle splinting for elbow contractures. J Bone Joint Surg Br 2000;82B:74–78.
35. Goldberg I, Peylan J, Yosipovitch Z, et al. Late results of excision of the radial head for an isolated closed fracture. J Bone Joint Surg Am 1986;68A:675–679.
36. Gordon M, Bullough PG. Synovial and osseous inflammation in failed silicone-rubber prosthesis. J Bone Joint Surg Am 1982;64A:574–580.
37. Green DP, McCoy H. Turnbuckle orthotic correction of elbow-flexion contractures after acute injuries. J Bone Joint Surg Am 1979;61A:1092–1095.
38. Grewal R, MacDermid JC, Faber KJ, et al. Comminuted radial head fractures treated

with a modular metallic radial head arthroplasty. Study of outcomes. J Bone Joint Surg Am 2006;88A:2192–2200.
39. Harrington IJ, Tountas AA. Replacement of the radial head in the treatment of unstable elbow fractures. Injury 1980;12:405–412.
40. Hastings H, Engles DR. Fixation of complex elbow fractures, part II: proximal ulna and radius fractures. Hand Clin 1997;13:721–735.
41. Heim U. Combined fractures of the upper end of the ulna and the radius in adults: a series of 120 cases. Rev Chir Orthop 1998;84:142–153.
42. Heim U. Kombinierte Verletzungen von Radius und Ulna im proximalen Unterarmsegment. Hefte Unfallchir 1994;241:61–79.
43. Heim U. Surgical treatment of radial head fracture. Z Unfallchir Versicherungsmed 1992;85:3–11.
44. Heim U, Pfeiffer KM. Internal Fixation of Small Fractures. 3rd ed. Berlin: Springer-Verlag, 1988.
45. Henry AK. Extensile Exposure. 2nd ed. Edinburgh: Churchill Livingstone, 1973.
46. Herbertsson P, Josefsson PO, Hasserius R, et al. Uncomplicated Mason type II and III fractures of the radial head and neck in adults. A long-term follow-up study. J Bone Joint Surg Am 2004;86A:569–574.
47. Hirvensalo E, Böstman O, Rokkanen P. Absorbable polyglycolide pins in fixation of displaced fractures of the radial head. Arch Orthop Trauma Surg 1990;109:258–261.
48. Hotchkiss RN. Displaced fractures of the radial head: Internal fixation or excision. J Am Acad Orthop Surg 1997;5:1–10.
49. Hotchkiss RN. Elbow contracture. In: Green DP, Hotchkiss RN, Pederson WC, eds. Green's Operative Hand Surgery. Philadelphia: Churchill-Livingstone, 1999:667–682.
50. Hotchkiss RN. Fractures and dislocations of the elbow. In: Rockwood CA, Green DP, Bucholz RW, et al, eds. Rockwood and Green's Fractures in Adults. 4th ed. Philadelphia: Lippincott-Raven, 1996:929–1024.
51. Hutchinson DT, Horowitz DS, Ha G, et al. Cyclic loading of olecranon fracture fixation constructs. J Bone Joint Surg Am 2003;85A:831–837.
52. Ikeda M, Fukushima Y, Kobayashi Y, et al. Comminuted fractures of the olecranon. J Bone Joint Surg Br 2001;83B:805–808.
53. Jobe FW, Stark H, Lombardo SJ. Reconstruction of the ulnar collateral ligament in athletes. J Bone Joint Surg Am 1986;68A:1158–1163.
54. Johnston GW. A follow-up of 100 cases of fracture of the head of the radius. Ulster Med J 1952;31:51–56.
55. Josefsson PO, Gentz CF, Johnell O, et al. Dislocations of the elbow and intraarticular fractures. Clin Orthop 1989;246:126–130.
56. Josefsson PO, Gentz CF, Johnell O, et al. Surgical versus nonsurgical treatment of ligamentous injuries following dislocation of the elbow joint. J Bone Joint Surg Am 1987;69A:605–608.
57. Josefsson PO, Johnell O, Wendeberg B. Ligamentous injuries in dislocations of the elbow joint. Clin Orthop 1987;221:221–225.
58. Judet T, Garreaue de Loubresse C, Piriou P, et al. A floating prosthesis for radial head fractures. J Bone Joint Surg Br 1996;78B:244–249.
59. Jupiter JB, Leibovic SJ, Ribbans W, et al. The posterior Monteggia lesion. J Orthop Trauma 1991;5:395–402.
60. Jupiter JB, Ring D. Operative treatment of posttraumatic proximal radioulnar synostosis. J Bone Joint Surg Am 1998;80A:248–257.
61. Jupiter JB, Ring D. Treatment of unreduced elbow dislocations with hinged external fixation. J Bone Joint Surg Am 2002;84A:1630–1635.
62. Kapandji IA. The Physiology of the Joints. 5th ed. Edinburgh: Churchill Livingstone, 1982.
63. Kocher T. Textbook of Operative Surgery. 3rd ed. London: Adam and Charles Black, 1911.
64. Linsheid RL, O'Driscoll SW. Elbow dislocations. In: Morrey BF, ed. The elbow and Its Disorders. 2nd ed. Philadelphia: WB Saunders, 1993:441–452.
65. Lyons FA, Rockwood CA. Migration of pins used in operations on the shoulder. J Bone Joint Surg Am 1990;72A:1262–1267.
66. Mansat P, Morrey BF. The column procedure: a limited lateral approach for extrinsic contracture of the elbow. J Bone Joint Surg Am 1998;80A:1603–1615.
67. Mason ML. Some observations on fractures of the head of the radius with a review of 100 cases. Br J Surg 1959;42:123–132.
68. Mast J, Jakob RP, Ganz R. Planning and Reduction Techniques in Fracture Surgery. Heidelberg: Springer-Verlag, 1979.
69. McArthur RA. Herbert screw fixation of the head of the radius. Clin Orthop 1987;224: 79–87.
70. McAuliffe JA, Wolfson AH. Early excision of heterotopic ossification about the elbow followed by radiation therapy. J Bone Joint Surg Am 1997;79A:749–755.
71. McKee MD, Bowden SH, King GJ, et al. Management of recurrent, complex instability of the elbow with a hinged external fixator. J Bone Joint Surg Br 1998;80B:1031–1036.
72. McKee MD, Jupiter JB, Bosse G, et al. The results of ulnar neurolysis for ulnar neuropathy during post-traumatic elbow reconstruction. Orthop Trans 1995;19:162–163.
73. McKee MD, Schemitsch EH, Sala MJ, et al. The pathoanatomy of lateral ligamentous disruption in complex elbow instability. J Shoulder Elbow Surg 2003;12:391–396.
74. Melhoff TL, Noble PC, Bennet JB, et al. Simple dislocation of the elbow in the adult: results after closed treatment. J Bone Joint Surg Am 1988;70A:244–249.
75. Miller GK, Drennan DB, Maylahn DJ. Treatment of displaced segmental radial head fractures: long-term follow-up. J Bone Joint Surg Am 1981;63A:712–717.
76. Moro JK, Werier J, MacDermid JC, et al. Arthroplasty with a metal radial head for unreconstructable fractures of the radial head. J Bone Joint Surg Am 2001;83A: 1201–1211.
77. Morrey BF. Anatomy of the elbow joint. In: Morrey BF, ed. The Elbow and Its Disorders. 2nd ed. Philadelphia: WB Saunders, 1995:16–52.
78. Morrey BF. Complex instability of the elbow. J Bone Joint Surg Am 1997;79A:460–469.
79. Morrey BF. Current concepts in the treatment of fractures of the radial head, the olecranon, and the coronoid. J Bone Joint Surg Am 1995;77A:316–327.
80. Morrey BF. Radial head fractures. In: Morrey BF, ed. The Elbow and Its Disorders. Philadelphia: WB Saunders, 1985:355.
81. Morrey BF. Surgical exposures of the elbow. In: Morrey BF, ed. The Elbow and Its Disorders. 2nd ed. Philadelphia: WB Saunders, 1993:139–166.
82. Morrey BF, Adams RA, Bryan RS. Total elbow replacement for posttraumatic arthritis of the elbow. J Bone Joint Surg Br 1991;73B:607–612.
83. Morrey BF, An KN. Articular and ligamentous contributions to the stability of the elbow joint. Am J Sports Med 1983;11:315–320.
84. Morrey BF, Tanaka S, An KN. Valgus stability of the elbow. A definition of primary and secondary constraints. Clin Orthop 1991;265:187–195.
85. Muller ME, Nazarian S, Koch P, et al. The Comprehensive Classification of Fractures of Long Bones. Berlin: Springer-Verlag, 1990.
86. Nestor BJ, O'Driscoll SW, Morrey BF. Ligamentous reconstruction for posterolateral rotatory instability of the elbow. J Bone Joint Surg Am 1992;74A:1235–1241.
87. O'Driscoll SW. Classification and spectrum of elbow instability: recurrent instability. In: Morrey BF, ed. The Elbow and Its Disorders. 2nd ed. Philadelphia: WB Saunders, 1993:453–463.
88. O'Driscoll SW. Technique for unstable olecranon fracture-subluxations. Oper Tech Orthop 1994;4:49–53.
89. O'Driscoll SW, Bell DF, Morrey BF. Posterolateral rotatory instability of the elbow. J Bone Joint Surg Am 1991;73A:440–446.
90. O'Driscoll SW, Jupiter JB, Cohen M, et al. Difficult elbow fractures: pearls and pitfalls. Instr Course Lect 2003;52:113–134.
91. O'Driscoll SW, Morrey BF, Korinek S, et al. Elbow subluxation and dislocation. A spectrum of instability. Clin Orthop 1992;280:186–197.
92. Osbourne G, Cotterill P. Recurrent dislocations of the elbow. J Bone Joint Surg Br 1966;48B:340–346.
93. Papagelopoulos PJ, Morrey BF. Treatment of nonunion of olecranon fractures. J Bone Joint Surg Br 1994;76B:627–635.
94. Patterson SD, Bain GI, Mehta JA. Surgical approaches to the elbow. Clin Orthop 2000; 370:19–33.
95. Pavel A, Pittman JM, Lance EM, et al. The posterior Monteggia fracture. A clinical study. J Trauma 1965;5:185–199.
96. Pearce MS, Gallannaugh SC. Mason type II radial head fractures fixed with Herbert bone screws. J R Soc Med 1996;89:340–344.
97. Pelto K, Hirvensalo E, Bostman O, et al. Treatment of radial head fractures with absorbable polyglycolide pins: a study on the security of fixation in 38 cases. J Orthop Trauma 1994;8:94–98.
98. Penrose JH. The Monteggia fracture with posterior dislocation of the radial head. J Bone Joint Surg Br 1951;33B:65–73.
99. Prayson MJ, Williams JL, Marshall MP, et al. Biomechanical comparison of fixation methods in transverse olecranon fractures: a cadaveric study. J Orthop Trauma 1997; 11:565–572.
100. Protzman RR. Dislocation of the elbow joint. J Bone Joint Surg Am 1978;60A:539–541.
101. Pugh DM, Wild LM, Schemitsch EH, et al. Standard surgical protocol to treat elbow dislocations with radial head and coronoid fractures. J Bone Joint Surg Am 2004;86A: 1122–1130.
102. Radin EL, Riseborough EJ. Fractures of the radial head. J Bone Joint Surg Am 1966; 48A:1055–1065.
103. Regan W, Morrey BF. Fractures of the coronoid process of the ulna. J Bone Joint Surg Am 1989;71A:1348–1354.
104. Ring D, Chin K, Jupiter JB. Nonunion of nonoperatively treated fractures of the radial head. Clin Orthop 2002;398:235–238.
105. Ring D, Doornberg JN. Fracture of the anteromedial facet of the coronoid process. Surgical technique. J Bone Joint Surg Am 2007;89A(suppl 2 Pt 2):267–283.
106. Ring D, Gulotta L, Jupiter J. Articular fractures of the distal part of the humerus. J Bone Joint Surg Am 2003;85A:232–238.
107. Ring D, Hannouche D, Jupiter JB. Surgical treatment of persistent dislocation or subluxation of the ulnohumeral joint after fracture-dislocation of the elbow. J Hand Surg [Am] 2004(29A):470–480.
108. Ring D, Jupiter J. The operative release of complete ankylosis of the elbow due to heterotopic bone in patients without severe injury of the central nervous system. J Bone Joint Surg Am 2003;85A:849–857.
109. Ring D, Jupiter JB. Fracture-dislocation of the elbow. J Bone Joint Surg Am 1998;80A: 566–580.
110. Ring D, Jupiter JB. Operative fixation and reconstruction of the coronoid. Tech Orthop 2000;15(2).
111. Ring D, Jupiter JB. Reconstruction of posttraumatic elbow instability. Clin Orthop 2000;370:44–56.
112. Ring D, Jupiter JB. Surgical exposure of coronoid fractures. Tech Shoulder Elbow Surg 2002;3:48–56.
113. Ring D, Jupiter JB, Gulotta L. Atrophic nonunions of the proximal ulna. Clin Orthop 2003;409:268–274.
114. Ring D, Jupiter JB, Gulotta L. Unstable nonunions of the distal humerus. J Bone Joint Surg Am 2003;85A:1040–1046.
115. Ring D, Jupiter JB, Sanders RW, et al. Transolecranon fracture-dislocation of the elbow. J Orthop Trauma 1997;11:545–550.
116. Ring D, Jupiter JB, Simpson NS. Monteggia fractures in adults. J Bone Joint Surg Am 1998;80A:1733–1744.
117. Ring D, Jupiter JB, Zilberfarb J. Posterior dislocation of the elbow with fractures of the coronoid and radial head. J Bone Joint Surg Am 2002;84A:547–551.
118. Ring D, Jupiter JB, Zilberfarb J. Roles of the medial collateral ligament and the coronoid in elbow stability. Reply to letter to the editor. J Bone Joint Surg Am 2003;85A: 568–569.
119. Ring D, Kloen P, Tavakolian J, et al. Loss of alignment after operative treatment of posterior Monteggia fractures: salvage with dorsal contoured plate fixation. J Hand Surg [Am] 2004;29:694–702.
120. Ring D, Quintero J, Jupiter JB. Open reduction and internal fixation of fractures of the radial head. J Bone Joint Surg Am 2002;84A:1811–1815.
121. Sanchez-Sotelo J, Romanillos O, et al. Results of acute excision of the radial head in elbow radial head fracture-dislocations. J Orthop Trauma 2000;14:354–358.
122. Sherman R. Soft-tissue coverage for the elbow. Hand Clin 1997;13:291–302.
123. Smith AM, Urbanosky LR, Castle JA, et al. Radius pull test: predictor of longitudinal forearm instability. J Bone Joint Surg Am 2002;84A:1970–1976.
124. Smith GR, Hotchkiss RN. Radial head and neck fractures: anatomic guidelines for proper placement of internal fixation. J Shoulder Elbow Surg 1996;5:113–117.
125. Soyer AD, Nowotarski PJ, Kelso TB, et al. Optimal position for plate fixation of complex fractures of the proximal radius: a cadaver study. J Orthop Trauma 1998;12:291–293.

126. Stevanovic M, Sharpe F, Itamura J. Treatment of soft tissue problems about the elbow. Clin Orthop 2000;370:127–137.

127. Taylor TKF, Scham SM. A posteromedial approach to the proximal end of the ulna for the internal fixation of olecranon fractures. J Trauma 1969;9:594–602.

128. van Riet R, Glabbeek FV, Neale PG, et al. The noncircular shape of the radial head. J Hand Surg Am 2003;28:972–978.

129. van Riet RP, Glabbeek FV, Verborgt O, et al. Capitellar erosion caused by a metal radial head prosthesis. A case report. J Bone Joint Surg Am 2004;86A:1061–1064.

130. Vanderwilde RS, Morrey BF, Melberg MW, et al. Inflammatory arthritis after failure of silicone rubber replacement of the radial head. J Bone Joint Surg Br 1994;76B:78–81.

131. Vince KG, Miller JE. Cross union complicating fracture of the forearm. Part I. J Bone Joint Surg Am 1987;69A:640–653.

132. Viola RW, Hanel DP. Early "simple" release of posttraumatic elbow contracture associated with heterotopic ossification. J Hand Surg 1999;24:370–380.

133. Weseley MS, Barenfeld PA, Eisenstein AL. Closed treatment of isolated radial head fractures. J Trauma 1983;23:36–39.

33

DISTAL HUMERUS FRACTURES

George S. Athwal

INTRODUCTION

Distal humerus fractures remain some of the most challenging injuries to manage. They are commonly multifragmented, occur in osteopenic bone, and have complex anatomy with limited options for internal fixation. Treatment outcomes are often associated with elbow stiffness, weakness and pain. A painless, stable, and mobile elbow joint is desired as it allows the hand to conduct the activities of daily living, most notably personal hygiene and feeding. Therefore, starting with a highly traumatized distal humerus and finishing with a stable, mobile, and pain-free joint requires a systematic approach. Thought is required in determining the operative indications, managing the soft tissues, selecting a surgical approach, obtaining an anatomic articular reduction, and creating a fixation construct that is rigid enough to tolerate early range of motion.

In 1913, Albin Lambotte challenged the leading opinions of conservative management for distal humerus fractures and advocated an aggressive approach that consisted of open reduction and internal fixation.[100] He described the principles of osteosynthesis and believed anatomic restoration of anatomy correlated with a better return to function. Unfortunately, surgical outcomes in that era were plagued with a high risk of infection and hardware failure. In 1937, Eastwood described the technique of closed reduction under a general anesthetic and brief immobilization in a collar and cuff.[40] He reviewed 14 patients treated with this technique and reported that 12 returned to their original occupation. He stated "a perfect anatomical reduction is not necessary in order to obtain a good result." Evans in 1953, termed this mode of treatment "bag of bones" and believed that although it may be appropriate for the elderly patient, it was not ideal for the young active patient.[44] The conflict between operative and nonoperative management continued for decades to follow. Riseborough and Radin, in 1969, reported that operative treatment was unpredictable and often associated with poor outcomes; therefore, they recommended

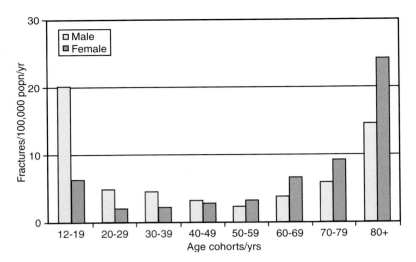

FIGURE 33-1 The age and gender related incidence of distal humerus fractures. (Data from Robinson CM, Hill RM, Jacobs N, et al. Adult distal humeral metaphyseal fractures: epidemiology and results of treatment. J Orthop Trauma 2003; 17(1):38–47.)

nonsurgical management.[168] Similarly, Brown and Morgan in 1971 reported satisfactory results with nonoperative management of 10 patients with distal humerus fractures.[22] Their patients were managed with early active motion and at final follow-up had an average arc of motion of 98 degrees.

In the last quarter century improved outcomes have been reported with surgery for distal humerus fractures. The principles set out by the Arbeitsgemeinschaft für Osteosynthesefragen (Association for the Study of Internal Fixation, AO-ASIF) group, including anatomic articular reduction and rigid internal fixation, allow for healing and early postoperative range of motion.* The last decade has seen advances in the understanding of elbow anatomy, improvements in surgical approaches, new innovative fixation devices and an evolution of postoperative rehabilitation protocols.

In younger patients, open reduction and internal fixation of distal humerus fractures using modern fixation principles is considered the gold standard. In elderly patients, restoration of the anatomy and obtaining rigid internal fixation may be difficult because of poor bone quality and comminution of the articular surface and metaphysis. In cases in which rigid internal fixation cannot be achieved to allow early range of motion, resultant prolonged immobilization often leads to poor outcomes.[4] Other complications associated with potentially poor outcomes include malunion, nonunion, contracture, avascular necrosis, heterotopic ossification, hardware failure, and symptomatic prominent hardware. In the elderly patient, the prolonged rehabilitation, propensity for stiffness, and increased reoperation rate associated with open reduction and internal fixation may convert a previously independent individual into a role of dependence.[171]

Primary total elbow arthroplasty has evolved to become a viable treatment option for elderly patients with articular fragmentation, comminution, and osteopenic bone.** Most recently, there has been a renewed interest in distal humerus hemiarthroplasty for the treatment of distal humerus fractures,[3,13,73,150] including fractures of the capitellum and trochlea.

*References 55,99,114,120,145,172,176.
**References 10,48,50,51,88,89,102,126.

EPIDEMIOLOGY

Approximately 7% of all adult fractures involve the elbow; of these, approximately one third involve the distal humerus.[8,146,173] Distal humerus fractures, therefore, comprise approximately 2% of all fractures. They have a bimodal age distribution,[146,147,171,172] with peak incidences occurring between the ages of 12 to 19 years, usually in males, and those aged 80 years and older, characteristically in females (Figure 33-1). In young adults, the fractures are typically caused by high-energy injures, such as motor vehicular collisions, falls from height, sports, industrial accidents, and firearms. In contrast, greater than 60% of distal humerus fractures in the elderly occur from low energy injuries, such as a fall from a standing height.[147,172]

Robinson and colleagues[172] reviewed a consecutive series of 320 patients with distal humerus fractures over a 10-year period. They calculated an overall incidence in adults of 5.7 cases per 100,000 in the population per year with a nearly equivalent male to female ratio. The most common mechanism of injury was a simple fall from a standing height (Table 33-1) and the most common fracture pattern was an extra-articular fracture accounting for just under 40% of all fractures. Bicolumn or complete intra-articular fractures were the second most common, accounting for 37%.

The overall incidence of distal humerus fractures is increasing, mimicking the increasing incidence in hip, proximal humerus and wrist fractures.[80,90,91] Palvanen et al.[146] studied trends in osteoporotic distal humerus fractures in Finish women. They reported a twofold increase in the age-adjusted incidence of distal humerus fractures from 1970 (12/100,000) to 1995 (28/100,000), and predicted an additional threefold increase by 2030. An aging population with increasing life expectancy combined with the fact that most of these fractures require surgical treatment is likely to result in increased health care expenditures. The identification and implementation of preventative strategies may help offset some of the economic impact of this injury. The mainstay of current fracture prevention strategy is to screen for osteopenia and osteoporosis with bone mineral density measurements and then to treat with medication therapy.[80] Other authors argue that a more important prevention strategy is to decrease the risk of falling. Falling is the greatest single risk factor for fracture,[90,91] and can be predicted based

TABLE 33-1	**Mechanism of Injury in 320 Distal Humeral Fractures**				
Mechanism of Injury	Number of Fractures (Number Open)	Average Age in Years (Range)	Males	Females	M:F Ratio
Simple fall	219 (68)	57.0 (12–99)	86	133	0.6:1
Fall from a height	5 (2)	27.0 (14–41)	3	2	1.5:1
RTA	42 (13)	33.2 (14–77)	27	15	1.8:1
Sport	41 (13)	22.9 (13–44)	34	7	4.9:1
Other	13 (4)	39.2 (14–92)	9	4	2.3:1
Total	320 (100)	48.4 (12–99)	159	161	1.0:1

RTA, road traffic accident
Data from Robinson CM, Hill RM, Jacobs N, et al. Adult distal humeral metaphyseal fractures: epidemiology and results of treatment. J Orthop Trauma 2003;17:38–47.

on clinical risk factors, such as age, weight, smoking, previous fracture and mother's hip fracture.[19]

PRINCIPLES OF MANAGEMENT

Mechanisms of Injury and Associated Injuries

The majority of distal humerus fractures occur in one of two ways: low-energy falls or high-energy trauma.[172] The most common cause is a simple fall in the forward direction.[147] In general, 70% of patients that sustain an elbow fracture fall directly on to the elbow because they are unable to break their fall with an outstretched arm.[147] High-energy injuries are the cause of most distal humerus fractures in younger adults. Motor vehicle collisions, sports, falls from heights, and industrial accidents predominate. These mechanisms are also associated with a higher likelihood of accompanying injuries, such as, open fractures, soft tissue injuries, other fractures in 16% of cases[55] and polytrauma (Table 33-2).

History and Physical Examination

The history should determine the mechanism of injury, the energy level, and the time since injury. In patients with high-

energy injuries, vigilance is required in identifying systemic injures and associated fractures. The pain from polytrauma and other concurrent issues such as inebriation and drug use may make identification of all injuries difficult; patients and their families should be pre-emptively counseled on the possibility of delayed identification of occult injuries.

Elderly patients, who comprise the majority of patients with distal humerus fractures, should be evaluated for the precipitants of the characteristic fall, as they may have undiagnosed cardiac arrhythmias, cerebrovascular disease, polypharmacy, or alcohol dependence. Special attention is directed toward identifying comorbidities and reversible illnesses that may impact upon the treatment recommendations and perioperative risk. Mental status, the ability to cooperate with rehabilitation, ambulatory status, and the requirement of walking aides should be assessed. Additionally, the preinjury functional abilities, demands, any limitations related to the upper extremities as well as the patient handedness may each affect treatment decision making.

A thorough physical examination should be conducted in all cases, particularly with high-energy trauma to identify systemic injuries and associated fractures. The injured extremity should be circumferentially examined for abrasions, bruising, swelling, fracture blisters, skin tenting, and open wounds. Open distal humerus fractures are not uncommon,[118,172] and should be treated with a standard open fracture protocol involving removal of gross contamination, covering of the wound with a sterile dressing, splinting, antibiotics, tetanus, possible wound culture, and early surgical irrigation and débridement.

A neurological exam must be performed and accurately documented preoperatively and postoperatively. Gofton et al. reported that 26% of patients with distal humerus fractures had an associated incomplete ulnar neuropathy at the time of presentation.[55] Vascular injuries, although rare in distal humerus fractures, should be assessed by examining the distal pulses, skin turgor, capillary refill, and color. Pulse diminution or other positive findings should be further examined with a brachial-brachial Doppler pressure index, which has been shown to be as specific and sensitive as arteriography in detecting brachial artery injuries.[43,122,170] The normal brachial-brachial Doppler pressure index is approximately 0.95 and it rarely falls below 0.85.[43,122,170] Patients with abnormal studies should be referred

TABLE 33-2	**The Relationship between Injury Mechanism and Soft-Tissue Injury**						
			Gustilo Grade				
Mechanism of Injury	Closed	Open (%)	I	II	IIIa	IIIb	
Simple fall	207	12 (5%)	4	4	4	0	
Fall from height	3	2 (40%)	0	0	2	0	
MVC	35	7 (17%)	2	4	0	1	
Sport	39	2 (5%)	0	2	0	0	
Other	13	0	0	0	0	0	
Total	297	23 (7%)	6	10	6	1	

MVC, Motor vehicle collision.
Data from Robinson CM, Hill RM, Jacobs N, et al. Adult distal humeral metaphyseal fractures: epidemiology and results of treatment. J Orthop Trauma 2003;17:38–47.

for vascular surgery consultation. Patients with excessive pain after high energy trauma should be examined for compartment syndrome of the forearm. Compartment pressures should be conducted when the clinical examination is inconclusive.[20] If compartment syndrome is diagnosed clinically or by pressure measurement, urgent surgical fasciotomies are required.[121]

Specific to elderly patients, when considering elbow arthroplasty the contraindications must be addressed. Absolute contraindications to elbow arthroplasty include active infection and inadequate soft tissue coverage. The patient history requires probing questions to rule out common infections, such as urinary tract infections and active diabetic ulcers. Open wounds in low energy distal humerus fractures are not an absolute contraindication to elbow arthroplasty, as they are typically small and clean. Such wounds, therefore, may undergo irrigation and débridement followed by staged elbow arthroplasty.

Imaging and Other Diagnostic Studies

Standard anteroposterior and lateral radiographs of the elbow are usually sufficient for diagnosis, classification, and surgical templating. However, initial radiographs obtained in plaster or a splint may obscure the fracture pattern and should be repeated. In some cases in which fracture shortening, rotation, and angulation distort the images, gentle traction views with appropriate analgesia or conscious sedation may improve the yield of the radiographs.

Computed tomography (CT) with three-dimensional reconstructions greatly improves the identification and visualization of fracture patterns. Although CT is not required for all cases, it is recommended for certain situations. In patients in whom a less invasive approach for open reduction and internal fixation is contemplated, such as a paratricipital approach rather than an olecranon osteotomy, a CT scan can assist with decision making and in identifying the locations of fracture fragments intraoperatively. In elderly patients with highly comminuted fractures, a CT scan may be useful in deciding whether an attempt should be made at ORIF versus proceeding directly to arthroplasty. When considering hemiarthroplasty for distal humerus fractures, a CT will confirm the articular fragmentation and the characteristics of the condylar fractures.

Diagnosis and Classification

Early classification schemes for fractures of the distal humerus were based on the anatomic location of the fracture and its appearance, using terms such as supracondylar, intracondylar, epicondylar, Y-type and T-type. In 1990, Müller defined the anatomic boundaries of a distal humerus fracture as one with an epicenter that occurs within a square whose base is the distance between the medial and lateral epicondyles on an anteroposterior radiograph (Figure 33-2).[134] The AO group devised the first comprehensive classification of distal humerus fractures, which was then adopted by the Orthopaedic Trauma Association (OTA) in 1996.[1] In 2007, the AO Classification Supervisory Committee and the OTA Classification, Database and Outcomes Committee updated the compendium to its present form.[110]

The AO/OTA classification is an alphanumeric system that assigns the first two digits of 13 to distal humerus fractures and classifies them based on location and degree of articular involvement (Figure 33-3). The system then further subclassifies fractures based on fracture line orientation, displacement direction and degree of fragmentation.[110] Type A fractures are extra-articular and may involve the epicondyles or occur at the

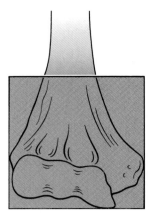

FIGURE 33-2 A distal humerus fracture is defined as a fracture with an epicenter that is located within a square whose base is the distance between the epicondyles on an anteroposterior radiograph.

distal humerus metaphyseal level. Although these fractures receive less attention in the literature than the more complex intra-articular type C fractures, they do account for one fourth of all distal humerus fractures.[172]

Type B fractures are termed partial articular, as there remains some continuity between the humeral shaft and the articular segment. Type B fractures include unicondylar fractures and sagittal plane or shear fractures of the articular surface involving the capitellum, trochlea, or both.

Single column fractures involve either the medial or lateral column, are intra-articular, and account for approximately 15% of all distal humerus fractures.[85,98,172] These fractures may also be classified by the Milch system,[124] which is based on whether the lateral portion of the trochlea remains attached to the humeral shaft. In a Milch type I fracture, the medial or lateral column can be fractured, but the lateral eminence of the trochlea remains attached to the humeral shaft. In a Milch type II fracture, the lateral eminence of the trochlea is apart of the column fracture.

A "divergent" single column fracture has also been described that occurs predominantly in younger patients who are predisposed to this injury because of a septal aperture (fenestration) in the olecranon fossa.[54,98] This fracture pattern is theorized to occur after an axial load is applied to the olecranon, which is then driven into the trochlea. A fracture occurs that splits the trochlea and propagates proximally between the columns to eventually exit either medially or laterally creating a "high" single column fracture.

Type C fractures are termed complete articular, meaning there is no continuity between the articular segments and the humeral shaft. Type C fractures have historically been called intracondylar fractures and the AO/OTA system further subclassifies them into simple (C1), simple articular with metaphyseal fragmentation (C2), and fragmentation of the articular surface and metaphyseal zone (C3). This system is widely used in the literature and trauma databases, and helps to standardize research protocols and treatment outcomes. Unfortunately, the classification system does have weaknesses as it does not account for factors such as the distal fragment height and amount of displacement, both of which may influence treatment.[67,164] The classification also does little to assist with the decision-making process between ORIF and arthroplasty, and finally it has been criticized as being overly complex.

(text continues on page 953)

Bone: humerus (1)

Location: Distal segment (13)

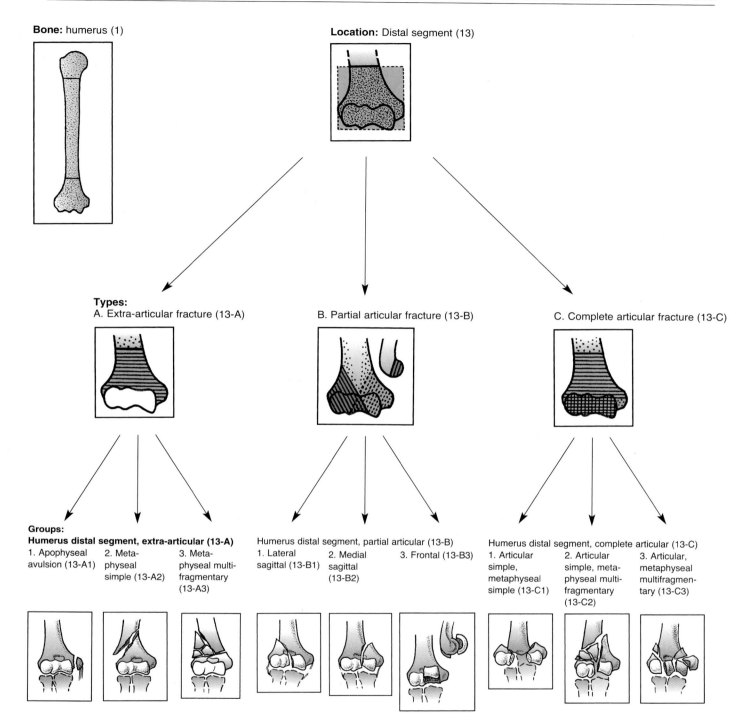

Types:

A. Extra-articular fracture (13-A)

B. Partial articular fracture (13-B)

C. Complete articular fracture (13-C)

Groups:

Humerus distal segment, extra-articular (13-A)

1. Apophyseal avulsion (13-A1)

2. Metaphyseal simple (13-A2)

3. Metaphyseal multifragmentary (13-A3)

Humerus distal segment, partial articular (13-B)

1. Lateral sagittal (13-B1)

2. Medial sagittal (13-B2)

3. Frontal (13-B3)

Humerus distal segment, complete articular (13-C)

1. Articular simple, metaphyseal simple (13-C1)

2. Articular simple, metaphyseal multifragmentary (13-C2)

3. Articular, metaphyseal multifragmentary (13-C3)

FIGURE 33-3 The AO/OTA Classification of Distal Humerus Fractures. (Redrawn from Marsh JL, Slongo TF, Agel J, et al. Fracture and dislocation classification compendium—2007: Orthopaedic Trauma Association classification, database, and outcomes committee. J Orthop Trauma 2007;21(10 Suppl):S1–133, with permission.)   (*continues*)

Subgroups and Qualifications:

Humerus, distal, extra-articular apophyseal avulsion (13-A1)

1. Lateral epicondyle (13-A1.1)

2. Medial epicondyle, nonincarcerated (13-A1.2)
(1) nondisplaced
(2) displaced
(3) fragmented

3. Medial epicondyle, incarcerated (13-A1.3)

A1

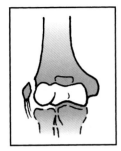
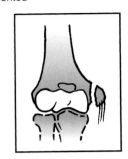
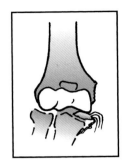

Humerus, distal, extra-articular metaphyseal simple (13-A2)

1. Oblique downward and inward (13-A2.1)

2. Oblique downward and outward (13-A2.2)

3. Transverse (13-A2.3)
(1) transmetaphyseal

(2) juxtaepiphyseal with posterior displacement (Kocher I)

(3) juxtaepiphyseal with anterior displacement (Kocher II)

A2

Humerus, distal, extra-articular metaphyseal multifragmentary (13-A3)

1. With intact wedge (13-A3.1)
(1) lateral
(2) medial

2. With fragmented wedge (13-A3.2)
(1) lateral
(2) medial

3. Complex (13-A3.3)

A3

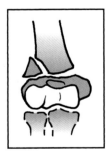
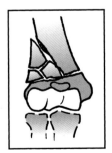

FIGURE 33-3 (*continued*)

Humerus, distal, partial articular, lateral sagittal (13-B1)

1. Capitellum (13-B1.1)
(1) through the capitellum (Milch I)
(2) between capitellum and trochlea

2. Transtrochlear simple(13-B1.2)
(1) medial collateral ligament intact
(2) medial collateral ligament ruptured
(3) metaphyseal simple (classic Milch II)
lateral condyle
(4) metaphyseal wedge
(5) metaphysio-diaphyseal

3. Transtrochlear
multifragmentary (13-B1.3)
(1) epiphysio-metaphyseal
(2) epiphysio-meta-
physeal-diaphyseal

B1

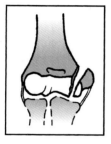
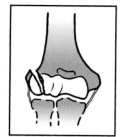
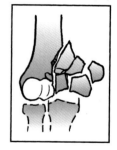
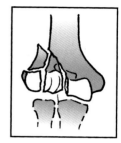

Humerus, distal, partial articular, medial sagittal (13-B2)

1. Transtrochlear simple, through
medial side (Milch I) (13-B2.1)

2. Transtrochlear simple, through
the groove (13-B2.2)

3. Transtrochlear multifragmentary
(13-B2.3)
(1) epiphysio-metaphyseal
(2) epiphysio-metaphyseal-diaphyseal

B2

Humerus, distal, partial articular, frontal (13-B3)

1. Capitellum (13-B3.1)
(1) incomplete (Kocher-Lorenz)
(2) complete (Hahn-Steinthal 1)
(3) with trochlear component
(Hahn-Steinthal 2)
(4) fragmented

2. Trochlea (13-B3.2)
(1) simple
(2) fragmented

3. Capitellum and trochlea (13-B3.3)

B3

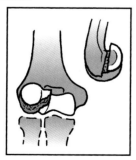
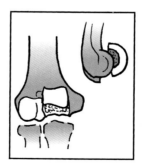
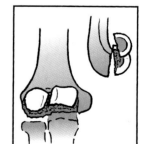

FIGURE 33-3 *(continued)*

Humerus, distal complete, articular simple, metaphyseal simple (13-C1)

1. With slight displacement (13-C1.1)	2. With marked displacement (13-C1.2)	3. T-shaped epiphyseal (13-C1.3)
(1) Y-shaped	(1) Y-shaped	
(2) T-shaped	(2) T-shaped	
(3) V-shaped	(3) V-shaped	

C1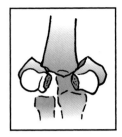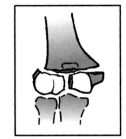

Humerus, distal, complete articular simple metaphyseal multifragmentary (13-C2)

1. With intact wedge (13-C2.1)	2. With a fragmented wedge (13-C2.2)	3. Complex (13-C2.3)
(1) metaphyseal lateral	(1) metaphyseal lateral	
(2) metaphyseal medial	(2) metaphyseal medial	
(3) metaphysio-diaphyseal-lateral	(3) metaphysio-diaphyseal-lateral	
(4) metaphysio-diaphyseal-medial	(4) metaphysio-diaphyseal-medial	

C2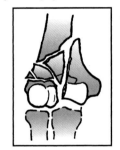

Humerus, distal, complete multifragmentary (13-C3)

1. Metaphyseal simple (13-C3.1)	2. Metaphyseal wedge (13-C3.2)	3. Metaphyseal complex (13-C3.3)
	(1) intact	(1) localized
	(2) fragmented	(2) extending into diaphysis

C3

FIGURE 33-3 (*continued*)

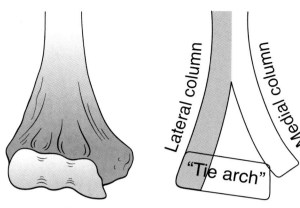

FIGURE 33-4 The medial and lateral columns support the articular segment. The distal most part of the lateral column is the capitellum and the distalmost part of the medial column is the nonarticular medial epicondyle. The trochlea is the medial part of the articular segment and is intermediate in position between the capitellum and medial epicondyle. The articular segment functions architecturally as a tie arch.

The Mehne and Matta classification of distal humerus fractures is also popular.[33,83] It is based on Jupiter's model[83] in which the distal humerus is composed of two divergent columns that support an intercalary articular segment (Figure 33-4), which is similar to the AO concept of condyles. The classifica-

tion has three main categories: intra-articular, extra-articular intracapsular, and extracapsular. The intra-articular group is further subdivided into bicolumn, single column, and articular fractures. The extra-articular intracapsular group consists of high and low transcolumn fractures and the extracapsular group has medial and lateral epicondyle fractures (Figure 33-5). This classification system has the same criticisms as the AO/OTA system with high complexity and poor intra-rater and inter-rater reliability. The classification also does not consider the specific types of articular fracture and the degree of fragment displacement. It is the author's opinion that the AO/OTA classification is preferred because it is more intuitive, it is ubiquitous and because it is the official classification of the OTA.

SURGICAL AND APPLIED ANATOMY AND COMMON SURGICAL APPROACHES

Surgical and Applied Anatomy

The elbow is anatomically a trocho-ginglymoid joint, meaning that it has trochoid (rotatory) motion through the radiocapitellar and proximal radioulnar joints and ginglymoid (hinge-like) motion through the ulnohumeral joint. An understanding of the complex bony anatomy of the elbow, soft tissue stabilizers, and

I. Intra-articular fractures
A. Single column

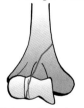
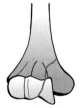

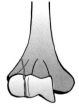
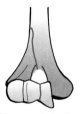

High medial column fracture (Milch type II)   Low medial column fracture (Milch type I)   High lateral column fracture (Mlch type II)   Low lateral column fracture (Milch type I)   Divergent single column fracture

B. Bicolumn

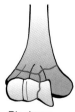

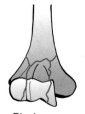
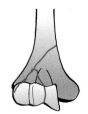
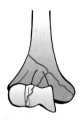

Bicolumn high T fracture   Bicolumn low T fracture   Bicolumn Y fracture   Bicolumn H fracture   Bicolumn medial lambda fracture   Bicolumn lateral lambda fracture

C. Articular surface fractures (capitellum, trochlea, or both)

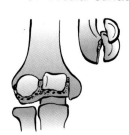

FIGURE 33-5 The Mehne and Matta classification of distal humerus fractures.   *(continues)*

II. Extra-articular intracapsular fractures

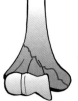

High flexion
transcolumn fracture
(anteroposterior view)

High flexion
transcolumn fracture
(lateral view)

Low extension
transcolumn fracture
(anteroposterior view)

Low extension
transcolumn fracture
(lateral view)

High abduction
fracture

High adduction
fracture

Low flexion transcolumn
fracture (anteroposterior view)

Low flexion transcolumn
fracture (lateral view)

High extension transcolumn
fracture (anteroposterior view)

High extension transcolumn
fracture (lateral view)

III. Extracapsular fractures

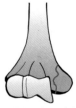

Medial epicondylar
fracture

Lateral epicondylar
fracture

FIGURE 33-5 (continued)

adjacent neurovascular structures is imperative when surgically treating distal humerus fractures.

The distal humeral shaft is triangular shaped in cross section, with its apex directed anterior. As the shaft approaches the distal humerus it bifurcates into two divergent cortical columns, termed the medial and lateral columns. The medial column diverges approximately 45 degrees from the humeral shaft in the coronal plane and terminates as the medial epicondyle. The lateral column, in the coronal plane, diverges at approximately 20 degrees from the shaft and as it extends distally it curves anteriorly creating approximately a 35- to 40-degree angle with the shaft in the sagittal plane (Figure 33-6). In the coronal plane, the trochlea is more distal than the capitellum resulting in a valgus alignment of 4 to 8 degrees. Overall, when including the ulna, the elbow has a valgus angle in extension of 10 to 17 degrees, termed the carrying angle. Axially, the distal humerus articular surface is internally rotated 3 to 8 degrees; therefore, as the elbow flexes it also internally rotates resulting in slight varus alignment.

The posterior aspect of the lateral column is relatively flat and wide, well suited for application of a posterolateral plate. The lateral column terminates in the capitellum anteriorly. The articular surface of the capitellum starts at the most distal aspect of the lateral column and encompasses an arc of approximately 180 degrees in the sagittal plane. Posterior fixation can be applied distally on the lateral column because of the absence of cartilage; however, lengths of screws directed anteriorly into the capitellum must be carefully scrutinized to prevent perforation into the radiocapitellar joint.

The trochlea, which is Greek for pulley, is the intervening segment of bone between the terminal ends of the medial and lateral columns that articulates with the greater sigmoid notch of the ulna. It is covered by articular cartilage anteriorly, inferiorly and posteriorly, creating an arc of almost 270 degrees. The trochlea is shaped like a spool with a central sulcus, which articulates with the central ridge of the greater sigmoid notch of the proximal ulna.

Superior to the trochlea and between the medial and lateral columns lies the olecranon fossa posteriorly and the coronoid fossa anteriorly. These fossae lie adjacent to each other and are separated by a thin bony septum. Occasionally this septum is absent and a septal aperture exists. The olecranon fossa is matched to the olecranon and accepts it during extension; similarly, the coronoid fossa is matched to the coronoid and accepts it during flexion. The tolerances of the fossae to accommodate their respective bony processes are narrow; therefore, screw placement through the fossae should be avoided as it may lead to impingement and decreased elbow range of motion. In distal humerus fractures with excessive metaphyseal comminution requiring supracondylar shortening, recreation of the fossae with a burr will improve range of motion.

In addition to the bony structures, there are several important soft tissue structures that require consideration when treating distal humerus fractures. The lateral collateral ligament

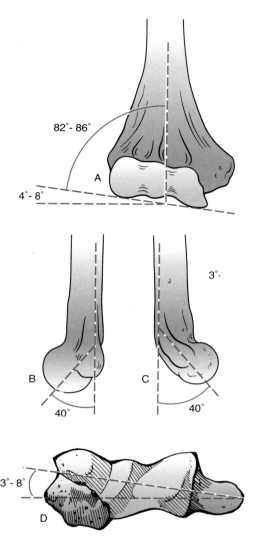

FIGURE 33-6 The distal humerus articular surface is aligned in 4 to 8 degrees of valgus relative to the shaft **(A)** and is angulated 35 to 40 degrees anteriorly in the sagittal plane. The medial epicondyle is the termination of the medial column and remains on the axis of the shaft in the sagittal view **(B)**, whereas the lateral epicondyle follows the capitellum into flexion **(C)**. Axially, the entire distal humerus articular surface is internally rotated 3 to 8 degrees **(D)**.

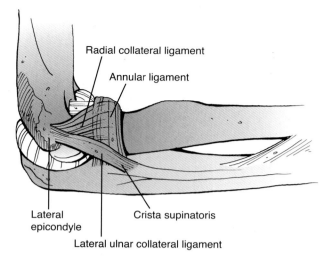

FIGURE 33-7 The lateral collateral ligament complex is an important restraint to varus and posterolateral rotatory instability and consists of the radial collateral ligament, the lateral ulnar collateral ligament, and the annular ligament. The annular ligament attaches to the anterior and posterior margins of the lesser sigmoid notch, whereas the radial collateral ligament originates from an isometric point on the lateral epicondyle and fans out to attach to the annular ligament. The lateral ulnar collateral ligament also arises from the isometric point on the lateral epicondyle and attaches to the crista supinatoris of the proximal ulna.

33-8). It originates from the anteroinferior aspect of the medial epicondyle, inferior to the axis of rotation, and inserts on the sublime tubercle of the coronoid. The MCL functions as an important restraint to valgus and posteromedial rotatory instability.[9,139] It is susceptible to injury at its origin during placement of a medial plate that curves around the medial epicondyle to lie on the ulnar aspect of the trochlea.

The ulnar, radial, and median nerves cross the elbow and knowledge of their precise locations is required to safely manage distal humerus fractures (Figure 33-9). The ulnar nerve pierces the medial intermuscular septum in the middle third of the arm to travel along side the medial head of triceps. The arcade of

(LCL) complex consists of the radial collateral ligament, the lateral ulnar collateral ligament and the annular ligament. The annular ligament attaches to the anterior and posterior margins of the lesser sigmoid notch, whereas the radial collateral ligament originates from an isometric point on the lateral epicondyle and fans out to attach to the annular ligament (Figure 33-7). The lateral ulnar collateral ligament also arises from the isometric point on the lateral epicondyle and attaches to the crista supinatoris of the proximal ulna. The LCL complex functions as an important restraint to varus and posterolateral rotatory instability.[39,78] The LCL complex is vulnerable to injury during application of a direct lateral plate; therefore, exposure of the lateral aspect of the distal lateral column should not extend past the equator of the capitellum.

The medial collateral ligament (MCL) consists of an anterior bundle, posterior bundle and transverse ligament. The anterior bundle is of prime importance in elbow stability (Figure

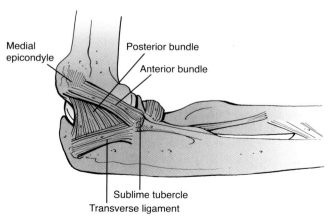

FIGURE 33-8 The medial collateral ligament functions as an important restraint to valgus and posteromedial rotatory instability. It consists of an anterior bundle, posterior bundle, and transverse ligament. The anterior bundle is of prime importance in elbow stability and it originates from the anteroinferior aspect of the medial epicondyle, and inserts on the sublime tubercle of the coronoid.

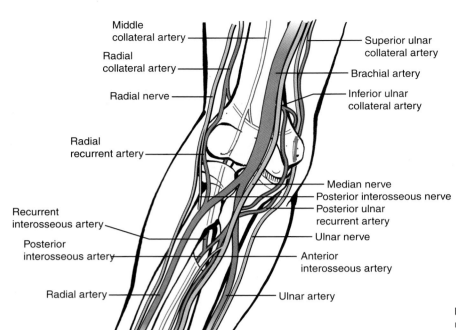

Middle collateral artery
Radial collateral artery
Radial nerve
Radial recurrent artery
Recurrent interosseous artery
Posterior interosseous artery
Radial artery
Superior ulnar collateral artery
Brachial artery
Inferior ulnar collateral artery
Median nerve
Posterior interosseous nerve
Posterior ulnar recurrent artery
Ulnar nerve
Anterior interosseous artery
Ulnar artery

FIGURE 33-9 Three peripheral nerves, the median, ulnar, and radial, cross the elbow joint along with a robust collateral blood supply.

Struthers, a musculofascial band present in 70% of the population,[186] is a potential area of nerve compression located approximately 8 cm proximal to the medial epicondyle. As the nerve approaches the elbow it travels behind the medial epicondyle to enter the cubital tunnel, a fibro-osseous groove bordered by the medial epicondyle superiorly, olecranon laterally and Osborne's ligament medially. When the nerve exits the cubital tunnel it travels between the two heads of the flexor carpi ulnaris muscle.

The radial nerve circles around the posterior aspect of the mid-humeral shaft in the spiral groove. On average, the nerve enters the spiral groove 20 cm proximal to the medial epicondyle (74% of the length of the humerus) and exits approximately 14 cm proximal to the lateral epicondyle (51% of the length of the humerus).[53] Along the lateral aspect of the humerus, two branches come off the nerve (nerve to the medial head of triceps and anconeus, and the lateral brachial cutaneous nerve) before it pierces the lateral intermuscular septum approximately 10 cm (36% of the length of the humerus) proximal to the lateral epicondyle.[53] The nerve then lies between brachialis and brachioradialis, where it bifurcates to the posterior interosseous nerve and the radial sensory nerve. The radial nerve is vulnerable to injury during exposure of distal humerus fractures with proximal shaft extension and during application of long posterolateral or direct lateral plates.

The median nerve travels with the brachial artery between the biceps and brachialis muscles in the anteromedial aspect of the arm. The nerve passes under the bicipital aponeurosis to enter the medial antecubital fossa, medial to the biceps tendon and brachial artery. The nerve then passes between the heads of pronator teres. During fixation of distal humerus fractures, the median nerve is relatively protected from direct injury by the robust brachialis muscle.

There is a consistent blood supply to the adult elbow, which can be organized into three vascular arcades: medial, lateral, and posterior.[207] The lateral arcade is formed by the interosseous

recurrent, radial recurrent, and radial collateral arteries and supplies the capitellum, radial head, lateral epicondyle, and lateral aspect of the trochlea. The medial arcade is formed by the superior and inferior ulnar collaterals and the anterior and posterior ulnar recurrent arteries and supplies the medial epicondyle and the medial aspect of the trochlea. The posterior arcade is formed by the medial collateral artery and contributions from the medial and lateral arcades and supplies the olecranon fossa and supracondylar area.

Common Surgical Approaches

There are several surgical approaches described for exposure and fixation of distal humerus fractures. They can be classified based on direction; posterior, lateral, medial, and anterior, and then further subclassified based on their specific anatomic intervals (Table 33-3). The ideal approach to a specific fracture pattern should provide sufficient exposure to allow anatomic reconstruction of the fracture and the application of the required internal fixation with minimal soft tissue or bony disruption to allow early mobilization. The selection of a surgical approach depends on multiple factors, including facture pattern, extent of articular involvement, associated soft tissue injury, rehabilitation protocols, and surgeon preference.[153]

Skin incisions about the elbow may be placed posterior, lateral, medial, or anterior depending on the surgical approach selected. Most posterior approaches benefit from a posterior longitudinal skin incision, which involves the elevation of full-thickness fasciocutaneous medial and lateral flaps.[36] The posterior skin incision can be straight or curve around the olecranon, medially or laterally, depending on surgeon preference. It is the author preference to conduct a relatively straight posterior skin incision that curves gently around the medial aspect of the olecranon (Figure 33-10A). The lateral approaches can be accessed via a direct lateral skin incision or by a posterior longitudinal skin incision with elevation of a lateral fasciocutaneous flap. Similarly, the medial approaches can be accessed by a direct

(text continues on page 960)

TABLE 33-3   Surgical Approaches to the Distal Humerus

Direction	Surgical Approach	Indications	Contraindications	Advantages	Disadvantages
Posterior	Olecranon Osteotomy[30,68, 106,162]	ORIF distal humerus and articular fractures (AO/OTA Type B and C)	Avoid if possibility of TEA	Best visualization of the articular surface for reduction and fixation	Nonunion and hardware prominence-related to osteotomy Limited visualization of anterior articular surfaces
	Paratricipital[7,179]	ORIF extra-articular and simple intra-articular (AO/OTA C1 and C2) fractures TEA	Comminuted intra-articular fractures	Avoids disruption of the extensor mechanism, no postoperative restrictions related to approach required	Limited visualization of the articular surfaces
	Triceps Splitting[25,59]	ORIF extra-articular and intra-articular fractures TEA	Anterior coronal shear fractures of capitellum or trochlea Prior olecranon osteotomy approach	Avoids complications associated with olecranon osteotomy	Limited visualization of anterior articular surfaces Risk of triceps insufficiency
	Triceps Reflecting[23]	ORIF intra-articular fractures	Anterior coronal shear fractures of capitellum or trochlea Prior olecranon osteotomy approach Traumatic triceps tendon tear	Avoids complications associated with olecranon osteotomy	Limited visualization of anterior articular surfaces Risk of triceps insufficiency
	TRAP[138]	ORIF intra-articular fractures TEA	Anterior coronal shear fractures of capitellum or trochlea Prior olecranon osteotomy approach Traumatic triceps tendon tear	Avoids complications associated with olecranon osteotomy Preserves nerve supply to anconeus	Limited visualization of anterior articular surfaces Risk of triceps insufficiency
	Van Gorder[199]	ORIF intra-articular fractures TEA	Anterior coronal shear fractures of capitellum or trochlea Prior olecranon osteotomy approach	Avoids complications associated with olecranon osteotomy	Limited visualization of anterior articular surfaces Risk of triceps insufficiency

(continues)

TABLE 33-3 **Surgical Approaches to the Distal Humerus (*continued*)**

Direction	Surgical Approach	Indications	Contraindications	Advantages	Disadvantages
Lateral	Kocher[96]	Lateral column fractures Lateral epicondyle fractures Capitellum ± lateral trochlear ridge fractures Fixation of associated radial head and neck fractures	Medial articular fractures (trochlea)	Good access to capitellum, and lateral column structures Improved access to medial joint by releasing LCL Good access to origin and insertion of LCL	No access to medial column
	EDC Split	Lateral column fractures Lateral epicondyle fractures Capitellum ± lateral trochlear ridge fractures Fixation of associated radial head fractures	Medial articular fractures (trochlea)	Good access to capitellum, and lateral column structures Improved access to medial joint by releasing LCL	No access to medial column
	Kaplan[92]	Capitellum ± lateral trochlear ridge fractures Fixation of associated radial head fractures	Medial articular fractures (trochlea) Lateral collateral ligament injuries	Avoids disrupting extensor origin on lateral epicondyle LCL is safe	No access to medial column Difficult access to lateral epicondyle for ORIF fracture or LCL repair Limited access to radial neck for fixation
Medial	Hotchkiss Over-the-Top[71]	Medial epicondyle and medial column fractures Trochlear fractures	Associated MCL tears requiring repair Complex medial and lateral articular fractures	Good access to medial column and anteromedial joint capsule	Difficult access to MCL for repair
	Taylor and Scham[195]	Medial epicondyle and medial column fractures Trochlear fractures MCL tears and coronoid fractures	Complex medial and lateral articular fractures	Good visualization of trochlea Good access to MCL for repair and coronoid for ORIF	Disruption of flexor-pronator origin
Anterior	Henry	Vascular injury Median nerve laceration	Requirement for plate fixation of columns or fixation of articular surface	Good access to brachial artery and median nerve	Limited access to medial and lateral columns

EDC, Extensor digitorum communis; LCL, lateral collateral ligament; MCL, medial collateral ligament; ORIF, open reduction and internal fixation; TEA, total elbow arthroplasty; TRAP, triceps reflecting anconeus pedicle.

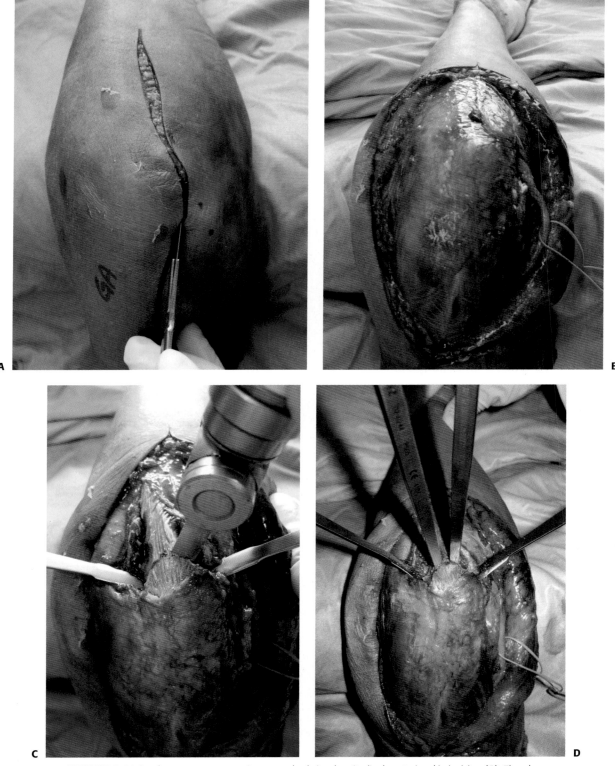

FIGURE 33-10 An olecranon osteotomy is approached via a longitudinal posterior skin incision **(A)**. The ulnar nerve is exposed and may be prepared for anterior subcutaneous transposition **(B)**. The subcutaneous border of the proximal ulna is exposed and the nonarticular portion of the greater sigmoid notch (the bare area) between the olecranon articular facet and the coronoid articular facet is clearly identified. This is accomplished by dissection along the medial and lateral sides of the olecranon to enter into the ulnohumeral joint. Medial and lateral retractors are then placed into the ulnohumeral joint and an apex distal chevron osteotomy entering into the bare area is marked on the subcutaneous border of the ulna. A microsagittal saw is used to complete two-thirds of the osteotomy **(C)** and two osteotomes, placed into each arm of the chevron, apply controlled leverage to fracture the remaining third **(D)**. *(continues)*

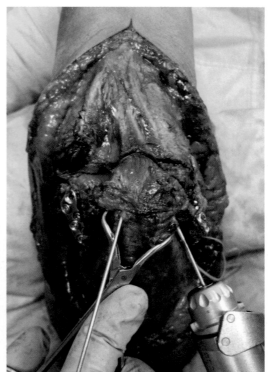

E

F

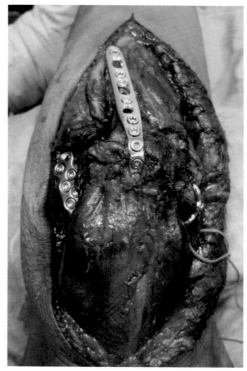

G

FIGURE 33-10 (*continued*) Once conducted, the olecranon fragment along with the triceps tendon and musculature can be bluntly dissected off the posterior aspect of the distal humerus **(E)**. At the completion of the case, provisional fixation of the olecranon fragment is done with crossing K-wires **(F)** followed by definitive compression plating **(G)**.

medial skin incision or a posterior longitudinal skin incision with elevation of a medial fasciocutaneous flap. There are several advantages to a direct midline posterior longitudinal skin incision, including access to both medial and lateral deep approaches and a decreased risk of cutaneous nerve injury.[36] The disadvantage of selecting a posterior longitudinal skin incision for isolated medial or lateral approaches is the increased risk of flap complications such as seromas and rarely necrosis.

Posterior Approaches

There are several posterior approaches and they can be classified into five general types: olecranon osteotomy, paratricipital (triceps-on), triceps splitting, triceps reflecting, and triceps dividing. The selection of a particular type of posterior approach depends on several factors, including: the degree of articular visualization required for anatomic reduction and internal fixation; the appropriateness of primary arthroplasty; patient factors (elderly, low demand); fracture characteristics (articular comminution); any associated injuries (i.e., triceps laceration or olecranon fracture) that may make one approach more favorable.

Olecranon Osteotomy. The olecranon osteotomy was first described by MacAusland[106] and has undergone several modifications.[26,49,162] When compared with other posterior approaches, osteotomy of the olecranon provides the best visualization of the distal humerus articular surface,[204] which is its main advantage. The main disadvantages of the approach are the complications associated with an osteotomy, including nonunion, malunion, and hardware irritation. Olecranon osteotomies are most commonly used for AO/OTA type C fractures, which require superior visualization of the articular fragments for anatomic reduction and internal fixation. An osteotomy can also be used for partial articular fractures (AO/OTA type B), especially if they are comminuted. Relative contraindications to an osteotomy are very anterior articular fractures (AO/OTA type B3), which can be difficult to visualize through an osteotomy and if a total elbow arthroplasty is planned as it may lead to problems with implant stability and osteotomy healing and fixation.

As for all posterior approaches, the ulnar nerve requires identification and protection to avoid iatrogenic nerve injury during fracture manipulation and fixation (Figure 33-10B). It remains unclear whether the ulnar nerve should be transposed or replaced in the cubital tunnel at the conclusion of the procedure.

Once the subcutaneous border of the proximal ulna is exposed, the nonarticular portion of the greater sigmoid notch (the "bare area") between the olecranon articular facet and the coronoid articular facet should be clearly identified. This is done by subperiosteally dissecting along the medial and lateral sides of the olecranon to enter into the ulnohumeral joint. Dissection should not proceed distally as it places the collateral ligament insertions at risk. Medial and lateral retractors are then placed into the ulnohumeral joint to protect the soft tissues and to allow direct visualization of the "bare area." An apex distal chevron osteotomy entering into the bare area is then marked on the subcutaneous border of the ulna (Figure 33-10C). A microsagittal saw is used to complete two thirds of the osteotomy. To avoid unpredictable propagation of the osteotomy, multiple perforations are carefully created through the remaining third using a Kirchner wire (K-wire). Two osteotomes, placed into each arm of the chevron, apply controlled leverage of the olecranon fragment causing fracture of the remaining third (Figure 33-10D). The fractured surface of the olecranon improves fragment interdigitation and facilitates anatomic reduction and stability during the repair. A chevron-shaped osteotomy provides rotation stability, increased surface area for healing, and protects the collateral ligament insertions.[151] A transverse olecranon osteotomy is also an option as it is technically simpler and can be performed more rapidly.[49,70] Following the osteotomy, the olecranon fragment along with the triceps tendon and musculature can be bluntly dissected off the posterior aspect of the distal humerus (Figure 33-10E). Typically, the anconeus muscle must be divided to reflect the triceps posteriorly which causes its denervation.[138] Anconeus muscle denervation can be avoided by reflecting the anconeus muscle posteriorly along with the olecranon fragment and triceps.[15] Once the osteotomy (Figure 33-10F,G) is conducted, flexion of the elbow is used to maximize visualization of distal humerus articular surface.

Fixation of the olecranon osteotomy can be achieved with tension band wiring,[111] screw/tension band constructs, or compression plating.[55] The author's preferred method of fixation is compression plating.[68] When using this method the plate is prefixed to the olecranon and then removed before conducting the osteotomy. This facilitates osteotomy reduction at the completion of the operative procedure. A 6.5- or 7.3-mm intramedullary compression screw may also be used for osteotomy fixation; however, care should be taken during screw insertion as malreduction is possible when the distal screw threads deflect into the normal varus bow of the ulna.[57]

Paratricipital Approach (Triceps-On). The paratricipital (bilaterotricipital, triceps sparing, or triceps-on) approach was first reported by Alonso-Llames in 1972 for the management of pediatric supracondylar fractures.[7] The approach involves the creation of surgical windows along the medial and lateral sides of the triceps muscle and tendon without disrupting its insertion on the olecranon.[179]

The approach starts with an extensile posterior skin incision and mobilization of the ulnar nerve. Along the medial side of the triceps, the interval between the triceps muscle and the medial intermuscular septum is developed (Figure 33-11A) and the triceps is elevated off the posterior aspect of the humerus (Figure 33-11B). Laterally, the triceps is elevated off the lateral intermuscular septum and the posterior humerus in conjunction with the anconeus muscle (Figure 33-11).[7,179] Distally, the paratricipital approach allows visualization of the medial and lateral columns, the olecranon fossa, and the posterior aspect of the trochlea. A modification of the paratricipital approach involves the creation of a third surgical window in Boyd's interval between the anconeus and lateral olecranon.[13] The third surgical window allows improved visualization of the distal humerus articular surface.

The paratricipital approach has several advantages, including, avoidance of an olecranon osteotomy, therefore the risks of nonunion and symptomatic olecranon hardware are avoided. Additionally, the triceps tendon insertion is not disrupted, allowing early active range of motion. This approach also preserves the innervation and blood supply of the anconeus muscle,[179] which provides dynamic posterolateral stability to the elbow. Finally, if further articular exposure is required, the paratricipital approach can be converted into an olecranon osteotomy. If further proximal exposure is required for associated fractures of the humeral shaft, the lateral side of the paratricipital approach can be converted into the Gerwin et al.[53] approach. This approach involves reflection of the triceps muscle unit from lateral to medial to expose 95% of the posterior humeral shaft and the radial nerve.

The disadvantage of the paratricipital approach is the limited visualization of the articular surface of the distal humerus; therefore, the approach is usually inadequate for fixation of type C3 fractures. The several advantages of this approach certainly indicate its use for AO/OTA types A2, A3, B1, B2, and possibly C1 and C2 fractures.[111,154,179]

In distal humerus fractures deemed unrepairable, in which the intent is to proceed directly to total elbow arthroplasty, the paratricipital approach is preferred because it avoids the problems associated with osteotomies and extensor mechanism healing in triceps detaching approaches. The approach is also useful in cases in which an initial attempt at ORIF is planned and there is a possibility of an intraoperative convertion to total elbow arthroplasty should fixation be deemed unsuccessful.

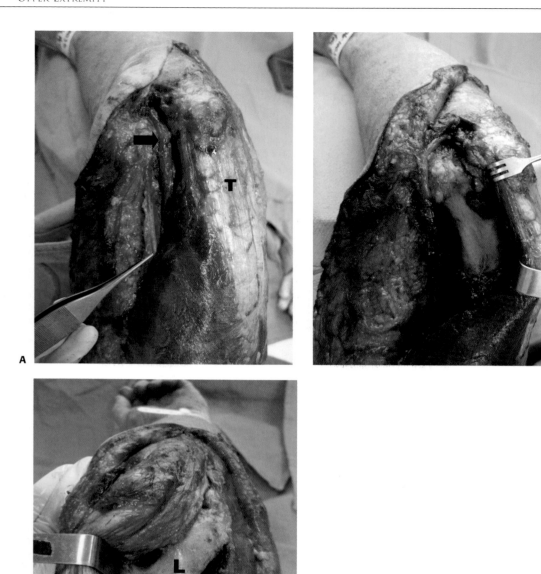

FIGURE 33-11 The paratricipital approach[7] is done through a longitudinal posterior skin incision. Medially **(A)**, the ulnar nerve (*black arrow*) is identified. The medial intermuscular septum (forceps) is excised and the triceps muscle is elevated off the posterior aspect of the distal humerus **(B)**. Laterally, the triceps muscle is elevated off the posterolateral aspect of the distal humerus allowing exposure of the lateral column, olecranon fossa and posterior aspect of the trochlea **(C)**. (L, lateral column; T, triceps.)

Triceps Splitting Approach. The triceps splitting approach described by Campbell involves a midline split through the triceps tendon.[25] The medial and lateral columns are exposed with subperiosteal dissection starting from the midline and moving outwards (Figure 33-12). Visualization of the articular surface of the distal humerus is challenging and can be improved by partial excision of the olecranon tip and flexion of the elbow. This approach can be extended proximally to the level of the radial nerve as it crosses the humeral shaft in the spiral groove. To expand the approach distally, the split can be extended through the triceps insertion to the subcutaneous border of the ulna. The triceps insertion is split midline, with release of

Sharpey fibers creating medial and lateral fasciotendinous sleeves. At the conclusion of the procedure, the triceps tendon is repaired to the olecranon via transosseous nonabsorbable braided sutures.

The advantages of the triceps splitting approach are its relative technical ease and the ability to convert from open reduction and internal fixation to total elbow arthroplasty with few consequences. The disadvantages of the approach include limited visibility of the articular surface, disruption of the extensor mechanism requiring postoperative protection and the risk of triceps dehiscence. In order to improve triceps healing, Gschwend et al.[59] modified the approach to incorporate a flake

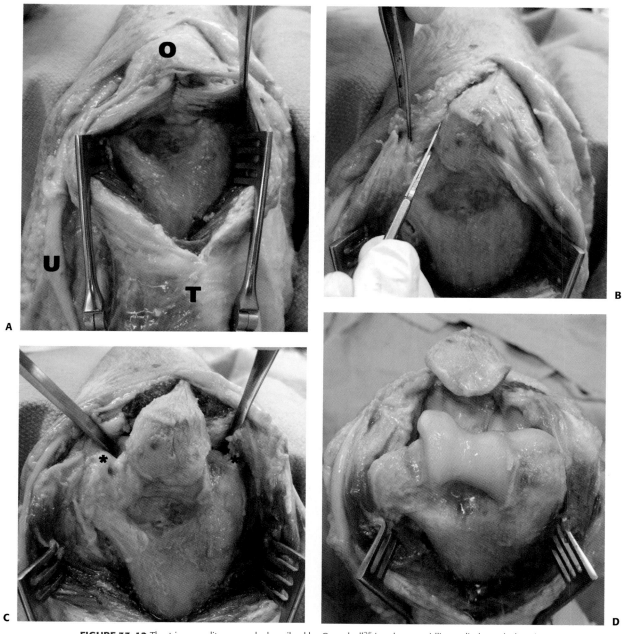

FIGURE 33-12 The triceps split approach described by Campbell[25] involves a midline split through the triceps tendon and medial head **(A)**. The approach can be extended distally by splitting the triceps insertion on the olecranon and raising medial and lateral full-thickness fasciotendinous flaps **(B,C)**. To gain further exposure of the posterior trochlea, the elbow is flexed and the olecranon tip may be excised. For ORIF, the medial and lateral collateral ligaments are preserved (*asterisk*); however, to obtain further exposure for TEA, they may be released **(D)**. (O, olecranon; T, triceps; U, ulnar nerve.)

of olecranon bone. McKee et al.[118] compared the extensor mechanism strength of patients treated with an olecranon osteotomy versus a triceps splitting approach and found no statistical significant difference, concluding that both approaches are effective.

Triceps Reflecting Approaches.

Bryan-Morrey Approach. The Bryan-Morrey approach[23] is commonly used for total elbow arthroplasty. The approach can be used for ORIF of distal humerus fractures; however, exposure

of the lateral column for the application of fixation is limited. The approach has been termed "triceps-sparing" which has led to confusion. The approach does not "spare" the triceps, but rather detaches the triceps tendon in continuity with the ulnar periosteum and anconeus creating a large reflection or sleeve.

The ulnar nerve is first identified and protected, and then the triceps insertion and the ulnar periosteum are sharply reflected off the proximal ulna in a medial to lateral direction (Figure 33-13). The sleeve of tissue created incorporates the anconeus muscle. As with the triceps splitting approach, careful

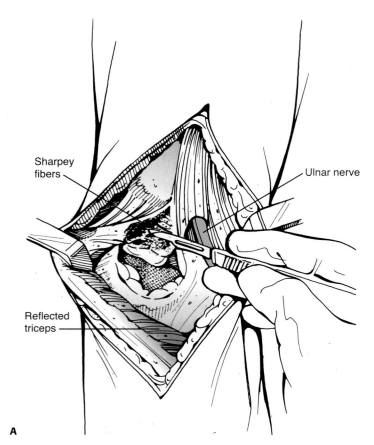

Sharpey fibers

Ulnar nerve

Reflected triceps

A

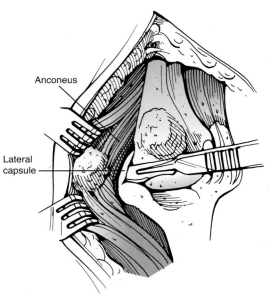

Anconeus

Lateral capsule

B

FIGURE 33-13 The Bryan-Morrey[23] approach is commonly used for total elbow arthroplasty. A posterior longitudinal skin incision is used and the ulnar nerve is identified and protected. The ulnar periosteum, triceps insertion and anconeus muscle are sharply reflected off the proximal ulna in a medial **(A)** to lateral **(B)** direction. To access the articular surfaces for arthroplasty, the collateral ligaments are released.

and solid repair of the triceps tendon is required via transosseous sutures. This approach is best suited for unrepairable distal humerus fractures in which primary elbow arthroplasty is planned.

Extended Kocher Approach. The extended Kocher approach may be used for total elbow arthroplasty and is seldom used for ORIF of distal humerus fractures. The approach is analogous to the Bryan-Morrey in that the triceps is reflected; however, the direction of reflection is lateral to medial.

Triceps Dividing Approaches.

Triceps Reflecting Anconeus Pedicle Approach. The triceps reflecting anconeus pedicle approach (TRAP) involves completely detaching the triceps from the proximal ulna with the anconeus muscle.[138] The approach is done through a longitudinal posterior skin incision after identification of the ulnar nerve. Kocher's interval is used to elevate the anconeus muscle and develop the distal lateral portion of the flap (Figure 33-14A). The medial portion of the flap is created by subperiosteal dissection from the subcutaneous border of the ulna. The anconeus flap is then reflected proximally to expose the triceps insertion, which is also sharply released (Figure 33-14B). The entire triceps-anconeus flap is then reflected proximally releasing the triceps muscle from the posterior aspect of the distal humerus (Figure 33-14C). This approach provides good exposure to the posterior elbow joint while protecting the neurovascular supply to the anconeus muscle. The TRAP approach also avoids the complications of an olecranon osteotomy and allows the use of the trochlear sulcus as a template to assist with articular reduc-

tion of the distal humerus. The major disadvantage of this approach is that the triceps is completely released from its insertion, therefore, there is a risk of triceps dehiscence and extensor weakness.

Van Gorder Approach (Triceps Tongue). The Van Gorder approach involves division of the triceps tendon at its musculotendinous junction.[199] The approach is most commonly used for total elbow arthroplasty and rarely for ORIF of distal humerus fractures. Transection of the triceps is done in the shape of a V, so that a V to Y plasty can be done if lengthening of the extensor mechanism is required. As the triceps is completely divided in this approach, it has the same risks as the TRAP approach. This approach is indicated for ORIF of distal humerus fractures when there is an associated complete or high grade partial triceps tendon laceration.

Lateral Approaches

Lateral approaches to the elbow can be accessed via a direct lateral skin incision or by a posterior longitudinal skin incision with elevation of a lateral fasciocutaneous flap. The approaches that will be discussed are the Kocher, Kaplan, and the extensor digitorum communis (EDC) split. Access to the radiocapitellar joint can also be obtained through a lateral epicondylar osteotomy or via a concurrent fracture of the lateral epicondyle.

The Kocher, Kaplan, and EDC split approaches are used to treat capitellar and radial head fractures. Proximal extension of these approaches can be used to access the lateral column, to treat partial articular lateral column fractures and some transcolumn fractures.

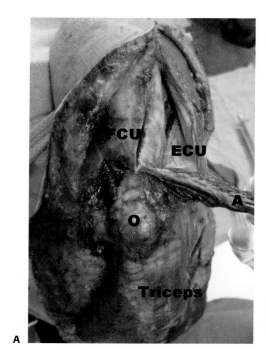

A

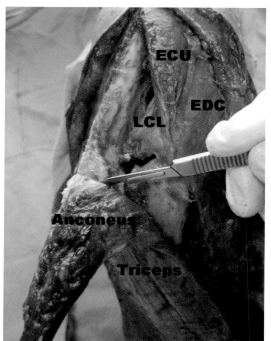

B

C

FIGURE 33-14 The triceps reflecting anconeus pedicle[138] (TRAP) approach is done through a longitudinal posterior skin incision after identification of the ulnar nerve. The interval between anconeus and extensor carpi ulnaris is used to elevate the anconeus muscle and develop the distal lateral portion of the flap. The medial portion of the flap is created by subperiosteal dissection from the subcutaneous border of the ulna. The anconeus flap is then reflected proximally **(A)** to expose the triceps insertion, which is also sharply released **(B)**. The entire triceps-anconeus flap is then reflected proximally releasing the triceps muscle from the posterior aspect of the distal humerus **(C)**. (A, anconeus; ECU, extensor carpi ulnaris; FCU, flexor carpi ulnaris; LCL, lateral collateral ligament; O, olecranon.)

The Kocher approach involves identification of the interval between extensor carpi ulnaris (ECU) and anconeus.[96] This interval can be identified by a thin fat stripe or by the perforating branches of the recurrent posterior interosseous artery (Figure 33-15A). The interval is developed by bluntly undermining the anconeus muscle, which will allow identification of the elbow joint capsule and the capsular thickening that is the lateral ulnar collateral ligament (LUCL) (Figure 33-15B,C). Some of the common extensor tendon origin will have to be elevated off the LUCL to allow an arthrotomy to be made anterior to the ligament (Figure 33-15D). The forearm is pronated during the approach, which moves the posterior interosseous nerve more anterior and distal. The radial neck is exposed by incising the annular ligament. This approach can be extended proximally by releasing the extensor carpi radialis longus (ECRL) and the brachioradialis off the anterolateral supracondylar ridge. To expose the posterolateral elbow joint and posterior aspect of the lateral column, another arthrotomy is made posterior to the LUCL and the triceps is elevated off the posterior lateral column.

An easier, and some believe safer, approach to the radiocapitellar joint is the extensor digitorum communis (EDC) split. This approach involves creation of a lateral elbow arthrotomy at the equator of the radiocapitellar joint (Figure 33-16). The site of the arthrotomy is chosen by palpating the capitellum

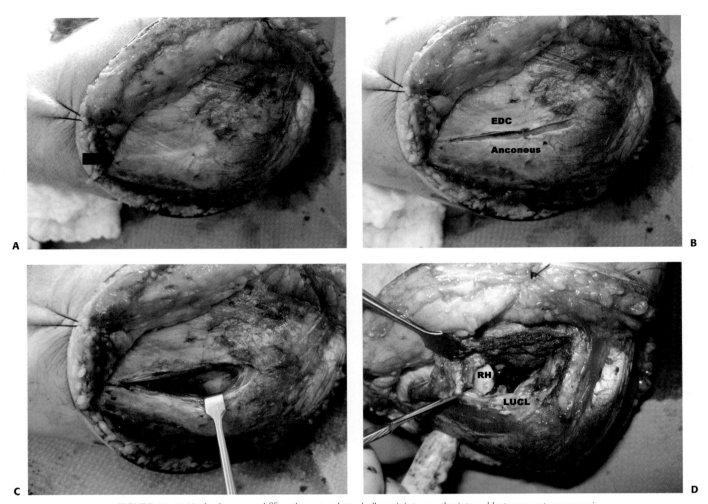

FIGURE 33-15 Kocher's approach[96] to the anterolateral elbow joint uses the interval between extensor carpi ulnaris (ECU) and anconeus **(A)**. This interval can be identified by a thin fat stripe (*black arrow*). The interval is developed by bluntly undermining the anconeus muscle, which allows identification of the elbow joint capsule and capsular thickening that is the lateral ulnar collateral ligament (LUCL) **(B,C)**. The posterior portion of the common extensor tendon origin has to be elevated off the LUCL to allow an arthrotomy to be made anterior to the ligament **(D)**. (RH, radial head.)

and radial head to determine the midequator. The structures below the equator include the LUCL and the posterolateral joint capsule, which should not be incised as they are important elbow stabilizers. The arthrotomy, therefore, is made in-line with the tendon fibers of EDC at the equator of the radiocapitellar joint and may be extended proximally along the anterolateral aspect of the lateral column. Dissection below the midequator is avoided, as it may disrupt the LUCL.

The Kaplan approach uses the interval between ECRL and EDC to access the radiocapitellar joint.[92] The approach provides good exposure of the radial head and capitellum and remains anterior to the lateral collateral ligament insertion. The forearm should be pronated during distal extension of the approach to maximize the distance to the posterior interosseous nerve.[32]

Medial Approaches

Medial approaches to the elbow can be accessed by a direct medial skin incision or a posterior longitudinal skin incision with elevation of a medial fasciocutaneous flap. When using a direct medial skin incision, care should be taken in identifying and protecting the branches of the medial antebrachial cutaneous nerve. The medial approaches can be used to treat isolated partial articular medial column fractures, trochlear fractures, coronoid fractures and fractures of the medial epicondyle.

Hotchkiss described the medial "over-the-top" approach, which starts with identification and transposition of the ulnar nerve.[71,151] The medial supracondylar ridge is identified and the flexor-pronator origin is release off the ridge to the level of the medial epicondyle. At the medial epicondyle, the flexor origin is split distally in-line with its fibers. Dissection directly inferior to the medial epicondyle is avoided, as it may disrupt the anterior bundle of the medial collateral ligament.

The medial coronoid, the anterior bundle of the medial collateral ligament (MCL) and the posteromedial ulnohumeral joint can be accessed through an approach that starts at the floor of the cubital tunnel. The humeral head of the flexor carpi ulnaris, palmaris longus, flexor carpi radialis, and pronator teres are bluntly elevated off the anterior bundle of the MCL and joint capsule in a posterior to anterior direction. Once exposed, an arthrotomy is made anterior to the anterior bundle of the MCL

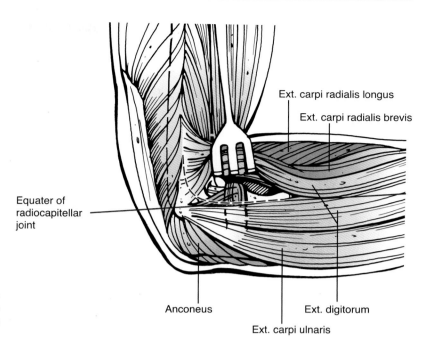

Ext. carpi radialis longus

Ext. carpi radialis brevis

Equater of
radiocapitellar
joint

Anconeus

Ext. digitorum

Ext. carpi ulnaris

FIGURE 33-16 The extensor digitorum communis (EDC) split approach. The EDC tendon is split anterior to the mid-equator of the radiocapitellar joint to avoid injury to the lateral ulnar collateral ligament.

to enter the anterior aspect of the ulnohumeral joint. The posteromedial aspect of the ulnohumeral joint is accessed by dividing the posterior and transverse bundles of the MCL. Taylor and Scham[195] described a similar approach with the only difference being that the ulnar head of FCU is elevated anteriorly with the other flexors.

Anterior Approach

The anterior approach to the elbow is rarely used for the internal fixation of adult distal humerus fractures[93,151] because it provides little access to the medial and lateral columns for the application of internal fixation. This approach may be used if access to the brachial artery or median nerve is required for repair or in release of posttraumatic elbow contractures.

CURRENT TREATMENT OPTIONS (AO/OTA TYPES A, B1, B2, AND C)

Nonoperative Treatment

In general, displaced distal humerus fractures should be managed with surgical intervention; however, circumstances exist where nonoperative management may be most appropriate. Nonoperative management techniques include above-elbow casting, olecranon traction, and collar and cuff treatment, the so-called "bag of bones" method.

The traction method involves the placement of a transolecranon traction pin that is attached to weights through a pulley system.[94] Traction is applied for 3 to 4 weeks, until there is sufficient early callous to allow cast bracing. The major disadvantages of this method are the complications associated with prolonged bed rest. Patients that are typically treated nonoperatively, the frail elderly, have significant medical comorbidities that put them at high risk of bed rest related complications, such as deep venous thrombosis, pulmonary embolism, and decubitus ulcers. The technique is largely of historical significance and has little use in modern distal humerus fracture care.

Collar and cuff treatment had been used for centuries before

it was first reported in modern medical literature in 1937 by Eastwood.[40] He described a closed reduction followed by application of a collar and cuff with the elbow between 90 and 120 degrees of flexion. The elbow is hung freely to allow gravity assisted reduction via a ligamentotaxis-type effect. Shoulder motion and active elbow flexion are initiated at 2 weeks and progressed.

Indications

Nonoperative management of distal humerus fractures in young patients is rarely recommended and it is generally reserved for patients deemed medically unfit to undergo surgery (Figure 33-17). Other circumstances are elderly patients with unrepairable distal humerus fractures in which arthroplasty is the most reasonable option, however, is contraindicated because of soft tissue compromise, such as skin loss. Once the soft tissue issues have been dealt with, delayed arthroplasty can be done if patients are sufficiently symptomatic.

Patients with nondisplaced fractures may also be managed with a trial of nonoperative management. These patients should be followed for the first 3 to 4 weeks with weekly serial radiographs to ensure displacement or angulation does not occur. Surgical fixation of these fractures, however, enhances stability, allows immediate motion, and obviously decreases the risk of delayed fracture displacement.

Results

In 1969, Riseborough and Radin[168] compared operative with nonoperative management in 29 patients with intra-articular distal humerus fractures. They reported better range of motion and less pain with nonoperative management, consisting of skeletal traction or manipulation and casting. The surgically treated group was plagued with early fracture displacement because of hardware failure from nonrigid fixation constructs. Brown and Morgan[22] in 1971 reported their results with nonoperative management of intra-articular distal humerus fractures in 10 patients at a mean follow-up of 2.5 years (range, 9 months to 4 years).

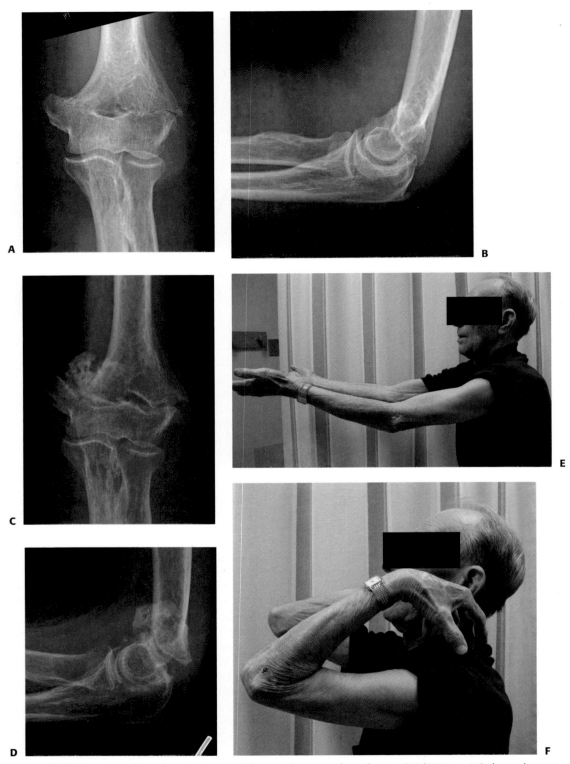

FIGURE 33-17 Radiographs of an 88-year-old man with a transcolumn fracture (AO/OTA type A2) deemed medically unfit for surgery because of severe congestive heart failure and inoperable coronary artery disease **(A,B)**. The patient was treated with a collar and cuff and early range of motion. Radiographs at 1-year follow-up **(C,D)**. The patient has no pain with a functional range of motion **(E,F)**.

At follow-up, the mean flexion was 128 degrees, the mean extension was 30 degrees, and the mean arc of motion was 100 degrees. Seven patients described no symptoms, whereas three complained of elbow aches in cold and damp weather.

Operative Treatment: Open Reduction and Internal Fixation

Indications

Anatomic reduction and rigid internal fixation is considered the gold standard for most displaced intra-articular distal humerus fractures (AO/OTA types B and C). Rigid internal fixation allows fracture healing to occur anatomically while permitting early range of motion to maximize functional recovery. The traumatized elbow is particularly prone to stiffness; therefore, early motion is vital, but not at the expense of fracture displacement. In cases in which sufficient fracture stability cannot be obtained to allow early motion, anatomic reconstruction of the articular surface and overall elbow alignment take precedence. An anatomically aligned stiff elbow with a healed articular surface can be subsequently managed with contracture release, but a fracture with hardware failure and articular nonunion or fragmentation may be difficult to manage with revision surgery.

Surgical treatment is also recommended for displaced or angulated extra-articular fractures (transcolumn) of the distal humerus (AO/OTA Type A2 and A3). Closed reduction and percutaneous K-wire fixation has been described for treatment of these injuries in adults.[82] The technique in adults is similar to the technique used pediatric supracondylar fractures with crossing K-wires inserted medially and laterally. In adults, this technique may be modified to exchange the K-wires for 3.5- or 4.5-mm cannulated screws. Closed reduction and percutaneous fixation has several disadvantages when used in adults. The fixation is semi-rigid and therefore requires supplementary splinting for up to 6 weeks, which may lead to elbow stiffness. K-wires are also inadequate for elderly patients with osteopenic bone. In general, the crossing K-wire or cannulated screw technique is not recommended for adult patients with AO/OTA Type A2 or A3 fractures.

Open reduction and internal fixation is the preferred fixation technique for these fractures (Transcolumn, AO/OTA Types A2 and A3). These fractures can be exposed through a paratricipital approach or a limited triceps split. Exposure of the articular surface, as obtained from an olecranon osteotomy, is not required for these extra-articular fractures. Bicolumnar fixation is recommended with orthogonal or parallel plating techniques. When the transcolumn fracture line is just proximal to the articular segment, the pattern can be referred to as a "low" transcolumn fracture. Low transcolumn fractures have limited bone available for distal fixation; therefore, bicolumn plating is necessary with plates applied as distal as possible with as many screws as possible in the distal fragment. Commercially available precontoured plates have extra screw holes distally to allow high-density screw insertion into the distal articular segment. In certain low transcolumn fractures in elderly patients with severe osteopenia or pre-existing arthritis, total elbow arthroplasty may be the most appropriate form of treatment. Elbow arthroplasty is discussed later in this chapter.

The commonly used classification systems do not account for fracture displacement, fracture angulation, or the severity of the soft tissue injury. These factors should be considered when deciding upon surgical management. In general, medically fit patients with distal humerus fractures with displacement or angulation meet the indications for surgical intervention.

Timing of Surgery

Surgical fixation of distal humerus fractures requires preoperative planning, specialized implants, instruments, and surgical expertise. Medically fit and stabilized patients with uncompromised soft tissues may be best managed with early surgery within 48 to 72 hours.[76] Early surgery may lead to decreases complications such as heterotopic ossification and stiffness. Polytrauma patients that are unstable or those with identified modifiable risk factors should be medically optimized preoperatively. In cases with injured soft tissues, such as excessive swelling, bruising, fracture blisters, or abrasions, delay of surgery may be most appropriate. Generally, patients admitted to the intensive care unit can be managed with a well-padded splint that is checked daily and removed every 2 to 3 days to examine the soft tissues for compromise and pressure points. In some cases, prolonged secondary surgical procedures may be contraindicated for several weeks because of medical issues. In these patients, static external fixation may be of benefit to stabilize the extremity for pain control, transfers, hygiene, and wound care. Ideally, external fixator pins should be placed as far away as possible from planned internal fixation implants to decrease the likelihood of infection. Although no literature exists to define a suitable delay, surgery should be conducted within 2 or 3 weeks. Delay beyond this time interval is possible; however, ORIF is made more difficult with increased surgical time, difficult fracture reductions owing to partial healing and callous, increased bleeding, and the increased risk of heterotopic ossification.

Fixation Principles

The goals in surgical treatment of distal humerus fractures are similar to those used for any periarticular fracture. The objectives are to obtain anatomic restoration of the articular surface and recreation of joint alignment with rigid internal fixation, stable enough to allow early range of motion.

Surgical Approach. The principles of fixation start with the selection of an appropriate surgical approach. The chosen approach should be accommodating to intraoperative findings, which may alter the surgical procedure. For example, a paratricipital approach may be used to initially access a noncomminuted intra-articular fracture (AO/OTA type C1 or C2); however, if the fracture proves difficult to reduce or if more comminution is present than expected, the approach can be converted to an olecranon osteotomy. Similarly, an olecranon osteotomy should not be the index approach for an elderly patient with a highly comminuted distal humerus fracture, which may be intraoperatively deemed unrepairable, necessitating total elbow arthroplasty. AO/OTA type B1 (lateral column) fractures can be surgically approached by Kocher's interval with proximal extension to expose the lateral column. AO/OTA type B2 (medial column) fractures can be approached via a Hotchkiss approach with proximal extension to expose the medial column. Single column fractures (medial and lateral) may also be exposed by the paratricipital approach that allows visualization

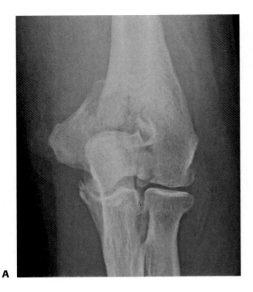
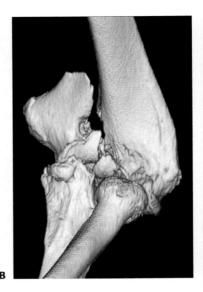
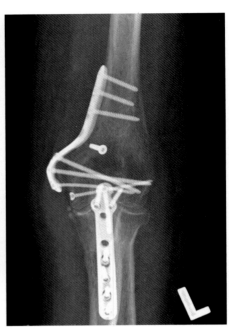

FIGURE 33-18 A 73-year-old woman with a comminuted intra-articular fracture of the medial column (AO/OTA type B1.3) treated with ORIF via an olecranon osteotomy **(A–C)**.

of the posterior aspects of both columns and the posterior aspect of the articular surface. In cases in which there is extensive articular comminution (AO/OTA types B1.3 and B2.3) an olecranon osteotomy may be required for improved visualization of the fracture and improved access for fixation (Figure 33-18).

AO/OTA Type A and C Fractures. For AO/OTA type C fractures, once the distal humerus articular surface is adequately exposed, the fracture hematoma is evacuated and the raw fracture surfaces are cleaned of loose debris. The origins of the common flexor and extensor tendons are preserved on the epicondyles, as are the collateral ligament origins. The fracture fragments can be manipulated manually or with small-diameter K-wires used as joy sticks. Once the fractured articular fragments are reduced and interdigitated, a large tenaculum can be used to hold the reduction until provisional transfixion with K-wires. Definitive fixation of the articular segment can be done with one or two centrally placed screws along the capitellar-trochlear axis (Figure 33-19) or by screws placed through plates that are applied in a parallel fashion (Figure 33-20). Ideally, intrafragmentary compression is best; however, not at the expense of shortening the trochlea in the medial–lateral plane. The trochlea is particularly susceptible to shortening when central comminution exists and lag screw fixation is used. In these instances, fully threaded (non-overdrilled) position screws rather than lag screws should be used to stabilize the articular segment.

Small articular fracture segments that cannot be incorporated into the greater fixation construct should be independently fixated. Supplementary implants should be available to address these small osteochondral fragments, such as minifragment plates, headless compression screws, countersunk small diameter screws, threaded K-wires, and bioabsorbable pins. These supplementary implants require strategic placement such that they do not interfere with trochlear fixation and bicolumnar plate application that will link the articular segment to the diaphysis.

The articular segment (AO/OTA type A fractures and AO/OTA Type C fractures after articular fixation), requires rigid attachment to the medial and lateral columns or distal humerus shaft. This can be accomplished by orthogonal,[67,84,181] parallel,[13b,174,175] or triple[55,111] plating. No clinical superiority of either method has been reported when comparing orthogonal with parallel plating techniques.

Orthogonal plating involves the placement of plates on both columns at 90-degree angles (Figure 33-21). Usually, the lateral plate is placed as distal as possible along the posterior aspect of the lateral column. The lateral plate should be contoured with a bend that matches the posterior curvature of the lateral column. To achieve maximum distal fixation, the end of the plate should lie just proximal to the posterior articular surface of the capitellum. Placement of the plate further distal may lead to impingement of the radial head on the plate in extension, resulting in pain and limited range of motion. Ideally, the lateral plate should be a 3.5-mm dynamic compression plate or equivalent. The medial plate is usually applied on the medial supracondylar ridge with contouring to curve around the medial epicondyle. The plate is typically a 3.5-mm reconstruction plate to allow easier bending; however, a 3.5-mm dynamic compression plate or a newer fracture-specific precontoured plate may be used.

Parallel plating also uses two plates; however, the plates are placed parallel to each other on their respective supracondylar ridges (Figure 33-22). Screws into the articular segment are preferentially placed through the plates to link the articular segment to the humeral shaft. Ideally, the longest possible screws should be inserted through the plate, to capture as many articular fragments as possible and engage fragments that are secured to the opposite column.[13b,136,137,174] This technique may be difficult to achieve and not always possible to perform. For example, longer screws can deflect and bend as they pass one another, causing displacement of tenuously stabilized osteochondral fragments.

Before definitive plate fixation, the elbow should be placed

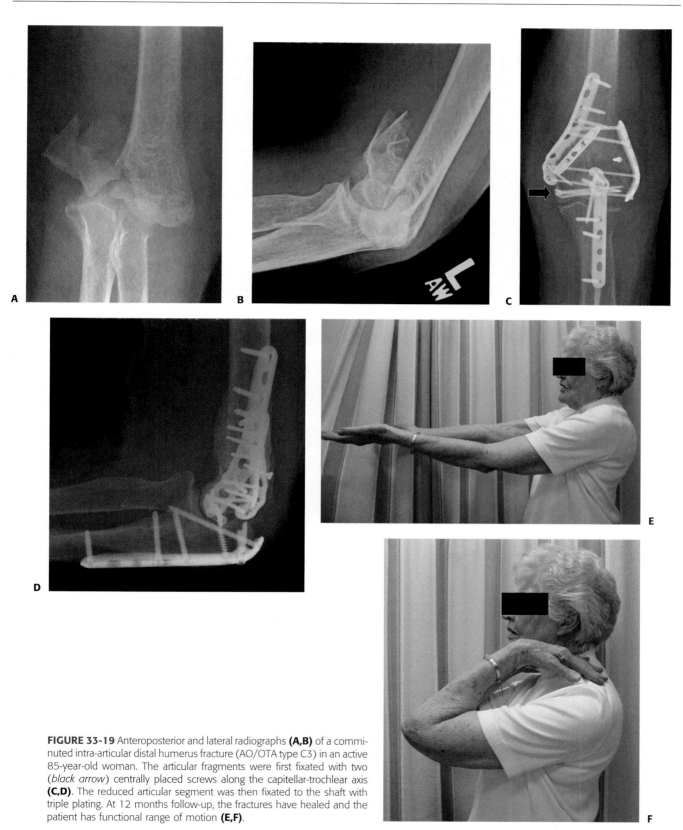

FIGURE 33-19 Anteroposterior and lateral radiographs **(A,B)** of a comminuted intra-articular distal humerus fracture (AO/OTA type C3) in an active 85-year-old woman. The articular fragments were first fixated with two (*black arrow*) centrally placed screws along the capitellar-trochlear axis **(C,D)**. The reduced articular segment was then fixated to the shaft with triple plating. At 12 months follow-up, the fractures have healed and the patient has functional range of motion **(E,F)**.

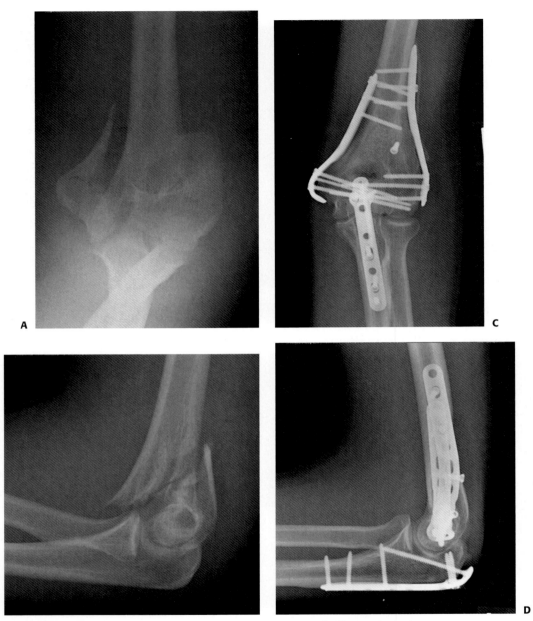

FIGURE 33-20 A bicolumn (AO/OTA type C1) fracture **(A,B)** treated with ORIF via an olecranon osteotomy. The distal humerus articular segment is fixated with three medial and three lateral screws placed through parallel plates **(C,D)**.

through a range of motion to ensure there is no hardware impingement. Also, an attempt should be made to dynamically compress the supracondylar level fracture with eccentrically placed screws through the medial and lateral plates.[136,137] If possible, the plates should end at different levels on the humeral shaft to minimize the stress riser effect and each plate should have at least three bicortical screws proximal to the metaphyseal comminution.[111,137]

Metaphyseal bone loss may be present in high-energy comminuted distal humerus fractures. This bone loss can be addressed with supracondylar shortening or bridge plating with autologous bone graft or allograft. Supracondylar shortening involves removing the comminuted fragments of metaphyseal bone and compressing the reconstructed articular segment to

the distal humeral shaft. Typically, the distal end of the shaft will require reshaping to increase the contact area between it and the articular segment.[140] If absolute rigid fixation cannot be achieved to allow early range of motion, triple plating should be considered as recommended by Gofton[55] and Jupiter.[83] Triple plating can also be useful for fixation of coronal plane fractures (Figure 33-19).

Fracture specific precontoured plates are now available for fixation of distal humerus fractures. Although these plates are marketed as precontoured, they generally still require some contouring to match distal humeral anatomy. Newer precontoured locking plates are also available and are of two types, fixed angle locking and variable angle locking. These plates may offer enhanced fixation in osteopenic bone; however, this has not

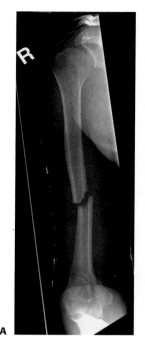
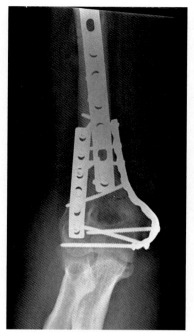
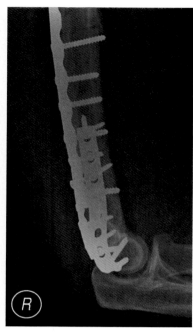

FIGURE 33-21 An AP injury radiograph **(A)** demonstrating a displaced intra-articular distal humerus fracture in association with an ipsilateral humeral shaft fracture. The fractures were exposed via a paratricipital approach extended proximally into a Gerwin et al.[53] approach. The patient's distal humerus fracture was fixated with orthogonal 3.5-mm dynamic compression plates **(B,C)** that were intra-operatively contoured. This technique has been popularized by the AO group and involves the placement of plates at 90-degree angles to each other. Usually, the lateral plate is placed as distal as possible along the posterior aspect of the lateral column. The medial plate is placed over the medial supracondylar ridge and curved around the medial epicondyle.

yet been shown to be clinically superior. The disadvantages of the fixed angle locking plates are the screws have predetermined trajectories, which may not accommodate all fracture patterns in all patients. In some plate designs, the predetermined screw trajectory aims toward the articular surface, which may predispose to joint penetration if screws are placed too long.

AO/OTA Type B1 and B2 Fractures. In general, the fixation principles and techniques used for AO/OTA type C (bicolumn) fractures are applicable to type B1 and B2 (single column) fractures. These fractures may be fixed with multiple screws or with single column plating.[85] Single column plating has the advantage of providing an antiglide construct at the proximal fracture line between the column and humeral shaft (Figure 33-18). In certain highly comminuted partial-articular fractures in elderly patients with osteopenia, total elbow arthroplasty may also be an appropriate treatment option. Elbow arthroplasty is discussed later in this chapter.

Implant Biomechanics
Controversy exists on which implant designs and plate configurations confer the greatest amount of stability when treating distal humerus fractures. Jacobson et al.[79] tested five different distal humerus plating constructs in cadaveric specimens. They reported that a medially applied 3.5-mm reconstruction plate along with an orthogonally applied posterolateral 3.5-mm dynamic compression plate provided the greatest sagittal plane stiffness, and equivalent frontal plane and torsion stiffness, when compared with other constructs which included parallel and triple plating.

Helfet and Hotchkiss[65] also found that orthogonal plating

provided greater rigidity and fatigue resistance when compared with a single Y plate or crossed screws.

In contrast, Schemitsch et al.[178] found that parallel plating with a medial 3.5-mm reconstruction plate and a lateral J plate had the greatest construct rigidity when compared to four other plate configurations, including orthogonal plating with 3.5-mm reconstruction plates. Self et al.[181] found that parallel plating trended towards having greater rigidity and load to failure than orthogonal plating, however, the differences did not reach statistical significance. Arnander et al.,[11] however, found that two 3.5-mm reconstruction plates applied in a parallel fashion did have statistically significant increased stiffness and strength in the sagittal plane when compared with two 3.5-mm reconstruction plates applied orthogonally.

Locking plates have several theoretical advantages, especially when used in patients with severe osteopenia. Schuster et al.[180] demonstrated that locking 3.5-mm reconstruction plates applied orthogonally had superior cyclic failure properties when compared with conventional nonlocked plates applied in a similar fashion in cadavers with low bone mineral density. Stoffel et al.[190] compared the mechanical stability of two different commercially available precontoured locking distal humeral plating systems. They reported significantly higher stability in compression, external rotation, and a greater ability to resist axial plastic deformation in the parallel plate system versus the orthogonal plate system. It should be noted that no clinical difference has yet be demonstrated between parallel and orthogonal plating, and more likely than not, both are acceptable as long as the principles of rigid internal fixation are met.

On the contrary, there is no debate in the use of one third tubular plates, which have been shown to have insufficient

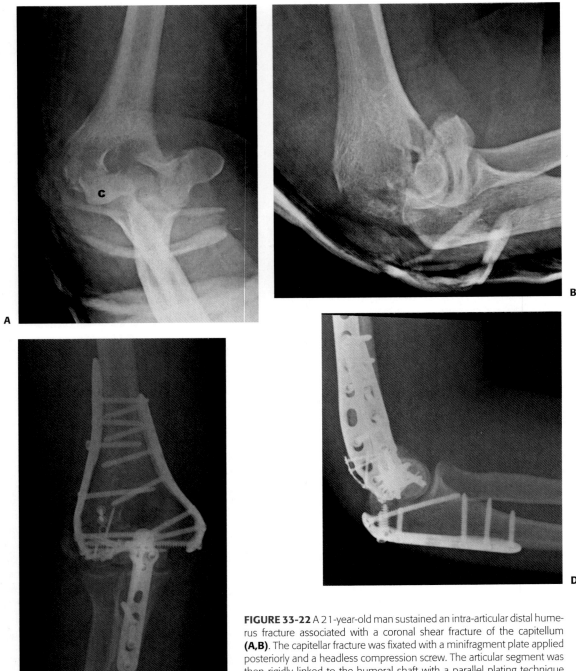

FIGURE 33-22 A 21-year-old man sustained an intra-articular distal humerus fracture associated with a coronal shear fracture of the capitellum **(A,B)**. The capitellar fracture was fixated with a minifragment plate applied posteriorly and a headless compression screw. The articular segment was then rigidly linked to the humeral shaft with a parallel plating technique **(C,D)**. (C, capitellum.)

strength and are susceptible to breakage.[70,136,137,196] These plates should not be used in the primary two-plate construct; however, they may be used as a supplementary third plate.

Results

When the principles of anatomic restoration of the joint surface, bicolumn plating, and rigid internal fixation to allow early range of motion are employed, good outcomes can be expected for patients with intra-articular distal humerus fractures* When

*References 6,12,35,41,48,58,60,72,143–145,171,174,185,196,208.

averaging the outcomes of 17 series published between 2002 and 2009 (Table 33-4), 85% of patients experienced good to excellent outcomes at a mean follow-up of 50 months. Doornberg et al.[35] have shown that the rate of good to excellent outcomes is durable in the long-term (12 to 30 years). Patients that sustain isolated intra-articular fractures of the distal humerus can expect some loss of elbow range of motion, although functional range of motion (30 to 130 degrees) is usually attained. As would be expected, patients who sustain distal humerus fractures in association with polytrauma or severe soft tissue injuries can anticipate worse outcomes.

TABLE 33-4   Summary of Outcomes of AO/OTA Type C (Intra-articular) Distal Humerus Fractures

Author	Year	Number of Fractures	Average Age of Patients (range)	Percentage of Open Fractures	Surgical Approach	Average Follow-Up in Months (range)	Outcome Assessment Used	Percentage with Excellent or Good Outcomes	Percentage with Satisfactory or Poor Outcomes
Pajarinen[145]	2002	18	44 (16–81)	28	OO[a]	25 (10–41)	OTA	56	44
Ozdemir[143]	2002	34	38 (20–78)	15	OO	82 (24–141)	Jupiter	62	38
Gupta[60]	2002	55	39 (18–65)	11	13 OO 42 TS	48 (24–108)	Aitken	93	7
Robinson[172]	2003	119	53 (13–99)	15	OO	19 (5–32)	n/a	n/a	n/a
Gofton[55]	2003	23	45 (14–89)	30	OO[a]	45 (14–89)	DASH, PRUNE, ASES-e, SF-36	93	7
Yang[208]	2003	17	41 (16–69)	29	OO	17 (13–38)	MEPS	88	12
Frankle[48]	2003	12	74 (65–86)	0	10 OO; 2 TS	57 (24–78)	MEPS	67	33
Allende[6]	2004	40	42 (16–77)	25	31 OO; 9 TR	47 (13–94)	Jupiter, OTA	85	15
Aslam[12]	2004	26	56 (18–82)	12	OO	35 (24–48)	Broberg/Morrey	70	30
Soon[185]	2004	12	43 (21–80)	0	5 OO; 7 TS	11 (2–21)	MESP	92	8
Huang[72]	2005	19	72 (65–79)	5	OO	97 (60–174)	Cassebaum, MEPS	100	0
Ozer[144]	2005	11	58 (16–70)	27	TRAP	26 (14–40)	OTA	91	9
Sanchez-Sotelo[b,174]	2007	34	58 (16–99)	41	17 TRAP 5 OO 8 PT 2 BM 2 TT	24 (12–60)	MEPS	84	16
Doornberg[35]	2007	30	35 (13–64)	30	20 OO	19 years (12–30 years)	DASH ASES-e MEPS	87	13
Ek[41]	2008	7	41 (12–73)	14	BM	35 (6–78)	MEPS, SF-36 DASH	100	0
Greiner[b,58]	2008	12	55 (21–83)	42	OO[a]	10 (6–14)	MEPS DASH	100	0
Athwal[13b]	2009	32	56 (19–88)	31	17 OO 12 TRAP	27 (12–54)	MEPS DASH	69	31
Total/Mean		501	50	21		49		84	16

[a]Olecranon osteotomy performed in most cases; [b]most fracture type C; BM, Bryan-Morrey; n/a: not applicable; OO, olecranon osteotomy; PT, paratricipital; TA, triceps split; TR, triceps reflecting; TRAP, triceps reflecting anconeus pedicle; TT, triceps tongue.

Gofton et al.[55] reported the patient-rated outcomes and physical impairments after orthogonal plating of AO/OTA Type C distal humerus fractures in 23 patients. The SF-36 scores of patients at final follow-up compared with age- and sex-matched controls showed no significant differences. Patients rated their overall satisfaction at 93% and on functional assessment indicated a 10% subjective loss of function when comparing the affected with unaffected limb. The mean score on the Disabilities of the Arm, Shoulder and Hand (DASH) questionnaire was 12, which is very close to the overall normative score of 10.1.[74] The isometric strength of the affected elbow was significantly reduced in all ranges, although, grip and pinch strength were not statistically different between affected and unaffected limbs. McKee and colleagues[120] also found decreased strength in the affected elbows and rated it at approximately 75% of normal. The mean DASH score was 20 points, indicating a mild residual impairment. Two of the eight parameters of the SF-36, physical function and role-physical, demonstrated small but significant differences among age-matched controls.

Open Fractures

Approximately 7% of distal humerus fracture are open,[172] and they are classified according to the system of Gustilo and Anderson.[61] The principles of open fracture treatment have remained unchanged for the last three decades. The priorities are wound irrigation and débridement, intravenous antibiotics, tetanus coverage, fracture stabilization and appropriate soft tissue management.[61,142] The common complications associated with open fractures include infection, nonunion, hardware failure, and wound problems.

The grade of open fracture varies with the mechanism of injury. Most blunt mechanisms of injury lead to grade I punctures, whereas blast or gun shots lead to grade III wounds.[172] Typically, most grade I puncture wounds are located posteriorly or posterolaterally on the elbow and are commonly associated with lacerations of the triceps tendon or muscle.[118,172] In cases of an intra-articular fracture with a triceps tendon laceration, the Van Gorder (triceps tongue) or triceps splitting approaches are preferred, as they prevent a second disruption of the extensor mechanism with an olecranon osteotomy.

Typically, in open injuries contaminated or devascularized bone and soft tissues are excised. This rule, however, does not hold absolutely true when dealing with large segments of articular surface. The risk of infection with retaining the fragments must be weighed against the risk of posttraumatic arthritis and potential need for secondary bone grafting or allograft reconstruction if the fragments are removed. Generally, an attempt should be made to preserve all articular segments with thorough cleansing and meticulous removal of all foreign material and contamination.

McKee et al.[118] reviewed 26 patients who underwent open reduction and internal fixation of open distal humerus fractures. According to the system of Gustilo and Anderson, 50% were grade I, 35% were grade II, and 15% were grade III. At follow-up, 15 patients (57%) had good to excellent outcomes based on the Mayo Elbow Performance score, and the mean DASH score was 24, indicating minimal to moderate disability. The mean elbow arc of flexion-extension motion was 97 degrees (range, 55 to 140 degrees). The overall infection rate was 11% (three patients), with only one patient sustaining a deep infection requiring operative débridement. Four patients (15%) were

diagnosed with delayed union (>16 weeks), with two patients going on to require revision surgery with bone grafting.

AUTHORS' PREFERRED TREATMENT

Open Reduction and Internal Fixation for Distal Humerus Fracture

Preoperative Planning. Anteroposterior and lateral radiographs of the elbow out of plaster are usually sufficient to determine the fracture pattern. If the radiographs are difficult to interpret or poorly demonstrate the articular fracture, I prefer a CT scan, with three-dimensional reconstructions, over traction radiographs requiring patient sedation. A CT scan can identify difficult fracture patterns, such as coronal fractures of the capitellum or trochlea, "low" fracture types, and segmental articular fractures (for example, a fracture between the medial trochlea and the medial epicondyle, producing a free medial trochlear fragment). In elderly patients with comminuted fractures in whom ORIF may not be possible and elbow arthroplasty is considered, a CT scan may assist with the preoperative decision making.

While awaiting surgery, patients are placed in a well-padded elbow splint and are encouraged to elevate the arm, ice the elbow, and maintain hand and finger range of motion. On the day of surgery, the skin and soft tissues are re-examined and the neurologic status is redocumented. Patients generally receive a general anaesthetic with an upper extremity regional block for postoperative pain control and therapy. Preoperatively, prophylactic antibiotics are administered intravenously.

Positioning. The patient is positioned supine with a bolster placed under the ipsilateral scapula and the elbow is supported by another bolster made of wrapped sterile sheet on the patient's chest (Figure 33-23A). The surgeon and assistant stand on the side of the injury while the scrub nurse and instruments are on the contralateral side, allowing the nurse to assist with arm positioning as required. A sterile tourniquet is used and the iliac crest is prepped and draped if bone grafting is anticipated. Portable (mini) fluoroscopy is used for all cases and is positioned on the operative side.

In circumstances in which there is no surgical assistant available, I prefer to position the patient in the lateral decubitus fashion on a bean-bag with a small axillary bolster. The elbow is then flexed over an elbow arthroscopy positioner (Figure 33-23B) and the scrub nurse and instrumentation are positioned on the same side. In the rare circumstance of bilateral fractures, when a second surgical team is available, the patient may be positioned prone with the elbows flexed over a positioner to allow simultaneous surgery.

Approach. An extensile posterior skin incision is used with elevation of full-thickness medial and lateral fasciocutaneous flaps. The ulnar nerve is exposed, tagged, and prepared for anterior subcutaneous transposition, which will be done at the completion of the procedure.

In patients with comminuted intra-articular AO/OTA type C3 fractures, I prefer a chevron-shaped osteotomy through the bare area, which is then fixated with a precontoured olecranon plate (*please see section on Olecranon Osteotomy*). The plate is preapplied to the olecranon before the osteotomy; this facilitates olecranon reduction and plate ap-

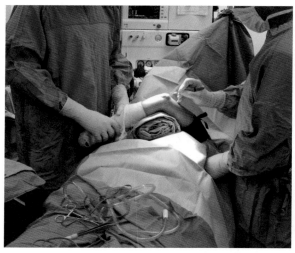
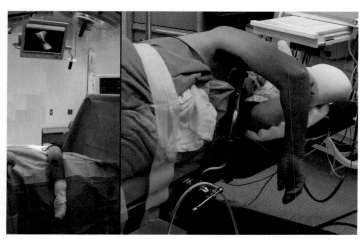

FIGURE 33-23 The patient may be positioned supine with a bolster placed under the ipsilateral scapula **(A)** or lateral decubitus on a bean-bag with the elbow flexed over an arthroscopy positioner **(B)**.

plication at the end of the operative procedure. For simple articular fractures (AO/OTA type C1 and C2) and extra-articular fractures (AO/OTA type A2 and A3), I prefer the paratricipital approach (Figure 33-11).[7] This approach allows bicolumn exposure and plating with preservation of the triceps mechanism. Simple intraarticular fractures can be reduced indirectly by anatomic reduction of the supracondylar level fracture. The articular reduction can be assessed with elbow flexion and direct visualization of the posterior aspect of the trochlea or fluoroscopy. The articular reduction may also be visualized directly by creation of a third surgical window in the Boyd interval, between the anconeus muscle and lateral olecranon.[13]

The paratricipital approach is also preferred for cases in which the reparability of the fracture will be determined intraoperatively. If the fracture is deemed fixable, it may be carried out through the paratricipital approach or the approach can be converted to an olecranon osteotomy. In cases in which the fracture is deemed irreparable, a total elbow arthroplasty may be done via the same approach.

Technique. Surgeons should be familiar with all plating techniques, including parallel, orthogonal, and triple plating, as some fractures will lend themselves to one technique over another. Generally, I prefer the technique of parallel plating; however, it does have its disadvantages. Thin and active patients may complain of hardware irritation from a prominent lateral plate. Therefore, in cases with a "high" lateral supracondylar level fracture, a posterolateral plate may be preferable (Figure 33-21).

After appropriate exposure, the joint and fracture fragments are irrigated and débrided of hematoma and fibrous tissue. The articular reduction proceeds first (Figure 33-24A–D). I prefer the use of K-wires, to function as joysticks, for manipulation of the fracture fragments. Typically, I place one K-wire through the fractured surface of the medial trochlea, aiming toward the medial epicondyle, running along the trochlear axis. This K-wire is then pulled out through the medial epicondyle until its tip lies flush and perpendicular to the fracture surface of the medial trochlea. A similar

K-wire is placed through the lateral articular fragment. These wires are then used to individually manipulate the fracture fragments, to reduce and interdigitate them. A large reduction tenaculum is used to hold the reduction and to provide compression until the medial K-wire can be drilled into the lateral fragment and the lateral K-wire drilled into the medial fragment. This provides provisional fixation of the articular segment. Next, I typically place a single fully threaded standard screw (2.7, 3.0, or 3.5 mm) along the axis of the articular segment to maintain the reduction (Figure 33-24E). This screw is usually inserted medial to lateral with its starting point located in the center of the medial trochlea. A small diameter axis screw is used to minimize its effect on other screws that will eventually be used to fixate the articular segment through plates to the diaphysis. When using small-diameter screws, my preference is not to use titanium as the resistance encountered during screw insertion in good quality bone has been known to shear off the screw heads.

If articular shear fractures or comminution exists, they are addressed before screw fixation of the large medial and lateral articular segments. These small articular fractures may be located anteriorly and can be exposed by internally rotating the appropriate column fragment. My preference is to fixate these small articular fragments with countersunk small-diameter screws (1.0-, 1.3-, 1.5-, or 2.0-mm) or with any small-diameter headless compression screw.

After the articular segment is reconstructed, longitudinal K-wires are used to temporarily fix it to the shaft (Figure 33-24F). Precountoured plates are then provisionally applied to the medial and lateral columns with K-wires placed distally and serrated bone reduction clamps proximally. Then, as many screws as possible are inserted through the plates into the articular segment (Figure 33-24G), ideally the screws should be as long as possible and engage as many articular fragments as possible. Screws should not be placed through the olecranon fossa as they may lead to impingement. The plates are then fixated to the humeral shaft with the first diaphyseal screws inserted in an eccentric fashion to provide supracondylar fracture compression.[136] Ideally, the plates

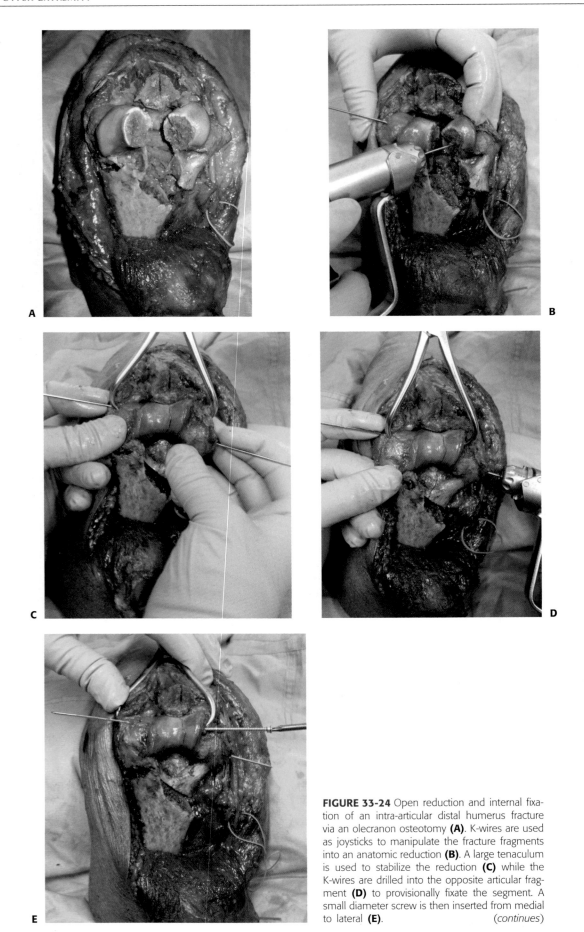

FIGURE 33-24 Open reduction and internal fixation of an intra-articular distal humerus fracture via an olecranon osteotomy **(A)**. K-wires are used as joysticks to manipulate the fracture fragments into an anatomic reduction **(B)**. A large tenaculum is used to stabilize the reduction **(C)** while the K-wires are drilled into the opposite articular fragment **(D)** to provisionally fixate the segment. A small diameter screw is then inserted from medial to lateral **(E)**. (*continues*)

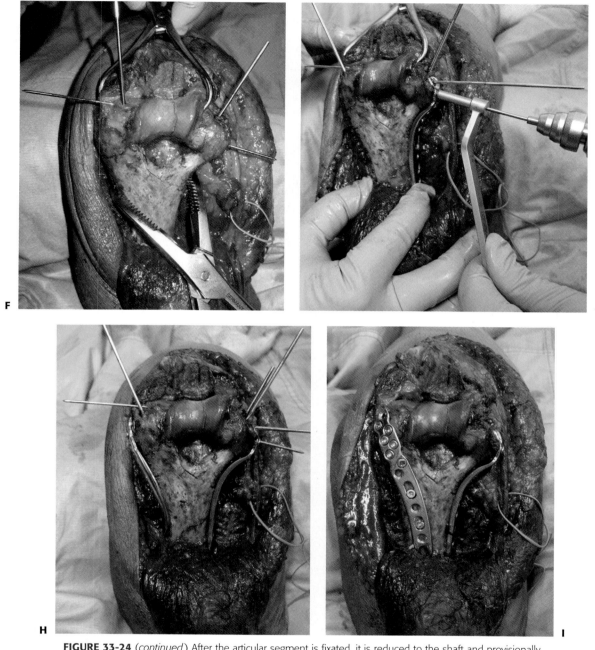

FIGURE 33-24 (*continued*) After the articular segment is fixated, it is reduced to the shaft and provisionally stabilized with long bicortical K-wires inserted up each column **(F)**. Definitive articular segment to shaft fixation is obtained with bicolumn plating in a parallel or orthogonal fashion **(G–I)**. Ideally, as many screws as possible are inserted through the plates into the articular segment, the screws should be as long as possible and they should engage as many articular fragments as possible. Screws should not be placed through the olecranon fossa as they may lead to impingement and decreased range of motion.

should end at different levels on the humeral shaft to minimize the stress riser effect (Figure 33-24H,I). Once ORIF of the distal humerus fracture is complete, the elbow is placed through a range of motion to ensure there is no impingement or instability.

Postoperative Care. Patients are placed in a well-padded plaster extension splint applied anteriorly and are encouraged to keep the arm elevated to minimize swelling. Active hand range of motion is started immediately. Elbow range of motion is started between days 2 and 7 postoperatively, depending on the status of the incision. Generally, active-assisted and active range of motion are encouraged (flexion, extension, pronation, and supination) for patients with a paratricipital approach or an olecranon osteotomy fixated with a plate. Passive extension is reserved for patients that underwent an extensor mechanism disrupting approach. Typically, a night extension splint is used for the first 6 weeks. At 6 weeks postoperative, passive stretching and

---

TABLE 33-5	Pearls and Pitfalls in the Management of Distal Humerus Fractures	
	Pearls	**Pitfalls**
Preoperative Evaluation	Recheck skin, soft tissues, and neurovascular status immediately before surgery	Missed skin tenting, excessive swelling, fracture blisters
	CT scan for complex fracture patterns (preferred) or traction radiographs	Unrecognized coronal shear fractures and articular comminution (fracture line between medial trochlea and medial epicondyle)
	If excessive comminution or bone loss, be prepare for bone grafting by adding it to the consent form and prep and draping iliac crest	Failure to recognize bone loss in open fractures
	In elderly patients with high comminution, be prepared for elbow arthroplasty by adding it to the consent form and having instrumentation available and industry representative (if required)	
	Intraoperative fluoroscopy available	
	Available headless compression screws, minifragment system or small diameter cannulated screws for articular comminution	
Exposure	Critically examine fracture pattern and chose an approach that balances required visualization for ORIF versus complications	Choosing an olecranon osteotomy in elderly patients who may require total elbow arthroplasty
	Recommend ulnar nerve transposition	
Surgery	Fix coronal shear fractures first with strategically placed hardware	Use of thin or narrow plates (i.e., one-third tubular)
	Use K-wires liberally for provisional fixation	Use of small diameter titanium screws in young dense bone: increased risk of screws head fracture on insertion and removal
	ORIF should progress from articular segment to columns	Radial nerve injury with placement of a long lateral plate
	Be prepare for triple plating in high comminuted columnar fractures	Inadequate fixation of "low" transcolumn fractures
	Place as many screws as possible into the distal articular segment	Screws placed across the olecranon fossa causing impingement
	Use fluoroscopy to ensure all hardware is extra-articular and of appropriate length	
	Once fracture stabilized, check elbow stability and range of motion to ensure no restriction	
Postoperative	Splint elbow in extension with anterior plaster to protect posterior incision and skin flaps	Active elbow extension is started too early in patients with triceps disrupting approaches
	Start early range of motion	

---

static progressive splinting are used if required. Strengthening may begin at 12 weeks providing there is evidence of radiographic union (Table 33-5).

Operative Treatment: Total Elbow Arthroplasty

Indications

Intra-articular distal humerus fractures are among the most challenging fractures to manage. Nonoperative treatment, although appropriate for some elderly patients, often leads to loss of motion and unsatisfactory functional outcomes. Open reduction and rigid internal fixation is considered gold standard; however, it may not be attainable in elderly patients with osteopenia, comminution, and articular fragmentation or in patients with pre-existing conditions of the elbow such as rheuma-

toid arthritis (Figure 33-25). In cases in which rigid internal fixation cannot be achieved to allow early range of motion, resultant prolonged immobilization often leads to poor outcomes.[4] Total elbow arthroplasty for such factures is a reliable treatment option with good outcomes*

Absolute contraindications to total elbow arthroplasty for distal humerus fractures include active infection and insufficient soft tissue coverage. The most important relative contraindication to elbow replacement for trauma is the younger active patient who is more appropriate for open reduction and internal fixation. Elderly patients with low-energy Gustilo and Anderson grade I open fractures are not an absolute contraindication to elbow arthroplasty. Generally, the wounds are punctures that

*References 10,48,51,64,87–89,102,126,133,157.

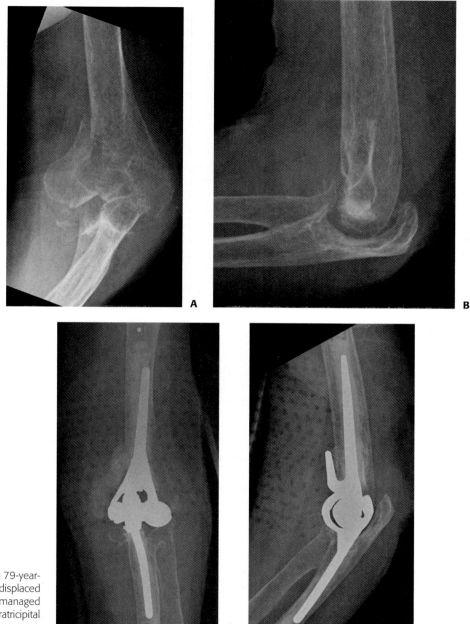

FIGURE 33-25 AP and lateral radiographs of a 79-year-old woman with rheumatoid arthritis and a displaced intra-articular medial column fracture **(A,B)** managed with a linked total elbow arthroplasty via a paratricipital approach **(C,D)**.

are small and clean. However, if there has been a time delay until open fracture management or the cleanliness of a wound is questioned, a staged procedure with initial irrigation and débridement followed by splinting and antibiotics until definitive surgery is deemed appropriate.

Technique

Total elbow arthroplasty is a technically demanding procedure and should be done by an experienced upper limb or trauma surgeon. Radiographs should be templated preoperatively to ensure implants of the appropriate size and lengths are available. The surgical approach starts with an extensile posterior skin incision and the elevation of medial and lateral fasciocutaneous flaps. The ulnar nerve requires identification and protection

during the surgical procedure as it is vulnerable to direct injury or indirect traction injury. Presently, the literature is unclear whether the ulnar nerve should be anteriorly transposed or returned to the cubital tunnel at the completion of the procedure.

In general, posterior approaches are preferred in the exposure of distal humerus fractures in preparation for elbow arthroplasty. Although all posterior approaches may be used for arthroplasty, some have advantages over others. The paratricipital approach has the advantage of maintaining complete integrity of the extensor mechanisms, whereas its disadvantage is that it increases the complexity of the procedure because it provides less visualization of the elbow joint. The triceps splitting, triceps reflecting, and triceps dividing approaches all provide good visualization of the elbow joint; however, they all disrupt the triceps insertion in one way or another and therefore require postoperative protection. Conducting a total elbow arthroplasty through an olecranon osteotomy is possible, however, not recommended. Ulnar component fixation may be compromised with certain implant designs. There are also concerns with osteotomy healing after disruption of the intramedullary blood supply by ulnar component cementation.

Generally, a linked design of total elbow arthroplasty should be used in the setting of distal humerus fracture. Unlinked designs may be used; however, great care must be taken in anatomically reducing and rigidly fixing the medial and lateral columns. Anatomic fixation of the columns allows appropriate tensioning of the medial and lateral collateral ligaments that are required for unlinked implant stability.

The key steps for insertion of a linked elbow arthroplasty are discussed via a paratricipital approach. McKee et al.[119] have shown that condylar resection during total elbow arthroplasty does not affect strength or functional outcome; therefore, through the medial arthrotomy while protecting the ulnar nerve, the medial collateral ligament is released and the medial fracture fragments are excised. Similarly, through the lateral arthrotomy the lateral collateral ligament complex is released and the lateral fracture fragments are excised. The distal humeral shaft with the remaining metaphyseal bone can now be delivered from under the triceps and ulna. The humerus is then prepared following the technical manual of the implant being used. Usually, the metaphyseal cutting blocks are not required as the fractured condyles have already been excised. The keys to judging correct humeral component rotation are to examine the trefoil shape of the distal humerus shaft, as the posterior cortex is parallel to the axis of elbow joint rotation, and to examine the insertions of the medial and lateral intermuscular septa, which are also parallel to the axis. Reaming and broaching of the humeral canal are done as described in the technical manual and the canal is sized for a cement restrictor. The length of the humerus and the level of the joint-line must also be recreated. This is done by placing the resected condyles onto the remaining humeral shaft to measure the location of the joint line. The tension in the soft tissues can also be used to judge appropriate humeral component length, once trial components are in place. Most humeral components are designed with an anterior flange that accepts a bone graft, which can be prepared from resected bone fragments.

Preparation of the ulna with the paratricipital approach requires strategic retractor and arm positioning. The proximal ulna is delivered medial to the humeral shaft to avoid excessive tension on the ulnar nerve. The forearm is then rotated 90 degrees, the elbow is flexed, and a rake retractor is used to draw back the triceps insertion to allow exposure of the greater sigmoid notch. The ulna is prepared as per the manufacturer's recommendations. As with the humerus, particular attention should be taken to ensure correct ulnar component placement. The correct rotation of the ulnar component can be determined by ensuring that the axis of rotation bisects the radial head and that the axis is parallel to the flat surface on the proximal dorsal ulna.[38]

It is recommend that antibiotic-laden bone cement be used and cement restrictors for the humeral and ulnar canals.[46] A cement gun with a small diameter injector nozzle is used to ensure complete filling of the intramedullary canal. The humeral and ulnar components can be cemented together at the same time or separately.

Results

The outcomes of total elbow arthroplasty for distal humerus fractures at short-term and mid-term follow-up have been reproducibly good (Table 33-6).* Most studies have used the Coonrad-Morrey implant (Zimmer, Warsaw, IN), which is

---

*References 10,48,51,64,87–89,102,126,133,157.

TABLE 33-6 **Summary of Outcomes of Total Elbow Arthroplasty for the Management of Distal Humerus Fractures[171]**

Author	Year	N	Average Age of Patients (range)	Surgical Approach	Average Follow-Up in Months	Range of Motion (arc)	Outcome Assessment Used	Percentage with Excellent or Good Outcomes	Complications
Gambirasio[50]	2001	10	85 (57–95)	Bryan-Morrey	18	101	MEPS	100%	1 HO, 1 CRPS
Garcia[51]	2002	16	73 (61–95)	Triceps Split	36	101	MEPS, DASH	100%	1 UN, 1 HO
Frankle[48]	2003	12	72 (65–88)	Bryan-Morrey	45	113	MEPS	100%	2 UN, 1 UP, 1 H, 1 DS
Kamineni[88]	2004	43	69 (34–92)	Bryan-Morrey	84	107	MEPS	93%	7 HO, 4 BW, 3 UIF, 1 HIF, 5 H, 1 DS
Lee[102]	2006	7	73 (55–85)	Bryan-Morrey	25	89	MEPS	100%	—
Kalogrianitis[87]	2008	9	73 (45–86)	Triceps Split	42	118	MEPS, LES	88%	1 SS
Prasad[157]	2008	15	78 (61–89)	Triceps Tongue	56	93	MEPS	85%	1 CRPS, 1 AS-U
Total/Mean		112	75		44	103		95%	

AS-U, Aseptic Loosening Ulna; BW, bushing wear; CRPS, complex regional pain syndrome; DS, deep infection; H, wound hematoma or dehiscence; HIF, humeral implant fracture; HO, heterotopic ossification; LES, Liverpool Elbow Score; MEPS, Mayo Elbow Performance Score; SS, superficial infection; UIF, ulnar implant fracture; UN, ulnar nerve palsy; UP: uncoupled prosthesis.

linked and described as semiconstrained because of its "sloppy" hinge.

In a retrospective study, Frankle et al. compared open reduction and internal fixation with elbow arthroplasty in 24 women over the age of 65 years with AO/OTA type C distal humerus fractures. They reported improved outcomes in the arthroplasty group at short-term follow-up. The small sample size and selection bias, however, confounds the interpretation of the results, as 8 of 12 patients in the arthroplasty group had rheumatoid arthritis (RA) and none had RA in the ORIF group. McKee and colleagues[113] presented preliminary data from a randomized prospective study comparing open reduction and internal fixation to elbow arthroplasty in elderly patients with comminuted distal humerus fractures. Outcomes were assessed with the Mayo Elbow Performance Score (MEPS) and Disabilities of the Arm, Shoulder, and Hand (DASH) score. Twenty-one patients were initially randomized into the two treatment groups; however, five patients randomized to ORIF were intraoperatively converted to arthroplasty. At 2 years follow-up, the MEPS was significantly better in the total elbow arthroplasty group; however, the DASH score was not significantly different between groups. The reoperation rate between the arthroplasty and the open reduction and internal fixation groups was also not significantly different.

At the present time, there are no midterm or long-term studies comparing the outcomes and complications of open reduction and internal fixation with total elbow arthroplasty for the treatment of complex distal humerus fractures in elderly persons. It is probable that the revision surgery rate would increase over time in patients treated with elbow arthroplasty, when compared with patients undergoing ORIF because of polyethylene wear, aseptic loosening, periprosthetic fracture, and infection.

AUTHORS' PREFERRED TREATMENT
Total Elbow Arthroplasty for Distal Humerus Fractures

Preoperative Planning. As with open reduction and internal fixation, anteroposterior and lateral radiographs of the elbow out of plaster are usually sufficient to determine the fracture pattern. If the feasibility of ORIF is questioned in an elderly patient, a CT scan may assist with preoperative decision making.

Preoperatively, elbow radiographs should be templated to ensure implants of the appropriate size and lengths are available. While awaiting surgery, patients are placed in a well-padded elbow splint and are encouraged to elevate the arm, ice the elbow, and maintain hand and finger range of motion. On the day of surgery, the skin and soft tissues are re-examined and the neurologic status is redocumented. Patients generally receive a general anaesthetic with an upper extremity regional block for postoperative pain control and therapy. Before starting the operative procedure and inflating the tourniquet, prophylactic antibiotics are administered intravenously.

Positioning. The patient is positioned supine with a bolster placed under the ipsilateral scapula and the elbow is supported by another bolster made of a wrapped sterile sheet on the patient's chest (Figure 33-23A). The surgeon and assistant stand on the side of the injury while the scrub nurse and arthroplasty instruments are on the contralateral side, allowing the nurse to assist with arm positioning as required. A sterile tourniquet is used.

Approach. My preferred approach for fractures deemed unreparable preoperatively, in which the surgical plan is to proceed directly to TEA is the paratricipital approach. This is also my preferred approach if an attempt at ORIF is planned for less comminuted articular fractures. In circumstances with high articular comminution in the elderly, in which a complete attempt at ORIF is planned, with the intraoperative bail-out being a TEA, I prefer the triceps split. The triceps split approach affords the best visualization of the joint for a complete attempt at ORIF, and still leaves the option open for a TEA if rigid internal fixation cannot be achieved.

Technique. I prefer the use of a linked total elbow arthroplasty for trauma and posttraumatic conditions. The ulnar nerve is identified, released, and prepared for anterior subcutaneous transposition. The medial and lateral fracture fragments, including the epicondyles, are excised and the distal end of the humeral shaft is delivered out from under the ulna and triceps. The humerus is prepared first with the appropriate rasps and broaches. Correct humeral component rotation is obtained by ensuring the axis of rotation of the component is parallel to the posterior cortex of the humeral shaft and parallel to the insertions of the medial and lateral intermuscular septa. The correct length of the humeral component is ensured by replacing the resected medial column fracture fragment on to the distal humerus. The location of the central axis of the humeral component should be at the approximate level of the distal aspect of the medial epicondyle.

Preparation of the ulna requires strategic retractor and arm positioning. The ulna is delivered medial to the distal humeral shaft to limit tension on the ulnar nerve. The forearm is then rotated 90 degrees, the elbow is flexed, and a rake retractor is used to retract the triceps insertion to allow exposure of the greater sigmoid notch. The ulna is prepared using rasps and broaches as per the implant's technical manual. The tip of the olecranon may be excised to improve visualization of the greater sigmoid notch. Correct rotation of the ulnar component is obtained by ensuring the center axis of the component bisects the radial head and is parallel to the flat spot of the dorsal ulna. A test reduction is done with the trial implants and the elbow is taken through a range of motion to ensure there is no impingement.

I prefer the use of antibiotic laden bone cement and cement restrictors in the humerus and ulna. Cement is inserted into the humerus first with a small-diameter nozzle and then into the ulna. The ulnar cement is manually pressurized and the component is inserted, followed by pressurization of the humerus and humeral component insertion. Excess bone cement is removed and the components are held still until the cement has cured. Elbow implants can also be cemented separately. Once cured, a wedge of bone graft fashioned from the resected articular segment is placed underneath the anterior flange of the humeral component. The components are then linked and the elbow is taken through a range of motion to ensure there is no impingement.

Postoperative Care. After the surgical procedure, the elbow is splinted in extension with an anteriorly applied slab of plaster. The arm is elevated for 24 hours and active hand range of motion is started immediately. Elbow range of motion is started between days 2 and 7 postoperatively, depending on the status of the soft tissues. Generally, unrestricted active range of motion is encouraged (flexion, extension, pronation, and supination) for patients with a paratricipital approach, while patients with a triceps split approach are restricted to gravity-assisted extension for 6 weeks to protect the triceps repair.

Operative Treatment: Hemiarthroplasty

Hemiarthroplasty is another surgical option for unreconstructable distal humerus fractures. This procedure has been described in the past,[123,182,191] and has recently experienced a renewed interest.[3,73,192] Two commercially available elbow arthroplasty systems have humerus implants that replicate the distal humeral articular surface, the Sorbie-Questor (Wright Medical Technology, Arlington, TN) and the Latitude (Tornier, Stafford, TX), and therefore can be used for hemiarthroplasty (Figure 33-26). The added benefit of the Latitude hemiarthroplasty is that it can be converted to a linked or unlinked total elbow arthroplasty. This is beneficial if intraoperative hemiarthroplasty stability cannot be achieved necessitating conversion to total elbow arthroplasty. Other systems that have nonanatomic humeral components, such as the Kudo (Biomet, Inc., Warsaw, IN),[3] have also been used for hemiarthroplasty. The use of nonanatomic components, however, is not recommended.

Indications

The indications for distal humerus hemiarthroplasty are virtually identical to total elbow arthroplasty. The theoretical ad-

vantage of a hemiarthroplasty is the absence of polyethylene wear debris and the associated osteolysis and aseptic loosening, which are common modes of failure with total elbow arthroplasties. Hemiarthroplasty, therefore, may function as an "in between" in those patients with unreconstructable distal humerus fractures who are deemed too young or too active for total elbow arthroplasty. It should be noted, however, that the believed benefits of hemiarthroplasty are completely speculative and no literature exists to support its use over total elbow arthroplasty.

Hemiarthroplasty of the distal humerus resurfaces the articular segments of the trochlea and capitellum. For it to function optimally to allow elbow stability and range of motion, it relies on the integrity of the primary and secondary elbow stabilizers.[73,135] Therefore, when considering hemiarthroplasty, the medial and lateral columns must be reconstructable (Figure 33-27), the radial head and coronoid must be intact, and the medial and lateral collateral ligaments must be repairable or intact on their respective condyles.[13,73]

The contraindications to distal humerus hemiarthroplasty are similar to those for total elbow arthroplasty. Additional contraindications include deficient medial or lateral column bone, deficient medial or lateral collateral ligaments, or fractures of the radial head or coronoid that cannot be rigidly stabilized. Chondral damage to the greater sigmoid notch or radial head are also relative contraindications, as patients may experience postoperative arthritic pain and limited motion. In these circumstances with deficient bone or soft tissue, linked total elbow arthroplasty should be considered.

Technique

As with total elbow arthroplasty, hemiarthroplasty is a technically demanding procedure and should only be conducted by surgeons experience in upper limb arthroplasty or complex trauma. Standard elbow radiographs are usually sufficient for assessing the fracture pattern and implant templating. Computed tomography (CT) will confirm the articular fragmentation, will identify occult fractures (such as fractures of the coronoid and radial head) and may assist with open reduction and internal fixation of the columns. Patients can be positioned su-

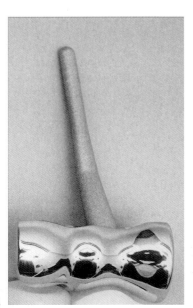

A

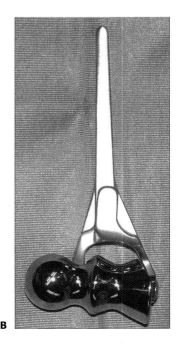

B

FIGURE 33-26 The Sorbie-Questor (Wright Medical Technology, Arlington, TN) **(A)** and the Latitude (Tornier, Stafford, TX) total elbow system **(B)** are two commercially available arthroplasty systems that have humeral implants that replicate the distal humeral articular anatomy, and therefore can be used for hemiarthroplasty.

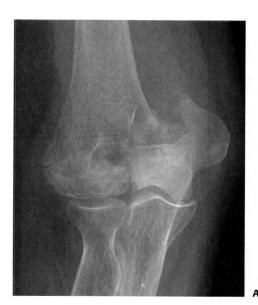
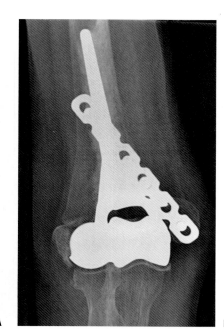

FIGURE 33-27 Distal humerus hemiarthroplasty with plate fixation of the medial column and suture fixation of the lateral epicondyle.

A   **B**

pine or in the lateral decubitus fashion. A sterile tourniquet is used and the approach starts with a longitudinal posterior skin incision. The ulnar nerve is identified, released, and prepared for anterior subcutaneous transposition. The options available for exposure of the elbow for hemiarthroplasty include: olecranon osteotomy, paratricipital approach, triceps split, triceps reflection, and triceps dividing approaches (please see section on surgical approaches). The most commonly used approaches for hemiarthroplasty are the olecranon osteotomy and the paratricipital approach. The olecranon osteotomy allows the best visualization of the joint, however, has a higher rate of complications if intraoperative conversion to a total elbow arthroplasty is required. The paratricipital approach maintains integrity of the extensor mechanism, however, affords less visualization of the articular surfaces. For hemiarthroplasty, the paratricipital approach can be modified by maintaining the collateral ligament attachments on the epicondyles and working through the fracture interval.

Once the facture is visualized, it should be carefully inspected to ensure open reduction and internal fixation is not possible. If hemiarthroplasty is deemed appropriate, sizing of the implant should be done next. The determination of correct humeral component size can be done three ways, preoperatively templating of contralateral elbow radiographs, piecing together the fractured trochlea and capitellum and comparing with the available trial implants, and placing trial implants into the greater sigmoid notch to select which one best aligns with the coronoid and radial head. The humeral canal is then entered by resecting the superior aspect of the olecranon fossa. The canal is reamed and broached to accept the chosen trial implant. The trial implant must be inserted to the correct depth to recreate the joint line. Local landmarks, such as the collateral ligament origins and condyles, are used to gauge correct implant length. Provisional fixation of one or both of the fractured columns with Kirschner wires may also assist with determination of the correct implant length. Conservative bone cuts are then made using the available cutting blocks. If use of the cutting blocks is not feasible, conservative free-hand cuts are made and

revised as necessary. The trial implant is then inserted into the humerus and the elbow is reduced and taken through a range of motion to ensure there is no restriction or impingement.

Once the appropriate orientation, length, and size of trial implant have been determined, the next step involves cementation of the true prosthesis and definitive fixation of the columnar fractures. This step can be done in one of several different orders: (i) the fractured columns can be definitively fixated in anatomic position with contoured plates/screws, or with K-wires/tension bands augmented with sutures (Figure 33-28) and then the implant cemented; (ii) the implant can be cemented first in anatomic position followed by columnar fracture fixation; (iii) the less comminuted column is definitively fixated first to allow easier fracture reduction and to assist with correct implant orientation and length. The implant is inserted and once the cement has hardened, the other column undergoes ORIF to the humeral shaft and stable implant. When conducting this procedure through an olecranon osteotomy, all the preceding methods are feasible; however, if using a paratricipital approach only the latter two are possible.

Before definitive implant insertion, a humeral cement restrictor is inserted and the canal is lavaged and dried. Antibiotic cement is inserted via a thin-nozzled pressurization gun. All excess cement is removed, especially around the medial and lateral column fracture surfaces. Once the implant has been cemented and columnar ORIF is complete, the elbow is placed through a range of motion and stability is checked. Postoperatively, the elbow is splinted for 2 to 3 days and then early active assisted range of motion is initiated.

Results

There is little information in the literature pertaining to the outcomes of distal humerus hemiarthroplasty for trauma.[3, 73,150,182] Adolfsson and Hammer reported on four cases using the non-anatomic Kudo (Biomet, Inc., Warsaw, IN) humeral prosthesis.[3] At a mean of 10 months follow-up (range, 3 to 14 months), the Mayo Elbow Performance Scores were excellent in three patients and good in one. The mean arc of elbow motion was 106 degrees and all patients described having no pain.

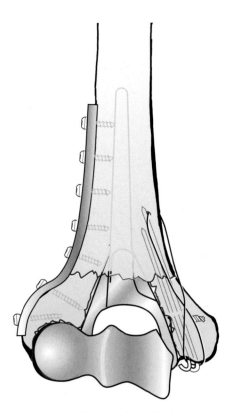

FIGURE 33-28 Medial and lateral column fixation in hemiarthroplasty for distal humerus fractures may be accomplished by plates and screws, sutures, and tension band constructs.

Parsons et al.[150] also reported on four patients undergoing hemiarthroplasty for acute fractures using the anatomic Sorbie-Questor implant (Wright Medical Technology, Arlington, TN). At early follow-up, they reported a mean ASES score of 83.5 and a mean elbow flexion of 130 degrees and extension of 16 degrees. Unfortunately, these two short-term follow-up studies are all that is available in the literature; therefore, further studies are required to determine if distal humeral hemiarthroplasty for acute trauma is feasible in the long-term.

COMPLICATIONS

Nonunion

Nonunions occur in approximately 6% (range, 0% to 25%) of distal humerus factures treated by modern doubling plating techniques.* Nonunions typically occur at the supracondylar level, are rarely intra-articular and are usually related to inadequate fixation.[5,66,112,148,163,183,184] Other risk factors for nonunion include "low" fracture types with limited distal bone for screw purchase, extensive comminution, and severe osteopenia. Patients typically present with pain, stiffness, and functional limitation. If there is associated failure of fixation, the patient may also present with abnormal motion owing to a mobile nonunion.

In patients presenting with nonunion after ORIF of distal humerus fractures, it is important to establish the cause of the nonunion. All patients should undergo infection screening blood work (complete blood count with differential, erythrocyte sedimentation rate, and C-reactive protein levels). Injury and postoperative radiographs should be examined critically to determine the initial facture pattern and the adequacy of initial ORIF. Examining postoperative radiographs in a serial fashion may reveal the cause of failure.

Treatment options for distal humerus nonunions include splinting, revision open reduction, and internal fixation and elbow arthroplasty. Splinting with externally applied bone stimulators, such as ultrasound, may be effective if fixation failure has not occurred. If surgical treatment is deemed necessary, a CT scan may be beneficial in examining the quality and quantity of the remaining distal humerus bone.

Revision open reduction and internal fixation should be the procedure of choice in healthy active patients. Revision procedures are technically demanding because of the altered anatomy, presence of failed hardware, excessive scarring, and generally poor bone quality. Because of these issues, an olecranon osteotomy is the preferred approach to allow the best access to the joint.[5,66,112,163] The goals of surgery are to obtain an anatomic articular reduction, rigid bicolumn fixation, and stimulate bone healing with autologous bone graft. Additional procedures that are usually required with revision ORIF of distal humerus fractures are anterior and posterior capsulectomy to address elbow stiffness and ulnar nerve neurolysis and transposition.[66,112,163] The outcomes of revision ORIF are generally satisfactory,[5,66,112,163] with bony union occurring in greater than 90% of patients.

In some nonunions, revision ORIF is not feasible, whether it is due to extensive bone loss or posttraumatic arthrosis. In these cases, total elbow arthroplasty is a reliable treatment option.[115,125,130] Patients that have a healed prior olecranon osteotomy can be approached via a paratricipital approach, Bryan-Morrey (triceps reflecting) approach, or by a triceps split. Patients with a nonunion of an olecranon osteotomy are approached through the osteotomy site. After elbow arthroplasty, the olecranon is fixated with a K-wire/tension band construct, plate/screws, or excision of the fragment and triceps advancement.[109] Other treatment options for distal humerus nonunions include arthrodesis,[159] resection arthroplasty, allograft distal humerus replacement,[2,31,197,198] vascularized bone grafting,[17] and Ilizarov methods.[21]

Stiffness and Heterotopic Ossification

Patients typically achieve functional range of motion after open reduction and internal fixation of distal humerus fractures. Risk factors for elbow stiffness and heterotopic ossification (HO) are head injury, polytrauma, severe soft tissue injury, delay to surgical intervention, prolonged postoperative immobilization, and open fractures.**

The reported incidence of HO after surgical treatment of distal humerus fractures varies from 0% to 49%.*** The majority of patients with HO do not experience any significant functional deficits; therefore, resection is not always necessary. Heterotopic ossification about the elbow can be classified by the system of Hastings and Graham (Table 33-7).[63] The incidence of elbow stiffness and contracture is difficult to determine as

---

*References 6,12,41,48,55,58,60,72,97,118,120,144,145,171,174, 185,196.

**References 52,76,86,111,149,164,165,174.
***References 6,12,41,58,60,144,174,185.

| TABLE 33-7 | \multicolumn{2}{l|}{**The Hastings Classification of Heterotopic Ossification**} |

Class	Subtype	Description
I		Radiographic heterotopic ossification without functional limitation
II	A	Limitation of flexion/extension
	B	Limitation of forearm pronation/ supination
	C	Limitation in both planes
III		Bony ankylosis of either the elbow or forearm

most all patients who undergo ORIF have some limitation in motion. The distinction between an elbow contracture and a normal postoperative outcome is dependent on several variables, including patient's expectations, activity level, age, and occupation. Morrey, in an effort to identify the etiology of elbow contractures, has classified them as intrinsic, extrinsic, and combined.[127–129] Intrinsic causes involve the articular surface, whereas extrinsic causes include capsular contracture and HO.

Primary prevention should be used by all surgeons to limit posttraumatic elbow contracture. For patients at high risk of HO, such as those with head injures, postoperative indomethacin, and/or radiation is recommended. For the treatment of elbow contractures, initial management should be nonoperative with physiotherapy, splints, and braces. Static progressive splinting under the direction of a physiotherapist has been reported as an effective method of regaining elbow range of motion.[34]

When splints and braces fail to obtain functional range of motion, the elbow may be treated surgically using either open or arthroscopic techniques. Generally, arthroscopy has a limited role in the treatment of contractures after distal humerus ORIF because of the often extensive internal fixation hardware that requires open removal. Open contracture releases may be done via a medial "over-the-top" exposure, a lateral column procedure or a combined approach.[127–129,194] The preoperative assessment of patients includes identification of prior surgical incisions, examination of the ulnar nerve, and clear localization of the pathology to determine the most appropriate surgical approach. The procedure typically involves ulnar nerve release, capsulectomy, débridement of the olecranon, coronoid and radial fossae, excision of symptomatic HO, and finally removal of internal fixation hardware. Postoperatively, patients are managed with continuous passive motion devices and static progressive splints. The routine use of indomethacin for HO prophylaxis after contracture release remains controversial.

The surgical excision of symptomatic HO should be delayed until its growth has ceased and it has become corticated. Preoperative or early postoperative single-dose radiation treatment has been recommended to decrease HO recurrence; however, there is little literature to support its use. The excision of HO is associated with significantly better gains in range of motion than release of soft-tissue only contractures.[149]

Wound Complications and Infection

Superficial wound infections are relatively common after ORIF of distal humerus fractures. Elbows should be examined to en-

sure there are no deep fluid collections that may indicate infected hematomas or seromas. The management of superficial infections consist of oral antibiotics, dressing changes and close observation.

Deep infections after ORIF of distal humerus fractures have a reported rate between 0% and 10%.* Management consists of surgical débridement and organism-specific intravenous antibiotics. Intraoperatively, fracture fixation is assessed to ensure it is stable. If stable, the patient is managed with serial surgical débridements as required and intravenous antibiotics until healing. If fracture stability is lost, staged revision ORIF is required along with intravenous antibiotics until healing.

Wound necrosis is also a complication that can occur after ORIF of distal humerus fractures. This is managed with surgical débridement to viable tissue. The remaining soft tissue defect is assessed to determine whether primary closure is possible or coverage is required. Coverage options depend on several variables, including size and depth of the defect, exposed hardware or vital structures, patient comorbidities, and potential donor site morbidity.[27,81] Consultation with a plastic or soft tissue reconstructive surgeon is recommended.

Ulnar Neuropathy

The ulnar nerve is the most commonly affected nerve in patients with distal humerus fractures. Injury can occur at the time of fracture, intraoperatively or postoperatively. At the time of fracture, the nerve may be injured by a direct impact or indirectly by traction owing to wide displacement of the fracture fragments. Intraoperatively, injury may occur by traction, manipulation of the nerve, or injury to its blood supply causing ischemia. Postoperatively, neuritis may occur by nerve "kinking" in flexion or extension, exuberant scarring, or irritation against fixation hardware.

Patients with preoperative neuropathy should undergo ulnar nerve exploration during the surgical procedure. The nerve should be decompressed and examined with loop magnification to ensure it is intact. If partially or completely lacerated, the nerve should undergo microsurgical repair. If the nerve is intact, a complete neurolysis should be done. The decision whether or not to transpose the nerve remains controversial.

Ulnar neuropathy that presents postoperatively, in a transposed nerve, can be managed with initial observation. The management of postoperative neuropathy in a nerve left in situ remains controversial. Some recommend observation, whereas others recommend acute decompression with anterior transposition. It is the author's practice to conduct a complete release and anterior subcutaneous transposition in all surgically treated distal humerus fractures.

The outcome of ulnar neuropathy with an intact nerve is good. Patients have a high rate of satisfaction, good return of intrinsic muscle strength, and a return of hand functionality.[117] Although the prognosis is generally good after ulnar neuropathy, patients do not return to completely normal.[16,117]

Olecranon Osteotomy Complications

An olecranon osteotomy affords the best visualization of the articular surface of the distal humerus, and therefore is a valua-

*References 6,12,41,48,55,58,60,72,97,99,118,120,144,145,164, 174,185,196.

ble approach for comminuted articular fractures. An olecranon osteotomy should be conducted in a systematic way to avoid complications, such as inadvertent fracture propagation, incorrect osteotomy location, and malreduction. Complications associated with olecranon osteotomies have been reported to occur in 0% to 31% of cases.*

Nonunion or delayed union of olecranon osteotomies have been reported in up to 10% of cases.** In many cases, the olecranon osteotomy requires more time to heal than the distal humerus fracture,[49] perhaps because of the ulna's unique blood supply.[205] The theorized risk factors for nonunion include use of a tension band technique, a transverse osteotomy, and single screw fixation, although, the literature does not support this. Three recent studies[30,68,162] on the outcomes of olecranon osteotomy looked at a total of 129 patients. All patients underwent an apex distal chevron osteotomy, although the types of fixation varied (plates, single medullary screws, and tension band constructs). There were no nonunions, one delayed union, three patients had early hardware failure require revision ORIF, and 18 patients (14%) had hardware removal specifically for irritation.

The management of olecranon nonunions includes ruling out infective causes and then revision plate ORIF with autologous bone grafting. In some cases when revision ORIF is not feasible because of the small size of the fragment or associated poor bone quality, the fragment may be excised with advancement of the triceps insertion.[109,200] Delayed unions of the olecranon are managed expectantly with consideration given to external bone stimulation devices.

Prominent symptomatic hardware is common after fixation of olecranon osteotomies. Patients may experience local pain, tenderness, or an inability to rest the elbow hard surfaces. These symptoms can be addressed by hardware removal after olecranon healing.

Total Elbow Arthroplasty Complications

Complications of total elbow arthroplasty include infection and wound healing, neuropathies, triceps insufficiency, instability, osteolysis and loosening, mechanical failure, periprosthetic fracture, and stiffness.

The rate of deep infection in total elbow arthroplasty ranges from 2% to 5%. The rate has been noted to be declining over time.*** The rate of infection can be minimized by meticulous surgical technique, use of perioperative antibiotics, sterile tourniquets, and antibiotic-laden cement. The consequences of deep infection can be devastating. The treatment often includes organism-specific intravenous antibiotics and surgical débridements with possible staged reconstruction. Organisms such as *Staphylococcus epidermidis* are particularly difficult to eradicate, and resection arthroplasty may be the consequence.

Ulnar neuropathy is common in traumatic conditions of the elbow. The probability of persistent ulnar neuropathy after total elbow arthroplasty for trauma is high, and is reported to occur in up to 28% of patients, with permanent dysfunction in up to 10%.**** Ulnar nerve exposure, complete neurolysis, and

anterior transposition is recommended, although transposition also has risks such as devascularization. The surgical approach used for elbow arthroplasty is also influential, as the extended Kocher approach has a higher risk of postoperative ulnar nerve palsy.[69,104]

Triceps insufficiency is a common problem after total elbow arthroplasty performed via an extensor mechanism disrupting approach, and is reported in up to 11% of patients.[131,152, 158,160,203] Surgical exposures that use a triceps-on approach such as the paratricipital approach, although more technically challenging, may avoid this complication. When using a triceps-disrupting approach, this complication can be minimized by solid anatomic repair of the triceps insertion and postoperative protection of the repair by avoiding active extension for 6 weeks. Many patients, such as those who use ambulatory aids or self-propelled wheelchairs, require a strong intact triceps mechanism. These patients may be best suited for the paratricipital approach. Patients who develop extensor mechanism insufficiency and rely on active extension may benefit from extensor mechanism revision repair or reconstruction with autograft or allograft.

Instability after total elbow arthroplasty is a problem associated with unlinked designs. These designs rely on correct implant positioning, preserved bony architecture, and intact soft tissue stabilizers. Typically, unlinked designs are not used for distal humerus fracture because of disrupted bony and soft tissue stabilizers; however, they may be used if these structures are anatomically repaired. Newer unlinked designs have several advantages. They have greater contact surface area in the ulno-humeral articulation providing increased constraint; some have the option of a radial head arthroplasty, which provides additional stability and others have the ability to convert to a linked implant. If intraoperative instability exists in an unlinked arthroplasty after repair of the bony structures and soft tissues, then conversion to a linked prosthesis should be performed.

Bearing wear in a total elbow arthroplasty is inevitable. Many implants allow for change of the bearing surface without revision of the components. Accelerated wear rates have been found in younger patients, in patients with posttraumatic conditions, and in cases with persistent postoperative malalignment or deformity.[75,101,108,125] The problem with polyethylene wear is the host reaction that causes osteolysis, which can lead to aseptic loosening and loss of bone stock.

Total elbow arthroplasty implants can also undergo fatigue fracture.[14] Metal fatigue most commonly affects titanium implants because of their notch sensitivity. Implants at risk are those with insufficient bony support of their metaphyseal segments caused by fractured or resected condyles or osteolysis. These at-risk implants experience high cantilever bending forces at the junction of the poorly supported metaphyseal segment and the well-fixed diaphyseal segment.

Periprosthetic fractures can occur intraoperatively and postoperatively. Risk factors for intraoperative fractures include osteopenic bone, excessive diaphyseal bowing with use of long stem implants, overly aggressive reaming, and revision cases. Fixation of condylar fractures when using a linked system is not required; however, shaft fractures require reduction and stabilization with some combination of long stem components with cerclage wires, allograft struts, or plate and screw fixation. Postoperative periprosthetic fractures can occur secondary to trauma or through pathological bone weakened by osteolysis. Periprosthetic fractures with unstable components likely require

---

*References 6,12,13b,30,48,55,60,68,162,185,208.
**References 6,12,13b,30,48,55,68,162,171,185,208.
***References 3,10,29,50,51,59,64,88,102,132,133,155,160,206.
****References 10,14,29,50,64,87,88,157,160,169,187,193.

revision arthroplasty in the medically fit patient. Periprosthetic fractures with stable components may be managed with immobilization or open reduction and internal fixation. Allograft strut grafts are useful adjuncts in these situations, especially in those with bone loss.

FRACTURES OF THE DISTAL HUMERUS AO/OTA TYPE B3

Introduction

Articular fractures of the distal humerus are a distinct group of fractures that involve the capitellum and/or trochlea with variable involvement of other periarticular structures, such as the epicondyles, radial head, medial collateral ligament, or lateral collateral ligament complex. These injuries are distal and do not extend proximal to the olecranon fossa to involve either column. They are typically caused by coronal shear forces, which fracture the anterior articular surfaces of the distal humerus. The capitellum is thought to be particularly susceptible to shear forces because its center of rotation is more anterior in reference to the humeral shaft. The most common mechanism of injury is a simple fall on the outstretched hand from a standing height.

Epidemiology

Isolated fractures of the capitellum are rare,[37,171,202] and isolated fractures of the trochlea are even more rare.[37,47] The reported annual incidence of articular fractures of the distal humerus is 1.5 per 100,000 population, with a marked female predominance.[202] In women, there is a bimodal distribution with peaks under the age of 19 and above 80 years. The increased prevalence of this injury in women over the age of 60 years is believed to be a result of the increase elbow carrying angle in women and osteoporosis.[56,202] In men there is a unimodal distribution with a peak incidence under the age of 19, with the mechanism of injury typically being high energy, such as motor vehicle collisions or falls from heights. Other associated injuries, such as ligament tears and radial head fractures, occur in up to 20% of cases.[37,167,171,201,202]

Principles of Management

A complete history and physical examination should be conducted in all cases as outlined in the beginning of this chapter. Anteroposterior and lateral radiographs of the elbow are usually sufficient to initially diagnose the injury; however, they may not be able to fully characterize complex articular fracture patterns. Computed tomography is strongly recommended if there is any suspicion of articular comminution or involvement of the epicondyles, radial head, posterior capitellum, or trochlea. It is the author's practice to routinely obtain CT scans for all articular fractures of the distal humerus.

Classification

In 1853, Hahn[62] described an isolated capitellar fracture, which now bears his name along with Steinthal's,[189] who described the injury in 1898. The Hahn-Steinthal or conventional type I fracture[24] involves the capitellar articular surface along with the subchondral bone (Figure 33-29). The Kocher[95]-Lorenz[105] or conventional type II fracture,[24] is rare and consists of the capi-

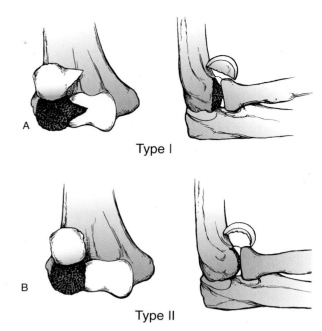

FIGURE 33-29 The Hahn-Steinthal (Type I) fracture of the capitellum involves the articular surface and a large portion of the subchondral bone **(A)**. The Kocher-Lorenz (Type II) fracture involves the articular surface of the capitellum with a thin layer of subchondral bone **(B)**.

tellar articular surface along with a thin shell of subchondral bone. Bryan and Morrey[24] modified this classification and added type III fractures, which are comminuted capitellar fractures. A fourth fracture pattern was added by McKee et al.,[116] which consisted of a type I fracture with medial extension to include the lateral half of the trochlea.

The AO/OTA comprehensive classification of fractures[1,110] classifies articular distal humerus fractures as type B3 (B3, 1) (Figure 33-3). Type B3 fractures are then further subclassified into capitellar, trochlear (B3, 2), and combined fractures (B3, 3).

Ring et al.[167] further examined articular shear fractures of the distal humerus and described them as a spectrum of injury. They observed that apparent isolated capitellar fractures on plain radiographs may turn out to be much more complex injuries when further imaged with CT. The authors identified five unique fracture patterns that progress in complexity (Figure 33-30).

Dubberly et al.[37] recently reported another classification for capitellar and trochlear fractures that was correlated to clinical outcome. The Dubberly et al.[37] classification has three types with a modifier for distal posterolateral column comminution. A type 1 fracture involves primarily the capitellum with or without the lateral trochlear ridge. A type 2 fracture involves the capitellum and most of the trochlea as one piece, whereas in the type 3 fracture the capitellum and trochlea are separate pieces. The authors found that as the complexity of the articular fractures increased, the outcomes worsened.

Current Treatment Options

Nonoperative Treatment

Nonoperative management of articular fracture of the distal humerus in young patients is rarely recommended and it is generally reserved for patients deemed medically unfit to undergo

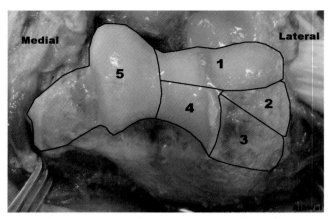

FIGURE 33-30 The Ring et al.[167] classification of distal humerus articular fractures has five patterns. A type 1 fracture involves the capitellum and the lateral portion of the trochlea. This fracture pattern has previously been described as a conventional type IV fracture. A type 2 fracture is described as a type 1 fracture that may be comminuted but includes a fracture of the lateral epicondyle. A type 3 fracture is a type 2 fracture that has comminution behind the capitellum with impaction of bone posteriorly. A type 4 fracture is a type 3 fracture with an additional fracture of the posterior trochlea. A type 5 fracture is a type 4 fracture that includes fracture of the medial epicondyle.

surgery. Nonoperative management techniques include above-elbow casting, and collar and cuff treatment with early mobilization, the so-called "bag of bones" method.

Closed Reduction and Casting

Closed reduction and casting is a described method for the treatment of displaced capitellar fractures.[141] The reduction maneuver involves placing the elbow into full extension and fore-arm supination, which usually results in the capitellum spontaneously reducing. If still displaced, manual pressure over the capitellum and a slight varus force to the elbow may assist with the reduction. If successful, the elbow is flexed so the radial head captures the capitellar fragment and then fluoroscopy is

used to confirm the reduction. The elbow is immobilized in an above-elbow plaster for 3 weeks with weekly radiographs to confirm maintenance of the reduction. If this technique is used, the author recommends postoperative CT imaging to confirm an anatomic reduction.

Open Reduction and Internal Fixation

Anatomic reduction and rigid internal fixation is considered the gold standard for most displaced articular fractures of the distal humerus. Rigid internal fixation allows fracture healing to occur anatomically while permitting early range of motion to maximize function. In cases in which sufficient fracture stability cannot be obtained to allow early motion, anatomic reconstruction of the articular surface and overall elbow alignment take precedence. An anatomically aligned stiff elbow with a healed articular surface can be subsequently managed with contracture release, but a fracture with hardware failure and articular nonunion or fragmentation may be difficult to manage with revision surgery.

Capitellum Fractures ± Lateral Trochlear Ridge (AO/OTA Type B3.1). Fractures of the capitellum with or without involvement of the lateral ridge of the trochlea can be approached through an extensile posterior skin incision or a direct lateral skin incision. The advantages of a posterior longitudinal skin incision are that it allows access both medially and laterally and decreases the risk of cutaneous nerve injury.[36] The deep lateral approach is via the Kocher interval[96] between anconeus and extensor carpi ulnaris. The arthrotomy is made anterior to the lateral ulnar collateral ligament and is extended proximally along the anterior aspect of the lateral supracondylar ridge, which then allows access to the fractured capitellum. The fragment is typically anteriorly displaced and is reduced by elbow extension, forearm supination, and application of a gentle varus force. Once an anatomic reduction is obtained the fragment is provisionally fixated with smooth small-diameter K-wires. Permanent rigid internal fixation is obtained by countersunk screws placed anterior to posterior through the articular surface (Figure 33-31), or by screws placed into the capitellum in a retrograde

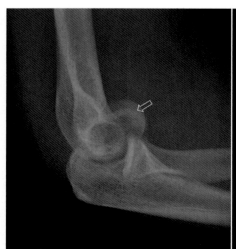
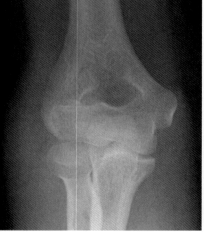
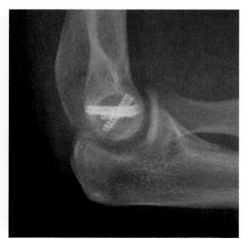

A   **B**

FIGURE 33-31 Fracture of the capitellum and the lateral ridge of the trochlea **(A)**. The double arc sign[116] is evident on the lateral radiograph (*arrow*). One arc represents the subchondral bone of the capitellum and the other arc represents the lateral ridge of the trochlea. This patient underwent open reduction and internal fixation with three headless compression screws inserted anterior to posterior **(B)**.

FIGURE 33-32 Fracture of the capitellum and lateral ridge of troch-lea associated with a radial head fracture **(A,B)**. Through a posterior longitudinal skin incision, the Kocher interval was used to approach the fractures for open reduction and internal fixation **(C,D)**. (C, capitellum; RH, radial head.)

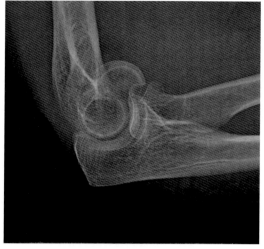

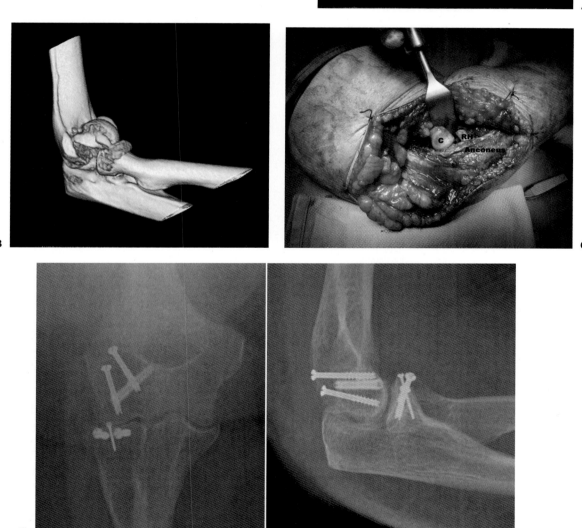

fashion from the posterior aspect of the lateral column or by a combined method (Figure 33-32). The placement of posterior to anterior screws has been shown to be biomechanically more stable and has the added benefit of not violating the articular surface.[42] In cases in which rigid internal fixation is obtained, early active range of motion can be initiated.

When there is comminution or impaction of the posterior aspect of the lateral column (Ring et al.,[167] type 3, and Dubberly et al.[37] type B), it may prevent anatomic reduction of the anterior capitellar fracture. These impaction fractures may require disim-paction and possibly bone grafting to fill the bony defects. In case with severe posterior comminution that may compromise anterior articular fixation, supplemental posterior lateral column plating may be required. Capitellar fractures that involve the lateral epicondyle (Ring et al. type 2) may be exposed by using the lateral epicondylar fracture as an osteotomy, reflecting the epicondylar fragment with the origin of the lateral collateral ligament distally (Figure 33-33). After fixation of the capitellum, the lateral epicondyle fracture may be fixated with screws or a plate, if large enough. If the fragment is too small to fixate, it is treated as a lateral ligament tear with repair through bone tunnels.

Rigid internal fixation of the Kocher[95]-Lorenz[105] or conventional type II osteochondral fractures is difficult, as the frag-ments are thin and may be comminuted. Treatment options for these fractures include attempted fixation with bioabsorbable pins, excision of the fragment, osteochondral grafts, or capitellar arthroplasty.

Isolated trochlear fractures (AO/OTA Type B3.2) are rare and should be treated with open reduction and internal fixation. Fixation may be done antegrade through the cartilage or retro-grade from posterior through a medial deep approach.

Capitellum and Trochlea Fractures (AO/OTA Type B3.3).
Capitellar fractures that involve a large portion of the trochlea

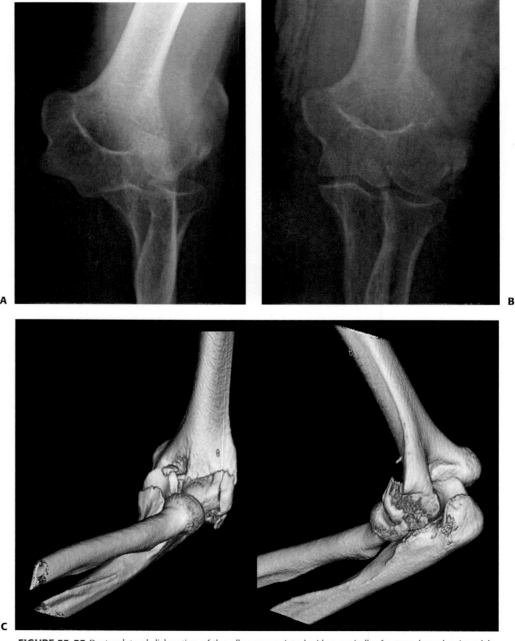

FIGURE 33-33 Posterolateral dislocation of the elbow associated with a capitellar fracture, lateral epicondyle fracture, and comminution and impaction of the posterior aspect of the lateral column **(A–C)**. (*continues*)

FIGURE 33-33 (*continued*) The lateral epicondyle fracture with the lateral collateral ligament (forceps) was reflected distally **(D)**, allowing access to the free capitellar fragment (*inset*). Because of the posterior comminution, a posterolateral plate was required to support the articular segment **(E)**.

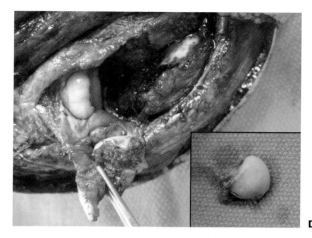

D

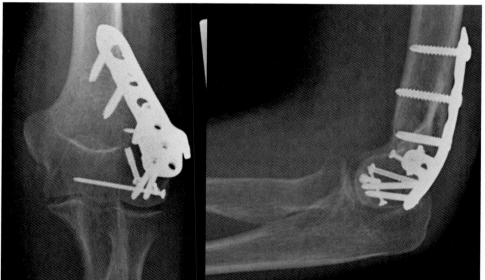

E

also require anatomic reduction and rigid internal fixation. Generally, these fractures require improved exposure of the medial trochlea and several surgical approach options exist. The lateral collateral ligament origin on the lateral epicondyle can be released, to allow the elbow to be hinged open laterally. By releasing the anterior and posterior joint capsules the distal humerus articular surface is booked open on the intact medial collateral ligament. A similar approach uses a lateral epicondylar fracture, which may be reflected distally to hinge open the elbow joint. Medial joint exposure can also be obtained by a separate medial approach, such as the flexor-pronator split or the Hotchkiss medial "over-the-top" approach. Finally, an olecranon osteotomy can be used to obtain optimum distal humerus articular exposure.

Once exposed, these fractures are rigidly secured with small-diameter headless compression or standard countersunk screws inserted antegrade, or with standard screws inserted retrograde. Fractures that are comminuted or have epicondylar involvement may benefit from additional plate application. Bone grafting may also be required for fractures that are comminuted or impacted.

Arthroplasty

In elderly patients with severe articular comminution and osteopenia, or in patients with pre-existing conditions of the elbow such as rheumatoid arthritis, open reduction and internal fixation may not be feasible. In such cases where rigid internal fixation cannot be achieved, elbow arthroplasty is a reliable treatment option. Total elbow arthroplasty can be done through a paratricipital approach using a linked implant. (Please see prior section on TEA insertion technique.) Distal humerus hemiarthroplasty is another surgical option for unreconstructable articular fractures (Figure 33-34). In cases with severe articular destruction with preserved columns and collateral ligaments, hemiarthroplasty presents an attractive option that resurfaces the damaged articulation. The theoretical advantage of a hemiarthroplasty is the absence of polyethylene wear debris and the associated osteolysis; however, it is a technically demanding procedure and no literature exists to support its use over total elbow arthroplasty. Further studies are required to determine the role of distal humerus hemiarthroplasty in elbow trauma.

Results

The outcomes after open reduction and internal fixation of capitellar fractures with or without involvement of the lateral troch-

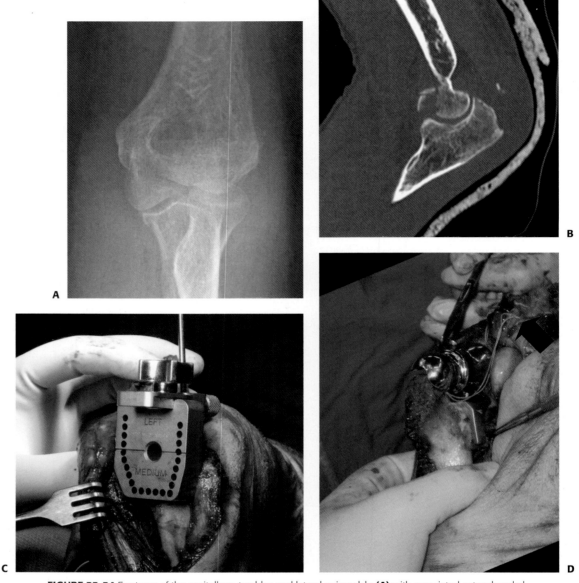

FIGURE 33-34 Fractures of the capitellum, trochlea and lateral epicondyle **(A)** with associated osteochondral fragmentation **(B)** in a 78-year-old active woman. As the fracture was deemed unrepairable intraoperatively, hemiarthroplasty was done via an approach that hinged open the elbow on the intact medial collateral ligament **(C,D)**. *(continues)*

lear ridge have been shown to be predictably good.* More complex fracture patterns with involvement of the anterior trochlea also have a relatively good prognosis;[37,116,167,188] however, Dubberley et al.[37] have shown that the outcomes do deteriorate with increasing fracture complexity.

The most common complication after surgical management of distal humerus articular fractures is elbow stiffness.[37,167] This is initially managed with nonoperative techniques, such as physiotherapy and splints. In refractory cases, open and arthroscopic contracture releases have proved successful. Other complications include nonunion,[166] malunion,[18] ulnar neuritis[167] and avascular necrosis.[37,103]

*References 28,37,45,56,77,107,156,161,167,177.

CONTROVERSIES AND FUTURE DIRECTIONS

Several implant-related advancements have been made over the last few years. The use precontoured and locking plates has become ubiquitous; however, no clinical advantages have been reported. Further study is required to determine if their additional cost leads to improved patient outcomes, especially in today's fiscally responsible health care environment.

Total elbow arthroplasty has certainly demonstrated predictably good outcomes in short to medium term follow-up; however, as with all total joints, the survivorship decreases over time. The role of hemiarthroplasty also requires further investigation to determine if it effectively functions as an intermediate to total joint replacement.

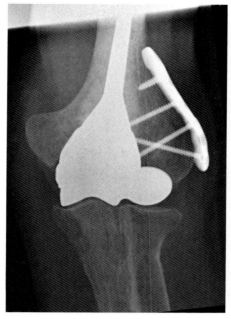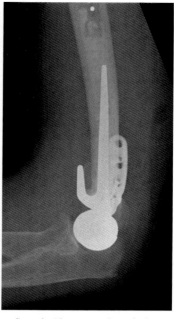

E   **F**

FIGURE 33-34 (*continued*)The lateral epicondyle fracture was fixated with sutures through the axis of the implant (*arrow*) and with a precontoured unicortical plate **(E,F)**.

ACKNOWLEDGMENTS

The author would like to thank Drs. C. Michael Robinson, Graham J.W. King, Kenneth J. Faber, Jennifer M. Wolf, Samir Mehta, and Eric Benson for their assistance with the preparation of this chapter.

REFERENCES

1. Fracture and dislocation compendium. Orthopaedic Trauma Association Committee for Coding and Classification. J Orthop Trauma 1996;10 Suppl 1:v–ix, 1–154.
2. Ackerman G, Jupiter JB. Nonunion of fractures of the distal end of the humerus. J Bone Joint Surg Am 1988;70(1):75–83.
3. Adolfsson L, Hammer R. Elbow hemiarthroplasty for acute reconstruction of intraarticular distal humerus fractures: a preliminary report involving four patients. Acta Orthop 2006;77(5):785–787.
4. Aitken GK, Rorabeck CH. Distal humeral fractures in the adult. Clin Orthop Relat Res 1986 Jun(207):191–197.
5. Ali A, Douglas H, Stanley D. Revision surgery for nonunion after early failure of fixation of fractures of the distal humerus. J Bone Joint Surg Br 2005;87(8):1107–1110.
6. Allende CA, Allende BT, Allende BL, et al. Intercondylar distal humerus fractures—surgical treatment and results. Chir Main 2004;23(2):85–95.
7. Alonso-Llames M. Bilaterotricipital approach to the elbow. Its application in the osteo-synthesis of supracondylar fractures of the humerus in children. Acta Orthop Scand 1972;43(6):479–490.
8. Anglen J. Distal humerus fractures. J Am Acad Orthop Surg 2005;13(5):291–297.
9. Armstrong AD, Dunning CE, Faber KJ, et al. Single-strand ligament reconstruction of the medial collateral ligament restores valgus elbow stability. J Shoulder Elbow Surg 2002;11(1):65–71.
10. Armstrong AD, Yamaguchi K. Total elbow arthroplasty and distal humerus elbow fractures. Hand Clin 2004;20(4):475–483.
11. Arnander MW, Reeves A, MacLeod IA, et al. A biomechanical comparison of plate configuration in distal humerus fractures. J Orthop Trauma 2008;22(5):332–336.
12. Aslam N, Willett K. Functional outcome following internal fixation of intraarticular fractures of the distal humerus (AO type C). Acta Orthop Belg 2004;70(2):118–122.
13. Athwal GS, Goetz TJ, Pollock JW, et al. Prosthetic replacement for distal humerus fractures. Orthop Clin North Am 2008;39(2):201–212, vi.
13b. Athwal GS, Hoxie SC, Rispoli DM, et al. Precontoured parallel plate fixation of AO/ OTA type C distal humerus fractures. J· Orthop Trauma 2009;23(8):578–580.
14. Athwal GS, Morrey BF. Revision total elbow arthroplasty for prosthetic fractures. J Bone Joint Surg Am 2006;88(9):2017–2026.
15. Athwal GS, Rispoli DM, Steinmann SP. The anconeus flap transolecranon approach to the distal humerus. J Orthop Trauma 2006;20(4):282–285.
16. Bartels RH, Grotenhuis JA. Anterior submuscular transposition of the ulnar nerve. For postoperative focal neuropathy at the elbow. J Bone Joint Surg Br 2004;86(7):998–1001.
17. Beredjiklian PK, Hotchkiss RN, Athanasian EA, et al. Recalcitrant nonunion of the distal humerus: treatment with free vascularized bone grafting. Clin Orthop Relat Res 2005 Jun(435):134–9.
18. Bilic R, Kolundzic R, Anticevic D. Absorbable implants in surgical correction of a capitellar malunion in an 11-year-old: a case report. J Orthop Trauma 2006;20(1):66–69.
19. Black DM, Steinbuch M, Palermo L, et al. An assessment tool for predicting fracture risk in postmenopausal women. Osteoporos Int 2001;12(7):519–528.
20. Boody AR, Wongworawat MD. Accuracy in the measurement of compartment pressures: a comparison of three commonly used devices. J Bone Joint Surg Am 2005;87(11):2415–2422.
21. Brinker MR, O'Connor DP, Crouch CC, et al. Ilizarov treatment of infected nonunions of the distal humerus after failure of internal fixation: an outcomes study. J Orthop Trauma 2007;21(3):178–184.
22. Brown RF, Morgan RG. Intercondylar T-shaped fractures of the humerus. Results in ten cases treated by early mobilisation. J Bone Joint Surg Br 1971;53(3):425–428.
23. Bryan RS, Morrey BF. Extensive posterior exposure of the elbow. A triceps-sparing approach. Clin Orthop Relat Res 1982 Jun(166):188–192.
24. Bryan RS, Morrey BF. Fractures of the distal humerus. In: Morrey BF, editor. The Elbow and Its Disorders. Philadelphia: WB Saunders, 1985, pp. 302–339.
25. Campbell WC. Incision for exposure of the elbow joint. Am J Surg 1932;15:65–67.
26. Cassebaum WH. Open reduction of T and Y fractures of the lower end of the humerus. J Trauma 1969;9(11):915–925.
27. Choudry UH, Moran SL, Li S, Khan S. Soft-tissue coverage of the elbow: an outcome analysis and reconstructive algorithm. Plast Reconstr Surg 2007;119(6):1852–1857.
28. Clough TM, Jago ER, Sidhu DP, Markovic L. Fractures of the capitellum: a new method of fixation using a maxillofacial plate. Clin Orthop Relat Res 2001 Mar(384):232–236.
29. Cobb TK, Morrey BF. Total elbow arthroplasty as primary treatment for distal humeral fractures in elderly patients. J Bone Joint Surg Am 1997;79(6):826–832.
30. Coles CP, Barei DP, Nork SE, et al. The olecranon osteotomy: a 6-year experience in the treatment of intraarticular fractures of the distal humerus. J Orthop Trauma 2006;20(3):164–171.
31. Dean GS, Holliger EHT, Urbaniak JR. Elbow allograft for reconstruction of the elbow with massive bone loss. Long-term results. Clin Orthop Relat Res 1997 Aug(341):12–22.
32. Diliberti T, Botte MJ, Abrams RA. Anatomical considerations regarding the posterior interosseous nerve during posterolateral approaches to the proximal part of the radius. J Bone Joint Surg Am 2000;82(6):809–813.
33. Doornberg J, Lindenhovius A, Kloen P, et al. Two- and three-dimensional computed tomography for the classification and management of distal humeral fractures. Evaluation of reliability and diagnostic accuracy. J Bone Joint Surg Am 2006;88(8):1795–1801.
34. Doornberg JN, Ring D, Jupiter JB. Static progressive splinting for posttraumatic elbow stiffness. J Orthop Trauma 2006;20(6):400–404.
35. Doornberg JN, van Duijn PJ, Linzel D, et al. Surgical treatment of intra-articular fractures of the distal part of the humerus. Functional outcome after 12 to 30 years. J Bone Joint Surg Am 2007;89(7):1524–1532.
36. Dowdy PA, Bain GI, King GJ, Patterson SD. The midline posterior elbow incision. An anatomical appraisal. J Bone Joint Surg Br 1995;77(5):696–699.

37. Dubberley JH, Faber KJ, Macdermid JC, et al. Outcome after open reduction and internal fixation of capitellar and trochlear fractures. J Bone Joint Surg Am 2006;88(1): 46–54.
38. Duggal N, Dunning CE, Johnson JA, et al. The flat spot of the proximal ulna: a useful anatomic landmark in total elbow arthroplasty. J Shoulder Elbow Surg 2004;13(2): 206–207.
39. Dunning CE, Zarzour ZD, Patterson SD, et al. Ligamentous stabilizers against posterolateral rotatory instability of the elbow. J Bone Joint Surg Am 2001;83-A(12): 1823–1828.
40. Eastwood WJ. The T-shaped fracture of the lower end of the humerus. J Bone Joint Surg Am 1937;19:364–369.
41. Ek ET, Goldwasser M, Bonomo AL. Functional outcome of complex intercondylar fractures of the distal humerus treated through a triceps-sparing approach. J Shoulder Elbow Surg 2008;17(3):441–446.
42. Elkowitz SJ, Polatsch DB, Egol KA, et al. Capitellum fractures: a biomechanical evaluation of three fixation methods. J Orthop Trauma 2002;16(7):503–506.
43. Ergunes K, Yilik L, Ozsoyler I, et al. Traumatic brachial artery injuries. Tex Heart Inst J 2006;33(1):31–34.
44. Evans EM. Supracondylar-Y fractures of the humerus. J Bone Joint Surg Br 1953;35-B(3):371–375.
45. Faber KJ. Coronal shear fractures of the distal humerus: the capitellum and trochlea. Hand Clin 2004;20(4):455–464.
46. Faber KJ, Cordy ME, Milne AD, et al. Advanced cement technique improves fixation in elbow arthroplasty. Clin Orthop Relat Res 1997 Jan(334):150–156.
47. Foulk DA, Robertson PA, Timmerman LA. Fracture of the trochlea. J Orthop Trauma 1995;9(6):530–532.
48. Frankle MA, Herscovici D Jr, DiPasquale TG, et al. A comparison of open reduction and internal fixation and primary total elbow arthroplasty in the treatment of intraarticular distal humerus fractures in women older than age 65. J Orthop Trauma 2003; 17(7):473–480.
49. Gainor BJ, Moussa F, Schott T. Healing rate of transverse osteotomies of the olecranon used in reconstruction of distal humerus fractures. J South Orthop Assoc 1995;4(4): 263–268.
50. Gambirasio R, Riand N, Stern R, et al. Total elbow replacement for complex fractures of the distal humerus. An option for the elderly patient. J Bone Joint Surg Br 2001; 83(7):974–978.
51. Garcia JA, Mykula R, Stanley D. Complex fractures of the distal humerus in the elderly. The role of total elbow replacement as primary treatment. J Bone Joint Surg Br. 2002; 84(6):812–816.
52. Garland DE, O'Hollaren RM. Fractures and dislocations about the elbow in the head-injured adult. Clin Orthop Relat Res 1982 Aug(168):38–41.
53. Gerwin M, Hotchkiss RN, Weiland AJ. Alternative operative exposures of the posterior aspect of the humeral diaphysis with reference to the radial nerve. J Bone Joint Surg Am 1996;78(11):1690–1695.
54. Glanville EV. Perforation of the coronoid-olecranon septum. Humeroulnar relationships in Netherlands and African populations. Am J Phys Anthropol 1967;26(1):85–92.
55. Gofton WT, Macdermid JC, Patterson SD, et al. Functional outcome of AO type C distal humeral fractures. J Hand Surg [Am] 2003;28(2):294–308.
56. Grantham SA, Norris TR, Bush DC. Isolated fracture of the humeral capitellum. Clin Orthop Relat Res 1981 Nov-Dec(161):262–269.
57. Grechenig W, Clement H, Pichler W, et al. The influence of lateral and anterior angulation of the proximal ulna on the treatment of a Monteggia fracture: an anatomical cadaver study. J Bone Joint Surg Br 2007;89(6):836–838.
58. Greiner S, Haas NP, Bail HJ. Outcome after open reduction and angular stable internal fixation for supra-intercondylar fractures of the distal humerus: preliminary results with the LCP distal humerus system. Arch Orthop Trauma Surg 2008;128(7):723–729.
59. Geschwend N, Simmen BR, Matejovsky Z. Late complications in elbow arthroplasty. J Shoulder Elbow Surg 1996;5(2 Pt 1):86–96.
60. Gupta R, Khanchandani P. Intercondylar fractures of the distal humerus in adults: a critical analysis of 55 cases. Injury 2002;33(6):511–515.
61. Gustilo RB, Anderson JT. Prevention of infection in the treatment of one thousand and twenty-five open fractures of long bones: retrospective and prospective analyses. J Bone Joint Surg Am 1976;58(4):453–458.
62. Hahn NF. Fall von einer besonderes varietat der frakturen des ellenbogens. Zeitsch-Wundartze Geburtshlefer 1853;6:185.
63. Hastings H 2nd, Graham TJ. The classification and treatment of heterotopic ossification about the elbow and forearm. Hand Clin 1994;10(3):417–437.
64. Hastings H 2nd, Theng CS. Total elbow replacement for distal humerus fractures and traumatic deformity: results and complications of semiconstrained implants and design rationale for the Discovery Elbow System. Am J Orthop 2003;32(9 Suppl):20–28.
65. Helfet DL, Hotchkiss RN. Internal fixation of the distal humerus: a biomechanical comparison of methods. J Orthop Trauma 1990;4(3):260–264.
66. Helfet DL, Kloen P, Anand N, et al. Open reduction and internal fixation of delayed unions and nonunions of fractures of the distal part of the humerus. J Bone Joint Surg Am 2003;85-A(1):33–40.
67. Helfet DL, Schmeling GJ. Bicondylar intraarticular fractures of the distal humerus in adults. Clin Orthop Relat Res 1993 Jul(292):26–36.
68. Hewins EA, Gofton WT, Dubberly J, et al. Plate fixation of olecranon osteotomies. J Orthop Trauma 2007;21(1):58–62.
69. Hodgson SP, Parkinson RW, Noble J. Capitellocondylar total elbow replacement for rheumatoid arthritis. J R Coll Surg Edinb 1991;36(2):133–135.
70. Holdsworth BJ, Mossad MM. Fractures of the adult distal humerus. Elbow function after internal fixation. J Bone Joint Surg Br 1990;72(3):362–365.
71. Hotchkiss RN. Elbow contractures. In: Green DP, Hotchkiss RN, Pederson WC, eds. Green's Operative Hand Surgery. Philadelphia: Churchill Livingstone, 1999, pp. 673–674.
72. Huang TL, Chiu FY, Chuang TY, Chen TH. The results of open reduction and internal fixation in elderly patients with severe fractures of the distal humerus: a critical analysis of the results. J Trauma 2005;58(1):62–69.
73. Hughes JSPM. Distal humeral hemiarthroplasty. In: Yamaguchi GK, McKee MD, O'Driscoll SW, eds. Advanced Reconstruction Elbow. Rosemont, NY: American Academy of Orthopaedic Surgeons, 2006, pp. 219–228.
74. Hunsaker FG, Cioffi DA, Amadio PC, et al. The American Academy of Orthopaedic Surgeons outcomes instruments: normative values from the general population. J Bone Joint Surg Am 2002;84-A(2):208–215.
75. Ikavalko M, Belt EA, Kautiainen H, Lehto MU. Souter arthroplasty for elbows with severe destruction. Clin Orthop Relat Res 2004 Apr(421):126–133.
76. Ilahi OA, Strausser DW, Gabel GT. Posttraumatic heterotopic ossification about the elbow. Orthopedics 1998;21(3):265–268.
77. Imatani J, Morito Y, Hashizume H, Inoue H. Internal fixation for coronal shear fracture of the distal end of the humerus by the anterolateral approach. J Shoulder Elbow Surg 2001;10(6):554–556.
78. Imatani J, Ogura T, Morito Y, et al. Anatomic and histologic studies of lateral collateral ligament complex of the elbow joint. J Shoulder Elbow Surg 1999;8(6):625–627.
79. Jacobson SR, Glisson RR, Urbaniak JR. Comparison of distal humerus fracture fixation: a biomechanical study. J South Orthop Assoc 1997;6(4):241–249.
80. Jarvinen TL, Sievanen H, Khan KM, et al. Shifting the focus in fracture prevention from osteoporosis to falls. BMJ 2008;336(7636):124–126.
81. Jensen M, Moran SL. Soft tissue coverage of the elbow: a reconstructive algorithm. Orthop Clin North Am 2008;39(2):251–264, vii.
82. Jones KG. Percutaneous pin fixation of fractures of the lower end of the humerus. Clin Orthop Relat Res 1967;50:53–69.
83. Jupiter JB, Mehne DK. Fractures of the distal humerus. Orthopedics 1992;15(7): 825–833.
84. Jupiter JB, Neff U, Holzach P, Allgower M. Intercondylar fractures of the humerus. An operative approach. J Bone Joint Surg Am 1985;67(2):226–239.
85. Jupiter JB, Neff U, Regazzoni P, Allgower M. Unicondylar fractures of the distal humerus: an operative approach. J Orthop Trauma 1988;2(2):102–109.
86. Jupiter JB, O'Driscoll SW, Cohen MS. The assessment and management of the stiff elbow. Instr Course Lect 2003;52:93–111.
87. Kalogrianitis S, Sinopidis C, El Meligy M, et al. Unlinked elbow arthroplasty as primary treatment for fractures of the distal humerus. J Shoulder Elbow Surg 2008;17(2): 287–292.
88. Kamineni S, Morrey BF. Distal humeral fractures treated with noncustom total elbow replacement. J Bone Joint Surg Am 2004;86-A(5):940–947.
89. Kamineni S, Morrey BF. Distal humeral fractures treated with noncustom total elbow replacement. Surgical technique. J Bone Joint Surg Am 2005;87 Suppl 1(Pt 1):41–50.
90. Kannus P. Preventing osteoporosis, falls, and fractures among elderly people. Promotion of lifelong physical activity is essential. BMJ 1999;318(7178):205–206.
91. Kannus P, Niemi S, Parkkari J, et al. Why is the age-standardized incidence of low-trauma fractures rising in many elderly populations? J Bone Miner Res 2002;17(8): 1363–1367.
92. Kaplan EB. Surgical approaches to the proximal end of the radius and its use in fractures of the head and neck of the radius. J Bone Joint Surg Am 1941;23:86.
93. Kelly RP, Griffin TW. Open reduction of T-condylar fractures of the humerus through an anterior approach. J Trauma 1969;9:901–914.
94. Keon-Cohen BT. Fractures at the elbow. J Bone Joint Surg Am 1966;48A:1623–1639.
95. Kocher T. Beitrage zur kenntniss einger praktisch wishctiger fraktur formen. Mitheil a Klin u Med Inst and Schweiz Basal, reihe. 1896:767.
96. Kocher T. Textbook of Operative Surgery. 3rd ed. London: Adam and Charles Black, 1911.
97. Korner J, Lill H, Muller LP, et al. Distal humerus fractures in elderly patients: results after open reduction and internal fixation. Osteoporos Int 2005;16(Suppl 2):S73–79.
98. Kuhn JE, Louis DS, Loder RT. Divergent single-column fractures of the distal part of the humerus. J Bone Joint Surg Am 1995;77(4):538–542.
99. Kundel K, Braun W, Wieberneit J, et al. Intraarticular distal humerus fractures. Factors affecting functional outcome. Clin Orthop Relat Res 1996 Nov(332):200–208.
100. Lambotte A. Chirurgie operatoire des fractures. Paris: Masson et Cie; 1913.
101. Lee BP, Adams RA, Morrey BF. Polyethylene wear after total elbow arthroplasty. J Bone Joint Surg Am 2005;87(5):1080–1087.
102. Lee KT, Lai CH, Singh S. Results of total elbow arthroplasty in the treatment of distal humerus fractures in elderly Asian patients. J Trauma 2006;61(4):889–892.
103. Liberman N, Katz T, Howard CB, et al. Fixation of capitellar fractures with the Herbert screw. Arch Orthop Trauma Surg 1991;110(3):155–157.
104. Ljung P, Jonsson K, Rydholm U. Short-term complications of the lateral approach for non-constrained elbow replacement. Follow-up of 50 rheumatoid elbows. J Bone Joint Surg Br 1995;77(6):937–942.
105. Lorenz H. Zur kenntnis der fractural capitulum humeri (Eminentiae Capitatae). Dtsche Ztrschr f Chir. 1905;78:531–545.
106. MacAusland WR. Ankylosis of the elbow: with report of four cases treated by arthroplasty. JAMA 1915;64:312–318.
107. Mahirogullari M, Kiral A, Solakoglu C, et al. Treatment of fractures of the humeral capitellum using herbert screws. J Hand Surg [Br] 2006;31(3):320–325.
108. Mansat P, Morrey BF. Semiconstrained total elbow arthroplasty for ankylosed and stiff elbows. J Bone Joint Surg Am 2000;82(9):1260–1268.
109. Marra G, Morrey BF, Gallay SH, et al. Fracture and nonunion of the olecranon in total elbow arthroplasty. J Shoulder Elbow Surg. 2006;15(4):486–494.
110. Marsh JL, Slongo TF, Agel J, et al. Fracture and dislocation classification compendium, 2007: Orthopaedic Trauma Association classification, database and outcomes committee. J Orthop Trauma 2007;21(10 Suppl):S1–133.
111. McCarty LP, Ring D, Jupiter JB. Management of distal humerus fractures. Am J Orthop 2005;34(9):430–438.
112. McKee M, Jupiter J, Toh CL, et al. Reconstruction after malunion and nonunion of intra-articular fractures of the distal humerus. Methods and results in 13 adults. J Bone Joint Surg Br 1994;76(4):614–621.
113. McKee MD. Randomized trial of ORIF versus total elbow arthroplasty for distal humerus fractures. AAOS 2007 February 16, 2007; San Diego; 2007.
114. McKee MD, Jupiter JB. A contemporary approach to the management of complex fractures of the distal humerus and their sequelae. Hand Clin 1994;10(3):479–494.
115. McKee MD, Jupiter JB. Semiconstrained elbow replacement for distal humeral nonunion. J Bone Joint Surg Br 1995;77(4):665–666.
116. McKee MD, Jupiter JB, Bamberger HB. Coronal shear fractures of the distal end of the humerus. J Bone Joint Surg Am 1996;78(1):49–54.
117. McKee MD, Jupiter JB, Bosse G, Goodman L. Outcome of ulnar neurolysis during post-traumatic reconstruction of the elbow. J Bone Joint Surg Br 1998;80(1):100–105.
118. McKee MD, Kim J, Kebaish K, et al. Functional outcome after open supracondylar

fractures of the humerus. The effect of the surgical approach. J Bone Joint Surg Br 2000;82(5):646–651.
119. McKee MD, Pugh DM, Richards RR, et al. Effect of humeral condylar resection on strength and functional outcome after semiconstrained total elbow arthroplasty. J Bone Joint Surg Am 2003;85-A(5):802–807.
120. McKee MD, Wilson TL, Winston L, et al. Functional outcome following surgical treatment of intra-articular distal humeral fractures through a posterior approach. J Bone Joint Surg Am 2000;82-A(12):1701–1707.
121. McQueen MM, Gaston P, Court-Brown CM. Acute compartment syndrome. Who is at risk? J Bone Joint Surg Br 2000;82(2):200–203.
122. Meissner M, Paun M, Johansen K. Duplex scanning for arterial trauma. Am J Surg 1991;161(5):552–555.
123. Mellen RHP. Arthroplasty of the elbow by replacement of the distal portion of the humerus with an acrylic prosthesis. J Bone Joint Surg Am 1947;29:348–353.
124. Milch H. Fractures and fracture dislocations of the humeral condyles. J Trauma 1964; 4:592–607.
125. Moro JK, King GJ. Total elbow arthroplasty in the treatment of posttraumatic conditions of the elbow. Clin Orthop Relat Res 2000 Jan(370):102–114.
126. Morrey BF. Fractures of the distal humerus: role of elbow replacement. Orthop Clin North Am 2000;31(1):145–154.
127. Morrey BF. Posttraumatic contracture of the elbow. Operative treatment, including distraction arthroplasty. J Bone Joint Surg Am 1990;72(4):601–618.
128. Morrey BF. The posttraumatic stiff elbow. Clin Orthop Relat Res 2005 Feb(431):26–35.
129. Morrey BF. Surgical treatment of extraarticular elbow contracture. Clin Orthop Relat Res 2000 Jan(370):57–64.
130. Morrey BF, Adams RA. Semiconstrained elbow replacement for distal humeral nonunion. J Bone Joint Surg Br 1995;77(1):67–72.
131. Morrey BF, Bryan RS. Complications of total elbow arthroplasty. Clin Orthop Relat Res 1982 Oct(170):204–212.
132. Morrey BF, Bryan RS. Infection after total elbow arthroplasty. J Bone Joint Surg Am 1983;65(3):330–338.
133. Müller LP, Kamineni S, Rommens PM, et al. Primary total elbow replacement for fractures of the distal humerus. Oper Orthop Traumatol 2005;17(2):119–142.
134. Müller M. The Comprehensive Classification of Fractures of Long Bones. Berlin: Springer-Verlag, 1990.
135. O'Driscoll SW. Elbow instability. Hand Clin 1994;10(3):405–415.
136. O'Driscoll SW. Optimizing stability in distal humeral fracture fixation. J Shoulder Elbow Surg 2005;14(1 Suppl S):186S–194S.
137. O'Driscoll SW. Supracondylar fractures of the elbow: open reduction, internal fixation. Hand Clin 2004;20(4):465–474.
138. O'Driscoll SW. The triceps-reflecting anconeus pedicle (TRAP) approach for distal humeral fractures and nonunions. Orthop Clin North Am 2000;31(1):91–101.
139. O'Driscoll SW, Morrey BF, Korinek S, An KN. Elbow subluxation and dislocation. A spectrum of instability. Clin Orthop Relat Res 1992 Jul(280):186–197.
140. O'Driscoll SW, Sanchez-Sotelo J, Torchia ME. Management of the smashed distal humerus. Orthop Clin North Am 2002;33(1):19–33, vii.
141. Ochner RS, Bloom H, Palumbo RC, Coyle MP. Closed reduction of coronal fractures of the capitellum. J Trauma 1996;40(2):199–203.
142. Olson SA, Rhorer AS. Orthopaedic trauma for the general orthopaedist: avoiding problems and pitfalls in treatment. Clin Orthop Relat Res 2005 Apr(433):30–37.
143. Ozdemir H, Urguden M, Soyuncu Y, et al. [Long-term functional results of adult intra-articular distal humeral fractures treated by open reduction and plate osteosynthesis]. Acta Orthop Traumatol Turc 2002;36(4):328–335.
144. Ozer H, Solak S, Turanli S, et al. Intercondylar fractures of the distal humerus treated with the triceps-reflecting anconeus pedicle approach. Arch Orthop Trauma Surg 2005; 125(7):469–474.
145. Pajarinen J, Bjorkenheim JM. Operative treatment of type C intercondylar fractures of the distal humerus: results after a mean follow-up of 2 years in a series of 18 patients. J Shoulder Elbow Surg 2002;11(1):48–52.
146. Palvanen M, Kannus P, Niemi S, Parkkari J. Secular trends in the osteoporotic fractures of the distal humerus in elderly women. Eur J Epidemiol 1998;14(2):159–164.
147. Palvanen M, Kannus P, Parkkari J, et al. The injury mechanisms of osteoporotic upper extremity fractures among older adults: a controlled study of 287 consecutive patients and their 108 controls. Osteoporos Int 2000;11(10):822–831.
148. Papaioannou N, Babis GC, Kalavritinos J, et al. Operative treatment of type C intra-articular fractures of the distal humerus: the role of stability achieved at surgery on final outcome. Injury 1995;26(3):169–173.
149. Park MJ, Kim HG, Lee JY. Surgical treatment of posttraumatic stiffness of the elbow. J Bone Joint Surg Br 2004;86(8):1158–1162.
150. Parsons M, O'Brien RJ, Hughes JS. Elbow hemiarthroplasty for acute and salvage reconstruction of intra-articular distal humerus fractures. Techn Shoulder Elbow Surg 2005; 6(2):87–97.
151. Patterson SD, Bain GI, Mehta JA. Surgical approaches to the elbow. Clin Orthop Relat Res 2000 Jan(370):19–33.
152. Pierce TD, Herndon JH. The triceps preserving approach to total elbow arthroplasty. Clin Orthop Relat Res 1998 Sep(354):144–152.
153. Pollock JW, Athwal GS, Steinmann SP. Surgical exposures for distal humerus fractures: a review. Clin Anat 2008;21(8):757–768.
154. Pollock JW, Faber KJ, Athwal GS. Distal humerus fractures. Orthop Clin North Am 2008;39(2):187–200, vi.
155. Potter D, Claydon P, Stanley D. Total elbow replacement using the Kudo prosthesis. Clinical and radiological review with 5- to 7-year follow-up. J Bone Joint Surg Br 2003; 85(3):354–357.
156. Poynton AR, Kelly IP, O'Rourke SK. Fractures of the capitellum—a comparison of two fixation methods. Injury 1998;29(5):341–343.
157. Prasad N, Dent C. Outcome of total elbow replacement for distal humeral fractures in the elderly: a comparison of primary surgery and surgery after failed internal fixation or conservative treatment. J Bone Joint Surg Br 2008;90(3):343–348.
158. Prokopis PM, Weiland AJ. The triceps-preserving approach for semiconstrained total elbow arthroplasty. J Shoulder Elbow Surg 2008;17(3):454–458.
159. Rashkoff E, Burkhalter WE. Arthrodesis of the salvage elbow. Orthopedics 1986;9(5): 733–738.
160. Ray PS, Kakarlapudi K, Rajsekhar C, et al. Total elbow arthroplasty as primary treatment for distal humeral fractures in elderly patients. Injury 2000;31(9):687–692.
161. Richards RR, Khoury GW, Burke FD, et al. Internal fixation of capitellar fractures using Herbert screws: a report of four cases. Can J Surg 1987;30(3):188–191.
162. Ring D, Gulotta L, Chin K, Jupiter JB. Olecranon osteotomy for exposure of fractures and nonunions of the distal humerus. J Orthop Trauma 2004;18(7):446–449.
163. Ring D, Gulotta L, Jupiter JB. Unstable nonunions of the distal part of the humerus. J Bone Joint Surg Am 2003;85-A(6):1040–1046.
164. Ring D, Jupiter JB. Complex fractures of the distal humerus and their complications. J Shoulder Elbow Surg 1999;8(1):85–97.
165. Ring D, Jupiter JB. Operative release of complete ankylosis of the elbow due to heterotopic bone in patients without severe injury of the central nervous system. J Bone Joint Surg Am 2003;85-A(5):849–857.
166. Ring D, Jupiter JB. Operative treatment of osteochondral nonunion of the distal humerus. J Orthop Trauma 2006;20(1):56–59.
167. Ring D, Jupiter JB, Gulotta L. Articular fractures of the distal part of the humerus. J Bone Joint Surg Am 2003;85-A(2):232–238.
168. Riseborough EJ, Radin EL. Intercondylar T fractures of the humerus in the adult. A comparison of operative and nonoperative treatment in twenty-nine cases. J Bone Joint Surg Am 1969;51(1):130–141.
169. Rispoli DM, Athwal GS, Morrey BF. Neurolysis of the ulnar nerve for neuropathy following total elbow replacement. J Bone Joint Surg Br 2008;90(10):1348–1351.
170. Roberts RM, String ST. Arterial injuries in extremity shotgun wounds: requisite factors for successful management. Surgery 1984;96(5):902–908.
171. Robinson CM. Fractures of the distal humerus. In: Bucholz RWHJ, Court-Brown C, Tornetta P, et al., eds. Rockwood and Green's Fractures in Adults. 6th ed. Philadelphia: Lippincott Williams and Wilkins, 2005, pp. 1051–116.
172. Robinson CM, Hill RM, Jacobs N, et al. Adult distal humeral metaphyseal fractures: epidemiology and results of treatment. J Orthop Trauma 2003;17(1):38–47.
173. Rose SH, Melton LJ 3rd, Morrey BF, et al. Epidemiologic features of humeral fractures. Clin Orthop Relat Res 1982 Aug(168):24–30.
174. Sanchez-Sotelo J, Torchia ME, O'Driscoll SW. Complex distal humeral fractures: internal fixation with a principle-based parallel-plate technique. J Bone Joint Surg Am 2007; 89(5):961–969.
175. Sanchez-Sotelo J, Torchia ME, O'Driscoll SW. Complex distal humeral fractures: internal fixation with a principle-based parallel-plate technique. Surgical technique. J Bone Joint Surg Am 2008;90(Suppl 2):31–46.
176. Sanders RA, Raney EM, Pipkin S. Operative treatment of bicondylar intra-articular fractures of the distal humerus. Orthopedics 1992;15(2):159–163.
177. Sano S, Rokkaku T, Saito S, et al. Herbert screw fixation of capitellar fractures. J Shoulder Elbow Surg 2005;14(3):307–311.
178. Schemitsch EH, Tencer AF, Henley MB. Biomechanical evaluation of methods of internal fixation of the distal humerus. J Orthop Trauma 1994;8(6):468–475.
179. Schildhauer TA, Nork SE, Mills WJ, Henley MB. Extensor mechanism-sparing paratricipital posterior approach to the distal humerus. J Orthop Trauma 2003;17(5):374–378.
180. Schuster I, Korner J, Arzdorf M, et al. Mechanical comparison in cadaver specimens of three different 90-degree double-plate osteosyntheses for simulated C2-type distal humerus fractures with varying bone densities. J Orthop Trauma 2008;22(2):113–120.
181. Self J, Viegas SF, Buford WL Jr, et al. A comparison of double-plate fixation methods for complex distal humerus fractures. J Shoulder Elbow Surg 1995;4(1 Pt 1):10–16.
182. Shifrin PG, Johnson DP. Elbow hemiarthroplasty with 20-year follow-up study. A case report and literature review. Clin Orthop Relat Res 1990 May(254):128–33.
183. Sodergard J, Sandelin J, Bostman O. Mechanical failures of internal fixation in T and Y fractures of the distal humerus. J Trauma 1992;33(5):687–690.
184. Sodergard J, Sandelin J, Bostman O. Postoperative complications of distal humeral fractures. 27/96 adults followed up for 6 (2–10) years. Acta Orthop Scand 1992;63(1): 85–89.
185. Soon JL, Chan BK, Low CO. Surgical fixation of intra-articular fractures of the distal humerus in adults. Injury 2004;35(1):44–54.
186. Spinner M, Kaplan EB. The relationship of the ulnar nerve to the medial intermuscular septum in the arm and its clinical significance. Hand 1976;8(3):239–242.
187. Spinner RJ, Morgenlander JC, Nunley JA. Ulnar nerve function following total elbow arthroplasty: a prospective study comparing preoperative and postoperative clinical and electrophysiologic evaluation in patients with rheumatoid arthritis. J Hand Surg [Am] 2000;25(2):360–364.
188. Stamatis E, Paxinos O. The treatment and functional outcome of type IV coronal shear fractures of the distal humerus: a retrospective review of five cases. J Orthop Trauma 2003;17(4):279–284.
189. Steinthal D. Die isolirte fraktur der eminenthia capetala in ellenbogengelenk. Zentralb Chir 1898;15:17.
190. Stoffel K, Cunneen S, Morgan R, et al. Comparative stability of perpendicular versus parallel double-locking plating systems in osteoporotic comminuted distal humerus fractures. J Orthop Res 2008;26(6):778–784.
191. Street DM, Stevens PS. A humeral replacement prosthesis for the elbow: results in ten elbows. J Bone Joint Surg Am 1974;56(6):1147–1158.
192. Swoboda B, Scott RD. Humeral hemiarthroplasty of the elbow joint in young patients with rheumatoid arthritis: a report on 7 arthroplasties. J Arthroplasty 1999;14(5): 553–559.
193. Tachihara A, Nakamura H, Yoshioka T, et al. Postoperative results and complications of total elbow arthroplasty in patients with rheumatoid arthritis: three types of nonconstrained arthroplasty. Mod Rheumatol 2008 May 29.
194. Tan V, Daluiski A, Simic P, Hotchkiss RN. Outcome of open release for posttraumatic elbow stiffness. J Trauma 2006;61(3):673–678.
195. Taylor TK, Scham SM. A posteromedial approach to the proximal end of the ulna for the internal fixation of olecranon fractures. J Trauma 1969;9(7):594–602.
196. Tyllianakis M, Panagopoulos A, Papadopoulos AX, et al. Functional evaluation of comminuted intra-articular fractures of the distal humerus (AO type C). Long-term results in twenty-six patients. Acta Orthop Belg 2004;70(2):123–130.
197. Urbaniak JR, Aitken M. Clinical use of bone allografts in the elbow. Orthop Clin North Am 1987;18(2):311–321.
198. Urbaniak JR, Black KE Jr. Cadaveric elbow allografts. A 6-year experience. Clin Orthop Relat Res 1985 Jul-Aug(197):131–140.

199. Van Gorder GW. Surgical approach in supracondylar "T" fractures of the humerus requiring open reduction. J Bone Joint Surg Am 1940;22:278.

200. Veillette CJ, Steinmann SP. Olecranon fractures. Orthop Clin North Am 2008;39(2): 229–236, vii.

201. Ward WG, Nunley JA. Concomitant fractures of the capitellum and radial head. J Orthop Trauma 1988;2(2):110–116.

202. Watts AC, Morris A, Robinson CM. Fractures of the distal humeral articular surface. J Bone Joint Surg Br 2007;89(4):510–515.

203. Weiland AJ, Weiss AP, Wills RP, et al. Capitellocondylar total elbow replacement. A long-term follow-up study. J Bone Joint Surg Am 1989;71(2):217–222.

204. Wilkinson JM, Stanley D. Posterior surgical approaches to the elbow: a comparative anatomic study. J Shoulder Elbow Surg 2001;10(4):380–382.

205. Wright TW, Glowczewskie F. Vascular anatomy of the ulna. J Hand Surg [Am] 1998; 23(5):800–804.

206. Yamaguchi K, Adams RA, Morrey BF. Infection after total elbow arthroplasty. J Bone Joint Surg Am 1998;80(4):481–491.

207. Yamaguchi K, Sweet FA, Bindra R, et al. The extraosseous and intraosseous arterial anatomy of the adult elbow. J Bone Joint Surg Am 1997;79(11):1653–1662.

208. Yang KH, Park HW, Park SJ, et al. Lateral J-plate fixation in comminuted intercondylar fracture of the humerus. Arch Orthop Trauma Surg 2003;123(5):234–238.

34

HUMERAL SHAFT FRACTURES

Michael D. McKee and Sune Larsson

GENERAL CONSIDERATIONS

A fracture of the humeral shaft is a common event, occurring more than 70,000 times a year in North America. It has been estimated previously as representing between 3% and 5% of all fractures,[17,120,148] but a more accurate figure is around 1% (see Chapter 3). Most will heal with appropriate conservative care, although a limited number will require surgery for optimal outcome.[42,50,148] Given the extensive range of motion of the shoulder and elbow, and the minimal effect from minor shortening, a wide range of radiographic malunion can be accepted with little functional deficit.[145] Current research in this area focuses on refining the indications for surgical intervention, decreasing the surgical failure rate through new implants and techniques, and optimizing the postinjury rehabilitation programs and thereby

minimizing the duration and magnitude of remaining disability.[17,153,154,160] The successful treatment of a humeral shaft fracture does not end with bony union; in the current emphasis on a holistic approach to patient care, the treating orthopaedic surgeon is frequently in an ideal position to intervene and improve a patient's life beyond what is traditionally recognized as the surgeons' role. Recognition of the injury as an osteoporotic fragility fracture in an elderly patient should prompt a referral for diagnostic investigations of, and potentially treatment for, an underlying osteoporotic condition. Similarly, fractures resulting from abusive domestic relationships or drug/alcohol addiction may represent opportunities to intervene. As with most orthopaedic injuries, the successful treatment of a humeral shaft fracture demands a knowledge of anatomy, surgical indications, techniques and implants, and patient function and expectations.

EPIDEMIOLOGY

The advent of comprehensive fracture databases at dedicated trauma units and the proliferation of capitated insurance contract populations have dramatically improved the information available regarding the epidemiology of fractures and dislocations. While in the past this was often of little importance, orthopaedic surgeons around the globe are increasingly aware that the complexity of economics and politics involved in the delivery of sound orthopaedic care is rapidly increasing. As those who know the most about the practical aspects and human side of this topic, it is important that orthopaedic surgeons take a leading role in this type of research.

A review by Tytherleigh-Strong et al.[160] provided an excellent picture of the epidemiology of humeral shaft fractures in the United Kingdom. This research was based at a single orthopaedic trauma center solely responsible for the fracture care of 600,000 people, thus providing a defined population for study. They found that there was a bimodal distribution of fractures (Fig. 34-1), with a peak (25 per 100,000 per year) in young, primarily male patients in the 21 to 30 age bracket and a larger peak (100 per 100,000 per year) primarily in older females 60 to 80 years old. They point out that high-energy trauma was responsible for the majority of injuries in young patients, and that this is the population that most of the orthopaedic literature focuses on. The fractures caused primarily by simple falls in older women (the second peak) thus represent a population intrinsically different from that described in reports on surgical intervention for these fractures. Only 5% of the injuries were associated with an open wound, and 63% were "simple" fracture patterns (AO/OTA type "A," Table 34-1). In a more recent study by Ekholm et al.[38] a similar bimodal distribution could be shown in a Swedish urban population, although with an even more pronounced rise in the incidence in elderly women. Again, this represents a fracture population different from most reports that concentrate on higher energy, open fractures.[137] This type of information has implications for resident training (relatively few "operative" fractures per center per year), resource management (the largest single group is elderly females with simple humeral fractures after falls), and research (to ensure comparisons of equivalent groups).[160]

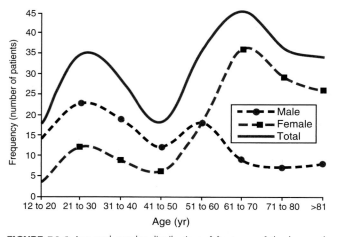

FIGURE 34-1 Age and gender distribution of fractures of the humeral shaft in 249 patients from Edinburgh. (From Tytherleigh-Strong G, Walls N, McQueen MM. The epidemiology of humeral shaft fractures. J Bone Joint Surg (B) 1998;80B(12):249–253, with permission.)

TABLE 34-1	**Fracture Pattern of 249 Fractures of the Humeral Shaft as Classified by the AO System**	
Type	Percentage	Average Age (yrs)
A1	29.2	
A2	10.8	
A3	23.3	
Total	63.3	56.5
B1	17.1	
B2	8.3	
B3	0.8	
Total	26.2	47.5
C1	5.4	
C2	3.3	
C3	1.7	
Total	10.4	56.2

From Tytherleigh-Strong G, Walls N, McQueen MM. The epidemiology of humeral shaft fractures. J Bone Joint Surg (B) 1998;80B(12):249–253.

Brinker et al.[17] examined prospectively gathered data from a capitated insurance contract where orthopaedic services for 135,000 (average annual enrollment) young (mean age 28.9 years) people were provided by a single physician group of 62 orthopaedic surgeons. The overall incidence of fractures was 847 per 100,000 people per year, with the incidence of humeral fractures being 13.1/100,000 people per year. As would be expected in a young population, males predominated in all fracture groups. This data is useful in estimating the orthopaedic resources required to service a young, active North American population.

ANATOMY

It is generally accepted that a humeral shaft fracture is one in which the main fracture line is distal to the surgical neck of the proximal humerus and proximal to the supracondylar ridge distally.[50,145,148] Proximally, the humerus is roughly cylindrical in cross section, tapering to a triangular shape distally.[49] The medullary canal of the humerus tapers to an end above the supracondylar expansion. This is different from the wide metaphyseal flares of the distal tibia and distal femur and has implications in intramedullary nailing of humeral shaft fractures.

The humerus is well enveloped in muscle and soft tissue, hence there is a good prognosis for healing in the majority of uncomplicated fractures. The medial and lateral intermuscular septa are tough fibrous bands that divide the arm into anterior and posterior compartments. The brachial artery, median nerve, and musculocutaneous nerves all remain in the anterior compartment for their entire course, while the ulnar nerve begins in the anterior compartment and passes through to the posterior compartment at the elbow. The radial nerve begins in the posterior compartment and passes through into the anterior compartment (Fig. 34-2).

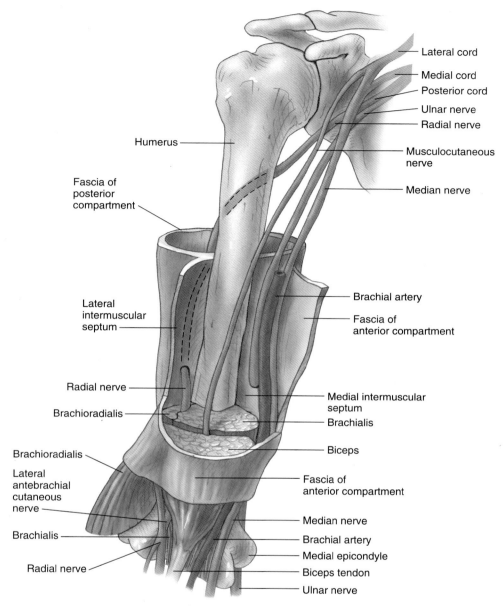

FIGURE 34-2 The neurovascular anatomy of the upper arm.

A thorough knowledge of anatomy is important for the successful treatment of humeral shaft fractures. By being aware of the insertion and direction of load of the various muscles attached to the humerus, it is easier to understand the fracture displacement and foresee potential problems in retaining the desired position following reduction. For instance, for fractures occurring proximal to the insertion of the pectoralis major, the proximal fragment will displace into abduction and external rotation due to unopposed muscles, while the distal fragment for the same reason often is displaced proximal and anterior.

DIAGNOSIS

History

As with most fractures, a careful and detailed history and physical examination provide critical information that serves as a starting point for treatment. The predominant causes of humeral shaft fractures include simple falls or rotational injuries in the older population and higher-energy mechanisms in the younger patient, including motor vehicle accidents, assaults, falls from a height, and throwing injuries. A history of minimal trauma causing fracture in the older patient may be the first point to alert the surgeon that the fracture may involve pathologic bone (be it from metastatic disease or severe osteoporosis) and prompt a thorough history (i.e., for prior cancer) and possibly a systemic work-up. In this situation, the treating surgeon has the potential to help the patient both in terms of the presenting fracture and the prevention of further fractures. Comorbidities, especially as they relate to the patient's suitability for a potential anaesthetic, should be elucidated. These may also be relevant with regard to the etiology of the fall that resulted in fracture: an unrecognized arrhythmia can cause recurrent falls and injuries. Thus, a clear description of the actual mechanism of the injury is important.

The described mechanism of injury should match the fracture type: while exceptions do occur, the presence of a spiral fracture indicates a rotational force (such as that which occurs when the arm is forcibly wrenched behind the back) that is not consistent with, for example, striking the arm against a door. Discordance between history and fracture type is a hallmark of domestic abuse, and again this may represent an opportunity to intervene in a potentially lethal situation.[167] Alcohol abuse, smoking, and/or illicit drug use are all potential risk factors for negative fracture outcome through repeat injury, noncompliance, or poor biology at the fracture site and represent an opportunity to improve outcome. For example, while it is unrealistic to expect uniform compliance, modern smoking cessation strategies have a success rate from 20% to 60%. It is also becoming apparent that the use of nonsteroidal anti-inflammatory drugs (NSAIDs), for years a standard treatment for pain and swelling after acute injury, is associated with prolonged fracture healing times.[84] Bhattacharyya et al.,[9] in a cohort study including almost 10,000 patients with humeral shaft fractures, showed that NSAID exposure within 60 to 90 days after fracture was significantly associated with nonunion. However, the authors also concluded that it is difficult from such a study design to prove whether the increased use was the cause to the nonunion or an effect of an already established painful nonunion. Burd et al.,[20] in a randomized clinical trial, investigated the effect of indomethacin on the prevention of heterotopic ossification in a group of polytrauma patients with acetabular fractures. One group received indomethacin, one group local irradiation, and the control group nothing. These patients also had a number of associated long bone fractures: the incidence of delayed and nonunion in the indomethacin-treated group was 26% versus 7% in the other two groups, a significantly higher rate ($P = 0.004$). We strongly discourage the use of NSAIDs in patients with humeral shaft fractures.[20,47]

Physical Examination

In the multiple trauma situation, history from the patient may be unobtainable, but any available information from the accident scene, paramedical personnel, or family members is important. In general, the treatment of a humeral fracture is a relatively low priority in the resuscitation of a severely injured patient, which should proceed according to the guidelines of the Advanced Trauma Life Support protocol.[2] Following stabilization of the patient, attention is turned to the affected arm. There is an increased incidence of open wounds, ipsilateral fractures, compartment syndromes, and neurovascular injuries in polytraumatized patients, and a careful assessment needs to be performed.[13,18,50,137,148] There is higher incidence of forearm compartment syndrome in patients, especially children, who have ipsilateral humeral and forearm fractures, the so-called "floating elbow" (Fig. 34-3A,B).[133] Associated injuries such as arterial ruptures, scapulothoracic dislocations, or hemo/pneumothoraces may be life-threatening (Fig. 34-4A,B). The presence or absence of a (usually radial) nerve injury is particularly important to document prior to any intervention.[46,64,76,118,128] In the prevailing medical-legal climate, it is generally assumed that the nerve is intact unless specifically noted otherwise. If a nerve injury exists but is not recorded prior to a reduction or any other procedure, the burden falls onto the physician to prove that he or she did not cause it. In cases where it is impossible

to clinically establish the function of the nerve (i.e., associated head injury), it should be clearly stated that the condition of the nerve cannot be determined.

A careful search for open wounds is very important, as the presence of an open fracture accelerates the urgency of the situation. Examination of the shoulder and elbow joint is mandatory: associated injuries or pre-existing joint pathology may be an indication for operative management as stiffness may transfer physiologic stress to the fracture site and increase healing time (Fig. 34-5).[147] This will have implications for treatment and counseling of the patient with regards to prognosis.

Imaging

Standard imaging for any humeral shaft fracture includes two radiographs at 90 degrees to each other that include the shoulder and elbow joints in each view. Further views can be ordered depending on the clinical examination and any abnormalities noticed on the initial films. For the typical humeral shaft fracture, it is rarely necessary to obtain further imaging. Exceptions to this would include shaft fractures with associated vascular injuries that should be investigated further with an angiogram (see Fig. 34-4) or computed tomographic (CT) scans of associated intra-articular injuries proximally or distally.[50,147,148] CT scanning may also be indicated in the rare situation where a significant rotational abnormality exists as rotational alignment is difficult to judge from plain radiographs of a diaphyseal long bone fracture. A CT scan through the humeral condyles distally and the humeral head proximally can provide exact rotational alignment, especially when compared to the normal side. Given the broad rotational range of the shoulder, fairly large degrees of rotational malalignment can be accepted.[145] However, severe degrees of rotational malalignment (>30 degrees) should be avoided as they have a deleterious effect on the functional "sphere of action" of the upper extremity. Hubner et al.[67] have advocated the use of ultrasound in developing countries.

CLASSIFICATION

Bone

There are a number of factors that are important to describe when a humeral shaft fracture is classified. These include the mechanism of injury (low-energy, high-energy, gunshot-associated), the location of the fracture (proximal, midshaft, distal) along with any potential periarticular or intra-articular extension, concomitant soft tissue wounds or lesions, associated nerve or vessel injury (radial nerve most commonly), the nature of the underlying bone (normal, osteopenic, pathologic), and the presence of any associated prosthesis. Descriptive terms such as these are useful in providing an overall picture of a particular humeral shaft fracture, although they may not lend themselves well to categorizing injuries for research or clinical trials. For this reason, more objective classification schemes have been developed to aid in such endeavors.

A popular and useful scheme is the Orthopaedic Trauma Association's Fracture and Dislocation Compendium, first published in 1996 and republished in 2007.[111,113,114] This system is based on the AO/ASIF Comprehensive Long Bone Classification, adds previously unclassified fractures, and reorders them in an alpha-numeric system. The humerus is designated bone "1" and is divided into proximal,[11] diaphyseal,[12] and distal[13] segments (Fig. 34-6). Fractures are divided into three types:

(text continues on page 1009)

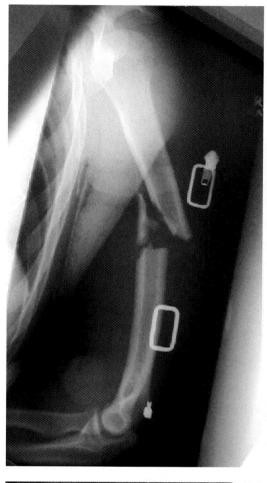

A

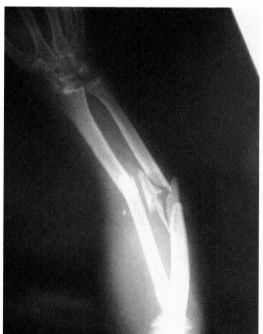

B

FIGURE 34-3 A,B. Three level upper extremity injury with closed humeral shaft fracture, comminuted open radial and ulnar shaft fractures, and associated compartment syndrome of the forearm and transscaphoid perilunate fracture dislocation of the wrist. **C,D.** Open reduction and internal fixation of all three injuries and a forearm fasciotomy allowed early postoperative motion and resulted in rapid union and reasonable functional outcome in this severely injured limb.

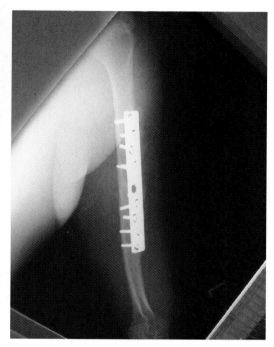

C

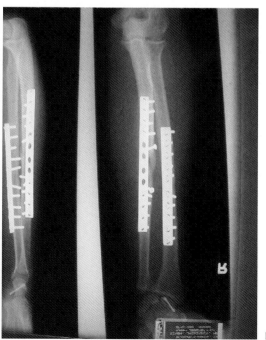

D

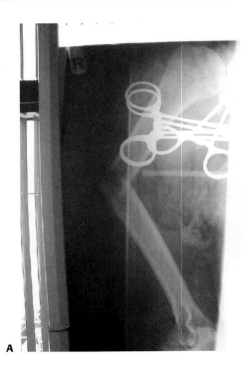

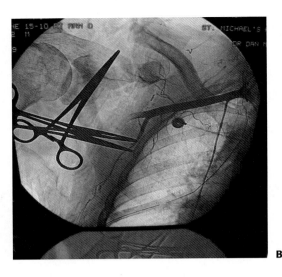

FIGURE 34-4 **A.** An angulated, open fracture of the humeral shaft in a patient from a roll-over motor vehicle accident. **B.** Angiogram demonstrates axillary artery injury with associated scapulo-thoracic dissociation (note the wide separation of the distal clavicle and acromion process).

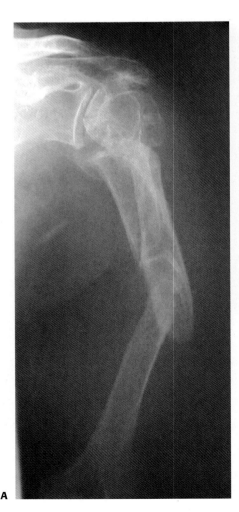

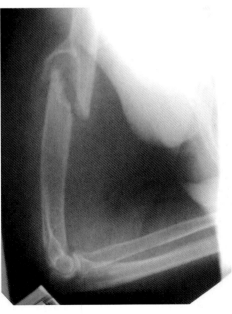

FIGURE 34-5 **A,B.** This elderly osteoporotic woman had previously sustained a humeral head and neck fracture treated conservatively that had resulted in a very stiff shoulder. She fell 4 years later and fractured the shaft of the humerus distal to the prior injury. Despite appropriate splinting, she developed a painful pseudarthrosis, as seen on the lateral radiograph **(B)**. Adjacent joint stiffness transfers much of the motion and stress of the limb to an ipsilateral fracture and increases the rate of delayed union and nonunion. This factor should be considered when deciding on treatment options.

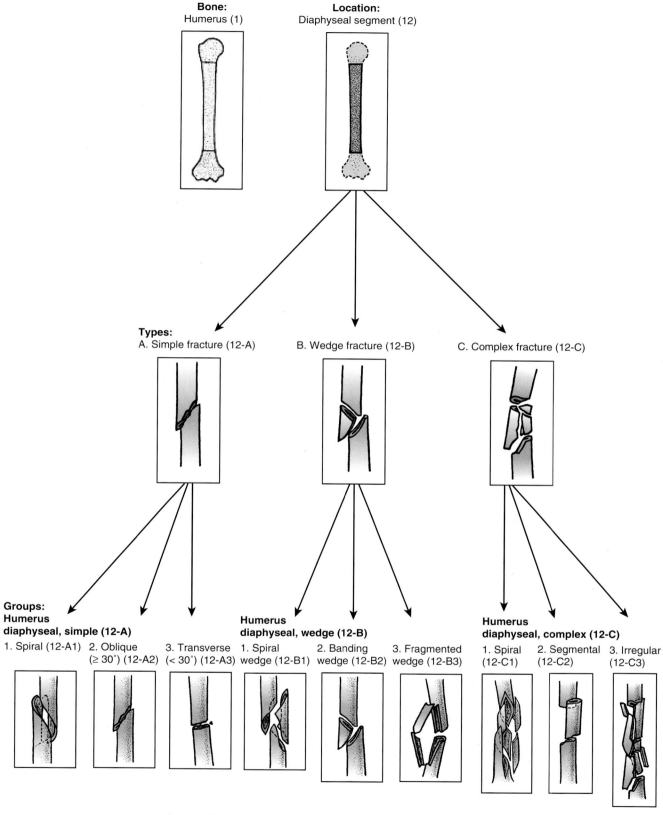

FIGURE 34-6 The OTA classification of humeral shaft fractures. (From Marsh JL, Slongo TF, Agel J, et al. Fracture and dislocation classification compendium—2007: Orthopaedic Trauma Association Classification, Database, and Outcomes committee. J Orthop Trauma 2007;21(10 Suppl), with permission.) *(continues)*

**Subgroups and qualifications:
Humerus diaphyseal, simple,
spiral (12-A1)**

1. Proximal zone (12-A1.1)

2. Middle zone (12-A1.2)

3. Distal zone (12-A1.3)

A1

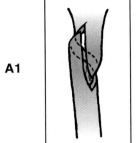
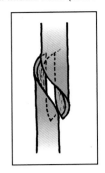

**Humerus diaphyseal, simple,
oblique (≥ 30°) (12-A2.2)**

1. Proximal zone (12-A2.1)

2. Middle zone (12-A2.2)

3. Distal zone (12-A2.3)

A2

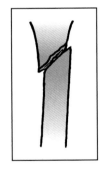
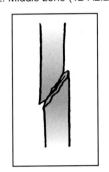

**Humerus diaphyseal, simple,
transverse (< 30°) (12-A3)**

1. Proximal zone (12-A3.1)

2. Middle zone (12-A3.2)

3. Distal zone (12-A3.3)

A1

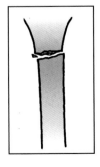
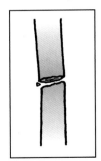
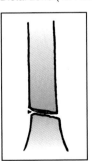

FIGURE 34-6 (*continued*)

Humerus diaphyseal,
wedge, spiral (12-B1)
1. Proximal zone (12-B1.1)   2. Middle zone (12-B1.2)   3. Distal zone (12-B1.3)

B1

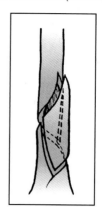

Humerus diaphyseal,
wedge, bending (12-B2)
1. Proximal zone (12-B2.1)   2. Middle zone (12-B2.2)   3. Distal zone (12-B2.3)

B2

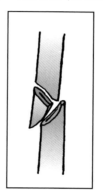

**Humerus diaphyseal,
wedge, fragmented (12-B3)**
1. Proximal zone (12-B3.1)   2. Middle zone (12-B3.2)   3. Distal zone (12-B3.3)

B3

FIGURE 34-6 (*continued*)

Humerus diaphyseal, complex, spiral (12-C1)
(1) Pure diaphyseal
(2) Proximal diaphylo-metaphyseal
(3) Distal diaphyslo-metaphyseal
1. With 2 intermediate fragments (12 -C1.1)

2. With 3 intermediate fragments (12-C1.2)

3. With more than 3 intermediate fragments (12-C1.3)

C1

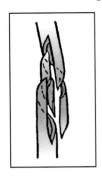
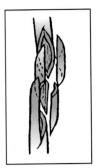

Humerus, diaphyseal, complex segmental (12-C2)
1. With 1 intermediate segmental fragment (12-C2.1)
(1) Pure diaphyseal
(2) Proximal diaphyslo-metaphyseal
(3) Distal diaphyslo-metaphyseal
(4) Oblique lines
(5) Transverse and oblique lines

2. With 1 intermediate segmental and additional wedge fragments (12-C2.2)
(1) Pure diaphyseal
(2) Proximal diaphyslo-metaphyseal
(3) Distal diaphyslo-metaphyseal
(4) Distal wedge
(5) Two wedges, proximal and distal

3. With 2 intermediate segmental fragments (12-C2.3)
(1) Pure diaphyseal
(2) Proximal diaphyslo-metaphyseal
(3) Distal diaphyslo-metaphyseal

C2

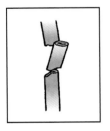

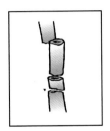

Humerus, diaphyseal, complex irregular (12-C3)
1. With 2 or 3 intermediate fragments (12-C3.1)
(1) 2 main intermediate fragments
(2) 3 main intermediate fragments

2. With limited shattering (< 4 cm) (12-C3.2)
(1) Proximal zone
(2) Middle zone
(3) Distal zone

3. With extensive shattering (> 4 cm) (12-C3.3)
(1) Pure diaphyseal
(2) Proximal diaphyslo-metaphyseal
(3) Distal diaphyslo-metaphyseal

C3

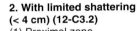

FIGURE 34-6 (*continued*)

"A" or "Simple" fractures of two main fragments, proximal and distal (cortical fragments of less than 10% of the circumference are ignored); "B" or "Wedge" fractures where there are one or more intermediate fracture fragments but, after reduction, there is contact between the main proximal and distal fragments; and "C" or "Complex" fractures, where there are one or more intermediate fragments such that, after reduction, there is no contact between the main fragments. These main types are then subdivided into groups based on fracture pattern (spiral, oblique, transverse) and subgroups based on proximal, middle, or distal zones of the diaphysis. The system is designed to reflect increasing fracture severity as one progresses from A to C types, and to help aid in treatment, prognosis, and research. The reliability and reproducibility of this type of scheme has not been critically assessed for the humeral shaft but has been looked at for both the proximal and distal segments of the bone. These investigators found that while there was poor inter- and intraobserver agreement for subgroup classification, there was "substantial" (kappa value 0.66) agreement for type (A, B, C) and "moderate" (kappa value 0.52) agreement for group designation.[150,165] Thus it seems reasonable to assume that (the anatomically simpler) humeral shaft fractures can reliably be classified at least as to type (simple, wedge, complex) and group (spiral, oblique, transverse).

Soft Tissue

Soft tissue lesions are classified by one of two schemes. The Gustilo classification divides wounds into three grades.[52] Grade I is a wound less than 1 cm (typically low-energy wounds caused by an inside-out puncture of the fragment end). A Grade II wound is greater than 1 cm and of higher energy. A Grade III wound has extensive soft tissue injury and/or periosteal stripping or a high-energy injury irrespective of the size of the wound. Depending on the severity of the stripping, Grade III lesions are subclassified into A, B, and C types, with B defined as an injury with extensive soft tissue loss and periosteal stripping usually associated with massive contamination. A Grade IIIC injury has an associated arterial injury that requires surgical repair for viability of the limb. Tscherne's[146] classification system of closed fractures has the advantage of including various degrees of closed soft tissue contusions and compartment syndromes as well. Type O fractures are from indirect violence (i.e., torsion) and have minimal soft tissue injury. Type I injuries have superficial abrasions or contusions caused by pressure from within. Type II injuries have deep abrasions with contused skin and/or muscle and may have an impending compartment syndrome. Type III injuries have extensive contusions or crushed muscle, subcutaneous avulsions, vascular injuries, and compartment syndromes. The reproducibility of soft tissue injury grading schemes has also been called into question.[19]

SURGICAL APPROACH

Although a number of surgical approaches to the humeral shaft have been described, there are two standard techniques that dominate most articles and reviews and are the most commonly used clinically: the posterior approach and the anterolateral approach.[36,49,50,62,65,148] Other described approaches that are useful in specific situations are the direct lateral approach and the direct medial approach.[71,75,103]

Anterolateral Approach

This approach is the preferred option for the majority of middle and proximal third humeral shaft fractures that require plate fixation (Fig. 34-7). The patient is positioned in the supine or semisitting position, a pad is placed behind the scapula to elevate the limb, and the arm is draped free to include access to the shoulder and elbow, if necessary. The limb can be supported on an adjustable covered Mayo stand or an arm board. The skin incision is centered over the fracture site and is performed longitudinally along the palpable lateral border of the biceps brachii. The proximal landmark for extension of the skin incision is the coracoid process, and distally it is anterior to the lateral supracondylar ridge. Next, the subcutaneous tissue and fascia are divided. Proximally, if necessary, dissection is performed between the pectoralis major muscle medially and the deltoid laterally, taking care to identify and protect the cephalic vein. If required, part of the broad deltoid insertion can be reflected posteriorly to gain access to the anterolateral shaft if needed for proper placement of a plate. In the midshaft region, the dissection plane is between the biceps and triceps, exposing the brachialis underneath, which is split longitudinally along its lateral portion. This muscle has dual innervation (radial nerve laterally, musculocutaneous nerve medially) and when correctly performed, this split is roughly in an internervous plane. When placing retractors around a midshaft fracture, it is important to avoid pressure on the radial nerve through the laterally placed

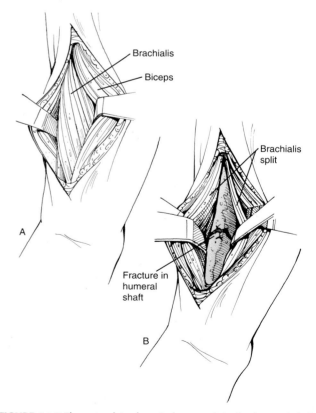

FIGURE 34-7 The anterolateral surgical approach to the humeral shaft. After skin and subcutaneous tissue dissection, the interval between the biceps anteriorly and the triceps posteriorly is developed. The shaft is identified distally by splitting the brachialis muscle in line with its fibers. The dissection can be extended into the delto-pectoral interval to gain access to the proximal humeral shaft and, if necessary, the humeral head.

retractor. Distally, dissection continues along the anterior aspect of the lateral supracondylar ridge between the brachialis medially and brachioradialis laterally. It is at this point that the radial nerve, as it wraps around the lateral aspect of the distal humerus, is closest to the dissection, and should be identified and protected.[27] It is in danger of being trapped underneath the distal, lateral corner of the plate: the surgeon should ensure that this corner is free of any soft tissue prior to closing (Fig. 34-8). The elbow range of motion should be examined to ensure there is no impingement from a very distal plate. The advantages of this approach include the favorable position of the patient, the ability to extend the incision proximally to deal with associated shoulder pathology or a proximal extension of the fracture, and identification of the radial nerve at the mid part or distally.[6] Disadvantages include technical difficulty in applying a plate distally along the (thin) lateral supracondylar ridge, the lack of access to any distal medial column pathology, and the noticeable scar that results.

Posterior Approach

The posterior approach is ideal for fractures that involve the distal third of the humerus, especially those that have an intra-articular extension or those that require an exploration and/or repair of an associated radial nerve injury.[50,76,118,148] The patient is typically positioned prone or in the lateral decubitus position with the affected side up. The arm is draped free over a bolster, and, depending on the proximal extent of the dissection

anticipated, a sterile tourniquet can be applied. A direct posterior skin incision is centered over the fracture site: It can extend from the tip of the olecranon distally to the posterolateral corner of the acromion proximally as required. After dissection of the subcutaneous tissue and superficial fascia, the triceps is sharply divided distally, taking care to identify and protect the radial nerve (and profunda brachii artery that runs with it) proximally.[80] The radial nerve crosses the posterior aspect of the humerus in the spiral groove roughly equidistant between the tip of the olecranon and the edge of the acromion and can be identified at the lateral edge of the attachment of the medial head of the triceps. Proximally, it is usually possible to identify an interval between the long and lateral heads of the triceps. The limit of proximal dissection is the overhanging cowl of the deltoid muscle posteriorly and the associated axillary nerve and posterior humeral circumflex artery. Distally, if fixation is anticipated on the medial column of the humerus, the ulnar nerve should be identified and protected. If required, the triceps can be elevated from the olecranon to gain access to the elbow joint. It should be firmly reattached through drill holes in the bone to prevent postoperative detachment (Fig. 34-9). The advantages of the posterior approach are mainly the ability to access both lateral and medial columns distally, the ease of fixing a shaft fracture with a distal extension, the flat posterior surface distally which is ideal for plate fixation, and the exposure of the radial nerve (Fig. 34-10). Paradoxically, its main disadvantage is the proximity of (and danger to) the radial nerve: plate extension past the midshaft of the bone must be done under the nerve, resulting in the awkward situation of having the nerve lying directly on the plate. Also, the prone or lateral position may not be favorable from an anaesthetic standpoint in a multiply-injured patient, and the humeral head and neck cannot be accessed safely through this approach.

Lateral Approach

The extended lateral approach, elucidated by Mills et al.,[103] consists of a lateral approach to the elbow that is extended proximally along the humeral shaft. It provides excellent exposure of the distal two thirds of the humerus and the radial nerve. It can be extended proximally into an anterolateral approach and distally along Kocher's interval distally to deal with lateral elbow pathology and has the advantage of being performed in the supine position. The skin incision follows a line from the deltoid insertion to the lateral epicondyle. After an incision through the superficial fascia, the triceps is reflected posteriorly and the brachialis and mobile wad of Henry are reflected anteriorly; muscle splitting is not necessary. The radial nerve is identified proximally as it wraps around the lateral aspect of the humerus; it is protected, as is the posterior antebrachial cutaneous nerve branch. The drawbacks of this approach are that access to the medial column distally is not possible and proximally, posterior access to the humeral shaft is limited by the deltoid muscle. The ideal indication for its use is a distal humeral shaft fracture that requires fixation and exploration of the radial nerve (i.e., a Holstein-Lewis fracture pattern).[64]

Anteromedial Approach

The anteromedial approach to the humerus provides exposure to the brachial artery and median and ulnar nerves. While it is rarely chosen for routine fracture fixation, it is an ideal approach

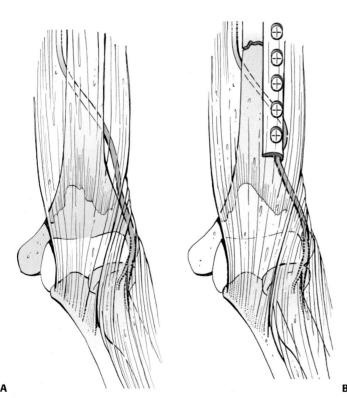

A   **B**

FIGURE 34-8 A. The radial nerve lies close to the humeral shaft as it exits from posterior to the shaft to anterior and is in danger of being entrapped underneath the distal, lateral corner of a compression plate applied through the anterolateral approach. **B.** During plate application the nerve and associated soft tissue is retracted laterally, and the corner of the plate should be checked prior to wound closure.

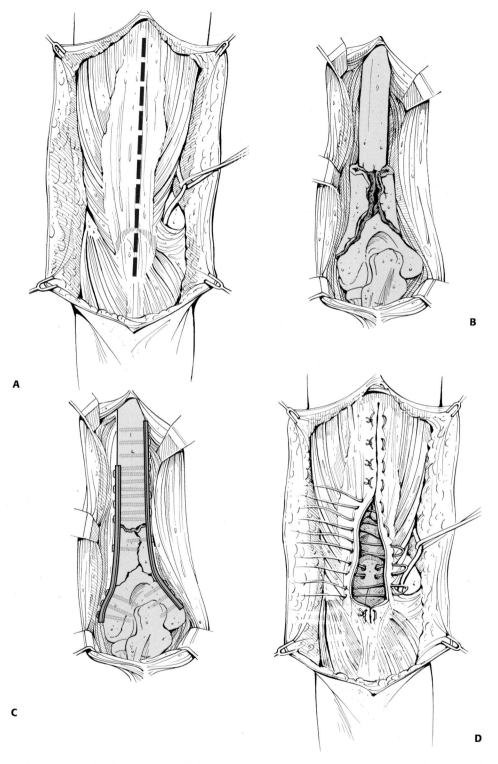

A

B

C

D

FIGURE 34-9 A–D. The posterior surgical approach to the humeral shaft. If necessary, the approach can be extended distally by reflecting the triceps from the olecranon, providing exposure of both medial and lateral columns. The triceps is then reattached through drill holes in the olecranon.

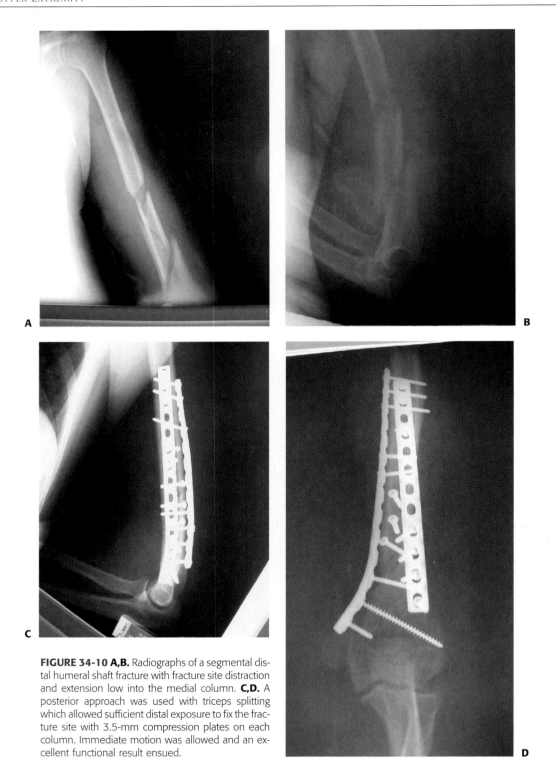

FIGURE 34-10 A,B. Radiographs of a segmental distal humeral shaft fracture with fracture site distraction and extension low into the medial column. **C,D.** A posterior approach was used with triceps splitting which allowed sufficient distal exposure to fix the fracture site with 3.5-mm compression plates on each column. Immediate motion was allowed and an excellent functional result ensued.

in the rare instance where there is a concomitant brachial artery injury that requires repair.[31,71,101] The surgical incision begins distally at the medial epicondyle and extends proximally along the posterior edge of the biceps brachii muscle. After dissection through the subcutaneous tissue and splitting of the superficial fascia, the ulnar nerve is identified and retracted posteromedially. The median nerve and brachial artery are identified and retracted anterolaterally. There are numerous small branches of the artery that require ligation. The medial inter-

muscular septum is then identified and can be partially resected to improve exposure and plate application. The triceps is stripped from the shaft and reflected posteriorly as required, and the origin of the coracobrachialis is reflected anteriorly. The main advantages of this approach are the excellent exposure of the neurovascular structures medially (especially if vascular repair is required) and the fact that the scar is well hidden when the arm is against the side, which makes it cosmetically appealing. However, it is a very "busy" anatomic area (including a number of cutaneous nerves such as the intercostobrachial nerve proximally and the medial cutaneous nerve of the arm distally), and neurovascular injury is a major concern. Also, proximal extension is very difficult: the axillary fold can be deceiving in how far it extends distally, especially in patients with an unfavorable body habitus (short, stocky, or obese).

NONOPERATIVE TREATMENT

Nonoperative treatment for fractures of the humeral shaft has a long and well-established history of success, with numerous authors reporting high rates of union with various types of splints, casts, and braces.[21,26,30,39,50,63,144,145,148,158] While anatomic reduction is rarely achieved with nonoperative treatment of these injuries, it is rarely necessary due to the wide range of motion of the shoulder and elbow, such that angulatory, axial, or rotational malunion is easily accommodated and functional limitation is minimal. The humeral shaft is well enveloped in muscle, has a robust blood supply,[80] does not bear weight, and is easily splinted, leading Sir John Charnley to state, "It is perhaps the easiest of the major long bones to treat by conservative methods."[26] Described techniques include hanging casts, "sugar tong" or coaptation splints, sling and swathes, long-arm casts, shoulder spica casts, and olecranon pin traction. However, while good results have been described with most of these methods, functional bracing has become the criterion standard for nonoperative treatment due to its ease of application, adjustability, low cost, allowance of shoulder and elbow motion, and reproducible record of success.[39,144,146,158] While a detailed description of nonoperative care is beyond the scope of this chapter, a review of functional bracing is an integral part of any description of humeral shaft fracture treatment.

Functional bracing was first described by Sarmiento[144] in 1977 and consisted of a custom-made, circumferential orthosis that allowed elbow and shoulder motion and was worn for a mean of 10 weeks in 51 patients with one nonunion. The device has been modified since and now is a prefabricated device with plastic supports and adjustable hook and loop straps that can be tightened as the swelling associated with the fracture recedes.[145] The device works on the principles of active muscle contraction correcting rotation and angulation, the "hydraulic" effect of soft tissue compression aligning the fracture fragments, and the beneficial effect of gravity on alignment. In the largest series to date of 922 patients (620 were followed to definitive outcome) with humeral shaft fractures treated with functional bracing, Sarmiento[145] reported union in 98% of 465 closed fractures and 94% of 155 low-grade open fractures. Open fractures took longer to heal than closed fractures (14 weeks versus 9.5 weeks). These results are consistent with those reported by Ostermann et al.[112] (4 nonunions of 191 fractures), Zagorski et al.[124] (3 nonunions of 170 fractures), and Ricciardi-Pollini (2 nonunions of 36 fractures).[171] However, the results in some other studies are not so favorable. In a study by Ekholm et al.,[39] 8 of 78 fractures did not heal when treated with a brace. Toivanen et al.[158] found a higher prevalence of nonunion with 21 of 93 fractures where bracing was not successful. Proximal shaft fractures were especially prone to healing problems. It is important to note that in these two studies, the time in a brace before converting to surgery was as low as 6 weeks in some cases, far less than the treatment time in Sarmiento's series.

Nevertheless, for properly selected patients, this technique results in a high rate of union. Given the early motion that is encouraged with this method, functional outcome of the elbow and shoulder is well maintained with 89% of patients losing 10 degrees of motion or less of the shoulder and 93% of patients losing 10 degrees of motion or less of the elbow in Sarmiento's series.[145] It should be noted, however, that many of the patients in this series were indigent and functional outcome data was rudimentary. For instance, elbow range of motion was recorded for only 301 of the original 922 patients.

Significant degrees of initial deformity are often surprisingly well corrected with this method under the influence of gravity, time, and the brace (Fig. 34-11). Sarmiento[145] reported that 55% of patients healed within 5 degrees of anatomic alignment following functional bracing of humeral shaft fractures, with varus being the commonest deformity: 42% of patients healed with 6 to 25 degrees of varus deformity. Eighty-six percent of patients healed within 10 degrees of anatomic alignment in the anteroposterior plane. These deformities did not seem to influence functional results. However, as mentioned, functional outcome data was minimal, and it is quite possible that subtle or delayed complications would not be detected. For example, recently the negative biomechanical and clinical effects of distal humeral varus malunion have been elucidated. Twenty patients with a mean varus malunion of 19 degrees developed posterolateral rotatory instability of the elbow a mean of 15 years after their initial distal humeral fracture.[109] It is unlikely this type of problem would have been elucidated in Sarmiento's study.

OPERATIVE TREATMENT

Operative Indications

The majority of isolated, simple humeral shaft fractures can be managed nonoperatively; however, there are specific operative indications that have been shown to enhance the outcome of the fracture or patient. These indications can be divided into three groups: fracture indications, associated injuries, and patient indications (Table 34-2). While some of these indications are absolute, such as an associated vascular injury or an associated higher grade open wound, many are relative indications where both patient and fracture features must be taken into consideration prior to deciding on treatment. For instance, although most segmental fractures are high-energy injuries with significant deformity, a segmental fracture in which both fracture lines are minimally displaced and the overall alignment is acceptable is a good candidate for a trial of conservative care with functional bracing. It is important to note that fracture comminution, in isolation, is *not* an indication for operative intervention. Although intuitively it would seem that such fractures are more likely to develop delayed or nonunion, this is not the case. In his large series of functional bracing, Sarmiento[145] found the median healing time was 11 weeks for the comminuted fractures and 12 weeks for the transverse fractures: others have reported similar findings. Some authorities have noted the relative propensity for delayed union in transverse or short oblique fractures managed nonoperatively in an active individual[147,148] and considered such injuries a relative indication for operative repair. Also, operative fixation of comminuted fractures is associated with a higher complication and mechani-

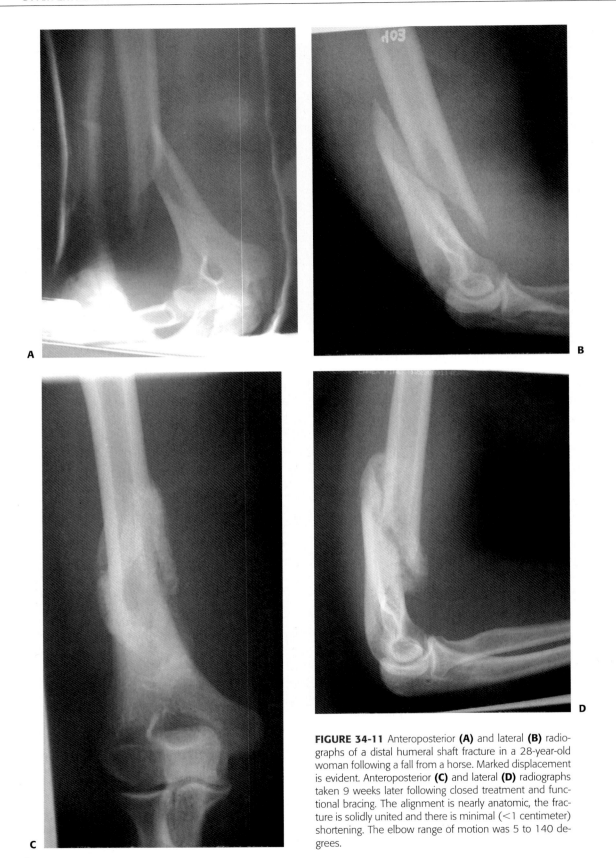

FIGURE 34-11 Anteroposterior **(A)** and lateral **(B)** radiographs of a distal humeral shaft fracture in a 28-year-old woman following a fall from a horse. Marked displacement is evident. Anteroposterior **(C)** and lateral **(D)** radiographs taken 9 weeks later following closed treatment and functional bracing. The alignment is nearly anatomic, the fracture is solidly united and there is minimal (<1 centimeter) shortening. The elbow range of motion was 5 to 140 degrees.

TABLE 34-2	Indications for Primary Operative Treatment of Humeral Shaft Fractures

Fracture Indications

- Failure to obtain and maintain adequate closed reduction
  - Shortening >3 cm
  - Rotation >30 degrees
  - Angulation >20 degrees
- Segmental fractures
- Pathologic fractures
- Intra-articular extension
  - Shoulder joint
  - Elbow joint

Associated Injuries

- Open wound
- Vascular injury
- Brachial plexus injury
- Ipsilateral forearm fractures
- Ipsilateral shoulder or elbow fractures
- Bilateral humeral fractures
- Lower extremity fractures requiring upper extremity weight bearing
- Burns
- High-velocity gun shot injury
- Chronic associated joint stiffness

Patient Indications

- Multiple injuries—polytrauma
- Head injury Glasgow Coma Scale ≤8
- Chest trauma
- Poor patient tolerance, compliance
- Unfavorable body habitus
  - Morbid obesity
  - Large breasts

cal failure rate, and thus is best avoided if conservative treatment is feasible.

Plate Osteosynthesis

Plate osteosynthesis remains the criterion standard of fixation of humeral shaft fractures against which other methods must be compared.[7,13,45,50,94,99,147,148,163] It is associated with a high union rate, low complication rate, and a rapid return to function. It can be used for fractures with both proximal and distal extension, is safe and effective in open fractures (see below), has essentially no elbow or shoulder morbidity, and is stable enough to allow early upper-extremity weight bearing in the multiply injured patient.[157] The surgical approaches, implants, and techniques are familiar to most orthopaedic surgeons, and it remains the procedure of choice at our institutions for humeral shaft fractures that require operative fixation (Fig. 34-12). Van der Griend et al.[163] reported union in 35 of 36 plated humeral shaft fractures with no shoulder or elbow mor-

bidity and one temporary radial nerve palsy. Bell et al.[7] had similar results (union in 37 of 39 fractures) as did Tingstad et al.[157] (union in 78 of 83 fractures). The union rate following open reduction and internal fixation of humeral shaft fractures averages 96% in a number of large series.[7,45,94,99,157,163] Complications are infrequent and include radial nerve palsy (2% to 5%, usually neurapraxic injuries which recover), infection (1% to 2% for closed fractures, 2% to 5% for open fractures) and refracture (1%).

Fractures in the middle or proximal third are best approached through an anterolateral incision. Fractures that extend into the distal third of the bone are best approached posteriorly. A broad 4.5 mm dynamic compression (DC) or limited contact compression (LCD) plate helps prevent longitudinal fracture or fissuring of the humerus because the screw holes in these plates are staggered.[147] In small individuals with thin humeri, a narrow 4.5 mm plate may be used. Inserted screws can be angled medially and laterally so they exit staggered on the opposite cortex, minimizing longitudinal stress. Other plates are not strong enough, especially in active individuals (Fig. 34-13). In the transition zone distally between the shaft and the supracondylar ridges, as the medial and lateral columns diverge, fixation can be achieved with two 3.5 mm compression plates along each column, avoiding plate impingement in the olecranon fossa (see Fig. 34-10). A lag screw placed across the main fracture line (either outside or through the plate) can increase construct strength by 30% to 40%, and if fracture or nonunion geometry permits, should be inserted (Fig. 34-14).[147] With a solid lag screw, three screws (six cortices) proximal and three screws (six cortices) distal constitute the minimum fixation; without a lag screw, at least four screws (eight cortices) proximally and distally are required. Fracture comminution, poor screw purchase, poor bone quality, or other negative factors should prompt longer plate application with more screws. Previously, it was recommended that a unicortical screw be placed in the last hole of the plate to minimize the stress-riser effect of the plate, provide a smoother transition of stress from plate to bone, and decrease the potential risk of fracture at the end of the implant. However, a biomechanical study by Davenport[34] showed no difference in stress between uni- and bicortical screws in the end of the plate, and this technique is no longer recommended.

There are several practical advantages to the use of the LCD plates over standard compression plates: they are easier to contour, allow for wider angle of screw insertion, and have bidirectional compression holes. Theoretical advantages include decreased stress shielding and improved bone blood flow due to limited plate-bone contact.[69] One study showed a 97% union rate in upper extremity injuries in which plate fixation was accomplished with LCD plates.[99]

Angle Stable

Even though conventional screw plate systems work very well in most patients when used for treatment of humeral fractures or nonunions, there are subgroups of patients where implant failure can be seen more frequently. Patients with osteopenic or osteoporotic bone are such a group where implant failure through screw loosening might be a problem. This is especially true if healing is slow and the patient uses a walking aid, and thereby is reliant on the upper extremity being able to take load.

Recently so-called angle stable or locked plating systems

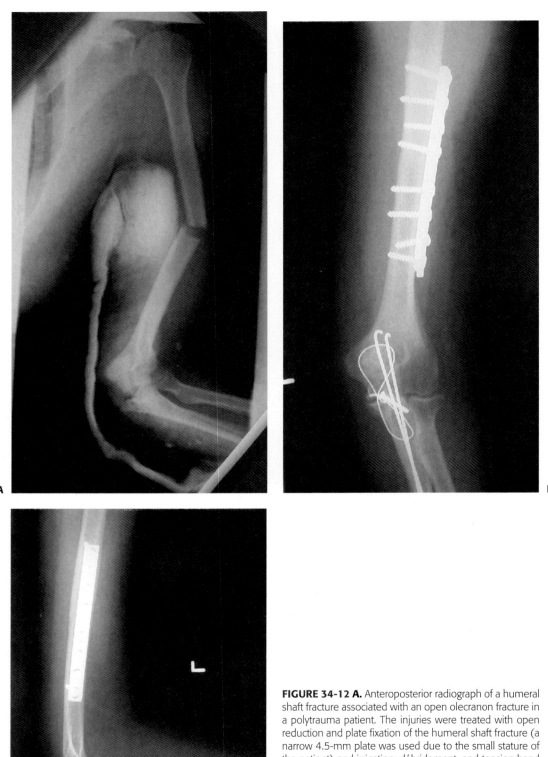

FIGURE 34-12 A. Anteroposterior radiograph of a humeral shaft fracture associated with an open olecranon fracture in a polytrauma patient. The injuries were treated with open reduction and plate fixation of the humeral shaft fracture (a narrow 4.5-mm plate was used due to the small stature of the patient) and irrigation, débridement, and tension-band wiring of the olecranon. Anteroposterior **(B)** and lateral **(C)** radiographs show healing of both fractures. An excellent functional outcome was the result, with an elbow range of motion of 20 to 135 degrees. Associated ipsilateral upper extremity fractures are one of the most common indications for primary operative fixation of humeral shaft fractures.

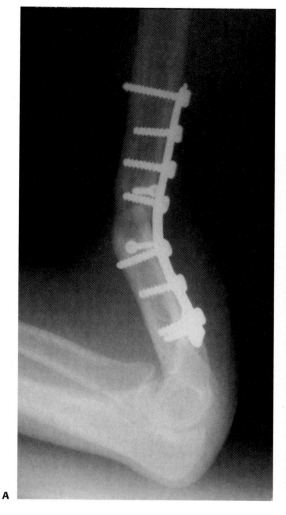
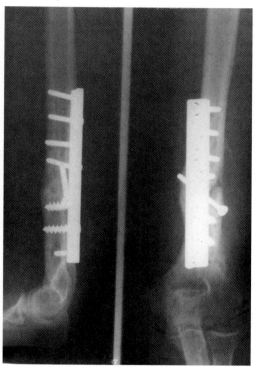

FIGURE 34-13 A. Proper plate selection is important in the fixation of humeral shaft fractures. This 18-year-old man had a displaced distal humeral shaft fracture fixed with a thin "T" plate placed directly posteriorly. This plate, with its thinnest dimension directly in the plane of motion of the elbow, was insufficient to withstand the forces applied to it in this muscular, active young man. An unacceptable 30-degree recurvatum deformity soon developed, with pain and instability at the fracture site. **B.** Revision with a lag screw and broad 4.5-mm compression plate restored local anatomy and resulted in rapid union. Compression plates are the implants of choice for humeral shaft fractures, especially in active young individuals.

have gained wide popularity. By locking the screws to the plate a number of mechanical advantages are gained, including a reduced risk for screw loosening and a stronger mechanical construct compared with conventional screws and plates. With locking plate systems, the pressure exerted by the plate on the bone is minimal as the need for exact anatomical contouring of the plate is eliminated. A theoretical advantage of this is less impairment of the blood supply in the cortical bone beneath the plate compared to conventional plates.

Despite clinical experience with locked plate systems being gained over the last few years, there remain very few published reports of their use in humeral fractures and nonunions. At the present time, there is some preliminary evidence that the improved fixation seen with locking devices may be advantageous in the humeral shaft, especially when dealing with osteopenic bone.[130,153] It is as yet difficult, due to the limited

number of publications, to define the exact role of and the proper indications for locking plates compared with conventional plate and screw systems.

Minimal Invasive Plate Osteosynthesis
Around the same time that angle stable systems were introduced into the market, the so-called minimal invasive plate osteosynthesis (MIPO) technique was popularized. Theoretically, the use of small skin incisions distant to the fracture site with submuscular plate insertion offers minimal soft tissue compromise. A prerequisite for the technique is indirect fracture reduction, using long spanning plates. The technique is widely used in tibial fractures as well as femoral fractures. For humeral shaft fractures, it has been considered too dangerous due to the risk of neurovascular injuries, particularly to the radial nerve. However, by using cadaver bones, different technical aspects have

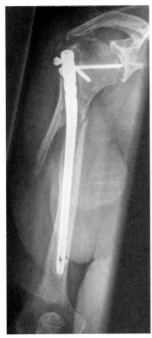
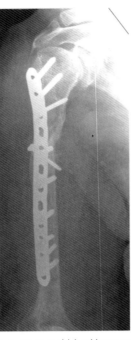

A

B

FIGURE 34-14 A. Aseptic nonunion in a 74-year-old healthy women 12 months following fixation with a locked nail. The fracture was never adequately reduced and one screw penetrated the joint. There were no signs of bone healing with instability in rotation and severe pain. **B.** Three months after reoperation with fixation with a compression screw and a locked plate and BMP for biologic stimulation. The fracture went on to uneventful healing.

been addressed in order to develop a useful and safe MIPO technique in humeral shaft fractures. Apivatthakakul et al.[3] showed that with the forearm in full supination the safe distance between the nerve and an anteriorly placed plate increased substantially. In 2004, Livani and Belangero[91] described their results when using the MIPO technique in 15 patients of whom 8 were polytraumatized and two were open fractures. Using an anterior plate position and 4.5 mm DC plates, they had no major complications, including no radial nerve palsies caused by the procedure. Fourteen of 15 fractures healed within 8 to 12 weeks, and two with varus alignment of 5 to 10 degrees. In 2007, two clinical series reported the use of a similar MIPO technique in 21 and 13 patients, respectively.[70,172]

In 21 patients with complex type C fractures, anterior placement of 4.5-mm large-angle stable-locking plates with 13 to 15 holes was used. There were no major complications during surgery, including no compromise of the radial nerve, and healing was obtained in 19 of 21 cases following the primary procedure.[70] Zhiquan et al.[172] reported on 13 patients with fractures through the mid or distal part of the shaft, with type B being the most common fracture type (10 of 13). The fractures were treated with a similar technique although with the use of narrow 4.5 mm DC plates with 10 to 12 holes for fixation. There were no nerve palsies resulting from the surgery. All fractures healed within 8 degrees of valgus and varus. The disadvantage of the MIPO technique in the humerus is a long operating time and increased radiation due to the need to check the reduction and the position of the implant during insertion and fixation. Future studies are awaited to confirm or refute any major advantages with its use in the humerus. Preliminary data and experience indicate a possible benefit in complex comminuted fractures.

Pearls and Pitfalls—Compression Plating

- Use an anterolateral approach for midshaft or proximal fractures, and a posterior approach for distal fractures.
- Use a broad 4.5-mm compression plate in most patients, with a minimum of 3 (and preferably 4) screws proximal and distal. A 4.5-mm narrow plate is acceptable for smaller individuals.
- Insert a lag screw between major fracture fragments, if possible.
- Check the distal corner of the plate for radial nerve entrapment prior to closure following the anterolateral approach.
- The intraoperative goal is to obtain sufficient stability to allow immediate postoperative shoulder and elbow motion.

Intramedullary Nailing

Locking, large-diameter humeral nails were introduced with the hope that the results from their use would parallel the clinical success seen with similar devices used for femoral and tibial fractures.[34,68,79,126,127,134,154] Previously available intramedullary implants for the humerus such as Rush pins or Enders nails, while effective in many cases with simple fracture patterns, had significant drawbacks such as poor or nonexistent axial or rotational stability.[1,57,121,135] Henley[59] reported a series of 49 patients with humeral shaft fractures treated with Ender nailing and had only one nonunion, and Brumback[18] reported a 94% union rate with Rush pins and Enders nails, although there was a significant rate of insertion site morbidity and backing out of the nails such that the "excellent" clinical success rate was much lower (62%). However, especially when used for comminuted or unstable fracture patterns, some form of additional stabilization was required, either internal (cerclage wire at the fracture site) or external (prolonged splinting). The construct that resulted was often not stable enough to allow early motion or upper extremity weight bearing in the case of the multiply injured patient with concomitant lower extremity injuries.

With the newer generation of nails came a number of locking mechanisms distally including interference fits from expandable bolts (Seidel nail) or ridged fins (Trueflex nail), or interlocking screws (Russell-Taylor nail, Synthes nail, Biomet nail). Unfortunately, despite favorable initial reports, these devices have not enjoyed the unparalled success of lower extremity locking nails. Problems such as insertion site morbidity, iatrogenic fracture comminution (especially in small diameter canals), and nonunion (and significant difficulty in its salvage) have been reported (Fig. 34-15).[40,97,98,140,151] In addition, some of the perceived advantages of nailing over compression plating (such as earlier upper-extremity ambulation and avoiding peri-implant fracture) have proven to be illusory.[68,98] A number of randomized clinical trials comparing these intramedullary implants to compression plating have been performed.[12,25,90,135] They have shown a higher reoperation rate and greater shoulder morbidity with the use of nails. At the present time, in our institutions, the use of locking nails is restricted to widely separate segmental fractures, pathologic fractures, fractures in patients with morbid obesity, and fractures with poor soft tissue over the fracture site (such as burns). A number of newer nails, designed to eliminate insertion site morbidity through an extra-articular start point, have been introduced (see below); it remains to be seen whether prospective, randomized trials will prove their advantages.

Original nail sizes were limited; thus, most locking humeral nails required reaming prior to insertion. While the reamings produced may improve fracture union, there are some draw-

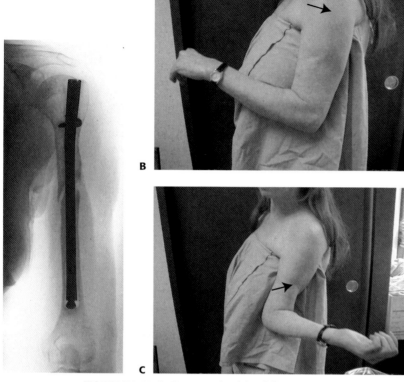

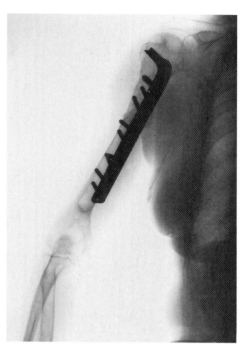

FIGURE 34-15 A. Gross rotational instability was present in a 41-year-old woman 7 months after having undergone reamed antegrade intramedullary nailing of a humeral shaft fracture. The distal interference fit of the nail failed. **B.** The incisional scar can be seen on the anterior aspect of her shoulder (*arrow*). The patient is facing straight ahead. **C.** It is possible for the patient to externally rotate her lower arm over 90 degrees without changing the orientation of her shoulder at all: the rotation occurs completely through the rotationally unstable nonunion. The skin and soft tissue can be seen bunching up at the midhumeral level of the nonunion (*small arrows*). **D.** Union following nail removal, bone grafting, judicious humeral shortening, and blade plate fixation.

backs. The fracture site must be kept closely apposed during reaming to prevent radial nerve damage. Also, the distal humeral canal tapers to a blind end above the olecranon fossa: it does not have a wide metaphyseal flare to vent debris or heat in front of an advancing reamer as does the femur or tibia. There is evidence that excessive reaming of the medullary canal can be detrimental. Reimer et al.[123] reported a 58% complication rate in patients undergoing Seidel humeral nailing when the humeral canal size was 9 mm or less, and postulated extensive reaming was one of the contributing factors. Others have reported extensive heat necrosis from excessive reaming, and we have experience with similar cases.[86,161] If there is not sufficient space, one risks distracting the fracture site as the nail wedges in the distal fragment during insertion (Fig. 34-16). One point emphasized in most series of large-diameter nails is that the humerus does not tolerate distraction. This is a risk factor for delayed and nonunion. In order to reduce the risk of distraction while at the same time improving the mechanical stability of the bone-implant construct, some nails offer the option to apply compression. One problem when applying compression has been related to breakage or bending of the locking screws leading to revision.[90,106] Newer nail designs have smaller (7-, 8-, or 9-mm) diameter implants that are better suited to small canal diameters. The smaller sized nails are usually solid, and they can often be inserted without reaming. Nailing is then turned into a very

quick procedure, an obvious advantage especially when dealing with polytraumatized patients. However, a major drawback with thinner nails is the reduced strength and the risk of implant breakage.

Antegrade Technique

The patient is placed in the beach-chair, semisitting position, with the affected arm draped free. The image intensifier is brought in directly laterally on the injured side, and the patient brought to the edge of the table, unless a radiolucent table is being used. The head is taped in place on a pad. Before proceeding, it is important to check and ensure a good radiographic picture of the entire humerus is possible. It may be necessary to have the patient lying partially off the table on a radiolucent support if the table is not radiolucent. The surgeon stands at the top of the bed looking down on the shoulder and the assistant stands below on the other side of the image holding the arm. A small incision is made at the anterolateral corner of the acromion, the deltoid is split, and any visible subdeltoid bursa is excised. The supraspinatus tendon is identified, and split for 1 to 2 cm in line with its fibers. The entry point for a standard antegrade nail is in the greater tuberosity, just lateral to the articular margin. A common mistake when learning nailing is that the entry point can be placed too lateral in the humeral head due to a feeling that the acromion prevents the surgeon

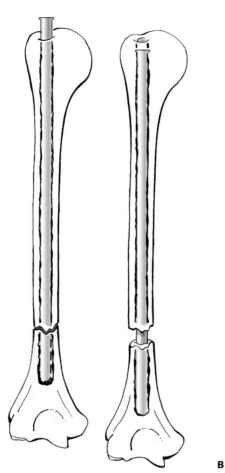

A   **B**

FIGURE 34-16 Fracture site distraction during intramedullary nailing. Since the humeral canal tapers to a blind end, if the nail is too long as it is impacted to avoid impingement in the shoulder **(A)**, it abuts the end of the canal and distracts the fracture site **(B)**. Fracture site distraction following humeral nailing is poorly tolerated and is a common finding in delayed unions and nonunions.

from reaching the correct position. In order to avoid an iatrogenic fracture of the proximal lateral cortex, it is crucial to reposition the insertion guide or the awl until it is in the desired position. The canal is then broached with either an awl or a starter reamer placed over a guidewire. If a reaming technique is used, a long guidewire is then passed to the fracture site, colinear with the medullary canal. The fracture is reduced with gentle longitudinal traction and manipulation, and the guidewire is passed across the fracture site. Extreme difficulty in reducing the fracture and passing the guidewire, especially in isthmal fractures, should alert the surgeon to the possibility of soft tissue (radial nerve) entrapment. In technology similar to that used for sciatic nerve monitoring during acetabular fracture fixation, Mills et al.[102] described using somato-sensory evoked potentials during closed humeral nailing to detect nerve injury. They found that they could detect signal change with impending nerve injury, and in at least one case, this prompted an open procedure with the finding of radial nerve entrapment in the fracture site.[102] However, this technology is not widely used at this time. Even so, the incidence of permanent radial nerve injury, despite its proximity to the humeral shaft, is surprisingly

low during closed nailing. If the fracture is open, the fracture site should be inspected visually to be sure it is free of soft tissue entrapment as the guidewire is passed. Using a combination of fluoroscopy and arm rotation, the guidewire is checked in two planes to ensure accurate placement.

We usually ream minimally, until the sound of cortical chatter is heard, and then insert a nail 1 to 1.5 mm smaller in diameter than the last reamer used. Care is taken to keep the fracture well reduced during the reaming process. The length of nail is carefully chosen and checked twice: if too long a nail is picked, one risks distracting the fracture site as the nail impacts the tapered end of the humeral canal as it is advanced in an attempt to seat it below the tuberosity proximally. Leaving the nail proud proximally will result in an increased incidence and severity of impingement (Fig. 34-17). Biomechanic studies have shown that nails locked with screws are axially and torsionally superior to so-called interference fit nail designs (Fig. 34-18).[10,92,173] The nail is then locked with screws using a jig proximally and a freehand technique distally. Distal anteroposterior or oblique locking, depending on the nail type used, is

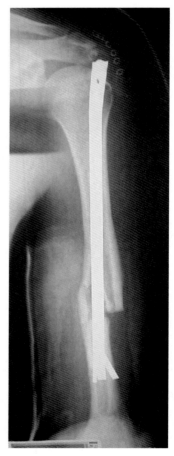

FIGURE 36-17 Anteroposterior radiograph following antegrade intramedullary nailing of a humeral shaft fracture. A number of sequential complications occurred: the distal fins of the nail deployed early, preventing proper seating of the nail and producing distraction at the fracture site. Thus, the surgeon was left with three choices: leave the nail proud at the shoulder, accept distraction at the fracture site, or restart with a shorter nail. The top of the nail was cut off but remained prominent causing intractable shoulder symptoms. Due to the prominence of the nail, the proximal locking screw could not be inserted, resulting in rotational instability. Multiple revision surgeries were the result.

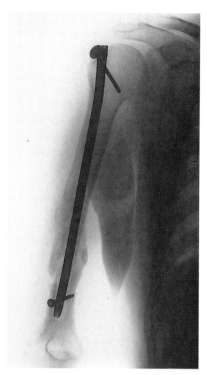

FIGURE 34-18 Uneventful union following a reamed, antegrade, interlocked humeral nail. Biomechanic and clinical data suggest that a device with both proximal and distal locking screws results in the best rotational and axial stability.

done through small open incisions; risk to the brachial artery, median nerve, and musculocutaneous nerve is minimized by the use of an open approach and by staying lateral to the biceps muscle and tendon. The radial nerve is at risk during lateral to medial locking.[14] While the nerve does not necessarily need to be seen and isolated, an incision with blunt dissection to bone, clear visualization of the tract and bony drill site, and use of a protective drill/screw insertion sleeve is mandatory. Anatomic studies have clearly shown that "blind" or percutaneous distal locking, as performed in the lower extremity, is not safe in the humerus.[41,119] Some authors advocate sectioning the coracoacromial ligament or performing a modest acromioplasty before closure in attempt to minimize impingement.[126,127] While this may be useful in the occasional case, there is no convincing evidence it is routinely successful. Any split in the rotator cuff should be repaired. A standard dressing is applied (a splint is not usually required), and the patient begins early active exercises under the supervision of a physiotherapist.

Retrograde Technique

This technique is best suited for fractures in the middle and distal thirds of the humerus. The patient is placed in a prone or lateral decubitus position with the arm over a bolster. The image intensifier is brought in from the ipsilateral side, and again it is important to ensure adequate imaging prior to proceeding. The arm is draped free, and an incision is made in the posterior midline from the tip of the olecranon proximally for 4 or 5 cm. The triceps is split down to bone and the olecranon fossa identified. There are two potential start points. The traditional one is in the midline, 2 cm above the olecranon fossa;

more recently, a start point through the superior aspect of the olecranon fossa itself has been advocated. This increases the effective working length of the distal segment, and provides a straighter alignment with the canal; however, it results in a greater reduction in resistance, especially to torque, compared to the more superior portal. A biomechanic study by Strothman et al.[155] showed a 29% reduction in load to failure for the superior portal and a 45% reduction for the olecranon fossa starting point. This weakness can result in iatrogenic or postoperative fracture. Lin et al.[89] changed their start point due to iatrogenic fracturing in a series of 39 retrograde nailings, and Rommens[136] reported 2 such fractures in his series of 39 cases. The same principles as with antegrade nailing apply for fracture reduction, guidewire passage, reaming, and nail insertion.[10] The nail should extend to a point where proximal locking can occur without risk of damage to the axillary nerve: this leaves the typical nail approximately 1.5 cm from the humeral head articular surface. The nail must be locked. If not, backing out into the elbow joint with subsequent loss of extension is possible. Prior to closure, it is important to wash out any residual bony debris from the reaming process: this may help prevent heterotopic ossification posteriorly (Fig. 34-19). The triceps is closed with interrupted sutures, and a dressing is applied. It is important to institute early elbow motion postoperatively to prevent stiffness, a complication of this procedure. Resisted extension should be avoided for 6 weeks postoperatively to protect the repair of the triceps split.

Pearls and Pitfalls—Intramedullary Nailing

- Avoid antegrade nailing in patients with pre-existing shoulder pathology or those who will be permanent upper extremity weight bearers (para- or quadriplegics).
- Use a nail locked proximally and distally with screws: use a mini-open technique for distal locking for all screws.
- Avoid intramedullary nailing in narrow diameter (<9 mm) canals: excessive reaming is not desirable in the humerus.
- Choose nail length carefully, erring on the side of a shorter nail:

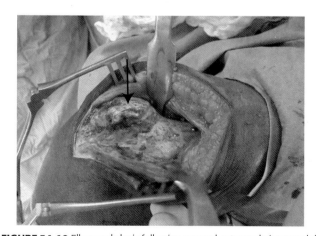

FIGURE 34-19 Elbow ankylosis following reamed, retrograde intramedullary nailing of a humeral shaft fracture. The intraoperative photograph is taken from a posterior approach, and the triceps has been split. The shoulder is to the right, the elbow is fixed at 90 degrees of flexion, and the forearm drops down to the left. The *arrow* marks a solid bridge of bone extending from the insertion point of the nail in the distal humerus to the olecranon. Resection of this osseous bridge followed by intensive physiotherapy resulted in a functional, but not normal, range of motion.

do not distract the fracture site by trying to impact a nail that is excessively long.

- Insertion site morbidity remains a concern: choose your entry portal carefully and use meticulous technique.

External Fixation

External fixation of the humerus is a suboptimal form of fixation with a significant complication rate and has traditionally been used as a temporizing method for fractures with contraindications to plate or nail fixation.[74,125] These include extensively contaminated or frankly infected fractures (Fig. 34-20), fractures with poor soft tissues (such as burns), or where rapid stabilization with minimal physiologic perturbation or operative time is required ("damage-control orthopaedics," see Chapter 9).[29,104,139] Most information in the literature is contained in case series describing the use of this technique for open humeral shaft fractures. Choong and Griffiths[29] treated seven "complex" open humeral shaft fractures with external fixation, and four went on to develop nonunion. Marsh and colleagues[93] used a monolateral external fixator to treat 15 patients with an open fracture of the humeral shaft. However, the complication rate was high: four patients required additional procedures prior to healing including two with breakage of the external fixator pins. Additionally, there were eight patients who required treatment for pin tract infections. Although Mostafavi and Tornetta[105] had good or excellent results in 12 of 18 of their patients treated with external fixation, the complication rate was high: three malunions, one delayed union, eight pin tract infections (two

with a sequestrum), and two refractures following fixator removal. While these results may indicate a selection bias, where only the worst injuries with the most extensive soft tissue damage were treated with this technique, in general, external fixation is cumbersome for the humerus and the complication rate is high. This is especially true for the pin sites, where a thick envelope of muscle and soft tissue between the bone and the skin and constant motion of the elbow and shoulder accentuate the risk of delayed union and malunion, resulting in significant rates of pin tract irritation, infection, and pin breakage.

AUTHORS' PREFERRED METHOD OF TREATMENT

Compression plate fixation is our treatment of choice for those humeral shaft fractures that have an operative indication (Table 34-2). We prefer the anterolateral approach unless the fracture is so distal that preoperative planning suggests it will not be possible to place four screws distally; if this is the case, a posterior approach is performed.[107] When dealing with open humeral shaft fractures, it is important to adhere to the principles of open fracture treatment. The open wound is inspected, any obvious debris (grass, clothing, dirt) is removed, and a sterile dressing is applied. The arm is splinted and prophylactic antibiotics started intravenously. Tetanus prophylaxis is given if required. The patient should be transferred emergently to the operating room where any associated life-threatening injuries take priority. Once these (or other orthopaedic injuries of greater urgency) are dealt with, attention is focused on the (open) humeral shaft fracture. Grossly contaminated wounds are subjected to a nonsterile scrub with copious sterile saline and a clorhexidene scrub brush. For the anterolateral approach, the patient is positioned sitting up 30 to 45 degree (favorable for polytrauma patients with abdominal, chest, or head injuries), and the arm is prepared in sterile fashion and draped free. An anterolateral approach is then performed (see "Surgical Approaches"); any open wounds are débrided, and if possible, included in the incision. The bone ends are exposed and thoroughly cleaned of debris and hematoma, taking care to preserve any soft tissue attachments to bony fragments. In open fractures, the medullary canal is carefully inspected as occasionally ground debris can be impacted far up the canal of the proximal fragment, especially in falls from a height, and this material must be removed. Completely devitalized cortical fragments are removed. For open fractures, the wound and incision are then copiously irrigated with a minimum of 9 liters of sterile saline. The radial nerve is identified distally between the brachialis and the brachioradialis and protected throughout the case. Care is taken not to pinch the nerve under the distal lateral corner of the plate (see Fig. 34-8). If radial nerve function is impaired or absent preoperatively, it is explored. This protects the nerve from further damage and adds useful prognostic information. If the nerve is found to be completely avulsed, the epineurium at the ends are tagged with a nonabsorbable, colored suture, for easier identification later, but primary repair (in blunt trauma cases) is usually not indicated.[46,76,118,128]

The fracture is then reduced and temporarily fixed with a 2-mm Kirschner wire. If possible, a lag screw is inserted

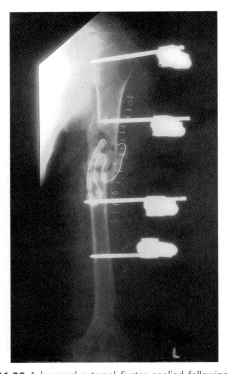

FIGURE 34-20 A humeral external fixator applied following hardware removal, irrigation, and débridement of a humeral shaft fracture treated initially by cerclage wiring and complicated by deep *Pseudomonas* infection. Antibiotic impregnated cement beads have been applied to the fracture site. External fixation is a useful temporizing method in this situation: following clinical and biochemical evidence of infection eradication, plating and bone grafting resulted in rapid union.

across the main fracture line. For most individuals, a broad 4.5-mm compression plate will be the implant of choice. The occasional small-boned patient may require a narrow 4.5-mm plate. A minimum six hole (with a lag screw) or eight hole (no lag screw) plate is contoured and applied. If the bone is osteoporotic or otherwise weak, a locking plate system should be considered. The fixation and radial nerve are checked, and an intraoperative radiograph is taken. Adjacent muscle is loosely approximated to obtain complete coverage of the plate, and a standard closure performed: drains are not typically necessary. Any open wounds are left open, and only the surgical extensions are closed. A sterile dressing and well-padded posterior splint are applied. The dressing and splint are removed at 48 hours postinjury. Wounds that have residual necrotic tissue, appear infected, have exposed bone, or require repeat débridement due to a high probability of residual contaminated material are returned to the operating room for repeat débridement and irrigation. The wound can then be closed in a delayed primary fashion if possible, or allowed to granulate in and heal by secondary intention. Larger defects may require a split-thickness skin graft to accelerate rehabilitation. More extensive soft tissue defects can be dealt with by a variety of local rotational (biceps) or pedicled (latissimus) flaps. Patients are encouraged to begin early, active motion of the shoulder and elbow under the supervision of a physiotherapist. If upper extremity weight bearing is required, an elbow gutter crutch is prescribed.

We reserve intramedullary nailing for patients with pathologic fractures, widely separate segmental fractures, or fractures with soft tissue conditions that would preclude or complicate plating, such as morbid obesity or local burns or some polytraumatized patients. While either plating or nailing is acceptable for most patients with humeral shaft fractures, we specifically avoid nailing in patients with preexisting shoulder pathology, those with narrow diameter humeral canals (<9 mm), those who will be permanent upper extremity weight bearers, and those with recognized radial nerve palsies. An antegrade approach is used for midshaft or proximal fractures, and a retrograde approach for distal fractures is ideal. We usually use a reamed nail locked with screws proximally and distally, though a thinner nail inserted without reaming is an option in selected cases. Reaming is done sparingly, stopping at the sound or feel of cortical chatter, and the nail inserted is 1 or 1.5 mm narrower than the last reamer. Great care is taken not to distract the fracture site with nail insertion. It is usually safer choosing a shorter rather than longer nail for this reason (see Fig. 34-16). An open approach should be used for the distal locking screws to avoid damage to neurovascular structures.[14,41,119] We no longer use small diameter flexible nails for humeral shaft fractures.

External fixation is useful in two situations. One is when rapid stabilization of the humerus is required, as in a critically ill patient with multiple injuries or in a fracture associated with a vascular injury where rapid stabilization can provide a stable platform for emergent vascular repair.[93,104,105,139] The other is when the associated soft tissue injuries or contamination (Gustilo type III) are so severe that plate fixation would result in exposed hardware or residual contamination. Using a large external fixator set, two pins are inserted from an anterolateral direction proximally and two pins distally (using a miniopen technique) and then connected with two straight bars. However, our recent experience with compression plating in these situations has been so favorable that the indications for external fixation have become very limited.

CLINICAL TRIALS OF PLATE FIXATION VERSUS INTRAMEDULLARY NAILING

There are numerous retrospective reviews of antegrade locked intramedullary nailing and compression plating in the literature.[7,13,34,45,68,94,99,126,134,157,163] Overall, they would suggest that the risk of shoulder pain is much less in patients treated with plates (essentially 0% versus 5% to 42% with antegrade nailing), and there is a trend towards a decreased nonunion rate with plating. However, these studies, like all retrospective studies, have inherent biases, including patient selection, a high lost to follow-up rate, incomplete outcome data and surgeon bias. Randomized clinical trials have been designed to overcome the biases inherent in prior observational studies, and are the criterion standard for evaluating treatment. There have been four randomized clinical trials that have compared locked intramedullary nailing to compression plating.[12,24,25,95] Although they are small in numbers, their design is solid and represents the best information on this topic. A recent meta-analysis conducted on three of those studies revealed that patients in the plated group had a lower rate of reoperation (6% versus 18%, $p = 0.03$), and a lower rate of shoulder pain (1% versus 21%, $p = 0.002$).[8] There were also more nonunions in the nail group (8/73, 11%) than in the plate group (5/83, 6%), although this difference did not reach statistical significance with the numbers available. These studies certainly did not confirm the theoretical advantages of locked intramedullary nailing of humeral shaft fractures and have re-established compression plating as the treatment of choice for the majority of these injuries (Table 34-3). In the most recent paper which was not available at the time of the meta-analysis, 47 patients were randomized to reamed nailing or DC plating. The union rates were similar between the groups, although the healing time was shorter in the intramedullary group. Shortening of the arm and restriction of shoulder movement was less in the plated group.[24]

HUMERAL FRACTURE ASSOCIATIONS

Radial Nerve Palsy

There is an intimate anatomic relationship between the radial nerve and the humeral shaft.[14,46,49] Thus, it is not surprising that the most common nerve palsy following a humeral shaft fracture is a radial nerve palsy. This is typically due to contusion and/or stretching of the nerve in the spiral groove at the moment of fracture. There is limited "give" in the nerve as it is tethered proximally as a terminal branch of the brachial plexus and distally as it exits through the lateral intermuscular septum. The incidence of radial nerve palsy is directly proportional to the degree of violence of the initial trauma. It ranges from 3% to 34% and increases with open fractures, polytrauma, vascular injury, and multiple ipsilateral fractures.[46,50,64,76,118,128,148]

| | TABLE 34-3 | Table of Advantages and Disadvantages of Plate Fixation, Intramedullary Fixation, and External Fixation of Humeral Shaft Fractures |

Parameter	Plate Fixation	Intramedullary Nails	External Fixators
Fracture around implant	−	−	+
Shoulder morbidity	+	−	+
Difficulty of reconstruction if primary treatment fails	+/−	−	+
Nonunion rate	+	−	−
Reoperation rate	+	−	−
Radial nerve injury	+/−	+/−	+/−
Small canal	+	−	+
Radiation exposure	+	−	−
Complex fractures	−	+	−
Intra-articular fracture extension	+	−	−

+, advantage; −, disadvantage

Tingstad et al.[157] reported an incidence of radial nerve palsy of 34% in 111 fractures predominantly in polytrauma patients, and Connolly[32] reported an incidence of 14 radial nerve injuries in 53 open fractures (26%). Fortunately, most of these lesions are neuropraxic injuries of the nerve: spontaneous recovery is the rule. Ogawa[110] reported 100% recovery in one large series, Pollock[118] reported a recovery rate of 90% in closed fractures, and Sarmiento[143] reported a 100% recovery rate in 85 patients with distal humeral shaft fractures. However, there is some evidence that the prognosis for recovery with high-energy or open fractures is not as good. Sanders et al.[142] presented twelve cases of open humeral shaft fractures associated with radial nerve injury; only four recovered function. Ring et al.[128] described six radial nerve transections in 24 patients with high-energy humeral shaft fractures with associated radial nerve palsy. Connolly[32] reported that four of fourteen radial nerve injuries in patients with open fractures did not recover and required nerve grafting.

Given the propensity for spontaneous recovery (and the lack of any evidence that early exploration improves matters), it is clear that, in general, the presence of a radial nerve injury in isolation is not an indication for operative management of a humeral shaft fracture (Fig. 34-21). In a systematic review of 1045 patients, it was concluded that based on available published data there is no significant difference in the final result of radial nerve palsy associated with fractures of the humeral shaft treated with initial expectancy or early exploration.[149] However, there are accepted indications for exploration of the radial nerve in the setting of a humeral shaft fracture. If there

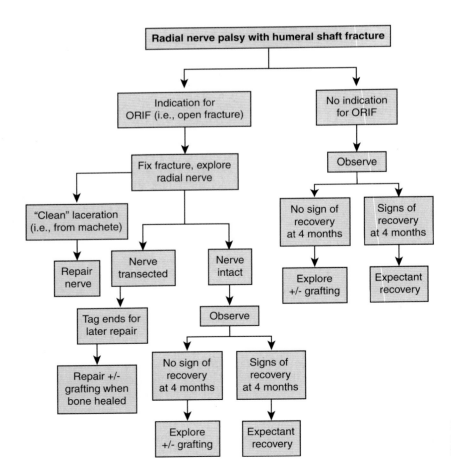

FIGURE 34-21 An algorithm for the management of radial nerve palsy in association with a humeral shaft fracture.

is another indication for operative repair, such as an open wound or an associated ipsilateral injury, then the injured nerve should be explored for a number of reasons. First, it is of prognostic value. While a contused or stretched nerve is the most likely finding, if a completely severed nerve is found then this helps guide early nerve reconstruction or tendon transfer after fracture healing.[128,142] Secondly, the nerve may be injured due to entrapment in the fracture site, compression by bony fragments, or other physical obstruction, and thus it is prudent to release and protect the nerve during fracture fixation. Third, in rare instances, primary repair of a completely lacerated nerve may be indicated. In most cases, extensive contusion and stretching make such an endeavor unrewarding, as the zone of injury of the nerve is often indistinct and the chance of recovery slim. For example, Ring et al.[128] reported that none of the five transected radial nerves repaired primarily in a series of high-energy humeral shaft fractures recovered. However, in instances where there is a clean laceration of the nerve from a bone fragment or sharp instrument (such as a machete), then primary repair may be successful, and Foster et al.[45] reported good results with primary nerve repair (four of five repaired nerves recovered).

Radial nerve palsies associated with low-velocity gunshot wounds may also recover spontaneously. Rather than being transected by the projectile, in most cases the nerve has been damaged by the concussive blast, shock-wave associated with the path of the bullet, or contused by bony fragments and is structurally intact.[145]

Following a radial nerve injury, the patient should be given a cock-up wrist splint and instructed to perform daily passive wrist, finger, and thumb range of motion exercises to prevent the development of a flexion contracture. Some authorities recommend that baseline electromyography and nerve conduction studies be performed at 3 weeks postinjury so that later studies can be compared to them.[11,156] The patient is observed clinically for any sign of recovery of the nerve, which is typically seen in the first muscles innervated distal to the injury: the brachioradialis and extensor carpi radialis brevis and longus. The electrical equivalent is the development of action potentials where complete denervation or fibrillation was noted before. One should expect to see nerve regeneration proceed at a rate of 1 inch per month. If no electrical or clinical activity can be identified by 4 months postinjury (depending on the site of the fracture), then surgical exploration of the nerve is indicated. Resection of the damaged portion of the nerve followed by cable graft reconstruction is usually required. If nerve reconstruction is unsuccessful or not indicated, tendon transfers are an ideal procedure to restore function, since the major contribution of the radial nerve to the hand is motor function.

Brachial Plexus Palsy

The successful outcome of functional bracing for humeral shaft fractures depends on a number of factors, including a compliant patient, an upright position, the "hydraulic" effect of a well-fitted splint, and the contraction of the associated muscles. Sarmiento points out that the muscle contraction during activity when the patient is in a splint helps to "align the fragments in a parallel direction, correcting the malrotation."[145] In patients with a significant brachial plexus palsy, this intrinsic muscle tone and contraction may be lost, resulting in a much higher

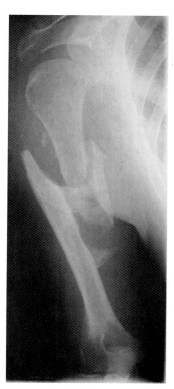

FIGURE 34-22 A humeral pseudarthrosis 14 months following a fracture complicated by a severe brachial plexus injury. Lacking normal muscle tension and tone, these injuries have a high rate of delayed and nonunion.

incidence of malunion and/or nonunion (Fig. 34-22). Also, the associated sensory loss may lead to ulceration of insensate skin under a tight splint or cast. There is relatively little in the literature regarding this topic, but Brien et al.[16] reported on 21 cases of humeral shaft fracture with associated brachial plexus palsy and reported superior results with plate fixation (three of three united). Of the eleven fractures treated nonoperatively, there were five nonunions, two delayed unions, and two malunions. The flail extremity interfered with rehabilitation and led to prolonged hospital stays. Additionally, only 2 of 21 patients showed any neurologic recovery. The authors described a much higher incidence of associated injuries in this patient population (eleven traumatic brain injuries), which often represent independent indications for operative intervention. Thus, an ipsilateral brachial plexus injury represents a strong relative indication for primary plate fixation of an associated humeral shaft fracture.

Pathological Bone

A metastatic deposit from a malignant neoplasm is the most common cause of a pathologic fracture of the shaft of a long bone in an adult.[78,82] The long bone most affected is the femur, followed by the humerus, which accounted for 96 of 588 pathological fractures (16%) in one large series.[53] These fractures usually occur late in the clinical course of the illness and are often a significant source of pain. The associated functional loss can be critically important in the typical older, debilitated patient and can result in a decreased quality of life, dependency upon others, possible hospitalization or institutionalization, and increased medical costs. While aggressive surgical treatment is not usually indicated in the moribund, cachetic patient, judicious intervention in a patient with a life expectancy measured in months or greater is often beneficial from both a patient-oriented and societal perspective.

Unfortunately, when dealing with pathologic humeral shaft fractures from malignant lesions, conservative care (consisting mainly of splinting and/or radiation) provides some symptomatic relief but rarely provides fracture healing or stability. Douglass et al.[37] reported dismal results in a series of patients with pathologic humeral shaft fractures treated with radiation and immobilization. Pain relief was evident in five of nine treated with radiotherapy and only 3 of 12 with immobilization. Flemming and Beals[43] reported on eight such patients treated conservatively and described poor pain relief with half having poor function. These unsatisfactory results have led other investigators to pursue operative avenues of treatment. For patients with a finite life expectancy, the ideal treatment would stabilize the entire shaft of the humerus, be performed through a small incision away from the metastatic disease (to allow radiotherapy without affecting incisional healing), minimize bleeding by not exposing the fracture site and tumor, and allow early motion and rapid return of function. Fracture healing per se is not as important as it is in a routine patient, and a stable mechanical construct that will last a finite period of time is the main goal. This discussion pertains to patients with established metastatic disease from an incurable systemic cancer; resection and reconstruction of primary malignant disease or an isolated metastasis with the potential for long-term survival (such as renal cell carcinoma) is beyond the scope of this chapter.

Harrington et al.[58] reported one of the first surgical experiences with a large number of patients with pathologic humeral fractures, and reported good results in 68 cases treated with Rush pinning and, in most cases, polymethlymethacrylate ce-

ment augmentation. In a series that originated from the Mayo Clinic, Lewallen et al.[88] (and later Yazawa et al.[170]) described a similar technique with good results: 48 of 55 patients in Lewallen's paper had good relief of pain. Lancaster[83] used a larger diameter Kuntscher nail and reported pain relief in 26 of 29 patients. However, they also had to open the fracture site and add polymethylmethacrylate cement to obtain rotational and axial stability. This is undesirable from a number of standpoints including increased blood loss, increased operative time, higher morbidity (from infection), and, if radiation is to be used, wound healing complications. The advent of larger diameter locking humeral nails has dramatically improved the care of patients with pathologic humeral shaft fractures. In a definitive article on the subject, Redmond et al.[122] performed closed, locked humeral nailing on 16 patients and reported good to excellent pain relief in all but 1 patient, with 14 extremities returning to "near normal" function within 3 weeks. Radiation was initiated at a mean of 7 days postoperatively in 14 humeri, with no infections, nerve palsies, or implant failures, and only one reoperation for the removal of a locking screw was required (Fig. 34-23). The rotational and axial control obtained by the locking screws eliminates the need to address stability at the fracture site directly. Thus, radiotherapy can be initiated earlier because there is no incision. In this specific situation, closed locked humeral nailing has significant advantages over compression plating and should be considered the treatment of choice for affected individuals.

Unreamed nailing can also be used for metastatic fractures of the humerus. In a study by Atesok and others,[4] 21 patients with 24 humeri fractured due to metastatic disease were treated with an unreamed nail. In 5 fractures, polymethylmethacrylate was used for augmentation. Pain relief was rated as good in 20

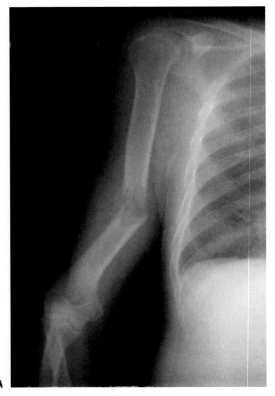

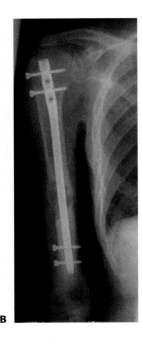

FIGURE 34-23 A. Pathologic humeral shaft fracture through a lytic defect caused by a deposit of metastatic carcinoma. **B.** Treatment with a statically locked closed humeral nail resulted in immediate stability and good pain relief; since there was no incision over the fracture site, early radiation therapy could be initiated. (Courtesy of Dr. Ralph B. Blasier.)

A   B

of their 21 patients. Bone union was achieved in 15 of the 17 patients who survived more than 3 months.

An open approach to the tumor site is best reserved for patients where tissue is required for diagnosis, or a definitive resection of the tumor mass is planned to gain sufficient local control to allow anticipated long-term survival (such as in isolated metastasis from renal cell carcinoma). In this situation, the technique of Chin et al.,[28] with segmental resection followed by metallic, cement, or allograft replacement and plating is recommended. Fractures in the metaphyseal region that are not amenable to stabilization with an intramedullary nail are best treated with prosthetic reconstruction.

Benign tumors or conditions (such as aneurysmal bone cysts or fibrous dysplasia) may weaken the bone sufficiently to result in a fracture from minimal force or trauma. In most cases, despite what may appear to be an unfavorable radiographic picture, closed treatment will result in healing. Often, the healing osseous response will obliterate or at least attenuate the lesion. Thus, the initial approach for the majority of pathologic fractures from benign tumors is nonoperative.

Open Wounds

Although present in less than 10% of humeral shaft fractures, an open wound complicates treatment, and there is relatively little specific information in the literature to aid in decision making. The patient with an open humeral shaft fracture has often sustained high-energy trauma and has an increased incidence of radial nerve palsy, fracture comminution, ipsilateral upper extremity fractures, and systemic injuries. Most information that is available is contained in larger series on the treatment of humeral shaft fractures that include a small percentage of fractures that had associated open wounds, and a variety of treatment techniques have been described.[7,45,94,99,157,163]

Open Reduction and Internal Fixation

Vandergriend and colleagues[163] reported on open reduction and internal fixation of 34 humeral shaft fractures, 13 of which were open. Although all 13 were plated and eventually healed without infection, only 5 had immediate plate osteosynthesis. The remaining 8 were plated secondarily after temporizing methods were used initially. In the only series dealing exclusively with the issue, Connolly et al.[32] reviewed 53 consecutive patients from a Level I trauma center managed with immediate plating of open humeral shaft fractures. Three patients underwent early amputation due to associated vascular injuries with mangled extremities, 3 were lost to follow-up, and 1 died. Forty-six patients were followed to definitive outcome, and they reported excellent results with no deep infections, no malunions, and nonunions. Forty fractures healed at an average of 18.6 weeks postinjury. There were six delayed unions that healed on average at 10.1 months postinjury, but none of these patients required other operative procedures to obtain union. The authors stressed the importance of a standard surgical protocol including thorough irrigation and débridement, stable fixation with broad 4.5 mm compression plates, a minimum of eight cortices transfixed proximal and distal to the fracture, leaving the wound open, and prophylactic antibiotics. In most cases, the plate was covered with local muscle and the wound allowed to granulate closed in a delayed fashion.

Intramedullary Nailing

Crates and Whittle[33] described a series of 73 acute humeral shaft fractures treated with antegrade nailing. Twenty-six of these fractures were open, and all healed without infection following locked antegrade nailing, although shoulder pain and impingement from prominent hardware was seen in over 10% of the patients. Sims and Smith[152] treated 22 acute fractures with intramedullary nailing; of the four open fractures, two went on to develop a nonunion. Rommens et al.[136] reported on 39 patients with humeral shaft fractures treated with locked retrograde humeral nailing. Four patients had open fractures. Although one developed a nonunion, none became infected. Other large series reporting on locked intramedullary nailing describe essentially similar results. Proper technique in these series included a thorough soft tissue irrigation and débridement, cleaning of the bone ends, open passage of the reaming guidewire followed by closure of the deep muscle layer to keep the osteogenic debris from the reaming around the fracture site. Although there may be problems with insertion site morbidity, it would appear that this technique has a low infection rate when used for open fractures of the humeral shaft.

External Fixation

A number of papers describe external fixation as a temporizing measure for severe open humeral shaft fractures with extensive soft tissue loss. However, the complication rate, including delayed and nonunion, is high. Choong and Griffiths[29] reported a 57% nonunion rate (4/7), Marsh and colleagues[93] had 4 reoperations in 15 cases, and Mostafavi and Tornetta[105] had good or excellent results in only 12 of 18 (67%) of their patients treated with external fixation. In general, this technique should be considered a temporary measure prior to definitive treatment.

Functional Bracing

In the largest series of functional bracing reported to date, Sarmiento and colleagues[145] were able to follow 620 patients treated with functional bracing for humeral shaft fractures at one of two university-affiliated hospitals with a large, uninsured, primarily indigent patient base. Of these, 155 had open fractures that were either Grade I or II injuries (37 patients) or caused by low-velocity gunshots (118 patients). The results in this series were remarkably good; the nonunion rate for open fractures was only 6%. There were no deep infections, although there were a significant number of patients lost to follow-up, and the authors stress that the patients they reported on are a specific subgroup. Individuals with multiple injuries (including ipsilateral fractures), higher grades of soft tissue damage, fractures caused by high-velocity gunshots, or with fracture complications were seen by other orthopaedic surgeons and were excluded from the study. Ostermann et al.[112] reported on 191 patients treated similarly, and Zagorski[171] described the results of 170 patients treated with functional bracing; both had nonunion rates of 2%. Although there are fewer patients in these studies, results were similar for the small percentage of individuals that had (low-grade) open injuries.

These studies suggest that isolated, low-grade open humeral shaft fractures (especially those that have resulted from low-velocity gunshots) can be managed safely and effectively with the use of functional bracing. The comminution often seen in such injuries is not, in isolation, an indication for surgical intervention. However, the most important aspect of electing to use this simple and straightforward technique for an open fracture is proper patient selection. Higher grades of soft tissue damage, polytrauma cases, associated ipsilateral fractures, fractures from high velocity gunshots, and fractures complicated by infection or malalignment in the brace are not suitable.

Requirement for Upper Extremity Weight Bearing

Due to the high incidence of associated lower extremity fractures (especially in polytrauma patients), the issue of whether a patient with a surgically repaired humeral shaft fracture can bear weight on it to aid in mobilization arises frequently. While most cases of fixation failure can be attributed to poor technique (i.e., too short a plate), the potentially deleterious effect of increased force from walking with a cane (25% body weight), a forearm crutch (45% body weight), or an axillary crutch (80% body weight) is a concern. It was originally felt that, similar to the lower extremity, a locked humeral nail would be a "load-sharing" device better suited to withstand the rigors of upper extremity weight bearing as compared to a "load-bearing" device such as a plate.[10,89,173]

However, biomechanic studies clearly show that a plate can restore excellent bending and torsional stiffness to the humerus.[60] Additionally, a clinical study by Tingstad et al.[157] examined the effect of immediate weight bearing in 82 patients with humeral shaft fractures treated with plate fixation. If necessary, due to lower-extremity injuries, patients were allowed to use platform crutches or a walker to ambulate. Ninety-four percent of the fractures healed primarily, and immediate upper extremity weight bearing had no effect on humeral fracture union, fixation failure, or alignment. The authors stressed the requirement for adequate fixation with a minimum of six cortices proximal and distal to the fracture site. Thus, it would appear that it is safe to allow immediate upper extremity weight bearing on a (properly performed) plated humeral shaft fracture. At our institutions, an elbow gutter crutch is typically used in this situation.

Humeral Prostheses

With the rising popularity of upper extremity arthroplasty and the aging demographics of the population, periprosthetic fractures of the humerus are increasing in incidence.[15,23,77,108,166] In a clinical situation similar to the lower extremity, a long rigid stemmed implant in an elderly, osteoporotic individual creates a stress riser that can result in fracture, especially if the stem is loose or complicated by osteolysis. Many of the treatment principles used in the upper extremity are extrapolated from extensive experience with periprosthetic femoral and tibial fractures. While not identical, this information serves as a basis for treatment until more accurate data is available. There are, however, some significant differences: There is less bone stock in the humerus, infection rates are higher, neurovascular structures are in closer proximity (and hence the incidence of iatrogenic injury is higher), and cemented stems are the standard.[15,23,77,108,166]

Total Elbow Arthroplasty

The incidence of periprosthetic fracture following total elbow arthroplasty has been estimated to be approximately 5%, and these injuries have been classified by Morrey and O'Driscoll.[108]

Type I fractures are isolated fractures of the humeral condyles. Type II fractures are around the stem of the humeral prosthesis and are divided into those with well-fixed or loose stems (subdivided into acceptable bone stock or severe bone loss). Type III fractures are fractures proximal to the stem. Type I injuries do not typically require active treatment, although they may be a harbinger of potential future problems due to osteolysis. Type III and Type II fractures associated with stable prostheses may be treated conservatively if there is reasonable alignment and bony apposition, and the patient can tolerate a prolonged period of time in a splint. Type II fractures associated with a loose stem and/or significant bone loss (which unfortunately is usually the case) require surgical intervention. In the largest series to date, Sanchez-Sotelo et al.[141] reported on 11 such patients treated with cortical strut allograft augmentation and revision arthroplasty with a long stem prosthesis. They found this procedure to be technically demanding and associated with a high complication rate, but had union of 10 of 11 fractures. We have had similar results with this method, which appears to be the treatment of choice for these fractures (Fig. 34-24). Technical points that are important include isolation and protection of both radial and ulnar nerves, careful removal of the old implant and cement (to prevent iatrogenic fracture), good fracture apposition (with humeral shortening if necessary), bone grafting of the fracture site, avoiding cement extrusion into the fracture site, and allograft strut placement that ensures fracture stabilization and graft/cement containment.

Total Shoulder Arthroplasty

There are a number of reports describing periprosthetic fractures following total shoulder arthroplasty, and the prevalence of such injuries has ranged from 1.6% to 2.4%.[15,23,77,166] As with other periprosthetic fractures, the quality of the bone, location of the fracture, and implant fixation are the main determinants of treatment and outcome. The available systems used to describe periprosthetic humeral fractures classify fractures based on the anatomic relation of the fracture to the stem.[96] A Type A fracture occurs at the tip of the stem extending proximally, Type B at the tip of the stem with or without some distal extension, and Type C distal to the tip of the stem.[166] The conservative treatment of Type C fractures is associated with a high success rate (Fig. 34-25). Campbell[23] reported healing in four of four such fractures, and the high union rate (five of six) of these fractures treated in a splint in the series by Kumar et al. led the authors to state that, "For Type C fractures, a trial of nonoperative treatment is recommended."[77] Type B fractures have a worse prognosis with conservative care. Six of seven did not heal in a series by Boyd et al.,[15] and four of five did not heal in the series of Kumar et al.[77] While a trial of conservative care in a well-aligned Type B fracture with a stable component may be reasonable, a lack of clear progression towards union should prompt operative intervention. Newer plates with the ability to enhance fixation proximally with cerclage wire mounts are useful in this regard. A fracture around a loose prosthesis should be treated with a long stem revision, with autogenous bone grafting of the fracture site. Type A fractures are usually associated with a loose stem, and if this is the case, require operative intervention similar to Type B fractures. In the unlikely event that the humeral component is stable, a trial of splinting is indicated. Groh et al.[51] reported on 15 fractures adjacent to humeral prostheses. Five type A fractures were

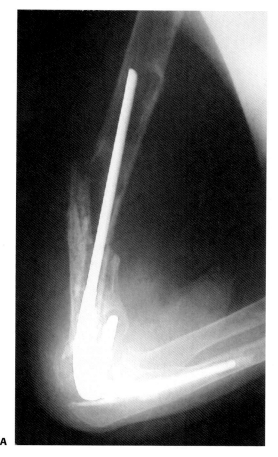

A

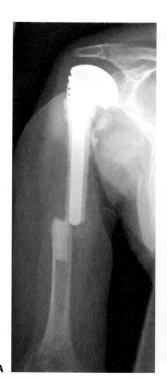

A

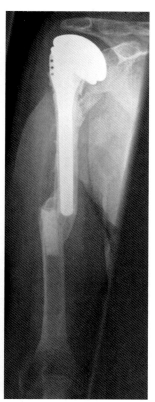

B

FIGURE 34-25 A. 65-year-old woman who 6 months following a hemiarthroplasty (due to a comminuted proximal humeral fracture) had a new fall and sustained a transverse fracture at the tip of the fixed stem. **B.** The fracture was treated with a functional brace. There was uneventful healing at about 9 weeks despite the presence of extensive cement at the fracture site.

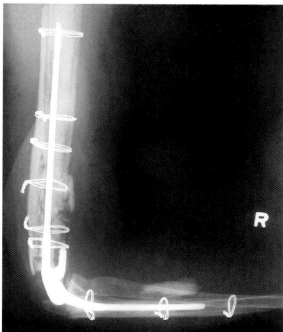

B

FIGURE 34-24 A. Lateral radiograph of a periprosthetic humeral fracture after trivial trauma 5 years following cemented total elbow arthroplasty for a distal humeral nonunion in a 67-year-old woman. The osteolysis and loosening of the humeral component is obvious. Like the lower extremity, this represents a risk factor for fracture. **B.** Lateral radiograph 2 years following revision with implant removal, allograft cancellous grafting, long stem revision, and allograft cortical strut grafting secured with cerclage wires. (The ulnar component was also loose and was revised.) A good result ensued.

treated nonoperatively with a brace while another 10, of which 5 were type C, were treated surgically with a long revision stem and cerclage. All fractures progressed to union.

COMPLICATIONS

Complications after Intramedullary Nailing

Insertion Site Morbidity

Insertion site pain and discomfort is a feature of many intramedullary nails, be it anterior knee pain following tibial nailing or shoulder pain after antegrade humeral nailing. Despite variations in insertion technique and implant design, persistent shoulder pain remains a problem following antegrade humeral nailing. Modifications of the insertion technique have ranged from mini incisions at the edge of the rotator cuff in an attempt to avoid cuff damage altogether to formal open approaches with partial anterior acromioplasty, division of the rotator cuff, insertion of the nail, and subsequent cuff repair.[34,68,126,127,134] The basic problem lies in the fact that the medullary canal is in line with the articular surface of the humeral head and the rotator cuff, and the insertion area is an anatomically limited one where any soft tissue swelling, nail protrusion, or other perturbation can result in painful impingement-like symptoms (see Fig. 34-17). In the initial enthusiasm for this technique, the incidence of shoulder problems was extremely variable, and, in general, underreported. Reimer[126] reported excellent shoulder function in 17 of 18 patients who underwent antegrade Seidel nailing. In 1991, Habernak and Orthner (in their original series on Seidel nailing of humeral shaft fractures) reported that, "all cases regained full shoulder movement with no functional impairment by an average of six weeks."[54] However, to their credit, the same authors later stated in a letter to the editor of the journal in which their work was published regarding antegrade humeral nailing through a standard portal, that, "This inevitably leads to damage of the cuff. . .When we reviewed the 19 active patients in 1991 we did not address their shoulders and this should have been addressed."[55] Subsequently, other authors reported much higher rates of shoulder pain and dysfunction following antegrade nailing including Robinson and his coauthors[134] (12 of 17 patients) and Ingman and Waters[68] (100%) causing a change to the retrograde technique.

With proper technique, the shoulder pain that is associated with the insertion of humeral nails is usually self-limiting and temporary. Proper technique includes minimizing damage to the cuff by protecting the edges during reaming, seating the nail well below the osseous surface, removing all reaming debris, carefully repairing the cuff upon completion of the procedure, and instituting early shoulder motion. However, despite all precautions, shoulder pain may be severe enough to warrant further surgical intervention, up to and including acromioplasty, subacromial bursectomy, nail removal, and cuff repair. Patients who will be permanent upper-extremity ambulators (such as those who are rendered para- or quadraplegic in the accident that causes their concomitant humeral shaft fracture) seem to be particularly vulnerable to violations of their subacromial space and rotator cuff. Intractable pain and impingement can be the result. Antegrade humeral nailing is relatively contraindicated in such individuals and in those with a prior history of impingement, and a humeral shaft fracture should be plated if an indication for operative intervention exists in these patients.

There have been two separate approaches to eliminating the insertion site morbidity seen with antegrade humeral nailing. One was to adopt a retrograde technique, where the nail is inserted through the olecranon fossa. There are several series that describe this technique.[10,68,89,136] However, complications include supracondylar fracture, elbow pain, triceps weakness, or elbow stiffness/ankylosis (see Fig. 34-19).

The other approach was to design humeral nails that avoid the articular surface and rotator cuff by having alterations in the proximal portion of the nail that allow an extra-articular start point, analogous to the proximal bend in a tibial nail. A report in 2003 by Stannard et al.[154] describes a titanium, flexible locking nail with a unique mechanism. Inserted in a flexible format, it allows an extra-articular starting point (1.5 cm distal to the greater tuberosity for antegrade insertion) and is tensioned by a screw in the end of the nail which stiffens the intercalated segments, producing a rigid construct. This is then locked in standard fashion. The Birmingham group reported on 42 treated with this device, and reported an excellent union rate.[154] Thirty-eight of 42 had no shoulder pain (mean constant score of 90 points, range 50 to 100). There were however, five major complications requiring reoperation (nonunion, hardware failure, deep infection), all associated with the smaller 7.5-mm version of the implant. The authors cautioned that, considering these complications, "options other than intramedullary fixation should be considered" in patients with canals 8 mm or less in diameter.[154] Analogous to previous reports of humeral nails however, these results need further confirmation before the device can be recommended for general use.

Fractures at the End of the Nail

A well-recognized complication of plating of humeral shaft fractures is the potential for fracture at the end of the plate due to the stress-concentrating effect of the screws or refractures following plate removal (Fig. 34-26).[147] It was thought that the introduction of locking humeral nails would lead to the elimination of this problem, as it has in the lower extremity with locked femoral and tibial nails. However, the anatomy of the distal humerus is fundamentally different from the tibia or femur; these lower extremity bones have a wide metaphyseal flare. The medullary canal of the distal humerus tapers rapidly to a narrow end above the olecranon fossa.[49,62] Thus, the tip of the nail ends in diaphyseal, rather than metaphyseal, bone. The juxtaposition of a long rigid implant with locking screws at the tip in diaphyseal bone leads to a significant stress riser effect, especially if there is a transcortical hole drilled for a missed distal locking screw. This is analogous clinically to the introduction of short locking nails for intertrochanteric and subtrochanteric fractures in the femur that were associated with a low but persistent incidence of femoral shaft fracture at the tip of the implant.[56,85] Similar fractures have been reported following locked humeral nailing.[98] These fractures were reported 8 to 26 weeks after the humeral shaft fracture had been treated. A sudden rotational motion was accompanied by an audible crack associated with an oblique or spiral distal humeral fracture at the distal end of the nail (Fig. 34-27). A number of factors result in delayed healing in this situation including the distal locking screw(s) and nail tip in the fracture site, the "Holstein-Lewis" pattern of fracture and the poor natural history of fractures at the end of long, rigid implants.[15,23,64,87] The limited number of reported cases makes treatment recommendations difficult. It would appear that these fractures are best treated with repeat operative intervention where the distal locking screws (and nail, if the shaft fracture is solidly healed) are removed and the fracture site reduced and then internally fixed. If the nail is left in place, then transcortical screws and/or cerclage wires will be required to augment proximal fixation.

Nonunion

Nonunion can occur following closed or operative treatment. Nonunion following operative repair is often the result of technical error, including inadequate plate size (see Fig. 34-13), fracture site distraction (see Figs. 34-15 and 34-16), inadequate screw purchase (Fig. 34-28), or mechanical failure from osteopenic bone.[32,45,94,107,147] Thus, careful attention to surgical technique and proper implant choice can reduce the incidence of nonunion. The treatment of nonunion is based on establishing mechanical stability and stimulating nonunion site biology.[48,66,72,73,81,115–117,129,131,138,162,168] Open reduction and internal fixation with iliac crest bone grafting has had consistently good results in the treatment of humeral shaft nonunion, regardless of the cause. Ring et al.[129] reported union in 24 of 25 humeral shaft nonunions treated in this fashion, and Otsuka et al.[115] reported union in all 25 patients from a similar series. Proper technique is essential and includes removal of all preexisting implants, débridement to bleeding healthy bone, reestablishing the medullary canals of the fragments, correction of

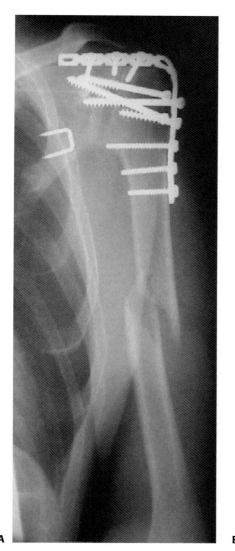

A

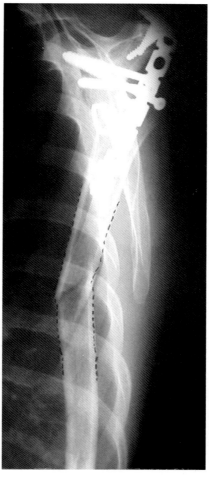

B

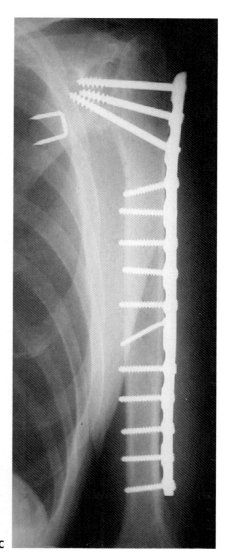

C

FIGURE 34-26 A. A 43-year-old man had a successful glenohumeral fusion following multiple failed surgical procedures for shoulder instability with subsequent arthritic change. He fell approximately 9 months postoperatively and sustained a humeral shaft fracture below the fusion plate. **B.** The lateral radiograph demonstrates the extension deformity at the fracture site (*dotted outline*). Operative intervention was recommended for two reasons: the long lever arm and shoulder fusion meant that there would be excessive force and motion at the fracture site, making a delayed or nonunion more likely. Second, the fracture would be very difficult to control in a splint, and the extension deformity would result in significant loss of function since compensatory motion through the shoulder was not available. **C.** Anteroposterior radiograph following open reduction and internal fixation. The old plate was removed and a long, broad large fragment plate was used for fixation. Extra screws were placed distally due to the increased stress anticipated, and fixation extended proximally to protect the arthrodesis.

deformity, stable fixation with compression, and bone grafting. Bone grafting is typically required for atrophic nonunions, as hypertrohic nonunions have favorable biology and will generally heal with mechanical stabilization alone. More recently, there has been increasing interest in the use of demineralized bone matrix (DBM) or synthetic bone graft substitutes in an attempt to eliminate the morbidity of autogenous bone grafting. In a retrospective study by Hierholzer et al.,[61] 78 patients with atrophic delayed union or nonunion were treated with open reduction and internal fixation with a plate. The first 45 also had autologous bone from the iliac crest added while the last 33 had DBM added instead of autologous bone. All procedures

were done by the same surgeon according to a strict protocol that was not altered during the study period. All cases except one in the DBM group healed. The authors concluded that the use of DBM prevented the 44% donor site morbidity seen in the bone grafted group, while providing consistently good healing. While there is some preliminary evidence that materials such as bone morphogenetic proteins (BMPs, i.e., BMP-7 or BMP-2) will provide sufficient biologic stimulus to produce union, it is important to use them properly.[164] They should form an integral part of a standard orthopaedic procedure (Fig. 34-29). For patients with bone loss of more than 5 to 6 cm or those who have failed conventional care, vascularized fibular grafting is a good

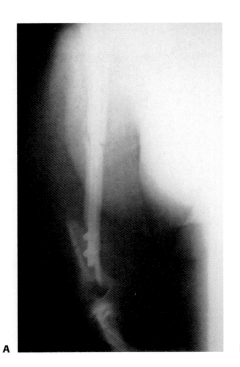

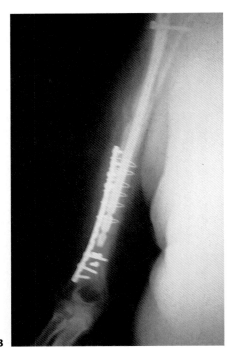

A

B

FIGURE 34-27 A. A fracture occurred at the distal tip of this interlocking humeral nail following a rotational injury 8 weeks after intramedullary nailing for a humeral shaft fracture. **B.** The fracture was repaired by removal of the interlocking screws from the fracture site, reduction of the fracture, and plate fixation with a combination of screws and cerclage wires.

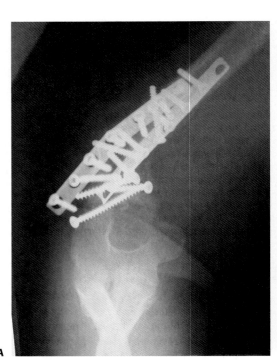

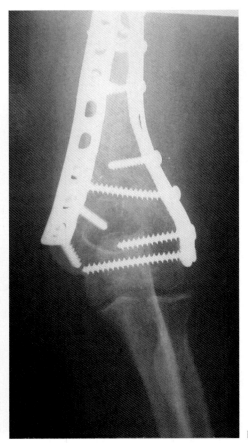

A

B

FIGURE 34-28 A. Inadequate distal purchase was a major technical error in the surgical treatment of this distal humeral shaft fracture in an obese 36-year-old woman. Using only three screws with marginal purchase distal to the fracture site resulted in early mechanical failure with varus collapse and pain. **B.** Radiograph following hardware removal, realignment, autogenous bone grafting, and repeat fixation with a precontoured plate laterally and a compression plate medially. The fracture healed promptly but the patient had an iatrogenic radial nerve palsy postoperatively that lasted 4 months. Revision surgery for humeral fractures carries with it a higher rate of complications, especially nerve injury.

FIGURE 34-29 This 77-year-old patient had had two attempts at fixation of a nonunion following conservative treatment of a humeral shaft fracture. **A.** There are two main problems: one is mechanical, with obvious loss of fixation in very osteopenic bone, and the second is biologic, with no evidence of callous formation or healing, an atrophic nonunion. **B.** Intraoperative photograph after realignment, débridement of the nonunion, re-establishment of the medullary canals, and plate fixation with a broad 4.5-mm compression plate. Following provisional fixation of the plate with one screw proximally and distally, a cortical strut allograft was applied medially and the remaining screws were inserted into it, dramatically enhancing fixation. rhBMP-7 was applied to the nonunion site (*arrow*) instead of autogenous bone (both anterior iliac crests had been harvested previously). With a stable arm and no bone graft donor site, the patient left the hospital the day after surgery. **C.** A follow-up radiograph taken at 4 months postoperatively revealing solid bony union. **D.** The steps in the procedure are depicted.

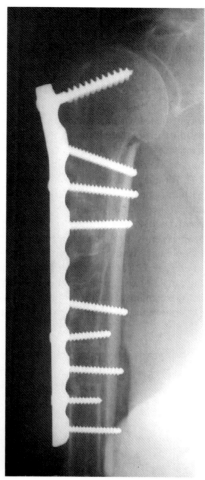

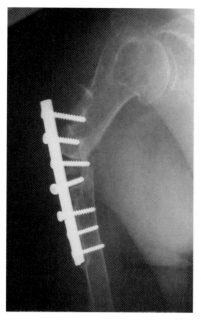

A

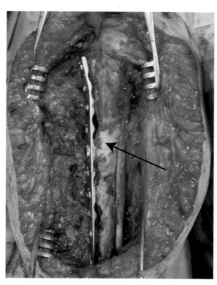

B

C

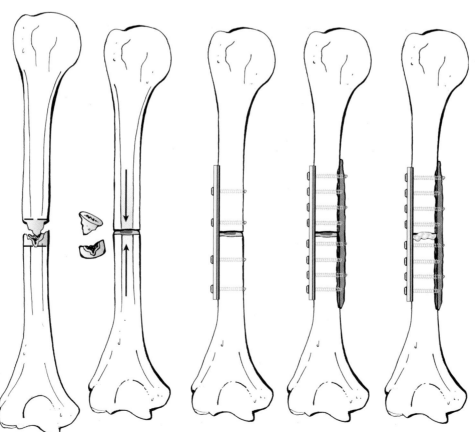

D

option; Jupiter[71] reported healing in 4 patients treated in this fashion.

Often nonunion is associated with severe osteopenia, be it as a cause of prior mechanical failure or as a result of prolonged disuse. There are several options for dealing with this situation: longer plates with more screws, cement augmentation of screw fixation, blade plate fixation, and the use of Schuli nuts for plate fixation.[22,72,116,131] Allograft can be used as intramedullary fixation or as cortical struts to aid in mechanical fixation (Fig. 34-29). Wright[168] reported success in 17 of 19 patients augmented with intramedullary allograft fibular fixation; Van Houwelingen and McKee[164] had union in all of six recalcitrant nonunions treated with onlay strut allografts to augment screw fixation. More recently, Ring et al.[130] reported on the use of a locking plate to enhance fixation in severely osteoporotic elderly patients (mean age 72 years) and had success with their primary procedure in 22 of 24 patients. This new technology has great promise in the treatment of fractures or nonunions with poor bone quality.

Nonunion following intramedullary nailing represents a unique problem. Originally, it was thought that exchange nailing would be routinely successful in this situation, just as it has been in the lower extremity. However, McKee et al.[97] found that exchange nailing was successful in only 4 of 10 such cases, and then had better success with nail removal, compression plating, and bone grafting (union in all nine cases). Similarly, Robinson et al.[134] had success with exchange nailing in only two of five cases. Nonunion associated with a loose nail is a difficult reconstructive problem and requires longer plates, liberal bone grafting or inductive bone graft substitute, and extensive dissection to remove the implanted nail. Wu and Shih[169] presented a comparative study on the use of intramedullary nails versus plates in the primary treatment of humeral nonunion, and found similar results in both groups (89.5% union in the plate group, 87.5% union in the nail group). However, if nailing is chosen as a treatment, bone grafting seems advisable.

Delayed union or nonunion following nonoperative treatment can be due to soft tissue interposition, displaced transverse fracture patterns, noncompliance with bracing (Fig. 34-30), un-

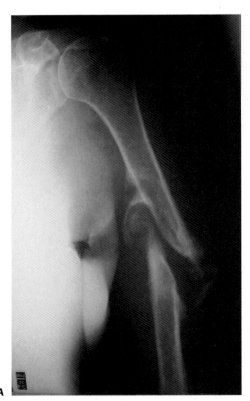

A

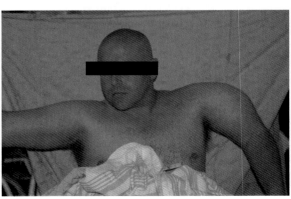

B

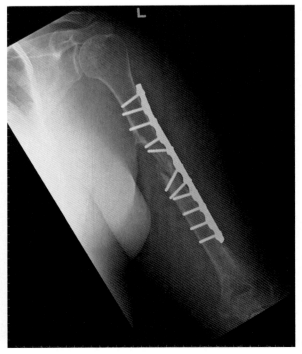

C

FIGURE 34-30 A synovial pseudarthrosis followed conservative treatment of a midshaft humeral fracture in a 38-year-old alcoholic who was noncompliant with treatment and did not wear his functional brace. Note the pseudoarticulation between the distal fragment and the reactive bone on the medial aspect of the proximal fragment. **B.** There was gross mobility at the nonunion site. This photograph also demonstrates why varus malalignment is common with these injuries. The intrinsic pull of the deltoid on the proximal fragment produces the typical deformity. Surgical tactics included excision of the interposed soft tissue and pseudocapsule, débridement of the bone ends to bleeding bone, re-establishment of the medullary canals with a drill, shortening, and reapproximation of the bony fragments. A broad, 4.5-mm plate was applied following lag screw fixation of the nonunion and rhBMP-7 was applied to the nonunion site to stimulate healing. **C.** Postoperative radiograph revealing excellent alignment and stable fixation. Early motion of the elbow and shoulder was allowed and union occurred.

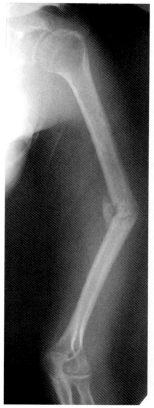
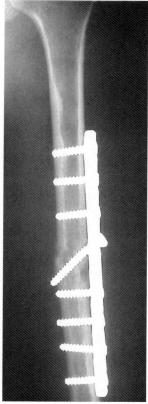

FIGURE 34-31 A. Unacceptable varus deformity and nonunion in a 22-year-old female student 6 months following a humeral shaft fracture treated conservatively. While a fairly broad range of angulatory, translational, and rotational malunion can be accepted in the humeral shaft due to the compensatory motion of the shoulder and elbow, this degree of deformity has functional and cosmetic consequences. The lack of osseous union caused ongoing pain at the nonunion site. **B.** Uneventful union following open reduction, correction of deformity, compression plating, and addition of bone morphogenetic protein.

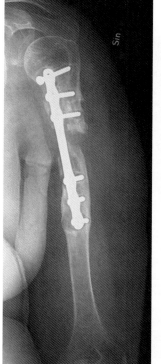
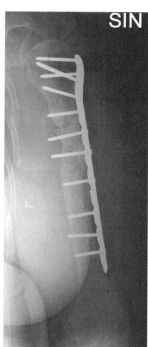

FIGURE 34-32 A. This 63-year-old female sustained a closed humeral fracture which was treated primarily with a brace. She developed a non-union, which was treated by plating and bone grafting at 9 months. Plate breakage 6 months later led to a reoperation with a new plate and another bone graft. This was complicated by postoperative infection. At time of referral, almost 2 years after the injury, the plate was loose with severe pain and instability. There was bone loss and no signs of healing. **B.** Five months following reoperation with slight shortening, revision of the sclerotic bone ends, and fixation with a new plate with compression and BMP to stimulate healing. Cultures were negative at time of revision. The fracture has healed uneventfully.

favorable body habitus (i.e., morbid obesity), or severe fracture angulation (Fig. 34-31). A true synovial pseudarthrosis can result (see Fig. 34-30), which requires extensive débridement at the time of surgical repair.

Some authorities have reported that nonunion of the upper extremity is relatively well-tolerated, compared to lower-extremity nonunion, especially in elderly patients or those with multiple medical comorbidities whose functional demands are limited. However, Ring et al.[132] showed that a humeral pseudarthrosis can be very debilitating in elderly patients whose independent functioning is often marginal and can often be the difference between independent living and institutionalization. They used the Enforced Social Dependency Scale to evaluate 22 elderly (mean age 72 years) patients with humeral nonunion and found a mean value of 39 points (0 = complete independence, 100 = complete dependency). The authors stated that 8 patients had been told there was nothing that could be done surgically for their problem. Following successful operative repair of the nonunion, the Enforced Social Dependency Score decreased to a mean of 9 points, reflecting a dramatic improvement in independent functioning. Recognition of the associated impairment and knowing about the improved implants and techniques for the operative repair of humeral nonunion in the

elderly population can lead to a more aggressive surgical approach to this problem; age alone should not be used as a contraindication to fixation (Fig. 34-32).[132]

Pearls and Pitfalls—Nonunion Treament

- Investigate for infection prior to initiating treatment
- Some bone shortening (<3 cm), in order to have apposition of healthy, viable bone ends, is acceptable in treatment of nonunion of the humeral shaft.
- Correction of deformity and compression plating is the treatment of choice.
- Add a bone graft or osteoinductive bone graft substitute to atrophic nonunions.
- A variety of techniques are available to deal with osteoporotic bone.

Infection

Fortunately, due to its excellent blood supply and thick soft tissue and muscle coverage, deep infection of the humerus is relatively rare, even in open fractures treated aggressively with immediate internal fixation. In our experience, infection in this setting is usually related to underlying medical co morbidities, especially diabetes or severe, mutilating injuries that are often near-amputations.

Where deep infection develops following fracture fixation, the general principles of treatment should be followed (see Chapter 24). Cultures are taken to establish the causative bacteria, appropriate antibiotics are administered intravenously, the patient's medical condition is optimized, and the infected fracture is débrided and irrigated. If the implanted fixation is solid, it is left in place; if not, it is removed and a spanning external fixator is applied (two pins proximal, two distal). We have had excellent success in augmenting standard techniques through the addition of an antibiotic impregnated, osteoconductive bone substitute at the fracture or infection site. It provided a very high local concentration of antibiotics and it then contributed to eradicating infection in 23 of 25 patients.[100] If necessary, serial débridements are performed. If the original plate or nail has been left in place, the hardware can be removed following union, if necessary. If an external fixator is used, repeat fixation with bone grafting can be performed when the wound is clean and the infection eradicated as evidenced clinically and microbiologically. In recalcitrant cases, the Ilizarov technique has been described as a useful salvage option.[44,81,117,159] However, in the humerus it is associated with a high complication rate, a prolonged period of time in the frame, and a significant risk of refracture.

CONCLUSION

Humeral shaft fractures are common. While most of these fractures can be treated nonoperatively with the expectation of a high degree of success, the alert orthopaedic surgeon can also use the interaction as an opportunity to intervene in other related health areas, such as the recognition, diagnosis, and referral for treatment of osteoporosis. There remains a consistent subset of these fractures that will have improved outcomes with operative intervention. Open reduction and compression plating has a consistent record of high union rates, low complication rates, and rapid functional restoration that makes it the standard against which other methods are compared. Locked intramedullary nailing is an attractive option in select fracture types or clinical situations. Future innovations, be they technique- or implant-related, should be subjected to rigorous, prospective randomized studies prior to universal acceptance or recommendation.

REFERENCES

1. Allen WC, Piotrowski G, Burstein AH, et al. Biomechanical principles of intramedullary fixation. Clin Orthop Rel Res 1968;60:13–20.
2. American College of Surgeons. Advanced Trauma Life Support (ATLS) Manual. Chicago: American College of Surgeons; 1993:17–46.
3. Apivatthakakul T, Arpornchayanon O, Bavornratanavech S. Minimally invasive plate osteosynthesis (MIPO) of the humeral shaft fracture. Is it possible? A cadaveric study and preliminary report. Injury 2005;36(4):530–538.
4. Atesok K, Liebergall M, Sucher E, et al. Treatment of pathological shaft fractures with unreamed humeral nail. Ann Surg Oncol 2007;14(4):1493–1498.
5. Bae H, Widmann RF, Hotchkiss RN. Extreme rotational malunion of the humerus. J Bone Joint Surg Am 2001;83(3):424–427.
6. Baker DM. Fracture of the humeral shaft associated with ipsilateral fracture dislocation of the shoulder: report of a case. J Trauma 1971;11:532–534.
7. Bell MJ, Beauchamp CG, Kellam JK, et al. The results of plating humeral shaft fractures in patients with multiple injuries. J Bone Joint Surg Br 1985;67:293–296.
8. Bhandari M, Devereaux PJ, McKee MD, et al. Compression plating versus intramedullary nailing of humeral shaft fractures—a meta-analysis. Acta Orthop 2006;77(2):279–284.
9. Bhattacharyya T, Levin R, Vrahas MS, et al. Nonsteroidal anti-inflammatory drugs and nonunion of humeral shaft fractures. Arthritis Rheum 2005;15(3):364–367.
10. Blum J, Machemer H, Baumgart F, et al. Biomechanical comparison of bending and torsional properties in retrograde intramedullary nailing of humeral shaft fractures. J Orthop Trauma 1999;13:344–350.
11. Bodine SC, Lieber RL. Peripheral nerve physiology, anatomy, and pathology In: Simon SR, ed. Orthopaedic Basic Science. Rosemont IL: AAOS, 1994:325–396.
12. Bolano LE, Iaquinto JA, Vasicek V. Operative treatment of humerus shaft fractures: a prospective randomized study comparing intramedullary nailing with dynamic compression plating. Presented at the Annual Meeting of the American Academy of Orthopaedic Surgeons 1995.
13. Bone L. Fractures of the shaft of the humerus. In: Chapman MW, ed. Operative Orthopedics. Vol 1. Philadelphia: J.B. Lippincott, 1988:221–234.
14. Bono CM, Grossman MG, Hochwald N, et al. Radial and axillary nerves. Anatomic considerations for humeral fixation. Clin Orthop Rel Res 2000;373:259–264.
15. Boyd AD, Thornhill TS, Barnes CL. Fractures adjacent to humeral prostheses. J Bone Joint Surg Am 1992;74:1498–1504.
16. Brien WW, Gellman H, Becker V, et al. Management of fractures of the humerus in patients who have an injury of the ipsilateral brachial plexus. J Bone Joint Surg Am 1990;72(8):1208–1210.
17. Brinker MR, O'Connor DP. The incidence of fractures and dislocations referred for orthopaedic services in a capitated population. J Bone Joint Surg Am 2004;86:290–297.
18. Brumback RJ, Bosse MJ, Poka A, et al. Intramedullary stabilization of humeral shaft fractures in patients with multiple trauma. J Bone Joint Surg Am 1986;68:960–969.
19. Brumback RJ, Jones AL. Interobserver agreement in the classification of open fractures of the tibia. The results of a survey of 245 orthopedic surgeons. J Bone Joint Surg Am 1994;76:1162–1166.
20. Burd TA, Hughes MS, Anglen JO. Heterotopic ossification prophylaxis with indomethacin increases the risk of long-bone nonunion. J Bone Joint Surg Br 2003;85(5):700–705.
21. Caldwell JA. Treatment of fracture of the shaft of the humerus by hanging cast. Surg Gynecol Obstet 1940;70:421–425.
22. Cameron U, Jacob R, Macnab I, et al. Use of polymethyl methacrylate to enhance screw fixation in bone. J Bone Joint Surg Am 1975;57:655–656.
23. Campbell JT, Moore RS, Iannotti JP, et al. Periprosthetic humeral fractures: mechanisms of fracture and treatment options. J Shoulder Elbow Surg 1998;7:406–413.
24. Changulani M, Jain UK, Keswani T. Comparison of the use of the humerus intramedullary nail and dynamic compression plate for the management of diaphyseal fractures of the humerus. A randomized controlled study. Int Orthop 2007;31(3):391–395.
25. Chapman JR, Henley MB, Agel J, et al. Randomized prospective study of humeral shaft fracture fixation: Intramedullary nails versus plates. J Orthop Trauma 2000;14:162–166.
26. Charnley J. The Closed Treatment of Common Fractures. Baltimore: Williams & Wilkins, 1961.
27. Chesser TJ, Leslie IJ. Radial nerve entrapment by the lateral intermuscular septum in trauma. J Orthop Trauma 2000;14:65–66.
28. Chin HC, Frassica FJ, Hein TJ, et al. Metastatic diaphyseal fractures of the shaft of the humerus. The structural strength evaluation of a new method of treatment with a segmental defect prosthesis. Clin Orthop Rel Res 1989;248:231–239.
29. Choong PF, Griffiths JD. External fixation of complex open humeral fractures. Aust NZ J Surg 1988;2:137–142.
30. Christensen S. Humeral shaft fractures: operative and conservative treatment. Acta Chir Scand 1967;133(6):455–460.
31. Connolly J. Management of fractures associated with arterial injuries. Am J Surg 1970;120:331.
32. Connolly S, Nair R, Waddell JP, et al. Immediate plate osteosynthesis of open fractures of the humeral shaft. Proceedings of the 55th Canadian Orthopaedic Association Annual Meeting, Edmonton, Alberta, Canada, June 3–6, 2000.
33. Crates J, Whittle AP. Antegrade interlocking nailing of acute humeral shaft fractures. Clin Orthop Rel Res 1998;350:40–50.
34. Crolla KMP, de Varis LS, Clevers GJ. Locked intramedullary nailing of humeral fractures. Injury 1993;24:403–406.
35. Davenport SR, Lindsey R, Leggon R, et al. Dynamic compression plate fixation: a biomechanical comparison of unicortical and bicortical distal screw fixation. J Orthop Trauma 1988;2:146–150.
36. DePalma AF. The Management of Fractures and Dislocations. Philadelphia: WB Saunders, 1970.
37. Douglass HO, Shukla SK, Mindell E. Treatment of pathological fractures of long bones excluding those due to breast cancer. J Bone Joint Surg Am 1976;58(8):839–847.
38. Ekholm R, Adami J, Tidermark J, et al. Fractures of the shaft of the Humerus. An epidemiological study of 401 fractures. J Bone Joint Surg Br 2006;88(11):1469–1473.
39. Ekholm R, Tidermark J, Törnkvist H, et al. Outcome after closed functional treatment of humeral shaft fractures. J Orthop Trauma 2006;20(9):591–596.
40. Farragos AF, Schemitsch ED, McKee MD. Complications of intramedullary nailing for fractures of the humeral shaft: a review. J Orthop Trauma 1999;13:258–267.
41. Faruqui NA, Hutchins PM. Humeral nailing—an anatomical study. J Bone Joint Surg Br 1997;79(Suppl 1):102.
42. Fears RL, Gleis GE, Seligson D. Diagnosis and treatment of complications: fractures of the diaphyseal humerus. In: Browner BD, Jupiter JB, Levine AM, et al, eds. Skeletal Trauma. 2nd ed. Toronto: WB Saunders Co., 1998:567–578.
43. Flemming JE, Beals RK. Pathologic fracture of the humerus. Clin Orthop Rel Res 1986;203:258–260.
44. Flinkkilä T, Ristiniemi J, Pajala A, et al. Salvage of humeral shaft nonunion with cortical thinning after failed intramedullary nailing using Ilizarov's technique: a report of seven cases. Injury 2005;36(10):1246–1251.
45. Foster RJ, Dixon JL, Bach AW, et al. Internal fixations of fractures and nonunions of the humeral shaft. J Bone Joint Surg Am 1985;67:857–864.
46. Garcia A Jr, Maeck BH. Radial nerve injuries of fractures of the shaft of the humerus. Am J Surg 1960;99:625–627.
47. Giannoudis PV, MacDonald DA, Matthews SJ, et al. Nonunion of the femoral diaphysis: The influence of reaming and non-steroidal anti-inflammatory drugs. J Bone Joint Surg Br 2000;5:655–658.
48. Gill DRJ, Torchia ME. The spiral compression plate for proximal humeral shaft non-

union: A case report and description of a new technique. J Orthop Trauma 1999;13(2): 141–144.
49. Goss CM, ed. Gray's Anatomy. 25th ed. Philadelphia: Lea & Febiger, 1950.
50. Gregory PR. Fractures of the humeral shaft. In: Bucholz RW, Heckman JD, eds. Rockwood and Green's Fractures in Adults. 5th ed. Philadelphia: Lippincott Williams & Wilkins, 2001:973–996.
51. Groh GI, Heckman MM, Wirth MA, et al. Treatment of fractures adjacent to humeral prostheses. J Shoulder Elbow Surg 2008;17(1):85–89.
52. Gustilo RB, Anderson JT. Prevention of infection in the treatment of 1025 open fractures of the long bones. Retrospective and prospective analysis. J Bone Joint Surg Am 1976; 58:453–458.
53. Habermann ET, Lopez RA. Metastatic disease of bone and treatment of pathological fractures. Orthop Clin N Am 1989;20:469–486.
54. Habernak H, Orthner E. A locking nail for fractures of the humerus. J Bone Joint Surg Br 1991;73(4):651–653.
55. Habernak H, Orthner E. A locking nail for fractures of the humerus—letter to the editor J Bone Joint Surg Br 1998;80:557.
56. Halder SC. The Gamma nail for peritrochanteric fractures. J Bone Joint Surg Br 1992; 74:340–344.
57. Hall RF, Pankovich AM. Ender nailing of acute fractures of the humerus. J Bone Joint Surg Am 1987;69:558–567.
58. Harrington KD, Sim FH, Enis JE, et al. Methylmethacrylate as an adjunct in internal fixation of pathological fractures. Experience with 375 cases. J Bone Joint Surg Am 1976;58:1047–1055.
59. Henley MB, Chapman JR, Claudi BF. Closed retrograde Hackethal nail stabilizaton of humeral shaft fractures. J Orthop Trauma 1992;6:18–24.
60. Henley MB, Monroe M, Tencer AF. Biomechanical comparison of methods of fixation of a midshaft osteotomy of the humerus. J Orthop Trauma 1991;5:14–20.
61. Hierholzer C, Sama D, Toro JB, et al. Plate fixation of ununited humeral shaft fractures: effect of type of bone graft on healing. J Bone Joint Surg Am 2006;88(7):1442–1447.
62. Hollinshead WH. Anatomy for Surgeons. Vol 3. New York: Hoeber-Harper, 1958.
63. Holm CL. Management of humeral shaft fractures. Fundamental nonoperative techniques. Clin Orthop Rel Res 1970;91:132–139.
64. Holstein A, Lewis GB. Fractures of the humerus with radial nerve paralysis. J Bone Joint Surg Am 1963;45:1382–1388.
65. Hoppenfeld S, De Boer P. Exposures in Orthopedics. Philadelphia: J.B. Lippincott, 1984:47–75.
66. Hornicek FJ, Zych GA, Hutson JJ, et al. Salvage of humeral nonunions with on lay bone plate allograft augmentation. Clin Orthop Rel Res 2001;386:203–209.
67. Hubner U, Schlicht W, Outzen S, et al. Ultrasound in the diagnosis of fractures in children. J Bone Joint Surg Br 2000;82:1170–1173.
68. Ingman AM, Waters DA. Locked intramedullary nailing of the humeral shaft fractures. J Bone Joint Surg Br 1994;76:23–29.
69. Jain R, Podworthy N, Hupel TM, et al. Influence of plate design on cortical bone perfusion and fracture healing in segmental tibia fractures. J Orthop Trauma 1999;13: 178–186.
70. Jiang R, Luo CF, Zeng BF, et al. Minimally invasive plating for complex humeral shaft fractures. Arch Orthop Trauma Surg 2007;127(7):531–555.
71. Jupiter JB. Complex nonunion of the humeral diaphysis: treatment with a medial approach, an anterior plate, and a vascularized fibular graft. J Bone Joint Surg Am 1990; 72:701–707.
72. Jupiter JB. Complex nonunion of the humeral diaphysis. J Bone Joint Surg Am 1990; 72:701–707.
73. Jupiter JB, von Deck M. Ununited humeral diaphyses. J Shoulder Elbow Surg 1998; 7:644–652.
74. Kamhin M, Michaelson M, Waisbrod H. The use of external skeletal fixation in the treatment of fractures of the humeral shaft. Injury 1977;9:245–248.
75. Kellar A. The management of gunshot fractures of the humerus. Injury 1995;26:93–95.
76. Kettlekamp DB, Alexander H. Clinical review of radial nerve injury. J Trauma 1967; 7(3):424–432.
77. Kumar S, Sperling JW, Haidukewych GH, et al. Periprosthetic humeral fractures after shoulder arthroplasty. J Bone Joint Surg Am 2004;86(4):680–689.
78. Kunec JR, Lewis RJ. Closed intramedullary rodding of pathological fractures with supplemental cement. Clin Orthop Rel Res 1984;188:183–186.
79. Kuntscher G. Practice of Intramedullary Nailing. Springfield, IL: Charles C. Thomas, 1967.
80. Laing PG. The arterial supply of the adult humerus. J Bone Joint Surg Am 1956;38: 1–105.
81. Lammens J, Bauduin G, Dreisen R, et al. Treatment of nonunion of the humerus using the Ilizarov external fixator. Clin Orthop Rel Res 1998;353:223–230.
82. Lancaster JM, Koman LA, Gristina AG, et al. Pathologic fractures of the humerus. Southern Med J 1988;81:52–55.
83. Lancaster JM, Koman AL, Gristina AG, et al. Treatment of pathologic fractures of the humerus. South Med J 1988;81:52–55.
84. Lancaster T, Stead L. Physician advice for smoking cessation. Coch Data Syst Rev 2004; 18(4):CD000165.
85. Leung KS, So WS, Shen WY, et al. Gamma nails and dynamic hip screws for peritrochanteric fractures: a randomized prospective study in elderly patients. J Bone Joint Surg Br 1992;74:345–351.
86. Leung M, Hertel R. Thermal necrosis after tibial reaming for intramedullary nail fixation. J Bone Joint Surg Br 1996;78(4):584–587.
87. Lewallen DG, Berry DJ. Periprosthetic fracture of the femur after total hip arthroplasty: treatment and results to date. Instr Course Lect 1998;47:2443–2449.
88. Lewallen RP, Pritchard DJ, Sim FH. Treatment of pathologic fractures or impending fractures of the humerus with Rush rods and methylmethacrylate. Experience with 55 cases in 54 patients 1968–1977. Clin Orthop Rel Res 1982;166:193–198.
89. Lin J, Inoue N, Valdevit A, et al. Biomechanical comparison of antegrade and retrograde nailing of humeral shaft fracture. Clin Orthop Rel Res 1998;351:203–213.
90. Lin J, Shen PW, Hou SM. Complications of locked nailing in humeral shaft fractures. J Trauma 2003;54:943–949.
91. Livani B, Belangero WD. Bridging plate osteosynthesis of humeral shaft fractures. Injury 2004;35(6):587–595.
92. Maher SA, Meyers K, Borens O, et al. Biomechanical evaluation of an expandable nail for the fixation of midshaft fractures. J Trauma 2007;63(1):103–107.
93. Marsh JL, Mahoney CR, Steinbronn D. External fixation of open humerus fractures. Iowa Orthop J 1999;19:35–42.
94. Mast JW, Spiegal PG, Harvey JP, et al. Fractures of the humeral shaft. Clin Orthop Rel Res 1975;12:254–262.
95. McCormack RG, Brien D, Buckley RE, et al. Fixation of fractures of the shaft of the humerus by dynamic compression plate or intramedullary nail: a prospective randomized trial. J Bone Joint Surg Br 2000;82:336–339.
96. McDonough EB, Crosby LA. Periprosthetic fractures of the humerus. Am J Orthop 2005;34(12):586–591.
97. McKee MD, Miranda MA, Reimer BL, et al. Management of humeral nonunion after the failure of locking intramedullary nails. J Orthop Trauma 1996;10:492–499.
98. McKee MD, Pedlow FX, Cheney PJ, et al. Fracture below the end of locking humeral nails: a report of three cases. J Orthop Trauma 1996;10(7):500–504.
99. McKee MD, Seiler J, Jupiter JB. The application of the limited contact dynamic compression plate in the upper extremity: an analysis of 114 cases. Injury 1995;26:661–666.
100. McKee MD, Wild LM, Schemitsch EH, et al. The use of an antibiotic-impregnated, osteoconductive, bioabsorbable bone substitute in the treatment of infected long bone defects. J Orthop Trauma 2002;16(9):622–627.
101. McNamara JJ, Brief DK, Stremple JF, et al. Management of fractures with associated arterial injury in combat casualties. J Trauma 1973;13:17–19.
102. Mills WJ, Chapman JR, Robinson LR, et al. Somatosensory evoked potential monitoring during closed humeral nailing: a preliminary report. J Orthop Trauma 2000;14(3): 167–170.
103. Mills W J, Hanel DP, Smith DG. Lateral approach to the humeral shaft: an alternative approach for fracture treatment. J Orthop Trauma 1996;10:81–86.
104. Modabber MR, Jupiter JB. Operative management of diaphyseal fractures of the humerus. Clin Orthop Rel Res 1998;347:93–104.
105. Mostafavi HR, Tornetta P. Open fractures of the humerus treated with external fixation. Clin Orthop Rel Res 1997;337:187–197.
106. Mückley T, Diefenbeck M, Sorkin AT, et al. Results of the T2 humeral nailing system with special focus on compression interlocking. Injury 2008;39(3):299–305.
107. O'Brien PJ, Guy P, Blachut P. Humeral shaft fractures-open reduction internal fixation. In: Wiss D, ed. Master Techniques in Orthopedic Surgery-Fractures. Philadelphia: Lippincott-Raven, 1998:63–80.
108. O'Driscoll SW, Morrey BF. Periprosthetic fractures about the elbow. Orthop Clin North Am 1999;30(2):319–325.
109. O'Driscoll SW, Spinner RJ, McKee MD, et al. Tardy posterolateral instability of the elbow due to cubitus varus. J Bone Joint Surg Am 2001;83(9):1358–1369.
110. Ogawa K, Ui M. Humeral shaft fracture sustained during arm wrestling: report on 30 cases and review of the literature. J Trauma 1997;42(2):243–246.
111. Orthopaedic Trauma Association Classification scheme for long bone fractures. J Orthop Trauma 1996;10(supp 1):1–158.
112. Ostermann PA, Ekkernkamp A, Muhr G. Functional bracing of shaft fractures of the humerus—an analysis of 195 cases. Orthop Trans 1993–1994;17:937.
113. OTA Classification: Fracture and Dislocation Classification Compendium. Orthopedic Trauma Association Committee for Coding and Classification. J Orthop Trauma 2007; 21(10 suppl):1–161.
114. Orthopaedic Trauma Association. Fracture and Dislocation Classification Compendium—2007. Available at: http://www.ota.org/compendium/compendium.html. Accessed June 24, 2009.
115. Otsuka NY, McKee MD, Liew A, et al. The effect of comorbidity and duration of nonunion on outcome after surgical treatment for nonunion of the humerus. J Shoulder Elbow Surg 1998;7:127–33.
116. Palmer SH, Handley R, Willett K. The use of interlocked customized blade plates in the treatment of metaphyseal fractures in patients with poor bone stock. Injury 2000; 31:187–191.
117. Patel VR, Menon DK, Pool RD, et al. Nonunion of the humerus after failure of surgical treatment: management using the Ilizarov circular fixator. J Bone Joint Surg 2000; 82(7):977–983.
118. Pollock FH, Drake D, Bovill EG, et al. Treatment of radial neuropathy associated with fractures of the humerus. J Bone Joint Surg Am 1981;63:239–243.
119. Port AM, Nanu AM, Cross AT. Windows for humeral interlocking nails—an anatomical study. J Bone Joint Surg Br 1997;79(Suppl 1):102.
120. Praemer A, Furner S, Rice DP. Musculoskeletal Conditions in the United States. Rosemont, IL: American Academy of Orthopaedic Surgeons, 1999.
121. Pritchett JW. Delayed union of humeral shaft fractures treated by closed flexible intramedullary nailing. J Bone Joint Surg Br 1985;67:715–718.
122. Redmond BJ, Biermann JS, Blasier RB. Interlocking intramedullary nailing of pathological fractures of the shaft of the humerus. J Bone Joint Surg Am 1996;78(6):891–896.
123. Reimer BL, Foglesong ME, Burke CJ, et al. Complications of Seidel nailing of narrow diameter humeral diaphyseal fractures. Orthopaedics 1994;17:19–29.
124. Ricciardi-Pollini PT, Falez F. The treatment of diaphyseal fractures by functional bracing. Italian J Orthop and Traumatology 1985;11:199–205.
125. Rich NM, Metz CW, Hutton JE, et al. Internal versus external fixation of fractures with concomitant vascular injuries in Vietnam. J Trauma 1971;11:463–473.
126. Riemer BL. Humeral shaft fractures-intramedullary nailing. In: Wiss D, ed. Master Techniques in Orthopedic Surgery—Fractures. Philadelphia: Lippencott-Raven, 1998: 81–94.
127. Riemer BL, D'Ambrosia R, Kellman JF, et al. The anterior acromial approach for antegrade intramedullary nailing of the humeral diaphysis. Orthopedics 1993;16: 1219–1223.
128. Ring D, Chin K, Jupiter JB. Radial nerve palsy associated with high-energy humeral shaft fractures. J Hand Surg Am 2004;29(1):144–147.
129. Ring D, Jupiter JB, Quintero J, et al. Atrophic ununited diaphyseal fractures of the humerus with a bony defect. J Bone Joint Surg Br 2000;82(6):867–871.
130. Ring D, Kloen P, Kadzielski J, et al. Locking compression plates for osteoporotic nonunions of the diaphyseal humerus. Clin Orthop Rel Res 2004;245:50–54.
131. Ring D, McKee MD, Perey BH, et al. The use of a blade plate and autogenous cancellous bone graft in the treatment of ununited fractures of the proximal humerus. J Shoulder Elbow Surg 2001;10:501–507.
132. Ring D, Perey B, Jupiter J. The functional outcome of operative treatment of ununited

fractures of the humeral diaphysis in older patients. J Bone Joint Surg Am 1999;81: 177–190.

133. Ring D, Waters PM, Hotchkiss RN, et al. Paediatric floating elbow. J Paediatr Orthop 2001;21(4):456–459.

134. Robinson CM, Bell KM, Court Brown CM, et al. Locked nailing of humeral shaft fractures. J Bone Joint Surg Br 1992;74:558–561.

135. Rodrigues-Merchan E. Carlos. Compression plating versus Hackethal nailing in closed humeral shaft fractures failing nonoperative reduction. J Orthop Trauma 2000;14: 162–166.

136. Rommens PM, Verbruggen J, Broos PL. Retrograde locked nailing of the humeral shaft fractures. J Bone Joint Surg Br 1995;77:84–89.

137. Rose SH, Melton LJ, Morrey BF, et al. Epidemiologic features of humeral fractures. Clin Orthop Rel Res 1982;168:24–30.

138. Rosen H. The treatment of nonunions and pseudarthroses of the humeral shaft. Orthop Clin North Am 1990;21:725–742.

139. Ruland WO. Is there a place for external fixation in humeral shaft fracture? Injury 2000;31(Suppl):27–34.

140. Rupp RE, Chrissos MG, Ebraheim N. The risk of neurovascular injury with distal locking screws of humeral intramedullary nails. Orthopedics 1996;19:593–595.

141. Sanchez-Sotelo J, O'Driscoll S, Morrey BF. Periprosthetic humeral fractures after total elbow arthroplasty: treatment with implant revision and strut allograft augmentation. J Bone Joint Surg Am 2004;84(9):1642–1650.

142. Sanders R, Yach J, Dipasquale T, et al. Radial nerve palsy associated with humeral fractures. Presented at the 16th Annual Meeting of the Orthopaedic Trauma Association, San Antonio, Texas, October 12, 2000.

143. Sarmiento A, Horowitch A, Aboulafia A, et al. Functional bracing for comminuted extra-articular fractures of the distal third of the humerus. J Bone Joint Surg Br 1990; 72(2):283–287.

144. Sarmiento A, Kinman PB, Calvin EG, et al. Functional bracing of fractures of the shaft of the humerus. J Bone Joint Surg Am 1977;59:596–601.

145. Sarmiento A, Zagorski JB, Zych G, et al. Functional bracing for the treatment of fractures of the humeral diaphysis. J Bone Joint Surg Am 2000;82:478–486.

146. Schandelmaier P, Krettek C, Rudolf J, et al. Outcome of tibial shaft fractures with severe soft tissue injury treated by unreamed nailing versus external fixation. J Trauma 1995; 39(4):707–711.

147. Schatzker J. Fractures of the humerus. In Schatzer J, Tile M, eds. The Rationale for Operative Fracture Care. 2nd ed. Berlin: Springer-Verlag, 1996:83–94.

148. Schemitsch EH, Bhandari M. Fractures of the diaphyseal humerus. In: Browner BD, Jupiter JB, Levine AM, et al, eds. Skeletal Trauma. 3rd ed. Toronto: WB Saunders Co., 2001:1481–1511.

149. Shao YC, Harwood P, Grotz MR, et al. Radial nerve palsy associated with fractures of the shaft of the humerus: a systematic review. J Bone Joint Surg Br 2005;87(12): 1647–1652.

150. Siebenrock KA, Gerber C. The reproducibility of classification of fractures of the proximal end of the humerus. J Bone Joint Surg Am 1993;75(12):1751–1755.

151. Simon P, Jobard D, Bistour L, et al. Complications of Marchetti locked nailing for humeral shaft fractures. Int Orthop 1999;23:320–324.

152. Sims SH, Smith SE. Intramedullary nailing of humeral shaft fractures. J South Orthop Assoc 1995;1:24–31.

153. Sommer C, Gautier E, Muller M, et al. First clinical results of the Locking Compression Plate (LCP). Injury 2003;34:S43–S54.

154. Stannard JP, Harris HW, McGwin G Jr, et al. Intramedullary nailing of humeral shaft fractures with a locking, flexible nail. J Bone Joint Surg Am 2003;85(11):2103–2110.

155. Strothman D, Templeman DC, Varecka T, et al. Retrograde nailing of humeral shaft fractures: a biomechanical study of its effects on the strength of the distal humerus. J Orthop Trauma 2000;14:101–104.

156. Swenson MR, Villasana DR. Neurologic evaluation of the upper extremity. In: Kasdan ML, ed. Occupational Hand and Upper Extremity Injuries and Diseases. Philadelphia: Hanley and Belfus, 1991:115–130.

157. Tingstad EM, Wolinsky PR, Shyr Y, et al. Effect of immediate weight-bearing on plated fractures of the humeral shaft. J Trauma 2000;49(2):278–280.

158. Toivanen JA, Nieminen J, Laine HJ, et al. Functional treatment of closed humeral shaft fractures. Int Orthop 2005;29(1):10–13.

159. Tomic S, Bumbasirevic M, Lesic A, et al. Ilizarov frame fixation without bone graft for atrophic humeral shaft nonunion: 28 patients with a minimum 2-year follow-up. J Orthop Trauma 2007;21(8):549–556.

160. Tytherleigh-Strong G, Walls N, McQueen MM. The epidemiology of humeral shaft fractures. J Bone Joint Surg Br 1998;80(12):249–253.

161. Utvag SE, Grundnes O, Reikeras O. Effects of degrees of remaining on healing of segmental fractures. J Bone Joint Surg Am 1998;12:192–199.

162. Valchanou VD, Michailov P. High-energy shock waves in the treatment of delayed and nonunion of fractures. Int Orthop 1991;15:181–184.

163. Van der Griend RA, Tomasin J, Ward EF. Open reduction and internal fixation of humeral shaft fractures. J Bone Joint Surg Am 1986;68:430–433.

164. Van Houwelingen AP, McKee MD. Treatment of osteopenic humeral shaft nonunion with compression plating, humeral cortical allograft struts and bone grafting. J Orthop Trauma 2005;19(1):36–42.

165. Wainwright AM, Williams JR, Carr AJ. Interobserver and intraobserver variation in classification systems for fractures of the distal humerus. J Bone Joint Surg Br 2000; 82:636–642.

166. Worland RL, Kim DY, Arrendondo J. Periprosthetic humeral fractures: management and classification. J Shoulder Elbow Surg 1999;8:590–594.

167. Worlock P, Stower M, Barbor P. Patterns of fractures in accidental and nonaccidental injury in children: a comparative study. British Med J 1986;293:100–102.

168. Wright TW, Miller GJ, Vander Griend RA, et al. Reconstruction of the humerus with an intramedullary fibular graft. J Bone Joint Surg Br 1993;75:801–807.

169. Wu CC, Shih CH. Treatment for nonunion of the shaft of the humerus: comparison of plates and Seidel interlocking nails. Can J Surg 1992;35:661–665.

170. Yazawa Y, Frassica FJ, Chao EYS, et al. Metastatic bone disease. A study of the surgical treatment of 166 pathologic humeral and femoral fractures. Clin Orthop Rel Res 1990; 251:213–219.

171. Zagorski JB, Latta LI, Zych GA, et al. Diaphyseal fractures of the humerus. Treatment with prefabricated braces. J Bone Joint Surg Am 1988;70(4):607–610.

172. Zhiquan A, Bingfang Z, Yeming W, et al. Minimally invasive plating osteosynthesis (MIPO) of middle and distal third humeral shaft fractures. J Orthop Trauma 2007; 21(9):628–633.

173. Zimmerman MC, Waite Am, Deehan M, et al. A biomechanical analysis of four humeral fracture fixation systems. J Orthop Trauma 1994;8:233–239.

PROXIMAL HUMERUS FRACTURES

C. Michael Robinson

INTRODUCTION

Fractures of the proximal humerus are common and debilitating injuries and are an increasing problem in the elderly. There is universal agreement that most stable fractures, which often occur in frail, elderly patients, are best treated nonoperatively. The major controversy surrounds the minority of more complex, displaced and multipart fractures. More ink than blood may have been spilt in the debate over these injuries, and their discussion in the orthopaedic literature is disproportionate to their prevalence. As a consequence, patients with similar injuries may receive widely different opinions about the severity of their fracture, its likely outcome, and its best treatment, depen-

dent on the unit in which they are treated and the surgeon who treats them.

Why is this? The first and major problem stems from the difficulty in assessing these injuries. There are substantial difficulties in classifying these injuries reliably and reproducibly and in evaluating their outcome. There is also considerable variation in the treatment expectations and likely outcome for different patients, dependent on their age and functional capabilities before their injury. There is a wide range of treatment options for these injuries, each with its advantages and disadvantages. It may be difficult to reconcile the risk of complications from one particular form of treatment against its likely benefits. Finally, over the past 10 years, there has been considerable expansion in the range of reconstructive implants available to treat these injuries. Their uncontrolled introduction, without clear evidence of superiority over existing techniques, further confounds any attempt at rational appraisal of relative merits of the different treatment options.

Four recent meta-analyses[21,112,173,197] of the existing literature have highlighted the paucity of Level I or II studies of these injuries. The need for prospective, randomized multicenter clinical trials comparing the available treatment options is clear, yet few such studies are ongoing at present. This lack of high-level scientific evidence confounds any attempt at consensus-based, protocol-driven management. The aims of this chapter are therefore to describe the assessment tools and treatment options that are currently available for these injuries and to highlight the major areas of controversy in their management.

EPIDEMIOLOGY

Proximal humeral fractures are one of the most common osteoporotic fractures, with an annual incidence of between 63 and 105 fractures per 100,000 population per year.[57,129,165,187,225,260] They account for 5% of all injuries to the appendicular skeleton.[55,187] The prevalence of these fractures is increasing in the elderly,[139,225] although whether this is a direct result of the shifting population demographic, or an age/sex–specific rise is unclear. The current exponential rise in incidence is set to continue, with one projection suggesting a trebling of the number of fractures in the elderly over the next three decades.[225]

Fractures of the proximal humerus follow a unimodal elderly distribution curve with a low incidence under the age of 40 years and an exponential increase thereafter.[55] Although most patients are typically in the younger aging population (aged between 65 and 75 years),[55,57,274] the skewed population demographics dictate that the age-/sex–adjusted incidence of fractures in the elderly is much higher[57,129,165,187,225,260] (Fig. 35-1). There are marked gender differences, with approximately 70% to 80% of fractures occurring in women,[55,57,165,187] in studies from North America, Scandinavia, the United Kingdom, France, southern Europe, Japan, and Australia.[11,57,109,129,187,226,260,268] These fractures are less common in the Japanese pop-

ulation compared with that of northern Europe or North America and are also less common in black Americans compared with white Americans.[10,109,260] The majority of fractures are undisplaced or stable two-, three-, and four-part fractures, and a detailed evaluation of their prevalence is provided in the classification section of this chapter.

MECHANISM OF INJURY

Fractures in adolescents and younger adults are usually produced by high-energy injuries, mainly from road traffic accidents, sports injuries, falls from height, or gunshot wounds. However, these are much less common than fractures in the elderly, which are usually low-energy osteoporotic injuries.[13,57,165,181,187] More than three quarters follow low-energy domestic falls,[57,165,187,260] and the risk of fracture is increased in sedentary individuals with low bone mineral density, a family history of osteoporotic fracture, frequent falls, and evidence of impaired balance.[174] Middle-aged patients who sustain low-energy fractures frequently have a predisposing medical comorbidity or are physiologically older through the effects of alcohol, drug, or tobacco overuse.[212,213] Any other condition that produces osteoporosis at an earlier age will also increase the risk of fracture; in females, an early menopause is probably the most common cause of this.

During impact on the shoulder, the head of the humerus is thought to fracture on the hard-packed bone of the glenoid, which acts as an anvil.[73] The interaction of this external force with the forces generated by the intrinsic shoulder musculature, and the quality of the proximal humeral bone stock, determines the initial fracture configuration and any ensuing displacement. Elderly patients, with advanced osteoporosis or with medical comorbidities, are more likely to have displaced fractures.[222] A proximal humeral fracture may occur from direct impact to the shoulder or indirectly by transmission of forces from a fall onto the outstretched arm. Depleted protective neuromuscular responses, because of a delayed reaction time, cognitive impairment, neuromuscular disorders, impaired balance, or acute intoxication, increase the risk of a fall directly onto the shoulder.[174,226,264] The nondominant arm is also affected in up to

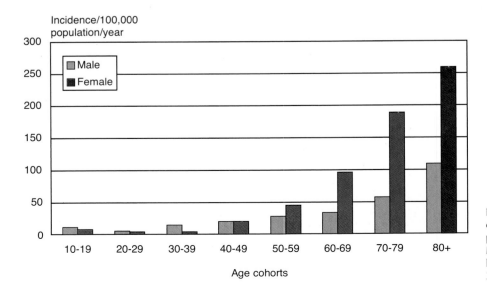

FIGURE 35-1 The age/gender-specific incidence of proximal humeral fractures in an urban population. (Data from CourtBrown CM, Garg A, McQueen MM. The epidemiology of proximal humeral fractures. Acta Orthop Scand 2001;72: 365–371.)

three quarters of cases,[196,324] suggesting an association with reduced strength and neuromuscular coordination. Diminished protective responses are an indirect measure of poor physiologic status, and this may explain why patients who sustain proximal humerus fractures from direct impact on the shoulder tend to be frailer than those who sustain wrist fractures,[142,222,274] where the arm is outstretched to break the fall.

A fracture that occurs after little or no trauma may be pathologic from metastatic tumor deposits or, rarely, caused by a primary bone tumor or infection. In contrast, persistence of shoulder pain after a significant injury with normal radiographs may be caused by an occult fracture (typically of the greater tuberosity) or a rotator cuff injury.[237,317] This may only be detectable using ultrasound or magnetic resonance imaging (MRI).[237,317]

CLINICAL ANATOMY

Bony Anatomy

The shoulder is the most mobile joint of the appendicular skeleton and is prone to instability. Fracture-dislocation is therefore more common in this area than in other juxta-metaphyseal fractures. The diaphysis expands into the surgical neck, which is just below the greater and lesser tuberosities at the metaphyseal flare (Fig. 35-2). The anatomic neck is the region immediately above the tuberosities and below the humeral articular surface.

The humeral articular segment occupies approximately one third of a sphere, with a diameter of curvature averaging 46 mm (with a range of 37 to 57 mm).[29,124,131] The inclination of the humeral head relative to the shaft averages 130 degrees (with a range of 123 to 136 degrees), and the geometric center of the humeral head is offset an average of 2.6 mm posteriorly (range of −0.8 to 6.1 mm) and 7 mm (range of 3 to 11 mm) medially from the axis of the humeral shaft.[29,124,131,243] The humeral head is normally retroverted by an average of 20 degrees, with respect to the distal humeral interepicondylar axis. However, the degree of retroversion may vary quite dramatically from between 10 degrees of anteversion to 60 degrees of retroversion.[29,124,167]

Cadaveric studies of bone mineral density have shown that the distribution of bone within the proximal humerus is not uniform. The subchondral bone beneath the articular surface is predictably dense cancellous bone, with bone mineral density decreasing progressively toward the geometric center of the humeral head and into the metaphyseal area of the surgical neck[265] (Fig. 35-3). The overall bone quality of the proximal humerus can be reliably predicted by the cortical thickness of the proximal diaphysis,[293] as well as the age of the patient.[313] Because most proximal humeral fractures occur from compressive and shear forces, these areas of relative bone paucity are prone to impaction, creating cancellous defects when the fracture is reduced. These may be filled by the use of bone grafts or bone graft substitutes.[106,169,253] The highest bone density is found in

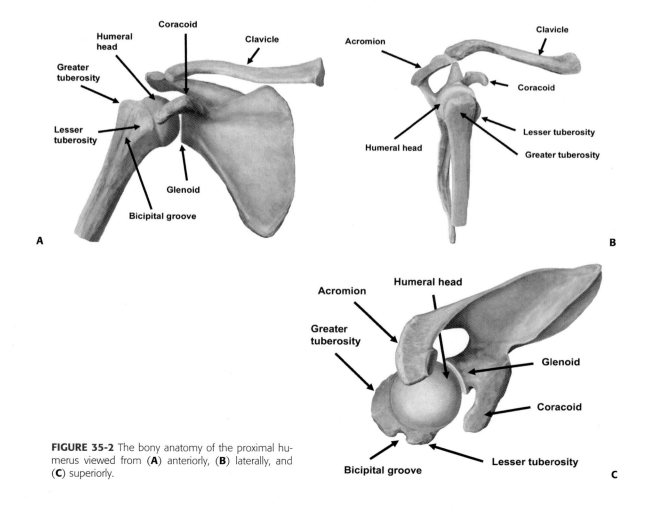

FIGURE 35-2 The bony anatomy of the proximal humerus viewed from (**A**) anteriorly, (**B**) laterally, and (**C**) superiorly.

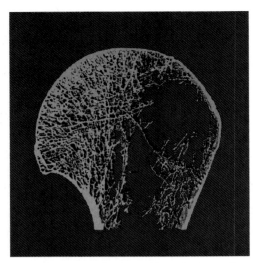

FIGURE 35-3 Microcomputed tomographic study of cancellous trabeculae in humeral head demonstrates marked porosity in greater tuberosity region and most dense bone just underneath humeral head. (Reprinted with permission from Meyer DC, Fucentese SF, Koller B, Gerber C. Association of osteopenia of the humeral head with full-thickness rotator cuff tears. J Shoulder Elbow Surg 2004;13:333–337.)

the subchondral bone immediately beneath the articular surface. There is also a progressive decrease in bone mineral density from superior to inferior and from posterior to anterior in the four quadrants of the humeral head.[120,293–295] The head is therefore analogous to a hen's egg, with a strong, compression-resistant exterior and a less mechanically robust interior. Knowledge of these areas of bone concentration is important to appreciate when operative plate or nail reconstructive techniques are used, because poor screw positioning in the head may compromise the rigidity of the surgical reconstruction, leading to early failure.

Soft Tissue Anatomy

The proximal humerus lies deep to the deltoid, periscapular musculature, and rotator cuff. The latter consists of the musculotendinous units of subscapularis, supraspinatus, infraspinatus, and teres minor. The tendinous long head of the biceps in its groove separates the lesser from the greater tuberosity. It is therefore a valuable surgical landmark for identifying these fracture fragments, and it serves as a "tramline" to the terminus at the superior pole of the empty glenoid in fracture-dislocations (Fig. 35-4).

The greater tuberosity has three separate facets for the attachment of the supraspinatus, infraspinatus and teres minor tendons.[199] The subscapularis tendon inserts into the lesser tuberosity, which is separated from the greater tuberosity by the bicipital groove. The displacement of the tuberosities when they are fractured is governed by their soft tissue attachments. The greater tuberosity is typically pulled medially, superiorly, and posteriorly by supraspinatus, infraspinatus, and teres minor tendons, whilst the lesser tuberosity is displaced anteriorly and medially by subscapularis. The pull of the rotator cuff muscles on their tuberosity attachments also explains why the humeral head is usually displaced posteriorly in a three-part greater tuberosity fracture, as a result of the unopposed pull of the subscapularis, whereas the head may be anteverted in the more

uncommon three-part lesser tuberosity fracture. If the periosteal attachments to the head are ruptured, the humeral shaft may be translated medially into the axilla, by the pull of the pectoralis major and latissimus dorsi tendons. Fracture of a tuberosity fragment defunctions the rotator cuff muscles that attach to it, and the tendon will regain function only once the fracture has healed. A tuberosity fragment that becomes displaced and heals with malunion may produce longer-term dysfunction of the attached cuff tendons or may give rise to subacromial or coracoid impingement.[105,206]

Blood Supply

The arterial supply to the intact proximal humerus arises from the axillary artery via its anterior and posterior circumflex humeral branches, which anastamose medially in the quadrilateral space, laterally in the area of the greater tuberosity, and in the humeral head through the rich network of interosseous anastamose (Fig. 35-5). The anterior circumflex artery contributes collateral branches, which feed the lesser tuberosity and the humeral head by entering along the line of anterior and inferior capsular reflection at the anatomic neck. The main branch of the anterior circumflex is an anterolateral ascending artery, which ascends the bicipital groove and enters the head just below the articular surface, to form the intraosseous arcuate artery. In the uninjured state, this provides the majority of the vessels that perfuse the humeral head, with the exception of the greater tuberosity and posteromedial aspect of the head, which are perfused by branches of the posterior circumflex artery.[35,104,172] This provides a leash of vessels, which enter the head along the line of the capsular insertion in the anatomic neck posteriorly and inferiorly.

Arterial perfusion has not been studied in vivo after a fracture, and alternate sources of vascularization to the humeral head may become important after injury. The observations that the humeral head may be perfused and that osteonecrosis does not inevitably occur after more complex three- and four-part fractures in which these vessels are damaged lend support to this argument.[14,103,123] It is likely that after fracture, additional sources of head perfusion may come from either of the tuberosities (if they are not fractured), via their soft tissue capsular and rotator cuff attachments, and from residual attachments of the capsule to the articular margin. In particular, the branches of the posterior circumflex humeral artery[35,71,194] that enter the head posteroinferiorly along the line of capsular reflection may maintain arterial perfusion to the head. These vessels are often intact in three- and four-part valgus fractures of the anatomic neck, provided the capsule remains intact and the medial periosteal hinge, which these vessels traverse and which connects the head to the shaft, has not been damaged.[71,123] Fractures of the anatomic neck where the head fragment has an appreciable intact spike of bone extending into the medial metaphysis are also at lower risk of osteonecrosis.[14,35,71,123,194] This may be because the fracture line is below the line of capsular reflection and the branches of the posterior circumflex artery are preserved. Extra-articular surgical neck fractures also have a low risk of osteonecrosis, because sources from both the anterior and posterior circumflex vessels are likely to be intact. In contrast, in certain three- and four-part fractures and fracture-dislocations, where the capsular attachments are completely disrupted, the risk of osteonecrosis is much higher.

If the branches of the circumflex humeral vessels are uninjured, they should be protected during reduction and fixation

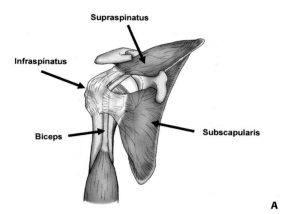

FIGURE 35-4 Soft-tissue anatomy of shoulder showing the rotator cuff musculature (**A**) and the neurovascular structures (**B**).

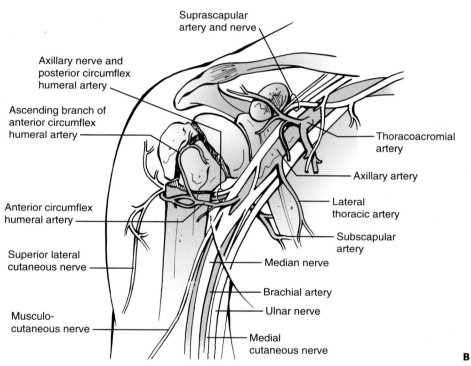

of the fracture to preserve this important source of blood supply. It is also important to avoid extensive dissection and soft tissue stripping, to reduce the risk of damaging other intact periosteal feeding vessels.

Nerve Supply

The innervation of the shoulder is derived from branches of the brachial plexus (C5–T1) (Fig. 35-4B). The trunks, divisions, cord, and branches of the plexus may be damaged by displaced fracture fragments or through traction injury. During operative treatment, most of these structures are usually protected from injury by the conjoined tendons of the short head of biceps and coracobrachialis, which mark the medial extent of surgical exposure through the deltopectoral approach. However, it is important to avoid prolonged traction on these tendons intraoperatively, as this may injure the musculocutaneous nerve. This pierces the conjoined tendon approximately 5 to 8 cm below the tip of the coracoid process.[80] The axillary nerve (C5–C6) is the main structure at risk during operative treatment of proximal humeral fractures. The nerve arises from the posterior cord

of the plexus and travels posterolaterally over the lower subscapularis to enter the quadrilateral space, where it is an immediate inferior relation of the glenohumeral joint capsule. It gives off a posterior branch that supplies the posterior deltoid and teres minor and provides sensation to the "badge area" of the upper arm. The anterior branch winds around the surgical neck deep to the deltoid muscle and has a somewhat variable course.[153] It innervates the anterior and middle thirds of the deltoid but has no cutaneous branches.

CLINICAL ASSESSMENT

History and Physical Examination

Fractures of the proximal humerus present with pain, swelling, and bruising of the upper arm, which is usually severe in the first 2 weeks postinjury. Since the fracture lies deep to the shoulder musculature, the revealed bruising and swelling are often most pronounced as it tracks anteroinferiorly into the lower arm. Although the degree of swelling is a poor marker of the severity

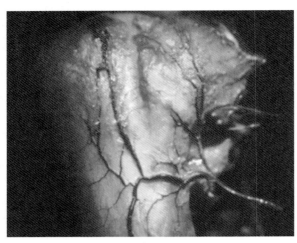

FIGURE 35-5 The major blood supply to the humeral head is derived from the anterior humeral circumflex artery. Its ascending branch is shown coursing lateral to the bicipital groove. (From Gerber C, Schneeberer AG, Vinh TS. The arterial vascularization of the humeral head. An anatomical study. J Bone Joint Surg Am 1990;72A:1486–1494, with permission.)

of the underlying bony injury, very severe swelling may denote an underlying vascular injury. Open fractures of the proximal humerus are relatively uncommon, although off-ended fractures with severe anterior displacement of the proximal shaft may occasionally produce pressure necrosis of an area of skin in the upper arm, leading to skin breakdown and infection. Careful reinspection of the anterior soft tissues is important in this group of patients, as the postinjury swelling settles.

It is perhaps surprising that major vascular injuries are only rarely associated with proximal humeral fractures,[46] given the proximity of the adjacent axillary vessels and the tethering of the surgical neck to the trifurcation of the two circumflex vessels and the subscapular artery. It is important to carefully assess the circulation distal to the fracture in every case.[232,321] In the presence of a vascular injury, only minimal and subtle signs of peripheral ischemia may be present, because of the rich collateral circulation. These are frequently missed initially, but a large or expanding hematoma, pulsatile external bleeding, unexplained hypotension, and an associated nerve trunk or plexus injury should increase the level of suspicion. Axillary arterial laceration may be produced by the displaced sharp edge of the medial shaft in a displaced two-part surgical neck fracture. Injury to the vessels is also relatively common in three- or four-part anterior fracture-dislocations, where direct injury to the vessels may be caused by either the displaced humeral head or the displaced shaft. Finally, intimal tears may be produced by injuries in which there is significant traction on the arm.

Any patient with a history of transient ischemia of the extremity or ongoing signs of vascular compromise should be referred for specialist vascular surgical advice. Doppler arterial pulse volume recordings may be useful, and a single-injection trauma angiography is usually accurate in the operating room setting. If more time is available, then a formal retrograde femoral arteriogram should be obtained. In addition, more sophisticated studies including digital subtraction angiography are now available to assess these injuries

A careful assessment of the neurologic status of the arm must also be made, as subtle deficits are commonly missed.[64] Most

neurologic injuries are either direct injuries to the brachial plexus from fracture fragments (by the same mechanisms as for vascular injury) or traction injuries to the axillary nerve (most commonly in two-part greater tuberosity anterior fracture-dislocations).[24,64,280,298,299] Careful assessment of the plexus and its branches must be undertaken after any proximal humeral fracture. Electromyography and nerve conduction studies should be requested to delineate the extent of nerve injury and the prospects for recovery.

Signs of rotator cuff dysfunction are difficult to elicit after an acute proximal humeral fracture. Cuff dysfunction is inevitable if there is a tuberosity fracture, because the attached cuff is defunctioned. The integrity of the cuff can only be assessed clinically when the fracture heals, allowing the tendon to function again. However, isolated rotator cuff avulsions and ruptures are commonly encountered,[89] even with fractures that do not involve the tuberosities. Imaging of the rotator cuff should be obtained at an early stage if signs persist, using ultrasound or preferably MRI. It is important to appreciate that many tears may predate the injury or be "acute-on-chronic" tears that have been aggravated by the injury.

Although most proximal humeral fractures are isolated injuries, it is important to assess for evidence of other systems injuries using Advanced Trauma Life Support (ATLS) secondary survey guidelines, particularly in the presence of a high-energy injury. Ipsilateral chest injuries (rib fractures, hemothorax, or pneumothorax) and cervical spine injuries are commonly associated with shoulder injuries in high-energy trauma. Intrathoracic and retroperitoneal fracture-dislocation of the humeral head have also been reported but are extremely rare.[281,310]

Proximal humeral fractures often occur with simultaneous fractures of the hip after low-energy injury. Simultaneous fractures of the wrist, forearm, or elbow are also relatively common and may be masked by the pain and swelling in the shoulder. Conversely, it is important to exclude a shoulder injury in any patient with shoulder pain associated with a more distal extremity fracture. Assessment may be particularly difficult in patients who have an ipsilateral humeral shaft fracture. Good-quality orthogonal radiographs, centered on the shoulder must always be obtained to exclude an associated fracture or dislocation.[157,216]

A thorough assessment of the patient's general state of health, fitness for anesthesia, and ability to cooperate with prolonged rehabilitation should be made. As with any other osteoporotic fracture, an assessment of the severity of osteoporosis should be undertaken. Secondary preventative treatment should be considered, aimed at reducing the risk of further osteoporosis-related falls and fractures. Dietary supplementation with calcium and vitamin D may also be of benefit in improving the rate of fracture healing.[69]

Imaging and Other Diagnostic Studies

The standard "trauma series" of conventional radiographs consists of anteroposterior and lateral radiographs, together with an axillary view. The latter may be uncomfortable to obtain after injury, and the Velpeau view[79] or modified axillary view[302] are considered acceptable substitutes, because these can be taken without removing the painful fractured arm from the sling (Fig. 35-6). Anteroposterior radiographs taken in the standard anatomic planes are often unsatisfactory, because the glenoid, coracoid, and acromion may overlap the proximal humeral frac-

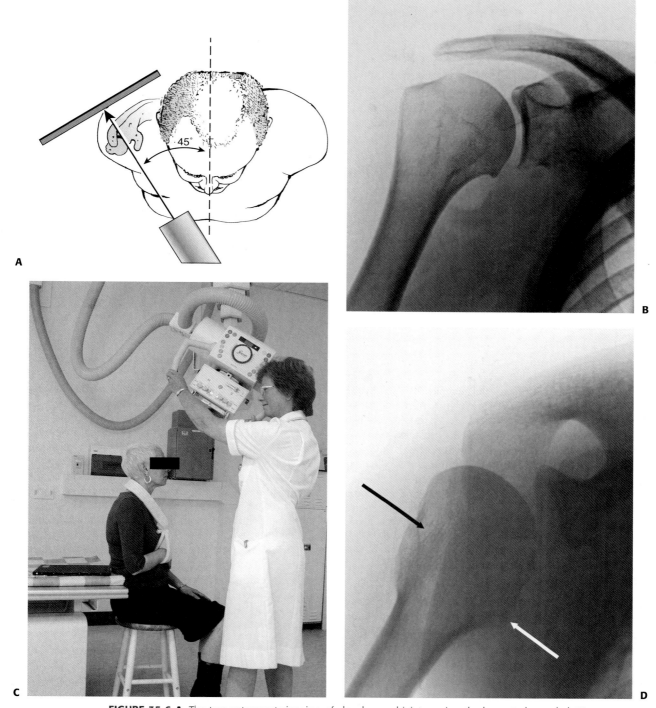

FIGURE 35-6 A. The true anteroposterior view of glenohumeral joint requires the beam to be angled 45 degrees from the sagittal plane. **B.** The true anteroposterior view in the plane of the scapula is orthogonal to the face of the glenoid to show the maximum amount of the humeral head articular surface possible. **C.** The modified axial view is obtained with the arm resting in a sling and the x-ray gantry tilted 45 degrees in the sagittal plane. **D.** The view clearly shows the outline of the greater tuberosity (*black arrow*) and lesser tuberosity (*white arrow*) and confirms congruent reduction of the humeral head.

ture. The best depiction of the fracture is therefore obtained if orthogonal views are taken in the plane of the glenoid. Since the scapula is protracted on the chest wall, the anteroposterior view is usually obtained by tilting the x-ray beam approximately 30 degrees medial to the normal anatomic plane (see Fig. 35-2).

Neer pointed out that the plane of maximal angulation and

displacement of the shaft with respect to the head in a proximal humeral fracture is typically anteromedial.[207] This deformity is therefore seldom adequately visualized on standard trauma series radiographs. Computed tomography (CT) scanning is being increasingly used to provide further detail of the complex fracture anatomy (Fig. 35-7).[73] Most modern spiral scanners have

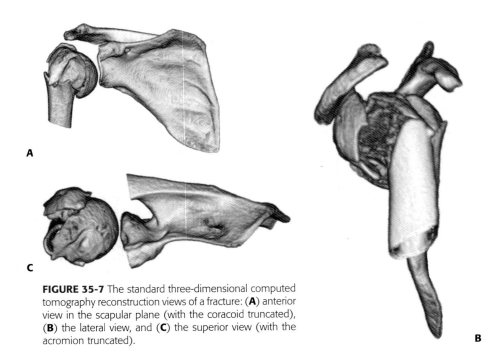

FIGURE 35-7 The standard three-dimensional computed tomography reconstruction views of a fracture: (**A**) anterior view in the scapular plane (with the coracoid truncated), (**B**) the lateral view, and (**C**) the superior view (with the acromion truncated).

the software facility for three-dimensional reformatting of the images,[137] to provide a better representation of the complex anatomy of these injuries. These images may also aid in the detection of articular surface injuries, which are often not visualized on conventional radiographs.[73]

MRI is not commonly used in initial fracture assessment, as it provides less detail about the bone architecture than CT. In addition, the deformity produced by the fracture may hinder interpretation of the soft tissue anatomy of the injury. MRI may be useful in imaging the integrity of the rotator cuff in patients who have complications after their initial treatment and require later reconstructive surgery.

CLASSIFICATION AND CLINICAL CHARACTERISTICS

Classification of any musculoskeletal injury should serve as a guide to treatment and predict outcome. Although classification of proximal humeral fractures has tended to focus on the fracture configuration, it is important to appreciate that there are important patient- and treatment-related factors that determine the outcome after these injuries.

The Injury

Classification systems for proximal humeral fractures that evaluated displacement and the presence of an associated shoulder dislocation had been described before the 1970s.[150] Codman recognized that the proximal humerus tends to fracture along its physeal lines of fusion into four principal fragments (the two tuberosities, the humeral head, and the shaft).[48] Neer subsequently refined these definitions to produce the classification that remains most widely used today.[207,208] Each of the four fragments are considered as unique parts only if they are separated by more than 1 cm or angulated by more than 45 degrees to one another (Fig. 35-8). These parameters were selected somewhat arbitrarily, and reproducible and reliable measure-

ment of the degree of displacement and angulation is difficult using conventional radiographs.[19,276,277]

According to this system of classification, undisplaced or minimally displaced fractures are termed *one-part fractures*. Displaced fractures are classified according to the number of displaced fragments, regardless of the number of secondary fracture lines, into *two-, three-,* or *four-part configuration*. Fracture-dislocations are also classified according to the direction of displacement of the humeral head (anterior or posterior), as well as according to the number of fracture fragments. Using these criteria, Neer suggested that 85% of fractures are minimally displaced, although more recent studies suggest a prevalence of closer to 50%.[57,129,316]

The AO/ASIF classification system of proximal humeral fractures[193,203] uses the familiar alphanumeric triads of fracture types to produce 27 main subgroups (Table 35-1). Although this system has been retained by the Orthopaedic Trauma Association in its recent fracture compendium,[193] it is not intuitive and is seldom used either in clinical practice or in the academic literature.

Other classifications have been produced,[14,73,123,291] but none has proved as robust over time or gained the general acceptance of the Neer classification. It has been criticized for lacking reproducibility,[19,276,277] and since it is an anatomic classification, it does not directly serve as a guide to treatment or directly predict outcome. The complex three-dimensional deformity of these fractures can only be adequately appraised at the time of surgery[291] or using CT with three-dimensional reconstructions.[73,266]

Despite these criticisms, the Neer classification has survived intact for the past 40 years, although at the time when the classification was first produced there was a limited range of treatment options available to treat proximal humeral fractures. The recent advances in the technology available to assess and treat these fractures, together with an improved appreciation of the factors associated with a more benign prognosis after reconstruction, have led to a refined description of some fracture

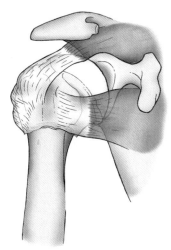

Undisplaced one-part

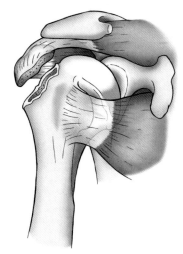

Two-part greater tuberosity

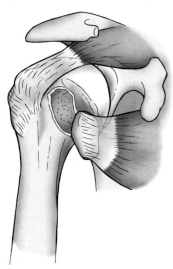

Two-part lesser tuberosity

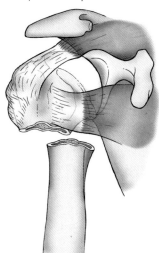

Two-part surgical neck

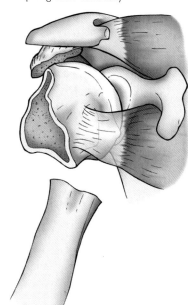

Three-part greater tuberosity

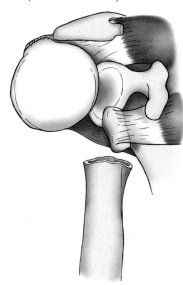

Three-part lesser tuberosity

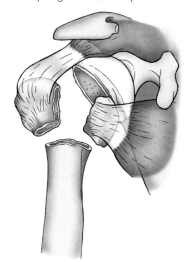

Four-part fracture

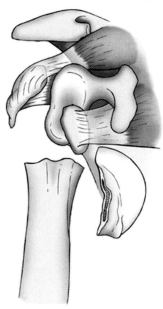

Four-part fracture-dislocation (may be anterior or posterior)

FIGURE 35-8 The main subgroups of Neer classification of proximal humerus fractures. (Modified from Neer CS. Displaced proximal humeral fractures: I. Classification and evaluation. J Bone Joint Surg Am 1970;52A:1077–1089, with permission.) The rarer articular surface fractures (head-splitting or impression fractures) are not depicted here, but are described freely in the text and depicted in Figures 35.12, 35.16, and 35.17.

TABLE 35-1 The OTA Classification of Proximal Humeral Fractures

Major Category	Subgroup
Extra-articular, unifocal fracture (11A)	Greater tuberosity (11A1) Surgical neck metaphysis impacted (11A2) Surgical neck metaphysis not impacted (11A3)
Extra-articular, bifocal fracture (11B)	Three-part surgical neck fracture, metaphysis impacted (11B1) Three-part surgical neck fracture, metaphysis not impacted (11B2) Extra-articular fracture with glenohumeral dislocation (11B3)
Articular fracture (11-C)	Slight displacement (11-C1) Marked displacement (11-C2) With glenohumeral dislocation or head-split (11-C3)

diagnosed late.[228,237,317] Undisplaced fractures tend to occur in a slightly younger, fitter group of patients,[57,86,156,221,222] possibly because they have better proximal humeral bone stock and a stronger and thicker periosteal sleeve of tissue preventing fracture displacement. Despite their prevalence, these injuries tend to receive less attention in the literature, because most are treated nonoperatively and have a good prognosis.

Minimally displaced fracture lines may be present in either the anatomic or surgical neck of the humerus and in one or both tuberosities (Fig. 35-9). Although secondary displacement is possible, especially if the head is not impacted on the shaft fragment, this is relatively unusual. Inferior subluxation of the humeral head may occasionally occur through hemarthrosis, muscle atony, or capsular injury. This almost always spontaneously resolves with nonoperative treatment over a period of a few weeks. Minimally displaced greater tuberosity fractures can be associated with rotator cuff tears, and this may be the source of persistent disability after fracture.[149] Arthroscopic debridement and repair may be successful in these patients.[149]

configurations. Some of these configurations did not feature in the original descriptive classification but nevertheless provide useful additional prognostic information. Until a more comprehensive classification is produced, which guides treatment and predicts outcome, it is best to view these as "descriptive modifiers" of the original Neer classification, which may alter the treatment and outcome for some of the fracture subtypes. For completeness, the AO/OTA classification is given together with the modified Neer classification in the following sections.

Classification of Individual Fracture Subtypes

Undisplaced or Minimally Displaced One-Part Fractures (OTA Types A, B, or C)

It is estimated that approximately 50% of proximal fractures are undisplaced, when Neer's criteria for displacement are strictly applied[57,86,156] (Table 35-2). Such estimations can only be approximate because of the difficulties in estimating angulation and displacement on conventional radiographs. Minor fractures may not reach the attention of orthopaedic services or may be

Two-Part Greater Tuberosity Fractures and Fracture-Dislocations (OTA Types A1.1, A1.2, and A1.3)

These injuries have received scant attention in the literature, but they are common, accounting for approximately 10% of all proximal humeral fractures[57] (Table 35-2). The recovery from this injury may be protracted because of the associated defunctioning or impingement of the rotator cuff, which they may produce. These injuries have a spectrum of severity: approximately half are isolated fractures, and the remainder are associated with glenohumeral dislocations and associated soft tissue injury, most commonly an associated nerve injury. Those associated with a glenohumeral dislocation tend to occur in the middle-aged and elderly, as distinct from isolated dislocations, which tend to occur in younger individuals. The "terrible triad" of the shoulder occurs when the tuberosity avulsion fracture is associated with anterior dislocation of the shoulder and an associated nerve or plexus injury.[108] This injury pattern is relatively common, although the exact prevalence has not been defined. It represents the most severe form of injury, from which functional recovery is often incomplete.

TABLE 35-2 The Relative Prevalence of Proximal Humeral Fractures According to the Neer Classification

Fracture Type			Proportion of All Fractures (%)	Mean Age (yr)
Isolated fractures	One-part		49.0	63
	Two-part	Greater tuberosity	4.0	67
		Lesser tuberosity	0.2	NS
		Anatomic neck	0.3	50
		Surgical neck	28.0	70
	Three-part		9.3	72
	Four-part		2.0	72
	Head-split		0.7	73
Fracture-dislocations	Two-part		5.2	59
	Three-part		0.2	64
	Four-part		1.1	72

From CourtBrown CM, Garg A, McQueen MM. The epidemiology of proximal humeral fractures. Acta Orthop Scand 2001;72: 365–371.

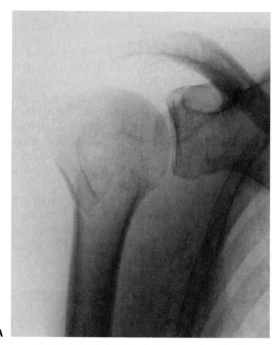 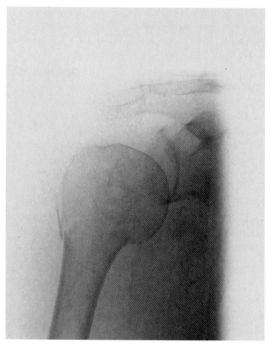

FIGURE 35-9 A,B. Undisplaced and stable fracture configurations are best treated nonoperatively in most elderly patients, as shown in these two examples.

Tuberosity fractures occurring in association with glenoid rim fractures may give rise to primary redislocation of the shoulder.[250] However, isolated greater tuberosity fractures are seldom associated with glenohumeral instability, possibly because there is an inferior capsular rupture rather than the typical anteroinferior labral detachment (Bankart lesion), which more commonly affects younger patients.[248,249,261]

The exact mechanism of injury for these fractures is uncertain and there may be several.[8,107] An injury produced by axial loading may produce a primary anatomic neck fracture via the same mechanism as for an impacted valgus fracture. The displacement of this fracture may be slight but sufficient to cause a secondary greater tuberosity fracture. The greater tuberosity fracture is often the most striking feature on the initial trauma series radiographs, and the anatomic neck fracture may not be visible if the correct anteroposterior views of the shoulder are not taken (Fig. 35-10). It is estimated that approximately 10% of isolated greater tuberosity fractures may have a concomitant

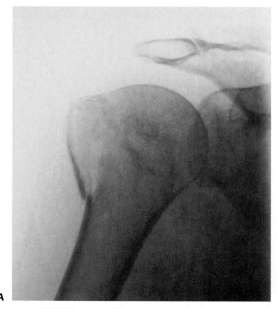 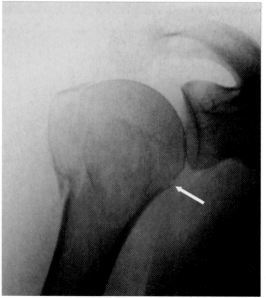

FIGURE 35-10 Many seemingly isolated greater tuberosity fractures (**A**) actually have undisplaced anatomic neck fracture lines (*arrow*), which are only seen when a correctly orientated anteroposterior view is taken (**B**).

anatomic neck fracture. Alternatively a tuberosity fracture may be produced by a traction injury, often during a glenohumeral dislocation. This may either be from a bony avulsion of the rotator cuff, or through propagation of an acute osteochondral fracture of the posterior humeral head (Hill-Sachs lesion), as it engages on the anterior glenoid.[8,73,107]

The anatomic configuration of the fracture can also vary quite widely, ranging from small, often multifragmentary injuries to larger single-fragment fractures (Fig. 35-11). The former should be regarded as a rotator cuff avulsion injury and has a tendency to retract over time because of the unopposed pull of the attached supraspinatus and infraspinatus tendons. The latter injury is less prone to redisplacement. While Neer considered 1 cm of displacement of any fracture fragment to be clinically significant, recently some authors have suggested that 5 mm of displacement should be considered a more appropriate threshold and indication for operative treatment for these injuries,

given the high risk of cuff dysfunction and impingement even with this degree of displacement.[31,81,224]

Two-Part Lesser Tuberosity Fractures and Fracture-Dislocations (OTA Type A1.3, Subgroup 4)

Displaced (two-part) lesser tuberosity fractures are very rare injuries but are probably more common than undisplaced (one-part) lesser tuberosity fractures, because of the tendency of the attached subscapularis tendon to retract the fragment medially (Fig. 35-12). They are atypical of other proximal humeral fractures, because they tend to occur in middle-aged adults, with a slight male predominance, and are usually produced by relatively high-energy injuries.[72,177,218,257]

Isolated lesser tuberosity fractures probably represent bony avulsions of the subscapularis tendon, usually from a forced external rotation injury.[257] These fractures may also occur in association with posterior glenohumeral dislocations. In these

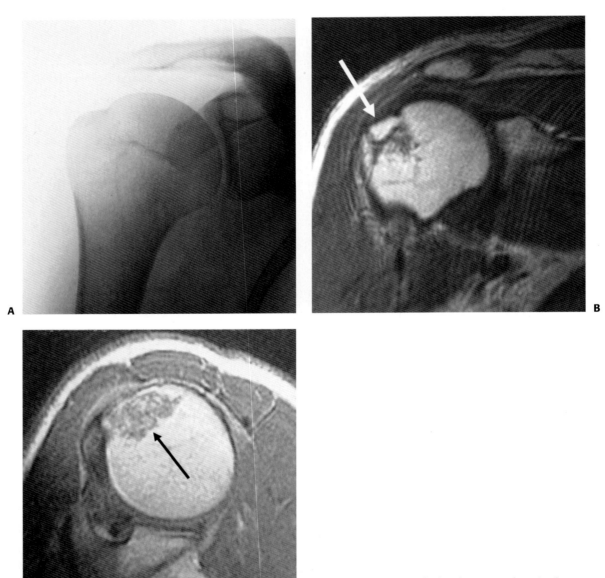

A

B

C

FIGURE 35-11 An undisplaced greater tuberosity fracture may not be visible on conventional radiography (**A**) and may only be seen on magnetic resonance imaging (**B,C**).

(continues)

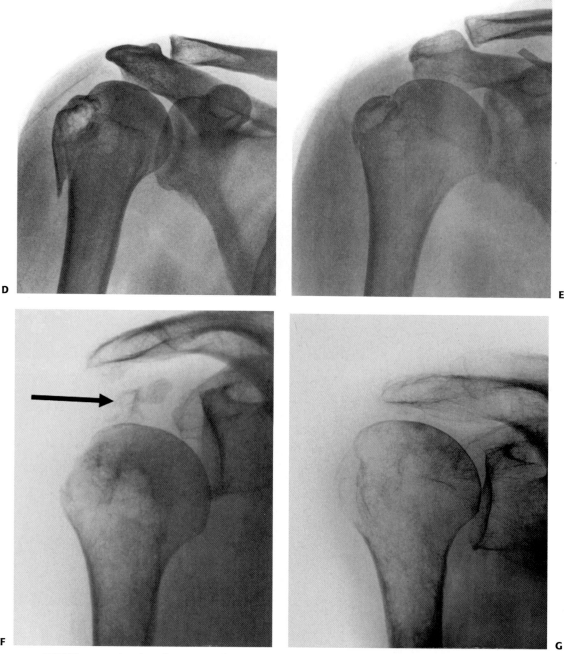

FIGURE 35-11 (*continued*) Greater tuberosity fractures vary widely in their size, ranging from larger fragments (**D**) to smaller avulsion-type injuries (**E**). These may displace in the same manner as a rotator cuff tear, with retraction of the tendon leading to progressive displacement of the bone fragment (*arrow*) (**F**). Untreated, this may lead to a rotator cuff–deficient shoulder with a high-riding humeral head and rotator cuff arthropathy (**G**).

circumstances, the fracture is caused by propagation of the acute osteochondral fracture of the anterior humeral head (reverse Hill-Sachs defect), as it engages on the posterior glenoid.[257]

Two-Part Extra-Articular (Surgical Neck) Fractures (OTA Types A2 and A3)

These fractures account for a quarter of proximal humeral fractures and they tend to occur in a slightly older group of individuals than the remainder of the proximal humeral fracture popu-

lation (Table 35-1). They are extra-articular fractures, although undisplaced secondary tuberosity fracture lines may be seen. Since the soft tissue attachments and blood supply to the humeral head and tuberosities are preserved, there is a low risk of osteonecrosis.

Neer described three types of surgical neck fractures: angulated, translated/separated, and comminuted[207] (Fig. 35-13). The angulated fracture may either be in neutral alignment, or such that the head and attached tuberosities are tilted into varus

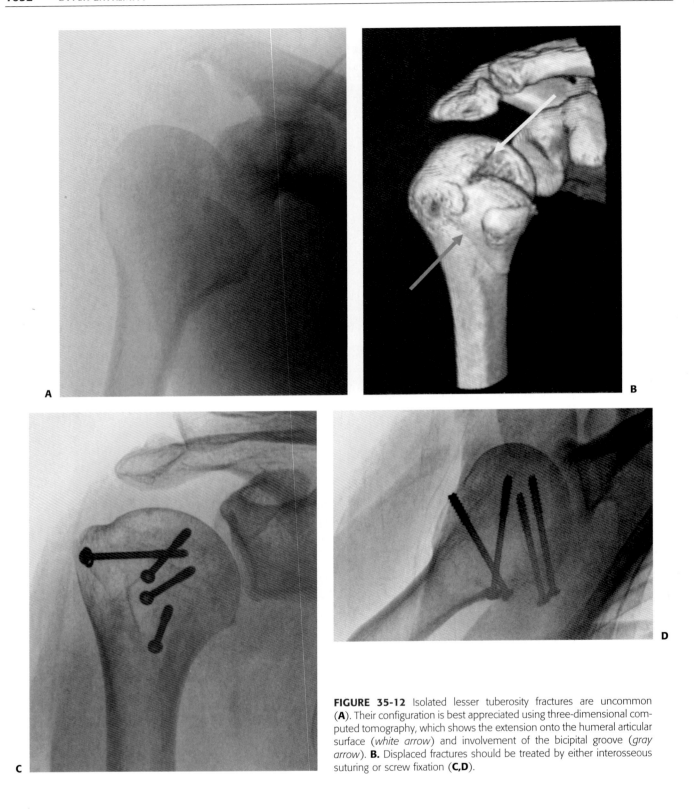

FIGURE 35-12 Isolated lesser tuberosity fractures are uncommon (**A**). Their configuration is best appreciated using three-dimensional computed tomography, which shows the extension onto the humeral articular surface (*white arrow*) and involvement of the bicipital groove (*gray arrow*). **B.** Displaced fractures should be treated by either interosseous suturing or screw fixation (**C,D**).

or valgus.[73] The shaft is usually impacted onto the humeral head, and the direction and extent of the head displacement are determined by the orientation of the shaft as it is driven up within the metaphysis and the manner in which the metaphyseal bone fails at the time of fracture. Because of their impaction, these fractures have a low risk of complete displacement and nonunion. However, the impacted varus fracture is unusual in

that the degree of angulation of the head on the shaft may increase with nonoperative treatment.[59]

Discontinuity of the humeral head from the shaft can be produced either by translation and separation of the shaft on the head or through extensive comminution of the metaphyseal area, leading to loss of cortical continuity.[207] Displacement may be incomplete, with some residual cortical contact, or the head

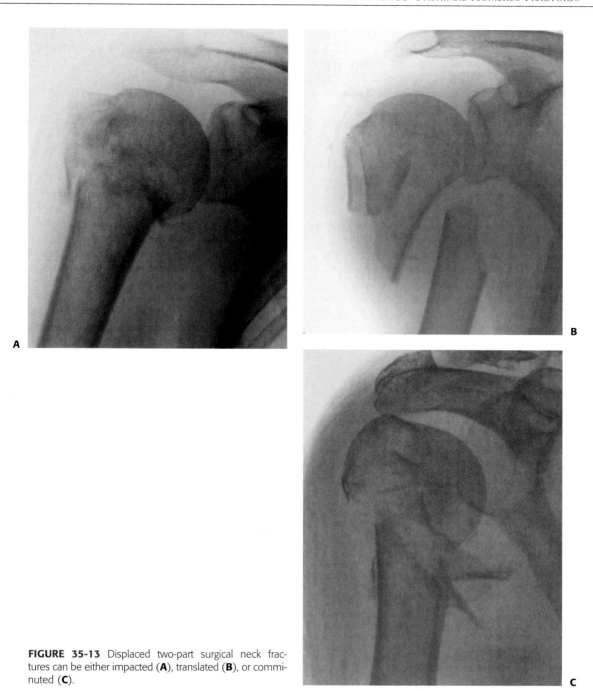

FIGURE 35-13 Displaced two-part surgical neck fractures can be either impacted (**A**), translated (**B**), or comminuted (**C**).

may be completely disconnected for the shaft.[58,73] The shaft tends to be pulled anteromedially, through the pull of the pectoralis major. With complete displacement, the head either adopts a neutral position or may progressively tilt into a varus position due the pull of the attached rotator cuff muscles. Spontaneous reduction of these fractures seldom occurs, and they have a higher risk of nonunion after nonoperative treatment.[58,60]

Two-Part Anatomic Neck Fractures (OTA Type C1.3)

Isolated anatomic neck fractures, with an enlocated humeral head, are extremely uncommon injuries[57] (Table 35-2). Any experience of their treatment and prognosis is likely to be anecdotal, although Neer described these fractures as having a high

rate of osteonecrosis.[207,208] This fracture configuration occurs most frequently in association with posterior dislocation of the fractured humeral head (see later).

Three- and Four-Part Fractures Without Dislocation (OTA Types B1, B2, C1, and C2)

The major area of confusion in classification arises from this group of multifragmentary injuries, which account for approximately 10% of proximal humeral fractures (Table 35-2). On initial inspection, they appear to be a diverse group, in which the extent of comminution and displacement of the three or four fracture fragments varies markedly. However, most of the variation in the fracture lines and their displacement can be explained by an understanding of the deforming forces that produce the constant feature of a primary fracture of the anatomic neck of the humerus.[73] Tuberosity fractures are thought to be a secondary phenomenon, which are caused by displacement of the humeral head relative to the shaft. The fracture configuration is determined by the direction and severity of displacement of the humeral head, and the deforming forces produced by the residual soft tissue attachments of each fracture fragment.

In the past, these injuries were regarded to have a high risk of osteonecrosis after nonoperative treatment or head-conserving reconstruction, because of the disruption of the soft tissue attachments to the humeral head. It is now recognized that conventional radiographs overestimate the degree of soft tissue and tuberosity detachment from the head, and the risk of humeral head ischemia and later osteonecrosis. Seeking additional descriptive evaluation of the fracture is therefore to be encouraged. This should include, in addition to evaluation of the number of fracture parts, a detailed assessment of the configuration and orientation of the fracture parts and an assessment of the potential viability of the humeral head and the extent of articular surface involvement. Definitive assessment of these parameters can only be made at the time of surgery, although preoperative

three-dimensional CT greatly facilitates evaluation and planning the reconstruction. These factors are discussed in more detail next.

Humeral Head Angulation and Displacement. As with two-part surgical neck fractures, in three- and four-part fractures, the humeral head may be either impacted on the shaft, or unimpacted, when it may translate or separate from the shaft. As with two-part surgical neck fractures, the humeral head may have a neutral, valgus, or varus angulation.

Neutral Angulation. In this fracture configuration, the humeral head occupies a neutral position in the coronal plane on anteroposterior view. It may be internally rotated in the horizontal plane, if there is a three-part greater tuberosity fracture, because of the pull of the subscapularis on the attached lesser tuberosity, whereas in four-part fractures, the head tends to adopt a neutral position.

Impacted-Valgus Fractures. In this fracture configuration, the fractured humeral head faces superiorly (in valgus), with the tuberosities splayed on either side of it (Fig. 35-14). Its anatomic

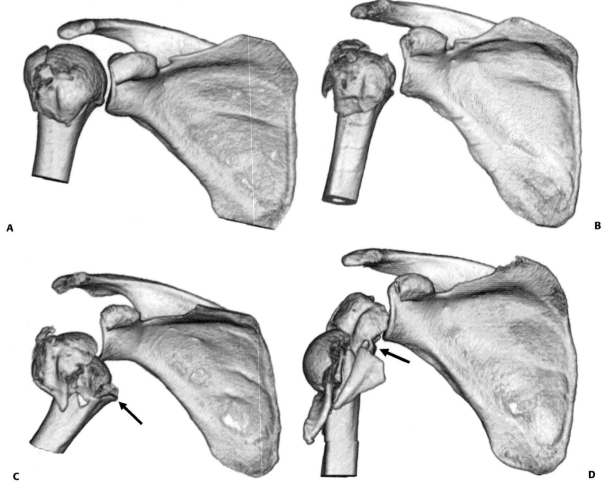

FIGURE 35-14 Three- and four-part impacted valgus fractures show considerable variation radiologically and on three-dimensional computed tomography reconstructions (as shown), ranging from fractures that are minimally displaced (**A**), through more severe valgus angulation (**B**) to displacement with lateral translation of the head, where the medial soft tissue hinge is disrupted (*arrow*) and the risk of osteonecrosis is higher (**C,D**).

features were described subsequent to the Neer classification,[207,289] and Jakob was the first to recognize its benign prognosis compared with other multipart fractures.[134] It is one of the more common patterns of fracture[56,57] and represents a spectrum of injury, with variation in the degree of humeral head angulation and displacement.[56,65] Recognition of this variation is important, because it is now realized that treatment aimed at preserving the native humeral head may not always produce satisfactory results.

The degree of valgus displacement of the humeral head may be slight and these fractures merge with the previously described two-part greater tuberosity fracture configuration. If the head is pushed farther into the metaphysis, there is a greater degree of valgus impaction.[73] The intact medial periosteal hinge and capsule between the head and the calcar is the axis around which displacement occurs and may act as a source of perfusion to the humeral head.

When the humeral head has assumed an extreme position with the articular surface facing directly superiorly, the sharp medial calcar is exposed and the medial hinge of periosteum begins to tear as it is stretched over the unyielding edge of the calcar. This causes lateral translation of the head relative to the calcar, resulting in further propagation of the tear in the periosteal hinge.

The degree of lateralization that the humeral head can tolerate before it becomes completely denuded of soft tissue attachments and at higher risk of osteonecrosis of the head is unclear. Cadaver studies suggest that the medial periosteal hinge completely ruptures at between 6 to 11 mm of lateral head displacement,[7,113,240,241] although it has been suggested that as little as 5 mm of displacement may be sufficient to cause complete disruption[272] (Fig. 35-14).

Two "end-stage" patterns of impacted valgus fracture are recognized, in which the humeral head is invariably devoid of soft tissue attachments and ischemic. The humeral head may remain attached to the shaft and dislocate anteroinferiorly. This injury pattern is discussed together with other fracture-dislocations below (see Type II anterior fracture-dislocations). Alternatively, the lateralization of the humeral head caused by the medial displacement of the shaft may progress such that the head becomes completely disengaged from the shaft. This pattern of injury may occur de novo or be produced iatrogenically through an attempted closed reduction of a lower grade fracture.[77,121,252]

Varus Fractures. Three- and four-part fractures in which the humeral head is tilted into varus have received less attention than valgus fractures but nevertheless constitute a substantial proportion of these injuries (Fig. 35-15). They are thought to represent a more severe end of the spectrum of two-part surgical neck impacted varus fractures, in which undisplaced fractures in the tuberosities open up and displace.[73] As with two-part surgical neck varus fractures, the humeral head has a tendency to tilt into a progressively greater degree of varus with nonoperative treatment.

Tuberosity Fracture Configuration and Displacement. The classic description of the two tuberosity fracture fragments has undergone some redefinition,[207] since it is now appreciated that most tuberosity fractures occur secondary to the displacement of the head fragment. Their degree of spatial displacement is

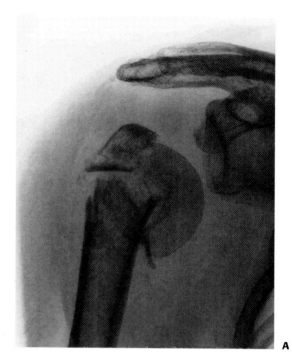

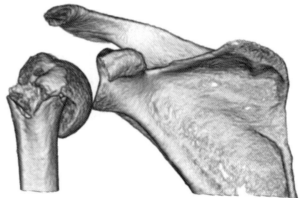

FIGURE 35-15 Three- and four-part varus fractures are less common than valgus injuries, and radiologically give rise to inferior subluxation of the humeral head on conventional radiography (**A**) and on three-dimensional reconstructions of computerised tomograms (**B**).

initially minimal, relative to their normal anatomic position. With nonoperative treatment, progressive displacement may occur because of the unopposed pull of the rotator cuff muscles.

Neer three-part lesser tuberosity fractures are extremely uncommon injuries, accounting for only 0.3% of all proximal humeral fractures,[57] and most of the remaining 10% of three-part fractures therefore involve the greater tuberosity (Table 35-1). The bicipital groove does not form a plane of cleavage between the tuberosities, as conceived in the original concept of the injury.[49,207] Instead, the characteristic initial tuberosity fracture line is located posterior to the hard cortical bone of the groove, in the softer bone of the anterior portion of the greater tuberosity, just lateral to the supraspinatus facet.[73] A separated greater tuberosity fragment may itself be comminuted and tends to retract posterosuperomedially because of the pull of the infraspinatus and teres minor tendons (Fig. 35-16).

In four-part fractures, the humeral head shears off from the

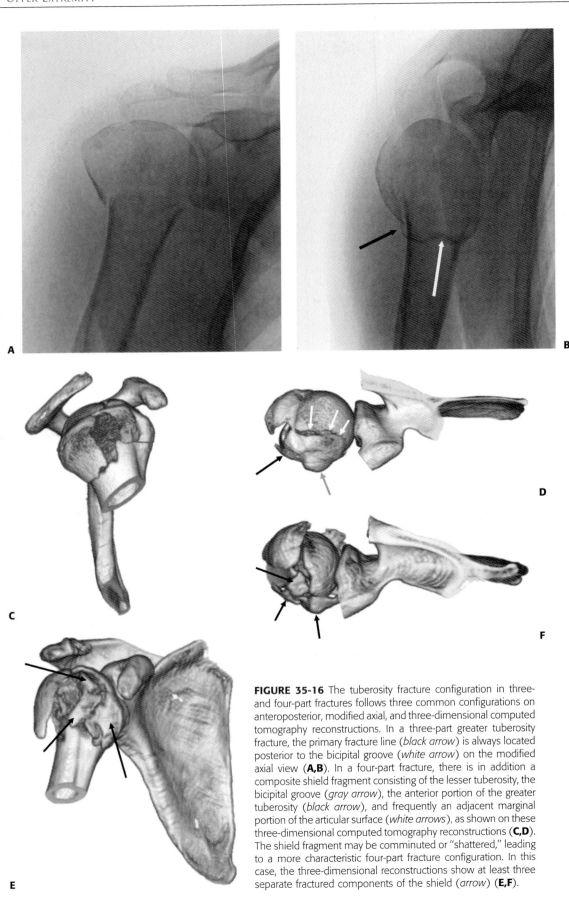

FIGURE 35-16 The tuberosity fracture configuration in three- and four-part fractures follows three common configurations on anteroposterior, modified axial, and three-dimensional computed tomography reconstructions. In a three-part greater tuberosity fracture, the primary fracture line (*black arrow*) is always located posterior to the bicipital groove (*white arrow*) on the modified axial view (**A,B**). In a four-part fracture, there is in addition a composite shield fragment consisting of the lesser tuberosity, the bicipital groove (*gray arrow*), the anterior portion of the greater tuberosity (*black arrow*), and frequently an adjacent marginal portion of the articular surface (*white arrows*), as shown on these three-dimensional computed tomography reconstructions (**C,D**). The shield fragment may be comminuted or "shattered," leading to a more characteristic four-part fracture configuration. In this case, the three-dimensional reconstructions show at least three separate fractured components of the shield (*arrow*) (**E,F**).

remaining composite tuberosity fragment, which comprises the anterior portion of the greater tuberosity, the bicipital groove, the lesser tuberosity, and often a portion of the adjacent articular surface (Fig. 35-16). This composite "shield" fragment may either be intact, comminuted with minimal separation of its component parts, or comminuted and separated ("the shattered shield"). Most four-part fractures, as conceived by Neer,[207] fall into the latter group and account for a small minority of all these fractures (Table 35-2). Although other fracture configurations have been described,[123,195,291] in practice these other types of two- and three-part fractures are extremely rare.

Recognition of the nuances of the tuberosity fracture configuration is important since a large shield fragment may produce an obstacle to gaining access to the displaced humeral head fragment, if operative treatment is selected. The predictable and progressive displacement of unhealed tuberosity fragments may lead to later problems from rotator cuff impingement and dysfunction.

Humeral Head Viability and Risk of Osteonecrosis. The risk of osteonecrosis of the humeral head after three- and four-part fractures prompted an attempt to identify factors that are predictive of this complication. Back-bleeding after bore-hole insertion in the cancellous bone of the humeral head and Doppler flowmetry to detect humeral head blood flow have been used to quantify the degree of humeral head ischemia at the time of surgery.[123] The presence of a longer posteromedial metaphyseal spike of bone attached to the humeral head (longer than 8 mm) may be associated with a high rate of intraoperative head perfusion, presumably through retained blood flow through capsular attachments in this area. In addition, preservation of a medial hinge in a valgus fracture, without lateralization of the head, is also associated with a greater likelihood of humeral head perfusion.[123] However, there is a poor correlation of the presence of intraoperative head blood flow with the later development of osteonecrosis.[14] Some humeral heads that are perfused at surgery later develop osteonecrosis, whereas some ischemic heads did not develop osteonecrosis after internal fixation. At present, there is no reliable method to accurately predict the development of osteonecrosis of the humeral head after fracture.

Articular Surface Involvement. In Neer's original description, articular surface fractures were regarded as a separate subgroup of fracture-dislocations. It is now recognized from CT studies that these injuries are more common than was previously appreciated. Fractures that involve the articular surface can occur through a variety of mechanisms: In the most severe and rare form, the larger surface area of the humeral head may be cleaved as it impacts against the narrow "anvil" of the glenoid into two or more large fragments in the true "head-splitting" fracture.

It is much more common for the tuberosity fragments in intra-articular fractures to carry peripheral portions of the articular surface with them as "marginal" fragments. This type of articular injury is particularly associated with larger shield fractures, which often have a portion of the adjacent superolateral humeral articular surface attached to them (Fig. 35-17). These fragments may be difficult to see on plain radiographs, although a "double shadow" of the articular surface is usually pathognomonic (Fig. 35-17). Failure to anatomically reduce these articular fragments may compromise the reconstruction and lead to early secondary osteoarthrosis.

The final type of articular surface fracture occurs through direct injury when the humeral head articular surface impacts on the anterior or posterior glenoid rim during a posterior or anterior glenohumeral dislocation, respectively. If the acute osteochondral fracture of humeral head (Hill-Sachs lesion or reverse Hill-Sachs lesion) propagates, this may produce a Type I anterior-fracture dislocation or a posterior fracture-dislocation. These are discussed in more detail in the next section.

Complex Fractures with Glenohumeral Dislocation (OTA Types B3 and C3)

These injuries are rare (Table 35-2), and anterior are much more common than posterior fracture-dislocations. The terminology that has been used to describe these injuries is confusing—in continental Europe, the term "dislocation" has often been used synonymously with "displacement."[119,145,211] To avoid ambiguity, the term "fracture-dislocation" is best reserved for injuries in which there is complete dissociation of the fractured humeral head from the glenoid.

The dislocation adds an extra level of difficulty to the treatment of complex multipart proximal humeral fractures, and they are traditionally regarded as representing the more severe end of the spectrum of multipart fractures, with a higher risk of osteonecrosis. However, there is evidence to suggest that the mechanism of injury and prognosis may be different for some anterior fracture-dislocations and the majority of posterior fracture-dislocations.[73,207,209,245,252]

Three- and Four-Part Anterior Fracture-Dislocations. The recognition that some anterior fracture-dislocations have a better prognosis following open reduction and internal fixation (ORIF) has led to classification into two subtypes, as follows.

Type I Injuries (Viable Humeral Head With Retained Capsular Attachments). Type I injuries tend to occur in younger males, who commonly sustain their fracture-dislocation during a high-energy energy.[252] The humeral head commonly retains capsular attachments through both an intact periosteal sleeve around the lesser tuberosity in a three-part fracture-dislocation and a retained extracapsular posteromedial bone spike attached to the head. The pathologic features of the injury resemble those of a first-time anterior dislocation of the glenohumeral joint,[248] because there is a soft tissue or bony avulsion of the anteroinferior capsulolabral complex (a soft tissue or bony Bankart lesion) and an acute osteochondral fracture of the posterior humeral head (Hill-Sachs lesion) caused by its impaction on the anterior glenoid rim. The fracture is produced by propagation of the Hill-Sachs lesion, through the anatomic neck of the humerus, and therefore occurs after the head has dislocated[252] (Fig. 35-18).

Type II (Nonviable Humeral Head Devoid of Significant Capsular Attachments). The Type II injury is more common, and mostly occurs in older females, who sustain their injuries in low-energy trauma. Radiologically, the fracture resembles a three- or four-part valgus fracture, but with the humeral head dislocated anteroinferiorly, and not engaged on the glenoid. The humeral head fractures in a valgus position and the exposed sharp medial calcar tears through the inferomedial capsule in the region of the axillary recess. The shaft displaces through this capsular rent, carrying the impacted humeral head with it

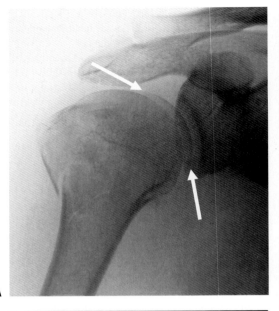

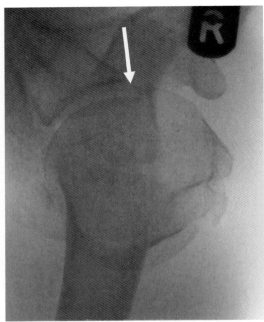

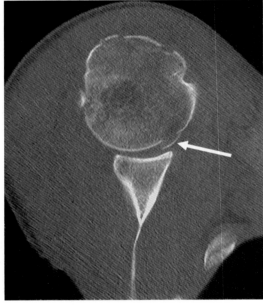

FIGURE 35-17 A. "Double-shadow" on the anteroposterior radiograph (*arrow*) is pathognomic of a head-split fracture. The split is also seen on the modified axial view (**B**) but the extent of head involvement is best assessed using a computed tomography scan (**C**). The *white arrows* show the head-split.

(Fig. 35-18). Any remaining capsular attachments to the head are torn during the dislocation. The importance of the recognition of this injury is that although the fracture configuration is similar to the valgus fracture (which typically has a benign prognosis), the dislocated humeral head is devoid of capsular attachments and blood supply and is therefore at much higher risk of osteonecrosis. The results of a head-salvaging reconstruction in this injury type are therefore poor.

In both types of anterior fracture-dislocations, undisplaced anatomic neck fractures are difficult to detect on standard radiographs, and these injuries are commonly initially mistaken for two-part greater tuberosity fracture-dislocations.[121,252] Secondary displacement of the head may be produced if an attempt is made to obtain a closed relocation by manipulation. CT should be performed for all anterior shoulder dislocations with a greater tuberosity fracture, where an undisplaced anatomic neck fracture is suspected on the trauma series radiographs.

Two-, Three-, and Four-Part Posterior Fracture-Dislocations. Posterior fracture-dislocations are a rare but important group of proximal humeral fractures, which occur in a relatively young, middle-aged group of predominantly male patients. This injury may be bilateral, when it is usually produced by a seizure, caused by either epilepsy, alcohol or drug withdrawal, or hypoglycemia.[245] Unilateral injuries typically occur from falls from height or road traffic accidents.

This injury is analogous to the Type I anterior fracture-dislocation: The fracture of the anatomic neck propagates from the area of an osteochondral fracture of the anterior humeral head (reverse Hill-Sachs lesion), as it engages on the posterior glenoid rim. The posterior dislocation of the humeral head avulses the posteroinferior capsulolabral soft tissue sleeve and produces a reverse Bankart lesion (capsulolabral avulsion of the posteroinferior glenoid rim) in all cases. However, the capsule and periosteal sleeve are in continuity, and the anatomic neck fracture

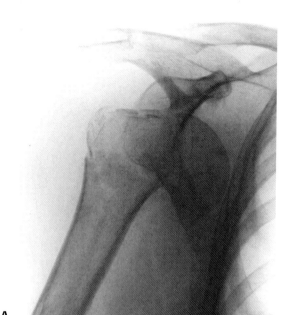

A

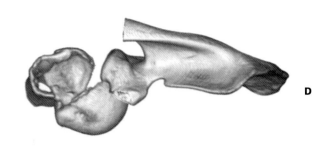

D

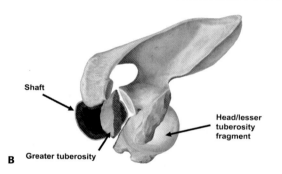

Shaft

Greater tuberosity

B

Head/lesser
tuberosity
fragment

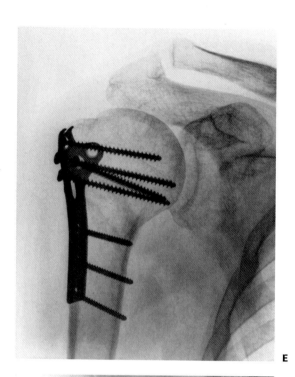

E

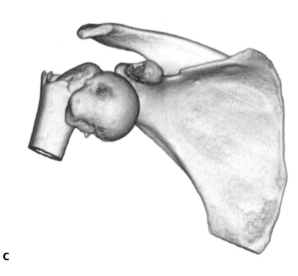

C

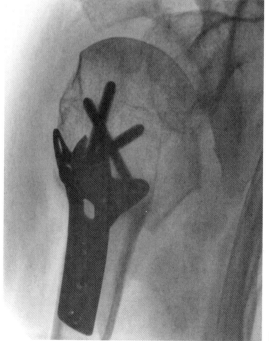

F

FIGURE 35-18 In Type I anterior fracture-dislocations, the humeral head is engaged on the anterior glenoid rim, as shown on the anteroposterior radiograph (**A**), the schematic diagram (**B**), and anteroposterior and superior three-dimensional computed tomography reconstructions (**C,D**). Internal fixation of these fractures is associated with a low risk of osteonecrosis (**E,F**). *(continues)*

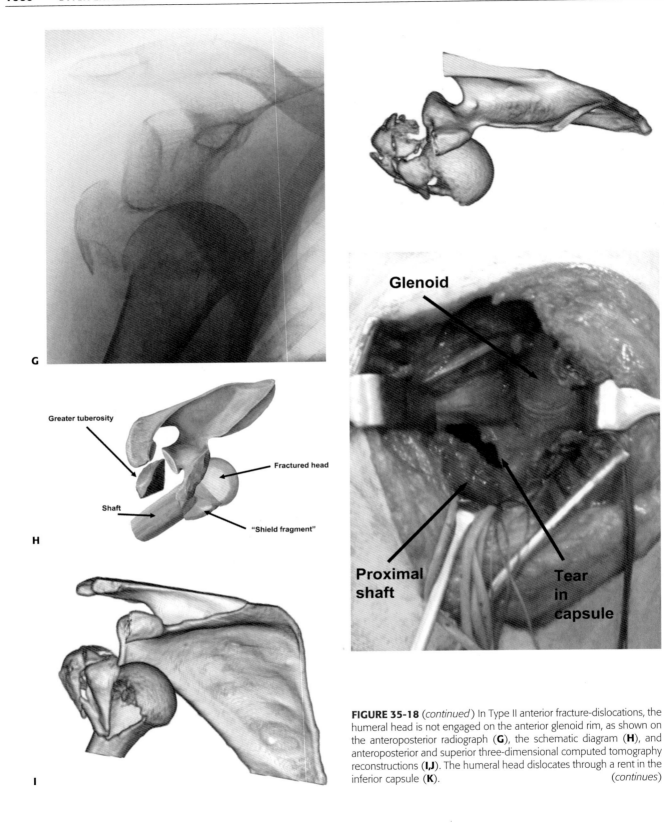

FIGURE 35-18 (*continued*) In Type II anterior fracture-dislocations, the humeral head is not engaged on the anterior glenoid rim, as shown on the anteroposterior radiograph (**G**), the schematic diagram (**H**), and anteroposterior and superior three-dimensional computed tomography reconstructions (**I,J**). The humeral head dislocates through a rent in the inferior capsule (**K**). (*continues*)

"hinges" on these structures. Three fracture subtypes are determined by the type and extent of "secondary" fractures lines in the tuberosities[245] (Fig. 35-19). Their recognition is important, because they serve as a guide to the technique of internal fixation that should be used.

OPERATIVE APPROACHES

The Deltopectoral Approach

Operative treatment of proximal humeral fractures, whether by ORIF or by arthroplasty, is most commonly performed using

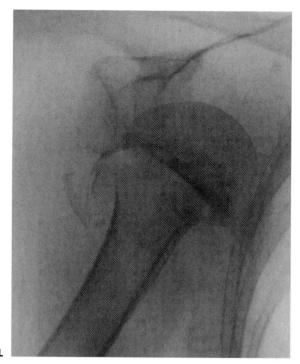
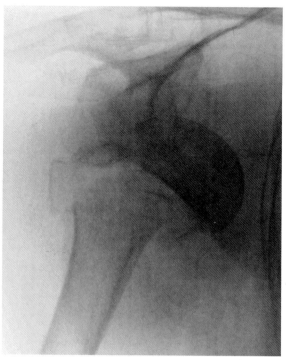

L   M

FIGURE 35-18 (*continued*) It is usually devoid of soft tissue attachments and at higher risk of osteonecrosis. Iatrogenic displacement of the initially impacted shaft from the head may occur during attempted relocation of the shoulder, as seen on these premanipulation and postmanipulation radiographs that were taken in the emergency department (**L,M**).

this "utility" approach,[106,159,255,305] which is extensile and follows normal anatomic planes. The cephalic vein should be identified and protected, and it is customary to reflect the vein laterally, as there are less feeding vessels to this side to be ligated. The traditional skin incision, which follows the surface markings of the deltopectoral interval, is now often replaced by a more cosmetic skin incision, which is in the line of the anterior axillary skin crease (along the line of the bra-strap in women). With more extensive elevation of the soft tissue flaps in the proximal and distal portions of this incision, similar access can be gained to that obtained with the traditional incision (Fig. 35-20). The approach is extensile (Henry approach) and can be continued distally as an anterolateral approach if there is a diaphyseal extension of the fracture. This skirts anterior to the deltoid insertion and extends as an anterolateral approach between the brachialis and triceps. In this situation, the radial nerve must be exposed distally, as it emerges between the brachialis muscle and brachioradialis muscles.

This approach provides good access to most of the front of the shoulder but only limited access to its posterolateral aspect. Visualization and manipulation of a large retracted greater tuberosity fragment may therefore be difficult in muscular individuals.

Deltoid-Splitting Approaches

The Limited Deltoid-Splitting Approach
The traditional "limited" deltoid-splitting approach has previously been used sparingly in shoulder fracture reconstruction[1,81,184] because of the perceived risk of injury to the anterior branch of the axillary nerve.[39,43,153,168] However, this approach provides good visualization of the posterolateral aspect of

the shoulder without the requirement for extensive soft tissue dissection or forcible retraction. Although the approach is widely used in shoulder arthroplasty surgery,[51,178,191] in posttraumatic reconstruction it has been mainly used to treat greater tuberosity fractures.[81]

The Extended Deltoid-Splitting Approach
Dissatisfaction with the deltopectoral approach for fracture surgery led to the development of novel extended deltoid-splitting approaches. These identify and preserve the anterior terminal branches of the axillary nerve, as they traverse the deep surface of the deltoid muscle.[153] The skin incision may be fashioned longitudinally as an extension of a traditional deltoid-splitting incision, in line with the fibers of the middle third of the deltoid.[92,93,96] However, the author prefers to use a shoulder strap incision, with its apex centered over the tip of the acromion,[146,244,245,251,253,254] because it follows the relaxed skin tension lines around the shoulder girdle[32] and therefore tends to heal more cosmetically. It also has the advantage that a simultaneous deltopectoral exposure may also be performed at its lower anterior extension, if required.[252] An extended longitudinal incision provides better exposure of the diaphysis and should be used for fractures with extension into the humeral shaft.

A distally based elliptical skin flap is formed, which allows full exposure of the superior deltoid muscle. This is then split in the line of its fibers at the junction of the anterior and middle portions of the muscle. This site is relatively bloodless, as it is a watershed area of the deltoid blood supply.[111,130,204] This superior split produces the upper "window" of the approach and with further dissection allows visualization of the whole

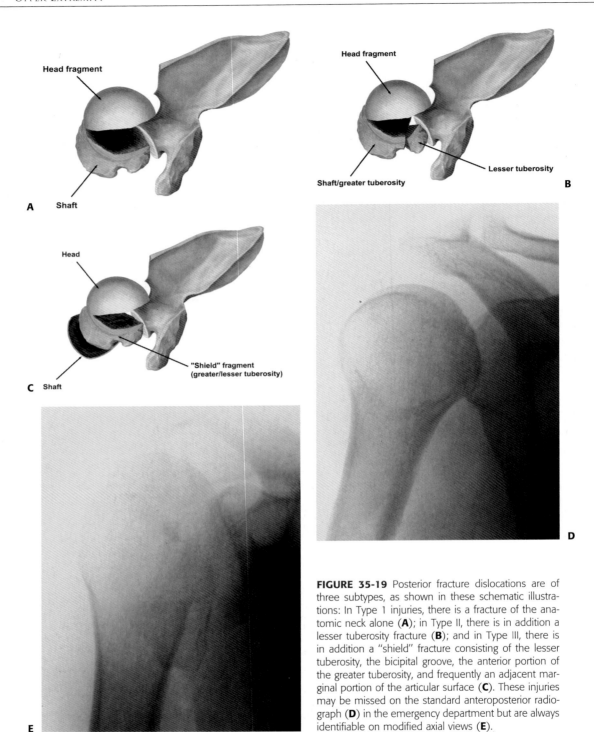

FIGURE 35-19 Posterior fracture dislocations are of three subtypes, as shown in these schematic illustrations: In Type 1 injuries, there is a fracture of the anatomic neck alone (**A**); in Type II, there is in addition a lesser tuberosity fracture (**B**); and in Type III, there is in addition a "shield" fracture consisting of the lesser tuberosity, the bicipital groove, the anterior portion of the greater tuberosity, and frequently an adjacent marginal portion of the articular surface (**C**). These injuries may be missed on the standard anteroposterior radiograph (**D**) in the emergency department but are always identifiable on modified axial views (**E**).

anterolateral and posterolateral aspect of the proximal humerus (Fig. 35-21).

The anterior branch of the axillary nerve and its accompanying vessels are then identified and protected.[251] The deltoid split is then continued distal to the nerve, producing a lower "window," to view the lateral diaphysis. The approach is versatile, allowing either ORIF or hemiarthroplasty to be performed through the same incision. At the end of the procedure, meticulous repair of the deltoid attachment to the acromion is important, to avoid later detachment. Recent cadaveric studies have confirmed the safety of deltoid-splitting surgical approaches that protect the anterior motor branch of the nerve,[92,93,96,146] although there remains theoretically an increased risk of injuring the nerve and of later deltoid detachment from the acromion. The risk of injuring these structures is also increased if secondary operative procedures are required.

Other Approaches

Open, posterior deltoid-splitting approaches[135,309] have been described for the exposure and treatment of posterior-fracture dislocations. Open, combined deltopectoral and deltoid-split-

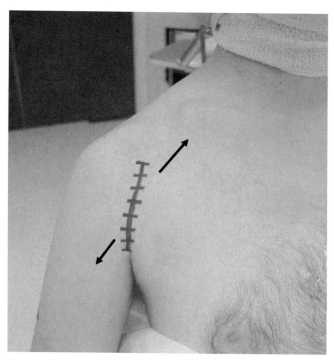

FIGURE 35-20 The deltopectoral approach should follow the anterior axillary crease for better cosmesis. Similar access to the traditional skin incision, which follows the surface markings of the interval, can be obtained by deep dissection of the skin flaps superolaterally anfd inferomedially (*arrow*).

ting surgical approaches have also been described for complex three- and four-part fractures where adequate exposure cannot be gained through a single incision.[90,179] Minimally invasive and arthroscopic approaches are described in more detail in later sections.

TREATMENT

General Considerations

The major goal in the treatment of proximal humeral fractures is to promote complication-free healing to recreate a pain-free, mobile, stable, and functional shoulder joint. In most instances, this is best achieved with nonoperative treatment. While functional normality may be reached in more innocuous injuries, with more severe injuries this is seldom attainable, and the patient should be appropriately counseled at an early stage. Three main groups of factors determine outcome, and these should be taken into consideration when deciding on treatment:

Patient Characteristics

Since the majority of stable proximal humeral fractures are treated nonoperatively, the choice of treatment in these injuries is not markedly influenced by the patient's physiologic status. The minority of patients who require surgical treatment can be safely treated operatively, with a low operative risk from anesthesia. However, nonoperative treatment should be considered in frail, elderly patients, with very limited functional expectations, or limited life expectancy, irrespective of the radiologic severity of the fracture.

Some studies have specifically assessed the predictive value of patient-related factors on outcome after proximal hume-

ral fracture following nonoperative treatment and hemi-arthroplasty.[25,56,58,59,255] The age of the patient is the most constant and well-defined determinant of outcome after treatment. The adverse effect of advanced age on clinical outcome is likely to be related to several factors commonly seen in the elderly and frail patient, including cognitive deficits,[25] rotator cuff tears,[200] osteoporosis,[61] and difficulty with postoperative rehabilitation.[25] Patients with a history of alcohol abuse have an increased risk of nonunion[300] and are less likely to be compliant with postoperative rehabilitation regimens.[25] Tobacco consumption also increases the risk of nonunion after proximal humerus fractures.[259] Other commonly encountered medical comorbidities, which should be considered as "modifiers" when deciding on treatment, are listed in Table 35-3. The multitude of patient-related factors that affect outcome makes their classification difficult, and currently there is no satisfactory overall method of assessing this.

Fracture Type

In their native format, none of the commonly used fracture classifications consider fracture displacement, the severity of the soft tissue injury, or the presence of other skeletal injuries. Their ability to guide treatment and predict outcome is therefore limited.

Surgical Expertise

Modern surgery for the more complex proximal humeral fractures requires considerable surgical expertise, and the full armamentarium of shoulder reconstructive implants, each with its technical advantages and drawbacks (Table 35-4). A technically poor, unstable reconstructive procedure will usually produce a worse outcome than nonoperative treatment. Referral to a center with a surgeon experienced in shoulder reconstructive procedures should always be considered for more complex injuries. This should particularly apply if local resources are limited or if the attending surgeon considers that they lack the experience to adequately treat the injury. Ideally, these injuries should be treated by surgeons who are experienced in both modern fracture reconstructive techniques and arthroplasty.

Assessment of Outcome

Although there are several key areas of controversy in the treatment of the more complex injuries, four recent meta-analyses[21,112,173,197] of the existing literature have highlighted the paucity of Level I, II, or III evidence. The quality of the published literature on the treatment of proximal humeral fractures is heterogeneous, and most studies are retrospective Level IV and Level V case-series studies. The patient group being described is often ambiguous, because of inconsistencies in classification and patient selection. Most series are also too small to support any statistical conclusions, and patients with different injuries are often combined to increase group size. General applicability may be uncertain as reports are often from a single surgeon reporting a single technique. Furthermore, the bulk of the published results emanate from centers of excellence, where the patterns of injury encountered may be different from everyday practice. The excellent results reported by shoulder specialists, working with modern facilities in tertiary referral centers, may or may not be reproducible in centers where expertise and resources are more limited. Inevitably, most papers report

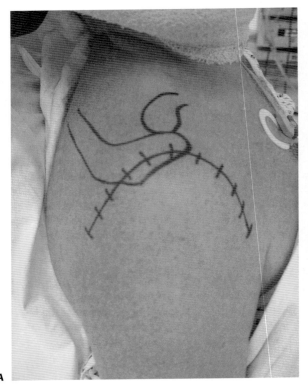

A

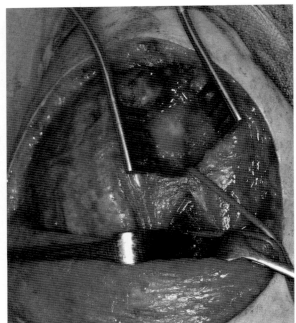

C

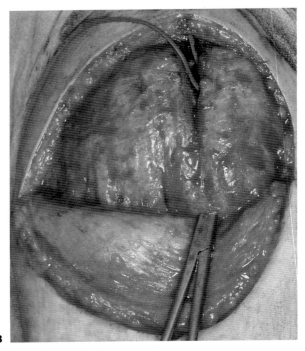

B

FIGURE 35-21 The extended deltoid-splitting approach uses a distally based skin flap to improve cosmesis and allow extension into the deltopectoral interval if required (**A**). Formation of the elliptical skin flap allows full exposure of the superior deltoid muscle, which is then split, creating an "upper window" proximal to the axillary nerve. A large artery forceps is inserted through the deltoid distal to the area of the nerve and is used to deliver an arterial sling around a cuff of soft tissue containing the axillary nerve (**B**). The "lower window" of the incision is created distal to the arterial sling protecting the axillary nerve by continuing the deltoid split, which then allows visualization of the lateral proximal humeral diaphysis with further dissection. The lower window is then exposed using hand-held retractors to allow insertion of lower plate screws into the proximal humeral diaphysis (**C**).   (*continues*)

successful results and this may not reflect the generality of experience with a particular treatment. Many of the operative series have reported on younger patients with more innocuous injuries, as a result of the selection bias and the same results may not be achieved in the elderly. Very few studies directly compare different treatment modalities, and there are only three randomized trials of surgical intervention in the literature.[164,289,324]

Most of the published results of treatment include an assessment of pain, range of movement, and ability to perform normal activities, which are usually collectively amalgamated to pro-duce a functional score. This score is then used to grade the outcome, usually into the four categories of "excellent," "good," "fair," and "poor." Some scores also incorporate a radiological assessment, but most studies consider this separately. The other surrogate outcome measure which has been used is the incidence of complications.

Assessment of Functional Outcome

The deficiency of many of the commonly used functional scores that have been used (such as the Neer, Constant, UCLA, and

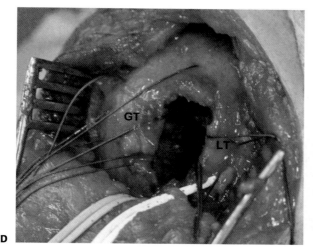

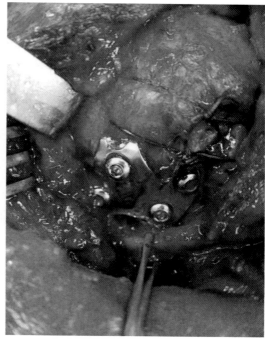

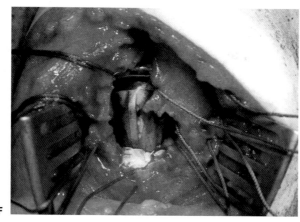

FIGURE 35-21 (*continued*) The tuberosities (GT and LT) are tagged and the fracture is reduced, creating a large cancellous void between the tuberosities, which requires bone grafting (**D**). Fractures may be treated by either internal fixation (**E**) or hemiarthroplasty (**F**) using this approach.

ASES scores) is that they are not sufficiently flexible to accommodate the variability in patients' own expectations from treatment. Entirely different results for the same patients may be obtained depending on the scoring system used.[34] Function is closely related to age and activity, and an outcome resulting in

TABLE 35-3	Summary of the Medical Comorbidities Commonly Associated with Increased Risk of Surgical Complications
Comorbidity	Operative Risk
Dementia/mental impairment	Poor compliance with rehabilitation
Diabetes mellitus	Deep infection
Immunocompromise	Nonunion/infection/osteonecrosis
Parkinson disease	Fixation failure
Rheumatoid arthritis	Nonunion/infection
Disseminated malignancy	Nonunion/infection
Steroid medication	Nonunion/infection/osteonecrosis
Heavy tobacco use	Nonunion/osteonecrosis
Alcohol abuse	Nonunion/osteonecrosis/poor compliance with rehabilitation

disability in a young and active patient may equate with entirely satisfactory function in the elderly patient.[181,196,316] More recently, newer audit tools have been produced, which attempt to address this deficiency by assessing the patient's own aspirations and feelings about their injury and its treatment. The newer tools are administered as questionnaires, which either selectively assess limb function (the DASH score and the Oxford score) or assess the patient's general health status in response to injury (the SF-36 and Musculoskeletal Function Assessment). Patients' assessments of their own outcomes are often significantly more favorable than their numerical scores would suggest.[125,236,323] The chief drawback of these is the difficulty in assessing the patient's functional status before their injury, to evaluate the efficacy of the treatment used. Although normative "control" values are available for the general population, the patients who sustain proximal humeral fractures may not be strictly comparable.

Biodex and Cybex machines can accurately and reproducibly assess components of shoulder function, but these have not been widely used in clinical studies to date.[144] Assessment of muscle strength and range of movement can also be made using commercially available muscle testing machines, which can selectively "isolate" muscle groups and produce computer-generated simulations of normal daily activities. The range of movement, strength, and endurance of the injured shoulder are compared with the normal uninjured side, thereby "controlling" for the effect of age and individual variation. These systems have the advantage of providing a quantitative evalua-

TABLE 35-4 **The Advantages and Disadvantages of the Techiques Used to Treat Displaced Proximal Humeral Fractures**

Technique	Advantages	Disadvantages

Nonoperative treatment	Function as good as operative treatment for many fractures
	
	Low risk of infection and other operative complications
		Malunion inevitable:
		  Cuff dysfunction/stiffness more likely
		  Later salvage surgery is more difficult
		Risk of nonunion increased

Minimally invasive techniques	Reduced injury to soft tissue envelope Lower infection risk	Steep learnng curve Risk of axillary nerve/vascular injury Less stable fixation
Intramedullary nailing	More stable fixation technique in osteoporotic bone Minimal dissection required for insertion	Rotator cuff dysfunction after anterograde insertion Poor results in multipart fractures High rate of late metalwork removal

Open reduction and plate fixation	Anatomic fracture reduction is possible:
	  Improved functional outcome
	  Later revision surgery easier
	Most stable method of fixation in multipart fractures:
	  Rigid implants
	  Adjuvant bone grafting techniques possible
		Open surgical approach required:
		  Increased risk of infection
		  Increased risk of ostenecrosis
		
		Top of plate may cause mechanical impingement

Hemiarthroplasty	Risk of nonunion, osteonecrosis, and symptomatic malunion removed Low reoperation rate	Poor functional outcome Late arthroplasty complications difficult to treat in the elderly

tion of function, and repeated testing allows appraisal of the recovery of function over time. The major drawback is that objective evidence of weakness may not correlate well with the patient's overall level of function and degree of satisfaction with their outcome. In addition, isolation of the individual components of shoulder movement is difficult because of the confounding affects of coexistent scapulothoracic movement. Nevertheless, this technology may prove to be increasingly useful in the future in the objective assessment of functional outcome.

Assessment of Radiologic Outcome

Radiologic assessment involves assessment of fracture union, the degree of malunion, and the presence of osteonecrosis and degenerative change. Assessing union may be difficult in many fractures because of the metaphyseal location of the fracture, which seldom results in much external callus formation. Union is therefore usually implied by lack of displacement of the fracture on sequential radiographs and diminution rather than widening of fracture lines. This is supported by lessening of shoulder pain and return of function. Assessment of union after anatomic reduction and internal fixation is even more difficult, although fixation failure or progressive loosening is always associated with nonunion. CT is useful in doubtful cases. Malunion may be assessed by measuring residual displacement of fracture fragments with respect to each other using conventional radiographs, but accurate assessment can only be made using CT.

Osteonecrosis may range from patchy sclerosis through partial head involvement to complete involvement and collapse. There is currently no generally accepted classification for osteonecrosis in the humeral head. The differential diagnosis is from osteoarthrosis of the head, which is classified using the system of Samilson and Prieto.[267] Collapse and deformity are usually not present in osteoarthrosis. CT and MRI are useful

where there is doubt about the diagnosis and to assess the degree and severity of head involvement.

Assessment of Complications

Complications of treatment occur relatively frequently during both operative and nonoperative treatment. The three major complications of treatment are nonunion, osteonecrosis, and rotator cuff dysfunction and stiffness. After operative treatment, one quarter of patients can expect to develop one or more significant complication during treatment, with 1 in 10 requiring further surgery. Complications of treatment may be inaccurately reported in retrospective studies, because of incomplete documentation in case records. Prospective cohort studies usually report higher incidences, and this may explain the wide variation in the published literature.

Some complications can occur with any method of treatment, and these are discussed at the end of the chapter. Complications that are specific to a particular method of treatment are discussed in the following treatment section. There are identifiable factors associated with an increased risk of specific complications (Table 35-5).

Most studies have focused on treatment techniques rather than particular fracture types. For this reason, in the following section treatment is discussed by technique rather than by fracture configuration.

The Expected Functional Outcome after Fracture

As a general rule, the majority of elderly patients, who have undisplaced or stable osteoporotic proximal humeral fractures, will have a pain-free shoulder that is functional to their requirements after nonoperative treatment, if they avoid the major complications of nonunion, osteonecrosis, and rotator cuff dysfunction. There is evidence to suggest that continued functional recovery may take place during the first 2 years after the injury.

TABLE 35-5	**Factors Associated with a Poorer Functional Outcome and Increased Risk of Complications after a Proximal Humeral Fracture**	
Category	Factor	Adverse Factors
Patient-related factors	Patient motivation/compliance*	Poor compliance/motivation
	Workers' Compensation claim*	Claim pending
	Age	Advanced age
	Osteoporosis	Poor bone stock leading to risk of nonunion
	Medical comorbidity	See Table 35-3
	Joint disease before injury	Degenerative joint disease
		Inflammatory joint disease
Injury-related factors	Fracture configuration	Fracture-dislocation
	Injury mechanism/injuries sustained	High-energy injury
		Multiple injuries
		Head injury
		Ipsilateral upper limb injury
	Soft tissue injury	Open fracture
		Skin/muscle loss
		Neurovascular injury
Surgery-related factors	Internal fixation	Nonrigid fixation
		Technical error
	Immobilization	Prolonged immobilisation
	Recovery	Postsurgical complications
		Reoperations
	Type of intervention	Nonoperative treatment
	Timing of surgery	Late surgery

*Although these factors adversely affect functional outcome, they probably do not increase the risk of complications after surgery.

However, the rate of recovery is rapid in the first 6 months, slows exponentially during the subsequent 6 months, and is minimal in the second year.[244,253,257] Complete functional normality is uncommon, but most patients have only minor complaints of activity-related ache and sensitivity to cold or damp weather ("barometric shoulder").

Operative treatment is often considered for the minority of patients with more complex fracture configurations, and those who are younger have higher functional demands on their shoulder. Careful preoperative counseling is therefore required, because the functional benefits from surgery are usually relative rather than absolute, and there is a substantial risk of complications.

Accomplishing the "essential" activities of daily living of feeding, washing, and maintaining perineal hygiene requires only a composite (at the glenohumeral joint and scapulothoracic articulation) pain-free arc of 60 degrees forward flexion, abduction, and internal rotation at the shoulder girdle. Some authors have suggested that such a result may be considered satisfactory in the elderly.[196,316] Even lesser degrees of movement may be tolerated in low-demand elderly individuals, whereas more movement is often required for function in younger, active patients. A wide range of intrinsic and extrinsic factors have been associated with poorer functional outcomes from treatment (Table 35-5).

Nonoperative Treatment

Indications

Nonoperative treatment is the mainstay of treatment for approximately 85% of proximal humeral fractures. The absolute indications for its use include minimal displacement (one-part fractures), advanced age (usually over the age of 85 years), dementia, and medical contraindications to operative intervention. However, in the majority of instances, nonoperative treatment is selected because in the surgeon's opinion the fracture pattern is stable. This usually implies that there is residual cortical contact between the shaft and the humeral head fragment, preferably with some impaction of the two fragments, and minimal tuberosity displacement. Such a configuration substantially reduces the risk of later nonunion, regardless of whether the fracture is of two-, three-, or four-part configuration.

Technique

Pain control is often difficult for the first few days after the injury, because adequate splintage across the fracture is not possible. The pain is typically aggravated by recumbency, and most patients find it most comfortable to sleep in a chair or recliner for the first week after the injury. In elderly patients, admission to hospital may be required, because many will be unable to cope with their normal daily activities, especially if they are living alone.

Oral analgesia, supplemented by topical ice/heat therapy, is prescribed, and a sling is used to rest the arm, which allows distraction of the fractured bone ends.[66] Hanging casts offer no demonstrable advantage[181,236,290] and may excessively distract the fracture, predisposing to nonunion. Prolonged immobilization does not improve healing rates or outcome,[156] and the functional recovery is better when physiotherapy commences early.[47,156,164,181,316]

The precise timing and type of exercises are important[79,156,181,200]: elbow, wrist and hand mobilization should begin immediately, with assisted passive shoulder rotation, flexion, and abduction ("pendular") exercises beginning at around 1 week.[127] Active shoulder isometric exercises are begun at 3 weeks, progressing to isotonic strengthening and stretching exercises at 6 to 12 weeks.[79,156] It is important that exercises continue during the first year after injury, because delayed restoration of movement may continue during this time. Prolonged supervised physiotherapy is often recommended,[156,181] although there is evidence that a single physiotherapy session with subsequent performance of exercises at home is just as effective.[20] Physiotherapy adjuncts, such as hydrotherapy[242] or pulsed electrotherapy,[188] do not improve outcome.

It is customary to monitor potentially unstable fractures, which are at risk of secondary redisplacement by repeat radiographs in the first 2 weeks. It is not uncommon to see transient inferior subluxation of the humeral head in stable fractures, which may be caused by hemarthrosis, deltoid inhibition, or rotator cuff dysfunction[233,315] (Fig. 35-22). Late radiographic monitoring should ideally be undertaken to ensure fracture healing and absence of signs of osteonecrosis during the first few years after the injury. In practice, this is seldom practicable and most patients are discharged from follow-up once their fracture is healed and they have regained satisfactory function.

Results

The functional outcome is satisfactory in the majority of patients with one-part fractures involving the surgical neck of the humerus,[47,86,144,156,164,196,316] one-part greater tuberosity fractures,[229] impacted two-part surgical neck,[58] varus two-part surgical neck,[59] and three- and four-part impacted valgus[56] fractures treated nonoperatively (Table 35-6). Union rates of up to 100% have been reported for minimally displaced fractures, with the vast majority of patients achieving a painless or only mildly painful shoulder.[56,58,59,86,156] The final range of motion achieved is up to 90% of the uninjured side,[156] and most patients are satisfied with their outcome.[316] The radiographic appearance often fails to correlate with the final clinical outcome.[197,316]

Nonoperative treatment of displaced, unstable, and multipart fractures and fracture-dislocations is more controversial.[74,175,181,182,220,236,273,323] Neer's influential series[207] established a poor reputation for nonoperative treatment, which was reinforced by similar contemporary reports.[290] Most studies of nonoperative treatment report poorer functional outcomes than for minimally displaced fractures[181,236] (Table 35-6). However, several of these studies comment on the high degree of patient satisfaction despite the poor functional score and poor radiologic appearance after treatment.[236,323] The studies that have compared nonoperative with operative treatment have produced conflicting results. Some show a benefit from operative intervention,[161] whereas the majority fail to demonstrate convincing benefits from operative intervention.[58,78,324]

As with other methods of treatment for proximal humeral fractures, nonunion, osteonecrosis, and symptomatic malunion, are the major complications which may occur after nonoperative treatment (Table 35-6). The risk of these complications is extremely low when nonoperative treatment is used for minimally displaced fractures[316] but is higher for older patients and those with displaced and multipart fractures.[181,182,220,273] Failed nonoperative treatment is not benign and subsequent operative reconstructive procedures are usually technically more difficult, resulting in a poorer outcome overall than when the operative intervention is performed primarily.[34]

Operative Treatment

For the minority of patients who require operative treatment, surgery can be deferred for 48 hours without deleterious effects.

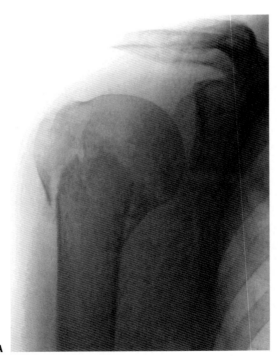
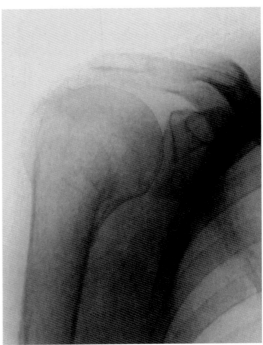

FIGURE 35-22 Inferior subluxation of the humeral ahead is not uncommon after impacted surgical neck of humerus fracture (**A**). This usually corrects spontaneously during the first 2 weeks after the injury (**B**).

TABLE 35-6   Summary of the Case Series Results of Nonoperative Treatment for Proximal Humeral Fractures in Series That Report Functional Outcome*

Fracture Type	Author	Year of Publication	No. of Patients	Fracture Type	Average Age of Patients (range) (yr)	Follow-Up (range) (mo)	Outcome Assessment	Percentage with Good or Excellent Results	Percentage with Fair or Poor Results	Complications
One-part (minimally displaced)	Clifford	1980	80	Majority minimally displaced	61 (NK)	24 (18–48)	Neer	81	19	Not reported
	Young	1985	64	Majority minimally displaced	66 (40–86)	6	Individual	56	44	MU-5 (8%), NE-2 (3%), NU-2 (3%), HO-1 (2%), SAI-1 (2%)
	Mills	1985	90	Majority minimally displaced	59 (22–93)	32.6 (NK)	Neer	52	48	Not reported
	Kristiansen	1989	85	Majority minimally displaced	NK	24	Neer	62	38	Not reported
	Koval	1997	104	All minimally displaced	63 (24–94)	41 (12–117)	Individual	77	13	None
	Gaebler	2003	376	All minimally displaced	63 (13–87)	12	Neer	87	13	None
	Keser	2004	27	All minimally displaced	51 (25–75)	25 (12–34)	Constant	74	26	SAI-6 (22%), RCT-5 (19%)
	Platzer	2005	135	One-part greater tuberosity	56 (18–88)	42 (24–240)	Constant	97	3	Not reported
Multipart and displaced	Leyshon	1984	42	Two-, three-, and four-part	65 (23–84)	88.9 (24–240)	Neer	57	43	ON-6 (14%), OA-3 (7%)
	Rusmussen	1992	42	Two-, three-, and four-part	77 (28–91)	24 (11–49)	Neer	29	71	None
	Zyto	1998	14	"Displaced multifragmentary"	70 (26–75)	120	Constant	Poor function but high patient satisfaction		ON-2 (14%), OA-1 (7%)
	Serin	1999	29	Two-, 3 three-, and four-part	54 (18–81)	42 (NK)	Neer	76	24	MU-5 (17%), HO-1 (3%), ON-1 (3%)
	CourtBrown	2001	109**	Two-part surgical neck	72 (<10–>90)	12	Neer	Fair (mean)		NU-5 (5%)
	Lill	2001	52	Two-, three-, and four-part	72 (31–88)	20 (3–93)	Constant	62	38	MU-23 (44%), OA-14 (27%), ON-8 (15%)
	CourtBrown	2002	125	Impacted valgus	71 (44–88)	12	Neer	81	19	None
	CourtBrown	2004	99	Impacted varus	68 (23–94)	12	Neer	79	21	None
	Olsson	2005	46	Mixed	59 (24–79)	NK (12–156)	Constant	83	17	MU-7 (15%), NU-1 (2%)
	Lefevre-Colau	2007	64	"Impacted and stable"	63.3 (NK)	6	Constant	Good (mean)		Not reported
	Edelson	2008	63	Two-, three-, and four-part	66 (37–87)	32 (24–84)	Simple shoulder test	82	18	ON-2/16 (13%), MU-63 (100%)
	Total		1537		63.5 (13–94)	24.3 (11–240)		77	23	

*Only English-language studies, or studies with an English-language translation, appearing in peer-reviewed journals during the last 30 years are shown.
**Eighteen were treated operatively.
NK, not known or not recorded; NU, nonunion; MU, malunion; ON, osteonecrosis; RCT, rotator cuff tear; SAI, subacromial impingement; HO, heterotopic ossification; NE, neurologic injury; OA, osteoarthritis.

If the patient has medical comorbidities, it is best to wait for these to be optimized in the first week after injury before the surgery is performed. There is no evidence to suggest that the timing of surgery affects the outcome. All procedures are performed under general anesthesia with broad-spectrum antibiotic and antithrombotic prophylaxis. A scalene block is often performed for postoperative analgesia.

Fluoroscopy should be available for all proximal humeral fracture surgery. The patient is positioned in a supine beachchair position, with a head rest and shoulder operating table "cut-away" to facilitate access for the fluoroscope from the opposite side of the table (Fig. 35-23). By rotating the C-arm, good anteroposterior and "modified" axial views[302] can be obtained during surgery.[253,254] It is important to secure all anesthetic tubing and make sure that equipment is cleared from the path of the C-arm to prevent intraoperative detachment. The whole arm is prepared and draped, to allow its free movement by the assistant during surgery. Appropriate instrumentation for both humeral head fixation and replacement should always be available in the operating theatre (Table 35-7).

Minimally Invasive Techniques

Percutaneous reduction and minimally invasive fixation techniques avoid the necessity for a formal surgical approach.[122,133,134,152,239,241] The potential advantages of these techniques are the same as for any other minimally invasive surgery, by improving cosmesis and reducing blood loss, postoperative pain, infection risk, and trauma to adjacent soft tissues. In the shoulder, avoiding surgical injury to the deltoid muscle is seen as a particular advantage because of the risk of dysfunction and pseudoparalysis of this muscle that can develop after open surgery. However, most of these techniques are technically demanding and have a protracted learning curve.

Closed Manipulation. Direct closed manipulative treatment under general anesthesia has been used to try to reduce displaced fractures. Typically an attempt is made to impact the shaft fragment onto the humeral head. Reduction of displaced tuberosity fragments cannot be achieved. Unfortunately, this technique is associated with a very high rate of redisplacement of the fracture fragments, even after a good initial reduction.[196,208,289,316] The technique is now seldom used alone, without some attempt at improving the stability of the reduction, typically using percutaneous fixation.

Percutaneous Pin or Screw Fixation.
Indications. These techniques have been described to treat most types of displaced proximal humeral fractures, with the exception of fracture-dislocations. Valgus three- and four-part fractures, and unimpacted two-, three-, and four-part fractures in which the shaft has translated or separated from the head fragment, are thought to be particularly suitable for the use of this technique.*

Technique. Fracture reduction is achieved under C-arm fluoroscopy, using a combination of closed manipulation and percutaneous introduction of instruments and pins to act as "joysticks" that manipulate fracture fragments. Detailed knowledge of the local anatomy is required to facilitate reduction and to avoid damaging the anterior branch of the axillary nerve, which is vulnerable to injury as it courses around the neck of the humerus laterally. Anatomic studies have confirmed the close relationship of the axillary nerve, long head of biceps, circumflex humeral vessels, and cephalic vein to the pins.[138,262]

Once reduction is achieved, definitive fixation is achieved using threaded K-wires or cannulated screws inserted across the key fracture fragments[122,133,240] (Fig. 35-24). Smooth and thin wires have a tendency to loosen, break, or migrate, and thick, terminally threaded K-wires are used to minimize the risk of pin migration.[122,152] The pins are inserted through small incisions, and a curved hemostat is used to dissect down to the periosteum and to mobilize soft tissue to avoid neurovascular injury. A protective sheath such as a drill guide should be used to prevent injury to the soft tissues. Two or three retrograde pins are placed from the shaft into the head fragment. The pin

*References 41,45,122,133,138,141,152,158,239,240,285,308.

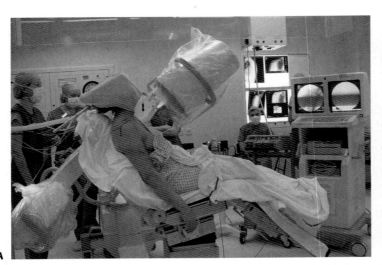
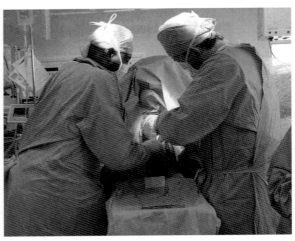

A **B**

FIGURE 35-23 The patient is positioned in the beach chair position for surgery. The fluoroscope is positioned on the opposite side of the operating table (**A**), to allow the surgeon and assistant to have free access to the shoulder throughout the procedure (**B**).

TABLE 35-7	Surgical Pearls: "Checklist" for the Reconstruction of Proximal Humeral Fractures
Admission checklist	Ensure no open wounds, skin tenting, or areas of skin necrosis around shoulder.
	Document any neurologic deficit.
	Ensure routine hematologic, biochemical, and cardiorespiratory workup is performed.
	Optimise of any comorbidities with medical treatment.
	Explain risks of surgery to patient and likely prognosis.
	Obtain informed consent.
	Draw up a fracture plan based on radiographs.
	Computed tomography scan with three-dimensional reconstruction for fracture treated operatively.
Preoperative	Discuss postoperative and regional analgesia with anesthetist.
	Confirm availability of an assistant(s) (preferrably "skilled").
	Antibiotic prophylaxis
	Radiographer and fluorosocopy available in operating room
	Position patient in beach-chair position: check supports and pressure areas, and ensure hips/knees flexed.
	Ensure free access to airway for the anaesthetist before draping.
	Ensure head and neck properly secured to headrest.
	Draw surgical landmarks with permanent marker.
	Ensure operating lights correctly positioned.
Equipment to be available in theater	Appropriate screw/plate sets
	Small cannulated screw set
	Bending pliers and press for plate contouring
	K-wires for temporary fixation
	Nerve slings
	Small oscillating saw
	Osteotomes
	Small and large reduction clamps
	Bolster for axilla
	Shoulder arthroplasty trays
Postoperatively	Liase with physiotherapist regarding rehabilitation plan.
	Update patient regarding surgical reconstruction obtained.
	Wound check before discharge.

entry point should be distal enough to the fracture line to gain adequate purchase of the intact humeral shaft cortex. The pins are inserted eccentrically to each other, from anterolateral to posteromedial (about 30 degrees), because of the anatomic retroversion of the humeral head.

If the tuberosities are fractured, they are secured with wires or cannulated screws. Pins are placed under fluoroscopic guidance through the greater tuberosity, from superolateral to inferomedial, approximately 1 cm distal to the rotator cuff insertion, engaging the medial cortex of the shaft fragment. At this point, care should be taken not to advance the pins past the medial cortex to avoid damaging the axillary nerve or posterior humeral circumflex artery. The pins are cut below the skin to reduce the risk of pin tract infection.

In patients with poor bone stock, the grip of the individual wires and screws is often poor, and percutaneous fixation does not provide absolute stability. To enhance the stability of the reconstruction, a "humerus block" may be inserted in a minimally invasive manner, which links together the head-shaft wires, improving the mechanical stability of the reconstruction.[238]

Results. Most series that have reported the use of percutaneous pin or screw fixation report satisfactory functional results (Table

35-8).* However, there is a substantial rate of complications, including fixation failure, malunion, nonunion, and osteonecrosis (Table 35-8). It is noteworthy that the use of this technique tends to be reported in selected younger patients, who would be expected to have a lower rate of these complications from operative treatment.

Arthroscopic Reconstruction. Arthroscopic techniques to repair rotator cuff tears have been adapted for the acute reduction and internal fixation of isolated lesser and greater tuberosity fractures[22,40,99,141,148,271] and selected more complex fractures.[6,63,99,141,143,297] This technique is promising, allowing minimally invasive direct visualization of the reduction of the displaced fragments rather than the indirect view afforded with percutaneous fixation under C-arm fluoroscopy. However, there is a protracted learning curve, and expertise in arthroscopic surgery is required.*

Arthroscopic techniques have also been used in the late treatment of complications, to treat the posttraumatic stiff shoulder,[12,37,128,180] to débride or repair cuff tears associated with

*References 41,45,122,133,134,141,152,239,285.
*References 22,40,99,141,143,148,269,271.

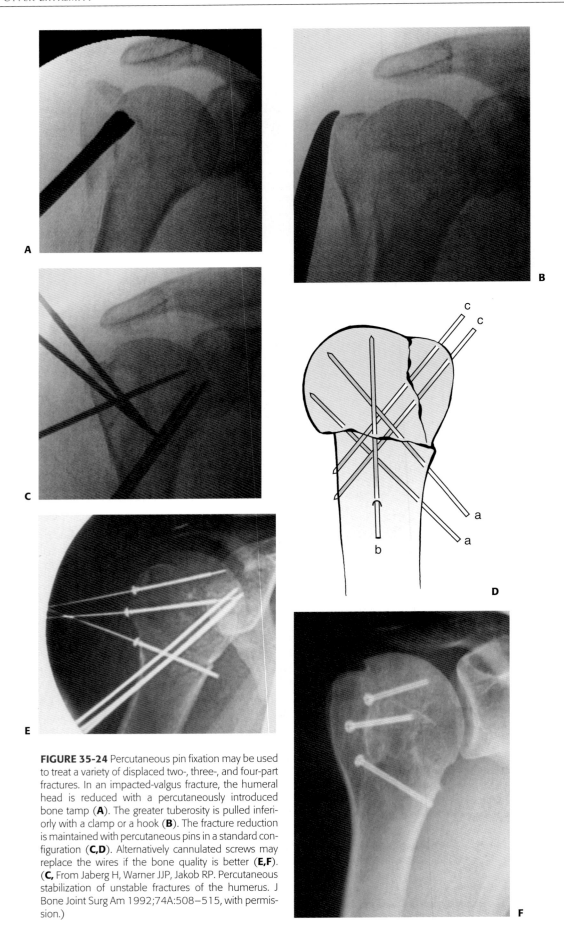

FIGURE 35-24 Percutaneous pin fixation may be used to treat a variety of displaced two-, three-, and four-part fractures. In an impacted-valgus fracture, the humeral head is reduced with a percutaneously introduced bone tamp (**A**). The greater tuberosity is pulled inferiorly with a clamp or a hook (**B**). The fracture reduction is maintained with percutaneous pins in a standard configuration (**C,D**). Alternatively cannulated screws may replace the wires if the bone quality is better (**E,F**). (**C,** From Jaberg H, Warner JJP, Jakob RP. Percutaneous stabilization of unstable fractures of the humerus. J Bone Joint Surg Am 1992;74A:508–515, with permission.)

TABLE 35-8 Summary of the Case Series Results of Minimally Invasive Techniques for Proximal Humeral Fractures in Series That Report Functional Outcome*

Author	Year of Publication	No. of Patients	Average Age of Patients (range) (yr)	Follow-Up (range) (mo)	Outcome Assessment	Percentage with Good or Excellent Results	Percentage with Fair or Poor Results	MU	AVN	Complications: Other
Kocialkowski	1990	22	61 (13–91)	19 (6–36)	Neer	38	62	0	1 (5%)	MF-9 (41%), SI-5 (23%), RS-2 (9%), NE-1 (5%), NU-1 (5%)
Jakob	1991	18	49.5 (24–81)	4.2 (2–10)	Neer	74	26	0	5 (26%)	
Jaberg	1992	48	63 (17–85)	36 (24–84)	Neer	71	29	13 (27%)	10 (21%)	RS-8 (17%), MF-5 (10%), SI-4 (8%), NU-2 (4%), DI-1 (2%)
Resch	1997	27	54 (25–68)	24 (18–47)	Constant	Good (mean)		5 (19%)	2 (7%)	RS-2 (7%), MF-1 (4%)
Chen	1998	19	43 (8–89)	21 (14–29)	Neer	84	16	1 (6%)	0	MF-2 (11%), NU-1 (6%)
Soete	1999	31	68 (29–82)	45 (25–67)	Constant	87	13	4 (13%)	5 (16%)	MF-1 (4%), SI-1 (4%)
Herscovici	2000	40	50 (23–88)	40 (12–68)	ASES	Fair (mean)		8 (20%)	3 (8%)	MF-5 (12%), RS-5 (12%), DI-1 (2%)
Keener	2007	27	61 (41–79)	35 (12–77)	Constant	58	42	4 (17%)	1 (4%)	ST-1 (4%), MF-1 (4%)
Calvo	2007	50	71 (45–89)	13.6 (12–26)	Constant	Fair (mean)		14 (28%)	4 (8%)	MF-18 (36%), RS-2 (4%), SI-2 (4%), NU-1 (2%)
Dimakopoulos**	2007	165	54 (18–75)	64.8 (36–132)	Constant	Excellent (mean)		8 (5%)	10 (6%)	HO-15 (9%), RS-7 (4%), SAI-4 (2%), OA-2 (1%), NU-2 (1%)
Total		474	58 (8–91)	40 (2–132)		69	31	57 (12%)	34 (7%)	

*Only English-language studies, or studies with an English-language translation, appearing in peer-reviewed journals during the last 30 years are shown; **n - number of patients.
***Transosseous suture fixation technique.
NU, nonunion; MU, malunion; SI, superficial infection; DI, deep infection; AVN, avascular necrosis; SAI, subacromial impingement; ST, stiffness; NE, neurologic injury; MF, movement of fixation; RS, revision surgery; OA, osteoarthritis.

fractures,[98,149,237] and to treat malunions.[6,98,126,143,231] Most of the published literature in this area is in the form of isolated case reports at present, and it is uncertain whether there are discrete advantages of their use over open surgical techniques.

Minimally Invasive Plating and Intramedullary Nailing. Many of the modern locked-plating and intramedullary nailing systems that have been introduced in the past 10 years have the facility for percutaneous insertion through small stab incisions. Screw insertion proximal and distal to the fracture is performed percutaneously using custom-made jigs. The techniques of reduction are the same as those used for percutaneous pin/screw fixation, and similar local soft tissue structures are at risk of injury. This technique tends to be reserved for simpler displaced two-part surgical neck fractures, where reduction of the two main fragments can be accomplished relatively easily.[170,284]

External Fixation. In the past, this technique has been used both as a solitary treatment[162,166] and as an adjunct to minimally invasive fixation.[161,163] However, the technique is now seldom used because of the poor fixation gained by half-pins in the humeral head, the high risk of pin track infection, and the availability of more rigid methods of definitive fixation. The Ilizarov method had also been used as a primary treatment for proximal humeral fractures[132,275] but is now usually reserved for the treatment of contaminated open fractures[140] and occasionally for nonunions with large bone defects.[42]

Open Reduction and Internal Fixation Techniques

ORIF techniques are more commonly used than minimally invasive approaches, because of the shorter learning curve, greater accuracy of articular reduction, and greater stability of fixation that can be achieved using more rigid internal fixation implants. The major drawbacks include the greater blood loss and risk of infection after an open surgical exposure. A large variety of implants have been used to provide definitive fixation, and techniques that have been used in more than one case series are discussed further.

Plate Fixation.

Indications. Plate fixation is currently the most commonly used method of internal fixation for displaced proximal humeral fractures. The aim is to provide secure fixation of the humeral head to the shaft, thereby preventing secondary torsional redisplacement of the shaft from the head and to provide additional fixation of reduced tuberosity fragments. This technique is the most widely used method to treat displaced but salvageable two-, three-, and four-part fractures. Several key steps are identified, which are critical to the success of the reconstruction.

Technique.

Surgical Approach and Exposure. The procedure can be performed through a deltopectoral or extended deltoid-splitting approach, identifying and protecting the anterior branch of the axillary nerve before any fracture manipulation or instrumentation. In three-part greater tuberosity and four-part fractures, the main split in the tuberosities is first located in the area immediately posterior to the bicipital groove. The space formed by this fracture line is developed to gain access to the humeral head and the glenohumeral joint. Both tuberosities are tagged

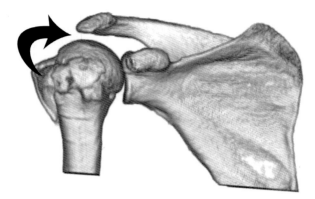

FIGURE 35-25 In an impacted-valgus fracture, the humeral head has to be elevated to achieve reduction (*arrow*).

with nonabsorbable interosseous sutures. If the bone quality is poor, these sutures should be placed intratendinously, through the rotator cuff tendon insertion in the tuberosity. It is customary to extend the split in the tuberosities by incising along the line of the rotator interval, to perform a limited arthrotomy. This allows inspection of the articular surface to assess any marginal articular fragments attached to the tuberosities, and any other articular pathology. In displaced two-part surgical neck fractures, none of these steps are required, unless there are undisplaced tuberosity fracture lines, which should be sutured at this stage to prevent later redisplacement.

Reduction of the Humeral Head on the Shaft. Regardless of the fracture configuration, reduction of the humeral head onto the shaft fragment must be achieved in all three planes of potential displacement (sagittal, coronal, and horizontal). Preoperative three-dimensional CT greatly facilitates understanding of the pattern of displacement and planning the reduction maneuvers. It is customary to reduce the fracture in the sagittal and coronal planes first: Varus and valgus deformities of the head can be corrected by the eccentric insertion of K-wires, elevators, or osteotomes into the humeral head (Figs. 35-25 and 35-26). These are then used as joysticks to correct the deformity. In the sagittal plane, it is customary for the head to tilt into slight flexion or extension, which is usually fairly easily corrected.

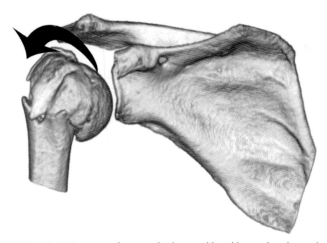

FIGURE 35-26 In a varus fracture, the humeral head has to be elevated from its inferiorly subluxed position to achieve reduction.

Once the head has been sagittally and coronally reduced, anatomic reduction can usually be achieved by correcting any translation of the shaft under the head. The shaft is characteristically displaced anteromedially, because of the pull of pectoralis major. Reduction is usually achieved by lateralizing the shaft, either directly by applying reduction forceps or indirectly by pressure in the axilla, using a custom-made "bolster," which helps avoids excessive manual handling in this potentially unsterile area.[254] Alternatively, there are a variety of indirect reduction techniques using the definitive plate osteosynthesis to "fine-tune" the reduction[287] (Fig. 35-27).

Correction of any residual rotational deformity is now undertaken. In two-part fractures, correct interdigitation of fracture lines in the head relative to the shaft confirms correction of any rotational deformity. In three- and four-part fractures, correction of rotation can be confirmed by ensuring satisfactory alignment of the bicipital groove (containing the biceps tendon) across the fracture.

In three- and four-part fracture-dislocations, the humeral head must be relocated into the glenoid before these reduction maneuvers can be performed. In Type I anterior-fracture dislocations and posterior fracture-dislocations, the humeral head must be first disengaged from the anterior or posterior glenoid rim, respectively, under direct vision. Relocation can then usually easily be achieved by rotation of the humeral head into the glenoid. In Type II anterior fracture-dislocations, the humeral head is not engaged on the glenoid. Relocation of the humeral head is achieved by delivering it back through the tear in the

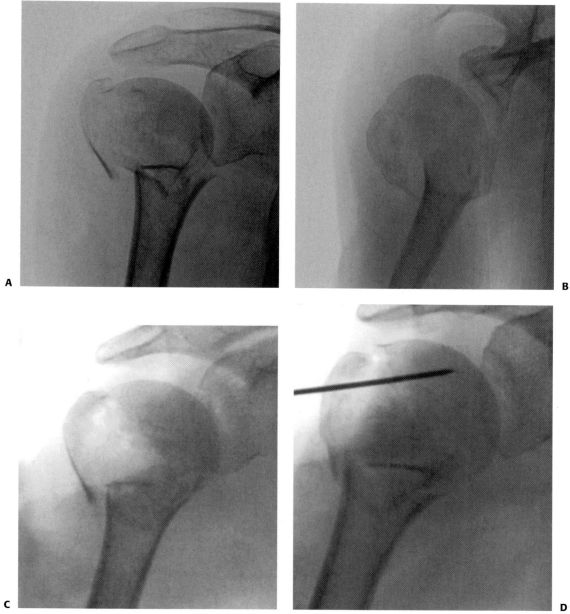

FIGURE 35-27 Indirect reduction techniques may be used to reduce fractures in which there is appreciable medial translation of the shaft fragment from the head (**A,B**). The head is disimpacted and reduced, leaving a large metaphyseal cancallous void (**C**), which is filled with femoral head allograft (**D**).　　　*(continues)*

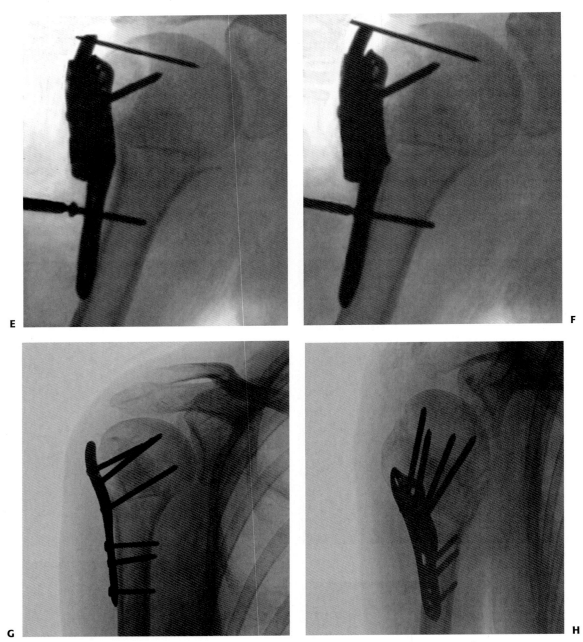

FIGURE 35-27 (*continued*) A locking plate is applied and secured to the head fragment with no attempt to reduce the shaft (**E**). Tightening a nonlocking screw distal to the fracture translates the shaft laterally to achieve reduction (**F**). The remaining head and shaft screws are now inserted to produce the final reconstruction (**G,H**).

anteroinferior capsule. Occasionally, the mobile humeral ahead cannot be relocated through the extended deltoid-splitting approach and a supplementary deltopectoral approach is required.

Adjuvant Stabilization of the Reduction. Once the head is reduced, it can be temporarily held with K-wires. In three- and four-part fractures, there is often an extensive metaphyseal void after reduction of the displaced humeral head fragment, which is then irrigated clear of blood and debris. The cancellous void may be ignored, but there is a trend toward filling these defects with bone graft or substitutes, to enhance stability and reduce the risk of redisplacement. Small cancellous defects (less than 20-mL) have been filled using bone substitutes, which are in-

jected in a semiliquid form and cure over a period of 10 to 20 minutes (Fig. 35-28). Where there is a greater metaphyseal void, impacted morselized autograft or allograft and structural allografts have been used to fill the defects[106,253,254,263,296] (Fig. 35-29).

The importance of the posteromedial calcar support to the stability of reduction has also recently been highlighted. If this area is fractured and comminuted, or is malreduced, there is potential for instability and acute redisplacement despite internal fixation. This frequently applies to two-, three-, and four-part fractures, where the head has displaced into varus. This is analogous to the posteroinferior comminution seen in intracapsular femoral neck fractures, which is frequently implicated in

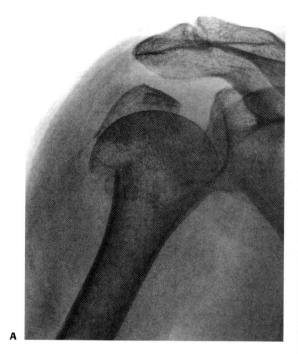

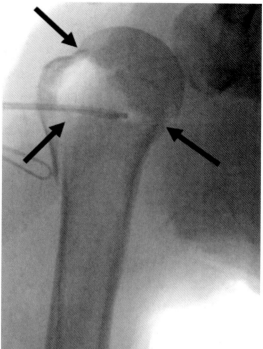

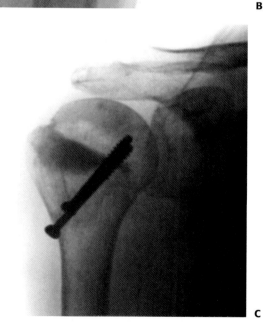

FIGURE 35-28 Large laterally based triangular metaphyseal defects are created after reduction of impacted valgus fractures (**A,B**). These can be filled with bone substitutes if the defect is small (**C**) or bone graft if the defect is more than 20 mL.

acute fixation failure after reduction and screw fixation. Where this support is compromised in proximal humeral fractures, the use of either a low inferomedial screw (Fig. 35-29) or a fibular strut graft has been advocated to restore stability.[91,95,97]

Bone grafting may also be required when there is a large reverse Hill-Sachs lesion associated with a two-, three-, or four-part posterior fracture-dislocation, which may lead to acute re-dislocation as the defect reengages on the posterior glenoid rim. Where there is a large residual osteochondral fragment with retained soft tissue attachment, this is treated by elevation of the osteochondral fragment, with insertion of morselized femoral head allograft to buttress the elevated fragment, with support from "positional screws."[244,245] Where the fragments are comminuted or loose, a femoral head osteochondral allograft is

sculpted to fill the defect.[102,244,245] Bone grafting of classic Hill-Sachs lesions associated with anterior fracture-dislocations is not usually required, because the shoulder is usually stable once reduced.

Another innovative approach to the treatment of large metaphyseal defects is to span the defect by inserting a modular humeral arthroplasty stem. The humeral head is then reattached to the cemented stem using a "Bilboquet" device, which is a circular staple, which is driven into the raw cancellous surface of the back of the humeral head.[70]

Tuberosity Fixation. In three- and four-part fractures, once the reduction is stabilized, the greater and lesser tuberosities are

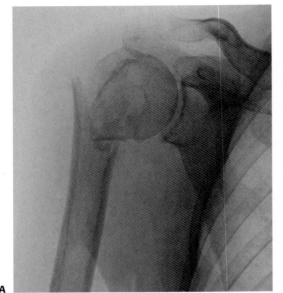

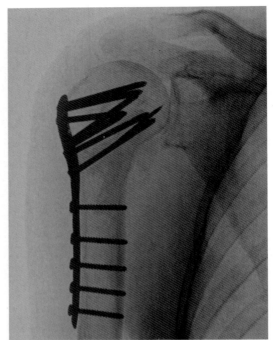

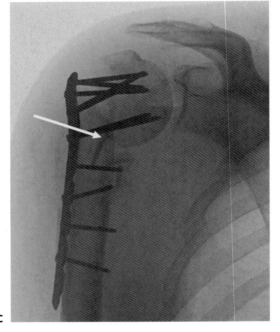

FIGURE 35-29 The defect produced after reduction of a varus displaced fracture (**A**) is larger on the side of the medial calcar (medially based triangular defect). These fractures require support from structural bone graft and low calcar screws as show in this case (**B**). In another case, failure to provide adequate calcar support (*arrow*) resulted in early failure of the locking plate with the head falling back into varus (**C**).

reduced and fixed. It is important to check at this stage that any marginal articular surface fragments attached to the tuberosities are reduced anatomically (Fig. 35-30). If these are unstable, supplementary subchondral screw or threaded wire fixation may be required to maintain stability. It is also important to confirm that both tuberosities are anatomically reduced relative to the humeral head and shaft.

The tuberosities are now fixed anatomically to prevent early "pull-off," using cancellous screws or an interosseous suturing technique, dependent on the bone quality and the extent of comminution(Fig. 35-31). Securing a tuberosity in a superior position may give rise to rotator cuff impingement, and advancing it too distally may defunction the rotator cuff.

Definitive Plate Fixation. It is important to appreciate that the function of the plate is only to reconnect the head to the shaft.

Tuberosity fragments must be fixed separately, because the fixation of these fragments provided by screws inserted through the plate will not provide sufficient stability to prevent their redisplacement. Generic cloverleaf, buttress, and simple semitubular plate fixation have been successfully used to treat both simple and complex proximal humeral fracture patterns for many years (Table 35-9). Over the past 10 years, proximal humeral locking plates have been introduced, which may help to provide more secure fixation in the osteoporotic bone of the humeral head, theoretically reducing the risk of fixation failure.[23,76,154,202] Many different designs of plate are now available, differing in their shape and the locking mechanism at the screw–plate interface.[303,304] Some plates permit only a fixed (monoaxial) orientation of each screw to the plate using a jig, while others allow a degree of freedom (polyaxial) in the angle at which the screws can be inserted.

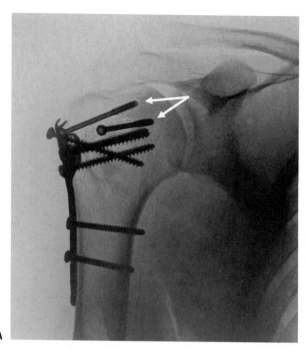

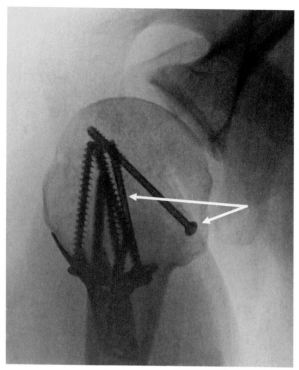

FIGURE 35-30 A,B. Articular surface fractures must be reduced and fixed separately using screws (*arrow*).

Most plates are designed to be inserted on the lateral wall of the proximal humerus (Fig. 35-27), and the orientation of the plate relative to the reduced greater tuberosity is critical: The anterior free edge of the plate should be placed just posterior to the bicipital groove to facilitate the insertion of the screws centrally or slightly posteriorly in the humeral head, which is offset

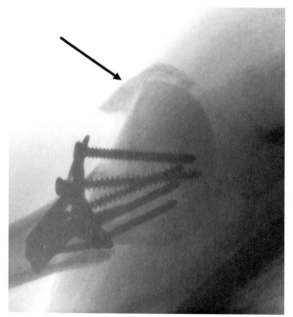

FIGURE 35-31 The tuberosities should be reduced and fixed with sutures, as well as screws through the plate to prevent tuberosity pull-off as depicted previously in Figure 36-21E. Failure to securely fix the greater tuberosity usually results in early redisplacement, as shown (*arrow*). This usually produces a symptomatic rotator cuff–deficient shoulder.

posteriorly and retroverted relative to the shaft. The plate must be cranial enough to allow screws to be inserted centrally into the head in the anterior projection but not so high that the top edge of the plate impinges against the acromion. The plate may be used to indirectly "fine-tune" the fracture reduction (Fig. 35-27).

Typically, three or four screws are inserted distal to the fracture, with four to six head screws proximally, dependent on the bone quality. It is essential to ensure that none of the head screws are inadvertently placed within the joint. The drill is inserted at low speed using a "push" technique until it can be felt to encounter resistance when it comes into contact with the hard subchondral bone of the humeral head. The screw length is measured at this point and should be between 40 and 50 mm in most cases. Once all screws are inserted, the shoulder is rotated under live fluoroscopy in both anteroposterior and modified axial views, to ensure no intra-articular screws are seen.

Results. Most reported case series focus on technical aspects of plate treatment and contain mixed subgroups of fractures. This prevents detailed analysis of the results for individual fracture subtypes using these implants (Table 35-9). The functional results are satisfactory using both conventional and locking plates, with a relatively low rate of the major complications of osteonecrosis, nonunion, and malunions. As a result, the rate of revision surgery is comparatively low in most series.

It is noteworthy that the initial enthusiasm for the use of proximal humeral locking plates[23,76,154,202] has recently been tempered by reports documenting a higher rate of fixation failure and screw cut-out.[4,75,223,259] It is apparent that stable reduction of the fracture is still required to prevent the risk of later fixation failure of these stiffer implants at the implant–bone

TABLE 35-9 Summary of the Case-Series Results of Plate Fixation Techniques for Proximal Humeral Fractures in Series That Report Functional Outcome*

Technique	Author	Year of Publication	No. of Patients	Average Age of Patients (range) (yr)	Follow-Up (range) (mo)	Outcome Assessment	Percentage with Good or Excellent Results	Percentage with Fair or Poor Results	ON	RS	Other
Conventional plates	Moda	1990	25	NK	NK	Neer	84	16	0	0	OA-2 (8%), SI-1 (4%), BT-1 (4%)
	Esser	1994	26	55 (19–62)	74 (12–144)	ASES	92	8	0	0	DIS-6 (23%), MF-1 (4%)
	Hessmann	1999	98	(<30–>80)	34 (24–72)	Constant	70	30	4 (4%)	9 (9%)	MU-15 (15%), DI-3 (3%), NE-1 (1%), NU-1 (1%)
	Hintermann	2000	38	72 (52–92)	40.8 (28.8–54)	Constant	79	21	2 (5%)	8 (21%)	ST-5 (13%), OA-3 (8%), MU-3 (8%), DI-1 (3%)
	Ring	2001	25	61 (22–80)	41 (26–72)	Constant	80	20	0	1 (4%)	NU-2 (8%), FR-1 (4%)
	Wijgman**	2002	60	48 (19–79)	120 (48–264)	Constant	87	13	22 (37%)	0	ST-5 (8%), SAI-1 (3%)
	Wanner	2003	60	62 (17–89)	17 (6–42)	Constant	Fair (mean)		2 (3%)	7 (12%)	MF-3 (5%), SAI-2 (3%), DIS-1 (2%), ST-1 (2%)
	Galatz***	2004	13	61 (25–77)	36 (12–125)	Neer	92	8	0	1 (8%)	MF-1 (8%), NU-1 (8%)
	Robinson	2003	25	67 (35–84)	12	Constant	Good (mean)		0	0	SAI-3 (12%), SI-2 (8%)
	Meier	2006	36	69 (23–88)	22 (13–28)	Constant	Fair (mean)		0	10 (28%)	MF-9 (25%), SI-2 (6%), MU-1 (3%)
	Total		381	60 (17–92)	48.6 (6–264)		83	17	30 (8%)	36 (9%)	
Custom locking plates	Bjorkenheim	2004	72	67 (27–89)	12	Constant	50	50	3 (4%)	2 (3%)	MU-3 (12%), SAI-3 (12%), MF-2 (8%), NE-2 (8%), DI-1 (4%)
	Fankhauser	2005	26	64.2 (28–82)	12	Constant	Good (mean)		2 (8%)	2 (8%)	SI-1 (6%), ST-1 (6%), MF-1 (6%)
	Koukakis	2006	18	61.8 (31–85)	16.2 (6–32)	Constant	55	44	1 (6%)	1 (6%)	MF-8 (13%), DI-6 (10%), SI-5 (8%), NE-2 (3%), NE-2 (3%)
	Machani	2006	62	61 (19–76)	19.2 (11–39)	HSS	60	40	0	0	
	Hirschmann	2007	119	67.6 (NK)	12	Constant	Fair (mean)		3 (3%)	26 (22%)	SAI-14 (12%), MF-5 (4%), NU-2 (2%), BT-1 (1%), SI-1 (1%)
	Moonot	2007	32	59.9 (18–87)	11 (3–24)	Constant	Fair (mean)		1 (3%)	4 (13%)	MF-3 (9%), MU-2 (6%), NU-1 (3%), SAI-1 (3%), NE-1 (3%)
	Agudelo	2007	153	62.3 (22–92)	2 (1–10)	ISS	N/A		7 (5%)	NK	MF-21 (14%), DI-7 (5%), RCT-5 (3%), ST-3 (2%), SAI-3 (2%), NU-1 (1%)
	Charalambous	2007	25	63 (30–83)	6 (3–18)	N/A	N/A		1 (4%)	4 (16%)	MF-11 (44%), MU-3 (12%), NU-3 (12%), ST-1 (4%), FR-1 (4%)
	Rose	2007	16	51 (18–78)	12 (6–20)	N/A	N/A		0	3 (19%)	NU-4 (25%)
	Handschin	2007	31	67 (27–87)	19 (11–24)	UCLA	77	23	2 (6%)	3 (10%)	SAI-2 (6%), DIS-1 (3%)
	Egol	2008	51	61 (NK)	16 (6–45)	N/A	N/A		1 (2%)	8 (16%)	NU-2 (4%), DI-1 (2%), HO-1 (2%)
	Hepp	2008	83	65 (18–88)	12	Constant	Fair (mean)		4 (5%)	9 (11%)	MF-13 (16%), MU-3 (4%), NU-3 (4%)
	Owsley	2008	53	52 (18–89)	12	qDASH	N/A	N/A	0	7 (13%)	MU-13 (25%), MF-12 (23%), NU-2 (4%), SAI-1 (2%)
	Laflamme	2008	27	64 (38–88)	19 (12–34)	Constant	Good (mean)		0	2 (7%)	MU-9 (33%)
	Total		496	63.6 (18–89)	13.4 (3–39)		58	42	25 (5%)	69 (14%)	

*Only English-language studies, or studies with an English-language translation, appearing in peer-reviewed journals during the last 30 years are shown; **n - number of patients.
**Cerclage wire internal fixation used also.
***Plate fixation performed on nonunions.
Nonunion (NU), Malunion (MU), Superficial infection (SI), Deep infection (DI), Osteonecrosis (ON), Subacromial impingement (SAI), Fracture (FR), Biceps tendonitis (BT), Stiffness (ST), Neurological injury (NE), Movement of fixation (MF), Revision surgery (RS), Osteoarthritis (OA).

interface.[183] Revision of the operative technique, with the increased use of bone grafts or supplementary calcar screws to improve the stability of the reduction, may result in further improvement in results.

Intramedullary Nailing.

Indications. Anterograde nailing of proximal humeral fractures has the advantage of reducing the surgical exposure required to obtain secure fixation. However, despite the more lateral entry point of some nails, there are concerns about the injury to the rotator cuff that is inevitably produced during nail insertion,[186] as for nailing of humeral diaphyseal fractures.[246] Due to the reduced fixation options proximal to the fracture, nailing has been mainly used to treat displaced two-part surgical neck fractures.[18,186,235] Newer nail designs allow multiple proximal screws to be inserted eccentrically through the nail, to fix three- and four-part fractures. Locking technology has also been used to allow screws to lock into the nail, improving the rigidity of the reconstruction.[62,185,198] However, when the greater tuberosity is fractured, there is a greater risk of redisplacing the fracture during nail insertion, and the results in more complex fractures have been poorer with a 45% reoperation rate.[3,18] For this reason, the current "ideal" indication for this technique is a more elderly patient with a displaced two-part surgical neck fracture, and the implant is not often used to treat more complex three- and four-part fracture configurations.

Technique. In most cases, where the nail is used to treat a fresh, displaced surgical neck fracture, a smaller deltoid-splitting incision is used to gain access to the nail entry portal. After a miniarthrotomy has been made through the supraspinatus, dependent on the nail design, the entry point for the nail is either through the anterior portion of the greater tuberosity or through the lateral articular surface just adjacent to it. After opening into the medullary canal, a guide wire is screened across the reduced fracture. Minimal reaming is usually required and the nail is the inserted by gentle pushing and twisting movements. Using a radiolucent targeting jig, proximal and distal locking screws are inserted (Fig. 35-32). The arthrotomy and rotator cuff are meticulously repaired at the end of the procedure.

Retrograde intramedullary devices have been used more infrequently for displaced extra-articular surgical neck fractures. They have the advantage of distal insertion, thereby avoiding dissection of the rotator cuff and capsule. Results have been reported from a number of centers internationally using Ender nails,[219] large K-wires,[234] and specially designed flexible pins[318-320] and nails[110] in the treatment of two-part neck fractures. Unfortunately, functional results are available from one only study.[234] The main complication of wire insertion (via the olecranon fossa) is restriction of elbow extension,[219] but early implant failure necessitating revision surgery is also reported in 25% of patients.[319]

Results. The reported functional results after both unlocked and locked nailing of proximal humeral fractures are satisfactory (Table 35-10). However, most series report substantial rates of fixation failure and malunion, especially for more unstable two-part fractures and multipart fractures.[3] There is also a substantial risk of rotator cuff dysfunction requiring secondary nail re-

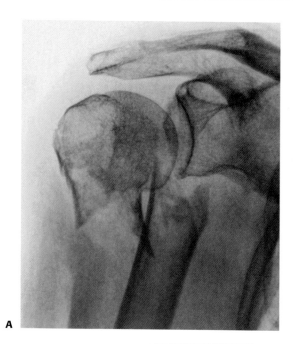

A

B

FIGURE 35-32 Translated and comminuted displaced surgical neck fractures (**A**) can be treated by locked intramedullary nailing in the older patient (**B**).

moval. These complications result in a high rate of revision surgery after the use of these implants.[3]

"Minimal-Fixation" (Screw and Osteosuturing Techniques).

Indications. Tension band principles are theoretically highly applicable in the proximal humerus where the tensile force of the rotator cuff attachments to the convexity of the anterolateral

TABLE 35-10 **Summary of the Case Series Results of Intramedullary Nailing Techniques for Proximal Humeral Fractures in Series That Report Functional Outcome***

	Author	Year of Publication	No. of Patients	Average Age of Patients (range) (yr)	Follow-Up (range) (mo)	Outcome Assessment	Percentage with Good or Excellent Results	Percentage with Fair or Poor Results	Complications
Unlocked nails	Zifko	1991	35	60 (20–84)	15	Neer	58	42	MU-3 (9%), NU-2 (6%), RS-1 (3%)
	Robinson	1993	23	(60–69 (80+))	18 (18–40)	Neer	69	31	MF-4 (17%), RS-4 (17%), SI-2 (9%)
	Ogiwara	1996	34	69.5 (48–86)	9.9 (6–22)	Individual	N/A	N/A	MU-12 (35%), MF-8 (24%), NU-1 (3%)
	Wachtl	2000	53	52 (3–91)	17 (4–30)	Constant	Fair (mean)		MF-22 (42%), AVN-7 (13%), OA-6 (11%), NU-5 (9%)
	Qidwai	2001	41	34 (17–62)	32.8 (18–51)	Neer	93	7	MF-6 (15%), RE-6 (15%), RS-1 (2%), AVN-1 (2%), MU-1 (2%)
	Takeuchi	2002	41	65 (18–95)	29 (24–48)	Neer	90	10	NU-1 (2%), RS-1 (2%), MF-1 (2%), FR-1 (2%)
	Tamai	2005	31	75 (58–91)	13 (6–32)	JOA	Good (mean)		MU-3 (10%), RS-2 (6%), NU-2 (6%), FR-2 (6%), MF-1 (3%)
	Park	2006	26	62 (27–79)	39 (24–59)	Neer	88	12	MU-6 (23%), RS-3 (12%), NU-1 (4%), AVN-1 (4%), MF-1 (4%)
	Total		284	58 (3–95)	21.6 (4–59)		80	20	
Locked nails	Lin	1998	21	65.8 (42–96)	19.2 (13–33)	Neer	86	14	None reported
	Bernard	2000	11	65.8 (45–83)	NK	NK	N/A		MF-5 (45.5%), RS-5 (45.5%)
	Rajasekhar	2001	25	61.4 (16–85)	18 (2–24)	Constant	80	20	RS-3 (12%), NU-1 (4%), AVN-1 (4%), ST-1 (4%), MF-1 (4%)
	Adedapo	2001	23	68.7 (27–100)	12	Neer	Good (mean)		MF-4 (17%), RS-4 (17%), AVN-1 (4%)
	Lin**	2003	15	55.1 (36–72)	13.8 (3–66)	Neer	87	13	MF-4 (27%), FR-2 (13%), NE-1 (7%), NU-1 (7%)
	Mittlmeier	2003	114	68.8 (25–97)	12	Constant	Good (mean)		RS-48 (43%), MF-26 (23%), AVN-9 (8%), ST-6 (5%), NU-3 (3%), DI-3 (3%), NE-1 (1%), DIS-1 (1%)
	Agel	2004	20	48 (18–80)	10 (4–28.3)	NK	N/A		MF-4 (20%), SI-1 (5%), SAI-1 (5%), RS-1 (5%)
	Kazakos	2007	27	65.9 (36–79)	12	Neer	78	22	ST-1 (4%), MF-1 (4%), AVN-1 (4%), RS-1 (4%)
	Sosef***	2007	28	66 (34–90)	12 (1–27)	Constant	89	11	RS-6 (21%), MF-4 (14%), AVN-1 (4%), NU-1 (4%), SAI-1 (4%)
	Mihara	2008	19	70.5 (60–83)	13.8 (6–48)	JOA	Good (mean)		MU-3 (16%)
	Total		196	67 (16–100)	13 (3–66)		85	15	

*Only English-language studies, or studies with an English-language translation, appearing in peer-reviewed journals during the last 30 years are shown.
**Intramedullary nail technique performed on nonunions.
***Mixed acute and late surgery.
NU, nonunion; MU, malunion; SI, superficial infection; DI, deep infection; AVN, avascular necrosis; FR, fracture (FR); RE, reduced elbow movement; NE, neurologic injury; MF, movement of fixation; RS, revision surgery; OA, osteoarthritis; ST, stiffness; DIS, dislocation.

humerus can be converted into compressive forces. Screw fixation either alone or combined with interosseous suture fixation techniques may be used in isolated two-part tuberosity fractures and some minimally displaced three- and four-part fractures.[106,253,254,296]

Technique. This technique was originally described using figure-of-eight wire suturing to treat three-part greater tuberosity fractures.[53,115,155,190,324] However, wire sutures are prone to breakage and loosening, and the technique was subsequently adapted with the incorporation of other implants such as Enders nails, K-wires, and supplementary screws to improve the rigidity of the reconstruction in osteoporotic bone.[247,306] The latest generation of high-strength cords and braided suture materials have now replaced wiring in the modern-day version of this technique.[67,106,217,227] Other adaptations have also been described to improve the mechanical stability of the reconstruction in osteoporotic bone, including impaction of the humeral head, a "parachute" suturing technique,[9] and augmentation of the fixation with external fixation.[151] Regardless of the technique used, it is important to stabilize the head to the shaft and fix any tuberosity fractures to both the head and the shaft.

Results. Although good functional results have been reported,[52,114–116,155,190] some series have documented a high fixation failure rate and poorer overall outcomes.[56,58,59,324] These techniques have been mainly used in the elderly, where conventional plate fixation was thought to be at high risk of failure from screw cut-out. It remains to be seen whether these procedures will continue to have a role, with the recent advances in plate and biomaterial technology to provide more stable fixation in osteoporotic bone.

Replacement Arthoplasty

Indications. The risk of osteonecrosis and nonunion was reported to be prohibitively high after three- and four-part fractures, with or without dislocation of the humeral head.[207,209] Neer popularized the use of replacement arthroplasty to treat acute fractures in the early 1970s, and this remains the main indication for the use of this technique today. Delayed arthroplasty has also been widely used to treat complications arising from both nonoperative and operative fracture treatment.[5,28]

Hemiarthroplasty has been much more widely used than total shoulder arthroplasty, except where the patient has degenerative joint disease affecting the glenoid. It is also customary to use cemented rather than uncemented implants, because of the poor potential for bone–implant integration in these osteoporotic fractures. The initial stemmed implants, such as the Neer prostheses (Mark I and II), were of monoblock design, but these have been superceded by modular designs, which allow adjustment of the height and offset of the prosthesis after cementation of the stem. Newer implants, such as the Tournier prosthesis, are now available that are specifically designed to treat fractures and have jigs for judging insertion, porous coating, and fenestrations to encourage tuberosity healing.

The goal of hemiarthroplasty is to restore the anatomic relationship of the humeral head to the tuberosities and to the shaft by achieving proper component height, off-set, and version. Anatomic healing of the tuberosities is often associated with a good functional outcome, while secondary displacement or nonunion is usually associated with a weak and poorly func-

tional shoulder. It is therefore critical not only to ensure optimal fixation of the tuberosities but also to prevent secondary displacement by postoperative protection of the shoulder. Postoperative stiffness in the presence of tuberosity healing is a manageable problem, whereas secondary tuberosity displacement and nonunion are untreatable.

Technique.

Conventional Arthroplasty. The patient is positioned in the beach-chair position, preferably with a cut-away to facilitate a full intraoperative range of movement of the shoulder. All procedures are performed under a standard antibiotic and antithrombotic prophylaxis regimen. The initial surgical approach is identical to that for an internal fixation procedure and can be achieved using either a deltopectoral approach or a deltoid-splitting approach. The tuberosities are mobilized, and heavy nonabsorbable braided sutures (Ethibond, Fibrewire, or Orthocord) are placed through the tendon around each tuberosity. The humeral head is extracted and is used to select the head implant size.

The prosthetic height may be judged according to the preoperative templating, or the calcar of the proximal humerus, which serves as a guide to the location of the anatomic neck of the humerus before the fracture. If the calcar is fractured, another useful internal reference point is the upper border of the pectoralis major insertion. The average distance from this point to the top of the humeral head has been shown to be 5 cm.[100] The greater tuberosity can also be used to check the height of the implant, as the neck of the prosthesis will have to lie exactly at the level of the insertion of the supraspinatus if it is anatomically reduced. After thorough medullary lavage, standard second-generation techniques are used to insert antibiotic-impregnated cement. The prosthesis should be cemented in 20 to 30 degrees of retroversion. This can be determined by placing the forearm in neutral rotation, with the transepicondylar axis of the elbow perpendicular to the trunk. The humeral head should face the glenoid with 20 to 30 degrees of retroversion in this position. The fin of the prosthesis of most implants is then located just posterior to the posterior lip of the bicipital groove. Excessive retroversion should be avoided to reduce the tension on the greater tuberosity repair and reduce the risk of secondary redisplacement (Fig. 35-33).

The tuberosities are sutured to each other, and to the proximal shaft of the humerus, using the previously inserted nonabsorbable sutures. The sutures may be passed through the holes in the prosthesis to act as a stable fixation point, although some surgeons prefer to attach the tuberosities directly to each other. The sutures are assembled such that the intertubercular sutures are orthogonal to the sutures that attach the tuberosities to the shaft. A circumferential suturing technique, passing round the medial prosthetic neck, has also been described.[82–84] Some surgeons perform bone grafting in the area of the tuberosities, or into the fenestrations of the newer prosthetic designs, using cancellous bone from the excised humeral head. Newer fracture stems also have a narrower metaphyseal segment and are hydroxyapatite coated, in an attempt to enhance fixation of the tuberosities to the implant. The high rate of tuberosity pull-off and nonunion has also generated renewed interest in other enhanced suturing techniques to try to encourage tuberosity healing.[2,160]

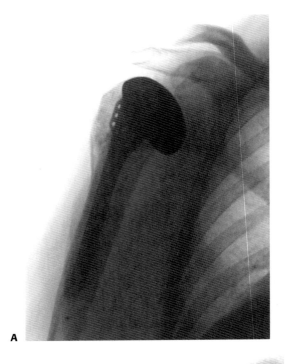

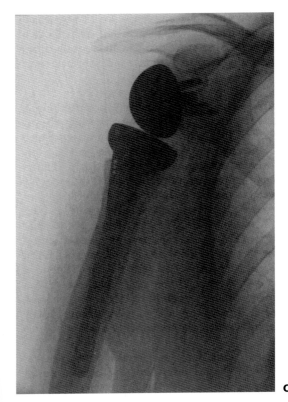

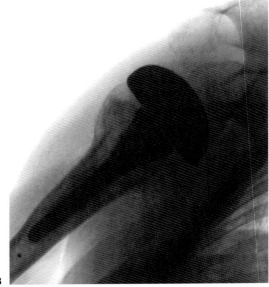

FIGURE 35-33 Nonreconstructable fractures may be treated with a humeral head arthroplasty. A conventional hemiarthroplasty may be associated with satisfactory shoulder function if the tuberosities heal, as shown in this case on anteroposterior and modified axial views (**A,B**). Reverse shoulder arthroplasty joint is a newer technique, which does not rely on the integrity of the rotator cuff for function. The results of the use of this technique for acute fractures are largely unknown at present (**C**).

Reverse Shoulder Arthroplasty. As an alternative strategy, the use of reverse total shoulder arthroplasty has also been recently advocated. This lateralizes the shoulder joint center of rotation, improving the mechanical advantage of the deltoid and compensating for rotator cuff deficiency. This is achieved by converting the glenoid into a spherical head and the head of the humerus into a socket, thus providing a stable fulcrum for cuff deficient shoulders (Fig. 35-33). The chief theoretical advantage of the technique is that tuberosity healing may not be as important in determining the functional outcome, because the prosthesis is designed to function in cuff-deficient shoulders.

Results. The reported outcomes after primary hemiarthroplasty for fractures are varied (Table 35-11). Satisfactory prosthetic survival rates have been reported, with a low rate of revi-

sion.[255] However, few studies have replicated the functional outcomes that were reported by Neer.[117,209] The results are best when the arthroplasty is performed as a primary treatment, in a younger patient,[255] and the tuberosities heal.[27,255] However, most patients who are treated with arthroplasty have a relatively weak, stiff, but pain-free shoulder.[27,159,255,322] This may be acceptable for an elderly frail patient but is frequently suboptimal in a younger, more active individual. It is notable that despite extensive product marketing, there is no evidence to suggest that the newer range of trauma arthroplasty implants produce a better functional outcome than the generic implants.[189]

Rotator cuff dysfunction from early tuberosity redisplacement or nonunion is probably the major reason for the unsatisfactory functional outcome (Fig. 35-34). Many patients are also unable to comply with an aggressive rehabilitation program after

TABLE 35-11 Summary of the Case-Series Results of Humeral Head Replacement Techniques for Proximal Humeral Fractures in Series That Report Functional Outcome*

Technique	Author	Year of Publication	No. of Publications	Early/Late**	Average Age of Patients (range) (yr)	Follow-Up (range) (mo)	Outcome Assessment	Percentage with Good or Excellent Results	Percentage with Fair or Poor Results	HO	RS	Other
Hemiarthroplasty	Neer	1970	43	A	NK	NK	Neer	91	9	6 (14%)	0	MU-2 (5%), SI-1 (2%)
	Tanner	1983	43	M	69 (47–86)	38 (24–120)	Individual		N/A	1 (2%)	1 (2%)	NU-4 (9%), RT-3 (7%), MU-2 (5%), DIS-2 (5%), NE-1 (2%), RD-1 (2%)
	Moeckel	1992	22	A	70 (49–87)	36 (29–46)	HSS	91	9	9 (41%)	2 (9%)	DIS-1 (5%), SAI-1 (5%)
	Hawkins	1993	19	A	64 (39–81)	40 (11–94)	UCLA	40	60	0	2 (10%)	OA-7 (37%), DIS-2 (10%), MF-2 (10%), NE-1 (5%)
	Goldman	1995	22	A	67 (48–86)	30 (12–66)	ASES	N/A	N/A	0	0	MF-7 (32%), SI-1 (5%)
	Norris***	1995	23	L	53.3 (18–79)	54 (24–108)	ASES	N/A	N/A	2 (9%)	5 (22%)	MU-3 (13%), NE-3 (13%), SI-1 (4%), FR-1 (4%)
	Dimakopoulos	1997	38	M	56 (35–79)	37 (12–48)	ASES	N/A	N/A	2 (5%)	0	RCI-2 (5%)
	Bosch	1998	25	M	64.5 (47–82)	42.4 (5–98)	Constant	24	76	2 (8%)	1 (4%)	DIS-1 (4%)
	Zyto***	1998	27	A	71 (48–91)	39 (12–94)	Constant	Poor (median)		1 (4%)	0	MU-3 (11%)
	Movin****	1998	29	M	71 (47–87)	36 (24–144)	Constant	0	100	0	2 (7%)	NE-1 (3%), MF-1 (3%), OA-1 (3%)
	Boileau***	2001	70	L	59 (30–87)	19 (12–48)	Constant	42	58	0	4 (6%)	FR-5 (7%), NU-4 (6%), SAI-3 (4%), DI-2 (3%), DIS-1 (1%), NE-1 (1%)
	Antuna***	2002	25	L	65 (31–85)	72 (24–180)	Neer	48	52	0	2 (8%)	NU-2 (8%), RD-2 (8%), MU-1 (4%)
	Prakash	2002	22	M	69 (45–86)	33 (6–93)	ASES	75	25	1 (5%)	0	MU-2 (9%), DIS-1 (5%), NU-1 (5%), MF-1 (5%)

(continues)

TABLE 35-11

Summary of the Case-Series Results of Humeral Head Replacement Techniques for Proximal Humeral Fractures in Series That Report Functional Outcome* (continued)

Technique	Author	Year of Publication	No. of Patients	Early/Late**	Average Age of Patients (range) (yr)	Follow-Up (range) (mo)	Outcome Assessment	Percentage with Good or Excellent Results	Percentage with Fair or Poor Results	Complications HO	RS	Other
	Becker	2002	27	M	67 (36–82)	45 (12–76)	Neer	63	27	15 (56%)	0	MU-62 (45%), SI-9 (7%), FR-3 (2%), DIS-1 (1%), DI-1 (1%), MF-1 (1%)
	Robinson	2003	138	A	65.8 (30–90)	75.6 (24–156)	Constant	Fair (median)		0	11 (8%)	MF-2 (3%), NU-2 (3%), MU-15 (21%), RCT-2 (3%), DI-1 (1%), RD-1 (1%)
	Mighell	2003	72	A	66 (39–89)	36 (12–89)	ASES	Fair (mean)		18 (25%)	4 (6%)	MU-2 (6%), SAI-1 (3%), RD-1 (3%), NE-1 (3%)
	Demirhan	2003	32	A	58 (37–83)	35 (8–80)	Constant	47	53	0	0	MU-28 (17%)
	Kralinger	2004	167	A	70 (22–91)	29 (12–88)	Constant	Poor (mean)		0	0	MU-5 (11%), SI-1 (2%), NE-1 (2%), DIS-1 (2%)
	Gronhagen	2007	46	A	72 (42–91)	53 (12–168)	Constant	Poor (mean)		25 (54%)	11 (24%)	DIS-1 (3%)
	Sosna	2008	33	L	58 (39–75)	24	Constant	Poor (mean)		0	1 (3%)	FR-1 (2%)
	Sosna	2008	43	A	57 (32–78)	24	Constant	Fair (mean)		0	1 (2%)	
	Antuna	2008	57	A	66 (23–89)	124 (60–264)	Neer	47	53	0	3 (5%)	SAI-3 (5%), DIS-1 (2%), MF-1 (2%)
	Total		1023		65.3 (18–91)	46 (0–264)		52	48			
Reverse arthroplasty	Levy	2007	29	L	69 (42–80)	NK	ASES	Poor (mean)		0	4 (14%)	DIS-4 (14%), MF-3 (10%), FR-3 (10%), DI-1 (3%)
	*Bufquin	2007	43	A	78 (65–97)	22 (6–58)	Constant	Fair (mean)		0	0	NU-14 (39%), FR-11 (26%), MU-6 (14%), NE-5 (12%), RD-3 (7%), DIS-1 (2%)
	Total		72		74 (42–97)	22 (6–58)						

*Only English-language studies, or studies with an English-language translation, appearing in peer-reviewed journals during the last 30 years are shown.
**A, acute; L, late; M, mixed.
***Mixed total and hemiarthroplasty performed.
NU, nonunion; MU, malunion; SI, superficial infection; DI, deep infection; RCT, rotator cuff tear; RCI, rotator cuff insufficiency; SAI, subacromial impingement; DIS, dislocation; FR, fracture; HO, heterotopic ossification; RD, reflex sympathetic dystrophy; NE, neurologic injury; MF, movement of fixation; RS, revision surgery; OA, osteoarthritis.

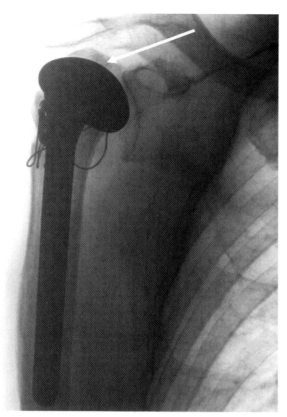

FIGURE 35-34 Tuberosity pull-off (*arrow*) is a frequent complication of conventional arthroplasty for acute fracture. This complication is usually associated with a poor functional outcome.

surgery, and this may result in the development of symptomatic periarticular adhesions and capsulitis.

The other complications associated with prosthetic arthroplasty include instability, dislocation, prosthetic loosening, late infection, and periprosthetic fracture. Most patients will not survive long enough to develop these complications; those who do should be treated as for a primary arthroplasty for degenerative joint disease.[36,230,311] Periprosthetic fractures are difficult to treat and the risk of this complication is increased in elderly, osteoporotic patients, who are unsteady on their feet and prone to further falls.[307] Nonoperative brace treatment may be used in frail patients,[147] whereas open reduction and plate fixation is required in younger and fitter patients, with a stable prosthesis. Revision to a long-stem prosthesis may be required if there is substantial prosthetic loosening.[312]

The reverse total shoulder arthroplasty has been used extensively to treat patients with rotator cuff arthropathy,[283] with reliably good results, and the poor functional outcome associated with traditional arthroplasty has led to its use being extended to acute three- and four-part fractures and fracture-dislocations. Encouraging early results have been reported using this technique in case series (Table 35-11), but there is currently a requirement for a comparative study with traditional arthroplasty implants to assess the relative merits of these two techniques. Reverse shoulder arthroplasty is associated with the same risk of complications as conventional arthroplasty. In addition, reverse arthroplasty is frequently complicated by notching of the scapular neck, which may occasionally result in scapu-

lar stress fracture. The longer-term risks associated with this complication are as yet unknown.

Postinjury Rehabilitation Regimes

Following operative treatment, most patients are advised to wear a shoulder immobilizer sling for 4 to 6 weeks. The period of immobilization depends on the stability of fixation after head-conserving techniques. Some surgeons prefer to rigidly immobilize the arm for the first 4 weeks after an arthroplasty procedure, to minimize the risk of tuberosity pull-off. Most surgeons prefer the patient to commence pendular exercises and elbow range of movement exercises immediately, with active-assisted range of motion exercises commencing at 2 weeks after the operation. Abduction of the shoulder beyond 90 degrees or external rotation beyond the neutral position is prohibited during this period.

Isometric rotator cuff exercises and graduated active range-of-motion exercises supervised by a physiotherapist, supplemented by a home exercise program, are commenced after removal of the sling and continued for at least 6 months after the operation.

AUTHORS' PREFERRED METHOD OF TREATMENT

General Treatment Philosophy

There is good evidence to support the use of nonoperative treatment for the majority of patients with proximal humeral fractures. The functional outcome in these patients will usually be sufficient to their needs, and the risk of complications is low. They are typically physiologically old, frail, and unable to comply with an aggressive shoulder rehabilitation program and have a fracture of a simple and stable configuration.

Given the lack of Level I and II evidence, the author believes that there is no incontrovertible evidence on which to guide a decision regarding the best management for the remaining minority of patients.[21,112,197] They are often younger and well motivated but have more complex injuries. An individualized approach is adopted for these patients, taking into account the patient-, injury-, and surgeon-related factors that have been discussed previously. Operative treatment is considered when the individual patient's functional outcome is likely to be significantly improved by the surgery or when nonoperative treatment would be associated with an unacceptably high risk of complications or severe functional impairment. The most common complications that give rise to this degree of functional disability are nonunion, osteonecrosis, and rotator cuff dysfunction. Although rare, any one of these complications will usually compromise the functional outcome for the patient. In contrast, if a fracture heals with a perfused head and a functional rotator cuff, the patient will usually have good shoulder function, regardless of the radiologic appearance.

Current evidence suggests that reconstructive surgery falls into two categories with distinctly different functional outcomes: Humeral head-conserving procedures should aim to anatomically reduce and fix the fracture in a stable manner. If this subsequently heals without osteonecrosis and with a functional rotator cuff, the patient will have a good functional outcome. This form of treatment should therefore be regarded as an "opportunity" for the patient to regain a pain-free, functional shoulder. The level of function may approach the preinjury state in younger, well-motivated individuals. In contrast, most of the contemporary literature suggests that the use of humeral head arthroplasty is associated with a pain-free but poorly functional shoulder, because of tuberosity pull-off or rotator cuff dysfunction and failure.

Based on this evidence, the author believes that ORIF should be the default primary operative treatment for the majority of complex proximal humeral fractures, where the humeral head appears viable and can be reconstructed. Primary arthroplasty is reserved for the minority of patients, where nonoperative treatment is likely to be associated with a high risk of complications, and a humeral head-conserving procedure is infeasible. The latter situation only arises if the humeral head is devoid of soft tissue attachments and has a high risk of osteonecrosis, or rarely when the fracture is technically unreconstructable. Therefore, if a surgical reconstruction is contemplated, it is the author's routine practice to evaluate the detailed anatomy of the fracture on spiral CT scanner with three-dimensional reconstructions, before surgery. In this way, a more informed decision can be made about whether the humeral head is likely to be salvageable at surgery. This allows better preoperative counseling about the likely form of surgical reconstruction and eventual outcome.

The author does not use percutaneous fracture fixation techniques, as it is believed that superior anatomic fracture reduction and stable fixation can be better achieved using open techniques (Table 35-12). The extended deltoid-splitting approach, through a shoulder-strap skin incision, is used in almost all cases. The approach is especially useful for of Type I anterior fracture-dislocations[73,252] and all posterior fracture-dislocations.[244,245] In Type II anterior fracture-dislocations, the humeral head is usually denuded of all soft tissue attachments and may be very mobile and difficult to retrieve into the wound through the deltoid split. In these circumstances, a separate limited deltopectoral approach is sometimes required, through the anterior portion of the shoulder strap incision to retrieve the humeral head. The only fracture in which a deltopectoral approach is used primarily is the two-part displaced lesser tuberosity fracture, where better access is provided through a direct anterior approach.[257] All humeral head arthroplasty procedures are also performed through a deltoid-splitting incision.

Treatment of Individual Injury Patterns

Undisplaced or Minimally Displaced One-Part Fractures (OTA Type A, B, or C)

These injuries are mostly managed nonoperatively as described previously. Routine radiologic screening of the fracture is undertaken at 1 to 2 weeks to ensure secondary displacement has not occurred, especially if there are multiple undisplaced fracture lines or if the shaft is not fully impacted on the humeral head and is thereby potentially unstable. Elbow, wrist, and hand mobilization begins immediately, with shoulder pendular exercises beginning when there is radiologic confirmation of maintenance of fracture reduction.

Active shoulder isometric exercises are begun at around 3 weeks, progressing to isotonic strengthening and stretching exercises at 6 to 12 weeks following injury. The patient is advised to continue shoulder exercises during the first year after injury, because delayed restoration of movement may continue during this time. Emphasis is placed on a patient-orientated home exercise program, rather than prolonged supervised physiotherapy. Outpatient monitoring continues until there is evidence of fracture union both clinically (absence of pain, restoration of function and range of motion) and radiologically. Prolonged radiologic reassessment thereafter is not logistically feasible in our unit, with the large numbers of patients treated. However, we advise patients to return for reassessment if they notice increased pain or worsening function in their shoulder.

Two-Part Greater Tuberosity Fractures and Fracture-Dislocations (OTA Types A1.1, A1.2, and A1.3)

All undisplaced greater tuberosity fractures are initially treated nonoperatively, as for other one-part fractures. However, repeat

TABLE 35-12 Goal-Orientated Treatment of Proximal Humeral Fractures

Goal of Treatment		Technique
Preserve function		Open reduction and internal fixation rather than arthroplasty, if possible
		Stable anatomic fracture reduction, wherever possible
		Stable internal fixation
		Early rehabilitation
Prevent complications	Osteonecrosis	Preserve the humeral head vascularity:
		Avoid dissection around bicipital groove
		Good soft tissue handling
		Preserve residual periosteal and capsular attachments to head
	Nonunion	Stable reduction and fixation of head-shaft segment
		Avoid excessive periosteal stripping
	Malunion	Anatomic reduction and fixation of head-tuberosity segments
		Repair of any associated rotator cuff tear

radiographs are obtained at 1 and 2 weeks postinjury, as secondary displacement may occur through the pull of the attached supraspinatus and infraspinatus tendons. In physiologically older and frail patients (usually older than 80 years) with limited functional expectations, a substantial degree of displacement is tolerated without recourse to operative treatment. These patients often have a poor outcome with attempted surgical reduction and fixation, because of their poor bone quality and preexisting cuff dysfunction, which precludes stable fixation. Although they will often have signs of continued cuff dysfunction from the tuberosity nonunion or malunion, their functional outcome will usually be adequate for their needs.

Operative treatment is advised for physiologically younger (typically younger than 65 years), active patients with fractures, which are either primarily displaced by more than 5 mm or become displaced by this amount within the first 2 weeks postinjury. In addition, selected older patients (typically aged between 65 and 80 years) with fragment displacement of 1 cm or more are offered operative reconstruction. When there is a substantial tuberosity fragment (greater than 2.5 cm), open reduction through a limited deltoid-splitting approach and internal fixation using partially thread cancellous 3.5-mm screws are performed. It is important to insert screws to transfix the fragment to both the humeral head and the medial cortex of the metaphysis. Meticulous repair of any associated rotator cuff injury is also performed.

When the fragment is smaller than 2.5 cm or if it is heavily comminuted, it is the author's policy to treat these injuries in the same manner as a rotator cuff avulsion. Arthroscopic assessment is performed and, if feasible, the small tuberosity fragments are repaired to their native bed, using a combination of cuff and interosseous sutures attached to suture anchors inserted at the margins of the cuff avulsion. As with all arthroscopic rotator cuff repairs, a "double-row" fixation to the "footprint" of the greater tuberosity is preferable to reduce the risk of later repair failure and to maximize the healing potential.[38,171] If arthroscopic repair is not possible, the tuberosity is reconstructed through a limited deltoid-splitting approach using a similar technique of transosseous repair.[81]

The relatively unusual injury pattern in which the tuberosity fracture is associated with a bony glenoid rim avulsion is often associated with acute instability of the shoulder.[250] For this reason, the author routinely treats both of these injuries with primary internal fixation.

Two-Part Lesser Tuberosity Fractures and Fracture-Dislocations (OTA Type A1.3, Subgroup 4)

Isolated lesser tuberosity fractures typically occur in younger or middle-aged patients and are displaced. Nonoperative treatment of these injuries risks later functional incapacity, because of subscapularis dysfunction. It is the author's policy to treat all these fractures operatively in medically fit patients. ORIF is performed through a standard deltopectoral approach. If there is a single large fragment, definitive internal fixation is performed using partially threaded 3.5-mm cancellous screws, inserted through the lesser tuberosity.[257] Judging accurate screw length (typically between 40 and 50 mm) is an important technical aspect of the procedure, to gain bicortical purchase. Where the fragment is 2.5 cm or less or if there is comminution, screw fixation risks secondary comminution or does not give sufficient stability. For these patients, the reduction is maintained by interosseous sutures, placed both through the tuberosity and through the bone–tendon junction, which are tied to the adjacent metaphyseal bone.[257]

In the minority of patients where the lesser tuberosity fracture is associated with a locked posterior dislocation, an attempt is initially made to obtain closed reduction of the dislocation under anesthesia. Where this is not possible, an open reduction is performed through an extended deltoid-splitting approach. After reduction of the shoulder has been obtained, the stability of the shoulder is assessed throughout a full range of internal and external rotation movement, both with the arm at the side and in 90 degrees of abduction. If the shoulder is acutely unstable because of reengagement of a reverse Hill-Sachs lesion on the posterior glenoid beyond neutral rotation, the reverse Hill-Sachs lesion is either elevated and bone-grafted or, if there is a larger defect, filled with a sculpted femoral head allograft, which is secured with two countersunk 3.5-mm partially threaded cancellous screws. The lesser tuberosity is then reattached anatomically, using the same techniques as for other isolated two-part fractures, using either two 3.5-mm partially threaded cancellous screws or interosseous sutures.

Two-Part Extra-Articular (Surgical Neck) Fractures (OTA Types A2 and A3)

Almost all fractures in which the shaft is impacted into the surgical neck are treated nonoperatively. A substantial degree of translation of these two fragments is usually tolerated, as long as there is residual cortical contact and impaction. Occasionally, if there is severe varus angulation of the head fragment in a physiologically younger individual (typically younger than 65 years), operative disimpaction, anatomic reduction, and plate fixation will be performed to reduce the risk of later impingement of the greater tuberosity in the narrowed subacromial space and dysfunction of the rotator cuff from its shortened lever arm.

It is the author's experience that separated and comminuted surgical neck fractures, where there is no appreciable contact of the humeral head with the shaft, are mechanically unstable and therefore prone to nonunion. In physiologically younger patients (typically aged under 65 years), open reduction and fixation is performed, using either a standard clover leaf or locking plate, dependent on the bone quality in the humeral head. Unfortunately, many of the patients who sustain these unstable injuries are either elderly, frail individuals (typically older than 80 years), or younger but with multiple medical comorbidities or alcohol-dependency problems. This type of injury is therefore often a "marker" of their poor physiologic status. These patients are still at a higher risk of nonunion, but operative treatment may be contraindicated because of either their high anesthetic risk or the likelihood of operative fixation failure. Although these patients are often treated nonoperatively, operative fixation should be offered if at all possible. This is because nonunion is almost always associated with pain and severe functional disability and operative treatment of the primary injury is always technically easier than the treatment of an established nonunion.

An attempt is made to reduce the fracture anatomically wherever possible. It is important to restore continuity of the medial calcar support to prevent acute fixation failure using either structural graft or a low inferomedial screw, which is inserted separate from the plate. Occasionally, if there is extensive metaphyseal comminution in an older patient, the risk of nonunion across the area of comminution is high. In these circumstances, shortening and impaction of the shaft fragment within the head is performed to produce a more stable configuration before plate application. If the bone quality in the humeral head is very poor, a short proximal humeral locked intramedullary nail will often provide more secure fixation than a plate. However, a locking plate is preferred for definitive fixation, if at all possible, to minimize the risk of the later rotator cuff dysfunction, which nailing usually produces.

Three- and Four-Part Fractures without Glenohumeral Dislocation (OTA Types B1, B2, C1, and C2)

Fractures that occur in physiologically older patients should be treated nonoperatively, if there is residual cortical continuity of the humeral head fragment on the shaft, the tuberosities are not too widely displaced, and humeral head appears viable. Although the outcome is often imperfect, after union these patients will usually have a pain-free shoulder, which has sufficient function for their everyday needs.

Operative treatment is offered to physiologically younger patients, where it is thought that the risk of nonunion, cuff dysfunction or osteonecrosis is high or where operative treatment is likely to provide a significant improvement in shoulder function over nonoperative treatment. In practice, this means that surgery to prevent nonunion or cuff dysfunction is often offered to patients with fractures in which the humeral shaft and tuberosities have significantly displaced from the humeral head. The risk of osteonecrosis is determined by the fracture configuration, with wide displacement of the head from the shaft with likely loss of the medial periosteal and capsular hinge, and the absence of a medial metaphyseal spike particularly associated with a higher risk of this complication. There are substantial functional gains from internal fixation for fractures in which the humeral head has displaced from its normal 130 degree head-shaft orientation to occupy an extreme position of varus (90-degree head-shaft angle) or valgus (180-degree head-shaft angle) or where there is marked humeral head articular surface incongruity from displaced marginal articular fragments attached to the tuberosities.

ORIF is performed whenever possible, and preoperative CT can provide an indication of the likelihood that this will be feasible. Operative technique follows the protocol previously described: The goal is to attempt anatomic or near-anatomic reconstruction, and the author freely uses bone substitutes and allograft to fill metaphyseal defects and supplementary screws to reduce and fix articular surface fragments that are attached to the tuberosities. Definitive internal fixation is performed, using either a cloverleaf or proximal humeral locking plate, dependent on the quality of the bone in the humeral head.

The patient is always preoperatively counseled that if the fracture is deemed to be unreconstructable, a cemented humeral head hemiarthroplasty will be performed. This is usually only indicated if the head is devoid of soft tissue attachments and shows no back bleeding. The patient is counseled that the likely outcome after an arthroplasty will be a pain-free but stiff shoulder. However, an arthroplasty is more likely to function well when it is performed as a primary, rather than as a salvage procedure.

Three- and Four-Part Fractures with Associated Glenohumeral Dislocation (OTA Types B3 and C3)

Type I Anterior Fracture-Dislocations. ORIF is attempted for all these fractures, as their risk of osteonecrosis is much lower. A closed manipulation of this type of injury should never be attempted, because of the risk of dislodging the head and damaging residual soft tissue attachments.[121,252] Through an extended deltoid-splitting approach, the fractured tuberosities are tagged with stay sutures and gentle traction allows exposure of the anterior glenoid margin to reveal the dislocated humeral head. Insertion of an osteotome or a blunt elevator between the anterior glenoid rim and the engaged Hill-Sachs lesion of the humeral head is required to disengage the two structures, after which reduction of the humeral head can be achieved, by translating it forward to face the glenoid. Following its relocation, the humeral head usually has retained anterior and inferior capsular attachments, but active arterial bleeding from drill holes inserted into the raw cancellous surface of the back of the humeral head confirms active perfusion. The fractures are then anatomically reconstructed using suturing of the tuberosities, locking-plate fixation, with filling of any metaphyseal defects using allograft or bone substitutes as described previously. Operative treatment is not required for either associated bony or soft tissue labral pathology, or the posterior humeral head defect, as anatomic reduction and fixation of the fracture usually restores full shoulder stability.

Type II Anterior Fracture-Dislocations. In these injuries, the humeral head is almost inevitably devoid of soft tissue attachments and there is no evidence of active arterial bleeding from the raw cancellous surface of the back of the humeral head following relocation. A head-salvaging reconstruction with plate fixation is therefore less likely to be successful, because of the risk of later osteonecrosis. It may be worth attempting this in a physiologically younger patient (typically younger than 65 years), accepting that the risk that a later humeral head arthroplasty may be required.

For most physiologically older patients, the choice of treatment rests between closed manipulation and humeral head arthroplasty. It is the author's policy to initially attempt a gentle closed manipulation of the shoulder under general anesthesia. Minimal traction is required, and instead an attempt is made to maneuver the head through the rent in the inferior capsule to achieve relocation against the glenoid. There is a substantial risk of disengaging the humeral head from the shaft,[121,252] but if a closed relocation of the head can be achieved, the injury is then usually stable and can be treated nonoperatively. The use of temporary percutaneous pinning of the dislocated head to the shaft may prevent their disengagement.[121] As with younger patients, there is a substantial risk of later osteonecrosis following a successful relocation, but many of these frail elderly patients may not develop these symptoms within their limited life span. If a closed relocation cannot be achieved or if the head becomes disengaged from the shaft, a standard cemented hemiarthroplasty is performed

Posterior Fracture-Dislocations. As with Type I anterior-fracture dislocations, it is the author's policy to attempt ORIF of all these fractures, as their risk of osteonecrosis is low. A similar operative approach is used: The engaged humeral head is disimpacted from the posterior glenoid rim with a bone lever.

Relocation is then achieved under direct vision by rotating the humeral head forward to face the glenoid. The reduced humeral head is almost invariably perfused, with residual capsular attachments and active arterial back-bleeding from its fractured cancellous surface.

The fracture is provisionally reduced and provisionally stabilized using two or three Kirschner wires to restore rotational stability and allow assessment of residual posterior instability. Judging the accuracy of the reduction of the primary fracture is often difficult, where marginal impaction has produced an acute osteochondral fracture of the humeral head (reverse Hill-Sachs lesion). However, the presence of the intact posterior capsule and periosteal "hinge" is a useful aid to reduction, serving as a template for "closing the door" to achieve the reduction.

Residual anterior osteochondral humeral head defects (reverse Hill-Sachs lesions) that persist after provisional reduction of the head and that are engaging the posterior glenoid rim with the shoulder in neutral rotation are considered to be a potential source of posterior instability. Where there is a large residual osteochondal fragment with retained soft tissue attachment, this is treated by elevation of the osteochondral fragment, with insertion of morselized femoral head allograft to buttress the elevated fragment and support from "positional screws." Where the fragments are larger, comminuted, or loose, a deep-frozen femoral head osteochondral allograft is sculpted on-table to fill the defect. These procedures usually restore full on-table stability, and repair of posterior soft tissue labral or bony glenoid rim fractures is seldom required.

The fracture is now definitively fixed according to its configuration. Two-part anatomic neck fractures are stabilized using 3.5-mm partially threaded cancellous lag screws. These are inserted perpendicular to the fracture line into the humeral head, through the intact lateral proximal humeral metaphysis. The humeral head component of the more complex three- and four-part fractures is fixed to the tuberosities, using either lag screws or interosseous sutures. This composite is then stabilized to the humeral shaft using either a cloverleaf or locking plate, dependent on the bone quality.

The usual postoperative rehabilitation protocol is modified slightly, and a foam pad or pillow is used to restrict the patient from internally rotating their shoulder beyond a neutral position for 4 weeks, to protect against potential posterior instability.

Fractures in Unusual Situations.
Severe Injuries. These rare but more severe injuries are usually seen after industrial or heavy machinery accidents, motor vehicle accidents, or gunshot/blast injuries. They are characterized by the severity of the soft tissue and bony injury to the shoulder, which is often associated with a neurovascular injury. They may occur in association with multiple injuries to other systems, as well as other orthopaedic injuries.

The patient is initially managed according ATLS guidelines, with life-threatening injuries managed first, before attention is turned to the shoulder injury. Any vascular injury to the shoulder takes priority and should be repaired immediately if there is acute ischemia. Vascular reconstruction may be contraindicated if the distal circulation is good through the collateral circulation, without an expanding hematoma, and there is a complete plexus avulsion, which is unreconstructable.

Débridement and washout of any open wounds is performed as for any other open fracture. Any dead or devitalized bone should be removed. Topical antibiotic beads and parenteral antibiotic therapy are provided, and repeated wound inspection and redébridement and soft tissue coverage with local flaps may be required. If there is more extensive fracture comminution or bone loss, temporary splintage and maintenance of length and alignment may be possible using temporary external fixation or fine wire fixation until soft tissue cover has been obtained. Delayed staged reconstruction can then be performed, using either internal fixation and bone grafting or Ilizarov techniques, dependent on the fracture configuration.

The optimal time of nerve injury repair is at approximately 2 to 3 months, but it depends on the nerves involved, the type of injury, and the age of the patient. Nerve recovery is better with younger patients and more distal injury. The recovery from a sharp injury is better than from a blunt injury. Early exploration and repair are usually indicated after a penetrating injury with complete motor loss in a given motor group.

Proximal humeral fractures may occur in patients with multiple injuries, and internal fixation of the fracture is frequently contemplated as part of early total care. However, these patients often have lower limb injuries that require them to use crutches. They therefore use their upper limbs more than normal during transfer and mobilization, and this can result in early fixation failure of the proximal humeral fracture. This is because these patients are placing nonphysiologic cyclic loads through their arm during weight-bearing. Early internal fixation of the proximal humeral fracture is therefore only recommended if the patient is able to rest his or her arm in a sling during subsequent rehabilitation.

Fractures Extending Into the Diaphysis. Extension of a proximal humeral fracture into the shaft is occasionally encountered, through either a long medial metaphyseal spike, extensive metaphyseodiaphyseal comminution, or a true segmental fracture. The proximal humeral fracture is commonly, but not invariably, extra-articular, with minimal tuberosity involvement. These uncommon injuries are unstable, and attempted nonoperative treatment is difficult since adequate splintage cannot be provided. There is a high risk of nonunion and late reconstructive surgery is complex because of the extensive fibrous union and the complex three-dimensional deformity.

Intramedullary nailing can be used to treat these injuries, but there is a substantial risk of rotator cuff dysfunction at the shoulder. Although the technique of helical plating has been used,[94,314] the early treatment of these injuries has recently been greatly simplified by the provision of longer proximal humeral locking plates, which allow bridging of comminuted areas and rigid fixation across segmental fractures (Fig. 35-35). This can be accomplished either through distal extension of a deltopectoral approach into an anterolateral approach to the humerus or through an extended deltoid-splitting approach. The deltoid insertion must be split to accommodate the longer plate, but this can be repaired after plate application without deleterious effects.

PROGNOSIS AFTER FRACTURE

The mean age of patients who sustain proximal humeral fractures is a decade younger than those who sustain hip fractures.[57,210,274] Most are living in their own homes when they

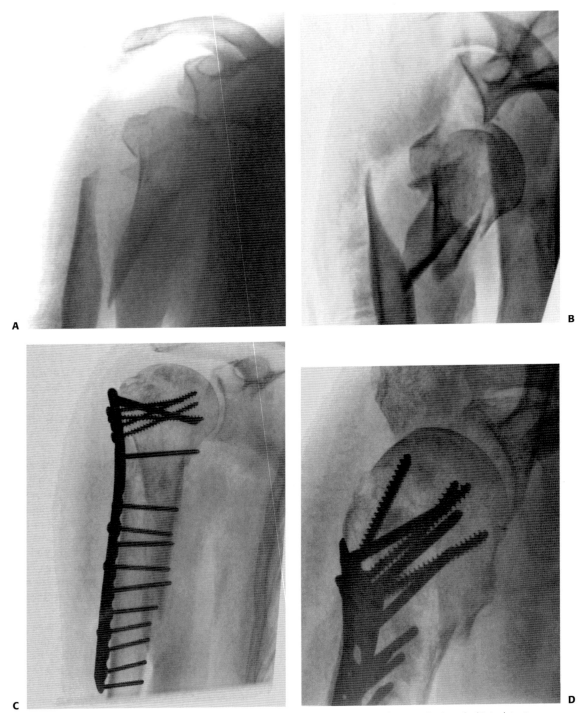

FIGURE 35-35 Fractures that extend into the diaphysis can be treated by the use of a long locking plate. In this fracture, there was also a dislocation of the humeral head with a significant humeral head-split (**A,B**). Following reduction and fixation with a long locking plate, the fracture healed without signs of osteonecrosis at 2 years (**C,D**).

sustain their injury,[57] and most are treated nonoperatively as outpatients. Despite this, 1 in 10 patients will have died within the first year after sustaining this injury, and 1 in 3 have died by 5 years.[220–222,274] The overall mortality in the first year is more than three times greater than that of the general population, and twice as great in the subsequent 4 years.[274] Paradoxically, although the highest mortality rate is seen in elderly patients following proximal humeral fracture, the risk of death

is higher in younger individuals compared with the general population. Many of the patients who sustain this injury at a younger age have risk factors for the development of premature osteoporosis including, most commonly, premature menopause, arthritides, immobility, malignancy, prolonged drug treatment (particularly steroid and anticonvulsant medication), medical comorbidities, excessive tobacco use, excessive alcohol ingestion, and neuromuscular disorders.[274,220–222] These prefracture comorbidities reflect a reduced physiological reserve in these younger patients, and this may be responsible for their curtailed survival, compared with their peers in the general population. Medical optimization of these comorbidities should be a key priority in the treatment of younger individuals who sustain low-energy fractures, especially if they require surgery to treat their fracture.

Persisting posttraumatic disability may tip patients who sustain proximal humeral fractures into social dependency[57] as a result of pain, loss of use of the limb, and reduced mobility, from difficulty in using walking aids. These patients are also at substantially greater risk of sustaining other osteoporotic fractures,[256] and careful consideration should be given to secondary preventative treatment to reduce this risk after the index proximal humeral fracture.

COMPLICATIONS

There are numerous complications of proximal humerus fractures that have been described, but most are rare. Complications may occur as an inevitable consequence of a more severe injury or as a result of treatment. The latter may be because of errors in procedure selection or in the surgery provided. Implant-specific operative complications have been described in the previous sections and will not be discussed further here.

Attempts have been made to classify complications after these fractures, for those patients receiving delayed treatment using an arthroplasty (Table 35-13). Some postinjury complications are not considered in this classification,[26] although it does serve to highlight the three most common sources of complications (osteonecrosis, nonunion, and tuberosity malunion causing cuff dysfunction), which may compromise the functional recovery after this injury, as well as highlighting the poor prognosis associated with arthroplasty procedures in which osteotomy of the greater tuberosity is required. These three complications are considered in detail, together with an overview of the range of other complications and their treatment, as follows.

Osteonecrosis

Humeral Head

Osteonecrosis of the humeral head occurs as a consequence of loss of perfusion of the articular surface and subchondral bone, which undergo involutional change, leading to articular collapse and fibrosis. This condition may or may not be symptomatic,[305] and the head may collapse completely, or there may be partial involvement, with or without articular collapse.[14,123] The spec-

trum of presentation, the lack of precise radiological guidelines for its assessment, and the wide range of treatments make estimation of its prevalence difficult (Tables 35-6, 35-8, 35-9, 35-10, and 35-11).

This complication may be an inevitable complication of the injury, because of the irrevocable injury to the head blood supply. Three- and four-part fractures and fracture-dislocations are therefore at higher risk than are one- and two-part fractures. It may also occur as a consequence of operative treatment, because of excessive fracture manipulation and stripping of soft tissues, which contain the residual vascularity to the articular segment. Some individuals may also be predisposed to this complication, either through their poor physiologic state, through their medical comorbidities and drug treatment, or through smoking and alcohol abuse. The pathophysiology of this condition is incompletely understood at present and other unknown factors may also be important. It does not invariably develop even if the head is completely denuded of blood supply,[14,103,123] whereas some cases appear to occur "sporadically" after a relatively innocuous injury.

The presentation is usually with pain, stiffness, and loss of function, typically after a "latent" period, where function has been satisfactory. Radiologically, the changes vary from patchy and segmental humeral head sclerosis, to complete humeral head resorption and collapse (Fig. 35-36). The differential diagnosis is from posttraumatic osteoarthrosis, in which the degree of collapse is usually less severe, and from chronic joint sepsis, which, if clinically suspected, should be excluded by bacteriologic examination of a joint aspirate. CT and especially MRI are useful in the evaluation of the extent and severity of head involvement.

In some cases, the osteonecrosis may not be associated with severe symptoms, and nonoperative treatment is advisable.[305] Core decompression may occasionally be indicated for patients who have early radiologic changes,[201] but most patients have advanced collapse and are symptomatic by the time they present.[101] Hemiarthroplasty is indicated where symptoms are debilitating and function is poor.[28,68] This technique is much more likely to be successful if there is no associated malunion that requires treatment.[101] If there are reciprocal glenoid changes, a total joint arthroplasty may be more successful in relieving pain and restoring motion.[68] Where there is a severe associated tuberosity malunion or cuff tear, reverse shoulder arthroplasty may provide better function, although comparative studies have not yet been performed to evaluate this.

Tuberosity

Osteonecrosis may also occur in one or both tuberosities after fracture, regardless of the viability of the humeral head (Fig.

TABLE 35-13	Boileau et al.'s Classification of Complications of Proximal Humeral Fractures and Their Recommended Treatment	
Class	Description	Recommended Treatment
1	Cephalic collapse (ostenecrosis)	Conventional arthroplasty
2	Neglected (locked) fracture-dislocations	Conventional arthroplasty
3	Nonunion of the head-neck segment	Plate and bone graft if possible. Reverse shoulder arthroplasty if not reconstructable
4	Head-tuberosity malunion or nonunion	Reverse shoulder arthroplasty

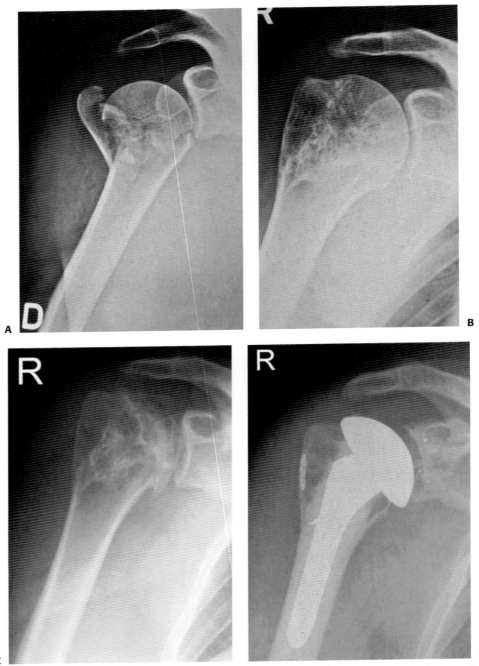

FIGURE 35-36 Osteonecrosis may occur after both nonoperative and operative treatment and is normally treated using a conventional hemiarthroplasty (**A–D**). *(continues)*

35-36). Resorption, sclerosis, and collapse may be seen after fracture of the greater tuberosity (the "disappearing tuberosity") and may also occur in the lesser tuberosity. It may occur after two-, three-, or four-part fractures and may follow nonoperative treatment, internal fixation, or arthroplasty. This complication is predictable, because until a fractured tuberosity unites, it only receives blood supply through residual periosteal attachments and its cuff attachments, which are often relatively avascular in elderly patients. The patient usually has debilitating shoulder pain and loss of function, with clinical signs of rotator cuff weakness and dysfunction. Subclinical forms probably occur frequently, and the precise pathology has not yet been fully elucidated. At present, there is no known treatment for this complication.

Nonunion

Nonunion of the head to the shaft of the proximal humerus is a rare but debilitating complication.[60] The normal time for clinical union of a proximal humeral fracture is typically 4 to 8 weeks. It is therefore logical to define nonunion to be present if a fracture site is still mobile 16 weeks postinjury, although 6 months has been used in some studies. In the only study to have evaluated the epidemiology of this complication, the over-

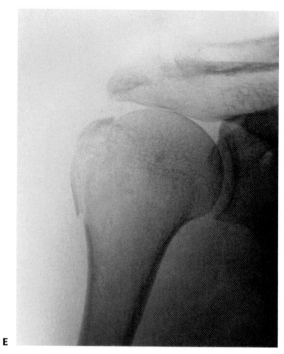
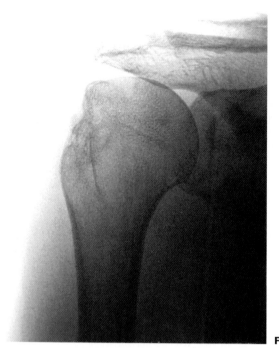

E   **F**

FIGURE 35-36 *(continued)* Osteonecrosis of the greater tuberosity (the "disappearing tuberosity") is also encountered, and is not amenable to treatment (**E** and **F**).

all reported incidence was 1.1%, although this rose to 8% if metaphyseal comminution was present and 10% if there was displacement of the surgical neck.[60] Nonunion of one or both tuberosities to the head is less common and is considered together with tuberosity malunions later section below.

Although nonunion may occur sporadically, in most instances there are identifiable patient-, fracture-, or treatment-related risk factors: Common patient-related factors include osteoporosis, poor physiologic state, medical comorbidities and drug treatment, heavy smoking, and alcohol abuse.[118,270,300] Shoulder inflammatory or degenerative joint disease, causing preinjury shoulder stiffness, may also predispose to nonunion.[258] The fractures most at risk of nonunion are two-, three-, or four-part displaced fractures, where there is no residual cortical contact between the humeral head and shaft, and those where there is marked metaphyseal comminution.[60] The complete disruption of periosteal sleeve leads to mechanical instability, and soft tissue interposition of periosteum, muscle, and the tendinous portion of the long head of biceps may also inhibit callus formation.[87,205] During nonoperative treatment, it is stated that the use of hanging casts, which distract the fracture, and overzealous shoulder mobilization may predispose to nonunion.[209] Poor surgical technique with extensive soft tissue stripping and a mechanically unstable fracture reduction and fixation may also predispose to nonunion.

In clinical practice the diagnosis of a nonunion is seldom a problem. Pain, stiffness, and loss of function in the arm are the most constant complaints. The pain tends to be severe and debilitating and is aggravated by use of the arm and shoulder, because most movement occurs at the site of the nonunion. This is not amenable to splinting, and use of a sling further compromises shoulder function. On examination, the patient often has a "pseudoparalysis" of the deltoid, rotator cuff, and periscapular muscles, with a flail arm. Attempted movement of

the shoulder is painful and any motion occurs in the fracture site rather than the glenohumeral joint. Radiologically, there is resorption and widening of the fracture line, often with massive bone resorption (Fig. 35-37).

Further investigation should include CT to confirm the nonunion and assess the state of the humeral head articular cartilage, the degree of separation and healing of any associated tuberosity fractures, and the feasibility of reduction and fixation of the fracture. If surgical reconstruction has been previously performed, infection should be excluded at the site of the nonunion by culture of an aspirate performed under ultrasound control.[68]

Sustained pain relief and restoration of function after the development of this complication can only be provided by operative treatment. This is technically challenging, because of capsular contractures and scarring from previous surgery, bone loss, distorted anatomy, and osteopenia of the humeral head.[87,88] Unfortunately, many patients with established nonunions are too elderly, frail, or medically unfit to undergo this type of surgery and the prolonged shoulder rehabilitation program thereafter. Pain management and activity modification are all that can be offered to these patients.

All medically fit patients should be offered a surgical reconstruction. Attempts have been made to classify these according to their anatomic site and the degree of bone loss.[44] In practice, the chief decision is whether the nonunion is amenable to an attempt at ORIF or whether a humeral head procedure is required. The decision as to which form of treatment is most appropriate is individualized, but absence of infection, adequate humeral head bone stock, lack of severe tuberosity malunion, and absence of degenerative change or collapse of the articular surface are mandatory for an attempted open reduction and plate fixation.

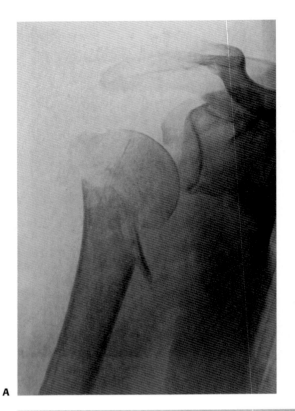

A

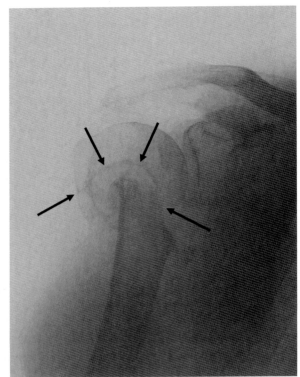

B

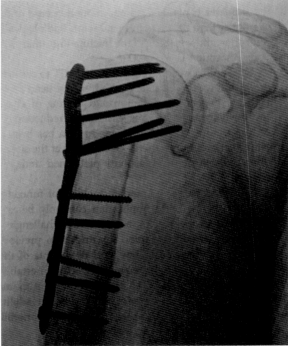

C

FIGURE 35-37 Nonunion after nonoperative treatment of a translated surgical neck fracture (**A**) at 3 months (**B**) is a debilitating complication. There is massive metaphyseal bone loss from the "windshield-wiper" effect of the shaft in the head (*arrow*). Reduction and internal fixation was achieved by excision of the nonunion and shortening to bayonet the shaft fragment into the humeral head (**C**).

Open Reduction and Internal Fixation

The use of intramedullary nailing with bone grafting has been described to treat nonunions,[118,205] but since this technique provides less rigid fixation at the site of the nonunion, the technique is less commonly used than open reduction and plate fixation. The exposure is similar to that used for primary plate fixation. The nonunion is exposed and taken down by excision of the fibrous union and pseudocapsule and removal of any devitalized bone fragments. Arthrolysis of a stiff joint may be required, which aids in subsequent rehabilitation and limits force transmission at the nonunion site.[118] However, care must be taken to avoid devitalization by excessive soft tissue stripping to expose the nonunion. It is essential to ensure that the bone ends are bleeding and the medullary canal is clear of fibrous debris.

If there is minimal bone loss, the bone ends may be reduced

in a relatively anatomic fashion. This is unusual, and more commonly there is extensive metaphyseal bone loss because of the "windscreen-wiper" effect of the shaft at the site of the mobile synovial nonunion. Satisfactory viable bone contact can usually only be achieved by impaling the relatively narrow bayonet of the shaft into the sheath of the wide humeral head metaphysis. The nonunion site is typically autografted with either cortico-cancellous strips of iliac crest bone graft, an intramedullary bone plug, or a fibular strut graft.[301] This may result in significant humeral shortening, but this is usually well tolerated. If maintenance of length is deemed to be important in a younger patient, this requires more extensive grafting of the metaphyseal defect, using autogenous bone, augmented with fibular strut grafts.

Provisional fixation is achieved with K-wires and definitive plate fixation is then performed. A locking proximal humeral plate is the ideal implant in this situation, given the relatively poor proximal humeral bone stock. Postoperative rehabilitation follows the standard guidelines as for primary fixation.

The treatment of any associated tuberosity fractures depends on whether they are healed and their degree of displacement. Ununited fragments may be amenable to reduction and stabilization using the osteosuturing techniques previously described, whereas healed, minimally displaced tuberosity fragments do not require adjuvant treatment. Tuberosity osteotomy may occasionally be used if there is a severe malunion, but this should be avoided if at all possible because of the risk of subsequent nonunion of the fragment.

Most series that have reported on head-conserving reconstruction of established nonunions have reported a high success rate in achieving union, often with a good eventual functional outcome.* However, a high rate of postoperative complications is to be expected, which may require further surgery, and the functional recovery time is usually prolonged.

Humeral Head Arthroplasty

This technique is preferred if there is poor humeral head and metaphyseal bone stock and cavitation, severe tuberosity malunion or displaced nonunion, or collapse and degenerative change of the humeral articular surface. The main aim of treatment is pain relief, and the eventual poor functional recovery is often worse than for a primary arthroplasty. Although hemiarthroplasty is most commonly used, total shoulder replacement may be indicated if there is glenoid articular surface wear or defects. The functional outcome is poor when osteotomy of the tuberosities is performed, and this should be avoided if possible.[26,27] It has been suggested that reverse shoulder arthroplasty may improve the shoulder function in patients with nonunions associated with severe tuberosity malunions,[26] although comparative studies have not yet been reported.

Most studies that have reported on the use of arthroplasty to treat nonunion suggest that the procedure may be effective in reducing or eliminating pain but with a high rate of complications, often requiring further surgery and a disappointing functional recovery.[5,26,118,205,214] It remains to be seen in future clinical studies whether the use of reverse shoulder arthroplasty will improve the outcome over conventional arthroplasty in the treatment of this challenging complication.[30] At present, an arthroplasty should only be considered for patients who have poorly controlled pain and have nonunions that are not amenable to reduction and internal fixation.

*References 5,87,88,118,185,205,270,282,300,301.

Malunion

Some degree of malunion is inevitable in displaced proximal humeral fractures that are treated nonoperatively. It may occur after surgery through intraoperative malreduction or through inadequate fixation that allows secondary redisplacement. Two types of malunion are distinguishable and often coexist: malunion of the head on the shaft either through impaction, translation, rotation, or angulatory deformity is common and is well tolerated in most patients. Malunion of one of both tuberosities is also common and well tolerated in older patients with limited functional expectations. However, in physiologically younger patients, the altered shoulder mechanics produced by the defunctioning and tearing of the rotator cuff tendons and mechanical impingement of the displaced tuberosity fragments often produces an unacceptable degree of pain and functional compromise. Where the two conditions coexist, it is therefore most often the tuberosity malunion that is symptomatic.

A symptomatic malunion will typically give rise to shoulder pain, which is typically localized over the anterior deltoid. The pain is typically aggravated by use of the arm, particularly in forward flexion, abduction, and internal rotation movements. This frequently results in impairment of the patient's ability to perform normal daily activities and leisure pursuits. It is important to try to distinguish the cause of symptoms on physical examination, because rotator cuff impingement and tears, post-traumatic shoulder stiffness, acromioclavicular joint dysfunction, biceps tendinopathy, and complex region pain syndromes may all be contributory to symptomatology. In addition to specific clinical testing of these structures, a good response to subacromial local anesthetic tends to localize symptoms to the subacromial space. If infection is suspected, appropriate hematologic studies and bacteriologic examination of a joint aspirate are warranted.

The complex anatomy of most malunions is best appreciated using CT with three-dimensional reconstructions. MRI may be useful in evaluating the state of the rotator cuff and capsule, but interpretation of images is frequently hampered by the distorted anatomy. It may be useful in detecting radiologically occult early osteonecrosis. As with nonunion, attempts have been made to classify this complication,[17,26] but most often treatment is individualized based on the patient's physiologic status and level of symptoms, the anatomy of the injury, and the likelihood of success from a surgical reconstructive procedure.

The results of corrective surgery are unpredictable, and for older patients a trial of nonoperative treatment is advisable. A shoulder rehabilitation program, pain management, and activity modification may reduce the symptoms to acceptable levels and improve function. The patients who remain symptomatic despite this treatment and request surgery should be carefully counseled about the likely limited gains from surgery, as well as the significant risk of complications. The technical details of the operative treatment according to the anatomic pattern of malunion are discussed next.

Two-Part Greater Tuberosity Malunion or Displaced Nonunion

Isolated malunions and nonunions of the greater tuberosity fracture are relatively common but are usually debilitating only in younger, physically active patients. The tuberosity retracts posterosuperomedially by the deforming forces of its attached cuff muscles, but the articular surface is unaffected. The posterior displacement may produce a bony block to external rotation, whilst superior displacement may block abduction and lead to subacromial impingement. Tuberosity malposition can also produce cuff dysfunction, attrition, and tears.[278] Arthroscopic assessment may provide useful extra information and may occasionally be amenable to arthroscopic mobilization and fixation in the presence of a relatively mobile nonunion.[98]

Surgical reconstruction is performed using a deltoid-splitting approach to gain access to the displaced tuberosity, which is usually fixed and immobile. The fragment is mobilized by excision of the fibrous nonunion or osteotomy of a malunion. An extensive posterior capsular release or excision and a rotator interval dissection are often required to mobilize the fragment sufficient for it to be reduced to its decorticated native bed. Fixation is achieved using either interosseous sutures or screw fixation, as for an acute fracture. It is important to test the repair by fully internally rotating the arm, to ensure the repair is not unduly tight. An acromioplasty and subacromial decompression should be performed if the subacromial space is narrowed, to reduce the risk of later impingement. If the repair is tight, the arm is immobilized for 4 weeks in neutral or slight external rotation, to reduce the risk of failure of the repair. The postoperative treatment protocol is otherwise identical to the treatment of an acute fracture. There are a few reports of the results of treatment of greater tuberosity malunions,[17] which report substantial pain relief and functional improvement but with prolonged recovery times.

Two-Part Lesser Tuberosity Malunion or Displaced Nonunion

Two-part lesser tuberosity fractures are frequently diagnosed late or missed at initial presentation.[72,176,215,218] The displaced fragment may block internal rotation or cause subscapularis weakness, and occasionally this may be amenable to arthroscopic treatment.[126] The fragment is exposed through a deltopectoral approach and mobilized with capsular releases as for malunion of the greater tuberosity. ORIF with anatomic reduction of associated articular involvement can be performed with heavy interosseous sutures or screws, dependent on the fragment size.

Two-Part Surgical Neck Malunion

An isolated surgical neck malunion is seldom a cause of severe debility unless the humeral head heals with a varus deformity sufficient to cause secondary cuff impingement or dysfunction.[15,68,278,279,286] The deformity is characteristically a complex angulatory (varus or rarely valgus) and internal rotational malunion, with translation of the shaft anteromedially.[17,68,278,279]

Operative treatment is seldom indicated except in younger patients who are still symptomatic after a prolonged shoulder rehabilitation program. If clinically indicated, osteotomy to correct the deformity and locking plate fixation are performed.[15,286] Open capsular release is usually performed if there is significant associated posttraumatic stiffness and the osteotomy is usually bone grafted. The results from this technique are satisfactory in most reported series.[17,286]

Three- and Four-Part Malunions

In a minority of cases where there is no osteonecrosis and the deformity is less severe, soft tissue releases and an osteotomy of the fracture fragments, followed by internal fixation, may be attempted. A successful outcome can only be achieved if there is a good correction of both osseous and soft tissue abnormalities.[16,17] However, most symptomatic malunions are complex three-dimensional deformities, which can usually only be treated by prosthetic replacement (Fig. 35-38). The integrity of the glenoid articular surface determines whether humeral hemiarthroplasty or total shoulder arthroplasty is performed. The chief indication is for pain relief and the functional gains are often minimal. Extensive capsular excision is usually required, and any associated rotator cuff tears should be repaired.

In some cases of tuberosity malposition, a greater tuberosity osteotomy can be avoided by using a small stem that is shifted in the medullary canal to compensate for the tuberosity malposition or by the use of an eccentric modular humeral head. If the normal relationship between the tuberosities and the humeral head cannot be achieved, either a tuberosity osteotomy and conventional arthroplasty, or a reverse shoulder arthroplasty should be performed. There may also be a role for the use of a resurfacing humeral hemiarthroplasty in selected cases, as this does not require the use of an intramedullary stem for fixation. Three quarters of the humeral head must remain after reaming for this technique to be used, to allow secure fixation and prosthetic bone ingrowth.

The available case-series literature for treatment of complex multipart malunions is scarce, but the results of prosthetic arthroplasty are inferior to those of prosthetic treatment of similar acute fractures. In particular, the requirement for tuberosity osteotomy is associated with a poor prognosis.[26] Pain relief is usually achieved, but shoulder range of motion and strength are often limited.* The results of the use of reverse shoulder arthroplasty for the treatment of severe malunion are still largely unknown in the longer term, although this is a promising new technique and the results of comparative outcome studies are awaited.[30]

Other Complications

Posttraumatic Shoulder Stiffness

The causes of posttraumatic shoulder stiffness are often multifactorial: Although capsular contracture is usually the main cause of refractory stiffness, other factors may include fracture malunion, complex regional pain syndrome, thoracic outlet syndrome, mechanical impingement of implants, and rotator cuff dysfunction from impingement or tears. These factors are poorly described in the contemporary literature but may nevertheless be contributory to persistent stiffness after fracture.

The most characteristic finding is of restriction of movement in a "capsular pattern," with generalized stiffness but selectively greater loss of shoulder abduction and external rotation. The initial treatment is nonoperative with shoulder rehabilitation to attempt to regain movement by selective stretching exercises. Most patients improve to a degree on this regime, and recovery of movement is often protracted over the first year after injury. A plateau in recovery is usually heralded by the presence of a firm "woody" feel on terminal stretching exercises, suggesting a mechanical block to movement. Distension arthrography is useful in stretching and rupturing the capsule in idiopathic ad-

---

*References 5,16,17,26,33,34,68,85,192,214,292.

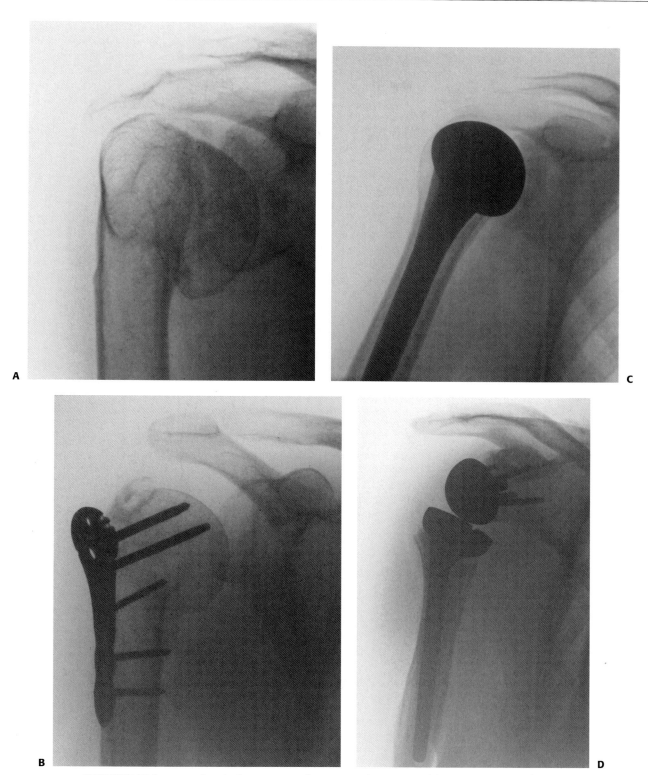

FIGURE 35-38 Symptomatic malunion may occur after nonoperative treatment (**A**) or poor operative reduction and fixation (**B**). In most instances, treatment should involve humeral head replacement avoiding osteotomy of the greater tuberosity if possible (**C**). In this case, treatment was followed by symptomatic loosening at 3 years with massive rotator cuff tear. A revision to a reverse shoulder arthroplasty was successful in eliminating shoulder pain and improving function (**D**).

hesive capsulitis, but it is the author's experience that this procedure is less effective in the post-traumatic shoulder.

In malunited fractures, it is important to distinguish whether the stiffness is because of soft tissue contracture or the malunion itself. An examination under anesthesia under fluoroscopy followed by an arthroscopic examination of the shoulder is often required to distinguish these apart. If the malunion is considered to be the cause of the stiffness, it is unlikely that a soft tissue release will be effective and consideration is given to corrective osteotomy as described previously.

In patients with refractory posttraumatic stiffness without malunion, treatment with manipulation under anesthesia is usually performed. This procedure is contraindicated in patients with uncertain fracture healing and in patients with severe osteoporosis, where there is a substantial risk of humeral shaft fracture during manipulation. If manipulation is unsuccessful in regaining sufficient movement, this should be followed by arthroscopic release of capsulitic tissue from the rotator interval, circumferential intra-articular capsular releases, subacromial decompression, and removal of impinging metalwork.[37,128,180] It is important to check for restoration of movement at each stage of the release and to measure the final on-table range of movement at the end of the procedure. The use of a continuous passive movement machine with regional anesthesia may be useful in retaining movement in the early postoperative period. Prolonged physiotherapy is often required thereafter to consolidate the improved range of movement.

Infection

Infection is relatively rare in the shoulder even after surgical repair using open methods. This is because of the rich vascularity to this region and the good soft tissue coverage.[50,136] The precise prevalence of this complication is difficult to evaluate, because most reported case series of operative treatment are retrospective. Although infection is usually regarded to be a postsurgical complication, it may occasionally develop after nonoperative treatment. This is more likely in thin, debilitated patients, either from infection of the fracture hematoma, or in those with displaced surgical neck fractures from pressure on the anterior soft tissues.

Most infections are encountered after surgery and the risk is likely to be increased in thin and debilitated patients, with a more severe soft tissue injury and grade of fracture, prolonged surgery time, poor surgical technique, and operator inexperience. It is important to distinguish superficial from deep infections. Superficial infections are common, confined to the integumental layers, and do not form a purulent collection. Superficial pin track infections are a particularly common complication of percutaneous pinning of fractures.[133,152] In contrast, deep infections often form a sinus with a deep purulent collection that extends to the implant. These fail to resolve without further surgical treatment. Ultrasound and MRI may be useful in assessing for the presence of a deep collection.

Superficial infections with a bacteriologically proved growth of pathogenic organisms invariably resolve with antibiotic therapy. It is often difficult to distinguish between a superficial infection and a wound hematoma, especially if cultures are equivocal. Broad-spectrum antibiotic therapy and topical dressings are frequently given empirically following discharge from hospital, and most superficial infections resolve on this regimen. More severe superficial infections should be treated with parenteral antibiotics, guided by wound cultures. An ultrasound-guided aspirate is useful in distinguishing a deep purulent infection from a sterile wound hematoma. Large sterile wound hematomas require surgical drainage, as wound dehiscence may otherwise occur, with the risk of subsequent bacterial colonization and deep infection.

Deep infections may occur either early or as a delayed phe-

TABLE 35-14   **Currently Unanswered Questions in the Treatment of Proximal Humeral Fractures**

Area of Controversy		Questions
Classification		What is the best method of classification for these fractures?
Outcome assessment		What is the best patient-orientated outcome measure?
Fractures	One-part	When should the patient be allowed to mobilize their shoulder after these fractures?
		What is the most appropriate rehabilitation program?
	Two-part greater tuberosity	What degree of displacement of the fracture should be the threshold for surgical stabilization?
		Which is the best operative technique to treat these injuries, screw fixation or interosseous suturing?
		Does the severity of the associated rotator cuff injury influence the outcome?
	Two-part surgical neck	Is operative treatment better than nonoperative treatment in the elderly?
		What is the best operative technique to treat these injuries, intramedullary nailing or open reduction and internal fixation?
	Impacted valgus fractures	What degree of valgus angulation should be the threshold for operative intervention?
	Varus fractures	What degree of varus angulation should be the threshold for operative intervention?
	Three- and four-part	Is operative treatment better than nonoperative treatment in displaced three- and four-part fractures in the elderly?
		Which is the best operative technique to treat these fractures, open reduction and internal fixation, minimally invasive fixation, or arthroplasty?
		Are locking plates better than conventional plates in the treatment of these injuries?
		What is the role of bone grafts and bone substitutes in the treatment of these injuries?
		Does reverse shoulder arthroplasty produce better results than conventional arthroplasty?

nomenon, as with any implant-related infection. Early sepsis with a stable implant should be treated with a protocol of repeated surgical irrigation and debridement and with prolonged parenteral and then oral antibiotic therapy. The sepsis may be refractory to this treatment protocol, and in these circumstances a radical débridement with implant removal may be required to eradicate the infection, thereby allowing later revision surgery.

Late deep infection may occur several years after a humeral head arthroplasty. It may follow a transient bacteremia, and the organism may be of low virulence or be antibiotic resistant.[54,288] Débridement, metalwork removal, spacer insertion, and antibiotic therapy may help to suppress or eradicate infection. Delayed reimplantation may be possible if the infection can be eradicated.[54,288]

FUTURE DIRECTIONS AND CONCLUSIONS

Most proximal humeral fractures are stable injuries of the aging population, which heal with a pain-free, functional shoulder after nonoperative treatment. There are many unanswered questions in the treatment of the minority of more complex injuries and those that occur in younger and more active patients (Table 35-14). To meet this challenge, the aim must be to produce more robust and reliable standardized systems of classification and patient-orientated outcome measures. Only when these are available will surgeons be able to collaborate to produce the well-designed comparative clinical outcome studies, to enable proper evidence-based management of these injuries.

ACKNOWLEDGMENT

The author wishes to thank Kenn C. Godley for his assistance in the preparation of this manuscript.

REFERENCES

1. Abbott L, Dec J, Saunders J, et al. Surgical approaches to the shoulder joint. J Bone Joint Surg Am 1949;31A:235–255.
2. Abu-Rajab RB, Stansfield BW, Nunn T, et al. Reattachment of the tuberosities of the humerus following hemiarthroplasty for four-part fracture. J Bone Joint Surg Br 2006; 88B:1539–1544.
3. Adedapo AO, Ikpeme JO. The results of internal fixation of three- and four-part proximal humeral fractures with the Polarus nail. Injury 2001;32:115–121.
4. Agudelo J, Schurmann M, Stahel P, et al. Analysis of efficacy and failure in proximal humerus fractures treated with locking plates. J Orthop Trauma 2007;21:676–681.
5. Antuna SA, Sperling JW, Sanchez-Sotelo J, et al. Shoulder arthroplasty for proximal humeral nonunions. J Shoulder Elbow Surg 2002;11:114–121.
6. As'ad M, Thet MM, Chambler AF. Arthroscopic treatment for malunion of a head-splitting proximal humeral fracture: the need for adequate initial radiologic investigation. J Shoulder Elbow Surg 2007;16:e1–e2.
7. Aschauer ERH. Four-part proximal humeral fractures: ORIF. In: Warner JJP, Iannotti JP, Gerber C, eds. Complex and Revision Problems in Shoulder Surgery. 2nd Ed. Philadephia: Lippincott-Raven Publishers, 2005, 289–309.
8. Bahrs C, Lingenfelter E, Fischer F, et al. Mechanism of injury and morphology of the greater tuberosity fracture. J Shoulder Elbow Surg 2006;15:140–147.
9. Banco SP, Andrisani D, Ramsey M, et al. The parachute technique: valgus impaction osteotomy for two-part fractures of the surgical neck of the humerus. J Bone Joint Surg Am 2001;83A(suppl 2, pt 1):38–42.
10. Baron JA, Barrett JA, Karagas MR. The epidemiology of peripheral fractures. Bone 1996; 183(suppl):209S–213S.
11. Baron YM, Brincat M, Galea R, et al. The epidemiology of osteoporotic fractures in a Mediterranean country. Calcif Tissue Int 1994;54:365–369.
12. Barth JR, Burkhart SS. Arthroscopic capsular release after hemiarthroplasty of the shoulder for fracture: a new treatment paradigm. Arthroscopy 2005;21:1150.
13. Bartlett CS III, Hausman MR, Witschi TH. Gunshot wounds to the shoulder. Orthop Clin North Am 1995;26:37–53.
14. Bastian JD, Hertel R. Initial postfracture humeral head ischemia does not predict development of necrosis. J Shoulder Elbow Surg 2008;17:2–8.
15. Benegas E, Zoppi FA, Ferreira Filho AA, et al. Surgical treatment of varus malunion

16. of the proximal humerus with valgus osteotomy. J Shoulder Elbow Surg 2007;16: 55–59.
16. Beredjiklian PK, Iannotti JP. Treatment of proximal humerus fracture malunion with prosthetic arthroplasty. Instr Course Lect 1998;47:135–140.
17. Beredjiklian PK, Iannotti JP, Norris TR, et al. Operative treatment of malunion of a fracture of the proximal aspect of the humerus. J Bone Joint Surg Am 1998;80A: 1484–1497.
18. Bernard J, Charalambides C, Aderinto J, et al. Early failure of intramedullary nailing for proximal humeral fractures. Injury 2000;31:789–792.
19. Bernstein J, Adler LM, Blank JE, et al. Evaluation of the Neer system of classification of proximal humeral fractures with computerized tomographic scans and plain radiographs. J Bone Joint Surg Am 1996;78A:1371–1375.
20. Bertoft ES, Lundh I, Ringqvist I. Physiotherapy after fracture of the proximal end of the humerus. Comparison between two methods. Scand J Rehabil Med 1984;16:11–16.
21. Bhandari M, Matthys G, McKee MD. Four-part fractures of the proximal humerus. J Orthop Trauma 2004;18:126–127.
22. Bhatia DN, de Beer JF, van Rooyen KS. The bony partial articular surface tendon avulsion lesion: an arthroscopic technique for fixation of the partially avulsed greater tuberosity fracture. Arthroscopy 2007;23:786.
23. Bjorkenheim JM, Pajarinen J, Savolainen V. Internal fixation of proximal humeral fractures with a locking compression plate: a retrospective evaluation of 72 patients followed for a minimum of 1 year. Acta Orthop Scand 2004;75:741–745.
24. Blom S, Dahlback LO. Nerve injuries in dislocations of the shoulder joint and fracture of the neck of the humerus. Acta Chir Scand 136, 461–466. 1970.
25. Boileau P, Caligaris-Cordero B, Payeur F, et al. [Prognostic factors during rehabilitation after shoulder prostheses for fracture]. Rev Chir Orthop Reparatrice Appar Mot 1999; 85:106–116.
26. Boileau P, Chuinard C, Le Huec JC, et al. Proximal humerus fracture sequelae: impact of a new radiographic classification on arthroplasty. Clin Orthop Relat Res 2006;442: 121–130.
27. Boileau P, Krishnan SG, Tinsi L, et al. Tuberosity malposition and migration: reasons for poor outcomes after hemiarthroplasty for displaced fractures of the proximal humerus. J Shoulder Elbow Surg 2002;11:401–412.
28. Boileau P, Trojani C, Walch G, et al. Shoulder arthroplasty for the treatment of the sequelae of fractures of the proximal humerus. J Shoulder Elbow Surg 2001;10: 299–308.
29. Boileau P, Walch G. The three-dimensional geometry of the proximal humerus. Implications for surgical technique and prosthetic design. J Bone Joint Surg Br 1997;79: 857–865.
30. Boileau P, Watkinson D, Hatzidakis AM, et al. Neer Award 2005: The Grammont reverse shoulder prosthesis: results in cuff tear arthritis, fracture sequelae, and revision arthroplasty. J Shoulder Elbow Surg 2006;15:527–540.
31. Bono CM, Renard R, Levine RG, et al. Effect of displacement of fractures of the greater tuberosity on the mechanics of the shoulder. J Bone Joint Surg Br 2001;83B: 1056–1062.
32. Borges AF. Relaxed skin tension lines. Dermatol Clin 1989;7:169–177.
33. Bosch U, Fremerey RW, Skutek M, et al. [Hemi-arthroplasty—primary or secondary measure for 3- and 4-fragment fractures of the proximal humerus in the elderly?]. Unfallchirurg 1996;99:656–664.
34. Bosch U, Skutek M, Fremerey RW, et al. Outcome after primary and secondary hemiarthroplasty in elderly patients with fractures of the proximal humerus. J Shoulder Elbow Surg 1998;7:479–484.
35. Brooks CH, Revell WJ, Heatley FW. Vascularity of the humeral head after proximal humeral fractures. An anatomical cadaver study. J Bone Joint Surg Br 1993;75B: 132–136.
36. Brown TD, Bigliani LU. Complications with humeral head replacement. Orthop Clin North Am 2000;31:77–90.
37. Burkhart SS. Arthroscopic subscapularis tenolysis: a technique for treating refractory glenohumeral stiffness following open reduction and internal fixation of a displaced three-part proximal humerus fracture. Arthroscopy 1996;12:87–91.
38. Burkhead WZ Jr, Skedros JG, O'Rourke PJ, et al. A novel double-row rotator cuff repair exceeds strengths of conventional repairs. Clin Orthop Relat Res 2007;461:106–113.
39. Burkhead WJ, Scheinberg RBG. Surgical anatomy of the axillary nerve. J Shoulder Elbow Surg 1992;1:31–36.
40. Cadet ER, Ahmad CS. Arthroscopic reduction and suture anchor fixation for a displaced greater tuberosity fracture: a case report. J Shoulder Elbow Surg 2007;16:e6–e9.
41. Calvo E, de Miquel I, de la Cruz JJ, et al. Percutaneous fixation of displaced proximal humeral fractures: indications based on the correlation between clinical and radiographic results. J Shoulder Elbow Surg 2007;16:774–781.
42. Cattaneo R, Catagni MA, Guerreschi F. Applications of the Ilizarov method in the humerus. Lengthenings and nonunions. Hand Clin 1993;9:729–739.
43. Cetik O, Uslu M, Acar HI, et al. Is there a safe area for the axillary nerve in the deltoid muscle? A cadaveric study. J Bone Joint Surg Am 2006;88A:2395–2399.
44. Checchia SL, Doneux P, Miyazaki AN, et al. Classification of nonunions of the proximal humerus. Int Orthop 2000;24:217–220.
45. Chen CY, Chao EK, Tu YK, et al. Closed management and percutaneous fixation of unstable proximal humerus fractures. J Trauma 1998;45:1039–1045.
46. Chervu A, Quinones Baldrich WJ. Vascular complications in orthopedic surgery. Clin Orthop Relat Res 1988;275–288.
47. Clifford PC. Fractures of the neck of the humerus: a review of the late results. Injury 1980;12:91–95.
48. Codman EA. The Shoulder. Rupture of the Supraspinatus Tendon and Other Lesions in or about the Subacromial Bursa. Boston: privately printed, 1934.
49. Codman EA. The Shoulder. Rupture of the Supraspinatus Tendon and Other Lesions in or about the Subacromial Bursa. Boston: Thomas Todd, 2008.
50. Connor PM, Flatow EL. Complications of internal fixation of proximal humeral fractures. Instr Course Lect 1997;46:25–37.
51. Copeland S, Levy O, Brownlaw W. Resurfacing arthroplasty of the shoulder. Techniques in shoulder and elbow surgery 2003;4:199–210.
52. Cornell CN. Tension-band wiring supplemented by lag-screw fixation of proximal humerus fractures. Orthop Rev 1994;(suppl):19–23.
53. Cornell CN, Levine D, Pagnani MJ. Internal fixation of proximal humerus fractures using the screw-tension band technique. J Orthop Trauma 1994;8:23–27.

54. Coste JS, Reig S, Trojani C, et al. The management of infection in arthroplasty of the shoulder. J Bone Joint Surg Br 2004;86B:65–69.

55. CourtBrown CM, Caesar B. Epidemiology of adult fractures: a review. Injury 2006;37: 691–697.

56. CourtBrown CM, Cattermole H, McQueen MM. Impacted valgus fractures B1.1. of the proximal humerus. The results of nonoperative treatment. J Bone Joint Surg Br 2002; 84B:504–508.

57. CourtBrown CM, Garg A, McQueen MM. The epidemiology of proximal humeral fractures. Acta Orthop Scand 2001;72:365–371.

58. CourtBrown CM, Garg A, McQueen MM. The translated two-part fracture of the proximal humerus. Epidemiology and outcome in the older patient. J Bone Joint Surg Br 2001;83:799–804.

59. CourtBrown CM, McQueen MM. The impacted varus A2.2. proximal humeral fracture: prediction of outcome and results of nonoperative treatment in 99 patients. Acta Orthop Scand 2004;75:736–740.

60. CourtBrown CM, McQueen MM. Nonunions of the proximal humerus: their prevalence and functional outcome. J Trauma 2008;64:1517–1521.

61. Cummings SR, Melton LJ. Epidemiology and outcomes of osteoporotic fractures. Lancet 2002;359:1761–1767.

62. Cuny C, Darbelley L, Touchard O, et al. [Proximal 4-part humerus fractures treated by antegrade nailing with self-stabilizing screws: 31 cases]. Rev Chir Orthop Reparatrice Appar Mot 2003;89:507–514.

63. Dawson FA. Four-part fracture dislocation of the proximal humerus: an arthroscopic approach. Arthroscopy 2003;19:662–666.

64. de Laat EA, Visser CP, Coene LN, et al. Nerve lesions in primary shoulder dislocations and humeral neck fractures. A prospective clinical and EMG study. J Bone Joint Surg Br 1994;76B:381–383.

65. DeFranco MJ, Brems JJ, Williams GR Jr, et al. Evaluation and management of valgus impacted four-part proximal humerus fractures. Clin Orthop Relat Res 2006;442: 109–114.

66. DePalma AF, Cautilli RA. Fractures of the upper end of the humerus. Clin Orthop Relat Res 1961;20:73–93.

67. Dimakopoulos P, Panagopoulos A, Kasimatis G. Transosseous suture fixation of proximal humeral fractures. J Bone Joint Surg Am 2007;89A:1700–1709.

68. Dines DM, et al. Posttraumatic changes of the proximal humerus: malunion, nonunion, and osteonecrosis: treatment with modular hemiarthroplasty or total shoulder arthroplasty. J Shoulder Elbow Surg 1993;2:11–21.

69. Doetsch AM, Faber J, Lynnerup N, et al. The effect of calcium and vitamin D3 supplementation on the healing of the proximal humerus fracture: a randomized placebo-controlled study. Calcif Tissue Int 2004;75:183–188.

70. Doursounian L, Grimberg J, Cazeau C, et al. A new internal fixation technique for fractures of the proximal humerus—the Bilboquet device: a report on 26 cases. J Shoulder Elbow Surg 2000;9:279–288.

71. Duparc F, Muller JM, Freger P. Arterial blood supply of the proximal humeral epiphysis. Surg Radiol Anat 2001;23:185–190.

72. Earwaker J. Isolated avulsion fracture of the lesser tuberosity of the humerus. Skeletal Radiol 1990;19:121–125.

73. Edelson G, Kelly I, Vigder F, et al. A three-dimensional classification for fractures of the proximal humerus. J Bone Joint Surg Br 2004;86:413–425.

74. Edelson G, Safuri H, Salami J, et al. Natural history of complex fractures of the proximal humerus using a three-dimensional classification system. J Shoulder Elbow Surg 2008.

75. Egol KA, Ong CC, Walsh M, et al. Early complications in proximal humerus fractures OTA types 11. Treated with locked plates. J Orthop Trauma 2008;22:159–164.

76. Fankhauser F, Boldin C, Schippinger G, et al. A new locking plate for unstable fractures of the proximal humerus. Clin Orthop Relat Res 2005;176–181.

77. Ferkel RD, Hedley AK, Eckardt JJ. Anterior fracture-dislocations of the shoulder: pitfalls in treatment. J Trauma 1984;24:363–367.

78. Fjalestad T, Stromsoe K, Blucher J, et al. Fractures in the proximal humerus: functional outcome and evaluation of 70 patients treated in hospital. Arch Orthop Trauma Surg 2005;125:310–316.

79. Flatow E. Fractures of the proximal humerus. In: Bucholz RW, Heckman JD, eds. Rockwood and Green's Fractures in Adults. 5th Ed. Philadelphia: Lippincott, Williams & Wilkins, 2001, 997–1040.

80. Flatow EL, Bigliani LU, April EW. An anatomic study of the musculocutaneous nerve and its relationship to the coracoid process. Clin Orthop Relat Res 1989;166–171.

81. Flatow EL, Cuomo F, Maday MG, et al. Open reduction and internal fixation of two-part displaced fractures of the greater tuberosity of the proximal part of the humerus. J Bone Joint Surg Am 1991;73A:1213–1218.

82. Frankle MA, Greenwald DP, Markee BA, et al. Biomechanical effects of malposition of tuberosity fragments on the humeral prosthetic reconstruction for four-part proximal humerus fractures. J Shoulder Elbow Surg 2001;10:321–326.

83. Frankle MA, Mighell MA. Techniques and principles of tuberosity fixation for proximal humeral fractures treated with hemiarthroplasty. J Shoulder Elbow Surg 2004;13: 239–247.

84. Frankle MA, Ondrovic LE, Markee BA, et al. Stability of tuberosity reattachment in proximal humeral hemiarthroplasty. J Shoulder Elbow Surg 2002;11:413–420.

85. Frich LH, Sojbjerg JO, Sneppen O. Shoulder arthroplasty in complex acute and chronic proximal humeral fractures. Orthopedics 1991;14:949–954.

86. Gaebler C, McQueen MM, CourtBrown CM. Minimally displaced proximal humeral fractures: epidemiology and outcome in 507 cases. Acta Orthop Scand 2003;74: 580–585.

87. Galatz LM, Iannotti JP. Management of surgical neck nonunions. Orthop Clin North Am 2000;31:51–61.

88. Galatz LM, Williams GR Jr, Fenlin JM Jr, et al. Outcome of open reduction and internal fixation of surgical neck nonunions of the humerus. J Orthop Trauma 2004;18:63–67.

89. Gallo RA, Sciulli R, Daffner RH, et al. Defining the relationship between rotator cuff injury and proximal humerus fractures. Clin Orthop Relat Res 2007;458:70–77.

90. Gallo RA, Zeiders GJ, Altman GT. Two-incision technique for treatment of complex proximal humerus fractures. J Orthop Trauma 2005;19:734–740.

91. Gardner MJ, Boraiah S, Helfet DL, et al. Indirect medial reduction and strut support of proximal humerus fractures using an endosteal implant. J Orthop Trauma 2008;22: 195–200.

92. Gardner MJ, Griffith MH, Dines JS, et al. The extended anterolateral acromial approach allows minimally invasive access to the proximal humerus. Clin Orthop Relat Res 2005; 123–129.

93. Gardner MJ, Griffith MH, Dines JS, et al. A minimally invasive approach for plate fixation of the proximal humerus. Bull Hosp Jt Dis 2004;621-2.:18–23.

94. Gardner MJ, Griffith MH, Lorich DG. Helical plating of the proximal humerus. Injury 2005;36:1197–1200.

95. Gardner MJ, Lorich DG, Werner CM, et al. Second-generation concepts for locked plating of proximal humerus fractures. Am J Orthop 2007;36:460–465.

96. Gardner MJ, Voos JE, Wanich T, et al. Vascular implications of minimally invasive plating of proximal humerus fractures. J Orthop Trauma 2006;20:602–607.

97. Gardner MJ, Weil Y, Barker JU, et al. The importance of medial support in locked plating of proximal humerus fractures. J Orthop Trauma 2007;21:185–191.

98. Gartsman GM, Taverna E. Arthroscopic treatment of rotator cuff tear and greater tuberosity fracture nonunion. Arthroscopy 1996;12:242–244.

99. Gartsman GM, Taverna E, Hammerman SM. Arthroscopic treatment of acute traumatic anterior glenohumeral dislocation and greater tuberosity fracture. Arthroscopy 1999; 15:648–650.

100. Gerber A, Warner JP. Hemiarthroplasty for Management of Complex Proximal Humerus Fractures: Preoperative Planning and Surgical Solutions. In: Warner JJP, Flatow EL, Iannotti JP, eds. Complex and revision problems in shoulder surgery. Philadelphia: Lippincott-Raven, 2005, pp. 2005.

101. Gerber C, Hersche O, Berberat C. The clinical relevance of posttraumatic avascular necrosis of the humeral head. J Shoulder Elbow Surg 1998;7:586–590.

102. Gerber C, Lambert SM. Allograft reconstruction of segmental defects of the humeral head for the treatment of chronic locked posterior dislocation of the shoulder. J Bone Joint Surg Am 1996;78A:376–382.

103. Gerber C, Lambert SM, Hoogewoud HM. Absence of avascular necrosis of the humeral head after posttraumatic rupture of the anterior and posterior humeral circumflex arteries. A case report. J Bone Joint Surg Am 1996;78A:1256–1259.

104. Gerber C, Schneeberger AG, Vinh TS. The arterial vascularization of the humeral head. An anatomical study. J Bone Joint Surg Am 1990;72A:1486–1494.

105. Gerber C, Terrier F, Ganz R. The role of the coracoid process in the chronic impingement syndrome. J Bone Joint Surg Br 1985;67B:703–708.

106. Gerber C, Werner CM, Vienne P. Internal fixation of complex fractures of the proximal humerus. J Bone Joint Surg Br 2004;86B:848–855.

107. Green A, Izzi J Jr. Isolated fractures of the greater tuberosity of the proximal humerus. J Shoulder Elbow Surg 2003;12:641–649.

108. Groh GI, Rockwood CA Jr. The terrible triad: anterior dislocation of the shoulder associated with rupture of the rotator cuff and injury to the brachial plexus. J Shoulder Elbow Surg 1995;41:51–53.

109. Hagino H, Yamamoto K, Ohshiro H, et al. Changing incidence of hip, distal radius, and proximal humerus fractures in Tottori Prefecture, Japan. Bone 1999;24:265–270.

110. Halder SC, Chapman JA, Choudhury G, et al. Retrograde fixation of fractures of the neck and shaft of the humerus with the "Halder humeral nail." Injury 2001;32: 695–703.

111. Hallock GG. The hemideltoid muscle flap. Ann Plast Surg 2000;44:18–22.

112. Handoll HH, Gibson JN, Madhok R. Interventions for treating proximal humeral fractures in adults. Cochrane Database Syst Rev 2003;CD000434.

113. Hausberger KH. Blood supply of intraarticular fractures of the humeral head: an anatomical and biomechanical study. In: Proceedings of the 14th Congress of the European Society for Shoulder and Elbow Surgery, Lisbon, 2000.

114. Hawkins RJ, Angelo RL. Displaced proximal humeral fractures. Selecting treatment, avoiding pitfalls. Orthop Clin North Am 1987;18:421–431.

115. Hawkins RJ, Bell RH, Gurr K. The three-part fracture of the proximal part of the humerus. Operative treatment. J Bone Joint Surg Am 1986;68A:1410–1414.

116. Hawkins RJ, Kiefer GN. Internal fixation techniques for proximal humeral fractures. Clin Orthop Relat Res 1987;77–85.

117. Hawkins RJ, Switlyk P. Acute prosthetic replacement for severe fractures of the proximal humerus. Clin Orthop 1993;156–160.

118. Healy WL, Jupiter JB, Kristiansen TK, et al. Nonunion of the proximal humerus. A review of 25 cases. J Orthop Trauma 1990;4:424–431.

119. Hente R, Kampshoff J, Kinner B, et al. [Treatment of dislocated 3- and 4-part fractures of the proximal humerus with an angle-stabilizing fixation plate]. Unfallchirurg 2004; 107:769–782.

120. Hepp P, Lill H, Bail H, et al. Where should implants be anchored in the humeral head? Clin Orthop Relat Res 2003;139–147.

121. Hersche O, Gerber C. Iatrogenic displacement of fracture-dislocations of the shoulder. A report of seven cases. J Bone Joint Surg Br 1994;76B:30–33.

122. Herscovici D Jr, Saunders DT, Johnson MP, et al. Percutaneous fixation of proximal humeral fractures. Clin Orthop Relat Res 2000;97–104.

123. Hertel R, Hempfing A, Stiehler M, et al. Predictors of humeral head ischemia after intracapsular fracture of the proximal humerus. J Shoulder Elbow Surg 2004;13: 427–433.

124. Hertel R, Knothe U, Ballmer FT. Geometry of the proximal humerus and implications for prosthetic design. J Shoulder Elbow Surg 2002;11:331–338.

125. Hessmann M, Baumgaertel F, Gehling H, et al. Plate fixation of proximal humeral fractures with indirect reduction: surgical technique and results utilizing three shoulder scores. Injury 1999;30:453–462.

126. Hinov V, Wilson F, Adams G. Arthroscopically treated proximal humeral fracture malunion. Arthroscopy 2002;18:1020–1023.

127. Hodgson SA, Mawson SJ, Stanley D. Rehabilitation after two-part fractures of the neck of the humerus. J Bone Joint Surg Br 2003;85B:419–422.

128. Holloway GB, Schenk T, Williams GR, et al. Arthroscopic capsular release for the treatment of refractory postoperative or post-fracture shoulder stiffness. J Bone Joint Surg Am 2001;83A:1682–1687.

129. Horak J, Nilsson BE. Epidemiology of fracture of the upper end of the humerus. Clin Orthop Relat Res 1975;250–253.

130. Hue E, Gagey O, Mestdagh H, et al. The blood supply of the deltoid muscle. Application to the deltoid flap technique. Surg Radiol Anat 1998;20:161–165.

131. Iannotti JP, Gabriel JP, Schneck SL, et al. The normal glenohumeral relationships. An anatomical study of 140 shoulders. J Bone Joint Surg Am 1992;74A:491–500.

132. Ilizarov GA, Sysenko I, Shved SI, et al. [Transosseous osteosynthesis in treating fracture-dislocations of the shoulder]. Ortop Travmatol Protez 1982;46–48.

133. Jaberg H, Warner JJ, Jakob RP. Percutaneous stabilization of unstable fractures of the humerus. J Bone Joint Surg Am 1992;74A:508–515.

134. Jakob RP, Miniaci A, Anson PS, et al. Four-part valgus impacted fractures of the proximal humerus. J Bone Joint Surg Br 1991;73B:295–298.
135. Jerosch J, Greig M, Peuker ET, et al. The posterior subdeltoid approach: a modified access to the posterior glenohumeral joint. J Shoulder Elbow Surg 2001;10:265–268.
136. Johansson O. Complications and failures of surgery in various fractures of the humerus. Acta Chir Scand 1961;120:469–478.
137. Jurik AG, Albrechtsen J. The use of computed tomography with two- and three-dimensional reconstructions in the diagnosis of three- and four-part fractures of the proximal humerus. Clin Radiol 1994;49:800–804.
138. Kamineni S, Ankem H, Sanghavi S. Anatomical considerations for percutaneous proximal humeral fracture fixation. Injury 2004;35:1133–1136.
139. Kannus P, Palvanen M, Niemi S, et al. Osteoporotic fractures of the proximal humerus in elderly Finnish persons: sharp increase in 1970 to 1998 and alarming projections for the new millennium. Acta Orthop Scand 2000;71:465–470.
140. Karatosun V, Alekberov C, Baran O, et al. Open fractures of the proximal humerus treated with the Ilizarov method: 12 patients followed 3 to 8 years. Acta Orthop Scand 2002;73:460–464.
141. Keener JD, Parsons BO, Flatow EL, et al. Outcomes after percutaneous reduction and fixation of proximal humeral fractures. J Shoulder Elbow Surg 2007;16:330–338.
142. Kelsey JL, Browner WS, Seeley DG, et al. Risk factors for fractures of the distal forearm and proximal humerus. The Study of Osteoporotic Fractures Research Group. Am J Epidemiol 1992;135:477–489.
143. Kendall CB, Tanner SL, Tolan SJ. SLAP tear associated with a minimally displaced proximal humerus fracture. Arthroscopy 2007;23:1362–1363.
144. Keser S, Bolukbasi S, Bayar A, et al. Proximal humeral fractures with minimal displacement treated conservatively. Int Orthop 2004;28:231–234.
145. Kettler M, Biberthaler P, Braunstein V, et al. [Treatment of proximal humeral fractures with the PHILOS angular stable plate. Presentation of 225 cases of dislocated fractures]. Unfallchirurg 2006;109:1032–1040.
146. Khan LA, Robinson CM, Will E, Whittaker R. Assessment of axillary nerve function and functional outcome after fixation of complex proximal humerus fractures using the extended deltoid-splitting approach. Injury 2008.
147. Kim DH, Clavert P, Warner JJ. Displaced periprosthetic humeral fracture treated with functional bracing: a report of two cases. J Shoulder Elbow Surg 2005;14:221–223.
148. Kim KC, Rhee KJ, Shin HD, et al. Arthroscopic fixation for displaced greater tuberosity fracture using the suture-bridge technique. Arthroscopy 2008;24:120–123.
149. Kim SH, Ha KI. Arthroscopic treatment of symptomatic shoulders with minimally displaced greater tuberosity fracture. Arthroscopy 2000;16:695–700.
150. Knight RA, Mayne JA. Comminuted fractures and fracture-dislocations involving the articular surface of the humeral head. J Bone Joint Surg Am 1957;39A:1343–1355.
151. Ko JY, Yamamoto R. Surgical treatment of complex fracture of the proximal humerus. Clin Orthop Relat Res 1996;225–237.
152. Kocialkowski A, Wallace WA. Closed percutaneous K-wire stabilization for displaced fractures of the surgical neck of the humerus. Injury 1990;21:209–212.
153. Kontakis GM, Steriopoulos K, Damilakis J, et al. The position of the axillary nerve in the deltoid muscle. A cadaveric study. Acta Orthop Scand 1999;70:9–11.
154. Koukakis A, Apostolou CD, Taneja T, et al. Fixation of proximal humerus fractures using the PHILOS plate: early experience. Clin Orthop Relat Res 2006;442:115–120.
155. Koval K, Sanders R, Zuckerman J, et al. Modified tension band wiring of displaced surgical neck fractures of the humerus. J Shoulder Elbow Surg 2, 85–92. 1993.
156. Koval KJ, Gallagher MA, Marsicano JG, et al. Functional outcome after minimally displaced fractures of the proximal part of the humerus. J Bone Joint Surg Am 1997;79A: 203–207.
157. Kozak TK, Skirving AP. Fracture dislocation with associated humeral shaft fracture. Injury 1995;26:129–130.
158. Kralinger F, Irenberger A, Lechner C, et al. [Comparison of open versus percutaneous treatment for humeral head fracture]. Unfallchirurg 2006;109:406–410.
159. Kralinger F, Schwaiger R, Wambacher M, et al. Outcome after primary hemiarthroplasty for fracture of the head of the humerus. A retrospective multicenter study of 167 patients. J Bone Joint Surg Br 2004;86B:217–219.
160. Krause FG, Huebschle L, Hertel R. Reattachment of the tuberosities with cable wires and bone graft in hemiarthroplasties done for proximal humeral fractures with cable wire and bone graft: 58 patients with a 22-month minimum follow-up. J Orthop Trauma 2007;21:682–686.
161. Kristiansen B, Kofoed H. Transcutaneous reduction and external fixation of displaced fractures of the proximal humerus. J Bone Joint Surg 1988;70B:821–824.
162. Kristiansen B. External fixation of proximal humerus fracture. Clinical and cadaver study of pinning technique. Acta Orthop Scand 1987;58:645–648.
163. Kristiansen B. Treatment of displaced fractures of the proximal humerus: transcutaneous reduction and Hoffmann's external fixation. Injury 1989;20:195–199.
164. Kristiansen B, Angermann P, Larsen TK. Functional results following fractures of the proximal humerus. A controlled clinical study comparing two periods of immobilization. Arch Orthop Trauma Surg 1989;108:339–341.
165. Kristiansen B, Barfod G, Bredesen J, et al. Epidemiology of proximal humeral fractures. Acta Orthop Scand 1987;58:75–77.
166. Kristiansen B, Kofoed H. External fixation of displaced fractures of the proximal humerus. Technique and preliminary results. J Bone Joint Surg Br 1987;69B:643–646.
167. Kronberg M, Brostrom LA, Soderlund V. Retroversion of the humeral head in the normal shoulder and its relationship to the normal range of motion. Clin Orthop Relat Res 1990;113–117.
168. Kulkarni RR, Nandedkar AN, Mysorekar VR. Position of the axillary nerve in the deltoid muscle. Anat Rec 1992;232:316–317.
169. Kwon BK, Goertzen DJ, O'Brien PJ, et al. Biomechanical evaluation of proximal humeral fracture fixation supplemented with calcium phosphate cement. J Bone Joint Surg Am 2002;84A:951–961.
170. Laflamme GY, Rouleau DM, Berry GK, et al. Percutaneous humeral plating of fractures of the proximal humerus: results of a prospective multicenter clinical trial. J Orthop Trauma 2008;22:153–158.
171. Lafosse L, Brozska R, Toussaint B, et al. The outcome and structural integrity of arthroscopic rotator cuff repair with use of the double-row suture anchor technique. J Bone Joint Surg Am 2007;89A:1533–1541.
172. Laing PG. The arterial supply of the adult humerus. J Bone Joint Surg Am 1956;38A: 1105–1116.
173. Lanting B, MacDermid J, Drosdowech D, Faber KJ. Proximal humeral fractures: a systematic review of treatment modalities. J Shoulder Elbow Surg 2008;17:42–54.
174. Lee SH, Dargent-Molina P, Breart G. Risk factors for fractures of the proximal humerus: results from the EPIDOS prospective study. J Bone Miner Res 2002;17:817–825.
175. Lefevre-Colau MM, Babinet A, Fayad F, et al. Immediate mobilization compared with conventional immobilization for the impacted nonoperatively treated proximal humeral fracture. A randomized controlled trial. J Bone Joint Surg Am 2007;89A:2582–2590.
176. Leslie A, Cassar-Pullicino VN. Avulsion of the lesser tuberosity with intra-articular injury of the glenohumeral joint. Injury 1996;27:742–745.
177. Levine B, Pereira D, Rosen J. Avulsion fractures of the lesser tuberosity of the humerus in adolescents: review of the literature and case report. J Orthop Trauma 2005;19: 349–352.
178. Levy O, Copeland SA. Cementless surface replacement arthroplasty of the shoulder: 5- to 10-year results with the Copeland mark-2 prosthesis. J Bone Joint Surg Br 2001; 83B:213–221.
179. Levy O, Pritsch M, Oran A, et al. A wide and versatile combined surgical approach to the shoulder. J Shoulder Elbow Surg 1999;8:658–659.
180. Levy O, Webb M, Even T, et al. Arthroscopic capsular release for posttraumatic shoulder stiffness. J Shoulder Elbow Surg 2008.
181. Leyshon RL. Closed treatment of fractures of the proximal humerus. Acta Orthop Scand 1984;55:48–51.
182. Lill H, Bewer A, Korner J, et al. [Conservative treatment of dislocated proximal humeral fractures]. Zentralbl Chir 2001;126:205–210.
183. Lill H, Hepp P, Korner J, et al. Proximal humeral fractures: how stiff should an implant be? A comparative mechanical study with new implants in human specimens. Arch Orthop Trauma Surg 2003;1232-3.:74–81.
184. Lill H, Hepp P, Rose T, et al. [The angle stable locking-proximal-humerus-plate LPHP. for proximal humeral fractures using a small anterior-lateral-deltoid-splitting-approach: technique and first results]. Zentralbl Chir 2004;129:43–48.
185. Lin J, Hou SM. Locked-nail treatment of humeral surgical neck nonunions. J Trauma 2003;54:530–535.
186. Lin J, Hou SM, Hang YS. Locked nailing for displaced surgical neck fractures of the humerus. J Trauma 1998;45:1051–1057.
187. Lind T, Kroner K, Jensen J. The epidemiology of fractures of the proximal humerus. Arch Orthop Trauma Surg 1989;108:285–287.
188. Livesley PJ, Mugglestone A, Whitton J. Electrotherapy and the management of minimally displaced fracture of the neck of the humerus. Injury 1992;23:323–327.
189. Loew M, Heitkemper S, Parsch D, et al. Influence of the design of the prosthesis on the outcome after hemiarthroplasty of the shoulder in displaced fractures of the head of the humerus. J Bone Joint Surg Br 2006;88B:345–350.
190. Lu CC, Chang MW, Lin GT. Intramedullary pinning with tension-band wiring for surgical neck fractures of the proximal humerus in elderly patients. Kaohsiung J Med Sci 2004;20:538–545.
191. Mackenzie D. The antero-superior exposure for total shoulder replacement. Orthop Traumatol 1993;2:71–77.
192. Mansat P, Guity MR, Bellumore Y, et al. Shoulder arthroplasty for late sequelae of proximal humeral fractures. J Shoulder Elbow Surg 2004;13:305–312.
193. Marsh JL, Slongo TF, Agel J, et al. Fracture and dislocation classification compendium—2007: Orthopaedic Trauma Association classification, database, and outcomes committee. J Orthop Trauma 2007;2110(suppl):S1–133.
194. Meyer C, Alt V, Hassanin H, et al. The arteries of the humeral head and their relevance in fracture treatment. Surg Radiol Anat 2005;27:232–237.
195. Meyer DC, Espinosa N, Hertel R. Combined fracture of the greater and lesser tuberosities with intact connection of the humeral head to the shaft. J Trauma 2006;61: 206–208.
196. Mills HJ, Horne G. Fractures of the proximal humerus in adults. J Trauma 1985;25: 801–805.
197. Misra A, Kapur R, Maffulli N. Complex proximal humeral fractures in adults: a systematic review of management. Injury 2001;32:363–372.
198. Mittlmeier TW, Stedtfeld HW, Ewert A, et al. Stabilization of proximal humeral fractures with an angular and sliding stable antegrade locking nail Targon PH. J Bone Joint Surg Am 2003;85A(suppl 4):136–146.
199. Mochizuki T, Sugaya H, Uomizu M, et al. Humeral insertion of the supraspinatus and infraspinatus. New anatomical findings regarding the footprint of the rotator cuff. J Bone Joint Surg Am 2008;90A:962–969.
200. Moda S, Chadha N, Sangwan S, et al. Open reduction and internal fixation of proximal humeral fractures and fracture dislocations. J Bone Joint Surg Br 1990;72B:1050–1052.
201. Mont MA, Maar DC, Urquhart MW, et al. Avascular necrosis of the humeral head treated by core decompression. A retrospective review. J Bone Joint Surg Br 1993;75B: 785–788.
202. Moonot P, Ashwood N, Hamlet M. Early results for treatment of three- and four-part fractures of the proximal humerus using the PHILOS plate system. J Bone Joint Surg Br 2007;89B:1206–1209.
203. Muller M, Nazarian S, Koch P, et al. The Comprehensive Classification of Fractures of Long Bones. New York, Springer, 1990.
204. Munnoch DA, Herbert KJ, Morris AM, et al. The deltoid muscle flap: anatomical studies and case reports. Br J Plast Surg 1996;49:310–314.
205. Nayak NK, Schickendantz MS, Regan WD, et al. Operative treatment of nonunion of surgical neck fractures of the humerus. Clin Orthop Relat Res 1995;200–205.
206. Neer CS. Impingement lesions. Clin Orthop Relat Res 1983;70–77.
207. Neer CS. Displaced proximal humeral fractures. I. Classification and evaluation. J Bone Joint Surg Am 1970;52A:1077–1089.
208. Neer CS. Four-segment classification of proximal humeral fractures: purpose and reliable use. J Shoulder Elbow Surg 2002;11:389–400.
209. Neer CS. Displaced proximal humeral fractures. II. Treatment of three-part and four-part displacement. J Bone Joint Surg Am 1970;52A:1090–1103.
210. Neer C. Four-segment classification of displaced proximal humeral fractures. Am Acad Orthop Surg Instr Course Lect 1975;chapter 9:160–168.
211. Neumann K, Muhr G, Breitfuss H. [Primary humerus head replacement in dislocated proximal humeral fracture. Indications, technique, results]. Orthopade 1992;21: 140–147.
212. Nguyen TV, Center JR, Sambrook PN, et al. Risk factors for proximal humerus, forearm, and wrist fractures in elderly men and women: the Dubbo Osteoporosis Epidemiology Study. Am J Epidemiol 2001;153:587–595.

213. Nordqvist A, Petersson CJ. Shoulder injuries common in alcoholics. An analysis of 413 injuries. Acta Orthop Scand 1996;67:364–366.
214. Norris TR, Green A, McGuigan FX. Late prosthetic shoulder arthroplasty for displaced proximal humerus fractures. J Shoulder Elbow Surg 1995;4:271–280.
215. Nove-Josserand L, Walch G, Levigne CH, et al. Fracture of the lesser tuberosity of the humerus in adults. About 17 cases. J Shoulder Elbow Surg 1995;4:S30–S33.
216. O'Donnell TM, McKenna JV, Kenny P, et al. Concomitant injuries to the ipsilateral shoulder in patients with a fracture of the diaphysis of the humerus. J Bone Joint Surg Br 2008;90B:61–65.
217. Ochsner PE, Ilchmann T. [Tension band osteosynthesis with absorbable cords in proximal comminuted fractures of the humerus]. Unfallchirurg 1991;94:508–510.
218. Ogawa K, Takahashi M. Long-term outcome of isolated lesser tuberosity fractures of the humerus. J Trauma 1997;42:955–959.
219. Ogiwara N, Aoki M, Okamura K, et al. Ender nailing for unstable surgical neck fractures of the humerus in elderly patients. Clin Orthop Relat Res 1996;330:173–180.
220. Olsson C, Petersson CJ. Clinical importance of comorbidity in patients with a proximal humerus fracture. Clin Orthop Relat Res 2006;442:93–99.
221. Olsson C, Nordqvist A, Petersson CJ. Increased fragility in patients with fracture of the proximal humerus: a case control study. Bone 2004;34:1072–1077.
222. Olsson C, Nordquist A, Petersson CJ. Long-term outcome of a proximal humerus fracture predicted after 1 year: a 13-year prospective population-based follow-up study of 47 patients. Acta Orthop 2005;76:397–402.
223. Owsley KC, Gorczyca JT. Displacement/screw cutout after open reduction and locked plate fixation of humeral fractures. J Bone Joint Surg Am 2008;90A:233–240.
224. Paavolainen P, Bjorkenheim JM, Slatis P, et al. Operative treatment of severe proximal humeral fractures. Acta Orthop Scand 1983;54:374–379.
225. Palvanen M, Kannus P, Niemi S, et al. Update in the epidemiology of proximal humeral fractures. Clin Orthop Relat Res 2006;442:87–92.
226. Palvanen M, Kannus P, Parkkari J, et al. The injury mechanisms of osteoporotic upper extremity fractures among older adults: a controlled study of 287 consecutive patients and their 108 controls. Osteoporos Int 2000;11:822–831.
227. Panagopoulos AM, Dimakopoulos P, Tyllianakis M, et al. Valgus impacted proximal humeral fractures and their blood supply after transosseous suturing. Int Orthop 2004; 28:333–337.
228. Patten RM, Mack LA, Wang KY, et al. Nondisplaced fractures of the greater tuberosity of the humerus: sonographic detection. Radiology 1992;182:201–204.
229. Platzer P, Kutscha-Lissberg F, Lehr S, et al. The influence of displacement on shoulder function in patients with minimally displaced fractures of the greater tuberosity. Injury 2005;36:1185–1189.
230. Plausinis D, Kwon YW, Zuckerman JD. Complications of humeral head replacement for proximal humeral fractures. Instr Course Lect 2005;54:371–380.
231. Porcellini G, Campi F, Paladini P. Articular impingement in malunited fracture of the humeral head. Arthroscopy 2002;18:E39.
232. Pretre R, Hoffmeyer P, Bednarkiewicz M, et al. Blunt injury to the subclavian or axillary artery. J Am Coll Surg 1994;179:295–298.
233. Pritchett JW. Inferior subluxation of the humeral head after trauma or surgery. J Shoulder Elbow Surg 1997;6:356–359.
234. Qidwai SA. Treatment of proximal humeral fractures by intramedullary Kirschner wires. J Trauma 2001;50:1090–1095.
235. Rajasekhar C, Ray PS, Bhamra MS. Fixation of proximal humeral fractures with the Polarus nail. J Shoulder Elbow Surg 2001;10:7–10.
236. Rasmussen S, Hvass I, Dalsgaard J, et al. Displaced proximal humeral fractures: results of conservative treatment. Injury 1992;23:41–43.
237. Reinus WR, Hatem SF. Fractures of the greater tuberosity presenting as rotator cuff abnormality: magnetic resonance demonstration. J Trauma 1998;44:670–675.
238. Resch H, Hubner C, Schwaiger R. Minimally invasive reduction and osteosynthesis of articular fractures of the humeral head. Injury 2001;32(suppl 1):SA25–SA32.
239. Resch H, Povacz P, Frohlich R, et al. Percutaneous fixation of three- and four-part fractures of the proximal humerus. J Bone Joint Surg Br 1997;79B:295–300.
240. Resch H, Hubner C. Percutaneous treatment of proximal humerus fractures. In: Levine WN, et al., eds. Fractures of the Shoulder Girdle. New York: Marcel Decker, 2003.
241. Resch H, Aschaver E, Poracz P, et al. Closed reduction and fixation of articular fractures of the humeral head. Tech Shoulder Elbow Surg 2000;3:154–158.
242. Revay S, Dahlstrom M, Dalen N. Water exercise versus instruction for self-training following a shoulder fracture. Int J Rehabil Res 1992;15:327–333.
243. Robertson DD, Yuan J, Bigliani LU, et al. Three-dimensional analysis of the proximal part of the humerus: relevance to arthroplasty. J Bone Joint Surg Am 2000;82A: 1594–1602.
244. Robinson CM, Aderinto J. Posterior shoulder dislocations and fracture-dislocations. J Bone Joint Surg Am 2005;87A:639–650.
245. Robinson CM, Akhtar A, Mitchell M, et al. Complex posterior fracture-dislocation of the shoulder. Epidemiology, injury patterns, and results of operative treatment. J Bone Joint Surg Am 2007;89A:1454–1466.
246. Robinson CM, Bell KM, CourtBrown CM, et al. Locked nailing of humeral shaft fractures. Experience in Edinburgh over a 2-year period. J Bone Joint Surg Br 1992;74B: 558–562.
247. Robinson CM, Christie J. The 2-part proximal humeral fracture: a review of operative treatment using two techniques. Injury 1993;24:123–125.
248. Robinson CM, Dobson RJ. Anterior instability of the shoulder after trauma. J Bone Joint Surg Br 2004;86B:469–479.
249. Robinson CM, Howes J, Murdoch H, et al. Functional outcome and risk of recurrent instability after primary traumatic anterior shoulder dislocation in young patients. J Bone Joint Surg Am 2006;88A:2326–2336.
250. Robinson CM, Kelly M, Wakefield AE. Redislocation of the shoulder during the first 6 weeks after a primary anterior dislocation: risk factors and results of treatment. J Bone Joint Surg Am 2002;84A:1552–1559.
251. Robinson CM, Khan L, Akhtar A, et al. The extended deltoid-splitting approach to the proximal humerus. J Orthop Trauma 2007;21:657–662.
252. Robinson CM, Khan LA, Akhtar MA. Treatment of anterior fracture-dislocations of the proximal humerus by open reduction and internal fixation. J Bone Joint Surg Br 2006; 88B:502–508.
253. Robinson CM, Page RS. Severely impacted valgus proximal humeral fractures. Results of operative treatment. J Bone Joint Surg Am 2003;85A:1647–1655.
254. Robinson CM, Page RS. Severely impacted valgus proximal humeral fractures. J Bone Joint Surg Am 2004;86A(suppl 1, pt 2):143–155.
255. Robinson CM, Page RS, Hill RM, et al. Primary hemiarthroplasty for treatment of proximal humeral fractures. J Bone Joint Surg Am 2003;85A:1215–1223.
256. Robinson CM, Royds M, Abraham A, et al. Refractures in patients at least 45 years old. A prospective analysis of 22,060 patients. J Bone Joint Surg Am 2002;84A:1528–1533.
257. Robinson CM, Teoh KH, Baker A, et al. Fractures of the lesser tuberosity of the humerus in the adult: epidemiology and functional outome after operative treatment. J Bone Joint Surg Am 2008.
258. Rooney PJ, Cockshott WP. Pseudarthrosis following proximal humeral fractures: a possible mechanism. Skeletal Radiol 1986;15:21–24.
259. Rose PS, Adams CR, Torchia ME, et al. Locking plate fixation for proximal humeral fractures: initial results with a new implant. J Shoulder Elbow Surg 2007;16:202–207.
260. Rose S, Melton J, Morrey B, et al. Epidemiological features of humeral fractures. Clin Orthop Relat Res 1982;168:24–30.
261. Rowe CR, Sakellarides HT. Factors related to recurrences of anterior dislocations of the shoulder. Clin Orthop 1961;20:40–48.
262. Rowles DJ, McGrory JE. Percutaneous pinning of the proximal part of the humerus. An anatomic study. J Bone Joint Surg Am 2001;83A:1695–1699.
263. Russo R, Visconti V, Lombardi LV, et al. The block-bridge system: a new concept and surgical technique to reconstruct articular surfaces and tuberosities in complex proximal humeral fractures. J Shoulder Elbow Surg 2008;17:29–36.
264. Sabick MB, Hay JG, Goel VK, et al. Active responses decrease impact forces at the hip and shoulder in falls to the side. J Biomech 1999;32:993–998.
265. Saitoh S, Natatsuchi Y, Latta L, et al. Distribution of bone mineral density and bone strength of the proximal humerus. J Shoulder Elbow Surg 1994;3:234–242.
266. Sallay PI, Pedowitz RA, Mallon WJ, et al. Reliability and reproducibility of radiographic interpretation of proximal humeral fracture pathoanatomy. J Shoulder Elbow Surg 1997;6:60–69.
267. Samilson RL, Prieto V. Dislocation arthropathy of the shoulder. J Bone Joint Surg Am 1983;65A:456–460.
268. Sanders KM, Seeman E, Ugoni AM, et al. Age- and gender-specific rate of fractures in Australia: a population-based study. Osteoporos Int 1999;10:240–247.
269. Schai PA, Hintermann B, Koris MJ. Preoperative arthroscopic assessment of fractures about the shoulder. Arthroscopy 1999;15:827–835.
270. Scheck M. Surgical treatment of nonunions of the surgical neck of the humerus. Clin Orthop Relat Res 1982;255–259.
271. Scheibel M, Martinek V, Imhoff AB. Arthroscopic reconstruction of an isolated avulsion fracture of the lesser tuberosity. Arthroscopy 2005;21:487–494.
272. Schmidt AH. Proximal humeral fractures: open reduction internal fixation. In: Wiss DA, ed. Master Techniques in Orthopaedic Surgery. Fractures. 2nd Ed. Philadelphia: Lippincott-Raven, 2006, 37–49.
273. Serin E, Karatosun V, Balci C, et al. Two-prong splint in the treatment of proximal humeral fracture. Arch Orthop Trauma Surg 1999;119:368–370.
274. Shortt NL, Robinson CM. Mortality after low-energy fractures in patients aged at least 45 years old. J Orthop Trauma 2005;19:396–400.
275. Shved SI, Sysenko I. [Treatment of fractures of the proximal end of the humerus in middle-aged and elderly patients by the Ilizarov method]. Vestn Khir Im I I Grek 1984; 132:80–82.
276. Sidor ML, Zuckerman JD, Lyon T, et al. The Neer classification system for proximal humeral fractures. An assessment of interobserver reliability and intraobserver reproducibility. J Bone Joint Surg Am 1993;75A:1745–1750.
277. Siebenrock KA, Gerber C. The reproducibility of classification of fractures of the proximal end of the humerus. J Bone Joint Surg Am 1993;75A:1751–1755.
278. Siegel JA, Dines DM. Proximal humerus malunions. Orthop Clin North Am 2000;31: 35–50.
279. Siegel JA, Dines DM. Techniques in managing proximal humeral malunions. J Shoulder Elbow Surg 2003;12:69–78.
280. Simeone FA. Neurological complications of closed shoulder injuries. Orthop Clin North Am 1975;6:499–506.
281. Simpson NS, Schwappach JR, Toby EB. Fracture-dislocation of the humerus with intrathoracic displacement of the humeral head. A case report. J Bone Joint Surg Am 1998; 80A:889–891.
282. Simpson NS, et al. Reconstruction of nonunion of the proximal humerus with a custom blade plate. Orthop Trans 1996;20:11–12.
283. Sirveaux F, Favard L, Oudet D, et al. Grammont inverted total shoulder arthroplasty in the treatment of glenohumeral osteoarthritis with massive rupture of the cuff. Results of a multicenter study of 80 shoulders. J Bone Joint Surg Br 2004;86B:388–395.
284. Smith J, Berry G, Laflamme Y, et al. Percutaneous insertion of a proximal humeral locking plate: an anatomic study. Injury 2007;38:206–211.
285. Soete PJ, Clayson PE, Costenoble VH. Transitory percutaneous pinning in fractures of the proximal humerus. J Shoulder Elbow Surg 1999;8:569–573.
286. Solonen KA, Vastamaki M. Osteotomy of the neck of the humerus for traumatic varus deformity. Acta Orthop Scand 1985;56:79–80.
287. Sperling JW, Cuomo F, Hill JD, et al. The difficult proximal humerus fracture: tips and techniques to avoid complications and improve results. Instr Course Lect 2007; 56:45–57.
288. Sperling JW, Kozak TK, Hanssen AD, Cofield RH. Infection after shoulder arthroplasty. Clin Orthop Relat Res 2001;206–216.
289. Stableforth PG. Four-part fractures of the neck of the humerus. J Bone Joint Surg Br 1984;66B:104–108.
290. Svend-Hansen H. Displaced proximal humeral fractures. A review of 49 patients. Acta Orthop Scand 1974;45:359–364.
291. Tamai K, Hamada J, Ohno W, et al. Surgical anatomy of multipart fractures of the proximal humerus. J Shoulder Elbow Surg 2002;11:421–427.
292. Tanner MW, Cofield RH. Prosthetic arthroplasty for fractures and fracture-dislocations of the proximal humerus. Clin Orthop Relat Res 1983;116–128.
293. Tingart MJ, Apreleva M, von Stechow D, et al. The cortical thickness of the proximal humeral diaphysis predicts bone mineral density of the proximal humerus. J Bone Joint Surg Br 2003;85B:611–617.

294. Tingart MJ, Bouxsein ML, Zurakowski D, et al. Three-dimensional distribution of bone density in the proximal humerus. Calcif Tissue Int 2003;73:531–536.

295. Tingart MJ, Lehtinen J, Zurakowski D, et al. Proximal humeral fractures: regional differences in bone mineral density of the humeral head affect the fixation strength of cancellous screws. J Shoulder Elbow Surg 2006;15:620–624.

296. Vandenbussche E, Peraldi P, Naouri JF, et al. [Four-part valgus impacted fractures of the upper extremity of humerus: ilium graft reconstruction. Apropos of 8 cases]. Rev Chir Orthop Reparatrice Appar Mot 1996;82:658–662.

297. Varghese J, Thilak J, Mahajan CV. Arthroscopic treatment of acute traumatic posterior glenohumeral dislocation and anatomic neck fracture. Arthroscopy 2006;22:676–672.

298. Visser CP, Coene LN, Brand R, et al. Nerve lesions in proximal humeral fractures. J Shoulder Elbow Surg 2001;10:421–427.

299. Visser CP, Coene LN, et al. Electromyographic findings in shoulder dislocations and fractures of the proximal humerus: comparison with clinical neurological examination. Clin Neurol Neurosurg 1999;101:86–91.

300. Volgas DA, Stannard JP, Alonso JE. Nonunions of the humerus. Clin Orthop Relat Res 2004;46–50.

301. Walch G, Badet R, Nove-Josserand L, et al. Nonunions of the surgical neck of the humerus: surgical treatment with an intramedullary bone peg, internal fixation, and cancellous bone grafting. J Shoulder Elbow Surg 1996;5:161–168.

302. Wallace WA, Hellier M. Improving radiographs of the injured shoulder. Radiography 1983;49:229–233.

303. Walsh S, Reindl R, Harvey E, et al. Biomechanical comparison of a unique locking plate versus a standard plate for internal fixation of proximal humerus fractures in a cadaveric model. Clin Biomech Bristol Avon 2006;21:1027–1031.

304. Weinstein DM, Bratton DR, Ciccone WJ, et al. Locking plates improve torsional resistance in the stabilization of three-part proximal humeral fractures. J Shoulder Elbow Surg 2006;15:239–243.

305. Wijgman AJ, Roolker W, Patt TW, et al. Open reduction and internal fixation of three- and four-part fractures of the proximal part of the humerus. J Bone Joint Surg Am 2002;84A:1919–1925.

306. Williams GR Jr, Copley LA, Iannotti JP, et al. The influence of intramedullary fixation on figure-of-eight wiring for surgical neck fractures of the proximal humerus: a biomechanical comparison. J Shoulder Elbow Surg 1997;6:423–428.

307. Williams GR Jr, Iannotti JP. Management of periprosthetic fractures: the shoulder. J Arthroplasty 2002;174(suppl 1):14–16.

308. Williams GR Jr, Wong KL. Two-part and three-part fractures: open reduction and

309. internal fixation versus closed reduction and percutaneous pinning. Orthop Clin North Am 2000;31:1–21.

309. Wirth MA, Butters KP, Rockwood CA Jr. The posterior deltoid-splitting approach to the shoulder. Clin Orthop Relat Res 1993;92–98.

310. Wirth MA, Jensen KL, Agarwal A, et al. Fracture-dislocation of the proximal part of the humerus with retroperitoneal displacement of the humeral head. A case report. J Bone Joint Surg Am 1997;79A:763–766.

311. Wirth MA, Rockwood CA Jr. Complications of shoulder arthroplasty. Clin Orthop Relat Res 1994;47–69.

312. Worland RL, Kim DY, Arredondo J. Periprosthetic humeral fractures: management and classification. J Shoulder Elbow Surg 1999;8:590–594.

313. Yamada M, Briot J, Pedrono A, et al. Age- and gender-related distribution of bone tissue of osteoporotic humeral head using computed tomography. J Shoulder Elbow Surg 2007;16:596–602.

314. Yang KH. Helical plate fixation for treatment of comminuted fractures of the proximal and middle one third of the humerus. Injury 2005;36:75–80.

315. Yosipovitch Z, Goldberg I. Inferior subluxation of the humeral head after injury to the shoulder. A brief note. J Bone Joint Surg Am 1989;71A:751–753.

316. Young TB, Wallace WA. Conservative treatment of fractures and fracture-dislocations of the upper end of the humerus. J Bone Joint Surg Br 1985;67B:373–377.

317. Zanetti M, Weishaupt D, Jost B, et al. MR imaging for traumatic tears of the rotator cuff: high prevalence of greater tuberosity fractures and subscapularis tendon tears. AJR Am J Roentgenol 1999;172:463–467.

318. Zifko B, Poigenfurst J, Pezzei C. [Intramedullary nailing of unstable proximal humeral fractures]. Orthopade 1992;21:115–120.

319. Zifko B, Poigenfurst J, Pezzei C, et al. Flexible intramedullary pins in the treatment of unstable proximal humeral fractures. Injury 1991;22:60–62.

320. Zifko B, Poigenfurst J. [Treatment of unstable fractures of the proximal end of the humerus using elastic curved intramedullary wires]. Unfallchirurgie 1987;13:72–81.

321. Zuckerman JD, Flugstad DL, Teitz CC, et al. Axillary artery injury as a complication of proximal humeral fractures. Two case reports and a review of the literature. Clin Orthop Relat Res 1984;234–237.

322. Zyto K. Nonoperative treatment of comminuted fractures of the proximal humerus in elderly patients. Injury 1998;29:349–352.

323. Zyto K, Ahrengart L, Sperber A, et al. Treatment of displaced proximal humeral fractures in elderly patients. J Bone Joint Surg Br 1997;79B:412–417.

324. Zyto K, Wallace WA, Frostick S, et al. Outcomes in hemiarthroplasty for three and four part fractures of the proximal humerus. J Shoulder Elbow Surg 1998;7:85–89.

36

CLAVICLE FRACTURES

Michael D. McKee

INTRODUCTION

Clavicle fractures are common injuries in young, active individuals, especially those who participate in activities or sports where high-speed falls (e.g., bicycling, motorcycles) or violent collisions (e.g., football, hockey) are frequent, and they account for approximately 2.6% of all fractures.* In contrast to most fractures, Robinson[137] reported in an epidemiologic study that the annual incidence in males was highest in the under-20 age group, decreasing with each subsequent age cohort (Fig. 36-1). The incidence in females was more constant, with peaks seen in teenagers (e.g., sports, motor vehicle accidents) and the elderly (e.g., osteoporotic fractures from simple falls). The annual incidence of fractures in their population was 29 per 100,000 population per year.[137]

*References 27–30,43,103,104,109,111,114.

The majority of clavicular fractures (80% to 85%) occur in the midshaft of the bone, where the typical compressive forces applied to the shoulder and the narrow cross section of the bone combine and result in bony failure[27–30,95,137,160] (Fig. 36-2). Distal third fractures are the next most common type (20%), and although they can result from the same mechanisms of injury as that seen with midshaft fractures, they tend to occur in more elderly individuals as a result of simple falls.[52,138,140,141,169] Medial third fractures are the rarest (5%), perhaps because of the difficulty in accurately imaging (and identifying) them.[150,163] One recent study of 57 such fractures reported that patients were typically men in their fifth decade and that the usual mechanism of injury was a motor vehicle accident.[163] These authors also noted a relatively high (20%) associated mortality rate from concomitant head and chest injuries.

Older studies suggested that a fracture of the shaft of the clavicle, even when significantly displaced, was an essentially

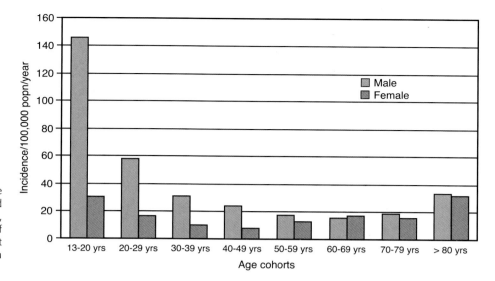

FIGURE 36-1 The epidemiology of clavicle fractures in Edinburgh, Scotland. (Adapted from Robinson CM, Court-Brown CM, McQueen MM, et al. Estimating the risk of nonunion following nonoperative treatment of a clavicle fracture. J Bone Joint Surg Am 2004;86A:1359–1365.)

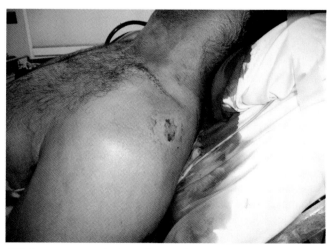

FIGURE 36-2 **A.** Mechanism of injury. Clavicle fractures are usually produced by a fall directly on the involved shoulder. **B.** Corresponding clinical photograph demonstrating posterior skin abrasion following displaced midshaft clavicle fracture.

benign injury with an inherently good prognosis when treated nonoperatively.[100–104] In a landmark 1960 study, Neer reported nonunion in only 3 of 2235 patients with middle-third fractures of the clavicle treated by a sling or figure-of-eight bandage.[100] Rowe[144] showed an overall incidence of nonunion of 0.8% in 566 clavicle fractures treated in a similar fashion. Thus, what was thought to be the most serious complication following clavicular fracture—nonunion—appeared to be extremely rare. Also, malunion of the clavicle (which occurred radiographically on a predictable basis in displaced fractures) was described as being of radiographic interest only, with little or no functional consequences. This thinking dominated the approach to clavicle fractures for decades.

More recently, there has been increasing evidence that the outcome of nonoperatively treated (especially displaced or shortened) midshaft fractures is not as optimal as was once thought.* In 1997, Hill et al.[62] were the first to use patient-oriented outcome measures to examine 66 consecutive patients with displaced midshaft clavicle fractures, and they found an unsatisfactory outcome in 31%, as well as a nonunion rate of 15%. In a metaanalysis of the literature from 1975 to 2005, Zlowodzki et al.[185] found that the nonunion rate for nonoperatively treated displaced midshaft clavicle fractures was 15.1%, exponentially higher than that previously described (Table 36-1). Other recent epidemiologic and prospective studies have supported these findings.† In addition, malunion of the clavicle has been clearly shown by multiple authors to be a distinct clinical entity with characteristic signs and symptoms that can be significantly improved by corrective osteotomy.[7,9,20,23,38,76,90,91] Potential explanations for the increased complication rate seen following the nonoperative care of these fractures may be because of changing injury patterns (especially from "extreme" sports such as mountain-bicycling, snowboarding, and all-terrain vehicle riding), increased expectations of the modern patient, comprehensive follow-up (including patient-oriented outcome measures), and focusing on adults (elimina-

*References 14,39,61,62,77,90,92,111–113.
†References 14,39,62,92,110–112,137–139.

TABLE 36-1	Metaanalysis of Nonoperative Treatment, Intramedullary Pinning, and Plate Fixation for Displaced Midshaft Fractures of the Clavicle From Series Published in 1975 through 2005			
Treatment Method	Percentage with Nonunion	Infections (Total)	Infections (Deep)	Fixation Failures
Nonoperative (n = 159)	15.1	0	0	0
Plating (n = 460)	2.2	4.6	2.4	2.2
Intramedullary pinning (n = 152)	2.0	6.6	0	3.9

Adapted from Zlowodzki M, Zelle BA, Cole PA, et al. Treatment of midshaft clavicle fractures: systemic review of 2144 fractures. J Orthop Trauma 2005;19:504–507.

ting children with their inherently good prognosis and remodeling potential).[‡]

Good results with a high union rate and a low complication rate have been reported from a variety of techniques for primary fixation of displaced fractures of the clavicle, dispelling some of the pessimism that surrounded prior studies where a poor understanding of soft tissue handling, a selection bias of patients, and inadequate implants combined to produce inferior results.[§] Zlowodzki et al.'s metaanalysis showed a relative risk reduction of 86% (from 15.1% to 2.2%) for nonunion with primary plate fixation compared with nonoperative treatment.[185]

While there is increasing interest in, and enthusiasm for, primary fixation of clavicle fractures, it is vital to remember that the majority of these fractures can and should be treated nonoperatively. The current research in this area should not provoke a swing of the operative pendulum into indiscriminate fixation of all clavicle injuries. Clinical and basic science research in this field adds objective information to this topic and is directed at prompting a thoughtful assessment of each injury based on these data and each case's individual merits such as the function and expectations of the patient, the location of the fracture, and the degree of displacement or comminution. Treatment is then based on this assessment, rather than pursuing either a blanket condemnation of fixation or an unreasoning rush to surgery.

PRINCIPLES OF MANAGEMENT

Mechanisms of Injury

A direct blow on the point of the shoulder is the most common reported mechanism of injury that produces a midshaft fracture of the clavicle.[15,95,137,160] This can occur in a number of ways, including being thrown from a vehicle or bicycle, during a sports event, from the intrusion of objects or vehicle structure during a motor vehicle accident, or falling from a height. A recent prospective trial of more than 130 completely displaced midshaft fractures of the clavicle identified motor vehicle/motorcycle accidents, bicycling accidents, skiing/snowboarding falls or collisions, sports injuries, and falls as the most commonly involved mechanisms.[15] As the shoulder girdle is subjected to compression force directed from laterally, the main strut maintaining position is the clavicle and its articulations (Fig. 36-3). As the force exceeds the capacity of this structure to withstand it, failure can occur in one of three ways. The acromioclavicular (AC) articulation may fail, the clavicle may break, or the sternoclavicular (SC) joint may dislocate. SC injuries are rare and are typically associated with more direct posterior blows against the medial clavicle (posterior dislocations) or anterior blows to the distal shoulder girdle (levering the proximal clavicle into an anterior dislocation).[81,158] Presumably, there are subtle nuances of the direction and magnitude of applied forces and local anatomy that dictate whether the failure occurs in the AC joint, or in the clavicle, and the magnitude of displacement that occurs. Most (85%) clavicle fractures occur in the midshaft of the bone where, as can be seen in a cross section, the bone is narrowest and enveloping soft-tissue structures (which may help dissipate injury force) are most scarce.[27–30,137,138] It is typical to see a large abrasion or contusion on the posterior aspect of the shoulder in patients with displaced midshaft clavicular fractures, especially those who fall from bicycles, motorcycles, or other vehicles: this force vector may also contribute to the location of the fracture. The direction of the initial deforming force and both gravitational and muscular forces on the clavicle are significant and result in the typical deformity seen after fracture, with the distal fragment being translated inferiorly, anteriorly, and medially (shortened) and rotated anteriorly (Fig. 36-4).

Simple falls from a standing height are unlikely to produce a displaced fracture in a healthy young person but can result in injury in elderly, osteoporotic individuals: these fractures are typically seen in the distal third of the clavicle. If the mechanism of injury is trivial and does not seem commensurate with the fracture depicted, then a careful investigation for a pathologic fracture should be performed[30,157] (Fig. 36-5).

[‡]References 65,70,86,89,113,128,139,162,171,180.
[§]References 2,15,22,39,49,56,74,82,107,125–127.

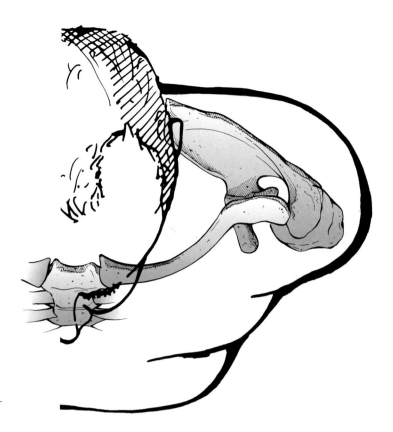

FIGURE 36-3 The strut function of the clavicle, the only bony articulation between the axial skeleton and the upper limb.

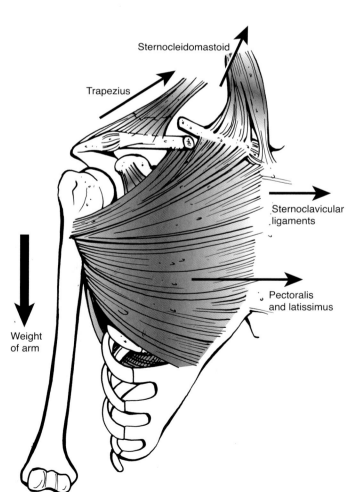

Sternocleidomastoid

Trapezius

Sternoclavicular ligaments

Pectoralis and latissimus

Weight of arm

FIGURE 36-4 Muscular and gravitational forces acting on the clavicle with resultant deformity. The distal fragment is translated anteriorly, medially, and inferiorly and rotated anteriorly. This results in the scapula being protracted.

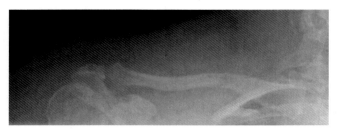

FIGURE 36-5 A 45-year-old previously well woman presented to the fracture clinic with shoulder pain following an episode of minor trauma. Radiographs revealed a fracture through a lytic lesion of the clavicle. This was the presentation of what subsequent investigation revealed to be a widely disseminated metastatic adenocarcinoma of unknown source.

Associated Injuries

Associated injuries are increasingly common in patients with fractures of the clavicle, compared with the incidence reported in older traditional studies.[36,40,41,89,162,183] There may be several reasons for this, including more liberal use of improved diagnostic techniques (i.e., computed tomography [CT] scanning), the greater speed and violence of many modern sports (e.g., motocross and snowboarding), and the improved survivorship of patients with significant chest trauma who would have died before the institution of comprehensive treatment of the trauma patient. In fact, several studies from Level I trauma centers have examined the characteristics of polytrauma patients with clavicle fractures and have noted a high mortality rate (20% to 34%) from associated chest and head trauma.[89,162] Presumably, these series of critically injured patients contain survivors who live to require treatment for the complications of their clavicle fractures who may not have survived without modern trauma care.

Patients who have been the victims of high-energy vehicular

trauma are more likely to have associated injures to the thoracic cage, including ipsilateral rib fractures, scapular and/or glenoid fractures, proximal humeral fractures, and hemothoraces/pneumothoraces[28,89,162] (Fig. 36-6). In addition to simply being good medicine, identification of these injuries is important for multiple reasons. Patients may require urgent treatment directed specifically at the associated injury (i.e., tube thoracostomy for pneumothorax), their presence may influence the treatment of the clavicle fracture (i.e., an associated displaced glenoid neck fracture, the "floating shoulder" [see later]), or (as objective information on this entity increases) they may give an indication of the likelihood of a negative outcome for the clavicle fracture (malunion, nonunion) that may have implications regarding primary fixation (Fig. 36-7). The clavicle can also be injured from penetrating trauma including projectiles, blasts, and sword or machete blows (Fig. 36-8). In this situation, diagnosing and treating underlying chest and/or vascular injuries are critically important, and the clavicle can be treated on its own merits.* However, if a vascular repair has been performed, clavicular fixation (if possible) provides an optimally stable environment for healing.

History

The history should delineate a number of aspects to optimize the patient's care. In addition to the standard demographic data, the details of the mechanism of injury are important. A clavicle fracture caused by a simple low-energy fall is unlikely to be associated with other fractures or intrathoracic injuries, whereas

*References 29,30,34,63,72,99,133,165.

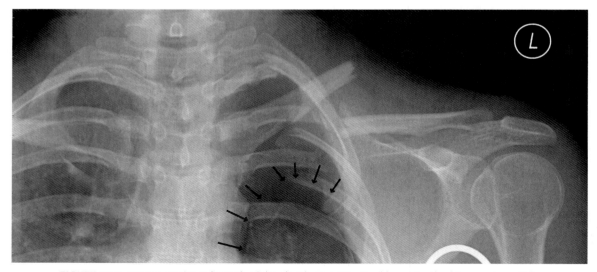

FIGURE 36-6 Anteroposterior radiograph of the clavicle in a 42-year-old man involved in a motor-vehicle collision. Associated injuries include multiple ipsilateral upper rib fractures, an ipsilateral pneumothorax (arrows outlining collapsed lung), and multiple lower extremity fractures. This patient has four relative indications for operative fixation: (i) the severe displacement of the clavicle fracture, (ii) the multiple upper rib fractures, which tend to destabilize the shoulder girdle, (iii) the associated lower extremity fractures and the resultant need for immediate upper extremity use, and (iv) the pneumothorax, which is indicative of the degree of trauma applied to the shoulder.

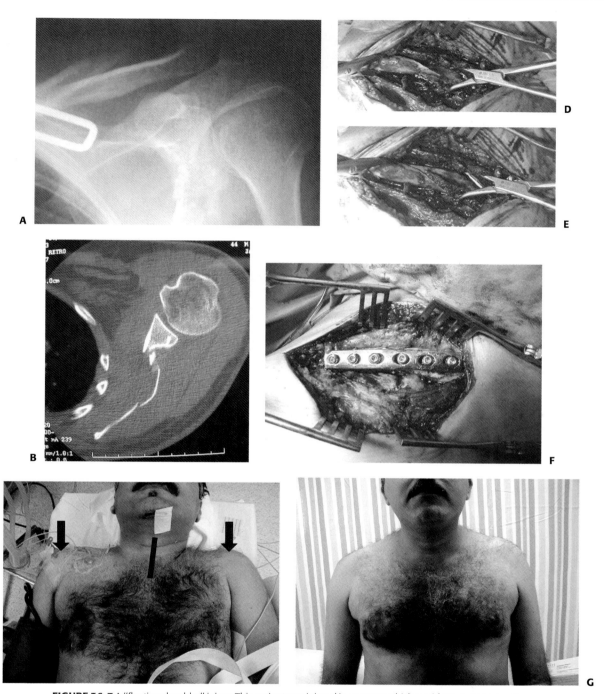

FIGURE 36-7 A "floating shoulder" injury. This patient was injured in a motor vehicle accident. **A.** Anteroposterior radiograph demonstrates a displaced, shortened left clavicle fracture. **B.** Computed tomography scan of the shoulder reveals a comminuted glenoid neck fracture. **C.** There is significant clinical deformity. **D.** Intraoperatively, the fracture is reduced with the aid of reduction clamps, and an anterior fixation plate is applied (**E**). Symmetry of the shoulder was restored by clavicle fixation alone (**F**), and it was not necessary to repair the glenoid fracture. **G.** There was an excellent clinical result with full restoration of motion and a Constant-Murley Shoulder Outcome Score of 95.

a fracture that occurs as a result of severe vehicular trauma or a fall from a height should prompt a search for other injuries. In my experience, clavicle fractures that result from falls while bicycling often have associated multiple ipsilateral upper rib fractures. At a Level I trauma center, McKee et al.[89] studied 105 polytrauma patients (multiple system injury and Injury Severity Score greater than 16) with fractures of the clavicular shaft and

found a mortality rate of 32%, mainly as a result of associated head and chest injuries. This high incidence of associated head and chest injuries mandates careful clinical and radiographic investigation. The physical mechanism of injury is important: while the majority of fractures will result from a blow to the shoulder, failure of the bone can also occur from a traction-type injury. This usually occurs in an industrial or a dockyard

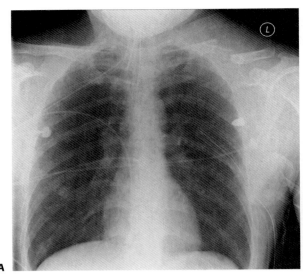

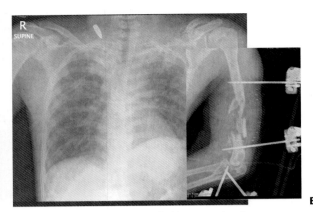

FIGURE 36-8 A. Comminuted clavicle fracture resulting from a low-velocity gunshot wound with an associated hemopneumothorax and a retained intrathoracic bullet, treated with tube thoracostomy. The degree of clavicular deformity and the associated injuries represent a relative indication for operative repair. **B.** Severe injuries in a 25-year-old soldier struck by a high-velocity (AK-47) bullet that fractured the humerus, struck the clavicle, shattering the midportion, lacerated the subclavian vein and artery (causing life-threatening hemorrhage), and came to rest in the soft tissues of the neck. In an austere military operating environment, the clavicle fragments were resected and a vascular repair was performed.

injury in which the involved arm is forcefully pulled away from the body as it is caught in machinery. It can also occur in vehicular trauma when the arm is pinned against or strikes a fixed object as the torso continues past it. This can lead to scapulothoracic dissociation, as the shoulder girdle fails in tension at the SC joint, the clavicle, or the AC joint. This is evident on the radiographs when a completely displaced, distracted fracture site is seen (as opposed to the typical overlapping fracture fragments) (Fig. 36-9). The high incidence of neurologic and vascular traction injuries seen in this setting mandates further investigation (i.e., angiography), because they can be limb threatening.[29,36,54,99,122,183]

If the clavicular fracture has occurred with minimal trauma, one must be alert to the possibility of a pathologic fracture (Fig. 36-5). Metabolic processes that weaken bone (i.e., renal disease,

hyperparathyroidism), benign or malignant tumors (i.e., myeloma, metastases), or pre-existing lesions (i.e., congenital pseudarthrosis of the clavicle) can result in pathologic fracture. In this setting, nonoperative treatment of the clavicle fracture is recommended initially, while intervention is directed toward diagnosis and treatment of the underlying condition. Once the primary diagnosis has been made and treatment initiated, the clavicle fracture is treated based on its individual aspects. Also, repetitive or unusual loads may induce a stress fracture of the clavicle, typically in bodybuilders or weightlifters.[119,143,152]

In the past, when treatment of all clavicular shaft fractures was consistently nonoperative, a detailed history of lifestyle, occupation, and medical conditions was usually perfunctory at best, since these factors did little to influence decision making. However, there is increasing evidence that operative intervention is superior in carefully selected cases of displaced clavicular shaft fracture, such that additional information gleaned from the history contributes to the risk/benefit analysis regarding possible surgery. Compliant patients in the 16-to-60 age group, who have active recreational lifestyles and/or physically demanding occupations (especially those that require throwing, repetitive overhead work, or recurrent lifting), are candidates for primary operative repair if they are medically fit and have completely displaced fractures with good bone quality.[15,96,125,167,185] Factors associated with noncompliance and a high rate of fixation failure, such as drug and alcohol abuse, untreated psychiatric conditions, homelessness, or uncontrolled seizure disorders, are contraindications for primary operative repair of clavicle fractures.[10]

Physical Examination

When nonoperative treatment was chosen for the vast majority of clavicle fractures, there was little emphasis placed on a careful physical examination of the shoulder girdle. However, there are

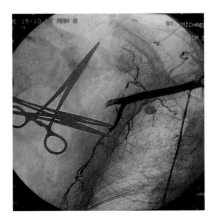

FIGURE 36-9 Emergency angiogram of a patient with scapulothoracic dissociation and wide distraction of a very distal clavicle fracture. There is an associated axillary artery avulsion, a complete brachial plexus injury, and multiple ipsilateral upper extremity fractures.

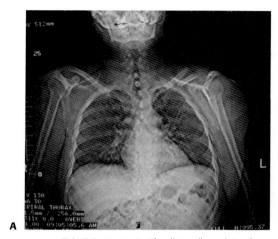 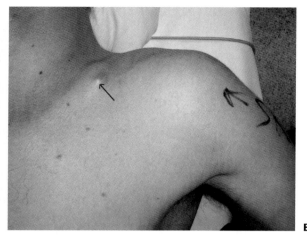

FIGURE 36-10 A. The "scout" portion of a computed tomography scan in a polytrauma patient with a displaced clavicle fracture demonstrates the typical deformity that occurs with these injuries. **B.** The corresponding clinical photograph demonstrates blanching of the skin over the medial fragment (*arrow*).

a number of findings that are important in surgical decision making. There is usually swelling, bruising, and ecchymosis at the fracture site, as well as deformity with displaced fractures. Visible deformity of the shoulder girdle, best seen when the patient is standing, is an important feature to recognize. The usual position seen with a completely displaced midshaft fracture of the clavicle has been described as shoulder "ptosis," with a droopy, medially driven, and shortened shoulder[57,68,122,135] (Fig. 36-10). In addition, the shoulder translates and rotates forward: this is a deformity that can best be seen by viewing the patient from above. Because of this malposition of the shoulder girdle, inspection of the patient from behind may reveal a subtle prominence of the inferior aspect of the scapula from scapular protraction as it moves with the distal fragment. Shortening of the clavicle should be measured clinically with a tape measure. A mark is made in the midline of the suprasternal notch and another is made at the palpable ridge of the AC joint: measuring this length gives the difference between the involved and normal shoulder girdle.[155]

A careful neurologic and vascular examination of the involved limb is mandatory, especially if surgical intervention is contemplated. If a deficit is not noted preoperatively, then it may be incorrectly attributed to the surgery, which has prognostic, medicolegal, and treatment implications.[27–30]

Surprisingly, given its subcutaneous nature and exposed position, open fractures of the clavicle are relatively rare. Most open fractures are associated with high-energy vehicular trauma, and recognition is important for a number of reasons: the fracture itself will require irrigation, debridement, and fixation, and there is a high incidence of associated injuries. In the largest series in the literature focusing on open clavicle fractures, Taitsman et al. described 20 patients with this injury: 15 patients had pulmonary injuries, 13 patients had head injuries, 8 patients had scapular fractures, 11 patients had facial trauma, and there were a variety of other injuries.[162]

Imaging and Other Diagnostic Studies

Simple anteroposterior (AP) radiographs are usually sufficient to establish the diagnosis of a clavicle fracture. The diagnosis

may also be made from a single AP chest radiograph, which may be the only available film in an urgent trauma setting. The chest radiograph can also be used to evaluate the deformity of the involved clavicle relative to the normal side and to look for associated skeletal injuries such as rib, glenoid, and scapular fractures. A measurement of length can be made on the chest radiograph comparing the injured to the uninjured side: shortening of 2 cm or more represents a relative indication for primary fixation. To best delineate a clavicular fracture, as when one is determining whether operative intervention is warranted, a radiograph should be taken in the upright position (where gravity will demonstrate maximal deformity). Ideally, the radiographic beam for the AP radiograph of the clavicle should be angled 20 degrees superiorly to eliminate the overlap of the thoracic cage and show the clavicle in profile.[27–30,134,170] Also, if the torso is internally rotated a similar 20 degrees (rotating internally when standing or by bumping up the opposite side while supine), this places the scapula and shoulder girdle parallel to the cassette for a true AP film. CT scanning of midshaft clavicular fractures is rarely performed in the clinical setting, although this imaging modality can demonstrate the complex three-dimensional deformity that affects the shoulder girdle with these injuries, including significant scapular angulation and protraction.[57] It is also useful for evaluating fractures of the medial third of the clavicle and the remainder of the shoulder girdle, such as the glenoid neck in cases of a "floating shoulder."[42,130,142]

Lateral clavicle fractures can be well visualized with AP radiographs. Centering the radiograph on the acromioclavicular joint and angling the beam in a cephalic tilt of approximately 15 degrees (the Zanca view) helps delineate the fracture well, by removing the overlap of the upper portion of the thoracic cage.[29,30] To accurately delineate the degree of fracture displacement, these radiographs should be taken with the patient standing and the arm unsupported by slings, braces, or the uninjured arm. On occasion, it may be useful to obtain a stress view to determine the integrity of the coracoclavicular ligaments (as this can influence the choice of fixation): a 5- to 10-pound weight is suspended from the wrist of the affected arm and then radiographs are taken. CT scanning of lateral clavicle fractures is rarely required clinically but can be useful in selected cases to determine intra-articular extension or displacement.

Fractures of the medial clavicle, especially those involving the SC joint, are notoriously difficult to accurately assess with plain radiographs. CT scanning is the radiographic procedure of choice when the anatomy of the fracture is unclear. This investigation can help distinguish between a medial epiphyseal fracture (common in individuals up to 25 years of age) and true SC dislocations[29,150,163,181] (Fig. 36-11).

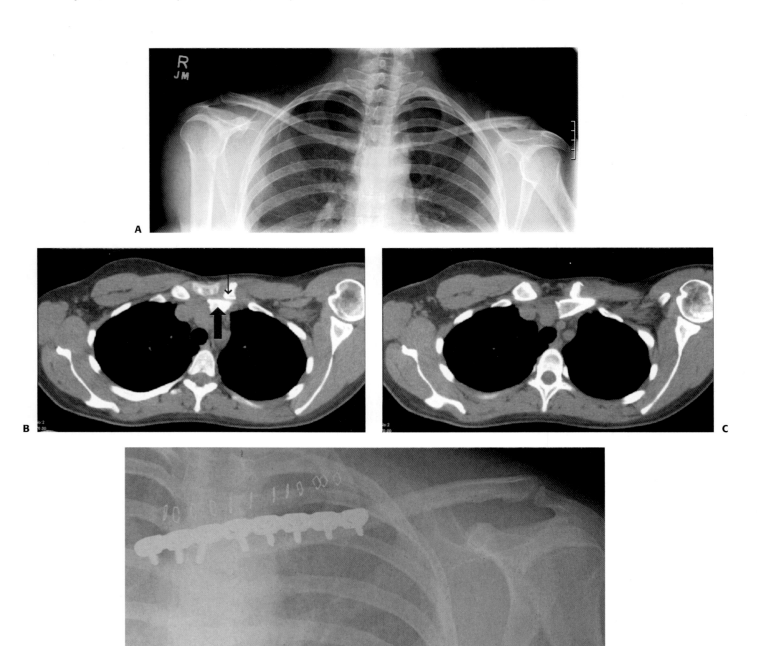

FIGURE 36-11 Fractures of the medial end of the clavicle are difficult to visualize with conventional radiography. This 32-year-old female equestrian sustained a medial clavicle fracture following a riding accident when her horse fell on her. **A.** The anteroposterior radiograph reveals some asymmetry of the clavicles, but it is difficult to define the exact nature of the injury due to the overlap of bony axial structures and the spinal column. **B.** Computed tomography scan clearly demonstrates the medial fracture with a small residual medial fragment (*small arrow*) and posterior displacement of the shaft (*large arrow*), (**C**) impinging on the mediastinal structures. **D.** Plate fixation was performed, with extension of the plate onto the sternum due to the small size of the medial fragment. Once bony union has occurred (between 3 and 6 months), the plate should be removed. (Case courtesy of Dr. Jeremy A. Hall.)

Diagnosis and AO/OTA Classification

A number of classification schemes have been proposed for fractures of the clavicle. These have traditionally been based on the position of the fracture, with the groups originally divided by Allman into proximal (group I), middle (group II), and distal (group III) third fractures. This general grouping has the advantage of corresponding to the clinical approach to these fractures of most orthopaedic surgeons.[29] Recognizing that this basic scheme does not take into account factors that influence treatment and outcome, such as fracture pattern, displacement, comminution, and shortening, various authorities have refined the classification to include other variables. Because of their high rate of delayed and nonunion, Neer[101] divided distal clavicle fractures into three subgroups, based on their ligamentous attachments and degree of displacement (type II was subsequently modified by Rockwood)[29]:

Type I: Distal clavicle fracture with the coracoclavicular ligaments intact
Type II: Coracoclavicular ligaments detached from the medial fragment, with the trapezoidal ligament attached to the distal fragment
    IIA (Rockwood): Both conoid and trapezoid attached to the distal fragment
    IIB (Rockwood): Conoid detached from the medial fragment
Type III: Distal clavicle fracture with extension into the AC joint

Ideally, a classification scheme should be reproducible with a low rate of interobserver and intraobserver variability, should help direct treatment, can be used to predict outcome, should be useful in both the clinical and research realms, and should be simple enough to be practically useful yet robust enough to include all fracture patterns. While at the present time there is no classification scheme that has been rigorously tested to meet all these objectives, modern schemes based on prospective, comprehensive population-based studies are available. Nordqvist et al.[111] examined more than 2035 fractures of the clavicle over a 10-year period and essentially expanded on Allman's original scheme by adding subtypes based on fracture displacement, including a comminuted category for midshaft fractures. In a similar population-based study in Edinburgh, Robinson[137] evaluated more than 1000 consecutive fractures of the clavicle and developed a classification scheme based on prognostic variables from the analysis of the data (Fig. 36-12). It continues the traditional scheme of dividing the clavicle into thirds and adds variables that are of proven diagnostic value (intra-articular extension, displacement, and comminution). However, a feature of this scheme is that it reverses the traditional numbering scheme, describing medial fractures as type I, middle third fractures as type II, and distal third fractures as type III. Because distal third fractures are firmly entrenched in the orthopaedic lexicon as "type II" fractures, this can lead to significant confusion. Despite this drawback, the Robinson classification is based on an extensive database that includes prospectively gathered, objective clinical data. For this reason, it is the classification I prefer to use clinically as it can help predict outcome and hence guide treatment, including the decision to operate and fixation methods chosen. The *AO/OTA Fracture and Dislocation Classification Compendium* was updated in 2007 to include recent developments including a unified numbering scheme and measures to improve observer reliability (Fig. 36-

13). The clavicle is designated as segment 15 and is divided into the standard medial metaphyseal, diaphyseal, and lateral metaphyseal fractures.[85] An important difference is that the metaphyseal fractures in this scheme are not one third of the length of the bone but are shorter segments, according to the AO "rule of squares." For the all-important diaphysis, there are simple (15-B1), wedge (15-B2), and complex (15-B3) subtypes.

SURGICAL AND APPLIED ANATOMY AND COMMON SURGICAL APPROACHES

Surgical and Applied Anatomy

Bony Anatomy

The clavicle is a relatively thin bone, widest at its medial and lateral expansions where it articulates with the sternum and acromion, respectively (Fig. 36-14). It has two distinct curves: the larger, obvious curve is in the coronal plane giving the bone its characteristic "S" shape (medial end convex anterior and lateral end concave anterior).[95] There is also a more subtle superior curve delineated in a cadaver study by Huang et al.[64] This milder superior bow had its apex laterally a mean of 37 mm from the acromial articulation, with a mean magnitude of 5 mm. The medial superior surface of the clavicle was found to be flat. This article also described the fit of a precontoured clavicular plate to 100 pairs of cadaver clavicles. The authors found that there were significant sex and racial differences in the fit of the plate from best (black male clavicles) to worst (white female clavicles). This article helps explain why intraoperatively it often is necessary to adjust or contour even "anatomic" plates for the clavicle to achieve an optimal fit.[64] The bone in the relatively thin diaphysis is typically hard cortical bone best suited for cortical screws, whereas the medial and lateral expansions are softer cancellous bone where larger pitch cancellous screws can be inserted without tapping.

Ligamentous Anatomy

Medial. There is relatively little motion at the SC joint, and the supporting soft tissue structures are correspondingly thick. Medially, the clavicle is secured to the sternum by the SC capsule, and although there are not easily demonstrable "ligaments," the thickening of the posterior capsule has been determined to be the single most important soft tissue constraint to anterior or posterior translation of the medial clavicle. There is also an interclavicular ligament that runs from the medial end of one clavicle, gains purchase from the superior aspect of the sternum at the sternal notch, and attaches to the medial end of the contralateral clavicle. Acting as a tension wire at the base of the clavicle, this ligament helps prevent inferior angulation or translation of the clavicle. In addition, there are extremely stout ligaments that originate on the first rib and insert on the undersurface or the inferior aspect of the clavicle.[18] A small fossa inferomedially, the rhomboid fossa, has been described as an attachment point for these ligaments, which are primary resistors to translation of the medial clavicle.

Lateral. The coracoclavicular ligaments are the trapezoid (more lateral) and conoid (more medial), which are stout ligaments that arise from the base of the coracoid and insert onto the small osseous ridge of the inferior clavicle (trapezoid)

Robinson Cortical Alignment Fracture (Type 2A)

Undisplaced (Type 2A1)

Angulated (Type 2A2)

Robinson Displaced Fractures (Type 2B)

Simple or single butterfly (Type 2B1)

Segmental or comminuted (Type 2B2)

Allman Group I
Craig Group I

Robinson Cortical Alignment Fracture (Type 3A)

Extra-articular (Type 3A1)
Neer Type I
Craig Type I

Intra-articular (Type 3A2)
Neer Type III
Craig Type III

Robinson Displaced Fractures (Type 3B)

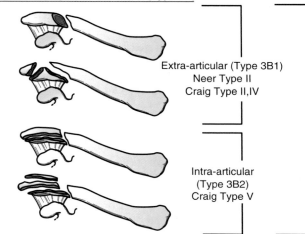

Extra-articular (Type 3B1)
Neer Type II
Craig Type II,IV

Intra-articular
(Type 3B2)
Craig Type V

Allman Group II
Craig Group II

Robinson Undisplaced Fractures (Type 1A)

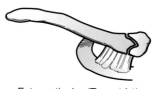

Extra-articular (Type 1A1)
Craig Type I

Intra-articular (Type 1A2)
Craig Type III

Robinson Displaced Fractures (Type 1B)

Extra-articular (Type 1B1)
Craig Type II

Extra-articular (Type 1B2)
Craig Type V

Allman Group III
Craig Group III

FIGURE 36-12 Robinson classification scheme of clavicle fractures.

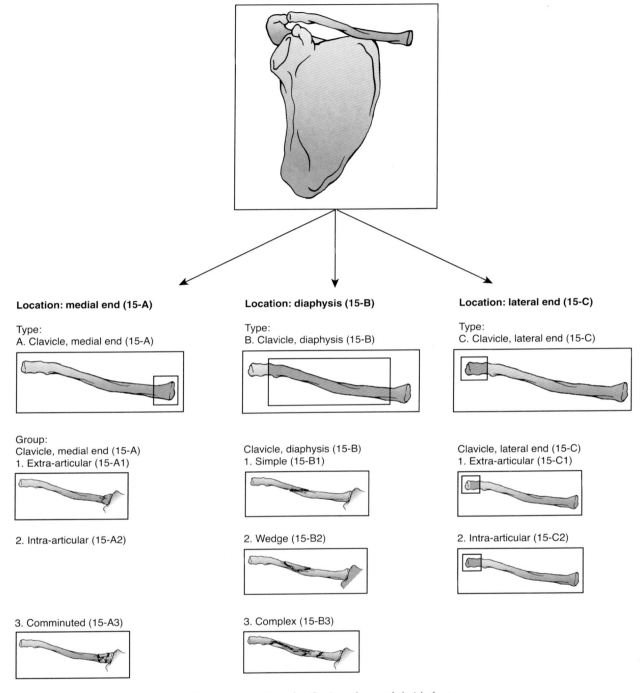

FIGURE 36-13 AO/OTA classification scheme of clavicle fractures.

and the clavicular conoid tubercle (conoid). These ligaments are very strong and are the primary resistance to superior displacement of the lateral clavicle. Their integrity, or lack thereof, plays an important role in the decision making and fixation selection for the treatment of displaced lateral third clavicle fractures. Clavicle fractures in this location will often have an avulsed inferior fragment to which these ligaments are attached, especially in younger individuals. Inclusion of these fragments in surgical fixation selection enhances the stability of the operative repair. The capsule of the AC joint is thickened superiorly and is primarily responsible for resist-

ing AP displacement of the joint. It is important to repair this structure, which is usually reflected surgically as part of the deep myofascial layer, when operating on the lateral end of the clavicle. If one is inserting a hook plate for fixation of a very distal fracture, a small defect can be made in the posterolateral aspect of the capsule for insertion of the hook portion into the posterior subacromial space.[22,39,75,169,182]

Muscular Anatomy

The clavicle is not as important as the scapula in terms of muscle origin but still serves as the attachment site of several large

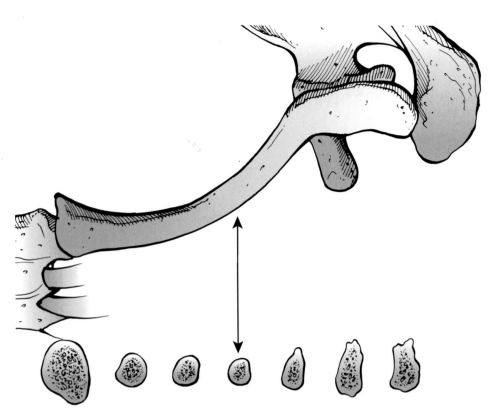

FIGURE 36-14 The cross-sectional and topographic anatomy of the clavicle. The clavicle is narrowest in its midportion, explaining the high incidence of fractures in this area.

muscles. Medially, the pectoralis major muscle originates from the clavicular shaft anteroinferiorly, and the sternocleidomastoid originates superiorly. The pectoralis origin merges with the origin of the anterior deltoid laterally, while the trapezius insertion blends superiorly with the deltoid origin at the lateral margin (Fig. 36-15). Muscle attachment plays a significant role in the deformity that results after fracture: the medial clavicular fragment is elevated by the unopposed pull of the SC muscle, while the distal fragment is held inferiorly by the deltoid and medially by the pectoralis major. The undersurface of the clavicle is the insertion site of the subclavius muscle, which is of little significance functionally but serves as a soft tissue buffer in the subclavicular space superior to the brachial plexus and subclavian vessels. The platysma, or "shaving muscle," is variable in terms of thickness and extent but usually envelopes the anterior and superior aspects of the clavicle and runs in the subcutaneous tissues, extending superiorly to the mandible and deeper facial muscles. It is divided during the surgical approach and is typically included in the closure of the superficial, or skin/subcutaneous, layer.

Neurovascular Anatomy
The supraclavicular nerves originate from cervical roots C3 and C4 and exit from a common trunk behind the posterior border of the sternocleidomastoid muscle. There are typically three major branches (anterior, middle, and posterior) that cross the clavicle superficially from medial to lateral and are at risk during surgical approaches. If they are divided, an area of numbness is typically felt inferior to the surgical incision, although this tends to improve with time. A more difficult problem can be

the development of a painful neuroma in the scar, which, although rare, can negatively affect an otherwise good surgical outcome. For this reason, some authorities recommend identification and protection of these nerves during operative repair.[69,70,154] More vital neurovascular structures lie inferior to the clavicle. The subclavian vein runs directly below the subclavius muscle and above the first rib, where it is readily accessible (for central venous access) and vulnerable (to inadvertent injury). More posteriorly lie the subclavian artery and the brachial plexus, separated from the vein and clavicle by the additional layer of the scalenus anterior muscle medially. The plexus is closest to the clavicle in its midportion, where the greatest care needs to be taken in not violating the subclavicular space with drills, screws, or instruments. Despite the proximity of these vital structures, iatrogenic injury is surprisingly rare (see later).

Common Surgical Approaches
Currently, there are two common surgical approaches applicable to the fixation of clavicle fractures, each with its own advantages and disadvantages, as follows:

Anterosuperior
Anterosuperior plating can reasonably be considered the most popular operative method for fixation of the clavicle.[11,12,15,24,31] Its advantages include a general familiarity with this approach in most surgeons' hands, the ability to extend it simply to both the medial and lateral ends of the clavicle, and clear radiographic views of the clavicle postoperatively. Its disadvantages include the trajectory of screw placement (from superior to infe-

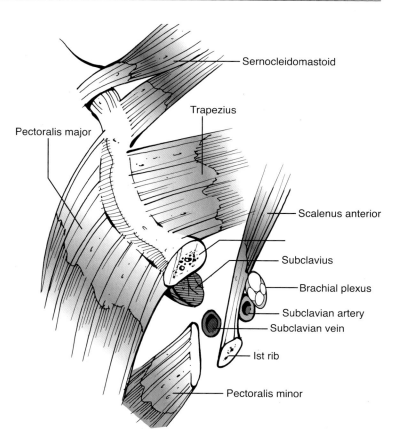

FIGURE 36-15 Applied anatomy of the clavicle. Anterosuperiorly, the pectoralis major muscle and fascia envelope the medial 60% of the clavicle, while the lateral 40% is covered by the deltoid muscle and its fascia. Posterosuperiorly, the trapezius muscle attaches to the clavicle.

rior), which can be difficult, and inadvertent "plunging" with the drill, which can place the underlying lung and neurovascular structures at risk. Also, the clavicle is fairly narrow in its supero-inferior dimension, and typically the length of screws inserted ranges from 14 to 16 mm in females to 16 to 18 mm in males. In thin individuals, hardware prominence can be problematic and may lead to hardware removal. The surgical approach and technique are detailed later (see "Authors' Preferred Method of Treatment").

Anteroinferior

Several groups have published large series on the advantages of anteroinferior plating of acute clavicle fractures.[25,74,153] Advantages of this technique include an easier screw trajectory with less likelihood of serious injury with inadvertent overpenetration of the drill (although the incidence of iatrogenic nerve injury is very low), the ability to insert longer screws in the wider AP dimension of the clavicle, and decreased hardware prominence. It is also technically easier to contour a small-fragment compression plate along the anterior border as opposed to the superior surface: however, the advent of precontoured plates has largely negated this particular advantage. Collinge et al. reported on the use of this technique in 58 patients and described one fixation failure, one nonunion, three infections, and only two hardware removals.[25] Potential disadvantages of this technique include the lack of general familiarity with the approach and that the plate tends to obscure the fracture site radiographically. Also, although there remains some controversy on the matter, biomechanical studies have in general shown that the most advantageous position for plate placement is the superior surface.

The procedure is performed with the patient in the supine position with a bump or pad between the scapulae to help restore length and improve exposure. The arm can be free-draped to aid in fracture reduction. The skin incision is centered over the fracture site along the inferior palpable edge of the clavicle, roughly in a line drawn from the sternal notch to the anteroinferior aspect of the AC joint. As experience with the technique grows, a smaller skin incision and extensive subcutaneous mobilization for exposure are possible. Any identifiable supraclavicular nerves are protected, and the clavipectoral fascia is incised and reflected inferiorly. The fracture site is identified, cleaned, and reduced with reduction forceps. A lag screw(s) is placed if possible, or the fracture can be temporarily secured with K-wires. Following this, fixation proceeds with the chosen plate being contoured to fit along the anteroinferior surface of the clavicle. Since the contouring of the plate is performed in the long axis of the plate, it is much simpler to contour a straight compression plate to the anterior, as opposed to the superior surface (Fig. 36-16). Additionally, it is usually possible to place screws that are 2 to 4 mm longer in the AP dimension of the clavicle. Following fracture fixation, a two-layer soft tissue closure is performed in as standard fashion. Postoperative care is similar to that instituted following anterosuperior plating.

CURRENT TREATMENT OPTIONS

A review article focusing on evidence-based medicine outlined treatment approaches to displaced midshaft fractures of the

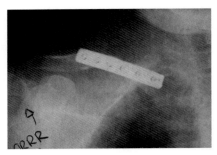

FIGURE 36-16 Anteroinferior plating of the clavicle with a conventional 3.5-mm compression plate. It is much simpler to contour a conventional straight plate in this plane compared with superior placement.

clavicle.[93] This resource summarizes the available objective evidence about recommendations for the optimal treatment of these injuries (Table 36-2). The grades of recommendation are as follows:

Grade A: Good evidence (high-quality prospective, randomized clinical trials [RCTs] with consistent findings) recommending for or against intervention

Grade B: Fair evidence (lesser-quality RCTs, prospective comparative studies, case-control series) recommending for or against intervention

Grade C: Poor-quality evidence (case series or experts' opinions) recommending for or against intervention

Grade I: There is insufficient or conflicting evidence, not allowing a recommendation for or against intervention

While there are an abundance of manuscripts detailing the treatment of clavicle fractures, most tend to be retrospective reviews, although there are an increasing number of prospective and/or randomized trials being published.[15,61,68,139] My personal recommendations for treatment must be considered in light of the evidence available in Tables 36-1 and 36-2.

Operative Indications for Clavicle Fractures

There are numerous large series that describe relatively good results following nonoperative treatment of clavicle fractures, and it is my opinion that the majority of clavicle fractures can, and should, be treated in this fashion.[3,40,47,72,100,144] However, there are serious deficiencies in these reports, including the inclusion of children (who have an intrinsically good result and remodeling potential), large numbers of patients lost to follow-up, and radiographic and/or surgeon-based outcomes that are insensitive to residual deficits. Recent evidence from prospective and randomized clinical trials has suggested that there is a subset of individuals who benefit from primary operative care[15,61,68,125,139,172] (Fig. 36-17). Operative repair in this setting should be reserved for medically well, physically active patients who stand to benefit the most from a rapid restoration of normal anatomy and stable fixation. There are multiple potential indications for primary operative fixation, outlined in Table 36-3.

Nonoperative Treatment

The earliest reported attempt at closed reduction of a displaced midshaft fracture of the clavicle was recorded in the "Edwin Smith" papyrus dating from the 30th century B.C. Hippocrates described the typical deformity resulting from this injury and emphasized the importance of trying to correct it.[1] It is usually possible to obtain an improvement in position of the fracture fragments by placing the patient supine, with a roll or sandbag behind the shoulder blades to let the anterior displacement and rotation of the distal fragment correct with gravity, followed by superior translation and support of the affected arm. Unfortunately, it is difficult or impossible to maintain the reduction achieved. For this reason, over the millennia that followed the first description of treatment of this fracture, there have been hundreds of descriptions of different devices designed to maintain the reduction, including splints, body jackets, casts, braces, slings, swathes, and wraps.[1,3,16,27,87] At the present time, there is no convincing evidence that any of these devices reliably maintains the fracture reduction or improves clinical, radio-

TABLE 36-2	Recommendations for the Optimal Treatment of Displaced Midshaft Fractures of the Clavicle		
Statement		Grade*	References
Young active patients with completely displaced midshaft fractures of the clavicle will have superior results with primary fracture fixation		B	15, 154, 185
Anteroinferior plating may reduce the risk of symptomatic hardware compared with superior plating.		C	25, 82
There is no difference in outcome between a regular sling and a figure-of-eight bandage when nonoperative treatment is selected.		B	3, 159
There is no difference in outcome between plating and intramedullary nailing of displaced midshaft clavicle fractures.		I	7, 24, 56, 67, 125, 185
Factors associated with poor outcome following nonoperative treatment of displaced midshaft clavicle fractures include shortening and increasing fracture comminution.		A	14, 61, 91, 113, 139, 154, 185

*Grade of recommendation.

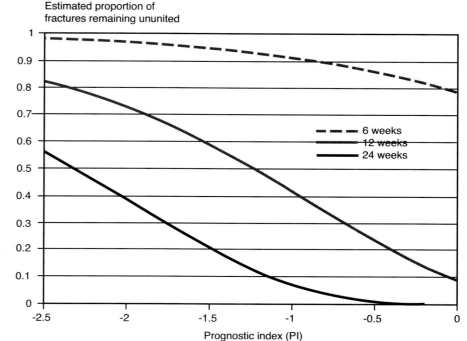

FIGURE 36-17 Probability of nonunion at various time points following a midshaft clavicle fracture. The PI (Prognostic Index) decreases with each of the following factors: increasing age, increasing comminution, increasing displacement, and female sex. (Adapted from Robinson CM, Court-Brown CM, McQueen MM, et al. Estimating the risk of nonunion following nonoperative treatment of a clavicle fracture. J Bone Joint Surg Am 2004;86A:1359–1365.)

graphic, or functional outcomes. For many years, the standard of care in North America was the "figure-of-eight" bandage: Andersen and colleagues[3] examined its utility in a prospective, randomized, controlled clinical trial comparing it to a simple sling in 60 patients. They could demonstrate no functional or radiographic difference between the two groups, and in general the patients preferred the sling (2 of 27 dissatisfied with the sling compared with 9 of 34 dissatisfied with the figure-of-eight bandage, P = 0.09). In a retrospective review of 140 patients

treated nonoperatively, Stanley and Norris[159] did not find any difference between a standard sling and a figure-of-eight bandage, a finding confirmed by other authors.[123,124] Also, I have seen several temporary lower trunk brachial plexus palsies from figure-of-eight bandages that resulted from overtightening. For this reason, in my practice, if nonoperative care is selected, a simple, conventional sling with a padded neckpiece is applied, and no attempt at reduction is made.

External Fixation

There are reports in the literature of various techniques of external fixation for clavicle fractures.[33,148,164] This method takes advantage of the intrinsic healing ability of the clavicle and allows restoration of length and translation without the scarring or morbidity of a surgical approach. Also, there is no retained hardware at the conclusion of treatment. Schuind et al.[148] reported on a series of 20 patients treated with external fixation for clavicular injuries, many of whom had local soft tissue compromise; union occurred in all. Tomic et al.[164] described the treatment of 12 patients with nonunion of the clavicular shaft by application of a modified Ilizarov device. Union was achieved in 11 of 12 patients with an increase in the mean Constant-Murley Shoulder Outcome Score from 30 preoperatively to 69 postoperatively. It is clear that this technique is technically possible to perform and may be useful in certain specific situations. Unfortunately, the practical difficulties associated with the position and prominence of the fixation pins, coupled with a lack of patient acceptance in the North American population, has resulted in minimal use of this technique.

Intramedullary Pinning

Intramedullary (IM) pinning of fractures of the shaft of the clavicle has several advantages. These are similar to the benefits seen with IM fixation of long bone fractures in other areas, although

---

TABLE 36-3 **Relative Indications for Primary Fixation of Midshaft Clavicle Fractures**

Fracture Specific
1. Displacement >2 cm
2. Shortening >2 cm
3. Increasing comminution (>3 fragments)
4. Segmental fractures
5. Open fractures
6. Impending open fractures with soft tissue compromise
7. Obvious clinical deformity (usually associated with items 1 and 2)
8. Scapular malposition and winging on initial examination

Associated Injuries
1. Vascular injury requiring repair
2. Progressive neurologic deficit
3. Ipsilateral upper extremity injuries/fractures
4. Multiple ipsilateral upper rib fractures
5. "Floating shoulder"
6. Bilateral clavicle fractures

Patient Factors
1. Polytrauma with requirement for early upper extremity weight bearing/arm use
2. Patient motivation for rapid return of function (e.g., elite sports or the self-employed professional)

this technique had not been as consistently successful in the clavicle as series in the femur or tibia have reported.[8,29,45,48,56,67,94] Advantages include a smaller, more cosmetic skin incision, less soft tissue stripping at the fracture site, decreased hardware prominence following fixation, technically straightforward hardware removal, and a possibly lower incidence of refracture or fracture at the end of the implant. Recently, modifications to the technique have included a radiographically guided completely "closed" technique.[24] Since, at the present time, there is no consistently reliable way to "lock" an IM clavicle pin, complications include those common to all unlocked IM devices, namely failure to control axial length and rotation, especially with increasing fracture comminution and decreasing intrinsic fracture stability. A biomechanical study of clavicular osteotomies by Golish et al.[53] comparing 3.5-mm compression plates to 3.8-mm or 4.5-mm IM pins showed that the plated constructs were superior in resisting displacement in a number of different testing modes (maximal load, cyclical stress) compared with both IM nail constructs.

The technique includes positioning the patient in a semisitting position on a radiolucent table, with an image intensifier on the ipsilateral side. By rotating the image 45 degrees caudal and cephalad, orthogonal views of the clavicle can be obtained. A small incision is then made over the posterolateral corner of the clavicle 2 to 3 cm medial to the AC joint (Fig. 36-18). The posterior clavicle at this point is identified and the canal breached with a drill consistent with the planned fixation device. A reduction of the fracture is then performed, either through a small open incision or, as experience increases, in a completely closed fashion using a percutaneous reduction clamp on the medial fragment and a "joystick" in the proximal fragment. Alternatively, the fixation device can be inserted using a "retrograde" technique where it is passed out from the fracture site through the lateral fragment. The fracture is then reduced and the IM device is inserted into the medial fragment under direct vision. It is important to accurately reduce length and rotation, although the latter can be quite difficult if done closed and no visual clues from the fracture configuration are available. A small incision may be necessary to reduce vertically oriented comminuted fragments and "tease" then back into alignment. Following this, the canal is drilled to the appropriate size to accept the planned IM device. Options include headed pins, partially threaded pins or screws, cannulated screws, and smooth wires. Although some series report favorable results with smooth wires, the North American experience with small-diameter smooth pin fixation includes breakage and migration and is, in general, dismal.[78,83,97,108] Smooth wires are contraindicated for fracture fixation about the shoulder in general and for the clavicle in particular. It is important not to distract the fracture site with the fixation device, which can occur as the pin is inserted into the unyielding opposite cortex as the S-shaped clavicle comes into contact with the end of the straight pin. If this occurs, the pin must be withdrawn slightly or a shorter pin used. The head of the pin or screw can be left prominent to facilitate early removal through a small posterior incision or can be left flush with the bone to decrease soft tissue irritation (Fig. 36-19). Some authors advocate leaving the pin in a prominent position subcutaneously for easy access in the clinic at the time of early (7 to 8 weeks postoperatively) hardware removal. This step depends on the type of fixation device used and the philosophy of the treating surgeon. The incisions are closed in a fashion similar to that used for plate fixation, although they are typically smaller. If the surgeon is confident with the stability of the repair, early motion is instituted similar to that performed following plate fixation.

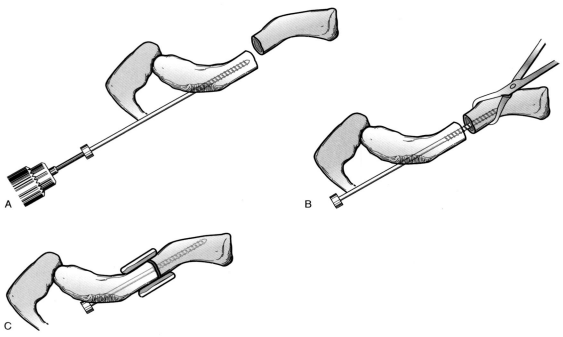

FIGURE 36-18 Intramedullary fixation with a headed, distally threaded pin (modified Haigie pin). **A.** Retrograde drilling of the distal fragment. **B.** Reduction and fixation of the fracture. **C.** Addition of bone graft or bone graft substitute.

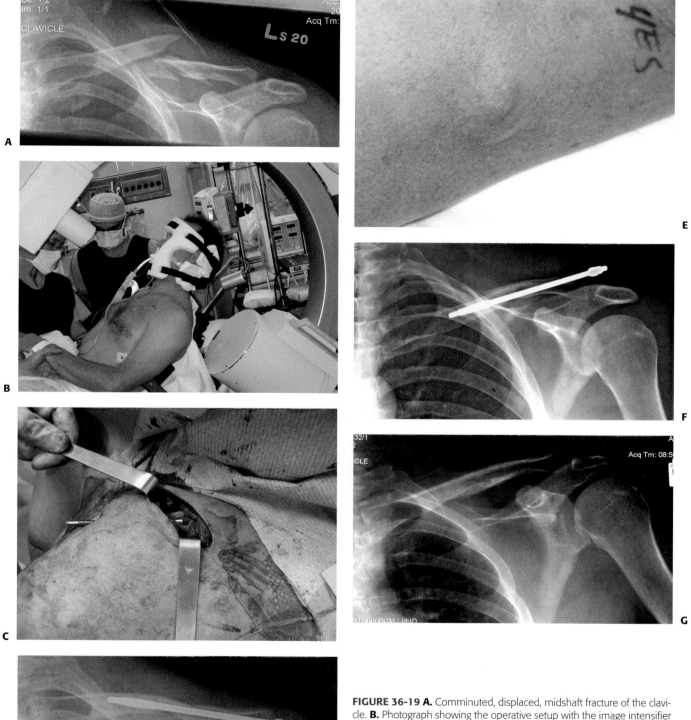

FIGURE 36-19 A. Comminuted, displaced, midshaft fracture of the clavicle. **B.** Photograph showing the operative setup with the image intensifier in place. **C.** Small incision is made and the fracture is reduced in an open fashion followed by retrograde insertion of the pin. **D.** Postoperative radiograph revealing reduction of the fracture. **E.** Radiograph demonstrating bony union. **F.** Skin irritation over prominent pin. **G.** Follow-up radiograph following uneventful union and pin removal. (Case courtesy of, and copyright by, Dr. David Ring.)

AUTHORS' PREFERRED METHOD OF TREATMENT

Use of a Precontoured Plate for Displaced Midshaft Fractures of the Clavicle

Preoperative Planning

While this section will describe the author's technique of operative repair of a midshaft clavicle fracture, it is important to remember that the majority of midshaft fractures can be treated nonoperatively. A careful physical examination (see earlier) is mandatory to rule out other injuries, which may influence the anesthetic (i.e., an ipsilateral pneumothorax) or the surgery (damaged skin or deficient soft tissue, neuro-vascular injury). The skin in this area is typically bruised, with extensive swelling, following a displaced midshaft fracture. Since the difficulty of reduction and fixation does not increase until approximately 2 weeks following injury, it may be prudent to delay operative intervention (as one would in other areas) until the soft tissue in the vicinity of the planned surgical approach is more robust. Radiographs of the injured clavicle are usually sufficient. The surgeon should observe the severity of the displacement, the number of fracture fragments, and the location of the main fracture line (Fig. 36-20). There is often a vertically oriented anterosuperior fragment, which may benefit from lag screw fixation, and mini-fragment screws should be available as this fragment may

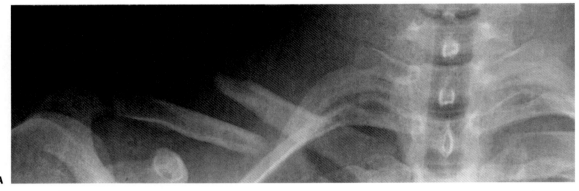

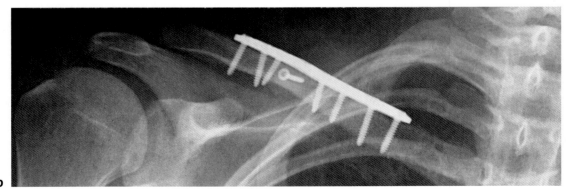

FIGURE 36-20 A. Anteroposterior radiograph of a displaced midshaft clavicle fracture. Note the difference in diameter of the proximal and distal fragments at the fracture site, suggesting that a significant degree of rotation has occurred. **B.** Intraoperative photograph of a displaced fracture, (**C**) reduced anatomically and held with a small fragment reduction forceps. **D.** Postoperative radiograph after open reduction and internal fixation with an anterior-to-posterior lag screw followed by fixation with an anatomic plate.

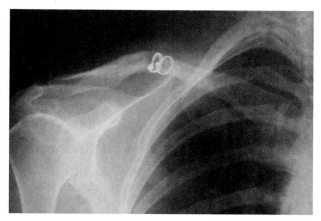

FIGURE 36-21 Cerclage wiring in isolation is inadequate to control the deforming forces at the site of a displaced clavicle fracture. It results in all of the risks of surgical intervention with few of the benefits and is to be avoided.

be quite narrow. Also, the number of screws that can be potentially placed into the distal fragment can be determined preoperatively, so that the appropriate plate can be available. Older series describing fixation of clavicle fractures have described poor results when inadequate fixation such as cerclage wires alone or plates of inadequate size or length are used[100,102,127,144] (Figs. 36-21 and 36-22). A fixation set that includes plates that are precontoured, or "anatomic," to fit the "S" shape of the clavicle is ideal. Although these plates may require some intraoperative adjustments, they typically save significant time associated with the extensive contouring required to make a straight plate fit the bone. They help to decrease the soft tissue irritation that occurs when the end of a straight plate protrudes past the end of the bone as the clavicle curves away.

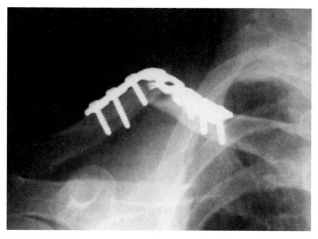

FIGURE 36-22 Anteroposterior radiograph of a 35-year-old man who weighed more than 200 pounds, whose clavicle nonunion was fixed with a 3.5-mm pelvic reconstruction plate. Early mechanical failure occurred through deformation of the plate. This type of plate may be suitable for smaller, low-demand individuals but has a higher failure rate when used in larger, more physically active patients, especially given the current availability of stronger, precontoured plates.

Patient Positioning

The patient is positioned in the "beach-chair" semisitting position on a regular operating room table with an attached foot-piece to support the legs. It has not been routinely necessary to use special tables or positioners. The head is placed on a round support and, if general anesthesia is to be used, the endotracheal tube is taped to the opposite side. The arm does not need to be free-draped for isolated injuries and is usually padded and strapped to the patient's side. It is helpful to place a small pad behind the involved shoulder to elevate it and check to ensure that the anticipated superior drill trajectory is free from obstruction. This is less of a concern if an anteroinferior plate application is chosen.

Surgical Approach

A superior approach and plating is my preferred technique because of the simplicity of the surgical approach, the well-proved clinical record of superior plate application, and several biomechanical studies that have suggested that the optimal location for plate placement is superior.[55,66] An oblique skin incision is made centered superiorly over the fracture site. The subcutaneous tissue and platysma muscle are kept together as one layer and extensively mobilized, especially proximally and distally. As experience with the technique increases, a smaller incision using "minimally invasive" principles can be used. Care is taken to identify, isolate, and protect any visible, larger branches of the supraclavicular nerves: smaller ones may need to be divided. It is usually wise to warn patients that they may experience some numbness inferior to the incision, which will typically improve with time. The myofascial layer over the clavicle is incised and elevated in one contiguous layer. Therefore, at the conclusion of the procedure, fracture site, and plate coverage are enhanced by having two soft tissue layers (skin/subcutaneous tissue, myofascial layer) to close. Care is taken to preserve the soft tissue attachments to any major fragments, especially the vertically oriented fragment of the anterosuperior clavicle that is often seen. It is not necessary to completely denude these fragments to reduce them.

Technique

The main fracture line and major fragments are clearly identified and cleaned of debris and hematoma, and a fixation strategy is formulated. If there is a free fragment of sufficient size to be structurally important (one third of the clavicle circumference or greater), it can be reduced to the proximal or distal clavicle from which it arose and fixed with a lag screw, simplifying the fracture to a simple pattern (Fig. 36-23). The proximal and distal fragments are then reduced with the aid of reduction forceps; they can be held temporarily with a K-wire or, ideally, with a lag screw. A precontoured plate of sufficient length is then applied to the superior surface. If a lag screw has been placed, then it is usually sufficient to secure the fracture with three bicortical screws (six cortices) both proximally and distally. If it is not possible to place a lag screw, then four screws should be inserted proximally and distally. If the main fracture line is of a stable configuration, compression holes can be used to apply compression. If the fracture is comminuted or of an unstable pattern, then the plate should be applied in a "neutral" mode.

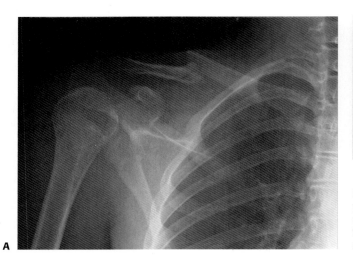

A

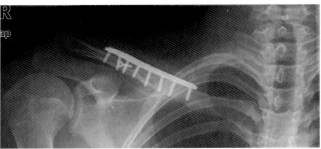

B

FIGURE 36-23 A. Displaced midshaft fracture of the clavicle in a 16-year-old boy, with abrasion and tenting of the skin, approximately 2.5 cm of shortening, and an obvious clinical deformity. **B.** The intervening fragments were fixed with a lag screw followed by plate fixation. Prompt, anatomic healing occurred, as might be expected in an adolescent.

Care must be taken not to violate the subclavicular space and the vital structures therein. If there is any concern intraoperatively about violation of the pleural space, a Valsalva maneuver should be performed to identify any leakage of air.

In general, surgical intervention is selected for only young active patients with high quality bone, and for this reason screw purchase is usually excellent, especially in the cortical area. Although there has been increasing interest in the use of locking-plate technology in this area, there have been few reports on this technique in the clavicle. Celestre et al.[19] reported that a superiorly placed locking plate was biomechanically superior to a conventional compression plate, although there is little clinical information regarding their use at the present time. One small retrospective series described their use in recalcitrant clavicular nonunions: all 11 fractures eventually healed. I have not found that locking plates are routinely necessary for the fixation of clavicle fractures, and I have no experience with them. Following fixation, it is important to close both soft tissue layers with interrupted, nonabsorbable sutures. Postoperative radiographs are taken in the recovery room.

Postoperative Protocol
The surgery can typically be done on an outpatient basis. Postoperatively, the arm is placed in a standard sling for comfort and gentle pendulum exercises are allowed, and the patient is seen in the fracture clinic at 10 to 14 days postoperatively. The wound is checked and radiographs are taken. The sling is discontinued, and unrestricted range-of-motion exercises are allowed, but no strengthening, resisted exercises or sporting activities are allowed. At 6 weeks postoperatively, radiographs are taken to ensure bony union. If acceptable, the patient is allowed to begin resisted and strengthening activities. If delayed union is evident, then more aggressive activities are avoided. It is generally advised that contact (football, hockey) and/or unpredictable (mountain biking, snowboarding) sports be avoided for 12 weeks postoperatively. However, compliance in this predominantly young, male population is variable and many individuals return to such activities earlier than recommended.

Hardware Removal
The clavicle has relatively poor soft tissue coverage, and hardware prominence following plate fixation is a clinical concern. Previously, prior to the advent of plates specifically designed for the clavicle, it was often necessary to contour a straight compression plate to fit the bone by twisting the plate on its long axis so that the plate faced the bone as the underlying clavicle curved away from it.[88,96] In addition to making screw placement difficult, this led to undue prominence of the ends of the plate and a high incidence of subsequent plate removal. With the current availability of stronger, curved, low-profile plates, symptomatic prominence of the plates is much lower and routine plate removal is not typically required.

Pearls and Pitfalls
- Patient selection is critical: operative intervention is reserved for young, healthy, physically active patients with good bone quality and completely displaced fractures who stand to benefit most from operative fixation with an intrinsically low complication rate.
- Noncompliance and substance abuse (be it alcohol, illicit drugs, or prescription narcotics) are contraindications to surgical intervention. No clavicular fixation is strong enough to withstand an unprotected fall down stairs or a physical altercation in the immediate postoperative period.[47,125,126]
- Clinically, a visibly deformed shoulder on inspection usually corresponds to a minimum of 2 cm of shortening radiographically (Fig. 36-24).
- It is critical to develop, protect, and securely close the two soft tissue layers. The superficial layer is the skin and subcutaneous tissue, and the deep layer is the deltotrapezial myofascial layer. This helps protect against deep infection and ensures plate coverage if there is a superficial infection.
- Comminuted fragments, especially the vertically displaced anterosuperior fragment often seen, should be gently "teased" back into position, maintaining soft tissue attachments. They can be secured with mini- or small-fragment screws. Reduction is important but not at the cost of denuding all of soft tissue attachment (Fig. 36-25).
- While typically it is not necessary to dissect in the subclavicular space to place protective retractors, it is very important not to

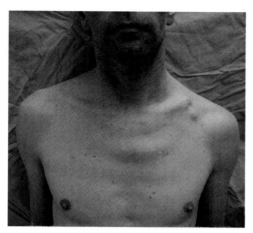

FIGURE 36-24 The typical clinical deformity following a displaced left midshaft clavicular fracture with a short, droopy, "ptotic" shoulder with anterior translation and rotation of the distal fragment and limb.

"plunge" into this area with drills or taps. If a lung injury is suspected intraoperatively, the wound is filled with saline and the anesthetist performs a Valsalva maneuver. The presence of air escape indicates pleural injury and should prompt a chest radiograph and consultation for pleural drainage (catheter or chest tube).

- A plate of size and strength commensurate with the patient's size and compliance should be used. In general, 3.5-mm compression plates or precontoured plates are ideal, especially for larger individuals (>150 pounds) or those who will rehabilitate aggressively.

Plate or Hook Plate Fixation of Displaced Fractures of the Lateral Clavicle

Preoperative Planning

A careful examination of the skin over the lateral clavicle and planned operative site is important. As with midshaft

fractures, temporizing until the soft tissue status improves may be prudent. The major technical challenges in these injuries are purchase in the distal fragment and resisting the primary displacing forces, which draw the proximal fragment superiorly and the distal fragment (secured by the AC and coracoclavicular ligaments to the coracoid and scapula) inferiorly.[4,22,39,71,75,116] Also, the cancellous bone of the distal fragment may be inferior in quality to that of the shaft, and there may be unrecognized comminution. The treating surgeon should template the fracture preoperatively to determine the number of screws that will have purchase in the distal fragment: there are a number of precontoured "anatomic" plates available for this purpose. If it is anticipated that there will be insufficient distal purchase, then alternative fixation strategies need to be considered. These can include augmenting fixation into the coracoid process or achieving purchase to or under the acromion. In this instance, the use of a hook plate (a precontoured plate with a projection or "hook" that is inserted posteriorly in the subacromial space) can be extremely useful, especially with very distal fractures.[48,52,182]

Patient Positioning

Patients are positioned in the "beach chair" or semisitting position, similar to the position used for midshaft fractures. A small pad or bump is placed behind the involved shoulder to elevate it into the surgical field. The head is placed on a round support and rotated out of the way of the operative field. Recently, frames and supports designed to give greater exposure of the shoulder (i.e., for shoulder arthroscopy) have become popular. This type of operative setup can also be used and may facilitate intraoperative radiography. It is not usually necessary to free-drape the involved arm, although this can be done if there is any difficulty anticipated with the reduction (i.e., if the fracture is severely displaced or greater than 2 to 3 weeks old).

Surgical Approach

The surgical approach is similar to that used for superior plating of the clavicle. A skin incision placed directly superiorly over the distal clavicle, extending approximately 1 cm

A

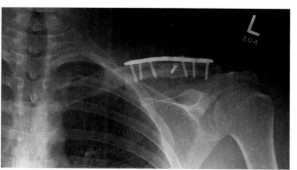

B

FIGURE 36-25 A. Anteroposterior radiograph with 20-degree cephalad tilt demonstrating a completely displaced midshaft clavicle fracture with shortening. There are often vertically oriented fracture fragments that arise from the anterosuperior surface of the clavicle at the site of displaced midshaft fractures, giving many fractures a "Z" pattern. If possible, they should be gently teased back into place and fixed with small or minifragment screws, followed by plate fixation. It is important not to denude the fragment when attempting to fix it. Reduction is performed by reducing the vertical intercalated fragment to the distal fragment and securing it with a 2.7-mm lag screw. The distal assembly is then reduced to the proximal assembly with the aid of two towel clip reduction forceps, followed by plate fixation with a precontoured plate. **B.** Postoperative radiograph revealing restoration of length and anatomic reduction.

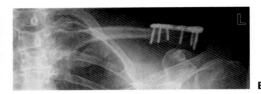

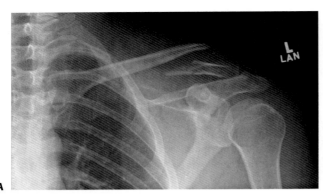

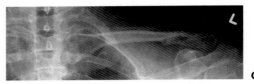

FIGURE 36-26 A. Anteroposterior radiograph of a displaced distal clavicle fracture in a 38-year-old patient after falling off a mountain bike at high speed. Although the fracture was closed, there was significant bruising and swelling over the shoulder. The degree of displacement of this fracture suggests a high likelihood that delayed union or nonunion would result with nonoperative treatment. After the soft tissue swelling had subsided 10 days postinjury, operative fixation was performed with a plate specifically designed for the distal clavicle, allowing for the placement of four screws in the small distal fragment (**B**). The fracture healed uneventfully and the patient was able to return to work within a week of the surgery. **C.** Final follow-up radiograph following hardware removal for local soft tissue irritation, a common problem in this area, shows solid union.

past the AC joint, is made. The skin and subcutaneous layer are developed, and the deltotrapezial myofascial layer is incised directly over the distal clavicle and reflected anteriorly and posteriorly. The AC joint is identified. This can be done by inserting an 18-gauge needle into the joint from the superior aspect, and an arthrotomy can be avoided. It is possible to use an anteroinferior approach for plate fixation of distal clavicle fractures, although in my experience this involves a significant amount of detachment of the deltoid and it is not possible to convert easily to coracoclavicular screw augmentation or hook plate fixation.[179]

Technique

The fracture site is identified and cleaned of debris and hematoma. The fracture is reduced, and it may be held with either a K-wire or a lag screw. Elevating the distal fragment to meet the proximal fragment may aid in reduction. If the main fracture line is in the coronal plane, it may be possible to lag the fracture from anterior to posterior through a small anterior stab incision separate from the primary incision.

Once the fracture is reduced and provisionally stabilized, the optimal type of plate is chosen. Anatomic plates that fit the distal clavicle are now available, and placing four bicortical, fully threaded, cancellous screws in the distal fragment should be the goal (Fig. 36-26). Following fixation, the surgeon must judge whether the number and quality of distal fragment screws are sufficient to provide stability until union occurs. If this is judged to be inadequate, there are several options at this point. Since the primary deforming force at the fracture site is superior displacement of the proximal fragment, it is possible to augment fixation by securing the proximal fragment to the coracoid with a longer screw inserted through one of the plate holes (Fig. 36-27). This screw, typically 30 to 40 mm long, helps secure the proximal fragment to the coracoid and prevent the superior displacement. Since there is some intrinsic motion between the clavicle and the coracoid and scapula, with time this screw either loosens or it may break, but it will give 6 to 8 weeks of stability and fracture healing before doing so. Alternatively, it may be necessary to augment fixation by using a hook

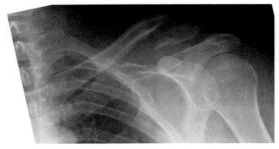

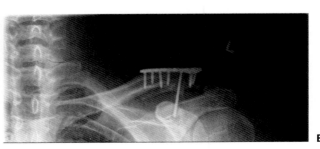

FIGURE 36-27 A. It is possible to augment fixation in distal clavicle fractures with poor-quality bone or a very small distal fragment by placing a screw through the plate into the coracoid process, which helps resist the forces that displace the fracture (superior displacement of the proximal fragment, inferior displacement of the distal fragment). Since there is 10 to 15 degrees of rotational motion between the clavicle and the coracoid, this fixation will eventually loosen (as it has in this case) or break (**B**). However, typically it provides augmented fixation for 6 to 8 weeks postoperatively, which is usually sufficient for the fracture to heal.

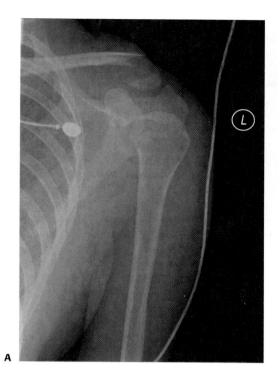

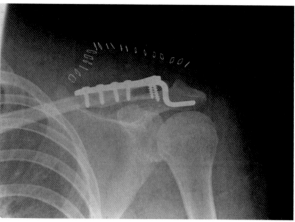

FIGURE 36-28 A. Anteroposterior radiograph of a very distal clavicle fracture in a 22-year-old female pedestrian struck by a street car. The fracture was open with significant soft tissue damage, near transection of the superior deltoid and trapezius, and severe instability of the shoulder girdle. It can be anticipated that conventional plating may be inadequate given the small size of the distal fragment and the associated shoulder girdle instability. **B.** Radiograph following irrigation and débridement, hook plate fixation, and deltoid/trapezial muscle repair. Early motion was initiated and an excellent result ensued.

plate with fixation under the acromion to prevent superior migration of the proximal fragment. This technique is selected when there is insufficient bony purchase in the distal fragment with conventional screws.[49,52,182] This may be readily apparent during preoperative planning (Fig. 36-28) or may only be realized intraoperatively. The advantage of subacromial fixation is that conventional plating can be rapidly converted to this technique intraoperatively. The AC joint is identified, and the posterior edge of the distal clavicle is dissected free. An entrance into the subacromial space is then made with a pair of heavy curved scissors that will create the path of the "hook" extension of the plate. It is important that this space is made posteriorly, so that there will be no impingement of the rotator cuff in the critically tight anterior subacromial space. Once this path has been created, the hook is placed in it and the plate reduced to the shaft of the clavicle. Several different hook depths and lengths for this plate are currently available, and trial reductions can be performed to determine the optimal plate type. Alternatively, the plate can be "walked down" onto the clavicular shaft by sequential placement of the screws from distal to proximal: this can be a very effective technique of fracture reduction as this maneuver "levers" the distal fragment to the proximal fragment. On occasion, it may be necessary to contour the shaft of the plate to prevent overreduction of the fracture; however, if excessive contouring appears to be required, a more likely explanation is that the fracture is not reduced and that there is residual superior angulation. It is possible to securely repair even very distal fractures (that are essentially AC joint fracture-dislocations) with this technique: minimal, if any, purchase is required in the distal fragment. Unlike static fixation across the AC joint, which is doomed to loosening or fatigue failure, hook plate fixation allows some intrinsic motion between the bones. A cadaver study revealed that this technique most closely reflected the

biomechanics of the native AC joint—namely, secure enough to provide reliable fixation yet physiologically flexible.[182] Following fixation, the wound is thoroughly irrigated and a two-layer closure similar to that for midshaft fractures is performed.

Postoperative Protocol
The arm is placed in a sling and the patient is allowed early active motion in the form of pendulum exercises. At 10 to 14 days postoperatively, the wound is checked and the stitches are removed. The sling is then discarded and full range-of-motion exercises are instituted; sling protection can be extended if the quality of fixation is questionable. At 6 to 8 weeks, if radiographs are favorable, resisted and strengthening exercises are instituted. Return to full contact or unpredictable sports (i.e., mountain biking) is usually discouraged until 12 weeks postoperatively. While hardware removal is typically optional for those with conventional plates, it can be anticipated that a high percentage of individuals with hook plate fixation will require plate removal to regain terminal shoulder flexion and abduction. This is usually performed at a minimum of 6 months postoperatively.

Pearls and Pitfalls
- The rate of delayed union and nonunion for completely displaced distal clavicle fractures treated nonoperatively is approximately 40%.
- Even minimally displaced fractures may take an excessive period of time to heal or may develop a fibrous union. However, without displacement, they are often not symptomatic enough to warrant surgical intervention.
- The technical challenge faced during operative treatment of distal clavicle fractures is fixation of the distal fragment; the surgeon should be prepared to deal with unexpected commi-

nution or poor screw purchase in the distal fragment using anatomic plates, coracoclavicular fixation, or hook plates.

- Hook plate fixation is an effective alternative to conventional plate fixation when faced with inadequate distal purchase. To avoid subacromial impingement, the hook should be placed just posteriorly
- A high percentage of patients treated with hook plate fixation will require plate removal to regain full range of shoulder motion.
- Rigid transacromial fixation has a high rate of loosening and fatigue failure because of the intrinsic motion at the AC joint and is therefore not routinely recommended

"FLOATING SHOULDER"

The combination of ipsilateral fractures of the clavicle and scapular neck has traditionally been called the "floating shoulder," which has been considered to be an unstable injury that may require operative fixation.[42,130,142,166,168,175,176] In fact, this injury pattern can be considered to be a subgroup of the "double disruption of the superior shoulder suspensory complex (SSSC)," a concept introduced by Goss.[54,122] This describes the bone and soft tissue circle, or ring, of the glenoid, coracoid process, coracoclavicular ligament, clavicle (especially its distal part), AC joint, and the acromion. This complex is extremely important biomechanically, as it maintains the anatomic relationship between the upper extremity and the axial skeleton. The clavicle is the only bony connection between the two, and the scapula is suspended from it by the coracoclavicular and AC ligaments. Thus, any injury that disrupts this ring at two or more levels is considered inherently unstable and one whose cumulative effect may be greater than the sum of its individual constituents.[178] Long-term functional problems have been reported following significantly displaced injuries of this nature, including shoulder weakness and stiffness, impingement syndrome, neurovascular compression, and pain.* Such injuries have been considered relative indications for operative intervention (Fig. 36-7). Combined scapular (or glenoid neck) and clavicle fractures are the commonest type of double disruptions of the SSSC, and there remains considerable controversy over optimal treatment.

A study by Leung and Lam described good or excellent results in 14 of 15 patients with this injury pattern following fixation of both the clavicle and glenoid fractures.[79] However, Herscovici et al.[59] described excellent results in seven of nine patients who had their floating shoulder treated with reduction and fixation of the clavicular fracture only. These findings were confirmed in a study performed by Rikli et al.,[135] who performed clavicle fixation in isolation in 11 patients with combined clavicle and glenoid fractures. They described an average Constant-Murley Shoulder Outcome Score in the operated shoulders of 95% of the unaffected side. These studies support the concept, in selected cases, of clavicular fracture reduction and fixation alone. It is postulated that reduction of the clavicle helps to reduce and stabilize the glenoid fracture, eliminating the requirement for operative fixation of the glenoid. This is an important point, since open reduction and internal fixation (ORIF) of the glenoid can be a difficult and complex procedure with a high complication rate, especially if the surgeon lacks experience in this anatomic area.

*References 29,40,42,58–60,79,130,142,166,168,175,176.

There are also reports that support nonoperative management of this injury. Ramos et al.[130] described the results of nonoperative treatment in 16 patients with ipsilateral fractures of the clavicle and glenoid. Eleven patients had a complete recovery to near normal status, although one had a significant malunion of the glenoid neck and three had significant shoulder asymmetry. Edwards et al.[40] reported good results ("pleased" or "satisfied") in 16 of 20 patients with floating shoulder injuries treated nonoperatively. There were four patients who were "dissatisfied" or "unhappy" with their outcome. While the outcome assessment of these patients was suboptimal, it would appear that nonoperative treatment may be considered, especially for minimally displaced fractures. Interestingly, two of the four patients with poor results had severely displaced clavicular fractures. In a clinical study, Williams and colleagues[176] evaluated 9 of 11 patients with a floating shoulder treated nonoperatively and found five excellent, one good, and three fair results. They found that the worse clinical results were strongly associated with 3 cm or more of medial displacement of the glenoid and recommended nonoperative care for lesser amounts of displacement. Similarly, van Nort et al.[166] performed a questionnaire review including 31 of 35 floating shoulder patients treated nonoperatively and found that only 3 required late operative reconstruction for clavicular malunion or nonunion. They found that results in the nonoperative group (a mean Constant-Murley Shoulder Outcome Score of 76) deteriorated with increasing degrees of glenoid displacement. Interestingly, they also found that three of the four patients who had their clavicle fracture fixed primarily had a poor result because of scapular malunion. They believed that this failure of indirect glenoid reduction following clavicular reduction and fixation was because of associated ligamentous injuries that caused a dissociation of the two structures.

There is some limited biomechanical evidence to support the intuitive clinical finding that increasing degrees of fracture displacement in floating shoulder injuries corresponds to poorer results if left unreduced. Williams et al.[175] performed a cadaver biomechanical study by establishing a scapular neck fracture and investigating the effect of an ipsilateral clavicle fracture, a coracoacromial ligament injury, and an AC ligament injury. They found that substantial instability (lack of resistance to a medially directed force) only occurred after associated ligamentous disruption. Although there are limitations to this study (such as the uniaxial direction of the applied deforming force), it remains one of the only biomechanical studies on this topic.

Unfortunately, given the variable and sporadic nature of this injury, there is a paucity of prospective, randomized, or comparative trials on which to base treatment recommendations. What is clear is that earlier recommendations for routine operative fixation for all floating shoulder injuries were too liberal and that poor results occur regularly with badly displaced fractures that are treated nonoperatively. In addition, the aggressiveness of treatment must be commensurate with the risk of intervention and the expected functional demands of the patient. Thus, an operative approach may be indicated in a young healthy individual who requires extensive overhead activity for work (painter, plasterer, electrician, etc.), whereas the same fracture pattern may be treated nonoperatively in an elderly, low-demand patient with multiple medical comorbidities. Further research in this area may help identify currently unknown factors that may predict outcome and hence guide treatment.[73] Current standard operative indications include the following:

1. A clavicle fracture that warrants, in isolation, fixation (see Operative Indications, earlier)
2. Glenoid displacement of greater than 2.5 to 3.0 cm
3. Displaced intra-articular glenoid fracture extension
4. Patient-associated indications (i.e., polytrauma with a requirement for early upper extremity weight bearing)
5. Severe glenoid angulation, retroversion, or anteversion greater than 40 degrees (Goss type II)
6. Documented ipsilateral coracoacromial and/or AC ligament disruption or its equivalent (i.e., coracoid fracture [AC joint disruption])

If operative intervention is chosen, then anatomic reduction and internal fixation of the clavicle is typically performed first, and the shoulder is then reimaged. If fixation of the clavicle results in indirect reduction of the glenoid such that its alignment is within acceptable parameters, then no further intervention is required apart from close follow-up. If the glenoid remains in an "unacceptable" position, then fixation of the glenoid neck, typically performed through a posterior approach, is indicated (see Chapter 37). Also, Oh et al.[117] reported the failure of isolated clavicle fixation in two cases of floating shoulder. If this first method is chosen in this setting, the clavicle may experience greater loads than with isolated fractures, and the size and length of the fixation device selected should be commensurate with these anticipated loads.[117]

COMPLICATIONS

Infection

Infection had traditionally been one of the most feared complications following fixation of displaced clavicular fractures, and earlier series described an unacceptably high rate of deep infection.[2,27,50,100] However, significant improvements have been made in a number of areas that are well recognized to decrease infection, including perioperative antibiotics, selective operative timing with regard to soft tissue conditions, better soft tissue handling, two-layer soft tissue closure, and fixation that is superior biomechanically.* In a recent metaanalysis that examined operative series from 1975 to 2005, Zlodwodzki et al. reported a superficial infection rate of 4.4%, and a deep infection rate of only 2.2%; these figures are significantly improved compared with earlier studies.[185] If infection does occur and it is superficial, then it is usually possible to temporize with local wound care and systemic antibiotics until fracture union has occurred. At this point, plate removal, débridement, and thorough irrigation have a high success rate in infection eradication.

Deep infection with unstable implanted hardware is a more complex problem. If it appears that there is progressive bone formation, then temporizing until union occurs followed by hardware removal and debridement may be successful. If there is no obvious progress toward union, then operative intervention is indicated. Hardware removal followed by radical débridement of infected bone and dead or devitalized tissue and subsequent irrigation is performed. At this point there are several options. If the patient is healthy without comorbidities (as is usually the

case) and the infecting organism is a sensitive one, then immediate reconstruction with plating, bone grafting, and local antibiotics may be warranted. Alternatively, especially with polymicrobial infections or resistant organisms (i.e., methicillin-resistant *Staphylococcus aureus*), local antibiotic–impregnated polymethylmethylacrylate cement beads or an antibiotic-impregnated bone substitute is implanted into any residual dead space following debridement and systemic antibiotics are administered until clinical and hematologic markers indicate the infection has been eradicated. Delayed reconstruction can then be performed. If there is a significant soft tissue deficiency, then the assistance of a plastic surgeon who can perform soft tissue coverage, typically with a rotational pectoralis major flap, is ideal.[161,174]

Nonunion

Traditionally, the rate of nonunion of the clavicle has been described as being less than 1% of all fractures. This was based on two sentinel studies—one by Neer[100] in 1960 that described 3 nonunions in 2235 patients and one by Rowe[144] in 1968 in which only 4 of 566 patients developed nonunion after a fracture of the clavicle. More recently, however, the nonunion rate following closed treatment of completely displaced midshaft fractures of the clavicle has been described as being exponentially higher, in the 15% to 20% range.[15,62,139,185] The reason for this difference is unclear but probably includes more complete follow-up in recent studies, the exclusion of children (with their inherently good natural history), changing mechanisms of injury (mountain biking, all-terrain vehicles, parachuting), and modern patients' intolerance of prolonged immobilization. In addition, several prospective population-based studies have been helpful in elucidating factors associated with the development of nonunion (Fig. 36-17). Robinson et al.[139] identified increasing age, female sex, fracture displacement, and comminution as risk factors for nonunion in midshaft fractures. Lateral third fractures had higher nonunion rates as patient age and fracture displacement increased.[138] Nowak et al.[113] prospectively followed 208 patients with radiographically verified clavicle fractures and, 9 to 10 years postinjury, found that 96 (46%) still had sequelae. They identified no bony contact between the fracture fragments as the strongest predictor for sequelae. Nonunion occurred in 15 patients (7%). Zlowodzki et al.[185] performed a metaanalysis of all series of displaced midshaft fractures from 1975 to 2005 and identified 22 published manuscripts. They found that, for the specific entity of completely displaced midshaft fractures of the clavicle, the nonunion rate with nonoperative treatment was 15.1%, while the nonunion rate following operative treatment was 2.2%. This represents a relative risk reduction (for nonunion) of 86% (95% confidence interval, 71% to 93%). This meta-analysis, in addition to recent prospective studies examining primary operative fixation of clavicle fractures, definitively terminated the postulation that primary fixation was associated with a higher, not lower, nonunion rate (Table 36-1). This observation was based on early operative studies with poor patient selection, inadequate fixation (Figs. 36-21 and 36-22), and inferior soft tissue management. Undoubtedly, there are other factors that contribute to the incidence of nonunion (i.e., associated fractures, soft tissue interposition, rotation at the fracture site) that have yet to be clarified.[129,159,171,173] Therefore, at the present time, factors associated with the development of nonunion include complete fracture displacement (no contact between the main proximal

---

*References 15,74,82,106,125,126,146,149.

FIGURE 36-29 Atrophic nonunion of the clavicle. The degree of bone loss demonstrated in this case suggests that an intercalary graft may be required to restore length and obtain union.

and distal fragments), shortening of greater than 2 cm, advanced age, more severe trauma (in terms of both mechanism of injury and associated fractures), and refracture. Primary operative fixation, however, is not associated with a higher nonunion rate.

Nonunion is defined as the lack of radiographic healing at 6 months postinjury (Fig. 36-29). While a significant percentage of distal nonunions may be asymptomatic, especially in the elderly,[109] the majority of midshaft nonunions in young active individuals will be symptomatic enough to require treatment.*

Treatment Options

A variety of methods have been described for the treatment of an established clavicular nonunion that is symptomatic enough to warrant operative intervention.[†] Successful nonunion repair usually decreases pain and improves function. Described methods range from noninvasive techniques such as electrical stimulation and low-intensity ultrasound to minimally invasive techniques (isolated bone grafting, screw fixation) to formal ORIF with iliac crest bone grafting. Apart from isolated case reports, or cases described in larger series of standard treatments, there is very little objective evidence to support the use of electrical stimulation or ultrasound in this area.[13,29,30] In rare cases where there is minimal deformity or shortening, a stable hypertrophic nonunion with good soft tissue coverage and no infection, and a biologically favorable host (i.e., no smoking or diabetes), such techniques may occasionally be successful in promoting union. However, the majority will require mechanical stabilization and biological stimulation.

There are two main techniques to achieve union: plate fixation and IM screw or pin fixation. The gold standard treatment against which other methods must be compared is ORIF with a compression plate and iliac crest bone graft. Reported success rates with this technique are high if appropriate size and length plates are used. Manske and Szabo[84] (10 of 10 healed), Eskola et al.[46] (20 of 22 healed), Jupiter and Leffert[69] (16 of 19 healed), Boyer and Axelrod[11] (7 of 7 healed), Olsen et al.[118] (16 of 17 healed), and Bradbury et al.[12] (31 of 32 healed) all describe excellent results with a low complication rate. It is important to note that the forces generated by deformity correction and the longer healing time will mean that the operative construct for a nonunion will require greater stability for a longer period of time than that for an acute fracture. Multiple authors stress that short four-hole plates, weak 1/3 tubular plates, or even 3.5-mm pelvic reconstruction plates in larger (>200 pounds) patients are inadequate for this type of fixation and have higher

failure rates (Fig. 36-22). A small fragment compression plate, a precontoured "anatomic" plate, or their equivalent with a minimum of three bicortical screws in each fragment is recommended* (see "Author's Preferred Method of Treatment," next).

There are many theoretical advantages to IM pinning with open bone grafting for the treatment of clavicular nonunions. A smaller incision with better cosmesis, less soft tissue stripping, decreased hardware irritation, and easier hardware removal (often under a local anaesthetic) are proposed benefits compared with plate fixation. There are several reports describing good results including Boehme et al.[8] (20 of 21 healed) and Enneking et al.[45] (13 of 14 healed). In the only comparative study of fixation techniques for clavicle nonunion, Wu et al.[178] described union in 9 of 11 patients treated with plate fixation and 16 of 18 of those treated with IM fixation. However, Wilkins and Johnston[173] reported pin failure in two of four patients treated in this fashion, and the two failed IM fixations in the series by Wu et al.[178] both healed with subsequent plate fixation. In addition to IM fixation being weaker biomechanically and not controlling length and rotation as well as a plate, others have reported difficulty with pin migration and breakage using this technique.[73,83,97,108] A randomized, prospective study comparing plate and IM fixation is required to define their respective roles in this setting.

Severe bone loss and/or poor bone quality, typically associated with multiple failed operative procedures and infection, can complicate the reconstruction of recalcitrant clavicular nonunions. The final treatment option in such circumstances is clavicular excision or claviculectomy (either partial or total).[29,30,177] Considering the important strut effect of the clavicle for upper extremity function and the availability of modern treatment options, this must be considered a salvage procedure. While reasonable results with retention of a full range of motion and relief of pain have been described in selected cases with severe preoperative pathology, a significant decrease in strength (especially overhead) and a loss of shoulder girdle stability typically result.

AUTHORS' PREFERRED METHOD OF TREATMENT
Midshaft Nonunion of the Clavicle

My preferred surgical treatment for a midshaft nonunion of the clavicle is ORIF with a precontoured anatomic clavicular plate with the addition of an iliac crest bone graft or osteoinductive bone graft substitute. Patient positioning and draping are similar to those used for the fixation of acute midshaft fractures, with the exception of having an iliac crest bone graft site prepared (typically the contralateral side) if bone grafting is anticipated (see later). The surgical approach is similar to that used for a fracture, taking care to reflect and preserve the myofascial layer for later closure, and the superior surface of the clavicle at the nonunion site is identified. The ends of the nonunion are identified, and judicious soft tissue dissection is performed around them to allow correction of deformity. This usually involves bringing the distal fragment out to length and translating it superiorly and posteriorly. The distal fragment is often rotated anteriorly, and derotating it brings the flat superior surface directly superi-

*References 5,13,37,46,80,84,115,118,147.
†References 11,12,29–31,37,46,69,70,84,173,178.

*References 11,12,29–31,37,46,69,70,84.

orly, facilitating plate placement on the superior surface. The sclerotic ends of the proximal and distal fragments are identified and a rongeur is used to clear them back to bleeding bone. It is rarely necessary to resect excessive bone to do this. The medullary canals are then reestablished with a drill to allow the free egress of osteoprogenitor cells to the nonunion site. Reduction forceps are then placed on the proximal and distal fragments and a reduction is performed. Remembering that there is a slight apex superior bow to the native clavicle, excess superior callous is rongeured away to allow the plate to fit on the superior surface of the clavicle. Any excess callous removed in the approach, débridement or deformity correction is saved, morcellized, and inserted into the fracture site at the conclusion of the procedure. If possible, the nonunion is then fixed with an anterior-to-posterior small- or mini-fragment lag screw (Fig. 36-30). The chance of success of this helpful step can be increased by recognizing the orientation of the nonunion line during the approach and debridement. Lag screw fixation helps hold the reduction while the plate is applied and also increases the construct stability. If this is not possible, then a 2.0-mm K-wire can be inserted to hold the reduction while a precontoured clavicle plate is applied to the superior surface. I typically use an eight-hole plate: this allows for one or even two empty holes at the nonunion site (often necessary because of bony configuration or lag screw interference) while providing for three bicortical screws both proximal and distal, which I consider to be the absolute minimum for fixation. If the nonunion is transverse in nature, the first screws on each side are inserted in a compression mode and tightened after the provisional K-wire has been removed. Although they are available, I have not found it routinely necessary to use locking screws or plates in the clavicle. If the nonunion is hypertrophic (the minority), then the morcellized autograft from the local bone is applied to the nonunion site and a standard closure, as for a fracture case, is performed. Thorough irrigation and hemostasis are achieved before closure, and drains are not used.

If the nonunion is atrophic, then either morcellized autograft from the iliac crest or an osteoinductive bone substitute, such as a bone morphogenic protein, is packed in and around the nonunion site. Bone substitutes with little osteoinductive capability, such as calcium phosphates or sulfates, allograft, or demineralized bone, are to be avoided. A structural or intercalary graft may be required in certain cases where there has been excessive loss of length or previous surgery has failed. Shortening can often be determined preoperatively by comparing the length of the clavicle radiographically to the measured clinical length. If there appears to be significant bone loss, then an intercalary graft, according to the technique of Jupiter and Ring,[70] can be used. Postoperative care is similar to that following malunion reconstruction or acute fracture fixation.

Malunion

Traditionally, it was believed that malunion of the clavicle (which was ubiquitous with displaced fractures) was of radiographic interest only, and success in the clinical setting was defined as fracture union. However, more recently, a number of investigators have described a fairly consistent pattern of patient symptomatology (with orthopaedic, neurologic, "functional," and cosmetic features) following malunion of displaced midshaft fractures of the clavicle.[7,20,57,68,76,90,122,135] While all of the factors that contribute to the development of this condition are unclear, it is typically diagnosed in young, active patients with significant degrees of shortening at the malunion site (Fig. 36-31). As could be reasonably anticipated, shortening of the shoulder girdle (with the typical inferior displacement and anterior rotation of the distal fragment) results in a variety of biomechanical and anatomic abnormalities that translate directly into patient complaints. Orthopaedically, shortening of the muscle–tendon units that traverse the malunion site results in a sense of weakness and rapid fatigability, with a loss of endurance strength. It has been previously shown that there are significant, objective deficits in maximal strength and endurance (especially of abduction) following the healing of displaced midshaft fractures of the clavicle treated nonoperatively[92,155] (Fig. 36-32). Narrowing and displacement of the thoracic outlet (the inferior border of which is the clavicle) result in numbness and paraesthesias, usually in the C8-T1 nerve root distribution, exacerbated by provocative overhead activities. Because of their deformity, patients complain of the appearance of their shoulder and difficulty with backpacks, hiking packs, military gear, and shoulder straps: this has been termed a deficit in "functional cosmesis." Patients with this condition also complain of upper back pain and periscapular aching, especially with repetitive activity. There is objective evidence that the displace-

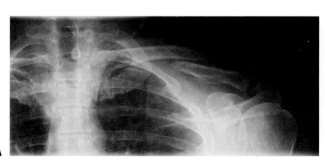
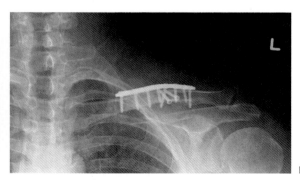

FIGURE 36-30 A. Atrophic nonunion 14 months following nonoperative care of a completely displaced fracture of the clavicle. **B.** Successful repair with correction of deformity, plate fixation, and the addition of bone morphogenetic protein to the nonunion site. The oblique nature of the nonunion in the coronal plane facilitated fixation with two anterior-to-posterior lag screws.

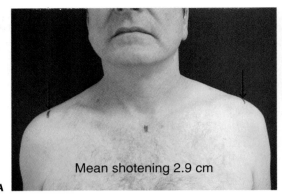
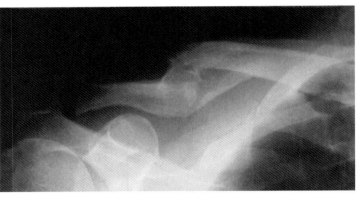

Mean shotening 2.9 cm

A

B

FIGURE 36-31 Typical clinical features of clavicle malunion (**A**) with a corresponding radiograph (**B**). Note the shoulder asymmetry and the difference in the position of the acromioclavicular joints (*arrows*).

ment of the distal fragment (to which the scapula is attached) results in malalignment of the scapulothoracic joint and a form of scapular winging: this produces periscapular muscle spasm and fatigue pain.[57,131]

It appears that the predominant risk factor for the development of this condition is shortening at the malunion site. Hill et al.[61] found that shortening of 2 cm or more was associated with poor functional outcome and a high rate of patient dissatisfaction. McKee et al.[90] described a series of 15 patients with a symptomatic clavicular malunion who had a mean degree of shortening of 2.9 cm, and Bosch et al.[9] described an "extension osteotomy" in four patients with shortening of 0.9 to 2.2 cm. In a retrospective study, Eskola et al.[47] reported on 83 patients with displaced fractures and found that shortening of 1.2 cm or more was associated with increased pain at final follow-up. However, this point remains controversial. In retrospective reviews, Nordqvist et al.[112] (225 midshaft clavicle fractures) and Oroko et al.[120] (41 midshaft clavicle fractures) could not demonstrate a relationship between shortening and a poor outcome. It is probable that length is just one component of a complex three-dimensional deformity, which, combined with the intrin-

sic variability of human response to skeletal injury, explains why some individuals with malunion function well and others determinedly seek operative correction. For patients with a symptomatic malunion who have failed a course of physiotherapy for muscle strengthening, the options are to accept the disability or have a corrective osteotomy.

AUTHORS' PREFERRED METHOD OF TREATMENT

Malunion of the Clavicle

Operative intervention is reserved for patients with signs and symptoms of malunion that are specific to the condition and sufficiently symptomatic to warrant surgery. A vague and generalized ache about the shoulder (especially in a patient with medicolegal or compensation issues) and a radiographic malunion is not necessarily an indication for surgery. Patients selected for surgery are typically young, active, and healthy with good bone stock. The primary goal of surgery is to correct the deformity, and preoperative planning is important (Fig. 36-33). Careful measurement both clinically

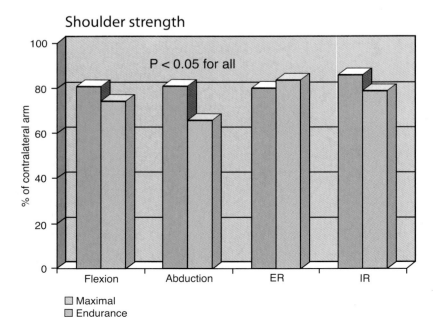

Shoulder strength

P < 0.05 for all

FIGURE 36-32 Objectively measured shoulder strength following nonoperative treatment of displaced midshaft fracture of the clavicle (maximal, endurance) compared with normal contralateral side. Patients were a minimum of 14 months postinjury, with a mean of 54 months.

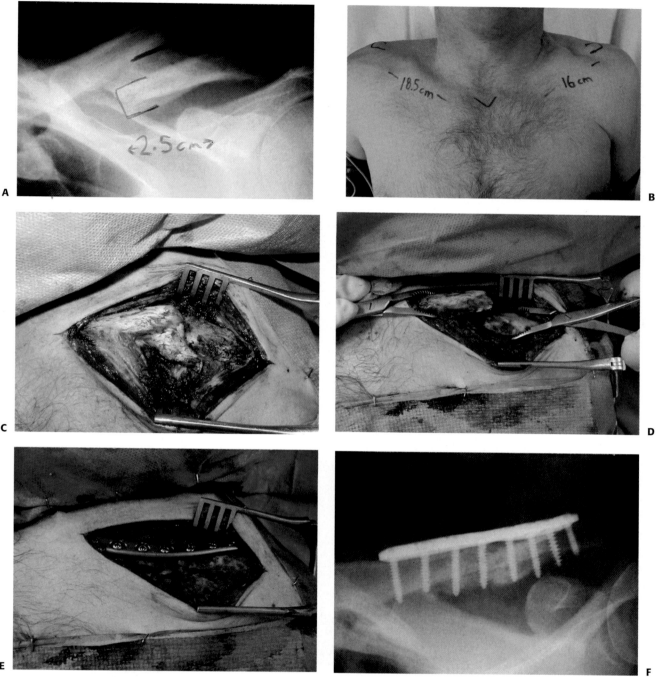

FIGURE 36-33 A. Anteroposterior radiograph of a symptomatic clavicle malunion with 2.5 cm of shortening. **B.** Corresponding clinical photograph shows the measurement of clavicular length from the sternal notch to the acromioclavicular joint. **C.** Intraoperative photograph of the malunion site demonstrates the typical displacement of the distal fragment with medial, inferior, and anterior translation. This also shows the abundant local bone that is usually present at the malunion site. While it is difficult to appreciate, there is often anterior rotation of the distal fragment as well. **D.** Intraoperative photograph following osteotomy of the malunion showing recreation of the original fracture line and rongeuring of excess callus (which will be used to graft the osteotomy site) and distraction of the fragments to their correct length and position. It is typically not necessary to perform an intercalary bone graft, as there is rarely absolute bone loss, and the original proximal and distal fragments can be reestablished using a combination of a microsagittal saw and osteotomes. **E.** Intraoperative photograph following reduction and plate fixation using an anatomic precontoured plate. **F.** Anteroposterior radiograph following union. The patient's preoperative symptoms resolved promptly.

and radiographically defines the degree of length to be restored. A posteroanterior thorax or chest radiograph that includes both clavicles has been shown to be a reliable way of comparing length to the opposite (normal) clavicle.[155] Inferior displacement and anterior rotation of the distal fragment is corrected by having the plate applied to the superior surface flush both medially and laterally; some contouring of the plate may be required in the anterosuperior plane as there is a slight caudal bow to the clavicle.

Patient positioning and the surgical approach are similar to those used for acute fracture fixation or nonunion repair.[91] The exception is that in certain cases it is prudent to have an iliac crest bone graft site prepared (see later). In general, it has not been routinely necessary to insert an intercalary graft to restore length. It is usually possible to identify the position of the proximal and distal fragments in most patients. The malunion site is cleared, a mark is made in the bone proximally and distally, and the length is measured. This enables the surgeon to calculate how much length has been gained by remeasuring the distance between the two marks at the conclusion of the osteotomy. Next, the osteotomy to recreate the original fracture and proximal and distal fragments is made with a combination of a microsagittal saw and osteotomes. Care is taken not to violate the subclavicular space. Following the osteotomy, the proximal and distal fragments are grasped with reduction forceps and gently distracted to the desired position. Routinely, it is not necessary to free-drape the arm for traction. For difficult cases, a mini-distractor can be used to correct length and maintain position while fixation is applied. Care must be taken to not overdistract the fragments as neurologic injury may result.[136] Depending on the configuration of the bone ends, after the osteotomy is performed it is often possible to fashion an interdigitating or step cut contour to improve intrinsic stability and increase the bony surface area for healing. The medullary canals are reestablished with a drill, and the osteotomy is temporarily secured with a Kirschner wire. It is then measured for correction of deformity and length. On occasion, an absolute bone deficit may be encountered, such that reduction of the fragments does not restore length. Options at this point include accepting some shortening or using an intercalary graft. This situation can be anticipated preoperatively when the measured clinical shortening (i.e., 3 cm) is significantly greater than the degree of shortening seen on the radiograph of the involved clavicle. Once deformity correction is confirmed, definitive fixation is performed: there are several precontoured "anatomic" plates designed for clavicular fixation that are ideal for this purpose.[64] If a lag screw can be placed across the osteotomy, then three additional screws both proximally and distally are usually sufficient. If not, four screws proximally and distally are recommended. Additional local bone can be morcellized and added to the osteotomy site. Wound closure and postoperative care are the same as those for acute fracture fixation or nonunion repair.

Neurovascular Injury

Despite the proximity of the brachial plexus and subclavian vessels, neurovascular injury is surprisingly rare, given the number of severely displaced clavicular shaft fractures seen in practice.* In general, neurovascular injuries associated with clavicle fractures can be divided into three groups: acute injuries, delayed injuries, and iatrogenic injuries.

Acute Injuries

A careful vascular and neurologic examination is critical with any clavicular injury, especially those associated with high-energy trauma. If the indications of vascular injury are present, an angiogram is indicated. In addition to being diagnostic, with the refinement of interventional techniques such as embolization and stenting, this procedure can also be therapeutic (Fig. 36-34). While direct impalement of bony fragments can occur, most neurovascular injuries occur from excessive traction, which in its most severe form is termed *scapulothoracic dissociation*. The unique feature of these injuries is that the associated clavicular fracture is typically distracted, rather than shortened. This can be a limb- or life-threatening injury: a study by Ebraheim et al.[36] reported 3 deaths in 15 patients, and Zelle et al.[183] described 3 deaths and 6 amputations in 22 patients in their series from a major European trauma center. If limb salvage is to be performed, shoulder girdle stabilization is indicated to create an optimal healing environment for the soft tissue structures. There have been case reports of direct neurologic injury from clavicular fracture fragments: in this situation, operative decompression of the brachial plexus by reduction and fixation of the clavicle fracture is indicated.[6,10,32,51,63,132,145]

Delayed Injuries

Delayed injuries tend to occur because of encroachment of the thoracic outlet, from either displacement of the borders (i.e., from clavicular displacement caused by malunion or nonunion) or encroachment from inferior callus formation (this phenomenon can be especially severe in patients with a concomitant head injury [Fig. 36-35]). In the case reports describing this entity, debridement of local callus with realignment and fixation of the clavicle injury is indicated.[24,44,132] The most common reason for brachial plexus irritation following clavicular fracture is the chronic thoracic outlet syndrome (TOS) that results from clavicular malunion (see earlier). In this setting, operative treatment should be directed toward reestablishing the preinjury dimensions of the thoracic outlet through a corrective clavicular osteotomy.[7,9,20,90] Simply removing the "bump" around the fracture site or conventional treatments for TOS such as first rib resection have a high failure rate. This is because the fundamental anatomic problem is the change in position, orientation, and contour of the thoracic outlet from the displacement of the distal clavicular segment, rather than from local impingement of callus or normal structures (i.e., the first rib). Connolly and Ganjianpour[26] reported the case of a patient with TOS following a clavicular malunion that was treated with first rib resection to no avail, while corrective clavicular osteotomy resulted in prompt resolution of symptoms. McKee et al.[90] reported resolution of TOS symptoms in 16 patients who underwent corrective clavicular osteotomy to treat a malunion. Chronic impingement of the thoracic outlet leading to TOS is probably the most common form of neurovascular "injury" following displaced clavicular fractures.

*References 6,10,17,21,32,35,51,63,132,136,145,165.

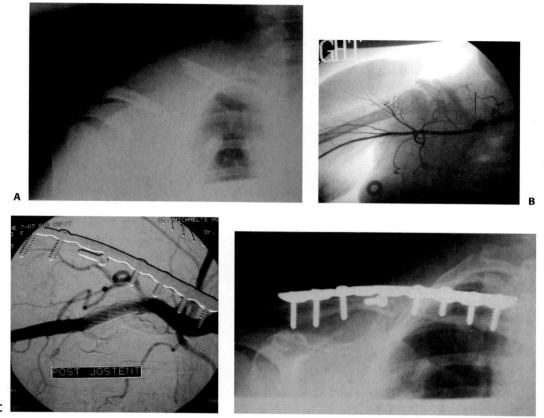

FIGURE 36-34 A. Anteroposterior radiograph of a morbidly obese 57-year-old woman who sustained a severely displaced midshaft fracture of the clavicle in a fall from a standing height. **B.** She also had a partial brachial plexus injury and a partial laceration of the subclavian artery with pseudoaneurysm formation (*arrow*), shown on the preoperative angiogram. **C.** The patient was treated with immediate stenting of the resultant pseudoaneurysm, followed by plate fixation of the fracture with a 3.5-mm limited contact dynamic compression plate. **D.** The indications for fixation included reducing the severe displacement and creating an optimal environment for neurologic and vascular healing. Uneventful bony and soft tissue healing ensued.

Iatrogenic Injury

Despite the proximity of the brachial plexus, catastrophic injury from intraoperative penetration by drills or taps is very rare. Shackford[151] reported a case of subclavian pseudoaneurysm formation with distal embolization from screw penetration after plate fixation of a clavicular nonunion, and Casselman et al.[17] described a similar case. Iatrogenic injury can occur, but it is thought to occur in specific situations where distraction can occur. Ring and Holovacs[136] described three cases of brachial plexus palsy after IM fixation of clavicle fractures. They postulated that the distraction of the fracture site (a prerequisite for reduction and pin insertion) and the delayed presentation (patients were diagnosed several weeks after their injury) led to a traction injury of the brachial plexus. Fortunately, all three patients with palsies recovered completely with nonoperative care. It appears that distraction of a shortened clavicular fracture, especially one that presents or is treated some weeks or months following initial injury, creates a risk for a traction-type injury to the adjacent brachial plexus. Overdistraction at the fracture site or any violation of the subclavicular space is to be avoided during operative repair of clavicular injuries. Fortunately, with the information presently available, these injuries are usually transient in nature and, with time, a full recovery can usually be expected.

Refracture

True refracture after healing of a fracture of a clavicle is surprisingly rare. It has been my experience that many individuals who have claimed to have sustained multiple fractures of the clavicle in fact, a nonunion following their initial fracture that never healed completely. Recurrent episodes of trauma prompt medical attention, and new radiographs are misinterpreted as showing a "refracture." The few cases that are reported describe a higher nonunion rate following "refracture": regardless of the exact etiology, patients with this condition should be counseled about the high rate of unsatisfactory outcome and that they may benefit from fixation.[15,29,30]

Given the increasing popularity of operative fixation of displaced clavicle fractures and the patient population involved, it is not surprising that fractures at the end of a plate used for fixation of a prior clavicle fracture are being encountered. This typically occurs from recurrent high-energy trauma. Large prospective series are not available and recommendations are based on only a few cases. In general, a fracture in the upper extremity that occurs at the end of a stable implanted diaphyseal plate has a poor natural history and a high chance of delayed union or nonunion. It is my experience that these fractures, if displaced, generally require repeat fixation. Attempts should be made to

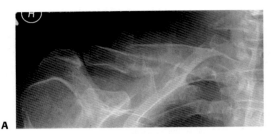

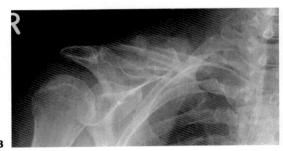

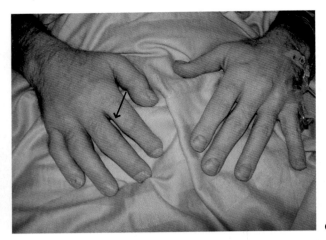

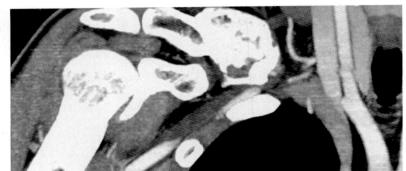

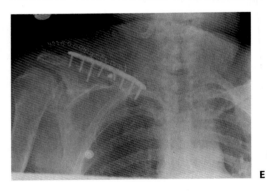

FIGURE 36-35 A. Initial anteroposterior radiograph of a 46-year-old polytrauma patient with a head injury demonstrates a displaced clavicle fracture. **B.** Anteroposterior radiograph at 6 weeks postinjury reveals abundant callus formation around the fracture. The patient had increasing neuralgic pain in the associated upper extremity with progressive objective muscle weakness in the hand. The involved hand (**C**, *arrow*) had signs of venous obstruction with swelling, loss of skin wrinkle definition, and violaceous discoloration. **D.** Computed tomography scan confirmed severe obstruction of the thoracic outlet due to a combination of severe shortening and displacement of the fracture site and exuberant callus formation. This patient was treated with operative correction of the deformity, complete resection of the supraclavicular callus, and judicious resection of infraclavicular callus followed by plate fixation. **E.** Prompt resolution of symptoms, complete neurologic recovery, and uncomplicated fracture union ensued.

fix the fracture and span the area of bone previously repaired (Fig. 36-36). If the fracture is minimally displaced, a trial of nonoperative care with the arm at rest in a sling is reasonable.

Scapular Winging

Winging of the scapula can take many different forms and may have multiple etiologies, and has been anecdotally reported to

occur following the nonoperative treatment of displaced midshaft fractures of the clavicle.[131] Rasyid et al.[131] reported two cases of winging of the scapula, one from a "neglected" fracture of the clavicle with 2 cm of shortening. The typical clavicle malunion or nonunion with deformity results in a shortened, protracted shoulder. Since the scapula moves with the distal end of the clavicle (through its only bony attachment at the AC

FIGURE 36-36 A. A 40-year-old professional motorcycle racer had plate fixation of a midshaft clavicle nonunion that developed following a displaced midshaft fracture. The nonunion healed uneventfully, but 2 years later, following another high-velocity crash, he sustained a fracture at the lateral end of the plate. **B.** This fracture also developed into a nonunion, and required repeat fixation with a longer plate. This is a potential risk for individuals with plate fixation of the clavicle who continue to participate in high-risk activities.

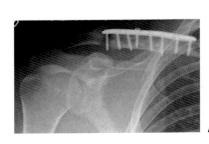

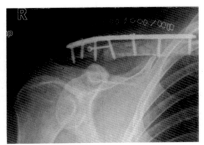

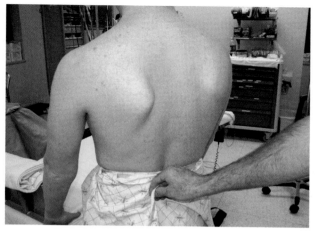

FIGURE 36-37 Clinical photograph of scapular winging of left shoulder associated with a midshaft clavicle malunion with 3 cm of shortening. There is a characteristic protrusion of the inferior angle of the scapula, produced as the scapula rotates and translates anteriorly with the distal clavicular fragment.

joint), this can lead to scapular malposition with a shortened, protracted shoulder (Fig. 36-37). This scapular malposition has recently been quantified in a series of patients with clavicle malunion by Hall et al.[57] using three-dimensional CT scanning in which mean clavicular shortening of 16 mm resulted in 10 mm of lateral scapular displacement, with anterior rotation of 8 degrees and 10 millimeters of elevation from the posterior chest wall (Fig. 36-38). They postulated that this rotation and displacement result in the winging seen in their patients.[57] The negative mechanical effects of this shoulder position are well documented, with a mean decrease in rotational strength ranging from 13% to 24% in one study.[156] This may also explain the characteristic periscapular muscular fatigue pain that these patients describe. Future research should elucidate the risk factors for and potential treatment of this condition.

OUTCOMES

Traditionally, clavicle fractures have been treated nonoperatively, but recent studies have shown that the union rate for

displaced midshaft fractures of the clavicle may not be as favorable as previously described. In a prospective series of 868 patients with clavicle fractures treated nonoperatively, Robinson et al.[139] reported a significantly higher nonunion rate (21%) in displaced comminuted midshaft fractures. An analysis of this paper by Brinker et al.[14] suggested a nonunion rate varying between 20% and 33% for displaced comminuted fractures in males. Hill et al.[62] studied 66 consecutive displaced midshaft clavicle fractures and found a 15% nonunion rate and a 31% rate of patient dissatisfaction with nonoperative care. Based on their data, they concluded that displacement of the fracture fragments of greater than 2 cm was associated with an unsatisfactory result. A metaanalysis of studies of clavicle fractures from 1975 to 2005 revealed that displaced midshaft clavicle fractures treated nonoperatively had a nonunion rate of 15.1%. This metaanalysis also showed that primary plate fixation was, contrary to prevailing opinion, a safe and reliable procedure.[185] Nowak et al.[113,114] examined the late sequelae in 208 adult patients with clavicle fractures at 10 years postinjury. Interestingly, 96 (46%) still had symptoms despite the fact that only 15 (7%) had an established nonunion. McKee et al. reported on a series of patients who has nonoperative treatment of a displaced midshaft clavicle fracture a mean of more than 4 years earlier. Objective muscle strength testing revealed significant strength deficits, especially of shoulder abduction and flexion, which help explain some of the patient dissatisfaction seen despite bony union.[92]

While it is unclear why such a dramatic difference exists in outcome between previous reports on clavicle fractures and contemporary studies, one possibility may be the inclusion of children in the older reports, which, because of their inherent healing abilities and remodeling potential, may artificially improve the overall results. Also, patient-oriented outcome measures, as used by Hill et al. and McKee et al., have been shown to reveal functional deficits in the upper extremity that have not been detected traditionally.[15,62,92] A focus on radiographic outcomes would not reveal such problems. Patient expectations and injury patterns are changing. Several studies that examined clavicular shaft fractures in polytrauma patients found that the presence of a clavicle fracture was associated with a 20% to 30% mortality rate (mainly from concomitant chest and head injuries), and that survivors displayed a significant level of residual disability in the involved shoulder.[89,161] Thus, there is a surviving patient population (with clavicle fractures) that has an intrinsically worse prognosis where long-term sequelae may be more common.

Although it is not typically an orthopaedic priority, cosmesis is important to patients, and an unsightly scar has been a traditional deterrent to operative treatment of clavicular fractures.[28–30,100,105,121,127] However, to a body image–conscious patient (predominantly young, male population), a droopy shoulder is also of significant cosmetic concern. In a recent randomized clinical trial (RCT) comparing operative and nonoperative treatment, despite the incidence of hardware prominence and incisional complications (numbness, sensitivity) in the operative group, more patients in this group answered "yes" to the question, "Are you satisfied with the appearance of your shoulder?" than in the nonoperative group (52 of 62 versus 26 of 49, $P = 0.001$; Table 36-4). This study also showed superior surgeon-based (Constant-Murley Shoulder Outcome Score and patient-based Disabilities of the Arm, Shoulder, and Hand [DASH] questionnaire) upper extremity outcomes.[15]

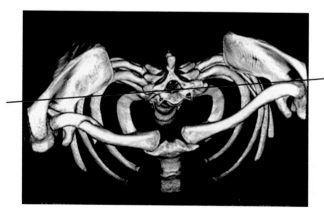

FIGURE 36-38 Three-dimensional computed tomography scan reconstruction of a patient with a right-sided clavicular malunion. A reference line through the coronal plane of the body reveals the significant anterior translation of the shoulder girdle.

TABLE 36-4	Cosmesis Following Operative versus Nonoperative Care

Complaint	Operative Care (n = 62)	Nonoperative Care (n = 49)	P Value
"Droopy" shoulder	0	10	0.001*
Bump/asymmetry	0	22	0.001*
Scar	3	0	0.253
Sensitive/painful fracture site	9	10	0.891
Hardware irritation/prominence	11	0	0.001*
Incisional numbness	18	0	0.001*
Satisfied with appearance of shoulder	52	26	0.001*

*$P < 0.05$.

In contradistinction to older case series, recent studies on the primary plate fixation of acute midshaft clavicle fractures have reported high success rates with union from 94% to 100% and low rates of infection and surgical complications. A recent metaanalysis of plate fixation for 460 displaced fractures revealed a nonunion rate of only 2.2%. With improved implants, prophylactic antibiotics, and better soft tissue handling, one can conclude that plate fixation is a reliable and reproducible technique.[15,74,125,126,185]

CONTROVERSIES AND FUTURE DIRECTIONS

Patient Selection for Operative Intervention

Recent studies have made it clear that there is a subset of patients, especially those with shortened, displaced fractures, who would benefit from primary operative repair of clavicular injuries.[15,62,139] However, these early interventions are not without risk and consume significant health care resources. Also, there are patients who appear to have multiple prognostic factors for a poor outcome following a clavicular fracture (i.e., displacement greater than 2 cm) and yet heal promptly (albeit in a "displaced" position) with minimal symptomatology and full function of the involved shoulder. While some of the explanation for this is undoubtedly due to the inherent variability of patient response to musculoskeletal injury, there may be other factors that are not clearly defined or understood at present. For example, while most studies use the magnitude of shortening when defining fracture displacement, this alone is a relatively simplistic linear measurement of what is typically a complex three-dimensional deformity. Since most of the major muscle groups of the shoulder have a scapular origin, it may be that the final position of the scapula relative to the trunk and upper arm (which is difficult to measure; see "Scapular Winging") may be the dominant factor in determining prognosis.[57] While the prognostic index published by Robinson et al.[139] is a dramatic advance in providing objective information and facilitating our ability to predict outcome, there are still significant improvements that can be made so that intervention can be selected specifically for those patients for whom the risk/benefit ratio of surgery is favorable. It is also clear that patient noncompliance,

especially when associated with substance abuse, is a clear contraindication for surgery. Bostman et al.,[10] in a study of 103 consecutive adults with acute, displaced midshaft fractures of the clavicle, stated, "Patient noncompliance with the postoperative regimen could be suspected to have been a major cause of the failures."

Method of Fixation

It remains unclear what the optimal method of fixation is for displaced midshaft clavicle fractures in individuals who are deemed appropriate for surgical fixation. There are proponents of both IM fixation and plate fixation. The method of plate fixation is also controversial, with some authorities recommending plate placement on the superior surface of the clavicle, while others recommend the anterior/inferior surface.[10,15,25,27,74,184] There are no direct comparative studies between these various operative techniques available at the present time, although it is hoped that prospective studies that are currently under way comparing these techniques will clarify the issue. While there are many theoretical advantages to IM fixation, it appears that the results of this method with currently available implants are more unpredictable than the results reported for plate fixation. Biomechanically, they appear to be inferior in resisting displacement compared with plate fixation.[55] Two clinical studies comparing IM fixation to nonoperative treatment failed to show any advantage in the IM fixation group. Grassi et al.[96] described a high complication rate with IM fixation including eight infections, three "refractures," two delayed unions, and two nonunions with hardware failure in 40 patients. Judd et al.,[68] in a randomized trial, failed to show an advantage of IM fixation over nonoperative care in 57 patients, with nearly half the operative group losing some degree of reduction. The metaanalysis by Zlowodzki et al.[185] did not reveal any significant differences between plate and IM fixation, although this analysis was hampered by the lack of any direct comparative studies. Conversely, Chuang et al.[24] described 100% union with no significant complications in a group of 34 patients with an acute midshaft fractures of the clavicle treated with an IM cannulated screw. At the present time, IM fixation does not appear to be as reliable in most series as plate fixation, and it remains to be seen whether refinements in this technique and the associated fixation devices can provide more consistent results.

It is probable that anteroinferior plating leads to less plate irritation than placement of the plate on the superior surface of the clavicle, at least with previously available plate systems. In the one direct comparison (nonrandomized) between the two techniques, Lim et al.[82] reported a significantly better pain visual analogue scale for patients in the anteroinferior fixation group ($P = 0.05$). This finding awaits confirmation from further studies.

Timing of Surgical Intervention

Conventional thinking has been that nonoperative treatment is appropriate for most, if not all, fractures of the clavicle, even severely displaced injuries, with the assumption that the reconstructive repair of those that developed nonunion or symptomatic malunion would produce results similar to that of primary operative repair of the original fracture. Since these injuries are nonarticular, and the reported "success" rate of reconstruction is high, this approach seems to have inherent merit. However, there is recent evidence that while operative reconstruction of malunion or nonunion is a reliable procedure, with increasing refinement of outcome measures and objective muscle strength testing, it is apparent that there are residual deficits compared with what primary operative repair can provide. Potter et al.[128] examined a cohort of 15 patients who had undergone late reconstruction with plate fixation for clavicular nonunion or malunion ("delayed group") a mean of 63 months postinjury and compared them to a similar cohort of 15 patients who had primary plate fixation of a clavicle fracture a mean of 0.5 month after injury ("acute group"). The groups were similar in age, sex, original fracture characteristics, and mechanism of injury. They found that there were subtle but significant differences between the two groups with regard to shoulder scores (a Constant-Murley Shoulder Outcome Score of 89 in the delayed group and 95 in the acute group, $P = 0.02$), and the delayed group demonstrated inferior endurance strength in the involved shoulder. They concluded that while late reconstruction is a reliable and reproducible procedure, there were subtle decreases in outcome compared with acute fixation and recommended that this information be used in decision making when counseling patients with displaced midshaft fractures of the clavicle. Rosenberg et al.[142] reported similar results in a group of 13 patients who had late reconstruction for clavicular malunion and nonunion. While osseous healing occurred in all cases, there was a mean 20-point deficit in Constant-Murley Shoulder Outcome Score (61 versus 81, $P = 0.01$) in the affected shoulders. The authors thought that "lasting functional impairment" was possible even with objective success. With time, significant adaptive changes (muscle atrophy, soft tissue contracture, bone loss) occur in the shoulder girdle of individuals with clavicular malunion or nonunion that will compromise the outcome of late reconstructive surgery to some degree compared with the results of primary plate fixation. This is useful, objective information in evaluating the risk/benefit ratio of early operative intervention.

CONCLUSION

Recent studies have provided objective information that enhances our knowledge and aids in the decision making regarding the treatment of fractures of the clavicle. While the majority of clavicle fractures will heal with nonoperative care (a simple sling is probably best) and a prompt return of near normal shoulder function can be expected, there is a subset of fractures that benefit from operative intervention. Poor prognostic signs include increasing fracture displacement (especially shortening), fracture comminution, and an increasing number of fracture fragments, especially in older patients. In prospective studies of carefully selected patients, operative plate fixation provides a more rapid return to a superior level of shoulder function with a consistently low complication rate compared with nonoperative care. Anteroinferior plate placement may have some advantages over superior plate positioning with respect to soft tissue irritation. IM fixation has many theoretical advantages and a high rate of success in skilled hands, although results in the literature remain inconsistent. While the difference is small, primary plate fixation provides significantly improved results in terms of strength and shoulder scores compared with delayed reconstruction. Malunion of the clavicle is a definite clinical entity that benefits from corrective osteotomy, which can usually be performed without a bone graft. Scapular winging is a common finding following the failure of primary nonoperative care and the development of a nonunion or a symptomatic malunion, and it can lead to significant patient symptoms. Future studies that are randomized, prospective, and comparative are needed to refine the indications for primary operative repair, investigate the role that scapular malposition plays, and determine the ideal method of fixation.

REFERENCES

1. Adams F. The genuine works of Hippocrates. New York: William Wood and Co., 1886.
2. Ali Khan MA, Lucas HK. Plating of fractures of the middle third of the clavicle. Injury 1978;9:263–267.
3. Andersen K, Jensen PO, Lauritzen J. The treatment of clavicular fractures: figure-of-eight bandage versus a simple sling. Acta Orthop Scand 1987;58:71–74.
4. Ballmer FT, Gerber C. Coracoclavicular screw fixation for unstable fractures of the distal clavicle. A report of five cases. J Bone Joint Surg Br 1991;73B:291–294.
5. Ballmer FT, Lambert SM, Hertel R. Decortication and plate osetosynthesis for nonunion of the clavicle. J Shoulder Elbow Surg 1998;7:581–585.
6. Barbier O, Malghem J, Delaere O, et al. Injury to the brachial plexus by a fragment of bone after fracture of the clavicle. J Bone Joint Surg Br 1997;79B:534–536.
7. Basamania CJ. Claviculoplasty [abstract]. J Shoulder Elbow Surg 1999;8:540.
8. Boehme D, Curtis RJ, DeHaan JT, et al. Nonunion of fractures of the midshaft of the clavicle. Treatment with a modified Haigie intramedullary pin and autogenous bone-grafting. J Bone Joint Surg Am 1991;73A:1219–1226.
9. Bosch U, Skutek M, Peters G, et al. Extension osteotomy in malunited clavicular fractures. J Shoulder Elbow Surg 1998;7:402–405.
10. Bostman O, Manninen M, Pihlajamaki H. Complications of plate fixation in fresh displaced midclavicular fractures. J Trauma 1997;43:778–783.
11. Boyer MI, Axelrod TS. Atrophic nonunion of the clavicle: treatment by compression plate, lag-screw fixation, and bone graft. J Bone Joint Surg Br 1997;79B:301–303.
12. Bradbury N, Hutchinson J, Hahn D, et al. Clavicular nonunion: 31/32 healed after plate fixation and bone grafting. Acta Orthop Scand 1996;67:367–370.
13. Brighton CT, Pollick SR. Treatment of recalcitrant nonunion with a capacitively coupled electrical field: a preliminary report. J Bone Joint Surg Am 1985;67A:577–585.
14. Brinker MR, Edwards TB, O'Connor DP. Letter to the editor. J Bone Joint Surg Am 2005;87AA:677–678.
15. Canadian Orthopaedic Trauma Society (MD McKee, principal investigator). Plate fixation versus nonoperative care for acute, displaced midshaft fractures of the clavicle. J Bone Joint Surg 2007;89A:1–11.
16. Carley S. Toward evidence-based emergency medicine: best BETS from the Manchester Royal Infirmary. Collar and cuff or sling after fracture of the clavicle. J Accid Emerg Med 1999;16:140.
17. Casselman F, Vanslembroek K, Verougstraete L. An unusual case of thoracic outlet syndrome. J Trauma 1997;43:142–143.
18. Cave AJ. The nature and morphology of the costoclavicular ligament. J Anat 1961;95:170–179.
19. Celestre P, Robertson C, Mahar A, et al. Biomechanical evaluation of clavicle fracture plating techniques: does a locking plate provide improved stability? J Orthop Trauma 2008;22:241–247.
20. Chan KY, Jupiter JB, Leffert RD, et al. Clavicle malunion. J Shoulder Elbow Surg 1999;8:287–290.
21. Chen CE, Liu HC. Delayed brachial plexus neuropraxia complicating malunion of the clavicle. Am J Orthop 2000;29:321–322.
22. Chen CH, Ch WJ, Shih CH. Surgical treatment for distal clavicle fractures with coracoclavicular ligament disruption. J Trauma 2002;52:7–8.

23. Chen DJ, Chuang DCC, Wei FU. Unusual thoracic outlet syndrome secondary to fractured clavicle. J Trauma 2002;52:393–398.
24. Chuang TY, Ho WP, Hsieh PS, et al. Closed reduction and internal fixation for acute midshaft clavicular fractures using cannulated screws. J Trauma 2006;60:1315–1321.
25. Collinge C, Devinney S, Herscovici D, et al. Anteroinferior plate fixation of middle third fractures and nonunions of the clavicle. J Orthop Trauma 2006;20:680–686.
26. Connolly JF, Ganjianpour M. Thoracic outlet syndrome treated by double osteotomy of a clavicular malunion. J Bone Joint Surg Am 2002;84A:437–440.
27. Craig EV. Fractures of the clavicle. In: Rockwood CA, Matsen FA, eds. The Shoulder. Philadelphia: WB Saunders, 1990:367–412.
28. Craig EV. Fractures of the clavicle. In: Rockwood CA, Green DP, Bucholz RW, Heckman JD, eds. Rockwood and Green's Fractures in Adults. Philadelphia: Lippincott-Raven, 1996:1109–1161.
29. Craig EV. Fractures of the clavicle. In: Rockwood CA, Matsen FA, eds. The Shoulder, 3rd ed. Philadelphia: WB Saunders, 1998:428–482.
30. Crenshaw AH. Fractures of the shoulder girdle, arm and forearm. In Willis CC, ed. Campbell's Operative orthopaedics, 8th ed. St. Louis: Mosby–Year Book, 1992: 989–995.
31. Davids PH, Luitse JS, Strating RP, et al. Operative treatment for delayed union and nonunion of midshaft clavicular fractures: AO reconstruction plate fixation and early mobilization. J Trauma 1996;40:985–986.
32. Della Santa D, Narakas A, Bonnard C. Late lesions of the brachial plexus after fracture of the clavicle. Ann Chir Main Memb Super 1991;10:531–540.
33. Demiralp B, Atesalp AS, Sehirlioglu A, et al. Preliminary results of the use of Ilizarov fixation in clavicular nonunion. Arch Orthop Trauma Surg 2006;126:401–405.
34. Dickson JW. Death following fractured clavicle. Br Med J 1952;2:666.
35. Dutta A, Malhotra SK, Kumar V. A fractured clavicle and vascular compression: a non-orthopedic indication of figure-of-eight bandage. Anesth Analg 2003;96:910.
36. Ebraheim NA, An HS, Jackson WT, et al. Scapulothoracic dissociation. J Bone Joint Surg Am 1988;70A:428–432.
37. Ebraheim NA, Mekhail AO, Darwich M. Open reduction and internal fixation with bone grafting of clavicular nonunion. J Trauma 1997;42:701–704.
38. Edelson JG. The bony anatomy of clavicular malunions. J Shoulder Elbow Surg 2003; 12:173–178.
39. Edwards DJ, Kavanagh TG, Flannery MC. Fractures of the distal clavicle: a case for fixation. Injury 1992;23:44–46.
40. Edwards SG, Whittle AP, Wood GW. Nonoperative treatment of ipsilateral fractures of the scapula and clavicle. J Bone Joint Surg Am 2000;82A:774–780.
41. Edwards SG, Wood GW, Whittle AP. Factors associated with Short Form-36 outcome in nonoperative treatment for ipsilateral fractures of the clavicle and scapula. Orthopedics 2002;25:733–738.
42. Egol KA, Connor PM, Karunakar MA, et al. The floating shoulder: clinical and functional results. J Bone Joint Surg Am 2001;83A:1188–1194.
43. Eiff MP. Management of clavicle fractures. Am Fam Physician 1997;55:121–128.
44. England JD, Tiel RL. AAEM case report 33: Costoclavicular mass syndrome. Am Assoc Electrodiagn Med Muscle Nerve 1999;22:412–418.
45. Enneking TJ, Hartlief MT, Fontijine WP. Rushpin fixation for midshaft clavicular nonunions: good results in 13/14 cases. Acta Orthop Scand 1999;70:514–516.
46. Eskola A, Vainionpaa S, Myllynen P, et al. Surgery for ununited clavicular fracture. Acta Orthop Scand 1986;57:366–367.
47. Eskola A, Vainionpaa S, Myllynen P, et al. Outcome of clavicular fracture in 89 patients. Arch Orthop Trauma Surg 1986;105:337–338.
48. Fann CY, Chiu FY, Chuang TY, et al. Transacromial Knowles pin in the treatment of Neer type 2 distal clavicle fractures. A prospective evaluation of 32 cases. J Trauma 2004;56:1102–1105.
49. Flinkkila T, Ristiniemi J, Hyvonen P, et al. Surgical treatment of unstable fractures of the distal clavicle: a comparative study of Kirschner wire and clavicular hook plate fixation. Acta Orthop Scand 2002;73:50–53.
50. Fowler AW. Treatment of fractured clavicle. Lancet 1968;1:46–47.
51. Fujita K, Matsuda K, Sakai Y, et al. Late thoracic outlet syndrome secondary to malunion of the fractured clavicle: case report and review of the literature. J Trauma 2001;50: 332–335.
52. Goldberg JA, Bruce WJ, Sonnabend DH, et al. Type 2 fractures of the distal clavicle: a new surgical technique. J Shoulder Elbow Surg 1997;6:380–382.
53. Golish SR, Oliviero JA, Francke EI, et al. A biomechanical study of plate versus intramedullary devices for midshaft clavicle fixation. J Orthop Surg 2008;3:28.
54. Goss TP. Scapular fractures and dislocations:diagnosis and management. J Am Acad Orthop Surg 1995;3:22–33.
55. Goswami T, Markert RJ, Anderson CG, et al. Biomechanical evaluation of a pre-contoured clavicle plate. J Shoulder Elbow Surg 2008;17:815–818.
56. Grassi FA, Tajana MS, D'Angelo F. Management of midclavicular fractures: comparison between nonoperative treatment and open intramedullary fixation in 80 patients. J Trauma 2001;50:1096–1100.
57. Hall JA, Farrugia M, Potter J, et al. The radiographic quantification of scapular winging following malunuion of displaced clavicular shaft fractures [abstract]. COA Abstract Supplement 2007;June 1:43.
58. Hashiguchi H, Ito H. Clinical outcome of the treatment of floating shoulder by osteosynthesis for clavicular fracture alone. J Shoulder Elbow Surg 2003;12:589–591.
59. Herscovici D Jr, Fiennes AG, Allgower M, et al. The floating shoulder: ipsilateral clavicle and scapular neck fractures. J Bone Joint Surg Br 1992;74B:362–364.
60. Herscovici D Jr, Sanders R, DiPasquale T, et al. Injuries of the shoulder girdle. Clin Orthop 1995;318:54–60.
61. Hill JM. Closed treatment of displaced middle-third fractures of the clavicle gives poor results [letter to the editor]. J Bone Joint Surg Br 1998;80B:558.
62. Hill JM, McGuire MH, Crosby LA. Closed treatment of displaced middle-third fractures of the clavicle gives poor results. J Bone Joint Surg Br 1997;79B:537–539.
63. Howard FM, Shafer SJ. Injuries to the clavicle with neurovascular complications. A study of 14 cases. J Bone Joint Surg Am 1965;47A:1335–1346.
64. Huang JI, Toogood P, Chen MR, et al. Clavicular anatomy and the applicability of precontoured plates. J Bone Joint Surg Am 2007;89A:2260–2265.
65. Hudak PL, Amadio PC, Bombardier C. Development of an upper extremity outcome measure: The DASH. Upper Extremity Collaborative Group (UECG). Am J Ind Med 1996;29:602–608.
66. Iannotti MR, Crosby LA, Stafford P, et al. Effects of plate location and selection on the stability of midshaft clavicle osteotomies: a biomechanical study. J Shoulder Elbow Surg 2002;11:457–462.
67. Jubel A, Andermahr J, Schiffer G, et al. Elastic stable intramedullary nailing of midclavicular fractures with a titanium nail. Clin Orthop Relat Res 2003;408:279–285.
68. Judd DB, Bottoni CR, Pallis MP, et al. Intramedullary fixation versus nonoperative treatment for midshaft clavicle fractures. In Proceedings of the 72nd Annual Meeting of the American Academy of Orthopaedic Surgeons. Washington DC, February 2005.
69. Jupiter JB, Leffert RD. Nonunion of the clavicle. Associated complications and surgical management. J Bone Joint Surg Am 1987;69A:753–760.
70. Jupiter JB, Ring D. Fractures of the clavicle. In: Iannotti JP, Williams GR, eds. Disorders of the Shoulder: Diagnosis and Management. Philadelphia: Lippincott Williams & Wilkins, 1999.
71. Kao FC, Chao EK, Chen CH, et al. Treatment of distal clavicle fracture using Kirschner wires and tension band wires. J Trauma 2001;51:522–525.
72. Khan SA, Shamshery P, Gupta V et al. Locking compression plate in longstanding clavicular nonunions with poor bone stock. J Trauma 2008;64:439–441
73. Kim KC, Rhee KJ, Shin HD, et al. Can the glenopolar angle be used to predict outcome and treatment of the floating shoulder? J Trauma 2008;64:174–178.
74. Kloen P, Sorkin AT, Rubel IF, et al. Anteroinferior plating of midshaft clavicular nonunions. J Orthop Trauma 2002;16:425–430.
75. Kona J, Bosse JM, Staeheli JW, et al. Type II distal clavicle fractures: a retrospective review of surgical treatment. J Orthop Trauma 1990;4:115–120.
76. Kuhne JE. Symptomatic malunions of the middle clavicle [abstract]. J Shoulder Elbow Surg 1999;8:539.
77. Ledger M, Leeks N, Ackland T, et al. Short malunions of the clavicle: an anatomic and functional study. J Shoulder Elbow Surg 2005;14:349–354.
78. Leppilahti J, Jalovaara P. Migration of Kirschner wires following fixation of the clavicle: report of 2 cases. Acta Orthop Scand 1999;70:517–519.
79. Leung KS, Lam TP. Open reduction and internal fixation of ipsilateral fractures of the scapular neck and clavicle. J Bone Joint Surg Am 1993;75A:1015–1018.
80. Leupin S, Jupiter JB. LC-DC plating with bone graft in posttraumatic nonunions in the middle third of the clavicle. Swiss Surg 1998;4:89–94.
81. Lewonowski K, Bassett GS. Complete posterior sternoclavicular epiphyseal separation. A case report and review of the literature. Clin Orthop 1992;281:84–88.
82. Lim M, Kang J, Kim K, et al. Anterior inferior reconstruction plates for the treatment of acute midshaft clavicle fractures. In proceedings from the 19th Annual Meeting of the Orthopaedic Trauma Society. Salt Lake City, Utah, October 2003.
83. Lyons FA, Rockwood CA Jr. Migration of pins used in operations on the shoulder. J Bone Joint Surg Am 1990;72A:1262–1267.
84. Manske DJ, Szabo RM. The operative treatment of midshaft clavicular nonunions. J Bone Joint Surg Am 1985;67A:1367–1371.
85. Marsh JL, Slongo TF, Agel J, et al. Fracture and dislocation classification compendium: 2007 Orthopaedic Trauma Association Classification, Database, and Outcomes Committee. J Orthop Trauma 2007;21:S1–S74.
86. Matsumoto K, Miyamoto K, Sumi H, et al. Upper extremity injuries in snowboarding and skiing: a comparative study. Clin J Sport Med 2002;12:354–359.
87. McCandless DN, Mowbray MA. Treatment of displaced fractures of the clavicle. Sling versus figure-of-eight bandage. Practitioner 1979;223:266–267.
88. McKee MD, Seiler JG, Jupiter JB. The application of the limited contact dynamic compression plate in the upper extremity: an analysis of 114 consecutive cases. Injury 1995;26:661–666.
89. McKee MD, Stephen DJG, Kreder HJ, et al. Functional outcome following clavicle fractures in polytrauma patients. J Trauma 2000;47:616.
90. McKee MD, Wild LM, Schemitsch EH. Midshaft malunions of the clavicle. J Bone Joint Surg Am 2003;85A:790–797.
91. McKee MD, Wild LM, Schemitsch EH. Midshaft malunion of the clavicle: Surgical technique. J Bone Joint Surg Am 2004;86A:37–44.
92. McKee MD, Pedersen EM, Jones C, et al. Deficits following non-operative treatment of displaced, midshaft clavicle fractures. J Bone Joint Surg Am 2006;88A:35–40.
93. McKee MD. Optimal treatment of displaced midshaft fractures of the clavicle. Phildelphia: Saunders, 2009;126–132.
94. Moore TO. Internal pin fixation for fracture of the clavicle. Ann Surg 1951;17:580–583.
95. Moseley HF. The clavicle: its anatomy and function. Clin Orthop 1968;58:17–27.
96. Mullaji AB, Jupiter JB. Low-contact dynamic compression plating of the clavicle. Injury 1994;25–45.
97. Naidoo P. Migration of a Kirschner wire from the clavicle into the abdominal aorta [letter]. Arch Emerg Med 1991;8:292–295.
98. Naidu SH, Heppenstall RB, Brighton CT, et al. Clavicle nonunion: results of treatment with electricity, AO dynamic compression plating and autogenous bone grafting, and excision of the nonunion in 43 patients. Orthop Trans 1994;18:1072.
99. Natali J, Maraval M, Kieffer E, et al. Fractures of the clavicle and injuries of the subclavian artery. Report of 10 cases. J Cardiovasc Surg (Torino) 1975;16:541–547.
100. Neer CS. Nonunion of the clavicle. JAMA 1960;172:1006–1011.
101. Neer CS. Fractures of the distal clavicle with detachment of the coracoclavicular ligaments in adults. J Trauma 1963;3:99–110.
102. Neer CS. Fractures of the distal third of the clavicle. Clin Orthop 1968;58:43–50.
103. Neer C. Fractures of the clavicle. In: Rockwood CA, Green DP, eds. Fractures in Adults, 2nd ed. Philadelphia: JB Lippincott, 1984:707–713.
104. Neviaser JS. The treatment of fractures of the clavicle. Surg Clin North Am 1963;43: 1555–1563.
105. Neviaser RJ. Injuries to the clavicle and acromioclavicular joint. Orthop Clin North Am 1987;18:433–438.
106. Neviaser RJ, Neviaser JS, Neviaser TJ. A simple technique for internal fixation of the clavicle. A long term evaluation. Clin Orthop 1975;109:103–107.
107. Ngarmukos C, Parkpian V, Patradul A. Fixation of fractures of the midshaft of the clavicle with Kirschner wires. Results in 108 patients. J Bone Joint Surg Br 1998;80B: 106–108.
108. Nordback I, Markkula H. Migration of Kirschner pin from clavicle into ascending aorta. Acta Chir Scand 1985;151:177–179.

109. Nordqvist A, Petersson C. The incidence of fractures of the clavicle. Clin Orthop 1994; 300:127–132.
110. Nordqvist A, Petersson C, Redlund-Johnell I. The natural course of lateral clavicle fracture. Fifteen (11–21) year follow-up of 110 cases. Acta Orthop Scand 1993;64: 87–91.
111. Nordqvist A, Petersson CJ, Redlund-Johnell I. Midclavicle fractures in adults: end result study after conservative treatment. J Orthop Trauma 1998;12:572–576.
112. Nordqvist A, Redlund-Johnell I, von Scheele A, et al. Shortening of clavicle after fracture. Acta Orthop Scand 1997;68:349–351.
113. Nowak J, Holgersson M, Larsson S. Can we predict long-term sequelae after fractures of the clavicle based on initial findings? A prospective study with 9 to 10 years follow-up. J Shoulder Elbow Surg 2004;13:479–486.
114. Nowak J, Mallmin H, Larson S. The aetiology and epidemiology of clavicular fractures. A prospective study during a 2-year period in Uppsala, Sweden. Injury 2000;35: 353–358.
115. O'Connor D, Kutty S, McCabe JP. Long-term functional outcome assessment of plate fixation and autogenous bone grafting for clavicular nonunion. Injury 2004;35: 575–579.
116. Ogden JA. Distal clavicular physical injury. Clin Orthop 1984;188:68–73.
117. Oh CW, Kyung HS, Kim PT, et al. Failure of internal fixation of the clavicle in the treatment of ipsilateral clavicle and glenoid neck fractures. J Orthop Sci 2002;6: 601–603.
118. Olsen BS, Vaesel MT, Sojbjerg JO. Treatment of midshaft clavicular nonunion with plate fixation and autologous bone grafting. J Shoulder Elbow Surg 1995;4:337–344.
119. Ord RA, Langdon JD. Stress fracture of the clavicle. A rare late complication of radical neck dissection. J Maxillofac Surg 1986;14:281–284.
120. Oroko PK, Buchan M, Winkler A, et al. Does shortening matter after clavicular fractures? Bull Hosp Joint Dis 1999;58:6–8.
121. O'Rourke IC, Middleton RW. The place and efficacy of operative management of fractured clavicle. Injury 1975;6:236–240.
122. Owens BD, Goss TP. The floating shoulder. J Bone Joint Surg Br 2006;88B:1419–1424.
123. Pedersen MS, Kristiansen B, Thomsen F, et al. [Conservative treatment of clavicular fractures.] Ugesker Laeger 1993;155:3832–3834.
124. Petracic B. [Efficiency of a rucksack bandage in the treatment of clavicle fractures.] Unfallchirurgie 1983;9:41–43.
125. Poigenfurst J, Rappold G, Fischer W. Plating of fresh clavicular fractures: results of 122 operations. Injury 1992;23:237–241.
126. Poigenfurst J, Reiler T, Fischer W. [Plating of fresh clavicular fractures. Experience with 60 operations.] Unfallchirurgie 1988;14:26–37.
127. Post M. Current concepts in the treatment of fractures of the clavicle. Clin Orthop 1989;245:89–101.
128. Potter J, Lones C, Wild LM, et al. Does delay matter? The restoration of objectively measured shoulder strength and patient-oriented outcome after immediate fixation versus delayed reconstruction of displaced midshaft fractures of the clavicle. J Shoulder Elbow Surg 2007;16:514–518.
129. Pyber JB. Nonunion of fractures of the clavicle. Injury 1978;9:268–270.
130. Ramos L, Mencia R, Alonso A, et al. Conservative treatment of ipsilateral fractures of the scapula and clavicle. J Trauma 1997;42:239–242.
131. Rasyid HN, Nakajima T, Hamada K, et al. Winging of the scapula caused by disruption of "sternoclavicular linkage": report of two cases. J Shoulder Elbow Surg 2000;9:144–147.
132. Reichenbacher D, Seiber G. Early secondary lesions of the brachial plexus: a rare complication following clavicular fracture. Unfallchirurgie 1987;13:91–92.
133. Renger RJ, de Bruijin AJ, Aarts HC, et al. Endovascular treatment of a pseudoaneurysm of the subclavian artery. J Trauma 2003;55:969–971.
134. Riemer BL, Butterfield SL, Daffner RH, et al. The abduction lordotic view of the clavicle: a new technique for radiographic visualization. J Orthop Trauma 1991;5:392–394.
135. Rikli D, Regazzoni P, Renner N. The unstable shoulder girdle: early functional treatment utilizing open reduction and internal fixation. J Orthop Trauma 1995;9:93–97.
136. Ring D, Holovacs T. Brachial plexus palsy after intramedullary fixation of a clavicle fracture. J Bone Joint Surg Am 2005;87A:1834–1836.
137. Robinson CM. Fractures of the clavicle in the adult. J Bone Joint Surg Br 1998;80B: 476–484.
138. Robinson CM, Cairns DA. Primary nonoperative treatment of displaced lateral fractures of the clavicle. J Bone Joint Surge Am 2004;86A:778–782.
139. Robinson CM, Court-Brown CM, McQueen MM, et al. Estimating the risk of nonunion following nonoperative treatment of a clavicle fracture. J Bone Joint Surg Am 2004; 86A:1359–1365.
140. Rockwood CA. Fractures of the outer clavicle in children and adults. J Bone Joint Surg Br 1982;64B:642.
141. Rokito AS, Eisenberg DP, Gallagher MA, et al. A comparison of nonoperative and operative treatment of type II distal clavicle fractures. Bull Hosp Joint Dis 2003;61: 32–39.
142. Rosenberg N, Neumann L, Wallace AW. Functional outcome of surgical treatment of symptomatic nonunion and malunion of midshaft clavicle fractures. J Shoulder Elbow Surg 2007;16:510–513.
143. Roset-Llobet J, Sala-Orfila JM. Sports-related stress fracture of the clavicle: a case report. Int Orthop 1998;22:266–268.
144. Rowe CR. An atlas of anatomy and treatment of midclavicular fractures. Clin Orthop 1968;58:29–42.
145. Rumball KM, Da Silva VF, Preston DN, et al. Brachial-plexus injury after clavicular fracture: case report and literature review. Can J Surg 1991;34:264–266.
146. Russo R, Visconti V, Lorini S, et al. Displaced comminuted midshaft clavicle fractures: Use of Mennen plate fixation system. J Trauma 2007;63:951–954.
147. Sakellarides H. Pseudarthrosis of the clavicle: a report of 20 cases. J Bone Joint Surg Am 1961;43A:130–138.
148. Schuind F, Pay-Pay E, Andrianne Y, et al. External fixation of the clavicle for fracture or nonunion in adults. J Bone Joint Surg Am 1988;70A:692–695.
149. Schwarz N, Hocker K. Osteosynthesis of irreducible fractures of the clavicle with 2.7-mm ASIF plates. J Trauma 1992;33:179–183.
150. Seo GS, Aoki J, Karakida O, et al. Case report: nonunion of a medical clavicular fracture following radical neck dissection: MRI diagnosis. Orthopedics 1999;22:985–986.
151. Shackford SR. Taming of the screw: a case report and literature review of limb-threatening complications after plate osteosynthesis of a clavicular nonunion. J Trauma 2003; 55:840–843.
152. Shellhaas JS, Glaser DL, Drezner JA. Distal clavicular stress fracture in a female weight lifter: a case report. Am J Sports Med 2004;32:1755–1758.
153. Shen WJ, Liu TJ, Shen YS. Plate fixation of fresh displaced midshaft clavicle fractures. Injury 1999;30:497–500.
154. Smith CA, Rudd J, Crosby LA. Results of operative versus nonoperative treatment for 100% displaced midshaft clavicle. Proceedings from the 16th Annual Open Meeting of the American Shoulder and Elbow Surgeons, March 18, 2000, p 41.
155. Smekal V, Deml C, Irenberger A et al. Length determination in midshaft clavicle fractures: validation of measurement. J Orthop Trauma 2008;22:458–462
156. Smith J, Dietrich CT, Kotajarvi BR, et al. The effect of scapular protraction on isometric shoulder rotation strength in normal subjects. J Shoulder Elbow Surg 2006;15: 339–343.
157. Spar I. Total claviculectomy for pathological fractures. Clin Orthop 1977;129:236–237.
158. Spencer EE, Kuhn JE. Biomechanical analysis of reconstructions for sternoclavicular joint instability. J Bone Joint Surg Am 2004;86A:98–105.
159. Stanley D, Norris SH. Recovery following fractures of the clavicle treated conservatively. Injury 1988;19:162–164.
160. Stanley D, Trowbridge EA, Norris SH. The mechanism of clavicular fracture. A clinical and biochemical analysis. J Bone Joint Surg Br 1988;70B:461–464.
161. Tarar MN, Quaba AA. An adipofascial turnover flap for soft tissue cover around the clavicle. Br J Plast Surg 1995;48:161–164.
162. Taitsman L, Nork SE, Coles CP, et al. Open fractures of the clavicle and associated injuries. J Orthop Trauma 2006;20:369–399.
163. Throckmorton T, Kuhn JE. Fractures of the medial end of the clavicle. J Shoulder Elbow Surg 2007;16:49–54.
164. Tomic S, Bumbasirevic M, Lesic A, et al. Modification of the Ilizarov external fixator for aseptic hypertrophic nonunion of the clavicle: an option for treatment. J Orthop Trauma 2006;20:122–128.
165. Tse DH, Slabaugh PB, Carlson PA. Injury to the axillary artery by a closed fracture of the clavicle. A case report. J Bone Joint Surg Am 1980;62A:1372–1374.
166. van Noort A, te Slaa RL, Marti RK, et al. The floating shoulder: a multicentre study. J Bone Joint Surg Br 2001;83B:795–798.
167. Verborgt O, Pittoors K, Van Glabbeek F, et al. Plate Fixation of middle-third factures of the clavicle in the semiprofessional athlete. Acta Orthop Belg 2005;71:17–21.
168. Veysi VT, Mittal R, Agarwal S, et al. Multiple trauma and scapula fractures: so what? J Trauma 2003;55:1145–1148.
169. Webber MC, Haines JF. The treatment of lateral clavicle fractures. Injury 2000;31: 175–179.
170. Weinberg B, Seife B, Alonso P. The apical oblique view of the clavicle: its usefulness in neonatal and childhood trauma. Skeletal Radiol 1991;20:201–203.
171. White RR, Anson PS, Kristiansen T, et al. Adult clavicle fractures: relationship between mechanism of injury and healing. Orthop Trans 1989;13:514–515.
172. Wick M, Muller EJ, Kollig E, et al. Midshaft fractures of the clavicle with a shortening of more than 2 cm predispose to nonunion. Arch Orthop Trauma Surg 2001;121: 207–211.
173. Wilkins RM, Johnston RM. Ununited fractures of the clavicle. J Bone Joint Surg Am 1983;65A:773–778.
174. Williams GR, Koffler K, Pepe M, et al. Rotation of the clavicular portion of the pectoralis major for soft-tissue coverage of the clavicle. An anatomical study and case report. J Bone Joint Surg Am 2000;82A:1736–1742.
175. Williams GR, Naranja J, Klimkiewicz J, et al. The floating shoulder: a biomechanical basis for classification and management. J Bone Joint Surg Am 2001;83A:1182–1187.
176. Williams GR Jr, Silverberg DA, Iannotti JP, et al. Nonoperative treatment of ipsilateral clavicle and glenoid neck fractures. American Shoulder and Elbow Surgeons 15th Open Meeting, Anaheim, CA, 1999.
177. Wood VE. The results of total claviculectomy. Clin Orthop 1986;207:186–190.
178. Wu CC, Shin CM, Chen WJ, et al. Treatment of clavicular aspectic nonunion: Comparison of plating and intramedullary nailing techniques. J Trauma 1999;45:512–516.
179. Yamaguchi H, Arakawa H, Kobayashi M. Results of the Bosworth method for unstable fractures of the distal clavicle. Int Orthop 1998;22:366–368.
180. Yian EH, Ramappa AJ, Arneberg O, et al. The Constant score in normal shoulders. J Shoulder Elbow Surg 2005;14:128–133.
181. Zaslav KR, Ray S, Neer CS 2nd. Conservative management of a displaced medial clavicular physeal injury in an adolescent athlete. A case report and literature review. Am J Sports Med 1989;17:833–836.
182. Zdero R, Yoo D, MacConnell A, et al. A biomechanical study of acromioclavicular joint fixation. J Orthop Trauma 2007;21:248–253.
183. Zelle BA, Pape HC, Gerich TG, et al. Functional outcome following scapulo-thoracic dissociation. J Bone Joint Surg Am 2004;86A:2–8.
184. Zenni EJ Jr, Krieg JK, Rosen MJ. Open reduction and internal fixation of clavicular fractures. J Bone Joint Surg Am 1981;63A:147–151.
185. Zlowodzki M, Zelle BA, Cole PA, et al. Treatment of midshaft clavicle fractures: systemic review of 2144 fractures. J Orthop Trauma 2005;19:504–507.

37

SCAPULAR FRACTURES

Arthur van Noort

INTRODUCTION

The scapula is an integral part of the connection between the upper extremity and the axial skeleton. This highly mobile, thin sheet of bone articulates in three different joints: with the humerus in the glenohumeral joint, with the clavicle in the acromioclavicular joint, and with the thorax in the scapulothoracic joint. To accomplish a full range of shoulder motion, a smooth coordination is required of motion in all three articulations. Therefore, a complex interaction of several muscles that envelope the scapula is necessary.[146] Besides its assistance in the movements of the arm in the shoulder joint, the scapula has two other functions. It is a mobile platform for the humeral head and upper extremity to work against, and it serves as a point of attachment for muscles, tendons, and ligaments.[62] No less than 18 different muscles insert on or originate from the scapula allowing six basic movements of the shoulder blade over the posterior chest wall: elevation, depression, upward rotation, downward rotation, protraction, and retraction.[63]

Scapular fractures are generally the result of a high-energy trauma with a high incidence of significant associated (local and remote) injuries.[3,67,79,115,116,169,184,191] These associated injuries are often major, multiple, and sometimes life-threatening, therefore needing priority in treatment. The relative infrequency (prevalence 1 %) and "benign characteristics" of a scapular fracture probably explain the limited attention in the literature.[78]

Historically, scapular fractures have been treated by closed means. One of the earliest descriptions of treating scapular fractures was published in 1805 in Desault's treatise on fractures. Since then, it has been suggested in the literature that over 90% of scapular fractures are non- or minimally displaced and do well with conservative treatment.[79,115,184] This observation, however, has been based on the treatment of scapular fractures in general and its relevance is therefore very limited. A more differentiated approach is necessary as good results are not guaranteed with exclusively conservative treatment.[8] Recent literature is more focussed on the results of conservative[79,115] or operative treatment[41,42,61,66,74,84,98,99,112,132,133,156] with regard to specific fracture types. This contrasts with publications before the 1990s which were particularly focussed on the trauma mechanism and associated injuries.[115,116,169,184] Specific types of scapular fractures are severe injuries that may result in significant shoulder dysfunction. There are a few reports on poor prognosis after conservative treatment of displaced glenoid, scapular neck, coracoid, and acromion fractures.[1,77,127] Along with technical refinement of diagnostic tools, more attention is currently paid to these fracture types as demonstrated by the rising number of publications on this subject.

PRINCIPLES OF MANAGEMENT

Mechanisms of Injury

Scapular fractures are caused by different mechanisms, of which blunt trauma is probably the most common.[1,3,8,115,116,169] This direct force may cause fractures in all anatomic areas of the scapula. Other mechanisms are indirect injuries: (i) traction by muscles or ligaments may induce avulsion fractures of the acromion or coracoid, which in rare cases are caused by a seizure or an electrical shock[110,166]; and (ii) impaction of the humeral head into the glenoid fossa which may induce glenoid and some scapular neck fractures.

As in general with high-energy trauma, traffic accidents are the main cause of scapular fractures (occupants of motor vehicles in about 50% of cases[1,8,115] and pedestrians in 20%[3,115]). Other causes are motorcycle accidents, fall from heights, crush injuries, or sporting activities (horseback riding, skiing, and contact sports).

Associated Injuries

Usually, high energy is required to fracture a scapula, hence scapular fractures are commonly associated with concomitant injuries. Research shows that 61% to 98% of scapula fractures have associated injuries.[1,3,17,21,79,97,115,116,165,169] These associated injuries may be multiple and may need priority in treatment. As a result, diagnosis and treatment of scapular injuries may be delayed or suboptimal.

A wide variety of regional and remote injuries have been reported that may be life-threatening, such as pneumothorax (9% to 38%),[3,45,118,169] pulmonary contusion (8% to 54%),[45,116,169] arterial injury (11%),[45,169] closed head injuries (20% to 42%),[79,115] and splenic or liver lacerations 3% to 5%.[116] Brachial plexus injury is present in 5% to 13%[3,45,79,115,169] and is often the most important prognostic factor with regard to the final clinical outcome, whether fracture treatment be conservative or otherwise. The reported mortality rate of patients with scapular fractures from the concomitant injuries varies between 2% and 15%.[115,169,191]

In a recent review article on the operative treatment of scapular fractures, Lantry[97] analyzed the associated injuries of 160 cases in 11 different studies. Rib fractures were the most common associated injury, followed by head and chest injuries. Fractures in remote anatomic areas were found in nearly 20% of patients. To determine the significance of scapular fractures in blunt trauma, Stephens[161] compared two matched groups of patients with and without scapular fractures. Except for a significantly higher incidence of thoracic injuries in the group with scapular fractures, he found no difference in mortality or incidence of neurovascular injuries. Veysi[179] reported in 2003 that patients with scapula fractures have more severe underlying chest injuries and overall injury severity scores (ISS). However, these findings, which were confirmed by other authors,[161,183] did not correlate with a higher rate of intensive therapy unit admission, length of hospital stay, or mortality. There is no clear correlation between the number and severity of associated injuries and the type of scapular fracture. Nevertheless, Tadros[165] found in a prospective study that the ISS and abbreviated injury score for chest injuries are higher and posterior structure injuries are more frequent in patients with fractures involving multiple scapular regions.

In summary, scapular fractures should alert the surgeon to the presence of other, sometimes very severe injuries. Severe chest injury should also raise suspicion of a possible scapular fracture.[108]

History and Physical Examination

A patient with a scapular fracture typically presents with the arm adducted along the body and will protect the injured shoulder from all movements.

Physical examination may reveal swelling, ecchymosis, crepitus, and local tenderness. The ecchymosis is in general less than expected probably because the scapula is protected by a thick layer of soft tissue. Active range of motion is restricted in all directions. Abduction in particular is very painful.

Neviaser[126] described in 1956 that the rotator cuff function is weak and very painful secondary to inhibition from intramuscular hemorrhage. This has been described as a "pseudorupture" of the rotator cuff and usually resolves within a few weeks. When a scapular fracture is diagnosed, it is important to perform a careful neurovascular examination to rule out arterial injury and/or brachial plexopathy.

Imaging and Other Diagnostic Studies

After initial assessment, according to Advanced Trauma Life Support (ATLS) principles, specific radiographic evaluation of the injured shoulder is indicated as soon as the patient is in a stable condition. Associated injuries requiring urgent treatment may force the treating surgeon, particularly in polytrauma patients, to evaluate the chest only by a routine supine chest radiograph. This is the earliest opportunity to identify a scapular fracture. Harris[68] pointed out in a retrospective analysis of 100 patients with major blunt chest trauma that the scapular fracture was diagnosed on the initial chest radiograph in only 57 of 100 patients and, although present, was not recognized in 43%. Particularly extensive associated chest injuries may overshadow the scapula with a delay in diagnosis as a result.[164]

Scapular fractures are notoriously difficult to visualize radiographically. Except for the chest radiograph, a true anteroposterior (AP) view, perpendicular to the plane of the scapula, a lateral, and an axillary view are recommended. A true axillary projection of the glenohumeral joint and scapula is ideally performed with the arm in 70 to 90 degrees of abduction, which might be very painful for the patient in the acute situation. Alternatives for this view are the Velpeau axillary lateral view[12] (see Fig. 39-6) or the trauma axillary lateral view,[170] which can be taken while the patient is supine. In case of a complex shoulder injury with a double disruption of the superior shoulder suspensory complex (SSSC) (Fig. 37-1), a weight-bearing AP projection of the shoulder is recommended by Goss.[60]

Most scapular fractures will be diagnosed by the three-view scapula trauma series, but special views may be necessary for selected fracture types. The Stryker notch view is useful for coracoid fractures (see Fig. 39-8) while the apical oblique view[48] and the West Point lateral view[147] are useful for glenoid rim fractures. In cases of scapular fractures with multiple frac-

FIGURE 37-1 A,B. A double disruption of the SSSC (fracture of the coracoid process and ipsilateral lateral clavicle fracture). **C,D.** After open reposition and internal fixation of both clavicle and coracoid process, both fractures healed. Despite the acromioclavicular joint subluxation, the patient had a maximum constant score of 100.

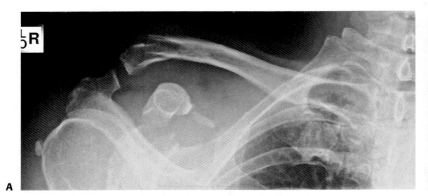

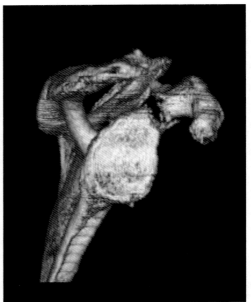

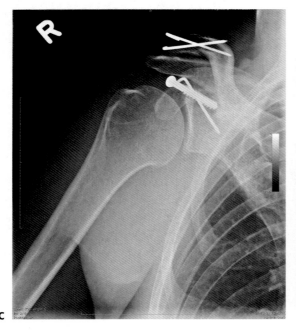

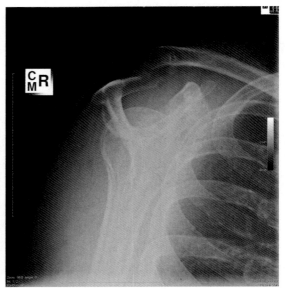

ture lines and particularly significant displacement, a computed tomography (CT) scan is recommended, although the additional value is not clear in every fracture type.[113] It is, however, useful to assess the size, location, and degree of displacement of fragments in coracoid, acromion, and glenoid fractures. In glenoid fractures, it is also helpful to evaluate the position of the humeral head in relation to the glenoid fossa or fracture fragment (Fig. 37-2). Finally, a three-dimensional CT scan can be very helpful in understanding complex fracture patterns and in preoperative planning.

Diagnosis and Classification

Scapular fractures are generally classified by anatomic area (body and spine, glenoid cavity, glenoid [scapular] neck, acromion, and coracoid).

Fractures of the body and spine are the most common (approximately 50%), followed by the scapular neck (approximately 25%), glenoid cavity (approximately 10%), acromion (approximately 8%), and coracoid process (approximately 7%).[1,79,115,127,184]

There are several other classification systems reported in the literature. Zdravkovic and Damholt[191] divided scapular fractures into three types: type 1, fractures of the body; type 2, fractures of the apophysis (including acromion and coracoid); and type 3, fractures of the superior lateral angle, including the glenoid neck and glenoid. Zdravkovic and Damholt[191] considered type 3 fractures, which represented only 6% of their series to be the most difficult to treat.

Thompson and colleagues[169] presented a classification system which also divided scapular fractures into three different classes:

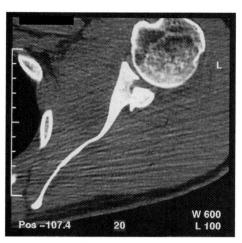

FIGURE 37-2 The humeral head is subluxed along with a posterior fracture fragment.

Class 1: acromion, coracoid, and minor fractures of the body
Class 2: glenoid and scapular neck fractures
Class 3: major scapular body fractures

In their opinion, classes 2 and 3 were much more likely to have associated injuries.

Wilber and Evans[184] divided scapular fractures into two groups. Group 1 included patients with fractures of the scapular body, scapular neck, and spine; group 2 included patients with fractures of the acromion, coracoid process, and glenoid. They reported poor functional outcome caused by loss of glenohumeral motion and residual pain in patients of group 2.

Finally, the Orthopaedic Trauma Association's (OTA) classification, which was originally published in 1996, has been revised for scapular fractures.[107] In this new format, the differences between the OTA and AO classification have now been eliminated by a unified alpha-numeric code (Fig. 37-3).

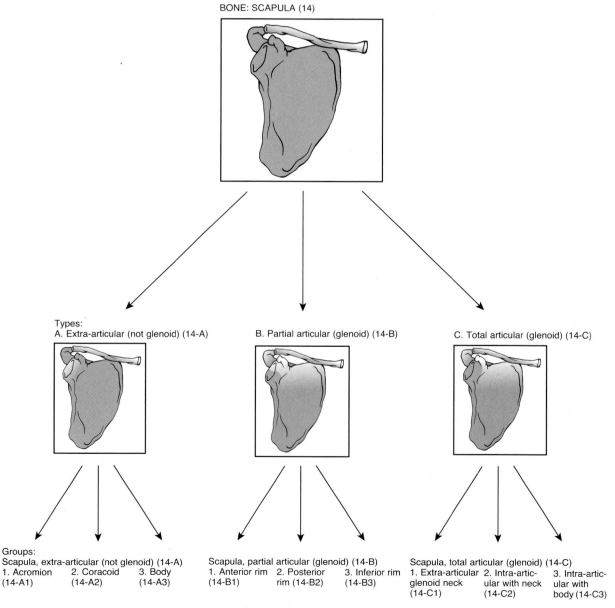

BONE: SCAPULA (14)

Types:
A. Extra-articular (not glenoid) (14-A)   B. Partial articular (glenoid) (14-B)   C. Total articular (glenoid) (14-C)

Groups:
Scapula, extra-articular (not glenoid) (14-A)
1. Acromion (14-A1)   2. Coracoid (14-A2)   3. Body (14-A3)

Scapula, partial articular (glenoid) (14-B)
1. Anterior rim (14-B1)   2. Posterior rim (14-B2)   3. Inferior rim (14-B3)

Scapula, total articular (glenoid) (14-C)
1. Extra-articular glenoid neck (14-C1)   2. Intra-articular with neck (14-C2)   3. Intra-articular with body (14-C3)

FIGURE 37-3 The OTA classification of scapular fractures.

Glenoid Fractures

The most commonly used classification scheme concerning glenoid fractures is the one devised by Ideberg et al.,[77,78] who described five different fracture types. Goss[60] modified this system by subdividing type 5 and introducing type 6, a stellate glenoid fracture with extensive intra-articular comminution (Fig. 37-4).

The diagnosis of glenoid neck fractures can be made with the standard three-view trauma series. The axillary radiograph combined with CT scanning is used to demonstrate any subluxation or displacement.

Scapular Neck Fractures

Scapular neck fractures are extra-articular fractures by definition. Although three fracture patterns have been described as scapular neck fractures,[62] only two run through the scapular neck (Fig. 37-5). One fracture pattern runs lateral from the origin of the coracoid to the lateral border of the scapula (anatomic neck), and the other runs medial from the coracoid to the lateral border of the scapula. According to the OTA, both are classified as type 14-C1 (see Fig. 37-3).

Diagnosis of a scapular neck fracture is reliably made by plain films, in contrast with assessment of the amount of fracture displacement and angulation.[26,113] A common method to determine angulation deformity and shortening, as described by Bestard,[10] is on an AP radiograph of the scapula (Fig. 37-6). Three-dimensional CT reconstruction images may be of more benefit in assessment of displacement and angulation, in contrast with the images of a conventional CT scan.[113]

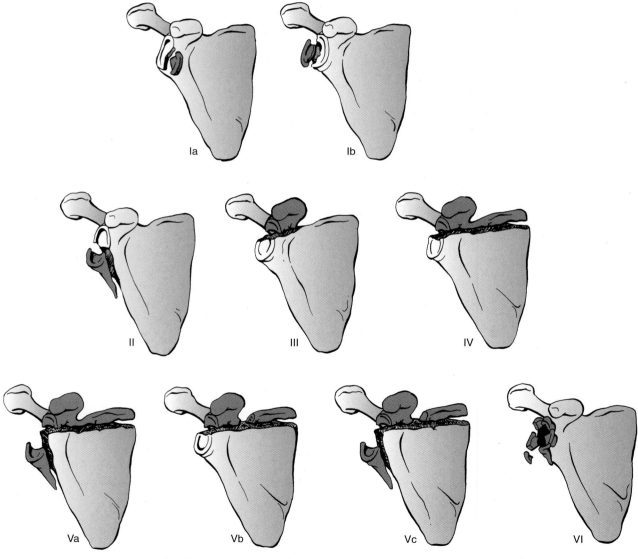

FIGURE 37-4 Classification of fractures of the glenoid cavity: type Ia, anterior rim fracture; type Ib, posterior rim fracture; type II, fracture line through the glenoid fossa exiting at the lateral scapular border; type III, fracture line through the glenoid fossa exiting at the superior scapular border; type IV, fracture line through the glenoid fossa exiting at the medial scapular border; type Va, combination of types II and IV; type Vb, combination of types III and IV; type Vc, combination of types II, III, and IV; type VI, comminuted fracture. (Goss TP. Scapular fractures and dislocations: diagnosis and treatment. J Am Acad Orthop Surg 1995;3(1):22–33, with permission.)

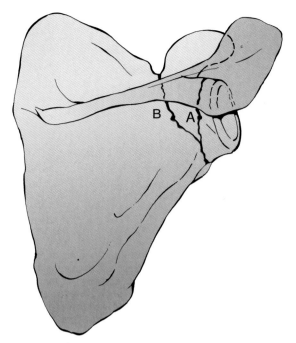

FIGURE 37-5 Line A is a fracture through the anatomic scapular neck. Line B is a fracture through the surgical scapular neck.

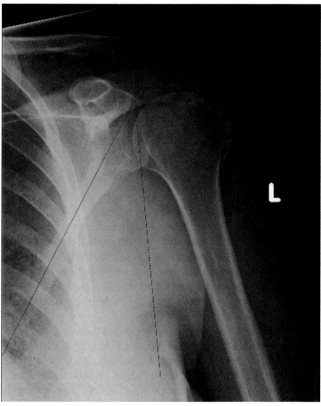

FIGURE 37-6 The GPA is the angle between the line connecting the most cranial with the most caudal point of the glenoid cavity and the line connecting the most cranial point of the glenoid cavity with the most caudal point of the scapular body. It provides a value for the obliquity of the glenoid articular surface in relation to the scapular body. A GPA ranging from 30 to 45 degrees is considered normal.[10]

Acromion Fractures

Kuhn[90] has proposed a subclassification of acromion fractures, which are classified by the OTA as type 14-A1 fractures, to help determine the need for operative intervention. According to the classification of Kuhn, type 1 are nondisplaced fractures, type 2 displaced fractures without reduction of the subacromial space, and type 3 displaced fractures with reduction of the subacromial space (Fig. 37-7).[90]

The diagnosis is radiographic. A three-view trauma series, including an AP view, a lateral view, and an axillary view of the scapula, will detect most acromial fractures. Caution should be used to differentiate an acromial fracture from an os acromiale. An axillary radiograph of the contralateral shoulder may be helpful, because an os acromiale is bilateral in approximately 45% to 62% of the cases.[38,101] Occasionally, a CT scan is necessary to define the configuration of the fracture precisely (Fig. 37-8B,C).

Coracoid Fractures

Ogawa,[133] who simplified the classification scheme of Eyres,[42] classified coracoid fractures into two different types. Type 1 is situated proximal to the coracoclavicular ligament attachment and type 2 distal to these ligaments (Fig. 37-9). Ogawa[133] suggested that a type 1 fracture may disturb the scapulothoracic connection (see Fig. 37-1).

The complex anatomy of the scapula makes defining the fracture type difficult. The coracoid process is not easily visualised on a radiograph. Apart from the usual three-view trauma series, an AP tilt view (35 to 60 degrees),[60] a Stryker notch view,[145] and a Goldberg posterior oblique 20-degree cephalic tilt view[53] may be helpful. A CT scan with three-dimensional reconstruction images will give more insight into the fracture pattern.

Scapulothoracic Dissociation

Damschen et al.[29] proposed a classification system for scapulothoracic dissociation in 1997 based on musculoskeletal, vascular, and neurologic impairment. Zelle et al.[192] modified the group of neurologic impairment of this classification scheme and added the group with a complete brachial plexus avulsion as the most severe type (Table 37-1).

The diagnosis of scapulothoracic dissociation is based on history, clinical findings, and radiography. The difficulty for the treating physician is that the severe associated injuries may divert attention away from the sometimes subtle clinical signs of the scapulothoracic dissociation.[94] The clinical signs may vary between swelling from a dissecting hematoma and a flail and pulseless extremity.

A well-centered chest radiograph will demonstrate lateral displacement of the scapula on the injured side, which is pathognomic of a scapulothoracic dissociation. The degree of lateralization can be quantified using the scapula index (Fig. 37-10).[86,134]

SURGICAL AND APPLIED ANATOMY AND COMMON SURGICAL APPROACHES

Surgical and Applied Anatomy

A thorough knowledge of the bony contours of the scapula and its related musculotendinous and neurovascular structures is

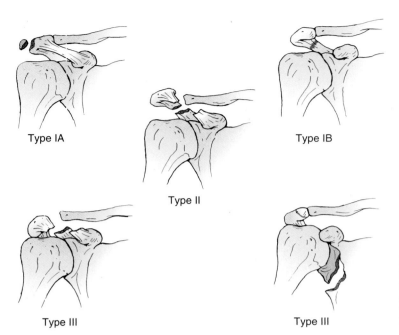

Type IA

Type IB

Type II

Type III

Type III

FIGURE 37-7 Kuhn classification of fractures of the acromion process. Type I undisplaced: Ia avulsion fractures and Ib true fractures. Type II displaced without reduction of the subacromial space. Type III displaced with reduction of the subacromial space. This reduction may be by inferior displacement of the acromion or by an association with a superiorly displaced glenoid neck fracture.

required for adequate treatment of patients with scapular fractures, particularly if operative treatment is considered. The scapula is a large, flat, triangular bone that connects the clavicle to the humerus. At least 18 different muscles originate from and insert into this highly mobile bone (Fig. 37-11).

Special attention should be given to neurovascular structures at risk when surgery (both anteriorly and posteriorly) is undertaken.

Brachial Plexus

The brachial plexus descends in the concavity of the medial two thirds of the clavicle, accompanies the axillary artery, and lies beneath the pectoralis minor muscle. The musculocutaneous nerve originates from the lateral cord and penetrates the conjoined tendon of biceps and coracobrachialis at a variable distance (average 5 cm) from the coracoid tip (Fig. 37-12).

Suprascapular Nerve

Beneath the trapezius and omohyoid muscle, the suprascapular nerve enters the supraspinous fossa under the transverse ligament (or suprascapular ligament). The nerve runs beneath the supraspinatus muscle and curves round the external corner of the spine of the scapula to the infraspinous fossa (Fig. 37-13). In the supraspinous fossa, it gives off two branches to the supraspinatus muscle, and in the infraspinous fossa, it gives off two branches to the infraspinatus muscle, besides some filaments to the shoulder joint and scapula.

The safe zone for avoiding suprascapular nerve injury during open surgical procedures require dissection of the posterior shoulder joint within 2.3 cm of the superior glenoid rim and within 1.4 cm of the posterior rim of the glenoid at the level of the base of the scapular spine (see Fig. 37-13).[157]

Axillary Nerve

Before entering the quadrilateral space, the axillary nerve runs together with the circumflex humeral artery overlying the subscapular muscle. The axillary nerve divides in this space and

sends a posterior branch to the teres minor muscle, together with a lateral brachial cutaneous nerve (see Fig. 37-13).[6] An anterior branch runs from this space approximately 5 cm below the edge of the acromion as the nerve passes anteriorly to innervate the anterior two thirds of the muscle.

The innervation of the posterior part of the deltoid is variable. In 70%, it is innervated by the posterior branch, in 27% by posterior and anterior branches, and 3% only by the anterior branch.[172] One should therefore be careful when performing a deltoid splitting approach in a posterior surgical approach.

The branch to the teres minor arises from the posterior branch of the axillary nerve immediately adjacent to the inferior aspect of the capsule at the level of the glenoid rim (see Fig. 37-13).[6]

Common Surgical Approaches

Posterior Approach

The most common surgical posterior approach to the scapula in the last decades was the one described by Judet.[83] It is an extensive approach which involves dissection of the infraspinatus muscle from the infraspinatus fossa with the risk of neurovascular damage (suprascapular nerve) and structural muscle damage. Nowadays, the advocated posterior approaches are less invasive, since no or minimal infraspinatus detachment is necessary when using the interval between the teres minor and infraspinatus muscle.[16,36,82,128,129]

For the posterior approach, the patient is placed in a prone or lateral decubitus position. As described by Ebraheim,[36] a skin incision is utilized along the scapular spine and then a vertical extension is made at the lateral border of the scapula (a "reverse Judet" skin incision) (Fig. 37-14). This allows the surgeon to reflect the complete posterior deltoid, if necessary, off the scapular spine. A medially based fascia flap is raised to expose the scapular musculature. The interval between the infraspinatus and teres minor muscles is entered with the infraspinatus muscle retracted cranially and the teres minor muscle laterally. This avoids any injury to the suprascapular nerve sup-

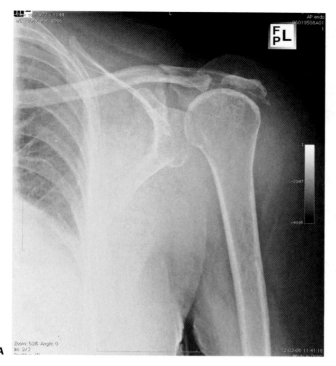

A

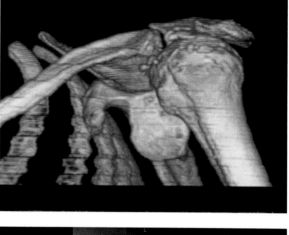

B

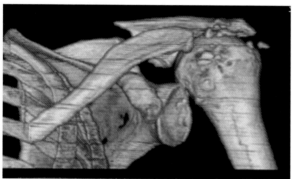

C

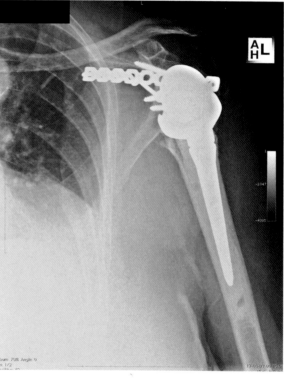

D

FIGURE 37-8 The radiograph **(A)** and CT **(B,C)** scan of an 80-year-old woman with a posterocranial glenohumeral luxation with a symptomatic pseudarthrosis of an acromion fracture. **D.** The patient underwent a plate osteosynthesis with bone graft and a reversed shoulder prosthesis.

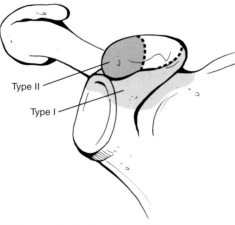

FIGURE 37-9 Ogawa classification of coracoid fractures. Type I is proximal to and type II is distal to the coracoclavicular ligaments.

TABLE 37-1	The Classification System for Scapulothoracic Dissociation as Proposed by Damschen et al.[29] and Modified by Zelle et al.[192]

Type	Clinical Findings
I	Musculoskeletal injury alone
IIa	Musculoskeletal injury with vascular injury
IIb	Musculoskeletal injury with incomplete neurologic impairment of the upper extremity
III	Musculoskeletal injury with incomplete neurologic impairment of the upper extremity and vascular injury
IV	Musculoskeletal injury with complete brachial plexus avulsion

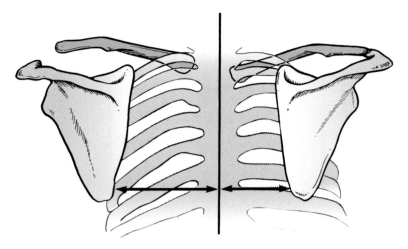

FIGURE 37-10 The diagnosis of scapulothoracic dissociation can be made on a nonrotated AP radiograph by comparing the distance from the medial border of the scapula with the spinous processes between the affected (*long arrow*) and unaffected (*short arrow*) sides. Kelbel et al.[86] created the scapula index and reported a normal value to be a ratio of 1.07 ± 0.04.[134]

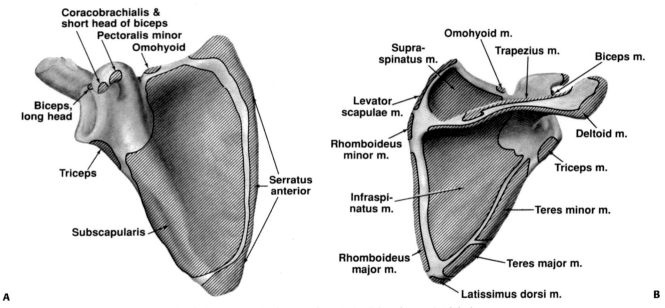

A

B

FIGURE 37-11 Muscle insertions onto the scapula. Anterior **(A)** and posterior **(B)** views.

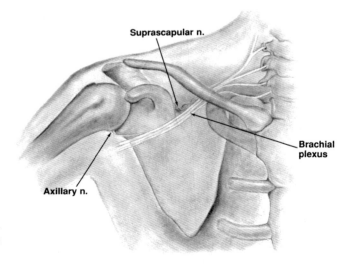

FIGURE 37-12 The position of the brachial plexus in relation to the anterior surface of the scapula. The supraclavicular and axillary nerves are also shown.

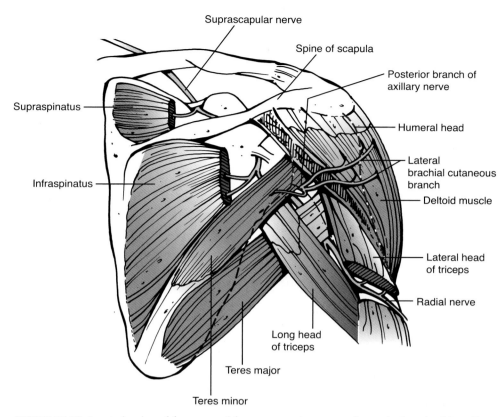

FIGURE 37-13 A posterior view of the course of the suprascapular nerve and posterior branch of the axillary nerve in relation to the scapula and overlying muscles.

plying the infraspinatus muscle as well as to the axillary nerve supplying the teres minor muscle. The lateral border of the scapula and the glenoid joint are then displayed, with the possibility of open reduction and internal fixation of scapular neck fractures and posterior glenoid fractures (types Ib, II, IV, and possibly V) (see Fig. 37-14).

A disadvantage of the described approach is the release of the posterior deltoid muscle off the scapular spine. Alternatives are described by Wirth[186] who described a posterior approach with splitting of the posterior deltoid in line with its fibers distally to the upper border of the teres minor. Splitting the deltoid muscle, however, endangers the integrity of the axillary nerve

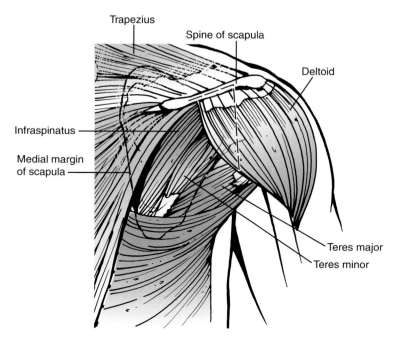

FIGURE 37-14 Posterior approach to the glenohumeral joint/scapular neck showing the skin incision.

at the level of the dense connective tissue of the subdeltoid fascia. Furthermore, the intramuscular nerve branches can occasionally be damaged within the lateral deltoid compartment.

Finally, Brodsky et al.[16] and Jerosch et al.[82] claim excellent exposure with their posterior subdeltoid approach to the posterior aspect of the glenohumeral joint and scapular neck (Fig. 37-15). After a vertical skin incision, the inferior border of the spinal part of the deltoid is identified and mobilized by blunt dissection. By abducting the free draped arm 60 to 90 degrees, it is easier to retract the mobilized deltoid muscle and enter the

interval between the infraspinatus and teres minor muscle as described above, allowing access to the posterior aspect of the glenoid and lateral border of the scapular body. Care should be taken to avoid injury to the circumflex scapular artery, which lies directly medial to the insertion of the long head of triceps, and the axillary and suprascapular nerves.

Anterior Approach

The anterior approach is used for coracoid and type Ia glenoid fractures. It is performed in the beach chair position, with the

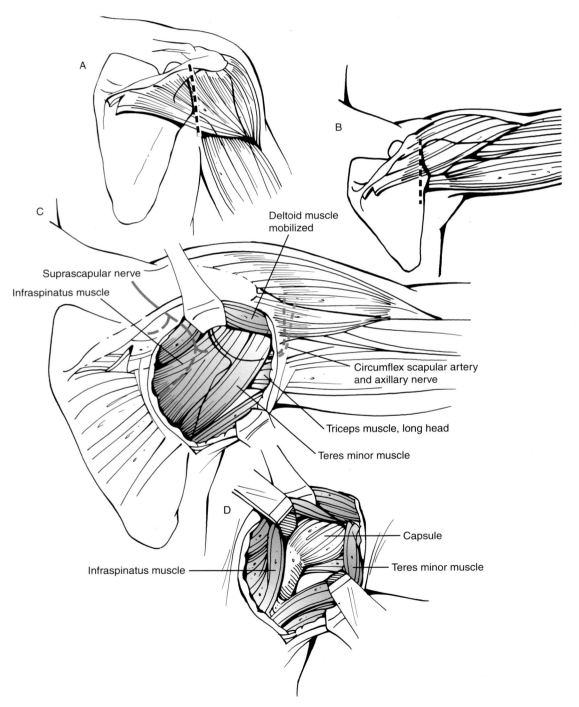

FIGURE 37-15 The posterior approach to the glenohumeral joint and scapula. **A.** Arm in adduction. **B.** Arm in 90 degrees of abduction. **C.** The underlying rotator cuff muscles. **D.** The capsular incision.

incision made in Langer lines over the coracoid process to the axillary fold. The deltopectoral groove is opened with the cephalic vein attached to the deltoid muscle. In the presence of an anterior glenoid rim (type Ia) fracture, the subscapularis tendon is dissected off the anterior glenohumeral capsule and turned back medially. The capsule is opened and a humeral retractor is inserted behind the posterior aspect of the glenoid to visualize the entire glenoid cavity. After reduction and internal fixation of the glenoid fracture, the capsule, which is usually not stretched by the injury, is closed without performing a capsular shift.

Superior Approach

A superior approach is indicated when a superior glenoid fragment (type III, type V glenoid fracture) or an anatomic neck fracture of the scapula is difficult to control or stabilize. This approach can be added to an anterior or posterior approach. It is performed in a beach chair position with the skin incision made midway between the scapular spine and clavicle, laterally over the edge of the acromion. The trapezius can then be split in the line of its fibers, taking care to protect the accessory nerve which runs from anterior to posterior. After identifying the suprascapular notch, the supraspinatus muscle can either be split or shifted to the anterior or posterior part of the supraspinatus fossa depending on whether access is required to the anterosuperior or posterosuperior aspect of the glenoid. Care should be taken to protect and avoid injury to the suprascapular nerve and vessels that lie medial to the coracoid process.

CURRENT TREATMENT OPTIONS

Glenoid Fractures

Glenoid fractures make up 10% of all scapular fractures. Only 10% of glenoid fractures are significantly displaced,[60] meriting surgical consideration. The majority (90%) are minimally displaced or undisplaced and should be treated nonoperatively. Fractures of the glenoid are commonly found in the middle aged, between 40 and 60 years, with a male prevalence,[78] and result most often from high-energy direct trauma.[1,57,79,112,115,150] They occur when the humeral head is driven with a substantial force against the glenoid fossa. This may be caused by a direct force on the shoulder or an axial force through the humerus. The direction of this axial force will predict the fracture pattern. The most common fracture type is the anterior chip fragment fracture (type Ia), which is often associated with an anterior shoulder dislocation.[78]

Many authors have reported good early functional outcome in patients treated nonoperatively with intra-articular fractures without associated instability.[20,77,144,151] Since the late 1980s, operative treatment of glenoid fractures has gained more attention.[4,8,74,84,89,98,156] There is a current trend towards arthroscopic techniques of glenoid fracture treatment, particularly in Ideberg type I fractures.[9,22,24,51,138,163,167]

Ideberg Type I

Fractures of the anterior or posterior margin of the glenoid (types Ia and Ib, respectively) may cause instability of the glenohumeral articulation. These fracture types are usually sustained during traumatic glenohumeral subluxation or dislocation.[76,77] After injury, the continuity between capsule, labrum, and frac-

ture fragment is usually maintained. Instability of the glenohumeral joint can be expected when the fragment is displaced more than 1 cm and if at least 25% of the glenoid cavity anteriorly or at least 33% of the glenoid cavity posteriorly is involved.[32] Although debate exists among surgeons about the amount of displacement and the size of the fragment that is acceptable, it is accepted that rim fractures associated with persistent or recurrent instability should undergo open reduction and internal fixation.[32,66,77,159] An axillary radiograph and CT scan will demonstrate whether the humeral head is centered exactly in the glenoid fossa or is displaced along with the fracture fragment. The latter is an indication for surgical treatment. The goal of surgery is to prevent morbidity secondary to glenohumeral instability or degenerative joint disease by accurate reduction of the articular surface. According to the literature of the last decade, open procedures can be replaced by arthroscopic fixation of fragments with promising results particularly in type I fractures[9,22,24,138,163,167]; most authors reported restoration of glenohumeral stability and good functional results.

Ideberg Type II

Type II fractures occur when the force through the humeral head is directed somewhat inferiorly, with a fracture line running from the glenoid fossa to the lateral border of the scapula body as a result. The amount of articular displacement and the degree of comminution determines the need for open reduction and internal fixation. Goss[60] advocates open reduction and internal fixation with displacement of more than 5 mm. This is based on the findings of Soslowsky et al.,[162] who demonstrated that the maximum thickness of glenoid articular cartilage is 5 mm. Schandelmaier[156] reviewed 22 patients with displaced glenoid fractures after a mean review period of 10 years: 9 had a type 2 fracture and were treated by open reduction and internal fixation through a posterior approach. He found a mean constant score of 94.

Ideberg Type III

A type III glenoid fossa fracture occurs when the force is directed superiorly, causing a fracture that involves the upper third of the glenoid fossa including the coracoid. The fracture runs from the glenoid fossa through the superior scapular body in the proximity of the scapular notch. According to Goss,[60,61] type III,V, and VI injuries in particular are prone to neurovascular injuries and damage to the SSSC. As with all other glenoid fractures, a type III injury is usually undisplaced and can be treated conservatively with good functional outcome in absence of associated neurologic injury. The indication for operative treatment is also displacement of more than 5 mm.

Ideberg Type IV

This type is caused by the humeral head being driven centrally into the glenoid fossa. A fracture line runs from the fossa directly across the scapula body to exit along its medial border and splits the glenoid fossa into two parts. Surgery is indicated when there is more than a 5-mm separation between the two parts. Surgery may prevent symptomatic degenerative joint disease, instability of the glenohumeral joint and, although extremely rare, nonunion of the fracture.

Ideberg Type V

Originally, Ideberg[76,77] described type V as a combination of a type II and IV injury, with a direct violent trauma as the mechanism of injury in most cases.[20] Goss[57] subdivided type 5 into three different subtypes (see Fig. 37-4). Type Va is a combination of type II and IV, Type Vb a combination of type III and IV, and type Vc a combination of type II, III, and IV. These subtypes are caused by more complex and probably greater forces than those causing the simpler fracture patterns.[57] The same indications used for type II, III, and IV should be applied when determining the need for open reduction.[19] Operative treatment of type V injuries does not uniformly lead to a good functional outcome, which is probably mostly related to associated neurovascular injuries and postoperative complications.[77,84,98,112,156]

Ideberg/Goss Type VI

Type VI fractures, introduced by Goss,[60] are caused by the most violent force and include all fractures with at least two articular fragments. Even if displacement of the fragments is substantial, with or without subluxation of the humeral head, open reduction and internal fixation is not indicated due to the extensive comminution.[60]

In general, Ideberg's experience with fracture type II through V indicates

1. Closed reduction under anesthesia is unsuccessful in improving position of the fracture fragment(s);
2. Secondary improvement of position of fracture fragments is possible after conservative treatment due to moulding of the fracture by muscle forces across the glenohumeral joint;
3. A good result occurred in 75% of the cases after early mobilization;
4. Open reduction and internal fixation may also lead to a good result in the absence of other significant ipsilateral shoulder fractures, nerve, or muscle injuries.[76–78]

Scapular Neck Fracture

A fracture of the neck of the scapula is the second most common scapular fracture.[3,79,115,116] The suggested mechanisms of trauma are a direct blow to the shoulder, a fall on the point of the shoulder, or a fall on the outstretched arm. The fracture line most often extends from the suprascapular notch area across the neck of the scapula to its lateral border inferior to the glenoid (surgical neck fracture) or, rarely, lateral from the origin of the coracoid to its lateral border inferior to the glenoid (anatomic neck) (see Fig. 37-5).

Scapular neck fractures, by definition extra-articular fractures, are sometimes accompanied by a fracture line through the coracoid process or may remain as an intact unit. If the scapular neck fracture is not associated with an ipsilateral shoulder lesion (of the SSSC), displacement is possible but rare.[31,58,176] According to the concept of the SSSC, isolated fractures of the scapular neck are considered stable fractures.[61]

The treatment of these fractures has historically been nonoperative, mostly with a favorable outcome.[79,83,103,115,116,177] Recommended methods of closed treatment include closed reduction and olecranon pin traction for 3 weeks followed by a sling,[32] closed reduction and a shoulder spica cast for 6 to 8 weeks,[7] and even the use of a traction suspension system for reduction of a displaced neck fracture.[177] Some authors doubt the usefulness of closed reduction in these fractures, advocating the use of a sling and suggest mobilizing the affected arm as soon as possible.[117] Lindholm and Leven[103] studied a series of

scapular neck and body fractures and concluded that if untreated, all fractures healed in the position displayed at the time of the original injury.

These studies, however, do not present data to justify these recommendations. A more differentiated approach is necessary as conservative treatment does not uniformly lead to a good result. Several authors noted fair to poor results after conservative treatment of severely displaced scapular neck fractures.[1,3,49,127,135,148] Displacement is defined as at least 1 cm of translation or 40 degrees of angulation (or a glenopolar angle [GPA] <20 degrees) in the AP plane of the scapula and separates minor from major injuries according to Zdravkovic,[191] Nordqvist and Petersson,[127] and Geel.[50]

Ada and Millar[1] reported on 24 patients with displaced scapular neck fractures. Of the 16 patients treated conservatively, 50% complained of pain at night, 40% had weakness of abduction, and 20% had decreased range of motion. Whether translational displacement of at least 1 cm remains a good criterion for surgical treatment of scapular neck fractures is controversial.[148,176] The criterion of angulation greater than or equal to 40 degrees (or a GPA <20 degrees) is probably less questionable. Several authors reported less favorable long-term outcome after conservative treatment of angulated scapular neck fractures, compared with scapular neck fractures without angular displacement.[15,88,148,173] Good to excellent results have been reported on open reduction and internal fixation of patients with displaced scapular neck fractures.[9,67,88,100] In these series, however, displaced scapular neck fractures are in most cases associated with ipsilateral clavicle fractures. According to Zlowodzki,[194] who performed a systematic review of 520 scapular fractures in 22 case series, excellent or good results can be achieved with nonoperative treatment of isolated neck fractures in 77% of the cases and in 88% of the cases with operative treatment. Universal guidelines for conservative or operative treatment are difficult to establish empirically because the available literature does not include randomized or nonrandomized comparative studies. Treatment should, therefore, be individualized.

The Superior Shoulder Suspensory Complex

Goss[61] described the SSSC, consisting of the glenoid, coracoid, acromion, distal clavicle, coracoclavicular ligaments, and acromioclavicular ligaments (Fig. 37-16). This bone–soft tissue ring maintains the normal, stable relationship between the upper extremity and the axial skeleton. Single disruptions of the SSSC, such as an isolated scapular neck fracture, are usually anatomically stable because the integrity of the complex is preserved, and nonoperative management yields good functional results. When the complex is disrupted in two places (double disruption), such as a scapular neck fracture with an acromioclavicular joint disruption, a potentially unstable anatomic situation is created. Because the SSSC includes the glenoid, acromion, and coracoid, many double disruption injuries involve the scapula. In the presence of a displaced fracture of the acromion, coracoid process, glenoid, or scapular neck, the possibility of another lesion of the SSSC (i.e., a double disruption) should be considered. According to Goss,[61] open reduction is indicated for double disruptions that are accompanied by significant displacement, which may lead to delayed union, malunion, or nonunion as well as long-term functional deficits.

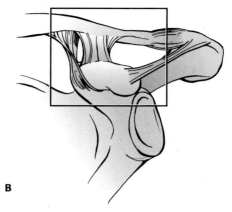

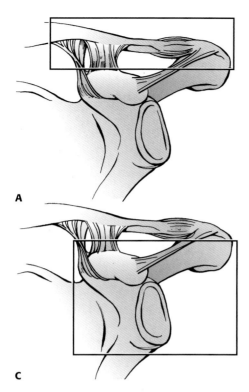

FIGURE 37-16 The SSSC **A.** Clavicle–acromioclavicular joint–acromion strut. **B.** Clavicle–coracoclavicular ligament–coracoid linkage. **C.** Three process-scapular body junction. (From Goss TP. Fractures of the scapula. In: Rockwood CA, Matsen FA, Wirth MA, et al., eds. The Shoulder. 3rd ed. Philadelphia: Saunders, 2004:413, with permission.)

The most common described double disruption of the SSSC is the ipsilateral glenoid surgical neck and midshaft clavicle fracture. This injury, although the terminology is criticized,[91] is also defined as a floating shoulder.

The Floating Shoulder

Ganz and Noesberger[46] were the first authors who described this injury in 1975. They suggested a loss of the stabilizing effect of the clavicle in the case of a combination of these two fractures. In contrast to isolated scapular fractures, they found more severe displacement of the scapular fracture when combined with an ipsilateral clavicle fracture. The weight of the arm and the combined contraction of the biceps, triceps, and coracobrachialis muscles may cause inferior and rotational displacement of the distal fragment resulting in a change in the contour of the affected shoulder, the so-called drooping shoulder (Fig. 37-17). Apart from this possible caudal and rotational displacement, it is also suggested, although criticized by some,[129,175] that the glenoid fragment is displaced anteromedially by contraction of the rotator cuff muscles (Fig. 37-18).[46,66,71] Translational displacement of the scapular neck will result in shortening of the lever arm of the rotator cuff musculature and threaten the functional balance of the glenohumeral joint.[66,158] This may result in loss of abduction strength,[1,20,66] although this is not necessarily synonymous with limitation of range of motion, as demonstrated in a biomechanical analysis.[25] Williams and colleagues[185] conducted the only cadaver study on this subject to determine the stability afforded by specific structures. They concluded that ipsilateral fractures of the scapular neck and the shaft of the clavicle do not produce a floating shoulder without additional disruption of the coracoacromial and acromioclavicular capsular ligaments. These findings have not yet been confirmed in clinical studies.

The rarity of the floating shoulder is also illustrated by the complete lack of well-performed, prospective studies with comparison of different treatment options. The literature on this subject is limited to data provided only by case reports and retrospective studies of small patient series.

Good clinical results are reported for both conservative and operative treatment (Table 37-2). Traditionally, floating shoulders were treated nonoperatively. However, over the last 2 decades, there has been increased interest in open reduction and internal fixation of these fractures.[40,66,69,71,93,99,141] Herscov-

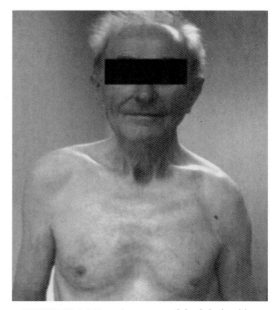

FIGURE 37-17 Drooping aspect of the left shoulder.

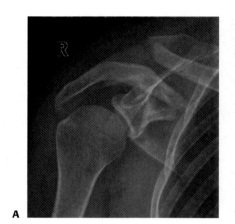
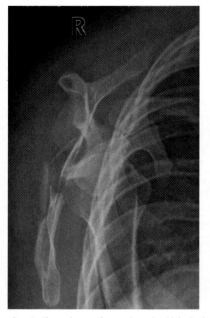
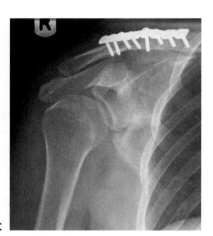

A   **B**   **C**

FIGURE 37-18 A,B. Radiographs of an ipsilateral scapular neck and midshaft clavicle fracture. **C.** The glenoid fossa is still not reduced despite open reduction and internal fixation of the clavicle.

ici[71] reported on nine patients: seven had been treated operatively (with osteosynthesis only of the clavicle) and the remaining two had been treated nonoperatively. Their good results led them to recommend open reduction and internal fixation of the clavicle only, in order to prevent malunion of the scapular neck. The authors presumed that the glenoid neck fracture would usually reduce and be stabilized indirectly. Rikli[141] retrospectively analyzed 12 cases, 11 with osteosynthesis of the clavicle alone, whereas one had both the clavicle and the glenoid neck

fractures fixed. The findings of Leung and Lam[99] are based on the treatment results in 15 cases in whom simultaneous fixation of the displaced scapular and clavicle fractures had been performed. All but one patient had a good, or excellent, functional result, according to the scoring system of Rowe.[151] All fractures healed at an average of 8 weeks postoperatively. Good results in seven operatively treated patients, by fixation of both the scapular neck and clavicle fractures, or disrupted acromioclavicular joint, have also been described in a retrospective study

TABLE 37-2   **Reported Results of Conservative and Operative Management of the Floating Shoulder**

	Number	Conservative	ORIF Clavicle	ORIF Clavicle and Scapula	Outcome Measure	Outcome Conservative (mean score)	Outcome Operative (mean score)
Edwards[39]	20	20	—	—	Constant[28]	96	
Egol[40]	19	12	—	7	American Shoulder and Elbow Surgeons[119]	80.2	88.7
Hashiguchi[69]	5	—	—	—	University of California, Los Angeles[41]	34.2	
Herscovici[71]	9	2	—	7	Herscovici	1 good; 1 poor	7 excellent
Labler[93]	17	8	6	3	Constant[28]	90	66 93 (ORIF both)
Leung[99]	15	—	—	15	Rowe[151]		84
Ramos[139]	13	13	—		Herscovici[71]	11 excellent; 1 good	
Rikli[141]	12	—	11	1	Constant[28]		Constant: 96%
van Noort[173]	35	28	7		Constant[28]	76	Constant: 71%

ORIF, open reduction and internal fixation.

by Egol et al.[40] Finally, in a study of Labler et al.,[93] six patients were treated with internal fixation of only the clavicle and three with fixation of both clavicle and scapular fractures.

Routine operative treatment of a floating shoulder without regard to displacement has recently been questioned. Edwards[39] reported excellent results in 17 and good results in 3 patients in whom all ipsilateral fractures of the scapula and clavicle had been treated nonoperatively by a shoulder immobilizer, until the associated injuries allowed mobilization of the shoulder. They recommend conservative treatment, especially in patients with less than 5-mm displacement. In a retrospective study, van Noort et al.[173] reported fair to good results in 28 patients treated conservatively (mean constant score: 76), with a well-aligned glenoid. The authors concluded that these rare shoulder lesions are not unstable by definition and that conservative treatment leads to a good functional outcome in the absence of caudal displacement of the glenoid. Caudal displacement was defined as an inferior angulation of the glenoid of at least 20 degrees.[174] Ramos et al.[139] in 1997 reviewed 13 patients with ipsilateral fracture of the clavicle and scapular neck treated conservatively. The average follow-up was 7.5 years. Using Herscovici's scoring method,[71] they reported 84.6% excellent, 7.7% good, and 7.7% fair results.

Based on both clinical and biomechanical studies, it remains unclear under which criteria a floating shoulder should be treated operatively. Current experience indicates that an undisplaced, or minimally displaced, ipsilateral clavicle and scapular neck fracture can be treated conservatively, with a good functional outcome. The amount of displacement that is acceptable at the fracture sites of the glenoid neck and clavicle is controversial.

Scapular Body Fracture

Approximately 50% of scapular fractures involve the scapular body and spine.[61] This fracture type is correlated with the highest incidence of associated injuries.[19,169] They are generally caused by indirect forces or by direct trauma. Wyrsch and co-workers[190] reported a scapular body fracture in a professional boxer who sustained the injury during an attempted punch. More rare causes are seizures, electrical shock treatments,[11,70,110,166] or stress fractures.[136] Scapular body fractures heal readily and do not merit operative intervention,[115,116,184] regardless of the number of fracture fragments. The fact that these fractures heal well without significant clinical symptoms is probably directly related to the protection of a thick layer of muscles surrounding the scapula. Several series of conservatively treated patients with scapular body fractures have been reported with union of the fracture and a good functional outcome.[3,79,103,115] Zlowodzki[194] reported in a systematic review of 520 scapular fractures in 22 case series, that 99% of all scapular body fractures had been treated nonoperatively. Excellent or good results were achieved with nonoperative treatment in 88% of the cases.

Nonetheless, painful scapulothoracic crepitus caused by malunion of the scapular body may have adverse mechanical and functional effects on shoulder movement. Excision of the bony prominence in these cases is usually curative.[44,45] Other clinical symptoms are pain, limited range of motion, and winging of the scapula by loss of the serratus anterior muscle.[64] Nordqvist and Petersson[127] found poor long-term results in

some patients with more than 10 mm of displacement. Nonunions are extremely rare. Two cases have been reported which were both treated successfully by open reduction, rigid internal fixation, and bone grafting.[43,64]

Acromial Fracture

The acromion provides one side of the acromioclavicular joint and serves as the point of attachment for the deltoid muscle and a number of ligaments. By forming the roof of the glenohumeral joint, it lends posterosuperior stability. Approximately 8% to 9% of all scapular fractures involve the acromion.[3,115,184]

There are four causes described for an acromial fracture:

1. A direct blow from the outside, in general a significant force.
2. A force transmitted via the humeral head from the inside. Traumatic superior displacement of the humeral head, which may also result in an associated rotator cuff tear, can cause an (superiorly displaced) acromial fracture. Another mechanism is rotator cuff arthropathy, in which an acromial fracture may occur by superior migration of the humeral head.[20]
3. An avulsion fracture is usually caused by an indirect force. Heyse-Moore and Stoker,[72] Rask and Steinbergh,[140] and Russo et al.[153] reported forceful contraction of the deltoid muscle resulting in an avulsion fracture of the acromion.
4. Stress fractures of the acromion have been reported, particularly in sports.[65,178,181] Subacromial decompression with significant thinning of the acromion may also lead to a stress fracture.[106,111,152,182]

A diversity of associated ipsilateral shoulder lesions with an acromion fracture is described. The brachial plexus is at risk particularly with an inferiorly displaced acromion fracture.[114,123] Other associated lesions, as reported earlier, are rotator cuff lesions.[104,145] Finally, ipsilateral acromioclavicular joint lesions, coracoid, clavicle, glenoid, and proximal humeral fractures and shoulder dislocations have been reported.[58,92,95,102,114,122,193]

Independent of the mechanism of trauma, when a fracture does occur, it is usually non- or minimally displaced. Nonoperative treatment in these cases will lead to union of the fracture with a good to excellent functional outcome.[61] Most acromion fractures are successfully treated simply by immobilization with a sling or Velpeau dressing until the pain has subsided, which is usually within 3 weeks.[1,81,90,92,102,114,120] Some authors have advocated the use of a spica cast with the shoulder in abduction.[122,184] Omission of a sling or another form of immobilization may cause secondary displacement of the fracture.[59]

According to the classification of Kuhn,[90] the group of non- or minimally displaced fractures are type I fractures and caused by indirect force (avulsion fracture-type Ia) or a direct trauma (type Ib). Nonoperative treatment is also advocated by Kuhn[90] in dislocated acromial fractures in which the subacromial space is not compromised (type II fracture). However, a poor clinical outcome or a symptomatic pseudarthrosis of patients with a type II fracture has been reported.[34,90] In type III displaced fractures in which the subacromial space is diminished by the inferior pull of the deltoid on the acromial fragment, open reduction with internal fixation is advocated by Kuhn[90] and Ogawa[132] to prevent secondary impingement. Most authors recommend open reduction and internal fixation for markedly displaced acromion fractures to reduce the acromioclavicular joint and prevent nonunion, malunion, and secondary impingement.[124,151] When surgery is performed, a variety of surgical techniques may be employed, including the use of tension band wiring, sutures, Kirschner wires, staples, lag screws, and plates.[8,30,61,66,81,182] Excision of the acromial fragment has been reported but is generally not recommended for fragments larger than half an inch because it can result in substantial weakness of the deltoid muscle.[90,120,123,130]

Coracoid Fracture

The most common mechanisms that have been described as a cause of a coracoid fracture are

1. A direct blow to the superior point of the shoulder;
2. A direct contact between the humeral head and coracoid process in case of an anterior shoulder dislocation;[47,168]
3. An avulsion fracture by a forceful contraction of the short head of the biceps, pectoralis minor, or coracobrachialis muscle;[5,149]
4. As part of an acromioclavicular dislocation;[180] and
5. Stress fractures have been reported: medial migration of the humeral head from rotator cuff arthropathy may result in a coracoid fracture.[14]

Coracoid fractures may be isolated, but in many cases are accompanied by ipsilateral shoulder injuries. Ogawa[133] reported acromioclavicular dislocations as the most common associated lesion, seen in 60 of the 67 described patients. Other common associated lesions are lacerations or abrasions over the posterolateral or lateral deltoid muscle, (lateral) clavicle fractures, shoulder dislocations, and rotator cuff tears.

Fractures in adults are most common at the base of the coracoid, whether or not with extension in the upper border of the scapula and/or the glenoid.[42,80,131,188] Other reported sites are the middle portion[33,137] and the tip.[75,121,193]

Many methods of treatment of coracoid fractures have been described. There is, however, no consensus in the literature about the preferred treatment of coracoid fractures. Many authors suggest that non- or minimally displaced fractures can be successfully treated by conservative treatment.[42,52,109,193] On occasion, however, these injuries may be significantly displaced and of functional importance, thus making surgical management a consideration. Fractures of the coracoid tip are avulsion injuries (Ogawa type 2) that may displace considerably. Despite the chance of nonunion,[117] this type of fracture can be treated conservatively with good functional outcome.[23,42,52,109,132] On occasion, operative treatment is indicated when the fractured coracoid tip impedes the reduction of an anterior dislocated humeral head.[42,189] Other indications for surgery include a painful nonunion after anterior shoulder dislocation.[47,85]

Treatment of fractures of the coracoid base (type 1) follow the same reasoning described for fractures of the coracoid tip. However, displacement of the fracture is more common which may be due to accompanying ipsilateral shoulder injuries (double disruptions of the SSSC). In these circumstances, or in cases with extension of the fracture into the glenoid fossa (with displacement), open reduction and internal fixation with screw fixation of the coracoid fracture is advocated.[42,61,133] Martin-Herrero,[109] however, described satisfactory outcome in conservative treatment in seven patients despite displacement of the fracture and associated ipsilateral shoulder injuries in six.

Scapulothoracic Dissociation

Scapulothoracic dissociation is characterized by a complete loss of scapulothoracic articulation and lateral displacement of the scapula, while the skin is usually intact. It is classically caused by a violent lateral distraction or rotational displacement of the shoulder girdle when the upper extremity is caught on a fixed object while the body is moving at high speed.[2] It is a rare, severe injury of the shoulder girdle with a high mortality rate (10%).[29] Some authors describe this injury, which is almost always associated with severe vascular injuries (prevalence 88% to 100%), as an internal forequarter amputation.[96,154,187,192] As well as lesions of the subclavian and axillary artery, associated complete or partial disruptions of the brachial plexus (prevalence up to 94%)[29] are frequent and well described in the literature. Other described associated lesions are osseous injuries to the shoulder girdle (particularly clavicle fractures, but also acromioclavicular or sternoclavicular dislocation), injury to muscles (deltoid, pectoralis minor, rhomboids, levator scapulae, trapezius, and latissimus dorsi), and massive soft tissue swelling in the shoulder region. Approximately 50% of the reported cases are the result of a motorcycle accident.[18]

The management of patients with scapulothoracic dissociation should follow the ATLS principles with cardiopulmonary stabilization and resuscitation being of paramount importance. Treatment recommendations have focused on the care of the accompanying neurovascular injury. In a hemodynamically stable patient, arteriography is used to determine the vascular integrity, followed by surgical repair if necessary. However, it should be appreciated that an extensive collateral network around the shoulder can protect against limb-threatening ischemia.[54,100,171] Sampson et al.[154] presented a series of 11 cases). They questioned the need for vascular repair in these patients, all of whom had a complete brachial plexus palsy, no radial pulse, and subclavian or axillary artery occlusion on arteriography. Of these 11 cases, 6 were revascularized and 5 were not. All 11 limbs remained viable, although none of the 11 patients regained any function. Zelle et al.[192] demonstrated that the extent of the neurologic injury is of paramount importance in predicting the functional outcome. All of their patients with a complete brachial plexus avulsion either had an amputation or had poor shoulder function at the time of follow-up. Partial plexus injuries, however, have a good prognosis, and most patients achieve complete recovery or regain functional use of the extremity.[60] If upper extremity function is not restorable, an immediate above-elbow amputation seems to result in better functional outcomes, lower complication rates, better relief of causalgia, and more successful return to work than a late amputation.[13,18,192] Many patients refuse a secondary amputation despite a flail, anesthetic upper extremity.[27,35,54,171]

The recommended treatment of associated osseous lesions in patients with scapulothoracic dissociation is unclear and should therefore be individualized. Nevertheless, Goss[61] advised open reduction and internal fixation of clavicle fractures and stabilisation of disrupted acromioclavicular or sternoclavicular joints for three reasons: to avoid delayed or nonunion, to restore as much stability as possible to the shoulder complex thus reducing long-term functional problems, and to protect the brachial plexus, subclavian, and axillary vessels from further injury caused by tensile forces.

AUTHORS' PREFERRED TREATMENT

Scapular Neck Fractures

Reduction of translational displacement (>1 cm) in an isolated scapular neck fracture is not necessary to obtain a good functional outcome with conservative treatment. One should be aware of the possibility of ipsilateral shoulder lesions (e.g., fractures, rotator cuff lesions, and intra-articular glenohumeral damage), which may influence the final functional outcome.[155,176] Symptomatic local care in a shoulder immobilizer followed by passive exercises as soon as the pain allows will not interfere with fracture healing and will result in a good to excellent functional outcome.

In case of an associated ipsilateral clavicle fracture (floating shoulder), there is a chance of further displacement of either or both of the fractures. Current experience indicates that undisplaced, or minimally displaced, ipsilateral clavicle and scapular neck fractures can be treated conservatively with a good functional outcome. In relatively young patients without comorbidities, open reduction and internal fixation by plate osteosynthesis should be considered in displaced, shortened, midshaft clavicle fractures because of the chance of nonunion (prevalence 15%)[73,142] or malunion. Fixation of the clavicle fracture may allow reduction of the glenoid neck fracture and restoration of the shoulder contour. However, despite anatomic reduction of the clavicle fracture, displacement of the scapular neck fracture may persist. In particular, rotational displacement of the scapular neck will compromise the functional outcome. In case of caudal angulation of the glenoid fossa of more than 20 degrees (or a GPA angle <30 degrees) (see Fig. 37-6), operative treatment should be considered through a posterior approach with plate osteosynthesis along the lateral border of the scapula (Fig. 37-19). However, caution should be employed to avoid surgical overtreatment in the absence of data to support an aggressive approach.

Glenoid Fossa Fractures

For type Ia fractures, surgical treatment is preferred where there is subluxation of the humeral head or in fractures likely to cause glenohumeral instability, which can be predicted if the fracture is displaced more than 5 mm or if a quarter or more of the glenoid cavity is involved. Exposure is performed through a standard deltopectoral approach with mobilization of the subscapularis muscle. A large fragment can be fixed with two screws, but smaller or comminuted fragments may require a buttress plate with smaller screws.

The same indications for surgery as for a type Ia fracture should be applied for a type Ib fracture except that the size of the posterior fragment which will predict instability is a third or more of the glenoid cavity. For posterior fractures, a posterior glenohumeral exposure is advocated with access to the glenohumeral joint through the interval between the infraspinatus and teres minor muscles. In both types Ia and Ib, there are possible advantages of arthroscopically controlled operative treatment using percutaneous screw fixation. This is typically dependable on the skill of the sur-

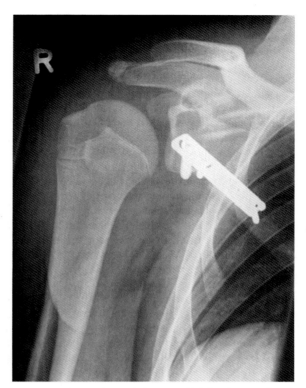

FIGURE 37-19 A scapular neck fracture which has been reduced and stabilized with a plate.

geon but also on the size and comminution of the fracture fragment.

Types II through V have poorly defined indications for operative treatment. However, on the basis of available reports, it seems reasonable to conclude that surgery has a definite role in the treatment of glenoid fossa fractures. When the humeral head is not centered in the major portion of the glenoid fossa and is subluxed along with the fracture fragment, open reduction and internal fixation of the fracture is indicated. Type II fractures are approached posteriorly, and type III by either a superior or combined posterior and superior approach. A cannulated interfragmentary compression screw (3.5-mm) is placed after a Kirschner wire positioned in the superior fragment is used to manipulate and reduce the fracture. A posterosuperior approach is usually required for the treatment of types III, IV, Vb, and Vc, so that the superior glenoid fragment can be reduced and fixed relative to the inferior aspect of the glenoid cavity. Care should be taken when using the posterosuperior approach which places the suprascapular nerve in some jeopardy as the nerve passes through the scapular notch, the supraspinatus muscle, the spinoglenoid notch, and the infraspinatus muscle.

Type VI fractures are managed nonoperatively. Passive exercises should be started as soon as possible in order to prevent the development of a stiff painful shoulder. These injuries have the highest chance of posttraumatic arthritis.

COMPLICATIONS

The available information with regard to the complications of scapular fractures and their treatment is very sparse. One should make a distinction between the complications of treatment and concomitant injuries associated with scapular fractures. The latter are sometimes life-threatening and may have more consequences with respect to the priorities of treatment and the overall functional outcome. On the other hand, regional complications such as nerve injuries may influence the functional outcome of the affected shoulder dramatically. An example is a brachial plexus injury, which is described by Rockwood,[143] after coracoid fracture. Suprascapular nerve injuries are reported following scapular neck fracture with extension into the suprascapular notch[37,160] and from coracoid base fractures.[143] Axillary nerve and brachial plexus injuries have been described in association with an acromion fracture.[114,115]

Reported complications after conservative treatment are in general uncommon and variable. Malunion and particularly nonunion of scapula fractures are very rare. In a recent search of the medical literature, Marek[105] discovered only 15 cases of scapula nonunion after nonoperative management. Malunion of particularly scapular body fractures is well tolerated, although painful scapulothoracic crepitus is described.[1,3,127] Displaced glenoid fractures may lead to glenohumeral arthritis and instability,[1,66] pain (in rest and with exertion), limitation in range of motion, and weakness.[1,3,127,191] Some authors suggest that displaced fractures of the glenoid neck can lead to altered mechanics of the surrounding soft tissues, giving rise to glenohumeral pain and dysfunction.[1,3,49,127,135,148]

With regard to complications of operatively treated patients with scapular fractures, Lantry[97] analyzed the postoperative complications of 212 cases described in 15 retrospective case series. The overall reported complication rate in these studies was fairly low. The most common complications were removal of implants in 7 % due to metal failure or local discomfort and infection in 4 %. Other mentioned complications were nerve injuries (2%), mostly involving the suprascapular nerve (4 out of 5), reoperation other than hardware removal for posttraumatic arthritis (2%), rotator cuff dysfunction (1%), and heterotopic ossification (1%). Nonunion after operatively treated scapular fractures is not cited as a complication except for one reported case by Marek.[105] Finally, an improper physical therapy rehabilitation program or a poor patient compliance may contribute to unnecessary postoperative shoulder stiffness.

FUNCTIONAL OUTCOME

In general, more than 90% of scapular fractures are non- or minimally displaced and do well clinically after conservative treatment.[79,115,184] This observation has been based on treatment of scapular fractures in general, and its relevance is therefore very limited. A more differentiated approach turned out to be necessary as conservative treatment does not uniformly lead to good results.[1,9,135] Literature regarding outcome of treatment of specific fracture types, however, is mostly comprised of case reports and small series and is therefore scarce. There is particularly concern about poor functional outcome after conservative treatment of displaced acromion, coracoid process (base), scapular neck, and glenoid fossa fractures.[1,3,49,127,135,148] With respect to functional outcome after operative treatment, most series concern glenoid fossa fractures[57,66,84,98,112,156] and scapular neck fractures with or without an ipsilateral clavicle fracture.[1,8,40,66,69,71,93,99,141,173] In a systematic review of 243 cases,

Lantry[97] pointed out that good to excellent functional results were obtained in approximately 85% of cases which mainly consisted of displaced glenoid fossa and scapular neck fractures. Limitations of interpreting these study results are the retrospective character of the case series (level IV) and the various outcome scales and scoring systems. In the above mentioned studies, the following shoulder scoring systems were used: American Shoulder and Elbow Surgeons,[40] constant score,[8,39,93,141,156,173,176] Herscovici score,[39,71,139] Neer score,[131,133] Rowe score,[98,99] University of California, Los Angeles, score,[69] or subjective scores based on the surgeon's assessment mainly based on pain and range of motion.[1,3,66,112,116,127]

CONTROVERSIES AND FUTURE DIRECTIONS

The problem with the management of scapular fractures in general is the lack of evidence-based treatment. The scientific knowledge is based on case series and expert opinion (level IV and V). The available literature includes neither randomized nor nonrandomized comparative studies. Apart from the different nonvalidated and nonspecific outcome measures and methodological limitations of many studies, the influence is of associated injuries on the final outcome is unclear.

The challenge for the future is to complete well-documented, methodologically correct, comparative studies on the fracture types that may benefit from surgical treatment, such as displaced glenoid and scapular neck fractures.

REFERENCES

1. Ada JR, Miller ME. Scapular fractures. Analysis of 113 cases. Clin Orthop Relat Res 1991;269:174–180.
2. Althausen PL, Lee MA, Finkemeier CG. Scapulothoracic dissociation: diagnosis and treatment. Clin Orthop Relat Res 2003;416:237–244.
3. Armstrong CP, Vanderspuy J. The fractured scapula: importance in management based on series of 62 patients. Injury 1984;15:324–329.
4. Aulicino PL, Reinert C, Kornberg M, et al. Displaced intra-articulair glenoid fractures treated by open reduction and internal fixation. J Trauma 1986;26:1137–1141.
5. Asbury S, Tennent TD. Avulsion fracture of the coracoid process: a case report. Injury 2005;36:567–568.
6. Ball CM, Steger T, Galatz LM, et al. The posterior branch of the axillary nerve: an anatomic study. J Bone Joint Surg 2003;85-A:1497–501.
7. Bateman JE. The Shoulder and Neck. Philadelphia: WB Saunders, 1978.
8. Bauer G, Fleischmann W, Dussler E. Displaced scapular fractures: indication and long-term results of open reduction and internal fixation. Arch Orthop Trauma Surg 1995;114:215–219.
9. Bauer T, Abadie O, Hardy P. Arthroscopic treatment of glenoid fractures. Arthroscopy 2006;22:569–576.
10. Bestard EA, Schvene HR, Bestard EH. Glenoplasty in the management of recurrent shoulder dislocation. Contemp Orthop 1986;12:47.
11. Beswick DR, Morse SD, Barnes AU. Bilateral scapular fractures from low-voltage electrical injury: a case report. Ann Emerg Med 1982;11:11–12.
12. Bloom MH, Obata WG. Diagnosis of posterior dislocation of the shoulder with use of the Velpeau axillary and angled up radiographic views. J Bone Joint Surg 1967;49-A:943–949.
13. Bondurant FJ, Cotler HB, Buckle R, et al. The medical and economic impact of severely injured lower extremities. J Trauma 1988;28:1270–1273.
14. Boyer DW. Trapshooter's shoulder: stress fracture of the coracoid process: case report. J Bone Joint Surg 1975;57-A:862.
15. Bozkurt M, Can F, Kirdemir V, et al. Conservative treatment of scapular neck fracture: the effect of stability and glenopolar angle on clinical outcome. Injury 2005;36:1176–1181.
16. Brodsky JW, Tullos HS, Gartsman G. Simplified posterior approach to the shoulder joint. J Bone Joint Surg 1987;69-A:773–774.
17. Brown CV, Velmahos G, Wang D, et al. Association of scapular fractures and blunt thoracic aortic injury: fact or fiction? Am Surg 2005;71:54–57.
18. Brucker PU, Gruen GS, Kaufmann RA. Scapulothoracic dissociation: evaluation and management. Injury 2005;36:1147–1155.
19. Butters KP. Fractures of the scapula. In: Buchholz RW, Heckman JD, eds. Fractures in Adults. 5th ed. Philadelphia: Lippincott Williams and Williams, 2002:1095.
20. Butters KP. The scapula. In: Matsen FA, ed. The Shoulder. Philadelphia, PA: WB Saunders Co, 1990:335–361.

21. Butters KP. The scapula. In Rockwood CA Jr, Matsen FA, eds. The Shoulder. Vol 1. Philadelphia: WB Saunders Co, 1998:391–427.
22. Cameron SE. Arthroscopic reduction and internal fixation of an anterior glenoid fracture. Arthroscopy 1998;14:743–746.
23. Carr AJ, Broughton NS. Acromioclavicular dislocation associated with fracture of the coracoid process. J Trauma 1989;29:125–126.
24. Carro LP, Nunez MP, Llata JI. Arthroscopic-assisted reduction and percutaneous external fixation of a displaced intraarticular glenoid fracture. Arthroscopy 1999;15: 211–214.
25. Chadwick EKJ, van Noort A, van der Helm FCT. Biomechanical analysis of scapular neck malunion-a simulation study. Clin Biomech 2004;19:906–912.
26. Churchill RS, Brems JJ, Katschi H. Glenoid size, inclination, and version: an anatomic study. J Shoulder Elbow Surg 2001;10:327–332.
27. Clements RH, Reisser JR. Scapulothoracic dissociation: a devastating injury. J Trauma 1996;40:146–149.
28. Constant CR, Murley AHG. A clinical method of functional assessment of the shoulder. Clin Orthop 1987;214:160–164.
29. Damschen DD, Cogbill TH, Siegel MJ. Scapulothoracic dissociation caused by blunt trauma. J Trauma 1997;42:537–540.
30. Darrach W. Fracture of the acromion process of the scapula. Ann Surg 1913;59: 455–456.
31. De Beer J, Berghs BM, van Rooyen KS, et al. Displaced scapular neck fracture: a case report. J Shoulder Elbow Surg 2004;13:123–125.
32. DePalma AF. Fractures and fracture-dislocations of the shoulder girdle. In: Jacob RP, Kristiansen T, Mayo K, et al., eds. Surgery of the Shoulder. 3rd ed. Philadelphia: JB Lippincott, 1983:366–367.
33. De Rosa GP, Kettelkamp DB. Fractures of the coracoid process of the scapula: a case report. J Bone Joint Surg 1977;59-A;696–697.
34. Dounchis JS, Pedowitz RA, Garfin SR. Symptomatic pseudarthrosis of the scromion: report of a case and review of the literature. J Orthop Trauma 1999;13:63–66.
35. Ebraheim NA, An HS, Jackson WT, et al. Scapulothoracic dissociation. J Bone Joint Surg 1988;70-A:428–432.
36. Ebraheim NA, Mekhail AO, Padanilum TG, et al. Anatomic considerations for a modified posterior approach to the scapula. Clin Orthop 1997;334:136–143.
37. Edeland HG, Zachrisson BE. Fracture of the scapular notch associated with lesion of the suprascapular nerve. Acta Orthop Scand 1975;46:758.
38. Edelson JG, Zuckerman J, Hershkovitz I. Os acromiale: anatomy and surgical implications. J Bone Joint Surg 1993;74-B:551–555.
39. Edwards SG, Whittle AP, Wood GW 2nd, et al. Nonoperative treatment of ipsilateral fractures of the scapula and clavicle. J Bone Joint Surg 2000;82-A:774–780.
40. Egol KA, Connor PM, Karunakar MA, et al. The floating shoulder: clinical and functional results. J Bone Joint Surg 2001;83-A:1188–1194.
41. Ellman H, Kay SP. Arthroscopic subacromial decompression for chronic impingement. Two- to 5-year results. J Bone Joint Surg 1991;73-B:395–398.
42. Eyres KS, Brooks A, Stanley D. Fractures of the coracoid process. J Bone Joint Surg 1995;77-B:425–428.
43. Ferraz IC, Papadimitriou NG, Sotereanos DG. Scapular body nonunion: a case report. J Shoulder Elbow Surg 2002;11:98–100.
44. Findlay RT. Fractures of the scapula and ribs. Am J Surg 1937;38:489–494.
45. Fischer RP, Flynn TC, Miller PW, et al. Scapular fractures and associated major ipsilateral upper-torso injuries. Current Concepts in Trauma Care 1985;1:14–16.
46. Ganz R, Noesberger B. Treatment of scapular fractures. Hefte Unfallheilkd 1975;126: 59–62.
47. Garcia-Elias M, Salo JM. Nonunion of a fractured coracoid process after dislocation of the shoulder. J Bone Joint Surg 1985;67-B:722–723.
48. Garth WP, Slappey CE, Ochs CW. Roentgenographic demonstration of instability of the shoulder: the apical oblique projection. J Bone Joint Surg 1984;66-A:1450–1453.
49. Gagey O, Curey JP, Mazas F. Recent fractures of the scapula. Apropos of 43 cases. Rev Chir Orthop Reparatrice Appar Mot 1984;70:443–447.
50. Geel CW. AO principles of fracture management. In: Rüdi TP, Murphy WM, eds. Scapula and Clavicle. Stuttgart: Thieme, 2000:260.
51. Gigante A, Marinelli M, Verdenelli A, et al. Arthroscopy-assisted reduction and percutaneous fixation of a multiple glenoid fracture. Knee Surg Sports Traumatol Arthroscopy 2003;11:112–115.
52. Gill JF, Haydar A. Isolated injury of the coracoid process: a case report. J Trauma 1991; 31:1696–1697.
53. Goldberg RP, Vicks B. Oblique angle to view coracoid fractures. Skeletal Radiol 1983; 9:195–197.
54. Goldstein LJ, Watson JM. Traumatic scapulothoracic dissociation: case report and literature review. J Trauma 2000;48:533–535.
55. Goodrich A, Crosland E, Pye J. Acromion fractures associated with posterior shoulder dislocation. J Orthop Trauma 1998;12:521–522.
56. Gorczyca JT, Davis RT, Hartford JM, et al. Open reduction internal fixation after displacement of a previously nondisplaced acromial fracture in a multiply injured patient: case report and review of literature. J Orthop Trauma 2001;15:369–373.
57. Goss TP. Double disruptions of the superior shoulder suspensory complex. J Orthop Trauma 1993;7:99–106.
58. Goss TP. Fractures of the glenoid cavity. J Bone Joint Surg 1992;74-A:299–305.
59. Goss TP. Fractures of the glenoid neck. J Shoulder Elbow Surg 1994;3:42–52.
60. Goss TP. Fractures of the scapula: diagnosis and treatment. In: Rockwood CA, Matsen FA, Wirth MA, et al., eds. The Shoulder. Philadelphia: Saunders-Elsevier, 2004: 413–454.
61. Goss TP. The scapula: coracoid, acromial, and avulsion fractures. Am J Orthop 1996; 25:106–115.
62. Goss TP. Scapular fractures and dislocations. J Am Acad Orthop Surg 1995;3:22–33.
63. Gray H. Descriptive and surgical anatomy. New York: Crown Publishers, 1977: 138–144.
64. Gupta R, Sher J, Williams GR Jr, et al. Nonunion of the scapular body. A case report. J Bone Joint Surg 1998;80-A:428–430.
65. Hall RJ, Calvert PT. Stress fracture of the acromion: an unusual mechanism and review of the literature. J Bone Joint Surg 1995;77-B:153–154.
66. Hardegger FH, Simpson LA, Weber BG. The operative treatment of scapular fractures. J Bone Joint Surg 1984;66-B:725–731.
67. Harmon PH, Baker DR. Fracture of the scapula with displacement. J Bone Joint Surg 1943;4:834–838.
68. Harris RD, Harris JH Jr. The prevalence and significance of missed scapular fractures in blunt chest trauma. Am J Roentgenol 1988;151:747–750.
69. Hashiguchi H, Ito H. Clinical outcome of the treatment of floating shoulder by osteosynthesis for clavicular fracture alone. J Shoulder Elbow Surg 2003;12:589–591.
70. Henneking K, Hofmann D, Kunze K. Skapula fracturen nach electrounfall. Unfallchirurgie 1984;10:149–151.
71. Herscovici D Jr, Fiennes AG, Allgower M, et al. The floating shoulder: ipsilateral clavicle and scapular neck fractures. J Bone Joint Surg 1992;74-B:362–364.
72. Heyse-Moore GH, Stoker DJ. Avulsion fractures of the scapula. Skeletal Radiol 1982; 9:27–32.
73. Hill JM, McGuire MH, Crosby LA. Closed treatment of isplaced middle-third fractures of the clavicle gives poor results. J Bone Joint Surg 1997;79-B:537–541.
74. Hoffmann R, Tarhan O, Petersen P. Schulterblattbrüche: welche müssen wann operiert werden. OP-Journal 2002;18:225–229.
75. Horn K. Beobachtung eines U berlastungsschadens der Schulterblattgrate und des Proc coracoideus. Wschr Unfallheilk 1942;49:53–59.
76. Ideberg R. Fractures of the scapula involving the glenoid fossa. In Welsh R, ed. Surgery of the Shoulder. Philadelphia, PA: BC Decker, 1984:63.
77. Ideberg R. Unusual glenoid fractures: a report on 92 cases. Acta Orthop Scand 1987; 58:191–192.
78. Ideberg R, Grevsten S, Carsson S. Epidemiology of scapular fractures. Incidence and classification of 338 fractures. Acta Orthop Scan 1995;66:395–397.
79. Imatani RJ. Fractures of the scapula: a review of 53 fractures. J Trauma 1975;15: 473–478.
80. Ishizuki M, Yamaura I, Isobe Y, et al. Avulsion fracture of the superior border of the scapula. J Bone Joint Surg 1981;63-A:820–822.
81. Izadpanah M. Osteosynthese bei den scapulafrakturen. Arch Orthop Unfallchir 1975; 83:153–164.
82. Jerosch J, Greig M, Peuker ET. The posterior subdeltoid approach: a modified access to the posterior glenohumeral joint. J Shoulder Elbow Surg 2001;10:265–268.
83. Judet R. Traitement chirurgical des fractures de l'omoplate. Acta Orthop Belg 1964; 30:673–678.
84. Kavanagh BF, Bradway JK, Cofield RH. Open reduction and internal fixation of displaced intraarticular fractures of the glenoid fossa. J Bone Joint Surg 1993;74-A: 479–484.
85. Kälicke T, Andereya S, Gekle J, et al. Coracoid pseudarthrosis caused by anterior shoulder dislocation with concomitant coracoid fracture. Unfallchirurg 2002;105:843–844.
86. Kelbel JM, Jardon OM, Huurman WW. Scapulothoracic dissociation. A case report. Clin Orthop Relat Res 1986;209:210–214.
87. Khallaf F, Mikami A, Al-Akkad M. The use of surgery in displaced scapular neck fractures. Med Princ Pract 2006;15:443–448.
88. Kim KC, Rhee KJ, Shin HD, et al. Can the glenopolar angle be used to predict outcome and treatment of the floating shoulder? J Trauma 2008;64:174–178.
89. Kligman M, Roffman M. Glenoid fracture: conservative treatment versus surgical treatment. J South Orthop Assoc 1998;7:1–5.
90. Kuhn JE, Blasier RB, Carpenter JE. Fractures of the acromion process: a proposed classification system. J Orthop Trauma 1994;8:6–13.
91. Kumar VP, Satku K. Fractures of clavicle and scapular neck. J Bone Joint Surg 1993; 75:509.
92. Kurdy NMG, Shah SV. Fracture of the acromion associated with acromioclavicular dislocation. Injury 1995;26:636–637.
93. Labler L, Platz A, Weishaupt D, et al. Clinical and functional results after floating shoulder injuries. J Trauma 2004;57:595–602.
94. Lahoda LU, Kreklau B, Gekle C, et al. Skapulothorakale dissoziation. Ein missed injury? Unfallchirurg 1998;101:791–795.
95. Laing R, Dee R. Acromion fractures. Orthop Rev 1984;13:17–20.
96. Lange RH, Noel SH. Traumatic lateral scapular displacement: an expanded spectrum of associated neurovascular injury. J Orthop Trauma 1993;7:361–366.
97. Lantry JM, Roberts CS, Giannoudis PV. Operative treatment of scapular fractures: a systematic review. Injury 2008;39:269–283.
98. Leung KS, Lam TP, Poon KM. Operative treatment of displaced intra-articular glenoid fractures. Injury 1993;24:324–328.
99. Leung KS, Lam TP. Open reduction and internal fixation of ipsilateral fractures of the scapular neck and clavicle. J Bone Joint Surg 1993;75-B:1015–1018.
100. Levin PM, Rich NM, Hutton JE Jr. Collateral circulation in arterial injuries. Arch Surg 1971;102:392–399.
101. Liberson F. Os acromial: a contested anomaly. J Bone Joint Surg 1937;19-A:683–689.
102. Lim KE, Wang CR, Chin KC, et al. Concomitant fracture of the coracoid and acromion after direct shoulder trauma. J Orthop Trauma 1996;10:437–439.
103. Lindholm A, Leven H. Prognosis in fractures of the body and neck of the scapula. A follow-up study. Acta Chir Scand 1974;140:33–36.
104. Madhavan P, Buckingham R, Stableforth PG. Avulsion injury of the subscapularis tendon associated with fracture of the acromion. Injury 1994;25:271–272.
105. Marek DJ, Sechriest VF 2nd, Swiontkowski MF, et al. Case report: reconstruction of a recalcitrant scapular neck nonunion and literature review. Clin Orthop Relat Res 2009;467(5):1370–1376.
106. Marr DC, Misamore GW. Acromion nonunion after anterior acromioplasty: a case report. J Shoulder Elbow Surg 1992;1:317.
107. Marsh JL, Slongo TF, Agel JNA, et al. Fracture and dislocation classification compendium—2007: Orthopaedic Trauma Association classification, database, and outcomes committee. J Orthop Trauma 2007;21:S1–S6.
108. Martin SD, Weiland AJ. Missed scapular fracture after trauma. A case report and a 23-year follow-up report. Clin Orthop 1994;299:259–262.
109. Martin-Herrero T, Rodriguez-Merchan C, Munuera-Martinez L. Fractures of the coracoid process: presentation of seven cases and review of the literature. J Trauma 1990; 30:1597–1599.
110. Matthews LS, Burkhead WZ, Gordon S, et al. Acromial fracture: a complication of arthroscopic subacromial decompression. J Shoulder Elbow Surg 1994;3:256–261.
111. Matthews RE, Cocke TB, D'Ambrosia RD. Scapular fractures secondary to seizures in patients without osteodystrophy. J Bone Joint Surg 1983;65-A:850–853.

112. Mayo KA, Benirschke SK, Mast JW. Displaced fractures of the glenoid fossa. Clin Orthop Relat Res 1998;347:122–130.
113. McAdams TR, Blevins FT, Martin TP, et al. The role of plain films and computered tomography in the evaluation of scapular neck fractures. J Orthop Trauma 2002;16:7.
114. McGahan JP, Rab GT. Fracture of the acromion associated with an axillary nerve deficit: a case report and review of the literature. Clin Orthop Relat Res 1980;147:216–218.
115. McGahan JP, Rab GT, Dublin A. Fractures of the scapulae. J Trauma 1980;20:880–883.
116. McGinnis M, Denton JR. Fractures of the scapula: a retrospective study of 40 fractured scapulae. J Trauma 1989;29:1488–1493.
117. McLaughlin HL. Trauma. Philadelphia: WB Saunders, 1959.
118. McLennen JG, Ungersma J. Pneumothorax complicating fractures of the scapula. J Bone Joint Surg 1982;64-A;598–599.
119. Michener LA, McClure PW, Sennett BJ. American Shoulder and Elbow Surgeons Standardized Shoulder Assessment Form, patient self-report section: reliability, validity, and responsiveness. J Shoulder Elbow Surg 2002;11:587–594.
120. Mick CA, Weiland AJ. Pseudoarthrosis of a fracture of the acromion. J Trauma 1983;23:248–249.
121. Montgomery SP, Loyd RD. Avulsion fracture of the coracoid epiphysis with acromioclavicular separation: report of two cases in adolescents and review of the literature. J Bone Joint Surg 1977;59-A:963–965.
122. Nakae H, Endo S. Traumatic posterior dislocation of the shoulder with fracture of the acromion in a child. Arch Orthop Trauma Surg 1996;66-A:758–763.
123. Neer CS II. Fractures about the shoulder. In: Rockwood Jr CA, Green DP, ed. Fractures. Philadelphia: JB Lippincott, 1984:713–721.
124. Neer CS II. Shoulder Reconstruction. Philadelphia: WB Saunders; 1990.
125. Neer CS II, Marberry TA. On the disadvantages of radical acromionectomy. J Bone Joint Surg 1981;63-A:416–419.
126. Neviaser J. Traumatic lesions: injuries in and about the shoulder joint. Instr Course Lect 1956;13:187–216.
127. Nordqvist A, Petersson CJ. Fracture of the body, neck, or spine of the scapula. Clin Orthop Relat Res 1992;283:139–144.
128. Norwood LA, Matiko JA, Terry GC. Posterior shoulder approach. Clin Orthop Relat Res 1985;201:167–172.
129. Obremskey WT, Lyman JR. A modified judet approach to the scapula. J Orthop Trauma 2004;18:696–699.
130. O'Donoghue DH. Injuries to the shoulder girdle. Instr Course Lect AAOS 1960;17:392–405.
131. Ogawa K, Inokuchi S, Matsui K. Fracture of the coracoid process. Acta Orthop Scand 1990;61:7–8.
132. Ogawa K, Naniwa T. Fractures of the acromion and the lateral scapular spine. J Shoulder Elbow Surg 1997;6:544–548.
133. Ogawa K, Yoshida A, Takahashi M, et al. Fractures of the coracoid process. J Bone Joint Surg 1997;79-B:17–19.
134. Oreck SL, Burgess A, Levine AM. Traumatic lateral displacement of the scapula: a radiographic sign of neurovascular disruption. J Bone Joint Surg 1984;66-A:758–763.
135. Pace AM, Stuart R, Brownlow H. Outcome of glenoid neck fractures. J Shoulder Elbow Surg 2005;14:585–590.
136. Parr TJ, Faillace JJ. Scapular body stress fracture—a case report. Acta Orthop Scan 1999;70:84–85.
137. Petty OH. Fracture of the coracoid process of the scapula caused by muscular action. Ann Surg 1907;45:427–430.
138. Porcellini G, Campi F, Paladini P. Arthroscopic approach to acute bony Bankart lesion. Arthroscopy 2002;18:764–769.
139. Ramos L, Mencia R, Alonso A, et al. Conservative treatment of ipsilateral fractures of the scapula and clavicle. J Trauma 1997;42:239–242.
140. Rask MR, Steinberg LH. Fracture of the acromion caused by muscle force: a case report. J Bone Joint Surg 1978;60-A:1146–1147.
141. Rikli D, Regazzoni P, Renner N. The unstable shoulder girdle: early functional treatment utilizing open reduction and internal fixation. J Orthop Trauma 1995;9:93–97.
142. Robinson CM, Court-Brown CM, McQueen MM, et al. Estimating the risk of nonunion following nonoperative treatment of a clavicle fracture. J Bone Joint Surg 2004;86-A:1359–1365.
143. Rockwood CA Jr. Dislocations about the shoulder. In: Rockwood CA Jr, Green DP, eds. Fractures in Adults. 2nd ed. Philadelphia: JB Lippincott, 1984:719–721.
144. Rockwood CA Jr. Management of fractures of the scapula. Orthop Trans 1986;10:219.
145. Rockwood CA Jr, Matsen FA. The scapula. In: Butters KP, ed. The Shoulder. Philadelphia: WB Saunders, 1990;345–353.
146. Rodosky MW. Traumatic injuries of the shoulder and shoulder girdle. In: Dee R, Hurst LC, Gruber MA, et al., eds. Principles of Orthopaedic Practice. 2nd ed. Columbus, OH: McGraw-Hill, 1997:398.
147. Rokous JR, Feagin JA, Abbott HG. Modified axillary roentgenogram. A useful adjunct in the diagnosis of recurrent instability of the shoulder. Clin Orthop Relat Res 1972;82:84.
148. Romero J, Schai P, Imhoff AB. Scapular neck fracture—the influence of permanent malalignment of the glenoid neck on clinical outcome. Arch Orthop Trauma Surg 2001;121:313–316.
149. Rounds RC. Isolated fracture of the coracoid process. J Bone Joint Surg 1949;31-A:662.
150. Rowe CR. Fractures of the scapula. Surg Clin North Am 1963;43:1565.
151. Rowe CR. The Shoulder. New York: Churchill Livingstone, 1987:373–381.
152. Rupp S, Seil R, Kohn DM. Surgical reconstruction of a stress fracture of the Acromion after arthroscopic subacromial decompression in an elite tennis player. Arthroscopy 1998;14:106–108.

153. Russo R, Vernaglia, Lombardi L, et al. Arthroscopic treatment of isolated fracture of the posterolateral angle of the acromion. Arthroscopy 2007;23:798.
154. Sampson LN, Britton JC, Eldrup-Jorgensen J, et al. The neurovascular outcome of scapulothoracic dissociation. J Vasc Surg 1993;17:1083–1089.
155. Schai PA, Hintermann B, Koris MJ. Preoperative arthroscopic assessment of fractures about the shoulder. Arthroscopy 1999;15:827–835.
156. Schandelmaier P, Blauth M, Schneider C, et al. Fractures of the glenoid treated by operation. A 5- to 23-year follow-up of 22 cases. J Bone Joint Surg 2002;84-B:173–177.
157. Shishido H, Kikuchi S. Injury of the suprascapular nerve in shoulder surgery: an anatomic study. J Shoulder Elbow Surg 2001;10:372–376.
158. Simpson NS, Jupiter JB. Complex fracture patterns of the upper extremity. Clin Orthop Relat Res 1995;318:43–53.
159. Sinha J, Miller AJ. Fixation of fractures of the glenoid rim. Injury 1992;23:418–419.
160. Solheim LF, Roaas A. Compression of the scapular nerve after fracture of the scapular notch. Acta Orthop Scand 1978;49:338.
161. Stephens NG, Morgan AS, Corvo P, et al. Significance of scapular fracture in the blunt-trauma patient. Ann Emerg Med 1995;26:439–442.
162. Soslowsky LJ, Flatow EL, Bigliani LU, et al. Articular geometry of the glenohumeral joint. Clin Orthop Relat Res 1992;285:181.
163. Sugaya H, Kon Y, Tsuchiya A. Arthroscopic repair of glenoid fractures using suture anchors. Arthroscopy 2005;21:635.
164. Tadros AM, Lunsjo K, Czechowski J, et al. Causes of delayed diagnosis of scapular fractures. Injury 2008;39:314–318.
165. Tadros AM, Lunsjo K, Czechowski J, et al. Multiple-region scapular fractures had more severe chest injury than single-region fractures: a prospective study of 107 blunt trauma patients. J Trauma 2007;63:889–893.
166. Tarquinio T, Weinstein ME, Virgilio RW. Bilateral scapular fractures from accidental electric shock. J Trauma 1979;19:132–133.
167. Tauber M, Moursy M, Eppel M, et al. Arthroscopic screw fixation of large anterior glenoid fractures. Knee Surg Sports Traumatol Arthrosc 2008;6:326–332.
168. Te Slaa RL, Verburg H, Marti RK. Fracture of the coracoid process, the greater tuberosity, and the glenoid rim after acute first-time anterior shoulder dislocation: a case report. J Shoulder Elbow Surg 2001;10:489–492.
169. Thompson DA, Flynn TC, Miller PW, et al. The significance of scapular fractures. J Trauma 1985;25:974–977.
170. Tietge RA, Ciullo JV. The CAM axillary x-ray. Orthop Trans 1982;6:451.
171. Tüzüner S, Yanat AN, Ürgüden M, et al. Scapulothoracic dissociation: a case report. Isr J Med Sci 1996;32:70–74.
172. Uz A, Apaydin N, Bozkurt M, et al. The anatomic branch pattern of the axillary nerve. J Shoulder Elbow Surg. 2007;16-A:240–244.
173. Van Noort A, te Slaa RL, Marti RK, et al. The floating shoulder, a Dutch multicenter study. J Bone Joint Surg 2001;83-B:795–798.
174. Van Noort A, te Slaa RL, Marti RK, et al. The floating shoulder, a Dutch multicenter study (correspondence). J Bone Joint Surg 2002;84-B:776.
175. Van Noort A, van der Werken Chr. The floating shoulder—review article. Injury 2006;37:218–227.
176. Van Noort A, van Kampen A. Fractures of the scapula surgical neck—outcome after conservative treatment in 13 cases. Arch Orthop Trauma Surg 2005;125:696–700.
177. Van Wellen PAJ, Casteleyn PP, Opdecam P. Traction-suspension therapy for unstable glenoid neck fracture. Injury 1992;23:57–58.
178. Veluvolu P, Kohn HS, Guten GN, et al. Unusual stress fracture of the scapula in a jogger. Clin Nucl Med 1988;13:531–532.
179. Veysi VT, Mittal R, Agarwal S, et al. Multiple trauma and scapula fractures: so what? J Trauma 2003;55:1145–1147.
180. Wang KC, Hsu KY, Shih CH. Coracoid process fracture combined with acromioclavicular dislocation and coracoclavicular ligament rupture. A case report and review of the literature. Clin Orthop Relat Res 1994;300:120–122.
181. Ward WG, Bergfeld JA, Carson WG Jr. Stress fracture of the base of the acromion process. Am J Sports Med 1994;22:146–147.
182. Warner JP, Port J. Stress fracture of the acromion. J Shoulder Elbow Surg 1994;3:262.
183. Weening B, Walton C, Cole PA, et al. Lower mortality in patients with scapular fractures. J Trauma 2005;59:1477–1481.
184. Wilber MC, Evans EB. Fractures of the scapula. An analysis of 40 cases and a review of the literature. J Bone Joint Surg 1977;59-A:358–362.
185. Williams GR Jr, Naranja J, Klimkiewicz J, et al. The floating shoulder: a biomechanical basis for classification and management. J Bone Joint Surg 2001;83-A:1182–1187.
186. Wirth MA, Butters KP, Rockwood CA Jr. The posterior deltoid-splitting approach to the shoulder. Clin Orthop Relat Res 1993;296:92–98.
187. Witz M, Korzets Z, Lehmann J. Traumatic scapulothoracic dissociation. J Cardiovasc Surg 2000;41:927–929.
188. Wolf AW, Shoji H, Chuinard RG. Unusual fracture of the coracoid process. A case report and review of the literature. J Bone and Joint Surg 1976:58-A:423–424.
189. Wong-Chung J, Quinlan W. Fractured coracoid process preventing closed reduction of anterior dislocation of the shoulder. Injury 1989;20:296–297.
190. Wyrsch RB, Spindler KP, Stricker PR. Scapular fracture in a professional boxer. J Shoulder Elbow Surg 1994;4:395–398.
191. Zdravkovic D, Damholt VV. Comminuted and severely displaced fractures of the scapula. Acta Orthop Scand 1974;45:60.
192. Zelle BA, Pape HC, Gerich TG, et al. Functional outcome following scapulothoracic dissociation. J Bone Joint Surg 2004;86-A:2–7.
193. Zilberman Z, Rejovitzky R. Fracture of the coracoid process of the scapula. Injury 1981;13:203–206.
194. Zlowodzki M, Bhandari M, Zelle BA, et al. Treatment of scapula fractures: systematic review of 520 fractures in 22 case series. J Orthop Trauma 2006;20:230.

38

GLENOHUMERAL JOINT SUBLUXATIONS, DISLOCATIONS, AND INSTABILITY

Young W. Kwon, Kevin J. Kulwicki, and Joseph D. Zuckerman

INTRODUCTION

The wide range of motion provided by the shoulder girdle allows the glenohumeral joint to be used as a stable fulcrum for placing the upper extremity at various positions in three-dimensional space. A consequence of this flexibility, however, is the propensity for the joint to become unstable. As such, the shoulder is believed to be the most commonly dislocated major joint in the human body, with the reported incidence being 8.2 to 23.9 per 100,000 persons per year.[128,196,203,251] Understandably, therefore, the diagnosis and the treatment of glenohumeral instability have been well documented in the history of mankind. The first description of shoulder dislocation is believed to

have occurred as early as 3000 BCE.[295] In addition, prehistoric drawings from 1200 BCE show figures that are extremely similar to a shoulder reduction maneuver commonly used today.[107] Detailed descriptions regarding the pathology and the treatment of shoulder instability can also be found in the teachings of Hippocrates who lived around 450 BCE.[25,92,93] To treat patients with shoulder instability, he recommended the judicious insertion of a hot iron poker into the axilla to form "eschar tissue."

With the recent enthusiasm for recreational and sporting activities, the incidence of glenohumeral instability may be increasing. In accordance, the amount of information in the orthopaedic literature regarding this condition has also seen a significant gain. Recent publications have greatly augmented the knowledge base on the diagnosis, natural history, treatment, and expected outcome of glenohumeral instability. Experiences with various repair techniques, including both open and arthroscopic, have also provided additional options in the surgical management of this condition. Thus, despite the fact that it has been widely recognized and treated over the long course of human history, treatment for glenohumeral instability is continuing to evolve.

PRINCIPLES OF MANAGEMENT

Mechanism of Injury

It is sometimes difficult to identify a clear mechanism of injury that resulted in shoulder instability. This may be true in patients with underlying ligamentous laxity or in patients whose shoulder musculature has been deconditioned. For these patients, the onset of instability can be associated with minimal or no significant trauma.[66,215,239] In most patients, however, shoulder instability occurs after a clear traumatic insult. According to one estimate, up to 96% of acute shoulder dislocations were traumatic in origin.[236] For these patients, it is important to estimate the amount of energy that produced the instability. Some cases of instability are the result of a violent high-energy trauma, and may be associated with other soft-tissue or bony damage.

Although direct trauma to the shoulder girdle can result in subluxations or dislocations, instability usually occurs after an indirect force is applied to the shoulder. In the cadet population at West Point, for example, subluxations are much more common than frank dislocations and are associated with activities including throwing punches, collisions, and falls.[203] As such, unexpected force to the arm when the glenohumeral joint is in a susceptible position is often the cause of instability. For many anterior shoulder dislocations, the shoulder is typically in some combination of abduction, external rotation, and extension when a sudden load is applied to the arm. For posterior instability, on the other hand, the shoulder is usually in flexion, adduction, and internal rotation when an axial load is applied (Fig. 38-1). Other much less common mechanisms such as seizures and electrical shock can also cause glenohumeral joint instability.[33,248] With these mechanisms, wherein all the muscles about the joint are cocontracted, the external rotators of the shoulder can overpower the internal rotators to cause posterior dislocations.

FIGURE 38-1 Mechanism of injury for posterior glenohumeral dislocation. An axial load to the arm when the shoulder is in flexion, adduction, and internal rotation places the humeral head in a position susceptible to posterior dislocation.

Associated Injuries

Various injuries can occur in association with shoulder instability. Most are thought to occur during the initial episode of dislocation or subluxation, and can involve either soft tissue or the bony structures. They include, but are not limited to, humeral head defects, tuberosity fractures, glenoid fractures, humeral neck fractures, rotator cuff tears, vascular compromise, and neurologic injuries. Identification of these injuries is extremely important because they can often affect patient management and outcome. As such, all patients must be scrutinized for any associated injuries. Of these, some occur more commonly and merit special attention.

Defects in the humeral head occur when the glenohumeral joint is dislocated.[91,158] With the trauma of the dislocation, the humeral head is forced upon the glenoid rim and the relatively soft bone of the humeral head is crushed. The end result is an impression of the glenoid rim that is made on the humeral head. As such, these defects are often referred to as "impression fractures." With subsequent muscle spasms, these fractures can enlarge. In patients with initial shoulder dislocations, the incidence of a humeral head defect is noted to be between 38% and 47%.[32,237] In patients with recurrent instability, the reported incidence is even higher at 50% to 67%.[259]

In anterior shoulder dislocations, the defects are created on the posterolateral aspect of the humeral head and are referred to as Hill-Sachs lesions (Fig. 38-2).[91] With posterior shoulder dislocations, the defects are created on the anteromedial aspect of the humeral head and are sometimes called reverse Hill-Sachs lesions. As such, location of these defects can demonstrate the direction of the instability. In addition, presence of these defects also suggests a traumatic dislocation as they are relatively uncommon in patients with nontraumatic instability. Although most small humeral head defects do not influence treatment, large defects warrant special attention as they may require specific surgical intervention.

The incidence of rotator cuff tears that occur in association with shoulder dislocations is unknown; however, it appears to increase dramatically with age. Although the overall rate of rotator cuff tear may be as low as 15%, its incidence in patients older than 40 years has been estimated to be between 35% and 40%.[210,286] In patients older than 60 years of age, the incidence of concomitant rotator cuff tears may be as high as 80%.[286] These patients typically present with weakness of shoulder abduction and external rotation. Often their presentation may be confusing and misdiagnosed as a neurologic injury.[119,192] Nonetheless, any patient who demonstrates weakness after shoulder dislocation must be evaluated for a rotator cuff tear because prompt identification and management is crucial to the overall outcome.[210]

Because of their close proximity to the glenohumeral joint, the axillary nerve and the brachial plexus are susceptible to injury during shoulder dislocations (Fig. 38-3). Based on electrophysiological findings, the rate of injury may be as high as 65%. The incidence of clinically evident neurologic injury, however, is believed to be much lower, with the reported rates between 5% and 25%.[26,47,172,260] These studies also demonstrated that the axillary nerve is the most commonly injured neurologic structure after a shoulder dislocation and that this rate of injury is increased in older individuals.

Typically, these patients demonstrate weakness and numb-

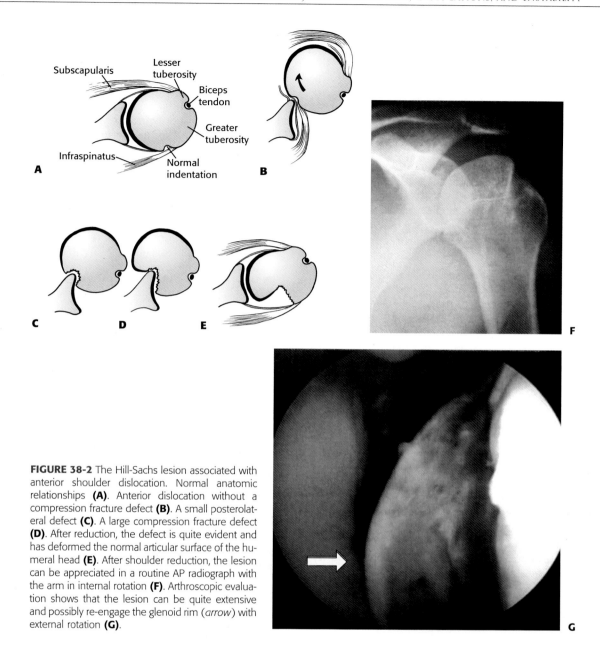

FIGURE 38-2 The Hill-Sachs lesion associated with anterior shoulder dislocation. Normal anatomic relationships **(A)**. Anterior dislocation without a compression fracture defect **(B)**. A small posterolateral defect **(C)**. A large compression fracture defect **(D)**. After reduction, the defect is quite evident and has deformed the normal articular surface of the humeral head **(E)**. After shoulder reduction, the lesion can be appreciated in a routine AP radiograph with the arm in internal rotation **(F)**. Arthroscopic evaluation shows that the lesion can be quite extensive and possibly re-engage the glenoid rim (*arrow*) with external rotation **(G)**.

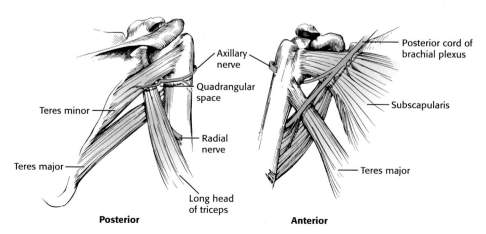

FIGURE 38-3 Anatomy of the axillary nerve as it passes through the "quadrangular space." Because of its nearby location, the axillary nerve is the most commonly injured neurologic structure after a shoulder dislocation.

ness. Nevertheless, as demonstrated in an electrophysiological study, some patients with axillary nerve injury exhibited completely normal sensation about the shoulder.[17] Therefore, relying on sensory testing alone for axillary nerve function may be misleading. Examination of the axillary nerve must include specific testing of both the sensory (sensation about the lateral deltoid area) and the motor (isometric contraction of the deltoid) components. If a neurologic injury is suspected, an electrophysiological examination should be obtained to establish the baseline of injury. For these patients, most authors typically recommend close observation rather than early surgical intervention because neurologic recovery over the course of 3 to 6 months is anticipated.[17,26,260] If repeated electrophysiological studies do not demonstrate signs of recovery by 2 to 3 months, nerve exploration may then be considered.[286]

History and Physical Examination

Presentation of Acute Dislocations

Initial management of shoulder dislocation begins with identification of the injury. Often the patient may be able to clearly recount the shoulder position as well as the direction of the applied force. In other instances, this information may be more clearly obtained from an eyewitness. Additional information regarding prior shoulder injury, prior episodes of instability, and prior treatments should all be documented. Hand dominance, occupation, activity level, and general health history should also be obtained. A general survey of the patient, including an adequate examination of the spinal column, should then be performed. Inspection of the shoulder may reveal an open wound, localized swelling, or a gross deformity. Often these deformities can be best visualized by inspecting the patient from behind, with the patient in a sitting position. With an anterior or posterior glenohumeral dislocation, the humeral head may be palpable beneath the skin.

A complete shoulder examination may not be possible because of pain and muscle spasms. Whenever possible, however, the limits of shoulder motion should be established as they may provide insight into both the severity and the direction of the instability. Patients with an anterior dislocation, for example, will typically demonstrate limitations in internal rotation and abduction. In contrast, patients with a posterior dislocation will often demonstrate limitations in external rotation. In very rare instances, referred to as *luxatio erecta humeri,* the patient may suffer from inferior glenohumeral dislocation with the arm locked in fully abducted position (Fig. 38-4).[45,268,292] Before any manipulation, a complete neurovascular examination of the upper extremity must be performed and documented. The axillary nerve is the most commonly injured nerve after an anterior glenohumeral dislocation, with some electrodiagnostic studies reporting rates as high as 60%.[17,260] Therefore, both the motor and the sensory component of this nerve must be examined (Fig. 38-5). Although quite rare, vascular injuries following shoulder dislocations have also been reported.[65,148]

Presentation of Instability

Patients with shoulder instability may present with a variety of clinical symptoms. Some may present for definitive care after being treated at a local emergency room for an acute shoulder dislocation. Some may present with a recent exacerbation of a recurrent instability. Others may present with a vague history of

pain without clinical suspicion or prior diagnosis of instability. Because of this variability in presentation, the importance of an accurate and complete history cannot be overemphasized.

As with all patients with a shoulder related complaint, general orthopaedic information should be obtained first. This includes age, occupation, hand dominance, level of sporting or recreational activity, presence of any previous injury or surgery, and functional impairments because of shoulder symptoms. If pain is the predominant complaint, its characteristics such as severity, location, duration, and precipitating position and/or activity must be clearly defined. In contrast, if instability is the predominant complaint, the frequency and the severity of the instability as well as the susceptible shoulder positions should be elicited. Often these patients have been avoiding specific tasks that involve placing their shoulder in a position vulnerable to dislocations. As such, details of their functional limitations may provide clues to the direction and the severity of the instability.

Whenever possible, the mechanism of shoulder instability should be defined clearly. This includes the timing, the amount of applied energy, the position of the shoulder at the time of the impact, and the degree of instability. For patients with recurrent instability, the severity of force associated with a recent exacerbation may be slight such as raising the arm or reaching for an object. Any history of previous shoulder instability should prompt questions regarding the nature of the injury as well as any prior treatments. Clinical evaluation of patients with recurrent instability should include questions regarding voluntary instability. Any issues regarding a secondary gain from shoulder instability should also be defined. If a patient can dislocate the shoulder voluntarily, it should be observed firsthand in order to identify the position of the arm, the amount of needed effort, and the direction of dislocation. In addition, these patients should be queried for any associated neurologic signs such as weakness, numbness, and tingling sensations.

Physical Examination

Examination of an unstable shoulder can be quite challenging. Some of the findings may be subtle, and the ultimate diagnosis may be difficult to establish. In patients who have suffered a recent instability episode, associated symptoms may be severe enough to preclude an adequate examination. For these patients, a basic examination to document glenohumeral joint reduction and neurologic status may be all that can be accomplished during the initial visit. If so, they should be evaluated more thoroughly at a later date when majority of the pain has subsided. A detailed neurologic examination of the upper extremity must be performed and documented during all clinical evaluations.

A thorough examination of the shoulder begins with inspection. Any abnormalities such as asymmetry, muscular atrophy, localized edema, or ecchymosis should be noted. This is usually followed by manual palpation for localized tenderness and bony defects. Range of motion of the affected shoulder should be obtained and compared with the contralateral shoulder. In addition, differences between active and passive range of motion should be noted. If possible, the etiology of this difference, whether caused by pain, weakness, or both, should be determined. General strength testing is performed with specific maneuvers to identify rotator cuff weakness. This is particularly important for an older individual, because the association be-

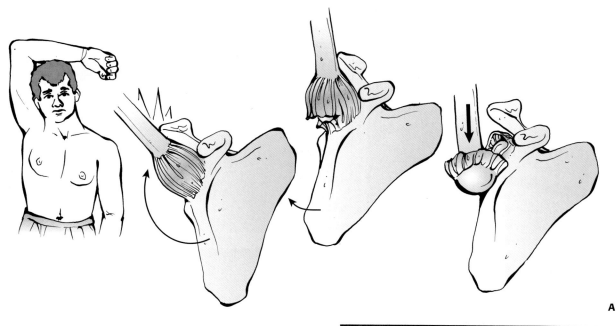

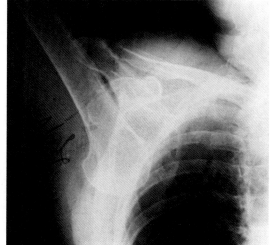

FIGURE 38-4 Locked inferior dislocation of the glenohumeral joint, also known as *luxatio erecta*. With hyperabduction of the arm, the lateral acromion acts as a lever against the proximal humerus to dislocate the shoulder inferiorly **(A)**. After dislocation, the humeral head is locked inferior to the glenoid rim **(B)**. In these patients the rotator cuff tendons are typically detached from the humeral head, and there may also be an associated fracture of the greater tuberosity.

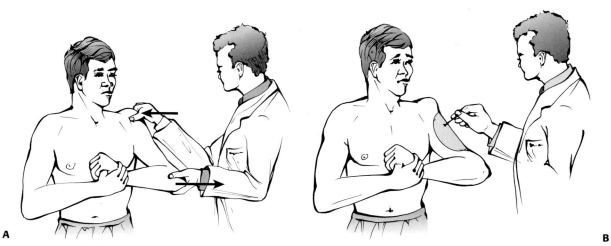

FIGURE 38-5 Technique for testing axillary nerve function. With the arm adducted and stabilized by the examiner, the patient is asked to actively abduct the arm. The motor component **(A)** of the axillary nerve is documented by observing or palpating deltoid muscle contraction. The sensory component **(B)** of the axillary nerve is documented by testing the sensation to the lateral aspect of the upper arm.

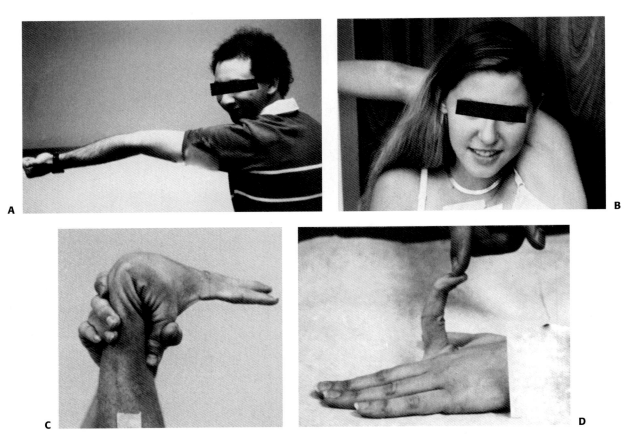

FIGURE 38-6 A–D. Examples of patients with generalized ligamentous laxity.

tween rotator cuff tears and shoulder dislocations increases significantly with age.[191] Findings consistent with a generalized systemic laxity are also noted. These include elbow hyperextension, hyperflexion of the wrist (thumb to forearm maneuver), hyperextension of the metacarpophalangeal joints, and knee hyperextension (Fig. 38-6). Provocative maneuvers for shoulder instability are typically reserved for the end of the examination as they may reproduce the clinical symptoms of pain and apprehension. For most techniques, the maneuver should be performed bilaterally to compare and contrast the symptomatic shoulder with the asymptomatic shoulder.

One of the most widely used examinations of instability is the "drawer" test. This maneuver can be performed either with the patient in the sitting or supine position. It can be used to assess both anterior and posterior instability. It has been suggested that this maneuver is most reliable if the arm is held in 80 to 120 degrees of abduction, 0 to 20 degrees of forward flexion, and 0 to 30 degrees of external rotation.[8] If the patient is supine, the entire shoulder should be off the table to allow free access to the shoulder girdle. While the shoulder girdle is manually stabilized with one hand, the other hand manipulates the humeral head for anterior translation (Fig. 38-7). For normal shoulders this translation should be smooth with a firm endpoint. If the translation is excessive in comparison with the contralateral shoulder, or if the maneuver reproduces the clinical symptoms of apprehension or pain, a presumed diagnosis of anterior instability can be established. This is a reliable test when the patient is able to relax the shoulder muscle sufficiently and allow the maneuver to be performed without tension.[55] In addition to anterior instability, the same maneuver can also be

adjusted to test for posterior instability. This is accomplished by manually translating the humeral head posteriorly. Again, posterior instability is suspected if the maneuver reproduces pain or apprehension. In this fashion, the "drawer" test can be used to test for instability in multiple directions.

A variant of the drawer test is the "load shift" test.[250] Unlike the "drawer" test, the arm is placed in 20 degrees of abduction and 20 degrees of forward flexion. Rotation is maintained at neutral, and longitudinal pressure is applied to the humeral head in order to load the glenohumeral joint. Similar to the "drawer" test, the humeral head is then grasped and translated in either the anterior or posterior direction to assess for laxity and pain.[8]

Although it is generally used to test for inferior laxity, the "sulcus" test is often positive in many patients with multidirectional instability (Fig. 38-8).[187] This maneuver is performed in the sitting position with the shoulder fully adducted. By manually placing downward traction on the arm, inferior translation of the humeral head is created. Significant translation will produce a noticeable "dimple" or "sulcus" at the lateral edge of the acromion. By placing the shoulder in external rotation, the sulcus test can also be used to estimate the integrity of the rotator interval structures such as the coracohumeral ligament and the superior glenohumeral ligament. External rotation of the shoulder should place these structures under tension and allow them to act as a restraint to inferior translation. As such, a positive sulcus sign with the shoulder in external rotation would suggest excessive laxity within the structures of the rotator interval.[8]

The "apprehension" test specifically examines anterior instability of the glenohumeral joint.[239] This maneuver is designed

FIGURE 38-7 The drawer test. While stabilizing the scapula with one hand, the other hand grasps the humeral head. A gentle pressure is then applied toward the center of the glenoid. At the same time, the humeral head is manually translated in the anterior and in the posterior direction.

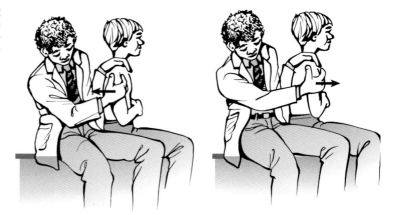

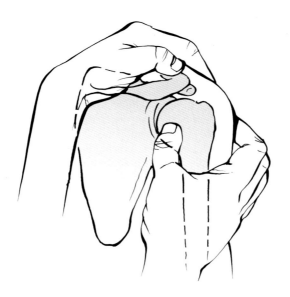

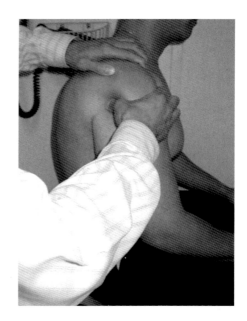

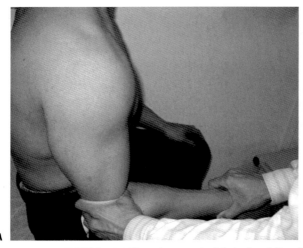
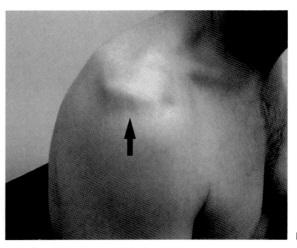

A   **B**

FIGURE 38-8 The sulcus test for inferior instability of the shoulder. With the patient in the sitting position, a downward traction is placed on the adducted arm **(A)**. With a positive test **(B)**, excessive inferior translation produces a dimple (*arrow*) on the lateral aspect of the acromion. By performing this test with the arm in external rotation, the maneuver can also be used to test the integrity of the rotator interval structures.

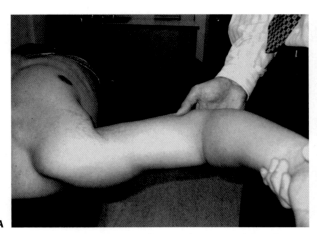

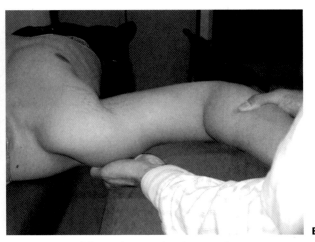

A   B

FIGURE 38-9 The apprehension and the fulcrum tests for anterior instability. In the apprehension test, the shoulder is abducted and externally rotated such that it is in a position vulnerable to dislocation with the patient in supine position **(A)**. Symptomatic patients will report the sensation of apprehension or "getting ready to dislocate." In the fulcrum test, this sensation of instability is accentuated by placing an anteriorly directed force on the posterior humeral head **(B)**.

to cause the feeling of imminent dislocation (apprehension) in patients as their shoulder is placed in a position that is vulnerable to dislocation. The patient is placed in the supine position with the shoulder slightly off of the table. The shoulder is then positioned in 90 to 100 degrees of abduction and neutral rotation. From this point, the shoulder is externally rotated until it reaches its maximal limit or until the feeling of apprehension is reported by the patient (Fig. 38-9A). Some patients may report pain instead of apprehension. Although pain may be used as an indicator for instability, it is typically not as specific or as reliable as apprehension in documenting anterior instability.[55,155] Modifications of this maneuver that try to either exaggerate or diminish the instability have also been described. As such, the "fulcrum" (Fig. 38-9B) and the "crank" test (Fig. 38-10) are similar to the "apprehension" test, but an anteriorly directed force is placed on the posterior aspect of the shoulder to exaggerate the instability. In contrast, in the "relocation test," a posteriorly directed force is placed on the anterior aspect of the shoulder to eliminate the feeling of apprehension (Fig. 38-11). Finally, the "surprise" test is another variation of the apprehension test where the examination starts with a posteriorly directed force on the anterior shoulder. As this force is manually stabilizing the glenohumeral joint, the patient does not experience apprehension even when the shoulder is placed in abduction and maximal external rotation. By abruptly removing this force, the patient will suddenly experience apprehension or pain. Although all these maneuvers can detect anterior instability, a recent study has suggested that the surprise test may be the most accurate.[155]

In contrast to these maneuvers that examine anterior instability, the "jerk" test is a provocative maneuver for posterior glenohumeral instability (Fig. 38-12).[133] This maneuver can be carried out with the patient in either the sitting or supine position. Again, if the patient is in the supine position, the shoulder should be slightly off the table. After elevating the shoulder to 90 degrees in the plane of the scapula, an axial load is placed on the humerus such that the humeral head is compressed against the glenoid. This can be easily accomplished by pushing

axially against the flexed elbow. By gradually adducting the shoulder, the humeral head may subluxate or even dislocate posteriorly and produce a sudden jerk. When the shoulder is taken out of adduction, the humeral head will abruptly reduce back onto the glenoid and produce another jerk. The findings from this test can be quite dramatic in patients with posterior instability. Because of guarding, however, a positive finding may be difficult to elicit in an awake patient. As such, instead of the jerk, the test can also be considered positive if the maneuver elicits the sensations of apprehension or pain.

Although all these provocative maneuvers can be informa-

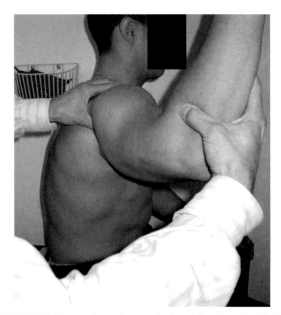

FIGURE 38-10 The crank test for anterior instability. The shoulder is abducted and externally rotated such that it is in a position vulnerable to anterior dislocation with the patient in sitting position. With an anteriorly directed force on the posterior humeral head, the instability is accentuated to cause the sensation of apprehension or "getting ready to dislocate."

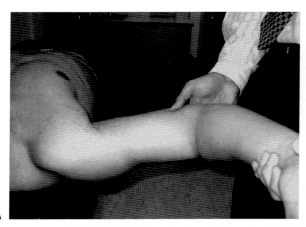
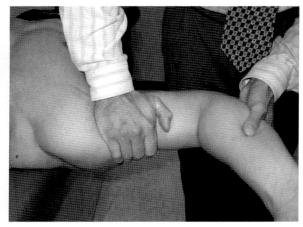

A   B

FIGURE 38-11 The relocation test for anterior instability. With the patient supine, the shoulder is abducted and externally rotated such that it is in a position vulnerable to dislocation **(A)**. With a positive relocation test, the apprehension is reduced with a posteriorly directed force on the shoulder **(B)**.

tive, voluntary or involuntary guarding may compromise the reliability of the examination. If a clear diagnosis of instability cannot be established, examination under anesthesia should be considered in select cases. After adequate anesthesia and sedation, patients are unable to guard against instability and the same provocative maneuvers can be performed in a controlled environment. In addition, even with an established diagnosis, examination under anesthesia should always be performed prior to initiating any surgical procedure in order to confirm the diagnosis.

Imaging and Other Diagnostic Studies

For all patients with suspected shoulder instability, routine radiographs should be obtained to assess the direction of the instability and to identify any associated fractures or bony defects.

Because of the oblique position of the scapula on the thorax, a routine anteroposterior (AP) radiograph will display the glenoid fossa as an ellipse (Fig. 38-13A). Therefore, in normal shoulders, the articular surface of the humeral head will overlap this elliptical shadow of the glenoid. A dislocated glenohumeral joint is suggested when this overlap is significantly altered. As such, a distance between the anterior glenoid rim and the humeral head that is greater than 6 millimeters is highly suggestive of a posterior shoulder dislocation, and is referred to as a "positive rim" or as a "vacant glenoid" sign.[6,231] A "true" AP radiograph of the shoulder is obtained when the x-ray beam is perpendicular to the plane of the scapula (Figure 38-13B).[231] Thus the x-ray beam is angled 35 to 45 degrees oblique to the sagittal plane of the body. In this view, the glenohumeral joint is profiled so that there is no overlap between the glenoid and the

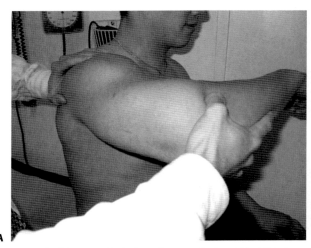
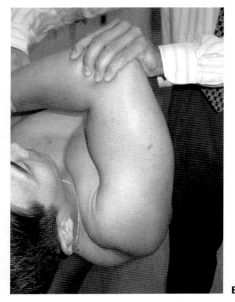

A   B

FIGURE 38-12 The jerk test for posterior instability. With the patient in either sitting **(A)** or supine **(B)** position, the arm is abducted and internally rotated. An axial load is then placed on the humerus while the arm is moved horizontally across the body. With a positive test, a sudden jerk occurs when the humeral head slides off of the back of the glenoid and when it is reduced back onto the glenoid.

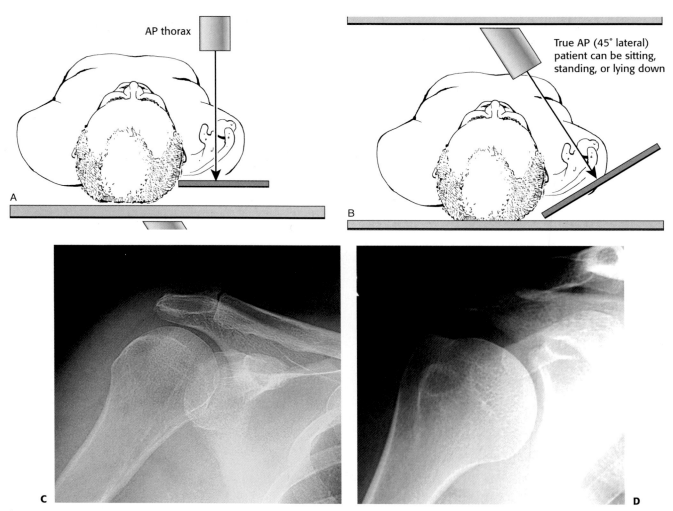

FIGURE 38-13 Technique for obtaining AP thorax **(A)** and true AP **(B)** radiographs of the shoulder. In an AP view, the radiograph actually represents an oblique view of the shoulder joint. In a true AP view, the x-ray beam is parallel to the joint so that there is minimal overlap between the humeral head and the glenoid surface. The radiographic views of the shoulder AP **(C)** and shoulder true AP **(D)** are demonstrated.

humeral head. In normal shoulders a concave contour of the glenoid fossa should match the convex articular surface of the humeral head. If any overlap between the glenoid and the humeral head is identified in this view, dislocation should be suspected.

It must be stressed that any AP radiograph of the shoulder must be accompanied by another orthogonal view to document the location of the humeral head. An axillary view radiograph is preferable because it can readily display the location of the humeral head relative to the glenoid, as well as allowing clear visualization of the bony anatomy. This radiograph is obtained by placing the cassette on the superior aspect of the shoulder while directing the x-ray beam between the thorax and the abducted arm (Fig. 38-14A).[145] For patients who cannot abduct the arm, two additional techniques have also been described. These modified radiographs, called the trauma axillary lateral view (Fig. 38-14B) and the Velpeau axillary lateral view (Fig. 38-15), require minimal abduction of the arm and provide comparable views of the shoulder.[18]

If an adequate axillary lateral radiograph cannot be obtained, a scapula lateral view radiograph may also display the location

of the humeral head.[170, 231] This radiograph is obtained by placing the cassette on the lateral aspect of the shoulder and directing the x-ray beam parallel to the spine of the scapula (Fig. 38-16). This view is orthogonal to the "true" AP view of the scapula, and outlines the scapula as the letter "Y" (Fig. 38-17A). Hence, the scapula lateral view is sometimes referred to as the scapula "Y" view. The two upper limbs of the letter Y represent the scapula spine and the coracoid process, respectively, whereas the inferior limb of the Y represents the scapula body. The glenoid fossa is located in the center of the Y where all the limbs intersect (Figure 38-17B). Therefore, the humeral head should reside within this central portion of the Y in normal shoulders (Figure 38-17C). In addition to the scapula lateral view, another lateral radiograph that can be obtained is the transthoracic lateral view. For this view the x-ray beam is directed through the thoracic cavity and projected onto a cassette that is placed lateral to the shoulder. As expected, this view is often difficult to interpret because of the presence of other anatomic structures. Hence it is typically not recommended for evaluation of an unstable shoulder.

In addition to the glenohumeral joint, radiographs must be

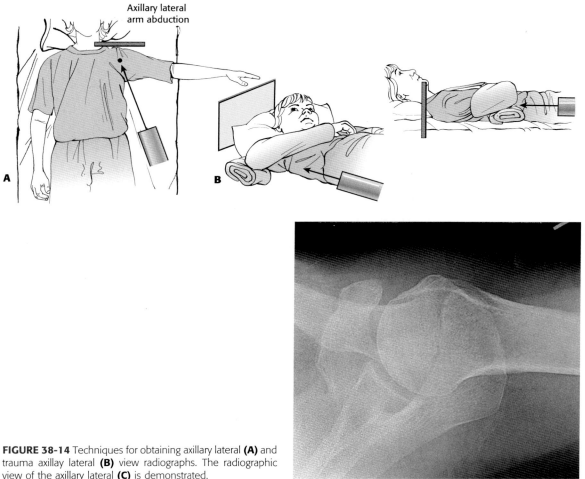

FIGURE 38-14 Techniques for obtaining axillary lateral **(A)** and trauma axillay lateral **(B)** view radiographs. The radiographic view of the axillary lateral **(C)** is demonstrated.

closely scrutinized for associated fractures and deformities. If other structural defects are suspected, additional radiographs must be obtained to fully characterize the injury. When a glenoid bony defect is suspected, the West Point axillary view should be considered (Fig. 38-18). This radiograph is taken with the patient in a prone position with the involved shoulder slightly elevated on a pillow. With the cassette placed on the superior aspect of the shoulder, the x-ray beam is directed toward the axilla in a 25 degrees downward and a 25 degrees inward direction. This radiograph provides a tangential view of the anterior glenoid and can be quite useful in identifying anterior glenoid rim fractures.[235] Another radiograph that can be helpful in detecting glenoid defect is the apical oblique view.[67] This radiograph is similar to the "true" AP view of the shoulder, but the x-ray beam is angled approximately 45 degrees downward (Fig. 38-19). In this fashion, a tangential view of the anterior glenoid rim can be obtained for analysis.

In some patients, a humeral head defect can be easily visualized on routine or "true" AP radiographs of the shoulder. Since a Hill-Sachs lesion is located in the posterolateral aspect of the humeral head, internal rotation of the shoulder should improve the visualization of the defect on an AP radiograph. For further characterization, a Stryker notch view can be considered (Fig. 38-20).[82] For this radiograph, the patient is placed supine, and the arm is forward flexed such that the elbow is directed over the face. The elbow is usually flexed so the hand can rest on top of the head. The x-ray beam is then angled approximately 10 degrees downward and projected onto a cassette that is placed on the posterior aspect of the shoulder. Studies have demonstrated that this view can greatly improve the ability to identify and characterize a Hill Sachs lesion.[82,240]

If radiographs are not sufficient, a computed tomography (CT) scan should be considered. In fact, for the majority of orthopaedic surgeons, CT scans have become the imaging modality of choice for characterizing associated fractures. CT scan images can provide details regarding the size and the extent of the bony defects. In addition, with the recent advances in CT technology, three-dimensional reconstructions of the shoulder can provide exquisite details of the bony anatomy and identify defects that were previously underappreciated.[257]

In contrast to radiographs and CT scans, magnetic resonance imaging (MRI) is the modality of choice for assessing soft tissue injuries. MRI provides high resolution images along different body axes to fully illustrate the defect. Multiple authors have reported on the usefulness of MRI for identifying rotator cuff tears as well as labral defects. According to one study, MRI showed 100% sensitivity and 95% specificity in the diagnosis of full thickness rotator cuff tears. In addition, MRI demonstrated 88% sensitivity and 93% specificity in the diagnosis of labral pathology.[111] A more recent study supported this finding as the authors observed 100% agreement between the MRI readings and the arthroscopic findings for the presence of an anterior

(text continues on page 1179)

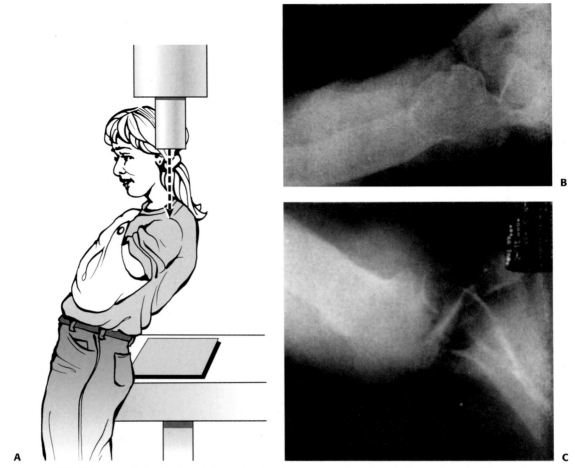

FIGURE 38-15 A. Positioning of the patient for the Velpeau axillary lateral view radiograph. **B.** Note the posterior dislocation of the humeral head. **C.** Note the posterior dislocation of the humeral head with reverse Hill-Sach lesion. (Part A modified with permission from Bloom and Obata. J Bone Joint Surg 1967;49-A: 943–949.)

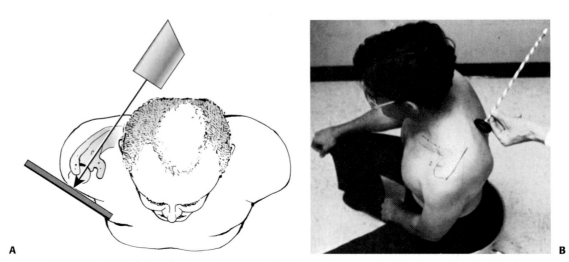

FIGURE 38-16 Technique for obtaining a scapula lateral, also known as the "Y", view radiograph. With the cassette placed on the anterior lateral aspect of the shoulder **(A)**, the x-ray beam is directed parallel to the plane of the scapula **(B)**.

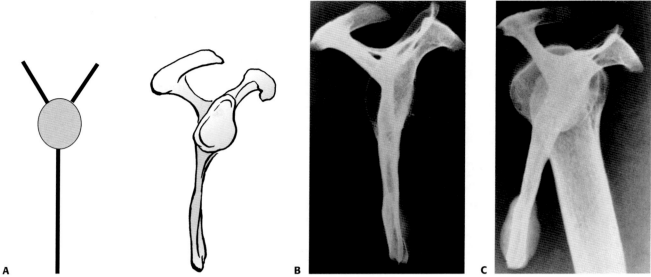

FIGURE 38-17 Interpretation of the scapula lateral, also known as the "Y" view radiograph. The obtained view of the scapula is projected as the letter Y. As shown in the schematic **(A)**, the lower limb represents the scapula body whereas the upper limbs represent the coracoid process and the scapular spine. Scapula lateral radiograph of a cadaveric scapula **(B)** highlights the fact that the glenoid surface lies in the middle of the letter Y. Therefore in these radiographs, the humeral head should lie directly over the glenoid in the middle of the Y **(C)**.

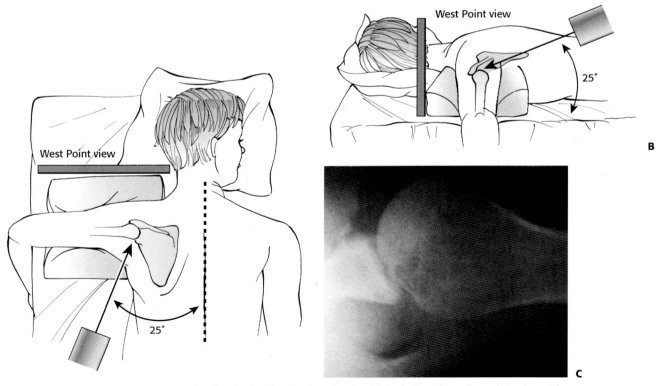

FIGURE 38-18 West Point view for the identification of a glenoid rim lesion. This radiograph is taken with the patient in the prone position. The beam is angled approximately 25 degrees from the midsagittal plane **(A)** in order to provide a tangential view of the glenoid. In addition, the beam is angled 25 degrees downward **(B)** in order to highlight the anterior and posterior aspects of the glenoid. In this fashion, the entire glenoid rim can be clearly visualized **(C)**.

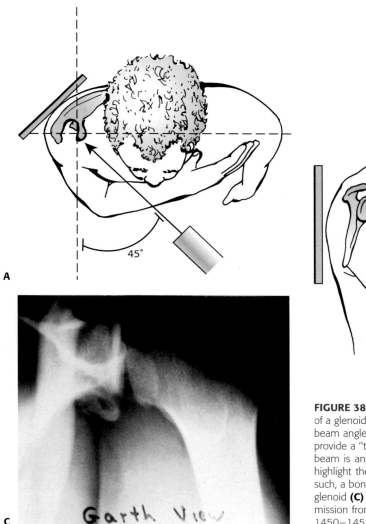

A

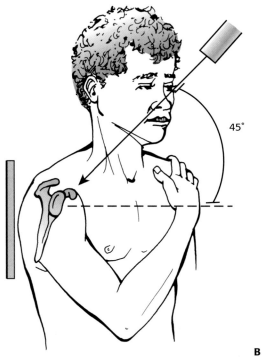

B

C

FIGURE 38-19 Apical oblique view for the identification of a glenoid rim lesion. This radiograph is taken with the beam angled approximately 45 degrees **(A)** in order to provide a "true AP" view of the glenoid. In addition, the beam is angled 45 degrees downward **(B)** in order to highlight the anterior inferior aspect of the glenoid. As such, a bony defect in the anterior inferior aspect of the glenoid **(C)** can be easily visualized. (Modified with permission from Garth et al. J Bone Joint Surg 1984;66-A: 1450–1455.)

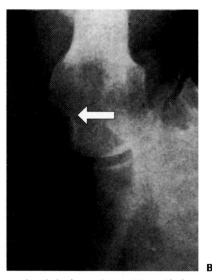

FIGURE 38-20 Stryker notch view for humeral head defects. The patient is in the supine position with the arm flexed to 120 degrees so that the hand can be placed on top of the head **(A)**. The x-ray beam is then angled approximately 10 degrees. The radiograph **(B)** can clearly reveal the presence of any osseous defects (*arrow*). (Modified with permission from Hall et al. J Bone Joint Surg 1959;41:489–494.)

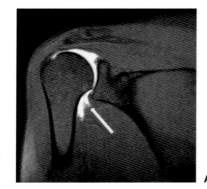
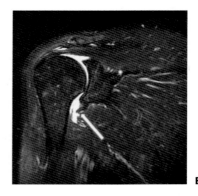

FIGURE 38-21 The humeral avulsion of the glenohumeral ligament, or HAGL Lesion. T1- **(A)** and T2-weighted **(B)** MRIs clearly demonstrate that the inferior glenohumeral ligament (*arrow*) is detached from the humeral neck.

labral lesion as well as a Hill-Sachs lesion.[134] Sensitivity of identifying intra-articular soft tissue lesions with an MRI may be augmented by the injection of intra-articular contrast. These studies, termed MR-arthrograms, can be very helpful in delineating structural defects within the joint and can be a useful adjunct for appropriate preoperative planning (Fig. 38-21).[36,84,272]

Diagnosis and Classification

Currently, there is no universally accepted classification system for glenohumeral instability (Table 38-1). In general, instability is classified based on severity (subluxation or dislocation), duration (acute or chronic), occurrence (single or recurrent), mechanism (traumatic or nontraumatic), and direction (anterior, posterior, or multidirectional). Because these classifications are mostly descriptive, multiple terms can be applied to a single patient. For example, glenohumeral instability in a patient may be described as an acute traumatic anterior dislocation or as a recurrent nontraumatic posterior subluxation.

Glenohumeral subluxation is defined as translation of the humeral head against the glenoid without a complete separation of the articular surfaces. As such, the joint will spontaneously reduce back to its anatomic position when the distracting force is no longer present. A certain amount of humeral head translation is expected during normal glenohumeral motion and thus, a precise definition for subluxation is difficult to establish. Nevertheless, excessive translation that causes symptoms of apprehension and pain should be considered abnormal. In contrast, glenohumeral dislocation is defined as excessive translation of the humeral head that results in complete separation of the articular surfaces. In these instances, even after the distracting force is eliminated, the joint will not spontaneously reduce

back to its anatomic position. In rare cases, some patients suffer from instability patterns that cannot be classified into either of these two categories. Such is the case when the humeral head translates against the glenoid surface and remains "perched" on the glenoid rim. Configuration of the deformity is stable so that no change will occur when the distracting force is eliminated. With minimal additional force, however, the humeral head can either completely dislocate or return back to its anatomic position. As such, this state of instability cannot be easily defined as either a subluxation or a dislocation.

Glenohumeral joint instability is considered to be acute if the condition has occurred within 24 to 36 hours of the initial medical evaluation. An attempt at closed reduction is more likely to be successful for an acute dislocation than a chronic dislocation. Thus, chronic dislocations, especially those greater than 4 weeks, are highly unlikely to be reduced in a closed manner.[74] If a patient has suffered multiple instability episodes, the instability is considered to be recurrent. This definition applies to both dislocations and subluxations.

Direction of shoulder instability can be obvious when a dislocation has occurred. In patients with anterior dislocations, the humeral head is often located inferior to the coracoid process. In addition to these subcoracoid dislocations, other anterior shoulder dislocations such as subglenoid, subclavicular, and intrathoracic have also been described.[45,72,244] In patients with less severe instability, the direction of instability may be subtle and more difficult to identify. Some patients may exhibit unidirectional instability in anterior, posterior, or inferior direction only. Others, however, may have generalized ligamentous laxity that results in multidirectional instability.[188] Although it may be difficult to establish, clear identification of the instability pattern is crucial to the formation of an appropriate treatment plan.

Recently, the Orthopaedic Trauma Association (OTA) has revised the comprehensive classification system for fractures and dislocations (Fig. 38-22) originally published in 1996.[161] This system can be applied to shoulder dislocations by utilizing a two digit numerical identifier of "10." The first digit of "1" specifies the shoulder girdle whereas the second digit of "0" specifies dislocation. Then, a letter is used to identify the specific joint ("A" = glenohumeral, "B" = sternoclavicular, "C" = acromioclavicular, "D" = scapulothoracic), followed by another number to describe the direction ("1" = anterior, "2" = posterior, "3" = lateral, "4" = medial, "5" = other). Thus, for example, an anterior glenohumeral dislocation would be classified as "10-A1" using the OTA classification system. Although

TABLE 38-1	Classifications of Shoulder Instability	
Severity	Mechanism	
Subluxation	Traumatic	
Dislocation	Atraumatic	
Duration	Direction	
Acute	Anterior	
Chronic	Posterior	
Occurrence	Multidirectional	
Single		
Recurrent		

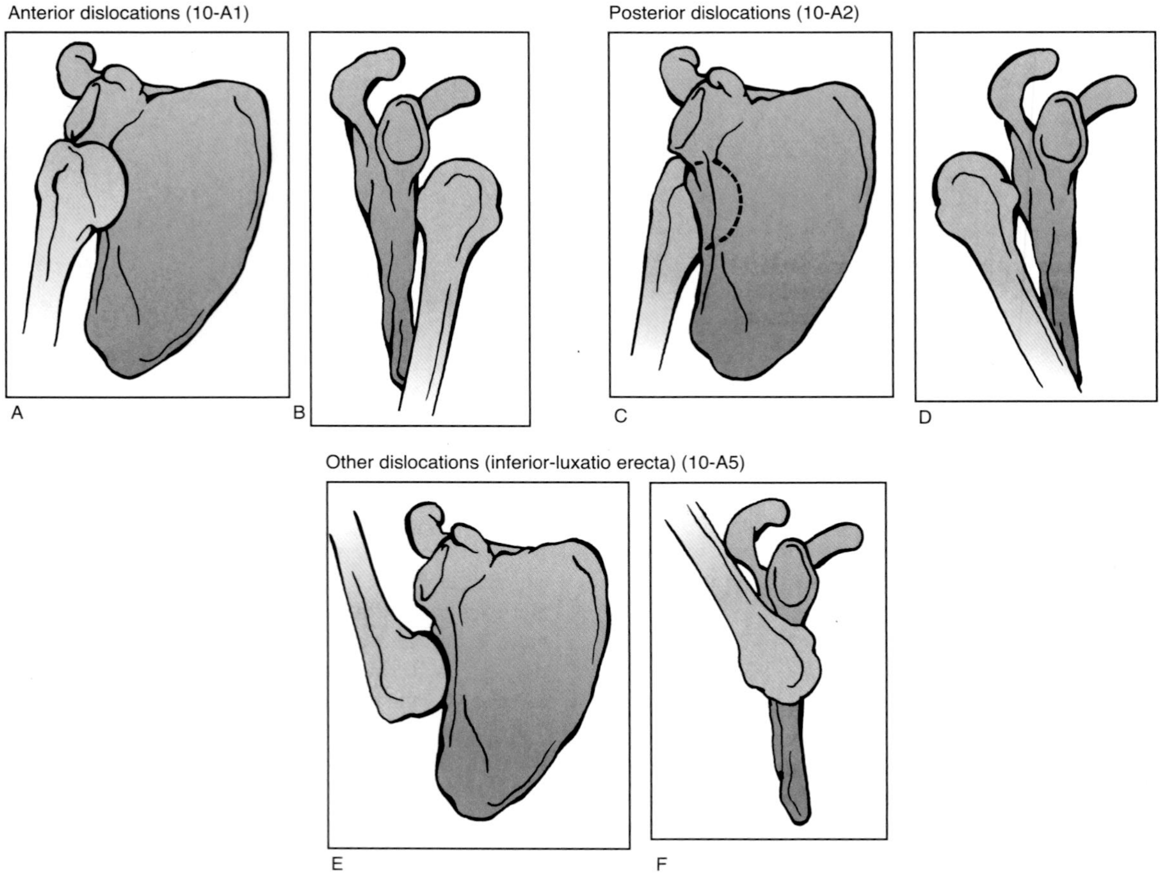

Anterior dislocations (10-A1)

Posterior dislocations (10-A2)

Other dislocations (inferior-luxatio erecta) (10-A5)

FIGURE 38-22 The Orthopaedic Trauma Association Classification for glenohumeral dislocations. The numeral "10" signifies the shoulder dislocation and the letter "A" specifies the glenohumeral joint. Anterior Dislocation is classified as 10-A1 **(A,B)**. Posterior Dislocation is classified as 10-A2 **(C,D)**. Lateral Dislocation, 10-A3 is theoretical and not seen clinically. Medial Dislocation classified as 10-A4, is also theoretical and not seen clinically. Inferior Dislocation, also known as *luxatio erecta,* is classified as 10-A5 **(E,F)**.

this system provides a simple method to describe a dislocation, it does not provide other relevant information regarding shoulder instability such as severity, duration, recurrence, and mechanism.

SURGICAL AND APPLIED ANATOMY AND COMMON SURGICAL APPROACHES

Surgical and Applied Anatomy

The essential function of the shoulder girdle is to act as a fulcrum for the use of the upper extremity in three-dimensional space. A critical element of establishing this fulcrum is the presence of a stable glenohumeral joint. Stability of the joint, in turn, is provided by various bony and soft tissue structures. Anatomic constraints to shoulder motion and translation are referred to as static stabilizers. In contrast, structures whose normal physiologic action creates a stabilizing effect on the shoulder are referred to as dynamic stabilizers. Ultimately, stability of the glenohumeral joint is the result of a complex interplay among these static and dynamic stabilizers.

Bony Anatomy

The scapula has a complex three dimensional structure. Notable parts of the scapula include the body, the spine, the acromion,

the glenoid, and the coracoid process (Fig. 38-23A). Parts of the scapula articulate with the distal clavicle and the humeral head to form the acromioclavicular and the glenohumeral joints, respectively. The scapula rests on the posterior aspect of the thoracic cage and is stabilized by the periscapular musculature. The glenoid surface is located on the lateral aspect of the scapula such that its surface has a slightly superior inclination relative to the vertical axis of the body. This inclination has been shown to play an important role in augmenting inferior stability of the glenohumeral joint.[115] In addition, the scapula is anteverted 30 to 40 degrees in respect to the coronal axis of the body, whereas the glenoid surface is roughly orthogonal to the plane of the scapula.[37] Therefore, the glenoid surface is anteverted 30 to 40 degrees and faces anterolaterally in respect to the coronal axis of the human body. This glenoid anteversion, in turn, is matched by the retroversion of the humeral head. With the humerus in neutral rotation (i.e., the forearm pointing forward in respect to the body), the humeral head faces posteromedially. In this fashion, the perpendicular axis of the humeral head corresponds to the perpendicular axis of the glenoid fossa in normal shoulders (Figure 38-23B).

The surface geometry of the glenoid was once believed to be elliptical, with a vertical diameter that is greater than its horizontal diameter. Unlike a typical symmetric ellipse, the infe-

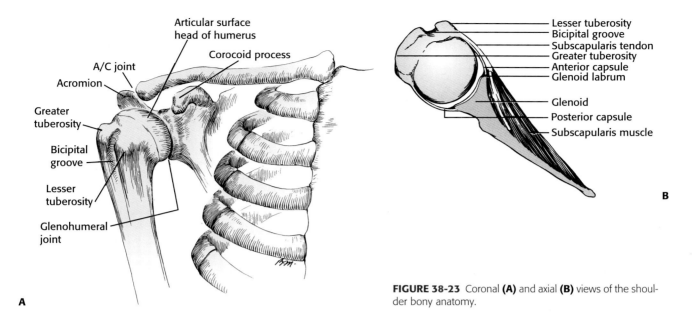

FIGURE 38-23 Coronal **(A)** and axial **(B)** views of the shoulder bony anatomy.

rior glenoid surface has a slightly greater horizontal dimension than the superior glenoid surface. In fact, the inferior 2/3 of the glenoid roughly approximates a circle, whereas the overall glenoid surface is "pear shaped."[108] The size of the humeral head can vary widely between individuals; however, there appears to be a direct correlation between height and the diameter of the humeral head such that a taller person typically has a larger humeral head.[110] Morphology of the humeral head is nearly spherical in shape, but the articular cartilage has variable thickness along different axes. Thus, the peripheral contour of its articular surface is also slightly elliptical.[110]

The interaction between the humeral head and the glenoid fossa has been intensely scrutinized and found to be very precise. For most shoulder movements, the center of the humeral head is located within 1 millimeter from the central axis of the glenoid cavity.[105] This is somewhat surprising because the overall size of the humeral head is significantly greater than that of the glenoid. As such, at any given position, the majority of the humeral head does not contact the glenoid and remain "uncovered."

In addition, the radius of curvature of the glenoid surface also does not correspond to that of the humeral head. On average, the radius of curvature of the glenoid is greater (less curved) by 2.3 millimeters.[110] Although this mismatch in size and radius of curvature may produce decreased joint stability, it also prevents impingement of the proximal humerus against the periphery of the glenoid. The end result, therefore, is increased range of shoulder motion.

Labrum and Capsule

The bony anatomy of the glenohumeral joint has minimal inherent constraints that allow for a large range of motion. The majority of glenohumeral stability, therefore, is provided by the various soft tissue structures that surround the joint. One of the most important of these stabilizing structures is the glenoid labrum. The labrum is a dense fibrous tissue which circumferentially surrounds the glenoid. It is contiguous with the glenoid rim and interacts with the glenohumeral ligaments and the

intra-articular synovium (Fig. 38-24). The importance of the labral tissue to the overall joint stability has been well described in the literature.[11,12,146] Correlation between traumatic anterior shoulder dislocations and an anteroinferior labral defect is extremely high. As such, this labral defect has been termed the "essential lesion."[11,12]

Despite the high association with instability, the mechanism by which the labrum confers stability to the glenohumeral joint is somewhat unclear. The anterior labrum may augment stability of the joint by providing a secure attachment site for the glenohumeral ligaments. Some earlier studies demonstrated that if the ligament attachment sites can be maintained, excision of the labrum did not seem to affect glenohumeral stability.[219,269] Anatomically, the labrum effectively enlarges and deepens the glenoid surface by 1 centimeter and 50%, respectively, and provides additional surface to interact against the humeral head.[104] Therefore, the labrum may provide stability to the joint by creating additional surface for humeral head translation. Recent cadaveric studies support this hypothesis as they demonstrated that if a labral defect is created, the humeral head is no longer centered within the glenoid fossa and the joint becomes increasingly unstable.[57,146]

The glenoid and the humeral head are enclosed within the glenohumeral capsule. The joint capsule is generally loose and redundant at most shoulder positions. At extremes of motion, however, the capsule tightens and provides stability to the joint. Thus, depending on the position of the shoulder, certain portions of the capsule will tighten and act as a restraint against humeral head translation. Studies have confirmed that different parts of the glenohumeral capsule can act as a primary or a secondary stabilizer against shoulder dislocation in all directions.[201,247]

The capsule completely encompasses the joint such that it maintains a stable and finite joint volume. In normal shoulders, this finite volume provides stabilizing force on the joint, as distracting the humeral head away from the glenoid will create a relative vacuum within the capsule. In fact, physiologic intra-articular pressure within the glenohumeral joint is slightly nega-

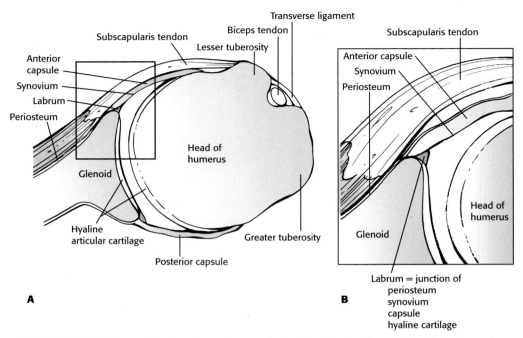

FIGURE 38-24 A. Cross-sectional anatomy of a normal shoulder. Note the close relationship between the subscapularis tendon and the anterior capsule. **B.** A magnified view of the anterior joint shows that the labrum is essentially devoid of fibrocartilage and is composed of tissues from nearby hyaline cartilage, capsule, synovium, and periosteum.

tive. Osmotic action of the synovium is believed to remove free fluid from the joint, thus creating a slightly negatively intra-articular joint pressure.[149] When the capsule is vented and opened to the atmosphere, the force necessary to translate the humeral head decreases significantly.[71,81,139] The stabilizing force generated by the finite joint volume and the associated negative intra-articular pressure may be as high as 146 N. During a dislocation, the capsule undergoes a plastic deformation, which may result in increased capsular volume.[49] This static stabilizing force has been demonstrated to be diminished in patients with shoulder instability.[81]

Glenohumeral Ligaments

The glenohumeral ligaments are some of the most important static stabilizers of the glenohumeral joint. They include the superior glenohumeral ligament, the middle glenohumeral ligament, the inferior glenohumeral ligaments, and the coracohumeral ligament. All three glenohumeral ligaments are intimately associated with the joint capsule. In fact, these ligaments were once believed to be *variable* thickenings within the joint capsule.[40] Multiple studies, however, have demonstrated that the glenohumeral ligaments are consistently present and that they are clearly distinguishable from the capsule.[171,220]

The superior glenohumeral ligament originates from the anterior superior aspect of the glenoid and extends to the anterior aspect of the humeral head just superior to the lesser tuberosity. Biomechanical studies have demonstrated that this ligament acts as the primary restraint to inferior translation in the adducted shoulder, and as a secondary restraint to posterior humeral head translation.[247,277] The middle glenohumeral ligament has a variable origin as it can arise from the supraglenoid tubercle, anterosuperior aspect of the labrum, or the scapular neck. It can

be quite dense and "cord-like" in some patients but practically nonexistent in others.[186] This ligament often becomes confluent with the tendon of the subscapularis muscle and attaches to the inferior aspect of the lesser tuberosity. In addition to acting as a secondary stabilizer against anterior humeral head translation, the middle glenohumeral ligament also appears to provide a restraint to excessive external rotation when the shoulder is in approximately 45 degrees of abduction.[247] The inferior glenohumeral ligament consists of three different components: the superior band, the anterior axillary pouch, and the posterior axillary pouch.[197] This ligament originates from the anteroinferior aspect of the labrum and extends to the inferior aspect of the lesser tuberosity. The inferior glenohumeral ligament complex has been compared to a hammock-like swing that surrounds and supports the humeral head when the shoulder is abducted.[199] As such, this ligament has been demonstrated to be the primary stabilizer against anterior and posterior translation of the humeral head, as well as being a restraint against excessive external rotation of the abducted shoulder.[23,198,219]

In a majority of the unstable shoulders, these ligaments are compromised from their origin at the glenoid. It has also been demonstrated, however, that the ligaments and the capsule may be damaged in midsubstance or at their insertion in the humeral head.[182,193] Both of these injuries may occur as an isolated entity or in conjunction with other lesions such as labral defects.[224]

In contrast to the glenohumeral ligaments, the coracohumeral ligament originates from outside the joint. It arises from the lateral aspect of the coracoid process, passes within the interval between the subscapularis and the supraspinatus tendons (i.e., the rotator interval), and attaches to the lesser and greater tuberosities.[124] This structure is tight when the shoulder is adducted and becomes loose when the shoulder is abducted.[13] Therefore, the coracohumeral ligament is believed to

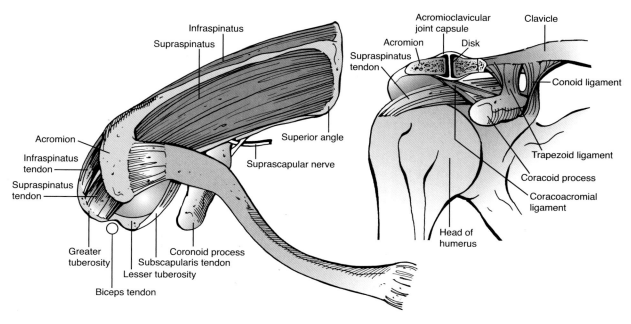

FIGURE 38-25 The glenohumeral anatomy and ligaments.

prevent excessive external rotation when the arm is adducted. In addition, this ligament is also believed to stabilize the joint against inferior subluxation when the arm is adducted.[13,202]

Rotator Cuff Muscles

The rotator cuff consists of the subscapularis, the supraspinatus, the infraspinatus, and the teres minor muscles (Fig. 38-25). Although these structures are generally considered to be dynamic stabilizers of the glenohumeral joint, their tendons surround the joint and often interdigitate with the joint capsule.[39] Therefore, even without muscle contractions, they can also act as static stabilizers of the glenohumeral joint.

During shoulder motion, muscle contractions may generate a displacing force across the glenohumeral joint. Contraction of the anterior deltoid muscle, for example, produces a posteriorly directed force on the humeral head. If left unbalanced, this force can create posterior shoulder instability. To counteract these forces, the rotator cuff muscles selectively contract to maintain the humeral head centered within the glenoid fossa. Thus, the rotator cuff muscles counterbalance the displacing forces created by the contractions of other shoulder girdle muscles. In this fashion, they act to dynamically stabilize the glenohumeral joint.[141,186,259]

In addition to countering displacing forces, contractions of the rotator cuff muscles also generate a medially directed force on the humeral head. This results in compression of the humeral head against the glenoid fossa, which in turn provides additional joint stability. Dynamic stability conferred by joint compression appears to be active throughout all shoulder motion.[147,154,276] In fact, sufficient joint compression can even overcome the destabilizing effects of ligament sectioning and joint venting.[276] Thus, dynamic stability provided by the rotator cuff muscles may be able to compensate for the loss of other stabilizing structures.

Biceps Tendon

The proximal biceps tendon originates from the supraglenoid tubercle, courses along the rotator interval, and exits the gleno-

humeral joint into the bicipital groove of the humerus. The physiologic role of the proximal biceps tendon has received much attention, but remains somewhat controversial. Experimental studies have shown that loading of the biceps tendon can decrease the tension on the inferior glenohumeral ligament.[233] Loading of the biceps tendon can also decrease humeral head translation in all directions, especially in the adducted shoulder.[113,204] In fact, a cadaveric study demonstrated that loading of the biceps tendon can prevent anterior shoulder dislocation even when the joint is destabilized by venting or by creating a labral lesion.[113] Thus, loading of the biceps tendon appears to provide a stabilizing effect on the glenohumeral joint. Notably, a recent electromyographic study demonstrated that when forearm position is controlled, the biceps muscle remains electrically silent during all shoulder motion.[152] This has led to the conclusion that, physiologically, the biceps tendon may not be under any significant tension during normal shoulder motion. Without significant loading, it is unclear whether the biceps tendon confers any additional stability to the glenohumeral joint.

Coracoacromial Arch

Superficial to the rotator cuff tendons, the shoulder is maintained within the confines of the coracoacromial arch. This arch is formed by the coracoid process, the coracoacromial ligament, and the acromion. These structural constraints limit the extent of anterosuperior, superior, and posterosuperior translation of the humeral head. In patients with a large rotator cuff tear, for example, this arch often represents the last restraint to anterosuperior glenohumeral dislocation. In normal shoulders with intact rotator cuff tendons, there also appears to be contact and load transfer between the coracoacromial arch and the rotator cuff tendons.[62,290] Therefore, during normal shoulder motion, a downward force is exerted by the coracoacromial arch, through the rotator cuff tendons, onto the humeral head to limit superior translation.

Common Surgical Approaches

Anterior Approach

The skin incision is placed on the anterior axillary line starting from the coracoid process and extending distally (Fig. 38-26A). In most patients, the surgical incision can be placed in line with the axillary fold for improved cosmesis. After the skin incision and subcutaneous dissection, the interval between the anterior deltoid and the pectoralis major muscle is identified. This area, also referred to as the deltopectoral interval, is outlined by the cephalic vein which must be dissected and retracted away from the surgical field (Fig. 38-26B). The cephalic vein is typically retracted laterally as most small feeding vessels originate from the deltoid muscle. The underlying clavipectoral fascia can then be incised to gain access to the shoulder (Fig. 38-26C). The overlying subscapularis tendon may be split in line with its fibers or it can be released just medial to its insertion at the lesser tuberosity (Fig. 38-26D). It must be stressed that rigid and anatomic repair of the subscapularis tendon must be completed at the end of the procedure as good surgical results correlate with subscapularis function.[243] At this

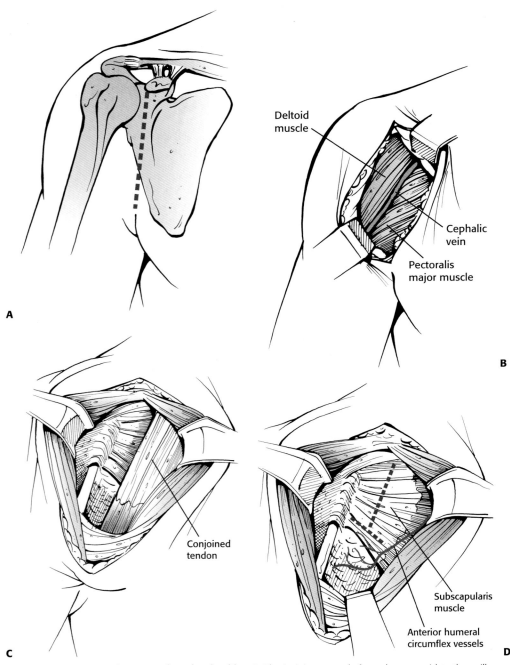

FIGURE 38-26 Anterior approach to the shoulder. **A.** The incision extends from the coracoid to the axillary fold. **B.** The deltopectoral interval is identified and developed, taking the cephalic vein laterally with the deltoid. **C.** The conjoined tendon and subscapularis are identified. **D.** A subscapularis tenotomy is made vertically, separating the subscapularis tendon from the underlying capsule.

point, the capsule is vertically incised to expose the joint and the anterior glenoid margin.

Posterior Approach

The skin incision is usually placed just medial to the posterolateral corner of the acromion, extending to the axillary crease. For access to the glenohumeral joint, traditional approaches have released the deltoid muscle from its origin on the acromion. Recent modifications of the approach, however, specifically avoid the release of the deltoid origin. For most patients, adequate exposure can be obtained by splitting the deltoid from the posterior acromion to the upper border of the teres minor (Fig. 38-27). The theoretical advantage of this modification is the preservation of strength and function of the posterior deltoid.[284] Once the rotator cuff tendons are exposed, the infraspinatus tendon can be incised and reflected medially. Excessive medial reflection should be avoided in order to prevent injury to the suprascapular nerve (Fig. 38-28). In situations where the infraspinatus tendon is very lax, it may be possible to simply retract the tendon superiorly instead of releasing it. The teres minor muscle fibers are then retracted inferiorly to gain exposure to the posterior capsule. Care must be taken when handling the teres minor because the axillary nerve and the posterior humeral circumflex vessels lie just inferior to this structure in the quadrilateral space. Once the posterior capsule is isolated, it is incised to expose the joint.

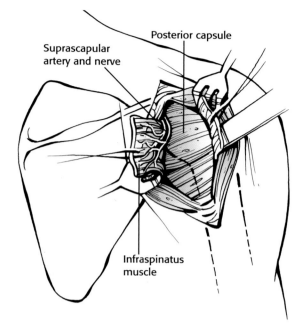

FIGURE 38-28 Anatomy of the suprascapular artery and nerve. During a posterior approach to the shoulder, excessive medial retraction of the rotator cuff tendons can damage these structures.

CURRENT TREATMENT OPTIONS

Treatment for patients with glenohumeral instability is based on a multitude of factors. For every patient, the potential for failing nonoperative therapy is considered against the risks of surgical intervention and its anticipated outcome. As such, nonoperative treatment is generally recommended for patients who should respond successfully to rehabilitation and have a low likelihood of developing symptomatic recurrent instability.

For patients with a first time traumatic shoulder dislocation, the overall rate of recurrent instability has been reported to be between 26% and 48%.[97,260] Recent 25-year follow-up data of 229 shoulders in 227 patients suggest that 42% of patients with a first time dislocation never have another event, whereas 7% have only one additional dislocation or subluxation event.[99] It has also been demonstrated that various factors affect the likelihood of developing recurrent instability. They include several patient-related factors such as age, level of sporting or recreational activity, compliance, and associated injuries. Of these, the single most important risk factor for developing recurrent instability appears to be age. In patients under 20 years of age, the incidence of recurrent dislocation has been reported to be between 55% and 95%.[95,172,173,236,260] In contrast, for patients older than 40 years of age, the reported rate of recurrent dislocation is less than 6%.[173,237,260] One recent study reported a 3% recurrence rate at 25-year follow-up in patients 30 to 40 years of age at the time of their initial dislocation.[99]

In addition to age, patient activity has also been identified as an independent factor for developing recurrent instability. As such, even in patients under 20 years of age, the rate of recurrent instability in nonathletic patients was only 30%. In contrast, in the same group of patients who did participate in athletic activities, the recurrence rate reached 80%. Because of this relatively high rate of recurrent instability after traumatic dislocation, for the young and active patients nonoperative treatment should be recommended with caution. To describe this group of patients, the acronym **TUBS** has been widely used (Table 38-2). This term represents patients who have been suffering from **T**raumatic **U**nidirectional instability that is often associated with a **B**ankart lesion, and whose treatment often requires **S**urgery.[262]

Because of these issues, optimal treatment for young and active patients with an acute shoulder dislocation is still de-

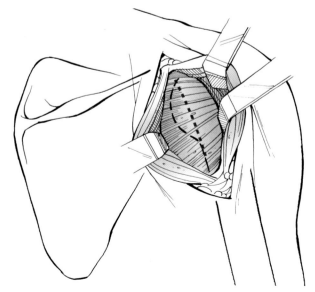

FIGURE 38-27 The posterior approach to the shoulder. After the skin incision, the deltoid muscle can be split along its fibers from the acromion to the upper border of the teres minor. Underlying rotator cuff tendons can then be incised to gain access to the shoulder capsule and joint.

| TABLE 38-2 | **Acronyms for Types of Recurrent Shoulder Instability** |

TUBS
  *T*raumatic
  *U*nidirectional
  *B*ankart lesion
  *S*urgery is often necessary

AMBRI
  *A*traumatic
  *M*ultidirectional
  *B*ilateral
  *R*ehabilitation is the primary mode of treatment
  *I*nferior capsular shift is often performed if surgery is indicated

(Reproduced with permission from Thomas S, Matsen F. An approach to the repair of glenohumeral ligament avulsion in the management of traumatic anterior glenohumeral instability. J Bone Joint Surg 1989;71-A:506–513.)

bated. In the cadet population of patients at West Point, for example, there is 85% to 92% rate of recurrent instability after an initial dislocation.[46,279] Therefore some authors have recommended immediate surgical stabilization of the shoulder in such high-risk patients.[122,230] In contrast, however, other authors have found that surgical stabilization is requested by only a minority of patients and recommended against immediate surgery.[242]

For patients who complain of multidirectional or bilateral shoulder instability, the onset of symptoms usually does not include a traumatic incident. Generally, these patients demonstrate signs of general systemic laxity, which in turn may also be associated with "loose" shoulder ligaments and capsule. As such, the glenohumeral ligaments may be incompetent, and predispose the patients to developing symptomatic shoulder instability. By strengthening the dynamic stabilizers, it should be possible to overcome the inherent glenohumeral joint laxity. Thus, for example, one study noted that 80% of patients with atraumatic shoulder instability were successfully treated with a specific set of exercises to strengthen the shoulder musculature.[31] According to another study, patients with unilateral instability, functional impairments, and higher grades of laxity were unlikely to respond to therapy, and patients who did respond to therapy typically demonstrated improvements within three months of starting their rehabilitation.[180] If physical rehabilitation does not provide adequate improvement, however, these patients often require surgical tightening of the entire shoulder capsule with the inferior capsular shift procedure. To describe this group of patients, another popular acronym of **AMBRI** has been developed (Table 38-2). The term represents patients who have been suffering from *A*traumatic *M*ultidirectional glenohumeral instability that can be *B*ilateral, and whose condition should be treated with *R*ehabilitation or, if necessary, *I*nferior capsular shift.[262]

In summary, the treatment of choice must be determined on an individual basis. The likelihood of developing recurrent instability as well as the likelihood of successful nonoperative management must be considered based on various patient related factors. Thus, for example, treatment of a 21-year-old professional basketball player with recurrent traumatic glenohumeral dislocations is likely to involve a surgical procedure.

On the other hand, initial treatment recommendation for a 35-year-old recreational tennis player who suffers from atraumatic multidirectional instability will primarily be nonoperative, focusing on physical rehabilitation.

Nonoperative Treatment

Closed Reduction Techniques for Acute Dislocation

An acute shoulder dislocation is a condition that requires emergent care. The joint should be reduced to its anatomic position as soon as possible, and a closed reduction should be attempted for most patients. In the select patients with concomitant proximal humerus fractures, however, reduction under anesthesia should be considered. The likelihood of a successful closed reduction is dependent on multiple factors, including the presence of muscle spasm, duration of the dislocation, presence of interposing structures, and the availability of adequate assistance.

To obtain adequate muscle relaxation and pain control during shoulder reduction, intravenous analgesic and sedation agents are often used. Although these agents can be extremely valuable, their use necessitates careful patient monitoring. In rare circumstances, excessive sedation may even lead to a respiratory compromise that requires formal airway protection. As such, administration of intravenous agents typically requires the use of significant clinical resources. Recently, some authors have reported that intra-articular injection of lidocaine, rather than intravenous agents, can be used to effectively control pain and muscle spasms during shoulder reduction. They demonstrated that closed reduction after intra-articular lidocaine injection had high rates of success, especially if the attempts were performed within 5.5 hours after the dislocation.[176] When compared with those who received intravenous agents, these patients were also shown to spend less time in the emergency room and incur less expense.[176]

After administration of either intra-articular or intravenous analgesia, a closed reduction can be attempted. A number of different reduction techniques and maneuvers have been described in the literature.[286] Some of the more commonly utilized techniques are described below. All of these techniques rely on appropriate positioning of the shoulder with gentle, slow, and sustained traction on the arm. Sudden or forceful manipulations are avoided because they can lead to significant complications. If initial shoulder reduction is unsuccessful, the degree of sedation and analgesia must be evaluated to ensure that adequate muscle relaxation has been obtained. If closed reduction is not successful, the patient should then be taken to the operating room on an emergent basis for either closed or open reduction. Once closed reduction is accomplished, anatomic reduction of the glenohumeral joint must be confirmed with radiographs. In addition, postreduction documentation of the neurovascular status must also be performed.

One of the earliest closed reduction techniques was originally described by Hippocrates (Fig. 38-29A).[92,93] This method utilizes the concept of traction and countertraction to distract the glenohumeral joint and is applicable for most shoulder dislocations. If performed by a single person, countertraction can be provided by a foot that is placed on the thorax just inferior to the axilla. If assistance is available, countertraction can also be provided by a sheet that is placed around the upper thorax and held steady by an assistant (Fig. 38-29B). Against this countertraction, slow and steady traction is applied to the arm

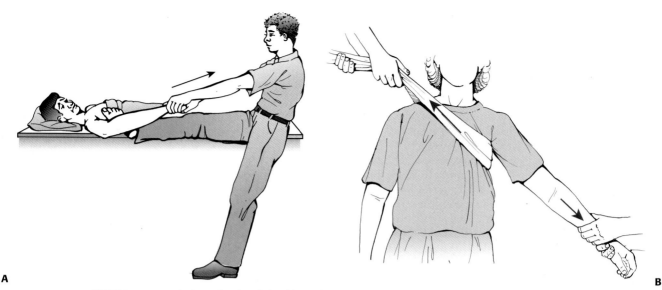

FIGURE 38-29 Techniques for closed shoulder reduction. The Hippocratic method **(A)** utilizes a downward traction on the arm against the countertraction provided by the foot on the thorax. Care must be taken to avoid placing the foot in the axilla as it can cause damage to the underlying neurovascular structures. A modification of this technique **(B)** uses a hand-held sheet around the thorax to provide countertraction.

to distract the humeral head away from the glenoid. Upon disengagement of the humeral head from the glenoid rim, the traction is released, and the joint is allowed to reduce back to its anatomic position. In some instances, gentle rotation or manipulation of the humeral head may be required to mobilize the humeral head.

A similar traction maneuver is also utilized in the Stimson technique.[255] Following its original description, this technique has undergone a few modifications. The patient is placed in prone position with the affected arm hanging free over a table (Fig. 38-30). In this manner, the table provides a stable base against which a gentle downward traction is placed on the arm. The traction can be applied manually or by attaching weights to the wrist. Typically, 5 pounds is sufficient for most patients. Depending on the size of the patient, however, the amount of weight can be varied accordingly. By applying this traction for a period of time (10 to 20 minutes), the shoulder musculature will fatigue and allow sufficient relaxation for humeral head disengagement. The traction is then released, and the joint is allowed to reduce back to its anatomic position.

Another commonly utilized reduction maneuver is the Milch technique, which is especially useful for anterior dislocations.[174] Unlike some of the other maneuvers, this technique relies on shoulder position rather than distraction. The maneuver can be performed with the patient in either supine or prone position. Upon administration of analgesia and moderate traction, the arm is abducted and externally rotated. The dislocated humeral head is then manually manipulated back into the joint. Various authors have reported that this method is associated with a high rate of success and with minimal complications.[142,241]

Definitive Nonoperative Treatment

After a successful closed reduction that is confirmed by radiographs, the arm should be immobilized for a period of time. Although most surgeons agree that a brief period of immobiliza-

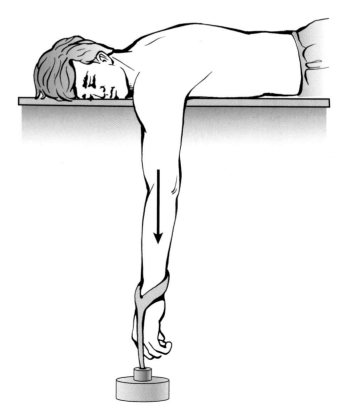

FIGURE 38-30 The Stimson technique for closed shoulder reduction. With the patient prone, weight is hung from the wrist to distract the shoulder joint. Eventually, with sufficient fatigue in the shoulder musculature, the joint easily reduces.

tion is required for patient comfort and protection, the exact protocol for immobilization is still controversial. Thus recommendations regarding the type, duration, and position of immobilization have yet to be firmly established.

In comparison to a simple sling, immobilization in a Velpeau dressing, which includes a sling and a swath, does not appear to alter the subsequent development of recurrent instability.[52] Therefore, since more rigid orthoses tend to be quite cumbersome, a simple sling is preferred for most patients. As for the duration of immobilization, some series have reported no correlation between the duration of immobilization and the development of recurrent instability.[98,172] In a prospective randomized study, for example, Hovelius and colleagues showed that the type and duration of initial immobilization had no affect on the development of recurrent instability.[97] In contrast, other studies have reported decreased rates of recurrent instability in patients whose shoulders were immobilized for a short period of time. For example, one study showed that patients who were immobilized for more than 1 week demonstrated a significantly decreased rate of recurrent instability in comparison with their nonimmobilized counterparts.[128] In other studies, the incidence of recurrent instability in patients who were immobilized for less than 3 weeks was nearly twice that of those who were immobilized for 3 weeks or longer.[136,256] One of these studies also demonstrated that the duration of immobilization affected recurrent instability only in patients younger than 30 years of age. For older patients immobilization had minimal impact on recurrent instability.[136] Therefore, age of the patient should also be considered when deciding on the duration of postreduction immobilization.

In addition to the type and duration of immobilization, the position of immobilization has also received significant attention. A simple sling places the shoulder in internal rotation. Some studies have suggested that this position may not be optimal in preventing recurrent instability. In patients who sustained a traumatic anterior shoulder dislocation, position of the anterior labrum after reduction appears to be more anatomic if the arm is positioned in slight external rotation.[116] This radiographic observation has been supported by a clinical study which demonstrated that, at a relatively short-term follow-up period of 15 months, patients immobilized in external rotation did not develop recurrent instability. In contrast, patients who were immobilized in the traditional internally rotated position demonstrated a recurrent dislocation rate of 30%.[112] This difference was even more striking for patients younger than 30 years of age, as the rates of recurrent dislocation in the external and the internal rotation groups were 45% and 0%, respectively.[112]

In contrast with these promising results, some of the more recent studies have demonstrated no such advantage for immobilization in external rotation. As such, a surgically created Bankart lesion placed in external rotation did not demonstrate any change in pressure between the glenoid and the capsulelabral complex.[153] Also, a recent study directly compared sling immobilization against external rotation immobilization after a primary dislocation event in patients less than 35 years old. Over 2-year follow-up, no significant difference was noted between the groups, with the sling group having 27% rate of recurrent instability and the external rotation group having a 23% rate of recurrent instability.[282] With seemingly contradictory data, it appears that the consequences of immobilization in external rotation are incompletely understood. Therefore,

further studies are still needed to optimize the postreduction immobilization protocol.

Nonoperative management of patients with glenohumeral instability relies on the principles of immobilization, protection, and rehabilitation. Immobilization allows for general recovery of the shoulder from the traumatic incident. In addition, immobilization also allows for the initial healing of the static stabilizers. As discussed in the previous section, the optimal protocol for the position and duration of immobilization has not been clearly defined.

The second principle of nonoperative treatment is protection. A brief period of immobilization is designed to protect the shoulder from additional episodes of instability. Subsequent to this initial phase, activity level of the patient must be modified to allow for the healing of the static stabilizers. Activity patterns are altered so that the shoulder is not placed in positions vulnerable to dislocation. Typically, this is accomplished by limiting the range of shoulder motion as well as refraining from participating in any high-risk activities. Experiments in primates demonstrated that 3 months were required to restore normal collagen structural patterns in the shoulder capsule, and that 4 to 5 months were required to restore normal tensile strength.[219] Therefore, this may provide a reasonable guideline for the period of protection.

The final principle of nonoperative treatment is rehabilitation. Dynamic stabilizers are strengthened to provide additional stability for the compromised joint. Compression of the glenohumeral joint by the rotator cuff muscles, for example, can overcome the destabilizing effects of ligament sectioning and joint venting.[276] As such, muscle rehabilitation may be able to compensate for the loss of some static stabilizers. Specific protocols for rehabilitation of the shoulder can vary; however, most protocols concentrate on strengthening the rotator cuff as well as the deltoid muscles.[31,286] In addition, some authors have also stressed the importance of strengthening the periscapular musculature, as they allow the scapula to function as a stable platform for shoulder motion.[31,73]

The likelihood of successful nonoperative treatment for shoulder instability can vary widely, depending on a multitude of factors. For example, those with associated injuries such as rotator cuff tear or a bony defect are less likely to be amenable to nonoperative management. Misamore evaluated nonoperative treatment of multi-directional instability and found that patients who were likely to improve with therapy did so within 3 months of initiating a therapy program. Patients who had unilateral symptoms, symptoms with activities of daily living, and high grades of laxity were likely to fail conservative treatment and require surgical intervention.[180] In a long-term follow-up study, Hovelius recently noted that 42% of patients treated with therapy had no recurrent instability, whereas an additional 7% had only one additional dislocation.[99]

Operative Treatment for Anterior Instability

Surgical stabilization for anterior shoulder instability is generally recommended for patients who have the following conditions: (i) failed appropriate nonoperative therapy, (ii) recurrent dislocation at a young age, (iii) irreducible dislocation, (iv) open dislocation, and (v) unstable joint reduction. In addition, even after a first time dislocation, young patients who actively participate in high-demand activities may also be considered for operative treatment. Again, although the general principles are clear, the exact indications for surgery are relatively arbitrary, and the specific criteria will likely vary among individual surgeons. In addition, patient expectations may also vary, as some would prefer an early surgical intervention rather than to continue with nonoperative management that may not be successful.

Once the decision for surgical stabilization has been made, a number of surgical options are available. They include arthroscopic techniques, open techniques with soft tissue repair or augmentation, and open techniques with bony augmentation. Traditionally, open anterior shoulder stabilization procedures have been the "gold standard," with many studies reporting good to excellent outcomes in the vast majority of patients. In comparison with these open procedures, early reports of arthroscopic stabilization procedures produced results that were notably inferior. With the development of newer instruments and techniques, however, the results of arthroscopic stabilizations have improved. As such, some recent studies of arthroscopic stabilizations have reported outcomes that are nearly equivalent to those after an open procedure.[53,127,129] Therefore, provided that the surgery is performed with adequate expertise, the choice between open and arthroscopic procedure may not significantly affect the overall outcome.

Reported and theoretical advantages of arthroscopic stabilization include shorter operative time, shorter hospitalization, decreased morbidity, lower incurred cost, less pain in the early postoperative period, and decreased rate of postoperative complications (Table 38-3).[19,53,78,162] It should be noted, however, that the amount of time required for adequate healing is not significantly altered with an arthroscopic technique. Therefore, these patients still need an adequate period of protection and rehabilitation similar to that after an open procedure.

There are few specific situations where most surgeons would preferentially utilize open techniques. They include situations where the procedure would involve isolation and fixation of a bony fragment. As such, for cases with either a large Hill-Sachs lesion or a substantial glenoid defect, open techniques are typically recommended. Another pathology that may not be optimal for an arthroscopic repair is the humeral avulsion of the glenohumeral ligament (HAGL lesion). Finally, for many surgeons, open procedures are preferred for patients whose anatomy has been altered because of deformity or previous surgery.[177]

Arthroscopic Procedures for Anterior Instability

The procedure begins with an arthroscopic examination of the entire joint to clearly identify the structural defects. Significant

---

TABLE 38-3	**Advantages and Disadvantages of Arthroscopic Stabilization for Anterior Shoulder Instability**[a]
Pros	Cons
Improved cosmesis	Technically demanding
Shorter operative time	Difficult in revision cases
Shorter hospital stay	Difficult w/ altered anatomy
Decreased morbidities	Cannot address bony defects
Decreased complications	
Lower cost	

[a](see text for details)

---

bony defects in the glenoid or the humeral head must be documented, as their presence may require conversion to an open procedure. According to some studies, a glenoid defect greater than 21% to 30% of the surface area or a Hill-Sachs defect that engages the anterior glenoid rim with abduction and external rotation is associated with a high likelihood of recurrent instability.[30,114,129] In addition, the labrum must be carefully examined for any damage, and the capsule should be assessed for redundancy and notable defects. Some surgeons have utilized the "drive thru" sign to describe a loose joint.[206,209] This sign is positive if the arthroscope can be easily passed from the posterior portal, through the joint, into the anteroinferior quadrant. Unfortunately, although this sign is associated with shoulder laxity, it is not specific for shoulder instability and its accuracy for diagnosing shoulder instability is less than 50%.[166] Upon completion of the diagnostic arthroscopy, the necessary portals are established. Although surgical techniques vary among surgeons, most tend to utilize the posterior portal for the arthroscope and anterior portals for the instruments. If an anteroinferior capsulolabral lesion, also known as the "Bankart" lesion, is identified, the defect must be repaired (Fig. 38-31A). The medially displaced labrum should be mobilized and reattached to the glenoid rim in its anatomic position (Fig. 38-31B,C). This surgery is often referred to as the arthroscopic Bankart procedure.

Early arthroscopic techniques utilized a metallic staple to reattach the labrum. Unfortunately, this technique was associated with relatively high rates of complications (12%) and recurrent instability (33%).[48,120,143] Others have described an arthroscopically assisted transglenoid suture technique to reattach the labrum. Although short-term follow-up data indicated excellent results with this procedure in the majority of patients, at a mid-term follow-up of 2 to 8 years, the results deteriorated with reported recurrent instability in 17% of the patients.[168,266] More recently, arthroscopic stabilization techniques have utilized suture anchors that can be placed at the anterior glenoid rim. These anchors provide a stable base to reattach the capsulolabral complex. Using suture anchors to address an isolated an anterior labral lesion and mild capsular redundancy, various authors have reported good to excellent results in the vast majority of patients, including those with a "high demand" shoulder such as collegiate and professional overhead athletes.[34,53,130,214,222] With relatively short-term follow-up, these studies also reported very low rates of recurrent instability between 0% and 10% for most patients and 12.5% to 16.5% for high-demand "collision" athletes.[34,53,130,164,265,355] At mid-term follow-up of 2 to 6 years, the rate of recurrent instability was still only 4% to 7%.[129,144,230] Negative prognostic factors for arthroscopic anterior stabilization include bone loss, inferior laxity or multidirectional instability, and total number of anchors used in the repair being less than four.[20]

In addition to the repair of the torn labrum, if associated defects are noted in the capsule or the humeral attachments of the ligaments, they must also be repaired as well. A midsubstance tear in the capsule can occur in up to 4% of the cases and require an anatomic repair for optimal results.[182,226] Similar to the midsubstance tears, HAGL lesions can occur in 1% to 9% of cases of recurrent shoulder instability and may be the defect responsible for persistent instability after surgical stabili-

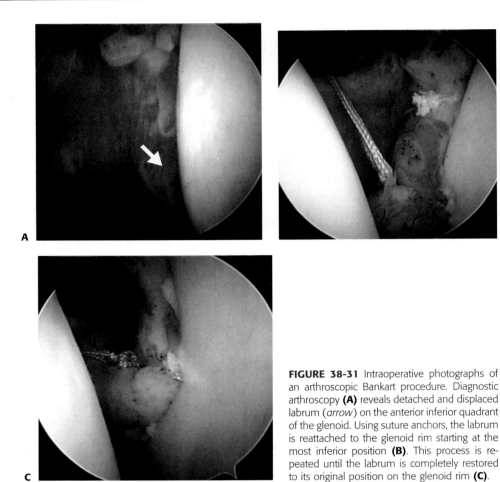

FIGURE 38-31 Intraoperative photographs of an arthroscopic Bankart procedure. Diagnostic arthroscopy **(A)** reveals detached and displaced labrum (*arrow*) on the anterior inferior quadrant of the glenoid. Using suture anchors, the labrum is reattached to the glenoid rim starting at the most inferior position **(B)**. This process is repeated until the labrum is completely restored to its original position on the glenoid rim **(C)**.

zation.[28,264,289] Although most surgeons would prefer repairing this defect using an open technique, some authors have described an arthroscopic repair of the lesion with early favorable outcome.[137,228,253]

With advancing technology and expertise in arthroscopy, a number of surgeons have recently reported on their experience performing arthroscopic surgeries on shoulders that were traditionally addressed with open techniques. As such, patients who have previously failed a surgical procedure have been stabilized with arthroscopic methods with reasonable outcomes.[22,189] Arthroscopic techniques have also been used to repair anterior glenoid bone defects associated with "bony Bankart" lesions.[258]

In addition to the capsule and the labrum, the rotator interval must also be scrutinized during any stabilization procedure. Biomechanical studies have demonstrated that these structures contribute to the stability of the humeral head against posterior translation, inferior translation, and excessive external rotation.[13,212,277,291] In addition, thermal shrinkage of the interval tissue has been shown to decrease anterior translation of the humeral head.[249] Thus, defects within the rotator interval may contribute to instability in multiple directions.[59,195] Several surgeons have described arthroscopic techniques for the evaluation and imbrication of the rotator interval tissue.[69,126,212,270] For patients with clinical or arthroscopic findings consistent with an interval defect, the rotator interval tissue should be imbricated. This should be performed at least 1 cm lateral to the glenoid surface in order to avoid tethering the coracohumeral ligament that can result in loss of external rotation.[212] In patients who continue to demonstrate symptoms consistent with instability without a prior dislocation, isolated interval closure may lead to good and excellent outcomes.[59] In the majority of the patients, however, rotator interval closure represents a supplemental stabilization technique that is performed in conjunction with repair of other lesions.[291]

Arthroscopic capsulorrhaphy can be quite cumbersome and requires significant surgical expertise. In order to simplify the procedure, an arthroscopic technique called thermal capsulorrhaphy was developed. By applying a source of heat, from either a laser or a radiofrequency probe, the capsular tissue can be caused to contract.[54,261] The end result of the process is to decrease capsular redundancy, decrease joint volume, and reduce glenohumeral translation.[274] Initial enthusiasm for thermal capsular shrinkage was due, in part, to the fact that the technology can be applied to all parts of the glenohumeral capsule and required less surgical expertise than other arthroscopic procedures. Hence even surgeons without extensive arthroscopic experience were able to use this technology to treat patients with shoulder instability. Unfortunately, however, the procedure has been associated with unpredictable outcomes.[178] Some authors have reported good to excellent clinical outcomes after a relatively short follow-up period.[181,223] Even for overhead athletes, good to excellent results were obtained in 88% of the patients.[223] In contrast, other authors have reported clearly inferior results with recurrent instability in 24% to 47% of the patients.[43,88,179,207] According to one prospective study, an unsatisfactory outcome was documented in 37% of the patients.[43] In addition, anatomic studies have raised concerns regarding possible thermal damage to the nearby axillary nerve.[80,165] Clinical studies have substantiated these concerns. In one study axillary nerve neuropathy was observed in 21% of the patients who were treated with thermal capsulorrhaphy.[179] In addition, significant capsular thinning or necrosis may also result, requiring soft tissue grafting.[3,178,207] Other noteworthy complications of this procedure include excessive stiffness as well as extensive chondrolysis (Fig. 38-32).[38,88,117,151,179] Because of these issues, thermal capsulorrhaphy has experienced a significant decline in popularity. Thus, although this technology may play a role in augmenting other stabilization constructs, most authors do not recommend its use as the primary procedure for shoulder stabilization.[88]

Open Soft Tissue Procedures for Anterior Instability

Among the numerous techniques that have been described to treat patients with anterior glenohumeral instability, the open Bankart procedure is perhaps the most commonly performed surgery. In this procedure, the anterior labral defect is identified, mobilized, and then reattached to its original anatomic site on the anterior inferior glenoid rim.[11,12] Reattachment of the labrum to the glenoid rim can be achieved using a number of different methods. In the original description by Bankart, drill holes in the glenoid were utilized. He reported no recurrent dislocations in 27 consecutive patients who were treated with this technique.[12] Other authors, utilizing the same technique, were also able to duplicate this success. The reported rate of recurrent dislocation after this procedure is roughly 2% with good to excellent results in the vast majority of patients.[103,225] Recently, instead of drill holes, surgeons have utilized suture anchors to reattach the labrum. Using this technique, good to excellent results have been reported in 88% to 94% of the patients, with recurrent dislocations in only 0% to 9.7% of the patients at short- to midterm follow-up.* With a long-term follow-up at 29 years, recurrent instability rate after this procedure was still low at 10%. Joint arthrosis was noted in surprisingly high 40% of the patients, but symptomatic in only 16.6% of the patients. Overall, despite the joint arthrosis, 100% of patients were satisfied with the surgery.[208]

In addition to the repair of the labrum, some authors have also recommended reduction of the capsular redundancy. Termed the "capsulolabral reconstruction," this technique utilizes a similar surgical approach to correct the pathoanatomic changes in both the labrum and the capsule.[118,140,183] After

*References 14,53,121,150,214,229.

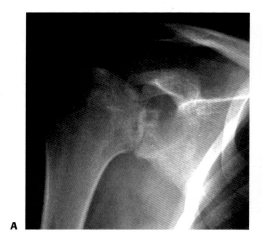

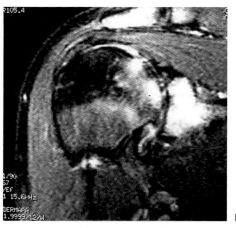

FIGURE 38-32 Iatrogenic complication of thermal capsulorrhaphy resulting in endstage arthrosis of the shoulder. Approximately 6 months after the procedure, an AP radiograph **(A)** and MRI **(B)** of the shoulder reveal a complete loss of articular cartilage that is later confirmed during the intraoperative examination **(C)**. (Copyright JP Iannotti, MD, PhD.)

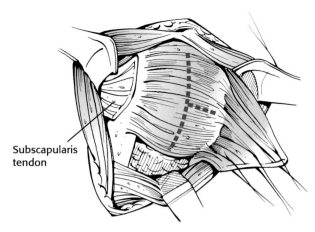

Subscapularis tendon

FIGURE 38-33 "T" capsular incision for anterior capsulorrhaphy.

standard anterior exposure, the capsule is isolated from the subscapularis. At this point a "T"-shaped incision is made on the capsule which includes both a horizontal and a vertical incision (Fig. 38-33). The vertical incision can be placed laterally near the humeral head or medially next to the glenoid rim depending on the specific technique to be performed. With the additional horizontal incision, two separate flaps of capsule, one superior and one inferior, are created. If a labral defect is present, it is repaired as described previously. The two flaps of the capsule are then imbricated onto each other by shifting the inferior flap superiorly and the superior flap inferiorly. In this fashion, parts of the capsule are overlapped on each other, and the overall capsular volume can be significantly reduced. It should be emphasized that the capsular plication is performed only to remove the redundancy in the tissue. Excessive anterior capsular tightening can alter the biomechanical characteristics of the joint, including increased posterior humeral head translation and increased joint contact forces with arm elevation, which in turn may lead to premature joint arthrosis.[275] Using this technique, various authors have reported good to excellent outcomes in the vast majority of patients with extremely low rates of recurrent dislocation. Even in patients with high functional demands, this procedure has been associated with good to excellent results in 92% to 96% of the patients, with recurrent dislocation in only 0% to 4% of the patients.[118,121,183,205]

For the capsulolabral reconstruction, the primary focus is to restore the normal anatomy of the capsulolabral complex. The subscapularis tendon is not imbricated during the procedure because it is not a part of the pathoanatomy. Rather, it is usually repaired back to its original length. In the Putti-Platt procedure, however, the capsular defects are essentially ignored. Rather, the primary focus is shifted to the subscapularis tendon, as it is divided at its midpoint and imbricated upon itself.[200] After making a vertical incision 2 to 3 centimeters medial to the lesser tuberosity, the lateral stump of the tendon is fixed to the glenoid rim with sutures around the capsule and the labrum. The medial stump is then laid on top and repaired to the lateral stump. In this fashion, the subscapularis tendon is significantly shortened, and the amount of external rotation is greatly reduced. Compared with the Bankart and the capsulolabral reconstruction procedures, results after the Putti-Platt procedure appear to be clearly inferior. As such, good to excellent results were found in only 55% to 85% of the patients, and recurrent instability

was observed in 9% and 35% of the patients.[63,135,138,294] This procedure is also associated with loss of shoulder strength and motion.[63,135,273,294] Although loss of external rotation can exceed 40 degrees in some patients, most studies have reported an average loss of 9 to 23 degrees.[41,135,273,294] Finally, long-term follow-up of patients who underwent the Putti-Platt procedure demonstrated a high incidence of progressive and symptomatic glenohumeral arthritis (Fig. 38-34). According to several studies, mild to moderate osteoarthritis was seen in 26% to 30% of the patients, and the severity of the arthritis correlated directly to the duration of follow up.[1,135,273] It has been suggested that the development of arthritis is related to the loss of external rotation and posterior subluxation secondary to overtightening of the anterior shoulder structures. Nonetheless, a recent study of patients who had the Putti-Platt procedure also showed that shoulders without a significant loss of motion can still develop symptomatic joint arthrosis.[86]

Another technique that alters the normal anatomy of the subscapularis tendon is the Magnuson-Stack procedure.[157] In this procedure, the insertion of the subscapularis tendon is transferred from the lesser tuberosity to a position that is lateral to the bicipital groove. With this technique, the primary goal

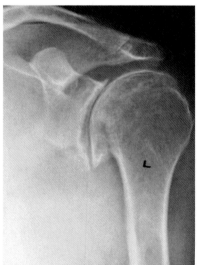

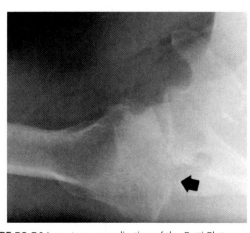

FIGURE 38-34 Long-term complication of the Putti-Platt procedure that resulted in endstage arthrosis of the shoulder. AP **(A)** and axillary **(B)** radiographs reveal large osteophytes and posterior subluxation with loss of joint space.

is to create a tight anterior soft tissue sling that will support the humeral head against anterior translation. Proponents of this procedure demonstrate that good to excellent results can be obtained in 90% to 97% of the patients, with low rates of recurrent dislocations.[2,89,175] Even with long-term follow-up, reported rates of recurrent instability have been less than 5%.[125,234] Although these results are impressive, nonphysiological means of shoulder reconstructions have generally fallen into disfavor since they alter the normal biomechanics of the glenohumeral joint and do not directly address the underlying pathoanatomy. As expected, the Magnuson-Stack procedure is associated with a loss of external rotation and forward elevation. In comparison with the patients who underwent the Putti-Platt procedure, however, this loss was fairly minimal at 5 to 10 degrees.[221,234] Other reported complications of the procedure include excessive anterior tightening with posterior glenohumeral subluxation, damage to the biceps tendon, and early joint arthrosis.[1,77,86]

Open Bony Procedures for Anterior Instability

In addition to the soft tissue techniques, a number of different bony procedures have been described to treat patients with anterior glenohumeral instability. Defects greater than 30% of the glenoid surface may be associated with persistent instability.[114,184] Therefore, if these defects are present, they can be addressed by placing a piece of bone on the glenoid neck in order to provide an additional surface to interact against the humeral head and to act as a buttress against anterior dislocation. Even without a glenoid bone defect, however, surgeons have utilized various bony procedures to stabilize the glenohumeral joint with varying degrees of success.

Because of its nearby location, the coracoid process has been utilized in two of the more commonly performed bony procedures. The first is the Bristow procedure in which the tip of the coracoid process, with the conjoined tendons attached, is transferred through a split in the subscapularis muscle and fixed onto the anterior inferior glenoid rim just outside the capsule.[90] A subsequent modification of the procedure transfers the coracoid process over the superior border of the subscapularis tendon.[267] Usually, the rim of the glenoid is exposed and decorticated in order to enhance bony union between the cut surface of the coracoid process and the glenoid rim. Because of the remaining capsule, however, some portion of the transferred bone will not directly interact with the exposed glenoid rim. Patient satisfaction rate at early and midterm follow up after this procedure has been reported to be between 82% and 97%.[10,58,267] Recurrent dislocations after the procedure were very uncommon, with the reported incidence between 0% and 6%.[58,96,156,267] If episodes of subluxations are also included, however, the rate of recurrent instability is much higher at 8.5% to 21%.[10,58,96,267] With an extended long-term follow up of 26 years, one study has demonstrated that both patient satisfaction and joint stability deteriorated to 70% and 85%, respectively.[245] In addition, the Bristow procedure is also associated with high rates of complications that include loss of external rotation, problems related to the screw fixation, residual pain, and graft nonunion.[58,267] In fact, the rate of screw-related complications was reported to be as high as 24% in one study.[194] Because of these concerns, some authors have recommended that the Bristow procedure not be performed for routine anterior stabilization of the shoulder.[245,293]

Another bony procedure that utilizes the coracoid process is the Latarjet procedure. In comparison with the Bristow procedure, a significantly larger portion of the coracoid process is transferred to the neck of the glenoid. The bone is placed in an extracapsular position, laid on its side, and fixed to the scapula with screws. At a long-term follow-up evaluation, good to excellent clinical results were found in 88% to 93% of the patients who were treated with this procedure.[4,252] Rates of recurrent instability, including both subluxation and dislocation, have been reported to be between 2% to 10%.[4,100] Ninety-eight percent patient satisfaction has been described at 15-year follow-up.[102] Despite these clinical results, however, the procedure is also associated with the subsequent development of joint arthrosis. Although the majority of the changes were classified as mild, glenohumeral arthrosis was reported in 30% to 71% of the patients.[4,100,101] In one study, moderate to severe arthrosis was described in 14% of patients with a Latarjet procedure at 15-year follow-up. [101]

Another of the more commonly used bony procedures is the Eden-Hybbinette procedure.[50,109] The original description as well as the modification of the procedure places an iliac crest bone graft on the anterior aspect of the glenoid. Therefore, the humeral head must translate further to dislocate. Long-term studies of this procedure have shown good to excellent results in 75% to 85% of the patients.[27,217,218] Reported rates of recurrent dislocations have been mixed, with some authors reporting only 4% and others reporting up to 33%.[27,138,218] Unfortunately, after long-term follow-up evaluation in excess of 15 years, several authors have reported joint arthrosis in 47% to 89% of the patients.[217,218] Thus the Eden-Hybbinette procedure has lost much of its popularity as a primary procedure for routine anterior shoulder stabilization.

In contrast to these procedures that place the bone outside the joint, another option is to place the bone graft within the joint. Intra-articular bone grafts are typically inserted to restore, rather than to enlarge, the glenoid surface. Although individual techniques can vary, most surgeons place the bone against decorticated glenoid neck and then fix the graft using several metallic screws. The fixed graft is subsequently contoured to match the surface of the native glenoid. Finally, the anterior capsule and the subscapularis tendon are restored to their anatomic position. A limited series of patients treated in this fashion demonstrated good results with absence of apprehension and return to preinjury level of athletic activities. The authors noted that intra-articular placement of grafts improved the likelihood of graft union as well as allowing improved matching of the glenoid surface.[278] Hence, although long-term clinical data are still lacking, this technique may provide a promising alternative to addressing symptomatic glenoid bony defects.

Operative Treatment for Posterior Instability

Indications

Isolated posterior instability is relatively rare and thought to comprise 2% to 12% of all shoulder instability cases.[21,24] As such, the clinical history and examination must be thoroughly reviewed in order to ensure that the instability is isolated to the posterior direction only. For these patients, indications for surgery include failure of nonoperative management, open dislocations, irreducible dislocations, and unstable reductions. In some patients, traumatic posterior dislocations may be associated with a large bony defect in either the glenoid or the anteromedial humeral head (reverse Hill-Sachs lesion). With these defects, even after a concentric reduction is obtained, joint stability may be compromised enough to warrant operative management.

Once the decision to proceed with an operation has been established, there are multiple available surgical options. Surgical stabilization may be performed arthroscopically, through an open anterior approach, or through an open posterior approach. To date, no single approach or technique has been associated with conclusively superior results. As such, the choice of any specific procedure should be based on patient expectations as well as surgeon-related factors such as familiarity, technical expertise, and available equipment and personnel.

Arthroscopic Procedures for Posterior Instability

The procedure starts with a diagnostic arthroscopy to identify and document any structural defects. Although specific protocols may vary among surgeons, most utilize an anterior portal for the arthroscope and two posterior portals for the instruments. If a posterior capsulolabral detachment is identified, it should be mobilized and reattached to the posterior glenoid rim. Recently use of suture anchors has become the technique of choice for capsulolabral reattachment. Unlike anterior instability, however, a posterior capsulolabral detachment is a much less common finding. For posterior instability, capsular redundancy seems to play a more critical role. As such, this redundancy should be addressed by performing arthroscopic posterior capsulorrhaphy.[21]

Using this arthroscopic technique, authors have reported good to excellent results in 86% to 96% of the patients at short- to midterm follow up.[131,281,288] Rates of recurrent instability in these studies have ranged from 0% to 12%.[21,24,75,131,216,281] One recent study confirmed that frank posterior dislocations after surgery were very rare; however, clinically significant posterior subluxations may be more common. In this study 11% of the patients failed clinical stability tests and 8% pursued revision surgery for persisting pain, instability, or decreased function.[24]

Similar to anterior and multidirectional instability, some authors have recommended the use of thermal capsulorrhaphy to reduce posterior capsular redundancy. As mentioned previously, however, this technology may be associated with unacceptable risks for clinical failures and complications, frequently resulting in persisting pain, instability, and damaged capsular tissue. As such, routine use of this technique as a primary stabilizing procedure has fallen into disfavor.

Open Anterior Procedures for Posterior Instability

In selective patients with atraumatic glenohumeral instability whose primary complaint is in the posterior direction, an anterior approach for posterior shoulder stabilization has been described.[285,286] This procedure is performed in a manner similar to the inferior capsular shift procedure for patients with multidirectional instability. The anterior deltopectoral approach is utilized to expose the shoulder. After releasing the subscapularis tendon and isolating the capsule, the capsule is released from the humeral neck as far posteriorly as possible. The capsule is then advanced anteriorly and superiorly in order to remove the redundancy in the anterior, inferior, and posteroinferior aspects of the joint. In addition to the capsular imbrication, the anterior

approach also provides an opportunity to address the concomitant laxity in the rotator interval. In this fashion, humeral head translation is reduced in all directions. At a midterm follow up of 5 years, a case series reported good to excellent results in 9 of the 10 patients who were treated with this technique.[285]

Following a traumatic posterior dislocation, a large bony defect in the anterior aspect of the humeral head (also known as the reverse Hill-Sachs lesion) may be present. If the defect is large, it may engage the posterior glenoid rim during internal rotation, resulting in recurrent episodes of instability. Therefore although an anatomic joint reduction can be initially obtained, stable and congruent motion may not be maintained. For these patients, the bony defect is the primary pathology and it can be addressed with the McLaughlin procedure (Fig. 38-35A). The original description of the procedure includes an anterior approach with release of the subscapularis tendon from the lesser tuberosity. The released tendon is then transferred into the bony lesion to fill the defect and to prevent the humeral head from engaging the posterior glenoid rim.[170] A modification of this procedure, described by Neer (Fig. 38-35B), does not release the subscapularis tendon. Rather, the lesser tuberosity is osteotomized with the attached tendon so that it can be transferred into the bony defect.[60,286] Although similarly filling the defect, this modification creates a more stable construct with improved potential for healing. Although only a few studies

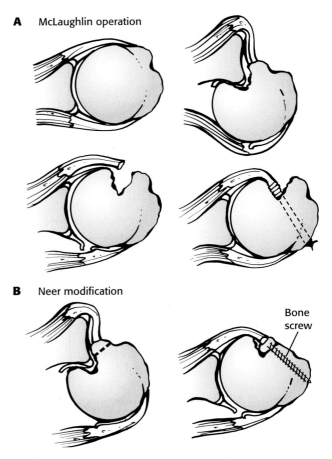

FIGURE 38-35 A. The McLaughlin operation. In the presence of a large anterior humeral head lesion, the subscapularis tendon can be transferred into the defect. **B.** A subsequent modification by Neer transfers the lesser tuberosity with the attached subscapularis tendon.

have been published, authors have reported stable shoulders with congruent motion in the majority of patients who were treated with this operation.[60,170]

Open Posterior Procedures for Posterior Instability

For patients with unidirectional posterior instability or for those with multidirectional instability whose primary symptoms are in the posterior direction, a posterior approach to the shoulder can be utilized. Upon exposure of the joint, if a clear capsulolabral detachment is present, it should be repaired. In addition, posterior capsular redundancy is addressed by performing posterior capsulorrhaphy in a manner similar to anterior capsulorrhaphy. For these procedures meticulous surgical technique must be utilized, because the posterior capsule is often very thin and fragile.

Some authors advocate posterior capsulorrhaphy using metallic staples for fixation. According to one series, however, unsatisfactory results were reported in 9 of the 20 (45%) patients.[263] The authors suggested that the high rate of failures may be related to general ligamentous laxity and unrecognized multidirectional instability.[263] Regardless, the use of a staple has been abandoned in favor of suture capsulorrhaphy.[263] Results following posterior suture capsulorrhaphy are more encouraging. Studies have reported good to excellent results in 80% to 92% of the patients who were treated with this procedure. Rates of recurrent instability have been reported to be between 11% and 23% in these studies.[16,64,227]

Several authors have suggested that patients with recurrent posterior instability may possess excessive glenoid retroversion, and that this retroversion may be responsible for the high rates of surgical failures.[64,106,132,287] If excessive retroversion (e.g., greater than 30 degrees) does exist, normal glenoid version can be restored by performing a posterior glenoid osteotomy. This procedure utilizes a similar surgical approach as described above. After exposing the joint, an opening wedge osteotomy is performed at the posterior scapular neck. The opening wedge can be stabilized with a bone graft from either the iliac crest or the posterior acromion. Surgical exposure of the scapular neck must be performed with caution as the suprascapular nerve lies in close proximity and is susceptible to injury during the procedure.

Case reports of glenoid osteotomy have mostly produced satisfactory results.[15, 287] A recent report of 32 patients who were treated with this procedure also noted good to excellent results in 82% of the patients.[76] Rates of recurrent instability after the procedure have been reported to be between 12% and 17%.[76,85] Unfortunately, however, this procedure is also associated with a variety of complications including anterior subluxation, coracoid impingement, glenohumeral arthrosis, and intra-articular glenoid fracture.[64,70,76,85] Therefore some authors have suggested that the procedure be performed only in patients whose glenoid shows significant retroversion in excess of 30 degrees.[286]

Operative Treatment for Multidirectional Instability

Indications

Multidirectional instability of the shoulder is often a difficult diagnosis to establish. In many instances, patients exhibit signs of generalized ligamentous laxity and the onset of their shoulder symptoms are not preceded by significant trauma. In other instances, however, patients exhibit signs of generalized ligamentous laxity but sustain an injury that produces unidirectional instability. As such, it is difficult to determine whether these patients should be categorized and treated in a manner similar to unidirectional or multidirectional instability. These nuances in establishing a clear diagnosis have contributed to the lack of a true consensus for surgical management of these patients.

Most surgeons do agree, however, that the primary treatment for patients with atraumatic multidirectional instability should be nonoperative, with a primary focus on shoulder rehabilitation. Strengthening of the dynamic shoulder stabilizers has the potential to compensate for the generalized laxity of the static shoulder stabilizers. Operative treatment for these patients is indicated only when nonoperative management has been unsuccessful. Although the specific indications may vary among surgeons, operative management is generally recommended for patients who suffer from continued pain and/or disability despite participation in a structured physical rehabilitation program for greater than 3 to 6 months.

Once the decision for an operative stabilization has been established, the procedure may be performed arthroscopically or as an open procedure. For open procedures, some surgeons preferentially utilize an anterior approach, whereas others utilize either an anterior or a posterior approach based on the primary direction of instability. The "gold standard" for surgical management of multidirectional instability has been the open stabilization. With recent technological advances, results after arthroscopic stabilizations are clearly improving. A recent study of arthroscopic capsulorrhaphy demonstrated a fairly low rate of instability at 10.5%.[160] Nevertheless, to date, long-term outcome studies after arthroscopic techniques are still lacking and have yet to replicate those of open surgery (Table 38-4).*

Arthroscopic Procedures for Multidirectional Instability

After performing an examination under anesthesia to confirm the diagnosis, a diagnostic arthroscopy is performed to document the pathology. In the vast majority of patients with atraumatic multidirectional instability, a clear capsulolabral detachment is not present. The most common finding is the presence of redundant capsule in the anterior, inferior, and posterior aspects of the joint, all of which must be addressed. For arthroscopic capsulorrhaphy in the anterior region, the arthroscope is typically placed through a posterior portal whereas the instruments and the sutures are managed through anterior portals. In contrast, for posterior capsulorrhaphy, the arthroscope is placed through the anterior portal whereas the instruments and the sutures are managed through posterior portals. Again, the capsulorrhaphy typically starts in the inferiormost aspect of the joint and progresses superiorly until the redundancy in the capsule has been sufficiently removed.

According to one study, arthroscopic capsulorrhaphy using transglenoid suture technique has been associated with 88% good to excellent results and 12% recurrent instability.[271] Subsequently, surgeons have slightly modified the technique to perform the entire capsulorrhaphy using suture tying techniques. With a relatively short follow up of approximately 3 years, two studies have reported good to excellent results in 94% to 95%

*References 9,35,42,68,83,169,187,213.

TABLE 38-4	Results after Arthroscopic and Open Stabilizations for Multidirectional Instability			
Author	No. Shoulders	Follow-up	Recurrent Instability	Successful Outcome
Arthroscopic Stabilization				
McIntyre et al., 1997	19	34 mo	5%	95%
Treacy et al., 1999	25	60 mo	12%	88%
Gartsman et al., 2001	47	35 mo	2%	94%
Open Stabilization				
Neer & Foster, 1980	40	a	3%	97%
Cooper & Brems, 1992	43	39 mos	9%	91%
Hamada et al., 1999	34	100 mos	26%	85%
Bak et al., 2000	26	54 mos	8%	92%
Pollock et al., 2000	49	61 mos	4%	94%
Choi & Ogilvie-Harris, 2002	53	42 mo	9%	89%

a8 shoulders, <12 mos; 15 shoulders, 12–24 mos; 17 shoulders, >24 mos

of the patients. In addition, they reported very low rates of recurrent instability at 2% to 5%.[68,169] Mid- and long-term follow-up studies of this technique, however, are still lacking. Rotator interval closure may be added to capsular plication in the setting of multidirectional instability in order to further limit humeral head translation.

Another arthroscopic technique that has been utilized to treat patients with multidirectional instability is thermal capsulorrhaphy. As noted in the previous sections, outcomes after this procedure have been mixed. Various studies have reported recurrent instability in 19% to 47% of the patients.[43,56,61,179] In addition to these high rates of recurrent instability, this procedure has also been associated with high rates of complications. Therefore, routine use of this technique for patients with multidirectional instability has fallen into disfavor.

Open Procedures for Multidirectional Instability

Some authors treat all patients with multidirectional instability through an open anterior approach. This procedure is performed in a manner similar to open anterior capsulolabral reconstruction, as described in the previous section. The primary difference, however, is the focus on the inferior aspect of the shoulder capsule. As such, inferior capsular redundancy must be addressed by first releasing the capsule from the humeral neck all the way to the posterior inferior quadrant of the joint. The released capsule is then advanced anteriorly and superiorly to remove the global capsular redundancy. The original description of this inferior capsular shift procedure was reported by Neer et al.[187] In their preliminary series, satisfactory results were reported in 39 of the 40 patients, with only one patient developing recurrent instability. Several subsequent studies have reported comparable results with good to excellent results in over 90% and recurrent instability in less than 10% of the patients.[9,42] In one report, the authors also noted that the failures occurred early and that the overall outcomes did not deteriorate over time.[42] Biomechanical analysis of the inferior capsular shift demonstrated that glenohumeral mechanics and contact pressures did not change significantly, compared with normal

joints.[275,280] Therefore, even with long-term follow-up, development of glenohumeral arthrosis will hopefully remain minimal.

Rather than utilizing an anterior approach in all patients, some surgeons recommend approaching the shoulder from the direction of primary instability. As such, if a patient exhibits signs of multidirectional instability but has a primary complaint of posterior instability, a posterior approach is suggested. A posterior capsular shift procedure is performed as described previously. Again, particular attention should be given to the inferior capsule in order to remove the global capsular redundancy. Utilizing either an anterior or a posterior approach based on the direction of primary instability, authors have reported good to excellent results in 85% to 94% of the patients.[35,83,213] Although the rate of recurrent instability was relatively low in two of these studies (4% to 9%), one study reported recurrent instability in 26% of the patients.[83] These authors also showed that the recurrent instability tended to occur early and that the successful results were maintained over time.[83]

AUTHORS' PREFERRED TREATMENT

Nonoperative Treatment

Closed Reduction Techniques for Acute Dislocation

Acute shoulder dislocations must be managed emergently. After adequate assessment is completed, closed reduction of the shoulder is attempted. In order to obtain muscle relaxation and pain control, we prefer the use of intra-articular lidocaine injection. If needed, light supplemental intravenous sedation can also be given. Although many different reduction techniques can be used, our initial technique of choice is the traction–countertraction method as described previously (see Fig. 38-29B). The maneuver is performed with slow and sustained traction. Sudden and forceful manipulations must be avoided because they can lead to additional injuries. Typically, a successful reduction is accompanied by a "clunk" sensation. Once completed, closed reduction is confirmed with postreduction radiographs.

If the initial attempt of closed reduction is unsuccessful, the patient is re-examined to determine the degree of muscle relaxation. If adequate muscle relaxation can be obtained, another closed reduction may be attempted. If the second reduction is still unsuccessful or if adequate muscle relaxation cannot be ensured, the patient will require general anesthesia in the operating room for either closed or open reduction.

If a qualified person observes the shoulder dislocation outside a clinical facility, it may be unclear whether the closed reduction should be attempted immediately or wait until a formal evaluation can be completed. Thus, for example, an orthopaedic surgeon who is on "the field" supervising a high level athletic competition may witness a player who sustains a shoulder dislocation. In this situation, after initial assessment and examination, the surgeon may consider immediate closed reduction. Possible advantages of immediate reduction include the relative ease of reduction prior to onset of muscle spasms, immediate relief of pain, and relief of pressure on the adjacent neurovascular structures. In contrast, possible disadvantages of immediate reduction include suboptimal assistance, potential damage to the neurovascular structures during the reduction maneuver, and displacement of unrecognized fractures. Without necessary personnel and equipment, it would be difficult to address any complications caused by improper reduction techniques. Therefore, if a clinical facility is readily available, a thorough evaluation of the injury, including radiographs, should be completed first. Attempts at a closed shoulder reduction can then be performed in a controlled environment with adequate analgesia. Emergent attempts of closed reduction on "the field" should only be considered in situations when transfer to a clinical facility is not readily available and/or the viability of the upper extremity is threatened by a vascular injury.

Definitive Nonoperative Treatment

Definitive nonoperative treatment is recommended for the following patients: (i) all patients who sustained a first time traumatic dislocation regardless of age, (ii) patients older than 40 years of age with recurrent instability, (iii) all patients who are suffering from atraumatic instability. In young and/or active patients with traumatic dislocations, however, the high likelihood of developing recurrent instability is thoroughly discussed. In addition, for older patients, rotator cuff tendon function is carefully examined to identify the possibility of an acute tear. If needed, an MRI is obtained to document the status of the rotator cuff tendons.

For patients younger than 30 years of age, the shoulder is immobilized for approximately 3 weeks. For patients between 30 and 40 years of age, the shoulder is immobilized for 1 to 2 weeks. For patient older than 40 years of age, the shoulder is immobilized for only 1 week. We believe that prolonged immobilization in the elderly patients should be avoided as it can readily lead to shoulder stiffness. For most patients, a simple sling is utilized for immobilization. For those with isolated posterior instability, the arm in placed in a "gunslinger" type of orthosis that places the arm in neutral rotation and 20 degrees of abduction. Patients are allowed to remove the immobilization for hygiene purposes. In addition, they are also allowed to perform simple and

nonstressful waist level activities such as writing and typing. For patients with atraumatic instability, immobilization is often not required unless they are experiencing significant pain. If so, their shoulders are immobilized in a similar pattern.

After this initial phase, patients are instructed to avoid positions that place their shoulders at risk for instability. As such, patients with anterior instability should limit external rotation to less than 30 degrees and abduction to less than 60 degrees. For patients with posterior instability, they are instructed avoid flexion greater than 60 degrees and internal rotation greater than 30 degrees. They are also specifically instructed to avoid cross body adduction. These restrictions are gradually decreased to provide additional motion over the course of 6 to 9 weeks. Typically, full range of motion is allowed by 3 months.

In addition to these restrictions, a regimen of strengthening exercises is instituted. Although supervised physical therapy may be useful, it must be stressed to patients that they take responsibility for their own rehabilitation and that the exercises are performed daily. During the rehabilitation phase, patients are instructed to avoid any sporting or other high-risk activities. Gradually, as they gain strength and stability in the shoulder, patients can return to low-demand recreational activities. They should not, however, return to high impact activities until adequate conditioning of the shoulder musculature is restored. For most patients, this will require at least 6 months of rehabilitation.

Operative Treatment for Anterior Instability

Indications

Surgical stabilization is indicated for those patients whose instability symptoms have become a disability despite adequate nonoperative therapy. In selected young patients with a high functional demand of the shoulder, immediate surgical stabilization may be considered without a course of nonoperative treatment because they possess a high risk of recurrent instability. Before the operative procedure, a complete examination under anesthesia is performed to confirm both the direction and the degree of the instability. By performing the sulcus test with the shoulder in external rotation, the integrity of the rotator interval is also examined. For most patients we prefer arthroscopic techniques for anterior stabilization of the shoulder. Open procedures are generally reserved for patients who have undergone previous shoulder surgery, those with a large bony defect in either the glenoid or the humeral head, and those with a HAGL lesion.

Arthroscopic Procedures

Arthroscopic stabilization begins with a complete examination of the joint. If there is a glenoid bony defect greater than 25% of the surface, the procedure is immediately converted to an open procedure. In addition, an open procedure is also preferred if the humeral head defect is large enough to clearly engage the anterior glenoid rim with abduction and external rotation. After examination of the joint, two anterior portals are established in the rotator interval. One portal is created immediately superior to the subscapularis tendon, whereas the other is placed at the superior edge of the rotator interval. These portals are used interchangeably for instruments and sutures. If these portals do not provide sufficient access to the inferior capsule, an accessory posterior inferior portal is also created.

At this point, the anterior inferior labrum is identified. In most patients with traumatic instability, the capsulolabral complex is typically detached and displaced medially. The complex must be released and mobilized from the glenoid neck until it can be easily advanced back onto its anatomic position on the anterior inferior glenoid rim. A suture anchor is then inserted onto the glenoid rim. Typically, the stabilization begins in the inferior portion of the joint and progress superiorly. In rare cases, the most inferior suture anchor cannot be adequately placed through the inferior portal. If so, a separate stab incision should be placed on the skin so that the anchor can be passed through the subscapularis tendon. Caution must be taken, however, to ensure that no instruments enter the joint inferior to the subscapularis tendon since the nearby axillary nerve may be injured. After the anchor has been placed, one of the suture ends is passed through the capsulolabral complex. For most patients capsular redundancy can be addressed simultaneously by grasping a portion of the capsule with the same suture. The sutures are then tied using various arthroscopic knot tying techniques. This process is repeated until the entire capsulolabral complex is restored onto its anatomic position on the glenoid rim. If preoperative examination is consistent with a rotator interval laxity (i.e., positive sulcus sign compared with contralateral shoulder with the arm in adduction and external rotation) and if there is excessive glenohumeral translation after the arthroscopic Bankart procedure, an arthroscopic rotator interval closure is then performed. In our experience, the sutures should be placed at least one centimeter lateral to the glenoid rim in order to avoid excessive tethering of the coracohumeral ligament which may, in turn, limit external rotation.

Open Procedures

For open stabilizations, the procedure is performed through the deltopectoral interval as described. Whenever the anatomy is difficult to decipher, the coracoid process is used as the defining landmark. It is termed the "lighthouse" of the anterior shoulder, and provides a palpable guide to the deltopectoral interval as well as the coracoacromial arch. The coracoid process is also the origin for the conjoined tendon of the coracobrachialis and the short head of the biceps muscles. The brachial plexus and the major vessels to the upper extremity lie immediately medial to this structure. As such, surgical exploration of the shoulder joint should remain lateral to the coracoid process and the conjoined tendon. After adequate exposure is achieved, additional dissection must be performed to isolate the glenohumeral capsule and the joint.

Our open procedure of choice is a capsulolabral reconstruction. This is carried out by first developing the interval between the subscapularis and the anterior capsule. This interval may be easier to define and develop near the glenoid, where the subscapularis is mostly muscular. The subscapularis tendon is then released near its insertion on the lesser tuberosity. An adequate stump of the tendon must be maintained laterally for a tendon to tendon repair at the end of the procedure. After isolation of the anterior capsule, a vertical incision is made laterally near the humeral head 5 to 7 millimeters medial to the site of subscapularis tenotomy. A horizontal incision is then created to expose the joint. In this fashion, a "T"-shaped incision is created on the capsule (see Fig. 38-33). The joint is then examined to identify the capsulolabral pathology. The displaced capsulolabral complex is mobilized and reattached to its anatomic position using suture anchors. Subsequently, the capsule is imbricated and closed. Redundancy in the capsule is removed during this imbrication. If a HAGL lesion is present, the repair can be completed at this stage as well. Typically, the shoulder is maintained in 45 degrees of abduction and 45 degrees of external rotation while the capsular repair is being performed. The subscapularis tendon is then repaired anatomically.

In patients with a substantial glenoid defect greater than 25%, our procedure of choice is to utilize an iliac crest bone graft to fill the defect (Fig. 38-36). We prefer an intracapsular graft placement in order to accurately fill the defect and to contour the surface appropriately. Appropriate sizing of the graft is important since an inappropriately large graft will prevent a complete closure of the capsule. The graft is then fixed to the scapula using metallic screws. Prior to final tightening of the screws, however, a suture is placed around each of the screw heads. These sutures are subsequently used to attach the capsulolabral complex onto the graft. Intraoperative fluoroscopy can be quite useful in assessing the length and the location of the screws. After fixation of the graft and imbrication of the capsule, the subscapularis tendon is repaired anatomically. Because of pliability of its muscle fibers, anatomic closure of the subscapularis tendon around the graft is typically not difficult.

Postoperative Care

After surgical stabilization for anterior instability, either arthroscopic or open, the involved shoulder is immobilized for approximately 4 to 6 weeks in a simple sling. Patients are allowed to remove the sling during this period to perform passive motion exercises and for hygiene purposes. The limits of passive motion may vary depending on the stability of the repair. Immediately after the procedure, however, flexion and external rotation are typically limited to 90 and 20 degrees, respectively. These limits are gradually increased to gain near full motion by 8 to 10 weeks. When the period of immobilization is completed, active motion is gradually instituted. Resistive strengthening exercises can be started by 10 to 12 weeks after the procedure. Patients are typically allowed full use of their shoulder by 6 months after the procedure; however, participation in high demand activities and contact sports may be delayed up to 9 months.

Operative Treatment for Posterior Instability

Indications

Unidirectional posterior instability is a relatively infrequent problem. As such, the diagnosis must be clearly established prior to initiating a specific treatment plan. Our indications for surgical stabilization include failure of nonoperative therapy, an unstable or incongruent reduction, and open dislocations. For all patients undergoing operative management, following induction of anesthesia, an examination must be performed to confirm the diagnosis of unidirectional posterior instability.

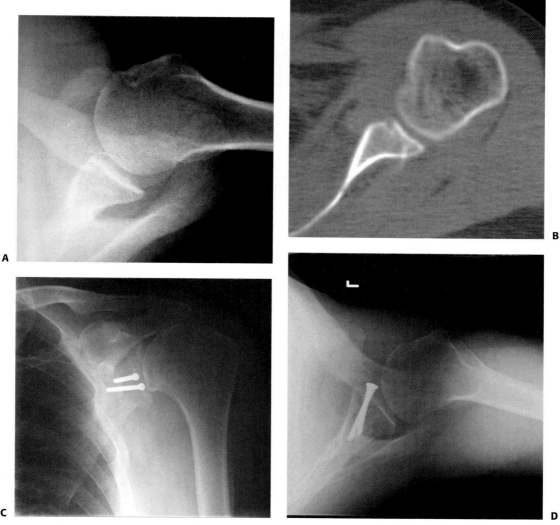

FIGURE 38-36 Radiographs of a patient with recurrent anterior shoulder instability caused by a glenoid rim defect. Axillary view radiograph **(A)** and CT-scan image **(B)** reveal an osseous defect in the anterior glenoid rim. Using a standard delto-pectoral approach, the defect was identified and filled with a tricortical iliac crest bone graft. Postoperative radiographs **(C,D)** show that the graft, fixed with two screws, is coplanar with the native glenoid.

Arthroscopic Procedures

For patients without sufficient bony defects, our preferred method of stabilization is arthroscopic posterior capsulorrhaphy. A diagnostic arthroscopy is first performed to document the structural defects. To gain better visualization of the posterior structures, the arthroscope is placed through an anterior portal. Typically, two portals are established on the posterior aspect of the shoulder for instruments and suture management. If a posterior capsulolabral detachment is identified, the displaced labrum is released and mobilized. After mobilization, it is reattached to its anatomic site on the glenoid rim using suture anchors. Sutures from these anchors are also passed through the capsule to perform a capsular plication. If a capsulolabral detachment is not present, an isolated capsular plication is performed using monofilament sutures. To augment the plication, these sutures are typically passed through the labrum for enhanced fixation.

Open Procedures

In revision surgical cases, or if arthroscopic capsulorrhaphy cannot be adequately performed, we prefer open posterior capsulorrhaphy using a posterior approach. For this procedure, the patient is placed in a lateral decubitus position. The affected shoulder is tilted slightly anteriorly so that clear visualization of the posterior shoulder is possible. After the skin incision, we typically split the deltoid muscle in line with its fibers. Sometimes, in patients whose deltoid muscle contains significant bulk and resting tone, adequate exposure of the shoulder may not be possible by simply splitting the muscle. In these rare circumstances, the posterior deltoid is released from its origin on the acromion, and then reattached at the end of the procedure using bone tunnels. Upon visualization of the rotator cuff tendons, the infraspinatus tendon is incised approximately 1 centimeter lateral to its musculotendinous junction. In this fashion subsequent repair can be performed through the tendinous portion, and its insertion at the greater tuberosity can be spared. The infraspinatus must be reflected with caution as the underlying capsule can be very thin and friable. The capsule is then incised vertically the midpoint between the humeral head and the glenoid rim. The incision must be extended in order to include the inferior aspect of the capsule. The medial capsular flap is then shifted laterally and superiorly, and imbricated to reduce any redundancy. At this point, if the infraspinatus tendon is felt to be excessively loose, it can also be slightly shortened by imbricating upon itself. Typically, capsular plication and infraspinatus repair are performed with the shoulder in neutral rotation.

We consider glenoid osteotomy only for patients with excessive glenoid retroversion. Since the procedure is associated with a high rate of complication, we often reserve its use for patients who have previously undergone a posterior capsulorrhaphy and failed. As such, glenoid osteotomy is considered for patients who have (i) glenoid retroversion greater than 20 degrees, (ii) failed extended and continuous nonoperative rehabilitation, and (iii) recurrent instability after previous posterior capsulorrhaphy. For patients who meet these criteria, computed tomography is routinely obtained for preoperative planning. The correction necessary to achieve neutral glenoid version is determined from the

images. Patient positioning and surgical procedure is performed as described by Rockwood and colleagues (Fig. 38-37).[286] Before performing the osteotomy, a straight blunt instrument is inserted into the joint so that it rests on the anterior and posterior glenoid rim. With the instrument held steady, the osteotomy is made parallel to this instrument approximately 8 to 10 millimeters medial to the glenoid rim. The initial cut of the osteotomy can be made with an osteotome or with an oscillating saw. Once the anterior cortex is engaged, an osteotome is used to complete the cut and the osteotomy site is opened to the desired correction. To stabilize the osteotomy site, we utilize a bone graft from the posterior corner of the acromion. Typically, insertion of the graft stabilizes the osteotomy, and the construct does not require additional fixation. After the osteotomy has been completed, a posterior capsulorrhaphy is also performed.

Postoperative Care

Upon completion of the surgical stabilization, patients are immobilized in an orthosis with the arm in neutral rotation for approximately 6 weeks. Patients who underwent a soft tissue procedure are allowed to remove the immobilization during this period for hygiene purposes and for daily passive motion exercises. They are instructed to avoid internal rotation beyond the neutral position. Patients who underwent

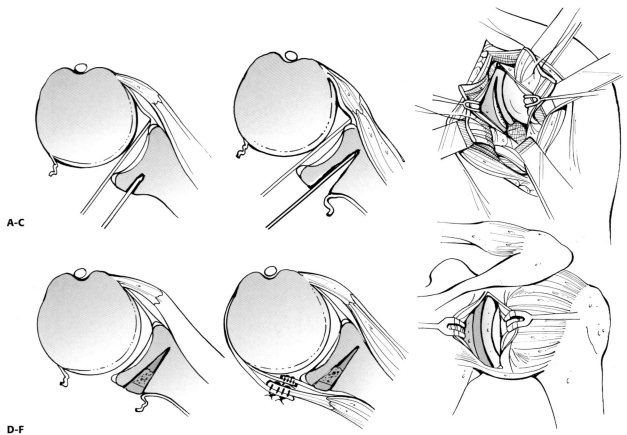

A-C

D-F

FIGURE 38-37 Posterior glenoid osteotomy. **A.** An osteotome is placed in the joint to use as a parallel guide. A second osteotome is then used to begin the osteotomy. **B.** The osteotome is advanced approximately 90% the distance across the glenoid, being sure to leave an anterior hinge of bone. **C.** The osteotome is removed. **D.** The osteotomy is then bone grafted to maintain the desired change in version. **E.** The posterior capsule and infraspinatus are repaired. **F.** Note the change in version which is maintained by the bone graft.

a bony procedure, however, are only allowed to remove their immobilization for personal hygiene and do not start passive motion exercises until 3 to 4 weeks after the procedure. The limits of passive motion may vary depending on the stability of the repair and/or construct. Immediately after the procedure, however, flexion and internal rotation are typically limited to 60 degrees and neutral, respectively. These limits are gradually increased to gain near full motion by 8 to 10 weeks. When immobilization is discontinued, active motion is gradually instituted. Active strengthening exercises are started by 10 to 12 weeks after the procedure. Patients are typically allowed to use their shoulder without restrictions by 6 to 8 months after the procedure; however, participation in high-demand activities and contact sports is prevented for at least 9 months in most patients.

Operative Treatment for Multidirectional Instability

Indications

For all patients with multidirectional instability, we stress the importance of nonoperative management with a structured and supervised rehabilitation program. Surgical stabilization is only considered if the patient has been compliant with the program for greater than 6 months and continues to be symptomatic. An examination under anesthesia is first performed to confirm the direction and degree of instability.

Open Procedures

Our preferred method of surgical stabilization is an open inferior capsular shift utilizing an anterior approach. After reflecting the subscapularis tendon from the underlying capsule, a horizontal capsulotomy is performed. Then, the capsule is incised vertically near its insertion on the humeral head. The capsule is released inferiorly along the humeral neck to the posterior inferior quadrant. Often, traction sutures are used to maintain tension on the capsule as it is being released. The capsule is then mobilized superiorly and laterally as to remove global capsular redundancy. The superior capsular flap is advanced inferiorly to place additional tension on the inferior capsule. The capsular advancement should be performed with the shoulder held at approximately 30 degrees of abduction and 30 degrees of external rotation. The subscapularis tendon is then repaired anatomically. Finally, the rotator interval is closed to further stabilize the joint. In our experience, sutures for rotator interval closure should be placed at least 1 centimeter lateral to the glenoid rim. Otherwise, the coracohumeral ligament may be tethered by the suture and limit external rotation.

Postoperative Care

Following surgical stabilization, the involved shoulder is immobilized in an orthosis in neutral rotation and 20 degrees of abduction for approximately 6 weeks. Patients are allowed to remove the immobilization during this period for hygiene purposes. Passive motion is instituted at 3 weeks after the surgery. The limits of motion may vary depending on the stability of the repair. Shortly after the procedure, however, flexion, external rotation, and internal rotation are typically limited to 90, 30, and 10 degrees, respectively. These limits are gradually increased to gain near full motion by 8 to 10

weeks. Upon removal of immobilization, active motion is instituted. Active strengthening exercises may be started by 10 to 12 weeks after the procedure. Patients are typically allowed full use of their shoulder by 6 months after the procedure; however, participation in high-demand activities and contact sports is prevented for at least 9 months in most patients.

Pearls and Pitfalls

Many recent studies have provided valuable information on the evaluation and treatment of glenohumeral instability. As such, management of patients with shoulder instability is continuing to evolve. Despite these changes, however, certain principles in the management of shoulder instability have remained constant and form the foundation for approaching this clinical problem. In our experience, the following "pearls and pitfalls" have been useful reminders to ensure appropriate evaluation and treatment of shoulder instability.

- When evaluating patients with acute dislocations, a complete set of radiographs must be obtained and evaluated. These radiographs should include orthogonal views of the joint in order to clearly identify the location of the humeral head.
- All closed reduction techniques should utilize slow, gentle, and sustained maneuvers. Any sudden and forceful manipulations can lead to additional injuries to the shoulder girdle.
- Both the motor and the sensory component of the axillary nerve function must be tested and documented. Intact sensation in the lateral aspect of the shoulder does not guarantee intact axillary nerve function.
- All patients with shoulder instability should be questioned regarding voluntary instability as this condition may have significant implications in the overall treatment plan and the anticipated outcome.
- All patients who sustained a traumatic shoulder dislocation should be carefully examined for a rotator cuff tear. This is especially important for patients older than 40 years of age, because the incidence of a concomitant rotator cuff tear is alarmingly high in this population. If the clinical examination is unclear, an MRI should be obtained to document clearly the status of the rotator cuff tendons.
- Initial treatment for patients with atraumatic multidirectional instability should focus primarily on physical rehabilitation. By strengthening the dynamic stabilizers, it should be possible to overcome the inherent glenohumeral joint laxity and obtain a stable shoulder.
- It is crucial to identify all the pathological defects that are associated with the instability. In addition to a detailed physical examination, imaging modalities such as MR-arthrogram are extremely helpful to clearly delineate the cause of instability.
- Prior to starting any surgical procedure, an examination under anesthesia should be performed to confirm the clinical diagnosis and document the direction and degree of instability.
- Surgical stabilization techniques should address all the underlying pathoanatomy responsible for the instability. If the structural defects are not adequately addressed, recurrent instability may occur.
- Although patients who underwent arthroscopic procedures may experience decreased pain and morbidity in the early post-operative period, healing of their repaired tissues is not likely to be substantially different than their counterparts who underwent open procedures. As such, arthroscopic procedures do not necessarily justify early or condensed rehabilitation.

- An appropriate postoperative protocol is crucial to the overall outcome. Initial periods of immobilization and protection should precede any aggressive rehabilitation. In addition, although supervised physical therapy can be very useful, we routinely stress to patients that they are responsible for their own rehabilitation and cannot rely solely on the therapists.

COMPLICATIONS

Infections

Regardless of the specific surgical approach, infection is an uncommon complication following a shoulder stabilization procedure. For example, review of all anterior shoulder stabilizations performed at the Mayo Clinic between 1980 and 2001 identified only six infections.[254] Similarly, review of the recent literature on arthroscopic shoulder stabilizations has demonstrated an infection rate less than 0.25%.[7,44,53,129,281] Because of this low incidence, etiological factors that may predispose patients to infection are difficult to identify. Nevertheless, potential predisposing factors could include inadequate skin preparation prior to the procedure, contamination during the procedure, and development of a postoperative hematoma. Although compromised immune status may also increase the likelihood of postoperative infection, the majority of the patients with shoulder instability are young and healthy, and do not possess such risk factors.

Despite this low incidence, the likelihood of a postoperative infection may be minimized even further by utilizing meticulous surgical technique. Another common prophylaxis against infection is the use of perioperative antibiotics. Since many of these surgeries are performed as an outpatient procedure, most patients only receive a single dose of intravenous antibiotics immediately before the start of the procedure. For those patients who stay overnight, a second and/or third dose may be given, but this is generally based on surgeon preference rather than empirical data.

Postoperatively, if a large hematoma is identified, an operative evacuation should be considered. Although the decision must be individualized for each patient, surgical evacuation may prevent the hematoma from being seeded with bacteria and becoming a source for deep abscess. If definite postoperative infection has been identified, it should be treated urgently. In order to prevent the development of septic arthritis and to protect the surgical construct, the underlying infection must be treated aggressively. For simple and isolated cellulitis, treatment with intravenous or oral antibiotics may be sufficient. On the other hand, if there is evidence to suggest a deeper infection, prompt irrigation and surgical débridement is indicated. This can be performed either arthroscopically or as an open procedure. In general, regardless of whether the initial stabilization surgery was performed arthroscopically or open, an arthroscopic evaluation should be considered. The joint can be irrigated and, based on the findings, a more invasive débridement can then be performed.

Neurologic Injuries

A nerve injury may occur as a result of excessive traction or direct injury. Neurological injury associated with an open anterior shoulder repair is a relatively uncommon complication.

According to one study, for example, a neurological injury occurred in 8.2% of the 282 patients who underwent an open anterior stabilization surgery.[94] The incidence of neurological deficit following an arthroscopic stabilization, however, has been variable. Some of the earlier studies report an incidence as high as 30%.[5,167,211,325] In these reports, predisposing factors include traction in the lateral decubitus position, compression secondary to fluid extravasation, and a tourniquet effect following excessively tight wrapping of the arm. Fortunately, most injuries were neuropraxias that resolved spontaneously.[232] In some of the recent series of arthroscopic stabilizations, the incidence of neurological injury has been reported to be approximately 3%.[68,75,129,131,214,281]

When a neurological deficit occurs following an open surgical repair, the musculocutaneous and the axillary nerves are commonly involved. The musculocutaneous nerve is likely to be injured due to excessive retraction on the conjoined tendons. In most instances, these injuries are neuropraxias that resolve spontaneously. Injury to the axillary nerve can occur during dissection of the shoulder capsule in the anterior inferior quadrant of the glenoid. When traction is the cause of the injury, spontaneous recovery can be expected. Nonetheless, direct injury to the axillary nerve has been reported, and the likelihood of a spontaneous recovery is less optimistic.[163] Minimizing the risk of injury to the axillary nerve can be accomplished by palpating or visually identifying the nerve during the procedure. In addition, placement of a retractor between the inferior capsule and the axillary nerve can generally protect the nerve from a direct injury. Less commonly, the suprascapular nerve can be injured. In anterior bone grafting surgeries, for example, screws that are used to fix the graft penetrate posterior superior aspect of the glenoid and can come within 4 mm of the nerve.[159] For open posterior approaches, this nerve can be injured if the surgical dissection is carried out significantly medial to the glenoid rim. For any of the nerves, if a direct injury or laceration is suspected, early exploration of the nerve should be considered.

Restricted Motion

Stiffness following shoulder stabilization can occur for a variety of reasons. Nonanatomic reconstructions, such as the Putti-Platt and the Magnusson-Stack procedures, are designed to restrict motion. As such, these procedures have fallen into disfavor and been replaced by capsular procedures that address the underlying pathoanatomy. Unfortunately, even the anatomic capsulolabral reconstruction procedures can result in stiffness. Immediately after the reconstruction, it is important to document that normal joint motion has been maintained and that excessive capsular tightening has not occurred. Although excessive tightening can also occur after arthroscopic repairs, it is generally believed to occur at a lower rate.[53,79,185]

Other common causes of stiffness following shoulder stabilization surgery include prolonged immobilization and poor compliance with the rehabilitation program. Duration of immobilization following shoulder surgery can vary widely depending on multiple factors. In addition, individual patients tend to display variable abilities in regaining normal shoulder motion. It is important to initiate a rehabilitation program that focuses on motion as soon as possible following the repair. The need for early motion, however, must be balanced against placing the underlying surgical construct at risk for failure. Patients are expected to regain their motion on a gradual basis during the first 3 months following shoulder surgery. Patients who do not regain the desired motion within 6 to 9 months should be considered for a surgical release. Although closed manipulation under anesthesia is widely utilized, we tend to avoid this procedure because of its uncontrolled nature and the risk of additional damage. Rather, we prefer an arthroscopic evaluation with controlled release of the scar tissue and any overly tightened structures.

As noted in the previous sections, nonanatomic and excessively tight reconstructions can lead to long-term complications. The Putti-Platt procedure, for example, has been associated with the development of symptomatic degenerative arthritis. Excessive tightening of the anterior structures is believed to result in permanent posterior humeral head subluxation and incongruent motion, which in turn leads to glenohumeral arthritis. In addition to the Putti-Platt procedure, any nonanatomic reconstructions causing excessive tightening of the anterior structures can, in theory, lead to the same long-term complications. The best approach to avoid this problem is prevention (i.e., avoiding excessive tightening of the anterior structures during the surgical repair).

Hardware Complications

Use of screws and staples for open capsular and noncapsular procedures has been associated with a significant rate of hardware complications.[296] Types of hardware complications can be broadly classified as (i) incorrect placement of the implant, (ii) migration after placement, (iii) loosening, and (iv) breakage of the device. In a series of 37 patients who developed complications related to the use of screws and staples, 35 patients underwent a procedure for anterior instability. Twenty-one patients had problems from the screws, whereas 14 patients had problems related to the use of staples (Fig. 38-38). Common complaints included shoulder pain, decreased motion, crepitus, and radiating paresthesias. The time interval between surgery and the onset of symptoms ranged from 4 weeks to 10 years. In this series, hardware had been incorrectly placed in 10 patients,

had migrated or loosened in 22, and fractured in 3. Thirty-two patients required a second surgical procedure to address these complications. At the time of the reoperation, 43% of the patients were noted to have significant injury to their articular cartilage. Fortunately, hardware-related complications from screws and staples are now fairly uncommon. This decrease is partly because of the fact that many surgeons, now being aware of the potential problems, have significantly decreased their use of these devices. In addition, as noncapsular procedures have been performed less frequently, the need for their use has also significantly decreased.

Increasing use of the capsulolabral reconstruction procedures and the advent of arthroscopic techniques have resulted in the development of new devices for shoulder surgery. Currently, one of the most commonly used devices for shoulder stabilization surgery is the suture anchor. Metallic suture anchors can be associated with similar hardware complications such as incorrect placement, migration, loosening, and breakage. Incorrect placement can be readily identified in postoperative radiographs, but may remain asymptomatic. Broken or loose hardware, however, tends to cause enough symptoms to warrant further evaluation and possible treatment. When symptoms related to metallic anchors are present, prompt evaluation must be performed in order to limit the potential for articular cartilage injury. Incorrectly placed or migrated anchors should be removed, which can often be accomplished arthroscopically. An anchor that has migrated and remains embedded in the inferior aspect of the joint, away from the articular cartilage, may not cause any additional damage. As such, if additional migration does not occur and the symptoms remain minimal, the anchor may not need to be removed. It must be stressed, however, that these patients must be monitored on a regular basis for at least 4 to 6 months to ensure that the anchor remains in a fixed position.

Recently, development of bioabsorbable suture anchors has decreased the risk of these hardware-related complications. Thus, for example, a loose anchor may be resorbed prior to causing any symptoms or permanent damage. Despite these

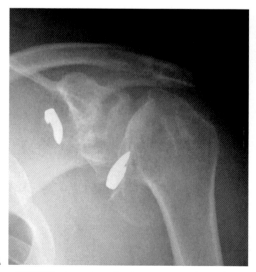 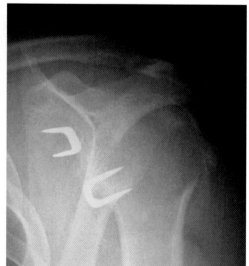

A **B**

FIGURE 38-38 Complications associated with the use of metallic staples. AP **(A)** and scapula lateral **(B)** views reveal loose staples, with the onset of joint arthrosis.

advantages, however, bioabsorbable anchors can still cause hardware complications including foreign body reaction.[29,51] Fortunately, this complication is believed to occur very infrequently with minimal long-term sequelae.

Chronic Dislocation

Clinical Presentation

Patients with a chronic shoulder dislocation usually report a history of traumatic incident. The trauma may involve fall from a height, motor vehicle accident, or less commonly, electrical shock or seizure episodes. These accidents cause an acute shoulder dislocation which is associated with significant pain. In most patients, this pain is sufficient enough to seek immediate medical attention. Chronic shoulder dislocations occur in situations when the initial dislocation was unappreciated or when the patient did not or could not seek adequate medical care. As such, chronic dislocations may be observed in patients with extremely high tolerance of pain, patients with decreased mental ability to recognize or verbalize their pain, and patients with additional injuries that are more obvious or life-threatening.

Several weeks after the injury, shoulder pain and edema will start to dissipate. With the resolution of symptoms, patients may start using their arm at waist level for functional activities. This improvement can often be mistaken as the initial step in their recovery. Despite these improvements, however, shoulder motion will continue to be limited. Patients with an anterior dislocation typically lack internal rotation and abduction, whereas those with a posterior dislocation often lack external rotation and abduction. If the humeral head remains engaged on the glenoid rim, shoulder motion will often be associated with a mechanical block as well as crepitus. Because of this limitation in motion, these patients can be misdiagnosed as having a posttraumatic adhesive capsulitis or a "frozen shoulder."[87,246] As the improvement in shoulder function reaches a plateau, a more serious injury is eventually suspected.

Patients with a chronic shoulder dislocation can suffer from varying degrees of pain. Thus, some patients may report surprisingly little pain whereas others will complain of excruciating pain. In addition, their functional capacity can also vary widely with some patients reporting fairly reasonable use of their arm, especially at waist level. As a general group, however, these patients suffer from significant shoulder dysfunction. Perhaps the most consistent of their symptoms include stiffness, crepitus, deformity, and failure to use the arm for overhead activities.

Nonoperative Treatment

Management of a chronic shoulder dislocation remains a challenge. Primary goals of treatment are satisfactory pain relief and optimization of functional recovery. It is crucial for the surgeon to establish reasonable expectations for the treatment. This information must be thoroughly discussed with the patient and family. Desire to perform aggressive, and often technically demanding, interventions should be tempered by the patient's expectations, general health, anticipated functional recovery, and ability to participate in postoperative rehabilitation.

Nonoperative treatment of chronic shoulder dislocations may be appropriate for patients with minimal pain and disability. Following the resolution of pain from the initial injury, elderly patients with a low functional demand may demonstrate excellent adaptation. With a functional contralateral upper ex-

tremity, these patients may be able to perform activities of daily living despite limitations in their shoulders. Nonoperative management may also be desirable for patients with an unacceptably high medical risk for surgery, patients with an uncontrollable seizure disorder, and patients who are physically or mentally unable to comply with postoperative instructions and rehabilitation. For these patients, initial treatments should concentrate on supportive care. As such, they should undergo a brief period of immobilization. Once they recover from the initial injury, gradual rehabilitation that focuses on the restoration of function should be instituted. As such, active assisted and active motion exercises should be augmented with occupational therapy that emphasizes activities of daily living. Aggressive passive stretching exercises should be avoided as they can lead to further injuries.

Most outcome studies of nonoperative treatment for chronic shoulder dislocations contain a small number of patients. As such, firm conclusions are difficult to establish. In general, however, these studies show that rarely is enough motion regained for overhead activities.[74,87,170] Patients with a chronic posterior dislocation appear to have a more favorable outcome than those with a chronic anterior dislocation. Because of these findings, it must be stressed to the patient that the treatment is based on achieving "limited goal" outcomes with tolerable pain and function. As such, unrealistic patient expectations for a normal shoulder must be addressed prior to the initiation of any treatment.

Operative Treatment

Surgical management of a chronic shoulder dislocation can vary widely. The choice to proceed with any specific procedure is dependent on multiple factors including the chronicity of the injury, associated bony injuries, and associated soft tissue injuries. Other patient-related factors such as age, hand dominance, vocational requirements, and medical comorbidities also play a significant role. Because of this variability, no single procedure has been preferentially used to treat patients with a chronic shoulder dislocation.

The primary goal of surgery is a concentric and stable joint. An attempt at closed reduction, even under general anesthesia, is unlikely to be successful.[74,246] If the joint cannot be reduced, an open surgical reduction can then be performed. In most situations, the deltopectoral interval is used for an anterior approach to the shoulder. After exploration of the joint and removal of any interposed tissues, the humeral head is reduced back onto the glenoid. Because of soft tissue contractures, joint reduction may not be stable. In these situations, appropriate soft tissue releases must be performed. In a classic article by Rowe and Zarins, appropriate soft tissue release and postoperative immobilization were sufficient to maintain concentric shoulder reduction.[238] For patients with chronic anterior dislocations, the arm was immobilized anterior to the coronal plane of the body after the surgical reduction. Conversely, for patients with chronic posterior dislocations, the arm was immobilized posterior to the coronal plane of the body. Of the seven shoulders that were treated in this fashion, they observed good to excellent results in five shoulders and fair results in two shoulders.[238]

Other authors, however, have recommended the use of supplemental fixation to maintain postoperative joint reduction.[74, 190,283] In a recent report of 10 patients with a chronic shoulder

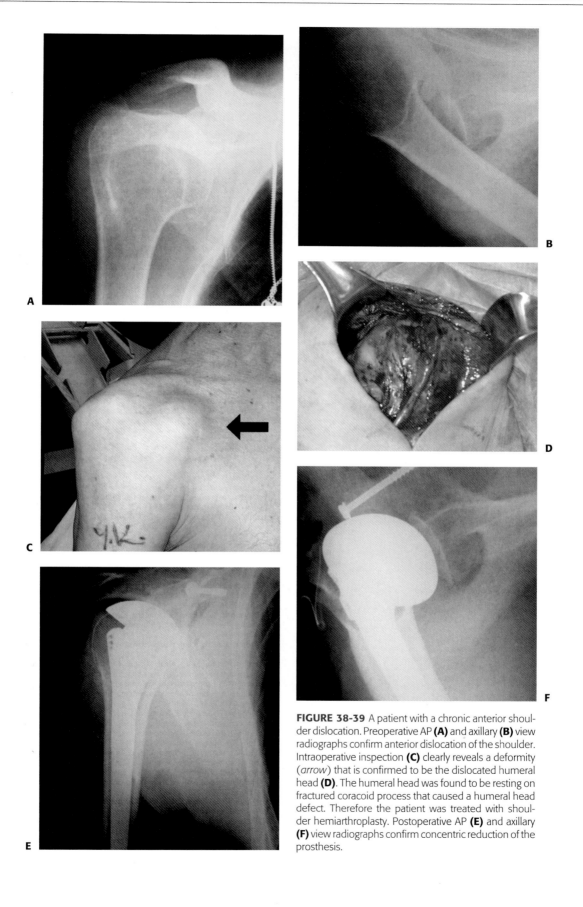

FIGURE 38-39 A patient with a chronic anterior shoulder dislocation. Preoperative AP **(A)** and axillary **(B)** view radiographs confirm anterior dislocation of the shoulder. Intraoperative inspection **(C)** clearly reveals a deformity (*arrow*) that is confirmed to be the dislocated humeral head **(D)**. The humeral head was found to be resting on fractured coracoid process that caused a humeral head defect. Therefore the patient was treated with shoulder hemiarthroplasty. Postoperative AP **(E)** and axillary **(F)** view radiographs confirm concentric reduction of the prosthesis.

dislocation, the shoulders were surgically reduced and then fixed with percutaneously placed Kirschner wires through the acromion into the humeral head. This construct was augmented with a Bristow procedure in all patients. The Kirschner wires were left in place for 4 weeks during which the patients were immobilized in a body bandage. At a follow up of greater than 2 years, the author reported stable joint reductions in all patients with a good to excellent clinical result in 8 of the 10 patients.[74]

If chronic shoulder dislocation is associated with a significant bony injury, the defect may need to be surgically addressed. Based on the location and the size of the defect, a number of different procedures may be considered. They include the McLaughlin procedure, disimpaction and bone grafting, and resection arthroplasty.[87,123,190,238] If degenerative changes are present within the joint, shoulder replacement surgery can also be considered (Fig. 38-39). Unfortunately, to date, no single procedure has clearly demonstrated a superior outcome compared to others for the chronically dislocated shoulder.

REFERENCES

1. Ahmad CS, Wang VM, Sugalski MT, et al. Biomechanics of shoulder capsulorrhaphy procedures. J Shoulder Elbow Surg 2005;14(1 Suppl S):12S–18S.
2. Ahmadain A. The Magnuson-Stack operation for recurrent anterior dislocation of the shoulder: a review of 38 cases. J Bone Joint Surg 1987;69-B:111–114.
3. Alcid JG, Powell SE, Tibone JE. Revision anterior capsular shoulder stabilization using hamstring tendon autograft and tibialis tendon allograft reinforcement: minimum two-year follow-up. J Shoulder Elbow Surg 2007;16(3):268–272.
4. Allain J, Goutallier D, Glorion C. Long-term results of the Latarjet procedure for the treatment of anterior instability of the shoulder. J Bone Joint Surg 1998;80-A:841–852.
5. Andrews J, Carson W, Ortega K. Arthroscopy of the shoulder: technique and normal anatomy. Am J Sports Med 1984;12:1–7.
6. Arndt J, Sears A. Posterior dislocation of the shoulder. Am J Roentgenol Radium Ther Nucl Med 1965;94:639–645.
7. Bacilla P, Field L, Savoie F. Arthroscopic Bankart repair in a high-demand patient population. Arthroscopy 1997;13:51–60.
8. Bahk M, Keyurapan E, Tasaki A, et al. Laxity testing of the shoulder: a review. Am J Sports Med 2007;35(1):131–144.
9. Bak K, Spring B, Henderson J. Inferior capsular shift procedure in athletes with multidirectional instability based on isolated capsular and ligamentous redundancy. Am J Sports Med 2000;28:466–471.
10. Banas M, Dalldorf P, Sebastianelli W, et al. Long-term follow-up of the modified Bristow procedure. Am J Sports Med 1993;21:666–671.
11. Bankart A. The pathology and treatment of recurrent dislocation of the shoulder joint. Br J Surg 1939;26:23–29.
12. Bankart A. Recurrent or habitual dislocaton of the shoulder-joint. Br Med J 1923;2:1132–1133.
13. Basmajian J, Bazant F. Factors preventing downward dislocation of the adducted shoulder joint. J Bone Joint Surg 1959;41-A:1182–1186.
14. Berendes TD, Wolterbeek R, Pilot P, et al. The open modified Bankart procedure: outcome at follow-up of 10 to 15 years. J Bone Joint Surg Br 2007;89(8):1064–1068.
15. Bessems J, Vegter J. Glenoplasty for recurrent posterior shoulder instability. Good results in 13 cases followed for 1 to 16 years. Acta Orthop Scand 1995;66:535–537.
16. Bigliani L, Pollock R, McIlveen S, et al. Shift of the posteroinferior aspect of the capsule for recurrent posterior glenohumeral instability. J Bone Joint Surg 1995;77–A:1011–1020.
17. Blom S, Dahlback L. Nerve injuries in dislocations of the shoulder joint and fractures of the neck of the humerus. A clinical and electromyographical study. Acta Chir Scand 1970;136(6):461–466.
18. Bloom M, Obata W. Diagnosis of posterior dislocation of the shoulder with use of Velpeau axillary and angle-up roentgenographic views. J Bone Joint Surg 1967;49–A(5):943–949.
19. Bohnsack M, Brinkman T, Ruhmann O, et al. [Open versus arthroscopic shoulder stabilization. An analysis of the treatment cost]. Orthopade 2003;32:654–658.
20. Boileau P, Villalba M, Hery JY, et al. Risk factors for recurrence of shoulder instability after arthroscopic Bankart repair. J Bone Joint Surg Am 2006;88(8):1755–1763.
21. Bottoni CR, Franks BR, Moore JH, et al. Operative stabilization of posterior shoulder instability. Am J Sports Med 2005;33(7):996–1002.
22. Bottoni CR, Smith EL, Berkowitz MJ, et al. Arthroscopic versus open shoulder stabilization for recurrent anterior instability: a prospective randomized clinical trial. Am J Sports Med Nov 2006;34(11):1730–1737.
23. Bowen M, Warren R. Ligamentous control of shoulder stability based on selective cutting and static translation experiments. Clin Sports Med 1991;10:757–782.
24. Bradley JP, Baker CL, 3rd, Kline AJ, et al. Arthroscopic capsulolabral reconstruction for posterior instability of the shoulder: a prospective study of 100 shoulders. Am J Sports Med 2006;34(7):1061–1071.
25. Brockbank W, Griffiths D. Orthopaedic surgery in the 16th and 17th centuries: Luxations of the shoulder. J Bone Joint Surg 1948;30-B:365–375.
26. Brown J. Nerve injuries complicating dislocation of the shoulder. J Bone Joint Surg 1952;34-B:526.
27. Brox J, Finnanger A, Merckoll E, et al. Satisfactory long-term results after Eden-Hybbinette-Alvik operation for recurrent anterior dislocation of the shoulder: 6 to 20 years' follow-up of 52 patients. Acta Orthop Scand 2003;74:180–185.
28. Bui-Mansfield LT, Banks KP, Taylor DC. Humeral avulsion of the glenohumeral ligaments: the HAGL lesion. Am J Sports Med 2007;35(11):1960–1966.
29. Burkhart A, Imhoff A, Roscher E. Foreign-body reaction to the bioabsorbable suretac device. Arthroscopy 2000;16:91–95.
30. Burkhart S, De Beer J. Traumatic glenohumeral bone defects and their relationship to failure of arthroscopic Bankart repairs: significance of the inverted-pear glenoid and the humeral head engaging Hill-Sachs lesion. Arthroscopy 2000;16:677–694.
31. Burkhead W, Rockwood C. Treatment of instability of the shoulder with an exercise program. J Bone Joint Surg 1992;74-A:890–896.
32. Calandra J, Baker C, Uribe J. The incidence of Hill-Sachs lesions in initial anterior shoulder dislocations. Arthroscopy 1989;5:254–257.
33. Carew-McColl M. Bilateral shoulder dislocations caused by electric shock. Br J Clin Prac 1980;34:251–254.
34. Carreira DS, Mazzocca AD, Oryhon J, et al. A prospective outcome evaluation of arthroscopic Bankart repairs: minimum 2-year follow-up. Am J Sports Med 2006;34(5):771–777.
35. Choi C, Ogilvie-Harris D. Inferior capsular shift operation for multidirectional instability of the shoulder in players of contact sport. Br J Sports Med 2002;36:290–294.
36. Chung CB, Sorenson S, Dwek JR, et al. Humeral avulsion of the posterior band of the inferior glenohumeral ligament: MR arthrography and clinical correlation in 17 patients. AJR Am J Roentgenol 2004;183(2):355–359.
37. Churchill R, Brems J, Kotschi H. Glenoid size, inclination, and version: an anatomic study. J Shoulder Elbow Surg. 2001;10:327–332.
38. Ciccone WJ 2nd, Weinstein DM, Elias JJ. Glenohumeral chondrolysis following thermal capsulorrhaphy. Orthopedics 2007;30(2):158–160.
39. Clark J, Harryman D. Tendons, ligaments, and capsule of the rotator cuff. Gross and microscopic anatomy. J Bone Joint Surg 1992;74-A:713–725.
40. Codman E. Rupture of the supraspinatus tendon and other lesions in or about the subacromial bursa. The Shoulder. Boston: Thomas Todd, 1934.
41. Collins K, Capito C, Cross M. The use of the Putti-Platt procedure in the treatment of recurrent anterior dislocation, with special reference to the young athlete. Am J Sports Med 1986;14:380–382.
42. Cooper R, Brems J. The inferior capsular shift procedure for multidirectional instability of the shoulder. J Bone Joint Surg 1992;74-A:1516–1521.
43. D'Alessandro D, Bradley J, Fleischli J, et al. Prospective evaluation of thermal capsulorrhaphy for shoulder instability: indications and results, 2- to 5-year follow-up. Am J Sports Med 2004;32:21–33.
44. D'Angelo G, Ogilvie-Harris D. Septic arthritis following arthroscopy, with cost/benefit analysis of antibiotic prophylaxis. Arthroscopy 1988;4:10–14.
45. Davids J, Talbott R. Luxatio erecta humeri. A case report. Clin Orthop 1990;252:144–149.
46. DeBerardino TM, Arciero RA, Taylor DC. Arthroscopic stabilization of acute initial anterior shoulder dislocation: the West Point experience. J South Orthop Assoc 1996;5(4):263–271.
47. DePalma A, Silberstein C. Results following a modified Magnuson procedure in recurrent dislocation of the shoulder. Surg Clin North Am 1963;43:1651–1653.
48. Detrisac D, Johnson L. Arthroscopic shoulder capsulorrhaphy using metal staples. Orthop Clin North Am 1993;24:71–88.
49. Dewing CB, McCormick F, Bell SJ, et al. An analysis of capsular area in patients with anterior, posterior, and multidirectional shoulder instability. Am J Sports Med 2008;36(3):515–522.
50. Eden R. Operation der habituellen schulterluxation unter mitteilung eines neuen verfahrens bei abriss am inneren pfannenrande. Dtsch Z Chir 1918;144:269–280.
51. Edwards D, Hoy G, Saies A, et al. Adverse reaction to an absorbable shoulder fixation device. J Shoulder Elbow Surg 1994;3:230–233.
52. Ehgartner K. [Has the duration of cast fixation after shoulder dislocations an influence on the frequency of recurrent dislocation? (author's translation)]. Arch Orthop Unfallchir 1977;89:187–190.
53. Fabbriciani G, Milano G, Demontis A, et al. Arthroscopic versus open treatment of Bankart lesion of the shoulder: a prospective randomized study. Arthroscopy 2004;20:456–462.
54. Fanton G. Arthroscopic electrothermal surgery of the shoulder. Oper Tech Sports Med 1998;6:139–146.
55. Farber AJ, Castillo R, Clough M, et al. Clinical assessment of three common tests for traumatic anterior shoulder instability. J Bone Joint Surg Am 2006;88(7):1467–1474.
56. Favorito P, Langenderfer M, Colosimo A, et al. Arthroscopic laser-assisted capsular shift in the treatment of patients with multidirectional shoulder instability. Am J Sports Med 2002;30:322–328.
57. Fehringer E, Schmidt G, Boorman R, et al. The anteroinferior labrum helps center the humeral head on the glenoid. J Shoulder Elbow Surg 2003;12:53–58.
58. Ferlic D, DiGiovine N. A long-term retrospective study of the modified Bristow procedure. Am J Sports Med 1988;16:469–474.
59. Field L, Warren R, O'Brien S, et al. Isolated closure of rotator interval defects for shoulder instability. Am J Sports Med 1995;23:557–563.
60. Finkelstein J, Waddell J, O'Driscoll S, et al. Acute posterior fracture dislocations of the shoulder treated with the Neer modification of the McLaughlin procedure. J Orthop Trauma 1995;9:190–193.
61. Fitzgerald B, Watson B, Lapoint J. The use of thermal capsulorrhaphy in the treatment of multidirectional instability. J Shoulder Elbow Surg 2002;11:108–113.
62. Flatow E, Soslowsky L, Ticker J, et al. Excursion of the rotator cuff under the acromion. Patterns of subacromial contact. Am J Sports Med 1994;22:779–788.
63. Fredriksson A-S, Tegner Y. Results of the Putti-Platt operation for recurrent anterior dislocation of the shoulder. Int Orthop 1991;15:185–188.
64. Fuchs B, Jost B, Gerber C. Posterior-inferior capsular shift for the treatment of recurrent, voluntary posterior subluxation of the shoulder. J Bone Joint Surg 2000;82-A:16–25.
65. Gardham J, Scott J. Axillary artery occlusion with erect dislocation of the shoulder. Injury 1980;11:155–158.
66. Garth W, Allman F, Armstrong W. Occult anterior subluxations of the shoulder in noncontact sports. Am J Sports Med 1987;15:579–585.
67. Garth W, Slappey C, Ochs C. Roentgenographic demonstration of instability of the

shoulder: the apical oblique projection. A technical note. J Bone Joint Surg 1450–1455 1984;66-A.
68. Gartsman G, Roddey T, Hammerman S. Arthroscopic treatment of multidirectional glenohumeral instability: 2- to 5-year follow-up. Arthroscopy 2001;17:236–243.
69. Gartsman G, Taverna E, Hammerman S. Arthroscopic rotator interval repair in glenohumeral instability: description of an operative technique. Arthroscopy 1999;15: 330–332.
70. Gerber C, Ganz R, Vinh T. Glenoplasty for recurrent posterior shoulder instability: an anatomic appraisal. Clin Orthop 1987;216:70–79.
71. Gibb T, Sidles J, Harryman D, et al. The effect of capsular venting on glenohumeral laxity. Clin Orthop 1991;268:120–127.
72. Glessner J. Intrathoracic dislocation of the humeral head. J Bone Joint Surg 1961;43–A: 428–430.
73. Glousman R, Jobe F, Tibone J, et al. Dynamic electromyographic analysis of the throwing shoulder with glenohumeral instability. J Bone Joint Surg 1988;70-A:220–226.
74. Goga I. Chronic shoulder dislocations. J Shoulder Elbow Surg 2003;12:446–450.
75. Goubier J, Iserin A, Duranthon L, et al. A four-portal arthroscopic stabilization in posterior instability. J Shoulder Elbow Surg 2003;12:337–341.
76. Graichen H, Koydl P, Zichner L. Effectiveness of glenoid osteotomy in atraumatic posterior instability of the shoulder associated with excessive retroversion and flatness of the glenoid. Int Orthop 1999;23:95–99.
77. Green A, Norris T. Shoulder arthroplasty for advanced glenohumeral arthritis after anterior instability repair. J Shoulder Elbow Surg 2001;10:593–545.
78. Green M, Christensen K. Arthroscopic Bankart procedure: 2- to 5-year follow-up with clinical correlation to severity of glenoid labral lesion. Am J Sports Med 1995;23(3): 276–281.
79. Green M, Christensen K. Arthroscopic versus open Bankart procedures: a comparison of early morbidity and complications. Arthroscopy 1993;9:371–374.
80. Greis P, Burks R, Schickendantz M, et al. Axillary nerve injury after thermal capsular shrinkage of the shoulder. J Shoulder Elbow Surg 2001;10:231–235.
81. Habermeyer P, Schuller U, Wiedemann E. The intra-articular pressure of the shoulder: an experimental study on the role of the glenoid labrum in stabilizing the joint. Arthroscopy 1992;8:166–172.
82. Hall R, Isaac F, Booth C. Dislocations of the shoulder with special reference to accompanying small fractures. J Bone Joint Surg 1959;41-A:489–494.
83. Hamada K, Fukuda H, Nakajima T, et al. The inferior capsular shift operation for instability of the shoulder. Long term results in 34 shoulders. J Bone Joint Surg 1999; 81-B:218–225.
84. Hasan SS, Fleckenstein C, Albright J. Open treatment of posterior humeral avulsion of the glenohumeral ligaments: a case report and review of the literature. J Shoulder Elbow Surg 2007;16(4):e3–5.
85. Hawkins R. Glenoid osteotomy for recurrent posterior subluxation of the shoulder: assessment by computed axial tomography. J Shoulder Elbow Surg 1996;5:393–400.
86. Hawkins R, Angelo R. Glenohumeral osteoarthrosis. A late complication of the Putti-Platt repair. J Bone Joint Surg 1990;72-A:1193–1197.
87. Hawkins R, Neer C, Pianta R, et al. Locked posterior dislocation of the shoulder. J Bone Joint Surg 1987;69-A:9–18.
88. Hawkins RJ, Krishnan SG, Karas SG, et al. Electrothermal arthroscopic shoulder capsulorrhaphy: a minimum 2-year follow-up. Am J Sports Med 2007;35(9):1484–1488.
89. Head S, Grimberg B, Chesar J, et al. [Magnuson Stack operation for chronic anterior shoulder instability]. Harefuah 1996;130:300–304.
90. Helfet A. Coracoid transplantation for recurring dislocation of the shoulder. J Bone Joint Surg 1958;40-B:198–202.
91. Hill H, Sachs M. The grooved defect of the humeral head. A frequently unrecognized complication of dislocations of the shoulder joint. Radiology 1940;35:690–700.
92. Hippocrates. Injuries of the shoulder. Dislocations. Clin Orthop 1989;246:4–7.
93. Hippocrates. Works of Hippocrates with an English translation by WHS Jones and ET Withington. London: William Heinemann, 1927.
94. Ho E, Cofield R, Balm M, et al. Neurologic complications of surgery for anterior shoulder instability. J Shoulder Elbow Surg 1999;8:266–270.
95. Hovelius L. Anterior dislocation of the shoulder in teenagers and young adults. Five-year prognosis. J Bone Joint Surg 1987;69-A:393–399.
96. Hovelius L, Akermark C, Albrektsson B, et al. Bristow-Laterjet procedure for recurrent anterior dislocation of the shoulder. A 2- to 5-year follow-up study on the results of 112 cases. Acta Orthop Scand 1983;54:284–290.
97. Hovelius L, Augustini B, Fredin H, et al. Primary anterior dislocation of the shoulder in young patients. A 10-year prospective study. J Bone Joint Surg 1996;78-A:1677–1684.
98. Hovelius L, Eriksson K, Fredin H, et al. Recurrences after initial dislocation of the shoulder. Results of a prospective study of treatment. J Bone Joint Surg 343–349 1983; 65-A(3).
99. Hovelius L, Olofsson A, Sandstrom B, et al. Nonoperative treatment of primary anterior shoulder dislocation in patients 40 years of age and younger: a prospective 25-year follow-up. J Bone Joint Surg Am 2008;90(5):945–952.
100. Hovelius L, Sandstrom B, Rosmark D, et al. Long-term results with the Bankart and Bristow-Latarjet procedures: recurrent shoulder instability and arthropathy. J Shoulder Elbow Surg 2001;10:445–452.
101. Hovelius L, Sandstrom B, Saebo M. One hundred eighteen Bristow-Latarjet repairs for recurrent anterior dislocation of the shoulder prospectively followed for 15 years: study II—the evolution of dislocation arthropathy. J Shoulder Elbow Surg 2006;15(3): 279–289.
102. Hovelius L, Sandstrom B, Sundgren K, et al. One hundred eighteen Bristow-Latarjet repairs for recurrent anterior dislocation of the shoulder prospectively followed for fifteen years: study I—clinical results. J Shoulder Elbow Surg 2004;13(5):509–516.
103. Hovelius L, Thorling J, Fredin H. Recurrent anterior dislocation of the shoulder: results after the Bankart and Putti-Platt operations. J Bone Joint Surg 1979;61-A:566–569.
104. Howell S, Galinat B. The glenoid-labral socket. A constrained articular surface. Clin Orthop 1989;243:122–125.
105. Howell S, Galinat B, Renzi A, et al. Normal and abnormal mechanics of the glenohumeral joint in the horizontal plane. J Bone Joint Surg 1988;70-A:227–232.
106. Hurley J, Anderson T, Dear W, et al. Posterior shoulder instability. Surgical versus conservative results with evaluation of glenoid version. Am J Sports Med 1992;20: 392–400.
107. Hussein M. Kocher's method is 3000 years old. J Bone Joint Surg 1968;50-B:669–671.
108. Huysmans PE, Haen PS, Kidd M, et al. The shape of the inferior part of the glenoid: a cadaveric study. J Shoulder Elbow Surg 2006;15(6):759–763.
109. Hybbinette S. De la transplantation d'un fragment osseux pour remedier aux luxations recidivantes de l'epaule: constatations et resultats operatoires. Acta Chir Scand 1932; 71:411–445.
110. Iannotti J, Gabriel J, Schneck S, et al. The normal glenohumeral relationships. J Bone Joint Surg 1992;74-A:491–500.
111. Iannotti J, Zlatkin M, Esterhai J, et al. Magnetic resonance imaging of the shoulder. Sensitivity, specificity, and predictive value. J Bone Joint Surg 1991;73-A:17–29.
112. Itoi E, Hatakeyama Y, Kido T, et al. A new method of immobilization after traumatic anterior dislocation of the shoulder: a preliminary study. J Shoulder Elbow Surg 2003; 12:413–415.
113. Itoi E, Kuechle D, Newman S, et al. Stabilising function of the biceps in stable and unstable shoulders. J Bone Joint Surg 1993;75-B:546–550.
114. Itoi E, Lee S, Berglund L, et al. The effect of a glenoid defect on anteroinferior stability of the shoulder after Bankart repair: a cadaveric study. J Bone Joint Surg 2000;82-A: 35–46.
115. Itoi E, Motzkin N, Morrey B, et al. Scapular inclination and inferior stability of the shoulder. J Shoulder Elbow Surg 1992;1:131–139.
116. Itoi E, Sashi R, Minagawa H, et al. Position of immobilization after dislocation of the glenohumeral joint. J Bone Joint Surg 2001;83-A:661–667.
117. Jerosch J, Aldawoudy AM. Chondrolysis of the glenohumeral joint following arthroscopic capsular release for adhesive capsulitis: a case report. Knee Surg Sports Traumatol Arthrosc Mar 2007;15(3):292–294.
118. Jobe F, Giangarra C, Kvitne R, et al. Anterior capsulolabral reconstruction of the shoulder in athletes in overhand sports. Am J Sports Med 1991;5:428–434.
119. Johnson J, Bayley J. Early complications of acute anterior dislocation of the shoulder in the middle-aged and elderly patient. Injury 1982;13:431–434.
120. Johnson L. Arthroscopy of the shoulder. Orthop Clin North Am 1980;11:197–204.
121. Jolles B, Pelet S, Farron A. Traumatic recurrent anterior dislocation of the shoulder: two to four year follow up of an anatomic open procedure. J Shoulder Elbow Surg 2004;13:30–34.
122. Jones KJ, Wiesel B, Ganley TJ, et al. Functional outcomes of early arthroscopic bankart repair in adolescents aged 11 to 18 years. J Pediatr Orthop 2007;27(2):209–213.
123. Jones R. Orthopaedic Surgery of Injuries, vol 1. Oxford: Oxford University Press, 1921.
124. Jost B, Koch PP, Gerber C. Anatomy and functional aspects of the rotator interval. J Shoulder Elbow Surg 2000;9(4):336–341.
125. Karadimas J. Recurrent traumatic anterior dislocation of the shoulder. Two hundred eighteen consecutive cases treated by a modified Magnuson-Stack procedure and follow for 2 to 18 years. Acta Orthop Scand Suppl 1997;275:69–71.
126. Karas S. Arthroscopic rotator interval repair and anterior portal closure: an alternative technique. Arthroscopy 2002;18:436–439.
127. Karlsson J, Magnusson L, Ejerhed L, et al. Comparison of open and arthroscopic stabilization for recurrent shoulder dislocation in patients with a Bankart lesion. Am J Sports Med 2001;29:538–542.
128. Kazar B, Relovszky E. Prognosis of primary dislocation of the shoulder. Acta Orthop Scand 1969;40:216–224.
129. Kim S, Ha K, Cho Y, et al. Arthroscopic anterior stabilization of the shoulder. Two- to six-year follow-up. J Bone Joint Surg 2003;85-A:1511–1518.
130. Kim S, Ha K, Kim K. Bankart repair in traumatic anterior shoulder instability: open versus arthroscopic technique. Arthroscopy 2002;18:755–763.
131. Kim S, Ha K, Park J, et al. Arthroscopic posterior labral repair and capsular shift for traumatic unidirectional recurrent posterior subluxation of the shoulder. J Bone Joint Surg 2003;85-A:1479–1487.
132. Kim SH, Noh KC, Park JS, et al. Loss of chondrolabral containment of the glenohumeral joint in atraumatic posteroinferior multidirectional instability. J Bone Joint Surg Am 2005;87(1):92–98.
133. Kim SH, Park JC, Park JS, et al. Painful jerk test: a predictor of success in nonoperative treatment of posteroinferior instability of the shoulder. Am J Sports Med 2004;32(8): 1849–1855.
134. Kirkley A, Litchfield R, Thain L, et al. Agreement between magnetic resonance imaging and arthroscopic evaluation of the shoulder joint in primary anterior dislocation of the shoulder. Clin J Sport Med 2003;13:148–151.
135. Kiss J, Mersich I, Perlaky G, et al. The results of the Putti-Platt operation with particular reference to arthritis, pain, and limitation of external rotation. J Shoulder Elbow Surg 1998;7:495–500.
136. Kiviluoto O, Pasila M, Jaroma H, et al. Immobilization after primary dislocation of the shoulder. Acta Orthop Scand 1980;51:915–919.
137. Kon Y, Shiozaki H, Sugaya H. Arthroscopic repair of a humeral avulsion of the glenohumeral ligament lesion. Arthroscopy 2005;21(5):632.
138. Konig D, Rutt J, Treml O, et al. Osteoarthritis and recurrences after Putti-Platt and Eden-Hybbinetter operations for recurrent dislocation of the shoulder. Int Orthop 1997;21: 72–76.
139. Kumar V, Balasubramaniam P. The role of atmospheric pressure in stabilizing the shoulder: an experimental study. J Bone Joint Surg 1985;67-B:719–721.
140. Kvitne R, Jobe F, Jobe C. Shoulder instability in the overhand or throwing athlete. Clin Sports Med 1995;14:917–935.
141. Labriola JE, Lee TQ, Debski RE, et al. Stability and instability of the glenohumeral joint: the role of shoulder muscles. J Shoulder Elbow Surg 2005;14(1 Suppl S):32S–38S.
142. Lacey T, Crawford H. Reduction of anterior dislocations of the shoulder by means of the Milch abduction technique. J Bone Joint Surg 1952;34-A:108–109.
143. Lane J, Sachs R, Riehl B. Arthroscopic staple capsulorrhaphy: a long-term follow-up. Arthroscopy 1993;9(190–194).
144. Law BK, Yung PS, Ho EP, et al. The surgical outcome of immediate arthroscopic Bankart repair for first time anterior shoulder dislocation in young active patients. Knee Surg Sports Traumatol Arthrosc 2008;16(2):188–193.
145. Lawrence W. New position in radiographing the shoulder joint. Am J Roentgenol Radium Ther Nucl Med 1915;2:728–730.
146. Lazarus M, Sidles J, Harryman D, et al. Effect of a chondral-labral defect on glenoid concavity and glenohumeral stability. A cadaveric model. J Bone Joint Surg 1996;78-A:94–102.
147. Lee S, Kim K, O'Driscoll S, et al. Dynamic glenohumeral stability provided by the

rotator cuff muscles in the midrange and end-range motion. A study in cadavera. J Bone Joint Surg 2000;82-A:849–857.
148. Lev-El A, Rubinstein Z. Axillary artery injury in erect dislocation of the shoulder. J Trauma 1981;21:323–325.
149. Levick J. Joint pressure-volume studies: their importance, design, and interpretation. J Rheumatol 1983;10:353–357.
150. Levine W, Richmond J, Donaldson W. Use of the suture anchor in open Bankart reconstruction. A follow-up report. Am J Sports Med 1994;22:723–726.
151. Levine WN, Clark AM, Jr., D'Alessandro DF, et al. Chondrolysis following arthroscopic thermal capsulorrhaphy to treat shoulder instability. A report of two cases. J Bone Joint Surg Am Mar 2005;87(3):616–621.
152. Levy A, Kelly B, Lintner S, et al. Function of the long head of the biceps at the shoulder: electromyographic analysis. J Shoulder Elbow Surg 2001;10:250–255.
153. Limpisvasti O, Yang BY, Hosseinzadeh P, et al. The effect of glenohumeral position on the shoulder after traumatic anterior dislocation. Am J Sports Med 2008;36(4): 775–780.
154. Lippitt S, Vanderhooft J, Harris S, et al. Glenohumeral stability from concavity-compression: a quantitative analysis. J Shoulder Elbow Surg 1993;2(1):27–35.
155. Lo I, Nonweiler B, Woolfrey M, et al. An evaluation of the apprehension, relocation, and surprise test for anterior shoulder instability. Am J Sports Med 2004;32:301–307.
156. Lombardo S, Kerlan R, Jobe F, et al. The modified Bristow procedure for recurrent dislocation of the shoulder. J Bone Joint Surg 1976;58-A(2):256–261.
157. Magnuson P, Stack J. Recurrent dislocation of the shoulder. JAMA 1943;123:889–892.
158. Malgaigne J. Traite des Fractures et des Luxations. Paris: Balliere, 1847.
159. Maquieira GJ, Gerber C, Schneeberger AG. Suprascapular nerve palsy after the Latarjet procedure. J Shoulder Elbow Surg 2007;16(2):e13–15.
160. Marquardt B, Potzl W, Witt KA, et al. A modified capsular shift for atraumatic anterior-inferior shoulder instability. Am J Sports Med 2005;33(7):1011–1015.
161. Marsh JL, Slongo TF, Agel J, et al. Fracture and dislocation classification compendium—2007: Orthopaedic Trauma Association classification, database, and outcomes committee. J Orthop Trauma 2007;21(10 Suppl):S1–133.
162. Matthews L, Vetter W, Oweida S, et al. Arthroscopic staple capsulorrhaphy for recurrent anterior shoulder instability. Arthroscopy 1988;4:106–111.
163. Matthews L, Zarins B, Michael R, et al. Anterior portal selection for shoulder arthroscopy. Arthroscopy 1985;1:33–39.
164. Mazzocca AD, Brown FM, Jr., Carreira DS, et al. Arthroscopic anterior shoulder stabilization of collision and contact athletes. Am J Sports Med 2005;33(1):52–60.
165. McCarty E, Warren R, Deng X, et al. Temperature along the axillary nerve during radiofrequency induced thermal capsular shrinkage. Am J Sports Med 2004;32: 909–914.
166. McFarland E, Neira C, Gutierrez M, et al. Clinical significance of the arthroscopic drive-through sign in shoulder surgery. Arthroscopy 2001;17:38–43.
167. McFarland E, O'Neill O, Hsu C. Complications of shoulder arthroscopy. J South Orthop Assoc 1997;6:190–196.
168. McIntyre L, Caspari R. The rationale and technique for arthroscopic reconstruction of anterior shoulder instability using multiple sutures. Orthop Clin North Am 1993;24: 55–58.
169. McIntyre L, Caspari R, Savoie F. The arthroscopic treatment of multidirectional shoulder instability: 2-year results of a multiple suture technique. Arthroscopy 1997;13: 418–425.
170. McLaughlin H. Posterior dislocation of the shoulder. J Bone Joint Surg 1952;34-A(3): 584–590.
171. McLaughlin H. Recurrent anterior dislocation of the shoulder: morbid anatomy. Am J Surg 1960;99:628–632.
172. McLaughlin H, Cavallaro W. Primary anterior dislocation of the shoulder. Am J Surg 1950;80:615–621.
173. McLaughlin H, MacLellan D. Recurrent anterior dislocation of the shoulder: II. A comparative study. J Trauma 1967;7:191–201.
174. Milch H. Treatment of dislocation of the shoulder. Surgery 1938;3:732–740.
175. Miller L, Donahue J, Good R, et al. The Magnuson-Stack procedure for treatment of recurrent glenohumeral dislocations. Am J Sports Med 1984;12(2):133–137.
176. Miller S, Cleeman E, Auerbach J, et al. Comparison of intra-articular lidocaine and intravenous sedation for reduction of shoulder dislocations: a randomized, prospective study. J Bone Joint Surg 2002;84-A:2135–2139.
177. Millett PJ, Clavert P, Warner JJ. Open operative treatment for anterior shoulder instability: when and why? J Bone Joint Surg Am 2005;87(2):419–432.
178. Miniaci A, Codsi MJ. Thermal capsulorrhaphy for the treatment of shoulder instability. Am J Sports Med Aug 2006;34(8):1356–1363.
179. Miniaci A, McBirnie J. Thermal capsular shrinkage for treatment of multidirectional instability of the shoulder. J Bone Joint Surg 2003;85-A:2283–2287.
180. Misamore GW, Sallay PI, Didelot W. A longitudinal study of patients with multidirectional instability of the shoulder with 7- to 10-year follow-up. J Shoulder Elbow Surg 2005;14(5):466–470.
181. Mishra D, Fanton G. Two-year outcome of arthroscopic Bankart repair and electrothermal assisted capsulorrhapy for recurrent traumatic anterior shoulder instability. Arthroscopy 2001;17:844–849.
182. Mizuno N, Yoneda M, Hayashida K, et al. Recurrent anterior shoulder dislocation caused by a midsubstance complete capsular tear. J Bone Joint Surg Am 2005;87(12): 2717–2723.
183. Montgomery W, Jobe F. Functional outcome in athletes after modified capsulolabral reconstruction. Am J Sports Med 1994;22:353–358.
184. Montgomery WH, Jr., Wahl M, Hettrich C, et al. Anteroinferior bone-grafting can restore stability in osseous glenoid defects. J Bone Joint Surg Am Sep 2005;87(9): 1972–1977.
185. Morgan C, Bordenstab A. Arthroscopic Bankart suture repair: technique and early results. Arthroscopy 1987;3:111–122.
186. Moseley H, Overgaard B. The anterior capsular mechanism in recurrent anterior dislocation of the shoulder. J Bone Joint Surg 1962;44-B(4):913–926.
187. Neer C, Foster C. Inferior capsular shift for involuntary inferior and multidirectional instability of the shoulder. A preliminary report. J Bone Joint Surg 1980;62-A:897–908.
188. Neer CSI. Involuntary inferior and multidirectional instability of the shoulder etiology, recognition, and treatment. Instr Cour Lect 1985;34:232–238.
189. Neri BR, Tuckman DV, Bravman JT, et al. Arthroscopic revision of Bankart repair. J Shoulder Elbow Surg 2007;16(4):419–424.
190. Neviaser J. Treatment of old unreduced dislocations of the shoulder. Surg Clin North Am 1963;43:1671–1678.
191. Neviaser R, Neviaser T, Neviaser J. Anterior dislocation of the shoulder and rotator cuff rupture. Clin Orthop 1993;291:103–106.
192. Neviaser R, Neviaser T, Neviaser J. Concurrent rupture of the rotator cuff and anterior dislocation of the shoulder in the older patient. J Bone Joint Surg 1988;70-A: 1308–1311.
193. Nicola T. Anterior dislocation of the shoulder: the role of the articular capsule. J Bone Joint Surg Am 1942;24:614–616.
194. Nielsen A, Nielsen K. The modified Bristow procedure for recurrent anterior dislocation of the shoulder. Results and complications. Acta Orthop Scand 1982;53:229–232.
195. Nobuhara K, Ikeda H. Rotator interval lesion. Clin Orthop 1987;223:44–50.
196. Nordqvist A, Petersson CJ. Incidence and causes of shoulder girdle injuries in an urban population. J Shoulder Elbow Surg 1995;4(2):107–112.
197. O'Brien S, Neves M, Arnoczky S, et al. The anatomy and histology of the inferior glenohumeral ligament complex of the shoulder. Am J Sports Med 1990;18:449–456.
198. O'Brien S, Schwartz R, Warren R, et al. Capsular restraints to anterior-posterior motion of the abducted shoulder: a biomechanical study. J Shoulder Elbow Surg 1995;4: 298–308.
199. O'Brien S, Warren R, Schwartz E. Anterior shoulder instability. Orthop Clin North Am 1987;18:395–408.
200. Osmond-Clarke H. Habitual dislocation of the shoulder: the Putti Platt operation. J Bone Joint Surg 1948;30-B:19–25.
201. Ovesen J, Nielsen S. Anterior and posterior shoulder instability: a cadaver study. Acta Orthop Scand 1986;57:324–327.
202. Ovesen J, Nielsen S. Experimental distal subluxation in the glenohumeral joint. Arch Orthop Trauma Surg 1985;104:78–81.
203. Owens BD, Duffey ML, Nelson BJ, et al. The incidence and characteristics of shoulder instability at the United States Military Academy. Am J Sports Med 2007;35(7): 1168–1173.
204. Pagnani M, Deng X, Warren R, et al. Role of the long head of the biceps brachii in glenohumeral stability: a biomechanical study in cadavera. J Shoulder Elbow Surg 1996;5:255–262.
205. Pagnani M, Dome D. Surgical treatment of traumatic anterior shoulder instability in American football players. J Bone Joint Surg 2002;84-A:711–715.
206. Pagnani M, Warren R. Arthroscopic shoulder stabilization. Oper Tech Sports Med 1993;1:276–284.
207. Park HB, Yokota A, Gill HS, et al. Revision surgery for failed thermal capsulorrhaphy. Am J Sports Med 2005;33(9):1321–1326.
208. Pelet S, Jolles BM, Farron A. Bankart repair for recurrent anterior glenohumeral instability: results at 29 years' follow-up. J Shoulder Elbow Surg 2006;15(2):203–207.
209. Peterson C, Altchek D, Warren R. Operative arthroscopy. In: Rockwood C, Matsen F, eds. The Shoulder. 2nd Ed. Philadelphia: WB Saunders, 1998.
210. Pevny T, Hunter R, Freeman J. Primary traumatic anterior shoulder dislocation in patients 40 years of age and older. Arthroscopy 1998;14:289–294.
211. Pitman M, Nainzedeh N, Ergas E, et al. The use of somatosensory evoked potentials for detection of neuropraxia during shoulder arthroscopy. Arthroscopy 1988;4:250–255.
212. Plausinis D, Bravman JT, Heywood C, et al. Arthroscopic rotator interval closure: effect of sutures on glenohumeral motion and anterior-posterior translation. Am J Sports Med 2006;34(10):1656–1661.
213. Pollock R, Owens J, Flatow E, et al. Operative results of the inferior capsular shift procedure for multidirectional instability of the shoulder. J Bone Joint Surg 2000;82-A:919–928.
214. Potzl W, Witt K, Hackenberg L, et al. Results of suture anchor repair of anteroinferior shoulder instability: a prospective clinical study of 85 shoulders. J Shoulder Elbow Surg 2003;12:322–326.
215. Protzman R. Anterior instability of the shoulder. J Bone Joint Surg 1980;62-A:909–918.
216. Provencher MT, Bell SJ, Menzel KA, et al. Arthroscopic treatment of posterior shoulder instability: results in 33 patients. Am J Sports Med 2005;33(10):1463–1471.
217. Rachbauer F, Ogon M, Wimmer C, et al. Glenohumeral osteoarthrosis after the Eden-Hybbinette procedure. Clin Orthop 2000;373:135–140.
218. Rahme H, Wikblad L, Nowak J, et al. Long-term clinical and radiologic results after Eden-Hybbinette operation for anterior instability of the shoulder. J Shoulder Elbow Surg 2003;12:15–19.
219. Reeves B. Acute anterior dislocation of the shoulder: clinical and experimental studies. Ann R Coll Surg Engl 1968;43:255–273.
220. Reeves B. Experiments on the tensile strength of the anterior capsular structures of the shoulder in man. J Bone Joint Surg 1968;50-B:858–865.
221. Regan W, Webster-Bogaert S, Hawkins R, et al. Comparative functional analysis of the Bristow, Magnuson-Stack, and Putti-Platt procedure for recurrent dislocations of the shoulder. Am J Sports Med 1989;17:42–48.
222. Reichl M, Koudela K. [Posttraumatic anterior shoulder instability—arthroscopic stabilization method using bone anchors]. Acta Chir Orthop Traumatol Cech 2004;71:37–44.
223. Reinold M, Wilk K, Hooks T, et al. Thermal assisted capsular shrinkage of the glenohumeral joint in overhead athletes: a 15 to 47 months follow-up. J Orthop Sports Phys Ther 2003;33:455–467.
224. Rhee YG, Cho NS. Anterior shoulder instability with humeral avulsion of the glenohumeral ligament lesion. J Shoulder Elbow Surg 2007;16(2):188–192.
225. Rhee YG, Ha JH, Cho NS. Anterior shoulder stabilization in collision athletes: arthroscopic versus open Bankart repair. Am J Sports Med 2006;34(6):979–985.
226. Rhee YG, Ha JH, Park KJ. Clinical outcome of anterior shoulder instability with capsular midsubstance tear: a comparison of isolated midsubstance tear and midsubstance tear with Bankart lesion. J Shoulder Elbow Surg 2006;15(5):586–590.
227. Rhee YG, Lee DH, Lim CT. Posterior capsulolabral reconstruction in posterior shoulder instability: deltoid saving. J Shoulder Elbow Surg 2005;14(4):355–360.
228. Richards DP, Burkhart SS. Arthroscopic humeral avulsion of the glenohumeral ligaments (HAGL) repair. Arthroscopy 2004;20(Suppl 2):134–141.
229. Richmond J, Donaldson W, Fu F, et al. Modification of the Bankart reconstruction with a suture anchor. Report of a new technique. Am J Sports Med 1991;19:343–346.

230. Robinson CM, Jenkins PJ, White TO, et al. Primary arthroscopic stabilization for a first-time anterior dislocation of the shoulder. A randomized, double-blind trial. J Bone Joint Surg Am Apr 2008;90(4):708–721.

231. Rockwood C, Wirth M. Subluxations and dislocations about the glenohumeral joint. In: Rockwood C, Green D, Bucholz R, et al., eds. Rockwood and Green's Fractures in Adults. Philadelphia: Lippincott-Raven, 1996; 1193–1339.

232. Rodeo S, Forster R, Weiland A. Neurological complications due to arthroscopy. J Bone Joint Surg 1993;75-A:917–926.

233. Rodosky M, Harner C, Fu F. The role of the long head of the biceps muscle and superior glenoid labrum in anterior stability of the shoulder. Am J Sports Med 1994; 22:121–130.

234. Rodriguez Merchan E, Ortega M. The Magnuson-Stack operation for recurrent anterior dislocation of the shoulder. A long-term follow-up of 44 operations. Int Orthop 1994; 18:356–358.

235. Rokous J, Feagin J, Abbott H. Modified axillary roentgenogram: a useful adjunct in the diagnosis of recurrent instability of the shoulder. Clin Orthop 1972;82:84–86.

236. Rowe C. Prognosis in dislocations of the shoulder. J Bone Joint Surg 1956;38-A(5): 957–977.

237. Rowe C, Sakellarides H. Factors related to recurrences of anterior dislocations of the shoulder. Clin Orthop 1961;20:40–47.

238. Rowe C, Zarins B. Chronic unreduced dislocations of the shoulder. J Bone Joint Surg 1982;64-A(4):494–505.

239. Rowe C, Zarins B. Recurrent transient subluxation of the shoulder. J Bone Joint Surg 1981;63-A:863–872.

240. Rozing P, DeBakker H, Obermann W. Radiographic views in recurrent anterior shoullder dislocation: comparison of six methods for identification of typical lesions. Acta Orthop Scand 1986;57:328–330.

241. Russell J, Holmes E, Keller D, et al. Reduction of acute anterior shoulder dislocations using the Milch technique. A study of ski injuries. J Trauma 1981;21:802–804.

242. Sachs RA, Lin D, Stone ML, et al. Can the need for future surgery for acute traumatic anterior shoulder dislocation be predicted? J Bone Joint Surg Am 2007;89(8): 1665–1674.

243. Sachs RA, Williams B, Stone ML, et al. Open Bankart repair: correlation of results with postoperative subscapularis function. Am J Sports Med 2005;33(10):1458–1462.

244. Saxena K, Stavas J. Inferior glenohumeral dislocation. Ann Emerg Med 1983;12: 718–720.

245. Schroder DT, Provencher MT, Mologne TS, et al. The modified Bristow procedure for anterior shoulder instability: 26-year outcomes in Naval Academy midshipmen. Am J Sports Med 2006;34(5):778–786.

246. Schultz T, Jacobs B, Patterson R. Unrecognized dislocations of the shoulder. J Trauma 1969;9:1009–1023.

247. Schwartz R, O'Brien S, Warren R, et al. Capsular restraints to anterior posterior motion in the shoulder. Orthop Trans 1988;12:727.

248. Segal D, Yablon I, Lynch J, et al. Acute bilateral anterior dislocation of the shoulders. Clin Orthop 1979;140:21–22.

249. Selecky M, Tibone J, Yang B, et al. Glenohumeral joint translation after arthroscopic thermal capsuloplasty of the rotator interval. J Shoulder Elbow Surg 2003;12:139–143.

250. Silliman JF, Hawkins RJ. Classification and physical diagnosis of instability of the shoulder. Clin Orthop Relat Res 1993(291):7–19.

251. Simonet WT, Melton LJ 3rd, Cofield RH, et al. Incidence of anterior shoulder dislocation in Olmsted County, Minnesota. Clin Orthop Relat Res 1984(186):186–191.

252. Singer G, Kirkland P, Emery R. Coracoid transposition for recurrent anterior instability of the shoulder. A 20-year follow-up study. J Bone Joint Surg 1995;77-B:73–76.

253. Spang JT, Karas SG. The HAGL lesion: an arthroscopic technique for repair of humeral avulsion of the glenohumeral ligaments. Arthroscopy 2005;21(4):498–502.

254. Sperling J, Cofield R, Torchia M, et al. Infection after shoulder instability surgery. Clin Orthop 2003;414:61–64.

255. Stimson L. An easy method of reducing dislocations of the shoulder and hip. Med Record 1900;57:356–357.

256. Stromsoe K, Senn E, Simmen B, et al. [Recurrence frequency after the first traumatic shoulder dislocation]. Helv Chir Acta 1980;47:85–88.

257. Sugaya H, Moriishi J, Dohi M, et al. Glenoid rim morphology in recurrent anterior glenohumeral instability. J Bone Joint Surg 2003;85-A:878–884.

258. Sugaya H, Moriishi J, Kanisawa I, et al. Arthroscopic osseous Bankart repair for chronic recurrent traumatic anterior glenohumeral instability. Surgical technique. J Bone Joint Surg Am 2006;88(Suppl 1 Pt 2):159–169.

259. Symeonides P. The significance of the subscapularis muscle in the pathogenesis of recurrent anterior dislocations of the shoulder. J Bone Joint Surg 1972;54-B:476–483.

260. te Slaa R, Wijffels M, Brand R, et al. The prognosis following acute primary glenohumeral dislocation. J Bone Joint Surg 2004;86-B:58–64.

261. Thabit G. The arthroscopically assisted holmium: YAG laser surgery in the shoulder. Oper Tech Sports Med 1998;6:131–138.

262. Thomas S, Matsen F. An approach to the repair of glenohumeral ligament avulsion in the management of traumatic anterior glenohumeral instability. J Bone Joint Surg 1989; 71-A:506–513.

263. Tibone J, Ting A. Capsulorrhaphy with a staple for recurrent posterior subluxation of the shoulder. J Bone Joint Surg 1990;72-A:999–1002.

264. Tirman PF, Steinbach LS, Feller JF, et al. Humeral avulsion of the anterior shoulder stabilizing structures after anterior shoulder dislocation: demonstration by MRI and MR arthrography. Skeletal Radiol 1996;25(8):743–748.

265. Tjoumakaris FP, Abboud JA, Hasan SA, et al. Arthroscopic and open Bankart repairs provide similar outcomes. Clin Orthop Relat Res 2006;446:227–232.

266. Torchia M, Caspari R, Asselmeier M, et al. Arthroscopic transglenoid multiple suture repair: 2- to 8-year results in 150 shoulders. Arthroscopy 1997;13:609–619.

267. Torg J, Balduini F, Bonci C, et al. A modified Bristow procedure for recurrent dislocation and subluxation of the shoulder. Report of 212 cases. J Bone Joint Surg 1987;69-A(6):904–913.

268. Tornetta P, Simon G, Stratford W, et al. Luxatio erecta: Persistent displacement of the greater tuberosity after reduction. Orthop Rev 1993;22:855–858.

269. Townley C. The capsular mechanism in recurrent dislocations of the shoulder. J Bone Joint Surg 1950;32-A:370–380.

270. Treacy S, Field L, Savoie F. Rotator interval capsule closure: an arthroscopic technique. Arthroscopy 1997;13:103–106.

271. Treacy S, Savoie F, Field L. Arthroscopic treatment of multidirectional instability. J Shoulder Elbow Surg 1999;8:345–350.

272. Tung GA, Hou DD. MR arthrography of the posterior labrocapsular complex: relationship with glenohumeral joint alignment and clinical posterior instability. AJR Am J Roentgenol 2003;180(2):369–375.

273. van der Zwaag H, Brand R, Obermann W, et al. Glenohumeral osteoarthrosis after Putti-Platt repair. J Shoulder Elbow Surg 1999;8:252–258.

274. Victoroff B, Deutsch A, Protomastro P, et al. The effects of radiofrequency thermal capsulorrhaphy on glenohumeral translation, rotation, and volume. J Shoulder Elbow Surg 2004;13:138–145.

275. Wang VM, Sugalski MT, Levine WN, et al. Comparison of glenohumeral mechanics following a capsular shift and anterior tightening. J Bone Joint Surg Am 2005;87(6): 1312–1322.

276. Warner J, Bowen M, Deng X, et al. Effect of joint compression on inferior stability of the glenohumeral joint. J Shoulder Elbow Surg 1999;8:31–36.

277. Warner J, Deng X, Warren R, et al. Static capsuloligamentous restraints to superior-inferior translation of the glenohumeral joint. Am J Sports Med 1992;6:675–685.

278. Warner JJ, Gill TJ, O'Hollerhan J D, et al. Anatomical glenoid reconstruction for recurrent anterior glenohumeral instability with glenoid deficiency using an autogenous tricortical iliac crest bone graft. Am J Sports Med 2006;34(2):205–212.

279. Wheeler JH, Ryan JB, Arciero RA, et al. Arthroscopic versus nonoperative treatment of acute shoulder dislocations in young athletes. Arthroscopy 1989;5(3):213–217.

280. Wiater JM, Vibert BT. Glenohumeral joint volume reduction with progressive release and shifting of the inferior shoulder capsule. J Shoulder Elbow Surg 2007;16(6): 810–814.

281. Williams R, Strickland S, Cohen M, et al. Arthroscopic repair for traumatic posterior shoulder instability. Am J Sports Med 2003;31:203–209.

282. Willits KR. A randomized evaluation of immobilization in external rotation after primary shoulder dislocation. Proceedings of the 75th Annual Meeting of the American Academy of Orthopaedic Surgeons. San Francisco, CA: AAOS; 2008.

283. Wilson J, McKeever F. Traumatic posterior (retrograde) dislocation of the humerus. J Bone Joint Surg 1949;31-A:160–172.

284. Wirth M, Butters K, Rockwood C. The posterior deltoid-splitting approach to the shoulder. Clin Orthop 1993;296:92–98.

285. Wirth M, Groh G, Rockwood C. Capsulorrhaphy through an anterior approach for the treatment of atraumatic posterior glenohumeral instability with multidirectional laxity of the shoulder. J Bone Joint Surg 1998;80-A:1570–1578.

286. Wirth M, Rockwood C. Subluxations and dislocations about the glenohumeral joint. In: Bucholz R, Heckman J, eds. Rockwood and Green's Fractures in Adults. Philadelphia: Lippincott Williams & Wilkins, 2001; 1109–1207.

287. Wirth M, Seltzer D, Rockwood C. Recurrent posterior glenohumeral dislocation associated with increased retroversion of the glenoid. A case report. Clin Orthop 1994;308: 98–101.

288. Wolf E, Eakin C. Arthroscopic capsular plication for posterior shoulder instability. Arthroscopy 1998;14:153–163.

289. Wolf EM, Cheng JC, Dickson K. Humeral avulsion of glenohumeral ligaments as a cause of anterior shoulder instability. Arthroscopy 1995;11(5):600–607.

290. Wuelker N, Plitz W, Roetman B. Biomechanical data concerning the shoulder impingement syndrome. Clin Orthop 1994;303:242–249.

291. Yamamoto N, Itoi E, Tuoheti Y, et al. Effect of rotator interval closure on glenohumeral stability and motion: a cadaveric study. J Shoulder Elbow Surg 2006;15(6):750–758.

292. Yamamoto T, Yoshiya S, Kurosaka M, et al. Luxatio erecta (inferior dislocation of the shoulder): a report of five cases and a review of the literature. Am J Orthop 2003;32: 601–603.

293. Young D, Rockwood C. Complications of a failed Bristow procedure and their management. J Bone Joint Surg 1991;73-A:969–981.

294. Zaffagnini S, Marcacci M, Loreti I, et al. Results of the original Putti-Platt procedure for shoulder instability: review of Putti's scholar experience. Knee Surg Sports Traumatol Arthrosc 2000;8:314–319.

295. Zimmerman L, Veith I. Great Ideas in the History of Surgery: Clavicle, Shoulder, and Shoulder Amputations. Baltimore: Williams & Wilkins, 1961.

296. Zuckerman J, Matsen F. Complications about the glenohumeral joint related to the use of screws and staples. J Bone Joint Surg 1984;66-A:175–180.

39

ACROMIOCLAVICULAR JOINT INJURIES

Leesa M. Galatz, Ronald F. Hollis Jr., and Gerald R. Williams Jr.

INTRODUCTION

The acromioclavicular (AC) joint is commonly involved in traumatic injuries that affect the shoulder. Treatment of these injuries has been controversial and continues to evolve to this day. Most injuries are related to falls onto the shoulder and to repetitive use of the shoulder, such as heavy labor and athletics. This chapter focuses primarily on the traumatic aspects of AC disorders and describes the anatomy, classification, biomechanics, diagnosis, and treatment of these injuries.

Dislocation of the AC joint, particularly its treatment, has been a subject of controversy from the earliest medical writings. Hippocrates[1] (460–377 BC) wrote:

> Physicians are particularly liable to be deceived in this accident (for as the separated bone protrudes, the top of the shoulder appears low and hollow), so that they may prepare as if for dislocation of the shoulder; for I have known many physicians otherwise not expert at the art who have done much mischief by attempting to reduce shoulders, thus supposing it as a case of dislocation.

Galen[1] (129–199 AD) obviously had paid close attention to Hippocrates, because he diagnosed his own AC dislocation received from wrestling in the palaestra. This famous physician of the Greco–Roman period treated himself in the manner of Hippocrates (i.e., tight bandages to hold the projecting clavicle down while keeping the arm elevated). He abandoned the treatment after only a few days because it was so uncomfortable. It is appropriate that one of the earliest reported cases in the literature was related to sports, because today participation in sports is certainly one of the most common causes of AC dislocations.

From the earliest publications through the time of Paul of Aegina (7th century), dislocations of the AC joint have become better recognized. Their treatment, however, has remained essentially unchanged. Hippocrates[1] stated that no impediment, small or great, will result from such an injury. He further stated that there would be a "tumefaction" or deformity, "for the bone cannot be properly restored to its natural situation." This statement apparently was, has been, and will be received by the orthopaedic community as a challenge. There is probably not another joint in the body that has been treated in so many different ways as the AC joint in attempts to "properly restore" it to "its natural situation."

The treatment of AC joint injuries has evolved and changed as our understanding of the nature of the problem and the biomechanics of the joint has developed. In 1917, Cadenat[18] described the transfer of the coracoacromial ligament, which was later popularized by Weaver and Dunn.[152] This remains the most commonly used and successful surgical treatment we have today for many complete AC dislocations. Surgical treatment was very common in the 1940s to the 1960s for complete dislocations.[144]

After further study, the complete dislocations (of the AC joint) according to older classification systems were broken down into more detailed groupings depending on the position of the clavicle and the degree of soft tissue injury.[121] Now, treatment addresses the specific pathology involved, and many of the injuries thought to need treatment in the past are successfully treated with conservative measures. Treatment remains controversial in many circumstances, as over the years numerous surgical methods have been described.

PRINCIPLES OF MANAGEMENT

Mechanism of Injury

Direct force is the most common mechanism of injury and is produced by the patient falling onto the lateral aspect of the shoulder with the arm in an adducted position (Fig. 39-1). The force drives the acromion downward and medially. Bearn[7] showed that downward displacement of the distal clavicle is primarily resisted through an interlocking of the sternoclavicular ligaments. If no fracture occurs, the force first sprains the AC ligaments (a mild sprain), then tears the AC ligaments (a moderate sprain) and stresses the coracoclavicular ligament, and finally—if the downward force continues—tears the deltoid and trapezius muscle attachments from the clavicle and ruptures the coracoclavicular ligaments (a severe AC sprain, which completes the dislocation). At this point, the upper extremity has lost its suspensory support from the clavicle and the scapula displaces inferiorly.

The mechanism for the inferior dislocation of the clavicle under the coracoid is thought to be a very severe direct force onto the superior surface of the distal clavicle, along with abduction of the arm and retraction of the scapula.[97] This type of AC joint dislocation is exceedingly rare.

Classically, the literature indicates that upward displacement of the clavicle is diagnostic of a complete AC dislocation. Although there may be a slight upward displacement of the clavicle by the pull of the trapezius muscle, the characteristic anatomic feature is actually inferior displacement of the shoulder and arm. The scapula and attached upper extremity are sus-

FIGURE 39-1 The most common mechanism of injury is a direct force that occurs from a fall on the point of the shoulder.

pended from the clavicle primarily by the coracoclavicular ligaments and secondarily through the AC ligament and the surrounding musculature. Therefore, when a severe downward force is applied to the point of the shoulder (assuming the sternoclavicular ligaments do not rupture and the clavicle does not fracture), the coracoclavicular ligaments rupture. The suspension system of the scapula and attached upper extremity from the clavicle is lost. Consequently, the arm displaces inferiorly (Fig. 39-2). Because the weight of the arm is no longer suspended from the clavicle, there may be a slight upward pull by the trapezius muscle on the clavicle. However, the major deformity seen in complete AC dislocation is a downward displacement of the shoulder.

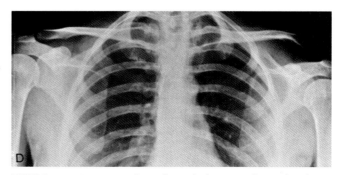

FIGURE 39-2 Anteroposterior radiograph demonstrating a chronic AC joint dislocation on the left upper extremity. Note that the clavicles are in the same position bilaterally, and the left scapula is displaced inferiorly. (From Rockwood CA, Young DC. Disorders of the acromioclavicular joint. In: Rockwood CA, Matsen F III, eds. The Shoulder. Philadelphia: WB Saunders, 1990:434.)

Associated Injuries

Scapulothoracic Dissociation

AC separations may be associated with other injuries about the shoulder. Scapulothoracic dissociations are characterized by lateral displacement of the scapula, a severe neurovascular injury, and an injury to bone (either an AC separation, a displaced clavicle fracture, or a sternoclavicular disruption). Scapulothoracic dissociations are usually clinically obvious. Injuries associated with AC separations, however, may be less obvious. The patient not only will have pain in the shoulder but also will complain of chest pain and pain in the periscapular and perithoracic region. Clinical examination demonstrates the AC deformity as well as marked tenderness in the periscapular and perithoracic region. An anteroposterior chest radiograph demonstrates an increased distance between the medial scapular border and the midline on the affected side compared with the unaffected side, as well as perhaps a pleural effusion. Magnetic resonance imaging of the thorax demonstrates increased signal in the periscapular and perithoracic muscles in addition to a pleural effusion.

Fractures

Fractures associated with AC separations may include fractures of the clavicle, the acromion process, the coracoid process, and the sternoclavicular joint. Wurtz and colleagues[157] reported 4 patients with a fracture of the middle third of the clavicle and dislocation of the AC joint. Various treatment methods were used and achieved good results in all four patients with 1- to 3-year follow-up. Barber[6] reported a patient with a type IV AC joint injury associated with a contralateral pneumothorax and an ipsilateral pulmonary contusion.

Brachial Plexus Abnormalities

Meislin and colleagues[98] have reported a patient who developed a brachial plexus neuropraxia 8 years after sustaining a type III AC separation. The patient responded well to coracoclavicular stabilization. Brachial plexus injuries associated with AC separations are not common. Sturm and Perry,[137] in a review of 59 patients with brachial plexus injuries, identified two patients with AC separations.

Coracoclavicular Ossification

Coracoclavicular ossification has been referred to as both ossification and calcification. Urist[146] demonstrated that bone does indeed form in the coracoclavicular interval. The calcification can be formed heterotopically around the area of injury, or it can form a bridge between the coracoid and the clavicle. Usually, it has no effect on the functional outcome.

Osteolysis of the Distal Clavicle

Osteolysis of the distal clavicle may follow an acute injury or may occur in persons who have repeated stress on the shoulder. Madsen[88] reported seven patients with the rare complication known as posttraumatic osteolysis of the distal clavicle. He identified eight cases in the literature at that time (1963), the first of which was reported by Werder in 1950. Cahill[19] reported 46 patients who were athletes, none of whom had an acute injury, but 45 of whom lifted weights as part of their training. He used technetium bone scans and a 35-degree cephalic tilt radiographic view to help make the diagnosis. Several authors have reported this condition in women.[92,99,112]

The radiographic findings are osteoporosis, osteolysis, and tapering of the distal clavicle. Usually, bony changes do not occur in the acromion. Changes usually occur only in the injured shoulder. If changes are noted in both shoulders, then other conditions should be considered, such as rheumatoid arthritis, hyperparathyroidism, and scleroderma. The differential diagnosis of a lesion in one shoulder should include Gorham's massive osteolysis, gout, and a neoplasm such as multiple myeloma. Microscopic studies of the distal clavicle have been reported by Murphy and coworkers[104] and Madsen.[88] They described demineralization, subchondral cysts, and erosion of the distal clavicle. Griffiths and Glucksman[56] performed a biopsy 8 months after injury that showed patches of necrotic and reactive woven bone.

History and Physical Examination

As with any orthopaedic evaluation, a thorough history should be obtained detailing the mechanism of injury as well as a complete discussion of patient symptoms. A complete evaluation of all injured extremities should be documented including a neurovascular examination. When AC joint injury is suspected, the patient should be examined, whenever possible, in the standing or sitting position. The weight of the arm stresses the AC joint and makes a deformity more apparent.

Type I Injury

In a type I injury, there is minimal to moderate tenderness and swelling over the AC joint without palpable displacement of the joint. Usually there is only minimal pain with arm movements. Tenderness is not present in the coracoclavicular interspace.

Type II Injury

With subluxation of the AC joint, moderate to severe pain is noted at the joint. If the patient is examined shortly after injury, the outer end of the clavicle may be noted to be slightly superior to the acromion. Motion of the shoulder produces pain in the AC joint. With gentle palpation, the lateral end of the clavicle is unstable in the anterior–posterior direction. If the mid-clavicle is grasped and the acromion stabilized, posterior–anterior motion of the clavicle in the horizontal plane can be detected. There should be little, if any, instability in the vertical plane. Tenderness is also noted when the physician palpates anteriorly in the coracoclavicular interspace.

Type III Injury

The patient with type III injury, complete dislocation of the AC joint, characteristically presents with the upper extremity held adducted close to the body and supported in an elevated position to relieve the pain in the AC joint. The shoulder complex is depressed when compared with the normal shoulder. The clavicle may be prominent enough to tent the skin (Fig. 39-3). Moderate pain is the rule, and any motion of the arm, particularly abduction, increases the pain.

Tenderness is noted at the AC joint, the coracoclavicular interspace, and along the superior aspect of the lateral fourth of the clavicle. The entire length of the clavicular shaft should be palpated to detect an associated clavicle shaft fracture. The lateral clavicle is unstable in both the horizontal and vertical

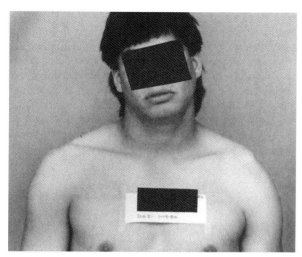

FIGURE 39-3 This patient has a complete type III dislocation of the left AC joint. The left shoulder is drooping, and there is prominence of the left distal clavicle. (From Rockwood CA, Young DC. Disorders of the AC joint. In: Rockwood CA, Matsen F III, eds. The Shoulder. Philadelphia: WB Saunders, 1990:425.)

planes. The key to the diagnosis of a type III injury is that the defect can be reduced with upward pressure under the elbow. A reducible injury is differentiated from a type IV or V injury, which cannot be reduced (see below).

Type IV Injury

The patient with a type IV injury has essentially all the clinical findings of a type III injury. In addition, examination of the seated patient from above reveals that the outline of the displaced clavicle is inclined posteriorly compared with the uninjured shoulder. The clavicle usually is displaced so severely posteriorly that it becomes "buttonholed" through the trapezius muscle and tents the posterior skin (Fig. 39-4). Consequently, motion of the shoulder is more painful than in a type III injury. The AC joint cannot be reduced manually in this situation.

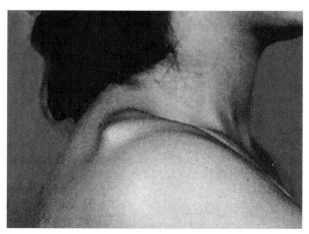

FIGURE 39-4 Patient with type IV AC joint injury. Note that the distal end of the clavicle is displaced posteriorly back into and through the trapezius muscle. (From Rockwood CA, Young DC. Disorders of the acromioclavicular joint. In: Rockwood CA, Matsen F III, eds. The Shoulder. Philadelphia: WB Saunders, 1990:446.)

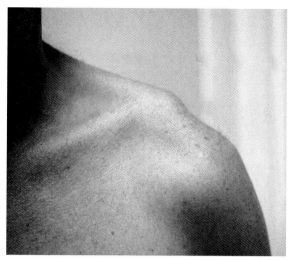

FIGURE 39-5 A photograph of a type V AC joint dislocation demonstrating the superior displacement of the clavicle relative to the shoulder.

The sternoclavicular joint should always be examined for an associated anterior dislocation.[126]

Type V Injury

The type V injury is an exaggeration of the type III injury in which the distal end of the clavicle appears to be grossly superiorly displaced and tenting the skin (Fig. 39-5). This apparent upward displacement is the result of downward displacement of the upper extremity. The patient has more pain than with a type III injury, particularly over the distal half of the clavicle. This is secondary to the extensive muscle and soft tissue disruption from the clavicle that occurs with this injury. The distal clavicle is subcutaneous and cannot be manually reduced. Occasionally, there is so much inferior displacement of the upper extremity that the patient will develop symptoms of traction on the brachial plexus.

Type VI Injury

Type VI injuries are very rare. The superior aspect of the shoulder has a flat appearance, as opposed to the rounded contour of the normal shoulder. With palpation, the acromion is prominent, and there is a definite inferior stepdown to the superior surface of the coracoid process. Because of the amount of trauma required to produce a subcoracoid dislocation of the clavicle, there may be associated fractures of the clavicle and upper ribs or injury to the upper roots of the brachial plexus. These associated injuries may produce so much swelling of the shoulder that the disruption of the AC joint may not initially be recognized. Vascular injuries secondary to the dislocation were not present in the patients presented by McPhee,[97] Schwarz and Kuderna,[130] and Gerber and Rockwood.[54] However, all the adult cases reported by McPhee[102] and Gerber and Rockwood[54] had transient paresthesias before reduction of the dislocation. After reduction, the neurologic deficits resolved.

Imaging and Other Diagnostic Studies

Good-quality radiographs of the AC joint require one third to one half the x-ray penetration required to image the glenohumeral joint. Radiographs of the AC joint taken using routine shoulder technique will be overpenetrated (i.e., dark), and small fractures may be overlooked. Therefore, the x-ray technician must be specifically requested to take radiographs of the "AC joint" rather than the "shoulder."

Anteroposterior Views

Routine anteroposterior views should be obtained with the patient standing or sitting, with the back against the x-ray cassette and the arms hanging unsupported at the side. Because of significant individual variation in AC joint anatomy and because the coracoclavicular interspace will vary with the angle of the x-ray beam and with the distance between the beam and the patient, both AC joints should be imaged simultaneously on one large (14- × 17-inch) cassette. Large patients with shoulders too broad to be visualized on a single cassette should have radiographs made with two smaller (10- × 12-inch) cassettes using identical technique.

The difficulty in evaluating AC joint injuries lies in the fact that with this projection, the distal clavicle and acromion are superimposed on the spine of the scapula. Subtle fractures of the distal clavicle are easily missed. Zanca[159] noted this during a review of 1000 radiographs of patients with shoulder pain. Therefore, he recommended a 10 to 15 degree cephalic tilt view to project an unobscured image of the joint (Fig. 39-6). This view is now routinely used in the evaluation of AC joint injuries and is particularly useful when there is suspicion of a small fracture or loose body on routine views (Fig. 39-7).

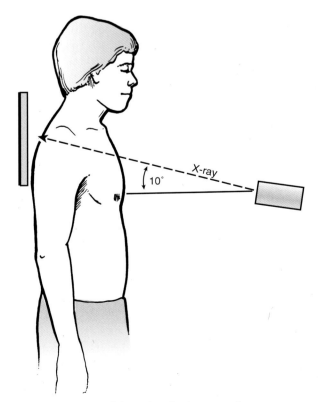

FIGURE 39-6 Position of the patient for the Zanca view—a 10- to 15-degree cephalic tilt of the standard view for the AC joint. (From Rockwood CA, Young DC. Disorders of the acromioclavicular joint. In: Rockwood CA, Matsen F III, eds. The Shoulder. Philadelphia: WB Saunders, 1990:428.)

Lateral Views

As with any musculoskeletal injury, a radiograph in one plane is not sufficient to classify an AC joint injury. An axillary lateral view should be taken of the injured shoulder when an AC dislocation is suspected. The cassette should be placed on the superior aspect of the shoulder and medial enough to expose as much of the lateral third of the clavicle as possible. This will reveal any posterior displacement of the clavicle as well as any small fractures that may have been missed on the anteroposterior view.

Stryker Notch View

A variant of an AC joint injury involves a fracture of the coracoid process. This injury should be suspected when there is an AC joint dislocation on the anteroposterior projection, but the coracoclavicular distance is normal, or equal to that on the opposite, uninvolved side. A Stryker notch view taken appropriately puts the coracoid in profile and is the best view for evaluating this injury. This is performed with the patient supine and the arm elevated over the head with the palm behind the head. The humerus must be parallel to the longitudinal axis of the body, with the elbow pointed straight toward the ceiling (Fig. 39-8).

Other Modalities

Schmid and Schmid[129] reported the use of ultrasonography in the diagnosis of 22 cases of type III AC dislocation. Ultrasound examination demonstrated visible instability of the distal clavicle, incongruity of the joint, hematoma formation, or visible ligament remnants in all cases. However, in spite of the advent of such sophisticated imaging modalities as ultrasonography, computed tomography (CT), and magnetic resonance imaging, plain radiography continues to be the most readily available, cost-effective method for routine investigation of injuries to the AC joint.

Diagnosis and Classification

Diagnosis

Normal Joints. The width and configuration of the AC joint in the coronal plane may vary significantly from individual to individual. This should be remembered so that a normal variant is not mistaken as an injury. In a study of 100 radiographs of normal shoulders, Urist[146] found that nearly half (49%) of the AC joints were inclined superolateral to inferomedial, with the articular surface of the clavicle overriding the acromion; 27% were vertical, and 3% were inclined superomedial to inferolateral, with the articular surface of the clavicle underriding the acromion. Another 21% of the joints were incongruent, with the clavicle lying either superior or inferior to the acromial articular surface.

The normal width of the AC joint in the coronal plane is 1 to 3 mm.[159] Petersson and Redlund-Johnell[115] measured AC joint width radiographically in 151 normal individuals and drew several conclusions: the AC joint space normally diminishes with increasing age, a joint space of 0.5 mm in a patient older than 60 years is conceivably normal, and a joint space of greater than 7 mm in men and 6 mm in women is pathologic.

The coracoclavicular interspace also exhibits significant individual variation. The average distance between the clavicle and the coracoid process ranges from 1.1 to 1.3 cm.[6] An increase in the coracoclavicular distance of 50% over the normal side

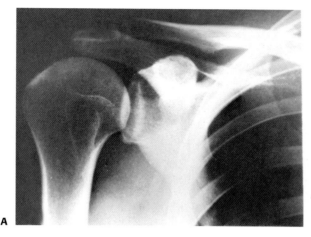

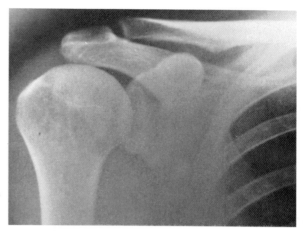

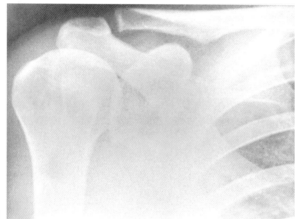

FIGURE 39-7 An explanation of why the AC joint is poorly visualized on routine shoulder x-rays. **A.** This routine anteroposterior view of the shoulder shows the glenohumeral joint well. However, the AC joint is too dark to interpret, because that area of the anatomy has been overpenetrated by the x-ray technique. **B.** When the exposure usually used to take the shoulder radiographs is decreased by two thirds, the AC joint is well visualized. However, the inferior corner of the AC joint is superimposed on the acromion process. **C.** Tilting the tube 15 degrees upward provides a clear view of the AC joint.

FIGURE 39-8 Technique for taking the Stryker notch view to demonstrate fractures of the base of the coracoid. The patient is supine with a cassette placed posterior to the shoulder. The humerus is flexed approximately 120 degrees so the patient's hand can be placed on top of the head. The x-ray beam is directed 10 degrees superior. (From Rockwood CA, Young DC. Disorders of the acromioclavicular joint. In: Rockwood CA, Matsen F III, eds. The Shoulder. Philadelphia: WB Saunders, 1990:433.)

signifies a complete AC dislocation.[6] Complete dislocation has been seen with as little as a 25% increase in the coracoclavicular distance.

Type I Injury. In a type I injury, the radiographs of the AC joint are normal, except for mild soft tissue swelling, as compared with the uninjured shoulder. There is no widening, no separation, and no deformity.

Type II Injury. In a type II injury, the lateral end of the clavicle may be slightly elevated. The AC joint, when compared with the normal side, may appear to be widened. The widening probably is the result of a slight medial rotation of the scapula and slight posterior displacement of the clavicle by the pull of the trapezius muscle. The coracoclavicular space of the injured shoulder is the same as that of the normal shoulder.

Type III Injury. In obvious cases of complete AC dislocations, the joint is totally displaced. The lateral end of the clavicle is displaced completely above the superior border of the acromion and the coracoclavicular interspace is significantly (25% to 100%) greater than in the normal shoulder (Fig. 39-9). Fractures may be noted involving the distal clavicle or the acromion process.

Rarely, complete AC dislocation will be accompanied by a fracture of the coracoid process rather than by disruption of the coracoclavicular ligaments. Although the fracture of the cor-

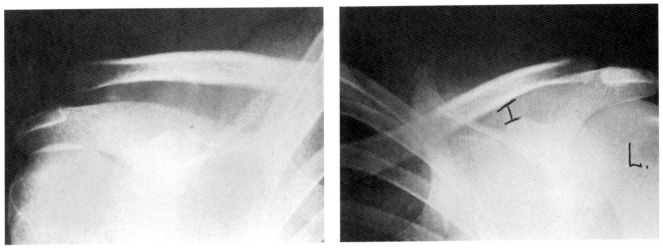

FIGURE 39-9 X-ray appearance of a grade III injury. Not only is the right AC joint displaced compared with the left, but, more significantly, notice the great increase in the coracoclavicular interspace on the injured right shoulder compared with the normal left shoulder.

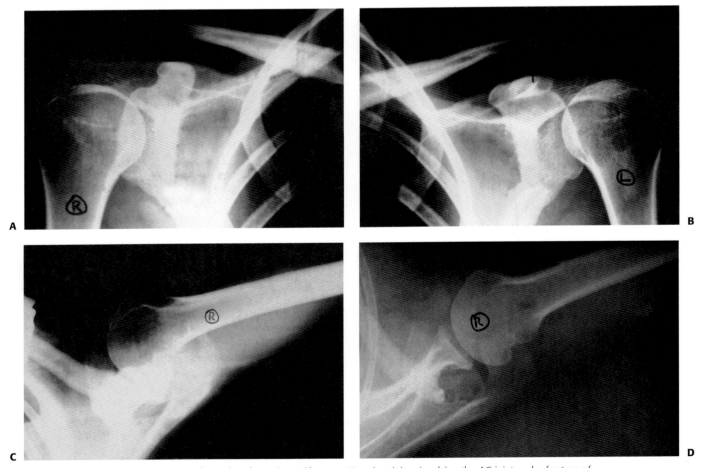

FIGURE 39-10 Radiographs of a patient with a type III variant injury involving the AC joint and a fracture of both the base and the tip of the coracoid. **A.** An anteroposterior radiograph of the injured right side. The coracoid injury is not visualized. **B.** A radiograph of the uninjured left side demonstrating that the coracoclavicular distance is equal on the injured and unaffected sides. **C.** An axillary view shows the tip fracture, but the fracture at the base is not easily detected. **D.** The West Point view clearly shows the fracture at the tip of the coracoid process. *(continues)*

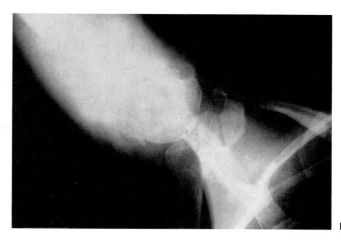

E

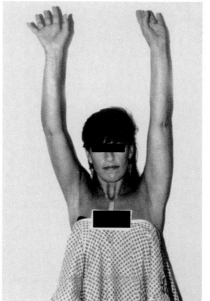

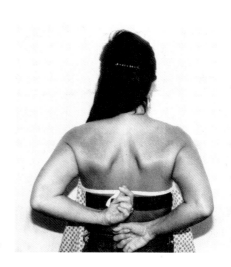

FIGURE 39-10 (*continued*) **E.** The Stryker notch view clearly shows the fracture at the base of the coracoid. **F.** Nonoperative treatment in this case led to an excellent result as evidenced by full overhead elevation. **G.** The patient regained near-normal internal rotation.

F   G

acoid process is difficult to visualize on routine radiographs, its presence should be suspected because of the presence of a complete AC separation and a normal coracoclavicular distance, as compared with the uninjured shoulder. The best special view for visualizing the coracoid fracture is the Stryker notch view (Fig. 39-10). The technique for obtaining this view is described above. A few unusual injury patterns uncommonly occur and are variations of type III injuries. Most often, complete separation of the articular surfaces of the distal clavicle and acromion is accompanied by complete disruption of the AC and coracoclavicular ligaments. Children and adolescents usually sustain a variant of complete AC dislocation. Radiographs reveal displacement of the distal clavicular metaphysis superiorly with a large increase in the coracoclavicular interspace. These injuries are most often Salter-Harris type I or II injuries in which the epiphysis and the intact AC joint remain in their anatomic locations while the distal clavicular metaphysis is displaced superiorly through a dorsal rent in the periosteal sleeve (Fig. 39-11).[11,30,40,43,66] The lateral epiphysis of the clavicle is barely visible because it is thin and appears and fuses over a short time period at approximately 19 years of age.

Eidman and coworkers[40] reported on 25 AC injuries in children treated surgically. In all patients younger than 13 years of age, there was a lateral Salter-Harris clavicular fracture rather than a true AC dislocation. The importance of recognizing this injury is that the intact coracoclavicular ligaments remain attached to the periosteal sleeve. Nonoperative management most often results in healing of the clavicular fracture and thus reestablishment of the integrity of the coracoclavicular ligaments. Those authors who recommend surgical repair in selected instances emphasize the importance of repairing the dorsal rent in the periosteal sleeve.[40,43]

A second variation of the type III injury involves complete separation of the AC articular surfaces combined with a fracture of the coracoid process.[20,76,91] This is an extremely uncommon injury. In most cases the coracoclavicular ligaments have remained intact and attached to the displaced coracoid process fracture, which most often occurs through the base. There are only two reported cases of complete AC separation—coracoclavicular ligament disruption and coracoid process fracture.[150,154] According to the authors, the mechanism of injury for this "triple lesion" is a simultaneous blow to the acromion and forcible

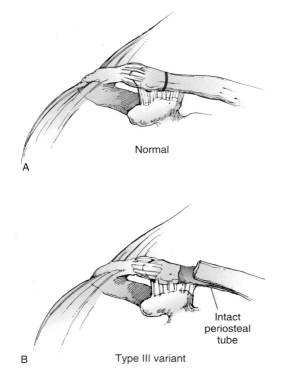

Normal

A

Type III variant

B

Intact
periosteal
tube

FIGURE 39-11 A. In children and adolescents, the distal clavicular physis lies medial to the AC capsular reflection. Injuries in this age group are often type II Salter-Harris fractures involving the physis rather than AC dislocations. **B.** The coracoclavicular ligaments remain attached to the intact periosteal sleeve while the medial clavicular fragment displaces through a dorsal periosteal rent.

elbow flexion against resistance. In both of these reported cases, the patients underwent operative repair.

Both operative and nonoperative methods of treatment have been described for combined AC dislocation and coracoid process fracture with intact coracoclavicular ligaments. Results

seem to be similar in both groups. Therefore, most authors recommend nonoperative treatment. Most often, the coracoid process fracture is extra-articular. However, we have encountered instances in which the coracoid fragment contains a significant portion of the glenoid fossa. The conjoined tendon rotates the coracoid process and glenoid inferolaterally and can result in substantial articular displacement. In this situation, open reduction and internal fixation may be necessary and is predicated on the amount of displacement of the articular fragment (Fig. 39-12).

Type IV Injury. Although the radiographic findings associated with a type IV injury include a relative upward displacement of the clavicle from the acromion and an increase in the coracoclavicular interspace, the most striking feature is the posterior displacement of the distal clavicle, as seen on the axillary lateral radiograph (see Fig. 39-13). In patients with heavy, thick shoulders or in patients with multiple injuries in whom an axillary lateral view of the shoulder or a scapular lateral radiographic view cannot be taken, a CT scan may be of great value in helping to confirm clinical suspicions of a posteriorly dislocated AC joint.

Type V Injury. The characteristic radiographic feature of type V injuries is a marked increase (100% to 300%) in the coracoclavicular interspace. The clavicle appears to be grossly displaced superiorly away from the acromion (Fig. 39-14). However, radiographs reveal that the clavicle on the injured side is actually at approximately the same level as the clavicle on the normal side, and the scapula is displaced inferiorly.

Type VI Injury. There are two types of inferior AC dislocation: subacromial and subcoracoid. In the subacromial type, radiographs reveal a decreased coracoclavicular distance (i.e., less than the normal side), and the distal clavicle is in a subacromial location. The subcoracoid dislocation is characterized by a reversed coracoclavicular distance, with the clavicle displaced inferior to the coracoid process (Fig. 39-15). Because this injury

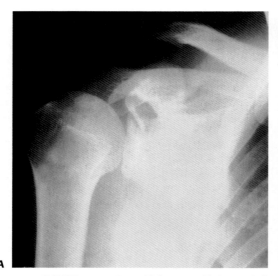

A

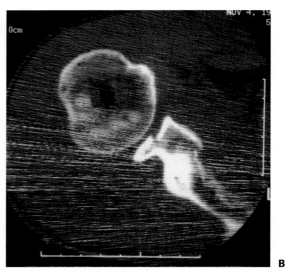

B

FIGURE 39-12 Coracoid fracture with intra-articular extension. **A.** Anteroposterior radiograph showing the fracture through the coracoid. **B.** A CT scan showing the glenoid displacement necessitating open reduction and internal fixation of the glenoid.

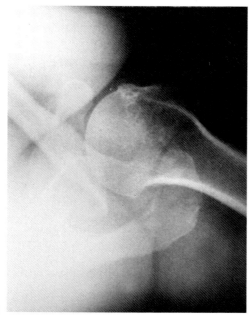
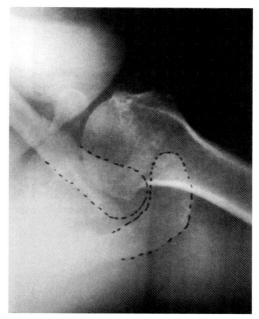

FIGURE 39-13 Type IV posterior dislocation of the AC joint. **A.** Axillary lateral radiograph of the right shoulder. **B.** Axillary view with the distal clavicle and acromion outlined.

usually is the result of severe trauma, it often is accompanied by multiple other fractures of the clavicle and ribs.

Classification

Acromioclavicular joint injuries are best classified according to the extent of damage inflicted by a given force. However, unlike other joints, the differential diagnosis of sprains of the AC joint is based on the severity of injury sustained by the capsular ligaments (AC ligaments) and extracapsular ligaments (coracoclavicular ligaments), as well as the supporting musculature (deltoid and trapezius muscles). Therefore, injuries to the AC joint are graded according to the amount of injury to the AC and coracoclavicular ligaments. Injuries in this anatomic area have always been referred to as "AC joint injuries," although the injuries have varying degrees of disruption between the scapula and the clavicle, not limited to the one particular joint.

The strength of any classification system depends on its ability to predict prognosis or the need for surgical intervention. Rockwood's group[154] developed the most widely accepted classification system, based on the original work of Tossy et al.[144] in 1963. It is an expanded, accurate classification system based on the anatomic severity of the injury. The modified classification is described below and is summarized in Table 39-1 and illustrated in Figure 39-16.

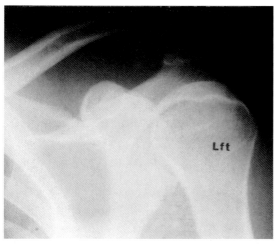

FIGURE 39-14 An anteroposterior radiograph of a type V dislocation shows the marked increase in the coracoclavicular interspace. The clavicle appears to be grossly displaced away from the acromion.

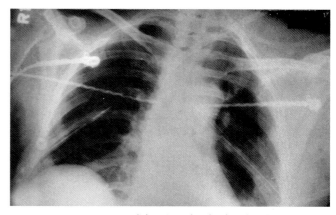

FIGURE 39-15 Type VI AC dislocation. The distal end of the left clavicle is in the subcoracoid position. The high-energy trauma causing this injury is evidenced by the bilateral chest tubes in this patient. (From Rockwood CA, Young DC. Disorders of the acromioclavicular joint. In: Rockwood CA, Matsen F III, eds. The Shoulder. Philadelphia: WB Saunders, 1990:447. Courtesy of R.C. Erickson and D. Massillion.)

TABLE 39-1	**Modified Acromioclavicular Joint Injuries Classification**			
Type	AC Joint	AC Ligament	CC Ligament	Deltoid and Trapezius Muscles
I	Intact	Sprain	Intact	Intact
II	Displaced	Torn	Sprain/Intact	Intact
III	Disrupted	Torn	Torn	Usually intact
IV	Disrupted	Torn	Torn	Detached
V	Disrupted	Torn	Torn	Detached
IV	Inferior displacement of clavicle (extremely rare)			

Type I. A mild force to the point of the shoulder produces a minor strain to the fibers of the AC ligaments. The ligaments remain intact, and the AC joint remains stable.

Type II. A moderate force to the point of the shoulder is severe enough to rupture the ligaments of the AC joint. The distal end of the clavicle is unstable in the horizontal plane (i.e., anteroposterior), but vertical (i.e., superoinferior) stability is preserved by virtue of the intact coracoclavicular ligament. The scapula may rotate medially, producing a widening of the AC joint. There may be a slight, relative upward displacement of the distal end of the clavicle secondary to stretching of the coracoclavicular ligaments.

Type III. A severe force is applied to the point of the shoulder which tears the AC and coracoclavicular ligaments resulting in a complete AC dislocation. The distal clavicle appears to be displaced superiorly as the scapula and shoulder complex droop inferomedially. Radiographic findings include a 25% to 100% increase in the coracoclavicular space in comparison to the normal shoulder.[121]

Type IV. Posterior dislocation of the distal end of the clavicle, or a type IV AC dislocation, is relatively rare. The clavicle is posteriorly displaced into or through the trapezius muscle as the force applied to the acromion drives the scapula anteriorly and inferiorly. Posterior clavicular displacement may be so severe that the skin on the posterior aspect of the shoulder becomes tented. The literature concerning posterior AC dislocations consists mostly of small series and case reports.[5,64,89,107,135] Some[5,89,135] refer to this injury as a "posterior dislocation of the clavicle," and others[64,107] prefer the term "anterior dislocation of the AC joint."

Type V. Type V AC dislocation is a markedly more severe version of the type III injury. The distal clavicle has been stripped of all its soft tissue attachments (i.e., AC ligaments, coracoclavicular ligament, and the deltotrapezius muscle attachments) and lies subcutaneously at the displaced AC joint. When combined with superior displacement of the clavicle owing to unopposed pull of the sternocleidomastoid muscle, the severe downward droop of the extremity produces a marked disfiguration of the shoulder. Radiographically, the coracoclavicular space is in-

creased greater than 100% in comparison to the opposite, normal shoulder.[121]

Type VI. Inferior dislocation of the distal clavicle, or type VI AC dislocation, is an exceedingly rare injury.[54,97,124] Gerber and Rockwood's[54] series of three patients is the largest one reported in the literature. The injury is often the result of severe trauma and is frequently accompanied by multiple injuries. The mechanism of dislocation is thought to be severe hyperabduction and external rotation of the arm, combined with retraction of the scapula. The distal clavicle occupies either a subacromial or a subcoracoid location.

In all reported cases of subcoracoid dislocation, the clavicle has become lodged behind an intact conjoined tendon. The AC ligaments are disrupted in either a subacromial or subcoracoid dislocation. The coracoclavicular ligament, however, is intact in a subacromial dislocation and completely disrupted in a subcoracoid dislocation. Likewise, the integrity of the deltoid and trapezius muscle attachments depends on the degree of clavicular displacement.

Incidence

Rowe and Marble[123] retrospectively reviewed the medical records of the Massachusetts General Hospital and found 52 AC joint injuries among 1603 shoulder girdle injuries. Most occurred in the second decade of life. Thorndike and Quigley[141] reported AC joint involvement in 223 of 578 athletes with shoulder injuries. AC injuries are among the most common injuries affecting hockey and rugby players.[31,35] AC dislocation is more common in males (5:1 to 10:1) and is more often incomplete than complete (approximately 2:1).

SURGICAL AND APPLIED ANATOMY AND COMMON SURGICAL APPROACHES

Surgical and Applied Anatomy

The AC joint is a diarthrodial joint located between the lateral end of the clavicle and the medial margin of the acromion process of the scapula. The articular surfaces initially are hyaline cartilage. A fibrocartilaginous disk of varying size and shape exists inside the joint. Viewed from the anterior–posterior direction, the inclination of the joint may be almost vertical, or it may be inclined from downward medially, with the clavicle overriding the acromion by an angle as large as 50 degrees (Fig. 39-17). There may be an underriding type of inclination, with the clavicle facet under the acromion process. The articular surface of the clavicle overrides the articular surface of the acromion approximately 50% of the time, and the articular surfaces are incongruent.

There are two types of fibrocartilaginous intraarticular disks—complete and partial (meniscoid). The disk varies greatly in size and shape.[33] With age, the meniscus undergoes degeneration until it is essentially no longer functional beyond the fourth decade.[33,114,125] The nerve supply to the AC joint is from branches of the axillary, suprascapular, and lateral pectoral nerves.

Acromioclavicular Ligaments

The AC joint is surrounded by a thin capsule reinforced above, below, anteriorly, and posteriorly by the superior, inferior, ante-

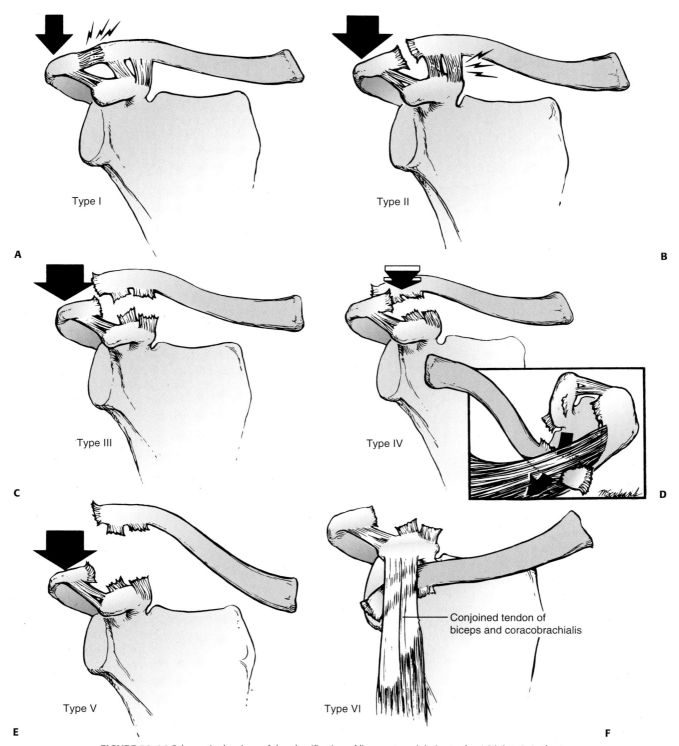

FIGURE 39-16 Schematic drawings of the classification of ligamentous injuries to the AC joint. **A.** In the type I injury, a mild force applied to the point of the shoulder does not disrupt either the AC or the coracoclavicular ligaments. **B.** A moderate to heavy force applied to the point of the shoulder will disrupt the AC ligaments, but the coracoclavicular ligaments remain intact (type II). **C.** When a severe force is applied to the point of the shoulder both the AC and the coracoclavicular ligaments are disrupted (type III). **D.** In a type IV injury, not only are the ligaments disrupted, but the distal end of the clavicle is also displaced posteriorly into or through the trapezius muscle. **E.** A violent force applied to the point of the shoulder not only ruptures the AC and coracoclavicular ligaments but also disrupts the muscle attachments and creates a major separation between the clavicle and the acromion (type V). **F.** This is an inferior dislocation of the distal clavicle in which the clavicle is inferior to the coracoid process and posterior to the biceps and coracobrachialis tendons. The AC and coracoclavicular ligaments are also disrupted (type VI).

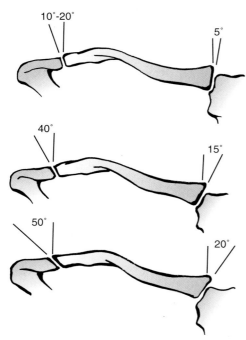

FIGURE 39-17 Variations of the inclination of the AC and the sternoclavicular joints. (Redrawn from DePalma AF. Surgery of the Shoulder. Philadelphia: JB Lippincott, 1973.)

rior, and posterior AC ligaments (Fig. 39-18). The fibers of the superior AC ligament, which is the strongest of the capsular ligaments, blend with the fibers of the deltoid and trapezius muscles, which are attached to the superior aspect of the clavicle and the acromion process. These muscle attachments are important in that they strengthen the weak and thin ligaments, thereby adding stability to the AC joint. The AC ligaments stabilize the joint in an anteroposterior direction (the horizontal plane).[32,125,146] Recent studies have shown the distance from the lateral clavicle to the insertion of the superior AC ligament and capsule to range from 5.2 to 7 mm in women and approximately 8 mm in men, much less than previously thought.[13,130] An AC resection that extends medial to the capsular insertion leads to instability in the horizontal plane.[12]

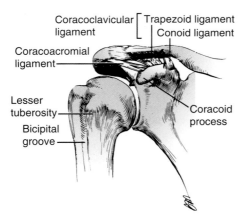

FIGURE 39-18 Normal anatomy of the AC joint.

Coracoclavicular ligament
Trapezoid ligament
Conoid ligament
Coracoacromial ligament
Lesser tuberosity
Bicipital groove
Coracoid process

Coracoclavicular Ligament

The coracoclavicular ligament is a very strong, heavy ligament whose fibers run from the outer, inferior surface of the clavicle to the base of the coracoid process of the scapula. The coracoclavicular ligament has two components: the conoid and the trapezoid ligaments (see Fig. 39-18). A bursa may separate these two portions of the ligament. The trapezoid ligament measures from 0.8 to 2.5 cm in length and from 0.8 to 2.5 cm in width. The conoid ligament varies from 0.7 to 2.5 cm in length and from 0.4 to 0.95 cm in width.[125] The distance from the lateral clavicle to the lateral most fibers of the trapezoid ligament measures as little as 10 mm.[13,62,63,120]

The conoid ligament, the more medial of the two, is cone shaped, with the apex of the cone attaching on the posteromedial side of the base of the coracoid process. The base of the cone attaches onto the conoid tubercle on the posterior undersurface of the clavicle. The conoid tubercle is located at the apex of the posterior clavicular curve, which is at the junction of the lateral third of the flattened clavicle with the medial two thirds of the triangular shaft.

The trapezoid ligament arises from the coracoid process, anterior and lateral to the attachment of the conoid ligament. This is just posterior to the attachment of the pectoralis minor tendon. The trapezoid ligament extends superiorly to a rough line on the undersurface of the clavicle. This line extends anteriorly and laterally from the conoid tubercle.

Biomechanics

The biomechanics of the AC joint involve static (ligamentous) stability, dynamic stability, and AC joint motion. This has been a topic of research for many years, and recently more sophisticated techniques in biomechanic research have elucidated the role of the various structures about the joint.

The only connection between the upper extremity and the axial skeleton is through the clavicular articulations at the AC and sternoclavicular joints. Bearn[7] stressed the importance of the sternoclavicular ligaments in supporting the distal end of the clavicle. Through anatomic dissections and selective divisions of the sternoclavicular ligaments, he demonstrated how these ligaments prevent downward displacement of the distal end of the clavicle. Hence, in the erect position, the strong sternoclavicular ligaments support the clavicles out, away from the body, like the wings off the body of an airplane. Furthermore, just as the jet engines are suspended from the underside of the wings, the upper extremities are suspended from the distal clavicles through the coracoclavicular ligament. Thus, the coracoclavicular ligament is the prime suspensory ligament of the upper extremity.

AC joint stability is maintained predominantly by the surrounding ligamentous structures, specifically the coracoclavicular ligaments (conoid and trapezoid) and the AC capsule and ligaments.

Urist[146] demonstrated that the distal clavicle could be completely dislocated anteriorly and posteriorly away from the acromion process following excision of the AC joint capsule. Only after the coracoclavicular ligaments were transected did vertical displacement of the clavicle relative to the acromion occur (Fig. 39-19). Fukuda and colleagues[48] performed load-displacement tests with a fixed displacement after sequential ligament sectioning in order to determine individual contributions of the various

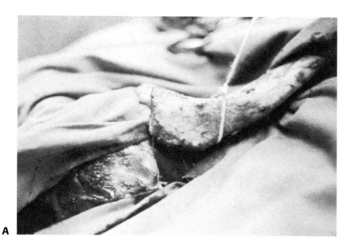

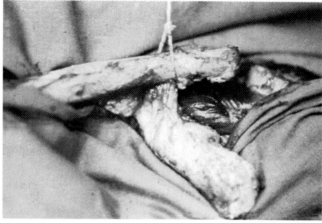

FIGURE 39-19 The importance of the AC and coracoclavicular ligaments for stability of the AC joint, demonstrated in a fresh cadaver. **A.** With the muscles and AC capsule and ligaments resected and with the coracoclavicular ligaments intact, the clavicle can be displaced anteriorly, as shown, or posteriorly from the articular surface of the acromion. **B.** However, because the coracoclavicular ligaments are intact, the clavicle cannot be displaced significantly upward. **C.** Following the transection of the coracoclavicular ligaments, the clavicle can be displaced completely above the acromion process. This suggests that the horizontal stability of the AC joint is accomplished by the AC ligaments, and vertical stability is obtained through the coracoclavicular ligaments.

ligaments to AC stability. The contribution of the AC, trapezoid, and conoid ligaments was determined at small and large displacements. At small displacements, the AC ligaments were the primary restraint to both posterior (89%) and superior (68%) translation of the clavicle—the most common failure patterns seen clinically. At large displacements, the conoid ligament provided the primary restraint (62%) to superior translation, while the AC ligaments remained the primary restraint (90%) to posterior translation. The trapezoid ligament served as the primary restraint to AC joint compression at both large and small displacements.

Studies have demonstrated that the trapezoid ligament has a greater role in resistance to posterior displacement of the clavicle and the conoid has a greater role in anterior displacement.[82,133] The role of the AC joint capsule and ligaments has been studied extensively with respect to distal clavicle resection.[15,32,45,46] Posterior abutment of the clavicle against the acromion is avoided with only 5 mm of bone removal. This preserves the capsule and ligaments, maintaining anteroposterior stability of the AC joint. Larger resections have been shown to result in excessive posterior translation.[12,75] Together, these experiments have led to the following conclusions:

- The horizontal stability is controlled by the AC ligament.
- The vertical stability is controlled by the coracoclavicular ligaments.

These statements are obviously oversimplifications. The motion and translations that occur at the AC joint are likely to be much more complicated than biplanar. Further work is clearly needed in this area.

The coracoclavicular ligament helps to couple glenohumeral abduction and flexion to scapular rotation on the thorax. Full overhead elevation cannot be accomplished without combined and synchronous glenohumeral and scapulothoracic motion.[22,70,73] As the clavicle rotates upward, it dictates scapulothoracic rotation by virtue of its attachment to the scapula—the conoid and trapezoid ligaments.

Motion of the Acromioclavicular Joint

Motion of the AC joint has been a subject of debate. The clavicle rotates upward 40 to 50 degrees with elevation of the shoulder.

Rockwood et al.[122] showed that there was only 5 to 8 degrees of rotation of the clavicle relative to the acromion. Although the clavicle rotates 40 to 50 degrees during full overhead elevation, this rotation is combined with simultaneous scapular rotation rather than with pure AC joint motion. This "synchronous scapuloclavicular" motion was originally described by Codman[22] and more recently by Flatow.[45]

Common Surgical Approaches

The patient is positioned in a beach chair configuration with the back of the table 15 to 20 degrees short of the vertical position. It is important to make sure that all potential points of pressure are well padded. A small roll or a 1 liter intravenous fluid bag is placed under the ipsilateral scapula to bring the shoulder forward. This allows good access to the superior aspect of the shoulder. The skin incision is approximately 6 cm in length and is made in Langer skin lines 2 to 3 cm medial to the AC joint. Full-thickness subcutaneous flaps are developed medially and laterally to expose the deltoid and trapezius aponeuroses the AC joint and the lateral 2 to 3 cm of the distal clavicle.

Electrocautery is used to incise the periosteum and deltotrapezius fascia parallel to the longitudinal axis of the clavicle in a medial-lateral orientation at the junction between the anterior one third and the posterior two thirds of the lateral clavicle (see Fig. 39-24). The incision starts approximately 2 to 3 cm medial to the AC joint and extends laterally to the acromial attachment of the AC capsule. The lateral clavicle is exposed subperiosteally by carefully elevating the deltotrapezius fascia, periosteum, and AC capsule in one layer starting at the medial-lateral incision and extending anteriorly and posteriorly. In most type III injuries, the AC capsule has been avulsed from the clavicle, leaving the acromial attachment intact. As the anterior and posterior subperiosteal flaps are being elevated from the lateral clavicle, the intact acromial attachment of the capsule is preserved. The specifics to further surgical procedures will be discussed later in the chapter.

CURRENT TREATMENT OPTIONS

Type I Injury

The type I injury is characterized by sprained but intact AC ligaments and normal coracoclavicular ligaments. There is no role for operative management in the acute setting.

Type II Injury

In a type II injury, the AC ligaments are torn and the coracoclavicular ligaments are stretched but intact. Nonoperatively treated type I and II injuries may lead to more chronic disability than previously recognized.[29] A recent series reported by Mouhsine et al.[107] found that 52% of patients with types I and II injuries remained symptomatic at an average 6 year follow-up. Radiographic changes at the AC joint were common.

Nonoperative Treatment

Acutely, all type II injuries are treated nonoperatively. The arm should be placed in a sling for 10 to 14 days or until the symptoms subside. This is followed by an early and gradual rehabilitation program. With this method of treatment, the subluxation is ignored. Heavy lifting or unprotected contact sports should be avoided for 8 to 12 weeks to allow complete ligament healing, because a second injury before complete ligament healing could convert the subluxation into a complete dislocation. However, an earlier return to sports may be facilitated by using a protective pad over the AC joint.

Operative Treatment

Persistent pain after a type II AC injury may be the result of posttraumatic osteolysis of the clavicle, posttraumatic arthritis, recurrent anteroposterior subluxation, torn capsular ligaments

trapped within the joint, loose pieces of articular cartilage, or a detached intraarticular meniscus. Meniscal derangement is uncommon and is characterized by displacement in and out of the joint like a torn meniscus in the knee. The type of operative treatment recommended for symptomatic, chronic type II injuries depends on the cause of the persistent symptoms. Surgical options include isolated meniscal débridement, distal clavicle excision, and AC reconstruction. AC reconstruction is only rarely indicated in instances of persistently painful anterior-posterior instability.

Type III Injury

Throughout recorded medical history, both nonoperative and operative methods of treatment of the complete AC dislocation have enjoyed cyclical popularity. During the 1950s, 1960s, and 1970s, surgical repair gained widespread popularity. In 1974, Powers and Bach[117] polled all chairmen of approved residency training programs in the United States about their treatment of complete AC injuries and reported the following findings; the majority of program chairmen treated type III injury by open reduction. Surgical treatment varied, but 60% used temporary AC fixation and 35% used coracoclavicular fixation. Nonoperative treatment was rarely advocated. As a result of these findings, Powers and Bach[117] concluded that surgical repair was the most popular method of treatment for complete AC dislocations.

Powers and Bach[117] used the classification of AC joint injuries described by Tossy et al.[144] A complete dislocation was described as a rupture of the coracoclavicular ligaments, the AC ligament, the capsule of the joint, and the fibers of the deltoid and trapezius musculature. This had been described as a "free-floating clavicle." This classification does not allow distinction between complete dislocations with varying degrees of soft tissue injury, such as disruption of AC ligaments and coracoclavicular ligaments with and without injury to the surrounding musculature. It was not until later that Rockwood[121] introduced his classification system, distinguishing among the severity of these injuries. This presents a problem when comparing the older literature to the new, because in older reports, a complete dislocation, or Tossy type III injury, likely includes what we now consider types III, IV, and V together.

In the early 1990s, Cox[27,28] performed a study similar to the Powers and Bach[117] study of 1974. Cox mailed surveys to two groups of orthopaedic surgeons: one group of 62 orthopaedic surgeons participating in the care of athletes on a regular basis, and the second group of 231 chairmen of orthopaedic residency training programs in North America. Fifty-one of the 59 orthopaedic surgeons in group 1 who responded (86.4%) preferred nonoperative management of type III AC dislocations. Of the surgeons, 30 preferred symptomatic treatment over attempts at manual reduction. Also, 135 of the 187 orthopaedic chairmen who responded (72.2%) preferred nonoperative management of type III injuries, and 97 of these advocated symptomatic treatment rather than attempts at closed manipulation. Most recently, Nissen et al.[108] in 2007 presented a similar study that included a mail-in survey sent to all members of the American Orthopaedic Society for Sports Medicine (AOSSM) and approved Accreditation Council for Graduate Medical Education orthopaedic program residency directors. Of the 664 respondents, 81% (71/87 AOSSM members) to 86% (502/577 directors) continue to treat uncomplicated type III AC separations conservatively. According to Cox[27,28] and Nissen et al.,[108] the current preference for treatment of type III AC injuries is nonoperative, involves symptomatic treatment, and represents a shift toward nonoperative treatment since the Powers and Bach[117] survey of 1974.

Many authors have reported successful nonoperative management for the type III AC dislocation.[3,5,10,34,50,81,96,116,118, 119,139,149,156] Bjerneld et al.[10] reported good to excellent results in the vast majority of patients treated conservatively in both type II and type III (complete) injuries. Dias et al.[34] followed 44 patients with a complete dislocation for 5 years. At that point, results were satisfactory in all the patients. In 1996, at an average of 12.5 years after injury, 30 of the original 44 patients were again reviewed.[119] All had a good outcome.

Galpin and colleagues[50] compared conservative treatment to surgical treatment with a Bosworth coracoclavicular screw.[14] The results of nonoperative treatment were equal if not superior to those of operative treatment. The nonoperative group had earlier return to work and sports. In a review of all AC injuries, Post[116] stated that almost all type III AC dislocations could be treated without operative intervention. Taft et al.[139] compared a group of patients treated nonoperatively with sling, taping, or a Kenny-Howard sling to a group treated operatively with AC or coracoclavicular fixation. Subjective ratings of pain and stiffness and objective ratings of strength and range of motion were similar in both groups. There was a much higher complication rate in the operative group. Press and colleagues[118] found benefits to both operative and nonoperative treatment, but earlier return to work and sports with nonoperative treatment. There were no significant differences with respect to shoulder range of motion, manual muscle strength, and neurovascular findings between the two groups.

Very few prospective, randomized studies of nonoperative versus operative treatment for AC dislocations have been performed. One of the few was by Larsen et al.,[81] who compared conservative treatment to operative treatment with AC fixation using two 2-mm threaded Kirschner wires across the joint. The rehabilitation period was significantly shorter with nonoperative treatment, and after 13 months there was no difference in the clinical results. They recommended operative treatment in thin patients who have a prominent lateral end of the clavicle, in those who do heavy work, and in patients whose work requires that the shoulder be held in abduction and flexion quite often.

The other randomized, prospective trial was by Bannister et al.,[4] in which nonoperative treatment was compared to fixation with a coracoclavicular screw. Conservatively treated patients regained movement significantly more quickly and fully, returned to work and sports sooner, and had fewer unsatisfactory results than those having early operation. In patients with a severe dislocation, defined as having displacement of greater than 2 cm, however, early surgery produced better results. Bannister et al.[4] later established a classification based on radiographic analysis. Injuries in which the clavicle was displaced 2 cm or more were associated with detachment of the origin of the anterior deltoid. These patients benefited from early surgery.

Several studies have documented no significant strength difference in patients when compared to the opposite side with complete AC separations who were treated nonoperatively.[87,118,142,149,156] Wojtys and Nelson's[156] study is unique in that both strength and endurance were tested. According to their study, both strength and endurance were comparable to the noninjured side. However, there was a trend (not statistically significant) toward a decrease in the expected strength and endurance advantage on the dominant shoulder in patients whose dominant shoulder was injured.

In 1997, McFarland et al.[96] surveyed 42 team orthopaedists representing all major league baseball teams to ascertain their treatment for a hypothetical starting rotation pitcher who had sustained a grade III AC joint separation 1 week before the start of the season. Twenty-nine (69%) reported they would treat the injury nonoperatively, while 13 (31%) stated they would operate immediately. Twenty (48%) of the physicians reported treating a total of 32 such injuries in baseball players. Twenty (62.5%) were treated nonoperatively, and 12 (37.5%) were treated operatively. There was not a major difference in outcome between the two groups.

A possible indication for operative treatment is in the polytrauma patient. A report by Gallay and colleagues[49] showed that a displaced AC joint injury in a polytrauma patient has a greater effect on shoulder function than isolated AC joint injuries when evaluated by both disease-specific and general health outcomes. Standard treatment methods may be inadequate in this population.

In summary, the management of the type III AC dislocation is still somewhat controversial, although the majority of current reports support nonoperative treatment. When reading the literature, one must consider that in most comparison studies between operative and nonoperative treatment the type of surgery varies. Rarely is there consistency between study groups and methods. In most patients with type III injuries, excellent functional results can be obtained with nonoperative management. Younger, more active patients with more severe degrees of displacement and laborers who use their upper extremity above the horizontal plane may benefit from operative stabilization.

Nonoperative Treatment

Numerous methods of nonoperative treatment of a complete AC dislocation have been reported including adhesive strapping, slings, bandages, braces, traction, pressure dressings, and plaster casts. Most commonly, patients are treated with short-term sling support followed by early range of motion. Devices used to maintain reduction by closed means are rarely used. They cause the patient much discomfort and have never proven to maintain the reduction. There is also no correlation between residual deformity and outcome.[139] Nonoperative treatment more commonly consists of short-term (1 to 2 weeks) sling support, symptomatic treatment with nonsteroidal anti-inflammatory medication, and early mobilization. Schlegel et al.[128] prospectively followed a group of acute type III injuries, with 80% favorable results. Of the 20 patients evaluated 1 year after injury, 4 felt their results were suboptimal. There was no difference in range of motion in any of the patients. Strength tests revealed equal strength between sides in all but the "bench press," which revealed a 17% decrease on the injured side.

Operative Treatment

Operative management of acute type III injuries is occasionally indicated.[83] During the 1800s and early 1900s, practically every conceivable operation for AC dislocation was performed. These procedures included AC repairs, coracoclavicular repairs, com-

TABLE 39-2	Pros and Cons of Operative Treatment Options for Acromioclavicular Joint Dislocations	
	Pros	Cons
Intra-articular AC Fixation	Anatomic reduction	• Hardware failure or migration • Distal clavicle osteolysis
Extra-articular Coracoclavicular Repairs	Superior strength of initial fixation (screw)	• Screw failure • Bone resorption secondary to hardware • Does not address soft tissue injury
Ligament Reconstruction	• Anatomic repair • No risk of metallic hardware failure or retention	• Less initial fixations strength • Harvest coracoacromial ligament

bined AC and coracoclavicular repairs, coracoclavicular fusion, and dynamic muscle transfers using the tip of the coracoid process and attached conjoined tendon.* Currently, the most popular methods of stabilization are coracoclavicular or intraarticular (i.e., AC) repairs (Table 39-2). Many of the specific procedures used today are combinations or modifications of previously described procedures (Fig. 39-20).

Intra-articular Acromioclavicular Fixation. Most modern, commonly used techniques employ some type of coracoclavicular fixation or reconstruction. However, many methods using intra-articular fixation are described in the literature. One should be cautious in using these techniques, as the placement of hardware across the AC joint can be problematic.

Most authors use small, smooth or threaded Steinmann pins. Lizaur and colleagues[85] advocate the use of two 1.8-mm percutaneous Kirschner wires to stabilize the joint, and they emphasized repair of the damaged deltoid and trapezius. These pins can be inserted from the lateral edge of the acromion through the joint and into the clavicle or from the joint out through the acromion and then back across the joint into the clavicle. Fama

*References 14,17,18,41,42,44,55,60,61,67–69,85,101,113,114,122, 133,137,144,146,148,149,153,160.

and Bonaga[44] reported the use of a smooth wire inserted laterally in the acromion, through the AC joint, out the posterior cortex of the clavicle, and through the skin posterior to the clavicle. The wire was then bent back on itself to meet the other end of the wire. The two ends were then fastened together like a safety pin to prevent migration. It must be emphasized that despite the fact that the pin is bent, it can break, migrate, and create serious consequences. (The section on complications, below, discusses pin migration to the spinal cord, lung, subclavian artery, pulmonary artery, mediastinum, heart, and other areas.)

A comparison of AC methods of fixation was reported by Eskola and coworkers.[41] They performed a prospective, randomized trial in 100 patients using three types of AC fixation: (a) smooth pins, (b) threaded pins, and (c) cortical screws. Thirteen of the 86 patients available for review developed symptomatic osteolysis of the distal clavicle. Eight of the 13 cases of osteolysis occurred among the 25 patients who underwent cortical screw fixation. In a 4-year follow-up on 70 of the 100 cases, the results were graded as good in 67 of the 70 patients.[42] These authors preferred the use of the threaded Kirschner wires.

Regardless of the method of fixation, the majority of authors report the use of other procedures as an adjunct to AC fixation. Neviaser[106] introduced superior AC ligament reconstruction through transfer of the coracoid attachment of the coracoacromial ligament to the superior aspect of the clavicle. He did not

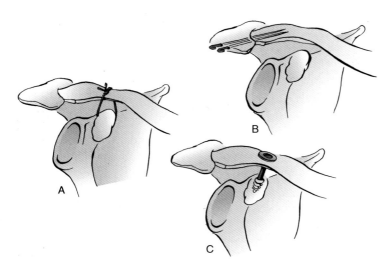

FIGURE 39-20 Various operative procedures for injuries to the AC joint. **A.** Suture between the clavicle and the coracoid process. **B.** Steinmann pins across the AC joint. **C.** A lag screw between the clavicle and the coracoid process.

recommend repair of the coracoclavicular ligament. Ho and colleagues[69] advocated reconstruction of the superior AC ligament using the coracoacromial ligament and reconstruction of the coracoclavicular ligament using Marlex tubing passed inferior to the coracoid and over the clavicle. These procedures were done alone or in combination. Paavolainen et al.[113] described AC fixation in combination with AC and coracoclavicular ligament repair.

More recently, a technique involving the use of a hook plate has been described.[60,61,132] This technique has a high complication rate, and a second procedure is always required to remove the plate. This plate does not offer any benefit over more commonly used procedures.

Extra-articular Coracoclavicular Repairs.

The technique of placing a screw between the clavicle and the coracoid was described by Bosworth[14] in 1941. The screw was placed percutaneously, using local anesthesia and fluoroscopic guidance (Fig. 39-21). With the patient in a seated position, a stab wound was made on the superior aspect of the shoulder, 3.8 cm medial to the distal end of the clavicle. After a drill hole was made in the clavicle, an assistant reduced the AC joint by depressing the clavicle and elevating the arm using a special clavicle-depressing instrument. An awl was used to develop a hole in the superior cortex of the base of the coracoid process, which was visualized using fluoroscopy. A regular bone screw was then inserted. The screw was left indefinitely, unless specific indications for removal developed. Bosworth[14] did not recommend either repair of the coracoclavicular ligaments or exploration of the AC joint. Bosworth[14] also developed a lag screw with a broad head, which he preferred to the original regular bone screw.

Percutaneous insertion of a cannulated coracoclavicular screw was reported by Tsou[145] in 1989, who placed a guide pin fluoroscopically from the clavicle to the coracoid process. After adequate positioning of the pin within the coracoid had been confirmed radiographically, a cannulated drill bit and screw were sequentially passed over the guide pin. Tsou[145] reported a 32% technical failure rate in 53 patients with complete AC dislocation using this technique. Accurate insertion of the screw is difficult to perform percutaneously. Furthermore, the percutaneous technique does not allow coracoclavicular ligament repair, deltoid and trapezius reattachment, or AC joint débridement.

Many other surgeons have reported the use of a Bosworth screw or a slight modification of the original technique.[4,50,138] Rockwood's group[59] presented a technique for the chronic, symptomatic dislocated AC joint in which the coracoacromial ligament was transferred from its acromial insertion into the medullary canal of the clavicle, along with temporary placement of a coracoclavicular screw to stabilize the clavicle until the ligament healed. The screw is usually removed 8 weeks postoperatively, necessitating a second procedure. A bioabsorbable screw may afford comparable strength to a steel screw,[140] and may obviate the need for removal.

Coracoclavicular fixation by methods other than a screw has been reported. Stam and Dawson[136] and Goldberg et al.[55] described the use of cerclage Dacron ligaments looped over the clavicle and under the coracoid. Verhaven et al.[148] utilized a double Dacron velour ligament for fixation in a prospective study in 28 consecutive patients with a mean follow-up of 5.1 years; 71% had good or excellent results. There was little correlation between the end result and the degree of residual dislocation, coracoclavicular ossification and posttraumatic arthritic changes, or osteolysis of the distal clavicle. Browne and associates[17] used 5-mm Mersilene (Ethicon, Somerville, NJ) tape for coracoclavicular fixation. Morrison and Lemos[101] reported 12 of 14 good and excellent results when using a synthetic loop placed through drill holes in the base of the coracoid and the anterior third of the clavicle.

Cerclage techniques using various synthetic materials have also been described.[23,67,68,74,110] Most of these authors also reported AC joint débridement, AC joint ligament repair or reconstruction, coracoclavicular ligament repair, and imbrication of the deltotrapezius fascia—either alone or in combination—in addition to the coracoclavicular fixation.

Ligament Reconstruction.

The majority of reconstructive procedures accepted today involve ligament reconstruction with or without augmentation with suture, tape, or hardware. The recent literature has focused on anatomic coracoclavicular reconstruction to more closely reproduce the intact ligamentous state, thus enhancing stability.[26,57,94,95] Costic et al.[26] found that anatomic coracoclavicular reconstruction more closely approximates the stiffness of the native ligamentous state than does a standard Weaver-Dunn repair. Mazzocca et al.[95] performed a biomechanic cadaver study comparing an anatomic coracoclavicular ligament reconstruction using a semitendinosis graft to

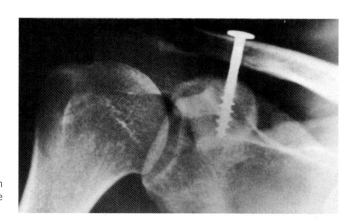

FIGURE 39-21 Postoperative anteroposterior radiograph of the shoulder with a Bosworth screw in place. Note that the AC joint has been reduced and the coarse lag threads of the screw are well seated into the coracoid process.

a modified Weaver-Dunn procedure and an arthroscopic technique using nonabsorbable suture material. Specimens were tested with a directionally applied force (anterior, posterior, and superior) as well as cyclic loading and load to failure to simulate physiologic states at the AC joint. These were compared to the intact ligamentous state. Results showed the anatomical coracoclavicular ligament reconstruction had significantly less anterior and posterior translation when compared to the other forms of reconstruction.[95] Superior displacement during cyclic loading was equal among the groups.[95] They concluded that anatomic ligamentous reconstruction more closely approximated the intact state, thus providing more stability than the other two forms of reconstruction. A similar study by Grutter et al.[57] also showed superior biomechanic results of anatomic ligament reconstruction when compared to a modified Weaver-Dunn technique when specimens were loaded to failure in the coronal plane. The authors further concluded that anatomic reconstruction recreated the tensile strength of the intact state when a flexor carpi radialis tendon was used.[57]

Type IV and V Injuries

Because of the severe posterior displacement of the distal clavicle in a type IV injury, and the gross superior displacement in the type V injury, most authors recommend surgical repair.[107,135] The posterior displacement of the clavicle into the trapezius in a type IV injury will lead to discomfort with motion. Therefore, surgical reduction of the deformity and stabilization of the clavicle are often necessary. The posterior displacement produces significant stripping of the deltotrapezial fascia from the distal clavicle. Its repair at the end of the stabilization procedure is a crucial step in augmenting distal clavicular stability.

Type V injuries require operative reduction and stabilization because they result in significant deltotrapezial stripping and resultant gross instability, which commonly leads to chronic pain and disability. Again, meticulous repair of the deltotrapezial fascia augments the repair.[111]

Type VI Injury

All type VI injuries described in the literature have been treated with surgery.[54,97,124] Initial attempts at closed reduction failed. In one instance, after open reduction by lateral retraction of the scapula, the clavicle was stabilized by suturing the deltoid and trapezius muscle avulsion and by repairing the AC joint capsule. In one patient, whose shoulder was operated on 2.5 months after injury, a Steinmann pin was used to stabilize the AC joint. After immobilization for 3 to 5 weeks, both of these patients had almost full range of motion and good power. One patient with a recurrent subcoracoid dislocation was treated by excision of the distal 1 cm of the clavicle, and at 5-year follow-up the patient had no complaints or weakness. Gerber and Rockwood[54] reported on using the extra-articular technique with a coracoclavicular lag screw combined with repair of the ligaments and imbrication of the deltotrapezius fascia over the top of the clavicle.

Type III Variants

AC dislocation with a fracture of the coracoid process is not a common injury in adults. The mechanism of injury may be essentially the same as for a type III AC dislocation, except the coracoclavicular ligaments do not fail and a fracture occurs through the base of the coracoid, allowing relative upward displacement of the distal clavicle. It is important to recognize that, in order for the coracoid fracture to be responsible for the AC displacement, the fracture must occur through the base. If the fracture occurs at the tip of the coracoid process, either concomitant coracoclavicular ligament injury or a second fracture through the coracoid base has occurred, allowing displacement of the AC joint (see Fig. 39-10). The isolated coracoid tip fracture, when it occurs in conjunction with an AC dislocation, is thought to result from a sudden pull on the coracoid process by the conjoined tendons.[150]

Coracoid process fractures may not always be easy to recognize, and it is important that good radiographs be obtained to look for this injury before surgical management. Although the axillary radiographic view can suggest a fracture of the coracoid process, the Stryker notch view or the CT scan can best indicate the site and degree of displacement of the fracture (see Fig. 39-12).

Placement of an interfragmentary screw across a fracture of the coracoid base with intact coracoclavicular ligaments is difficult. Therefore, the need for surgery is one of the few indications for placement of pins across the AC joint. If the fracture involves the tip of the coracoid and there is significant displacement, then screw fixation may be indicated for the coracoid fracture and the AC joint may be stabilized by a coracoclavicular loop.[150] Conversely, fibrous unions of the tip of the coracoid process are often asymptomatic. Consequently, a combined AC dislocation and fracture of the tip of the coracoid process may be treated nonoperatively using methods similar to those prescribed for isolated type III injuries.

Bernard and associates[9] reported 4 cases of combined AC dislocation and fracture of the coracoid base and reviewed 13 cases from the literature. They concluded that although surgery could produce good results, equally satisfactory function and minimal residual deformity could be achieved by immobilization of the shoulder in a sling for 6 weeks. Kumar[76] had good short-term success with conservative treatment as well.

Chronic Acromioclavicular Injuries

Patients with types I and II AC joint injuries may develop late degenerative changes.[8,29,102] The meniscus and articular cartilage often sustain an injury that leads to these degenerative changes. Chronic pain after types I and II injuries is treated with mild analgesics such as nonsteroidal anti-inflammatory medication, avoidance of painful activity or positions, and intra-articular injection with corticosteroid preparations. Many will resolve with this conservative treatment.

Patients with chronic type I injuries who do not respond to conservative care may require operative excision of the distal clavicle to provide relief of pain. This can be performed using an open or an arthroscopic technique.[47,51,52,58,103,134] The important aspect of either technique is preservation or repair of the AC joint capsule to maintain anteroposterior stability of the joint.[15]

In patients with chronic pain after type II AC sprains, the initial conservative regimen is the same as for type I injuries. If conservative, symptomatic treatment fails, surgery may be indicated. Isolated distal clavicle excision after a type II injury may fail because of anteroposterior instability of the distal clavicle and resultant posterior abutment of the clavicle on the scapular spine. Therefore, the patient should be examined carefully for increased anteroposterior translation of the clavicle relative to the acromion during surgical planning. If indeed, anteroposterior instability exists, distal clavicle excision may be combined with AC capsular reconstruction or coracoacromial ligament transfer.[152]

Chronic pain and instability after complete AC dislocations (types III, IV, and V) should not be treated with isolated distal clavicle excision. This merely shortens the clavicle without stabilizing it and is often associated with persistent postoperative symptoms. Therefore, distal clavicle excision should be combined with stabilization in chronic, symptomatic, complete AC injuries. The most popular reconstructive procedure is transfer of the acromial attachment of the coracoacromial ligament to the resected surface of the distal clavicle and concurrent coracoclavicular stabilization. Coracoclavicular stabilization greatly increases the strength of the construct.[36,59,62,63,77,78,118,131,142,151,153]

AUTHORS' PREFERRED TREATMENT

Type I Injury

Nonoperative Treatment

Usually, the symptoms subside after 7 to 10 days of rest. The application of an ice bag for the first 12 to 24 hours, whenever convenient, will help to ease the discomfort. A sling can be worn to support the arm and to remind the patient and others that the shoulder is injured. We encourage the patient to rest the shoulder and to resume a normal range of motion as the symptoms subside. Heavy stresses, lifting, and contact sports should be delayed until there is a full range of motion and no pain to joint palpation. This usually takes 2 weeks.

Operative Treatment

Surgical treatment is indicated if symptomatic AC arthritis develops late as a result of a prior type I AC injury. Surgery is also indicated after a type I injury in the absence of radiographic degenerative findings when internal derangement of the joint is suspected as the etiology of pain. If the patient has failed 3 to 6 months of nonoperative treatment (e.g., nonsteroidal anti-inflammatory medication, rest, activity modification, corticosteroid injections), distal clavicle excision is recommended. This can be performed using either open or arthroscopic techniques.[72] Overzealous excision of bone should be avoided in order to preserve the AC ligaments. We prefer arthroscopic excision of 0.5 to 0.7 cm of bone.[13,120]

Type II Injury

Nonoperative Treatment

As in a type I injury, rest is an important factor. An ice pack is used during the first 12 to 24 hours. The patient is given a sling to rest and support the arm. The sling is worn for 1 to 2 weeks, depending on the age of the patient, the symptoms, and the circumstances. We encourage the patient to begin gentle range-of-motion exercises of the shoulder and allow use of the arm for dressing, eating, and necessary activities of daily living when symptoms permit, which is usu-

ally on about the seventh day. The typical patient is instructed not to use the shoulder for any heavy lifting, pushing, pulling, or contact sports for at least 6 weeks. We do not want the patient to have another injury or stress the AC joint to convert a type II problem to a type III problem. However, earlier return to athletics can be facilitated through the use of protective padding over the superior aspect of the joint. For the average patient who only occasionally puts stress on the AC joint, the development of chronic problems is uncommon and usually can be resolved with anti-inflammatory drugs, moist heat, and judicious use of intra-articular corticosteroids.

Operative Treatment

There is no role for operative management in acute type II AC injuries. However, patients with symptomatic chronic type II injuries that have not responded to 3 to 6 months of nonoperative treatment are surgical candidates. If the primary complaint is pain, radiographs reveal AC arthritis with a normal coracoclavicular distance, and the pain is relieved with intra-articular injection of a local anesthetic, we prefer isolated distal clavicle excision. Although this can be accomplished by open as well as arthroscopic means, arthroscopic excision allows for relative preservation of the soft tissue envelope surrounding the distal clavicle and AC joint (i.e., the deltotrapezius fascia and the AC capsule). Arthroscopic distal clavicle excision can be performed by the direct superior approach.[46] However, the subacromial approach is easier and more familiar to most surgeons. It also allows inspection of the bursal side of the rotator cuff.[72] Regardless of the operative technique utilized, however, excision of excessive amounts of bone may result in symptomatic anteroposterior subluxation. Therefore, excision is limited to 0.5 to 1.0 cm.

Isolated excision of the intra-articular meniscus or joint débridement without distal clavicle excision is rarely indicated. It is unlikely that the meniscus could be damaged without some injury occurring to the articular surfaces. Furthermore, patients with no radiographic degenerative changes and chronic pain and tenderness over the AC joint following a type II AC injury most commonly will demonstrate anteroposterior subluxation and be candidates for AC reconstruction.

Recurrent, symptomatic anteroposterior subluxation as a late complication of an acute type II AC subluxation can be very subtle. Moreover, the decision to perform surgical reconstruction of the AC ligaments, as opposed to an isolated distal clavicle excision, can be a difficult one. If the patient presents years after the original injury, the type of AC injury originally sustained may not be obvious. If the joint reveals advanced degenerative changes, with large periarticular osteophytes, increased anteroposterior translation may not be demonstrable on physical examination. Under these circumstances, particularly if the coracoclavicular distance is radiographically normal, isolated arthroscopic distal clavicle excision may be indicated. However, if anteroposterior translation is increased compared to the normal side, AC reconstruction is a better choice.

In most cases, reconstruction of the AC ligaments is combined with distal clavicle excision. Transfer of the acromial attachment of the coracoacromial ligament into the medullary canal of the resected distal clavicle is most commonly performed for correction of superoinferior instability associated with chronic disruption of the coracoclavicular ligaments. However, it can also be used to correct recurrent anteroposterior subluxation associated with chronic AC capsular disruption. The traditional technique is modified, however, so that the coracoacromial ligament is transferred to the posterior corner of the resected clavicle, rather than to the center of the medullary canal. This places the transferred ligament in a more anteroposterior orientation, which theoretically provides better resistance to anteroposterior translation.

The consequences of coracoacromial ligament transfer are not known. However, subsequent development of rotator cuff insufficiency in a patient who has undergone coracoacromial ligament transfer potentially could result in anterosuperior subluxation of the glenohumeral joint. Therefore, prior to transferring the coracoacromial ligament, we attempt to perform plication of the AC joint capsule. If the capsular repair is stable, we forgo coracoacromial ligament transfer.

Surgical Technique—Chronic Type II Injury.. A 5- to 6-cm incision is made in Langer's lines approximately 1.5 to 2.0 cm medial to the AC joint (Fig. 39-22). Full-thickness subcutaneous flaps are developed medially and laterally to expose the AC joint, deltoid and trapezius aponeuroses, and the distal 2 cm of the lateral clavicle. With care, it is possible to separate the deltoid and trapezius aponeuroses from the underlying posterior, superior, and anterior AC capsule. The AC capsule is then exposed by sharply, individually dissecting the deltoid and trapezius away from the capsule and distal clavicle.

The AC joint is identified by placing a needle through the capsule into the articular space. The periosteum of the lateral clavicle is scored with an electrocautery perpendicular to the long axis of the clavicle approximately 1.5 cm medial to the joint line. The AC capsule is then incised in a medial to lateral direction at the midportion of the joint. The clavicular attachment of the capsule along with the periosteum up to the previously placed score mark are sharply elevated with a #15 scalpel in one continuous layer. This detachment starts at the medial-lateral capsular incision and continues anteriorly and posteriorly to expose the AC joint and distal clavicle. Typically, the capsule remains strongly attached to the acromion. Additionally, the capsule is usually redundant anteriorly and posteriorly because of recurrent anteroposterior subluxation.

The distal clavicle is excised using a combination of a microsagittal saw and an osteotome. Our goal is to resect 0.5 to 1.0 cm of bone with as little disruption of the inferior capsule as possible. Therefore, a small drill is used to perforate the distal clavicle in two or three places. A microsagittal saw is then used to saw through the clavicle up to the inferior cortex. An osteotome is placed in the osteotomy site and twisted. This will crack the inferior cortex through the previously placed drill holes. The lateral fragment is excised and a power burr is used to smooth the cortical margins of the resected distal clavicle.

The capsular flaps are inspected to determine whether they are of adequate quality and length to plicate and reattach to the resected distal clavicle. If the capsule is of sufficient quality and will reach to the resected surface of the distal

clavicle, a series of four small, unicortical drill holes are made along the lateral margin of the resected distal clavicle approximately 2 to 3 mm from the edge. Nonabsorbable sutures are passed through these drill holes and exit the medullary canal just inferior to the superior cortical surface. The posterior capsular flap is shifted anteriorly and sutured to the edge of the distal clavicle with the two most posterior sutures; the anterior capsular flap is shifted posteriorly and sutured to the edge of the distal clavicle using the two most anterior sutures. After the knots are tied, the free ends of the most anterior and posterior sutures are used to reattach the reflected deltoid and trapezius aponeuroses, respectively. The excess suture is then excised.

If the capsular flaps are insufficient to allow plication and secure reattachment to the resected surface of the distal clavicle, the acromial attachment of the coracoacromial ligament must be transferred (Fig. 39-23). A small portion of the anterior deltoid is released from the anterior acromion to expose the acromial attachment of the coracoacromial ligament. The ligament is then released from the acromion and mobilized distally to its attachment on the coracoid process. Two sutures are placed in the free end of the ligament. Two unicortical drill holes are placed in the posterosuperior surface of the distal clavicle. These drill holes exit the medullary canal of the clavicle and are oriented from a posterosuperior to an anteroinferior direction. The coracoacromial ligament sutures are then passed through these clavicular drill holes and tied over the posterosuperior cortical bridge. Additional drill holes are placed along the superior and anterosuperior surfaces of the clavicle for reattachment of the deltoid and trapezius aponeuroses.

Postoperative rehabilitation is the same, regardless of the method of reconstruction. The arm is immobilized in an abduction orthosis or abduction pillow for 3 weeks. Pendulum and passive external rotation exercises are then initiated and continued for 2 to 3 weeks. The arm continues to be supported in the abduction pillow or orthosis until 5 to 6 weeks postoperatively. Passive mobilization in all planes along with active and active assisted range of motion are instituted 5 to 6 weeks postoperatively. When active range of motion is 80% to 85% of the normal side (usually 6 to 8 weeks postoperatively), strengthening exercises are begun. Return to sports activities is allowed at 4 to 6 months postoperatively.

Type III Injury

Nonoperative Treatment

We recommend nonoperative treatment for the vast majority of acute type III injuries. A sling is used for comfort for 1 to 2 weeks. Ice and rest during the first 24 to 48 hours after injury decrease the discomfort associated with the soft tissue injury. Patients are encouraged to remove the sling and use the shoulder actively within their limits of pain. Patients will often avoid overhead use of the arm for the first week to 10 days. Within 3 to 4 weeks, the range of motion is usually within 80% of the opposite shoulder and strengthening exercises are instituted. Return to full activity may take as long as 3 to 4 months. However, athletic activity may be allowed

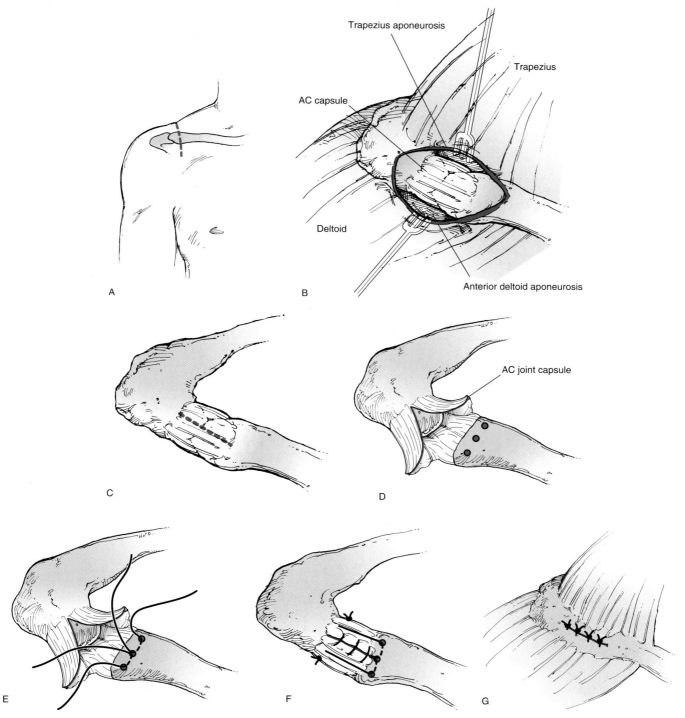

FIGURE 39-22 Surgical repair of a chronic type II AC joint injury. **A.** A 5- to 6-cm skin incision is made in Langer lines approximately 1.5 to 2 cm medial to the AC joint. **B.** The anterior deltoid aponeurosis is reflected anteriorly off of the AC joint capsule. **C.** The AC joint capsule is incised in a medial to lateral direction at the midportion of the joint. **D.** Anterior and posterior flaps are elevated to expose the AC joint and distal clavicle. Drill holes are placed 5 mm from the articular margin and 5 mm of distal clavicle is excised using a microsagittal saw. **E.** Additional drill holes are placed 1 to 2 mm medial to the resectional margin; sutures are placed through the drill holes. **F.** The capsule is repaired back to the distal clavicle. **G.** The deltoid and trapezius are repaired over the capsule.

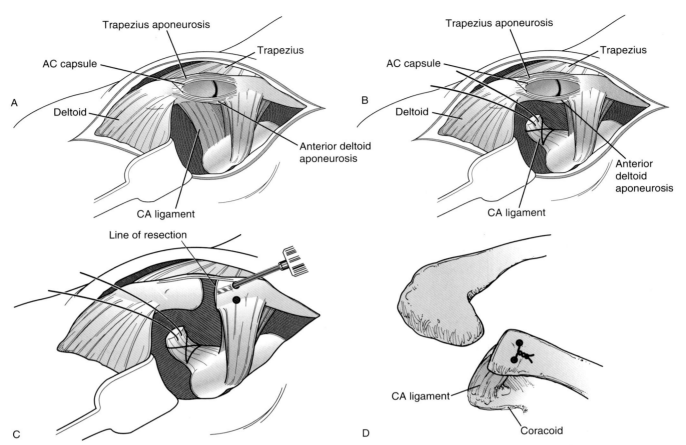

FIGURE 39-23 Transfer of the acromial attachment of the coracoacromial ligament. **A.** A small portion of the anterior deltoid is reflected from the anterior acromion to expose the coracoacromial ligament. **B.** The ligament is released from the acromion and sutures are placed in the end. **C.** Two unicortical drill holes are placed in the posterosuperior surface of the distal clavicle, exiting through the medullary canal. **D.** The coracoacromial ligament is transferred to the medullary canal. The sutures are placed through the drill holes and tied over the top of the clavicle.

much sooner, if necessary, through the use of a protective pad over the AC joint or specifically modified athletic equipment.

Operative Treatment

Acute Injury. Operative stabilization of type III injuries is considered in heavy manual laborers, patients with a concomitant brachial plexus injury, or overhead athletes when the injury involves the dominant arm. In order for surgical intervention to occur, the patient must understand that return to full activities will not be permitted for 4 to 6 months postoperatively. In addition, the postoperative protocol, including the use of an abduction pillow for 3 to 6 weeks, is discussed in detail. If the patient agrees, operative stabilization is performed. This represents 5% or less of all type III AC injuries seen by our service.

The initial surgical approach and dissection are detailed earlier in this chapter under "Common Surgical Approaches." Once the dissection is complete with the distal clavicle and AC joint exposed, any remnant of the intraarticular disk is excised. The distal clavicle is delivered into the wound and the articular surface is inspected (Fig.

39-24). If the articular surface is intact, the distal clavicle is not excised. This is the exception rather than the rule, and if there is any concern, the meniscus is removed and the distal clavicle is excised in order to eliminate it as a potential source of chronic pain. The anterior deltoid, which has been elevated from its clavicular origin with the anterior subperiosteal flap, is retracted anteriorly. The clavicle is retracted posteriorly to expose the coracoid process. If the torn coracoclavicular ligaments can be identified, they are preserved for later repair. The base of the coracoid process protrudes almost perpendicularly from the scapula. After a short distance, it makes a direct lateral turn and proceeds laterally to its termination at the tip. The base of the coracoid process is exposed subperiosteally. Two bone anchors are loaded with heavy nonabsorbable sutures, one through each anchor. It is important that the nonabsorbable sutures are passed through drill holes in the clavicle and not around the clavicle. Passage around the clavicle has been associated with erosion, fracture, and loss of fixation. Use of suture anchors in the base of the coracoid to achieve coracoclavicular fixation is a recent development replacing the passage of sutures around the undersurface of the coracoid. After the perios-

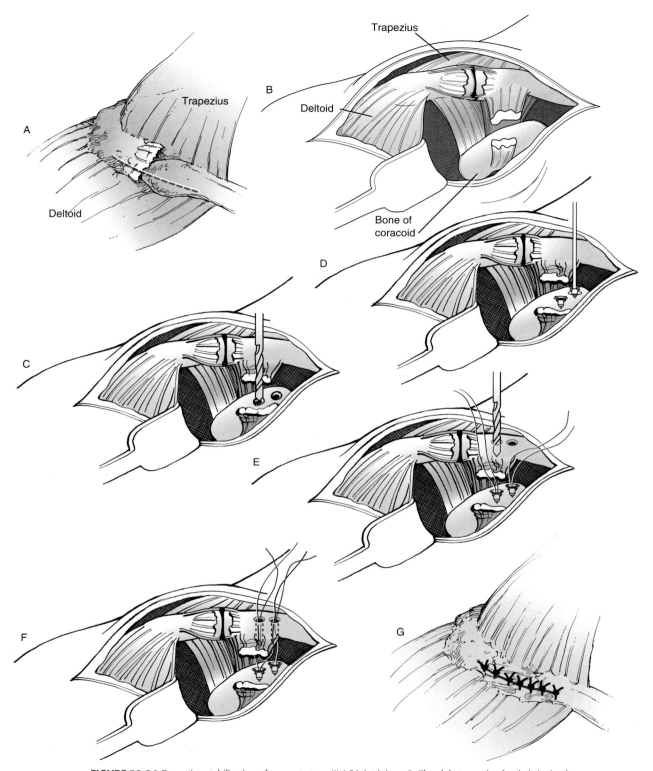

FIGURE 39-24 Operative stabilization of an acute type III AC joint injury. **A.** The deltotrapezius fascia is incised in a medial-lateral orientation superior to the AC joint. **B.** The clavicle is delivered into the wound after reflecting the anterior deltoid and trapezius. **C.** Two holes are drilled in the base of the coracoid in preparation for anchor insertion. **D.** Suture anchors are inserted in the base of the coracoid. **E.** Two drill holes are placed through the clavicle for passage of the sutures. **F.** Two to three suture anchors are placed along the lateral clavicular margin. The sutures are used to reattach the AC joint capsule and the deltotrapezial aponeurosis. **G.** The deltotrapezial aponeurosis is repaired.

teum at the base of the coracoid has been removed for exposure, the holes are drilled and the anchors inserted according to the manufacturer's instructions. We typically use Mitek (DePuy Mitek, Inc., Raynnam, MA) G4 anchors (Fig. 39-25). The strength of suture anchors was compared to sutures around the base of the coracoid for the treatment of AC joint separations in a cadaver study by Breslow et al.[16] They found no difference in laxity between the two methods after repeated cycling. Suture anchors offer the advantages of a decreased risk of neurovascular injury and reduced surgical time.

After the suture anchors have been placed at the base of the coracoid, the coracoclavicular interspace is inspected for any remnants of the coracoclavicular ligaments. If any portions of the ligaments can be identified and are of sufficient quality, a suture is passed between the torn ends, but is not tied until after the clavicle has been reduced and fixed.

Drill holes must be placed in the clavicle for passage of the coracoclavicular sutures (see Fig. 39-24). The AC joint is reduced by pushing up on the elbow to bring the acromion to the clavicle. With the joint reduced, the entry points for the drill holes are identified. The drill holes should be bicortical and placed at the junction of the anterior one third and posterior two thirds of the clavicle in the anterior–posterior direction. A suture passer is then used to pass one limb of the suture from each anchor through each hole so that there are two sutures through each hole. Each suture is then tied to itself over the bone bridge between the drill holes. It is helpful to color the ends of one suture with a skin marker before passing them through the bone; the colored suture facilitates differentiation between the two once they are passed through the clavicle. The AC joint is held in a reduced or slightly overreduced position by applying an axial, compressive load to the humerus. The coracoclavicular sutures are then tied. If any sutures were placed in the coracoclavicular ligament remnants, they are also tied.

If the AC joint capsule is identifiable and repairable, the tissue is imbricated over the superior aspect of the joint. Suture anchors placed along the lateral clavicular margin in an anterior to posterior direction approximately 5 mm from the articular surface may facilitate reconstruction of the capsule (see Fig. 39-24). These anchors are then used to reattach the medial (clavicular) aspect of the AC capsule, as well as

the deltoid and trapezial aponeuroses, to the lateral aspect of the clavicle. The deltotrapezius aponeurosis and clavicular periosteum, medial to the reattached AC capsule, are also closed. The subcutaneous tissue and skin are then closed in a standard fashion.

Postoperative management is conservative in order to minimize stress across the repair. The shoulder is immobilized in a sling for 6 weeks, with removal for elbow, wrist, and hand range of motion. Overhead elevation, both active and passive, is contraindicated for 6 weeks to avoid rotational forces across the AC joint. The procedure is extraarticular, therefore, long-term stiffness of the glenohumeral joint is unusual.

Chronic Injury.. Many patients with chronic type III injuries are asymptomatic. However, when symptoms are present, they typically take the form of trapezius fatigue, AC joint pain, and brachial plexus irritation. Under these circumstances, AC reconstruction is indicated.

Patient positioning is similar to the method previously described for reconstruction of the chronic type II injury. The detailed incision and approach has also been described in the surgical approach section of this chapter.

A longitudinal incision is made centering about 2 cm medial to the AC joint. Full-thickness flaps are developed both medially and laterally to expose the deltotrapezial fascia. Adequate exposure should include the AC joint as well as 2 to 3 cm of the distal clavicle for optimal visualization. Electrocautery is used to incise the periosteum and deltotrapezial fascia in a parallel fashion to the longitudinal axis of the clavicle (Fig. 39-26). The incision should start approximately 2 to 3 cm medial to the AC joint and extend laterally to the acromial portion of the AC joint. The lateral clavicle is exposed subperiosteally by carefully elevating the deltotrapezial fascia, periosteum, and AC capsule in one layer starting at the medial-lateral incision and extending anteriorly and posteriorly. Any remnant of the intra-articular disk is excised.

The distal clavicle is delivered into the wound and excision of roughly 1 cm of the distal clavicle is performed with a saw. The anterior deltoid, which has been elevated from its clavicular origin, with the anterior subperiosteal flap is retracted anteriorly. The clavicle is retracted posteriorly to

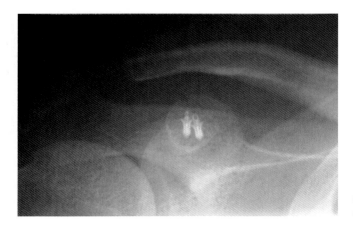

FIGURE 39-25 Postoperative radiograph after reconstruction using suture anchors at the base of the coracoid.

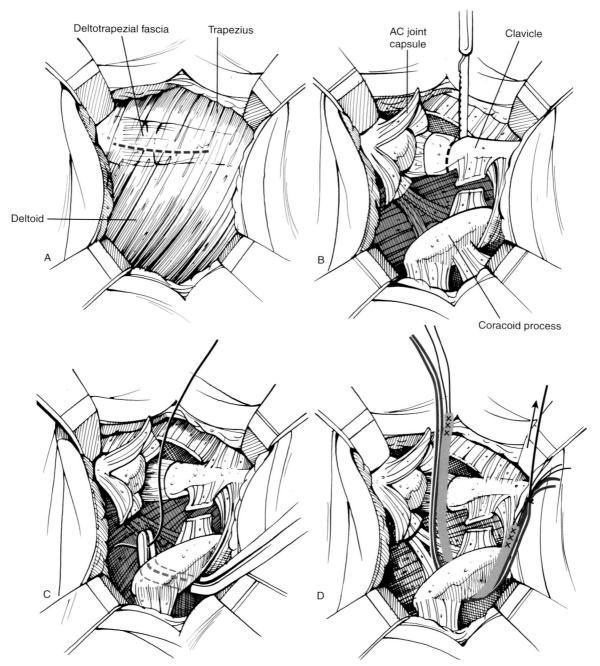

FIGURE 39-26 Treatment of a chronic type III AC joint injury with distal clavicle resection and anatomic coracoclavicular ligament reconstruction. **A.** The deltotrapezial fascia is incised parallel to the longitudinal axis of the clavicle. **B.** Excision of roughly 1 cm of the distal clavicle is performed with a saw. **C.** A Satinsky vascular clamp is placed around the undersurface of the coracoid and a shuttle stitch is passed. **D.** Nonabsorbable sutures and a biological graft are shuttled around the base of the coracoid.   (*continues*)

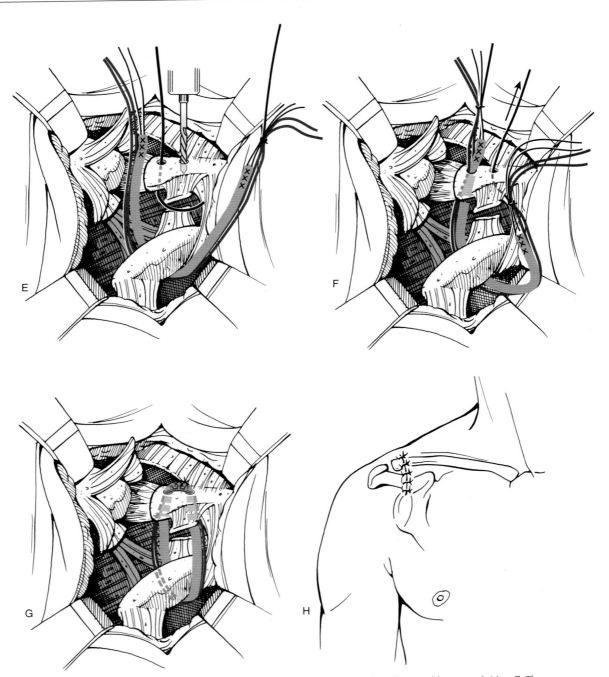

FIGURE 39-26 (*continued*) **E.** Two drill holes are placed in the clavicle with a roughly 1.5-cm bridge. **F.** The shuttle suture is used to bring the sutures and graft through the holes in clavicle. **G.** The two nonabsorbable sutures are then tied to each other to hold the clavicle reduced and then the graft is secured. **H.** The subcutaneous tissue and skin are repaired as described previously.

allow exposure of the coracoid. The base of the coracoid is exposed subperiosteally. It is important to make sure good exposure both medially and laterally are achieved to aid in the passage around the base of the coracoid. A Satinsky vascular clamp is placed around the undersurface of the coracoid, in a medial to lateral fashion, staying on bone all the way around in order to protect the neurovascular structures below. A suture is placed into the open clamp and pulled around the base of the coracoid (see Fig. 39-26). This suture is used to shuttle three heavy nonabsorbable sutures and a biologic graft around the base of the coracoid (see Fig. 39-26). We often use a semitendinosus allograft, but the surgeon can use any autograft or allograft tendon of similar strength. A whipstitch is placed in both ends of the graft to aide in passage of the tendon.

Once the suture and graft are in position around the base of the coracoid, two drill holes are placed in the clavicle for passage of the sutures and graft. One drill hole is placed around 1 cm from the lateral edge of the clavicle and one is placed around 2.5 cm from the lateral edge (see Fig. 39-26). These holes are also drilled from slightly anterior to posterior through the clavicle, which will help translate the clavicle slightly anteriorly when it is secured. After the holes are drilled, sutures are placed through the holes in the clavicle and used to shuttle the respective suture ends up through the clavicle. The AC joint is then reduced by pushing up on the elbow to bring the acromion to the clavicle. The two nonabsorbable sutures are then tied to each other to hold the clavicle securely reduced before securing the graft. The third nonabsorbable suture is not tied and is used as a back-up shuttle stitch as needed. The graft can be secured by one of two methods. Bioabsorbable anchors can be placed adjacent to the graft in each tunnel or the graft may be tied over itself in a simple fashion and the knot sutured with nonabsorbable material for security. Either method provides adequate security of the graft while it heals to the bone tunnels. Only moderate tension is needed when securing the graft as the heavy sutures are supplying the main source of tension.

Thorough irrigation of the wound should be completed. Closure of the incised deltotrapezial fascia is performed in a pants-over-vest fashion using heavy nonabsorbable sutures. Any remaining AC joint capsule should be repaired as well whenever possible. The subcutaneous tissue and skin are repaired as described previously.

Type IV, V, and VI Injuries

These injuries nearly always require operative treatment. The surgical technique and aftercare are similar to the methods described for the acute or chronic type III injury above as dictated by the timing of the surgery after injury. The subcoracoid subtype of the type VI injury may require a deltopectoral incision to extricate the dislocated clavicle. The reconstruction then proceeds as previously described.

Type III Variants

We treat pseudodislocations with a nonoperative approach. They nearly always recover without incident, and rarely have any further sequelae. AC injuries associated with fractures of the coracoid process are treated nonoperatively in most cases. The fractures usually occur at the tip or the base of the coracoid. As long as the deltotrapezial fascia is not disrupted to a large extent, and there is not severe coracoid displacement, we treat them in the same manner as a type III injury (see Fig. 39-10).

If the fracture of the coracoid extends intra-articularly into the glenoid, we consider surgery. This depends largely on the amount of intra-articular displacement. We use 5 mm or more of glenoid displacement as our criterion for surgical treatment. A CT scan is often helpful in evaluating this fracture as the glenoid component is much more easily appreciated with this study (see Fig. 39-13).

Pearls and Pitfalls

A thorough understanding of coracoclavicular and AC anatomy is essential to the safe and effective treatment of AC joint injuries. Table 39-3 lists some tips that may help assist the surgeon during reconstruction of the AC joint as well as help to stay away from some of the common pitfalls associated with this procedure.

COMPLICATIONS

An inferiorly and medially directed force applied to the dorsum of the acromion most often results in injury to the AC articulation, the sternoclavicular articulation, or the shaft of the clavicle. However, combined injuries have been reported. Wurtz and associates[158] and Lancourt[80] have reported combined AC dislocation and clavicle fracture. Several reports exist of simultaneous dislocations of both the sternoclavicular and AC ends of the clavicle or bipolar dislocations.[2,25,39,53,71,127] Bipolar clavicular dislocation (i.e., combined AC and sternoclavicular dislocation) is a rare injury that has been sparsely reported in the literature.[2,127] When this injury does occur, it is most often a posterior or type IV AC dislocation associated with an anterior sternoclavicular dislocation.[127] This underscores the importance of a thorough evaluation of any patient with an AC joint injury with particular attention being paid to the sternoclavicular joint.

Many complications result from operative treatment of AC

TABLE 39-3 *Pearls and Pitfalls*

- While exposing the clavicle, create thick, intact deltotrapezial flaps to assist closure at the end of the case
- Clear the medial and lateral margins of the coracoid to assist passage of suture and graft under it
- Use a Satinsky vascular clamp to pass the shuttle suture under the coracoid from medial to lateral
- Keep an adequate bone bridge between the drill holes in the clavicle to reduce the risk of fracture
- Clear tissue from drill holes on the undersurface of the clavicle to ease passage of the graft
- Push up on the elbow to reduce the acromion to the clavicle before securing the repair

dislocations. Besides the obvious wound infection and osteomyelitis that might develop from the operative procedure, several other complications occur (e.g., a fracture through a drill hole, loss of purchase of the internal fixation, metal failure, and migration of the fixation device to other parts of the body). The incidence of recurrent deformity is probably higher than routinely expected. This should not be very surprising. There is nowhere else in the body where the weight of an entire extremity is supported through so little fixation (Fig. 39-27). In addition, the potential planes of motion at the injured AC joint are numerous and result in complex loading of the reconstruction. For these reasons, we advocate longer and more aggressive immobilization than is commonly described.

Migration of Pins

Pins used to stabilize the AC joint have a colorful, interesting history of migration into remote, life-threatening locations such as the lung,[93] the spinal cord,[109] the neck[84] posterior to the carotid sheath, and the pleura or close to it.[38] Vessels in the thorax and neck have also been the recipients of pin migration injury (Fig. 39-28).

In most instances, pin migration can be prevented by bending a hook on the portion of the pin that protrudes from the acromion process. However, the pins can break, and then part of the pin is free to migrate. Patients must be prepared and forewarned of the possible necessity of pin removal and the complications of pins that are not removed.

Lyons and Rockwood[86] reviewed 37 reports of pin migration in operations about the shoulder. They recommended that pin use should be avoided in operations about the shoulder. When pins are utilized, they should be bent or have restraining devices to decrease the risk of migration. The patient should be informed of the risks. Close follow-up should be performed and the pins should be removed at the conclusion of therapy or whenever migration is noted. Pin migration may have devastating consequences. Eight patients have died.

Failure of Soft Tissue Repairs

In the treatment of a ligamentous injury to the AC joint, the simple repair of the coracoclavicular and AC ligaments without

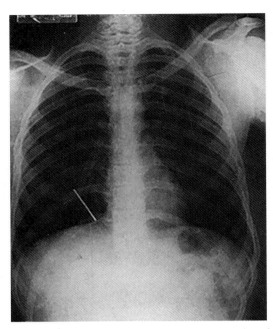

FIGURE 39-28 A broken Steinmann pin has migrated into the right lung field from its previous location in the right AC joint.

the additional support of coracoclavicular sutures, screws, or internal fixation, the AC fixation will likely fail. This is particularly true in chronic injury to the AC and coracoclavicular ligaments, and there is often a major separation between the clavicle and the coracoid. Transfer of the acromial attachment of the coracoacromial ligament onto or into the medullary canal of the distal clavicle alone is not strong enough. It must be supplemented with additional fixation as recommended in the treatment section.

Failure of soft tissue repairs can also result from suture breakage, suture anchor pullout, or screw breakage. If failure is noticed early in the postoperative period, reoperation to correct the problem is usually indicated. If failure occurs weeks to months after surgery, infection should be suspected and ruled out.

Complications Related to Nonabsorbable Tape or Suture

Coracoclavicular fixation using grafts or synthetic material has been associated with various complications. Goldberg and colleagues[55] recognized erosion of a Dacron graft through the distal clavicle in some cases (Fig. 39-29). Moneim and Balduini[100] noted a coracoid fracture after reconstruction of the coracoclavicular ligaments through two drill holes in the clavicle. Fractures of the distal clavicle secondary to the use of loop sutures between the coracoid and the distal clavicle have been reported.[37,90] Other complications include aseptic foreign body reactions[23] and infections.[105] Neault et al.[105] reported three cases in which nonabsorbable tape or suture was directly related to a postoperative infection. Two infections occurred within a year, but one was 5 years after repair of a type III injury. Colosimo et al.[23] reported two cases of aseptic foreign body reactions to Dacron graft material 2 and 4 years after surgery. Microscopic examination revealed chronic

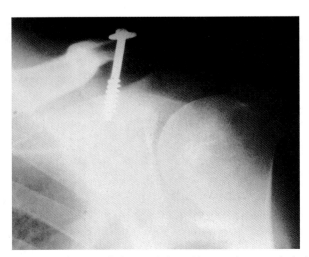

FIGURE 39-27 Radiograph showing failure of fixation of a coracoclavicular screw.

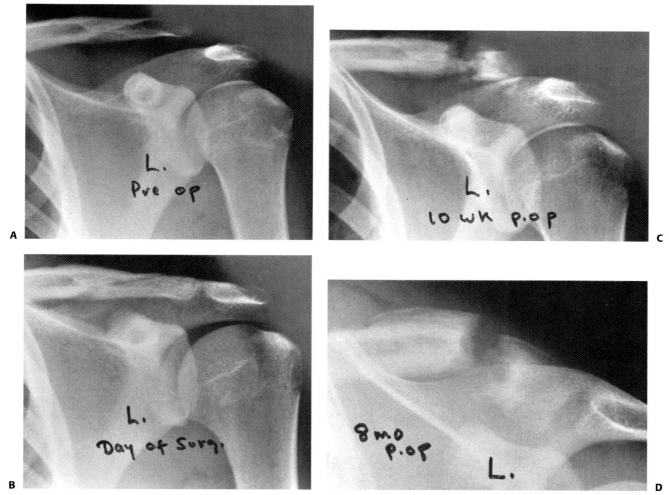

FIGURE 39-29 Complications from using cerclage material as a loop around the top of the clavicle and under the coracoid process for treatment of complete AC dislocations. **A.** Preoperative radiograph demonstrating the type III dislocation of the AC joint. **B.** The postoperative radiograph demonstrates near anatomic reduction using a 6-mm soft Dacron vascular graft loop. **C.** Gradual erosion of the Dacron graft completely through the distal clavicle can be seen. **D.** Note the superior migration of the shaft of the clavicle.

inflammation with a foreign body giant cell reaction. Both patients improved after removal of the Dacron material and were back to work in 10 days.

Acromioclavicular Arthritis

Symptomatic arthritis of the AC joint may occur after surgical fixation. Weaver and Dunn[152] recommended distal clavicle excision and transfer of the coracoacromial ligament for both acute and chronic AC separations. In a review article, Cook and Heiner[24] recommend distal clavicle excision as part of the acute surgical management of patients with AC separations. They reported that postoperative degenerative changes in the AC joint may be as high as 24% and that primary excision of the distal clavicle was associated with little morbidity. Conversely, the vast majority of series reporting the results of surgical management of AC separations do not advocate primary excision of the distal clavicle.[66] Therefore, there is no consensus regarding primary distal clavicle excision and coracoacromial ligament transfer for acute AC injuries.

CONTROVERSIES AND FUTURE DIRECTIONS

The Role of Arthroscopy in the Treatment of Acromioclavicular Joint Injuries

Recent literature has proposed an increased role for the use of arthroscopy in the treatment of AC joint injuries. Wolf and Pennington[155] described an all-arthroscopic technique of AC joint reconstruction. The coracoid is visualized through the subcoracoid recess in the anterior aspect of the joint. An anterior cruciate ligament guide is used to drill a hole through the clavicle and coracoid, and SecureStrand cable (Surgical Dynamics, Norwalk, CT) is used for fixation. They reported a series of 4 patients with no recurrence of deformity. Lafosse et al.[80] published an all-arthroscopic technique for coracoclavicular ligament reconstruction, which releases the coracoacromial ligament from the undersurface of the acromion and transfers it to the inferior clavicle. Proponents of arthroscopic reconstruction claim the benefits of this more minimally invasive technique are less violation of deltotrapezial fascia, faster postoperative recovery, less pain, and fewer complications.

Although many different arthroscopic techniques have been proposed, few clinical outcome studies have been published. Chernchujit et al.[21] published a series of 13 patients who had an arthroscopic reconstruction following AC joint disruption using suture anchors and a titanium plate. These patients were followed for a mean of 18 months. Twelve patients returned to work without pain within 3 months after the operation and the average constant score at last follow-up was 95. Postoperative radiographs confirmed an anatomic reduction in 10 patients, residual subluxation in two patients, and redislocation of the joint in one patient. Given this, as well as evolving surgical techniques, we may see an expanding role for arthroscopy in the future for the management of these injuries.

REFERENCES

1. Adams FL. The Genuine Works of Hippocrates. Vols 1 and 2. New York: William Wood, 1886.
2. Arenas AJ, Pampliega T, Iglesias J. Surgical management of bipolar clavicular dislocation. Acta Orthop Belg 1993;59:202–205.
3. Bannister GC, Wallace WA, Stableforth PG, et al. A classification of acute acromioclavicular dislocation: a clinical, radiological, and anatomical study. Injury 1992;23:194–196.
4. Bannister GC, Wallace WA, Stableforth PG, et al. The management of acute acromioclavicular dislocation. A randomized prospective controlled trial. J Bone Joint Surg 1989;71B:848–850.
5. Barber FA. Complete posterior acromioclavicular dislocation: a case report. Orthopedics 1987;10:493–496.
6. Bearden JM, Hughston JC, Whatley GS. Acromioclavicular dislocation: method of treatment. J Sports Med 1973;1:5–17.
7. Bearn JG. Direct observations on the function of the capsule of the sternoclavicular joint in clavicular support. J Anat 1967;101:159–170.
8. Bergfeld JA, Andrish JT, Clancy WG. Evaluation of the acromioclavicular joint following first and second-degree sprains. Am J Sports Med 1978;6:153–159.
9. Bernard TNJ, Brunet ME, Haddad RJ. Fractured coracoid process in acromioclavicular dislocations: report of four cases and review of the literature. Clin Orthop 1983;175:227–232.
10. Bjerneld H, Hovelius L, Thorling J. Acromioclavicular separations treated conservatively. A 5-year follow-up study. Acta Orthop Scand 1983;54:743–745.
11. Black GB, McPherson JAM, Reed MH. Traumatic pseudodislocation of the acromioclavicular joint in children: a 15-year review. Am J Sports Med 1991;19:644–646.
12. Blazar PE, Iannotti JP, Williams GR. Anteroposterior instability of the distal clavicle after distal clavicle resection. Clin Orthop 1998;348:114–120.
13. Boehm TC. The relation of the coracoclavicular ligament insertion to the acromioclavicular joint. A cadaver study of relevance to lateral clavicle resection. Acta Orthop Scand 2003;74(6):718–721.
14. Bosworth BM. Acromioclavicular separation: new method of repair. Surg Gynecol Obstet 1941;73:866–871.
15. Branch TP, Burdette HL, Shahriari AS, et al. The role of the acromioclavicular ligaments and the effect of distal clavicle resection. Am J Sports Med 1996;24:293–297.
16. Breslow MJ, Jazrawi LM, Bernstein AD, et al. Treatment of acromioclavicular joint separation: suture or suture anchors? J Shoulder Elbow Surg 2002;11(3):225-229.
17. Browne JE, Stanley RF, Tullos HS. Acromioclavicular joint dislocations: comparative results following operative treatment with and without primary distal clavisectomy. Am J Sports Med 1977;5:258–263.
18. Cadenat FM. The treatment of dislocations and fractures of the outer end of the clavicle. Int Clin 1917;1:145–169.
19. Cahill BR. Osteolysis of the distal part of the clavicle. J Bone Joint Surg 1982;64A:1053–1058.
20. Carr AJ, Broughton NS. Acromioclavicular dislocation associated with fracture of the coracoid process. J Trauma 1989;29:125–126.
21. Chernchujit B, Tischer T, Imhoff AB. Arthroscopic reconstruction of the acromioclavicular joint disruption: surgical technique and preliminary results. Arch Orthop Trauma Surg 2006;126:575–581.
22. Codman EA. Rupture of the supraspinatus tendon and other lesions in or about the subacromial bursa. In: Codman EA, ed. The Shoulder. Boston: Thomas Todd, 1934:32–65.
23. Colosimo AJ, Hummer CD 3rd, Heidt RS Jr. Aseptic foreign body reaction to Dacron graft material used for coracoclavicular ligament reconstruction after type III acromioclavicular dislocation. Am J Sports Med 1996;24:561–563.
24. Cook DA, Heiner JP. Acromioclavicular joint injuries. Orthop Rev 1990;14:510–516.
25. Cook F, Horowitz M. Bipolar clavicular dislocation: report of a case. J Bone Joint Surg 1987;64A:145–147.
26. Costic RS, Labriola JE, Rodosky MW. Biomechanical rationale for development of anatomical reconstructions of coracoclavicular ligaments after complete acromioclavicular joint dislocations. Am J Sports Med 2004;32:1929–1936.
27. Cox JS. Acromioclavicular joint injuries and their management principles. Ann Chir Gynecol 1991;80:155–159.
28. Cox JS. Current method of treatment of acromioclavicular joint dislocations. Orthopedics 1992;15:1041–1044.
29. Cox JS. The fate of the acromioclavicular joint in athletic injuries. Am J Sports Med 1981;9:50–53.
30. Curtis RJ. Operative management of children's fractures of the shoulder region. Orthop Clin North Am 1990;21:315–324.
31. Daly P, Sim FH, Simonet WT. Ice hockey injuries: a review. Sports Med 1990;10:122–131.
32. Debski RE, Parsons IM, Woo SL, et al. Effect of capsular injury on acromioclavicular joint mechanics. J Bone Joint Surg Am 2001;83A:1344–1351.
33. DePalma AF. The role of the disks of the sternoclavicular and the acromioclavicular joints. Clin Orthop 1959;13:222–233.
34. Dias JJ, Steingold RF, Richardson RA, et al. The conservative treatment of acromioclavicular dislocation. Review after 5 years. J Bone Joint Surg 1987;69B:719–722.
35. Diaz JJ, Gregg PJ. Acromioclavicular joint injuries in sport: recommendations for treatment. Sports Med 1991;11:125–132.
36. Dumontier C, Sautet A, Man M, et al. Acromioclavicular dislocations: treatment by coracoacromial ligamentoplasty. J Shoulder Elbow Surg 1995;4:130–134.
37. Dust WN, Lenczner EM. Stress fracture of the clavicle leading to nonunion secondary to coracoclavicular reconstruction with Dacron. Am J Sports Med 1989;17:128–129.
38. Eaton R, Serletti J. Computerized axial tomography: a method of localizing Steinmann pin migration. Orthopedics 1981;4:1357–1360.
39. Echo BS, Donati RB, Powell CE. Bipolar clavicular dislocation treated surgically: a case report. J Bone Joint Surg 1988;70A:1251–1253.
40. Eidman DK, Siff SJ, Tullos HS. Acromioclavicular lesions in children. Am J Sports Med 1981;9:150–154.
41. Eskola A, Vainionpaa S, Korkala O, et al. Acute complete acromioclavicular dislocation. A prospective randomized trial of fixation with smooth or threaded Kirschner wires or cortical screw. Ann Chir Gynaecol 1987;76:323–326.
42. Eskola A, Vainionpaa S, Korkala S, et al. Four-year outcome of operative treatment of acute acromioclavicular dislocation. J Orthop Trauma 1991;5:9–13.
43. Falstie-Jensen S, Mikkelsen P. Pseudodislocation of the acromioclavicular joint. J Bone Joint Surg 1982;64B:368–369.
44. Fama G, Bonaga S. [Safety pin synthesis in the cure of acromioclavicular luxation]. Chir Organi Mov 1988;73:227–235.
45. Flatow EL. The biomechanics of the acromioclavicular, sternoclavicular, and scapulothoracic joints. Instr Course Lect 1993;42:237–245.
46. Flatow EL, Cordasco FA, Bigliani LU. Arthroscopic resection of the outer end of the clavicle from a superior approach: a critical, quantitative, radiographic assessment of bone removal. Arthroscopy 1992;8:55–64.
47. Flatow EL, Duralde XA, Nicholson GP, et al. Arthroscopic resection of the distal clavicle with a superior approach. J Shoulder Elbow Surg 1995;4:41–50.
48. Fukuda K, Craig EV, An KN, et al. Biomechanical study of the ligamentous system of the acromioclavicular joint. J Bone Joint Surg 1986;68A:434–440.
49. Gallay SH, Hupel TM, Beaton DE, et al. Functional outcome of acromioclavicular joint injury in polytrauma patients. J Orthop Trauma 1998;12:159–163.
50. Galpin RD, Hawkins RJ, Grainger RW. A comparative analysis of operative versus nonoperative treatment of grade III acromioclavicular separations. Clin Orthop 1985;193:150–155.
51. Gartsman GM. Arthroscopic resection of the acromioclavicular joint. Am J Sports Med 1993;21:71–77.
52. Gartsman GM, Combs AH, Davis PF, et al. Arthroscopic acromioclavicular joint resection. An anatomical study. Am J Sports Med 1991;19:2–5.
53. Gearen PF, Petty W. Panclavicular dislocation: report of a case. J Bone Joint Surg 1982;64A:454–455.
54. Gerber C, Rockwood CA. Subcoracoid dislocation of the lateral end of the clavicle: a report of three cases. J Bone Joint Surg 1987;69A:924–927.
55. Goldberg JA, Viglione W, Cumming WJ, et al. Review of coracoclavicular ligament reconstruction using Dacron graft material. Aust NZ J Surg 1987;57:441–445.
56. Griffiths CJ, Glucksman E. Post traumatic osteolysis of the clavicle: a case report. Arch Emerg Med 1986;3:129–132.
57. Grutter PW, Petersen SA. Anatomical acromioclavicular ligament reconstruction: a biomechanical comparison of reconstructive techniques of the acromioclavicular joint. Am J Sports Med 2005;33:1723–1728.
58. Gurd FB. The treatment of complete dislocation of the outer end of the clavicle: a hitherto undescribed operation. Ann Surg 1941;113:1094–1098.
59. Guy DK, Wirth MA, Griffin JL, et al. Reconstruction of chronic and complete dislocations of the acromioclavicular joint. Clin Orthop 1998;347:138–149.
60. Habernek H, Schmid L, Walch G. [Management of acromioclavicular joint dislocation with the Wolter hook-plate. One year follow-up of 35 cases]. Unfallchirurgie 1993;19:33–39.
61. Habernek H, Weinstabl R, Schmid L, et al. A crook plate for treatment of acromioclavicular joint separation: indication, technique, and results after 1 year. J Trauma 1993;35:893–901.
62. Harris RI, Vu DH, Sonnabend DH, et al. Anatomic variance of the coracoclavicular ligaments. J Shoulder Elbow Surg 2001;10(6):585–588.
63. Harris RI, Wallace AL, Harper GD, et al. Structural properties of the intact and the reconstructed coracoclavicular ligament complex. Am J Sports Med 2000;28(1):103–108.
64. Hastings DE, Horne JG. Anterior dislocation of the acromioclavicular joint. Injury 1979;10:285–288.
65. Havranek P. Injuries of distal clavicular physis in children. J Pediatr Orthop 1989;9:213–215.
66. Hawkins RJ, Warren RF, Noble JS. Suture Repair Technique for Acute and Chronic Acromioclavicular Dislocations. Rosemont, IL: American Academy of Orthopaedic Surgeons videotape series, 2005.
67. Hessmann M, Gotzen L, Gehling H. Acromioclavicular reconstruction augmented with polydioxanonsulphate bands. Surgical technique and results. Am J Sports Med 1995;23:552–556.
68. Hessmann M, Gotzen L, Gehling H, et al. [Results of reconstruction of acromioclavicular joint rupture with PDS implants]. Unfallchirurg 1997;100:193–197.

69. Ho W-P, Chen J-Y, Shih C-H. The surgical treatment of complete acromioclavicular joint dislocation. Orthop Rev 1988;27:1116–1119.
70. Inman VT, Saunders M, Abbott LC. Observations on the function of the shoulder joint. J Bone Joint Surg 1944;26:1–30.
71. Jain AS. Traumatic floating clavicle: a case report. J Bone Joint Surg 1984;66B:560–561.
72. Kay SP, Ellman H, Harris E. Arthroscopic distal clavicle excision. Technique and early results. Clin Orthop 1994;301:181–184.
73. Kennedy JC, Cameron H. Complete dislocation of the acromioclavicular joint. J Bone Joint Surg 1954;36B:202–208.
74. Kiefer H, Claes L, Burri C, et al. The stabilizing effect of various implants on the torn acromioclavicular joint. A biomechanical study. Arch Orthop Trauma Surg 1986;106: 42–46.
75. Klimkiewicz JJ, Williams GR, Sher JS, et al. The acromioclavicular capsule as a restraint to posterior translation of the clavicle: a biomechanical analysis. J Shoulder Elbow Surg 1999;8:119–124.
76. Kumar A. Management of coracoid process fracture with acromioclavicular joint dislocation. Orthopaedics 1990;13:770–772.
77. Kumar S, Sethi A, Jain AK. Surgical treatment of complete acromioclavicular dislocation using the coracoacromial ligament and coracoclavicular fixation: report of a technique in 14 patients. J Orthop Trauma 1995;9:507–510.
78. Kutschera HP, Kotz RI. Bone-ligament transfer of coracoacromial ligament for acromioclavicular dislocation. A new fixation method used in six cases. Acta Orthop Scand 1997;68:246–248.
79. Lafosse L, Baier GP, Leuzinger J. Arthroscopic treatment of acute and chronic acromioclavicular joint dislocation. Arthroscopy 2005;21:1017–1028.
80. Lancourt JB. Acromioclavicular dislocation with adjacent clavicular fracture in a horseback rider: a case report. Am J Sports Med 1990;18:321–322.
81. Larsen E, Bjerg-Nielsen A, Christensen P. Conservative or surgical treatment of acromioclavicular dislocation. A prospective, controlled, randomized study. J Bone Joint Surg 1986;68A:552–555.
82. Lee KW, Debski RE, Chen CH, et al. Functional evaluation of the ligaments at the acromioclavicular joint during anteroposterior and superoinferior translation. Am J Sports Med 1997;25:858–862.
83. Lemos MJ. The evaluation and treatment of the injured acromioclavicular joint in athletes. Am J Sports Med 1998;26:137–144.
84. Lindsey RW, Gutowski WT. Migration of a broken pin following fixation of the acromioclavicular joint. Orthopedics 1986;9:413–416.
85. Lizaur A, Marco L, Cebrian R. Acute dislocation of the acromioclavicular joint. Traumatic anatomy and the importance of deltoid and trapezius. J Bone Joint Surg 1994; 76B:602–606.
86. Lyons FA, Rockwood CA. Migration of pins used in operations on the shoulder. J Bone Joint Surg 1990;72A:1262–1267.
87. MacDonald PB, Alexander MJ, Frejuk J, et al. Comprehensive functional analysis of shoulders following complete acromioclavicular separation. Am J Sports Med 1988; 16:475–480.
88. Madsen B. Osteolysis of the acromial end of the clavicle following trauma. Br J Radiol 1963;36:822.
89. Malcapi C, Grassi G, Oretti D. Posterior dislocation of the acromioclavicular joint: a rare or an easily overlooked lesion? Ital J Orthop Traumatol 1978;4:79–83.
90. Martell JR. Clavicular nonunion complications with the use of Merselene tape. Am J Sports Med 1992;20:360–362.
91. Martin-Herrero T, Rodriguez-Merchan C, Munuera-Martinez L. Fracture of the coracoid process: presentation of seven cases and review of the literature. J Trauma 1993;30: 1597–1599.
92. Matthews LS, Simonson BG, Wolock BS. Osteolysis of the distal clavicle in a female body builder: a case report. Am J Sports Med 1992;21:50–52.
93. Mazet RJ. Migration of a Kirschner wire from the shoulder region into the lung: a report of two cases. J Bone Joint Surg 1943;25A:477–483.
94. Mazzocca AD, Arciero RA, Bicos J. Evaluation and treatment of acromioclavicular joint injuries. Am J Sports Med 2007;35:316–329.
95. Mazzocca AD, Santangelo SA, Johnson ST. A biomechanical evaluation of an anatomical coracoclavicular ligament reconstruction. Am J Sports Med 2006;34:236–246.
96. McFarland EG, Blivin SJ, Doehring CB, et al. Treatment of grade III acromioclavicular separations in professional throwing athletes: results of a survey. Am J Orthop 1997; 26:771–774.
97. McPhee IB. Inferior dislocation of the outer end of the clavicle. J Trauma 1980;20: 709–710.
98. Meislin RJ, Zuckerman JD, Nainzadeh N. Type III acromioclavicular joint separation associated with late brachial plexus neurapraxia. J Orthop Trauma 1992;6:370–372.
99. Merchan EC. Osteolysis of the distal clavicle in a woman: case report and a review of the literature. Ital J Orthop 1992;18:561–563.
100. Moneim MS, Balduini FC. Coracoid fracture as a complication of surgical treatment by coracoclavicular tape fixation. A case report. Clin Orthop 1982;168:133–135.
101. Morrison DS, Lemos MJ. Acromioclavicular separation. Reconstruction using synthetic loop augmentation. Am J Sports Med 1995;23:105–110.
102. Moushine E, Garofalo R, Crevoisier X, et al. Grade I and II acromioclavicular dislocations: results of conservative treatment. J Shoulder Elbow Surg 2003;12(6):599–602.
103. Mumford EB. Acromioclavicular dislocation. J Bone Joint Surg 1941;23:799–802.
104. Murphy OB, Bellamy R, Wheeler W, et al. Posttraumatic osteolysis of the distal clavicle. Clin Orthop 1975;109:108–114.
105. Neault MA, Nuber GW, Marymont JV. Infections after surgical repair of acromioclavicular separations with nonabsorbable tape or suture. J Shoulder Elbow Surg 1996;5: 477–478.
106. Neviaser JS. Acromioclavicular dislocation treated by transference of the coracoacromial ligament: a long-term follow-up in a series of 112 cases. Clin Orthop 1968;58:57–68.
107. Nieminen S, Aho AJ. Anterior dislocation of the acromioclavicular joint. Ann Chir Gynaecol 1984;73:21–24.
108. Nissen CW, Chatterjee A. Type III acromioclavicular separation: results of a recent survey on its management. Am J Orthop 2007;36;89–93.
109. Norell H, Llewellyn RC. Migration of a threaded Steinmann pin from an acromioclavicular joint into the spinal canal. J Bone Joint Surg 1965;47A:1024–1026.
110. Nuber GW, Bowen MK. Disorders of the acromioclavicular joint: pathophysiology, diagnosis, and management. In: Iannotti JP, Williams GR, eds. Disorders of the Shoulder: Diagnosis and Management. Philadelphia: Lippincott Williams & Wilkins, 1999: 739–764.
111. Nuber GW, Bowen MK. Disorders of the acromioclavicular joint: pathophysiology, diagnosis, and management. In: Iannotti JP, Williams GR, eds. Disorders of the Shoulder: Diagnosis and Management. Philadelphia: Lippincott Williams & Wilkins, 1999: 739–762.
112. Orava S, Virtanen K, Holopainen YVO. Posttraumatic osteolysis of the distal ends of the clavicle: a report of three cases. Ann Chir Gynaecol 1984;73:83–86.
113. Paavolainen P, Bjorkenheim JM, Paukku P, et al. Surgical treatment of acromioclavicular dislocation: a review of 39 patients. Injury 1983;14:415–420.
114. Petersson CJ. Degeneration of the acromioclavicular joint. Acta Orthop Scand 1983; 54:434–438.
115. Petersson CJ, Redlund-Johnell I. Radiographic joint space in normal acromioclavicular joints. Acta Orthop Scand 1983;54:431–433.
116. Post M. Current concepts in the diagnosis and management of acromioclavicular dislocations. Clin Orthop 1985;200:234–247.
117. Powers JA, Bach PJ. Acromioclavicular separation: closed or open treatment. Clin Orthop 1974;104:213–233.
118. Press J, Zuckerman JD, Gallagher M, et al. Treatment of grade III acromioclavicular separations. Operative versus nonoperative management. Bull Hosp Jt Dis 1997;56: 77–83.
119. Rawes ML, Dias JJ. Long-term results of conservative treatment for acromioclavicular dislocation. J Bone Joint Surg 1996;78B:410–412.
120. Renfree KJ, Riley MK, Wheeler D, et al. Ligamentous anatomy of the distal clavicle. J Shoulder Elbow Surg 2003;12(4):355–359.
121. Rockwood CA. Injuries to the acromioclavicular Joint. In: Rockwood CA, Green DP, eds. Fractures in Adults. Vol 1. 2nd ed. Philadelphia: JB Lippincott, 1984:860.
122. Rockwood CA, Williams GR, Young CD. Injuries to the acromioclavicular joint. In: Rockwood CA, Green DP, Bucholz RW, Heckman JD, eds. Fractures in Adults. Vol 2. 4th ed. Philadelphia: Lippincott-Raven, 1996:1341–1414.
123. Rowe CR. In: Cave EF, ed. Fractures and other injuries. Chicago: Year Book Medical; 1961.
124. Sage J. Recurrent inferior dislocation of the clavicle at the acromioclavicular joint. Am J Sports Med 1982;10:145–146.
125. Salter EG, Nasca RJ, Shelley BS. Anatomical observations on the acromioclavicular joint and supporting ligaments. Am J Sports Med 1987;15:199–206.
126. Salter EG, Shelley BS, Nasca R. A morphological study of the acromioclavicular joint in humans. Anat Rec 1985;211:353(abst).
127. Sanders JO, Lyons FA, Rockwood CA. Management of dislocations of both ends of the clavicle. J Bone Joint Surg 1990;72A:399–402.
128. Schlegel TF, Burks RT, Marcus RL, et al. A prospective evaluation of untreated acute grade III acromioclavicular separations. Am J Sports Med 2001;29(6):699-703.
129. Schmid A, Schmid F. [Use of arthrosonography in diagnosis of Tossy III lesions of acromioclavicular joints]. Aktuel Traumatol 1988;18:957–962.
130. Schwarz N, Kuderna H. Inferior acromioclavicular separation: report of an unusual case. Clin Orthop 1988;234:28–30.
131. Shoji H, Roth C, Chuinard R. Bone block transfer of coracoacromial ligament in acromioclavicular injury. Clin Orthop 1986;208:272–277.
132. Sim E, Schwarz N, Hocker K, et al. Repair of complete acromioclavicular separations using the acromioclavicular-hook plate. Clin Orthop 1995;314:134–142.
133. Skjeldal S, Lundblad R, Dullerud R. Coracoid process transfer for acromioclavicular dislocation. Acta Orthop Scand 1988;59:180–182.
134. Snyder S, Banas M, Karzel R. The arthroscopic Mumford procedure: an analysis of results. Arthroscopy 1995;11:157–164.
135. Sondergard-Petersen P, Mikkelsen P. Posterior acromioclavicular dislocation. J Bone Joint Surg 1982;64B:52–53.
136. Stam L, Dawson I. Complete acromioclavicular dislocations: treatment with a Dacron ligament. Injury 1991;22:173–176.
137. Sturm JT, Perry JFJ. Brachial plexus injuries from blunt trauma—a harbinger of vascular and thoracic injuries. Ann Emerg Med 1987;16:404–406.
138. Sundaram N, Patel DV, Porter DS. Stabilization of acute acromioclavicular dislocation by a modified Bosworth technique: a long-term follow-up study [published erratum appears in Injury 1992;23(5):359]. Injury 1992;23:189–193.
139. Taft TN, Wilson FC, Oglesby JW. Dislocation of the acromioclavicular joint. An end-result study. J Bone Joint Surg 1987;69A:1045–1051.
140. Talbert TW, Green JR 3rd, Mukherjee DP, et al. Bioabsorbable screw fixation in coracoclavicular ligament reconstruction. J Long Term Eff Med Implants 2003;13(4): 317–323.
141. Thorndike AJ, Quigley TB. Injuries to the acromioclavicular joint: a plea for conservative treatment. Am J Surg 1942;55:250–261.
142. Tibone J, Sellers R, Tonino P. Strength testing after third-degree acromioclavicular dislocations. Am J Sports Med 1992;20:328–331.
143. Tienen TG, Oyen JF, Eggen PJ. A modified technique of reconstruction for complete acromioclavicular dislocation. Am J Sports Med 2003;31:655–659.
144. Tossy JD, Mead NC, Sigmond HM. Acromioclavicular separations: useful and practical classification for treatment. Clin Orthop 1963;28:111–119.
145. Tsou PM. Percutaneous cannulated screw coracoclavicular fixation for acute acromioclavicular dislocations. Clin Orthop 1989;243:112–121.
146. Urist MR. Complete dislocation of the acromioclavicular joint: the nature of the traumatic lesion and effective methods of treatment with an analysis of 41 cases. J Bone Joint Surg 1946;28:813–837.
147. Verhaven E, Casteleyn PP, De Boeck H, et al. Surgical treatment of acute type V acromioclavicular injuries. A prospective study. Acta Orthop Belg 1992;58:176–182.
148. Verhaven E, DeBoeck H, Haentjens P, et al. Surgical treatment of acute type-V acromioclavicular injuries in athletes. Arch Orthop Trauma Surg 1993;112:189–192.
149. Walsh WM, Peterson DA, Shelton G, et al. Shoulder strength following acromioclavicular injury. Am J Sports Med 1985;13:153–158.

150. Wang K, Hsu K, Shih C. Coracoid process fracture combined with acromioclavicular dislocation and coracoclavicular ligament rupture: a case report and review of the literature. Clin Orthop 1994;300:120–122.

151. Warren-Smith CD, Ward MW. Operation for acromioclavicular dislocation. A review of 29 cases treated by one method. J Bone Joint Surg 1987;69B:715–718.

152. Weaver JK, Dunn HK. Treatment of acromioclavicular injuries, especially complete acromioclavicular separation. J Bone Joint Surg 1972;54A:1187–1194.

153. Weinstein DM, McCann PD, McIlveen SJ, et al. Surgical treatment of complete acromioclavicular dislocations. Am J Sports Med 1995;23:324–331.

154. Williams GR, Nguyen VD, Rockwood CR. Classification and radiographic analysis of acromioclavicular dislocations. Appl Radiol 1989;12:29–34.

155. Wolf EM, Pennington WT. Arthroscopic reconstruction for acromioclavicular joint dislocation. Arthroscopy 2001;17(5):558-563.

156. Wojtys EM, Nelson G. Conservative treatment of grade III acromioclavicular dislocations. Clin Orthop 1991;268:112–119.

157. Wurtz LD, Lyons FA, Rockwood CA Jr. Fracture of the middle third of the clavicle and dislocation of the acromioclavicular joint. A report of four cases. J Bone Joint Surg 1992;74A:133–137.

158. Wurtz LO, Lyons FA, Rockwood CA. Fracture of the middle third of the clavicle and dislocation of the acromioclavicular joint. J Bone Joint Surg 1992;74A:133–136.

159. Zanca P. Shoulder pain: Involvement of the acromioclavicular joint: analysis of 1000 cases. AJR 1971;112:493–506.

40

STERNOCLAVICULAR JOINT INJURIES

Anil K. Dutta, Michael A. Wirth, and Charles A. Rockwood Jr.

INTRODUCTION

In Sir Astley Cooper's 1824 text, sternoclavicular (SC) injuries are discussed as injuries that can essentially be managed with a sling and swathe.[41] The first case reports of sc injury are attributed to Rodrigues[166] who described a patient with posterior dislocation presenting with signs of suffocation following a compression injury between a wall and a cart. Isolated nineteenth century reports in Europe were followed by those of American authors in the 1920s and 1930s.[55,118] SC joint injuries are uncommon and are usually relatively benign injuries. However, the more severe posterior injury patterns can represent true medical emergencies and require the orthopaedic surgeon to be knowledgeable regarding the proper steps in diagnosis and treatment. Computed tomography (CT) scan remains the imaging modality of choice. Early and prompt reduction is indicated for posterior dislocations and posterior physeal injuries.

A variety of reconstructive techniques are available if needed, but are rarely required.

PRINCIPLES OF MANAGEMENT

Mechanisms of Injury

Either direct or indirect force can produce a dislocation of the SC joint. Because the SC joint is subject to practically every motion of the upper extremity and because the joint is small and incongruous, one would think that it would be the most commonly dislocated joint in the body. However, the ligamentous supporting structure is strong and so designed that it is, in fact, one of the least commonly dislocated joints. A traumatic dislocation of the SC joint usually occurs only after tremendous forces, either direct or indirect, have been applied to the shoulder.

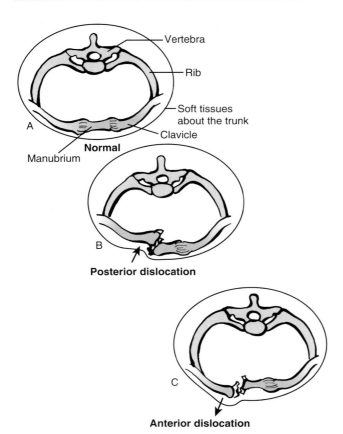

FIGURE 40-1 Cross sections through the thorax at the level of the SC joint. **A.** Normal anatomic relations. **B.** Posterior dislocation of the SC joint. **C.** Anterior dislocation of the SC joint.

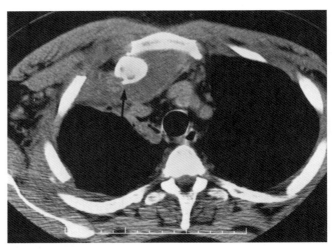

FIGURE 40-2 Computed axial tomogram of a posterior SC joint dislocation that occurred when the driver's chest impacted the steering wheel during a motor vehicle accident. The steering wheel was fractured from the driving column and the vehicle was totally destroyed.

Direct Force

When a force is applied directly to the anteromedial aspect of the clavicle, the clavicle is pushed posteriorly behind the sternum and into the mediastinum (Fig. 40-1). This may occur in a variety of ways: an athlete lying on his back on the ground is jumped on and the knee of the jumper lands directly on the medial end of the clavicle, a kick is delivered to the front of the medial clavicle, a person lying supine is run over by a vehicle, or a person is pinned between a vehicle and a wall (Fig. 40-2). Anatomically, it is essentially impossible for a direct force to produce an anterior SC dislocation.

Indirect Force

A force can be applied indirectly to the SC joint from the anterolateral or posterolateral aspects of the shoulder. This is the most common mechanism of injury to the sternoclavicular joint. Mehta and coworkers[131] reported that three of four posterior SC dislocations were produced by indirect force, and Heinig[86] reported that indirect force was responsible for eight of nine cases of posterior SC dislocations. If the shoulder is compressed and rolled forward, an ipsilateral posterior dislocation results; if the shoulder is compressed and rolled backward, an ipsilateral anterior dislocation results (Fig. 40-3).

Most Common Cause of Injuries

The most common cause of dislocation of the SC joint is vehicular accidents; the second is an injury sustained during participa-

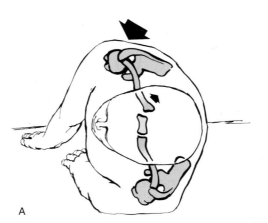
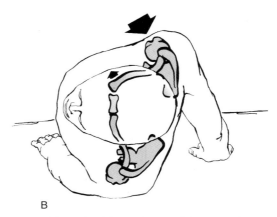

FIGURE 40-3 Mechanisms that produce anterior or posterior dislocation of the SC joint. **A.** If the patient is lying on the ground and a compression force is applied to the posterolateral aspect of the shoulder, the medial end of the clavicle will be displaced posteriorly. **B.** When the lateral compression force is directed from the anterior position, the medial end of the clavicle is dislocated anteriorly.

tion in sports.[139,143,195] Omer,[143] in his review of patients from 14 military hospitals, found 82 cases of SC joint dislocations. He reported that almost 80% of these occurred as the result of vehicular accidents (47%) or in athletics (31%).

Incidence of Injury

The incidence of SC dislocation, based on the series of 1603 injuries of the shoulder girdle reported by Cave and associates,[38] is 3%. (Specific incidences in the study were glenohumeral dislocations at 85%, acromioclavicular injuries 12%, and SC injuries 3%.) In the series by Cave et al.,[38] and in our experience, dislocation of the SC joint is not as rare as posterior dislocation of the glenohumeral joint.

In a study of 3451 injuries during alpine skiing, Kocher and Feagin[105] showed that injuries involving the shoulder complex accounted for 39.1% of upper extremity injuries and 11.4% of all alpine skiing injuries. Of the 393 injuries involving the shoulder complex, SC separations accounted for 0.5%.

The largest series from a single institution was reported by Nettles and Linscheid,[139] who studied 60 patients with SC dislocations (57 anterior and 3 posterior). Fery and Sommelet[67] found a ratio of 40 anterior to 8 posterior dislocations. Waskowitz[195] reviewed 18 cases of SC dislocations, none of which were posterior. However, in our series of 185 traumatic SC injuries, there were 135 patients with anterior dislocation and 50 patients with a posterior dislocation.

Associated Injuries

SC injury can be accompanied by significant damage to the critical surrounding structures in the neck and thorax and/or by other musculoskeletal injuries. Significant concomitant injuries of the mediastinum must be considered to avoid catastrophic outcomes. These injuries almost always occur in the setting of posterior SC fractures and dislocations and include:

1. Tracheal compression: from the initial case report of Rodriques[166] to multiple case reports in recent articles, the trachea can be displaced by the posteriorly displaced medial aspect of the clavicle. Acute airway compromise or subacute dyspnea are key symptoms.[121,137]
2. Pneumothorax: pleural violation by the clavicle has been noted with SC dislocation and should be especially considered in high-energy direct trauma.[147]
3. Laceration of the great vessels: the great vessels of the mediastinum can be directly transected and case reports have included the pulmonary artery,[204] brachiocephalic vein,[42] and superior vena cava.[147] Compression of any of the great vessels without frank laceration can also occur as a complication of injury.[140,144]
4. Esophageal perforation/rupture: cases of esophageal rupture are often described in relation to local sequelae. Howard[90] reported a case of rupture complicated by osteomyelitis of the clavicle. Wasylenko[196] reported on a fatal tracheoesophageal fistula.

Associated Orthopaedic Injuries

Bilateral Dislocations

In 1896, Hotchkiss[88] reported a bilateral traumatic dislocation of the SC joint. The senior author has treated four cases of bilateral SC dislocation. Bilateral subluxation has also been reported.[77]

Dislocations of Both Ends of the Clavicle

When dislocation of both ends of the clavicle occurs, the SC dislocation is usually anterior.[74,145] To our knowledge the first reported case of dislocation of both ends of the clavicle was by Porral[154] in 1831. In 1923, Beckman[15] reported a single case and reviewed 15 cases that had been previously reported. With the exception of this patient, all patients had been treated conservatively with acceptable function. Dieme et al.[53] reported three cases of "floating clavicle." In 1990, Sanders et al.[170] reported 6 patients who had a dislocation of both ends of the clavicle. Two patients who had fewer demands on the shoulder did well with only minor symptoms after nonoperative management. The other 4 patients had persistent symptoms that were localized to the acromioclavicular (AC) joint. Each of these patients had a reconstruction of the AC joint, which resulted in a painless, full range of motion and a return to normal activity (Fig. 40-4). AC dislocation can also accompany medial clavicle epiphyseal fracture/dislocation.[75] Wade et al.[194] reported a trapped posterior inferior AC dislocation associated with a medial epiphyseal fracture which required open reduction of the AC joint and exploration of the SC injury with a good result.

Combinations of Sternoclavicular Dislocations and Fractures and Dislocations of the Clavicle

Fracture of the midshaft of the clavicle with either anterior or posterior dislocation of the SC joint has been noted. It is important to assess the AC joint and the SC joint in the face of the more obvious midshaft clavicle fracture to avoid a delay in diagnosis. Tanlin,[183] Arenas et al.,[4] Friedl and Fritz,[70] and Thomas[184] have all reported patients who had an anterior dislocation of the SC joint and a fracture of the midclavicle. Allen et al.,[3] Nakazato,[138] and Mounasamy[136] each reported on a skeletally immature patient who had an ipsilateral clavicle fracture and a posterior dislocation of the SC joint. Velutini and Tarazona[192] reported a bizarre case of posterior dislocation of the left medial clavicle, the first rib, and a section of the manubrium. Elliott[58] reported on a tripartite injury about the clavicle region in which the patient had an anterior subluxation of the right SC joint, a type II injury to the right AC joint, and a fracture of the right midclavicle. Pearsall and Russell[149] reported a patient who had an ipsilateral clavicle fracture, an anterior SC joint subluxation, and a long thoracic nerve injury. All of these injuries involving the SC joint and the clavicle were associated with severe trauma to the shoulder region.

Combination of Sternoclavicular Dislocation and Scapulothoracic Dissociation

Tsai and Swiontowski[187] reported a patient with SC dislocation associated with scapulothoracic dissociation. This patient had also sustained a transection of the axillary artery and an avulsion of the median nerve. Following a vascular repair and an above the elbow amputation, this patient was left with a complete brachial plexopathy.

Treatment of Combined Injuries

Bilateral dislocations are managed based on the criteria for treatment of each individual dislocation separately. When patients have dislocations of both ends of the clavicle, we recommend stabilization of the AC joint with appropriate surgical techniques for type III, IV, V, and VI separations. The SC dislocation is generally treated nonoperatively with the exception of the

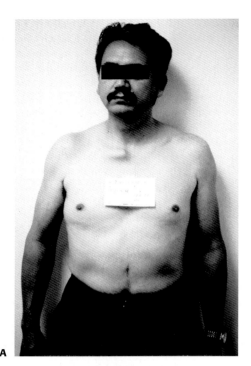

FIGURE 40-4 Dislocation of both ends of the clavicle. **A.** Clinical view demonstrating anterior dislocation of the right SC joint. **B.** The axillary radiograph reveals posterior dislocation of the AC joint. **C.** These injuries are generally treated by AC joint repair/reconstruction with return of near normal function.

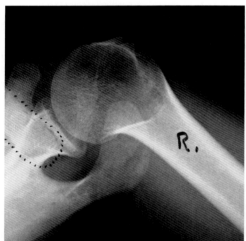

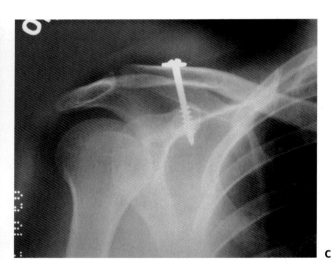

unreduced posterior dislocation which is treated following the guidelines outlined later in this chapter. When the clavicle is fractured with an SC dislocation, the clavicle should be stabilized with internal fixation for posterior injuries and treated as appropriate for an isolated clavicle fracture when the SC dislocation is anterior. In the rare case of a scapulothoracic disassociation and SC dislocation, only the exclusive criteria for SC management can be applied in isolation.

History and Physical Examination

Elucidating the mechanism of injury can alert the initial treating physician to associated injuries and to the direction of dislocation. The patient should be questioned about pain in the adjacent AC joint and glenohumeral joint. The patient with a posterior dislocation has more pain than a patient with an anterior dislocation, and the anterosuperior fullness of the chest produced by the clavicle is less prominent and visible when compared with the normal side. The usually palpable medial end of the clavicle is displaced posteriorly. The corner of the sternum is easily palpated as compared with the normal SC joint. Venous congestion may be present in the neck or in the upper extremity.[80] Symptoms may also include a dry irritating cough and hoarseness.[59,150] Breathing difficulties, shortness of breath, or a choking sensation may be noted. Circulation to the ipsilateral arm may be decreased, although the presence of pulses does not exclude vessel injury. The patient may complain of difficulty in swallowing or a tight feeling in the throat or may be in a state of complete shock or possibly have a pneumothorax. The distal neurologic exam may reveal diminished sensation or weakness secondary to brachial plexus compression. Complete nerve deficits suggest more severe injury patterns. The exam should include assessment of the Wynne-Davies signs[205] of generalized ligamentous laxity as these patients are predisposed to atraumatic anterior SC joint subluxation. We have seen a number of patients who clinically appeared to have an anterior dislocation of the SC joint but on x-ray studies were shown to have complete posterior dislocation. The point is that

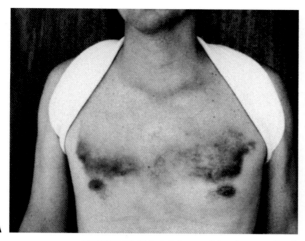
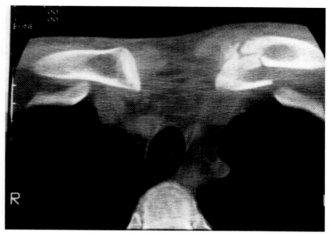

FIGURE 40-5 A. A 34-year-old patient was involved in a motorcycle accident and sustained an anterior blow to the chest. Note the symmetric anterior chest wall ecchymosis. **B.** CT reveals a left medial clavicle fracture without disruption of the SC joint.

one cannot always rely on the clinical findings of observing and palpating the joint to make a distinction between anterior and posterior dislocations.

Radiographic Imaging

Anteroposterior Views

Occasionally, the routine anteroposterior or posteroanterior radiographs of the chest or SC joint suggest something is wrong with one of the clavicles, because it appears to be displaced as compared with the normal side. McCulloch et al.[128] reported that on nonrotated frontal radiographs, a difference in the relative craniocaudal positions of the medial clavicles of greater than 50% of the width of the heads of the clavicles suggests dislocation. It would be ideal to take a view at right angles to the anteroposterior plane, but because of the anatomy, it is impossible to obtain a true 90-degree cephalic-to-caudal lateral view. Lateral radiographs of the chest are at right angles to the anteroposterior plane, but they cannot be interpreted because of the density of the chest and the overlap of the medial clavicles with the first rib and the sternum. Regardless of a clinical

impression that suggests an anterior or posterior dislocation, radiographs and preferably a CT scan must be obtained to confirm one's suspicions (Fig. 40-5).

Special Projected Views

There have been numerous special radiographic projections recommended for the SC joint.[63,66,86,87,97,110,160,172,186] While the serendipity view is frequently obtained as a front line image for evaluation of the SC joint, the Heinig and Hobbs views are rarely obtained if CT is available. However, the Heinig and Hobbs views can be useful when suspicion is high on clinical exam and confirmation is needed before referral for CT, especially in the outpatient setting when delayed presentation often leads to misdiagnosis.

Heinig View. With the patient is a supine position, the x-ray tube is placed approximately 30 inches from the involved SC joint and the central ray beam is directed tangential to the joint and parallel to the opposite clavicle. The cassette is placed against the opposite shoulder and centered on the manubrium (Fig. 40-6).

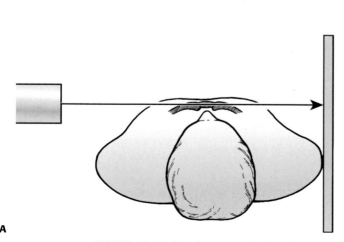
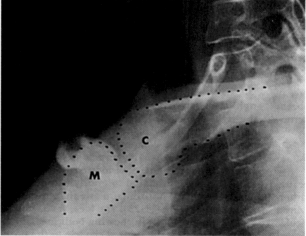

FIGURE 40-6 Heinig view. **A.** Positioning of the patient for x-ray evaluation of the SC joint, as described by Heinig. **B.** Heinig view demonstrating a normal relationship between the medial end of the clavicle (*C*) and the manubrium (*M*).

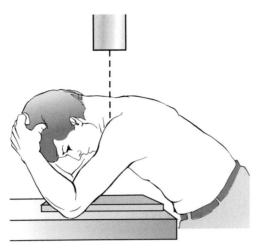

FIGURE 40-7 Hobbs view. Positioning of the patient for x-ray evaluation of the SC joint, as recommended by Hobbs. (From Hobbs DW. Sternoclavicular joint: a new axial radiographic view. Radiology 1968;90:801–802.)

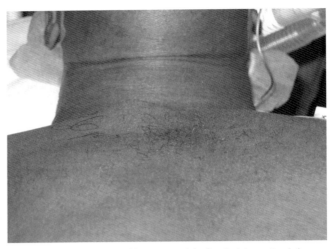

FIGURE 40-9 When viewed from around the level of the patient's knees, it is apparent that the left clavicle is dislocated anteriorly.

Hobbs View. In the Hobbs view, the patient is seated at the x-ray table, high enough to lean forward over the table. The cassette is placed on the table, and the lower anterior rib cage is against the cassette (Fig. 40-7). The patient leans forward so that the nape of his flexed neck is almost parallel to the table. The flexed elbows straddle the cassette and support the head and neck. The x-ray source is above the nape of the neck, and the beam passes through the cervical spine to project the sternoclavicular joints onto the cassette.

Serendipity View. The "serendipity view" is rightfully named because that is the way it was developed. The senior author accidentally noted that the next best thing to having a true cephalocaudal lateral view of the SC joint was a 40-degree cephalic tilt view. The patient is positioned on his back squarely and in the center of the x-ray table. The tube is tilted at a 40-degree angle off the vertical and is centered directly on the sternum (Figs. 40-8 to 40-11). A nongrid 11- × 14-inch cassette is placed squarely on the table and under the patient's upper shoulders and neck so that the beam aimed at the sternum will project both clavicles onto the film.

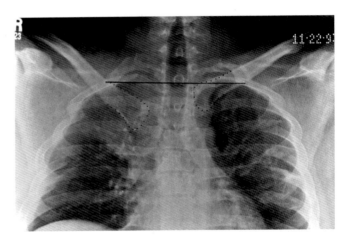

FIGURE 40-10 Posterior dislocation of the right medial clavicle as seen on 40-degree cephalic tilt serendipity radiograph. The right clavicle is inferiorly displaced as compared to the normal left clavicle.

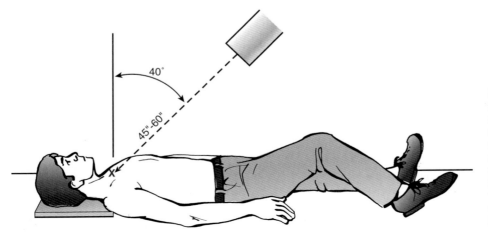

FIGURE 40-8 Serendipity view. Positioning of the patient to take the "serendipity" view of the SC joints. The x-ray tube is tilted 40 degrees from the vertical position and aimed directly at the manubrium. The nongrid cassette should be large enough to receive the projected images of the medial halves of both clavicles. In children, the tube distance from the patient should be 45 inches; in thicker-chested adults, the distance should be 60 inches.

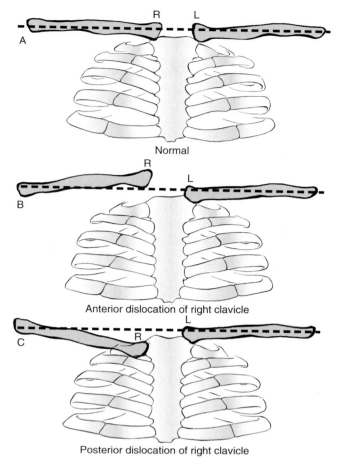

FIGURE 40-11 Interpretation of the cephalic tilt (serendipity view) x-ray films of the SC joints. **A.** In the normal person, both clavicles appear on the same imaginary line drawn horizontally across the film. **B.** In a patient with an anterior dislocation of the right SC joint, the medial half of the right clavicle is projected above the imaginary line drawn through the level of the normal left clavicle. **C.** If the patient has a posterior dislocation of the right SC joint, the medial half of the right clavicle is displaced below the imaginary line drawn through the normal left clavicle.

(Figure labels within image: R, L, Normal, Anterior dislocation of right clavicle, Posterior dislocation of right clavicle)

Special Techniques

Tomograms. Tomograms can be very helpful in distinguishing between a SC dislocation and a fracture of the medial clavicle. They are also helpful in questionable anterior and posterior injuries of the SC joint to distinguish fractures from dislocations and to evaluate arthritic changes.

In 1959, Baker[8] recommended the use of tomography and said it was far more valuable than routine radiographs and the fingertips of the examining physician. In 1975, Morag and Shahin[135] reported on the value of tomography, which they used in a series of 20 patients, and recommended that it be used routinely to evaluate problems of the SC joint. From a study of normal SC joints, they pointed out the variation in the x-ray appearance in different age groups.

Computed Tomography Scans. Without question, the CT scan is the best technique to study problems of the sternoclavicular joint (Fig. 40-12). It clearly distinguishes injuries of the joint from fractures of the medial clavicle and defines minor subluxations of the joint. One must remember to request CT scans of both *SC joints and the medial half of both clavicles* so the injured side can be compared with the normal side. Numerous authors have reported on the value of using a CT scan as the method of choice for radiographic evaluation of the SC joint.[30,43,44,51,52,54,111,114,120] Lucet et al.[120] used CT scans to evaluate the SC joints in 60 healthy subjects homogeneously distributed by sex and decade of life from 20 to 80 years old. They reported that 98% of the subjects had at least one sign of various abnormalities, such as sclerosis, osteophytes, erosion, cysts, and joint narrowing. The number of signs increased with age and the number of clavicular signs was greater than those in the sternum.

Magnetic Resonance Images. Brossman et al.[26] correlated magnetic resonance imaging (MRI) scans with anatomic sections in 14 SC joints from elderly cadavers. They concluded that MRI did depict the anatomy of the SC joint and surrounding soft tissues (Fig. 40-13). T2-weighted images were superior to T1-weighted images in depicting the intra-articular disk. Magnetic resonance arthrography allowed the delineation of perforations in the intra-articular disk. In children and young adults when there are questions of diagnosis between dislocation and

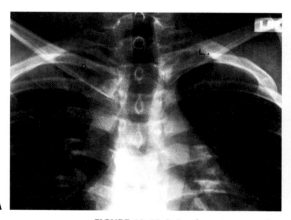

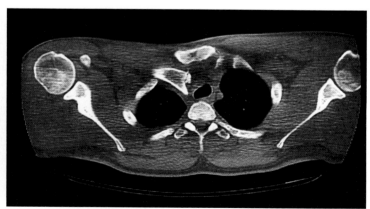

FIGURE 40-12 A. Routine anteroposterior radiograph of posteriorly dislocated right SC joint. **B.** The anteroposterior view is suggestive of a posterior dislocation. However, the CT scan clearly demonstrates the posteriorly displaced right medial clavicle. Note the displacement of the trachea.

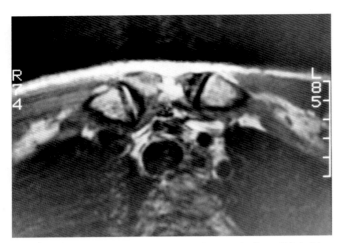

FIGURE 40-13 MRI of the SC joint. The epiphysis on both medial clavicles is clearly visible.

SC joint or physeal injury, the MRI scan can be used to determine if the epiphysis has displaced with the clavicle or is still adjacent to the manubrium. Benitez et al.[15] evaluated 41 patients with SC trauma at an average of 9 months postinjury and found an 80% incidence of articular disk injury and a 59% incidence of subluxation. MRI may be useful in this light to better understand the in vivo mechanisms of injury of the SC joint and to elucidate causes of pain well after the traumatic event.[16]

Ultrasound. Pollock et al.[153] reported the use of ultrasound in the diagnosis of two posterior dislocations of the SC joint. Siddiqui and Turner[175] illustrated the use of intraoperative ultrasound to confirm whether a closed reduction has been successful or not.

Diagnosis and Classification

Two methods can be used to classify SC joint subluxations and dislocations: the anatomic position of the injury and the etiology of the problem. The Orthopaedic Trauma Association Classification is simply based on the direction of the dislocation and not on etiology.

Orthopaedic Trauma Association Classification

The anterior and posterior dislocations are well described. A recent case report confirms the possibility of a superior dislocation which occurred after and indirect force mechanism. The authors noted that only the interclavicular and intra-articular disc ligaments were ruptured (Fig. 40-14).[115]

Anatomic Classification

Anterior Subluxation and Dislocation. Anterior dislocations are the most common. The medial end of the clavicle is displaced anteriorly or anterosuperiorly to the anterior margin of the sternum.

Posterior Dislocation. Posterior SC dislocation is uncommon. The medial end of the clavicle is displaced posteriorly or posterosuperiorly with respect to the posterior margin of the sternum (see Fig. 40-19A,B).

Etiologic Classification

Traumatic Injuries.

Mild Sprain. In a mild sprain, all the ligaments are intact and the joint is stable. There may be local damage to the capsule and the joint may develop an effusion, but there is no translation of the clavicle or loss of congruity.

Moderate Sprain (Subluxation). In a moderate sprain, there is subluxation of the SC joint. The capsular ligaments, the intra-articular disk, and costoclavicular ligaments may be partially disrupted. The subluxation is usually anterior but posterior subluxation can occur.

Acute Dislocation. In a dislocated SC joint, the capsular and intra-articular ligaments are ruptured. Occasionally, the costoclavicular ligament is intact but stretched out enough to allow dislocation of the joint.

Recurrent Dislocation. If the initial acute traumatic dislocation does not heal, mild to moderate forces may produce recurrent dislocations; this is rare.

Unreduced Dislocation. The original dislocation may go unrecognized, it may be irreducible, or the physician may decide not to reduce certain dislocations.

Atraumatic Problems.

Spontaneous Subluxation or Dislocation. The condition usually occurs in the late teens and in young adults and more often in women.

While both SC joints can be affected,[77] usually one joint is more of a problem than the other (Fig. 40-15). It usually occurs in patients who have generalized ligament laxity of other joints. In middle-aged women, spontaneous anterior or anterior/superior subluxation can occur and may be in association with condensing osteitis of the clavicle.[191] In some patients, the atraumatic anterior dislocation of the SC joint is painful and is associated with a snap or pop as the arm is elevated overhead, and another snap occurs when the arm is returned to the patient's side. Atraumatic posterior dislocation[126] and subluxation have been reported.[127]

Other Conditions of the Sternoclavicular Joint. It is important to consider other pathologies particular to the SC joint during the diagnostic process. Infection may mimic trauma and should especially be considered in patients with history of intravenous drug abuse, immunocompromise, or indwelling subclavian catheters. SC hyperostosis is an inflammatory condition of the SC joint and medial ribs which results in new bone formation and even ankylosis of the SC joint. It is associated with Japanese ethnicity and dermatologic lesions in the palms and plantar regions. Three conditions which predominate in women are condensing osteitis, Friedreich disease, and osteoarthritis.[201] Condensing osteitis of the medial clavicle typically occurs in women of late child-bearing age and presents as a painful joint with sclerosis on radiographs, similar to condensing osteitis of the ilium and pubis seen in the same demographic group. Friedreich's disease is osteonecrosis of the medial clavicle. Osteoarthritis typically manifests in the postmenopausal years and can appear as a pseudosubluxation anteriorly.[23]

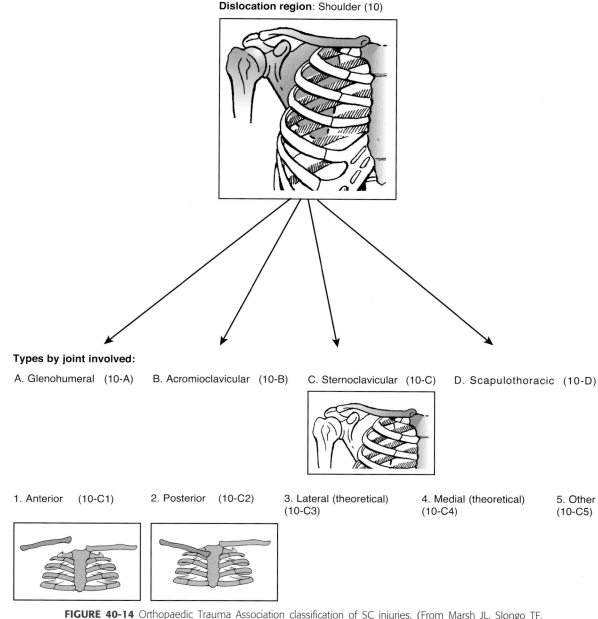

Dislocation region: Shoulder (10)

Types by joint involved:

A. Glenohumeral (10-A)   B. Acromioclavicular (10-B)   C. Sternoclavicular (10-C)   D. Scapulothoracic (10-D)

1. Anterior   (10-C1)   2. Posterior   (10-C2)   3. Lateral (theoretical)   4. Medial (theoretical)   5. Other
                                                        (10-C3)   (10-C4)   (10-C5)

FIGURE 40-14 Orthopaedic Trauma Association classification of SC injuries. (From Marsh JL, Slongo TF, Agel J, et al. Fracture and dislocation classification compendium—2007: Orthopaedic Trauma Association classification, database, and outcomes committee. J Orthop Trauma. 2007;21(10 Suppl):S104–107, with permission.)

SURGICAL AND APPLIED ANATOMY

Surgical Anatomy

The surgeon who is planning an operative procedure on or near the SC joint should be completely knowledgeable about the vast array of anatomic structures immediately posterior to the SC joint. There is a "curtain" of muscles (the sternohyoid, sternothyroid, and scaleni) posterior to the SC joint and the inner third of the clavicle, and this curtain blocks the view of the vital structures. Some of these vital structures include the innominate artery, innominate vein, vagus nerve, phrenic nerve, internal jugular vein, trachea, and esophagus (Fig. 40-16). It is important to remember that the arch of the aorta, the superior vena cava, and the right pulmonary artery are also very close to the SC joint. Another structure to be aware of is the anterior jugular vein, which is between the clavicle and the curtain of muscles.

Applied Anatomy

The SC joint is a diarthrodial joint and is the only true articulation between the upper extremity and the axial skeleton. The articular surface of the clavicle is much larger than that of the sternum, and both are covered with hyaline cartilage. The enlarged bulbous medial end of the clavicle is concave front to back and convex vertically and therefore creates a saddle-type joint with the clavicular notch of the sternum.[81,164] The clavicular notch of the sternum is curved, and the joint surfaces are not congruent. Cave[37] demonstrated that in 2.5% of patients,

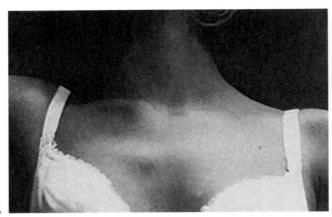
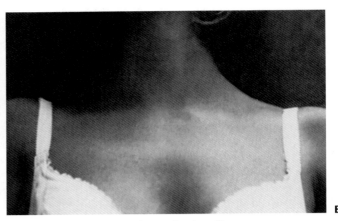

A   B

FIGURE 40-15 Spontaneous anterior subluxation of the SC joint. **A.** With the arm in the overhead position, the medial end of the right clavicle spontaneously subluxates anteriorly without any trauma. **B.** When the arm is brought back down to the side, the medial end of the clavicle spontaneously reduces. Usually this is not associated with significant discomfort. (From Rockwood CA, Matsen F III, eds. The Shoulder. Philadelphia: WB Saunders, 1990, with permission.)

there is a small facet on the inferior aspect of the medial clavicle, which articulates with the superior aspect of the first rib at its synchondral junction with the sternum.

Because less than half of the medial clavicle articulates with the upper angle of the sternum, the SC joint has the distinction of having the least amount of bony stability of the major joints of the body.

Ligaments of the Sternoclavicular Joint

There is so much joint incongruity that the integrity of the SC joint has to come from its surrounding ligaments: the intra-articular disk ligament, the extra-articular costoclavicular ligament (rhomboid ligament), the capsular ligament, and the interclavicular ligament.

Intra-articular Disk Ligament. The intra-articular disk ligament is a very dense, fibrous structure that arises from the synchondral junction of the first rib and the sternum and passes through the SC joint. It divides the joint into two separate spaces.[81,164] The upper attachment is on the superior and posterior aspects of the medial clavicle. DePalma[48] has shown that the disk is perforated only rarely; the perforation allows a free communication between the two joint compartments. Anteriorly and posteriorly, the disk blends into the fibers of the capsular ligament. The disk acts as a checkrein against medial displacement of the inner clavicle.

Costoclavicular Ligament. The costoclavicular ligament, also called the rhomboid ligament, is short and strong and consists of an anterior and a posterior fasciculus.[14,36,81] Cave[36] reported that the average length is 1.3 cm, the maximum width is 1.9 cm, and the average thickness is 1.3 cm. Bearn[14] has shown that there is always a bursa between the two components of the ligament. Because of the two different parts of the ligament, it has a twisted appearance.[81] The costoclavicular ligament attaches below to the upper surface of the first rib and at the adjacent part of its synchondral junction with the sternum. It attaches above to the margins of the impression on the inferior surface of the medial end of the clavicle, sometimes known as the rhomboid fossa.[81,164] Cave[36] has shown, in a study of 153

clavicles, that the attachment point of the costoclavicular ligament to the clavicle can be one of three types: (i) a depression, the rhomboid fossa (30%), (ii) flat (60%), or (iii) an elevation (10%).

The fibers of the anterior fasciculus arise from the anteromedial surface of the first rib and are directed upward and laterally. The fibers of the posterior fasciculus are shorter and rise lateral to the anterior fibers on the rib and are directed upward and medially. The fibers of the anterior and posterior components cross and allow for stability of the joint during rotation and elevation of the clavicle. The two-part costoclavicular ligament is in many ways similar to the two-part configuration of the coracoclavicular ligament on the outer end of the clavicle.

Bearn[14] has shown experimentally that the anterior fibers resist excessive upward rotation of the clavicle and that the posterior fibers resist excessive downward rotation. Specifically, the anterior fibers also resist lateral displacement, and the posterior fibers resist medial displacement.

Interclavicular Ligament. The interclavicular ligament connects the superomedial aspects of each clavicle with the capsular ligaments and the upper sternum. According to Grant,[79] this band may be comparable to the wishbone of birds. This ligament helps the capsular ligaments to produce "shoulder poise," that is, to hold up the shoulder. This can be tested by putting a finger in the superior sternal notch; with elevation of the arm, the ligament is quite lax, but as soon as both arms hang at the sides, the ligament becomes tight.

Spencer et al.[179] have shown experimentally that the costoclavicular and interclavicular ligaments have little effect on anterior or posterior translation of the SC joint. In an anatomic study, Tubbs et al.[189] found that the interclavicular ligament prevented superior displacement of the clavicle with shoulder adduction and depression and failure occurred at 53.7N.

Capsular Ligament. The capsular ligament covers the anterosuperior and posterior aspects of the joint and represents thickenings of the joint capsule. The anterior portion of the capsular ligament is heavier and stronger than the posterior portion.

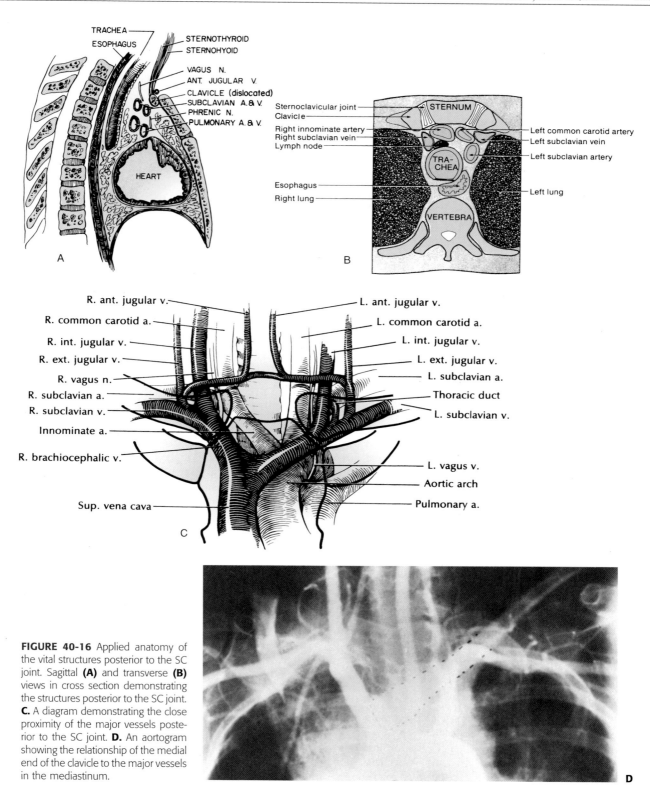

FIGURE 40-16 Applied anatomy of the vital structures posterior to the SC joint. Sagittal **(A)** and transverse **(B)** views in cross section demonstrating the structures posterior to the SC joint. **C.** A diagram demonstrating the close proximity of the major vessels posterior to the SC joint. **D.** An aortogram showing the relationship of the medial end of the clavicle to the major vessels in the mediastinum.

According to the original work of Bearn,[14] this may be the strongest ligament of the SC joint, and it is the first line of defense against the upward displacement of the inner clavicle caused by a downward force on its distal end. The clavicular attachment of the ligament is primarily onto the epiphysis of the medial clavicle, with some secondary blending of the fibers into the metaphysis. The senior author has demonstrated this,

as have Poland,[152] Denham and Dingley,[47] and Brooks and Henning.[25] Although some authors report that the intra-articular disk ligament greatly assists the costoclavicular ligament in preventing upward displacement of the medial clavicle, Bearn[14] has shown that the capsular ligament is the most important structure in preventing upward displacement of the medial clavicle. In experimental postmortem studies, he determined, after

FIGURE 40-17 Motions of the clavicle at the SC joint. **A.** With full overhead elevation, the clavicle elevates 35 degrees. **B.** With adduction and extension, the clavicle displaces anteriorly and posteriorly 35 degrees. **C.** The clavicle rotates on its long axis 45 degrees, as the arm is elevated to the full overhead position.

cutting the costoclavicular, intra-articular disk, and interclavicular ligaments, that they had no effect on clavicle poise. However, the division of the capsular ligament alone resulted in a downward depression on the distal end of the clavicle. Bearn's[14] findings have many clinical implications for the mechanisms of injury of the SC joint.

Through a cadaver study, Spencer et al.,[179] measured anterior and posterior translation of the SC joint. Anterior and posterior translation were measured in intact specimens and following transection of randomly chosen ligaments about the SC joint. Cutting the posterior capsule resulted in significant increases in anterior and posterior translation. Cutting the anterior capsule produced significant increases in anterior translation. This study demonstrated that the posterior SC joint capsule is the most important structure for preventing both anterior and posterior translation of the SC joint, with the anterior capsule acting as an important secondary stabilizer.

The Subclavius Muscle

Reis et al.[158] studied the function of the subclavius muscle and found that the basic function of the subclavius was to stabilize the SC joint. They also stated that the subclavius could act as a substitute for the ligaments of the SC joint. We believe that this is an important study as it might explain why some people, after loss of the medial clavicle and the SC ligament, do not have instability of the medial end of the clavicle. It also gives a reason for leaving the subclavius muscle intact during operations on the SC joint.

Range of Motion of the Sternoclavicular Joint

The SC joint is freely movable and functions almost like a ball-and-socket joint with motion in almost all planes, including rotation.[19,119] In normal shoulder motion the clavicle, via mo-

tion through the SC joint, is capable of 30 to 35 degrees of upward elevation, 35 degrees of combined forward and backward movement, and 45 to 50 degrees of rotation around its long axis (Fig. 40-17). It is likely the most frequently moved joint of the long bones in the body, because almost any motion of the upper extremity is transferred proximally to the SC joint.

Epiphysis of the Medial Clavicle

Although the clavicle is the first long bone of the body to ossify (during the fifth intrauterine week), the epiphysis at the medial end of the clavicle is the last of the long bones in the body to appear and the last physis to close (Fig. 40-18). The medial clavicular epiphysis does not ossify until the 18th to 20th year,

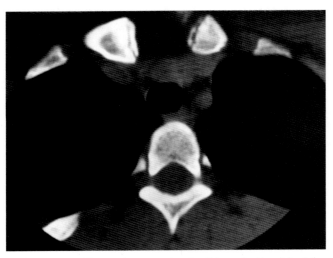

FIGURE 40-18 CT scan demonstrating the thin, wafer-like disk of the epiphysis of the medial clavicle.

and it fuses with the shaft of the clavicle around the 23rd to 25th year.[79,81,152] Webb and Suchey,[198] in an extensive study of the physis of the medial clavicle in 605 males and 254 females at autopsy, reported that complete union may not be present until 31 years of age. This knowledge of the epiphysis is important, because many of the SC dislocations in adults are injuries through the physeal plate.

CURRENT TREATMENT OPTIONS

The majority of injuries to the SC joint can be successfully managed by nonoperative measures (observation or closed reduction). This includes most of the acute and chronic anterior subluxations and dislocations, the acute traumatic posterior subluxations and dislocations, and, remembering that the physis of the medial clavicle does not close until the 23rd to 25th year, the acute traumatic anterior and posterior physeal injuries of the medial clavicle.

It is the chronic posterior dislocation and the acute, irreducible posterior dislocation that may require a surgical procedure. Some authors also recommend the open reduction and internal fixation of acute and chronic anterior dislocations.

Traumatic Injuries—Anterior

Subluxation

The treatment of subluxation is nonoperative. Application of ice is recommended for the first 12 hours, followed by heat for the next 24 to 48 hours. The joint may be subluxated anteriorly or posteriorly, which may be reduced by drawing the shoulders backward as if reducing and holding a fracture of the clavicle. For both anterior and posterior subluxations that are stable, a clavicle strap can be used to hold the reduction. A sling and swath can also be used to hold up the shoulder and to prevent motion of the arm. The patient should be protected from further injury for 4 to 6 weeks. Immobilization can be accomplished with a soft figure-of-eight bandage with a sling for temporary support.

Dislocation

There still is some controversy regarding the treatment of acute anterior dislocation of the SC joint. A large series of SC injuries was published in 1988 by Fery and Sommelet.[67] They reported on 40 anterior dislocations, 8 posterior dislocations, and 1 unstable SC joint. They ended up treating 15 injuries closed, but because of problems, had to operate on 17 patients; 17 patients were not treated. They had good and excellent results with both the closed and operative treatment, but recommended that closed reduction should be initially undertaken. In 1990, de Jong and Sukul[46] reported long-term follow-up results in 10 patients with traumatic anterior SC dislocations. All patients were treated nonoperatively with analgesics and immobilization. The results of treatment were good in 7 patients, fair in 2 patients, and poor in 1 patient at an average follow-up of 5 years. Most acute anterior dislocations are unstable following reduction, and many operative procedures have been described to repair or reconstruct the joint. At this time, the mixed results of these procedures have not clearly advanced a case for their use instead of observation.

Nonoperative Treatment

Method of Closed Reduction. Closed reduction of anterior dislocation of the SC joint may be accomplished with local or general anesthesia or, in stoic patients, without anesthesia. Most authors recommend the use of narcotics or muscle relaxants. The patient is placed supine on the table, lying on a 3- to 4-inch-thick pad placed between the shoulders. In this position, the joint may reduce with direct gentle pressure over the anteriorly displaced clavicle. However, when the pressure is released, the clavicle usually dislocates again. Occasionally, the clavicle will remain reduced. Sometimes, the physician will need to push both of the patient's shoulders back to the table while an assistant applies pressure to the anteriorly displaced clavicle.

Postreduction Care. After reduction, to allow ligament healing, the shoulders should be held back for 4 to 6 weeks with a figure-of-eight dressing or one of the commercially available figure-of-eight straps used to treat fractures of the clavicle.

Operative Treatment

Although some authors have recommended operative repair of anterior dislocations of the SC joint, we believe that the operative complications are too great and the end results are too unsatisfactory to consider an open procedure.

Traumatic Injuries—Posterior

Subluxation

In mild sprains, the ligaments remain intact and the patient complains of moderate discomfort. The joint may be swollen and tender to palpation. Care must be taken to rule out the more significant posterior dislocation, which may have initially occurred and spontaneously reduced. When in doubt, it is best to protect the SC joint with a figure-of-eight bandage for 2 to 6 weeks. As with all injuries to the SC joint, it must be carefully evaluated by CT scan.

Dislocation

As a general rule, when even a posterior dislocation of the SC joint is suspected, the physician must perform a very careful examination of the patient to rule out damage to the structures posterior to the joint such as the trachea, esophagus, the brachial plexus, the great vessels, and the lungs. Not only is a careful physical examination important, but special radiographs must be obtained. A CT scan of both medial clavicles allows the physician to compare the injured side with the normal side, and this is the recommended imaging study. Occasionally, when vascular injuries are suspected, the CT scan will need to be combined with an arteriogram of the great vessels.

Certainly in young adults under the age of 22 or 23, in whom many if not most of the injuries are physeal fractures, a nonoperative approach of closed reduction should be strongly considered.

General anesthesia is usually required for reduction of a posterior dislocation of the SC joint because the patient has pain and muscle spasms. However, for the stoic patient, some authors have performed the reduction under intravenous narcotics and muscle relaxants.

From a review of the earlier literature, it would appear that the treatment of choice for posterior SC dislocation was operative. However, since the 1950s, the treatment of choice has been closed reduction.[33,40,44,65,83,86,129,130,134,148,169,181]

Nonoperative Treatment

Methods of Closed Reduction. Most posterior SC dislocations are successfully reduced closed if accomplished within 48 hours of injury. A variety of techniques have been described.

Abduction Traction Technique. For the abduction traction technique,[49,65,99,125,129,134,161] the patient is placed on his or her back with the dislocated shoulder near the edge of the table. A 3- to 4-inch-thick sandbag is placed between the shoulders (Fig. 40-19). Lateral traction is applied to the abducted arm, which is then gradually brought back into extension. This may be all that is necessary to accomplish the reduction. The clavicle usually reduces with an audible snap or pop, and it is almost always stable. Too much extension can bind the anterior surface

of the dislocated medial clavicle on the back of the manubrium. Occasionally, it may be necessary to grasp the medial clavicle with one's fingers to dislodge it from behind the sternum. If this fails, the skin is prepared, and a sterile towel clip is used to grasp the medial clavicle to apply lateral and anterior traction (Fig. 40-20).

Adduction Traction Technique. In this technique,[29] the patient is supine on the table with a 3- to 4-inch bolster between the shoulders. Traction is then applied to the arm in adduction, while a downward pressure is exerted on the shoulder (Fig. 40-21). The clavicle is levered over the first rib into its normal position. Buckerfield and Castle[29] reported that this technique was successful in 7 patients when the abduction traction technique had failed.

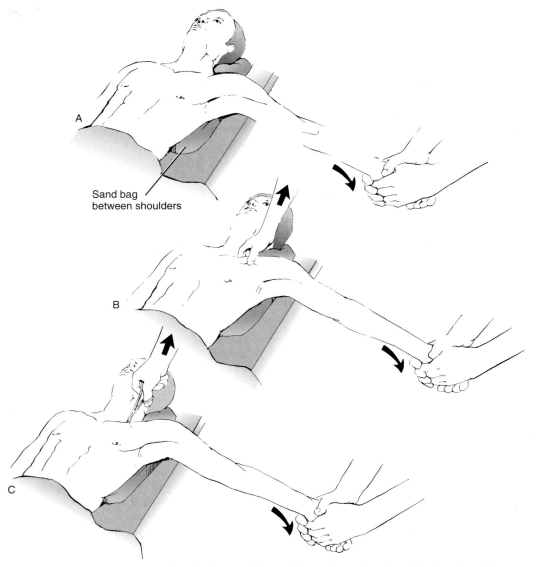

Sand bag between shoulders

FIGURE 40-19 Technique for closed reduction of the SC joint. **A.** The patient is positioned supine with a sandbag placed between the two shoulders. Traction is then applied to the arm against countertraction in an abducted and slightly extended position. In anterior dislocations, direct pressure over the medial end of the clavicle may reduce the joint. **B.** In addition to the traction, it may be necessary to manipulate the medial end of the clavicle with the fingers to dislodge the clavicle from behind the manubrium. **C.** In stubborn posterior dislocations, it may be necessary to sterilely prepare the medial end of the clavicle and use a towel clip to grasp around the medial clavicle to lift it back into position.

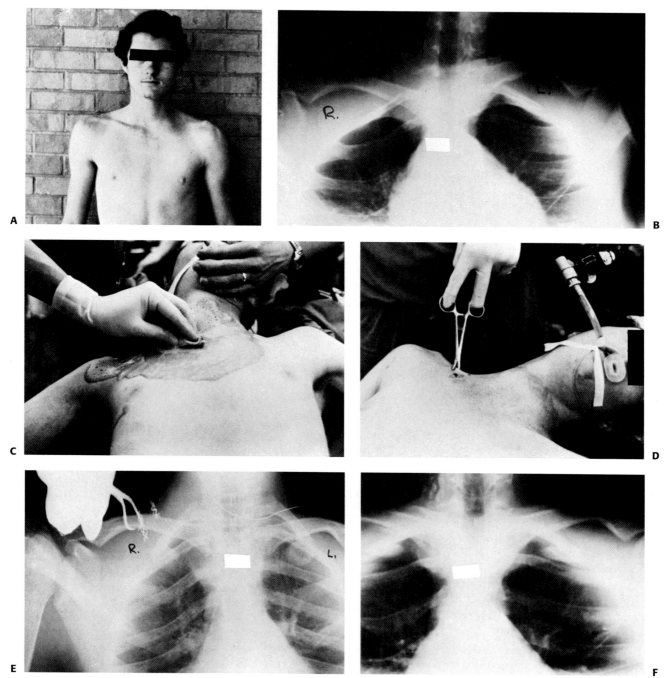

FIGURE 40-20 Posterior dislocation of the right SC joint. **A.** A 16-year-old boy has a 48-hour-old posterior dislocation of the right medial clavicle that occurred from a direct blow to the anterior right clavicle. He noted immediate onset of difficulty in swallowing and some hoarseness in his voice. **B.** A 40-degree cephalic tilt radiograph confirmed the posterior displacement of the right medial clavicle as compared with the left clavicle. Because of the patient's age, this was considered most likely to be a physeal injury of the right medial clavicle. **C.** Because the injury was 48 hours old, we were unable to reduce the dislocation with simple traction on the arm. The right shoulder was surgically cleansed so that a sterile towel clip could be used. **D.** With the towel clip placed securely around the clavicle and with continued lateral traction, a visible and audible reduction occurred. **E.** Postreduction radiographs showed that the medial clavicle had been restored to its normal position. The reduction was quite stable, and the patient's shoulders were held back with a figure-of-eight strap. **F.** The right clavicle has remained reduced. Note the periosteal new bone formation along the superior and inferior borders of the right clavicle. This is the result of a physeal injury, whereby the epiphysis remains adjacent to the manubrium while the clavicle is displaced out of a split in the periosteal tube.

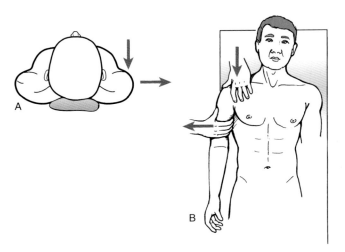

FIGURE 40-21 The Buckerfield-Castle technique. **A,B.** The patient is lying on the table with a bolster between the shoulders. Traction is applied to the arm in adduction while a downward force is applied on the shoulder.

Postreduction Care. After reduction, to allow ligament healing, the shoulders should be held back for 4 to 6 weeks with a figure-of-eight dressing or one of the commercially available figure-of-eight straps used to treat fractures of the clavicle.

Operative Treatment

Rarely, closed reduction maneuvers are unsuccessful in maintaining stability of the posterior dislocation of the SC joint. A delay in reduction of 48 hours may make closed reduction impossible, reinforcing the importance of early diagnosis.[35] In these situations, open reduction and acute repair of the soft tissues is warranted. The first option is direct repair of the anterior and posterior capsule, intra-articular disk ligament, and costoclavicular ligament. The surgeon can also employ one of the various techniques that are available for ligament reconstruction for an unreduced or chronic dislocation, especially if additional stability is required due to the disruption of native tissues.

Recurrent, Chronic, or Unreduced Dislocation

Nonoperative Treatment

Chronic or unreduced anterior dislocations can be reconstructed, but do not generally require such procedures. Occasionally, following conservative treatment of a subluxation of the SC joint, the pain lingers on and the symptoms of popping and grating persist. Joint exploration may be required as several authors have reported symptom relief following joint exploration, removal of the torn or degenerated intra-articular disk, along with a capsulorraphy.[6,12,55] Many authors have included chronic or unreduced anterior dislocations with posterior dislocations in their series of operative patients. This makes it difficult to understand the true benefits of surgery in this situation. Postoperatively, recurrent instability,[67] limitations of activity,[7] and pain[61] often occur, and patient expectations should be adjusted accordingly. While most chronic posterior SC fracture-dislocations require open procedures, a singular exception is young adults who may have no symptoms, and the physician can wait to see if the physeal plate remodeling process removes the posteriorly displaced bone.[163]

Operative Treatment

Should closed maneuvers fail to reduce the posterior displacement of the medial clavicle in the adult, an operative procedure should be performed, because most adult patients cannot tolerate posterior displacement of the clavicle into the mediastinum. Complications accompanying unreduced posterior dislocations include late thoracic outlet syndrome, late and significant vascular problems, respiratory compromise, and dyspnea on exertion.[24,73,117,186] We have treated patients with a medial clavicle resection and reconstruction who have had complaints of swelling and arm discoloration, in addition to signs and symptoms of effort thrombosis and dysphagia secondary to a posteriorly displaced medial clavicle.

If adults younger than 25 years of age have symptoms from the pressure of the posteriorly displaced clavicle into the mediastinum and closed reduction is unsuccessful, an operative procedure should be performed. If the patient is under 25 and without symptoms after the initial obligatory attempt at closed reduction, then close observation is acceptable as remodeling potential still exists.

Surgical Reconstructions for Anterior or Posterior Dislocations

There are several procedures described to maintain the medial end of the clavicle in its normal articulation with the sternum (Table 40-1). Much like the AC joint, the recent literature has focused on case reports of technique descriptions and modifications of existing surgeries. Given the rarity of the injury and even rarer necessity for surgery, there is no large experience with any of the techniques. Nonetheless, certain basic principles should be adhered to in the midst of this creative atmosphere.

The operative procedure should be performed in a manner that disturbs as few of the anterior ligament structures as possible. If the procedure can be performed with the anterior ligaments intact, then, with the shoulders held back in a figure-of-eight dressing, the reduction may be stable. If all the ligaments are disrupted, a decision has to be made whether to try to stabilize the SC joint or to resect the medial 1 to 1.5 inches of the medial clavicle and anatomically stabilize the remaining clavicle to the first rib. Resection alone cannot be performed in the setting of disrupted ligaments and may worsen the instability of the residual medial clavicle, requiring even greater attention to the need for ligament reconstruction in such a scenario.[17]

Once faced with the need for reconstruction, the surgeon has to embrace a surgical strategy from the existing armamentarium. Procedures can be viewed from two different perspectives: tissue and stabilization. With regards to tissue, options are: (a) local ligaments and capsule, (b) tendon transfers (subclavius or sternocleidomastoid), or (c) grafts. With regards to stabilization, options are: (a) stabilize to first rib, (b) stabilize to manubrium, or (c) stabilize to the first rib and the manubrium. Fixation is generally provided by soft tissue tensioning and suture, although augmenting with pins, plates, or screws have all been proposed.

Three broad technical philosophies have been characterized by Spencer and Kuhn[179]: (i) intramedullary ligament transfer, (ii) costoclavicular ligament reconstruction, and (iii) SC ligament reconstruction. Spencer and Kuhn,[179] through a biomechanic analysis, evaluated the three different reconstruction techniques in a cadaver model. The intramedullary ligament,[164] the

TABLE 40-1	**Surgical Techniques for Sternoclavicular Reconstruction**
1. Open Excision with intramedullary ligament repair	Uses intra-articular disk ligament as a transfer into medial clavicle; reinforced with local tissue repair[154]
2. Semitendinosus graft with figure-of-eight reconstruction	Reconstitutes capsular ligaments with graft[33,149]
3. Subclavius tenodesis: technique of Burrows	Use a slip of subclavius to reconstruct the costoclavicular ligament-modification is to use graft (fascia lata) to re-create costoclavicular ligament[31]
4. Sternocleidomastoid reconstruction to first rib and clavicle	Use a partial slip of sternocleidomastoid through first rib and clavicle to recreate costoclavicular ligament[18]
5. Partial sternocleidomastoid transfer to clavicle and manubrium	Use a partial slip of sternocleidomastoid to recreate capsular ligaments; no exposure of first rib[5,26]
6. Plate stabilization	Balser plate inserted into manubrium; repair of local capsule; plate removal required[66]
7. Screw fixation	Transfixing screws across SC joint; removal required[24]
8. Suture anchor repair	Anchors in manubrium used to imbricate capsule and passed through bone tunnels in clavicle; no exposure of first rib[1]
9. Interposition arthroplasty	Use a bone-tendon allograft as an interposition and fix to resected medial clavicle with screws[125]
10. Medial clavicle resection	Simple removal of 1.0 cm of medial clavicle; repair local tissue[17,156]

subclavius tendon transfer,[32] and a semitendinosus graft placed in a figure-of-eight fashion through drill-holes in the clavicle and manubrium were used to reconstruct the SC joint. Each of the three reconstruction methods was subjected to anterior or posterior translation to failure, and the changes in stiffness compared with the intact state were analyzed statistically. The figure-of-eight semitendinosus reconstruction showed superior initial mechanical properties to the other two techniques. The authors believed that this method reconstructs both the anterior and posterior joint capsules providing an initial stiffness that is closer to that of the intact sternoclavicular joint (Figs. 40-22 and 40-23). This technique has now been described with some success in young adults with refractory anterior instability.[7,34,157] A plethora of other techniques abound in the literature. Some of the literature from the 1960s and 1970s recommended stabilization of the SC joint with Kirschner wires (K-wires) or Steinmann pins.[25,28,47,49,59] These techniques have become largely historical due to their high complication rate as will be discussed later. Other authors recommended the use of various types of suture wires across the joint,[9,31,70,84,98,142,151,156,181,182] reconstruction using local tendons,[10,19,122,124] or the use of a special plate.[85] Fascia lata, suture, screw fixation across the joint, subclavius tendons, osteotomy of the medial clavicle, and resection of the medial end of the clavicle have also been advocated.[2,9,10,27,32,81,102,118,122,133,143,164,177]

Transfer of the sternocleidomastoid has been revisited in different forms. Booth and Roper[19] described transferring the sternal head of the tendon around the first rib and through the clavicle and back upon itself. Brown[27] used the clavicular head of the sternocleidomastoid as an anterior sling across the SC joint augmented with pins. Armstrong et al.[5] modified the use of the sternocleidomastoid by using only a slip of the sternal head and passing it through a medial clavicle bone tunnel. The

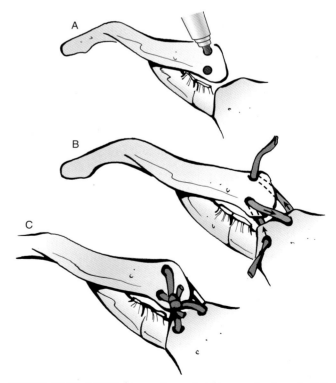

FIGURE 40-22 Semitendinosus figure-of-eight reconstruction. **A.** Drill holes are passed from anterior to posterior through the medial part of the clavicle and the manubrium. **B.** A free semitendinosus tendon graft is woven through the drill holes such that the tendon strands are parallel to each other posterior to the joint and cross each other anterior to the joint. **C.** The tendon ends are tied in a square knot and secured with suture. (From Spencer EE, Kuhn JE. Biomechanical analysis of reconstructions for sternoclavicular joint instability. J Bone Joint Surg 2004;86A(1):98–105.)

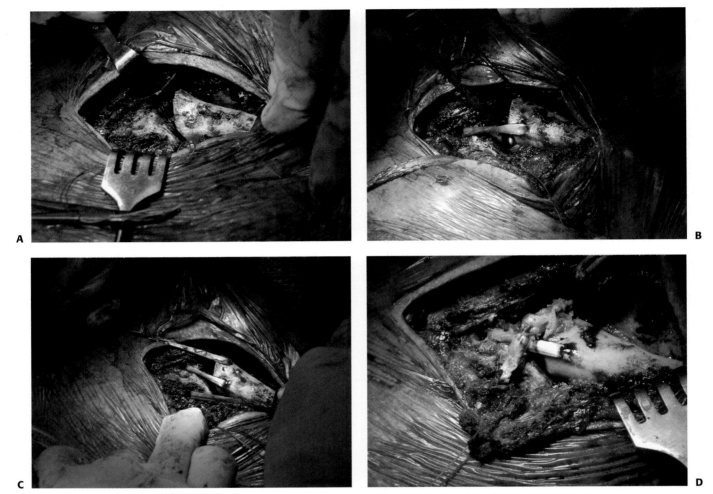

FIGURE 40-23 Semitendinous figure-of-eight reconstruction **A.** Reduction of the SC joint. **B.** Passing the tendon graft through bone tunnels with suture passer. **C.** Tensioning of the graft. **D.** Completed figure-of-eight construct. (Courtesy of Charles E. Rosipal, MD, and T. Kevin O'Malley, MD.)

graft is sutured to itself to recreate the anterior SC ligament without exposure of the first rib.

More recently, Thomas et al.[185] reported a safe surgical technique for stabilization of the SC joint with the use of suture material. Their technique involved tying the suture material on the superficial aspects of the medial clavicle and manubrium. This avoids the exposure of the first rib and avoids drilling through the inner cortex of the clavicle and manubrium. Recently Abiddin[1] has described a similar technique with the use of suture anchors in the manubrium and drill holes in the clavicle. While smooth pin and wire fixation is now taboo, fixation of the SC joint with other metal implants is still considered a valid option, although the implants do require removal. Franck et al.[69] reported an alternative therapy for traumatic SC instability using a plate for stabilization. A Balser plate was contoured to match the shape of the clavicle and the hook of the plate was used for sternal fixation. A retrosternal hook position was used for seven anterior dislocations and an intrasternal position was used for three posterior dislocations. For each patient, the plate was attached to the clavicle with screws and the torn ligaments were repaired. All plates were removed by 3 months. At 1-year follow-up, 9 of 10 patients had excellent results with no cases of redislocation. One patient developed a postoperative

seroma that required surgical drainage, and one patient developed arthrosis (Fig 40-24). In 1997, Brinker et al.[24] described another technique of hardware fixation across the joint. The authors used two 75-mm cannulated screws to stabilize an unstable posterior dislocation of the SC joint. The screws were removed at 3 months, and at 10 months the patient had full range of motion without pain and returned to college level football.

Interpositional arthroplasty techniques have also emerged in recent years. Battaglia et al.[13] presented three cases of an Achilles tendon allograft and bone plug used to treat anterior instability in 2 patients and a medial clavicle fracture nonunion in one. The graft was fixed to a trough in the medial clavicle resection with screws, passed through bone tunnels in the manubrium and sutured upon itself.[23] Meis et al.[132] reported using an intramedullary transfer of the sternocleidomastoid as an interposition for degenerative SC joint pain after resection.

Since 1982, various authors have recommended open reduction and internal fixation for acute injuries, as well as for chronic problems. In 1982, Pfister and associates[150,151] recommended open reduction and repair of the ligaments over nonoperative treatment. In 1988, Fery and Sommelet[67] reported 49 cases of dislocations of the SC joint. In these patients, if closed reduction

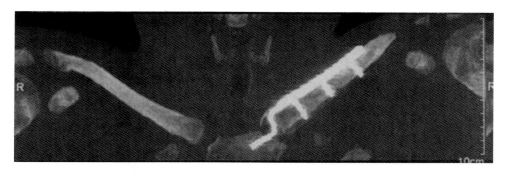

FIGURE 40-24 CT scan of manubrium showing intrasternal plate insertion. (From Franck WM, Jannasch O, Siassi M, et al. Balser plate stabilization: an alternate therapy for traumatic sternoclavicular instability. J Shoulder Elbow Surg 2003;12(3):276–281.)

was not successful, they performed open reduction. In symptomatic chronic unreduced dislocations, they either performed a myoplasty or excised the medial end of the clavicle if the articular surfaces were damaged. They were able to follow 55% of their patients for an average of more than 6 years. They had 42% excellent results among the operative cases. Of those patients who were treated with closed reduction, 58% were satisfied. Ferrandez and colleagues[64] reported 18 subluxations and dislocations of the SC joint. Seven had moderate sprains and 11 had dislocations. Of the 3 patients with a posterior dislocation, all had symptoms of dysphagia. All of the subluxations were treated nonoperatively with excellent results. The remaining 10 patients with dislocations were treated with surgery (i.e., open reduction with suture of the ligaments and K-wires placed across the clavicle and the sternum). The wires were removed 3 to 4 weeks following surgery. At 1- to 4-years follow-up, most of the operative cases had a slight deformity. In 2 patients, migration of the K-wires was noted but was without clinical significance.

Eskola and associates[61,62] strongly urged operative repair of dislocations of the SC joint. In 1989, they reported on 12 patients treated for painful SC joints. The average time from injury was 1.5 years, and the average follow-up after surgery was 4.7 years. In 5 patients, the SC joint was stabilized with a palmaris longus or plantaris tendon graft placed between the first rib and the manubrium; in 4 patients, the medial 2.5 cm of the clavicle was resected without any type of stabilization; and in 3 patients, the clavicle was fixed to the first rib with a fascia lata graft. They reported good results in four patients, three treated with tendon grafts and one with a fascia lata graft. They had four fair results and four poor results in those patients who had only resection of the medial clavicle. There was little discussion of the patients' preoperative symptoms, work habits, or range of motion, or the degree of joint reduction following the surgery. In 1990, Tricoire and colleagues[186] reported six retrosternal dislocations of the medial end of the clavicle. They recommended reduction of these injuries to avoid the possible complications arising from protrusion of the clavicle into the mediastinum. SC capsulorrhaphy was performed in 2 patients and a subclavius tenodesis was used in the remaining 4 patients. All joints were temporarily stabilized with SC pins for 6 weeks. Results were satisfactory in all cases at a mean follow-up of 27 months.

Resection of the Medial End of the Clavicle

McLaughlin,[130] Breitner and Wirth,[22] Pridie,[155] Bateman,[11,12] and Milch[133] have all recommended excision of the medial clavicle when degenerative changes are noted in the joint. If the medial end of the clavicle is to be removed because of degenera-

tive changes, the surgeon should be careful not to damage the costoclavicular ligament (Fig. 40-25).

Recently, using the results of an anatomic study of 86 cadavers, Bisson et al.[18] recommended a safe resection length that would result in no or minimal disruption of the costoclavicular ligament of 1.0 cm in men, and 0.9 cm in women.

Arthrodesis

Arthrodesis was once reported[159] in the treatment of a habitual dislocation of the SC joint. However, this procedure should *not* be done because it prevents the previously described normal elevation, depression, and rotation of the clavicle. The end result would be a severe restriction of shoulder movement (Fig. 40-26).

Postoperative Care

In most situations, the shoulders are held back with a figure-of-eight bandage for 4 to 6 weeks. When K-wires or Steinmann pins are used, the patient should avoid vigorous activities until the pins are removed. The pins should be carefully monitored with radiographs until they are removed.

Treatment of Physeal Injuries of the Sternoclavicular Joint

Many so-called dislocations of the SC joint in adults are not dislocations but physeal injuries. Most of these injuries will heal without surgical intervention. In time, the remodeling process

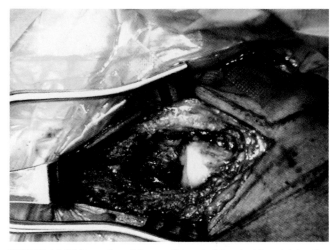

FIGURE 40-25 Resection of the medial end of the clavicle, retaining the costoclavicular ligament.

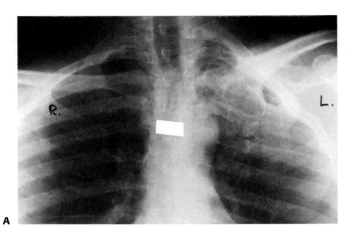

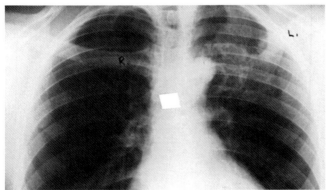

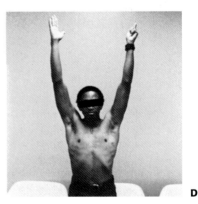

FIGURE 40-26 The effect of an arthrodesis of the SC joint on shoulder function. **A.** As a result of a military gunshot wound to the left SC joint, this patient had a massive bony union of the left medial clavicle to the sternum and the upper three ribs. **B.** Shoulder motion was limited to 90-degrees of flexion and abduction. **C.** Radiograph after resection of the bony mass and freeing up the medial clavicle. **D.** The motion of the left shoulder was essentially normal after the elimination of the SC arthrodesis.

eliminates any bone deformity or displacement. Anterior physeal injuries can certainly be left alone without problem. Posterior physeal injuries should be reduced. If the posterior dislocation cannot be reduced by closed means and the patient is having *no significant symptoms*, the displacement can be observed while remodeling occurs (Fig. 40-27). It is only in this

regard that posterior physeal injuries differ from posterior SC dislocations in adults. If the posterior displacement is symptomatic and cannot be reduced closed, the displacement must be reduced surgically as is required for posterior SC dislocations in adults (Fig. 40-28).

Indeed, as with other physeal injuries, the potential for re-

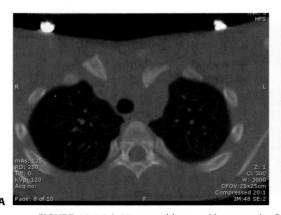

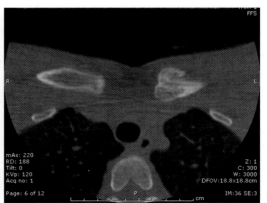

FIGURE 40-27 A 17–year-old man with a posterior SC physeal injury. **A.** The initial injury CT scan displays a physeal fracture-dislocation. The patient had no symptoms of mediastinal compression and was treated with observation after initial attempts at closed reduction were unsuccessful. **B.** Six months after injury, the CT scan shows healing with remodeling and a reduced SC joint. The patient remained asymptomatic and returned to normal activities.

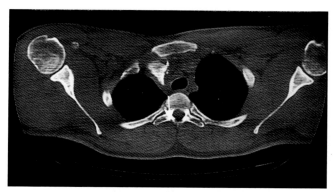

FIGURE 40-28 CT scan of a 19-year-old patient who was involved in a motor vehicle accident and presented with complaints of chest pain and a "choking sensation" that was exacerbated by lying supine. Note the physeal injury of the medial clavicle and compression of the trachea.

modeling is significant and may extend until the 23rd to 25th year. The senior author[162] has demonstrated a similar mechanism to support conservative treatment of adolescent AC joint injuries or "pseudodislocations," in which there is a partial tear of the periosteal tube containing the distal clavicle. The coracoclavicular ligaments remain secured to the periosteal tube. Because of its high osteogenic potential, spontaneous healing and remodeling to the preinjury "reduced" position occur within this periosteal conduit. Waters et al.[197] reported successful operative treatment of 13 traumatic posterior SC fracture-dislocations in children and adolescents, and other authors have reported the successful treatment of posteriorly displaced medial clavicle physeal injuries in adolescents.[91,206,207]

Anterior Physeal Injuries of the Medial Clavicle

If the anterior physeal injury is recognized or if the patient is younger than 25 years, closed reduction, as described for anterior dislocation of the SC joint, should be performed. The shoulders should be held back in a clavicular strap or figure-of-eight dressing for 3 to 4 weeks, even if the reduction is stable. Healing is prompt, and remodeling will occur at the site of the deformity.

Posterior Physeal Injuries of the Medial Clavicle

Closed reduction of a posterior displacement of the medial clavicle should be performed in the manner described for posterior dislocation of the SC joint. The reduction is usually stable with the shoulders held back in a figure-of-eight dressing or strap. Immobilization should continue for 3 to 4 weeks. If the posterior physeal injury cannot be reduced, the patient is not having symptoms, and the patient is younger than 23 years, the physician can wait to see if remodeling eliminates the posterior displacement of the clavicle.

Treatment of Spontaneous Subluxation or Dislocation of the Sternoclavicular Joint

Atraumatic Anterior Instability

As with the classification of glenohumeral joint instability, the importance of distinguishing between traumatic and atraumatic instability of the SC joint must be recognized if complications

are to be avoided. C. R. Rowe (personal communication, 1988) described several patients who had undergone one or more unsuccessful attempts to stabilize the SC joint. In all cases, the patient was able to voluntarily dislocate the clavicle after surgery. Rockwood and Odor's[165] study of 29 patients with spontaneous subluxation treated nonoperatively with no failures further reflects the appeal of avoiding surgery in this population.

Crosby and Rubino[45] reported a case of spontaneous atraumatic anterior dislocation secondary to pseudoarthrosis of the first and second ribs. Despite a 6-month course of conservative treatment, this 14-year-old girl was still painful. A CT scan of the chest with three-dimensional reconstruction was performed. The scan revealed a pseudoarthrosis anteriorly between the first and second ribs underlying the medial part of the clavicle. Resection of the anterior portions of the first and second ribs containing the pseudoarthrosis relieved her symptoms and allowed the patient to return to her normal activities. The authors recommended chest radiographs and a possible CT scan with three-dimensional reconstruction to completely evaluate an underlying congenital condition if the subluxation is rigid and unresponsive to nonoperative care.

Atraumatic Posterior Instability

Spontaneous posterior subluxation/dislocation has only been noted in a few isolated case reports. Martin et al.[126] described a case of spontaneous atraumatic posterior dislocation of the SC joint. This occurred in a 50-year-old previously healthy woman who awoke one morning with a painful SC joint. A CT scan confirmed the posterior dislocation. She later developed dysphagia, and a closed reduction was unsuccessful. At 1 year without any other treatment, she was back to playing golf and was asymptomatic. More recently, Martinez et al.[127] reported on the operative treatment of a 19-year-old woman with a symptomatic spontaneous posterior subluxation. The posteriorly displaced medial clavicle was stabilized with a figure-of-eight suture technique with the use of a gracilis autograft. At follow-up the patient was pain free; however, a repeat CT scan demonstrated posterior subluxation of the medial clavicle with erosion of the clavicle and manubrium. In light of the recurrence of subluxation after reconstruction, the authors recommended conservative treatment of atraumatic posterior subluxation of the SC joint.

AUTHORS' PREFERRED METHOD OF TREATMENT

Traumatic Injuries

Anterior

Subluxation.. For mild sprains, we recommend the use of cold packs for the first 12 to 24 hours and a sling to rest the joint. Ordinarily, after 5 to 7 days, the patient can use the arm for everyday activities.

In addition to the cold pack, for subluxations we may use a soft, padded figure-of-eight clavicle strap to gently hold the shoulders back to allow the SC joint to rest. The harness can be removed after a week or so. Then the arm is placed in a sling for about another week, or the patient is allowed to return gradually to everyday activities.

Dislocation. In general, we manage anterior dislocations of the SC joint in adults by either a closed reduction or by "skillful neglect." Most of the anterior dislocations are unstable, but we accept the deformity since we believe it is less of a problem than the potential problems of operative repair and internal fixation.

Method of Reduction. In most instances, even knowing that the anterior dislocation will be unstable, we still try to reduce the anterior displacement. Muscle relaxants and narcotics are administered intravenously, and the patient is placed supine on a table with a stack of three or four towels between the shoulder blades. While an assistant gently applies downward pressure on the anterior aspect of both of the patient's shoulders, the medial end of the clavicle is pushed backward where it belongs. On some occasions, rare as they may be, the medial clavicle may stay adjacent to the sternum. However, in most cases, either with the shoulders still held back or when they are relaxed, the anterior displacement promptly recurs. We explain to the patient that the joint is unstable and that the hazards of internal fixation are too great, and we prescribe a sling for a couple of weeks and allow the patient to begin using the arm as soon as the discomfort is gone.

Most of the anterior injuries that we have treated in patients up to 25 years of age are not dislocations of the SC joint. Rather, they are type I or II physeal injuries, which heal and remodel without operative treatment. Patients older than 25 years with anterior dislocations of the SC joint do have persistent prominence of the anterior clavicle. However, this does not seem to interfere with usual activities and, in some cases, has not even interfered with heavy manual labor.

We wish to re-emphasize that *we do not recommend open reduction* of the joint and would *never* recommend placing transfixing pins across the SC joint.

Postreduction Care of Anterior Dislocations.. If the reduction is stable, we place the patient in either a figure-of-eight dressing or in whatever device or position the clavicle is most stable. If the reduction is unstable, the arm is placed into a sling for a week or so, and then the patient can begin to use the arm for gentle everyday activities.

Posterior
Dislocation. It is important to obtain a careful history and perform a careful physical examination in the patient with a posterior SC dislocation (Table 40-2). For every patient,

---

TABLE 40-2 **Keys to the Diagnosis of Posterior Sternoclavicular Dislocation**

- History of a violent injury
- Painful SC joint
- Difficulty in swallowing
- Difficulty in breathing
- Decreased range of motion of the upper extremity
- Palpable step-off of the SC joint
- Positive "serendipity view" radiograph
- Posterior displacement seen on CT scan

---

the physician should obtain radiographs and/or a CT scan. If the patient has distention of the neck vessels, swelling of the arm, a bluish discoloration of the arm, or difficulty swallowing or breathing, then the patient should be evaluated by using a CT scan with contrast of the vascular structures. It is also important to determine if the patient has a feeling of choking or hoarseness. If any of these symptoms are present, indicating pressure on the mediastinal structures, the appropriate cardiovascular or thoracic specialist should be consulted.

We do not believe that operative techniques are usually required to reduce acute posterior SC joint dislocations. Furthermore, once the joint has been reduced by closed means, it is usually stable.

Although we used to think that the diagnosis of an anterior or posterior injury of the SC joint could always be made on physical examination, one cannot rely on the anterior swelling and firmness as being diagnostic of an anterior injury as the posterior injuries may create a significant anterior fullness. Therefore, we recommend that the clinical impression always be documented with appropriate imaging studies, preferably a CT scan, before a decision to treat or not to treat is made.

Method of Closed Reduction. The patient is placed in the supine position with a 3- to 4-inch-thick sandbag or three to four folded towels placed between the scapulas to extend the shoulders. The dislocated shoulder should be near the edge of the table so that the arm and shoulder can be abducted and extended. If the patient is having extreme pain and muscle spasm and is quite anxious, we use general anesthesia; otherwise, narcotics, muscle relaxants, or tranquilizers are given through an established intravenous route in the normal arm. First, gentle traction is applied on the abducted arm in line with the clavicle while countertraction is applied by an assistant who steadies the patient on the table. The traction on the abducted arm is gradually increased while the arm is brought into extension (see Fig. 40-19). If reduction cannot be accomplished with the patient's arm in abduction, then we will use the adduction technique of Buckerfield and Castle[29] that is described above (see Fig. 40-21).

Reduction of an acute injury may occur with an audible pop or snap and the relocation can be noted visibly and by palpation. If the traction techniques are not successful, an assistant grasps or pushes down on the clavicle in an effort to dislodge it from behind the sternum. Occasionally, in a stubborn case, especially in a thick-chested person or a patient with extensive swelling, it is impossible to obtain a secure grasp on the clavicle with the fingers alone. The skin should then be surgically prepared and a sterile towel clip used to gain purchase on the medial clavicle percutaneously (see Fig. 40-20). The towel clip should encircle the shaft of the clavicle as the dense cortical bone prevents the purchase of the towel clip into the clavicle. Then the combined traction through the arm plus the anterior lifting force on the towel clip will reduce the dislocation. Following the reduction, the SC joint is usually stable, even with the patient's arms at the side. However, we always hold the shoulders back in a well-padded figure-of-eight clavicle strap for 3 to 4 weeks to allow for soft tissue and ligamentous healing.

Surgical Procedure. The complications of an unreduced posterior dislocation are numerous: thoracic outlet syndrome,[73] vascular compromise,[21] and erosion of the medial clavicle into any of the vital structures that lie posterior to the SC joint. Therefore, in adults over the age of 23, if closed reduction fails, an open reduction should be performed. It is critical that a thoracic surgeon is immediately available when the patient is taken to the operating room to intervene if needed.

When operating on the SC joint, care must be taken to evaluate the residual stability of the medial clavicle. It is the same analogy as used when resecting the distal clavicle for an old AC joint problem. If the coracoclavicular ligaments are intact, an excision of the distal clavicle is indicated. If the coracoclavicular ligaments are gone, then, in addition to excision of the distal clavicle, one must reconstruct the coracoclavicular ligaments with a SC injury. If the costoclavicular ligaments are intact, the clavicle medial to the ligaments should be resected and beveled smooth. If the ligaments are torn, the clavicle must be stabilized to the first rib. If too much clavicle is resected, or if the clavicle is not stabilized to the first rib, an increase in symptoms can result (Fig. 40-29).

The patient is placed supine on the table, and three to four towels or a sandbag should be placed between the scapulae. The upper extremity should be draped out free so that lateral traction can be applied during the open reduction. In addition, a folded sheet around the patient's thorax should be left in place so that it can be used for countertraction when traction is applied to the involved extremity. An anterior incision is used that parallels the superior border of the medial 3 to 4 inches of the clavicle and then extends downward over the sternum just medial to the involved SC joint (Fig. 40-30). The trick is to try to remove sufficient soft tissues to expose the joint but to leave the anterior capsular ligament intact. The reduction can usually be accomplished with traction and countertraction while lifting up anteriorly on a clamp placed around the medial clavicle. Along with

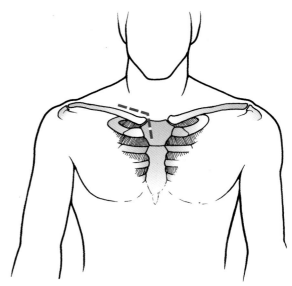

FIGURE 40-30 The proposed skin incision used for open reduction of a posterior SC dislocation.

the traction and countertraction, it may be necessary to use an elevator to pry the clavicle back to its articulation with the manubrium.

When the reduction has been obtained, with the shoulders held back, the reduction will be stable if the anterior capsule has been left intact. If the anterior capsule is damaged or is insufficient to prevent anterior displacement of the medial end of the clavicle, we recommend excision of the medial 1 to 1.5 inches of the clavicle and securing the residual clavicle anatomically to the first rib with 1-mm polyester fiber tape. The medial clavicle is exposed by careful subperiosteal dissection (Fig. 40-31). When possible, any remnant of the capsular or intra-articular disk ligaments should be identified and preserved as these structures can be used to help stabilize the medial clavicle. The capsular ligament covers the anterosuperior and posterior aspects of the joint and represents

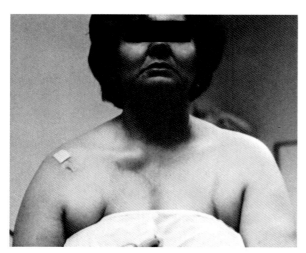

FIGURE 40-29 This postmenopausal, right-handed woman had a resection of the right medial clavicle because of a preoperative diagnosis of "possible tumor." The postoperative microscopic diagnosis was degenerative arthritis of the right medial clavicle. After surgery, the patient complained of pain and discomfort, marked prominence, and gross instability of the right medial clavicle.

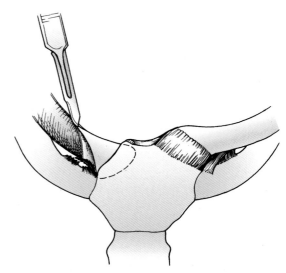

FIGURE 40-31 Subperiosteal exposure of the medial clavicle. Note the posteriorly displaced medial end of the clavicle.

thickenings of the joint capsule. This ligament is primarily attached to the epiphysis of the medial clavicle and is usually avulsed from this structure with posterior SC dislocations. The intra-articular disk ligament is a very dense, fibrous structure and may be intact. It arises from the synchondral junction of the first rib and sternum and is usually avulsed from its attachment site on the medial clavicle. If the sternal attachment sites of the intra-articular or capsular ligaments are intact, a nonabsorbable no. 1 cottony polyester fiber suture is woven back and forth through the ligament so that the ends of the suture exit through the avulsed free end of the tissue. The medial 1- to 1.5-inch end of the clavicle is resected, being careful to protect the underlying vascular structures, and being careful not to damage any of the residual costoclavicular (rhomboid) ligament. The vital vascular structures are protected by passing a curved Crego elevator or ribbon retractor around the posterior aspect of the medial clavicle to isolate them from the operative field during the bony resection.

Excision of the medial clavicle is facilitated by creating drill holes through both cortices of the clavicle at the intended site of clavicular osteotomy. Following this step, an air drill with a side-cutting burr is used to complete the osteotomy (Fig. 40-32). The anterior and superior corners of the clavicle are beveled smooth with an air burr for cosmetic purposes. The medullary canal of the medial clavicle is drilled and curetted to receive the transferred intra-articular disk ligament (Fig. 40-33). Two small drill holes are then placed in the superior cortex of the medial clavicle, approximately 1 cm lateral to the site of resection (Fig. 40-34). These holes communicate with the medullary canal and will be used to secure the suture in the transferred ligament. The free ends of the suture are passed into the medullary canal of the medial clavicle and out the two small drill holes in the superior cortex of the clavicle (Fig. 40-35). While the clavicle is held in a reduced anteroposterior position in relationship to the first rib and sternum, the sutures are used to pull the ligament tightly into the medullary canal of the clavicle (Fig 40-36). The suture is tied, thus securing the

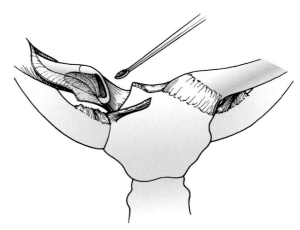

FIGURE 40-33 The medullary canal of the medial clavicle is curetted in preparation for receiving the transferred intra-articular ligament.

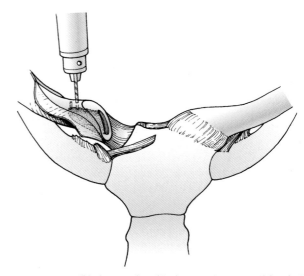

FIGURE 40-34 Drill holes are placed in the superior cortex of the clavicle, approximately 1 cm lateral to the osteotomy site.

FIGURE 40-32 Resection of the medial clavicle and identification of the intra-articular ligament tagged with a suture. (Courtesy of Charles E. Rosipal, MD, and R. Michael Gross, MD.)

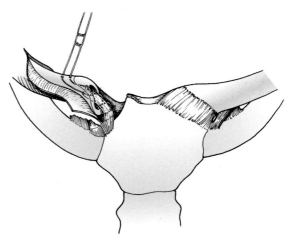

FIGURE 40-35 The free ends of the suture are passed into the medullary canal and out the two holes in the superior cortex.

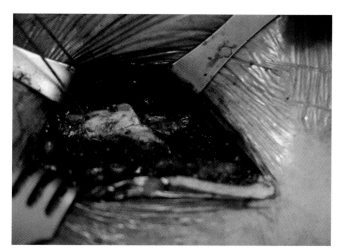

FIGURE 40-36 Passage of the intra-articular disc ligament into the medullary canal. (Courtesy of Charles E. Rosipal, MD, and R. Michael Gross, MD.)

FIGURE 40-38 Passage of sutures through the clavicle and sutures through the periosteal sleeve. (Courtesy of Charles E. Rosipal, MD, and R. Michael Gross, MD.)

transferred ligament into the clavicle (Fig. 40-37). The stabilization procedure is completed by passing multiple (five or six) 1-mm cottony polyester fiber sutures around the reflected periosteal tube, the clavicle, and any of the residual underlying costoclavicular ligament and periosteum on the dorsal surface of the first rib (Figs. 40-38 to 40-40). The intent of the sutures passed around the periosteal tube and clavicle and through he costoclavicular ligament and periosteum of the first rib is to anatomically restore the normal space between the clavicle and the rib. To place sutures around the clavicle and the first rib and pull them tight would decrease the space and could lead to pain. We usually detach the clavicular head of the sternocleidomastoid, which temporarily eliminates the superior pull of the muscle on the medial clavicle. Postoperatively, the shoulders should be held back in a figure-of-eight dressing for 4 to 6 weeks to allow for healing of the soft tissues.

Pearls and Pitfalls

We do not recommend the use of K-wires, Steinmann pins, or any other type of metallic pins to stabilize the SC joint. The compli-

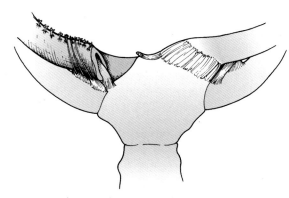

FIGURE 40-39 Closure of the periosteal sleeve around the medial clavicle and secure fixation of these structures to the costoclavicular ligament.

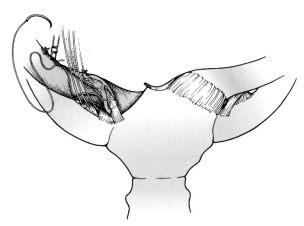

FIGURE 40-37 The transferred ligament is secured into the medial clavicle by tying the sutures exiting from the superior cortex of the clavicle.

FIGURE 40-40 Intraoperative photograph showing polyester fiber sutures around the reflected periosteal tube, the clavicle, and the residual underlying costoclavicular ligament and periosteum on the dorsal surface of the first rib. (Courtesy of Charles E. Rosipal, MD, and R. Michael Gross, MD.)

cations can be very serious and are discussed in the section on complications.

In 1997, Rockwood and associates[164] reported on a series of 23 patients who had undergone a resection of the medial end of the clavicle. The patients were divided into two groups: group I, those who underwent resection of the medial end of the clavicle with maintenance or reconstruction of the costoclavicular ligament; and group II, those who had a resection without maintaining or reconstructing the costoclavicular ligament. The outcome in all but 1 of the 7 patients in group II was poor, with persistence or worsening of preoperative symptoms. The only patient of this group with a successful result had a posterior epiphyseal separation in which the costoclavicular ligament remained attached to the periosteum, thus preventing instability. All of the 8 patients in group I who had a primary surgical resection of the medial end of the clavicle with maintenance of the costoclavicular ligaments had an excellent result. When the operation was performed as a revision of a previous procedure with reconstruction of the costoclavicular ligament, the results were less successful, but only 1 patient of 7 was not satisfied with the outcome of treatment.

Postreduction Care of Posterior Dislocations. If open reduction is required, a figure-of-eight dressing is used for 6 weeks and this is followed by a sling for another 6 weeks. During this time, the patient is instructed to avoid using the arm for any and all strenuous activities of pushing, pulling, or lifting. They should not elevate or abduct the arm more than 60 degrees during the 12-week period. They can use the involved arm to care for bodily needs (i.e., eating, drinking, dressing, and toilet care). This prolonged immobilization will allow the soft tissues a chance to consolidate and stabilize the medial clavicle to the first rib. After 12 weeks, the patient is allowed to gradually use the arm for usual daily living activities, including over the head activities. *However, we do not recommend that the patients, after resection of the medial clavicle and ligament reconstruction, return to heavy laboring activities.*

Physeal Injuries of the Medial Clavicle.. We still perform the closed reduction maneuvers as described above for a suspected anterior or posterior injury. Open reduction of the physeal injury is seldom indicated, except for an irreducible posterior dislocation in a patient with significant symptoms of compression of the vital structures in the mediastinum. After reduction, the shoulders are held back with a figure-of-eight strap or dressing for 3 to 4 weeks.

Before the epiphysis ossifies at the age of 18, one cannot be sure whether a displacement about the SC joint is a dislocation of the SC joint or a fracture through the physeal plate. Despite the fact that there is significant displacement of the shaft with either a type I or type II physeal fracture, the periosteal tube remains in its anatomic position and the attaching ligaments are intact to the periosteum (i.e., the costoclavicular ligament inferiorly and the capsular and intra-articular disk ligaments medially) (Fig. 40-41).

Unreduced Traumatic Dislocation of the Sternoclavicular Joint
Anterior Dislocation. As previously described, most patients with an unreduced and permanent anterior dislocation of

the SC joint are not very symptomatic, have almost a complete range of motion, and can work and even perform manual labor without many problems. Because the joint is so small and incongruous and because the results in patients who have had the attempted reconstructions are so inconsistent, we recommend a plan of "skillful neglect."

If the patient has persistent symptoms of traumatic arthritis for 6 to 12 months following a dislocation or a previous arthroplasty, and if the symptoms can be completely relieved by injection of local anesthesia into the SC joint region, we perform an arthroplasty of the SC joint (Fig. 40-42).

Posterior Dislocation.. In the adult, because of the potential problems that can be associated with the clavicle remaining displaced posteriorly into the mediastinum, an arthroplasty is performed as previously described (Fig. 40-43).

Atraumatic Problems—Spontaneous Subluxation or Dislocation

We have seen a number of patients with spontaneous subluxation or dislocation of the SC joint. About the only symptom they have is that the medial end of the clavicle subluxates or dislocates anteriorly when they raise their arms over their head (see Fig. 40-15).[165] This occurs without any history of trauma. Many of these patients have the characteristic finding of generalized ligamentous laxity (i.e., hyperextension of the elbows, knees, and fingers as well as hypermobility of the glenohumeral joints) (Fig. 40-44). We have never seen a spontaneous posterior subluxation of the SC joint. Only occasionally does the patient with atraumatic anterior displacement complain of pain during the displacement. Because it is difficult to stabilize the joint and prevent the subluxation or dislocation and end up with a pain-free range of motion, we manage the problem with skillful neglect.

In the review by Rockwood and Odor[165] of 37 patients with spontaneous atraumatic subluxation, 29 were managed without surgery and 8 were treated (elsewhere) with surgical reconstruction. With an average follow-up of more than 8 years, all 29 patients treated nonoperatively were doing fine without limitations of activity or lifestyle. The 8 patients treated with surgery had increased pain, limitation of activity, alteration of lifestyle, persistent instability, and significant scars. In many instances, before reconstruction or resection, these patients had minimal discomfort, excellent range of motion, and only complained of a "bump" that slipped in and out of place with certain motions. Postoperatively, these patients still had the bump, along with scars and painful range of motion (Fig. 40-45).

COMPLICATIONS
Nonoperative Complications

The only complications that occur with anterior dislocation of the SC joint are a cosmetic bump or late degenerative changes.[201–203] The serious complications that occur at the time of dislocation of the SC joint are primarily limited to the poste-

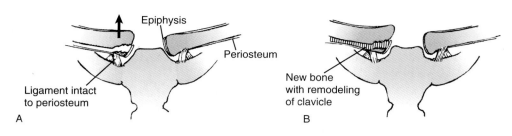

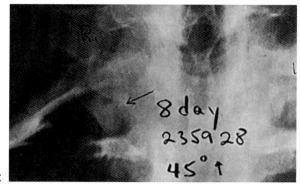

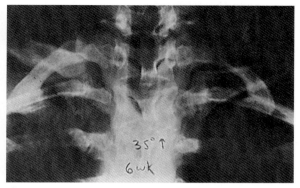

C

D

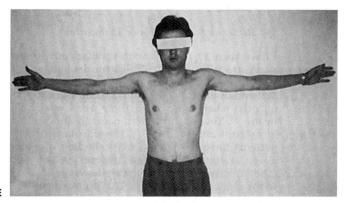

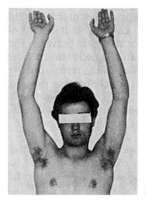

E

F

FIGURE 40-41 A. A schematic of the healing process with a type II physeal injury of the medial clavicle. The medial clavicle splits out of the periosteal tube, leaving a small fragment (Thurstan Holland sign) behind. The costoclavicular ligament is intact to the inferior periosteal tube. **B.** Through remodeling from the retained epiphysis and the periosteal tube, the fracture heals. **C.** A radiograph at 8 days reveals that the right medial clavicle is displaced superiorly from the left clavicle. The inferior medial corner of the clavicle is still located in its normal position adjacent to the epiphysis. **D.** A radiograph at 6 weeks reveals new bone formation along the inferior periosteal tube. Note the thin epiphyseal plate of the normal left medial clavicle. **E,F.** Clinically, at 8 weeks the physeal injury has healed and the patient has a full range of motion. (From Rockwood CA, Matsen F III, eds. The Shoulder. Philadelphia: WB Saunders, 1990, with permission.)

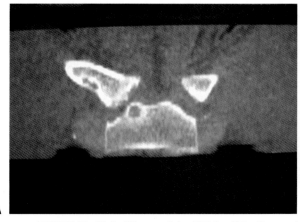

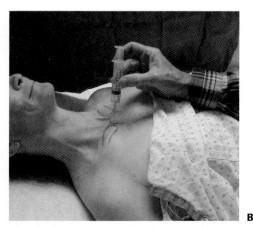

A

B

FIGURE 40-42 A. CT scan of the SC joint. This 42-year-old patient had a symptomatic chronic anterior SC joint dislocation. Note joint space narrowing, medial clavicle osteophytes, and manubrial cysts. **B.** This patient's symptoms were completely relieved by injection of local anesthesia into the SC joint.

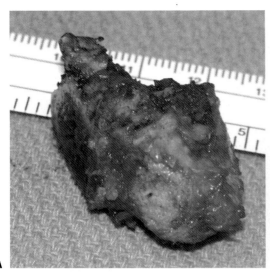

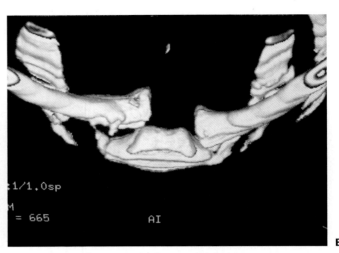

A

B

FIGURE 40-43 Chronic posterior SC joint dislocation. **A.** An osteophyte projecting from medial clavicle corresponds to the area of capsular injury. **B.** Three-dimensional reconstruction CT scan demonstrating the osteophyte.

rior injuries (see Fig. 40-45). Many complications have been reported secondary to the retrosternal dislocation: right pulmonary artery laceration[204]; transected internal mammary artery and lacerated brachiocephalic vein[42]; pneumothorax and laceration of the superior vena cava[147]; tracheal stenosis and respiratory distress[137,186]; venous congestion in the neck, rupture of the esophagus with abscess and osteomyelitis of the clavicle[20]; pressure on the subclavian artery in an untreated patient[90,140,180]; occlusion of the subclavian artery late in a patient who was not treated[180]; obstruction of the subclavian vein caused by an unreduced type II Salter-Harris injury of the medial clavicular physis[60]; compression and thrombosis of the brachiocephalic vein[103]; myocardial conduction abnormalities[186]; compression of the right common carotid artery by a fracture-dislocation of the SC joint[90]; pseudoaneurysm of the right subclavian artery (Fig. 40-46); brachial plexus compression[129] and hoarseness of the voice, onset of snoring, and voice changes from normal to falsetto with movement of the arm[20,98,134,169,190]; fatal tracheoesophageal fistula[196]; mediastinal compression[95]; and severe thoracic outlet syndrome with swelling and cyanosis of the upper extremity.[73,92]

Worman and Leagus,[204] in their excellent review of the complications associated with posterior dislocations of the SC joint, reported that 16 of 60 patients reviewed from the literature had suffered complications of the trachea, esophagus, or great vessels.[82,98,152]

Complications Following Operative Procedures

The Use of Pins to Stabilize the Sternoclavicular Joint

There have been numerous reports of deaths and three near-deaths from migrations of intact or broken K-wires or Steinmann pins into the heart, pulmonary artery, or the aorta.* Numerous other authors have reported complications from pin migration into the pulmonary artery,[27,113,115] aorta,[141] heart,[57,94,167,171] subclavian artery,[174] mediastinum,[64,78,109,193] and breast.[77]

In 1990, Lyons and Rockwood[123] published data on the migration of pins from the SC joint in 21 patients. They reported that pins from the SC joint had migrated into the chest, heart, mediastinum, subclavian vein, and lung. They recommended that large, small, smooth, threaded, bent, or straight pins *not* be used for fixation of the SC joint because of their potential to migrate into vital structures and even cause death. Further, they recommended that any time pins were used to manage any problems about the shoulder (i.e., clavicle fractures or

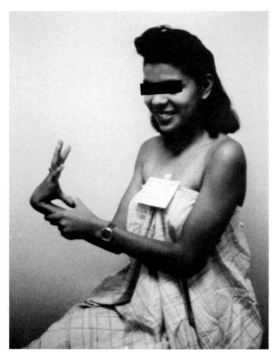

FIGURE 40-44 This patient has developed spontaneous subluxation of her SC joint. She also has generalized ligamentous laxity of the wrists, fingers, and elbows.

*References 39,68,71,76,80,93,96,100,106,107,113,116,139,146,170, 176,188.

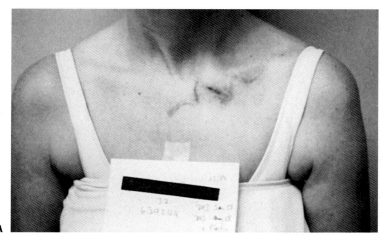
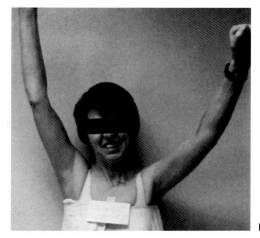

FIGURE 40-45 Patients treated with surgery for spontaneous, atraumatic subluxation of the SC joint often have increased pain, limitation of activity, alteration of lifestyle, persistent instability of the joint, and a significant scar. **A,B.** Not only was the cosmetic scarring a problem, but motion and pain were worse than before the reconstruction. (From Rockwood CA, Matsen F III, eds. The Shoulder. Philadelphia: WB Saunders, 1990, with permission.)

injuries to the AC joint), the pins be monitored very closely with radiographs and that they should always be removed (Fig. 40-47).

Residual Instability

After reduction of a posterior dislocation, there may be some increased laxity which should normalize with time. A case report of anterior subluxation after closed reduction of a posterior dislocation noted that the residual anterior instability resolved with observation.[199] Even with reconstructive procedures, the joint may remain subluxed or subjectively unstable with motion. This is particularly true of patients who were treated surgically for atraumatic instability. Excessive resection

of the medial clavicle without successful stabilization can create a challenging instability of the residual medial clavicle for which few options exist (Fig. 40-48). In such cases, total claviculectomy may be the only option.[108] An islandized hemipectoralis muscle flap has been also suggested as a means for filling a large medial clavicular defect and may prove useful in these cases.[173]

THE STERNOCLAVICULAR JOINT—THE PAST, PRESENT, AND FUTURE

Injuries of the SC joint are rare and, therefore, no one has lots of experience with them. As a result, many of the problems go

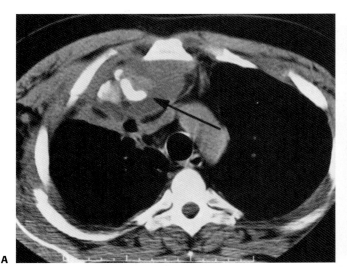
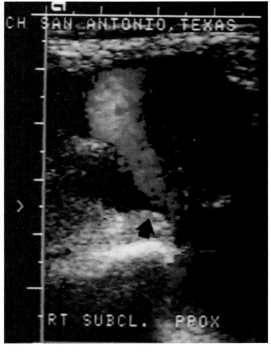

FIGURE 40-46 A. CT scan revealing a posterior fracture-dislocation of the SC joint with significant soft tissue swelling and compromise of the hilar structures. **B.** Duplex ultrasound study revealing a large pseudoaneurysm of the right subclavian artery. Note the large neck of the pseudoaneurysm, which measured approximately 1 cm in diameter (*arrow*).

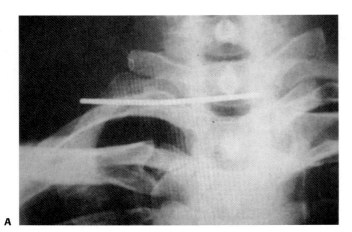

FIGURE 40-47 Migration of pins from the SC joint. **A,B.** Migration of Steinmann pin into the spinal canal. **C.** Migration of Steinmann pin into the mediastinum.

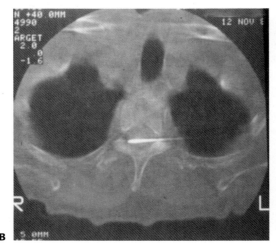

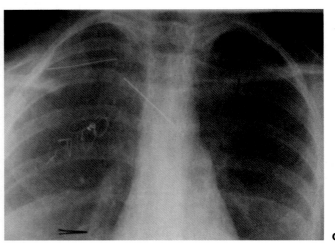

unrecognized or are treated inappropriately. Only an occasional publication cites the SC joint and because of the rarity of the problem, it can almost be called the "forgotten joint." It is one of the strongest and most stable joints, and when it dislocates it is difficult to stabilize. If more orthopaedic surgeons would write up their treatment of this rare condition, there would be more data for orthopaedic surgeons to review and to help

understand the problem. After years of experience in publications, we still have not read of the ultimate stabilizing procedure for dislocations of the SC joint. Most surgeons leave anterior dislocations of the joint alone as patients can function nicely after despite some instability. The question is: why shouldn't we be able to reduce it and hold it and keep it in place until the ligaments are healed? One thing that is for certain in the twenty-first century is that we understand that the SC dislocation should not be stabilized with K-wires, Steinmann pins, or similar devices. Simple pinning of the joint with or without repairing the ligaments usually results in pin migration to the chest, mediastinum, abdominal organs, and even to the spinal canal. Many deaths have been reported from intracardiac penetration of migrating pins. Recently, the use of a combination clavicle plate with intrasternal hook has been reported but long-term results are needed before this is a commonly accepted procedure.

Management of posterior dislocations of the SC joint is a challenge. Certainly, we must recognize the condition in adults because the continued displacement of the clavicle can cause erosion into the great vessels and mediastinum and can produce severe complications. If the clavicle is removed from the mediastinum, the question is what to do next? Does one try to stabilize it, pin it, plate it, or does one resect the medial 2 cm and then stabilize the residual clavicle down to the first rib to prevent anterior/superior and/or continued posterior displacement?

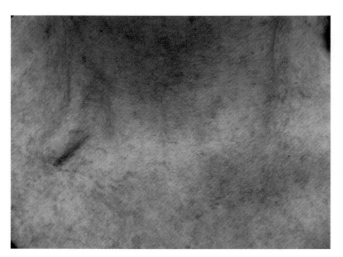

FIGURE 40-48 Excessive resection of the medial clavicle resulting in residual instability of the medial clavicle with adduction.

While dislocations are a problem, so are the patients with anterior/posterior spontaneous subluxation of the SC joint. Does one stabilize it, excise the medial clavicle, or continue to observe the patient? So far, the literature reflects that this condition occurs in young people and the symptoms gradually disappear with aging. Again, if there were more publications on this complex problem, then more orthopaedists would understand it.

What can one look forward to in the diagnosis and treatment of traumatic and atraumatic conditions of the SC joint? The use of SC pin fixation should be of historical interest only and we can hope that some type of safe anterior or posterior stabilization procedure can be developed for the unstable joint. Hopefully, we will see more and more publications in the orthopaedic literature that will educate orthopaedic surgeons in the management of problems of the SC joint.

REFERENCES

1. Abiddin Z, Sinopidis C, Grocock CJ, et al. Suture anchors for treatment of sternoclavicular joint instability. J Shoulder Elbow Surg 2006;15:315–8.
2. Allen AW. Living suture grafts in the repair of fractures and dislocations. Arch Surg 1928;16:1007–1020.
3. Allen BF, Zielinski CJ. Posterior fracture through the sternoclavicular physis associated with a clavicle fracture: A case report and literarture review. AJ Ortho 1999;28(10): 598–600.
4. Arenas AJ, Pampliega T, Iglesias J. Surgical management of bipolar clavicular dislocation. Acta Orthop Belg 1993;59(2):202–205.
5. Armstrong AL, Dias JJ. Reconstruction for instability of the sternoclavicular joint using the tendon of the sternocleidomastoid muscle. J Bone Joint Surg Br 2008;90:610–3.
6. Aumann U, Brüning W. Die Discopathie des sternoclaviculargelenkes. Chirurg 1980; 51:722–726.
7. Bae DS, Kocher MS, Waters PM, Micheli LM, Griffery M, Dichtel L. Chronic recurrent anterior sternoclavicular joint instability: results of surgical management. J Pediatr Orthop. 2006;26:71–4.
8. Baker EC. Tomography of the sternoclavicular joint. Ohio State Med J 1959;55:60.
9. Bankart ASB. An operation for recurrent dislocation (subluxation) of the sternoclavicular joint. Br J Surg 1938;26:320–323.
10. Barth E, Hagen R. Surgical treatment of dislocations of the sternoclavicular joint. Acta Orthop Scand 1983;54:746–747.
11. Bateman JE. The Shoulder and Neck. Philadelphia: WB Saunders, 1972.
12. Bateman JE. The Shoulder and Neck. 2nd ed. Philadelphia: WB Saunders, 1978.
13. Battaglia TC, Pannunzio ME, Abhinav CB, et al. Interposition arthroplasty with bone-tendon allograft: A technique for treatment of the unstable sternoclavicular joint. J Orthop Tr 2005;19:124–129.
14. Bearn JD. Direct observation on the function of the capsule of the sternoclavicular joint in clavicular support. J Anat 1967;101:159–180.
15. Beckman T. A case of simultaneous luxation of both ends of the clavicle. Acta Chir Scand 1923;56:156–163.
16. Benitez CL, Mintz DN, Potter HG. MR imaging of the sternoclavicular joint following trauma. Clin Imaging 2004;28:59–63.
17. Bicos J, Nicholson GP.Treatment and results of sternoclavicular injuries. Clin Sports Med 2003;22:359–70.
18. Bisson LJ, Dauphin N, Marzo JM. A safe zone for resection of the medial end of the clavicle. J Shoulder Elbow Surg 2003;12(6):592–594.
19. Booth CM, Roper BA. Chronic dislocation of the sternoclavicular joint: an operative repair. Clin Orthop 1979;140:17–20.
20. Borowiecki B, Charow A, Cook W, et al. An unusual football injury (posterior dislocation of the sternoclavicular joint). Arch Otolaryngol 1972;95:185–187.
21. Borrero E. Traumatic posterior displacement of the left clavicular head causing chronic extrinsic compression of the subclavian artery. Physician Sports Med 1987;15:87–89.
22. Breitner S, Wirth CJ. [Resection of the acromial and sternal ends of the clavicle.] Z Orthop 1987;125:363–368.
23. Brenner RA. Monarticular, noninfected subacute arthritis of the sternoclavicular joint. J BoneJoint Surg 1959;41B:740–3.
24. Brinker MR, Bartz RL, Reardon PR, et al. A method for open reduction and internal fixation of the unstable posterior sternoclavicular joint dislocation. J Orthop Trauma 1997;11:378–381.
25. Brooks AL, Henning GD. Injury to the proximal clavicular epiphysis. J Bone Joint Surg 1972;54A:1347–1348(abst).
26. Brossman J, Stabler A, Preidler KW, et al. Sternoclavicular joint: MR imaging—anatomic correlation. Radiology 1996;198(1):193–198.
27. Brown JE. Anterior sternoclavicular dislocation: a method of repair. Am J Orthop 1961; 31:184–189.
28. Brown R. Backward and inward dislocation of sternal end of clavicle: open reduction. Surg Clin North Am 1927;7:1263.
29. Buckerfield C, Castle M. Acute traumatic retrosternal dislocation of the clavicle. J Bone Joint Surg 1984;66A:379–385.
30. Burnstein MI, Pozniak MA. Computed tomography with stress maneuver to demonstrate sternoclavicular joint dislocation. J Comput Assist Tomogr 1990;14(1):159–160.
31. Burri C, Neugebauer R. Carbon fiber replacement of the ligaments of the shoulder

girdle and the treatment of lateral instability of the ankle joint. Clin Orthop 1985;196: 112–117.
32. Burrows HF. Tenodesis of subclavius in the treatment of recurrent dislocation of the sternoclavicular joint. J Bone Joint Surg 1951;33B:240–243.
33. Butterworth RD, Kirk AA. Fracture dislocation sternoclavicular joint: case report. Va Med 1952;79:98–100.
34. Castropil W, Ramadan LB, Bitar AC, et al. Sternoclavicular dislocation-reconstruction with semitendinosus tendon autograft: a case report. Knee Surg Sports Traumatol Arthrosc 2008;17.
35. Carmichael KD, Longo A, Lick S, et al. Posterior sternoclavicular epiphyseal fracture-dislocation with delayed diagnosis. Skeletal Radiol 2006;35:608–12.
36. Cave AJE. The nature and morphology of the costoclavicular ligament. J Anat 1961; 95:170–179.
37. Cave EF. Fractures and Other Injuries. Chicago: Year Book Medical, 1958.
38. Cave ER, Burke JF, Boyd RJ. Trauma Management. Chicago: Year Book Medical, 1974: 409–411.
39. Clark RL, Milgram JW, Yawn DH. Fatal aortic perforation and cardiac tamponade due to a Kirschner wire migrating from the right sternoclavicular joint. South Med J 1974; 67:316–318.
40. Collins JJ. Retrosternal dislocation of the clavicle. J Bone Joint Surg 1972;54B:203(abst).
41. Cooper AP. The Lectures of Sir Astley Cooper on the Principles and Practices of Surgery. Philadelphia: E.L. Carey & A. Hart, 1935:559.
42. Cooper GJ, Stubbs D, Waller DA, et al. Posterior sternoclavicular dislocation: a novel method of external fixation. Injury 1992;23:565–567.
43. Cope R. Dislocations of the sternoclavicular joint. Skeletal Radiol 1993;22:233–238.
44. Cope R, Riddervold HO. Posterior dislocation of the sternoclavicular joint: report on two cases, with emphasis on radiologic management and early diagnosis. Skeletal Radiol 1988;17:247–250.
45. Crosby LA, Rubino LJ. Subluxation of the sternoclavicular joint secondary to pseudoarthrosis of the first and second ribs. J Bone Joint Surg 2002;84A(4):623–626.
46. de Jong KP, Sukul DM. Anterior sternoclavicular dislocation: a long-term follow-up study. J Orthop Trauma 1990;4:420–423.
47. Denham R Jr, Dingley AF Jr. Epiphyseal separation of the medial end of the clavicle. J Bone Joint Surg 1967;49A:1179–1183.
48. DePalma AF. The role of the discs of the sternoclavicular and the acromioclavicular joints. Clin Orthop 1959;13:222–233.
49. DePalma AF. Surgery of the Shoulder. 2nd ed. Philadelphia: JB Lippincott, 1973: 328–340.
50. DePalma AF. Surgical anatomy of acromioclavicular and sternoclavicular joints. Surg Clin North Am 1963;43:1541–1550.
51. Destouet JM, Gilula LA, Murphy WA, et al. Computed tomography of the sternoclavicular joint and sternum. Radiology 1981;138:123–129.
52. Deutsch AL, Rexnick D, Mink JH. Computed tomography of the glenohumeral and sternoclavicular joints. Orthop Clin North Am 1985;16(3):497–511.
53. Dieme C, Bousso A, Sane A, Sané JC, Niane M, Ndiaye A, Sy MH, Seye S. Bipolar dislocation of the clavicle or floating clavicle. A report of 3 cases. Chir Main 2007;26: 113–6.
54. Djerf K, Tropp H, Asberg B. Case report: retrosternal clavicular dislocation in the sternoclavicular joint. Clin Radiol 1998;53:75–76.
55. Duggan N. Recurrent dislocation of sternoclavicular cartilage. J Bone Joint Surg 1931; 13:365.
56. Durpekt R, Vojácek J, Lischke R, et al. Kirschner wire migration from the right sternoclavicular joint to the heart: a case report. Heart Surg Forum 2006;9:E840–2
57. Echlin PS, Michaelson JE. Adolescent butterfly swimmer with bilateral subluxing sternoclavicular joints. Br J Sports Med 2006;40:e12.
58. Elliott AC. Tripartite injury of the clavicle. S Afr Med J 1986;70:115.
59. Elting JJ. Retrosternal dislocation of the clavicle. Arch Surg 1972;104:35–37.
60. Emms NW, Morris AD, Kaye JC, et al. Subclavian vein obstruction caused by an unreduced type II Salter Harris injury of the medial clavicular physis. J Shoulder Elbow Surg 2002;11(3):271–273.
61. Eskola A. Sternoclavicular dislocation—a plea for open treatment. Acta Orthop Scand 1986;57:227–228.
62. Eskola A, Vainiopaa S, Vastamaki M, et al. Operation for old sternoclavicular dislocation. J Bone Joint Surg 1989;71B:63–65.
63. Fedoseev VA. Method of radiographic study of the sternoclavicular joint. Vestn Rentgenol Radiol 1977;3:88–91.
64. Ferrandez L, Yubero J, Usabiaga J, et al. Sternoclavicular dislocation, treatment, and complications. Ital J Orthop Traumatol 1988;14:349–355.
65. Ferry AM, Rook FW, Masterson JH. Retrosternal dislocation of the clavicle. J Bone Joint Surg 1957;39A:905–910.
66. Fery A, Leonard A. Transsternal sternoclavicular projection: diagnostic value in sternoclavicular dislocations. J Radiol 1981;62:167–170.
67. Fery A, Sommelet J. Dislocation of the sternoclavicular joint: a review of 49 cases. Int Orthop 1988;12:187–195.
68. Fowler AW. Migration of a wire from the sternoclavicular joint to the pericardial cavity (letter). Injury 1981;13:261–262.
69. Franck WM, Jannasch O, Siassi M, et al. Balser plate stabilization: an alternate therapy for traumatic sternoclavicular instability. J Shoulder Elbow Surg 2003;12(3):276–281.
70. Friedl W, Fritz T. Die PDS-Kordefixation der Sternockavikularen Luxation und Para-artikularen Klavikulafrankturen. Unfallchirurg 1994;97:263–265.
71. Fueter-Töndury M. Drahtwanderung nach Osteosynthese. Schweiz Med Wochenschr 1976;106:1890–1896.
72. Gale DW, Dunn ID, McPherson S, et al. Retrosternal dislocation of the clavicle: the "stealth" dislocation: a case report. Injury 1992;23:563–564.
73. Gangahar DM, Flogaites T. Retrosternal dislocation of the clavicle producing thoracic outlet syndrome. J Trauma 1978;18:369–372.
74. Garretson RB III, Williams GR Jr. Clinical evaluation of injuries to the acromioclavicular and sternoclavicular joints. Clin Sports Med 2003;22:239–254.
75. Gaudernak T, Poigenfurst J. Simulatenous dislocation-fracture of both ends of the clavicle. Unfallchirurgie 1991;17:362–4.
76. Gerlach D, Wemhoner SR, Ogbuihi S. On two cases of fatal heart tamponade due

to migration of fracture nails from the sternoclavicular joint. Z Rechtsmed 1984;93: 53–60.
77. Gleason BA. Bilateral, spontaneous, anterior subluxation of the sternoclavicular joint: a case report and literature review. Mil Med 2006;171:790–2.
78. Grabski R. Unusual dislocation of a fragment of Kirschner wire after fixation of the sternoclavicular joint. Wiad Lek 1987;40:630–632.
79. Grant JCB. Method of Anatomy. 7th ed. Baltimore: Williams & Wilkins, 1965.
80. Grauthoff Von H, Klammer NI. Komplihationem durch Drahtvenderungen nach Kirschnerdracht-Sprakungen on der Klavikula. Fortschr Geb Rontgenstr Nuklearmed Erganzungsband 1978;128:591–594.
81. Gray H. Osteology. In: Goss CM, ed. Anatomy of the Human Body. 28th ed. Philadelphia: Lea & Febiger, 1966:324–326.
82. Greenlee DP. Posterior dislocation of the sternal end of the clavicle. JAMA 1944;125: 426–428.
83. Gunther WA. Posterior dislocation of the sternoclavicular joint: report of a case. J Bone Joint Surg 1949;31A:878–879.
84. Habernek H, Hertz H. [Origin, diagnosis and treatment of sternoclavicular joint dislocation.] Aktuelle Traumatol 1987;17(1):23–28.
85. Haug W. Retention Einer Seltenen Sternoclavicular Lluxationsfrktur Mittels Modifizierter Y-platte der AO. Aktuel Traumatol 1986;16:39–40.
86. Heinig CF. Retrosternal dislocation of the clavicle: early recognition, x-ray diagnosis, and management. J Bone Joint Surg 1968;50A:830(abst).
87. Hobbs DW. Sternoclavicular joint: a new axial radiographic view. Radiology 1968;90: 801–802.
88. Hotchkiss LW. Double dislocation of the sternal end of the clavicle. Ann Surg 1896; 23:600.
89. Howard FM, Shafer SJ. Injuries to the clavicle with neurovascular complications: a study of fourteen cases. J Bone Joint Surg 1965;47A:1335–1346.
90. Howard NJ. Acromioclavicular and sternoclavicular joint injuries. Am J Surg 1939;46: 284–291.
91. Hsu HC, Wu JJ, Lo WH, et al. Epiphyseal fracture—retrosternal dislocation of the medial end of the clavicle: a case report. Chin Med J 1993;52:198–202.
92. Jain S, Monbaliu D, Thompson JF. Thoracic outlet syndrome caused by chronic retrosternal dislocation of the clavicle. J Bone Joint Surg [Br] 2002;84B:116–118.
93. Janssens de Varebeke B, Van Osselaer G. Migration of Kirschner pin from the right sternoclavicular joint resulting in perforation of the pulmonary artery main trunk. Acta Chir Belg 1993;93:287–291.
94. Jelesijevic V, Knoll D, Klinke F, et al. [Penetrating injuries of the heart and intrapericardial blood vessels caused by migration of a Kirschner pin after osteosynthesis.] Acta Chirg Iugosl 1982;29:274–276.
95. Jougon JB, Denis JL, Dromer CEH. Posterior dislocation of the sternoclavicular joint leading to mediastinal compression. Ann Thoacic Surg 1996;61:711–713.
96. Kahle M, Filler RL, Forster R. Luxations in the sternoclavicular joint. Aktuel Traumatol 1990;20:83–86.
97. Kattan KR. Modified view for use in roentgen examination of the sternoclavicular joints. Radiology 1973;108:8.
98. Kennedy JC. Retrosternal dislocation of the clavicle. J Bone Joint Surg 1949;31B:74–75.
99. Kennedy PT, Mawhinney JD. Retrosternal dislocation of the sternoclavicular joint. JR Coll Surg Edinb 1995;40:208–209.
100. Keferstein R, Frese J. Intrathoracic dislocation of a metal-piece after the use of wires in bone-surgery. Unfallchirurgie 1980;6(1):56–61.
101. Kennedy PT, Mawhinney HJD. Retrosternal dislocation of the sternoclavicular joint. JR Coll Surg Edinb 1995;40:208–209.
102. Key JA, Conwell HE, eds. The Management of Fractures, Dislocations, and Sprains. 5th ed. St. Louis: CV Mosby, 1951:458–461.
103. Kiroff GK, McClure DN, Skelley JW. Delayed diagnosis of posterior sternoclavicular joint dislocation. MJA 1996;164(19):242–243.
104. Klein MA, Spreitzerm AM, Miro PA, et al. MR imaging of the abnormal sternoclavicular joint—a pictorial essay. Clin Imaging 1997;21:138–143.
105. Kocher MS, Feagin JA Jr. Shoulder injuries during alpine skiing. Am J Sports Med 1996;24:665–669.
106. Konstantinov B, Cherkes-Zade D. Case of injury to the aorta by a Kirschner pin during osteosynthesis of the sternoclavicular joint. Ortop Travmatol Protez 1972;33:73–74.
107. Kremens V, Glauser F. Unusual sequela following pinning of medial clavicular fracture. AJR Radium Ther Nucl Med 1956;76:1066–1069, 1956.
108. Krishnan SG, Schiffern SC, Pennington SD, et al. Functional outcomes after total claviculectomy as a salvage procedure. A series of six cases. J Bone Joint Surg Am 2007; 89:1215–9.
109. Kumar P, Rees GM, Godbole R, et al. Intrathoracic migration of a Kirschner wire. JR Soc Med 2002;95:198–199.
110. Kurzbauer R. The lateral projection in roentgenography of the sternoclavicular articulation. AJR 1946;56:104–105.
111. Laurencin CT, Senatus P, Patti J, et al. Dislocation of the sternoclavicular joint. Evaluation using paraxial computed tomographic reconstruction. Orthop Rev 1993;22(1): 101–103.
112. Lemire L, Rosman M. Sternoclavicular epiphyseal separation with adjacent clavicular fracture: a case report. J Pediatr Orthop 1984;4:118–120.
113. Leonard JW, Gifford RW. Migration of a Kirschner wire from the clavicle into pulmonary artery. Am J Cardiol 1965;16:598–600.
114. Levinsohn EM, Bunnell WP, Yuan HA. Computed tomography in the diagnosis of dislocations of the sternoclavicular joint. Clin Orthop 1979;140:12–6.
115. Little NJ, Bismil Q, Chipperfield A, et al. Superior dislocation of the sternoclavicular joint. J Shoulder Elbow Surg 2008;17:e22–3.
116. Liu HP, Chang CH, Lin PJ, et al. Migration of Kirschner wire for the right sternoclavicular joint into the main pulmonary artery: a case report. Chang Keng I Hsueh 1992; 15(1):49–53.
117. Louw JA. Posterior dislocation of the sternoclavicular joint associated with major spinal injury: a case report. S Afr Med J 1987;71:791–792.
118. Lowman CL. Operative correction of old sternoclavicular dislocation. J Bone Joint Surg 1928;10:740–741.
119. Lucas DB. Biomechanics of the shoulder joint. Arch Surg 1973;107:425–432.
120. Lucet L, Le Loet X, Menard JF, et al. Computed tomography of the normal sternoclavicular joint. Skeletal Radiol 1996;25:237–241.
121. Luhmann JD, Bassett GS. Posterior sternoclavicular epiphyseal separation presenting with hoarseness: A case report and discussion. Ped Emerg Care 1998;14:130–132.
122. Lunseth PA, Chapman KW, Frankel VH. Surgical treatment of chronic dislocation of the sternoclavicular joint. J Bone Joint Surg 1975;57B:193–196.
123. Lyons F, Rockwood CA Jr. Current concepts review. Migration of pins used in operations of the shoulder. J Bone Joint Surg 1990;72A:1262–1267.
124. Maguire WB. Safe and simple method of repair of recurrent dislocation of the sternoclavicular joint. J Bone Joint Surg 1986;68B:332(abst).
125. Marker LB, Klareskov B. Posterior sternoclavicular dislocation: an American football injury. Br J Sports Med 1996;30(1):71–72.
126. Martin SD, Altchek D, Erlanger S. Atraumatic posterior dislocation of the sternoclavicular joint. Clin Orthop 1993;292:159–164.
127. Martinez A, Rodriguez A, Gonzalez G, et al. Atraumatic spontaneous posterior subluxation of the sternoclavicular joint. Arch Orthop Trauma Surg 1999;119:344–346.
128. McCulloch P, Henley BM, Linnau KF. Radiographic clues for high-energy trauma: Three cases of sternoclavicular dislocation. AJR 2001;176:1534.
129. McKenzie JMM. Retrosternal dislocation of the clavicle: a report of two cases. J Bone Joint Surg 1963;45B:138–141.
130. McLaughlin H. Trauma. Philadelphia: WB Saunders, 1959:291–292.
131. Mehta JC, Sachdev A, Collins JJ. Retrosternal dislocation of the clavicle. Injury 1973; 5:79–83.
132. Meis RC, Love RB, Keene JS, Orwin JF. Operative treatment of the painful sternoclavicular joint: a new technique using interpositional arthroplasty.J Shoulder Elbow Surg 2006;15:60–66.
133. Milch H. The rhomboid ligament in surgery of the sternoclavicular joint. J Int Coll Surg 1952;17:41–51.
134. Mitchell WJ, Cobey MC. Retrosternal dislocation of the clavicle. Med Ann DC 1960; 29:546–549.
135. Morag B, Shahin N. The value of tomography of the sternoclavicular region. Clin Radiol 1975;26:57–62.
136. Mounasamy V, Fleming M, Birnbaum M. Eur J Orthop Surg Traumatol 2006;16: 351–353.
137. Nakayama E, Tanaka T, Noguchi T, et al. Tracheal stenosis caused by retrosternal dislocation of the right clavicle. Ann Thorac Surg 2007;83:685–7.
138. Nakazato T, Wada I, Tsuchiya D, et al. Clavicle fracture and posterior sternoclavicular dislocation in a newborn. Ortho 2001;24(12):1169–1170.
139. Nettles JL, Linscheid R. Sternoclavicular dislocations. J Trauma 1968;8:158–164.
140. Noda M, Shiraishi H, Mizuno K. Chronic posterior sternoclavicular dislocation causing compression of a subclavian artery. J Shoulder Elbow Surg 1997;6(6):564–569.
141. Nordback I, Markkula H. Migration of Kirschner pin from clavicle into ascending aorta. Acta Chir Scand 1985;151:177–179.
142. Nutz V. [Fracture dislocation of the sternoclavicular joint.] Unfallchirurg 1986;89: 145–148.
143. Omer GE. Osteotomy of the clavicle in surgical reduction of anterior sternoclavicular dislocation. J Trauma 1967;7:584–590.
144. Ono K, Inagawa H, Kiyota K, et al. Posterior dislocation of the sternoclavicular joint with obstruction of the innominate vein: case report. J Trauma 1998;44(2):381–383.
145. Pang KP, Yung SW, Lee TS, Pang CE. Bipolar Clavicular Injury. Med J. Malaysia 2003; 58:621–4.
146. Pate JW, Wilhite J. Migration of a foreign body from the sternoclavicular joint to the heart: a case report. Am Surg 1969;35:448–449.
147. Paterson DC. Retrosternal dislocation of the clavicle. J Bone Joint Surg 1961;43B: 90–92.
148. Peacock HK, Brandon JR, Jones OL. Retrosternal dislocation of the clavicle. South Med J 1970;63:1324–1328.
149. Pearsall AW, Russell GV. Ipsilateral clavicle fracture, sternoclavicular joint subluxation, and long thoracic nerve injury: an unusual constellation of injuries sustained during wrestling. AJ Sports Med 200;28(6):904–908.
150. Pfister U, Ode E. Die Luxation im sterno-clavicular-gelenk. Unfallmed Arbeit 1983(October).
151. Pfister U, Weller S. Luxation of the sternoclavicular joint. Unfallchirurgie 1982;8: 81–87.
152. Poland J. Traumatic Separation of Epiphyses of the Upper Extremity. London: Smith, Elder, 1898:135–143.
153. Pollock RC, Bankes MJK, Emery RJH. Diagnosis of retrosternal dislocation of the clavicle with ultrasound. Injury 1996;27(9):670–671.
154. Porral MA. Observation d'une double luxation de la clavicule droite. J Univ Hebd Med Chir Prat 1831;2:78–82.
155. Pridie K. Dislocation of acromioclavicular and sternoclavicular joints. J Bone Joint Surg 1959;41B:429(abst).
156. Prime HT, Doig SG, Hooper JC. Retrosternal dislocation of the clavicle. Am J Sports Med 1991;19:92–93.
157. Qureshi SA Shah AK, Pruzansky ME. Using the semitendinosus tendon to stabilize sternoclavicular joints in a patient with Ehlers-Danlos syndrome: a case report. Am J Orthop 2005;34:315–8.
158. Reis FP, de Camargo AM, Vitti M, et al. Electromyographic study of the subclavius muscle. Acta Anat 1979;105:284–290.
159. Rice EE. Habitual dislocation of the sternoclavicular articulation: a case report. J Okla State Med Assoc 1932;25:34–35.
160. Ritvo M, Ritvo M. Roentgen study of the sternoclavicular region. AJR 1947;53:644–650.
161. Rockwood CA Jr. Dislocation of the sternoclavicular joint. In: Rockwood CA Jr, Green DP, eds. Fractures, 1st ed, vol 1. Philadelphia: JB Lippincott, 1975:756–787.
162. Rockwood CA Jr. Injuries to the Sternoclavicular Joint. In: Rockwood CA Jr, Green DP, eds. Fractures. 2nd ed, vol 1. Philadelphia: JB Lippincott, 1984:910–948.
163. Rockwood CA Jr. The shoulder: facts, confusions, and myths. Int Orthop 1991;15: 401–405.
164. Rockwood CA Jr, Groh GI, Wirth MA, et al. Resection arthroplasty of the sternoclavicular joint. J Bone Joint Surg 1997;79(3):387–393.
165. Rockwood CA Jr, Odor JM. Spontaneous atraumatic anterior subluxation of the sternoclavicular joint. J Bone Joint Surg 1989;71A:1280–1288.
166. Rodrigues H. Case of dislocation, inwards, of the internal extremity of the clavicle. Lancet 1843;1:309–310.

167. Rubenstein ZR, Moray B, Itzchak Y. Percutaneous removal of intravascular foreign bodies. Cardiovasc Intervent Radiol 1982;5:64–68.

168. Sadr B, Swann M. Spontaneous dislocation of the sternoclavicular joint. Acta Orthop Scand 1979;50:269–74.

169. Salvatore JE. Sternoclavicular joint dislocation. Clin Orthop 1968;58:51–54.

170. Sanders JO, Lyons FA, Rockwood CA Jr. Management of dislocations of both ends of the clavicle. J Bone Joint Surg 1990;72A:399–402.

171. Schechter DC, Gilbert L. Injuries of the heart and great vessels due to pins and needles. Thorax 1969;24:246–253.

172. Schmitt WGH. Articulatis Sternoclavicularis: Darstellung in Einer Zweiter Ebene. Rontgenpraxis 1981;34:262–267.

173. Schulman MR, Parsons BO, Lin H, et al. Islandized hemipectoralis muscle flap for sternoclavicular defect. J Shoulder Elbow Surg 2007;16:e31–4.

174. Sethi GK, Scott SM. Subclavian artery laceration due to migration of a Hagie pin. Surgery 1976;80:644–646.

175. Siddiqui AA, Turner SM. Posterior sternoclavicular dislocation: The value of intraoperative ultrasound. Injury 2003;34:448–453.

176. Smolle-Juettner FM, Hofer PH, Pinter H, et al. Intracardiac malpositioning of a sternoclavicular fixation wire. J Orthop Trauma 1992;6:102–105.

177. Speed K. A textbook of Fractures and Dislocations. 4th ed. Philadelphia: Lea & Febiger, 1942:282–290.

178. Spencer EE, Kuhn JE. Biomechanical analysis of reconstructions for sternoclavicular joint instability. J Bone Joint Surg 2004;86A(1):98–105.

179. Spencer EE, Kuhn JE, Huston LJ, et al. Ligamentous restraints to anterior and posterior translation of the sternoclavicular joint. J Shoulder Elbow Surg 2002;11(1):43–47

180. Stankler L. Posterior dislocation of clavicle: a report of 2 cases. Br J Surg 1962;50:164–168.

181. Stein AH. Retrosternal dislocation of the clavicle. J Bone Joint Surg 1957;39A:656–660.

182. Tagliabue D, Riva A. Le lussazioni sterno-claveari. Minerva Orthop 1985;36:876–871.

183. Tanlin Y. Ipsilateral sternoclavicular joint dislocation and clavicle fracture. J Orthop Trauma 1996;10(7):506–507.

184. Thomas CB Jr, Friedman RJ. Ipsilateral sternoclavicular dislocation and clavicle fracture. J Orthop Trauma. 1989;3:355–7.

185. Thomas DP, Williams PR, Hoddinott HC. A "safe" surgical technique for stabilization of the sternoclavicular joint: a cadaveric and clinical study. Ann R Coll Surg Engl 2000; 82:432–435.

186. Tricoire JL, Colombier JA, Choiron P, et al. Retrosternal dislocation of the clavicle: a report of six cases. Fr J Orthop Surg 1990;1:107–112.

187. Tsai DW, Swiontkowski MF, Kottra CL. A case of sternoclavicular dislocation with scapulothoracic dissociation. AJR 1996;167:332.

188. Tubbax H, Hendzel P, Sergeant P. Cardiac perforation after Kirschner wire migration. Acta Chir Belg 1989;89:309–311.

189. Tubbs RS, Loukas M, Slappey JB, et al. Surgical and clinical anatomy of the interclavicular ligament. Surg Radiol Anat 2007;29:357–60.

190. Tyler HDD, Sturrock WDS, Callow FM. Retrosternal dislocation of the clavicle. J Bone Joint Surg 1963;45B:132–137.

191. van Holsbeeck M, van Melkebeke J, Dequeker J, et al. Radiographic findings of spontaneous subluxation of the sternoclavicular joint. Clin Rheumatol 1992;11:376–81.

192. Velutini J, Tarazona P. Fracture of the minubrium with posterior displacement of the clavicle and first rib. Int Orthop 1998;22:269–271.

193. Venissac N, Alifano M, Dahan M, et al. Intrathoracic migration of Kirschner pins. Ann Thoracic Surg 2000;69:1953–1955.

194. Wade AM, Barrett MO, Crist BD, et al. J Orthop Trauma 2007;21:418–21.

195. Waskowitz WJ. Disruption of the sternoclavicular joint: an analysis and review. Am J Orthop 1961;3:176–179.

196. Wasylenko MJ, Busse EF. Posterior dislocation of the clavicle causing fatal tracheoesophageal fistula. Can J Surg 1981;24:626–627.

197. Waters PM, Bae DS, Kadiyala RK. Short-term outcomes after surgical treatment of traumatic posterior sternoclavicular fracture-dislocations in children and adolescents. J Pediatr Orthop 2003;23(4) ;464–469.

198. Webb PA, Suchey JMM. Epiphyseal union of the anterior iliac crest and medial clavicle in a modern multiracial sample of American males and females. Am J Phys Anthropol 1985;68:457–466.

199. Wettstein M, Borens O, Garofalo R, et al. Anterior subluxation after reduction of a posterior traumatic sterno-clavicular dislocation: a case report and a review of the literature. Knee Surg Sports Traumatol Arthrosc 2004;12:453–6.

200. Winter J, Sterner S, Maurer D, et al. Retrosternal epiphyseal disruption of medial clavicle: case and review in children. J Emerg Med 1989;7:9–13.

201. Wirth MA, Rockwood CA. Chronic conditions of the acromioclavicular and sternoclavicular joints. In: Chapman MW, ed. Operative Orthopaedics, part XI. 2nd ed. Philadelphia: JB Lippincott, 1992:1683–1693.

202. Wirth MA, Rockwood CA. Complications following repair of the sternoclavicular joint. In: Bigliani LU, ed. Complications of the shoulder. Baltimore: Williams & Wilkins, 1993:139–153.

203. Wirth MA, Rockwood CA. Complications of treatment of injuries to the shoulder. In: Epps CH, ed. Complications in Orthopaedic Surgery. 3rd ed. Philadelphia: JB Lippincott, 1994:229–253.

204. Worman LW, Leagus C. Intrathoracic injury following retrosternal dislocation of the clavicle. Trauma 1967;7:416–423.

205. Wynne-Davies R. Familial Joint Laxity. Proc R Soc Med 1971;64:689–90.

206. Yang J, Al-Etani H, Letts M. Diagnosis and treatment of posterior sternoclavicular joint dislocation in children. AJ Ortho 1996;25(8):565–569.

207. Zaslav KR, Ray S, Neer CS. Conservative management of a displaced medial clavicular physeal injury in an adolescent athlete. Am J Sports Med 1989;17(6):833–836.

INDEX

Note: Page numbers followed by an *f* indicate figures; page numbers followed by a *t* indicate tables.